A BIOGRAPHICAL DICTIONARY OF

BRITISH ARCHITECTS

1600–1840

A BIOGRAPHICAL DICTIONARY OF BRITISH ARCHITECTS 1600–1840

THIRD EDITION

* * *

Howard Colvin

PUBLISHED FOR THE PAUL MELLON
CENTRE FOR STUDIES IN BRITISH ART BY
Yale University Press
NEW HAVEN AND LONDON
1995

10 9 8 7 6 5 4 3 2

Set in Linotron Plantin by Best-set Typesetter Ltd., Hong Kong, and printed and bound in Great Britain by St Edmundsbury Press Ltd., Bury St Edmunds, Suffolk.

Library of Congress Cataloging-in-Publication Data

Colvin, Howard Montague.
A biographical dictionary of British architects, 1600–1840 / Howard Colvin. — 3rd ed.
p. cm.
Includes bibliographical references and indexes.
ISBN 0–300–06091–2 (hbk.)
ISBN 0–300–07207–4 (pbk.)
1. Architects—Great Britain—Biography—Dictionaries. I. Title.
NA996.C6 1995
720′.92′241—dc20 94–39135
[B] CIP

Contents

Preface

I AM GRATEFUL to the Paul Mellon Centre and Yale University Press for giving me the opportunity to publish a new edition of this Dictionary. Its scope and format remain unchanged, but continuing research, both by myself and by others, has called for many amendments, for the incorporation of much new information about individual architects and their works, and sometimes for a reassessment of their place in British architectural history. Over 160 additional biographical notices will be found, and more than 2000 buildings whose architects have been newly identified have been added to the lists. Some persons included in 1978 have been omitted in 1995, either because it has become clear that, like the 'antiquary' and connoisseur Daniel Lock, the Catholic priest Fr. Lovi, or the master bricklayer Samuel Westbrook, they did not after all qualify as architects, or because a review of their careers showed that, like John Cunningham (1799–1873) or John Elliott (*c.*1812–1891), what they did before 1840 was so much outweighed by what they did after that date that their inclusion in a dictionary of pre-Victorian architects could no longer be justified. Their names are given in Appendix B, and information about some of them will be found in the *Directory of British Architects 1834–1900* recently published by the British Architectural Library.

As a work of biographical reference for the period 1600–1840 this edition is therefore both more comprehensive and more consistent than its predecessor. But of course it is still far from definitive: of many of the architects included far too little is at present known to make their careers intelligible, and there are still numerous buildings of importance whose designers remain unidentified. To what extent does it even constitute a complete nominal record of those architects who in principle qualify for inclusion? So far as professional architects of the late eighteenth and early nineteenth centuries are concerned, the answer is that it is probably virtually complete, though more builder-architects of this period undoubtedly remain to be identified. Taking the eighteenth century as a whole, it is unlikely that the name of any architect of national importance is missing, but the entries for Hoare and John Read show how imperfect our knowledge still is of some Georgian architects, while for the seventeenth century it is possible to point to a dozen names (e.g. Duddell, Elder, Anthony Ellis, Lancelot Freson, Hancock, Hawkins, Mackline, Scott, Vezy), whose association with a single building is all that is known at present about what may have been a lifetime's involvement in architectural practice. Some of these men may eventually emerge as recognizable personalities with a known *oeuvre*, but most of them will probably remain as a reminder of how little we know (or are ever likely to know) about the lesser architects of the seventeenth century. For this period no systematic programme of further biographical research can easily be prescribed, but for the Georgian period many records both public and private remain to be fully exploited, while from about 1790 onwards, directories and newspaper advertisements, used in conjunction with Census returns, probate records and other sources now readily available in County Record Offices and elsewhere, could form the basis of further regional studies on the lines of the *Dictionary of Architects of Suffolk Buildings 1800–1914* by Brown, Haward and Kindred (1991).

Although such local records have by no means been neglected either by myself or by those who have been good enough to pass on to me the fruits of their researches, it is beyond the capacity of a single person fully to assimilate the information available about every provincial builder-architect. Nevertheless, in concluding a work which, in its successive editions, has now occupied me on and off for some fifty years, I hope that, imperfect though it is, it will provide both a reliable source of reference for all those interested in Stuart, Georgian and early nineteenth-century architecture in England, Scotland and Wales, and a basis for further research by British architectural historians.

OXFORD
December 1993

The opportunity afforded by the present reprint has been taken to correct a number of misprints and some simple errors of fact.

A fuller list of corrections, together with addenda, will be found in *Architectural History*, vol. 39 (1996), pp. 236–241, and it is intended to publish further additions and corrections in subsequent editions of that periodical.

December 1996

Preface to Second Edition

AFTER TWENTY YEARS in print, *A Biographical Dictionary of English Architects 1660–1840* needed a new lease of life if it were to serve another generation of architectural historians. For those twenty years have seen a sustained activity in extending our knowledge of British architecture equalled only by the collaborative enterprise which between 1852 and 1892 produced the Architectural Publication Society's *Dictionary*. In this activity *A Biographical Dictionary of English Architects 1660–1840* has played its part by attempting to provide that hard foundation of ascertainable fact without which no historical edifice can safely be erected. But by 1974 scarcely a page that was printed in 1954 could stand without amplification or correction. Not only did many bald and inadequate notices need expansion, but many new ones called for inclusion, and some old ones for exclusion.

This is, however, rather more than merely a revised edition of the 1954 Dictionary. Its scope has been extended both in time and in space. Chronologically the starting date is now 1600 instead of 1660, and biographies of Scottish and Welsh as well as of English architects have been included for the first time. The name of Inigo Jones is perhaps enough in itself to justify the extra sixty years, and the careers of Campbell, Gibbs, Adam, Mylne and Burn serve to demonstrate the close links which existed between English and Scottish architectural practice from the Union onwards, if not before. For the continued exclusion of Irish architects no excuse is needed, since a comprehensive Dictionary of Irish Architects is in active preparation by a consortium of Irish architectural historians. As for the years after 1840, my determination to stray no further into the reign of Victoria will be fully justified by the publication of a companion *Dictionary of Victorian Architects* by Dr. J. Mordaunt Crook and Mr. Paul Joyce.*

Apart from these chronological and topographical extensions, in what ways does this book differ from its predecessor? In principle very little, but the intervening twenty years have made it possible to investigate many new sources and to exploit some old ones in a much more systematic manner than could be attempted in the 1950s. Many documents that then had to be arduously sought out in the muniment rooms of remote country houses are now readily accessible in County Record Offices. Many drawings that were once hidden in the recesses of the R.I.B.A. Library have now been made the subject of an admirable catalogue. Twenty years travelling about the British Isles has also enabled me to see many buildings whose architectural character

* Of the Irish dictionary only the seventeenth-century volume by Dr. Rolf Loeber was in fact published (1981). The projected *Dictionary of Victorian Architects* has been superseded by the *Directory of British Architects 1834–1900* published by the British Architectural Library in 1993.

was at best imperfectly known to me in 1954, and thus to form a clearer idea of the stylistic personality of many individual architects. Too marked an expression of personal opinion would be out of place in a work of reference, but I hope that the attempt to indicate (however briefly and inadequately) the character and quality of the work of at least the more notable architects in this book will meet with the approval of its readers. In forming these brief assessments I have often had recourse to Sir Nikolaus Pevsner's *Buildings of England*, and the photographic archives of the two National Monuments Records in London and Edinburgh have been of great value.

Although more comprehensive in coverage and more consistent in treatment than its predecessor, this Dictionary is of course far from being definitive. Anyone who is familiar with the processes of historical research will be aware that a work of this kind can be no more than a stopping-place on a road that has no end. The more one knows, the more possibilities for further research open before one, and no one is more conscious than myself that the sources for the biography of British architects between 1600 and 1840 have not been exhausted by this book. This is particularly true of the many provincial architects whose careers can only be investigated on a local basis. J. D. Bennett's *Leicestershire Architects 1700–1850* (1968), David Walker's article on the Stirlings of Dunblane, and the catalogue (by Angus Taylor and Jeffrey Haworth) of the recent Webster Exhibition at Kendal show in different ways what can be achieved by painstaking local research to reconstruct the careers of those provincial architects who did so much to shape our towns and villages. Much more work of this sort remains to be done. And there are many individual buildings of importance whose architects have yet to be identified. If the designers of, say, Lees Court, Kent, the Castle Ashby screen, Tredegar House, Barnsley Park, or Shobdon Church could be established, some of the biographies in this Dictionary might read very differently. Here it may be appropriate to say that in this book, as in its predecessor, I have been cautious in admitting attributions based solely on stylistic criteria. In general, such attributions have been included only when they have seemed to me to be so compelling as to amount almost to certainty, and only when documentary evidence appears to be lacking. To clear away the undergrowth of irresponsible attribution that impeded British architectural scholarship earlier in this century was one of the main objectives of *A Biographical Dictionary of English Architects 1660–1840*, and (without of course denying that stylistic attribution has its place in architectural research) a book such as this is no place for speculative guess-work.

In *A Biographical Dictionary of English Architects* it was stated that my aim had been to include everyone 'who habitually made, or may be presumed to have made, architectural designs'. Broadly speaking that still remains true of the present work. But in the state of knowledge prevailing in 1954 it was necessary to include the names of many men for whose architectural activity there was no more evidence than a single exhibit at the Royal Academy, or an ambiguous reference in some document where the distinction between 'architect' and 'builder' was far from clear. Their *bona fides* as architects was in many cases uncertain, and their inclusion in the Dictionary was provisional. After the lapse of twenty years, some of them have emerged as authentic architectural personalities. Others, however, can now be presumed to have died young, to have abandoned architecture for some other career, or to have been in reality no more than executant craftsmen. As such they have now been excluded together with many more of their kind whose names have come to light since 1954. To have included all these architectural nonentities would have encumbered the pages of this Dictionary to little purpose. They have accordingly been omitted, but for convenience of reference their names have been printed in Appendix B, together with a codified indication of the reason for their exclusion. Their places have been more than filled by the names of some 400 English and 250 Scottish and Welsh architects who did not find a place in the 1954 Dictionary.

Many mistakes in *A Biographical Dictionary of English Architects* have been corrected, but in a work of this size new errors will inevitably have arisen, and I can only beg the indulgence of those who may detect inaccuracies that have escaped my vigilance.

OXFORD
December 1975

Acknowledgements

THE WRITER of a dictionary of this kind incurs many obligations: to fellow scholars, to archivists and librarians, and to private owners. Many of those whose help is acknowledged in the previous editions of 1954 and 1978 have continued liberally to volunteer information and patiently to answer queries, notably Dr. Lindsay Boynton, Miss Nancy Briggs, Mrs. Bridget Cherry, Prof. J. Mordaunt Crook, Mr. J. G. Dunbar, Dr. Terry Friedman, Prof. Andor Gomme, Mr. John Harris, Mr. Richard Hewlings, Mr. Gervase Jackson-Stops, Mr. Peter Howell, Mr. Frank Kelsall, Dr. Peter Leach, Dr. Derek Linstrum, Prof. Michael McCarthy, Mr. Julian Orbach, Mr. Peter Reid, Mr. Bernard Pardoe, Mr. Michael Robbins, Dr. J. M. Robinson, Prof. Alistair Rowan, Mr. Derek Sherborne, Prof. A. A. Tait, Mr. Nigel Temple, Dr. Eric Till and Mr. David Walker.

Local correspondents with special knowledge of a particular locality have continued to give invaluable assistance. To those named in 1978 must be added Mrs. Elizabeth Beaton (N.E. Scotland), Mr. Maxwell Craven (Derbyshire), Mrs. Grace McCombie (Northumberland), Dr. Michael McGarvie (Somerset), Dr. Norman Scarfe (Suffolk) and Mr. David Whitehead (Worcestershire and Herefordshire). Mr. David Cubitt has for many years sent me architectural items extracted from the Norfolk and Norwich newspapers. Mr. Thomas Lloyd has provided much important information about Welsh architects.

Among the many archivists and librarians to whom I am indebted for help I should like particularly to mention Dr. Robert Bearman of the Shakespeare Birthplace Trust Records Office, Dr. Iain Gordon Brown of the National Library of Scotland, Mr. R. J. Chamberlain-Brothers and Mr. Michael Farr of the Warwickshire Record Office, Mr. Robin Harcourt-Williams at Hatfield House, the Revd. Timothy Parry of Lambeth Palace Library, Mr. C. J. Pickford of the Bedfordshire Record Office, Mr. Colin Shrimpton at Alnwick Castle, Mrs. P. A. Smith (Sherborne Castle Estates), Miss M. M. Stewart of the Dumfries Archives Centre, and Mr. Peter Vasey of the Scottish Record Office. At the Royal Institute of British Architects Miss Jill Lever, Mr. Neil Bingham and Mr. Tim Knox have given me the freedom of the Drawings Collection, while Dr. Ruth Kamen and her staff readily provided information about former Fellows and Associates. At Sir John Soane's Museum Mr. Peter Thornton, Mrs. Margaret Richardson, Miss Christine Scull and Miss Susan Palmer have been equally helpful. In Scotland I have continued to benefit from the immense fund of knowledge accumulated at the National Monuments Record by Miss Catherine Cruft and Mr. Ian Gow. Miss Ierne Grant has kindly provided me with references to (and sometimes with transcripts of) a number of documents in the Scottish Record Office, while Mr. John Gifford has generously shared with me the results of his researches for several volumes of the *Buildings of Scotland.* In Lancashire Dr. Janet Gnosspelius and Mrs. S. M. Lewis very helpfully established for me the dates of death of many architects practising in Manchester, Liverpool and elsewhere in that county.

For important information about individual architects I am indebted to Mr. David Blissett (Sir Charles Barry), Mr. Alistair Forsyth (Stowey and Jones), Mr. Richard Garnier (Sir Robert Taylor), Prof. Andor Gomme (Francis Smith), Mr. W. R. H. Hakewill (the Hakewills), Mrs. Sally Jeffery (John James), Dr. M. Kerney (George Smith), Dr. David King (Robert and James Adam), Mr. A. R. Lewis (James Craig), Mr. Peter Meadows (Joseph and Ignatius Bonomi), Miss Moira Rudolf (Thomas Harrison), Mr. Edward Saunders (Joseph Pickford), Mr. David Sturdy (the Townesends), Mr. Angus Taylor (William Lindley and the Websters of Kendal) and Mr. Christopher Webster (R. D. Chantrell).

Others whose help in various ways I gratefully acknowledge are Mr. David Alexander, Mr. Nicholas Antram, Mr. John Archer, Mr. Bruce Bailey, Dr. T. A. Barnard, Mr. K. N. Bascombe, Mrs. H. Basford, Mr. Brian Blackwood, Dr. J. N. L. Booker, Mr. G. K. Brandwood, Mr. Alan Brooks, Mr. W. J. Brushe, Dr. Tristram Clarke, Dr. Rosalys Coope, Mr. Stephen Croad, Mr. J. A. K. Dean, Miss Brenda Doyle, Mr. Donald Findlay, Mr. C. F. Fisher, Mr. Angus Fowler, Dr. Eileen Harris, Dr. Frances Harris, Mr. Philip Heath, Mr. Ralph Hyde, Miss Jean Imray, Mr. Peter Inskip, Mr. Louis Jebb, Dr. D. A. Johnson, Mr. Jonathan Kewley, Mr. Nicholas Kingsley, Mrs. Lesley Lewis, Mr. Carl Lounsbury, Dr. James Macaulay, Mr. Aonghus MacKechnie, Mr. V. V. Millett, Mr. K. S. Mills, Mr. Anthony Mitchell, Mr. Richard Morris, Mr. W. Mostyn-Owen, Dr. Timothy Mowl, Mr. Philip Nokes, Mr. Hugh Pagan, Mr. D. R. Perriam, Miss Anne Riches, Mr. Frank Salmon, Dr. Cinzia Sicca, Mr. John Simmons, Mrs. Julia Abel Smith, Mr. Cyril Stael, Dr. John Stables, Mr. Peter Thornborrow, Dr. J. W. Turley, Miss Ann Turner, Mr. Nigel Tringham, Dr. Gerard Vaughan, Dr. David Watkin, Mr. Andrew Wells, Mr. R. Williams, Dr. C. Wilson, and Dr. Giles Worsley.

For access to drawings or documents in private archives or libraries I am grateful to the Duke of Montrose, the Duke of Norfolk, the Duke of Northumberland, the Marquess of Salisbury, the Earl of Elgin, the Earl of Mansfield, the Earl of Radnor, the Earl and Countess of Rosebery, the Earl of Shelburne, the Dowager Countess of Craven, Lord Shuttleworth, Lady Wrenbury, the late Sir John Fitzherbert, Bart., Mr. Keith Adam, Mr. C. H. Bagot, Mrs. V. E. Betti, Mr. Patrick Buchanan of Touch, Mr. J. A. Burdon-Cooper, Mr. J. J. Eyston, the late Mr. Henry Harpur-Crewe, Mr. Michael Johnson-Fergusson, Mr. Michael Pratt, Mrs. D. L. Pringle of Torwoodlee, Miss Riddell of Cheeseburn Grange, Commander Michael Saunders Watson, Mr. Lewis Smith, Major Patrick Telfer-Smollett of Bonhill, Mr. Ben Weinreb, Mr. D. P. White and Dr. Penry Williams; to the Librarians of

Caius, St. John's and Trinity Colleges, Cambridge, and of All Souls, Christ Church, Corpus Christi, Trinity and Worcester Colleges, Oxford, the Librarians of Gray's Inn and the Royal Academy of Arts, and the archivists of Hoare's Bank and the Bank of England.

Guide to Contents

THE PURPOSE of this book is sufficiently indicated by its title, but there are certain matters of method which require explanation, notably the chronological and topographical scope of the work and the principles upon which individual architects have qualified for inclusion.

My aim has been to include every architect – and by 'architect' I mean anyone, whether amateur, tradesman or professional, who habitually made architectural designs – the major part of whose career falls within the limiting dates. Thus Decimus Burton (1800–1881) has been included because most of his work was done before he was 40, whereas George Edmund Street, who died in the same year, has not because he was active chiefly in the 1850s and 1860s. Inevitably there have been borderline cases, in some of which no doubt another writer would have made different decisions. But I hope that in this as in other respects the element of personal preference has not been sufficiently great to impair the value of this book as a comprehensive record of British architects who practised between 1600 and 1840.

For the purposes of this Dictionary a 'British' architect is one who, irrespective of national origin, practised in England, Scotland or Wales. Architects domiciled in Ireland have been excluded, but many buildings erected in Ireland to the designs of English or Scottish architects have been noted. Architects of British origin whose careers were spent entirely overseas, e.g. in India, have not usually been included, but entries will be found for some who emigrated after an initial period of practice in Britain. Many amateur architects have been given a place, but a man whose architectural activity was limited to designing his own house has not normally qualified for inclusion.

So far as possible the works of each architect have been placed in chronological order. When this has not been practicable they have been listed alphabetically. Whenever it has seemed desirable public and private buildings have been listed separately. The dates printed are normally those of construction (rather than of the whole process of design and construction), but in many cases only an approximate date can be given. No attempt has been made to list unexecuted designs on the same basis as executed ones, but attention has often been drawn to important unexecuted designs either in the body of the biography or in a separate section. Dates of demolition and alteration have been stated so far as it has been possible to ascertain them, and an attempt has been made to indicate the employment of Gothic and other non-classical styles, though in neither case is it claimed that the information given is complete. The county boundaries referred to are those in force before the Local Government Act of 1972 (soon to be rendered obsolete by further legislation) and therefore correspond closely to those in use during the historical period covered by this Dictionary.

The authority for each entry in the lists will be found either at the head of the list (where one source is common to all entries) or (more often) within *square brackets* immediately after that entry. References given within *round brackets* are to books and articles which describe or illustrate the building in question but which are not cited as authorities. *'Attributed'* means that the evidence is largely or wholly stylistic. In this edition, as in its predecessors, such purely stylistic attributions have been sparingly made, partly because my purpose has been to provide a body of authentic information uncompromised by speculation and partly because in a dictionary there is no room in which to argue controversial cases of attribution.

Abbreviations

A.P.S.D.	*The Dictionary of Architecture*, ed. Wyatt Papworth for the Architectural Publication Society, 8 vols., 1852–92.
Arch. Hist.	*Architectural History.*
Arch. Rev.	*The Architectural Review.*
Architectural Mag.	*The Architectural Magazine*, ed. J. C. Loudon, 5 vols., 1834–8.
B.L	British Library.
C. Life	*Country Life.*
C.R.O.	County Record Office.
C.U.L.	Cambridge University Library.
D.N.B.	*The Dictionary of National Biography.*
dem.	demolished.
exhib.	exhibited.
Gent's Mag.	*The Gentleman's Magazine*, 1731–1868.
G.L.R.O.	Greater London Record Office.
G.R.	The card-index of nineteenth-century churches and their architects compiled by the late H. S. Goodhart-Rendel (R.I.B.A. Library and National Monuments Record).
Hist. MSS. Comm	Historical Manuscripts Commission.
History of the King's Works	*The History of the King's Works*, ed. H. M. Colvin, 6 vols., 1963–82.
I.C.B.S.	Records of the Incorporated Church Building Society (Lambeth Palace Library).
Jnl.	*Journal.*
N.L.S.	National Library of Scotland, Edinburgh.
N.L.W.	National Library of Wales, Aberystwyth.
N.M.R.	National Monuments Record (England).
N.M.R.S.	The National Monuments Record of Scotland.
N. and Q.	*Notes and Queries.*
N.R.A.S.	National Register of Archives for Scotland.
N.S.A.	*The New Statistical Account of Scotland*, 15 vols., 1845.
O.S.A.	*The 'Old' Statistical Account of Scotland*, by Sir J. Sinclair, 21 vols., 1791–9.
P.C.C.	Prerogative Court of Canterbury (wills in Public Record Office).
P.R.O.	Public Record Office, London.
Port	M. H. Port, *Six Hundred New Churches*, 1961.
R.A.	The Royal Academy of Arts.
R.C.A.M.	The Royal Commission on the Ancient and Historical Monuments of Scotland or the Royal Commission on Ancient Monuments in Wales.
R.C.H.M.	The Royal Commission on Historical Monuments (England).
R.I.B.A.	The Royal Institute of British Architects.
R.I.B.A.D.	The Royal Institute of British Architects Drawings Collection.
R.O.	Record Office.
S.R.O.	The Scottish Record Office, Register House, Edinburgh.
V.&A.	Victoria and Albert Museum, London.
V.C.H.	*The Victoria County History of England.*

Vitruvius Britannicus	*Vitruvius Britannicus, or the British Architect*, by Colen Campbell, 3 vols., 1715, 1717 and 1725; continued by J. Woolfe and J. Gandon, vol. iv, 1767, vol. v., 1771.
W.A.M.	Westminster Abbey Muniments.
Willis & Clark	R. Willis and J. W. Clark, *The Architectural History of the University of Cambridge*, 3 vols., 1886.
Wren Soc.	*The Wren Society*, 20 vols., 1924–43.

[ ] a reference in square brackets gives the source or authority for the preceding statement or statements.

( ) a reference in round brackets is to a book or article which describes or illustrates the building in question but is not cited as an authority.

The Practice of Architecture, 1600–1840

IT IS APPROPRIATE to begin a biographical dictionary of professional men by giving some account of the history of their profession. Indeed, the history of British architecture is bound up with its own practice, and the careers of those architects and master workmen who figure in this dictionary would scarcely be intelligible without some idea of the conditions under which they designed and built. For many of them architecture was a craft rather than an art: it is therefore with the building trades that the first part of this introduction is concerned. The second attempts to trace the rise of the architectural profession in Britain, a process that falls within – indeed very nearly coincides with – the chronological limits of this book. For in 1600 there were no architects in the sense in which we understand the term today. By 1840 there was an established architectural profession, based on a regular system of pupilage and held together by the newly founded Institute of British Architects. This new profession had come into being through the labours and aspirations of those whose names appear in this volume, and a summary of its history may not inappropriately serve to introduce their careers.[1]

THE BUILDING TRADES

> *'As to the Masters, most of them live handsomely; and some, who employ many Hands, and undertake large works, commonly called* Master-builders, *obtain good Estates; but then they are such who not only have Money at Command, but take great Pains to qualify themselves for Projecting, drawing Plans, surveying and Estimating Buildings'*
>
> (A General Description of all Trades, 1747).

In its building organization, as in so much else, Britain in the seventeenth century was still dependent on the methods of the medieval past. Today, building is managed by a 'contractor' who makes himself responsible for the engagement of workmen skilled in bricklaying, carpentry, masonry and so forth; then, it was in the hands of the individual master workman, for there were as many masters as there were trades, and the bricklayer, the mason, the carpenter, the joiner, the plumber, the glazier, the painter, the smith and the pavior was each the proprietor of a separate yard or workshop, in which he carried on his appropriate craft. These men served an apprenticeship of seven years, then worked as journeymen, and eventually achieved the status of

[1] Frank Jenkins, *Architect and Patron*, 1961, is a general study of the architectural profession in England, Barrington Kaye, *The Development of the Architectural Profession in Britain*, 1960, a sociological one. See also J. Wilton-Ely, 'The Rise of the Professional Architect in England', in *The Architect*, ed. S. Kostof, New York 1977. For Scotland see H. Colvin, 'The beginnings of the architectural profession in Scotland', *Arch. Hist.* 29, 1986.

independent master craftsmen. In London at least, the masters of the principal building trades were members of City Companies which still discharged functions which they had inherited from the medieval craft guilds. The Masons' Company, for instance, still carried out searches for 'false' – that is, defective – workmanship, and endeavoured to restrain 'foreign' masons who were not freemen of the City from carrying on their trade in London. But the Great Fire of 1666 did much to break down this always precarious monopoly, for in order to attract labour Parliament enacted that 'foreigners' should be permitted to work in the City, and that if they remained for seven years, they should enjoy the same liberty as freemen for the rest of their lives. The Companies' control, once lost, was never effectively restored, and by the middle of the eighteenth century they had degenerated into societies whose activities were chiefly sociable and charitable.[2]

In any case, the mason's craft was never centred wholly upon the towns. In the seventeenth and early eighteenth centuries it was still closely connected with the quarries from which the stone was derived. Quarrying villages, like Ketton in Rutland and Painswick in Gloucestershire, were nurseries of masons throughout the period, and many of the best-known master builders traced their origins to some small place of this sort. It was from Raunds in Northamptonshire that the Grumbolds came to work on the Cambridge colleges in the seventeenth century, and it was only the proximity of the Headington quarries that gave Oxford its flourishing school of masons in that and the following century.[3] The Strongs of Taynton, the Platts of Rotherham, and the Woodwards of Chipping Campden are further examples of masons whose fortunes were laid in the freestone quarries of the Midlands and north of England. The most successful firms were generally those whose capital and experience was handed on from one generation to another, as was the case with the Smiths of Warwick and the Mylnes of Edinburgh: but even within a single lifetime it was possible for a master mason to make a substantial fortune. Samuel Fulkes, for instance, who worked as a mason in London at 2s. 6d. a day in 1664, took small contracts of £9, £14, £117 and £613 in the 1670s, then much larger ones of £1888, £1946, £3204 and £3335 in the 1680s, and ended as one of the principal masonry contractors for St Paul's Cathedral.[4] Andrews Jelfe, who was one of the builders of Westminster Bridge, left a country house, a flourishing business, considerable London property, and over £30,000 when he died in 1759. Like most of his type, he combined sculpture with building, and the elaborate monuments with which

[2] For the masons, see E. Conder, *The Hole Craft and Fellowship of Masons*, 1894, and D. Knoop & G. P. Jones, *The London Mason in the Seventeenth Century*, 1935: for the carpenters, E. B. Jupp & W. W. Pocock, *Historical Account of the Company of Carpenters*, 2nd ed., 1887, and B. W. E. Alford & T. C. Barker, *A History of the Carpenters Company*, 1968. For the incorporation of building tradesmen in other towns, see D. Knoop & G. P. Jones, *The Mediaeval Mason*, 1933, pp. 229–33. For Scotland, see H. Carr, *The Mason and the Burgh*, 1954, and David Stevenson, *The First Freemasons*, Aberdeen 1988.

[3] For the Headington quarries, see W. J. Arkell, *Oxford Stone*, 1947.

[4] D. Knoop & G. P. Jones, 'The Rise of the Mason Contractor', *R.I.B.A. Jnl.* ser. 3, vol. 43, No. 20, 1936, 1063.

it was the custom to commemorate the dead were a profitable source of income to the eighteenth-century master mason. Their production occupied his yard during the three or four months of the year when building in the open was at a standstill,[5] and they gave him scope to exercise his inventiveness as a designer. Some ability as a draughtsman was essential to his craft: 'he must learn Designing, and to draw all the five Orders of Architecture, according to their several Proportions', wrote Campbell in his *London Tradesman*; 'his skill in Drawing is likewise employed in taking down with his Chalk upon the Block of Stone, from the Architect's Plan, the Out-lines of any Figure, Moulding, or Scroll, that is to be cut; In a word, without Drawing and Figures he cannot make a Stone-Mason, unless he is to be employed only in cutting and squaring Flag-Stones. It is an ingenious genteel Craft, and not unprofitable. The Master may be ranked among the first Rank of Tradesmen; and the Journeyman, when employed, makes Three Shillings a Day, or at least Half a Crown.'[6]

Equally profitable were the trades of the bricklayer and the carpenter – the latter being in many cases combined with that of the joiner.[7] The former, in 1600, was chiefly to be found in the neighbourhood of London, and in counties such as Norfolk and Suffolk, where stone was not readily accessible: but his influence was to spread rapidly as the use of his material became general in the eighteenth century, and the London Rebuilding Act of 1667 set a standard in domestic brickwork which soon affected building practice throughout the country.[8] The extension of the bricklayer's trade to districts such as Herefordshire and Cheshire was to some extent achieved at the expense of the master carpenter, whose 'black-and-white' architecture had hitherto been the rule in those counties. Certainly there is no example in the eighteenth century of a master carpenter such as John Abel of Hereford (d. 1675), whose timber-framed market-houses are among the outstanding monuments of his craft. But the bricklayer could not dispense with the services of the carpenter altogether. He could and did undertake to 'build by the great' – that is, 'to make an estimate of the total expence of a House . . . and contract for the execution of the whole for the amount of (his) estimate'.[9] But it must be remembered that the training and equipment of an eighteenth-century master workman were confined to his own craft: 'if he was a bricklayer, he would have to sublet the carpentry: if he was a carpenter he

[5] 'They are idle about four Months of the Year, unless they have some skill in sculpture, in which they may be employed all the Year', says Campbell in *The London Tradesman*, 1747, 159.

[6] R. Campbell, *The London Tradesman*, 1747, 158–9.

[7] 'Carpentry and Joinery . . . are often performed by the same Persons though the work of these is much lighter and generally reckoned more curious than that of the Carpenters, for a good Joiner can often do both well, but every Carpenter cannot work at Joinery, especially the nicer Parts of it' (*A General Description of all Trades*, 1747, 124). The plumbing and glazing trades were also frequently combined.

[8] On this subject, cf. G. F. Webb in *R.I.B.A. Jnl.* 27 May 1933, 580, and *The Journeys of Celia Fiennes*, ed. C. Morris, 1949, 179 (a new brick house 'in the exact forme of the London architecture'), 183 (houses at Liverpool 'new built of brick and stone after the London fashion').

[9] Thos. Mortimer, *The Universal Director*, 1763.

must sublet the bricklaying; and in either case he must put all the minor trades into other hands'.[10]

This subcontracting was often accomplished by a species of barter whereby one tradesman aided another in the performance of his appropriate task, thus reducing cash payments to the minimum and making it possible for a group of tradesmen to undertake considerable enterprises with much less capital than would otherwise be necessary. Thus, in speculative building, it was not uncommon for the chief promoter or 'undertaker' to offer his associates a share in the new development in return for work performed or materials delivered. Richard Frith, the builder of the London street which bears his name, adopted this expedient in 1687–8 in connection with a project for laying out a new street of houses on the site of the Royal Mews in St. James's Park. The list of his associates, which has been preserved, includes a mason, a brickmaker, a bricklayer, a carver, and two joiners, each of whom was to receive a plot in the 'new intended streete' in proportion to the amount of 'worke [by him] wrought, or goods sold and delivered'.[11] Speculative building brought great rewards, but it was also attended with great risks, and the names of its victims figure prominently in eighteenth-century bankruptcy lists. 'Both Carpenters and Joiners' – to quote Campbell once more – 'are Undertakers in Building as well as the Master-Bricklayers; and are liable to split upon the same Rock of Building-Projects: But a Gentleman who wants to build with Security as well as Beauty, would do well not to trust entirely to their Skill.'[12] There was, in fact, general agreement among seventeenth- and eighteenth-century architectural writers that to put all the work into the hands of a single 'undertaker' was to court disaster.[13] Sir Roger Pratt warned his readers against it,[14] and so did Sir Christopher Wren.

> There are 3 ways of working [he wrote to the Bishop of Oxford in 1681]: by the Day, by Measure, by Great; if by the Day it tells me when they are Lazy. If by measure it gives me light on every particular, and tells me what I am to provide. If by the Great I can make a sure bargain neither to be

[10] John Summerson, *Georgian London*, 1945, 60.

[11] B.L., Add. MS. 16370, f. 115. It was by similar methods that in 1819–20 John Nash built the Regent Street Quadrant as a personal speculation (John Summerson, *John Nash*, 1935, 220).

[12] *The London Tradesman*, 1747, 161.

[13] The practice was forbidden by the Carpenters' Company in 1607 on the ground that 'the King's majesty's subjects being owners of the building are very much and often deceived of true and substantial stuff and workmanship' thereby (Jupp & Pocock, *Historical Account of the Company of Carpenters*, 2nd ed. 1887, 149). The Fellows of St. John's College, Cambridge, found too late that it was a 'way of building not so allowable in works intended for posterity' when they entrusted the erection of their Second Court to two undertakers in 1598–1602 (Willis and Clark, ii, 249), and it was bitter experience of the ways of a contractor (the architect-builder Thomas Johnson) which led the Justices of Warwick to resolve in 1790 'that no contract for building the whole Gaol shall be made with one person' (Warwickshire County Records, Q.S. Class 24 (h)).

[14] 'We shall not only do great prejudice to our building but also in putting out our work by the great, be most exceedingly abused, and overreached by our workmen' (*The Architecture of Sir Roger Pratt*, ed. R. T. Gunther, 1928, 48).

overreached nor to hurt the undertaker: for in things they are not every day used to, they doe often injure themselves, and when they begin to find it, they shuffle and slight the worke to save themselves. I think the best way in this business is to worke by measure: according to the prices in the Estimate or lower if you can, and measure the work at 3 or 4 measurements as it rises. But you must have an understanding trusty Measurer, there are few that are skilled in measuring stone worke, I have bred up 2 or 3.[15]

The first method advocated by Wren was the direct labour system, which can be traced back to early medieval practice. Thus when the churchwardens of Marlow rebuilt their Church House in 1717 they found the materials (which cost them £48:16:2½) themselves, and paid the workmen employed by the day. Thomas Gray, bricklayer, received £4:4:2 for 50 days' work at 20d. a day, and the other men employed were engaged on a similar basis.[16] Building 'by measure' was probably less troublesome, but involved the expense of employing a measurer or surveyor. Most architects were prepared to act as measuring surveyors and although the engagement of a surveyor did not necessarily mean going to him for the design,[17] the two functions were so intimately associated that the terms 'architect' and 'surveyor' were almost synonymous in eighteenth-century parlance.[18] Master builders too were not infrequently employed in this capacity, and according to *A General Description of all Trades* (1747) many of them made it their 'chief business' to 'survey and estimate other Men's Works'. In Edinburgh an experienced master mason or master wright could aspire to become one of the 'sworn measurers'. These were public officials who were licensed to measure building work at a rate fixed by the City Council. Some at least of the applicants for these posts were examined on behalf of the Council by the Professor of Mathematics at the University.[19]

That master builders both English and Scottish made designs, both for themselves and for one another, there is abundant evidence, and the author of *The City and Countrey Purchaser and Builder's Dictionary* (1703) was of the opinion that 'there be many Master-workmen that will contrive a Building and draw a Draught, or Design thereof, as well as most (and better than some) Surveyors'. But in the seventeenth century it was still not uncommon – especially in country circles – for the builder to be told to take an existing building as his model. When the tower of Crondall Church in Hampshire was

[15] *Wren Soc.* v, 20. See also Pratt, *op. cit.*, 141.

[16] *Records of Bucks.* xv, 1947, 6.

[17] Thus William Baker (*q.v.*) frequently acted as surveyor of churches and other buildings which he did not design.

[18] A good surveyor of Building, or such as we call Architects' (Roger North, *Of Building*, f. 7[v]); 'architects and surveyors (the terms are now synonymous)' (J. Noble, *The Professional Practice of Architects*, 1836, 19). Johnstone's *Commercial Street Directory* of 1817 gives 108 men who called themselves 'Architect and Surveyor', or 'Surveyor and Architect', but only one who called himself simply 'Architect'. He was Sir John Soane, whose views on the subject were printed in *The Artist* xiv, 13 July 1807.

[19] Colvin, as in n. 1, 173.

rebuilt in 1659, the churchwardens 'went about looking at other towers, and eventually fixed upon the tower of Battersea Church as the best pattern to go by'. They then sent their workmen to measure it up and build their own in similar fashion.[20] And contracts not infrequently specify that a chimney-stack or an ornamental feature shall be 'like unto or better than' some chosen example of its kind.[21]

It was in this way that the ideas of the London architect percolated slowly into the consciousness of the local master builder. Reminiscences of the Banqueting House in Whitehall, for instance, can be seen in buildings erected in many parts of the country during the seventeenth century. But Inigo Jones's carefully composed façade did not lend itself easily to the rule-of-thumb methods of the country builder, and at Brympton D'Evercy in Somerset (*c.*1680) the mason has managed his fenestration so clumsily that the terminal pediment at one end is segmental in form while that at the other is triangular. The more empirical, less uncompromisingly Italianate architecture of Wren and his contemporaries adapted itself more readily to imitation by the master builder, and the employment of large numbers of country workmen in the rebuilding of London did much to impress the salient features of the new style upon their minds.[22]

But the degree of control even in the case of works erected under the immediate supervision of the Surveyor-General or one of his colleagues was often far from complete, and it is necessary to distinguish carefully between those few buildings for which he made working drawings and those many others for which he merely 'gave a model' to be interpreted 'in the ordinary language of the London builders'.[23] Wren's City churches, in particular, were the result of cooperation between the Surveyor-General and the highly competent craftsmen whom he employed – men who were quite capable of designing and building a church without the supervision of a member of the Royal Society. And to a great extent they actually did so: the ceilings, altar-pieces, pulpits and other furnishings were usually designed by those who executed them. Sometimes they submitted a drawing or a model to Wren or one of his colleagues: but more often they did not, and it is a tribute to the high standard of contemporary craftsmanship that the resultant interiors were so rarely disharmonious.

[20] C. D. Stokes, *A History of Crondall and Yateley*, 1905, 8.

[21] 'The workmanship of the front next the Street not to be inferior to Mr. Honylove's building in ornament' (contract, dated 1668, to build a house in Gracechurch Street, London, among archives of St. John's College, Oxford); 'The Frontespeice and Lucron windowes [and other details] to be like them at Battlesdon' (contract, dated Feb. 1673/4, to build Holme Lacy House, Herefordshire: P.R.O., Chancery Masters' Exhibits, Duchess of Norfolk deeds, Box M, Bundle 24, No. 7789); the water-table, stools of windows of upper stories to be of Portland stone, 'moulded as the Earl of Ranelagh's at Chelsea' the 'severall stackes of chimneys shall be headed with Portland stone as they are at Arlington House' (contract, dated Nov. 1692, to build a house at Petersham for the Earl of Rochester: Surrey C.R.O., S.C. 13/26/102).

[22] For a striking example of this, see the account of the rebuilding of Newent Church, below, p. 959. See also *Wren Soc.* vii, 72.

[23] The quotation is from an unpublished paper by Sir John Summerson on the architecture of the London Temple, which he kindly allowed me to read in MS.

It was doubtless inevitable that an architect with so many churches in course of erection at the same time should exercise but a loose control over the details of their execution, especially as the interior fittings were the financial responsibility of the parishes concerned. But that precisely the same methods were followed by a fashionable country-house architect of the period is shown by the papers of Captain William Winde, the architect of Hampstead Marshall (1663 onwards), Combe Abbey (1682–5) and Castle Bromwich (1685–90). Having determined the architectural features of the building in consultation with his client, he assembled a team of craftsmen who submitted designs for the decorative features – ceilings, pediments and gateways – which they were prepared to execute. Their 'draughts' were then signed and dated by the architect to show that they had been 'allowed'.[24] Pierce the carver and Goudge the plasterer both designed their own work in this way and their draughtsmanship is, if anything, more accomplished than that of Winde himself.[25]

Buildings of the period between 1660 and 1720 represent one of the high-water marks of English architectural craftsmanship. How long it was capable of maintaining itself at this level it is impossible to conjecture, for once more the skill of the master workman had to adjust itself to a change of taste – one which was in the long run to prove fatal to his artistic self-sufficiency. There was no room in the Palladian dictatorship initiated by Lord Burlington for the individualism of a Pierce or a Goudge: Vitruvian precedent took the place of personal inventiveness, and although the craftsmanship remains of the highest quality, from about 1730 it is doing the will of the architect to an extent which it had never done before. The pressure of this new architectural discipline was to increase until, by the end of the eighteenth century, the craftsman had sunk to the level of a mere executant, dependent for every detail upon the working drawings supplied by the architect.

But if the master builder was henceforth to be subordinate to the architect, he could still attempt to keep abreast of current taste by the intelligent use of pattern-books. Leoni's edition of *Palladio*, Campbell's *Vitruvius Britannicus* and Kent's *Designs of Inigo Jones* were the text-books of the new Palladianism, and the printed lists of subscribers include the names of a number of masons, carpenters and joiners. James Gibbs followed suit with his *Rules for Drawing the Several Parts of Architecture*, in which he taught a simplified method of measurement calculated to appeal to the practical builder, who could scarcely be expected to grasp the mysteries of modular proportion. Within a few years, the building craftsman had at his disposal an astonishing number of these manuals, many of them written by men of his own class, like William Halfpenny and Batty Langley, who seem to have

[24] 'Letters and papers relating to the rebuilding of Combe Abbey', ed. H. Colvin, *Walpole Soc.* 1, 1984.

[25] In 1688 Winde told Lady Bridgeman of Castle Bromwich that Goudge had 'bine employed by mee this 6 or 7 yeares, is an excelent draufftsman and mackes all his desines himeselfe' (letter quoted by G. W. Beard in *Decorative Plasterwork in Great Britain*, 1975, 48). For Pierce, see below, pp. 754–5.

found their production more profitable even than building. The bibliography of the architectural pattern-books is, indeed, enormous, and their diffusion does more than anything else to explain the high standard of provincial building in the mid-eighteenth century. Most of them are nowadays exceedingly rare, and the condition of surviving copies suggests that in many cases they were literally thumbed to pieces in the builders' yards.

The pattern-book made it possible for the builder-architect to survive well into the second half of the eighteenth century. But with the reign of George III the tides of British taste began to ebb and flow with ever-increasing rapidity, and as the neo-classical challenged the Palladian, and the Grecian confronted the Gothic, it became yearly more difficult for the builder-architect to hold his own against the professional. While his artistic self-sufficiency was thus being imperilled, his status as an independent craftsman was being jeopardized by economic causes beyond his control. How he reacted to the economic crises of the late eighteenth century has yet to be determined.[26] Nor is it clear how far the Napoleonic wars, by curtailing both public and private building, may have affected the fortunes of the smaller building businesses. What is certain is that the extensive architectural activity of the early nineteenth century – the era of 'metropolitan improvement' in London, of the 'second New Town' in Edinburgh, and of much building and rebuilding of churches and country houses throughout the two kingdoms – brought opportunities for a new type of builder who was more of an entrepreneur than a craftsman. For these were the years which saw the rise of the building contractor, who, without being the master of any specific trade himself, engaged a full staff of workmen on a permanent wage basis, and was able to take on contracts which before would have been divided between two or three independent master builders. When contracts were not forthcoming, he developed land in order to keep his men employed. The first of this new type of general builder was Thomas Cubitt, whose methods became the model for the great Victorian contractors.[27] Many who a generation earlier would have set up as independent master builders were now content to accept the position of employees and shelter themselves under the wing of a Cubitt or a Peto. Thus economic change, combined with the growing eclecticism of nineteenth-century taste, brought about the decline of the independent master builder, leaving the field to the building contractor on one hand and to the architect on the other. In early Victorian Britain intelligent and enterprising builder-architects were still to be found, such as the Carlines of Shrewsbury, the Smiths of Darnick or the Owens of Haverfordwest, but they were the last of their kind.

[26] The effect of these crises on the volume of building (though not on the structure of the building trades) has been studied by T. S. Ashton, *Economic Fluctuations in England 1700–1800*, 1959, 84–105.

[27] For these developments see E. W. Cooney, 'The Origins of the Victorian Master Builders', *Economic History Review*, 2nd ser. viii, 1955, and M. H. Port, 'The Office of Works and Early 19th-century Building Contracts', *ibid.* xx, 1967. For Cubitt himself see below, pp. 282–4.

'You must be aware that Architecture is the profession of a Gentleman, and that none is more lucrative when it is properly attended to'
Mrs James Wyatt to her son Philip, 1808 (B.L., Egerton MS. 3515)

The architect as we know him today is a product of the Renaissance. This does not mean that the architect, in the sense of 'one who both furnishes the designs and superintends the erection of buildings',[28] had been unknown in the Middle Ages. But the medieval architect was a master craftsman (usually a mason or a carpenter by trade), one who could build as well as design, or at least 'one trained in that craft even if he had ceased to ply his axe and chisel'.[29] He was a master workman whose skill was based on a technical experience of building rather than on a theoretical knowledge of architecture as an art. The word 'architect' itself, used by the ancients in much the same sense as it is by ourselves, came in the Middle Ages to be regarded as the equivalent of 'master mason' or 'master carpenter'.[30]

It was, then, the mason and the carpenter who were the architects of the Middle Ages. That some of them were men of genius cannot be denied, and even if architecture did not rank as a 'liberal art', there is evidence that those who practised it as masters enjoyed a certain status in the society of their time. The recognition that there were able men in the medieval building world, and that those men deserve the name of 'architect', does not, however, imply that their functions were identical with those of architects in modern times. Architectural practice has evolved together with the society which it serves. A modern architect is a professional man set aside from the building trade by education and specialized training. His architectural expertise is acquired by academic instruction rather than by practical experience, and his approach to design is theoretical rather than empirical. When he designs a building he envisages it as a whole and works it out in detail on paper before transmitting the drawings to the executant builder. The medieval architect, on the other hand, was normally a craftsman by training, and frequently acted as one of the executants of the buildings he himself designed. That he was capable of envisaging a building as a whole we cannot doubt, and there is abundant evidence that he could express his ideas on the drawing-board. But in the Middle Ages the processes of design and construction were much more closely linked than is the case today. Much more was left to be worked out on the spot than is normal in modern architectural practice, and even major churches were sometimes begun without any clear idea how they were to be completed. That the technical achievement of the great Gothic churches was possible at all was due partly to the accumulated experience of the Romanesque age, and partly to the rediscovery of Greek science in the thirteenth century. The science of most utility to architecture was of course

[28] *A.P.S.D., s.v.* 'ARCHITECT'.
[29] D. Knoop & G. P. Jones, *The Mediaeval Mason,* 1933, 197.
[30] N. Pevsner, 'The Term Architect in the Middle Ages', *Speculum* xvii, 1942, 549–62.

geometry, and it was above all a knowledge of geometry that distinguished the medieval master mason or master carpenter from his subordinates. That knowledge might find expression in drawn 'patrons' and 'patterns', of which many examples survive on the continent, though few have been preserved in British archives. But it was also more widely disseminated in the form of simple geometrical formulae which made it possible to develop many of the elevational features of a building from a given plan in accordance with predetermined rules of proportion, without the intervention of working drawings.[31]

Another difference between medieval and modern architectural practice must be emphasized. All that we know of the medieval craftsman suggests that it was very rare for a master mason, however eminent, to dictate to a master carpenter, or *vice versa*. Each was supreme in his own sphere, and solved his own problems in accordance with the traditions of his own craft. Each trade was a distinct 'mistery', understood only by its own practitioners, and applied independently to each new commission. Common patronage, common experience and common artistic conventions enabled one trade to work harmoniously beside another, but it was rare for any one individual to exercise that technical and aesthetic control over every component of a building which modern architects have come to take for granted. In studying the careers of medieval architects it is therefore necessary to think of them as members of a team working in collaboration rather than as architects in the sense in which the term has been understood in modern times.

In Italy – and to a lesser extent in France – the authority of the architect was already asserting itself in the sixteenth and early seventeenth centuries. But in Tudor and Stuart Britain medieval practice was still the norm in architectural matters. The great Elizabethan houses were assembled piecemeal rather than designed as artistically coherent entities. 'The plan might come from one source, the details from a number of others. Designs could be supplied by one or more of the craftsmen actually employed on the building; or by an outside craftsman; or by the employer; or by a friend of the employer; or by a professional with an intellectual rather than a craft background.'[32] Though Renaissance detailing might be one ingredient of the whole it was seen as a decorative dressing rather than as a discipline which pervaded the entire design of the building. So those (often of foreign birth) who purveyed it had not yet usurped the functions of the craftsmen architects who still dominated the British architectural scene at the beginning of the seventeenth century. The way was not yet clear for the genius of a Wren or for the dictatorship of taste of an Earl of Burlington to impose itself on the architecture of an age.

The change, when it came, was the doing, not so much of the builder-

[31] See P. Frankl, 'The Secret of the Mediaeval Masons', *Art Bulletin* xxvii, 1945, and Lon R. Shelby, 'The Geometrical Knowledge of Mediaeval Master Masons', *Speculum* xlvii, 1972.

[32] Mark Girouard, *Robert Smythson and the Architecture of the Elizabethan Era*, 1966, 22–3. See also E. Mercer, *English Art 1553–1625*, 1962, 53–9.

architects as of their patrons. The modern architect did not evolve, as if by an involuntary process, out of the traditional master workman. It is true that changing economic conditions were having their effect on the building trades, notably in releasing them gradually from the restrictions of medieval craft-regulation and in encouraging the growth of the contract system that had made its appearance long before.[33] But neither of these developments did anything to modify their functions in the matter of architectural design. The emergence of the modern architect was therefore due less to changing economic conditions than it was to changing tastes, and in Britain it was the more sophisticated taste of the Stuart court that first allowed a man of genius to exercise the full functions of an architect in the modern sense. That man was Inigo Jones, and it was he who first imposed Italian discipline on English architecture, taking his ideas direct from the Italian masters instead of through the indirect medium of French buildings and German and Flemish pattern-books. The Palladian architecture which Inigo Jones introduced into England was based on a highly sophisticated theory of design which could not well be studied outside Italy, and was beyond the intellectual grasp of the average master builder. Moreover, its execution demanded that the craftsman should subordinate himself to a single controlling mind in a way which he had never been required to do before. It demanded, in fact, the employment of someone whose education had included the conscious study of design, and whose functions were to be supervisory rather than executive: in other words, the architect.

As Surveyor of the Royal Works Inigo Jones was paramount for over twenty years. But he was essentially a court architect, and the extinction of court life during the Civil War and Commonwealth meant a serious setback for his personal influence. Nevertheless, the taste for Italian culture had taken firm root even in the minds of those who were of the parliamentary persuasion, and after the Restoration there was a general demand among the English aristocracy for houses in what Roger North called 'the Grand maniere of Jones'. Although there were one or two master builders who were tolerably well versed in the new style of architecture,[34] they were in a minority, and a person who wished his house to be in a correct taste had either to educate his workmen himself,[35] or, as Sir Roger Pratt advised, to

> get some ingenious gentleman who has seen much of that kind abroad and been somewhat versed in the best authors of Architecture: viz. Palladio, Scamozzi, Serlio, etc. to do it for you, and to give you a design of it in paper, though but roughly drawn, (which will generally fall out

[33] D. Knoop & G. P. Jones, 'The Rise of the Mason Contractor', *R.I.B.A. Jnl.* xliii, 1936.

[34] E.g. Peter Mills and the sons of Nicholas Stone.

[35] As Sir James Pytts had done in 1618 when he lent his mason 'one booke of Architecture . . . which he hath promissed to redeliver unto me' ('The Building of the Manor-House of Kyre Park, Worcestershire', in *The Antiquary* xxii, 1890, 53), and as Sir Roger Townshend did in 1620 when he took his master mason abroad before setting him to build Raynham Hall (below, p. 330).

better than one which shall be given you by a home-bred Architect for want of his better experience, as is daily seen) . . .[36]

The demand thus created was sufficiently general to give employment to a small number of men who specialized in architectural design and supervision. Hugh May, William Samwell and Captain William Winde were architects of the type described by Pratt, gentlemen by birth who supplemented modest private incomes by acting as architects and artistic advisers. In a sense they were the founders of the English architectural profession, but in their lifetimes the conception of such a profession was still in the future, for there was no form of architectural education other than apprenticeship to a building trade, and those who called themselves architects had usually been grounded in some other art or discipline. Inigo Jones himself may have begun life as a painter; so, perhaps, did Hugh May;[37] Balthazar Gerbier was a diplomatist and teacher of aristocratic exercises who merely counted the arts of design among his manifold accomplishments, William Winde a military engineer, and Wren a Professor of Astronomy. Only Webb, who had been 'brought up by his Unckle Mr. Inigo Jones upon his late Maiestyes command in the study of Architecture, as well that wch relates to building as for masques, Tryumphs and the like', could claim to have received a specifically architectural training, and he himself had no disciple. It was the accident of the Great Fire which made Robert Hooke a practising architect, and there must have been others who, like John Evelyn and Roger North, were equally well versed in architectural matters, but who did not 'pretend either to great publick designes, nor new models of great houses'. Even in the eighteenth century it was still possible for a soldier like Vanbrugh or a painter like Kent to achieve celebrity as an architect, and the century was to be well advanced before the system of apprenticeship to a practising architect provided the established basis of a professional training comparable to that offered by the Law or even the Church.[38]

Most people, indeed, still thought it unnecessary to consult anyone but a master workman when undertaking building operations, and some, like Roger North, preferred to make the designs themselves without professional assistance. 'For a profest architect is proud, opiniative and troublesome, seldome at hand, and a head workman pretending to the designing part, is full of paultry vulgar contrivances; therefore be your owne architect, or sitt still', was his advice.[39] It is not surprising, therefore, that very few seventeenth-century architects lived exclusively upon their earnings. Some, like Samwell and Pratt, had small private incomes; others, like Wren and Hooke, enjoyed academic posts; while for Ryder and Webb (and later for Wren) it was the Office of His Majesty's Works which gave them a basic income in return for official duties which left them ample time for private practice.

[36] *The Architecture of Sir Roger Pratt*, ed. R. T. Gunther, 1928, p. 60.

[37] His early connection with Lely at least suggests such a possibility: see p. 647.

[38] R. Campbell, in his *London Tradesman* (1747), says of architects that 'I scarce know of any in England who have had an Education regularly designed for the Profession.'

[39] *Of Building* (B.L., Add. MS. 32540), f. 23.

The importance of the Office of Works in the history of the English architectural profession cannot easily be over-emphasized. In the seventeenth and eighteenth centuries it provided by far the greatest number of posts open to architects in the form of surveyorships and clerkships of the works.[40] The most famous architects of the day sat on its Board, and it was through the agency of the King's Works that so many skilled master craftsmen became acquainted with the latest ideas in design and decoration – ideas which in due course they incorporated in buildings for their own private clients. The Office of Works was, in fact, a kind of unacknowledged substitute for a royal academy of architecture such as Colbert established in France, and it retained its importance as the focus of English architectural activity well into the latter part of the eighteenth century. So long, moreover, as the clerkships of the Works remained in the gift of the Surveyor-General (which they did at least until 1782), the latter was able to find places for his chosen subordinates, and it is in the exercise of this patronage that the 'school' of Wren or Chambers must be sought, rather than in the idea of private pupilage.[41] It was by capturing the Office of Works in the 1730s that Lord Burlington was able to impose his Palladian formula upon the public buildings of London, and so create a tradition of official architecture which lasted to the Second World War.

The importance of the Office of Works in maintaining the tenuous thread of architectural experience is shown by the number of eighteenth-century architects who were either 'bred up in the King's Works' or held office under the Surveyor-General. But outside the royal palaces there was no body of persons trained in architectural drawing and supervision as there is today, and it was not until about the middle of the century that it became possible for a young man to take up architecture as a career, to enter the office of a practising architect, and to learn to design without previously having learned to build. Fortunes were nevertheless to be made by those who had somehow acquired the requisite knowledge and skill to practise the art. 'Few men who have gained any reputation [as architects] but have made good estates,' declared Campbell in 1747,[42] and George Vertue, writing in 1749, placed architecture at the head of the artistic professions. 'I must own,' he said, '[that] the branch of the art of building in Architecture is much improved and many men of that profession has made greater fortunes . . . than any other branch of Art whatever – their manner of undertakings is so profitable, by their agreements at so much per cent for drawings and direction of works of building. . . . Indeed this profession of building has many profitable advantages which makes it worth while to study, travel and labour.'[43]

[40] See Appendix C.

[41] Thus James Elmes observes that Chambers 'educated no pupils – that is to say, as the word is now understood. . . . His only followers or pupils were bred in the office of the Board of Works, in which he held the situation of surveyor-general' ('History of Architecture in Great Britain', in *Civil Engineer and Architect's Jnl.* x, 1847, 300).

[42] *The London Tradesman*, 1747, 157.

[43] Walpole Society, *Vertue Note Books* iii, 146, 150.

The first English architect who was in the habit of taking pupils appears to have been Sir Robert Taylor, of whom it was said that he and James Paine 'nearly divided the practice of the profession between them' until the advent of the brothers Adam.[44] His rival followed his example, and by the third quarter of the eighteenth century it was usual for the London architect to have in his office one or more young men who were at once his pupils and his assistants. Their status was that of articled clerks, unless they had sufficient experience to rank as 'improvers', in which case they would receive a small weekly wage in addition to board and lodging. Such an apprenticeship, commencing at the age of 16, lasted for five or six years,[45] and in the course of it the intelligent pupil had ample opportunity to learn the essentials of architectural draughtsmanship and professional practice. He would, at the same time, seek to attend the lectures of the Professor of Architecture at the Royal Academy, and would show the best of his own essays in design at the annual exhibition under the address of his tutor and master. He might even gain one of the medals (two silver and one gold)[46] offered annually by the Academy for students' work, or gain a 'premium' from the Society of Arts. At the end of his apprenticeship, he aspired to travel – certainly to Rome and northern Italy, if possible to Sicily and Greece, perhaps even to Asia Minor and the Levant. There, for two or three never-to-be-forgotten years, he measured, drew and sometimes excavated the monuments of antiquity, forming a collection of sketches and measured drawings upon which he could draw for inspiration in the future, and some of which he would later work up for future Royal Academy exhibitions. Thus at the age of 25 or 26 the young architect was fully equipped for professional practice. If he was lucky, he obtained a post as surveyor to a corporation, a charity, a fire insurance office or a private estate until such time as, through friends, influence, or success in a public competition, he laid the foundations of a successful private practice and began to take pupils of his own. If he was unlucky – and the indications are that by the beginning of the nineteenth century architecture was attracting more aspirants than it could gainfully employ – he spent his life as an assistant in another architect's office, combined architecture with some other occupation, or gave it up altogether. A good many casualties of this sort will be found in the pages of this Dictionary, but successful careers were open to those in whom creative skill was matched by business ability. The worldly wealth of Sir Robert Taylor, Sir William Chambers or Henry Holland was

[44] Hardwick's 'Memoir of Sir William Chambers', prefaced to Gwilt's edition of *A Treatise on the Decorative Part of Civil Architecture*, 1825.

[45] See the terms of apprenticeship to Sir John Soane, given by A. T. Bolton, *Architectural Education a Century Ago* (Soane Museum Publication No. 12): see also R.I.B.A. *Sessional Papers*, 1855–6, p. 1, for Sir William Tite's statement that a six years' apprenticeship was normal in the early nineteenth century.

[46] For a list of the gold medallists, see J. E. Hodgson & F. A. Eaton, *History of the Royal Academy*, 1905, Appendix VII. A travelling studentship was also offered, but as it was tenable for several years, and awarded alternately from those attending the Schools of Painting, Sculpture and Architecture, the chances of obtaining it were small. The architects who held it during the period 1769–1840 were John Soane (1777), George Hadfield (1790), Lewis Vulliamy (1818), Samuel Loat (1828) and John Johnson (1837).

not derived exclusively from professional fees, but in the next generation Sir John Soane made a fortune strictly by professional activity, and the Probate records show that by the reign of Victoria a leading London architect could expect to leave a substantial estate to his heirs.[47] Architecture had, in fact, become a reputable and remunerative occupation which an ambitious parent could contemplate with favour for his son – one which no longer depended upon the uncertainties of aristocratic patronage or the doubtful devices of speculative building. The architect had at last taken his place alongside the doctor and the lawyer, and it would not be long before he began to formulate his own standards of professional conduct and to create an organization through which they could be enforced.

In Scotland the development of an architectural profession took essentially the same course. Here, as in England, it was from the ranks of the building tradesmen that the professional architect began to emerge in the course of the eighteenth century. In Edinburgh competence in draughtsmanship had been a necessary qualification for membership of the Incorporation of Masons at least since the early seventeenth century. Thus when James Smith, soon to be Edinburgh's leading architect, applied for admittance in 1680, he was required to draw plans of a large three-storey, double-pile house with four pavilions and a Doric doorway (the last to be drawn to a larger scale). In this way the expertise gained through apprenticeship to an established master was formally tested in a way that was unique to Scotland. On the other hand, the lack after the Union of a Scottish Office of Works meant that there was no established hierarchy of posts to which the leading Scottish architects could aspire, which helps to explain why so many of them chose (like the Adam brothers) to seek employment in England. In Scotland, even more than in England, cultivated gentry played a large part in the formation of architectural taste, but architects like James Smith and William Adam have their place in the history of the Scottish Enlightenment, and by the reign of George III Robert Adam, Robert Mylne and James Playfair were pre-eminent as neo-classical architects in England as well as in their native country. That they thought of themselves very much as professionals is clear from a letter that the Adam brothers wrote to an English client in the 1770s: 'it is of little consequence to us what the practice is, among professional builders. We are not builders by profession, but Architects and Surveyors, & live by those Branches.'[48]

By the accession of George III, there was in Britain the nucleus of an architectural profession, but the implications of professional status had hardly begun to make themselves felt in the minds of the architects themselves, still less in those of their patrons. Most architects supplemented their incomes by building speculations, and were thought none the worse of for

[47] Sir Robert Smirke's estate was valued for probate at £90,000. Barry and Blore both left £80,000, Decimus Burton and Lewis Vulliamy £60,000, Burn £40,000 and C. R. Cockerell £35,000.

[48] H. Colvin, 'The beginnings of the architectural profession in Scotland', *Arch. Hist.* 29, 1986.

doing so;[49] nearly all were prepared to contract for the erection of the buildings which they designed;[50] and some acted in the additional capacity of house- and estate-agents. Moreover, there was still no provision for the academic study of design, no place for the exhibition of drawings and models, no forum in which architects could exchange ideas and enjoy one another's society. A few architects had, it is true, been admitted to artists' clubs, like the *Society of Virtuosi of St. Luke,* which counted William Talman, James Gibbs, Christopher Wren, junior, and William Kent among its members; but the activities of such societies were chiefly convivial and their existence was often brief.[51] The 'Society for the improvement of knowledge in Arts and Sciences' to which Robert Morris read his *Lectures on Architecture* in about 1730 was presumably a more serious affair, but seems to have been equally short-lived. Some architects were Fellows of the Royal Society, and the profession has always been well represented in the Society of Antiquaries, but neither body took more than an indirect interest in architectural matters and none in contemporary architectural practice.

In France architecture was catered for by its own Academy, founded by Colbert in 1671, but in spite of frequent pleas for an artistic academy in this country,[52] it was not until 1768 that the idea came to fruition in the Royal Academy of Arts. The truth is, that in the early eighteenth century England was still too dependent upon foreign artists to justify the creation of a national academy, while the political atmosphere was not favourable to the establishment of an institution so closely associated elsewhere with royal absolutism.[53] It was, characteristically, through the agency of a private but highly aristocratic body that England nearly achieved her academy of the arts in the middle of the century. The *Society of Dilettanti* acquired a site in Cavendish Square for the purpose, and in 1755 entered into negotiations with a committee of artists who submitted a detailed plan for the management of the proposed academy. As no less than six of them were architects,[54] it may be presumed that architecture would have been adequately represented in an academy established under the patronage of the Society which sponsored the publication of the *Antiquities of Athens*. But the project came to nothing,

[49] Wren's Bridgewater Square, Barbican, Paine's Salisbury Street, Strand, Holland's Hans Town, Chelsea, and the Adams' Adelphi Buildings are major examples of speculative building by architects.

[50] 'The Architect either undertakes the whole work for a certain Sum, or is paid for superintending the work only' (R. Campbell, *The London Tradesman,* 1747, 155).

[51] Whitley, *Artists and Their Friends in England, 1700–1799* i, 1928, 68–70, 74–7; ii, 241–4.

[52] Cf. Stephen Switzer, *The Nobleman, Gentleman and Gardener's Recreation*, 1715, 237; George Vertue, *Note Books* (Walpole Society) ii, 150–5; iii, 74; John Gwynn, *An Essay on Design including Proposals for Erecting a Public Academy to be supplied by Voluntary Subscription (until a Royal Foundation can be obtain'd) for Educating British Youth in Drawing*, 1749; Nesbitt, *Essay on the Necessity of a Royal Academy*, 1755. Matthew Brettingham junior's scheme for a British Academy is outlined in a letter, dated 27 May 1753, in Holkham MS. 744, ff. 136–9.

[53] N. Pevsner, *Academies of Art*, 1940, 126.

[54] John Gwynn, Robert Taylor, James Stuart, Isaac Ware, Nicholas Revett and Thomas Sandby.

partly (as the younger Matthew Brettingham reported)[55] because of the difficulty of raising money, and partly because the Dilettanti demanded a dominant share in the government of the Academy, which the artists were not prepared to concede.[56]

In 1754 architecture received encouragement from a somewhat different quarter. This was the foundation of the *Society for the Encouragement of Arts, Manufactures, and Commerce,* now known as the Royal Society of Arts.[57] Although its primary concern was the encouragement of industrial art, it also sought to promote the 'polite arts' (which included architecture), on the ground that 'the Art of Drawing is absolutely necessary in many employments, trades and manufactures.' So far as architecture was concerned, it did this chiefly by offering small monetary awards for promising designs by student architects. A considerable number of young men received encouragement in this way, and the 'Register of Premiums' includes the names of Edward Stevens, James Gandon, John Plaw, Robert Baldwin and George Richardson.[58]

The Society also provided wall-space for the first public exhibition of paintings in this country, held in April 1760. It was intended to make this an annual event, and to maintain with the proceeds a fund for old and infirm artists. But as the Society would not permit any charge to be made for admission, and also interfered with the hanging of the pictures, the majority of the artists soon seceded and founded their own Society of Artists (incorporated in 1765), which held exhibitions in a room at Spring Gardens from 1761 onwards. Both the *Incorporated Society of Artists* and the rival *Free Society of Artists* (as those who continued to hold exhibitions with the Society of Arts called themselves) had architects among their members, and both admitted architectural drawings to their exhibitions.[59] Architects were, moreover, prominent in the management of the Incorporated Society, and Chambers and Paine both played a leading part in the internal dissensions which led to its eventual dissolution. Paine was one of those who did his best to keep it in being, while Chambers took the initiative in founding a new body to take its place.[60] This was the Royal Academy of Arts (founded in 1768), which in due course rendered both the older societies redundant, the Free Society holding its last exhibition in 1783, the Incorporated Society in 1791.

The *Royal Academy*, with its royal charter and its rooms in Somerset House alongside the Royal and Antiquarian Societies, represented the first

[55] Holkham MS. 744, f. 136.

[56] Whitley, *Artists and Their Friends* i, 157–8; L. Cust, *History of the Society of Dilettanti*, ed. Colvin, 1898, 53–5.

[57] H. T. Wood, *A History of the Royal Society of Arts*, 1913. Its early members included George Dance, senior, Robert Mylne, James Paine, Sir William Chambers and the three Adam brothers.

[58] See the *Register of Premiums* awarded between 1754 and 1776, printed in 1778.

[59] See A. Graves, *The Society of Artists of Great Britain and the Free Society of Artists*, 1907, and Horace Walpole's notes printed by H. Gatty in *Walpole Society* xxvii, 1938–9.

[60] Whitley, *Artists and their Friends in England* i, 1928, 248, where the degree of personal rivalry between Chambers and Paine is, however, greatly exaggerated.

official recognition of the place which native artists and architects had created for themselves in the life of the nation. Five of the thirty-six original Academicians were architects,[61] and the post of Treasurer was given to Sir William Chambers, whose successors in office were, for over a hundred years, to be members of his profession.[62] Architectural drawings were hung at the annual exhibitions, and the designs for almost every building of importance erected during the latter part of the period covered by this book were shown at the Royal Academy.[63] Moreover, the Instrument by which the Academy was established provided for the appointment of a Professor of Architecture, 'who shall read annually six public lectures, calculated to form the taste of the Students, to instruct them in the laws and principles of composition, to point out to them the beauties or faults of celebrated productions, to fit them for an unprejudiced study of books, and for a critical examination of structures'.[64] Although these professorial lectures could hardly be said to create a school of architecture, admission to the 'Royal Academy Schools' was eagerly sought by young men serving their time in an architect's office, and for more than fifty years formed a regular part of almost every architect's education. So far as his seniors were concerned, election as A.R.A. or R.A. was the acknowledged recognition of professional eminence.

But the handful of architect R.A.s was inevitably in a permanent minority in a body composed mainly of painters, and even Sir William Chambers, dominant though he was in its counsels for nearly thirty years, showed no wish to increase their number or in any way to associate the Academy with the interests of the architectural profession as such.[65] It was inevitable, therefore, that the first steps towards a professional association should have come from outside the Academy, though it was not until nearly twenty-five years after its foundation that the leading architects practising in London became sufficiently conscious of their mutual interests to form a society composed exclusively of members of their own profession. *The Architects' Club*, as it was called, was founded in 1791 by James Wyatt, George Dance, Henry Holland and S. P. Cockerell, and met once a month at the Thatched House Tavern in St. James's.[66] Its composition was highly select, for no one could be a member who was not an R.A., A.R.A. or Gold Medallist, or a member of the Academies of Rome, Parma, Florence or Paris.[67] Moreover, a

[61] Sir William Chambers, John Gwynn, Thomas Sandby, W. Tyler and George Dance, junior.

[62] His immediate successors were John Yenn (1796–1820), Sir Robert Smirke (1820–50), Philip Hardwick (1850–61) and Sydney Smirke (1861–74).

[63] See A. Graves, *The Royal Academy of Arts, 1769–1804*, 8 vols., 1907.

[64] For holders of the Professorship, see Appendix C.

[65] Cf. Dr. H. M. Martienssen's unpublished London Ph.D. thesis on *The Architectural Theory and Practice of Sir William Chambers*, 1949, 143–6.

[66] The original members, in addition to the four founders, were Sir William Chambers, Robert Adam, Robert Mylne, Richard Jupp, James Lewis, Richard Norris, John Soane, John Yenn, Thomas Hardwick, Robert Brettingham and James Paine, junior (T. Mulvany, *Life of James Gandon*, 1846, 295–7).

[67] The insistence upon foreign travel was abandoned in 1803 owing to the Napoleonic War (*The Farington Diary*, ed. J. Greig, ii, 123).

single black ball was sufficient to exclude a candidate from admission.[68] Honorary membership was reserved for those whose place of residence was outside London.[69]

Although primarily a dining club, the Architects' Club was not without a sense of its responsibilities as an association of professional men.[70] In 1792 some of its members met in order 'to define the profession and qualifications of an architect',[71] and in 1796 Mylne laid before it a resolution forbidding one architect from interfering in another's commission.[72] In the previous year it had appointed a committee to go into the question of architects' charges. This was a matter upon which Soane held strong views, and his refusal to accept the majority decision to make a measuring charge of 2½ per cent, in addition to the customary 5 per cent for designs and supervision, led to his estrangement from the other members of the Club.[73] This was by no means the only matter over which the Club was divided, and Soane told Farington early in 1796 that he did not think it would last long, 'the members consisting only of persons who are too much in a state of rivalship and frequently crossing each other'.[74] In fact, it survived for at least thirty years.[75] But little more is heard of its activities, and it is clear that so exclusive a body could never adequately represent the interests of a rapidly growing profession.[76]

It is not surprising, therefore, that attempts were made to establish other associations of a more representative character. The first of these was the *Surveyors' Club,* founded in 1792 by sixteen surveyors who met at the Shakespeare Tavern to discuss 'the propriety of forming a meeting of Surveyors on some general and beneficial principles'. But its objects were chiefly of a social and charitable nature, and only three or four of its twenty-four original members were in practice as architects.[77] The rest were District Surveyors appointed under the Act of 1774, or men of the type described in

[68] George Hadfield, a Gold Medallist of the Royal Academy, was so excluded in 1795, much to the annoyance of James Wyatt, who was one of his proposers (*The Farington Diary*, ed. J. Greig, i, 85).

[69] John Carr, Nicholas Revett and Thomas Sandby were the first Honorary Members. James Gandon was elected in Dec. 1791.

[70] W. L. Spiers, 'The Architects' Club', *R.I.B.A. Jnl.*, 3rd ser., xviii, 1911, 240.

[71] A. T. Bolton, *Portrait of Sir John Soane*, 67.

[72] Barrington Kaye, *The Development of the Architectural Profession in Britain*, 1960, 59.

[73] A. T. Bolton, *Portrait of Sir John Soane*, 76–7. A skit by Soane on the members of the Club and their pretensions is preserved in MS. in the Soane Museum (Envelope F. Div. 14, No. 40). It is in the form of a dialogue between a representative of the Club and a cadidate for membership.

[74] *The Farington Diary*, ed. J. Greig, i, 137.

[75] See the lists of members published in the *British Imperial Kalendar* between 1812 and 1824.

[76] In 1834 its members were invited to participate in the foundation of an architectural institute, but declined 'altering the character or extending the views of the club' (*A Plain Statement of Facts connected with the Coalition between the Society for the Promotion of Architecture and Architectural Topography and the Society of British Architects*, 1834, 11).

[77] E.g. William Purser, Edward Mawley and Peter Upsdell. Other members were James Burton, the builder, and Henry Hurle, a carpenter who founded the 'Ancient Order of Druids'.

contemporary directories as 'Surveyor and Builder'.[78] More important for the history of the architectural profession was the *London Architectural Society,* founded in 1806. The reason given for its establishment was that 'among the Institutions so liberally established in this city there is not one calculated for the encouragement of Architecture. The feeble protection afforded by the Royal Academy can hardly be deemed an exception.[79] The lectures have long ceased,[80] and medals privately distributed, and the use of a library for a few hours one day in the week, and at a time when it is hardly possible for the student in architecture to attend . . . cannot be deemed of much value', while the 'few clubs which have been formed by persons in the profession, are rather to enjoy the pleasures of good fellowship among men engaged in the same pursuit, than for the advancement of the art'.[81] The method proposed for the advancement of the art was to require every member to produce annually an original architectural design, under forfeiture of two guineas, and an essay, under forfeiture of half a guinea. The Society met once a fortnight in order to discuss these productions, and anyone who was absent from two successive meetings was fined 5s. The designs and essays were to remain the property of the Society, which undertook to publish such as were considered worthy of the honour. The Society attracted some of the more literary members of the profession, such as Joseph Woods, its president, James Elmes and James Peacock, and it published at least two volumes of its essays.[82] But rules of such severity were hardly calculated to attract a large membership, and the life of the Society was earnest but short.

A somewhat more genial association was the *Architects' and Antiquaries' Club*, which was founded in December 1819 by ten gentlemen who, having observed the value of foreign academies of architecture, 'could not resist the mortifying contrast which was presented, in comparing the state of Architecture in those cities with that of this kingdom'. The society was to consist of twenty members, and there were to be six dinners annually at the Freemasons' Tavern. Each member was expected 'occasionally to furnish the Society with an Essay on a Subject of Antient Architecture, or some branch of Antiquity connected with domestic economy or the fine Arts'. The members included Edward Cresy, Joseph Gwilt, Augustus Pugin, J. Sanders (its first president) and G. L. Taylor (his successor). The antiquary John Britton acted as Treasurer and Honorary Secretary, and there were two Honorary

[78] I am indebted to the officers of the Surveyors' Club for their courtesy in allowing me to examine its records.

[79] The Academy's attitude towards its architectural responsibilities is strongly criticized in *The Library of the Fine Arts* iv, 1832, 213–19; see also John Britton's complaint in *Portrait of Sir John Soane*, 317.

[80] Dance, who held the Chair of Architecture from 1798 to 1805, delivered no lectures.

[81] From the preface to *Essays of the London Architectural Society*, 1808.

[82] For some account of the Society, see *The Builder* xxi, 1863, 86, 112–13, 140. Other members were James Savage (vice-president), C. A. Busby (secretary), Edmund Aikin, W. H. Ashpitel, Samuel Beazley, J. G. Bubb, the sculptor, Coade, the artificial stone manufacturer, and Josiah Taylor, the architectural publisher.

and Corresponding Members, John Foster of Liverpool and S. T. Whitwell of Leamington.[83]

But, however profitable this intercourse between the architects and the amateurs may have been, it was no substitute for a professional association, the lack of which continued to be deplored both by those in practice, who needed its protection against inadequate remuneration and unfair competition, and by their pupils, who compared the meagre ration of instruction which they received at the Royal Academy with the life-classes and other facilities enjoyed by the more favoured students of painting and sculpture.[84] Three figures stand out in this period of uncertainty during which the architectural profession was slowly feeling its way towards that Insitute of British Architects which all realized was the ultimate goal: Sir John Soane, who by his personal example set a standard of professional conduct which all respected and some emulated; James Elmes, better known as a writer than as a practising architect, who in either capacity lost no opportunity of impressing the need for association both upon his fellow-architects and upon the general public; and Thomas Leverton Donaldson, the leader of the younger generation, who was to live to become President of the Institute of British Architects, and to hear himself hailed as 'father of his profession' by the Prince of Wales.[85]

It was on Elmes's initiative that the first serious attempt to create a professional organization took place in 1810. A meeting of architects was held in his house, in order to take steps to establish a Royal Academy of Architecture, with a Library and a Museum of Models. Details of the scheme were sent to all the leading architects in London, and favourable replies were received from 'Messrs. Nash, Jeffry and Lewis Wyatt, Ware, Gwilt, Hardwick, Porden, Gandy, Tatham, Bond, Beazley, Lewis and other eminent professors'. Elmes afterwards 'drew it out in the shape of a letter' to Thomas Hope, which he published in *The Pamphleteer*.[86] But, as he afterwards confessed, 'little was done, except in private compliments to me, and one Review which noticed it'.[87]

[83] Records of the Society are preserved in the Bodleian Library, Gough Adds. London 8° 405.

[84] See an article 'On the Condition of the Architectural Students in the Royal Academy of London compared with those of other Nations' in *Annals of the Fine Arts* ii, 1817, 19, and cf. *Monthly Magazine*, July 1809.

[85] Donaldson was the founder of the *Architectural Students' Society*, whose members were in the habit of meeting together 'to make a design or a sketch from a given subject, or to discuss a paper'. In 1817, as a young man of 26, he organized a meeting of architectural students in Pall Mall to petition the Royal Academy 'to form a School of Architecture and allow them a further extension of the use of their Library'. The Academicians received this demonstration 'in good part', and agreed to open the Library twice a week in term-time instead of only once. But nothing was done to meet the more important demand that Architecture should be placed on the same footing as Sculpture and Painting in the Royal Academy Schools. (*Annals of the Fine Arts* ii, 1817, 124, 258, 340; *The Farington Diary*, ed. J. Greig, viii, 114, 115; R.I.B.A. *Sessional Papers*, 1855–6, 2; R.I.B.A. Library, Pam. Q.11, No. 2.)

[86] 'A Letter to Thomas Hope Esq. on the insufficiency of the existing establishments for promoting the Fine Arts towards that of Architecture and its Professors', *The Pamphleteer* iii, 1814, 330.

[87] *Annals of the Fine Arts* ii, 1817, 261–2.

Much the same happened in 1819 when a fresh series of meetings was held in order to discuss a 'Proposed Institution for the Cultivation and Encouragement of Architecture'. Elmes was appointed secretary, and a number of resolutions were passed which were published in *Annals of the Fine Arts*[88] – a periodical which (under Elmes's editorship) consistently championed the cause of architecture.

There, it would seem, the matter rested until 1831, when a renewed attempt to unite the profession resulted in the formation of the *Architectural Society*, whose ultimate ambition was 'to form a British School of Architecture, affording the advantages of a Library, Museum, Professorships and periodical exhibitions'.[89] It began with a membership of over forty, and attracted some eminent Victorian architects.[90] The Duke of Sussex agreed to become its patron, and in 1835 Sir John Soane signified his approval of its aspirations by the gift of £250.[91] But in spite of all that it did to provide improved facilities for architectural students, the Architectural Society did not satisfy the urgent need for an association which would seek to define the obligations of an architect towards his client, and at the same time to gain for its members a status in business and society comparable to that enjoyed by other professional men. It was with these objects that, in 1834, a committee was formed which included the names of P. F. Robinson (its chairman), T. L. Donaldson (its chief organizer), Charles Fowler, J. Goldicutt, H. E. Kendall, James Savage and James Noble.[92] Its purpose was to draw up a scheme for the formation of an institute 'to uphold the character and improve the attainments of Architects'. The result of its deliberations was a prospectus explaining the need for such an institute, defining its objects, and setting out its proposed constitution. There was to be a 'Library of works of every kind connected with Architecture' and a 'Museum of Antiquities, Models and Casts'; there were to be 'periodical meetings of the members for the purpose of discussion and improvement by lecture, essay, or illustration', and provision was to be made for the instruction of students in 'the various branches of Science connected with Architecture in addition to those attainable in an Architect's Office, and not provided by any existing Institution'. Membership was to be divided into two classes – Fellows, who were to be elected from architects who had been established in practice for not less than five years, and Associates, who were to be admitted by examination.[93]

[88] Vol. iv, 1819, 348–51.

[89] A copy of its printed *Laws and Regulations* is in Sir John Soane's Museum. Its first president was W. B. Clarke, and the members of the committee were T. H. Wyatt, Benjamin Ferrey, A. W. and J. H. Hakewill, T. M. Nelson, Thomas Walker, George Moore and George Mair. Reports of its meetings were published in Loudon's *Architectural Magazine* and in the *Gent's Mag.*

[90] Including David Brandon, G. E. Street, Ewan Christian and Sir William Tite (President, 1838–42).

[91] A. T. Bolton, *Portrait of Sir John Soane*, 514.

[92] Author of a work on *The Professional Practice of Architects*, 1836.

[93] The prospectus is printed by Bolton, *Portrait of Sir John Soane*, 509–12. See also the 'Address and Regulations of the Institute of British Architects, explanatory of their Views and Objects', printed in the *Architectural Magazine* ii, 1835, 305–6.

This prospectus was sent to a number of leading architects, who agreed to become original members, and Sir John Soane, the lifelong advocate of professional standards in architecture and the most distinguished member of his profession, was offered the presidency. This he was obliged to decline owing to a rule prohibiting Royal Academicians from becoming members of any other society of artists, but he indicated his approval of the Institute's programme by a gift of £750. At the same time he presented the sum of £250 already mentioned to the Architectural Society, expressing a hope that the two bodies might before long be united – an event which eventually took place in 1842, largely through the efforts of Sir William Tite.

Meanwhile, Earl de Grey had consented to give the Institute the benefit of his social and political influence, and it was under his presidency that the first meeting was held on 3 June 1835. T. L. Donaldson, now Honorary Secretary, was able to announce that the Institute already counted eighty members, that contacts had been established with several foreign academies, and that the nucleus of a library had been formed. In 1836 the Institute began the publication of its *Transactions*, and in 1837 it received the final recognition of a royal charter of incorporation.[94]

With the foundation of the *Institute of British Architects*, architecture had at last achieved its acknowledged place among the professions, and although much remained to be done – both from within the Institute and from without – to work out all the implications of that status, its attainment marks the end of the process which it has been the object of this Introduction to trace. No Victorian barrister would have dared to question a Fellow of the Institute of British Architects in the terms in which counsel is reported[95] to have addressed himself to Daniel Asher Alexander:

> 'You are a builder, I believe?'
>
> 'No, sir; I am not a builder; I am an architect.'
>
> 'Ah well, builder or architect, architect or builder – they are pretty much the same, I suppose?'
>
> 'I beg your pardon; they are totally different.'
>
> 'Oh, indeed! Perhaps you will state wherein this difference consists.'
>
> 'An architect, sir, conceives the design, prepares the plan, draws out the specification – in short, supplies the mind. The builder is merely the machine; the architect the power that puts the machine together and sets it going.'

[94] It was not, however, until 1866 that the Institute was officially authorized to add the epithet 'Royal' to its title. The Royal Gold Medal had been instituted by Queen Victoria in 1848. For the Institute's subsequent history see *The Growth and Work of the R.I.B.A 1834–1934*, ed. J. A. Gotch, 1934. An *Institute of the Architects of Scotland* was founded in 1840 under the presidency of the 5th Duke of Buccleuch, but collapsed almost immediately owing to a dispute over the eligibility for membership of David Bryce, who was not yet in independent practice. It was refounded in 1850 as the *Architectural Institute of Scotland*, again with the Duke of Buccleuch as President.

[95] *Builder* xx, 795. The interrogator is said to have been Sir James Scarlett (1769–1844), and the case was probably that of Chapman, Gardiner and Upward *v.* De Tastet (1817), reported in *Annals of the Fine Arts* iii, 1818, 560–65, in which Scarlett appeared for the defendant.

'Oh, very well, Mr. Architect, that will do. A very ingenious distinction without a difference. Do you happen to know who was the architect of the Tower of Babel?'

'There was no architect, sir. Hence the confusion.'

In fact, the Victorian architect, if he were a man of any ability or enterprise, was well able to make a living without maintaining that connection with the building trade which had been the chief resource of so many of his Georgian predecessors. Churches, prisons, town halls, bridges, warehouses and factories were going up apace in the industrial towns of the Midlands and the north, while country houses and suburban villas continued to provide rich commissions for the domestic architect. The improvement in communications meant that the new professional architect, while retaining his London office, could personally supervise the erection of half a dozen buildings at once, in a way that had been quite impossible for his eighteenth-century predecessor, who supplied a plan and elevation, answered queries by letter, and relied on the experience and discretion of his master craftsmen to give satisfaction to his client and observe the established rules of sound building. The Industrial Revolution, which provided the professional architect with so many new opportunities, also provided him with the means to exploit them, and his triumph came in the 1840s and 1850s with the railways, which enabled a Gilbert Scott to rebuild half the parish churches of England in accordance with his own conception of Gothic architecture, and finally destroyed the autonomy of the local builder.

With the fruits of these developments this Introduction is not concerned, for they are part of the history of Victorian architecture, and as such lie outside the chronological scope of this book. Most of the men whose biographies it contains saw England from the road, not from the rail, and there were few of them who had no connection with the building trade in one or other of its forms, from the Smiths of Warwick, who were builders first and architects last, to Sir Jeffry Wyatville, the 'honourable augmentation' of whose name did not conceal the fact that he was descended from a typical eighteenth-century building family, or that he himself was 'taken into a profitable partnership by John Armstrong, a large builder of Pimlico'.[96] Sir William Chambers was the contractor for, as well as the architect of, the houses which he built at Peper Harow and Roehampton, and most architects of his generation were prepared to submit an estimate upon which they obtained advances of money, making contracts with the tradesmen, and not infrequently taking a discount or percentage from them in addition to whatever remuneration they obtained from their employer.[97] But this was a very

[96] *D.N.B.*

[97] *A.P.S.D.*, *s.v.*, 'ARCHITECT' and 'CONTRACTOR'. Such practices were denounced in vain by Robert Morris in *The Qualifications and Duty of a Surveyor, explained in a Letter to the Rt. Hon. the Earl of* ——, 1752, and in *A Second Letter to the Rt. Hon. the Earl of* —— *concerning the Qualifications and Duty of a Surveyor*, 1752. See also the anonymous article 'On the Present State of the Professions of Architect, Surveyor, and of the Building Trade in England' in Loudon's *Architectural Magazine* i, 1834, 12–16.

different matter from the earlier identity of builder and designer which had survived from the Middle Ages. It opened the way for dishonesty and shoddy building, and it made Sir John Soane's definition of an architect's duties, uncompromising in its rejection of the past, the only possible basis upon which the new profession was to achieve the respect of the public:

> The business of the Architect is to make the designs and estimates, to direct the works, and to measure and value the different parts; he is the intermediate agent between the employer, whose honour and interest he is to study, and the mechanic, whose rights he is to defend. His position implies great trust; he is responsible for the mistakes, negligences, and ignorance of those he employs; and above all, he is to take care that the workmen's bills do not exceed his own estimates. If these are the duties of an Architect, with what propriety can his situation, and that of the builder or the contractor, be united?

When this was first published in 1788[98] Soane's was a voice crying in the wilderness, but by 1835, when it was reprinted in his memoirs, he was preaching to the converted. Jeffry Wyatville had found to his mortification that, despite his extensive practice, he was allowed to remain a candidate for admission to membership of the Royal Academy for twenty years, because the 'union of the tradesman with the architect was deemed, by the Royal Academicians, a sufficient bar to the advancement of Mr. Jeffry Wyatt to be one of their society'.[99] When the founders of the Institute of British Architects drew up their prospectus, they had no hestitation in decreeing that divorce between Architecture and Building which subsequent practice made absolute. No architect was to be eligible for membership who received 'any pecuniary consideration, or emolument, from Tradesmen, or who had any interest or participation in any Trade or Contract connected with Building'. Henceforth no architect would be able to supplement his income by speculative building, nor even by measuring and valuing works on behalf of builders. But whatever he may have lost in financial opportunity, he gained in social status and respectability: for henceforth he would rank as a gentleman, a scholar and an artist, clearly distinguished from the 'mechanic' who called himself a builder. For his client the gain was equally great: for now he could entrust his architectural affairs to his architect with the same confidence with which previously he had been accustomed to place his legal affairs in the hands of his lawyer. No longer would he be subjected to the confusion, the expense, above all the exasperation, which (as anyone who is familiar with the minutes of eighteenth-century building committees will know) so often resulted from the haphazard methods and ill-defined responsibilities of the time when the architectural profession was still in the making.

[98] In his *Plans, Elevations and Sections of Buildings executed in several Counties*, p. 7.
[99] *Gent's Mag.* xiii, 1840, 546.

A

ABEL, JOHN (*c.*1578–1675), was a master carpenter who was responsible for several notable examples of the ornamental timber-framed architecture characteristic of the West Midlands in the sixteenth and seventeenth centuries. He lived at Sarnesfield near Leominster in Herefordshire, where a table-tomb in the churchyard refers to him as an 'architector' and records his death in 1674 in his 97th year.[1] The parish register shows that he was buried on 31 January 1674/5.

According to the collections for a history of Herefordshire made by Thomas Blount (d. 1679), Abel built the timber-framed market houses at BRECON, 1624 (dem.), KINGTON,[2] 1654 (dem. 1820), and LEOMINSTER, 1633 (dismantled 1861 and rebuilt as a house called 'Grange Court'), and distinguished himself during the Civil War by constructing a corn-mill for use by the royalist forces besieged in Hereford in 1645. [Camden's *Britannia*, ed. Gough, ii, 1789, 460, citing Blount MSS.]

In 1625 Abel contracted to build the plain stone GRAMMAR SCHOOL at KINGTON for £240 [*The History of Kington, by a member of the Mechanics Institute,* Kington, 1845, 164–5]. In 1633 he was employed by Lord Scudamore to 'Survay the woorkes for reparing' ABBEY DORE CHURCH, HEREFS., and surviving accounts show that he performed the structural carpentry of the roofs himself. Presumably he also designed the handsome wooden screen [H. M. Colvin, 'The Restoration of Abbey Dore Church in 1633–4', *Trans. Woolhope Naturalists' Field Club* xxxii, 1948, 235–7]. In March 1652/3, as 'John Abell of Sarnesfield, carpenter', he contracted to erect a 'new building' at TYBBERTON COURT, HEREFS., for William Greene [Hereford R.O., L. C. Deed 880 and Brydges Papers 3471]. This does not survive. The attribution to Abel of various other buildings, including the very elaborate timber-framed Market Hall at Hereford (late sixteenth century, dem. 1862) cannot be substantiated. [R. A. Ford, 'John Abel, a 17th century Architector', *Trans. Woolhope Naturalists' Field Club*, 1963–8, pp. cvii–cix; N. Drinkwater, 'The Old Market Hall, Hereford', *ibid.* xxxiii, 1949–51, 1–13.]

ABRAHAM, ROBERT (1774–1850), was the son of a builder, and became a pupil of the surveyor James Bowen. It was as a London building surveyor that he began his professional life, and it was not until after the Napoleonic War that, in middle age, he developed a successful practice as an architect. He was fortunate enough to be employed by 'some of the chief Roman Catholic families in England', and many of his most important commissions were due to the patronage of the 12th Duke of Norfolk. He was a competent practitioner in the diverse styles expected of an English architect in the early nineteenth century, but his reputation rested on reliability rather than originality as a designer. His best-known work, the County Fire Office at the top of Lower Regent Street, was an effective re-creation of the south front of Old Somerset House, then believed to be the work of Inigo Jones.

Abraham's extensive knowledge of building practice was passed on to a number of pupils, including his son H. R. Abraham (who died in 1877, aged 73), G. Alexander, H. Flower, J. Lockyer, Thomas Little, T. Mackintosh, R. E. Philips, M. J. Stutely, C. Verelst and J. Woolley. His eldest daughter married Richard Bethell, Baron Westbury, Lord Chancellor 1861–5, whose influence procured for H. R. Abraham the commission for the Middle Temple Library. Abraham died on 11 December 1850, and was buried in the extension of Hampstead churchyard. His wife Eliza (d. 1818), the daughter of the botanical artist Peter Brown, was an accomplished flower-painter. [*Builder* viii, 1850, 598, 602; *A.P.S.D.*; *Gent's Mag.* 1818 (ii), 644; T. A. Nash, *Life of Richard Lord Westbury*, 1888, i, 44, 49, ii, 13.]

KENTON LANE FARM, WEALDSTONE, MIDDLESEX, for William Loudon, *c.*1808; dem. [J. C. Loudon, *Observations on Laying Out Farms in the Scotch Style*, 1812, 75n.].

WOODHALL FARM, PINNER, MIDDLESEX, remodelled for William Loudon, *c.*1808–9 [*ibid*].

LONDON, COUNTY FIRE OFFICE, REGENT STREET, 1819; dem. 1924 [*Builder, ut supra*] (measured drawings in *Arch. Rev.* lvi, 1924, 243–8).

LONDON, Nos. 176–86 REGENT STREET, for J. Carbonell, wine-merchant, 1820; dem. [*Builder, ut supra*; drawing by Abraham reproduced in *C. Life*, 26 Oct. 1961, Supplement, 22].

LONDON, NORFOLK HOUSE, ST. JAMES'S SQUARE, alterations and stables in Charles Street for 12th Duke of Norfolk, 1819–20 [*Builder, ut supra; Survey of London* xxix, 193]. According to Wheatley and Cunningham, *London Past and Present* ii, 1891, 600, he was also responsible for the addition of the portico

[1] The inscription was recut in 1858, when the date 1674 was inadvertently altered to 1694. The tomb itself was repaired in 1886.

[2] Gough prints 'Knighton', but this is almost certainly a mistake for 'Kington'.

and balcony for the 13th Duke of Norfolk in 1842. Norfolk House was dem. 1938.

LONDON, THE CRAVEN CHAPEL, FOUBERT'S PLACE, 1821–2 [*Survey of London* xxxi, 200–1].

MILDENHALL SCHOOL, WILTS., 1823–4, Gothic [J. Britton, *Beauties of Wiltshire* iii, 1825, 268; inscription on building].

FORNHAM HALL, SUFFOLK, works for 12th Duke of Norfolk *c.*1824; dem. *c.*1951 [*Builder, ut supra*].

ALTON TOWERS, STAFFS., conservatories and garden buildings for 15th Earl of Shrewsbury (d. 1827) [J. C. Loudon, *Encyclopaedia of Cottage, Farm and Villa Architecture,* 1846, 784–9] (*C. Life*, 2 June 1960). Some of his drawings for Alton were sold by Quaritch, 9 April 1879, lots 688–92, and there is one in R.I.B.A. Drawings Coll.

HAYLING ISLAND, HANTS., building development for William Padwick, who bought the land from the Duke of Norfolk in 1825 [printed handbill offering building leases and naming Abraham as architect in charge].

LONDON, THE WESTERN SYNAGOGUE, ST. ALBAN'S PLACE, off JERMYN STREET, 1827–8; dem. 1914 [*Builder, ut supra*].

TOOTING, SURREY, rebuilt NATIONAL SCHOOLS, 1829–30 [W. E. Morden, *History of Tooting Graveney*, 1897, 227, 232–3].

WORKSOP MANOR, NOTTS., works for the Earl of Surrey, afterwards 13th Duke of Norfolk, including a gardener's cottage [*Builder, ut supra; Gardener's Magazine* vi, 1830, 34–5].

WESTMINSTER BRIDEWELL, TOTHILL FIELDS, 1830–4; dem. 1885 [*Builder, ut supra*; T. L. Donaldson, *Handbook of Specifications*, 1860, 68].

HARLOW, ESSEX, THE FAWBERT AND BARNARD SCHOOL, 1836 [*Architectural Magazine* iii, 1836, 532].

LONDON, OXFORD STREET, houses on the Berners estate, 1836 [*A.P.S.D.*].

THAME PARK, OXON., reconstructed medieval chapel for Baroness Wenman, 1836, Gothic [*Building News*, 30 March 1888, 457].

ARUNDEL, SUSSEX, THE TOWN HALL, for 12th Duke of Norfolk, 1836, Gothic [drawings in W. Sussex C.R.O., BO/AR/53/1].

ARUNDEL, SUSSEX, CONGREGATIONAL CHAPEL (now Union Church), TARRANT STREET, 1836–8, Romanesque [*Evangelical Mag.* 1837, 30–1].

LONDON, THE COLLEGE OF HERALDS, QUEEN VICTORIA STREET, designed RECORD ROOM, 1842–4 [W. H. Godfrey and others, *The College of Arms*, Survey of London Monograph No. 16, 1963, 26 and pl. 11: see p. 24 for Abraham's earlier scheme for rebuilding the College in the West End].

ACTON, SAMUEL (*c.*1773–1837), was the nephew and pupil of Nathaniel Wright (*q.v.*). He entered the Royal Academy Schools in 1790 at the age of 17 and won the Silver Medal in 1794. He exhibited at the Royal Academy from 1791 to 1802. He held the post of Surveyor to the Commissioners of Sewers for the City of London. In 1822 he was President of the Surveyors' Club, and left £500 to found a Charitable Fund for the benefit of its members and their dependants. He died in Jan. 1837 at Hill House, Chalfont St. Peter, Bucks. [records of the Surveyors' Club].

ADAM, JAMES (1732–1794), born in Edinburgh on 21 July 1732, was the third son of William Adam (*q.v.*) and the younger brother of Robert Adam (*q.v.*). Sketch-books at Penicuik House show that he was already making competent architectural drawings in his early twenties. Among these are a design for CUMNOCK CHURCH, AYRSHIRE, dated 1753, which corresponds almost exactly to that church as built 1754 (dem. 1864), and a plan and elevation of GUNSGREEN HOUSE, EYEMOUTH, BERWICKSHIRE, as built *c.*1755. His architectural education was completed by a tour of Italy, upon which he set out in 1760 accompanied by the draughtsman George Richardson. In Venice he was joined by Clérisseau, who accompanied him to Rome. He subsequently visited Naples and Paestum, but projects to visit Greece and Sicily came to nothing. The journal which he kept was printed in *The Library of the Fine Arts* ii, nos. 9–10, 1831, where it was mistakenly attributed to his brother. It shows the critical attitude towards Palladio and the interest in 'grotesque' and Pompeian decoration which was later to find expression in the introduction to *The Works of Robert and James Adam.* On his return in 1763 he joined the family partnership in London.

Although an elegant draughtsman and a competent architect, James Adam lacked both the drive and the genius of his elder brother, and was content to act as his junior partner rather than attempt to establish himself in independent practice. By 1763, when he returned to England, Robert had already worked out the essentials of the Adam style, and James's contribution to its genesis appears to have been slight. As Robert's partner he does, however, share the credit for the many buildings which they jointly designed and erected, and his achievement must not be judged merely by the few buildings which he seems to have designed independently. Besides the two early works mentioned above, these included the Ionic entrance gateway at CULLEN HOUSE, BANFFSHIRE, for the 3rd Earl of Seafield, 1767 [drawing in private hands, photo at N.M.R.S. and references to designs by James in letters from John Adam to Lord Seafield in S.R.O. GD 248/982/1], and HERTFORD SHIRE AND TOWN HALL, 1767–9, altered *c.*1885 [A. T. Bolton, 'The Shire Hall, Hertford', *Arch. Rev.*, 1 April 1918, vol. 43, 68–73]. James must also have been largely, if not wholly, responsible for four buildings in GLASGOW which were all built after Robert Adam's death in 1792, namely THE ROYAL INFIRMARY, 1792–4, dem. *c.*1910, THE TRON OR LAIGH CHURCH, now a theatre, 1794, THE BARONY CHURCH, 1793–4, dem. 1886, and THE ASSEMBLY ROOMS, 1796–8, dem. *c.*1890. 'Robert and James Adams' were named as architects of the Infirmary on the foundation-stone, but 'the late Mr. James Adams' is alone credited with the design of the Tron Church and the Assembly Rooms in *The Picture of Glasgow*, 1812, 87, 125. James Adam also signs the drawings for the Gothic ST. GEORGE'S EPISCOPAL CHAPEL, YORK PLACE, EDINBURGH, built in 1792–4, and was doubtless also responsible for the adjoining castle-style manse.

In 1769 James Adam succeeded his brother as Architect of the King's Works upon the latter's election as M.P. for Kinross, retaining the post until its abolition in 1782. Having in the 1770s acquired an estate in Essex, he interested himself in agriculture, and in 1789 published *Practical Essays on Agriculture*, 'carefully collected and digested from the most eminent authors' (2nd ed. 1794) – a compilation from previous writers which, according to a notice in the *Monthly Review*, 'could not be ranked in the class of useful performances'. He also projected a treatise on architecture which was never completed. He died in London on 20 October 1794. Portraits by Allan Ramsay, *c.*1754, and Pompeo Batoni, painted in Rome in 1763, are illustrated by Fleming, pls. 22 and 88. The former is in the Laing Art Gallery at Newcastle. Prominent in the latter portrait is the 'Britannic Order' which James Adam invented. A sketch by him for a 'Chapiteau Ecossais' also exists.

Three of James Adam's architectural sketch-books are among the Clerk papers at Penicuik House, Midlothian (photos. at N.M.R.S.), and several early designs by him are in vol. vii of the Adam drawings in Sir John Soane's Museum. His unexecuted designs for an enormous castellated house for the Earl of Lonsdale at Lowther, Westmorland, dated 1767, are in the Cumbria Record Office at Carlisle, together with alternative schemes by Robert Adam dated 1767 and 1771. [*A.P.S.D.; Gent's Mag.* 1794 (ii) 1056; A. T. Bolton, *The Architecture of Robert and James Adam*, 2 vols., 1922; John Fleming, *Robert Adam and his Circle*, 1962; John Fleming, 'James Adam in Naples', in *Oxford, China and Italy, Writings in Honour of Harold Acton*, ed. Chaney & Ritchie (1984).

ADAM, JOHN (–1790), is supposed to have been a relative of Robert and James Adam. He appears in the Glasgow Directories as 'mason and architect', and he was Deacon of the Glasgow Masons in 1769. His known buildings are in a plain early eighteenth-century style with details similar to the work of William Adam. In 1768–72 he built the NEW (JAMAICA) OR BROOMIELAW BRIDGE at GLASGOW (dem. 1833–5) to the designs of Robert and William Mylne. He also built the range of houses facing Argyle Street from St. Enoch's Burn westwards, including ADAM'S COURT (dem.), which was named after him. In about 1767 he designed and built PETERSHILL HOUSE, nr. GLASGOW (dem.) for Alexander Williamson. He died at Glasgow on 30 June 1790. [*Scots Mag.* 1790, 311; *Extracts from the Records of the Burgh of Glasgow*, ed. Renwick, vii–viii, *passim*; Jas. Cleland, *Annals of Glasgow* i, 1816, 448; *The Old Country Houses of the Glasgow Gentry*, Glasgow 1870, pl. lxxxi and text; Senex, *Glasgow Past and Present* ii, 1884, 12, 433; information from Mr. David Walker.]

ADAM, JOHN (1721–1792), was the eldest son of William Adam (*q.v.*). He attended Dalkeith Grammar School, but the demands of the family business prevented him from going on to Edinburgh University. During the 1740s he was gradually taking over the control of his father's affairs, and when William Adam died in 1748 John succeeded him as laird of Blair Adam and as Master Mason to the Board of Ordnance. He immediately took his brother Robert into partnership and in the course of the next ten years they completed the very profitable works at Fort George and elsewhere in the Highlands which their father had undertaken after the rebellion of 1745. They also inherited his extensive architectural practice, which, until Robert established himself in London in 1758, continued to be a family partnership. To this partnership John Adam contributed business ability rather than artistic distinction, but he was nevertheless a competent architect who relied on the established formulae of English Palladianism to direct his taste. Of the buildings listed below, those erected before about 1760 must be regarded as the joint work of a firm in which John was the senior partner: when they are illustrated in *Vitruvius Scoticus* they normally appear above the plural signature *Adam's Architects*.

After about 1770 John Adam was eclipsed as an architect by his brilliant brother and appears to have given up practice. In 1772 he even got Robert and James to make designs (never carried out) for rebuilding his own house at Blair Adam (see Bolton, *Architecture of R. and J. Adam* i, 12). He continued, however, to be very much involved in his brothers' affairs. Indeed, it was chiefly to relieve his financial embarrassment after the failure of Fairholme's bank in 1764 that the firm of 'William Adam & Co.' was established in that year, and when the Adelphi speculation ended in disaster in 1772 he was obliged to mortgage the Blair Adam estate in order to avoid bankruptcy. His own business activities included the sale of stone from the Aberdeen quarries and a partnership in the Carron Iron Works. He died on 25 June 1792, leaving Blair to his only surviving son William Adam (1751–1839), barrister and M.P. A portrait by Francis Cotes at Blair Adam is illustrated by Fleming, pl. 21, and a portrait medallion by James Tassie dated 1791 is in the Scottish National Portrait Gallery. A sketch-book containing drawings of buildings seen by John Adam in England in 1748 is in the R.I.B.A. Drawings Collection. In the same collection there is also a drawing by John Adam for a scheme to unite the old and new towns at Edinburgh dated 1752. [John Fleming, *Robert Adam and his Circle*, 1962; T. C. Barker, 'The Aberdeen Quarries', *Arch. Rev.*, Feb. 1958; R. H. Campbell, *Carron Company*, Edinburgh, 1961, *passim*; L. Namier & J. Brooke, *The House of Commons 1754–1790* ii, 1964, 8–10; I. R. M. Mowat, 'John Adam as Town Planner', *Scottish Georgian Soc's Bulletin* No. 10, 1983; David King, *The Complete Works of Robert & James Adam*, 1991, Appendix C: 'Works done by John Adam on his own'.]

EDINBURGH, house in CANONGATE for Andrew Fletcher, Lord Milton, *c.*1745/50; dem. [*Vit. Scot.*, pl. 45].

BANFF CASTLE, BANFF, rebuilt for Lord Deskford, 1750–2 [S.R.O., GD 248/984/4 and 1169–70].

EDINBURGH, TWEEDDALE LODGING, No. 14 HIGH STREET, alterations for 4th Marquess of Tweeddale, *c.*1750–3 [National Library of Scotland, Yester Papers, MS. 14551, ff. 114 *et seq.*]

HOPETOUN HOUSE, WEST LOTHIAN, completion for 2nd Earl of Hopetoun, 1750–4 [Alistair Rowan in *Arch. Hist.* 27, 1984, 194–9].

BUCHANAN HOUSE, STIRLINGSHIRE, alterations to house and gardens for 2nd Duke of Montrose, 1751; largely destroyed by fire 1850 [payments to John Adam 'for drawing plans &c A^0. 1751' in S.R.O., GD 220/6, vol. 106: cf. *Scots Peerage* vi, 268].

INVERARAY, ARGYLLSHIRE, works for 3rd Duke of Argyll, including ARGYLL ARMS HOTEL, 1751–55, the CHERRY PARK offices, 1760–1, and Gothic Bridge over R. Aray, 1758–60; collapsed 1772 [*Vit. Scot.*, pl. 74, signed 'John Adam Architect'; I. G. Lindsay & Mary Cosh, *Inverary and the Dukes of Argyll*, 1973, 136–7, 156–7]. John Adam appears also to have designed the elliptical GARDEN, or FREW'S, BRIDGE, 1759–61, though in *Vitruvius Scoticus* it is ascribed to James Adam [Lindsay & Cosh, *op. cit.*, 372 n. 47].

EDINBURGH, GREYFRIARS CEMETERY, mausoleum to William Adam, 1753–5, wrongly dated 1750 by inscription added 1827, probably designed in association with R. and J. Adam: see D. King, *Complete Works of R. & J. Adam*, 359–60.

CASTLE GRANT, MORAYSHIRE, additions for Sir Ludovic and James Grant, 1753–6 and 1765 [S.R.O., GD 248/176, 177 *passim* and GD 248/108].

EDINBURGH, THE ROYAL EXCHANGE (now City Chambers), 1753–61 [W. Forbes Gray, 'The Royal Exchange', *Book of the Old Edinburgh Club* xxii, 1938, 12–13].

LEITH, CUSTOM HOUSE, enlarged 1754; dem. 1812 [Edinburgh University Library, MS. Laing II, 135].

ARNISTON, MIDLOTHIAN, dining- and drawing-rooms on W. side for Robert Dundas, Lord Arniston, 1754–8 [Mary Cosh, 'The Adam Family and Arniston', *Arch. Hist.* 27, 1984].

DUMFRIES HOUSE, AYRSHIRE, for 4th Earl of Dumfries, 1754–9 [*Vit. Scot.*, pls. 19–21] and bridge in grounds, 1760–2 [T. Ruddock, *Arch Bridges 1735–1835*, 1979, 118].

EDINBURGH, DRUMSHEUGH, house for James Erskine, Lord Alva, 1755; dem. *c.*1822 [payments to 'Mr. Adams' in National Library of Scotland, MS. 5158, f. 24].

INVERARAY, ARGYLLSHIRE, THE TOWN or COURT HOUSE, 1755–7 [I. G. Lindsay & Mary Cosh, *Inveraray and the Dukes of Argyll*, 1973, 158–62].

EDINBURGH, conversion of Lord Lovat's house in High Street into an office for the Commissioners for Annexed Estates, 1756 [S.R.O., E 727/3 and E 727/8/1].

HAWKHILL VILLA, SOUTH LEITH, EDINBURGH, for

Andrew Pringle, Lord Alemoor, 1757; dem. 1971 [*Vit. Scot.*, pl. 123, signed 'John Adam, Architect'; James Simpson, 'Lord Alemoor's Villa at Hawkhill', *Bull. Scottish Georgian Soc.* i, 1972].

DOUGLAS CASTLE, LANARKS., for the Duke of Douglas, 1757–61, Gothic; dem. 1937–51 [*Vit. Scot.*, pl. 135] (T. Hannam, *Famous Scottish Houses: the Lowlands*, 1928, 90–1).

YESTER HOUSE, E. LOTHIAN, interior of great saloon for 4th Marquess of Tweeddale, *c.*1758–61 [J. G. Dunbar, 'The Building of Yester House 1670–1878', *Trans. E. Lothian Antiquarian Soc.* xiii, 1972, 42–4].

?PAXTON HOUSE, BERWICKS., for Patrick Home, *c.*1758–61 [Alistair Rowan in *C. Life*, 17, 24 Aug. 1967].

BALLOCHMYLE HOUSE, AYRSHIRE, for Allan Whitefoorde (d. 1767), *c.*1760; remodelled in Jacobean style 1887–8 [*Vit. Scot.*, pl. 63].

WHIM, PEEBLESSHIRE, added library (forming S. wing) for 3rd Duke of Argyll, 1761 [*R.C.A.M. Peeblesshire* ii, 327].

MOFFAT HOUSE, MOFFAT, DUMFRIESSHIRE, for 2nd Earl of Hopetoun, 1761–3 [accounts at Hopetoun House in name of 'Mr. Adam', *ex. inf.* Mr. Basil Skinner].

EDINBURGH, HERIOT'S HOSPITAL, gateway and porter's lodge on N. side, 1762; dem. [W. Steven, *History of George Heriot's Hospital*, 1872, 123].

KERSE (or ZETLAND HOUSE), STIRLINGSHIRE, designed offices for Sir Lawrence Dundas, Bart., 1763 [estimate among Zetland papers in N. Yorkshire R.O.] It is not known whether these offices were built. Kerse was dem. *c.*1958.

EDINBURGH, ADAM SQUARE, two houses, later the Watt Institution, 1763–4; dem. 1871 [*Edinburgh Evening Courant*, *ex. inf.* Mr. J. Gifford] (J. Grant, *Old & New Edinburgh* i, 1882, 377).

MOY HOUSE, MORAYSHIRE, internal alterations for James Grant, 1763–5 [S.R.O., GD 248/49/3/11 & 16 and 248/178/2].

BUCHANAN (MILTON OF BUCHANAN) CHURCH, STIRLINGSHIRE, 1764 [S.R.O., GD 220/6/8, *sub anno* 1761 and 220/6/50].

BANFF, THE TOLBOOTH STEEPLE, 1764–7 by 'Mr. Adam' [*Annals of Banff*, ed. W. Cramond i, 1891, 311].

PORTSOY, BANFFSHIRE, granary at Shorehead for 3rd Earl of Seafield, 1765 [S.R.O., GD 248/3443, letter of 19 May 1765].

DUNROBIN CASTLE, SUTHERLAND, designed quadrangular stables for 17th Earl of Sutherland, 1766 [N.M.R.S., photos of drawings signed by John Adam]. If built, these stables were destroyed by fire in 1790: cf. W. Fraser, *The Sutherland Book* i, 1894, 471.

CULLEN HOUSE, BANFFSHIRE, minor works for 3rd Earl of Seafield in conjunction with James Adam, 1767–9 [letters in S.R.O., GD 248/982/1].

CRAIG CASTLE, AUCHINDOIR, ABERDEENSHIRE, new wing for John Gordon, 1768–9; dem. [drawings in Scott of Gala papers, temporarily deposited in S.R.O. 1978].

ADAM, ROBERT (1728–1792), was born at Kirkcaldy in Fife on 3 July 1728. He was the second surviving son of William Adam (*q.v.*), architect, builder and entrepreneur. In Edinburgh, where he attended the High School, and in 1743 matriculated at the University, Robert met some of the leading figures in Scottish intellectual life, among them William Robertson, the historian (who was his cousin), Adam Smith, the political economist (himself a native of Kirkcaldy), David Hume, the philosopher, and Adam Ferguson, another philosopher who was to become his 'particular friend'. In 1745 or 1746 he left the University prematurely in order to join his father's drawing-office at a time when it was under serious strain. When William Adam died in 1748, Robert and his elder brother John entered into partnership in order to carry on their father's business as an architect and contractor. So lucrative was this that by 1754 Robert had a capital of £5000 – more than enough to enable him to embark on that extended Grand Tour from which he hoped to return with fresh architectural ideas derived from a systematic study of the principal monuments of antiquity.

Robert left Edinburgh in October 1754. In Brussels he joined his travelling-companion the Hon. Charles Hope (younger brother of the Earl of Hopetoun, for whom John Adam was then completing Hopetoun House), whose friendship would automatically give him the entrée to aristocratic society wherever they went. In Florence he persuaded the French architectural designer Clérisseau to join him, thus acquiring the services of a brilliant draughtsman with a strong interest in the neo-classical. He reached Rome in February 1755. There, under Clérisseau's guidance, he studied drawing and antiquity assiduously, acquiring the knowledge and expertise that would enable him to set up in practice as a fashionable architect. Among his Italian acquaintances was another pioneer of neo-classical taste, G. B. Piranesi, who later dedicated his account of the Campus Martius to *Roberto Adam Britann. Architecto Celeberrim.* In the summer of 1757 he set sail from Venice with Clérisseau and two other draughtsmen in order to explore and measure the ruins of the great late Roman palace of Diocletian at Split in Dalmatia. Owing to the difficulties raised by the Venetian governor, it was clear that a prolonged stay was out of the question, and it was only by 'unwearied application' that the task was completed within the space of five weeks. The result was the publication in 1764 of the *Ruins of the Palace of the Emperor Diocletian at Spalatro*, a magnificent volume sumptuously engraved by Bartolozzi and others.

Robert Adam returned to England by way of the Rhineland during the winter of 1757–8, arriving in London in January. He established himself in a house in Lower Grosvenor Street, where he was soon joined by his two sisters and his brothers James and William. The decision to set up practice in London had already been taken while Robert was in Italy. 'Scotland', he wrote in 1755, 'is but a narrow place. [I need] a greater, a more extensive and more honourable scene, I mean an English life.' It was with the object of equipping himself for English practice that, according to his own reckoning, he had spent between £800 and £900 a year in Italy, and the time had now come to realize his ambition to become the leading architect, not merely in Scotland, but in England as well. Henceforth he was to be the principal director of the family firm.[1] There can be no doubt that it was he who made it famous by his brilliance as a designer and his enormous capacity for work: but the less spectacular abilities of James and the business acumen of William also contributed to its success, while John Adam provided capital from his estate at Blair Adam. In addition to these private resources, Robert Adam could count on support from his fellow-countrymen in London, including the Duke of Argyll and Lord Bute, George III's first minister, who, although unfriendly at first, in 1761 procured for Adam one of the two newly created posts of Architect of the King's Works, with a salary of £300 p.a. The other went to Sir William Chambers, the king's architectural mentor and Adam's principal rival. Adam was already a member of the Society of Arts, to which he had been elected immediately after his return from Italy, and in 1761 he became a Fellow of the Royal Society. Thus established in practice, Adam set out to revolutionize English domestic architecture, which for thirty years had followed the pattern laid down for it by Lord Burlington. In place of the strict grammar of the orders as described by Vitruvius and interpreted by Palladio, he substituted a new and elegant repertoire of architectural ornament based on a wide variety of classical sources ranging from antiquity to the Cinquecento. The success of the new style was immediate, and within a very few years it had taken the place of the prevailing Palladianism and become the common property of the London builder. Among architects, only Sir William Chambers remained resolute in his refusal to have anything to do with Adam's 'affectations', and there can be no doubt that it was owing to his disapproval that Robert Adam never became a Royal Academician. Adam, for his part, ignored the Academy, sending none of his designs for exhibition at Somerset House. He did not, however, lack advertisement, for his publication of the *Ruins at Spalatro* was a claim to the archaeological scholarship that was now one of the credentials of a serious neo-classical architect, and in 1773 there appeared the first elegantly engraved volume of the *Works in Architecture of Robert and James Adam*.[1] The second volume followed in 1779, the third posthumously in 1822. By 1773 the Adam manner had already been successfully imitated by others, and the preface to the first volume was intended to assert the brothers' claim 'to have brought about . . . a kind of revolution in the whole system' of English architecture. In particular, they claimed to have brought back the principle of 'movement', which (in their own words) 'is meant to express the rise and fall, the advance and recess with other diversity of form, in the different parts of a building, so as to add greatly to the picturesque of the composition'. This quality they recognized and admired in the works of Sir John Vanbrugh, though at the same time deploring the 'barbarisms and absurdities' which made his bold designs so different from their own refined and polished compositions. The picturesque approach to architectural design revealed by this passage is illustrated by the romantic landscape compositions, of which Robert Adam left a large number executed in pen and

[1] For the firm of 'William Adam & Co.' set up in 1764 see Alistair Rowan in *Journal of the Royal Society of Arts* cxxii, 1974, 659–78. It was a firm of developers and builders' merchants whose operations included the building of the Adelphi, the management of brickworks in London and Essex, and the quarrying of Aberdeen granite. Despite numerous financial vicissitudes it remained in business until 1801. Robert and James Adam kept a separate account for the profits of their joint architectural practice.

[1] There are reprints by Thezard 1902, by Tiranti 1939 and 1959, by Academy Editions 1975, and by Dover Publications 1980. In 1821 a small quarto volume was published by Priestley and Weale entitled *Designs for Vases and Foliage, composed from the Antique, by Robert Adam*, consisting of fourteen engravings without any letterpress.

wash, and even more by the dramatic massing of such castellated mansions as Seton and Culzean Castles, whose picturesque (yet always symmetrical) grouping, assisted by a minimum of Gothic detail, was to be imitated by a whole generation of Scottish country-house architects: but it is also apparent in more orthodox buildings such as Gosford House or Edinburgh University. Here the architectural vocabulary remains strictly classical, but effects of surprise or movement are achieved that in other hands or at other periods might be classed as baroque.

It was, however, in interior design that the Adam revolution made its greatest impact. Here ingenious and imaginative planning ensured a progression of varied and interesting shapes in place of the simple rectangular rooms of earlier Georgian architecture, and walls, ceilings, chimney-pieces, carpets and furniture – down even to details like door-knobs and candlesticks – were designed as part of an elegant, varied and highly sophisticated decorative scheme incorporating neo-classical and Renaissance motifs such as griffins, sphinxes, altars, urns and putti. Plasterwork (often embellished with panels painted by artists such as Cipriani, Zucchi and Rebecca) played a large part in every Adam interior. Joseph Rose (1745–99) was the plasterer who gave actuality to many of Adam's designs with unfailing technical skill.

The immense output of the Adam office was made possible only by the employment of a number of highly skilled draughtsmen. Of these the most important were the Scottish George Richardson (*q.v.*), the Liègois Laurent-Benoît Dewez (1731–1812, subsequently the leading Belgian architect), and the Italians Agostino Brunias, Joseph Bonomi, Giuseppe Manocchi and Antonio Zucchi. Manocchi (*q.v.*), who returned to Italy in 1773, considered that he had been badly treated by the Adams, but in the introduction to his *Book of Ceilings* (1776) George Richardson spoke with gratitude of the eighteen years he had spent as an assistant in the Adam office.

Although for nearly thirty years Robert Adam was one of the two or three busiest architects in England, he was given few opportunities for monumental design on a large scale. By the time of his return from Italy, the great country mansions which reflected the ascendancy of the Whig aristocracy had already been built, and in many cases it was left to him only to remodel their interiors in accordance with modern taste. Too rarely was he permitted to design an important house from the foundation up, and it was not until the end of his life that major public commissions were entrusted to him at Cambridge and Edinburgh Universities. The former, however, came to nothing, while the latter, unfinished at the time of his death, was subsequently completed in a very different way from what its architect had intended. Only the Register House remains as the nearest approach to a monumental building in the list of Adam's works.

It is to 'the desire to raise a great building of a semi-public nature in the monumental manner' that the Adelphi scheme is, in part at least, to be attributed. In 1768 the brothers took a ninety-nine-year lease of an extensive area on the north bank of the river Thames, upon which they proposed to erect twenty-four first-rate houses, treated as a single architectural composition and raised on a terrace whose vaulted interior was intended to be let as warehouses. As a development it was admirable, but as a speculation it was unprecedented, and in June 1772 work was halted by a national credit crisis. On 27 June David Hume wrote to Adam Smith:

> Of all the sufferers I am most concern'd for the Adams. . . . But their undertakings were so vast that nothing cou'd support them: they must dismiss 3000 workmen, who, comprehending the materials must have expended above 100,000 a year. They have great funds; but if these must be dispos'd of, in a hurry and to disadvantage, I am afraid the remainder will amount to little or nothing. . . . To me, the scheme of the Adelphi always appeared so imprudent, that my wonder is, how they cou'd have gone on so long.

Having failed to raise sufficient funds by a loan raised on the security of the Blair Adam estate, and by the sale of many of the works of art that they had brought back from Italy,[1] the brothers retrieved themselves from financial disaster by disposing of the whole property by means of a lottery (1774). Meanwhile in 1773 they had become involved (though not as principals) in another great town-planning venture in Marylebone, where they proposed to build a series of detached private palaces on either side of Portland Place. This time the outbreak of the War of American Independence led to the abandonment of the project in its original form, and blocks of houses took the place of the independent mansions originally proposed. The façades were designed by James Adam, but each house was built as an independent speculation.

A prominent feature of the Portland Place

[1] They were sold at Christie's 25–27 Feb. and 1–2 March 1773.

houses was the use of stucco for the central features on either side. Having acquired the patents in two stucco compositions – one invented by a Mr. David Wark of Haddington, the other by a Swiss clergyman named Liardet – the brothers obtained in 1776 an Act of Parliament vesting in the patentees the exclusive right to manufacture what they called 'Adam's new invented patent stucco'. A rival composition was put on the market by John Johnson (*q.v.*), who maintained that it was based on a stucco invented before either Wark or Liardet had come on the scene. The Adams, however, claimed that Johnson had infringed their patent, and went to law (1778). The case was heard before Lord Chief Justice Mansfield, who, as a client and fellow-countryman of the plaintiffs, laid himself open to the charge of partiality when he gave judgement in favour of the Messrs. Adam. The case attracted considerable publicity, and was the subject of two pamphlets.

From about 1760 to 1780 Robert Adam was the most fashionable architect in Britain, but in the 1780s he began to be eclipsed by James Wyatt, and during the last ten years of his life his practice was almost confined to his native Scotland, where Wyatt found no patrons. Here he developed the picturesque castle style – an indeterminate synthesis of Gothic and classical forms – which was characteristic of his later domestic work, and which may be seen as his answer to Wyatt's success as a Gothic designer.

Robert Adam died suddenly on 3 March 1792, and was buried in the south transept of Westminster Abbey. The funeral was 'private', but the pall-bearers were the Duke of Buccleuch, the Earl of Coventry, the Earl of Lauderdale, Viscount Stormont, Lord Frederick Campbell and William Pulteney of Westerhall. The only official position which Adam held at the time of his death was the surveyorship of Chelsea Hospital, to which he had been appointed in 1765. He had relinquished the post of Architect of the King's Works in 1769, when he entered parliament as M.P. for Kinross-shire. The death of his brother James in 1794 meant the end of the firm, though William Adam survived to submit designs for the completion of Edinburgh University in 1815. He died in 1822 at the age of 84. He had gone bankrupt in 1801, and in 1818 and 1821 sold all his brothers' pictures, furniture, antiques and other possessions.[1]

In 1833 the bulk of the architectural drawings made by Robert and James Adam, nearly 9000 in number, were purchased from the family by Sir John Soane, and now form one of the principal treasures of the Museum which bears his name. Other drawings are in the collections of the Victoria and Albert Museum, the National Gallery of Scotland and the R.I.B.A., while some remain at Blair Adam and Penicuik houses in Scotland. For those in American collections see John Harris, *A Catalogue of British Drawings for Architecture . . . in American Collections*, 1971. It was apparently in the last years of Robert's life that drawings were made in the Adams' Edinburgh office for a volume of engraved designs for classical villas and castle-style houses. This was never completed, but formed the basis of Alistair Rowan's *Designs for Castles and Country Villas by Robert and James Adam* (Phaidon 1985).

The only certainly authentic portraits of Robert Adam are an ivory plaque at Blair Adam and the portrait in the National Portrait Gallery in London, formerly attributed to Zoffany and now to David Martin. Three medallions in paste-relief by James Tassie are in the Scottish National Portrait Gallery, but two at least are posthumous.

[*Gent's Mag.* 1792 (i), 282–3; John Swarbrick, *Robert Adam and his Brothers: their Lives, Work and Influence on English Architecture*, 1915; A. T. Bolton, 'Robert Adam as a Bibliographer, Publisher and Designer of Libraries', *Trans. Bibliographical Soc.* xiv, 1915–17; A. T. Bolton, *The Architecture of Robert and James Adam*, 2 vols., 1922, with detailed index to the drawings in Sir John Soane's Museum; J. Steegman & C. K. Adams, 'The Iconography of Robert Adam', *Arch. Rev.* xci, 1942; J. Lees-Milne, *The Age of Adam*, 1947; John Fleming, *Robert Adam and his Circle*, 1962; Eileen Harris, *The Furniture of Robert Adam*, 1963; Namier & Brooke, *The House of Commons 1754–1790* ii, 1964, 7–8; Damie Stillman, *The Decorative Work of Robert Adam*, 1966; Clifford Musgrave, *Adam and Hepplewhite Furniture*, 1966; Damie Stillman, 'Robert Adam and Piranesi', *Essays in the History of Architecture presented to Rudolf Wittkower*, ed. D. Fraser, 1967; John Fleming, 'Robert Adam's Castle Style', *C. Life*, 23–30 May, 1968; John Fleming, 'A retrospective View by John Clerk of Eldin, with some comments on Adam's Castle Style', in *Concerning Architecture*, ed. J. Summerson, 1968; Alistair Rowan, 'After the Adelphi: Forgotten years in the Adam brothers' practice', *Journal of the Royal Society of Arts* cxxii, 1974, 659–710; James Macaulay, *The Gothic Revival*, 1975, chap. vi ('Robert Adam's Northern Castles'); A. A. Tait, 'The Sale of Robert Adam's Drawings', *Burlington Mag.*

[1] The catalogue of the 1818 sale is printed in *Sale Catalogues of Libraries of Eminent Persons* iv, ed. Watkin, 1972, 135–92.

120, July 1978; I. G. Brown, 'Commemorative portraits of Robert Adam', *ibid.*; G. Beard, *The Work of Robert Adam* (Edinburgh 1978); G. Beard, 'Robert Adam and his Craftsmen', *Connoisseur* July 1978; James Simpson, 'Robert Adam – the Scottish Family Backgound', *Bull. Scottish Georgian Soc.* No. 5, 1978; M. B. Gerson, 'A Glossary of Robert Adam's neo-classical Ornament', *Arch. Hist.* 24, 1981; Margaret Richardson, 'Robert Adam's last visit to Scotland, 1791', *Arch. Hist.* 25, 1982; Frank Kelsall, 'Liardet versus Adam', *Arch. Hist.* 27, 1984; J. & A. Rykwert, *The Brothers Adam*, 1985; A. Rowan, *Robert Adam* (Catalogue of Architectural Drawings in the Victoria & Albert Museum), 1988; Eileen Harris, *British Architectural Books and Writers 1556–1785*, 1990, 71–94; D. King, *The Complete Works of Robert & James Adam*, 1991; Margaret H. B. Sanderson, *Robert Adam and Scotland*, Scottish Record Office 1992; I. G. Brown, *Monumental Reputation. Robert Adam and the Emperor's Palace*, N.L.S. 1992, 'Robert Adam's Drawings: Edinburgh's Loss, London's Gain', *Book of the Old Edinburgh Club*, N.S. 2, 1992; A. A. Tait, *Robert Adam: Drawings and Imagination*, 1993.]

The following list of the executed works of Robert and James Adam is a corrected version of the one in the 1978 edition of this *Dictionary*, collated with the list published by Dr. David King in his *Complete Works of Robert & James Adam* (1991), in which references will be found to the original drawings in Sir John Soane's Museum which (unless otherwise stated) constitute the basic authority in each case. All the buildings listed by Dr. King are illustrated in his book and many other illustrations of buildings by the Adam brothers will be found in Bolton's *Works of R. and J. Adam* (1922) and Rowan's *Designs for Castles and Country Villas by R. and J. Adam* (1985).

PUBLIC BUILDINGS, ETC.

LONDON, screen-wall to THE ADMIRALTY, WHITEHALL, 1760; mutilated by G. L. Taylor 1827–8, restored 1923 (*Works* i, iii)

QUARNDON, DERBYSHIRE, KEDLESTON HOTEL, for 1st Lord Scarsdale, *c.*1760–2.

HIGH WYCOMBE, BUCKS., rebuilt the SHAMBLES AND BUTTER MARKET, 1761. The present lantern was added *c.*1900.

LONDON, BUCKINGHAM HOUSE, architectural transparency in honour of King George III's birthday, 1762 (*Works* i).

CROOME CHURCH, WORCS., Gothic interior decoration of church designed by L. Brown (*q.v.*) for 6th Earl of Coventry, 1763.

EDINBURGH, THE RIDING SCHOOL, NICOLSON STREET, 1763–4; dem. 1830 [W. Forbes Gray in *Book of the Old Edinburgh Club* 20, 1935].

HERTFORD, THE SHIRE AND TOWN HALL, 1767–9 [A. T. Bolton, 'The Shire Hall, Hertford', *Arch. Rev.* 43, 1 April 1918, 68–73].

GUNTON CHURCH, NORFOLK, for Sir William Harbord, Bart., completed 1769 (faculty 1766); choir formed 1894.

BATH, SOMERSET, PULTENEY BRIDGE for William Pulteney, 1769–74; shops much altered at various times (W. Ison, *The Georgian Buildings of Bath*, 1948, 65–9).

LONDON, WHITEHALL, remodelled house (No. 1) as Board Room for Paymaster-Ceneral and Commissioners of Chelsea Hospital, 1771; dem. 1909 (*Works* i; *Survey of London* xvi, pls. 96–8).

KINROSS COUNTY BUILDINGS, architectural embellishment of S. front, 1771. Inscription: 'This County House was repaired by the Crown. A.D. 1771. Robert Adam, Knight of the Shire, decorated this front at his own expense.'

LONDON, THE ROYAL SOCIETY OF ARTS, JOHN STREET, 1772–4 [John Summerson in *Jnl. Royal Soc. of Arts* cii, 1954, 920–33; D. G. C. Allan, *The Houses of the Royal Society of Arts*, 1974, 6–16] (*Works* i).

?DERBY, THE ASSEMBLY ROOMS, may have designed interior completed 1774; destroyed by fire 1963 [inconclusive correspondence in Curzon of Kedleston papers].

EDINBURGH, THE REGISTER HOUSE, 1774–92; rear portion completed by Robert Reid (*q.v.*) 1822–30 [A. A. Tait, 'The Register House: the Adam Building', *Scottish Historical Review* liii, 1974, 115–23] (*Works* i).

BURY ST. EDMUNDS, SUFFOLK, THEATRE AND MARKET CROSS (later Town Hall, now Art Gallery), 1775–80; ground floor enclosed 1840.

LONDON, DRURY LANE THEATRE, altered and refronted, 1775–6; rebuilt by H. Holland (*q.v.*) 1791–4.

PONTEFRACT, YORKS., remodelled RED LION INN for Sir Rowland Winn, Bart., 1776.

MISTLEY CHURCH, ESSEX, remodelled church of 1735 for Richard Rigby, 1776; dem. except for twin towers 1870 (*Works* ii)

LONDON, CHELSEA HOSPITAL, redecorated Council Chamber, 1776, and other minor works [C. G. T. Dean, *The Royal Hospital Chelsea*, 1950, 65].

EDINBURGH, THE UNIVERSITY, commenced to Adam's designs, 1789–93; completed to modified designs by W. H. Playfair 1817–26; dome added by Sir Rowand Anderson 1887 [A. G. Fraser, *The Building of Old*

College, Edinburgh, 1989] (*Works* iii).

EDINBURGH, THE BRIDEWELL PRISON, CALTON HILL, 1791–5; dem. *c.*1884.

GLASGOW, THE TRADES HOUSE, GLASSFORD STREET, 1791–4; outer bays added later, interior much altered.

GLASGOW, THE ROYAL INFIRMARY, CATHEDRAL SQUARE, 1792–4; dem. 1907.

EDINBURGH, ST. GEORGE'S EPISCOPAL CHAPEL AND MANSE, YORK PLACE, 1792–4, Gothic, now a warehouse [J. Stark, *Picture of Edinburgh*, 1823, 220; R.C.A.M., *City of Edinburgh*, 187].

LASSWADE CHURCH, MIDLOTHIAN, as built 1793 (dem. 1956) was in some way related to a much more elaborate Greek Cross design made by the Adams in 1791 (plan as built in G. Hay, *Architecture of Scottish Post-Reformation Churches*, 1957, 94).

GLASGOW, rebuilt THE TRON KIRK, 1793–4; now a theatre.

GLASGOW, THE ASSEMBLY ROOMS, INGRAM STREET, erected 1796–8 to designs made before 1794; terminal pavilions added by H. Holland, 1807; dem *c.*1889. Part of the Adam façade was re-erected as the McLellan Arch on the Green at the end of Charlotte Street (G. Richardson, *New Vitruvius Britannicus* i, 1802, pls. 8–9).

LONDON: DOMESTIC ARCHITECTURE

LITTLE WALLINGFORD HOUSE, WHITEHALL, entrance screen for 8th Earl of Kinnoull, 1761; dem. 1786 [*Works* i, view of Whitehall and text].

LANSDOWNE HOUSE, BERKELEY SQUARE, begun *c.*1762 for 3rd Earl of Bute, who sold it unfinished to 2nd Earl of Shelburne, later 1st Marquess of Lansdowne, a condition of the sale being the completion of the house by Adam at Bute's expense. It was completed in 1768, except for the gallery, which was subsequently fitted up as a library by G. Dance, jnr., and remodelled as a picture-gallery by Robert Smirke (see D. Stillman in *Art Bulletin* lii, 1970, 75–80). The house was dem. in 1936. The interior of the drawing-room is now in the Museum of Arts at Philadelphia, U.S.A., that of the dining-room in the Metropolitan Museum of Art, New York.

BUCKINGHAM HOUSE, ceiling and chimney-piece for Queen Charlotte, *c.*1762; ceiling destroyed and chimney-piece now in Queen's Presence Chamber, Windsor Castle.

ARLINGTON STREET, No. 19, alterations and decorations for Sir Lawrence Dundas, Bart., 1763–6; dem. (*C. Life*, 17 Sept. 1921).

GROSVENOR SQUARE, No. 18 (later 19), alterations for 8th Earl of Thanet, 1764–5; dem. 1933 (*C. Life*, 1–8 March 1919: *Survey of London* xl, 136).

PICCADILLY, COVENTRY HOUSE, No. 29 (now 106), interiors for 6th Earl of Coventry, 1765–6.

PALL MALL, No. 34 (later 35), for Andrew Millar, 1765–6; dem. [*Survey of London* xxix, 325–6].

HILL STREET, No. 23 (now 31), alterations to interior for Mrs. Elizabeth Montagu, 1766 [*Mrs Montagu's Letters*, ed. R. Blunt i, 1923, 152–3].

FIFE HOUSE, WHITEHALL, interior of a room for 2nd Earl of Fife, 1766–7; dem. [letter from W. Donn to T. Estcourt *c.*1774 in Glos. C.R.O., D 1571/E 356, giving his charges for executing Adam's design for Lord Fife's room, and drawing in Verney archives at Claydon House, Bucks., of the 'ceiling of Lord Fife's Great Room at Whitehall', endorsed 'Mr. Donn to be left at the Inn Aylesbury'].

HANOVER SQUARE, No. 16 (later 18), added library for Lord Le Despenser, 1766–8; dem.

GREEN PARK, DEPUTY RANGER'S LODGE, 1768; dem. 1841 (*Works* iii).

MANSFIELD and DUCHESS STREETS, house for General Robert Clerk, 1768–71; damaged by fire 1771 and rebuilt by the Adams for Clerk and his wife, the Dowager Countess of Warwick, 1771–5; enlarged and remodelled by Thomas Hope (*q.v.*), *c.*1800; dem. 1851 [King, 268–70; building accounts, etc. in B.L., Add. MS. 40714, ff. 110–14].

THE ADELPHI BUILDINGS, STRAND, with JOHN, ROBERT, WILLIAM and JAMES STREETS, 1768–72; dem. 1936 except 1–3 Robert Street, 6–10 Adam Street and 2–4 John Street.

PICCADILLY, No. 79 (No. 1, Stratton St.), ceiling for 11th Earl of Eglinton, 1769; dem. 1929.

BERKELEY SQUARE, No. 15 (later 38), ceilings for Robert Child, 1769–70 and 1776; dem. 1939, one ceiling re-erected at Hinton Ampner House, Hants.

GROSVENOR SQUARE, No. 25 (later 28), probably designed interior decoration for Sir Robert Rich, Bart., 1769–70; dem. 1957 [*Survey of London* xl, 145].

HERTFORD STREET, No. 10, interior decoration for General John Burgoyne, 1769–71.

SACKVILLE STREET, No. 29, ceiling in drawing-room for John Parker, cr. Lord Boringdon, 1770.

NORTHUMBERLAND HOUSE, STRAND, interior decorations, including the Glass Drawing Room, for 1st Duke of Northumberland, 1770–5; dem. 1874, but parts reassembled in Victoria and Albert Museum [D. Owsley & W. Rieder, *The Glass Drawing Room*, Victoria & Albert Museum, 1974].

MANSFIELD STREET, speculative development of houses, 1770–4.

HARRINGTON HOUSE, ST. JAMES'S STABLE YARD, design for Dressing Room for 2nd Earl of Harrington, *c.*1770, probably executed.

CHANDOS HOUSE, CHANDOS and QUEEN ANNE STREETS, PORTLAND PLACE, for 3rd Duke of Chandos, 1770–1.

BRITISH COFFEE HOUSE, COCKSPUR STREET, *c.*1770; dem. 1886 (*Works* ii; *C. Life*, 25 Aug. 1917).

ST. JAMES'S SQUARE, No. 33, for Hon. George Hobart, later 3rd Earl of Buckinghamshire, 1770–2 [*Survey of London* xxix, 206–10].

SOHO SQUARE, No. 20, remodelled for Baron Grant, 1771–2; dem. 1924 (*C. Life*, 7 July 1917).

CURZON STREET, No. 30, internal alterations for Hon. H. F. Thynne, 1771–2.

ST. JAMES'S SQUARE, No. 20, for Sir Watkin Williams-Wynn, 1771–4; extended by Mewès & Davis in 1936 to incorporate No. 21, which was given an identical façade [*Survey of London* xxix, 164–74] (*Works* i, ii, iii).

APSLEY HOUSE, PICCADILLY, for 2nd Earl Bathurst, *c.*1772–8; enlarged and refaced by B. and P. Wyatt, 1828–9.

CHARLOTTE STREET, No. 8 (now Bloomsbury St., No. 10), ceilings, etc. for George Keate, 1773; cf. Lysons, *Environs of London* ii (2), 1811, 467, for Keate's lawsuit with the Adam brothers.

DERBY HOUSE, No. 23 (later 26), GROSVENOR SQUARE, remodelled interior for Lord Stanley, later 12th Earl of Derby, 1773–4; dem. 1861 (*Works* ii; *Survey of London* xl, 142–4).

ASHBURNHAM HOUSE, No. 19 (later 30), DOVER STREET, alterations for 2nd Earl of Ashburnham, 1773–6, including entrance gates and lodge; dem. (*Works* ii).

HOME HOUSE, No. 17 (now 20), PORTMAN SQUARE, for Elizabeth, Countess of Home, 1773–6 [Margaret Whinney, *Home House*, 1969; *Apollo* Aug. 1987].

ST. JAMES'S SQUARE, No. 11, refronted and some redecoration for Sir Rowland Winn, Bart., 1774–6; portico and balcony added 1877 [*Survey of London* xxix, 123–4].

FREDERICK'S PLACE, OLD JEWRY, a square containing 'eight capital Dwelling houses', 1775–6 [M. J. Chandler, 'Frederick's Place', *Arch. Rev.* Feb. 1958; *R.I.B.A. Drawings Catalogue, A*, 15].

ROXBURGHE (afterwards HAREWOOD) HOUSE, HANOVER SQUARE, remodelled for 3rd Duke of Roxburghe, 1776; dem. 1908 (W. H. Godfrey, 'Harewood House', *Arch. Rev.* 37–8, 1915).

BOLTON HOUSE, No. 2 SOUTHAMPTON ROW (later Nos. 66–7 Russell Square), interior decoration for 6th Duke of Bolton, 1776–7; dem. (features now in New York, *ex inf.* Dr. Eileen Harris).

PORTLAND PLACE, street of 68 houses, 1776–90; many altered or rebuilt.

DRUMMOND'S BANK, CHARING CROSS, alterations for Messrs. Drummond, 1777–8; dem. 1877.

NEW BURLINGTON STREET, No. 10, remodelled interior for Sir John Griffin Griffin, 1778–9; dem. *c.*1920 [*Survey of London* xxxii, 493–4; J. D. Williams in *Essex Jnl.* 18, 1983].

HILL STREET, No. 31 (now 17), drawing-rooms for Sir Abraham Hume, Bart., 1779; since altered (*C. Life* 17 March 1917).

?GREAT RUSSELL STREET, BLOOMSBURY, library for Topham Beauclerk, 1779; dem. 1788. Adam is stated to have designed this library for Beauclerk in the report of its demolition in *The World*, 21 March 1788. For its erection see Horace Walpole's *Letters* (to Lady Ossory, 14 Nov. 1779). No drawings survive, but in 1770 Beauclerk had employed Adam to make designs for an observatory on Muswell Hill (Bolton, Appendix, 23).

CUMBERLAND (formerly YORK) HOUSE, 86 PALL MALL, alterations for Henry Frederick, Duke of Cumberland, 1780–1; dem. 1908–12 [*Survey of London* xxix, 367].

HANOVER SQUARE, No. 21 (later 23), internal alterations and addition of balconies for Sir John Hussey Delaval, Bart., 1781–2; dem. *c.*1939 [Tyne & Wear Archives, Newcastle, Hussey-Delaval Papers, Box 19 (i); Northumberland C.R.O., 2 DE/23/1].

HARLEY STREET, No. 1 (now 2), alterations for 2nd Earl of Hopetoun, probably *c.*1787.

FITZROY SQUARE, south and east sides, 1790–4; S. side reconstructed internally after damage by bombing in 1940s.

EDINBURGH: DOMESTIC ARCHITECTURE

BELLEVUE, DRUMMOND PLACE (later THE EXCISE OFFICE), for Major General John Scott of Balcomie, 1775; dem. *c.*1840.

CHARLOTTE SQUARE, designed in 1791 and executed, with modifications (especially to the east and west sides), between 1792 and 1807.

QUEEN STREET, No. 7 (now 8), for Chief Baron Robert Ord, 1770–1.

GLASGOW: DOMESTIC ARCHITECTURE

COLLEGE HOUSES, Nos. 169–77 and 179–85 HIGH STREET, 1793; dem.

DUBLIN: DOMESTIC ARCHITECTURE

LANGFORD HOUSE, MARY STREET, ceiling of drawing-room, etc. for Hercules Rowley, 1765; dem.

COUNTRY HOUSES

HAREWOOD HOUSE, YORKS. (W.R.), modified John Carr's designs 1758 and designed interiors for Edwin Lascelles, cr. Lord Harewood, 1765–71: for further details see below under Carr, John.

GORDON HOUSE (later Seaton House and now Maria Grey Training College), ST. MARGARET'S ROAD, ISLEWORTH, MIDDLESEX, enlarged for General Humphry Bland, 1758–9.

HATCHLANDS, SURREY, interiors for Admiral Edward Boscawen, 1758–61 (*C. Life*, 17 Sept., 1 Oct. 1953).

SHARDELOES, nr. AMERSHAM, BUCKS., portico, interior decorations and stables for William Drake, 1759–63.

CROOME COURT, WORCS., interiors of house, also orangery and garden building called 'the Owl's Nest', for 6th Earl of Coventry, 1760 onwards [G. W. Beard, 'Robert Adam and Croome Court', *Connoisseur*, Oct. 1953].

KEDLESTON HALL, DERBYSHIRE, completed house for 1st Lord Scarsdale after Matthew Brettingham and James Paine had begun the central block and quadrants. The Adams were responsible for the S. front, the saloon, the interior decoration, the bridge, fishing house, and other minor buildings on the estate, *c.*1760–70 (*Vitruvius Britannicus* iv, 1767, pls. 45–51; *C. Life*, 26 Jan., 2, 9 Feb. 1978).

PAINSHILL, SURREY, probably designed ceiling of Temple of Bacchus for the Hon. Charles Hamilton, 1761; dem. [N. Kitz in *C. Life*, 13 Dec. 1979].

BOWOOD HOUSE, WILTS., altered portico, designed interiors and remodelled office-block for 2nd Earl of Shelburne, 1761–70: also designed mausoleum in grounds, completed 1764. The main body of the house was dem. 1956 (*C. Life*, 6 Sept. 1913).

COMPTON VERNEY, WARWICKS., rebuilt N. and S. wings, added portico, formed great hall, etc., and probably designed orangery (dem.) for 14th Lord Willoughby de Broke, *c.*1761–7.

WITHAM PARK, SOMERSET, new house for William Beckford, begun *c.*1762 (date of drawings) but abandoned after Beckford's death in 1770 [J. Collinson, *History of Somersetshire* ii, 1791, 235; *Vitruvius Britannicus* v, 1771, pls. 38–42].

MERSHAM-LE-HATCH, KENT, for Sir Wyndham Knatchbull, 1762–5 (*C. Life*, 26 March 1921).

SYON HOUSE, ISLEWORTH, MIDDLESEX, remodelled interior for 1st Duke of Northumberland, 1762–9, and designed entrance-screen, built 1773 (*Works* i, ii, iii; *C. Life*, 16 April 1992).

UGBROOKE PARK, DEVONSHIRE, rebuilt for 4th Lord Clifford, 1763–71, castle style [A. Rowan in *C. Life*, 20, 27 July, 3 Aug., 5 Oct. 1967].

OSTERLEY PARK, MIDDLESEX, remodelled for Robert Child, 1763–80.[1] The Adams also designed the entrance lodges, bridge and garden houses (J. Hardy and M. Tomlin, *Osterley Park House*, V. & A. Museum, 1985).

MOOR PARK, HERTS., designed gateway, tea-pavilion and perhaps also ceiling of gallery for Sir Lawrence Dundas, 1763–5 (J. Harris, The Dundas Empire', *Apollo*, Sept. 1967, 176).

AUDLEY END, ESSEX, interior decoration for Sir John Griffin Griffin, later 4th Lord Howard de Walden, 1763–5; three-arched bridge, 1764; Temple of Victory on Ring Hill, 1772; Palladian bridge and tea-house, 1782–3 [J. D. Williams, *Audley End: the Restoration of 1762–97*, Chelmsford 1966] (*C. Life*, 24 July 1925).

KIMBOLTON CASTLE, HUNTS., gatehouse, entrance-screen and St. Neot's road gates for 4th Duke of Manchester, 1764–5.

NOSTELL PRIORY, YORKS. (W.R.), remodelled hall and decorated principal rooms for Sir Rowland Winn, Bart., 1765–75. The Adams designed new wings, the northern of which was built between 1776 and 1785, when work was suspended: it was finally completed in 1875. The southern wing was never begun. They also designed the Featherstone, Foulby, Huntwick and perhaps also the Wragby Gates and the S. and W. sides of the stable block, including the Riding House, for which a drawing from the Adam office exists (Nostell archives, C 3/1/4/75). The N. and E. sides are by Pritchett and Watson, 1829, but making use of the Adams' design for the cupola [drawings and accounts at Nostell and the Soane Museum].

STRAWBERRY HILL, TWICKENHAM, MIDDLESEX, Gothic ceiling and chimney-piece in Round Drawing Room for Horace Walpole, 1766–7.

WIMBLEDON HOUSE, SURREY, interior decor-

[1] The west side of the house, including the Gallery, had already been remodelled for Francis Child before his death in 1761.

ation designed, and probably executed, for Sir Ellis Cunliffe, 1766–7; dem.

AUCHENCRUIVE HOUSE, AYRSHIRE, interiors for Richard Oswald, 1766–7; castellated tea-house tower, 1778 (*C. Life*, 17 Dec. 1932).

WHITEHAVEN CASTLE (formerly Flatt Hall, later a hospital), CUMBERLAND, enlarged and remodelled for Sir James Lowther, 1766–*c.*1770, castle style [B. Tyson in *Trans. Ancient Monuments Soc.* N.S. 28, 1984, 62–3].

LUTON HOO, BEDS., for 3rd Earl of Bute, 1767–74; left unfinished; altered by R. Smirke, *c.*1825 onwards; reconstructed by S. Smirke after a fire in 1843; interior remodelled by Mewès & Davis, 1903–7. The Adams probably also designed the stables. [M. Hall in *C. Life*, 16–23 Jan. 1992] (*Works* i).

HALSWELL PARK, SOMERSET, interior decoration of Ionic temple for Sir Charles Kemeys Tynte, Bart., 1767.

LEYTON, ESSEX, THE GREAT HOUSE, remodelled principal rooms for Thomas Oliver, *c.*1767–9; dem. 1905 [*V.C.H. Essex* vi, 191].

KENWOOD HOUSE, HAMPSTEAD, LONDON, remodelled house and added library and portico for 1st Earl of Mansfield, 1767–9 (*Works* i).

NEWBY HALL, YORKS. (W.R.), remodelled interior of south wing (containing sculpture gallery) and designed library for William Weddell, 1767–74 (*C. Life*, 19, 26 June 1937, 7, 14, 21 June 1979).

SALTRAM HOUSE, DEVON, redecorated saloon and library for John Parker, cr. Lord Boringdon, 1768–9 (*C. Life*, 4, 11 May, 14 Sept. 1967).

LOWTHER VILLAGE, WESTMORLAND, layout of model village for Sir James Lowther, carried out *c.*1770–5 on the basis of plans made by the Adams in 1766 [R. W. Brunskill, 'Lowther Village and Robert Adam', *Trans. Ancient Monuments Soc.* N.S. xiii, 1967].

MELLERSTAIN, BERWICKSHIRE, for the Hon. George Baillie, *c.*1770–8, incorporating wings by W. Adam, castle style (*C. Life*, 28 Aug., 4 Sept. 1968).

ALNWICK CASTLE, NORTHUMBERLAND, interior decoration of keep in the Gothic style for 1st Duke of Northumberland, *c.*1770–80; destroyed *c.*1854. The Adams succeeded James Paine (*q.v.*) as the duke's architects. The principal rooms for which they were responsible were the saloon, drawing-room and library. For plans of the castle in the 18th century see *Castles of Alnwick & Warkworth etc. from sketches by C. F. Duchess of Northumberland*, privately printed 1823 and *R.I.B.A. Sessional Papers 1856–7*, 14. The Adams also designed ALNWICK BRIDGE for the duke in 1773 [Alnwick archives, U.I. 46] and the Gothic BRIZLEE TOWER in Hulne Park, 1777–83 [*ibid.* and drawings in Soane Museum].

CASTLE HOUSE, CALNE, WILTS., rebuilt garden front for David Bull, 1770; dem. *c.*1960.

HITCHIN PRIORY, HERTS., designs for John Radcliffe, 1770–3. Adam drawings exist both for a new house on a different site and for remodelling the old house. Neither was carried out, but a new south front was built in 1770–3 by Richard Dixon, carpenter, and Joseph Dixon, mason, both of London. In Sept. 1772 Radcliffe paid 'Messrs. Adams' £140, and in December he paid £26 16s. to 'Mr. Nasmith Foreman to Messrs. Adams for plans' [Herts. C.R.O., DE 4422/2]. It would therefore appear that the new front with the Drawing and Music Rooms was based on drawings by the Adams (*C. Life*, 17–24 Oct. 1925).

WEDDERBURN CASTLE, DUNS, BERWICKSHIRE, for Patrick Home, 1771–5, castle style [A. Rowan, 'Wedderburn Castle', in *The Country Seat*, ed. Colvin & Harris, 1970, and in *C. Life*, 8 Aug. 1974].

STOWE HOUSE, BUCKS., designs for rebuilding S. front for 1st Earl Temple, 1771, executed with modifications by Thomas Pitt (*q.v.*), 1772–7.

FOXLEY, HEREFS., internal alterations for Sir Uvedale Price, Bart., 1772–3; dem. 1948 [drawings in Soane Museum and MS. notes in copy of Gibbs's *Book of Architecture* formerly at Foxley, recording Adam's employment, copied by the late B. Little].

HEADFORT HOUSE, CO. MEATH, IRELAND, interiors for 1st Earl of Bective, 1772–5 [J. Harris, *Headfort House and Robert Adam*, R.I.B.A. 1973] (*C. Life*, 21–28 March 1936).

ANCASTER HOUSE, RICHMOND, SURREY, probably designed house as built for 3rd Duke of Ancaster, 1773; since enlarged and altered.

LETTERFOURIE HOUSE, BANFFSHIRE, for James Gordon, 1773.

CALDWELL HOUSE, AYRSHIRE, for William Mure, 1773–4, castle style.

ST. EDMUND'S HILL (now MORETON HALL), BURY ST. EDMUNDS, SUFFOLK, for John Symonds, 1773–6.

THE OAKS, CARSHALTON, SURREY, temporary pavilion in garden for Lord Stanley, later 12th Earl of Derby, for *fête-champêtre* held on 9 June 1774 (cf. *Gent's Mag.* 1774, 264–5 and *Works* iii). The Adams were also responsible for castellated additions to the house (dem. 1957–60) carried out for Lord Derby *c.*1777–8 but never completed (D.

Hughson, *London* v, 1808; J. P. Neale, *Views of Seats* ii, 1819) [A. Rowan in *Burlington Mag.* Oct. 1985].

ARDINCAPLE CASTLE, DUNBARTONSHIRE, castellated addition for Lord Frederick Campbell, 1774; dem. 1957.

HAMPTON, MIDDLESEX, alterations to David Garrick's villa, probably including the remodelling of the portico, 1775.

WOOLTON HALL, LANCS., greatly enlarged for Nicholas Ashton, *c.*1775 [S. A. Harris. 'Robert Adam and Woolton Hall', *Trans, Hist. Soc. of Lancs. and Cheshire*, cii, 1950].

THE ELMS, EPSOM, SURREY, alterations and additions for Anthony Chamier, 1775; dem. *c.*1825.

COMBE BANK, SUNDRIDGE, KENT, addition of two wings with domed pavilions for Lord Frederick Campbell, one built *c.*1775–7, the other later; since much altered (*C. Life*, 28 Sept. 1972, 723).

HENDON PLACE (later TENTERDEN HALL), HENDON, MIDDLESEX, new front for William Aislabie, 1776; dem. 1936.

KNOWSLEY, LANCS., dairy for 12th Earl of Derby, 1776–7; dem.

WENVOE CASTLE, GLAMORGANSHIRE, for Peter Birt, 1776–7, castle style; dem. (except stables) after a fire in 1910. The Adams' plan and elevations were carried out with modifications. There are, however, no Adam drawings for the interiors. A statement in *Gent's Mag.* 1785 (ii), 937, that the architect was Henry Holland (then engaged at Cardiff Castle) may indicate that he was employed to execute the Adams' designs and it is likely that he designed the stables, as suggested in R.C.A.M. *Glamorganshire, The Greater Houses*, 1981, 346. A letter to Birt from Thomas Roberts (apparently the builder) in the National Library of Wales (MS. 20656 B) confirms the date of erection but throws no light on the identity of the architect employed.

MAMHEAD, DEVON, probably enlarged for 1st Earl of Lisburne, 1777; dem. 1830.

WORMLEYBURY, HERTS., interior decoration for Sir Abraham Hume, Bart., 1777–9 (*C. Life*, 30 Jan. 1915).

CULZEAN CASTLE, AYRSHIRE, for 10th Earl of Cassilis, 1777–92, castle style (*C. Life*, 4–11 Sept. 1915).

WEALD HALL, ESSEX, decoration of dining-room for Christopher Tower, 1778: dem. 1950–1 (*C. Life*, 3 Oct. 1914).

LANGSIDE, RENFREWSHIRE, for Thomas Brown, 1778; dem. *c.*1955 [drawings in Soane Museum inscribed 'Aikenhead'].

BYRAM HALL, YORKS. (W.R.), decoration of library, etc., for Sir John Ramsden, Bart., 1780; dem. *c.*1922.

MISTLEY HALL, ESSEX, alterations for Richard Rigby, *c.*1780; dem. 1835; also the Swan Fountain and adjacent cottages.

OXENFOORD CASTLE, MIDLOTHIAN, remodelled for Sir John Dalrymple, Bart., 1780–2, castle style; altered and enlarged by W. Burn, 1842 (*C. Life*, 15 Aug. 1974).

MOCCAS COURT, HEREFS., ceiling, etc. of circular drawing-room for Sir George Cornewall, Bart., 1781. The house was built 1776–83 to designs by A. Keck (*q.v.*) that resembled an unexecuted design by the Adams made in 1775 (*C. Life*, 18–25 Nov. 1976).

JERVISTON HOUSE, HOLYTOWN, LANARKSHIRE, for James Cameron, 1782; dem. 1966.

CASTLE UPTON, CO. ANTRIM, IRELAND, alterations for 1st Lord Templetown (d. 1785), begun 1783; further alterations and castellated stables for 2nd Lord Templetown, 1788–9; house altered by E. Blore, 1836–7.

BRASTED PLACE, KENT, for Dr. John Turton, 1784–5; roof heightened, etc., 1871.

ASHBURNHAM PLACE, SUSSEX, entrance lodges for 2nd Earl of Ashburnham, 1785 [accounts formerly at Ashburnham Place].

SUNNYSIDE HOUSE (now KINGSTON GRANGE), LIBERTON, MIDLOTHIAN, for Patrick, later Sir Patrick Inglis, Bart., 1785–7; S. side enlarged (A. Rowan in *Architectural Association Files*, No. 4, 1983).

BRIGHTON, SUSSEX, MARLBOROUGH HOUSE, OLD STEINE, rebuilt for W. G. Hamilton, 1786 [Drawings in Soane Museum, one wrongly titled as for 'Genl. Hamilton'].

GLASSERTON HOUSE, WIGTOWNSHIRE, for Admiral Keith Stewart, 1787; porch added by W. Elliot *c.*1820; dem. *c.*1950 (J. P. Neale, *Views of Seats*, 2nd ser. v, 1829).

KIRKDALE HOUSE, KIRKCUDBRIGHTSHIRE, for Sir Samuel Hannay, Bart., 1787–8; central block reconstructed internally after fire in 1893. The bridge is also by the Adams and so probably is the octagonal farmstead.

MILBURN, CLAREMONT LANE, ESHER, SURREY, for Sir John Hussey Delaval, Bart., later 1st Lord Delaval, 1787–90; since much altered [Hussey Delaval Papers in Northumberland C.R.O., 2 DE/23/1 and 3].

BARHOLM (or BALHAZY), nr. CREETOWN, KIRKCUDBRIGHTSHIRE, for John McCulloch, 1788; dem. 1960. The earlier design illustrated in *Vitruvius Scoticus*, pl. 94, was not carried out.

RUSCOMBE HOUSE, HARE HATCH, BERKS., probably remodelled for Sir James Eyre, 1789; dem. 1830.

YESTER HOUSE, EAST LOTHIAN, remodelled centre of N. front for 7th Marquess of Tweeddale, 1789–90 [J. G. Dunbar, 'The Building of Yester House 1670–1878',

Trans. E. Lothian Antiquarian Soc. xiii, 1972, 35–6] (*C. Life*, 23–30 July 1932 and 9, 16, 23 Aug. 1973).

NEWLISTON HOUSE, WEST LOTHIAN, for Thomas Hogg, 1789–90; wings added by D. Bryce, 1845 (*C. Life*, 26 Feb. 1916).

DALQUHARRAN CASTLE, AYRSHIRE, for Thomas Kennedy, 1789–90, castle style; enlarged 1881; gutted (except offices) 1971 (*C. Life*, 22 Aug. 1974, 494–5).

WYRESIDE, nr. GARSTANG, LANCS., alterations, including addition of portico, for J. F. Cawthorne, *c.*1789–90; rebuilt 1843 (engraving in *The Lonsdale Magazine or Provincial Repository* ii, 1821, 201).

TULLOCH CASTLE, ROSS & CROMARTY, castellated folly called CAISTEAL GORACH, for Duncan Davidson, 1790 [drawings in Soane Museum, vol. 48, 103–6, identified by Mr. John Gifford].

FULLARTON CASTLE, AYRSHIRE, castellated stables and farm buildings for Col. William Fullarton, *c.*1790.

UDNY HOUSE, TEDDINGTON, MIDDLESEX, probably added picture gallery for Robert F. Udny (d. 1802), perhaps *c.*1790; dem. *c.*1825 (W. Niven, 'Robert Udny's Villa at Teddington', *Home Counties Mag.* 1899).

SETON HOUSE, EAST LOTHIAN, for Alexander Mackenzie, 1790–1, castle style.

AIRTHREY CASTLE, STIRLINGSHIRE, for Robert Haldane, 1790–1, castle style.

ARCHERFIELD HOUSE, EAST LOTHIAN, remodelled interior for William Nisbet, 1790–1 [accounts in S.R.O., GD 6/1644].

DUNBAR CASTLE (later Castle Park Barracks), EAST LOTHIAN, for 8th Earl of Lauderdale, 1790–2.

BELLEVILLE (or BALAVIL) HOUSE, INVERNESS-SHIRE, for James Macpherson, 1790–6 (J. Fleming, 'Balavil House' in *The Country Seat*, ed. Colvin & Harris, 1970, 178–80).

GLENCARSE HOUSE, PERTHSHIRE, for Thomas Hunter, begun 1790s; additions 1889.

WALKINSHAW HOUSE, nr. PAISLEY, RENFREWSHIRE, for Dayhort Macdowall, 1791; dem. 1920.

GOSFORD HOUSE, EAST LOTHIAN, for Francis Charteris, titular Earl of Wemyss, 1791–*c.*1800; wings dem. *c.*1810; house remodelled and new wings built 1883–91 to designs of W. Young; centre block gutted 1940; N. wing unroofed *c.*1950; S. wing rehabilitated 1951 (G. Richardson, *New Vitruvius Britannicus* i, 1802, pls. 43–50; *C. Life*, 21 Oct., 4 Nov. 1971).

DALKEITH HOUSE, MIDLOTHIAN, bridge ('Montagu Bridge') over R. Esk in grounds for 3rd Duke of Buccleuch, 1792 [drawing in Scottish National Gallery Print Room, signed by R. Adam and dated 1791; set of drawings at Drumlanrig Castle]; entrance gates from Dalkeith, 1794 [drawing in Soane Museum li, 62, signed by James Adam and dated 1794].

STOBS CASTLE, ROXBURGHSHIRE, for Sir William Elliott, Bart., 1792–4, castle style.

MAULDSLEY CASTLE, LANARKSHIRE, for 5th Earl of Hyndford, 1792–6, castle style; altered by David Bryce, 1860; dem. 1959.

BALBARDIE HOUSE, BATHGATE, WEST LOTHIAN, for Alexander Majoribanks, 1793; dem. *c.*1960 except one pavilion, since dem. [T. P. Marwick, 'Balbardie House and Robert Adam', *Arch. Rev.* xlviii, 1920, 81–5].

BARNTON CASTLE, MIDLOTHIAN, remodelled for George Ramsay, *c.*1794, castle style; enlarged by David Hamilton, *c.*1810; dem. *c.*1920 (J. Small, *Castles & Mansions of the Lothians* i, 1883).

MAUSOLEA AND MONUMENTS

YESTER, MIDLOTHIAN, probably designed Gothic façade to truncated church to serve as burial place for 4th Marquess of Tweeddale, 1753 [J. G. Dunbar in *Trans. E. Lothian Antiquarian Soc.* xiii, 1972, 31–2].

BOWOOD, WILTSHIRE, mausoleum in memory of 1st Earl of Shelburne, 1761–4.

KING'S LYNN, NORFOLK, ST. NICHOLAS' CHAPEL, monument to Sir Benjamin Keene (d. 1757), erected 1762 [H. Colvin in *Arch. Hist.* 21, 1978, 94].

ST. MICHAEL PENKEVIL CHURCH, CORNWALL, monument to Admiral Edward Boscawen (d. 1761), erected 1763, J. M. Rysbrack, sculptor [signed].

MERSHAM CHURCH, KENT, tablet to Sir Wyndham Knatchbull (d. 1763).

KEDLESTON CHURCH, DERBYSHIRE, monument to Sir Nathaniel Curzon (d. 1758), erected 1763, J. M. Rysbrack, sculptor [signed].

ROMSEY ABBEY CHURCH, HANTS., tablet to Lady Palmerston (d. 1769).

WORCESTER CATHEDRAL, monument to Bishop James Johnson (d. 1774), Joseph Nollekens, sculptor.

MILTON ABBEY CHURCH, DORSET, table-tomb to Lady Milton, 1775, A. Carlini, sculptor [M. I. Webb in *Arch. Rev.* May 1958, 331].

KELBURNE CASTLE, AYRSHIRE, pyramidal monument to 3rd Earl of Glasgow (d. 1775); 1775.

EDINBURGH, OLD CALTON BURYING GROUND, monument to David Hume (d. 1776), erected 1778.

EDINBURGH, BOTANIC GARDENS, urn to memory of Carl Linnaeus, 1778.

DUMFRIES, column in memory of 3rd Duke of Queensberry (d. 1778), 1780.

DUMFRIES, ST. MICHAEL'S CHURCHYARD, probably designed monument to Hugh Lawson (d. 1781) [D. King, *The Complete Works of R. & J. Adam*, 408 (Addendum)].

HESTON CHURCH, MIDDLESEX, monument to Robert Child (d. 1782), P. M. Van Gelder, sculptor.

CASTLE UPTON, CO. ANTRIM, IRELAND, mausoleum in memory of the Hon. Arthur Upton (d. 1768), erected 1789.

ALVA CHURCHYARD, CLACKMANNANSHIRE, Johnstone family mausoleum for John Johnstone, 1790–1.

WESTERKIRK CHURCHYARD, DUMFRIESSHIRE, Johnstone family mausoleum for Sir James Johnstone, 1790–1.

WESTMINSTER ABBEY, LONDON, monuments to Lt. Col. Roger Townshend (d. 1759); James Thomson (d. 1748, erected 1762); Mary Hope (d. 1767); Elizabeth, Duchess of Northumberland (d. 1776); Major John André (d. 1780).

ADAM, WILLIAM (1689–1748), was the leading Scottish architect of his day. Though his forbears, as hereditary proprietors of a small estate near Forfar, had long ranked as minor gentry, William's father John Adam made a living as a builder in Kirkcaldy, where William was born on 30 October 1689. Of his early life nothing certain is known, but he was probably educated locally. By the 1730s he had made himself 'the universal architect' of a country whose belated emergence from a backward and impoverished past offered great opportunities to an enterprising man. In the words of John Clerk of Eldin, William Adam was 'a man of distinguished genius, inventive enterprise and engaging address' who was on excellent terms both with the Scottish aristocracy and with some of the leading figures of the 'Scottish Enlightenment'. Unlike Sir William Bruce and James Smith, the two leading architects of the previous generation, whose sympathies had been Jacobite, Adam was a Presbyterian Whig and therefore acceptable both to the government and to men of influence such as the 2nd Earl of Stair (who was his particular patron).

Although he always styled himself 'Architect', William Adam was not only a building contractor on a large scale, but also an entrepreneur who engaged in a variety of business enterprises. In 1728 Sir John Clerk of Penicuik 'could not enough admire the enterprising temper of the proprietor who had at that time under his own care near to twenty general projects – Barley Mills, Timber Mills, Coal Works, Salt Pans, Marble Works, Highways, Farms, houses of his own a-building and houses belonging to others not a few'. Although there were times when his friends thought that he had overreached himself ('As for Adams', wrote the Marquis of Annandale in 1724, 'he has so many Real, and so many imaginary projects, that he minds no body nor no thing to purpose'), he made a substantial fortune which he invested partly in house property in Edinburgh and partly in the estate of Blair Crambeth in Kinross-shire, the nucleus of which he bought in 1731 for £8010 Scots and renamed Blair Adam. In 1728 he took up residence in Edinburgh, when he was made a burgess gratis in recognition of the 'good services' which he had rendered to the city. During the previous year Lord Stair had almost succeeded in persuading Walpole to revive for Adam the post of Surveyor of the King's Works in Scotland previously held by James Smith in the reign of Queen Anne, but the proposal fell through because of the king's death. However, in 1728 Adam became Clerk and Storekeeper of the Works in Scotland, and in 1730 he was appointed Mason to the Board of Ordnance in North Britain, a post which brought him large contracts for military fortifications after the '45.

The extent of William Adam's architectural practice can be judged from the list of buildings printed below. In addition he often acted as a landscape gardener, e.g. at Newliston (1731), Taymouth (*c.*1732), Craigston (1733) and Buchanan House (1745). His vigorous and eclectic architectural style did not turn its back on the Scottish past, while drawing on a variety of recent classical architecture both English and continental. Despite his friendship with Sir John Clerk, the Scottish Lord Burlington, in whose company he visited London in 1727, he had 'little taste for the severities of the English neo-Palladian School'. On the contrary, he deployed architectural forms from a variety of sources with a freedom of invention which is sometimes bizarre but never dull. Arched windows, channelled masonry, richly carved tympana, prominent swags and other such features give a lively and sometimes slightly over-dressed character to his elevations which contrasts strongly with the restraint of most contemporary English architecture. Gibbs and Vanbrugh were undoubtedly influential in the formation of Adam's style, but there is evidence of an early visit to the Low Countries (whence, according to John Clerk of Eldin, he introduced the manufacture of pantiles into Scotland) which may have given him first-hand experience of continental baroque and his library included copies of Montano, Vignola, Ruggieri, Marot, Le Pautre and Decker.

In 1727 Adam began to solicit subscriptions for a volume of engravings illustrating the works of himself and other contemporary Scottish architects, but he never brought the project to fruition and, although the drawings and engravings were made, the book was still unpublished at the time of his death. John Adam issued proposals for printing it by subscription in 1766, but this too proved abortive, and it was not until 1811 that *Vitruvius Scoticus* was at last published by John Adam's son William. It contains 179 plates, of which over 100 illustrate Adam's own designs and ten (added by John Adam) some of the earlier works of his sons. There is no text or introduction.

In 1716 William Adam married Mary Robertson, daughter of William Robertson of Gladney, by whom he had four sons and six daughters. The eldest son John (*q.v.*), succeeded his father as the laird of Blair Adam, and carried on the various family businesses in Edinburgh. Robert and James (*qq.v.*), born in 1728 and 1732, left Scotland to go into partnership in London, whither they were followed by the fourth son William (1738–1822), who had a chequered business career in the City.

William Adam died on 24 June 1748, and is commemorated by a bust (illustrated by J. Swarbrick, *Robert Adam*, 1915, 35) in the family mausoleum in the Greyfriars Churchyard, Edinburgh. Another bust probably of William Adam is in the Scottish National Portrait Gallery, and there is a duplicate in the collection of Mr. John Harris. A portrait by William Aikman at Blair Adam is reproduced by Fleming and Gifford.

[John Fleming, *Robert Adam and his Circle*, 1962; *Vitruvius Scoticus*, ed. James Simpson, Edinburgh 1980; James Macaulay, *The Classical Country House in Scotland 1660–1800*, 1987; John Gifford, *William Adam*, Edinburgh 1989; *Architectural Heritage* i (1990), containing papers on William Adam; Eileen Harris, *British Architectural Books and Writers 1556–1785* (1990), 94–104.] In 1743 there was a lawsuit between William Adam and Lord Braco over his remuneration for designing and building Duff House, Banffshire. The printed *Depositions* incidental to this case throw considerable light on Adam's architectural practice.

PUBLIC BUILDINGS, ETC.

ABERDEEN, enlarged THE TOWN HOUSE, 1729–30; dem. 1865 [*Aberdeen Fifty Years Ago*, Aberdeen 1868, 65].

ABERDEEN, ROBERT GORDON'S HOSPITAL, 1730–2; altered and enlarged by John Smith 1830–3, now part of Robert Gordon's School [*Vit. Scot.*, pls. 107–8].

HAMILTON CHURCH, LANARKSHIRE, 1731–4; interior remodelled 1926 [*Vit. Scot.*, pls. 12–13].

STONEHAVEN, KINCARDINESHIRE, BRIDGE over COWIE WATER, 1732 [*Caledonian Mercury, ex inf.* Mr. J. Gifford].

DUNDEE, THE TOWN HOUSE, 1732–4; dem. 1932 [*Vit. Scot.*, pl. 104].

GLASGOW, THE UNIVERSITY LIBRARY, 1732–45; enlarged 1782; dem. *c.*1887 [*Vit. Scot.*, pls. 155–7].

ABERFELDY, PERTHSHIRE, THE TAY BRIDGE, 1733–5 [*Vit. Scot.*, pl. 122].

EDINBURGH, THE ORPHANS' HOSPITAL, 1734–5; dem. 1845 [*Vit. Scot.*, pls. 139–40].

SANQUHAR, DUMFRIESSHIRE, THE TOWN HOUSE, 1735–7 [S.R.O., Buccleuch Papers, GD 224/1638].

ABERUTHVEN, PERTHSHIRE, mausoleum for 1st Duke of Montrose, 1736–8 [S.R.O., GD 220/6/1384/30].

FALKIRK CHURCH, STIRLINGSHIRE, octagonal steeple, 1738 [S.R.O., CH2/242/13, p. 234].

EDINBURGH, GEORGE WATSON'S HOSPITAL, 1738–41; rebuilt by David Bryce as the Royal Infirmary, 1870–9 [*Vit. Scot.*, pl. 151; N.L.S., MS. 17871, ff. 17–22].

EDINBURGH, THE ROYAL INFIRMARY, 1738–48; partly dem. 1884 [*Vit. Scot.*, pls. 149–50; R. Thin, 'The Old Infirmary', *Book of the Old Edinburgh Club* xv, 1927].

HADDINGTON, EAST LOTHIAN, THE TOWN HOUSE, 1742–5; Assembly Rooms added 1788, steeple 1830–1 [Town Council Minutes in S.R.O., 10 June 1742].

EDINBURGH, ROYAL BANK OF SCOTLAND, OLD BANK CLOSE, HIGH STREET, plans accepted 1744, but carried out 1750–4 by S. Neilson to a revised plan; dem. [J. Fleming, *op. cit.*, 336].

DOMESTIC ARCHITECTURE

FLOORS CASTLE, ROXBURGHSHIRE, for 1st Duke of Roxburghe, 1721–6; remodelled by W. H. Playfair 1837–45 [*Vit. Scot.*, pls. 48–9; building accounts in Charter Room at Floors] (*C. Life*, 11–18 May 1978).

HOPETOUN HOUSE, MIDLOTHIAN, enlarged and remodelled for 1st and 2nd Earls of Hopetoun, 1721–6 [*Vit. Scot.*, pls. 14–21; A. Rowan, 'The Building of Hopetoun', *Arch. Hist.* 27, 1984].

MAVISBANK HOUSE, LOANHEAD, MIDLOTHIAN, for Sir John Clerk (*q.v.*), 1723–7; gutted by fire 1973 [*Vit. Scot.*, pls. 46–7; Gifford, *op. cit.*, 90–5].

LAWERS HOUSE, PERTHSHIRE, reconstructed 1724–6 for Col. Sir James Campbell [*Vit.*

Scot., pls. 158–9; bills attested by Adam in S.R.O., GD 237/99]. Further works in 1737–44, for which bills survive *ibid.*, were also by Adam: see his letter of 1737 about the design of the N. front (N.R.A.S., list 631, Bute Papers 2, Bdl. 1737 and 17, Bdl. 1742 (1)).

DALMAHOY (formerly BELVEDERE) HOUSE, RATHO, MIDLOTHIAN, for George Dalrymple, 1725–8 [*Vit. Scot.*, pl. 72].

MELLERSTAIN, BERWICKSHIRE, wings for George Baillie, 1725–9: part of a design for a complete new house, for which drawings attributable to William Adam are preserved at Mellerstain, together with letters from him (*C. Life*, 28 Aug., 4 Sept. 1958).

NEWLISTON HOUSE, WEST LOTHIAN, stables, offices and garden layout for 2nd Earl of Stair, *c.*1725–35 [*Braco Case Depositions*, 1743, 22, 24–5; plan for gardens by Wm. Adam in Muniment Room at Blenheim Palace, Oxon.]. The design for a new house illustrated in *Vit. Scot.* was not carried out.

GARVALD MANSE, EAST LOTHIAN, 1726 [N.L.S., MS. 14666, f. 109].

THE DRUM, LIBERTON, MIDLOTHIAN, for James Lord Somerville, 1726–30 [*Vit. Scot.*, pls. 37–8] (*C. Life*, 9 Oct. 1915).

ARNISTON, MIDLOTHIAN, for Robert Dundas, later Lord Arniston, 1726–32 [*Vit. Scot.*, pls. 39–44; A. A. Tait, 'William Adam and Sir John Clerk: Arniston and the Country Seat', *Burlington Mag.* March 1969; Mary Cosh, 'The Adam Family and Arniston', *Arch. Hist.* 27, 1984] (*C. Life*, 15–22 Aug. 1925).

DUN HOUSE, ANGUS, for David Erskine, Lord Dun, 1730–*c.*1740 [*Vit. Scot.*, pls. 69–70] (*C. Life*, 20 Nov. 1986, 22 June 1989). *Vit. Scot.*, pls. 57–8 represents an earlier scheme. The design of 1722 illustrated by Fleming, *op. cit.*, pl. 8, is by the Earl of Mar.

CRAIGIEHALL, WEST LOTHIAN, alterations, including new front doorway (removed 1852) and additions, including N.E. pavilion (remodelled 1828) for the Hon. Charles Hope, *c.*1730 [*Vit. Scot.*, pls. 86–7 and cf. later survey plan in portfolio at Dalmeny House]; also bridge in grounds [Percy Letters at Alnwick Castle, vol. 32, f. 79v].

RED BRAES, BONNINGTON, MIDLOTHIAN, for Hew Crawfurd, Clerk to the Signet, *c.*1730; dem. 1927 [S.R.O., GD 1/51/37, a sketch-plan by R. Mylne 1781 of 'A House designed by old Adam for Mr. Crawfurd, for Red Brae near Poutherhall']. See James Grant, *Old and New Edinburgh* iii, *c.*1880, for view of rear elevation and cf. *Book of the Old Edinburgh Club* xix, 170–1.

BALGREGAN HOUSE, STONEYKIRK, WIGTOWNSHIRE, remodelled for John McDowall, *c.*1730; dem. 1966 [*Vit. Scot.*, pls. 127–8].

YESTER HOUSE, EAST LOTHIAN, alterations including new roof and addition of pilasters and attic to centre of N. front for 4th Marquess of Tweeddale, 1730. The centre of the N. front was again altered to its present form by R. Adam in 1788 [*Vit. Scot.*, pls. 27, 30; J. G. Dunbar, 'The Building of Yester House 1670–1878', *Trans. E. Lothian Antiquarian Soc.* xiii, 1972, 26–7] (*C. Life*, 23–30 July 1932, 16–23 Aug. 1973).

CUMBERNAULD HOUSE, DUNBARTONSHIRE, for 6th Earl of Wigtown, 1731; reconstructed internally after fire in 1877 [*Vit. Scot.*, pls. 125–6].

CHATELHERAULT, LANARKSHIRE, for 5th Duke of Hamilton, 1731–43 [*Vit. Scot.*, pl. 160; accounts in S.R.O., GD 31/554; A. A. Tait, 'William Adam at Chatelherault', *Burlington Mag.* June 1968].

HADDO HOUSE, ABERDEENSHIRE, for 2nd Earl of Aberdeen, 1732–5; redecorated internally 1880 [*Vit. Scot.*, pls. 34–6] (*C. Life*, 18–25 Aug. 1966).

HOLYROODHOUSE, EDINBURGH, repairs 1733–4 [Edinburgh University Library, MS. Laing II, 88].

FALA HOUSE (or HAMILTON HALL), MIDLOTHIAN, for Thomas Hamilton, *c.*1735; dem. *c.*1830 [*Vit. Scot.*, pl. 121; *Braco Case Depositions*, 1743, 10, 19, 25–6] (Sir Hew Hamilton Dalrymple, *A Short Account of the Hamiltons of Fala, and of Fala House*, 1907, with plate).

NIDDRIE HOUSE, MIDLOTHIAN, additions for Andrew Wauchope, 1735; enlarged by W. Burn, 1823; dem. after fire in 1959 [*Braco Case Depositions*, 1743, 27, where Andrew Wauchope states that 'Mr. Adams built a Pavilion and Colonnades, and Office-houses for the Deponent, as also a Family Burial-Place, and Court before it of cut stone']. The design in *Vit. Scot.*, pls. 114–15 was not carried out.

BRUNSTANE HOUSE, DUDDINGSTON, MIDLOTHIAN, S. range rebuilt and office court added for Andrew Fletcher, Lord Milton, 1735–44 [N.L.S., MSS. 16555, ff. 6, 8; 17477, ff. 216–17, 225–8; 16564, ff. 4–5; 16559, f. 11; 16572, f. 7; 17478, f. 60, and framed drawing in Acc. 10444].

DUFF HOUSE, BANFFSHIRE, for William, Lord Braco, later 1st Earl of Fife, 1735–41 [*Vit. Scot.*, pls. 146–8; *Vitruvius Britannicus* v, 1771, pls. 58–60]. For Adam's lawsuit with Lord Braco in 1743 see the printed *Petitions* and *Depositions*, from which it appears that he also designed a temple on Downhill and a triumphal arch on an island in the River Deveron.

HAMILTON PALACE, LANARKSHIRE, temple on bowling-green for 5th Duke of Hamilton, 1736–7; dem. [Duke of Hamilton's archives at Lennoxlove, TD 80/100/21].[1]

EDINBURGH, TWEEDDALE LODGING, NO. 14 HIGH STREET, stables and coach-house for 4th Marquess of Tweeddale, 1736–7 [N.L.S., Yester Papers, MS. 14551, ff. 51–2].

TINWALD, DUMFRIESSHIRE, for Charles Erskine, 1738–40; interior destroyed by fire 1946 and reconstructed to a different design 1948 [*Vit. Scot.*, pls. 152–3; *Braco Case Depositions*, 1743, 23, 24, 28–9; letters from Adam in N.L.S., MS. 5074, ff. 153, 195].

MINTO HOUSE, ROXBURGHSHIRE, for Sir Gilbert Elliot, Lord Minto, *c.*1738–43; porch, offices, etc. added by A. Elliott *c.*1810; further alterations by M. Wardrop 1859; gutted 1973, dem. 1992–3 [plan, drawings, accounts, etc. in N.L.S., Minto papers] (plan and elevation dated 1766 in Bodleian Library, Gough Maps 39, f. 28).

BALVENY HOUSE, BANFFSHIRE, repaired roof for William, Lord Braco, 1739; dem. 1929 [Braco Case, *Petition for Lord Braco*, 1743, 4–5].

EDINBURGH, MINTO HOUSE, CHAMBERS STREET, for Sir Gilbert Elliot, Lord Minto, *c.*1739–40; dem. *c.*1845 [*Vit. Scot.*, pls. 59–60].

MURDOUSTOUN CASTLE, LANARKSHIRE, for Alexander Inglis, *c.*1735/40; heightened and partly rebuilt *c.*1800 [*Braco Case Depositions*, 1743, 10, 23, 46].

CARNOUSIE, BANFFSHIRE, addition for Arthur Gordon, 1740; dem. [*Braco Case Depositions*, 1743, 32; *An Exact Copy of the Depositions of the Witnesses adduced by William Lord Braco*, 1743, 1] (W. D. Simpson in *Trans. Banffshire Field Club*, 1936).

HOLYROODHOUSE, EDINBURGH, decoration of apartment for 5th Duke of Hamilton, 1740 [S.R.O., GD 31/554, John Adam *v.* Duke of Hamilton, 1770].

ELIE HOUSE, FIFE, work including carved pediment for Sir John Anstruther, *c.*1740 [*Braco Case Depositions*, 1743, 19, 20, 22]. The design for a new house in *Vit. Scot.*, pls. 88–9, was not carried out.

CAROLINE PARK, MIDLOTHIAN, offices for John, 2nd Duke of Argyll, 1740–2 [Mary Cosh in *C. Life*, 13 July 1972, 81].

GARTMORE HOUSE, PERTHSHIRE, for Nicol Graham, *c.*1740/5; altered by J. Baxter, 1779–80; remodelled 1901–2 [*Vit. Scot.*, pl. 83].

DALKEITH HOUSE, MIDLOTHIAN, stables, coach-houses, gardener's cottage and bridge over South Esk for 2nd Duke of Buccleuch, 1741–2 [S.R.O., accounts formerly at Dalkeith Palace].

TAYMOUTH CASTLE, PERTHSHIRE, addition of wings and other alterations for 3rd Earl of Breadalbane, *c.*1742; rebuilt in 19th century [*Vit. Scot.*, pl. 51; *Braco Case Depositions*, 13].

CULLEN HOUSE, BANFFSHIRE, bridge over ravine adjoining house, for 2nd Earl of Seafield, 1743 [letter from Adam to Lord Tweeddale, 4 June 1743, in N.L.S., MS. 14551, f. 89] (*C. Life*, 15 Sept. 1906).

CASTLE DOUNIE, INVERNESS-SHIRE, begun for 12th Lord Lovat, 1745, but abandoned after rebellion of 1745 [Fleming, *op. cit.*, 63–4].

INVERARAY CASTLE, ARGYLLSHIRE, supervised construction to designs of Roger Morris for 3rd Duke of Argyll, 1745–8 [I. G. Lindsay & Mary Cosh, *Inveraray and the Dukes of Argyll*, 1973, 32, 46, etc.].

The dates of the following works are uncertain

AIRDRIE, FIFE, works, probably including the addition of wings (dem.), for Col. Sir Philip Anstruther [*Braco Case Depositions*, 1743, 2].

BARNTON CASTLE, CRAMOND, MIDLOTHIAN, 'repairs and other works' for William Hamilton, Lord Daer (d. 1742); remodelled by R. Adam *c.*1794; dem. *c.*1927 [*Braco Case Depositions*, 1743, 24, 27].

BROXMOUTH, EAST LOTHIAN, a bridge, cascades and repairs to house for 1st Duke of Roxburghe [*Braco Case Depositions*, 1743, 2].

EGLINTON CASTLE, AYRSHIRE, rebuilt S. side and built kitchen and back court for 9th Earl of Eglinton (d. 1729); rebuilt 1798–1800; dem. 1925 [*Braco Case Depositions*, 1743, 16, 22].

THE HIRSEL, BERWICKSHIRE, work for 8th Earl of Home [*Braco Case Depositions*, 1743, 23].

LONMAY, ABERDEENSHIRE, for James Frazer. Only the pavilions shown in *Vit. Scot.*, pl. 95, appear to have been built, and one of these has since been demolished.

MAKERSTOUN HOUSE, ROXBURGHSHIRE, perhaps altered house for —— Makdougal in accordance with drawings now belonging to Mr. C. Scott of Gala House, Selkirkshire; remodelled *c.*1800; restored 1973.

NEWHALL HOUSE, GIFFORD, EAST LOTHIAN, for

[1] Adam was employed at Hamilton Palace from 1727 to 1743, making plans for the gardens and designing the church and dog-kennel (Chatelherault), etc., but appears to have been responsible only for minor repairs and alterations to the Palace itself, for the enlargement of which he made an unexecuted design illustrated in *Vitruvius Scoticus*.

Lord William Hay (d. 1723); dem. 1909 [*Vit. Scot.*, pls. 73–4; *Braco Case Depositions*, 1743, 2]. Alterations or additions by the Adam firm were contemplated in 1756 [S.R.O., GD 248/177/41/32].

The following designs by William Adam do not appear to have been carried out: AIRTH HOUSE, STIRLINGSHIRE, for James Graham, *c.*1720 [*Vit. Scot.*, pls. 64–5]; BELHAVEN HOUSE, EAST LOTHIAN, for 4th Lord Belhaven [*Vit. Scot.*, pl. 154]; BUCHANAN HOUSE, STIRLINGSHIRE, for 1st Duke of Montrose [*Vit. Scot.*, pls. 135–6], presumably the 'plan and estimate of the intended buildings at Buchanan A⁰ 1741' for which Adam was paid £315 [S.R.O., GD 220/6, vol. 4] and cf. GD 220/6/33, p. 826 and RHP 6150, a 'General Plan of the House, Gardens and Parks at Buchanan as proposed for His Grace the Duke of Montrose', signed 'William Adam 1745'; CALLY, KIRKCUDBRIGHTSHIRE, for Alexander Murray [*Vit. Scot.*, pls. 111–13]; a garden temple at CASTLE KENNEDY, WIGTOWNSHIRE, for 2nd Earl of Stair [*Vit. Scot.*, pls. 120–1]; CRAIGDARROCH, DUMFRIESSHIRE, for Alexander Ferguson, *c.*1726 [*Vit. Scot.*, pls. 77–8 and estimate in S.R.O., GD 77/204/1]. The existing house dated 1729 bears only a general resemblance to Adam's published design and must have been the work of a less sophisticated master builder; FASQUE CASTLE, KINCARDINESHIRE, for Sir Alexander Ramsay [*Vit. Scot.*, pl. 100]; KENMURE CASTLE, KIRKCUDBRIGHTSHIRE [*Vit. Scot.*, pls. 51–3]; PRESTON HALL, MIDLOTHIAN, for the Duchess of Gordon [*Vit. Scot.*, pls. 107–8]; SAUGHTON HOUSE, MIDLOTHIAN, for James Watson [*Vit. Scot.*, pls. 116–17]; TORRANCE HOUSE, LANARKSHIRE, for Col. James Stewart [*Vit. Scot.*, pls. 139–40; drawings in N.L.S., MS. 8222], with the possible exception of the wings.

POLLOK HOUSE, RENFREWSHIRE (now GLASGOW) is a doubtful case. It was built 1747–52 for Sir John Maxwell. A memorandum among the Maxwell Papers in the Mitchell Library, Glasgow [T-PM 106/243] refers (3 June 1734) to the promise of 'Mr. Adams Architect' to 'finish the plan of a house for me', and W. Fraser, *Memoirs of the Maxwells of Pollok*, 1863, i, 98, states that Adam made a design for the house in 1737. But nothing was done for ten years, and there is no evidence that the design adopted in 1747 was the one made in 1737. However, the house has features characteristic of Adam's work, and the elevation has affinities with an unexecuted design for Mellerstain attributed to him. If the design was his, its execution would presumably have devolved on his sons after his death in 1748 (*C. Life*, 25 Jan. 1913; Juliet Kinchin, *Pollok House*, Glasgow Museums & Art Galleries, 1983).

ADAMS, JAMES (1785–1850), son of James Adams, a Plymouth surveyor, was a pupil of Sir John Soane from 1806 to 1809. He was admitted to the Royal Academy Schools in 1808, winning the Gold Medal in 1809. By 1818 he was established in Portsmouth, where he practised for the rest of his life. His recorded works are: some additions to MOUNT EDGCUMBE HOUSE, CORNWALL, for 2nd Earl of Mount Edgcumbe [exhib. R.A. 1818]; the GENERAL DISPENSARY at DEVONPORT, 1815 [exhib. R.A. 1818]; a transeptal addition to SHEDFIELD CHURCH, HANTS., 1834, dem. *c.*1875 [I.C.B.S.]; THE CONGREGATIONAL CHAPEL at FAREHAM, HANTS., 1836, Perp. Gothic [*Evangelical Mag.* 1837, 272]; and ST. THOMAS'S CHURCH, ELSON, nr. GOSPORT, HANTS., 1845, in the Early English style [G.R.]. A. F. Livesay of Portsmouth was his pupil.

ADAMS, JOHN EASTRIDGE (– 1849), of Plymouth, is described in local directories as a builder, surveyor and hydraulic engineer. He designed the Greek Revival FREEMASONS' HALL in CORNWALL STREET, PLYMOUTH, 1828, illustrated as his work in J. Britton & E. W. Brayley's *Devonshire Illustrated*, 1829, 43.

ADDISON, EDWARD (1656–1705), was born at Kirkby Thore in Westmorland, where he was baptized on 2 October 1656. He became one of the leading master masons in Cumberland and Westmorland, and according to the antiquary Thomas Machell (*q.v.*), who held the living of Kirkby Thore from 1677 to 1698, he (Machell) and Addison were 'the first introducers of Regular building into these Parts'. Machell adds that 'Hutton Hall in the County of Cumberland was Altered by Addison' [Machell MSS., Cathedral Library, Carlisle, vol. I, p. 538]. HUTTON-IN-THE-FOREST, CUMBERLAND, has a classical frontispiece which is evidently the work for which Addison was responsible. This part of the house was built by Sir George Fletcher (d. 1700), and is in a style somewhat similar to the work of Addison's contemporary William Thackeray (*q.v.*). Its exact date is not known, but it was probably built *c.*1685 (*Archaeological Jnl.* cxv, 1958, pl. 26; *Country Life*, 4–8 Feb. 1965). In 1692–4 Addison executed the masonry of LOWTHER HALL, WESTMORLAND, for Sir John Lowther, Bart. [accounts in Cumbria Record Office], but it is not clear who designed this locally important classical house (see p. 953).

Addison was buried at St. Lawrence's Church, Appleby, on 4 February 1704/5. His surname was a common one in the villages between Appleby and Penrith, and a freemason of King's Meaburn named Robert Addison, reputed to be one of 'the best workmen' in the county of Westmorland, made a font for Bampton Church in 1726 [M. E. Noble, *The History of Bampton*, 1901, chap. xi]. John Addison, of Marwood Park, near Barnard Castle, Co. Durham, mason, who in 1684 contracted to enlarge Ewan Christian's tower-house at UNERIGG or EWANRIGG, nr. Maryport in CUMBERLAND (dem. 1903), 'according to a draught or modell thereof by the said John Addison to the [said] Ewan now delivered' (and still attached to the document), was no doubt a member of the same family [Cumbria Record Office, D/Cu/compt. 11] (B. Tyson, 'Unerigg Hall', *Trans. Ancient Monuments Soc.* N.S. 26, 1982).

AIKIN, EDMUND (1780–1820), was the youngest son of Dr. John Aikin, physician and author. He was articled to James Carr (*q.v.*) and entered the Royal Academy Schools in 1801. Shy, nervous and physically delicate, he hardly had the constitution for independent architectural practice, and a good deal of his time was devoted to literary projects. Together with the artist George Dawe he was employed by Thomas Hope (*q.v.*) to prepare the finished drawings for the latter's *Household Furniture* (1807), and in 1808 he published *Designs for Villas and other Rural Buildings*, with a dedication to Hope, and an *Essay on Modern Architecture* (in the *Essays* of the London Architectural Society, of which he became secretary). His *Essay on the Doric Order*, 1810, was the first work to provide comparative plates of the various exemplars of the Greek Doric orders drawn to the same scale. He also wrote the account of St. Paul's Cathedral for Britton's *Fine Arts of the English School* (1809–12), and an essay on Elizabethan architecture appended to his sister Lucy Aikin's *Memoirs of the Court of Queen Elizabeth* (1818). During this period Aikin's only architectural work appears to have been the PRESBYTERIAN CHAPEL in JEWIN STREET, LONDON, which he designed for Dr. A. Rees, 1808–9, dem. *c.*1890 [J. Britton, *Original Picture of London*, 27th ed. *c.*1832, 122, with engraving].

For two or three years (*c.*1810–13) Aikin assisted General Sir Samuel Bentham, the naval engineer and architect, in his designs for works at Sheerness, Portsmouth, and other dockyards. His success in winning the competition[1] for the WELLINGTON ASSEMBLY ROOMS (now the Irish Centre, 127 Mount Pleasant) at LIVERPOOL (1815–16) induced him to settle there in 1814. He was subsequently employed to adapt an existing house in Colquitt Street for the premises of the LIVERPOOL ROYAL INSTITUTION (opened 1817; dem.: see illustration in *The Stranger in Liverpool*, 1837, 22), and designed various other buildings in Liverpool, including some 'elegant villas'. His only other recorded work appears to have been a villa at TOTTERIDGE, HERTS., illustrated in his *Designs for Villas*, pls. 24–5. In 1819 his health broke down and he died at his father's house at Stoke Newington on 11 March 1820.

As the Wellington Rooms at Liverpool show, Aikin was a fastidious and scholarly Greek Revival architect. Although, under pressure from a client, he designed a row of Gothic shop-fronts in Bold Street, Liverpool, which are said to have 'exhibited great originality and picturesque effect', he regarded the Gothic Revival with disapproval, and rather perversely attempted in his *Designs for Villas* to advocate the merits of Islamic architecture as a possible alternative. [Memoir prefaced to 1835 edition of *Designs for Villas*; Lucy Aikin, *Memoir of John Aikin, M.D.* i, 1823, 267–72; *A.P.S.D.*; W. J. Pinks, *History of Clerkenwell*, ed. Wood, 1851, 268; J. A. Picton, *Memorials of Liverpool* ii, 1875, 212; numerous references in Thomas Rickman's diary.]

AINGER, ALFRED (1797–1859), was the son of Samuel Ainger, a carpenter and surveyor of London. He entered the Royal Academy Schools in 1816 and took up the freedom of the City of London in 1826. He was Surveyor to the Trustees of the Charities of the parish of St. Augustine and St. Faith in the City, and in 1830–1 he and J. H. Taylor repaired the church of ST. AUGUSTINE, OLD CHANGE and rebuilt the upper part of the spire [Guildhall Library, MSS. 8881, 8898]. His practice was not extensive as he possessed private means, and his only major work was the NORTH LONDON (later UNIVERSITY COLLEGE) HOSPITAL, 1833, rebuilt 1897–1906 to the designs of Alfred Waterhouse. He also designed a large conservatory in the Royal Horticultural Society's Gardens at Chiswick, Middlesex, in 1838 [*A New Survey of London*, published by John Weale 1853, ii, 484]. Ainger was the author of *Suggestions towards an Amendment of the Building Act*, 1825, and of *The Building and other Acts relating to Building*, 1836. He was the father of Canon Alfred Ainger (1837–1904), Master of the Temple.

[1] The other competitors were Eyes, Gandy, Gwilt, Jay, Lugar and Rickman.

[*Builder* xvii, 1859, 765; Guildhall Library, MSS. 2738/1 and 2; E. Sichel, *The Life and Letters of Alfred Ainger*, 1906, in which a portrait of the architect is reproduced.]

AIRD, —, described as 'Master of Works', designed the INFIRMARY, DUNCAN STREET, GREENOCK, RENFREWSHIRE, 1808–9, enlarged 1869 [D. Weir, *History of the Town of Greenock*, Greenock 1829, 32].

AITCHISON, GEORGE (1792–1861), was the son of a carpenter and builder at Leyton in Essex. He was first (1808) apprenticed to his father, and then became (1813) a pupil of H. H. Seward, with whom he remained until 1823, when he became principal clerk to Thomas Hardwick. In 1826 he moved to the office of Thomas Lee, but in the following year obtained the appointment of surveyor or clerk of works to the St. Katherine's Dock Company. He was also architect to the Founders' Company and to the London and Birmingham Railway Company, for whom he designed TRING STATION, HERTS., in 1838 [exhib. at R.A. 1840]. For the Union Bank of London he enlarged their premises in Pall Mall and designed a branch office in Fleet Street. He is said to have been equally competent as architect, engineer and surveyor, and to have been 'not only excellent at arrangement and construction, but one of the most beautiful draughtsmen of his day'. Both sides of his professional activity were represented in the drawings that he exhibited at the Royal Academy. He was a member of the Society called 'Freemasons of the Church' (for which see p. 105) and in 1842 was given the title of 'Professor of Concreting and Opus Incertum' [*Builder* i, 1843, 24]. He died on 12 June 1861. His son George Aitchison, R.A. (1825–1910), was President of the R.I.B.A. in the years 1896–9. [*Minutes of Proceedings of the Institution of Civil Engineers* xxi, 1861–2, 569–71.]

AITKINS, JOHN, was the architect (otherwise unknown) who was employed by Thomas Stonor to carry out alterations in the Gothic style to the interior of the hall of STONOR PARK, OXON., in 1758–9 [*V.C.H. Oxon.* viii, 142] (*C. Life*, 13 Oct. 1950).

AKROYD, JOHN (1556–1613), was a Yorkshire master mason who achieved celebrity as the builder of the Schools Quadrangle at Oxford University. John Akroyd was the eldest son of William Akroyd, a mason living at Warley in the parish of Halifax, where he was born in November 1556. His only documented work in Yorkshire is the GRAMMAR SCHOOL at HEATH (1598–1601, dem.), but the chairman of the governors at the time was Sir John Savile (d. 1607) of Bradley and Methley Halls, and circumstantial evidence suggests that Akroyd designed or altered both these houses, and that he may also have been employed at Howley Hall by another member of the Savile family: Sir John, afterwards Lord Savile (d. 1630). It was Sir Henry Savile (younger brother of Sir John Savile of Methley) who, as Warden of Merton College, first brought Akroyd to Oxford at a time when there was a dispute between the university and the newly incorporated Company of Freemasons, Carpenters, Joiners and Slaters of Oxford. At Merton, Akroyd and his partner John Bentley (a freemason from Elland, nr. Halifax) undertook the masonry of the GREAT or FELLOWS' QUADRANGLE in January 1608/9 for £570 and completed it in 1610. The carpenter was another Yorkshireman, Thomas Holt. In August 1611 the College gave Akroyd a gratuity of £20, 'because he had faithfully carried out the work of erecting the new quadrangle'.[1]

In 1610–11 Akroyd was employed by Sir Thomas Bodley to build the ARTS END of THE BODLEIAN LIBRARY, and in March 1613 he and his partner John Bentley undertook to build the adjoining SCHOOLS QUADRANGLE (not completed until *c.*1620). Akroyd, however, died in September 1613, long before the building was finished. In the register of St. Mary's Church, where he was buried, he is commemorated as 'Mr. John Acroid, chief builder of the Schools', His partner Bentley died only three months later at the age of 40 (December 1613), and was buried at St. Peter's in the East, where a monument (now destroyed) described him as *Johannes Bentleius Eboracensis novae partis bibliothecae novarumque scholarum architectus peritissimus.*[2] The direction of the works seems then to have passed to John Bentley's brother Michael, who died at Oxford in June 1618, and was also buried at St. Peter's in the East. Thomas Holt, the carpenter, survived until 1624, and (having settled in Oxford) was buried in

[1] 'Eodem tempore allocavimus Johanni Acroide architecto viginti libras preter alias 20 li. quas antea accepit quod fidelem operam lavaverat in constructione novi aedificii quadrangularis' (Merton College *Registrum Annalium*, 1567–1731, p. 236).

[2] In 1611 Sir Edward Pytts of Kyre Park, Worcs., 'brought John Bentley ffreemason from Oxford (where he wrought the newe addition to Sir Thomas Bodleigh his famous library) with me as I came from London to Kyer to take instructions from me by veuinge the place to draw me a newe platte . . .' (Mrs. Baldwyn-Childe, 'The Building of Kyre Park', *The Antiquary* xxi, 1890).

Holywell churchyard, where Anthony Wood records an inscription *in memorian Thomae Holt Eborac. Scholarum publicarum architecti.*

In the absence of any regular series of accounts for the building of the Schools Quadrangle it is impossible to cite any evidence which demonstrates conclusively that Akroyd (or anyone else) was responsible either for the design of the building as a whole or for that of its most ambitious feature, the Tower of the Five Orders. Undoubtedly Sir Henry Savile, whose judgement was to Bodley 'as the judgement of a mason', must have been closely involved in the general conception. But in England the idea of towers ornamented with superimposed orders, though deriving ultimately from French architecture of the mid-sixteenth century, seems to have found particular favour in the northern counties, notably at Howley Hall, Yorks. (*c.*1590), Stonyhurst, Lancs. (*c.*1592–5), and Browsholme Hall, Yorks. (*c.*1605–10). It is therefore possible to see the Merton tower and its successor in the Schools Quadrangle as a Yorkshire idea which Sir Henry Savile imported to Oxford together with his masons, and if so John Akroyd no doubt made the necessary drawings from which they were built. Badly integrated into the traditional Gothic quadrangles in which they are set, they certainly show the limited comprehension of classical architecture that might be expected of a Yorkshire master mason.

[T. W. Hanson, 'Halifax Builders in Oxford', *Trans. Halifax Antiquarian Soc.*, 1929, 253–317; Rachel Poole, 'The Architect of the Schools and the Tower of the Five Orders', *Bodleian Quarterly Record* iii, 1922, 263–4; I. G. Philip, 'The Building of the Schools Quadrangle', *Oxoniensia* xiii, 1948; Catherine Cole, 'The Building of the Tower of Five Orders', *Oxoniensia* xxxiii, 1968; *V.C.H. Oxon.* iii, 45–7, 102.]

ALBON, WILLIAM (*c.*1797–1870), was admitted to the Royal Academy Schools in 1822 at the age of 25, and exhibited architectural drawings at the Academy from various London addresses from 1817 to 1852. Some of his exhibits were of a topographical character, and his career as an architect remains obscure. He died in South Molton Street on 19 May 1870 [Principal Probate Registry, Calendar of Probates].

ALDERSON, MOSES ATHA (1801–1869), was born at Holbeck, nr. Leeds, and appears subsequently to have practised as an architect and engineer at Birmingham, where he died in 1869. He was a member of the Royal Society of Arts and of the London Mechanics' Institution. In 1834 he published *An Essay on the Nature and Application of Steam*. He competed for the Houses of Parliament in 1835. His design is described in the *Catalogue of the Designs for the New Houses of Parliament*, 6th ed., 65. The two Houses were each to be octagonal, surmounted by a Gothic lantern. An album containing designs by Alderson for ROSE VILLA, THISTLE GROVE, BROMPTON, for E. R. Clarke, *c.*1841, is in the R.I.B.A. Drawings Collection.

ALDERSON, WILLIAM (–*c.*1835), of Chelsea, was a member of the Society of Friends. His principal recorded work was THE MIDDLESEX COUNTY LUNATIC ASYLUM (now ST. BERNARD'S HOSPITAL), HANWELL, MIDDLESEX, 1829–31; wings added 1838 [G.L.R.O., M.A./AJ/1] (description in Weale's *New Survey of London* ii, 1853, 601–7). In 1828 he told the committee of magistrates responsible for the Asylum that he had recently designed a School for the Society of Friends at WIGTON, CUMBERLAND. Later the same year he showed Thomas Rickman his designs for the Asylum and for FRIENDS' MEETING HOUSES at HODDESDON, HERTS. and STOKE NEWINGTON, MIDDLESEX. The latter, built in 1827–8, was dem. in 1957 (*Arch. Rev.* April 1946, 113). He is referred to as 'the late Mr. Alderson' in Loudon's *Architectural Magazine* for July 1835, and his will was proved in June 1836 [P.C.C. 333 STOWELL]. Unexecuted designs by Alderson for lodges for Woodfold Park, Lancs., are in the Lancashire R.O. (DDX 949/2/9).

ALDHOUSE, FRANCIS, was a surveyor practising in Little Titchfield Street, London, in the early nineteenth century. He was concerned in the remodelling of BAYFORDBURY, HERTS., for William Baker in 1809–12. Plans made by him in 1809 are referred to in correspondence among the Baker family papers in the Hertfordshire Record Office (Nos. 401–8), and no record of any other architect has been found. The elegant Greek Doric additions are illustrated in *C. Life*, 17, 23 Jan. 1925. From the same correspondence it appears that Aldhouse had recently been involved in building SACOMBE PARK, HERTS., for George Caswall.

ALDRICH, HENRY (1648–1710), the son of Henry Aldrich (d. 1683), later auditor to the Duke of York, was born in January 1647/8. He was educated at Westminster School and at Christ Church, Oxford, taking his B.A. in 1666 and his M.A. in 1669. In 1682 he became a Canon of Christ Church and received his B.D. and D.D. Finally in 1689 he succeeded to the office of Dean. From 1692 to 1695 he served as Vice-Chancellor.

Aldrich had a reputation for learning in many fields, and his writings included editions of Greek and Latin texts, ecclesiastical tracts, and books on logic, mathematics, heraldry, music and architecture. His library contained many books on antiquities and a large collection of architectural and other engravings. He left his books to Christ Church Library, but all his personal papers were destroyed in accordance with his will, so that little is known about his architectural activities. There is, however, reason to think that he had visited France and Italy, and according to Dallaway's edition of Walpole's *Anecdotes* he had spent 'a considerable time' in the latter country, where he associated with 'the eminent in architecture'. He was certainly regarded as an 'able judge in architecture' by his contemporaries, as is shown by the direction of Sir Edward Hannes, who in 1710 left £1000 for the building of the Westminster School dormitory, 'in contriving whereof he desired Sir Christoper Wren and Dr. Aldrich should be consulted'. At the time of his death he was engaged in compiling an *Elementa Architecturae*, 'intended to have been divided into two parts treating respectively of Civil and Military Architecture'. Each part was to consist of three books, but only Book 1 and part of Book 2 of the Civil section were completed. A few copies of the first 44 pages of the text were printed during the author's lifetime[1], but the first edition (in Latin and English) was not published until 1789 as *Elementa Architecturae Civilis* (2nd ed. 1818). 'It is a scholarly rather than a practical work, and contains many quotations from Vitruvius and Palladio, the authors whom he accepted as his chief authorities.' Aldrich was buried in Christ Church Cathedral, where a monument was erected twenty years later by Dr. George Clarke (*q.v.*), his former friend and colleague. His portrait by Kneller is in Christ Church Hall and there is a marble bust in the library. Other portraits at Christ Church and in the Bodleian are listed by Mrs. Poole, *Catalogue of Oxford Portraits* (Oxford Historical Society) i, 78, and iii, 40–2.

Architecture was only one of Aldrich's attainments, and even in Oxford very few buildings can be attributed to him. Indeed, the only building which he is known definitely to have designed is the PECKWATER QUADRANGLE at his own college of CHRIST CHURCH, built by William Townesend between 1706 and 1714. On the foundation-stone laid by the Earl of Salisbury, Aldrich was formally described as its 'architect' [Bodleian, Tanner MS. 338, f. 315]. The fourth side of the quadrangle, intended by Aldrich to contain further sets of rooms, was eventually completed as a library in 1717–38 to the designs of Dr. George Clarke [Hist. MSS. Comm., *Portland* vii, 217, and cf. the engravings showing Aldrich's original scheme reproduced by Colvin, *Unbuilt Oxford*, fig. 22]. A scheme to adorn Tom Quadrangle at Christ Church with a 'piaza' or colonnade in place of the intended Gothic cloister, reported in 1705 to have been recently abandoned, was no doubt due to Aldrich [Bodleian Library, MS. Top. gen. c. 66, ff. 31–64]. Peshall's statement, in his edition of Wood's *City of Oxford*, 1773, 41, that Aldrich was the architect of ALL SAINTS CHURCH, OXFORD, 1701–10, has generally been accepted, and he was certainly concerned in its erection, for his name appears among the list of trustees on the design engraved by M. Burghers which was circulated to appeal for funds after the fall of the tower of the old church in March 1700. The steeple of the new church was not, however, completed until 1718–20, and its design as executed represents a compromise between Aldrich's original proposal and an alternative one submitted by Nicholas Hawksmoor after the Dean's death [H. M. Colvin, 'The Architects of All Saints Church, Oxford', *Oxoniensia* xix, 1954]. In 1675–6 Aldrich had supervised the repair of ST. MARY'S CHURCH, OXFORD, in conjunction with Maurice Wheeler, rector of St. Ebbe's [*Letters of H. Prideaux*, Camden Soc. 1875, 50].

Three other Oxford buildings have been attributed to Aldrich with less certainty. In the case of TRINITY COLLEGE CHAPEL (1691–4) all that is definitely known is that he was one of the 'able judges in architecture' whose advice the College took before deciding to rebuild 'wholly upon new foundations'. There is no contemporary evidence to support the conjecture that he was the author of the design submitted to Wren's criticism by the President, Dr. Bathurst [*Wren Soc.* v, 15], but the possibility cannot be dismissed. According to Dallaway's edition of Walpole's *Anecdotes of Painting* iv, 1827, 75, Aldrich designed the FELLOWS' BUILDING at CORPUS CHRISTI COLLEGE, 1706–12. Here the design may have been due to William Townesend, the contracting mason, but the façade bears sufficient

[1] According to a note in the sale catalogue of James West's library (1773) only ten copies were printed, 'and those never perfected, the author's death preventing'. There is a copy (B.n.9) in Worcester College Library that was given to Dr. George Clarke by Aldrich in 1708. With it are (B.n.8) the original drawings for 39 of the plates, with a note by Dr. Clarke that they were from the Dean's own hand.

resemblance to Peckwater to suggest that Aldrich may have had some influence on it. On the strength of an otherwise unknown engraved design for its elevation in his collection, it has been suggested that Aldrich may have been the architect of QUEEN'S COLLEGE LIBRARY (1693–4), but engraved designs were commonly circulated to attract subscriptions and the survival of one in Aldrich's extensive collection proves nothing.

What is remarkable about Aldrich's one authenticated work is its conscious classicism. The façades of Peckwater Quadrangle (though awkwardly juxtaposed) anticipate those of Queen Square, Bath, by some twenty years, and entitle Aldrich to be regarded as one of the forerunners of the Palladian movement which he did not live to see. In this connection it is worth drawing attention to the fact that it was Aldrich who persuaded C. Fairfax to undertake the Latin translation of Palladio's *Antichità di Roma* that was published by the Clarendon Press in 1709 (cf. *Hearne's Collections*, ed. Dobie, viii, 103) and that in the preface Fairfax states that Aldrich acknowledged Palladio as his professed master in architecture. Further evidence of Aldrich's Palladian interests is afforded by a drawing in Worcester College Library. This is a copy in Aldrich's hand of Webb's drawing of Palladio's Teatro Olimpico at Vicenza.

That Aldrich was a skilled draughtsman is shown by two volumes of his drawings preserved at Christ Church. These are mostly copies of engravings, and many of them are derived from published illustrations of churches and other buildings in the Holy Land. At the Clarendon Press there is a volume of designs for initial letters and decorations which have been attributed to Aldrich by Miss H. M. Petter. The original drawings at Christ Church for the Oxford Almanacs of 1676 and 1689 appear to be in his hand. The latter has an architectural setting; but the only strictly architectural designs by Aldrich that have so far been identified are the drawings for his *Elementa Architecturae Civilis* in Worcester College Library (see p. 70, n. 1), a plan and elevation for All Saints Church that is presumably by him (reproduced in *Oxoniensia* xix, 1954, pl. v), and three drawings among the unexecuted projects for enlarging All Souls College that also appear to be in his hand (see H. M. Colvin, *Catalogue of Architectural Drawings in the Library of Worcester College, Oxford*, 1964, pls. 49–50, where they are wrongly attributed to John James).

[*D.N.B.*; *Hearne's Collections*, ed. Dobie, iii, Oxford Historical Soc. 1889, 89–90; E. F. A. Suttle, 'Henry Aldrich, Dean of Christ Church', *Oxoniensia* v, 1940; W. G. Hiscock, 'Henry Aldrich, Book Collector, Musician, Architect', in *A Christ Church Miscellany*, 1946; W. G. Hiscock, *Henry Aldrich*, 1960; Howard Colvin, *Unbuilt Oxford*, 1983, chap. 4; Eileen Harris, *British Architectural Books and Writers 1556–1785*, 1990, 109–13.]

ALEFOUNDER, JOHN (1732–1787), was the son of John Alefounder (d. 1763), a well-to-do carpenter and builder of Colchester. He practised as an architect and surveyor in London, where in 1774 he was appointed District Surveyor of the parish of St. Luke, Old Street [Middlesex County Records]. His son John, born 1758, entered the Royal Academy Schools in 1776 as an architectural student, but became a portrait and miniature painter, and died at Calcutta in 1795 [information from Mr. J. Bensusan-Butt; *Gent's Mag.* 1795 (ii), 880].

ALEXANDER, SIR ANTHONY (– 1637), was second son of William Alexander, 1st Earl of Stirling (d. 1640). He was educated at Glasgow University, and in July 1626 had licence to travel abroad for three years. On his return he was appointed (1 April 1629) Master of Work to the King in Scotland jointly with James Murray (*q.v.*). Anthony must have owed the appointment to his father, at that time Secretary of State for Scotland, but in the warrant he is stated to have acquired 'eruditione et peregrinando sufficientem peritiam in architectura'. The office was confirmed after Murray's death in 1634, but Alexander himself died at London on 17 September 1637. He had been knighted in 1635. [J. Balfour Paul, *The Scots Peerage* viii, 178.]

ALEXANDER, DANIEL ASHER (1768–1846), a native of London, was educated at St. Paul's School, and became a pupil of Samuel Robinson. He entered the Royal Academy Schools in 1782, and won the Silver Medal the same year. In 1796 he was appointed surveyor to the London Dock Company, for whom he designed very extensive ranges of warehouses at Wapping, 'capacious in size, convenient in arrangement, and magnificent in design and execution'. From 1796 to 1822 he was also Surveyor to the Fishmongers' Company. In 1807 he became surveyor to Trinity House, and designed a number of lighthouses for the Brethren.

Alexander specialized in the designing of large utilitarian buildings such as prisons and warehouses. He was an able and resourceful engineer, and handled large expanses of stone- or brick-work with a sense of drama which reflected his admiration for Piranesi's engravings. The interiors of Maidstone Gaol, in particular, are said to remind the architectural visitor forcibly of the *Invenzioni di Carceri*. His practice was extensive, but his reputation suffered from the revelation of frauds perpetrated by the clerk of works and tradesmen employed at Maidstone Gaol, which he failed to detect, and for which he was obliged to accept responsibility.

In London, Alexander moved in artistic as well as professional circles. Flaxman and Chantrey were his intimate friends, and in their company he made annual visits to France from 1815 onwards. Edward I'Anson (*q.v.*) was at first his assistant and afterwards his partner. His eldest son, Daniel Alexander (*c*.1796–1843), had an architectural training in his father's office, but in 1820 gave up architecture for the Church.[1] His pupils included W. H. Ashpitel, James Beek, C. A. Busby, J. P. Pritchett, James Savage, Richard Suter, John Wallen, John Walters, John Whichcord and Joseph Woods. He retired in the 1820s, moving first to Yarmouth in the Isle of Wight, and then to Exeter, where he died. He was, however, buried at Yarmouth, where he had gratuitously designed the church tower as a memorial to his third son Henry, who died in 1829, aged 19. There is a portrait by John Partridge in the Port of London Authority's Building, and one by Chantrey in the Victoria and Albert Museum [*Gent's Mag*. 1846 (ii), 210; *Builder* xx, 1862, 795; *A.P.S.D.*; *D.N.B.*; A. E. Richardson, 'The Architect of Dartmoor', *Arch. Rev.* April 1918; information from Mr. Robert Adams].

LONDON, HIGHBURY HILL HOUSE, for Dr. William Saunders, *c*.1790; dem. [*A.P.S.D.*]

SOUTHWARK, SCOTT'S WAREHOUSES, BANKSIDE, *c*.1790 [*A.P.S.D.*]

LONDON, PURDAY'S WAREHOUSES, No. 48 MARK LANE, *c*.1790; dem. [*A.P.S.D.*]

THE MOTE, nr. MAIDSTONE, KENT, for 1st Earl of Romney, 1793–1801 [MS. accounts in Kent Archives Office].

LONDON DOCK BUILDINGS and WAREHOUSES, WAPPING, 1796–1820; dem. 1970s except part of New Tobacco Warehouse, converted into a shopping centre etc. 1986 [*A.P.S.D.*]

ROCHESTER BRIDGE, widened and formed two centre arches into one, 1798 [Nichols, *Literary Illustrations* vi, 736–7; exhib. at R.A. 1799].

ROCHESTER CATHEDRAL, repaired fabric 1799–1803 and made plan for improvement of Close, 1801 [B.L., *King's Maps* xvii, 8; information from Mrs. Mary Covert].

CAMER COURT, MEOPHAM, KENT, proposed alterations to offices for William Smith, 1801 [Kent Archives Office, drawings in U 1127/P23/1–2].

LONGFORD CASTLE, WILTS., alterations and extensive additions (including three new towers) for 2nd Earl of Radnor, 1802–17, closely following a scheme made by J. Wyatt in 1796 [*A.P.S.D.*]

BRISTOL, BAPTIST COLLEGE, STOKES CROFT, 1806–12; dem. 1972 [*A.P.S.D.*, *s.v.* 'Bristol'].

DARTMOOR PRISON OF WAR, PRINCETOWN, DEVONSHIRE, 1806–9; since much altered [*A.P.S.D.*]

GREENWICH, QUEEN'S HOUSE, addition of flanking blocks and colonnades for Royal Naval Asylum, 1807–10 [P.R.O., ADM 80/111].

MAIDSTONE, COUNTY GAOL, 1811–19 [*Gent's Mag*. 1813 (ii), 32–4, 68, 134–5, 329–32, 645–8].

DOWNTON CHURCH, WILTS., alterations for 2nd Earl of Radnor, 1812–15 [*A.P.S.D.*].

LONDON, ALL HALLOWS CHURCH, BARKING, repaired 1813 [*Gent's Mag*. 1813 (i), 526–7].

TONBRIDGE, KENT, THE LOWER BRIDGE, plans dated 1814 [Kent County Records, Q.S., Sundry Plans, S.1.].

OLD LONDON BRIDGE, survey and report with Dance and Chapman, 1814 [*A.P.S.D.*].

COLESHILL HOUSE, BERKS., repairs for 2nd Earl of Radnor, 1814–16; destroyed by fire 1952 [*A.P.S.D.*].

BEDDINGTON HOUSE, SURREY, alterations (with his son) to south wing (including library) for Mrs. A. P. Gee, 1818; dem. *c*.1865 [*A.P.S.D.*].

COMBE BANK, nr. SUNDRIDGE, KENT, alterations [*A.P.S.D.*].

YARMOUTH, ISLE OF WIGHT, designed upper part of church tower, 1831, Gothic (executed by Joseph Squire) [I.C.B.S.; inscription in church].

Lighthouses at ANGLESEY (SOUTH STACK, 1809), FARNE ISLANDS (1809), HELIGOLAND (1811), HURST (1812), HARWICH (1818), LUNDY (1820).

ALEXANDER, GEORGE, was an 'architect and builder' at Golspie in Sutherland in the early nineteenth century. A crude unexecuted design for a church at Wick by 'Mr. Alexander' [S.R.O., RHP 12363] is presumably his work. In 1818–21 he was employed to remodel the W. front of BALNAGOWAN CASTLE, ROSS-SHIRE, for Sir Charles Lockhart Ross [S.R.O., SC 34/23/3, pp. 3, 148, 204–5, 266,

[1] His only independent works were the library at Beddington House, Surrey (dem.), and rebuilding the tower and nave of Walton-on-the-Hill Church, Surrey (Gothic, again rebuilt 1895), both for Mrs. A. P. Gee, 1818 [*A.P.S.D.*].

270], and in 1820–1 he designed and built the ASSEMBLY ROOMS at the corner of HIGH STREET and NORTH STREET, ELGIN [R. Young, *Annals of Elgin*, 1879, 267, 400]. A 'smart cottage-farmhouse' by him at INVERBRORA, nr. BRORA, SUTHERLAND, 1820–1, is mentioned by J. Gifford, *Highlands & Islands*, Buildings of Scotland, 1992, 561.

ALEXANDER, GEORGE, was described as 'Master of the City's Works and Architect in Perth' in 1820, when he inspected the buildings of Kilspindie School, Perthshire [S.R.O., HR 417/1]. In the Perth Art Gallery there is a survey plan by him of Perth Tolbooth and Council Chamber (dem. 1839), dated 1810.

ALFRAY, ROBERT, appears to claim the authorship of SOMERSBY HALL, LINCS., a small house built in 1722 in the style of Sir John Vanbrugh. Among the Nattes Drawings in Lincoln City Library there is (vol. III, 309) a wash drawing of 'SUMMERSBY HALL in the County of Lincoln the seat of Robert Burton Esq[r]. built 1722. Rob[t]. Alfray Inv[t].: delin.' Robert Burton was a Londoner who had married Katherine Langhorne of Somersby in 1706 [John Harris in *Archaeological Jnl.* cxxxi, 1974, 314]. Alfray is otherwise known only as one of the subscribers to West & Toms' *Views of All the Ancient Churches etc in the Cities of London and Westminster*, 1736–9, where he is described as 'Surveyor'. He may have been a member of the armigerous family of Alfrey seated as Westdean in Sussex (cf. W. Berry, *County Genealogies: Sussex*, 1830, 244–5).

ALLANSON, ROBERT (*c.*1735–1773), is said to have designed PENCARROW, CORNWALL, for Sir John Molesworth, Bart., 1765–75 (*C. Life*, 8–16 July 1954). According to a later paper among the Molesworth archives, he was a descendant of Sir William Allanson, Lord Mayor of York in the reign of Charles I, and 'came down from Yorkshire a young man as Architect to Pencarrow the Family seat of the Molesworths', settled at Egloshayle and died there at the age of 38 in 1773. The date of Allanson's death is confirmed by the Egloshayle parish register, but no further evidence of his architectural activities at Pencarrow or elsewhere has been found.

ALLASON, THOMAS (1790–1852), was a pupil of William Atkinson. He entered the Royal Academy Schools in 1808, and won the Silver Medal in 1809. In 1810 he was awarded a gold palette by the Society of Arts for a design for an Academy of Arts. He travelled in Greece in 1814 as draughtsman to Messrs. John and Edward Spencer Stanhope, for their publications on *The Battle of Platœa*, 1817, and *The Actual State of the Plain of Olympia, and of the Ruins of the City of Elis*, 1824. On his return, he published *Picturesque Views of the Antiquities of Pola in Istria*, 1817, and an etching of Milan Cathedral. He claimed to be the first to observe the entasis of columns in Greek architecture, a discovery for which the credit was in fact due equally to Haller and C. R. Cockerell, with whom Allason discussed the problem on the spot in Athens, and to whom he was indebted for accurate drawings: see his paper 'On the Columns of the Athenian Temples' in *Quarterly Jnl. of Science and Arts* x, 1821, 204–6.

Allason was surveyor to the Stock Exchange, the Alliance Fire Office, the Pollen estate, Westminster, the Ladbroke estate, Notting Hill, the Pitt estate, Kensington, and the d'Este estate, Ramsgate. In Notting Hill he was responsible for the development of the Ladbroke estate from 1823 onwards and for the design of many of the houses, including those in Linden Gardens, where he built LINDEN LODGE (dem. *c.*1875) for his own occupation. The Pitt estate in Kensington was also developed under his direction from 1844 onwards, and his name is commemorated in ALLASON'S TERRACE, Nos. 67–81 Kensington High Street. The development of the d'Este estate at Ramsgate remains to be investigated, but it presumably included Allason's own house, Augusta Lodge.

Allason's chief public building was THE ALLIANCE FIRE OFFICE in BARTHOLOMEW LANE, LONDON, 1841, dem. 1932. Loudon regarded him as an 'eminent villa architect' and illustrated Linden Lodge in his *Encyclopaedia of Cottage, Farm and Villa Architecture*, 1846, pp. 826–34 (and cf. pp. 99–1001). At ALTON ABBEY (later TOWERS), STAFFS., he designed additions to the house and garden buildings for the 15th Earl of Shrewsbury, and thereafter was much employed as a landscape gardener. In 1841 he carried out extensive repairs to BLENHEIM PALACE, OXON., for the 6th Duke of Marlborough. His last works were the Italianate PYRGO PARK, nr. ROMFORD, ESSEX, for Robert Field, 1851–2 (enlarged by E. M. Barry, 1862; dem. 1938), and SULHAMSTEAD PARK, BERKS., for M. G. Thoyte, M.P. His only pupil was Charles Day. One of his three sons, Thomas (d. 1868), succeeded to most of his appointments, and rebuilt the Stock Exchange in Capel Court in 1853–4. [*A.P.S.D.*; obituary in *Builder* x, 1852, 241; *Survey of London* xxxviii, 1973, *passim.*]

ALLEN, GEORGE (1798–1847), was a native of Brentford. He became a pupil of James Elmes, entered the Royal Academy Schools in

1818, and won the Silver Medal in 1820. His practice was largely commercial, consisting of warehouses and the like. He was much employed in making valuations for railway, gas and dock companies, and was surveyor to the Haberdashers' Company, the Deptford Creek Bridge Company and the parishes of St. Olave, Southwark, and St. Nicholas, Deptford. In 1844 he was appointed District Surveyor for Rotherhithe and Hatcham. In 1827–8 he prepared and published *Plans and Designs for the Future Approaches to the New London Bridge*, making several suggestions that were adopted by the Bridge Committee. He became a Fellow of the R.I.B.A. and exhibited at the Royal Academy between 1820 and 1840. His office was in Tooley Street, Southwark. [*A.P.S.D.*; *Builder* v, 1847, 311–12.]

PENSHURST, KENT, restoration of HARDEN COTTAGE 'in the ancient English style', exhib. at Royal Academy, 1826.

BERMONDSEY, ST. JAMES'S CHURCH, in conjunction with James Savage, who was responsible for the design, 1827–8 [*A.P.S.D.*].

SOUTHWARK, THE BRIDGE HOUSE HOTEL for John Humphery, M.P., 1834 [exhib. at Royal Academy, 1835].

SOUTHWARK, UNION WORKHOUSE, for the parishes of St. Olave and St. John, 1836 [Brayley, *History of Surrey* v, 1848, 389].

BRENTFORD, MIDDLESEX, THE INFANT SCHOOL, 1837 [*A.P.S.D.*].

EALING, MIDDLESEX, villa for J. T. Sleap, *c.*1840 [exhib. at Royal Academy].

SOUTHWARK, ST. OLAVE'S CHURCH, restoration after the fire of 1843; dem. 1926 [*A.P.S.D.*].

SOUTHWARK, ST. JOHN'S GIRLS' SCHOOL, 1845 [*A.P.S.D.*].

BERMONDSEY, CHRISTCHURCH, with W. B. Hays, 1847, Romanesque; dem. *c.*1966 [*A.P.S.D.*].

Several wharves, warehouses, etc., in Southwark, including Fenning's Wharf, 1836; those on the north side of Southwark Cathedral, for John Humphery, 1838; Cotton's Wharf, for Messrs. Scovell; Topping's Wharf (after 1843); and Davis's Wharf [Brayley, *Topographical History of Surrey* v, 356, 373, 389 n.].

ALLEN, JAMES, statuary and architect of Bristol, was the son of John Allen, a joiner. In 1752 he was apprenticed to the mason and sculptor James Paty [P.R.O. Apprenticeship Register], and in 1780 was admitted to the freedom of the city as a carver. He was one of the three City Surveyors appointed under the Act of 1788, but resigned in 1792. In the following year he became bankrupt and his house and yard were sold. He subsequently practised as an architect and drawing master [W. Ison, *The Georgian Buildings of Bristol*, 1952, 30–1].

In 1787 Allen submitted a design for St. Paul's Church, Bristol, which was not accepted. Subsequently he designed ST. THOMAS'S CHURCH, BRISTOL, incorporating the medieval tower, 1790–3 [Ison, *op. cit.*, 84–5] and WINFORD CHURCH, SOMERSET, incorporating the medieval tower, 1796 [churchwardens' accounts in Somerset C.R.O.]. In 1796 he repaired ST. MARY REDCLIFFE CHURCH, BRISTOL [John Evans, *Chronological History of Bristol*, 1824, 302]. A drawing by him of gatepiers at HINTON ST. GEORGE, SOMERSET, is in the Yale Center for British Art.

ANDERSON, ADAM (*c.*1780–1846), was a scientific polymath who was Rector of Perth Academy from 1809 until 1837, when he became Professor of Natural Philosophy at St. Andrews. While at Perth he was involved in many schemes of public improvement, among them the provision of an adequate water-supply. He was not only the engineer of the new water system installed in 1830–2, but also the architect of the Waterworks, a prominently sited circular domed building of the Doric order which is now the Tourist Office [K. J. Cameron, *The Schoolmaster Engineer*, Abertay Historical Society, Dundee 1988].

ANDERSON, JAMES (–*c.*1856), 'engineer and architect', was admitted a burgess of Edinburgh in 1825 [*Roll of Edinburgh Burgesses*, Scottish Record Soc. 1933, 10]. Thereafter he appears in the directories as 'civil engineer and architect' or 'surveyor' until 1856/7. In 1826 he submitted a design for St. Andrew's Place U.P. Church, Leith [*St. Andrew's Place United Presbyterian Church, Leith*, 1888, 38]. He lived in Shandwick Place, and must be distinguished from James Anderson, a wright of West Maitland Street, who appears to have designed and built the R.C. CHAPEL at DRIMNIN (BONNAVOULIN), ARGYLLSHIRE, in 1838 [R.C.A.M. *Argyllshire* 3, 191n].

ANDERSON, JOHN, designed two churches in County Durham for the Church Building Commissioners, one at WEST RAINTON, 1825,[1] the other at HETTON-LE-HOLE, 1832 [Port, 177]. The former was rebuilt in 1864, the latter in 1898.

[1] The I.C.B.S. Certificate for this church is, however, signed by Thomas Nicholson, a surveyor and builder at Hexham.

ANDERSON, WILLIAM, *see* HENDERSON, WILLIAM.

ANDERTON, THOMAS (1777–1834), of Gargrave nr. Skipton, made designs in 1817 for rebuilding CARLTON-IN-CRAVEN RECTORY, YORKS. (W.R.) [Borthwick Institute, MGA 1817/4]. In 1819 he made the designs (in a Georgian Gothic style) for rebuilding KETTLEWELL CHURCH, YORKS. (W.R.) [I.C.B.S.; Borthwick Institute, Fac. 1819/2]. The church was again rebuilt in 1882–5. Thomas was the father of William Anderton, described as 'architect and mason' of Gargrave, to whose designs the church of ST. JAMES, BARNOLDSWICK, YORKS. (W.R.) (dem. 1960), was built in the lancet style in 1842 [I.C.B.S.] [Gargrave Parish Register in N. Yorkshire C.R.O.].

ANGELL, SAMUEL (1800–1866), was the son of William Sandell Angell, deputy alderman of Cornhill Ward, London. He became a pupil of Thomas Hardwick, and entered the Royal Academy Schools in 1816. In 1821–3 he travelled in Italy and Sicily with William Harris (*q.v.*), discovering at Selinus a series of metopes from the Greek temples there. Harris died of malaria in Palermo, but Angell returned to England to publish, in conjunction with Harris's brother-in-law Thomas Evans (*q.v.*), *Sculptured Metopes discovered amongst the Ruins of the Temples of the Ancient City of Selinus in Sicily* (1826).

In 1824 Angell became surveyor to the Clothworkers' Company, for whom he was responsible for the development of their Islington estate from 1846 onwards. Here his name was commemorated in Angell Terrace, now Nos. 7–21 St. Peter's Street [*V.C.H. Middlesex* viii, 23]. Angell was also surveyor to the Saddlers' Company, and from 1831 was one of the London District Surveyors. He became a fellow of the R.I.B.A., and exhibited at the Royal Academy between 1817 and 1850. George Judge and Herbert Williams were his pupils. He died at Abbey Lodge, Chertsey, on 28 November 1866. F. W. Porter appears to have taken over his practice. [F. Boase, *Modern English Biography* iv, 1908, 135; *Gent's Mag.* 1847 (i), 180–1, 1867 (i), 250; *Builder* 1859, 304].

LONDON, LAMB'S CHAPEL and ALMSHOUSES, MONKWELL STREET, for the Clothworkers' Company, 1824–5, Elizabethan style; dem. 1872 [J. Timbs, *Curiosities of London*, 1867, 212].

KING'S LYNN, NORFOLK, THE WEST NORFOLK HOSPITAL, 1834–5; enlarged 1847, 1852, etc. [*Norwich Mercury*, 20 Dec. 1834, *ex inf.* Mr. David Cubitt].

TOTTENHAM, MIDDLESEX, schools on SCOTLAND GREEN, 1836 [*Architectural Mag.* iii, 1836, 190].

ST. THOMAS'S CHURCH, OLD KENT ROAD, 1837–8; dem. 1868 [*Companion to the Almanac*, 1838, 220].

ST. VEDAST'S CHURCH, FOSTER LANE, LONDON, repairs to steeple, 1837 [see below, under Davy, Christopher].

ST. JAMES'S CHURCH, MUSWELL HILL, MIDDLESEX, 1842, Gothic; enlarged 1874–5; dem. 1902 [G. Watson & L. C. Kent, *The Church on the Hill*, 1951].

LONDON, THE COUNTESS OF KENT'S ALMSHOUSES, DANBURY STREET, ISLINGTON, for the Clothworkers' Company, 1854 [*Builder* 1859, 304].

LONDON, CLOTHWORKERS' HALL, MINCING LANE, 1856–60, Italianate; destroyed by bombing 1940 [T. L. Donaldson, *Handbook of Specifications*, 1860, 481].

ANGUS, GEORGE (1792–1845), a native of Meikleour in Perthshire, practised in Edinburgh. He was a competent but eclectic architect, who adapted his style to circumstances. His Dundee High School is in a Greek Revival style similar to Hamilton's Edinburgh High School, but all his churches are Gothic. In Dundee he was responsible for an important piece of town-planning – the formation of Reform Street, with the portico of his High School as the terminal feature. In 1833 he won the competition for the new gaols, police office and sheriff courthouse at Dundee. Owing to financial difficulties the court-house, whose Tuscan portico was to have formed the principal architectural feature, had to be dropped, but it was eventually built in the 1860s with a façade based on Angus's original design. After the advent of James Black (*q.v.*) as Town's Architect of Dundee in 1833 the corporation ceased to employ Angus, but he also designed the Watt Institution and prepared feu-plans for an extensive layout of villas on the lands of Dudhope which proved largely abortive because of depression in the 1840s. A stone in the Warriston Cemetery in Edinburgh records his death on 8 June 1845 at the age of 53.

EDINBURGH, THE SUBSCRIPTION BATHS AND DRAWING ACADEMY (now Masonic Lodge), 17–19a HILL STREET, 1825–8 [Edinburgh Dean of Guild Plans, 10 May 1825].

DUNDEE, THE PUBLIC SEMINARIES or HIGH SCHOOL, 1832–4 [C. Mackie, *Historical Description of Dundee*, 1836, 142].

KINROSS CHURCH, KINROSS-SHIRE, 1832, Gothic [*N.S.A.* ix, *Kinross-shire*, 21].

KINGSKETTLE CHURCH, FIFE, 1832–4, Gothic [*ibid.*]

TULLIALLAN CHURCH, KINCARDINE-ON-FORTH, FIFE, 1833, Gothic [*ibid.*]

DUNDEE, REFORM STREET, all elevations, and also interiors of the three S.E. blocks, 1833 [David Walker, *Architects and Architecture in Dundee 1770–1914*, Abertay Historical Soc.'s Publication No. 3, 1955, 9–10].

DUNDEE, THE GAOLS AND BRIDEWELL, 1833–6, enlarged 1843–4; dem. [James Thomson, *History of Dundee*, 1847, 152; David Walker, *op. cit.*, 10–11].

ALLOA HOUSE, CLACKMANNANSHIRE, rebuilt for 9th Earl of Mar, 1834–8, in Greek Revival style; remodelled in Tudor style *c.*1865; dem. *c* 1954 [S.R.O., GD 17/423/2, 3, 4, 8, 9].

DUNDEE, THE WATT INSTITUTION (now Y.M.C.A.), 1838–9 [Dundee Public Library, minutes of Watt Institution, *ex inf.* Mr. David Walker].

ALLOA EPISCOPAL (subsequently R.C.) CHURCH, CLACKMANNANSHIRE, 1839–40, Gothic [*N.S.A.* viii, *Clackmannanshire*, 43].

KIRRIEMUIR, ANGUS, THE BRITISH LINEN BANK, 45–47 HIGH STREET, 1841–3 [plans at Bank of Scotland dated 16 July 1839, *ex inf.* Mr. David Walker].

TAIN, ROSS-SHIRE, THE BRITISH LINEN BANK (now Bank of Scotland), 1845 [contracts advertised in *Aberdeen Jnl.* 30 April 1845, *ex inf.* Mr. David Walker].

APPLETON, ROBERT (1791–1854), was born in Lancashire and began life as a carpenter and joiner but eventually established himself as an architect and surveyor at Halesworth in Suffolk. He had a local practice designing vicarages and schools in the 1840s and 1850s. In 1823 he enlarged HALESWORTH CHURCH [I.C.B.S.] and in 1827–9 he designed ST. JAMES'S CHURCH, DUNWICH (chancel added 1881) in a classical style [I.C.B.S.] [C. Brown *et al.*, *Dictionary of Architects of Suffolk Buildings 1800–1914*, Ipswich 1991, 28–9].

ARCHER, JOHN LEE (1791–1852), was the son of a civil engineer practising in Ireland. In 1812 he obtained employment as a draughtsman in the London office of John Rennie, but left in 1818 in order to set up practice on his own as an architect and engineer. He exhibited at the Royal Academy from time to time, but does not appear to have secured any important commission. In 1826 he obtained the post of Civil Engineer to the government of Van Diemen's Land (now Tasmania), where he designed a number of public buildings of considerable merit, including the Customs House in Hobart, now the Parliament House. In 1838 his department was abolished, and he was given alternative employment as a Police Magistrate. He served in this capacity for fourteen years, dying at Stanley in December 1852. [Roy Smith, *John Lee Archer*, Tasmanian Historical Research Association, 1962; information from Mr. E. R. Pretyman.]

ARCHER, THOMAS (*c.*1668–1743), was the youngest son of Thomas Archer of Umberslade in Warwickshire, a country gentleman who represented his county in parliament in 1660. He was educated at Trinity College, Oxford, from 1686 to 1689 and subsequently travelled abroad for four years. Of his itinerary nothing is known beyond the fact that he was in Padua in December 1691. It may, however, be conjectured that he visited Germany and Austria on his way to Italy [*Architectural Review*, Sept. 1957, 344]. In 1705 he obtained the court post of Groom Porter, which gave him control of gaming tables in the royal palaces, and was reputed to be worth £1000 a year: this he probably owed to the Duke of Devonshire, then Lord Steward of the Household. In 1715 he was in addition given the sinecure comptrollership of customs at Newcastle. Archer was one of the Commissioners for building Fifty New Churches under the Act of 1711, and in 1713 he sought unsuccessfully to obtain the post of Comptroller of the Works after Vanbrugh's dismissal. No appointment was made as Harley was contemplating a reform of the Office of Works in which the comptrollership would have been abolished, and on the change of government in 1714 Vanbrugh was reinstated.

In 1715 Archer purchased an estate at Hale in Hampshire, where he proceeded to rebuild the house and enlarge the church, and at the time of his death he owned considerable property in Warwickshire, Worcestershire and Dorset as well as in London. His first wife, Eleanor, daughter of John Archer of Welford, Berks., died of smallpox within a year of her marriage. His second wife was Anne, daughter of John Chaplin of Tathwell, Lincs., who survived him. They had no children. Archer died at his house in Whitehall on 22 or 23 May 1743, aged 74, and was buried at Hale in a vault under the north transept of the church, and opposite the monument which he had erected, probably to his own design, in 1739. A portrait attributed to Kneller hangs in the former church of St. John, Smith Square. Another belongs to Lord Plymouth.

Archer was an amateur architect in the sense that he did not depend upon architectural practice for his livelihood, and worked chiefly for fellow-members of the English aristocracy. He was, however, an able and active designer and a competent (if hardly an elegant) draughtsman. Nothing is known of his architectural training, but it is evident that his foreign tour must have been crucial in the development of his architectural style. The influence of Bernini and Borromini is obvious in many of his designs, and Archer's work has more in common with continental baroque than that of any other English architect. This is apparent not only in his use of standard baroque motifs such as eared architraves and broken pediments, but in his handing of space and above all in his fondness for convex and concave planes. Whereas Vanbrugh and Hawksmoor created an insular baroque which had few immediate continental precedents, Archer brought a direct experience of European baroque to England. It is this that gives his work a unique place in English architectural history. Among his most accomplished and characteristic works are St. Paul's Church, Deptford, Heythrop House, and the domed garden pavilion at Wrest Park in Bedfordshire. His influence is seen in the work of the master builder Nathaniel Ireson (*q.v.*), whom he employed at Hale as a young man, and in that of the Bastard brothers (*q.v.*) of Blandford.

[Marcus Whiffen, *Thomas Archer*, 1950; information from Mr. Peter Wayne.]

HOUSES

CHATSWORTH HOUSE, DERBYSHIRE, N. front for 1st Duke of Devonshire, 1704–5 [Francis Thompson, *A History of Chatsworth*, 1949, 77–8]. The Cascade House (1702) has long been attributed to Archer on stylistic grounds and is explicitly stated to have been 'built by Archer' in the diary of William Freeman in Sir John Soane's Museum, under the year 1724.

CLIVEDEN HOUSE, BUCKS., addition of wings and quadrant colonnades for 1st Earl of Orkney, before 1717, perhaps *c.*1705; colonnades dem. 1849, wings altered in nineteenth century [*Vitruvius Britannicus* ii, 1717, pls. 70–4; G. Jackson-Stops, 'The Cliveden Album; drawings by Archer, Leoni and Gibbs', *Arch. Hist.* 19, 1976].

WEST SHEEN, RICHMOND, SURREY, added stable and office wings for John Jeffreys, M.P., *c.*1705; dem. [Northants. C.R.O., Buccleuch (Shrewsbury) papers, no. 77, f. 68: 'Mr. Archer . . . the Architect for Heythrop . . . did not want fancy in Mr. Jeffrey's his stable and offices'].

HEYTHROP HOUSE, OXON., for Duke of Shrewsbury, 1707–10. The interior was destroyed by fire 1831 and rebuilt 1870 by Alfred Waterhouse, who demolished Archer's wings [letters from Duke of Shrewsbury in B.L., Add. MS. 40776, ff. 55, 61, 63; H. Walpole, *Anecdotes of Painting*, ed. Dallaway & Wornum, ii, 1862, 687] (*Vitruvius Britannicus* v, 1771, pls. 82–5].

attributed: remodelling of AYNHO PARK, NORTHANTS., for Thomas Cartwright, 1707–11, including addition of library, conservatory, stables and coach-house [stylistic attribution]. The library and conservatory were altered by Sir J. Soane in 1800–1 (*C. Life*, 2–16 July 1953).

WREST PARK, BEDS., domed garden pavilion for Duke of Kent, 1709–11 [*Vitruvius Britannicus* i, 1715, pl. 33] (*C. Life*, 4 Aug. 1917). The demolished Cain Hill House, another garden building erected *c.*1712–15, can also be attributed to Archer.

ROEHAMPTON HOUSE, WANDSWORTH, SURREY, for Thomas Cary, 1710–12, now part of Queen Mary's Hospital; wings added by Lutyens 1910 [*Vitruvius Britannicus* i, 1715, pls. 80, 81].

HALE HOUSE, HANTS., for himself soon after 1715; much altered by Henry Holland 1770 (*C. Life*, 8 Aug. 1941; *Wren Soc.* xvii, pls. xliv, xlv).

attributed: CHETTLE HOUSE, DORSET, for George Chafin, *c.*1715; roof with split pediment removed *c.*1846 [G. F. Webb in *C. Life*, 6 Oct. 1928; Arthur Oswald, 'A Plan of Chettle', in *The Country Seat*, ed. Colvin & Harris, 1970, 85–7].

attributed: LONDON, RUSSELL HOUSE, No. 43 KING STREET, COVENT GARDEN, for Admiral Edward Russell, Earl of Orford, 1716–17 [*Survey of London* xxxvi, 166–78].

attributed: LONDON, MONMOUTH HOUSE, SOHO SQUARE, new façade and other alterations for Sir James Bateman, *c.*1717–18; dem. 1773 [*Survey of London* xxiii, 109–12].

attributed: MARLOW PLACE, BUCKS., probably for John Wallop, Viscount Lymington, afterwards 1st Earl of Portsmouth, *c.*1720 [H. M. Colvin in *Records of Bucks.* xv, 1947, 8] (measured drawings in *Arch. Rev.* xxvii, 170–5, xxviii, 282–4, 1910).

HARCOURT HOUSE, No. 1 CAVENDISH SQUARE, LONDON,[1] for 1st Viscount Harcourt, *c.*1725; dem. J. Rocque's engraving of 'The Original Design of ye Rt. Honble ye Ld Harcourt's House in Cavendish Square, as it was drawn by Mr. Archer, but Built and Altered to what it now is by Edward Wilcox

[1] Not to be confused with the house on the opposite (west) side of the square built by Lord Bingley, which was known as Harcourt House from 1773, when it was acquired by the 1st Earl Harcourt, until its demolition in 1906.

Esqr. *Ex Autographis Architecti*' is in B.L. *King's Maps* xxvii, 6.

Note: there is no reason to think that Archer designed Umberslade Hall, Warwicks., built by his brother Andrew *c.*1693–5, as suggested in *A.P.S.D.* and *Wren Soc.* xvii, p. xlii (see below, p. 886). It is doubtful whether any of his designs for rebuilding Hurstbourne Park, Hants., for the 1st Earl of Portsmouth, were carried out, but see T. Mowl, 'Thomas Archer and the Hurstbourne Park Bee House', *Arch. Hist.* 30, 1987. Serle's House, Southgate Street, Winchester (*c.*1720), shows many characteristics of Archer's style, but may have been designed by a master builder rather than by Archer himself.

CHURCHES

BIRMINGHAM, ST. PHILIP (now CATHEDRAL), 1710–15; tower 1725; chancel enlarged by J. A. Chatwin 1883–4, exterior refaced 1864 and 1911 [*Vitruvius Britannicus* i, 1715, pls. 10–11; B. Walker, 'St. Philip's Church, Birmingham', *The Central Literary Mag.* xxx, 1931, with references to the book of 'Orders, Memorandums and Agreements of the Commissioners', now lost].

LONDON, ST. PAUL, DEPTFORD, 1713–30 [original plans in B.L., *King's Maps* xviii, 18 e–i; *The Commissions for Building Fifty New Churches*, ed. M. H. Port, London Record Soc. 1986, *passim*] (G. Pinkerton, 'The Parish Church of St. Paul, Deptford', *Arch. Rev.* 51, 1922, with measured drawings). The rectory designed by Archer was dem. *c.*1885.

WESTMINSTER, ST. JOHN, SMITH SQUARE, 1713–28; interior gutted 1742 and reconstructed 1744–5 by James Horne, who removed the internal columns; interior rearranged 1824–5 by W. Inwood; again gutted 1941 and rebuilt to original design by Marshall Sisson, 1965–8 [*Wren Soc.* xvii, pl. xl, showing Archer's original design for the towers; J. E. Smith, *Parochial Memorials of St. John's Westminster*, 1892; *The Commissions*, as above; W. A. Eden in *C. Life*, 1 March 1962].

HALE PARISH CHURCH, HANTS., rebuilt chancel and added transepts at his own expense, 1717 [inscription on monument and memo. in Parish Register]. A central bell-cupola was removed in 1895, when the roof was rebuilt and the modillioned cornice added (*Wren Soc.* xvii, pl. xlv).

MONUMENTS

Archer designed the monument in ROUS LENCH CHURCH, WORCS., to Sir Francis Rous (d. 1687). It was erected in 1719 in accordance with the will of Lady Frances Rous (d. 1715), who was Archer's sister [E. A. B. Barnard, 'The Rouses of Rous Lench', *Trans. Worcs. Arch. Soc.*, N.S., viii, 1931, 55–8].

Archer probably designed the monument at HAMPTON, MIDDLESEX, to Susannah Thomas, died 1731, whose will directs him to erect it as her executor [P.C.C. 105 ISHAM]. It is signed 'W. Powell Ft.'

He no doubt designed his own monument at HALE, which he erected in 1739 during his lifetime (*Wren Soc.* xvii, pl. xlv),[1] and he may have designed that at TANWORTH, WARWICKS., to his father, Thomas Archer, and his mother, Anne, which was erected by his brother Andrew (*Wren Soc.* xvii, pl. xliii).

ARMSTRONG, WILLIAM (–1858), was an architect and civil engineer of Bristol. He was one of the building surveyors for that city from 1836 until his death in October 1858. He had the reputation of being a practical man whose abilities lay in sound construction rather than in the art of design. In 1829 he was one of the unsuccessful competitors for the bridge over the Avon Gorge at Clifton. He enlarged RADSTOCK CHURCH, SOMERSET, in 1832 [I.C.B.S.] and altered ST. PHILIP AND ST. JACOB'S CHURCH, BRISTOL, in 1839–41 [I.C.B.S.]. He designed THE CONGREGATIONAL CHAPEL in BRUNSWICK SQUARE, BRISTOL, in 1835 [W. Ison, *The Georgian Buildings of Bristol*, 1952, 205] and THE INDEPENDENT CHAPEL, GLENDOWER STREET, MONMOUTH, in 1844 [*Monmouthshire Merlin*, 7 June 1844]. In *c.*1850 he reconstructed part of the former Dominican Friary at BRISTOL as THE FRIENDS' SCHOOL [*Builder* viii, 1850, 91]. E. W. Godwin was his pupil.

ARNOLD, WILLIAM (–1637?), was an important master mason in Somerset in the early seventeenth century. In 1617 he was living at Charlton Musgrove, nr. Wincanton, and he appears to have been identical with William Arnold, *alias* Goverson, who was a churchwarden of Charlton Musgrove in 1600, 1601 and 1622, and who died there in March 1636/7. The name Arnold was associated in the seventeenth century with the freestone quarries at Ketton in Rutland, and in 1621 Arnold Goverson supplied large

[1] The supposed 'design for monument to Thomas Archer' by P. Scheemakers in the Soane Museum, illustrated on the same plate, is, in fact, for the monument to Sir Christopher Powell at Boughton Monchelsea, which is signed by that sculptor. There is no evidence to connect Scheemakers with Archer's monument.

quantities of Ketton stone for the building of Raynham Hall in Norfolk. It is probable, therefore, that William Arnold was a member of the Ketton family who had moved to Somerset.

William Arnold's first recorded work was the remodelling of CRANBORNE HOUSE, DORSET, for Robert Cecil, 1st Earl of Salisbury, between 1608 and 1612. In December 1609 he was paid £5 for 'drawing a plott for Cranborne house', and in November 1610 'Arnold the freemason' received £40 'in part of £250 agreed upon to build a tarryce & a kitchen'. What is almost certainly this 'plot', showing the 'tarris', the new kitchen and other proposed additions, is preserved at Hatfield House (Oswald, *Country Houses of Dorset*, pl. 149). Among the additions made to the house at this time (and shown on the plan) are the two porches, which are treated as *loggie*, with Tuscan columns supporting open arches. The very similar porch at WAYFORD MANOR, DORSET, can confidently be attributed to Arnold, and similarities between Cranborne and Wayford on the one hand, and MONTACUTE HOUSE, SOMERSET, on the other, make it very probable that Arnold was also the designer of the last-named house, built by Sir Edward Phelips during the last decade of the sixteenth century.

In 1609 Arnold received an important commission from the executors of Nicholas Wadham, whose will provided for the building of the Oxford college which bears his name. As there were difficulties about obtaining masons in Oxford it was decided to send a team of masons from Somerset, with William Arnold at their head. Wadham's widow, writing to her half-brother Lord Petre, praised Arnold as 'an honest man, a perfect workman, and my neere neighboure'. He had, she said, been 'commended' to her by Sir Edward Phelips – further evidence that he had been employed at Montacute. Phelips' good opinion of Arnold was shared by Sir Edward Hext of Low Ham, another Somerset landowner, who considered him 'the absolutest and honestest workeman in England'. Arnold was accordingly engaged to 'be imployed in the provysyon of tymber & stones for Wadham Colledge as also for drawyng of a plott & for the byldyng of yt'. His 'plott' was shown to the King, the Archbishop of Canterbury, the Lord Chancellor and the Lord Treasurer (Robert Cecil), and was carried out under his direction between 1610 and 1612 [T. G. Jackson, *Wadham College, Oxford*, 1893, 29–51; Nancy Briggs, 'The Foundation of Wadham College', *Oxoniensia* xxi, 1957, 63, 67–8].

One other documented work of Arnold's is recorded. In 1617 he agreed to supply George Luttrell with a 'plott' and an 'upright' for remodelling the south side of DUNSTER CASTLE, SOMERSET, and to oversee the work. Despite Arnold's 'great experience in architecture', Luttrell was dissatisfied with the result, and a lawsuit ensued in the Court of Chancery. Arnold's work at Dunster was much altered by Salvin in 1869 [H. C. Maxwell Lyte, *History of Dunster* ii, 1909, 366 (*C. Life*, 16, 23 July 1987).

Though essentially traditional in character, Arnold's architecture is enlivened by the introduction of classical features with mannerist detailing derived from Flemish sources such as the publications of Hans Vredeman de Vries (1527–1606). [Arthur Oswald, *Country Houses of Dorset*, 2nd ed. 1959, 25–30.]

ARROW, JAMES (–1791), of Westminster, was a carpenter and joiner by trade. He held the post of Surveyor to the Victualling Office and Inspector of Repairs to the Admiralty from 1774 to 1785, and in 1783 designed extensive new buildings at the ROYAL VICTUALLING YARD, DEPTFORD [P.R.O., ADM 111/93, 17 Feb. 1783; drawings in R.I.B.A. Collection dated 1786 and 1788]. In 1768 he was one of the unsuccessful applicants for the surveyorship of the East India Company. Designs for a fireproof arch, submitted by Arrow to the Society of Arts in 1772, are in the R.I.B.A. Drawings Collection. A monument to Ann Littlejohn (d. 1771) in the church of St. Andrew, Halfway Tree, Jamaica, bears the signature of *Jas. Arrow, Archt. and Sefn. Alken, Sculpt.* [*C. Life*, 25 Jan. 1968, correspondence]. James Hunter was his pupil, exhibiting a 'Design for a temple dedicated to the Cardinal Virtues' at the Royal Academy in 1776 from 'Mr. Arrow's, Tothill Fields, Westminster'. Arrow died at his house in Tothill Fields on 28 August 1791 [*Gent's Mag.* 1791 (ii), 874].

ARUNDALE, FRANCIS VYVYAN JAGO (1807–1853), was a pupil of the elder Pugin. He accompanied Pugin on his tour of Normandy and (together with G. B. Moore, Benjamin Ferrey and Talbot Bury) helped to make the drawings published as *Specimens of the Architectural Antiquities of Normandy*, 1828. In 1829 he was admitted to the Royal Academy Schools on Pugin's recommendation. In 1832 he went out to Egypt as a draughtsman to assist Robert Hay in his archaeological investigations. When Hay returned to England in 1833 Arundale joined Catherwood and Joseph Bonomi in an expedition to Palestine. He eventually returned to England by way of Asia Minor, bringing with him a large collection of drawings, many of which he exhibited at the Royal Academy in subsequent years. In 1837 he published *Illustrations of Jerusalem and Mount Sinai* and in 1842 he contributed to Birch's *Gallery of Antiquities selected from the British Museum.* Col. Howard Vyse's *Operations carried out at the Pyramids of Gizeh in 1837*, 3 vols. 1840–2, was illustrated by his drawings. Arundale was also the author of a folio volume entitled *The Edifices of Andrea Palladio, forming a selection from his most admired buildings* [1832], based on measurements made by himself and J. B. Atkinson of York, and of *Examples and Designs of Verandahs* (1851).

Arundale never practised as an architect, and the only building he is known to have designed was a boat-house at HAMS HALL, WARWICKS., for Charles Bowyer Adderley, the design for which he exhibited at the Royal Academy in 1839. He married the daughter of H. W. Pickersgill, R.A. His portrait by William Brockedon is in the National Portrait Gallery. [*Builder* xii, 1854, 83; S. Tillett, *Egypt Itself*, 1984.]

ASHPITEL, WILLIAM HURST (1776–1852), was a pupil of D. A. Alexander, whom he assisted in his works in the London Docks. He was also for some time an assistant of John Rennie, under whom he was concerned in the construction of the Kennet and Avon Canal. He afterwards entered into partnership with James Savage, and later practised for some time alone. Ashpitel was elected a member of the Surveyors' Club in 1806. He quitted practice early and thereafter 'gave his attention chiefly to improvements upon his own property' at Clapton. He was the father of the architect Arthur Ashpitel (1807–69). He died on 20 April 1852, aged 75.

Memorandum books in the Royal West of England Academy at Bristol and the Avery Architectural Library of Columbia University, New York, throw considerable light on Ashpitel's practice as a London surveyor. His principal architectural works were ST. JOHN'S CHURCH, S. HACKNEY, LONDON (with J. Savage), 1806–10, dem. 1845 (illustrated in W. Robinson, *History of Hackney* ii, 1843, 171); work (probably the addition of a dining-room) for Sir Charles Talbot at CHART PARK, nr. DORKING, SURREY, demolished in 1819 by Thomas Hope in order to enlarge his park at Deepdene [D. & E. Mercer, *Chart Park, Dorking*, Dorking 1993, 31]; THE GROVE, WORTH, SUSSEX; SHENLEY RECTORY, HERTS., and repairs to NORTH MIMMS CHURCH and alterations to NORTH MIMMS HOUSE, HERTS. A fantastic design by him for a Gothic 'Belle Vue', exhibited at the Royal Academy in 1800, is illustrated in the 3rd Catalogue of Paul Grinke of London, 1971, item 14. [*A.P.S.D.*; John Harris, *A Catalogue of British Drawings for Architecture etc. in American Collections*, 1971, 16–18.]

ASHWELL, THOMAS, was a carpenter and builder of Tottenham in Middlesex. In 1835 he designed and built JESUS CHURCH, FORTY HILL, ENFIELD, MIDDLESEX, imitating (at the patron's request) James Savage's Holy Trinity, Tottenham [E. H. A. Koch, *Forty Hill Church and Parish*, 1935; W. Robinson, *History and Antiquities of Tottenham*, 2nd ed. 1840, i, 155, ii, 134, 355].

ASTLEY, JOHN (?1730–1787), was a spendthrift portrait-painter who is said to have had some ability as an architect. In 1759 he married a rich widow, Lady Duckenfield Daniell, who first settled on him the estate of Over Tabley in Cheshire, and then died (1762), leaving him, on the death of her daughter (which occurred soon after), the Duckinfield estate near Stockport, worth some £5000 a year. Tabley he soon sold (though not before he had 'decorated' and 'built' there), but Duckinfield he retained, building there DUKINFIELD LODGE (dem.), 'two stone bridges over the Tame for the accommodation of the village, and a handsome circus of brick houses, divided into semi-circles by the road'. In 1769 he acquired the lease of SCHOMBERG HOUSE, PALL MALL, LONDON, which he divided into three, occupying the central house himself. He also had a house overlooking the river in the Terrace at Barnes in Surrey, afterwards occupied by Lady Archer.

> In the structure and decoration of small buildings . . . Astley's architecture was preeminent; Pall Mall is one instance; Lady Archer's saloon and conservatory, at Barnes, is another; Duckenfield is yet finer than either. The saloon, the loggio in front, the chambers on each side, and the great octagon, are all as exquisite as original, from the first idea to the last (W. Betham, *Baronetage of England* ii, 1802, 378–9.)

As (with the possible exception of some plasterwork at Schomberg House, illustrated in *Survey of London* xxx, pl. 208) nothing now remains of any of 'Beau Astley's' architectural works, it is difficult to judge his skill as a designer. He died at Dukinfield Lodge on 14 November 1787, leaving the estate to his son (by a later marriage) Francis Duckenfield Astley. [S. Redgrave, *Dictionary of Artists*, 1878, 14–15; *D.N.B.*; *Gent's Mag.* 1759, 606; J. Dugdale, *The New British Traveller* i, 1819, 325.]

ATKINSON, JOHN (*c.*1799–1856), was the son of a mason and paviour of the same name. The elder Atkinson had a yard at 100 Goswell Road, London, where in about 1815 he was joined in partnership by Thomas Whitfield Browne. As contracting masons, Atkinson and Browne built Salters' Hall (1823–7) and the New Hall of Christ's Hospital (1824). As a statuary mason Atkinson signs tablets at Haverhill, Suffolk (1815) and Overstone, Northants. (1830). The younger Atkinson practised as an architect. In 1833 he was responsible for rebuilding CODDINGTON CHURCH, CHESHIRE, in an undistinguished Gothic style [I.C.B.S.] and in 1834 for repairing and refitting BODENHAM CHURCH, HEREFS. [I.C.B.S.]. The patron of Bodenham was John Arkwright (a grandson of the industrialist Sir Richard Arkwright), and in 1832 or 1833 John Atkinson had succeeded William Atkinson (*q.v.*), to whom he may have been related, as Arkwright's professional adviser in the remodelling of HAMPTON COURT, HEREFS., to the designs of the amateur architect Charles Hanbury Tracy (*q.v.*), carried out between 1835 and 1841. Many letters to and from Atkinson are preserved among Arkwright's papers in the Herefordshire Record Office (A 63/135).

From about 1836 Atkinson was living at Beulah House, Upper Norwood, and in that year he exhibited at the Royal Academy his designs for a proposed crescent at Beulah Spa. The design for a 'church for Camberwell' which he exhibited in 1842 must have been an unsuccessful submission for St. Giles' Church there, built to the designs of Scott and Moffatt in 1842–44. Atkinson died at Frindsbury, Kent on 5 April 1856, aged 57 [*Gent's Mag.* 1856, 660; records of the Bank of England; R. Gunnis, *Dictionary of British Sculptors*, 1953, 21].

ATKINSON, PETER (1735–1805), born at or near Ripon, was brought up as a carpenter, but became an assistant to John Carr of York, by whom he was employed at Buxton, Harewood and elsewhere. In 1786 he was appointed receiver or steward to the City of York, with responsibility for the maintenance of corporation property, and on Carr's retirement soon afterwards he succeeded to his exensive practice in Yorkshire and the north of England. He died on 19 June 1805, aged 70, and was buried in the churchyard on the north side of the church of St. Mary Bishophill Senior. He was a competent practitioner in the conservative Georgian manner that he had learned from Carr. [*A.P.S.D.*; York Reference Library, MS. Notes on York artists by J. W. Knowles, i, 9.]

YORK, No. 18 BLAKE STREET, for Mrs. Elizabeth Woodhouse, *c.*1789 [*R.C.H.M. York* v, 110].

YORK, MONK BRIDGE, 1794; widened 1924–6 [*V.C.H. York*, 519].

HACKNESS HALL, YORKS. (N.R.), for Sir R. V. B. Johnstone, Bart., 1797 [*A.P.S.D.*]. The interior was gutted by fire in 1910 and reinstated by W. H. Brierley (*C. Life*, 19 March 1921, where Carr is wrongly described as the architect).

HAINTON HALL, LINCS., rebuilt west front for George Heneage, 1800 [signed drawings preserved in house].

WORTLEY HALL, YORKS. (W.R.), stable-block for James Archibald Stuart Wortley (afterwards 1st Lord Wharncliffe), *c.*1800 [Wortley papers in Sheffield Archives, Wh. M. 58/45–6, *ex inf.* Mr. Richard Hewlings].

ORMSBY HALL, SOUTH ORMSBY, LINCS., additions at rear for Charles Burrell Massingberd, 1803 [drawings in Lincs. Record Office signed *Peter Atkinson & Son, 1803*].

YORK, BOOTHAM HOUSE (now SCHOOL), No. 51 BOOTHAM, for Sir R. V. B. Johnstone, Bart., 1803–4 [R.C.H.M., *York* iv, 60].

HAREWOOD HOUSE, YORKS. (W.R.), gateway and farm buildings for 1st Earl of Harewood, *c.*1803 [R. B. Wragg in *Archaeological Jnl.* cxxv, 1968, 342 n. 4; J. M. Robinson, *Georgian Model Farms*, 1983, 126].

BROCKFIELD HALL, WARTHILL, YORKS. (N.R.), for Benjamin Agar, 1804–7 [Giles Worsley in *C. Life*, 9 March 1989].

ATKINSON, PETER, junior (*c.*1776–1843), son and pupil of the above, became his father's partner in 1801, and succeeded to his practice in 1805. He was surveyor and steward to the York Corporation for many years. At first Atkinson was in partnership with Matthew Phillips (*q.v.*), but the partnership was dissolved in 1819, and from that year until 1827 he was in partnership with his former pupil Richard Hey Sharp (*q.v.*). He was afterwards assisted by his sons John Bownas Atkinson (1807–74) and William Atkinson (1811–86). He retired soon after 1833, and lived abroad during the last years of his life, dying in Calcutta on 13 January 1843. A portrait of him, attributed to Martin Archer Shee, hangs in the City Art Gallery at York. It shows him holding a view of the Ouse Bridge, a work for which his design was accepted as a result of an open competition judged by Thomas Harrison of Chester [*A.P.S.D.*].

Atkinson designed some stylish Greek Revival buildings, but the numerous Commissioners' churches for which he was responsible are somewhat dreary buildings with wide, bleak naves usually lighted by lancet windows. His unexecuted designs for a rectory at Foston in Yorkshire for the Revd. Sydney Smith are in the Borthwick Institute of Historical Research at York (MGA 1813/1).

SECULAR BUILDINGS

YORK, THE CITY GAOL, 1802–7; dem. 1880 [*A.P.S.D.*].

YORK, enlarged the FEMALE PRISON (now the CASTLE MUSEUM) in THE CASTLE, adding the end bays to match Carr's Assize Courts, 1802 [W. Hargrove, *History of York* ii, 1818, 241–2; R.C.H.M., *City of York* ii, 85].

MIDDLETON-ON-THE-WOLDS RECTORY, YORKS. (E.R.), *c.*1810 [Glebe Terrier in Borthwick Institute, York, mentions Atkinson as architect, *ex inf.* Dr. David Neave].

YORK, THE COUNCIL CHAMBER at THE GUILDHALL, 1810–11 [W. Hargrove, *op. cit.*, 436].

YORK, THE OUSE BRIDGE, 1810–20 [W. Hargrove, *op. cit.*, 198–200].

YORK, THE FOSS BRIDGE, 1811–12 [W. Hargrove, *op. cit.*, 288–9].

YORK, THE SUBSCRIPTION LIBRARY, ST. HELEN'S SQUARE, 1811–12 [W. Hargrove, *op. cit.*, 443].

YORK, THE HOUSE OF CORRECTION, 1814; dem. *c.*1840 [W. Hargrove, *op. cit.*, 179].

BOLTON ABBEY, YORKS (W.R.), S. range of Hall for 6th Duke of Devonshire, *c.*1814, Gothic [P. Leach, 'Lord Burlington in Wharfedale', *Arch. Hist.* 32, 1989].

BRADFORD, YORKS. (W.R.), completed the GRAMMAR SCHOOL to designs of W. Bradley (*q.v.*), 1818–20; dem. 1871 [D. Linstrum, *West Yorkshire Architects and Architecture*, 1978, 250].

*YORK, the CONCERT ROOM adjoining the Assembly Rooms, 1824–5; dem. 1974 [*A.P.S.D.*, *s.v.* 'York'; R.C.H.M. *City of York* v, 102].

NABURN, YORKS. (E.R.), THE LOCK or BANQUETING HOUSE, 1824–5 [York City Archives, Ouse Navigation Trustees' Account Book, Jan. 1824, July 1826; *ex inf.* Mr. I. H. Gordon].

*YORK, THE NEW RESIDENCE (now PUREY-CUST CHAMBERS), DEAN'S PARK, 1824–7 [Hargrove's *Guide to York*, 1838, 96].

*BRADFORD, YORKS. (W.R.), THE DISPENSARY, DARLEY STREET, 1826–7; altered 1903 [W. Cudworth, *The Bradford Infirmary*, 1880, 5].

YORK, THE LAYERTHORPE BRIDGE, 1829; widened 1926 [*V.C.H. York*, 519].

CHURCHES

SPROATLEY, YORKS. (E.R.), reconstructed 1819–20, Gothic; altered 1886 [I.C.B.S.: 'we have the same architect as the Wainfleet people, Lincolnshire', but William Hutchinson acted as 'surveyor' and responsibility for the design is not clear].

WAINFLEET ALL SAINTS CHURCH, LINCS., 1820–1, Gothic [I.C.B.S.; B.L., Add. MS. 36369, no. 139].

†*STANLEY, YORKS. (W.R.), 1821–4, Gothic; largely rebuilt by W. D. Caröe 1912–13 after a fire [Port, 138].

†*ALVERTHORPE, YORKS. (W.R.), 1823–5, Gothic [Port, 138].

†*WOODHOUSE MOOR, nr. LEEDS., YORKS. (W.R.), ST. MARK, 1823–5, Gothic [Port, 138].

*ROTHWELL, YORKS. (W.R.), repaired and enlarged 1824–6 [I.C.B.S.].

†*SCARBOROUGH, YORKS. (N.R.), CHRIST CHURCH, 1826–8, Gothic; chancel added 1873; dem. [Port, 164].

†*LINTHWAITE, YORKS, (W.R.), 1827–8, Gothic; chancel added 1895 [Port, 168].

†SOUTH CROSLAND, YORKS. (W.R.), 1827–9, Gothic [Port, 166].

†GOLCAR, YORKS. (W.R.), 1828–9, Gothic; roof rebuilt by R. D. Chantrell 1844 [Port, 166].

†NEW MILL, YORKS. (W.R.), 1829–30, Gothic; remodelled 1882 [Port, 168].

†BIRKENSHAW, YORKS. (W.R.), 1829–30, Gothic; chancel added 1892–3 [Port, 166].

†MANCHESTER, ST. ANDREW, TRAVIS STREET, 1829–31, Gothic; dem. [Port, 132].

†HECKMONDWIKE, YORKS. (W.R.), 1830–1, Gothic, chancel added 1916 [Port, 166].

†CLECKHEATON, YORKS (W.R.), 1830–1, Gothic; chancel added 1864 [Port, 166].

STAVELEY, YORKS. (W.R.), 1831, Gothic; rebuilt 1864 [I.C.B.S.].

ATKINSON, THOMAS (?1729–1798), was one of the leading architects in Yorkshire during the reign of George III. Nothing is known of his early life or of his architectural training, but he was probably the Thomas, son of Thomas Atkinson, mason, who was baptized at Holy Trinity, King's Court, York, on 22 June 1729 [*Yorks. Parish Record Soc.* lxxxv, 1928, 65]. His father may have been connected with a family of bricklayers of the same name with interests in both York and Selby. Thomas Atkinson himself has been identified with Thomas Atkinson of Selby, bricklayer,

---

* Designed in partnership with R. H. Sharp.

† Built for the Commissioners for Building New Churches.

who became a freeman of York in 1758, but as he was a statuary mason by trade, he is more likely to have been the Thomas Atkinson, 'stonecutter', who took up his freedom in 1760 [R. Davies, *The Freeman's Roll*, York 1835, 3]. About the same time he appears to have become a convert to Catholicism, and found a number of patrons among the Catholic gentry of Yorkshire. Plans in Sheffield Archives (E.BV.263(11) and 266(1–2)) show that in 1766 he was employed by the 9th Duke of Norfolk to lay out part of his Sheffield estate for building.

Thomas Atkinson had four sons, James, Joseph, John and Thomas, the first three of whom were all masons by trade. Atkinson 'dropped down dead near his own door' in St. Andrewgate, York, on 4 May 1798, aged 70. He died insolvent, but his business was continued by his son John, who erected a tablet to his memory in St. Saviour's Church, York (J. B. Morrell, *York Monuments*, pl. lxxv *c*).

Atkinson was an able architect in both Gothic and classical styles. Bishopthorpe Palace and the chancel of Coxwold Church are elegant and effective essays in the rococo Gothic of the 1760s, and at Brandsby Church and the chapel of the Bar Convent at York he used the classical orders to achieve interesting and original spatial effects. For his work as a monumental sculptor see Rupert Gunnis, *Dictionary of British Sculptors*, 2nd ed. 1968, 22. A design by him for an Ionic greenhouse will be found in Richard Steele, *An Essay upon Gardening*, York 1793, at end. [*A.P.S.D.*; J. C. H. Aveling, *Catholic Recusancy in the City of York 1558–1791*, Catholic Record Soc. 1970, 150, 371–2; information from the late Dr. E. A. Gee.]

BISHOPTHORPE PALACE, YORKS. (W.R.), designed Gothic gatehouse 1763–5, and remodelled house in Gothic style for Archbishop Robert Hay Drummond, 1766–9 [Anon., *Eboracum: or the History of the City of York* ii, 1788, 169 note; *Beauties of England and Wales* xvi, 1812, 247] (J. P. Neale, *Views of Seats*, 1st ser., v, 1822; *C. Life*, 12 Jan. 1929).

attributed: BISHOPTHORPE CHURCH for Archbishop Robert Hay Drummond, 1766, Gothic; altered 1842 and dem. 1899 except west front.

?HOUGHTON HALL, YORKS. (E.R.), for Philip Langdale, *c.*1765 [cf. letter from Beaumont Hotham to Thomas Atkinson printed in A. M. W. Stirling, *The Hothams* i, 1918, 310, and referring to his engagement with 'Mr. Langdale' in 1769] (*C. Life*, 23–30 Dec. 1965).

YORK, THE BAR CONVENT AND CHAPEL, BLOSSOM STREET, Chapel 1766–9, first block complete 1775, street front 1786 [Bar Convent archives, *ex inf.* the late Dr. E. A. Gee].

BRANDSBY CHURCH, YORKS. (N.R.), 1767–70, mainly at the expense of Francis Cholmeley [*V.C.H. Yorks. N.R.* ii, 104, 106].

WARTER HALL, YORKS. (E.R.), alterations for Sir Joseph Pennington, 1768 [correspondence in Pennington–Ramsden papers, Hull University Library].

TIXALL HALL, STAFFS., designs, perhaps not executed, for alterations for the Hon. Thomas Clifford, *c.*1770 [G. F. Webb in *C. Life*, 3 Sept. 1932, 270]. The house was dem. *c.*1925.

DALTON HALL, SOUTH DALTON, YORKS. (E.R.), rebuilt for Sir Beaumont Hotham, Bart. (d. 1771) and his son Sir Charles Hotham, Bart., 1771–5; altered 1873–4 [letters in Hull University Library, DDHO(3) 48/1, *ex inf.* Dr. David Neave].

BROUGH HALL, YORKS. (N.R.), addition of wings and other alterations for Sir John Lawson, Bart., 1772–5 [W. Angus, *Select Views of Seats*, pl. xxii, 1790] (*C. Life*, 12–19 Oct. 1967).

BURTON CONSTABLE, YORKS. (E.R.), Billiard Room, *c.*1773 (converted into chapel 1830), Blue Drawing Room, 1776, and Orangery, 1788–9, for William Constable [Ivan Hall in *C. Life*, 13 May 1982; drawings at Burton Constable].

CARLTON HALL (now TOWERS), YORKS. (W.R.), work, including new E. wing containing stables and chapel, *c.*1774–7, and Home Farm, *c.*1778, for Thomas Stapleton [Mark Girouard in *C. Life*, 26 Jan. 1967; J. M. Robinson, 'A Catalogue of the Architectural Drawings at Carlton Towers, Yorkshire,' *Arch. Hist.* 22, 1979].

SHEFFIELD, SHREWSBURY HOSPITAL, octagonal chapel, 1776–7; dem. 1825 [reference to Atkinson as architect in the journal of John Platt, the mason who built the chapel: J. D. Potts, *Platt of Rotherham*, Sheffield 1959, 14] (engraving in Joseph Hunter, *History of Hallamshire*, 1868, 179; description in John Wesley's *Journal*, 15 Aug. 1781).

COXWOLD CHURCH, YORKS. (N.R.), rebuilt chancel for 2nd Earl of Fauconberg, 1777, Gothic [B.L., Add. MS. 41135, f. 17].

SHEFFIELD, ST. PETER'S CHURCH (now CATHEDRAL), added N.E. chapel (converted into an organ-chamber 1878–80), 1777 [R. E. Leader, *Surveyors and Architects of Sheffield*, 1903].

SHEFFIELD, surveying new streets and drawing plans and elevations for them, 1779 [Sheffield City Library, R. E. Leader's notes, 141, p. 38].

attributed: YORK, NO. 20, ST. ANDREWGATE, for

himself, *c.*1780–90 [R.C.H.M. *City of York* v, 202].

TERREGLES HOUSE, KIRKCUDBRIGHTSHIRE, for W. H. Maxwell Constable (of Everingham, Yorks.), 1788; enlarged 1831; dem. 1964 [Hull University Library: letters in Constable Maxwell papers, EV 60/20].

YORK, THE WORKHOUSE, MARYGATE, 1792 [*York Herald*, 7 April 1792].

HALSHAM, YORKS. (E.R.), MAUSOLEUM for Edward Constable of Burton Constable, 1794–1802 [N. Higson, 'The Building of the Halsham Mausoleum', *Trans. E. Yorkshire Georgian Soc.* v (2), 1961–3].

ATKINSON, THOMAS WITLAM (1799–1861), was the son of a mason at Cawthorne, Yorkshire, and began life as a builder's labourer. Having shown an aptitude for carving, he executed sculpture on churches at Barnsley and Ashton-under-Lyne and was introduced to Westmacott by John Spencer Stanhope of Cannon Hall (where his mother had been a housemaid). From sculpture he graduated to architecture by acting as clerk of the works for Basevi at St. Thomas's Stockport, and for H. E. Kendall at St. George's, Ramsgate. At the same time he was making a close study of Gothic detail, particularly in the churches of Lincolnshire, and in 1829 he published *Gothic Ornaments selected from the different Cathedrals and Churches in England*, with plates drawn and lithographed by himself and Charles Atkinson (who was probably his brother and was certainly in partnership with him about this time; see *The Literary Blue Book*, 1830, 88).

In 1827 Atkinson settled in London and began to practise as an architect. A Gothic altar-tomb in CAWTHORNE CHURCH, YORKS. (W.R.), in memory of Walter Spencer Stanhope (d. 1821), exhibited at the R.A. in 1830, was one of his first works. In conjunction with Charles Atkinson he reconstructed BOWERS GIFFORD CHURCH, ESSEX, in 1829–30 [Essex C.R.O. D/P 387/6/1 and I.C.B.S. plan in Society of Antiquaries' Library] and designed HYDE CHURCH, CHESHIRE, 1831–2, Gothic [Port, 140, 177]. ST. NICHOLAS, LOWER TOOTING, SURREY, consecrated 1833, was another early work in the Gothic style. Several commissions in Manchester induced him to move there in about 1835. Here his principal work was the MANCHESTER & LIVERPOOL DISTRICT BANK in SPRING GARDENS, 1834, an astylar Italianate building (now demolished) whose erection, according to Atkinson's obituary notice in *The Builder*, 'was as important in the architectural history of Manchester, as that of the Travellers' Club was in London'. In ST. LUKE'S, CHEETHAM HILL, MANCHESTER, 1836–9 (dem. except tower *c.*1980), he made use of his Gothic studies to produce a church that was exceptionally scholarly for its date. Other works were ST. BARNABAS, OPENSHAW, LANCS., 1838–40, dem.; THE MANCHESTER & LIVERPOOL DISTRICT BANK, HANLEY, STAFFS., 1833, Gothic, dem. 1881 [signed lithograph in William Salt Library, Stafford, iv. 266]; Italianate villas in the neighbourhood of Manchester for Messrs. Heelis, Slater, Bradshaw and others; houses at ASHTON and STALYBRIDGE for Messrs. Swire, Lea and Harrison;[1] HOUGH HILL PRIORY, STALYBRIDGE, for David Cheetham, 1832, and a house near STOCKPORT for a Mr. Walmsley.[2] Atkinson exhibited at the Royal Academy between 1830 and 1842. F. T. Bellhouse and Edward Hall were in his office as pupils, and J. E. Gregan (1812–55) was his assistant until 1840.

'After some reverses, owing perhaps to a too liberal expenditure on works of art', Atkinson returned to London, and in 1844 went to Hamburg to compete unsuccessfully for the church of St. Nicholas, which was awarded to Gilbert Scott. After this he abandoned architecture for the pursuits of an explorer and topographical artist, in which he achieved some celebrity. His best-known works were *Oriental and Western Siberia: a Narrative of Seven Years' Explorations and Adventures* (1858), and *Travels in the Upper and Lower Amoor and the Russian Acquisitions on the Confines of India and China* (1860). He died in Kent on 13 August 1861. [Obituary in *Builder* xix, 1861, 590; *A.P.S.D.*; *D.N.B.* (*Supplement*); A. M. W. Stirling, *The Letter-Bag of Lady Elizabeth Spencer-Stanhope* ii, 1913, 95–6.]

ATKINSON, WILLIAM (*c.*1773–1839), was born at Bishop Auckland, Durham, and began life as a carpenter. He was probably a son of another William Atkinson who was employed as a builder at Auckland Castle in the 1760s, and is doubtless the 'Atkinson, Junr.' who signs drawings connected with James Wyatt's works at the Castle for Bishop Barrington in the 1790s [John Cornforth in *C. Life*, 3 Feb. 1972]. Through Bishop Barrington's good offices he became a pupil of Wyatt and moved to London, where he entered the Royal Academy Schools in 1796, winning the Gold Medal in 1797. He subsequently exhibited regularly at the Academy until 1811. In 1805 he published a volume of

[1] Probably William Harrison (d. 1853), of West Hill, Stalybridge.

[2] Probably John Walmsley of Wallnut Cottage, Heaton Norris.

Views of Picturesque Cottages. The Roman cement known as 'Atkinson's cement' was introduced by him to the London market, the raw material being shipped to his own wharf in Westminster from Lord Mulgrave's estates near Whitby. The cement could be used both as an external rendering and to form mouldings. It was through the favour of Lord Mulgrave, then Master General of the Ordnance, that in 1813 Atkinson succeeded James Wyatt as architect to the Board of Ordnance, a post which he retained until the abolition of his department in 1829.

In 1812–16 Atkinson appears to have had an office in Manchester: it was from Manchester that in February 1812 he wrote to the Duke of Devonshire's London agent about projected works at Burlington House [letter at Chatsworth, *ex inf.* Mr. P. A. Bezodis]; it was also from Manchester that in 1813 and 1814 he exhibited at the Liverpool Academy, and his name appears in the Manchester directories for 1815 and 1816.

Atkinson was primarily a country-house architect, and he specialized in the design of picturesque Gothic houses, usually based on an irregular, asymmetrical plan, with a profusion of battlemented towers and pinnacled gables. He was not a very sensitive architect, and his Gothic detail has lost the elegant charm of the eighteenth century without achieving the scholarship of the nineteenth. Of his few classical works, the interiors of Broughton Hall are the most successful, and show that he could rival some of the best Regency designers.

Atkinson was a keen geologist and botanist. The gardens of his villa at Grove End, Paddington, were planted with rare trees and embellished with 'specimens of the varieties of English stone'. In about 1830 he bought an estate of 170 acres at Silvermere, nr. Cobham in Surrey, where he built himself a house, and was able to indulge in his 'favourite pursuits of horticulture and planting' on a large scale. Here he died on 22 May 1839, and was buried at Walton-on-Thames. He left two sons, William and Henry George Atkinson, the younger of whom was also an architect. His pupils included T. Allason, R. R. Banks, P. H. Desvignes, M. Habershon and J. B. Watson, while Thomas Tredgold, C.E., spent ten years in his office between 1813 and 1824. [*A.P.S.D.*; *Farington Diary*, ed. J. Greig, vii, 205; J. T. Smith, *A Book for a Rainy Day*, 1905, 312–13; E. W. Brayley, *Topographical History of Surrey* ii, 1841, 368; letter about planting at Silvermere in N.L.S., MS. 587, no. 1202; will, P.C.C. 339 VAUGHAN.]

HOUSES

CASTLE EDEN, CO. DURHAM, castellated lodge and gateway for Rowland Burdon, *c.*1800 [exhib. at R.A. 1800].

SCONE PALACE, PERTHSHIRE, reconstructed for 3rd Earl of Mansfield, 1803–12, Gothic [exhib. at R.A. 1808, 1811; J. P. Neale, *Views of Seats*, 1st ser., v, 1822; J. Cornforth in *C. Life*, 18 Aug. 1988]. Atkinson also designed the stables (1810) and the mausoleum may be attributed to him.

BROADWELL GROVE, nr. BURFORD, OXON., for William Hervey, soon after 1804, Gothic; altered later in 19th century [exhib. at R.A. 1810].

FOOTS CRAY, KENT, house for J. Olive, *c.*1804 [exhib. at R.A. 1804].

MULGRAVE CASTLE, YORKS. (N.R.), remodelled for 1st Earl of Mulgrave, *c.*1804–11, castle style [exhib. at R.A. 1804; J. P. Neale, *Views of Seats*, 2nd. ser. ii, 1825].

HAREWOOD HOUSE, HEREFS., alterations for Sir Hungerford Hoskyns, Bart., probably *c.*1805; dem. 1952 [letter from Atkinson 3 Nov. 1818, mentioning former work here, in Herefs. R.O., D 52/4/8, *ex inf.* Mr. D. Whitehead].

CHIDDINGSTONE CASTLE, KENT, remodelled for Henry Streatfield, *c.*1805–10, Gothic; completed by H. E. Kendall *c.*1837–8 [exhib. at R.A. 1805].

BRETTON HALL, YORKS. (W.R.), Doric lodge and gateway for Col. T. R. Beaumont, 1807 [exhib. at R.A. 1807].

TWYFORD ABBEY, WEST TWYFORD, MIDDLESEX, for Thomas Willan, 1807–9, Gothic [*Beauties of England & Wales* x (2), 1816, 353; *A.P.S.D.*].

ROSSIE PRIORY, PERTHSHIRE, for 8th Lord Kinnaird, 1807–15, Gothic; partly dem. 1949 [J. P. Neale, *Views of Seats*, 2nd ser. ii, 1825].

PANSHANGER, HERTS, for 5th Earl Cowper, 1807–20, Gothic (succeeding Samuel Wyatt); dem. 1953–4 [*A.P.S.D.*] (*C. Life*, 11–18 Jan. 1936).

BROUGHTON HALL, YORKS. (W. R.), added pedimented wings and made other alterations for Stephen Tempest, 1809–11 [C. Hussey in *C. Life*, 31 March, 7, 14 April 1950].

BIEL HOUSE, EAST LOTHIAN, additions (since dem.) for W. H. Nisbet, *c.*1810–12, Gothic [*N.S.A.* ii, 57] (J. Small, *Castles and Mansions of the Lothians* i, 1883; *C. Life*, 30 Aug. 1902).

LISMORE CASTLE, CO. WATERFORD, IRELAND, repairs and alterations for 6th Duke of Devonshire, 1811 [Mark Girouard in *C. Life*, 6–13 Aug. 1964].

BOWHILL, SELKIRKSHIRE, additions for 4th

Duke of Buccleuch, 1813–17 [*A.P.S.D.*; John Cornforth in *C. Life*, 5 June 1975] (R.C.A.M., *Selkirkshire*, 65–6).

DITTON PARK, BUCKS., for Lord Montagu, 1813–17, Gothic [J. P. Neale, *Views of Seats*, 1st ser., i, 1818] (*C. Life*, 11 Jan. 1990).

CLAPHAM LODGE (later INGLEBOROUGH HALL), CLAPHAM, nr. SETTLE, YORKS. (W.R.), for James Farrer, *c.*1814 [exhib. at Liverpool Academy, 1814].

ABBOTSFORD, ROXBURGHSHIRE, for Sir Walter Scott, Bart., 1814–24, Gothic, incorporating suggestions by Edward Blore [N.L.S., MS. 3889, f. 17; *The Letters of Sir Walter Scott*, ed. H. J. C. Grierson, 1934, iv, 333–6, 526–7, vii, 208; C. Wainwright in *C. Life*, 9 June 1989].

GARNONS, HEREFORDSHIRE, enlarged and remodelled for Sir J. G. Cotterell, Bart., 1815–*c.*1830 [J. P. Neale, *Views of Seats*, 2nd ser. iv, 1828]; largely dem. 1957–8 except one wing (itself remodelled *c.*1900).

GORHAMBURY, HERTS., rebuilt N. wing 1816–17, demolished S. wing and made other alterations 1826–8 for 1st Earl of Verulam [J. C. Rogers in *C. Life*, 25 Nov. 1933].

TULLIALLAN CASTLE, FIFE, for Viscount Keith, 1817–20, Gothic [*A.P.S.D.*].

THE DEEPDENE, nr. DORKING, SURREY, remodelled for Thomas Hope, 1818–19 and 1823; dem. 1967 [David Watkin, *Thomas Hope*, 1968, 166, 288].

TAYMOUTH CASTLE, PERTHSHIRE, extensive Gothic additions for 4th Earl of Breadalbane, 1818–21 and 1827–8 [*A.P.S.D.*; Alistair Rowan in *C. Life*, 8–15 Oct. 1964].

HYLANDS, nr. CHELMSFORD, ESSEX, works, chiefly greenhouses, etc., for P. C. Labouchère, 1819–25 [*Trans. Horticultural Soc. of London* viii, 1828, 402; *Gardener's Mag.* iii, 1828, 399; E. Abraham, *Hylands*, Chelmsford 1988, 9, 16].

LONDON, GROVE END, PADDINGTON, for himself, *c.*1818; dem. [J. T. Smith, *A Book for a Rainy Day*, 1905, 312–13].

LONDON, HOPE HOUSE, DUCHESS STREET, PORTLAND PLACE, added FLEMISH PICTURE GALLERY to designs of Thomas Hope, 1819–20; dem. 1851 [D. Watkin, *Thomas* Hope, 1968, 122] (Britton & Pugin, *Public Buildings of London* i, 1825, 310–12).

DABTON HOUSE, THORNHILL, DUMFRIESSHIRE, for 5th Duke of Buccleuch, as residence for his Agent, 1820 [photos at N.M.R.S. of signed drawings in Buccleuch archives].

CHEQUERS, BUCKS., alterations (removed 1909) for R. Greenhill Russell, 1823, Tudor style [*A.P.S.D.*] (J. G. Jenkins, *Chequers*, 1967).

LONDON, No. 34 BURLINGTON GARDENS, enlarged for Col. the Hon. H. F. C. Cavendish, 1823 [*A.P.S.D.*].

SWALLOWFIELD HOUSE, BERKS., alterations for Sir Henry Russell, Bart., 1824–6 [Lady Constance Russell, *Swallowfield and its Owners*, 1901; family correspondence in Bodleian Library, MS. Eng. lett. c. 151].

HIMLEY HALL, STAFFS., enlarged for 4th Viscount Dudley & Ward, 1824–7 [*A.P.S.D.*] (*C. Life*, 1 Dec. 1934, 570).

THE MYNDE PARK, MUCH DEWCHURCH, HEREFS., remodelled exterior for J. H. Symons, 1825 [letter from carpenter to Atkinson 31 July 1825 *penes* Mr. W. A. Twiston Davies and cf. unexecuted designs for internal alterations by Atkinson in N.L.W., Mynde collection, 5273–4].

LONDON, DUDLEY HOUSE, No. 100 PARK LANE, for 4th Viscount Dudley & Ward, 1827–8 [*A.P.S.D.*; *Survey of London* xl, 278].

LONDON, BREADALBANE HOUSE, No. 21 PARK LANE, minor work for 4th Earl of Breadalbane, 1827–8; dem. 1876–7 [S.R.O., GD 112/20/6].

HOLME LACY, HEREFS., alterations, including new N. entrance front, for Sir Edwyn Scudamore Stanhope, Bart., 1828–32 [letter from Atkinson to John Arkwright, 25 Sept. 1832, Herefordshire C.R.O., A 63/135].

MONTREAL, RIVERHEAD, KENT, added extensions on each side of house for 1st Earl Amherst, 1829; dem. [drawings in Kent Archives Office, U 1350, P.21].

SILVERMERE, nr. COBHAM, SURREY, for himself, *c.*1830 [E. W. Brayley, *Topographical History of Surrey* ii, 1841, 368].

WOBURN ABBEY, BEDS., kitchen garden, pinery, etc., for 6th Duke of Bedford, before 1833 [James Forbes, *Hortus Woburnensis*, 1833, 297–403, *passim*].

CHURCHES

BISHOP AUCKLAND, CO. DURHAM, ST. ANNE'S CHAPEL in Market Place, added Gothic W. tower *c.*1800, probably based on a design made by James Wyatt in 1796 and preserved at Auckland Castle; dem. 1847 [Brayley & Britton, *Beauties of England & Wales* v, 1803, 219].

TWYFORD CHURCH, MIDDLESEX, reconstructed for Thomas Willan, 1808, Gothic; incorporated as chancel of enlarged church, 1958 [*A.P.S.D.*].

DURHAM CATHEDRAL, repaired central tower, 1809–12 [*A.P.S.D.*, *s.v.* 'Durham'].

NEWTON HEATH, nr. MANCHESTER, rebuilt ALL SAINTS CHURCH, 1814–16, Gothic; enlarged at E. end, 1844; chancel 1880 [by

'Atkinson': Thomas Rickman's diary, 24 Aug. 1817].

CANONBIE CHURCH, DUMFRIESSHIRE, 1822, Gothic [S.R.O., Buccleuch Muniments, Chamberlain's accounts 1824–5, p. 42].

DITTON CHAPEL, BUCKS., repairs for 5th Duke of Buccleuch, 1823–6 [Buccleuch Muniments formerly at Dalkeith Palace VI, 1, now S.R.O.].

RICKMANSWORTH CHURCH, HERTS., rebuilt except tower, 1825–6, Gothic; rebuilt 1890 [I.C.B.S.].

FINLARIG, PERTHSHIRE, Breadalbane family mausoleum, 1829–30 [S.R.O., GD 112/20/6].

PUBLIC BUILDINGS

As architect to the Board of Ordnance (1813–29) Atkinson is said to have been responsible for works (probably minor) at THE ORDNANCE OFFICE, PALL MALL, LONDON (dem. *c.*1910), THE TOWER OF LONDON and WOOLWICH ARSENAL. In 1823 he designed RANSOM & CO'S BANK, 1 PALL MALL, EAST (dem.) and in 1822–3 erected some buildings in the HORTICULTURAL SOCIETY'S GARDENS at CHISWICK [*A.P.S.D.*].

In 1814 Atkinson made designs for public buildings for the Corporation of BOSTON, LINCS. Of these the FISH MARKET was built 1815–16. The ASSEMBLY ROOMS, built 1820–2 under the direction of Jeptha Pacey (*q.v.*) may have been based on a design made by Atkinson in 1813 [Boston Corporation Records, *ex inf.* Mr. Richard Hewlings].

ATTERBURY, LUFFMAN (1740–1796), was a carpenter by trade, but was also prepared to act as an architect or surveyor. Music was, however, his great interest, and as a composer he gained a degree of celebrity that he never attained as a designer of buildings. Lord Le Despenser appears to have been one of his principal patrons, for it was an oratorio composed by Atterbury that was performed in West Wycombe church in 1775 when Paul Whitehead's heart was buried in the adjoining mausoleum, and in 1780 Atterbury was employed by Lord Le Despenser to supervise the building of the Rectory (now Mere House) at Mereworth in Kent in accordance with designs made by Nicholas Revett. Letters from Atterbury complaining, *inter alia*, of the inadequacy of Revett's drawings, are among the Dashwood papers in the Bodleian Library (MSS. D. D. Dashwood B 11/13/26a, B 15/1/6a).

ATWOOD, THOMAS WARR (*c.*1733–1775), was a prosperous plumber and glazier of Bath. He was a member of a family that was prominent in local affairs, and was himself a member of the Common Council from 1760 onwards. Although there appears to be no evidence that he ever held any formal appointment as city architect or surveyor, he played a leading part in directing the Corporation's building policy and on 3 July 1775 was formally thanked 'for his attention . . . in the management of the business relative to the Public improvements in this City'. Public service and private profit went hand in hand, for Atwood himself contracted for much of the ensuing work, and was also in a position to obtain leases of Corporation property upon which he built the PARAGON CRESCENT (1768) and OXFORD ROW (1773). For the city he designed the PRISON in GROVE STREET (1772–3), and the GUILDHALL was being rebuilt by him when he was accidentally killed on 15 November 1775 'by the sudden falling of a decayed floor' in an old house that he was examining on the site of the new building. The Guildhall was subsequently completed under the directions and to the designs of his assistant Thomas Baldwin (*q.v.*), who is also believed to have designed the very elegant monument to Atwood in the churchyard at Weston, nr. Bath. Atwood was a competent though conservative architect whose elevations are excellent examples of the English Palladian tradition as applied to street architecture. A miniature portrait by Van Diest is in the City Art Gallery. [Bath City Council Minutes 1760–1775; W. Ison, *The Georgian Buildings of Bath*, 1948, 35–7, 2nd ed. 1980, 11–13.]

AUDUS, JAMES (1781–1867), was the son of John Audus (1752–1809), a wealthy merchant who came to live at Selby in Yorkshire in 1771. After a visit to Bath the father determined to erect a crescent in Selby similar to John Palmer's Lansdown Crescent in that city, and obtained a 99-year lease of a site on the south side of the abbey church from Lord Petre. His death in 1809 prevented the full accomplishment of his plan, but THE CRESCENT was completed by his son, who was an amateur architect, and designed several buildings in Selby, including the AUDUS ALMSHOUSES which he founded and endowed in Gowthorp in 1833, the COURT HOUSE, 1855, the WESLEYAN CHAPEL in JAMES STREET, and ST. JAMES'S CHURCH, 1866. In 1824 SELBY ABBEY CHURCH was repewed under his direction. Having held 'every office of honour and responsibility in the town of Selby', Audus died there on 14 May 1867. [E. Parsons, *The Tourist's Companion from Leeds and Selby to Hull*, 1835, 107, 108, 109–10, 132–3; W. B. Morrell, *History of Selby*, 1867, 230, 254–8.]

AUSTIN, GEORGE (1787–1848), born at Woodstock, was the son of George Austin, a surveyor of that place, who was employed in connection with the rebuilding of the tower of Woodstock Church in 1784, and by the Duke of Marlborough at Blenheim Palace. In *c.*1820 he became surveyor to CANTERBURY CATHEDRAL, which he found in a dangerous condition. In order to save it, he carried out extensive repairs, including the rebuilding of the vault and gable of the south-east transept, resetting the groining of the choir, and restoring the north nave aisle to the perpendicular. After consultation with Thomas Rickman (*q.v.*), he took down the decayed north-west tower, and between 1832 and 1841 erected the present tower to correspond with that at the south-west angle. He designed a new altar screen and the archiepiscopal throne (illustrated in *Builder* vi, 1848, 139). He was buried in a vault under the north-west tower, where a bronze tablet and a stained-glass window were erected to his memory. His son, H. G. Austin (1823–92), succeeded him as surveyor to the cathedral fabric. [Obituary in *Builder*, vii, 1849, 205; *A.P.S.D.*; Oxfordshire C.R.O., Bishop's Transcripts of Woodstock Parish Register.]

AXTELL, FRANCIS, was the surveyor employed to supervise the repair of LUDLOW CASTLE, SHROPSHIRE, after twenty years of neglect during the Interregnum. Between 1662 and 1667 over £2000 was spent under his direction in rehabilitating the castle as the headquarters of the Council in the Marches of Wales [P.R.O., AO 1/2520/611].

AYERS, CHARLES ROBERT (*c.*1788–1845), practised from Lower Grosvenor Street and John Street (Berkeley Square), London, during the early nineteenth century. From the drawings which he exhibited at the Royal Academy it appears that he designed the mansion at TREHILL, nr. EXETER, for J. H. Ley, 1827, a Gothic house at PETWORTH, SUSSEX, for J. J. King, 1828, CANONTEIGN HOUSE, DEVON, for the Hon. Capt. P. B. Pellew, M.P. (afterwards 2nd Viscount Exmouth), 1828, and alterations and additions to COLEBROOK PARK, nr. TUNBRIDGE WELLS, KENT, for Sir Edward Colebrooke, Bart., 1829, dem. *c.*1870. Trehill and Canonteign are stuccoed houses with Greek Revival detail. Ayers died at Brighton in October 1845, aged 57 [*Gent's Mag.* 1845 (ii), 662].

AYTON, WILLIAM (–1643?), belonged to a family of masons to whom there are numerous references in the minute book of a Masons' lodge meeting at Aitchison's Haven, nr. Musselburgh in Midlothian, extracts from which were printed in *Ars Quatuor Coronatorum* xxiv, 1911, 34–41. William Ayton, senior and junior, were prominent members of the lodge in 1598, but the man who is the subject of this entry was probably the William, son of John Ayton, mason in Musselburgh, who was apprenticed to John Brown, mason of Edinburgh, in January 1598/9. He subsequently became the foreman or assistant of William Wallace (*q.v.*). On Wallace's death in 1631 Ayton succeeded him as master mason of HERIOT'S HOSPITAL, EDINBURGH, begun in 1628 and still incomplete. He undertook 'to prosecute and follow forth the Modell, Frame, and Building of the said wark, as the same is alredy begun, and to devyse, plott, and set down what he shall think meittest for the decorement of the said wark'. It was he who brought the building to a state of near completion in the 1640s. In 1633 he was working at Holyroodhouse, and in about 1640 he designed INNES HOUSE, MORAYSHIRE, for the laird of Innes, whose accounts include a payment of £26 13s. 4d. 'to Wm. Aitoun, Maister Maissoun at Herriott his work, for drawing the form of the House on paper'. Innes is a house on the traditional Scottish L-plan with Anglo-Flemish detail similar to that of Heriot's Hospital (*C. Life*, 4 Nov. 1976).

Ayton did not become a burgess of Edinburgh until August 1640. In 1643 John Mylne succeeded him as master mason of Heriot's Hospital and he died in 1645. His portrait, inscribed 'Measter Meason to Heriot's Vorke', belongs to the Hospital. [*A.P.S.D.*; D. MacGibbon & T. Ross, *The Castellated and Domestic Architecture of Scotland*, 1887–92, ii, 203, iv, 144, v, 560–1; H. Carr, *The Mason and the Burgh*, 1954, 38; *Register of Edinburgh Apprentices 1583–1666*, Scottish Historical Soc., 1906, 9; Alistair Rowan, 'George Heriot's Hospital, Edinburgh', *C. Life*, 6 March 1975; testament in S.R.O., CC 8/8/61, f. 301].

B

BACHOP, BAUCHOP, or **BAAK,** TOBIAS (–1710), was the most prominent member of a family of masons working in the neighbourhood of Alloa in Clackmannanshire in the late seventeenth and early eighteenth centuries. Tobias appears to have been the son of Thomas Bachup of Alloa, and was probably apprenticed to his father. In 1680 he was concerned in some extensive repairs to ALLOA CHURCH [D. MacGibbon & T. Ross, *The Castellated and Domestic Architecture of Scotland* v, 1892, 378–9], and in 1684 he contracted to reconstruct LOGIE CHURCH, STIRLINGSHIRE, 'conforme to ane draught drawn be the said Tobias himself' [contract printed in Scottish History Soc., *Miscellany* xi, 1990, 308–10]. These two churches (both now in ruins) were buildings of traditional character, but soon afterwards Bachop came into contact with Sir William Bruce, the pioneer of Scottish classicism, who employed him first at KINROSS HOUSE (1686–90) [S.R.O., Bruce of Kinross papers, GD 29/1982 and Mylne papers, GD 1/51/62], and subsequently at HOPETOUN (1698 onwards), CRAIGIEHALL (1699) and MERTOUN (now HARDEN) HOUSE, BERWICKSHIRE (1703) [J. G. Dunbar, *Sir William Bruce*, exhibition catalogue 1970, nos. 154, 165; S.R.O., Register of Deeds, Durie, vol. 124, pp. 213–15]. Bruce evidently thought highly of Bachop and in 1692 recommended him to the 3rd Duke of Hamilton when the latter was about to build Hamilton Palace, though in the event the house was built not by Bachop but by James Smith (*q.v.*) [Rosalind K. Marshall, *The Days of Duchess Anne*, 1973, 193]. In 1697 Bruce's right-hand man Alexander Edward (*q.v.*) witnessed the contract whereby Bachop undertook to enlarge KINLOCH HOUSE, PERTHSHIRE, for Dame Margaret Graham [S.R.O., RH 12/39/155]. This contract mentions chimneys built by Bachop at PANMURE HOUSE, ANGUS, where he had recently carried out alterations and additions for the 4th Earl of Panmure in which Edward had also been concerned [S.R.O., GD 45/18/614].

In about 1690 Bachop built (and probably designed) THE OLD CROSS, ALLOA, and in 1705 he undertook to build the TOWN HALL and STEEPLE at DUMFRIES after John Moffat of Liverpool (*q.v.*) had furnished 'a modall' but declined to execute it himself. The committee accordingly 'resolved to send for one Tobias Bachup, a master builder now at Abercorn' (i.e. Hopetoun), 'who is said to be of good skill'. Bachop is subsequently referred to as 'our architect' and as 'architect and builder of the steeple and council house', and he claimed to have spent six weeks making drawings and moulds for the building. However in the steeple at least he appears to have followed Moffat's design, which was itself based on the steeple of the College at Glasgow [W. McDowall, *History of Dumfries*, Edinburgh 1867, 539–42; S.R.O., CS 228/B/1/42].

Other records show Bachop working at a house called ARGATY near DOUNE in PERTHSHIRE in 1687 [S.R.O., GD 29/1982/8], apparently involved in alterations to CORTACHY CASTLE, ANGUS, in 1696 [S.R.O., GD 16/34/272], making a monument to Provost J. McCulloch (d. 1698) in HOLYRUDE CHURCHYARD, STIRLING [S.R.O., CS 181/626], working at STIRLING CASTLE, where he built a three-gun battery in 1689 and was engaged in alterations to the Palace buildings from 1699 onwards [R.C.A.M. *Stirlingshire* i, 188], and advising the 1st Duke of Montrose about his Glasgow house in 1708 [S.R.O., GD 220/6/26, p. 59]. He was presumably the 'Mr. Boak, a contractor at Stirling', to whose plan Sir John Shaw, Bart., intended to rebuild the MANSION HOUSE at GREENOCK, LANARKS. in 1702 had he not died soon afterwards [MacGibbon & Ross, *op. cit.* iii, 486].

Bachop died on 26 April 1710. The house which he had built for himself in Kirkgate, Alloa, still exists, and bears the date 1695, with the initials of himself and his wife Margaret Lapsley. The well-designed symmetrical façade with classical detailing shows an intelligent understanding of the new architectural vocabulary which Bachop would have learned from Bruce.

[J. Crawfurd, *Memorials of the Parish of Alloa*, 1874, 61; D. MacGibbon & T. Ross, *The Castellated and Domestic Architecture of Scotland* v, 1892, 127–8, 377–8; *Masterton Papers* (Scottish History Soc. 1893), 483.]

BACKHOUSE, R— WILLIAM, of London, exhibited designs for a dock at COVE, nr. CORK, IRELAND, at the Society of Artists in 1791, and for 'the Custom-house and Exchange to be built on the new pier' there, at the Royal Academy in 1806. In 1818 he exhibited a design for alterations to SANDBECK HOUSE, YORKS. (W.R.), for the 6th Earl of Scarbrough, and in 1826, when he applied unsuccessfully for the position of surveyor to the Commissioners for Building New Churches, he named the Earl of Scarbrough as a referee, others being the Earl of Coventry, General Isaac Gascoyne, and Messrs. Jolliffe and Banks, the building contractors [Church Commissioners records, file 21744, pt. 5]. In his will, William Jolliffe, M.P. (d. 1802), directed that he was to be buried in Merstham Church, Surrey, in a vault 'to be prepared according to a plan by – Backhouse, architect' [P.C.C. 465 KENYON]. Among Jolliffe papers in the P.R.O. [C 107/93], there is a plan showing alterations to the DOLPHIN INN, PETERSFIELD, HANTS., signed 'R.W.B. architect, London, 1819'. An elevation of BALLS PARK, HERTS., in the R.I.B.A. Drawings Collection, signed by R. W. Backhouse and dated 1786, may indicate that he was employed to alter that house for the Dowager Viscountess Townsend.

BACON, CHARLES (1784–1818), younger son of the sculptor John Bacon, R.A., was a pupil of J. T. Groves of the Office of Works, with whom he remained for some years after the expiration of his articles. In 1811 he succeeded Groves as Clerk of the Works at Whitehall, Westminster and St. James's, and in 1815 he also became responsible for the Mews at Charing Cross. In 1816 he became architect to Ely Cathedral, and in July of the same year was appointed architect to Princess Charlotte. He also held the post of surveyor to the county of Middlesex from September 1816 until his death on 10 June 1818, at the age of 34 [*Gent's Mag.* 1818 (i), 574]. His diary for 1816–17 is in the Essex Record Office [D/DQ 14/42]. The volume for 1813–15 was sold at Sotheby's 24 July 1957, lot 471, and that for 1817–18 is in private possession.

As a private architect, Bacon's principal works appear to have been the Gothic entrance gateway to WOODFORD HALL, ESSEX, for J. Maitland, M.P., 1810 [exhib. at R.A.], and a library at the same house, 1816 [Diary]; the rebuilding of WOODFORD CHURCH, ESSEX, 1816, altered 1889 [*V.C.H. Essex* vi, 354; drawing in R.I.B.A. Drawings Collection]; alterations to WALTHAMSTOW CHURCH, ESSEX, 1817–18 [*V.C.H. Essex* vi, 290]; the enlargement of WOODFORD LODGE (now HALL), NORTHANTS., for Charles Arbuthnot, M.P., *c.*1813 [*A.P.S.D.*; Diary]; and OAKLANDS, nr. OKEHAMPTON, DEVON, for Albany Savile, M.P., a Greek Revival house begun *c.*1816 and completed after Bacon's death by his pupil Charles Vokins [R. Ackermann, *Repository of Arts*, 3rd ser. viii, 1826, 249–50; J. C. Loudon, *Encyclopaedia of Rural Architecture*, 1846, 915]. In 1809 he shared with J. A. and G. S. Repton the first prize for the design of public buildings then intended to be erected in Westminster [P.R.O., WORK 8/10B, 24]. He designed the Gothic monument in BYLAUGH CHURCH, NORFOLK, to Sir John Lombe, Bart. (d. 1817), which was executed by his brother [Diary].

BADGER, JOSEPH (1738–1817), was born at Hathersage in Derbyshire, but established himself in Sheffield, where he conducted a successful business as a carpenter, joiner, builder and architect from his yard in Orchard Street.

In 1776 he was employed by Francis Hurt Sitwell to superintend the conversion of the Great Chamber in the Jacobean RENISHAW HALL, DERBYSHIRE, into a drawing-room in the Adam style, and between 1793 and 1808 he enlarged and remodelled the house for Sir Sitwell Sitwell, Bart., with interiors in the same style. He almost certainly designed the stables built in 1794 [C. Hussey in *C. Life*, 7–14 May 1938]. The dining-room and staircase at THE OAKS, NORTON, nr. SHEFFIELD, bear a marked resemblance to his work at Renishaw, and were probably designed by him for Sir William Chambers Bagshawe early in the nineteenth century.

In 1784 Badger surveyed ECCLESALL BIERLOW CHURCH, YORKS. (W.R.), with John Bishop, mason, preparatory to its rebuilding [*Yorks. Arch. Jnl.* xvii, 68], and in 1788 he measured work done by John Platt (*q.v.*) at WORTLEY HALL, YORKS, (W.R.) [Wortley papers in Sheffield City Library, WhM. 58/26]. In 1801 he was employed to lay out the new MARKET PLACE at ROTHERHAM, YORKS. (W.R.), and to design elevations for the buildings [J. Guest, *Historic Notices of Rotherham*, 1879, 542]. He was presumably the 'Thomas Badger' who, according to W. Odom, *Memorials of Sheffield, its Cathedral and Churches*, 1992, 86, designed and built ST. JAMES'S CHAPEL, SHEFFIELD, in 1786–9, dem. 1940. His designs for a Sessions House, with adjoining Bailiff's and Gaoler's houses, made for the Duke of Norfolk, are in Sheffield Archives [No. 15263], where there are also a plan by him for proposed additions to a house at Wards End dated 1796 [Wheat Collection 1791], and an agreement to build a coffee house dated 1793 [No. Wil. D.260]. Badger was active as a speculative builder in and around Sheffield, and among the houses he is known to have built were WESTBOURNE HOUSE, CROOKESMOOR, described as 'lately erected' in 1807, and TAPTON GROVE, RANMOOR, both demolished.

Badger died on 15 July 1817, aged 79. His wife is said to have been the mistress of the 5th ('Wicked') Lord Byron. His son Joseph Badger, junior, was in James Wyatt's office in 1793, when he exhibited a design for a villa at the Royal Academy, but did not survive his father, dying in 1807 at the age of 33.

In the 1820s the family was represented by another Joseph Badger, a carpenter, and by Jonathan Badger, a carpenter and joiner who died on 18 March 1834, aged 63. These were probably the sons of Joseph Badger's younger brother Jonathan.

[Sheffield Archives, Arthur Jackson's MS. copy of the inscriptions in Sheffield Parish Churchyard, 1894, nos. 518, 2826; R. E. Leader, *Surveyors and Architects of the Past in Sheffield*, 1903; information from Mr. John Titterton.]

BAILEY, CHARLES (*c.*1767–1855), of Haywood in Nynehead, Somerset, was a land surveyor and agent to the Sanford family [P. Eden, *Dictionary of Land Surveyors and Car-*

tographers, 1975, 26]. He appears also to have acted as an architect, for he signs the designs for rebuilding SIR JOHN POPHAM'S ALMSHOUSES (now R.C. Church) at WELLINGTON, SOMERSET, 1833 [P.R.O., C 108/322]. He died in September 1855 at the age of 88 [Nynehead Parish Register in Somerset C.R.O.]

BAILEY, GEORGE (1792–1860), entered Sir John Soane's office as a pupil in 1806, and remained as an assistant until Soane's death in 1837. He was admitted to the Royal Academy Schools in 1813 and exhibited at the Royal Academy in 1811, 1822 and 1823. In 1837 he became the first curator of Sir John Soane's Museum, in accordance with Soane's will, and remained in charge of the museum until his death. He was one of the two Hon. Secretaries of the Institute of British Architects. [Obituary in *Builder*, xviii, 1860, 842; A. T. Bolton, *Architectural Education a Century Ago* (Soane Museum Publication No. 12), 16.]

BAILEY, JAMES (*c.*1771–1850), was primarily a surveyor. He lived and practised in Lambeth, at first in partnership with John Middleton (d. 1833/4) and afterwards with his former pupil R. Willshire. In Lambeth he acted as local surveyor to the Duchy of Cornwall, and designed ST. MARK'S SCHOOL, HARLEYFORD ROAD, KENNINGTON, 1824 [*Survey of London* xxvi, 25–7]. In conjunction with Willshire he built the TRINITY HOMES, ACRE LANE, STOCKWELL, for Thomas Bailey in 1822 [*ibid.*, 98–9]. He is perhaps to be identified with the 'Mr. Bailey, an architect of London', who designed COCK'S SAUCE ESTABLISHMENT, DUKE STREET, READING, *c.*1820, and who at the same time was 'engaged with extensive alterations at Caversham Park Mansion' for Col. Marsac [*Reminiscences of Reading, by an Octogenarian*, 1888, 95], and may have been the J. Bailey who signs a perspective drawing of William Wilkins's design for Downing College, Cambridge, that is preserved at Downing (C. Sicca, *Committed to Classicism. The Building of Downing College Cambridge*, 1987, fig. 35). Bailey was President of the Surveyors' Club in 1812 and 1848, and died on 24 Sept. 1850, aged 79 [*Gent's Mag.* 1850 (ii), 558]. The practice was continued by R. Willshire in partnership with R. Parris. Charles Barry was a pupil of Middleton and Bailey from 1810 to 1816.

BAINE, JOHN, was the author of a scheme for the development of the area to the north of the New Town at Edinburgh, which he submitted to the city authorities in 1801. It was rejected in favour of a layout designed by Robert Reid and William Sibbald, but the 'explanatory memoir' is preserved in Edinburgh University Library (MS. Laing II, 415). It shows that Bain was familiar with town-planning in England and abroad, but throws no light on his origins or occupation. He must, however, be the 'Bain' mentioned in Alexander Campbell's *Journey from Edinburgh through parts of North Britain* ii, 1802, 278, as one of the architects Scotland could boast of.

BAIRD, JAMES, was a master mason of Govan, nr. Glasgow. In 1724 he rebuilt KILBARCHAN CHURCH, RENFREWSHIRE [R. D. Mackenzie, *Kilbarchan*, Paisley 1902, 152–3], and in 1736–8 THE LOW CHURCH at PAISLEY [R. Brown, *History of Paisley* i, 1886, 404].

BAIRD, JOHN (1798–1859), was born at Dalmuir in Dunbartonshire. He was apprenticed to an architect or builder of Glasgow called Shepherd, to whom he was related. When Shepherd died in 1818 Baird, barely 20 and not yet out of his apprenticeship, took over the office and by hard work built up a practice second only to that of David Hamilton. Refusing to take part in public competitions, he acquired a reputation for shrewdness and probity which in later life earned him many commissions as a valuer of property and as an arbitrator in building disputes.

Baird's architecture is marked by a classical reserve from which he rarely deviated. His buildings are always logical and business-like. His style matured early, and, once established, it never changed. Although he lived well into the reign of Victoria he made few concessions to changing fashions. Romanesque, Gothic and Italian were little to his taste, but he did produce several churches in the perfunctory Gothic of the time, and his design for the new University buildings at Woodlands, commissioned in 1846, but never carried out, was 'chiefly in the style of Heriot's Hospital'. Even in his later Gothic work he clung tenaciously to the style of the 1820s, his mansion at Urie (1855) being in the late Tudor idiom evolved by Wilkins and Burn forty years earlier. On the other hand the possibilities of iron made a strong appeal to his essentially practical mind. As early as 1827 he designed an iron hammer-beam roof for the Argyle Arcade, and in 1855–6 built in Jamaica Street one of the outstanding iron warehouses of the nineteenth century.

Baird died in December 1859. He had a younger brother Anthony who practised independently until 1834/5, when he took up accountancy. For some years before his death

Baird was assisted by James Thomson (1835–1905), who ultimately became his partner and continued his practice under the name of 'Baird and Thomson'. Alexander ('Greek') Thomson (1817–1875) was in Baird's office from 1836 to 1849, when he left to form a partnership with another John Baird (1816–93), who was Thomson's brother-in-law, but apparently no relation of his namesake. Baird's portrait by Daniel Macnee (1857) hangs in Glasgow Art Gallery. Gildard describes him as 'a large and well-built man' who 'had a presence as of one that ought to be in authority'.

[James Maclehose, *One Hundred Eminent Glasgow Men*, Glasgow 1886, i, 21–4; Thomas Gildard, 'An Old Glasgow Architect on some Older Ones', *Trans. Royal Philosophical Soc. of Glasgow* xxvi, 1895; A. Gomme & D. Walker, *The Architecture of Glasgow*, 1987, 285; information from Mr. David Walker.]

GLASGOW: COMMERCIAL AND DOMESTIC ARCHITECTURE

THE ARGYLE ARCADE, 98–102 ARGYLE STREET, 1827–8; new entrance 1962 [*A.P.S.D.*, *s.v.* 'Glasgow'].

THE WELLINGTON ARCADE, SAUCHIEHALL STREET, *c.*1830; new entrance 1861; dem. [*A.P.S.D.*]

SOMERSET PLACE, SAUCHIEHALL STREET, 1840; end block rebuilt 1962 [A. Gomme & D. Walker, *The Architecture of Glasgow*, 1987, 285].

CLAREMONT (now BERESFORD) HOUSE and TERRACE, WOODLANDS, 1842–7 [Maclehose, 21–2].

WOODLANDS TERRACE, WOODLANDS, 1849–50 [Gomme & Walker, 285].

WEST NILE STREET, premises of Messrs. Wilson, Kay & Co., 1851; dem. [Senex, *Glasgow Past and Present* i, 1884, 232].

MACDONALD'S MUSLIN WAREHOUSE, INGRAM, HANOVER and QUEEN STREETS, for Messrs. J. & D. MacDonald, 1854; dem. [*A.P.S.D.*]

PRINCE OF WALES'S BUILDINGS, 34–8 BUCHANAN STREET, 1854 [*A.P.S.D.*]

TOBACCO WAREHOUSE, JAMES WATT STREET, 1854; enlarged 1911 [Gomme & Walker, 1987, 315].

SIR JAMES CAMPBELL'S WAREHOUSE, 115–37 INGRAM STREET and 111–28 BRUNSWICK STREET, 1854; planned by Baird, but on Sir James Campbell desiring baronial elevations, they were, at Baird's suggestion, designed by R. W. Billings [Maclehose, 23].

GARDNER'S WAREHOUSE, 36 JAMAICA STREET, 1855–6 [*A.P.S.D.*]

SMITH & SONS' WAREHOUSE, 208–16 ARGYLE STREET, 1856; dem. [*A.P.S.D.*]

CHURCHES

GLASGOW, GREYFRIARS UNITED PRESBYTERIAN CHURCH, ALBION STREET, 1821; dem. *c.*1967 [Maclehose, 22; J. Pagan, *Sketch of the History of Glasgow*, 1847, 186].

GLASGOW, U.P. CHURCH, WELLINGTON STREET, BLYTHSWOOD, 1825; dem. 1909 [*A.P.S.D.*]

BONHILL, DUNBARTONSHIRE, 1835–6 [contract drawings in S.R.O., RHP 8164–8171].

GLASGOW, CAMBRIDGE STREET CHURCH, 1834; altered 1846 and 1868; dem. *c.*1975 [Gomme & Walker, 1987, 285].

GLASGOW, ANDERSTON U.P. (later 'OLD PARISH') CHURCH, HEDDLE PLACE, 1839–40; dem. 1967 [Gomme & Walker, 1987, 285].

GREENOCK, GEORGE SQUARE CONGREGATIONAL CHURCH, 1839–40, Gothic [W. M. Brownlie, *History of the George Square Congregational Church*, 1956, 33].

DUNFERMLINE, FIFE, CONGREGATIONAL CHURCH, CANMORE STREET, 1841–2, Gothic [specification in Dunfermline Public Library, *ex inf.* Mr. J. Gifford].

GLASGOW, ERSKINE U.P. (later BRISBY MEMORIAL) CHURCH, 45 SOUTH PORTLAND STREET, 1842, Gothic; dem. [Senex, *Glasgow Past and Present* i, 1884, 148].

KIRKCALDY, FIFE, ST. PETER'S EPISCOPAL CHURCH, TOWNSEND PLACE, 1844, Gothic; dem. 1975 [*The Scottish Episcopal Church Year Book*, 1973–4, 280].

GLASGOW, SHAMROCK STREET U.P. CHURCH, *c.*1850; Gothic; dem. [Senex, *Glasgow Past and Present* i, 1884, 148].

COUNTRY HOUSES

CLOBER HOUSE, NEW KILPATRICK, DUNBARTONSHIRE, enlarged for Alexander Dunlop in Tudor style, 1833 [*N.S.A.* viii, 49].

CAIRNHILL HOUSE, AIRDRIE, LANARKS., for G. M. Nisbett, 1841, Jacobethan [H. M. Nisbett & S. C. Agnew, *Cairnhill*, Edinburgh 1949, 201].

CARBETH GUTHRIE, STIRLINGSHIRE, additions for William Smith, 1835 [*The Old Country Houses of the Glasgow Gentry*, 1870, pl. xviii].

STONEBYRES HOUSE, LESMAHAGOW, LANARKS., extensive additions for James Monteath, 1844; altered *c.*1900; dem. 1934 [J. B. Greenshields, *Annals of the Parish of Lesmahagow*, 1864, 83].

VIEWPARK HOUSE, UDDINGSTON, LANARKS., probably for William Robertson, *c.*1840 [Maclehose, 23].

BIRKWOOD HOUSE, LESMAHAGOW, LANARKS., for J. G. McKirdy, *c.*1840, castellated [Maclehose, 23] (J. G. Greenshields,

Annals of the Parish of Lesmahagow, 1864, plate at p. 101).

URIE HOUSE, FETTERESSO, KINCARDINESHIRE, reb. 1855 for Alexander Baird in Tudor style; enlarged 1883–4; gutted [Maclehose, 23].

MONUMENT

GLASGOW NECROPOLIS, monument to James Ewing (d. 1853) [G. Baird, *Sketches of Glasgow Necropolis*, 1857, 182].

BAKER, —, of St. Michael's Mount, described as 'the Superintendent of Sir J. St. Aubyn's late improvements at his castle there', surveyed Crowan Church, Cornwall, in 1831 [I.C.B.S.]. He was doubtless the 'John Baker Esq.' listed as a resident at St. Michael's Mount in Pigot's *Directory* of 1830.

BAKER, CHARLES (1791–1861), of Painswick, Glos., described in Pigot's *Directory* as 'architect, civil engineer and land-surveyor', and on his trade-card [Gloucester Public Library, R.229, 56] as 'Land and Timber Surveyor, Land Agent and Civil Engineer', had a local practice in all these capacities. From about 1834 to 1844 he had an office in Cheltenham and was in partnership with E. H. Shellard (d. 1885), later of Manchester. A plan in the Cheltenham Art Gallery indicates that Baker and Shellard were responsible for the layout of the Bayshill estate at Cheltenham in *c.*1838 and perhaps for some of the street elevations (e.g. the Royal Well and Bayshill Terraces in St. George's Road) [information from Mr. A. S. Brooks and Mr. J. V. Garrett].

Baker became the owner of the mansion in Painswick called Castle Hale (whose front he rebuilt *c.*1837) by marrying the daughter of its previous owner, but by the 1840s he was in financial difficulties and was obliged to let the house and live elsewhere. His account- and letter-books for the years 1836–9 and 1829–49, respectively, are in the Gloucestershire Record Office (D 3917/1–2).

Baker's recorded architectural works include minor Gothic churches at SLAD, 1831–4 [I.C.B.S.] and CAINSCROSS, 1835–7 [*Gent's Mag.* 1837 (i), 311], both illustrated in A. Smith, *Ecclesiastical Edifices in the Borough of Stroud*, 1838; the classical BEDFORD STREET CONGREGATIONAL CHURCH, STROUD, 1835–7, with staircase in the form of a tempietto [R. Nott, *The Bedford Street Congregational Church 1837–1937*, 1937, 18–19]; THE STROUD UNION WORKHOUSE, 1837 [*Gloucester Jnl.*, 28 Jan. 1837] and WHITESHILL VICARAGE, GLOS., 1841, Gothic [Gloucester Diocesan Records F 4/1]. The CHURCH OF ST. PHILIP & ST. JAMES in LECKHAMPTON, GLOS., was built to the designs of Baker and Shellard in 1838–40 and rebuilt in 1879–82 [*Gloucester Jnl.*, 28 April 1838]. The attribution to Baker of THE OAKLANDS (now Whitfield School), CHARLTON KINGS, nr. CHELTENHAM, 1837, rests on inadequate evidence as set out in *Charlton Kings Local History Bulletin* No. 7, 1982.

BAKER, JOHN, was surveyor to the Haberdashers' Company during the last decade of the eighteenth century and a small volume of plans and elevations of London properties made by him in that capacity is in the R.I.B.A. Drawings Collection (*Catalogue: B*, 12–13 and G. Worsley, *Architectural Drawings of the Regency Period*, 1991, 142–3). He was presumably the man of the same name who was surveyor to the Mercers' Company from 1778 to 1784, when he was dismissed for 'repeated instances of inattention and irregularity'.

BAKER, RICHARD (1743–1803), son of William Baker of Highfields, Cheshire (*q.v.*), was educated at Repton School. His father's will indicates that at the time of his death in 1771 Richard was helping him in his 'architectural affairs'. Richard lived for a number of years at Leominster, where, however, he used his wife's surname of Hassall 'for the sake of peace and quietness'. He subsequently moved to Stratford-on-Avon, where he died in 1803 [P.C.C. 757 MARRIOTT]. As owner of Highfields he was succeeded by his son William Baker (d. 1863).

The Shropshire Quarter Sessions Records show that Richard Baker was frequently employed to survey churches for the purpose of obtaining Briefs, but the only church that is known to have been rebuilt to his designs is ADDERLEY, SALOP., 1801 [MS. churchwardens' accounts and vestry minutes]. It is a cruciform Gothic building with traceried windows of cast iron.

BAKER, WILLIAM (1705–1771), of Highfields, nr. Audlem in Cheshire, was an architect and surveyor much employed in Shropshire, Staffordshire and the adjoining counties in the middle of the eighteenth century. He was the son of Richard Baker of London and Leominster, and was born in London in 1705. It is likely that he is to be identified with a William Baker who was employed by Francis Smith of Warwick (*q.v.*) in the early 1730s. In 1737 he married Jane Dod, daughter and heiress of George Dod of Highfields, a direct descendant of William Dod, who built the house in 1567. For some years after their marriage William Baker and his wife appear to have lived at Bridgnorth, where all their four children were baptized, but by 1748 he was established at Highfields, where he combined the profession of an architect with that of a gentleman farmer. The survival of his account-book and diary for the years 1748–59 sheds considerable light on the practice of a minor Georgian provincial architect, and shows that in the course of the twelve years which it covers he designed or altered a number of country houses, surveyed churches in need of repair or rebuilding, and also designed several funerary monuments. His most important work was probably the Butter Cross or Market at Ludlow, a robust but unpolished classical building whose façade forms an effective termination to the main street. Like other works of Baker's (e.g. Patshull House), it is strongly influenced by Gibbs (cf. the latter's *Book of Architecture*, pl. 62). A plan and elevation of the Butter Market are shown in Baker's hand in his portrait, reproduced in *C. Life*, 31 Jan. 1991, 48. Designs by Baker for a Town Hall at Bishops Castle, Salop., made in 1745, are among the Powis papers in the Shropshire Record Office [552/14/box 465]. They differ from the building as erected *c.*1745/50, but it may nevertheless have been designed by Baker. Baker is also known to have made unexecuted designs for the Shropshire Infirmary, 1745 [minute book of the Infirmary in Shropshire C.R.O., 9 Aug. 1746], for Hosyer's Almshouses at Ludlow, 1756 [*V.C.H. Salop.* ii, 109], and for the improvement of the English Bridge at Shrewsbury in 1765 [minute book of the Bridge Trustees in Shropshire C.R.O., 20 Nov. 1765].

William Baker died on 29 November 1771, aged 66, and was buried at Audlem, where there is a tablet to his memory in the south aisle of the church. His elder son Richard (*q.v.*) followed his father's profession [Arthur Oswald, 'William Baker of Audlem, Architect', in *Collections for a History of Staffordshire* (Staffordshire Record Soc.), vol. for 1950–1 (1954); J. M. Robinson, 'Highfields, Audlem, Cheshire', *C. Life*, 31 Jan. 1991; R. Morrice, 'The Payment Book of William Baker of Audlem', in *English Architecture Public and Private: Essays for Kerry Downes*, ed. Bold & Chaney, 1993].

PUBLIC BUILDINGS

LUDLOW, SALOP., THE BUTTER CROSS, 1743–4 [signed plan and elevation formerly in Ludlow Museum].

MONTGOMERY, THE MARKET HALL, 1748; upper part rebuilt 1828 [J. D. K. Lloyd, 'Montgomery Town Hall and its Architect', *Montgomeryshire Collections* iv, 1958].

HEREFORD, COLLEGE OF THE VICARS CHORAL, repairs and alterations, 1750 [Baker's account-book, 1750].

HOUSES

Baker's account-book shows that he was constantly employed in surveying and altering houses, though it is not always clear exactly what was done. Unless otherwise stated, it is the source for the following list.

LUDLOW, SALOP., 52 BROAD STREET, for Richard Salwey, 1743; dem. 1879 [Morrice, *op. cit.*, 245, citing drawing in Shropshire C.R.O., 2505–7].

PENN HALL, nr. WOLVERHAMPTON, STAFFS., drawings and surveying for Thomas Bradney, 1748–54.

'BEVERLEY', i.e. BEVERÉ, CLAINES, WORCESTER, drawing and surveying for Richard Brodribb, 1748–9.

MORVILLE HALL, SALOP., work for Arthur Weaver, 1748. Baker was probably responsible for the addition of the two office wings and for alterations to the house itself (*C. Life*, 15–22 Aug. 1952). The house was again altered *c.*1770, when features attributable to Baker were removed. A painting showing these features is illustrated by J. Harris, *The Artist and the Country House*, 1979, fig. 212.

LIVERPOOL, houses in HANOVER STREET for Messrs. Pardoe, Fletcher and Cunliffe, 1748; dem.

MAWLEY HALL, SALOP., unspecified work, probably to the stables, for Sir Edward Blount, Bart., 1748.

RANTON ABBEY, STAFFS., surveying for Sir Jonathan Cope, Bart., 1748–9 and 1752–3; gutted *c.*1940.

POWIS CASTLE, MONTGOMERYSHIRE, unspecified work (probably general repairs) for 1st Earl of Powis, 1748–54.

OAKLY PARK, SALOP., alterations for 1st Earl of Powis, 1748–58; remodelled by C. R. Cockerell, 1819–36 [cf. estimate and drawings in N.L.W., Powis, 21129–45].

ENVILLE, STAFFS., unspecified plans for 4th Earl of Stamford, perhaps for the Home Farm, 1748–50.

ALDENHAM HOUSE, MORVILLE, SALOP., stables for Sir Richard Acton, Bart., 1750–1 (*C. Life*, 30 June 1977).

TIXALL HALL, STAFFS., probably rebuilt quadrangle for 5th Lord Aston, 1750–1; dem. *c.*1925.

DARLASTON HALL, STAFFS., plans of or for a house for John Jervis, 1751; dem. 1953.

ACTON BURNELL HALL, SALOP., enlarged for Sir

Edward Smythe, Bart., 1753–8.

WOOD EATON, STAFFS., THE HALL FARMHOUSE for the Revd. William Astley, headmaster of Repton School, 1753–6.

WINGERWORTH HALL, DERBYSHIRE, work for Sir Henry Hunloke, Bart., 1753–4; dem. *c.*1930.

WOODHOUSE FARM, PEPLOW, nr. HODNET, SALOP., for Charles Pigot, 1754–6.

SWYNNERTON HALL, STAFFS., an outbuilding for Thomas Fitzherbert, 1754–6.

PATSHULL HOUSE, STAFFS., completion of house for Sir John Astley, Bart., 1754–8. Baker succeeded James Gibbs (d. 1754) as Astley's architect, and references in his diary to the parlour, library, stables and chapel show that he designed the flanking pavilions and forecourt which contain these buildings. The entrance gateway is also his work [*V.C.H. Staffs.* xx, 165–7].

HANKELOW HALL, CHESHIRE, alterations, including drawing-room, for Mr. Wettenhall, 1755–7.

EGGINTON HALL, DERBYSHIRE, plans for the Revd. Sir John Every, Bart., 1756, probably those carried out by B. Wyatt and sons 1758–61; dem. 1955.

TERRICK HALL, WHITCHURCH, SALOP., plan for Mr. Watson, 1756.

WHITMORE HALL, STAFFS., surveying for Edward Mainwaring, 1765; for possible alterations to this house by Baker see G. Nares in *C. Life*, 6 June 1957.

BRAND HALL, NORTON-IN-HALES, SALOP., minor alterations to interior for Robert Davison, 1756.

HANMER HALL, FLINTSHIRE, additional building for Humphrey Hanmer, 1756.

ASTBURY RECTORY, CHESHIRE, repairs and alterations for the Revd. Joseph Crewe, 1757–9.

KEELE HALL, STAFFS., alterations to S. front for Ralph Sneyd, 1757–9; rebuilt by A. Salvin, 1854–60.

DORFOLD HALL, CHESHIRE, repairs and alterations for James Tomkinson, 1757–9 (*C. Life*, 31 Oct. 1908).

WOODHOUSE or WODEHOUSE, nr. WOMBOURNE, STAFFS., plans for Samuel Hellier, 1758–9, probably for the stable-block as built.

SIDWAY HALL, nr. MAER, STAFFS., altered or rebuilt for – Eld, 1758–9; since much altered.

TEDDESLEY HALL, nr. PENKRIDGE, STAFFS., unidentified work, probably to wings or outbuildings, for Sir Edward Littleton, Bart., *c.*1759; dem. 1954.

CHURCHES

Baker was employed as surveyor in connection with the repair or rebuilding of several churches. He supervised the building of the Gothic STONE CHURCH, STAFFS., 1754–8, and the classical ST. JOHN'S CHURCH, WOLVERHAMPTON, STAFFS., 1756–9. The former was designed by William Robinson (*q.v.*), the latter apparently by T. F. Pritchard (*q.v.*). In 1754–6 he was employed as 'Inspector of the work' by the churchwardens of SEIGHFORD, STAFFS., the tower and part of the nave of whose church were rebuilt in the Gothic style [churchwardens' accounts in Wm. Salt Library, Stafford and his own diary, which records the laying of the foundation stone]. In Jan. 1757 he surveyed ELLENHALL CHURCH, STAFFS., and made a plan and estimate (£1053) for its repair to support the parishioners' application for a Brief. In March 1757, after the upper part of the tower of ACTON CHURCH, nr. NANTWICH, CHESHIRE, had been blown down into the nave, Baker agreed 'to Inspect the repair of the church' for £42. In 1758 he surveyed the leaning tower of WYBUNBURY CHURCH, CHESHIRE, and reported that the 'chancel should be new rooft'. In January 1759 he received 6 guineas from the 3rd Earl of Breadalbane (whose wife came from a Staffordshire family) 'for plans of a Kirk', probably that of KENMORE, PERTHSHIRE, which was built by the Earl in 1760 and is in the Gothic style. In addition to these church commissions recorded in his account-book, Baker is said to have been the 'undertaker' employed in 1765 to case in brick the tower of UPPER PENN CHURCH, nr. WOLVERHAMPRTON, STAFFS., with some Gothic detailing.

MONUMENTS

ACTON SCOTT CHURCH, nr. CHURCH STRETTON, SALOP., monument to Edward Acton (d. 1747), executed by 'Mr. Hiorn' in 1751.

LEIGHTON CHURCH, SALOP., monument to Elizabeth Leighton (d. 1754).

NORTON-IN-HALES CHURCH, SALOP., monument to Samuel and Barbara Davison, erected 1757.

BALDWIN, ROBERT (–*c.*1804), was the son of a builder or surveyor. After serving an apprenticeship with Matthew Brettingham (d. 1769) he hoped to complete his architectural education by a visit to Italy, but was 'hindered by my father' [*curriculum vitae* in *The several petitions . . . for and against a bill to remove Chelmsford Gaol*, 1771, Essex C.R.O., D/DBe 01, p. 49]. In February 1763 he was engaged by Robert Mylne at £50 p.a., and remained in his office as the clerk responsible for Blackfriars Bridge until 1766 [Robert Mylne's diaries, 28 Feb. 1763 and 13 Sept. 1766]. From 1762 onwards he exhibited numerous designs at the Society of Artists and the Free Society of Artists, and in 1764 and 1765 he was awarded premiums for architectural drawings by the Society of Arts. In 1768 he became an assistant of George Dance, the City Surveyor, but subsequently caused trouble by claiming to be Dance's partner [Dorothy Stroud, *George Dance*, 1971, 89–90].

Baldwin appears never to have established himself in independent practice and in later life was in receipt of charity from Sir John Soane. No building is known to have been erected from his designs, but several unexecuted schemes are recorded. They include an engraved design for a Record Office in Edinburgh made in collaboration with the Earl of Morton, then Lord Clerk Register, and published in 1767 (S.R.O., RHP 6082 and Bodleian, Gough Maps 38, f. 62[b]), a set of drawings for a new house at Wardour in Wiltshire (1768) among the Arundell family papers in the Wiltshire C.R.O., and an engraved design for a gaol in the county of Essex, n.d. probably 1770 (B.L., *King's Maps*, xiii, 11f). An elegantly drawn *trompe l'oeil* section of the church of St. Stephen, Walbrook, presented by him to Sir John Soane, is in the Soane Museum (AL, Folio 1, 7). In 1769 Baldwin published *The Chimney-Piece Maker's Daily Assistant*, vol. ii, in continuation of vol. i of the same title published by John Crunden and others in 1766, and in 1787 *Plans, Elevations and Sections of the Machines and Centering used in erecting Black-Friars Bridge*, consisting of 7 double-page plates and a large folding plan [Eileen Harris, *British Architectural Books and Writers*, 1990, 116].

BALDWIN, THOMAS (1568–1641), Comptroller of the King's Works from 1606 until his death in 1641, came from a family of Hertfordshire gentry with property at Watford (where he was born) and Berkhamsted (where he was buried). Nothing is known of his career before his appointment as Comptroller in 1606, and in office he appears to have been more of an administrator than an architect. Nevertheless there is some evidence that on occasion he designed and supervised buildings for private clients. In 1623 he provided the Fishmongers' Company with a 'devise' for the JESUS HOSPITAL at BRAY, BERKSHIRE. This is a quadrangular brick building in the vernacular style, 'devoid of Jonesian influence' [*History of the King's Works* iii, 131]. In 1632–3 Baldwin appears to have been consulted by Oxford University about the building of the SELDEN END of the BODLEIAN LIBRARY. The Vice-Chancellor's accounts record a payment of £9 'to the king's controllour for his coach-hire and in other expences in coming hither to give directions about the staircase', but another document refers (probably by mistake) to 'Mr. Controller of His Majesty's Household', and it may be noted that there was a separate payment of £12 to an unnamed 'surveyor' 'for drawing of modells and three severall journeys about the same business' [*Wood's Life and Times*, ed. A. Clark, Oxford Historical Soc. iv, 1895, 53]. Another building for which the nature of Baldwin's responsibility is ill-defined was a large addition to the west side of HOLLAND HOUSE, KENSINGTON, built in 1638–40 by Henry Rich, Earl of Holland. The accounts [Leeds Archives, TN/EA/13/74, ff. 34–5] show that over £5000 were 'Received by the forsaid workmen of Mr. Baldwin'. This addition was demolished in 1704 and no representation of it appears to be known.

Baldwin is commemorated by a monument in Berkhamsted Church carved by Nicholas Stone [*Walpole Soc.* vii, 136 and viii ('A Lost Monument by Nicholas Stone')]. As Comptroller he was succeeded by his nephew Francis Wetherid.

BALDWIN, THOMAS (*c.*1750–1820), began his career as a speculative builder in Bath. From 1776 onwards he held the post of City Architect and Surveyor. This appointment followed the death in November 1775 of Thomas Warr Atwood (*q.v.*), who for some years had been in effective control of the city's building activities. In 1779 Baldwin was in addition appointed Deputy Chamberlain. In 1787 he was appointed Inspector of the Baths, and in 1789 his plans for their development were authorized by the 'Bath Improvement Act'. He was also responsible for planning Bathwick New Town for the Pulteney family, and undertook much of the building himself. In 1791, following irregularities in his accounts, he was dismissed from his post as Deputy Chamberlain and in 1793 from that of City Architect and Surveyor. Bankruptcy ensued, from which he was eventually discharged in 1802. Although finished as a town-planner and speculative builder, he continued to practise as an architect until his death on 7 March 1820, aged 70.

Baldwin was one of the principal creators of Georgian Bath, and designed several of its most celebrated buildings. His public buildings were in a basically Palladian style with elegant neo-classical ornament derived from the Adam brothers, but his Cross Bath was remarkable for combining walls of baroque curvature with the most refined neo-classical detailing. The façades of his speculative street developments were cleverly designed to provide architectural incident by economical means. [Bath City Council Minutes, 1776–1792; W. Ison, *The Georgian Buildings of Bath*, 1948, 37–40, 2nd ed. 1980, 13–15; Jane Root, 'Thomas Baldwin: His Public Career in Bath', *Bath History* v, 1994].

The following were Baldwin's principal works in BATH:

THE GUILDHALL, 1775–9.
NORTHUMBERLAND BUILDINGS, *c.*1778–80.
SOMERSETSHIRE BUILDINGS, MILSOM STREET, 1781–3.
THE CROSS BATH and PUMP ROOM, 1783–4; enlarged by J. Palmer 1797–8; converted into a swimming-bath by C. E. Davis 1886 [Jean Marco, 'The Cross Bath', *Bath History* ii, 1988, 68–74].
COLONNADE in front of OLD PUMP ROOM, 1786.
PAVILION over KING'S BATH SPRING, *c.*1788; dem. early 19th century.
THE NEW PRIVATE BATHS, 1788–9.
ARGYLE BUILDINGS (now STREET), *c.*1789.
LAURA PLACE, *c.*1789.
GREAT PULTENEY STREET, *c.*1789.
SYDNEY PLACE, Nos. 1–14 and houses in BATHWICK STREET, 1788–92.
THE ARGYLE CONGREGATIONAL CHAPEL, BATHWICK, 1788–9; enlarged by H. E. Goodridge 1821.
UNION STREET, *c.*1790.
CHEAP STREET, refronted *c.*1790.
STALL STREET, refronted *c.*1790.
BATH STREET, 1791.
THE GREAT PUMP ROOM, 1790–1; completed by J. Palmer 1793–4.
LAURA CHAPEL, BATHWICK, 1795; dem.

Elsewhere, Baldwin designed:

HAFOD HOUSE, CARDIGANSHIRE, for Thomas Johnes, 1786–8 [James E. Smith, *A Tour to Hafod*, 1810, 11]. Hafod was gutted by fire in 1807 and rebuilt by Baldwin, with some alterations. It was subsequently altered and enlarged and finally dem. *c.*1960. An engraving in S. R. Meyrick, *History of Cardiganshire*, 1810, 351, probably shows the house as originally built.
BATHFORD CHURCH, SOMERSET, added S. transept 1803; extended as aisle 1817–18; rebuilt 1870 [A. Craig, *Some History of St. Swithun's Church, Bathford*, p.p. 1980, 4–5].
DEVIZES, WILTS., THE TOWN HALL, 1806–8 [J. Waylen, *Chronicles of the Devizes*, 1839, 316].
RAINSCOMBE HOUSE, nr. OARE, WILTS., remodelled for the Revd. James Rogers, *c.*1816 [account for professional services in Wilts. C.R.O., 754/141; *V.C.H. Wilts.* x, 130 and plate].

BALFOUR, ROBERT (*c.*1770–1867), was the son of a farmer at Kilmany in Fife. He is said to have worked as a mason in Edinburgh for the Adam brothers before establishing himself at St. Andrews, where the Town Council minutes show that in August 1799 he petitioned for a piece of ground near Shore Bridge for a workshop and yard. He lived in BALFOUR HOUSE, THE SHORE, which he built for himself, and was probably responsible for several other houses in St. Andrews which show marked Adam influence. He appears to have retired in the 1830s, but lived on until 1867, when he died, almost completely blind, at the age of 97.

Balfour's principal works were the addition of a S. wing (subsequently remodelled) to BALCARRES, FIFE, for Robert Lindsay, 1804 [Anne Riches, 'Balcarres', *The St. Andrews Area*, Royal Archl. Inst. 1991, 45]; the addition of a new front to STRATHTYRUM HOUSE, nr. ST. ANDREWS, for the Cheape family, *c.*1805 [Paterson of Carpow papers, St. Andrews University Library, MS. 36220]; CARPOW HOUSE, ABERNETHY, PERTHSHIRE, for the Paterson family, *c.*1807, dem. [*ibid.*]; the repair and enlargement of KINGSBARNS CHURCH, FIFE, 1811 [S.R.O., HR 184/1]; alterations to LEUCHARS (1812–14), CRAIL (1815) and SCOONIE (1822) CHURCHES, all in FIFE [S.R.O., HR 154/1, 242/1, 764/1]; and the refronting of PITMILLY, KINGSBARNS, FIFE, for David Monypenny, Lord Pitmilly, 1818; dem. [St. Andrews Univ. Muniments UC 400, an application by Balfour to quarry stone for the house] (A. H. Millar, *Fife: Pictorial and Historical* i, 1895, 362–3).

[R. G. Cant, 'St. Andrews Architects', *St. Andrews Preservation Trust Year Book* for 1966, 16–17; information from Dr. R. G. Cant and Mr. David Walker.]

BALL, JAMES HOWELL (1790–1857), practised in Plymouth during the first half of the nineteenth century. In 1828–9 he refitted the interior of the CHARLES CHURCH there, gutted 1941 [G. Wightwick, *Nettleton's Guide to Plymouth etc.*, 1836, 24]. He also designed the ELDAD CHAPEL, PLYMOUTH, 1829, in a 'mixed Gothic' style [Wightwick, 25], ST. LUKE'S CHURCH, TAVISTOCK PLACE, PLYMOUTH, 1828–9 [R. N. Worth, *History of Plymouth*, 2nd ed. 1890, 245], and SALCOMBE CHURCH, DEVON, 1843, in a coarse 'Early English' style [I.C.B.S.]. He died on 21 August 1857, aged 67 [monumental inscription in Plymouth cemetery].

BAMPFYLDE, COPLESTONE WARRE (1720–1791), of Hestercombe House, nr. Taunton in Somerset, was a talented country gentleman of whom it was said *nihil tetigit* *quod non ornavit*. Best known as a landscape-painter, he was also on occasion an amateur architect. His principal achievement in this capacity was the TOWN HALL at TAUNTON, which was built to his designs in 1770–2. He presumably designed the Doric temple which he erected in his own grounds at Hestercombe in 1786, and among the Arundell family papers in the Wiltshire C.R.O. there is a set of designs for a Palladian mansion at Wardour in Wiltshire 'drawn by Mr. Bampfylde'. [*D.N.B.; Procs. Somerset Archaeological Soc.* xviii, 1872, 163–6, lxxxv, 1939, 97; J. Savage, *History of Taunton*, 1822, 581; Kenneth Woodbridge, *Landscape and Antiquity*, 1970, 60.]

BANCKES, MATTHEW (–1706), was an eminent master carpenter of the age of Wren. Probably a son of Matthew Banckes, Master of the Carpenters' Company in 1637,[1] he was apprenticed to John Scott, carpenter to the Ordnance Office, and married a daughter of John Grove, Master Plasterer in the Office of Works. In 1683 he became Master Carpenter in the Office of Works and in 1698 he was Master of the Carpenters' Company. He died in 1706, having previously resigned his official post in favour of his son-in-law John Churchill [*Cal. Treasury Books* xx, 108, 285, 646; xxi, 64]. John James (*q.v.*) was his apprentice, receiving from him 'ten years' instruction in all the practical parts of building' [Hist. MSS. Comm., *Portland* x, 120–1].

In addition to his official work at the royal palaces, Banckes carried out the carpenter's work at six of the City churches, and was employed as executant surveyor in connection with several buildings designed by Wren, notably TRINITY COLLEGE LIBRARY, CAMBRIDGE, where he supervised the construction of the elaborately trussed floor in 1685–6 [Willis & Clark ii, 540; *Wren Soc.* v, 40, 42–3] and the UPPER SCHOOL at ETON COLLEGE, where he was paid £86 'for Surveying and Advising and Examining and Correcting the Workmen's accounts' in 1689–91 [*Wren Soc.* xix, 108–10]. At Eton he subsequently acted as architect, the Provost and Fellows resolving in 1699 to refit the choir 'according to the modell designed by Mr. Banks their Surveyor' [Willis & Clark i, 447]. The reredos and screen which he designed were removed in 1847. Banckes's reputation is shown by the fact that in 1693 the 3rd Duke of Hamilton consulted him about the designs for HAMILTON PALACE. 'I am now consulting with one Banks that carries on the buildings at Hampton Court, who is the best at contriving of any in England', he told the Duchess, and in 1694 Banckes was paid £11 'for drawing some draughts of the Palace of Hamilton at several times' [Rosalind K. Marshall, *The Days of Duchess Anne*, 1973, 193–4].

In 1692–3 Banckes contracted with Laurence, Earl of Rochester, to rebuild the latter's house at PETERSHAM, SURREY, in two stages, according to an unsigned drawing still attached to the contract. Many of the architectural details were to correspond with those at Ranelagh House, Chelsea, and the Earl of Ranelagh (*q.v.*) was to act as arbitrator in the event of any dispute [Surrey C.R.O., SC 13/26/102–3]. The house, which is illustrated by J. Kip, *Britannia Illustrata* i, 1714, pl. 33, was destroyed by fire in 1721. In 1700 Banckes performed the carpentry of WINSLOW HALL, BUCKS., a house probably designed by Wren [*Wren Soc.* xvii, 67–70]. His estimate for making a promenade 130 feet long for the 2nd Duke of Beaufort at BEAUFORT HOUSE, CHELSEA (dem. 1739), is in the British Library [Sloane MS. 4066, f. 260].

Banckes had two sons who were successful master craftsmen. Henry (*c.*1679–1716), a mason by trade, was in partnership with Edward Strong, junior, and with him had contracts at Blenheim Palace, Marlborough House, London, and Cannons House, Middlesex. Matthew (*c.*1682–1714), a carpenter like his father, worked at Blenheim from 1706 onwards, and was responsible, with his partner John Barton, for 'roofing all the grand Pile' and for making the centering for the great bridge. Banckes's daughters Anne, Mary and Patience married, respectively, Charles Hopson, Master Joiner to the Office of Works, John Churchill, Master Carpenter, and Henry Wise, Master Gardener [will in P.R.O., PROB 11/489/164].

BARCLAY, THOMAS, was a master mason of Balbirnie, nr. Markinch in Fife, where in 1785–6 he reconstructed the manse [S.R.O., HR 59/6]. He was probably responsible for the rebuilding of MARKINCH CHURCH in 1786, but this cannot be proved as the Heritors' minutes do not begin until 1788. In 1793 he submitted a design for Monimail Church, Fife, at the request of Lord Balgonie, but a proposal by Thomas Faulkner, a Cupar mason, was preferred [S.R.O., HR 432/1]. His most important work was probably the de-

[1] In 1633 the elder Banckes was, with Edmund Kinsman (*q.v.*), concerned in the rebuilding of the City Church of ST. ALBAN, WOOD STREET, subsequently destroyed in the Great Fire. In Jan. 1633/4 he was paid £3 'for his drawing of plotts measuringe ye church & comming several tymes' (Churchwardens' Accounts in Guildhall Library, MS. 7673/1).

lightful classical TOWN HOUSE at FALKLAND, FIFE, built by him to his own designs in 1801–2 [S.R.O., B 25/5/2, Minutes of Falkland Town Council 28 Nov. 1800 and 9 Feb. 1801]. He appears also to have designed the MANSE at FALKLAND in 1806–7 [S.R.O., HR 416/1, p. 89, and 416/7].

When the Markinch Heritors wanted to enlarge their church in 1806 they wrote to James Barclay of Edinburgh, who designed and built the north aisle. He was evidently related to Thomas Barclay, for the contract was accepted by the Heritors on condition that it was countersigned by Thomas and George Barclay. In 1807 James designed a new spire which was built by Thomas [S.R.O., HR 59/1]. James Barclay was also employed at BALBIRNIE HOUSE, where in 1815–21 he enlarged the house to the designs of Richard Crichton and himself designed some cottages [Alistair Rowan in *C. Life*, 6 July 1972]. [Information from Mr. David Walker.]

BARDWELL, WILLIAM (1795–1890), born at Southwold in Suffolk, was a pupil of George Wyatt and of George Maddox. In a letter in the Cambridge University Archives (F.M.1) he stated that he 'afterwards studied nearly two years at Paris' and was concerned in the 'building of the chapelle expiatoire' in the crypt of the church of St. Denis, presumably as a pupil of François Debret, who was in charge of the restoration of St. Denis from 1813 to 1846. He began to exhibit at the Royal Academy in 1829, and also exhibited at the Society of British Artists in 1834 and 1837. In 1835 he competed unsuccessfully for the Houses of Parliament and for the Fitzwilliam Museum at Cambridge. His design for the former building was intended to embody all the successive styles of English medieval architecture: the Royal Entrance was under a 'Norman tower', the House of Lords was in the style of Becket's Crown in Canterbury Cathedral, the House of Commons was an elongated octagon 'in the florid style', and other features were Tudor Gothic. In 1832 he had been responsible for an elborate town-planning scheme for West-minster, inspired by a Select Committee appointed 'to inquire into the most economical and eligible mode of improving the approaches to the Houses of Parliament, . . . and also of improving the immediate neighbourhood of Buckingham Palace'. This proved abortive, but Bardwell's plan anticipated the construction of Victoria Street, planned in 1844 and opened in 1851 [B. Kitchin, 'An 1832 Town-Planning Scheme for Westminster', *Arch. Rev.* xxxii, 1912, 251–2; P.R.O., MPD 87].

In 1868 Bardwell listed his principal executed works as GLENSTAL CASTLE, CO. LIMERICK, IRELAND, a large and ambitious essay in the Norman style designed for Matthew Barrington and built in 1838–9 (*C. Life*, 3 Oct. 1974); the PRIOR'S CHAPEL in LIMERICK CATHEDRAL, presumably about the same date; 'Picture Galleries, Pall Mall', presumably alterations to the British Institution's Galleries at 52 Pall Mall, demolished in 1868; model cottages for the Labourer's Friend Society at SHOOTERS HILL, KENT (illustrated by J. C. Loudon, *Encyclopaedia of Cottage, Farm and Villa Architecture*, 1846, 237–8); 'Healthy Homes' in the district of St. James's Westminster (contract advertised in *Builder* xiv, 1856, 321); 'dwellings at ENFIELD for the Board of Ordnance'; and 'various country houses'. His designs for an Italianate parsonage and a Grecian villa are illustrated by Loudon, *op. cit.*, 853, 877.

Bardwell was the author of *Temples, Ancient and Modern, or Notes on Church Architecture*, 1837, in which he argued that as Gothic was essentially a mason's architecture, modern churches built in brick ought to be classical in style; *Westminster Improvements: a brief account of ancient and modern Westminster . . . by one of the architects of the Westminster Improvement Company*, 1839; *A Brief Historical Narrative of the Royal Church and Parish of St. Margaret, Westminster*, n.d.; *Healthy Homes and How to Make Them*, 1858; and *What a House should be* [1875]. He died on 8 July 1890, aged 94, and was buried in the churchyard at Southwold, where there is a monument to his family. [*The Architect's, Engineer's and Building Trades' Directory*, 1868, 99.]

BARKER, JOHN (1668–1727), of Rowsley in Derbyshire, a carpenter and joiner by trade, was active as an architect and builder in the north Midlands during the early years of the eighteenth century. He was the son of Henry Barker (d. 1705), a joiner of Darley, nr. Bakewell in Derbyshire, to whom he was apprenticed in 1681 [Sheffield Archives, Barker papers, D. 654]. The 'Mr. Barker, joyner' who was employed in the remodelling of THORESBY HOUSE, NOTTS., in 1684–5 was no doubt his father [B.L., Egerton MS. 3539, ff. 153–63]. He was presumably the John Barker who in 1698 made a survey plan of Henderskelfe in Yorkshire, the future site of Castle Howard [K. Downes, *Vanbrugh*, 1977, 20], and in 1700/1 one of Chatsworth House, Derbyshire [Francis Thompson, *A History of Chatsworth*, 1949, 160 and pl. 28]. The proximity of Rowsley to Haddon Hall must have brought Barker into contact with the Manners family, and in 1704–5 he and two masons contracted to build the STABLES at BELVOIR CASTLE, LEICS., for the 1st Duke of Rutland [Belvoir Castle muniments, Misc. MS. 67]. The simple and rather old-fashioned design was probably due to Barker, for among the drawings for HOPTON HALL, DERBYSHIRE, in the Derbyshire Record Office (D 258/36/12) there is a design for a similar block of offices and stables 'drawn for Sr. Phillipp Gell [d. 1719] by John Barker'. In 1709–12 Barker contracted to build ST. ANN'S CHURCH, MANCHESTER. He is referred to as 'the undertaker' of the church in a letter dated 16 May 1710, and on 27 February 1709/10 he wrote from Rowsley directing a correspondent to address a letter 'to my Lodging near the New Church in Manchester or to be left with any of my men the Carpenters there' [Cheshire Record Office, Cholmondeley papers, L 31]. The designer of this large classical church is not known, but Barker must be regarded as a possible candidate, for after the collapse of WHITCHURCH CHURCH, SALOP., in 1711 an estimate was made for rebuilding it 'according to a designe drawn by John Barker to be after the doricke Order the church to be 88 ft. long & 62 ft. wide within'. As the existing church built in 1712–13 by William Smith of Tettenhall corresponds to these dimensions and is decorated with Doric pilasters, it would appear that Barker's design was accepted. The churchwardens' accounts show that in 1711 there was a meeting with 'Mr. Smiths and Mr. Barker', and that when the accounts for building the church were finally settled, John Barker was paid for 'additional' carpenter's and joiner's work. As Smith, a mason or bricklayer by trade, had contracted to erect the entire building 'by the great', it is probable that Barker undertook the woodwork as a sub-contractor [MS. churchwardens' accounts; Shropshire Record Office, Bridgewater collection, 212/1–6]. In 1711 Barker contracted with the 2nd Duke of Devonshire to rebuilt the BATHS at BUXTON according to drawings made by him and still attached to the articles of agreement [Sheffield Archives, Barker papers, D 666]. In 1712 Barker made a design for reconstructing the chapel at CHOLMONDELEY, CHESHIRE, for the Earl of Cholmondeley, that was not proceeded with, but the drawing is preserved among the Cholmondeley papers in the Cheshire Record Office (cf. Lord Cholmondeley to Adams, 28 Jan. 1711/12). Barker is also mentioned as builder or architect at TATTON PARK, CHESHIRE (rebuilt 1780–91) [*Tatton Park*, National Trust 1982, 58] and in connection with alterations to Lord Gower's stables at COTTESMORE HALL, RUTLAND (dem. 1974) in 1716 [Staffordshire C.R.O., D/593/P/16/2/2/7].

Besides acting as a carpenter, joiner and architect, Barker lent money and may have had some experience in the management of property. In 1723 the 3rd Duke of Rutland (for whose grandfather he built the stables at Belvoir) made Barker his steward. He moved from Rowsley to Belvoir, and was buried at Bottesford when he died in 1727. His elder son John was educated at Wadham College, Oxford, and became a physician. His second son Thomas (1709–54) and his grandson John (1731–95) succeeded him as stewards to the Dukes of Rutland, and were the founders of the family which figures in Burke's *Landed Gentry* as 'Barker of Brooklands'. [Sheffield Archives, Barker papers, especially D. 595, 634, 654–5, 828, pp. 82–6, 88, etc.; information from Mr. Edward Saunders.]

BARLOW, THOMAS (–1730), was a master carpenter who was active as a speculative builder in London during the reigns of Queen Anne and George I. He is known to have built houses in Albemarle Street (*c.*1700), Southampton Street (1708) and New Bond Street (where he lived), and Barlow Place (formerly Mews) off Bruton Street is named after him. He was involved in the development of the 1st Earl of Scarbrough's estate round Hanover Square (*c.*1715), and from 1720 until his death he was employed as surveyor of the Grosvenor estate. In that capacity he was responsible for the layout of Grosvenor Square and the adjoining streets, but probably exercised only a general control over the elevations. Barlow, who was a director of the Westminster Fire Office and a vestryman of St. George's Church, Hanover Square, died in January 1730, leaving a substantial estate to his son Richard, who died in 1740, 'having greatly wasted and outrun his fortune'. [*Survey of London* xxxix, 11–12.]

BARNARD, JOHN (–1762), was a carpenter by trade. Together with James King (*q.v.*), he contracted in 1738 to build, to King's design, the timber superstructure originally envisaged for Westminster Bridge, but subsequently abandoned in favour of a completely stone bridge [R. J. B. Walker, *Old Westminster Bridge*, 1979, 78, 82, 119]. Barnard later designed the wooden bridge which was built over the Thames at KEW in 1758–9; dem. 1783 [engraving signed 'John Barnard Archt.' in Bodleian, Gough Maps 30, ff. 30^{v}–31]. Barnard was one of the competitors for Blackfriars Bridge in 1760.

BARNES, DAVID, 'Architect and Surveyor' of Broadstairs, and proprietor of a library and reading-room there [*The Watering Places of Great Britain and Fashionable Directory*, 1833, 42], designed HOLY TRINITY CHURCH, BROADSTAIRS, KENT, 1828–30 [I.C.B.S.]. This small church in the lancet style was remodelled in 1914–15. In 1819 Barnes had subscribed to Peter Nicholson's *Architectural Dictionary* from an address in Cornhill, London.

BARNES, PHILIP, practised in Norwich. He was Secretary of the Norwich Society of Artists in 1817–21 and President in 1825. From 1832 to 1835 he was a member of the Norwich Sewers Commission. In 1820, in collaboration with J. T. Patience, he submitted a design for a Court House for the county of Norfolk which received a premium but was not executed. In 1823, in collaboration with Edward Brown, he submitted three designs for the new City Gaol. None of them was accepted, but Barnes was employed to supervise the execution of the new Gaol at the end of St. Giles' Street from the winning designs of Richard Brown of London, 1824–7 (dem.). [Information from Mr. A. P. Baggs.]

BARRIE, ANDREW, was a mason of Montrose in Angus. He designed and was the principal contractor for building the NORTH ESK BRIDGE, nr. Montrose, in 1770–5, with help and advice from John Smeaton and John Adam, who are named with him as 'architects' of the bridge in the prominent inscription [T. Ruddock, *Arch Bridges and their Builders*, 1979, 87]. In the Register House in Edinburgh there is a design by Barrie for a house in High Street, Montrose, for Lieut. Strachan dated 1778 [RHP 6006]. Another design for a house in the same town [RHP 6007] is probably by him.

BARROW, R—— J——, *see* LONG, FREDERICK.

BARRY, SIR CHARLES (1795–1860), the fourth son of a prosperous Westminster stationer, was articled at the age of 15 to Messrs Middleton and Bailey, a firm of surveyors in Lambeth, with whom he remained for six years. From them he learned the practical side of his profession, but in other respects was largely self-taught. On coming of age in 1816, he decided to spend a modest legacy from his father on an architectural tour of the Continent. He left England in 1817, travelling alone through France and Italy, and in Greece and Turkey in company with C. L. Eastlake (d. 1865) and W. Kinnard (*q.v.*), who was collecting material for a supplementary volume of the *Antiquities of Athens*. He was about to return to England when David Baillie, an archaeological traveller from Cambridge, who had met him in Athens and admired his drawings, offered to take him to Egypt and Syria and to pay him £200 a year for his sketches of the architecture and scenery of those countries.[1] In 1819–20 he returned to England by way of Cyprus, Rhodes, Malta, Sicily and Italy, where he met his lifelong friend J. L. Wolfe (*q.v.*). It was with Wolfe's help that in Rome and Florence he made those studies of Renaissance architecture that were to be so important in the formation of his architectural style.

On his return to London Barry established himself in Ely Place, Holborn, and, after a rapid study of Gothic, obtained (perhaps through the good offices of Soane, who knew his fiancée) the job of designing two of the Commissioners' churches then being erected in the neighbourhood of Manchester. Other commissions followed, notably the Royal Institution of Fine Arts at Manchester, which gave him an opportunity to demonstrate his ability as an orthodox Grecian architect. This was fortunate, for, although Barry could appreciate the dramatic possibilities of Gothic, as St. Peter's, Brighton, shows, he was not in sympathy with the more extreme revivalists, considering that 'deep chancels, high roodscreens and (in a less degree) pillared aisles . . . belong to the worship and institutions of the past rather than the present.' These were not sentiments which would lead to ecclesiastical commissions in the future, and while his contemporaries were taking advantage of the spate of Victorian church building, Barry applied himself to the more congenial task of designing public buildings and altering country mansions, in which he could make use both of his Italian studies and of his considerable skill in planning. By now he had renounced the Greek Revival in favour of the Italianate manner that was to make his fortune as an architect. His success in adapting the features of the Italian *palazzo* to English architecture – first displayed in the Travellers' Club in Pall Mall – provided an acceptable alternative to the extremes of Greek and Gothic hitherto offered to prospective builders, and established him as the leading London architect for club-houses and similar institutions. The Italianate style also permitted a greater richness of detail that

[1] Some of these drawings are now in the Griffith Institute, Ashmolean Museum, Oxford. Barry's own travel sketch-books are in the R.I.B.A. Drawings Collection.

Barry did not fail to exploit, and that appealed strongly to a generation tired of the 'chaste' (but often arid) simplicity of the Greek Revival. Barry was not, however, wedded to his Italian formula. 'Grandeur of outline' and 'richness of detail' were the two keynotes of his style, and he was equally ready to provide them in Tudor Gothic (as at Canford Manor), in Jacobethan (as at Highclere and Horsley Towers) or even in Scottish Baronial (as at Dunrobin Castle). But it was the Travellers' Club that made him famous, and it was the Italianate style that represented his personal contribution to the repertoire of Victorian architecture. With rich clients – and some of Barry's clients were very rich indeed – it was a style that could easily become overblown and a little vulgar, and Barry cannot be absolved from contributing to the coarsening of architectural taste that is apparent in the 1840s. In gardening, too, he ranks as one of the creators of Victorian taste, surrounding his opulent mansions with elaborate architectural flower-gardens in place of the subtler Georgian conception of the house as an integral part of a carefully composed landscape.

Many of Barry's early commissions were gained in competition, and in 1836 he won the biggest architectural competition of the century by obtaining the first prize for his design for the new Houses of Parliament. The style was, as the authorities demanded, 'Gothic or Elizabethan', but according to his son Barry 'would have preferred the Italian style', and the underlying discipline of the design is classical rather than Gothic. The prominent towers did, however, give the otherwise symmetrical building a picturesque quality that was recognizably medieval in inspiration, and the employment of A. W. N. Pugin to design much of the detail ensured that it was based on authentic Gothic prototypes. The competition design (for which the drawings are lost) was considerably modified both in plan and in elevational treatment before it was carried out, and many drawings survive (in the P.R.O., House of Lords Record Office, R.I.B.A. Drawings Collection and Society of Antiquaries' library) to illustrate the process. They were the work of a team of draughtsmen which, besides A. W. N. Pugin, included Barry's pupils John Gibson and George Somers Clarke and his sons Charles and Edward Middleton Barry. The difficulties of carrying on so vast a building were exacerbated for Barry by the need to satisfy not only committees of both Houses of Parliament, impatient to see their respective Chambers finished, but also the commissioners appointed in 1848 to supervise the whole operation on behalf of the government, and the Royal Fine Arts Commission set up in 1841 to decorate the interior with the works of contemporary artists. In addition Barry found himself fighting a running battle with Dr. Reid, an expert on ventilation whose failure to cooperate with the architect caused serious difficulties as the work proceeded. Drainage, the great clock, and finally Barry's own remuneration led to further controversy and vexation. It is not surprising therefore that the supervision of this great work became a full-time task which almost eliminated Barry's private practice during the latter part of his life. In 1852, after the Royal Entrance had been used for the first time by the Queen, Barry was knighted, but the building as a whole was incomplete at the time of his death, and was finished by his son E. M. Barry.

Barry was a compulsive worker who allowed himself little relaxation; indeed for him 'work without interruption was relaxation', and when he was designing the Houses of Parliament he slept for barely five hours out of the twenty-four. This exceptional capacity for work was one of the secrets of Barry's professional success, but in the end it led to the heart disease which caused his sudden death on 12 May 1860, at his home, Elm House, Clapham Common. He was buried in Westminster Abbey. A statue by J. H. Foley was erected to his memory in the Palace of Westminster in 1864. There is a portrait by J. P. Knight in the National Portrait Gallery and a bust by P. Park at the Reform Club. Barry was an R.A. and an F.R.S. and a Vice-President of the R.I.B.A., having refused the presidency on the death of Earl de Grey in 1859. He received the Royal Gold Medal of the R.I.B.A., and was a member of many foreign academies, including the American Institute of Architects. Of his four sons two, Charles (1824–1900) and Edward Middleton (1830–1880), followed their father's profession. From 1848 the former was in partnership with R. R. Banks.

[A. Barry, *The Life and Works of Sir Charles Barry*, 1867; obituary in *Builder* xviii, 1860, 305–7; memoir by M. D. Wyatt in *R.I.B.A. Trans*, 1859–60, 118–137, and *Builder* xviii, 1860, 322, 342; biographical notes by J. L. Wolfe in R.I.B.A. Library; *D.N.B.*; A. R. Dent, 'Barry and the Greek Revival', *Architecture*, 5th ser., iii, 1924–5, 225, 320; Marcus Whiffen, *The Architecture of Sir Charles Barry in Manchester* (Royal Manchester Institution, 1950); H.-R. Hitchcock, *Early Victorian Architecture in Britain* i, 1954, chaps. vi–vii; Peter Fleetwood-Hesketh, 'Sir Charles Barry', in *Victorian Architecture*, ed. P. Ferriday, 1963; Mark Girouard, 'Charles Barry: A Centenary Assessment', *C. Life*, 13

Oct. 1960; Marcus Binney, 'The Travels of Sir Charles Barry', *C. Life*, 28 Aug., 4, 11 Sept. 1969; *Catalogue of the R.I.B.A. Drawings Collection: B*, 1972, 18–54.]

Unless otherwise stated, the following list of Barry's executed works is based on Appendix A of A. Barry's *Life and Works of Sir Charles Barry*, where a list of unexecuted works will also be found.

CHURCHES

PRESTWICH, LANCS., ALL SAINTS, STAND, 1822–5, Gothic.

MANCHESTER, ST. MATTHEW, CAMPFIELD, 1822–5, Gothic; dem. 1951.

RINGLEY, LANCS., 1824, Gothic; rebuilt 1851–4.

BRIGHTON, ST. PETER, 1824–8, Gothic; Barry subsequently designed a spire that was not built; chancel added by Somers Clarke 1900.

BRIGHTON, HOLY TRINITY, SHIP STREET, alterations including addition of classical bell-turret, 1825–6; since Gothicized [J. L. Wolfe's MS. memoir] (A. Dale, *Fashionable Brighton*, 1947, pl. 10).

LONDON, HOLY TRINITY, CLOUDESLEY SQUARE, ISLINGTON, 1826–8, Gothic.

LONDON, ST. PAUL, BALLS POND, ISLINGTON, 1826–8, Gothic.

LONDON, ST. JOHN, UPPER HOLLOWAY, ISLINGTON, 1826–8, Gothic.

LONDON, ST. MARTIN OUTWICH, repaired and altered, 1827; dem. 1874.

PETWORTH, SUSSEX, rebuilt tower, added spire and altered nave for 3rd Earl of Egremont, 1827–30. The nave was altered again in 1903 and the spire was removed in 1947.

HOVE, SUSSEX, THE BRUNSWICK CHAPEL (now ST. ANDREW'S CHURCH), for the Revd. E. Everard, 1827–8, Italianate; chancel added by C. Barry, junior, 1882.

LONDON, ST. MARY, STOKE NEWINGTON, remodelled church and added spire, 1827–9; damaged by bombing 1940 and restored 1953, when the N. aisle was rebuilt, minus an additional N. aisle added by Barry.

LONDON, ST. PETER, SAFFRON HILL, HOLBORN, 1830–2, Gothic; gutted 1940; dem. 1955.

LONDON, ST. PETER, ISLINGTON, 1834–5, Gothic; enlarged by Gough & Roumieu, 1842–3 [I.C.B.S.; S. Lewis, *History of Islington*, 1842, 359–60].

WRINGTON, SOMERSET, reredos, 1832 [*Procs. Somerset Archl. Soc.* N.S. xiii, 1887, 15].

MANCHESTER, UNITARIAN CHAPEL (closed 1921), UPPER BROOK STREET, 1837–9, Gothic (*The Unitarian Heritage*, 1986, 55, 69).

HURSTPIERPOINT, SUSSEX, rebuilt 1843–5, Gothic.

TRENTHAM, STAFFS., reconstructed 1844 for 2nd Duke of Sutherland, Gothic.

PUBLIC BUILDINGS

MANCHESTER, THE ROYAL INSTITUTION OF FINE ARTS (now City Art Gallery), 1824–35.

BRIGHTON, THE SUSSEX COUNTY HOSPITAL, 1826–8; subsequently enlarged.

LONDON, ST. JOHN'S NATIONAL SCHOOLS, ISLINGTON, 1830.

LONDON, THE TRAVELLERS' CLUB, PALL MALL, 1830–2 (W. H. Leeds, *The Travellers' Club*, 1839; *Survey of London* xxix, 399–408).

DULWICH COLLEGE, alterations and additions, 1831, Gothic; largely destroyed in the reconstruction by C. Barry, junior, 1858 onwards.

BIRMINGHAM, KING EDWARD VI'S GRAMMAR SCHOOL, 1833–7, Gothic; enlarged by E. M. Barry 1860; dem. 1936 (drawings in R.I.B.A. and Birmingham Reference Library, MS. 617).

LONDON, ROYAL COLLEGE OF SURGEONS, LINCOLN'S INN FIELDS, remodelled 1835–7, retaining but altering G. Dance's portico; further additions by Barry 1854–5; attic storey added 1888–9.

MANCHESTER, THE ATHENAEUM (now Annexe to Art Gallery), 1837–9.

LONDON, THE REFORM CLUB, PALL MALL, 1838–41 (*Survey of London* xxix, 408–15).

LONDON, TRAFALGAR SQUARE, layout and fountains, 1840; fountains removed 1948 and re-erected at Ottawa, Canada.

KENMARE, CO. KERRY, IRELAND, MARKET-HOUSE for 3rd Marquess of Lansdowne, *c.*1840 [drawings in Moulton-Barrett volume, R.I.B.A.D.]

PALACE OF WESTMINSTER and HOUSES OF PARLIAMENT, 1840–60; completed by E. M. Barry 1860–70 (M. H. Port, *The Houses of Parliament*, 1976).

LONDON, PENTONVILLE PRISON, ISLINGTON, designed architectural features in accordance with plan made by Major Joshua Jebb, surveyor-general of convict prisons, 1841–2 [*History of the King's Works* vi, 1972, 630–1].

DULWICH GRAMMAR SCHOOL, 1841–2, Tudor Gothic.

OXFORD, UNIVERSITY COLLEGE, extension at W. end of High Street front, 1842, Tudor Gothic.

LONDON, WHITEHALL, reconstructed BOARD OF TRADE and PRIVY COUNCIL OFFICES, 1844–5.

ISTANBUL, TURKEY, THE BRITISH EMBASSY, 1845–7, built by W. J. Smith following sketches made by Barry [*History of the King's Works* vi, 1972, 634–8].

DEVONPORT, DEVON, ROYAL NAVAL FACTORY at MORICE TOWN, KEYHAM, 1847–8; dem.

GOLSPIE, SUTHERLAND, fountain in memory of Elizabeth, Duchess of Sutherland (d. 1839), 1850–1 [*Building Chronicle* i. 74, 16 Sept. 1854].

DOWLAIS SCHOOL, GLAMORGANSHIRE, for Sir John Guest, 1853–5.

EDINBURGH, consultant architect for THE LIFE ASSOCIATION OF SCOTLAND'S offices, PRINCES STREET, designed by David Rhind, 1855–8; dem. [J. Grant, *Old and New Edinburgh* ii, 1882, 123; J. L. Wolfe's MS. memoir].

HALIFAX, YORKS. (W.R.), TOWN HALL, 1859–62; executed by E. M. Barry, who designed the interiors and the roof.

DOMESTIC ARCHITECTURE

SOUGHTON HALL, FLINTSHIRE, alterations for W. J. Bankes, *c.*1825/30; largely rebuilt by J. Douglas, 1867–9 [E. Hubbard, *Clwyd* (Buildings of Wales), 1986, 408–9].

BUILE HILL, nr. MANCHESTER, house (now Salford Mining Museum) for Sir Thomas Potter, 1825–7; enlarged *c.*1865.

BRIGHTON, SUSSEX, No. 47 GRAND PARADE, added library at rear for Mrs. Ann Dulaney, 1826. The house itself, recently built by A. & A. H. Wilds, proved to be so badly constructed that it had to be rebuilt to Barry's designs in 1827–8 [papers of Henry Lloyd, Mrs. Dulaney's agent, in archives of Lloyd's Bank, London].

BRIGHTON, SUSSEX, house (later Xaverian College) in QUEEN'S PARK for Thomas Attree, 1829–30; dem. 1971: part of an extensive housing scheme that was never carried out (*C. Life*, 11 Aug. 1917, supplement).

LONDON, Nos. 16–17 PALL MALL (shops and living accommodation) for Thomas Ashton, 1833–4; dem. 1913 [*Survey of London* xxix, 325 and pl. 271].

HORSLEY PLACE (now HORSLEY TOWERS), EAST HORSLEY, SURREY, for William Currie, 1834, Tudor Gothic; tower, hall, library, etc., added by 1st Earl of Lovelace, 1847–8.

BOWOOD HOUSE, WILTSHIRE, works for 3rd Marquess of Lansdowne, including the Derry Hill Gateway (1834–8), the clock tower and alterations to the house (*c.*1830–48, dem.1956) and gardens; also the Lansdowne Monument on Cherhill Down, 1845 [*Builder*, 6 Oct. 1849, 474; A. T. Bolton, *Architecture of R. & J. Adam* i, 1922, 210–11; J. Cornforth in *C. Life*, 22 June 1972; for the Monument see letter in *Wiltshire Times*, 13 Nov. 1981, citing account, specification and contract in Lansdowne family archives].

TRENTHAM HALL, STAFFS., reconstructed for 2nd Duke of Sutherland, 1834–40 and 1840–9; dem. 1910 (*Companion to the Almanac*, 1837, 247–50; *C. Life*, 25 Jan., 1, 8 Feb. 1968). Barry also designed the monument at Tittensor on the Trentham estate to the 1st Duke of Sutherland (d. 1833), 1834, with a statue by Chantrey [drawing in private possession].

LILLESHALL, SALOP., Tudor and half-timbered lodges for 2nd Duke of Sutherland, 1835, of which at least two, the HEATH HILL LODGE and the SHERIFFHALES LODGE (immediately W. of Sheriffhales Church) were built and still exist [drawings in private possession].

BROOK STREET HOUSE, ASH-BY-SANDWICH, KENT, alterations for J. J. Godfrey, *c.*1835 [J. L. Wolfe's MS. memoir].

KINGSTON LACY, DORSET, recased and internally remodelled for W. J. Bankes, 1835–41 (A. Oswald, *Country Houses of Dorset*, 1959, 144–7; *Kingston Lacy*, National Trust, 1990).

WALTON HOUSE (later MOUNT FELIX), WALTON-ON-THAMES, SURREY, reconstructed for 5th Earl of Tankerville, 1835–9; dem. 1973.

LONDON, STAFFORD (now LANCASTER) HOUSE, ST. JAMES'S, alteration of lantern and redecoration of staircase for 2nd Duke of Sutherland, *c.*1838–41 [H. M. Colvin, 'The Architects of Stafford House', *Arch. Hist.* i, 1958, 28–9].

KIDDINGTON HALL, OXON., remodelled for Mortimer Ricardo, *c.*1840–50.

LONDON, No. 1 ADDISON ROAD, KENSINGTON, alterations for Col. Charles Richard Fox, 1841–2; dem. *c.*1875.

HIGHCLERE CASTLE, HANTS., remodelled for 3rd Earl of Carnarvon, 1842–9 (Mark Girouard, *The Victorian Country House*, 1971, 68–70; *C. Life*, 30 June 1988). Barry also remodelled the circular Ionic temple in the park [drawings at Highclere dated 1838].

EYNSHAM HALL, nr. WITNEY, OXON., remodelled for 5th Earl of Macclesfield, 1843; dem. 1904 (*V.C.H. Oxon.* xii, 109).

DUNCOMBE PARK, YORKS. (N.R.), alterations including addition of wings and forecourt for 2nd Lord Feversham, 1843–51 (*C. Life*, 24–31 May 1990).

HAREWOOD HOUSE, YORKS. (W.R.), altered interior and remodelled exterior for 3rd Earl of Harewood, 1843–50. Barry also laid out the formal gardens.

LONDON, ST. JOHN'S LODGE, REGENT'S PARK, consultant architect for alterations and additions by Ambrose Poynter for Sir Isaac Lyon Goldsmid, especially interior of ballroom, 1844–7 [cf. A. T. Bolton in University of London: Institute of Archaeology's *First Annual Report*, 1937, 15].

LONDON, No. 1 CLEVELAND SQUARE, flank wall for Lord Sydney, 1845; dem. 1895 [*Survey of London* xxx, 495].

?LONDON, Nos. 12, 18–19 and 20 KENSINGTON PALACE GARDENS, for Messrs. Grissell & Peto, 1845–7 [*Survey of London* xxxvii, 167–70, 179–81].

DUNROBIN CASTLE, SUTHERLAND, greatly enlarged for 2nd Duke of Sutherland, 1845–50 in collaboration with W. Leslie of Aberdeen, Barry's role being largely that of consultant architect; interiors of principal rooms destroyed by fire in 1915.

LONDON, BRIDGEWATER HOUSE, GREEN PARK, for 1st Earl of Ellesmere, 1846–51 (*Survey of London* xxx, 496–504).

CANFORD MANOR, DORSET, enlarged for Sir John Guest, 1848–52, Tudor Gothic.

SHRUBLAND PARK, SUFFOLK, alterations and additions, including formal gardens, for Sir W. F. Middleton, Bart., 1849–54 (*C. Life*, 24 Sept., 19, 26 Nov. 1953).

CLIVEDEN HOUSE, BUCKS., rebuilt for 2nd Duke of Sutherland, 1850–1 (*C. Life*, 7, 14 Dec. 1912, with plan).

GAWTHORPE HALL, LANCS., altered and restored for Sir James Kay-Shuttleworth, Bart., 1850–2 (*C. Life*, 4, 11 Sept. 1975)

EDGBASTON HALL, WARWICKS., alterations for 4th Lord Calthorpe, 1852.

LONDON, No. 2 SOUTH STREET, refronted for David Lyon, 1852; dem. *c.*1928 [*Survey of London* xl, 338].

LONDON, No. 41 BROOK STREET, refronted for Robert Nasmyth, 1853 [*Survey of London* xl, 23].

BARTHOLOMEW, ALFRED (1801–1845), was the son of a watchmaker in Clerkenwell. He was intended by his parents for a commercial career, and 'received only the moderate education of a middle-class school'. But a strong aptitude for mathematics led to his being articled to J. H. Good (*q.v.*). He afterwards taught perspective 'to the younger branches of a noble family', before starting practice. Writing and journalism were, however, to be his real *métier*, and his only architectural work of importance was the (classical) FINSBURY SAVINGS BANK in SEKFORDE STREET, CLERKENWELL, 1840 [*Civil Engineer* iii, 1840, 217]. His design for rebuilding the KENTISH TOWN EPISCOPAL CHAPEL, described in the *Civil Engineer* for 1842, was not carried out.

Bartholomew was keenly interested in church worship, and his first publication was a translation of the psalms, entitled *Sacred Lyrics, being an attempt to render the psalms of David more applicable to parochial psalmody*, 1831. He was one of the founders of a society called the 'Freemasons of the Church', whose object was 'the recovery, maintenance, and furtherance of the true principles and practice of architecture', and (although not hostile to classical architecture) was an enthusiastic advocate of the structural rationality of Gothic, which he expounded in the *Essay on the Decline of Excellence in the Structure of Modern English Buildings* which he appended to his *Specifications for Practical Architecture*, 1840, 2nd ed. 1846. He was also the author of *Hints relative to the Construction of Fire-Proof Buildings – and on the failure to produce sound and estimable Architecture by the means at present usually adopted*, 1839, and of a *Cyclopaedia of the New Metropolitan Building Act*, 1844, previously published in the *Builder*, of which he had become editor some time after its foundation in 1843. In 1844 he obtained the post of district surveyor of Hornsey, but died of bronchitis in January 1845, aged 44. The flower-painter Valentine Bartholomew was his elder brother. [Obituaries in *Builder* iii, 1845, 29, and *Gent's Mag.* 1845 (i), 320–1; *A.P.S.D.*; *D.N.B.*; G. G. Pace, 'Alfred Bartholomew, a pioneer of functional Gothic', *Arch. Rev.* Oct. 1942; C. L. Eastlake, *History of the Gothic Revival*, 1872, 214–16.]

BARTLETT, J— E—, was the author of *An Essay on Design, as applied generally to Edifices, both Private and Public, intended as a guide to Persons engaged in the Study of Architecture and containing pleasing information to private Gentlemen*, published at Lymington, Hants., in 1823. The book contains designs for castellated mansions. Bartlett designed the SOLENT SEA BATHS at LYMINGTON, *c.*1830 [*Views of the Principal Seats and Scenery in the Neighbourhood of Lymington* drawn by L. Haghe and published by R. A. Grove, 1832]. This building, which was surmounted by a hexagonal reading-room overlooking the sea, has been demolished.

BASEVI, GEORGE (1794–1845), was of Jewish birth. His father, George Basevi, senior, was a brother-in-law of Isaac D'Israeli, and was also related to the Ricardos. After attending Dr. Burney's school at Greenwich, Basevi became in 1811 a pupil of Sir John Soane, who thought highly of his ability. In 1816, on the expiry of his articles, he set out on a tour of Italy and Greece which lasted three years, and included a visit to Constantinople. Avidly studying buildings of every age from Ancient Greece to the High Renaissance, Basevi gradually emancipated himself from the influence of Soane, and returned well equipped to serve the increasingly eclectic taste of George IV's England. In 1820 he established himself in practice in the Albany, and in the following year he became surveyor to the newly formed Guardian Assurance Company. Between 1825 and 1840 he was employed by the financiers W. and G. Haldimand to superintend the erection of the houses in Belgrave Square, all of which, with the exception of the large mansions which occupy the angles, were built to his designs. In 1829 he was appointed surveyor to the trustees of Smith's Charity estate in Brompton, and laid out Pelham Crescent, Sydney Place, part of Brompton Crescent, and the adjoining streets. He also acted as surveyor to the Thurloe estate in South Kensington, then being developed by its owner, John Alexander, and designed the handsome houses in Thurloe Place, Thurloe Square, etc., built early in the 1840s.

In 1833 Basevi was one of the architects invited to submit plans for rebuilding the House of Commons (see *Parliamentary Papers*, 1833). By 1835, when he won the competition for the Fitzwilliam Museum at Cambridge, he was established as one of the leading English architects. Two important commissions, which he shared with Sydney Smirke, were the Conservative Club in St. James's Street and the Carlton Club in Pall Mall. The former was completed to their joint designs, but Basevi did not live to carry out the latter, for on 16 October 1845, while inspecting the western tower of Ely Cathedral, he fell through the floor of the belfry, and was killed on the spot. He was buried in the cathedral, where there is a brass to his memory in the north choir aisle. A plaster bust by an unknown sculptor is in the Fitzwilliam Museum: there is a cast in the R.I.B.A. Drawings Collection. Basevi is said to have been 'cold and somewhat haughty in manner', but scrupulously just in his professional activities. He was a Fellow of the R.I.B.A., the Royal Society and of the Society of Antiquaries. Francis Dollman (1812–1899) was in his office from 1833 to 1845. His son James Palladio Basevi (1832–71) was an officer in the Royal Engineers.

Basevi was probably the most successful of Soane's many pupils. Like other architects of his day, he was prepared to design Gothic churches and Tudor almshouses when required, but it was as a classical architect that he made his mark. In the Fitzwilliam Museum he produced one of the major works of the Early Victorian period, offering to a taste tired of the arid grandeur of the British Museum an opulent display of Graeco-Roman detailing. His London houses in Kensington and Belgravia show a similar (but more discreet) desire to liven up the anonymous uniformity of Georgian street architecture.

[Obituary in *Builder* iii, 1845, 510–11; *A.P.S.D.* (article by Sydney Smirke); *D.N.B.*; A. T. Bolton, *The Portrait of Sir John Soane*, 1927, 271–8; W. H. F. Basevi, 'The Grand Tour of an Architect', *The Architect*, 7 July–1 Sept. 1922.]

PUBLIC BUILDINGS

WATFORD, HERTS., THE MORRISON ALMSHOUSES, 1824; dem. 1964–5 [signed drawings in Guildhall Library, MS. 19227/31].

OXFORD, BALLIOL COLLEGE, building on west side of Garden Quadrangle, 1826–7; upper storey added by E. P. Warren 1926. In 1841 Basevi made designs for rebuilding the main front of the College facing Broad Street, but they were rejected. The original drawings are in the College Library [*V.C.H. Oxon.* iii, 94–5].

STAMFORD, LINCS., DR. FRYER'S ALMSHOUSES, Tudor Gothic, 1832 [signed].

STAMFORD, LINCS., TRUESDALE'S HOSPITAL, Tudor Gothic, 1832 [signed].

STROUD, GLOS., THE SUBSCRIPTION ROOMS, 1833–4. Basevi furnished the designs gratuitously, and they were carried out by Charles Baker of Painswick [P. H. Fisher, *Notes and Recollections of Stroud*, 1871, 161; specification in Glos. R.O., D. 1347].

LONDON, enlarged THE MIDDLESEX HOSPITAL, MORTIMER STREET, 1834; dem. 1928 [*A.P.S.D.*].

CAMBRIDGE, THE FITZWILLIAM MUSEUM, 1836–45, completed (with some alterations to the design) by C. R. Cockerell, 1845–8, and by E. M. Barry, 1870–5 [Willis & Clark, iii, 198–228].

HOVE, SUSSEX, ST. MARY'S HALL SCHOOL, EASTERN ROAD, for the Revd. H. V. Elliott, 1836, Tudor Gothic [A. Dale, *Fashionable Brighton*, 1947, 139].

TWICKENHAM, MIDDLESEX, THE NATIONAL (ARCHDEACON CAMBRIDGE'S) SCHOOLS, 1840–1; dem. [*A.P.S.D.*].

LONDON, THE CONSERVATIVE CLUB-HOUSE, ST. JAMES'S STREET, in association with S. Smirke, 1843–4. The exterior was the joint design of the two architects: in the interior the decoration of the ground floor is said to have been due to Basevi, that of the first floor to Smirke [*A.P.S.D.*; *Survey of London* xxx, 478–84].

LITTLEPORT, CAMBS., NATIONAL SCHOOL, 1844 [*Norfolk Chronicle*, 1 June, 1844].

ELY, CAMBS., PARSON'S ALMSHOUSES, ST. MARY STREET, 1844–5, Tudor Gothic [*A.P.S.D.*].

ELY, CAMBS., addition to the GAOL, 1845 [*A.P.S.D.*].

WISBECH, CAMBS., THE NEW GAOL or HOUSE OF CORRECTION, 1845–6; dem. [Gardner's *History, Gazeteer and Directory of Cambridgeshire*, 1851, 613].

CHURCHES

STOCKPORT, CHESHIRE, ST. THOMAS, 1822–5; chancel added 1890 [Port, 132].

GREENWICH, KENT, ST. MARY, 1823–4; dem. *c.*1935 [Port, 134; *Gent's Mag.* 1829 (ii), 395–7] (*Greenwich and Lewisham Archaeological Soc.'s Trans.*, 1936).

HOVE, SUSSEX, OLD PARISH CHURCH, reconstruction in Norman style, 1833–6 [*A.P.S.D.*].

CHELSEA, ST. SAVIOUR, WALTON PLACE, 1839–40, Gothic; north aisle added 1878, chancel 1890 [Port, 152].

TWICKENHAM, MIDDLESEX, HOLY TRINITY, 1840–1, Gothic; chancel and transepts added by F. T. Dollman 1863 [*A.P.S.D.*].

OXFORD, BALLIOL COLLEGE CHAPEL, plaster Gothic ceiling, 1841; dem. 1856 [*V.C.H. Oxon.* iii, 91].

CHELSEA, ST. JUDE, 1843–4, Gothic; dem. 1933 [Port, 152].

EYE, NORTHANTS., 1845–6, Gothic; steeple built posthumously 1857 by F. T. Dollman [*Gent's Mag.* 1847 (i), 646].

MONUMENT

KENSAL GREEN CEMETERY, family tomb of J. A. Hankey, 1838 [A. W. Hakewill, *Modern Tombs gleaned from the Public Cemeteries of London*, 1851, pl. 2].

LONDON HOUSES

BELGRAVE SQUARE, designed the houses (excluding those at the angles) for W. & G. Haldimand, 1825–40 [*A.P.S.D.*]. No. 31 is signed 'G. Basevi, Archt. 1827'.

SOUTH KENSINGTON, laid out the Thurloe estate for John Alexander (d. 1831) and his son H. B. Alexander, designing ALEXANDER SQUARE, etc., 1827–30, and THURLOE SQUARE, etc., *c.*1839–45 [Dorothy Stroud, *The Thurloe Estate*, 1959].

SOUTH KENSINGTON, designed PELHAM CRESCENT, PELHAM PLACE, BROMPTON (now EGERTON) CRESCENT and WALTON PLACE for the Trustees of Smith's Charity from 1833 onwards [Dorothy Stroud, *The South Kensington Estate of Henry Smith's Charity*, 1975].

PICCADILLY, No. 144, alterations for T. W. Beaumont, *c.*1836; dem. [*A.P.S.D.*].

COUNTRY HOUSES

According to Sydney Smirke (in *A.P.S.D.*) Basevi was employed 'more or less extensively' on the following houses:

ASHGROVE (now WEST HEATH SCHOOL), nr. SEVENOAKS, KENT, additions for W. Haldimand, *c.*1828.

BITTON GROVE (now Council Offices), nr. TEIGNMOUTH, DEVON, remodelled for W. Mackworth Praed, *c.*1835.

BLAKE HALL, ESSEX, remodelled for George Capel Cure, 1822; enlarged 1855 [cf. *V.C.H. Essex* iv, 14].

BRETTON HALL, YORKS. (W.R.), where he designed the stables for T. W. Beaumont in 1842 [archives of Lord Allendale, *ex inf.* Dr. D. Linstrum] (*C. Life* 21–28 May 1938).

FOX HILLS, OTTERSHAW, nr. CHERTSEY, SURREY, for J. I. Briscoe, *c.*1840, Tudor style; interiors altered 1923.

GATCOMBE PARK, GLOS., alterations (probably including stables, conservatory and interior of library), for David Ricardo, *c.*1820.

LONGHILLS HALL, nr. LINCOLN, for the Revd. P. Curtois, 1838.

NEWBERRIES PARK, RADLETT, HERTS., for Capt. R. W. Phillimore; dem. *c.*1950.

PAINSWICK HOUSE, GLOS., alterations, including addition of wings, for W. H. Hyett, Basevi's brother-in-law, 1827–32 (*C. Life*, 1 Sept. 1917).

SHERE MANOR HOUSE, SURREY, for Reginald Bray (who did not, however, inherit the estate from his brother until 1866).

TAPLOW HOUSE, BUCKS., enlarged for 2nd Marquess of Thomond, *c.*1840.

TITNESS PARK, nr. SUNNINGHILL, BERKS., for Sampson Ricardo, Tudor Gothic; dem. *c.*1950.

WATFORD, HERTS., house 'near' for Stewart Marjoribanks, presumably BUSHEY GROVE or WATFORD PLACE, probably in 1820s.

In addition Basevi designed COULSDON RECTORY, SURREY, 1841–3, Tudor Gothic [signed drawings in G.L.R.O., Diocese of Winchester Office Papers, 1841/10]. He no doubt designed BEECHWOOD, HIGHGATE, LONDON, for his brother Nathaniel Basevi, 1834 [C. Hussey in *C. Life*, 7 March 1952], and it may be conjectured that Basevi was the architect employed by Osman (son of David) Ricardo to reconstruct BROMSBERROW PLACE, GLOS., *c.*1825. His unexecuted design for Dinder Rectory, Somerset, for Dr. Richard Jenkyns, Master of Balliol College, Oxford, is illustrated in *C. Life*, 20 Oct. 1977, 1104, fig. 2.

BASIL, SIMON (–1615), was Surveyor of the King's Works from 1606 to 1615. His recorded career begins in 1590, when he was employed by the surveyor Robert Adams to draw a plan of Ostend. During Adams's brief tenure of office as Surveyor of the Works, Basil was Clerk of Works at Richmond. Just before his death Adams recommended him to Lord Burghley as competent to design fortifications, and in 1597 he is mentioned in connection with a 'modell' of Flushing. After Burghley's death in 1598, Robert Cecil (afterwards Earl of Salisbury) employed him at SALISBURY HOUSE in the Strand (1601), at THE NEW EXCHANGE in the Strand (1608–9) and at HATFIELD HOUSE, HERTS. (1607–12). Although he was in effective control of the operations at all three buildings, it does not necessarily follow that he made the designs. At Hatfield House these were certainly made, not by Basil but by Robert Liminge (*q.v.*). In the case of the other two buildings the authorship of the designs must be left in doubt, but Basil was no doubt closely involved in working them out even if he did not draw them himself. The only evidence of his activities elsewhere is a plan at Hatfield of Sir Walter Raleigh's house, SHERBORNE CASTLE, DORSET, made some time between 1600 and 1609.

In 1597 Basil became Comptroller of the Works, and in April 1606 he succeeded Sir David Cuningham as Surveyor. His surveyorship was marked by important administrative reforms, but he does not appear to have been a designer of any distinction, and even before his death the artistic initiative in the royal works was passing to Inigo Jones. Basil died in September 1615 and was buried at St. Martin's-in-the-Fields. His son Simon (1612–63) followed his father's profession and his career as a Clerk of the Works at Greenwich and Eltham before the Civil War and at Hampton Court after the Restoration was recorded on a memorial tablet formerly in Isleworth Church. [John Summerson in *History of the King's Works* iii, 1975, 108–20, etc.; Lawrence Stone, 'The Building of Hatfield House', *Archaeological Jnl.* cxii, 1955; Lawrence Stone, 'Inigo Jones and the New Exchange', *Archaeological Jnl.*, cxiv, 1957; Lawrence Stone, *Family and Fortune*, 1973, *passim*; A. P. Baggs, 'Two designs by Simon Basil', *Arch. Hist.* 27, 1984.]

BASKETT, WILLIAM (1782–1842), of Camberwell, was the architect employed by Fiennes Wykeham-Martin to rebuild the house within LEEDS CASTLE, KENT, in the Tudor Gothic style in 1822–5. The Wykeham-Martin papers in the Kent Archives Office show that he had previously worked with John Haverfield (*q.v.*) and had been employed by the Wykeham-Martins at their former residence, Chacombe Priory, Northants. In 1826 he designed the VICARAGE at ARRETON, ISLE OF WIGHT, a place where the Wykeham-Martin family had property. He died at Camberwell on 10 June 1842, aged 60 [David Cleggett, 'The rebuilding of Leeds Castle in 1822', *Building Technology and Management*, Oct. & Dec. 1982: further information from Mr. Cleggett].

BASNETT, CHARLES HENRY (*c.*1784–1859), was the only son of John Basnett of Wokingham, Berks. He became a pupil of Jeffry Wyatville, from whose office he exhibited at the Royal Academy in 1804–7. He subsequently moved to Bath, whence he sent architectural drawings to the R.A. exhibitions between 1815 and 1821. Nothing further has been ascertained about his career until his death in Brock Street, Bath, on 18 July 1859, at the age of 75 [*Gent's Mag.* 1859 (ii), 314].

BASSETT, HENRY (1803–?1847), was the son of George Bassett, who exhibited at the Royal Academy as a painter in 1829 and 1832, but who figures in *Pigot's Directory* of 1837–8 as a house agent and surveyor and in the *Literary Blue Book* of 1830 as an architect. Henry was admitted to the Royal Academy Schools in 1822 at the age of 19. In 1823 he won the Gold Medal of the Society of Arts for a design for a British Museum, and in 1825 he was awarded the Gold Medal of the Royal Academy. By 1839 he was employed on the Southampton estate in Bloomsbury, giving as his address the Southampton Estate Office in Fitzroy Square. His principal recorded work is BURTON PARK, nr. PETWORTH, SUSSEX, for John Biddulph, an assertively Grecian house of which he exhibited a perspective view at the Royal Academy in 1831 (*C. Life*, 11 July 1936; N. Pevsner, *Sussex*, 123–4). In 1833 he designed a villa, THE EAGLES, 33 WEST HILL, for Thomas Clark on Lord Southampton's estate at Highgate [*Catalogue of the R.I.B.A. Drawings Collection: B*, 60 and fig. 43]. In 1844 he exhibited a model of a pair of Italianate villas then being built to his designs in GLOUCESTER ROAD, REGENT'S PARK, probably to be identified as 'Gloucester Villas', dem. 1972. He disappears from the London directories after 1845, dying probably in 1847.

BASTARD, a family of architects and master builders based on Blandford in Dorset, and active in that county throughout the greater part of the eighteenth century. The founder of the firm was THOMAS BASTARD

(d. 1720), a joiner by trade, who is described on his monument in Blandford Church as 'a man useful, and industrious in his generation . . . and eminent for his skill in Architecture'. Little is known about his architectural work, most of which must have perished in the fire which destroyed Blandford in 1731, but it is likely that he was responsible for the fine woodwork in the church at CHARLTON MARSHALL, nr. BLANDFORD, rebuilt by the rector, Dr. Charles Sloper, in 1713, and perhaps for SPETTISBURY RECTORY, rebuilt by the same Dr. Sloper in 1716. Thomas may also have supervised the reconstruction of the neighbouring churches of WINTERBORNE STICKLAND and ALMER, DORSET, about this time, but there is no documentary evidence to show that he was consulted.

After Thomas Bastard's death in 1720 his business was continued by three of his sons, Thomas, John and William. Thomas died in 1731 and it was his younger brothers JOHN (*c.*1688–1770) and WILLIAM (*c.*1689–1766) whose partnership produced a number of handsome buildings mostly designed in a vernacular baroque style of considerable merit though of no great sophistication. A favourite motif that recurs often in their work is a capital with inturning volutes derived from Borromini. This had been used by Archer in the 1720s, and its reappearance in the work of the Bastards may well have been due to personal contact with Archer, who lived only twenty miles away at Hale, nr. Fordingbridge. As carvers and joiners the Bastards often employed rococo motifs, and a sketch-book in a private collection contains designs by them for furniture, chimney-pieces, picture-frames, etc., many of which were copied from the first English rococo manual, Brunetti's *Sixty Different Sorts of Ornaments*, 1731.

It was the fire which destroyed Blandford in 1731 that gave the Bastard brothers the opportunity to leave their mark on this small country town. Their principal works were the TOWN HALL of 1734, which is Palladian in style, and the CHURCH of 1735–9, whose plan (with short transeptal projections) reflects the influence of some of the Fifty New Churches in London. The spire which the Bastard brothers designed was not executed, the existing wooden cupola being due to 'other hands', but the sumptuous Mayor's Seat and other woodwork remain to demonstrate the excellence of their joinery. The chancel was extended in 1896. Galleries, inserted in 1836–7, were removed in 1970. According to the inscription on their monument, John and William Bastard were also responsible for 'several other Publick & Private Edifices'. One of these must have been the GREYHOUND INN (1734–5), now a bank, which was their property, and the RED LION INN can confidently be attributed to them on stylistic grounds. A 'survey book' of John Bastard's now in the County Record Office shows that the two houses (forming a single architectural composition) at the junction of East Street and the Market Place were built by him and his brother, and that they themselves occupied the house on the east side of the entrance (No. 75 East Street). In 1760 John Bastard, as 'a considerable sharer in the general Calamity', erected the Doric Pump-house near the church 'in Remembrance of God's dreadful Visitation by Fire . . . And to prevent, by a timely supply of Water (With God's Blessing) the fatal Consequences of FIRE hereafter'.

Outside Blandford the firm is known to have executed carver's and joiner's work of high quality at HAZLEGROVE HOUSE, SOMERSET, for C. H. Mildmay in 1732 (illustrated in *C. Life*, 18 May 1929) [bill printed in *C. Life*, 18 Jan. 1930, 99], and at LULWORTH CASTLE, DORSET, much of the interior of which (destroyed by fire in 1929) they redecorated and refurnished for Edward Weld, *c.*1727–58 [J. Marco & F. Kelly, 'Lulworth Castle from 1700', *Arch. Hist.* 34, 1991]. At CRICHEL HOUSE, DORSET, John Bastard was employed (together with the master-mason Francis Cartwright) in rebuilding the house for Sir William Napier, Bart., after a fire in 1742 [John Cornforth, 'The Building of Crichel', *Arch. Hist.* 27, 1984]. There is also documentary evidence that the Bastard brothers built, and probably designed, a house (now a School of Art) in MARKET STREET, POOLE, for Sir Peter Thompson, in 1746–9. A monument to John Dirdoe (d. 1724) in Gillingham Church, Dorset, is signed 'John Bastard & Co.'

The two Bastard brothers are commemorated by a monument in Blandford Church, and by a stone obelisk in the churchyard, which records their 'Skill in Architecture and Liberal Benefactions to this Town'. Their portraits hang in the Town Hall. Neither was married, and their partnership was continued by their nephews, Thomas Bastard 'the elder' (1720–71) and Thomas Bastard 'the younger' (1724–91). The former does not appear to have been responsible for any architectural work of significance, but payments to the latter by Humphrey Sturt in 1771–3 show that he was involved in the enlargement of CRICHEL HOUSE, DORSET, at that time, certainly as builder and possibly as the designer of the shell and exterior of the new rooms that were to be decorated by James Wyatt [John

Cornforth, *op. cit.*] (*C. Life*, 16 May 1925).

BENJAMIN BASTARD (*c*.1698–1772), fifth son of Thomas Bastard (d. 1720), was apprenticed in 1712 to William Townesend, the Oxford master mason (*q.v.*). He subsequently established himself as a mason at Sherborne in Dorset. Soon after 1720 he or another member of his family designed the large stone-built house in St. Swithin's Street, 'erected chiefly by Henry Seymour Portman', which is now the Digby School for Girls [Hutchins, *History of Dorset* iv, 1861, 282]. A monument in the cloister of Wells Cathedral, erected in 1749 to the memory of Peter Davis, Recorder of Wells, and signed 'Benj. Bastard, Sherborne, Fecit', shows that he was also a monumental sculptor. In 1753–4 he refronted the old SHIRE HALL at DORCHESTER (rebuilt 1796–7) and supplied the furniture for the Grand Jury Room [Dorset County Records]. A payment of 1 guinea to him by the 6th Lord Digby in 1758 'for drawing a plan of the stables' suggests that he designed the STABLES at SHERBORNE CASTLE, built in 1759 [account-book 1753–63 in Dorset C.R.O., D/SHC 1262]. In 1765 the W. tower of WEST COKER CHURCH, SOMERSET, was heightened under his direction [M. Nathan, *Annals of W. Coker*, 1957, 412]. When he died in 1772, he owned two inns and other property in Sherborne. He was buried at Castleton, where a tablet (now illegible) commemorated both him and his son Thomas, who died the same year, aged 42.

In 1738 Benjamin Bastard took as an apprentice his nephew JOHN BASTARD (1722–1778), who established himself as a mason in London, and is known to have executed masonry at Stoneleigh Abbey, Warwicks., 1764 [W. A. Thorpe in *Connoisseur*, March 1947, 19], the Dashwood Mausoleum at West Wycombe, Bucks., 1764–5 [Bodleian Library, MS. D.D. Dashwood B 12/6/1], the Middlesex Hospital [Hospital Records], and Greenwich Hospital [P.R.O., ADM 68/876]. On his tomb in Tarrant Keynston churchyard he is described as 'late of the Parish of St. Mary le Bone . . . , Mason and Architect'.

JOSEPH BASTARD (d. 1783), sixth and youngest son of Thomas Bastard (d. 1720), is described in Hutchins's *History of Dorset* as a 'builder and surveyor' of Basingstoke, Hants. In legal documents he is always referred to as of Sherborne St. John, a village a few miles from Basingstoke, where he died in 1783.

[H. M. Colvin, 'The Bastards of Blandford', *Archaeological Jnl.* 104, 1948; Arthur Oswald, *Old Towns Revisited*, 1952, 73–96; Arthur Oswald, *Country Houses of Dorset*, 1959, 30–8; John Adams, 'The Bastards of Blandford', *Arch. Rev.* June 1968, 445–50; R.C.H.M. *Dorset* iii (1), 16–40 (for Blandford); Polly Legg, 'A Bastard Barometer', *Procs. Dorset Nat. Hist. & Archl. Soc.* 107, 1985; contract with plan and elevation for premises in Blandford in Dorset C.R.O., D 856/7/3.]

BATEMAN, a firm of architects practising in Birmingham throughout the nineteenth century. Its founder appears to have been Joseph Bateman, a joiner by trade, who died in 1811. The practice was continued by Thomas and Joseph Bateman, whose relationship is uncertain. Soon after 1830 they separated, Thomas dying in 1837. Meanwhile Joseph had taken into partnership George Drury (*c*.1807–1851) and established a second office in Leamington. After his death or retirement Drury took his son John Jones Bateman into partnership, thus establishing the firm of 'Drury and Bateman'. After Drury's death in 1851 J. J. Bateman acquired a new partner in Benjamin Corser (d. 1918). J. J. Bateman died in 1903 at the age of 85, leaving a son, C. E. Bateman, F.R.I.B.A., to carry on the practice into the 1930s. The bulk of its records are now in the Reference Library at Birmingham (MS. 1542).

In LEAMINGTON SPA, Joseph Bateman designed THE WARNEFORD HOSPITAL, 1832–4, and VICTORIA PLACE, 1834, drawings of which he exhibited at the Birmingham Society of Artists in 1834. According to Fairfax's *Guide and Directory to Leamington Spa* (1838), 151, he also designed EASTNOR TERRACE, demolished in 1849–50 to make way for a railway station. In BIRMINGHAM Bateman and Drury designed GREENWAY TERRACE, BORDESLEY, 1836 [Reference Library, MS. 1542, Box 39, bundle 3], and in 1837–8 the LICHFIELD & TAMWORTH BANK'S OFFICE [*Architectural Mag.* iv, 1837, 80]. They also rebuilt the N. aisle of CHILVERS COTON CHURCH, WARWICKS., in 1837–8 [I.C.B.S.]. The principal works of Drury and Bateman were THE QUEEN'S HOSPITAL, BATH ROW, BIRMINGHAM, 1840–1, the QUEEN'S COLLEGE (now College Chambers), BIRMINGHAM, 1843–4, Gothic, refronted 1904, and the NEW WORKHOUSE, BIRMINGHAM HEATH, 1850–2, Tudor Gothic, dem. [Cornish's *Guide to Birmingham*, 1867, 65–7, 72–3].

[*A.P.S.D.*, *s.v.* 'Birmingham'; *Aris's Birmingham Gazette*, 1 July 1811, May 1851].

BATLEY, WILLIAM (*c*.1594–1674). A monument now built into the outside wall of the vestry of Wellingborough Church, Northants., commemorates William Batley, 'architect', who died in November 1674, aged 80 [J. G. Nichols, *Literary Illustrations of the*

Eighteenth Century, v, 601]. In February 1654/5 a builder or surveyor called Batley made an estimate for alterations to SYDENHAM HOUSE, DEVON, for Edward Wise [*Trans. Devonshire Assoc.* xli, 1909, 144–5] (*C. Life*, 28 June 1956).

BATTLEY, JOHN, is said to have been 'of some local eminence in Leeds, where he erected the theatre and several considerable buildings in the town and neighbourhood'. His principal works were 'executed about 1770–80' [S. Redgrave, *Dictionary of Artists of the English School*, 1878, 32].

BATTY, EDWARD (*c.*1740–1807), of Lancaster, is variously described as 'wood merchant and house carpenter' (1781), 'joiner and cabinet maker' (1794) and (in his will) as 'architect and house carpenter'. In 1801 he stated that he had 'followed the Business of Architect and Surveyor of Buildings and Estates all his life time and hath resided at Lancaster near 40 years' [Lancs. Record Office, Marton of Capernwray uncatalogued legal papers, *ex inf.* Mr. Richard Hewlings]. A plan signed by him shows that he laid out DALTON SQUARE, LANCASTER for building in 1783 [A. White, *The Buildings of Georgian Lancaster*, Lancaster 1992, 8]. A tablet on the external E. wall of St. John's Church, Lancaster, records the death of 'Edward Batty of this Town Architect' on 22 February 1807, aged 67.

BAUCHOP, TOBIAS, *see* BACHOP, TOBIAS.

BAUD, BENJAMIN (*c.*1807–1875), was a pupil of Francis Goodwin. He entered the Royal Academy Schools in 1829 at the age of 22, and exhibited at the Academy from 1826 to 1851. From 1826 to 1840 he assisted Sir Jeffry Wyatville in the rebuilding of Windsor Castle, and in 1842, in conjunction with Michael Gandy (*q.v.*), he published *Architectural Illustrations of Windsor Castle*, with text by John Britton. His portrait forms the frontispiece to that work.

In 1835 Baud was one of the unsuccessful competitors for the new Houses of Parliament, but in 1838 he won the competition for the WEST LONDON CEMETERY at BROMPTON, and during the next few years designed the domed chapel, main entrance lodge and catacombs for the cemetery's proprietors. In 1844 he was dismissed by the company and appears thereafter to have been chiefly engaged in alterations and additions to private houses, but in 1857 he was employed by the 2nd Earl of Lonsdale to design the LONSDALE MAUSOLEUM in LOWTHER CHURCHYARD, WESTMORLAND [W. Whellan, *History & Topography of Cumberland & Westmorland*, 1860, 798]. Baud died at Richmond, Surrey, on 17 April 1875, aged 69 [obituary in *Builder* xxxiii, 1875, 402; J. S. Curl, *The Victorian Celebration of Death*, 1972, 115–29].

BAXTER, JOHN (–*c.*1770), was an Edinburgh master mason of considerable repute. He enjoyed the confidence and patronage of Sir John Clerk of Penicuik (*q.v.*) through whose influence he was employed to build a number of large country houses in Scotland in the 1730s and '40s. He could draw as well as build, and understood the plain Palladian style favoured by his patron. His earliest recorded contracts were MAVISBANK HOUSE, MIDLOTHIAN, which he began to build for Clerk in 1723 'according to a design concocted between me [Clerk] and Mr. [William] Adams', and HADDO HOUSE, ABERDEENSHIRE, a house designed by William Adam for the 2nd Earl of Aberdeen under Clerk's direction and built by Baxter in 1732–5 [bills in Aberdeen University Library; Christopher Hussey in *C. Life*, 18–25 Aug. 1966]. In 1738–9 he was building a house for the Master of Ross, presumably HAWKHEAD PARK, RENFREWSHIRE [S.R.O., GD 18/5246/6/41], and in 1740 began GALLOWAY HOUSE, WIGTOWNSHIRE, for Lord Garlies. Here the design was a collaborative effort on the part of Sir John Clerk, the architect John Douglas and the client, and Baxter's share in it appears to have been slight, though he made and altered drawings for the building he was to execute [J. Macaulay, *The Classical Country House in Scotland 1660–1800*, 1987, 102]. In 1745–9 Baxter built ORMISTON HALL, EAST LOTHIAN (now a ruin), for John and George Cockburn [S.R.O., Register of Deeds, 1751], and in 1756–9 was employed by Francis Charteris, titular Earl of Wemyss, to build AMISFIELD HOUSE, EAST LOTHIAN (dem. *c.*1928), to the design of Isaac Ware [see payments to 'John Baxter, Architect' in the building accounts cited by C. Hussey, *C. Life*, 15 July 1965, 184]. Meanwhile at PENICUIK HOUSE, MIDLOTHIAN, he had in 1753 carried out some alterations for Sir John Clerk's son, James Clerk, and after Sir John's death in 1755 the new baronet, himself an amateur architect, completely rebuilt the house (1761–9) with Baxter as executant architect and builder [Alistair Rowan in *C. Life*, 15–22 Aug. 1968; below, p. 255].

In 1753 Baxter had built MAYSHADE HOUSE, nr. LOANHEAD, MIDLOTHIAN, for his own occupation [S.R.O., Edinburgh Sasines]. By 1769 he was in poor health and more or less retired, for on 25 Feb. his son John Baxter, junior (*q.v.*), wrote that his father had been so much indisposed that he 'has given up business to me, ever since my return from Italy' [S.R.O., GD 44/49/16]. The date of his death has not been ascertained, but it must have occurred in about 1770.

[Ann M. Simpson, 'The Architectural Work of the Baxter Family in Scotland 1722–98', Edinburgh University, unpublished thesis, 1971.]

BAXTER, JOHN (–1798), was the son and successor of John Baxter (*q.v.*). In 1761 his father sent him and his brother Alexander to Italy to study architecture. Here John 'became a figure of some standing' among the foreign artists resident in Rome. He competed for at least one architectural prize, and in March 1766 he was admitted a full member of St. Luke's Academy. In 1767, very shortly before his return to Scotland, he was joined by the painter Alexander Runciman, another protégé of Sir James Clerk, who was to decorate the ceiling of 'Ossian's Hall' at Penicuik on his return. In the Vatican there is a painting of the two Baxters, with Runciman and another artist (reputedly Fuseli), which must date from this year. While in Rome Baxter had some chimney-pieces made to his designs by Italian sculptors, probably for Penicuik, but they were all 'broke in pieces in carriage for Scotland' [B.M. Print Room Sc. A. 5.9]. Back in Scotland, he almost immediately took over the family business from his ailing father, and continued to combine the functions of architect and contracting mason throughout his life. Like Robert Adam, Baxter undoubtedly acquired a more sophisticated style of draughtsmanship and design in Rome than he could ever have learned in Edinburgh. But lacking Adam's ambition and genius, he was responsible for no spectacular innovation in Scottish architecture. Indeed, both his Town House at Peterhead and his Bellie Church at Fochabers (the centre-piece of a new town which he laid out for the Duke of Gordon) are surmounted by steeples of a traditional Scottish type derived ultimately from Gibbs, while his elegant Merchants' Hall in Hunter Square, Edinburgh, is a competent performance in the style of Adam himself.

The principal source of information about Baxter's architectural works is the catalogue of drawings and other works of art that were sold after his death:[1] it included a large collection of prints, numerous 'Old Master' drawings, some paintings by Alexander and John Runciman, and a quantity of busts, basso relievos, antique plaster figures, etc. There were also many architectural drawings by Baxter himself, including a set of designs for a 'sepulchral chapel' made in Rome, probably for the 1764 *concorso* of the Academy at Parma. Among the Gordon Cumming papers in the National Library of Scotland there is a set of plans, signed 'John Baxter Architect 1778', for adding wings and a portico to an unidentified Scottish country house (in portfolio catalogued as 'Bound volumes No. 51'). In 1791 he submitted three designs for a new development near Edinburgh to be called 'Picardy Village', but they were not accepted [*Book of the Old Edinburgh Club* xxv, 29–30]. Baxter died at Edinburgh in July 1798. He left a son John who was in the service of the East India Company. [Ann M. Simpson, 'The Architectural Work of the Baxter Family in Scotland 1722–98', unpublished thesis, Edinburgh University, 1971; Ann & James Simpson, 'John Baxter, Architect, and the Patronage of the Fourth Duke of Gordon', *Bull. Scottish Georgian Soc.* ii, 1973; D. Stillman, 'British Architects and Italian Architectural Competitions, 1758–1780', *Jnl. Society of Architectural Historians* (of America), xxxii, 1973, 56–7.]

[1] The only known copy is in Edinburgh Public Library (Cowan bequest). The account book of the sale is in the Beinecke Library at Yale (Osb. shelves f.c.11).

COUNTRY HOUSES

HALLHEAD HOUSE or CASTLE, ABERDEENSHIRE, repairs or alterations for Sir Robert Gordon, Bart., before 1769, probably in connection with its use as a farm-house [S.R.O., GD 44/43/14: 'It was this young man who drew the plan and directed the work at Hallhead Castle'; cf. D. MacGibbon & T. Ross, *The Castellated and Domestic Architecture of Scotland* iv, 1892, fig. 870].

PENICUIK HOUSE, MIDLOTHIAN, minor alterations for Sir James Clerk, *c.*1770–78, including remodelling of three central windows of rear elevation [Alistair Rowan in *C. Life*, 15 Aug. 1968].

MORTONHALL HOUSE, LIBERTON, MIDLOTHIAN, for Thomas Trotter, *c.*1769 ['plans and elevation of the house of Mortonhall' in Sale Catalogue] (J. Small, *Castles and Mansions of the Lothians* ii, 1883; R.C.A.M., *City of Edinburgh*, 1951, 236–7 and fig. 421).

GORDON CASTLE, MORAYSHIRE, remodelled for 4th Duke of Gordon, 1769–82, castellated; dem. 1961 [S.R.O., drawings (RHP 1056–1071) and accounts (esp. GD 44/49/16) among Gordon papers; 'various designs for Gordon Castle . . . built by Mr. Baxter' in

Sale Catalogue] (Neale, *Seats*, ser. i, vol. i). Baxter also designed some farmhouses on the estate, for which drawings by him survive [S.R.O., RHP 2378].

GORDONSTOUN HOUSE, MORAYSHIRE, probably responsible for alterations (chiefly internal) for Sir Robert Gordon, Bart., 1772–6 ['plans and elevations of Gordonstoun House' in Sale Catalogue]. The date and authorship of the circular office-court have not yet been established.

EGLINTON CASTLE, AYRSHIRE, castellated gateway for 11th Earl of Eglinton, 1780 [National Library of Scotland, MS. 580, No. 397 (f. 116)]. Baxter's sale included a set of unexecuted designs for rebuilding the Castle itself, photos of which are at N.M.R.S.

GARTMORE HOUSE, PERTHSHIRE, alterations for Robert Graham, 1779–80; remodelled 1901–2 [payments in account-book among Graham papers in S.R.O. (GD 22/1/468) and 'south and north elevation of Gartmore House' in Sale Catalogue] (*Scottish Field*, Nov. 1958).

ELLON CASTLE, ABERDEENSHIRE, alterations for 3rd Earl of Aberdeen, 1781–7; largely dem. 1851 [drawings dated 1781 at N.M.R.S.; accounts at Haddo House, *ex inf.* Mrs. Simpson; 'Plans and Elevations of Ellon Castle' in Sale Catalogue].

DUNS CASTLE, BERWICKSHIRE, stables (1792–4), Gothic gateway (1791) and proposed alterations to house (1794) for Robert Hay, 1791–4 [N.M.R.S., photos. of drawings at Duns].

AVONTOUN HOUSE, WEST LOTHIAN, for Robert Blair, 1792–4; dem. *c.*1970 [papers belonging to Miss Alice Maconochie; designs in Sale Catalogue].

BALMUTO HOUSE, FIFE, additions (dem. 1962) for Claud Boswell, 1797 [S.R.O., GD 66/1/275, account of mason work by John Baxter & Co.].

GLENFIDDICH LODGE, BANFFSHIRE, alterations for 4th Duke of Gordon, 1798; subsequently rebuilt to designs by J. Plaw [S.R.O., Gordon papers, GD 44/32/10].

OTHER BUILDINGS

KENMORE BRIDGE, PERTHSHIRE, for the Commissioners for Annexed Estates, 1774 [S.R.O., E 732/18/1–2, GD 112/48 and RHP 971/1].

CALLANDER CHURCH, PERTHSHIRE, for the Commissioners for Annexed Estates, 1771–3; dem. [S.R.O., E 732/18/2; E 777/169/11(2)].

TUGNET, SPEYMOUTH, MORAYSHIRE, WAREHOUSE, etc. for Steuart of Tannachy, 1772 [S.R.O., GD 44/Sec. 52/37, pp. 325, 343, *ex. inf.* Mrs. E. Beaton].

GARTCHONZIE BRIDGE over R. Teith nr. CALLANDER, PERTHSHIRE, for the Commissioners for Annexed Estates, 1774 [S.R.O., E 732/18/1 and 2/1].

DALNACARDOCH INN, BLAIR ATHOLL, PERTHSHIRE, for the Commissioners for Annexed Estates, 1774 [S.R.O., E 732/18/2].

FOCHABERS NEW TOWN, MORAYSHIRE, for 4th Duke of Gordon, 1775–90 [S.R.O., GD 44/32/10].

CULLEN HOUSE, BANFFSHIRE, internal alterations for 4th Earl of Seafield, 1777 [S.R.O., GD 248/800/4].

EDINBURGH, houses in GREENSIDE WELL (below Calton Hill), as a personal speculation, 1780–3 [S.R.O., Edinburgh Sasines].

EDINBURGH, TRON CHURCH, alterations 1785–7 for road-widening in connection with the South Bridge and Hunter Square. Baxter shortened the church by one bay to east and west and reduced the south aisle to a slight pedimented projection with detail carefully matched to the original [Edinburgh Town Council Minutes, 3 June 1788] (plan showing Baxter's alterations in G. Hay, *Architecture of Scottish Post-Reformation Churches*, 1957, fig. 15).

EDINBURGH, MERCHANTS' HALL, 3–4 HUNTER SQUARE, 1788. The ground floor was altered 1898 to form premises for the Royal Bank of Scotland [R.C.A.M., *City of Edinburgh*, 101–2, citing Minute Book of the Edinburgh Merchant Co.] (A. T. Bolton, *The Architecture of R. and J. Adam* ii, 1922, 250).

PETERHEAD, ABERDEENSHIRE, THE TOWN HOUSE (with steeple), 1788 [J. T. Findlay, *History of Peterhead*, Aberdeen 1933, 274].

FEARN ABBEY CHURCH, ROSS-SHIRE, monument to Admiral Sir John Lockhart Ross (d. 1790) [design in Sale Catalogue].

INVERESK CHURCHYARD, MIDLOTHIAN, monument to Sir Archibald Hope, 1794 [design in Sale Catalogue].

BELLIE CHURCH, FOCHABERS, MORAYSHIRE, for 4th Duke of Gordon, 1795–7 [drawings in S.R.O., RHP 8531–4; accounts in S.R.O., GD 44/32/10; L. Shaw, *History of the Province of Moray*, ed. Gordon, i, 1882, 71] (G. Hay, *Architecture of Scottish Post-Reformation Churches*, 1957, fig. 28).

BAXTER, JOHN (–1837), usually referred to in contemporary documents as 'John Baxter, junior, Architect', was the son of John Baxter, a builder of Portobello, nr. Edinburgh. So far as is known they were not related to John Baxter of Edinburgh (d.

1798). The father built Nos. 1–8 BAXTER'S PLACE, a block of houses in Leith Walk, Edinburgh, below Calton Hill, on a site feued to him in 1800 [S.R.O., Edinburgh Sasines]. In 1809 the two Baxters were among the trustees for building Portobello Church (designed by W. Sibbald) [W. Baird, *Annals of Duddingston and Portobello*, 1898, 321], and in 1813 the son was sufficiently highly esteemed to be one of the architects invited to judge the competition for laying out the Calton Grounds [S.R.O., GD 113/322; A. J. Youngson, *The Making of Classical Edinburgh*, 1966, 149]. He subsequently laid out and developed ROSEFIELD PLACE, ROSEFIELD AVENUE, EAST AND WEST BRIGHTON CRESCENT and 3–8 SANDFORD GARDENS, PORTOBELLO, from 1823 onwards [S.R.O., Edinburgh Sasines]. He died on 30 May 1837 [S.R.O., SC 70/1/61, p. 730].

BEACHCROFT, SAMUEL (*c.*1801–1861), entered the Royal Academy Schools in 1823 at the age of 22. He was a pupil of H. H. Seward, and exhibited at the Academy from 1818 to 1822. In 1825 he became District Surveyor for Chelsea. An inscription in MORTLAKE CHURCH, SURREY, records that the church was enlarged to his designs in 1840, but his work was destroyed when the nave was rebuilt in 1906. Beachcroft became a Fellow of the (R.)I.B.A. in 1835, retired in 1853, and died at Putney in 1861. CHARLES BEACHCROFT, who entered the R.A. Schools in 1835, used Samuel Beachcroft's address when he exhibited at the Academy in 1833. He died in 1866.

BEALES, ROBERT, is described as a builder or surveyor of Lawford in Essex in Pigot's *Directories* of the period 1823 to 1832. Drawings signed 'R. Beales, Lawford' show that he remodelled CROWE HALL, STUTTON, SUFFOLK, in a picturesque Gothic style for John Page Reade *c.*1825–6 (*C. Life*, 26 Dec. 1957) [information from Mr. Roger White].

BEARD, the name of a family of minor architects practising in Somerset in the early nineteenth century. In 1813 'Mr. Beard of Somerton' provided the designs for GLASTONBURY TOWN HALL, a simple classical building built in 1818 [H. F. Scott-Stokes, *Annals of Glastonbury Corporation 1705–1834*, 1925, 17]. In 1821 the nave and chancel of NORTHOVER CHURCH, SOMERSET, were rebuilt in a basic Gothic style under the direction of 'Mr. Beard' [*V.C.H. Somerset* iii, 230, n. 67]. In what was presumably the next generation, JAMES BARON BEARD, 'surveyor and builder of Langport', designed or remodelled two Somerset rectories, at KINGSDOWN, 1836, and LIMINGTON, 1838 [Somerset C.R.O., D/D/Bb m, 66, 70], while JOHN BARON BEARD, architect of Taunton, reconstructed the nave of ASHCOTT CHURCH, SOMERSET, in 1833 [I.C.B.S.] According to Pigot's *Directory* an architect called Joseph Beard was practising in Bath in 1830.

BEARE, ROBERT SPENCE, started to practise in Norwich in 1812 [*Norwich Mercury* 4 Jan. 1812] and exhibited architectural designs at the Norwich Society of Artists in 1812–14. They included 'a Cottage for Samuel Parkinson, Esq.' (1812), a house for Mrs. Hook of Chapelfield, Norwich (1812), and a 'Design for a Theatre proposed to be erected at Lynn' (1813).

BEAUMONT, JOHN (*c.*1769–1799), practised in Doncaster until his death in 1799 at the age of 30. A competently drawn elevation of a house, signed 'J. Beaumont inv[t]. et del. 1792. Devonshire Street, Portland Place, London', suggests a London training. [information from Mr. Guise Beaumont, Grahamstown, S. Africa].

BEAZLEY, CHARLES (*c.*1760–1829), was a pupil of Sir Robert Taylor. He is said to have deputized for the latter as surveyor to the Bank of England during the last seven years of his life, and succeeded him as steward of the Bank's estates when he died in 1788. For nearly fifty years Beazley was District Surveyor to the parishes of St. James and St. John, Clerkenwell. As architect to the Goldsmiths' Company he made designs in 1804 for a new Hall, but they were not executed. He exhibited at the Royal Academy between 1787 and 1806. He died at West End, Hampstead, on 6 January 1829, aged 69 according to the *Gentleman's Magazine* (65 according to *A.P.S.D.*). Samuel Beazley, George Draper, George Maliphant, J. Medland, George New, William Rogers and W. F. Pocock were his pupils. Beazley's surviving works suggest that he was a competent but not particularly interesting exponent of the plain English neo-classical style of the early nineteenth century. [*A.P.S.D.*; *Gent's Mag.* 1829 (i), 92; Walpole, *Anecdotes of Painting* v, ed. F. W. Hilles & P. B. Daghlian, 1937, 199.]

SPELDHURST CHURCH, KENT, rebuilt 1794–5; rebuilt 1870–1 [churchwardens' accounts in Kent Record Office, P 344/5/3/, *ex inf.* Mr. D. Findlay].

FAVERSHAM CHURCH, KENT, Gothic tower and spire similar to that of St. Dunstan's in the East, London, 1799 [exhib. at R. A. 1799].

MAIDSTONE, KENT, triumphal arch in honour

of King George III, 1799 [engraving in B.L., *King's Maps* xvii, 2.2, c].

OSPRINGE PLACE, nr. FAVERSHAM, KENT, for Isaac Rutten, *c.*1799 [exhib. at R.A. 1799].

SHERNFOLD PARK, nr. FRANT, SUSSEX, a pavilion for C. E. Pigou, 1799 [exhib. at R.A. 1799].

HOLLINGBOURNE HOUSE, KENT, for B. D. Duppa, 1799–1800 [exhib. at R.A. 1799 and 1801].

TODDINGTON HOUSE, GLOS., repaired south wing for Charles Hanbury Tracy, later Lord Sudeley, after a fire in 1800; dem. *c.*1820 [*A.P.S.D.*].

CRANFORD PARK, MIDDLESEX, bridge for 5th Earl of Berkeley [original drawings in B.L., *King's Maps* xxix, 8; exhib. at R.A. 1806].

THE GOLDSMITHS' ALMSHOUSES, ACTON, MIDDLESEX, 1811 [*A.P.S.D.*].

Note: The statement in *A.P.S.D.* that Beazley and George Smith jointly designed the Jewin Street Presbyterian Chapel for Dr. A. Rees in 1808 appears to be incorrect (see under Aikin, William), but they may have designed a Wesleyan Methodist Chapel that stood in the same street and was demolished in 1878. For the possibility that Beazley designed the Presbyterian Chapel in Little Chapel Street, Soho, 1822–4, dem. 1894, see *Survey of London* xxxiii, 295.

BEAZLEY, SAMUEL (1786–1851), was the son of an army accoutrement maker of Westminster, and received his architectural training in the office of his uncle, Charles Beazley. He served as a volunteer in the Peninsular War, and, among other exploits, claimed to have rescued the Duchesse d'Angoulême from the Napoleonic forces in Bordeaux in 1815. For the remainder of his life he combined the professions of architect and playwright. As a schoolboy he had distinguished himself by writing a comedy and then constructing the stage upon which he and his friends performed it, and in later life he continued both to write plays and to design their architectural setting. He was the author of over a hundred operas, farces and other dramatic performances of a similar character, many of which he staged himself. He also published two novels, *The Roué*, 1828, and *The Oxonian*, 1840. He was well-known for his lively and witty conversation, and lived a fashionable life at his London house in Soho Square.

Beazley was the leading specialist of his day in the design of theatres, of which he built a considerable number in London and elsewhere. Towards the end of his life he became architect to the South-Eastern Railway Company, for which he designed the stations on the North Kent Railway, the Lord Warden Hotel at Dover, and a new town at Ashford for the employees in the locomotive works. Stylistically he was an eclectic designer in a variety of styles, from 'Grecian' to 'Norman', from neo-classical to 'Louis Quatorze'. His writings included a paper on 'The Rise and Progress of Gothic Architecture', in the *Essays of the London Architectural Society*, 1808, and a small book entitled *A General View of the System of enclosing Waste Lands; with particular reference to the proposed Enclosure at Epsom in Surrey*, 1812. He exhibited frequently at the Royal Academy. F. R. Beeston was a pupil. Beazley died suddenly on 12 October 1851 at his country house, Tonbridge Castle, Kent, aged 65. [*A.P.S.D.*; *D.N.B.*; obituary in *Builder* ix, 1851, 694; Dudley Harbron, 'Samuel Beazley', *Arch. Rev.* lxxix, 1936, 131; *Gent's Mag.* 1851, 559, 1852, 2.]

THEATRES

LONDON, THE ROYAL LYCEUM THEATRE, 1816 [Britton & Pugin, *Public Buildings of London* i, 1825, 273–8]; this was destroyed by fire in 1830, and rebuilt by Beazley, 1831–4 [*Builder* v, 489, 507; *R.I.B.A. Jnl.* 3rd ser. i, 1894, 655]; the theatre was subsequently redecorated in an Italianate style, and in 1902 it was reconstructed, with the exception of the portico.

BIRMINGHAM, THE THEATRE ROYAL, NEW STREET, was rebuilt under his direction between 6 Jan. 1820, when the former building was destroyed by fire, and 14 Aug. of the same year: the façade of 1780, by Samuel Wyatt (*q.v.*), was, however, preserved; dem. 1956 [*A.P.S.D.*].

DUBLIN, THE THEATRE ROYAL, HAWKINS STREET, 1821; destroyed by fire 1880 [G. N. Wright, *Historical Guide to Dublin*, 1821, 271].

LEAMINGTON SPA, WARWICKS., THE COUNTY LIBRARY AND READING ROOMS, ETC., BATH STREET, for Mr. Elliston, 1820–1 [Moncrieff's *Guide to Leamington Spa*, 1833, 51].

LEAMINGTON SPA, WARWICKS., THE ROYAL ASSEMBLY ROOMS, BATH STREET, *c.*1820; dem. 1968 [Moncrieff's *Guide to Leamington Spa*, 1833, 57].

LONDON, THE DRURY LANE THEATRE, remodelled interior, 1822; he also added the colonnade in Little Russell Street, 1831 [Britton & Pugin, *Public Buildings of London* i, 1825, 247; *Survey of London* xxxv, 64–5].

LONDON, THE ROYAL SOHO (afterwards ROYALTY) THEATRE, DEAN STREET, for Miss Fanny Kelly, 1834–7; rebuilt 1882; dem.

1954 [*Survey of London* xxxiii, 215–17].

LEICESTER, THE THEATRE, 1836; dem. 1958 [*Architectural Mag.* iii, 1836, 584, correcting a statement on p. 482 that it was designed by William Parsons] (R. Leacroft, 'The Theatre Royal, Leicester', *Trans. Leics. Arch. Soc.* xxxiv, 1958).

LONDON, THE ST. JAMES'S THEATRE, KING STREET, for John Braham, 1835; dem. 1957–8 [*A.P.S.D.*].

LONDON, THE CITY OF LONDON THEATRE, NORTON FOLGATE, BISHOPSGATE, 1837; dem. [*A.P.S.D.*].

LONDON, THE ADELPHI THEATRE, STRAND, rebuilt the façade, 1841; the theatre was rebuilt by T. H. Wyatt in 1858; dem. [*A.P.S.D.*].

Beazley also made the designs for theatres erected in Belgium, South America and India. His unexecuted designs for The Casino in Leicester Square, London, are illustrated in *Survey of London* xxxiv, pl. 33.

OTHER WORKS

CASTLE BERNARD, CO. OFFALY, IRELAND, designs for park entrance and school for Thomas Bernard, M.P., 1811 [exhib. at R.A.].

EAST DENE, BONCHURCH, ISLE OF WIGHT, for – Surman, *c.*1825, 'Elizabethan' style [W. B. Cooke, *Bonchurch, Shanklin and the Undercliff*, 1849, 29].

BOGNOR, SUSSEX, THE CLARENCE HOTEL and 'NEW CRESCENT', *c.*1830 [*The Bognor Guide*, Petworth, 1838].

LEYS CASTLE, INVERNESS-SHIRE, for Col. John Baillie, 1832–4, castle style [building papers in N.L.S., Acc. 9135; exhib. at R.A. 1833].

STUDLEY CASTLE, WARWICKS., for Sir Francis L. Holyoake Goodricke, Bart., 1834, Norman style [exhib. R.A. 1835].

BRETBY PARK, DERBYSHIRE, design for a boudoir for the Countess of Chesterfield, exhibited at R.A. 1838, now in R.I.B.A. Drawings Coll.

CAHIR CASTLE, CO. TIPPERARY, IRELAND, alterations for the 2nd Earl of Glengall, *c.*1838–40 [exhib. at R.A. 1838].

LONDON, D'OYLEY'S WAREHOUSE, 346 STRAND, 1838 [exhib. at R.A. 1838].

BEDFORD, proposed improvements to BARHAM ESTATE, exhibited at R.A. 1840.

LONDON, THE AMICABLE LIFE ASSURANCE OFFICE, 50 FLEET STREET, 1843; dem. 1911 [exhib. at R.A. 1843; cf. *N. and Q.*, 11th ser., vi, 67].

LONDON, THE PARTHENON CLUB'S LIBRARY, 16 REGENT STREET, 1844; dem. [exhib. at R.A. 1844].[1]

DOVER, improvements on CASTLE HILL, 1847 [exhib. at R.A. 1847].

DOVER, THE PILOT HOUSE, 1848; dem. [*Builder* vi, 1848, 414, with illustration].

DOVER, THE LORD WARDEN HOTEL, 1848–53 [*Civil Engineer* xiv, 519; exhib. at R.A. 1846].

BEECH HILL HOUSE, HIGH BEECH, ESSEX, for Richard Arabin, *c.*1848 [*A.P.S.D.*].

HILLERSDON HOUSE, CULLOMPTON, DEVON, for W. C. Grant, 1848–9 [exhib. at R.A. 1848].

THEDDINGWORTH, LEICS., cottages for 4th Earl Spencer, 1851 [*Associated Architectural Societies' Reports and Papers*, 1850–1, 32].

ASHFORD, KENT, housing estate for South-Eastern Railway Co., 1851 [*A.P.S.D.*].

BONN, GERMANY, addition to UNIVERSITY BUILDINGS [*A.P.S.D.*].

RAILWAY STATIONS for the South-Eastern Railway Co., including part of the terminus at LONDON BRIDGE, 1850–1; dem. 1969 [*A.P.S.D.*].

BEDFORD, FRANCIS OCTAVIUS (1784–1858) was the son of JOHN BEDFORD (1741–1805) of Acton Green, Middlesex, who changed his name from Tubb to Bedford by deed poll in 1785. The father, though described in 1783 as 'upholder', exhibited architectural drawings at the Royal Academy in 1793 and was presumably the author of a volume of architectural drawings in Sir John Soane's Museum (AL 5D) that includes a design for a hospital in Marylebone signed 'J. Bedford' and dated 1793. He evidently designed Bedford House, Bedford Corner, Acton Green, for which there is a drawing on f. 34.

Francis Bedford may perhaps have been a pupil of William Porden, of whose will he was an executor. In 1811–13 he and J. P. Gandy were engaged by the Society of Dilettanti to accompany Sir William Gell as architectural draughtsmen on an expedition to Greece and Asia Minor. Their discoveries were published in 1817 as *The Unedited Antiquities of Attica*, and in 1840 as the third volume of the *Antiquities of Ionia*. [*Historical Notices of the Society of Dilettanti*, 1855, 46–52]. The publication of a further volume was delayed by the death of William Wilkins, and the plates which had been engraved for this purpose

[1] This appears in the R.A. Catalogue as 'The Pantheon Library, erected in Regent Street', but Mr. John Harris informs me that the original drawing is inscribed 'The Parthenon Club House Library'. The Parthenon Club's premises were John Nash's former house at 14–16 Regent Street.

were forgotten until 1912, when their rediscovery led to the publication of part V of the *Antiquities of Ionia* under the editorship of W. R. Lethaby (see *Catalogue of the R.I.B.A. Drawings Collection: B*, 63).

Bedford's recorded architectural works are almost all churches designed for the Parliamentary Commissioners. Four of them are scholarly Greek Revival versions of the St. Martin-in-the Fields formula, with effectively composed steeples rising above a Doric or Corinthian portico. The rest are Gothic and characteristic of the pre-ecclesiological period in which they were built.

Bedford exhibited occasionally at the Royal Academy from 1814 onwards. In the 1820s he was living in Camberwell, where he designed some houses in NORTH TERRACE, PECKHAM ROAD, for a Mr. Spence [Church Building Commissioners, Surveyors' Reports I, 30, *ex inf.* Prof. M. H. Port], but towards the end of his life he moved to Crayland House, nr. Greenhithe, Kent, where he died on 13 March 1858 [Principal Probate Registry, Calendar of Probates]. Many of the drawings that he made in Greece and Asia Minor are in the R.I.B.A. Drawings Collection, together with a sketch-book and notes.

Francis was the father of Francis Bedford, junior (1815–1894), an artist who exhibited drawings of a topographical character at the Royal Academy. [information about the Bedford family from Mr. Lawrence Duttson].

LONDON, ST. GEORGE, WELLS STREET, CAMBERWELL, 1822–4; converted into flats 1992 [Port, 134].

LONDON, ST. JOHN, WATERLOO ROAD, LAMBETH, 1823–4; damaged by bombing 1940–1 [Port, 134] (*Survey of London* xxiii, 32–6).

LONDON, HOLY TRINITY, NEWINGTON, 1823–4; converted into Henry Wood Concert Hall 1973–5 [Port, 136] (*Survey of London* xxv, 109–12).

LONDON, ST. LUKE, WEST NORWOOD, 1823–5; altered by G. E. Street 1870–9 [Port, 134] (*Survey of London* xxvi, 173–4).

LONDON, ST. MARY THE LESS, LAMBETH, 1827–8; dem. 1967, Gothic [Port, 154] (*Survey of London* xxiii, 144).

NEWCASTLE-UNDER-LYME, STAFFS., ST. GEORGE, 1827–8, Gothic [Port, 160].

LONDON, HOLY TRINITY, LITTLE QUEEN STREET, HOLBORN, 1829–31, Gothic; dem. 1910 [Port, 152].

RIDDINGS, DERBYSHIRE, ST. JAMES, 1830–1, Gothic [Port, 142].

HORWICH, LANCS., HOLY TRINITY, 1830–1, Gothic [Port, 148].

TUNSTALL, STAFFS., CHRIST CHURCH, 1830–1; chancel, etc., added 1885; Gothic [Port, 160].

BEDFORD, THOMAS (1772–1817), elder brother of F. O. Bedford (*q.v.*), was also an architect and was presumably the person of this name who was employed as a clerk by Sir John Soane in 1797–8. He subsequently practised in Carmarthenshire, where he designed CARMARTHEN BOROUGH GAOL, 1811; dem. [Carmarthen Corporation Records]; a villa called CAPEL ISA, nr. LLANDEILO for Thomas Lewis, 1811 [Carmarthen Record Office, Mansel-Lewis 1920 and 1590]; and repaired LLANGATHEN CHURCH, 1811 [*ibid.*, Cawdor papers, box 2/74] [all *ex inf.* Mr. Thomas Lloyd]. Bedford died at Great Yarmouth in March 1817 [information from Mr. Lawrence Duttson].

BEGG, JAMES, is known only as the builder and probable designer of Nos. 1–6 GAYFIELD PLACE and 33 GAYFIELD SQUARE, EDINBURGH, 1791 [S.R.O., Edinburgh Sasines, vol. 433, p. 158]. An otherwise unknown architect called William Begg signs some architectural drawings in private possession in Edinburgh. They are dated in the 1820s.

BELASYSE, THOMAS, 4TH VISCOUNT FAUCONBERG (1699–1774), succeeded to the estate of Newburgh Priory, Yorkshire, in 1719. Though brought up a Catholic, he conformed to the Established Church in 1734, and was a Lord of the Bedchamber to King George II. He was made an Earl in 1756. He was responsible for extensive alterations at NEWBURGH PRIORY and, at least in those carried out after a fire in 1757, was evidently his own architect, for on 23 August 1757 he wrote to the Duke of Manchester that he had 'settled the Design for rebuilding the consumed Roomes, which are now copying by a tolerable Draughtsman', and sent him a design for a greenhouse to be built at Kimbolton Castle, Hunts. A portrait by Andrea Soldi at Newburgh Priory shows him holding a plan of the former Dining Room there. [J. Cornforth in *C. Life*, 7, 14 March 1974; letter to Duke of Manchester in Hunts. C.R.O., DDM 49/7, *ex inf.* Mr. R. Hewlings].

BELK, EDWIN, exhibited architectural drawings at the Society of Artists and the Free Society of Artists between 1762 and 1768, and at the Royal Academy between 1772 and 1786. They included an 'Elevation of a tomb for an officer' (1773), an 'Elevation of the principal front designed for the town hall at Bath' (1776) and an 'Elevation of a small villa, designed for a gentleman in Flanders' (1786).

BELL, HENRY (1647–1711), was the son of Henry Bell, a prosperous merchant of King's Lynn in Norfolk. After attending the local Grammar School, Bell went to Caius College, Cambridge, where he took his B.A. degree in 1665. A period of foreign travel followed, in the course of which he visited 'most of the politer parts of Europe'. In 1686, on his father's death, Bell inherited his property in Lynn, and continued his business as a producer and exporter of linseed oil and other commodities. In 1690 he became an alderman, and in 1692 and 1703 served as mayor. In 1702 he thought of standing for Parliament as M.P. for King's Lynn, but was induced to withdraw in favour of Robert Walpole. Bell died on 11 April 1711, aged 64, leaving an ample endowment of land and property to his wife and family. On his monument, formerly in St. Margaret's Church, he was described as *vir ingenii admodum capacis, variis artibus, Picturâ praesertim et Architecturâ instructissimus*. This is borne out by his will (P.C.C. 99 YOUNG), in which he mentions paintings by Holbein, Rembrandt, Heemskerk senior and junior, Goltzius and others, books on painting, sculpture, architecture, mathematics, perspective and surveying, and copper plates, engravings, prints and maps. A small number of engravings signed by Bell are preserved in the British Museum and the Bodleian Library (Gough Maps 24 and 44 and MS. Gough Norfolk 21). They are all topographical in character and portray scenes and buildings in King's Lynn. At the time of his death he left a manuscript which was published posthumously in 1728 as *An Historical Essay on the Original of Painting*, 'by Henry Bell, Architect, late of Lynn-Regis, Norfolk, Esq.' To it is prefixed a brief memoir which is one of the principal authorities for his life.

Like his neighbour, Sir Roger Pratt, Bell was an educated gentleman who took up architecture as a serious pastime, and who had had the benefit of a Grand Tour. According to the author of his memoir his travels 'conduced very much to his Improvement in that particular Science'. 'The Town of Northampton' – he continues – 'which was Rebuilt agreeable to his Plan, and pursuant to his own Direction, is a Testimony sufficient to evince his Masterly Hand in that Noble Science to succeeding Ages. The Place of his Nativity may likewise furnish us with Buildings sufficient to demonstrate the skill of the deceased Architect.'

Further evidence of Bell's responsibility for the rebuilding of Northampton after the fire of September 1675 comes from an entry in Robert Hooke's diary which records his meeting in August 1676 'one Bell from Mr. Francis Morgan, an ingenious architect, . . . a witt', for Francis Morgan was one of the commissioners for rebuilding Northampton, and the purpose of the meeting was no doubt for Hooke to pass on some of his experience in the reconstruction of London after the Great Fire of 1666. The minutes of the commissioners are lost, but a document in the Northamptonshire Record Office records a meeting on 18 January 1676/7 at which it was 'Order'd and Agreed that Mr. Henry Bell and Mr. Edward Edwards, two experienc'd Surveyors now residing in the said Town of Northampton', should be employed as 'managers' for the rebuilding of ALL SAINTS CHURCH, NORTHAMPTON (1677–80). The portico was added in 1701 (presumably to Bell's own designs), and the statue of Charles II in 1711–12. Bell may also have been concerned in the design of the adjoining SESSIONS HOUSE, 1676–88,[1] and it is likely that he was responsible at least for the façades of some of the rebuilt houses (e.g. one that survives on the south side of the Market Place).

Bell's other documented works are all in KING'S LYNN. They comprise the CUSTOMS HOUSE, built in 1683 as an Exchange at the expense of Sir John Turner, for which Bell's responsibility is established by an engraving in which he gave his name as architect; the MARKET CROSS, 1707–10, dem. 1831, an elaborate domed structure inscribed 'HENRICO BELL ARCHITECTO'; and the altarpieces of ST. MARGARET'S and ST. NICHOLAS'S CHURCHES, set up in 1684 and 1704 respectively, but both since removed, the former to North Runcton church [Bodleian, MS. Gough Norfolk 21, f. 101]. To these may probably be added THE DUKE'S HEAD INN built by Sir John Turner *c.*1684; the house of his brother Charles Turner (d. 1711) in the Market Place, destroyed by fire 1768; the conversion of ST. JAMES'S CHAPEL into a Hospital or Children's Home, 1682–3; and NORTH RUNCTON CHURCH, NORFOLK, for whose rebuilding in 1703–13 Bell was one of the trustees. Bell's responsibility for the last building is confirmed by a notebook of the Revd. Thomas Kerrich, an eighteenth-century antiquary who was a native of Norfolk. In a notebook in the Northamptonshire Record Office he lists Bell's works as 'The Market Cross & Shambles, the Custom House, Mr. Baggs's House, Mr.

[1] See, however, pages 334 and 248 for payments to Edwards and C. G. Cibber in connection with the Sessions House.

Mayor's House, [and] some other Houses' at King's Lynn, and 'the Church of North Runcton'. Only stylistic evidence suggests that Bell may perhaps have been concerned in the design of EUSTON CHURCH, SUFFOLK, 1676, the interior of the courtyard at KIMBOLTON CASTLE, HUNTS., *c.*1685 (?), STANHOE HALL, NORFOLK, built in 1703 by Thomas Archdale, a relation by marriage of the Turners of King's Lynn, and NARFORD HALL, NORFOLK, for Andrew Fountaine, 1702–4.

As an architect neither of the Court (like Wren and May), nor of the landed gentry (like Winde and Pratt), but of the mercantile community from which he sprang, Bell has a distinctive place in English architectural history. His style was a vigorous reflection of that of the capital, perhaps with some direct influence from Holland. Jarman's Royal Exchange appears to have been the prototype of his Customs House (designed as an Exchange), Wren's St. Mary-at-Hill of the Greek Cross plans of All Saints, Northampton, and North Runcton Church.

[E. M. Beloe, *King's Lynn: Our Borough, Our Churches*, 1899; H. L. Bradfer-Lawrence, 'The Merchants of Lynn', in *A Supplement to Blomefield's Norfolk*, ed. C. Ingleby, 1929, 156–60; E. B. Chancellor, *Lives of the British Architects*, 1909, 159–62; G. F. Webb, 'Henry Bell of King's Lynn', *Burlington Magazine* xlvii, July 1925, 24–33; J. F. Howes, 'Bell of Lynn: a Contemporary of Sir C. Wren', *R.I.B.A. Jnl.*, 3rd ser., xxxv, 13 April 1929; H. M. Colvin and L. M. Wodehouse, 'Henry Bell of King's Lynn', *Architectural History* iv, 1961; Martin Archdale, 'Henry Bell as a Country House Architect', *C. Life* 15, 29 Sept. 1966.]

BELL, HENRY (1767–1830), best known as the pioneer of steam navigation, was for some years an architect and builder in Glasgow. He was the son of a millwright living at Torphichen Mill, nr. Linlithgow, and was apprenticed to his father. Subsequently he became a pupil of an engineer called Inglis, and then went to London to work for Rennie. In 1790 he settled in Glasgow, and in the following year entered into partnership with James Paterson to form the firm of Bell and Paterson, builders. This lasted until about 1800, when Bell turned his attention to the problems of steam navigation. The only building known to have been designed by him is CARLUKE CHURCH, LANARKS., for which the designs of Henry Bell, 'Architect in Glasgow', were adopted by the Heritors in 1799 [S.R.O., HR 179/1]. It is an unpretentious essay in basic Gothic. [*D.N.B.*; Edward Morris, *The Life of Henry Bell*, 1844.]

BELL, JOHN (–1784), was a builder and architect of Durham. In his *Plans, Elevations and Sections of Noblemen and Gentlemen's Houses* (2nd ed. 1783), James Paine states that Axwell Park, Durham, 'and several other of my designs were carried into execution by Mr. John Bell'. In the 1760s Bell was employed at ALNWICK CASTLE, NORTHUMBERLAND, under Paine's direction [Alnwick MSS. 94, f. 31 and 187A, vol. ii], and in the Yorkshire Archaeological Society's Library (MS. 349) there are sketches of Wressell Castle, Yorkshire, 'by Mr. Bell the architect imploy'd in restoring Alnwick Castle 1765'. His knowledge of Gothic architecture was strikingly demonstrated in 1768, when he was commissioned by the corporation of Alnwick to design THE POTTERGATE TOWER, a remarkably ambitious gate-tower with openwork battlements and a 'crown' supported by flying arches like that of St. Nicholas, Newcastle [G. Tate, *History of Alnwick* ii, 1848–9, 287]. The crown was removed after storm-damage in 1812 and was not replaced. In 1781 Bell designed ST. ANNE'S CHAPEL, BISHOP AUCKLAND, CO. DURHAM, to which a tower was added later by W. Atkinson (*q.v.*) [MS. history of the church in Durham C.R.O., *ex inf.* Mr. D. Findlay]. Bell's burial at the church of St. Mary le Bow, Durham, is recorded in the parish register on 16 Feb. 1784.

BELL, SAMUEL (1739–1813), was the son of John Bell, a wright of Dundee, where he was born on 6 May 1739. He followed his father's trade, but also practised as an architect, and designed most of Dundee's public buildings between 1770 and his death on 23 January 1813 [New Register House, Edinburgh, Dundee Register; *Scots. Mag.* lxxv, 1813, 238]. Though 'provincial and not very up-to-date', he provided Dundee with some attractive buildings in a late Georgian style of basically Palladian character with some Adamesque trimmings [David Walker, *Architects and Architecture in Dundee 1770–1914*, Abertay Historical Society's Publication No. 3, 1955, 4–6].

DUNDEE

ST. ANDREW'S CHURCH, 1772–4 [Town Council Minutes 10 Feb. 1772, *ex inf.* Mr. David Walker].

THE TRADES' HALL, 1776–8; dem. [J. Maclaren, *History of Dundee*, 1874, 184].

THE ENGLISH EPISCOPAL CHAPEL (later UNION HALL), HIGH STREET, 1783–4; dem. 1876 [A. C. Lamb, *Dundee, its Quaint and Historic Buildings*, Dundee 1895, pl. xiii].

ST. CLEMENT'S CHURCH, 1786–8, Gothic; damaged by fire 1841 [Town Council Minutes 15 Jan. 1787, *ex inf.* Mr. David Walker].

attributed: THE SAILORS' HALL or TRINITY HOUSE, YEAMAN SHORE, 1790; dem. 1888 [stylistic attribution, see illustration in *Dundee Delineated*, Dundee 1822, 123].

THE THEATRE ROYAL (now offices), CASTLE STREET, 1807–9 [F. Boyd, *Records of the Dundee Stage*, Dundee 1886, 14].

FORFAR OLD KIRK: Bell was closely involved in the building of this church in 1788–91. In Jan. 1788 John Gibson, 'architect of St. Cyrus', was invited to design a church, but in March a plan submitted by James Millar, mason of Bridgeton, was approved, 'and recommended to Mr. Samuel Bell Architect in Dundee to make out the dimensions for every part of the work'. In 1790 Bell was invited to inspect the old steeple and to receive instructions for a new one. Nothing, however, was done until 1813, when the Town Council 'advertised for contractors for the new steeple to be built to the plans of the late Samuel Bell'. Although the existing steeple built in 1813–14 bears the name of 'Patrick Brown Architect', the design is identical with one of Bell's drawings for the steeple of Monifieth Church, and Brown must only have been the executant [S.R.O., HR 415/3; D. T. Adam, *Review of the Administration of the Town's Affairs by successive Town Councils between 1660 and 1965*, Forfar 1967, 29–30; S.R.O., RHP 7929–32, tracings of drawings of the church made by Bell in 1795].

TANNADICE MANSE, ANGUS, 1797–8 [S.R.O., HR 465/1].

KINNETTLES CHURCH, ANGUS, 1811–12 [advt. in *Dundee Advertiser*, 28 June 1811, *ex inf.* Mr. David Walker].

MONIFIETH CHURCH, ANGUS, 1812, Gothic [drawings in S.R.O., RHP 35188].

BELL, THOMAS, was a Lincolnshire builder. The tower of WELTON-BY-LINCOLN CHURCH, LINCS., bears the date 1768 and the name 'Thomas Bell Builder', while the tower of BASSINGHAM CHURCH, LINCS., is inscribed 'Thomas Bell, Architect, 1783'.

BELL, WILLIAM, designed the classical JUNCTION ROAD CHURCH AT LEITH in 1824–5 [*Junction Road U.P. Church*, by one of the Elders, 1896, 13]. In 1826 he submitted a design for St. Andrew's Place U.P. Church, Leith [*St. Andrew's Place United Presbyterian Church Leith*, 1888, 38].

BELLAS, or **BELLHOUSE,** HENRY (*c.*1724–1777), a master carpenter of Appleby, Westmorland, probably designed, and certainly supervised the building of HILLBECK HALL, nr. BROUGH, WESTMORLAND, for John Metcalfe, 1775–7 [accounts, etc. in Cumbria C.R.O., D. Lons. C 13/1]. The fenestration is in a Gothic manner derived from Batty Langley, and in the main street of Appleby there is a house with virtually identical features which may therefore be attributed to Bellas, who died in 1777, aged 53 [*Trans. Ancient Monuments Soc.* N.S. 32, 1988, 117].

BELWOOD, WILLIAM (1739–1790), was the son of a shoemaker in York. He was apprenticed to a carpenter and took up his freedom in 1761. In 1763–5 he was working at Syon House, Middlesex, under Stiff Leadbetter, the master carpenter employed to carry out Robert Adam's designs there [account in Alnwick Castle archives, U.III. 5]. This presumably brought him to Adam's attention and led to his employment at Harewood House, Yorkshire, where he superintended the execution of Adam's interiors from 1765 onwards. In 1774 he established himself in independent practice in York, advertising in the *York Courant* that 'having conducted several capital buildings under the great masters in architecture, Robert and James Adam, Esquires', he 'proposes making designs for buildings from the plainest to the most elegant . . . also temples and ornamental buildings, bridges, &c . . .'

Belwood's competence as an architectural designer in the Adam manner is demonstrated by the stables at Newby Hall, which in the past have been unhesitatingly attributed to the Adam brothers themselves. Elsewhere his elevations were more in the manner of Chambers than that of Adam, and at Ripley Castle he designed a Gothic building with a classical interior. Belwood died at York on 21 May 1790, aged 50 [Jill Low, 'William Belwood: Architect and Surveyor', *Yorkshire Archl. Jnl.* 56, 1984, where authority will be found for all the following works].

NEWBY HALL, YORKS. (W.R.), the stables for William Weddell, *c.*1777. Belwood was also responsible for heightening the wings, for internal alterations, chiefly to the first floor, and for the lodge and main porch (*C. Life*, 7–14 June 1979).

BURTON LEONARD CHURCH, YORKS. (W.R)., 1779–80; rebuilt 1877–8.

NEWBY (NOW BALDERSBY) PARK, YORKS. (N.R.), alterations to façade, new staircase and remodelling of interior for Thomas Robinson, 2nd Lord Grantham (*q.v.*), 1780–6; interior rebuilt after fire, 1902.

YORK, ALL SAINTS PAVEMENT CHURCH, rebuilt E.

end, 1781–3, Gothic.

NORTON CONYERS, YORKS. (N.R.), stable-block and alterations to house for Sir Bellingham Graham, Bart., 1781–6 (*C. Life*, 9–16 Oct. 1986).

RIPLEY CASTLE, YORKS (W.R.), alterations to house and new Gothic stable-block, for Sir John Ingilby, Bart., 1783–6 (*C. Life*, 13–20 Aug. 1932).

BENETT, JOHN (1773–1852), a Wiltshire country gentleman and M.P., is stated by Sir Richard Colt Hoare to have rebuilt his family seat, PYTHOUSE, nr. TISBURY, WILTS., in 1805 'from his own designs', and also to have erected in the grounds 'an elegant little chapel, copied from the style of a part of Canterbury Cathedral' [R. Colt Hoare, *Modern Wiltshire: Dunworth Hundred*, 1829, 131]. According to some contemporary MS. notes on the 'District round Shaftesbury', 'Mr. Benett . . . arranged his own plans and supervised the execution of them from the beginning to the completion, rising at 5 o'clock every morning for that purpose.' The house is a handsome building in the Palladian tradition with an Ionic portico. The Gothic chapel is now in ruins. Benett is also recorded to have designed a range of stables at STOCKTON HOUSE, WILTS., for Henry Biggs soon after 1800. They are in a traditional style to harmonize with the Jacobean house [Marcus Binney in *C. Life*, 9 Feb. 1984]. Colt Hoare states that the top stage of the central tower of TISBURY CHURCH, WILTS., was designed by Benett's father Thomas (d. 1797), so two generations of the family would appear to have been amateur architects. An estimate 'of the mason's work to execute the plan of the new Tower for Tisbury Church' is preserved among the Benett papers in the Wiltshire Record Office (413/474).

BENHAM, SAMUEL HENRY, was practising in Oxford in 1823, when he designed a coffee-room at ALL SOULS COLLEGE [All Souls MS. CCCC(d), 17 Dec. 1823] and enlarged WESTON-ON-THE-GREEN VICARAGE, OXON. [*V.C.H. Oxon.* vi, 347], but by 1833 he was established in Brighton [*The Watering Places of Great Britain and Fashionable Directory*, Joseph Robins, London 1833]. He altered NEW SHOREHAM CHURCH, SUSSEX, *c.*1829 [I.C.B.S.], and in 1832 designed a Gothic clock-tower intended to be erected in South Street, Worthing, Sussex, but not executed [*Architectural Mag.* i, 1834, 245; cf. *V.C.H. Sussex* vi(i), 117]. He competed for the Houses of Parliament in 1835, submitting a design in the 'collegiate style of the 14th., 15th. and 16th. centuries' as seen at 'Christ Church, Magdalen and New College, Oxford'. His unexecuted design for remodelling the New Buildings at Magdalen College in the Grecian style, is preserved in the College archives.

BENHAM, THOMAS, of Southampton, designed the churches of SHEDFIELD, HANTS., 1829, rebuilt 1875–80, and COPYTHORNE, or NORTH ELING, HANTS., 1834, altered and enlarged by Butterfield in 1891–2 [I.C.B.S.].

BENNISON, APPLETON (*c.*1750–1830), was a mason and architect of Hull, where he died on 25 March 1830, aged 80 [*Gent's Mag.* 1830 (i), 381]. In 1801 he advertised in the *Hull Advertiser*: 'Plans and Elevations drawn at shortest notice; Marble Chimney Pieces and Monuments executed in the neatest manner.' From 1792 to 1810 he was engaged in carrying out works at BRIDLINGTON HARBOUR, and in 1804–5 he rebuilt the bridge over the R. Hull at TICKTON, YORKS. (E.R.), to the designs of William Chapman [*ex inf.* Prof. A. W. Skempton]. In 1800 he contracted to build the REGISTER OFFICE at BEVERLEY, and in 1804–14 he erected the COURT HOUSE and GAOL there to the designs of Charles Watson [G. Poulson, *Beverlac* i, 1829, 426]. His designs for rebuilding ROUTH RECTORY, YORKS. (E.R.), made in 1815, are in the Borthwick Institute at York (MGA 1815/4). In 1819 he designed the ZION CONGREGATIONAL CHAPEL AT COTTINGHAM, YORKS. (E.R.) [*Hull Advertiser*, 1 Oct. 1819]. He refitted the interior of SKIRLAUGH CHURCH, YORKS. (E.R.), in 1819 [*ibid.*, 6 Aug. 1819] and rebuilt the nave of BISHOP BURTON CHURCH, YORKS. (E.R.), in 1820–1 [*V.C.H. E. Riding* iv, 9]. The name of 'Stephen Bennison, Architect', found in a bottle when the chancel (rebuilt 1778) of NORTHALLERTON CHURCH, YORKS. (N.R.), was again rebuilt in 1884, may have been a misreading of 'Appleton' [J. L. Saywell, *History and Annals of Northallerton*, 1885, 221–2]. Two memorial tablets signed by Bennison can be seen in Kirk Ella Church, Yorks. (E.R.).

BENSON, ROBERT, LORD BINGLEY (*c.*1676–1731), was the son of a successful Yorkshire attorney, who left him a substantial estate. In 1702 he entered parliament as member for Thetford and subsequently represented the city of York from 1705 until 1713, when he was elevated to the peerage. At first a Whig, he later became a moderate Tory. As such he was appointed a lord of the Treasury in Harley's government (1710) and was Chancellor of the Exchequer from 1711 to 1713. During the last year of his life he was

Treasurer of the Household to George II.

Benson had the reputation of being an authority on architectural matters. In Edward Oakley's *Magazine of Architecture* (1730) he is bracketed with Lords Burlington and Herbert as noble experts in architecture, and there are many references in contemporary sources to his architectural knowledge. His advice was sought both by Lord Strafford when building Wentworth Castle and by the Duke of Chandos at Cannons. In 1713 it was even rumoured that he was 'to have the care of seeing Whitehall rebuilt'. How far Benson was a practising architect rather than merely a well-informed patron is uncertain: a drawing (in private hands) for remodelling Ledston Hall, Yorks., in Palladian style for Lady Elizabeth Hastings, is inscribed in pencil, 'Lord Bingley's plan for finishing Ledstone', but is almost certainly in the hand of a draughtsman. If, as seems likely, Benson himself designed the country house which he built as BRAMHAM PARK, YORKS. (W.R.), *c*.1705–10, he was an architect of ability. The house is illustrated in *Vitruvius Britannicus* ii, 1717, 81–2, and *C. Life*, 20–27 Feb., 12–19 June 1958.[1] The central block was gutted by fire in 1828 and restored by Detmar Blow *c*.1910. Benson also owned a smaller house called THE NUNNERY at CHESHUNT, HERTS. (dem.), where he was responsible for various improvements to the buildings and garden.

In 1725–6 Benson built himself a house (dem. 1906) on the west side of Cavendish Square which was described by Ralph in 1734 as 'one of the most singular pieces of architecture about town', and by Timbs as 'having the appearance of a Parisian mansion'. From 1773, when it was bought by Lord Harcourt, it was known at Harcourt House, and must not be confused with the house on the opposite side of the square designed by Archer for an earlier Lord Harcourt in *c*.1725.

[*D.N.B.*; G.E.C., *Complete Peerage; The Westminster Abbey Registers*, ed. Chester, 1876, 331; *The Wentworth Papers 1705–39*, ed. J. Cartwright, 1883, 85, 133, 200, 442; C. H. & M. I. Collins Baker, *James Brydges, Duke of Chandos*, 1949, 140–1, 302; T. R. Collick, 'The Patronage of Robert Benson', *Arch. Rev.*, Dec. 1965; D. Linstrum, *West Yorkshire Architects and Architecture*, 1978, 61–4.]

BENSON, WILLIAM (1682–1754), was the eldest son of Sir William Benson, a wealthy iron merchant who was Sheriff of London in 1706–7. As a young man he made a continental tour which included Hanover and Stockholm. When in 1707 he married the daughter of a Bristol merchant, the settlement made by his father included the purchase of lands in Wiltshire to the value of £5000. No house was included, and in February 1708 Benson obtained a 21-year lease of Amesbury Abbey from its owner Lord Bruce [Wilts. Record Office, Antrobus Deeds 283/44, *ex inf.* Dr. T. P. Connor]. However he almost immediately began to build a house for himself on a nearby property of his own. Conceived as a villa, and with a façade directly inspired by Amesbury (then believed to be the work of Inigo Jones), WILBURY HOUSE (*C. Life*, 3–10 Dec. 1959; see also J. Harris, *The Design of the English Country House 1620–1920*, 1985, 112–13) was a remarkably precocious building for its date. According to Colen Campbell, who illustrated it in *Vitruvius Britannicus* i, 1715, pls. 51–2, the house was 'invented and built' by Benson himself. Even if this was polite flattery, Benson was clearly an architectural patron with advanced ideas. He also appears to have been interested in hydraulics. It was the piped water supply with which he provided the inhabitants of Shaftesbury that helped to secure his election as Whig M.P. for that borough in 1715, and in 1716 he ingratiated himself with George I by 'giving directions' for a 'curious waterwork' in the gardens at Herrenhausen in Hanover. As he was 'a favourite of the Germans' at Court, and the author of a well-known anti-Tory pamphlet, Benson was an obvious candidate for preferment by a Whig government, and in 1718 he persuaded the ministry to dismiss the octogenarian Wren from the surveyorship of the Works and appoint himself to the post. The appointment was not, however, to be permanent, for it was to last only 'until the said William Benson shall be in possession of one of the two offices of Auditor of the Imprests and Foreign Accounts' (of which he had obtained a reversionary grant in the previous year).

Benson's surveyorship lasted for fifteen months, in the course of which he sacked his ablest subordinates, declared war on his closest colleagues, infuriated the Treasury and finally brought down upon himself the wrath of the House of Lords for falsely insisting that their Chamber was in imminent danger of collapse. Though apparently the result of incompetence, there is evidence that this extraordinary episode was really a plot on the part of Benson and Colen Campbell (whom he had appointed Deputy Surveyor) to pull down the old Houses of Parliament in order to give them the opportunity to design a magnificent new Palladian building. As it was, the

[1] For the possibility that Thomas Archer was involved in the design of Bramham see G. W. Beard in *C. Life*, 11 Dec. 1958, 1421.

only architectural fruit of Benson's surveyorship was the new state rooms at Kensington Palace (1718–20), which were probably designed by Colen Campbell.

In July 1719 Benson was obliged to relinquish his post, having (to quote Hawksmoor) 'got more in one year (for confusing the King's Works) than Sr. Chris. Wren did in 40 years for his honest endeavours'. Financially he was compensated by the assignment of a considerable debt due to the Crown in Ireland, and after Edward Harley's death in 1735 he enjoyed the profits of the auditorship of the Imprests which he had been promised in 1717. There is some evidence of a continuing interest in architecture. In 1719 Benson was in some way involved in the building of Stourhead House, Wiltshire, by his brother-in-law Henry Hoare to the designs of Colen Campbell, and in 1723 the two men were jointly responsible for the new chancel of the parish church at QUARLEY, HANTS. (a Hoare property), for the Venetian east window is inscribed GUILIELMUS BENSON & HENRICUS HOARE ARM. F[ECERUNT] A.D. 1723. In about 1720 Benson purchased the island of Brownsea near Poole in Dorset and converted the Tudor artillery fort there into a house for himself [Hutchins, *History of Dorset* i, 1861, 650–1]. The character and extent of his alterations have been obscured by later extensions.

In 1734 Benson sold Wilbury to his nephew Henry Hoare II, and retired to Wimbledon, where he died on 2 Feb. 1754, aged 72. A portrait of him hangs in the hall at Stourhead. There is a copy of the sale catalogue of his library in the British Library (S.C.S. 2(4)).

[*D.N.B.*; *History of the King's Works* v, chap. v; K. Woodbridge, *Landscape and Antiquity: Aspects of English Culture at Stourhead*, 1970, 18–21; *Survey of London* i (Bromley-by-Bow), 8–9.]

BENTLEY, JOHN (*c.*1573–1613), *see* AKROYD, JOHN.

BENTLEY, RICHARD (1708–1782), son of Dr. Richard Bentley, the celebrated scholar, has a place in architectural history as a member of the 'Committee of Taste' which superintended the erection of Horace Walpole's Gothic villa at STRAWBERRY HILL, TWICKENHAM, MIDDLESEX. The hall and staircase, the screen in the Holbein Chamber, several chimney-pieces and various other details were designed by him between 1751 and 1761, when he quarrelled with Walpole. His drawings for Strawberry Hill are now in the Lewis Collection at Farmington, Connecticut, U.S.A. They are bound up in a volume which contains a number of other architectural drawings by Bentley, with annotations by Walpole. Among them are a Gothic gateway (not executed) for Dr. Trevor, Bishop of Durham, at Bishop Auckland; 'a Triangular Chinese Building designed for the Rt. Honble. Henry Fox at Holland House' (not executed); a 'Design of a fictitious steeple for Nic. Hardinge, Esq. at Kingston', showing a Gothic spire superimposed on the roof of an existing building; a 'Design of a Chimney in the style of Architecture in the reign of James the first' (probably the one designed for Lord Strafford mentioned by Walpole in his letter to Bentley of 27 March 1755); a 'Design (not executed) of a Gothic Columbarium at the Vine' (cf. Walpole to Montagu, 25 Aug. 1757); and an unexecuted design for a fancifully Gothic farmhouse for Sir Thomas Sebright of Beechwood, Herts.

Several other light-hearted designs of this character, made by Bentley for Walpole's friends, are mentioned in the latter's correspondence. Among those that were executed were a Gothic cloister added to Richard Bateman's villa at OLD WINDSOR, BERKS., subsequently dismantled by Lord Bateman after his uncle's death in 1774 [H. W. to Montagu, 24 Sept. 1762];[1] ST. HUBERT'S PRIORY, a Gothic farm with a steeple for Henrietta, Countess of Suffolk, on her estate at MARBLE HILL, TWICKENHAM, 1758, pulled down after her death in 1767 [drawing at Farmington]; a Gothic monument to Sir Horace Mann's brother Galfridus Mann (d. 1756) in LINTON CHURCH, KENT [H.W. to Mann, 24 Oct. 1758]; a Gothic 'umbrello' in Menagerie Wood, WENTWORTH CASTLE, YORKS., for the 2nd Earl of Strafford, designed 1756, executed 1759, now collapsed, but illustrated in *C. Life*, 25 Oct. 1924, 641, fig. 15 [Walpole to Strafford, 30 Oct. 1759, to Lady Ailesbury, Aug. 1760, and to Montagu, 1 Sept. 1760]; 'a very pretty Gothic room' for the 4th Earl of Holdernesse in Yorkshire, 1760, presumably at HORNBY CASTLE (largely dem.) [H.W. to Montagu, 4 July 1760]; and a Gothic stable at CHALFONT HOUSE, BUCKS., for Lady Mary Churchill, *c.*1760 [*ibid.*].

Bentley was a clever draughtsman rather than an architect, a Georgian Rex Whistler whose decorative talents were equally suited to Gothic follies or to book-illustration. In the latter capacity his principal achievement was

[1] The drawing illustrated by W. S. Lewis in *Metropolitan Museum Studies* v (i), 1934, fig. 18, as a design for the Strawberry Hill cloister is, as Mr. John Harris and Prof. M. J. McCarthy have pointed out, more likely to be a design for the one at Old Windsor.

the set of drawings which he provided to illustrate the first edition of Gray's poems printed at the Strawberry Hill Press in 1753. After his rupture with Walpole he turned his attention to play-writing, but his tragedy, *Philodamus*, was received with laughter; and his comedies seldom lasted for more than two or three nights. Bentley was brought up to no profession, and, having no regular source of income, was constantly in financial difficulties. For several years he was compelled to live abroad, partly in France and partly in Jersey, and among the drawings at Farmington is an unexecuted design for the façade of a town hall at St. Helier, dated 1755. He ended his life in retirement at Westminster. An engraved portrait is reproduced in Cunningham's edition of Walpole's letters, ii (1857), 296.

[*D.N.B.*; the Yale edition of *Horace Walpole's Correspondence*, ed. W. S. Lewis, vol. 35, 1973, 129–272; W. S. Lewis, 'The Genesis of Strawberry Hill', *Metropolitan Museum Studies*, v (i), 1934; John Harris, *A Catalogue of British Drawings for Architecture, Decoration, Sculpture etc. in American Collections*, New Jersey 1971, 19–29 and pls. 15–18.]

BENWELL, SAMUEL, was a nephew of John Plaw, and became a pupil of J. B. Papworth in 1803. His exhibits at the Royal Academy between 1803 and 1817 included 'The lawn front of a cottage, erected for Mr. Vernon, at Crouch End, Hornsey, Middlesex' (1809), a 'Design for a chapel intended to be built in the neighbourhood of Fitzroy Square' (1810) and 'One of a series of designs made for Ombersley Church, Worcestershire, by direction of the Marchioness of Downshire' (1815). Ombersley Church was not in fact built to Benwell's designs, but to those (1825–9) of Rickman and Hutchinson. Benwell's only other recorded work appears to be THE WESLEYAN CHAPEL, BANBURY, OXON., 1811–12 (now a warehouse) [*V.C.H. Oxfordshire* x, 119]. He died young. [W. Papworth, *J. B. Papworth*, 1879, 14, 96.]

BERRY, THOMAS, of Gainsborough, a carpenter by trade, made designs in 1792 for rebuilding GAINSBOROUGH RECTORY, LINCS. [Lincolnshire Record Office, Gilbert's Act Mortgage papers No. 13]. Two or three years later the church of STAINTON-BY-LANGWORTH, LINCS., was rebuilt to his designs [Nottingham University Library, Pierrepont papers, 3337].

BEST, R— H—, exhibited a 'Design for a Police Office and other buildings forming a quadrangle in front of Covent Garden Theatre and opening a view of that structure from a proposed street connecting Waterloo Bridge with Holborn' at the Royal Academy in 1827. A 'Mr. Best' is mentioned in the minutes of the East India Company in April 1807, when it was agreed that alterations should be made to HERTFORD CASTLE (then occupied by the East India College) according to his estimate [*ex inf.* Miss Dorothy Stroud].

BEVANS, JAMES, of London, appears to have specialized in the design of prisons and asylums on Benthamite principles. The *Report of the Committee on Madhouses in England* published by the House of Commons in 1815 (*Parliamentary Papers* 1814–15 (iv)) contains engraved plates drawn by him of a design on the panopticon principle for a proposed London Asylum for the insane, a plan of the Asylum at Guy's Hospital, and a plan of an intended Asylum for Insane Paupers at Wakefield, Yorks. *The Account of all the Gaols, Houses of Correction etc. in England, Wales, Ireland and Scotland* (*Parliamentary Papers* 1819 (vii)) contains 4 plates illustrating his design for a penitentiary for 600 prisoners. In 1818 he exhibited at the Royal Academy a design for 'an octagonal building 86 feet in diameter, with a cast-iron roof, designed for the Chrestomathic day-school to be erected in the city of Westminster'.

BEVANS, JOHN, a Quaker builder and surveyor of Plaistow, Essex, designed a number of buildings for the Society of Friends, including THE DEVONSHIRE HOUSE MEETING HOUSES, CAVENDISH COURT, BISHOPSGATE STREET, LONDON, 1789 [W. Beck & T. F. Ball, *The London Friends' Meetings*, 1869, 376]; THE FRIENDS' RETREAT, FULFORD, YORK, 1794–6, an asylum for the insane run by Quakers and illustrated in S. Tuke, *Description of the Retreat, York*, 1813 [*V.C.H. York*, 471; R.C.H.M., *York* iv, 51]; THE FRIENDS' MEETING HOUSE, ST. HELEN'S STREET, DERBY, 1808 [R.C.H.M., *Nonconformist Chapels and Meeting-Houses in Central England*, 1988, 45]; and THE QUAKER MEETING HOUSE at GUILDFORD, SURREY, 1805–6 [H. Rowntree, *Early Quakerism in Guildford*, 1952, 28–30].

BICKERTON, FRANCIS, of York, was one of the surveyors who examined GAINSBOROUGH CHURCH, LINCS., in 1734–5, and a report condemning the church, signed by him and Francis Smith of Warwick, is in the Record Office at Lincoln (Fac. 9/68). In 1732–3 he was paid a total of £20 for 'directing and supervising the finishing of the Great Room in the Lord Mayor's House', i.e. the MANSION HOUSE, YORK, built in 1725–7 [York City Archives: Chamberlains' Rolls, *ex. inf.* the late Dr. E. A. Gee]. In March 1737/8 'Mr. Bickerton' paid the carver Henry Watson for work at WENTWORTH WOODHOUSE, YORKS (W.R.), on behalf of Lord Malton [Bodleian, MS. Eng. misc. f. 383, fo. 139], and he is again mentioned in connection with works there in 1743 [Sheffield Archives, Wentworth Papers, Letter Book, 2 June 1743]. A person of this name was Clerk of the Works at Richmond (New Park Lodge) from 1749 to 1754, and at the Queen's House, Greenwich, from 1754 to 1768.

BIGGS, RICHARD (–1776), held the post of Clerk of the Works at Windsor Castle from 1745 until his death in 1776. As 'Richard Biggs, Architect', he subscribed in 1739 to part 2 of R. West & H. W. Tom's *Views of All the Ancient Churches in the Cities of London and Westminster.* In 1749 he was one of the arbitrators appointed in connection with a dispute over the repair of Chertsey Bridge [Surrey County Records, Q.S. 5/7, pp. 67–72]. In 1755 Henry Grenville, brother of Lord Temple, told Sanderson Miller that 'Mr. Biggs' had submitted an unacceptably high estimate for a building which he had intended to erect at a place called 'Beechly Mount' that was probably on his property at Shrub Hill near Dorking [Warwickshire C.R.O., CR 125 B/378–9]. Designs by Biggs for additions to a house at HARE HATCH, nr. WARGRAVE, BERKS., for Mrs. Pritchard, dated 1757, are in Sir John Soane's Museum (Drawer 43, v), together with others for Gothic alterations to a house at BRAY, BERKS., for R. Bidleson, dated 1762. With them are three designs for the Countess of Pomfret's remarkable Perpendicular Gothic house in ARLINGTON STREET, LONDON, built 1757–9 (dem. 1920), and attributed by Horace Walpole to Sanderson Miller. As a resident in Arlington Street himself, Walpole is unlikely to have been mistaken, but the derivation from St. George's Chapel, Windsor, of several features of the interior confirms Biggs's involvement in the design, as argued by John Harris in *Georgian Group's Journal*, 1991, 45–9. By his will, dated 10 December 1775, Biggs left a gold ring to Thomas Ripley, senior, and a perspective view of Windsor Castle in straw to Horatio Ripley [P.C.C. 6 COLLIER].

BILBY, WILLIAM (1776–1848), was the founder of a family firm of builders at Melton in Suffolk which continued into the twentieth century. He designed or altered several local parsonage houses, including those of DALLINGHOO, 1832, BREDFIELD, 1836, MARTLESHAM, 1837 and BOYTON, 1846, and also designed small National Schools at BUCKLESHAM, 1844, MELTON, 1845 and DALLINGHOO, 1847. [C. Brown, B. Haward & R. Kindred, *Dictionary of Architects of Suffolk Buildings 1800–1914*, 1991, 39–40.]

BILLING, the name of a family of builders and architects of Reading, of which there appear to have been at least three generations. The founder of the business was RICHARD BILLING I (*c.*1747–1826), who designed ST. MARY'S CHAPEL, CASTLE STREET, READING, 1798–9; portico and chancel added 1840–2 [J. Doran, *History of Reading*, 1835, 170–1]. He was succeeded by his eldest son RICHARD BILLING II (*c.*1785–1853), who evidently became a pupil of Samuel Robinson and D. R. Roper, for it was from their office in Southwark that he exhibited a design for a town hall at the Royal Academy in 1806. Richard Billing II was a prominent figure in the municipal life of Reading in the early nineteenth century, held office as surveyor to the Corporation of which he was a member, and took advantage of his position to further his own interests and those of his clients. It was, for instance, on Corporation land, leased to himself for ninety-nine years on his own valuation, that he built Albion Place as a speculation [*Reading Mercury,* 14 Oct. 1833]. In about 1851 he went bankrupt, and thereafter practised only as a surveyor and valuer. He was killed in a road accident at Watlington on 25 July 1853, in his 69th year [*Gent's Mag.* 1853 (ii), 324]. He had three sons, all of whom were in the architectural profession: RICHARD BILLING III (1814–1884), JOHN BILLING (1816–1863) and ARTHUR BILLING (1824–1896). Richard carried on the family practice in Reading, while John and Arthur both established offices in London. In addition Richard Billing I had a younger son John who died in 1808 aged 20 [*Reading Mercury*, 8 Aug. 1808]. This was the J. Billing of Reading who in 1807 had exhibited at the R.A. a 'Design for a house built in Berkshire'. [information from the late Canon B. F. L. Clarke.]

The following works are by Richard Billing II or III, either independently or in conjunction:

READING, SOUTHAMPTON PLACE, 1813–18 [P. H. Ditchfield, *Reading Seventy Years Ago*, 1887, 6, 81].

READING, ST. GILES'S CHURCH, enlarged and mostly rebuilt by R. Billing and son, 1821–2 [Parish Records].

EAST WOODHAY CHURCH, HANTS., rebuilt 1823, Gothic; chancel added 1850. A tablet on the tower is inscribed 'Rebuilt 1823 Billing

& Son Architects & Builders'.

READING, ALBION PLACE, 1825–35 [*Reading Mercury,* 14 Oct. 1833].

BEENHAM VICARAGE, BERKS., altered or rebuilt, 1826 [Salisbury Diocesan Records].

READING, house in The Butts for Mr. Higgs, 1831 [*Reading Mercury,* 14 Oct. 1833].

BLEDLOW RIDGE, BUCKS., Chapel of Ease, 1834; dem. 1868 [Lipscomb, *History of Bucks.* ii, 1847, 122].

BILLINGTON, a family of architects and builders at Wakefield, of whom the following appear to have been the principal members.

JOHN BILLINGTON (–1773) was Surveyor of Bridges to the West Riding of Yorkshire from 1771 until his death [W. Riding Quarter Sessions Order Books]. He was presumably the carpenter of the same name who was employed at SERLBY HALL, NOTTS., between 1760 and 1773 [Serlby archives, *ex inf.* Dr. Peter Leach], and was probably the J.B. who initialled designs among the Nostell Priory archives [C 3/4/4, 1–3] for building stables and adding wings to THORNTON HALL, THORNTON CURTIS, LINCS., for Sir Rowland Winn of Nostell. Stables more or less corresponding to the drawing were built in 1766, and similar wings were built in 1769 (*C. Life,* 2 Jan. 1986). John Billington, described as a carpenter of Fowlby (on the Nostell estate), signs an undated contract 'to execute and finish the inside of the stables' of HICKLETON HALL, YORKS. (W.R.), for Godfrey Wentworth, 'according to the plan that he hath sent' [Yorkshire Archaeological Soc., Wentworth of Woolley MSS., *ex inf.* Dr. Peter Leach].

JOHN BILLINGTON (*c.*1780–1835), of Wakefield, was a joiner by trade, but in 1812 advertised that he was starting business as a builder and surveyor, and is subsequently described as an architect. He died in February 1835, aged 55 [information from Mr. John Goodchild of Wakefield Library]. He was presumably the architect surnamed Billington who added a portico to the STAFFORD ARMS HOTEL in WAKEFIELD in 1830 [J. W. Walker, *Wakefield* ii, 1939, 530].

WILLIAM BILLINTON may have been the son of John Billington (d. 1835), who had a son William baptized in Sept. 1807, but spelled his name without a 'g'. He practised in Wakefield as an architect and civil engineer from the mid-1830s until the 1850s. In 1834 he exhibited at the Northern Society for the Encouragement of the Fine Arts at Leeds, showing a design for an intended Savings Bank at Wakefield and a 'bird's eye view of the New Cemetery at Leeds' (presumably an unexecuted design for the Woodhouse Cemetery there). He was engineer to the Wakefield Waterworks Company and contractor for a mile of railway through the town [*ex inf.* Mr. John Goodchild]. As an architect he designed the neo-Norman MONK BRETTON CHURCH, YORKS. (W.R.), 1838–9; rebuilt 1877 [I.C.B.S.], the Greek Revival ATHENAEUM in FAWCETT STREET, SUNDERLAND, CO. DURHAM, 1839–41 [W. Fordyce, *History of the County of Durham* ii, 1855, 477], and a row of houses in BOND STREET, WAKEFIELD, called BOND TERRACE, which he built as a personal speculation in 1840 [J. Goodchild, *Wakefield Town Trail,* 1975, 6]. In the extra-illustrated copy of Whitaker's *Loidis and Elmete* in Leeds Public Library there is (vol. ii) a lithograph showing Billinton's unexecuted design for the Proprietary School at Wakefield, submitted in competition in 1833.

BILLINGTON, JOHN, was the author of *The Architectural Director, being an approved guide to architects, draughtsmen, etc. in the study, employment and execution of architecture,* 1829, 2nd ed. 1834, a work of somewhat similar character to Gwilt's *Encyclopaedia of Architecture.* He is described on the title-page as 'of the Royal Academy of Architecture at Paris'. The book received a hostile review in Loudon's *Architectural Magazine* i, 1834, 84, where it is suggested that 'Billington' was a *nom-de-plume.*

BINGLEY, LORD, *see* BENSON, ROBERT.

BINNING, A— M—, signs a perspective drawing dated 1832 showing a castellated design for rebuilding ARDKINGLASS HOUSE, ARGYLLSHIRE, the seat of Sir James Campbell, after its destruction by fire in 1831. The design was not carried out. The author can probably be identified as Alexander Munro Binning, an Edinburgh lawyer who was a member of the Association for the Promotion of the Fine Arts in Scotland. The drawing, formerly at Ardkinglass, is now in the National Monuments Record for Scotland.

BIRCH, J—, of London, appears to have designed GNATON HALL, NEWTON FERRERS, DEVON, for in 1826 he exhibited a 'Villa about to be erected at Gnaton, Devon, for H. R. Roe, Esq.' at the Society of British Artists.

BIRD, JOHN, designed and built the GOLDSMITHS' ALMSHOUSES at HACKNEY, 1705, with a simple pedimented front [T. Longstaffe-Gowan in *Georgian Group Jnl.* 1992, 82–3] and in 1706 built a new Vestry House for the parish of St. Anne & St. Agnes, Gresham Street, London [W. McMurry, *The Records of*

Two City Parishes, 1925, 401]. He was a member of the Brewers' Company.

BIRD, JOHN (1768–1829), of Liverpool, 'was one of those self-taught scholars who are more indebted to native genius than to early instructions'. He began life as a landscape-artist. As early as 1789 he provided a drawing (of Lleweny Hall, Denbighshire) for Angus's *Views of Seats*. In 1810 he joined the Liverpool Academy, and was its secretary in 1810–11. He subsequently practised as an architect and surveyor, but his only recorded work in this capacity appears to be ST. NICHOLAS (R.C.) CHURCH, LIVERPOOL, *c.*1810, Gothic; dem. 1972 [J. A. Picton, *Memorials of Liverpool* ii, 1875, 214]. He was concerned in a publication entitled *The Carpenters' and Joiners' Price Book . . . containing the prices of wood and work . . . with new and useful tables . . . by Isaac Harrison, Robert Jackson, Matthew Nelson, William Potts . . . and examined and approved by John Bird, Architect and Surveyor* (Liverpool, 1811), of which there is a copy in the National Library of Wales (MS. 4982 c). He died at Whitby on 5 February 1829, aged 61. [*Gent's Mag.* 1829 (i), 190; H. C. Marillier, *The Liverpool School of Painters*, 1904, 63–4; information from the late S. A. Harris.]

BIRD, WILLIAM, *see* BYRD, WILLIAM.

BIRKHEAD, BENJAMIN (*c.*1780–1858), was a pupil of Thomas Leverton, to whom he was apprenticed in 1799 [P.R.O., IR 1/37, p. 214]. He exhibited at the Royal Academy in 1805 and 1808. He was elected to the Surveyors' Club in 1807, and was also a member of the London Architectural Society [*Builder* xxi, 1863, 86]. He died in Hans Place, Chelsea, on 7 October 1858, aged 78 [*Gent's Mag.* 1858 (ii), 541].

BISBROWN, CUTHBERT (–1788), was an enterprising builder in Liverpool. In Gore's *Directory* of 1766 he is described as 'builder and cabinet maker', but in 1774 as 'surveyor'. In 1766 he borrowed nearly £12,000 to finance building developments in Liverpool, and in 1771–4 he was the promoter of a scheme for a 'new town' on the Earl of Sefton's estate in Toxteth Park. This was to be called 'Harrington' in compliment to the Countess of Sefton, who was a daughter of the 2nd Earl of Harrington. A church (St. James, Toxteth Park) and a few houses were built, but the scheme ended in failure and Bisbrown's bankruptcy (1776). He was described as 'architect' in the register of St. James's church when he was buried there in February 1788. [J. A. Picton, *Memorials of Liverpool* ii, 1875, 459–61; James Boardman, *Liverpool Table Talk*, 1871, 35; C. W. Chalklin, *The Provincial Towns of Georgian England*, 1974, 110–11; *Gent's Mag.* 1776, 95; register of St. James, Toxteth Park, *ex. inf.* Dr. Janet Gnosspelius.]

BLACK, ALEXANDER (*c.*1701–1761), 'architect', is said by S. Redgrave in his *Dictionary of Artists*, 1878, 43, to have 'attained eminence by his works in Edinburgh, where he practised', and to have died there on 19 February 1761, aged 60.

BLACK, JAMES (–1841), was Town's Architect of Dundee from 1833 until his death. He stated in 1835 that he had been in practice since 1805, but nothing is known of his career before 1817, when he came to Dundee. In 1833 he succeeded David Neave as Town's Architect, but found that he had a serious rival in George Angus of Edinburgh, who (despite Black's intrigues) won both the Reform Street competition of 1832 and the Prison and Bridewell competition of 1833. Though quite an able designer, Black had to be content with the relatively minor commissions listed below. He died on 24 May 1841. [David Walker, *Architects and Architecture in Dundee 1770–1914*, Abertay Historical Society's Publication No. 3, 1955.]

Some of Black's papers are preserved in the Albert Institute at Dundee. They include a design for a *cottage orné* and a study for Somerville Place. In the Kinfauns Estate Office at Rockdale there is an unexecuted design by him for a Gothic burying place for the Gray family in the churchyard at Fowlis Easter, Angus, dated 1819 (photograph at N.M.R.S.).

DUNDEE

ST. GEORGE'S CHURCH, SCHOOL WYND, 1824–5; dem. [Walker, 9].

ST. AIDAN'S CHURCH, BROUGHTY FERRY, 1824–6, Gothic [Walker, 9].

BUILDINGS in W. DOCK STREET, DOCK STREET, SOUTH UNION STREET and CRAIG STREET, 1824–5; dem. [*Dundee Advertiser*, 21 Oct, 1824, *ex. inf.* Mr. David Walker].

CHARLES STREET, tenements for the Dundee Joint Stock Co., 1824–5 [*ibid.*, 4 Nov. 1824].

SOMERVILLE PLACE, Nos. 1–4, 1830 [Walker, 9].

THE HOWFF, BARRACK STREET GATEWAY, 1833–4 [Walker, 11].

U.P. CHURCH, W. BELL STREET (now Regional Music Centre), 1840 [Walker, 11].

Black was also responsible for the layout of

SOUTH COMMERCIAL STREET, 1828; LINDSAY STREET and PANMURE STREET, 1839.

ABROATH, THE ACADEMY or HIGH SCHOOL, 1821 [G. Hay, *History of Arbroath*, 1876, 365].

FORFAR, THE MANSE, 1828 [S.R.O., HR 415/3/2].

GRANGE HOUSE, MONIFIETH, ANGUS, 1829 [Walker, 9].

BLACK, ROBERT (*c.*1800–1869), practised in Glasgow, where from 1843 to about 1854 he was in partnership with James Salmon (1805–1888). According to *The Architect's, Engineer's and Building Trades' Directory* of 1868 he had designed 'upwards of twenty churches' and several banks and warehouses. His earlier works included THE MECHANICS' INSTITUTION, NORTH HANOVER STREET, GLASGOW, 1831 [J. Pagan, *Sketch of the History of Glasgow*, 1847, 186]; THE CITY OF GLASGOW BANK, VIRGINIA STREET, 1838, dem. [J. Pagan, *op. cit.*, 174]; a terrace in ADELAIDE PLACE, BATH STREET, begun 1839 [*The Architect's . . . Directory*, 1868]; and a Grecian monument to Prof. John Dick (d. 1833) in THE NECROPOLIS, 1838, which has Black's signature [J. Pagan , *op. cit.* 184; wrongly attributed to Thomas Hamilton in G. Blair, *Sketches of Glasgow Necropolis*, 1857, 98]. For works designed in partnership with Salmon see T. Gildard in *Trans. Phil. Soc. of Glasgow* xxvi, 1894–5, 121.

BLACKBURN, WILLIAM (1750–1790), was born in Southwark, where his father was a tradesman. His mother was a Spaniard. He was apprenticed to a surveyor, but is said to have 'derived very few advantages' from his instruction. At the age of 19 he competed for the Royal Exchange at Dublin [*Builder* xxvii, 1869, 781]. He became a student at the Royal Academy Schools in 1772, and was awarded the Silver Medal in 1773. In 1775 he exhibited a 'garden seat' and a 'stable building', both 'designed for a gentleman in Surrey'. In 1782 the course of his life was changed by his success in winning the first premium offered by the commissioners appointed to erect prisons under the Penitentiary Act of 1779. In the event these prisons were never built, but Blackburn's success led to numerous commissions to design other prisons. He became intimate with John Howard, the prison reformer, and had the reputation of being the only architect who had Howard's confidence. He was in fact a pioneer of radial planning in prison design, and his prisons incorporated the latest thinking on solitary confinement, segregation, 'useful labour', etc. Their façades were appropriately and effectively designed.

In 1776 Blackburn was appointed Surveyor to the Watermen's Company. He also held the posts of Surveyor to St. Thomas's and Guy's Hospitals, and to the County of Surrey. His career was cut short by his early death, which occurred at Preston in Lancashire on 28 October 1790, while he was on his way to Glasgow to make designs for a new gaol in that city. Some of his commissions were completed by his brother-in-law William Hobson, a Southwark builder with whom he had been closely associated.

[*D.N.B.*; John Chambers, 'Collections for Biography of English Architects' in R.I.B.A. Library; will, P.C.C. 5 BEVOR; obituaries in *Gent's Mag.* 1790, p. 1053, and *Caledonian Mercury*, 9 Dec. 1790; J. Howard, *Account of the Principal Lazarettos in Europe*, 1789; *Report from the Committee of Aldermen appointed to visit several gaols in England*, 1816, 72, 91, 106, 117; Gloucestershire County Records, Q/AG 2–5, 7; T. A. Markus, 'Pattern of the Law', *Arch. Rev.* Oct. 1954; Helen Rosenau, *Social Purpose in Architecture*, 1970, 84.]

PRISONS

OXFORD, THE COUNTY GAOL (in the Castle), begun *c.*1785, completed by Daniel Harris 1805; enlarged 1850–2 [Howard, *Lazarettos*, 170; R. Gardner, *History, Gazeteer and Directory of Oxfordshire*, 1852, 331].

OXFORD, THE CITY GAOL, GLOUCESTER GREEN, 1786–9; enlarged 1870; dem. 1879 [Howard, *Lazarettos*, 171].

LIVERPOOL, THE NEW BOROUGH GAOL, 1786–7; dem. 1855 [*Report from the Committee of Aldermen*, Appendix A, 106].

IPSWICH, SUFFOLK, THE COUNTY GAOL, 1786–90 [*Report from the Committee of Aldermen*, Appendix A, 91; Howard, *Lazarettos*, 155].

SALFORD, LANCS., THE NEW BAILEY PRISON, 1787–90; enlarged 1816; dem. *c.*1872 [record of inscription on foundation-stone in Nostell Priory library; Howard, *Lazarettos*, 206].

NORTHLEACH, GLOS., THE HOUSE OF CORRECTION (now Museum), 1787–91 [J. R. S. Whiting, *Prison Reform in Gloucestershire*, 1975, chap. 12].

LITTLEDEAN, GLOS., THE HOUSE OF CORRECTION (now Record Office), 1787–91 [Whiting, *op. cit.*, chap. 10].

HORSLEY, GLOS., THE HOUSE OF CORRECTION, 1787–91; dem. 1880 [Whiting, *op. cit.*, chap. 13].

BRISTOL, THE GLOUCESTERSHIRE COUNTY BRIDEWELL, LAWFORD'S GATE, 1787–91; destroyed by rioters 1831 [Whiting, *op. cit.*, chap. 11].

GLOUCESTER, THE COUNTY GAOL, 1788–91; enlarged 1845–55 [Whiting, *op. cit.*, chap. 3].

MONMOUTH, THE COUNTY GAOL, 1788–90 [Monmouthshire County Records, QS/MB.: 0003 and C. Bu. 1; Howard, *Lazarettos*, 177].

PRESTON, LANCS., THE COUNTY BRIDEWELL, 1789; governor's house rebuilt 1834 [Howard, *Lazarettos*, 205].

LIMERICK GAOL, IRELAND, *c.*1789 [J. Chambers, *op. cit.*; Howard, *Lazarettos*, 91].

LEWES, SUSSEX, THE HOUSE OF CORRECTION, 1789–93; enlarged 1814; dem. 1967 [E. Sussex Record Office, QAP/2/11 and QAP 12/E12].

DORCHESTER, DORSET, THE COUNTY GAOL, 1789–95 [M. B. Weinstock, 'Dorchester Model Prison 1791–1816', *Procs. Dorset Nat. Hist. and Arch. Soc.* lxxviii, 1956].

EXETER, THE DEVON COUNTY GAOL, 1789–95; dem. 1853 [Devon County Record Office, Gaol Committee Book, 1788–95; Howard, *Lazarettos*, 186n.].

STAFFORD, THE COUNTY GAOL, *c.*1789–93 [*V.C.H. Staffs.* vi, 204].

DUBLIN, alterations to the NEWGATE GAOL; dem. *c.*1880 [*D.N.B.*].

OTHER BUILDINGS

LONDON, WATERMEN'S HALL, ST. MARY AT HILL, 1778–80 [H. Humpherus, *History of the Watermen's Company* ii, n.d., 321 *et seq.*] (*C. Life*, 14 Nov. 1974, 1488).

CAMBERWELL, NO. 154 DENMARK HILL, for Edward Henshaw, 1785–6 [J. Edwards, *A Companion from London to Brightelmston*, 1801, Part I, 17, § xviii] (*Survey of London* xxvi, 146–9, pls. 52–3).

BRISTOL, THE UNITARIAN CHAPEL, LEWIN'S MEAD, 1788–91 [W. Ison, *The Georgian Buildings of Bristol*, 1952, 81–4].

LONDON, GUY'S HOSPITAL, SOUTHWARK, alterations, *c.*1788 [Howard, *Lazarettos*, 136].

BLOGG, WILLIAM (1767–1815), was the son of Samuel Blogg, a bricklayer of Norwich. In 1791, at the age of 24, he entered the Royal Academy Schools, winning the Silver Medal in 1792. For a short time in 1791 he was a pupil of Sir John Soane, but in 1793 he was in James Wyatt's office. For a few years he practised in London, exhibiting at the Academy a 'Design for improving the front of Heatherton House' (either Heatherden House, nr. Hurst Green, Sussex, or Heatherton Park, Somerset) (1797), a 'Design for the east front of a new street at Brighton' (1797) and 'Designs for cottages for Sir Christopher Hawkins' of Trewithen, Cornwall (1798). In 1802 he went bankrupt [*European Mag.* 1802], and in August 1803 he was back in Norwich advertising his services as an 'Architect and Surveyor' [*Norwich Mercury*, 6 Aug. 1803]. In 1807–8 he supervised repairs to the town walls and the demolition of several of the medieval gateways [Norwich City Archives, Minutes of the Tonnage Committee]. He died in All Saints parish in April 1815 [*Norfolk Chronicle*, 15 April 1815, *ex inf.* Mr. David Cubitt].

BLONDEL, GEORGES FRANÇOIS (*c.*1730 – after 1791), was the son of Jacques François Blondel (1705–74), best known as the author of several important architectural books, and as the founder of a celebrated École des Arts in Paris. After a training in his father's school Georges spent some time in Rome before returning to Paris to teach architecture and drawing. He arrived in London in about 1764, the year he signed a red chalk view of the interior of St. Paul's Cathedral, now at the Courtauld Institute. He exhibited various works, chiefly mezzotints, at the Society of Artists and the Free Society in 1765–7 and 1774, and in 1772 held an exhibition of his architectural and other designs in Covent Garden. The printed catalogue shows that he hoped to establish a school of design on the lines of his father's Parisian establishment, but nothing came of the project, and Blondel appears to have returned to France in 1774, the date of his father's death. He himself died some time after 1791. During his stay in England Blondel was employed by Lord Temple at STOWE HOUSE, BUCKS., making a number of designs for which he claimed payment in 1774 (B.L., Add. MS. 41136, ff. 6–7). Few of them were executed, but he may have remodelled Gibbs's Lady's (now Queen's) Temple. What appear to be some of Blondel's original drawings for Stowe remain in an extra-illustrated copy of Lysons' *Buckinghamshire* belonging to the late Capt. R. W. Morgan-Grenville. [Campbell Dodgson, 'The Mezzotints of G. F. Blondel', *Print Collector's Quarterly* ix, 1922, 303–14; Jeanne Lejeaux, 'G. F. Blondel, Engraver and Draughtsman', *ibid.*, 1936, 260–77; John Harris, 'Blondel at Stowe', *Connoisseur*, March 1964; Laurence Whistler & others, *Stowe, a Guide to the Gardens*, 1968; Michael McCarthy, 'The Rebuilding of Stowe House, 1770–1777', *Huntington Library Quarterly* xxxvi, 1973.]

BLORE, EDWARD (1787–1879), was the eldest son of Thomas Blore, F.S.A., a lawyer of antiquarian tastes. His early years were spent at Stamford, where he developed the enthusiasm for Gothic architecture and the skill as a topographical artist that remained with him for life. Before he was 20 he had drawn the illustrations for his father's *History of Rutland* (1811), and he was afterwards employed to make the architectural drawings for many other topographical works, such as Surtees' *Durham*, Baker's *Northamptonshire* and Clutterbuck's *Hertfordshire*. He was also employed by John Britton to make the drawings of York and Peterborough for his *Cathedrals* series, and for portions of his *Architectural Antiquities*. Among his early acquaintances were Sir James Hall, whose *Essay on the Origin, History and Principles of Gothic Architecture* (1813) he helped to illustrate, and Thomas Rickman, with whom he corresponded. In 1816 he was introduced to Sir Walter Scott, who was about to rebuild Abbotsford with the help of the architect William Atkinson. Blore made some sketches which pleased Scott 'as being less Gothic & more in the old fashioned Scotch stile' than Atkinson's. Both plan and execution remained, however, in Atkinson's hands and Blore was only one of several contributors to the final design. He cannot therefore be regarded in any strict sense as the architect of Abbotsford. The principal result of Blore's friendship with Scott was his employment as 'manager' of *The Provincial Antiquities and Picturesque Scenery of Scotland*, a work for which he provided all the architectural drawings. Owing to Scott's financial difficulties, only two volumes were issued (1819–26). In 1824–6 Blore published his best-known work, *The Monumental Remains of Noble and Eminent Persons*, containing a fine collection of engravings of medieval brasses and effigies.

By the 1820s Blore had made the transition from an antiquarian draughtsman to a practising architect. How he acquired his practical knowledge of building construction is not clear, but he soon gained the reputation of being a thoroughly trustworthy architect whose estimates were to be relied upon. It was his reputation as 'the cheap architect' that led in 1832 to his employment by the government to complete Buckingham Palace after Nash's extravagance had caused his dismissal. Although never a member of the Office of Works, Blore was also employed to carry out various works at Windsor Castle and Hampton Court. From 1827 to 1849 he was surveyor to Westminster Abbey, where he refitted the choir and rescued the thirteenth-century retable from misuse. He was a Fellow of the Society of Antiquaries and of the Royal Society, and was one of the founders of the Royal Archaeological Institute. In 1834 Oxford gave him an honorary D.C.L., but he refused the knighthood which he was offered on the completion of his work at Buckingham Palace.

Energetic and reliable, Blore built up an extensive practice both as a country-house architect and as a designer and restorer of churches. The 'Tudor' and 'Elizabethan' styles were his speciality, and the elevations of nearly all his numerous country houses were based on his studies of fifteenth- and sixteenth-century domestic architecture. As a church architect he experimented with the Romanesque and the Early English, but was more at home with the Decorated and the Perpendicular. He rarely used the Greek or Roman orders, which were then normal for civic or commercial building,[1] and most of his public commissions were for buildings such as schools for which the 'Tudor Collegiate' style was appropriate. Although his knowledge of medieval precedent was probably quite as extensive as Pugin's, Blore lacked the genius which might have transformed his antiquarian expertise into living architecture. A dull competence pervades all his work, and none of his churches count for much in the history of the Gothic Revival. Indeed, the *Ecclesiologist* considered him to be 'entirely unacquainted with the true spirit of Pointed Architecture' (vol. iii, 1843, 99, 2nd ed.).

Blore gave up practice in 1849, but lived on in retirement until his death at his house in Manchester Square on 4 September 1879 at the age of 91. He left 48 volumes of antiquarian drawings, now in the British Library (Add. MSS. 42000–42047), 'the result of more than seventy years' unremitting labour', and including 'almost every example of ancient castellated and domestic architecture remaining in England'. Other drawings are in the Society of Antiquaries' Library and the R.I.B.A. Drawings Collection, but the principal collection of his architectural designs is in the Print Room of the Victoria and Albert Museum. Account-books recording most of his commissions as an artist and architect from 1817 onwards are in Cambridge University Library (Add. MSS. 3954–3956), together with separate volumes relating to his principal architectural works (Add. MSS. 3922–3953) and some letters from his clients (Add. MS. 8170). Letters to Blore from his publishers and others are in the John Rylands Library at Manchester (MS. 1305), together with his own memoirs of Sir Walter Scott (MS. 1257).

F. C. Penrose (1817–1903), Frederick Marrable (1818–72), Henry Clutton (1819–

[1] His only considerable classical works were Buckingham Palace and Haveringland Hall, Norfolk.

93), William Mason (1810–97), George Moore (*q.v.*) and William Burges (1827–81) were among his pupils.

Portraits of Blore are reproduced in *Illustrated London News* lxxv, 1879, 280, *C. Life*, 14 Dec. 1945, 1058, and *The History of the King's Works* vi, pl. 5. A reputed portrait by William Hilton, R.A., at the University Press, Cambridge, is reproduced by E. A. Crutchley, *History and Description of the Pitt Press*, 1938, 8. A bust by John Ternouth (1845), formerly at the same institution, was transferred to Abbotsford in 1969.

[Obituaries in *Proceedings of the Society of Antiquaries*, 2nd ser., viii, 1879–81, 347–52, and *Builder* xxxvii, 1879, 1019; C. L. Eastlake, *History of the Gothic Revival*, 1872, 138–41; *D.N.B.*; *Three Howard Sisters*, ed. Maud, Lady Leconfield & J. Gore, 1955, 156; *Catalogue of the R.I.B.A. Drawings Collection: B*, 90–93; correspondence with Sir Walter Scott in N.L.S., especially MSS. 3029 and 3134, no. 172.]

PUBLIC BUILDINGS, ETC.

LONDON, THE CHARTERHOUSE, PREACHER'S and PENSIONERS' COURTS, 1825–30 [W. J. D. Roper, *Chronicles of Charter House*, 1847, 168–9].

OXFORD, completed north wing of UNIVERSITY PRESS, WALTON STREET, 1829–30, classical [*V.C.H. Oxon.* iii, 57].

WOBURN, BEDS., MARKET HOUSE for 6th Duke of Bedford, 1830 [*Description of Woburn and its Abbey*, Woburn 1845, 108].

WARMINSTER, WILTS., TOWN HALL and buildings on opposite corner, 1830 [*V.C.H. Wilts.* viii, 95].

WILTON, WILTS., ST. MARY MAGDALENE'S HOSPITAL, 1831–2 [drawings at Wilton House; C.U.L., Add. MS. 3954, f. 65[v]].

CAMBRIDGE, THE PITT PRESS, 1831–2 [Willis & Clark, iii, 140–44; R.I.B.A.D.].

OXFORD, WADHAM COLLEGE, alterations to Warden's Lodgings, new entrance gates, etc., 1832 [T. G. Jackson, *Wadham College, Oxford*, 1893, 125, 147].

RETFORD, NOTTS., TRINITY HOSPITAL, 1832–3 [A. Jackson, *History of Retford*, Retford 1971, 69; R.I.B.A.D.; C.U.L., Add. MS. 3954, f. 61[v]].

BEDFORD, principal front of THE ENGLISH (later the COMMERCIAL, then the MODERN) SCHOOL, HARPUR STREET, 1833–37 [J. Godber, *The Harpur Trust 1552–1973*, 1973, 39; R.I.B.A.D.].

GREENOCK, THE WATT INSTITUTION AND GREENOCK LIBRARY, UNION STREET, 1835–7; completed 1846 [*N.S.A.* vii, 423; R.I.B.A.D.].

TAVISTOCK, DEVON, THE GRAMMAR SCHOOL, for 6th Duke of Bedford, 1837 [J. C. Loudon, *Gardener's Mag.* xviii, 1842, 550].

OXFORD, MERTON COLLEGE, reconstructed entrance tower, 1837–8 [A. Vallance, *The Old Colleges of Oxford*, 1912, 21, 23].

OXFORD, SHELDONIAN THEATRE, new cupola, 1837–8 [Gardner's *History, Gazeteer and Directory of Oxfordshire*, 1852, 248; C.U.L., Add. MS. 3956, f. 42].

PENN, BUCKS., THE GIRLS' SCHOOL, for 1st Earl Howe, 1838–9 [C.U.L., Add. MS. 3956, f. 59[v]].

MANCHESTER, offices for the Bridgewater Trust, 1840 [C.U.L., Add. MS. 3955, f. 16].

CHELSEA, ST. MARK'S TRAINING COLLEGE, STANLEY GROVE, 1843–7, 'Byzantine' and 'Norman' styles [*Survey of London* iv, 44].

MARLBOROUGH COLLEGE, WILTS., new buildings, including Chapel (dem. 1884), Dining Hall, Master's Lodge, A House and B House, 1845–8 [A. G. Bradley & others, *History of Marlborough College*, 1893, 83, 104].

LONDON, DEAN'S YARD, WESTMINSTER, enlarged offices of Queen Anne's Bounty, 1847–8 [C.U.L., Add. MS. 3955, f. 86].

DOMESTIC ARCHITECTURE

ABBOTSFORD, ROXBURGHSHIRE, for Sir Walter Scott, contributed ideas for external treatment of house designed by W. Atkinson 1816–23 [*The Letters of Sir Walter Scott*, ed. H. J. C. Grierson, iv, 1932, 289, 333–7, 339, etc.; N.L.S., MS. 3029].

COREHOUSE, LANARKSHIRE, for George Cranstoun, Lord Corehouse, 1824–7 [J. M. Leighton, *Select Views on the River Clyde*, 1830, 17; R.I.B.A.D.].

FREELAND HOUSE, PERTHSHIRE, remodelled for 6th Lord Ruthven, 1825–6 [C.U.L., Add. MS. 3954, ff. 45[v], 53[v]–54; perspective in R.I.B.A.D.]. This house is given to W. Burn in *R.I.B.A. Trans.* 1869–70, and drawings at N.M.R.S. indicate that he was concerned in its building, but as Blore made some 50 working drawings for Freeland he must be regarded as its principal architect.[1]

WESTON HOUSE, nr. LONG COMPTON, WARWICKS, for Sir George Philips, Bart., 1826–30; dem. 1932 [Warwicks. C.R.O., Philips papers, Box 25; exhib. at R.A. 1828; R.I.B.A.D.].

CANFORD MANOR, nr. WIMBORNE, DORSET, re-

[1] In Sept. 1830 Burn complained to Rickman (then in Edinburgh) 'of Blore for supplanting him in some places'. No doubt Freeland was one of them.

constructed for William Ponsonby, cr. Lord de Mauley, 1826–36; afterwards much altered and enlarged by Sir Charles Barry [Eastlake; C.U.L., Add. MSS. 3922–6; R.I.B.A.D.].

GOODRICH COURT, HEREFS., for Sir Samuel Rush Meyrick, 1828–31; altered and enlarged *c.*1880; dem. 1950 [Eastlake; C.U.L., Add. MS. 3927; V. & A. 182 r; R.I.B.A.D.; H. Meller, 'The Architectural History of Goodrich Court', *Trans. Woolhope Naturalists' Field Club* xlii (2), 1977].

NORMAN COURT, HANTS., unspecified work for C. B. Wall, 1829 [C.U.L., Add. MS. 3954, f. 72].

LAMBETH PALACE, rebuilt residential wing, converted Great Hall into Library and remodelled Chapel (to which he added a stone vault), for Archbishop William Howley, 1829–48 [C.U.L., Add. MSS. 3928–34; V. & A. 182 o; R.I.B.A.D.; *Survey of London* xxiii, 81–103].

ST. ASAPH, N. WALES, enlarged BISHOP'S PALACE for Bishop William Carey, 1830–1 [C.U.L., Add. MS. 3935; V. & A. 182 s; R.I.B.A.D.].

KEELE HALL, STAFFS., stables (now Principal's House) and alterations to house for Ralph Sneyd, 1830–3 [C.U.L., Add. MS. 3955, ff. 5–6; C. Hussey in *C. Life*, 14 Jan. 1960].

MOUNTEVIOT, CRAILING, ROXBURGHSHIRE, new house for 7th Marquess of Lothian, begun *c.*1830 but never completed [C.U.L., Add. MS. 3954, f. 71v; R.I.B.A.D.].

MIDDLETON PARK, MIDDLETON STONEY, OXON., lodge for 5th Earl of Jersey, *c.*1830 [C.U.L., Add. MS. 3955, f. 4v].

BUCKINGHAM PALACE, LONDON, completed palace designed by J. Nash, 1832–7, adding attic on garden front; converted S.E. conservatory into Chapel 1842–3; added E. wing facing Mall (refronted by Sir Aston Webb 1913), 1847–50 [M. H. Port in *History of the King's Works* vi, 277–92].

ISLEWORTH (now NAZARETH) HOUSE, MIDDLESEX, for Sir William Cooper, 1832 [W. Keane, *Beauties of Middlesex*, 1850, 66; C.U.L., Add. MS. 3939].

CROSBY HALL, BISHOPSGATE, LONDON, repaired Great Hall, *c.*1832 [H. J. Hammon, *The Architectural Antiquities of Crosby Place, London*, 1844, 12].

MERTON HALL, NORFOLK, repairs for 4th Lord Walsingham, 1832–5 and enlarged for 5th Lord Walsingham, 1846–8; mostly destroyed by fire 1956 [*Proc. Soc. Antiq.*, obituary; C.U.L., Add. MSS. 3937–8; R.I.B.A.D.].

CROM, or CRUM, CASTLE, CO. FERMANAGH, IRELAND, for 3rd Earl of Erne, 1832–8, and repaired to original designs after major fire in 1841 [*Proc. Soc. Antiq.*, obituary; R.I.B.A.D.; G. Jackson-Stops in *C. Life*, 26 May, 2 June, 1988].

VALE ROYAL, CHESHIRE, rebuilt S.E. wing for 1st Lord Delamere, 1833–4 [C.U.L., Add. MS. 8170, no. 49; MS. account of alterations at Vale Royal since 1810, formerly at Vale Royal].

HINCHINGBROOKE, HUNTS., reconstruction after fire (1830) for 7th Earl of Sandwich, 1833–6 [C.U.L., Add. MS. 3956, f. 31; *V.C.H. Hunts.* ii, 136] (*C. Life*, 6–13 April 1929).

LATIMERS, CHESHAM, BUCKS., rebuilt for the Hon. Charles Compton Cavendish, afterwards Lord Chesham, 1834–8 [C.U.L., Add. MS. 3936; R.I.B.A.D.; G. G. Scott, *Recollections*, 1879, 51; B. Burgess, 'Latimer', *Records of Bucks.* vi, 1887, 35].

OTFORD COURT, SHOREHAM, KENT, for H. St. J. Mildmay, 1834–8; dem. *c.*1955 [C.U.L., Add. MSS. 3940, 3956, f. 32].

PULL (now WELLS) COURT, BUSHLEY. WORCS., for the Revd. E. C. Dowdeswell, 1834–9 [C.U.L., Add. MSS. 3942–3; R.I.B.A.D.].

GOPSALL HALL, LEICS., alterations to offices for 1st Earl Howe, 1835; dem. 1951 [C.U.L., Add. MSS. 3944, 3956, f. 35].

KIRKLANDS, ANCRUM, ROXBURGHSHIRE, for John Richardson, *c.*1835; rebuilt 1907–8 [C.U.L., Add. MS. 3956, f. 30; R.I.B.A.D.; *N.S.A.* iii, 1845, 245].

ESCRICK PARK, YORKS. (E.R.), repairs and alterations for Lord Wenlock, *c.*1835 [C.U.L., Add. MS. 3955, f. 7v; *Proc. Soc. Antiq.*, obituary]; cf. R.I.B.A.D. for an unexecuted scheme for further alterations *c.*1839.

CHILLINGHAM, NORTHUMB., estate cottages, etc. for 6th Earl of Tankerville, *c.*1836 [drawings in Tankerville papers, Northumb. C.R.O.; C.U.L., Add. MS. 3956, f. 22].

CASTLE UPTON, CO. ANTRIM, IRELAND, enlarged for 1st Lord Templetown, 1836–7 [C.U.L., Add. MS. 3956, f. 41; V. & A. 182 s].

HARLAXTON MANOR, LINCS. Blore's accounts [C.U.L., Add. MS. 3956, f. 47] show that in 1837 he was employed by Gregory de Ligne Gregory 'to examine the state of the house and arrange plans for carrying on the work'. The house had been begun in 1831 to the designs of Anthony Salvin, but he was dismissed in 1837. Blore's association with the house was brief, for in 1838 William Burn (*q.v.*) took over: cf. *Civil Engineer and Architect's Jnl.* ii, 1839, 39 (where Blore's role is stated to have been advisory only), *C. Life*, 11 April 1957, and C. Hussey, *English Country Houses: Late Georgian*, 1958, 242, where, however, Gregory

Gregory (d. 1860) is confused with his father George (d. 1822).

MALLOW CASTLE, CO. CORK, IRELAND, design for adding a tower for D. Jephson, 1837 [C.U.L., Add. MS. 3956, f. 49].

COMBERMERE ABBEY, CHESHIRE, stables for 1st Viscount Combermere, 1837 [C.U.L., Add. MS. 3956, f. 19].

DORFOLD HALL, CHESHIRE, chimney-pieces in drawing- and dining-rooms for Revd. James Tomkinson, 1837–8 and 1843; since removed [C.U.L., Add. MS. 3955, f. 8v] (*C. Life*, 31 Oct. 1908).

BALLYDRAIN, CO. ANTRIM, IRELAND, for Hugh Montgomery, 1837–8; damaged by I.R.A. *c.*1972 [C.U.L., Add. MS. 3956, f. 40; V. & A. 182 r].

MILTON ABBOT VICARAGE, DEVON, for the Revd. S. L. Hammick, 1837–8 [C.U.L., Add. MS. 8170, f. 5].

LODSWORTH HOUSE, SUSSEX, for Hasler Hollist, 1837–8 [C.U.L., Add. MS. 3947; V. & A. 182 r].

CREWE HALL, CHESHIRE, repairs and alterations for 3rd Lord Crewe, 1837–43; interior destroyed by fire 1866 and rebuilt by E. M. Barry [C.U.L., Add. MSS. 3945–6; R.I.B.A.D.; *Proc. Soc. Antiq.*, obituary].

ALOUPKA, CRIMEA, villa for Prince Michael Woronzow, 1837–40 [R.I.B.A.D.; V. & A. 182 q; *Builder* viii, 1850, 354–5; J. Mordaunt Crook in *C. Life*, 2 March 1972].

SYDNEY, NEW SOUTH WALES, AUSTRALIA, GOVERNOR'S HOUSE, 1837–45 [J. M. Herman, *The Early Australian Architects and their Work*, 1954, 202–3, 219–20; R.I.B.A.D.].

RAMSEY ABBEY, HUNTS., remodelled for Edward Fellowes, 1838–9 [*Proc. Soc. Antiq.*, obituary; C.U.L., Add. MS. 3949] (*V.C.H. Hunts.* ii, 192–3).

MEREVALE HALL, WARWICKS., for W. S. Dugdale, 1838–44 [*Proc. Soc. Antiq.*, obituary; V. & A. 182 f and g) (*C. Life*, 13–20 March, 1969).

HAMPTON COURT PALACE, MIDDLESEX, restoration works, 1838–48 [M. H. Port in *History of the King's Works* vi, 333–5].

CONINGTON CASTLE, HUNTS., internal alterations for J. M. Heathcote, 1839–40 [C.U.L., Add. MS. 3956, f. 58v; *V.C.H. Hunts.* iii, 145].

BOTLEYS, nr. CHERTSEY, SURREY, alterations for Robert Gosling, 1839–40 [C.U.L., Add. MS. 3956, f. 60v].

STOWE HOUSE, BUCKS., designed LAMPORT and WATER STRATFORD LODGES, rebuilt BELL GATE, remodelled BOURBON TOWER and carried out minor alterations to house for 2nd Duke of Buckingham, 1839–43 [drawings and bills in Stowe papers, Huntington Library, San Marino, California, *ex inf.* Mr. Gervase Jackson-Stops].

CAPESTHORNE HALL, CHESHIRE, remodelled 1839–42 for Edward Davies Davenport; damaged by fire 1861 and rebuilt by A. Salvin 1865–8 [*Proc. Soc. Antiq.*, obituary] (*C. Life*, 1–8 Sept. 1977).

HAVERINGLAND HALL, NORFOLK, for Edward Fellowes, 1839–43; dem. 1946, 'Grecian' [*Proc. Soc. Antiq.*, obituary; accounts in Norfolk Record Office; V. & A. 182 d] (J. H. Mason, *Norfolk Photographically Illustrated*, 1865).

WISTON PARK, SUSSEX, alterations for Charles Goring, *c.*1840–3 [V. & A. 182 i; C.U.L., Add. MS. 3956, f. 70].

SHADWELL PARK, NORFOLK, S. wing for Sir Robert John Buxton, *c.*1840–3 [C.U.L., Add. MSS. 3950–1; V. & A. 182 e; B.L., Add. MS. 42027, ff. 92–3] (*C. Life*, 2–9 July 1964).

WORSLEY NEW HALL, LANCS., for Lord Francis Egerton, 1840–5; dem. 1945–6 [C.U.L., Add. MS. 3951; drawings and account in R.I.B.A.D.] (*Builder* viii, 1850, 270–1).

WORSLEY PARSONAGE, LANCS., for Lord Francis Egerton, 1841–3 [C.U.L., Add. MS. 3951].

THE GROVE, WATFORD, HERTS., repairs for 4th Earl of Clarendon, 1841–2 [C.U.L., Add. MS. 3955, f. 12v; *Proc. Soc. Antiq.*, obituary].

COOLHURST, nr. HORSHAM, SUSSEX, additions for C. S. Dickens, 1841–4 [C.U.L., Add. MS. 3955, f. 26v].

GREAT MORETON HALL, CHESHIRE, for G. H. Ackers, 1841–6 [Ormerod, *History of Cheshire*, ed. Helsby iii, 1875, 46; V. & A. 182 b] (P. de Figuereido & J. Treuherz, *Cheshire Country Houses*, 1988, 103–6).

WINDSOR CASTLE, BERKS., alterations to Upper Ward for Queen Victoria, 1841–7, and reconstructed Lodgings of Military Knights in Lower Ward, 1840–7 [M. H. Port in *History of the King's Works* vi, 392–3; W. H. St. J. Hope, *Architectural History of Windsor Castle*, 1913, 533, 567, etc.].

HATCHFORD, nr. COBHAM, SURREY, remodelled for Lord Francis Egerton, 1842–3; dem. [C.U.L., Add. MS. 3955, ff. 24, 79].

CASTLE HILL, DEVON, additions for 2nd Earl Fortescue, 1842–5 [*Proc. Soc. Antiq.*, obituary; C.U.L., Add. MS. 3955, f. 27] (*C. Life*, 17–24 March 1934).

WILLERSLEY CASTLE, DERBYSHIRE, alterations for Peter Arkwright, 1843 [C.U.L., Add. MS. 3955, f. 43].

CRAKAIG, SUTHERLAND, sketch design for 2nd Duke of Sutherland, 1843, executed 1845 [Staffs. R. O., Leweson-Gore MSS., K.1. 10-4; C.U.L., Add. MS. 3955, f. 43].

KINGSTON HALL, NOTTS., for 1st Lord Belper, 1843–5 [C.U.L., Add. MS. 3952].

THICKET PRIORY, YORKS. (E.R.), for the Revd. Joseph Dunnington-Jefferson, 1844–7 [*Proc. Soc. Antiq.*, obituary; drawings in B.L., Add. MS. 47,610; C.U.L., Add. MS. 3955, f. 45].

NORTH MIMMS PARK, HERTS., alterations, including new entrance hall and staircase, for Fulke Greville, 1845–6 [C.U.L., Add. MS. 3955, f. 50].

THE FRYTHE, nr. WELWYN, HERTS., for William Wilshere, 1845–6 [*Proc. Soc. Antiq.*, obituary; C.U.L., Add. MS. 3955, f. 51].

HECKFIELD PLACE, HANTS., alterations for Charles Shaw Lefevre, 1847; dem. [C.U.L., Add. MS. 3955, f. 75].

CHURCHES

WINCHESTER CATHEDRAL, organ case in choir, 1824 [Eastlake, 140; cf. Blore's printed *Report to the Dean of Winchester on the proposed removal of the organ from the side to the centre of the Cathedral*, 1823].

BATTERSEA, ST. GEORGE, 1827–8; chancel added 1874; dem. [Port, 150–1; V. & A. 182 o].

PLAISTOW, ESSEX, ST. MARY, 1828–9; dem. 1889 [Port, 144–5; R.I.B.A.D.].

PETERBOROUGH CATHEDRAL, refitted choir 1828–32; Blore's stone organ-screen dem. and stalls removed to St. Dominic's R.C. Church, Newcastle-upon-Tyne, 1890s [*A.P.S.D.*, *s.v.* 'Peterborough'; R.I.B.A.D.; C.U.L., Add. MS. 3955, ff. 3–4].

WARRINGTON, LANCS., ST. PAUL, 1829–31; dem. 1984 [Port, 150–1; V. & A. 182 p; unsigned drawings in R.I.B.A.D.].

RIPON MINSTER, YORKS., restoration of choir, 1829–31 [*Gent's Mag.* 1830 (ii), 355; 1831 (ii), 168; V. & A. 182 p].

WOBURN CHURCH, BEDS., rebuilt tower, 1830; dem. *c.*1865 [*History and Description of Woburn and its Abbey*, Woburn 1845, 109].

CANFORD MAGNA CHURCH, DORSET, westward extension of nave, *c.*1830; replaced by a new extension 1876–8 [I.C.B.S.; *R.C.H.M. Dorset* ii, 197; C.U.L., Add. MS. 3955, f. 2].

OXFORD, WADHAM COLLEGE CHAPEL, restored roof and erected stone reredos, 1831–2 [T. G. Jackson, *Wadham College, Oxford*, 1893, 156–7; V. & A. 182 p; R.I.B.A.D.].

CAMBRIDGE, TRINITY COLLEGE CHAPEL, alterations, 1831–2 [Willis & Clark, ii, 986].

GREAT BRINGTON CHURCH, NORTHANTS., south porch for 2nd Earl Spencer, 1832 [*Architectural Notices of the Archdeaconry of Northants.*, 1849, 262].

WALTHAM CROSS, HERTS., HOLY TRINITY, 1831–2 [Port, 146–7].

OTTERY ST. MARY CHURCH, DEVON, restored stone altar screen, *c.*1832 [W. Spreat, *Churches of Devon*, Exeter 1842].

LEYTONSTONE, ESSEX, ST. JOHN BAPTIST, 1832–3 [I.C.B.S.; Eastlake, 140; V. & A. 182 p].

CROFT, LANCS., CHRIST CHURCH, 1832–3 [Port, 148–9; V. & A. 182 o].

LONGFLEET CHURCH, DORSET, 1833–5; enlarged 1864; rebuilt 1915 [I.C.B.S.] (ill. J. Sydenham, *History of Poole*, 1839, 462).

STRATFORD LANGTHORNE, ESSEX, ST. JOHN THE EVANGELIST, 1833–4; chancel added 1882 [Port, 144–5; V. & A. 182 p].

EASEBOURNE CHURCH, SUSSEX, monumental chapel at east end of south aisle, for W. S. Poyntz, 1834–6 [C.U.L., Add. MS. 3956, f. 34].

POTTERS BAR, MIDDLESEX, ST. JOHN, 1835, 'Norman'; dem. [C. Mackeson, *Guide to the Churches of London*, 1894–5, 69].

BATH ABBEY CHURCH, stone choir screen, 1835; removed *c.*1860 [*A.P.S.D.*, *s.v.* 'Bath'; V. & A. 182 o].

WESTMINSTER, ST. MARY THE VIRGIN, VINCENT SQUARE, 1836–7; dem. 1923 [Port, 156–7].

STEPNEY, ST. PETER, MILE END ROAD, 1837–8, 'Norman' [C. Mackeson, *Guide to the Churches of London*, 1894–5, 69].

CHELSEA, CHRIST CHURCH, 1838; altered by W. D. Caröe 1900–1 [*Companion to the Almanac*, 1838, 220; V. & A. 182 o].

OXFORD, MERTON COLLEGE CHAPEL, restored roofs of choir and transepts, 1838–43 [*V.C.H. Oxon.* iii, 101; V. & A. 182 p].

LONDON, ST. LUKE, BERWICK STREET, SOHO, 1838–9; dem. 1936 [*Survey of London* xxxi, 226–7].

LAMBETH, HOLY TRINITY, 1838–9; destroyed by bombing *c.*1941 [Port, 154–5].

LONDON, CHRIST CHURCH, HOXTON, 1839, 'Norman'; destroyed by bombing 1944 [*Gent's Mag.* 1839 (ii), 303].

OXFORD, ST. MARY MAGDALEN, restored south aisle, 1839 [*Companion to the Almanac*, 1842, 201].

BARKINGSIDE, ESSEX, HOLY TRINITY, 1839–40, 'Norman' [Port, 144–5].

ASWARBY CHURCH, LINCS., rebuilt chancel for Sir Thomas Whichcote, Bart., 1839–41 [C.U.L., Add. MS. 3956, f. 61].

NORWICH CATHEDRAL, repaired west front, *c.*1840 [*A.P.S.D.*, *s.v.* 'Norwich'; V. & A. 182 p; C.U.L., Add. MS. 3956, f. 76v].

THORNEY ABBEY, CAMBS., new east end at expense of 6th Duke of Bedford, 1840–1, 'Norman' [Gardner's *History, Gazeteer and Directory of Cambridgeshire*, 1851, 560; V. & A. 182 p; C.U.L., Add. MS. 3956, f. 69].

CONINGTON CHURCH, HUNTS., pews, pulpit, etc., 1841 [V. & A. 182 h].

ELY CATHEDRAL, 'improvements partly executed and partly abandoned', 1840–1 and 1844 [C.U.L., Add. MS. 3955, f. 69v].

LATIMER CHAPEL, BUCKS., at expense of the Hon. C. C. Cavendish, 1841–2; east end by G. Scott 1867 [J. J. Sheahan, *History of Buckinghamshire*, 1862, 842].

LONDON, ST. JAMES THE GREAT, BETHNAL GREEN, 1841–4; converted into flats [C. Mackeson, *Guide to the Churches of London*, 1894–5, 65; V. & A. 182 a].

LONDON, ST. THOMAS, CHARTERHOUSE GARDENS, GOSWELL STREET ROAD, 1841–2, 'Norman'; dem. 1909 [*Christian Guardian* 1841, 180; V. & A. 182 o].

WINDSOR, BERKS., HOLY TRINITY, 1842–4; altered 1875 [*Ecclesiologist* ii, 1843, 136; V. & A. 182 p; R.I.B.A.D.]

ADDINGTON CHURCH, SURREY, repairs and alterations for William Howley, Archbishop of Canterbury, 1843 [C.U.L., Add. MS. 3955, ff. 32v, 70v; V. & A. 182 o].

OXFORD, ST. JOHN'S COLLEGE CHAPEL, reconstructed 1843 [*V.C.H. Oxon.* iii, 263; V. & A. 182 h].

BUSHLEY CHURCH, WORCS., at expense of Revd. E. C. Dowdeswell, 1843 [C.U.L., Add. MS. 3955, f. 32v; V. & A. 182 a].

CINDERFORD CHURCH, GLOS., 1843–4 [P.R.O., F17/101].

RAMSEY ABBEY CHURCH, HUNTS., restoration, 1843 [*Builder* xxxvii, 1879, 1019; V. & A. 182 h].

WESTMINSTER ABBEY, canons' stalls and choir fittings, 1843–8; restoration of exterior of north side of nave, 1849 [*A.P.S.D.*, *s.v.* 'Westminster Abbey'].

BRANDISTON CHURCH, NORFOLK, restoration, 1844 [*Builder* ii, 1844, 93].

GLASGOW CATHEDRAL, restoration, 1846 onwards (executed by William Nixon) [V. & A. 182 o; E. L. G. Stones, 'Notes on Glasgow Cathedral', *Innes Review* xxi (2), 140–52].

OXFORD, ST. MARY THE VIRGIN, began restoration of steeple, 1848, but was superseded by J. C. & C. Buckler, 1850 [J. G. Jackson, *St. Mary the Virgin, Oxford*, 1897, 144–6].

LONDON, SAVOY CHAPEL, font and font cover, 1865 [H. White, *Memorials of the Savoy*, 1878, 238; V. and A. 182 j].

DUDLEY, WORCS., ST. THOMAS, font and font cover, 1867 [*Builder* xxv, 1867, 679–80].

MONUMENTS

WADHAM COLLEGE, OXFORD, monuments to Wardens John Wills (d. 1806) and William Tournay (d. 1833) [J. Ingram, *Memorials of Oxford* ii, 1837, Wadham section, 15].

CASTLE ASHBY CHURCH, NORTHANTS., monument to 1st Marquess of Northampton (d. 1828), 1843 [V. & A. 182 h; C.U.L., Add. MS. 3955, f. 30v].

BISHOP MIDDLEHAM CHURCH, DURHAM, monument to Robert Surtees (d. 1834) [F. Whellan & Co.'s *History, Topography and Directory of Durham*, 1894, 244].

BLICKING CHURCH, NORFOLK, monument to 7th Marquess of Lothian (d. 1841), 1842 [V. & A. 182 h; C.U.L., Add. MS. 3955, f. 32].

LINCOLN CATHEDRAL, monument to William Hilton, R.A., 1864 [*Builder* xxiii, 1865, 227].

KENSAL GREEN CEMETERY, monument to General Foster Walker, 1866 [*Builder* xxiv, 1866, 306].

BLOXHAM, JOHN (–1715), was a carpenter and surveyor of Banbury. At present his only known work is ADDERBURY RECTORY (now 'The Grange'), OXON., which he contracted to rebuild in 1682 in accordance with 'a draught drawn by the sayd John Bloxham' and still attached to the document. Bloxham is described as 'Surveyor' in the entry of his burial in Banbury parish register [*Cake and Cockhorse*, the journal of the Banbury Historical Society, March 1965, 207–11].

BLYTH, JOHN (1806–1878), entered the Royal Academy Schools in 1827, and in 1833 exhibited a design for a monument to the Revd. Robert Hall, a celebrated Baptist minister at Bristol. In 1828 he gratuitously supervised the building of the CLERKENWELL PAROCHIAL SCHOOLS to the designs of W. C. Mylne [W. J. Pinks, *History of Clerkenwell*, 1881, 577, 711]. He repaired the church of ST. BARTHOLOMEW THE GREAT, SMITHFIELD, LONDON, after a fire in 1830, and restored the blocked-up triforium [G. Godwin, *The Churches of London* i, 1838, 10]. His only other recorded works appear to be NICHOLSON & CO'S DISTILLERY, ST. JOHN STREET, CLERKENWELL, 1828 [Pinks, *op. cit.*, 683], the NORTHAMPTON TABERNACLE (now SS. Peter & Paul R.C. Church), AMWELL STREET, CLERKENWELL, 1835, and the CITY OF LONDON LITERARY AND SCIENTIFIC INSTITUTION, 165 ALDERSGATE STREET, 1837–8; dem. [*Architectural Mag.* iii, 41; v, 135–6]. Blyth was President of the Surveyors' Club in 1867. R. C. Carpenter was his pupil. He died in Albert Road, Regent's Park, on 17 Feb. 1878, aged 71.

BOAG, JAMES, had an extensive business as a builder and architect in Sutherland and Easter Ross during the reign of George III. He was a carpenter by trade, and came from the Lowlands, but established himself in

Sutherland, first at Golspie and later at Dornoch. Among the many churches which he designed and built were those of RESOLIS or KIRKMICHAEL, ROSS-SHIRE, 1767, and KILDONAN, SUTHERLAND, 1786–8. He also erected the SPINNINGDALE MILL, SUTHERLAND, 1794, destroyed by fire in 1806. He was a rough man, who 'terrified all the school-boys, as well as every inmate of his own house, by the violence of his temper and his readiness to take offence'. His buildings were in the simplest style of eighteenth-century Scottish vernacular. [Donald Sage, *Memorabilia Domestica; or Parish Life in the North of Scotland*, 2nd ed., Wick 1899, 57, 121–22; *Scotland's Magazine*, July 1965, 24.]

BODT, or **BOTT,** JOHANN VON (1670–1745), was the son of a German father and a French mother. He was born and brought up in Paris, but as a Protestant he was obliged to leave France after the revocation of the Edict of Nantes in 1685. He went to Holland, where he entered the service of the Prince of Orange as a military engineer. In this capacity he came to England and served in William III's army in Ireland in 1690–1 and in Flanders in 1692–5. He held the rank of a captain of artillery in the Royal Engineers until August 1699, when he resigned to enter the service of the King of Prussia. In this employment he designed and erected several important buildings in Potsdam, including the Arsenal and the steeple of the Parochialkirche (which may have been influenced by Wren's St. Vedast, Foster Lane). In 1728 he transferred to Saxony, rose to the rank of general, and died at Dresden in 1745.

While in England Bodt made designs, which have apparently not survived, for rebuilding Whitehall Palace for William III. These were probably made soon after the fire which destroyed the old palace in 1698. Bodt also made designs for a grandiose royal hospital in the style of Bruand's Invalides which were probably intended for Greenwich. Neither of these schemes was, of course, carried out, but in *c.*1710–20 it was to Bodt's designs that the east wing of WENTWORTH CASTLE (STAINBOROUGH HALL), YORKS. (W.R.), containing a magnificent gallery, was built by the 1st Earl of Strafford. The Earl was Ambassador to Prussia from 1706 to 1711, and directed the building operations at Wentworth Castle by letter from Berlin. Horace Walpole, who was a friend of the family, refers to Bodt as the architect in a letter to Bentley of August 1756, and in 1773 the 2nd Earl remembered that the front had been designed by the architect of the Arsenal at Potsdam [*The Letters and Journals of Lady Mary Coke*, Edinburgh 1896, iv, 234]. There is an engraving of it dated 1713 (B.L., *King's Maps* xlv, 29c) made from a drawing by Charles Holzendorf, who was then secretary to the Embassy at Berlin, and it is illustrated in *Vitruvius Britannicus* i, 1715, pls. 92–4. What appear to be Bodt's original designs, differing in several respects from the building as executed, are in the Victoria and Albert Museum (D.212, 1890 and E.307–8, 1937).[1] The interior was eventually completed in 1724 under the direction of James Gibbs, but the exterior remains as a remarkable and almost unique example of Franco-Prussian architecture in Georgian England.[2]

[Nikolaus Pevsner, 'John Bodt in England', *Arch. Rev.* July 1961; John Harris, 'Bodt and Stainborough', *ibid.*; E. F. Sekler, *Wren and his Place in European Architecture*, 1956, 191.]

BOND, JOHN LINNELL (1764–1837), received instruction in architectural drawing from James Malton. He entered the Royal Academy Schools in 1783, aged 19, winning the Silver Medal in 1784 and the Gold Medal in 1786. He was an accomplished draughtsman and enjoyed drawing such compositions as 'the Temple of Jupiter at Olympia, with the procession of the conquerors in the games', which he exhibited at the Academy in 1803. Despite his considerable talents he was too modest and retiring to make a name for himself, and preferred 'to confine his labours to the gratification and service of the few friends who had discernment enough to appreciate his merits'. His chief patron appears to have been Sir Gerard Noel, M.P., for whom he designed the nucleus of EXTON HALL, RUTLAND, 1811, and the imposing neo-classical STAMFORD HOTEL at STAMFORD, LINCS., *c.*1810–29. His other works, as exhibited at the R.A., were an unidentified villa at Wimbledon (1796), an anatomical theatre and museum in Blenheim (now Ramillies) Street, London, for Joshua Brookes, F.R.S. (1806), a shop-front 'lately erected' to Messrs. Tatham & Bailey's premises, Nos. 13–14 Mount Street, Grosvenor Square (1808), 'a room erecting at Southampton Castle for the Marquis of Lansdowne, after the manner of the Moorish architecture of Granada' (1809), and a villa at Bushey, Herts. (1814). He also made designs for the Strand (*i.e.* Waterloo) Bridge for George Dodd, the engineer at first

[1] These drawings came from the Talman Collection. One of them is inscribed 'W. T. del & inv.', but it is not in William Talman's hand, and the inscription appears to have been due to a later owner who was unaware of its real authorship.

[2] Kettlethorpe Hall, nr. Wakefield (dated 1727), is another, but the identity of its architect is unknown.

employed by the Bridge Company, but it was eventually built by John Rennie to his own designs.

In 1818–21 Bond travelled in Italy and Greece. He contributed to the *Literary Gazette* articles on architectural subjects, and left in manuscript a translation of Vitruvius that had occupied him for some twenty years. He exhibited regularly at the Royal Academy from 1782 to 1814, and also at the Society of British Artists in 1833. Drawings of details of Henry VII's Chapel, made by him in 1807, are in the British Library (Add. MS. 15529). His portrait by H. Singleton is in the R.I.B.A. Collection. [*Literary Gazette* 1837, 724; *Gent's Mag.* 1837, 655; *A.P.S.D.*; *D.N.B.*]

BONNAR, THOMAS (–*c.*1832), was the son of John Bonnar, a painter of Edinburgh, and was admitted a burgess of the city in June 1795 [*Roll of Edinburgh Burgesses*, Scottish Record Soc., 1933, 20]. He became a Sworn Measurer in 1807 and was appointed Superintendent of Public Works in December 1809, but was dismissed in December 1818, when he was made the scapegoat for the bungled hanging of Robert Johnston for highway robbery, which ended in a riot [Edinburgh Town Council Minutes, vols. 177–8; *Scots Mag.* N.S. iv, 1819, 49–54]. From 1810 Bonnar also acted as surveyor to Heriot's Hospital. As an architect he was much engaged in laying out streets in the New Town. He probably died in 1832, when his name disappears from the Edinburgh directories.

EDINBURGH[1]

DRUMMOND PLACE, partly revised elevations designed by Robert Reid, 1817–18.

HERMITAGE PLACE, LEITH, Nos. 1–14, 1817–25 [*Edinburgh Evening Courant*, 15 Oct. 1825].

BELLEVUE CRESCENT, 1819–32; completed 1882–4.

GLOUCESTER PLACE, Nos. 4–15, 1822.

LONDON STREET, Nos. 42–54, 1823.

EAST CLAREMONT STREET, Nos. 1–85, for the Heriot Trust, 1824–30. Nos. 1–11 Bellevue Terrace were built in a uniform style 1834–56.

ATHOLL CRESCENT and PLACE, and Nos. 3–25 TORPHICHEN STREET, for the Heriot Trust, 1824–31.

QUEEN STREET GARDENS,, gardener's house, 1819 [Heriot Trust records, drawing dated 6 August 1819].

[1] Unless otherwise stated this list is based on the Scottish Development Department's duplicated *List of Buildings of Special Architectural or Historical Interest in Edinburgh*, 1971, where references are given to the relevant Sasines, etc. Several drawings by Bonnar are preserved among the records of the Heriot Trust.

BONOMI, IGNATIUS (1787–1870), was the second surviving son of Joseph Bonomi (*q.v.*), in whose office he was trained. The Napoleonic Wars would have interfered with any plans for an Italian tour, and his father's death in 1808 obliged him to start practice on his own at the age of 21. The decision to move to the north of England must have been due, at least indirectly, to his father's employment at Lambton Castle, Ignatius's first private commission of any consequence being for John Wharton of Skelton Castle, brother-in-law of the owner of Lambton. Established in Durham, Bonomi soon built up an extensive practice second only to that of John Dobson of Newcastle. Not only did he have a considerable clientèle among the local aristocracy, and the clergy both Anglican and Catholic, but from 1813 he also held the post of Surveyor of Bridges for the county. It was 'Mr. Bonomi's experience in building bridges' that led the Stockton & Darlington Railway Company to employ him to design one of the first railway bridges in England (at Skerne, nr. Darlington) in 1824. In 1831 he took as a pupil J. L. Pearson, who stayed on as an assistant after the expiry of his articles. Pearson hoped in due course to be taken into partnership, but left in 1841, when Bonomi decided instead to enter into partnership (1842) with John Augustus Cory (1819–1887), a pupil of J. J. Scoles. Bonomi retired in 1850, leaving Durham in 1856 to settle near his brother Joseph at Wimbledon, where he lived on until 1870. Cory continued to practise in Durham until 1856, when he went into partnership with Scott's pupil C. J. Ferguson (d. 1904) at Carlisle. A portrait in oils of Bonomi by Charles Martin, painted in Florence in 1861, is in private ownership in Vancouver, B.C.

Bonomi was a competent designer in both neo-classical and Gothic styles, but his output was less impressive either in quality or in quantity than that of his only rival, John Dobson. His most interesting secular works were Burn Hall, whose channelled masonry and mansard roof suggest the influence of recent French architecture, and the singular house in Wimbledon (called 'The Camels') which in old age he designed for himself and his Egyptologist brother Joseph. Joseph had been Curator of Sir John Soane's Museum, and the interior of 'The Camels' reflected some of the eccentricities of Soane's house. Otherwise Bonomi offered the standard alternatives of Greek Revival or picturesque Gothic current at the time. Although some of his early churches (e.g. Redcar) are not unattractive, most of those he designed from about 1830 onwards are in a stereotyped lancet style, and the credit for the more varied and enterprising churches of his later years must be given to his partner Cory. The archaeologically correct reproduction of the thirteenth-century Archbishop's Chapel at York which he built at Brough Hall was effectively designed by Sir William Lawson, the owner of Brough, and John Brown, the historian of York Minster, and Bonomi merely supervised its erection.

[A. F. Sealey & D. Walters, 'The First Railway Architect', *Arch. Rev.* May 1964; J. H. Crosby, *Ignatius Bonomi of Durham, Architect*, Durham 1987; Peter Meadows, 'Ignatius Bonomi: An Architect in Cleveland', *Cleveland and Teesside Local History Society's Bulletin* 50, 1986; Peter Meadows, 'Palatinate Patronage' (Bonomi as a country-house architect), *C. Life*, 14 Dec. 1989; information from Mrs. J. Crosby and Mr. Peter Meadows (in the following list of works sources marked 'P. M.'. are *ex inf.* Mr. Meadows).]

PUBLIC AND DOMESTIC ARCHITECTURE

LONDON, ARGYLL HOUSE, ARGYLL STREET, proposed internal alterations for 4th Earl of Aberdeen, 1808; dem. 1864–5 [B.L., Add. MS. 43229, f. 314, letter from Bonomi].

SKELTON CASTLE, YORKS. (N.R.), works for John Wharton, including lodge, staircase and castellated entrance-front, 1810–17 [P. Meadows, 1986, 38–41].

DURHAM, completed the COUNTY GAOL and COURTHOUSE, 1810–11, superseding F. Sandys (*q.v.*), and extended Gaol, 1815–19 and later [W. Fordyce, *History of Durham* i, 1857, 292–3; *Durham Advertiser*, 25 Feb. 1815].

EGGLESTON HALL, MIDDLETON-IN-TEESDALE, CO. DURHAM, for William Hutchinson, *c.*1810/15 [*The Early Life of Clement Burlison*, Durham, n.d., 4].

DARLINGTON, CO. DURHAM, THE FREE GRAMMAR SCHOOL (LEADYARD SCHOOL), 1813; dem. 1875 [N. Sunderland, *History of the Free Grammar School, Darlington*, 1963; C. P. Nicholson in *Darlington & Stockton Times*, 12 May 1923, *ex inf.* P. M.].

?BEAMISH HALL, CO. DURHAM, remodelled for M. J. Davison, *c.*1813–16; enlarged 1897 and 1909 [references in Shafto papers, Durham University (Prior's Kitchen), 614 suggest that Beamish Hall was by the same architect as Eggleston, *ex inf.* P. M.].

MELBOURNE (ROSSMOOR) LODGE, MELBOURNE, YORKS. (E.R.), for General James Wharton, *c.*1816 [plans in Bonomi's hand among his drawings for Skelton Castle and Normanby Hall, *ex inf.* P. M.].

LAMBTON CASTLE, CO. DURHAM, works including lodges (*c.*1815), Lamb Bridge over R. Wear (1819–20) and enlargement and remodelling of house in Gothic style (*c.*1820–8) for J. G. Lambton, afterwards 1st Earl of Durham; severely damaged by subsidence 1854 and largely rebuilt by J. Dobson and S. Smirke 1857–62; partly dem. 1930 [Neale, *Seats*, ser. i, ii; C. Hussey in *C. Life* 24–31 March 1966].

BRIGHTON, SUSSEX, No. 17 CLARENCE PLACE for Prince Hoare, 1816–19; dem. [letters from Prince Hoare to I. Bonomi in Bonomi family papers, *ex inf.* P. M.].

NORMANBY HALL, nr. MIDDLESBROUGH, YORKS. (N.R.), for William Ward Jackson, 1817–25 [P. Meadows, 1986, 41–2].

STANHOPE HOUSE, STANHOPE, CO. DURHAM, for the London Lead Company, 1818 [*Durham Advertiser*, 19 June 1818, *ex inf.* P. M.].

CROFT, YORKS. (N.R.), terrace of houses for Sir William Chaytor, Bart., 1819 [Chaytor Papers in N. Yorks. R.O., *ex inf.* P. M.].

SHERBURN HOSPITAL, nr. DURHAM, fifteen houses for the brethren, 1820 [*Durham Advertiser*, 20 May 1820, *ex inf.* P. M.].

STANHOPE RECTORY, CO. DURHAM, for Dr. Henry Phillpotts, 1821 [*The Early Life of Clement Burlison*, Durham, n.d., 5].

DURHAM, SUBSCRIPTION LIBRARY and NEWSROOM, 1821–2 [*Durham Chronicle*, 27 April 1822, *ex inf.* P. M.].

BURN HALL, CO. DURHAM, for B. J. Salvin, 1821–34 [MS. autobiography of F. H. Salvin in private possession; drawings and letters formerly at Burn Hall].

WINDLESTONE HALL, CO. DURHAM, for Sir Robert Eden, Bart., 1821–34 [H. Conyers Surtees, *History of Coundon with . . . Windlestone*, 1924, 12; design for ceiling 'for Sir Robert Eden's library' by Bonomi dated 1822 in Bonomi family papers].

MARTON HOUSE, LONG MARTON, WESTMORLAND, for Robert Stagg, Agent to the London Lead Co., *c.*1822–3 [*The Early Life of Clement Burlison*, Durham, n.d., 11].

SUNDERLAND, CO. DURHAM, THE INFIRMARY (now part of University of Sunderland), 1822–4 [W. Robinson, *Story of the Royal Infirmary, Sunderland*, Sunderland 1934, 46–7].

NEWTON HOUSE, nr. BEDALE, YORKS. (N.R.), for 3rd Earl of Darlington (later Marquess and 1st Duke of Cleveland), 1822–3; dem. 1956 [R. Hird, *Annals of Bedale*, ed. L. Lewis, N. Yorks, R.O. 1975, iv, 526–31].

MIDDLETON-IN-TEESDALE, CO. DURHAM, cottages in Masterman Place for the London Lead Co., 1823–4 [E. Mackenzie & M.

Ross, *History of the County Palatine of Durham* ii, 1834, 252].

CROSS BECK HOUSE, NORMANBY, YORKS. (N.R.), alterations for Miss Jane Lambton, 1823–4 [Ward Jackson diaries, Middlesbrough Reference Library, *ex inf.* P. M.].

DINSDALE SPA BATHS, CO. DURHAM, for J. G. Lambton, later 1st Earl of Durham, *c.*1823–4 [Lambton papers at Lambton Castle, *ex inf.* P. M.].

STANHOPE CASTLE, CO. DURHAM, alterations or additions for Cuthbert Rippon, *c.*1823–35 [MS. list of Bonomi's works in family archives; reference in letter from I. Bonomi to Joseph Bonomi dated 15 March 1835, *ibid.*].

?COULBY MANOR, nr. HEMLINGTON, YORKS. (N.R.), for Mr. Bewicke, 1824–5 [Ward-Jackson diaries, as above, *ex inf.* P. M.].

DINSDALE PARK HOTEL (later Retreat for Mental Invalids), CO. DURHAM, for J. G. Lambton, later 1st Earl of Durham, 1824–6 [W. Fordyce, *History of Durham* i, 1857, 509].

WITTON CASTLE, CO. DURHAM, minor alterations, including entrance, for Sir William Chaytor, Bart., *c.*1824–40 [Chaytor papers, N. Yorks. R.O., *ex inf.* P. M.].

BLAGDON, NORTHUMBERLAND, added *porte cochère* to S. front, 1826, and portico to E. front, 1830, for Sir Matthew White Ridley, Bart., both removed after fire in 1944 [Hodgson, *History of Northumberland* ii (2), 328; C. Hussey in *C. Life*, 18 July 1952].

CROFT SPA BATHS, YORKS. (N.R.), for Sir William Chaytor, Bart., *c.*1827; dem. 1958 [Chaytor papers, N. Yorks. R.O., *ex inf.* P. M.].

LONDON, No. 10 CARLTON HOUSE TERRACE, interior for Sir Matthew White Ridley, Bart., 1827; since remodelled by Detmar Blow [*Life & Letters of Cecilia Ridley*, ed. Viscountess Ridley, 1958, 47].

ELVET HILL, nr. DURHAM, for himself, 1827–9 [M. Apperley, *History of Elvet Hill*, 1913; Ward-Jackson diaries as above].

NEWCASTLE, THE PRIORY (now ST. ANNE'S CONVENT), WESTGATE, for Cuthbert Rippon, 1828 [*Newcastle Chronicle*, sale advt. 9 Dec. 1837, *ex inf.* P. M.].

NUNWICK, SIMONBURN, NORTHUMBERLAND, alterations including Tuscan portico and dining-room, for R. L. Allgood, 1829 [*History of Northumberland* xv, 199; G. Nares in *C. Life*, 12–19 July 1956].

THE HERMITAGE, CHESTER-LE-STREET, CO. DURHAM, for Thomas Cookson, before 1830 [MS. list of works in Bonomi family papers].

DURHAM, THE DEANERY, alterations and internal redecoration for Dean Jenkinson, 1830 [Deanery records, Durham University (Prior's Kitchen), *ex inf.* P. M.].

KIRKLEY HALL, NORTHUMBERLAND, altered and enlarged for Revd. J. S. Ogle, 1832; largely rebuilt after fire in 1928 [MS. list of works in Bonomi family papers].

EASINGTON RECTORY, YORKS. (N.R.), additions 1832–3 [Borthwick Institute, York, MGA 1832/3].

LOFTUS HOUSE, YORKS. (N.R.), addition to offices for Sir Robert Dundas, 1834–7 [Dundas papers, N. Yorks. R.O., *ex inf.* P. M.].

CROFT SPA HOTEL, YORKS. (N.R.), added ASSEMBLY ROOMS for Sir William Chaytor, Bart., 1835 [N. Yorks. R.O., Chaytor papers, E. 252].

HOVINGHAM, YORKS. (N.R.), THE SPA (now a private house), for Sir William Worsley, Bart., 1835 [drawings nos. 219–20 at Hovingham Hall in Bonomi's hand, dated Durham March 1835].

BEDLINGTON VICARAGE, NORTHUMBERLAND, 1836 [Northumberland R.O., Q.A.B. Mortgage Papers, *ex inf.* P. M.].

UPLEATHAM HALL, YORKS. (N.R.), additions for 1st and 2nd Earls of Zetland, *c.*1836–40; dem. 1897 [Bonomi family papers, letter of I. Bonomi to Joseph Bonomi, 1 Feb. 1836; Chaytor Papers, N. Yorks R.O., letter of I. Bonomi to Chaytor, 15 May 1840, *ex inf.* P. M.].

UPLEATHAM, YORKS. (N.R.), NATIONAL SCHOOL for 1st Earl of Zetland, *c.*1837; dem. *c.*1895 [J. W. Ord, *History of Cleveland*, 1846, 360].

YORK, MARYGATE, ST. MARY'S ABBEY GATEHOUSE LODGE, conversion into house for Prof. John Phillips, 1839 [Bonomi family correspondence, *ex inf.* P. M.].

CLERVAUX CASTLE, CROFT, YORKS. (N.R.), for Sir William Chaytor, Bart, 1839–44; dem. 1951 [N. Yorks. R.O., Chaytor papers E. 253–4].

ASKE HALL, nr. RICHMOND, YORKS. (N.R.), alterations for 2nd Earl of Zetland, *c.*1840 onwards [Giles Worsley in *C. Life*, 8 March 1990].

PEPPER ARDEN, SOUTH COWTON, YORKS. (N.R.), work for the Hon. Richard Pepper Arden, 1840 [letter from Charlotte Bonomi to Joseph Bonomi, 4 May 1840, in Bonomi family papers, mentioning I. Bonomi's visit to the house, *ex inf.* P. M.].

WHITWORTH, CO. DURHAM, NATIONAL SCHOOL, for Revd. R. Gray, *c.*1840, Gothic [J. L. Pearson's 'Studies and Examples of Modern Architecture', *ex inf.* P. M.].

HARPERLEY PARK, CO. DURHAM, alterations, probably including staircase hall, for G. H. Wilkinson, *c.*1840 [MS. list of Bonomi's works in family papers].

REDCAR VICARAGE, YORKS. (N.R.), *c.*1840; dem. [J. W. Ord, *History of Cleveland*, 1846, 360].

RICHMOND UNION POORHOUSE, YORKS. (N.R.), enlarged 1841 [N. Yorks. R.O., Poor Law papers, *ex inf.* P. M.].

DURHAM, THE MECHANICS' INSTITUTE, CLAYGATE, 1841–2; extended 1849 [*Durham Advertiser*, 6 April 1849, *ex inf.* P. M.].

DUNSA MANOR, DALTON, nr. RICHMOND, YORKS. (N.R.), for William Lister, 1841–2 [N. Yorks. R.O., Chaytor papers, *ex inf.* P. M.].

*WYNYARD PARK, CO. DURHAM, restoration after fire for 3rd Marquess of Londonderry, 1841–2 [P. Meadows, 1986, 46–9].

*STOKESLEY MANOR, YORKS. (N.R.), enlarged for Col. R. Hildyard, 1843–4 [P. Meadows, 1986, 49].

*LOFTUS-IN-CLEVELAND RECTORY, YORKS. (N.R.), for Revd. H. S. Hildyard, 1844–5 [J. W. Ord, *History of Cleveland*, 1846, plate facing p. 277; Borthwick Institute, York, MGA 1845/6].

*WILTON VICARAGE, YORKS. (N.R.), for Sir John Lowther, Bart., 1844–5 [Hildyard papers, *ex inf.* P. M.].

*CROFT, YORKS. (N.R.), NATIONAL SCHOOL, 1844–5, Tudor Gothic [C. Dodgson, *A Short Account of the first establishment of the Croft National School*, Darlington 1846].

*BIDDLESTONE HALL, NORTHUMBERLAND, chapel (R.C.) for Walter Selby, 1845 [letter from I. Bonomi to Joseph Bonomi, 1845, in family papers, *ex inf.* P. M.].

*BLAKE HALL, MIRFIELD, YORKS. (W.R.), additions for Joshua Ingham, *c.*1845; dem. 1954 [letter from John Cory to Joseph Bonomi, 15 Feb. 1870, *ibid.*, *ex inf.* P. M.].

*HESLEYSIDE, nr. BELLINGHAM, NORTHUMBERLAND, alterations, including addition of clock-tower, for W. H. Charlton, *c.*1847 [*Recollections of a Northumberland Lady*, ed. L. E. O. Charlton, 1949, 178–9; *C. Life*, 18 May 1989].

*STOKESLEY, YORKS. (N.R.), MARKET BUILDINGS, 1849 [*Durham Chronicle*, 27 April 1849, *ex inf.* P. M.].

WIMBLEDON, SURREY, house called 'THE CAMELS' in PRINCES ROAD for himself and his brother Joseph Bonomi, 1865–6; dem. [Bonomi family papers].

BRIDGES

The principal bridges designed by Bonomi for the County of Durham were at HAUGHTON-LE-SKERNE, 1813; WOLSINGHAM, 1816; CHESTER-LE-STREET, 1819; and SHINCLIFFE, 1824–6 [J. Crosby, *Ignatius Bonomi*, 1987, 76–80.] He also designed the SKERNE RAILWAY BRIDGE, nr. DARLINGTON, for the Stockton & Darlington Railway Co., 1824–5 [A. F. Sealey & D. Walters in *Arch. Rev.* May 1964].

* Designed in partnership with J. A. Cory.

CHURCHES

(all Gothic unless otherwise stated)

REDCAR, YORKS. (N.R.), 1823–9; chancel 1888 [J. W. Ord, *History of Cleveland*, 1846, 360].

DURHAM, ST. CUTHBERT (R.C.), 1826–7; tower added 1869 [E. Mackenzie & M. Ross, *History of the County Palatine of Durham* ii, 1834, 402].

DARLINGTON, ST. AUGUSTINE (R.C.), 1826–7; altered by J. A. Hansom 1865 [Mackenzie & Ross, *op. cit.* ii, 1834, 402].

WINLATON, CO. DURHAM, 1827–9 [Mackenzie & Ross, *op. cit.* i, 1834, 197].

DURHAM CATHEDRAL, repairs to S. gable of Chapel of the Nine Altars and gable of S. transept, *c.*1828 [*A.P.S.D.*, *s.v.* 'Durham'; cf. *Catalogue of R.I.B.A. Drawings Coll.: B*, 95].

FERRYHILL, CO. DURHAM, ST. LUKE, 1828–9; dem. *c.*1853 [Mackenzie & Ross, *op. cit.*, ii, 1834, 310].

CHESTER-LE-STREET, CO. DURHAM, Earl of Durham's pew or chapel, 1828–32 [Mackenzie & Ross, *op. cit.* i, 1834, 114].

SATLEY, CO. DURHAM, tower, 1829 [I.C.B.S.].

DUDDO, NORTHUMBERLAND, 1832, neo-Norman; converted into a school 1881 [*The British Magazine* iii, 1833, 602].

DURHAM, ST. OSWALD, ELVET, reconstructed 1834 [*A.P.S.D.*, *s.v.* 'Durham'].

HUTTON, BERWICKSHIRE, 1834–5, neo-Norman [S.R.O., HR 146/2, 189–99].

BROUGH HALL, YORKS. (N.R.), supervised erection of ST. PAULINUS' CHAPEL (R.C), for Sir William Lawson, 1834–7 [Lawson's diaries in N. Yorks. R.O., *ex inf.* P. M.] (*C. Life*, 19 Oct. 1967).

SUNDERLAND, CO. DURHAM, ST. MARY (R.C.), 1835; chapel added 1852 [W. Fordyce, *History of Durham* ii, 1857, 444].

UPLEATHAM, YORKS. (N.R.), 1834–5, neo-Norman [J. W. Ord, *op. cit.*, 360; I.C.B.S.].

WIGTON, CUMBERLAND, ST. CUTHBERT (R.C.), 1837 [W. Whellan, *Cumberland & Westmorland*, 1860, 277].

DENTON, CO. DURHAM, addition of N. transept, 1836; rebuilt 1891 [I.C.B.S.].

ANCROFT, NORTHUMBERLAND, addition of N. transept, 1836; dem. 1869 [I.C.B.S.].

NORHAM, NORTHUMBERLAND, tower 1836–8, rebuilt aisles and added N. transept, 1844 [Northumberland C.R.O., parish records, *ex inf.* P. M.].

HOUGHTON-LE-SPRING, CO. DURHAM, ST. MICHAEL (R.C.), 1837 [M. A. Richardson, *The Local Historian's Table-Book*, 1841–6, iv, 401].

BELLINGHAM, NORTHUMBERLAND, ST. OSWALD (R.C.), 1837–9 [Northumberland C.R.O., transcripts of records of Hexham & Newcastle R.C. Diocese, *ex inf.* P. M.].

DODDINGTON, NORTHUMBERLAND, restoration and new chancel, 1838; altered 1888–97 [*History of Northumberland* xiv, 148–9].

BATTYEFORD (MIRFIELD), YORKS. (W.R.), CHRISTCHURCH, 1838–40; dem. *c.*1975 [I.C.B.S.].

CORNHILL, NORTHUMBERLAND, rebuilt 1840; chancel added 1866 [I.C.B.S.].

BARTON, YORKS. (N.R.), 1840–1; altered 1910 [I.C.B.S.].

CROOK, CO. DURHAM, 1840–3; enlarged 1885 [I.C.B.S.].

SCREMERSTON, NORTHUMBERLAND, 1840–3, with vicarage and school [I.C.B.S.; R.I.B.A.D.].

*LOW DINSDALE, CO. DURHAM, W. tower, 1843 [parish records in Durham C.R.O.].

*INGLETON, CO. DURHAM, 1843–4 [I.C.B.S.].

*GILLING WEST, YORKS. (N.R.), new N. aisle, etc., 1844–5 [I.C.B.S.].

*BRANXTON, NORTHUMBERLAND, 1844–9, neo-Norman [I.C.B.S.].

*NENTHEAD, CUMBERLAND, 1845; reroofed, etc.1907 [I.C.B.S.].

*UPPER HOPTON, YORKS. (W.R.), 1845–6 [I.C.B.S.].

*PITTINGTON, CO. DURHAM, enlarged 1846–7 [I.C.B.S.].

*DEWSBURY, YORKS. (W.R.), ST. MATTHEW, WEST TOWN, 1847–8 [I.C.B.S.].

*KING'S STERNDALE, DERBYSHIRE, 1848–9 [I.C.B.S.].

*OXENHOPE, YORKS. (W.R.), 1848–9, neo-Norman [I.C.B.S.].

*SOHAM, CAMBS., restoration of chancel for Pembroke College, Cambridge (of which Cory's brother was a Fellow), 1848–9 [R. Gardner, *History, Gazetter & Directory of Cambridgeshire*, 1851, 393].

*TORRE PELLICE, PIEDMONT, ITALY, WALDENSIAN CHURCH, 1849, perhaps based on a design supplied by General Charles Beckwith; somewhat altered in execution [plan signed by Bonomi & Cory in private ownership in Italy, *ex inf.* P. M.; R. Bounous & M. Lecchi, *I templi delle valli valdesi*, Turin 1988, 139–43].

MONUMENTS

HAYES, KENT, monument in churchyard and tablet in church to Sir Vicary Gibbs (d. 1820), carved by C. H. Smith, 1822 [letters from Prince Hoare to Bonomi in family papers, *ex inf.* P. M.].

CHISLEHURST, KENT, monument in churchyard and tablet in church to Mary and Anne Hoare, carved by C. H. Smith, 1824–5 [*ibid.*]

WHITTINGHAME, E. LOTHIAN, Gothic monument in Old Burial Ground to Hay family, for Robert Hay, 1837 [R.I.B.A., L 5/14/1–2].

BONOMI, JOSEPH (1739–1808), was born in Rome on 19 January 1739. His father, whose family came from Asiago in the Veneto, acted as agent to many of the Roman nobility. Joseph was educated at the Collegio Romano and became a pupil (according to his son Ignatius) of the architect Antonio Asprucci, though the *A.P.S.D.* says he was a pupil of the Marchese Teodoli, a nobleman who devoted himself to the study and practice of architecture. There is also evidence that he was taught draughtsmanship by Clérisseau. In 1767 he came to England to work for the brothers R. and J. Adam, who had met him in Rome, and in whose London office he remained until 1781. Failing to obtain any substantial commissions on his own, he decided in 1783 to return to Italy. Here he became an associate of the Clementine Academy at Bologna and of the Academy of St. Luke at Rome. However, in 1784 he returned to England and this time quickly established himself in practice in London. In 1789 he was elected A.R.A. by the casting vote of Sir Joshua Reynolds. In the following year Reynolds made an unsuccessful attempt to secure his election as a full Academician in order to qualify him for the vacant professorship of Perspective, and it was the opposition to this proposal that led to Reynolds's temporary resignation of the presidency in February 1790. In 1800 Bonomi was offered the appointment of architect to the King of Naples, but nothing came of this tempting proposal owing to the fall of Zurlo, the minister concerned. In 1804 he was made an honorary architect to St. Peter's, Rome, for which he had in 1776 made an unexecuted design for a sacristy.

Bonomi was an accomplished architectural draughtsman and exhibited regularly at the Royal Academy from 1783 onwards. He soon achieved a considerable reputation as a designer of country houses, and is alluded to as a fashionable architect in Jane Austen's *Sense and Sensibility.* Externally his houses have a severity that may be neo-classical in intention but is apt to be somewhat arid in effect unless relieved (as it was at Longford, Eastwell and Laverstoke) by a bold portico designed to act as a *porte cochère.* A large 'Diocletian' window was a favourite motif. Bonomi's decorative style was in some respects similar to that of the Adam brothers, but his interiors are often more robust and architectural in character and more overtly antique in style. At Packington the rich decoration of the gallery, based on Ponce's *Description des Bains de Titus* (1786), reflects the personal taste of his patron the Earl of Aylesford, and the remarkable church, with its primitive Greek columns supporting a vault derived from the Roman baths, was probably due as much to Lord Aylesford's own studies of the antique originals as to Bonomi's neo-classical sympathies, which did not lie in the direction of Greece (though he had visited Paestum). In interpreting his patron's wishes Bonomi did, however, produce a building as radical as anything by Gilly or Ledoux, though there is no evidence that he knew or was influenced by French neo-classical architects or their work. For the Gothic style Bonomi had absolutely no sympathy: writing to the Earl of Buchan in 1807 he denounced it as having caused the 'total corruption' of medieval architecture throughout Europe except at Rome, and lamented 'the revival of such absurdities in this country' (N.L.S., MS. 14835).

Bonomi married in 1775 Rosa Florini, a cousin of Angelica Kauffmann. They had four sons, the second of whom is noticed above. The youngest, Joseph Bonomi, junior (1796–1878), was distinguished as an Egyptologist, and became the second curator of Sir John Soane's Museum.[1] Joseph Bonomi died on 9 March 1808, aged 69, and was buried in the Marylebone cemetery (inscription in Lysons, *Environs of London* ii, 1811, 547). There are portraits by Rigaud and Dance at the Royal Academy. A large collection of Bonomi's architectural drawings was presented to the R.I.B.A. by his descendants in 1991.

['The Life and Works of Joseph Bonomi', *Architect, Engineer and Surveyor*, 1843, 70–1; memoir by Wyatt Papworth in *R.I.B.A. Transactions* 1868–9, 123–134; J. E. Hodgson & F. A. Eaton, *The Royal Academy*, 1905, 37ff; ; *The Farington Diary*, ed. J. Greig, vii, 124; memoir of Joseph Bonomi, junior, in *Transactions of the Society for Biblical Archaeology* for 1879; will, P.C.C. 41 ELY; Peter Meadows, *Joseph Bonomi Architect* (R.I.B.A. 1988) and 'Perspectives by Joseph Bonomi', *C. Life*, 28 April 1988; Peter Meadows & John Cornforth, 'Draughtsman Decorator', *C. Life*, 19 April 1990.]

[1] It was Joseph Bonomi, junior, not his brother Ignatius, who in 1842 (not 1838) helped a local architect, James Combe, to design the Egyptian façade of the Temple Mills, Leeds. See *Companion to the Almanac*, 1844, 241–2, obituary in *Trans. Soc. Biblical Archaeology* as above, and B.L., Add. MS. 38094, ff. 166–77.

LONDON, No. 51 UPPER BROOK STREET, work for William Locke; 1782, dem. 1905 [design for a chimney-piece inscribed 'for Wm Lock's Esqr in Upper Brook Street / Joseph Bonomi Archit Febry 1782' in possession of W. A. Brandt, Esq., 1969].

PACKINGTON HALL, WARWICKS., interiors, including the Pompeian Gallery (1785–8), for 4th Earl of Aylesford, 1784 onwards [Marcus Binney in *C. Life*, 16–23 July 1970; Desmond Fitz-Gerald in *Connoisseur*, Sept. 1972, 8–9; Meadows, 1988, 20–2].

DALE PARK, SUSSEX, for Sir George Thomas, Bart., 1784–8; dem. 1959 [Neale, *Seats*, ser. 2, v].

LONDON, UXBRIDGE HOUSE, BURLINGTON GARDENS, assisted John Vardy, junior, 'in the disposition of the south front' for 1st Earl of Uxbridge, *c.*1785–9 [Britton & Pugin, *Public Buildings of London* i, 1825, 82; *Survey of London* xxxii, 461–3].

STANSTED HOUSE, SUSSEX, remodelled, with James Wyatt, for Richard Barwell, 1786–91; destroyed by fire 1900 [J. Dallaway, *Western Division of Sussex* ii, 1815, 159].

FISHERWICK PARK, STAFFS., interior of drawing-room for 1st Marquess of Donegal, 1787; dem. 1814–16 ['Memoir of J. F. Rigaud', ed. Pressly, *Walpole Soc.* 50, 1984, 74].

THE FOREST HALL, MERIDEN, WARWICKS., 1787–8; enlarged 1845 [*Records of the Woodmen of Arden*, privately printed 1885, 7–8].

LONDON, THE BAVARIAN EMBASSY CHAPEL, WARWICK STREET, 1789–90 [J. Britton, *The Original Picture of London*, 27th ed. *c.*1832, 123] (G. Houghton-Brown, 'The Bavarian Chapel, London', *Arch. Rev.* Aug. 1947, 67; *Survey of London* xxxi, 170–2).

GREAT PACKINGTON CHURCH, WARWICKS., for 4th Earl of Aylesford, 1789–92 [R.I.B.A.D.; Marcus Binney in *C. Life*, 8 July 1971].

LONGFORD HALL, SALOP., for Ralph Leeke, 1789–92 [exhib. at R.A., 1797; G. Richardson, *New Vitruvius Britannicus* i, 1802, pls. 15–16] (*C. Life*, 16 Aug. 1962).

LONDON, MONTAGU (later PORTMAN) HOUSE, PORTMAN SQUARE, Great Room etc. for Mrs. Elizabeth Montagu, 1789–90; destroyed by bombing 1941 [exhib. at R.A. 1790; R.I.B.A.D.].

LANGLEY PARK, nr. BECKENHAM, KENT, additions for Sir Peter Burrell, afterwards Lord Gwydyr, 1790; destroyed by fire 1913 [*A.P.S.D.*].

ASHTEAD PARK, SURREY, for Richard Howard, 1790, executed by Samuel Wyatt [*Some*

Records of the Ashtead Estate, 1873, 169].

SPRINGFIELD HOUSE, KNOWLE, WARWICKS., for Richard Moland, 1790–1, remodelled internally *c.*1900 [R.I.B.A.D.].

HORSLEY PLACE (later TOWERS), SURREY, greenhouse, stables and coach-houses for William Currie, 1792; dem. [exhib. at R.A. 1794; R.I.B.A.D.].

BURWOOD PARK, WALTON, SURREY, remodelled for Sir John Frederick, Bart., *c.*1792 [R.I.B.A.D.].

PONSBOURNE PARK, HERTS., for Stephen Sullivan, 1792–3; remodelled 1876 [R.I.B.A.D.].

BARRELLS, WARWICKS., for Robert Knight, 1792–4; portico removed 1856; in ruins since fire in 1933 [exhib. at R.A.; R.I.B.A.D.].

COWICK HALL, YORKS. (W.R.), alterations for 5th Viscount Downe, including W. staircase and stables, 1792–*c.*1808 (drawings in N. Yorks. C.R.O. and R.I.B.A.D.; John Killeen, *A Short History of Cowick Hall*, 1967].

KING'S LANGLEY CHURCH, HERTS., monument to Mary E. Crawford (d. 1793), executed by R. Westmacott [signed].

LONDON, THE SPANISH CHAPEL, MANCHESTER SQUARE, 1793–6; enlarged 1846; dem. 1880 [exhib. at R.A. 1793; drawing of interior by Bonomi in vestry of St. James's, Spanish Place; R.I.B.A.D.].

EASTWELL PARK, KENT, for George Finch Hatton, 1793–1800; enlarged by W. Burn 1849; remodelled 1895; dem. 1926 [exhib at R.A. 1794 and 1799; G. Richardson, *New Vitruvius Britannicus* i, 1802, pls. 39–41].

BLICKLING PARK, NORFOLK, pyramidal mausoleum to memory of 2nd Earl of Buckinghamshire, 1794–6 [exhib. at R.A. 1794; drawings at Blickling and R.I.B.A.D.].

SANDLING HOUSE, nr. HYTHE, KENT, for W. Deedes, 1795–7; bombed 1943 and dem. 1945–6 [exhib. at R.A. 1799; R.I.B.A.D.].

SUTTONS, STAPLEFORD TAWNEY, ESSEX, greenhouse for Charles Smith, 1796 [R.I.B.A.D.].

LITTLE LONDON or HILLINGDON PARK, MIDDLESEX, house for Count Peter de Salis, 1796–7; dem. *c.*1835 [R.I.B.A.D.].

LAMBTON HALL (now CASTLE), CO. DURHAM, rebuilt for W. H. Lambton, *c.*1796–7; work interrupted by Lambton's death in 1797, completed 1801; enlarged and castellated by I. Bonomi, *c.*1820–8; rebuilt 1860–4 [exhib. at R.A. 1798, 1800, 1802] (*C. Life*, 24–31 March 1966).

STAPLEFORD TAWNEY CHURCHYARD, ESSEX, monument to wife of Charles Smith, 1797 [R.I.B.A.D.].

LAVERSTOKE PARK, HANTS., for Henry Portal, 1796–9; altered in 19th century [exhib. at R.A. 1799; R.I.B.A.D.].

NEW YORK, NORTH AMERICA, house probably No. 59 BROADWAY, for J.B. Church, 1797; dem. [drawing of the house 'now building' formerly in family collection].

PIERCEFIELD, nr. CHEPSTOW, MONMOUTHSHIRE, saloon and staircase (now destroyed) and addition of wings for Sir Mark Wood, Bart., 1797 [Ackermann, *Repository of the Arts*, ser. 3, v, 1825, 313].

HATCHLANDS, nr. GUILDFORD, SURREY, alterations, including new entrance, for W. B. Sumner, 1797 [H. S. Goodhart-Rendel, *Hatchlands*, National Trust guidebook 1948, 5–7] (*C. Life*, 17 Sept., 1 Oct. 1953, 20 Sept. 1989).

EDEN HALL, CUMBERLAND, partly rebuilt for Sir John C. Brisco, *c.*1797–1800; rebuilt by Smirke 1821 [papers in Cumbria R.O., Carlisle, *ex inf.* P. Meadows].

THE ORCHARD, BLACKHEATH, KENT, stables for Viscount Lewisham (later 3rd Earl of Dartmouth), 1801; dem. *c.*1898 [R.I.B.A.D.].

ROSNEATH, DUNBARTONSHIRE, for 5th Duke of Argyll, 1803–6; gutted by fire 1947, dem. 1961 [exhib. at R.A. 1806; G. Richardson, *New Vitruvius Britannicus* ii, 1808, pls. 15–16; *R.I.B.A. Trans.* 1868–9, 129–33].

LONDON, No. 121 LONG ACRE, architectural additions to decorative paintings by Sir James Thornhill for John Hatchett, n.d.; dem. [E. Croft-Murray, *Decorative Painting in England* ii, 1970, 173].

Bonomi's unexecuted designs included proposed Saloon, Drawing Room and Book Room at BURLEY-ON-THE HILL, RUTLAND, for 8th Earl of Winchilsea, 1782 [R.I.B.A.D.]; a scheme for fitting up the unfinished gallery at LANSDOWNE HOUSE, LONDON, 1786 [drawings at Bowood and R.I.B.A.D.]; a sculpture gallery at TOWNELEY HALL, LANCS., for Charles Towneley, 1789 [R.I.B.A.D.]; alterations to SUTTON PLACE, SURREY, for J. Webbe Weston [F. Harrison, *Annals of an Old Manor-House*, 1899, 146]; a new wing at WOOLBEDING, SUSSEX, 1791 [Arthur Oswald in *C. Life*, 15 Aug. 1947, 330]; rebuilding RÛG, MERIONETHSHIRE, 1797 [R.I.B.A.D.]; a Gothic gateway at MERRION PARK, DUBLIN, for 7th Viscount Fitzwilliam, 1803 [R.I.B.A.D.]; and various works at INVERARAY CASTLE, ARGYLLSHIRE, for 6th Duke of Argyll, 1806–7 [I. G. Lindsay & Mary Cosh, *Inveraray and the Dukes of Argyll*, 1973, 311].

BOORER, JOHN, obtained the second premium in the competition for rebuilding

London Bridge in 1823. He exhibited a design for a new hall for the Fishmongers' Company at the Royal Academy in 1834: it was not executed.

BOOTH, JAMES, was a master mason at Stony Middleton in Derbyshire. He was employed to build the stables at Chatsworth to the designs of James Paine in 1758–63, and the stables behind the Crescent at Buxton to those of John Carr in 1779–85. In 1767 he was among the subscribers to Paine's *Plans . . . of Noblemen and Gentlemen's Houses.* In his *Churches of Derbyshire* ii, 1877, 247, J. C. Cox records that STONY MIDDLETON CHURCH was believed to have been rebuilt in 1759 by 'the same architect' who 'designed the stables at the back of the Crescent at Buxton, the stables at Chatsworth, the rectory at Eyam, and Stoke Hall'. STOKE HALL, nr. Stony Middleton, was built in 1757 for the Revd. John Simpson, and Booth was probably the architect as well as the builder, though he may have been assisted by Paine. EYAM RECTORY was built for the Revd. E. Seward *c.*1765. Simpson and Seward were also among the subscribers to Paine's book. Stoke Hall and the octagonal church at Stony Middleton are both buildings of some architectural pretensions which suggest that their designer was a man of ability.

BOOTH, JOHN (1759–1843), the son of a bricklayer, practised as an architect and surveyor in Devonshire Street, London, and later in Red Lion Square. He was a member of the Drapers' Company, of which he was Master in 1821, and was President of the Surveyors' Club in 1802. He died in 1843, aged 83 [*Gent's Mag.* 1843 (i), 442]. In 1817–18 he remodelled ST. GEORGE'S CHURCH, QUEEN SQUARE, LONDON, adding Doric porticos that were removed by S. S. Teulon in 1867–8 [G.L. Record Office P82/GEO/75/2], and in 1821 the S. aisle of ORE CHURCH, SUSSEX, was rebuilt to his designs [I.C.B.S]. He was the father of W. J. Booth (*q.v.*).

BOOTH, WILLIAM JOSEPH (*c.*1796–1871), was the younger son of John Booth (*q.v.*). He became a pupil of George Maddox, and entered the Royal Academy Schools in 1819. A tour of Italy and Greece followed, and in 1822 he exhibited at the Academy a 'View of the Temple of Theseus, taken on the spot in . . . 1820'. In 1822 he became surveyor to the Drapers' Company (of which he and his father were members), for whom he designed various buildings on their Irish property at DRAPERSTOWN and MONEYMORE, CO. DERRY, including the classical Market House and the neo-Norman church at the latter place. What appears to be his signature (rather than his father's) on a drawing in the Lloyd-Baker Estate Office may indicate that he designed the houses in Lloyd Square, Lloyd-Baker Street and Granville Square, Clerkenwell, *c.*1820–40 [J. S. Curl, *Moneymore and Draperstown*, Ulster Architectural Heritage Soc.1979, 66–8]. Booth retired in 1855 to Torquay, dying there on 24 December 1871 [Principal Probate Registry, Calendar of Probates; *R.I.B.A. Procs.* 1872–3, 9].

BORLACH, JOHN, was, as James Gibbs (d. 1754) states in his will, 'for many years' his draughtsman. He made the drawing of Sir William Bruce's house at Kinross that was later engraved in Adam's *Vitruvius Scoticus.* The American architect Charles Bulfinch (1763–1844) owned a collection of 20 engraved plates, intended for publication and entitled *Designs of Architecture for Arches or Gates* . . . by John C. Borlach, Architect'. This (apparently unique) copy now belongs to the Massachusetts Institute of Technology. The title-page is illustrated in T. Friedman, *James Gibbs* (1984), 25.

BORRA, GIOVANNI BATTISTA (1713–1770), was a Piedmontese architect who was employed in England in the 1750s. Born at Dogliani in December 1713 (not 1712), he was a pupil of Vittone, and is best known for the interior of the Racconigi Palace near Turin (1756–7), for the façade of the Teatro Carignano and for the church of San Sudario in that city. In 1749 he was to have accompanied Lord Charlemont (then in Italy) on his expedition to the Levant, but was persuaded instead to join Robert Wood and James Dawkins as draughtsman on their celebrated tour of Asia Minor and Syria in 1750–1. Together with them he returned to England in the autumn of 1751 and prepared the finished drawings for the engraved plates of their two folio volumes on Palmyra and Baalbec, published in 1753 and 1757, respectively. The plates are variously signed 'J. B. (i.e. John Baptist) Borra', 'J. P. Borra' (presumably a misprint) and 'Borra'. Borra's surviving sketch-books are in the London University Institute of Classical Studies, and the original finished drawings were presented to the R.I.B.A. by a descendant of Dawkins in 1907 and are now in its Drawings Collection. According to the article on 'Civil Architecture' in the *Edinburgh Encyclopaedia* (written by Thomas Telford, who had his information from Dawkins's nephew), Borra tried to abscond with these drawings. 'By immediate and active pursuit, those relating to the architectural parts were all recovered; but twenty-six finely executed landscapes in Egypt, Greece and Asia Minor, were, only a few years ago, accidentally discovered and purchased by the present Mr. Dawkins, in a public auction room in London.' Some further drawings, of unknown provenance, exist in a private collection (see Francis Russell in *C. Life*, 4 Nov. 1976).

In 1755 'Mr. Bora' was employed by the 9th Duke of Norfolk to design the decoration of some of the principal rooms in NORFOLK HOUSE, ST. JAMES'S SQUARE, recently built under the direction of Matthew Brettingham. Norfolk House was demolished in 1938, but the interior of the Music Room was re-erected in the Victoria and Albert Museum (see Desmond Fitz-Gerald, *The Norfolk House Music Room*, V. & A. Museum, 1973). Borra's work at Norfolk House is highly accomplished and presents an unusual combination of Italianate rococo with motifs derived from Palmyra. Similar decoration is found in some of Borra's buildings in Piedmont (notably the Racconigi Palace), and in England at STRATFIELD SAYE, HANTS. (drawing- and dining-room ceilings, date uncertain), and STOWE HOUSE, BUCKS. (State Bedroom and Dressing-room as redecorated for Lord Temple in 1760). No documentary evidence of Borra's responsibility for work at Stratfield Saye has so far been found, but the employment of 'Signor Borra' at Stowe is well attested by papers now in the Huntington Library in California, which include eight letters from Borra, dated from London in 1752 and 1754. At Stowe he not only redecorated the two rooms already mentioned, and designed the double flight of steps on the S. front, but was responsible for the neo-classicizing of several of the early Georgian garden buildings. In 1752 he was making drawings, under Lord Temple's directions, for the Temple of Concord and Victory. The Rotondo was altered to his designs in 1752, the Boycott Pavilions in 1758, the Oxford Gate *c.*1760, and the twin Lake Pavilions soon afterwards. He made an unexecuted design, engraved by Bickham in 1753, to dress up the south front of the house in neo-classical style. [Laurence Whistler, 'Signor Borra at Stowe', *C. Life*, 29 Aug. 1957; John Harris, 'Blondel at Stowe', *Connoisseur*, March 1964; Michael McCarthy, 'Eighteenth-Century Amateur Architects and their Gardens', in *The Picturesque Garden and its Influence outside the British Isles*, ed. Pevsner, Dumbarton Oaks, Washington, 1974; information from Mr. Michael Gibbon.]

Exactly when Borra left England for good is uncertain, but by 1756 he was fully employed in Piedmont, and he continued to practise there as an architect and civil engineer until his death in November 1770 (not 1786).

[Information from Dr. Olga Zoller of Bonn, whose doctoral thesis has established the correct dates of Borra's birth and death; *The Edinburgh Encyclopaedia* vi, 1830, 550–1; C. A. Hutton, 'The Travels of Palmyra Wood, 1750–1', *Jnl. of Hellenic Studies* xlvii, 1927; T. H. Clarke, 'The Discovery of Palmyra', *Arch. Rev.* March 1947; Eileen Harris, *British Architectural Books and Writers 1556–1785*, 1990, 492.]

BOSTOCK, H—, exhibited at the Royal Academy from Kensington between 1833 and 1841. His works included a 'Design for a private chapel proposed to be erected for a gentleman in Essex' (1833) and 'Alterations and additions lately completed to the villa of H. D. Raincock Esq. of Croydon, Surrey' (1837).

BOTHAM, JOSEPH, practised both in Manchester and in Sheffield, where in 1826 he took Samuel Worth (*q.v.*) into partnership. His works included the BRUNSWICK METHODIST CHAPEL, LEEDS, 1824–5, dem. 1984, with a handsome classical façade [D. Linstrum, *West Yorkshire Architects and Architecture*, 1978, 203]; the EASTBROOK WESLEYAN CHAPEL, LEEDS ROAD, BRADFORD, 1825, Gothic, dem. 1902 [*Bradford Observer*, 19 July 1902]; and ST. GEORGE'S (later HOLY TRINITY) CHURCH, LONDON ROAD, DERBY, 1836, Gothic, dem. 1904 [S. Glover, *History & Directory of Derby*, 1849, 27]. The EBENEZER WESLEYAN METHODIST CHAPEL, SHALEMOOR, SHEFFIELD, *c.*1823, Gothic, can also be attributed to him. The church in Derby was built as a speculation which ended in Botham's bankruptcy in 1838 [Glover, *loc.cit.*]. His son J. R. Botham practised as an architect in Birmingham in the 1850s.

BOTT, JOHANN VON, *see* BODT.

BOTTOMLEY, JOSEPH (–1796/7), of 42 Wood Street, Cheapside, exhibited architectural drawings at the Royal Academy from 1791 to 1795. They were mostly of existing buildings, but the 'Elevation of Denton Court near Canterbury' which he showed in 1795 may indicate that he had some responsibility for the recent rebuilding of that house by Sir Samuel Egerton Brydges. As 'Joseph Bottomley, Architect', he was among the subscribers to George Richardson's *New Designs in Architecture*, 1792. He died in the winter of 1796/7 [P.R.O., PROB 11/1284, f. 248]. In

1794 he published from 42 Wood Street a collection of designs for metal fanlights, skylights, stair rails, etc., of which there is a copy in the Soane Museum, and he was presumably the founder of the firm of 'Joseph Bottomley, fanlight manufacturers', which operated from 8 Beech Street, Barbican, up to the 1830s.

BOWEN, JOHN (1785–1853), of Bridgwater, Somerset, was the son-in-law of Peter Nicholson (*q.v.*). After a chequered career he became an employee of Trinity House as engineer in charge of lighthouse construction around the coast of India. He incidentally undertook to supervise the erection of an iron bridge at Lucknow that had been manufactured by the Butterley Ironworks to the designs of John Rennie. Returning to Bridgwater in 1815, he became engineer to the Bridgwater Turnpike Trust, edited a local newspaper, and engaged in controversy over the New Poor Law. He appears also to have designed the circular classical MARKET HOUSE built in 1826–7 [*V.C.H. Somerset* vi, 217, citing *Robson's Somerset Directory*, 1839; see also S. G. Jarman, *History of Bridgwater*, 1889, 131]. [Margaret Allen, 'John Bowen of Bridgwater', *Studies in Somerset History* (typescript), Somerset Record Office, 1971; information from Mr. M. McGarvie.]

BOWEN, THOMAS (*c.*1788–1859), of Swansea, was a mason and builder by trade. In 1820 he designed and built the TOWN HALL at NEATH, GLAMORGANSHIRE, 'a major and ambitious work . . . with twin flights of steps rising to a pillared loggia', and in 1825 he made a similar design for SWANSEA TOWN HALL which he proceeded to build with the Gloucester architect John Collingwood as supervisor on behalf of the burgesses. Collingwood found Bowen's plans incorrect and his specification inadequate and bankruptcy ensued. This was probably the end of Bowen's career as an architect, but he was apparently still in business as a builder at the time of his death in 1859. Swansea Town Hall was remodelled in 1847 by Thomas Taylor of London [Thomas Lloyd, 'The Architects of Regency Swansea', *Gower* 41, 1990; C. F. Cliff, *The Book of South Wales*, 1854, 152].

BOWIE, ALEXANDER (–*c.*1829), was a builder-architect of Stirling, where he was responsible for building several elegant and distinctively detailed houses in Allan Park between 1818 and 1827. CRAIGS HOUSE, STIRLING, built before 1820 for Robert Gillies, may also be attributed to him [David Walker in *C. Life*, 28 Aug. 1969]. He was presumably the Alexander Bowie who enlarged the Romanesque DUNNING CHURCH, PERTHSHIRE, in 1810 [S.R.O., HR 560/1]. Bowie made his will in May 1829 and appears to have died soon afterwards.

BOYCE, GIDEON ACLAND (*c.*1797–1861), practised at Tiverton in Devon, where he restored the GREENWAY CHAPEL in the PARISH CHURCH in 1829, as recorded by an inscription. In TIVERTON he also designed the MASONIC HALL, ANGEL HILL, 1834 [*Exeter Flying Post*, 11 Sept. 1834], ST. JOHN'S CHURCH (R.C.), 1836–8, Gothic [W. Harding, *History of Tiverton*, 2, 1847, 67] and a Tudor Gothic school for John Heathcoat adjoining his mill, 1841 [G. Jackson-Stops in *C. Life*, 18 July 1985, 162]. PETTON CHAPEL, DEVON, 1847–8, was his work [I.C.B.S.]. He died at Tiverton on 16 Jan. 1861, aged 64, and is commemorated on the family monument in the churchyard.

BOYD, GEORGE, exhibited a view of 'Shoreham manor-house, the seat of T. Barnett' (a misprint for 'T. Borrett') at the Royal Academy in 1805, and in 1807 'An elevation for a new manor-house at Shoreham, Kent, the seat of Sir W. Stirling, Bart.' Whether Sir Walter Stirling adopted Boyd's design is not known. Boyd's exhibit in 1810 was a 'Design for a country residence in the Gothic style, about to be built in Gloucestershire'. He continued to practise as an architect and surveyor in London until the late 1830s.

BOYD, JOHN, of Glasgow, began life as a mason. After attempting unsuccessfully to set himself up as a builder, 'he turned architect and inspector, and taught drawing at his house in Jamaica Street'. One of his pupils records that 'more fun than work went on in the school'. This was in the 1830s [James Cruikshank, *Sketch of the Incorporation of Masons*, Glasgow, 1879, 80]. He was presumably the John Boyd who designed the front of the FREE CHURCH at STRANRAER, WIGTOWNSHIRE, in 1845 [S.R.O., CH 3/1382/2, 8 July 1845].

BOYD, THOMAS (*c.*1753–1822), practised in Dumfries, where he died on 23 Sept. 1822, aged 69 [W. McDowall, *Memorials of St. Michael's Churchyard, Dumfries*, 1876, 233]. He was a competent provincial designer, usually in a somewhat old-fashioned Palladian manner. His bridge at Dumfries was ornamented with pairs of Ionic columns copied from Mylne's Blackfriars Bridge. In 1801–5 he made designs for a new bridge over the R. Eden nr. Carlisle, but was eventually superseded by Smirke [M. I. M. MacDonald, 'The Building of the New Eden Bridge at Carlisle', *Trans. Cumberland and Westmorland Arch. Soc.* N.S. lxxi, 1971].

GLENAE, DUMFRIESSHIRE, for Robert Dalzell, 1789 [*Scottish Field*, April 1964, 51, citing contract] (J. G. Dunbar, *Historic Architecture of Scotland*, 1966, fig. 55).

DUMFRIES, THE THEATRE, 1790–2 [W. McDowall, *History of Dumfries*, 1867, 703].

DUMFRIES, THE NEW (BUCCLEUCH STREET) BRIDGE (R. Nith), 1791–4; widened 1893 [W. McDowall, *Memorials of St. Michael's Churchyard, Dumfries*, 1876, 233; signed plan and elevation at Drumlanrig Castle dated 1792].

CALLY HOUSE, KIRKCUDBRIGHTSHIRE, raised wings and corridors for James Murray, 1794 [*Catalogue of R.I.B.A. Drawings Coll.: B*, 99, figs. 73–4].

DUMFRIES, THE TRADES' HALL, 134 HIGH STREET, 1804–6 [W. McDowall, *History of Dumfries*, 1867, 743].

BOYD, WILLIAM (–1795), 'formerly an eminent architect and builder at Gibraltar', died at his house in Exeter on 9 Nov. 1795 [*Gent's Mag.* 1795 (ii), 1055].

BOYERS, D[ANIEL?], a builder and surveyor of Horncastle, Lincs., published *The Art of Conducting and Measuring Buildings, by a Simple Method*, Horncastle 1807. The book was reissued by a London publisher in 1831.

BOYLE, RICHARD, 3RD EARL OF BURLINGTON and 4TH EARL OF CORK (1694–1753), was born on 25 April 1694. He succeeded his father, the 2nd Earl, in 1704 at the age of 10, and inherited extensive estates in Yorkshire and Ireland. He had a country house at Londesborough in the East Riding, a town house in Piccadilly and a suburban seat at Chiswick in Middlesex. His status as a major landowner in Ireland and Yorkshire was recognized by George I, who in 1715 appointed him Lord Treasurer of Ireland and Lord Lieutenant of the East and West Ridings of Yorkshire, while George II made him a Privy Councillor (1729) and a Knight of the Garter. In May 1733, however, he resigned all his posts when a promised 'white staff' (the symbol of high office under the Crown) was not forthcoming, and went into opposition. According to Lord Hervey, Burlington let it be known that 'his resignation did not proceed from any dislike to the measures of the Administration, or any quarrel with the ministers', but only from his resentment at the King's failure to honour his word. While her husband withdrew from the court, Lady Burlington retained her own office of Lady of the Bedchamber to the Queen.

Exactly what lay behind this breach between Burlington and the King may never be known, but it has been claimed that he was a Jacobite, and if so the conflict of loyalties might well explain his withdrawal from court. His family background was one of devotion to the Stewarts and there are circumstances in his life which could suggest that, although ostensibly a loyal subject of the Hanoverian regime, he was in fact an active supporter of the Pretender. If so, he avoided any overt act of treason, and in the critical year of 1715 appears to have carried out his duties as Lord Lieutenant in Yorkshire in a manner satisfactory to the government. The evidence for clandestine activity is of its nature apt to be inconclusive, and is certainly so in Burlington's case. If, however, his Jacobitism were to be proved, then several aspects of his life as a student and patron of the arts might appear in a new light. Contacts with exiled Jacobites would become as important a feature of his foreign travels as architectural inquiry, and his cult of Palladianism, far from reflecting any Whig ideology, could be seen as a conscious reversion to the architectural ideals of the early Stuart court during the surveyorship of Inigo Jones.

Whatever political ideology may have lain behind Lord Burlington's espousal of Palladian principles, his dedication to architecture was remarkable in an eighteenth-century nobleman. His taste in painting and gardening had already been praised by Macky in 1714, but it was apparently not until 1716, when he was 22, that Burlington became seriously interested in architecture. How far this interest was stimulated by buildings seen in the course of his foreign tours[1] it is difficult to say. Even if most of his foreign itineraries were to be explained in terms of clandestine contact with exiled Jacobites rather than of planned architectural tourism, an observant eye can take in a lot in the intervals of social or conspiratorial meetings, and when he was in the Veneto in 1719 he made careful notes on the architectural detailing of several of Palladio's buildings in his copy of the *Quattro Libri*. By this time his role as a patron of the arts was clearly formulated. He was a prominent supporter of the Royal Academy of

[1] Burlington made four foreign tours: in 1714–5 to the Netherlands, Germany, Rome and the principal North Italian cities, including a short visit to Venice; in 1717 to Paris and Flanders; in 1719 to Paris and Italy, including 10 or 12 days in the Veneto; and in 1726 to France.

Music recently established in London, with Handel and Bononcini as composers. William Kent had joined his entourage as a history painter. He had also undertaken to support the Italian sculptor Guelfi, and with Colen Campbell as his architect he hoped to restore Palladian architecture to the position it had held in England in the time of Inigo Jones. Campbell took the place of James Gibbs, who in 1716 had begun to transform Burlington's house in Piccadilly into 'the only town residence really fit for a British nobleman' by rebuilding the forecourt, and Kent was set to work to adorn the interior. But Burlington's dependence on Campbell appears to have become less close in the early 1720s, when he began to act as his own architect without professional advice, assisted only by Henry Flitcroft ('Burlington Harry'), a young man of humble origin whom he had recently taken into his service, Daniel Garrett, and a draughtsman named Samuel Savill. As early as 1717 he had designed a garden pavilion in the grounds of Chiswick House, and it is possible that he was himself responsible for the semicircular colonnade at Burlington House. It was in 1722 that he laid the foundation stone of his first public work, the Dormitory of Westminster School. Drawings for this had already been made by Wren and Dickinson, the surveyors of Westminster Abbey, and the adoption in their place of Burlington's Palladian design therefore marked the first victory of his campaign against the empirical classicism of Wren. Burlington's mission was to reinstate in Augustan England the canons of Roman architecture as described by Vitruvius, exemplified by its surviving remains, and practised by Palladio, Scamozzi and Jones. As he did not himself investigate the antique remains in Italy he was largely dependent for his knowledge of them on Palladio's drawings and engravings, which provided the sources for many favourite Anglo-Palladian motifs such as the tripartite window from the Baths of Diocletian, the coffered vaults of the Roman temples, and the close-set columns of the 'Egyptian Hall'. Palladio's villas and palaces and the Jones–Webb drawings were Burlington's remaining sources. Neither was used indiscriminately: indeed Burlington and his colleagues set a standard of classical correctitude in which there was no room either for Palladio's occasional excursions into mannerism or for the Jacobean deviations disclosed in some of the Jones–Webb drawings. Radical though Burlington's architectural programme was, it appealed to an aristocracy nurtured on classical literature and ready to demonstrate that emancipation from contemporary European taste recently called for by Lord Shaftesbury.

During the 1720s and 1730s almost all the characteristic features of English Palladianism appear in buildings erected to Burlington's designs. It was at Tottenham Park that the pavilion towers from Wilton were first decorated with Venetian windows: it was at Chiswick that the same Venetian windows were first placed in arched recesses: and it was at York, in Burlington's Assembly Rooms, that Palladio's Egyptian Hall was reconstructed with doctrinaire exactitude. By the early 1730s the conventions of the new Palladianism had become established as the accepted style for English country houses and public buildings. As for Burlington himself, his authority as 'il Palladio e il Jones de' nostri tempi'[1] was absolute. For more than thirty years he was the acknowledged arbiter of English architectural taste. He was consulted by everyone, from fellow peers like the Duke of Richmond and the Earl of Leicester to the aldermen of London and York. When Wentworth Woodhouse was building, Sir Thomas Robinson reported that 'the whole finishing will be entirely submitted to Lord Burlington'. Even Hawksmoor's designs for the mausoleum at Castle Howard were subjected to Burlington's censorship, and given, at his behest, a flight of steps like those at Chiswick. By now Burlington's chief architectural ally was William Kent. Kent, who began his career as a history painter, had, under Burlington's patronage, found his true vocation as an architect, and became the most influential of those who interpreted his ideas. As Horace Walpole put it, Lord Burlington was 'the Apollo of the Arts', and William Kent was his 'proper priest'. By securing posts for his protégés in the Office of Works, Burlington was able to influence public as well as private architecture, and Kent's designs for the Horse Guards, the Royal Mews and the Treasury Buildings were, like his projects for a Royal Palace and for rebuilding the Houses of Parliament, directly inspired by Burlington's ideas.

Burlington's enthusiasm for Palladio was equalled only by his devotion to Inigo Jones, and besides repairing the portico of St. Paul's, Covent Garden, in 1727, and the Barber-Surgeon's Hall in Monkwell Street, because they were the work of Jones, he purchased a gateway designed by the same architect, which he removed from Beaufort House to his grounds at Chiswick (cf. B.L., Add. MS. 4055, f. 349). In 1720–1 he bought from John Talman a

[1] The phrase was inscribed by the Italian poet Scipione Maffei in a copy of Sanmichele's *Five Orders* which he presented to Burlington.

large collection of drawings by Inigo Jones and Webb, and arranged for their publication by William Kent as the *Designs of Inigo Jones* (1727), with the addition of 'Some few Designs of Buildings' by the Earl himself. With them were the drawings by Palladio that Inigo Jones had purchased in Italy in 1614. Burlington had already acquired Palladio's drawings of the Roman baths and other ancient buildings, which had been the property of the Barbaro-Trevisan family since the architect's death at their Villa Maser in 1580. These drawings were evidently intended to illustrate a book on Roman architectural antiquities which Palladio never completed. Burlington hoped to recover the manuscript and publish the entire work, but the text (if it ever existed) has never come to light, and in the end he printed for private circulation only a few copies of the engraved drawings of the Roman baths as *Fabbriche Antiche disegnate da Andrea Palladio*. Despite the date 1730 on the title-page the book was not in fact issued until several years later. Pope's *Epistle to Lord Burlington* (1731) was written to celebrate what at that date was still envisaged as a more complete edition of Palladio's drawings. Unpublished drawings in Burlington's collection were used by Isaac Ware in his *Designs of Inigo Jones and Others* (1743), and by John Vardy in *Some Designs of Mr. Inigo Jones and Mr. William Kent* (1744). Ware also acknowledged his assistance in the preface to his *Palladio* (1738), which he dedicated to Burlington.

The drawings which Burlington collected descended through his only surviving daughter to the Dukes of Devonshire. Some of them remain at Chatsworth, but the greater part is on permanent loan to the R.I.B.A. Drawings Collection in London. Among them are a number of Burlington's own drawings which prove beyond doubt that he could 'draw and design as well as pay the bill', and it is clear that, as Wittkower has said, 'he must be assigned a decisive share in the development of English neo-classicism, not only as a patron of artists . . . but as a practising architect.'

Burlington died on 4 December 1753, and was buried in the family vault at Londesborough (for the inscribed coffin-plate see *C. Life*, 19 Dec. 1947). At least a dozen portraits of Burlington are known or recorded (see John Wilton-Ely in *Arch. Hist.* 27, 1984). Among the most important are one in the National Portrait Gallery attributed to Jonathan Richardson (*c.*1718), and that by George Knapton (1743) at Chatsworth.

[*A.P.S.D.*; *D.N.B.*; G.E.C., *Complete Peerage* ii, 432–3; will (P.R.O., P.C.C. 333 SEARLE); MS. Letters at Chatsworth and B.L., Althorp Papers; *Walpole Soc.* xix, 160–1; *Vertue Note Books* (Walpole Soc.) iii, 55–6, 73, 139–40; H. Walpole, *Anecdotes of Painting*, ed. Dallaway & Wornum, 1862, iii, 773–6; Fiske Kimball, 'Burlington Architectus', *R.I.B.A. Jnl.* xxxiv–xxxv, 1927; James Lees-Milne, 'Lord Burlington in Yorkshire', *Arch. Rev.* July 1945; R. Wittkower, 'Lord Burlington and William Kent', *Archaeological Jnl.* cii, 1945, reprinted in *Palladio and English Palladianism*, 1974; R. Wittkower, *The Earl of Burlington and William Kent* (York Georgian Soc's Occasional Papers No. 5, 1948); R. Wittkower, 'Un libro di Schizzi di Filippo Juvarra a Chatsworth', in *Bollettino Soc. Piemontese d'Archeologia e di Belle Arti*, 1949, reprinted in *Studies in the Italian Baroque*, 1975; J. Lees-Milne, *Earls of Creation*, 1962, 103–56; Pat Rogers, 'The Burlington Circle in the Provinces: Alexander Pope's Yorkshire Friends', *Durham University Jnl.* 67, 1974–5; *History of the King's Works* v, 1976, 419–20 (for Burlington's involvement in the scheme for new Houses of Parliament in 1731–3); *Lord Burlington and his Circle* (papers given at a Georgian Group Symposium, 1982); C. Sicca, 'Lord Burlington at Chiswick: Architecture and Landscape', *Garden History* 10 (1), 1982; Peter Leach, 'Lord Burlington in Wharfedale', *Arch. Hist.* 32, 1989; Jane Clark, 'The mysterious Mr. Buck' [Burlington as a Jacobite], *Apollo*, May 1989; C. Sicca, 'The Architecture of the Wall; Astylism in the Architecture of Lord Burlington', *Arch. Hist.* 33, 1990; Eileen Harris, *British Architectural Books and Writers 1556–1785*, 1990, 348–351; Jane Clark, 'Palladianism and the Divine Right of Kings', *Apollo*, April 1992; Jacques Carré, *Lord Burlington*, Clermont-Ferrand, 1993].

CHISWICK HOUSE, MIDDLESEX, Casina or Bagnio, 'the first essay of his Lordship's happy invention', 1717; dem. 1778 [*Vitruvius Britannicus* ii, 1725, pl. 26].

LONDON, BURLINGTON HOUSE, PICCADILLY. According to Fiske Kimball (*R.I.B.A. Jnl.* xxxiv, 687, note §), Burlington himself designed the semicircular colonnade, dem. 1868 and removed to Battersea Park, but never re-erected. The E. side of the forecourt was designed by Gibbs in 1716, and the refronting of the house, carried out in 1719, was entrusted to Campbell, who also designed the gateway to Piccadilly, illustrated in *Vitruvius Britannicus* iii, 1725, pl. 25. Conclusive evidence as to the authorship of the colonnade is lacking, but as Campbell does not claim the credit for it either for his patron or for himself, the possibility that it was designed by Gibbs cannot be excluded [*Survey of London* xxxii, 398].

TOTTENHAM PARK, WILTS., for Charles, Lord Bruce, 1721 onwards; wings added to Burlington's designs *c.*1730; enlarged and remodelled by T. Cundy 1826. Flitcroft was the executant architect [R. Wittkower in *Archaeological Jnl.* cii, 1945, 154; the Earl of Cardigan in *Wilts. Arch. Mag.* lii, 1948, 176–83; J. Harris, 'The Building Works of Lord Viscount Bruce', in *Lord Burlington and his Circle*, 1982]. Burlington also appears to have designed ornamental buildings in the park, including a Banqueting House, 1743; dem. 1824 (recorded in Marquess of Ailesbury's archives, drawing 361).

LONDON, GREAT (now OLD) BURLINGTON STREET, No. 30 for 6th Earl of Mountrath, *c.*1721; dem. 1935 [R.I.B.A.D. VI/4; *Survey of London* xxxii, 505–8].

WESTMINSTER SCHOOL, THE DORMITORY, 1722–30; altered 1895 by T. G. Jackson, who cut windows through alternate niches; gutted by bombing 1940/1, since restored [*Wren Soc.* xi, 35–45, pls. 8–28].

LONDON, GREAT (now OLD) BURLINGTON STREET, No. 29 for General George Wade, 1723; dem. 1935 [*Vitruvius Britannicus* iii, 1725, pl. 10; *Survey of London* xxxii, 500–4; T. Knox & T. Longstaffe-Gowan, 'General Wade's house', *Georgian Group's Jnl.* 1991].

LONDON, QUEENSBERRY HOUSE, No. 7 BURLINGTON GARDENS, gateway for 3rd Duke of Queensberry, *c.*1723; dem. 1785 [W. Kent, *Designs of Inigo Jones* i, 1727, pl. 59, left; *Catalogue of R.I.B.A. Drawings Coll: B*, 199].

OATLANDS, WEYBRIDGE, SURREY, probably designed 'villa' (a garden building) for 7th Earl of Lincoln, *c.*1725; dem. [*Arch. Hist.* 25, 1982, 9, 17].

WALDERSHARE PARK, KENT, THE BELVEDERE TOWER, for Sir Robert Furnese, 1725–7. A plan from Chatsworth appears to establish Burlington's authorship of this tower, which bears a remarkable but presumably fortuitous resemblance to one of the tower mausolea at Palmyra (cf. R. Wood, *The Ruins of Palmyra*, 1753, pl. lvi). Furnese was a connoisseur who subscribed to all the Palladian publications. His accounts (Kent Archives Office, U 471, A.17) show that it cost over £1000 to build, but throw no light on the origin of the design, which on purely stylistic grounds might be attributed to Colen Campbell.

CHISWICK HOUSE, MIDDLESEX, refronted the existing house (later dem.) and designed and built the adjoining Villa, *c.*1725–9. The wings, added in 1788, were dem. 1952. In addition to the Casina (above), Burlington designed the Circular Temple, a Pavilion (dem.), and an Orangery (dem.), all of which are shown on Roque's engraving of 1736 [W. Kent, *The Designs of Inigo Jones* i, 1727, pls. 70–3] (H. A. Tipping, *English Homes*, Period V, i, 1921, 139–54; K. Downes, 'Chiswick Villa', *Arch. Rev.* Oct. 1978; R. Hewlings, *Chiswick House and Gardens*, English Heritage 1989).

LONDON, WARWICK HOUSE, WARWICK STREET, ST. JAMES'S, internal alterations for Charles, Lord Bruce, 1726–7; dem. 1827 [Marquess of Ailesbury's archives, nos. 1827–33].

ROUND COPPICE, IVER HEATH, BUCKS., for Charles, Lord Bruce, 1726–7; dem. 1954 [drawings from Chatsworth, B.21, C.3–4; John Harris as above under Tottenham Park].

CASTLE HILL, DEVONSHIRE, remodelled for Lord Clinton (afterwards 1st Lord Fortescue) by Roger Morris, working under the direction of Lord Burlington and Lord Herbert, 1729–*c.*1740. Morris's contract for the Portland stonework of the exterior, dated 22 Feb. 1728/9, specifies that the proportions of the entablature 'shall be made as the Earl of Burlington or the Lord Herbert shall direct' [Devon C.R.O., Fortescue Papers, E 1/93], and on 7 June 1730 Lord Clinton wrote to Lord Burlington asking for a promised drawing of the inside of the hall, 'that cannot be begun till your Lordship is so good as to send me the draught' [Chatsworth letters 198.0]. The centre was gutted by fire in 1934, and subsequently restored (*C. Life*, 17, 24 March 1934, 29 Oct. 1938).

NORTHWICK PARK, WORCS. (now GLOS.), E. front and entrance hall for Sir John Rushout, Bart., *c.*1730–2 [R. Wittkower, 'Lord Burlington at Northwick Park', in *The Country Seat*, ed. Colvin & Harris, 1970, 121–30].

FOXHALL, CHARLTON, SUSSEX, a banqueting house for members of the Charlton Hunt, among whom the Duke of Richmond was prominent, *c.*1730; dem. [D. Defoe, *Tour through Great Britain* i, 1738, 205; Earl of March, *Records of the Old Charlton Hunt*, 1910, 25, quoting contemporary verses].

YORK, THE ASSEMBLY ROOMS, 1731–2; new entrance front by J. P. Pritchett & W. Watson, 1828. In 1735 Burlington provided designs for an additional building, completed in 1739 but dem. 1860 [*Vitruvius Britannicus* iv, pls. 78–81; R. Wittkower, *The Earl of Burlington and William Kent*, York Georgian Soc. Occasional Paper No. 5, 1948; R. Wittkower, 'Burlington and his Work in

York' (1954), reprinted in *Palladio and English Palladianism*, 1974; H. Goodall, 'Lord Burlington's York Piazza', York Georgian Soc's *Annual Report* 1970].

CHISWICK, MIDDLESEX, house formerly of Sir Stephen Fox and later of the Earl of Morton, altered hall for 1st Earl of Wilmington, 1732; dem. *c.*1812 [Chatsworth, BC B.12: 'Section of a hall which I altered for my Lord Wilmington at Chiswick 1732'].

LONDON, RICHMOND HOUSE, WHITEHALL, for 2nd Duke of Richmond, 1733–4; altered by James Wyatt 1782; destroyed by fire 1791 [H. Walpole, *Anecdotes of Painting* v, ed. F. W. Hilles & P. B. Daghlian, 1939, 161; *Walpole Soc.* xix, 160; bound vol. of drawings at Goodwood (Small Library A4) on loan to R.I.B.A.D.; drawings from Chatsworth, D.17, 18 and probably D.6A; T. P. Connor, 'Architecture and Planting at Goodwood 1723–50', *Sussex Archl. Colls.* 117, 1979, 187].

PETERSHAM LODGE, SURREY, for 1st Earl of Harrington, *c.*1733; wings terminating in polygonal pavilions added by E. Shepherd *c.*1740; altered by 1st Lord Camelford *c.*1785; dem. *c.*1835 [*Walpole Soc.* xix, 160] (engraving by T. Lightoler in B.L., *King's Maps* xl, 29a).

HOLKHAM HALL, NORFOLK. According to Matthew Brettingham, junior, 'the general ideas . . . were first struck out by the Earls of Burlington and Leicester, assisted by Mr. William Kent', *c.*1734 [*The Plans and Elevations of the late Earl of Leicester's House at Holkham*, 2nd ed. 1773]. Features specifically attributed to Burlington in that book are the ceiling of the portico (pl. 18) and the ceiling of the north dressing-room (pl. 24).

WOBURN FARM, nr. CHERTSEY, SURREY, octagonal temple for Philip Southcote, 1743; dem. [drawing from Chatsworth, B.15].

COLESHILL HOUSE, BERKS. An inscription dated 31 Dec. 1748 recorded that the chimney-stacks at the angles of the house were 'rebuilt for Sr Mark Pleydell Bt. in 1744 by ye Direct[s]. of ye Earls of Burlington and Leicester'. Lord Burlington employed Isaac Ware to make drawings of the ceilings here. The house was destroyed by fire 1952.

KIRBY HALL, OUSEBURN, YORKS. (W.R.), elevation for Stephen Thompson,[1] in association with Roger Morris, 1747–*c.*1755; dem. 1920 [contemporary engraving by Basire inscribed 'Elevation by R. Morris Arch[t]. and the Earl of Burlington: Executed, & the inside finishings, by J. Carr, Architect. Plans by the Owner, S.T.' (B.L., *King's Maps* xlv, 24–1); *Vitruvius Britannicus* v, 1771, pls. 70–1, inscribed 'E. of Burlington and R. Morris Ar.'; letters from Stephen Thompson to Thomas Grimston in E. Yorks. Record Office, DDGR/41].

EUSTON HALL, SUFFOLK, wooden bridge in the park for 2nd Duke of Grafton; dem. [described by Sir Thomas Robinson in 1731: Hist. MSS. Comm., *Carlisle*, 87; plan and estimate from Chatsworth, B.22].

BOYNTON HALL, YORKS. (E.R.), designs for alterations to south and west fronts for Sir William Strickland, Bart. (d. 1735), inaccurately carried out by a local builder. In 1768 Sir Thomas Robinson related how 'L[d] Burlington gave him a beautiful design, with a Palladian roof, and an Attic Story, instead of the old wretched and ugly roof of our Gothick ancestors – when the house was compleated, Sir W[m]. went down . . . when alas he found the old fashioned roof, and many other material alterations from the plan' [*Arch. Rev.* Aug. 1926, 51; Francis Johnson, 'Boynton Hall', *Trans. E. Yorks. Georgian Soc.* iii (3), 1954; Arthur Oswald in *C. Life*, 22–29 July 1954].

LONDESBOROUGH HOUSE, YORKS. (E.R.), alterations to his own country house, for which the only specific evidence appears to be a design for a garden gateway from Chatsworth dated 1735 (B.13); dem. 1811.

CLIFTON HALL, NOTTS., Belvedere summer-house for Sir Robert Clifton, Bart.; dem. 1969 ['Travel Journal of Philip Yorke', ed. J. Godber, *Beds. Hist. Rec. Soc.* xlvii, 1968, 126, 11 Aug. 1744, when he saw the 'Summer house designed by Lord Burlington']. Sir Robert Clifton was a guest at Londesborough in Sept. 1735 [Chatsworth Letters, 127.10].

Burlington's unexecuted designs included a house for Col. James (not William) Gee (d. 1751) at BISHOP BURTON, YORKS. (E.R.) [R.I.B.A.D. VI/1]; and a house for William Pulteney (cr. Earl of Bath 1742) [*ibid.*, VI/3], which was published by Kent, *Designs of Inigo Jones* ii, 1727, pl. 12, as 'a House with an Arcade, Design'd by the Earl of Burlington'. THE SCHOOL AND ALMSHOUSES AT SEVENOAKS, KENT, as built in 1727, differ too considerably from Burlington's designs [R.I.B.A.D. VI/8 and Kent, *op. cit.* ii, pls. 52–3], to be regarded as his, and although the Duke of Richmond was pressing for his drawings for the COUNCIL HOUSE at CHICHESTER in 1730 [Chatsworth letters, 201.0 and 201.2], the building erected in 1731 does not correspond exactly to either of

[1] The house was built by Stephen Thompson during the lifetime of his father Henry Thompson, who did not die until 1760, aged 83.

Burlington's alternative designs [R.I.B.A.D.]. Vertue was no doubt correctly informed in attributing it to Roger Morris, who was associated with Burlington at Kirby Hall, Yorks. (above) and may well have been concerned in Sevenoaks School too.

BRADBERRY, THOMAS, entered the Royal Academy Schools in 1820. He was awarded the Silver Medal in 1821 and the Gold Medal in 1823. In 1820 he exhibited a 'View of St. John's Church, Westminster' at the Royal Academy. Directories show that he subsequently practised as an architect from 8 Langbourn Chambers, Fenchurch Street. He drew several plates for Britton & Pugin's *Public Buildings of London*, 1826–8, but no architectural work of his has so far been identified.

BRADFORD, JOHN, 'Architect of Coventry', was employed to rebuild the N. and S. aisles of MERIDEN CHURCH, WARWICKS., in 1826–7 [Vestry Minutes in Warwicks. C.R.O.]. He also designed LEEK WOOTTON VICARAGE, WARWICKS., in a sub-Georgian style in 1824/30 [Lichfield Joint Record Office, B/A/13].

BRADIE, JOHN, of London (otherwise unrecorded, but cf. 'Brodie, John' below), designed a lodge or cottage at STOKE PARK, WILTS., for Joshua Smith in 1800. It survives as the lodge south of the main road, and the original drawing is in the Cooper Union Museum, New York [J. Harris, *Catalogue of British Drawings for Architecture etc. in American Collections*, 1971, 34].

BRADLEY, THOMAS (1753–1833), of Halifax, began life as a joiner, but had a successful career as a canal engineer and also practised as an architect. At the age of 22 he probably designed the HALIFAX PIECE HALL, a monumental building of almost Roman grandeur built in 1775–9. His was certainly the design accepted in 1775, and he is stated to have been the 'architect' of the building in White's *Directory of the West Riding*, published only four years after his death. On the other hand, one of the Hopes of Manchester (*q.v.*) is referred to as 'The Architect' in a contemporary song sheet celebrating the completion of the building, and an estimate made in 1775 is signed by 'Samuel and John Hope'. The loss of the minutes of the responsible committee makes it difficult to establish the respective roles of Bradley and the Hopes in the design and construction of the building, but a careful examination of the evidence has suggested that the Hopes were brought in to work out and supervise the realization of a design made by an inexperienced young man [Philip Smithies, *The Architecture of the Halifax Piece Hall*, Halifax, 1988].

Bradley's only other recorded work as an architect is CROWNEST HOUSE, LIGHTCLIFFE, YORKS. (W.R.), for William Walker, 1788 (dem.), an elegant Georgian house in the style of John Carr and indeed 'virtually a copy' of his neighbouring 'Pye Nest' [G. Richardson, *New Vitruvius Britannicus* i, 1802, pls. 64–5]. In 1789 an engraving of THE SQUARE INDEPENDENT CHAPEL, HALIFAX, was published in Jacob's *History of Halifax* from a drawing made by Bradley in 1772, but it is unlikely that he was the architect of this chapel, built in 1771–2.

In 1792 Bradley was appointed Superintendent Surveyor of the Calder & Hebble Navigation, and the rest of his life was spent on canal work. According to the inscription on his gravestone in the Square Church graveyard, he 'discharged the duties of that Situation with great ability as well as the utmost integrity and zeal of the interest of his employers' [Reginald Spink, 'Thomas Bradley', *Halifax Evening Courier*, 22 April 1978].

BRADLEY, WILLIAM (*c.*1777–1854), originally of Halifax and later of Poppleton, son of the above, appears in Pigot's 1828–9 *Directory* as a joiner, but subscribed as 'Architect' to several early nineteenth-century architectural books. His only recorded work is COLEY CHURCH, YORKS. (W.R.), 1816, Gothic, described by Pevsner as 'a remarkably serious design for its date' [Borthwick Institute, York, Fac. 1816/2]. Miss Anne Lister, who thought of employing Bradley at Shibden Hall, was told that he was 'not a man to be depended on – very idle [and] not fit to be an architect' [R. Spink, 'William Bradley', *Halifax Evening Courier*, 29 April 1978; D. Linstrum, *West Yorkshire Architecture and Architects*, 1978, 372].

BRADSHAW, WILLIAM (*c.*1728–1801), was a builder and surveyor of Henley-on-Thames. In 1781 his design for a new stone bridge at Henley was rejected, but he supervised the construction of the existing bridge designed by William Hayward (*q.v.*) and built in 1782–6 [Francis Sheppard, 'Henley Bridge and its Architect', *Arch. Hist.* 27, 1984], and in 1789 he supervised the rebuilding of Great Marlow Bridge to the designs of R. F. Brettingham [Bridge Commissioners' records in Bucks. C.R.O.]. In 1795–6 he designed and built HENLEY-ON-THAMES TOWN HALL, pulled down and re-erected as a private house at Crazies Hill in 1899 [Henley Borough Minute-book 1722–99 in Oxon. C.R.O.].

He died in 1801, aged 73 [Henley parish register].

BRADWELL, DAVID (*c.*1735–1813), was the first of three bricklayers and builders in Cambridge who bore this name. He was succeeded by David Bradwell II (d. 1836, aged 66), whose son David Bradwell III predeceased his father, dying in 1835 at the age of 35 [monumental inscription at St. Andrew the Great Church, Cambridge, *ex inf.* Mrs. M. E. L. Clifford]. In 1785 David Bradwell I and a carpenter named Kaye designed and built a lecture-room (dem.) in the Botanic Garden [Willis & Clark, iii, 153]. Either he or his son signs drawings of ROPSLEY PARSONAGE, LINCS., dated 1803, in the Lincs. R.O. (Fac. 5/16).

BRAINE, WILLIAM, was a carpenter living at 43 East Street, Manchester Square. In 1813 he exhibited a design for a villa at the Royal Academy. F. E. Braine, of the same address, exhibited 'a Design for a public bath' in 1822.

BRAMBLE, BENJAMIN (*c.*1789–1857), was an architect and builder of Portsmouth. His principal work was the Greek Revival GUILDHALL, PORTSMOUTH (afterwards the Museum and Art Gallery), 1837–8; dem. after bombing 1940/1 [R. East, *Extracts from the Portsmouth Records*, 1891, 809] (J. Summerson, *The Bombed Buildings of Britain*, 1942, 99). He also designed HOLY TRINITY CHURCH, WEST COWES, ISLE OF WIGHT, for Mrs. S. Goodwin, 1832, in the lancet Gothic of the period [G.R.]. He died at Southsea on 18 November 1857, aged 68 [*Gent's Mag.* 1857 (ii), 691].

BRASH, JOHN (–1848), practised in Glasgow. Very little is known about him, but such of his works as have been identified show that he was an architect of some ability. The elder James Salmon (1805–88) was his pupil. He retired to Falkirk and died there on 12 Feb. 1848 [S.R.O., SC 67/36/28, p. 154; A. Gomme & D. Walker, *Architecture of Glasgow*, 1987, 75, 286].

STRATHBLANE CHURCH, STIRLINGSHIRE, rebuilt 1803, Gothic [S.R.O., HR 371/1, p. 15].

GLASGOW, TOLCROSS RELIEF (now CENTRAL) CHURCH, 1805–6; steeple added 1834–5 [Gomme & Walker, 286].

GALSTON OLD CHURCH, AYRSHIRE, 1808–9 [S.R.O., HR 797/3 and RHP 14293–8].

GLASGOW UNIVERSITY, THE HAMILTON BUILDING, 1811–13, altering earlier design by Peter Nicholson; dem. [J. Coutts, *History of the University of Glasgow*, Glasgow 1909, 357].

GLASGOW, MCMILLAN CALTON CHURCH (originally First Reformed Presbyterian Congregation), CALTON, 1819; dem. [W. J. Couper, *A Century of Congregational Life*, Glasgow 1919, 30].

SHOTTS CHURCH, LANARKS., 1820, modifying a design by J. Gillespie Graham. Brash was asked to produce 'a corrected plan divested of every sort of unnecessary ornament' [S.R.O., HR 739/2].

GLASGOW, BLYTHSWOOD SQUARE, E., W. and S. sides, 1823, N. side 1829, perhaps following an outline plan by J. Gillespie Graham [Gomme & Walker, 75, 286, fig. 53].

BRASIER, EDWARD BARWELL (1753–), was the son of Edward Brasier, a London banker [P.R.O., PROB 11/1175/74]. He was admitted to the Royal Academy Schools in 1778. A Colchester poll-book of 1788 shows that he had a vote there, but in the same year he used his father's address to exhibit at the Royal Academy a design for an entrance to Callendar Park, Stirlingshire, for William Forbes. The original drawing is illustrated in the Christopher Wood Gallery's 1984 Catalogue: see also S.R.O., GD 171/15/30/7.

BRAY, JOEL (*c.*1787–1846), practised in London. He was President of the Surveyors' Club in 1835 and died on 23 December 1846, aged 59 [records of the Surveyors' Club]. A volume in private ownership entitled 'Bray's Designs for Cottages and Villas' includes a villa 'at HAYES [END], MIDDLESEX, for John Gurney, Designed and Executed 1823', and another at NEW HAMPTON, MIDDLESEX, 'Design'd and Executed 1825'.

BREAM, SAMUEL, was a cabinet-maker of Great Yarmouth, Norfolk, who at least occasionally made architectural designs. In 1771 he made an unexecuted design for a stone bridge of one arch over Yarmouth Haven, of which an engraving was published in *Gent's Mag.* 1771 (104–5 and cf. 487–8). In 1782 he was among those who submitted designs for rebuilding the Theatre at Birmingham [Minutes of the Proprietors in Birmingham Reference Library, Lee Crowder Collection 387].

BREES, SAMUEL CHARLES (–1865), won the Gold Medal of the Society of Arts in 1830 for his design for a village church. In 1835 he competed for the Houses of Parliament in conjunction with Joseph Griffiths. Their joint design was described as 'Gothic, of various periods, embracing the early castellated, palatial, and Tudor styles' [*Catalogue of the Designs for the New Houses of Parliament*, 6th ed. 1836, 39–40]. Brees exhibited topographical drawings at the Royal Academy from 1833 to 1837. He subsequently practised as a civil engineer in Croydon, dying on 3 May 1865 [Principal Probate Registry, Calendar of Probates]. His *Railway Architecture* (1837) is a collection of designs for bridges and other railway works by Robert Stephenson, John Rennie and others, supplemented by some singular designs of his own for tunnel fronts, etc.

BREREWOOD, FRANCIS (*c.*1699–1781), was the younger son of Thomas Brerewood, a wealthy linen-draper descended from a family well known in Chester. His brother Thomas (d. 1748) married a daughter of the 4th Lord Baltimore, and spent most of his life in Maryland. Francis first appears in 1715 as the author of a translation of the Abbé Terraçon's *Discourse on the Iliad of Homer*, but subsequently made a somewhat precarious living as a painter and architect. A portrait of Benedict Leonard Calvert, Governor of Maryland, in the Baltimore Museum of Art, is the chief extant evidence of his ability as a painter. All that is at present known of his architectural activities is that he altered PLACE HOUSE, HORTON, nr. COLNBROOK, BUCKS. (dem. 1785), for his father in about 1725, and worked between 1753 and 1758 at WOODCOTE PARK, nr. EPSOM, SURREY, for the 6th Lord Baltimore, where he added a cupola and other embellishments to the house and landscaped the grounds. In 1736 he was sufficiently well established in England to decline a flattering invitation to visit Maryland and design a Governor's House and other buildings, but towards the end of his life he was in poor circumstances. He died in July 1781 at the age of 82. [*Gent's Mag.* 1791 (ii), 713–16, with engraving of a view of Place House painted by Brerewood; Mrs. Russell Hastings, 'The Versatile Francis Brerewood', *Antiques*, Jan. 1934, 15–16; John Harris, 'Woodcote Park', *Connoisseur*, May 1961; will, P.C.C. 329 WEBSTER.]

BRETTINGHAM, MATTHEW (1699–1769), was the second son of Launcelot Brettingham (1664–1727), a bricklayer or mason of Norwich. He was apprenticed to his father, and took up his freedom as a bricklayer in 1719, on the same day as his elder brother Robert (*q.v.*).[1] He built up a considerable business as a surveyor and building contractor in East Anglia. From 1734 onwards he was employed by the Earl of Leicester to supervise the building of Holkham Hall to the designs of William Kent, and received a salary of £50 a year for 'taking care of his Lordship's buildings' there until the Earl's death in 1759. According to a letter written by his son Matthew, he 'considered the building of Holkham as the great work of his life'. In 1761, when he published *The Plans Elevations and Sections of Holkham in Norfolk, the Seat of the late Earl of Leicester*, he inscribed his own name as 'Architect' on the plates, without any reference to Kent, and his portrait by Heins (1749) shows him proudly holding a drawing of Kent's triumphal arch in the park. His son attempted to justify this conduct by saying that the original designs 'were departed from in every shape and he that had conducted the laying of every Brick from the foundation to the Roof thought he had a better claim to the Reputation of the Fabrick than he who only gave the designs, but never once attended the execution of any part of the work'. However true this may have been – and the architectural history of Holkham has not yet been worked out in detail – the fact remains that Brettingham 'had not the modesty to own that it was built after the design of Kent', and it was left to his son, who brought out a second and enlarged edition of the book in 1773, to admit at least that 'the general ideas were first struck out by the Earls of Burlington and Leicester, assisted by Mr. William Kent.'

It is less clear how much importance should be attached to a letter addressed by a certain William Ingram to the Mayor of Lynn in 1745, in which he claimed to be 'the person who has been employed [by Brettingham] to copy Mr. Kent's works at Holkham and other things of that nature; The drawing of ye Church which he has shown to ye gentlemen of Lynn, and to ye Committee of ye House of Commons, was don by me (tho' its a very poor design as much like a Barn as a Church) in short all the drawings he flashes about the country with, are mine, or of some other person's doing, he being entirely ignorant of drawing or measuring . . .' For Ingram was a man with a grievance against his employer, who owed him money, and his abusive letters were deliberately intended to damage Brettingham's reputation as an architect. There can be no doubt, however, that Brettingham's employment at Holkham led, in the words of his epitaph in St. Augustine's

[1] The statement in *D.N.B.* that as a young man Brettingham 'travelled on the continent of Europe', and published *Remarks on Several Parts of Europe . . . collected upon the spot since the year 1723*, in 4 vols., fol., 1723–38, is incorrect, as the author of this work was really J. D. Breval (d. 1738).

Church at Norwich, 'to the Patronage and esteem of the Nobility, the most distinguish'd for their love of *Palladian* Architecture', and his son testified that 'So early as the year 1740 he had a numerous Acquaintance with the Gentlemen of the County, S[r]. William Harbord, S[r]. Beauchamp Proctor, a Colonel Earle, a Squire Doughty, of Hannow, Mrs. Townsend, of Hunningham, all imploy'd him, and this Lord Orford's father invited him to Houghton, but died before anything could be done there.' He was also 'consulted in all Public Works, built several Bridges in the County, employ'd by Bishop Gooch and the Dean, to direct the Repairs of the Cathedral, erected the Shire house on the Castle Hill, and put on the battlements to the Castle, for which business he never got fully paid for his trouble, through the opposition of some of the County Gentlemen, and the ill behaviour of his Brother Robert, who did the flint stone work of the Shire house'. The building of the Shire house was in fact an episode from which neither Brettingham nor his brother emerged with credit. Their accounts were unsatisfactory, if not actually fraudulent, and had to be submitted to arbitration. As a result of this affair Matthew lost the confidence of the magistrates, who had hitherto employed him as surveyor of the county bridges.

By this time, however, Brettingham's practice as an architect was extending beyond the bounds of East Anglia. In London he designed in the course of the next few years important houses for members of the aristocracy as exalted as the Dukes of York and Norfolk, the Earl of Strafford and the Earl of March, and his account-book (P.R.O., C 108/362) shows that in the 1750s and '60s he was being consulted by the owners of country houses in counties as far afield as Warwickshire, Westmorland and Sussex. Through Lord Leicester's good offices he even became a member of White's Club, where, 'being a man of mild manners and an excellent player at cards', he soon became popular, and earned the nickname of 'Rectitude'.

The idea of publishing a volume containing the designs for Holkham originated with the 1st Earl of Leicester, whose death in 1759 left Brettingham to produce it on his own. In the preface he stated that he intended to follow this work with a collection of designs for country houses made by himself in collaboration with the Earl of Leicester. 'This', he says, 'was our joint study and amusement in the country, and the drawings for this work have been made by me near twenty years; but they were not to appear in print, till after the publication of Holkham: if leisure permits they may possibly be engraved next year, together with the Earl of Leicester's intended plans for a new house in town.'[1]

Brettingham was an orthodox but unenterprising Palladian whose dull, well-bred façades betray neither the intellect of a Burlington nor the fancy of a Kent. No masterpiece stands out from the list of his works, but in nearly all of them the solid virtues of mid-Georgian architecture are evident.

Brettingham retired to his house outside St. Augustine's Gate at Norwich, where he died on 19 August 1769, aged 70. The epitaph on his monument in St. Augustine's Church is given by Chambers, *Norfolk Tour*, 1829, 1236, and by Wearing, *Georgian Norwich: its Builders*, 1926, 4. His portrait by Heins, dated 1749, is in the R.I.B.A. Drawings Collection. His will mentions property at Weston in Norfolk and a leasehold estate in London held of the Earl of Leicester. He had three sons, the eldest of whom, Matthew, followed his father's profession. The second, Robert, a worsted manufacturer, was the grandfather of another Matthew Brettingham (1792–1826), who is described as a surveyor of No. 1 South Crescent, Bedford Square, London, in his will (P.C.C. 8 STOWELL). The Matthew who is the subject of this entry had a sister Elizabeth who married one of the De Carle family of masons, and for many years he maintained 'his sister Decarle, her old husband, and son'. This circumstance no doubt explains why one of his brother-in-law's family was christened Robert Brettingham De Carle (d. 1791), and why the name of Brettingham was likewise borne by three generations of the Sowerby family of botanists after Robert Brettingham De Carle's daughter Anne married its founder James Sowerby (1757–1822).

Robert Baldwin and Richard Edwin are stated to have been Brettingham's pupils in the *Register of Premiums* of the Society of Arts (1778). William Newton was also in his office for a time.

[Family letters in Bodleian, MS. Eng. misc. c. 504; account-book 1747–64 in P.R.O., C 108/362; *Norfolk Chronicle*, 2 Sept. 1769 (deaths of Matthew Brettingham and of his son Robert); will, P.C.C. 300 BOGG; *A.P.S.D.*; *The Farington Diary*, ed. J. Greig, i, 294; T.W.F., 'Matthew Brettingham, the Architect of Holkham', *East Anglian* ii, 1866, 131–2; S. J. Wearing, *Georgian Norwich: its Builders*, Norwich 1926, 2–5; C. W. James,

[1] In the R.I.B.A. Drawings Collection there is a set of drawings for a town house for the Earl of Leicester 'near Berkeley Square' which should be attributed to the elder Brettingham (rather than to his son, as in *Catalogue of R.I.B.A. Drawings Coll.: B*, 102–3).

Chief Justice Coke, 1929, chap. 36; H. L. Bradfer-Lawrence, 'The Merchants of Lynn', in *A Supplement to Blomefield's Norfolk*, ed. C. Ingleby, 1929, 194–5 (for W. Ingram); D. E. Howell James, 'Matthew Brettingham and the County of Norfolk', *Norfolk Archaeology* xxxiii, 1962–5; Walter Brettingham, 'The Brettingham Family of Norfolk', *Blackmansbury* vi, nos. 3–4, 1969; D. E. Howell James, 'Matthew Brettingham's Account Book', *Norfolk Archaeology* xxxv, 1971; Eileen Harris, *British Architectural Books & Writers 1556–1785*, 1990, 123–4.]

COUNTRY HOUSES

HOLKHAM HALL, NORFOLK. Besides acting as executant architect for the 1st Earl of Leicester from 1734 onwards, Brettingham claimed to have designed the North Lodges, the Temple, the Arch Gate to the gardens, the Seat in the Orangery, the Bridge at the head of the Lake, and the East Lodge [*The Plans Elevations and Sections of Holkham*, 2nd ed. 1773, pls. 54–58, 60, 67].

HONINGHAM HALL, NORFOLK, work for Mrs. (Henrietta) Townshend, between 1738 and 1749; dem. 1967 [see p. 155 for source] (J. J. Sambrook, 'Honingham Hall', *Norfolk Archaeology* xxxiv, 1968).

HEYDON HALL, NORFOLK, minor alterations for Augustine Earle, 1740 [J. Cornforth in *C. Life*, 29 July 1982, 320].

HANWORTH HOUSE, NORFOLK, alterations, probably including drawing-room, for Robert Doughty, *c.*1742–3 [Richard Haslam in *C. Life*, 15 June 1987].

LANGLEY HALL, NORFOLK, work, perhaps including addition of wings, for Sir William Beauchamp Proctor, *c.*1742–5 [see p. 155 for source] (*East Anglian* ii, 1866, 271; *C. Life*, 2 July 1927).

GUNTON HALL, NORFOLK, for Sir William Harbord, after 1742; enlarged by J. Wyatt *c.*1785; centre gutted by fire 1882; reconstructed 1981 [see p. 155 for source] (Neale's *Seats*, 1st ser. iii; *C. Life*, 8 May 1986, 21 Dec. 1989).

GOODWOOD, SUSSEX, work for 2nd Duke of Richmond, perhaps including the W. front, 1750 [T. P. Connor, 'Architecture and Planting at Goodwood 1723–50', *Sussex Archl. Colls.* cxvii, 1979, 191].

MARBLE HILL, TWICKENHAM, MIDDLESEX, alterations (chiefly interior of dining-room) for Henrietta Howard, Countess of Suffolk, 1750–1 [Marie P. G. Draper, *Marble Hill House*, 1970, 43–4].

EUSTON HALL, SUFFOLK, remodelled house and added new offices for 2nd Duke of Grafton, 1750–56 [P.R.O., C 108/362] (*C. Life*, 10, 17, 24 Jan. 1957).

MOOR PARK, HERTS., alterations for 1st Lord Anson, 1751–4 [P.R.O., C 108/362].

PETWORTH HOUSE, SUSSEX, works for 2nd Earl of Egremont, 1751–63, including Sculpture Gallery (1754–63), Stables (after 1756) and Lodges [G. Jackson-Stops, 'The Building of Petworth', *Apollo* cv, 1977, 330; C. Rowell in *Apollo* cxxxviii, 1993, 30].

KEDLESTON HALL, DERBYSHIRE, designed new house for Sir Nathaniel Curzon, Bart. (cr. 1st Lord Scarsdale), *c.*1757–8, of which only the wings were built as part of a revised design by James Paine [J. Paine, *Plans ... of Noblemen's Houses* ii, 1783, 14].

WORTLEY HALL, YORKS. (W.R.), probably designed E. wing built by John Platt (*q.v.*) for Edward Wortley Montagu in 1757–9; altered *c.*1870 [Wortley Montagu's accounts in Sheffield Archives (Wh.M. 142, p. 133) show that in April 1759 he paid 'Mr. Brettingham' (i.e. Matthew Brettingham, jnr.) 10 guineas 'for his Journey into Yorkshire' and 5 guineas 'for Draughts & other business done by his father'].

SHORTGROVE, nr. SAFFRON WALDEN, ESSEX, new bridge, lodge, etc. for Percy Wyndham O'Brien, Earl of Thomond, 1758–62 [P.R.O., C 108/362].

WAKEFIELD LODGE, NORTHANTS., repairs and alterations for 2nd Duke of Grafton, 1759 [P.R.O., C 108/362].

BENACRE HALL, SUFFOLK, remodelled for Sir Thomas Gooch, Bart., 1763–4; interior damaged by fire 1926 [P.R.O., C 108/362; H. Davy, *Views of the Seats of Noblemen and Gentlemen in Suffolk*, 1827].

PUTNEY HEATH, SURREY, house for Sir William Fordyce, M.D., *c.*1764 [autobiography of Henry Couchman, *q.v.*].

PACKINGTON HALL, WARWICKS., remodelled for 3rd Earl of Aylesford, 1766–72. The clerk of works was Henry Couchman (*q.v.*), whose MS. autobiography describes Brettingham as architect [M. Binney in *C. Life*, 9, 16, 23 July 1970].

LONDON

RICHMOND HOUSE, WHITEHALL, alterations and additions for 2nd Duke of Richmond, 1744; destroyed by fire 1791 [*Walpole Soc.* xlix, 1983, 39, 48].

ST. JAMES'S SQUARE, No. 5, for 2nd Earl of Strafford, 1748–9 [*Survey of London* xxix, 100–2] (*C. Life*, 3 Nov. 1988).

NORFOLK HOUSE, ST. JAMES'S SQUARE, for 9th Duke of Norfolk, 1748–52; portico added 1842; dem. 1938 [*Survey of London* xxix,

192–202].

ST. JAMES'S SQUARE, No. 13, unspecified work for 1st Lord Ravensworth, in or before 1753 [*Survey of London* xxix, 136].

LINCOLN'S INN, unspecified work, 1756 [P.R.O., C 108/362].

DOVER STREET, work for Percy Wyndham O'Brien, afterwards Earl of Thomond, 1754 [P.R.O., C 108/362].

EGREMONT HOUSE, No. 94 PICCADILLY (afterwards Cambridge House and from 1866 to 1992 the Naval and Military Club), for 2nd Earl of Egremont, 1756–63 [P.R.O., C 108/362 and Petworth House archives, 6618] (*C. Life*, 20 June 1991).

PICCADILLY, house (Nos. 138–9) for William Douglas, 3rd Earl of March and 4th Duke of Queensberry, *c.*1760–4; dem. [P.R.O., C108/362; autobiography of Henry Couchman (*q.v.*)].

PALL MALL, No. 104 for 2nd Earl of Egmont, 1761–2; dem. 1838 [printed evidence of Brettingham's pupil Robert Baldwin in connection with Bill to remove Chelmsford Gaol, 1771, Essex C.R.O., D/DBe 01, p. 49].

YORK (afterwards CUMBERLAND) HOUSE, No. 86 PALL MALL, for Edward Augustus, Duke of York, 1761–3; dem. 1908–12 [*Survey of London* xxix, 364–7; *Vitruvius Britannicus* iv, 1767, pls. 5–7].

SPRING GARDENS, house for Thomas Anson, before 1764; dem. [P.R.O., C 108/362].

PICCADILLY, No. 80, for Sir Richard Lyttelton, 1764–6; dem. [Bridgwater papers in Herts. C.R.O., AH 1297–1336].

PRIVY GARDENS, WHITEHALL, alterations to house for the Hon. Hans Stanley, 1765; dem. *c.*1820 [autobiography of Henry Couchman (*q.v.*); *Survey of London* xiii, 242–3].

OTHER WORKS

LENWADE BRIDGE, WITCHINGHAM, NORFOLK (R. Wensum), 1741 [plan and elevation initialled MB in Norfolk Record Office, Rye MS. 17, vol. 1, 153].

KING'S LYNN, ST. MARGARET'S CHURCH, rebuilt nave, crossing, and north and south transepts after fall of spire of south-west tower, 1742–6, Gothic [King's Lynn Corporation Archives, Ae 31; *Commons' Jnls.*, 6 Dec. 1744].

NORWICH, THE SHIREHOUSE, 1747–9; dem. 1822; Gothic [D. E. Howell James in *Norfolk Archaeology* xxxiii, 1965, 346–9; Bodleian Library, MS. Eng. Misc. c. 504, f. 2].

NORWICH, repairs to CASTLE, including new battlements, 1747–9 [Bodleian Library, MS. Eng. Misc. c. 504, f. 1].

NORWICH, the following houses are referred to as his work in a letter from his son printed in *East Anglian* ii, 1866, 131–2:

House in SURREY COURT, SURREY STREET, for James Crowe; dem. *c.*1901 (*Norfolk Archaeology* xxiv, 1930, pl. facing p. 74).

House in SURREY STREET for Dr. Peek.

House in ST. GILES for Mr. Stannard.

Ironmonger's shop at corner of Dove Lane for Mr. Pattison.

UNEXECUTED DESIGNS

Several apparently unexecuted works are mentioned in Brettingham's account-book in the P.R.O. They include 'intended alterations' at BLICKLING HALL, NORFOLK, for the 1st Earl of Buckinghamshire, 1753–5; plans for a new house at BELMONT, nr. WARNEFORD, HANTS., for the 11th Earl of Clanricarde, 1754; designs for a large mansion at LOWTHER HALL, WESTMORLAND, for Sir James Lowther, 1759–63 (*Architectural Drawings from Lowther Castle*, ed. Colvin *et al.*, Society of Architectural Historians of G.B., 1980, figs. 12–18); a plan and elevation for an 'intended alteration' to BEECHWOOD PARK, HERTS., for Sir Thomas Sebright (drawing still at Beechwood, 1967); and plans and drawings for John Buxton of SHADWELL LODGE, NORFOLK, 1760. The 'business' which he transacted for the 2nd Earl Poulett at HINTON ST. GEORGE, SOMERSET, and for the 1st Earl Gower at BILL HILL, BERKS., cannot readily be identified.

BRETTINGHAM, MATTHEW (1725–1803), was the eldest son of the architect Matthew Brettingham (d. 1769). He went to Italy in 1747, joined forces with Stuart and Revett and discussed with them the project to explore the architectural antiquities of Athens which they carried out in 1750–1. Brettingham himself remained in Italy until 1754, studying architecture and sculpture and buying statues and pictures for Lord Leicester, Lord Dartmouth and others. A manuscript notebook, containing an 'account of Monies Received on My Lord the Earl of Leicester's account and of my Father's, Beginning from my first setting out of England, August 1747', is preserved at Holkham (MS. 744), and much of the antique sculpture now in the house was collected by him. He returned by way of Germany and Holland, bringing with him a collection of moulds of ancient sculpture, from which he proposed to take casts for sale. He also hoped to find subscribers who would support a project for the establishment of 'an Academy of Design in

England', and made plans for a building in which to house it. At the same time, he was 'preparing to enter on the stage of business' as an architect, although, as he admitted in a letter to a former patron, he had so far had little experience 'in the practical part of Building'. In the late 1750s, however, when his father, 'having much business in Town, could not at that period give up so much of his time to a single building' (i.e. Holkham), Matthew junior 'was stationed there frequently to make up deficiencies of attendance'.

He was subsequently employed by Charles, 2nd Earl of Egremont (d. 1763), a member of the Society of Dilettanti, to buy statues for the gallery at Petworth, and in 1761, when Egremont was appointed British Plenipotentiary to the Congress of Augsburg, Brettingham supervised the housing of him and his embassage in that city. He was also patronized by Lord North, who had met him in Rome, and who, according to Joseph Farington, would have appointed him to the Comptrollership of the Works but for the King's determination to give the post to Chambers. Lord North then made him President of the Board of Green Cloth, a sinecure whose value was somewhat reduced as a result of Burke's Act of 1782, whereupon North made him Deputy Collector of the Cinque Port duties, which (according to Farington) gave him an income of between £400 and £500 a year. He lived at Norwich, and became a freeman of the city in 1769.

The income derived from his sinecures seems largely to have relieved Brettingham from the need to develop an extensive architectural practice. Immediately after his return to England he made a 'plan and elevations' (no doubt for a house in Ireland) for Ralph Howard, later Viscount Wicklow, but it does not appear to have been built [letter to Howard in Holkham MS. 744, f. 133v]. Letters to his sisters in the Bodleian Library [MS. Eng. Misc. c. 504, ff. 8–10] show that in 1767–9 he was working at Packington, Benacre and Shortgrove, evidently on behalf of his father, and the only important independent commission with which he can be credited was for the 12th Earl of Suffolk at CHARLTON HOUSE, WILTS. Here in 1772–6 he rebuilt the north and east fronts and remodelled the interior, filling the central quadrangle with a domed hall in an elegant neo-classical style. Even here the hall was left unfinished at Lord Suffolk's death in 1779, and was still in an incomplete state in the early nineteenth century [*C. Life*, 14–21 Oct. 1933, and 4 Nov., p. 483, for inscription on roof recording that 'This edifice was rendered such as it is under the skilful direction of Matthew Brettingham Architect and the careful superintendence of James Darley Clerk of the Works. Begun A.D. 1772. Finished A.D. 1776']. For the 3rd Earl of Egremont he converted the State Bedchamber at PETWORTH HOUSE, SUSSEX, into the White Library in 1774–6 [G. Jackson-Stops, 'The Building of Petworth', *Apollo* cv, 1977, 332].

In 1771 Brettingham was among the architects who were invited to submit designs for rebuilding part of Lincoln's Inn [*Records of the Society of Lincoln's Inn: the Black Books* iii, 407; iv, 5, 7]. His drawings were not accepted; long mislaid, they are now preserved in the library of the Inn. A sketch-book dating from *c.*1750 is in the R.I.B.A. Drawings Collection. It contains several sketches of buildings in Rome and a number of designs in the English Palladian tradition. A recurring theme is, however, a domed hall of the kind he was eventually to build at Charlton Park. In Sir John Soane's Museum there are (4D, ff. 36–73) a number of drawings, mostly designs for houses, which are stated to be 'principally by M. Brettingham'.

Brettingham died in Norwich on 18 March 1803, aged 78. His will is P.C.C. 293 MARRIOTT. [C. W. James, *Chief Justice Coke*, 1929, 286–9; *East Anglian* ii, 1866, 131–2; S. J. Wearing, *Georgian Norwich: its Builders*, Norwich 1926, 4–5; H. A. Wyndham, *A Family History 1688–1837*, 1950, 141, 169; Farington's Diary, 4 Dec. 1800; J. G. Nichols, *Illustrations of Literary History* iii, 725; Lesley Lewis, *Connoisseurs and Secret Agents in Eighteenth Century Rome*, 1961, 151–4; *Catalogue of the R.I.B.A. Drawings Collection*: *B*, 102–6; J. Kenworthy-Browne, 'Matthew Brettingham's Rome Account-Book 1747–1754', *Walpole Soc.* xlix, 1983.]

BRETTINGHAM, ROBERT (1696–1768), was the eldest son of Launcelot Brettingham of Norwich. He took up his freedom in 1719 as a bricklayer and apprentice of his father. He executed the flint stonework of the Shirehouse at Norwich designed by his brother Matthew (*q.v.*). In August 1753 he advertised in the *Norwich Mercury* that, as he 'is leaving off his business of Mason, he intends to act in the character of an Architect, in drawing plans and elevations, giving estimates, or putting out work, or measuring up any sort of building, for any Gentleman in the County'. In October 1753 he was appointed architect and surveyor to the committee for building the Octagon Chapel at Norwich, but he was afterwards superseded by Thomas Ivory, who designed the existing Chapel. Advertisements in the *Norwich Mercury* in 1757 and 1760 show that Brettingham was acting as a house and estate agent. He was sheriff of Norwich in 1764, and is buried under an inscribed slab in St. Giles' Church [S. J. Wearing, *Georgian Norwich: its Builders*, Norwich 1926, 6–10].

BRETTINGHAM, ROBERT WILLIAM FURZE (*c*.1750–1820), was the son of Michael Savary Furs, who married a daughter of the architect Matthew Brettingham, senior. He was therefore grandson of the elder, and nephew of the younger Brettingham, and adopted their surname, 'supposing that professionally it might be of service to him'. He entered the Royal Academy Schools in 1775, and travelled in Italy from 1778 to 1782. The young John Soane was his companion on the outward journey. In 1783 he exhibited at the Royal Academy a drawing of an 'antique fragment' from the garden of the Villa Medici. He began practice soon after, and in 1790, upon the death of William Blackburn, succeeded him as the architect of several prisons. He does not appear ever to have designed a building of major importance, and difficulties with more than one of his clients suggest either an awkward character or some lapses in professional competence. His surviving or recorded works indicate a classical style comparable to that of James Wyatt.

From 1794 until 1805, when he resigned, Brettingham held the post of Resident Clerk in the Office of Works. He was one of the original members of the Architects' Club on its foundation in 1791, but in 1799 he failed to obtain election as A.R.A. In 1800 he married Mrs. Smith, widow of the banker Samuel Smith, thus obtaining 'a good fortune'. He appears to have retired from practice soon afterwards. Even before his marriage he could afford to live in Berkeley Square. After it he moved to his wife's house, 32 Grosvenor Place, and later to Petersham, where he died in 1820. Brettingham had several pupils, but the only one 'to continue in the profession' was George Smith (*q.v.*), who supplied information for the somewhat inaccurate account of Brettingham's career in the A.P.S. *Dictionary*.[1] There is a portrait by George Dance in the British Museum. [*A.P.S.D.*; will, P.C.C. 653 KENT; *The Farington Diary*, ed. J. Greig, i, 80, 294, ii, 80; A. T. Bolton, *The Portrait of Sir John Soane*, 1927, 5, 16, 20, 42–3; W. T. Whitley, *Artists and their Friends in England* ii, 1928, 236; Walter Brettingham, 'The Brettingham Family of Norfolk', *Blackmansbury* vi, nos. 3–4, 1969.]

[1] T. J. R. Jackson and S. Woolley were pupils who did not persist.

KINGSTON LACY, DORSET, alterations for Henry Bankes, 1784–9 [*Kingston Lacy*, National Trust 1990, 57–8].

LONDON, No. 91 PALL MALL, alterations for 1st Marquess of Buckingham, 1785–6; rebuilt as Buckingham House by Soane in 1792–5 [*A.P.S.D.*; *Survey of London* xxix, 360].

'Improved elevations to an old house in the West of England' [exhib. at R.A. 1786]; possibly for TREWITHEN, CORNWALL, for which unexecuted drawings endorsed 'Brettingham's Plans' are in Cornwall R.O.

READING, DUKE STREET BRIDGE (R. Kennet), 1787–8 [*Reading Mercury*, 12 March 1787].

FELBRIGG HALL, NORFOLK, minor alterations for William Windham, 1787–9 [Windham's *Diary*, ed. Baring, 1866, 117–19, 190; bills in B.L., Add. MS. 39,917, ff. 142–6, 212–13].

'Hermitage built in Middlesex' [exhib. at R.A. 1788].

BENHAM PLACE, BERKS., bridge in the park for 6th Lord Craven, 1789; dem. [exhib. at R.A. 1790].

GREAT MARLOW BRIDGE, BUCKS. (R. Thames), 1790 (a wooden bridge replaced in 1830) [*Reading Mercury*, 4 Sept. 1786].

DOWNPATRICK GAOL, CO. DOWN, IRELAND, 1789–96 [*A.P.S.D.*].

LONDON, LITTLE DEAN'S YARD, WESTMINSTER, three houses on the south side, 1789. Of these, Grant's and the house of the Master of the King's Scholars survive. The third, Rigaud's, was dem. in 1896 [L. E. Tanner, *Westminster School*, 1923, 56].

LONGLEAT HOUSE, WILTS., unspecified work for 1st Marquess of Bath, *c*.1790 [*A.P.S.D.*; Christopher Hussey in *C. Life*, 29 April 1949].

AUDLEY END, ESSEX, TEMPLE OF CONCORD, for 4th Lord Howard de Walden, 1790 [exhib. at R.A. 1792, 1793 and 1798; J. D. Williams, *Audley End: the Restoration of 1762–97*, Chelmsford 1966, 47–8].

SAFFRON WALDEN CHURCH, ESSEX, repairs and alterations, 1790–2 [exhib. at R.A. 1799; Lord Braybrooke, *History of Audley End and Saffron Walden*, 1836, 205; Essex C.R.O., Braybrooke papers, Annual Accounts, 1793].

NORTHAMPTON COUNTY GAOL, 1791–4; rebuilt *c*.1840 [*A.P.S.D.*; *Gent's Mag.* 1818 (ii), 499].

LONDON, No. 21 ST. JAMES'S SQUARE (afterwards Winchester House), for 5th Duke of Leeds, 1791–5; completed by Sir J. Soane after a disagreement between Brettingham and his client; dem. 1934 [*Survey of London*, xxix, 175–80, pl. 191].

LONDON, BAKER STREET, a house, 1792 [contract between R.B. and John Lane, builder, to erect a house in Baker Street, 9 Feb. 1792, advertised in catalogue of Jantzen of East Grinstead, Sussex, 1966, item no. 181; cf *Blackmansbury* vi, 1969, 39].

'A gentleman's house near Southampton' [exhib. at R.A. 1793].

READING COUNTY GAOL, 1793–4; rebuilt 1842 [Berks. C.R.O., Q.S. Order Book 1791–5, 317–20, 439].

TAPLOW LODGE, BUCKS., enlarged or rebuilt for John Fryer, *c.*1795 [Farington's Diary, 6 May 1795].

DOWNPATRICK CATHEDRAL, CO. DOWN, IRELAND, design for refitting choir [exhib. at R.A. 1795, and by Brettingham's pupil S. Woolley in 1798].

HILLSBOROUGH HOUSE, CO. DOWN, IRELAND, enlarged for 2nd Marquess of Downshire, *c.*1795–7 [exhib. at R.A. 1797; E. R. R. Green & E. M. Jope in *Ulster Journal of Archaeology* xxiv–v, 1961–2, 145–151].

DOWNSHIRE HOUSE, ROEHAMPTON, SURREY, work for 2nd Marquess of Downshire, presumably *c.*1795 [*A.P.S.D.*].

LONDON, CURZON STREET, No. 19, library for Sir John Sebright, Bart., 1802 [this commission ended in a lawsuit between Brettingham and Sebright: see *The Farington Diary*, ed. Greig, ii, 80, and correspondence in Sir John Soane's Museum, Soane Case, 'Misc. MSS. relating to Architecture', I].

WALDERSHARE PARK, KENT, work for the Earl of Guilford [*A.P.S.D.*]. Brettingham probably designed the single-storey outer wings, containing library and kitchen, for the 3rd Earl of Guilford (d. April 1802), for their parapets carry suitable neo-classical detail, and they are shown on a plan in the author's possession initialled by Brettingham and dated 12 March 1802.

LONDON, BERKELEY SQUARE, No. 42 (later No. 9), 'a fine room' at the rear for himself; dem. [*A.P.S.D.*]. Brettingham lived here from 1792 to 1801.

BREWSTER, JAMES (1805–*c.*1845), was the son of the Revd. Dr. James Brewster, minister of Craig, nr. Montrose. He came to Dundee in 1832, when his competition designs for the new seminaries were much admired and only narrowly beaten by those of George Angus (*q.v.*). Later that year he was entrusted with the layout of Euclid Crescent in consultation with Angus. In 1833 he competed for the Gaols and Bridewell, but was again defeated by Angus. He had left Dundee by 1840, and was dead by 1848. In Dundee Public Library there is a ground plan of his design for the seminaries and an unexecuted design for a hearse house for the Constitution Road Cemetery. [Hew Scott, *Fasti Ecclesiae Scoticanae* v, 386; *Builder* vi, 1848, 553; information from Mr. David Walker.]

DUNDEE, WARD CHAPEL, CONSTITUTION ROAD, 1833, Gothic [C. Mackie, *Historical Description of the Town of Dundee*, 1836, 128].

FORFAR, ST. JAMES'S CHURCH, 1835–6, lancet Gothic [contract in *Dundee Advertiser*, 24 April 1835].

KIRRIEMUIR, ANGUS, WEBSTER'S SEMINARY, 1837–8, Jacobethan style [A. Reid, *Regality of Kirriemuir*, 1909, 177].

MONTROSE, DORWARD HOUSE, 1838, Italianate [advt. in *Dundee Advertiser*, 28 June 1838].

BRIANT, HENRY, of Reading, was the author of the winning designs in the competition for the ROYAL BERKSHIRE HOSPITAL, READING, in 1837. He submitted two designs, one in the Gothic, the other in the Grecian style, both of which were among the first three selected by George Basevi, the assessor. The handsome Greek design was executed in 1837–9, but with internal modifications based on the Gothic plan [*Reading Mercury*, 11 Feb. 1837; *Architectural Mag.* iv, 151–3]. The portico of ST. MARY'S CHAPEL, CASTLE STREET, READING, was designed in 1840 by Messrs. Henry & Nathaniel Briant, of 164 Friar Street, Reading [*Reading Mercury*, 7 and 14 March 1840]. According to N. Pevsner, *Berkshire* (Buildings of England, 1966), they also designed the Italianate BARCLAYS (formerly SIMONDS) BANK in KING STREET, READING, 1838–9. W. N. Briant, of 25 Sydney Terrace, Reading, exhibited architectural designs at the Royal Academy in 1842–3.

Briant is said to have given up architecture for the church, and if so he must have been the Revd. Henry Briant, of Queens' College, Cambridge, who was ordained in 1843, had a living at Macclesfield, and died at Manchester on 20 May 1884, aged 71 [Venn, *Alumni Cantabrigienses 1752–1900* i, 1940, 374].

BRIDEL, W—, exhibited at the Royal Academy from 1795 to 1797. His drawings included 'a villa erecting for Governor Blunt in America' (1796), and 'A view of the British Magazine at St. Petersburg' (1797).

BRIDGENS, RICHARD HICKS (1785–1846), was a pupil of the sculptor and modeller George Bullock, from whose premises in Liverpool he exhibited drawings at the Liverpool Academy in 1810, 1811 and 1812. They included a design for a monument, a restoration of the screen in Sefton Church, and a chimney-piece in Speke Hall. In 1813 he began to exhibit at the Royal Academy from

London addresses, and the two drawings of Joseph Ridgway's house at RIDGMONT, HORWICH, LANCS., which he sent to the Liverpool Academy in 1814 may have represented his first architectural commission. In 1822 he published a folio volume of engravings of the medieval church at Sefton in Lancashire. He may have visited Italy about this time, for in the same year he exhibited at the Royal Academy 'an attempt to improve the restoration of the Barberini candelabrum now erecting in bronze', and a 'View in the Forum in Rome – showing the excavation made at the charge of Her Grace the Duchess of Devonshire'. He subsequently attempted to establish himself in practice in Birmingham, where James Watt of Aston Hall employed him to design some oak furniture in a Jacobean style to match the house. In 1826 Bridgens exhibited drawings for the restoration of Aston Hall, but they were not carried out, and in 1825 Watt told C. R. Cockerell that Bridgens had been obliged to leave Birmingham for lack of employment there [Cockerell's diary, *sub anno*]. Soon afterwards he went out to the West Indies, publishing in 1836, soon after his return, *West Indian Scenery . . . from Sketches during a residence of seven years in Trinidad.* Watt continued to employ him at Aston Hall, where in about 1836 a porch (dem. 1856) was built to his designs. All that is known about his subsequent career is that in 1838 he published a volume entitled *Furniture with Candelabra and Interior Decoration designed by R. Bridgens*. This contains designs for furniture in both Gothic, classical and Elizabethan styles. [J. C. Corson, *Notes and Index to Sir Herbert Grierson's Edition of the Letters of Sir Walter Scott*, 1979, 385, for dates of birth and death; Virginia Green, 'George Bullock, Richard Bridgens and James Watt's Regency furnishing schemes', *Furniture History* xv, 1979.]

BRIDGES, JAMES, practised in Bristol from 1757 to 1763. Nothing is known of his origins, but he appears to have come to Bristol from the American colonies. In 1757 he submitted three designs to the commissioners for rebuilding Bristol Bridge, describing them in detail in a pamphlet entitled *Four Designs for Rebuilding Bristol Bridge*, which he published two years later. Other designs were submitted, including one by Ferdinando Stratford for a single-arch bridge, and a controversy arose over their respective merits. In 1762 Bridges published a second pamphlet, entitled *Reasons for Building a Bridge of Three Arches on the Old Foundations with his Objections to the Single Arch Plan*, and it was his design for a three-arch bridge that was eventually completed in 1768. It was executed under the direction of Thomas Paty, for Bridges himself had sailed for the West Indies in October 1763, disgruntled at the treatment he had received from the commissioners. The design was inspired by Labelye's Westminster Bridge of 1739–50. Widening in 1861 and 1873 has effectively destroyed it as a work of architecture.

Bridges' best-preserved work in Bristol is the house known as the ROYAL FORT, which he designed for a wealthy merchant named Thomas Tyndall shortly before 1760. He refers to the model (still preserved in the building) which he made for the Royal Fort in an 'advertisement' appended to his earlier pamphlet, and the house is also mentioned as his in a valedictory letter written by one of his supporters and printed in *Felix Farley's Bristol Journal* for 22 Oct. 1763. The exterior is a handsome though not particularly discriminating composition in the Anglo-Palladian style, but the interior is remarkable for exuberant rococo decoration by Thomas Paty (*C. Life*, 27 May 1916).

During his stay in Bristol Bridges was responsible for two churches: ST. WERBURGH, whose nave and chancel he rebuilt on the old footings in 1758–61, reusing much of the medieval masonry, including the windows, and ST. NICHOLAS, which he offered to rebuild in 1760 on a plan similar to one he had seen executed in Pennsylvania. His designs were eventually accepted in 1762, and the church was completed in 1769 by Thomas Paty, who took charge when Bridges left Bristol in 1763. St. Nicholas was a large stone box pierced with simplified 'Perpendicular' windows and decorated with rococo plasterwork. It was gutted by bombing in 1940 and subsequently reconstructed as a museum. St. Werburgh's was taken down in 1878 and rebuilt in Mina Road, Baptist Mills.

[W. Ison, *The Georgian Buildings of Bristol*, 1952, 31–2, 65–70, 114–23; Eileen Harris, *British Architectural Books and Writers 1556–1785*, 1990, 124–6; Vestry Minutes and contracts for St. Werburgh's Church in Bristol Record Office.]

BRIGDEN, EDWARD, was employed early in the 1820s to superintend the building of Sir Robert Smirke's churches at Chatham and Bristol [Church Building Commissioners' Minute Books, 22 May 1827, *ex inf.* Prof. M. H. Port]. He subsequently practised in Bristol, where his name is found in the Directories from 1825 to 1834. DR. WHITE'S HOSPITAL, TEMPLE STREET, BRISTOL, was rebuilt to his designs in 1824; dem. *c.*1970 [Bristol City Archives, Dr. White's Hospital Accounts, *ex* *inf.* Miss Joanna Tolmie]. In 1827 he rebuilt EASTON-IN-GORDANO CHURCH, SOMERSET, again rebuilt 1871–2 [G.R.]. Later he became surveyor to the Dowlais Iron Company in South Wales [P. Eden, *Dictionary of Land Surveyors and Local Cartographers*, 1975, 45].

BRIGGS, JOHN, was a builder and surveyor at Chepstow in Monmouthshire. In 1829 he added an aisle to WOOLASTON CHURCH, GLOS., rebuilt 1859 [I.C.B.S.], and in 1830 he designed a sturdy new tower for ST. BRIAVEL'S CHURCH, GLOS. [Vestry Minutes in Glos. C.R.O.].

BRINE, THOMAS, practised in the Isle of Man in the early nineteenth century. He was responsible for alterations and additions to BISHOP'S COURT for the Hon. George Murray, Bishop of Sodor and Man, 1814, Gothic; and to the Gaol and Rolls Office in CASTLE RUSHEN, *c.*1815 and 1827 [P.R.O., H O 98/75; *Archaeologia* xciv, 1951, 19], and for designing ST. MARY'S CHURCH, CASTLETOWN, 1826, Gothic; gutted 1985 and converted into offices [information from Mr. B. R. S. Megaw].

BRISTOW, JOHN, exhibited architectural drawings at the Royal Academy from Sun Street, Bishopsgate, in 1792 and 1793. His son, J. J. Bristow, junior, was admitted to the R. A. Schools in 1794 at the age of 19. He exhibited at the Academy from 1793 to 1802, including a 'view of a seat designed to be erected in Scotland' (1802).

BROAD, RICHARD, of Worcester, was admitted a freeman of that city in February 1752. In 1766 he submitted designs for the new Worcester Infirmary which were rejected in favour of those of Anthony Keck (*q.v.*) [Worcester County Record Office, Infirmary Book of Orders 1745–1800]. In 1768 he made a plan of Worcester. Two large tablets in coloured marbles to Henry (d. 1738) and Mary Wolstenholme (d. 1749) at STOKE EDITH CHURCH, HEREFS., bear his signature. [Information from Mr. D. Whitehead.]

BROADBENT, JOHN (1803–1842), was the son of George Broadbent of Walton Breck, nr. Liverpool. He became a pupil of Thomas Rickman, but did not get on with his master. He subsequently practised in Liverpool until his early death at the age of 39 on 5 March 1842. He worked chiefly for commercial and mercantile clients in Liverpool, but in 1837 he designed a house in Ireland for a Mr. Cullen. His most important works appear to have been the churches of ST. AUGUSTINE, SHAW STREET, LIVERPOOL, 1829–30, Greek Revival, dem.; ST. ANTHONY (R.C.), SCOTLAND ROAD, 1832–3, a large Gothic building in a lancet style derived from Rickman; and the tower of WALTON-ON-THE-HILL CHURCH, LANCS., 1831–2, Gothic. Working drawings for St. Augustine's and St. Anthony's are in the R.I.B.A. Drawings Collection. Further details of Broadbent's practice are afforded by his business diaries for 1837 and 1840, now in Liverpool Public Library. [J. A. Picton, *Memorials of Liverpool* ii, 1875, 327, 343.]

BRODIE, JOHN (otherwise unrecorded, but cf. 'Bradie, John' above), signs a design for the Stables at FIRLE PLACE, SUSSEX, as built for the 3rd Viscount Gage, 1801 [drawing at Firle, *ex inf.* Mr. R. Hewlings].

BROMFIELD, JOSEPH (*c.*1743–1824), of Shrewsbury, was a plasterer by trade, but frequently acted in the capacity of an architect or surveyor. As Joseph Bromfield, 'Ornamental Plasterer', he was admitted to the Shrewsbury Carpenters' and Bricklayers' Company in 1777, but it was not until 1792 that he became a burgess of the town. He served as Mayor in 1809, and died on 6 June 1824, aged 81. His will [P.C.C. 581 ERSKINE], in which he describes himself as 'architect', shows that he owned a good deal of property in Shrewsbury, including the houses forming the Crescent (on the south side of Town Walls), and a house at Llandrillo in Merionethshire called Brannas Lodge. He lived in St. Julians Friars, probably at No. 37, a Georgian house whose octagonal dining-room has an elaborately decorated plaster ceiling. 'Books, prints, busts, statues and pictures' are mentioned in his will.

Examples of Bromfield's workmanship as a plasterer can be seen at St. Chad's Church in Shrewsbury, at Oakley Park, Salop. (dining-room ceiling), and in Bishop Hurd's Library at Hartlebury Castle, Worcs. (where he was working to designs by James Smith of Shifnal). He was clearly an able craftsman capable of elegant work. As an architect he appears to have been competent but unremarkable.

[Shrewsbury Public Library: records of the Carpenters' and Bricklayers' Co. (13487); *The Shrewsbury Burgess Roll*, ed. H. E. Forrest, 1924, 40; *Salop. Arch. Soc. Trans.* 4th ser. ix, 1923–4, 9; information from Miss M. C. Hill.]

WALCOT HALL, SALOP., acted as 'superintendent' of alterations and additions (including a new portico) for 2nd Lord Clive, 1784–90 [Salop. Record Office, Powis 552/9/290]

(*C. Life*, 14 Oct. 1939). James Byres (*q.v.*) was involved.

attributed: SHREWSBURY, THE CRESCENT, TOWN WALLS, *c.*1790 [three of the four houses forming this crescent were insured by Bromfield with the Salop. Fire Office in 1791 and 1815; all four are described as his property in his will].

APLEY CASTLE, SALOP., for St. John Charlton, 1791–4; dem. 1955, portico re-erected as an eye-catcher at Hodnet Hall [Salop. Record Office, Apley Castle records, Box 19/1–8] (S. Leighton, *Shropshire Houses*, 1901, 11).

STYCHE HALL, SALOP., alterations and additions, including canted bays flanking entrance, for the Hon. Robert Clive, 1796–8 [Salop. Record Office, Powis 552/9/50].

ATTINGHAM PARK, SALOP., lodges, marble bath in house, and unexecuted design for picture-gallery for 2nd Lord Berwick, 1796–9 [Salop. Record Office, 112, Box 45, vouchers, *ex inf.* Mr. James Lawson].

CAERYNWCH, MERIONETHSHIRE, for (Sir) Richard Richards, 1801 [N.L.W., Glansevern 5471].

NANHORON, CAERNARVONSHIRE, for Col. Richard Edwards, 1797; enlarged 1834 [papers at Nanhoron, *ex inf.* Dr. J. M. Robinson].

RÛG, MERIONETHSHIRE, probably designed new house for Col. Edward Vaughan Salusbury, *c.*1802–5 [N.L.W., Glansevern 5470, 5472, 5492, and Richard Haslam in *C. Life*, 13 Oct. 1983].

GLANSEVERN, MONTGOMERYSHIRE, for Sir Arthur Davies Owen, 1803–7; dem. 1978 [N.L.W., Glansevern 5469–5589, also a signed drawing for a fireplace].

BERRINGTON RECTORY (now HALL), SALOP., for the Hon. and Revd. Richard Noel Hill, 1805 [*V.C.H. Salop.* viii, 25].

NANNAU, MERIONETHSHIRE, additional wing (dem.) for Sir Robert Vaughan, Bart., 1806 [N.L.W., Glansevern 5484]. As Bromfield's letters (Glansevern 5470–1) show that he was at Nannau in Aug.–Sept. 1801, he may have designed the house itself, built *c.*1800, as well as the wing added in 1806.

ACTON SCOTT HALL, SALOP., remodelled for Thomas Stackhouse Acton, *c.*1810/20 [*V.C.H. Salop.* x, forthcoming].

CHURCHSTOKE CHURCH, MONTGOMERYSHIRE, 1814–15; remodelled *c.*1881 [Shropshire C.R.O., Vestry Minutes 1739–1847 and contract dated 1814].

BROOKES, WILLIAM McINTOSH (1800–1849), entered Peterhouse, Cambridge, in October 1823, and took his B.A. in 1829. At the same time he was attending the Royal Academy Schools in London and learning to draw under George Maddox. Between 1829 and 1838 he exhibited at the Academy from 6 Adam Street, Adelphi. He became a Fellow of the R.I.B.A. His works included a dull Tudor Gothic court at his own college, a Romanesque church at Albury, Surrey, the Perpendicular Gothic Irvingite church at the same place, designed in association with William Wilkins, and the formidable Greek Doric octastyle portico of the demolished Shire Hall at Bury St. Edmunds. Brookes died in the Adelphi on 13 December 1849 [Venn, *Alumni Cantabrigienses*, Pt. II, i, 396; *Gent's Mag.* 1850 (i), 222].

CAMBRIDGE, PETERHOUSE, THE GISBORNE COURT, 1825–6, Tudor Gothic [Willis & Clark, i, 39].

CAMBRIDGE, THE TOWN GAOL, PARKER'S PIECE, 1828, castellated; dem. [Willis & Clark, i, 39].

HACKNEY, LONDON, THE CHURCH OF ENGLAND GRAMMAR SCHOOL, 1829, Gothic [exhib. at R.A. 1831].

LONDON, ST. MICHAEL, WOOD STREET, repairs, 1831, when the west tower was 'thrown open to the body of the church'; dem. 1894 [G. Godwin, *The Churches of London* i, 1838; the builder's contract is Guildhall Library MS. 2259].

EAST HAM VICARAGE, ESSEX, rebuilt 1832 [exhib. at R.A. 1834].

DORKING CHURCH, SURREY, rebuilt 1835–7, Gothic; rebuilt by H. Woodyer, 1872 [E. W. Brayley, *History of Surrey* v, 95].

THAMES DITTON CHURCH, SURREY, added N. aisle, 1836, Gothic [Faculty in G.L.R.O., DW/OP/1835/6; Vestry Minutes].

IPSWICH, SUFFOLK, THE COUNTY COURTS, 1836–7, Tudor Gothic [J. Wodderspoon, *Memorials of Ipswich*, 1850, 7].

ALBURY, SURREY, THE CATHOLIC APOSTOLIC CHURCH, for Henry Drummond, Gothic; designed in association with William Wilkins, *c.*1837, and completed by Brookes after the latter's death in 1839 [drawings in possession of the Trustees, signed jointly by Wilkins and Brookes, 1837–9 and subsequently by Brookes alone: photos at N.M.R.]

LONDON, ST. ANNE & ST. AGNES CHURCH, GRESHAM STREET, alterations and repairs, 1838–9 [W. McMurray, *A City Church Chronicle*, 1914].

ALBURY CHURCH, SURREY, for Henry Drummond, 1840–1, Romanesque style based on church of Thaon, Normandy; chancel added 1869 [E. W. Brayley, *History of Surrey* v, 95].

BURY ST. EDMUNDS, SUFFOLK, THE SHIRE HALL, 1841–2; dem. 1906 [W. Suffolk Record Office, Q.S. Order Books, 17 March 1841; cf. W. White, *History, Gazetteer & Directory of Suffolk*, 1844, 644 (H. R. Barker, *West Suffolk Illustrated*, 1907, 62).

EPSOM, SURREY, CHRIST CHURCH, EPSOM COMMON, 1844, Gothic; rebuilt 1877 [E. W. Brayley, *History of Surrey* iv, 365].

EPSOM, SURREY, THE VICARAGE, CHURCH STREET, for Revd. B. B. Bockett [E. W. Brayley, *History of Surrey* iv, 369].

BROOKS, JOSEPH (1707–1788) and JONATHAN, of Liverpool, 'were the great builders of the town' in the mid-eighteenth century. They also carried on business as timber merchants, lime-burners, rope-makers, etc., and owned an extensive yard between Wood Street and the present Bold Street, the site of which for its whole length was their rope-walk. There are considerable payments to them for work on Liverpool Exchange, built to the designs of John Wood, 1749–54 [Liverpool Treasurers' Books, Picton Reference Library]. Joseph was president of the Infirmary in 1771, and took much interest in the welfare of the poor, having been for some time treasurer of the Workhouse on Brownlow Hill (rebuilt 1846), which he had built in 1769–70, and where his portrait by R. Caddick still, in 1875, hung in the boardroom. He was a Nonconformist, and there was a tablet in his memory in the Key Street Chapel. His name is preserved in Brooks Street, where for many years stood his brickyard. In 1774–5 the body of ST. NICHOLAS CHURCH, LIVERPOOL, was rebuilt under his direction in a simple Georgian Gothic style: it was gutted in 1940–1 and rebuilt to a different design. His will (P.C.C. 229 CALVERT) shows that Jonathan predeceased him. [J. A. Picton, *Memorials of Liverpool* ii, 38, 39, 59, 135–6, 154; *Liverpool Vestry Books*, ed. H. Peet, i, 1912, 218 and *passim.*]

BROOKS, WILLIAM (1786–1867), was a pupil of D. R. Roper. He entered the Royal Academy Schools in 1808, and exhibited at the Academy from 1803 to 1815. He was a zealous Nonconformist and anti-Papist, a keen supporter of the movement for the abolition of slavery, and a persistent writer of letters to the newspapers on these and other topics. He was a member of the Goldsmiths' Company. Poor health led him to retire early. He died at Headington on 11 December 1867, aged 80. His son, C. W. Shirley Brooks, was a well-known editor of *Punch.* C. Dyer and L. W. Lloyd were his pupils.

Brooks designed at least two buildings of some distinction – the Finsbury Unitarian Chapel and the ingeniously planned and elegantly detailed London Institution. The 'numerous private edifices' mentioned in his obituary have yet to be identified. [*Gent's Mag.* 1868, 254–5; G. S. Layard, *A Great 'Punch' Editor: the Life of Shirley Brooks*, 1907, 2, 7, 90–1.]

GREAT HOLLAND RECTORY, ESSEX, design for the Revd. H. Rice [exhib. at R.A. 1812].

HARROW-ON-THE-HILL, MIDDLESEX, house for the vicar, the Revd. J. M. Cunningham [exhib. at R.A. 1815].

LONDON, THE LONDON INSTITUTION, FINSBURY CIRCUS, 1815–19; dem. 1936 [Britton & Pugin, *The Public Buildings of London* i, 1825, 186–92; contracts and specifications in Guildhall Library, MS. 2751] (*C. Life*, 11 April 1936).

DUDLEY, WORCS., ST. THOMAS, 1816–17, Gothic [*Gent's Mag.* 1868, 254; J. Noake, *The Rambler in Worcestershire* ii, 1848, 62].

LONDON, THE UNITARIAN CHAPEL, SOUTH PLACE, FINSBURY, 1824; dem. [J. Elmes, *Metropolitan Improvements*, 1831, 163 and plate].

BRISTOL, THE FEMALE ORPHAN ASYLUM (now Salvation Army Home), HOOK'S MILLS, ASHLEY HILL (with C. Dyer), 1827–9 [*Gent's Mag.* 1868, 254].

ISLINGTON, COLLEGE OF THE CHURCH MISSIONARY SOCIETY, *c.*1828; dem. [J. Elmes, *Metropolitan Improvements*, 1831, 145 and plate].

BROUGHTON, JAMES (*c.*1647–1711), was appointed surveyor to the Dean and Chapter of Westminster on 14 January 1696/7, in succession to Robert Hooke. In March 1699, in accordance with the Act of Parliament for the repair of the Abbey Church, he became under-surveyor of the fabric at a salary of £50 per annum, the chief surveyor being Sir Christopher Wren. He retained both posts until his death on 31 January 1710/11, aged 63. He is buried in the east cloister, where there is a monument to his memory [Westminster Abbey Muniments; Bodleian Library, MS. Gough Westminster 1, p. 50; his will is P.C.C. 19 YOUNG].

BROWN, GEORGE, was a minor Northumbrian architect of the reign of George III. Among the drawings at Wallington Hall is a design by him for a new kitchen wing there dated 1769 (not executed). In 1772–3 he was employed by the County to report on the state of its bridges after the great flood of 1771, and made designs for a new bridge at Alnwick that were not carried out [Northumberland

Record Office, Q.S. Order Books 10, p. 567, 11, p. 37].

BROWN, JAMES (*c.*1729–1807), was an Edinburgh architect-builder and a wright by trade. He is best known as the designer and builder of GEORGE SQUARE, the first large-scale house-building scheme in eighteenth-century Edinburgh, and the first true square. Built in 1766–85, and named after his brother George, laird of Elliestown and Receiver-General of Excise in Scotland, it consisted of sixty-one houses on sites sub-feued by him to speculative masons and wrights. Only the W. side now remains more or less intact. A few years earlier he had built BROWN SQUARE, a much smaller development now absorbed into Chambers Street, and he subsequently built most of the houses in CHARLES STREET, CRICHTON STREET, WINDMILL STREET (dem. 1963) and BUCCLEUCH PLACE (1780–92) [W. N. Boog Watson, 'George Square, Edinburgh, 1766–1966', *University of Edinburgh Jnl.* 22, 1965–6; *Book of the Old Edinburgh Club* v, 26, and xxvi, *passim*; A. J. Youngson, *The Making of Classical Edinburgh*, 1966, 68].

In 1770 Brown was consulted by the Heritors of Kelso about the state of their church [S.R.O., HR 651/3]; in 1779 he provided a design for PEEBLES PARISH CHURCH (completed 1784; dem. 1885), but it was not fully adhered to in execution [Gunn, *Parish Church of Peebles*, 1917, 6–7; J. W. Buchan, *History of Peeblesshire*, 1864, 268]; in 1789 he probably designed the wings containing library and kitchen that were added by Alexander Smollett to CAMERON HOUSE, STIRLINGSHIRE; destroyed by fire 1865 except the library wing, incorporated in new house 1868 [Smollett papers at Cameron House, 1982]; in 1793 he was one of several architects who submitted designs for St. Cuthbert's Manse in Edinburgh [S.R.O., HR 152/2], and in 1796 he built a porch (since dem.) at the E. end of ST. CUTHBERT'S CHURCH [W. Sime, *History of the Church and Parish of St. Cuthbert*, 1829, 152].

In 1775 Brown published anonymously a pamphlet entitled *The Importance of the Cowgate Bridge etc. considered* [Bodleian Library, Gough Scotland 260 (10)], and he was probably the 'J. Brown' who drew the engravings illustrating *A Plan for erecting a new Prison and Bridewell in the City of Edinburgh*, published by the Lord Provost and Archibald Cockburn in 1782 [Bodleian, Godwin Pamphlet 1813 (14)]. Brown died at his house in George Square on 8 December 1807, aged 78 [*Scots Mag.* 69, 1807, 960; Burial Register of Buccleuch Relief Church Burial Ground].

BROWN, LANCELOT (1716–1783), was born at Kirkharle in Northumberland, and educated in the village school at Cambo. At the age of 16 he was engaged as a gardener by Sir William Loraine of Kirkharle, where he was later entrusted with laying out an addition to the grounds. After small landscape commissions at Benwell and other nearby places he left Northumberland in 1739. His first design in the South was a lake at Kiddington Park in Oxfordshire. In 1741 he moved to Stowe as head gardener to Lord Cobham, becoming virtually clerk of the works for building as well as gardening. Here he came into contact with William Kent, the first great exponent of English landscape gardening, in collaboration with whom he 'naturalized' the formal layout of what was already one of the most celebrated of English parks. As Kent's assistant and Lord Cobham's gardener, his advice was in due course asked by other gentlemen anxious to improve their grounds, and when his employer died in 1749 Brown gave up his post at Stowe and began to practise as a consulting landscape gardener. In the course of the next thirty years he was called upon to exercise his art in every part of the country, and by the time of his death in 1783 his characteristic landscapes, with their serpentine lakes and scattered clumps of trees, had become one of the most familiar features of the English countryside.

In Brown's hands the house, which before had dominated the estate, became an integral part of a carefully composed landscape intended to be seen through the eye of a painter, and its design could not be divorced from that of the garden. So architecture as well as horticulture necessarily formed a part of Brown's professional equipment. In addition to his fame as a gardener, Brown did, in fact, enjoy a considerable reputation as an architect, and in his *Theory and Practice of Landscape Gardening*, Humphry Repton bears witness to the 'comfort, convenience, taste, and propriety of design in the several mansions and other buildings which he planned'. Croome Court, his earliest architectural work, probably owed something to the advice of Sanderson Miller, and closely resembled the house which the latter soon afterwards designed for Lord Lyttelton at Hagley. Newnham Paddox, another of Brown's early works, followed a similar Palladian model, and Fisherwick was in the same tradition. Elsewhere Brown designed stables and other subsidiary buildings in a Gothic style reminiscent of William Kent. Much of his architectural work was executed by Henry Holland, a master builder of Fulham, with whom he became acquainted soon after leaving Stowe. In 1771 Brown took

Holland's son Henry into a kind of informal partnership, introducing him to his clients, and gradually handing over to him the architectural side of his practice. In 1773 the younger Holland married Brown's daughter Bridget, and when Brown made his will in 1779 he named his son-in-law as one of his executors.

In 1764 Brown was appointed Master Gardener at Hampton Court, a post which brought him an official residence at Hampton known as Wilderness House. He died on 6 February 1783, at the age of 67, and was buried at Fenstanton in Huntingdonshire, where he had bought a small estate in 1767. A volume of Brown's correspondence is in the British Library (Add. MS. 69795).

The earliest list of Brown's architectural works was printed by Humphry Repton in his *Theory and Practice of Landscape Gardening* (1803), from information supplied by Holland. *Capability Brown*, by Dorothy Stroud (1950; new edition 1975) is a comprehensive study of his work as landscape gardener and architect. See also Peter Willis, 'Capability Brown in Northumberland', *Garden History* 9, 1981, and 'Capability Brown's account with Drummond's Bank', *Arch. Hist.* 27, 1984.

Unless otherwise stated, the following list of Brown's architectural works is based on Miss Stroud's book, where full references will be found.

STOWE HOUSE, BUCKS., THE COBHAM MONUMENT for 1st Viscount Cobham, 1747–8 [letter from Brown to George Bowes, 22 Oct. 1750, Durham C.R.O., D/St. 347/37].

CROOME COURT, WORCS., remodelled for 6th Earl of Coventry, 1751–2, probably following a design by Sanderson Miller (*q.v.*).

WARWICK CASTLE, alterations for 1st Earl of Warwick, including rebuilding of porch to Great Hall, 1753–5, and wooden bridge over R. Avon, 1758 [*V.C.H. Warwicks.* viii, 461, 471].

NEWNHAM PADDOX, WARWICKS., largely rebuilt for 5th and 6th Earls of Denbigh, 1754–68; remodelled by T. H. Wyatt 1876–9; dem. 1952 [A. Wood, 'Lancelot Brown and Newnham Paddox', *Warwickshire History* i (1), 1969].

BURGHLEY HOUSE, NORTHANTS., works for 9th Earl of Exeter, including alterations to S. front of house, Gothic stables, greenhouse and bath-house, 1756–78; bridge in park 1774–7 [E. Till, 'Capability Brown at Burghley', *C. Life*, 16 Oct. 1975].

CROOME CHURCH, WORCS., for 6th Earl of Coventry, 1758–63, Gothic. The interior decoration was designed by Robert Adam.

PRIOR PARK, BATH, an unidentified 'additional building' for Ralph Allen (d. 1764), probably *c.*1760.

LONGLEAT HOUSE, WILTS., gateway to flower-garden for 3rd Viscount Weymouth, 1760.

CHILLINGTON HALL, STAFFS., bridge in park for Thomas Giffard, before 1761.

CORSHAM COURT, WILTS., enlarged house for Paul Methuen, 1761–4; altered by Nash and Repton 1797–8 and by Bellamy 1844–9; also designed Gothic Bath House in North Avenue and an orangery there (dem.) [F. J. Ladd, *Architects at Corsham Court*, 1978, 45–69].

SPRING HILL, nr. BROADWAY, WORCS., for 6th Earl of Coventry, 1763; remodelled in 19th century.

BLENHEIM PALACE, OXON., remodelled High Lodge and designed façade to Park Farm for 4th Duke of Marlborough, 1764–5, Gothic.

BURTON PYNSENT, SOMERSET, THE COLUMN, for 1st Earl of Chatham, 1765 (*C. Life*, 10 Sept. 1987).

CASTLE ASHBY, NORTHANTS., bridge, ?temple and dairy for 8th Earl of Northampton, *c.*1765.

BROADLANDS, nr. ROMSEY, HANTS., remodelled for 2nd Viscount Palmerston, 1766–8; entrance portico, etc. added by Holland 1788–92; entrance front altered 1859 (*C. Life*, 31 March, 7 April 1923, 4, 11, 18 Dec. 1980).

FISHERWICK PARK, STAFFS., for 5th Earl (later 1st Marquess) of Donegal, 1766–74; dem. 1814–16 (*C. Life*, 28 July 1983).

ASHBURNHAM PLACE, SUSSEX, work for 1st Earl of Ashburnham, including greenhouse and alteration to offices, *c.*1767.

COMPTON VERNEY, WARWICKS., probably designed Bridge, 1770–2, and Chapel, 1776–8, for 6th Lord Willoughby de Broke.

REDGRAVE HALL, SUFFOLK, remodelled for Rowland Holt, *c.*1770; dem. 1946.

SLANE CASTLE, CO. MEATH, IRELAND, the stables for 1st Viscount Conyngham, *c.*1770, Gothic [A. Rowan, 'Georgian Castles in Ireland', *Bull. Irish Georgian Soc.* vii (i), 1964, 16–17].

*CLAREMONT HOUSE, nr. ESHER, SURREY, for 1st Lord Clive, 1771–4 [G. Richardson, *New Vitruvius Britannicus* i, 1802, pls. 61–3; *Surrey Archl. Colls.* lxv, 1968, 91–2].

BURTON CONSTABLE, YORKS. (E.R.), the S. (office) courtyard for William Constable, 1772–3, Gothic.

BROCKLESBY PARK, LINCS., alterations for 1st Lord Yarborough, 1773; damaged by fire 1898 and subsequently reconstructed; partly dem. *c.*1955.

SCAMPSTON HOUSE, YORKS. (E.R.), bridge for Sir

William St. Quintin, Bart., 1773.

MILTON ABBAS, DORSET, model village for 1st Lord Milton, *c.*1774–80. But see below under Sir William Chambers, who also made designs for the new village.

*BENHAM PLACE, BERKS., for 6th Lord Craven, 1774–5; attic storey added and pediment removed *c.*1870.

*LONDON, No. 75 SOUTH AUDLEY STREET, alterations for 3rd Earl of Bute, 1775–6 [*Survey of London* xl, 312–3].

*CADLAND, nr. SOUTHAMPTON, HANTS., for the Hon. Robert Drummond, 1775–8; wing added by Holland 1782; enlarged by Wyatville 1837; dem. *c.*1955.

*TRENTHAM HALL, STAFFS., alterations for 2nd Earl Gower, 1775–8; reconstructed by Barry 1834–40 and 1840–9; dem. 1910 (*C. Life*, 25 Jan. 1968, fig. 8). For the lodges designed by Brown (not by Pickford) see P. du Prey, *John Soane*, 1982, 255.

CLANDON PARK, SURREY, stables for 1st Earl of Onslow, *c.*1775; dem. *c.*1974.

CHILHAM CASTLE, KENT, lodges, etc. for Thomas Heron, 1777; dem. 1862.

*CARDIFF CASTLE, GLAMORGANSHIRE, reconstructed in Gothic style for Lord Mount Stuart, 1777–8; rebuilt 1875 (*C. Life*, 6 April 1961).

*LONDON, No. 34 BERKELEY SQUARE, internal alterations for Lady Mary Coke, 1780; dem. 1879 [*Survey of London* xl, 318].

STANSTEAD PARK, SUSSEX, alterations for Richard Barwell, 1781–3, perhaps not executed.

*NUNEHAM PARK, OXON., alterations including heightening of wings for 2nd Earl Harcourt, 1781–2 [M. L. Batey, *Nuneham Courtenay, Oxfordshire*, 1970, 11–12].

WYNNSTAY, DENBIGHSHIRE, the Dairy for Sir Watkin Williams-Wynn, Bart., 1782 [P. Howell in *C. Life*, 6 April 1972, 853 and fig. 8].

ASKE HALL, YORKS. (N.R.), bridge in park for Sir Lawrence Dundas, Bart. (d. 1781).

BROWN, RICHARD, practised in London, but appears from his early exhibits at the Royal Academy to have had some connection with Devonshire. In 1804 he showed 'A design for a villa with distant view of the Catwater, Plymouth, Devon', in 1807 'A Cottage designed for Sir M. Lopez, Bart., to be built in Devonshire' (probably at Maristow, Lopez's seat), in 1808 a 'Design for rebuilding Warleigh House, the seat of J. Radcliff, Esq. Devon' (not carried out), and in 1812 a view of 'Oldaport Farm, Modbury, Devon'. Subsequent exhibits included 'A proposed design for the Regency Park' (1812), a 'Military Chapel and Officers' apartments, erecting by the Royal African Society at Cape Castle, on the Gold Coast of Africa' (1818), and 'A Market House, designed for Great Yarmouth, Norfolk' (1827: not built).

In 1823, in collaboration with W. Cubitt of Ipswich, Brown submitted the winning design in the competition for a new GAOL AND HOUSE OF CORRECTION, ST. GILES GATES, NORWICH. However, in 1824 he withdrew from further participation in this work, and most of the building (dem.) was carried out under the direction of Philip Barnes [information from Mr. A. P. Baggs]. In 1831 Brown designed for the 3rd Lord Holland a lodge at the Kensington High Street entrance to HOLLAND HOUSE [Lord Ilchester, *Chronicles of Holland House 1820–1900*, 1937, 368–71]. The only other building that he is known to have designed is the INDEPENDENT CHAPEL, TOPSHAM, DEVON, a feeble Gothic structure signed 'R^{D}. BROWN Architect 1839'.

Brown evidently taught drawing, for he frequently called himself 'Architect and Professor of Perspective'. He was the author of *The Principles of Practical Perspective or Scenographic Projection*, 1815, 2nd. ed. 1815, with dedication to Sir John Soane; *Domestic Architecture, containing a History of the Science and the Principles of Designing Public Edifices, Private Dwelling-Houses, Country Mansions and Suburban Villas*, with a section on Landscape Gardening, 1842 (an indiscriminately eclectic work which includes designs for houses in every European style and several oriental ones as well); *Sacred Architecture, its Rise, Progress and Present State embracing the Babylonian, Indian, Egyptian, Greek, and Roman Temples, – the Byzantine, Saxon, Lombard, Norman and Italian Churches, with an analytical inquiry into the Origin, Progress, and Perfection of the Gothic Churches in England; and practical directions for restoring these dilapidated Christian Edifices to their primitive beauty*, 1845, and other works. His travels in France (1822), Switzerland and Italy are mentioned in *Domestic Architecture* (pp. 277, 279, etc.). His London office was at 23 Wells Street, Oxford Street, but he probably retired to Devonshire, for the preface to *Domestic Architecture* is dated from Topsham, and the preface to *Sacred Architecture* from Exeter. M. A. Nicholson, Clark Rampling and J. Tarring were his pupils. An engraved portrait forms the frontispiece to *Domestic Architecture*.

BROWN, ROBERT (–1832), practised in Edinburgh, where he was responsible for laying out a number of building estates in the New Town. In 1813 he was one of the archi-

* In collaboration with H. Holland.

tects who submitted designs for the Calton Hill town-planning scheme [A. J. Youngson, *The Making of Classical Edinburgh*, 1966, 149]. Then in 1815 he acted as Robert Reid's assistant at the Signet Library [S.R.O., E 343/2, p. 197; E 343/3, p. 24]. Between 1810 and 1830 he was engaged in laying out streets: PITTVILLE (formerly PITT) STREET and MELVILLE (now BELLFIELD) STREET, on the Marquess of Abercorn's estate in PORTOBELLO, *c.*1810–18; 1–16 BRANDON STREET, 1–7 EYRE PLACE and 1–8 HUNTLEY STREET on James Eyre's estate, 1822–5; MELVILLE CRESCENT, MELVILLE STREET, WALKER STREET and MANOR PLACE for the Walker Trust, 1822–5; 1–22 ANNANDALE STREET, 1–8 and 17–32 HADDINGTON PLACE and 7–8 and 17–18 HOPETOUN CRESCENT for Major John Hope, 1825–7; 11–22 CIRCUS PLACE N.W. and ST. STEPHEN STREET, 1825–6; 1–32 CLARENCE STREET and 109–119 HENDERSON ROW for James Peddie, 1829–36; and 70–88 HAMILTON PLACE, 1830 [Scottish Development Dept., duplicated *List of Buildings of Special Architectural or Historical Interest in Edinburgh*, 1971, with reference to Sasines, etc.].

Brown also designed NEWINGTON AND ST. LEONARD'S CHURCH (originally HOPE PARK CHAPEL and now QUEEN'S CONCERT HALL), CLERK STREET, EDINBURGH, 1823 [J. Stark, *Picture of Edinburgh*, 5th. ed. 1835, 226], and the BURGHER CHURCH in ROSE STREET, EDINBURGH, 1829 [minutes of the Burgher Congregation, *ex inf.* Mr. W. S. M. Lucas and Mr. David Walker]. In 1827 he largely rebuilt REDNOCK HOUSE, PERTHSHIRE, for General Graham Stirling [plans at Rednock, photos. at N.M.R.S.], and in 1830 he rearranged the interior of YESTER HOUSE, EAST LOTHIAN, for the 8th Marquess of Tweeddale [J. G. Dunbar, 'The Building of Yester House 1670–1878', *Trans. E. Lothian Antiquarian Soc.* xiii, 1972, 37–8]. Brown died on 30 December 1832 [S.R.O., SC 70/1/53, pp. 602–8].

Brown's son Robert Brown, junior (*c.*1804–1860), joined his father's practice in 1830, and took it over after his death. In 1838–9 he added a *porte cochère* to YESTER HOUSE [J. G. Dunbar, *op. cit.*], and in 1835–6 he designed KIRK YETHOLM CHURCH, ROXBURGHSHIRE, in a somewhat crude Gothic style [S.R.O., HR 189/2]. In the 1840s he enlarged and remodelled DUNVEGAN CASTLE, SKYE, for Norman MacLeod, adding, among other features, the existing castellated porch [*The Book of Dunvegan*, ed. R. C. MacLeod, 3rd Spalding Club 1938, i, p. xxxvii].

The younger Brown died on 4 December 1860, aged 56, and is commemorated by a monument in St. Cuthbert's churchyard, Edinburgh. He married the daughter of a builder named Henderson, and left a son Robert who became a civil engineer and died at Bombay in 1869 at the age of 36.

BROWN, SAMUEL (1756–), of Derby, was descended from a family of masons in that town, his father Samuel and his grandfather Solomon (d. 1726) both being masons, as were his uncles Solomon (d. 1756), Sacheverell and Henry and his nephew Sacheverell Brown, junior. Samuel had a builder's yard in Derby and also practised as an architect. He was employed to make the working drawings for the GENERAL INFIRMARY at DERBY, built in 1806–9 to the designs of the industrialist William Strutt [R. Simpson, *History & Antiquities of Derby* i, 1826, 466; S. Glover, *History of the County of Derby* ii (1), 1833, 506]. For Sir Henry Harpur, Bart., of Calke Abbey he designed an elegant CASINO on the banks of the R. Trent at SWARKESTON, *c.*1808 (dem.); a grotto, cascade and Gothic bridge (dem.) at CALKE ABBEY, 1809–10, and remodelled REPTON PARK in Gothic style, 1810–11; dem. 1890s [H. Colvin, *Calke Abbey, Derbyshire*, 1985, 51–2, 122; information about the Brown family from Mr. Maxwell Craven].

BROWN, THOMAS, of Renfrew, directed the building of ROSS-DHU HOUSE, DUNBARTONSHIRE, for Sir James Colquhoun, Bart., in 1773–4. The house is said, probably correctly, to have been designed by Sir James Clerk of Penicuik (*q.v.*) and if so Brown would only have been responsible for supervising its execution. Several payments to 'Mr. Thomas Brown, Architect at Renfrew, for his attendance &c about my Buildings' are found in an account-book formerly at Ross-dhu.

BROWN, THOMAS (–1840), *see* HAYLEY, WILLIAM.

BROWN, THOMAS (*c.*1781–1850), practised in Edinburgh, where he first appears as a surveyor and drawing-master in about 1810. He held the post of Superintendent of the City Works from 1819 until 1847, when he retired on a pension of £150. He died on 5 June 1850, aged 69, and is commemorated by a monument in the Greyfriars Cemetery. David Cousin (1809–78) was his principal assistant and succeeded him as City Architect. John Cunningham (1799–1873) was his pupil. [City Archives; James Brown, *Epitaphs and Monumental Inscriptions in Greyfriars Churchyard*, 1867, 273.]

Brown's son Thomas Brown, junior, became architect to the Prison Board of

Scotland in 1837 and designed, *inter alia*, the County Prison at Inverness, 1845, and the Debtors' Prison on Calton Hill, completed 1846, dem. *c.*1884. In 1848 or 1849 he took James Maitland Wardrop (1824–82) into partnership, thus founding the firm in which Charles Reid, H. M. Wardrop and Rowand Anderson were subsequently partners. There are plans of prisons by him in the Scottish Record Office (RHP 21327 *et seq.*), and the National Library of Scotland (MS. 354, B. and C.).

LEITH, EXCHANGE BUILDINGS, CONSTITUTION STREET, 1809–10, incorporating Assembly Rooms of 1783 [Edinburgh Dean of Guild plans, elevation initialled 'T B 2nd. October 1809', *ex inf.* Mr. David Walker].

LEITH, TRINITY HOUSE, 1816–17 [John Mason, *History of Trinity House of Leith*, Glasgow 1957, 173–5].

NORTH LEITH ASSOCIATE BURGHER (later N. LEITH U.P. and ultimately ST. NINIAN'S) CHURCH, COBURG STREET, 1818, Gothic; dem. *c.*1960 [Edinburgh Dean of Guild plans, 1818].

EDINBURGH, INFIRMARY STREET U.P. CHURCH (now University Works Dept.), 1822 [Edinburgh Dean of Guild plans].

EDINBURGH, ST. MARY, BELLEVUE CRESCENT, 1823–6 [*A.P.S.D.*, *s.v.* 'Edinburgh'; Town Council Minutes, 26 March 1823].

LEITH, THE PRISON, 1824; dem. [*The Scotsman*, 12 Aug. 1824].

LUFFNESS HOUSE, EAST LOTHIAN, additions, 1825 (kitchen) and 1841 (W. front, dem. 1959) for General Sir Alexander Hope and George William Hope, respectively [C. McWilliam, *Lothian*, Buildings of Scotland, 1978, 318, based on drawings at Luffness].

EDINBURGH, COMELY BANK, 1817–18 [elevation in S.R.O., RHP 4429]; FETTES ROW, 1821; layout of INVERLEITH ROW, 1823; CUMBERLAND STREET, 1823; PRESTON STREET WEST, 1824; NEWINGTON PLACE WEST and 58–68 NEWINGTON ROAD, *c.*1825; ROYAL CRESCENT, 1825–9; INVERLEITH PLACE, 1826 [all from Sasines].

EDINBURGH, ST. GILES' CATHEDRAL, fitted up nave as a parish church, 1842 [*History of the King's Works* vi, 254].

BROWN, THOMAS (–1833), lived at Uphall in Midlothian, where he died on 11 June 1833 [S.R.O., SC 41/53/1]. Both he and his successor THOMAS BROWN II (1806–1872) appear to have specialized in the designing of farm buildings, etc., and were employed for that purpose on the Hopetoun estates. In 1814 the elder Brown was responsible for a 'New Addition' (including a dining-room) to NEW SAUGHTON or CAMMO HOUSE, MIDLOTHIAN, for James Watson, dem. after a fire in 1977 [S.R.O., GD 150/3352–3, esp. 3353/77], in 1827–30 he designed additions to ORMISTON HALL, E. LOTHIAN, for the 5th Earl of Hopetoun [S.R.O., SC 40/67/7, voucher 189, *ex inf.* Miss C. Cruft], and in 1828–9 he altered and repaired OVER RANKEILLOUR HOUSE, FIFE, for General Sir Alexander Hope [S.R.O., SC 20/44/5, 69, 87]. Early in the 1830s either he or his son worked for William Adam (d. 1839) at BLAIR ADAM in KINROSS-SHIRE, where he designed the Memorial (1833) and various gates and lodges [Blair Adam archives, *ex inf.* Prof. A. A. Tait]. TEMPLE CHURCH, MIDLOTHIAN, converted into a house in 1977, was built in 1832 to the designs presumably of the elder Brown [S.R.O., HR 774/1, 5 June 1830], and the younger one altered CARRINGTON CHURCH, MIDLOTHIAN, in 1836 [S.R.O., HR 460/1, 16 Nov. 1838]. The latter is commemorated by a tombstone in Uphall churchyard.

BROWN, WILLIAM, was described as 'architect' when he was admitted to the Incorporation of Wrights at Glasgow in 1831 [*The Incorporation of Wrights in Glasgow*, Glasgow 1880, 48]. He designed THE LYCEUM, SOUTH ALBION STREET, GLASGOW (dem.), an establishment containing a subscription library and news room [*The Picture of Glasgow*, Glasgow 1812, 147–8].

BROWN, WILLIAM (1778–1851), was a native of Mendham, Norfolk. He practised in Ipswich as an architect and surveyor, and at the same time established a firm of timber merchants that lasted until the 1980s. He designed several public and private buildings, often with Greek Revival detailing. He spent the last ten years of his life in an Asylum. Robert Brown (*c.*1806–1876), Norwich's leading Victorian architect, was his nephew and pupil. [C. Brown, B. Haward & R. Kindred, *Dictionary of Architects of Suffolk Buildings 1800–1914*, 1991, 53.]

IPSWICH, HOUSE OF CORRECTION (for Women), 1802; altered 1823 to become Borough Gaol [C. Brown *et al.*, *op. cit.*].

IPSWICH, THE PROVISION MARKET, consisting of an inner and an outer quadrangle surrounded by a piazza, the inner having as its centre a fountain surmounted by an obelisk, 1810–11; dem. 1897 [*Ipswich Jnl.*, 17 March 1810; J. Dugdale, *The British Traveller* iv, 1819, 301; J. Wodderspoon, *Memorials of Ipswich*, 1850, 11] (J. Glyde, *Illustrations of Old Ipswich*, 1889, 69).

THE NORFOLK LUNATIC ASYLUM, THORPE-NEXT-

NORWICH, 1811–14 [C. Mackie, *Norfolk Annals* i, 1901, 89, 116].

HARLESTON CHURCH, NORFOLK, enlarged 1819; dem. 1872 [account in parish records in Norfolk C.R.O., PD 295/66].

BARKING, SUFFOLK, THE RECTORY (now PARKWOOD HOUSE), 1819–20 [Suffolk C.R.O., Suffolk Archdeaconry Records FF1/5/1].

EARL STONHAM RECTORY, SUFFOLK, rebuilt 1820 [*ibid.*, FF 1/30/1].

IPSWICH, NEW ASSEMBLY ROOMS, NORTHGATE STREET (now a shop), 1820–1 [C. Brown *et al.*, *op. cit.*].

IPSWICH, terrace of houses (Nos. 27–35) in LOWER BROOK STREET, 1825 [*Ipswich Jnl.*, 31 Dec. 1825, *ex inf.* Mr. J. Bensusan-Butt].

BROWNE, ADAM (–1655), held the post of Surveyor to Westminster Abbey from 1639 until his death in 1655. Among the Westminster Abbey Muniments there are surveys of repairs needed at the Abbey drawn up by Browne, and estimates by him for making a gallery and altering the pews during the Commonwealth [W.A.M. 9908, 9909, 5320, 9828, 24852, 24854, 24855, 24857, 42687, etc.]. Browne was a joiner by trade, and in 1629 he had made the mannerist chimney-piece in the Jerusalem Chamber at the Abbey [W.A.M. 6612]. In the 1630s he was much employed by Archbishop Laud, and at Arbury Hall, Warwickshire, there is a fine cabinet in a style similar to the chimney-piece which bears Laud's arms as Bishop of London (1628–31) and which may well have been made for him by Browne.

In 1633–4 University College, Oxford, bought 800 old boards from 'Mr. Browne Joyner of London', who is also described as 'Mr. Brown joyner to my Ld. Grace of Cant.' [University College records]. At that time Browne was being employed by Laud at St. John's College, where in 1632 he made a screen 'to part the upper end of the Chappell' [P.R.O., S. P. Dom. Charles I, 226, no. 21]. At Lambeth Palace Browne made an altar and other joinery work for Laud in 1633 [P.R.O., S. P. Dom. Charles I, 246, no. 88], and in Laud's accounts there are payments to him for picture-frames, three 'cedar chests', a press for copes, work in 'Your Grace's study', etc. [P.R.O., E 101/547/5, *passim*]. At Laud's trial in 1644 'Browne, his Joyner' was a reluctant witness, giving evidence about 'Popish' windows ordered by Laud for his houses at Lambeth and Croydon and put up under Browne's direction [*Laud's Works*, ed. Bliss, iv, 1854, 209, 228; W. Prynne, *Canterburies Doome . . .*, 1644, 61].

Browne was also concerned in building the Canterbury Quadrangle at St. John's College, which was paid for by Laud. The accounts for its erection show that in Feb. 1632/3 he was paid £5 'for his paines in comming downe [from London] & drawing the Drafts, & making the Moulds'. Besides providing drawings and moulds he negotiated with masons on the College's behalf and drew up a contract with the carpenter [St. John's College Muniments, lxxxi, 2, pp. 81–2]. The drawings in question were probably for the upper parts of the two classical frontispieces, which there is reason to think were completed in a different and more baroque style than that originally envisaged. If these frontispieces can be attributed to him he must rank as one of the leading English architectural designers of the 1630s. The design of the frontispieces is, however, closely linked to the contemporary architecture of Antwerp, and Browne may have been only the executant architect of a design brought over from that city, or made by someone like Sir Balthasar Gerbier (*q.v.*) who was in touch with architects and artists in Antwerp [H. Colvin, *The Canterbury Quadrangle, St. John's College, Oxford*, 1988, 33–8, 45–6].

BROWNE, ARTHUR (*c.*1757–1840), practised in the Close at Norwich. He was a founder-member of the Norwich Society of Artists in 1805, and was its President in 1807. He exhibited at the Society from 1805 to 1833. In 1799 the *Gentleman's Magazine* illustrated a design made by him for an octagonal domed mansion 'intended to be erected at Burnham Market, Norfolk, as a residence for Lord Nelson'. A design for a 'Temple of Victory', published in the same magazine in 1800, appears also to have been made by him, and he signs unexecuted designs for a gaol at Bury St. Edmunds, and for an obelisk in honour of Lord Nelson, which appeared in the *Gentlemen's Magazine* in August 1801 and August 1807, respectively. All these designs are of a markedly neo-classical character. Intwood Hall and Magdalene Bridge are, however, Gothic, and it was no doubt a Gothic design that was expected in 1825, when Wilkins, Browne and Rickman were invited to compete for the new building at St. John's College, Cambridge, by its fellows (one of whom was Browne's son Arthur, afterwards vicar of Mendham, Norfolk) [Willis & Clark, ii, 278]. Browne died at his house in the Close at Norwich on 18 March 1840, aged 83 [*Bury & Norwich Post*, 25 March 1840, *ex inf.* Mr. David Cubitt]. According to an obituary in the *Norwich Mercury* (21 March 1840), he had taken up architecture 'at a late period in his life'. In the list of his works which follows all references to the exhibitions of the Norwich Society of Artists (N.S.A.) have been provided by Mr. A. Paget Baggs.

LITTLE PLUMSTEAD, NORFOLK, Gothic house or *cottage orné* for Francis Gostling, *c.*1806 [exhib. at N.S.A. 1806; cf. J. Chambers, *Norfolk Tour* i, 1829, 6].

NORWICH, GUILDHALL, remodelled THE COMMON COUNCIL CHAMBER, 1806 [*Norwich Mercury*, 27 Feb. 1808, *ex inf.* Mr. David Cubitt].

INTWOOD HALL, NORFOLK, for J. S. Muskett, *c.*1807, Tudor Gothic [exhib. at N.S.A. 1810].

NORWICH, CARROW BRIDGE (cast iron), 1810; dem. [exhib. at N.S.A. 1810].

NORWICH, CARROW HILL, supervised gratuitously laying out of road, as recorded on a plaque fixed to wall of Black Tower.

COSTESSEY, NORFOLK, THE PILGRIMS' WELL (obelisk, etc.), *c.*1810 [drawing in Todd Collection, Norwich Castle Museum, Forehoe Hundred].

NORWICH, ST. ANDREW'S PLACE, house for P. J. Knights, *c.*1811 [exhib. at N.S.A. 1811].

CAMBRIDGE, four houses near Pembroke College, *c.*1816 [exhib, at N.S.A. 1816].

SWAFFHAM, NORFOLK, design for 'addition to the house of a gentleman', exhib. at N.S.A. 1816.

HORNING VICARAGE, NORFOLK, 1820 [Norfolk C.R.O. DN/DPL/1/2/34].

HEPWORTH RECTORY, SUFFOLK, 1820 [Suffolk C.R.O. (Bury), 806/2/10].

NORWICH, Triumphal Arch in Market Place to commemorate coronation of King George IV, 1821 [J. Chambers, *Norfolk Tour* iii, 1829, 1104].

NORWICH, ST. STEPHEN'S CHURCH, monument to W. Stevenson, F.S.A. (d. 1821), executed by De Carle [J. Chambers, *Norfolk Tour* iii, 1829, 1094].

CAMBRIDGE, MAGDALENE BRIDGE (cast iron), 1823 [signed 'Arthur Browne Archt. 1823'].

NORWICH, ST. PETER MANCROFT CHURCH, monument to Revd. C. J. Chapman (d. 1826), executed by William Allen [J. Chambers, *Norfolk Tour* iii, 1829, 1097].

CAMBRIDGE, EMMANUEL COLLEGE, enlarged kitchen and remodelled its W. elevation in Tudor Gothic style, 1828 [Willis & Clark ii, 716]. Browne may also have been responsible for the N. range of the New Court, built in 1824.

EAST BILNEY RECTORY, NORFOLK, 'Elizabethan', 1837–40 [Norfolk C.R.O., DN/DPL/1/1/9].

NORWICH CATHEDRAL, fittings of St. Luke's Chapel [J. Chambers, *Norfolk Tour* iii, 1829, 1104].

BROWNE, EDWARD HENRY, of London, exhibited at the Royal Academy between 1831 and 1843, including the 'Facade of the new fire station house about to be erected for the London Fire-Engine Establishment in Chandos Street, St. Martin's Lane' (1836), the 'St. John's National Schools, now erecting at Walham Green' (1836), 'A cottage, erecting in Upper Harmer Street, Gravesend, for George Kiallmarll, Esq.' (1843), and 'A cottage erecting in Millfield Lane, Highgate, for Albert Walls, Esqr.' (1843). A design by him for an Italianate villa is in the R.I.B.A. Drawings Collection. He appears to have died or retired soon after 1850, when his practice at 13 Beaufort Buildings, Strand, was taken over by Samuel Field.

BROWNE, JOSEPH, was primarily a purveyor of marble and scagliola. His premises were in University Street, Bloomsbury, where in 1830 he exhibited a large collection of antique marble and other works of art. He made chimney-pieces and monumental tablets, and acted occasionally as an architect [R. Gunnis, *Dictionary of British Sculptors 1660–1851*, 1968, 65–6]. In 1814 he enlarged the dining-room (now the library) at RABY CASTLE, CO. DURHAM, for the 3rd Earl of Darlington, with a screen of Ionic scagliola columns [A. Rowan in *C. Life*, 22 Jan. 1970, 187], and he signs two architectural drawings among the Gordon Castle papers in the Scottish Record Office, one a design for a mausoleum (RHP 2378, no. 42), the other for a Grecian temple (RHP 2413). Both were probably made for the 5th Duke of Gordon (d. 1836).

BROWNE, ROBERT (1756–1827), junior, was the son of Robert Browne, senior, who was one of the joint clerks of works at Somerset House under Chambers from 1776 onwards, and held the post of Clerk of the Works at the Tower, Newmarket, Winchester and Greenwich from 1790 until his death in 1796. The son entered the Royal Academy Schools in 1776, and exhibited drawings at the Academy from 1778 to 1798. In 1793 he showed 'A pavilion erected at Ampton', presumably a domed Doric temple at AMPTON HALL, SUFFOLK, that is recorded in photographs. In 1789 he obtained a post in the Office of Works as Clerk of the Works at Windsor Castle, and from 1790 to 1815 held a similar post at Richmond and Kew Palaces. In 1805 he carried out alterations to KEW CHURCH, SURREY, for King George III, including the addition of the west portico and the south aisle [plans in Surrey Archdeaconry Records]. In 1811–12 he designed a wooden bridge over the Thames at DATCHET, BUCKS., dem. 1851 [*Oxford Herald*, 9 March 1811]. In 1815 he was promoted to the office of Assistant Surveyor-General and Cashier, from which he retired in 1822. The arrangements for the coronation of George IV in 1820 were under his direction [A. T. Bolton, *The Portrait of Sir John Soane*, 353]. He died on 14 August 1827, aged 72, and is commemorated by a monument in the churchyard at Kew. R. C. Kidd was his pupil.

BROWNING, BRYAN (1773–1856), was a native of Thurlby, Lincs. Nothing is known of his architectural training, but as early as 1817 he made designs for rebuilding RINGWOOD VICARAGE, HANTS. [Winchester Diocesan Records]. From about 1820 to 1830 he was in partnership with George Woolcott (*q.v.*) in Doughty Street, London, as 'Builders and Surveyors'. In 1824 they built STRENSHAM COURT, WORCS., for John Taylor to designs probably made for them by George Maddox (*q.v.*) and in 1825–7 they were the contractors for YORK (now LANCASTER) HOUSE, LONDON, for which Benjamin Wyatt was the architect [*A.P.S.D.*, *s.v.* 'Maddox, George' and contract for Strensham in Birmingham Reference Library, 434264 Dv. 576]. The records of the Foundling Hospital (G.L.R.O.), show that in 1825 they were concerned in building houses on the north side of MECKLENBURGH SQUARE to the designs of Joseph Kay (*q.v.*).

By 1834 Browning was back in Lincolnshire as a practising architect, living at Northorpe (between Bourne and Thurlby). He had already, in 1821, designed the SESSIONS HOUSE at BOURNE, LINCS., whose small but effective façade ingeniously combines an external staircase and a columnar screen [*The Lincoln, Rutland and Stamford Mercury*, 4 and 11 May, 26 Oct. 1821], and in 1828 he competed unsuccessfully for the new Sessions House at Sleaford [*Arch. Hist.* 27, 1984, 345, 348, pl. 2a]. By 1838 he was established in Stamford, where in the 1840s he was retained by Lord Exeter at £180 p.a. Here he designed the WORKHOUSE, 1835 (dem.), the Greek Revival STAMFORD INSTITUTION on ST. PETER'S HILL, 1842, and GRANT'S IRON FOUNDRY, 1845, of which the portal survives in Wharf Road. He also remodelled BARN HILL HOUSE for the Marquess of Exeter, 1843, and laid out the Blackfriars estate for Lord Brownlow in 1840 [R.C.H.M., *Stamford*, 1977, lxxxiv, 51, 63, 69, 162].

In 1824–5 Browning designed THE HOUSE OF CORRECTION at FOLKINGHAM, LINCS., with a dramatic façade suggestive of Vanbrugh or Ledoux [unsigned drawings in Lincs. C.R.O., Kesteven Q.S. Records, endorsed 'Mr. Browning's plans']. Later works by him are STOKE DRY RECTORY, RUTLAND, 1840, and THE NATIONAL SCHOOL at TITCHMARSH, NORTHANTS, 1840–1, both Tudor Gothic [Northants. C.R.O., Peterborough Diocesan Records and School plans 68], and the nave of THRAPSTON CHURCH, NORTHANTS., 1841–3 [I.C.B.S.]. In 1846–8 he was responsible for alterations to APETHORPE, NORTHANTS., for the 11th Earl of Westmorland [R.C.H.M., *Northants.*, vi, 1984, 8]. In the Lincolnshire Record Office there are plans by him for altering or rebuilding the parsonages at ALWALTON, HUNTS. (1833), FLETTON, HUNTS (1835), GREATFORD, LINCS. (1838) and DEEPING ST. JAMES, LINCS. (1839).

Browning died on 1 October 1856, and is commemorated by a monument in the cemetery at Stamford. His son Edward Browning (1816–82) appears to have been in partnership with him towards the end of his life, and succeeded to his practice. In 1847–9 STAMFORD BRIDGE was rebuilt 'by Messrs. Browning' together with the adjoining Conservative Club, originally a toll-house [M. E. C. Walcott, *Memorials of Stamford*, 1867, 31]. The Jacobean-style block at the corner of Red Lion Square and High Street (1848) and the rebuilding of BYARD HOUSE, No. 19 ST. PAUL'S STREET (1851), following the 17th-century style of the previous building on the site, were other products of the Browning office during this period [R.C.H.M. *Stamford*, 113, 148]. Edward, who was a pupil of George Maddox, worked at both Burghley and Apethorpe and was responsible for the Jacobean remodelling of Barrington Hall, Essex, in 1863 [*The Architect's, Engineer's and Building Trades' Directory*, 1868, 103]. Bryan had a younger son Henry (1822–1907), who began life in the family office, but in 1851 went to Cambridge, graduated, was ordained and held the living of St. George's with St. Paul's Stamford from 1862 to 1890.

BROWNING, L—, exhibited at the Royal Academy from South Molton Street, London, between 1812 and 1815, showing in 1815 his design for 'the alteration and improvements of Bunny Park, Nottinghamshire, now executing for Lord Rancliffe'.

BRUCE, SIR WILLIAM (*c.*1630–1710), was the younger son of Robert Bruce of Blairhall, a Perthshire laird who was closely connected with other and more prominent branches of the Bruce family, including those represented by the Earls of Kincardine and of

Elgin and Ailesbury. The date of his birth is not known, but it is likely that he was born in about 1630. A William Bruce was, however, admitted to St. Salvator's College at St. Andrews for the academic year 1637–8, and if this was the future baronet, he must have been born in the 1620s. Nothing certain is known about his early life. Whatever ability he may have shown as a young man, it was primarily to political services that he appears to have owed his subsequent advancement. According to Sir Robert Douglas's *Baronage of Scotland* (1798) Bruce played a part in converting General Monk to the Royalist cause in 1659, and the existence of a passport for Bruce signed by Monk on 7 Sept. 1659 certainly suggests that he may have been involved in the negotiations which preceded the Restoration, for it not only permits him 'to passe about his occasions on this side the Fryth [of Forth] & other parts of Scotland', but also refers to his impending 'returne to Holland', where the royal court was then in exile. The Clarendon State Papers afford further evidence that Bruce was employed as a confidential messenger between the Scottish lords and Charles II in the months immediately preceding the Restoration. Soon after the Restoration he was knighted, and through the patronage of the Earl (later Duke) of Lauderdale obtained various employments, including those of Clerk of the Bills,[1] receiver of fines, and commissioner of excise in Fife. From March 1672 he also enjoyed the farm of the Scottish customs and had various commercial interests, such as a share in the Royal Fishery Company of 1670. By 1665 he was in a position to acquire a small estate at Balcaskie in Fife, and in 1675 a larger one at Kinross on the shores of Loch Leven. In 1668 his new status as a landed gentleman was recognized by the grant of a baronetcy, and subsequently a peerage may even have been talked of. As it was, he was a landowner, a Justice of the Peace (1673), parliamentary commissioner for Kinross-shire, and for a few months (April 1685 to May 1686) a member of the Privy Council for Scotland.

With the death of Charles II (1685) Bruce's good fortune failed him. For the rest of his life he was politically suspect. James II distrusted him and the governments of William III and Queen Anne, believing him (with some justification) to be a Jacobite sympathizer, placed him under confinement on more than one occasion. After 1686 he devoted most of his energies to the management of his estates, and to the completion of a country seat at Kinross. But, deprived of the financial rewards of office, Bruce found that his works could be continued only by burdening his estate with debt. By 1700 he reckoned that he had spent upwards of £10,000 on building operations, and even when they were concluded the cost of maintaining the elaborate formal gardens was still heavy. It was, therefore, only with difficulty that Bruce created the magnificant house which he hoped to hand on to his successors in the baronetcy.

Of Bruce's architectural education there is no record, but 'it is reasonable to suppose that an inherent interest in the subject was developed both by theoretical studies and by travel' (Dunbar). His visits to Holland during the Interregnum may well have extended to France, and he is known to have made a 'foreign journey' in 1663. He was also in England on various occasions, and although France may have been the dominant influence in the formation of his architectural style, several of his country houses conform to the 'double-pile' formula popularized by May and Pratt soon after the Restoration.

Bruce's career as an official architect was limited to the years 1671–8, when he held the post of 'Surveyor-general and overseer of the King's Buildings in Scotland'. This was a revival of the ancient office of 'Master of Work' to the Scottish Crown, vacant since 1668, but with a new title and an enhanced salary (£300 instead of £100). The appointment was specifically for the purpose of rebuilding the palace of Holyroodhouse, and apart from some repairs to Edinburgh and Stirling Castles and to the fortifications on the Bass Rock, there is no evidence that Bruce carried out any other architectural works for the Crown. The whole scheme appears to have originated with the all-powerful Lauderdale, and it may have been due to political differences between Bruce and Lauderdale that in May 1678 his warrant was revoked on the ground that the reconstruction of Holyroodhouse was finished. In 1671 Holyroodhouse had consisted of an irregular cluster of buildings, of which the sixteenth-century north-west tower was the principal architectural feature. Assisted by Robert Mylne, the King's Master Mason, Bruce created a symmetrical front by erecting a duplicate tower to the south and linking the two together by means of a lower balustraded range incorporating a Doric entrance-portico. The whole design, including the incorporation of late Gothic towers into a formal composition, is thoroughly French in character. Within the main courtyard the restrained classicism of the principal elevations is also French in derivation, and 'introduced a

[1] In December 1681 he resigned this post in favour of James Anstruther (Sir John Lauder, *Historical Notices of Scottish Affairs* i, 1848, 344).

completely new idiom into Scottish architecture', hitherto addicted to the mannerist exuberance of buildings like Heriot's Hospital. The interior decoration was, however, carried out in the rich Anglo-Dutch style of Restoration England.

Apart from his brief tenure of the Surveyor's office, Bruce was essentially a gentleman architect, whose designs were nearly all made for fellow members of the Scottish aristocracy. Defoe called him the 'Kit Wren of Scotland', but Hugh May and Sir Roger Pratt were the English architects with whom it is most appropriate to compare him. The number of country houses for which he was directly responsible is not large, but his architectural influence was much more extensive than the short list of his authenticated works might suggest. His advice was often sought by his friends and their relatives even when there was no question of his assuming direct control over their building operations. In this way he was consulted about designs for new houses by the Earl of Tweeddale in 1670 and by the Earl of Cassilis in 1673–4. A few years later when the Duke of Queensberry proposed to remodel Drumlanrig he made a memorandum that the papers were 'to be looked over and advised be Sr. Wm. Bruice', and in 1692 the Duke of Hamilton did not begin work at Hamilton Palace before he had obtained Bruce's advice about the best man to employ. Bruce's influence was further extended by those who worked with him. To call them his pupils would be misleading, but it was undoubtedly from Bruce that the master masons Robert Mylne and Tobias Bachop (*qq.v.*) learned a more classical vocabulary. In the case of James Smith (*q.v.*) the exchange of expertise may have been almost as much to Bruce's advantage as to Smith's, but Smith's importance as an exponent of Bruce's style is evident. Alexander Edward, minister of Kemback (*q.v.*), seems to have begun his architectural career as Bruce's draughtsman, before developing a practice of his own.

Bruce rightly ranks as the effective founder of classical architecture in Scotland. Before him Scottish domestic architecture was still dominated by the basic forms of the late medieval castle overlaid with mannerist decoration from France and the Low Countries. Though highly picturesque, the result was an architectural idiom far removed from the classical conventions which by 1660 were generally accepted (if not always understood) in England. It was Bruce's function to design unfortified houses for the first generation of Scottish lairds to realize that the tower-house was an anachronism, and to persuade them to abandon corbel and crow-step in favour of cornice and pediment. Not all Bruce's houses were built on new foundations. Often it was a case of adapting an old fabric to modern uses, and here some compromise with the past was inevitable. At his own house of Balcaskie, at Lauderdale's castle of Thirlestane, at his grandson's seat of Craighall, he was obliged to improvise in a manner which hardly suggests the mastery of his later works. At Holyroodhouse he was even prepared, in the interests of symmetry, to duplicate a sixteenth-century tower block complete with its conical roofs and battlements. But at Dunkeld, Moncreiffe and Kinross he adapted the compact formula developed in England by architects like Webb and Pratt and gave it a dignity and a presence that it rarely attained in English hands. At Craigiehall and Mertoun a basically conventional façade is made interesting by subtle variations in fenestration, while Hopetoun shows that he could handle a more complex design with equal assurance. Not only, therefore, was Bruce, in the words of Sir John Clerk of Penicuik, 'the chief introducer of Architecture in this country': as a designer of country houses he was fully the equal of his English contemporaries.

For Bruce house and garden were part of a single conception. At Kinross in particular the nobility of the architecture is enhanced by the magnificent formality of the setting. At the same time the deliberate alignment of the main vista on the ruins of Lochleven Castle suggests that Bruce, like Vanbrugh, has a place in the prehistory of the picturesque. Although architecture was his dominant interest, Bruce's fondness for horticulture, music and painting is shown by numerous surviving accounts of personal expenditure from 1665 onwards. He may also have been something of a linguist, for besides owning books published in French and Italian, as well as in Latin and Greek, he appears to have had a reading knowledge of German and Dutch.

Bruce was twice married, first in about 1660 to Mary, daughter of Sir James Halket of Pitfirrane, and secondly (in 1700) to Magdalen (Scott), the widow of an Edinburgh merchant named Clerk. He died on 1 January 1710, 'at a very advanced age', and was buried in the family vault at Kinross. His property was inherited, first by his son John, and then by his daughter Anne, who married Sir Thomas Hope of Craighall. A portrait by Michael Wright, painted in 1664, is in the Scottish National Portrait Gallery. Another version of this portrait hangs at Kinross House. At Holyroodhouse there is a portrait of Bruce in old age by Sir John Medina. Some of his papers remain at

Kinross House. Others are in the Register House at Edinburgh.

[S.R.O., Bruce of Kinross papers (GD 29); B.L., Lauderdale papers, especially Add. MSS. 23134, f. 170, and 23135, ff. 32–6; *Cal. S.P. Domestic 1663–4*, 265, *1671*, 295–6, *1678*, 197; *Acts of the Privy Council of Scotland* i–xii, *passim*; *The Acts of Parliament of Scotland* xii (index), 258; *The Clarendon State Papers*, ed. Routledge; Hist. MSS. Comm., *House of Lords*, N.S. viii, 87, 92, 111, 149, 152–3, 182–3, 191, 195, 199, *Laing* i, 349–50; *Journal of the Hon. John Erskine of Carnock 1683–7*, ed. W. Macleod, Scottish History Soc. 1893, 154 (reference to Bruce as 'Viscount of Kinross'); Joseph Robertson, 'Notice of a Volume of the Accounts of Sir William Bruce', *Proc. Soc. Ant. Scotland* iii, 1862, 113–17; David Marshall, 'Three Contracts for the Reparation of Holyrood Palace, etc', *Proc. Soc. Ant. Scotland*, N.S. ii, 1880, 324–37; R. S. Mylne, *The Master Masons to the Crown of Scotland*, 1893: Sir Wm. Fraser, *The Earls of Melville and Leven*, 1890, i, 272, iii, 237, 239; H. F. Kerr in *Quarterly of the Royal Incorporation of Architects of Scotland*, 1924; T. C. Smout, *Scottish Trade on the Eve of Union*, 1963, 75; John Lowrey, 'Bruce and his Circle at Craigiehall 1693–1708', in *Aspects of Scottish Classicism*, ed. Frew & Jones, St. Andrews 1988; J. G. Dunbar, *The Architecture of Scotland*, 1978, 75–89; Hubert Fenwick, *Architect Royal*, Kineton 1970; J. G. Dunbar, *Sir William Bruce*, exhibition catalogue published by the Scottish Arts Council, 1970. The last is by far the best account of Bruce's work in print.]

PUBLIC BUILDINGS

HOLYROODHOUSE, EDINBURGH, enlarged and remodelled for King Charles II, 1671–9 [*Cal. S.P. Domestic 1671*, 295–6; R. S. Mylne, *The Master Masons to the Crown of Scotland*, 1893, chaps. 9–10; drawings and contracts in B.L., Egerton MSS. 2870–1; building accounts in S.R.O.].

LAUDER CHURCH, BERWICKSHIRE, for 1st Duke of Lauderdale, 1673 [letter from Lauderdale in S.R.O., GD 29/1897/9] (G. Hay, *Architecture of Scottish Post-Reformation Churches*, 1957, fig. 21 and pl. 8b).

EDINBURGH, five cisterns or fountains in the city as part of a new system of water-supply, 1674–5 [*Extracts from the Records of the City of Edinburgh 1665–80*, ed. M. Wood, xlii–xliii, 427].

EDINBURGH, THE EXCHANGE, PARLIAMENT CLOSE, for Thomas Robertson, 1680–1; destroyed by fire 1700 [R. Miller, *The Municipal Buildings of Edinburgh*, Edinburgh 1895, 126–7; Marguerite Wood, 'All the Statelie Buildings of Thomas Robertson', *Book of the Old Edinburgh Club* xxiv, 1942, 137].

KINROSS, SOUTH QUEICH BRIDGE, *c.*1694, since replaced [R. Sibbald, *The History of Fife and Kinross*, 1803 ed., 274].

EDINBURGH, THE PARLIAMENT HOUSE, fitted up library for Faculty of Advocates in the Laigh Hall, 1702 [I. G. Brown, *Building for Books*, Aberdeen 1989, 31].

STIRLING, THE TOWN HOUSE, 1703–5 [R.C.A.M., *Stirlingshire* ii, 293].

attributed: ABERCORN CHURCH, WEST LOTHIAN, THE HOPE AISLE, for 1st Earl of Hopetoun, 1707–8 (*C. Life*, 20 Oct. 1966).

COUNTRY HOUSES

LESLIE HOUSE, FIFE, supervised enlargement and remodelling by Robert Mylne (*q.v.*) for 7th Earl (1st Duke) of Rothes, 1667–72; largely destroyed by fire 1763 [J. Dunbar, *Sir William Bruce* (exhibition catalogue), 10, citing Rothes papers in Kirkcaldy Museum; *Vitruvius Scoticus*, pls. 66–8].

BALCASKIE HOUSE, FIFE, enlarged and altered for himself, *c.*1670–74 [J. Dunbar, *Sir William Bruce* (exhibition catalogue), 10–11, citing S.R.O., Bruce of Kinross papers, and in Royal Archaeological Institute, *The St. Andrew's Area*, 1991, 46–8, with plan] (*C. Life*, 2 March 1912; 25 May 1989).

THIRLESTANE CASTLE, BERWICKSHIRE, supervised remodelling by Robert Mylne (*q.v.*) for 1st Duke of Lauderdale, *c.*1670–77; altered 1840–1 [J. G. Dunbar, 'The Building-activities of the Duke and Duchess of Lauderdale, 1670–82', *Archaeological Jnl.* cxxxii, 1975] (D. MacGibbon & T. Ross, *Castellated and Domestic Architecture of Scotland* iv, 1892, 334–9).

HAM HOUSE, SURREY, gateways for Elizabeth, Countess of Dysart (afterwards Duchess of Lauderdale), 1671 and 1675 [J. G. Dunbar, 'The Building-activities of the Duke and Duchess of Lauderdale, 1670–82', *Archaeological Jnl.* cxxxii, 1975].

PANMURE HOUSE, ANGUS, gateway for 3rd Earl of Panmure, 1672 [S.R.O., GD 45/18/599].

BRUNSTANE HOUSE, MIDLOTHIAN, enlarged and remodelled for 1st Duke of Lauderdale, *c.*1672–5; S. range rebuilt by W. Adam 1735–44 [J. G. Dunbar, 'The Building-activities of the Duke and Duchess of Lauderdale, 1670–82', *Archaeological Jnl.* cxxxii, 1975].

LETHINGTON (now LENNOXLOVE), EAST LOTHIAN, alterations for 1st Duke of Lauderdale, 1673–4 and 1676–7, including new stableblock [J. G. Dunbar, 'The Building-activities of the Duke and Duchess of Lauderdale, 1670–82', *Archaeological Jnl.* cxxxii, 1975].

DUNKELD HOUSE, PERTHSHIRE, for 1st Marquess of Atholl, *c.*1676–84; dem. 1830 [J. G. Dunbar, *Sir William Bruce* (exhibition catalogue), 14].

attributed: MONCREIFFE HOUSE, PERTHSHIRE, for Thomas Moncreiffe, 1679; destroyed by fire 1957 [J. G. Dunbar, *Sir William Bruce* (exhibition catalogue), 14].

?INVERMAY HOUSE, PERTHSHIRE, for James and David Drummond, 1686; dem. *c.*1805 [building contract of 19 May 1686 specifies that the house is to be designed 'be Sir William Bruce of Kinross or . . . Mill architector, or any other relevant architector that the lairds shall think fit': Scottish History Society, *Miscellany* xi, 1990, 312–4].

KINROSS HOUSE, KINROSS-SHIRE, for himself, 1686–93 [*Vitruvius Scoticus*, pls. 61–2; Mark Girouard in *C. Life*, 25 March, 1 April 1965; J. G. Dunbar, 'Kinross House', in *The Country Seat*, ed. Colvin & Harris, 1970; S.R.O., Bruce of Kinross papers, GD 29/263, and accounts in Mylne papers, GD 1/51/62].

CRAIGIEHALL HOUSE, WEST LOTHIAN, for 2nd Earl of Annandale, *c.*1695–1708; altered by W. Adam *c.*1730, W. Burn 1828, D. Bryce 1852 and R. Lorimer 1926–7 [letters in S.R.O., GD 29/1955/2 and at Raehills (NRA Scotland, list 2171) and variant design in portfolio at Dalmeny House].

CRAIGHALL, nr. CUPAR, FIFE, alterations and additions for Sir William Hope (then a minor in Bruce's guardianship), 1697–9; long ruinous, finally dem. *c.*1955 [accounts in S.R.O., Bruce of Arnot papers, GD 242, box 27; J. G. Dunbar, *Sir William Bruce* (exhibition catalogue), 16].

KINNAIRD CASTLE, ANGUS, unexecuted design for remodelling house for 4th Earl of Southesk, 1698 [J. G. Dunbar, 'Two late 17th-century designs for Kinnaird Castle' in *Scottish Country Houses 1600–1914* (Essays in Honour of Kitty Cruft), ed. Gow & Rowan, 1995].

HOPETOUN HOUSE, WEST LOTHIAN, for Charles Hope, afterwards 1st Earl of Hopetoun, 1699–1702 and further works 1706–10; remodelled by William, John and Robert Adam, 1721–56 [*Vitruvius Scoticus*, pls. 14–19; *Vitruvius Britannicus* ii, 1717, pls. 75–77; John Fleming in *C. Life*, 5–12 Jan. 1956; Alistair Rowan, 'The Building of Hopetoun', *Arch. Hist.* 27, 1984].

AUCHENDINNY, MIDLOTHIAN, for John Inglis, 1702–7 [attributed to Bruce by Henry Mackenzie (1745–1831), who lived at Auchendinny: see *The Anecdotes and Egotisms of Henry Mackenzie*, ed. H. W. Thompson, 1927, 216].

MERTOUN (or HARDEN) HOUSE, BERWICKSHIRE, for Sir William Scott, begun 1703; wings added by W. Burn 1843, removed by I. G. Lindsay 1953–5 [*Vitruvius Scoticus*, pl. 142] (*C. Life*, 2–9 June 1966).

HOUSE OF NAIRNE, PERTHSHIRE, for 2nd Lord Nairn, *c.*1709–12; dem. 1760. Several people were consulted, including the Earl of Mar and Alexander McGill, and the extent of Bruce's responsibility for the building is uncertain: see J. G. Dunbar, *Sir William Bruce* (exhibition catalogue), 20; S.R.O., GD 112/40/7 and GD 124/15/788; *Chronicles of the Atholl and Tullibardine Families*, compiled by the 7th Duke of Atholl, ii, 1908, 109].

Note: The attribution to Bruce of WEMYSS HALL (or HILL OF TARVIT), nr. CUPAR, FIFE, for John Wemyss, 1696, though not implausible, is not at present supported by any documentary evidence, and is not sufficiently compelling on stylistic grounds to justify inclusion in the list of Bruce's authenticated works.

Bruce was very likely responsible for the remodelling of his birthplace, BLAIRHALL, nr. CULROSS (formerly PERTHSHIRE, now FIFE), for his elder brother Thomas Bruce, in about 1690 [Marcus Dean, 'Blairhall and Sir William Bruce', *Jnl. and Annual Report of the Architectural Heritage Soc. of Scotland*, 1987, no. 14].

In 1697 Bruce made a design for MELVILLE HOUSE, FIFE, which may or may not have been the one executed by James Smith (*q.v.*) [see his letters in S.R.O., GD 26/13/272, 440].

For an anecdote suggesting that BROOMHALL, FIFE, as originally built in 1702, was designed by Bruce, see John Ramsay of Ochtertyre, *Scotland and Scotsmen*, ed. A. Allardyce ii, 1888, 95 n.

EDINBURGH AND GLASGOW

EDINBURGH, TWEEDDALE COURT, HIGH STREET, alterations and improvements during Bruce's possession of the property, *c.*1664–70. In 1670 he sold it to the Earl of Tweeddale [N.L.S., MSS. Acc. 3495 and Acc. 4862, 99/1 and 99/2].

GLASGOW, GIBSON'S LAND, SALTMARKET STREET, for Walter Gibson, *c.*1690; collapsed 1823 [John MacUre, *View of the City of Glasgow*, 1736, 149]. Though early enough to deserve respect, this attribution cannot be regarded as authoritative.

BRYAN was a family of masons and carvers whose business was based on the quarries at

Painswick in the Cotswolds. In 1766 George Shirley of Ettington in Warwickshire noted that 'Thomas [*sic*] Bryan lives in Painswick & owns the Quarry' [account-book in Warwicks. C.R.O.]. The principal members of the family were John (1716–87) and Joseph (1718–79), sons of Joseph Bryan of Painswick (1682–1730). John is described as 'late of this town, carver', on his pyramidal monument in Painswick Churchyard. Joseph established himself in Gloucester, where he died in 1779. His son John married his uncle John's daughter and succeeded to the family business.

The firm was responsible for many tablets and churchyard memorials of excellent quality (for further details see R. Gunnis, *Dictionary of British Sculptors 1660–1851*, revised ed. 1968). They were also masonry contractors. In July 1750 John Bryan of Painswick and Joseph Bryan of Gloucester, masons, together with William Clark of Leonard Stanley, carpenter, undertook to rebuild the west tower of GREAT WITCOMBE CHURCH, GLOS., for £80 [contract among Hicks Beach family papers]. The tower is of traditional Gothic design, with battlements and pinnacles. In 1747–8 John Bryan received 10 guineas for a pair of gate-piers for the entrance to Painswick Churchyard [Painswick Parish Records]. In 1776 Joseph and John Bryan made a proposal for rebuilding the spire of ST. NICHOLAS' CHURCH, GLOUCESTER, which was out of alignment, but nothing was done until 1783, when John Bryan contracted to take down the top of the steeple as far as the coronet and to erect a copper ball and pinnacles thereon, thus giving it its present termination [extracts from Vestry Minutes in Gloucester Public Library, MS. NF. 5.3].

BRYCE, JOHN (1805–1851), was a younger brother of David Bryce (1803–1876), the pupil and assistant of William Burn. They were the sons of William Bryce, a builder of Edinburgh. William Bryce, junior, who was practising as an architect in Edinburgh in the early 1820s, appears to have been an elder son. He died on 5 September 1823 [*Scots Mag.* 1823, 512]. John Bryce practised in Glasgow, where he designed the DUKE STREET REFORMATORY or HOUSE OF REFUGE, *c.*1825; dem.; the column, etc., in the JEWS' BURIAL GROUND at THE NECROPOLIS, 1833; a monument (1834) in THE NECROPOLIS to William McGavin (d. 1832); QUEEN'S CRESCENT, ST. GEORGE'S, 1840; 55–71 ASHLEY STREET, ST. GEORGE'S, 1849; 4–26 BOTHWELL STREET, BLYTHSWOOD (with Alexander Kirkland), 1849; and QUEEN'S TERRACE, 61–127 WEST PRINCES STREET, ST. GEORGE'S, 1850. Unlike his younger brother he remained generally faithful to the Scottish classical tradition. [J. Pagan, *Sketch of the History of Glasgow*, 1847, 180, 183; A. Gomme & D. Walker, *Architecture of Glasgow*, 1987, 286].

BUCKLE, GEORGE, is listed as an architect practising in London in Pigot's *Directory* of 1827–8 and in *The Literary Blue Book* of 1830.

BUCKLER, JOHN (1770–1851), was born at Calbourne in the Isle of Wight. According to the obituary in the *Oxford Herald*, he 'commenced life as clerk to Mr. R. B. Fisher, steward of Magdalen College, Oxford, and for many years held the appointment of bailiff or collector of rents to that society'. In 1849, when he retired, it was stated that he had been in the service of the College for sixty years as the bailiff of its London property. As a boy, he was fond of drawing, and he 'employed all his leisure time when engaged at the College in that pursuit'. At the end of his life he calculated that he had made over 13,000 sketches, mainly of topographical subjects, and his careful drawings of ancient buildings form an invaluable record of much that has since been altered or destroyed. Forty-two volumes of original sketches by himself and his sons are preserved in the British Library (Add. MSS. 36356–97). They include a systematic record of most of the parish churches and other ancient buildings in Buckinghamshire, Hertfordshire, Oxfordshire, Somerset, Staffordshire, Wiltshire and Yorkshire. From these sketches Buckler was commissioned to produce sets of finished drawings for private patrons. Among these were T. L. Parker, of Browsholme Hall, Yorkshire, for whom he drew 'Ancient Castles and Domestic Architecture' (vol. 2 of which is now in the Yale Center for British Art); Lord Grenville, for whom he prepared an extra-illustrated copy of Lysons' *Buckinghamshire* in 8 vols. (now in the possession of the Morgan-Grenville family); Sir Richard Colt Hoare, for whom he worked in Wiltshire and Wales; J. H. Smyth-Pigott and the Bishop of Bath and Wells, for whom he made drawings of Somerset; Dr. T. D. Whitaker and Francis Maude, who employed him in Yorkshire; John Morier and William Knight, for whom he made a large number of drawings in Hertfordshire; and William Salt and Lord Bagot, for whom he did the same in Staffordshire. A number of his drawings of the latter county are in the William Salt Library at Stafford, and 750 Hertfordshire drawings are in the County Record Office at Hertford (for their acquisition see R. L. Hine, *Confessions of an Uncommon Attorney*, 1946, 124–7). Those of

Somerset, made for Smyth-Pigott, are now in the Museum at Taunton, and the Wiltshire drawings made for Colt Hoare (sold from Stourhead in 1883) are in the Devizes Museum (see *Wilts. Arch. Mag.* xl, 148–90). There are several volumes of Berkshire and Oxfordshire drawings by the Bucklers in the Bodleian Library (MSS. Top. Berks. c.49, 50, 51; Top. Oxon. a. 65–9 and don. a. 2, 3 and 7). One volume of Welsh drawings made for Colt Hoare is in the National Library of Wales.

Buckler occasionally practised as an architect. As early as 1792 he drew plans and elevations for the development of the Magdalen College estate off Tooley Street, Southwark (on the site of London Bridge Station), which were carried out as a speculation by one Robert Tyler and the surveyor and builder C. T. Cracklow (*q.v.*) [Magdalen College archives, Steer Maps 89 and CP 8/61]. In 1822 he designed a Gothic tablet to Benjamin Tate in MAGDALEN COLLEGE ANTE-CHAPEL [*Gent's Mag.* 1823 (i), 133 and engraving]; in 1825 a similar tablet to George Tate in MITCHAM CHURCH, SURREY [Wimbledon Public Library, extra-illustrated copy of Brayley's *Surrey* iii (3), 314]; and in 1828 TATE'S ALMSHOUSES, MITCHAM, SURREY [B.L., Add. MS. 36388, ff. 259–61]. In 1828 he repaired and repainted Bishop Waynflete's monument in WINCHESTER CATHEDRAL for Magdalen College. His most substantial architectural works appear to have been HALKIN CASTLE, FLINTSHIRE, for the 2nd Earl Grosvenor, 1824–7, Tudor Gothic; enlarged by J. Douglas 1886 [exhib. at R.A. 1827–8; cf. *Views of Eaton Hall* for views of the house by Buckler]; the tower of THEALE CHURCH, BERKS., built in thirteenth-century style in 1827–8 to correspond with the nave designed by Edward Garbett a few years before [drawings in B.L., Add. MS. 36357]; GLASTONBURY PRIORY or ABBEY HOUSE, SOMERSET, for J. F. Reeves, 1829–30, Tudor Gothic [exhib. at R.A. 1830; drawings in B.L., Add. MS. 36381]; and POOL PARK, DENBIGHSHIRE, an early essay in the half-timbered style for the 2nd Lord Bagot, *c.*1828 [exhib. at R.A. 1830]. It is also likely that he had some hand in the Gothic remodelling of BLITHFIELD HOUSE, STAFFS., for Lord Bagot in 1822–3 [Arthur Oswald in *C. Life* 28 Oct., 4–11 Nov. 1954 and cf. drawings by Buckler in B.L., Add. MS. 36385, ff. 126–151]. All these were buildings in which Buckler's antiquarian knowledge was put to good use by like-minded patrons, but for general architectural practice he had little inclination. As he wrote in 1849, 'to build, repair, or survey warehouses and sash-windowed dwellings, however profitable, was so much less to my taste than perspective drawing with such subjects before me as Cathedrals, Abbeys, and ancient parish churches, that I never made any effort to increase the number of my employers as an architect, and as the engagements of my old patrons ceased, my occupations in that capacity ceased also . . .' He finally gave up practice in about 1830, but his eldest son JOHN CHESSELL BUCKLER (1793–1894) and his youngest son GEORGE BUCKLER (1811–86) both became architects. The former shared his enthusiasm for sketching, and his pencil drawings of ancient buildings are almost indistinguishable in technique from those of his father. In 1822 he published *Views of the Cathedral Churches of England and Wales*, a collection based on a series of large prints previously issued individually by his father between 1799 and 1814, and in 1826 he and his father published *Views of Eaton Hall in Cheshire*.

In the early 1820s the two Bucklers were involved in the controversy over the reconstruction of the Cloister Quadrangle at Magdalen College, Oxford. John Buckler was among the many architects who were consulted, but his advice was not followed and in 1823 his son published an anonymous pamphlet (*Observations on the Original Architecture of St. Mary Magdalen College, Oxford, and on the Innovations anciently or recently attempted*) deploring the unnecessarily destructive manner in which the Quadrangle was rebuilt by J. T. Parkinson [T. S. R. Boase, 'An Oxford College and the Gothic Revival', *Jnl. Warburg and Courtauld Institutes* xviii, 1955]. J. C. Buckler's later publications included *Sixty Views of Endowed Grammar Schools*, 1827, *An Historical and Descriptive Account of the Royal Palace at Eltham*, 1828, a *History of the Architecture of the Abbey Church at St. Albans*, 1847, and *A Description and Defence of the Restorations of Lincoln Cathedral*, 1866. In 1836 he obtained the second prize in the competition for rebuilding the Houses of Parliament, and he designed a number of buildings in the Gothic or Elizabethan styles, including COSTESSEY HALL, NORFOLK, 1826, dem. 1920, BUTLEIGH COURT, SOMERSET, 1845, DUNSTON HALL, NORFOLK, 1859, THE CHORISTERS' HALL (now the Library) at MAGDALEN COLLEGE, OXFORD, 1849–51, and the Turl Street front of JESUS COLLEGE, 1854–6. His son CHARLES ALBAN BUCKLER (1824–1905) also practised as an architect, chiefly for Catholic clients.

John Buckler exhibited regularly at the Royal Academy from 1796 onwards. He was elected F.S.A. in 1810. He died on 6 December 1851, aged 81. There is an engraved portrait of him by Sir W. Newton.

[Family papers and drawings in Bodleian Library, MSS. dep. a. 38–41, c.410; letters to Dr. Routh in Magdalen College Library; C. A. Buckler, *Bucleriana: Notices of the Family of Buckler*, privately printed 1886 (the author's own copy, with additions, is B.L., Add. MS. 37123); *D.N.B.*; W. D. Macray, *Registers of Magdalen College*, N.S. vi, 1909, 33, 43; obituaries in *Gent's Mag.* 1852 (i), 103–4, and *Builder* x, 1852, 7; C. Eastlake, *A History of the Gothic Revival*, 1872, 110–11; R. D. Middleton, *Dr. Routh*, 1938, 180–6; obituary of J. C. Buckler in *Jackson's Oxford Jnl.*, 13 Jan. 1894.]

BULL, SIMEON THOMAS (1789–1847), was a pupil of George Gwilt. He exhibited at the Royal Academy from Gwilt's office in 1809–10 and subsequently practised from Holles Street, Cavendish Square. He was President of the Surveyors' Club in 1824. The evidence of directories and his will (P.R.O. PROB 11/2057, f. 453) combine to show that he died in 1847.

BULLAR, GEORGE, was apprenticed to Messrs. Middleton & Bailey of Lambeth in 1799 [P.R.O., Apprenticeship Registers, IR 1/72]. He exhibited at the Royal Academy from 1803 to 1808, including a 'Design for the Britannia General Country Fire Insurance Office about to be erected in one of the eastern counties' (1804), a 'Perspective of one side of a square, being part of a series of designs (about to be put in execution) for the improvement of a large estate in the vicinity of the metropolis' (1805), the 'Garden front of a villa to be erected on the banks of the river Orwell at Ipswich' (1807), and the 'South elevation of a nobleman's mansion erecting in the vicinity of Southampton' (1808).

BULLAR, GEORGE THOMAS, was an architect who specialized in the design of prisons. For some years he was secretary to the Society for the Improvement of Prison Discipline and was responsible for the model radial prison plans which it published in 1826. The prison for juvenile offenders built at Parkhurst in the Isle of Wight in 1839 appears to be Bullar's only recorded work [R. Evans, *The Fabrication of Virtue: English Prison Architecture 1750–1840*, Cambridge 1983, 277, 410, etc.]. A plan and description by Bullar of 'a Gaol or House of Correction designed to contain 250 prisoners', dated 1827, are reported to be in the Central State Archives (Ts GADA) in Moscow (Fond 1261, op. 1, dolo 2359).

BUNCE, SAMUEL (*c.*1765–1802), was a pupil of James Wyatt, from whose office he exhibited at the Royal Academy in 1786–88. Soon afterwards he went to Rome, where he became intimate with Flaxman. He returned to England in the spring of 1790 and established himself in Hatton Garden. One of the fruits of his Italian expedition was a drawing of the Temple of Apollo at Cori which he exhibited at the Academy in 1797. In March 1796 he was appointed to the newly established post of Architect to the Admiralty, which he held until his death in October 1802 [J. C. Sainty, *Admiralty Officials 1660–1870*, 1975, 91, 113].

In 1797–8 Bunce designed the gallery which the painter George Romney added to his newly acquired house on Hollybush Hill, Hampstead, and a small 'marine villa' at Felpham, Sussex, for Romney's friend William Hayley. Both these buildings survive, the former as ROMNEY HOUSE, HAMPSTEAD, the latter as THE TURRET, FELPHAM, described by Pevsner as 'pasteboard stucco Tudor'. In 1797 Bunce collaborated with Jeremy Bentham in producing designs for a 'Panopticon House of Industry', a revolutionary workhouse built almost entirely of iron and glass with continuous ribbons of windows like a twentieth-century factory.

[*The Farington Diary*, ed. J. Greig, iii, 53; A. B. Chamberlain, *George Romney*, 1910, 207–9, 214–16; J. Romney, *Life of George Romney*, 1830, 251; R. Evans, *The Fabrication of Virtue: English Prison Architecture 1750–1840*, Cambridge 1983, 222–3.]

BUNN, JOHN, was a carpenter and builder of Norwich. In 1802 he made a design for alterations and additions to HARESFOOT, BERKHAMSTEAD, HERTS. (dem.) [R.I.B.A.D.], and in 1833 he designed KESSINGLAND VICARAGE, SUFFOLK [Norfolk C.R.O., DN/DPL/1/3/36]. His son, John Bunn, junior, announced in 1840 that he was starting practice in Norwich after ten years 'under Architects of eminence' [*Norfolk Chronicle*, 11 April 1840, *ex inf.* Mr. David Cubitt]. The younger Bunn succeeded J. T. Patience as City Surveyor of Norwich in 1843 and in 1849 designed THE CORN EXCHANGE at HARLESTON, NORFOLK [*Norwich Mercury*, 1 Sept. 1849].

BURCHELL, STEPHEN (1806–?1843), son of Joseph Burchell of Leatherhead, was a pupil of Sir John Soane from 1823 to 1828 [A. T. Bolton, *The Works of Sir J. Soane*, Appendix C, p. xlvi]. He entered the Royal Academy Schools in 1825, and won the Silver Medal in 1828 with drawings of Smirke's General Post Office that are now in the R.I.B.A. Drawings Collection. In 1835 he competed for the Houses of Parliament in association with J. Thrupp. They submitted a design in the late Gothic style [*Catalogue of Designs for the New Houses of Parliament*, 6th ed. 1836, 29–30]. Burchell made the drawings for the lithographs of Prior Birde's Oratory at Bath published by E. Davis in 1834. The original drawings are in the R.I.B.A. Collection. A person of this name died in Abergavenny in 1843.

BURGESS, WILLIAM, of Exeter, designed ST. SIDWELL'S CHURCH, EXETER, 1812–13, Gothic, dem. 1942 [inscription recorded by B. F. Cresswell, *Exeter Churches*, Exeter 1908, 158]; THE ROYAL PUBLIC ROOMS, EXETER, 1820, dem. [*A.P.S.D.*, *s.v.* 'Exeter']; THE NEW MARKET HALL, TAUNTON, SOMERSET, 1821, dem. [J. Savage, *History of Taunton*, 1822, 582]; CULLOMPTON VICARAGE, DEVON, 1820 [Devon C.R.O., Diocesan Records]; and MEETH RECTORY, DEVON, 1825 [*ibid.*]. In 1825 he partly rebuilt the nave of ILMINSTER CHURCH, SOMERSET [I.C.B.S.]. He was presumably the 'Mr. Burges' who designed HAREFIELD HOUSE, LYMPSTONE, DEVON, for — Gattey in a somewhat crude Soanean style [R. Ackermann, *Views of Seats* i, 1830, 95].

BURLINGTON, EARL OF, *see* BOYLE, RICHARD.

BURN, GEORGE, was the brother of James Burn of Haddington (*q.v.*). In the Scottish Record Office there is a design by him for BILSDEAN BRIDGE, OLDHAMSTOCKS, EAST LOTHIAN, dated 1797 [RHP 5504]. Subsequently he moved to N. E. Scotland, where he was employed by the Duke of Gordon. S.R.O., RHP 2008/8 is a design by him for a one-arched bridge dated 'Huntly Lodge 16 July 1800', and drawings by him exist for an unexecuted pedimented building, apparently a chapel, on the Gordon estates, dated 1802 [S.R.O., GD 44/48/70]. In 1803 he was described as 'of Fochabers' when his estate was sequestrated [*Aberdeen Jnl.*, 15 Nov. 1803]. This was only a temporary setback, for between 1800 and 1814 Burn built at least six bridges: at THURSO, CAITHNESS, 1800 [*Edinburgh Evening Courant*, 4 Sept. 1800]; BRIDGE OF AVON, BALLINDALOCH, BANFFSHIRE, for General James Grant, 1800 [inscription]; SPEY BRIDGE, FOCHABERS, MORAYSHIRE, *c.*1801–5, partially destroyed in the great flood of 1829 [drawings in S.R.O., RHP 2008/1]; NAIRN, 1804 [contract in N.L.S., Gordonstoun papers, Box 92]; WICK, CAITHNESS, 1806–7 (dem. 1877) [Jean Dunlop, *The British Fisheries Society 1786–1893*, 1978, 159]; and LOVAT BRIDGE over the R. Beauly in Inverness-shire, to the designs of Thomas Telford 1811–14 [A. R. B. Haldane, *New Ways through the Glens*, 1973, 129]. Burn also designed and built DINGWALL CHURCH, ROSS-SHIRE, 1800–1 [S.R.O., Presbytery Records, 19 Dec. 1799, *ex inf.* Mrs. E. Beaton]. He was concerned in harbour works at PULTENEYTOWN (WICK), CAITHNESS, in 1808 and at KIRKWALL, where he built the E. Pier in 1809–11. A design by him for a harbour office at Pulteneytown dated 1817 is in the S.R.O. (RHP 11803), and a design for an unidentified house is in N.M.R.S.

BURN, JAMES (–1816) was an architect and builder of Haddington in East Lothian. He was a wright by trade, and became a burgess of Haddington in July 1777. In 1784 he bought Kinloch House in Market Street, where he established his yard [*ex. inf.* Mr. David Walker]. According to John Martine's *Reminiscences of the Royal Burgh of Haddington* (1883) he 'built a great number of excellent family houses in Haddington and throughout the county, among which may be mentioned Mr. Roughead's and the late Mr. Banks's houses in High Street; Mr. Todrick's in Hardgate; as also the Hopes House, and Newbyth House'. At NEWBYTH, EAST LOTHIAN (1817–18), Burn was rebuilding the house to the designs of Archibald Elliot (*q.v.*). It is likely, however, that he himself designed as well as built Captain Hay's elegant villa at HOPES, nr. GIFFORD, EAST LOTHIAN, in about 1825, as he evidently had CAPONFLAT, nr. HADDINGTON, for Robert Veitch, 1797–8, dem. *c.*1946 [S.R.O., SC 40/67/3, *ex inf.* Miss C. Cruft]. In Haddington, where he was known as 'Old Timmer', Burn designed and built THE FLESHMARKET in 1804 [Martine, 63], and in 1808 made designs for altering and refitting the interior of the CHURCH that were carried out in 1810–11 in a modified form, with James and Archibald Elliot as consultant architects [S.R.O., HR 101/1–2].

During the first decade of the nineteenth century Burn obtained several commissions in ABERDEEN, including THE ABERDEEN BANK on the south side of Castle Street, 1801 (later extended down Marischal Street by William Smith); THE BRIDEWELL, UNION STREET, 1809, dem. 1868; and the balustraded parapet of the UNION BRIDGE, 1805, replaced by another design when the bridge was widened in 1905–8 [W. Thom, *History of Aberdeen* ii, 1804, 59; *Aberdeen Fifty Years Ago*, Aberdeen 1868, 28–9, 57–8; G. M. Fraser, 'Archibald Simpson and his Times', chap. vi, *Aberdeen Weekly Jnl.* 10 May 1918]. The Bank (one of the first buildings of dressed granite in the city) has a well-composed façade of Doric pilasters; the Bridewell was designed in a bleak but not inappropriate version of Adam's castle style.

Burn also designed the IMAGE BRIDGE in the grounds of BRECHIN CASTLE, ANGUS, for William Maule, cr. Lord Panmure, 1797 (the piers remain but Burn's timber spans were later replaced by iron) [David Walker in *C. Life*, 19 Aug. 1971], a one-arch bridge over the Birns Water at MILTON FORD, SALTOUN, EAST LOTHIAN, 1805 [drawing in N.L.S., MS. 17874, no. 3], and the BRIDGE OF DYCE, ABERDEENSHIRE, consisting of a wooden arch of 109 ft. span over the R. Don, 1803; rebuilt 1850, dem *c*.1970 [*N.S.A.* xii, 128] (*Edinburgh Encyclopeadia* iv, 1830, pl. lxxxviii).

Burn died on 27 Jan. 1816 [S.R.O., SC 70/1/15, p. 616]. According to Martine his business 'was carried on by his relation Mr. Hay Walker'.

BURN, ROBERT (1752–1815), was a mason by trade. According to a family tree he was born in 1752 and was 'of Jessfield' (Portobello). The earliest reference to him that has so far been noted shows that in 1775 he was acting as overseer of the masonry of St. Cuthbert's Church, Edinburgh, then being completed by the contractor James Weir (*q.v.*) [S.R.O., GD 69/210]. On 4 April 1782 he was admitted a burgess of Edinburgh [*Roll of Edinburgh Burgesses*, Scottish Record Soc. 1933, 28]. His best-known work as an architect is the Nelson Monument on Calton Hill, a castellated tower which has more the character of a private folly than a public monument.

Burn, who was the father of the better-known William Burn (*q.v.*), died on 5 June 1815 and was buried in the Calton Cemetery in a Gothic burial place erected in 1816 'by his widow and twelve surviving children'. At the N.M.R.S. there is a photograph of a portrait of Robert Burn and his son William as a young man. The original was in 1956 in private possession at St. Andrews. [*Scots. Mag.* 1815, 559; *Gent's Mag.* 1815 (i), 647; information from the late Colin McWilliam.]

EDINBURGH, THE PUBLIC DISPENSARY, RICHMOND STREET, 1776; dem. [engraving in Bodleian Library, Gough Maps 39, f. 11, signed 'R. Burn invt. et delint'].

CAIRNESS HOUSE, ABERDEENSHIRE, for Charles Gordon of Cairness, 1782–3; dem. 1791 to make way for new house by James Playfair [David Walker & Colin McWilliam in *C. Life*, 28 Feb. 1971].

? THE HERMITAGE OF BRAID, MORNINGSIDE, EDINBURGH, for Charles Gordon of Cluny, *c*.1785, castellated [Burn is described as 'architect to the late Mr. Gordon' in an inventory of papers belonging to Col. John Gordon of Cluny among the Claeson Gordon family papers, *ex inf.* Prof. A. Rowan].

EDINBURGH, Nos. 141–171 LEITH STREET, 1790–1800 [S.R.O., Edinburgh Sasines, vol. 516 under 'Greenside Place'].

TEVIOT BANK (then THE KNOWES), ROXBURGHSHIRE, for David Simpson, *c*.1791; rebuilt 1833 [drawing at Teviot Bank, *ex inf.* N.M.R.S.].

?NETHERURD, PEEBLESHIRE, for William Lawson, 1791–4. In the building contract it is stipulated that the completed work shall be inspected by Burn and James McLeran, both described as 'architects', and in the event of any dispute Burn is to act as arbitrator [S.R.O., GD 120/415, dated 25 March 1791].

ORBIESTON HOUSE, BELLSHILL, LANARKS., *c*.1795; dem. [advt. in *Edinburgh Evening Courant*, 21 Nov. 1795] (*Old Country Houses of the Old Glasgow Gentry*, 1870, pl. 79).

ST. GILES' CATHEDRAL, EDINBURGH, alterations (masons' work), 1796–7 [J. Cameron Lees, *St. Giles', Edinburgh*, 1889, 402].

CAIRNFIELD HOUSE, BANFFSHIRE, for Adam Gordon, 1799–1804 [NRA(S), Gordon of Cairnfield papers, bundle 131, Burn's account].

ABERDOUR MANSE, FIFE, 1803 [S.R.O., GD 150/1818b/12–14].

EDINBURGH, PICARDY PLACE, Nos. 1–12 UNION STREET, FORTH STREET (excluding Nos. 4–10) and BROUGHTON STREET, designed 1800, built *c*.1804–10 [*Book of the Old Edinburgh Club* xxv, 30–3].

EDINBURGH, GILLESPIE'S HOSPITAL (THE ROYAL BLIND ASYLUM), GILLESPIE CRESCENT, 1800–1, castellated; enlarged by MacGibbon & Ross 1883–4 and 1892; dem. 1975 [signed drawings in N.M.R.S.].

EDINBURGH, THE ROYAL BANK OF SCOTLAND, HIGH STREET, design for new entrance, 1803 [S.R.O., RHP 5556].

SALTOUN HALL, EAST LOTHIAN, proposed alterations for General John Fletcher Campbell, 1803 [drawings in N.L.S., MS. 17873].

SALTOUN MANSE, EAST LOTHIAN, court of offices, 1804 [drawings in N.L.S., MS. 17874, no. 4].

LEITH, THE GRAMMAR SCHOOL or ACADEMY, 1804–6; dem. 1896 [Alexander Mackay, *A Sketch of the History of Leith Academy*, Leith 1934, 21–2] (J. Grant, *Old and New Edinburgh* iii, 165).

INVERMAY, nr. FORTEVIOT, PERTHSHIRE, for J. H. Belshes, 1806 [correspondence in Fettercairn papers, National Library of Scotland, *ex inf.* Prof. A. A. Tait].

DUMFRIES, layout of CASTLE STREET and GEORGE STREET, 1806 [titles at A. Curtis Wolfe, Gatehouse of Fleet, 1977, *ex inf.* N.M.R.S.].

EDINBURGH, THE NELSON MONUMENT, CALTON HILL, 1807–14 [Storer's *Views of Edinburgh*, 1820–2; *Edinburgh Evening Courant*, 28 July 1808, progress report of the Committee]. The custodian's house was built 1814–16 under the direction of Thomas Bonnar.

EDINBURGH, LANCASTERIAN SCHOOL, NICOLSON STREET, 1812 [advt. for tenders in *Edinburgh Evening Courant*, 13 July 1812].

BURN, WILLIAM (1789–1870), was the son of Robert Burn (*q.v.*), a builder and architect of Edinburgh, where he was born on 20 December 1789. After an education at the High School he was sent in 1808 to London to become a pupil in Robert Smirke's office. In 1811 or 1812 he returned to Edinburgh and began practice from the family building yard in Leith Walk. By 1813 he was sufficiently well known to be one of the architects invited to report on the plans submitted for the layout of the Calton Hill area, and in 1814 he established an office of his own in George Street (at first at No. 78, later at No. 131). In 1816 his narrow defeat in the competition for the completion of the Edinburgh University buildings inaugurated a 'long and in time bitter rivalry' between himself and the successful competitor, W. H. Playfair.

Burn's earliest works were public buildings, but in 1817–18 he obtained the first commissions for the country houses which were to be his speciality for the rest of his long working life. He soon gained a reputation for skill in domestic planning which secured him the patronage first of the Scottish, and ultimately of the English, aristocracy. By 1830 he had a bigger practice than any other Scottish architect, and could count among his clients the Dukes of Hamilton and Buccleuch, the Earls of Haddington and Kinnoull, and many other influential persons. By 1840 he had already designed or altered over ninety country houses, besides thirty churches and twenty-five public buildings of various sorts. Overwork probably contributed to the serious breakdown in health which in 1841 induced him to take his pupil and assistant David Bryce into partnership. In 1844 he moved to London (6 Stratton Street) in order to take advantage of the numerous commissions he was now receiving from English clients, leaving Bryce in charge of the Edinburgh office. The partnership soon began to show signs of strain and was finally dissolved in 1850. Towards the end of his life Burn formed a fresh partnership with his nephew J. MacVicar Anderson (1834–1915), who continued his practice after his death. Burn died on 15 February 1870, aged 80, and was buried in Kensal Green Cemetery. His estate was valued for probate at 'under £40,000'. He married Eliza MacVicar, by whom he had several children.

Burn was a man of vigorous and independent character, frank and plain spoken, but very patient in meeting the wishes of his wealthy and sometimes idiosyncratic clients. Secure in the patronage of the great, he could afford to shun the ordinary media of nineteenth-century architectural publicity, the exhibition drawing and the professional journal. He never exhibited at the Royal Academy, and after his initial failure in 1816 he waited forty years before entering for another public competition.[1] He did, however, join the Institute of British Architects on its foundation in 1835, and in 1840 he agreed to become Vice-President of a proposed Institute of Architects in Scotland, but resigned almost immediately because of a quarrel with the committee over the eligibility for membership of his assistant Bryce. In the 1850s he acted as Consulting Architect to the Government in Scotland, and in 1865 he was one of the three assessors of the controversial competition for the Foreign Office in Whitehall.

Burn's early public buildings are in the style of his master Smirke. John Watson's School and the Merchant Maiden Hospital are representative of this early phase. They are competent but conventional essays in Greek Doric. But by 1834, when he designed the New Club in Edinburgh, he was pioneering the Italian palazzo style for city buildings that was later to be exploited by his partner Bryce and others. As a church architect his classical parish church at North Leith and his Gothic Episcopal Church in Edinburgh are well-designed buildings which compare favourably with the best works of contemporary English architects, but most of his country churches are of slight architectural merit. At first his country houses were derivative in character. Saltoun, with its Gothic lantern lighting a central hall, resembled Archibald Elliot's Taymouth Castle; Dundas Castle was 'a weakly detailed essay in Smirke's early Lowther idiom'; while Blairquhan (*c.* 1820–4), Carstairs (1822–4) and Garscube (1826–7) owed their Tudor Gothic dress to Wilkins's Dalmeny. The Grecian Camperdown House (1824–6) was an Ionic version of Wilkins's Grange Park. But at Carstairs some of the gables were treated in a manner more

[1] For the Caledonian Railway Station at Glasgow, 1858. None of the plans submitted was carried out.

Jacobean than Tudor, and by about 1825 Burn had made the Jacobethan manor-house his speciality. Riccarton (1823–7) and Strathendry (1824) were the first complete houses in this style which (like the Tudor Gothic) gave ample freedom for Burn to deploy the elaborate internal arrangements for which he was becoming celebrated. By 1830 Burn was experimenting with the Scottish vernacular style which he introduced at Faskally (1829) and Milton Lockhart (1829–36), and in that year corbelled angle turrets made their appearance at Tyninghame. Thereafter the progression to the fully developed 'Scottish Baronial' style was inevitable, though it was Burn's pupil Bryce rather than Burn himself who was to be its most celebrated exponent. Burn himself continued to turn out innumerable houses in Elizabethan, Jacobean or Scottish vernacular dress as the occasion required. If necessary he could also provide very competent designs in a classical, or even a Georgian, manner (Prestwold Hall, 1843, Swanbourne House, 1864), and in his interiors he showed considerable virtuosity in recreating quite different 'period' styles – Italian Renaissance at Prestwold, Flemish Mannerist and Louis XV at Stoke Rochford, High Baroque at Harlaxton and Revesby (though for the two last Bryce's assistance may have been important). For his great patron the 5th Duke of Buccleuch he provided an appropriate forecourt to the seventeenth-century mansion at Drumlanrig, a Jacobean conservatory and two Gothic churches at Dalkeith, an addition to Bowhill in the late Georgian style, and a French Renaissance château in Whitehall.

Despite his immense professional success and his remarkable versatility as a designer, Burn cannot be ranked as a great architect. It is tempting to dismiss him (in the words of the younger Charles Barry) as 'more a man of business than an artist'. Although (as Barry recognized) this would not be altogether fair, Burn's output is more remarkable for its quantity than for its quality. Among the long list of his works not a single building stands out as a masterpiece. His early Grecian buildings were among the pioneer works of their kind in Scotland. But they were heavily dependent on the examples of Wilkins and Smirke and showed great competence rather than originality. Up to about 1840 his Gothic churches are generally 'Perpendicular' in style and recognizably Scottish in character, but after that date they are routine products of the Gothic Revival. As for his Tudor and Jacobethan mansions, their dry, repetitive detailing rarely succeeds in recapturing the charm of their prototypes: what commended them to Burn's clients was the convenience of their planning – above all, the care taken to safeguard the owner's privacy from both servants and guests – rather than what Robert Kerr called 'the obsolete forms of a barbarous style'. Nevertheless Burn is a remarkable figure in British architectural history, epitomizing in a single career the whole course of nineteenth-century architecture from Greek Revival to Scottish Baronial.

There is a marble bust of Burn by Thomas Campbell dated 1834 at the Royal Incorporation of Architects of Scotland. The R.I.B.A. Drawings Collection has a plaster cast presented by the sculptor in 1836. For Burn's professional charges see a letter to Sir John Forbes of Craigievar in S.R.O., GD 250/41. David Bryce, Norman Shaw and W. E. Nesfield were Burn's most celebrated pupils. Shaw and Nesfield both left in 1853 for Salvin's office. Other pupils and assistants were W. B. Colling, James (son of T. L.) Donaldson, David MacGibbon, M. L. Moffatt, J. W. Penfold and J. C. Walker.

A large collection of Burn's drawings was acquired by the R.I.B.A. Drawings Collection in 1950. Many Scottish drawings were subsequently transferred to the Scottish National Monuments Record, and some working drawings were distributed to English County Record Offices.

[Obituaries in *Builder*, 1870, 189, 231, and *Building News*, 1870, 245; memoir by T. L. Donaldson in *R.I.B.A. Trans.* 1869–70, 121–9; John MacLachlan, 'Edinburgh Architects', in *Builder*, 1882, 667–8; *D.N.B.*; R. Kerr, *The English Gentleman's House*, 1864, 476–7; Mark Girouard, *The Victorian Country House*, 1971, 22–4, 32; David Walker, 'William Burn: the country house in transition', in *Seven Victorian Architects*, ed. Jane Fawcett, 1976, and 'William Burn' in 'Scottish Pioneers of the Greek Revival', *Scottish Georgian Soc's Journal* 11, 1984.]

In the following list 'T.L.D.' stands for the list of Burn's principal works compiled by T. L. Donaldson and printed in *R.I.B.A. Trans.* 1870, 125–8. Original drawings in the R.I.B.A. Collection and the Scottish National Monuments Record are indicated by 'R.I.B.A.D.' and 'N.M.R.S.' A dagger (†) indicates works designed in partnership with David Bryce.

PUBLIC BUILDINGS

GREENOCK, RENFREWSHIRE, THE ASSEMBLY ROOMS (EXCHANGE BUILDINGS), 1812–14; dem. [R.I.B.A.D.].

EDINBURGH, THE MERCHANT MAIDEN HOSPITAL,

LAURISTON LANE, 1816–19; dem. [T. H. Shepherd, *Modern Athens*, 1829, 61; N.M.R.S.].

GREENOCK, RENFREWSHIRE, THE CUSTOM HOUSE, 1817–18 [Chapman, *Picture of Glasgow*, 1822, 366–7; R.I.B.A.D.; T.L.D.].

EDINBURGH, GEORGE WATSON'S HOSPITAL, additions, 1820; dem. 1870 [*Edinburgh Evening Courant*, 12 Oct. 1820].

PORT GLASGOW, RENFREWSHIRE, CUSTOM HOUSE, 1821; dem. [N.M.R.S.].

TRANENT, EAST LOTHIAN, GEORGE STIEL'S INSTITUTION (now St. Joseph's School), 1821–2 [N.M.R.S.; *N.S.A.* ii, 302].

ELGIN, THE TRINITY LODGE OF MASONS, 1821–2; [*Aberdeen Jnl.*, 14 Feb. 1821, *ex inf.* Mr. David Walker].

PERTH, MURRAY'S ROYAL ASYLUM FOR THE INSANE 1822–7 [D. Peacock, *Perth, its Annals and its Archives*, Perth 1849, 498; T.L.D.].

DUNDEE, THE UNION (now ROYAL) BANK, 53 MURRAYGATE, 1823; since altered [T.L.D.; N.M.R.S.].

EDINBURGH, THE ACADEMY, HENDERSON ROW, 1823–36 [T. H. Shepherd, *Modern Athens*, 1829, 75–6; N.M.R.S.].

EDINBURGH, GASWORKS AT TANFIELD, CANONMILLS, 1824, later the Tanfield Hall; largely dem. [K. F. Schinkel's diary of his visit of Britain in 1826: *Arch. Rev.* May 1945, 134] (James Grant, *Old and New Edinburgh* iii, 89).

LEITH, THE CUSTOM HOUSE, additions and alterations, 1824–5 [N.M.R.S.].

EDINBURGH, JOHN WATSON'S HOSPITAL (now SCOTTISH GALLERY OF MODERN ART), BELFORD ROAD, 1825–8 [T.L.D.; drawings in N.M.R.S. and S.R.O., RHP 38221].

KIRKCALDY TOWN HOUSE, FIFE, 1826–32, Romanesque; dem. [N.M.R.S.].

EDINBURGH, SIR WILLIAM FORBES' (later UNION) BANK, 2 PARLIAMENT SQUARE, 1827–30; converted into Courts 1885 [T.L.D.].

GLASGOW, THE BANK OF SCOTLAND, INGRAM STREET, 1828; since mutilated [T.L.D.; N.M.R.S.].

CURRIE, MIDLOTHIAN, PAROCHIAL SCHOOL, 1829–30, Gothic [*The Scotsman*, 19 Sept. 1829; S.R.O., CH 2/83/6].

DUNDEE, THE LUNATIC ASYLUM, alterations and additions, 1830 and 1839; dem. [J. Maclaren, *History of Dundee*, 1874, 285].

EDINBURGH, THE THEATRE ROYAL, new façade and other alterations, 1830; dem. 1859 [T.L.D.].

SCHAW'S HOSPITAL (now Mary Murray Institute), PRESTONPANS, EAST LOTHIAN, 1830–1, Jacobethan [T.L.D.; N.M.R.S.].

ST. ANDREW'S, FIFE, MADRAS COLLEGE, 1832–4, Jacobethan [T.L.D.; N.M.R.S.].

HADDINGTON, EAST LOTHIAN, THE COUNTY COURT HOUSE, 1833, Tudor Gothic; enlarged 1911 and 1956 [James Miller, *History of Haddington*, 1900, 228; N.M.R.S.; T.L.D.].

STIRLING, THE BANK OF SCOTLAND, 22–4 KING STREET, 1833 [T.L.D.; N.M.R.S.] (*C. Life*, 28 Aug. 1969, 504, fig. 6).

KIRKCALDY, FIFE, THE BANK OF SCOTLAND, 226 HIGH STREET, 1833 [T.L.D.].

EDINBURGH, SIGNET LIBRARY, remodelled W. H. Playfair's staircase in order to open communication between Lower and Upper Libraries, 1833. The Ionic columns, the stairs and the ironwork are by Burn [*History of the Society of Writers to the Signet*, 1890, 439].

DUMFRIES, THE CRICHTON INSTITUTION (lunatic asylum), 1835–9; enlarged by W. B. Moffat and others [T.L.D.; R.I.B.A.D.].

INVERNESS, THE SHERIFF COURT ('THE CASTLE'), 1834–5, castellated [T.L.D.; G. Cameron, *History of Inverness*, Inverness 1847, 69].

EDINBURGH, THE NEW CLUB, 85 PRINCES STREET 1834; dem. 1966 [T.L.D.; R.I.B.A.D.].

CUPAR, FIFE, COUNTY BUILDINGS, enlarged by internal remodelling of an adjoining building, 1835–6 [T.L.D.; N.M.R.S.].

GREENOCK, RENFREWSHIRE, BANK OF SCOTLAND, 1837; since altered [T.L.D.; N.M.R.S.].

MONTROSE, ANGUS, BANK OF SCOTLAND, at corner of HIGH STREET and JOHN STREET, 1839 [N.M.R.S.].

ELGIN, MORAYSHIRE, COLUMN in memory of 5th Duke of Gordon (d. 1836), 1839; statue added 1854–5 [*Elgin Courant*, 15 Feb. 1839, *ex inf.* Mrs. E. Beaton].

EDINBURGH, THE LUNATIC ASYLUM (WEST HOUSE), MORNINGSIDE TERRACE, 1839–40; enlarged 1852, 1867, 1874, etc. [T.L.D.; *A.P.S.D.*, *s.v.* 'Edinburgh'].

EDINBURGH, NORTH BRITISH ASSURANCE OFFICE, 64–5 PRINCES STREET, 1841; dem. *c.*1901 [T.L.D.; N.M.R.S.].

DUNDEE, BANK OF SCOTLAND, REFORM STREET, 1842 [T.L.D.; N.M.R.S.].

†EDINBURGH, THE ASSEMBLY ROOMS, GEORGE STREET, addition of MUSIC HALL, 1843 [T.L.D.; N.M.R.S.].

†BANFF, THE FIFE ARMS HOTEL, 1843–4 [*Edinburgh Evening Courant*, 7 Dec. 1844].

†EDINBURGH, EDINBURGH LIFE ASSURANCE OFFICE (now Royal Society), 22–4 GEORGE STREET, 1843 [T.L.D.].

†GLASGOW, WESTERN BANK, MILLER STREET, addition, 1845; dem. [T.L.D.; N.M.R.S.].

†EDINBURGH, THE BRITISH LINEN BANK, ST. ANDREW'S SQUARE, 1846–51 [C. A. Malcolm, *History of the British Linen Bank*, 1950, 127, 170–1].

---

† Wholly or partly by D. Bryce.

†EDINBURGH, THE EDINBURGH & GLASGOW BANK, HANOVER STREET, extension to No. 69 (doubling the elevation) and house at No. 71, 1847 [Edinburgh Dean of Guild plans, 1847].

SOUTH STOKE, LINCS., almshouses for Christopher Turnor, 1850–1 [R.I.B.A.D.].

COCKSHUTT, SALOP., NATIONAL SCHOOL, 1855 [drawings in Salop. C.R.O. 1564/67–73].

GLASGOW, THE POST OFFICE, MANHATTAN BUILDINGS, GEORGE SQUARE, 1855–6, Italianate; dem. [*A.P.S.D.*, *s.v.* 'Glasgow'].

CHURCHES

(All Gothic unless otherwise stated)

KEIR, DUMFRIESSHIRE, 1813–14 [S.R.O., CH 2/298/10, p. 152].

NORTH LEITH, MIDLOTHIAN, 1814–16; classical [A. Campbell, *The Present State of Leith*, 1827, 294; R.I.B.A.D.; N.M.R.S.] (G. Hay, *The Architecture of Scottish Post-Reformation Churches*, 1957, fig. 49).

EDINBURGH, ST. JOHN (EPISCOPAL), PRINCES STREET, 1816–18; apse added 1879–82 [T. H. Shepherd, *Modern Athens*, 1829, 72].

DUNFERMLINE, FIFE, THE NEW ABBEY CHURCH, 1818–21 [E. Henderson, *Annals of Dunfermline*, 1879, 598; N.M.R.S.].

CUPAR, FIFE, EPISCOPAL CHAPEL, 1819–20; dem. 1866 [Vestry Minutes, *ex inf.* Mr. Tristram Clarke].

DUNDEE, alterations to TOWN'S CHURCHES, 1823; destroyed by fire 1841 [N.M.R.S.].

ST. ANDREWS, FIFE, EPISCOPAL CHURCH, NORTH STREET, 1824–5; new front by Sir G. G. Scott 1854; dem. 1870 and re-erected at Buckhaven [N.M.R.S.].

KINGARTH, BUTESHIRE, 1824–6 [N.M.R.S.].

KINNOUL, PERTHSHIRE, 1826 [*N.S.A.* x, 942; N.M.R.S.].

ABDIE, FIFE, 1827, with Italianate bellcote, adapting a design by James Milne [*N.S.A.* ix, 54; S.R.O., HR 649/1, pp. 79–84].

ST. MONANS, ABERCROMBIE, FIFE, reconstructed 1827–8 [*N.S.A.* ix, 351; N.M.R.S.; S.R.O., HR 25/1, p. 69].

ARDNAMURCHAN (KILCHOAN), ARGYLLSHIRE, 1827–31 [*N.S.A.* vii, 148].

CORSTORPHINE, MIDLOTHIAN, largely rebuilt 1828; altered 1903–5 [S.R.O., HR 588/1, p. 177; N.M.R.S.].

CRAMOND, MIDLOTHIAN, repairs and alterations, 1828 [S.R.O., HR 713/5].

STENTON, EAST LOTHIAN, 1829 [*N.S.A.* ii, 57; T.L.D.].

EDINBURGH, ST. GILES' CATHEDRAL, reconstructed exterior, 1829–33 [drawings in N.M.R.S. and P.R.O., MPD 193].

†EDINBURGH, LOTHIAN ROAD U.P. CHURCH, 1830–1, classical; designed by David Bryce as Burn's assistant [*Builder*, 3 June 1882, 668].

PEEBLES, ST. PETER'S EPISCOPAL CHURCH, 1830–3 [N.M.R.S.].

THURSO, CAITHNESS, ST. PETER & ST. ANDREW, 1830–3 [S.R.O., E 329/1, ff. 104–5, 130–2, T.L.D.].

NEWBURGH, FIFE, 1833; dem. [*N.S.A.* ix, 71; N.M.R.S.].

TYNRON, DUMFRIESSHIRE, 1835–7 [N.M.R.S.].

MINNIGAFF, KIRKCUDBRIGHTSHIRE, 1836 [*N.S.A.* iv, 134].

RESTALRIG, MIDLOTHIAN, restoration, 1836–7 [W. Burnett, 'Restalrig and its Collegiate Church', *Trans. Scottish Ecclesiological Soc.* ii, part 2, 1907–8, 286].

EDINBURGH, ST. LUKE'S FREE CHURCH, YOUNG STREET, 1836; dem. [N.M.R.S.].

KIRKCUDBRIGHT, 1836–8 [N.M.R.S.].

NORTHESK, MUSSELBURGH, MIDLOTHIAN, 1838 [*N.S.A.* i, 285].

ETTRICK BRIDGE, SELKIRKSHIRE, chapel for 5th Duke of Buccleuch, 1838–9 [N.M.R.S.].

GLADSMUIR, EAST LOTHIAN, 1838–9; destroyed by fire 1886 [S.R.O., HR 115/2; N.M.R.S.].

ST. ANDREWS, FIFE, ST. MARY'S (now Victory Memorial Hall), 1839 [N.M.R.S.].

HAWICK, ROXBURGHSHIRE, EAST BANK CHURCH, for 5th Duke of Buccleuch, 1839 [T.L.D.].

MORTON, THORNHILL, DUMFRIESSHIRE, 1839–41, Romanesque [N.M.R.S. and drawings at Drumlanrig Castle].

PENNINGHAME, NEWTON STEWART, WIGTOWNSHIRE, 1840 [*N.S.A.* iv, 178].

DALKEITH, MIDLOTHIAN, WEST CHURCH, for 5th Duke of Buccleuch, 1840 [T.L.D.].

PORTPATRICK, WIGTOWNSHIRE, 1840–2 [T.L.D.].

†LANGHOLM, DUMFRIESSHIRE, 1842–3 [T.L.D.; R.I.B.A.D.].

DUNDEE, SOUTH and EAST CHURCHES, 1842–4 and 1846–7, respectively [J. Maclaren, *History of Dundee*, 1874, 218].

†DALKEITH, MIDLOTHIAN, ST. MARY'S EPISCOPAL CHURCH, for 5th Duke of Buccleuch, 1844–6 [N.M.R.S.].

†DALKEITH, MIDLOTHIAN, ST. NICHOLAS (EAST) CHURCH, restoration, 1848–51 [drawings in S.R.O., RHP 7041–4, and at Drumlanrig Castle].

STOKE ROCHFORD or SOUTH STOKE CHURCH, LINCS., restoration, 1847 [*Gent's Mag.* 1847 (i), 527].

†FALKLAND, FIFE, 1849–51 [S.R.O., GD 152/57/1/1–22].

---

† Wholly or partly by D. Bryce.

COUNTRY HOUSES

GALLANACH HOUSE, ARGYLLSHIRE, for Dugald MacDougall, 1814–17, castellated; enlarged *c.*1903 [R.C.A.M., *Argyll* ii, 255].

CASTLE FRASER, ABERDEENSHIRE, redecoration of hall, etc., for Col. Charles Mackenzie Fraser, 1816–18; since altered [H. Gordon Slade, 'Castle Fraser', *Proc. Soc. Antiq. Scot.* 109, 1977–8, 260].

CRAIGIELANDS, nr. MOFFAT, DUMFRIESSHIRE, for William Younger, 1817 [unsigned drawings in Burn's hand in collection of Royal Incorporation of Architects of Scotland].

DUNDAS CASTLE, WEST LOTHIAN, rebuilt for James Dundas, 1818, castellated [R.I.B.A.D.; Neale, *Seats*, 2nd ser. ii, 1825; unsigned drawings in Burn's hand in S.R.O., RHP 12672 *et seq.*].

SALTOUN HALL, EAST LOTHIAN, enlarged for Andrew Fletcher, 1818–26, castellated [signed drawings in N.L.S., MS. 17873].

BARROGILL CASTLE (now CASTLE OF MEY), CANISBAY, CAITHNESS, enlarged for 12th Earl of Caithness, 1819; altered 1954 [drawings formerly at N.M.R.S., presented to the Queen Mother 1953].

ADDERSTONE HALL, nr. BELFORD, NORTHUMBERLAND, for Thomas Forster, 1819, Greek Revival [R.I.B.A.D.].

MOUNT STUART, ISLE OF BUTE, lodge for 2nd Marquess of Bute, *c.*1820 [C. M. Armet, guidebook to Mount Stuart, n.d., 5].

BLAIRQUHAN, STRAITON, AYRSHIRE, for Sir David Hunter Blair, 1820–4, Tudor Gothic [T.L.D.; R.I.B.A.D.; Neale, *Seats*, 2nd ser., iii; Alistair Rowan in *C. Life*, 19–26 April 1973] (A. H. Millar, *Castles and Mansions of Ayrshire*, 1885).

CARSTAIRS HOUSE, LANARKSHIRE, for Henry Monteith, 1822–4, Tudor Gothic [T.L.D.; R.I.B.A.D.; Neale, *Seats*, 2nd ser. i, 1824] (plans and elevations in P. Nicholson's *New Practical Builder*, 1823, 566).

BURNTISLAND MANSE (later Forth Hotel, altered 1843), FIFE, 1823 [S.R.O. HR 126/1, p. 42].

CAMPERDOWN HOUSE, nr. DUNDEE, ANGUS, for 2nd Viscount Duncan, cr. 1st Earl of Camperdown, 1824–6, Greek Revival [T.L.D.; N.M.R.S.].

NIDDRIE HOUSE, MIDLOTHIAN, castellated additions for Col. William Wauchope, 1823; dem. after fire 1959 [T.L.D.; R.I.B.A.D.].

LOCHEND HOUSE, nr. DUNBAR, EAST LOTHIAN, for Sir George Warrender, Bart., 1823, Gothic [T.L.D.; R.I.B.A.D.]; added offices 1851 [T.L.D.].

LENNOXLOVE, EAST LOTHIAN, minor alterations to tower and roof for 11th Lord Blantyre, 1823–5 [drawings at Lennoxlove, photos at N.M.R.S.].

RICCARTON, MIDLOTHIAN, enlarged for Sir William Gibson Craig, 1823–7, Jacobethan; dem. 1956 [T.L.D.] (J. Small, *Castles and Mansions of the Lothians* ii, 1883).

STRATHENDRY, LESLIE, FIFE, for the Hon. Mrs. Douglas, 1824, Jacobethan [T.L.D.; R.I.B.A.D.; N.M.R.S.].

RATHO HOUSE (now PARK), MIDLOTHIAN, for John Bonar, 1824, Jacobethan [T.L.D.; R.I.B.A.D.].

BRODIE CASTLE, MORAYSHIRE, new wing for William Brodie, 1824–8, Jacobethan; altered by James Wylson 1845–6 [T.L.D.; correspondence at Brodie *ex inf.* Mr. David Walker] (*C. Life*, 26 Aug. 1916, 14 Aug. 1980).

SNAIGOW HOUSE, PERTHSHIRE, for James Keay, 1824–7, Tudor; dem. 1962 [T.L.D.; R.I.B.A.D.; N.M.R.S.].

PINKIE HOUSE, MIDLOTHIAN, alterations and additions for Sir John Hope, Bart., 1825 [T.L.D.].

PITFOUR CASTLE, PERTHSHIRE, additions for Sir J. S. Richardson, 1825 [T.L.D.].

DRUMFINN (later AROS HOUSE), ARGYLLSHIRE, for Hugh Maclean, 1825, Tudor Gothic; altered 1875; dem. *c.*1960 [T.L.D.; R.I.B.A.D.] (R.C.A.M., *Argyllshire* iii, pl. 78c).

TEASSES, CERES, FIFE, for Robert Christie, 1825; Jacobethan; remodelled 1879 [R.I.B.A.D.].

BALNAMOON HOUSE, ANGUS, addition for James Carnegy Arbuthnot, 1825 [plan and specification at Balnamoon, *ex inf.* Mr. David Walker].

FREELAND HOUSE, PERTHSHIRE, see under Blore, Edward, 1825–6.

HODDAM CASTLE, DUMFRIESSHIRE, alterations and castellated additions for General Matthew Sharpe, 1826; these additions dem. 19— [T.L.D.; R.I.B.A.D.].

FETTERCAIRN, LAURENCEKIRK, KINCARDINESHIRE, reconstructed for Sir William Forbes, 1826 [T.L.D.; N.M.R.S.].

DUNTRUNE, ANGUS, for William Stirling Graham, 1826, Tudor Gothic [N.M.R.S.].

GARSCUBE, DUNBARTONSHIRE, rebuilt for Sir Archibald Campbell, Bart., 1826–7, Tudor Gothic; dem. 1955 [T.L.D.; *N.S.A.* viii, 49; R.I.B.A.D.; N.M.R.S.] (J. Irving, *The Book of Dumbartonshire* iii, 1874).

DALHOUSIE CASTLE, MIDLOTHIAN, alterations and additions for 9th Earl of Dalhousie, 1826–8 [T.L.D.; R.I.B.A.D.: cf. accounts in S.R.O., GD 45/19/188] (J. Small, *Castles and Mansions of the Lothians* i, 1883).

LAURISTON CASTLE, MIDLOTHIAN, enlarged for Thomas Allan, 1827 [T.L.D.; R.I.B.A.D.; J. A. Fairley, *Lauriston Castle*, 1925, 173]

(*C. Life*, 30 Nov. 1990).

PITCAIRNS, DUNNING, PERTHSHIRE, for J. Pitcairn, 1827, Tudor Gothic [R.I.B.A.D.; N.M.R.S.].

BALCASKIE, FIFE, alterations and additions for Sir Ralph Anstruther, Bart., including bridge in park, 1827–8, work on house, 1830–2, and West (Carnbee) Lodge, 1843 [T.L.D.; *N.S.A.* ix, 348; S.R.O. SC 20/44/6, *passim, ex inf.* Mr. John Gifford] (*C. Life*, 2 March, 1912, 25 May, 1989).

WHITTINGHAME HOUSE, EAST LOTHIAN, alterations and additions for James Balfour, 1827 [T.L.D.; N.M.R.S.].

CLIVEDEN HOUSE, BUCKS., for Sir George Warrender, Bart., 1827–30, early Georgian style; destroyed by fire 1849 [T.L.D.; R.I.B.A.D., wrongly catalogued as 'Clifden, Co. Galway'].

PILRIG HOUSE, MIDLOTHIAN, additions for James Balfour, 1828; removed *c.*1960 [Barbara Balfour-Melville, *The Balfours of Pilrig*, Edinburgh 1907, 214].

CRAIGIEHALL, WEST LOTHIAN, addition to E. and W. fronts for James Hope-Vere, 1828 [drawings in portfolio at Dalmeny House].

DALKEITH PALACE, MIDLOTHIAN, lodge and gateway for 5th Duke of Buccleuch, 1828 [N.L.S., MS. 3906, f. 141], followed in *c.*1830 by an unexecuted scheme for remodelling the house, illustrated in *R.I.B.A. Drawings Catalogue: B*, fig. 119, and in 1832–4 by the Chamberlain's House and the polygonal Jacobethan conservatory [T.L.D.; R.I.B.A.D.; Buccleuch papers now in S.R.O.].

DUPPLIN CASTLE, PERTHSHIRE, for 10th Earl of Kinnoull, 1828–32, Jacobethan; dem. 1967 [T.L.D.; *N.S.A.* x, 878; R.I.B.A.D.; N.M.R.S.; A. H. Millar, *Castles and Mansions of Scotland: Perthshire and Forfarshire*, 1890, 125–137].

GILMERTON HOUSE, EAST LOTHIAN, alterations and new stables for Sir David Kinloch, Bart., 1828–9 [N.M.R.S.].

FASKALLY, PERTHSHIRE, for Archibald Butter, 1829, Scottish vernacular style [T.L.D.; N.M.R.S.]; further alterations and additions 1837 [R.I.B.A.D.].

ST. FORT, FORGAN, FIFE, for Capt. Robert Stewart, 1829, Jacobethan; dem. 1952 [T.L.D.; R.I.B.A.D.; N.M.R.S.] (A. H. Millar, *Fife, Historical and Pictorial* ii, 1895, 280).

TYNINGHAME HOUSE, EAST LOTHIAN, remodelled for 9th Earl of Haddington, 1829–30, Scottish vernacular style [T.L.D.; R.I.B.A.D.; N.M.R.S.] (*C. Life*, 16 Aug. 1902; A. Hannam, *Famous Scottish Houses of the Lowlands*, 1928, 181–4).

MILTON LOCKHART, CARLUKE, LANARKSHIRE, for William Lockhart, 1829–36, Scottish vernacular style; dem. 1956 [T.L.D.; *N.S.A.* vi, 582; R.I.B.A.D.; N.M.R.S.] (G. V. Irving & A. Murray, *Upper Ward of Lanarkshire* ii, 1864, 486).

PITCAPLE CASTLE, ABERDEENSHIRE, restoration for Hugh Lumsden, *c.*1830 [John Davidson, *Inverurie*, 1878, 417].

AYTOUN HOUSE, BRIDGE OF EARN, PERTHSHIRE, for — Murray, 1830 [N.M.R.S.].

DUNSKEY HOUSE, WIGTOWNSHIRE, enlarged or rebuilt for Forbes Hunter Blair, 1830 [R.I.B.A.D.; N.M.R.S.].

BLANERNE, nr. DUNS, BERWICKSHIRE, designs (? executed), *c.*1830; gutted 1895 [R.I.B.A.D.].

DRUMLANRIG CASTLE, DUMFRIESSHIRE, repairs and alterations for 5th Duke of Buccleuch, including a new gardener's house and probably including the forecourt wings, *c.*1830–4 [T.L.D.; *N.S.A.* iv, 506; J. C. Loudon in *Gardener's Mag.* ix, 2, and *Architectural Mag.* i, 94. For Burn's letter to Sir Walter Scott soliciting this job see N.L.S., MS. 3906, f. 141] (*C. Life*, 25 Aug., 1–8 Sept. 1960).

EDMONSTONE HOUSE, MIDLOTHIAN, drawing-room for Col. John Wauchope, 1830; dem. [J. Small, *Castles and Mansions of the Lothians* i. 1883].

SPOTT HOUSE, DUNBAR, EAST LOTHIAN, reconstructed for James Sprot, 1830, Scottish vernacular style [T.L.D.] (J. Small, *Castles and Mansions of the Lothians* ii, 1883).

RAEHILLS, DUMFRIESSHIRE, enlarged for J. J. Hope Johnstone, 1830–4 [drawings at N.M.R.S. dated 1829–30, but Loudon, *Gardener's Mag.* ix, 1833, 5, and *N.S.A.* iv, 158–9, show that the work was in progress in 1833–4].

BOWHILL, SELKIRKSHIRE, enlarged for 5th Duke of Buccleuch, 1831 onwards [T.L.D.; R.I.B.A.D.; N.M.R.S.; R.C.A.M., *Selkirkshire*, 65–6; John Cornforth in *C. Life*, 5–26 June 1975].

ARDGOWAN HOUSE, RENFREWSHIRE, enlarged for Sir Michael Shaw-Stewart, 1831–2 [T.L.D.; accounts, etc. in Strathclyde Regional Archives, T-ARD 1/6/181].

URRARD, nr. BLAIR ATHOLL, PERTHSHIRE, for Alston Stewart, 1831 [Lord Cockburn, *Circuit Journeys*, 1889, 38].

DAWYCK HOUSE, PEEBLESSHIRE, for Sir John Nasmyth of Posso, Bart., 1831–2; enlarged 1898; Scottish vernacular style [T.L.D.; R.I.B.A.D. under 'Posso'; S.R.O., GD 35/196 (4)].

AUCHMACOY HOUSE, LOGIE BUCHAN, ABERDEENSHIRE, rebuilt for James Buchan, 1831–3; Jacobethan [R.I.B.A.D.; N.M.R.S.]; completed by John Smith (*q.v.*).

KILCONQUHAR CASTLE, FIFE, remodelled for Sir Henry Bethune, Bart., 1831–9; damaged by fire 1978 [T.L.D.; R.I.B.A.D.; N.M.R.S.; A. H. Millar, *Fife, Pictorial and Historical* ii, 1895, 18–19].

ABERDALGIE MANSE, PERTHSHIRE, for 10th Earl of Kinnoull, 1832 [*N.S.A.* x, 880].

NEWBYTH HOUSE, EAST LOTHIAN, addition of kitchen offices, with connecting corridor and castellated tower, for Sir David Baird, Bart., 1832 [S.R.O., SC 40/67/8, *ex inf.* Miss C. Cruft].

CHARLETON HOUSE, KILCONQUHAR, FIFE, added dining-room for John Anstruther Thomson, 1832 [W. Kay in *C. Life*, 22 Feb. 1990]. For an unexecuted scheme by Burn to remodel the house in 1818 see S.R.O., SC 20/44/3, pp. 363–5, 393–414 and drawings in scrap-book at Charleton.

KIRKMICHAEL HOUSE, DUMFRIESSHIRE, for J. S. Lyon, 1832–3, Jacobethan [R.I.B.A.D.; J. C. Loudon in *Gardener's Mag.* ix, 1833, 5].

AUCHTERARDER HOUSE, PERTHSHIRE, for Capt. James Hunter, 1832–3, Jacobethan; remodelled 1886–9 [T.L.D.; R.I.B.A.D.; N.M.R.S.].

SPOTTISWOODE HOUSE, WESTRUTHER, BERWICKSHIRE, for John Spottiswoode, 1832–4, Jacobethan; dem. *c.*1928 [T.L.D.; R.I.B.A.D.; N.M.R.S.].

GOSFORD, EAST LOTHIAN, remodelled old manor-house as temporary residence for 6th Earl of Wemyss, 1832; dem. [T.L.D.; N.M.R.S.] (J. Small, *Castles and Mansions of the Lothians* i, 1883).

NEW INVERAWE (now ARDANAISEIG HOUSE), KILCHRENAN, ARGYLLSHIRE, for James Archibald Campbell, 1833 [N.M.R.S.; R.C.A.M., *Argyll* ii, 247].

TEVIOT BANK (formerly THE KNOWES), HAWICK, ROXBURGHSHIRE, rebuilt for William Scott, 1833 [R.I.B.A.D.; *N.S.A.* iii, 372].

THE GART, CALLANDER, PERTHSHIRE, for Capt. Houston Stewart, 1833 [T.L.D., R.I.B.A.D.].

NETHERBY HALL, CUMBERLAND, additions for Sir James Graham, Bart., 1833 [T.L.D.; R.I.B.A.D.] (*C. Life*, 21–28 Jan. 1949).

HANLEY LODGE, CORSTORPHINE, MIDLOTHIAN, 1834; dem. ? 1948 [N.M.R.S.].

THURSO CASTLE, CAITHNESS, alterations and additions for Sir John Sinclair, Bart., 1834; dem. *c.*1875 [T.L.D.].

MARCHMONT, BERWICKSHIRE, alterations for Sir H. P. Hume Campbell, Bart., 1834 [T.L.D.] (*C. Life*, 28 Feb., 7 March 1925).

MEIGLE HOUSE, PERTHSHIRE, additions for Patrick Murray, 1834, Tudor [R.I.B.A.D.].

MONKRIGG, nr. HADDINGTON, EAST LOTHIAN, for the Hon. Capt. William Keith, R.N., 1834–5; enlarged *c.*1863 [T.L.D.; R.I.B.A.D.; N.M.R.S.; S.R.O., GD 35/196 (4)].

MACBIEHILL HOUSE, PEEBLESSHIRE, remodelled for the Revd. J. I. Beresford, 1835, Scottish vernacular style; dem. [R.I.B.A.D.; N.M.R.S.] (W. Chambers, *History of Peeblesshire*, 1864, 502).

TYNEHOLME HOUSE, PENCAITLAND, EAST LOTHIAN, for Patrick Dudgeon, 1835, Jacobethan [T.L.D.; R.I.B.A.D.].

PARKHILL HOUSE, POLMONT, STIRLINGSHIRE, alterations for — Henderson, 1835 [R.I.B.A.D.].

ABOYNE CASTLE, ABERDEENSHIRE, alterations and additions (since removed) for 9th Marquess of Huntly, 1835 [T.L.D.; R.I.B.A.D.; N.M.R.S.].

BOWERHOUSE, nr. DUNBAR, EAST LOTHIAN, for Col. J. Carfrae, *c.*1835–6 [S.R.O., GD 35/196 (4)].

CARMYLE COTTAGE (now HOUSE), 138 CARMYLE AVENUE, CARMYLE, LANARKS., for John Sligo, 1836 [N.M.R.S.].

STENHOUSE, STIRLINGSHIRE, enlarged for Sir Michael Bruce, Bart., 1836; dem. *c.*1965 [T.L.D.; R.I.B.A.D.].

ANTON'S HILL, COLDSTREAM, BERWICKSHIRE, for General Sir Martin Hunter, 1836 [T.L.D.; N.M.R.S.].

ARTHURSTONE HOUSE, MEIGLE, PERTHSHIRE, new wing for Patrick Murray, 1836, Jacobethan; taken down 1855 and re-erected as a new house at Cardean (since dem.) ['Mr. Burn' noted as architect on survey plan at Arthurstone, *ex inf.* Mr. David Walker; A. Mackay, *Meigle Past and Present*, 1876, 46–7].

NEWBATTLE ABBEY, MIDLOTHIAN, added attic storey with gables to E. front for 7th Marquess of Lothian, 1836 [photos of drawings at N.M.R.S.].

KNOWSLEY HALL, LANCS., boat-house, bridges, etc. for 13th Earl of Derby, 1836–9 [T.L.D.; R.I.B.A.D.].

DUNCRUB PARK, PERTHSHIRE, rebuilt for 8th Lord Rollo, 1836–7; rebuilt 1870; dem. 1950 [T.L.D.; R.I.B.A.D.].

IRVINE HOUSE, LANGHOLM, DUMFRIESSHIRE, enlarged for 5th Duke of Buccleuch (A. H. Maxwell, tenant), 1836–7 [Buccleuch papers now in S.R.O.].

CRAIGNISH CASTLE, ARGYLLSHIRE, partly rebuilt for James Campbell, 1837, Elizabethan style [R.I.B.A.D.].

BRANXHOLM CASTLE, ROXBURGHSHIRE, alterations for 5th Duke of Buccleuch, 1837 [R.I.B.A.D.; N.M.R.S.].

INVERGOWRIE HOUSE, ANGUS, additions for Alexander Clayhills, 1837, Scottish vernacular style [*N.S.A.* xi, 578; R.I.B.A.D.; N.M.R.S.].

LUDE, nr. BLAIR ATHOLL, PERTHSHIRE, for J. P.

McInroy, 1837–40, Jacobethan [T.L.D.; R.I.B.A.D.; N.M.R.S.].

HARLAXTON MANOR, LINCS., completion of house for Gregory de Ligne Gregory, 1838 onwards, following A. Salvin (1831–7) and Edward Blore (1837) [T.L.D.; cf. *Civil Engineer and Architect's Jnl.* ii, 1839, 39] (C. Life, 11 April 1957; C. Hussey, *English Country Houses: Late Georgian*, 1958, 242, and A. Grogan in *Archaeological Jnl.* cxxxi, 1974, 324–9).

ARDDARROCH HOUSE, DUNBARTONSHIRE, for John MacVicar, 1838 [N.M.R.S.] (J. Irvine, *Book of Dumbartonshire* iii, 1879).

JURA HOUSE, ISLE OF JURA, ARGYLLSHIRE, additions, including offices, for Colin Campbell, 1838; dem. [*N.S.A.* vii, 540].

FINNART HOUSE, FORTINGAL, PERTHSHIRE, for Donald McLaren, 1838; Jacobethan [R.I.B.A.D.; N.M.R.S.].

CASTLE MENZIES, PERTHSHIRE, alterations and additions for Sir Neil Menzies, Bart., 1839–40 [T.L.D.; N.M.R.S.] (A. H. Millar, *Castles and Mansions of Scotland: Perthshire and Forfarshire*, 1890, 43–63).

BALCARRES, FIFE, enlarged for Col. James Lindsay, 1839–43, Scottish vernacular style [T.L.D.; R.I.B.A.D.] (*C. Life*, 9 Aug. 1902).

MUCKROSS ABBEY, CO. KERRY, for H. A. Herbert, 1839–43, Jacobethan style; enlarged by David Bryce 1853 [T.L.D.; R.I.B.A.D.].

NINEWELLS HOUSE, CHIRNSIDE, BERWICKSHIRE, for Elizabeth Hume, 1839–41; dem. 1964 [N.M.R.S.].

FALKLAND HOUSE, FIFE, for O. Tyndall Bruce, 1839–44, Jacobethan style [T.L.D.; R.I.B.A.D.].

WHITEHILL HOUSE (now ST. JOSEPH'S HOSPITAL), LASSWADE, MIDLOTHIAN, for R. B. Wardlaw Ramsay, 1839–44, Jacobethan style [T.L.D.; *N.S.A.* i, 612; R.I.B.A.D.; N.M.R.S.] (J. Small, *Castles and Mansions of the Lothians* ii, 1883).

CARDRONA HOUSE, TRAQUAIR, PEEBLESSHIRE, for Miss Alison Williamson, 1840 [N.M.R.S.] (W. Chambers, *History of Peeblesshire*, 1864, 396).

REDCASTLE, ROSS-SHIRE, additions for Col. Hugh Duncan Baillie, 1840, Scottish vernacular style; now in ruins [R.I.B.A.D.].

DUNACH, nr. OBAN, ARGYLLSHIRE, for James Forsyth, *c.*1840, Jacobethan [printed sale particulars of 1860].

THIRLESTANE CASTLE, BERWICKSHIRE, alterations and addition of wings for 9th Earl of Lauderdale, 1840–3 [T.L.D.; R.I.B.A.D.] (*C. Life*, 11–18 Aug. 1983).

STOKE ROCHFORD HOUSE, LINCS., for Christopher Turnor, 1841–3; Jacobethan [T.L.D.; R.I.B.A.D.] (*C. Life*, 9 Nov. 1901; M. Girouard, *The Victorian Country House*, 1971, pl. 27).

†SEACLIFFE HOUSE, NORTH BERWICK, EAST LOTHIAN, for George Sligo, 1841; dem. [T.L.D.] (J. Small, *Castles & Mansions of the Lothians* ii, 1883).

OXENFOORD CASTLE, MIDLOTHIAN, castellated additions for 8th Earl of Stair, 1842 [T.L.D.; R.I.B.A.D.; N.M.R.S.] (J. Small, *Castles and Mansions of the Lothians* ii, 1883; *C. Life*, 15 Aug. 1974).

GALLOWAY HOUSE, WIGTOWNSHIRE, alterations for 9th Earl of Galloway, 1842–6 [T.L.D.; N.M.R.S.] (F. O. Morris, *Picturesque Views of Seats* iv, 35).

SOUTH RAUCEBY HALL, LINCS., for Anthony Willson, 1842, Elizabethan style [T.L.D.; R.I.B.A.D.].

PRESTWOLD HALL, LEICS., remodelled for Charles William Packe, 1843, classical [T.L.D.; R.I.B.A.D.] (*C. Life*, 16–23 April 1959; Mark Girouard, *The Victorian Country House*, 1971, 71–2).

CAIRNHILL or CARNELL HOUSE, CRAIGIE, AYRSHIRE, alterations and additions for John Ferrier Hamilton, 1843, Scottish vernacular style [T.L.D.; R.I.B.A.D.; N.M.R.S.].

MERTOUN (now HARDEN) HOUSE, BERWICKSHIRE, addition of south wing (dem. 1953) for Lord Polwarth, 1843–4 [T.L.D.] (*C. Life*, 2–9 June 1966).

RABY CASTLE, DURHAM, alterations and additions for 2nd Duke of Cleveland, 1843–7, castle style [T.L.D.; R.I.B.A.D.; Alistair Rowan in *C. Life*, 22 Jan. 1970].

BAMFF HOUSE, PERTHSHIRE, alterations and additions for Sir James Ramsay, Bart., 1844, Scottish vernacular style [T.L.D.; contract in S.R.O., GD 83/961; N.M.R.S.].

REVESBY ABBEY, LINCS., for J. Banks Stanhope, 1844, Jacobethan [T.L.D.; R.I.B.A.D.].

†CARRADALE HOUSE, ARGYLLSHIRE, for Richard Campbell, 1844, Scottish vernacular style [T.L.D.].

DARTREY, CO. MONAGHAN, for Lord Cremorne, cr. Earl of Dartrey, 1844–6, Jacobethan; dem. [T.L.D.; R.I.B.A.D.] (F. O. Morris, *Picturesque Views of Seats* iii, 57).

REDRICE HOUSE, HANTS., remodelled for the Revd. Thomas Best, 1844; altered *c.*1911 and *c.*1933; classical [T.L.D.].

†INCHDAIRNIE, KINGLASSIE, FIFE, alterations and additions for Mrs. M. A. Aytoun, 1845, Scottish vernacular style; destroyed by fire [T.L.D.] (A. H. Millar, *Fife, Pictorial and Historical* ii, 1895, 82).

†LENY HOUSE, CALLANDER, PERTHSHIRE, alterations and additions for J. B. Hamilton,

† Wholly or partly by D. Bryce.

1845, Scottish vernacular style [T.L.D.].

†CLATTO, nr. ST. ANDREWS, FIFE, for Col. John Law, 1845, Scottish venacular style; altered and partly dem. [T.L.D.].

†LADYKIRK HOUSE, BERWICKSHIRE, alterations and additions for David Robertson, 1845; dem. 1966 [T.L.D.].

EATON HALL, CHESHIRE, alterations and additions for 2nd Marquess of Westminster, 1846–51; rebuilt 1870 onwards by A. Waterhouse; dem. 1963 [T.L.D.; R.I.B.A.D.] (for views of the principal front as altered by Burn see Eastlake, *History of the Gothic Revival*, 1872, 77, and F. O. Morris, *Picturesque Views of Seats* i, 31).

CALWICH ABBEY, STAFFS., for the Hon. and Revd. A. Duncombe, 1846, Jacobethan; dem. 1926 [T.L.D.].

CREEDY PARK, nr. CREDITON, DEVON, for Col. Sir Henry R. Ferguson-Davie, Bart., 1846, classical; destroyed by fire 1915 [T.L.D.] (F. J. Snell, *Devonshire*, Mate's County Series, Bournemouth 1970, 40).

BANGOR CASTLE (now Town Hall), CO. DOWN, for R. E. Ward, 1847, Jacobethan [T.L.D.].

LINCOLN, THE DEANERY (now Cathedral School), 1847 [Lincolnshire Record Office, MGA 315].

GORHAMBURY, HERTS., alterations and additions for 2nd Earl of Verulam, 1847 onwards [T.L.D.; R.I.B.A.D.].

ARUNDEL CASTLE, SUSSEX, alterations and additions, including main gateway, wall facing town and new lodges for 13th Duke of Norfolk, 1847–53 [T.L.D.; R.I.B.A.D.; drawings at Arundel Castle; J. M. Robinson, 'Gothic Revival at Arundel', *Connoisseur*, March 1978].

IDSWORTH HOUSE, HANTS., for Sir J. Clarke-Jervoise, 1848–52, Jacobethan; altered by H. S. Goodhart-Rendel 1912–14 [T.L.D.; R.I.B.A.D.].

MOOR PARK, HERTS., alterations for Robert Grosvenor, cr. 1st Lord Ebury, 1849 [T.L.D.].

EASTWELL PARK, KENT, large addition in Jacobean style for 10th Earl of Winchilsea, 1849; dem. 1926 [T.L.D.] (F. O. Morris, *Picturesque Views of Seats* vi, 45).

POLTALLOCH HOUSE (or CALLTON MÓR), ARGYLLSHIRE, for Neil Malcolm, 1849–53, Jacobethan; gutted 1957 [T.L.D.; R.I.B.A.D.; N.M.R.S.] (R.C.A.M. *Argyllshire* vii, 351–3).

BEECHWOOD PARK, HERTS., remodelled Great Hall and other alterations for Sir Thomas Sebright, Bart., *c.*1850–4 [T.L.D.; drawings in Herts. C.R.O., D/Ex 45 B.2] (*C. Life*, 12–19 Nov. 1938).

PEPPER ARDEN, SOUTH COWTON, YORKS. (N.R.), alterations and additions for 3rd Lord Alvanley, 1850 [T.L.D.].

SURRENDEN DERING, nr. ASHFORD, KENT, alterations and additions for Sir Edward Dering, Bart., *c.*1850; destroyed by fire except west wing 1952 [T.L.D.].

BABWORTH HALL, NOTTS., alterations and additions for H. Bridgman Simpson, 1850 [T.L.D.].

ROEHAMPTON GROVE, SURREY, added Italianate wing for S. Lyne Stephens, 1851 [T.L.D.].

STONELEIGH ABBEY, WARWICKS., conservatory and other works for 2nd Lord Leigh, 1851 [T.L.D.].

THE HIRSEL, BERWICKSHIRE, lodges, etc., for 11th Earl of Home, 1851 [T.L.D.].

DUNIRA, COMRIE, PERTHSHIRE, for Sir David Dundas, Bart., 1851–2, Scottish vernacular style; dem. [T.L.D.; R.I.B.A.D.; N.M.R.S.].

ORWELL PARK, NACTON, SUFFOLK, alterations and additions for George Tomline, 1851–3 [T.L.D.; R.I.B.A.D.].

RAMPTON MANOR, NOTTS., for the Revd. C. W. Eyre, 1851–3, Elizabethan style ['Office Book' in R.I.B.A.D.].

HOLKHAM HALL, NORFOLK, stables, north and south gates, etc., for 2nd Earl of Leicester, 1851–5 [T.L.D.; R.I.B.A.D.].

SANDON HALL, STAFFS., for 2nd Earl of Harrowby, 1852–5, Jacobethan style [T.L.D.; R.I.B.A.D.] (*C. Life*, 13 June 1991).

KILRUDDERY HOUSE, CO. WICKLOW, conservatory, etc., for 11th Earl of Meath, 1852 [T.L.D.].

BRANKSOME TOWER, POOLE, DORSET, for C. W. Packe, 1852, Tudor Gothic; dem. [T.L.D.].

KINMEL PARK, DENBIGHSHIRE, work for H. R. Hughes, who succeeded 1852 [T.L.D.]. Burn's surviving drawings [Bangor University Library, Hughes papers, 1794] relate to a gate lodge (1858), gamekeeper's house (1862) and agent's house (1865), but the Palladian stable block, apparently built between 1852 and 1854, is attributed to Burn by M. Girouard, *The Victorian Country House*, 1971, 137 and pl. 283. It is mentioned as existing in Burke's *Visitation of Seats*, 2nd ser., i, 1854, 2.

GODMERSHAM PARK, KENT, alterations (removed 1935) for Edward Knight, 1853 [T.L.D.] (*C. Life*, 16–23 Feb. 1945).

ABBOTSFORD, ROXBURGHSHIRE, added south-west wing for J. R. Hope Scott, 1853–5 [T.L.D.; N.M.R.S.].

CASTLEWELLAN, CO. DOWN, for 4th Earl of

† Wholly or partly by D. Bryce.

Annesley, 1854, castellated [T.L.D.; R.I.B.A.D.].

BUCHANAN HOUSE, STIRLINGSHIRE, for 4th Duke of Montrose, 1854–8, Scottish vernacular style; dem. 1954 [T.L.D.; R.I.B.A.D.] (plan in M. Girouard, *The Victorian Country House*, 1971, 23).

PATSHULL HOUSE, STAFFS., alterations for 5th Earl of Dartmouth, 1855 [T.L.D.].

TAPLOW COURT, BUCKS., refronted for C. Pascoe Grenfell, 1855–6, Tudor Gothic [T.L.D.].

AMPORT HOUSE, HANTS., for 14th Marquess of Winchester, 1855–7, Elizabethan style [T.L.D.].

BRAWL (or BRAAL) CASTLE, HALKIRK, CAITHNESS (a shooting lodge), for Sir George Sinclair, 1856 [R.I.B.A.D.].

FONTHILL ABBEY, WILTS., for 2nd Marquess of Westminster, 1856–9, Scottish baronial style; dem. 1955 [T.L.D.; R.I.B.A.D.] (*C. Life*, 28 Dec. 1901).

LYNFORD HALL, NORFOLK, for S. Lyne Stephens, 1856–61, Jacobethan; interior gutted 1928 [T.L.D.; R.I.B.A.D.].

HAMILTON PALACE, LANARKS., minor alterations for 11th Duke of Hamilton, 1856–7 [N.M.R.S.].

SANDBECK PARK, YORKS. (W.R.), internal alterations for 9th Earl of Scarbrough, 1857 [T.L.D.; drawings in Sheffield Archives, AP 49] (*C. Life*, 7, 14 and 21 Oct. 1965).

CHEVELEY PARK, CAMBS., alterations and additions for 6th Duke of Rutland, 1858; dem. [T.L.D.].

TUSMORE HOUSE, OXON., alterations for 2nd Earl of Effingham, 1858; dem. 1961 [T.L.D.] (*C. Life*, 30 July, 6 Aug. 1938).

WISHAW HOUSE, LANARKSHIRE, alterations and additions for 8th Lord Belhaven and Stenton, 1858; dem. 1953 [T.L.D.; N.M.R.S.].

BALINTORE CASTLE, ANGUS, for David Lyon, 1859, Scottish baronial style; dismantled [T.L.D.; R.I.B.A.D.] (H. R. Hitchcock, *Early Victorian Architecture*, 1954, pl. viii, 33).

STANWAY MANOR, GLOS., additions for 6th Earl of Wemyss, 1859–60; partly dem. 1948–9 [T.L.D.; C. Hussey in *C. Life*, 3–17 Dec. 1964].

RYDE, ISLE OF WIGHT, house for Gilbert Smith, 1859–60, picturesque gabled style [R.I.B.A.D.].

BLITHFIELD, STAFFS., minor works for 3rd Lord Bagot, 1860 [T.L.D.] (*C. Life*, 28 Oct., 4, 11 Nov. 1954).

CLANDEBOYE, CO. DOWN, HELEN'S TOWER, for 5th Baron (afterwards 1st Earl of) Dufferin, designed 1848, built *c.*1860–2, castellated [T.L.D.; R.I.B.A.D.; M. Bence-Jones in *C. Life*, 1 Oct. 1970].

DOGMERSFIELD PARK, HANTS., alterations and additions for Sir Henry Mildmay, Bart., 1860 [T.L.D.].

TEHIDY PARK, CORNWALL, alterations and additions for J. F. Basset, 1861; dem. 1919 [T.L.D.; drawings in Cornwall C.R.O.].

LAMPORT HALL, NORTHANTS., rebuilt north front for Sir Charles Isham, Bart., 1861–2 [Sir Gyles Isham, 'The Architectural History of Lamport', *Northants. Architectural and Archaeological Soc.* lvii, 1951, 27].

THE LEYS, GANAREW, HEREFS., for John Bannerman, 1861–2, Jacobethan [R.I.B.A.D.].

EILDON HALL, ROXBURGHSHIRE, alterations for 5th Duke of Buccleuch, 1861–7 [N.M.R.S.].

PACKINGTON HALL, WARWICKS., conservatory (dem.) and carriage-porch (dem. 1965) for 6th Earl of Aylesford, 1862 [G. C. Tyack in *Archaeological Jnl.* cxxviii, 1971, 242].

POLMAISE, STIRLINGSHIRE, for Col. John Murray, 1863, Scottish vernacular style; dem. [T.L.D.].

GANTON HALL, YORKS. (E.R.), for Sir F. D. Legard, Bart., 1863 [T.L.D.].

SHIRBURN CASTLE, OXON., stables for 6th Earl of Macclesfield, 1863 [T.L.D.; drawings at Shirburn Castle].

BLICKLING HALL, NORFOLK, alterations to W. range for 8th Marquess of Lothian, 1864 [T.L.D.].

KIMBOLTON CASTLE, HUNTS., alterations for 7th Duke of Manchester, 1864 [T.L.D.].

SWANBOURNE HOUSE, BUCKS., for Sir Thomas Fremantle, Bart., 1864–5, Georgian style [T.L.D.; R.I.B.A.D.].

SPYE PARK, WILTS., for J. W. G. Spicer, 1864-8; gutted by fire 1974 [T.L.D.].

POWERSCOURT, CO. WICKLOW, alterations and additions for 7th Viscount Powerscourt, 1865 [T.L.D.].

WHITTLEBURY LODGE, NORTHANTS., for 2nd Lord Southampton, 1865–8, Jacobethan; recons. after fire 1871; dem. 1972 [T.L.D.].

WESTON PARK, STAFFS., alterations and additions, including new entrance and orangery, for 3rd Earl of Bradford, 1866 [T.L.D.] (*C. Life*, 9, 16 and 23 Nov. 1945).

WICKHAM COURT, WEST WICKHAM, KENT, alterations for Col. Farnaby Lennard, 1866 [T.L.D.].

HIGHWOODS, MORTIMER, BERKS., for Dr. Walter Bryant, 1866, picturesque gabled style [R.I.B.A.D.].

WORTLEY HALL, YORKS. (W.R.), alterations and additions for 1st Earl of Wharncliffe,

1867–73 [drawings in Sheffield Archives, AP 51].

OAKLANDS PARK (now LOCKERLEY HALL), HANTS., for F. G. Dalgety, 1867–8 [T.L.D.].

OTTERSHAW PARK, SURREY, new wing for Sir Edward Colebrooke, Bart., 1868; dem. 1908 [T.L.D.].

BROCKLESBY PARK, LINCS., alterations and additions for 3rd Earl of Yarborough, 1868; reconstructed after fire in 1898; partly dem. *c.*1955 [T.L.D.].

RENDLESHAM HALL, SUFFOLK, for 5th Lord Rendlesham, 1868–71, Jacobean style; dem. *c.*1950 [T.L.D.].

CRICHEL, DORSET, additions for H. G. Sturt, 1869 [T.L.D.].

SOMERLEY, HANTS., alterations and additions for 3rd Earl of Normanton, 1869–70, continued by J. MacVicar Anderson 1870–4; partly dem. *c.*1955 [T.L.D.; R.I.B.A.D.; C. Hussey in *C. Life*, 16–23 Jan. 1958].

TOWN HOUSES, ETC.

EDINBURGH, Nos. 6–8 and 10–32 MORRISON STREET (originally ST. ANTHONY'S PLACE) and Nos. 112–116 LOTHIAN ROAD, 1821 [S.R.O., Edinburgh Sasines].

EDINBURGH, Nos. 7–22 CLAREMONT CRESCENT, *c.*1823 [S.R.O., Edinburgh Sasines].

EDINBURGH, Nos. 2–28 and 32–42A HENDERSON ROW, Nos. 162–168 DUNDAS STREET and Nos. 1A, 2–4 PERTH STREET, for the Heriot Trustees, 1825–6 [S.R.O., Edinburgh Sasines].

LONDON, MONTAGU HOUSE, PRIVY GARDENS, WHITEHALL, for 5th Duke of Buccleuch, 1853–9, French Renaissance style; dem. [*Survey of London* xiii, 218–19; T.L.D.; R.I.B.A.D.].

LONDON, No. 22 ARLINGTON STREET, alterations and additions (including the neo-Georgian street façade, dem. 1978) for 11th Duke of Hamilton, 1854–6 [T.L.D.; R.I.B.A.D.].

LONDON, No. 18 CARLTON HOUSE TERRACE, for 5th Duke of Newcastle, 1863–4 [T.L.D.; R.I.B.A.D.].

LONDON, No. 17 (later 18) GROSVENOR SQUARE, for 3rd Earl Fortescue, 1865–6; dem. 1934 [T.L.D.; R.I.B.A.D.].

LONDON, No. 7 GROSVENOR PLACE, for Lord George Manners, 1866; dem. [T.L.D.; R.I.B.A.D.].

DUNDEE, layout of UNION STREET, 1825 [David Walker, *Architects and Architecture in Dundee*, Abertay Historical Soc.'s Publication No. 3, 1955, 8].

MONUMENTS, MAUSOLEA, ETC.

EDINBURGH, OLD CALTON BURYING GROUND, Gothic monument to his father Robert Burn, 1816 [*Edinburgh Annual Register* ix, 1816, p. ccccl xxxvi].

EDINBURGH, THE MELVILLE MONUMENT, ST. ANDREW SQUARE, 1821 [N.M.R.S.].

KIRKPATRICK IRONGRAY, KIRKCUDBRIGHTSHIRE, monument to Helen Walker (d. 1791), the original of Jeanie Deans in *The Heart of Midlothian*, erected at the expense of Sir Walter Scott, 1831 [Scott's *Journal*, 5 May 1831].

HOPETOUN, WEST LOTHIAN, Hope family mausoleum, 1831, Gothic [N.M.R.S.].

ERSKINE HOUSE, RENFREWSHIRE, obelisk in memory of Lord Blantyre, 1831 [N.M.R.S.].

KILLEARNADALE KIRK, ARGYLLSHIRE, mausoleum for Colin Campbell, 1838, Gothic [*N.S.A.* vii, 540].

BEN BHRAGIE, GOLSPIE, SUTHERLAND, pedestal for Chantrey's colossal statue of the 1st Duke of Sutherland, 1837 [J. Barron, *The Northern Highlands in the Nineteenth Century* ii, 1907, 203].

STOKE ROCHFORD, LINCS., obelisk in memory of Sir Isaac Newton, for Christopher Turnor, *c.*1840 [R.I.B.A.D.].

STAINDROP CHURCHYARD, CO. DURHAM, mausoleum for 2nd Duke of Cleveland, 1850 [R.I.B.A.D.].

ROEHAMPTON, SURREY, mausoleum (in grounds of Roehampton Grove adjoining churchyard) to S. Lyne Stephens, 1864 [J. Thorne, *Handbook to the Environs of London* ii, 1876, 512; drawings in Surrey C.R.O.].

BURNELL, THOMAS, was probably a member of a family of sculptors and masons, one of whom, Thomas Burnell, had been Master of the Masons' Company in 1783. He was a pupil of Sir Robert Taylor [H. Walpole, *Anecdotes of Painting* v, ed. F. W. Hilles & P. B. Daghlian, 1939, 198], and exhibited at the Royal Academy in 1802 and 1806, including the (Gothick) 'W. front and conservatory to Berrymede Priory, Acton, Middlesex, one of the seats of Col. Clutton' (dem. 1977), the 'Front next the Thames, on Hammersmith Mall, [of] the seat of W. Lewis, Esq.', and 'Walnut Tree Lodge, E. Moulsey [Surrey], the seat of R. Bradstreet, Esq.' He was still practising in Chancery Lane in 1814.

BURNS, THOMAS (–1858), was a builder and architect of Glasgow. He went bankrupt in 1827, but was still active in the 1830s and 1840s. According to Gildard he designed 'several *quoad sacra* churches before the Disruption'. His identified works included CAMBUSNETHAN CHURCH, LANARKS., 1839–40, Gothic [S.R.O., HR 712/1], KILMUN CHURCH, ARGYLLSHIRE, 1841, Gothic [*N.S.A.* vii, 611], and THE FREE CHURCH NORMAL SEMINARY, COWCADDENS, GLASGOW, 1846, Tudor Gothic; dem. 1973 [*A.P.S.D.*, *s.v.* 'Glasgow']. Burns died on 14 November 1858 [S.R.O., SC 36/48/44, p. 636].

BURRELL, JOHN, practised in Camberwell for over thirty years. He exhibited at the Royal Academy from 1817 to 1854, including a 'Mausoleum to the memory of Sir T. Picton' (1818), 'A castellated mansion to be erected in Ayrshire' (1820), and 'Alterations and additions for W. H. Child, Esq. at Dulwich' (1828). In 1835 he and Robert Lugar entered a joint design for rebuilding the Houses of Parliament [*Catalogue of the Designs for the New Houses of Parliament*, 6th ed. 1836, 12–13]. He designed a BAPTIST CHURCH in COLDHARBOUR LANE, DENMARK HILL, 1823 [*Survey of London* xxvi, 151].

BURROUGH, Sir JAMES (1691–1764), was the son of Dr. James Burrough, a physician of Bury St. Edmunds in Suffolk. He was educated at the Grammar School at Bury, and at Gonville and Caius College, Cambridge, where he took his M.A. in 1716. In 1727 he became one of the Esquire Bedells of the University, and in 1754 was elected Master of his college. As an amateur architect, he may be compared with Dean Aldrich and Dr. George Clarke at Oxford, and, like them, he 'was a great virtuoso in painting, prints and medals, of which he had a very choice and valuable collection'.

One of the earliest architectural works with which Burrough is known to have been associated was the SENATE HOUSE at CAMBRIDGE, which was intended to form part of a larger complex of university buildings. He was a member of the syndicate responsible for its erection, and himself furnished a design which is said to have been not unlike that submitted by James Gibbs, except that it was 'upon Rustick Pillars' [Hist. MSS. Comm., *Portland* v, 630; *Wren Soc.* xvii, 46–7]. On 8 March 1721/2 he was among those who signed an order that Gibbs should 'take with him to London Mr. Burrough's Plan of the Intended publick Buildings and make what improvements he shall think necessary upon it'. It is not clear to what extent the design eventually adopted was based on his, for, although his friend William Cole, writing shortly after his death, implies that he was the architect, Gibbs published the plan and elevation as his own. On the whole, it seems probable that, as Willis concluded, 'Burrough had no other share in the work than that of suggesting the general arrangement, and of taking an active part in the promotion and management of the building'. In 1752 he made a design, based on Gibbs's scheme of 1722, for rebuilding the east front of the University Library adjoining the Senate House, but this was rejected through the influence of the Duke of Newcastle, then Chancellor, who gave £500 towards the cost, and persuaded the Syndics to adopt an elevation made by his own architect, Stephen Wright. This slight to Burrough caused a good deal of ill-feeling in the University, and, according to Cole, it was 'in order to cajole and bring into temper Mr. Burrough' that the Duke 'soon after procured him a Knighthood'. The actual occasion of this honour was, however, the presentation to George II of an Address on the coming of age of the Prince of Wales in 1759. Burrough's design was engraved and published by James Essex in 1775 [Willis & Clark, iii, 43–70, 536–7].

Burrough was much in demand as an architectural adviser in eighteenth-century Cambridge, and most of his executed works were in that university. In 1733, however, he designed an altarpiece for Canterbury Cathedral, and he is stated in a contemporary letter to have designed the 'apartments' in the Assembly Rooms at Norwich, built by Thomas Ivory in 1754. This is confirmed by a note in a sketch-book of Sir William Chambers in the Victoria and Albert Museum. In 1757 he was consulted by the corporation of Wisbech as to the merits of the plans for a new bridge submitted by Messrs. Swaine and Sharman [N. Walker & J. Craddock, *History of Wisbech*, 1849, 419].

Although some of his buildings (notably the range at Peterhouse) are Palladian in character, Burrough was not a strict follower of the Anglo-Palladian school. Like Gibbs he often designed in a chastened baroque style that is as sober in effect as most Palladian work, but belongs to the early rather than to the mid eighteenth century. His elaborate internal decoration is also pre-Palladian in character and almost rococo in feeling, though not in motif.

Being, as Cole tells us, 'a very large and corpulent Man, who lived freely and used no Exercise', Burrough's health was poor, and towards the end of his life he suffered from a variety of complaints. He maintained his interest in architecture to the last, and on the very day of his death 'Mr. Essex (the Builder) was with him after Dinner for half an Hour, talking upon that Business.' He was buried in the antechapel at Gonville and Caius College, where there is a ledger-stone in his memory. His portrait by Heins is in the Master's Lodge. He left the College his collection of Greek and Roman coins and 'all such of my books as they have not already in the Library'. Among the College MSS. (No. 620) is a copy of Aldrich's *Elementa Architecturae* presented by him. None of his drawings appear to have survived. [*D.N.B.*; J. Venn, *Biographical History of Gonville and Caius College* iii, 1901, 127; Willis & Clark, iii, 536–40; J. Nichols, *Literary Illustrations of the Eighteenth Century* iv, 91 n.]

STANWICK RECTORY, NORTHANTS., for Dr. Peter Needham, 1717 [Richard Cumberland, *Memoirs* i, 1807, 50].

GONVILLE AND CAIUS COLLEGE, CAMBRIDGE. Burrough probably designed the cupola erected over the Combination Room in 1728, and in 1729 he directed repairs and improvements in the Master's Lodge. He probably directed the ashlaring of the Gonville Court, 1751–4 [Willis & Clark, i, 188, 201–2].

QUEENS' COLLEGE, CAMBRIDGE, remodelled interior of hall in classical style, 1732–1734: Burrough's ceiling was removed 1846, and in 1861 his fireplace was taken down [Willis & Clark, ii, 46].

CANTERBURY CATHEDRAL, designed classical altarpiece, erected 1733, removed 1820 [C. E. Woodruff & W. Danks, *Memorials of Canterbury Cathedral*, 1912, 347–8; *A.P.S.D.*, *s.v.* 'Canterbury'].

EMMANUEL COLLEGE, CAMBRIDGE. Burrough received 7 guineas in 1735 'for his assistance in beautifying ye Chappell', but the details of the work are not recorded. In 1752 he made designs for rebuilding part of the College which were not executed [Willis & Clark, ii, 709, 713–15].

BURY ST. EDMUNDS, SUFFOLK, THE 'MANOR HOUSE' (now Museum) for the Countess of Bristol, 1736–8 [*The Letter-Books of John Hervey, First Earl of Bristol*, ed. S.H.A.H., iii, 1894, 151–3].

PETERHOUSE, CAMBRIDGE, Burrough's Building, designed 1736, executed 1738–42; refronted the main quadrangle 1754–6 [Willis & Clark, i, 35–8].

CORPUS CHRISTI COLLEGE, CAMBRIDGE, altarpiece in chapel, 1742; dem. 1823 [Willis & Clark, i, 295].

TRINITY HALL, CAMBRIDGE, remodelled hall and quadrangle, 1742–5, and made unexecuted design for a new Library Court [Willis & Clark, i, 228–9].

SIDNEY SUSSEX COLLEGE, CAMBRIDGE, remodelled interior of hall, 1749–52; designed stone gateway to Hall Court 1761–2, removed to Jesus Lane 1831 [R. C. Smail, 'Sir James Burrough at Sidney', *Cambridge Review*, 30 April 1960; Peter Salway in *C. Life*, 25 Feb. 1960].

CAMBRIDGE, GREAT ST. MARY'S CHURCH, Doctors' Gallery in the chancel, 1754; removed 1863 [Willis & Clark, iii, 538; C. H. Cooper, *Annals of Cambridge* iv, 1852, 291] (*V.C.H. Cambs.* iii, 131).

NORWICH, ASSEMBLY ROOMS, designed interior of building, 1754 [J. Nichols, *Literary Illustrations* vi, 1831, 804; note by Sir W. Chambers in album in Victoria and Albert Museum, 93 B. 21, f. 90, no. 382].

CLARE COLLEGE, CAMBRIDGE, designed new chapel, 1763; completed by James Essex 1764–9, after his death [Willis & Clark, i, 115].

BURTON, DECIMUS (1800–1881), was the tenth son of James Burton (*q.v.*). He was educated at Tonbridge School and received practical training in his father's office. According to a note left by his father, he 'left school in September 1816 and became my assistant in the office'. At the same time he was being taught architectural draughtsmanship by George Maddox, and in 1817 he began to attend the Royal Academy Schools under the professorship of Sir John Soane. He was evidently a precocious pupil, for as early as 1817–18 he appears to have assisted his father to design the latter's villa in Regent's Park, and in 1818–19 he designed South Villa for a private client. Soon afterwards he was allowed by Nash to design Cornwall (1821) and Clarence (1823) Terraces in Regent's Park, of which his father was the builder. He started independent practice in April 1823, 'and found himself, before he had completed his 24th year, in the full tide of professional work'. One of his earliest clients was G. B. Greenough, M.P. and founder of the Geological Society, for whom he designed another villa in Regent's Park. The wealthy and influential Greenough was to be responsible for bringing him several commissions in later years.

Burton's first public building was the Colosseum in Regent's Park (1823–7). 'A Greek version of the Pantheon', with a dome slightly larger than that of St. Paul's, this was regarded as a remarkable achievement for a young man of 23, and he soon obtained important commissions in the Royal Parks from the Office of Woods and Forests. These included the Hyde Park screen and the arch on Constitution Hill. It was through Greenough that Burton was commissioned to design the Athenaeum Club, of which he was an early member, and where he was to meet many of his future clients. He enjoyed great success both as a designer of villas and small country houses and as a town planner specializing in the kind of picturesque layout of which Regent's Park had been the prototype. Of this the Calverley Estate at Tunbridge Wells was a particularly attractive example. He also had a considerable reputation as an expert in the construction of glass and iron conservatories, of which he designed notable examples at Chatsworth, Regent's Park and Kew.

Although he may be classed as a Greek Revivalist, Burton was by no means an archaeological purist. His knowledge of the principal antique monuments was based on the published works of others rather than on personal investigation and discovery. His use of the orders is always correct, but he showed a lack of pedantry in their application that sets him apart from some of his more doctrinaire contemporaries, such as Hamilton and Smirke. From Nash he had learned to combine the classical and the picturesque, and it is the picturesque that is predominant in much of his later work. For the Gothic Revival he felt no enthusiasm. He did, it is true, design some houses with pointed windows and turrets, and even some Gothic churches, but his lack of sympathy for the style is apparent enough in the arid interiors and coarse detailing of the churches, which are among the least attractive of their period.

Burton travelled extensively both in Europe and in North America. Details of his tours are lacking, but he is known to have visited France and Spain in 1826, Holland in 1846 and Germany in 1850. He was a Fellow of the Royal Society, of the Society of Antiquaries and of the R.I.B.A., of which he was at one time Vice-President, and a member of several other learned societies. He retired in 1869, and lived partly at St. Leonard's, where he had built himself a small house (The Cottage, Maze Hill), and partly in London (1, Gloucester Houses, Hyde Park), where he died unmarried on 14 December 1881. His practice was continued by his nephew Henry Marley Burton (1813–80). John Crake, Henry Currey, George Mair, A. W. Hakewill and George Williams were his pupils. E. J. May (d. 1941) joined his office shortly before he retired. A portrait in oils attributed to Sir William Beechey is known only from a photograph. A photographic portrait taken in 1873 is preserved at the Athenaeum Club and was used as the basis of an engraving in *Illustrated London News* lxxix, 1881, 650. A number of Burton's drawings are in the Victoria and Albert Museum (C. J. Richardson Collection), and there are others in the Hastings Museum, the R.I.B.A. Drawings Collection and the Architectural Association's Library.

[Obituaries in *Builder* xli, 1881, 779, and *Jnl. Royal Society* xxxiv, 1882–3, viii–ix; *D.N.B.*; R. P. Jones, 'The Life and Works of Decimus Burton', *Arch. Rev.* xvii, 1905; Philip Miller, *Decimus Burton*, Exhibition Catalogue 1981; information from Mr. Neil Cooke.]

Unless otherwise stated the source of the following list of Burton's works is *Builder* xli, 1881, 779.

PUBLIC BUILDINGS, ETC.

London

THE COLOSSEUM, REGENT'S PARK, for Thomas Hornor, 1823–7; altered by W. Bradwell 1845; dem. 1875 (J. Britton & A. Pugin, *The Public Buildings of London* ii, 1828, 271–5; *C. Life*, 2 Jan. 1953).

HYDE PARK, Ionic screen at Hyde Park Corner, lodges at Stanhope, Grosvenor and Cumberland Gates, 1824–5; lodge at Prince of Wales Gate, 1846.

PARLIAMENTARY MEWS, PRINCE'S STREET, WESTMINSTER, 1825–6; remodelled as Stationery Office 1853–4; dem. 1950 [*History of the King's Works* vi, 1973, 536–7] (J. Elmes, *Metropolitan Improvements*, 1831, plate).

ZOOLOGICAL SOCIETY, REGENT'S PARK, buildings and gardens, 1826–41. Burton's original plan for the layout is P.R.O., MPE 906. See also *A Series of Ten Views of the Southern Portion of the Gardens of the Zoological Society in Regent's Park laid out to the Designs of D. Burton, Esq., drawn on Stone by James Hakewill*, 1831.

BUCKINGHAM PALACE, archway on Constitution Hill, 1827–8; originally intended as a Royal Entrance to the palace from the north, but moved to its present position 1883 (W. H. Leeds, *Supplement* to Britton & Pugin, *Public Buildings of London*, 1838, 124–34); and enclosure of palace forecourt, 1850–1.

THE ATHENAEUM CLUB, WATERLOO PLACE, 1827–30; attic storey added 1899–1900 (*Survey of London* xxix, 386–99).

THE ROYAL NAVAL CLUB, 160 BOND STREET, 1828–31.

BEULAH SPA, UPPER NORWOOD, pump-room, layout of grounds, etc., 1828–31 [E. Walford, *Old and New London* vi, n.d., 315].

THE JUNIOR UNITED SERVICE CLUB, CHARLES STREET, ST. JAMES'S, alterations, 1830; dem. 1855 (*Survey of London* xxix, 291–2).

THE ROYAL SOCIETY OF LITERATURE, ST. MARTIN'S PLACE, 1830–1; dem.

HYDE PARK, remodelled store-house or magazine for the Grenadier Guards, *c.*1830.

NORTHUMBERLAND STREET, STRAND, No. 1, warehouse for Messrs. Gilpin & Co., Army clothiers, 1830–2.

CLIFFORD'S INN, FLEET STREET, alterations, 1830–4; dem. 1934.

CHARING CROSS HOSPITAL, 1831–4; enlarged 1877, 1881 and 1904.

CLUB CHAMBERS, LOWER REGENT STREET, 1838–9; dem. (*Companion to the Almanac*, 1840, 246).

ROYAL BOTANIC SOCIETY'S GARDENS, REGENT'S PARK, conservatory (1845–6, dem. 1932) and other buildings, 1840–59 (*A New Survey of London*, J. Weale, 1853, ii, 487–94; measured drawings of the conservatory were published in *Architect and Building News*, 1 April 1932 ('Obituaries of Buildings', No. 25)). Burton's report on the layout of the gardens is printed in *Gardeners' Mag.* xvi, 1840, 514–16.

THE UNION CLUB, TRAFALGAR SQUARE, addition of attic storey, etc., 1841–50.

THE ORIENTAL CLUB, HANOVER SQUARE, additions, 1852–4.

THE ROYAL GEOGRAPHIC SOCIETY, 15 WHITEHALL PLACE, 1854–55; dem. [letters at Royal Geographic Soc., *ex inf.* Mr. Neil Cooke].

THE UNITED SERVICE CLUB, WATERLOO PLACE, enlargement on east side and alterations to principal elevations, including addition of frieze, 1858–9 (*Survey of London* xxix, 392–4).

Elsewhere

ABERSYCHAN IRONWORKS, MONMOUTHSHIRE, 1826; dem.

ST. LEONARD'S, HASTINGS, SUSSEX, probably designed Assembly Rooms, Baths, hotels, etc. for his father James Burton, 1828 onwards: see p. 200.

ABERDEEN, the Ionic screen to St. Nicholas Churchyard in Union Street was built by John Smith (*q.v.*) in 1830, apparently following designs supplied by Burton in 1829 [G. M. Fraser in *Aberdeen Weekly Journal*, 21 June 1918].

BATH, SOMERSET, report on Public Baths, 1829, and designed THE TEPID SWIMMING BATH, executed by G. P. Manners, 1830; dem. 1923 [W. Ison, *The Georgian Buildings of Bath*, 1948, 64].

DUBLIN, PHOENIX PARK, lodges, etc., 1834–49. There are drawings by Burton in National Library of Ireland, Portfolio 26.

PARIS, BRITISH EMBASSY (HÔTEL CHAROST), alterations and repairs, 1841–50 [*History of the King's Works* vi, 1972, 633–4].

KEW, SURREY, ROYAL BOTANIC GARDENS, Palm House, entrance gates to Kew Green and 'Campanile' (water-tower and chimney), 1845–8; Museum of Economic Botany, 1855–7; Temperate House, 1859–62, wings added 1895–7, restored 1977–82 [*History of the King's Works* vi, 442–5; E. T. Diestelkamp, 'Richard Turner and the Palm House at Kew Gardens', *Newcomen Soc.'s Trans.* 54, 1982–3] (G. Godwin, *Buildings and Monuments, Modern and Mediaeval*, 1850, 25–8).

EAST RETFORD, NOTTS., FREE GRAMMAR SCHOOLS (in South Retford), 1855–7, Elizabethan.

CHURCHES

TUNBRIDGE WELLS, KENT, HOLY TRINITY (now Arts Centre), 1827–9, Gothic.

SOUTHBOROUGH, KENT, for John Deacon, 1830–1, Gothic; steeple by E. Christian 1883.

RIVERHEAD, KENT, 1831, Gothic; chancel by Sir A. W. Blomfield, 1882. There is an elevation by Burton in the Kent Archives Office, U 1350 P. 23.

GORING, SUSSEX, rebuilt for David Lyon, 1836–8, Gothic.

EASTBOURNE, SUSSEX, HOLY TRINITY, 1837–9, Gothic; aisles by B. Ferrey 1855; remodelled 1909.

FLIMWELL, SUSSEX, 1839–40, Gothic; spire added 1873, chancel 1879.

BOBBINGWORTH, ESSEX, tower and porch, 1840, Gothic [*V.C.H. Essex* iv, 15].

FLEETWOOD, LANCS., for Sir Peter Hesketh-Fleetwood, Bart., 1840, Gothic; chancel added 1880.

LONDON, TEMPLE CHURCH, restoration with Sydney Smirke, 1841–3 [J. Mordaunt Crook, 'The Restoration of the Temple Church', *Arch. Hist.* viii, 1965, 41–3].

BRADFORD PEVERELL, DORSET, rebuilt for H. N. Middleton, 1849–51, Gothic.

LAUNCESTON, CORNWALL, repewing, 1851–3 [I.C.B.S.].

BUILDING ESTATES, ETC.

TUNBRIDGE WELLS, KENT, THE CALVERLEY ESTATE, for John Ward, 1828 onwards; Burton's own house, BASTON COTTAGE, was dem. *c.*1900 (plans and engravings in J. Britton, *Descriptive Sketches of Tunbridge Wells and the Calverley Estate*, 1832, and Colbran's *New Guide to Tunbridge Wells*, ed. J. Phippen, 1840, 53–9).[1]

---

[1] According to the 1847 edition of Colbran's *Guide* Burton had by then planned an estate at Tunbridge Wells for the Marquess Camden, but

BRIGHTON, SUSSEX, QUEEN ADELAIDE CRESCENT, for (Sir) Isaac Lyon Goldsmid, 1830–4, Only the east wing was built under Burton's direction [A. Dale, *Fashionable Brighton*, 1947, 151–2].

LIVERPOOL, LANCS., building estate (unidentified) for R. A. Barton, 1834–5.

EASTBOURNE, SUSSEX, planned an estate for 2nd Earl of Burlington (afterwards 7th Duke of Devonshire), which was not executed, with the exception of a villa for the owner, 1835–40.

GRAVESEND, KENT, layout of 'a large plot adjoining the high road, for building', 1836 [*Gent's Mag.* 1836 (i), 654].

FLEETWOOD, LANCS., scheme for new town, including church, North Euston Hotel, Queen's Terrace, Custom House and two lighthouses, partially executed for Sir Peter Hesketh-Fleetwood, Bart., 1836–43.

GLASGOW, Kelvinside building estate for Mathew Montgomerie, 1840.

FOLKESTONE, KENT, planned estate for 3rd Earl of Radnor, 1843; not proceeded with, drawings in Radnor Estate Office, Folkestone.

QUEENSTOWN (now COBH), CO. CORK, IRELAND, improvements and sea-wall for 5th Viscount Midleton, 1843–50.

HILL OF HOWTH, CO. DUBLIN, IRELAND, unexecuted project for building for 3rd Earl of Howth, 1845–6.

BOURNEMOUTH, HANTS., succeeded Benjamin Ferrey as architect to the Gervis Estate *c.*1845, and advised on development until 1859. For further details see C. H. Mate & C. Riddle, *Bournemouth: 1810–1910*, Bournemouth 1910, 90–92, etc.

DOMESTIC ARCHITECTURE

London

THE HOLME, REGENT'S PARK, probably assisted James Burton to design villa for himself, 1817–18: see below, p. 200. (J. Britton & A. Pugin, *The Public Buildings of London* i, 1825, 83–8).

SOUTH VILLA, REGENT'S PARK, for David Lance, 1818–19; rebuilt 1879–83 [Ann Saunders, *The Regents Park Villas*, Bedford College 1981, 16; sale particulars of 1820 in S.R.O., GD 112/20/7].

GROVE HOUSE (now NUFFIELD LODGE), REGENT'S PARK, for G. B. Greenough, 1822–4 (J. Britton & A. Pugin, *The Public Buildings of London* ii, 1828, 1–4; J. Elmes, *Metropolitan Improvements*, 1831, 30–2 and pl.).

PALL MALL EAST, house (No. 8) and warehouse for Messrs Hibbert & Co., Army clothiers, *c.*1825; dem.

ST. DUNSTAN'S LODGE, REGENT'S PARK, for 3rd Marquess of Hertford, 1825–8; dem. 1936 (J. Elmes, *Metropolitan Improvements*, 1831, plate). Burton's original drawings are at the Architectural Association.

PALL MALL EAST, house and shops for Sir H. F. Cooke, 1826–7; dem.

HANOVER LODGE, REGENT'S PARK, for Col. Sir Robert Arbuthnot, *c.*1827; remodelled by Lutyens 1911; restored as a students' hostel 1961–4 [Ann Saunders, *The Regents Park Villas*, Bedford College 1981, 27].

SPRING GARDENS, Nos. 10, 12, 14, *c.*1827, occupied chiefly by himself as house and office; dem. [*Survey of London* xx, 68, pl. 48].

CARLTON HOUSE TERRACE, No. 3 for Lord de Clifford, 1829–31; No. 4 (dem. 1929) for Lord Stuart de Rothesay.

PALL MALL, alterations to house (No. 80) for (Sir) John Kirkland, army agent, 1830 (cf. *Survey of London* xxix, 377).

WHITEHALL GARDENS, No. 6, additions for Cuthbert Ellison, 1831–2; dem. (*Survey of London* xiii, pls. 89–92).

HOLFORD HOUSE, REGENT'S PARK, for (Sir) James Holford, 1832–3; afterwards Regent's Park College; destroyed by bombing 194–.

HOLLAND HOUSE, KENSINGTON, restoration for 3rd Lord Holland, 1833; destroyed by bombing 1940.

ST. JOHN'S LODGE, REGENT'S PARK, alterations and additions for (Sir) Isaac Lyon Goldsmid, 1833–5 [P.R.O., CREST 13208, *ex inf.* Mrs. Susan Beattie].

GROSVENOR STREET, additions to No. 18 for the dowager Duchess of Roxburghe and her second husband Col. W. F. O'Reilly, 1835–6.

BELGRAVE SQUARE, additions to No. 10 for 2nd Earl of Burlington (afterwards 7th Duke of Devonshire), 1839–40.

HYDE PARK GARDENS, No. 18 for Mrs. Drummond, 1841–2.

DEVONSHIRE HOUSE, PICCADILLY, portico, hall and staircase for 6th Duke of Devonshire, 1843; dem. 1924 (*Builder* i, 1843, 5; B.M., Crace Views, Portfolio x, 96).

GREAT STANHOPE STREET, additions to No. 6 for A. Mitchell, 1853–4.

THE FERNS, VICTORIA ROAD, KENSINGTON, alterations and additions for E. W. Cooke, R.A., 1864 [E. W. Cooke's MS. diaries, *ex inf.* Mr. Andrew Saint].

Camden Park does not appear to have been laid out until *c.*1853, and the five Italianate houses built by 1863, when work stopped, were probably designed by another architect.

Country

BRIGHTON, SUSSEX, villa for H. Fauntleroy, 1822–3; dem.

ALDBURY GROVE, CHESHUNT, HERTS., additions for J. S. Jessop, 1822–4.

ELM BANK, LEATHERHEAD, SURREY, addition for Capt. William Stanley Clarke, 1822–5; largely rebuilt since war-damage.

BASTON HOUSE, HAYES, KENT, additions for S. N. Ward, 1823–5.

HOLWOOD HOUSE, KESTON, KENT, for John Ward, 1823–6 [drawing in Victoria & Albert Museum, D 1894–1907] (J. P. Neale, *Views of Seats*, 2nd ser., iv, 1828).

LIVERPOOL, LANCS., house at WEST DINGLE for J. B. Yates, 1827; dem. 1959 (*Portfolio of Measured Drawings*, Liverpool School of Architecture i, 1906, xxvii, xxviii).

MITCHELLS (now HOLMEWOOD), LANGTON GREEN, TUNBRIDGE WELLS, KENT, for C.H. Okey and J. Carruthers, 1827; burned 1837 and rebuilt to a different design.

HARROW, MIDDLESEX, Nos. 7 and 17 LONDON ROAD, two Gothic villas for General A. M. McGregor of Harrow Park, 1827.

THE GROVE, WEST MOLESEY, SURREY, additions for J. W. Croker, after 1828.

THE GROVE, PENSHURST, KENT, for F. Allnutt, 1828–33.

BECKENHAM, KENT, villa for B. Oakley, 1829.

GREAT CULVERDEN HOUSE, TUNBRIDGE WELLS, KENT, for J. J. Fisher, 1829–30; dem. 1956 (C. Greenwood, *Epitome of County History: Kent*, 1838, plate p. 124).

SPRING GROVE, PEMBURY, KENT, for A. B. Belcher, 1829–30; dem. 1871 [plans in Kent R.O., U 1050].

MABLEDON PARK, QUARRY HILL, TONBRIDGE, KENT, addition for John Deacon, 1829–31, Gothic (C. Greenwood, *Epitome of County History: Kent*, 1838, plate p. 125). This was the house originally built by James Burton as his own residence.

PARK HATCH, HASCOMBE, SURREY, conservatory, etc., for Joseph Goodman, 1830; dem.

GREAT WOOLSTONE, BUCKS., parsonage for the Revd. Dr. Weeden Butler, 1830; rebuilt *c.*1855.

CHATSWORTH, DERBYSHIRE, works including Home Farm and Great Conservatory (designed in association with Joseph Paxton 1836–40, dem. 1920) for 6th Duke of Devonshire, 1830–48. For the question of the responsibility for the design see Francis Thompson in *Derbyshire Countryside* xxi, Aug.–Sept. 1956, and G. F. Chadwick, *The Works of Sir Joseph Paxton*, 1961, 78–80.

SEVENOAKS, KENT, THE RECTORY, for the Revd. Thos. Curteis, 1831–2, Tudor Gothic; dem. 1959.

PAINSHILL, SURREY, additions (including a conservatory, since dem.) for W. H. Cooper, 1831–2 (*C. Life*, 2 Jan. 1958).

EAST CLIFFE HOUSE, RAMSGATE, KENT, additions for Sir Moses Montefiore, 1831–2; dem. 1954.

BURY HILL, nr. DORKING, SURREY, addition for C. Barclay, 1831–3; partly dem. *c.*1950; observatory for A. K. Barclay 1847–8.

COOMBE LODGE, COOMBE, nr. KINGSTON, SURREY, for W. O. Hunt, 1831–4.

BROOM HILL, nr. TONBRIDGE, KENT, for David Salomons, 1831–8.

BURRSWOOD HOUSE, SPELDHURST, KENT, for David Salomons, 1831–8, Elizabethan style.

BENTHAM HILL, nr. TONBRIDGE, KENT, for A. Pott, 1832–3, Elizabethan style.

WORTH PARK, SUSSEX, additions for Joseph Montefiore, 1833; destroyed by fire 1847.

BRIGHTON, SUSSEX, FURZE HILL VILLA, for (Sir) Isaac Lyon Goldsmid, 1833; dem. 1938 [exhib. at R.A. 1833; A. Dale, *Fashionable Brighton*, 1947, 152].

STOCKGROVE, GREAT BRICKHILL, BUCKS., rebuilt for Col. Henry Hanmer, *c.*1834; dem.

GLEVERING HALL, SUFFOLK, addition (including orangery) for A. Arcedekne, 1834–5.

GREAT BRICKHILL, BUCKS., THE RECTORY, for the Revd. H. Foulis, 1834–5.

OAKLANDS, SEDLESCOMBE, SUSSEX, for Hercules Sharpe, 1834–7.

CHISWICK HOUSE, MIDDLESEX, lodges and gates for 6th Duke of Devonshire, 1835.

CHISWICK, MIDDLESEX, GROVE HOUSE, alterations for 6th Duke of Devonshire, *c.*1835.

CHISWICK, MIDDLESEX, SUTTON COURT, alterations for 6th Duke of Devonshire, *c.*1835; dem. 1896.

HOLLANDS, or HOLLANDS FARM, SPELDHURST, KENT, for the Revd. H. Cholmondeley, 1835–6.

VEN HOUSE, MILBOURNE PORT, SOMERSET, added wings and conservatory and designed new drawing-room for Sir W. Medlycott, 1835–6 [volume of drawings seen at Ven in 1967].

KENNINGTON PLACE, nr. ASHFORD, KENT, additions for Dr. H. W. Carter, 1835–7.

COGHURST PLACE, GUESTLING, SUSSEX, for Musgrave Brisco, 1835–40; dem.

TUNBRIDGE WELLS, BLACKHURST, PEMBURY ROAD, for Ford Wilson, 1836–8 (C. Greenwood, *Epitome of County History: Kent*, 1838, plate p. 124).

PUTNEY PARK HOUSE, SURREY, additions for Robert Hutton, 1837–8.

HARROW SCHOOL, MIDDLESEX, house for the Revd. J. W. Colenso, 1838–9; dem.

BLACKHEATH, now LONDON, MORDEN HILL,

DARTMOUTH GROVE, for James Traill, 1838–40.

THE HOOKE, CHAILEY, SUSSEX, additions (largely dem. 1958) for R. W. Blencowe, 1838–44.

GREENSTEAD, ESSEX, parsonage for the Revd. P. W. Ray, 1839–40.

WOODHAYS, SURREY, additions for William Brown, 1839–41.

STANWICK PARK, YORKS. (N.R.), additions, chiefly to N. and E. sides, for Lord Prudhoe, afterwards 4th Duke of Northumberland, *c.*1839 onwards; dem. 1923 (*C. Life*, 17 Feb. 1900). At Alnwick Castle there are designs by Burton for works at Stanwick in 1840–2, including a greenhouse, an orangery and a domed entrance hall.

HARROW SCHOOL, MIDDLESEX, Headmaster's House, 1840, and enlarged 1845–6; altered.

ALVERBANK, STOKES BAY, nr. GOSPORT, HANTS., for J. W. Croker, *c.*1840.

GRIMSTON PARK, YORKS. (W.R.), rebuilt for 2nd Lord Howden, 1840–50 (*C. Life*, 9–16 March 1940).

HAYDON HILL, BUSHEY, HERTS., for T. G. Fonnereau, 1841–3.

STAPLETON HOUSE, nr. BRISTOL (now COLSTON'S SCHOOL), additions and alterations for the Ecclesiastical Commissioners, 1841–4, to convert it into residence for the Bishop of Gloucester and Bristol.

HEMINGFORD HOUSE, HEMINGFORD ABBOTS, HUNTS., for the Revd. J. Linton, 1842–3.

BAY HOUSE, ALVERSTOKE, HANTS. (later GOSPORT GRAMMAR SCHOOL), for 1st Lord Ashburton, 1844, Tudor Gothic.

TUNBRIDGE WELLS, KENT, BELLEVUE, for Aretas Akers, 1845.

WHIPS CROSS, WALTHAMSTOW, ESSEX, house for John Masterman, junior, 1845–7.

SYON HOUSE, ISLEWORTH, MIDDLESEX, river terrace, ornamental dairy, etc., for 4th Duke of Northumberland, after 1847.

BRADFORD PEVERELL HOUSE, DORSET, for H. N. Middleton, 1850–4; rebuilt by Henry Marley Burton 1863–7.

BOLNORE HOUSE, CUCKFIELD, SUSSEX, additions for Miss Dealtry, 1852–5.

CALSTOCK, CORNWALL, rectory for the Revd. C. L. Pemberton, 1853–4.

BEARWOOD, nr. WOKINGHAM, BERKS., alterations and additions for John Walter, 1853–8; rebuilt to designs of Robert Kerr 1865–74.

SENNOWE HALL, NORFOLK, additions for Trustees of Edmond Wodehouse under Court of Chancery, 1855–6; largely rebuilt 1905–7 (*C. Life*, 24–31 Dec. 1981).

HIGHAMS, nr. CHOBHAM, SURREY, additions for the Hon. Mrs. Seymour Bathurst, 1855–6.

NORTH COURT, FINCHAMPSTEAD, BERKS., for the Revd. T. Mozley, 1857–8; enlarged 1873; dem. 1970.

BINEHAM, CHAILEY, SUSSEX, rebuilt for J. G. Blencowe, 1858–60; dem.

BURTON, *alias* **HALIBURTON,** JAMES (1761–1837), was the son of William Haliburton (d. 1784), a Scottish builder who had migrated from Roxburghshire to London. In 1776 he was articled to a surveyor named James Dalton, with whom he later entered into a short-lived partnership. In 1785 he began his career as a speculative builder by erecting four 'third-rate' houses on a site in Southwark and subsequently did much building in London and the south-east of England.[1] He soon became the most enterprising and successful London builder of his time, and was largely responsible for the development of the Foundling Hospital, Skinners' and Bedford estates in Bloomsbury, where he built Russell Square (1800–14) and the adjoining streets, the east side of Tavistock Square (dem. 1938), Burton Street and Burton (now Cartwright) Crescent, as well as several of Nash's terraces round Regent's Park, a large part of Regent Street, and Waterloo Place. His readiness to take sites in this way did much to make the Regent Street scheme a financial success. In 1828 Burton turned his attention to St. Leonard's-on-Sea in Sussex, for whose development as a high-class seaside resort he was responsible. Among the buildings which he erected there were the Greek Doric Assembly Rooms (now a Masonic Hall), the Baths, a church and three hotels. By 1833 St. Leonard's was said 'to present the most unique collection of elegant buildings of any watering place on the British coast', and in 1834 a ten-weeks' visit by the Duchess of Kent and Princess Victoria did much to establish the town as a fashionable resort.

To what extent James Burton was his own architect at St. Leonard's and elsewhere, and to what extent he relied on his son Decimus for architectural assistance is not clear. According to the *A.P.S. Dictionary* (*s.v.* 'Parkinson') he had as early as 1788–9 both designed and built the LEVERIAN MUSEUM

[1] Burton's diary mentions several country houses where he was employed as builder and perhaps also as architect. They include alterations to MOOR PARK, SURREY for William Timson (the tenant), 1794–7; LEISTON OLD ABBEY, SUFFOLK, for William Tatnall, 1795; the enlargement of STREATHAM MANOR HOUSE, SURREY (dem. 1982) for Lord William Russell, 1797, and STONEWALL PARK, CHIDDINGSTONE, KENT, for John Woodgate, 1806.

(afterwards the SURREY INSTITUTION) in BLACKFRIARS ROAD, SOUTHWARK (dem.) for James Parkinson, and Elmes states that the RUSSELL INSTITUTION in GREAT CORAM STREET, 1802 (dem.), was erected 'by and from the designs of James Burton, Esq.' [*Metropolitan Improvements*, 1832, 132 and plate]. But at St. Leonard's the new town is said in a contemporary source (Robson's *Commercial Directory* of 1838) to have been built 'upon the plans of Decimus Burton, the Architect', and here only ST. LEONARD'S CHURCH (1831–4, dem. 1944), an elementary essay in lancet Gothic, is known to have been designed by James himself. According to Elmes (*op. cit*, 29) Burton's London villa, THE HOLME in REGENT'S PARK, built 1817–18, was designed by Decimus, but as he was only 17 at the time it seems likely that it was a case of collaboration between father and son. The country house which he built for himself at QUARRY HILL, nr. TONBRIDGE, in about 1803–5 appears to have been designed for him by J. T. Parkinson (*q. v.*), son of the proprietor of the Leverian Museum. It is illustrated in Brayley's *Beauties of England and Wales* viii, 1808, 1295, where it is described as 'erected with the appropriate materials of the country, as a fragment of a castle, but replete with modern conveniences'.

Burton was Master of the Tylers' and Bricklayers' Company in 1801–2. He was a magistrate in Kent and Sheriff of the county in 1810. He died at St. Leonard's on 31 March 1837, and is commemorated both by a monument in the burial-ground there and by a later memorial by the side of the roadway at the junction of Marina and Grand Parade. The third of his twelve children, James, became a pupil of Sir John Soane for a few months, but gave up architecture for the law, and subsequently took up Egyptology. His tenth son, Decimus, is noticed above. The eleventh, Alfred (1802–77), gained some architectural experience in his brother's office, and exhibited a few drawings at the Royal Academy in 1827–31, but succeeded in 1837 to his father's interest and property in St. Leonard's and spent the rest of his life there.

A copy of part of a notebook and diary kept by Burton from 1784 to 1811 is in the Hastings Museum, as is a portrait by E. U. Eddis. There is a copy of the sale catalogue of his library in the British Library (S.C.W. 33 (6)).

[R. Dobie, *The History of the United Parishes of St. Giles in the Fields and St. George Bloomsbury*, 1829, 144–9; *The Watering Places of Great Britain and Fashionable Directory*, Joseph Robins, London 1833, 104–9; John Summerson, *Georgian London*, 1945, 152–6; J. Manwaring Baines, *Burton's St. Leonards*, Hastings 1956; D. J. Olsen, *Town Planning in London*, Yale 1964, 52–3; Christopher Monkhouse, 'St. Leonard's', *C. Life*, 21–28 Feb. 1974; J. Summerson, *The Life and Work of John Nash*, 1980, 82, 85, 118–22; information from Mr. Neil Cooke.]

BUSBY, CHARLES AUGUSTIN (1786–1834), was the eldest son of Dr. Thomas Busby (1755–1838), musician and writer. He became a pupil of D. A. Alexander, from whom he learned the skills not only of building but also of engineering, especially in the use of cast iron for construction. At the same time he studied in the Royal Academy Schools, where he won the Gold Medal in 1807. He exhibited at the Academy every year but one from 1801 (when he was only 15) to 1811. In 1804 he became secretary to the London Architectural Society, a newly-formed association of young architects dissatisfied with the instruction provided by the Royal Academy. Each member was expected to produce an annual essay, and one of Busby's formed the introduction to his first publication, entitled *A Series of Designs for Villas and Country Houses adapted with Economy to the Comforts and to the Elegancies of Modern Life, with Plans and Explanations to Each*, 1808. Several commissions for villas were followed in 1810 by Busby's first public building, the Commercial Rooms at Bristol, intended as a social centre for the mercantile and professional community of the city. Busby's design offered an elegant Ionic temple-front to the street and provided an interior dominated by a 14-foot wide lantern supported by caryatids. In 1812 Busby gained the second premium of £100 in the competition for the design of a new Penitentiary on Millbank, and in 1813 he patented a design for a canal lock.

The lock was not, however, adopted by the Regent's Canal Company, to whom it was offered by Busby, and in 1816 the collapse of a roof designed by him 'on a new principle' threatened to terminate his career as an architect. In 1817 he migrated to North America, where he settled in New York and became a vocal member of the Historical and other societies. He travelled round the eastern seaboard inspecting buildings and studying steamboats (for which he constructed a new form of paddle-wheel, described in 'An Essay on the Propulsion of Navigable Bodies' which he published in the *American Monthly Magazine*, 1818). However, only one major architectural commission (for a theatre in Virginia) came his way, and in 1820 he returned to England. Lacking the means to establish himself in independent practice, he was obliged to accept employment in the office of Francis Goodwin, then busy designing Commissioners' churches. Goodwin, who had solicited more commissions for churches from local committees than the Commissioners would allow one architect to undertake, proposed to pass some of them on to others, including Busby, on the understanding that they would share the fee with him. In this way Busby came to submit designs in his own name for churches at Leeds (Quarry Hill) and Oldham. These were rejected by the Commissioners on the advice of Smirke and Nash, who declared Busby's roofs to be 'extremely weak and insecure'. Busby retaliated by publishing a broadsheet in which his roofs were approved by eight well-known London engineers, but the Church Building Commissioners did not relent.

Dissatisfied with his treatment by Goodwin, Busby left his office in 1822 and in 1823 moved to Brighton, where he entered into partnership with Amon Henry Wilds (*q. v.*). The fashionable and rapidly expanding seaside resort offered great opportunities to the two architects. The principal product of their partnership was the creation of Kemp Town on the eastern outskirts of Brighton, funded by the local landowner Thomas Read Kemp. They were also responsible for the layout of Brunswick Town, Hove, on the estate of the Revd. Thomas Scutt, a project for which Busby was primarily responsible, though a view of it exhibited at the Royal Academy in 1825 bore their joint names. Their relations were, however, unhappy, and the partnership was dissolved in 1825. Busby continued to be the principal architect of Brunswick Town (with the formal status of Surveyor from 1832) and himself engaged in some speculative building which in 1833 ended in bankruptcy. His early death on 18 September 1834 at the age of 48 terminated a career full of vicissitudes, but one that left a legacy of handsome classical terraces in Brighton that gives him an important place in its architectural history.

Besides his *Designs for Villas* (of which there was a second edition in 1835), Busby also published *A Collection of Designs for Modern Embellishments, suitable to Parlours and Dining Rooms, Folding Doors, Chimney Pieces, Verandas, Frizes, etc., on 25 Plates*, 1810.

A miniature portrait of Busby by J. Fruman dated 1807 is in the Victoria and Albert Museum (P. 44–1936). A large collection of architectural drawings by him was acquired by the R.I.B.A. Drawings Collection in 1986.

[*Gent's Mag.* 1811 (ii), 84 (marriage), 1834 (ii), 446 (death); Farington's Diary, 10 Dec. 1807; *Builder* xxi, 1863, 113; A. Dale, *Fashionable Brighton*, 1947, *passim*; Michael Port, 'Francis Goodwin . . . and his Quarrel with C. A. Busby', *Arch. Hist.* i, 1958; Neil Bingham, *C. A. Busby, The Regency Architect of Brighton & Hove*, R.I.B.A. Heinz Gallery 1991; further information from Mr. Bingham.]

CLAPHAM COMMON, SURREY (now LONDON), NIGHTINGALE COTTAGE, NIGHTINGALE LANE, for W. Nunn, 1807 [exhib. at R.A. 1808; Dale, 23].

CLAPHAM COMMON, SURREY (now LONDON), No. 44 SOUTH SIDE, *c.*1808 [R.I.B.A.D., ill. Bingham, 31].

CLAPHAM COMMON, SURREY (now LONDON), design for a villa near, for Mr. Strongitharm, [exhib. at R.A. 1808].

WINDSOR, BERKS., design for a villa to be erected for S. Dixon, exhib. at R.A. 1809.

BRISTOL, THE COMMERCIAL ROOMS, CORN STREET, 1810–11 [exhib. at R.A. 1810; B. Little in *C. Life*, 23 Sept. 1976; Bingham, 32–3].

SERGE HILL HOUSE, nr. ABBOTS LANGLEY, HERTS., 1810 [exhib. at R.A. 1811; Bingham, 35–6].

LONDON, CHAPEL & SCHOOL in CAMBRIDGE HEATH ROAD, BETHNAL GREEN, for the London Society for promoting Christianity among the Jews, 1813–14, with G. Maliphant; dem. 1895 [exhib at R.A. by Maliphant 1814; Bingham, 39–40].

SOMERLEY, HANTS., conservatory and keeper's cottage, for Henry Baring, 1811 [Bingham, 41].

GWRYCH CASTLE, near ABERGELEY, DENBIGHSHIRE, Gothic design for L. B. Hesketh, exhibited at R.A. 1814. This house was designed by Hesketh for himself over a period of years, with assistance from several architects, including Busby, Rickman, Welch and Kennedy. Drawings in the National Library of Wales show that little of Busby's design was executed. See also E. Hubbard, *Clwyd* (The Buildings of Wales), 175–6 and Bingham, 41–2 and pl. VI.

LONDON, THE ROYAL SOCIETY OF ARTS, redecorated the Great Room, 1814–15 [D. G. C. Allan, *The Houses of the Royal Society of Arts*, 1974, 19].

SIDMOUTH, DEVON, POWYS COTTAGE, for Mrs. Powys Floyd, 1815; enlarged 1870s [Bingham, 42–3].

PETERSBURG, VIRGINIA, U.S.A., BOLLINGBROOKE THEATRE, 1817; altered 1860s after a fire; dem. 1920s [Bingham, 48–9].

KEMP TOWN, BRIGHTON, SUSSEX (i.e. SUSSEX SQUARE, LEWES CRESCENT, ARUNDEL TERRACE and CHICHESTER TERRACE), for T. R. Kemp,

1823–*c.*1850, with A. H. Wilds [A. Dale, *Fashionable Brighton*, 1947, chaps. IV–VII; Bingham, chap. 4].

BRUNSWICK TOWN, HOVE, SUSSEX (i.e. BRUNSWICK SQUARE, BRUNSWICK TERRACE, BRUNSWICK STREET EAST and WEST, LOWER BRUNSWICK PLACE, S. end of LANSDOWNE PLACE, LANSDOWNE SQUARE, WESTERN ROAD N. of Brunswick Square, BRUNSWICK MARKET), 1823–*c.*1834 [A. Dale, *op. cit.*, chaps. VIII–X; Bingham, chap. 4].

MAIDENHEAD, BERKS., ST. MARY'S CHURCH, 1824–5, Gothic; chancel added 1877–8; dem. 1964 [J. W. Walker, *History of Maidenhead*, 1931, 32; MS. Vestry Minutes].

BRIGHTON, SUSSEX, ST. GEORGE'S CHAPEL, for T. R. Kemp, 1824–5 [Dale, *op. cit.*, 91]. A complete set of drawings of this chapel is in the P.R.O. (CO 323/144).

BRIGHTON, SUSSEX, PORTLAND PLACE and HOUSE, for Major Villeroy Russell, *c.*1824–28 [exhib. at R.A. 1830; Bingham, 69–70].

BRIGHTON, CAVENDISH PLACE, for the Count of St. Antonio, 1825 [Bingham, 71].

BUSH, THOMAS, was a London surveyor much employed as a measurer. His chief claim to notice appears to be the fact that Sir Robert Smirke (1780–1867) was his pupil. J. W. Higgins (1783–1854) was also articled to him. The evidence he gave to the Commissioners of Military Enquiry on the measurement of barracks in 1805 will be found in their *Fourth Report*, appendices 39 and 48 (*Parliamentary Papers*, vol. 7, part i, 1807).

BUTTERWORTH, JOSEPH (–1849), of Manchester, is at present known only as the architect of OLDHAM TOWN HALL, LANCS., 1840–1, enlarged 1879–80 [*Oldham: Jubilee of its Incorporation*, 1899, *ex inf.* Mr. W. J. Smith]. In the 1830s he was in partnership with A. W. Mills, but by 1843 Slater's *Directory of Manchester* gives 'Butterworth & Whitaker' as architects practising in partnership. Butterworth died intestate on 12 Jan. 1849 [Administration in Lancs. C.R.O., *ex inf.* Dr. Janet Gnosspelius].

BUXTON, JOHN (1685–1731), was a Norfolk squire who had some ability as an amateur architect. He was the son and heir of Robert Buxton (d. 1691) of Channons Hall, Tibenham (between Norwich and Diss), and Shadwell, nr. Thetford, and also inherited the Earsham estate near Bungay from his mother Elizabeth (*née* Gooch). Buxton's architectural skill is attested both by local historians and by a quantity of sketches which remain among his papers, now in Cambridge University Library. According to Thomas Harrison, the author of *Postwick and Relatives* (written in the mid-eighteenth century, but not published until 1858), Buxton was 'a fine genius very curious in such designs' and designed BIXLEY HALL, NORFOLK (dem. *c.*1900), for his cousin Sir Edward Ward, Bart., besides rebuilding his own house at EARSHAM. In 1721 he sold Earsham to Col. Windham and moved to Channons, but subsequently (1727–30) built a new house for himself at Shadwell called SHADWELL LODGE (completely rebuilt in the nineteenth century by Blore and Teulon and now known as 'Shadwell Park'). At CHANNONS HALL (largely demolished 1784) he carried out extensive repairs, modernized the interior and built new stables in 1721–4. Earsham, his only surviving house, is a plain red-brick building with recessed centre and hipped roofs. To judge from an engraving of Bixley (B.L., Add. MS. 23025, f. 203) and a watercolour of Shadwell (reproduced in *C. Life*, 2 July 1964), they were of similar architectural character.

[Burke's *Landed Gentry, s.v.* 'Buxton of Shadwell'; T. Harrison, *Postwick and Relatives*, 1858; Armstrong, *History of Norfolk*, 1781, 149; R. W. Ketton-Cremer, *Norfolk Portraits*, 1944, 79; Mark Girouard, 'Shadwell Park', *C. Life*, 2–9 July 1964; A. P. Baggs, 'Channons Hall', *Norfolk Archaeology* xxxiv, 1966; Buxton papers in Cambridge University Library, especially Box 29; information from Mr. A. P. Baggs.]

BYFIELD, GEORGE (*c.*1756–1813), is said to have been a pupil of Sir Robert Taylor [*Civil Engineer and Architect's Jnl*, iii, 1840, 147], but it was John Plaw (*q. v.*) to whom he was apprenticed in March 1771 [Freedom Register of the Tylers' & Bricklayers' Company, Guildhall Library MS. 3053/4, p. 62]. He exhibited regularly at the Royal Academy from 1780 onwards. In 1794, and again in 1799, he stood for election as an A.R.A., but without success. From 1803 onwards he acted as surveyor to the estates of the Dean and Chapter of Westminster. He was in partnership with H. H. Seward from 1810 until his death, which took place at his house in Craven Street on 9 August 1813, in his 58th year. J. Mills and J. Phillips were his pupils and John Coney, the architectural draughtsman, was in his office from 1805 to 1808.

At the time of his death Byfield was described as 'an eminent architect, who has built several Gaols, and for many years has made this branch of his profession his particular study'. In addition to the three prisons listed below, he is known to have made designs in 1801 for the new County Gaol at Worcester, but those of Francis Sandys were ultimately preferred. His plans for Downing College, Cambridge, submitted in 1804 to satisfy an order of the Court of Chancery requiring a second design in addition to those of James Wyatt, were also unsuccessful [C. M. Sicca, *Committed to Classicism: the Building of Downing College, Cambridge*, 1987, 140–1]. His country houses have (or had) elegant interiors in the Adam manner, but Brockhampton Chapel is Gothick and the Sessions House at Canterbury shows Greek Revival influence.

[*Gent's Mag.* 1783 (ii), 1064 (marriage); 1813 (ii), 299, 332 (death).]

DOMESTIC ARCHITECTURE

BASSINGBOURNE HALL, TAKELEY, ESSEX, 'a villa now building' and 'new-built lodges' for Sir Peter Parker in Essex were exhib. by Byfield at the R.A. in 1784. Parker had recently bought Bassingbourne Hall (*c.*1750; dem.), but does not appear to have rebuilt it. The lodges still exist on the A120 road.

PERDISWELL PARK, nr. WORCESTER, for Henry Wakeman, 1787–8; destroyed by fire 1956 [exhib. at R.A. 1787–8].

LONDON, No. 4 ST. JAMES'S SQUARE, internal alterations for Marchioness de Grey, 1790 [*Survey of London* xxix, 90–1].

CRAYCOMBE HOUSE, FLADBURY, WORCS., for George Perrott, 1791 [exhib. at R.A. 1790] (*C. Life*, 6 July 1940).

KINNERSLEY CASTLE, HEREFS., 'design for the intended alteration' for Thomas Clutton, exhib. at R.A. 1793.

BOSTON, U.S.A., 'design for a villa to be erected near', exhib. at R.A. 1795.

SALWARPE PARSONAGE, WORCS., alterations, 1795 [signed plan in Diocesan Records, Worcestershire C.R.O.].

COFTON HALL, COFTON HACKETT, WORCS., alterations for Robert Biddulph, 1796 [exhib. at R.A. 1796; signed drawings in Worcestershire C.R.O.].

BRIGHTON, SUSSEX, 'Design for a crescent on the West Cliff', exhib. at R.A. 1797, apparently not executed.

HURLINGHAM HOUSE (now the Hurlingham Club), FULHAM, MIDDLESEX, additions, including façade to river, for John Ellis, 1797–8 [exhib. at R.A. 1798; G. Richardson, *New Vitruvius Britannicus* ii, 1808, pls. 23–4].

MADRESFIELD COURT, WORCS., alterations for William Lygon, cr. Earl Beauchamp, 1799; remodelled 1864–75 by P. C. Hardwick [Farington's Diary, 20 July 1799].

GAYNES HALL, nr. ST. NEOTS, HUNTS., for J. Duberley, *c.* 1800 [exhib. at R.A. 1800].

MICHEL GROVE, nr. POLING, SUSSEX, alterations and additions (Gothic) for Richard Walker, 1801; dem. 1832 [exhib. at R.A. 1801; drawings at Arundel Castle dated 1801].

KENSINGTON, NOEL HOUSE, KENSINGTON GORE, for George Aust, 1804 [T. Faulkner, *History of Kensington*, 1820, 392 and plate].

SPETCHLEY PARK, WORCS., improvements for Robert Berkeley, 1807; rebuilt 1811 [exhib. at R.A. 1807].

PAPWORTH HALL, CAMBS., for C. Madryll Cheere, 1809 [exhib. at R.A. 1808, 1809, 1811].

WESTMINSTER, completed houses on south side of Dean's Yard built by George Hoare in 1758 for Samuel Cox, but left unfinished (with the exception of that in the centre), 1809 [designs in Westminster Abbey Muniments, 52408–9 and P. 29].

PERRIDGE HOUSE, DEVONSHIRE, for H. L. Toll (d. 1844) [R. Ackermann, *Repository of Arts*, 3rd ser., x, 1828, 311].

?WICK HOUSE, ST. JOHN IN BEDWARDINE, WORCESTER, for Thomas Bund (of which 'the two intended new fronts' were exhibited at the R.A. by Byfield's pupil John Phillips in 1790).

PUBLIC BUILDINGS, ETC.

WORCESTER, GUILDHALL, alterations to COUNCIL CHAMBER, 1791 [J. Chambers, *General History of Worcester*, 1819, 302].

WORCESTER, THE HOUSE OF INDUSTRY, 1793–4 [V. Green, *History of Worcester* ii, 1796, 13].

BROCKHAMPTON CHAPEL, nr. BROMYARD, HEREFS., for J. Barnaby, *c.*1799, Gothic [exhib. at R.A. 1799] (*C. Life*, 4 Jan. 1989).

CAMBRIDGE, COUNTY GAOL, 1802–7; dem. 1930 [exhib. at R.A. 1803].

BURY ST. EDMUNDS, SUFFOLK, COUNTY GAOL, 1803 [*Report of the Committee of Aldermen appointed to visit Several Gaols in England*, 1816, 44].

BURY ST. EDMUNDS, SUFFOLK, improvements to courts in SHIRE HALL, 1804; dem. [*Norfolk Chronicle*, 21 Jan. 1804, *ex inf.* Mr. David Cubitt].

KNIGHTSBRIDGE, LONDON, CANNON BREWERY, 1804; dem. 1841 [exhib. at R.A. 1804].

CANTERBURY, KENT, COUNTY GAOL AND SESSIONS HOUSE, LONGPORT, 1806–10 [exhib. at R.A. 1806].

BYRD, or **BIRD,** WILLIAM (1624–), was born in Gloucester and served an apprenticeship of eight years to Walter Nicholls, a mason of that city. He came to Oxford in or about 1647, for in 1681, when giving evidence in a lawsuit, he stated that he had worked in Oxford for thirty-four years. He had a yard in Holywell, and did a considerable business as a monumental sculptor. But he also took large masonry contracts, and in 1689 he stated that 'he hath often been employed in drawing of ground plotts, uprights and making estimates of the same'. On another occasion he said that 'since he has been a Master workman [he] hath in diverse Counties work'd at severall noble buildings too many to be here mentioned and lately in Oxford he built the Arch at New College [over New College Lane] and Edmund Hall Chappell'. The latter was consecrated in 1682, but was not finally completed until 1685–6. Other works carried out by Byrd in Oxford were the stone-carving for Wren's Sheldonian Theatre, 1666–9, including the fourteen 'termains', better known as 'the Emperors' heads', the new doorway into the Divinity School opposite the Theatre, which he made in 1668–9, perhaps under Wren's direction, and the fountain and bason in Tom Quad. at Christ Church in 1670 [R.A. Beddard, 'Christ Church under John Fell', supplement to *Christ Church Annual Report* 1976/77]. In 1683 he contracted to erect the south wing of Winchester Palace to Wren's designs, and it is probable that the plan of the palace, with its stepped-back wings, influenced the Garden Quadrangle at New College, of which Byrd built the inner portion on a similar plan in 1682–4 (the south-east block was added in 1700, and the north-east block in 1707). He was no doubt the 'Mr. Bird' who repaired William of Wykeham's monument in Winchester Cathedral in 1664, and who was employed to restore a defective pier on the south side of Winchester College Chapel in 1671. In 1672–3 he was paid £16 2s. for work on the east window of Worcester Cathedral [Treasurer's Accounts of the Dean and Chapter of Worcester, *ex inf.* Mr. David Whitehead].

Byrd was a prolific and successful monumental sculptor, and in 1658, according to Anthony Wood, he invented a process for painting or staining marble. The date of his death is not known, and it has not been established whether or not the sculptor Francis Bird (1667–1731) was his son. Thomas Wood (*q.v.*) was his apprentice.

[Mrs. J. C. Cole, 'William Byrd, Stonecutter and Mason', *Oxoniensia* xiv, 1949; Mrs. J. C. Cole, 'The Painting or Staining of Marble as practised by William Byrd of Oxford and Others', *Oxoniensia* xvii-xviii, 1952–3; *Oxoniensia* xxiv, 1959, 65; Rupert Gunnis, *Dictionary of British Sculptors*, revised ed. 1968, 55; T. F. Kirby, *Annals of Winchester College*, 1892, 219, 353; *Wren Soc.* vii, 23, 26, 34–6, 61–6; xix, 92–3, 95–6; Oxford University Archives, Vice-Chancellor's Court, 1688/9, Easter Term, 54.]

BYRES, JAMES (1734–1817), was the eldest son of Patrick Byres of Tonley, Aberdeenshire, a Scottish laird of Jacobite principles and Catholic beliefs. Patrick fled to France after the rebellion of 1745, taking with him his son, then twelve years old. James was brought up in France, and served for a time in the French army in Ogilvy's regiment. In 1756 he returned to Britain, but two years later set out for Italy in order to become a painter. In February 1758 Robert Mylne reported that 'a student of painting one Mr. Byers' was on his way from Aberdeen to Rome, and his arrival in May was noted by Hayward. He became a pupil of Raphael Mengs, but did not prove to have sufficient talent to become a successful painter in oils, and after a short period as a miniaturist turned to architecture. This evidently suited him better, for in 1762 he won a prize in the *Concorso Clementino* at the Academy of St. Luke. His design (for a palace) still survives in the Academy's archives. Despite this success (all the more notable because of his foreign nationality) Byres failed to establish an architectural practice, and although he designed buildings for several influential persons, very few of them are known to have been carried out. It is possible that he lacked the temperament to achieve success as a practical architect, but his preference for grandiose compositions in the late Roman baroque tradition of Fuga and Vanvitelli must have put him at a disadvantage in comparison with more up-to-date neo-classical architects such as Mylne and Chambers: certainly the vast columned halls which he designed for his British patrons were unlikely to commend themselves to a generation which was not yet inured to the cold austerities of the Greek Revival.

Instead, Byres became one of the most successful of the cicerones who displayed Rome to English milords on the Grand Tour. It was he who in 1764 spent several weeks showing Edward Gibbon the remains of the Imperial capital, and other celebrated Englishmen who employed him as a guide included Charles Towneley, Lord Clive, and the Dukes of Hamilton, Northumberland and Grafton. Like other 'antiquaries' Byres was an active dealer in antiquities and works of art, and the Portland Vase and Poussin's *Seven Sacraments* both passed through his hands. His explorations were not confined to Rome. In 1766 he toured southern Italy and Sicily in company with one of the Wilbrahams.[1] His jour-

[1] Probably George Wilbraham of Nantwich (1741–1813), afterwards M.P. for Bodmin.

nal, now in the National Library of Scotland (MS. 10339), shows that they visited Pompei, Paestum and other Greek sites. Byres's special interest was, however, in Etruscan antiquities. In 1767 he attempted unsuccessfully to publish a work on the *Etruscan Antiquities of Corneto*. This pioneer venture failed to gain enough support, but the plates, engraved for Byres by Christopher Norton, were eventually published in 1842 by Frank Howard, as *Hypogaei, or Sepulchral Caverns of Tarquinia, by the late James Byres, Esq. of Tonley*. Although chiefly known as an authority on classical antiquity, Byres was consulted by Sir James Hall in connection with his *Essay on Gothic Architecture* of 1813, and Bishop Percy was indebted to him for information about old Italian romances.

For over thirty years Byres was resident in Rome, where he lived close to the Piazza di Spagna. He is known, however, to have visited England from time to time; and in 1779 and again in 1783 he made the long journey from Rome to Scotland and back. His career as a cicerone was brought to an end by the effects of the French Revolution. In 1790 he withdrew to his Aberdeenshire seat of Tonley, where he lived on until his death in September 1817 at the age of 83.

Several portraits of Byres exist, including an oil-painting at the Accademia di S. Luca dated 1767; a paste medallion by Tassie in the Scottish National Portrait Gallery dated 1779; a family group by F. Smuglewicz in the same gallery; a similar painting by the same artist in the collection of Sir Brinsley Ford; an engraved portrait by J. Bogle dated 1782; and a portrait by Raeburn painted at the age of 77 (see J. Greig, *Sir Henry Raeburn*, 1911, 40).

[A. J. M. Gill, *The Families of Moir and Byres*, 1835; Burke's *Landed Gentry, s. v.* 'Moir-Byres'; John Fleming, 'Some Roman Cicerones and Artist-Dealers', *Connoisseur Year-Book*, 1959, 24–6; Basil Skinner, *Scots in Italy in the Eighteenth Century*, National Gallery of Scotland, 1966; D. Stillman, 'British Architects and Italian Architectural Competitions, 1758–1780', *Jnl. Society of Architectural Historians* (of America), xxxii, 1973, 51–4; *I disegni di architettura dell' Archivo storico dell' Accademia di San Luca*, 1974, nos. 605–11; Brinsley Ford, 'James Byres', *Apollo* xcix, 1974, 446–60; Francis Russell, 'Batoni's portrait of Mrs. Sandilands and other portraits from the collection of James Byres', *Burlington Mag.* Feb. 1978, 114–17; Brinsley Ford, 'The Byres Family by Franciszek Smuglewicz', *National Art Collections Fund Review*, 1984, 111–15; H. G. Slade, 'James Byres of Tonley', *Architectural Heritage* ii, 1991; letters in N.L.S., deposit 184; letters from Fr. Thorpe to Lord Arundell of Wardour in Arundell archive in Wilts. C.R.O.]

SLEAT CHURCH, SKYE, monument to Sir James Macdonald (d. 1766), 1768 [signed: Macdonald died in Rome, and in his *Tour to the Hebrides* Boswell records that the monument was made in Rome.]

BROCKLESBY, LINCS., three monuments (to Sir William Pelham, d. 1587, Francis Anderson, d. 1758 and Charles Pelham, d. 1763), made in Rome in 1769–72 for Charles Anderson Pelham, later 1st Lord Yarborough and later erected in the Mausoleum built in 1788–94 to the designs of James Wyatt [J. Lord, 'The Building of the Mausoleum at Brocklesby', *Church Monuments* vii, 1992].

BADMINTON HOUSE, GLOS., chimney-piece in Drawing Room for the Dowager Duchess of Beaufort, 1773 [G. Jackson-Stops in *C. Life*, 9 April 1987, 132].

FYVIE CASTLE, ABERDEENSHIRE, two chimney-pieces (of which that in the Drawing Room survives) for the Hon. William Gordon, 1773 [H. G. Slade, *op. cit.*, 24–5].

WALCOT HALL, SALOP. In 1787–90 Byres was responsible for alterations and additions (including a new portico) for the 2nd Lord Clive, with whom he returned from Italy in 1787 [B.L. Add. MS. 36495, f. 201]. These were modifications to works already in progress under Joseph Bromfield (*q.v.*). Additional expenditure incurred as a result of 'the Plan of Stone Stairs being alter'd by Mr. Byers' is mentioned in the accounts [Salop. C.R.O., Powis 552/9/290]. The stairs were dem. *c.*1935 but the portico survives (*C. Life*, 14 Oct. 1939).

AQUAHORTHIES, nr. INVERURIE, ABERDEENSHIRE, R.C. Seminary (now house), for Bishop George Hay, 1796–99 [H. G. Slade, *op. cit.*, 24].

CLUNY, ABERDEENSHIRE, FRASER FAMILY MAUSOLEUM in churchyard, 1808 [in his will dated 13 Aug. 1811, Byres directs his trustees to erect a mausoleum at Tough, Aberdeenshire, 'exactly similar to one I erected at Cluny for Miss Fraser'. This direction was cancelled by an eke or codicil dated 9 Sept 1816].

Byres' unexecuted designs include a house in ST. ANDREW'S SQUARE, EDINBURGH, for Sir Lawrence Dundas, 1768 (R.I.B.A.D.); a circular domed library for THE COLLEGE OF PHYSICIANS, EDINBURGH, 1768 (College of Physicians, Edinburgh); a mansion at WYNNSTAY, DENBIGHSHIRE, for Sir Watkin Williams-Wynn, 1770 (Wynn Estate Office, Denbigh, illustrated in *C. Life*, 23 March 1972, 689); an altar at WARDOUR CASTLE, WILTSHIRE, for 8th Lord Arundell, 1771 (Wilts. C.R.O.); KING'S COLLEGE, ABERDEEN, 1773 (drawings in King's College Library attributed to Byres by Mr. David Walker); HENHAM HALL, SUFFOLK, for Sir John Rous, cr. Earl of Stradbroke, 1774 (E. Suffolk C.R.O., see Hugh Honour, 'James Byres's Designs for rebuilding Henham Hall', in *The Country Seat*, ed. Colvin & Harris, 1970); CHARLEVILLE FOREST, CO. OFFALY, for the Earl of Charleville, 1789 (sold at Christie's, 15 Dec. 1987).

BYROM, WILLIAM (–1836), was the son-in-law of John Hope of Liverpool (*q. v.*), and succeeded to his practice, which he later handed on to his nephew Samuel Rowland (*q. v.*). He designed the Ionic BRUNSWICK CHAPEL, MOSS STREET, LIVERPOOL, opened 1811, dem.; the UNITARIAN CHAPEL, RENSHAW STREET, LIVERPOOL, 1811, dem.; and a house for himself in PRIORY ROAD, EVERTON, 1812, dem. *c.*1868 [*Builder* xxvii, 1869, 803–4; J. A. Picton, *Memorials of Liverpool* ii, 1875, 241, 368, 423; *Lancs. & Cheshire Record Soc.* 120, 1980, 23 for will proved 1836].

C

CABANEL, RUDOLPH, junior (*c.*1763–1839), was a native of Aix-la-Chapelle (according to some accounts of Liège), who lived in England from his boyhood. He designed the stage of DRURY LANE THEATRE, 1793–4, burned 1809; the ROYAL CIRCUS, afterwards the SURREY, THEATRE, BLACKFRIARS ROAD, 1805–6, erected under the superintendence of James Donaldson, burned 1865 (plate in J. Elmes, *Metropolitan Improvements*); and the ROYAL COBOURG THEATRE (afterwards the 'Old Vic'), WATERLOO ROAD, LAMBETH, 1816–18, reconstructed 1924. In 1794 he was consulted by George Saunders, the architect of the Theatre at Birmingham, 'respecting the Machinery of the Stage', and in 1814 he was employed to carry out alterations by the Proprietors [Minutes of the Proprietors in Birmingham Reference Library]. He was of 'an ingenious and inventive turn of mind', and invented a form of roof which bore his name, besides various mechanical appliances. [Obituary in *Civil Engineer and Architect's Jnl.* 1839 (ii), 118; *Gent's Mag.* 1839 (i), 329; *A.P.S.D.*; Brayley, *Surrey* iii, 399, v, 323.]

CAINE, Captain JOHN, was Master of the Tylers' and Bricklayers' Company in 1675–6 and 1697–8. In 1670–3 he built BREWERS' HALL, ADDLE LANE, LONDON, to the designs of Thomas Whiting (*q.v.*) [building accounts in Guildhall Library, MS. 5502]. He himself designed the TALLOW-CHANDLERS' HALL on DOWGATE HILL, which was built in 1671–3 under his direction [Guildhall Library, MS. 6153/4, Minutes of the Tallow-Chandlers Company; *Builder* cxiii, 10 Aug. 1917] (R.C.H.M., *London* (*City*), 101–3).

CAIRNCROSS, HUGH (–1808) and his son GEORGE (–1819) practised in Edinburgh during the reign of George III. Hugh probably came from Selkirkshire, where a master mason of the same name was active as a bridge-builder in the previous reign. He was a pupil or assistant of Robert Adam, under whom he acted as clerk of works at Culzean and Dalquharran Castles. In December 1791 Adam appointed him to be clerk of works for the new University Building in Edinburgh in place of John Paterson, and he continued in this employment until work stopped in 1795 [A. G. Fraser, *The Building of Old College*, Edinburgh 1989, 119–20].

In 1797 Hugh Cairncross designed ARDGOWAN HOUSE, RENFREWSHIRE, for Sir John Shaw-Stewart, Bart., as stated in Neale's *Views of Seats* vi, 1823, and confirmed by the original drawings signed by Cairncross, now at the Yale Center for British Art. In 1801 he was paid 'for measuring & valuing the work in the finishing of the English and Gaelic Churches at Inveraray' [I. G. Lindsay & Mary Cosh, *Inveraray and the Dukes of Argyll*, 1973, 394, n. 13], and in 1801 he submitted a design for rebuilding Falkirk Church which was not adopted owing to a dispute among the parishioners [S.R.O., GD 171/122]. In 1807 he designed Nos. 12–32 GAYFIELD SQUARE, EDINBURGH [S.R.O., Edinburgh Sasines]. At Dalmeny House there is an unexecuted design by him for developing land on the shores of the Forth at Newhall east of Queensferry.

Hugh Cairncross died at Melrose on 21 July 1808 [*Scots Mag.* lxxi, 1808, 640]. In 1815 his son provided the Lord Provost with a copy of Robert Adam's elevation for the west side of the University Building [Fraser, *op. cit.*, 139], and in the same year 'Mr. Cairncross, an Ordained Measurer', measured work at the new Signet Library [S.R.O., Minutes of the Trustees for Public Buildings, E 343/2, p. 197]. George Cairncross died in January 1819 and was buried in the Greyfriars Cemetery [Register in New Register House, Edinburgh, f. 292].

CALDWELL, ROBERT, was the son of Thomas Caldwell, a builder of Edinburgh.

He practised in Inverness until 1839, when he became a burgess of Edinburgh and opened an office in that city [*Roll of Edinburgh Burgesses*, Scottish Record Soc. 1933, 29]. Advertisements for tenders indicate that he designed CANTRAY HOUSE, CROY, INVERNESS-SHIRE (dem.) for Hugh Davidson in 1833 and BRACKLA HOUSE, nr. CAWDOR, NAIRNSHIRE, for Capt. William Fraser in 1835 [*Inverness Courier*, 7 Jan. 1833, 4 Nov. 1835, *ex inf.* Mr. John Gifford]. In 1836 his designs for PETTY CHURCH, INVERNESS-SHIRE, were superseded by others made by 'an architect from Edinburgh', but he was employed to supervise the execution of the latter [S.R.O., CH 2/553/11, pp. 94, 105–7, 119]. Caldwell also designed THE WEST CHURCH, HUNTLY STREET, INVERNESS, 1837–40, with a clumsy Ionic façade [S.R.O., CH 2/720/14, p. 145].

CALL, Sir JOHN (1732–1801), was a Cornish landowner who had made his fortune in India as a military engineer in the service of the East India Company. He returned to England in 1770, sat in the House of Commons as M.P. for Callington from 1784 to 1801, and took an active interest in agricultural affairs. His experience as a military engineer gave him sufficient competence as an architect to design BODMIN GAOL, CORNWALL, 1779, with Thomas Jones of Exeter (*q.v.*) as executant [*The Bodmin Register*, 1838, 111]. The gaol (rebuilt in the 19th century) is shown in the background of a portrait of Call sold at Sotheby's on 16 July 1986. Call probably designed his own residence, WHITEFORD HOUSE, STOKE CLIMSLAND, CORNWALL, 1775, a plain Georgian house dem. in 1913 [*D.N.B.; The House of Commons (History of Parliament) 1790–1820* iii, 1986, 359; Alistair Forsyth, 'Whiteford House', Duchy of Cornwall *Digest* iv, 1984, 30–37; further information from Mr. Forsyth].

CALVERT, JOHN (–*c.*1795), was an architect and builder of Swansea, where he repaired the parish church, paved the market-place, built a theatre (*c.*1785) and left his name in Calvert Street. As a builder he erected SLEBECH PARK, PEMBROKESHIRE, for John Symmons, probably to another's designs. In 1779 a lawsuit between himself and Symmons over his charges was settled in his favour [*Hereford Jnl.* 1779]. In 1782 he made plans for alterations to GOLDEN GROVE, CARMARTHENSHIRE, for John Vaughan [*Trans. Cymmrodorion Soc.* 1966 (i), 201], and a volume of drawings formerly in the collection of Sir Albert Richardson (dispersed by sale, 1983) contained designs probably by him for various houses including CASTELLAU, GLAMORGANSHIRE (cf. R.C.A.M. Wales, *Glamorgan* iv, 318–23). Calvert advertised a 'patent slating' in the *Hereford Journal* in 1784 and projected a tunnel under the River Severn at Aust. He died some time between 1794 and 1798 [T. Lloyd, 'The Architects of Regency Swansea', *Gower* 41, 1990; further information from Mr. Lloyd].

CAMELFORD, LORD, *see* PITT, THOMAS.

CAMERON, CHARLES (1745–1812), was the son of Walter Cameron, a carpenter and builder of Scottish origin established in London. He was apprenticed to his father in 1760, but subsequently became a pupil of the architect Isaac Ware who, like his father, was a member of the London Carpenters' Company. When Ware died in 1766, Cameron decided to carry out a project which Ware had formed for a new edition of Lord Burlington's *Fabbriche Antiche.* Unlike Ware, however, Cameron proposed to go to Rome in person in order to correct and complete the imperfect drawings of the Roman baths by Palladio which Burlington had used in his publication. In 1767 at the Free Society of Artists exhibition he showed six 'proof prints of ancient Thermae, intended for the work which is publishing', and by 1768 he was busy examining and drawing the original structures in Rome in a spirit of serious archaeological inquiry. Not only did he survey the remains of the 'Baths of Titus' (actually those of Trajan), but he penetrated into some parts of the Golden House of Nero beneath that were not rediscovered until the early twentieth century. The drawings which Cameron eventually published in 1772 as *The Baths of the Romans explained and illustrated, with the Restorations of Palladio corrected and improved*, with identical English and French texts, was a careful and scholarly work which served, as it was intended to do, as a text-book of neo-classical ornament and design. It was dedicated to Lord Bute, whose patronage Cameron no doubt hoped to attract. New issues of the book appeared in 1774 and 1775.

While in Rome Cameron appears to have claimed Jacobite sympathies and connections which had no basis in fact, but were calculated to gain him credit both in the Vatican and among influential exiles such as the Abbé Grant.

Apart from the publication of his book, and the exhibition of some of the original drawings at the Society of Artists (1772), Cameron's activities between his return from Italy (apparently in 1769) and his departure to Russia (probably in 1778) are by no means clear. The authenticity of a portrait painted by Robert Hunter in Dublin in 1771 or 1773 is too doubtful to be taken as proof of a sojourn in Ireland. In 1774, when he applied for one of the new district surveyorships in Middlesex he was not interviewed, 'being absent'. In 1775 he published two etchings, one of a silver vessel found in Rome, the other of a design for a shell-shaped vessel by Giulio Romano (Yale Center for British Art). Of his employment as an architect during this period the only evidence relates to a house in Hanover Square (No. 15, dem.) built by his father and others in 1770–4 for Jervoise Clarke. One of the bills is signed 'Charles Cameron Architectus' [Hants. C.R.O., 6 M 59]. It is an account for marble supplied by the statuary mason Thomas Carter, and in 1774 Carter was one of those who sponsored Cameron's application for the district surveyorship. A design for an Adam-type ceiling in the Soane Museum (xliv, set 9, no. 15), signed by Cameron, was very likely for this house. Subsequent litigation between Jervoise Clarke and Walter Cameron over property in White House Street, Piccadilly, ended to the latter's disadvantage, and in his financial difficulties he sold a large number of books, prints, busts and pictures belonging to his son, which the latter valued at £1500. Failing to recover them, Charles took proceedings against his father which resulted in the latter's imprisonment in the Fleet. This affair, and some story of Cameron's misbehaviour with one of Ware's daughters, were to be remembered to his disadvantage when in 1791 he was considered for honorary membership of the newly established Architects' Club, but was rejected by those 'who wished we might have only men of moral character and high reputation'.

By 1779 Cameron had begun a new life as architect to the Empress Catherine of Russia. The Empress was an enthusiastic patron of artists from Western Europe, and Cameron, whose book would have made his name known in architectural circles abroad, appears to have gone to Russia by invitation. Thus by 1779 the Empress had secured the services of one whom she subsequently described as 'Mr. Cameron, écossais de nation, Jacobite de profession, grand dessinateur, nourri d'antiquités, connu par un livre sur les bains romains'. For the rest of his life Cameron was a Russian court architect. For Catherine he worked chiefly at the PALACE OF TSARSKOE SELO, nr. ST. PETERSBURG, to which he made extensive additions, including the Cold Baths, the Agate Pavilion, the colonnaded gallery known as the 'Cameron Gallery', the Empress's private apartments and other important buildings later demolished. Simultaneously Cameron was designing the adjoining town of SOFIA (demolished with the exception of the neo-classical cathedral), and also the palace and village of PAVLOVSK for the Grand Duke Paul.

Tsarskoe Selo, Sofia and Pavlovsk together formed a vast urban and landscape development, much of which was destroyed by Catherine's successors, Paul and Alexander I. In the Crimea Cameron carried out important alterations to the Empress's palace of BAKHTCHI-SERAI, probably in connection with her visit in 1787. In 1793 J. L. Bond (*q.v.*) exhibited at the Royal Academy a drawing of a triumphal arch 'to be erected in the Crimea by C. Cameron Esq., architect to the Empress of Russia'. This was probably the one at Bakhtchi-serai. In 1795 Cameron designed a gallery and triumphal arch to be erected at Gatchina, but Catherine died before either had been built.

After Catherine's death in 1796 Cameron was dismissed by the Emperor Paul, who had already quarrelled with him over the cost of the work at Pavlovsk and was determined to reverse all his mother's policies. Unemployed and deprived even of his house, Cameron was for a time in considerable financial difficulties. He may have found private employment in the provinces, and there is an unauthenticated story that he returned to England for a period. By 1800, however, he appears to have been back at Pavlovsk, where soon afterwards he designed the elegant Ionic Pavilion of the Three Graces for the Empress Marie-Feodorovna. In 1803 the new Emperor, Alexander I, gave him the post of Architect to the Admiralty, in which capacity he designed a number of buildings, of which the most important was the NAVAL HOSPITAL at ORANIENBAUM, 1803–5. A design for a NAVAL CATHEDRAL at KRONSTADT in a mannered neo-classical style was still on the drawing-board when Cameron was dismissed in 1805 and succeeded by A. D. Zakharov. Early in 1812 he died at St. Petersburg, leaving a widow who later in the year dispersed his library and drawings by sale.

Despite the destruction of so much of what he built round Tsarskoe Selo, it is clear that Cameron was one of the major urban architects of the eighteenth century. He was also an accomplished designer and decorator in a neo-classical style that has affinities with that of Robert Adam. Like Adam he had first-hand knowledge of the Roman sources of neo-classical ornament, and although he may well have seen some of Adam's early works in England, his style is sufficiently individual to exonerate him from the imputation of being merely an imitator. Like Adam he insisted on designing every detail of furniture in the buildings for which he was responsible. At Tsarskoe Selo he produced some of the most exquisitely elegant interiors in eighteenth-century Europe. His use of colour was particularly effective. In the Agate Pavilion he set red agate columns with gilt bronze capitals against green jasper walls to achieve a rich polychromatic effect. Although in some respects still a Palladian, Cameron was a pioneer of the Greek Revival in Russia, notably in the Greek Doric Temple of Friendship at Pavlovsk, designed *c.*1780.

The main collection of Cameron's surviving architectural drawings is in the Hermitage Museum at St. Petersburg. Other drawings in Russian collections are listed on p. 27 of the Arts Council catalogue (see below) or mentioned by Shvidkovski. A portrait by A. O. Orlovsky, dated 1809, is illustrated by Isobel Rae and others.

[G. Loukomski, *Charles Cameron*, 1943; D. Stroud, *Henry Holland*, 1966, 135–6; *Charles Cameron*, catalogue of the Arts Council Exhibition, 1967–8, with text by Tamara Talbot-Rice and A. A. Tait; Isobel Rae, *Charles Cameron*, 1971; A. A. Tait, 'Cameron and the beginning of Neo-Classicism in Russia', *Architectural Association Files* i, 1981–2; Dmitri Shvidkovski, 'Cameron Discoveries', *Arch. Rev.* Dec. 1982, 'The Empress and the Architect', *C. Life*, 16 Nov. 1989; J. M. Robinson, 'Charles Cameron, the lost early years', *Apollo*, Jan. 1992; F. Salmon, 'Charles Cameron and Nero's Domus Aurea', *Arch. Hist.* 36, 1993.]

CAMPBELL, COLEN (1676–1729), began life as a Scottish lawyer. He was the eldest son of Donald Campbell, a younger brother of Sir Hugh Campbell of Cawdor Castle in Nairnshire. Donald Campbell was the laird of Boghole and Urchany, two small Nairnshire estates which had been given to him by his brother. These estates Colen Campbell inherited at the age of four when his father died in 1680. Of his subsequent upbringing there appears to be no record, but he was reputed to have had 'a liberal education' and he may have been the Colin Campbell who graduated from Edinburgh University in July 1695. It is much less likely that he was the person of the same name who signed the Visitors' Book of Padua University in 1697.[1] But he had probably been to Italy, for in 1715 or 1716, in a petition to King George I, he stated that he had 'studied Architecture here and abroad for several years'. What is certain is that in 1702 he was admitted to the Faculty of Advocates at Edinburgh, having 'past his tryalls as ane lawier' with the reputation of being 'the best civilian that past since the Revolutione'. For the next few years he practised as a lawyer in Edinburgh. He was still described as 'Doctor of Laws' when he designed the Rolls House in London in 1717, but by then he was already established as an architectural designer and publicist.

Exactly how Campbell made the transition from law to architecture is not known. There are, however, indications that he was in some way associated with James Smith (*c.*1645–1731, *q.v.*), whom he was to describe in *Vitruvius Britannicus* as 'the most experienced architect' in Scotland. Together with the drawings by Campbell himself in the R.I.B.A. Drawings Collection there are a number of drawings which are almost certainly by Smith (see below, p. 894). Some of these drawings relate to buildings known to have been designed by Smith, others were drawn for, or at least formed the basis of, plates in *Vitruvius Britannicus*, and others are studies on Palladian themes. None is dated, but as Smith was Campbell's senior by thirty years, there is a strong probability that Campbell was in some sense his pupil. Moreover, the presence of the Palladian studies, and the fact that Smith is known to have travelled in Italy, may suggest that he not only instructed Campbell in the practice of architecture, but also directed his attention to the architecture of Palladio. However this may be, it was as the propagandist of the Palladian movement in British architecture that Campbell made his name. *Vitruvius Britannicus* was conceived in about 1713 as a printsellers' publication akin to Kip's *Britannia Illustrata* (1707), but of a more strictly architectural character, with plans and elevations rather than perspective views. Campbell was brought in at a late stage when it was thought expedient to add a fashionably Palladian content to a book otherwise devoted to English baroque buildings, and his name was clumsily added to a title-page that had already been engraved without any author's name. Campbell introduced a number of his own designs, both executed and unexecuted, and wrote a polemical introduction that says little about the buildings by other contemporary architects that are illustrated, but extols those of a Palladian character. In the notes to individual plates he is, however, complimentary to Wren, Hawksmoor and other architects who had

[1] Mr. J. G. Dunbar kindly informs me that the Colin Campbell in question was probably an illegitimate son of the Earl of Breadalbane. This Colin Campbell was tutor to a gentleman named William Moncreiffe who signed the Visitors' Book at the same time.

contributed drawings of their works, especially Vanbrugh, but his rival Gibbs is studiously ignored and by implication criticized as the chief English exponent of the 'affected and licentious' forms of Italian baroque that he held up for condemnation. In this way what was ostensibly a representative collection of plates of modern British architecture, both public and private, became partly an advertisement for Campbell himself and partly a means of advocating the superiority of the 'Antique Simplicity' represented by Palladianism. The 'renowned Palladio' and the 'famous Inigo Jones' were held up for admiration, and the works (both authentic and reputed) of the latter figured prominently in the three folio volumes which were published by subscription in 1715, 1717 and 1725. They were reissued in 1731, and an extra plate of Umberslade Hall, Warwickshire, is found in this edition of the third volume. There is a modern reprint by Benjamin Blom, with an index volume by Paul Breman (1972).

The first volume of *Vitruvius Britannicus* was dedicated to George I, who acknowledged the compliment with two gifts, one of 30 guineas in 1717, the other of £30 in 1725. It was, however, to private rather than royal patronage that Campbell was chiefly indebted. As early as December 1708 he had made a first bid for architectural office. The post which he then coveted appears to have been the office of Master of Works in Scotland, previously held by Sir William Bruce and after him by James Smith. Nothing came of this attempt, and ten years elapsed before William Benson, having supplanted Wren as Surveyor of the King's Works, made Campbell Chief Clerk and Deputy Surveyor (Sept. 1718). Benson, though a disastrous failure as head of the Office of Works, had genuine architectural interests, and Campbell may possibly have had something to do with his country house in Wiltshire, an early essay in Jonesian revivalism dating from 1710 and duly illustrated in *Vitruvius Britannicus*. In July 1719 Campbell shared in Benson's disgrace, losing both his offices. His appointment in December 1719 as Architect to the Prince of Wales does not appear to have carried with it any salary and did not lead to any important commission for the prince, though Campbell found several new clients among the members of his court. But in Lord Burlington he soon found a new patron for whom building was a ruling passion. The publication of *Vitruvius Britannicus* probably helped to rouse Burlington's interest in architecture, and in 1719 he employed Campbell to remodel his town house in the Palladian style. Later Burlington dropped Campbell in favour of Kent and Flitcroft, but Campbell's subsequent patrons included such rich and influential men as Sir Robert Walpole, Henry Hoare, John Aislabie and the Earl of Pembroke. In 1726 he succeeded Vanbrugh as Surveyor of Greenwich Hospital, and in 1728 he published an improved translation of Palladio's *First Book of Architecture*. This was reissued the following year as *Palladio's Five Orders of Architecture*, with the addition of 5 plates of Campbell's own designs at the end.

Campbell was taken ill in Norfolk in the summer of 1729, and died at his house in Brook Street, London, on or about 13 September. He was buried in the south cloister of Westminster Abbey without any memorial. His estate, which included two London houses, was reputed to be worth £12,000. It was disputed between his wife Jane and his sister Henrietta Grant, who claimed that though Jane lived with Campbell as his wife, they were never legally married. A portrait of Campbell is mentioned in Jane Campbell's will (1738), but its present location is unknown. The head of an architect which forms part of the plaster decoration of Compton Place, Sussex, is supposed (probably rightly) to represent Campbell.

Although he came late to architecture and died in middle age, Campbell was one of the oustanding figures in English eighteenth-century architecture. But for Benson's fall, Campbell, as his Deputy, might have led the Palladian revolution in the Office of Works. As it was, the only royal work that can be attributed to him is the new suite of State Apartments at Kensington Palace, and the evidence for this is by no means conclusive (see *History of the King's Works* v, 196). As a country-house architect, however, Campbell was responsible for some of the key buildings of the Palladian movement. At Wanstead he provided the Palladian answer to Blenheim and Castle Howard – a country house of the first rank conceived in strictly classical terms. It was, in Summerson's words, 'to prove a classic statement by which English country houses were influenced, directly or indirectly, for more than a century', and among its more obvious progeny were Wentworth Woodhouse, Prior Park and Nostell Priory. At Houghton he Palladianized the standard English country house of the late seventeenth century, accenting its principal features with a portico, Venetian windows and (in the engraved design) pedimented towers from Wilton, in a manner that was to be imitated at Lydiard Tregoze, Croome Court, Hagley, Newnham Paddox, Fisherwick and elsewhere. At Mereworth he built 'the first and closest of the four English reproductions of Palladio's Villa Capra at Vicenza', and at Newby and Stourhead he designed the first of a new generation of relatively small but highly finished country houses based on the model of the Palladian villa. Thus between 1715 and 1725 Campbell established the prototypes from which the Palladian country house was to develop. When he died in 1729 the Palladian revolution was accomplished, and although it had complex origins, it was to Campbell that it owed some of its most characteristic architectural forms.

In 1750 'the Original Drawings of Gentlemen's Seats, with Plans and Elevations, &c., by that Great Architect, Collin Campbell', were advertised for sale by auction in London [*General Advertiser*, 13 Dec. 1750], and in 1966 a large collection of drawings by Campbell was found in two Yorkshire country houses – Newby Hall and Studley Royal. These drawings, which appear to have belonged to Earl de Grey (*q.v.*), were in 1967 presented to the R.I.B.A. Drawings Collection by the Wates Foundation. A further collection of original drawings for *Vitruvius Britannicus*, formerly at Nostell Priory, was given to the same Collection in 1973. Both collections are described in the *R.I.B.A. Drawings Catalogue*.

[*A.P.S.D.*; H. E. Stutchbury, *The Architecture of Colen Campbell*, Manchester 1967; G. L. M. Goodfellow, 'Colin Campbell', *Arch. Rev.* Aug. 1966; *Arch. Rev.* Feb. 1967, 95 (correspondence); G. L. M. Goodfellow, 'Colin Campbell's Last Years', *Burlington Mag.* cxi, April 1969, 185–191; H. M. Colvin, 'A Scottish Origin for English Palladianism?' with note by T. P. Connor on 'Colen Campbell Abroad', *Arch. Hist.* xvii, 1974; T. P. Connor, 'The Making of Vitruvius Britannicus', *Arch. Hist.* xx, 1977; T. P. Connor, 'Colen Campbell as Architect to the Prince of Wales', *Arch. Hist.* xxii, 1979; Eileen Harris, 'Vitruvius Britannicus before Colen Campbell', *Burlington Mag.* May 1986; Eileen Harris, *British Architectural Books and Writters 1556–1785*, 1990, 139–47, 359–61; *The History of the King's Works* v, 1976, *passim*; letters at Cawdor Castle, *ex inf.* Mr. J. G. Dunbar and Mr. T. P. Connor; Privy Purse Accounts of George I in Worcs. C.R.O.; Bodleian Library, MS. Rawlinson D. 923, f. 34 (dispute over estate); will (P.C.C. 243 ABBOTT).]

GLASGOW, SHAWFIELD MANSION, for Daniel Campbell, M.P., 1711–12; dem. 1792 [*Vitruvius Britannicus* ii, pl. 51; G. L. M. Goodfellow, 'Colin Campbell's Shawfield Mansion in Glasgow', *Jnl. Soc. Architectural Historians* xxiii, 1964].

WANSTEAD HOUSE, ESSEX, for Sir Richard Child, cr. Earl of Tylney, *c.*1714–20; dem. 1824 [*Vitruvius Britannicus* i, pls. 21–2 (the first design), 23–6 (the second design, more or less as executed); iii, pls. 39–41 (the third design, showing unexecuted additions)]. For views of the house as built see a sheet of engravings by Rocque dated 1735, Watts's *Seats* (1783) and Angus's *Seats* (1800). For the gardens see I. Dunlop & Fiske Kimball in *C. Life*, 28 July 1950. Some fittings are now at Wanstead House, Cambridge, and there are two chimney-pieces at Chillingham Castle, Northumberland.

CHESTER-LE-STREET, CO. DURHAM, house for John Hedworth, 1716, probably not built [*Vitruvius Britannicus* ii, pl. 88]. A detailed but undated 'Explanation' by Vanbrugh of his design for a house for Mr. Hedworth, sold at Sotheby's on 24–5 Jan. 1955 (now at Getty Center, California), may represent a rival scheme. The former seat of the Hedworth family at Harraton Hall, nr. Chester-le-Street, had passed by marriage to the Lambtons in 1688, and John Hedworth's branch of the family lived at the house called Chester Deanery.

BEVERLEY, YORKS. (E.R.), house in Eastgate for Sir Charles Hotham, Bart., 1716–20; dem. *c.*1760 [*Vitruvius Britannicus* ii, pl. 87; building accounts among Hotham papers in E. Yorks. R.O.]. A sketch of the house in Bodleian, Gough Maps 229, f. 273, shows that Campbell's design was not exactly followed in execution: in particular the rusticated arches linking the wings to the centre were omitted.

LONDON, THE ROLLS HOUSE, CHANCERY LANE, 1717–24; dem. 1895–6 [*Vitruvius Britannicus* iii, pls. 44–5; *History of the King's Works* v, 358] (chimney-pieces illustrated in *Arch. Rev.* xlviii, 1920, 23, 76).

EBBERSTON LODGE, nr. SCARBOROUGH, YORKS. (N.R.), for William Thompson (of Humbleton), 1718 [*Vitruvius Britannicus* iii, pl. 47] (S. D. Kitson in *Arch. Rev.* xxvi, 1909, 231; Arthur Oswald in *C. Life*, 7–14 Oct. 1954).

LONDON, BURLINGTON HOUSE, PICCADILLY, remodelled the front and designed the gateway to Piccadilly for 3rd Earl of Burlington, 1718–19; gateway dem. and front remodelled by E. M. Barry 1868 [*Vitruvius Britannicus* iii, pls. 22–5; *Survey of London* xxxii, 390–429 and illustrations].

LONDON, Nos. 31, 32, 33 and 34 OLD BURLINGTON STREET, 1718–23 [*Survey of London* xxxii, 508–17 and illustrations].

LONDON, CHANCERY LANE, nine houses on the Rolls Estate for Sir Joseph Jekyll, Master of the Rolls, 1719; dem. [*History of the King's Works* v, 358].

LONDON, THE BURLINGTON SCHOOL FOR GIRLS, BOYLE STREET, 1719–21; dem. 1937. Campbell was involved in this building as the representative of Lord Burlington, but how far (if at all) he was responsible for the design is not clear [*Survey of London* xxxii, 541–2].

WIMBLEDON, SURREY. In 1720 Colen Campbell and John Gould received £70 as 'overseers' of a new house here for Sir Theodore Janssen, Bart., which was unfinished at the seizure of his estates in 1721. Its subsequent history is not clear. [*The Particulars and Inventories of the Estates of the Late . . . Directors of the South-Sea Company*, 1721, 43–4].

LONDON, LEICESTER HOUSE, LEICESTER SQUARE, minor alterations for George, Prince of Wales, 1720–4; dem. 1792 [*Survey of London* xxxiv, 447].

MEREWORTH CASTLE, KENT, for the Hon. John Fane, afterwards 7th Earl of Westmorland, *c.*1720–5 [*Vitruvius Britannicus* iii, pls. 35–8]. The detached wings were built *c.*1740. (*C. Life*, 12, 19, 26 June 1920; H. A. Tipping, *English Homes, Period V*, vol. i, 1921, 39–66; C. Hussey, *English Country Houses: Early Georgian*, 1955, 58–65).

NEWBY (now BALDERSBY) PARK, YORKS. (N.R.), for Sir William Robinson, Bart., 1720–8; interior rebuilt after fire in 1902 [*Vitruvius Britannicus* iii, pl. 46; Lindsay Boynton in *The Country Seat*, ed. Colvin & Harris, 1970, 97–105].

STOURHEAD, WILTS., for Henry Hoare, *c.*1720–4; wings added 1793–5; portico (to Campbell's original design) 1841; centre restored after fire in 1902 [*Vitruvius Britannicus* iii, pls. 41–3; K. Woodbridge, *Landscape and Antiquity*, 1970, chap. 1] (C. Hussey, *English Country Houses: Mid Georgian*, 1956, 234–8).

HOUGHTON HALL, NORFOLK, for Sir Robert Walpole, begun 1722 to Campbell's designs under the supervision of T. Ripley, and completed 1735 with some modifications (e.g. to the towers by Gibbs and to the interior by Kent) [*Vitruvius Britannicus* iii, pls. 27–34] (Isaac Ware, *The Plans, Elevations and Sections of Houghton*, 1735; *C. Life*, 1, 8, 15, 22 Jan. 1921; H. A. Tipping, *English Homes, Period V*, vol. i, 1921, 67–110; C. Hussey, *English Country Houses: Early Georgian*, 1955, 72–86). For the possible involvement of Gibbs at an early stage, see J. Harris, 'Who designed Houghton?', *C. Life*, 2 March 1989.

WAVERLEY ABBEY, SURREY, for John Aislabie, *c.*1723–5; wings added by T. O. Hunter *c.*1750; centre altered or rebuilt by Sir Robert Rich *c.*1780; further alterations after fire in 1833 [T. P. Connor, 'A late villa by Colen Campbell', *Burlington Mag.* June 1982, 361–2].

LONDON, PEMBROKE HOUSE, WHITEHALL, for Henry Herbert, afterwards 9th Earl of Pembroke, 1724; rebuilt 1757; dem. 1913 [*Vitruvius Britannicus* iii, pl. 48; *Survey of London* xiii, 167–75]. An original elevation, dated August 1723, is in the Lister Collection in the Treasury Library, Whitehall, no. 52b. For an alternative design by William Dickinson dated 1723 see *Wren Soc.* xvii, pl. xlviii.

NOTTINGHAM, house in Stoney Street (north side of St. Mary's Churchyard), for John Plumptre, M.P., 1724; dem. 1853 [*Vitruvius Britannicus* iii, pl. 55]. For drawings connected with this house in Nottingham City Library see Stutchbury, *op. cit.*, Appendix vi.

HALL BARN, nr. BEACONSFIELD, BUCKS., the GREAT ROOM (Garden House) for Edmund Waller, 1724; largely destroyed by fire *c.*1840, but doorway and windows survive reset [*Vitruvius Britannicus* iii, pls. 49–50] (*C. Life*, 27 March 1942). For Waller's relationship to John Aislabie see R. Sedgwick, *The House of Commons 1715–54* ii, 1970, 505–6.

GOODWOOD HOUSE, SUSSEX, kitchen for 2nd Duke of Richmond, 1724, followed by an unexecuted design for a new house published in *Vitruvius Britannicus* iii, 1725, pls. 51–4 [T. P. Connor, 'Architecture and Planting at Goodwood', *Sussex Archl. Colls.* 117, 1979].

LONDON, Nos. 76 and 78 BROOK STREET, 1725–6. No. 76, which survives, was Campbell's own house, and his designs for the interiors are illustrated in his *Five Orders of Architecture* (1729) [G. L. M. Goodfellow in *Burlington Mag.* cxi, April 1969, 185–6; *Survey of London* xl, 16–17].

COMPTON PLACE, EASTBOURNE, SUSSEX, reconstructed for Sir Spencer Compton, cr. Lord (later Earl of) Wilmington, 1726–7 [H. A. Tipping, *English Homes, Period V*, vol. i, 134–7; C. Hussey, *English Country Houses, Early Georgian*, 1955, 87–96; G. L. M. Goodfellow in *Burl. Mag.* cxi, April 1969, 186–9].

HACKNEY, MIDDLESEX, house for Stamp Brooksbank, 1728; dem. *c.*1796 [plates in Campbell's *Five Orders of Architecture*, 1729] (view in W. Robinson, *History of Hackney*, 1842, 117).

STUDLEY ROYAL, YORKS. (W.R.), designs and

architectural advice for John Aislabie, *c.*1729. Campbell is known to have given advice about the quadrangular Palladian stables (completed 1731) just before his death in 1729, and the Banqueting House can probably be attributed to him on stylistic grounds [G. W. Beard in *C. Life* 10 Aug. 1961; G. L. M. Goodfellow in *Burlington Mag.* cxi, April 1969, 187–9; G. Worsley in *C. Life*, 1 Oct. 1987].

UNEXECUTED DESIGNS

Included in *Vitruvius Britannicus* are various designs for houses based on Palladian sources identified in Stutchbury, *op. cit.*, Appendix V; a design for a large and monumental domed church in Lincoln's Inn Fields, made 'at the desire of some Persons of Quality and Distinction' in 1712 (i, pls. 8–9); and a design for Westminster Bridge, *c.*1722 (iii, pl. 56).

In 1712 Campbell is recorded to have submitted designs for churches to the Commissioners for building Fifty New Churches (Minutes of the Committee in Lambeth Palace Library, 25 July 1712, MS. 2693, 11–12). These may possibly be the church designs in the R.I.B.A. Collection.

Unexecuted projects for country houses include a pair of plans (based on Palladio's Villa Emo) for ARDKINGLAS HOUSE, ARGYLLSHIRE, preserved at Inveraray Castle, the scheme for GOODWOOD HOUSE, SUSSEX, mentioned above, and designs for LOWTHER CASTLE, WESTMORLAND, published in *Architectural Drawings from Lowther Castle*, ed. Colvin, Crook and Friedman, Society of Architectural Historians of G.B. Monograph No. 2, 1980.

An important design for a uniform palatial treatment of 'seven new intended Houses on the East Side of Grosvenor Sqr.' is represented by an engraved plan and elevation, signed and dated 1725, in the volume of prints in the Gibbs Collection at the Ashmolean Museum, Oxford.

CAMPBELL, DUGAL (–1757) was a military engineer by profession. His recorded career begins in 1734, when he became a Sub-Engineer in the Civil Branch of the Ordnance. In 1739 he was appointed clerk of works to the Ordnance establishment in the Tower of London. In 1742 he was promoted to the rank of Engineer Extraordinary, in 1744 to that of Engineer in Ordinary, and in 1757 to that of Major, with the appointment of Chief Engineer in North America. He took part in the campaign against the Jacobites in Scotland in 1745–6, and served in Flanders in 1746–7 and at Louisbourg in Nova Scotia in 1757. He died in October of that year while on passage from Halifax to New York. His sister Janet was the wife of Leonard Smelt, a military engineer well known in eighteenth-century society. [T. W. J. Conolly, *Roll of Officers of the Corps of Royal Engineers from 1660 to 1898*, Chatham 1898; P.R.O., WO 54/204, pp. 120, 153; *Scots Mag.* xix, 1757, 614; will in P.R.O., PROB 11/834, f. 351.]

Dugal Campbell's official work for the Ordnance is represented by drawings in the Public Record Office, the Register House at Edinburgh and the National Library of Scotland, including designs for works at EDINBURGH CASTLE 1742, FORT WILLIAM 1744–6 and THE TOWER OF LONDON [P.R.O., WORK 31/129–131, etc.; N.L.S., Z2/4a, 6a, 28, 30a]. In 1743 he gave evidence about William Adam's contracts with the Ordnance in the lawsuit between Adam and Lord Braco [*Depositions in Adam v. Braco*, 1743, 26] and in 1752 he made a report on the Irish Barracks in the Tower which is now in the British Library (*King's Maps* xxiv, 23, m. 2). In the Duke of Argyll's archives there is a set of drawings by him for rebuilding INVERARAY CASTLE 'in the Castle stile', that is as a polygonal fort, complete with fosse and covered way. This remarkable design, one of the earliest of its kind, must have been made before the 3rd Duke began to build the castle to the designs of Roger Morris in 1746 [I. G. Lindsay & Mary Cosh, *Inveraray and the Dukes of Argyll*, 1973, 45 and fig. 19]. In the Public Library at Northampton there is a drawing signed by Dugal Campbell showing LYVEDEN NEW BUILDING (one of the eccentric structures built by Sir Thomas Tresham of Rushton *c.*1600) completed with a cupola as a house for the titular 'Lord Goreing', i.e. Sir Charles Goring of Highden, Sussex.

CAMPLING, JAMES (*c.*1741–), of Marylebone, exhibited at the Free Society of Artists from 1770 to 1774, including 'The principal front of a building now erecting for a gentleman in Russia' (1772), and a design for a church at Marylebone (1774). In 1774 he was an unsuccessful candidate for a district surveyorship. He was then 33 years of age. [Middlesex County Records, General Orders No. 10, f. 15 *et seq.*]

CANTWELL, JOSEPH (*c.*1750–1828), was apprenticed in 1764 to Robert Palmer, a tiler and bricklayer of London [Guildhall Library, MS. 3053/4, p. 33]. He practised chiefly as a surveyor, and held one of the London district surveyorships. He 'realised a handsome fortune, and retired from practice many years before his death'. In 1792 he founded the

Surveyors' Club, of which he was President in 1797. In 1807–8 he was Master of the Tylers' and Bricklayers' Company. He died at Stanwell on 7 August 1828, in his 79th year, leaving his house in Great Marlborough Street, London, to his son Robert (*q.v.*). [J. W. Penfold, *A Century of Surveyors*, 1892, 17; *Gent's Mag.* 1828 (ii), 189; *Survey of London* xxxvi, 108–110, 157n.; *Minutes of Proceedings of the Institution of Civil Engineers* xix, 1859–60, 186; will in P.C.C. 576 SUTTON.]

CANTWELL, ROBERT (*c.*1792–1858), was the son of Joseph Cantwell (*q.v.*), and continued to occupy his father's house at 20 Great Marlborough Street, London, for many years, though he was living in Wimpole Street at the time of his death on 6 October 1858, aged 66 [*Gent's Mag.*, N.S. v, 1858, 541]. Like his father, he had an extensive practice as a surveyor, and was much employed as an arbitrator. According to his obituary in the *Minutes of Proceedings* of the Institution of Civil Engineers (of which he became an Associate Member in 1841) he 'did not hold any public appointments, nor did he execute any important works'. He did, however, design ROYAL CRESCENT on the Norland Estate in KENSINGTON, a drawing of which he exhibited at the R.A. in 1839. This large crescent of stuccoed houses with Doric porches and cast-iron balconies is described and illustrated in *Survey of London* xxxvii, where Cantwell's responsibility for houses on the adjoining Ladbroke Estate, notably Nos. 2–6 and 24–28 HOLLAND PARK AVENUE and 1–4 LADBROKE TERRACE, is discussed. In 1851 John Spedding employed him to add a Drawing Room to MIREHOUSE, CUMBERLAND [J. M. Robinson, *Guide to the Country Houses of the North-West*, 1991, 124].

Cantwell appears to have had some connection with J. B. Papworth (*q.v.*), for a drawing for the Ladbroke Terrace houses is among the latter's drawings in the R.I.B.A. Collection, and in 1847 Cantwell was among those who presented a silver inkstand to Papworth on his retirement [Wyatt Papworth, *J. B. Papworth*, 1879, 94]. The Drawings Collection also contains designs by Papworth for alterations to the Marquis Bonneval's château, nr. Rouen in Normandy, marked 'for Mr. Cantwell to build'. Papworth's diary shows that these were made in 1826.

CAPON, WILLIAM (1757–1827), architectural draughtsman, was the son of a portrait-painter at Norwich. At first he studied under his father, but an interest in architecture led to him becoming a pupil of Michael Novosielski (*q.v.*), whom he assisted in the erection of the Italian Opera House in the Haymarket (1790–1). As Novosielski's assistant he learned the art of theatrical scene-painting which was to be his main occupation in life. He also designed the theatre 'and some other buildings' at Ranelagh Gardens. In 1780 he 'erected a small theatre in the court adjoining Wells Street, Oxford Street', and in 1794 he designed a theatre for Lord Aldborough at Belan House, Co. Kildare. On the completion of the Drury Lane Theatre in 1794 he was engaged by Kemble as scene-painter, and produced many elborate architectural sets in which considerable antiquarian knowledge was displayed. He excelled in medieval scenes, such as an 'Anglo-Norman hall' for *Hamlet*, or (for *Jane Shore*) 'a correct and beautiful restoration of the Council Chamber of Crosby House'. All his Drury Lane sets were destroyed in the fire of 1809, but illustrations of two characteristic scenes, from surviving drawings by Capon now at Stratford, will be found in the *Magazine of Art* xviii (1894–5). He also worked for some of the provincial theatres, notably for the Bath Theatre from 1805 onwards.

In his spare time Capon was an enthusiastic topographical and antiquarian artist. For over thirty years he lived in Westminster, and, like his friend John Carter (*q.v.*), made the antiquities of the Palace and Abbey his special study. All his more important drawings were carefully coloured, and he was one of the first antiquarian draughtsmen to use colour in order to distinguish the work of one period from that of another (cf. the perspective drawing of the half-demolished Painted Chamber reproduced as the frontispiece to vol. i of the *History of the King's Works*). The key to his work on the Palace of Westminster was his great coloured ground-plan, which formed the basis of an engraved plan published by the Society of Antiquaries in 1828. Many of his drawings are now in the Local History Collection of Westminster City Library. Some of them were reproduced by the London Topographical Society in 1923–4 as *Views of Westminster by William Capon*, and others by H. M. Colvin in 'Views of the Old Palace of Westminster', *Architectural History* ix, 1966.

At one time Capon hoped to become Surveyor to Westminster Abbey, but this ambition was never realized. In June 1804 he was appointed Architectural Draughtsman to the Duke of York. He was a regular exhibitor at the Royal Academy from 1788 onwards, showing chiefly architectural and topographical drawings. He also exhibited at the Society of Artists, the British Institution and the Society of British Artists. Though Gothic architecture was his main interest, his last work of importance is said to have been a design for a Doric church. He died on 26 September 1827, aged 70. His portrait by W. Bone is engraved in *Gent's Mag.* xcviii (i), 1828, 105. It shows in the background his design for a pyramidal building 205 feet high, to be erected on Shooter's Hill, Kent, as a 'national monument'. There is a copy of the sale catalogue of his drawings, etc., in the Bodleian Library (Douce CC. 284).

[*Gent's Mag.* 1827 (ii), 374–7; 1828 (i), 105–7; 1829 (i), 227; *D.N.B.*; W. J. Lawrence, 'Art in the Theatre. The Pioneers of Modern English Stage Mounting: William Capon', *Magazine of Art* xviii, 1894–5, 289–92.]

CARLINE, JOHN (1761–1835), was a mason and architect of Shrewsbury. His father, John Carline I (1730–1793), was a native of Lincoln, where his family is commemorated in Carline Road (formerly Carline Place). His mother was the daughter of John Hayward, another Lincoln mason (see p. 484). John Carline I moved to Shrewsbury, where he became foreman of the masons who built the English Bridge to the designs of John Gwynn between 1769 and 1774.

John Carline II had a flourishing business as an architect, builder and statuary mason. He lived in the Abbey Foregate in a house which he built for himself on the site of the Technical College. For some time he was in partnership with a bricklayer named John Tilley, but Tilley appears to have died in 1796, and in 1797 Carline entered into a new partnership with Tilley's stepson Henry Linell.

In 1790–2 Carline and Tilley built MONTFORD BRIDGE, SALOP., to the designs of Telford, and after the flood of 1795 they were again employed by Telford to rebuild the bridge over the Rea Brook at COLEHAM HEAD, SHREWSBURY. In 1793–5, however, it was to their own designs that they built the important WELSH BRIDGE at SHREWSBURY.

Many monuments, often in the Gothic style, were executed by John Carline and his sons, and the lions at the base of Lord Hill's Column, erected in 1814–16, were carved by the firm. An order-book, now in the County Record Office (Longueville Collection, Box 20), gives details of a number of tombstones, chimney-pieces and other jobs carried out in the years 1800–2.

John Carline was the father of John Carline III, architect (*q.v.*), Thomas Carline, sculptor (1799–1868), and of Jane Carline, wife of the Shrewsbury artist Philip Corbet. Thomas, after a period of initial success, failed to maintain his early reputation as a sculptor, and ended his life as Surveyor of Bridges to the North Riding of Yorkshire.

[R. Carline, 'Corbet and the Carlines–Shrewsbury Painters, Sculptors and Architects of the Early 19th. Century', *Shropshire Magazine*, March 1958; *Catalogue of an Exhibition of Works of the Corbet and Carline Families* (Shrewsbury Art Gallery, 1958); J. L. Hobbs, 'Carlines – Architects, Builders and Sculptors', *Shropshire Magazine*, March 1960; A. W. Ward, *The Bridges of Shrewsbury*, 1935, 89–90, 144–9; R. Gunnis, *Dictionary of British Sculptors 1660–1851*, revised ed. 1968.]

BORETON FARMHOUSE, CONDOVER, SALOP., 1782 [*V.C.H. Salop.* viii, 35].

ADDERLEY HALL, SALOP., built portico of new house for Sir Corbet Corbet, Bart., 1787–8; dem. 1877. The evidence [Shropshire Record Office, 327/Box 269, letter of 5 Sept. 1787] does not make it clear by whom the house was designed.

SHREWSBURY, designed and built THE WELSH BRIDGE, 1793–5 [A. W. Ward, *The Bridges of Shrewsbury*, 1935, 144–9].

SHREWSBURY, designed and built ST. ALKMUND'S CHURCH, 1794–5, Gothic [D. H. S. Cranage, *Churches of Shropshire* vi, 895].

WROCKWARDINE CHURCH, SALOP. repairs, etc., 1808 [D. H. S. Cranage, *Churches of Shropshire* ii, 647].

PRADOE, SALOP., designed and built dining-room for the Hon. Thomas Kenyon, 1810 [plan, specification and estimate in scrap-book No. 1 at Pradoe, *ex inf.* Shropshire Record Office].

SHADWELL HALL, nr. CLUN, SALOP., designed for William Botfield, 1812 [Shropshire Record Office, Garnett-Botfield Collection, 539].

TOTTERTON HALL, SALOP., alterations for the Rev. J. B. Bright, 1814 [Shropshire Record Office, 807/612].

PELLWALL HOUSE, MARKET DRAYTON, STAFFS., built new house for Purney Sillitoe to the designs of Sir John Soane, 1822–8 [D. Stroud, *The Architecture of John Soane*, 1961, 133].

SHREWSBURY, CLAREMONT BUILDINGS (a terrace) and CARLINE'S FIELDS (cottages) [Ward, 90].

CARLINE, JOHN (1792–1862), was the son and successor of John Carline II (*q.v.*). Like his father, he combined the practice of architecture with the business of a builder and monumental mason. He was prominent in municipal life as a Conservative councillor, and was also interested in ecclesiology and archaeology. Although most of his works are in the Romanesque or Gothic styles, he is said to have made copies of the Elgin Marbles which were later in Shrewsbury Museum, and the monument to Sir John Hill (d. 1824) in Prees Church by his brother Thomas is in a style 'much influenced by the Elgin marbles' (Pevsner).

In about 1835 he took a builder named Richard Dodson into partnership, but Dodson withdrew in 1845. About this time Carline lost heavily over the restoration of Hereford Cathedral, which he contracted to carry out under the direction of L. N. Cottingham (*q.v.*), and his financial position was aggravated by a large sum of money owed to him by his brother Thomas. Discouraged by these difficulties he went to Lincoln to live with his brother Richard, a successful solicitor. The business at Shrewsbury was carried on for a time by his clerk, James Hewitt, but was eventually wound up. Carline died at Lincoln in 1862. His unexecuted designs for rebuilding Skellingthorpe Church, Lincs., dated 1853, are in the local collection in Lincoln Public Library. [For sources see J. Carline (1761–1835).]

All the following buildings appear to be by John Carline III, but some uncertainty arises over the authorship of those built during the lifetime of his father (d. 1835).

SHREWSBURY, THE DRAPERS' ALMSHOUSES, 1825, Gothic [H. Pidgeon, *Memorials of Shrewsbury*, 2nd ed. 1851, 187].

IGHTFIELD RECTORY, SALOP., 1828–9 [Lichfield Joint Record Office, B/A/13].

SHREWSBURY, ST. MICHAEL'S CHURCH, 1829–30, Gothic; chancel 1873–4 [*Gent's Mag.* 1831 (i), 596].

SHREWSBURY, ST. MARY'S AND ST. MICHAEL'S PAROCHIAL SCHOOLS, ABBEY FOREGATE, 1832; enlarged 1840; Gothic [Pidgeon, *op. cit.*, 194].

SHREWSBURY, ST. MARY'S CHURCH, stone screen at west end of nave, 1834 (destroyed 1894) and large Gothic monument to Revd. J. B. Blakeway (d. 1826) [Pidgeon, *op. cit.*, 72–3, 82].

GRINSHILL CHURCH, SALOP., 1839–40; neo-Norman [I.C.B.S.]

ALBRIGHTON CHURCH, SALOP., 1840–1; neo-Norman [signed drawings in Shrewsbury School archives, Box A, bundle 8, *ex inf.* Mr. J. B. Lawson].

SHREWSBURY ABBEY CHURCH, neo-Norman altar-screen, *c.*1840; removed 1886 [Pidgeon, *op. cit.*, 115].

SHREWSBURY, ST. GILES' CHURCH, pulpit, pews, etc., *c.*1840 [Pidgeon, *op. cit.*, 126].

CARLOW, SAMUEL STEWART TOWNSEND (*c.*1815–1854), exhibited two architectural designs at the Royal Academy in 1837. He became a member of the Institute of British Architects in 1838, but resigned in 1849, probably on going out to Australia, where he died on 12 July 1854, aged 39 [*Gent's Mag.* 1858, 646].

CARMICHAEL, MICHAEL, was an Argyllshire builder-architect of the reign of George III. He was employed as a builder at Inveraray Castle in 1799–1800 [Duke of Argyll's archives, General Accounts, etc.], but the only building he is known to have designed is the very simple church at COLONSAY, 1802 [J. de Vere Loder, *Colonsay and Oronsay*, Edinburgh 1935, 166].

CARR, HENRY (*c.*1772–1828), was the son of James Carr (*q.v.*) and continued his practice in Clerkenwell, where he owned a number of houses in St. James' Street and Walk. He was elected a member of the Surveyors' Club in 1801 and died on 3 March 1828, aged 56. As Surveyor to the Salters' Company Carr designed SALTERS' HALL, ST. SWITHIN'S LANE, LONDON, 1823–7; dem. 1951. A competition was held in 1821, the first three prizes being awarded to J. C. Mead, Francis Pouget and Maximilian Godefroy (*qq.v.*). Carr then incorporated features from all three designs in a final version of his own which was executed in 1823–7. The attribution to George Smith by James Elmes in his *Metropolitan Improvements* appears to be without foundation. [*A.P.S.D.*; R. L. Alexander, *The Architecture of Maximilian Godefroy*, Baltimore 1974, 163–4; will P.C.C. 133 SUTTON.]

CARR, JAMES (*c.*1742–1821), was an architect and builder of Clerkenwell, where he lived in a house (No. 12) on the north side of Albemarle Street. He was presumably the James Carr who was President of the Surveyors' Club in 1798. His only known architectural works are ST. JAMES'S CHURCH, CLERKENWELL, 1788–92, a competent but old-fashioned design with a steeple in the Gibbs tradition, and NEWCASTLE PLACE, CLERKENWELL, a terrace of brick houses which he built as a speculation *c.*1793 [W. J. Pinks, *History of Clerkenwell*, ed. Wood, 1881, 51, 97, 268]. In 1803 he repaired the church of ST. MARTIN ORGAR in the City (dem. 1820) [Guildhall Library, MS. 975].

Carr retired to Cheshunt in Hertfordshire, where he is commemorated by a monument which records his death on 12 January 1821, aged 79 [J. E. Cussans, *History of Hertfordshire* ii, 1878, 228]. He was the father of Henry

Carr (*q.v.*) and Edmund Aikin and Samuel Ware were his pupils.

CARR, JOHN (1723–1807), was for more than half a century the principal architect practising in Yorkshire and the north of England. Although largely self-taught, and without the advantages either of a regular architectural education or of foreign travel,[1] Carr became one of the most competent and successful of Georgian architects. His practice was based on the patronage of the Yorkshire gentry, and country houses formed the bulk of his work. 'It was', as T. D. Whitaker wrote, to Carr's 'good taste' that 'so many families in the county of York are indebted for the comforts and elegancies of their dwellings.' Like his rival James Paine he assimilated in early life the conventions of the Palladian style propagated by Lord Burlington, to which he remained more or less faithful throughout his life. As a young man he had been involved in the building of a house (Kirby Hall) designed in part by Lord Burlington himself, and characteristic features of his architecture such as the Serlian window, the treatment of wings as subordinate pavilions, and the adoption of Vitruvian systems of proportion were no doubt due to the example of Burlington and to the written precepts of Robert Morris, a copy of whose *Select Architecture* he is known to have owned. The basically Palladian character of Carr's architecture was, however, modified in his earlier works by the rich rococo stucco-work which was provided for him by the York plasterers, and in his later ones by highly accomplished imitations of the elegant neo-classical interiors introduced by Robert Adam. Of the earlier style Heath Hall is perhaps the finest example; of the latter, the Assembly Room in the Crescent at Buxton. Carr could also Gothicize when the occasion required–notably at Raby Castle in Durham, where he designed a dramatic Gothic hall, and at Grimston Garth, where he provided his client with a charmingly romantic occasional residence in the form of a triangular tower with a central hexagonal dining-room.

Carr was, however, more than just a provincial representative of the Palladian school and an adroit imitator of Robert Adam. His Assize Court at York was a distinguished classical design of which neither Chambers nor Gandon would have been ashamed, and at Constable Burton (*c.*1762–8) his bold elimination of an architrave from the entablature of the portico was in the forefront of neo-classical taste not merely in England but in Europe (Robert Adam did the same at Compton Verney in 1761–7, Jacques Gondoin at the École de Chirurgie in Paris in 1771–6). Carr's election to the London Architects' Club (of which he was the only provincial member), and the number of his works that figure both in Woolfe and Gandon's *Vitruvius Britannicus* (vols. iv and v) and in Richardson's *New Vitruvius Britannicus*, shows that he was known and respected in the most sophisticated architectural circles.

John Carr was a stonemason by training. His father Robert (1697–1760), his grandfather John (1668–1736), and his great-grandfather Robert Carr (1644–1689) all worked as masons at Horbury, nr. Wakefield, where they owned quarries. Robert Carr, John's father, acted as one of the two Surveyors of Bridges to the West Riding. On his monumental inscription he is dignified with the name of 'Architect', and like other master workmen of his day, he was no doubt capable of making simple architectural designs. The fact that his wife, Rose Lascelles, was the daughter of a gentleman[1] indicates a modest degree of social advancement. John (born in May 1723) was the eldest of his six sons. Educated at the village school, he was probably apprenticed to his father, whom he certainly assisted in the quarry, on buildings for whose masonry the elder Carr had contracted, and in making (1752–3) a survey of the county bridges for the West Riding magistrates. He does not appear to have received any more formal instruction in architecture than was afforded by this practical experience, supplemented by standard manuals such as Morris's *Select Architecture*, Carr's own copy of which is now in Sir John Soane's Museum. Until the death of the elder Carr in 1760 John and his father frequently worked together, but by about 1750 John had already begun to develop an architectural practice. Huthwaite Hall was built to his designs in 1748, and several other houses followed during the next few years. In 1752 the Corporation of York voted to pay £88 to Carr for erecting an ornamental building over the Pikeing Wellhead. On its completion he was (1757) admitted a freeman of the city, in which he had by now taken up residence. Meanwhile he had achieved local celebrity by submitting a design for the grandstand on Knavesmire race-

[1] There is, however, evidence of a visit to Paris in 1771 (Ivan Hall, 'A Neoclassical Episode at Chatsworth', *Burlington Mag.* June 1980, 403).

[1] Though her father, John Lascelles of Norton-in-the-Clay, was described as 'gentleman', there is apparently no evidence that he was related to the Harewood Lascelles (Mary Mauchline, *Harewood House*, 1974, 175–6, n. 56).

course which was chosen in preference to one made by James Paine, hitherto the leading architect in the north of England. This work, which was much admired, brought Carr to the notice of the gentry attending the York races. Many private commissions followed, and for the next forty years Carr was busy designing country houses and public buildings throughout the northern counties. In 1760 he succeeded his father as one of the two Surveyors of Bridges for the West Riding, but resigned in 1773 soon after his appointment (1772) to the better-paid post of Surveyor of Bridges to the North Riding.

Despite the extent of his business, Carr found time to play a part in the municipal life of York. In 1766 he was appointed one of the city chamberlains, and in the following year he was elected one of the sheriffs of the city, but paid the usual fine to be excused from serving. In 1769 he was elected an alderman, and in 1770 served as Lord Mayor, an office which he is said to have performed 'with becoming dignity and hospitality'. In 1785, on the death in office of the then Lord Mayor, Carr filled the office for the remainder of the year. In the same year he was appointed one of the magistrates for the West Riding. By now his many commissions, added to his profits as a builder, and to the salary of £100 a year which he received from the North Riding magistrates for inspecting their bridges, had made him a wealthy man. In 1791–3 he rebuilt the church in his native village at his own expense, and in 1789 purchased a house there which he renamed Carr Lodge. This was intended for the residence of his nephew John Carr, for he himself had had no children by his wife Sarah Hinchcliffe, whom he married in 1746. Towards the end of his life he retired to Askham Richard, a village near York, where he purchased a mansion and estate. He retained his vivacity to the last, making long tours round the country to show his buildings to his great-nieces. He died on 22 February 1807, at the age of 83, and was buried in the church at Horbury, where there is a monument to his memory. His place as the leading architect in York was taken by his assistant Peter Atkinson (d. 1805), whose practice was continued by his son Peter (d. 1842) and his grandsons J. B. and W. Atkinson. The firm still exists under the name of Brierley, Leckenby, Keighley & Groom.

A portrait of Carr by William Beechey, presented by himself to the Corporation of York in 1803, hangs in the Mansion House. Another portrait by Beechey, dated 1791, formerly at Browsholme Hall,[1] now belongs to the National Portrait Gallery and is exhibited at Beningborough Hall, Yorkshire. A bust by Nollekens dated 1800 is in the York Art Gallery, together with a pastel by John Russell. A pencil portrait by George Dance made in 1796 is reproduced in W. Daniell, *A Collection of Portraits sketched from the Life* (1808–14). The silver tea-caddy which Carr presented to the City of York in 1796 is illustrated in *Country Life*, 1 July 1954, 44.

A large quantity of Carr's original drawings, bound up in folio volumes, was offered for sale by the London booksellers Priestly & Weale in 1825, but their present ownership is unknown. A small collection of ceiling designs by Carr is in the Victoria & Albert Museum (93 H.23). Carr's copy of Robert Morris's *Select Architecture* (1755) in Sir John Soane's Museum contains several sketches of his own designs. An illustrated survey of the county bridges built by Carr in the North Riding was presented by him to the magistrates in 1806 and is now in the North Yorkshire Record Office. Among unexecuted designs by Carr attention may be drawn to those for enlarging Busby Hall, Yorks. (N.R.), in the North Yorkshire Record Office (*c.*1760); for a race-stand at Kelso, Roxburghshire (1778), in the National Library of Scotland (MS. 13233, ff. 112–21); for the addition of castellated offices to Glamis Castle, Angus (drawings at Glamis); for Wetherby Grange, Yorks. (W.R.), in the Leeds Archives Office; and for a mausoleum for Richard Robinson, Archbishop of Armagh (d. 1794) in Armagh Cathedral Library.

[*A.P.S.D.*, article based on information supplied by J. B. Atkinson; R. Davies, 'A Memoir of John Carr', *Yorkshire Arch. Jnl.* iv, 1877; S. D. Kitson, 'Carr of York', *R.I.B.A. Jnl.*, 22 Jan. 1910; Anon., 'A Great Yorkshire Architect', *The Yorkshire Post*, 25 June 1919; R. B. Wragg, 'John Carr: Gothic Revivalist', *Studies in Architectural History*, ed. Singleton, ii, 1956; R. B. Wragg, 'John Carr: Bridgemaster', *York Georgian Society's Report*, 1957; R. B. Wragg, 'John Carr of York', *Jnl. W. Yorkshire Society of Architects*, Dec. 1957 and March 1958; R. B. Wragg, 'Stables Worthy of Stately Homes', *C. Life*, 1 Nov. 1962; John Ingamells, 'Portraits of John Carr', *City of York Art Gallery Quarterly* xxxiv, 1971; Ivan Hall, 'John Carr: A New Approach', *York Georgian Society's Report*, 1972; *The Works in Architecture of John Carr* (a list prepared by the York Georgian Society, York

[1] In 1845 Mary Anne Carr, the heiress of the Carr property, married Thomas G. Parker of Browsholme Hall, nr. Whalley.

1973); *John Carr of York* (duplicated catalogue by John Bradshaw & Ivan Hall of an exhibition at the Ferens Art Gallery, Hull, 1973); W. A. Eden & R. B. Wragg, 'John Carr, Stonecutter Extraordinary, and the Architectural Virtuosi', *Trans. Ancient Monuments Soc.* N.S. 24, 1979–80; Giles Worsley, 'John Carr's Last Tour', *C. Life*, 30 April 1987, 'Attributing Carr', *C. Life*, 5 May 1988.]

PUBLIC BUILDINGS

YORK, THE PIKEING WELL-HOUSE, NEW WALK, for the Corporation of York, 1752–6 [York Corporation Records, House Book 43, 318, 417] (R.C.H.M., *York* iv, 53).

YORK, GRANDSTAND ON KNAVESMIRE RACECOURSE, 1755–6; dem. but lower storey survives re-erected in the Paddock [R. B. Wragg, 'The Stand House on the Knavesmire', *York Georgian Soc's Report*, 1965–6; R.C.H.M., *York* iii, 50–1 (*C. Life*, 3 Sept. 1910).

PRESTON, LANCS., THE GUILDHALL, 1760–2; dem. 1862 [P. Whittle, *History of Preston* ii, 1837, 59].

BEVERLEY, YORKS. (E.R.), ASSEMBLY ROOMS, 1761–3; dem. *c.*1938 [E. Yorks, C.R.O., DDBC/21/92–105].

WAKEFIELD, YORKS. (W.R.), THE HOUSE OF CORRECTION, 1766–70, in association with John Watson; dem. [sources cited in *The Works in Architecture of John Carr*, 1973, 34].

LEEDS, THE GENERAL INFIRMARY, 1768–71; wings added 1782 and 1786; dem. 1893 [sources cited in *The Works in Architecture of John Carr*, 1973, 19].

OPORTO, PORTUGAL, THE HOSPITAL OF SAN ANTONIO (or MISERICORDIA), begun 1770, opened 1799, work continued intermittently until 1843, but never fully completed [R. B. & M. Wragg, 'Carr in Portugal', *Arch. Rev.* Feb. 1959; R. Taylor, 'John Carr e O Hospital de Santo António Do Porto, *Belas Artes*, No. 15, Lisbon 1960; R. Taylor, 'The Architecture of Port-Wine', *Arch. Rev.* June 1961].

YORK, COUNTY LUNATIC ASYLUM (now BOOTHAM PARK HOSPITAL), 1774–7; altered 1814 [sources cited in *The Works in Architecture of John Carr*, 36; R.C.H.M., *York* iv, 47–8].

NEWARK, NOTTS., TOWN HALL AND ASSEMBLY ROOMS, 1773–6 [G. Richardson, *New Vitruvius Britannicus* ii, 1808, pls. 11–14] (Ivan Hall, 'Newark Town Hall', *Georgian Group Jnl.* 1991).

YORK, ASSIZE COURTS IN THE CASTLE, 1773–7 [G. Richardson, *New Vitruvius Britannicus* ii, 1808, pls. 1–4].

LINCOLN, THE COUNTY HOSPITAL (now BISHOP'S HOSTEL), 1776–7 [Minute Book in Lincolnshire Record Office, pp. 43–105, *passim*].

NOTTINGHAM RACECOURSE GRANDSTAND, 1777; dem. 1910 [R. Thoroton, *The Antiquities of Nottinghamshire*, ed. Throsby, ii, 1790, 68 and plate (p. 151); *The Stretton Manuscripts*, ed. G. C. Robertson, 1910, p. ii].

DONCASTER, YORKS. (W.R.), RACECOURSE GRANDSTAND, 1777–81, altered 1804 and 1824; dem. 1969 [J. Tomlinson, *Doncaster*, 1887, 207–8] (E. Miller, *History of Doncaster*, 1804, 158, plate).

NOTTINGHAM, ASSEMBLY ROOMS, LOW PAVEMENT, 1778 [J. Orange, *History of Nottingham* ii, 1840, 940–1]; alterations by Carr 1790 [*The Stretton Manuscripts*, ed. G. C. Robertson, 1910, 181]; further alterations 1807; rebuilt 1836.

YORK, THE FEMALE PRISON (now CASTLE MUSEUM), 1780–3, to match Carr's Assize Courts. The builders were Messrs. Wilkinson & Prince of York, who submitted a plan and elevation which was approved in 1779. It was probably made for them by Carr, who was subsequently paid 'for his trouble in designing and conducting the building in the Castle Yard' [North Riding Q.S. Order Book, *ex inf.* Mr. R. B. Wragg]. Only the central portion was built under Carr's direction, the end bays being added by Peter Atkinson in 1802 [R.C.H.M., *York* ii, 85].

BUXTON, DERBYSHIRE, THE ASSEMBLY ROOMS in the Crescent, for 5th Duke of Devonshire, *c.*1780–90 [see below].

NORTHALLERTON, YORKS. (N.R.), COURT HOUSE AND HOUSE OF CORRECTION (now H.M. Prison) for North Riding, 1784–8 [N. Riding Q.S. Orders 1782–7, pp. 105, 342].

CHESTERFIELD, DERBYSHIRE, TOWN HALL for 3rd Duke of Portland, 1787–8; dem. [G. Hall, *History of Chesterfield*, 1839, 185].

CHURCHES

RAVENFIELD, YORKS. (W.R.), for Mrs. Elizabeth Parkin, 1756, Gothic [J. Hunter, *South Yorkshire* i, 1828, 398].

KIRKLEATHAM, YORKS. (N.R.), rebuilt for William Turner, *c.*1760–3, retaining the mausoleum of 1740 by J. Gibbs. Turner's account book for 1758–64 (in private hands) shows that Carr was paid £24 3s. 0d. 'for a Draft of the Church at Kirkleatham' in 1759. It was built by Robert Corney (*q.v.*), a local master carpenter, who according to J. W. Ord's *History of Cleveland*, 1846, 374, was 'both architect and builder' of the church. He may have modified Carr's design.

DEWSBURY, YORKS. (W.R.), rebuilt tower and north and south aisles, 1765–7, Gothic; altered by G. E. Street in nineteenth century [churchwardens' accounts cited by R. B. Wragg, 'John Carr: Gothic Revivalist', 18–19].

BIERLEY CHAPEL (now CHURCH), YORKS. (W.R.), for Dr. Richard Richardson, 1766; enlarged 1828 [W. Hiles, *History of the Parish of Bierley*, 1925, 19].

attributed: BOYNTON, YORKS. (E.R.), rebuilt 1768–70, Gothic [unsigned drawings published by A. R. Dufty in *Archaeological Jnl.* cv, 1948, 85, and attributed to Carr by Arthur Oswald in *C. Life*, 22 July 1954, and by R. B. Wragg, 'John Carr; Gothic Revivalist', 20–1].

YORK MINSTER, surveyed fabric and repaired choir roofs, 1770–3; repairs to transepts 1794–7 [J. Wylson, 'York Minster: its Fires and Restorations', *Builder* iii, 1845, 158; Fabric Accounts cited in *The Works in Architecture of John Carr*, 37].

SHEFFIELD, ST. PETER (now CATHEDRAL), repairs and alterations to south and east sides of chancel, 1773–5, Gothic [R. B. Wragg, 'John Carr: Gothic Revivalist', 21–2, and further sources cited in *The Works in Architecture of John Carr*, 30].

ROKEBY, YORKS. (N.R.), completed (1777–8) church begun by Sir Thomas Robinson (d. 1777) for J. S. Morritt [MS. notebook cited in *The Works in Architecture of John Carr*, 29].

attributed: DENTON, YORKS. (W.R.), for Sir James Ibbetson, Bart., 1776, Gothic [stylistic attribution combined with the fact that Carr was building Denton Park at the same time].

OSSINGTON, NOTTS., for Robert Denison, 1782–3, including a domed mausoleum at the east end, dem. 1838 [Denison papers in Nottingham University Library, De 2P/11].

HORBURY, YORKS (W.R.), 1791–3, at his own expense [inscription and sources cited in *The Works in Architecture of John Carr*, 17].

BRIDGES

As Surveyor of Bridges to the North Riding of Yorkshire from 1772 to 1803 Carr left a detailed survey-book of the county bridges recording those that he had built or repaired (see A. Booth, 'Carr of York and the Book of the Bridges', *Yorkshire Archaeological Jnl.* xxxviii, 1954, and *The Works in Architecture of John Carr*, 1973, on which the following list is based).

In the *North Riding* Carr designed or remodelled bridges at AYSGARTH (R. Ure), 1788, AYTON (R. Derwent), 1775; BAINBRIDGE (YORE BRIDGE, R. Ure), BIRDFORTH, 1798, dem. 1971; BOW BRIDGE, nr. RIEVAULX, 1789; CATTERICK (R. Swale), 1792; CRAMBECK, 1785; CROFT (R. Tees), 1795; DANBY WISKE, 1782; DOWNHOLME (R. Swale), 1773; EAST ROW, SANDSEND, nr. WHITBY, 1777; ELLERBECK, nr. OSMOTHERLEY, 1790, dem.; GRETA, nr. ROKEBY, 1773; GRINTON (R. Swale), 1797; HAWNBY, 1800; KILVINGTON, 1774, dem. 1970; LOW BOURN (R. Burn), nr. MASHAM, 1775; MORTON ON SWALE, 1800–3; SOUTH OTTERINGTON (R. Wiske), 1776; REETH (over Arkle Beck), 1772–3; RICCAL, nr. HELMSLEY, 1803; RICHMOND (R. Swale), 1789; RUTHERFORD (R. Greta), south of BARNARD CASTLE, 1773; SKIPTON ON SWALE, 1781; STRENSALL, 1798; THIRKLEBY, 1799, rebuilt 1931; THIRSK MILL, MILLGATE (over Cod Beck), 1789; YORK, YEARSLEY BRIDGE (R. Foss), 1794–5, since rebuilt.

In the *West Riding* where he was one of the two Surveyors of Bridges from 1761 to 1772, Carr designed bridges at CARLTON FERRY, nr. SNAITH (R. Aire); CONISTON COLD (R. Aire), 1763; FERRYBRIDGE, 1797–1804; HAREWOOD (R. Wharfe), 1771; MARLE BRIDGE (R. Dearne), nr. DARFIELD, 1766; and was one of the committee responsible for the wooden bridge at SELBY, opened 1795.

Ferrybridge, Richmond, Morton and Rutherford Bridges were among Carr's most notable bridge-works. Greta Bridge was probably the most elegantly designed and was certainly the one most often painted, notably by J. S. Cotman.

For other bridges widened or repaired by Carr see the two works cited above.

DOMESTIC ARCHITECTURE

The following list is confined to documented or otherwise well-authenticated works, supplemented by a small number of stylistic attributions which are regarded by the author as virtually certain. For doubtful and unexecuted works and a few less certain attributions see the list of *Works in Architecture of John Carr* published by the York Georgian Society in 1973. References to 'Chivers' are to the diary of Miss Elizabeth Chivers, formerly in the possession of the late Wilfred Partington. Miss Chivers was a neighbour of Carr's at Askham and knew him well. In 1803, 1804 and 1805 she made tours with her parents which were recorded in her diary, and carefully noted whenever she saw a building 'designed by our good neighbour Mr. Carr'. Similar diaries kept by Carr's great-nieces

Harriet and Amelia Clark in 1795 and 1796 are in York Minster Library (MSS. 328/1–3), and another of 1805 is described by Giles Worsley in *Country Life*, 5 May 1988. 'Davies' refers to the list of Carr's works given by Robert Davies in his memoir of Carr in *Yorkshire Archaeological Jnl.* iv, 1877.

KIRBY HALL, OUSEBURN, YORKS. (W.R.), employed on erection of house designed for Stephen Thompson by Lord Burlington and Roger Morris, 1747–*c.*1755; dem. 1920 except stables [contemporary engraving by Basire in B.L., *King's Maps* xlv, 24–1, recording that the house was 'Executed, & the inside finishings, by J. Carr, Architect'] (*Vitruvius Britannicus* v, 1771, pls. 70–1).

HUTHWAITE HALL, THURGOLAND, nr. PENISTONE, YORKS. (W.R.), for John Cockshutt, 1748 [*A.P.S.D.*] (*The Works in Architecture of John Carr*, 1973, pl. 1).

ASKHAM HALL, ASKHAM RICHARD, YORKS. (W.R.), additions for W. Garforth, *c.*1750; rebuilt 1889 (now H.M. Prison) [letter from Carr cited by Davies, 212].

THORP ARCH HALL, YORKS. (W.R.), for William Gossip, 1750–4 [W. Yorks. Archives, Leeds, Thorp Arch Estate Papers, box 21, references to Carr in Day Book 1749–51, *ex inf.* Mr. Peter Thornborrow of W. Yorks Archaeology Service].

ARNCLIFFE HALL, INGLEBY ARNCLIFFE, YORKS. (N.R.), for Thomas Mauleverer, *c.*1750–4; E. wing 1841 [*A.P.S.D.*; J. Whellan, *History and Topography of York and the North Riding* ii, 1859, 734] (*C. Life*, 25 Dec. 1920).

YORK, No. 47 BOOTHAM, for Mrs. Mary Thompson, 1752 [*A.P.S.D.*].

CAMPSMOUNT, nr. DONCASTER, YORKS. (W.R.). Payments to Carr indicate that he probably designed the house built for Thomas Yarborough, 1752–5; dem. 1940. Surviving drawings signed by Carr show that he subsequently designed the adjoining castellated farmyard; dem. 1972–3 [T. Connor, 'The Building of Campsmount', *Yorks. Archl. Jnl.* xlvii, 1975].

LEEDS, YORKS. (W.R.), town house for J. Dixon,[1] 1753 [*A.P.S.D.*].

NORTHALLERTON, YORKS. (N.R.), house, No. 84 HIGH STREET, for D. Mitford, *c.*1754 [*A.P.S.D.*].

HEATH HALL, nr. WAKEFIELD, YORKS. (W.R.), remodelled house and designed stable blocks for John Smyth, senior and junior, 1754–80 [W. Watts, *Seats of the Nobility and Gentry*, pl. lxxxiv, 1786] (*C. Life*, 19, 26 Sept., 3 Oct. 1968).

YORK, PETERGATE, house for J. Mitchell, 1755; dem. *c.*1860 [*A.P.S.D.*].

YORK, FAIRFAX HOUSE, No. 27 CASTLEGATE, remodelled interior for 9th Viscount Fairfax, *c.*1755–62 [R.C.H.M. *York* v, 112; John Cornforth in *C. Life*, 7–14 March 1985].

GILLING CASTLE, YORKS. (N.R.), repairs and minor alterations for 9th Viscount Fairfax, 1755–6 [Fairfax papers in North Yorkshire C.R.O., ZDV (F), misc. 1129].

PLOMPTON, nr. KNARESBOROUGH, YORKS. (W.R.), new house begun for Daniel Lascelles *c.*1755 but not finished except stables (subsequently partially converted into a house) [Steward's correspondence 1754–62 in Harewood archives; drawing of 'Plompton, S. front as it is executed for Daniel Lascelles 11 May 1761. J.C.' formerly in collection of Sir Albert Richardson]. For the Gothic farmhouse see R. B. Wragg, 'John Carr: Gothic Revivalist', 15.

attributed: YORK, GARFORTH HOUSE, No. 54 MICKLEGATE, for the Revd. Edmund Garforth, *c.*1755–7 [R.C.H.M., *York* iii, 76–7].

LYTHAM HALL, LANCS., for Thomas Clifton, 1757–64 [*A.P.S.D.* and accounts in Lancs. C.R.O. cited in *The Works in Architecture of John Carr*, 20] (*C. Life*, 21–28 July 1960).

NEWBY HALL, YORKS. (W.R.), alterations, including addition of wings, for William Weddell, *c.*1758–60; S. wing (sculpture gallery) internally remodelled by R. Adam 1767–74, both wings heightened by W. Belwood *c.*1775 [Chivers; drawings in Compton papers at Newby, *ex inf.* Miss Jill Low] (*C. Life*, 7, 14, 21 June 1979).

EVERINGHAM PARK, YORKS. (E.R.), for William H. Constable Maxwell, 1758–64; enlarged in 19th century; restored *c.*1965 [R. B. Wragg, 'Everingham Park: Carr's Work Authenticated', *Trans. East Yorks. Georgian Soc.* iv (2), 1955–6; Arthur Oswald in *C. Life*, 15–22 Feb. 1968].

KIRKLEES HALL, YORKS. (W.R.), alterations, including new staircase and external arcade, for Sir George Armytage, Bart., 1759–60 [D. Nortcliffe, 'The Re-styling of Kirklees Hall 1753–1790', *Halifax Antiquarian Soc's Transactions*, 1982].

HAREWOOD HOUSE, YORKS. (W.R.), for Edwin Lascelles, cr. Lord Harewood, 1759–71. The plan and exterior were substantially Carr's design, but the interior decoration of the principal rooms was wholly by R. & J. Adam. Both exterior and interior were

[1] This may have been the house said to have been built by Jeremiah Dixon in Boar Lane in 1750 (R. Thoresby, *Ducatus Leodiensis*, ed. Whitaker, 1816, 5), but the identification is not certain.

considerably altered by Sir C. Barry in 1843–50, when the portico was removed. Carr was also responsible for much of Harewood village, for a Temple of Venus, 1780 (dem.), and for the stables built in 1755–8, for which Chambers had made a rejected design in 1755. For the possibility that Carr, rather than Peter Atkinson, designed the triumphal arch gateway see G. Worsley in *C. Life*, 5 May 1988. [*Vitruvius Britannicus* v, pls. 25–8; R. B. Wragg in *Archaeological Jnl.* cxxv, 1968, 342–7; Mary Mauchline, *Harewood House*, 1974] (A. T. Bolton, *Architecture of R. & J. Adam* i, 157–77; C. Hussey, *English Country Houses: Mid Georgian*, 1956, 61–9).

attributed: KIRKLAND HALL, nr. GARSTANG, LANCS., for Alexander Butler, 1760 [stylistic attribution] (P. Fleetwood-Hesketh, *Murray's Lancashire Architectural Guide*, 1955, 71).

RAVENFIELD HALL, nr. ROTHERHAM, YORKS. (W.R.), altered house shown in Badeslade & Rocque, *Vitruvius Brittanicus* (*sic*) iv, 1739, pls. 108–9, possibly for Mrs. Elizabeth Parkin *c.*1760 and certainly for her cousin and heir Walter Oborne, 1767–70; dem. [*A.P.S.D.* and payments in W. Oborne's accounts in Sheffield City Library, OR 11].

ARTHINGTON HALL, YORKS. (W.R.), probably altered interior for Thomas Arthington, *c.*1760–70 [Giles Worsley, 'Attributing Carr', *C. Life*, 5 May 1988].

TABLEY HOUSE, CHESHIRE, for Sir Peter Leicester, Bart., *c.*1760–7 [*Vitruvius Britannicus* v, pls. 16–19, where it is called Oakland House; C. Hussey in *C. Life*, 21–28 July 1923] (C. Hussey, *English Country Houses: Mid Georgian*, 1956, 55–60).

HORNBY CASTLE, YORKS. (N.R.), rebuilt S. and E. ranges and added offices for 4th Earl of Holdernesse, *c.*1760–70; dem. 1930s except S. range. To Carr may also be attributed model farmhouses on the estate, built 1766–7 [Harriet Clark's journal, 1795, York Minster Library MS. 328/3, p. 32; Giles Worsley in *C. Life* 29 June 1989; J. M. Robinson, *Georgian Model Farms*, 1983, 127–8].

WENTWORTH WOODHOUSE, YORKS. (W.R.), works for 2nd Marquess of Rockingham (d. 1782) and his successor the 4th Earl Fitzwilliam, *c.*1760 onwards, including Stables, 1766–89; Keppel's Column, 1776–81; Rockingham Mausoleum, 1785–91; North Lodge, 1793; Rainborough Lodge, 1798; Lion Gate (Brampton Lodge), 1804; and various alterations to the house, notably the raising of the wings and the addition to them of the engaged porticos for the 4th Earl [A. Booth, 'The Architects of Wentworth Castle and Wentworth Woodhouse', *R.I.B.A. Jnl.*, 3rd ser., xli, 25 Nov. 1933, 71–2; M. & R. B. Wragg, 'Admiral Keppel's Column', *C. Life*, 27 Dec. 1958; R. B. Wragg on the stables in *C. Life*, 1 Nov. 1962; Juliet Allan in *Archaeological Jnl.* 137, 1980, 393–6; drawings, accounts and correspondence among Wentworth Woodhouse Muniments in Sheffield Archives] (*C. Life*, 20 Sept.–11 Oct. 1924, 17–24 March 1983, 24 Jan. 1991 (temples, etc.); C. Hussey, *English Country Houses: Early Georgian*, 1955, 147–54).

CLINTS HALL, nr. RICHMOND, YORKS. (N.R.), alterations for (Sir) Charles Turner of Kirkleatham, 1762–3; dem. *c.*1845 [accounts in Kirkleatham records in N. Yorks. C.R.O., ZK 6565] (W. Angus, *Seats of the Nobility and Gentry*, pl. xxiv, 1790).

YORK, CASTLEGATE HOUSE, CASTLEGATE, for Peter Johnson, 1762–3 [Davies] (R.C.H.M. *York* v, 114–15).

CAMPSALL HALL, YORKS. (W.R.), alterations for Bacon Frank, 1762–4 [letters from Carr in Sheffield Archives, BFM 1314–1318, *passim*].

STAPLETON PARK, YORKS. (W.R.), for Edward Lascelles, later Earl of Harewood (d. 1820), *c.*1762–4; dem. *c.*1930 [mentioned in letters from Carr to Bacon Frank of Campsall in Sheffield Archives, BFM 1314/67, 1316/6 and 22].

GROVE HALL, nr. RETFORD, NOTTS., remodelled for Anthony Eyre, in or soon after 1762; dem. 1952 [R. Thoroton, *Antiquities of Nottinghamshire*, ed. J. Throsby, iii, 1790, 264; H. A. Johnson & A. Cox, 'The Architecture of Grove Hall', *Trans. Thoroton Soc.* 89, 1985].

CONSTABLE BURTON, YORKS. (N.R.), for Sir Marmaduke Wyvill, Bart., *c.*1762–8 [*Vitruvius Britannicus* v, pls. 36–7; Farington's Diary, 21 May 1809] (*C. Life*, 28 Nov. 1968).

ESCRICK PARK, YORKS. (E.R.), enlargement of house and new stables for Beilby Thompson, 1763–5 [E. Riding C.R.O., DDFA/37/28; David Neave & Ivan Hall in *York Georgian Society's Annual Report*, 1971].

WHITE WINDOWS, SOWERBY BRIDGE, YORKS. (W.R.), alterations for John Priestley, 1763–8 [*A.P.S.D.*].

WELBECK ABBEY, NOTTS., alterations for 3rd Duke of Portland: chapel, 1763; stables, 1774; E. front, 1775–7 [A. S. Turberville, *Welbeck Abbey and its Owners* ii, 1938–9, 454; Nottingham University Library, Portland papers, PwF2, 540, etc.].

CANNON HALL, nr. BARNSLEY, YORKS. (W.R.), addition of wings and other alterations for John Spencer, 1764–7; further works, including stables and heightening of wings, for Walter Spencer-Stanhope, 1778 onwards [A. M. W. Stirling, *Annals of a Yorkshire House*, 1911, i, 146–8, ii, 116–18, 314–5; accounts in Sheffield City Library cited in *The Works in Architecture of John Carr*, 5].

GOLDSBROUGH HALL, nr. KNARESBOROUGH, YORKS. (W.R.), remodelled interior for Daniel Lascelles, 1764–5 [Harewood archives, Steward's correspondence and Letter-book 5, pp. 130, 152, 161].

SWINTON PARK, nr. MASHAM, YORKS. (N.R.), alterations for William Danby, 1764–7 [John Cornforth in *C. Life*, 7, 14, 21 April 1966].

KIRKLEATHAM HALL, YORKS. (N.R.), alterations to Jacobean house for Sir Charles Turner, 1764–7, externally Gothic; dem. 1954–6 [Arthur Young, *Six Months Tour through the North of England* ii, 1770, 107; R. B. Wragg, 'John Carr: Gothic Revivalist', 23–5].

TANFIELD HALL, YORKS. (N.R.), repairs and alterations for 2nd Lord Bruce, 1765; dem. 1816 [N. Yorks. C.R.O., ZJX 7/26/9, 10, 13, *ex inf.* Dr. G. Worsley].

?SWARLAND HALL, nr. FELTON, NORTHUMBERLAND, for D. R. Grieve, 1765; dem. 1934. Among the sketches in Carr's copy of Morris's *Select Architecture* in the Soane Museum is the plan of a house 'Designed for Mr. Grive, Northumberland'. The elevation of Swarland Hall (recorded by Sir John Summerson in *Architect and Building News*, 15 June 1934) does not correspond to this plan, but represents a design that may well have been by Carr.

attributed: COURTEENHALL, NORTHANTS., stables for Sir William Wake, Bart., after 1765 [Giles Worsley in *C. Life*, 30 Oct. 1986].

YORK, SKELDERGATE, his own house, 1765–9; dem. 1945 [*A.P.S.D.*; Davies; and sources cited in *The Works in Architecture of John Carr*, 38].

ASKE HALL, YORKS. (N.R.), alterations and additions to house and new stables for Sir Lawrence Dundas, Bart., *c.*1765–9 [accounts, etc. in Zetland archives, N. Yorks. C.R.O.] (*C. Life*, 1–8 March, 1990).

BOYNTON HALL, nr. BRIDLINGTON, YORKS. (E.R.), alterations for Sir George Strickland, Bart., *c.*1765–80 [Strickland papers cited in *The Works in Architecture of John Carr*, 4] (*C. Life*, 22–29 July 1954). The CARNABY TEMPLE built by Sir George Strickland may also be attributed to Carr.

HALIFAX, YORKS. (W.R.), house and warehouse in George Street for John Royds, 1766; later Rawson's Bank and now office, but partly dem. [*A.P.S.D.*; Davies; and references cited in *The Works in Architecture of John Carr*, 14].

TOWNELEY HALL, LANCS., interiors of drawing-rooms in S.E. wing for Charles Towneley, 1766–7; remodelled by Jeffry Wyatville *c.*1814 [Susan Bourne, *An Introduction to the Architectural History of Towneley Hall*, Burnley 1979, 19–20].

attributed: GLEDHOW HALL, ALLERTON, YORKS. (W.R.), for Jeremiah Dixon, 1766–7 [stylistic attribution, supported by Dixon's possible employment of Carr to design his town house in Leeds] (plan in *R.I.B.A. Jnl.*, 22 Jan. 1910, 253).

PYE NEST, nr. HALIFAX, YORKS. (W.R.), for John Edwards, 1767; dem. 1934 [*A.P.S.D.*; *A Series of Picturesque Views of Castles and Country Houses in Yorkshire*, Bradford 1885] (J. B. Burke, *A Visitation of Seats and Arms*, 2nd ser. i, 1854, 210, plate).

THORESBY HOUSE, NOTTS., for 2nd Duke of Kingston, 1767–71; dem. 1868; and remodelling of stables, etc. for Lord Newark, 1789–1804 [*Vitruvius Britannicus* v, pls. 11–13; J. H. Hodson, 'The Building and Alteration of the Second Thoresby House, 1767–1804', *Thoroton Society's Record Series* xxi, 1962, 16–20].

attributed: BISHOP AUCKLAND CASTLE, CO. DURHAM, S. wing (Gothic) for Bishops Richard Trevor and John Egerton, *c.*1767–72 [J. Cornforth in *C. Life*, 3 Feb. 1972; J. Macaulay, *The Gothic Revival*, 1975, 139–40].

RABY CASTLE, CO. DURHAM, alterations and additions, including Gothic entrance hall (1781–5), for 2nd Earl of Darlington, 1768–88 [Alistair Rowan, 'Gothic Restoration at Raby Castle', *Arch. Hist.* xv, 1972].

LEEDS, YORKS. (W.R.), BRIDGE END, house (now a shop) for Mr. Green, before 1769 [letter of 13 Feb. 1769 in Leeds Infirmary letter-book cited in *The Works in Architecture of John Carr*, 19].

KILNWICK HALL, YORKS. (E.R.), internal alterations for John Grimston, 1769–72; further alterations for Thomas Grimston, 1781; dem. 1951 [M. E. Ingram, *Leaves from a Family Tree*, 1951, 67–70, 113, and sources cited in *The Works in Architecture of John Carr*, 18].

THE SHAY, nr. HALIFAX, YORKS. (W.R.), probably for John Caygill, *c.*1770; dem. [*A.P.S.D.*; cf. *The Works in Architecture of John Carr*, 30].

BYRAM HALL, nr. FERRYBRIDGE, YORKS. (W.R.), extensive additions, including stables, for Sir John Ramsden, Bart., probably c.1770 (interior decoration by R. Adam, 1780); dem. [*A.P.S.D.*].

attributed: GLEDSTONE HALL, nr. SKIPTON, YORKS. (W.R.), begun by Richard Roundell (d. 1772) *c.*1770 and completed by the Revd. William Roundell; dem. 1928 except stables [stylistic attribution; see Kitson in *R.I.B.A. Jnl.*, 22 Jan. 1910 and C. Hussey in *C. Life*, 13 April 1935] (plate in T. D. Whitaker, *History of Craven*, 1812, 72, 1878 ed., 94).

ASTON RECTORY, nr. ROTHERHAM, YORKS. (N.R.), for the Revd. William Mason, *c.*1770 [sketch-plan of 'Revd. Mr. Mason's house at Aston' in Carr's copy of R. Morris's *Select Architecture* in Sir John Soane's Museum; M. & R. B. Wragg in *C. Life*, 12 April 1956].

SEDBURY PARK, nr. RICHMOND, YORKS. (N.R.), alterations for Robert D'Arcy Hildyard, *c.*1770; dem. [Grimston papers, letter dated 1770 from Sir Robert Hildyard to John Grimston in which he refers to Carr's recent work at Sedbury for his son, *ex inf.* Mr. R. B. Wragg].

DENTON PARK, YORKS. (W.R.), for Sir James Ibbetson, Bart., 1770–81 [G. Richardson, *New Vitruvius Britannicus* i, pls. 54–6; *C. Life*, 4 Nov. 1939].

CHESTERS, nr. HEXHAM, NORTHUMBERLAND, for John Errington, 1771; altered by J. Dobson in 1830s and remodelled by Norman Shaw 1893 [sketch-plan of house 'Designed for — Errington, Esqr.' in Carr's copy of R. Morris's *Select Architecture* in Sir John Soane's Museum; R. B. Wragg, 'Chesters', *Archaeologia Aeliana*, 4th ser. xxxvi, 1958].

ASTON HALL (now Aughton Hospital), nr. ROTHERHAM, YORKS. (W.R.), for 4th Earl of Holdernesse, 1771–2 or earlier; new staircase inserted by J. Platt (*q.v.*) *c.*1776 [T. Allen, *History of the County of York* iii, 1834, 145; sketch-plan of 'Aston House' in Carr's copy of R. Morris's *Select Architecture* in Sir John Soane's Museum; M. & R. B. Wragg in *C. Life*, 12 April 1956].

THIRSK HALL, YORKS. (N.R.), addition of wings and attic storey for Ralph Bell, 1771–3 [accounts in N. Riding C.R.O., ZAG 22].

LONDON, BURLINGTON HOUSE, PICCADILLY, alterations to interior, including the dining-room, for 3rd Duke of Portland, then the tenant of the house, *c.*1771–5 [letters from Carr in Nottingham University Library, Portland papers, PwF2, 539, 546; for the Duke's tenancy see *Survey of London* xxxii, 406].

attributed: ORMESBY HALL, nr. MIDDLESBROUGH, YORKS. (N.R.), front range of the stables for Sir James Pennyman, Bart., 1772 [Arthur Oswald in *C. Life*, 26 Feb. 1959].

REDBOURNE HALL, LINCS., works (probably including castellated gateway) for the Revd. Robert Carter Thelwall, 1773 [payment to Carr in accounts in Lincolnshire Archives Office, Red. 3/1/4/6].

BLYTH HALL, NOTTS., alterations for William Mellish, 1773–6; dem. 1972 [Barclay's Bank Ltd., ledgers of Gosling's Bank, *ex inf.* Mr. R. B. Wragg].

LEVENTHORPE HALL, nr. LEEDS, YORKS. (W.R.), for Richard Green, 1774; wings dem. and interior stripped [inscription giving Carr's name; Chivers].

CASTLE HOWARD, YORKS. (N.R.), the stables for 5th Earl of Carlisle, 1774–82 [J. H. Jesse, *George Selwyn and his Contemporaries*, 1843–4, iii, 17; account at Castle Howard cited in *The Works in Architecture of John Carr*, 6] (*C. Life*, 25 June 1927, 1 Nov. 1962).

PANTON HALL, nr. WRAGBY, LINCS., addition of wings for Edmund Turnor, 1775; dem. 1960 [T. Allen, *History of Lincolnshire* ii, 1834, 70; H. M. Colvin in *Lincolnshire Historian* No. 7, 1951, but note that demolition revealed evidence of Carr's additions not visible in 1951].

attributed: RIBSTON HALL, nr. KNARESBOROUGH, YORKS. (W.R.), interior of saloon and stables for Sir John Goodricke, Bart., *c.*1775 [Gervase Jackson-Stops in *C. Life*, 18 Oct. 1973].

NORTON PLACE, BISHOP NORTON, LINCS., for John Harrison, 1776 [J. Britton, *Beauties of England and Wales* ix, 1807, 670] (*C. Life*, 30 Sept. 1976).

BILLING HALL, GREAT BILLING, NORTHANTS., for Lord John Cavendish, 1776; dem. 1956 [G. Baker, *History of Northamptonshire*, 1822–30, i, 22].

BASILDON HOUSE, BERKSHIRE, for Sir Francis Sykes, Bart., 1776; alterations to interior by J. B. Papworth, 1839–44 [G. Richardson, *New Vitruvius Britannicus* i, pls. 12–14; *Arch. Rev.* lxviii, 1930, 113–19; *C. Life*, 5, 12, 19 May 1977].

COLWICK HALL, NOTTS., remodelled for John Musters, 1776 [R. Thoroton, *History of Nottinghamshire*, ed. Throsby, iii, 1790, 8].

MIDDLETON LODGE, MIDDLETON TYAS, YORKS. (N.R.), for George Hartley, 1777–80 [building contract in N. Yorkshire C.R.O., ZKU].

CASTLE FARM, SLEDMERE, YORKS. (E.R.), for Sir Christopher Sykes, 1778, castellated [John Popham in *C. Life*, 16 Jan. 1986].

CLIFTON HALL, NOTTS., alterations and additions for Sir Gervase Clifton, 1778–97 [accounts, now in Nottingham University Library, cited by C. Hussey in *C. Life*, 25 Aug. 1923]. The octagonal domed hall was built by Sir Robert Clifton *c.*1750 and did not form part of Carr's works.

BOLLING HALL, nr. BRADFORD, YORKS. (W.R.), remodelled E. wing for Capt. Charles Wood, R.N., 1779–80 [Wood papers at Garrowby Hall, *ex inf.* the late Major T. Ingram, and sources cited in *The Works in Architecture of John Carr*, 3] (*Picturesque Views of Castles and Country Houses in Yorkshire*, Bradford 1885).

THORNES HOUSE, nr. WAKEFIELD, YORKS. (W.R.), for James Milnes, 1779–81; dem. after fire in 1951 [G. Richardson, *New Vitruvius Britannicus* i, pls. 51–3].

LANGFORD HALL, NOTTS., for Charles Duncombe, *c.*1780 [Chivers].

BADSWORTH HALL, YORKS. (W.R.), alterations for 2nd Marquess of Rockingham, *c.*1780; [Fitzwilliam papers in Sheffield City Library, *ex inf.* Mr. R. B. Wragg].

NEW LODGE, WAKEFIELD ROAD, BARNSLEY, YORKS. (W.R.), for occupation of his nephew John Clark, *c.*1780 [Chivers and sources cited in *The Works in Architecture of John Carr*, 23].

WIGANTHORPE HALL, nr. MALTON, YORKS. (N.R.), for William Garforth, *c.*1780; dem. 1955 [plans in possession of Mr. R. B. Wragg; designs for ceilings in Victoria & Albert Museum, 93 H.23, nos. 8, 10 and 11].

BUXTON, DERBYSHIRE, THE CRESCENT and STABLES (the latter now the Devonshire Royal Hospital), for 5th Duke of Devonshire, 1780–90 [Ivan Hall, 'Buxton: The Crescent', *Georgian Group Jnl.* 1992].

GRIMSTON GARTH, nr. ALDBOROUGH, YORKS. (E.R.), for Thomas Grimston, 1781–6, castellated Gothic [M. E. Ingram, 'John Carr's Contribution to the Gothic Revival', *Trans. E. Riding Georgian Soc.* ii (3), 1949; M. E. Ingram & Francis Johnson in *C. Life*, 17 Oct. 1952].

CHATSWORTH HOUSE, DERBYSHIRE, redecoration of private apartments for 5th Duke of Devonshire, *c.*1782–4 [Ivan Hall, 'A neoclassical episode at Chatsworth', *Burlington Mag.*, June 1980].

CLIFTON HOUSE, ROTHERHAM, YORKS. (W.R.), for Joshua Walker, 1783 [J. Guest, *Historic Notices of Rotherham*, 1879, 681; *Minutes relating to Messrs. Samuel Walker & Co. 1741–1829*, ed. A. H. John, 1951, 21].

HOLKER HALL, nr. CARTMEL, LANCS., unidentified addition *c.*1783 and a garden temple *c.*1787 (dem.) for Lord George Cavendish [Clive Aslet in *C. Life*, 26 June 1980 and letter of 16 July 1787 from Carr in Lancs. C.R.O., DDCA/22/9/9].

WORKINGTON HALL, CUMBERLAND, extensive alterations for John Christian Curwen, 1783–91; mostly destroyed *c.*1972 [D. & S. Lysons, *Magna Britannia* iv, 1816, 173; Curwen's General Ledgers 1770–1792 in Cumbria Record Office] (plan in J. F. Curwen, *Workington Hall*, *c.*1910).

SAND HUTTON PARK, YORKS. (N.R.), for William Read 1786; much altered in 19th century; dem. 1971 [*A.P.S.D.*; Davies].

EASTWOOD HOUSE, ROTHERHAM, YORKS. (W.R.), for Joseph Walker, 1786–7; dem. [J. Guest, *Historic Notices of Rotherham*, 1879, 681; *Minutes relating to Messrs. Samuel Walker & Co. 1741–1829*, ed. A. H. John, 1951, 22].

FARNLEY HALL, nr. OTLEY, YORKS. (W.R.), addition of large new wing for Walter Hawksworth Fawkes, 1786–90 [J. P. Neale, *Views of Seats* v, 1822] (*C. Life*, 20–27 May 1954).

CASTLE WILLIAM, BUDBY, NOTTS., for Lord Newark, *c.*1789, a small castellated house on the Thoresby estate [J. H. Hodson in *Thoroton Society's Record Series* xxxi, 1962, 16–20].

DURHAM CASTLE, remodelled gateway for Bishop Shute Barrington, 1791: described by Harriet Clark in 1795 as 'a new Gothick Gateway . . . design'd by my uncle' [York Minster Library, MS. 328/1].

BRETTON HALL, YORKS. (W.R.), remodelled Dining Room and Library for Col. T. R. Beaumont, 1793, and designed garden temples, etc. [D. Linstrum, *West Yorkshire Architects and Architecture*, 1978, 79].

WOOD HALL, nr. WETHERBY, YORKS. (W.R.), for Fenton Scott, *c.*1795 [Giles Worsley in *C. Life*, 5 May 1988].

FAWLEY COURT, BUCKS., designs for gateway and stucco-work for his friend Strickland Freeman, 1797–9, perhaps not executed [Gloucestershire C.R.O., Strickland Freeman papers, D.1245, FF 38].

BELLE VUE, nr. HAWKSHEAD, LANCS., octagonal temple or summerhouse overlooking Lake Windermere, for the Revd. William Braithwaite of Belmont, Hawkshead, *c.*1799; subsequently enlarged, now ruinous [described as 'from a design of Alderman Carr's of York' in sale advt. in *Carlisle Pacquet*, Sept. 1800, *ex inf.* Mr. Angus Taylor].

COOLATTIN PARK (MALTON HOUSE), in SHILLELAGH, CO. WICKLOW, for 4th Earl Fitzwilliam, 1800–1808. The former house, then undergoing alteration to designs supplied by Carr, was burnt during the Rebellion of 1798, and work started on the new building in 1800 [Sheffield Archives, Fitzwilliam papers, MP 33, plans and elevations; letter of Jan. 1796 to Benjamin Hall referring to his designs 'for the house at Malton in Ireland'; letter of 22 Jan. to Lord Fitzwilliam; accounts in National Library of Ireland, MSS. 6012–6025, *ex inf.* Dr. E. McParland].

MILTON HOUSE, nr. PETERBOROUGH, NORTHANTS., alterations for 4th Earl Fitzwilliam, including new library (now dining room), *c.*1803 [Northants. C.R.O., Fitzwilliam papers, plan no. 126 (watermark 1802) in Carr's hand, and cf. letter referred to by C. Hussey in *C. Life*, 1 June 1961, 1273] (*C. Life*, 25 May 1961, fig. 8 and 1 June 1961, figs 7 and 9).

UPLEATHAM HALL, YORKS. (N.R.), refronted and enlarged for Sir Thomas Dundas, Bart., cr. Lord Dundas, date uncertain; dem. 1897 [Zetland papers in N. Yorkshire C.R.O., cited in *The Works in Architecture of John Carr*, 33].

TANKERSLEY PARK, YORKS. (W.R.), 'temple', presumably the 'Lady's Folly' (dem.), for the Fitzwilliam family, date uncertain ['design'd . . . by my Uncle Carr', Harriet Clark's 1795 journal, York Minster Library, MS. 328/1].

OBELISKS

Among the drawings in Carr's copy of R. Morris's *Select Architecture* in Sir John Soane's Museum there is a design for an obelisk inscribed 'design'd pr. J.C. and built by the Ld. primate of all Ireland 1782'. The Irish primate in 1782 was Richard Robinson, Archbishop of Armagh, and son of William Robinson of Rokeby, Yorkshire. In 1782–3 he erected an obelisk on KNOX'S HILL, ARMAGH, to commemorate his friendship with the Duke of Northumberland. Elizabeth Chivers records that Carr designed an obelisk in BRAMHAM PARK, YORKS. (W.R.), for George Fox, Lord Bingley (d. 1773).

CARTER, CHARLES JOHN (1784–1851), appears to have originated in Staffordshire, for the plan for Louth Vicarage which he made in 1832 is by 'Charles John Carter of Brereton, Staffs., surveyor'. Thereafter he was resident in Louth, where he died in 1851 [R. W. Goulding, *Epitaphs in St. Mary's Churchyard, Louth*, 1921, 41].

In Lincolnshire Carter designed TRINITY CHURCH, LOUTH, in 1834 (rebuilt 1866) [J. E. Swaby, *History of Louth*, 1951, 261] and EASTVILLE CHURCH, PARSONAGE and SCHOOL in 1839–40 [Lincs. Archives Office, 2CC 59/14752]. In 1837 he remodelled THE SYCAMORES, WESTGATE, LOUTH, for the Revd. Augustus Hobart-Hampden, with shaped gables, etc., in a style that has been described as 'a kind of latter-day Artisan Mannerism' [drawings in private possession, *ex inf.* Mr. N. Sharpley], and he is reported to have made designs for a new gate at SCRIVELSBY COURT, LINCS. [N. Pevsner & J. Harris, *Lincolnshire*, Buildings of England, 1989, 631]. He repaired the Lincolnshire churches of WELTON-LE-WOLD, 1837–9, ASHBY-CUM-FENBY, 1847–8 and NORTH THORESBY, 1848–9 [all I.C.B.S.]. In the Lincolnshire Archives Office there are designs by Carter for parsonage houses at LOUTH (1832), GAYTON-LE-MARSH (1834), WELTON-LE-WOLD (1834), BURGH-UPON-BAIN (1834) and LITTLE CARLTON (1843) in LINCOLNSHIRE, and at MILTON ERNEST in BEDFORDSHIRE (1835).

CARTER, EDWARD (–1663), was the younger son of Francis Carter, Chief Clerk of the King's Works (*q.v.*). Nothing is known of his early life, but from 1633 to 1641 he was employed as Inigo Jones's deputy in the great repair of ST. PAUL'S CATHEDRAL then in progress [cf. *Documents illustrating the History of St. Paul's*, ed. Simpson, Camden Soc. 1880, 142, and Nicholas Stone's *Note-Book*, ed. Finberg, Walpole Soc. 1919, 128]. He appears also to have acted as the Earl of Bedford's surveyor in COVENT GARDEN, where he signed the account for the new church built in 1631–2 to Inigo Jones's designs [*Survey of London* xxxvi, 28]. In 1643, in circumstances that are not altogether clear, Carter took the place of the absent Inigo Jones as Surveyor of the King's Works, 'thrusting out' John Webb, whom Jones had nominated as his deputy [*History of the King's Works* iii, 156, 161]. Until 1653, when he was superseded by John Embree, the Sergeant Plumber, Carter was responsible for the maintenance of the royal houses in circumstances that gave him no opportunities for original architectural work.

Nicholas Stone's nephew Charles Stoakes told George Vertue that Carter 'lived in Covent Garden and dyd soon after the Restoration' [*Vertue's Note Books*, Walpole Soc. ii, 53]. This was correct, for in 1633 Carter had built a large house for himself on the Earl of Bedford's estate in King Street, Covent Garden, and was subsequently prominent in parish affairs during the Commonwealth and Protectorate. The fact that in 1645–8 he was one of the 'triers' of candidates for eldership in the Presbyterian organization of London churches is doubtless indicative of his religious sympathies [*Survey of London* xxxvi, 28, 101]. His burial in March 1662/3 is recorded in the register of St. Paul's, Covent Garden [*Harleian Soc.* xxxvi, 1908, 27].

If he was the 'Cartor Surveyor' to whom a

payment of £8 is recorded in the accounts of the 2nd Earl of Northampton in September 1631, Edward Carter may have been responsible for the entrance screen then being built at CASTLE ASHBY, NORTHANTS. This is an ambitious classical structure whose deviations from Palladian propriety make it unlikely that it was designed by Inigo Jones himself [G. Jackson-Stops in *C. Life*, 30 Jan. 1986]. In 1642–9 he was employed to supervise extensive alterations to NORTHUMBERLAND HOUSE, STRAND (dem. 1874), for the 10th Earl of Northumberland, who had just acquired the house by his marriage to Lady Elizabeth Howard [J. Wood, 'The Architectural Patronage of the 10th Earl of Northumberland' in *English Architecture Public and Private. Essays for Kerry Downes*, ed. Bold & Chaney, 1993, 59–71], and in 1651 'Mr. Carter' in London made a design for the town house (dem.) which Lord Fairfax built in BISHOPHILL, YORK [B.L., Add. MS. 71448, nos. 1–4].

From his dismissal in 1653 until his death in 1663 all that is known of Carter's activities is that in 1656–8 'Carter' (presumably Edward) was paid £20 for surveying a new building erected by the Inner Temple in Temple Lane [*Calendar of Inner Temple Records*, ed. Inderwick ii, 1898, 325, 328]. The Treasurer of the Inner Temple at the time was Edmund Prideaux, who in 1649 had acquired FORDE ABBEY, DORSET, and it has been suggested that Carter may have been the architect who in the 1650s remodelled that house for Prideaux with several classical features, including a small loggia [J. J. West in *Archaeological Jnl.* 140, 1983, 27–8]. On the other hand, the suggestion that Carter might have designed HIGHNAM COURT, GLOS. (? 1658) (*C. Life*, 12–19 May 1950), has no foundation either in record or in family tradition. It was first made in 1791 in his *History of Gloucestershire* by Bigland, who, finding that Inigo Jones (then the reputed architect of the house) had died in 1652, concluded that it must have been designed by his successor.

The only unequivocal evidence at present available of Carter's architectural ability is a design for a house among the Trumbull papers in the Berkshire Record Office (D/ED P.5), endorsed as a 'Plot for the new building of East Hampsted Lodge by Mr. Edward Carter,' and dating apparently from some time after 1628, when William Trumbull acquired the estate. This shows a rectangular house with hipped roof, pedimented dormer windows, restrained classical detailing and other features (including an Italianate loggia) of a kind which it would be hard to parallel at this date outside Inigo Jones's office. Edward Carter is, therefore, a figure who may have had an important place in English architectural history as a disseminator of the classical style associated with Inigo Jones.

CARTER, FRANCIS (–1630), was a senior officer in the royal works during the surveyorship of Inigo Jones. He began his official career in 1610 as a clerk of works to Henry, Prince of Wales. After the prince's death in 1612 he became (22 Feb. 1614) Chief Clerk of the King's Works, a post which he retained until his death. He was a carpenter by training, and his first recorded work is the timber-work, including the screen, of the hall at TRINITY COLLEGE, CAMBRIDGE, which he performed in 1604–5 [Willis & Clark, ii, 491–2]. The screen is an elaborate classical structure with Jacobean mannerist ornament (R.C.H.M., *Cambridge*, pl. 257). In 1612 Sir Edward Pytts of Kyre (Worcs.), paid 40s. 'to Carter of St. Giles' Lane by Charing Cross . . . for drawing the upright of the fore part of my house at London' [Mrs. Baldwyn-Childe, 'The Building of Kyre Park, Worcs.', *The Antiquary* xxii, 1890, 51]. In 1613–14 Francis Carter was responsible as 'Surveyor or Contriver of buildings' for the design of the new aisle, doorway and cloister of the chapel at CHARTERHOUSE, LONDON, another building in the mannerist style, but of a more sophisticated character than the Trinity screen [Arthur Oswald, *C. Life*, 15 Oct. 1959]. It was in his official capacity that in 1618 he made an estimate of the cost of repairing PONTEFRACT CASTLE, YORKS. (W.R.), for King James I [*History of the King's Works* iii, 289–90]. In 1618 he provided the estimate – and therefore probably also the design – for the SALISBURY CHAPEL which the 2nd Earl of Salisbury added to HATFIELD CHURCH, HERTS. This has Gothic windows and a Tuscan arcade [Hatfield House, Cecil papers, vol. 143, f. 142]. Salisbury employed him again in 1627 to convert the shops in the upper floor of THE NEW EXCHANGE in THE STRAND into living accommodation [L. Stone, *Family and Fortune*, 1973, 106].

Carter's will shows that at the time of his death in 1630 he was living in St. Martin's Lane and that he owned property and silver plate of considerable value. He had three sons, Samuel (who predeceased him), William and Edward. To William he left 'my Cabinet in my closet with tabell dorins and bookes of Architeckter that belong to me and those above in his chamber and study that belong to him self' [P.C.C. 110 SCROOPE]. No more is known of William Carter, but Edward Carter's career is described above. A family group, formerly at Blenheim Palace, and now in the National Gallery of Ireland, was reported by Vertue to be 'said to be' either 'Carter Architect, deputy to Inigo Jones before Mr. Webb' or 'Lilly the Mathematician' [*Vertue's Note Books*, Walpole Soc. i, 53; iv, 140]. As the principal figure is holding a pair of compasses over a large terrestrial globe, his identification with the architect seems questionable.

Francis Carter is notable as one of the few subordinates of Inigo Jones in the Office of Works who had any ability as an architectural designer. His style, though far from Palladian, nevertheless 'exhibits a new sophistication, somewhere between the Elizabethan mode and the pure classicism of Jones' [John Summerson in *History of the King's Works* iii, 133].

CARTER, FRANCIS (*c.*1773–1809), is an architect of whom little would be known but for the survival in the Public Record Office of his account-book, covering the years 1789–98 (C 217/82/1). He appears to have been the son of a surveyor of the same name, for in 1798 he wrote to a debtor for payment due to him 'for surveying business done by my late Father', and it was as 'Francis Carter, Junior' that he exhibited at the Royal Academy in 1788, 1791, 1795 and 1800. At that time he was living in Moorfields and Finsbury, but in 1804 his address was given as Mare Street, Hackney. He was presumably the Francis Carter, of Hanover Street, Newington, who died on 1 November 1809, aged 36, and whose tombstone, formerly in the churchyard of St. Mary's Newington, described him as 'architect'.

The account-book shows that Carter had commissions as a surveyor or architect in counties as far distant as Berkshire and Lincolnshire. As an architect his most important work was the country house at MARDEN HILL, TEWIN, HERTS., which he designed for Robert Mackay in 1790–4. This reveals him as a competent designer in the spare late Georgian style of architects such as Leverton and Mylne. It was altered by Sir John Soane in 1819 (*C. Life*, 22 Aug. 1941). In 1791 Carter designed a chapel (since dem.) for HERTFORD GAOL [plans in Hertfordshire Record Office]. He was presumably responsible for the ROYAL FREEMASONS' CHARITY SCHOOL FOR GIRLS in ST. GEORGE'S FIELDS, SOUTHWARK (dem.), a drawing of which he exhibited at the R.A. in 1795. Other works recorded in the account-book are a house in London for Charles Fricker, 1794–5; two houses in ABINGDON, BERKS., for George Knapp, 1795–6; a gallery in ST. HELEN'S CHURCH, ABINGDON, 1796–7; alterations to WIGTOFT VICARAGE, LINCS., for the Revd. S. Partridge, 1797; alterations to a villa at KIRTON-IN-HOLLAND, LINCS., for Samuel Fydell, 1798–9; and two new houses at SOUTH END, BOSTON, LINCS., for Thomas Fydell, 1798–9.

CARTER, JOHN (1748–1817), was the son of Benjamin Carter, a mason and monumental sculptor in Piccadilly. When his father died in 1766 he became an assistant of Joseph Dixon, a mason and surveyor in Lambeth, from whom he received some architectural instruction. From 1768 onwards he made drawings for Henry Holland the elder, and according to one of his obituarists he was for a time employed by James Wyatt as a clerk of works. In 1774 he undertook to make the drawings for the *Builder's Magazine*, a serial work projected by the bookseller Newbery, and continued to do so until it ceased publication in 1778.[1] The 185 plates constituted a repertoire of architectural designs, mostly in a fanciful neo-classical style, but with some equally fanciful Gothic examples. The *Builder's Magazine* does not suggest that Carter was an architectural designer of much ability, an impression that his few executed buildings do nothing to modify. They are nearly all in the Gothic style of which he was a careful student and a passionate admirer, but they show that, despite his scorn for the Gothic work of his contemporaries, he had in practice little success in recreating medieval forms in a convincing manner. A precursor of Pugin as a Gothic propagandist, he lacked Pugin's ability to translate his vision of a medieval revival into reality.

Nervous, irascible and eccentric, Carter was ill-suited to regular architectural practice, and he made a living mainly by drawing medieval antiquities for such publications as Gough's *Sepulchral Monuments* (1786), and for private patrons like Horace Walpole and Sir Richard Colt Hoare. For the latter's *Itinerary of Archbishop Baldwin through Wales* (1806) he wrote a supplementary essay on architecture that was published separately in 1830 as *The Progress of Architecture, illustrated in a series of drawings taken from existing remains in South Wales*. He was also employed by the Society of Antiquaries, of which he became a Fellow in 1795, and at whose expense his plans, elevations, sections and details of Bath Abbey, St. Stephen's Chapel,

[1] For the bibliography of this publication see Eileen Harris, *British Architectural Books and Writers 1556–1785*, 1990, 130–3. There were several later editions up to 1823.

Westminster, and of Exeter, Durham, St. Albans and Gloucester Cathedrals were published between 1795 and 1813. Between 1780 and 1794 he published his *Specimens of Ancient Sculpture and Painting* (new edition 1838, reprinted 1887), and in 1786–93 six very small volumes of *Views of Ancient Buildings in England*, republished in 4 vols. as *Specimens of Gothic Architecture* in 1824. All the plates for these works were etched by himself. His major work was *The Ancient Architecture of England* (1795–1814), an attempt to set out 'in a regular manner' the 'Orders of architecture during the British, Roman, Saxon and Norman Æras', and, in particular, to demonstrate the English origin of 'the Pointed Arch style of Architecture'. A second edition with notes by John Britton was published in 1845. The original drawings are in the British Library (Add. MS. 30092). He was also the author of *Specimens of English Ecclesiastical Costume . . . selected from Sculptures, Paintings and Brasses* (1817), containing illustrations originally published in Fosbrooke's *British Monachism*.

Although Carter's drawings and engravings have a permanent value as a pioneer record of English medieval antiquities, his views on architectural history were frequently vitiated by his ignorance of foreign examples and by his inability to read any language other than his own. In England, however, he had the reputation of being 'Antiquity's most resolute friend', and from 1798 onwards he contributed to the *Gentleman's Magazine* a remarkable series of articles entitled 'Pursuits of Architectural Innovation', in which he inveighed ceaselessly against the thoughtless destruction and misguided restoration of ancient buildings. It was due to Carter's protests that the Galilee and the Neville screen at Durham were saved from destruction in 1796, and both here and elsewhere he persistently opposed the activities of James Wyatt as an 'improver' of ancient buildings.

In 1805 Carter described himself as 'a man lost in two extremes, one for the Antiquities of England, and the other for the Divine Melodies of the immortal Handel'. He was, in fact, passionately fond of music, and composed 'two operas founded upon the History, Ancient Manners and Customs of this Country', entitled *The White Rose* and *The Cell of St. Oswald*, for which he painted the appropriate scenery.

Carter died on 8 September 1817, and was buried at Hampstead. He never married, though as a young man he had an unhappy love-affair of which he published an extraordinary account (illustrated by an engraving of his *inamorata* in the nude) under the pseudonym of 'John Ramble'.[1] In later life he had a young female servant who (according to Britton) 'occasionally accompanied him on his sketching excursions, dressed in boy's clothes'.

Carter's drawings were sold at Sotheby's on 25 February 1818 and fetched £1695 (catalogue in Bodleian Library, Douce CC.284). Twenty volumes of his topographical drawings are in the British Library (Add. MSS. 29925-44), and there are many at Westminster City Library and in the Gough Collection in the Bodleian Library, including a fine set of Dorchester Abbey (Gough Maps 227). His original drawings for the *Builder's Magazine* are at the Canadian Centre for Architecture at Montreal. Other drawings are in the R.I.B.A. Drawings Collection, Durham Cathedral Library, Stonyhurst College and the Victoria and Albert Museum (D.18-1886 is a design for a Gothic reredos in his hand). Designs by Carter for extensive additions to Bywell Hall, Northumberland, made in 1777, are preserved at that house: see also *Builder's Magazine*, pl. lxxx, and lot 176 in the sale catalogue for designs for a large classical villa for J. Fenwick of Bywell.

[Obituaries in *Gent's Mag.* 1817 (ii), 363–6 and 366–8 (the latter by J. C. Buckler); 1818 (i), 273–6, 382; 1822 (i), 102–3; memoir by John Britton in *Builder* viii, 1850, 302–4; will in P.C.C. 472 EFFINGHAM; C. L. Eastlake, *A History of the Gothic Revival*, 1872, 103–8; *D.N.B.*; Joan Evans, *History of the Society of Antiquaries*, 1956, 206–14; M. E. Roberts, 'John Carter at St. Stephen's Chapel', in *England in the Fourteenth Century*, Harlaxton Symposium 1985, published 1986.]

MIDFORD CASTLE, nr. BATH, SOMERSET, was built *c.*1775 for H. Disney Roebuck after a design for 'a Gothic Mansion' published by Carter in the *Builder's Magazine*, but it is not known whether he was actually concerned in its erection [C. Hussey in *C. Life*, 3–10 March 1944].

PETERBOROUGH CATHEDRAL, Gothic altar-screen and organ-screen, 1780; removed 1832 [J. Britton, *History and Antiquities of Peterborough Cathedral*, 1828, 73; B.L., Add. MS. 29925, f. 81].

ELTON HALL, HUNTS., Gothic additions and alterations for 1st Earl of Carysfort, *c.*1790 [J. Britton, *History and Antiquities of Peterborough Cathedral*, 1828, 74; drawings by

[1] *The Scotch Parents; or, the Remarkable Case of John Ramble written by himself*, 1773. The B.L. copy has a contemporary inscription identifying the author as 'Mr. Carter, son of a statuary in Piccadilly', and Soane told John Britton that John Ramble was John Carter (*Builder* viii, 303 n.).

Carter in B.L., Add. MS. 29930, ff. 74–9] (*V.C.H. Hunts.* iii, 157, for views; also *C. Life*, 21 Feb., 7 March 1957).

CANTERBURY CATHEDRAL, designs for alterations to choir, 1791 [John Britton, *op. cit.*, 73].

WINCHESTER, ST. PETER'S CATHOLIC CHAPEL, JEWRY STREET (restored 1987 as MILNER HALL), for the Revd. John Milner, 1792, Gothic [J. Milner, *History of Winchester* ii, 1798, 230].

DEBDEN CHURCH, ESSEX, octagonal Gothic chapel and monument designed by Carter for R. M. T. Chiswell, 1792–3, but 'not executed under his entire direction' [J. P. Neale, *Views of Seats* ii, 1819, under 'Debden Hall'].

OATLANDS HOUSE, SURREY, Gothic detailing for the new front designed by Henry Holland for Frederick, Duke of York, 1794–1800; dem. [J. Carter, *The Ancient Architecture of England*, frontispiece; *Gent's Mag.* 1808 (i), 9; 1817 (ii), 365; B.L., Add. MSS. 29942, ff. 94, 103–5, 108–9, 29943, ff. 260, 262].

STOURHEAD, WILTS., ornamental cottage for Sir Richard Colt Hoare, Bart., 1806 [K. Woodbridge, *Landscape and Antiquity*, 1970, 146–7].

WROTHAM, KENT, HELEN BETENSON'S ALMSHOUSES, ST. MARY'S ROAD, 1806, Gothic [*Gent's Mag.* 1817 (ii), 365].

SUNDRIDGE CHURCH, KENT, alterations for Lord Frederick Campbell, *c.*1810 and Gothic monument for Lord Frederick (d. 1817) and his wife (d. 1807), for which the original designs are in B.L., Add. MS. 29941, ff. 45, 61–4 [J. Britton, *Descriptive Sketches of Tunbridge Wells and the Calverley Estate*, 1832, 10].

EXETER CATHEDRAL: the great west window, executed in Coade stone under the supervision of Sir John Soane *c.*1810, 'was from designs made by Mr. Carter' [*Gent's Mag.* 1817 (ii), 365].

LEA CASTLE, WORCS. Carter's designs for a house in the Norman style for John Knight, who acquired the site in 1809, are in the Metropolitan Museum of Art, New York. [T. Mowl, 'Designs by John Carter for Lea Castle, Worcs.', *Arch. Hist.* 25, 1982]. In B.L., Add. MS. 29942, ff. 136–8, there are designs by Carter for a 'Saxon' ice-house here, dated 1816. Lea Castle (dem. *c.*1945) was a castellated building differing in many respects from Carter's designs, but the existence in Kidderminster Public Library of a view of the house as built in Carter's hand suggests that he may have been responsible for the executed design as well as for the rejected one.

SEVENOAKS, KENT, a Gothic chapel 'now completing near Sevenoaks', 1817 [*Gent's Mag.* 1817 (ii), 365].

WESTMINSTER, Gothic details for Edward Hussey Delaval's house nr. Parliament Stairs; dem. [J. T. Smith, *A Book for a Rainy Day*, 1905 ed., 173–4].

CARTER, OWEN BROWNE (1806–1859), was born in London. Nothing is known of his early life beyond his own statement in 1834 that he had had fifteen years' experience 'in every branch of his profession, ten of which were spent with the late Mr. William Garbett', i.e. William Garbett of Winchester (*q.v.*). By 1829 he was sufficiently accomplished as an architectural draughtsman to be taken to Egypt by Robert Hay to participate in his archaeological survey, but illness obliged him to return to England in the winter of 1830/1 and it was not until Garbett's death in 1834 that he started his own architectural practice in Winchester.

Some of the drawings which Carter made in Egypt are in the Print Room of the British Museum and many of them were reproduced in the two folio volumes of lithographs entitled *Illustrations of Cairo* which Hay published in 1840. At Winchester Carter was active as an architectural topographer, supplementing his income as an architect by providing illustrations for P. Hall's *Memorials of Winchester* (1830) and publishing a set of four lithographs as *Picturesque Views in and near Basingstoke* (1841). He also wrote articles on local ecclesiastical antiquities for Weale's *Quarterly Papers on Architecture* (1844–5). Only a few numbers were published of a projected series of views of Wiltshire churches, but 63 of Carter's original drawings are preserved in the library of the Wiltshire Archaeological Society. In 1845, when the Archaeological Institute visited Winchester, Carter acted as one of the secretaries, and was thanked for the drawings which he made for the occasion. In 1847, 1849 and 1851 he exhibited at the Royal Academy.

Carter's practice appears to have failed in the 1850s and he died in poverty at Salisbury on 30 March 1859, aged 53. G.E. Street was in his office from 1841 to 1844, but moved on to 'a master of greater pretentions' in the person of Gilbert Scott. John Colson was also his pupil.

Carter's Gothic churches are typical of their period, despite some attempt to achieve authenticity of detail by copying windows and bell-turrets from medieval originals. His Winchester Corn Exchange is an attractive and effective classical design with a 'Vitruvian Tuscan' portico inspired by that of Inigo Jones's church in Covent Garden.

[*Gent's Mag.* 1859 (i), 550; *D.N.B.*; L. Binyon, *Catalogue of Drawings by British Artists in . . . the British Museum* i, 1898, 199–201; 'Drawings of Churches by O. B. Carter, 1847–50', *Wiltshire Archl. Mag.* xl, 1918–19, 190–1; S. Tillett, *Egypt Itself* (1984); R. Freeman, *The Art and Architecture of Owen Browne Carter*, Hampshire County Council 1991.]

NORK HOUSE, BANSTEAD, SURREY, designs for minor additions for 2nd Lord Arden, 1836; dem. 1929 [John Harris, *Catalogue of British Drawings for Architecture, etc. in American Collections*, 1970, 46–7].

WAREHAM, DORSET, WORKHOUSE (now Hospital), CHRISTMAS CLOSE, 1836, with H. Hyde [R.C.H.M., *Dorset* ii (2), 317].

WINCHESTER, THE CORN EXCHANGE (now Public Library), JEWRY STREET, 1836–8 [*Companion to the Almanac*, 1839, 246–7].

OTTERBOURNE CHURCH, HANTS., 1837–9, Gothic, in conjunction with William Yonge, squire of Otterbourne [*Gent's Mag.* 1839 (ii), 304; Georgina Battiscombe, *Charlotte Mary Yonge*, 1943, 50].

WINCHESTER, CHERNOCKE PLACE, SOUTHGATE STREET (a terrace of 8 houses), 1837–40 [Freeman, *op. cit.*, 4].

AMPFIELD CHURCH, HANTS., 1838–40, Gothic [*Gent's Mag.* 1839 (ii), 304].

WALLOP HOUSE, NETHER WALLOP, HANTS., for the Revd. Walter Blunt, 1838, Tudor style [signed lithograph published by Carter].

OVINGTON CHURCHYARD, HANTS., monument to Sir T. R. Dyer, Bart. (d. 1838), 1839 [*Gent's Mag.* 1839 (ii), 160].

WINCHESTER CEMETERY, CHAPELS, etc., 1840; dem. [Freeman, *op. cit.*, 8–9].

OAKLEY CHURCH, HANTS., added N. transept, 1840–1; rebuilt 1869 [I.C.B.S. plan in Library of Society of Antiquaries, London].

COLEMORE CHURCH, HANTS., alterations 1845 [I.C.B.S.]

HYDE, nr. WINCHESTER, HANTS., SCHOOL, 1845; dem. [Freeman, *op. cit.*, 8].

SOUTHAMPTON, ST. PETER'S CHURCH, COMMERCIAL ROAD, 1845–6, Romanesque; converted into offices *c.*1984 [P. Brannon, *Picture of Southampton*, 1850, 44].

WINCHESTER CASTLE, restored GREAT HALL 1845 and reconstructed GRAND JURY CHAMBER 1849–52 in Tudor Gothic style; altered 1872–3 [Freeman, *op. cit.*, 14–16].

WINCHESTER CATHEDRAL, designed curved steps to, and canopy of, choir pulpit, 1848 [Freeman, 21–22].

GRATELEY CHURCH, HANTS., restoration, 1850–1 [I.C.B.S.].

SALISBURY, POULTRY CROSS, restoration, 1852–4 [Freeman, *op. cit.*, 22].

CARTWRIGHT, FRANCIS (*c.*1695–1758), was a master builder living at Bryanston, nr. Blandford in Dorset. He is described as 'carver' in his will, but his monument in Blandford St. Mary Church shows that he also acted as an architect, for on it are carved a T-square, dividers and rule, and the incised elevation of a house. He died on 24 April 1758, aged 63, leaving a newly erected house in Blandford St. Mary, and directing that all his stock of 'Stone, Marble, Timber and Boards . . . with all Tools Engines and Implements belonging to my trade' should be sold for the benefit of his wife and daughter.

In 1738–41 Cartwright was responsible for alterations to CREECH GRANGE, DORSET, for Dennis Bond, including the rebuilding of the south front 'in a modest country version of the current Palladian style' [Arthur Oswald, *The Country Houses of Dorset*, 1959, 86]. What appears to be the original design for this front is in the R.I.B.A. Drawings Collection (K 4/24(1)). In 1746–50 he designed and built KING'S NYMPTON PARK, DEVON, for James Buller [contract and accounts in Cornwall Record Office, Buller papers, bundles 134 and 689]. This house is a Palladian villa whose general form and principal façade are based on Roger Morris's Marble Hill at Twickenham. CAME HOUSE, nr. DORCHESTER, DORSET, can also be attributed to Cartwright, for the north front closely resembles the elevation incised on his monument. The house was built by John Damer in 1754.

In 1744–6 Cartwright was employed (with John Bastard of Blandford) in rebuilding CRICHEL HOUSE, DORSET, for Sir William Napier, Bart., after a fire [Napier account at Hoare's Bank, *ex inf.* Mr. John Cornforth]. In 1754 he remodelled the E. and W. fronts of HALSWELL HOUSE, SOMERSET, for Sir Charles Kemeys Tynte, Bart. [G. Jackson-Stops in *C. Life*, 9 Feb. 1989], and in the same year he largely remodelled the interior of the Hon. James Everard Arundell's house at ASHCOMBE, TOLLARD ROYAL, WILTS. [Wilts. C.R.O., Arundell papers, Inventories and Household Accounts II].

Cartwright's work at Creech Grange, King's Nympton and Came establishes him as a competent provincial designer in the Palladian manner. His work as a carver needs further investigation, but it was presumably in that capacity that he was working for Henry Hoare at Stourhead in 1749–55. In 1742–3 he received over £20 from the churchwardens of Blandford Forum for unspecified work, presumably in the church.

[Arthur Oswald, *Country Houses of Dorset*, 1959, 34–5, 86, 158; R.C.H.M., *Dorset* ii (2), 270–1, 384–6, iii (1), pl. 119 (illustration of monument); Stourhead archives in Wiltshire Record Office, account-book 383/6; Blandford Parish records; P.C.C. 211 HUTTON.]

CARTWRIGHT, THOMAS (–1702), was one of the leading London mason-contractors during the latter part of the seventeenth century. He served his apprenticeship in the 1630s and was by 1663 a Liveryman of the Masons' Company, subsequently serving as Warden (1671) and twice as Master (1673 and 1694). After the Great Fire he was much employed in the City, rebuilding Moorgate, 1672, dem. 1760 (measured drawing in Bodleian Library, MS. Gough Drawings a. 1, f. 6) and undertaking masonry at the Weavers' Hall (1667–9); the Haberdashers' Hall (1669–71); the Drapers' Hall (completed 1671); the Tallow-Chandlers' Hall (1672–3) and Mercers' Hall (completed 1672). He was the mason-contractor for three of Wren's City churches – St. Benet Fink (1670–8), St. Mary le Bow (1670–80) and St. Antholin (1678–82). He was also the contracting mason for the new Royal Exchange and after Edward Jerman's death in 1668, 'declared himselfe master of the wholle designe intended for that buildinge'. No new surveyor was appointed in place of Jerman, and on 26 March 1670 Cartwright himself 'presented to the committee a draft of the frontispiece to Cornhill and the cupilo as he advised to build it, of which they approved'. The building was completed in 1671, in which year Cartwright dedicated an engraving of it to the Lord Mayor and Corporation (B.L., *King's Maps* xxiv, 11a, 1). It was destroyed by fire in 1838.

From about 1680 to 1702 Cartwright was engaged in rebuilding ST. THOMAS'S HOSPITAL, SOUTHWARK, whose 'frontispiece', ornamented with a statue of King Edward VI and four cripples, he designed and carved. He was also the mason employed to build ST. THOMAS'S CHURCH, SOUTHWARK, in 1700–2, and very likely made the design.

Though evidently capable of architectural design, Cartwright was primarily a mason and carver. In the latter capacity his most notable works were the monuments to Sir John Langham at Cottesbrooke, Northants. (1676), and to Sir John Lewys at Ledsham, Yorks. (W.R.) (1677). Several other tombs are mentioned in what is almost certainly his account-book in the Bodleian Library (MS. Rawlinson C.495, wrongly ascribed in the previous edition of this *Dictionary* to John Young, *q.v.*). For further details of his work as a sculptor see R. Gunnis's *Dictionary of British Sculptors 1660–1851*, revised ed. 1968, 86–7.

[D. Knoop & G. P. Jones, *The London Mason in the Seventeenth Century*, 1935, 38; *Wren Soc.*, *passim*; *A.P.S.D.*, *s.v.* 'Jerman'; Guildhall Library, MS. 184/4.]

CARVER, JOHN (–1858), was a builder-architect who established himself at Meigle in Perthshire, where either he or his successor built the house called 'Carverfield'. He designed BALHARY HOUSE, ALYTH, PERTHSHIRE, for John Smyth in 1817 [drawings preserved in the house, *ex inf.* Mr. David Walker], and a steading at LEGERTLAW, PERTHSHIRE, in 1830 [Seggieden Letter-Book, 1813–30]. He died on 27 February 1858 [S.R.O., SC 49/31/65–6]. He was presumably the father of John Carver (1834–96), an architect who is commemorated by a tombstone in Meigle churchyard, and the uncle of the latter's cousin David Carver (1803–78), who practised as an architect at Kinloch.

CARVER, RICHARD (*c.*1792–1862), was presumably the 'R. Carver' who was a pupil of Sir Jeffrey Wyatville, exhibiting architectural designs at the Royal Academy from Wyatville's office in 1811 and 1812. He established himself in practice at Taunton in Somerset, where he held the post of county surveyor. Carver's numerous churches, though occasionally showing some originality in plan (e.g. Theale, and the octagonal Blackford), are poorly detailed, and were despised by serious Gothic Revivalists. Mr. Carver 'has proved himself entirely ignorant of the principles of Ecclesiastical Architecture' declared the *Ecclesiologist* in 1844. Carver retired from the county surveyorship in 1857, and died at Wilton, nr. Taunton, on 1 September 1862, aged 70. [*Ecclesiologist* iii, 1844, 158; *Builder* xv, 1857, 78; monumental inscription.]

FAIRFIELD HOUSE, STOGURSEY, SOMERSET, alterations for (Sir) John Acland, *c.*1815 [*V.C.H. Somerset* vi, 140–1].

WILLETT HOUSE, ELWORTHY, SOMERSET, for Richard Blommart, *c.*1816 [*V.C.H. Somerset* v, 71].

CHAPEL CLEEVE HOUSE, SOMERSET, for John Halliday, 1818–23, Tudor Gothic; enlarged 1913–14 [*V.C.H. Somerset* v, 44].

BLACKFORD CHURCH, nr. WEDMORE, SOMERSET, 1823, Gothic [I.C.B.S.].

BRIDGWATER, SOMERSET, TOWN HALL, JUDGES' LODGINGS, etc. (now council offices), 1823 [*V.C.H. Somerset* vi, 202].

STOGURSEY CHURCH, SOMERSET, restoration, 1824 [*V.C.H. Somerset* vi, 156].

MAUNSEL HOUSE, NORTH PETHERTON, SOMERSET, alterations for Sir John Slade,

Bart., *c.*1835 [*V.C.H. Somerset* vi, 296].
BISHOP'S HULL CHURCH, SOMERSET, rebuilt nave, 1826 [I.C.B.S.].
WIVELISCOMBE CHURCH, SOMERSET, 1827–9, Gothic [inscription on W. gallery].
THEALE CHURCH, SOMERSET, 1828 [I.C.B.S.].
SUTTON MALLET CHURCH, SOMERSET, rebuilt 1829 except tower, Gothic [I.C.B.S.].
WELLINGTON, SOMERSET, HOLY TRINITY CHURCH, 1831, Gothic (cruciform); dem. [*Gent's Mag.* 1840 (ii), 307].
HATCH BEAUCHAMP CHURCH, SOMERSET, added S. aisle and vestry transept, 1834, Gothic [I.C.B.S.].
CHARD, SOMERSET, THE TOWN HALL, 1834–5 [Somerset C.R.O., Chard Corporation Minute Book 1779–1835].
MILVERTON, SOMERSET, THE SCHOOL-HOUSE, 1835 [accounts of the Trustees of the Mary Lambe Charity, Milverton, *ex inf.* Miss Mary Dunbar].
ST. AUDRIES HOUSE, WEST QUANTOXHEAD, SOMERSET, alterations for Sir Peregrine Fuller-Palmer-Acland, *c.*1835 [*V.C.H. Somerset* v, 131].
BURROWBRIDGE CHURCH, SOMERSET, 1836, Gothic [I.C.B.S.].
WILTON CHURCH, nr. TAUNTON, SOMERSET, rebuilt chancel and E. end of nave, 1837–8, Gothic [I.C.B.S.].
EAST HORRINGTON CHURCH, SOMERSET, 1838, Gothic [I.C.B.S.].
BURTLE CHURCH, SOMERSET, 1838–9, Gothic [I.C.B.S.].
COXLEY CHURCH, nr. WELLS, SOMERSET, 1838, Gothic [I.C.B.S.].
BURNHAM CHURCH, SOMERSET, added N. aisle, 1838–9 [I.C.B.S.].
BRIDGWATER, SOMERSET, HOLY TRINITY CHURCH, 1839–40, Gothic; dem. 1958 [*Gent's Mag.* 1840 (ii), 307; I.C.B.S.].
BULLAND LODGE, CHIPSTABLE, SOMERSET, enlarged *c.*1840 [*V.C.H. Somerset* v, 27].
CANNINGTON CHURCH, SOMERSET, internal rearrangement, 1840 [*V.C.H. Somerset* vi, 89].
LYNG VICARAGE, SOMERSET, *c.*1840 [*V.C.H. Somerset* vi, 63].
CHEDINGTON CHURCH, DORSET, 1840–1, Gothic [I.C.B.S.].
OVER STOWEY CHURCH, SOMERSET, enlarged 1840, Gothic [Church Commissioners, Church Building Commissioners' records, File 21744, pt. 8].
TAUNTON, SOMERSET, HOLY TRINITY CHURCH, 1842, Gothic [I.C.B.S.].
TAUNTON, SOMERSET, ST. MARY MAGDALENE CHURCH, repairs and restoration (with Benjamin Ferrey), 1842–3 [J. Cottle, *St. Mary Magdalene, Taunton*, 1845, 6].
EASTON (ST. PAUL) CHURCH, SOMERSET, refurnishing, 1845 [*Ecclesiologist* iv, 1845, 292].
HEMYOCK CHURCH, DEVON, extensive alterations, with C. E. Giles, 1846–7 [I.C.B.S.].
WELLINGTON CHURCH, SOMERSET, repaired and enlarged with C. E. Giles, 1849–50 [I.C.B.S.].
BEAMINSTER, DORSET, HOLY TRINITY CHURCH, with C. E. Giles, 1849–51, Gothic [R.C.H.M. *West Dorset*, 21].

Carver rebuilt or enlarged parsonage houses in DEVON at SILVERTON, 1839 [Devon C.R.O., Exeter Faculty papers]; and in SOMERSET at WEST QUANTOXHEAD, 1815, CUTCOMBE, 1833, EAST BRENT, 1838, MONKSILVER, 1838, WESTON ZOYLAND, 1839, PITMINSTER, 1840 and ISLE BREWER, 1846 [Somerset C.R.O., D/D/Bbm].

CARWITHAM, THOMAS, of Twickenham, was a pupil of Sir James Thornhill and a decorative painter. He appears to have specialized in architectural ornament, for he was the author of a small treatise entitled *The Description and Use of an Architectonick Sector* (1723), and at the end there is an advertisement: 'History and Architect Painting done by the Author'. There was a second edition in 1733. He should not be confused with John Carwitham, an engraver who published *Various Kinds of Floor Decorations represented both in plano and perspective. Being useful designs for ornamenting the floors of halls, rooms, summer houses &c . . . in twenty-four copper plates* [1739]. [E. Croft-Murray, *Decorative Painting in England* ii, 1970, 32; J. Harris, *Catalogue of British Drawings for Architecture . . . in American Collections*, 1971, 48; Eileen Harris, *British Architectural Books and Writers 1556–1785*, 1990, 149.]

CASSON, JOHN WHITESIDE (1767–1842), was the son of a joiner in Liverpool, and practised there throughout his working life. He probably designed No. 62 RODNEY STREET, LIVERPOOL, for John Gladstone in 1792, as the builder's contract specifies that the work was to be done 'to the satisfaction of J. W. Casson surveyor, who is to give directions from time to time as to the manner of executing the whole work' [St. Deiniol's Library, Hawarden, Gladstone papers, Box 178/15]. MELLING CHURCH, LANCS., 1834, Gothic, appears to be his only other recorded work [I.C.B.S.]. [information from Dr. Janet Gnosspelius].

CASTELL, ROBERT (–1728), appears to have been a scholarly gentleman rather than a practising architect, but nothing is known of his life before 1727, when proposals were published for a volume by him reconstructing and illustrating the two Roman villas described in the letters of Pliny the Younger. This was to be a preliminary to an edition of Vitruvius by Castell, illustrated by engravings from drawings in Lord Burlington's collection by Palladio and others. However, in June 1728 Castell was imprisoned for debt in the Fleet Prison in London, where he died of smallpox on 12 December. His ill-treatment by Bambridge, the Warden of the Fleet, became a national scandal, and was debated in the House of Commons. According to the Commons' *Journal* (xxi, 277), Castell was 'born to a competent estate', but died 'leaving all his affairs in the greatest confusion, and a numerous family of small children in the utmost distress'.

Castell's account of Pliny's villas was published posthumously in 1729 as *The Villas of the Ancients Illustrated*, with a dedication to Lord Burlington, but nothing more was heard of the edition of Vitruvius, although it was said to be 'ready for the Press' in 1728. *The Villas of the Ancients* was a serious attempt to reconstruct Pliny's villas from the literary evidence, and an improvement on earlier attempts by Scamozzi and Félibien. Castell printed his sources in the original Latin with an English translation, and accompanied them with elaborate engraved plates. These purport to show not only the villas but also their surroundings, and the layouts have interesting affinities with English landscape-gardening of the period. There were at least two reprintings, one a cheaper 'trade edition' omitting the Latin texts. [Eileen Harris, *British Architectural Books and Writers 1556–1785*, 1990, 149–54.]

CATHERWOOD, FREDERICK (1799–1854), was born in London, and was a pupil from 1815 to 1820 of Michael Meredith. Between 1821 and 1825 he made an extensive tour in Italy, Greece and Egypt. On his return, he began to practise his profession, designing a large glasshouse near Westminster Bridge, and some houses at Pentonville. It was, however, as an archaeological draughtsman that he was to make his name, and in this capacity he left England again in 1831 as a member of Robert Hay's expedition to investigate and record the antiquities of the Nile Valley. In company with Francis Arundale and Joseph Bonomi, he also explored Palestine and Arabia, and, disguised as an Egyptian officer, made measured drawings of the Dome of the Rock in Jerusalem. In the course of his travels he obtained the materials for a series of panoramas which he afterwards exhibited in London and New York. In 1836 he set up in practice in New York in partnership with Frederick Diaper, a pupil of Sir Robert Smirke who became a well-known American architect. But three years later he set out to investigate the Maya cities of Central America in company with J. L. Stephens, and it was his pioneer work in this field which gave him a place in the history of American archaeology which he never attained in that of architecture. His principal publication was the *Views of Ancient Monuments in Central America, Chiapas and Yucatán*, 1844. He also superintended the building of railways in Demarara, Panama and California. He returned to England in 1853, but was involved in the loss of the steamer *Arctic* while returning to America in the following year [V. W. Von Hagen, *Frederick Catherwood, Architect*, 1950]. Drawings by Catherwood were sold at Christie's on 14 July and 15 Dec. 1987.

CATLEY, THOMAS, an architect of Hastings, designed ST. CLEMENT'S CHURCH, HALTON, nr. HASTINGS, SUSSEX, 1838, dem. *c.*1970, in the 'Early English' style [*V.C.H. Sussex* ix, 25; *The Watering-Places of Great Britain and Fashionable Directory*, Joseph Robins, 1833, 24].

CATLYN, WILLIAM (1628–1709), of Hull, was the son of John Catlyn (d. 1658), a bricklayer who was Warden of the Hull Bricklayers' Company in 1628. The elder Catlyn was admitted a freeman of York in 1651, at the request of the 3rd Lord Fairfax [*Register of the Freemen of York*, Surtees Soc. 102, 1859, 111], which suggests that he may have been involved in the building of Fairfax's houses in Bishophill, York, and at Nunappleton, Yorks. (W.R.) (for the latter cf. correspondence in *Times Literary Supplement*, 28 Jan. and 11 Feb. 1972). William Catlyn was admitted a freeman of Hull in 1658 and was Warden of the Bricklayers' Company in 1667. In 1663 he enlarged the hospital at the CHARTERHOUSE, Hull's leading charitable institution, and built the master's house there. In 1673 he designed a new chapel at the Charterhouse (dem. 1778–80) and in 1681–2 he was engaged in 'beautifying' the GUILDHALL for the Corporation, perhaps adding the pedimented façade (dem. 1806). In 1682 he also oversaw the building of the MARKET CROSS (dem. 1762), a domed classical building probably designed by Richard Roebuck, the contracting mason.

The accounts for Catlyn's work at the Charterhouse were presented to the Council by Alderman George Crowle, who in 1664 built CROWLE HOUSE, HIGH STREET, HULL, in the local variety of Artisan Mannerism known as the 'Humber brick style'. Crowle also founded and built an almshouse called CROWLE HOSPITAL in SEWER LANE in 1668 and this was a building in a similar style. It is likely that Catlyn designed and built both Crowle's house and his hospital, and if so he may well have been responsible for other buildings of this character, including the front of WILBERFORCE'S HOUSE (*c.*1660), and the WORLABY HOSPITAL at WORLABY in LINCOLNSHIRE, built in 1663 by Lord Bellasis, the Governor of Hull, whose demolished house at Worlaby was another 'Artisan Mannerist' building. In 1674 Catlyn referred to his 'great undertakings in Lincolnshire', one of which was the GRAMMAR SCHOOL at BRIGG, which he contracted to build in July of that year [Lincs. Archives Office, Amcotts 6/C/40/3]. The Brigg school is a more restrained building, without Mannerist detailing, which suggests that Catlyn had by then assimilated the conventions of English Restoration architecture. Catlyn, who was Sheriff of Hull in 1683, died in 1709, leaving 'A Book of Architecture of Ancient Rome' to the library of Holy Trinity church.

[David Neave, 'William Catlyn of Hull', *Bulletin E. Yorks. Local History Soc.* Autumn 1983; I. & E. Hall, *Georgian Hull*, 1978/9, 14; information from Mr. J. A. Booth.]

CATT, BENJAMIN BATLEY (*c.*1783–1867), the son of a carpenter, was educated at Ipswich school and practised in that town as an architect, builder, auctioneer and timber merchant. He was a Bailiff of the borough in 1828, 1830 and 1832 and a Common Councillor in 1815 and was reported in 1835 to have used his position to his private advantage [C. Brown, B. Haward and R. Kindred, *Dictionary of Architects of Suffolk Buildings 1800–1914*, 1991, 63–4]. In Ipswich he designed the TOWN HALL, with a Palladian façade, 1818–19, dem. 1867, as recorded by the inscription on the foundation stone given by Dugdale, *British Traveller* iv, 1819, 298, and was associated with William Brown (*q.v.*) in the design of the PROVISION MARKET, 1810–11, dem. 1897 [G. R. Clark, *History and Description of Ipswich*, 1830]. Catt also designed HELMINGHAM RECTORY, SUFFOLK, 1812–13, with a Gothick front, his original drawing for which [Suffolk C.R.O., FF 1/44/1] is illustrated by Brown *et al.*, *op. cit.*, fig. 31.

CAUSFIELD, GEORGE, a mason of Seaton Sluice, Northumberland, contracted in 1739 to rebuild the tower of GATESHEAD CHURCH, CO. DURHAM [Durham C.R.O., EP/Ga SM/5/1, f. 439, *ex inf.* Dr. T. Friedman]. According to E. Mackenzie, *History of Newcastle* ii, 1827, 751, 'Causfield, the architect, was ruined by the undertaking.'

CAVELER, WILLIAM, was the author of a collection of measured drawings of details, etc., of medieval English architecture entitled *Select Specimens of Gothic Architecture*, 4 vols. 1835–6, 2nd ed. in 1 vol. 1839. He also published in 1850 *Architectural Illustrations of Warmington Church, Northamptonshire.* In 1837 he entered a Roman Doric design for the Royal Berkshire Hospital competition [*Reading Mercury*, 11 Feb. 1837] and he exhibited at the Royal Academy in 1844 and 1850. From about 1845 onwards he was practising in Margate, Kent, where he restored the parish church [*Builder* iv, 1846, 532].

CHALKLEY, C—, appears to have been a pupil of Jeffry Wyatville, from whose address he exhibited a 'Design for a Lodge' at the R.A. in 1800. In the W. Sussex Record Office there are two elevations of West Dean Park, Sussex, dated 1805 and endorsed as by Chalkley. West Dean Park was then in course of erection to the designs of James Wyatt.

CHALMERS, JOHN (–*c.*1814), lived at Chamberfield, nr. Dunfermline in Fife. In 1792 DUNFERMLINE TOWNHOUSE (dem.) was enlarged in accordance with a plan 'made out by' John Chalmers [S.R.O., B 20/13/13, 30 April 1792], and in the same year a design for QUEEN ANNE STREET CHAPEL, DUNFERMLINE, by 'Mr. John Chalmers Architect' was accepted but was not in the event proceeded with [S.R.O., CH 3/568/13]. In 1802–4 CARNOCK MANSE, FIFE, was built to his designs [S.R.O., CH 2/105/13, pp. 194–6]. He is referred to as the 'late Mr. Chalmers Architect' in 1814 [S.R.O., CH 2/105/14, pp. 128–9]. The death on 20 Feb. 1822 of John Chalmers, surveyor, 'fourth son of the late John Chalmers of Chamberfield, architect, Esqr.', is recorded in *Edinburgh Magazine* x, 1822, 560. The younger Chalmers practised in Edinburgh and in 1822 made a very competent set of plans and elevations of ST. GILES' CATHEDRAL [S.R.O., RHP 6512/8–12].

CHAMBERLAIN, PETER, a carpenter by trade, was admitted a freeman of Norwich in 1748 [*The Freemen of Norwich 1714–1752*, ed. Millican, Norfolk Record Soc. 52, 16]. In 1769 he advertised in the *Norwich Mercury* that he had had upwards of 30 years' experience of mensuration and architecture, and 'makes Estimates, draws Plans and Elevations, measures, values and superintends Buildings' [*Norwich Mercury*, 11 Feb. 1769, *ex inf.* Mr. David Cubitt].

CHAMBERS, ROBERT (*c.*1710–1784), was a mason by trade and a native of Gloucestershire. Horace Walpole describes him as 'carver, architect and stainer of marble'. Although best known in the first and last capacities, he did exhibit architectural drawings at the Free Society of Artists, e.g. 'A design in architecture of a plan and elevation of a grotesque building with its tessellated floor' (1763), plans and sections of the royal vault in Westminster Abbey (1769), and plans of the harbour and pier at Dover (1778, 1782). Designs by him for 'a Bone-House, to be built at the North East Corner of St. Mary's Church in Dover' (1773) and for a new window in the south wall of the same church 'near the font' (1772–3) are preserved in the British Library (*King's Maps*, xvi, 48). For his work as a sculptor and stainer of marble see R. Gunnis's *Dictionary of British Sculptors*, revised ed. 1968, 90–1. Some designs by Chambers for chimney-pieces at CLAYDON HOUSE, BUCKS., are among the Verney papers there.

CHAMBERS, SIR WILLIAM (1723–1796), was the son of John Chambers, a Scottish merchant established at Gothenburg in Sweden, where he was born on 23 February 1723. His father had him educated in England, sending him to Ripon, where he presumably attended the grammar school. At the age of 16 he returned to Sweden to begin a mercantile career in the Swedish East India Company. In 1740–2 he made his first voyage as a cadet on one of the Company's ships bound for Bengal. In 1743–5 a second voyage took him to Canton, and in 1748–9 he again travelled to China in the capacity of a 'supercargo' on the ship *Hoppet*. His commercial duties were not, however, onerous, and in an autobiographical note among the archives of Uppsala University he recalled that on these voyages he found time to study 'modern languages, mathematics and the free arts, but chiefly civil architecture, for which latter I have from my earliest years felt the strongest inclination'. Moreover, between voyages he was able to visit 'England, Scotland, Holland, Flanders and a part of France'. While in Canton, he had made sketches of Chinese buildings, and some of his European excursions appear to have been architectural in character. By 1749 he had enough capital to abandon his mercantile career and make architecture his 'sole study and profession'.

It was in J. F. Blondel's École des Arts in Paris that Chambers began his professional training and there he would have met some of the young men who were to be the leaders of French neo-classicism in the 1760s and 1770s. In the autumn of 1750 he set out for Italy, where he was to spend five years, chiefly in Rome, though he 'also visited . . . Naples, Florence, Bologna, Venice, Vicenza, Genoa, Milan, Turin etc., collecting in all these places all that could serve me and increase my knowledge [of] the science I had chosen for my study'. At Rome he appears to have received tuition from the French drawing-masters Clérisseau and Pécheux, and besides studying a wide variety of buildings, ancient and modern, he was strongly influenced by the neo-classical ideas of French designers such as Le Geay and Le Lorrain. His reputation among the visiting English as 'a prodigy for Genius, for Sense & good taste' was reported by his rival Robert Adam, who thought that he 'in great measure deserves their encomium'.

In 1755 Chambers returned to England to begin practice. He was accompanied by a wife and an infant daughter. Apart from the fact that she was born Catherine More and came from Bromsgrove, nothing certain is known of the origins of the woman Chambers had married in Rome in March 1753. Joseph Wilton (who met them both in Rome) told Farington that she was 'a milliner girl [who] followed him to Paris'. In London they took lodgings next to Tom's Coffee House in Russell Street, Covent Garden. Although at first he had few commissions, Chambers soon had the good fortune to be recommended to Lord Bute as a suitable person to become architectural tutor to the Prince of Wales, afterwards King George III, an appointment that laid the foundations of the royal favour which he was subsequently to enjoy. While at Rome he had made grandiose designs for a mausoleum to the memory of the prince's father, Frederick, Prince of Wales, and in 1757 the Dowager Princess employed him to lay out the grounds of her house at Kew, and to embellish them with a variety of temples and garden buildings, some classical, others oriental in style. In 1763 he advertised this royal patronage by the publication of a handsome folio dedicated to the princess and entitled *Plans, Elevations, Sections and Perspective Views of the Gardens and Buildings at Kew in Surrey*. A collection of the original drawings bound up by Chambers for presentation to Lord Bute is now in the Metropolitan Museum at New York. This was not Chambers's first book, for in 1757 he had published *Designs of Chinese Buildings, Furniture, Dresses, etc.*, and in 1759 he produced the first part of a projected *Treatise on Civil Architecture*, a work in which he set out 'to collect into one volume what is now dispersed in a great many, and to select, from mountains of promiscuous Materials, a Series of Sound Precepts and good Designs'. The result became the standard English treatise on the use of the Orders and their enrichments, largely superseding Isaac Ware's less discriminating *Complete Body of Architecture*. There was a second edition in 1768, and a third, 'considerably augmented', in 1791, when the title was altered to *A Treatise on the Decorative Part of Civil Architecture*, as the 'constructive' part was never written. There were later editions by Joseph Gwilt (1825) and J. B. Papworth (1826). The former was reissued by W. H. Leeds in 1862. A facsimile reprint of the 1791 edition was published in 1968.

By 1760 Chambers was well established in professional practice, and in the following year he joined the Office of Works as one of the two joint Architects appointed by the Crown at a salary of £300 p.a., the other being Robert Adam. By 1769, when he succeeded Flitcroft as Comptroller of the Works, he had become the effective head of the department, and when it was reorganized in 1782 he became the first holder of the new combined office of Surveyor-General and Comptroller. As head of the royal works Chambers proved to be an able and humane administrator as well as a distinguished government architect. Apart from remodelling Buckingham House for George III, and designing the State Coach that is still in use for coronations, his principal achievement as a public architect was Somerset House. Begun in 1776, and not quite finished at the time of his death, Somerset House became the great preoccupation of Chambers's later life, and absorbed nearly all his energies from the date of its commencement until his death twenty years later. In it he exemplified all the precepts that he laid down in the *Treatise*, making it one of the show-pieces of English architectural design and craftsmanship in the reign of George III. In 1770 he was made a Knight of the Polar Star by King Gustav of Sweden, and was later permitted by George III to assume the rank and title of an English knight. In 1766 he was elected a member of the Swedish Academy of Sciences, and he was also a member of the Florentine Academy (1752), a corresponding member of the French Academy of Architecture (1763) and a Fellow of the Royal Society (1776).

Chambers exhibited at the Society of Arts from 1761 to 1768, and in the latter year played a leading part in bringing about the foundation of the Royal Academy of Arts, of which he became the first Treasurer. For nearly thirty years he was the dominant figure in the councils of the Academy, at times overshadowing even the President (Sir Joshua Reynolds), who is said to have declared on one occasion that 'Sir William was Viceroy over him.' He exhibited at the Academy from 1769 to 1777. He was also a member of the Architects' Club, which began its meetings in 1791 at the Thatched House Tavern.

Chambers's architectural style was a sophisticated compound of French neo-classicism and English Palladianism. It was the former that was predominant when he returned from Italy in the 1750s, but it proved to be too novel for his conservative English clients, and for most of his private commissions he found it expedient to substitute a refined Palladianism. However, Chambers kept in touch with French architects such as Le Roy and de Wailly, and a second visit to Paris in 1774 enabled him to resume contact with French neo-classicism at source, with results that are clearly apparent in Somerset House. Despite his fastidious, almost academic, approach to architectural design, Chambers was far from being a pedant. He studied Michelangelo and Bernini as well as Palladio and Scamozzi, and there is a judicious balance in his advice to a pupil to 'correct that luxuriant, bold, and perhaps licentious style, which you will have acquired at Rome, Florence, Genoa and Bologna, by the simple, chaste, but rather tame manner [of the two latter architects]'. The Grecian innovations of Stuart and Revett were, however, little to his liking, and he signified his distaste for 'Attic Deformity' both in some lectures 'written for the use of the Royal Academy soon after its institution at a time when the indisposition of the Professor of Architecture [Thomas Sandby] rendered him unfit either to compose or deliver lectures', and in the introduction to the third edition of his *Treatise on Civil Architecture* (1791). With the contemporary fashion for Gothic he had equally little sympathy. Milton Abbey, his only experiment in that style, was designed to please its owner, Lord Milton, and more than one reference in his correspondence to 'this vast ugly Gothic house in Dorset' shows that he disliked the commission as much as he did 'this unmannerly imperious Lord, who treats me as he does every body, ill'. In Kew Gardens, however, Chambers showed that he was capable of the fanciful as well as of the grand manner. The Alhambra, the Moorish mosque and the Chinese pagoda were celebrated examples of their kind, and the fact that Chambers was the only English architect who had actually seen a Chinese town seemed to give him an authority in such matters which he himself was anxious not to exaggerate. His *Designs of Chinese Buildings* came when the vogue for such things was almost over, but had some importance as a source-book for authentic illustrations of Chinese architecture. As for the *Dissertation on Oriental Gardening* which he published in 1772, it was primarily an attack on the bare style of landscape-gardening associated with 'Capability' Brown,[1] and the oriental dress was merely a literary camouflage. To Chambers's embarrassment his supposed championship of the Chinese garden as a model for imitation was taken seriously by the public, obliging him in 1773 to publish a second edition with an 'Explanatory Discourse'. Worse still, the *Dissertation* brought down on him the effective ridicule of a well-aimed reply, published anonymously as *An Heroic Epistle to Sir William Chambers* (1773), but now known to have been written by the poet Mason with the connivance of Horace Walpole.[2]

From 1758 to 1765 Chambers lived in Poland Street, but in the latter year he moved to a house which he had built for himself in Berners Street. In 1765 he also acquired a lease of the Palladian villa at Whitton, near Hounslow, which Roger Morris had built for the Duke of Argyll. Towards the end of his life he moved to a small house in Norton (now Bolsover) Street, where he died on 8 March 1796. He was buried in the south transept of Westminster Abbey, under an inscribed slab.

Chambers's pupils and assistants included James Gandon, Edward Stevens, John Yenn, Thomas Hardwick, Robert Browne, Willey Reveley, Thomas Whetten, John Rudd and Richard Ripley. A list of over a dozen portraits is given by Harris (p. 173). The most important are those by Carl Frederik Von Breda (R.I.B.A.), Francis Cotes (Scottish National Portrait Gallery) and Sir Joshua Reynolds (Royal Academy and National Portrait Gallery). For a complete list of surviving drawings see Harris, p. 397. The most important collections are in the R.I.B.A. Drawings Collection, Sir John Soane's Museum, the Victoria and Albert Museum and the Royal Library at Windsor. A large collection of Chambers's letters is in the R.I.B.A. Library, and four letter-books containing copies of his professional correspondence from November 1769 to 1775 are in the British Library (Add. MSS. 41133–6).

A full bibliography will be found in John Harris's *Sir William Chambers*, 1970, which supersedes all previous biographical notices. T. Hardwick's 'Memoir of the Life of Sir William Chambers', prefixed to Gwilt's edition of the *Treatise on Civil Architecture* (1825), must, however, be mentioned as a basic source, and H. M. Martienssen, 'Chambers as a Professional Man', *Arch. Rev.* April 1964, supplements Harris. The sale catalogue of Chambers's library is printed in *Sale Catalogues of Libraries of Eminent Persons* iv, ed. Watkin, 1972, 107–34.

The following list of works is based on the 'Catalogue Raisonné' in Harris's biography, where full references to the relevant letters, drawings and other sources for each commission will be found. References are, as usual, given in round brackets to illustrations or descriptions of the individual buildings, H. indicating an illustration in Harris, *C.A.* an engraving in Chambers's *Treatise on Civil Architecture*. Particulars of various doubtful or very minor works omitted from the list below will be found in Harris, *op. cit.*

PUBLIC BUILDINGS, ETC.

LONDON, LITTLE DENMARK COURT, STRAND, alterations and additions to the premises of the Society of Arts, including the Great Room, 1759–60; dem.

WOODSTOCK, OXON., THE TOWN HALL, for 4th Duke of Marlborough, 1766 (H.).

LONDON, THE GERMAN LUTHERAN CHURCH in THE SAVOY, the interior, 1766–7; dem. 1875 (H.).

RICHMOND, SURREY, OBSERVATORY in OLD DEER PARK, for King George III, 1768 (H.).

RICHMOND, SURREY, temporary PAVILION for the reception of King Christian VII of Denmark, 1769 (H.).

HULL, YORKS. (E.R.), TRINITY HOUSE CHAPEL, 1772; dem. 1844.

LIVERPOOL, THE THEATRE ROYAL, 1772; dem. 1802 (R. Brooke, *Liverpool in the Last Quarter of the Eighteenth Century*, 1853).

DUBLIN, TRINITY COLLEGE, designed facing blocks containing Theatre (or Examination School) on south and Chapel on north, 1775. The Theatre was built 1777–86 under the direction of Graham Myers of Dublin, the Chapel in 1787–*c.*1800 (H.). These buildings formed part of a more extensive scheme designed by Chambers but not executed (see Harris, pl. 149).

LONDON, SOMERSET HOUSE, STRAND, 1776–96; completed by James Wyatt 1796–1801. The east wing containing King's College was added by R. Smirke in 1830–5, the west wing containing the Inland Revenue offices by J. Pennethorne in 1851–6. [See, in addition to the references given by

[1] Chambers is said to have submitted designs for Claremont which were rejected in favour of those of Brown. Personal pique at the loss of Lord Clive's patronage may therefore have embittered (though it cannot be supposed to have inspired) Chambers's attack on a style of gardening of which he disapproved on aesthetic grounds.

[2] See *Satirical Poems by William Mason*, ed. Paget Toynbee, 1926.

Harris, *The History of the King's Works* v, 1976, 363–80, and vi, 1973, 480–4.]

COUNTRY HOUSES

WILTON HOUSE, WILTS., works for 10th Earl of Pembroke, 1757–9, including Triumphal Arch (originally in park facing south front, removed to forecourt *c.*1800), Casina, Rock Bridge (dem.) and interior of library (dem.) (*C.A.*; H.) In 1772–4 Chambers designed a Tennis Court (dem.).

KEW GARDENS, SURREY, works for Augusta, Dowager Princess of Wales, including Bridge to 'House of Confucius', 1757 (dem.); Gallery of Antiques, 1757 (dem.); Orangery, 1757–61 (royal arms and cartouches with letter 'A' added 1842); Temple of Pan, 1758 (dem.); Temple of Arethusa, 1758 (dem.); Alhambra, 1758 (dem.); Stables, 1758 (dem.); Temple of Victory commemorating the Battle of Minden, 1759 (dem.); Ruined Arch, 1759; Theatre of Augusta, 1760 (dem.); Temple of Bellona, 1760 (rebuilt on different site); Menagerie, 1760 (dem.); Mosque, 1761 (dem.); Temple of the Sun, 1761 (dem.); Pagoda, 1761–2; Temple of Peace, 1763 (not completed); Temple of Æolus, before 1763 (rebuilt 1845); Temple of Solitude, before 1763 (dem.); Palladian Bridge, before 1763 (dem.) (W. Chambers, *Plans, Elevations, Sections and Perspective Views of the Gardens and Buildings at Kew in Surrey*, 1763; *C. Life*, 31 May 1930).

GOODWOOD HOUSE, SUSSEX, added south wing, stables and gate-piers (dem.) for 3rd Duke of Richmond, 1757–60 (H.).

MARINO HOUSE, nr. DUBLIN, alterations, additions and gate-piers for 1st Earl of Charlemont, *c.*1758–75; dem. *c.*1920.

MARINO HOUSE, nr. DUBLIN, THE CASINO, for 1st Earl of Charlemont, 1758–76 (*C.A.*; H.; *C. Life*, 4–11 Feb. 1988; J. Howley, *The Follies and Garden Buildings of Ireland*, 1993, 160–8).

CASTLE HILL (later DUNTISH COURT), DORSET, for Fitz Foy, *c.*1760; dem. 1965 (*Vitruvius Britannicus* v, pls. 61–3; plan in R.C.H.M., *Dorset* iii (1), 51).

THE HOO, KIMPTON, HERTS., bridge, gateway and internal alterations to house (dem. 1957) for Thomas Brand, *c.*1760–4 (illustration of bridge in *Vitruvius Britannicus* iv, pl. 18).

CASTLETOWN HOUSE, CO. KILDARE, work for Thomas Conolly, including internal decoration and probably also the gate-piers, *c.*1760 (*C. Life*, 3 April 1969; *The Georgian Society Records of Eighteenth-Century Domestic Architecture, etc.* v, 1913).

ROEHAMPTON, SURREY, villa known successively as PARKSTEAD, BESSBOROUGH HOUSE and MANRESA HOUSE, for 2nd Earl of Bessborough, 1760–*c.*1768 (*Vitruvius Britannicus* iv, pls. 11–13; H.; J. P. Alcock, 'Sir William Chambers and . . . Parkstead House, Roehampton', *Surrey Archl. Colls.* 72, 1980).

THE HYDE, nr. INGATESTONE, ESSEX, entrance-hall and staircase for Thomas Brand (afterwards Brand-Hollis), 1761; dem. 1982 after a fire (J. Disney, *Memoirs of Thomas Brand Hollis*, 1805, plates; H.).

COLEBY HALL, LINCS., TEMPLE OF ROMULUS AND REMUS, for Thomas Scrope, 1762 (H.).

STYCHE HALL, SALOP., house and stables for 1st Lord Clive, 1762–6; alterations in 1796–8 included addition of canted bays flanking entrance.

DUDDINGSTON HOUSE, MIDLOTHIAN, for 8th Earl of Abercorn, including stables and temple, 1763–8 (*Vitruvius Britannicus* iv, pls. 14–17; *C. Life*, 24 Sept. 1959).

WALCOT HALL, SALOP., remodelled for 1st Lord Clive, 1764–7 (*C. Life*, 14 Oct. 1939).

KIRKLEATHAM HALL, YORKS. (N.R.), gallery for (Sir) Charles Turner, *c.*1765; dem. 1955. The extent of Chambers's responsibility for this gallery is uncertain. It was probably built under the direction of John Carr, who may have modified Chambers's design.

TEDDINGTON GROVE, MIDDLESEX, for Moses Franks, *c.*1765; dem. (J. C. Loudon, *Gardener's Magazine* xv, 1839, 424–6).

NEWBY (now BALDERSBY) PARK, YORKS. (N.R.), Pheasantry, Menagerie, etc., for Sir Thomas Robinson, 1st Lord Grantham, *c.*1765; dem.

POSTON COURT, HEREFS., Casino for Sir Edward Boughton, Bart., date uncertain, probably *c.*1765; wings added *c.*1882.

WHITTON PLACE, MIDDLESEX, alterations and garden buildings for himself, *c.*1765 onwards; dem. *c.*1847.

HOUGHTON HOUSE, nr. AMPTHILL, BEDS., internal alterations for the Marquess of Tavistock, 1765; dismantled 1794, now a ruin, in which nothing remains of Chambers's work.

PEPER HAROW, SURREY, for 3rd and 4th Viscounts Midleton, *c.*1765–75. The stables had already been built to Chambers's designs in 1763 as an addition to the old house. The porch was added by C. R. Cockerell in 1843 (*C. Life*, 26 Dec. 1925; C. Hussey, *English Country Houses: Mid Georgian*, 1956, 111–14).

WREST PARK, BEDS., the Chinese Pavilion may have been designed by Chambers for 2nd Earl of Hardwicke, *c.*1766. According to D. & S. Lysons, *Magna Britannia* i, 1806, 86, the 'Roman Temple' over the Cold Bath was designed by Chambers, but see Stevens, Edward, p. 925.

BLENHEIM PALACE, OXON., works for 4th Duke of Marlborough, including internal decoration, the ornamentation of the East Gate (to the kitchen court), the Bladon Bridge, the Temples of Flora and Diana, the Tuscan gateway to the kitchen garden, and an ornamental tripod carved by Joseph Wilton, *c.*1766–75 (*C.A.*, 3rd ed. 1791, pl. 52, design for tripod; D. Green, *Blenheim Palace*, 1951). See also Hilary Young, 'Sir William Chambers and the Duke of Marlborough's Silver', *Apollo*, June 1987.

STANMORE HOUSE or PARK, MIDDLESEX, completion of a new house designed by John Vardy (d. 1765) for Andrew Drummond, 1766–9; further works for John Drummond 1769–70; dem. 1938 (H.).

BARTON HALL, GREAT BARTON, SUFFOLK, library for Sir Charles Bunbury, 1767–8; destroyed by fire 1914.

ANSLEY HALL, WARWICKS., Chinese temple for John Ludford, 1767; dem.

COBHAM HALL, KENT, general restoration and alterations including extension of attic storey on west front of Cross Wing, for 3rd Earl of Darnley, *c.*1767–70.

WOBURN ABBEY, BEDS., rebuilding of south wing, interiors including Eating Rooms and Library, and Basin Bridge, for 4th Duke of Bedford, 1767–72. In 1788–9 Holland raised the level of the terrace in front of the south front, set the end windows in arched recesses, and remodelled Chambers's interiors. The bridge has been shorn of its ornaments (H.).

ADDERBURY HOUSE, OXON., alterations for 3rd Duke of Buccleuch, *c.*1768; largely dem. 1808. (*V.C.H. Oxon.* ix, 8, for plan).

AMPTHILL PARK, BEDS., added wings and redecorated principal rooms for 2nd Earl of Upper Ossory, 1768–72; converted into flats 1979 (H.).

HENSINGTON HOUSE, WOODSTOCK, OXON., for 4th Duke of Marlborough, as residence for his agent, 1768–9; dem. *c.*1927 [*V.C.H. Oxon.* xii, 20].

attributed: THE PAGODA, PAGODA GARDENS, BLACKHEATH, KENT (now LONDON), for 3rd Duke of Buccleuch, *c.*1770; enlarged *c.*1840 and *c.*1900.

CASTLE HOWARD, YORKS. (N.R.), the Exclamation Gate for 5th Earl of Carlisle, *c.*1770.

PARTILLE SLOT, GOTHENBERG, SWEDEN, for his brother-in-law, David Sandberg, 1770 (H.).

SKELTON CASTLE, YORKS. (N.R.), minor internal work for John Hall Stevenson, *c.*1770.

DANSON HILL, KENT, internal alterations, timber Palladian bridge (dem.) and Doric temple for (Sir) John Boyd, *c.*1770. The temple was removed to Walden Bury House, Herts., in 1961.

RATHFARNHAM CASTLE, CO. DUBLIN, interiors for 4th Viscount Loftus, afterwards Earl of Ely, 1770–1 (*The Georgian Society Records of Eighteenth-Century Domestic Architecture, etc.* v, 1913; *C. Life*, 9 Sept. 1982).

KNIGHTSBRIDGE, LONDON, house for John Calcraft, 1770–2; dem. *c.*1838.

MILTON HOUSE, nr. PETERBOROUGH, NORTHANTS., alterations and interior decorations (including the Gallery) for 4th Earl Fitzwilliam, 1771–3; also a Corinthian temple, 1773, since dismantled, and the Doric orangery (*C. Life*, 1 June 1961).

RICHMOND, SURREY, WICK HOUSE, for Sir Joshua Reynolds, 1771–2; since much altered.

MILTON ABBEY HOUSE, DORSET, for 1st Lord Milton, incorporating medieval Great Hall, 1771–6, Gothic (*C. Life*, 16, 23 and 30 June, 21, 28 July 1966; R.C.H.M., *Dorset* iii (2), 191–7). Chambers and L. Brown both made designs for the model village built by Lord Milton *c.*1774–80. The evidence does not make it clear to which of them the final result should be ascribed, but the basic layout seems to have been Chambers's work [Arthur Oswald in *C. Life*, 29 Sept. 1966].

INGRESS ABBEY, KENT, work for John Calcraft, including a Doric temple to house a collection of Roman altars, before 1772; dem. The temple is now at Cobham Hall, Kent, where it was re-erected in 1820.

KEW, SURREY, THE WHITE HOUSE, alterations for King George III, 1772–3; dem. 1802.

AMESBURY HOUSE, WILTS., altered or redecorated Chinese temple for the Duchess of Queensberry, 1772 [evidence cited by Michael Cousins in *Follies* 4 (2), 1992, 15].

LUCAN HOUSE, CO. DUBLIN, designs for Agmondesham Vesey, who is said to have built the house 'on a plan of his own', 1773–5. The façade at least is likely to be by Chambers (*C. Life*, 31 Jan. 1947; Desmond Guinness & William Ryan, *Irish Houses and Castles*, 1971, 131–8).

TRENT PLACE, ENFIELD, MIDDLESEX, alterations for Sir Richard Jebb, *c.*1777; dem. (H.).

HEDSOR LODGE, BUCKS., for 2nd Lord Boston, 1778; dem. 1865 (H.).

WINDSOR CASTLE, BERKS., THE QUEEN'S LODGE, 1776–9 (dem. 1823), and LOWER LODGE, 1779–82 (remodelled as 'Burford Lodge', 1842), for King George III, both castellated (H.; *History of the King's Works* v).

HOUSES IN LONDON

RICHMOND HOUSE, WHITEHALL, works for 3rd Duke of Richmond, including gate to Privy Gardens (*C.A.*) and decoration of gallery, 1759–60; destroyed by fire 1791.

PEMBROKE HOUSE, WHITEHALL, internal decorations for 10th Earl of Pembroke, 1759–60, and riding-house, 1773; dem. 1913 (*C. Life*, 19 Sept. 1936, 294; *Survey of London* xiii, 167–75, pls. 67–88).

BUCKINGHAM HOUSE (later PALACE), remodelling of main façade, interior decoration, addition of north and south wings, Great or West Library, South Library, Octagon Library, East Library and Riding House, for King George III and Queen Charlotte, 1762–73; all dem. or remodelled 1825–36 [*History of the King's Works* v, 134–7].

BERKELEY SQUARE, No. 45, internal redecoration for 1st Lord Clive, 1763–7 (*C. Life*, 2 Jan, 1937).

BERNERS STREET, Nos. 13–22, 44, 45(?), 46, 47, 48–53(?), 54–58, built as a speculation in partnership with Thomas Collins, 1764–70; dem. Chambers occupied No. 13 himself.

GRANTHAM HOUSE, WHITEHALL, alterations for Sir Thomas Robinson, 1st Lord Grantham, *c.*1765(?); dem. *c.*1896 (*Survey of London* xiii, 160–1, pl. 47).

GOWER (afterwards CARRINGTON) HOUSE, WHITEHALL, for 2nd Earl Gower, 1765–74; dem. 1886 (*Survey of London* xvi, 176, pls. 94–5).

GROSVENOR SQUARE, No. 20 (formerly 19), alterations and interior decoration for 3rd Duke of Buccleuch, *c.*1767; dem. 1855.

CHEYNE WALK, No. 6, bath-house for Dr. Bartholomew Dominiceti, *c.*1768; dem.

ARLINGTON STREET, No. 21, repairs and alterations for 3rd Viscount Weymouth, 1769 [B.L., Add. MS. 41133, f. 29].

NEWMAN STREET, No. 85, for Mr. Gray, *c.*1769; dem.

MILTON HOUSE, PARK LANE, additions, including entrance gates and screen, for 1st Lord Milton, 1769–71; dem. (J. Carter, *The Builder's Magazine* ii, 1774, pl. x).

CLEVELAND ROW, house (now Warwick House) for Henry Errington, 1770–1; altered in nineteenth century (*Survey of London* xxx, 506–7 and pl. 232).

PICCADILLY, No. 79 (No. 1 STRATTON STREET), addition of attic storey for 4th Earl Fitzwilliam, 1770–1; dem. 1929.

ST. JAMES'S SQUARE, No. 22, alterations for Thomas Brand, junior, 1771; dem. 1847 (*Survey of London* xxix, 180–1; xxx, pl. 133).

MARLBOROUGH HOUSE, ST. JAMES'S, addition of attic and internal alterations for 4th Duke of Marlborough, 1771–4; altered 1865 (*C. Life*, 17 April 1937).

MELBOURNE HOUSE, PICCADILLY, for 1st Lord Melbourne, 1771–4; enlarged and reconstructed by Henry Holland and A. Copland as Albany Chambers 1803–4 (*Survey of London* xxxii, 367–89 and pls. 111–19; H.).

GEORGE STREET, No. 15, alterations, including Doric entrance doorway, for 2nd Earl Fauconberg, 1774.

GROSVENOR STREET, No. 28, alterations for (Sir) Charles Turner, 1774–5; rebuilt 1906 [*Survey of London* xl, 40].

HOUSE IN DUBLIN

CHARLEMONT HOUSE, RUTLAND SQUARE (now the Municipal Gallery of Modern Art), for 1st Earl of Charlemont, 1763–75. The portico is an addition and the interior has been remodelled (*The Georgian Society Records of Eighteenth-Century Domestic Architecture, etc.* iv, 1912, pls. vii–xi).

HOUSES IN EDINBURGH

ST. ANDREW'S SQUARE, No. 26, for Gilbert Meason, 1769–72; balustraded parapet added *c.*1840; north elevation 1878.

DUNDAS HOUSE (now Royal Bank of Scotland), ST. ANDREW'S SQUARE, for Sir Lawrence Dundas, 1771–4; porch added 1828; internal alterations 1825 and 1857–9.

MONUMENTS

attributed: EAST BARNET CHURCHYARD, HERTS., monument to John Sharpe (d. 1756).

attributed: CHELSEA CHURCHYARD, LONDON, monument to Sir Hans Sloane (d. 1753), 1764, Joseph Wilton, sculptor.

CHENIES CHURCH, BUCKS., monument to 2nd Duke of Bedford (d. 1711), 1769, Joseph Wilton, sculptor (signed) (H.).

WESTMINSTER ABBEY, monument in St. John's Chapel to 6th Earl and Countess of Mountrath, 1771, Joseph Wilton, sculptor (H.).

UNEXECUTED

Among many unexecuted designs listed by Harris, attention may be drawn to the following: a mausoleum in memory of Frederick, Prince of Wales, 1751–2 (H.); a new house at HAREWOOD, YORKS. (W.R.), for Edwin Lascelles, afterwards Lord Harewood, 1756 (H.); BLACKFRIARS BRIDGE, LONDON, 1759 (R. S. Mylne, *The Master Masons to the Crown of*

Scotland, 1893, 264); YORK HOUSE, PALL MALL, LONDON, for Edward Augustus, Duke of York, 1759 (H.,); successive projects for a palace at RICHMOND, SURREY, for King George III, 1762 onwards [*History of the King's Works* v, 225–7]; a house at HEADFORT, CO. MEATH, for 1st Earl of Bective, 1765 [*C. Life*, 21 March 1936, 303]; a palace at SVARTSJÖ, SWEDEN, for the Dowager Queen Louisa of Sweden, *c.*1769–70 (H.); a new house at ENVILLE, STAFFS., for 5th Earl of Stamford and Warrington, *c.*1770 [G. W. Beard, 'A New Design by Chambers', *Arch. Rev.* Sept. 1953]; a church for the parish of ST. MARYLEBONE, LONDON, 1770–4 (H.); stables at CASTLE HOWARD, YORKS. (N.R.), for 5th Earl of Carlisle, 1771; a steeple for WOODSTOCK CHURCH, OXON., 1776 [H. M. Colvin, 'The Rebuilding of Woodstock Church Tower', *Oxfordshire Archaeological Society's Report* No. 87, 1949]; and a bridge at DALKEITH HOUSE, MIDLOTHIAN, *c.*1790 [signed drawings in the Duke of Buccleuch's archives].

CHANTRELL, ROBERT DENNIS (1793–1872), was the son of Robert Chantrell, an English businessman living in 1793 in Newington (Southwark), but later in Bruges. From 1807 to 1814 he was a pupil of Sir John Soane. By 1818 he was established in Halifax, but in the following year his success in winning the competition for the Public Baths at Leeds led him to move to that city, where he built up a successful practice, particularly as an ecclesiastical architect. His public buildings were in the Greek Revival style, and included the ambitious South Market, which cost £22,000, and had as its focus a striking neo-classical feature in the form of a circular Doric temple or *tholos*. But it was as a designer of Gothic (and occasionally of neo-Norman) churches that Chantrell was best known in Yorkshire. Between 1823 and 1850 he designed some twenty-five new churches, several of them for the Commissioners for Building New Churches. The smaller ones were often in the lancet style, but in some of the larger ones (notably St. Peter's, the parish church of Leeds), Chantrell used a 'Decorated' or 'Perpendicular' vocabulary to good effect. His churches show a progressive development from the thin Georgian elegance of Christ Church, Leeds, with its cast-iron piers, to the more scholarly – but still hardly Puginesque – Gothic of St. Peter's, and ultimately to the serious medievalism of his later churches, in which he employed a system of geometrical proportions derived from a careful study of English Gothic churches (see his paper on the subject in *Builder* v, 1847, 300–2).

In 1846 Chantrell returned to London, where he subsequently became one of the architects who vetted plans for the Incorporated Church Building Society. In 1863 he moved to Eastbourne, and in the following year to Rottingdean. His membership of the R.I.B.A. ceased in 1868, and he died on 4 January 1872 at a hotel in Norwood. R. W. Moore and Thomas Healey were pupils. Chantrell exhibited at the Royal Academy in 1812–14, and at the Northern Society for the Encouragement of the Fine Arts in Leeds from about 1820 onwards. His son John Boham Chantrell was trained in his father's office. From 1842 to 1845 he was in partnership with Thomas Shaw of Leeds and from 1845 to about 1850 with his father, but appears to have been a failure as an architect.

[C. Webster, *R. D. Chantrell, Architect: His Life and Work in Leeds*, Thoresby Society, 2nd ser. 2, 1991; Bodleian Library, MS. Clarendon dep. c.19, ff. 149–52; *Gent's Mag.* 1847 (ii), 68–9.]

SECULAR BUILDINGS

LEEDS, THE PUBLIC BATHS, WELLINGTON ROAD, 1819–20; dem. [S. Lewis, *Topographical Dictionary* iii, 1831, 47].

LEEDS, THE PHILOSOPHICAL & LITERARY SOCIETY'S HALL, PARK ROW, 1819–20; alterations to museum by Chantrell, 1839–41; enlarged 1861–2; dem. [S. Lewis, *op. cit.*, 46].

LEEDS, Nos. 4, 5, 6, and 7 BOND STREET, shops for William Hey 1820 [Webster, *op. cit.*, 4].

LEEDS, THE MUSIC HALL, internal improvements, 1821, 1824–1825, 1840 [Webster, *op. cit.*, 151].

BRAMLEY PARSONAGE, nr. LEEDS, 1823 [Borthwick Institute, York, MGA 1823/3].

LEEDS, THE SOUTH MARKET, 1823–4; dem. [H. Schroeder, *The Annals of Yorkshire*, Leeds 1851, ii, 20].

RUDDING PARK, YORKS. (W.R.), repairs and alterations for Sir Joseph Radcliffe, Bart., after 1824 [Webster, *op. cit.*, 151].

ARMITAGE BRIDGE HOUSE, YORKS. (W.R.), for William Brooke, 1828 [C. A. Hulbert, *Annals of Almondbury*, 1882, 275–6].

LEEDS, THE COURT HOUSE, alterations 1834 [J. C. Loudon, *Architectural Mag.* i, 1834, 211] and 1840–1 [Webster, *op. cit.*, 150]; dem. 1901.

KIRKSTALL PARSONAGE, nr. Leeds, 1834–5; dem. [Webster, 150].

LEEDS, THE CONSERVATIVE PAVILION (temporary), 1838 [*Catalogue of R.I.B.A. Drawings Coll., C–F*, 21].

LEEDS, PAVILION, (temporary) for Yorkshire Agricultural Society, 1839 [Webster, *op. cit.*, 151].

Unidentified private houses at LEEDS (1825), BIRSTWITH (1840), HEADINGLEY (1842), WOODHOUSE LANE (1842) and LOWER WORTLEY (1844), for all of which tenders were advertised in the *Leeds Intelligencer* in those years, *ex inf.* Mr. Webster.

SCHOOLS in LEEDS for parishes of ST. MARY (1829), ST. MARK (1832) and CHRIST CHURCH (1841) and at HOLBECK (1840), HUNSLET (1840–3), and DEWSBURY (1842), YORKS. (W.R.) [parish records and *Leeds Intelligencer*, *ex inf.* Mr. Webster].

CHURCHES

HALIFAX, YORKS. (W.R.), ST. JOHN, repairs, 1818–20 [*Builder* v, 1847, 300].

LEEDS, CHRIST CHURCH, MEADOW LANE, 1823–6, Gothic; dem. 1972 [R. V. Taylor, *The Churches of Leeds*, 1875, 503].

HUNSLET, YORKS. (W.R.), ST. MARY, inserted galleries, 1826 [I.C.B.S.]; added W. tower (classical), 1832–3; dem. 1862 [Webster, *op. cit.*, 150].

KIRKSTALL, YORKS. (W.R.), 1828–9, Gothic [R. V. Taylor, *The Churches of Leeds*, 1875, 443] and repairs after damage by lightning, 1833 [I.C.B.S.]; altered 1863 and 1894.

LOCKWOOD, nr. HUDDERSFIELD, YORKS. (W.R.), 1828–9, Gothic, and chancel 1848–9 [Port, 179].

NETHERTHONG, YORKS. (W.R.), 1829–30, Gothic; remodelled 1877 [Port, 179].

NEW MILLS, DERBYSHIRE, 1829–30, Gothic [Port, 143].

MORLEY, YORKS. (W.R.), 1829–30, Gothic; chancel added 1885 [Port, 179].

HOLBECK, YORKS. (W.R.), ST. MATTHEW, 1829–32, Gothic; spire and chancel added by J. W. Hill, 1860 [R. V. Taylor, *The Churches of Leeds*, 1875, 373].

GLOSSOP, DERBYSHIRE, reconstructed (except steeple), 1831–2, Gothic; nave rebuilt 1914–15, chancel 1923 [I.C.B.S.].

GUISELEY, YORKS. (W.R.), added N. aisle and refitted interior, 1832–3 [I.C.B.S.].

PONTEFRACT, YORKS. (W.R.), ALL SAINTS, partial reconstruction of ruined church, 1832–3 [I.C.B.S.].

BRAMLEY, YORKS. (W.R.), enlarged 1833; rebuilt by Perkin & Backhouse 1863 [I.C.B.S.].

ARMLEY, YORKS. (W.R.), rebuilt (except chancel), 1834–5, Gothic; dem. *c.*1880 [I.C.B.S.].

SKIPTON, YORKS. (W.R.), CHRIST CHURCH, 1836–9, Gothic [*Gent's Mag.* 1839 (ii), 532].

HEADINGLEY, YORKS. (W.R.), ST. MICHAEL, 1837–8, Gothic; rebuilt 1884 [Bothwick Institute, York, Fac. 1836/3].

LEEDS, ST. PETER, rebuilt 1837–41, Gothic [J. Rusby & J. G. Simpson, *St. Peter's at Leeds*, 1896; plans at Borthwick Institute, York, Fac. 1837/5 and Society of Antiquaries, London]; monument to Ralph Thoresby in chancel, *c.*1841 [Webster, *op. cit.*, 106].

LOTHERSDALE, YORKS. (W.R.), 1838, Gothic; chancel added 1886 [I.C.B.S.].

FARNLEY TYAS, YORKS. (W.R.), 1838–40, Gothic [C. A. Hulbert, *Annals of Almondbury*, 1882, 263].

LEEDS, HOLY TRINITY, rebuilt classical steeple after damage by storm, 1839 [R. S. Shapley, 'Holy Trinity Church, Leeds', *Jnl. W. Yorks. Soc. of Architects* xiv (4), 1955, 3].

ADEL, YORKS. (W.R.), addition of bellcote, 1839, and restoration of chancel, 1843 [*Procs. Yorks. Architectural Soc.* 1888, 103 *et seq.*].

POOL, YORKS. (W.R.), 1839–40, Gothic; altered 1880 [C. L. Eastlake, *History of the Gothic Revival*, 1872, 377].

CHAPEL ALLERTON, YORKS. (W.R.), altered and repaired, 1839–40; dem. 1900 [Borthwick Institute, York, Fac. 1839/1].

BRUGES, BELGIUM, ST. SAUVEUR CATHEDRAL, rebuilt roof after fire, 1839–40 and added two upper storeys to Romanesque tower, with R. Buyck, 1844–6 [*Ecclesiologist* xi, 1850, 174; A. Van de Abeele & C. Webster, 'Architect Robert D. Chantrell en de Kathedraal van Brugge', *Brugs Ommeland* xxvi, 1986].

BATLEY CARR, YORKS. (W.R.), 1840–1, Gothic [R. V. Taylor, *The Churches of Leeds*, 1875, 166].

BIRKENSHAW, YORKS. (W.R.), repairs after storm damage, 1840–1 [I.C.B.S.].

SHADWELL, YORKS. (W.R.), 1841–2, neo-Norman [G. E. Kirk, *A Short History of the Parish Church of Thorner with some notice of the chapel and new parish church of Shadwell*, 1935, 25].

HONLEY, YORKS. (W.R.), 1842–3, Gothic [I.C.B.S.].

GOLCAR, YORKS. (W.R.), rebuilt defective roof, 1843–4 [I.C.B.S.].

LEVEN, YORKS. (E.R.), 1843–5, Gothic [*Gent's Mag.* 1843 (ii), 301; *Builder* v, 1847, 301–2].

DENHOLME GATE, YORKS. (W.R.), ST. PAUL, 1843–6, Gothic [I.C.B.S.].

RISE, YORKS. (E.R.), 1845, Gothic [*Builder* iii, 1845, 585; v, 1847, 302].

LUND, YORKS. (E.R.), chancel, 1845–6, Gothic [inscription on underside of altar, *ex inf.* Mr. I. H. Goodall].

MIDDLETON, nr. LEEDS, YORKS. (W.R.), 1845–6, Gothic [*Builder* v, 1847, 302], and Vicarage (dem.).

HALIFAX, YORKS. (W.R.), ST. PAUL, KING CROSS,

1845–7, Gothic; dem. *c.*1912 except steeple [*Builder* v, 1847, 302].

LEEDS, ST. PHILIP, 1845–7, Gothic; dem. [*Builder* v, 1847, 302, 485, 508].

KEIGHLEY, YORKS. (W.R.), rebuilt 1846–8, Gothic [W. H. Hatton, *The Churches of Yorkshire* i, 1880, 38].

ARMITAGE BRIDGE, YORKS. (W.R.), 1847–8, Gothic [*Builder* v, 1847, 302, vi, 1848, 249].

FANGFOSS, YORKS. (E.R.), rebuilt 1849–50, neo-Norman [*Architect and Building Gazette*, 24 Aug. 1850, 399].

BARMBY MOOR, YORKS. (E.R.), rebuilt except tower, 1850–2, Gothic [*V.C.H. Yorks. E. R.* iii, 145].

MALTON (NEW), YORKS. (N.R.), ST. MICHAEL, new chancel, 1858, neo-Norman [T. Whellan, *History & Topography of York and the N. Riding*, ii, 1859, 218].

PEASENHALL, SUFFOLK, rebuilt nave and chancel, 1860–1, Gothic [*Ipswich Journal*, 13 July 1861, 5].

CHAPLIN, ROBERT, practised as an architect and surveyor at Ashby-de-la-Zouch in Leicestershire from about 1820 to 1850. For many years he occupied a house in RAWDON TERRACE, of which he may have been the architect. His principal works in Ashby were the ambitious Greek Doric IVANHOE BATHS, 1822–5, dem. 1962 (*C. Life*, 5 March 1959, 451); and the HASTINGS (now ROYAL) HOTEL, 1826 [Wayte's *Descriptive and Historical Guide to Ashby-de-la-Zouch*, Ashby 1831, 120, 135]. Chaplin was probably the architect of MOUNT PAVILION, COLWICH, STAFFS. (now ST. MARY'S ABBEY), a Gothic house begun *c.*1830 for Viscount Tamworth, but not finished, and converted into a Benedictine nunnery in 1836. A plan signed by Chaplin is preserved at the Abbey [*ex inf.* the late Bryan Little]. Chaplin disappears from the local directories after 1850, but no record of his death has been found [J. D. Bennett, *Leicestershire Architects 1700–1850*, Leicester 1968].

CHAPMAN, JOHN, was the mason employed to rebuild HORTON CHURCH, DORSET, 1722–3. There are many payments in the churchwardens' accounts to him 'for Mason work', 'on account of Rebuilding ye Tower', etc. No surveyor is mentioned, and Chapman probably made the design himself. The tower shows the influence of Eastbury House (Sir John Vanbrugh, architect), upon which Chapman may perhaps have been employed [*C. Life*, 18 Feb. 1949, Correspondence].

CHAPMAN, ROBERT (*c.*1754–1827), was an architect and surveyor practising from 26 Wormwood Street, London. In 1803 the tower and chancel of ST. PETER'S CHURCH, ST. ALBANS, HERTS., were rebuilt to his designs, but they were much altered by Lord Grimthorpe in 1893 [E. W. Brayley, *The Beauties of England and Wales* vii, 1808, 97–8; W. C. Morgan, 'St. Peter's Church, St. Albans', *Trans. of the St. Albans and Herts. Architectural and Archaeological Soc.* i (2), 1897–8]. In 1806 he enlarged OFFCHURCH VICARAGE, WARWICKS. [signed plans in Warwick C.R.O., DR 302]. ST. HELEN'S CHURCH, BISHOPSGATE, LONDON, was repaired under his direction in 1807–9 [J. E. Cox, *Annals of St. Helen's, Bishopsgate*, 1876, 209, 216], and he repaired and reroofed ST. MARY, ALDERMANBURY, in 1808–10 [P. C. Carter, *The History of St. Mary Aldermanbury*, 1913, 23].

In 1811 Chapman entered into partnership with his nephew and pupil J. B. Gardiner (*q.v.*) and a young man named J. W. Upward. Upward gave up practice in 1815 to become a stockbroker, and Chapman retired soon afterwards. He died at Park Cottage, Camberwell Grove, on 30 March 1827, at the age of 73 [*Annals of the Fine Arts* iii, 1818, 560; *Gent's Mag.* 1827 (i), 377].

CHAPMAN, SAMUEL (1799–   ), was the son of the head gardener at Harewood House, Yorkshire [*ex inf.* Dr. J. H. Harvey]. He practised in Leeds in the 1820s. He designed ST. MARY'S CHURCH, LOW HARROGATE, YORKS. (W.R.), 1822–5, Gothic, dem. *c.*1903 [W. Grainge, *History of Harrogate*, 1882, 245], and the Greek Revival CORN EXCHANGE at LEEDS, 1827–8, dem. [J. Allen, *History of the County of York* ii, 1831, 537].

CHAPPLE, CHARLES, practised in Stonehouse, Devon, during the second quarter of the nineteenth century. In Pigot's 1830 *Directory* he is described as 'architect and surveyor, house and land agent, and registrar of marriages'. Plans in the Cornwall County Record Office signed by him include Valletort Terrace, Hotel and Baths, Stonehouse (1825), a design for public rooms in Stonehouse (1833), five houses to be built in Caroline Place, Stonehouse (*c.*1835), and proposed improvements on the Battery Hill at Stonehouse (1835). He designed the Greek Revival ST. CHARLES' CHAPEL, PLYMOUTH, 1828–9, dem. [Church Building Commissioners, Minute Books, 26 Aug. 1828, *ex inf.* Prof. M. H. Port], a school (Greek Doric, dem.) in PLYMOUTH [G. Wightwick, *Nettleton's Guide to Plymouth, etc.*, 1836, 14], and ST. KEW PARSONAGE, CORNWALL, 1837 [Devon C.R.O., Faculty papers].

CHASSEREAU, PETER, was the son of a naturalized Huguenot and lived in Berwick Street, Soho, London. Though primarily a cartographer and land surveyor, he styled himself 'Architect' on several of his maps, and included architectural design and the measurement of artificers' work among the services which he advertised in the *Gentleman's Magazine* for 1741 (p. 336). No building designed by him is known, but in 1740 he measured painter's work done at POLESDEN LACY, SURREY, for William Moore [Bodleian Library, MS. North b. 14, f. 55]. His last known map was one of the city of York which was engraved and published by J. Rocque in 1750. [A. Stuart Mason, 'The 1745 Parish Map of Shoreditch', *The Terrier. The Friends of Hackney Archives Newsletter* No. 16, 1989.]

CHATTERTON, JOHN, is at present known only as the author of an unexecuted design for the principal front of HANBURY HALL, WORCS., made *c.*1700 [J. Lees-Milne in *C. Life*, 4 Jan. 1968, fig. 6].

CHAWNER, THOMAS (1774–1851), was a pupil of Sir John Soane from 1788 to 1793. He entered the Royal Academy Schools in 1797, and exhibited at the Academy from 1791 to 1800. He obtained a post in the Land Revenue Department and when, in 1810, it was amalgamated with the Office of Woods and Forests, he was appointed one of the surveyors to the combined department. In 1832, when the Office of Woods, Forests and Land Revenues was merged with that of Works, Chawner and his colleague Rhodes continued to deal with the Land Revenue side. He retired in 1845, and died on 6 June 1851, aged 76 [*A.P.S.D.*].

As a Civil Servant, Chawner had few opportunities for architectural design. In 1811 he and Leverton (then the other Land Revenue surveyor) were asked to prepare plans for the layout of Marylebone (afterwards Regent's) Park. Their proposals, unimaginative in character, were rejected in favour of those of John Nash [John Summerson, *John Nash*, 106–9]. Their scheme of 1815 for building houses on the site of St. James's Palace also came to nothing [*History of the King's Works* vi, 367]. The attribution to Chawner of the design of Richmond Terrace, Whitehall, is without foundation (see below, p. 465), and his only official works of any consequence appear to have been BRIXTON PRISON, begun in 1819 (*Survey of London* xxvi, 103–5], an entrance (dem.) to St. James's Park at the north end of the former Duke Street (Whitehall), designed in conjunction with Rhodes in 1834 [*Architectural Mag.* i, 1834, 316], and stabling at CLAREMONT HOUSE, SURREY, at a time (1842) when it was occupied by the royal family [*History of the King's Works* vi, 322]. Numerous survey plans drawn by him are among the Land Revenue records in the Public Record Office. In a private capacity Chawner enlarged and altered MERTON PLACE, SURREY (dem.) for Lord Nelson, 1804–5 [J. Russell, *Nelson and the Hamiltons*, 1972, 437–8, 446, 484], completed (1807–8) the rebuilding of CHERTSEY CHURCH, SURREY, after the original architect, Richard Elsam, had been dismissed [E. W. Brayley, *History of Surrey* ii, 194], and surveyed (1811) KINGSTON CHURCH, SURREY, designing a new window (since removed) at the east end of St. James's Chapel 'to correspond as nearly as possible with that above the altar' [MS. Vestry Minutes]. Designs by him for altering the front of No. 6 CHEYNE WALK, CHELSEA, for John Gregory, 1817, are in the Cooper Hewitt Museum in New York (see J. Harris, *Catalogue of British Drawings for Architecture etc. in American Collections*, 62–3). In conjunction with Henry Rhodes he designed COX'S HOTEL, Nos. 53–55 JERMYN STREET, 1836–7; dem. 1923–4 [*Survey of London* xxix, 275], and some stabling at the corner of HAYMARKET and COVENTRY STREET [*A.P.S.D.*, *s.v.* 'Rhodes, Henry'].

Chawner was a member of the Surveyors' Club and acted as its President in 1811. W. S. Inman and George Porter were his pupils. He lived in Guilford Street and had a country residence in Surrey called Addlestone Cottage [Brayley, *op. cit.* ii, 220].

CHEESMAN, GEORGE, and Son, were builders and surveyors at Brighton, where they built houses in BRUNSWICK SQUARE, *c.*1828, and in PERCIVAL and CLARENDON TERRACES *c.*1848 onwards. In BRIGHTON they designed the churches of CHRIST CHURCH, MONTPELIER ROAD, 1837–8 (Gothic), dem. 1982, and ST. JOHN THE EVANGELIST, CARLTON HILL, 1840 (Greek Doric), and in LEWES that of ST. JOHN SUB CASTRO, 1839–40 (Gothic), all provincial works of little merit [*V.C.H. Sussex* vii, 37, 260–1; A. Dale, *Fashionable Brighton*, 1947, 52, 117, 169]. The younger Cheesman retired to St. Florence, Pembrokeshire, where he died on 25 March 1882, aged 68 [Principal Probate Registry, Calendar of Probates; monumental inscription at St. Florence, *ex inf.* Mr. T. Lloyd].

CHEFFINS, CHARLES FREDERICK (1807–1861), was the son of an employee of the New River Company living at Hoddesdon in Hertfordshire. He had a successful career as a civil engineer, but also acted occasionally as a surveyor and architect and ran a business in Holborn as a 'mechanical draughtsman and lithographer' specialising in the publication of railway maps. His principal recorded work as an architect was a house for J. G. Stokes at HODDESDON, exhibited at the R.A. in 1843. In the same exhibition a design for the NATIONAL SCHOOL at HODDESDON was shown by 'G. and C. Cheffins'. G. A. Cheffins, who may have been an elder brother, had exhibited architectural drawings at the R.A. from a Pentonville address in 1827–8, but was practising in Manchester in 1840 [*Gardener's Mag.* xvi, 1840, 321–2]. Joshua Cheffins was a 'carpenter, builder and surveyor' at Bishops Stortford in the 1830s. A 'Mr. Cheffins' was one of the competitors for the Fitzwilliam Museum at Cambridge in 1835 [Willis & Clark, iii, 204]. C. F. Cheffins died at 15 Gloucester Terrace on 22 October 1861, leaving two sons, Charles Richard and George Alexander, the former of whom continued his practice as a civil engineer [*Minutes of Proceedings of the Institution of Civil Engineers* xxi, 1861–2, 578–80; Principal Probate Registry, Calendar of Probates].

CHENEY, JOHN, signs designs dated 1795 for extensive alterations to the main block of STOKE BRUERN PARK, NORTHANTS. [B.L., Add. MS. 32352, f. 225]. They do not appear to have been carried out (cf. a photograph of the house as it existed before the fire of 1886 in *C. Life*, 9 March 1967, 526). Cheney had been clerk of works to S. P. Cockerell at Daylesford House, Glos., in 1788–93 [B.L., Add. MS. 29231, ff. 59–60], and was among the subscribers to Richardson's *New Vitruvius Britannicus* in 1802.

CHESHIRE, JOHN (–1812), a master mason of Over Whitacre, nr. Coleshill in Warwickshire, was well known as a 'steeple-mender'. In 1789 his skill in this kind of work was the subject of a letter to the *Gentleman's Magazine*, in which 'Gothicus' stated that after several conversations with Cheshire he was convinced 'that he is capable to execute any edifice in the Gothic taste', but that so far 'his abilities have been confined to the rebuilding of some ruinated spires, or new modelling ill-proportioned ones. The spires of the old church at Birmingham, St. Mary's at Leicester, and lately the new-erected spire at Hinckley, are standing objects of his performance' [*Gent's Mag.* 1789 (i), 214]. In November 1792 Cheshire was declared a bankrupt [*European Mag.* xxii], but either he or another member of his family continued to rebuild spires for another thirty years.

The following are churches whose spires are recorded to have been wholly or partially rebuilt by Cheshire or his successor: ASTON, WARWICKS., 1776–7 [A. E. Everitt, 'Aston Church', *Trans. Birmingham Archaeological Soc.*, 1872, 24]; WALSALL, STAFFS., 1777 [F. W. Willmore, *History of Walsall*, 1887, 148]; BIRMINGHAM, ST. MARTIN, 1781 [J. T. Bunce, *Old St. Martin's Church, Birmingham*, 1875, 20]; LEICESTER, ST. MARY, 1785 [G. K. Brandwood, *The Anglican Churches of Leicester*, Leicester 1984, 18]; HINCKLEY, LEICS. [*Gent's Mag.* 1789 (i), 214]; SHREWSBURY, ST. ALKMUND, 1788 [H. Owen & J. B. Blakeway, *History of Shrewsbury* i, 1825, 301]; COVENTRY, HOLY TRINITY, 1802 [T. Sharp, *Illustrations of the History of Holy Trinity Church, Coventry*, 1818, 33]; SHUSTOKE, WARWICKS., 1802 [memorandum in parish register in Warwicks. C.R.O.]; BRIXWORTH, NORTHANTS., 1808 [churchwardens' accounts 1787–1823, f. 39 in Northants. C.R.O., *ex inf.* Mr. David Parsons]; OLD SWINFORD, WORCS., 1809 [parish records, *ex inf.* Mr. H. J. Haden]; ADDERBURY, OXON., 1815 [H. J. Gepp, *Adderbury*, 1924, 92]; THAXTED, ESSEX, 1822 [Neale & Le Keux, *Views of Collegiate and Parish Churches in Great Britain* i, 1824].

CHILD, JOHN, (*c.*1790–1868), practised in Leeds, where he designed three Roman Catholic churches: ST. PATRICK, YORK ROAD, 1831–2, Gothic (converted into a school *c.*1892) [*Catholic Mag.* ii, 1832, 219–20, 574–5], ST. ANNE, PARK ROW, 1837–8, Gothic (since rebuilt) [lithograph in extra-illustrated copy of *Ducatus Leodiensis* in Leeds City Library, vol. v] and ST. JOSEPH, 1859–60 [D. Linstrum, *West Yorkshire Architects and Architecture*, 1978, 374]. His designs (1830) for a Rectory at PUDSEY, YORKS. (W.R.), are at the Borthwick Institute in York [MGA 1830/2]. It is likely that he designed several houses in HEADINGLEY, including THE PRIORY, CUMBERLAND ROAD, his own residence in the 1830s. By the 1850s he had been joined in practice by his son Henry Paul Child. He died at Knaresborough on 22 October 1868 [Principal Probate Registry, Calendar of Probates]. He should not be confused with Charles Child (d. 1862), of Eastwood, nr. Todmorden, and later of Halifax, who was in practice from about 1830 onwards, and designed, *inter alia*, churches at BRADSHAW (OVENDEN) and CRAGG, both in the West Riding [Port, 179], and the ODD-FELLOWS HALL at HALIFAX, 1840 [Linstrum, *op. cit.*, 374].

CHISHOLME, JOHN (*c.*1780–1808), was a native of Aberdeen and was educated at that university. As a very young man he submitted a design for the building of Union Street which was not adopted, although he was the first to propose a single arch for the Union Bridge. He subsequently went to London, where he became a pupil and assistant of John Rennie. While in Rennie's office he is said to have designed the western entrance to the East India Docks. In 1803 he began to exhibit at the Royal Academy, showing a project for a wooden bridge over the R. Don in Aberdeenshire, and in 1808 a design for Assembly Rooms at Aberdeen. In 1807 he joined Telford, and he was engaged in superintending the construction of Telford's new Court House at Carlisle when he died suddenly of heart failure on 2 November 1808, aged only 28. [G. M. Fraser, 'Archibald Simpson, Architect, and his Times', *Aberdeen Weekly Jnl.* 17 May 1918; *Gent's Mag.* 1808 (ii), 1044.]

CHUTE, JOHN (1701–1776), was the fifth and youngest son of Edward Chute of The Vyne, Hants. He was educated at Eton, and spent much of his time abroad until 1754, when he inherited the family property on the death of his brother Anthony. He was an amateur architect of considerable ability, and Horace Walpole, who had met him in Florence in 1740, described him as 'an able Geometrician, and . . . an Exquisite Architect, & of the purest taste both in the Grecian & Gothic Styles'. He played a prominent part in the designing of Walpole's Gothic villa at STRAWBERRY HILL, and when he died in 1776, Walpole wrote that he was 'my oracle in taste, the standard to whom I submitted my trifles, and the genius that presided over poor Strawberry!' The elevation of the house was largely Chute's work, and his surviving drawings show that the design of the 'South Tower' was influenced by one at The Vyne. It was also Chute who helped to design the detached Gothic Chapel built for Walpole in 1772 by the mason Thomas Gayfere [W. S. Lewis, 'The Genesis of Strawberry Hill', *Metropolitan Museum Studies* v (i), 1934; see also Michael McCarthy, *The Origins of the Gothic Revival*, 1987].

In 1752 Chute made Italianate designs (based partly on Serlio, book VII, 49) for rebuilding HAGLEY HALL, WORCS., for Sir George (afterwards Lord) Lyttelton, but they were rejected in favour of a more conventionally Palladian design by Sanderson Miller [Michael McCarthy, 'The Building of Hagley Hall', *Burlington Mag.*, April 1976]. A few years later (*c.*1755) he helped to remodel CHALFONT HOUSE, BUCKS., for Charles and Lady Mary Churchill, in the style of Strawberry Hill [Walpole's *Letters*, ed. Toynbee, iii, 317] (see Angus's *Seats* for a view of the house before successive alterations by Nash and Salvin). His most considerable and successful essay in the Gothic style was DONNINGTON GROVE, nr. NEWBURY, BERKS., designed in 1763 for the antiquary James Pettit Andrews, for which the original designs are in the W. S. Lewis Collection at Farmington (*C. Life*, 18, 25 Sept., 2 Oct. 1958).

At THE VYNE itself Chute made two notable alterations: the construction (1770) of a dramatic new classical staircase and the addition to the chapel of a Gothic Tomb Chamber in order to receive a monument to his ancestor Chaloner Chute (d. 1659), which was eventually erected after his death by his cousin T. L. Chute 'from the Design of his Precedessor'. The recumbent effigy, which is in the style of the seventeenth century, was executed by Thomas Carter [C. W. Chute, *A History of the Vyne*, 1888; Hants. C.R.O., Account of The Vyne by Horace Walpole, 31 M57/652, and 'Inventionary of Alterations to be made at the Vine July 1st. 1755' (633); Sir Charles Chute, 'A Monument by Thomas Carter', *C. Life*, 27 May 1954; Michael McCarthy, 'John Chute's Drawings for The Vyne', *National Trust Year Book 1975–76*, 70–9] (*C. Life*, 14, 21, 28 May 1921).

Both his drawings and his executed works show that Chute was a talented architectural designer. The staircase at The Vyne is a theatrical *tour de force* that has no parallel in English country-house architecture, and at Strawberry Hill Chute played a leading part in the creation of one of the key buildings in the history of the Gothic Revival.

Several portraits of Chute are preserved at The Vyne, including one by Gabriel Mathias showing him holding a Gothic design for the south front. Some of the architectural books in the library have sketches by Chute on the flyleaves, e.g. Langley's *Gothic Architecture* (1747) and *The City and Country Builder and Workman's Companion* (1756). Two folders of his drawings in the Hants. Record Office contain numerous sketches for The Vyne. An album of 64 drawings for Donnington Grove, Hagley, Strawberry Hill and The Vyne is in the W. S. Lewis Collection at Farmington, Connecticut, U.S.A. It was once in Walpole's library at Strawberry Hill. See J. Harris, *Catalogue of British Drawings for Architecture, etc., in American Collections*, 65–72.

Chute's correspondence with Horace Walpole is printed in vol. 35 of the Yale edition of *Walpole's Correspondence*. For a biographical sketch see Warren Hunting Smith, *Originals Abroad*, Yale 1952, 157–76.

CIBBER, CAIUS GABRIEL (1630–1700), was the son of a cabinet-maker to the King of Denmark, and was born at Flensborg in Schleswig. He was sent to Italy in order to improve a natural talent for sculpture, and came to England some time before the Restoration to work for John Stone in the yard in Long Acre where he was carrying on the business founded by his father Nicholas. As a sculptor, Cibber's most celebrated works were the relief on the base of the Monument (1673–5) and the two figures of 'Raving' and 'Melancholy Madness' (now in the Victoria and Albert Museum) which flanked the entrance to the Bethlehem Hospital (1680). He also executed important work at Thoresby (1685–7), at Chatsworth (1687–91), where he designed the marble altar-piece in the chapel, and at Hampton Court (1694–8), where he carved the pediment of the east front and the enrichments of the south front.

Cibber was employed as surveyor for rebuilding the Steel-Yard after the Great Fire, and the Arms of the Hanseatic League carved by him for this building (dem. 1863) are now in the Museum of London. After Edward Jarman's death in 1668 he was among those who applied to the Gresham Committee for the post of 'surveyor for carrying on the work at the Royal Exchange'. He was not chosen, but was employed as sculptor of several of the statues of kings which stood in niches round the court. In 1672 he was probably responsible for designing the GERMAN LUTHERAN CHURCH, LITTLE TRINITY LANE, LONDON (rebuilt 1772, dem. 1875), as he offered to act as architect *gratis* [Susan Gold in *Trans. Ancient Monuments Soc.* N.S. 28, 1984]. At Northampton he was in some way concerned in the building or decoration of the Sessions House (1676–88), for in 1683 it was ordered that £10 should be paid to 'Mr. Caius Gabrell Sibber for his paines in contriveing of the Sessions House' [Northants. County Records, rough Q.S. Order Book].

Cibber's chief architectural work was the DANISH CHURCH, WELLCLOSE SQUARE, LONDON, 1694–6; dem. 1869. This was erected for the use of Danish and Norwegian merchants and sailors, mainly at the expense of King Christian V of Denmark. Cibber, who gave his services free, superseded Thomas Woodstock as surveyor of the church, and his name appears as architect on two engravings of it published by Kip in 1697. Four baroque figures of saints in wood, carved by Cibber for the reredos, are now divided between the Danish Church in Ming Street, Poplar, and the Danish Church (formerly St. Katherine's) in Regent's Park. The church also contained a marble monument erected by Cibber to his second wife, Jane Colley, but this has been lost, together with any inscriptions to Cibber himself and to his son Colley, the actor and dramatist, who were both buried here. According to Vertue, 'he was a Gentleman-like man and a man of Good sense but died poor'.

[H. Faber, *Caius Gabriel Cibber*, 1926; R. Gunnis, *Dictionary of British Sculptors 1660–1851*, 101–3; John Physick, *Designs for English Sculpture 1680–1860*, 1969, figs. 11, 28; Margaret Whinney, *Sculpture in Britain 1530–1830*, 1964, 48–51; Walpole Society, *Vertue Note Books* i, 39, 91, 99, ii, 36, iv, 165; 'An Account of the Buildings, Charges and Finishing, etc. of the Danish Church in Wellclose Square MDCXCVI', *N. and Q.*, 9th ser., v, 1900, 492; Francis Thompson, *A History of Chatsworth*, 1949; Guildhall Library MSS. 337–8.]

CLARK, —, received £740 for rebuilding the detached tower of BERKELEY CHURCH, GLOS., in traditional Gothic style in 1750–2. No architect was employed, and in 1747 there was a payment of £1 7s. 6d. 'To the Masons for giving in a plan for the Tower and Expenses at meeting the same time' [MS. Churchwardens' Accounts]. In 1742 a master builder named William Clark was among those who reported unfavourably on the repairs recently carried out to TETBURY CHURCH, GLOS. [Gloucester Public Library, MS. R.R. 300. 1, p. 13]. This may, however, have been William Clark of Leonard Stanley, Glos., a carpenter who, together with John Bryan of Painswick and Joseph Bryan of Gloucester, masons, contracted in 1750 to rebuild the tower of GREAT WITCOMBE CHURCH, GLOS. [M. M. Cox & E. M. Clifford, *A History of the Parish of Great Witcombe*, 1954, 12–15]. 'Jo. Clerk' was one of the 'Gloucester masons' employed to rebuild the Perpendicular east window of WORCESTER CATHEDRAL in 1660–2 [Worcester Cathedral Archives, A. lxxiii].

CLARK, or **CLARKE,** JOHN (*c.*1585–1624), was one of the Yorkshire masons who came to Oxford in the reign of James I to work on the Schools Quadrangle, and died there in 1624. In 1617, when he was admitted to the freedom of the Oxford company of building craftsmen, his age was stated to be 32. His wife Prudence was almost certainly the daughter of John Akroyd (*q.v.*), the master mason in charge of the new Schools building. In Oxford Clark's most important work was the CARFAX CONDUIT, the elaborately carved terminal of the new water-supply provided at the expense of the lawyer Otho Nicholson, erected in 1616–17 and removed to Lord

Harcourt's park at Nuneham in *c.*1790. In London Clark was the mason responsible for rebuilding LINCOLN'S INN CHAPEL, a work in which Nicholson was also concerned. It may, indeed, have been on Nicholson's recommendation that Clark was employed, for in May 1618 'Mr. Otho Nicholson' was called in to advise on 'what manner of windows are most fit for the chappel' and also 'on the merits of Oxford freestone'. In November John Clark was asked to draw 'the platforme of the . . . modell', and in 1619–23 he built the existing chapel in a traditional Gothic style that was then still normal in Oxford, though soon to be rendered obsolete in London by the example of Inigo Jones's church in Covent Garden. It may have been as a consequence of his employment at Lincoln's Inn that Clark was, by 1620, a member of the London Masons' Company. He was presumably the John Clarke to whom Edward Marshall (d. 1675) was apprenticed. [Catherine Cole in *Oxoniensia* xxvi–xxvii, 1961–2, 231, 235–6; and on 'Carfax Conduit', *Oxoniensia* xxix–xxx, 1964–5, 144; John Summerson, 'Lincoln's Inn Chapel and its Designer', *Trans. Ecclesiological Soc.* N.S. iii, 1953, 39–41.]

CLARK, JOHN (–1857), was a native of Edinburgh, where he must have received his architectural training. In 1826 he won the competition for the Commercial Buildings at Leeds, defeating Barry, Chantrell, Salvin, Taylor and Goodwin with a Greek Revival design in the manner of Thomas Hamilton. This led him to settle in Leeds, where he practised until a few years before his death. His handsome classical buildings 'show the change from the purely Greek to the mixed Greek-Italianate of the late 30s and the 40s'. In 1835 he competed unsuccessfully for the Houses of Parliament with a Gothic design in which 'the earlier and later eras' were 'slightly intermingled . . . so as to form a harmonious combination with the existing palatial buildings'. [Obituary in *Building Chronicle*, May 1857, 197; Derek Linstrum, *Historic Architecture of Leeds*, 1969, 31–33, *West Yorkshire Architects and Architecture*, 1978, 332, 374]. In the following list *B.C.* refers to the *Building Chronicle*.

LEEDS, THE COMMERCIAL BUILDINGS or EXCHANGE, 1826–9; dem. 1872 [*B.C.*] (Linstrum, *Leeds*, 35, *W. Yorks.*, 333).

ROUNDHAY PARK (now Mansion House), nr. LEEDS, for Thomas Nicholson, 1826 [Goodall's *Illustrated Royal Handbook to Roundhay Park*, 1872, 3].

LEEDS, THE GRAMMAR SCHOOL, library and master's house, 1830, Tudor Gothic; dem. [Leeds City Archives, DB/187/263, *ex inf.* Dr. D. Linstrum].

AIREDALE COLLEGE, UNDERCLIFFE, BRADFORD, YORKS. (W.R.), 1831–4; dem. 1893–4 [*B.C.*; *Congregational Mag.* 1831, 581 with illustration].

HARROGATE, THE VICTORIA BATHS, 1832; dem. *c.*1870 [*B.C.*].

BRADFORD, YORKS. (W.R.), ST. PETER'S CHURCH (now Cathedral), reconstructed S. aisle, S. clerestorey and S. porch, 1832–3 [John Ayers, *Architecture in Bradford*, 1973, 28].

LEEDS, BANK MILLS for Messrs. Hives & Atkinson, 1833; dem. [*B.C.*].

LEEDS, THE TRUSTEE SAVINGS BANK, 30 BOND STREET, 1834; dem. 1971–2 [*B.C.*].

HULL, YORKS. (E.R.), THE WILBERFORCE COLUMN, originally in Victoria Square, now in Queen's Gardens, 1834 [J. Greenwood, *Picture of Hull*, 1835, 189].

MEANWOOD HALL (now Meanwood Park Hospital), nr. LEEDS, alterations for Christopher Beckett, *c.*1834 [*B.C.*].

LEEDS, WOODHOUSE CEMETERY CHAPELS and LODGES, 1835 [*B.C.*].

HARROGATE, YORKS. (W.R.), THE ROYAL CHALYBEATE SPA, 1835; dem. 1939 [*B.C.*].

GLEDHOW GROVE (now Chapel Allerton Hospital), nr. LEEDS, for John Hives, *c.*1835 [*B.C.*].

LEEDS, THE YORKSHIRE DISTRICT BANK, BOAR LANE, 1836; dem. [*B.C.*].

LEEDS, ST. GEORGE'S CHURCH, MOUNT PLEASANT, 1836–8, Gothic; apse, etc. added 1900–1 [*B.C.*].

OULTON HALL, YORKS. (W.R.), stables for John Blayds, 1837 [drawings in Leeds Archives, *ex inf.* Mr. Angus Taylor].

LEEDS, ST. JOHN'S CHURCH, repairs, 1837–8 [*B.C.*].

ST. CATHERINE'S (now Doncaster Infirmary), nr. DONCASTER, YORKS. (W.R.), for George Banks, 1838, Gothic [drawings in private possession, *ex inf.* Dr. T. F. Friedman].

LEEDS, two houses (now WAVERLEY HOUSE) on W. side of WOODHOUSE SQUARE, 1840 [D. Linstrum, *W. Yorks. Architects*, 105].

LEEDS, WOODHOUSE MOOR, ALMSHOUSES nr. Church, *c.*1840, Gothic [*B.C.*].

LEEDS, mills for John Wilkinson, 1842; dem. [*B.C.*].

ROSSINGTON CHURCH, YORKS. (W.R.), rebuilt (except tower), 1843–4, Gothic [*Builder* ii, 1844, 289].

BATLEY CARR, YORKS. (W.R.), parsonage, 1846 [Nettleton papers in Leeds Archives, *ex inf.* Dr. D. Linstrum].

RAWDON, YORKS. (W.R.), BENTON PARK CHAPEL, 1846, Gothic [*Congregational Year Book*, 1847, 170–1].

RAWDON, YORKS. (W.R.), farmhouse, etc. for

Robert Milligan, 1847 [Nettleton papers cited above].

APPERLEY BRIDGE, YORKS. (W.R.), house for J. Richardson, 1848 [*ibid.*].

CLARKE, GEORGE (1661–1736), was the son of Sir William Clarke, Secretary at War to Charles II, and was educated at Brasenose College and the Inner Temple. In 1680 he was elected to a fellowship at All Souls, where he 'showed brisk parts in the examination'. He took his M.A. in 1683, and later obtained the degreés of B.C.L. and D.C.L. His parliamentary career began in 1685, when he was elected as Member for the University of Oxford. He subsequently represented the University from 1717 until his death. Politically he was what Hearne called 'a Hanoverian Tory'. His first office was that of Judge Advocate-General (1682–1705). Later he was Secretary at War (1692–1704), secretary to Prince George of Denmark, and joint Secretary to the Admiralty (1702–5). In 1705 he was ejected from all his posts by the Whig government, but when the Tories returned to power in 1710 he was made a Lord of the Admiralty. After the death of Queen Anne he held no further offices and retired to Oxford, where he had retained his college fellowship. For the rest of his life he was a prominent and highly respected figure in academic society. When he died in 1736 he was buried in All Souls Chapel, where a monument commemorates his handsome features, his courtly manners and his 'taste in architecture, poetry and painting'. There is a bust by Cheere in the Codrington Library, a portrait after Kneller in the college hall, and another by Kneller in the Warden's Lodgings which shows him as Prince George's secretary. At Worcester College there are four further portraits and a miniature.

Well known in Oxford as a virtuoso and man of taste, particularly in architectural matters, Clarke was frequently consulted by those in charge of building operations at a time when many important works were in progress in the university. Unfortunately the short autobiography which he left is almost entirely political, and as little of his private correspondence has survived, his architectural activities have to be reconstructed largely from the numerous drawings which he left to Worcester College Library. From these, and from other sources, it is, however, clear that he has a place in the architectural history of Oxford comparable to that of Sir James Burrough (*q.v.*) at Cambridge. At Oxford Clarke stepped into the shoes of Dean Aldrich of Christ Church, the leading figure in Oxford architecture during the first decade of the eighteenth century. It was probably in 1710 – the year of Aldrich's death – that Clarke was consulted by the Vice-Chancellor about the design for the Clarendon Building, and it is among his collections that various alternative designs by Hawksmoor and others are preserved, as well as Thornhill's sketches for the statues of the Muses that crown the roof. In 1716 he revised Aldrich's project for a monumental building on the south side of Peckwater Quadrangle at Christ Church, retaining the giant Corinthian order which the Dean had envisaged, but reducing the number of bays from nine to seven, and introducing the lower order of Doric pilasters derived from Michelangelo's Capitoline palace. Thus Christ Church Library, as built between 1717 and 1738, is largely Clarke's design.

Surviving drawings make it clear that in conjunction with Hawksmoor Clarke also played an important part in the planning of the Queen's College (1710–21). At All Souls he built (1706) at his own cost (and evidently to his own designs) a new house for the Warden, on condition that he might occupy it during his lifetime;[1] refitted the chapel (1713–16); and was throughout deeply involved in the scheme for a new northern quadrangle which was eventually carried out to Hawksmoor's designs between 1715 and 1740. At University College too he was concerned in the building of the Radcliffe Quadrangle (1717–19) and with an unfulfilled project for a new Master's Lodging.

The last college to benefit from Clarke's architectural advice was the new foundation of Worcester. In disgust at the quarrels which divided his own college, it was to Worcester that he eventually left not only his library, but also the bulk of his fortune, which was to be devoted to the endowment of additional fellowships and the completion of its buildings. The new hall, chapel and library had already been begun in his lifetime, and the basic design seems to have been his, though modified and interpreted by Hawksmoor. To complete the college Clarke envisaged wings projecting westwards to north and south of the library with a new Provost's Lodging at the west end of the north wing. This scheme was published in Williams's *Oxonia Depicta* (1732), but in a codicil to his will Clarke left instructions that an alternative plan and elevation should be followed instead. Part of the north range was duly erected by his trustees between 1753 and 1759, but the corresponding range on the south was never built, and the remainder of the north range, including the Provost's

[1] The present front to High Street is a refacing of 1825 by Daniel Robertson.

Lodging, was built between 1773 and 1776 to modified designs by Henry Keene.[1]

Outside Oxford Dr. Clarke's only known architectural works are the Rectory at KINGSTON BAGPUIZE, BERKS., which he designed for Richard Blechynden, Provost of Worcester, in about 1723, and some alterations to COKETHORPE HOUSE, OXON., for the 1st Viscount Harcourt, *c.*1710. His architectural activities were thus largely confined to the circle of his Oxford acquaintances. But as the patron and collaborator of Hawksmoor and as the purchaser of that part of the Jones-Webb drawings that did not pass into the hands of Lord Burlington[2] he is a figure of considerable importance in English architectural history. Moreover, like Aldrich, he has some claim to be regarded as a precursor of the English Palladian revival. Though his architectural taste was more catholic than Aldrich's (Kingston Bagpuize Rectory has a doorway in the style of Giulio Romano), some of his unexecuted designs show markedly Palladian tendencies. As a draughtsman he was clumsy and inelegant, but he could convey an architectural idea to paper well enough to make it comprehensible, and when the need arose he could rely on Hawksmoor and Townesend to act as his architectural amanuenses and interpreters. His architectural library was one of the best of his time, and happily remains intact at Worcester College together with his large collection of prints and drawings.

[*D.N.B.*; autobiography printed in Hist. MSS. Comm., *Leybourne-Popham MSS.*, 1899, 259–89; M. Burrows, *The Worthies of All Souls*, 1874; F. A. Inderwick, *Records of The Inner Temple* iii, 107; W. G. Hiscock, *A Christ Church Miscellany*, 1946; Kerry Downes, *Hawksmoor*, 1959; H. M. Colvin, *Catalogue of Architectural Drawings of the 18th. and 19th. Centuries in the Library of Worcester College, Oxford*, 1964, *Unbuilt Oxford*, 1983; for Clarke's literary interests see the note by C. H. Wilkinson in Marvell's *Poems and Letters*, ed. H. M. Margoliouth, 3rd ed. 1971, 432–5.]

CLARKE, ISAAC, practised in London from the 1820s onwards. He was an assistant of John Walters, whose office in Fenchurch Street he took over when the latter died in 1821 [*A.P.S.D.*, *s.v.* 'Walters'; London directories]. He appears to have been the London architect called Clarke who designed two Greek Revival chapels in Brighton that were projected by a speculator called Barnard Gregory: ST. MARGARET'S, 1824 (dem. 1959) and ST. MARY'S, 1827 (dem. 1878). Both commissions seem to have been taken over by C. A. Busby and his partner A. H. Wilds, for according to *The Watering-Places of Great Britain and Fashionable Directory* of 1833, the latter chapel was 'completed under the direction of Mr. Wilds', while working drawings for the former are preserved among Busby's drawings in the R.I.B.A. Collection [A. Dale, *Fashionable Brighton*, 1947, 43; Neil Bingham, *C. A. Busby*, 1991, 73]. Clarke later designed the Gothic ST. BARNABAS, KENNINGTON, LONDON, 1848–50, in association with James Humphreys [Bridget Cherry & Nikolaus Pevsner, *London: South*, Buildings of England, 1983, 334]. He gave up practice soon after 1870, dying probably in 1885.

CLARKE, JAMES, was a carpenter and master builder of Newbury in Berkshire, where he or his firm built the TOWN HALL, 1742, dem. 1908 (ill. *Newbury District Field Club Trans.* v, 1895–1911, 230), the BRIDGE, 1769, the building in the London Road now known as THE DOWER HOUSE (formerly 'the King's Arms'), 'and most of the principal houses in Newbury of that date' [W. Money, *History of Newbury*, 1887, 353]. The Dower House is boldly designed in an almost Vanbrughian style. He may have been the James Clarke whose burial on 7 December 1773 is recorded in Newbury parish register.

CLARKE, THOMAS HUTCHINGS, appears to have been chiefly employed as an illustrator of architectural books. He was the author of *The Domestic Architecture of the Reigns of Elizabeth and James I* (1833) and of a volume of plans, sections and views of Eastbury House, Barking, Essex (1834). In 1839 he contributed a 'descriptive account' of the minster to W. B. Killpack's *History and Antiquities of the Collegiate Church of Southwell* (1839). In 1833 he exhibited at the Royal Academy his unsuccessful design for the new Grammar School at Birmingham. A drawing

[1] Two monuments which Clarke erected in Oxford should also be mentioned, since he presumably designed them, or at least dictated their general form. One, in St. Mary's Church, commemorates his cousin Elizabeth Cary (d. 1723/4) and is signed 'G.C.F.'. It consists of a portrait medallion set against baroque drapery. The other, in the Cathedral, commemorates Dean Aldrich and was set up in 1732. It incorporates a bust by Cheere.

[2] The date when Clarke acquired these drawings is not known, but it was before 1718, when Edward Southwell wrote to Lord Dartmouth to ask if he would lend a design for Whitehall Palace in his possession for comparison with Clarke's (Staffordshire Record Office, D 1778/L/2/529). In a letter in the Kent Archives Office dated May 1713, William Emmett says that the Whitehall design had recently been acquired by Clarke.

by him of the interior of the Palace of Madura in India, dated 1830, is in the British Library (Add. MS. 31343 Q). This appears to have been copied from another artist's work and does not prove that Clarke had visited India himself.

CLARKE, WILLIAM, wrote a detailed and scholarly account of *Pompeii* for the Library of Entertaining Knowledge, 1831–2. When a second edition was published in 1846 it was described as being 'chiefly from the MS. journals and drawings of William Clarke, Esq., architect'. He may perhaps have been the William Clarke who was a pupil in C. R. Cockerell's office from 1822 to 1827 [David Watkin, *C. R. Cockerell*, 1974, 42].

CLARKE, WILLIAM BARNARD, of Chapel Street, Bedford Row, London, exhibited a 'design for the proposed botanical garden on Primrose Hill' at the R.A. in 1832.[1] In 1834 he restored THE ELEANOR CROSS at WALTHAM, HERTS., in a manner criticized in *Architectural Mag.* iii, 280 (see also *Gent's Mag.* 1832 (ii), 105). According to the *Companion to the Almanac* for 1838 he was the architect employed to design the new watering-place at SOUTH HAYLING on HAYLING ISLAND, HANTS. He was President of the Architectural Society for several years, but resigned in 1839 on going abroad [*Gent's Mag.* 1839 (i), 81]. He is known to have been in Rome for some years in the 1840s, but was back in London in 1855–8.

CLAVERING, ROBERT, a builder (probably a carpenter by trade), was the author of *An essay on the construction and building of chimneys, including an enquiry into the common causes of their smoaking*, 1779, 2nd ed. 1788, 3rd ed. 1793. In the preface he states that his thoughts 'first turned to this subject in 1764', when he attempted to provide smoke-free chimneys in some houses that he was then building. Clavering also published in 1776 *The Carpenter's and Joiner's Vade Mecum*, a systematic guide to the valuation of building materials. [Eileen Harris, *British Architectural Books and Writers 1556–1785*, 1990, 165–6.]

CLAYTON, ALFRED BOWER (1795–1855), intended at first to become a painter, and studied under Etty, who is said to have 'expressed a high opinion of his talents'. He ultimately decided to be an architect, and was for some time in the office of D. R. Roper (*q.v.*). As Roper's assistant he is said to have been the effective architect of the Greek Revival church of St. Mark at Kennington, and of the well-proportioned Lambeth Shot Tower which was one of the landmarks of the South Bank until its demolition after the Second World War. From Roper's office he moved in about 1827 to that of George Smith (*q.v.*). H. C. Barlow, a pupil of Smith's at the time, remembered that his advent marked the introduction of a 'new style'. Of this the principal example was the London Corn Exchange in Mark Lane, an interesting Greek Revival building which Smith built in 1827–8 with Clayton's assistance. Clayton appears to have been in independent practice by 1833. In 1837 he migrated to Manchester, where he became Bridgemaster to the Hundred of West Derby. In 1842 he gave his address as Ormskirk, and in 1845 as Liverpool. He died at Everton in April 1855, of delayed shock after falling from a building he was examining at West Derby [*Builder* xiii, 1855, 216; xxvii, 1869, 65].

Clayton exhibited regularly at the R.A. from 1814 to 1837, showing pictorial compositions as well as architectural designs. He also exhibited at the Society of British Artists in 1824 and 1828 and at the Liverpool Academy of Arts in 1837, 1842 and 1845. His designs included a 'sketch of a villa, designed for and proposed to be erected on the estate of Tatnal Boone Esq. [at] Lewisham', 1833; a design for a farmhouse 'now erecting for W. Gambier Esq.' at Harrold, Beds., 1833; a design for a church at Herne Bay, 1834, probably CHRIST CHURCH, HERNE BAY, KENT, 1834, Gothic; an unexecuted design for the Town Hall at Penzance, 1835: 'a country residence now in progress near the Reculvers, Kent', 1836, probably BROOK, nr. RECULVER, KENT, for R. Collard; a 'design for a parsonage house to be erected near Whitstable, Kent, for the Rev. C. Plater', 1836; and 'alterations and additions' to NORLEY HALL, CHESHIRE, for Samuel Woodhouse, described as 'now erecting' in 1845. The last building, illustrated in Twycross's *Mansions of England: Cheshire* i, 1850, 127, is in the Tudor Gothic style.

CLEARE, or **CLEERE,** WILLIAM (–1690), was one of the leading London joiners at the end of the seventeenth century. He was presumably the William Cleere who was admitted to the freedom of the Joiners' Company in June 1654 on the termination of his apprenticeship, probably at the age of 21 [Guildhall Library, MS. 8051/1, f. 6]. He was employed at St. Paul's Cathedral, Chelsea Hospital and many of the London City Churches designed by Sir Christopher Wren. Both the first model of Wren's design for St.

[1] See lithograph of this in B.L., 1802 c. 17, vol. II, 65.

Paul's and the Great Model of 1672 were made by him [*Wren Soc.* xx, 45; G. W. Beard, *Craftsmen and Interior Decoration in England 1660–1820*, 1981, 251]. A master craftsman of Cleere's standing would have been accustomed to making designs both for himself and others, and it was in accordance with a drawing 'delivered and contrived' by 'William Cleare, gent.', that STOWE HOUSE, BUCKS., was to be built for Sir Richard Temple, Bart., in 1676 [G. Clarke & M. Gibbon in *Arch. Hist.* 1978, 93]. An original elevation for the 13-bay north front is illustrated in *C. Life*, 11 July 1957, 68.

CLEAVE, WILLIAM, is stated in Neale's *Seats* to have been responsible for extensive alterations to STAPLETON PARK, YORKS. (W.R.), dem. *c.*1930, for the Hon. Edward Petre, and this is confirmed by the fact that in 1820 he exhibited a 'south-east view of improvements made at Stapleton Park' at the R.A., giving his address as 'Brewer's Green, Westminster'. Reference to Pigot's *Directory* shows that William Cleave of this address was listed as a 'timber-merchant' in 1827–8.

CLEGHORN, CLAUD, 'builder', was admitted a burgess of Edinburgh in April 1800 [*Roll of Edinburgh Burgesses*, Scottish Record Soc., 1933, 35]. He was doubtless the author of a set of unexecuted drawings in the Center for British Art at Yale for ARDGOWAN HOUSE, RENFREWSHIRE, signed 'C. Cleghorn. Edin. 1797'. They represent a competent late Georgian design.

CLELAND, JAMES (1770–1840), was one of the outstanding figures in the life of Glasgow during the first three decades of the nineteenth century. He was a native of the city and a wright by trade, and ran a successful business as a builder. What was remarkable about Cleland was his intellectual ability, his public spirit and his activity in promoting schemes for the improvement of the city. For many years he was a prominent member of the Town Council and in 1831 became a J.P. In 1814 he was appointed Superintendent of Public Works, a post which he held until 1834, and whose duties he performed in an exemplary fashion. In 1819 he carried out a classified census of the population of Glasgow, the first of its kind ever taken in the United Kingdom. He subsequently published several historical and statistical works relating to Glasgow, of which the best known were his *Annals of Glasgow* (1816) and *An Historical Account of the Bills of Mortality, and the Probability of Human Life in Glasgow and Other Large Towns* (1836). His statistical achievements earned him an honorary LL.D from Glasgow University in 1826. When he retired in 1834 a building known as 'the Cleland Testimonial' was erected at the south-east corner of Sauchiehall Street and Buchanan Street and presented to him as a token of public esteem.

Cleland gained his celebrity as a public administrator rather than as an architect. But he was responsible for the design of the following buildings in Glasgow: THE POST OFFICE, NELSON STREET, 1810; THE MAGDALEN ASYLUM, 1812; THE BAZAAR adjoining the City Hall, 1817; and THE HIGH SCHOOL, UPPER MONTROSE STREET, 1820; all dem. In 1812 he purchased the old gaol or tolbooth in Trongate and erected in its place 'a handsome building' for commercial purposes designed by David Hamilton. At ARDROSSAN, AYRSHIRE, he designed in 1807 the domed BATHS (dem.), illustrated in a booklet by himself entitled *Description of that Part of Ardrossan . . . on which Baths are to be built by Tontine: as also an explanation of the Plans, and Specification of the various kinds of Work* (Glasgow 1807).

[*Extracts from the Records of the Burgh of Glasgow*, ed. Renwick, ix and x, *passim*; G. Eyre-Todd, *History of Glasgow* iii, 1934, 424–7; Joseph Irving, *The Book of Scotsmen*, 1881, 72; *D.N.B.*; R. Chapman, *The Picture of Glasgow*, 1812, 170, 190; Senex, *Glasgow Past and Present*, 1884, i, 392, ii, 129, 389; memoir by J. Cleland Burns prefixed to J. Cleland, *The History of the High School of Glasgow*, Glasgow 1878.]

CLEPHAN, JAMES, practised in London in the 1830s. The name Clephan or Clephane is a North Country one, and James may have been related to William Clephan, an architect and builder at Stockton-on-Tees who died in 1868. Between 1834 and 1839 Clephan acted as executant architect at WREST PARK, BEDS., which Earl de Grey (*q.v.*) was building to his own designs in a French *dix-huitième* style (*C. Life*, 25 June, 2 July 1970). In a MS. account of his works at Wrest Earl de Grey recalled that, when he engaged Clephan, the latter had 'just terminated a similar engagement with Lord Barrington, whose house was built by an amateur architect, his brother [-in-law], Tom Liddell. Clephan had been his superintendent, exactly in the sort of way that I required. I engaged him . . . and from that day to this [he] has given me the greatest satisfaction' [Bedfordshire Record Office, CRT 190/45/2, pp. 1–19]. Clephan had in fact been clerk of works at the Liddells' own castle of Ravensworth in Durham as early as 1815 [see the Coade Stone Co.'s letter-book, P.R.O., C 111/106], and had evidently fulfilled the same function at Beckett Park, Berks., whose reconstruction Thomas Liddell (*q.v.*) completed for his brother-in-law Lord Barrington in 1834. Clephan also designed the WORKHOUSE (now THE CEDARS) at AMPTHILL, 1835–6 [Bedfordshire Record Office, Minutes of the Ampthill Poor Law Union, p. 79], and competed unsuccessfully for one at Bideford in 1837 or 1838 [*Trans. Devonshire Assoc.*, 1, 1918, 552]. In 1838 he designed HOLDERNESS HOUSE, YORKS. (E.R.), for B. M. & W. E. Jalland in an Elizabethan style [J. J. Sheahan, *History of Hull*, 1864, 625] (G. Poulson, *History of Holderness*, 1840–1, 322, 341). He ceased practice soon after 1850.

CLERK, SIR JOHN (1676–1755), of Penicuik in Midlothian, was Scotland's chief arbiter of taste in matters architectural during the second quarter of the eighteenth century. He was the third generation of a family whose wealth had been founded by John Clerk (1611–1674), an enterprising merchant and art-dealer who bought the Penicuik estate in 1654. His father, Sir John Clerk (d. 1722), had been created a baronet in 1679, and gave his son a legal education, first at Glasgow and later at Leyden, followed in 1697–8 by a Grand Tour. He was admitted to the Scottish Bar in 1700 and subsequently achieved some success as an advocate. From 1702 to 1707 he represented Whithorn in the Scottish Parliament. Politically a Whig and an Anglophile, he was in 1706–7 a commissioner for the Union and was returned as a member of the first Parliament of Great Britain. In the following year he was made a Baron of the newly constituted Court of the Exchequer of Scotland, which brought him the then substantial salary of £500 p.a. He was a prominent figure in the intellectual society of Edinburgh after the Union and had many friends among the English intelligentsia of the day, including Lord Burlington, Lord Pembroke and the antiquaries Roger Gale and William Stukeley. He was a Fellow of the Society of Antiquaries and of the Royal Society and Vice-President of the Edinburgh Philosophical Society. 'At home, whether in Edinburgh or at his country-house at Penicuik, he gathered round himself a miniature *Accademia dell'Arcadia* of which the poet Allan Ramsay, the antiquarian Alexander Gordon and the architect William Adam were the principal ornaments; and through them and his other protégés he exerted a wide influence on the development of Scottish art and letters' (Fleming).

Among Clerk's many interests, architecture and landscape-gardening were prominent if not paramount. That they were an inherited taste is demonstrated by the survival of drawings made by his father for a house which he thought of building on his property at Mavisbank, nr. Loanhead, in 1696–8, by letters which show that in 1703–4 both father and son were helping their neighbour (Sir) David Forbes to design and build a country house at NEWHALL, MIDLOTHIAN [S.R.O., GD 18/5188, nos. 17–29] and, most notably, by the pyramidally roofed mausoleum which the 1st baronet designed and built in PENICUIK CHURCHYARD in 1683–4 in a form consciously recalling Antique tombs [S.R.O., GD 18/1752; H. Colvin, *Architecture and the After-Life*, 1991, 303–6].

In 1710 Clerk bought a house and estate at CAMMO, nr. Cramond, which he subsequently sold in 1726. The house was less than twenty years old, and Clerk's only addition to it appears to have been some stabling [S.R.O., GD 18/1679]. In 1722 he inherited his father's estates and began a new house at MAVISBANK, which he designed in collaboration with William Adam. His journal records that he laid the foundations in 1723 'according to a design concocted between me and Mr. Adams'. Adam was not at first employed as the builder, but (as Clerk explained in 1743) 'after the work had been carried on some time, and not to [his] mind, he then employed Mr. Adams to perfect what was undone' [*Depositions in the Cause William Adam v. Lord Braco*, 1743, p. 46]. Mavisbank was conceived as the small but elegant retreat of a man of affairs rather than as a major country seat. As such it had obvious affinities with the Palladian villa, and as such it was an important innovation in Scottish architecture, setting 'a new architectural fashion for Scottish country mansions of the middle rank' (Dunbar). In 1727, the year Mavisbank was finished, Clerk paid a visit to London, where he made contact with the leader of the English Palladian Revival, Lord Burlington, who not only entertained him at Chiswick, but presented him with two drawings by Inigo Jones from his collection. Clerk also saw Wilton, Wanstead and other important Palladian buildings in the south.

Back in Scotland, Clerk assumed something of the role of a Scottish Burlington. In a long manuscript poem entitled *The Country Seat* (1727) he expounded in sadly pedestrian verse much the same principles of design in architecture and landscape gardening as those that were being disseminated in England by Burlington and Kent. In architecture he insisted that 'the antient Greek and Roman structures, or the Designs of them by Palladio and others ought to be standards fit for the imitation of our modern Architects', while his views on landscape-gardening show that he was moving away from formality towards the 'naturalism' that was soon to transform English gardening.

Though hardly a single building can be attributed to Clerk in its entirety, his advice was often decisive in the choice of architect or design. At ARNISTON, MIDLOTHIAN, the house built by William Adam for Lord President Dundas in 1726–38 has been seen as a direct reflection of the precepts of *The Country Seat*. At HADDO HOUSE, ABERDEENSHIRE (1732–5), though William Adam was again the executant architect, the Palladian restraint of the design was undoubtedly due to Clerk's intervention: indeed, he claimed that 'I myself contributed not a little [to this 'modern regular building'] by concerting with the Earl [of Aberdeen] a plan & model for it & afterwards employing men to execute them' [S.R.O., GD 18/2110]. Apart from Adam, the man principally employed at Haddo was the master mason John Baxter (*q.v.*), who became something of a protégé of Clerk and who subsequently, with Clerk's advice, designed and built GALLOWAY HOUSE, WIGTOWNSHIRE (1740–2), for Clerk's friend Lord Garlies [S.R.O., GD 18/5011]. In 1738 Clerk gave advice to Charles Erskine before the latter built TINWALD HOUSE, DUMFRIESSHIRE [S.R.O., GD 18/5008], and in 1737 he was summoned by the Earl of Morton to ABERDOUR HOUSE, FIFE, where 'his lordship had invited me to advise him about the situation of a house which he intends to build near the old seat', though in the event nothing was done [S.R.O., GD 18/2113]. At DRUMLANRIG CASTLE, DUMFRIESSHIRE, he designed a cascade for the 2nd Duke of Buccleuch in 1732 [Tait, 137, n. 41 and fig. 40], and in the Register House there is an unsigned sketch by him for a 'Town House' or City Hall to be built on a site adjoining the Parliament House at Edinburgh [S.R.O., RHP 3865].

At PENICUIK HOUSE itself, although Clerk carried out extensive 'improvements' in the grounds, his only strictly architectural work seems to have been the circular tower which he built on Knight's Law between 1748 and 1751. It was left to his son SIR JAMES CLERK (1709–83), the 3rd baronet, to build, in 1761–9, a new house with the aid of the faithful Baxter. Like his father, Sir James was a cultivated man and a competent amateur architect. He studied law at Leyden in 1731–2 and visited Rome in 1732–4. Surviving drawings show that at Penicuik he designed not only the house itself (whose Palladian façade, though faithful to his father's principles, was a little old-fashioned for the 1760s), but also the quadrangular stable-block, whose two entrances are marked, one by a Gibbsian steeple,[1] the other by a full-scale reproduction of a domed Roman building called 'Arthur's Oven' that had stood intact in Stirlingshire until the eighteenth century, but, to the chagrin of Scottish antiquaries, had been pulled down in 1743. At Penicuik the replica serves as a dovecote. Other drawings represent a circular 'Pantheon' library that was never built. Penicuik House, enlarged by the addition of wings (designed by David Bryce in 1857), survives only as a ruin, having been gutted by fire in 1899 (*C. Life*, 15–22 Aug. 1968).

Other buildings probably designed by Sir James Clerk are PENICUIK KIRK, with a Doric portico, 1771; HAILES HOUSE, COLINTON, MIDLOTHIAN, for which a plan survives inscribed 'To James Carmichael Esqr. of Hils by S^{r}. Jas. Clerk'; and ROSS-DHU HOUSE, DUNBARTONSHIRE, built for Sir James Colquhoun in 1773–4, which is stated in A. Whyte & D. Macfarlane's *General View of the Agriculture of the County of Dumbarton*, 1811, 26, to have been 'built upwards of 30 years ago, from a design said to have been given by Sir J. Clerk of Pennycuik' (for a view see J. Irving, *Book of Dumbartonshire* iii, 1876). Drawings at Penicuik show an unexecuted design by him for rebuilding ELIE HOUSE, FIFE.

Portraits of Sir John Clerk (by Medina and Aikman) and of Sir James (attributed to William Denune) are preserved at Penicuik.

[Clerk family papers in S.R.O. GD 18 and drawings at Penicuik; *Memoirs of the Life of Sir John Clerk, Bart.*, ed. J. M. Gray, Scottish Hist. Soc., xiii, 1892; *D.N.B.*; Stuart Piggott, *William Stukeley*, 1985; Stuart Piggott, 'The Ancestors of Jonathan Oldbuck', *Antiquity* xxix, 1955; John Fleming, *Robert Adam and his Circle*, 1962; Alistair Rowan, 'Penicuik House, Midlothian', *C. Life*, 15–22 Aug. 1968; A. A. Tait, 'William Adam and Sir John Clerk: Arniston and "The Country Seat"', *Burlington Mag.* March 1969; Stuart Piggott, 'Sir John Clerk and "The Country Seat"', in *The Country Seat*, ed. Colvin & Harris, 1970; William Spink, 'Sir John Clerk of Penicuik', in *Furor Hortensis*, ed. P. Willis, Edinburgh 1974; Iain Gordon Brown, 'Sir John Clerk of Penicuik: Aspects of a Virtuoso Life', unpublished Ph.D. thesis, Cambridge 1980 and *The Clerks of Penicuik*, Edinburgh 1987, with further bibliography.]

[1] Penicuik is not unique in its steepled stable. Other eighteenth-century examples can be seen at Blackadder Mount, Berwickshire, at Tarvit House, nr. Cupar, Fife, and elsewhere in Scotland.

CLERK, WILLIAM and ANDREW, were described as the 'Architects' of CRATHIE CHURCH, ABERDEENSHIRE, 1804, dem. *c.*1893–4, in an inscription recorded by John Stinton, *Crathie and Braemar,* Aberdeen 1926, 264. There are very similar churches at ECHT (1804) and SKENE (1801).

CLINTON, GEORGE (–1850), was practising at Aberystwyth when he designed two churches in CARDIGANSHIRE at LLANDDEINIOL, 1832–4 (altered 1883), and EGLWYSFACH, 1833 [I.C.B.S.]. He was presumably the 'Mr. Clinton, architect, formerly of Shrewsbury and now of Cardiff', who according to Loudon's *Architectural Magazine* iv, 1837, 550, designed the classical church of HOLY TRINITY, COLEHAM, SHREWSBURY, 1836–7, rebuilt 1885–7 (illustrated in H. Pidgeon's *Memorials of Shrewsbury,* 1851, 136). The minutes of the building committee [Shropshire C.R.O., 3598/Ch./9] show that there was a competition in which Clinton submitted two designs, one classical, the other Gothic, both of which were rejected in favour of another ostensibly by a local builder called Joseph Stant, but possibly in fact by Clinton, who made the copies of 'Mr. Stant's plans' that were submitted to the Incorporated Church Building Society. George Clinton of Cardiff also designed the MARKET HOUSE at LLANDOVERY, CARMARTHENSHIRE, in 1840 [*Civil Engineer & Architect's Jnl.* iii, 1840, 39], and an elevation by him of a small Gothic house in the National Library of Wales [Ac. PZ 4512] has been identified by Mr. Thomas Lloyd as for TYCLWYDAU at LLANTRISANT COMMON, GLAMORGANSHIRE, for a member of the Williams family. Clinton died at Cardiff on 5 December 1850 [Principal Probate Registry, Calendar of Probates, 1869].

CLOAKE, GEORGE (*c.*1761–1812), 'architect', died at Kensington on 10 September 1812, in his 52nd year [*Gent's Mag.* 1812 (ii), 302]. In 1777 he had been apprenticed to a surveyor called Thomas Drew [P.R.O., Apprenticeship Registers, IR 1/29, 78].

COBB, JOHN (–1863) was a carpenter and builder of Chetwynd End, Newport, Shropshire, in the second quarter of the nineteenth century. By 1851 he was described as 'builder and architect'. In 1821 he was employed by the Haberdashers' Company to carry out an extensive repair and partial rebuilding of ADAM'S SCHOOL and ALMSHOUSES at NEWPORT, apparently to his own designs [Guildhall Library, Records of the Haberdashers' Company, MS. 15881, ff. 61–2, 84, etc.]. Cobb died in November 1863 [Principal Probate Registry, Calendar of Probates].

COCK, WALTER BROWN (*c.*1776–1840), was a mason and builder at Great Torrington, Devon. In 1828 he rebuilt the Gothic west tower and spire of TORRINGTON CHURCH, apparently to his own designs [contract in parish chest, 1960]. His death on 13 July 1840 at the age of 64 is recorded on a tombstone in the churchyard. In 1841–2 his son Walter Brown Cock, junior (*c.*1806–1874) and William Dunk, a carpenter, designed and built the classical MARKET HOUSE in the same town [Torrington corporation minute-books].

COCKERELL, CHARLES ROBERT (1788–1863), was the second son of S. P. Cockerell (*q.v.*). He was born in London on 27 April 1788 and was educated first at a private school and then at Westminster. At the age of 16 he began his architectural training in his father's office, where he remained for four or five years. In 1809 he moved to the office of his father's friend Robert Smirke, then engaged in rebuilding Covent Garden Theatre, but in the following year his father decided that the time had come for him to complete his education by a period of foreign travel. France and Italy were enemy territory, and it was in the temporary capacity of a King's Messenger with despatches for Constantinople that Cockerell began his Grand Tour. He reached Turkey after an adventurous voyage that included the capture of a prize off the French coast. Three months later, accompanied by another young architect, John Foster of Liverpool, he left for Athens. Here they found congenial company in the German archaeologists Haller and Linckh, together with whom they discovered the famous Ægina Marbles in the spring of 1811. Cockerell hoped to secure these for the British Museum, but much to his disappointment they eventually went to Munich. The Phigaleian Marbles which Cockerell and his friends soon afterwards discovered at Bassae in Arcadia were, however, purchased by the British government in 1813. In 1811–12 Cockerell and Foster joined the Hon. Frederick North on a tour of Hellenistic sites in Asia Minor. At Smyrna he met Captain Francis Beaufort, commanding H.M.S. *Fredericksteen,* who was engaged in surveying the southern shores of Asia Minor, and who invited Cockerell to accompany him. He parted with Beaufort in Malta in order to visit Sicily, where he spent three months measuring the temple of Jupiter Olympius at Girgenti (Agrigento). After a serious illness in Malta he returned to Greece by way of Albania, and, untiring as usual in his search for classical antiquities, proceeded on a tour of the Peloponnesus and the Archipelago. The abdication of Napoleon in April 1814 now made it possible for Cockerell to extend his tour to Italy, and he spent the winter of 1815–16 in Rome. In the spring of 1816 he visited Florence (where he made a clever pedimental restoration of the Niobe group in the Uffizi) and northern Italy before returning home in 1817 to begin architectural practice at the age of 29.

As a classical archaeologist Cockerell now had a considerable reputation. He had shared in some of the major discoveries of antique sculpture, investigated some important Greek temples, and been (with Haller) the first to observe the entasis of Greek columns. Of architectural practice he had, however, had little experience. His attempt, in 1816, to design a palace for the Duke of Wellington had shown how much he had to learn in that direction, and his fastidious nature recoiled from the drudgery of an architect's office: in a moment of depression he even announced his intention of 'living on a crust of bread' as an artist – a proposal from which he was eventually dissuaded by his father. Although he was soon established in independent practice, he continued to devote much of his time to preparing finished drawings of Greek antiquities for exhibition at the Royal Academy, and as illustrations for a projected history of Greek art, planned in conjunction with Haller, and abandoned only after the latter's death in 1818. In 1819 he exhibited the 'Idea of a Restoration of the Capitol and Forum of Rome . . . from the existing remains, the authorities of ancient writers, and the dissertations of Piranesi, Nardini, Venuti, and others', and in 1824 a companion restoration of Athens, 'as it may have been in the time of the Antonines'. It was, however, not until 1860 that he at last published his *magnum opus*, *The Temples of Jupiter Panhellenius at Ægina and of Apollo Epicurius at Bassae*. For, although 'drawing was to him as natural a mode of expression as speech', he found writing an effort, and the book, so his son tells us, 'was a load on his conscience all his life'.

Meanwhile in 1819 he had taken his father's place as Surveyor of St. Paul's Cathedral, and by 1822 he was well enough known to be chosen by a Scottish committee to design the National Monument in Edinburgh, intended by its sponsors to be a replica of the Parthenon. In 1833 he succeeded Soane as architect to the Bank of England. He was elected A.R.A. in 1829, R.A. in 1836, and Professor of Architecture in 1840. In 1848 he was the first recipient of the Royal Gold Medal of the R.I.B.A., and in 1860 he succeeded Earl de Grey as the Institute's first professional president. He was a Chevalier of the Legion of Honour, a Member of the Institut de France, of the Academy of St. Luke at Rome, and of many other foreign academies, and Oxford gave him an honorary degree in 1844. He retired from his professorship at the Royal Academy in 1857, and from practice in 1859. He died on 17 September 1863, aged 75, and was buried in the crypt of St. Paul's Cathedral, where a monument to his memory was erected by his son and successor, F. P. Cockerell (illustrated in *Wren Soc.* ix, 5). He married in 1828 Anna, daughter of the civil engineer John Rennie, by whom he had ten children. As a young man Cockerell was the subject of a fine drawing by Ingres, and the R.I.B.A. has a convincing portrait of him in old age by Sir William Boxall. Other portraits will be found in *Illustrated London News* xliii, 1863, 341–2, and on the podium of the Albert Memorial, where he stands between Pugin and Barry as a representative of Victorian architecture.

Cockerell was at once the most fastidious and the least pedantic of English neo-classical architects. For him as a practising architect scholarship was a servant, not a master, and the influence of his archaeological researches is shown in refinement of detail rather than in the literal reproduction of Greek or Roman architectural monuments. Nor did he disdain to learn from the more recent past. In Italy he had looked appreciatively at the buildings of the sixteenth and seventeenth centuries: as Surveyor of St. Paul's he became an enthusiastic student not only of Wren but also of Vanbrugh and Hawksmoor, whose powerful designs he admired long before anyone else.[1] In consequence his own work is a unique synthesis of neo-classical and baroque, of Greek Revival and English 'Renaissance'. The result is a personal style of great beauty and distinction which stands out clearly from the conflicting trends of early Victorian architecture. Boldly conceived in scale and recession, enlivened by the introduction of authentic but unhackneyed antique details such as his favourite 'Bassae' order, and planned with the

[1] Cf. Cockerell's designs for the Houses of Parliament (1835), which he described as 'composed in the Italian and Flemish manner of that day [i.e. the sixteenth century], and with reference to Wren, Vanbrugh, and our own great masters, so as to vary and to discover new combinations of the group at every step' (*Catalogue of the Designs offered for the New Houses of Parliament now exhibiting in the National Gallery*, 6th ed. 1836, 6).

best French neo-classical prototypes in mind, Cockerell's architecture is rich without being vulgar, eclectic without being imitative. One of its characteristic features is a generous but judicious use of sculptural decoration. 'Sculpture', wrote Cockerell, 'is the language of architecture', and his skill in drawing the human figure enabled him to design appropriate sculpture himself. He also made effective use of different-coloured materials, avoiding in this way the drabness of much Greek Revival architecture when seen in the dull light of northern Europe. Cockerell's style was best deployed in public buildings such as the Ashmolean Museum at Oxford and the unfinished University Library at Cambridge (whose interior, had it been completed, would have been his masterpiece) and his monumental banks established an architectural tradition that lasted into the twentieth century. As a country-house architect he was less successful, but the small houses which he built at Hinchwick in Gloucestershire and Enstone in Oxfordshire deserve to be noted as remarkably sensitive essays in the vernacular style of their region. Though Gothic architecture interested him as a scholar, it did not inspire him as an artist, and he designed nothing of much importance in that style. Lampeter College and the Seckford Hospital at Woodbridge are no more than competent performances in Tudor Gothic. At Killerton (Devon), Athens (Greece) and Longborough (Glos.), he designed chapels in the Romanesque, 'Early English' and 'Perpendicular' styles, respectively. Though Cockerell was recognized as one of the leading architects of his time, several important commissions eluded him. Among the buildings for which he competed unsuccessfully were the National Gallery (1833), the Houses of Parliament (1835), the Reform Club (1837), the Royal Exchange (1839) and the Carlton Club (1844). The National Monument at Edinburgh was never completed, and only one wing of his Cambridge University Library was built. All his public buildings in London have now been demolished, and his most important surviving works are the Ashmolean Museum at Oxford and the branch Banks of England at Manchester, Liverpool and Bristol.

Though Cockerell chose to take few if any pupils into his office,[1] the authority of his scholarship and the distinction of his personality made him one of the most revered figures in nineteenth-century British architecture. His Royal Academy lectures, illustrated by his views and restorations of Greek and Roman architecture, attracted much attention, and are described by a contemporary as filled with Academicians and students eager to hear him speak of the 'glories of Athens, Syracuse or Rome'. Though he exhibited only intermittently at the Academy, two of the drawings which he showed became famous. One was the 'Tribute to the Memory of Sir Christopher Wren', showing all Wren's works assembled in a single group (1838). The other was entitled 'The Professor's Dream: A Symposium of the principal architectural monuments of Modern and Ancient times, drawn to the same scale', and was exhibited in 1849.

Cockerell's principal publications were *Antiquities of Athens and other Places of Greece, Sicily, etc.*, supplementary to *The Antiquities of Athens* by Stuart & Revett, London 1830 (German translation 1829); *The Temple of Jupiter Olympius at Agrigentum*, 1830; 'The Architectural Works of William of Wykeham', *Proceedings of the Archaeological Institute at Winchester*, 1845; 'Ancient Sculptures in Lincoln Cathedral', 1848, reprinted in *Proceedings of the Archaeological Institute*, 1850; *Iconography of the West Front of Wells Cathedral*, 1851; 'On the Painting of the Ancients', *Civil Engineer and Architect's Jnl.* xxii, 1859, 42–44, 88–91; *The Temples of Jupiter Panhellenius at Ægina, and of Apollo Epicurius at Bassae*, 1860;[1] 'Architectural Accessories of Monumental Sculpture', *Civil Engineer and Architect's Jnl.* xxiv, 1861, 333–6; and *A Descriptive Account of the Sculptures of the West Front of Wells Cathedral photographed for the Architectural Photographic Association*, 1862. Cockerell's Royal Academy lectures were reported at length in the *Athenaeum* and in the *Builder* from 1843 onwards. The diary of his early travels was published in 1903 as *Travels in Southern Europe and the Levant, 1810–1817*, ed. S. P. Cockerell. A notebook with sketches of English country houses, etc., visited by Cockerell, entitled by him 'Ichnographica Domestica', was published by John Harris in *Architectural History* xiv, 1971. The manuscript was broken up and sold at Sotheby's in 1988, 55 sheets being now in the R.I.B.A. Drawings Collection.

The principal collections of Cockerell's drawings are at the Victoria and Albert Museum and the R.I.B.A. His MS. diaries for the years 1821–30 and 1832 are in the R.I.B.A. Library and a MS. scrap-book com-

[1] His principal assistants were James Noble (*q.v.*) and J. E. Goodchild. J. L. Clemence of Lowestoft described himself in 1868 as a former pupil of Cockerell.

[1] The original drawings for this book are in the Yale Center for British Art.

plied by his assistant J. E. Goodchild in 1889 and entitled 'Reminiscences of twenty-six years association with the late Professor C. R. Cockerell' is in the Drawings Collection. For other drawings and MS. sources see David Watkin, *The Life and Work of C. R. Cockerell*, 1974, which includes a full bibliography. The other principal authorities for Cockerell's life are obituaries in *Gent's Mag.* xv, 1863, 785–91, and *Builder* xxi, 1863, 683–5, 705; S. Smirke, 'Some Account of the Professional Life and Character of the Late Prof. C. R. Cockerell', *R.I.B.A. Transactions*, 1863–4; G. Aitchison, 'C. R. Cockerell', *R.I.B.A. Transactions*, N.S. vi, 1890, 255–61; J. M. Brydon, 'The Work of Prof. Cockerell, R.A.', *R.I.B.A. Jnl.* 3rd ser. vii, 1899–1900, 349–68; R. P. Cockerell, 'The Life and Works of C. R. Cockerell, R.A.', *Arch. Rev.* xii, 1902, 43–7, 129–46; R. P. Spiers, 'Cockerell's Restorations of Ancient Rome', *Arch. Rev.* xxix, 1911, 123–8; *D.N.B.*; and E. M. Dodd, 'Charles Robert Cockerell', in *Victorian Architecture*, ed. P. Ferriday, 1963.

PUBLIC BUILDINGS

SEVENOAKS, KENT, LADY BOSWELL'S CHARITY SCHOOL, 1818; the two flanking entrances were later heightened [R.I.B.A.D.].

BANBURY CHURCH, OXON., completed tower and portico, modifying original design by S. P. Cockerell, 1818–22 [*V.C.H. Oxon.* x, 102–3].

HARROW SCHOOL, MIDDLESEX, new wing containing Speech Room, 1819–20, Tudor style to form symmetrical composition with Old Schools [E. D. Laborde, *Harrow School*, 1948, 69–71] (*C. Life*, 14 July 1934).

LONDON, ST. PAUL'S CATHEDRAL, restoration including replacement of ball and cross on dome, 1821–22 [Diary].

LONDON, No. 49 PALL MALL, remodelled for the Travellers' Club, 1821–2; dem. *c.*1895 [Diary, and cf. Watkin, 160 n.].

OLDCASTLE, CO. MEATH, IRELAND, School, 1821–2 [Watkin, 168].

BRISTOL, THE LITERARY AND PHILOSOPHICAL INSTITUTION (later Masonic Hall), PARK STREET, 1821–3; gutted by bombing 1940 [exhib. at R.A. 1821; R.I.B.A.D.].

LONGBOROUGH CHURCH, GLOS., north transept, or 'Sezincote aisle', for Sir Charles Cockerell, Bart., 1822–3, Gothic [Diary].

ST. DAVID'S COLLEGE, LAMPETER, CARDIGANSHIRE, 1822–7, Tudor Gothic [exhib. at R.A. 1829; drawings at R.I.B.A., Lampeter and Royal Library, Windsor].

LONDON, THE HANOVER CHAPEL, REGENT STREET, 1823–5; repaired (by Cockerell) 1845–6; dem. 1896 [Britton & Pugin, *The Public Buildings of London* ii, 1828, 276–82; V. & A.] (P. Waterhouse, 'Hanover Chapel', *R.I.B.A. Jnl.*, 3rd ser., iv, 1897, 111–14; G. L. Carr, 'C. R. Cockerell's Hanover Chapel', *Jnl. Soc. of Architectural Historians* xxxix, 1980).

LONDON, ARCHBISHOP TENISON'S CHAPEL (ST. THOMAS), REGENT STREET, rebuilt west front as façade to Regent Street, 1824; Cockerell's façade was remodelled in 1854 and demolished in 1903. The church was demolished in 1973 [*Survey of London* xxxi, 183–4].

EDINBURGH, THE NATIONAL MONUMENT, CALTON HILL, in collaboration with W. H. Playfair, 1824–9 (unfinished) [correspondence with Playfair in National Library of Scotland, MS. 639].

MIDDLE CLAYDON, BUCKS., designed school for Sir Harry Calvert Verney, Bart., 1827, perhaps the building now used as the Post Office [Diary].

BRISTOL, HOLY TRINITY CHURCH, HOTWELLS, 1829–30; interior gutted by bombing 1940 and reconstructed to a different design 1958 [W. Ison, *The Georgian Buildings of Bristol*, 1952, 88–9].

LONDON, THE WESTMINSTER LIFE AND BRITISH FIRE OFFICE, STRAND, 1831–2; dem. 1908 [exhib. at R.A. 1832; R.I.B.A.D.; V. & A.].

LONDON, THE BANK OF ENGLAND, reconstructed the Dividend, Warrant and Cheque Offices and Accountant's Drawing Office, 1834–5. In 1848–50 these were remodelled by Cockerell as a new and enlarged Private Drawing Office. After the Chartist Troubles of 1848 he was employed to reconstruct the attic storey of the Bank as a fortified parapet-walk. In 1835 he published a set of 4 plates entitled *Plan and Section of the New Dividend Pay and Warrant Offices*, etc. See also *Architectural Mag.* iii, 1836, 109–12, and H. R. Steele & F. R. Yerbury, *The Old Bank of England, London*, 1930, chap. 7.

PLYMOUTH, DEVON, designs for BRANCH BANK OF ENGLAND, 1835, perhaps not executed (see below, 1842) [Watkin, 216].

WOODBRIDGE, SUFFOLK, THE SECKFORD HOSPITAL, 1835–40, Tudor Gothic [*R.I.B.A. Trans.*, N.S. vi, 1890, 259; drawings in Goodchild Album]. The lodge and gates were designed by Cockerell's assistant, J. Noble, in 1841–2 [Seckford Hospital archives, *ex inf.* Mr. Norman Scarfe].

LONDON, THE LONDON AND WESTMINSTER BANK, LOTHBURY, in collaboration with Sir William Tite, who designed the interior,

1837–9; dem. 1928 [see Tite's account of the partnership in *R.I.B.A. Trans.*, 1863–4, 24; drawings at R.I.B.A. and V. & A.] (measured drawings in *Architect and Building News*, 1 March 1935).

CAMBRIDGE, THE UNIVERSITY LIBRARY, north wing only executed, 1837–40 [Willis & Clark, iii, 103–21; Watkin, chap. xi; D. Watkin, 'Newly discovered drawings by C. R. Cockerell for Cambridge University Library', *Arch. Hist.* 26, 1983].

PORTSMOUTH, HANTS., remodelled BRANCH BANK OF ENGLAND, No. 26 HIGH STREET, 1838–9 [Watkin, 216–17].

HARROW SCHOOL, MIDDLESEX, Chapel, 1838–9, Tudor Gothic; dem. 1853 [E. D. Laborde, *Harrow School*, 1948, 92–5].

KILLERTON, DEVON, chapel, 1840–1, see under 'Domestic Architecture' below.

ATHENS, ENGLISH PROTESTANT CHURCH, 1840–3, Gothic (executed in modified form) [*Builder* xxi, 1863, 705; C. W. J. Eliot, 'Who designed the Anglican Church of St. Paul in Athens?', in *Polis & Imperium, Studies in Honour of Edward Togo Salmon*, Toronto 1974].

LONDON, SUN FIRE OFFICE, THREADNEEDLE STREET, 1841–2; remodelled 1895; dem. 1971 [R.I.B.A.D.; V. & A.].

OXFORD, THE ASHMOLEAN MUSEUM AND TAYLORIAN INSTITUTION, 1841–5 [*V.C.H. Oxon* iii, 57; drawings at R.I.B.A., V. & A. and Oxford University Archives].

PLYMOUTH, BRANCH BANK OF ENGLAND, COURTNEY STREET, 1842 [Watkin, 217].

OXFORD, THE QUEEN'S COLLEGE, conversion into library of arcaded space beneath Upper Library, 1843–5 [*V.C.H. Oxon.* iii, 143].

MANCHESTER, BRANCH BANK OF ENGLAND, KING STREET, 1844–5 [R.I.B.A.D.].

BRISTOL, BRANCH BANK OF ENGLAND, No. 12 BROAD STREET, 1844–6; interior rebuilt [R.I.B.A.D.].

LIVERPOOL, BRANCH BANK OF ENGLAND, CASTLE STREET, 1844–7 [V. & A.].

CAMBRIDGE, FITZWILLIAM MUSEUM, completion after death of G. Basevi, 1845–7. Cockerell's principal contribution, the entrance-hall and staircase, were respectively remodelled and replaced by E. M. Barry in 1870–5 [WILLIS & CLARK, III, 215–7; V. & A.].

LONDON, NATIONAL DEBT REDEMPTION OFFICE, OLD JEWRY, additions, 1846; dem. *c.*1900 [*R.I.B.A. Trans.*, N.S. vi, 1890, 259].

LONDON, ST. BARTHOLOMEW'S CHURCH, MOOR LANE, 1849–50, incorporating the fittings of Wren's St. Bartholomew Exchange: dem. 1902 [R.I.B.A.D.: V. & A.].

LONDON, UNIVERSITY COLLEGE, arrangement, in collaboration with T. L. Donaldson, of the Flaxman Gallery to receive the plaster models of Flaxman's sculpture given to the college in 1848, 1849–50 [*Architect and Building Gazette* ii, 1850, 568].

LIVERPOOL, BANK CHAMBERS, COOK STREET, 1849–50; dem. 1959 [Watkin, 219].

LIVERPOOL, ST. GEORGE'S HALL, completion of interiors after death of H. L. Elmes, 1851–4. Cockerell also designed the sculpture in the pediment executed by W. G. Nicholl [R.I.B.A.D.; Goodchild Album; *Builder* xiii, 1855, 126–7].

LIVERPOOL, LIVERPOOL AND LONDON INSURANCE COMPANY'S OFFICES, DALE STREET, assisted by F. P. Cockerell, 1856–7 [Watkin, 229–31].

WESTMINSTER SCHOOL, designed the scenery for the Latin play, 1858 [*A Naval Career: the Life of Admiral John Markham*, 1883, 14, n. 7].

DOMESTIC ARCHITECTURE

LONDON, NORTHUMBERLAND HOUSE, STRAND, survey and report for 3rd Duke of Northumberland, 1819 [Alnwick Castle MS. 94, f. 6 *et seq.*].

LONDON, No. 32 ST. JAMES'S SQUARE, for William Howley, Bishop of London, 1819–21, in collaboration with S. P. Cockerell [*Survey of London* xxix, 203–4].

OAKLY PARK, SHROPSHIRE, remodelled for the Hon. R. H. Clive, 1819–36 [C. Hussey in *C. Life*, 1–8 March 1956; C. Hussey, *English Country Houses: Late Georgian*, 1958, 151–60] (*C. Life*, 22 March 1990).

LONDON, GLOUCESTER HOUSE, PARK LANE, repairs to roof for William Frederick, Duke of Gloucester, 1821; dem. [Watkin, 249].

LONDON, ALBANY COTTAGE (later NORTH VILLA, now Islamic Cultural Centre), REGENT'S PARK, for T. B. Lennard, 1821; altered 1920s [Watkin, 249].

ABERGWILI PALACE, CARMARTHENSHIRE, repairs for the Bishop of St. David's, 1821 [Watkin, 249].

WOOLMERS, HERTINGFORDBURY, HERTS., alterations for Sir Gore Ouseley, Bart., 1821 [Diary].

LOUGH CREW, CO. MEATH, IRELAND, for J. L. Naper, 1821–9; dem. *c.*1965, but classical lodge and gates survive [Diary; R.I.B.A.D.].

KINTURK, CASTLE POLLARD, CO. MEATH, IRELAND, alterations, including addition of portico, for W. D. Pollard, 1821–5 [Diary].

BOWOOD HOUSE, WILTS., chapel, library and breakfast-room for 3rd Marquess of Lansdowne, 1822–4 [list of works in R.I.B.A. *Sessional Papers*, 1863–4, 27] (*C. Life*, 15 June 1972).

LONDON, No. 33 BROOK STREET, GROSVENOR

SQUARE, alterations for Henry Trail, 1823–4; rebuilt internally 1909–10 [Watkin, 250].

LONDON, No. 1 UPPER GROSVENOR STREET, alterations for his brother John Cockerell, 1822–3; dem. 1957 [Watkin, 250].

GRANGE PARK, HANTS., additions for Alexander Baring (afterwards 1st Lord Ashburton), including dining-room (dem. 1972) and conservatory (rebuilt *c.*1880 except for the Ionic portico), 1823–5 [J. M. Crook, 'Grange Park Transformed', in *The Country Seat*, ed. Colvin & Harris, 1970, 223–6].

GREENMOUNT, CO. ANTRIM, IRELAND, remodelled for Mrs. Anna Thompson, *c.*1823–5; now gutted and used as Northern Ireland Agricultural College [Diary].

SEZINCOTE HOUSE, GLOS., two lodges for Sir Charles Cockerell, Bart., one known formerly as Worcester Lodge, now as Beehive Lodge, 1823 [Diary].

DERRY ORMOND, nr. LAMPETER, CARDIGANSHIRE, for John Jones, 1824–5; enlarged 1860; dem. 1953 [list of works in R.I.B.A. *Sessional Papers*, 1863–4, 27; specification in N.L.W.].

PENTRE, BONCATH, PEMBROKESHIRE, alterations for Dr. Davies, 1824–5 [Diary].

CWMCYNFELIN, nr. ABERYSTWYTH, CARDIGANSHIRE, stables (now converted into dwellings) for J. Lloyd Williams, 1825 [Diary].

HINCHWICK FARM (now MANOR), CONDICOTE GLOS., for Sir Charles Cockerell, Bart., 1826 [Diary].

LONDON, EATON SQUARE, interior of house for Capt. W. A. Clifford, R.N., 1827 [Hermione Hobhouse, *Thomas Cubitt*, 1971, 274 n.; Watkin, 251].

LONDON, EATON SQUARE, interior of house for Mrs. Belli, Cockerell's aunt, 1828 [Diary].

SEZINCOTE HOUSE, GLOS., office wing for Sir Charles Cockerell, Bart., 1827 [Diary].

WYNNSTAY, DENBIGHSHIRE, altered Great Room (dem. 1858) and designed lodge for Sir Watkin Williams-Wynn, Bart., 1827–8 [Peter Howell & T. W. Pritchard in *C. Life*, 30 March, 6 April 1972].

LANGTON HOUSE, nr. BLANDFORD, DORSET, for J. J. Farquharson, 1827–33; dem. 1949 except for stables [list of works in R.I.B.A. *Sessional Papers*, 1863–4, 27].

LYNFORD HALL, NORFOLK, alterations and additions for Sir Richard Sutton, Bart., 1828; rebuilt by W. Burn 1863 [Diary].

NORTH WEALD BASSET VICARAGE, ESSEX, for his brother, the Revd. Henry Cockerell, 1828–9, Tudor style [Diary].

LANGLEYS, ESSEX, advised J. J. Tufnell, 1827, perhaps suggesting formation of entrance-hall by bringing forward three central bays [Diary; cf. Watkin, 251] (*C. Life*, 9 Jan. 1942).

ENSTONE VICARAGE, OXON., 1832–3 [Oxford C.R.O., MS. Oxford Dioc. papers b. 103, no. 2 b].

BLAISE CASTLE, nr. BRISTOL, picture-room (with Ionic portico) for J. S. Harford, 1832–3 [Alice Harford, *Annals of the Harford Family*, 1909, 54] (*C. Life*, 31 March 1900).

WYTHER GRANGE, ARMLEY, LEEDS, YORKS. (W.R.), alterations for John Gott, *c.*1835 [correspondence in possession of Mr. J. Goodchild].

KILLERTON, DEVON, private chapel in park for Sir T. D. Acland, Bart., 1840–1, Romanesque style [R.I.B.A.D.].

BURTON HILL HOUSE, MALMESBURY, WILTS., for his brother John Cockerell, 1842; rebuilt after a fire in 1846, presumably to Cockerell's designs, Tudor Gothic [MS. list of works at R.I.B.A.].

PEPER HAROW, SURREY, addition of porch and balustrade in front of the attics for 5th Viscount Midleton, 1843 [*R.I.B.A. Trans.*, N.S. vi, 1890, 259] (*C. Life*, 26 Dec. 1925).

CAVERSFIELD HOUSE, OXON., for the Revd. R. B. Marsham, 1842–5; dem. after fire 1976 [*R.I.B.A. Trans.*, N.S. vi, 1890, 259].

MONUMENTS

NEWCASTLE, ST. NICHOLAS CHURCH (now Cathedral), Admiral Lord Collingwood (d. 1810), 1821, executed by J. C. F. Rossi [R. Welford, *Monuments of St. Nicholas Newcastle*, 1880, pl. xiii].

HAMPTON CHURCH, MIDDLESEX, John Deverell, 1821, executed by J. C. F. Rossi, but apparently now lost or destroyed [Watkin, Appendix B].

HENBURY CHURCH, nr. BRISTOL, Mrs. H. Battersby, 1823, executed by J. C. F. Rossi [Watkin, Appendix B].

PIDDLETRENTHIDE CHURCH, DORSET, John Bridge (d. 1834), Gothic, executed by W. G. Nicholl [signed].

KENSAL GREEN CEMETERY, Lady Pulteney, 1849 [A. W. Hakewill, *Modern Tombs gleaned from the Public Cemeteries of London*, 1851, pl. 23].

ROYAL HOSPITAL, CHELSEA, granite obelisk to commemorate Victory of Chillianwallah, 1849 [Watkin, Appendix B].

ROYAL HOSPITAL, CHELSEA, catafalque for lying-in-state of the Duke of Wellington, 11–17 Nov. 1852 [*R.I.B.A. Trans.*, N.S. vi, 1890, 259].

BRIGHTON CEMETERY, H. J. Prescott, Governor of the Bank of England (d. 1856), 1858

[*R.I.B.A. Trans.*, N.S. vi, 1890, 259].

ROYAL HOSPITAL, CHELSEA, monument in chapel to the officers and men killed in the Indian Mutiny, 1858 [*R.I.B.A. Trans.*, N.S. vi, 1890, 259].

COCKERELL, SAMUEL PEPYS (1753–1827], was the son of John Cockerell of Bishop's Hull, Somerset.[1] Through his mother he was related to the family of the diarist Samuel Pepys. He began his architectural career as a pupil of Sir Robert Taylor, whose benevolent tutelage he was to acknowledge many years later in his will, where he refers to him as 'the affectionate prop and support of my early steps and to whom . . . I was chiefly indebted for my first advancement in life'. In 1774 Cockerell obtained his first appointment as District Surveyor for the parish of St. George's, Hanover Square. In 1775 he joined the Office of Works as Clerk of Works at the Tower of London, and in 1780 was also given the clerkship at Newmarket. Though regarded as 'very able in his profession' and 'very diligent and regular in His Majesty's service', he lost both posts as a result of the reorganization of the Office of Works in 1782. However, in 1785 he was appointed Inspector of Repairs to the Admiralty, and on Sir Robert Taylor's death in 1788 Cockerell succeeded to the surveyorships of the Foundling and Pulteney estates in London. In 1791 he obtained the surveyorship to the Victualling Office, and in 1806 that of the East India Company. He was also surveyor to the sees of Canterbury and London, and Surveyor of St. Paul's Cathedral from 1811 to 1819.

As surveyor to the governors of the Foundling Hospital, Cockerell was responsible for the development of their Bloomsbury estate, preparing in 1790 a report which summarized 'the cardinal principles of Georgian town-planning'. During the next fifteen years building proceeded under Cockerell's direction, but some of the governors were not satisfied that his supervision was adequate, and attempted to have him dismissed. Although the General Court appears to have been satisfied with his conduct, Cockerell eventually resigned in April 1808, his place being taken by his pupil Joseph Kay (for further details see D. J. Olsen, *Town Planning in London*, Yale 1964, 74–89). As surveyor to the Bishop of London Cockerell prepared plans for developing his Paddington estate, but they had been only partially implemented at the time of the architect's death, and the area was eventually laid out for building on the basis of a new scheme by his successor George Gutch (see Gordon Toplis, 'The History of Tyburnia', in *C. Life*, 15 Nov. 1973).

In 1824 Cockerell was the architect for another abortive scheme. This was for a new square on the Mortimer estate in Bloomsbury to be called 'Carmarthen Square'. In the event the site was bought for the building of University College (see sale particulars printed in *Trans. Carmarthenshire Antiq. Soc.* pt. 16, 1909–10, 52).

Cockerell was an able architect whose work is often interesting and original. Some of his designs show 'very marked French influence of an advanced kind', notably the destroyed church of St. Martin Outwich, the somewhat eccentric tower of St. Anne's, Soho, and the façade of Gore Court, Kent. At Daylesford and Sezincote he skilfully grafted oriental details on to basically English architectural forms for the benefit of Indian 'nabobs'; and at Tickencote in Rutland he made a serious if not very scholarly attempt to restore a twelfth-century church in a Romanesque style.

If Cockerell visited France or Italy the journey does not appear to have been recorded, but he is known to have gone to Ireland in July 1795, presumably for a professional purpose [P.R.O., CREST 2/918; Farington's Diary, 15 July 1795]. He lived in a house in Old Burlington Street, and latterly at Westbourne House, Paddington, the former residence of Isaac Ware, where he died on 12 July 1827, aged 74. He left a considerable estate, including the manor of Woolley in Huntingdonshire, which he had acquired in 1803. There are portraits of Cockerell and his wife by George Dance in the British Museum, and a half-length portrait by Beechey was engraved by Thomas Hodgetts (1834). His pupils included Joseph Kay, Benjamin Latrobe, Thomas Martyr, James Noble, William Porden, Robert Sibley, C. H. Tatham, and his (second) son C. R. Cockerell, who gave him considerable assistance during his last years. Some of his drawings are in the R.I.B.A. Collection. His unexecuted design for the Connaught Chapel, Paddington (1827), is in the Victoria and Albert Museum (E 2115, 1909). It is reproduced in *C. Life*, 15 Nov. 1973, p. 1527, fig. 3.

[*A.P.S.D.*; *D.N.B.*; *History of the King's Works* vi, 25; P.R.O., ADM 111/123, 1 Sept. 1791 (surveyorship of Victualling Office); John Summerson, *Architecture in Britain*

[1] According to the account of the family in Debrett's *Baronetage*, 1836, 348, S. P. Cockerell was born on 15 Feb. 1754, but in his diary C. R. Cockerell implies that his father was born on 6 Jan. 1753. This is consistent with his death in 1827 at the age of 74.

1530–1830, 1991, 539, n. 5; diaries of C. R. Cockerell; *Gent's Mag.* 1827 (ii), 93; P.C.C. 470 HEBER; *V.C.H. Hunts.* iii, 126; *Arch. Hist.* xiv, 1971, fig. 14b (plan of Cockerell's house at Westbourne Green).]

PUBLIC BUILDINGS

LONDON, SAUNDERS'S CHOCOLATE HOUSE, later the Albion Club House, 85 ST. JAMES'S STREET, 1786; dem. 1862 ['this Club built by my Father 30 years ago': C. R. Cockerell's diary, 10 Sept. 1823; *Survey of London* xxx, 468].

BANBURY CHURCH, OXON., rebuilt 1792–7; tower and portico completed to modified design by C. R. Cockerell 1818–22 [exhib. at R.A. 1792; *V.C.H. Oxon.* x, 102–3, with plan and illustration of S. P. Cockerell's original design for the tower].

BLOXHAM CHURCH, OXON., gratuitously supervised repair of spire, 1792 [Gardner's *History, Gazeteer and Directory of the County of Oxford*, 1852, 618; *V.C.H. Oxon*, ix, 76].

TICKENCOTE CHURCH, RUTLAND, rebuilt in Norman style, incorporating twelfth-century chancel, at expense of Eliza Wingfield, 1792 [*Gent's Mag.* 1806 (i), 34].

NORMANTON CHURCH, RUTLAND, proposed decorations for Sir Gilbert Heathcote, Bart., exhib. at R.A. 1793; rebuilt 1911.

LONDON, ST. MARTIN OUTWICH CHURCH, BISHOPSGATE STREET, rebuilt 1796–8; dem. 1874 [exhib. at R.A. 1797, 1798, 1799; C. W. F. Goss, 'St. Martin Outwich', *London and Middlesex Arch. Soc.'s Trans.*, N.S. vi, 1929] (external view in G. Godwin & J. Britton, *The Churches of London* ii, 1839; plan in W. Thornbury, *Old and New London* i, n.d., 534).

LONDON, ST. MARGARET'S CHURCH, WESTMINSTER, new roof, ceiling, galleries, and extensive repairs and redecoration, 1799–1802, Gothic [exhib. at R.A. 1799, 1801; MS. Minutes of the Committee for the Repair of the Church, 1798–1803, Westminster City Library, No. 2625] (H. F. Westlake, *St. Margaret's Westminster*, 1914, pls. vi, ix).

LONDON, WORSHIP STREET, SHOREDITCH, entrance to stables of the Light Horse Volunteers, *c.*1800 [exhib. at R.A. 1801].

LONDON, ST. ANNE'S CHURCH, SOHO, tower, 1802–3 [*Survey of London* xxxiii, 262–3, 270].

LONDON, THE WESTMINSTER GUILDHALL or SESSIONS HOUSE, 1804–5; dem. [J. Elmes, *Metropolitan Improvements*, 1831, 155, with illustration].

CONGLETON, CHESHIRE, THE GUILDHALL, 1804–5 (dem. 1868), may have been the 'Town Hall and Market House in Cheshire' which Cockerell exhibited at the R.A. in 1803: see illustration in R. Head, *Congleton Past and Present*, 1887, 137.

LONDON, ST. GEORGE'S CHURCH, SOUTHWARK, survey in 1806 prior to repair in 1808 [Surrey Archdeaconry Records].

TENBY, PEMBROKESHIRE, PUBLIC BATHS, for Sir William Paxton, 1811 (now known as Laston House and converted into flats) [J. Dugdale, *British Traveller* iv, 1819, 729].

SEVENOAKS CHURCH, KENT, restoration, including clerestory and plaster vault to nave, 1812 [J. Rooker, *Guide to Sevenoaks Church*, 1910].

LONDON, EAST INDIA HOUSE, LEADENHALL STREET, additions, 1822–3 (assisted by C. R. Cockerell); dem. 1861–2 [C. R. Cockerell's diary].

WINCHESTER, HOSPITAL OF ST. CROSS, restoration, 1827, completed by John Nash [John Summerson, *John Nash*, 1935, 286].

PADDINGTON, LONDON, added four dwellings to parish almshouses in Harrow Road; dem. 1860 [W. Robins, *Paddington Past and Present*, 1853, 67].

DOMESTIC ARCHITECTURE

WHITE KNIGHTS, nr. READING, BERKS., entrance gates and bridge for W. Byam Martin, *c.*1785 [exhib. at R.A. 1785].

LONDON, WHITEHALL, ADMIRALTY HOUSE, as residence for the First Lord of the Admiralty, 1786–8 [*Survey of London* xvi, 35–9 and pls. 46–57].

WATERSTOCK HOUSE, OXON., for Sir W. H. Ashurst, 1787–90; dem. 1956 [Bodleian Library, MS. d.d. Ashurst d.10, where the architect is called 'Sir Richard Cockerell'; J. Dale & P. H. Ditchfield, *Oxfordshire and Berkshire: County Biographies* (*c.*1900), where he is called 'Sir C. Cockerell'].

DAYLESFORD HOUSE, nr. MORETON-IN-MARSH, GLOS., remodelled for Warren Hastings, 1789–93; S. and E. fronts altered in 1850s [A. Ginger, 'Daylesford House and Warren Hastings', *Georgian Group's Report & Jnl.* 1989; N. Kingsley, *The Country Houses of Gloucestershire* ii, 1992, 113–17].

SALISBURY, ST. EDMUND'S COLLEGE (now Council House), addition of N. wing for H. P. Wyndham, 1790 [R.C.H.M., *Salisbury* i, 49].

ALDERBURY HOUSE, WILTS., for G. Y. Fort, 1791–6 [building accounts among Fort family papers in possession of Lady Wrenbury].

PIERREMONT HALL (now Council Offices), nr. BROADSTAIRS, KENT, for Thomas Forsyth, 1792 [*A.P.S.D.*].

LITTLE KINETON, WARWICKS., house for Richard Hill, begun 1792, but never completed [estimate dated 15 March 1792 in Sir John Soane's Museum].

MIDDLETON HALL, CARMARTHENSHIRE, for Sir William Paxton, 1793–5; gutted by fire 1931 and dem. 1951 [G. Richardson, *New Vitruvius Britannicus* ii, 1808, pls. 62–4]; also a tower in the park in memory of Lord Nelson, *c.*1815 [*The Beauties of England and Wales* xviii, 1815, 332] (S. Barton, *Monumental Follies*, 1972, 254).

LONDON, GREAT PULTENEY STREET, small house for Sir William Pulteney, Bart., *c.*1794 [C. R. Cockerell's diary, 22 March 1827].

GORE COURT, TUNSTALL, KENT, for G. Harper, 1792–5; dem. *c.*1925 [G. Richardson, *New Vitruvius Britannicus* i, 1802, pl. 11].

LONDON, PICCADILLY, No. 144, for (Sir) Drummond Smith, Bart., 1795; dem. [*A.P.S.D.*].

LONDON, PICCADILLY, No. 145, for Sir John Smith-Burges, Bart., 1795; dem. [*A.P.S.D.*].

HERRIARD PARK, HANTS., alterations for G. P. Jervoise, *c.*1797; dem. 1965 [S. Jeffery in *Arch. Hist.* 28, 1985, 45].

BUXTED PARK, SUSSEX, proposed alterations and additions for Sir George Shuckburgh Evelyn, Bart., 1801, perhaps not carried out; damaged by fire 1940 [letters in B.L., Add. MS. 38480, ff. 141–2] (*C. Life*, 21–28 April 1934).

NUTWELL COURT, nr. EXETER, DEVON, for 2nd Lord Heathfield, 1802 [exhib. at R.A. 1802].

LONDON, No. 13 HARLEY STREET, rooms for Sir William Beechey [Farington's Diary, 13 Oct. 1803].

SEZINCOTE HOUSE, nr. MORETON-IN-MARSH, GLOS., for his brother Sir Charles Cockerell, Bart., *c.*1805–20, Indian style [B.L., Add. MS. 29231, ff. 59–60; *Catalogue of the R.I.B.A. Drawings Coll.: C–F*, 34 and (for Thomas Daniell's designs for the Indian garden ornaments, etc.) 64–5] (*C. Life*, 13, 20 May 1939; C. Hussey, *English Country Houses: Late Georgian*, 1958, 66–73).

attributed: LONDON, NELSON SQUARE, SOUTHWARK, *c.*1807–10 [*Survey of London* xxii, 129–30].

TOFT HALL, CHESHIRE, added Dining Room, Library and twin towers for Ralph Leycester, 1810–13 [P. de Figueredo & J. Treuherz, *Cheshire Country Houses*, 1988, 187].

FULHAM PALACE, MIDDLESEX, rebuilt east front for William Howley, Bishop of London, 1814–15 [C. J. Fèret, *Fulham Old and New* iii, 1900, 114] (*C. Life*, 9 Feb. 1929).

LONDON, No. 32 ST. JAMES'S SQUARE, for William Howley, Bishop of London, 1819–21, in collaboration with C. R. Cockerell [*Survey of London* xxix, 203–4].

BROUGHTON RECTORY, OXON., added bow-windowed drawing-room, 1820 [*V.C.H. Oxon.* ix, 86].

CANON HILL, BRAYWICK, BERKS., classical greenhouse for James Law, date uncertain [B.L., Add. MS. 18674, f. 6].

COCKSEDGE, or **COXEDGE,** JOSEPH (*c.*1751–1839), was a native of King's Lynn who became 'an eminent architect and builder' in London. Francis Goodwin (*q.v.*) was his pupil. He retired in about 1810, and lived latterly in Edwardes Square, Kensington, where he died on 23 November 1839, in his 90th year [*Norwich Chronicle*, 30 Nov. 1839, *ex inf.* Mr. David Cubitt; *Gent's Mag.* 1840 (i), 104; *A.P.S.D.*, *s.v.* 'Goodwin'; sale catalogue of his library (1820) in B.L. S.C.L. 10 (12)].

COKE, THOMAS (1675–1727), was the son of John Coke (d. 1692), from whom he inherited the mansion and estate of Melbourne in Derbyshire. He was educated at New College, Oxford, and subsequently spent some time in the Low Countries. He sat in Parliament as Member for Derbyshire from 1698 to 1710, and for the rotten borough of Grampound from 1710 to 1714. Politically he was a Tory and a supporter of Harley, but retained the Court post of Vice-Chamberlain, to which he was appointed in 1707, throughout the reign of George I.

Coke was a connoisseur and man of taste. When his possessions were sold after his death there were 127 lots of pictures, 443 lots of prints and 1068 lots of books (including many architectural works). We have Vanbrugh's testimony that he was 'a great lover of musique and promoter of operas' [*Letters*, ed. Webb, 20], and at Melbourne, with some advice form Henry Wise, he laid out a formal garden which is one of the best surviving examples of its kind in the country. The muniments at Melbourne afford evidence that Coke was also an amateur architect. A notebook survives containing extracts from Vignola, notes about gardening and memoranda about various internal alterations to the house at Melbourne for which he was responsible.[1] There is also a description in Coke's

[1] Although Thomas Coke made a plan for remodelling the house with a façade facing the church, it remained basically a fabric of the sixteenth and seventeenth centuries until his son G. L. Coke employed William Smith to rebuild the east (garden) front in 1743–4. In a MS. *Description of Derbyshire*

hand of a design, evidently made by himself, of 'a House for the Duke' (presumably of Marlborough, with whom he was 'well acquainted'), and there are drawings and sketches by him for fitting up the interior of the chapel at DRAYTON HOUSE, NORTHANTS., for Lady Betty Germain, and for rebuilding CRANFORD HOUSE, MIDDLESEX, *c.*1725, for a fellow-courtier, the 3rd Earl of Berkeley. The designs for Cranford are mostly in a plain early Georgian style, with a Vignolesque front doorway, but some of the elevations attempt ineffectively to emulate Vanbrugh. Cranford, as rebuilt in 1722 (dem. 1944), resembled (though it did not exactly correspond to any of) Coke's drawings, so it is possible that he should be regarded as its architect. In 1726 Francis Smith of Warwick submitted an estimate for building a gatehouse at Melbourne for Coke 'according to his Honour's Draught'. An accompanying drawing (by Smith) shows that it was designed to be in the form of a simplified triumphal arch (Lothian archives, 219/1/28). Though apparently built, it was demolished before the end of the eighteenth century.

Coke died on 17 May 1727. His library and pictures were sold by auction in London in February 1728 (sale catalogue in B.L., C 119.h.3(7). His portrait by Michael Dahl hangs at Melbourne.

[Lothian archives at Melbourne Hall; Hist. MSS. Comm., *Cowper* iii; J. Talbot Coke, *Coke of Trusley*, privately printed 1880, 72–4; Lindley Scott in *C. Life*, 7 April 1928; David Green, *Gardener to Queen Anne*, 1956, 41–8; *Survey of London* xxx, 514–15; P. Heath, 'Melbourne Hall Reconsidered', *Georgian Group's Report & Journal*, 1988.]

COKER, FULLER, junior, was an architect and builder at Shipdam in Norfolk from about 1820 to about 1845. His designs for parsonages at CRANWICH, 1820, RYBURGH, 1821, SOUTH RAYNHAM, 1822, HARPLEY, 1829, and CRANWORTH, 1839, are in the Norfolk Record Office [DN/DPL/1/2–3]. An inscription in WATTON CHURCH, NORFOLK, records that the aisles were rebuilt by Coker in 1840 in an insensitive Gothic style.

COLE, CHARLES (*c.*1738–1803), was born at Peterborough, and lived for a time at Stamford. It was, however, in London that he established himself as a builder and surveyor. Here he became Assistant or Deputy Surveyor to the Office of Woods and Forests, in which capacity he successfully repaired the breach in the retaining banks of Virginia Water caused by a storm in 1768. He was, however, dismissed in about 1790 because his charges were considered unreasonable. As a builder his principal venture was the laying out of ELY PLACE, HOLBORN, in 1776, on the site of the Bishop of Ely's palace, which had been sold to him in accordance with an Act of Parliament obtained in 1772 (for further details see P.R.O., WORK 6/19, p. 127). The 'handsome and uniform' street which he erected in conjunction with the bricklayer John Gorham is the subject of unfavourable comment in Pugin's *Contrasts*. Cole was Master of the Tylers' and Bricklayers' Company in 1801–2, and died on 24 February 1803, aged 65, leaving a considerable estate. [*A.P.S.D.*; J. Chambers, MS. *Collections for a Biography of English Architects* at R.I.B.A.; *Obituary and Records of Lincolnshire, Rutland and Northants 1800–1850*; W. Stevenson, *Supplement to Bentham's Ely*, 1817, 82; *Gent's Mag.* 1803 (i), 199, 1816 (i), 395; P.C.C. 188 MARRIOTT.]

COLE, MATTHEW (–1692), of Clipston, Northants., was a carpenter by trade. In 1668 he designed and built the SCHOOL AND HOSPITAL (or almshouse) at CLIPSTON, a symmetrical gabled building in the local vernacular style. He died at an advanced age in October 1692 [Sir Gyles Isham, *Clipston School and Hospital*, 1956, 17–18].

COLE, WILLIAM (1800–1892), was the third architect of his name to practise in Chester. His father and his grandfather were primarily builders, and are not known to have designed any building of importance, though in 1784 William Cole I was the runner-up to Thomas Harrison in the competition for the new gaol at Chester. 'William Cole, junior' (as the subject of this entry was generally called) was born in Chester on 19 June 1800, and at the age of 14 became a pupil of Thomas Harrison. In 1829 he succeeded Harrison as county surveyor, and had the responsibility of completing the Grosvenor Bridge to the latter's designs. In 1833 he visited Italy, Greece, Asia Minor, Egypt and Morocco, and on his return published a volume entitled *Select Views of the Remains of Ancient Monuments in Greece, from drawings taken and coloured on the spot* (1835). In 1840 he moved to Birkenhead, an expanding town in whose development he played an important part, both as an architect, as a commissioner

by William Woolley (*c.*1715) in the College of Arms (Pegge MS. 15), it is stated that although Coke had 'made very curious Gardens, Fishponds etc., . . . the House being all or part of it seated on lands that Belong to the Cathedral of Carlisle . . . he has not yet thought fit to rebuild it'.

under the Improvement Act of 1833, and as a member of the Birkenhead Dock and Warehouse Company. Despite his training under one of the leading members of the Greek Revival and his foreign travels, Cole is chiefly known today as the designer of a castellated country house and two undistinguished Gothic churches.

A tall, handsome, man, Cole was twice married and had seventeen children. He died on 8 October 1892, aged 92. His portrait by Thomas Hargreaves is in the R.I.B.A. Collection. [F. Simpson, 'A Few Cheshire Worthies', *Jnl. Chester and North Wales Antiquarian Soc.*, N.S. xxviii, 1928, 116–24; *The Architect's, Engineer's and Building Trades' Directory*, 1868, 106.]

TATTON PARK, CHESHIRE, garden feature based on the Choragic Monument of Lysicrates, for Wilbraham Egerton, *c.*1820 [Arthur Oswald in *C. Life*, 30 July 1964, 295 and fig. 4].

CHESTER, ST. OSWALD'S CHURCH (south transept of the Cathedral), gallery, etc., 1826; removed 1880 [Simpson, *op. cit.*, 118; I.C.B.S.].

CHESTER, ST. BRIDGET'S CHURCH, 1827–8, Greek Doric; dem. 1892 [Simpson, *op. cit.*, 119].

CHESHIRE COUNTY LUNATIC ASYLUM (now Deva Hospital), UPTON, 1827–9 [J. Hemingway, *History of Chester* ii, 1831, 226, with plan and view].

BOLESWORTH CASTLE, CHESHIRE, rebuilt for George Walmsley, 1829, castellated Gothic; remodelled internally by C. Williams-Ellis 1921–3 [exhib. at R.A. 1831] (Twycross, *Mansions of England and Wales: Cheshire* i, 1850, 45; P. de Figueredo & J. Treuherz, *Cheshire Country Houses*, 1988, 35–8).

CHESTER, ST. PAUL'S CHURCH, BOUGHTON, 1829–30, classical; rebuilt 1876 [*A.P.S.D.*, *s.v.* 'Chester'].

CHESTER INFIRMARY, remodelled interior, 1830 [J. Hemingway, *History of Chester* ii, 1831, 208; W. Cole, *Plans and Sections of Chester Infirmary*, 1831].

CHESTER, THE METHODIST NEW CONNEXION CHAPEL, PEPPER STREET, 1835, Corinthian [Simpson, *op. cit.*, 121].

BIRKENHEAD, ST. ANNE'S CHURCH, 1846–50, Gothic [*A.P.S.D.*, *s.v.* 'Birkenhead'].

BIRKENHEAD, OXTON ROAD CONGREGATIONAL CHURCH, 1857–8, Gothic [*The Architect's . . . Directory*, *loc. cit.*].

BIRKENHEAD, BAPTIST CHAPEL, GRANGE ROAD, 1857–8, Doric [Simpson, *op. cit.*, 123].

COLEBATCH, GEORGE, a pupil in 1805 of W. R. Laxton (*q.v.*), exhibited at the Royal Academy between 1805 and 1809. He appears in the London directories in the 1830s and 1840s as a surveyor and builder in the Minories. G. Santler was his pupil in 1810.

COLEMAN, WILLIAM (–1718), a carpenter and joiner by trade, was the chief master builder employed in the execution of Sir John Vanbrugh's designs for remodelling KIMBOLTON CASTLE, HUNTS., from 1707 onwards. He had previously made plans himself which were set aside in favour of Vanbrugh's, but the latter had a high opinion of him as a builder, and told the Earl of Manchester that 'if we had such a Man at Blenheim he'd save us a Thousand pounds a Year'. Coleman died in 1718, leaving considerable property in Kimbolton, Wellingborough and elsewhere to his sons Joseph and Thomas. [*The Works of Sir John Vanbrugh* iv, *The Letters*, ed. Webb, 1928, 13, 15, 17, 20, 21, 24; Laurence Whistler, *The Imagination of Sir John Vanbrugh*, 1954, 135–7; building accounts in Hunts. County Record Office, especially dd. MIA.]

COLLARD, RICHARD, practised as an 'architect and surveyor' at Broadstairs in Kent in the 1820s and 1830s. No building by him has so far been identified, but his unexecuted designs for an episcopal chapel at Broadstairs in either Gothic or classical style are in the Kent Archives Office at Ramsgate [N. Yates, *Buildings, Faith and Worship*, Oxford 1991, 121].

COLLIE, JAMES (–*c.*1881) practised in Scotland. In the 1820s he was in Aberdeen, where he appears to have had some connection with John Smith (*q.v.*), one of whose account-books he signs [N.M.R.S., Abstract Book No. ix, 1829]. In the 1830s and 1840s, however, he was practising in Glasgow. In 1835 he published an *Historical Account of the Cathedral of Glasgow*, with plans and elevations (London, folio), and in about 1847 a similar work on *The Royal Palace of Linlithgow*. He designed THE ROYAL INFIRMARY, MONTROSE, a competent Greek Revival design of 1837–9 [*The Imperial Gazetteer of Scotland*, ed. J.M. Wilson, ii, 446]; the BRIDGE STREET terminal of the Glasgow & South-Western Railway, with a handsome Doric portico (dem. 1971) [Gildard's MS. notes, *ex inf.* Mr. David Walker]; and THE BLYTHSWOOD TESTIMONIAL SCHOOL at RENFREW, 1842 [Renfrew Town Council Minutes, *ex inf.* Mr. Walker]. In 1839 he competed unsuccessfully for the Blind Asylum at Aberdeen [G. M. Fraser in *Aberdeen Weekly Jnl.*, 30 Aug. 1918]. In 1850–1 he made a very competent survey of

Dundee. He was still active in 1869, when he was employed to carry out alterations to the eastern part of HOLY RUDE CHURCH, STIRLING [R.C.A.M., *Stirlingshire* i, 130]. At that date he was living at Bridge of Allan, where he had designed BELLMOIR HOUSE for his own occupation [information from Mr. Walker]. In 1842 he was made an Honorary Fellow of the London Society called the 'Freemasons of the Church' [*Builder* i, 1843, 24].

COLLINGWOOD, JOHN (*c.*1760–1831), practised first in Worcester and later in Gloucester, where he held the post of county surveyor from about 1820. He died in Gloucester on 14 March 1831, aged 71 [*Monmouthshire Merlin*, 19 March 1831, *ex inf.* Mr. A. G. Chamberlain].

In WORCESTER Collingwood designed THE DEPOT OF ARMS, QUEEN STREET, 1807 [*Worcester Jnl.*, 26 March 1807], and the octagonal BARBOURNE TOLL HOUSES (one of which survives as a shop), 1814 [*Worcester Jnl.*, 6 June 1814]. In 1811 the tower of ST. HELEN'S CHURCH was taken down under his direction, but it was not until 1819 that it was rebuilt [MS. Vestry Minutes]. Surveys of property in the city by him are in the P.R.O. (MPE 466) and the County Record Office (609:1). [information from Mr. D. Whitehead].

In GLOUCESTER Collingwood designed THE DEBTORS' PRISON, *c.*1820 [G. W. Counsel, *History of Gloucester*, 1829, 173], and erected THE COUNTY LUNATIC ASYLUM (now Horton Road Hospital) to the designs of William Stark of Edinburgh, who had died in 1813 [Ann Bailey, 'The Founding of the Glos. County Asylum', *Trans. Bristol and Glos. Arch. Soc., etc.*, 1971, 184].

Elsewhere, Collingwood enlarged APPERLEY COURT, GLOS., for Mrs. Strickland, *c.*1817–18 [Glos. C.R.O., D.1245 E.3] and in 1826–8 designed THE HOUSE OF CORRECTION at SWANSEA, GLAMORGANSHIRE [Glamorgan Record Office, QGP. 70], where he had recently supervised the erection of the Town Hall to the designs of Thomas Bowen (*q.v.*).

COLLINS, JAMES, of Birmingham, advertised in *Aris's Birmingham Gazette*, on 24 March 1746, that he 'undertakes Building in its whole Study and Practice, according to the most modern Rules of Architecture'. Soon after 1750 he rebuilt THE WHITE LION INN, STRATFORD-ON-AVON (now Nos. 16, 17 and 18 HENLEY STREET) [*V.C.H. Warwicks.* iii, 231].

COLLINS, JOB (–1800), was the son of Thomas Collins of Warwick. In *c.*1726 he was apprenticed to John Dunkley, mason of Warwick [Guildhall Library, index to Apprenticeship Registers in P.R.O.]. He was one of the contractors who rebuilt the Shire Hall, Warwick, in 1754–7 to the designs of Sanderson Miller [accounts in County Record Office]. In 1760 he was employed to rebuild the central tower of WOLSTON CHURCH, WARWICKS., after it had collapsed [R. Norton, *Wolston Church*, 1952, 11]. In 1774 the parishioners of ST. NICHOLAS, WARWICK, employed 'Messrs. Collins and London, Surveyors', to report on the condition of the north aisle of their church [Vestry Minutes in County Record Office]. According to W. Field, *History of Warwick*, 1815, 131, the church was rebuilt in 1779–80 'under the direction of Job Collins, an architect of Warwick', but the Vestry Minutes show that the architect and builder was Thomas Johnson (*q.v.*). Collins's burial on 20 June 1800 is recorded in the register of St. Nicholas' Church.

COLLIS, JAMES (*c.*1806–1886), practised in London. He exhibited at the Royal Academy in 1836–9, and designed THE KEMBLE TAVERN (dem.) at the corner of Bow Street and Long Acre, a quite pretentious classical building illustrated in *The Companion to the Almanac*, 1837, 242. He was the author of *The Builders' Portfolio of Street Architecture*, 1837, consisting of designs for the façades of terrace houses, a hotel, a club and a public house, etc. There is a copy at the Yale Center for British Art. Collis is also said to have published *Remarks on Street Architecture*, 1838, an untraced work whose title may merely be a paraphrase of *The Builders' Portfolio* [J. Archer, *The Literature of British Domestic Architecture 1715–1842*, MIT Press 1985, 274]. Collis was District Surveyor of Lee, Charlton and Kidbrooke from 1844 until his death in 1886 [*Builder* li, 1886, 906].

COLUMBANI, PLACIDO (*c.*1744–), was a Milanese architect who appears to have spent the greater part of his life in England. He was a competent designer in the neoclassical manner and a popularizer of the decorative style associated with the brothers Adam and Pergolesi. According to the *Encyclopaedia Britannica*, 11th ed. (*s.v.* 'Columbani'), his engraved designs were much used by English furniture designers of the late eighteenth century. He was presumably in England by 1766, when designs by him appeared in *The Chimney-piece Maker's Daily Assistant . . . from the original drawings of Thomas Milton, John Crunden and Placido Columbani.* His independent publications were *Vases and Tripods* (n.d.), *A New Book of Ornaments, containing a Variety of Elegant Designs for Modern Pannels, commonly executed in Stucco, Wood or Painting, and used in Decorating Principal Rooms* (1775), and *Variety of Capitals, Freezes and Corniches, and how to increase and decrease them, still retaining the same proportion as the original* (1776). In 1775 he exhibited a 'perspective view of a gentleman's villa' at the Society of Artists, and in 1786, at the age of 42, he obtained admission to the Royal Academy Schools.

As a practising architect, Columbani is known to have had the following commissions: the embellishment of MOUNT CLARE, nr. ROEHAMPTON, SURREY, with a Doric portico 'and many Architectural Ornaments' for Sir John Dick, Bart., soon after 1780 [W. Watts, *Views of Seats*, pl. lxii, 1784; Anne Riches, 'Mount Clare, Roehampton', *Arch. Hist.* 27, 1984, 259–60] (*C. Life*, 26 Jan., 2 Feb. 1935); making drawings for the interiors of AUDLEY END, ESSEX, for the 4th Lord Howard de Walden from 1781 onwards [accounts in Essex Record Office]; supervising works at DOWNHILL, CO. DERRY, for the 4th Earl of Bristol and Bishop of Derry, 1783–5 [P. Rankin, *Irish Building Ventures of the Earl Bishop of Derry*, Ulster Architectural Heritage Soc. 1972, 14–15]; designing a walled garden 209 feet square at ANTONY HOUSE, CORNWALL, for Reginald Pole-Carew (1793); making (1794) working drawings of Humphry Repton's design for a lodge at the same house, and (in 1801) plans of Pole-Carew's London house at No. 7 New Cavendish Street [letters and accounts at Antony]; designing a villa in PUTNEY LANE, PUTNEY, SURREY, for Godschall Johnson, 1793 [mentioned in letter at Antony, CE/E 25, 26]; and repairing the church of ST. KATHERINE BY THE TOWER, LONDON, 1799–1800, dem. 1825 [C. Jamison, *St. Katherine's Hospital*, 1952, 126].

COOK, ANDREW GEORGE, 'Architect and Builder', was the author of *The New Builder's Magazine*, a work containing an abstract of the Building Act of 1774, a list of prices 'allowed by the most eminent surveyors in London', an alphabetical glossary of architectural terms, and 177 engravings of architectural designs by John Carter. The latter were reprinted from the plates of the original *Builder's Magazine*, published between 1774 and 1778. Cook's edition was published without a date in *c.*1810, and again in 1819 and 1820.

COOK, JOHN, practised at Wooler, Northumberland, as a 'Civil Engineer and Architect' in the 1830s. In 1835 he enlarged WOOLER CHURCH on the N. side in a plain Gothic style [I.C.B.S.; parish records in Northumberland C.R.O.].

COOK, T—M—, was a pupil of Henry Hakewill. He entered the Royal Academy Schools in 1801 and exhibited at the Royal Academy from 1799 to 1802. A drawing of the Woodstock Gate to Blenheim Park, Oxon., signed 'T. M. Cook Oct. 4th 1794' is in the Avery Library of Columbia University, U.S.A. [John Harris, *Catalogue of British Drawings for Architecture etc. in American Collections*, 1971, 76].

COOK, THOMAS (–1803), 'of the City of Gloucester, Architect', was employed in 1787 to erect a temporary prison preparatory to the rebuilding of the Gloucester County Gaol to the designs of William Blackburn [Gloucestershire County Records]. According to J. Chambers's MS. *Collections for a Biography of English Architects* in the R.I.B.A. Library he died at Swansea in 1803.

COOK, THOMAS (*c.*1777–1842), practised in Leicester, where he died on 1 November 1842, aged 65. He was responsible for alterations to WYGGESTON'S HOSPITAL, LEICESTER, 1805, dem. 1875; alterations to LEICESTER INFIRMARY, 1815; enlarging FRIAR LANE BAPTIST CHAPEL, LEICESTER, 1878, dem.; for STAPLETON RECTORY, SALOP., 1827–30 [Lichfield Joint Record Office, B/A/13]; and for several workhouses in Leicestershire and Derbyshire. His most important work appears to have been the GRAMMAR SCHOOL at MARKET BOSWORTH, LEICS., 1827–8, in the Tudor Collegiate style. His unexecuted designs for St. Nicholas Church, Leicester (1824), are in the Record Office at Leicester [J. D. Bennett, *Leicestershire Architects 1700–1850*, Leicester 1968; letter in Warwick C.R.O., H.R. 29].

COOKE, JAMES, of Gloucester, was primarily a statuary mason, who signs a number of monumental tablets in the county between 1811 and 1836 (Rupert Gunnis, *Dictionary of British Sculptors*, 1968, 112). The only architectural work of any consequence that he is known to have undertaken was the rebuilding in 1826 of the nave of ST. MARY DE LODE CHURCH, GLOUCESTER, in stuccoed Gothic with cast-iron columns [*Gent's Mag.* 1826 (ii), 506]. In 1838 he remodelled COWLEY RECTORY, GLOS. [Gloucestershire C.R.O., GDR/F4/1].

COOPER, GEORGE, exhibited at the Royal Academy from various London addresses between 1792 and 1830. His earliest exhibits were architectural designs, but from about 1800 onwards he showed views of buildings in England and on the Continent. In 1807 he published a set of engraved designs for neo-classical chimney-pieces entitled *Designs for Decorative Architecture*, of which there is a copy in the Print Room of the Victoria & Albert Museum. In the same year he published a volume of engravings entitled *Architectural Reliques, or the Present State of Ancient British Architecture and Sculpture*, containing illustrations of Llandaff Cathedral and Tintern Abbey. Some sketches of Llandaff Cathedral made by him in 1805 are in Sir John Soane's Museum (AL 26, 1–5). Many of the illustrations in W. M. Wade's *Walks in Oxford* (Oxford 1817) were engraved from drawings by Cooper.

COOPER, JOHN (1745–1818), was a builder and surveyor at Derby, where three of his four sons were also in the construction industry, Joseph (1775–1835) as a builder and surveyor, Thomas as a stone and marble mason, and William as a plumber and glazier. All four were primarily builders, working for local landowners such as Sir Henry Harpur of Calke Abbey and erecting the new public buildings in Derby designed by Francis Goodwin and Robert Wallace. But John Cooper was both architect and builder for the enlargement of OCKBROOK CHURCH, DERBYSHIRE, in 1814–15; while Joseph designed a stuccoed villa in DERBY called PARKFIELDS HOUSE for Henry Cox *c.*1825; and Joseph is said to have built 'several of the best houses in Derby', including a stone-fronted terrace, Nos. 47–51 FRIAR GATE, 1840, and several villas on VERNON ROAD, all or most of which were probably designed by himself or his brother Joseph. [S. Glover, *History & Gazetteer of the County of Derby* ii (1), 1833, 595, *History & Directory of the Borough of Derby*, 1843, 50; Lichfield Joint Record Office, Faculties, for Ockbrook Church; information from Mr. Maxwell Craven.]

COOPER, JOHN, was probably a native of Staffordshire, and began his career as an associate of Samuel Wyatt (*q.v*), under whom he worked as a carpenter at Winnington Hall in Cheshire in 1775. He was subsequently employed by Wyatt as assistant at Baron Hill in Anglesey, and in 1778 established himself as a builder and architect at Beaumaris. Here he designed BODORGAN HALL for Owen Meyrick, 1779–82, and a house called THE FRIARS for Sir Hugh Williams, for whom he may also have remodelled LLANIDAN HALL. He also carried out alterations to PLAS NEWYDD for the 1st Earl of Uxbridge in 1783–5 [V. E. Mapp, 'The Rebuilding of Bodorgan Hall', *Trans. Anglesey Antiquarian Soc.* 1983; information from Mr. J. D. K. Lloyd]. In 1790 Cooper left Anglesey for the mainland, and in 1796 Sir Christopher Sykes noted that he was in charge of alterations at CHIRK CASTLE, DENBIGHSHIRE, for Richard Myddelton, including the interior of the Dining Room [National Library of Wales, MS. 2258 C]. To judge from Bodorgan and the interiors at Chirk Castle, Cooper's architectural style was closely modelled on that of the Wyatts.

COOPER, JOHN, was admitted to the Royal Academy Schools in 1816 at the age of 23. He was evidently the J. Cooper who exhibited architectural designs at the Academy from 1813 to 1827, giving as his address 13 Castle Street, Berners Street. This was the address of Samuel Cooper, 'architect and surveyor', who was presumably his father.

COOPER, JOHN, was an architect and builder at Canterbury. In 1811 his designs for rebuilding Strood Church, Kent, were set aside in favour of those of Robert Smirke [H. Smetham, *History of Strood*, 1899, 55–75]. In 1825 he enlarged HARBLEDOWN CHURCH, KENT, and in 1827 ASHFORD CHURCH, KENT, and refitted the latter's interior [I.C.B.S.]. He was the father of George Cooper, a monumental mason of Canterbury who was responsible (*inter alia*) for the obelisk at BILSINGTON, KENT, in memory of Sir Richard Cosway (d. 1835). For further details of G. Cooper's works see R. Gunnis, *Dictionary of British Sculptors*, 1968, 113.

COOPER, JOHN JAMES (–1839), of Reading, combined the functions of architect, surveyor and auctioneer. He designed an Italianate BAPTIST CHAPEL in the KING'S ROAD, READING, 1833–4; dem. *c.*1988 [*Reading Mercury*, 15 April 1833], and designed and built the CASTLE STREET CONGREGATIONAL CHAPEL, opened in 1837 [W. Fletcher, *Reading Past and Present*, 1839]. He also designed a Nonconformist Chapel at SINDLESHAM, BERKS., in 1834, rebuilt 1868 [*Reading Mercury*, 22 Feb. 1834], and in 1837 entered an Ionic design in the competition for the Royal Berkshire Infirmary [*Reading Mercury*, 11 Feb. 1837]. The QUEEN'S ROAD 'was formed under (his) superintendence' in about 1833 [W. Darter, *Reminiscences of Reading by an Octogenarian*, 1888. 109], so he may possibly have been responsible for designing the elegant Bath stone houses which form QUEEN'S CRESCENT. He was the father of the Reading architect J. O. Cooper (1822–1912).

COOPER, T—, of 13 Warren Street, designed the BAYSWATER CHAPEL, ST. PETERSBURG PLACE, NOTTING HILL, LONDON, for Edward Orme, 1818 (dem. 1881), exhibiting the design at the Royal Academy the same year. In 1819 he exhibited a view of the interior of the Royalty Theatre in Wellclose Square.

COOPER, THOMAS (–1854), of Brighton, was the son of a local builder who died in 1826 at the age of 70, as a result of falling from a house under construction in Brunswick Square. Cooper designed the following buildings in Brighton: a CHAPEL in Church Street for George Faithful, the dissenting minister, *c.*1826; THE BEDFORD HOTEL, 1829, dem.; and THE TOWN HALL, 1830–2. The hotel was a striking but unorthodox composition with Greek Revival detailing. [A. Dale, *Fashionable Brighton*, 1947, 61, 118, 179–80; *The Watering-Places of Great Britain and Fashionable Directory*, Joseph Robins, 1833, 33–5.]

COOPER, WILLIAM, was on 29 June 1727 admitted a member of the Company of Carpenters, Tylers and Brickmakers of Shrewsbury [Shrewsbury Public Library, MS. 13486]. He was presumably 'that ingenious Architect, Mr. William Cooper, Jun., of Salop.' who rebuilt MONTFORD CHURCH, SALOP., in 1735–8 [D. H. S. Cranage, *The Churches of Shropshire* ii, 1903, 766], and the William Cooper who rebuilt MYDDLE CHURCH, SALOP., in 1744 [Churchwardens' Accounts]. Both are small country churches of no architectural pretensions.

COOPER, WILLIAM, surveyed the church of ST. KATHERINE COLEMAN, LONDON, in 1739, and submitted drawings and an estimate for rebuilding it [Guildhall Library, MS. 1133, minutes of the trustees for rebuilding the church]. He may have been the William Cooper who was Bricklayer to the Commissioners of Sewers in 1738 [S. Perks, *History of the Mansion House*, 1922, 178], and in 1741–2 Master of the Tylers' and Bricklayers' Company.

COOPER, WILLIAM HENDERSON (*c.*1786–1850), practised in London from the 1820s until his death on 25 April 1850, aged 64 [*Gent's Mag.* 1850 (i), 685]. He designed THE BOOKSELLERS' RETREAT, KING'S LANGLEY, HERTS., 1845–6, a group of Tudor Gothic almshouses for retired members of the book trade [*Builder* iv, 1846, 358].

COPLAND, ALEXANDER (1774–1834), was the son of a builder and told a parliamentary committee in 1806 that he had been 'educated as a builder under Mr. Richard Holland' [*Fourth Report of the Commissioners of Military Inquiry*, 1806–7, Appendix 47, p. 235]. His training evidently included architectural drawing, for he entered the Royal Academy Schools as a student in 1788 and in 1817 he figures in a list of architects practising in London (*Annals of the Fine Arts* ii, 585). However, he was better known as one of the partners in a flourishing firm of builders and timber merchants of which the other members were the architect Henry Holland (Richard Holland's cousin) and his nephew Henry Rowles. Their yard in Horseferry Road was the centre of a large-scale building enterprise which made a fortune in building barracks during the Napoleonic Wars. With its own brickworks, sawpits and building tradesmen, it to some extent anticipated the better-known firm of Thomas Cubitt (*q.v.*), established in 1815 [E. W. Cooney, 'The Origins of the Victorian Master Builders', *Economic History Review*, 2nd ser., viii, 1955]. As 'Copland, Rowles & Co.' the firm was still in existence in the 1830s, but Copland died on 12 July 1834, aged 61 [*Gent's Mag.* 1834 (ii), 219]. His library was sold at Sotheby's on 6 December 1837 (catalogue in Bodleian Library, Mus. Bibl. III 8° 416). In 1801 he had bought the greater part of the Gunnersbury estate near Brentford, on which he built himself the existing GUNNERSBURY PARK, subsequently much enlarged by its later Rothschild owners [J. Thorne, *Handbook to the Environs of London* i, 1876, 160] (*C. Life*, 24 Nov. 1900). Frank Copland, who was in Sir John Soane's office from 1817 to 1820, was his son. Some of the latter's drawings are in the Soane Museum (Drawer 5, 8) [A. T. Bolton, *The Portrait of Sir John Soane*, 268 n., 287–9].

CORFIELD, THOMAS (–1833), 'surveyor and architect' of Park Street, Grosvenor Square, committed suicide in Greenwich Park on 30 June 1833 [*Gent's Mag.* 1833 (ii), 186].

CORNEY, ROBERT (*c.*1707–1774), of East Cotham, nr. Redcar, Yorks. (N.R.), is said in J. W. Ord's *History of Cleveland*, 1846, 374, to have been 'both architect and builder' of KIRKLEATHAM CHURCH, YORKS. (N.R.), *c.*1760–3, but the accounts indicate that a design had been made by John Carr (*q.v.*). Corney, who was a carpenter and joiner by trade, was also employed in building KIRKLEATHAM HOSPITAL from 1741 onwards [accounts in N. Yorks. Record Office]. In 1764–6 he rebuilt BUSBY HALL, YORKS. (N.R.), for Jane Turner in accordance with a drawing apparently made by himself and now in the N. Riding Record Office (ZDU). A chest-tomb in Kirkleatham Churchyard records his death on 19 January 1774, aged 67.

CORNISH, ROBERT (*c.*1760–1844), held the post of Surveyor to Exeter Cathedral from 1800 until his retirement in 1838. He was then presented with a piece of plate 'as a Token of the Respect of the Chapter and of the high sense they entertain of the value of his Services'. He died on 9 January 1844 in his 84th year [*Flying Post*, 11 Jan. 1844]. As cathedral architect he was succeeded by his eldest son ROBERT STRIBLING CORNISH (1788–1871), whom Gilbert Scott remembered as 'a very kindly and excellent old gentleman, and a thoroughly practical man' [*Recollections*, 1876, 345]. The younger Cornish was a Councillor and Alderman of Exeter, and held the office of Mayor in 1852–3. He married the daughter of John Powning of Exeter (*q.v.*), and died on 10 February 1871 [obituary in *Flying Post*, 15 Feb. 1871]. J. M. Allen (1809–83) and Edward Ashworth (1815–96) were pupils either of the father or of the son.

HOLY TRINITY CHURCH, EXETER, was rebuilt in 1820–1 by 'Cornish & Sons, Architects and builders' [I.C.B.S.]. ST. EDMUND'S CHURCH, EXETER, appears to have been rebuilt by Messrs. Cornish and Julian (i.e. G. H. Julian, afterwards City Surveyor) in 1834 [Diocesan Faculty papers]. Both these are in the elementary Perpendicular Gothic of the period. Messrs. Cornish and Julian also designed FREMINGTON VICARAGE, DEVON, in 1830 [Diocesan Registry, bundle 339], and repewed ST. PANCRAS CHURCH, EXETER, in 1831 [I.C.B.S.]. The younger Cornish designed THE NEW CITY PRISON at EXETER, 1819 [*The Exeter Guide*, 1836, 47] and parsonages at LYNTON, 1834, and HEANTON PUNCHARDON, DEVON, 1836 [Diocesan Registry, bundle 339]. The designs for the latter are in the Greek Revival style, with incised pilasters of the kind which ornament many early nineteenth-century houses in the suburbs of Exeter.

CORSTORPHINE, JOHN (1759–1826), of Kingsbarns in Fife, is listed in Pigot's *Directory* of 1825–6 among the 'Nobility and Gentry', but appears to have acted as both builder and architect. In 1797 he designed a new school at Kingsbarns, and in 1810–11 he and Robert Balfour (*q.v.*) were jointly responsible for the repair and enlargement of KINGSBARNS CHURCH to the latter's designs [S.R.O., HR 184/1]. His occupancy and reconstruction of KINGSBARNS HOUSE are recorded by the date 1794 and a panel of architect's instruments in the frieze. He died on 23 August 1826, and is commemorated by a wall monument in Kingsbarns Churchyard.

COTES, PHILIP B—, was apprenticed to Peter Upsdell (*q.v.*) in March 1795 for 5½ years [P.R.O., IR 1/36, p. 156], but he was 'at Mr. J. Malton's' when he first exhibited at the Royal Academy in 1798, and subsequently (1801–5) in the office of Jeffry Wyatt and his partner John Armstrong. Nothing further is known of him.

COTTINGHAM, LEWIS NOCKALLS (1787–1847), born at Laxfield in Suffolk, was the son of a farmer 'of an ancient and respectable family'. He was apprenticed to a builder at Ipswich, and was subsequently an architect's clerk in London until 1814, when he started practice on his own. In 1822 he became surveyor to the Cooks' Company, and in 1825 he was engaged by the dean and chapter of Rochester to carry out repairs to their Cathedral, including the rebuilding of the central tower (see G. H. Palmer, *The Cathedral Church of Rochester*, 1899, for an illustration of Cottingham's tower before its replacement in 1904). He was subsequently much employed in works of this character, and among the churches which he restored were those of THEBERTON, SUFFOLK, 1836; ASHBOURNE, DERBYSHIRE, 1839–40; ST. MARY at BURY ST. EDMUNDS, 1840–3; MILTON BRYANT, BEDS. (to which he added a new tower), 1841–3; GREAT CHESTERFORD, ESSEX, 1842; ROOS, YORKS. (E.R.), 1842; HORRINGER (*alias* HORNINGSHEATH), SUFFOLK, 1845; CLIFTON, NOTTS., 1846; and MARKET WESTON, SUFFOLK, 1844 (see *Builder* ii, 1844, 378). He repaired (1844) the spire of LOUTH CHURCH, LINCS., after damage by lightning, and restored the ABBEY CHURCH OF ST. ALBANS, 1833 (see details in *British Magazine* ii, 1832, 207–8; iii, 1833, 112), and the NORMAN GATEWAY at BURY ST. EDMUNDS (cf. his report in *Gent's Mag.* 1842 (ii), 302, and in *Architect, Engineer and Surveyor* iv, 1843, 22). He was also employed at ELVASTON CASTLE, DERBYSHIRE, by the Earl of Harrington, for whom he remodelled the E. front in the 1830s, at BROUGHAM HALL, WESTMORLAND., by Lord Brougham, at ADARE MANOR, CO. LIMERICK (*C. Life*, 15, 22 and 29 May 1969) by the Earl of Dunraven, and at COMBE ABBEY, WARWICKS., by the Earl of Craven. At the last house he designed a 'Louis XIV drawing room' which he exhibited at the Royal Academy in 1834 but it is doubtful whether it was carried out. He refitted the chapel of MAGDALEN COLLEGE, OXFORD, in

1830–2, and almost rebuilt ARMAGH CATHEDRAL in 1834–7. Among the comparatively few new buildings which he designed were SNELSTON HALL, DERBYSHIRE, for John Harrison, 1828, an elaborate Gothic house demolished in 1951 but illustrated in Burke's *Visitation of Seats and Arms*, series 2, i, 1854, 228, for which the original drawings are in the Derbyshire Record Office, D157 M, 3030–50, and a Tudor Gothic SAVINGS BANK (now flats) in CROWN STREET, BURY ST. EDMUNDS, 1846. In 1840 he exhibited at the Royal Academy a design for 'a village church now erecting in Derbyshire', described in *Gent's Mag.* 1840 (ii), 68, as cruciform, with a square tower, and almost certainly to be identified as STANTON-IN-THE PEAK CHURCH, built in 1838–9 at the expense of W. P. Thornhill of Stanton Hall.

In 1841 Cottingham began the restoration of HEREFORD CATHEDRAL, carried out, according to Gilbert Scott, 'with the most scrupulous regard for evidence, and with the least possible displacement of old stone' (see *Gent's Mag.* 1842 (i), 193–6, and J. Merewether, *A Statement of the Condition and Circumstances of the Cathedral Church of Hereford*, 1842, which contains the text of several testimonials in Cottingham's favour). Owing to the long illness which caused his death in 1847, much of the work at Hereford was carried out under the supervision of his son, who designed the reredos.

Cottingham's careful restorations of buildings that were often in a serious state of decay were more respectful of the surviving medieval fabric than the more doctrinaire restorations of later Gothic Revivalists such as Scott, and at Hereford, Armagh and the Norman Gateway at Bury St. Edmund's he showed considerable technical skill in dealing with formidable structural problems. His restoration of Magdalen College Chapel has an honourable place in the history of the Gothic Revival, and his Snelston Hall, though less effectively picturesque than Shaw's Ilam (1821–6) and less convincingly medieval than Blore's Goodrich Court (1828–31), was nevertheless a serious attempt to build an authentic Gothic mansion.

In about 1825 Cottingham was employed by Mr. John Field to lay out the latter's extensive estate on the south side of Waterloo Bridge. Some of his designs for houses on this estate are in the British Museum (Crace Views, xxxv, 65–7). He built a house (No. 43) for himself in Waterloo Bridge Road, with a museum specially designed to receive his collection of medieval woodwork, Gothic carvings, and plaster-casts of capitals, bosses and sculpture. This collection, of which a *Descriptive Memoir* was published in 1850, was dispersed after his death, but part of it formed the nucleus of the Royal Architectural Museum in Tufton Street, which was afterwards absorbed into the South Kensington Museum. Cottingham was a friend of John Carter and William Capon, and he published several works on medieval architecture, the most important of which were *Plans, etc. of Westminster Hall*, 1822, and *Plans, etc. of King Henry VII's Chapel*, 1822–9 (2 vols.). He also published an influential pattern-book for ornamental ironwork entitled *The Ornamental Metal Worker's Director*, 1823, enlarged and reissued in 1824 as *The Smith and Founder's Director, containing a Series of Designs and Patterns for Ornamental Iron and Brass Work*. A later edition entitled *The Smith's, Founder's and Ornamental Metal Worker's Director* appeared in 1845. Other publications were *Working Drawings of Gothic Ornaments, etc., with a Design for a Gothic Monsion*, 1824, and *Grecian and Roman Architecture, in 24 large folio plates*. Six of Cottingham's sketch-books are in the Avery Library of Columbia University, New York. The designs which he submitted in the competition for the Houses of Parliament in 1835 are in the R.I.B.A. Collection. They are in the style 'which prevailed in the reigns of Edward III and Richard II'.

Cottingham died on 13 October 1847, and was buried at Croydon, where he is commemorated by a brass in the parish church. F. R. Wilson of Alnwick, George Truefitt (1824–1902) and Calvert Vaux of New York (1824–1895) were his pupils. His practice was continued by his elder son Nockalls Johnson Cottingham (born 1823), who 'after a rather chequered career' perished in 1854 in the wreck of the steamer *Arctic* on his way to New York. [Obituaries in *Builder* v, 1847, 502, *Art Union* 9, 1847, 377, and *Gent's Mag.* 1847 (ii), 648–50; *A.P.S.D.*; *D.N.B.*]

COTTON, HENRY CHARLES (*c.*1805–1873), was admitted to the Royal Academy Schools in 1824 at the age of 19. He practised in London, dying in Highbury Place on 17 May 1873 [Principal Probate Registry]. His son Henry Robert Cotton was also an architect and surveyor. H. C. Cotton was presumably the Henry Cotton who is said to have designed LIVERPOOL TERRACE, WORTHING, SUSSEX, *c.*1830 [A. Dale, *Fashionable Brighton*, 1948, 35] – a composition praised by Pevsner for its 'powerfully organised unbroken rhythm of bow fronts accented with plain ironwork' [*Sussex*, Buildings of England, 1965, 388].

COTTON, ROBERT TURNER (*c.*1774–1850), is listed in the London directories as an architect and surveyor from the 1820s until his death on 10 March 1850 at the age of 76 [*Gent's Mag.* 1850 (i), 550].

COUCHMAN, HENRY (1738–1803), was the son of a carpenter at Ightham in Kent. After working for some years as a journeyman carpenter in Kent and London he was employed as a foreman by the builder Joseph Dixon, and then as a clerk of works by the architect Matthew Brettingham. In 1766 Brettingham sent him to Packington in Warwickshire to supervise the reconstruction of the Earl of Aylesford's country house. An inscription on the lead roof records that 'This house . . . was cased with stone and enlarged by Heneage Earl of Aylesford in the year 1772. Henry Couchman Surveyor of the Work.' Couchman's diligence made a favourable impression on Lord Aylesford, who used his influence to obtain for him a lease of Temple House, Temple Balsall, together with the appointment (1776) of Bailiff to the Trustees of Balsall Hospital.

For the rest of his life Couchman practised as an architect and surveyor in Warwickshire. In 1775 he designed THE DRAPERS' HALL at COVENTRY, dem. 1830. His design for the Assembly Room in this building, now in the Pierpont Morgan Library, is illustrated by J. Harris, *Catalogue of British Drawings for Architecture, etc. in American Collections*, pl. 55. After the death of Henry Keene in 1776, Couchman was employed by Sir Roger Newdigate to complete the Gothicization of ARBURY HALL, WARWICKS. Sir Roger was to some extent his own architect, and Couchman's function seems to have been to act as surveyor and draughtsman under his employer's supervision [A. C. Wood, 'The Diaries of Sir Roger Newdigate', *Trans. Birmingham Archaeological Soc.* lxxviii, 1962] (*C. Life*, 15, 29 Oct. 1953). He fulfilled the same function when Sir Roger Newdigate built HAREFIELD LODGE, MIDDLESEX, in 1786, the name of 'Hen. Couchman Archit.' appearing on the foundation-stone [Warwick County Record Office, Sir Roger Newdigate's diaries, CR 136/A 617]. In 1782 Couchman reconstructed the octagonal central tower of ATHERSTONE CHURCH, WARWICKS. [*ex inf.* the late P. B. Chatwin], and HIGHAM-ON-THE-HILL CHURCH, LEICS., was rebuilt to his designs in 1791 [Leicester Archdeaconry records, Fac. 173]. Couchman's unexecuted designs for a new church at ETTINGTON, WARWICKS., are among the Shirley family papers in the County Record Office. They show a small classical church with an apsidal chancel and cupola'd bell turret.

In 1783 Couchman designed a new House of Correction in Warwick, built under his supervision between 1784 and 1789, and since converted into a police-station. In 1790–3 he enlarged the Gaol towards Barrack Street, taking in the site of the former House of Correction [Warwick C.R.O., Class 24 (672, 677); extracts from Q.S. Records, Class 24 (h)]. His elevation to Barrack Street was retained when the County Gaol was reconstructed as the County Council Offices in 1929–32.

Couchman died at Temple House in 1803, and is commemorated by a brass tablet in Temple Balsall Church. He left a son, Henry Couchman, junior (1771–1838), who in 1802 succeeded his father as bailiff to Temple Balsall Hospital and also held the post of 'Bridgemaster' to the County of Warwick. A portrait, believed to be that of the elder Couchman, was in 1954 in the possession of Dr. H. J. Couchman of Morland, Ferndown, Dorset. [*Gent's Mag.* 1803 (i), 94; photocopy of autobiographical fragment in Warwick County Record Office; information from the late P. B. Chatwin.]

COULTHART, or **COULTHARD,** WILLIAM (–1833), practised in Lancaster from the 1820s until his death in 1833 [*Lancaster Gazette*, 9 Nov. 1833]. He was one of the Surveyors of Bridges for the Hundred of Lonsdale from 1825 to 1829 and was employed in connection with works to the gaols at Lancaster and Appleby. At LEVENS HALL, WESTMORLAND, there are designs by him for a village school dated 1823–4 and for chimneys (unexecuted) to be added to the Howard Tower at Levens. Sketch-plans by him in the Farrer papers, Manchester Central Library (L 1/1/6/4–8) suggest that he designed HALL GARTH, OVER KELLETT, LANCS., for G. Ainslie, 1826, with a small Greek Revival portico. Coulthart also designed HALTON RECTORY, LANCS., in the Elizabethan style, *c.*1832 [Liverpool Library, Binns Collection, vol. 2, f. 116] (E. Baines, *History of Lancashire* iv, 1836, 584). [Information from Mr. Angus Taylor and Dr. A. J. White.]

COULTHART, WILLIAM RITSON, appears in Leamington directories in the early 1830s as 'architect, surveyor and auctioneer', but had moved to Aberystwyth by 1836 and continued to practise there until he left Wales in 1849. At LEAMINGTON he designed the houses on the N. side of WARWICK STREET and those on the E. side of BEAUCHAMP SQUARE [Moncrieff's *Guide to Leamington Spa*, 1833, 75–6]. In Wales he rebuilt LLANAFAN CHURCH, CARDIGANSHIRE, 1836–41, altered 1862–7 [I.C.B.S.], designed ABERYSTWYTH TOWN

HALL, 1849 'in the Grecian style' [Hunt & Co's *Directory of Aberystwyth*, 1849], and supervised the enlargement of HAFOD HOUSE, CARDIGANSHIRE, to the designs of Anthony Salvin for Henry de Hoghton from 1847 onwards [*The Welshman*, 2 July 1847, *ex inf.* Mr. Thomas Lloyd]. In the National Library of Wales there are drawings by him for alterations to NANTEOS, CARDIGANSHIRE, for W. E. Powell, some of which may have been carried out early in the 1840s [N.L.W., Nanteos Plans 20–23, 105].

COUSE, KENTON (1721–1790), 'was bred an Architect under Mr. Flitcroft of the Board of Works, into which he was introduced as soon as a regular vacancy occurred'. He was apprenticed to Flitcroft in 1735 or 1736, and began his official career in 1746 as Labourer in Trust at Whitehall. In 1748 he became a Writing Clerk in the Office in Scotland Yard, and in June 1750 was promoted to the Clerkship of the Works at Newmarket, but in July of the same year changed places with James Paine, becoming Clerk of the Works at Charing Cross, etc. In 1762, on Thomas Kynaston's death, Flitcroft, now Comptroller of the Works, made Couse his personal clerk. He subsequently became Clerk of the Works at Whitehall, Westminster and St. James's (1766), and in 1775 Secretary to the Board, Clerk Itinerant and Clerk of the Works at the Queen's Palace (Buckingham House). In 1782 he lost all his offices as a result of Burke's Act, but became the first holder of the new post of Examining Clerk, which he retained until his death. For some years he was also Surveyor to the Goldsmiths' Company. A competent and conscientious official, Couse spent his life in the public service, and had comparatively little time or opportunity for private practice. The architectural works listed below show him as a faithful disciple of Flitcroft, maintaining in the age of Adam and Chambers the basically Palladian style of the previous generation. He died at his house in Scotland Yard on 10 October 1790, in his 70th year, and was buried at Lambeth. His wife Sarah was not, as stated in Collins' and other peerages (under 'Abercorn'), the daughter of the Hon. Charles Hamilton (d. 1786), but of a minor court official of the same name whose elder daughter married the author Edward Moore. By her he had a son and two daughters. His library was sold in 1791 with that of Francis Hiorne (catalogue in B.L. 129, 1.19). Written surveys of the Bishop of Durham's houses at Durham and Auckland Castle made in 1750–1 by Couse and Thomas Shirley are in the B.L. (Add. MS. 9815). [*A.P.S.D.*; *D.N.B.*; Guildhall Library, index to Apprenticeship Registers in P.R.O.; *Gent's Mag.* 1790 (ii), 959; J. Nichols, *Literary Anecdotes* iii, 1812, 642–3; John Chambers, MS. *Collections for a Biography of English Architects* in R.I.B.A. Library; *History of the King's Works* v and vi, *passim.*]

HAMPTON WICK, MIDDLESEX, house for Robert Lee, 1757–8 [Lambeth Palace Library, Court of Arches, Ff 221/21].

LONDON, ST. MARGARET'S CHURCH, WESTMINSTER, west gallery, 1757; repairs and reconstruction of east end 1758 in form of a Gothic apse with sedilia, incorporating stained-glass window from Waltham Abbey [Westminster City Library, MSS. 2421 and 135 (Vestry Minutes and Churchwardens' Accounts)].

NORMANTON PARK, RUTLAND, alterations and additions for Sir Gilbert Heathcote, Bart., 1763–7; dem. [Lincolnshire Record Office, Heathcote papers in Ancaster Collection].

NORMANTON CHURCH, RUTLAND, for Sir Gilbert Heathcote, Bart., 1764; tower added by T. Cundy 1826, nave and chancel rebuilt 1911 [Lincolnshire Record Office, *loc. cit.*].

LONDON, No. 29 (formerly 26), GROSVENOR SQUARE, enlarged for Sir Gilbert Heathcote, Bart., 1764; dem. 1957 [*Survey of London* xl, 146].

BOTLEYS, nr. CHERTSEY, SURREY, for Sir Joseph Mawbey, Bart., 1765; altered by E. Blore 1839–40 [*Vitruvius Britannicus* v, pls. 56–7; drawings in Minet Library, Camberwell].

LONDON, No. 10 DOWNING STREET, rebuilt front to street, 1766–75; altered 1959–60 [*History of the King's Works* v, 442] (*Survey of London* xiv, pls. 108–9).

LONDON, HOUSES OF PARLIAMENT, continued the STONE BUILDING southwards, forming new entrance to House of Commons, Committee Rooms, etc., 1766–9; dem. *c.*1880 [*History of the King's Works* v, 429–30].

COLNEY (CHAPEL) HOUSE, SHENLEY, HERTS., house begun for P.C. Crespigny, *c.*1770, but abandoned on death of his wife and ultimately completed by Charles Bourchier, Governor of Madras, *c.*1785; destroyed by fire *c.*1880 [plan by Couse *c.*1775 in Bodleian Library, Gough Herts. 13, f. 64] (E. W. Brayley, *Beauties of England and Wales* vii, 1806, 283; Neale's *Views of Seats*, 2nd. ser., ii).

LONDON, No. 2 GROSVENOR SQUARE, repairs and redecoration for the Marquess of Carmarthen, later 5th Duke of Leeds, 1774–5; dem. 1858 [*Survey of London* xl, 118].

RICHMOND BRIDGE, SURREY (R. Thames), in collaboration with James Paine, 1774–7; widened 1937 [James Paine, *Plans etc.* ii, 1783, pls. lxxii, lxxiii].

CLAPHAM, SURREY, HOLY TRINITY CHURCH, 1774–6; portico altered 1812, chancel added 1902 [Parish records; drawings by Couse in Surrey Archdeaconry records, Surrey C.R.O., R.I.B.A. Drawings Coll., and Avery Library, Columbia University, New York. The last are reproduced by J. Harris, *Catalogue of British Drawings for Architecture etc. in American Collections*, 1971, pls. 57–8].

WIMPOLE HALL, CAMBS., work for 2nd Earl of Hardwicke, 1777, probably including the apsidal Eating Room, since remodelled [R.C.H.M., *West Cambridgeshire*, 216].

BARNES, SURREY, THE WORKHOUSE (afterwards Manor House Hotel), 1778 [MS. Vestry Minutes].

OXFORD, THE QUEEN'S COLLEGE, internal reconstruction of west wing after fire in December 1778, carried out by George Shakespear (*q.v.*) with John Gwynn as surveyor in charge [*Letters of Radcliffe & James*, ed. Evans, Oxford Historical Soc. 1888, 270–2].

LONDON, DOWNING STREET, house on south side facing St. James's Park; dem. [Northumberland County Record Office, ZBU B5/6 (13): 'Plan of Mr. Sargent's house built by Couse'].

COWAN, GEORGE, held the post of Superintendent of Public Works in Edinburgh from 1747 until 1758, when he was dismissed for non-attendance [Edinburgh Town Council Minutes]. In the Canongate Churchyard there is a monumental inscription to Alexander Cowan, Builder, who died on 8 March 1776 aged 66, and his son George Cowan, Architect, who died on 23 October 1843.

COWLEY, WILLIAM (–1826), designed CROFT HOUSE (now No. 230, STAMFORD STREET), ASHTON-UNDER-LYNE, LANCS., for Samuel Heginbottom in 1810 [B. Burke, *Visitation of Seats* i, 1852, 123 and Twycross, *Mansions of England* iii, 1847, 89]. Although described as 'esquire' by Burke, the architect of Croft House was presumably the same as William Cowley, of Fairfield in Droylesdon (near Ashton-under-Lyne), who was described as 'architect and builder' in his will proved in September 1826 [*Lancs. & Cheshire Record Soc.* 113, 1972, 29].

COWPER, JOHN, was an architect and builder of Lewes in Sussex. In 1808 he was appointed clerk of works for the building of the County Hall at Lewes to the designs of John Johnson [*Sussex Archl. Colls.* 100, 1962, 5]. Cowper designed DANE HILL CHURCH, SUSSEX, 1836, Gothic; rebuilt 1892 [I.C.B.S.].

COX, H—, of Tooley Street, Southwark, exhibited the 'elevation of a villa now building in Hampshire' at the Royal Academy in 1797.

CRACKLOW, CHARLES THOMAS, was a London surveyor best known as the author of *Views of the Churches and Chapels of Ease in County of Surrey*, published in parts between 1823 and 1827. In 1791–4 he and one Robert Tyler undertook a speculative development on the Magdalen College estate in Southwark in accordance with a plan drawn up by John Buckler (*q.v.*) on behalf of the College. In 1788–9 he supervised the rebuilding of the tower of SHEARSBY CHURCH, LEICS. [advt. in *Leics. & Notts. Jnl.*, 27 Sept. 1788, *ex inf.* Mr. W. J. Brushe], and in 1804 he contracted to rebuild the upper part of the tower of CRAWLEY CHURCH, SUSSEX [W. Sussex C.R.O., Par. 60/4/1]. In 1796 he was the author of one of the schemes for the improvement of the Port of London considered by the commissioners. He advocated the construction of new docks at Rotherhithe [Sir Joseph Broodbank, *History of the Port of London* i, 1921, 86].

CRAIG, CHARLES ALEXANDER (1753–1833), spent the greater part of his life in the Office of Works. Born in Rochester, he became a pupil of Sir Robert Taylor, and was appointed Labourer in Trust at the Charing Cross Mews in 1776. In 1786 he became Resident Clerk, and in 1793 Examining Clerk. He retired when the Office was reorganized in 1814 after the death of James Wyatt. An 'industrious mediocrity', Craig had been largely responsible for the day-to-day running of the Office of Works during the surveyorship of the negligent Wyatt. As an architect he designed little or nothing, but occupied himself as Surveyor to the Commissioners of Westminster Bridge (1801–29), Surveyor, Clerk and Treasurer to the Commissioners for Paving Westminster, and District Surveyor of Lambeth and Newington under the Act of 1774. He died on 11 January 1833, in his 80th year. [*Gent's Mag.* 1833 (i), 91; *History of the King's Works* vi, 50–1 and *passim*; Farington's Diary, 12 April 1816.]

CRAIG, JAMES (1744–1795), was born in Edinburgh on 31 October 1744. He was the son of William Craig, a merchant, and his mother was a sister of the poet James Thomson, a relationship of which Craig was inordinately proud. His early life is obscure. He is said to have attended the High School, but it is likely that he was the boy of this name from George Watson's Hospital who was apprenticed to a mason called Patrick Jameson in 1759, and that, like so many other Scottish architects, he was therefore a mason by training. The earliest evidence of his acting in an architectural capacity appears to be in 1763, when he was employed to draw out for engraving a plan and elevation of the proposed North Bridge, made apparently by George Fraser (*q.v.*). This was intended to attract tenders and was published in *Scots Mag.* 25, 1763, 362.

In August 1766 Craig achieved celebrity as the author of the winning design for the layout of the New Town of Edinburgh. Seven plans were received, and Craig's was judged the best by the assessors. It was not, however, thought good enough to be adopted, and it was not until December that a 'rectified plan' was approved. Although this plan was drawn by William Mylne (probably under the direction of the assessors, who included Sir James Clerk and John Adam), it appears to have been a revised version of Craig's plan, and he continued to be involved in working it out in detail. What appear to be small-scale copies both of Craig's original plan and of the adopted one figure in successive editions of John Laurie's Plan of Edinburgh, published in 1766. The main difference was the substitution of two squares, one at each end of the New Town, for a single central square from which diagonal streets would have radiated to the corners of the built-up area. Although not particularly enterprising, the adopted plan was undoubtedly more realistic than Craig's original submission, with its awkward triangular plots, and was carried out from 1768 onwards. As the successful competitor Craig duly received the gold medal and the freedom of the city that had been promised, and in October 1767 he went to London and presented a copy of the revised plan to King George III. This is now in the British Library (*King's Maps*, xlix, 65). In 1786 he published a further plan for the layout of the roads leading to the South Bridge in a pamphlet entitled *Plan for improving the City of Edinburgh.* Incorporating both a crescent and an octagon, this showed a more imaginative approach to town-planning than his scheme for the New Town, but it would have involved extensive demolition and was not adopted.

For the architecture, as opposed to the plan, of the New Town Craig had no responsibility. He was, however, the architect as well as the planner of St. James' Square, commissioned in 1773 by Walter Ferguson, W.S., as a private speculation, but not completed for many years. The elevations were treated as a uniform composition, with severe but elegant detailing. He also designed the Physicians' Hall in George Street, with a handsome façade in the Palladian manner.

Craig was also employed as a town-planner in Glasgow, where the grid of streets in Blythswood and Meadowflatt appears to have originated in plans made by him in 1792 for Col. Campbell of Blythswood and the City authorities, but no development took place until after 1800, and Graig had no responsibility for its architectural character.

Despite the éclat which he gained as the planner of the New Town, Craig failed to develop an extensive practice and never became a fashionable architect like Robert Mylne or the Adams. After 1781 he was constantly borrowing money, and he died in debt. This lack of success appears to have been due in large measure to his own arrogant and intractable character. According to the *Scottish Register* of 1795 'he was unfortunate, owing chiefly, perhaps, to some visionary idea of consequence which he fancied he was entitled to indulge on account of his relationship to Thomson the Poet, a connection which he vainly flattered himself was to procure him consideration and employment, and to supersede in him the necessity of prosecuting those sober plans for success in life which prudence requires of other men.'

Craig died in Edinburgh on 23 June 1795. He is commemorated by a modern tombstone in the Greyfriars Cemetery. There is a portrait by David Allan in the Scottish National Portrait Gallery.

[New Register House, Edinburgh Birth Register; *Scots Mag.* 1795, 411; S.R.O., CC 8/130/1 (testament and probate inventory); *D.N.B.*; A. J. Youngson, *The Making of Classical Edinburgh*, Edinburgh 1966, 77–9, 98, 117–19, 288–9; M. K. Meade, 'Plans of the New Town of Edinburgh', *Arch. Hist.* xiv, 1971; Stuart Harris, 'New Light on the First New Town', *Book of the Old Edinburgh Club*, N.S. 2, 1992; *Extracts from the Records of the Burgh of Glasgow*, ed. R. Renwick, viii, 475; *Order and Space in Society*, ed. T. A. Markus, Edinburgh 1982, 177–8; information from Mr. A. R. Lewis.]

EDINBURGH, No. 35 ST. ANDREW'S SQUARE, for Alexander Crosbie, 1769; staircase and other alterations by A. Elliot, 1819 [Ian Gow in *C. Life*, 13 Sept. 1990].

EDINBURGH, ST. JAMES' SQUARE, for Walter Ferguson, W.S., 1773 onwards; dem.

[M. K. Meade, *op. cit.*; S.R.O., RHP 101–102, 4170, 6080].

ST. ANDREWS, ST. SALVATOR'S (then ST. LEONARD'S) CHURCH, alterations, comprising the replacement of the vault by a timber roof, 1773 [R. G. Cant, 'St. Andrews Architects', *St. Andrews Preservation Trust Year Book*, 1966–7, 16; elevation by Craig at Culzean Castle, no. 75].

EDINBURGH, MERCHANT STREET, plan and elevation for building on feus offered 1774 [*Edinburgh Evening Courant*, 25 June 1774].

EDINBURGH, THE PHYSICIANS' HALL, GEORGE STREET, 1776–8; dem. *c.*1843 [minutes of Coll. of Physicians in N.L.S., Acc. 3439/3, pp. 1452–1581, *passim*, *ex inf.* Mr. A. R. Lewis] (T. Shepherd, *Modern Athens*, 1829, 61).

INVERESK CHURCH, MIDLOTHIAN, monument to John Fullerton, d. 1775 [signed 'Craig ARCHT.'].

EDINBURGH, THE OLD OBSERVATORY (now OBSERVATORY HOUSE), CALTON HILL, 1776–92 [J. Stark, *Picture of Edinburgh*, 1823, 182].

EDINBURGH, ST. GILES' CATHEDRAL, refitted interior of High Church (i.e. Choir) with Gothic pulpit, galleries, etc., 1780; removed *c.*1880 [account in Edinburgh City archives, Bay C, shelf 24, pp. 253–4, *ex inf.* Mr. A. R. Lewis]; cf. earlier scheme of 1777 in N.L.S. MS. 502.

LEITH, GUN-BATTERY, NORTH FORT STREET, LEITH, 1780–1 [Edinburgh City Archives, Letters, vol. viii, nos. 110, 111; accounts in Bay 4, Shelf 14, *ex inf.* Mr. A. R. Lewis].

GLASGOW, TRONGATE, building for the Tontine Society at the rear of the Tontine Building, containing the Sugar Sampling Room, 1789–90; converted into a warehouse 1829; dem. [C. D. Dunlop, 'The Tontine Building', *Regality Club* ii, 1863, 77 and illustration].

KILLEARN, STIRLINGSHIRE, THE BUCHANAN MONUMENT, an obelisk in memory of George Buchanan, 1788 [R.C.A.M., *Stirlingshire* ii, 323 and pl. 51A].

The following unexecuted or unverified designs have been noted: designs for altering or rebuilding MOUNT STUART HOUSE, ISLE OF BUTE, for 3rd Earl of Bute, 1768–9 [payment in Mount Stuart archives 'to boarding of Mr. Craig, architect, during the five weeks he staid at Mountstuart measuring and making plans of the house']; ST. ANDREW'S CHURCH, DUNDEE, *c.*1768–9 [Town Council Minutes, *ex inf.* Mr. David Walker]; alterations to MOUNTQUHANIE HOUSE, FIFE, 1770 [S.R.O., RHP 9360, copy of elevation at Mountquhanie signed 'Jas. Craig 1770']; proposed addition of wings to DALKEITH HOUSE, MIDLOTHIAN, 1775 [in portfolio at Bowhill House]; design for an urn in memory of Provost Kincaid in GREYFRIARS CHURCHYARD, 1777 [Scottish National Gallery, Print Room, D. 384]; a library for the Writers to the Signet, 1778–9 [*History of the Society of Writers to the Signet*, Edinburgh 1890, 409–11]; internal alterations to CALLENDAR HOUSE, STIRLINGSHIRE, for William Forbes, 1785 [R.C.A.M., *Stirlingshire* ii, 350; S.R.O., RHP 14409, 14410]; a projected square in Edinburgh for Robert Hope, 1788 [S.R.O., RHP 11128]; the improvement of KIRKCALDY HARBOUR, 1788 [plan in Kirkcaldy Museum, KIRMG 1968.14.1].

CRAIG, JOHN (–*c.*1745), was a wright by trade. He lived in Glasgow, where he had a considerable business as a builder. He appears to have had some sort of business relationship with Allan Dreghorn (*q.v.*) [see *Extracts from the Records of the Burgh of Glasgow 1718–38*, ed. Renwick, 414, 423, 494, etc.]. In 1732 they submitted a joint design for Glasgow University Library, but it was not carried out [Glasgow University, Senate Minutes]. In 1735 Craig was appointed 'town's wright' or carpenter to the municipality of Glasgow, but the appointment was rescinded the following year [*Extracts*, as above, 435–6, 472]. Craig must have died shortly before 15 January 1745, when his heirs received a belated payment for his library design of 1732 [Glasgow University Faculty Minutes, vol. 36, f. 168].

CRAIG, JOHN, of Glasgow, was the son of William Craig, a prosperous timber-merchant of that city. In the Glasgow directories of 1787 and 1789 he is described as 'architect to his Royal Highness the Prince of Wales', but how he obtained this (presumably honorary) designation is not known. He visited Italy and was well known in Glasgow as a man of taste who could speak Italian and play the fiddle [Senex, *Glasgow Past and Present* ii, 1884, 278, 330]. In 1787 he married Sarah, sister of William Stark (*q.v.*), but she died at Barcelona in 1792 'on her way to Italy for the recovery of her health' [*Scots Mag.* xlix, 1787, 620; lv, 1793, 50]. His daughter Margaret married General Sir George Napier. He should not be confused with a wright named John Craig who built a house (No. 42) in Miller Street in 1775 [Senex, *op. cit.* ii, 415] and appears to have died in 1783 [Glasgow City Archives, Register of the Incorporation of Masons]. He was still alive in 1815, when he wrote a postscript to the text of Stark's report on the Calton Hill development at

Edinburgh in the *Scots Magazine* (vol. lxxvii, 582).

In Glasgow Craig designed THE GRAMMAR SCHOOL (later the Andersonian Institution), ST. GEORGE'S STREET, 1787–8, and THE SURGEONS' HALL, ST. ENOCH'S SQUARE, 1791, both demolished, in an elegant Adamesque style [R. Chapman, *Picture of Glasgow*, 1812, 125, 127]. A drawing formerly at Newhailes, Midlothian, and now in the National Library of Scotland (Acc. 7228/509), shows that he designed a court of offices for Andrew Stirling at DRUMPELLIER HOUSE, LANARKSHIRE, in 1790. An almost identical stable-block was afterwards built at NEWHAILES, probably by Miss Dalrymple (who inherited the estate in 1792), who evidently obtained the drawing in order to copy it in her own building.

CRAIK, WILLIAM (1703–1798), was the laird of Arbigland in Kirkcudbrightshire from 1743 until his death in 1798. He was distinguished as an agriculturalist and was also a competent amateur architect, rebuilding ARBIGLAND for himself and designing MOSSKNOWE, KIRKPATRICK FLEMING, DUMFRIESSHIRE, for Dr. William Graham in 1767. These are both small country houses in the Palladian tradition. Craik also designed KIRKBEAN CHURCH, KIRKCUDBRIGHTSHIRE, 1776, described as 'a model for a country parish' [*N.S.A.* iv, 238] [P. H. McKerlie, *History of the Lands and their Owners in Galloway* iv, 1878, 154–5; letters, etc. at Mossknowe, *ex inf.* Miss Anne Riches].

CRAKE, JOHN (*c.*1811–1859), was presumably related to Michael Crake, 'statuary, surveyor and builder', for whose sculpture see Rupert Gunnis's *Dictionary of British Sculptors*, revised ed. 1968, 116. John Crake became a pupil of Decimus Burton. He entered the Royal Academy Schools in 1831, and was awarded the Silver Medal the same year. He afterwards visited Italy, and on his return commenced practice in London. His exhibits at the Royal Academy indicate that he made designs for the terrace of houses in HYDE PARK GARDENS, 1836, and for an entrance lodge to DEENE PARK, NORTHANTS., for the 7th Earl of Cardigan, 1841. The latter may not have been built, as another design for a lodge at Deene was exhibited at the R.A. by T. H. Wyatt and David Brandon in 1850.

From 1842 to 1844 Crake was a member of council of the R.I.B.A. His marriage to a wealthy lady enabled him to retire from practice in 1852, and he took up residence at Datchet, where a churchyard monument records his death on 27 December 1859, in his 49th year. His widow survived until 1900. A student's design for a triumphal arch by him is in the R.I.B.A. Drawings Collection. [Obituary in *Builder* xviii, 1860, 6.]

CRANESON, W—, designed the PUBLIC BATHS, NEWCASTLE, opened in 1781, of which he published an engraved plan and elevation dedicated to the Mayor and Corporation (B.L., *King's Maps* xxxii, 57 m). Before taking up architecture, he had been 'an actor belonging to the Newcastle company of comedians' [M. A. Richardson, *The Local Historian's Table Book* ii, 1842, 268].

CRESWELL, or **CRISWELL,** WILLIAM (–1819), was Surveyor to the Armourers' and Brasiers' Company until his death in 1819. He was President of the Surveyors' Club in 1800, and in 1820 William Wickings presented the Club with an engraved portrait of Cresswell, 'an old and respected Member, whose integrity, rectitude, and abilities will always be had in remembrance' [J. W. Penfold, *A Century of Surveyors*, 1892, 13; *A.P.S.D.*, *s.v.* 'Good, J. H.'].

CRESY, EDWARD (1792–1858), was born at Dartford, Kent, and was educated at Rawes's academy at Bromley in the same county. He became a pupil of J. T. Parkinson, and afterwards spent two years in the office of George Smith. In 1816, accompanied by his friend and fellow-pupil G. L. Taylor, he made a walking tour through England in order to measure and draw the principal architectural monuments. In 1817 Cresy and Taylor, accompanied from 1818 by John Sanders, undertook a tour of Europe which occupied the next three years. Travelling mainly on foot, they visited France, Switzerland, Italy, Greece, Malta and Sicily before returning home by way of Italy and France in 1819. The results of their researches appeared in 1821–2 as *The Architectural Antiquities of Rome, measured and delineated by G. L. Taylor and E. Cresy*, 2 vols. (there was a later edition in 1874), and in 1829 they published a work on *Architecture of the Middle Ages in Italy illustrated by views . . . of the Cathedral, etc. of Pisa*. A third work on the architecture of the Renaissance was intended, but, after the publication of two parts, it was abandoned owing to lack of encouragement.

Partly as a result of this disappointment, Cresy accepted a professional engagement in Paris in 1829–30, and it was some time before he became well established in England. He refused to take part in competitions at a time when they were the usual way of securing important public commissions, and his practice was, in consequence, 'almost entirely of a private character'. Very little is known of his architectural works, but in 1824 he added a library to THE PRIORY, LEATHERHEAD, SURREY, for William Cotton [Brayley, *History of Surrey* iv, 437]. He also designed HULSWOOD VILLA, WILMINGTON, KENT, for John Hayward in the style of a 'Burgundian château', *c.*1835 [C. Greenwood, *Epitome of the History of Kent*, 1838, 70], added a Gothic porch to DARTFORD CHURCH in 1846 [S. K. Keyes, *Dartford, Further Historical Notes*, Dartford 1938, 385], and designed the NATIONAL SCHOOLS at HORTON KIRBY in 1857 [drawings in Kent Archives Office].

Cresy lived from 1824 until 1830 at No. 6 SUFFOLK STREET, LONDON, a house which he designed himself with a façade in imitation of Palladio's house at Vicenza [J. Elmes, *Metropolitan Improvements*, 1831, 123]. In 1828 he began building THE TOWERS at SOUTH DARENTH, nr. DARTFORD (dem.), as his own residence. The chimney-pieces were executed in Paris, in accordance with a design 'suggested by fragments I saw in the gallery of the Louvre'. It was at South Darenth that he died on 12 November 1858.

Cresy held strongly the view that architecture and engineering were a single profession, and himself became well known as a sanitary engineer. As superintending inspector under the Board of Health, he gave important evidence before the Health of Towns Commission of 1843 and in 1844 before the Commissioners for enquiring into the State of Large Towns and Populous Districts (*Parliamentary Papers*, 1844, xvii, 144). At Dartford he superintended the construction of the Gasworks in 1826–7. He published *A Practical Treatise on Bridge Building*, 1839, and *An Encyclopedia of Civil Engineering*, 1847 (2nd ed. 1856). He also published, in conjunction with C. W. Johnson, a work *On the Cottages of Agricultural Labourers, with Economical Working Plans* [1847].

Cresy became an F.S.A. in 1820, and was also a member of the British Archaeological Association, to whose proceedings he contributed several papers. In 1840 the London Topographical Society published his *Illustrations of Stone Church, Kent, with an historical account.* His wife translated into English Milizia's *Memorie degli Architetti antichi e moderni*, with Notes and Additional Lives, 2 vols., 1826. His eldest son, Edward Cresy (d. 1870), followed his father's profession. A small MS. notebook belonging to Cresy is preserved in the Kent Archives Office. It contains notes on the building of his house at South Darenth, and on local antiquities, etc. Extracts from it were published in the *Trans. of the Dartford Antiquarian Soc.* ii.

[Obituary in *Builder* xvi, 793, xvii, 166; G. L. Taylor, *Memoirs of an Octogenarian Architect*, 1870–2; *D.N.B.*].

CREW, JOHN THISTLEWOOD, entered the Royal Academy Schools in 1834. He exhibited at the Royal Academy from 1833 to 1859, including a number of views of Rome, and in 1841 'Caversham, the seat of William Crawshaw, Esq., shewing the additional colonnades now erecting'. It is probable that he was the architect employed by Crawshaw to enlarge CAVERSHAM PARK, OXON., at about this time.

CRICHTON, RICHARD (*c.*1771–1817), was the son of James Crichton, an Edinburgh mason who died in 1797. In early life he worked as a draughtsman for the Adam brothers in Edinburgh. In May 1797 he was admitted a burgess of Edinburgh. He was a competent and versatile architect who carried on the traditions established by the brothers Adam in their extensive Scottish practice. Thus Gask, Lawers and the Bank of Scotland on the Mound at Edinburgh are in the restrained classical style of Adam's later years; Rossie Castle was an essay in Adam's distinctive castle style. But Abercairny Abbey was an elaborately Gothic house in the manner of Porden, while the classical Dunglass was a remarkably early essay in picturesque asymmetry, and Balbirnie shows the influence of the Greek Revival.

In 1813 Crichton competed for the important town-planning scheme in the neighbourhood of Calton Hill, Edinburgh. He shared the prize with William Reid of Glasgow and Alexander Nasmyth (*qq.v.*), but none of their proposals were in fact carried out, and in 1814–15 the commission for the associated Calton Bridge went to Archibald Elliot instead of to himself. His design for the bridge is illustrated in the *Scots Magazine* for June 1814. Other unexecuted designs by Crichton were for the Merchant Maiden Hospital in Edinburgh [*Book of the Old Edinburgh Club* xxix, 24], and for a monument to Nelson at Forres [Robert Douglas, *Annals of Forres*, Elgin 1934, 318].

Crichton's career was cut short by his early death at the age of 46 on 17 August 1817. He is commemorated by an inscription added to the Graeco-Egyptian monument which he had erected to the memory of his father in St. Cuthbert's Churchyard. His practice was continued by his nephews R. & R. Dickson (*q.v.*)

[*A.P.S.D.*; *Roll of Edinburgh Burgesses*, Scottish Record Soc. 1933, 41; A. J. Youngson,

The Making of Classical Edinburgh, 1966, 142, 307 n. 36.]

ROSSIE CASTLE, ANGUS, for Hercules Ross, *c.*1795–1800, castle style; dem. 1957 [*Scots. Mag.* Sept. 1807; J. P. Neale, *Views of Seats*, 1st. ser. v; Soane Museum, Designs, vol. iv, pp. 48–52, copies made in 1795 of designs by Crichton dated 1793] (F. O. Morris, *Picturesque Views of Seats* v, 1889, 73).

CRAIG CHURCH, ANGUS, for Mrs Hercules Ross, *c.*1797–9, Gothic [advt for tender in *Edinburgh Evening Courant*, 4 June 1796].

COLINTON HOUSE, MIDLOTHIAN, drew elevation to correspond to plan provided by Thomas Harrison (*q.v.*), for Sir William Forbes, Bart., 1801 [drawings in Crichton's hand among Fettercairn papers in N.L.S. and cf. Acc. 4796/47/3].

GASK HOUSE, PERTHSHIRE, for Laurence Oliphant, 1801– [J. P. Neale, *Views of Seats*, 1st ser., iv, 1821].

EDINBURGH, THE BANK OF SCOTLAND on THE MOUND, jointly with Robert Reid, 1802–6 [Bank of Scotland Minutes, 29 Oct. 1800: 'Resolved to employ Robert Reid and Richard Chrichton, Architects in Edinburgh, jointly']; remodelled by D. Bryce 1865–70 (T. H. Shepherd, *Modern Athens*, 1829, plate at p. 74).

attributed: GELSTON CASTLE, KIRKCUDBRIGHTSHIRE, for Sir William Douglas, Bart., *c.*1805, castle style, now gutted [stylistic attribution].

ABERCAIRNY ABBEY, PERTHSHIRE, begun *c.*1805 for Col. Charles Moray Stirling (d. 1810), completed to an enlarged plan by R. & R. Dickson for James Moray (d. 1840) and William Moray (d. 1850), Gothic; dem. 1960 [J. P. Neale, *Views of Seats*, 1st ser., vi, 1823; Mark Girouard in *C. Life*, 9–16 March 1961; S.R.O., RHP 1017/22, 36 and 41].

STIRLING, COURT HOUSE AND GAOL, 1806–11 [R.C.A.M., *Stirlingshire* ii, 293; S.R.O., RHP 1884/2–5, 7–9].

INVERKEITHING CHURCH, FIFE, repairs and alterations, 1807–8; rebuilt 1826 [S.R.O., HR 279/1, 13 Feb. 1807–22 July 1808].

DUNGLASS, EAST LOTHIAN, for Sir James Hall, Bart., 1807–11; dem. 1947 [J. P. Neale, *Views of Seats*, 1st ser., iv, 1821, where it is stated that the architect was 'greatly assisted by the taste and judgment of the proprietor'; S.R.O., GD 206/2/160 and 206/5/106] (*C. Life*, 12 Sept. 1925).

BLAIR DRUMMOND, PERTHSHIRE, 'house for a smith or carpenter', now known as Blair Drummond Corner, 1813 [drawings at Blair Drummond Estate Office].

KINCARDINE-IN-MENTEITH CHURCH, PERTHSHIRE, 1814–16, Gothic [*N.S.A.* x, 1265; specification in S.R.O., GD 24; plans in Blair Drummond Estate Office].

LAWERS HOUSE, PERTHSHIRE, added Ionic portico, etc., for D. R. W. Ewart, *c.*1815 [J. P. Neale, *Views of Seats*, 1st ser., v, 1822] (*C. Life*, 10 Oct. 1925).

BALBIRNIE HOUSE, FIFE, enlarged and remodelled for General Robert Balfour, 1815–19 [J. P. Neale, *Views of Seats*, 1st ser., v, 1822; Alistair Rowan in *C. Life*, 29 June–6 July 1972].

CARRIDEN MANSE, WEST LOTHIAN, 1816 [advt. for tenders in *Edinburgh Evening Courant*, 28 Dec. 1816].

COCKPEN CHURCH, MIDLOTHIAN, designed 1816, built 1817–20 by R. & R. Dickson under supervision of A. Elliot [Heritors' minutes in S.R.O., CH 2/452/29; contract in HR 333/6; Crichton named as architect in *Edinburgh Mag.* iv, 1819, 368 and *Edinburgh Evening Courant*, 17 Jan. 1820].

CRISWELL, WILLIAM, *see* CRESWELL WILLIAM.

CROCKER, EDWARD (1758–1836), served the Office of Works in different capacities for more than forty years, ending his career as Clerk of the Works at Whitehall from 1818 to 1829, when he retired at the age of 71. He was a measuring surveyor rather than an architect and is best known for the careful coloured drawings, now in the Ashmolean Museum at Oxford, which he made of the medieval wall-paintings in the Painted Chamber at Westminster [*History of the King's Works* i, 499; vi, 59, 115, 116, 119, etc.].

CROMBIE, ALEXANDER (*c.*1709–1785), was the founder of a family of masons and architects in Dumfries. A native of Haddingtonshire, he came to Dumfries as a young man in order to work at Tinwald House under William Adam, took a lease of the Castledykes Quarry, and soon became one of the leading builders in the locality. In 1752 he and James Harley, Deacon of the Squaremen, built MOORHEAD'S HOSPITAL, and in 1770 he built the BUTCHER MARKET. His son Alexander (*c.*1757–1828) and grandson Andrew Crombie (*c.*1799–1855) were also leading builders and monumental masons in the town, and the latter's nephew Alexander (1812–80) and grand-nephew James (1845–1909) were in practice as architects during the second half of the nineteenth century. [W. McDowall, *Memorials of St. Michael's Churchyard, Dumfries*, Edinburgh 1876, 262–

4; *The Architect's, Engineer's and Building Trades' Directory*, 1868, 107].

CROSS, RICHARD (*c*.1790–1837), a native of Newcastle, was killed by a fall from his horse on 4 July 1837, aged 47 [*Newcastle Courant*, 7 July 1837; *The Hull, Rockingham Gazette*, 22 July 1837]. For the 6th Earl of Tankerville he designed stables and other offices at CHILLINGHAM CASTLE, NORTHUMBERLAND, 1823, altered CHILLINGHAM CHURCH in 1828–9, and designed cottages and farmhouses in 1836 [*Newcastle Chronicle*, 15 Nov. 1823, *Courant*, 27 Feb., 12 March 1836, *ex inf.* Mr. R. Hewlings; drawings for church in Northumberland C.R.O.].

CROWE, WILLIAM (1745–1829), Fellow of New College, Oxford, was born at Midgham in Berkshire, where his father was a carpenter. He became Public Orator of the University of Oxford in 1784, and was also known as a poet and preacher. He was interested in architecture, and occasionally lectured on that subject at New Colege. A printed syllabus of 16 lectures on the subject in Bodleian Library, G.A. Oxon. b. 111 (110) is probably his. In 1804 he lectured on Civil Architecture at the Royal Institution in London [Farington's Diary, 28 June, 1804]. Crowe is sometimes said to have designed the Library of Exeter College, erected in 1779 and demolished in 1859. But in fact John Townesend was both architect and builder, and Crowe did no more than 'suggest a few amendments in the details' [J. Ingram, *Memorials of Oxford* i, 1837, 14]. For a full account of Crowe's career see *D.N.B.*

CRUNDEN, JOHN (*c*.1741–1835), was born in Sussex and became an architect and surveyor in London. He exhibited at the Society of Artists from 1766 to 1777, and competed for the Royal Exchange at Dublin in 1769. In 1774 he was appointed District Surveyor for the parishes of Paddington, St. Pancras and St. Luke, Chelsea. Although dismissed in 1807 after a disagreement with the Middlesex magistrates (see John Coggan, *A Letter to the Magistrates of the County of Middlesex*, 1807), he was reinstated, retaining his three surveyorships until he resigned in 1824. When he died in 1835 he was in his 95th year. His will shows that he had been a keen archer.

Crunden is best known as the author of several popular architectural pattern-books. In 1765 he collaborated with J. H. Morris in publishing *The Carpenter's Companion for Chinese Railing and Gates* and contributed two plates to Robert Manwaring's *Carpenter's Companion to . . . Gothic Railing*. Then in 1766 he was one of the three authors of *The Chimney-Piece Maker's Daily Assistant*, the others being Thomas Milton and Placido Columbani. In 1765 he published *The Joyner and Cabinet-Maker's Darling, or Pocket Director*, containing forty designs for 'Gothic, Mosaic, and Ornamental Frets', and twenty designs for fanlights (later editions in 1770 and 1786), and in 1767 *Convenient and Ornamental Architecture, consisting of Original Designs [from] the Farm House . . . to the most grand and magnificent Villa*, with a dedication to the Duke of Newcastle (seven later editions in 1770, 1785, 1788, 1791, 1797, 1805, 1815). *Convenient and Ornamental Architecture* proved to be the most successful pattern-book of its kind, providing in a manageable form and at a reasonable price, designs for a wide range of domestic buildings in a basically Palladian style that continued to be popular for the rest of the eighteenth century.

Although Crunden's pattern-books made no attempt to be original or avant-garde, some of his executed buildings show him developing a more elegant style akin to that of the brothers Adam. Thus Boodle's Club was clearly inspired by Adam's Royal Society of Arts building in the Adelphi, and Belfield is described by Pevsner as 'an Adamesque essay with rooms of contrasted shapes'. Crunden's reputation even gained him a place in a foreign publication, J. Ch. Krafft's *Plans des plus beaux jardins pittoresques de France, d'Angleterre et d'Allemagne* (Paris 1809), the first two plates of which are devoted to a Gothic garden pavilion 'executé dans un parc, sur la route de Westminster près de Londres, d'après les dessins du célèbre Jean Grunden (*sic*)', and believed to have been situated near Fulham.

[*A.P.S.D.*; A. T. Bolton, *The Portrait of Sir John Soane*, 1927, 181–2; Dorothy Stroud, *Henry Holland*, 1966, 24, 26–7; *Builder* xxvii, 1869, 781; will, P.C.C. 471 GLOUCESTER; Eileen Harris, *British Architectural Books and Writers, 1556–1785*, 1990, 171–3.]

BROOKLANDS, WEYBRIDGE, SURREY, for George Payne, 1767; dem. Crunden was 'imploy'd to direct' the building of this house by Henry Holland, senior, and may or may not have been responsible for the design, which was illustrated in *Convenient and Ornamental Architecture*, pl. 36 [D. Stroud, *Henry Holland*, 23–4].

HALTON PLACE, nr. HELLIFIELD, YORKS. (W.R.), 1770 [N.M.R., photos. of drawings at Halton] (T. D. Whitaker, *History of Craven*,

1812, 439).

PORTSWOOD HOUSE, nr. SOUTHAMPTON, HANTS., for — Taylor, *c.*1770; dem. 1852 [E. W. Brayley & John Britton, *The Beauties of England & Wales* vi, 1805, 121].

SOUTHAMPTON, THE AUDIT HOUSE, 1771–3; dem. [*The Southampton Guide*, 1787, 32] (*Arch. Rev.* xlv, Feb. 1919, 33).

WOOLCOMBE HALL, MELBURY BUBB, DORSET, for Laurence Cox, *c.*1772; dem. before 1815 [exhib. at R.A. 1772; there is also an engraving signed 'J. Crunden, Architect'].[1]

BUSBRIDGE, nr. GODALMING, SURREY, improvements for Gen. Sir Robert Barker, 1775; dem. 1906 [W. Angus, *Views of Seats*, 1787, pl. vi].

LONDON, BOODLE'S (originally the Savoir Vivre) CLUB, ST. JAMES'S STREET, 1775–6; ground-floor rooms remodelled by J. B. Papworth 1821–4 [T. Malton, *A Picturesque Tour of London and Westminster*, 1791] (*C. Life*, 24 Dec. 1932; *Survey of London* xxx, 441–9).

BRIGHTON, SUSSEX, THE ASSEMBLY ROOMS of the CASTLE HOTEL for Mrs. Shergold, *c.*1776; converted into the Chapel Royal 1821–2; dem. 1851 and rebuilt in Montpelier Place as St. Stephen's Chapel, now secularized [H. D. Roberts, *History of the Royal Pavilion, Brighton*, 1939].

BELFIELD, nr. WEYMOUTH, DORSET, for Isaac Buxton, *c.*1775–80 [G. D. Squibb, *Belfield and the Buxtons*, privately printed 1954, 2; R.C.H.M. *Dorset* ii (2), 340 and plates].

LONDON, houses in PARK STREET and HEREFORD STREET, 1778; dem. 1865 [*Survey of London* xxxix, pl. 13c, xl, 174].

LONDON, No. 45 ST. PAUL'S CHURCHYARD, for Francis Newbery, 1778–9; dem. [Charles Welsh, *A Bookseller of the Last Century*, 1885, 143–4].

CUBITT, LEWIS (1799–1883), was the youngest of the Cubitt brothers, and according to family tradition, 'the laziest and least satisfactory of the three'. He was, however, much the most talented as an architect. Born in September 1799, he was apprenticed to his eldest brother Thomas (*q.v.*) in 1815, and became a member of the Carpenters' Company in 1822. He also received some architectural training in the office of H. E. Kendall, whose daughter Sophia he married. He was in partnership with his brothers by 1824, when 'Messrs. T. W. and L. Cubitt' repaired LEYTON CHURCH, ESSEX [J. Kennedy, *History of the Parish of Leyton*, 1894]. Thomas and William dissolved their partnership in 1827, and Lewis eventually left the former brother for the latter in 1832. Later in the 1830s he set up as an architect in independent practice at 77 Great Russell Street.

Lewis appears to have designed many of the houses in Bloomsbury and Belgravia which were built by the Cubitts in the 1820s. In 1837–9 he designed and built, as an independent speculation, a block of Italianate houses on the south side of LOWNDES SQUARE (plans and elevation in *The Surveyor, Engineer and Architect*, 1841, 154, 198). In the 1840s he entered on a successful career as a railway architect, designing in particular the BRICKLAYERS' ARMS STATION in BERMONDSEY (dem.) in 1842–4 and in 1851–2 the KING'S CROSS terminal of the Great Northern Railway (*Builder* ix, 1851, 739). The large scale and expressive simplicity of the latter station show that Lewis Cubitt was capable of something more than the genteel façades of Belgravia.[1] Another railway commission was a large Italianate building at COLCHESTER, begun as THE VICTORIA HOTEL, but eventually completed in 1843 as a Lunatic Asylum (THE ROYAL EASTERN COUNTIES INSTITUTION) [H. E. von Stürmer, *Historical Guide to Colchester*, 1852, 7].

Little appears to be known about Lewis Cubitt's career after 1852. He received a legacy of £10,000 under Thomas Cubitt's will in 1855, and himself lived on to the age of 84, dying at Brighton on 9 June 1883. His estate was valued for probate at £77,900. A portrait is reproduced by Hobhouse, pl. 104. [Sir Stephen Tallents, *Man and Boy*, 1943, 32; Hermione Hobhouse, *Thomas Cubitt, Master Builder*, 1971, 271 and *passim*.]

CUBITT, THOMAS (1788–1855), was the eldest son of Jonathan Cubitt, a native of Norfolk who moved to London at the end of the eighteenth century. Thomas began life as a journeyman carpenter, and as a young man made a voyage to India as a ship's carpenter. Returning to London in about 1809, he used such money as he had been able to save to set up business as a master carpenter. His first work of importance was to rebuild the defective roof of the Russell Institution in Great Coram Street. In 1814 he became a member of the Carpenters' Company, and was joined in business by his younger brother

[1] Plate 25 of *Convenient and Ornamental Architecture* shows a 'House designed for Lawrence Cox, Esq. to be built at Keston in Kent'. This does not appear to have been built.

[1] For the probable source of Cubitt's design for the screen-wall – a design for a bourse published by J. N. L. Durand in 1802 – see John Summerson, *Victorian Architecture: Four Studies in Evaluation*, 1970, 29–30 and fig. 7.

William (1791–1863). It was in the following year that he took the step that was to make him famous in the history of building. Having contracted to build the London Institution in Moorfields, he decided to set up a comprehensive building establishment of his own instead of following the normal practice of performing the carpenter's work himself and sub-contracting the other trades. 'Thomas Cubitt, bound by his contract under penalty to finish the new building by a certain date, was determined not to be left at the mercy of this complicated and inefficient system.' He accordingly bought some ground in Gray's Inn Road, built himself workshops upon it, 'purchased horses, carts and material, and engaged . . . gangs of carpenters, smiths, glaziers, bricklayers and other workers'. Although such arrangements may not have been wholly without precedent, Cubitt's enterprise was a pioneer venture of its kind, and its success gained him the reputation of having established the first modern building firm.

As a builder with a large labour force on a permanent wage basis, Cubitt could not afford to wait for work to be offered to him. In order to keep his men fully employed he took the initiative by engaging in speculative building on a large scale. In 1815 he began to develop land on the Calthorpe estate on the east side of Gray's Inn Road. In the early 1820s he built several 'genteel and commodious villas' in Highbury Park, and more in Stoke Newington (Albion Road), Islington (Barnsbury Park) and Bloomsbury (south side of Tavistock Square, in association with the stockbroker Benjamin Oakley). In 1824 he began to develop a further tract of ground on the Duke of Bedford's Bloomsbury estate, on which he built the west side of Tavistock Square, Woburn Place, Endsleigh Street, the greater part of Gordon Square, and part of the south side of Euston Square. The workmanship was excellent, and the competent architectural designing was done in Cubitt's own drawing office, for characteristically he preferred to be independent of architects as he was of other building tradesmen. For this side of the firm's activities his youngest brother Lewis (*q.v.*), who had had an architectural training, appears to have been responsible. The family partnership, however, began to break up in 1827, when William Cubitt left the firm in order to carry on the safer contracting side of the business from the Gray's Inn Yard, and Lewis eventually joined him in 1832.

The scene of Cubitt's greatest building enterprise was in the south-west of London, where the conversion of Buckingham House into a royal palace pointed out the Grosvenor estates as an area for development. In 1824 he took a lease from Lord Grosvenor of the district known as the 'Five Fields', and began to convert the swampy ground bordering the Westbourne river into the substantial squares of Belgravia. Belgrave Square itself was built by George and William Haldimand, the financiers, to the designs of George Basevi, but elsewhere Cubitt built for himself, and largely to his own designs, or those of his brother Lewis. The earlier part of Eaton Square (Nos. 103–18) is definitely attributed to 'T. & L. Cubitt' by Britton & Pugin, *The Public Buildings of London* ii, 1828. Further north, Cubitt built the two great houses which stand on either side of Albert Gate, the eastern of which he sold to George Hudson, the railway magnate, for £15,000. After Belgravia, he built Pimlico (where his Thames Bank works were established), while further afield he was responsible for the laying out of Clapham Park, on land sold to him by Major Atkins Bowyer, the lord of the manor, in 1824.

Meanwhile he was already engaged in building houses in Brighton for Thomas Read Kemp, and in 1828 he was one of the Committee of Management elected by the proprietors 'to superintend the general works and improvements to be done at Kemp Town'. He continued to serve on it until his death in 1855, and played a part in the history of the estate second only to that of Kemp himself.

Although mainly engaged in these great schemes of urban development, Cubitt built a few large houses for private clients either to his own designs or to those of his brothers William and Lewis. Conventionally 'Palladian' or Italianate in style, they were well appointed and substantially built, but somewhat undistinguished as works of architecture. They included POLESDEN LACEY HOUSE, GREAT BOOKHAM, SURREY, for the stationer Joseph Bonsor, 1821–3 [Brayley, *History of Surrey* iv, 472; Hobhouse, 50]; the remodelling of LINTON PARK, KENT, for 5th Earl Cornwallis, *c.*1825, for which William Cubitt acted as architect [see his evidence in the *Report of the Select Committee on the Office of Works, Parliamentary Papers* 1828, iv, 409] (*C. Life*, 29 March, 5 April 1946); additions to NORTHERWOOD, nr. LYNDHURST, HANTS., for John Pulteney, 1830–1 [G. F. Prosser, *Select Illustrations of Hampshire*, 1834]; alterations to the interior of NETLEY PLACE, nr. GUILDFORD, SURREY, for J. Fraser, 1847, destroyed by fire 1848 [*Gent's Mag.* 1848 (i), 76]; and No. 14 KENSINGTON PALACE GARDENS, for Edward Antrobus, 1849–51 [Hobhouse, 464–5]. The rebuilding of No. 12 ST. JAMES'S SQUARE in

1836 for Lord King, later 1st Earl of Lovelace, is attributed to Cubitt on stylistic grounds [*Survey of London* xxix, 134]. In 1845–8 he designed and built OSBORNE HOUSE, ISLE OF WIGHT, for Queen Victoria under the direction of the Prince Consort (plan in R. Kerr, *The Gentleman's House*, 1864, pl. 17). In 1846–50 he built the new east front of BUCKINGHAM PALACE to the designs of Edward Blore, and in 1852–6 added the Ball-room, etc., on the south side to those of Sir James Pennethorne (plans in *History of the King's Works* vi, 279, 288). In about 1830 he built a large house for himself in Clapham Park, and in 1850–4 a still larger one at DENBIES, nr. DORKING, SURREY (dem. 1953), where he died on 20 December 1855.

Cubitt left over £1,000,000, a will (then the longest on record) covering 30 skins of parchment, and a reputation for enterprise, integrity and public spirit which made him one of the great figures of early Victorian England. For, besides conducting building schemes on a larger scale than any hitherto known, Cubitt found time to take an active interest in such matters as the disposal of London's sewage, the provision of public parks, and the control of smoke. The creation of Battersea Park was due largely to his initiative, and when the success of the Great Exhibition of 1851 was in doubt, he became one of its guarantors. He frequently gave evidence to parliamentary committees investigating the problems of a rapidly expanding metropolis, and played a leading part in the preparation of the Metropolitan Buildings Act of 1855.

[Sir Stephen Tallents, *Man and Boy*, 1943, 30–6; Hermione Hobhouse, *Thomas Cubitt, Master Builder*, 1971, with full references to obituaries and other sources; *Catalogue of the R.I.B.A. Drawings Coll., C–F*, 54–5.]

CULLEN, —, designed the TOWN HALL at SOUTH MOLTON, DEVONSHIRE, in 1739, as appears by an entry in the building accounts (now in the Town Museum): 'gave Mr. Cullen for drawing the moddell of the Towne Hall £1–ls.' The building is an attractive example of provincial Georgian architecture.

CUMBERLEGE, CHARLES NATHANIEL (*c.*1807–1859), was admitted to the Royal Academy Schools in 1827 at the age of 20. He was recommended by his uncle Samuel Ware, to whose practice he succeeded on the latter's retirement in about 1840. He became a Fellow of the R.I.B.A. in 1845 and died in 1859. In 1834 he exhibited a design for 'proposed alterations' to WYDDIAL HALL, HERTS., at the R.A. He competed for the Houses of Parliament in 1835, submitting a design whose elevations were 'free from elaborate ornaments, the whole being intended to be faced with Portland stone'.

CUNDY, THOMAS, senior (1765–1825), was the eldest son of Peter Cundy, the owner of a small estate at Restowrick, St. Dennis, Cornwall. He left home early after a disagreement with his father, and, after a period of apprenticeship to a builder in Plymouth, decided to seek his fortune in London. Here he obtained employment as clerk of works to S. P. Cockerell, and educated himself by private study and attending evening lectures. In 1795 and 1796 he exhibited student's exercises at the Royal Academy. Eventually he set up business as an architect and builder in Ranelagh Street, Pimlico. Here he prospered, and in 1821 obtained the important post of surveyor to Lord Grosvenor's estates in Belgravia and Pimlico, then about to be laid out for building. By then he already had a considerable practice, especially as a designer of country houses either in a picturesque Gothic style reminiscent of Nash, or else in a conventional classical manner calculated to appeal to patrons who disliked the deviations of Dance or Soane. He exhibited some of his designs at the Royal Academy, and many of his works are shown in a small sketchbook now in the R.I.B.A. Collection, containing drawings apparently made by his son while in his father's office (see the *Catalogue* for a detailed list of its contents).

In 1816 Cundy visited Rome together with his son Thomas. He died in Ranelagh Street on 28 December 1825, aged 60, and was buried in the churchyard at Richmond in Surrey, where there is a tomb to his memory. His eldest son Thomas (*q.v.*) succeeded to his practice. James Cundy (1793–1826), his second son, was a statuary mason, and had a son named Samuel (d. 1867) who ran a marble-works in Pimlico and was employed by Gilbert Scott as a mason at St. Albans Abbey and elsewhere [obituary in *Builder* xxv, 1867, 464]. Joseph Cundy (1795–1875), third son of Thomas Cundy, senior, was an architect and speculative builder in Belgravia, and was the father of Thomas Syson Cundy, who became agent to the Fountaine-Montagu family of Ingmanthorpe Hall in Yorkshire and Papplewick, Notts., a position in which he was succeeded by his son and grandson. Nicholas Wilcox Cundy, born in 1778, was a younger brother of Thomas Cundy the elder. He practised as a civil engineer, but his works included the reconstruction of the

Pantheon in Oxford Street as a theatre in 1811–12.[1]

A portrait of Thomas Cundy was in the possession of the late T. J. Cundy of Brant Broughton, Lincs., together with a MS. account of the family written by Osbert F. Cundy, F.R.C.S., in 1874.

[*D.N.B.*; MS. by Osbert F. Cundy.]

The following list sets out the works of Thomas Cundy senior and junior up to the time of the former's death in 1825. 'Sketch-book' refers to the sketch-book in the R.I.B.A. Drawings Collection.

NORMANTON, RUTLAND, farmyard for Sir Gilbert Heathcote, Bart., 1795 (? executed) [sketch-book, p. 65].

RICHMOND, SURREY, ice-house and farmyard (? executed) for 1st Earl of Leicester, 1800 [sketch-book, pp. 15, 67].

BRIXTON LODGE, BRIXTON, SURREY, for J. Pitter, 1803; dem. [exhib. at R.A. 1803; sketch-book, p. 93, reproduced in *C. Life*, 9 March 1945, 418].

BEECHWOOD PARK, HERTS., interior of library for Sir John Sebright, Bart., 1804 [drawings formerly at Beechwood, together with a rejected design by Soane] (*C. Life*, 12–19 Nov. 1938).

LONDON, No. 22 (now 37) HILL STREET, BERKELEY SQUARE, interior for Robert Heathcote, before 1805 [*Gent's Mag.* 1805 (i), 275].

LONDON, No. 24 HILL STREET, BERKELEY SQUARE, perhaps designed picture gallery for Sir John Leicester (afterwards Lord de Tabley), *c.*1806; dem. Leicester formed the gallery out of an existing library soon after purchasing the house in 1805. No documents connected with the works of *c.*1806 appear to survive, but among the Leicester-Warren papers in the Cheshire Record Office [DLT/C3/41–61] there is an estimate by Cundy dated 24 June 1809 for converting the room under the gallery into an eating-room, etc., and it is possible that he had also been employed to design the gallery itself. This (very Soanean) gallery is illustrated by W. Carey, *Memoir of the Patronage and Progress of the Fine Arts in England*, 1826, 129 and in *Walpole Soc.* xxxviii, 1960–2, 62.

MIDDLETON PARK, MIDDLETON STONEY, OXON., altered and refaced house with stone, added Ionic portico and designed stables, etc., for 5th Earl of Jersey, 1806–10; dem. 1938 [exhib. at R.A. 1806–7; sketch-book, pp. 25–7, 63, 113, 115; *V.C.H. Oxon.* vi, 243, with illustration] (Neale's *Views of Seats*, 2nd ser., v).

BESSINGBY HALL, YORKS. (E.R.), for Harrington Hudson, 1807 [exhib. at R.A. 1807].

BETCHWORTH HOUSE, SURREY, alterations for Charles Henry Bouverie, 1808 [sketch-book, p. 17].

WYTHAM ABBEY, BERKS., remodelled for 5th Earl of Abingdon, 1809–10, Gothic [sketch-book, p. 21; exhib. at R.A. 1808–9].

HAWARDEN CASTLE (formerly Broadlane House), FLINTSHIRE; remodelled for Sir Stephen Glynne, Bart., 1809–10; castellated [Neale's *Views of Seats*, 2nd ser., v, 1829; exhib. at R.A. 1810] (*C. Life*, 15–21 June 1967).

WYCOMBE ABBEY, BUCKS., greenhouses for 1st Lord Carrington, 1811 [sketch-book, p. 69, reproduced in *Catalogue of R.I.B.A. Drawings Coll.: C–F*, fig. 44].

LONDON, COVENTRY HOUSE, No. 29 (now 106) PICCADILLY (now ST. JAMES'S CLUB), alterations for 7th Earl of Coventry, 1810–11 [papers at Croome Estate Office, F68].

WASSAND HALL, nr. BEVERLEY, YORKS. (E.R.), for the Revd. Charles Constable, 1813–14 [sketch-book, p. 31] (*Trans. E. Yorks. Georgian Soc.* v (i), 1958–61).

HEWELL GRANGE, WORCS., alterations for 6th Earl of Plymouth, including addition of portico, 1815–16; reduced to a ruin *c.*1890 [sketch-book, pp. 3, 5] (Neale's *Views of Seats* vi, 1823).

TARDEBIGGE VICARAGE, WORCS., alterations for 6th Earl of Plymouth, including bowfronted sitting-room, 1815 [sketch-book, p. 12].

COOLMORE, CARRIGALINE, CO. CORK, lodge, etc. for W. H. Newenham, 1815 [sketch-book, pp. 23, 37, 96–99].

FAWSLEY PARK, NORTHANTS., alterations for Sir Charles Knightley, Bart., 1815–16 [sketch-book, p. 7; exhib. at R.A. 1816].

MIDDLETON STONEY RECTORY, OXON., for 5th Earl of Jersey, 1816–17, Tudor Gothic, based on a design made for Lord Jersey by Henry Hakewill in 1812. The stables were added in 1819 to Cundy's design [sketch-book, pp. 120–3; *V.C.H. Oxon.* vi, 244].

WIMBORNE ST. GILES HOUSE, DORSET, alterations for 6th Earl of Shaftesbury, 1816–20, probably including roof of the Stone Hall [R.C.H.M., *Dorset*, v, 95–6].

HANWORTH PARK (now Hotel), MIDDLESEX, Gothic lodges, 1817–18 (? executed)

[1] He had some difficulty in doing this to the satisfaction of the Lord Chamberlain, for whom the building was surveyed by James Wyatt as Surveyor-General, assisted by Thomas Hardwick, George Saunders, John Soane and S. P. Cockerell [Blenheim Palace archives, F.I. 38].

[sketch-book, pp. 116–19].

MONTREAL, nr. WESTERHAM, KENT, rustic cottage for 2nd Lord (afterwards 1st Earl) Amherst, 1818 (? executed).

TOTTENHAM PARK, WILTS., stables for 1st Marquess of Ailesbury, 1818–20 [sketch-book, pp. 110–11, designs dated 1818].

LONDON, NORTHUMBERLAND HOUSE, STRAND, new staircase and rebuilding of garden front for 3rd Duke of Northumberland, 1818–24; dem. 1874 [plan by Cundy of new garden front in Evidence Room at Syon House, B. xv 2. g; *Survey of London* xviii, 17 and pls. 3(b) and 7(b); 'Historical Description of Northumberland House' at Alnwick Castle (C. xiii 1. g)].

SYON HOUSE, ISLEWORTH, MIDDLESEX. Cundy is stated in *D.N.B.* to have carried out works at Syon. As he was being employed at Northumberland House by the 3rd Duke of Northumberland in 1818–24, he was probably the architect responsible for casing the exterior of Syon House in Bath stone in 1819–26. This is supported by the existence in the Evidence Room at Syon of an unexecuted design by Cundy dated 1824 for altering the north side of the house (B. xiii 2. u).

ALTHORP HOUSE, NORTHANTS., THE 'GOTHIC LIBRARY', for 2nd Earl Spencer, 1819–20; dem. 1853 [drawings and correspondence at Althorp].

GARBALLY PARK, BALLINASLOE, CO. GALWAY, for 2nd Earl of Clancarty, *c.*1819 [Northumberland County Record Office ZM1 s. 76/27/44: letter from Lord Clancarty dated 7 July 1819: 'I hear from Garbally that my buildings are proceeding apace; indeed some complaints have reached me that their construction goes on even more rapidly than Mr. Cundy's designs'].

LONDON, BELGRAVE HOUSE, Nos. 15 & 16 GROSVENOR SQUARE, reconstructed for Viscount Belgrave, 1823–4; divided into two houses 1848–9; dem. 1935–40 [*Survey of London* xl, 131].

TOTTENHAM PARK, WILTS., enlarged and remodelled for 1st Marquess of Ailesbury, *c.*1823–6 [Lord Cardigan, *The Wardens of Savernake Forest*, 1949, 296; drawings in Ailesbury family archives].

HAWSTEAD PLACE, SUFFOLK, alterations and additions (chiefly to offices) for Philip Metcalfe (d. 1818), date unknown; dem. [sketch-book, p. 13].

BAYHAM ABBEY, SUSSEX, lodge for 1st Marquess Camden, date uncertain [sketch-book, pp. 100–101].

Note: The additions and alterations designed by Cundy for STANLEY HALL, SALOP., and BURTON HALL, LINCS., were not carried out.

CUNDY, THOMAS, junior (1790–1867), was the eldest son of Thomas Cundy, senior (*q.v.*). As a young man he worked in his father's office, and with him visited Rome in 1816. After his father's death in 1825 he succeeded to his practice and to his position as surveyor of the Grosvenor estate in London. He held this position for forty-one years, in the course of which Belgravia and Pimlico were transformed into a fashionable residential area, largely owing to the speculative enterprise of Thomas Cubitt (*q.v.*).

The two Cundys appear to have formed a single architectural firm, so that until the father's death in 1825 it is impossible to distinguish the son's contribution to the partnership. Though it records works carried out by the elder Cundy as early as 1795, the sketch-book in the R.I.B.A. Collection bears the signature of 'Thomas Cundy junior', and was apparently his work. It may be added that views of BESSINGBY HALL (1807), WYTHAM ABBEY (1809–10) and HAWARDEN CASTLE (1809–10) were exhibited at the Royal Academy under his name, though at the time he was still only in his teens. According to the information supplied to the *D.N.B.* by his son Thomas Cundy III, he was responsible for the works at TOTTENHAM PARK (*c.*1823–6) listed above, and also for alterations to MOOR PARK, HERTS., for his employer the 1st Marquess of Westminster (*c.*1830), and for the embellishment of GROSVENOR HOUSE, UPPER GROSVENOR STREET, LONDON (dem. 1927), first by the enlargement of the picture gallery (1825–7) and then by the addition of the Doric entrance-screen (1842–3), both for the same nobleman [*Survey of London* xl, chap. xiii]. The façade of the GROSVENOR ESTATE OFFICE, No. 53 DAVIES STREET, as remodelled in the late 1830s, must also have been designed by him [*Survey of London* xl, 7, 12].

Another work for which the younger Cundy, rather than his father, was presumably responsible, since it was built in 1826, the year after the elder Cundy's death, was the tower of NORMANTON CHURCH, RUTLAND. This unusual and effective design was copied from a baroque source, the towers of Archer's church of St. John, Smith Square, with which Cundy must have been very familiar [drawings in parish chest in 1947].

From the late 1840s onwards Cundy was assisted by his third son Thomas (1820–95), who eventually succeeded to his practice and surveyorship. Thomas Cundy III had some share in the design of most of the Gothic churches built by his father, namely ST. PAUL,

WILTON PLACE, KNIGHTSBRIDGE, 1840–3; HOLY TRINITY, PADDINGTON, 1844–6, dem. 1984, ST. MICHAEL, CHESTER SQUARE, 1844; ST. MARK, HAMILTON TERRACE (ST. JOHN'S WOOD), 1846–7; ST. BARNABAS, PIMLICO, 1847–50; ST. GABRIEL, WARWICK SQUARE, 1851–3; and ST. SAVIOUR, PIMLICO, 1864. The earlier churches were pre-Puginesque in character: St. Mark's, Hamilton Terrace, was, in Goodhart-Rendel's words, no more than 'a large broad Gothic riding-school'. By 1847, however, the Cundys had produced in St. Barnabas, Pimlico, what the St. Paul's Ecclesiological Society regarded as 'the most sumptuous and correctly fitted church erected in England since the Reformation'.

Towards the end of his life Cundy retired to Bromley in Kent. He died on 15 July 1867, aged 77. [*D.N.B.*; obituary in *Builder* xxv, 1867, 607; *Building News*, 30 Aug. 1867, 598.]

CUNNINGTON, JOHN, was a builder of Spalding in Lincolnshire. In about 1813 he built five terrace houses in LONDON ROAD, SPALDING, followed by eleven more some years later. These were probably the late Georgian houses in WELLAND TERRACE [R. Harmstone, *Notices of Remarkable Events connected with Spalding*, 1846, 41]. In 1820 he designed and built a church at WHAPLODE DROVE, LINCS., which proved to be unsafe, and had to be rebuilt the following year by J. Pacey and W. Swansborough [I.C.B.S.].

CUSTANCE, WILLIAM (–1831), at first a builder and surveyor of Cambridge, was later a surveyor and land agent in London. In 1798 he published a plan of Cambridge, based on that of Loggan (1688), but brought up to date. In Cambridge he was employed by Pembroke College in 1814 to build some houses (dem. 1871) on a site adjoining the college, and he probably designed and built the villas named PEMBERTON'S GROVE LODGE and THE GROVE. The latter is dated 1814 and the rainwater heads have the initials W.C. [Willis & Clark, i, 128; R.C.H.M. *Cambridge*, cxxix, 347, 354 and pl. 299; *Dictionary of Land Surveyors*, ed. P. Eden, 1975, 77.]

CUSWORTH, JOSEPH, was a pupil of Thomas Johnson of Leeds. He afterwards had five years' experience in the office of Peter Atkinson & Matthew Phillips at York. [F. Beckwith, *Thomas Taylor*, Thoresby Society 1949, 89]. He practised in Leeds from about 1815 until after 1840. He enlarged CHAPEL ALLERTON CHURCH, YORKS. (W.R.), in 1819 [Borthwick Institute, York, Fac. 1819/1].

D

DADFORD, THOMAS (–1801), was a canal engineer whose address is at different times given as Wordesley, nr. Stourbridge, Worcs. (1776), Cobridge, Staffs. (1780), Wolverhampton (1800) and Crickhowell, Breconshire (1801). He was elected to membership of the Smeatonian Society of Civil Engineers in 1783 [*Trans. Newcomen Society* xliv, 1971–2, 36]. He was a Roman Catholic, who in 1780 contributed towards the cost of building the Catholic ST. PETER'S CHAPEL at COBRIDGE, dem. 1936 [*Catholic Mag.* v, 1834, 429], for which he may have provided the designs, and in 1800–1 he designed a chapel for the R.C. SCHOOL at SEDGLEY PARK, nr. WOLVERHAMPTON, STAFFS. [F. C. Husenbeth, *History of Sedgley Park School*, 1856, 62; Bryan Little, *Catholic Churches since 1623*, 1966, 53]. He died in 1801 and was buried at Llanarth, Monmouthshire [*Catholic Record Soc.* 12, 1913, 252].

DANCE, GEORGE, senior (1695–1768), was the son of Giles Dance, a mason of London and a member of the Merchant Taylors' Company. Besides building work, Giles executed monumental sculpture, an example of which can be seen in the church of Wotton-under-Edge, Glos. (monument to Richard Dawes, d. 1712). He died in 1751. In his will he is described at being in partnership with his son, and in the 1720s 'Messrs. Dance & Co.' carried out masonry at South Sea House worth over £700. George Dance was born in London in 1695, and was made free of the Merchant Taylors' Company on 2 June 1725. In 1719 he had married Elizabeth, daughter of the surveyor James Gould (*q.v.*), and in 1725–8 he and his father formed part of a consortium of masons who built the church of St. Botolph, Bishopsgate, to the designs of his father-in-law [Guildhall Library MS. 21,130]. In 1735 Dance succeeded the negligent George Smith as Clerk of the Works to the City of London and surveyor of the Bridge House estate. The post, though not then salaried, gave its holder a virtual monopoly of the City's architectural work, together with the appropriate fees, and it was Dance's official position, as much as any other qualifications, that in 1737 led to the acceptance of his designs for the Mansion House in preference to those of Gibbs, James and Leoni. To provide a building of sufficient consequence on an awkwardly constricted site was a difficult task, and it cannot be said that Dance was wholly successful in solving the problem. Externally the result was 'cramped and overdressed' (Summerson), but the interior was more successful and the 'Egyptian Hall' is not without grandeur. Dance's other buildings are respectable but unremarkable Georgian performances in which the influences of Wren, Gibbs and contemporary Palladianism can all be detected. Of these, the church of St. Leonard's, Shoreditch, with a steeple derived from St. Mary-le-Bow, is the most ambitious.

Dance's 'diligence and integrity' as Clerk of the City's Works was rewarded in 1746 by a regular salary of £50 p.a. in addition to his fees. Early in 1768, within a few days of his death on 11 February, he resigned his office in favour of his youngest son George (*q.v.*). He was buried in the church of St. Luke's Old Street on which he had worked as a mason forty years earlier. His eldest son James (1722–74) proved to be indolent and irresponsible, but eventually had some success as an actor under the name of Love. His third son was Sir Nathaniel Dance (afterwards Dance-Holland), R.A. (1735–1811).

A portrait of Dance in his sixties by Francis Hayman is in the Fitzwilliam Museum at Cambridge (reproduced by Stroud, pl. 1). A later portrait by Nathaniel Dance hangs in the Mansion House, to which it was presented by Viscount Bearsted in 1934 (reproduced by S. Perks, *History of the Mansion House*, frontispiece). A number of his drawings for the Mansion House and other buildings are in Sir John Soane's Museum.

[*A.P.S.D.*; *D.N.B.*; Dorothy Stroud, *George Dance, Architect, 1741–1825*, 1971, chaps. 1–2; *George Dance the elder and younger*, catalogue of exhibition at the Geffrye Museum, Shoreditch, 1972.]

For a list of minor and unexecuted works see Stroud, Appendix ii.

LONDON

THE FLEET MARKET, 1736–7; dem. 1829 [A. Stratton, 'Two Forgotten Buildings by the Dances', *Arch. Rev.* xl, 1916, 21].

ST. LEONARD'S CHURCH, SHOREDITCH, 1736–40; galleries removed 1857; altered 1870; restored 1938; damaged 1944 [H. Ellis, *History of the Church of St. Leonard, Shoreditch*, 1798, 9].

SKINNERS' HALL, DOWGATE HILL, decoration of staircase, etc., 1737 [J. F. Wadmore, *Account of the Skinners' Company*, 1902, 133].

THE MANSION HOUSE, 1739–42. For the alterations by George Dance, junior, in 1795–6, including the removal of the attic over the Egyptian Hall, see below, p. 290. The attic over the ballroom was removed in 1842 [*Vitruvius Britannicus* iv, pls. 41–4; S. Perks, *The History of the Mansion House*, 1922].

ST. BOTOLPH'S CHURCH, ALDGATE, 1741–4; altered internally by J. F. Bentley 1888–91 [G. Godwin, *The Churches of London* ii, 1839; drawings in Soane Museum].

ST. MATTHEW'S CHURCH, BETHNAL GREEN, 1743–6; interior remodelled 1859–61 after a fire, when upper stage was added to tower; repaired 1953 after war-damage, when upper stage of tower was removed [drawings in Soane Museum].

LAMB'S CONDUIT, HOLBORN, rebuilt 1746; dem. [Stroud, 43–4].

THE CORN MARKET, MARK LANE, 1747–50; extended 1853; dem. 1881 [Stroud, 42; *Builder* xi, 1853, 340] (*Gent's Mag.* 1753, 111).

COWPER'S COURT, SMITHFIELD, TOM'S COFFEE-HOUSE, THE RAINBOW COFFEE-HOUSE, and two dwelling-houses, for 2nd Earl Cowper, 1748; dem. [plan and elevation in Herts. County Record Office, 1/20029].

ST. LUKE'S HOSPITAL, OLD STREET, 1750–1; rebuilt 1782 [Stroud, 49–50].

LONDON BRIDGE, removal of houses, replacement of two central arches by a single arch, and erection of balustrades and parapets, in collaboration with Sir Robert Taylor, 1756–66; dem. 1831 [Stroud, 52].

THE GREAT SYNAGOGUE, DUKE'S PLACE, ALDGATE, enlarged 1765–6; dem. 1790 [Stroud, 77–8].

ST. MARTIN OUTWICH CHURCH, repairs and rebuilding of steeple after fire, 1766; dem. 1796 [Paul Jeffery, 'The later History of St. Martin Outwich', *London Jnl.* 14 (2), 1989].

ELSEWHERE

COLERAINE, CO. LONDONDERRY, MARKET HOUSE, *c.*1740–3; dem. 1857 [R. Smith, *The Irish Society 1613–1963*, 1966, 82].

CANTERBURY CATHEDRAL, KENT, rebuilt gable of south-east transept, 1751; again rebuilt *c.*1825 [C. E. Woodruff & W. Danks, *Memorials of Canterbury Cathedral*, 1912, 349].

FAVERSHAM CHURCH, KENT, rebuilt nave, 1754–5 [Stroud, 50–1].

DANCE, GEORGE, junior (1741–1825), was the fifth and youngest son of George Dance, senior (*q.v.*). At the age of 17 he went to Italy at his father's expense, sailing from Gravesend in December 1758, and eventually arriving in Rome the following May with his elder brother Nathaniel, whom he had joined in Florence. When he returned to England in December 1764 George had had six years' architectural training in Italy in the course of which he had not only learned to draw very competently but had also absorbed the principles of the new neo-classicism. These are already evident in the design for 'a Public Gallery for Statues, Pictures, etc.', with which he won the gold medal at Parma in 1763. He had also been admitted to the Academy of St. Luke at Rome and had become a member of the Society of Arcadia, a fashionable body of Italian intellectuals.

In England Dance almost immediately obtained a commission for a city church (All Hallows, London Wall) which demonstrated his ability as a practical architect, and in 1768 he succeeded his father as Clerk of the City Works. This post brought him a steady flow of routine municipal work, but it also gave him the opportunity to design his most famous building, Newgate Prison. As city architect he was actively engaged in a number of important town-planning schemes, and for nearly fifty years exercised an enlightened supervision over the growth and redevelopment of the City. Besides the schemes for which he was directly responsible (by no means all of which came to fruition) he effected many minor improvements which cumulatively did much to modify the medieval street plan of London. The first developments for which he was personally responsible were America Square, Minories, and its adjoining Crescent and Circus (1768), and Finsbury Square (1777) and Finsbury Circus (designed 1802, but not carried out until *c.*1814). He also planned Skinner Street, Holborn (1790), Pickett Street, Strand (1793), and Alfred Place, off Tottenham Court Road (1802–10). In 1785 he provided James Hedger, the lessee of the Bridge House property in St. George's Field's, Southwark, with a design for a huge crescent to be built there and named in honour of John Howard, the prison reformer. This was published in the *Gentleman's Magazine* (Sept. 1786), but the development was vetoed by the landlords, and nothing was done until the expiration of Hedger's lease in 1810. In anticipation of this Dance was instructed in 1807 to prepare plans for laying out the property for the Bridge House Committee, and produced two schemes for a series of crescents, circles and polygons filling the spaces between the roads laid out by Robert Mylne on the aproaches to Blackfriars Bridge. For various reasons very little of Dance's plan materialized, but the buildings round St. George's Circus were erected in accordance with his directions. In about 1790 he made designs for the 1st Earl Camden for the layout of the Camden estate in Kentish Town, but after the building of Camden High Street this degenerated into haphazard development. A recurrent feature of Dance's town-planning schemes is the circus and crescent layouts which he transplanted from John Wood's Bath, and which subsequently became a commonplace of London's building development in the late eighteenth and early nineteenth centuries.

From 1796 onwards Dance prepared a series of bold and imaginative designs for the improvement of the Port of London with new docks and warehouses and, in place of the old and narrow London Bridge, two parallel bridges with a drawbridge in each, to enable traffic to cross on one while the drawbridge was raised in the other to give passage to ships. These schemes, illustrated in an appendix to the *Report of the Select Committee upon the Improvement of the Port of London* (*Parliamentary Reports* xiv, 1803, 574–6), found realization only as the subject of a fine engraving by William Daniell (1802), but the simple, monumental character of the warehouses envisaged by Dance was not without influence on the design of those subsequently built by Alexander and others. With Sir Robert Taylor, Dance is said to have been responsible for drafting the Building Act of 1774, which so largely determined the character of London street architecture for the next seventy years, and in 1815, when improvements in the City gaols were contemplated, he visited a number of prisons throughout the country, publishing in 1816 a *Report on Inspection, with a Committee of Aldermen, of Several Gaols of this Kingdom.*

In 1768 Dance was one of the original members of the newly founded Royal Academy. In 1798 he was elected Professor of Architecture, but failed to deliver any of the statutory lectures and resigned in 1805. He was also a Fellow of the Royal Society and of the Society of Antiquaries, and a member of the Architects' Club. In 1794 he was Master of the Merchant Taylors' Company, of which his father and grandfather had both been Freemen. Architecture was by no means Dance's only interest. He played well on the violin, flute and 'cello, and in later life spent much of his time making skilful but rather stereotyped pencil portraits of his contemporaries. Seventy-two of these were engraved by Daniell and published in two volumes in 1808–14 as *A Collection of Portraits sketched from the Life since the Year 1793*, but a further eighty-four prints were made and remain in proof in the British Museum, together with the original drawings. Portraits of fifty-three Royal Academicians by Dance are in the possession of the Royal Academy. For both collections see W. Roberts, 'Portraits by

George Dance' in *Notes and Queries*, 9th ser. iv, 1899, 1–3.

Sir John Soane was Dance's principal pupil. James Peacock was his assistant for many years, and William Mountague was his clerk. When Peacock died in 1814, Mountague took his place as assistant Clerk of the City Works, and when Dance himself retired in 1815, Mountague succeeded him. Dance died at his house in Gower Street on 14 January 1825, and was buried in St. Paul's Cathedral. A portrait by Sir Thomas Lawrence is in the Guildhall Art Gallery and there is an engraved portrait by S. W. Reynolds (1820) after J. Jackson. A self-portrait is reproduced by Stroud (frontispiece). A bust by Rossi was in the possession of the Poynder family (descendants of one of Dance's nieces) in the nineteenth century. There is a plaster version of it in Sir John Soane's Museum.

It is as a pioneer of neo-classicism that the younger Dance has his place in English architectural history. In All Hallows, London Wall (1765–7), an elegant simplification of the entablature demonstrates his awareness of current thinking by Laugier and other French theorists. Already in the '70s he was experimenting with those pendentive vaults which were later to form so characteristic a feature of Soane's personal style. In some of his later works (notably Coleorton Hall and Ashburnham Place) he attempted a curious stripped Gothic style which is more interesting than beautiful, but which (in the age of Wyatt and Nash) amply demonstrates his original and independent approach to architectural design. In Newgate Prison he designed a monumental building of the first rank. In spirit its forbidding walls, unbroken save for blind niches and chain-festooned doorways, were evocative of the *Invenzioni di Carceri* of Piranesi (whom Dance had in fact met in Rome). But Piranesi's fantastic interiors afforded no guidance to the designer of a real prison in which the architectural expression must necessarily be concentrated in the exterior, and here Dance combined themes from Palladio and Giulio Romano to create a façade that forcibly expressed the drama of retributive justice. The result, in contemporary opinion, was a building whose 'nobleness and grandeur approaches the true sublime in architecture'.

There is a large collection of Dance's drawings in Sir John Soane's Museum. This relates chiefly to his private practice. Drawings made by him and his assistants for the City of London's works are in the City Record Office. A copy of Leoni's edition of Palladio in the R.I.B.A. Collection contains a number of architectural sketches by Dance (see the *Catalogue*). Dance's library was sold in 1837. The catalogue is printed in *Sale Catalogues of Libraries of Eminent Persons* iv, ed. Watkin, 1972, 193–216.

[*Gent's Mag.* 1825 (i), 184–5; S. Angell, 'Sketch of the Professional Life of George Dance', *Builder* v, 1847, 333; *A.P.S.D.*; *D.N.B.*; J. Nichols, *Literary Anecdotes* ix, 1815, 522–3; The Farington Diary, *passim*; Sir R. Blomfield, 'The Architect of Newgate', in *Studies in Architecture*, 1905; Helen Rosenau, 'George Dance the Younger', *R.I.B.A. Jnl.* 3rd ser. liv, Aug. 1947, 502–7; John Summerson, *Heavenly Mansions*, 1949, 103–5 (on Dance's town-planning); M. Hugo-Brunt, 'George Dance as Town-Planner', *Jnl. Society of Architectural Historians* (of America), xiv, 1955, 13–22; *Survey of London* xxv (*St. George's Fields*), chap. 6; Dorothy Stroud, *George Dance, Architect, 1741–1825*, 1971; *George Dance the elder and younger*, catalogue of exhibition at the Geffrye Museum, Shoreditch, 1972; Georges Teyssot, *Città e utopia nell' illuminismo inglese: George Dance il giovane*, Rome 1974.]

PUBLIC BUILDINGS IN LONDON

ALL HALLOWS CHURCH, LONDON WALL, 1765–7 [Stroud, 74–77, citing minutes now in Guildhall Library].

WHITECROSS STREET, Coach Houses and Stables for Lord Mayor and City Officers, 1769–71; dem. [Stroud, 87].

SESSIONS HOUSE, OLD BAILEY, 1769–74; dem. 1902 [Stroud, 100–3].

NEWGATE PRISON, 1770–80; damaged in Gordon Riots 1780 and repaired with alterations 1780–4; altered internally 1835 and 1858; dem. 1902 [Stroud, chap. 5; 'Newgate Gaol: Catalogue of Drawings in Sir John Soane's Museum', *Arch. Hist.* ii, 1959] (Britton & Pugin, *The Public Buildings of London* ii, 1828, 54–66; A. E. Richardson, *Monumental Classic Architecture in Great Britain*, 1914, 29).

BRIDGE HOUSE, SOUTHWARK, alterations including new muniment room, 1771–2; dem. [City Records *ex inf.* Mr. H. D. Kalman].

MANSION HOUSE, added small portico to west door, 1775 (removed 1845); roofing over of cortile, removal of Grand Staircase and lowering roof of Egyptian Hall, 1795–6. The plain coffered ceiling inserted in the Egyptian Hall by Dance was enriched by J. B. Bunning in the 1840s [S. Perks, *History of the Mansion House*, 1922, 195–8].

GUILDHALL, new COMMON COUNCIL CHAMBER, 1777–8 (dem. 1908); CHAMBERLAIN'S COURT and OFFICES, 1787–9 (dem. 1882); rebuilt south façade in quasi-oriental style 1788–9; Justice Rooms on west side of

Guildhall Yard 1795–7 (dem. 1969); fitted up banqueting hall for entertainment of the allied sovereigns 1814 (see *Gent's Mag.* 1814 (ii), 179, and the painting by Daniell in the Guildhall Art Gallery) [Stroud, chap. 6 and pp. 219–20].

ST. LUKE'S HOSPITAL, OLD STREET, 1782–9; converted into Bank of England Printing Works 1917–20; dem. *c.*1955–60 [Stroud, 141–2].

SOUTHWARK, THE BOROUGH COMPTER (Debtors' Prison), TOOLEY STREET, 1785–7; dem. 1855 [Stroud, 108–9].

THE GILTSPUR STREET COMPTER (Debtors' Prison), 1787–91; dem. 1855 [Stroud, 109–10; A. Stratton, 'Two Forgotten Buildings by the Dances', *Arch. Rev.* xl, 1916, 23; Dorothy Stroud, 'The Giltspur Street Compter', *Arch. Hist.* 27, 1984].

HONEY LANE MARKET, 1788–9; dem. [Stroud, 147–8].

THE SHAKESPEARE GALLERY, No. 52 PALL MALL, for Alderman John Boydell, 1788–9; from 1805 the British Institution; dem. 1868–9 [A. Stratton, 'Boydell's Shakespeare Gallery', *Arch. Rev.* xli, 1917, 49; *Survey of London* xxix, 335–7; Stroud, 160–2].

ST. BARTHOLOMEW-THE-LESS CHURCH, SMITHFIELD, rebuilt in timber with an octagonal nave, retaining medieval tower, 1789–90, Gothic; rebuilt in stone by Thomas Hardwick, 1823–5, following Dance's plan [Stroud, 158–9].

ST. BARTHOLOMEW'S HOSPITAL, Surgeons' Theatre and other buildings, 1791–6; dem. [Stroud, 157].

MARTIN'S BANK, No. 68 LOMBARD STREET, 1793–5; dem. 1930 [Stroud, 159–60].

LEADENHALL MARKET, alterations, *c.*1795; dem. [Stroud, 149].

SOUTHWARK, COURT HOUSE, TOOLEY STREET, reconstruction of façade, 1796; dem. [Stroud, 109].

BILLINGSGATE MARKET HOUSE, 1798; dem. [Stroud, 149].

BRIDGE HOUSE YARD, WAREHOUSES, 1802–4; dem. [P.R.O., MR 80 (elevation); information from Mr. H. D. Kalman].

ROYAL COLLEGE OF SURGEONS, LINCOLN'S INN FIELDS, in collaboration with James Lewis, 1806–13; rebuilt 1835–7 by Sir Charles Barry, who retained the portico but fluted the columns [Stroud, 193–5].

PUBLIC BUILDINGS ELSEWHERE

BATH, THE THEATRE ROYAL, BEAUFORD SQUARE, elevation and interior of auditorium, 1804–5, for John Palmer, who was responsible for the remainder; interior rebuilt after fire in 1862 [W. Ison, *Georgian Buildings of Bath,* 1948, 102–4; Stroud, 205–6].

MICHELDEVER CHURCH, HANTS., rebuilt nave at expense of Sir Francis Baring, Bart., 1808–10, Gothic; altered 1881 [Winchester Diocesan records, Faculty papers; drawings in Soane Museum].

EAST STRATTON CHURCH, HANTS., wholly or partly rebuilt at expense of Sir Francis Baring, Bart., 1810, Gothic; dem. 1885 [Winchester Diocesan records, Faculty papers: 'according to designs by Sir Francis Baring's architect'; drawings in Soane Museum].

COUNTRY HOUSES

PITZHANGER MANOR, EALING, MIDDLESEX, additions for Thomas Gurnell, 1768; remodelled by Sir John Soane 1800–2 [Stroud, 87–9 and pls. 20–1].

ISLEWORTH, MIDDLESEX, house for Mr. (probably John) Franks, *c.*1770 [statement by Robert Baldwin (*q.v.*) in *The several petitions . . . for and against a bill to remove Chelmsford Gaol,* 1771, Essex C.R.O., D/DBe O1, p. 50].

unidentified house for — Webb, 1772 [Stroud, 92 and pl. 27a].

CRANBURY PARK, HANTS., remodelled principal rooms for Thomas Dummer, *c.*1780 [Stroud, 93–5 and pls. 23–6] (*C. Life,* 25 Oct., 8, 15 Nov. 1956).

CAMDEN PLACE, CHISLEHURST, KENT (now Golf Club House), alterations for 1st Earl Camden, *c.*1788 [J. Newman, *West Kent,* Buildings of England, 1976, 221]; further alterations for Thomson Bonar, 1807 [Stroud, 211].

LANGDOWN HOUSE, HYTHE, HANTS., designs (perhaps not executed) for George Tate, soon after 1790; dem. 1961 [Stroud, 239].

BOWOOD HOUSE, WILTS., minor alterations for 1st Marquess of Lansdowne, *c.*1795; dem. [Stroud, 164].

PAUL, CORNWALL, house designed for (Sir) Rose Price, 1797, but abandoned after foundations had been laid, when Price purchased an existing house at Trengwainton instead [Stroud, 245 and pl. 76b; D. Gilbert, *Parochial History of Cornwall* iii, 1838, 289].

WILDERNESS (now DORTON HOUSE), nr. SEVENOAKS, KENT, alterations, probably for 2nd Earl Camden, *c.*1800; remodelled 1855 [Stroud, 245].

STRATTON PARK, HANTS., remodelled for Sir Francis Baring, Bart., 1803–6; dem. (except portico) 1960 [Stroud, 200–3 and pls. 64–5].

MOUNT STEWART, CO. DOWN, IRELAND, W. wing, including staircase, for 1st Marquess of Londonderry, 1804–5 [G. Jackson-Stops in *C. Life*, 6 March, 1980].

COLEORTON HALL, LEICS., for Sir George Beaumont, Bart., 1804–8, Gothic; upper storey added by F. P. Cockerell 1862 [inscription on roof of porch; D. Stroud, 'George Dance and Cole Orton House', in *The Country Seat*, ed. Colvin & Harris, 1970].

LAXTON HALL, NORTHANTS., entrance hall for George Freke Evans, *c.*1812 [Neale, *Views of Seats*, 2nd ser., i; Stroud, 216].

ASHBURNHAM PLACE, SUSSEX, extensive alterations and additions for 3rd Earl of Ashburnham, 1813–17, externally Gothic; refaced in red brick 1853; dem. 1959; also bridge in park [Stroud, 216–19] (*C. Life*, 16, 23 and 30 April 1953).

KIDBROOKE PARK, nr. EAST GRINSTEAD, SUSSEX, rebuilt south front, with colonnade, for Charles Abbot (later Lord Colchester), 1815 [Abbot's diaries for 1814–15 in P.R.O., Gifts and Deposits, 30/9/35].

DOMESTIC ARCHITECTURE IN LONDON

LANSDOWNE HOUSE, BERKELEY SQUARE, alterations for 1st Marquess of Lansdowne, 1788–91, including library (remodelled by Smirke as a gallery 1816–19); dem. [Stroud, 163–5].

ST. GEORGE-IN-THE-EAST RECTORY, alterations for the Rev. Robert Farington, 1802–4 [Stroud, 206].

HILL STREET, MAYFAIR, No. 33, alterations to Sir Francis Baring's house, 1803; dem. [Stroud, 204].

PICCADILLY, No. 143, for Sir Nathaniel Dance-Holland, 1807–9 [Stroud, 210–11].

ST. JAMES'S SQUARE, No. 10, new kitchen, etc. in garden for Thomas F. Heathcote, 1810 [Hampshire C.R.O., 63 M 84/106] and proposed decoration of octagonal room in house [*Survey of London* xxix, 123].

MONUMENTS

PUTNEY COMMON, obelisk to commemorate the invention of David Hartley's fire-plates, 1788 [Stroud, 241].

WESTMINSTER ABBEY CLOISTER, tablet to Scipio and Alexander Duroure, 1766 [signed] (Stroud, pl. 15).

KEW CHURCH, SURREY, monument to Jeremiah Meyer, R.A., 1790 [signed drawing in B.M. Print Room, reproduced in Geffrye Museum Catalogue, 38].

UNEXECUTED WORKS

For doubtful and unexecuted works see Stroud, 238–45. Dance's designs for LOWTHER CASTLE, WESTMORLAND (1803), are in the Record Office at Carlisle. They do not resemble the sketches illustrated by Stroud (pl. 71c), and it is doubtful whether the latter are connected with Lowther.

Dance's design for the Bedford Charity School (Stroud, p. 238) was not carried out.

DANCE, THOMAS (–1733), is described in his obituary in the *London Magazine* of 1733 as 'an eminent Surveyor and Master-Builder, who built Guy's Hospital in Southwark'. The Minute Books of the Hospital show that on 14 April 1725 it was 'Resolved that Mr. Dance be continued in the employment of Surveyor of the Buildings necessary to this Hospital on the same conditions and with the same salary of Fifteen Guineas per Quarter as was agreed on with him in the Lifetime of Thomas Guy Esq.' The central building (1722–5) which he designed still exists, but was refronted in stone in 1777–8. The east wing was added in 1738–9 by James Steer, the west wing in 1774–7 by R. Jupp (see *Survey of London* xx, 1950, 37–8, where, however, Dance's name is wrongly given as 'Lane' – an error due to a misprint in *Gent's Mag.* 1733, 439). In his will, dated 8 December 1732, Dance is described as living in the parish of St. Paul, Covent Garden, and as being a plasterer by trade. He left considerable property, and made many charitable bequests. He mentions his brothers Richard, William and Joseph, and his nephew Richard Dance, but there is no indication that he was related to Giles Dance (d. 1751) or to his son George [S. Perks, *The History of the Mansion House*, 1922, 218; R. A. Cawson & T. H. E. Orde, 'The Design and Building of Mr. Guy's Hospital', *Guy's Hospital Reports*, vol. 118, 1969, 223–6]. On 21 December 1725 the *Daily Post* reported that 'a fine large Square, to be call'd Leman Square, is to be built in Goodman's Fields [Whitechapel], after a plan drawn by Mr. Dance of Covent Garden', but nothing came of this project. For Thomas Dance's connections with the Pulteney estate in Westminster see *Survey of London* xxxi, 9.

DANGERFIELD, EDWIN JAMES, was presumably the 'J. Dangerfield' who exhibited student's drawings at the Royal Academy in 1808 and 1809. He was then a pupil of either George or Lewis Wyatt, giving their Albany office as his address. In the 1830s he was practising in London as an architect and surveyor. His only known work is the clumsy Greek Revival CLOCK TOWER on the promenade at HERNE BAY, KENT, 1837, which bears the signature 'Edwin J. Dangerfield' (J. M. Crook, *The Greek Revival*, 1972, pl. 213).

DARLEY, JAMES (–1822), was employed as clerk of works at CHARLTON HOUSE, WILTS., during the alterations by Matthew Brettingham (*q.v.*) in 1772–6. An inscription formerly on the roof mentioned Darley's 'careful superintendence' of the works. In 1787–8 he and John Cox were paid over £4000 for landscaping the park at AVINGTON, HANTS., including making a new lake, and at about this time Darley submitted drawings and an estimate for 'intended additions' to the house for the 3rd Duke of Chandos to cost £3952 [Huntington Library, California, ST. BF. 13, *ex inf.* Mr. Edward Saunders and Maps & Plans, 12, *ex inf.* Mr. John Harris]. In 1788 Darley made an estimate for the repair of MALMESBURY ABBEY CHURCH, WILTS. [*Trans. Royal Historical Soc.* x, 1882, 49]. He died at Hullavington, Wilts., in 1822, leaving all his books and architectural drawings to his son John Darley [information from Mr. R. C. Hatchwell].

John Darley practised as an architect, surveyor and land agent in Chippenham. In 1824 he was concerned in proposed alterations to BOX CHURCH, WILTS. [Wiltshire C.R.O., WRO 789/26]. 'John Darley and Sons (R. & J. Darley)' of High Street, Chippenham, are listed as architects in the *Architect's, Engineer's and Building Trades' Directory* of 1868.

DARLY, MATTHIAS, 'Teacher and Professor of Ornament', was primarily an engraver of caricature and ornament. He published, *inter alia*, *A New Book of Chinese Designs*, 1754; *A New Book of Ceilings*, 1760; *The Ornamental Architect . . . consisting of the Five Orders drawn with their Embellishments*, 1770, reissued in 1773 as *A Compleat Body of Architecture* [Eileen Harris, *British Architectural Books and Writers 1556–1785*, 1990, 176–8].

DAUNEY, WILLIAM, was a native of Aberdeen, but spent some time in Jamaica, where he practised as an architect. He returned to Aberdeen in later life and lived in Marischal Street, where he is believed to have designed the house nos. 28–32 (*c.*1770). Archibald Simpson (*q.v.*) was his nephew. [G. M. Fraser, 'Archibald Simpson, Architect, and his Times', *Aberdeen Weekly Jnl.*, 19 April 1918]. In 1802–3 FRASERBURGH OLD CHURCH, ABERDEENSHIRE, was built by William Dauney, builder of Aberdeen [S.R.O., HR 345/5/5].

DAVENPORT, JOHN (–1795) of Burlton Grove near Wem in Shropshire, practised as a landscape gardener and architect during the latter part of the eighteenth century. Evidence of his career comes chiefly from letters he wrote to Warren Hastings in 1790–1 protesting against his dismissal from the latter's employment at DAYLESFORD HOUSE, GLOUCESTERSHIRE [B.L., Add. MS. 29172, ff. 98–9, 155, 198–201, 210–11, 226, 241, 264]. He said in November 1790 that he had then been in business for 22 years, and had been 'imployd in conciderable Buildings of Houses for gentlemen as well as their Grounds &c'. However, 'Hothouses, green Houses &c.' were his speciality, and it was to design garden buildings and to form a lake that he was employed at Daylesford. Here the existing Gothic Orangery appears to have been his work rather than that of S. P. Cockerell, the architect who was simultaneously remodelling the house for Hastings [A. Ginger, 'Daylesford House and Warren Hastings', *Georgian Group's Report & Jnl.* 1989, 97]. Davenport was at CLYTHA HOUSE in MONMOUTHSHIRE for ten days in July 1790 [Add. MS. 29172, ff. 98–99], and the accounts of William Jones of Clytha in the Gwent Record Office [M 413/2114] suggest that it was Davenport and not Nash (*q.v.*) who designed the Gothic folly known as CLYTHA CASTLE which Jones built in 1790, some of whose details resemble those of the Daylesford Orangery [Julia Abel Smith in *Georgian Group Jnl.* 1994, 81–3].

In 1790–1 Davenport was also working at MAWLEY HALL, SHROPSHIRE (Sir Walter Blount, Bart.), BETTISFIELD PARK, FLINTS. (Sir Thomas Hanmer, Bart.) and SCARTHINGWELL HALL, YORKS. (W.R.) (Lord Hawke), where he made a large lake and designed a bridge to cross it. Other clients by whom he claimed to have been employed were the Revd. Thomas Leigh of ADLESTROP PARK, GLOS., Mr. Pennington, and Sir John Read Scott, and he is known to have made plans for alterations at ALLENSMORE COURT, HEREFORDSHIRE, in 1783–4 [N. Kingsley in *C. Life*, 12 Jan. 1989, 112]. In the Gloucestershire County Record Office and the National Library of Wales there are unexecuted plans by Davenport for landscaping at Batsford Park, Glos., and Nanteos, Cardiganshire, respectively, and a collection of drawings for garden buildings connected with MAWLEY HALL (in private possession) includes three by him, one for a classical greenhouse, one for a hothouse and one for a gateway in the style of William Kent. Davenport died at Burlton in March 1795 [Loppington parish register].

DAVIDSON, WILLIAM, was a builder-architect working in Caithness. He added a north 'aisle' with a small cupola to LATHERON CHURCH, CAITHNESS, in 1821–2 [S.R.O., HR 51/1, 6 & 10 April 1821] and designed BOWER CHURCH, CAITHNESS, in 1847–8 [S.R.O., HR 665/1, pp. 14–15].

DAVIES, HUGH, was a master mason in Oxford in the reign of Charles I, but probably came from London, for in 1622–4 a mason of this name was paid £4 for making a dial for LINCOLN'S INN CHAPEL [*The Black Books of Lincoln's Inn*, ed. Baildon, ii, 1895, 451] and in 1625–6 he was working in Whitehall [P.R.O., E 351/3259]. In 1632 Hugh Davies was one of the original (but unsatisfactory) contractors for the building of the CANTERBURY QUADRANGLE at ST. JOHN'S COLLEGE, and in 1636 as 'statuarist' he was employed at BRASENOSE COLLEGE to carve statues of that college's founders [*V.C.H. Oxfordshire* iii, 215, 262]. In 1632–4 Davies was concerned in the design for the western extension of the BODLEIAN LIBRARY, and made a 'great model' of a projected staircase which he took up to London to show to the Chancellor (Archbishop Laud) and the Comptroller of the King's Works (Thomas Baldwin). In the event this was not built, and in December 1640 Davies, described as 'of the Citie of Oxford . . . Architector', disclaimed any further payment 'for all the modills, labours, paynes, travills, care, advise, & skill, by me. . . . bestowed. . . . about the buyldings . . . of . . . the said Universitie' [I. G. Philip, 'The Building of the Schools Quadrangle', *Oxoniensia* xiii, 1948, 47–8; Oxford University Archives WP β 5(5)]. In view of this evidence of his architectural skills, it is possible that Davies had some responsibility for the design of the Canterbury Quadrangle at St. John's as envisaged in 1632, but later modified by an unknown architect [H. Colvin, *The Canterbury Quadrangle, St. John's College, Oxford*, 1988, 44–5].

DAVIES, JOHN (1796–1865), was a pupil of George Maddox [*A.P.S.D.*, *s.v.* 'Maddox']. He began to exhibit at the Royal Academy in 1819, and travelled in Italy in 1820–1 in company with Samuel Paterson (*q.v.*). He subsequently practised from an office in the City of London and became a Fellow of the R.I.B.A. In 1858 he made a second visit to Italy. He died at Grove Hill, Woodford, Essex on 30 April 1865 [Principal Probate Registry, Calendar of Probates; monumental inscription on exterior of Woodford Church]. He was District Surveyor for Tower Hamlets from 1839 until his death.

Davies was a very competent architectural draughtsman. In 1821 the Italian engraver Rossini made a fine etching of the temples at Paestum from a drawing by Davies, and several of the plates in the *A.P.S. Dictionary* were from drawings provided by him. Examples of his draughtsmanship, and evidence of his foreign travels, were provided by the contents of an album sold at Sotheby's on 18 November 1971, and subsequently broken up. Davies was an able designer in the eclectic styles expected of an early nineteenth-century architect. His best works appear to have been Highbury College (Greek Ionic), the Synagogue in Great St. Helen's (with a rich classical interior) and the Baptist Chapel at Abingdon (with a bold façade of the Tuscan order). In 1832 he won the second prize in the competition for Fishmongers' Hall.

HIGHBURY COLLEGE (for Dissenters), ISLINGTON, 1825–6; dem. [exhib. at R.A. 1825; S. Lewis, *History of Islington*, 1842, 191–2, with engraving].

SOUTHGATE, MIDDLESEX, ST. PAUL'S CHAPEL, WINCHMORE HILL, 1827–8, Gothic [exhib. at R.A. 1828].

IPSWICH, SUFFOLK, probably designed THE CONGREGATIONAL CHURCH, ST. NICHOLAS STREET, 1828–9 [*Memoir of Thomas Wilson*, by his son, 1846, 413, 417].

NORTHAMPTON, THE COMMERCIAL STREET CONGREGATIONAL CHAPEL, 1829 [letter-book preserved in the church, *ex inf.* Mr. V. A. Hatley].

RICHMOND, SURREY, THE CONGREGATIONAL CHAPEL, 1830, 'Norman' [*Congregational Mag.* Feb. 1833, 65–71; *Memoir of Thomas Wilson*, by his son, 1846, 417].

FINCHLEY, MIDDLESEX, probably designed THE CONGREGATIONAL CHAPEL, 1830; since much altered [*Memoir of Thomas Wilson*, by his son, 1846, 417–18].

WEST WYCOMBE CHURCH, BUCKS., repairs, 1832 [I.C.B.S.].

STOCKWELL GRAMMAR SCHOOL, LAMBETH, 1833–4, Tudor Gothic [exhib. at R.A. 1833; *Companion to the Almanac*, 1835, 238–42, with illustrations].

THE GROVE, COOKHAM, BERKS., for W. H. Fleming, 1834 [exhib. at R.A. 1834].

BOSSINGTON HOUSE, HANTS., for J. M. Elwes, 1834, Tudor [exhib. at R.A. 1834].

BURE HOMAGE, MUDEFORD, HANTS., for Baroness de Feuchères, 1836; dem. 1956 [exhib. at R.A. 1836 by S. Gompertz as 'erecting from the designs and under the superintendence of Mr. J. Davies', but cf. Donthorne, W. J.].

LONDON, ST. SWITHIN'S LANE, offices for

Solomon Rothschild, 1836 [*Architectural Mag.* iii, 1836, 40; exhib. at R.A. 1836].

LONDON, CORNHILL, MARINE INSURANCE OFFICE, 1837; dem. [*Civil Engineer and Architect's Jnl.* i, 29; exhib. at R.A. 1837].

LONDON, NEW SYNAGOGUE, GREAT ST. HELEN'S, BISHOPSGATE, 1837–8; dem. [*Companion to the Almanac*, 1839, 223; exhib. at R.A. 1837] (*A New Survey of London*, John Weale 1853, ii, 535, view of interior).

LONDON, CROSBY HALL, BISHOPSGATE, restoration of medieval hall and design of new buildings (dem.), *c.*1837–40 [H. J. Hammon, *The Architectural Antiquities of Crosby Place, London*, 1844, 12–13].

ABINGDON, BERKS., THE OCK STREET BAPTIST CHAPEL, 1841 [*Baptist Mag.* 1841, 642].

LONDON, CAMDEN TOWN CONGREGATIONAL CHAPEL, 1843 [*Congregational Mag.*, 1843, 69 and frontispiece].

LONDON, ST. MARTIN ORGAR CHURCH, rebuilt tower, 1851–2[1] [P. Norman, *The London City Churches*, 1923, 29; exhib. at R.A. 1853].

LONDON, ST. MARTIN ORGAR RECTORY, ST. MARTIN'S LANE (E.C.), 1852 [exhib. at R.A. 1853].

LONDON, No. 14 CANNON STREET, façade for Messrs. Fisher, 1854; dem. [drawing sold at Sotheby's 18 Nov. 1971, inscribed 'Fisher's stone front, 14 Cannon Street West erected 1854, J. Davies Archt.'].

DAVIES, REES (–1850), practised at Aberythan, Llandysul, Cardiganshire. He repaired and reseated LLANDYSUL CHURCH in 1829–31 [I.C.B.S.]; designed CAPEL DEWI CHURCH, LLANDYSUL, 1833–6 (altered 1886) [I.C.B.S.]; enlarged BETTWS BLEDRWS RECTORY, CARDIGANSHIRE, 1842–4 [N.L.W., St. David's Bounty, plan 7]; and restored LLANFIHANGEL RHOS-Y-CORN CHURCH, CARMARTHENSHIRE, in 1848–50 [I.C.B.S.]. Davies's son John succeeded to his practice [information from Mr. Thomas Lloyd].

DAVIS, DANIEL (–1819), was a surveyor with an office in Bloomsbury Square, London. In 1809 he exhibited at the Royal Academy a design for rebuilding Covent Garden Market 'with the Piazza restored agreeably to the original intention of Inigo Jones'. His death was reported in *Gentleman's Magazine* 1819 (ii), 187. H. J. Elmes was his pupil.

DAVIS, EDWARD (*c.*1802–1852), was a pupil of Sir John Soane from 1824 to 1826. Soane subsequently described him as 'a very modest, unassuming young man' [A. T. Bolton, *The Portrait of Sir John Soane*, 1927, 226]. He was awarded a medal by the Society of Arts in 1825, and exhibited at the Royal Academy from 1828 to 1844. He practised in Bath, dying there on 30 April 1852, aged 50 [*Gent's Mag.* 1852 (i), 637]. C. E. Davis, City Architect of Bath from 1862 to 1902, was related to him and may have been his nephew.

Davis's earliest recorded work was the Gothic houses on ENTRY HILL, BATH, which he exhibited at the R.A. in 1828 as 'now building'. He subsequently occupied one of them himself. He laid out VICTORIA PARK, BATH, opened 1830, with a Gothic farmhouse and an entrance-screen in the manner of Soane [W. Ison, *The Georgian Buildings of Bath*, 1948, 45]. In 1833 he restored PRIOR BIRDE'S CHAPEL in BATH ABBEY CHURCH, subsequently (1834) publishing a series of engravings entitled *Gothic Ornaments, etc., of Prior Birde's Oratory*, from drawings by S. Burchell (*q.v.*). His exhibits at the R.A. show that he also designed TWERTON HOUSE, nr. BATH, for Charles Wilkins, 1838, and BARCOMBE, PAIGNTON, S. DEVON, for N. H. Nugent, 1838, dem. 1988, and that he remodelled MARSTON BIGOT CHURCH, SOMERSET, in the Norman style for the Hon. and Revd. R. C. Boyle, 1844–5. It was for the latter that in 1836–8 he designed MARSTON BIGOT RECTORY, a substantial house in a free classical style reminiscent of H. E. Goodridge [M. McGarvie in *Ancient Monuments Soc's Trans*, N.S. 26, 1982, 101–2]. In 1846 Davis won the competition for rebuilding LLANDEILO CHURCH, CARMARTHENSHIRE [*Builder* iv, 1846, 329], but the commission eventually went to Gilbert Scott.

DAVIS, JOSEPH GORDON, 'of London', is at present known only for works in Argyllshire: KILMORY CASTLE, which he rebuilt for Sir John Orde, Bart., 1828–36 [Pigot's *Directory of Scotland*, 1837, 230; *N.S.A.* vii, 686–7]; DUNTROON CASTLE, where he carried out various works, including the building of an ice-house at Crinan Ferry, for Neil Malcolm of Poltalloch, 1833–5 [Poltalloch papers, formerly S.R.O., GD 43/80/83 and 85, now Argyll & Bute District Archives, Lochgilphead]; and KILMARTIN CHURCH, a 'perpendicular' Gothic building erected to his designs in 1834–5 [S.R.O., HR 369/1, where his first name is given as 'James'].

DAVIS, VALENTINE (1784–1869), was a pupil of Samuel Robinson and probably also of D. R. Roper. A note in the R.I.B.A. Drawings Collection records that he was the

[1] The church itself had been demolished in 1830. The tower and the adjoining rectory were rebuilt by Davies as one structure.

son of Richard Davis of Davis's Wharf, Horselydown. According to the same source he 'built Portleven Harbour' and 'was much employed by Rennie, MacAdam & Lord Lowther, but till about 40 years of age was not required to follow his profession'. His exhibits at the Royal Academy included a view of Davis's Wharf (1807) and several designs for villas. In the R.I.B.A. Drawings Collection there is a set of drawings of Crosby Hall, Bishopsgate, made by Valentine Davis and Frederick Nash in about 1804 [*Catalogue: C–F*, 76]. Davis died in Islington in 1869, aged 84.

DAVISON, WILLIAM, exhibited at the Royal Academy in 1797 and 1798 from 3 Swinton Street, Battle Bridge, London. In 1816 he published a folio volume entitled *A Series of Original Designs for Shop-Fronts*. In the Avery Library of Columbia University there is an album of 59 designs for public and private buildings dating from about 1825 and entitled 'Memorandum of Mr. William Davison's Designs for Buildings' [John Harris, *Catalogue of British Drawings for Architecture, etc., in American Collections*, 1971, 94].

DAVY, CHRISTOPHER (*c.*1803–1849), practised as an architect and civil engineer in Furnival's Inn, Holborn, where he died on 18 February 1849, aged 46 [*Gent's Mag.* 1849 (i), 439]. He was the author of two architectural publications: *The Architect, Engineer and Operative Builders' Constructive Manual*, 1839, 2nd ed. 1841, and *Architectural Precedents*, 1841. The latter work contains an account of the Building Acts and specifications and working drawings of various typical buildings, including John Newman's Girls' School in Southwark, H. E. Kendall's Spilsby Gaol and Sessions House, an engine factory at Bromsgrove, and the steam-kitchen at the Reform Club.

Davy's own works, as recorded in his exhibits at the Royal Academy, were the Romanesque ST. THOMAS'S CHURCH in THE LIBERTY OF THE ROLLS, CHANCERY LANE, in association with J. Johnson, 1842, dem. 1886 (see *The Surveyor, Engineer and Architect*, 1843, plates at 257); offices at OUNDLE, NORTHANTS., for the Oundle Union Brewery Company, 1841; and the entrance to the EQUITABLE GAS COMPANY'S WORKS in LUPUS STREET, VAUXHALL, 1843. Between 1833 and 1846 he also exhibited several drawings of a topographical character, including (1838) an elevation and section of the steeple of St. Vedast's Church, Foster Lane, 'taken from actual measurement during the recent repairs (1837) under the direction of Mr. S. Angell'.

DAWSON, JOSHUA (*c.*1812–1856), practised in Preston until his death on 7 December 1856, aged 44 [Lancs. C.R.O., Preston Burial Register, PR1 2845/56]. His principal recorded work is ST. BARTHOLOMEW'S R.C. CHURCH, RAINHILL, LANCS., an ambitious classical building erected in 1838–40 at the expense of Bartholomew Bretherton of Rainhill House; campanile added 1849 [*London & Dublin Orthodox Jnl.*, no. 272, 12 Sept. 1840, 174–5] (N. Pevsner, *South Lancashire*, pls. 48–9). For the Earl of Derby Dawson designed buildings in the southern portion of LANCASTER ROAD, PRESTON, for which there is an original elevation in the County Record Office (DD PR 141/9) [C. Hardwick, *History of Preston*, 1857, 427].

DAY, CHARLES, was the only pupil of Thomas Allason (*q.v.*) [*A.P.S.D.*, *s.v.* 'Allason']. He was perhaps the son of a surveyor of the same name who was involved in building DORSET SQUARE and GLOUCESTER PLACE, MARYLEBONE, in the 1820s [deeds in Middlesex Land Registry, *ex inf.* Mr. A. F. Kelsall]. He practised in Worcester, where in the 1830s he held the post of County Surveyor. His principal work there was THE SHIRE HALL, 1834–8, an orthodox Greek Revival design in the manner of Smirke [exhib. at R.A. 1835 and 1838]. He designed two Roman Catholic churches: ST. FRANCIS XAVIER at HEREFORD, 1837–8, and ST. EDMUND, WESTGATE STREET, BURY ST. EDMUNDS, SUFFOLK, 1838 [both exhib. at R.A. 1838]. These are both Grecian designs, but the Chapel which he designed for the nuns of STANBROOK ABBEY, POWICK, WORCS., is said to have been in the 'Georgian Nonconformist' manner [B. Little, *Catholic Churches since 1623*, 1966, 110]. In BURY ST. EDMUNDS he also designed an inn, for which tenders were invited by an advertisement in the *Norfolk Chronicle*, 22 Oct. 1836, *ex inf.* Mr. David Cubitt].

Day's practice was continued by Henry Day (d. 1869), who was probably his son. Henry Day was succeeded in turn by his nephew Ernest Augustus Day (1846–1915) [information from Mr. B. Brotherton].

DAY, JOHN, of Lancashire Hill, Stockport, is described in Baines's *Directory of Lancashire* of 1825 as 'Surveyor of masons' and bricklayers' work'. He rebuilt HAYFIELD CHURCH, DERBYSHIRE, except the tower, in 1818 [Lichfield Joint Record Office, Faculty Papers, 1817], and in association with 'Goldsmith' designed *c.*1810 a simple Grecian villa at COMPSTALL, CHESHIRE (originally called GREEN HILL and now COMPSTALL HALL) for

George Andrew, a calico manufacturer [Twycross, *Mansions of Cheshire*, 1850, ii, 130; P. de Figueiredo & J. Treuherz, *Cheshire Country Houses*, 1988, 226].

DEANE, JAMES (*c.*1699–1765), was a carpenter of Colchester. He was the 'ingenious . . . Mr. James Deane' who drew the plates for Morant's *History of Colchester* (1748), and a volume of architectural drawings in the Essex County Record Office (D/DRc 227) has been identified as his work. It contains designs for farmhouses, barns, cottages and similar buildings, with estimates. Deane is known to have designed the west wing which was added to HOLLYTREES HOUSE, COLCHESTER, for Charles Gray, M. P., in 1748 [Essex C.R.O., D/DRe], and in his will [P.C.C. 327 RUSHWORTH] he bequeathed his books to Gray for the Castle Book Club. They are still preserved in Colchester Public Library, and include editions of Serlio and Palladio, Perrault's *Vitruvius* (1673) and Batty Langley's *Ancient Masonry*. Deane died in August 1765, aged 66, and was buried at All Saints Church, Colchester [information from Mr. J. Bensusan-Butt].

DEANE, JOHN, 'of Reading, surveyor', was paid £10 by the 6th Duke of Somerset in 1683/4 'for surveying and drawing of a Platforme in order to the building a new house' at MARLBOROUGH CASTLE, WILTS. This appears to establish John Deane as the probable designer of the large house which now forms the nucleus of Marlborough School [*Report of the Marlborough College Natural History Soc.* no. 99, 1958–9, 47, 72].

It is possible that John Deane of Reading was related to a family of masons of this name from Uffington in Berkshire, of whom Edward was active in the reign of Charles I and Anthony in that of Charles II, when he undertook several important contracts, e.g. for Horseheath Hall, Cambs., in 1663 [*The Architecture of Sir Roger Pratt*, ed. Gunther, 1928, 119] and Holme Lacy House, Herefs., in 1674 [below, p. 648]. Another John Deane was Master Mason to the City of London from 1696 until his death in 1705. In this capacity he was responsible for all the masonry of the EMANUEL ALMSHOUSES, TOTHILL FIELDS, LONDON (dem. 1893), in 1699–1701, and just before his death for work at the GUILDHALL [R. Gunnis, *Dictionary of British Sculptors 1660–1851*, 1968, 123]. In 1704 he contracted to carry out the masonry of a new house for William Cowper at COLE GREEN, HERTS. (dem. 1801) [L. Stone, 'Cole Green Park' in *The Country Seat*, ed. Colvin & Harris, 1970, 77] and the possibility that he designed this house is discussed by John Brushe in *Arch. Hist.* 24, 1981, 55.

DEARN, THOMAS DOWNES WILMOT (1777–1853), was presumably the Thomas Dearn who was apprenticed to William Thomas (*q.v.*) in 1793 [P.R.O., IR1/36, p. 44], and who exhibited designs for mausolea at the Royal Academy in 1798 and 1799. As 'T. D. W. Dearn' he exhibited in 1806 'a frame containing six designs: a private bath, a cenotaph to the memory of the late Marquis Cornwallis, Gothic entrance, Grecian entrance, villa in the castle style, private chapel and cemetery', and in 1808 a picture entitled 'Tomb of Geraldus, in the Castle court of St. Davids'. He practised at Cranbrook in Kent, where he died on 17 January 1853 [information from Mr. B. R. D. Price].

Dearn was the author of the following works: *Sketches in Architecture, consisting of Original Designs for Public and Private Buildings*, 1806, on the title-page of which he describes himself as 'Architect to the Duke of Clarence'; *Sketches in Architecture, consisting of Designs for Cottages and Rural Dwellings*, 1807; *The Bricklayer's Guide*, 1809, with a dedication to Sir John Soane; *Designs for Lodges and Entrances to Parks, Paddocks and Pleasure-Grounds*, 1811, 1823, dedicated to Sir Walter James, Bart.; *An Historical, Topographical and Descriptive Account of the Weald of Kent*, Cranbrook 1814; and *Hints on an Improved Method of Building*, 1821. He also published an engraving of the interior of Cranbrook Church, 1810 (B.L., Add. MS. 32359, ff. 167, 169), and an aquatint of the Surrey Chapel, Blackfriars Road, 1812 (B.L., *King's Maps* xxvii, 60 *c*). He designed a lodge (illustrated in *Designs for Lodges*, pl. ix) at ANGLEY, nr. CRANBROOK, for Sir Walter James, Bart., in 1809, and in 1808 exhibited at the R.A. his designs for a house called ATTWATERS at HAWKHURST, KENT, for J. D. Mercer. This does not appear to have been built.

DE BERLAIN, D—, submitted a 'Memorial' to the Mayor and Corporation of London in November 1735, in which he stated that 'Having had the honour to serve the Nation above 40 years, and being a Mathematician, Engineer, and Architect', he wished to submit a design for the new Mansion House, in which he had introduced 'the Corinthian, the Britannical, or Protestant, and the Dorick Orders'. He attended in person with his plan, but the Committee 'did not think fit to Receive it, and the same was delivered back to him and he was dismist' [S. Perks, *The History of the Mansion House*, 1922, 169].

At Christ Church, Oxford, there is a design for a large house presented to General John Guise by D. De Berlain in October 1734.

DE CAUX, or **CAUS,** ISAAC, was a native of Dieppe and either a son or a nephew of Salomon de Caux (*c.*1577–1626), a French garden-designer and hydraulic engineer who was in the service of Queen Anne of Denmark and of her son Henry, Prince of Wales, in 1611–12. After Prince Henry's death in November 1612 Salomon de Caux returned to the Continent, and was employed by the Elector Palatine and his English wife Princess Elizabeth to lay out the elaborate gardens at the Castle of Heidelberg (described in De Caux's *Hortus Palatinus a Friderico Rege Boemiae Electore Palatino Heidelbergae exstructus*, Frankfurt, 1620). He eventually died at Paris in 1626 [*D.N.B.*; Thieme-Becker; *History of the King's Works* iii, 124–5]. Isaac de Caux, however, remained in England, where he was naturalized in 1634 [*Huguenot Society's Publications* xviii, 1911, 53]. Like Salomon, he was primarily a designer of gardens and waterworks, but he described himself as 'ingenyeur et architecte', and there is evidence that in the latter capacity he had connections with Inigo Jones. In 1623–4 he constructed a grotto in the basement of Jones's Banqueting House in Whitehall [Per Palme, *Triumph of Peace*, 1957, 66], and in 1633–4 he appears to have been acting as the executant architect of the houses in Covent Garden designed by Jones for the 4th Earl of Bedford. He himself lived from 1630 to 1634 in a newly built house on the Bedford estate in (Little) Russell Street [*Survey of London* xxxvi, 28]. In 1630–3 he designed a grotto in the garden of SOMERSET HOUSE for Queen Henrietta Maria [P.R.O., LR 6/191], and the still existing grotto at WOBURN ABBEY, BEDS., can be attributed to him, for it was constructed for the Earl of Bedford in about 1630, and is unlikely to have been designed by anyone else.

From the service of the Earl of Bedford De Caux moved to that of the 4th Earl of Pembroke, who in 1636 employed him to rebuild the south front of WILTON HOUSE, WILTS., and to lay out an elaborate formal garden in front of it. De Caux's employment at Wilton is documented by a warrant dated 14 March 1635/6 in which the Earl authorizes him 'to take down . . . that side of Wilton House which is towards the Garden and such other parts as shall bee necessary & rebuild it anew with additions according to the Plott which is agreed'. Here, as at Covent Garden, there is reason to think that Inigo Jones was in the background, for John Aubrey says that it was on Jones's recommendation that De Caux ('an ingeniouse architect') was employed, and that the latter performed his task 'very well; but not without the advice and approbation of Mr. Jones'. The grand scheme for a classical façade nearly 400 feet in length (made probably before the death of Pembroke's son Charles in January 1634/5) is represented by a drawing in the library of Worcester College, Oxford. Only half of it was carried out, in the form of the existing south front with its pavilion towers, originally apparently with low pyramidal roofs, as in the likely Italian source, an engraving in Scamozzi's *Idea della Architettura Universale* of 1615. This building was gutted by fire in 1647 or 1648, after which the interior was rebuilt by John Webb, again 'by the advice of Inigo Jones'. Though the façade of the house was curtailed, the garden layout was fully carried out, and a few years later De Caux published a set of 26 engravings entitled *Wilton Garden* (n.d.). He presumably designed the grotto illustrated in *Vitruvius Britannicus* ii, pl. 65 [H. M. Colvin, 'The South Front of Wilton House', *Archaeological Jnl.* cxi, 1955; A. A. Tait, 'Isaac de Caus and the South Front of Wilton House', *Burlington Mag.* cvi, 1964, 74; Glenys Popper & John Reeves, 'The south front of Wilton House', *Burlington Mag.* cxxiv, 1982; John Bold, *Wilton House and English Palladianism*, R.C.H.M. 1988; H. Colvin, 'Isaac de Caus, Dominick Pyle and the Gardens at Wilton House', *Wiltshire Archaeological Mag.* 85, 1992].

In 1639 Nicholas Stone (*q.v.*) supplied 11½ feet of white marble cornice for the Earl of Pembroke by De Caux's order, no doubt for use at Wilton, and in 1637 it was also by De Caux's order that he made a black and white marble chimney-piece for the Countess of Home's house in Aldersgate Street, London [*The Note-Book of Nicholas Stone*, ed. W. L. Spiers, *Walpole Soc.*, 1918–19, 117, 127].

The only other building for which De Caux is known to have furnished designs is STALBRIDGE PARK, DORSET. In 1638 the 1st Earl of Cork gave £5 to 'Monsieur decon [*sic*] the french architect who belongs to my L. chamberleyn [i.e. Pembroke] . . . for drawing me a plott, for contriving my new intended buylding over the great sellar at Stalbridge' [*Lismore Papers*, ed. A. B. Grosart, 1st ser., v, 1886, 64]. Nothing remains of the seventeenth-century house at Stalbridge, and no representation of it has so far come to light.

According to Aubrey the Earl of Pembroke rewarded De Caux with a pension 'of, I think, a hundred pounds per annum for his life, and lodgings in the house'. Aubrey adds that he 'died about 1656' and that 'his picture is at Mr. Gauntlet's house at Netherhampton' [*The Natural History of Wiltshire*, ed. Britton, 1847, 83–4]. The will of his mother Mary de Caus, dated 18 July 1655, shows that he was still alive in that year [P.C.C. 377 AYLETT].

In 1644 De Caux had published a book entitled *Nouvelle Invention de lever l'eau plus hault que sa source avec quelques machines mouvantes par le moyen de l'eau et un discours de la conduite d'icele, par Isaac de Caus, Ingenyeur, natif de Dieppe. Imprimé à Londre l'an 1644.* An English translation by John Leak was published in London in 1659. The original drawing for the title-page of 1644 is in the Burlington-Devonshire Collection in the R.I.B.A. Drawings Collection, together with an elevation for the south front of Wilton House attributed to De Caux. The attribution is supported by the existence in a private library of a copy of De Caux's *Wilton Garden* with an extra plate which is an engraved version of this drawing without the stairs, the balustrade or the dormer windows, and with a pedimented attic feature which is roughly erased in the drawing. Other drawings attributed to De Caux are in the Clarke Collection at Worcester College, Oxford.

DECKER, P—, 'Architect', is the name on the title-pages of two pattern-books published in 1759, one entitled *Chinese Architecture, Civil and Ornamental. . . . adapted to this Climate*, the other *Gothic Architecture Decorated, consisting of a large Collection of Temples, Banqueting, Summer and Green Houses, etc. . . . likewise Designs of the Gothic Orders . . . and Rules for Drawing them.* Most of the plates in the former work were reused from *A New Book of Chinese Designs* by Edwards and Darly, published in 1754, while the Gothic designs resembled those of Halfpenny, Charles Over and Stephen Wright. No architect of this name has been identified, and it is possible that 'P. Decker' was a fictive name to cover a piece of derivative publishing [Eileen Harris, *British Architectural Books and Writers 1556–1785*, 1990, 178].

DEERING, J. P., see GANDY, J. P.

DEFFERD, JAMES (*c.*1750–1813), is said to have come of a Somerset family, but to have settled near Bangor in about 1790 and to have worked on the Penrhyn estate. According to J. Evans, *The Beauties of England and Wales* xvii (i), 1812, 245, 257, he designed PENRHOS HALL, ANGLESEY (dem.), for Lady Stanley, and added wings to BODORGAN, ANGLESEY, for O. P. Meyrick. Plans by him for PENNANT, DENBIGHSHIRE, are in the National Library of Wales [*ex inf.* Mr. T. Lloyd]. In 1795–6 ABERGLASLYN BRIDGE at BEDDGELERT, CAERNARVONSHIRE, was widened under his direction [R.C.A.M., *Caernarvonshire* iii, 127–8]. Defferd died at Llandegai in 1813 [*Gent's Mag.* 1814 (i), 523; Llandegai Parish Register in National Library of Wales].

DE GOMME, Sir BERNARD, *see* GOMME, Sir Bernard de.

DE GREY, EARL, *see* GREY, THOMAS PHILIP.

DE KEYSER, WILLEM (1603–), was one of the three sons of Hendrik de Keyser, architect and sculptor of Amsterdam. He was a talented sculptor and was for some years Master Mason to the city of Amsterdam. He came to England in 1621, probably to be apprenticed to Nicholas Stone (who had married his elder sister Maria in 1613), and while in this country married Walburga Parker. He returned to Amsterdam in 1640, but was back in England at the time of the Restoration [*Nicholas Stone's Note-Book*, ed. Spiers, *Walpole Soc.* vii, 32–3; Thieme-Becker, xx, 235; Elizabeth Neurdenburg, *De Zeventiende Eeuwsche Beeldhouwkunst in de Noordelijke Nederlanden*, Amsterdam 1948, 143–52]. Very little is known about his work in England, much of which was probably monumental sculpture, but in 1661 he was paid £2 by the Paymaster of the King's Works 'for drawing the draughts with the uprights for the intended Building at Greenwich' [P.R.O., WORK 5/2, under Whitehall, July 1661]. This was an abortive scheme for Charles II's intended palace at Greenwich, afterwards superseded by John Webb's design of 1663. Willem was still living in London in 1674, and in 1678 was admitted to the Masons' Company as a 'foreign member' [D. Knoop & G. P. Jones, *The London Mason in the Seventeenth Century*, 1935, 71], but the place and date of his death are not known.

DE LABRIÈRE, ALEXANDRE LOUIS, *see* LABRIÈRE, A.L. de.

DE LA ROCHE, PETER, a native of Geneva, was the author of *An Essay on the Orders of Architecture*, published in 1769, in which he put forward a new version of the Composite Order and also a 'Britannic Order' commemorating the Battle of Crécy. In the introduction he explained that, although he had received no architectural training, he had always been interested in architecture and now intended to devote himself to it [Eileen Harris, *British Architectural Books and Writers*

1556–1785, 1990, 179–80]. He competed for the Royal Exchange in Dublin in 1769 [*Builder* xxvii, 1869, 781].

DELIGHT, EZEKIEL, was appointed one of the District Surveyors for London in 1774. He became Surveyor to the Amicable Assurance Company, and designed their premises in Serjeants' Inn, Fleet Street, in 1793 [*N. and Q.*, 11th ser., vi, 67; records of the Amicable Assurance Co. now in possession of the Norwich Union Life Insurance Society]. This very competently designed building, with a façade in the style of Chambers, is illustrated in *The Parlour Book of British Scenery, Architecture and Antiquities*, 2nd ser., 1828, and in A. E. Richardson & C. L. Gill, *London Houses from 1660 to 1820*, 1911, pl. lxxx. The death of Delight's wife was reported in *Gent's Mag.* 1805 (ii), 1182.

DEMPSTER, GEORGE, of Greenock, was a wright by trade. He designed and built the GAELIC CHURCH, CAMPBELTOWN, ARGYLLSHIRE, 1803–6. The original steeple was destroyed by lightning in 1830 and partially rebuilt in 1884–5 [S.R.O., HR 67/1, pp. 44, 46–8; R.C.A.M., *Argyll* i, 105 and pl. 20B].

DEMPSTER, JAMES, is listed as Greenock's only architect in Pigot's *Directory* of 1825–6. In GREENOCK he designed the BLACKHALL STREET CHAPEL, 1823, and the EPISCOPAL CHAPEL, GOUROCK STREET, 1824, Gothic [Daniel Weir, *History of Greenock*, Greenock 1829, 20]. He was also the architect of KILMACOLM PARISH CHURCH, RENFREWSHIRE, 1830–1 [S.R.O., HR 306/1, p. 72, etc.], and (it is said) of CATHCART PARISH CHURCH in the same county, 1830–1, Gothic, dem. except tower *c.*1929. In 1828–9 he superintended the building of MAUCHLINE CHURCH, AYRSHIRE, to a Gothic design made by a local gentleman, William Alexander of Southbar, and made some modifications that were approved by the heritors [S.R.O., HR 443/2]. The BUTE COUNTY BUILDINGS at ROTHESAY were erected to his designs in 1832–3 in a castellated style; enlarged 1865–7 [Scottish Civic Trust, *Historic Buildings at Work*, 1983, 169, citing Argyll & Bute District Archives].

DENHAM, Sir JOHN (1615–1669), Surveyor-General of the King's Works from 1660 to 1669, was 'a celebrated Poet, and an eminent Royalist'. It was as a reward for his loyalty that he obtained the surveyorship, which he claimed had been promised to him by Charles II in 1649. Evelyn, who disagreed with Denham over the siting of Greenwich Palace, described him as 'a better poet than architect', and John Webb, who as Jones's pupil and deputy had hoped to succeed to the latter's post at the Restoration, protested that 'though Mr. Denham may, as most gentry, have some knowledge of the theory of architecture, he can have none of the practice, but must employ another'. The person so employed was Webb himself, who is referred to as Denham's deputy in May 1664 [P.R.O., WORK 5/5], and who, in November 1666, was placed in charge of the works at Greenwich Palace as Denham's assistant, 'to execute, act, and proceed there, according to your best skill and judgment in Architecture'. In March 1669, at the King's request, Denham made Wren his 'sole Deputy', and it was Wren who took his place at the Board of Works when he died two weeks later [*History of the King's Works* v, chap. 1].

Though Denham appears (until his mental illness in 1666) to have been a competent administrative head of the Office of Works, there is no evidence that he ever attempted to design a building. During his surveyorship Webb and Samwell acted as the King's architects for Greenwich and Newmarket, respectively, and the house which Denham began to build in Piccadilly in 1665 (afterwards Burlington House) was probably designed by one of his subordinates in the Office of Works [*Survey of London* xxxii, 391]. It is, therefore, only because he held the same office as Inigo Jones and Sir Christopher Wren for eight and a half years that Denham figures in this *Dictionary*. For a full account of his career as a poet and politician see *D.N.B.* and *The Poetical Works of Sir John Denham*, ed. T. H. Banks (Yale 1928).

DENSTONE, JAMES (1724–1780), of Derby, was a member of a family of plasterers, of whom the best-known was his brother Abraham (d. 1779), who worked for Robert Adam at Kedleston. James was apprenticed to Solomon Brown, a mason and bricklayer, became a freeman of Derby in 1748, and was buried at All Saints Church on 17 September 1780. He is described in local records as 'builder' or 'architect'. Circumstantial evidence suggests that he may have designed and built MARKEATON HALL, a rather clumsy Georgian house near Derby (dem. 1965), for Wrightson Mundy (d. 1762) [information from Mr. Maxwell Craven; G. Beard, *Craftsmen & Interior Decoration in England 1660–1820*, 1981, 256].

DENT, JOHN, 'a native of this town', is stated by John Askew in his *Guide to Cockermouth*, Cockermouth 1866, 6, to have designed the MARKET HALL at COCKERMOUTH, CUMBERLAND, 1835–8. It was in the style of John Foster's St. John's Market in Liverpool. Masons called John and Arthur Dent had been employed in rebuilding the chancel (subsequently destroyed by fire) of HOLM CULTRAM CHURCH, CUMBERLAND, in 1603 [Cumberland C.R.O., PR/122/34].

DERING, HENEAGE (1665–1750), was a wealthy and well-connected clergyman who, after serving as secretary to Archbishop Sharp of York, obtained a number of ecclesiastical preferments, including a canonry at York and the deanery of Ripon, to which he was appointed in 1711 [*D.N.B.*]. Dering was an able and intelligent man who published two poems in Latin verse, and there is some reason to think that he was an amateur architect. Among the Brewster papers in the North Yorkshire Record Office there are plans for a new house at ALDBY PARK, YORKS. (E.R.), the seat of John Brewster, endorsed 'Doct. Dering's Plan for a House'. They are accompanied by a letter from Dering in which he calls himself 'a well wisher to Architecture' and from which it is clear that he drew them himself. They were not adopted when Aldby was rebuilt in 1726, and the name of the architect employed is not known (*C. Life*, 13–20 Feb. 1986). Some further evidence of Dering's building activities is afforded by his autobiographical memoranda, printed in *Surtees Society* lxv (1875). Immediately after his institution to the rectory of SCRAYINGHAM, YORKS. (E.R.), in 1704 he 'began to rebuild the parsonage house, the old one being ruinous'. Later the same year he 'staid at BISHOPTHORPE, and took care of the alterations then making in the house' (by Archbishop Sharp). At the DEANERY in RIPON he was responsible for 'the brick building towards the garden', completed in 1715.

DESVIGNES, PETER HUBERT (1807–1883), was born in London in April 1807 and became a pupil of William Atkinson (*q.v.*). He entered the Royal Academy Schools in 1823, and was awarded a premium by the Society of Arts for an architectural design the same year. He exhibited at the R.A. from 1824 to 1832, and competed for the Houses of Parliament in 1835. No building designed by him in Britain has so far been identified, but in the late 1830s and 1840s he was working for the Prince of Liechtenstein, for whom he designed, *inter alia*, the rococo interiors of the PALAIS LIECHTENSTEIN in VIENNA, 1836–47, and a glass-house at LEDNICE, MORAVIA, 1842–8, based on English examples like that of the Duke of Devonshire at Chiswick [R. Wagner-Riezer, *Wiens Architektur im 19 Jahrhundert*, Vienna 1970, 135–6 and D. Kusák, *Lednice*, Prague, 1986].

A volume of drawings by Desvignes, mainly of stage sets in an accomplished eighteenth-centry style, was seen on the London art-market in 1985. He died at Hither Green, nr. Lewisham, on 27 December 1883, leaving an estate valued at £21,000 [Principal Probate Registry, Calendar of Probates].

DEWHURST, JOHN (1806–?1886), practised in Preston, where in 1841 he was living in Dewhurst Street, presumably a speculative development of his own building. He was then Surveyor of Bridges of the Hundred of Leyland. In Preston he designed a POLICE STATION (dem.) in AVENHAM STREET, 1832 [P. Whittle, *History of Preston* ii, 1837, 140], and the castellated GOVERNOR'S HOUSE of THE PRISON in STANLEY STREET in 1834 [C. Hardwick, *History of Preston*, Preston 1857, 440]. He also designed the Lancashire churches of BLEASDALE, 1835–6, and OUT RAWCLIFFE, 1837–8 [I.C.B.S.], and was presumably the 'Dewhurst' who was the builder and probably the designer of AINSWORTH CHURCH, LANCS., 1831–2 [I.C.B.S.]. Bleasdale Church is in the lancet style, but Out Rawcliffe is described by Pevsner as being 'a very individual building, Prussian rather than English', with two tiers of small round-arched windows and four corner-turrets (*North Lancashire*, Buildings of England, 185). Dewhurst was presumably the 'John Dewhurst, gentleman,' of Preston, whose death on 14 June 1886 is recorded in the Calendar of Probates of the Principal Probate Registry.

DE WILSTAR, JOHN JACOB, was a surveyor frequently employed by the Corporation of Bristol in the second quarter of the eighteenth century. In 1740 he submitted a design for a new Exchange, but it was not accepted [W. Ison, *The Georgian Buildings of Bristol*, 1952, 96]. De Wilstar's drawing of the garden front of REDLAND COURT, nr. BRISTOL, is in the British Library (*King's Maps* xiii, 77-3-*b*). In 1723 he made 'A new dessein' for rebuilding HEPPINGTON HOUSE, NACKINGTON, KENT, for Bryan Faussett, but the house (dem. *c.*1970) was not rebuilt until 1732. De Wilstar's drawings are preserved in a scrapbook in the possession of the Godfrey-Faussett family in the Isle of Wight [*ex. inf.* the late Rupert Gunnis].

De Wilstar may possibly have been identical with a Norwegian architect called 'Devolster' who is said in a pamphlet by a Bristolian called Josias Bateman (*A Just and*

True Relation of Josias Bateman's Case, 1732) to have been sent over to Lismore in Ireland by Lord Burlington in the 1720s [*ex inf.* Dr. T. A. Barnard].

DEYKES, JOHN, was a native of Great Malvern, where his father, Samuel Deykes, appears to have been a builder. He became a pupil of George Smith (*q.v.*) in London, and exhibited student's designs at the Royal Academy between 1810 and 1815. He subsequently practised in London, carrying out alterations to the east end of ST. BRIDE'S CHURCH, FLEET STREET, in 1822–3 [W. H. Godfrey, *The Church of St. Bride, Fleet Street*, Survey of London 1944, 54]. A statue of Guy, Earl of Warwick, in Warwick Lane, London, restored by 'J. Deykes, Archt.' in 1817, is illustrated by T. H. Shepherd in *London in the Nineteenth Century* (1829). In GREAT MALVERN the elder Deykes designed the FOLEY ARMS HOTEL in 1810 and was active in developing the town as a resort, while the son designed THE BATHS, THE ASSEMBLY ROOMS and THE CIRCULATING LIBRARY, 1819–23. Described by Britton and Pugin (*Public Buildings of London* i, 1825, 127) as 'the tasteful improver of Great Malvern', John Deykes is also credited with the design of a number of houses in that town, including Oriel House, Spa Lodge, Edith Lodge, Graham Place and houses in Worcester Road. [Mary Southall, *A Description of Malvern*, 1822 and 1825; B. S. Smith, *A History of Malvern*, Leicester 1964, 178–9, 181, 219].

DICKINSON, WILLIAM (*c.*1671–1725), is presumed to have been the son of William Dickinson, Chief Clerk of the King's Works from 1660 until his death in 1702, but there is no proof that the two Dickinsons were related. In November 1696 the younger Dickinson was appointed Clerk of the Works at Greenwich Palace, a post which came to an end in 1701 or 1702 following the establishment of the Royal Hospital. It is also in 1696 that he first appears in the accounts of St. Paul's Cathedral as assisting John Oliver, Wren's deputy, as a measurer. He continued in this employment after Oliver's death in 1701, and was described in 1711 as 'clerk for taking the accounts of several materials for the said building' [Hist. MSS. Comm., *Portland* x, 106]. During the early years of the eighteenth century he acted as Wren's assistant in connection with the rebuilding of the City churches, and his entertainment is mentioned in the records of several parishes. He was also, as Wren's deputy, employed in measuring the repairs to Westminster Abbey from 1700 onwards [Bodleian Library, MS. Gough Westminster 1], and in February 1710/11 he succeeded James Broughton both as Deputy Surveyor of the Fabric and as Surveyor to the Dean and Chapter of Westminster. In this dual capacity he was responsible between 1719 and 1722 for the repair of the north transept of the Abbey Church, including the reconstruction of the rose window and porch, and in 1722 for the erection of iron railings 'in the Gothick manner' across the latter. His drawing of the transept, as approved by Wren, is reproduced in *Wren Soc.* xi, pl. ii, and he initials a design for a proposed central tower over the crossing (pl. v). He also made a number of designs (the earliest dated 1711) for the new Dormitory of Westminster School, which was eventually built in 1722 to Lord Burlington's design (*Wren Soc.* xi, pls. x–xxi).

In 1711 Dickinson was, with Nicholas Hawksmoor, appointed one of the Surveyors to the Commissioners for Building Fifty New Churches in London. In January 1712/13 he 'laid two Models of Churches before the Commissioners', and the plan for a proposed church on the site of St. Mary le Strand (*Wren Soc.* x, pl. 13) is in his hand, but none of the new churches were built to his designs, and in 1713 he resigned to return to the Office of Works as Clerk of the Works at Whitehall, St. James's and Westminster. Two years later he lost this post in the purge following the introduction of Lord Halifax's Orders, but he retained his position as Surveyor to Westminster Abbey until his death on 24 January 1724/5, at the age of 54. He was buried outside the north porch of the Abbey, under a stone (now destroyed) with the inscription: H.S.E./GULIELMUS DICKINSON ARM. ARCHITECTUS;/QUALIS! SUSPICE./OBIIT 24° DIE JANUARII A.D. 1724/SUAEQUE AETATIS 54. The Chapter Book records the payment of 15 guineas to his widow for some of his drawings, including the surviving design for a central tower and one for a 'West Tower', now lost.

Dickinson was, like Hawksmoor, a pupil of Wren, and in a letter to the Duchess of Marlborough written in 1711, Wren's son described him as 'a person that has served [my father] with great fidelity, diligence and skill' [B.L., Add. MS. 61357, ff. 11–12]. Most of his working life was spent in the performance of the duties of a surveyor or clerk of works rather than in designing new buildings. Few important commissions appear to have come his way, and as a creative architect he has consequently to be judged almost entirely from his unexecuted designs. These make it clear that he was a competent, though not particularly adventurous, designer of the English baroque school. Most of his surviving drawings are to be found in the Gough Collection in the Bodleian Library. Besides many drawings connected with WESTMINSTER ABBEY (Gough Maps 23 and 41 G, ff. 14–19), attention may be drawn to the following: Baron Shutte's house (? in Westminster), 1705 (Gough Maps 22, f. 72); a design for a country house for Sir Charles Pye at CLIFTON CAMPVILLE, STAFFS., 1710 (Gough Gen. Top. 63, p. 440); an unexecuted design for WITNEY RECTORY, OXON., for Dr. Robert Freind, headmaster of Westminster School, 1711 (MS. Top. Oxon. a. 39, ff. 162–4); a plan of a church at LEEDS, 1722 (Gough Maps 227); a plan of Captain Tufnell's house at NORWOOD (Gough London 127, p. 322); and a miscellaneous sketchbook (MS. Gough Misc. Ant. 17). Two drawings in the Soane Museum show his own (rejected) and Colen Campbell's (successful) designs for PEMBROKE HOUSE, WHITEHALL, side by side (*Wren Soc.* xvii, pl. xlviii, where the building is wrongly identified as Ashburnham House). The design for a pair of houses reproduced in *Architectural History*, vol. 10, fig. 102, and a plan and elevation of a church reproduced by J. Harris, *Catalogue of British Drawings for Architecture etc. in American Collections*, pl. 66, have been attributed to him. Dickinson's interest in Gothic is shown by a number of drawings in that style for Westminster Abbey, and by an unexecuted design by him for a Gothic tower for ST. MICHAEL'S, CORNHILL (*Wren Soc.* x, pl. 9). Similarities between the pinnacles of the tower of ST. MARY, ALDERMARY and those envisaged in Dickinson's design for the central tower of Westminster Abbey suggest that at least the detailing of the former tower was due to him. [*Wren Soc., passim* (see index); *History of the King's Works*, v, *passim; Westminster Abbey Registers*, ed. J. L. Chester, Harleian Soc. 1876, 312; J. Dart, *Westmonasterium*, vol. i, book 2, chap. 3, 58; *V.C.H. Essex* vi, 191, n. 91 (for his marriage); will in Westminster City Library, No. 1895; Timothy Benton, 'Wren, Dickinson and the Westminster Abbey Repairs', in *A Gothic Symposium*, Georgian Group, 1983.]

DICKSON, RICHARD (1792–1857) and ROBERT (*c.*1794–1865), were the sons of John Dickson (1766–1828), an Edinburgh builder. Their mother was Mary Crichton, daughter of James Crichton, mason, and sister of the architect Richard Crichton (*q.v.*). Richard and Robert Dickson were probably pupils of their uncle, and took over his practice at 10 James Street, Edinburgh, when he died in 1817.

Like their predecessor, the two Dicksons were able designers in a variety of styles. They provided their clients with Gothic churches, Grecian academies or castellated houses with equal facility. Their Gothic work is richly detailed but not at all scholarly, and quite unaffected by Puginesque principles. On the other hand their Town Hall at Leith is a most successful synthesis of Renaissance and Greek Revival motifs in the manner of which C. R. Cockerell was the master. Their destroyed Veterinary College in Edinburgh appears to have been a building of similar quality.

Richard Dickson and his parents are commemorated by a monument in the Old Calton Burial Ground in Edinburgh. For the relationship of the Dickson and Crichton families see also Scottish Record Society, *Roll of Edinburgh Burgesses*, 1933.

CHURCHES AND PUBLIC BUILDINGS

KILCONQUHAR CHURCH, FIFE, 1820–1, Gothic [*N.S.A.* ix, 333]. The Heritors' Records show that they wanted the church to be copied from the new church at Cockpen, Midlothian, which the Dicksons were then building to the designs of Richard Crichton [S.R.O., HR 194/3].

EDINBURGH, CHURCH (later ST. DAVID'S) in GARDNER'S CRESCENT, 1827; dem. [S.R.O., CS 96/746/1].

LEITH, MIDLOTHIAN, THE TOWN HALL, 1827–8 [signed 'R. & R. DICKSON ARCHITECTS'] (A. E. Richardson, *Monumental Classic Architecture in Great Britain*, 1914, pl. xxxiv).

EDINBURGH, TRON CHURCH, rebuilt steeple after fire (1824), 1828 [*A.P.S.D., s.v.* 'Edinburgh'].

THE BATHGATE ACADEMY, BATHGATE, WEST LOTHIAN, 1831–3 [Thomas Davidson, *Bathgate Academy 1833–1933*, Bathgate 1933, 20–1].

EDINBURGH, THE VETERINARY COLLEGE, CLYDE STREET, 1833; destroyed by fire 1953 [O. Charnock Bradley, *History of the Edinburgh Veterinary College*, Edinburgh 1923, 31].

MUTHILL, PERTHSHIRE, ST. JAMES'S EPISCOPAL CHURCH, 1836 [*The Scottish Episcopal Church Year Book*, 1973–4, 284].

LEITH, MIDLOTHIAN, DR. BELL'S SCHOOL, GREAT JUNCTION STREET, 1839, Tudor Gothic; recons. 1890–2 [advt. for tenders in *Edinburgh Evening Courant*, 19 Nov. 1838].

COLLESSIE CHURCH, FIFE, 1839, Gothic [S.R.O., HR 36/1, p. 101, etc.].

DUNKELD, PERTHSHIRE, THE DUCHESS OF ATHOLL'S INDUSTRIAL SCHOOL, 1853 [drawings at Blair Castle].

KINCARDINE SCHOOL, PERTHSHIRE, 1855–6 [S.R.O., HR 275/1].

BLAIR ATHOLL, PERTHSHIRE, THE 'ATHOLL ARMS'

HOTEL, 1856 [drawings at Blair Castle].

LOGIERAIT, PERTHSHIRE, school for 6th Duke of Atholl, 1863 ['by the Duke of Atholl's architect', S.R.O., HR 38/2].

DOMESTIC ARCHITECTURE

EDINBURGH, NORTH BRIDGE, row of shops, 1817 [drawings in City Architect's Office].

ABERCAIRNY ABBEY, PERTHSHIRE, completed house, begun by R. Crichton, for James Moray (d. 1840) and William Moray (d. 1850), Gothic; dem. 1960 [Mark Girouard in *C. Life*, 9–16 March 1961].

CORTACHY CASTLE, ANGUS, addition of Gothic porch for 8th Earl of Airlie, 1820–1. This porch was demolished *c.*1873. [S.R.O., GD 16/27/446 and RHP 5167/1–3] (Jones's *Views of Scottish Seats*, *c.*1830; A. H. Millar, *Castles and Mansions of Scotland: Perthshire and Forfarshire*, 1890, 307–27).

COUL HOUSE, ROSS-SHIRE, for Sir George Stewart Mackenzie, Bart., 1820–1 [S.R.O., SC 25/67/2, pp. 11, 194–6].

WHITEHAUGH, NEWCASTLETON, ROXBURGHSHIRE, for Walter Scott of Whitehaugh, 1822–3 [S.R.O., SC 62/71/3, *ex inf.* Miss C. Cruft].

attributed: MILLEARNE, PERTHSHIRE, for J. G. Home Drummond, 1826–35, Gothic; dem. 1969 [Alistair Rowan in *C. Life*, 24 Feb.–2 March 1972].

BALBIRNIE HOUSE, FIFE, west lodge for General Robert Balfour, 1824 [payment in accounts formerly at Balbirnie, *ex. inf.* Prof. Alistair Rowan].

EDINBURGH, Nos. 1–25 GARDNER'S CRESCENT and 91–107, 109–115 MORRISON STREET, 1826 [S.R.O., Edinburgh Sasines].

EDINBURGH, addition of shop-fronts to Nos. 1–3 BAXTERS PLACE and new buildings adjoining in GREENSIDE LANE, 1830–5; dem. [photographs of drawings in N.M.R.S.].

BLAIR DRUMMOND, PERTHSHIRE, additions to East Lodge for Henry Home Drummond, 1836 [drawings at Blair Drummond].

ARBUTHNOTT HOUSE, KINCARDINESHIRE, estate buildings for 8th Viscount Arbuthnott, 1839 [drawings at Arbuthnott House, *ex inf.* Mr. J. G. Dunbar].

DUNIMARLE CASTLE, CULROSS, FIFE, for Mrs. Magdalene Shairpe-Erskine, 1839–45 [drawings at Dunimarle Castle, *ex inf.* Prof. Alistair Rowan].

BLAIR ATHOLL, PERTHSHIRE, BLAIR COTTAGES, 1840 [drawings at Blair Castle].

GARRYSIDE VILLAGE, PERTHSHIRE, for 6th Duke of Atholl, 1856 [drawings at Blair Castle].

DIGBY, WILLIAM, 5th LORD DIGBY (*c.*1662–1752), was the son of Kildare, 2nd Lord Digby, of Coleshill House, Warwicks., where he was born. He was educated at Magdalen College, Oxford. As the Digby peerage was Irish, he was able to sit in the House of Commons as Tory M.P. for Warwick from 1689 until 1698, when he succeeded his cousin John Digby, 3rd Earl of Bristol, as the owner of Sherborne Castle, Dorset. He was one of the commissioners for rebuilding the town of Warwick after its destruction by fire in 1694, and for building St. Philip's Church, Birmingham, in 1708. Digby's knowledge of architecture is attested both by the fact that he told Alexander Pope that CASTLETON CHURCH, SHERBORNE, DORSET, which he rebuilt in a simple Gothic Gothic style in 1714–15, largely at his own expense, 'was of his own architecture', and by the very professional advice which he gave to the fellows of Magdalen College, Oxford, about the design and construction of their New Building in 1728–34. He is one of the figures shown examining the plans in the *Oxford Almanack* for 1730. Digby does not, however, appear to have built anything significant either at Coleshill House (dem. *c.*1870) or at Sherborne Castle. There are several portraits of him at Sherborne. [G.E.C., *Complete Peerage* iv, 354; *The Correspondence of Alexander Pope*, ed. Sherburn, ii, 1956, 239; archives of Magdalen College, Oxford; H. M. Petter, *The Oxford Almanacks*, 1974, 57.]

DINGLEY, ROBERT (1710–1781), merchant and philanthropist, was the son of a prosperous London goldsmith and jeweller. He and his brother Charles were partners in a successful trade with Russia, Charles being based at St. Petersburg and Robert in London. Robert was a leading member of the Russia Company and for some years a Director of the Bank of England. As a philanthropist he was best known as a governor of the Foundling Hospital and as one of the founders of the Magdalen Hospital for penitent prostitutes. His first wife was Elizabeth, daughter of Henry Thompson of Kirby Hall, Yorkshire. After her death at Charlton in 1759 he married Esther Spencer and moved to Lamorbey near Bexley in Kent. His City residence was in St. Helen's Place, Bishopsgate.

Dingley was a keen connoisseur of the arts, and his wealth enabled him to form a fine collection of coins, antique gems and drawings. He was one of the original members of the Society of Dilettanti, from 1734 to 1748 a Fellow of the Society of Antiquaries, and from 1748 onwards of the Royal Society. Although he did not subscribe to any of the major architectural publications of his time, his skill as an amateur architect is attested by several engraved designs which bear his initials as their author. One of these is a design for the Magdalen Hospital (Bodleian Library, Gough Maps 20, f. 60v) signed 'R.D. inv. & del.' and presumably made about 1763, when a site for the hospital was found in Lambeth. However, Dingley's grand Palladian design, with a domed chapel on the principal axis, flanked by colonnaded wings, bore no resemblance to the more utilitarian design by Joel Johnson (*q.v.*) that was eventually carried out in 1769–72. Further evidence of Dingley's activity as an amateur architect are some engraved designs for temples among the architectural drawings at West Wycombe Park (the house of Sir Francis Dashwood, a fellow Dilettante), three proof engravings of designs for rustic buildings in the R.I.B.A. Drawings Collection, and an elaborate scheme for rebuilding the King's and Queen's Baths at Bath, engraved for presentation to the Corporation soon after 1766 and posthumously published by I. & J. Taylor in 1786 or 1787. The architecture is again Palladian in character [Eileen Harris, *British Architectural Books & Writers 1556–1785*, 1990, 183–5]. If any building was actually erected to Dingley's designs it has yet to be identified, but a letter in the E. Yorks. Record Office (DD/GR 42/4) shows that in 1754 he had a hand in John Carr's design for the Knavesmire race-stand at York. [J. H. Appleby, 'Robert Dingley, F.R.S., Merchant, Architect and Pioneering Philanthropist', *Notes & Records of the Royal Society* 45 (2), 1991; H.F.B. Compston, *The Magdalen Hospital*, 1917.]

DINNINGHOF, BARNARD, was a glazier by trade, and doubtless a Fleming or German in origin. In 1586 he became a freeman of York, and he was still working in Yorkshire in 1618. At Gilling Castle, Yorks. (N.R.), the heraldic glass in the Great Chamber is signed 'Bærnard Dinninckhoff fecit Anno 1585'. Among the Temple Newsam papers at Leeds there is a set of competently drawn plans by Dinninghof for a projected house at Sheriff Hutton for Thomas Lumsden, accompanied by a letter dated 2 October 1618 offering to build it for £440. In another document of this date he describes himself as 'of Follifoot Mote in the parish of Wichell', i.e. Wigtoft. [S. D. Kitson, 'Barnard Dinninghof', *Jnl. British Society of Master Glass-Painters* iii, 1929, 55–8; *Freemen of the City of York* ii, Surtees Soc. 1900; Leeds Archives, Temple Newsam Papers, SH A 3/1–2; information from the late Dr. E. A. Gee.]

DIXON, CORNELIUS (–1826), was an architectural decorator and theatrical scene-painter. A note by Horace Walpole records the fact that he studied in Rome under Clérisseau [A. Graves, *The Royal Academy of Arts, a Dictionary of Exhibitors* ii, 1905, 80]. In 1793–4 he was employed by Walpole at STRAWBERRY HILL, MIDDLESEX, 'new painting the paper of the staircase' and 'the ceiling under the stairs' [*Strawberry Hill Accounts*, ed. P. Toynbee, 1927, 20]. At No. 15 ST. JAMES'S SQUARE in 1794 he painted 'pilaster pannels', etc., for Thomas Anson under the direction of Samuel Wyatt [E. Croft Murray, *Decorative Painting in England* ii, 1970, 202]. A few years later James Wyatt employed him to paint the pillars in the dining-room at CANWELL HALL, STAFFS., 'in imitation of Italian marble', and he subsequently 'executed similar ones on a smaller scale in Mr. Boulton's dining-room' in his house at SOHO, nr. BIRMINGHAM [S. Shaw, *History of Staffordshire* ii, 1801, 22*]. His firm was still active in the 1820s, when 'Cornelius Dixon & Son' were paid £100 for painting the interior of the new COUNTY COURT HOUSE at CARLISLE [Cumbria Record Office, Q.S. Records, 1822] and 'Messrs. Dixon' were employed to paint the east wing of the BRITISH MUSEUM [*History of the King's Works* vi, 411, n. 4]. Dixon was living at 20, Alpha Cottages, Marylebone, at the time of his death in 1826 [P.R.O., PROB 11/1708. f. 74].

According to E. W. Brayley's *Historical and Descriptive Accounts of the Theatres of London*, 1833, Dixon was the architect as well as the scene-painter of a theatre in the East End of London, apparently the Royalty Theatre, Wellclose Square, built in 1785–7 and destroyed by fire in 1826. The scenes that he painted for this theatre were highly praised, but there appears to be no evidence that he designed the building itself. Some crudely drawn plans of a theatre in the Enthoven Collection in the Victoria and Albert Museum that are inscribed on the back with the names of Dixon and Capon do not correspond to the Royalty, although said to represent it [cf. R. Southern, *The Georgian Playhouse*, 1948, 26, pls. 10–13]. In 1792 Dixon did, however, receive the first premium of 20 guineas for his designs for rebuilding the Theatre Royal in Birmingham, but they were subsequently set aside in favour of plans by George Saunders [MS. Minutes of the Proprietors in the Birmingham Reference Library].

DIXON, HENRY (*c*.1783–1859), was a surveyor working in Oxford in the early nineteenth century, and primarily concerned with enclosure, drainage and the valuation of property. From 1820 onwards he was employed by St. John's College to lay out BEAUMONT and ST. JOHN'S STREETS, but the elevations may have been drawn by William Garbett (*q.v.*) [Tanis Hinchcliffe, *North Oxford*, 1992, 19–20]. However, Dixon certainly designed Nos. 15–19 BANBURY ROAD, OXFORD, for which his drawings and specification, dated 1847, are in the archives of University College. In the Bodleian Library (MS. Top. Oxon. a. 22(R)), there is a set of plans of Oxford Colleges made in 1848 'under the supervision of Mr. Henry Dixon of Oxford'. Dixon died at Leamington on 21 January 1859 according to J. M. Davenport's 'Obituary Book' in the Oxon. C.R.O. The Leamington Register gives his age as 76.

DIXON, JOHN, of Hull, was employed by the Corporation of Lincoln in 1762 to examine the Fish and Butchers' Shambles, and 'to draw a plan of a new Butchers' Shambles and bring in an estimate thereof'. In June 1765 it was decided to build a conduit over the High Bridge 'in the Form of an Obelisk', and on 6 July Dixon was ordered to erect it 'agreeable to the Plan and Estimate delivered in by him' [Lincoln Corporation Minutes, 1710–1800, pp. 442, 444–6] (for an engraving of the obelisk see Thomas Allom, *The Counties of Chester, Derby, Nottingham, Leicester, Rutland and Lincoln Illustrated*, 1836, 28). Dixon was employed by Sir John Hussey Delaval to measure plasterers' and joiners' work executed at Doddington Hall, Lincs., in 1760–2 [Bodleian Library, MS. Top. Lincs. c. 14, ff. 41–5, 56, 63–5, 70].

DIXON, JOHN, was an assistant of James Wyatt. Farington described him in 1794 as 'the artist who is employed by Wyatt to draw for him', and noted that he had been with Wyatt 'from the time of the building of the Pantheon' (opened in 1772). From 1781 to 1796 Dixon exhibited architectural designs at the Royal Academy, but in 1796 Smirke told Farington that 'Wyatt . . . will not allow Dixon to exhibit, as he says the designs are borrowed from his drawings' [Farington's Diary, 21 Jan. 1794, 4 Aug. 1796]. However, Dixon did exhibit again in 1801 and 1803, the subject in the latter year being 'a design for a Gothic hall'. A drawing of Wyatt's New Park, Wilts., formerly in an extra-illustrated copy of Britton's *Beauties of Wiltshire* in the library at Coleshill House, Berks., was stated to be 'by J. Dixon at Mr. Wyatt's': it was probably the view of this house that Dixon exhibited at the Academy in 1784. The name of 'John Dixon Clerk to Jas. Wyatt' is among those inscribed on the plate commemorating the completion of the Radcliffe Observatory, Oxford, to Wyatt's designs in 1794. At the time of Wyatt's sudden death in 1813 he was reported to owe Dixon £900 [Farington's Diary, 18 Sept. 1813]. What became of Dixon subsequently has not been discovered. He had a nephew, Joseph Dixon, who was admitted to the Royal Academy Schools in 1796 at the age of 20 and was awarded the Silver Medal in 1797.

DIXON, JOSEPH (–1787), appears to have been one of the sons of Joseph Dixon, a carpenter of Stamford who died in 1777. He established himself in London, where he was active as a mason and surveyor during the third quarter of the eighteenth century. According to the MS. autobiography of Henry Couchman (*q.v.*), who as a young man was one of his employees, he lived at first in Air Street, Piccadilly, but afterwards built himself a house and yard in Pimlico near the Chelsea waterworks. Other sources, however, give his address as St. Alban's Street (south of Pall Mall). In 1760–9 he built Blackfriars Bridge to the designs of Robert Mylne, and in 1770 he began to build a new bridge over the R. Exe at Exeter to his own designs, but his workmanship proved defective, and it was swept away by a flood in 1775 before it was complete [G. Oliver, *History of Exeter*, 1861, 169–172].[1] Couchman records that in 1764–5 Dixon built Almack's Rooms in King Street, St. James's to the designs of Robert Mylne, and a house in Piccadilly for the Earl of March to those of Matthew Brettingham. About this time he was also working at Burghley House, Northants., and erecting 'a new house in Gloucestershire'. In 1766 he enlarged COKER COURT, SOMERSET, for William Helyar, adding the rooms forming the Georgian E. range [Somerset C.R.O., DD/WHh Addenda 16 and DD/WHh (previously unlisted) 2].

In several of his works Dixon was associated with his brother Richard Dixon, a carpenter who became surveyor to the Westminster Lying-in Hospital (built in 1765–7 and dem. *c.*1830) [*Survey of London* xxiii, 42]. Together they were involved in building houses in Pall Mall in the 1760s [*op. cit.* xxix, 328–9]. This was a development in which Henry Holland was involved, and his account-book in Sir John Soane's Museum shows that he often employed Joseph Dixon as a mason. In 1770–2 Joseph and Richard

[1] A new bridge was then built (1776–8) under the direction of John Goodwin, 'who had been an assistant in the former erection' (*A.P.S.D.*, *s.v.* 'Exeter'). This in turn was rebuilt in 1905.

Dixon built the new south wing at Hitchin Priory, Herts., to the designs of R. & J. Adam [Herts. C.R.O., DE 4422/2]. In 1775–7 they were responsible for rebuilding ST. MARY'S CHURCH, BATTERSEA, Joseph as architect and surveyor, Richard as building contractor [J.G. Taylor, *Our Lady of Batersey*, 1925, 99–113]. By then Joseph Dixon was living in Battersea, but Richard was described as 'of Pimlico'. Joseph went bankrupt in March 1778, Richard in November [*Gent's Mag.* 1778, 142, 551]. Joseph Dixon died at Battersea in 1787 [Taylor, *op. cit.*, 120]. In his will [P.C.C. 171 MAJOR] he is described as 'Senior Bridge Master of London Bridge'. John Carter (*q.v.*) was for some years Dixon's pupil and assistant.

In his diary C.R.Cockerell recorded (14 May 1825) that a house near Aberystwyth in Cardiganshire called CWMCYNFELIN was 'built by Mr. Davis grandfather to [the then owner] from designs of a Mr. Dixon in London'. This was presumably either Joseph or Richard.

DIXON, JOSEPH, 'Carpenter and House Joyner', 'who had for several years past serv'd Mr. Thomas Ivory in the capacity of Foreman', announced in the *Norwich Mercury* of 11 October 1756 that he had taken over Mr. Thomas Ivory's yard and stock in St. Martin's at Oak, 'where he intends to carry on the said Business in all its Branches'. He was prepared to make 'Plans and Estimates for Gentlemen if required' [S. J. Wearing, *Georgian Norwich: its Builders*, 1926, 58–9].

DOBSON, JOHN (1787–1865), was born at Chirton, North Shields, Co. Durham, where his father was a prosperous market-gardener. He showed an early talent for drawing, and at the age of 15 became a pupil of David Stephenson, then the leading architect in Newcastle. At the same time he studied perspective under an Italian refugee artist called Boniface Musso, John Martin being his fellow-pupil. On the conclusion of his apprenticeship to Stevenson in 1809 he went to London, where he sought instruction from John Varley, the celebrated water-colour painter. Varley was so impressed by his ability that he agreed to give him lessons at five o'clock each morning – that being the only time he could spare. A painting entitled 'Dobson's Dream' was the product of this early morning tuition, for it represented the master's version of a dream recounted to him by his recently-awakened pupil. While in London Dobson formed a friendship with the artist Robert Smirke, R.A., who attempted, without success, to dissuade him from returning to the north. Once established in Newcastle, he found that 'although he was (with the exception of Mr. Bonomi of Durham) the only professional architect between Edinburgh and York . . . the demand for his services had to be created', and that the employment of builder-architects such as Dodds and Stephenson was still the rule. By characteristic patience and hard work, however, he soon built up a practice for himself in the new industrial towns. Professionally he was unusually well equipped. From Varley he had acquired an enviable facility in producing enticing water-colour perspectives of his designs (though, as his practice grew, he increasingly employed a professional water-colourist called Carmichael for this purpose). To the skill of an artist he added the resourcefulness of an engineer and the practical competence of a surveyor. According to his daughter he 'never exceeded an estimate, and never had a legal dispute with a contractor'. His technical ability was shown in securing the foundations of Lambton Hall, which had been rendered insecure by mining subsidence, and he was equally successful in underpinning and restoring the tower of St. Nicholas Church, Newcastle, when it was in imminent danger of collapse. As an engineer his outstanding achievement was the Central Railway Station at Newcastle, which embodied several structural innovations, one of which earned him a medal at the Paris Exhibition of 1858. He also designed wharves, warehouses, and a graving dock at St. Peter's Shipyard, Newcastle.

Although Dobson was involved in several developments in and around Newcastle in the 1820s, it was the speculative builder Richard Grainger who was responsible for the major town-planning schemes which transformed the city in the second quarter of the nineteenth century. Dobson's contribution to Grainger's new streets appears to have been limited to the façades of Eldon Square and of part of the east side of Grey Street south of the Theatre Royal. But the Royal Arcade and the New Markets were designed by Dobson, and his numerous other public buildings, including the Schinkelesque entrance to the General Cemetery and the grand portico of the Central Station, give him a prominent place among the architects who made Newcastle one of the most handsome Victorian cities in England.

In 1828 Dobson was commissioned by the 3rd Marquess of Londonderry to make plans for the new town which was intended to complement a new harbour which the marquess was building at Seaham, Co. Durham. Although the first stone of the first house was ceremonially laid on 28 November, the marquess's finances proved insufficient to build both harbour and town simultaneously, and in the event Dobson's layout was abandoned in favour of haphazard development. His plans remain among the Londonderry papers in the Durham County Record Office (D/Lo. P.596/3 and 6).

Dobson's practice as a designer of churches and country houses in the north of England was very extensive. In the course of a long career he designed or altered over sixty churches or chapels and more than a hundred houses. His earliest churches were mostly classical in style. But from the 1820s onwards he was designing churches in the meagre lancet style of the period and occasionally in a mechanical neo-Norman. By the 1850s, however, he could produce a conventional 'Decorated' church such as Otterburn that satisfied all the standards of Victorian ecclesiology. His restorations (notably that of Hexham Priory church) were apt to be drastic and controversial. As a country-house architect Dobson worked largely for the beneficiaries of the industrial revolution, designing new houses for wealthy manufacturers like Sir William Armstrong or embellishing old ones for established county families enriched by coal royalties. To both he offered Greek Revival or Tudor Gothic dress with equal facility. Though he was probably as competent a purveyor of domestic Gothic as Burn or Blore, it is his classical houses that are most revealing of Dobson's stature as an architect. Carefully sited, and superbly built of meticulously accurate masonry, their sensible planning soon earned for their architect the reputation of 'having the secret of keeping out the cold'. The detailing is always scholarly and precise, but the scale is apt to be overlarge and the effect is sometimes rather bleak. As Pevsner observes, the staircase at Meldon Park is 'the size of one in a London club'. Nevertheless they are handsome and habitable houses, and agreeably free from the stereotyped pedantry of so many English Greek Revival houses of the same date.

Dobson never visited the Mediterranean, but as a young man he travelled in England and France. He was a Fellow of the R.I.B.A. and in 1859 became the first President of the Northern Architectural Association. His youngest son Alexander had an architectural training with Sydney Smirke (who had married Dobson's eldest daughter), but died prematurely in 1854 in the explosion at Gateshead. Dobson himself was incapacitated by a stroke about two years before his death at Newcastle on 8 January 1865. A bust of Dobson is reproduced in his daughter's *Memoir*, and two oil portraits in the Laing Art Gallery at Newcastle are illustrated by Faulkner and Greg. A number of drawings by Dobson are in the same gallery.

[Margaret Jane Dobson, *A Memoir of John Dobson*, 1885; obituaries in *Builder* xxiii, 1865, 27 and *Newcastle Daily Journal*, 16 Jan. 1865; R. Welford, *Men of Mark 'twixt Tyne and Tweed* ii, 1895, 81–4; L. Wilkes & G. Dodds, *Tyneside Classical: The Newcastle of Grainger, Dobson and Clayton*, 1964; Mark Girouard, 'Dobson's Northumbrian Houses', *C. Life*, 17 and 24 Feb. 1966; Lyall Wilkes, *John Dobson*, 1980; T. Faulkner & A. Greg. *John Dobson, Newcastle Architect*, Tyne & Wear Museums Service, 1987. The last supersedes all previous biographies of Dobson.]

Unless otherwise stated, the list that follows is based on the long but very unreliable list of Dobson's works printed by his daughter in her *Memoir*. F. & G. stands for Faulkner & Greg. *op. cit.*, *N.D.J.* for the obituary in *Newcastle Daily Journal*, 16 Jan. 1865.

NEWCASTLE: PUBLIC AND COMMERCIAL BUILDINGS AND STREET ARCHITECTURE

THE ROYAL JUBILEE SCHOOLS, CITY ROAD, 1810–11 and alterations, 1854 [E. Mackenzie, *Newcastle* ii, 1837, 452; F. & G. citing *Newcastle Chronicle*, 29 Dec. 1854].

TYNE BREWERY, ST. MARY'S STREET, SANDGATE, 1816.

THE CUSTOM HOUSE, alterations, 1817; dem. *c.*1840.

THE OLD THEATRE, alterations to entrance, 1817; dem. 1836.

SANDYFORD BRIDGE, 1818.

TOBACCO WAREHOUSE, QUAYSIDE, for Benjamin Sorsbie, 1818–19.

ST. NICHOLAS CHARITY (or CLERGY JUBILEE) SCHOOL, 1819–20; dem. [E. Mackenzie, *Newcastle* ii, 1827, 446–7].

THE GUILDHALL or EXCHANGE, SANDHILL, added rounded extension to E. end containing Fish Market on ground floor, 1823–6, and rebuilt Merchants' Court, *c.*1830.

THE GAOL AND HOUSE OF CORRECTION, CARLIOL SQUARE, 1823–8 and major additions, 1859–61; dem. *c.*1929 [F. & G. citing drawings in Tyne & Wear Archives].

BLACKETT STREET, 1824 onwards [E. Mackenzie, *Newcastle* ii, 1827, 188–9].

THE LUNATIC ASYLUM, BATH LANE, reconstructed 1824 [E. Mackenzie, *Newcastle* ii, 1827, 525–6].

THE LYING-IN HOSPITAL (now Broadcasting House), NEW BRIDGE STREET, 1825–6, Tudor style.

ELDON SQUARE, façades for Richard Grainger, 1825–31; dem. *c.*1970 [*N.D.J.*].

THE NORTHERN ACADEMY OF ARTS, No. 41 BLACKETT STREET, 1827–8; dem. 1974.

ARTHURS HILL, streets and elevations for Isaac Cookson, 1827–33 [F. & G. citing Tyne & Wear Archives].

ST. MARY'S PLACE (terrace), 1829, Tudor Gothic.

SANDHILL, offices at north-east end of Tyne Bridge, 1830 [F. & G. citing *Newcastle Courant*, 19 June 1830].

THE ROYAL ARCADE, 1831–2; dem. 1963 (*Arch. Hist.* ii, 1959, 81–93).

VEGETABLE & BUTTER MARKETS, NEVILLE STREET, 1831–4.

THE NORTHERN COUNTIES CLUB, 1833.

THE GENERAL CEMETERY, JESMOND ROAD, Chapel and Entrance Gates, 1834–6.

GREY STREET, façades of E. side, between High Bridge and Mosley Street, for Richard Grainger, 1834–7 [F. & G. citing drawings in Laing Art Gallery, etc.].

NEVILLE STREET, planned 1828, built *c.*1835 [*N.D.J.*].

POLICE OFFICES, MANOR CHARE, 1836, Tudor Gothic.

THE SUNDERLAND & DURHAM UNION JOINT STOCK BANK, MOSLEY STREET, 1836.

QUAY between Broad Chare and the Swirle, 1837 [T. L. Donaldson, *Handbook of Specifications*, 1860, 824–30].

COACHMAKERS' MANUFACTORY, for Messrs. Atkinson & Philipson, 1837; dem. *c.*1920 [*N.D.J.*].

THE PUBLIC BATHS, RIDLEY PLACE, NORTHUMBERLAND ROAD, 1837–9.

DISPENSARY, NELSON STREET, 1839 [*N.D.J.*].

ASYLUM FOR BLIND, NORTHUMBERLAND STREET, 1840; dem. [*N.D.J.*].

ELSWICK, staithe for Elswick Lead Works, *c.*1840 [*N.D.J.*].

TRINITY HOUSE, BROAD CHARE, restoration of gateway, 1841 [Grace McCombie in *Archaeologia Aeliana* 5th ser. xiii, 1985, 180 and n. 76].

THE CASTLE, restoration of keep, 1847.

THE RIDING SCHOOL, 1847.

FLAX MILLS, OUSEBURN, for R. Plummer, 1847–8.

THE CENTRAL RAILWAY STATION, 1847–8 and added portico 1861–3.

THE MANORS STATION and GOODS WAREHOUSE, 1849–50; dem.

ST. MARY'S ALMSHOUSES, RYE HILL, School and Chapel, 1851, Gothic [F. & G. citing *Newcastle Chronicle*, 22 Aug. 1851].

STATION HOTEL, NEVILLE STREET, 1851 [F. & G. citing *Newcastle Courant* 11 July 1851].

BRICKLAYERS' HALL, CASTLE GARTH, 1851 Gothic; dem. [*N.D.J.*].

THE SURGEONS' HALL, VICTORIA STREET, 1851.

THE COLLEGE OF MEDICINE, NEVILLE STREET, 1851–2, Gothic; dem. *c.*1889.

THE INFIRMARY, new wing, 1852–5; dem. 1954.

RAGGED & INDUSTRIAL SCHOOLS, 1853–4 and additions 1858; dem.

NEWCASTLE COURANT OFFICE, GEORGE YARD, 1858; dem. [F. & G. citing *Newcastle Courant*, 12 Feb. 1858].

LITERARY & PHILOSOPHICAL SOCIETY, WESTGATE STREET, added Lecture Theatre, 1859 [*Builder* xvii, 1859, 275].

GAS COMPANY'S OFFICE, NEVILLE STREET, 1861–2, Italianate; dem. *c.*1971 [*N.D.J.*].

MECHANICS' INSTITUTE, ELSWICK, for Sir William Armstrong, 1862 [F. & G. citing *Newcastle Courant*, 2 Sept. 1862].

PUBLIC AND COMMERCIAL BUILDINGS ELSEWHERE

WALLSEND, NORTHUMB., planned HOWDEN DOCKS and designed staithes, 1814.

NORTH SHIELDS, NORTHUMB., docks for Michael Robson, 1816 [*N.D.J.*].

LIVERPOOL, CUSTOMS HOUSE, alterations 1817; dem. *c.*1830.

GLASGOW, CUSTOMS HOUSE, alterations 1817; dem.

TYNEMOUTH CASTLE, fortifications 1817.

SOUTH SHIELDS, CO. DURHAM, glass-works for Isaac Cookson, 1817.

PONTELAND, NORTHUMB., SCHOOL, 1817.

MORPETH, NORTHUMB., COUNTY GAOL and SESSIONS HOUSE, 1822–31, castellated; partly dem. [E. Mackenzie, *Northumberland* ii, 1825, 188–9, with plan; drawings in Percy archives, Alnwick Castle].

BELFORD, NORTHUMB., COUNTY PRISON, 1823, Tudor style [F. & G. citing *Newcastle Chronicle*, 22 Nov. 1823].

WOOLER, NORTHUMB., COUNTY PRISON, 1823 [*ibid.*]

HAMSTERLEY BRIDGE, CO. DURHAM, 1825.

HARBOTTLE BRIDGE, NORTHUMB., 1825.

HALTWHISTLE BRIDGE, NORTHUMB., 1826 [F. & G. citing *Newcastle Courant*, 29 April 1826].

WALBOTTLE BRIDGE, NORTHUMB., 1827.

MORPETH, NORTHUMB., GRAMMAR SCHOOL, restoration 1827 [F. & G. citing *Newcastle Courant*, 24 Feb. 1827].

MORPETH, NORTHUMB., bridge at High Ford, 1828 [F. & G. citing *Newcastle Courant*, 6 April 1828].

HENDON (SUNDERLAND), CO. DURHAM, SCHOOL, 1831; dem. [Fordyce, *Durham* ii, 1855, 466].

CHOLLERTON, NORTHUMB., SCHOOL, 1831, Tudor; largely dem.

STAMFORDHAM, NORTHUMB., SCHOOL, 1832, Tudor.

CULLERCOATS, NORTHUMB., building sites for

sale to elevations by Dobson, 1833 [F. & G. citing *Newcastle Chronicle*, 16 Nov. 1833].

GATESHEAD, CO. DURHAM, CEMETERY, 1834 [F. & G. citing *Newcastle Courant*, 11 Oct. 1834].

MONKWEARMOUTH, CO. DURHAM, planning development of Monkwearmouth Shore, etc. for Sir Hedworth Williamson, 1835 [F. & G. citing *Newcastle Journal*, 3 Oct. 1835].

TYNEMOUTH, NORTHUMB., HOUSE OF CORRECTION, additions, 1835 [F. & G. citing *Newcastle Courant*, 31 Jan. 1835].

GATESHEAD, CO. DURHAM, ELLISON SCHOOLS, 1836–7; dem. [F. & G. citing *Newcastle Chronicle*, 15 Oct. 1836].

HEXHAM, NORTHUMB., SAVINGS BANK, 1837 [F. & G. citing *Newcastle Courant*, 7 July 1837].

MONKWEARMOUTH, CO. DURHAM, DOCK OFFICE, North Dock, for Sir Hedworth Williamson, *c.*1837; dem. [F. & G.].

TYNEMOUTH, NORTHUMB., CROWN HOTEL, BATHS, etc., 1838 [F. & G. citing *Newcastle Courant*, 2 Nov. 1838].

GATESHEAD, CO. DURHAM, VIADUCT for Brandling Junction Railway Co., 1840–1.

MONKWEARMOUTH, CO. DURHAM, BATHS, TERRACE and HOTEL, ROKER TERRACE, 1840–1 [F. & G. citing *Newcastle Courant*, 17 April 1840].

CARLISLE, CUMBERLAND, RAILWAY STATION, LONDON ROAD, for the Newcastle & Carlisle Railway Co., 1841; dem.

NORTH SHIELDS, NORTHUMB., TOWN HALL, etc., 1844–5, Tudor [J. Latimer, *Local Records 1832–57*, Newcastle 1857, 202].

CULLERCOATS, NORTHUMB., rebuilding of breakwater, 1846 [F. & G. citing *Newcastle Courant*, 27 Nov. 1846].

NORTH SHIELDS, NORTHUMBERLAND, WAREHOUSE for North Shields & Tynemouth Railway, 1848 [F. & G. citing *Newcastle Chronicle*, 16 May 1848].

WELTON, NORTHUMB., Keeper's Cottage and Directors' Rooms for Whittle Dean Water Co., 1848, Tudor [*N.D.J.*].

SOUTH SHIELDS, CO. DURHAM, NORMAL SCHOOLS for J. Stevenson, *c.*1848; dem. [*N.D.J.*].

GATESHEAD, CO. DURHAM, RAILWAY STATION for York, Newcastle & Berwick Railway Co., 1849; dem. [F. & G. citing *Newcastle Courant*, 27 April 1849].

WELTON, NORTHUMB., RESERVOIR for Whittle Dean Water Co., 1850 [R. W. Rennison, *Water to Tyneside*, 1979, 57–61].

LYMM, CHESHIRE, SCHOOL, 1850.

TYNEMOUTH, PRIOR'S TERRACE, *c.*1850 [*N.D.J.*].

MONKWEARMOUTH, CO. DURHAM, planned housing estate for Sir Hedworth Williamson, 1851–7; dem. [Fordyce, *Durham* ii, 1855, 480].

SOUTH SHIELDS, CO. DURHAM, ST. STEPHEN'S NATIONAL SCHOOL, 1852–3; dem. [*Builder* xi, 1853, 167].

WHIXLEY, YORKS. (W.R.), SCHOOL, 1853.

BISHOPWEARMOUTH, CO. DURHAM, RECTORY PARK SCHOOLS, 1854, Tudor; dem.

HARTLEPOOL, CO. DURHAM, WEST VIEW CEMETERY, chapels and entrance, 1854–5; dem.

BENSHAM, CO. DURHAM, ST. CUTHBERT'S SCHOOL, 1855; dem. [F. & G. citing *Newcastle Courant*, 5 Jan. 1855].

WARRINGTON, LANCS., LIBRARY & MUSEUM, built 1855–6 as a modified version of design made by Dobson in 1853 [F. & G. citing minutes of Warrington Council and drawings in Library & Museum].

LIVERPOOL, warehouses, 1856.

SUNDERLAND, CO. DURHAM, SOUTH DOCK GRAIN WAREHOUSE for George Hudson, 1856–8 [F. & G. citing *Newcastle Courant*, 13 June 1856].

CHATTON, NORTHUMB., bridges, 1857 [F. & G. citing *Newcastle Courant*, 23 Jan. 1857].

LEEDS, YORKS. (W.R.), STATION HOTEL, 1857.

WHITBY, YORKS. (N.R.), Hotel, East Terrace and Royal Crescent for George Hudson, 1857.

MIDDLESBROUGH, YORKS. (N.R.), FREEMASONS' LODGE, 1858–61; dem. [*Builder* xix, 1861, 84].

BRANDON, CO. DURHAM, SCHOOL, 1859 [F. & G. citing *Newcastle Courant*, 12 Aug. 1859].

NORTH SHIELDS, NORTHUMB., office and workers' cottages for Tyne Improvement Commissioners, 1859–61; cottages dem. [F. & G. citing *Newcastle Courant*, 27 May 1859].

CHURCHES

(Gothic unless otherwise stated)

NORTH SHIELDS, NORTHUMB., SCOTCH PRESBYTERIAN CHURCH, HOWARD STREET, 1811, Doric.

NEWCASTLE, NEW ROAD WESLEYAN METHODIST CHAPEL, 1812–13, classical; dem.

NEWCASTLE, ALL SAINTS, repaired steeple, 1816 [E. Mackenzie, *Newcastle*, 1827, 305].

ST. JOHN LEE, nr. HEXHAM, NORTHUMB., rebuilt E. end, 1818–19; altered 1885.

GOSFORTH, NORTHUMB., added aisles 1819, Tuscan; enlarged 1884 and 1913.

WHITBURN, CO. DURHAM, restoration, 1819.

WHICKHAM, CO. DURHAM, restoration, 1819; enlarged 1862 by A. Salvin.

NEWCASTLE, ST. NICHOLAS (now CATHEDRAL), rebuilt N. window of N. transept, 1823–4; repaired (with J. Green) foundations of W.

tower, 1832–3; rebuilt E. gable of chancel with new window, 1859 [H. L. Honeyman, 'St. Nicholas, Newcastle', *Archaeologia Aeliana* 4th. ser. ix, 1932, 140–5].

SUNDERLAND, CO. DURHAM, INDEPENDENT CHAPEL, 1825 [*N.D.J.*].

ALNWICK, NORTHUMB., restoration, 1825.

NEWCASTLE, ST. JAMES'S PRESBYTERIAN CHAPEL, BLACKETT STREET, 1826, Greek Doric; dem. 1859.

GREENHEAD, NORTHUMB., 1826–8; chancel added 1900.

MONKWEARMOUTH, CO. DURHAM, SCOTCH PRESBYTERIAN CHURCH, 1826–7, classical; dem. [M. A. Richardson, *The Local Historian's Table-Book* iii, 356].

NEWCASTLE, QUAKERS' MEETING-HOUSE, off PILGRIM STREET, 1827.

BELFORD, NORTHUMB., largely rebuilt 1827–9 [I.C.B.S.] (F. R. Wilson, *Churches in the Archdeaconry of Lindisfarne*, 1870, with plan).

NEWCASTLE, ST. THOMAS, BARRAS BRIDGE, 1828–9 (B. Allsopp, *Historic Architecture of Newcastle*, 1967, 66–7, with plan).

NEWCASTLE, ST. JOHN, restorations 1829 and 1848 and designed reredos, etc., 1855.

STAMFORDHAM, NORTHUMB., restoration 1830; further restoration by B. Ferrey, 1848.

BENWELL, NORTHUMB., ST. JAMES, 1831–2; neo-Norman; chancel etc. added 1895 [R.I.B.A.D.].

MINSTERACRES, NORTHUMB., R.C. CHAPEL, 1834; replaced 1852–4 by new chapel by J. A. Hansom.

DINNINGTON, NORTHUMB., 1834–5 [*Builder* xxiii, 1865, 27].

GATESHEAD, CO. DURHAM, HOLY TRINITY CHAPEL, restoration 1837; enlarged on N. side 1893–4 [J. Latimer, *Local Records 1832–1857*, 1857, 80].

COWPEN, NORTHUMB., ST. CUTHBERT (R.C.), 1840.

NEWCASTLE, ST. PETER, OXFORD STREET, 1840–3; tower and spire completed 1860; dem. *c.*1936 [I.C.B.S., with plan].

LONG HORSLEY, NORTHUMB., ST. THOMAS (R.C.), 1841.

FELLING, nr. GATESHEAD, CO. DURHAM, ST. PATRICK (R.C.), 1841; rebuilt 1893–5.

WEST BOLDON, CO. DURHAM, restoration 1842 [*N.D.J.*].

BIRTLEY, CO. DURHAM, ST. MARY & ST. JOSEPH (R.C.), with Presbytery and School, 1842–3.

MORPETH, ST. MARY, restoration of nave, 1843 [*N.D.J.*].

NEWCASTLE, ST. ANDREW, designed neo-Norman S. transept and restored N. transept and chancel, 1844–6.

NORTH SHIELDS, NORTHUMB., BAPTIST CHAPEL, 1845–6, neo-Norman.

WARWICK BRIDGE CHURCH, CUMBERLAND, for Peter Dixon, 1845–6, neo-Norman.

BENSHAM (GATESHEAD), CO. DURHAM, ST. CUTHBERT, 1846–8, neo-Norman; N. aisle added 1875 [drawings and specification in library of Society of Antiquaries, London].

MONKWEARMOUTH, CO. DURHAM, ALL SAINTS, 1846–9.

NEWCASTLE, TRINITY PRESBYTERIAN CHURCH, NEW BRIDGE STREET, 1847; dem.

ALSTON, CUMBERLAND, repairs 1847; rebuilt 1869–70.

SOUTH SHIELDS, CO. DURHAM, PRESBYTERIAN CHURCH, FREDERICK STREET, 1847–9; dem. 1977.

WINSTON, CO. DURHAM, restoration 1848.

STELLA, CO. DURHAM, SS. MARY & THOMAS AQUINAS (R.C.), enlarged 1848–9.

MELDON, NORTHUMB., restoration 1849.

BYWELL ST. PETER, NORTHUMB., restoration 1849.

SHOTLEY BRIDGE, CO. DURHAM, ST. CUTHBERT, BENFIELDSIDE, 1849–50; enlarged 1881–6 [I.C.B.S.].

BISHOPWEARMOUTH, CO. DURHAM, addition of transepts, 1849–50 [W. Fordyce, *Durham* ii, 1857, 429; I.C.B.S., with plan].

EMBLETON, NORTHUMB., extended aisles westwards and rebuilt N. Transept ('Craster aisle'), 1850 (F. R. Wilson, *Churches of the Archdeaconry of Lindisfarne*, 1870, 134–5, with plan).

LYMM, CHESHIRE, rebuilt 1850–1; W. tower added 1888–90 [*Builder* x, 1851, 631].

HENDON, CO. DURHAM, ST. PAUL, 1851–2.

NEWCASTLE, JOHN KNOX PRESBYTERIAN CHURCH, CLAYTON STREET WEST, 1852; dem. *c.*1896 [F. & G. citing *Newcastle Courant*, 24 Sept. 1852].

TYNEMOUTH PRIORY CHURCH, NORTHUMB., restored PERCY CHAPEL, 1852.

FORD, NORTHUMB., restoration, 1852–3.

NEWCASTLE, UNITARIAN CHURCH, NEW BRIDGE STREET, 1852–4; dem.

CHATTON, NORTHUMB., Gothicization of church of 1770 (F. R. Wilson, *Churches of the Archdeaconry of Lindisfarne*, 1870, 67).

GATESHEAD, CO. DURHAM, restoration after damage by explosion, 1854–5.

OTTERBURN, NORTHUMB., 1855–7 (F. R. Wilson, *Churches of the Archdeaconry of Lindisfarne*, 1870, 105, with plan).

NORTH SHIELDS, NORTHUMB., ST. COLUMBA'S PRESBYTERIAN CHURCH, NORTHUMBERLAND SQUARE, 1856–7, Italianate [J. Latimer, *Local Records 1832–1857*, 1857, 388].

NORTH SHIELDS, NORTHUMB., WESLEYAN CHAPEL, HOWARD STREET, 1856–7, Palladian [J. Latimer, *op. cit.*, 381].

NEWCASTLE, ST. PAUL, ELSWICK, 1857–9.

HOUGHTON-LE-SPRING, CO. DURHAM, restoration 1858–9.

HEXHAM PRIORY CHURCH, NORTHUMB., restoration of choir and E. end, 1858–60.

JESMOND CHURCH, NEWCASTLE, 1858–61.

KIRKNEWTON, NORTHUMB., reconstructed nave and added N. aisle, 1860 [I.C.B.S., including objections from A. Salvin] (F. R. Wilson, *Churches in the Archdeaconry of Lindisfarne*, 1870, 71–3).

WARKWORTH, NORTHUMB., restoration of nave, 1860.

SUDBROOKE, LINCS., 1860–2, neo-Norman, for R. Ellison.

SOUTH SHIELDS, CO. DURHAM, ST. MARY'S TYNE DOCK, 1861–3; dem. 1982.

DOMESTIC ARCHITECTURE

CHEESEBURN GRANGE, NORTHUMB., remodelled for Ralph Riddell, *c.*1813 onwards, Gothic. Dobson also designed the private Catholic chapel [drawings at Cheeseburn Grange]. An E. wing added by J. A. Hansom *c.*1860 was dem. *c.*1985.

EARSDON, NORTHUMB., house for J. Nicholson, 1813 [*Builder* xxiii, 1865, 27].

BRADLEY HALL, nr. RYTON, CO. DURHAM, alterations for 1st Lord Ravensworth, 1813.

FIELD HOUSE, nr. GATESHEAD, CO. DURHAM, for George Barras, 1813; dem. 1931.

SEATON DELAVAL, NORTHUMB., restoration of W. wing (gutted by fire 1752) for Sir Jacob Astley, Bart., 1814–15; reroofed central block (gutted by fire 1822), for 2nd Lord Hastings, 1860. For Dobson's unexecuted scheme of 1814–17 for the addition of wings, see F. & G., 16–17.

BACKWORTH HALL, NORTHUMB., alterations for R. W. Grey, 1815 [*N.D.J.*].

HAMSTERLEY HALL, CO. DURHAM, alterations for Anthony Surtees, 1815, Gothic [*N.D.J.*].

WATERVILLE HOUSE, NORTH SHIELDS, NORTHUMB., for R. Rippon, 1815; dem.

FALLODEN HALL, NORTHUMB., additions for Sir George Grey, Bart., 1815; rebuilt in early 20th century after a fire.

CRAMLINGTON HALL, NORTHUMB., for A. M. de C. Lawson, *c.*1815; dem. 1950s [*Builder* xxiii, 1865, 27].

PRESTWICK LODGE, nr. PONTELAND, NORTHUMB., for P. Fenwick, 1815.

UNTHANK HALL, NORTHUMB., additions for Robert Pearson, 1815, and for Dixon Dixon, 1860.

BIRTLEY HALL, CO. DURHAM, for J. Warwick, 1815; dem. *c.*1916.

BENWELL GROVE, nr. NEWCASTLE, for Charles Cook, 1816; dem.

MINSTERACRES, nr. HEXHAM, NORTHUMB., enlarged for George Silvertopp, 1816.

ELAND HALL, PONTELAND, NORTHUMB., for William Barkley, 1816.

WHICKHAM, CO. DURHAM, house for J. Errington, 1816.

NEWCASTLE, STRAWBERRY PLACE, house for J. Harvey, *c.*1816 [*N.D.J.*].

BOLAM HALL, NORTHUMB., layout of gardens and lake for Hon. W. H. Beresford, 1816–18 [*N.D.J.*].

WEST JESMOND HOUSE (later JESMOND TOWERS), NEWCASTLE, additions for Sir Thomas Burdon, 1817; further additions for Robert Burdon Sanderson, 1823–7; much enlarged by subsequent owners; now La Sagesse Convent School, Gothic.

AXWELL PARK, CO. DURHAM, alterations and additions for Sir John Clavering, Bart., including garden temple, 1817–18.

JESMOND GROVE, NEWCASTLE, for James Losh, 1817.

VILLA REALE (later SANDYFORD PARK), JESMOND, NEWCASTLE, for Capt. John Dutton, 1817 [*N.D.J.*].

DOXFORD HALL, NORTHUMB., for William Taylor, 1817–18.

BELFORD HALL, NORTHUMB., alterations and additions for William Clark, 1817–18.

JESMOND VILLA (or HOUSE), NEWCASTLE, additions for Armorer Donkin, 1818.

BLACK DENE (afterwards JESMOND DENE) HOUSE, JESMOND, NEWCASTLE, for T. E. Headlam, M.D., 1818; rebuilt by Dobson for William Cruddace, 1851, and subsequently by Norman Shaw.

CHIPCHASE CASTLE, NORTHUMB., restoration of fenestration and other alterations for John Reed, 1819 (*C. Life*, 21 June 1956).

PRESTON VILLA, NORTH SHIELDS, NORTHUMB., for John Fenwick, 1819; dem.

ROCK TOWER, NORTHUMB., restoration and alterations for Charles Bosanquet, 1819.

HEXHAM ABBEY HOUSE, NORTHUMB., alterations for T. R. Beaumont, 1819 (presumably repairs after fire in 1818).

HEBBURN HALL, CO. DURHAM, alterations for Cuthbert Ellison, 1819.

WEST CHIRTON HOUSE, NORTH SHIELDS, NORTHUMB., for Michael Robson, 1819; dem.

BROOME PARK, NORTHUMB., alterations for William Burrell, 1820; dem. 1953.

BIDDLESTONE HALL, nr. ROTHBURY, NORTHUMB., alterations for Walter Selby, 1820; dem. *c.*1965.

HAWTHORN DENE HOUSE, nr. SEAHAM, CO. DURHAM, for Major Anderson, 1821, Gothic; remodelled as Hawthorn Tower by Thomas Moore of Sunderland *c.*1850; dem. or ruinous.

SOUTH HILL HOUSE, PLAWSWORTH, CO. DURHAM., for Thomas Fenwick, 1821; since altered.

SWANSFIELD HOUSE, nr. ALNWICK, NORTHUMB., alterations (?) for Henry Collingwood Selby, 1823; dem. 1975.

NEWTON-ON-THE-MOOR, NORTHUMB., house for Thomas Jamieson, 1823 [*N.D.J.*].

HALTWHISTLE, NORTHUMB., house for Revd. N. J. Hollingsworth, 1823.

NEWBROUGH HALL, NORTHUMB., for Revd. H. W. Wastell, 1823.

SHERIFF HILL HALL, GATESHEAD, CO. DURHAM, for R. Plummer, 1823; dem. [*N.D.J.*].

THE KNELLS, HOUGHTON, nr. CARLISLE, CUMBERLAND, for John Dixon, 1824 and/or 1845.

LONGHIRST HOUSE, nr. MORPETH, NORTHUMB., for William Lawson, 1824–8 (*C. Life*, 17 Feb. 1966).

FLOTTERTON HOUSE, NORTHUMB., for C. Weallans, 1825 [Mackenzie, *Northumberland*, ii, 1825, 485].

NUNNYKIRK HALL, NORTHUMB., rebuilt for William Orde, 1825 (*C. Life*, 17 Feb. 1966).

SHAWDON HALL, NORTHUMB., alterations and additions for William Pawson, 1825 [*N.D.J.*] and for W. J. H. Pawson, 1858, probably including E. Lodge and gates (*C. Life*, 5 March 1959).

ARCOT HALL, CRAMLINGTON, NORTHUMB., additions for George Shum Storey, *c.*1825 [*N.D.J.*].

GORTANLOISK, nr. DUNOON, ARGYLLSHIRE, shooting lodge for Sir John Fife, Bart., 1827.

BELLISTER CASTLE, NORTHUMB., alterations for John Kirsop, 1827; restored after fire 1901 [*N.D.J.*].

MATFEN, NORTHUMB., alterations (probably to the Dower House) for Sir Edward Blackett, Bart., 1828.

EMBLETON VICARAGE, NORTHUMB., Tudor Gothic additions to pele tower for Revd. G. D. Grimes, 1828 [*N.D.J.*].

LILBURN TOWER, nr. WOOLER, NORTHUMBERLAND, for H. J. W. Collingwood, 1829–37, Tudor Gothic; stables, etc. added for E. J. Collingwood, 1843–4 [G. Jackson-Stops in *C. Life*, 8 Nov. 1973].

WOOLSINGTON HALL, NORTHUMB., alterations for Matthew Bell, 1828.

MITFORD HALL, NORTHUMB., for B. O. Mitford, 1828–9 (designed 1823) (*C. Life*, 17 Feb. 1966).

HARBOTTLE CASTLE HOUSE, NORTHUMB., alterations for T. F. Clennell, 1829.

RIDLEY HALL, NORTHUMB., alterations for John Davison, 1829.

GLANTON PIKE, WHITTINGHAM, NORTHUMB., additions for Henry Collingwood, 1829.

TREWHITT HOUSE, nr. ROTHBURY, NORTHUMB., alterations (?) for J. Smart, 1830.

BENWELL TOWER (since 1881 Bishop of Newcastle's house), nr. NEWCASTLE, for Thomas Crawhall, 1830–1, Tudor Gothic; chapel added 1881.

BRINKBURN PRIORY HOUSE, NORTHUMB., additions for Major William Hodgson-Cadogan, 1830–7.

CHESTERS, nr. HEXHAM, NORTHUMB., additions for John Clayton, 1832 and 1837; remodelled by Norman Shaw 1893.

BLENKINSOPP HALL, NORTHUMB., additions (removed mid-20th century) for Col. J. B. Coulson, 1832 and 1837.

MELDON PARK, NORTHUMB., for Isaac Cookson, 1832 (*C. Life*, 24 Feb. 1966).

DARLINGTON, CO. DURHAM, house for J. Wilson, 1832–4.

HOLME EDEN, CUMBERLAND, for Peter Dixon, 1833–7, Tudor Gothic.

NEASHAM HALL, CO. DURHAM, large additions in Elizabethan style for J. S. Cookson, 1834–7; dem. 1970.

HIGH WARDEN, nr. HEXHAM, NORTHUMB., additions for John Errington, 1834.

BEAUFRONT CASTLE, NORTHUMB., rebuilt for William Cuthbert, 1837–41, Gothic (*C. Life*, 29 Jan.–5 Feb. 1976).

CRASTER TOWER, NORTHUMB., minor alterations for Thomas Wood-Craster, 1839 [*N.D.J.*; drawings in Northumberland C.R.O.].

TYNEMOUTH, NORTHUMB., crescent and villas for Messrs Dawson & Bowes, 1839 [F. & G. citing *Newcastle Advertiser*, 2 Feb., 1 June 1839].

SWINBURNE CASTLE, NORTHUMB., alterations for Thomas Riddell, 1840; dem.

EAST BOLDON HOUSE, CO. DURHAM, alterations for William Gray, 1840.

NEWCASTLE, JESMOND HIGH TERRACE, *c.*1840; dem. 1960s.

NEWCASTLE, ST. THOMAS'S PLACE (terrace), *c.*1840; dem. 1960s [*N.D.J.*].

NEWCASTLE, JESMOND ROAD, houses, including CARLTON TERRACE (Nos. 29–49), *c.*1840–5; some dem. [*N.D.J.* and sources cited by F. & G., 104].

ANGERTON HALL, NORTHUMB., for Ralph Atkinson, 1842, Tudor Gothic [F. & G. citing *Newcastle Journal*, 15 Jan. 1842].

BAMBURGH CASTLE, NORTHUMB., restoration for Lord Crewe's Trustees, 1843.

HACKWOOD HOUSE (formerly 'The Hags'), HEXHAM, NORTHUMB., for Charles Head, 1843.

HAUGHTON CASTLE, NORTHUMB., restoration for William Smith, 1844–5.

LINETHWAITE, nr. WHITEHAVEN, CUMBERLAND, for H. Harrison, 1845 [*Builder* xxiii, 1865, 27].

CLEADON COTTAGE, nr. SUNDERLAND, CO.

DURHAM, for Robert Swinburne, 1845; dem. 1981.

CHATTON VICARAGE (incorporating a pele tower) for Revd. Matthew Burrell, 1845 [F. & G. citing *Newcastle Courant*, 10 Jan. 1845 and drawings in Northumberland C.R.O., Queen Anne's Bounty Mortgage Papers].

THE BANK HOUSE, NEWBIGGIN, nr. MIDDLETON-IN-TEESDALE, CO. DURHAM, for J. H. Hinde, 1845.

SETTRINGTON RECTORY, YORKS. (E.R.), for Revd. C. M. Long, soon after 1846 [*Builder* xxiii, 1865, 27].

SANDHOE HOUSE, nr. HEXHAM, NORTHUMB., for Sir Rowland Errington, Bart., 1846–7, Jacobean.

CHOLLERTON VICARAGE (now GRANGE), NORTHUMB., additions 1847 [F. & G. citing drawings in Northumberland C.R.O., Queen Anne's Bounty Mortgage Papers].

SCAR HOUSE, ARKENGARTHDALE, YORKS. (N.R.), for John Gilpin, 1847–55 (*C. Life*, 25 Feb. 1988).

STOCKTON-ON-TEES, CO. DURHAM, HOLY TRINITY VICARAGE, 1850–1 [*N.D.J.*; drawings in Durham C.R.O., Queen Anne's Bounty Mortgage Papers, 39].

PENNYTHORNE HOUSE, MIDDLESBROUGH, YORKS. (N.R.), for A. Topham, 1851.

HIGH CROSS (hamlet), BENWELL, NORTHUMB., 1851; dem.

RYTON, CO. DURHAM, extensive additions to house for R. Leadbitter, 1851.

BENFIELDSIDE VICARAGE, CO. DURHAM, 1851, Tudor Gothic [F. & G. citing *Newcastle Journal*, 11 Jan. 1851; drawings in Durham C.R.O., Queen Anne's Bounty Mortgage Papers, 38].

NEWTON HALL, nr. BYWELL, NORTHUMB., alterations for W. F. Blackett, 1851.

OATLANDS HOUSE, OATLANDS PARK, SURREY, for W. C. Hewitson, 1851, Tudor Gothic; dem. 1972.

WINDSOR, BERKS., CHURCH HOUSE, for Revd. Stephen Hawtrey, 1851.

SUDBROOKE HOLME, LINCS., additions in Tudor style for Richard Ellison, 1851; dem. For a Tudor estate cottage here designed by Dobson see Loudon's *Encyclopaedia of Cottage, Farm & Villa Architecture*, 1846, ed., 1176.

FRIEDELHAUSEN, HESSEN, GERMANY, NEUES SCHLOSS, designs for Gothic castle for Baron von Nordeck zur Rabenau and his English wife, erected 1852–6 under the direction of the German architect Martin Unger [drawings and correspondence in Hessisches Staatsarchiv Marburg, Bestand 340, Nordeck zur Rabenau Acc. 1972/38, V 9, *ex inf.* Mr. Angus Fowler].

HENDON, SUNDERLAND, CO. DURHAM, ST. PAUL'S RECTORY, 1851; dem.

DILDAWN HOUSE, nr. CASTLE DOUGLAS, KIRKCUDBRIGHTSHIRE, alterations for Revd. Dr. Cowan, 1852, probably including addition of porch.

THE LEAZES, nr. HEXHAM, NORTHUMB., rebuilt for William Kirsopp, 1853.

CLEADON MEADOWS, nr. SUNDERLAND, CO. DURHAM, for Robert Shortridge, 1853; dem.

BISHOPWEARMOUTH RECTORY, CO. DURHAM, alterations 1853.

WALLINGTON HALL, NORTHUMB., the Central Hall for Sir Walter Trevelyan, Bart., 1853–4 (*C. Life*, 30 April 1970).

SEGHILL PARSONAGE, NORTHUMB., 1855.

WHITBURN HALL, CO. DURHAM, alterations (including Entrance Hall and Drawing Room) for Sir Hedworth Williamson, Bart., 1856; dem. 1980.

LAMBTON CASTLE, CO. DURHAM, major structural repairs and rebuilding for 2nd Earl of Durham, 1857–62, completed by Sydney Smirke, 1862–6, partly dem. 1930 [Dobson, *Memoir*, 32–4; F. & G. citing *Newcastle Courant*, 9 Oct. 1857 and drawing in Laing Art Gallery, Newcastle] (*C. Life*, 24–31 March 1966).

HOLEYN HALL, NORTHUMB., additions for Edward James, 1858.

INGLETHORPE HALL, nr. WISBECH, NORFOLK, for Charles Metcalfe, 1858–60.

JESMOND DENE HOUSE, NEWCASTLE, additions and detached banqueting house for Sir William G. Armstrong, 1860–2; dem. 1920s.

GREENWOOD, nr. EASTLEIGH, HANTS., for George Palmer, 1861; dem.

Domestic Works of Uncertain Date

CASTLETOWN HOUSE, ROCKCLIFFE, CUMBERLAND. According to the obituary in *N.D.J.* Dobson was employed at this house by 'Mounsey, Esq.' in 1847. An enlargement by Robert Mounsey (d. 1842) is recorded by the date 1831 over a door at the back of the house, but his successor G. G. Mounsey may have further altered the house in 1847 (*C. Life*, 7 Sept. 1989).

GIBSIDE, CO. DURHAM. According to his daughter Dobson made 'large additions' to this house for Lord Strathmore in 1813, 1815 and 1856. An unexecuted design by Dobson for additions dated 1814 is in the Durham C.R.O., D. St.x.46. By 1856 the owner was Sir William Hutt, M.P., who had married the widow of the 9th Earl in 1831. The house is now a ruin.

GOSFORTH HOUSE, NORTHUMBERLAND. According to his daughter Dobson made 'large additions to this house for 'Ralph

Brandling' in 1818, but according to the obituary in *N.D.J.* he made 'alterations to the north front' and designed a gateway for 'C. H. Brandling, Esq.'. The owners of the house during the first half of the 19th century were C. J. Brandling (d. 1826) followed by the Revd. Ralph Henry Brandling (d. 1853). The latter sold the contents of the house in 1836 and the whole property in 1852. The house was burnt by suffragettes in 1914 and rebuilt in 1921.

MONUMENTS, ETC.

HOLY ISLAND, Cross in Market Place for Henry Collingwood Selby, 1829 [*Proc. Soc. Antiquaries of Newcastle-on-Tyne*, 3rd. ser. iii, 1907–8, 286].

TYNEMOUTH, NORTHUMB., THE COLLINGWOOD MONUMENT, 1842–5; pedestals for guns added 1849.

Funerary Monuments: BAMBURGH CHURCH, NORTHUMB., William Clark (d. 1837), Gothic; DONCASTER, YORKS. (W.R.), ST. GEORGE, female member of Ellison family, probably Harriet Ellison (d. 1849), destroyed; NEWCASTLE, ST. NICHOLAS (CATHEDRAL), Robert Williamson (d. 1835) and James Archbold (d. 1849); NEWCASTLE GENERAL CEMETERY, Archibald Reed (d. 1842), Gothic [F. & G. 103–7 and sources there cited].

DODDS, JOHN (–1801), was a builder and architect of Newcastle-on-Tyne. In 1784 he was employed by John Reed to carry out minor alterations to CHIPCHASE CASTLE, NORTHUMBERLAND [Gordon Nares in *C. Life*, 14–21 June, 1956], and in 1788 he made an unexecuted design for rebuilding LAMBTON HALL, CO. DURHAM, for General John Lambton [C. Hussey in *C. Life*, 24 March 1966, 667]. In 1786 he and David Stephenson surveyed the church of ALL SAINTS, NEWCASTLE, and decided that it must be completely rebuilt. He submitted designs for a new church, but they were rejected in favour of Stephenson's [T. Sopwith, *An Historical and Descriptive Account of All Saints Church, Newcastle*, 1826, 19, 47]. In 1786–8 a W. tower was added to CHRIST CHURCH, NORTH SHIELDS, NORTHUMBERLAND, by Dodds and in 1792–3 the rest of the church was rebuilt to his designs [*Newcastle Courant*, 19 Aug. 1786, 21 April 1792, *ex inf.* Mrs. G. McCombie]. GOSFORTH CHURCH, NORTHUMBERLAND, was rebuilt to his designs in 1798–9 [*History of Northumberland* xiii, 336]. His death on 27 June 1801 was reported in the *Newcastle Advertiser* on 4 July of that year.

DONALDSON, JAMES (*c.*1756–1843), was a member of an Ayrshire family, and eventually inherited an estate in that county called Williamshaw (in Stewarton parish). In 1774 he was apprenticed to Thomas Leverton, and later married his niece Jane (daughter of Andrew) Leverton [P.R.O., Apprenticeship Registers; *V.C.H. Essex* vi, 268, n. 59]. It was 'from Mr. Leverton's' that in 1777 he exhibited his first drawing at the Royal Academy – 'a design for a temple'. In 1782 Robert Mylne engaged him as a clerk, and he remained in Mylne's office for some years. From 1809 until his death he held one of the district surveyorships for the City of London. He lived in Bloomsbury, and in 1793 exhibited at the Royal Academy a 'Design for the new schoolroom now building in Bloomsbury Churchyard, with an elevation of the Church'. In the British Library there is (*King's Maps* xxvii, 29 (3)) 'An Ideographical View of the New Chapel, Tavistock Place, Russell Square', signed 'J. Donaldson del. scul. etc. 1802.' The Tavistock (afterwards St. Andrew's) Chapel was built by James Burton in 1801 and demolished in 1900. A survey plan of Culzean Castle, Ayrshire, by James Donaldson, dated 1818, is preserved in a portfolio there. His designs for enlarging CLUTTON RECTORY, SOMERSET, 1817, are in the Somerset C.R.O. [D/D/Bbm, 45]. Donaldson died in Bloomsbury on 8 October 1843, aged 87 [*Gent's Mag.* 1843 (ii), 553; P.R.O. PROB 11/1988, 759].

Donaldson's elder son James supervised the erection of the SURREY THEATRE, BLACKFRIARS ROAD, to the designs of R. Cabanel in 1805–6, but 'fell a sacrifice to his great exertions and anxiety to get the theatre finished within the time that he had engaged', and died in 1806 at an early age [J. Elmes, *Metropolitan Improvements*, 1831, 135]. The most distinguished member of the family was his younger son Thomas Leverton Donaldson (1795–1885), who as a teacher, scholar and virtual founder of the R.I.B.A. was a prominent figure in the Victorian architectural scene. Regarded as 'the father of the profession', he was President of the R.I.B.A. in 1863–4, and was awarded the Royal Gold Medal in 1851. In 1842 he became the first Professor of Architecture at University College London, and held the post for over twenty years (see Sandra Blutman in *R.I.B.A. Jnl.* Dec. 1967, 542–4, for a fuller account of his career). As a practising architect he was less distinguished, but his works included HOLY TRINITY CHURCH, BROMPTON, 1826–9, Gothic (criticized in *Gent's Mag.* 1830 (i), 579–80, and made ecclesiologically more correct by Blore in 1843); the handsome classical library of UNIVERSITY COLLEGE LONDON, 1848–9; UNIVERSITY HALL (now Dr. Williams's Library), GORDON SQUARE, LONDON, 1848–9, Tudor Gothic; the centre of DALBY HALL, LEICS., for E. B. Hartopp, 1837–8, dem. 1951 [exhib. at R.A. 1837]; LAMBOURNE PLACE, BERKS., for Henry Hippisley, 1846, Jacobethan, dem. [exhib. at R.A. 1846]; and the refronting of SHOBROOKE PARK, DEVON, for J. H. Hippisley, 1845, dem. 1947 [*Builder*, 8 Aug. 1885, 179].

DONALDSON, THOMAS LEVERTON (1795–1885), *see* DONALDSON, JAMES.

DONN, WILLIAM, appears to have been a pupil of Lancelot Brown, for in a letter to a client about architects' charges he refers to 'Messrs. Adam, Sr. Wm. Chambers, Paine, Taylor, [and] my old master Browne'. He competed for the Royal Exchange, Dublin, in 1769, and exhibited his design at the Royal Academy in 1770. He also exhibited at the Free Society of Artists in 1770 and 1775. From 1769 to 1773 he was Surveyor to the Westminster Commission of Sewers. In 1774 he was living at Turnham Green in Middlesex.

One of Donn's patrons was the 2nd Earl of Fife, who in 1766–7 employed him to execute a design by Robert Adam for a 'Great Room' at FIFE HOUSE, WHITEHALL (dem. 1869). In 1774 Donn informed Thomas Estcourt that he had been paid £1508 for executing it, and among the drawings at Claydon House, Bucks., there is one of the 'Ceiling of Lord Fife's Great Room at Whitehall', endorsed 'Mr. Donn to be left at the Inn, Aylesbury'. In 1767 Lord Fife was also employing Donn to make drawings for proposed alterations to INNES HOUSE, MORAYSHIRE [*Lord Fife and his Factor*, ed. A. & H. Tayler, 1925, 42], where he may have designed the Georgian wings (dem. *c.*1860) illustrated in *C. Life*, 4 Nov. 1976, fig. 6.

Letters and drawings preserved at CLAYDON HOUSE, BUCKS., show that in the 1770s Donn was employed by Lord Verney to complete the ball-room and rotunda designed by Sir Thomas Robinson, and that at the same time he was engaged in altering the interior of APPULDURCOMBE HOUSE in the ISLE OF WIGHT for Sir Richard Worsley. Here he may have been supervising the execution of designs made by James Wyatt [L. O. J. Boynton, *Appuldurcombe House*, H.M.S.O. 1986, 31]. In 1774 Donn made designs for remodelling ESTCOURT PARK, GLOS. (dem. 1963) for Thomas Estcourt, but they do not appear to have been adopted [Glos. C.R.O., D 1571/E 356]. A reference in one of Donn's letters to Estcourt to his plans for Mr. Master's house indicates that he probably designed THE ABBEY, CIRENCESTER, GLOS., for Thomas Master, *c.*1774, dem. 1964.

DONOWELL, JOHN, appears to have made a living chiefly as an architectural draughtsman until he eventually became surveyor to the Earl of Salisbury. In 1754 he issued proposals for engraving and publishing by subscription a series of 'Perspective Views of the Colleges and other Public Buildings of Oxford' [*Jackson's Oxford Jnl.* 9 Nov. 1754], and eight prints, signed 'J. Donowell Arch.', were issued the following year. Other drawings of his which were engraved include two of St. Giles-in-the-Fields Church (1753), six of the gardens of Chiswick House (1753), two of Cliveden House (1753),[1] one of Ironmongers' Hall (1753), and one of Marylebone Gardens (1761) [cf. Michael Symes, 'John Donowell's Views of Chiswick and other Gardens', *Jnl. of Garden History* vii, 1987]. He exhibited at the Free Society of Artists (1761), at the Society of Artists at Spring Gardens (1762–70), and at the Royal Academy (1778–86). Many of his exhibits were of a topographical character, but they included a design for Skinners' Hall (1781), several for noblemen's houses, and a 'Sketch of a Design for a Palace'.

The plan and elevation of WEST WYCOMBE PARK, BUCKS., in the fifth volume of *Vitruvius Britannicus* (1771) are subscribed 'J. Donowell Archt.' Payments by the hand of J. Donowell are recorded under the year 1755 in the manuscript account-book of Banister Watts, a High Wycombe mason, who was employed by Sir Francis Dashwood in the house and grounds. Moreover, there is among the Dashwood papers a letter from Donowell about the purchase of Portland stone, dated 22 Sept. 1763, and there are payments to 'Mr. Donowell's men' in the West Wycombe accounts for 1761–3. He appears to have been employed to remodel the house under Dashwood's supervision, acting as draughtsman and clerk of works rather than as an autonomous architect. Even in this subordinate capacity he failed to give satisfaction and was dismissed in 1764. A friend of Dashwood commented: 'I believe the man is honest & does to the best of his Abilities, but these I am afraid from the experience I have had of him are not very extensive' [Bodleian Library,

[1] A drawing by Donowell of the S. front of Cliveden House is in the Print Room of the British Museum.

MSS. D. D. Dashwood, B 11/12/42, B 11/8/2a].

In the 1770s Donowell was employed by the 6th Earl of Salisbury as surveyor of his London estate, making in 1775 plans for urban development on the earl's property in Bermondsey. For the 7th Earl, who succeeded in 1780, he continued to act in this capacity for some years. In 1780–2 he carried out a 'complete repair' of the earl's country seat, HATFIELD HOUSE, HERTS. At the same time he designed the 'Pepper-Pot Lodges' there, which are remarkable as probably the earliest buildings in England in a neo-Jacobean style (cf. *C. Life*, 1 Dec. 1983, fig. 6). In 1783–4 he was responsible for repairs and alterations to Salisbury's London house, No. 20 ARLINGTON STREET (rebuilt *c.*1870 and since dem.), for which in 1787 he designed a new staircase, and in 1788 he designed a WORKHOUSE at HATFIELD, dem. *c.*1985 [Hatfield House archives, C.P.M. Supp. 58–9; drawings, vol. 14333; Accounts 106/12; Bills 566; 'Family Papers Supplement', vol. 4, f. 111; Pennant, *Journey from Chester to London*, 1782, 411; information from Mr. R. Harcourt-Williams]. According to Hutchins, *History of Dorset* ii, 1863, 443, the bridge at WEYMOUTH, DORSET, built in 1770 (dem. 1824) was 'executed by Mr. John Donowell'.

DONTHORN, WILLIAM JOHN (1799–1859), was born at Swaffham in Norfolk, where his father was a hatter. He became a pupil of Jeffry Wyatville (1817–20), and subsequently practised from 18 Hanover Street, London. He exhibited regularly at the Royal Academy from 1817 to 1853 and at the Norwich Society of Artists from 1815 onwards. He was a founder member of the R.I.B.A. E.J. Payne was his pupil. He died at Hastings on 18 May 1859, and is commemorated by a tablet in the north aisle of Swaffham Church. A large collection of his drawings is in the R.I.B.A. Drawings Collection. It was originally bound in four volumes entitled 'Classic Mansions', 'Gothic Mansions', 'Parsonage Houses' and 'Plans', and appears to have been intended for publication.

Donthorn had an extensive practice as a designer of country houses and parsonages, especially in his native county of Norfolk. His classical houses were remarkably uncompromising essays in a simplified Greek Revival style from which ornament was almost eliminated in order to create austere compositions of plain rectangular blocks. When carried out in pale East Anglian brick, Donthorn's classical houses were not calculated to appeal to any but the most sophisticated taste, and all of them have been demolished with the exception of Upton Hall (Notts.), which has more of the character of a villa by Decimus Burton. As a purveyor of Tudor Gothic Donthorn inherited Wyatville's picturesque style, but imposed on it a mannered verticality of his own. Although he joined the Cambridge Camden Scoiety in 1843 he failed to satisfy the standards of the ecclesiologists and despite many commissions for parsonage houses he designed only three new churches and 'restored' a fourth. His design for a new square adjoining Westminster Abbey, exhibited at the R.A. in 1846, was condemned in the *Gentleman's Magazine* (1846 (ii), 292) as an outmoded 'resuscitation of Wyatt's darling fancies', and it was noted as typical of his approach to Gothic design that the turrets of his parsonage houses often did duty as chimneys.

In 1844 Donthorn won the competition for the Leicester Memorial at Holkham by methods that were criticized both in the correspondence columns of the *Builder* (ii, 1844, 12, 23, 36), and in the *Narrative* of the proceedings that was subsequently printed. The design (derived from Nelson's Column in Trafalgar Square) consisted of a fluted column surmounted by a wheatsheaf and standing on a pedestal adorned with sculptures symbolizing Coke of Norfolk's agricultural achievements.

[*Gent's Mag.* 1859 (ii), 659; *Builder* xvii, 1859, 367; *Ecclesiologist* iii, 1843, 44; *Catalogue of the R.I.B.A. Drawings Collection: C–F*, 83–9; R. O'Donnell, 'W. J. Donthorn', *Arch. Hist.* xxi, 1978.]

DOMESTIC ARCHITECTURE

MARHAM HOUSE, NORFOLK, added dining-room and circular drawing-room for Henry Villebois, *c.*1822; dem. [R.I.B.A.D., which includes a rejected Gothic design] (R. H. Mason, *Norfolk Photographically Illustrated*, 1865).

WESTACRE HIGH HOUSE, NORFOLK, altered house and designed stables for Anthony Hammond, *c.*1823–9 [R.I.B.A.D.].

HILLINGTON HALL, NORFOLK, remodelled for Sir William Browne Ffolkes, Bart., 1824–8, Gothic; dem. *c.*1946 except stables and lodges [R.I.B.A.D.; exhib. at R.A. 1824, 1825, 1828, 1841 and at Norwich Soc. of Artists 1823, 1824, 1825].

FELBRIGG HALL, NORFOLK, castellated Gothic stables for Admiral William Windham, 1825, and north corridor 1831 [R.I.B.A.D.; drawings at Felbrigg; exhib. at R.A. 1826 and at Norwich Soc. of Artists 1830].

TWICKENHAM, MIDDLESEX, ULLESWATER COTTAGE, for C. Dufour, 1827 [exhib. at R.A. 1827].

CROMER HALL, NORFOLK, for George Thomas Wyndham, 1827; destroyed by fire 1829 and rebuilt to Donthorn's designs; altered by D. Brandon 1875; Gothic [R.I.B.A.D.; exhib. at Norwich Soc. of Artists 1830; R. W. Ketton-Cremer, *Felbrigg*, 1962, 232].

PICKENHAM HALL, NORFOLK, remodelled for W. L. Wiggett Chute, 1829; rebuilt 1903–4 [R.I.B.A.D.; exhib. at R.A. 1829 and at Norwich Soc. of Artists 1830] (R. H. Mason, *Norfolk Photographically Illustrated*, 1865).

WATLINGTON HALL, NORFOLK, for Charles Berners Plestow, 1830; destroyed by fire *c.*1943 [R.I.B.A.D.; exhib. at Norwich Soc. of Artists 1830].

ELMHAM HALL, NORFOLK, remodelled for the Hon. G. J. Milles, 1830; dem. *c.*1925 [R.I.B.A.D.; exhib. at Norwich Soc. of Artists 1830] (R. H. Mason, *Norfolk Photographically Illustrated*, 1865).

UPTON HALL, nr. SOUTHWELL, NOTTS., for Thomas Wright, *c.*1830 [R.I.B.A.D.].

HIGHCLIFFE CASTLE, HANTS., remodelled for Lord Stuart de Rothesay, incorporating the materials of the French 'Hotel des Andelys', 1830–4, Gothic [R.I.B.A.D.; exhib. R.A. 1835, 1838; letters printed by Augustus J. C. Hare in *The Story of Two Noble Lives* i, 1893, 177–9] (*C. Life*, 24 April, 1–8 May 1942, where 'Pennethorne' is a mistake for 'Donthorn').

WOOLLAND HOUSE, DORSET, alterations and additions for G. C. Loftus, 1833; dem. [R.I.B.A.D.; exhib. at R.A. 1833].

BURE HOMAGE, MUDEFORD, HANTS., remodelled for Baroness de Feuchères, *c.*1835; dem. 1956 [R.I.B.A.D.; exhib. at R.A. 1835]. But cf. J. Davies.

STANGROUND, HUNTS., alterations to house for the Revd. William Strong (d. 1842) or for his son the Revd. William Strong [R.I.B.A.D.].

PETERBOROUGH, THE DEANERY (now PRIOR'S GATE), remodelled 1842, and Tudor Gothic houses in Close flanking entrance to Bishop's Palace [R.I.B.A.D.; exhib. at R.A. 1842] (*C. Life*, 3 April 1958).

FOLKINGTON PLACE, SUSSEX, for Thomas Sheppard, 1844, Tudor Gothic [R.I.B.A.D.; exhib. at R.A. 1844] (*C. Life*, 3 April 1958).

CUCKFIELD PARK, SUSSEX, alterations for Warden Sergison, *c.*1850 [R.I.B.A.D.] (*C. Life*, 15–22 March 1919).

SHELFORD HOUSE, GREAT SHELFORD, CAMBS., for Capt. Robert G. Wale, *c.*1850, Gothic [R.I.B.A.D.].

HERONDEN HALL, TENTERDEN, KENT, for W. Whelan, 1853, Tudor Gothic [R.I.B.A.D.].

WALLINGTON HALL, NORFOLK, lodges for Edmund Peel, 1853 [exhib. at R.A. 1853].

PUBLIC BUILDINGS, ETC.

attributed: HILLINGTON CHURCH, NORFOLK, rebuilt 1823–4, Gothic.

PETERBOROUGH, GAOL and SESSIONS HOUSE, 1841–2 [exhib. at R.A. 1841].

SOUTH RUNCTON CHURCH, NORFOLK, Gothic monument to Robert Peel of Wallington Hall (d. 1842) [*Norwich Mercury*, 28 Feb. 1843, *ex inf.* Mr. David Cubitt].

UPPER DICKER, SUSSEX, HOLY TRINITY CHURCH, 1843, neo-Norman [I.C.B.S.].

HOLKHAM, NORFOLK, THE LEICESTER MONUMENT (a column in memory of Thomas Coke, Earl of Leicester), 1845–50 [*Narrative of the Proceedings regarding the Erection of the Leicester Monument*, Norwich 1850].

STOKE FERRY CHURCH, NORFOLK, restoration, 1847–8 [*Ecclesiologist* viii, 1848, 396].

KINGSTHORPE CHURCH, NORTHANTS., rebuilt chancel, 1850, Gothic [*Builder* viii, 1850, 557].

BAGTHORPE CHURCH, NORFOLK, 1853–4, Gothic [*Norfolk Chronicle*, 20 Aug. 1853].

PARSONAGES

Donthorn appears to have designed or altered the following rectories and vicarages, for nearly all of which there are drawings in the R.I.B.A. Collection. The dates of erection have usually been ascertained from other sources. The style is normally Tudor Gothic: CHIGWELL VICARAGE, ESSEX, *c.*1850; DUMMER RECTORY, HANTS., 1850; FINCHAM RECTORY, NORFOLK; FONTMELL RECTORY, DORSET; HALLATON RECTORY, LEICS., 1844; HOLME HALE RECTORY, NORFOLK, 1846; HORNBY VICARAGE, YORKS. (N.R.), 1827–8 [exhib. at R.A. 1828]; MOULTON ST. MICHAEL RECTORY, NORFOLK, 1831–2 (Italianate); OUNDLE VICARAGE, NORTHANTS., *c.*1845; PEASMARSH RECTORY (now HOUSE), SUSSEX, 1839; RUSHBURY RECTORY, SALOP., *c.*1852; THRAPSTON RECTORY, NORTHANTS., 1837; TITCHWELL RECTORY, NORFOLK, after 1824 (classical, dem.); TRUNCH RECTORY, NORFOLK, 1832; WEYBRIDGE RECTORY, SURREY.

WORKHOUSES

THRAPSTON, NORTHANTS., 1836 [*Architectural Mag.* iii, 1836, 482]; WISBECH, CAMBS., 1836, dem. [*Norfolk Chronicle*, 22 Oct. 1836];

SWAFFHAM, NORFOLK, 1836, dem. [*ibid.*, 28 Nov. 1835]; DOWNHAM MARKET, NORFOLK, 1836, dem. [*ibid.*, 17 Sept. 1836]; GAYTON, NORFOLK, 1836 [*ibid.*, 12 March 1836]; ELY UNION, 1837–8 [*ibid.*, 13 Oct. 1838]; AYLSHAM, NORFOLK, 1848–9 [*ibid.*, 1 April 1846]; WEST BECKHAM, NORFOLK, 1848–51 [*Builder* vi, 1848, 503] (references to *Norfolk Chronicle ex inf.* Mr. A. P. Baggs, Mr. R. O'Donnell and the late Mr. D. C. Young).

DORMER, HENRY (–1727), was an architect and land-surveyor who was active in Northamptonshire and Leicestershire during the reign of William III. Several estate surveys bearing his name are in the Northamptonshire Record Office. Towards the end of his life he became Master of the Jesus Hospital at Rothwell, Northants., where he died in 1727. Over the door of the hospital is a rhymed inscription signed 'Henry Dormer, Principal, 1721'.

The earliest evidence of Dormer's architectural work is in 1686, when he was paid for 'measuring a room of wainscot . . . wrought . . . by Henry Jones joyner' at LAMPORT HALL, NORTHANTS. [Sir Gyles Isham, 'Architectural History of Lamport', *Northants. Architectural and Archaeological Soc.'s Report* for 1951, 19]. In the same year he may have been concerned in the rebuilding of the top of the tower of CARLTON CURLIEU CHURCH, LEICS. [*V.C.H. Leics.* v, 80]. In 1693–4 the chapel of ST. MARY IN ARDEN, MARKET HARBOROUGH, LEICS., was rebuilt to his designs [Lincolnshire Record Office, Fac. 9/73]. It is now roofless and disused. From 1694 until early in 1697, when his place was taken by John Lumley, Dormer was employed by the 2nd Earl of Nottingham to supervise the rebuilding of BURLEY-ON-THE-HILL, RUTLAND, but his share (if any) in the design is uncertain[1] [H. J. Habakkuk, 'Daniel Finch, 2nd Earl of Nottingham: his House and Estate', in *Studies in Social History*, ed. J. H. Plumb, 1955, 148]. In 1706 Dormer made 'the modell of a new steeple' for BURTON OVERY CHURCH, LEICS. [Lincolnshire Record Office, Fac. 9/59]. Though considered 'very proper', it was not carried out. Dormer's original drawing is among the Wake Letters in the Library of Christ Church, Oxford (vol. iii). It shows a traditional battlemented tower with classical west door and cupola. St. Mary in Arden has round-headed windows with simplified tracery of a type that probably derived from Henry Bell's All Saints Church, Northampton.

DOTCHEN, JOHN, was a minor London architect whose existence is known almost exclusively from his exhibits at the Society of Artists (1772 and 1774) and the Royal Academy (1775–1810). They included 'a villa designed for a gentleman in Middlesex' (1776), 'a small villa just finished for a gentleman in Buckinghamshire' (1781), and 'a design for a Shire Hall in the North of England' (1784). In 1808 he won the third premium in the competition for the New Bethlehem Hospital.

DOUGLAS, JOHN (–*c.*1778?), practised as an architect in Edinburgh in the middle of the eighteenth century. In 1743 he stated that 'since the year 1730 he has built several Houses . . . for private Gentlemen' and that 'he has made Draughts of several Houses, which he has been afterwards imployed to build' [*Depositions in the cause William Adam v. Lord Braco*, 1743, 26]. In 1746 he was described as 'one John Douglas at Edinburgh, next in character to Mr. Adams, [who] has built several houses' [I. G. Lindsay & Mary Cosh, *Inveraray and the Dukes of Argyll*, 1973, 354, n. 40]. He was, in fact, a builder-architect of the same sort as his contemporary William Adam, but his practice was evidently on a smaller scale, and the list of recorded works given below does not include any major new country house or public building.

A collection of 38 drawings by Douglas in the National Monuments Record for Scotland throws some light on his architectural style. It includes several plans and elevations of country-house designs copied from Gibbs's *Book of Architecture*, Douglas's copy of which is in the same collection. Although the influence of Gibbs is apparent in some of Douglas's own designs, they are recognizably Scottish in such features as the larger proportion of wall to window and the use of turnpike stairs. In general, Douglas's architectural repertoire was not very different from that of Adam, but a distinctive feature of his work is a fondness for the polygonal: an octagonal church at Killin, octagonal steeples at

[1] From the papers in the Leicestershire Record Office (especially DG 7/1/128) it appears that Lord Nottingham was to a large extent his own architect. Before starting work he had obtained some advice from Wren and had measurements taken at Berkeley and Montagu Houses in London. Sir Henry Sheeres, the military engineer, also volunteered 'some Directions for my Lord Nottingham's building' dated 5 July 1695 (B.L., Sloane MS. 3828, ff. 176–80). Not only did Nottingham probably determine the design himself, he also drew up memoranda for the workmen's agreements and concerned himself with the minutiae of construction. When his brother Heneage was building at Albury in Surrey in 1698, Nottingham was able to give him some highly professional advice about his plans (see their correspondence in Leics. R.O., bundle 22).

Leuchars and Lochmaben, a canted bow at Archerfield, and large faceted urns as a decorative feature.

In 1734 the mason John Baxter, who was then building a house at Haddo in Aberdeenshire for the Earl of Aberdeen, reported to Sir John Clerk of Penicuik that John Douglas had been there and had annoyed him by criticizing his workmanship. Douglas, he told Clerk, was 'apt to break his toas on stons that lyes not in his road'. He was 'sorry to see such a cub who could nevor work a peice of good work all his days sett up for a Judge'. Douglas had given him a 'hint' of a design he had made for rebuilding Glasserton House, Wigtownshire (then recently destroyed by fire), and the new Galloway House that Baxter eventually built for its owner, Lord Garlies, on a different site, was at least partly based on drawings by Douglas [J. Macaulay, *The Classical Country House in Scotland 1660–1800*, 1987, 102]. In 1735–6 Douglas was involved in the enlargement of Quarrell, a house in Stirlingshire, to a design due ultimately to James Gibbs himself (see p. 405), and in 1736 he made designs for remodelling Blair Castle, Perthshire, for the 2nd Duke of Atholl in a classical style. These were not carried out but are preserved at Blair. In 1748 Douglas was responsible for two unexecuted schemes: one for the partial rebuilding of Holy Trinity Church at St. Andrews [S.R.O., CH 2/1132/5, pp. 324–6], the other for a plan for altering or rebuilding Dysart House, Fife, that was abandoned after John, Lord Sinclair's death in 1750 [S.R.O., GD 164/689, no. 12].

The John Douglas whose career can be followed from 1734 to 1757 was presumably the same as John Douglas, architect of Leith, who became a burgess of Edinburgh in 1745, and was still living in Leith in 1773–4 (see Williamson's *Edinburgh Directory* for that year), and with 'John Douglas of Pinkerton, Architect', whose will, dated at Leith on 26 March 1773, was proved in June 1778 [S.R.O., Edinburgh Testaments CC 8/8/124(2)].

ABERCAIRNY HOUSE, PERTHSHIRE, extensive repairs for James Moray, 1737–8 [S.R.O., GD 24/1/624].

KILLIN CHURCH, PERTHSHIRE. Douglas's plan for this church is mentioned in a letter of 1743 from Lord Breadalbane's chamberlain [N.R.A. Scotland, Survey 657, bundle 2], and he presumably designed the octagonal church built in 1744 by Thomas Clark, mason of Dunkeld.

LEUCHARS CHURCH, FIFE, octagonal tower, 1744 [contract in parish records, *ex inf.* Mr. W. Murray Jack].

LOCHMABEN, DUMFRIESSHIRE, THE TOLBOOTH, 1745; altered by D. Bryce, 1878 [this building closely resembles a design for a tolbooth in N.M.R.S., Douglas Drawings no. 36].

ARCHERFIELD HOUSE, EAST LOTHIAN, work for William Nisbet of Dirleton, 1745–6 [S.R.O., GD 6/1594, account for 1741–9, p. 22], and in June 1747 he contracted to build an addition (probably on the N. side) and two pavilions for £2360 sterling [contract at N.M.R.S.].

FINLAYSTON HOUSE, RENFREWSHIRE, contracted to build a new house of 3 storeys onto the W. end of the N. front for 13th Earl of Glencairn, 1746; remodelled *c.*1900 [S.R.O., GD 39/6/3/4/1 and cf. N.M.R.S. Douglas Drawings, nos. 27–35].

TAYMOUTH CASTLE, PERTHSHIRE, alterations for 2nd Earl of Breadalbane, 1746–50. Douglas's 'plans of the Dining Room, Entry to the House, & other things' are mentioned in the accounts of Lord Glenorchy, who was supervising the estate on behalf of his octogenarian father [S.R.O., GD 112/21/78].

HOLYROOD HOUSE, EDINBURGH, repairs 1754–7 [Edinburgh University Library, MS. Laing II, 88], and estimate for repairing the roof of the Abbey Church that might have been carried out but for the death of the 6th Duke of Hamilton, hereditary keeper of the palace [N.L.S., MS. 5371, ff. 196–209].

ST. ANDREWS, ST. SALVATOR'S COLLEGE, arcaded building on N. side, 1754–7; dem. *c.*1845 [R. G. Cant, 'St. Andrews Architects', *St. Andrews Preservation Trust Year Book* for 1966–7, 15].

DALHOUSIE CASTLE, MIDLOTHIAN. According to Sir Walter Scott the castle was 'mangled by a fellow called I believe Douglas, who destroyed as far as in him lay its military and baronial character and roofd it after the fashion of a Poor's house' (*Journal*, ed. W. E. K. Anderson, 1972, 403). A pyramidal Georgian roof is visible in views of the castle prior to Burn's restoration of 1826–8. The 8th Earl of Dalhousie, who succeeded in 1764, heads the list of executors in Douglas's will of 1773.

DOUGLAS, JOHN (*c.*1800–1862), though born in Northampton, was for most of his life a builder and surveyor at Sandiway, Weaverham, Cheshire. He was the father of John Douglas (1830–1911), the leading architect of Victorian Chester. The only building known to have been designed by the elder Douglas is HARTFORD LODGE (now WHITEHALL), HARTFORD, CHESHIRE, for Thomas Firth, 1835 [Twycross's *Mansions of England: Cheshire* i, 1850, with illustration;

Edward Hubbard, *The Work of John Douglas*, 1991, 1–2].

DOULL, WILLIAM (1791–1847), was the younger son of Alexander Doull, a Scottish plumber and glazier established in Greenwich. He became a pupil of Sir Robert Smirke, entered the Royal Academy Schools in 1814, and won the Silver Medal the following year. In 1819 he submitted designs for St. Peter's, Eaton Square, London, but they were not accepted [Westminster City Library, minutes of Building Committee among records of St. George's, Hanover Square]. In 1821 he exhibited at the Royal Academy a design for a church at Gibraltar. From 1836 to 1846 he was surveyor or assistant surveyor to the Westminster Commissioners of Sewers.

DOUTHWAITE, RICHARD W—, was in 1788 a pupil of James Paine, from whose office he exhibited a design for a temple at the Royal Academy in that year. In the following year Robert Mylne engaged him as a clerk at £40 p.a., and he remained in Mylne's office until Christmas 1800 [Robert Mylne's diary], exhibiting further designs at the Academy between 1791 and 1796. In 1820 he was acting as assistant to D. A. Alexander [Fishmongers' Company's records, *ex inf.* the late Priscilla Metcalf]. He subsequently became surveyor to the London Dock Company. A reference in one of Rickman's workbooks (B.L., Add. MS. 37801, f. 79[v]) suggests that he was still alive in 1832.

DOVE, JOHN (–1773), described as 'sometime of London, thereafter of Edinburgh, Architect', was presumably established in the latter city by 1763, when he married the daughter of an Edinburgh merchant. In 1772–3 he built, and no doubt designed, LADY GLENORCHY'S CHAPEL, EDINBURGH, dem. 1845. On 18 August 1773 he and his foreman were both killed when the scaffolding collapsed. Dove left substantial property in West Smithfield, London, and Lauriston Place, Edinburgh [*Scots Mag.* 1772, 580, 1773, 499–500; S.R.O., GD 237/256/2].

DOVE, THOMAS (*c.*1737–1811), of Scholes Green, was appointed County Surveyor of Norfolk in 1801. He was a member of the Norwich Tonnage Committee, and in that capacity supervised the building or repair of several bridges in the city. Designs by him for new buildings in Norwich Bridewell (1794 and 1803) are in Norwich City Archives [*ex inf.* Mr. A. P. Baggs]. As County Surveyor Dove was succeeded in 1806 by Francis Stone (*q.v.*), who in a MS. work on bridges in the County of Norfolk stated that his predecessor had designed those at BUNGAY and DITCHINGHAM DAM [B. Weinreb, *Catalogue No. 9, Bridges*, no. 88]. Dove died in Norwich in June 1811, aged 74 [*Norwich Mercury*, 22 June 1811, *ex inf.* Mr. David Cubitt].

DOWBIGGIN, the name of a family of London joiners and surveyors, of which at least three generations are recorded. LAUNCELOT DOWBIGGIN (*c.*1689–1759) was the son of Lawrence Dowbiggin of St. Andrew's Holborn, 'gentleman'. After apprenticeship to a joiner he was admitted to the freedom of the Joiners' Company in 1711 and was Master of the Company in 1756. In 1737 he was accused of intriguing to get the Common Council to reverse its decision to accept George Dance's designs for the Mansion House, but nevertheless was subsequently employed to carry out some of the joiner's work in the building [Sally Jeffery, *The Mansion House*, 1993, 51]. In 1747–8 he rebuilt the tower of ST. MARY'S CHURCH, ROTHERHITHE, possibly to his own design, but perhaps in general conformity to a design previously made by John James, the architect who had rebuilt the body of the church in 1714–15 [P. & S. Jeffery in *C. Life*, 20 April 1989]. But Dowbiggin himself designed ST. MARY'S CHURCH, ISLINGTON, built 1751–4 by Samuel Steemson [parish records in G.L. Record Office, and summary of expenditure, with plans, in Guildhall Library, MS. 474]. The church was destroyed by bombing in 1940, but Dowbiggin's attractive though somewhat unsophisticated classical steeple survives. A project by him for a bridge over the Thames at Blackfriars, made in 1753, is illustrated in *London Magazine* xxv, 1756, 160. He died on 24 July 1759, aged 70, and was buried at St. Mary's, Islington.

SAMUEL DOWBIGGIN (1726–1809), son of the above, took the livery of the Joiners' Company in 1754. In 1765 his were among the rejected designs for rebuilding the Church of All Hallows, London Wall [C. Welch, *Churchwardens' Accounts of All Hallows, London Wall*, 1912]. In 1773 he was one of the surveyors employed to inspect Banbury Church, Oxon. [A. Beesley, *History of Banbury*, 1841, 532–3]. He died on 19 November 1809, leaving considerable property in London and a farm in Hertfordshire to his sons Launcelot and Samuel [P.C.C. 815 LOVEDAY]. Samuel Dowbiggin signs an unexecuted and rather old-fashioned design for CHISELHAMPTON HOUSE, OXON., built in 1767–8 by a City merchant, Charles Peers [Arthur Oswald in *C. Life*, 28 Jan., 4 Feb.

1954).[1] The executed designs (which are better drawn as well as more up to date) are signed by 'Dowbiggin junior', presumably Samuel's son Launcelot Dowbiggin, who is listed as a surveyor of 53 Paternoster Row in *The Univeral British Directory of Trade and Commerce* of 1790. In the Soane Museum there is an undated estimate for a house at WINCHMORE HILL, MIDDLESEX, for John Gray, to be built 'agreeable to the several plans and elevations . . . drawn by Lancelot Dowbiggin of Paternoster Row'.

Thomas Dowbiggin & Co., a well-known firm of cabinet-makers and upholsterers in business during the second quarter of the nineteenth century, were no doubt members of the same family.

[H. L. Phillips, *Annals of the Worshipful Company of Joiners*, 1915, 111; S. Lewis, *History of Islington*, 1842, 210, 233.]

DOWN, RICHARD, is listed in Pigot's *Directory* of 1830 as 'Architect and Surveyor' of Eastover, Bridgwater, Somerset. He designed DODINGTON RECTORY, SOMERSET, in 1832 [Somerset C.R.O., D/D/Bb m, 59], and in the following year 'Down & Son' of Bridgwater remodelled HOLFORD RECTORY, SOMERSET [*ibid.*, 61]. The son was Edwin Down (d. 1880), who designed a Baptist chapel in Bridgwater in 1837 [*V.C.H. Somerset* vi, 236]. The practice was continued by the latter's son Evan Roberts Down.

DOWNE, EDWARD, is referred to as an 'architect' of Truro in the sale catalogue of the furniture from Caerhays Castle (1789) [*ex inf.* Mr. H. L. Douch]. William Downe was a builder-architect in Truro in the early nineteenth century. He designed CAMBORNE RECTORY, CORNWALL, in 1818 [Exeter Diocesan Faculty papers in Devon C.R.O.].

DRAPER, GEORGE (*c.*1796–after 1861), was a pupil of Charles Beazley from 1811 to 1813. He established himself in Chichester, whence he exhibited at the Royal Academy from 1827 to 1841. Some of his works (e.g. Chichester Infirmary and St. Bartholomew's Church) are in a somewhat old-fashioned Georgian style; others in the Gothic of the day. He was perhaps the George Draper who published engraved views of Beeleigh Abbey, Essex, in 1818.

FISHBOURNE CHURCH, SUSSEX, enlarged 1821 [I.C.B.S.].

LITTLEHAMPTON, SUSSEX, ST. MARY'S CHURCH, rebuilt 1826, Gothic [I.C.B.S.]; chancel added 1889; whole church rebuilt 1933–4.

NETLEY FORT, HANTS., tower for W. Chamberlayne, 1827 [exhib. at R.A.].

SOUTHAMPTON, PUBLIC BATHS, 1826 [exhib. at R.A. 1827].

WEST PARK, nr. FORDINGBRIDGE, HANTS., column commemorating Sir Eyre Coote, 1827 [*Civil Engineer and Architect's Jnl.* iii, 1840, 288].

MILLBROOK CHURCH, HANTS., rebuilt 1828, octagonal, incorporating old tower and chancel [I.C.B.S.]; dem. *c.*1880.

CHICHESTER INFIRMARY (now Royal West Sussex Hospital), 1828; enlarged 1839, reconstructed 1913 [*A.P.S.D.*].

CHICHESTER, ST. BARTHOLOMEW, MOUNT LANE, WESTGATE (now Theological College Chapel), 1830–2 [*Gent's Mag.* 1830 (ii), 219].

GOODWOOD, SUSSEX, THE RACE STAND, 1830 [W. H. Mason, *Goodwood, its House, Park and Grounds*, 1839, 183 and plate].

IRON ACTON RECTORY, GLOS., 1831–2 [Gloucestershire C.R.O., GDR/F4/1].

WEST DEAN VICARAGE, SUSSEX, 1833, Tudor Gothic [W. Sussex C.R.O., Ep. I 41/12].

LYMINGTON, HANTS., OBELISK commemorating Admiral Sir Harry Burrard-Neale (d. 1840), 1841 [exhib. at R.A.].

DREGHORN, ALLAN (1706–1765), was the son of Robert Dreghorn, a prosperous Glasgow wright who died in 1760. Allan followed his father's trade, but also had extensive business interests as a timber- and lead-merchant. He was a partner in the Smithfield Iron Company, and one of the founders of the first Glasgow bank. As a member of the ruling oligarchy of merchants he held the municipal offices of treasurer (1739) and bailie (1741). When he died in October 1765 at his country house at Ruchill he was a wealthy man, remembered as the owner of the first four-wheeled carriage to be kept by a citizen of Glasgow. His heir was his nephew Robert Dreghorn, who has a place in Glasgow folklore as the womanizing 'Bob Dragon'.

The number of buildings whose design can at present be ascribed to Dreghorn is small. The plans which he and John Craig (*q.v.*) submitted for the University Library in 1732 were not accepted [Glasgow University, Senate Minutes]. In 1736–8 he was involved in the building of the TOWN HALL, TRONGATE, extended 1758–60, remodelled as the Tontine Hotel 1781 and demolished *c.*1914. The municipal records contain no explicit reference to the authorship of this building, whose façade was based on Webb's gallery at Somerset House, London, but Dreghorn was em-

[1] Peers had also built Chiselhampton Church in 1763. There is no evidence to show who designed it.

ployed to measure the masonry and may have been responsible for the design [A. Gomme & D. Walker, *Architecture of Glasgow*, 1987, 52–3, 291; *Extracts from the Records of the Burgh of Glasgow* v, *1718–38*, 495, see also vi, *1739–59*, 14]. His principal architectural work was ST. ANDREW'S CHURCH, 1740–56, a handsome version of Gibbs's St. Martin's-in-the-Fields with a steeple based on another of Gibbs's published designs [*Extracts, etc.* vi, *1739–59*, 72–3, 420] (plan in G. Hay, *Architecture of Scottish Post-Reformation Churches*, 1957, 102). It may be presumed that he also designed the substantial town house which he built for himself in Clyde Street in 1752. For long used as a warehouse, it was finally demolished in 1976, but a water-colour reproduced in *Extracts from the Records of the Burgh of Glasgow* vii, 1912 (frontispiece), shows a handsome mansion in the style of Gibbs.

[*Extracts from the Records of the Burgh of Glasgow*, ed. Renwick, v–vii, *passim*; Senex, *Glasgow Past and Present*, 1884, i, 44, 470–1, ii, 330–1, 528–9, iii, 89; G. Eyre-Todd, *History of Glasgow* iii, 1934, 180–1; *The Regality Club*, 1st ser., 1889, 54–73; testamentary proceedings in S.R.O., CC 9/7/65, p. 453.]

DRINKWATER, —. In 1688, when extensive alterations were made to GREAT PARK HOUSE, AMPTHILL, BEDS., by the 2nd Earl of Ailesbury, £3 was paid to 'Mr. Drinkwater coming down and making draughts for the house before the building began' [MS. accounts in Marquess of Ailesbury's archives]. The house was subsequently sold to Lord Ashburnham, and rebuilt by him. 'Mr. Drinkwater' was probably a London master carpenter called Robert Drinkwater who was concerned in the erection of Lord Ailesbury's house on the north side of Leicester Square [*Survey of London* xxxiv, 460].

DRIVER, EDWARD (*c.*1784–1852), and GEORGE (*c.*1795–1855), were the third generation of a family of surveyors practising originally from the Old Kent Road, London, and later from Richmond Terrace, Whitehall. The firm had been founded by their grandfather Samuel Driver (d. 1779), a nurseryman and landscape gardener who had made plans for garden layouts at Adlestrop Park, Glos., in 1759 [Shakespeare's Birthplace Records Office, Stratford, DR 18/25/1a] and Swakeleys Park, Middlesex, in 1774 [Uxbridge Library, map 251]. He was succeeded by his sons Abraham and William Driver, who developed the site of their father's nursery for building, and were themselves surveyors and land agents of repute. Abraham's sons Edward and George were among the leading land surveyors of their time, doing much work for the Crown, and sometimes calling themselves architects. Their practice in the latter capacity was probably incidental and unimportant (cf. a design for an inn at Ilford in P.R.O., L.R.R.O. 1/765), but as a young man George Driver exhibited designs for schools, a museum and a combined temple and boathouse at the Royal Academy in 1813–20. S. T. Driver, described as 'architect', who died in December 1797 [*Gent's Mag.* 1798, 536] was presumably a member of the family. [F. M. L. Thompson, *Chartered Surveyors*, 1968, 49, 94; *Maps & Plans in the Public Record Office* i, 1967, *passim*; *Gent's Mag.* 1852 (ii), 659, 1855 (ii), 110.]

DUBISSON, THOMAS (–1775), of French Protestant origin, held the office of Clerk of the Works at Winchester Palace from 1725 until his death on 8 May 1775. He acted as clerk of the works at Stanmer Park, Sussex, under Nicholas Dubois in 1722–3 [accounts in E. Sussex C.R.O.] and was presumably the 'Dubuison' who, like Dubois, was involved in the building of Hanover Square, London (cf. Hugh Phillips, *Mid Georgian London*, 1964, 301, under No. 11A). In the 1730s he was surveyor to the London property of Lord Guilford [Bodleian Library, MS. North c. 11, ff. 97–9, 106, 108, 114, 118]. He was a Director of the FRENCH PROTESTANT HOSPITAL in LONDON (N. of Old Street, dem. 1865), to which additions were made to his designs in 1731–3 and 1737–9 [*Huguenot Society's Proceedings*, Quarto Ser. 56, 1983, 60–1].

DUBOIS, NICHOLAS (*c.*1665–1735), an architect of French birth, was probably a Huguenot refugee who left his country after the Revocation of the Edict of Nantes in 1685. According to his obituary in the *Gentleman's Magazine* for 1735, he 'was appointed by King William III one of the Tutors to the Prince of Friezeland, father of the present Prince of Orange'. In Queen Anne's reign he was serving in the British army. In 1706 he was a bombardier in the artillery train in Spain, and on 2 April was promoted to the rank of Captain. In May 1707 he was appointed quartermaster in the Queen's Own Regiment of Dragoons. From 1709 to 1711 he served as an Engineer in Marlborough's army in Flanders, 'where he exposed his life in many sieges'. After the Treaty of Utrecht (1713) he was retired on half-pay [C. Dalton, *English Army Lists and Commission Registers* vi, 1904, 35, 306; P.R.O., WORK 6/15, p. 36].

Hitherto a military engineer, Dubois now turned his attention to architectural practice in London. His choice as the translator of

Leoni's edition of *The Architecture of Andrea Palladio* (1715–18) associated him with one of the key books of the English Palladian Revival, but the Translator's Preface which he wrote scarcely suggests that he approached the task in the spirit of a Palladian missionary. In May 1718 he entered into partnership with the Italian architect Alessandro Galilei, with whom he was to be a 'Copartner & Joint Dealer . . . in all Designs, Buildings, Architecture, Drawings, both Military and Civil', for five years. The contract was witnessed by Galilei's patrons John Molesworth and Thomas Hewett [Ilaria Toesca, 'Alessandro Galilei in Inghilterra', *English Miscellany*, ed. Praz, iii, 1952, 212]. The partnership was, however, short-lived, for Galilei returned to Italy the following year. In November 1719 Dubois was appointed Master Mason in the Office of Works in succession to Benjamin Jackson. This appointment, which made Dubois a member of the Board of Works, was presumably due to Thomas Hewett, who had recently become Surveyor of the King's Works. In March 1720/1 Dubois appointed as his deputy the surveyor James Horne, who occasionally took his place at the Board.

Dubois was actively engaged in speculative building in London. Between 1717 and 1720 he was involved in the development of HANOVER SQUARE and ST. GEORGE STREET, on land leased from the Earl of Scarbrough. Deeds in the Middlesex Land Registry show that he was concerned in at least five sites in the Square, Nos. 19–21 on the W. side (of which 19 has been demolished, 20 altered and 21 remodelled) and Nos. 8 and 9 on the E. side (both demolished) [*ex inf.* Mr. A. F. Kelsall]. It was from Dubois that the 1st Duke of Montrose bought No. 20 in 1720 [S.R.O. GD 220/6, vol. 2, p. 22 and 220/5/834/12], and as Col. John Fane's house (No. 18, of which the original elevation is among the architectural drawings at West Wycombe Park) had a façade uniform with No. 21, it is probable that Dubois designed all four houses on the W. side of the square between Tenterden Street and Little Brook Street. Dubois also designed the double-fronted house, No. 15 St. George Street, for Samuel Hayes [P.R.O., C 11/1805/9 and deeds in Middlesex Land Registry, *ex inf.* Mr. F. Kelsall].

In 1720 Dubois attempted to set up a Builders' Company with a monopoly of building in London granted by Royal Charter or Patent. The scheme had the support of the Duke of Bridgwater, Charles Dubourgay (who had financed Dubois in Hanover Square) and James Horne. The company took land in Petty France near Bishopsgate for building, but ran out of funds and failed to secure its patent [P.R.O., C 11/1998/15 and 1999/14; C 78/1486/5, and records in the Guildhall Record Office, *ex inf.* Mr. A. F. Kelsall]. In the 1720s Dubois was involved in building developments on Lord Burlington's estate, and himself took a house in Old Burlington Street in which he lived from *c.*1726 to 1729 [*Survey of London* xxxii, 451]. He had previously built himself a house in Brewer Street, in which he lived from 1718 to 1721 [*op. cit.*, xxxi, 121–2]. In 1724 a house was to be built for Sir Thomas Webster, Bart., in JERMYN STREET 'to the satisfaction of Mr. Nicholas Dubois Architect and Surveyor' [MS. builder's notebook at Royal Institution of Chartered Surveyors, 17 Feb. 1723/4].

In 1720 Dubois was one of the architects who submitted designs for rebuilding the church of St. Martin-in-the-Fields, but on 21 July he voluntarily withdrew them [MS. Minutes of the Commissioners for Rebuilding St. Martin's Church, f. 6]. His unexecuted design for some extensive barracks in Hyde Park for the Foot Guards, made *c.*1716, and signed 'Nicholas Dubois Architect and Engineer', is illustrated in *R.I.B.A. Trans.*, 1880–1, pl. 1.

In 1718–19 Dubois carried out alterations to LEICESTER HOUSE, LEICESTER SQUARE (dem. 1792), for the Prince of Wales [*Survey of London* xxxiv, 447]. In 1719–20 he was being employed by the 1st Earl of Tankerville at DAWLEY HOUSE, MIDDLESEX, which the Earl was then partly rebuilding [payments in 'Mr. Robertson's 1st Book' in P.R.O., C 104/82, pp. 157, 160, 195]. In 1721 he was invited by the widowed Lady Stanhope to supervise the completion of the alterations to CHEVENING HOUSE, KENT, begun by Thomas Fort for the 1st Earl Stanhope, but hesitated to accept because Governor Pitt (Lady Stanhope's father) 'has employed another surveyor, Mr. James'. However, a note added to his letter by Grizel Lady Stanhope in 1797 states that 'Captain Dubois' was 'the person directed about the great (geometrical) staircase at Chevening, one of the same kind at his House in Brewer Street being liked' [Chevening archives and H. A. Tipping in *English Homes, Period V*, i, 23]. Between 1722 and 1727 Dubois designed STANMER PARK, SUSSEX (*C. Life*, 2 Jan. 1932), for Henry Pelham (d. 1725) and his brother and heir Thomas. Dubois' correspondence with the Pelhams shows that he had trouble with the servants at Stanmer, who called him 'the french son of a Bitch', and on 12 August 1727 he protests that he has never 'acted contrary to the rules of a liberal Education, a man of Honour, an old officer to the King, and a Gentleman born, as I am' [B.L., Add. MS. 33085, ff. 59, 112, 235, 285–6, 295, 351–2]. In the course of the correspondence he refers to visits, evidently professional, to 'my lady Effingham in Surry' and to 'Mr. Howard at Audley End in Essex', both in 1726. For the recently widowed Countess of Effingham he was evidently building EASTWICK PARK, GREAT BOOKHAM, SURREY (dem., see engraving in Brayley, *History of Surrey* iv, 470), stated in 1728 to have been recently completed by her 'for a new husband' (Sir Conyers Darcy), and at AUDLEY END he was presumably directing the demolition of a substantial part of the Jacobean house for Charles Howard [P. J. Drury in *Arch. Hist.* 27, 1980, 25]. Dubois' only other recorded work appears to be the bridge at LEWES, SUSSEX, built in 1727, and widened in 1932, which has his name and that of Arthur Morris, the mason, on the keystone [*V.C.H. Susssex* iii, 9].

Dubois died on 14 June 1735, aged 70 [*Gent's Mag.* 1735, 333]. In his will he appointed his wife Anna and the Earl of Essex as guardians of his sons Henry and Richard [P.C.C. 119 DUCIE]. As an architect he has to be judged chiefly by Stanmer Park, the most considerable work by him that is known to survive. This is a plain early Georgian house, competently designed, but not suggesting that Dubois was an architect of any great originality or distinction, still less that he was a convinced Palladian.

DUDDELL, —, was a late seventeenth-century architect of whom nothing is at present known except that in 1694 he went (apparently from London) to STONYHURST, LANCS., where Sir Nicholas Shireburn, Bart., was carrying out improvements. His visit is mentioned in Sir Nicholas's accounts, and among the Shireburn papers in the archives of the Weld family of Lulworth Castle there are two coloured elevations for remodelling Stonyhurst which are endorsed 'Mr. Duddell'. Neither was carried out. [J. Gerard, S.J., in *Stonyhurst Centenary Record*, 1894, 52 n. 3, 69 n. 2, 74–5.]

DUFOUR, ALEXANDER, 'architect', published in 1800 a *Letter to the Nobility and Gentry composing the Committee for raising the Naval Pillar, or Monument . . . in answer to the Letter of John Flaxman*, in which he protested against Flaxman's proposals for a colossal statue, 'in preference to an architectural monument'. In 1799 he exhibited at the Royal Academy a 'View of the Queen's new Guard House, St. James's Park', and in 1800 a 'Design for a town gate to record four Naval Victories'. He cannot have been the French architect of the same name (*c.*1760–1835) who was employed by Napoleon I at Versailles, but may have been related to a painter of portraits named William Dufour who exhibited at the R.A. between 1765 and 1770.

DUGDALE, J—, is stated in Virtue's *Picturesque Beauties of Great Britain: Kent* (1832), 11–12, to have been 'the principal architect employed' in designing HADLOW CASTLE, KENT, for W. B. May. The architectural history of this fantastic Gothic house (now mostly demolished) is obscure, but as early as 1821 the young J. B. Bunning had exhibited a design for the south front at the Royal Academy. The 170-foot Gothic tower was added later to the designs of G. L. Taylor (*q.v.*). No other work by Dugdale is known, but as he is described as 'esq.' he may have been an amateur. Virtue particularly commends his 'taste in the gothic style'.

DUMMER, EDMUND (–*c.*1712), was Surveyor to the Navy in the reign of William III. His connection with the navy began in 1682, when he was sent to Tangier as a midshipman-extraordinary and returned in 1685 with an illustrated journal containing 'The Viewes and Descriptions of . . . remarkable Lands, Cities, Towns and Arsenalls' in the Mediterranean, 'their severall Planes, and Fortifications, with divers Perspectives of Particular Buildings' (now B.L., King's MS. 40). He was subsequently employed in the dockyard at Chatham, where his ability as a draughtsman was noted by Pepys, and in June 1692 he succeeded Sir John Tippetts as Surveyor to the Navy. In this capacity his principal achievement was the planning and construction of the new dockyard at Hamoaze near Plymouth (*c.*1690–5), which included the first stone-lined dry dock in the British Isles, and the construction of a similar dock at Portsmouth. Dummer's report on the works at Plymouth, presented to the Navy Commissioners in December 1694, contains a detailed account of the Dockyard and its buildings, with a series of engraved 'draughts' showing the officers' dwelling-houses, the great storehouse, rope-house, etc. (B.L., Lansdowne MS. 847). From the text (esp. p. 22) it seems that Dummer designed this extensive complex of buildings himself, though the main block was clearly influenced by Hooke's Bethlehem Hospital, and Hooke's assistance cannot wholly be ruled out, for he had designed the Navy Office in 1674, and there is a set of the engraved designs for the dockyard among his drawings in B.L., Add. MS. 5238.

The contractor at Portsmouth was John Fitch (*q.v.*), and it was accusations of bribery by Fitch that led to Dummer's dismissal from his post in 1699. In 1700 he contracted to organize a packet service to Spain and the Leeward Islands, but the enterprise proved to be ill-advised, and after some of his boats had been taken by the French Dummer went bankrupt in February 1711/12, dying shortly afterwards in the Fleet Prison. He had in 1708 built a large house at South Stoneham in Hampshire, perhaps to the designs of Nicholas Hawksmoor, with whom he would have been well acquainted as a Director of Greenwich Hospital from 1695 and a member of its Fabric Committee. 'Twelve designs for Mr. Dummer's house' were in the sale of Hawksmoor's drawings in 1726. In 1698 Dummer made a general survey of the royal dockyards (B.L., King's MS. 43), and in the same year a survey of the ports on the south coast of which there are copies in the National Maritime Museum (P. 34 *a* and *b*), the Yale Center for British Art and the Library of Worcester College, Oxford. Edmund Dummer must be distinguished from his kinsman Edmund Dummer of Swaythling, a successful lawyer who died in 1724 and is buried in South Stoneham Church.

[N. Luttrell, *Brief Historical Relation* iv, 1857, 576, 645, 658; Christ Church Library, Oxford, MS. Diary of Sir John Evelyn, 10 July 1714; J. Ehrman, *The Navy in the War of William III*, 1953, 416–25, 644; B. Pool, *Navy Board Contracts 1660–1832*, 1966, 49, 75–6; E. G. R. Taylor, *The Mathematical Practitioners of Tudor and Stuart England*, Cambridge 1967, 272; *Wren Soc.* vi, 30–63, *passim*.]

DUNCKLEY, SAMUEL (–1714), was a mason of Warwick. He was one of the surveyors appointed to supervise the rebuilding of the town after the fire of 1694, and was himself employed in the rebuilding of ST. MARY'S CHURCH, where he rebuilt the damaged entrance to the BEAUCHAMP CHAPEL in an elaborate and remarkably convincing Gothic style. According to a *Brief Description of the Collegiate Church of Warwick* published in 1757 he 'designed, carved, built and finished' this portal himself, and this is confirmed by accounts cited by P. B. Chatwin in *Trans. Birmingham Archaeological Soc.* lxv, 1943–4, 37. William Stukeley records that Dunckley 'designed and built' the HIGH CROSS erected near WIBTOFT, WARWICKS., in 1712 to commemorate the site of the Roman VENONAE [Bodleian Library, Gough Maps 16, f. 43, and cf. engraving in Stukeley's *Itinerarium Curiosum*, 1776, 110]. Dunckley, who was a Baptist, appears to have died in 1714 [*The Restoration of the Beauchamp Chapel*, ed. Sir W. Dugdale, Roxburghe Club, 1956, 8 n.; *The Great Fire of Warwick*, ed. M. Farr, Dugdale Soc. 1992, *passim*].

DYER, CHARLES (1794–1848), was the son of a surgeon in Bristol, and became a pupil of William Brooks (*q.v.*). He practised in London, where he was a Fellow of the (R.)I.B.A., and frequently exhibited at the Royal Academy, but designed many buildings in his native city. His Victoria Rooms, with their handsome octastyle Corinthian portico, were his best-known and most ambitious building. He died on 29 January 1848, aged 54, of 'paralysis induced by too close application'. [*Builder* vi, 1848, 54; *A.P.S.D.*]

BRISTOL, THE FEMALE ORPHAN ASYLUM (later Salvation Army Home), HOOK'S MILLS, ASHLEY HILL (with W. Brooks), 1827–9; dem. *c.*1970 [*Gent's Mag.* 1868, 254].

BRISTOL, ST. PAUL'S CHURCH, BEDMINSTER, 1829–31, Gothic; chancel added 1892; gutted 1941 and rebuilt 1958 retaining tower [exhib. at R.A. 1828–9].

BRISTOL, THE SAVINGS BANK, ST. STEPHEN'S AVENUE, 1831; dem. [*A.P.S.D.*].

CLIFTON, BRISTOL, LITFIELD HOUSE, 1830 [signed 'Charles Dyer, Architect, 1830'].

CLIFTON, BRISTOL, CAMP (now ENGINEERS') HOUSE, for Charles Pinney, 1831 [signed 'Charles Dyer, Architect, 1831'].

ALDBOURNE VICARAGE, WILTS., altered or rebuilt 1833 [Salisbury Diocesan Records].

WALTHAM-ON-THE-WOLDS RECTORY, LEICS., 1833, Tudor Gothic [Lincolnshire C.R.O., Gilbert's Act mortgages, No. 167; *Civil Engineer & Architect's Jnl.* ii, 1839, 449].

BATTLEFIELDS HOUSE, GLOS. (5 miles N. of Bath), Gothic gate-lodge, 1836 [signed 'Charles Dyer, Architect, 1836'].

BRISTOL, THE BISHOP'S COLLEGE and CHAPEL, 1835–9, Tudor Gothic; dem. 1905 [exhib. at R.A. 1837] (Arrowsmith's *Dictionary of Bristol*, 1906, 165, plate). This building was designed for the Trustees of the Red Maids' School, but was sold on completion to the Trustees of the Bishop's College (W. A. Simpson, *History of the Red Maids' School*, 1908, 50–2).

CLIFTON, BRISTOL, SAVILE PLACE, Nos. 6–11, 1838 [signed 'Charles Dyer, Architect, 1838'].

LONDON, DYERS' HALL, No. 10 DOWGATE HILL, 1839–40; front altered 1856 [*A.P.S.D.*].

BRISTOL, THE VICTORIA ROOMS (now part of Bristol University), 1839–41 [exhib. at R.A. 1838–9; *Companion to the Almanac*, 1839, 243–6, with plan].

LONDON, OLD JEWRY CHAMBERS, OLD JEWRY, 1841–2 [*Civil Engineer and Architect's Jnl.* v, 333].

CLIFTON, BRISTOL, CHRIST CHURCH, CLIFTON DOWN ROAD, begun 1841, cons. 1844, Gothic; steeple 1859; N. and S. aisles 1885 [*A.P.S.D.*].

CLIFTON, BRISTOL, villa for Thomas Wentle, 1842 [exhib. at R.A. 1842].

BRISTOL, TYNDALL'S PARK, abortive scheme for layout, 1844 [*Builder* ii, 1844, 185].

WICK CHURCH, GLOS., 1845–8; completed by W. Butterfield 1849–50, Gothic [*A.P.S.D.*; Paul Thompson, *William Butterfield*, 1971, 442].

GREAT WALTHAM, ESSEX, NATIONAL SCHOOL, 1847, 'Elizabethan' [exhib. at R.A. 1847].

BRISTOL, ST. MARK, EASTON, 1848; completed by S. B. Gabriel, neo-Norman [*A.P.S.D.*].

DYER, a family of builders and surveyors of Alton in Hampshire from the end of the eighteenth century to the beginning of the twentieth. According to W. Curtis, *History of Alton*, 1896, 154, the firm was founded in 1784 by John Dyer, a carpenter, who was probably George Dyer's father. In 1812 John Dyer and George Parfect of Headley, bricklayer, rebuilt the nave of FROYLE CHURCH, HANTS., under the direction of James Harding, surveyor of Farnham [MS. 'Orders of Vestry for rebuilding, etc.']. The simple Gothic tower of NEWTON VALENCE CHURCH, HANTS., has an inscription recording that it was rebuilt in 1813 by 'JOHN DYER & GEORGE PARFECT BUILDERS.' George and William Dyer were responsible for alterations to PELHAM PLACE, HANTS., in 1834 [Pelham Place documents in County Record Office], enlarged HAWKLEY CHURCH, HANTS. (rebuilt 1865) in 1828 [I.C.B.S.], altered or rebuilt PATNEY RECTORY, WILTS., in 1833 [Salisbury Diocesan records], added a south aisle to BENTLEY CHURCH, HANTS., in 1835 [I.C.B.S.], and in 1838 rebuilt the nave of CHAWTON CHURCH, HANTS., destroyed by fire 1872 [W. A. Leigh & M. G. Knight, *Chawton Manor and its Owners*, 1911, 62].

DYER, NATHANIEL (*c.*1752–1833), of Nailsworth, Glos., designed NAILSWORTH EPISCOPAL CHAPEL, 1793–4, rebuilt 1898–1900 [MS. building accounts at vicarage, 1946]. In 1800 the roof of the nave of WOTTON-UNDER-EDGE CHURCH, GLOS., was rebuilt under his direction, with a Gothic plaster vault [V. R. Perkins, *Guide to the Church of St. Mary, Wotton-under-Edge*, 1912, 15]. In 1815 he gave an estimate and plan gratis for rebuilding the south aisle of WOODCHESTER CHURCH, GLOS., again rebuilt 1863–4 [Vestry minutes in Gloucestershire C.R.O.]. According to A. Smith, *Ecclesiastical Edifices in the Borough of Stroud*, 1838, Dyer also 'built several seats in this neighbourhood'. He was buried in a field behind 'The Lawns' at Nailsworth, where his name is inscribed on a stone slab. A tablet in the present church records his benefactions to the parish. In contemporary directories he is described as 'gentleman'.

DYMOND, GEORGE (*c.*1797–1835), architect of Bristol, died at his house in Castle Green on 29 August 1835 at the age of 38 [*Architectural Mag.* iii, 1836, 48]. He was a member of the Society of Friends.

In 1827–8 Dymond and R. S. Pope were jointly responsible for the Greek Doric Court of Justice and offices added to the left of Smirke's COUNCIL HOUSE in CORN STREET, BRISTOL [City Archives]. His major work was the extensive HIGHER MARKET at EXETER, with monumental Greek Doric façades very ably composed. Begun in 1835, the Market was completed after Dymond's death by Charles Fowler. It is fully described and illustrated in *Architectural Mag.* iii, 1836, 12–30.

E

EADS, JOHN, of Headley, Hants, was probably a bricklayer by trade. In 1803–4 he designed and built DOGMERSFIELD CHURCH, HANTS., for Sir Henry St. John Mildmay, Bart. [Hants. Record Office, 15 M 50/1294–8]. It is a small brick building with pointed windows. In 1803 Eads submitted plans for rebuilding CHAWTON RECTORY, HANTS. [Winchester Diocesan Records, Faculty papers].

EARLE, JOHN (*c.*1779–1863), was a mason, sculptor and architect of Hull, where his name first appears in the directories in 1810/11. In 1812 he was working at GRIMSTON GARTH, YORKS. (E.R.), for Thomas Grimston in connection with the castellated gatehouse, then in course of erection, but in what capacity is not clear [M. E. Ingram, *Leaves from a Family Tree*, 1951, 124]. In Hull Earle designed THE PILOT OFFICE, QUEEN STREET, 1819 [*Hull Advertiser*, 25 Dec. 1819, *ex inf.* Mr. A. G. Chamberlain]; FERRIES' HOSPITAL, PRINCE'S DOCK STREET, 1822 [*V.C.H. Yorks. E. Riding* i, 407]; THE ASSEMBLY ROOM, NORTH STREET, 1823; dem. [*Hull Advertiser*, 4 July 1823, *ex inf.* Mr. A. G. Chamberlain]; and ST. CHARLES R.C. CHURCH, JARRATT STREET, 1828–9, remodelled by J. J. Scoles 1834–5 [*V.C.H. Yorks. E. Riding* i, 331].

Earle appears to have been a competent provincial practitioner in a late Georgian classical style. As a sculptor he is represented by numerous monumental tablets in local churches. He died on 11 December 1863, aged 84 [J. J. Sheahan, *History of Kingston-upon-Hull*, 1864, 655]. His son Thomas Earle (1810–76) was a successful Victorian sculptor.

EATON, GEORGE (–1689), was a joiner resident at Etwall in Derbyshire who died in 1689 leaving a substantial estate [parish register in Derbyshire C.R.O. and will in Lichfield Joint Record Office]. He was presumably the 'surveyor' of this name who was employed to supervise the building of THE COUNTY HALL, DERBY, in 1657–9 [Derbyshire C.R.O., archives of Chandos-Pole of Hopton Hall, 60/3]. This is a classical building of some quality, with two mannerist doorways facing the courtyard. No other work by Eaton is at present recorded, but the west doorway of the Chapel at LOCKO PARK, DERBYSHIRE, dated 1669 (*C. Life*, 5 June 1969, fig. 4), has affinities with the architecture of the Shire Hall. Eaton's eldest son Thomas made survey plans of Etwall Hospital in 1695 and 1701 [Calendar of Records of Etwall Hospital in Bodleian Library, MS. Top. Derbys. *c.* 4, 99, 100].

EAYRE, THOMAS (1691–1757), of Kettering in Northamptonshire, was a versatile man whose activities included clockmaking, bell-founding and surveying. Over 200 bells cast by Thomas Eayre or his son of the same name (d. 1762/70) are recorded, together with a number of turret and long-case clocks. As a surveyor he was responsible for a MS. plan of the town of Peterborough, and for the first large-scale map of Northamptonshire, published in 1779. As a topographical draughtsman he was employed by John Bridges to make several drawings (now in the British Library, Add. MS. 32467) intended as illustrations for the latter's *History of Northamptonshire*. As an architect he designed a simple classical church at STOKE DOYLE, NORTHANTS, built 1722–5, for which his (variant) drawings, together with his account for making them, are among the Hunt of Boreatton papers in Shrewsbury Public Library. In 1744 he advised the antiquary William Stukeley about the construction of the Gothic bridge which the 2nd Duke of Montagu contemplated building in the park at BOUGHTON, NORTHANTS., to Stukeley's design [*Family Memoirs of the Revd. Wm. Stukeley*, Surtees Soc., i, 1882, 368–9].

After the death of Thomas Eayre and the bankruptcy of his son in 1762, the bell-founding business was continued by his brother Joseph Eayre (1707–72) at St. Neot's in Huntingdonshire. Joseph Eayre was also an ingenious man, whose 'invention for weighing a loaded waggon' was exhibited at the Royal Society in Feb. 1748/9. In 1741 he gave Stukeley a 'model' of a method of securing the steeple of ST. MARY'S CHURCH, STAMFORD, then in danger of collapse [*Family Memoirs, op. cit.* ii, 216–20, 329], and in 1762 the steeple of ST. MICHAEL'S CHURCH, STAMFORD (dem. 1832), was rebuilt 'with a neat tower and six bells agreeable to Mr. Eayre's plan' [MS. Vestry Minutes]. In the Storer Collection in Eton College Library (vol. ii) there is a rather crude design for a bridge at Blackfriars, signed 'Joseph Eayre, St. Neot's Oct. 3, 1759' [P. I. King, 'Thomas Eayre of Kettering and other Members of his Family', *Northamptonshire Past and Present* i, no. 5, 1952, 11–23, and no. 6, 10].

EBBELS, ROBERT (–1860), was active as a church architect in the 1830s. He lived at Trysull, nr. Wolverhampton, until 1841, when he moved to Spring Well Cottage, Tettenhall Wood, near the same town. In the 1850s he retired to Dawlish, where he died in August 1860 [Principal Probate Registry, Calendar of Probates]. He is described as 'a dapper, energetic little gentleman' by Mark Norman (*Random Recollections*). Most of his churches were undistinguished buildings with wide naves lighted by lancet windows, but his tower at Ewhurst Church is an effective essay in Norman revivalism. Nothing is known about his training as an architect, but in 1829 he exhibited two drawings at the Birmingham Society of Artists which appear to have been student's work: 'the archway and bridge across the approach to the Deepdene' (in Surrey), and an 'Entrance lodge at Garnons' in Herefordshire. As both these houses were designed by William Atkinson, Ebbels may have been his pupil.

SHIRLEY CHURCH, WARWICKS., 1832, Gothic; enlarged 1883 [I.C.B.S.].

WOLVERHAMPTON, ST. PAUL'S CHURCH, 1834, Gothic [Steen & Blackett's *Wolverhampton Guide*, 1871, 46].

ETTINGSHALL CHURCH, SCHOOLS and PARSONAGE, STAFFS., 1835–7, built in half-timber; the church was rebuilt 1874 [*Civil Engineer and Architect's Jnl.* i, 1837–8, 57].

GUILDFORD, SURREY, ST. NICHOLAS CHURCH, rebuilt 1836–7, Gothic; rebuilt 1870–6 [inscription in church].

READING, BERKS., ST. JOHN'S CHURCH, 1836–7, Gothic; rebuilt 1872 [*Reading Mercury*, 29 April 1837].

VENTNOR, ISLE OF WIGHT, ST. CATHERINE'S

CHURCH, for John Hambrough, 1836–7, Gothic; chancel added 1849, south aisle 1897–8 [*Civil Engineer and Architect's Jnl.* i, 1837–8, 57].

HAWLEY CHURCH, HANTS., 1837, Gothic; altered by J. B. Clacy 1857, chancel added 1863, steeple 1882 [*Civil Engineer and Architect's Jnl.* i, 1837–8, 57].

EWHURST CHURCH, SURREY, partial rebuilding, with new central tower in 'Norman' style, 1837–8; also Gothic Rectory for Revd. C. A. Stewart [Brayley, *Surrey* v, 179–80, with views].

WINDLESHAM CHURCH, SURREY, enlarged church and remodelled tower, 1837–8. Ebbels also designed the Gothic Rectory [Brayley, *Surrey* i, 467, 469].

TIPTON, STAFFS., ST. PAUL'S CHURCH, 1838–9, Gothic; altered 1899 [*Civil Engineer and Architect's Jnl.* i, 1837–8, 57].

WOLVERHAMPTON PARISH CHURCH, repairs, 1838–9 [G. P. Mander, *The Wolverhampton Antiquary*, 1933, 256].

HANDSWORTH, STAFFS., ST. JAMES'S CHURCH, 1838–40; enlarged 1895 [*Civil Engineer and Architect's Jnl.* i, 1837–8, 57].

SUNNINGDALE, BERKS., HOLY TRINITY CHURCH, 1839–40; chancel added by G. E. Street 1861, nave rebuilt by J. O. Scott 1887–8 [F. C. Hodder, *A Short History of Sunningdale*, 1937, 119].

WOMBORNE CHURCH, STAFFS., enlarged 1840–1, Gothic; rebuilt 1867 [*V.C.H. Staffs.* xx, 220].

WEST BROMWICH, STAFFS., ST. JAMES'S CHURCH, 1839–41, Gothic; tower added *c.*1890; dem. 1989 [I.C.B.S.].

COVENTRY, ST. PETER'S CHURCH, 1840–1, Gothic [B. Poole, *History of Coventry*, 1870, 223].

UPPER GORNAL CHURCH, STAFFS., 1840–1, Gothic [Port, 160–1].

CWMAMAN, CARMARTHENSHIRE, CHRIST CHURCH, 1841, Gothic [Port, 170–1].

OLD SWINFORD CHURCH, WORCS., rebuilt nave, 1843, Gothic [J. Noake, *The Rambler in Worcestershire*, 1848, 210].

TRYSULL CHURCH, STAFFS., enlarged 1843–4, Gothic [*V.C.H. Staffs.* xx, 194].

WONERSH HOUSE, SURREY, terrace and conservatory for 3rd Lord Grantley, *c.*1840; dem. 1935 [Brayley, *Surrey*, v, 151].

EBDON, CHRISTOPHER (1744–1824), was the son of Thomas Ebdon, a cordwainer of Durham, where he was born in October 1744. In 1761 he was apprenticed to James Paine [P.R.O., Apprenticeship Register I.R. 1/22], and it was from Paine's address in Salisbury Street, Strand, that he exhibited views of the interior of Durham Cathedral at the Society of Artists in 1767 and 1768. One of them was subsequently engraved by Tobias Miller. Early in the 1770s Ebdon was working for Henry Holland as a draughtsman [P. du Prey, *John Soane*, 1982, 29]. In 1776 he was in Rome and Florence, and was elected a member of the Florentine Academy [*Walpole Soc.* xxxii, 51; *Burlington Mag.* Aug. 1990, 537; letter to Henry Holland dated from Rome 8 Aug. 1776 in V. & A. Museum 92 D.28, f. 2]. In 1778, 1780 and 1783 he exhibited views of Roman temples at the Society of Artists, giving his address as 'at Earl Cowper's, Great George Street, Hanover Square'. Eventually he obtained several commissions in the south-west of England, for in 1783 he exhibited designs for lodges at TEHIDY PARK, CORNWALL, for Sir Francis Basset, Bart.; the Carew papers at Antony House, Cornwall, show that in 1787 he was paid £26 5s. 'for designs for a chapel at Tor Point' (apparently not carried out); and in the County Museum at Truro there are designs by him for the ASSEMBLY ROOMS at TRURO, opened in 1787. However, he evidently failed to establish himself in practice there, for between 1789 and 1792 he was more than once employed by Sir John Soane as a draughtsman [A. T. Bolton, *The Works of Sir John Soane*, 1924, Appendix C, xli], and in June 1793 he told Soane that he was 'going down into the North again . . . to continue there for good' [Sir John Soane's Museum, private correspondence, XVA.6]. In Durham he obtained the post of Surveyor of Bridges for the County which he held until 1813. In 1805 he was paid £15 for making plans for unspecified alterations at WYNYARD PARK [Giles Worsley in *C. Life*, 28 Aug. 1986, 616], and in 1810 he designed the FREEMASONS' LODGE, OLD ELVET, DURHAM, dem. 1868 [M. A. Richardson, *The Local Historian's Table Book* iii, 1843, 105]. Ebdon died at Durham in 1824 aged 80. John Downman, A.R.A., drew his portrait in 1812 [*Gent's Mag.* 1824 (ii), 572; J. Nichols, *Literary Anecdotes* viii, 698; G. C. Williamson, *John Downman*, 1907, lix; Durham C.R.O., parish register of St. Oswald's Church, Durham; monumental inscription in churchyard].

EBORAL, WILLIAM (–1795), was 'an eminent builder' of Warwick. In 1786–8 he designed and built the Gothic Greenhouse at WARWICK CASTLE containing the 'Warwick Vase' [*V.C.H. Warwicks.* viii, 463]. According to W. Field's *History of Warwick*, 1815, 81–2, he was the 'architect' of the GREAT BRIDGE at WARWICK, built by him in 1789–93 to a design closely resembling Robert Mylne's Leafield Bridge nearby. He died suddenly on 16 January 1795 [*Gent's Mag.* 1795 (i), 348].

EDGAR, WILLIAM (–1746) is described as 'Architect' on the plan of Edinburgh which he published in 1742. He appears to have been the William Edgar who was apprenticed to an Edinburgh wright in 1717 and admitted a burgess in 1726, but his few recorded activities are those of a land surveyor rather than an architect. He is said to have been with the Duke of Cumberland in the '45, and to have 'died of fatigue' in the Highlands in 1746. [W. Cowan, *The Maps of Edinburgh 1544–1929*, Edinburgh 1932, 30–5; M. K. Meade, 'Plans of the New Town of Edinburgh', *Architectural History* xiv, 1971, 43–4; E. G. R. Taylor, *The Mathematical Practitioners of Hanoverian England*, 1966, 205.]

EDGE, CHARLES (*c.*1801–1867), was one of the leading architects in Birmingham from about 1827 until his death in 1867. He began as a designer in the late Georgian Grecian style, but 'ended as a Victorian architect working in Italianate and Gothic'. After the bankruptcy of Messrs. Hansom & Welch in 1834 he was employed to complete the Town Hall. Besides the public buildings listed below he designed a number of commercial premises in Birmingham and several private houses in Edgbaston. Outside his own town his only important work was the CRESCENT at FILEY in YORKSHIRE, designed for the Birmingham solicitor J. W. Unett in 1835–8. In the 1840s he was for a time in partnership with an architect called Avery. Yeoville Thomason and his son C. A. Edge were his pupils. Four large volumes of drawings by Charles Edge and his son are in the Birmingham Reference Library. He died in Edgbaston on 21 July 1867. [Cornish's *Guide to Birmingham*, 1864, *passim*; Bryan Little, *Birmingham Buildings*, 1971, 124–5.]

BIRMINGHAM: PUBLIC BUILDINGS, ETC.

THE WESLEYAN METHODIST CHURCH, CONSTITUTION HILL, 1827–8; enlarged 1836 [drawings 1–6].

THE PUBLIC OFFICE, MOOR STREET, extended elevation, 1829–30; dem. 1911 [drawings 7–24].

THE BANK OF BIRMINGHAM (afterwards Branch Bank of England), BENNETT'S HILL, *c.*1832 [drawings 29–30; Cornish, 118].

THE MARKET HALL, HIGH STREET, 1832–5; dem. 1940 [drawings 75–87].

THE SCOTTISH PRESBYTERIAN CHURCH, BROAD STREET, 1834, Gothic; rebuilt 1848–9 by J. R. Botham [church minutes in Birmingham Reference Library Archives PC 2/3, 17 July 1834].

THE NORWICH UNION OFFICE, BENNETT'S HILL, 1834 [drawings 88–100].

ST. PETER'S CHURCH, DALE END, reconstruction, 1834–7, after fire; dem. 1899 [drawings 101–4].

THE GENERAL CEMETERY, KEY HILL, THE CHAPEL, 1835–6; dem. 1966 [drawings 118–129].

THE BIRMINGHAM AND MIDLAND BANK, UNION STREET, 1836 [drawings 167–78].

THE TOWN HALL, completion of building designed by J. A. Hansom and Edward Welch, 1836 onwards [drawings 131–66].

THE NATIONAL PROVINCIAL BANK, BENNETT'S HILL, *c.*1840 [Cornish, 119].

THE POST OFFICE, 93 NEW STREET, reconstruction of existing premises for use by Post Office, 1841–2; dem. [drawings 228–40].

ST. PAUL'S SCHOOL, WHARSTONE LANE, 1844 [drawings 272–6].

THE SAVINGS BANK, 31 CANNON HILL, *c.*1850; dem. [drawings 321–3].

ASTON, WATERWORKS ENGINE HOUSE, 1851 [drawing 329].

ST. GEORGE'S CHURCH, CALTHORPE ROAD, EDGBASTON, addition of chancel, 1856, Gothic [drawings 349–52].

ELSEWHERE

FILEY, YORKS. (E.R.), THE CRESCENT, for J. W. Unett, 1835–8 [drawings 107–15].

DUDLEY, WORCS., THE INDEPENDENT CHAPEL, KING STREET, 1839 [drawings 204–8].

EDGE, WILLIAM (*c.*1584–1643), was a freemason living at Raynham in Norfolk, where he died in his 60th year in 1643. From 1619 onwards he was engaged in building RAYNHAM HALL for Sir Roger Townshend, Bart. Townshend was to a large extent his own architect, and employed Edge as draughtsman as well as master mason. Moreover Edge twice accompanied Sir Roger to London, and in 1620 was paid for twenty-eight weeks attending him 'in England and out of England'. The markedly Jonesian character of Raynham's architecture may have been due to the study by Sir Roger and his mason of buildings by Inigo Jones which they inspected in London and Newmarket. Masons named Robert and John Edge were employed at Raynham in 1621, and in his will William Edge refers to his son William and his nephews Robert and William, sons of his brother Robert. [H. L. Bradfer-Lawrence, 'The Building of Raynham Hall', *Norfolk Archaeology* xxiii, 1926–8; John Harris,

'Raynham Hall, Norfolk', *Archaeological Jnl.* cxviii, 1961; Linda Campbell, 'The Building of Raynham Hall', *Arch. Hist.* 32, 1989.]

William Edge was also employed by Sir Hamon L'Estrange at HUNSTANTON HALL, NORFOLK, where considerable alterations were in process from 1625 to the early 1640s. In 1625 William Edge and his brother were paid 5s. 'for their travell from Raynham', and in the following year 5s. were again paid to William Edge 'when Sr. Roger Townshend sent him to see the Buylding'. William, Richard, Thomas and John Edge were all employed as masons at Hunstanton during the next fifteen years. Precisely what they did is not clear from the accounts, but, apart from alterations to the house itself, it probably included the octagonal park building illustrated in *Country Life*, 10 April 1926, fig. 6, which is said (no doubt correctly) to have been built in 1640. This elegant classical building is, like Raynham Hall, a notable reflection of the Court style of Inigo Jones in a remote country setting. They were not responsible for the classical gateway, with strapwork cresting, at the entrance to the courtyard, which is dated 1623, and was the work of Thomas Thorpe of Kingscliffe, Northants. (d. 1625/6), a master mason who was then engaged in building Blickling Hall for Chief Justice Hobart (cf. Summerson, *The Book of Architecture of John Thorpe*, Walpole Soc. 1966, 4). [Norfolk Record Office, L'Estrange papers, General Account 1613–1645, *passim*.]

EDGECOMBE, EDWARD (*c.*1756–1822) was a member of a family who had been builders at Tewkesbury in Gloucestershire at least since the reign of George II. In his *History of Tewkesbury* (1798), W. Dyde records that in 1795 'our ingenious townsman, Mr. Edward Edgecombe, now resident at Ellesmere in Shropshire', had made designs for refitting the interior of TEWKESBURY ABBEY CHURCH with new pews, galleries and a pulpit 'of peculiarly light and elegant construction' which were executed by J. Keyte of Kidderminster. Dyde also illustrates the MARKET HOUSE at Tewkesbury as the work of 'Rd. Edgecombe, Archt.', that is presumably Richard Edgecombe, described as 'Cabinet-maker and Builder' of Tewkesbury in *The Universal British Directory* of 1793–8. In 1788–9 Edward Edgecombe had designed WELSHAMPTON CHURCH, SHROPSHIRE (rebuilt 1863), with a striking octagonal tower [Shropshire C.R.O. 2608/381, *Shrewsbury Chronicle* 18 July 1789, and information from Mr. C. Jobson]. He died at Ellesmere in December 1822, aged 66 [Ellesmere parish register]. George Edgecombe, who designed STOAK CHURCH, CHESHIRE, 1827, Gothic, may have been a relation [*The Cheshire Sheaf* xxxvi, 1941, 23–30].

EDGERLY, EDWARD (*c.*1743–1806), of Hurley, Berks., is stated in the *Picturesque Views of Seats*, published by Harrison & Co. in 1787–8, to have built BEAR PLACE, HARE HATCH, BERKS. for M. Ximenes 'about four years since'. His death in 1806 at the age of 63 is recorded in Hurley parish register, where he is described as 'a Builder and Carpenter'.

EDMESTON, JAMES (1791–1867), was the architect to whom Gilbert Scott was articled in 1827. He was chosen more on account of his piety than of his distinction as an architect, which was slight. Although an Independent by descent, he joined the Anglican Church at a comparatively early age, and was the author of numerous hymns, including 'Lead us, Heavenly Father, lead us'. He lived at Homerton and had his office at Salvador House in Bishopsgate Street. His works included HACKNEY GRAMMAR SCHOOL, *c.*1830, Gothic; dem. [J. C. Loudon, *Architectural Mag.* v, 1838, 70, where his unexecuted Greek Ionic design for another school at Islington is illustrated]; ST. BARNABAS' SCHOOL, HOMERTON, 1855–6 [*Builder* xiii, 1855, 504; xiv, 1856, 320]; ST. PAUL'S CHURCH, ONSLOW SQUARE, 1859–60 [Dorothy Stroud, *The South Kensington Estate of Henry Smith's Charity*, 1975, 39]; and a Gothic dissenting chapel at LEYTONSTONE, ESSEX. His design (1835) for a lodge for W. G. D. Tyson at FOLEY HOUSE, nr. MAIDSTONE, KENT, is in the R.I.B.A. Drawings Collection. His design for a 'Protestant Church', shown at the Free Architectural Exhibition in 1850, was ridiculed in the *Ecclesiologist* xi, 1850, 173. His pupils included his son James Edmeston, junior (d. 1898), E. H. Springbett and W. B. Moffatt (afterwards Scott's partner). [G. G. Scott, *Personal and Professional Recollections*, 1879, 53–67; J. Julian, *A Dictionary of Hymnology*, 1907, 321–2.]

EDMONDS, CHRISTOPHER (*c.*1774–1853), exhibited at the Royal Academy from Southwark addresses between 1795 and 1801. He was surveyor to the Clink Paving Commissioners, and Master of the Tylers' and Bricklayers' Company in 1837–8. In 1801 he exhibited 'An addition to Tidmarsh House (Berks.), new building for R. Hopkins, Esq.' In 1815 he carried out internal alterations to MILTON CHURCH, nr. GRAVESEND, KENT [typed notes in church]. He designed ST. PAUL'S CHURCH, CLAPHAM, a plain brick building consecrated in 1815; chancel added 1879

[C. T. Cracklow, *Views of the Churches in the County of Surrey*, 1827], and ST. PETER'S CHURCH, SUMNER STREET, BANKSIDE, SOUTHWARK (dem. 1940), together with the adjoining ST. SAVIOUR'S SCHOOL, 1838–9 (dem.). The church was an undistinguished Gothic building whose interior is described in the *Companion to the Almanac*, 1840, 228, as 'not only exceedingly bald and plain, but mean and ugly; sufficiently dismal without being at all solemn'. The school was Elizabethan in style: a medal commemorating its erection is illustrated by J. Taylor, *The Architectural Medal*, 1978, 110.

Edmonds died on 23 August 1853, aged 79 [*Gent's Mag.* 1853 (ii), 428]. His practice was continued by his son Christopher William Crawford Edmonds.

EDMUNDS, WILLIAM, of Margate, Kent, was probably a son of Thomas Edmunds, a builder of the same place. At MARGATE he designed HOLY TRINITY CHURCH, 1825–9, Gothic (dem.); the LIGHTHOUSE (in the form of a Doric column) on the pier, 1828 (dem.); and the OFFICES of the Pier Company (dem.). At DOVER he designed HOLY TRINITY CHURCH, 1833–5, Gothic (dem.), and in 1839 the temporary pavilion erected for the banquet given to the Duke of Wellington by the Cinque Ports. It measured 130 × 120 feet and accommodated some 2000 persons. [S. Lewis, *Topographical Dictionary* iii, 1831, 254–5; M. H. Port, *Six Hundred New Churches*, 1961, 146–7; *Gent's Mag.* 1839 (ii), 416.]

EDWARD, ALEXANDER (1651–1708), was a dispossessed Scottish minister who turned to architecture and landscape-gardening and was a figure of some importance in the Scottish architectural scene at the end of the seventeenth century. His father, Robert Edward, minister of Murroes in Angus, was an ingenious man, interested in astronomy, dialling and cartography, who enjoyed the patronage of the Maule family (Earls of Panmure). Alexander, who shared his father's interests, graduated M.A. at St. Andrews in 1670 and entered the Church. He held the living of Kemback in Fife from 1682 until 1689, when he was dispossessed as an Episcopalian [Hew Scott, *Fasti Ecclesiae Scoticanae* v, 1925, 206].

The earliest evidence of Edward's architectural activities connects him with Sir William Bruce, the key figure in Scottish architecture after the Restoration. It consists of three plans of Bruce's seat at Kinross in Fife, one of the house itself, one of the gardens, and one of the policies in general.[1] These drawings are attributable to Edward because of their similarity to a garden layout for Hamilton Palace[2] which bears Edward's signature. As the drawing of the house shows it substantially as built, but with minor differences of detail, it must date from *c.*1685, shortly before work began. Although the design for Kinross must have been Bruce's own work, Edward thus appears to have been acting as his architectural assistant or draughtsman [J. G. Dunbar, 'Kinross House', in *The Country Seat*, ed. Colvin & Harris, 1970, 65–9]. Ten years later he is found in the same role in connection with Bruce's designs for Melville House, Fife. In a letter dated 21 April 1697 Sir William Bruce informed the Earl of Melville that Edward was hard at work 'extending' (i.e. drawing out) his designs for Melville House and would be sent to explain them to the Earl before he proceeded to 'extend the draught of the garden and courts' [S.R.O., GD 26/13/272 and 440]. Drawings[3] made in 1698 for remodelling Kinnaird Castle, Angus, for the Earl of Southesk to Bruce's designs are likewise in Edward's hand.

Between 1696 and 1708 Edward was personally responsible for the remodelling of BRECHIN CASTLE, ANGUS, for the 4th Earl of Panmure [David Walker & John Dunbar in *C. Life*, 12 Aug. 1971 and cf. plans in S.R.O., RHP 35166-8]. In October 1697 he witnessed the contract whereby the mason Tobias Bachop undertook to build an addition to KINLOCH HOUSE, PERTHSHIRE, 43 feet long and 22½ feet wide 'conform to the present house', with chimney-tops 'conform to the work of the chimneys the sd. Tobias built at Panmure' [S.R.O., RH 12/39/155]. In 1699 he witnessed another contract between Henry Maule of Kellie (the Earl of Panmure's younger brother) and a wright named Hendrie to panel the interior of the principal rooms at KELLIE CASTLE, ANGUS, 'conforme to the lyning of the waiting-room at Panmure' and (in the case of the Drawing Room) 'according to a draught to be given to the said Hendrie with a compleat capitall' [S.R.O., GD 45/18/1233]. He was still giving architectural advice about work at Kellie Castle in 1705 [S.R.O., GD 45/14/332a]. In 1699 he made a 'Draught of the Low Palace at Falkland' (Fife) for its hereditary keeper, the

[1] The first two plans belong to the Edinburgh College of Art; the third is among Sir John Clerk's papers at Penicuik House (PH 34).

[2] At Lennoxlove.

[3] At Kinnaird Castle. They were not carried out owing to the Earl's death in 1699. With them are plans by Edward for laying out the gardens, dated from 1695 to 1697.

2nd Marquess of Atholl [Blair Castle Muniments, Box 41, iv, 3]. A surviving letter [S.R.O., GD 45/26/140, loose in pocket] shows that in February 1700 he was concerned in the building of a house (now dem.) at ROSSIE in ANGUS for Patrick Scott. Later Edward assisted Bruce with the layout of the formal gardens at HOPETOUN HOUSE, WEST LOTHIAN [R. Sibbald, *History of the Sheriffdoms of Linlithgow and Stirling*, 1707, 20–1], and in 1708 he made the plan for laying out the grounds of HAMILTON PALACE, LANARKSHIRE, that has already been mentioned. At the same time he was concerned in alterations to the house and grounds at the Duke of Hamilton's English seat, ASHTON HALL, LANCS. In June 1706 he was reported to be 'goeing to take care of the D. of Hamilton's Gardens &c. at Ashton' [*Trans. Cumberland & Westmorland Arch. & Antiq. Soc.*, N.S. iii, 1903, 50], and a letter to Edward from an employee of the Duke, written from Ashton in July 1708, reports on the progress of masonry and joiner's work there [Hamilton archives at Lennoxlove, TD 81/100/7]. In 1704 Edward had designed the grand architectural monument in DUNKELD CATHEDRAL to the 1st Marquess of Atholl (d. 1703) [*Chronicles of the Atholl & Tullibardine Families*, by the 7th Duke of Atholl, ii, 1908, 43–5].

In 1701–2 Edward undertook a journey to London, Paris and the Low Countries on behalf of a group of Scottish noblemen (mostly of Jacobite sympathies), which included the Earls of Mar, Loudoun, Strathmore, Panmure, Hopetoun, Northesk and Southesk, the Marquess of Annandale, the Master of Balmerino, Sir John Shaw of Greenock and Hercules Scott of Brotherton. He undertook to 'view, observe and take draughts of the most curious and remarkable Houses, Edifices, Gardings, orchards, parks, plantations, land improvements, coall works, mines, water works and other curiosities of nature or art' [S.R.O., GD 124/16/24]. The list of houses he was to inspect included Chatsworth, Lowther, Belvoir and 'Earl Carlil's new designs near Yorke' (i.e. Castle Howard). The Earl of Mar particularly wanted drawings of Ranelagh House, Chelsea, and of the Earl of Rochester's house at Petersham. As soon as he reached London Edward was to write to various of his patrons, including the Earls of Panmure, Mar and Northesk, and 'to Alex Izit' (a joiner employed by Bruce at Hopetoun and elsewhere) 'about lyning of rooms'. He carried with him a letter of introduction from Sir Robert Sibbald to Sir Hans Sloane in which he was described as having 'acquired much fame by his skill in Architecture and drawing plans of houses and gardens' [B.L., Sloane MS. 4038, f. 167]. His visiting list also included Kneller, Knyff, Robert Kidwell the mason, and several map-sellers. In Paris he purchased prints and noted that the south-east front of the Louvre, the façade of St. Gervais and the Val-de-Grâce were 'the best architecture in Paris'. His itinerary included Versailles, Marly and St. Cloud, and he carried letters in cypher to the Pretender's Court at St. Germain. The notebook which he took with him on the journey is among the Panmure (Dalhousie) papers in the Register House at Edinburgh [S.R.O., GD 45/26/140], and a volume of engravings formerly at Hopetoun House and now in the library at Barnbougle (Dalmeny House) may represent those which he collected for the Earl of Hopetoun. It contains a number of seventeenth-century engravings of French palaces and gardens, an invitation to attend the funeral of the French architect Aubry at St. Eustache, Paris, on 25 December 1701, and a drawn plan of the parterre at the Palais Royal with an explanatory inscription in Edward's hand.

Most of the other drawings which Edward made in France appear to be lost, but a plan of Marly by him is among James Gibbs's drawings in the Ashmolean Museum at Oxford (III, 49, reproduced in *Gazette des Beaux-Arts*, ser. vi, ci, 54–6), and some drawings of topiary work in the gardens at Versailles annotated in his hand are in an album from Cliveden House, Bucks., on loan to the R.I.B.A. Drawings Collection. A letter to the Earl of Mar dated from Le Havre on 7 July 1702 also survives [S.R.O., GD 124/15/219].

Edward died in Edinburgh on 16 November 1708, aged 57, and was buried in the Greyfriars Churchyard. Sir Robert Sibbald (B.L., MS. *cit.*) characterized him as a 'Great Master in Architecture, and contrivance of Avenues, Gardens and Orchards'. His importance as Bruce's architectural adjutant is clear. Brechin Castle, his principal independent work so far identified, shows that stylistically he was Bruce's follower, but as an adaptation it does not necessarily reveal his full ability as an architectural designer. His garden layouts are in the formal grand manner of the period.

J. Lowrey, *Alexander Edward* (Crawford Centre for the Arts, University of St. Andrews, 1987), is a short account of Edward written to accompany an exhibition.

EDWARDS of Liverpool. Several architects of this name were practising in Liverpool in the first half of the nineteenth century. JAMES EDWARDS appears in the directories as an architect from 1811 to 1829 and may have died in 1834 [administration in *Lancs. & Cheshire Record Soc.* 120, 1980, 39]. From 1811 to 1823 his address was Copperas Hill, but he subsequently lived in Hawke Street. He was for some time an assistant in the office of John Foster *(q.v.)* [Lancs. C.R.O., PR 2307/19], and according to Picton's *Memorials of Liverpool* ii, 1875, 243, rumour gave him the credit for being the real designer of Foster's only Gothic church, St. Luke's, Liverpool (cons. 1831). EDWARD EDWARDS of Lawton Street is listed as an architect from 1810 to 1824 and died in 1826 [*Lancs. & Cheshire Rec. Soc.* 113, 1972, 36]. HENRY EDWARDS, born at Newport, Monmouthshire, *c.*1791 (1851 Census), had started his career as an architect and builder in Gloucester, but was in practice in Liverpool from about 1827 onwards, first in Dryden Street and later in Dale Street. In the 1830s and early 1840s he was in partnership with his son HENRY TURBERVILLE EDWARDS (born *c.*1817), but by 1849 he was living in retirement at Everton. His only architectural work so far identified is the handsome Greek Revival church of ST. JOHN, LISCARD ROAD, WALLASEY, CHESHIRE, 1832–33 [information from the late Edward Hubbard].

In the 1830s STEPHEN LANE EDWARDS was in partnership with Arthur Y. Williams (*q.v.*). They designed ST. JOHN'S CHURCH, KNOTTY ASH, LANCS., 1836, and CHRIST CHURCH, ACCRINGTON, LANCS, 1838–40, both Gothic [*Architectural Mag.* iv, 1837, 401–2]. In 1837 they exhibited at the Liverpool Academy of Arts their unexecuted design for the Liverpool Mechanics' Institute in Mount Street (built in 1835–7 under the direction of J. A. Picton, with a façade designed by A. H. Holme: see H. J. Tiffin, *History of the Liverpool Institute Schools*, 1935, 38).

EDWARDS, EDWARD, was a surveyor involved in the rebuilding of the town of Northampton after the great fire of 1675. Together with Henry Bell (*q.v.*) he appears to have been responsible for the two most important public buildings – ALL SAINTS CHURCH (1677–80) and the SESSIONS HOUSE (1676–88). A document in the County Record Office dated 18 January 1676/7 directs 'that Mr. Henry Bell and Mr. Edward Edwards, two experienced Surveyors now residing in the said Towne of Northampton be imployed as Managers' of the works at the church, and 'Mr. Edward Edwards, Surveyor', received £100 in connection with the rebuilding of the Sessions House [C. Markham, *County Buildings of Northampton*, 1885, 40]. It is possible that Edwards, like Bell, came from Norfolk, for a notebook of Sir Edward Turner offered for sale by Jantzen of East Grinstead in 1972 (Catalogue no. 112, item 42) refers to the measurement of a house at Winterton in that county in 1676 'by Mr. Edwards'. The churchwardens' accounts of BLETCHLEY CHURCH, BUCKS., record that in *c.*1709 one Edwards 'made divers Draughts of the Church in order to alter it, viz. drawings for an Altar piece and screen etc.' [W. Bradbrooke, 'The Reparation of Bletchley Church in 1710', *Records of Bucks.* xii, 1927–33, 248].

EDWARDS, FRANCIS (1784–1857), was born in Southwark and was apprenticed to a cabinet-maker in Moorfields. He showed a strong talent for architectural drawing, and in 1806 entered Soane's office as an 'improver'. He was admitted to the Royal Academy Schools in 1808, was awarded the Silver Medal the same year for measured drawings of the gallery of the British Institution in Pall Mall, and in 1811 won the Gold Medal for his design for a theatre. He exhibited at the Academy between 1809 and 1830. He left Soane's office in 1810, and assisted his former fellow-pupil H. H. Seward (then in partnership with George Byfield) for four days a week until 1823, when he devoted all his time to his own practice. Seward, on retiring soon afterwards, transferred many clients to him. Edwards was much employed in connection with arbitrations, valuations and similar work. He was responsible for the whole of the building and engineering work of the Imperial Gas Company from its incorporation in 1823, and received many commissions from Messrs. Goding, the brewers, for whom he designed the Lion Brewery which for more than a century was one of the landmarks of the South Bank. He was a Fellow of the Institute of British Architects and died on 15 August 1857 [*A.P.S.D.*].

HOXTON, IMPERIAL GAS COMPANY'S WORKS, 1824 onwards; dem. [*A.P.S.D.*].

HOXTON, ST. JOHN BAPTIST'S CHURCH, 1824–6 [drawings in R.I.B.A. Coll.].

HOLMBUSH, nr. CUCKFIELD, SUSSEX, for Thos. Broadwood, 1826, Gothic [T. W. Horsfield, *History of Sussex* ii, 1835, 222, and see *Builder* xvii, 1859, 708, for a tower in the park designed by Edwards].

ISLINGTON, layout of Milner-Gibson estate, 1828, and architecture of houses in GIBSON SQUARE and S. side of THEBERTON STREET, 1829–31 [Mary Cosh, *The Squares of Islington* ii, 1993, 89–95].

WOTTON HOUSE, SURREY, additions for W. J. Evelyn, 1830–53 [*A.P.S.D.*].

DEPTFORD, houses on the Evelyn estate, 1832–57 [*A.P.S.D.*].

CANNON BREWERY, KNIGHTSBRIDGE, additions for T. Goding, *c.*1835; dem. [*A.P.S.D.*].

LION BREWERY, GOLDEN SQUARE, additions for Messrs. Goding & Broadwood; dem. [*A.P.S.D.*].

LION BREWERY, BELVEDERE ROAD, LAMBETH, for Messrs. Goding & Co., 1836; dem. 1950 [drawings in R.I.B.A. Coll.].

PUBLIC HOUSES, for Messrs. Goding & Co. [*A.P.S.D.*].

No. 12 ST. GEORGE'S PLACE, HYDE PARK CORNER, for Thos. Goding, 1837 [*A.P.S.D.*].

ROMFORD, ESSEX, UNION WORKHOUSE, 1839, and subsequent additions [*A.P.S.D.*].

ROEHAMPTON, SURREY, additions to MOUNT CLARE for Sir Chas. Ogle, 1840 [*A.P.S.D.*] (*C. Life*, 26 Jan., 2 Feb. 1935).

CHELSEA, WELLINGTON SQUARE, KING'S ROAD, completion of square for Thomas Goding, 1840–7 [G.L. Record Office, Westminster Commissioners of Sewers, plans, vol. 38/1207].

VAUXHALL, additions and alterations to Messrs. Burnett's distillery, 1841–57 [*A.P.S.D.*].

BROADWOOD'S PIANO MANUFACTORY, 69 HORSEFERRY ROAD, WESTMINSTER, 1856; dem. [*A.P.S.D.*].

EDWARDS, THOMAS (–1775), lived at Greenwich, but enjoyed an extensive practice as an architect in Cornwall, where he also had mining interests. Nothing is certainly known of his early life. According to the author of the *Parochial History of Cornwall* (who wrongly gives his Christian name as William) he was 'a self-educated architect, the son of a small farmer'. But he may have been the Thomas, son of Thomas Edwards of St. Martin-in-the-Fields, who was apprenticed to John James (*q.v.*) in 1725.[1] James was Clerk of Works at Greenwich Hospital, and Edwards was living at Greenwich in 1753, when he appears among the subscribers to Francis Price's book on Salisbury Cathedral as 'Mr. Thomas Edwards, Architect of Greenwich'. He is similarly described in the subscription list to Borlase's *Natural History of Cornwall*, published in 1758. The latter book contains engravings of several of the country houses which Edwards is said to have designed.

Edwards's best-documented work is TREWITHEN, a country house about seven miles north-east of Truro which was under construction in the 1730s. An account 'for the buildings at Trewithen' in 1738–40 contains regular payments to 'Mr. Edwards Surveyor'. The money was generally paid 'per Potter', i.e. John Potter, who appears to have been either Edwards's agent or a builder. Edwards and Potter also appear in association at NANSWHYDEN, nr. St. Columb Major, the former seat of the Hoblyn family, for one early nineteenth-century writer says it was 'from the designs of Potter', while another attributes it to Edwards. This Potter may conceivably be the carpenter of the same name (*q.v.*) who owned and built the Little Theatre in the Haymarket in 1720.

Two other important houses which Edwards is stated to have designed by the author of the *Parochial History* and by other topographical writers are TEHIDY PARK, nr. Illogan, for J. P. Basset (1736), and CARCLEW, nr. Penryn. The latter house was begun by Samuel Kempe in the 1720s, but was still incomplete in 1749 when it was sold to the mine-owner William Lemon. Lemon is said to have employed Edwards to add the portico and offices to the central block built by Kempe.

The 'London builder renovating the mansion at Carclew' who 'undertook the reconstruction' of ST. GLUVIAS CHURCH, nr. PENRYN, 'after his own plans' can hardly be other than Edwards, and the accounts for rebuilding HELSTON CHURCH in 1756–61 show that the work was done by John Bland of Truro under the direction of Thomas Edwards, 'who is reckoned a very skilful architect'.

Edwards's last work was the addition of the Gothic tower and spire to ST. MARY'S CHURCH, TRURO. In 1765 the Corporation agreed to contribute £500 towards the cost of a steeple 'to be erected and built according to the plans of Mr. Thomas Edwards'. The builder was John Bland and the steeple was finished in 1769. It was not, however, until July 1775 that the Corporation resolved to pay Edwards £70 'for planning and directing the building of the tower at St. Mary's Church'. About thirty years later a local antiquary named Taunton recorded that 'the steeple was built by Mr. Edwards, architect of London', and that 'Mr. Bland was his agent to manage in his absence'. He added that Edwards was 'also the builder of Tehidy, Nanswydden, Mr. Daniell's and Mr. Lemmon's at Truro'. The last-named house was the residence of William Lemon, the builder of Carclew, who

[1] I owe this information to Mr. Edward Martin. If Edwards was apprenticed to James at the usual age of 14 he can hardly have been the 'Thomas Edwards Esq.' who subscribed to Gibbs's *Book of Architecture* in 1728. Mr. Martin has pointed out that as Surveyor to St. Paul's Cathedral James would have been well known to the Dean, Dr. Henry Godolphin, whose Cornish connections might have led to Edwards's employment in that county.

died in 1760. It was then the largest and most handsome house in Truro, but soon after Lemon's death his former agent Thomas Daniell, who had married Ralph Allen's niece, bought up Lemon's mining and mercantile interests, and built an equally imposing house in the same street, employing Edwards as his architect.

That Edwards and Daniell were well acquainted appears from the former's will, in which he directs that his mines are to be sold by his executors 'as Mr. Thomas Daniel of Truro in the County of Cornwall shall advise'. Where these mines were is not stated, but it seems likely the Edwards, like Daniell, acquired his mining interests through his association with William Lemon of Carclew. The will is dated 22 April 1773, and has a codicil witnessed by Mary Potter. It mentions a leasehold estate in Conduit Street and other property, including a share in Covent Garden Playhouse and an eighth share in the East Indiaman *Devonshire*. These were to be sold for the benefit of his wife and his sons John, Francis, James and Thomas. Edwards died at Greenwich on 30 October 1775, and was buried at St. Alphege's Church there on 5 November.

Edwards was a competent Georgian architect, though not a designer of much originality. His country houses derive from the style of Gibbs, while Helston Church exhibits several features borrowed directly from Hawksmoor's St. Alphege's, Greenwich. Of his two town houses the earlier is in the Gibbs style, with rich plaster decoration in the interior, while the later adopts the plainer sort of elevation fashionable in London and Bath in the third quarter of the eighteenth century.

[*The Parochial History of Cornwall*, 1867–72; Taunton MSS. at Royal Cornwall Institution; P.C.C. 415 ALEXANDER; *Gent's Mag.* 1775, 551; St. Alphege's, Greenwich, burial register; H. Dalton Clifford & Howard Colvin, 'A Georgian Architect in Cornwall', *C. Life*, 4 and 18 Oct. 1962.]

TEHIDY, CORNWALL, for J. P. Basset, 1736; altered and enlarged by Wm. Burn 1861; dem. after a fire 1919 [*Parochial History* ii, 228].

TREWITHEN, CORNWALL, completion of house for the heirs of Philip Hawkins, *c.*1738–40; altered by Sir Robert Taylor *c.*1763–4 [Hawkins documents in County Record Office] (*C. Life*, 2–9 April 1953).

CARCLEW, CORNWALL, completed house for William Lemon after 1749; colonnades added 18—; gutted 1934 [*Parochial History* iii, 395] (Richardson & Gill, *Regional Architecture of the West of England*, 1924, 92–3).

NANSWHYDEN, CORNWALL, for Robert Hoblyn (d. 1756); burned 1803 [Taunton MS.] (W. Borlase, *Natural History of Cornwall*, 1758, pl. 9).

ST. GLUVIAS CHURCH, CORNWALL, rebuilt *c.*1750; rebuilt 1883 [*Parochial History* ii, 85].

TRELOWARREN, CORNWALL, alterations for Sir Richard Vyvyan, Bart., including remodelling of interior of hall and south parlour, 1754–60 [Vyvyan papers, *ex inf.* Mrs. D. Fenwick].

TRURO, PRINCE'S HOUSE, PRINCE'S STREET, for William Lemon (d. 1760), now occupied by Farm Industries Ltd. [Taunton MS.].

TRURO, house in PRINCE'S STREET for Thomas Daniell, 1755–62, now known as the Mansion House [Taunton MS.] (Richardson & Gill, p. 96).

HELSTON CHURCH, CORNWALL, 1756–61 [H. S. Toy, *History of Helston*, 1936, 334–40; accounts in Cornwall Record Office, DD.90. 244–6].

TRURO, ST. MARY'S CHURCH, added Gothic tower and spire, 1766–9; dem. 1880 [F. W. Bullock, *History of the Church of St. Mary Truro*, Truro 1948, 80–1].

EDWARDS, WILLIAM (1719–1789), is celebrated as a bridge-builder in South Wales. He was the youngest son of a farmer at Eglwysilan, nr. Caerphilly in Glamorganshire, and began life as an agricultural labourer. His enterprise and intelligence led him first to learn the technique of dry-stone walling, at which he became adept, and then the art of a mason. Though entirely self-taught, he became so skilled at his trade that in 1746 he contracted to build a bridge of three arches over the R. Taff at PONT-Y-PRYDD, GLAMORGANSHIRE, and to maintain it for seven years. When it was destroyed by a flood two years later Edwards boldly decided to replace it by a single span of 140 feet that would offer no obstruction to the flood-waters of the Taff. This bridge was nearly complete when the weight of the masonry in the haunches forced out the keystones and thus caused the arch to collapse. Undaunted, Edwards determined to try again. In order to reduce the mass of masonry he pierced large cylindrical holes through the haunches. Whether this expedient was empirically devised by Edwards or not, it proved entirely successful and the bridge, completed in 1756, still stands today (plans and elevation in *Builder* iii, 1845, 427). Its elegant profile was as much admired as the ingenuity of its constructor, and he subsequently built many other bridges in South Wales. Among the more important were USK BRIDGE, MONMOUTHSHIRE (rebuilt 1836);

PONT-AR-TAWY, about 10 miles above Swansea, of one arch of 80 feet span; BETTWS BRIDGE, GLAM. (one arch, 45 feet span); LLANDOVERY BRIDGE, CARMARTHENSHIRE (one arch, 84 feet span, with one perforation in the haunches); WYCHTREE BRIDGE, over the R. Tawy near Morriston (one arch, 95 feet span, with two perforations); ABERAVON BRIDGE, GLAMORGANSHIRE (one arch, 70 feet span, without perforations); and GLASBURY BRIDGE, over the R. Wye near Hay, of five arches on high piers, afterwards destroyed by a flood. Some of these later bridges represented a considerable technical improvement on the first one at Pont-y-Prydd, whose roadway was so inconveniently steep that the nearby ford remained in use until the middle of the nineteenth century. For Edwards found that, where sufficient abutment was assured, it was possible to construct arches of much larger radius and lower rise than was commonly thought necessary.

Besides building bridges, Edwards continued to erect smelting houses, forges and other industrial buildings, and to carry on the business of a farmer. From 1745 onwards he also officiated as an Independent minister. He died in 1789, leaving six children. A portrait by a miniature-painter called Hill was exhibited at the Royal Academy in 1779.

Three of Edwards's four sons followed their father's trade, and David, the second, continued the bridge-building business. Among the bridges which he erected were those at LLANDEILO, CARMARTHENSHIRE (R. Tywi, 1771, replaced 1848), EDWINSFORD, CARMARTHENSHIRE (R. Cothy); PONTLOERIG, nr. Whitland, CARMARTHENSHIRE (R. Taf); BEDWAS, MONMOUTHSHIRE (R. Rhymney); and the five-arch bridge over the Usk at NEWPORT, MONMOUTHSHIRE, completed in 1801, dem. 1927. He lived at Beaupre, St. Mary Church, nr. Cowbridge.

[*Gent's Mag.* 1764, 564–5; B. H. Malkin, *The Scenery, Antiquities and Biography of S. Wales*, 1804, 84–94; Samuel Smiles, *The Lives of the Engineers* i, 1861, 266–75; *A.P.S.D.*; *D.N.B.*; *The Dictionary of Welsh Biography*, 1959, 198–9; W. B. Coventry, *A History of Pont-y-ty-Prydd* 1902; E. I. Williams, 'Pont-y-ty-pridd: A Critical Examination of its History', and S. B. Hamilton, 'Pont-y-ty-pridd: Notes on the Technical Significance of a Remarkable Bridge', *Transactions of the Newcomen Soc.* xxiv, 1943–5; T. Ruddock, *Arch Bridges and their Builders 1735–1835*, Cambridge 1979, 48–53.]

EDWIN, RICHARD (–1778), was a pupil of Matthew Brettingham in 1764, when he was awarded a premium of 7 guineas by the Society of Arts [*Register of Premiums*, 1778]. He competed for the Royal Exchange at Dublin in 1769 [*Builder* xxvii, 1869, 781]. He exhibited at the Society of Artists in 1770, and at the Royal Academy in 1774, 1776 and 1777. For the Hon. Edward Stratford, later 1st Earl of Aldborough, he designed in 1773–5 the Adamsian STRATFORD PLACE, OXFORD STREET, a 'longitudinal elevation' of which he exhibited at the Academy in 1774 [A. T. Bolton, 'Stratford Place', *London Topographical Record* xii, 1920; Dorothy Stroud, *George Dance, Architect*, 1971, 90–1]. He also appears to have designed the HANOVER SQUARE CONCERT ROOMS on the east side of HANOVER SQUARE, opened in 1775 by the dancing-master Sir John Gallini, and demolished *c.*1875, for in 1776 he exhibited 'a longitudinal section of the Concert Room in Hanover Square'. Edwin, who lived in Marylebone, died in October 1778 [P.C.C. 399 HAY].

EGLINGTON, a family of masons and stone-carvers working in the Midlands in the eighteenth century, most of whom were descended from Benjamin Eglington of Badby in Northamptonshire. He had several sons who were brought up as masons. The eldest, Benjamin (*c.*1730–1768), was the foreman mason at the building of the Derby Assembly Rooms to the designs of Joseph Pickford in 1763–4 and died in Derby in 1768. John (1733–1787) established himself in Birmingham. Samuel (1742–1788) moved to Ashbourne. He was primarily a stone-carver, but in 1771 submitted a jejune design for the Moot Hall at Wirksworth that was rejected in favour of one by Joseph Pickford [E. Saunders, 'The Moot Hall, Wirksworth', *Derbyshire Life*, Dec. 1978]. Joseph (1746–1810) went to Coventry, where he established a successful business as a builder-architect and enjoyed the status of a gentleman at the time of his death. Between 1775 and 1787 he rebuilt several windows at HOLY TRINITY CHURCH, COVENTRY, and recased the east end [T. Sharp, *Illustrative Papers on the History and Antiquities of Coventry*, 1871, 107]. He designed THE COUNTY HALL, COVENTRY, 1783–4, a conventional classical design of its time [T. Sharp, *The Coventry Guide*, 1823–4, 53], and in 1792 LEEK WOOTTON CHURCH, WARWICKS., was rebuilt to his designs in a Gothic style, incorporating the medieval tower [Shakespeare's Birthplace Record Office, Stratford, Leigh papers, Leek Wootton 25].

In the next generation Samuel (son of Benjamin) was a mason at Kineton in Warwickshire, where he died in 1816. In 1773–4 he and a carpenter named John Mantun contracted to rebuild LIGHTHORNE

CHURCH, WARWICKS., in a plain Gothic style [Churchwardens' accounts in Warwicks. C.R.O.]. Their work at Lighthorne was largely paid for by Lord Willoughby de Broke, who also employed both Eglington and Mantun at COMPTON VERNEY HOUSE, e.g. in building the Chapel to the designs of L. Brown in 1776–8 [Shakespeare's Birthplace as above, Willoughby de Broke papers]. At Birmingham, where an 'Eglington Senr.' of that city signs a large wall-tablet in ASTON CHURCH to Edward Brandwood (d. 1731), the family was still represented in the 1790s by Samuel and John Eglington, masons of Edmund Street.

[Wills in Lichfield Joint Record Office and Worcester C.R.O.; information from Mr. Edward Saunders.]

ELDER. Payments to 'Mr. Elder, Surveyor, for his Journey from London', occur at the beginning of the building accounts of ST. CATHARINE'S HALL, CAMBRIDGE, in 1674, but it is uncertain whether he was the designer of the new buildings that were erected during the next thirteen years [Willis & Clark, ii, 101].

ELGER, JOHN (1802–1888), was the younger son of the Bedford carpenter Isaac Elger (d. 1806), and had a successful career as a builder in London. His Bedford connections secured him the surveyorship of the Harpur Charity estate in Holborn, which he held from 1826 to 1846. His yard was on the Grosvenor Estate in South Street (E. of South Audley Street) and he was active as a speculative builder both on that estate in the 1830s and in Knightsbridge in the 1840s and 1850s. Although he had in 1829 submitted a classical design for the Harpur School in Bedford which was rejected in favour of a Gothic one by Blore, he appears to have been less of an architect than his brother T. G. Elger (*q.v.*), preferring to employ the young H. L. Elmes (*q.v.*), whose father James Elmes had designed the Bedford prison built by his brother in 1819. It was for Elger that H. L. Elmes made designs (unexecuted) for Assembly Rooms, etc., at Biggleswade in 1842, and Elmes designed the façades for most of Elger's speculations, including the imposing terrace of houses at PRINCES GATE, built *c.*1845 onwards, and 'chambers built in the garden and stable-yard of a mansion in Hanover Square', identifiable as HANOVER CHAMBERS, 23 HANOVER SQUARE (dem.). To Elmes may also be attributed the Gothic villa on Putney Heath called SCIO HOUSE which Elger built for his own occupation *c.*1845. He appears to have retired before 1860 and died at Brighton on 12 August 1888, aged 87, leaving an estate valued at over £115,000 [*A.P.S.D.*, *s.v.* 'Elmes'; J. Godber, *The Harpur Trust 1555–1973*, Bedford 1973, 39, 160, pl. 10; *Survey of London* xxxix, 131; *R.I.B.A. Drawings Catalogue C–F*, 103–4; information about Scio House from Mr. Roger White; Principal Probate Registry, Calendar of Probates].

ELGER, THOMAS GWYN (1794–1841), was the elder son of Isaac Elger (d. 1806), a carpenter of Bedford. He was apprenticed to a carpenter in London and at the same time gained some experience in drawing and surveying. In 1815 he returned to Bedford to take charge of the family business, and for the rest of his life ranked as Bedford's principal carpenter and builder. In 1819 the contract to build the new prison brought him into contact with its architect, James Elmes, with whose son his brother John (*q.v.*) was later to collaborate. Although primarily a builder, Elger acted from time to time as an architect. In 1825 it was to his designs that the BEDFORD LUNATIC ASYLUM was enlarged and in 1836–7 he designed SPRINGFIELD HOUSE, KEMPSTON, BEDS., as a private asylum for Dr. John Harris. In 1834 he designed THE BEDFORD ROOMS (now the 'Harpur Suite') in HARPUR STREET, with an impressive Doric temple-front; in 1835–6 the BIGGLESWADE UNION WORKHOUSE (now 'The Limes' in London Road); and in 1838 he refronted TINGRITH MANOR, BEDS (dem.). for the Misses Trevor. Elger was for many years a trustee of the Harpur Trust and served several times as Mayor of Bedford. He died of typhus on 8 April 1841 [C. Pickford, 'The Origins of the Architectural Profession in Bedfordshire', *Bedfordshire Mag.* 1992].

ELISON, THOMAS, 'Architecte du Prince de Wallis', is the name which appears on the title-page of a book entitled *Décorations pour Parcs et Jardins* which was published at Leipzig early in the nineteenth century. This book appears to have been a reprint of *Decorations for Parks and Gardens*, published in London by J. Taylor in *c.*1810, and usually attributed to Charles Middleton (*q.v.*).

ELLINS, JAMES, succeeded Thomas Dixon as foreman of Lady Oxford's works at WELBECK ABBEY, NOTTS., in 1743. Several architectural designs by him figure in a list of drawings made in 1764, and some of these drawings survive. Most of them are marked as 'not executed'. [Nottingham University Library, Pwf 10052; information from the late Francis Needham; R. W. Goulding,

'Henrietta Countess of Oxford', *Trans. Thoroton Soc.* xxvii, 1924.]

ELLIOT, ARCHIBALD (1760–1823) and JAMES (1770–1810), were the sons of a carrier at Ancrum in Roxburghshire. Archibald was born there in August 1760, James in April 1770. Archibald is said to have been brought up as a joiner, and to have been employed as a draughtsman by a cabinet-maker in London. There is a story that he worked at Douglas Castle, Lanarkshire, where, upon 'a difference arising between the architect and the proprietor, Elliot took up and completed the work'. He is also said either to have built Castle Mona in the Isle of Man to the designs of James Steuart, or to have completed it after Steuart's death in 1806. James Elliot's ability as a 'draughtsman and designer' is mentioned in a letter from Alexander Trotter of Dreghorn to Lord Breadalbane dated 13 September 1800, in which he says that James 'proposes to join in business with a Brother . . . in London . . . who has had a regular education there and much experience under the best masters' [S.R.O., GD 112/20/7]. Archibald was exhibiting architectural designs at the Royal Academy between 1794 and 1799, and the brothers were in partnership as architects soon after 1800. Archibald had an office in London, while James remained in Scotland to supervise the firm's work there. James's death in October 1810 at the age of 40 brought the partnership to an end, and thereafter Archibald appears to have divided his time between London (Osnaburgh Street) and Edinburgh (Calton Hill). He died in Edinburgh on 16 June 1823, and was buried in the New Calton Graveyard, where he is commemorated by a fluted column topped by a draped urn. His practice was continued by his son Archibald (*q.v.*).

Archibald Elliot was one of the leading Edinburgh architects during the first quarter of the nineteenth century. His Regent Bridge and County Hall were among the best Greek Revival buildings in the 'Modern Athens', and until his death he was strongly favoured by those who wanted a native Scotsman to be chosen as the architect of the National Monument on Calton Hill. An engraved plan of his design (N.L.S., MS. 13420, f. 101) shows a Pantheon-like 'Inscription Hall' 100 feet in diameter, with a hexastyle portico and an encircling colonnade, and attached to it at the rear a rectangular church with another hexastyle portico.

As a country-house architect, Elliot specialized in castellated houses with Gothic detailing. Externally, these houses are symmetrically designed in a manner which usually derives either from Inveraray (Taymouth and Stobo) or from the Adam castle style (Loudoun and Dreghorn). Often the interiors are classical, but at Taymouth, Lindertis and Newbyth the Elliots provided elaborate Gothic rooms in the style of Wyatt and Atkinson. [Ancrum parish register in New Register House, Edinburgh; *A.P.S.D.*; *Scots Mag.* 1810, 879; testament of Archibald Elliot in Commissariot of Edinburgh, 28 June 1825.]

PUBLIC BUILDINGS

†KIRKCALDY OLD CHURCH, FIFE, rebuilt (incorporating old tower), 1806–7 [S.R.O., HR 239/1, pp. 46, 47, 49, etc.]

DUNFERMLINE, FIFE, THE GUILDHALL, converted 1849–50 into COUNTY BUILDINGS, 79 HIGH STREET, 1807–11 [signed plans formerly in possession of the late James Shearer, R.S.A., *ex inf.* Mr. David Walker].

GLENORCHY CHURCH, DALMALLY, ARGYLLSHIRE, 1810–11, octagonal Gothic, by James Elliot [*N.S.A.* vii, 100–1; R.C.A.M. *Argyll* ii, 132].

HADDINGTON CHURCH, EAST LOTHIAN, consultant architects for alterations by James Burn (*q.v.*), including plaster vault in nave, 1810–11 [S.R.O., HR 101/2].

DUNKELD CATHEDRAL, PERTHSHIRE, fitted up choir as parish church, 1814 [drawing at Blair Atholl; N.L.S., MS. 13249, ff. 18–19].

EDINBURGH, THE NEW PRISONS, CALTON HILL, 1815–17, castellated; dem. *c.*1938 except Governor's house [*A.P.S.D.*] (T. H. Shepherd, *Modern Athens*, 1829, 44–5 and plates).

EDINBURGH, THE REGENT BRIDGE, 1815–19 [signed 'ARCHIBALD ELLIOT ARCHITECT'; A. J. Youngson, *The Making of Classical Edinburgh*, 1966, 142–7].

WATERLOO MONUMENT, PENIEL HEUGH, MONTEVIOT, ROXBURGHSHIRE, 1816 (after collapse of monument erected on an adjacent site to the design of W. Burn) [Kitty Cruft, 'The Building of the Peniel Heugh Monument', *Scottish Georgian Soc's Bulletin* No. 9, 1982].

EDINBURGH, ST. PAUL'S EPISCOPAL CHURCH, YORK PLACE, 1816–18, Gothic; chancel 1892 [*A.P.S.D.*; W. M. Gilbert, *Edinburgh in the Nineteenth Century*, 1901, 60].

EDINBURGH, THE COUNTY HALL, 1816–19; dem. *c.*1900 [*Scots Mag.* Nov. 1816; T. H. Shepherd, *Modern Athens*, 1829, 74 and plate].

EDINBURGH, PARLIAMENT HOUSE, COURT ROOMS

† In conjunction with James Elliot.

for LORDS ORDINARY at S. end of Parliament Hall, 1818–19 [S.R.O., E 343/3, pp. 7–94, Minutes of the Trustees for Public Buildings].

EDINBURGH, THE CALTON CONVENING ROOMS, WATERLOO PLACE, 1818–19 [part of Waterloo Place, for which see below, under 'Domestic Architecture'].

PAISLEY, RENFREWSHIRE, THE COUNTY BUILDINGS, 1818–20, castellated; enlarged 1850; dem. 1970 [C. Mackie, *Abbey and Town of Paisley*, Glasgow 1835, 148].

EDINBURGH, No. 35 ST. ANDREW'S SQUARE, alterations, including staircase, for Royal Bank of Scotland, 1819 [Ian Gow in *C. Life*, 13 Sept. 1990, 216].

INVERKEITHING, FIFE, PARISH SCHOOL, 1819 [S.R.O., HR 279/1, 10 Sept. 1819].

EDINBURGH, BROUGHTON PLACE CHURCH (Dr. Brown's Chapel), 1820–1, interior altered 1870 [Anon., *History of Broughton Place U.P. Church*, 1872, 151; Minutes of the Managers in S.R.O., CH 3/564/12, pp. 149, 160].

JEDBURGH, ROXBURGHSHIRE, THE COUNTY PRISON, 1820–3, castellated [Iain Macivor, *Jedburgh Castle, A Georgian Prison*, Jedburgh 1972].

BLAIR ATHOLL CHURCH, PERTHSHIRE, 1823–5 [S.R.O., CH 2/430/8].

DOMESTIC ARCHITECTURE, ETC.

LOUDOUN CASTLE, AYRSHIRE, for the Countess of Loudoun and her husband the 2nd Earl of Moira (afterwards 1st Marquess of Hastings), 1804–11, castellated; gutted in 1941 and now in ruins [exhib. at R.A. 1806; G. Richardson, *New Vitruvius Britannicus* ii, 1808, pls. 51–6].

†DREGHORN CASTLE, COLINTON, MIDLOTHIAN, enlarged and remodelled for Alexander Trotter, *c.*1805, castellated; dem. 1958 [*Scots Mag.* 1808, 243] (*The Beauties of Scotland* i, 1805, 443; J. Small, *Castles and Mansions of the Lothians* i, 1883).

†STOBO CASTLE, PEEBLESSHIRE, for Sir James Montgomery, Bart., 1805–11, castellated [W. Chambers, *History of Peeblesshire*, 1864, 438–9, R.C.A.M., *Peeblesshire* ii, 308–9].

†AUCHMORE HOUSE, KILLIN, PERTHSHIRE, altered and enlarged for 4th Earl (1st Marquess) of Breadalbane, 1806–7; rebuilt *c.*1870 [S.R.O., GDH 112/20/2].

†TAYMOUTH CASTLE, PERTHSHIRE, for 4th Earl (1st Marquess) of Breadalbane, 1806–10, castellated; subsequently enlarged by W. Atkinson and J. Gillespie-Graham [Alistair Rowan in *C. Life*, 8–15 Oct. 1964].

MINTO HOUSE, ROXBURGHSHIRE, rebuilt for 1st Earl of Minto, 1809–14; dismantled 1973, dem. 1992–3 [N.L.S., MSS. 13457, 13249, 11911, etc.; working drawings in N.M.R.S.; cf. *N.S.A.* iii, 367]. The new house followed the unusual V plan of the former one, and incorporated part of its fabric; cf. plan of the former house in Bodleian, Gough Maps 39, f. 28.

DUNKELD HOUSE, PERTHSHIRE, works for 4th Duke of Atholl, including castellated gateway and stables (dem.), 1809, restoration of the Low Wing after fire in 1814, and lodges, *c.*1815 [John, 7th Duke of Atholl, *Chronicles of the Atholl and Tullibardine Families* iv, 1908, 234, 261, 264; drawings at Blair Atholl].

LINDERTIS HOUSE, ANGUS, for Gilbert Laing Meason, 1815–16, castellated; dem. [J. P. Neale, *Views of Seats*, 1st ser., ii] (*Forfarshire Illustrated*, 1843, 114).

CALLENDAR HOUSE, STIRLINGSHIRE, Grecian Mausoleum in grounds for trustees of the late William Forbes, 1816 [S.R.O., GD 171/Box 78/5] (R.C.A.M., *Stirlingshire*, pl. 50).

NEWBYTH HOUSE, EAST LOTHIAN, for David Baird, 1818–19, castellated; interior rebuilt as flats after fire in 1972 [*A.P.S.D.*; contract in S.R.O., SC 40/67/5, p. 315; exhib. at R.A. 1819 by Archibald Elliot, junior].

LOCHNELL HOUSE, ARGYLLSHIRE, enlarged in castellated style for Lt. Gen. Duncan Campbell, 1818–20 [S.R.O., SC 51/60/1, 8 Feb. 1821; R.C.A.M., *Argyll* ii, 266].

EDINBURGH, WATERLOO PLACE, 1819 (designed 1815) [A. J. Youngson, *The Making of Classical Edinburgh*, 1966, 145].

LOCHNAW CASTLE, WIGTOWNSHIRE, enlarged for Sir Andrew Agnew, Bart., 1819–20; this addition since dem. [S.R.O., GD 154/499/1–2 and 6; T. M'Crie, *Memoirs of Sir Andrew Agnew*, 1850, 63–4].

LEITH, MIDLOTHIAN, feu-plan and elevations of houses in COMMERCIAL STREET, opposite Custom House, 1820 [*Edinburgh Evening Courant*, 17 April 1820, *ex inf.* Mr. J. Gifford].

THE HAINING, SELKIRKSHIRE, enlarged for John Pringle, *c.*1820 [J. P. Neale, *Views of Seats*, 1st ser., iv] (R.C.A.M., *Selkirkshire*, 49–50).

EDINBURGH, RUTLAND PLACE, STREET and SQUARE were built in 1830–4 to designs by John Tait based on plans made by Elliot in 1819 [S.R.O., Edinburgh Sasines].

ELLIOT, ARCHIBALD, junior (– 1843), was the son and successor of Archibald Elliot (*q.v.*). He exhibited at the Royal Acad-

† In conjunction with James Elliot.

emy in 1817–20, showing drawings of recent works by his father. Subsequently he practised in London from Osnaburgh Street, where he was in partnership with his brother Alexander. He altered THE ROYAL BANK OF SCOTLAND (formerly DUNDAS HOUSE), ST. ANDREW'S SQUARE, EDINBURGH, 1825–8, and designed the grand Greek Revival ROYAL BANK OF SCOTLAND, GLASGOW, 1827, and the MILITARY ACADEMY, LOTHIAN ROAD, EDINBURGH, 1829–30; dem. [*A.P.S.D.*; N. Munro, *History of the Royal Bank of Scotland*, Edinburgh 1928, 193–4]. For the 2nd Earl of Minto he designed the monument in REIGATE CHURCH, SURREY, erected in 1826 to the memory of William Elliot, M.P. (d. 1818) [N.L.S., MSS. 11913, f. 101, 11957, f. 116].

ELLIOT, WILLIAM (1761–*c.*1830), was an architect and builder at Kelso in Roxburghshire. He was the son of Thomas Elliot, the minister of Cavers near Hawick, a man who 'possessed considerable attainments as a mathematician and astronomer' [Lady Eliott & Sir Arthur Eliott, *The Elliots*, 1974, pedigree opp. p. 370].

In 1794–5 Elliot built the TEVIOT BRIDGE near KELSO, probably to the designs of Alexander Stevens (*q.v.*) [*Edinburgh Encyclopaedia* iv, 1830, 486]. He is otherwise known to have designed several minor but attractive country houses in the Border area of Scotland. Chesters is a conventional Georgian house with flanking wings, Ladykirk a simplified version of Chambers's Dundas House in Edinburgh, Crailing a compact and elegantly detailed villa.

Elliot was still in practice in Kelso in 1825, but by 1837 his place had been taken by his son Walter, who designed (*inter alia*) the BRITISH LINEN BANK in KELSO, 1839 [Bank of Scotland, Minutes of the British Linen Co., 6/6/16, p. 107, 4 June 1839, *ex inf.* Mrs E. Beaton]. Drawings in the R.I.B.A. Collection for gateways and lodges at Blackadder in Berwickshire, initialled W E, and dating from the early nineteenth century, can more plausibly be attributed to either William or Walter Elliot than to the Welsh architect William Edwards, as suggested in the *Catalogue*, *C–F*, 95.

CHESTERS HOUSE, ROXBURGHSHIRE, for Thomas Elliot Ogilvie, 1787–90 [G. Tancred, *Annals of a Border Club*, Jedburgh 1899, 336].

YAIR, SELKIRKSHIRE, for Alexander Pringle, 1788–9 [S.R.O., GD 246/30/2, parts 3 & 5] (R.C.A.M., *Selkirkshire*, 45–6).

LADYKIRK HOUSE, BERWICKSHIRE, for William Robertson, 1797–9; altered by W. Burn 1845; dem. 1966 [drawings formerly at Ladykirk].

WILTON CHURCH, ROXBURGHSHIRE, enlarged on north side, 1800 [S.R.O., HR 390/2].

CRAILING HOUSE, ROXBURGHSHIRE, for James Paton, 1803 [G. Tancred, *Annals of a Border Club*, Jedburgh 1899, 348] (*C. Life*, 14 June 1962).

DRUMLANRIG CASTLE, DUMFRIESSHIRE, restoration for 4th Duke of Buccleuch, 1813 [Mark Girouard in *C. Life*, 8 Sept. 1960, citing accounts at Drumlanrig].

KELSO CHURCH, ROXBURGHSHIRE, internal alterations (chiefly substitution of flat ceiling for domed one), 1823 [S.R.O., HR 651/4].

ELLIS, ANTHONY (1620–1671), built and presumably designed ALTHORP HOUSE, NORTHANTS., as remodelled by the 2nd Earl of Sunderland in 1666–8, and illustrated in *Vitruvius Britannicus* ii, pls. 95–7. The first stone was laid in February 1665/6, and between then and October 1668 Anthony Ellis, 'freemason and surveyor', received at least £2800 'towards the new building' [Blenheim Palace muniments, Box XVI/56 and B.L., Add. MS. 61489, ff. 139, 140, 155].

Anthony Ellis was a pupil of Nicholas Stone, to whom he was apprenticed in about 1635 and whose will he witnessed in 1641 [*The Note-Book of Nicholas Stone*, ed. Spiers, Walpole Soc., vii, 1918–19, 30, 147, etc.]. Like Stone, he was a sculptor as well as a builder, and his signature appears on the monument to Sir John Wentworth (d. 1651) at SOMERLEYTON, SUFFOLK. His will [P.C.C. 121 DUKE] shows that he lived in the parish of St. Martin-in-the-Fields, Westminster, and died in 1671.

ELLIS, ROBERT, a carpenter and builder of Fleet in Lincolnshire, designed and built ST. JOHN'S CHURCH in the parish of HOLBEACH, LINCS., 1839, Gothic [G. W. Macdonald, *A Brief Account of the Parish of Holbeach*, n.d., 56].

ELLIS, THOMAS, a carpenter of Sherborne, Dorset, rebuilt SPARKFORD CHURCH, SOMERSET, in a simple Gothic style in 1824, apparently to his own designs [I.C.B.S.].

ELMES, HARVEY LONSDALE (1814–1847), born at Oving, nr. Chichester, was the only son of James Elmes (*q.v.*), and godson of James Lonsdale, the artist, who was his father's intimate friend. He studied architecture under his father and his uncle Henry

John Elmes;[1] also with John Elger (*q.v.*), a speculative builder, for whom he later made a number of designs. In 1831 he was admitted as a student at the Royal Academy Schools, and in 1834 he became an assistant to H. E. Goodridge, in whose office at Bath he remained for three years. After this he returned to London and assisted his father in designing some houses in Queen Anne's Gate, and in the decoration of one of them for the Turkish ambassador.

In July 1839 he obtained the first premium of 250 guineas for the design of St. George's Hall, Liverpool, out of a total of seventy-five competitors. Soon afterwards the Corporation decided to build new Assize Courts, and a premium of £300 was offered for the best design: eighty-nine competitors entered, and Elmes was again successful (April 1840). It was then proposed to unite the two buildings, and Franklin, the city architect, was directed to adapt Elmes's plans. Fortunately he had the generosity not to stand in the way of the young architect, and it was a new design by Elmes himself which was approved on 27 October 1840. It comprised a great central hall, with the crown court at one end, the civil court at the other, and an elliptical concert room beyond it at a higher level. Work began in 1841, but the architect, whose already poor health had begun to deteriorate under the strain of preparing detailed drawings for this great edifice without adequate assistance, was advised to go abroad, leaving the engineer Robert Rawlinson in charge of the works. In 1842 he visited Belgium and Germany with his friend William Earle, whose account of the tour is printed in R.I.B.A. *Sessional Papers*, 1863–4, p. xi. In the course of it he was able to see some of the new monumental buildings by von Klenze and Schinkel which, through illustrations, may already have influenced his own approach to neo-classical design. On his return, he resumed work on St. George's Hall, but the worry and responsibility involved in its completion – and in particular the problem of vaulting the 73-foot span of the Great Hall – further impaired his health. He was obliged to leave his office, first for Ventnor and then for Jamaica, where he died on 26 November 1847, at the age of 34. The main structure of the building was finished by Rawlinson in the course of the next four years, and between 1851 and 1854 C. R. Cockerell completed the interior, largely to his own designs. The total cost was £400,000.

St. George's Hall is one of the major monuments of neo-classical architecture, 'holding its own in comparison with any classical building of these years in Europe' (Pevsner). The complexity of the brief and the insularity of the site (exposing all the elevations to view) set the architect a problem, both in planning and in composition, which he brilliantly solved. His approach, though controlled by scholarship, was very different from the archaeological pedantry which had inspired much Greek Revival architecture. For Elmes, like Cockerell, the classical orders represented an architectural vocabulary to be manipulated with intelligent understanding rather than a set of rigid precepts to be followed with absolute respect. The result is a building of monumental strength and grandeur in which the architectural vocabulary of Imperial Rome is most successfully used to symbolize the civic pride of a great Victorian industrial city. For a young man still in his twenties it was an astonishing achievement, only to be equalled by the equally precocious performance of Giles Gilbert Scott in the competition for the Anglican Cathedral in 1903.

Before his early death Elmes had time to design only a few other buildings: a large Tudor Gothic school of no special distinction, and several private houses in the Liverpool area. A number of his drawings (including those for St. George's Hall) are in the R.I.B.A. Collection, together with some letters and a MS. memoir by his father.

[Obituaries by his father in *Builder* xiii, 1855, 53–4, and *Building Chronicle* i, 1855, 213; others in *Builder* vi, 1848, 24, 71; J. T. Kilpin, 'The Late Mr. Elmes and St. George's Hall', *Trans. Historic Soc. of Lancs. and Cheshire*, N.S. ix, 1868–9 (giving the text of Elmes's correspondence with Robert Rawlinson); *A.P.S.D.*; R. P. Jones, 'The Life and Work of Harvey Lonsdale Elmes', *Arch. Rev.* xv, 1904, 231; *R.I.B.A. Drawings Coll. Catalogue: C–F*, 103–9.]

LIVERPOOL, ST. GEORGE'S HALL AND ASSIZE COURTS, designed 1840, begun 1841, structure completed 1847–51 by R. Rawlinson, interior by C. R. Cockerell 1851–4 [*Companion to the Almanac*, 1842, 221–6; *Builder* xiii, 1855, 1–5, 23, 26–8, 126–7].

LIVERPOOL, THE COLLEGIATE INSTITUTION, SHAW STREET, 1840–3, Gothic [*Companion to the Almanac*, 1842, 226–7; David Wainwright in *Arch. Rev.* May 1959].

LONDON, KENSINGTON, façades of houses in ENNISMORE GARDENS and PRINCE'S GATE, for John Elger, speculative builder, *c.*1843–6 [drawings in R.I.B.A. Coll.].

RABY HALL, ROCK FERRY, BIRKENHEAD, CHESHIRE, for William Irlam, 1845 [men-

[1] H. J. Elmes had an architectural training under Daniel Davis (*q.v.*), but he made a living as a builder in London rather than as an architect.

tioned in his father's memoir as 'a villa at Rock Ferry for William Irlam'].

WALLASEY, CHESHIRE, REDCLIFFE, WELLINGTON ROAD, NEW BRIGHTON, for Daniel Neilson, 1845, Tudor style [drawings in R.I.B.A. Coll.; N. Pevsner & E. Hubbard, *Cheshire*, 1971, 374].

WALLASEY, CHESHIRE, a villa at NEW BRIGHTON for G. H. Lawrence of Liverpool, *c.*1845 [MS. memoir by James Elmes, second version, p. 76].

attributed: SCIO HOUSE, PUTNEY HEATH, SURREY, for John Elger, *c.*1845, Gothic [see under 'Elger, John'].

ALLERTON TOWER, ALLERTON, LANCS., for Sir Hardman Earle, 1846; dem. 1937 [*A.P.S.D.*].

WOOLTON, LANCS., 'DRUID'S CROSS', villa for Joseph Hornby, 1846–7; dem. 1977 [drawings in R.I.B.A. Coll.] (P. Fleetwood-Hesketh, *Murray's Lancashire Architectural Guide*, 1955, 100).

THINGWALL HALL, KNOTTY ASH, nr. LIVERPOOL (now St. Edward's Orphanage), for Samuel Henry Thompson, *c.*1846–7 [letter from Elmes to Thompson in the author's possession].

LANCASHIRE COUNTY LUNATIC ASYLUM, RAINHILL, LANCS., executed by William Moseley, 1847–51; enlarged 1859–60 and 1886 [*A.P.S.D.*; exhib. posthumously at R.A. 1853].

LONDON, HANOVER CHAMBERS, 23 HANOVER SQUARE, for John Elger; dem. [*A.P.S.D.*].

ELMES, JAMES (1782–1862), was born in London. His father Samuel and his grandfather John Elmes were both builders by trade and members of the Tylers' and Bricklayers' Company. James was educated at Merchant Taylors' School and subsequently became a pupil of George Gibson. In 1804 he entered the Royal Academy Schools, winning the Silver Medal in 1805. He exhibited at the Royal Academy from 1801 to 1842. He became Surveyor to the Port of London, and enjoyed a moderate practice in London and in Sussex, where he had a house at Oving, near Chichester. He was best known, however, as a prolific writer on artistic and architectural topics, and, in particular, as the editor of Shepherd's *Metropolitan Improvements*. He was Vice-President of the London Architectural Society (founded 1806), lectured on architectural subjects at the Surrey and Russell Institution, and edited a pioneer art journal entitled *Annals of the Fine Arts* (1816–20). He was a friend of Haydon, and through him of Keats, some of whose sonnets first appeared under Elmes's editorship in *Annals of the Fine Arts*. Although essentially an architectural and literary antiquary, whose own writings show no great power of criticism, Elmes has a place in the history of architectural scholarship as the author of the first documented life of Wren, and it was from him that Sir John Soane purchased the important Wren manuscript known as the 'Court Orders' (*Wren Soc.* xviii). Failing sight obliged Elmes to give up practice in 1848. He died at Greenwich on 2 April 1862. His portrait by his friend James Lonsdale (1777–1839), now at the R.I.B.A., is reproduced in *Wren Soc.* xviii, frontispiece. Apart from his more famous son, Elmes's known pupils were John Haviland, Samuel Paterson and George Allen.

The following were Elmes's principal publications: 'A letter to T. Hope . . . on the insufficiency of the existing establishments for promoting the fine arts towards that of Architecture', in *The Pamphleteer* iii, 1813; *Hints for the Improvement of Prisons . . . partly founded on the principles of John Howard*, 1817; *Lectures on Architecture*, 1821, 2nd ed. 1823; *Memoirs of the Life and Works of Sir Chr. Wren, with a View of the Progress of Architecture in England, from the Reign of Charles I to the End of the Seventeenth Century*, 1823; *The Arts and Artists: or, anecdotes and relics of the Schools of Painting, Sculpture and Architecture*, 3 vols., 1825; *A General and Bibliographical Dictionary of the Fine Arts*, 1826; *A Practical Treatise on Architectural Jurisprudence*, 1827; the 'Historical, Topographical and Critical' introductions to *Metropolitan Improvements* and *London in the Nineteenth Century*, by T. H. Shepherd, 1827–9; *A Practical Treatise on Ecclesiastical and Civil Dilapidations*, 1829 (3rd ed.); *London Bridge . . . with a particular account of the new London Bridge*, 1831; *A Topographical Dictionary of London*, 1831; *A Scientific, Historical and Commercial Survey of the Harbour and Port of London*, 1838; and 'A History of Architecture in Great Britain' in *The Civil Engineer and Architect's Jnl.* x, 1847. [*Builder* xx, 1862, 275; *Gent's Mag.* 1862 (i), 784–5; *Autobiography of B. R. Haydon*, ed. T. Taylor, i, 1926, 248–9.]

SHERIFF'S COURT, ISLE OF THANET, KENT, 'new principal front, in the Egyptian style of architecture', exhib. as 'to be built' in 1805; probably not built.

STOCKWELL, SURREY, two villas, built 1805–6 [exhib. at R.A. 1807].

OAKWOOD HOUSE, nr. CHICHESTER, SUSSEX, 1809–12 [exhib. at R.A. 1811].

CHICHESTER, KING'S HOLME (KINGSHAM), 'design for', exhib. at R.A. 1811.

CHICHESTER, ST. JOHN'S CHAPEL, 1812–13, erected under the supervision of John Haviland during Elmes's illness [*A.P.S.D.*, *s.v.* 'Haviland'; *V.C.H. Sussex* iii, 163].

CHICHESTER CATHEDRAL, rebuilt upper part of spire, 1813–14 [*Civil Engineer and Architect's Jnl.* x, 1847, 237].

BEDFORD, THE NEW GAOL, 1819–20; dem. [*Annals of the Fine Arts* iv, 1819, 353; *Notes and Extracts from the Beds. County Records* i [*c.*1905], 194, 196].

WATERFORD, IRELAND, THE HOUSE OF CORRECTION, 1820 [*Annals of the Fine Arts* v, 1820, 438–9].

LONDON, SOCIETY OF BRITISH ARTISTS, SUFFOLK STREET, interior (with J. Nash), *c.*1823 [J. Summerson, *John Nash*, 1935, 216].

LONDON, BAKERS' HALL, No. 16 HARP LANE, repairs, 1825 [J. Timbs, *The Curiosities of London*, 1867, 410].

RAVENSCOURT, nr. HAMMERSMITH, MIDDLESEX, a cottage, 1824 [exhib. at R.A. 1824].

LONDON, FARRINGDON STREET, obelisk to Robert Waithman, 1833; moved to Bartholomew Close 1951 [*Architectural Mag.* ii, 1835, 94].

WESTMINSTER, Nos. 6–12 (even) QUEEN ANNE'S GATE (BIRDCAGE WALK), of which No. 6 was for the PARLIAMENTARY AGENCY OFFICES, 1837 [*Architectural Mag.* iv, 75].

WESTWOOD HALL, nr. LEEK, STAFFS., alterations and additions for John Davenport, M.P., 1837; rebuilt 1850–2 [exhib. at R.A. 1837].

ELSAM, RICHARD, was a pupil of Robert Browne, Clerk of the Works at Kew Palace. He was living at Richmond at the time of his marriage, in 1793, to Miss Crawley, of Ipswich [*Gent's. Mag.* 1793 (ii), 1050]. He exhibited at the Royal Academy between 1797 and 1807 from an address in Newington Butts. For some years (until *c.*1803) he was employed in the Barrack Department of the War Office. A design by James Johnson (*q.v.*) for barracks for 2500 officers and men (B.L., *King's Maps* xxvi, 7 tt and uu), dated 1795, is signed by Elsam as draughtsman.

Elsam appears to have been a quarrelsome character, whose career was marked by frequent disagreements with his clients and others. In 1803 he published *An Essay on Rural Architecture, being an attempt, also to refute the Principles of Mr. James Malton's Essay on British Cottage Architecture*, in which he illustrated several of his executed works, and incidentally accused C. A. Craig, the District Surveyor for Lambeth, of having unreasonably condemned some villas which Elsam had designed for a speculative builder in Vauxhall, on the ground that they were not in conformity with the Building Act of 1774. In 1804 he began to rebuild Chertsey Church, 'but after the general incorrectness of his estimates had been proved by the great outlay, he was superseded by the trustees', and the church was completed by Thomas Chawner. Soon after this episode Elsam emigrated to Northern Ireland, where he set up in practice in Londonderry. It was from Londonderry that in 1808 he published *The Gentleman and Builders Assistant*, 'containing a list of prices of the several artificers works, usually employed in building, together with some Observations on the Customs of Measuring in Ireland, which, in many instances, tend not only to injure the employer but the employed'. The frontispiece shows his Gothic design for 'the Free School now erecting at Londonderry', but he appears to have quarrelled with the authorities soon after, for in 1814 the building was completed in a 'Regency classical style' by John Bowden [Ulster Architectural Heritage Soc., *List of Buildings in the City of Derry*, 1970, 60]. Elsam subsequently practised in Dublin, but by 1818 he was back in England as surveyor to the Corporation of Dover, for whom he designed a new gaol in 1820–1. But 'owing to litigation with the architect . . . the cost to the corporation was very considerable, and is still a charge on the poor-rates'.

After this Elsam disappears from record. He had, however, published three further books: *Hints for improving the Condition of the Peasantry, with Plans, Elevations and Descriptive Views of Characteristic Designs for Cottages*, with a dedication to Thomas Coke of Holkham (1816), *A Brief Treatise on Prisons, illustrated with an enlarged design of the New Gaol about to be erected at Dover* (1818), and *The Practical Builder's Perpetual Price-Book* (1825) which contains some designs for houses by the author. Various of his designs are also illustrated in Nicholson's *Practical Builder*. Unexecuted designs by him for a church at Roscrea, Co. Tipperary, 1813, and for a gaol at Monaghan, 1814, are in the National Library of Ireland (MS. 8821(S) 115) and the Dublin Castle records (S.P.O. 558/423/31 and CSORP 1821/547), respectively (*ex inf.* Dr. E. McParland). His exhibits at the R.A. show that he made unexecuted designs for Finborough Hall, Suffolk (1804), and Wilton Castle, Yorks (1805). Elsam's published designs reveal him as a self-conscious seeker after ingeniously geometrical plans clothed either in neo-classical or picturesque Gothic dress. A bust of him by Turnerelli was exhibited at the R.A. in 1814.

IPSWICH, SUFFOLK, a pair of semi-detached Gothic houses for Mr. J. Doughty, 'about to be erected' in 1803 [*Essay on Rural Architecture*, 1803, pl. 14].

HALSTEAD, ESSEX, SLOE FARM, for Charles Hanbury [*Essay on Rural Architecture*, 1803, pls. 17, 18].

GOSFIELD PLACE, ESSEX, enlarged for J. G. Sparrow, *c.*1800; dem. *c.*1940 [*Essay on Rural Architecture*, 1803, pl. 27] (*Excursions in the County of Essex* ii, 1819, 152).

WALMER, KENT, 'Marine pavilion now erecting for A. Gram, Esq.' [*sic* in R.A. Catalogue 1805]; perhaps Walmer Cottage, later the property of J. Gaunt.

LONDON, KENNINGTON, houses in CARDIGAN PLACE built by Thomas Evans, 1806 [*The Practical Builder's Price-Book*, 1825, pl. 5].

CHERTSEY CHURCH, SURREY, 1806–7, Gothic; completed by T. Chawner [Brayley, *Topographical History of Surrey* ii, 193–4].

TUNBRIDGE WELLS, KENT, 'Mr. Baker's chateau', exhib. at R.A. 1807, perhaps Mount Calverley Lodge, later the property of A. St. John Baker.

CAVAN, IRELAND, THE COUNTY PRISON, 1810 [P. Nicholson, *Treatise on the Five Orders of Architecture*, 1834, pls. lxiv, lxv. See also *A Description of Cavan Gaol*, 1810, by R. Elsam or James Neild].

IRELAND, a cottage nr. DEVIL'S BIT, CO. TIPPERARAY, for Daniel Ryan, 1813 [*Hints on improving the Condition of the Peasantry*, 1816, No. x].

DOVER, THE GAOL, 1820–1 [*The Watering-Places of Great Britain and Fashionable Directory*, 1833, 175].

DOVER, THE ROUND HOUSE, for John Shipdem, the Town Clerk; dem. 1945 [J. M. Richards, *The Bombed Buildings of Britain*, 2nd ed. 1947, 186].

ELSDEN, WILLIAM, was an English military engineer who designed the UNIVERSITY OF COIMBRA in PORTUGAL in 1773–7. This large building, designed in a neo-classical style influenced by English Palladianism, is Elsden's only recorded architectural work. All that is known of his career is that he taught mathematics at the Portuguese Royal Military Academy and in 1771 was appointed Quartermaster General with the rank of Lieutenant Colonel [John Bury in *C. Life*, 17 Sept. 1987, correspondence].

ELVINS, THOMAS (–1802), described as 'an eminent architect of Birmingham', died on 27 August 1802 [*Gent's Mag.* 1802 (ii), 879]. He was presumably the Thomas Elvins who had been apprenticed to Thomas Fewster of Birmingham, carpenter, in 1753 [P.R.O., Apprenticeship Register I R 1/51/275].

EMBREE, JOHN, a plumber by trade, held the post of Surveyor of Works under the Protectorate government. He had become Sergeant Plumber in Feb. 1639/40, and was put in charge of the Office of Works in March 1653, holding the post until the Restoration of Charles II in 1660. Although there was considerable expenditure on the Protector's residences, little is known of Embree's activity as Cromwell's Surveyor. In 1655 he bought some of the buildings of Exeter Cathedral, including the cloisters, for whose demolition he appears to have been directly or indirectly responsible. Of his career after 1660 nothing is known. [*History of the King's Works* iii, 165–8].

EMETT, THOMAS (*c.*1771–1826), 'senior' of Preston, is listed as an architect in Baines's Lancashire directory of 1825. He was no doubt related to John Emett, an architect or surveyor who is said to have designed the column erected in the Market Place at Preston in 1782, and to Charles Emett, listed as a 'Joiner and Builder' of Preston in Pigot's *Directory* of 1828–9. Thomas Emett was presumably the 'Mr. Emett' who is stated in Twycross's *Mansions of England and Wales: Cheshire* ii, 1850, 114, to have designed SHRIGLEY HALL nr. PRESTBURY, CHESHIRE, for William Turner, M.P. for Blackburn, in 1825. This is a large house designed in a conservative neo-classical style reminiscent of the Wyatts. Emett died on 18 August 1826, aged 55 [obituary notice in local newspaper, *ex inf.* Mr. Colin Stansfield].

EMLYN, HENRY (*c.*1729–1815), architect and builder of Windsor, was probably related to the family of Emblin or Emlyn, several of whom were builders at Maidenhead, Berks., in the eighteenth century. He himself was apprenticed in 1744 to William May of Windsor, carpenter [P.R.O., Apprenticeship Register I.R. 1/17/103]. The records of the Office of Works show that he was employed as a carpenter at Windsor Castle from 1761 onwards. From 1784 to 1791 he was also the official carpenter to the Dean and Chapter of Windsor. Between 1787 and 1792 ST. GEORGE'S CHAPEL was restored under his direction at the expense of King George III. He designed the elaborate Gothic organ gallery executed in Coade stone, the organ case, the Sovereign's and Prince of Wales's stalls and the pulpit, showing considerable skill in imitating the spirit of the fifteenth-century craftsmen's work, especially in his series of incidents from the life of George III (for illustrations see M. R. James, *St. George's Chapel, Windsor: the Woodwork of the Choir*, 1933) [W. H. St. J. Hope, *History of Windsor Castle*, 389–95]. Engravings of Edward IV's vault in St. George's Chapel by him were published in

1796 by the Society of Antiquaries, of which he had become a Fellow in the previous year (*Vetusta Monumenta* iii, pls. 7–9).

It is probable that Emlyn was the designer of the Gothic screen (in Coade stone) of the Kederminster Chapel in LANGLEY MARISH CHURCH, nr. WINDSOR, for Sir R. Bateson Harvey, 1792. In 1789–90 the spire of ST. GILES' CHURCH, READING, was rebuilt in Riga fir, covered with copper, under his direction. [MS. Churchwardens' Accounts]. His work was destroyed when the church was largely rebuilt in 1871–2. He repaired the tower of HUNGERFORD PARISH CHURCH in 1795–6 [MS. Churchwardens' Accounts]. It was subsequently rebuilt in 1812. In 1809–11 WINDSOR PARISH CHURCH was repewed under his direction [MS. Churchwardens' Accounts].

In 1781 Emlyn published *A Proposition for a New Order of Architecture, with rules for drawing the several parts* (2nd ed. 1784, 3rd ed. 1797). This 'British' Order consisted of a shaft that at one-third of its height divided itself into two, so that there were twin capitals supporting the entablature. The foliage of the capitals was represented by knightly plumes, with the star of the Order of the Garter between the volutes. In the frieze the Prince of Wales's feathers served as triglyphs and acorns were substituted for conventional guttae. In 1786 Emlyn incorporated his order into a scheme for a new Lower Ward at Windsor. Nothing came of this, but according to Elmes George III allowed Emlyn to execute a specimen of the order which was later removed. An example of it can still be seen in the portico of BEAUMONT LODGE nr. WINDSOR, a house designed by Emlyn for Henry Griffiths, *c.*1790 [Neale, *Seats* i, 1818; Sandra Blutman, 'Beaumont Lodge and the British Order', in *The Country Seat*, ed. Colvin & Harris, 1970, 181–4].

Emlyn died on 10 December 1815, at the age of 86. There is a tablet to his memory in the Bray Chantry in St. George's Chapel. A portrait by A. Livesey in private ownership shows him standing by a bust of Inigo Jones, with Beaumont Lodge in the background.

[*A.P.S.D.*; *D.N.B.*; *Gent's Mag.* 1815 (ii), 573; Shelagh M. Bond, 'Henry Emlyn of Windsor', *C. Life*, 13 Sept. 1962, reprinted with additions in *Report of the Society of Friends of St. George's Chapel, Windsor* iv, No. 3, 1962; Eileen Harris, *British Architectural Books and Writers 1556–1785*, 1990, 186–8.]

EMMETT, MAURICE (*c.*1646–1694), master bricklayer, was the son of Maurice Emmett, who briefly held the post of Master Bricklayer in the Office of Works at the Restoration in 1660, but was almost immediately superseded by Isaac Corner. However, on Corner's death in 1677, Maurice Emmett, junior (the subject of this entry), took his place, and retained it until his own death in 1694.

As a master bricklayer Emmett was employed at Chelsea Hospital from 1682, at Winchester Palace in 1683–4, at Windsor in 1685–6, at Whitehall in 1685–7 and at Kensington Palace in 1689–90 (see *Wren Soc.* xx, 65, index). At Hampton Court in 1689 he was involved in the collapse of some brickwork, which led Wren to declare himself 'very ill used' by Emmett [*Wren Soc.* xviii, 202–3]. His rates for building Sir Philip Warwick's house in St. James's (for which see *Survey of London* xxix, 427–8) are given in *The Architecture of Sir Roger Pratt*, ed. Gunther, 1926, 231. There is considerable evidence of his ability as an architectural draughtsman. In 1665–6 either he or his father made a plan of AUDLEY END [P.R.O., E 351/3379], and in 1667–8 he was paid for making unspecified 'draughts and designs' for the King [E 351/3281]. He appears both to have designed and built THE COLLEGE OF ARMS in the City of London, begun in 1671 [W. H. Godfrey & A. Wagner, *The College of Arms*, 1963, 11–12], and he was concerned in the reconstruction of WINDSOR CASTLE by Hugh May between 1674 and 1684. There are several payments to him 'for making sundry draughts concerning the Repairs of the said Castle', for his 'Extraordinary Service in drawing the draughts of the Duke's apartment . . . and of severall other Roomes and Lodgings, takeing several Admeasurements and setting out the Ground for the New Lodgings and other like services' [W. H. St. John Hope, *History of Windsor Castle*, 312–22, 541]. A 'model of a house designed by my father Emmett' was among his son William's possessions in 1714 [inventory in Kent Archives Office].

Emmett died in November 1694, aged 48, and is commemorated by a monument on the N. wall of St. Margaret's Church, Westminster. He left two sons, William (*q.v.*) and Maurice. The latter was educated at Merton College, Oxford, and the Inner Temple, and was admitted a Fellow of the Royal Society in March 1697/8 [*The Record of the Royal Society*, 1940, 387]. William Emmett, who executed much carving for royal and other buildings in the 1680s, and who made the altar-piece for the TEMPLE CHURCH, was his elder brother.

[N. Davenport, 'A Note on the Emmetts', in *Wren Soc.* xiv, p. xxiii; *Walpole Soc.* xxxi, 48, n. 2.]

THE EMMETT FAMILY

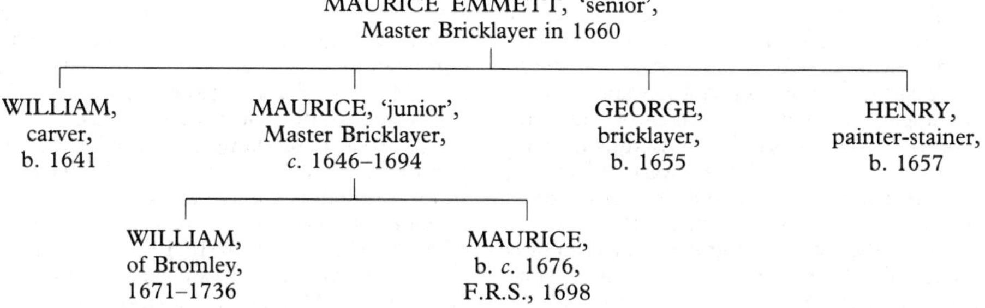

EMMETT, WILLIAM (1671–1736), eldest son of the above, was baptized at St. Margaret's Church, Westminster, on 14 December 1671. Nothing is known of his upbringing, but in 1694 he was appointed to be Registry Clerk to the Court of Exchequer at a salary of £200 a year with an annuity. In 1698 he sold this place for £500 and went to live at Bromley in Kent. In 1702, when applying for a faculty for a private pew in the parish church, he was stated to be 'a person of very good note and repute', to enjoy 'a plentiful Estate', and to live 'in a very large mansion house which he hath lately rebuilt in the said parish of Bromley'. This may have been Redwood House in the High Street (demolished in 1905), where he was living towards the end of his life. He took an active part in parish affairs, and in 1731 made the plans for a new workhouse, demolished in 1845. He married Eleanor, daughter of John Thornhill of Rossby, Lincs., and died at Bromley on 11 May 1736.

In 1702 Emmett published a series of engravings of St. Paul's Cathedral (*Wren Soc.* xiv, pls. xiii–xvii), and others of the Middle Temple Hall (Bodleian Library, Gough Maps 19, ff. 7 and 9). He also engraved mezzotint portraits of Queen Anne, Prince George of Denmark and Princess Sophia. These engravings were published from a house in New Street, London, which belonged to his younger brother Maurice. He had in his possession some designs for Whitehall Palace attributed to Inigo Jones which Colen Campbell published in *Vitruvius Britannicus* ii, 1717, pls. 2–19. These were given to the British Museum by one of Emmett's descendants in 1848 and are now in the Print Room. With them is the elevation of an unpublished design for the same palace made by Emmett himself between 1710 and 1714. It is in an elaborate but somewhat unsophisticated Italian baroque style. Some of Emmett's papers, including a manuscript treatise on the Orders and a glossary of architectural terms, are among the Norman family papers in the Kent Archives Office at Maidstone.

[N. Davenport, 'Note on the Emmetts', *Wren Soc.* xiv, p. xxiii; *Walpole Soc.* xxxi, 48, n. 2; E. L. S. Horsburgh, *Bromley, Kent*, 1929, 419–20; 'Monumental Inscriptions of Bromley, Kent', in *The British Archivist: Miscellanea*, ed. R. Holworthy; Rochester Diocesan Registry: Muniment Book, 1683–1717, f. 69; *Middle Temple Records*, ed. C. H. Hopwood, iii, 1490; Thieme-Becker, *Künstler-Lexikon* x, 505; British Museum, *Catalogue of British Drawings* i, 1960, 304–6 and pl. 119a.]

ERLAM, SAMUEL, was apprenticed in 1801 to a surveyor in Paddington named Henry Cooper [P.R.O., Apprenticeship Registers, IR 1/38, 204]. He subsequently engaged in speculative building on the Grosvenor estate in London during the period 1815–30. Houses built by him survive in Davies Street (Nos. 55–61 odd), and he lived for some time in one of the houses he had built in Green Street [*Survey of London* xl, 69, 76, 186, 255]. He exhibited architectural drawings at the Royal Academy in 1815 and 1817, and probably in 1825 and 1828, when 'J' Erlam may be a misprint in the catalogue. John S. Erlam, who exhibited in 1842 and was a candidate for a surveyorship at Brighton in 1847 [*Builder* v, 1847, 161], may have been his son.

ERSKINE, JOHN, 11TH EARL OF MAR (1675–1732), was the eldest son of the 10th Earl. Of his youth little is known except that he was educated at Edinburgh and Leiden and made the Grand Tour. On his father's death in 1689 he inherited the family seat at Alloa in Clackmannanshire, and an estate much depleted by the heavy debts contracted by his royalist grandfather as well as by his Jacobite father. In these circumstances he prudently adopted a policy of political conformity which enabled him to take his seat in the Scottish parliament in 1698 and secured his appointment as a member of the Privy Council of Scotland. He subsequently supported the Union, and was rewarded first with the office of one of the two Secretaries of State for Scotland (1705) and then with the Keepership of the Scottish Signet. In 1707 he was made a Privy Councillor in England. Despite his second marriage to the daughter of the Whig Duke of Kingston, he accepted office from the Tory government in 1713, and in 1715, finding himself treated with suspicion by the Hanoverians, he put himself at the head of the Pretender's forces in Scotland. His defeat at Sheriffmuir meant exile, attainder and loss of his peerage, penalties only slightly mitigated by the dukedom conferred upon him in 1715 by the grateful James Stuart. In 1717 Mar went to Italy. In 1719 he returned to France by way of Geneva, where for some time he was held under arrest at the behest of the English government. He resided in Paris until 1729, when bad health sent him to Aix-la-Chapelle, where he died in May 1732 at the age of 57.

Two passions appear to have dominated Mar's life in exile: political intrigue and architectural design. With the former this *Dictionary* is not concerned, except to record the fact that in 1724 he lost the Pretender's confidence, and in the following year severed his connection with the Jacobite Court, without, however, reconciling himself with the Hanoverian one. How Mar developed his interest in architecture and landscape-gardening is not recorded: it is not known, for instance, whether he was in any way a friend or disciple of Sir William Bruce (*q.v.*). But in 1701 Mar figured prominently among the Scottish magnates who sent Alexander Edward (*q.v.*) on his visit to London and Paris in search of botanical and architectural information, and Edward had for many years been Bruce's right-hand man. In 1712 the Earl of Ranelagh (*q.v.*), himself an amateur architect, left Mar the 'scriptore' in his closet at Chelsea, together with 'all the Mathematicall Instruments Rulers and perspective glasses . . . which are in the scriptore'. Mar's patronage of James Gibbs in the days of his political influence is well attested. Already in 1709 Gibbs regarded him as 'very much my friend', and when Gibbs died in affluence in 1754 his sense of obligation to Mar was such as to induce him to leave £1000, three houses and all his plate to Mar's impoverished son Lord Erskine.

Though (as he wrote to his son) Mar was 'never rich enough to undertake the building of a new house all at once', he altered and improved his seat at Alloa so as to make it 'a tolerable good and agreeable one within, tho' not very beautiful and regular without'. The great formal plantations with which he surrounded the castle are described by Macky, and illustrated by a map of Alloa engraved by L. Sturt in 1710 from a survey by Bernard Lens (copy in S.R.O., RHP 13258, no. 2). In his *Journey through England* Macky also mentions the small house at Twickenham, formerly Sir Thomas Skipwith's, which 'was improv'd and inhabited by that great Architect the late Earl of Marr' and had 'hanging gardens to the River'. It was called Copt Hall and was demolished in the nineteenth century (R. S. Cobbett, *Memorials of Twickenham*, 1872, 356–8).[1] According to John Ramsay of Ochtertyre (*Scotland and Scotsmen*, ed. A. Allardyce, ii, 1888, 97, n. 2), Mar was reputed to have designed Tullibody and Tillicoultry Houses in Clackmannanshire and Blair Drummond in Perthshire. The last was in fact designed by Alexander McGill (*q.v.*), but he may have had the benefit of Mar's advice. Tullibody (dem.) appears to have dated from the reign of George I. Tillicoultry was rebuilt in 1806 and nothing is known of the previous house.

Of Mar's architectural activity in exile there is abundant evidence. In April 1716 he wrote to Gibbs from Avignon asking him to take care of his drawings, and in January 1718 he got Gibbs to send him a case of drawing instruments. On one occasion two sheets of his 'large drawing paper' were requisitioned by the Pretender, and when he was received in audience by the Pope it was a bound volume of plans of St. Peter's that he took away as a present. Although it is not quite true that (as Sir Robert Douglas wrote) 'his only amusement during his exile was to draw plans and designs for the good of his much beloved native country', it was undoubtedly his principal solace. 'I am', he told a correspondent in 1717, 'infected with the disease of building and planting.' Through English or Scottish

[1] Among Mar's drawings there are two maps showing a projected house at Twickenham on a different site corresponding approximately to that where Lady Suffolk's Marble Hill was to be built in the 1720s. One of them is dated 1711, before his exile, the other 1719 (RHP 13258, nos. 67–8). Mar also made a design for improving Secretary Johnston's Orleans House nearby (no. 84).

correspondents he kept in touch with architectural events in Britain, supplying sketches for Gibbs to develop, making suggestions for the improvement of designs that were sent to him for criticism, even contributing (under the guise of 'a person of quality') a grandiose design for a palace to William Adam's projected *Vitruvius Scoticus*. Whigs as well as Tories benefited from these thoughts from abroad, for the large collection of Mar's surviving drawings (S.R.O., Mar and Kellie papers, RHP 13256–8) includes proposals for Wolterton (1725), the Norfolk seat of Horatio Walpole, the British representative at Paris, for Sir Thomas Robinson's at Rokeby (1730), and for Sir William Wentworth's at Bretton Park, Yorks (1730). Among the papers of his relations the Erskines of Dun (Angus) there is a set of designs for a new house made by him in Paris in 1723, with a note that 'the copier has done no honour by these Draughts to the Designe, but Mr. M[c][Gil]l will understand them' [S.R.O., RHP 13288].[1] As early as 1726 he composed a paper in which he suggested building bridges on the north and south sides of the Old Town of Edinburgh. He had in fact envisaged the principal features of the improvements of the late eighteenth century – the North Bridge, the South Bridge and the siting of George Street, the backbone of the New Town. He also proposed the formation of a navigable canal between the Forth and the Clyde. To the improvement of his own forfeited house and estate at Alloa he devoted an immense amount of thought, drawing plan after plan for intersecting avenues of ever-increasing complexity, and devising a remarkable addition to the parish church incorporating an elaborate family pew and a memorial to himself and his family in the form of a black marble obelisk free-standing beneath a top-lighted dome. Among his more grandiose schemes were plans (anticipating the similar idea of Robert Adam for Syon) for filling the internal quadrangles of Wilton, Longleat and Drumlanrig with domed polygonal halls. Abroad, too, he was ready with designs for acquaintances like a Captain de Wilde, for whose house in Antwerp he devised an ingenious new entrance, the Marquis de Tessé, for whom he designed a Palladian country seat at Chatou, near St. Germain, or the Jacobite Lord Falkland, whose house at Mézières, nr. Orléans, he offered to improve in 1726.[1]

Mar's designs reflect an extensive knowledge of French and Italian, as well as of English and Scottish architecture. Dated at Paris, Urbino, Spa or Geneva, they show an acquaintance with the work of architects as diverse as Bramante, Palladio, Le Pautre and Guarini. There are many studies based on Mansart's Marly, and it was a domed version of Marly that he sent to William Adam for publication in *Vitruvius Scoticus*. Although the character of most of these designs is markedly baroque, neo-classical influence is sometimes apparent. As early as 1718 Mar told John Stewart of Innernity that he was designing a house whose elevations were based on the Maison Carrée at Nîmes, and complained that Italian architects 'will be originals and leave the example [of antiquity] and all its noble simplicity for trifling gimcrack insignificant ornaments worthy of nobody but Vanbruge'.

As an architect in exile the Earl of Mar is a unique figure in British architectural history. Though a nostalgic fantasy runs through so many of his designs, no one can examine them without recognizing an able and fertile imagination, or fail to conclude that if Scotland lost a lord of dubious political integrity in 1715, she also lost an amateur architect of some distinction.

[*D.N.B.*; Sir Robert Douglas, *Peerage of Scotland*, 2nd ed. Edinburgh 1813, ii, 217–19; *Macfarlane's Geographical Collections*, ed. Mitchell, Scottish History Soc. i, 309, and J. Macky, *A Journey through Scotland*, 1723, 181–3 (for descriptions of Mar's gardens at Alloa); J. Macky, *A Journey through England* i, 1724, 61–2 (for his house at Twickenham); *The Earl of Mar's Legacies to Scotland and to his Son, Lord Erskine*, ed. S. Erskine, Scottish History Soc. xxvi, 1896, including (192–3) directions for his monument in Alloa Church and (201–2) his scheme for the improvement of Edinburgh; J. Crawford, *Memorials of the Town and Parish of Alloa*, 1874, 89–91; Hist. MSS. Comm., *Egmont* ii, 235–6; *Portland* vi, 120–1, x, 301–2; *Dartmouth* i, 319; *Stuart Papers* ii, 92–3, iv–vi, *passim*; T. C. Smout, 'The Erskines of Mar and the Development of Alloa', *Scottish Studies* vii, 1963; A. J. Youngson, *The Making of Classical Edinburgh*,

[1] One of these drawings was reproduced by John Fleming, *Robert Adam and His Circle* (1962), pl. 8, but without recognizing its authorship. There are further designs for this house dated April 1731 in the Mar and Kellie Collection. The house was actually built to the designs of William Adam and bears the date 1730.

[1] Capt. de Wilde's house, for which the designs are dated 1729–30, was in the Vieille Rue de la Monie in Antwerp, near the church of St. Georges. Mar also designed a house for the Bishop of Namur at La Plante, nr. Namur (1731), and one for M. Roëttier at Choisy-le-Roi (1721). The design for the Marquis de Tessé is dated 1728.

1966, 13–14; T. Friedman, 'A "Palace worthy of the grandeur of the King": Lord Mar's designs for the Old Pretender', *Arch. Hist.* 29, 1986; Margaret C. H. Stewart, 'An Exiled Jacobite's Architectural Activities: Lord Mar's "House J"', *Jnl. and Annual Report of the Architectural Heritage Soc. of Scotland*, 1987; N.L.S., MS. 5156, ff. 129–32; S.R.O., Mar and Kellie papers, especially GD 124/14, *passim.*]

ESPIN, THOMAS (1767–1822), the son of a farmer, was born at Holton in Lincolnshire, and educated at Wragby. He took up schoolmastering, and in 1790 was appointed Master of a small school at Louth founded in 1677 under the will of Dr. Mapletoft, Dean of Ely. Here he also conducted a private 'Mathematical, Architectural, Nautical and Commercial Academy'. His interests were architectural and antiquarian, and he became a competent topographical artist and draughtsman. A number of his drawings were engraved to illustrate such books as Howlett's *Views in the County of Lincoln* (1805). In 1805 he supervised the rebuilding of the belfry windows in the tower of Louth Church, and in 1815 he was invited by the Corporation to make designs for a new Town Hall. In the event this was not built, but Espin had his plans printed as *Plans and Elevations of the New Town Hall which was intended to have been erected in the Market-Place at Louth, Lincolnshire* (Louth 1815). A copy with the original drawings inserted is in the possession of the Louth Natural History and Antiquarian Society. His design for a gallery in Louth Church dated 1817 is in the Lincolnshire Record Office (Fac. 9/44).

For his own occupation Espin designed in 1818 a picturesque Gothic house called Priory Cottage. He died at Louth in 1822, and was buried in a Gothic mausoleum which he had built in the grounds of his house.

A portrait of Espin belongs to the Corporation of Louth. Another, then in private possession, was reproduced by R. W. Goulding in *Notes on Books and Pamphlets printed at Louth 1801–50* (Louth 1920), which contains a short biography. See also R. W. Goulding, *Louth Parish Church*, 1916, 19; E. J. Willson's Lincolnshire Collections in the Library of the Society of Antiquaries; and *Gent's Mag.* 1822 (ii), 570–1.

ESSEX, JAMES (1722–1784), was the son of James Essex (d. 1749), a carpenter and joiner of Cambridge, who executed much of the woodwork in the University during the first half of the eighteenth century and of whom an account will be found in Willis & Clark's *Architectural History of the University of Cambridge* iii, 540–1. He was educated at the grammar school attached to King's College, and afterwards studied architecture under Sir James Burrough, with whom he collaborated in designing several Cambridge buildings. At the same time he continued to practise his father's trade, and in 1749–50, after the latter's death, he built the wooden bridge at Queens' College to the designs of W. Etheridge. He was, however, anxious to establish himself as an architect, and when, in 1748, the Revd. Robert Masters, Fellow and Bursar of Corpus Christi College, who had employed Essex to make a design for a proposed new building at that college, had the plan printed and circulated as his own, Essex promptly issued proposals for engraving and printing it himself. Masters replied by asserting that 'Essex was no otherwise employ'd therein than copying out his [Masters'] Design', but in a *Letter to his Subscribers*, published in 1749, Essex was able to demonstrate that this was not the case, and that he was the real author of the design.[1]

Essex was subsequently to carry out many works in Cambridge in the classical style which he had learned from Burrough, but it is as a Gothic architect that he is chiefly remarkable: for, unlike his contemporaries, who regarded Gothic merely as a decorative style, a kind of indigenous rococo with romantic associations, Essex fully appreciated its structural character and had an archaeologist's knowledge of its detail. He was, in fact, the first practising architect to take an antiquarian interest in medieval architecture, and his knowledge of Gothic construction remained unique until the ecclesiological movement of the early nineteenth century. As early as 1756 he issued *Proposals for publishing Plans Elevations and Sections of King's College Chapel, in Fifteen Plates with Observations on the Original Contracts* (printed in Gough's *British Topography* i, 237). This work was never published, but the measured drawings made by Essex are preserved among his papers in the British Library. He subsequently contributed several pioneer papers on medieval architecture to *Archaeologia*, the journal of the Society of Antiquaries of London, of which he was elected a Fellow in 1772, and he was the author of an unpublished 'History of Gothic Architecture in England', of which the manuscript and drawings are now in the British Library. He was the friend of Gough, Tyson, Bentham, Cole, Kerrich and other anti-

[1] The design circulated by Masters in 1748 and a revised version of it published by Essex in 1773 are both illustrated in *C. Life*, 17 Oct. 1931, 425.

quaries, and Horace Walpole employed him at Strawberry Hill. At Ely and Lincoln he carried out technically skilful and for the most part aesthetically judicious restorations in a manner that was unique in the eighteenth century. At Ely he saved the east end from threatened collapse and carried out a major repair of the Octagon in a very competent manner, somewhat modifying its external appearance but adhering faithfully to its general form and character. Only in the choir was he guilty of a rearrangement which entailed the destruction of the twelfth-century pulpitum, the mutilation of a number of tombs, and the removal of some of the original stalls. At Lincoln, where he was well served by an excellent mason (John Hayward) and carver (James Pink), his repairs were effective and his own additions to the fabric have a scholarly character that sets them apart from other contemporary essays in the Gothic style. Indeed, the cresting with which he crowned the central tower, the arch which he built across the west end of the nave, and the apse which he added to the north choir transept are frequently mistaken for medieval work.

Essex lived in a house (now dem.) opposite St. Catharine's Hall. He married the daughter of a Cambridge bookseller named Thurlbourn, by whom he had a son, who died in infancy, and a daughter, who married a former fellow of Queens' College. A miniature portrait of Essex from Bowtell's MSS. at Downing College is reproduced in the Cambridge Antiquarian Society's Octavo Publications, vol. 24, together with a silhouette group of Essex, his wife and daughter by Francis Torond that is in private possession. He died at Cambridge on 14 September 1784, of a paralytic stroke, and was buried in St. Botolph's Churchyard, where a tomb commemorates him and his family. There is also a tablet to his memory in the north aisle of the church. His MSS. were presented to the British Library by the Revd. T. Kerrich, to whom they had been bequeathed on his death, and now form Add. MSS. 6761–73, 6776 and 42569. His original letters to Richard Gough are preserved among the latter's correspondence in the Bodleian Library (MS. Gough Gen. Top. 46, ff. 139–261). Some of them were published by J. Nichols in his *Illustrations of Literary History* vi, 284–310, and there are many references to Essex in Horace Walpole's correspondence (see especially the Yale edition of Walpole's correspondence with Cole). His 'Journal of a Tour through part of Flanders and France in August, 1773' is printed in the Octavo Publications of the Cambridge Antiquarian Society, vol. 24, 1888, with a biographical introduction by W. M. Fawcett.

His own publications were: *Mr. James Essex's Letter to his Subscribers to the plan and elevation of an intended addition to Corpus Christi College in Cambridge* (Feb. 1748/9); a 'Letter to Dr. Ducarel, containing observations on Canterbury Cathedral', February 1768, in Nichols, *Bibl. Top. Brit.* i, 470; the 'Plan of the Original Cathedral Church of Ely' and the 'Account of the Old Conventual Church at Ely', in Bentham's *Ely*, 1812, Addenda, pp. 1–10; 'Remarks on the Antiquity and the Different Modes of Brick and Stone Buildings in England', in *Archaeologia* iv, 1776; 'Some Observations on Lincoln Cathedral', *ibid.*; 'Observations on the Origin and Antiquity of Round Churches; and of the Round Church at Cambridge in particular', in *Archaeologia* vi, 1782; 'Observations on Croyland Abbey and Bridge', in Nichols, *Bibl. Top. Brit.* xxii, 1784; 'A Description and Plan of the Ancient Timber Bridge at Rochester', in *Archaeologia* vii, 1785; a description and plan of Denny Abbey, Cambs., 'extracted from Mr. Essex's MSS.', and printed in Lysons, *Magna Britannia* (Cambridgeshire), 1808, 272–4. For his views on the origins of Gothic architecture see T. Kerrich in *Archaeologia* xvi, 1812, 306–10. A list of his engraved designs is given by W. M. Fawcett in the introduction to Essex's 'Tour'.

[*A.P.S.D.*; *D.N.B.*; *Gent's Mag.* 1784 (ii), 718; Willis & Clark, iii, 540–6; J. Nichols, *Literary Anecdotes* v, 117, vi, 624–5, vii, 128, viii, 578, ix, 341–2; J. Nichols, *Illustrations of Literary History* iv, 482, vi, 284–310, 400; D. R. Stewart, 'James Essex', *Arch. Rev.* Nov. 1950; T. H. Cocke, 'James Essex, Cathedral Restorer', *Arch. Hist.* xviii, 1975, *The Ingenious Mr. Essex* (exhibition catalogue, Fitzwilliam Museum, Cambridge, 1984), 'James Essex', in *The Architectural Outsiders*, ed. R. Brown, 1985.]

CAMBRIDGE UNIVERSITY

Unless otherwise stated, Willis & Clark's *Architectural History of the University of Cambridge* is the authority for all the following works.

CHRIST'S COLLEGE, ashlared and regularized interior of First Court, 1758–75.

CLARE COLLEGE, executed Chapel designed by Sir James Burrough (d. 1764), 1764–9.

EMMANUEL COLLEGE, refaced and refitted Hall, 1760–4; rebuilt W. range (street front) of Chapel Court to revised design, 1771–5.

GREAT ST. MARY'S CHURCH, built Doctors' Gallery in church to design of Sir J. Burrough, 1754; removed 1863 (*V.C.H. Cambs.* iii, 131).

JESUS COLLEGE, refitted Combination Room, 1762–3.

KING'S COLLEGE, repaired Chapel, designed Gothic reredos and altar-piece (dem. 1897) and paved ante-chapel, 1770–6 [A. Doig in *Arch. Hist.* 21, 1978, 79–82].

QUEEN'S COLLEGE, built wooden bridge to design by W. Etheridge (*q.v.*); designed chambers at S.W. angle of college, 1756–60; remodelled interior of Chapel, 1772–5 (altered 1845).

ST. CATHARINE'S HALL (now COLLEGE), THE RAMSDEN BUILDING at E. end of S. Range, 1757–*c.*1760.

ST. JOHN'S COLLEGE, refaced and altered S. Range of First Court, 1773–5; repaired foundations of Third Court, 1777; repaired Library roof, 1783 [A. C. Cook, *From the Founder to Gilbert Scott*, Cambridge 1980, 58, 66–71, supplementing Willis & Clark].

SENATE HOUSE, completed exterior of W. end (hitherto faced in brick) in stone with pilasters, 1766–8 (cf. drawings in B.L., Add. MS. 6776, ff. 94–6).

SIDNEY SUSSEX COLLEGE, rebuilt E. range of S. court, containing Chapel and Library, 1776–82; chapel altered *c.*1920; S. front refaced *c.*1833.

TRINITY COLLEGE, supervised reconstruction of N. and S. sides of Nevile's Court to modified version of original design, 1755–8; stone bridge (R. Cam), 1763–5; new building at S. end of W. range of Great Court, including Combination Room, 1771–4; since altered internally.

TRINITY HALL, rebuilt Garret Hostel Bridge (R. Cam) in timber on brick piers, 1769; replaced 1837 by iron bridge designed by W. C. Mylne.

UNIVERSITY LIBRARY, fitted up 'dome room' for manuscripts, 1750–1.

OTHER WORKS

CAMBRIDGE, rebuilt THE GREAT BRIDGE (R. Cam), 1754; dem. 1823 [*V.C.H. Cambs.* iii, 114].

ELY CATHEDRAL, restored E. front to the perpendicular, reroofed the choir, repaired the Octagon, 1757–62. Under his direction the choir stalls were moved to the presbytery in 1769–71 and a new Gothic choir screen and organ loft were built. The screen was removed in 1844 and the Octagon was restored to its original form by Scott from 1860 onwards. [P. Lindley in *Arch. Hist.* 30, 1987, 83–112].

MADINGLEY HALL, CAMBS., minor alterations for Sir John Hynde Cotton, Bart., and re-erection of former gateway of Schools building at Cambridge as Gothic entrance to Stable Court, *c.*1759–60 [Nichols, *Literary Anecdotes* vi, 625].

LINCOLN CATHEDRAL, carried out extensive repairs, designed Gothic arch at W. end of nave, apse to northernmost chapel of N. choir transept, and arches at W. end of choir aisles (carved by James Pink), repaved the church, repaired the choir screen, designed altar-piece, bishop's throne, and battlements and spires of central tower, 1762–5. [Two volumes of designs, estimates and letters in archives of the Dean and Chapter of Lincoln; B.L., Add. MS. 6772, ff. 271–82; T. Cocke in *Medieval Art & Architecture at Lincoln Cathedral*, British Archl. Assn. 1986, 151–3].

THAXTED CHURCH, ESSEX, altered E. end and designed Gothic altar-piece, 1765–7; dem. [MS. Churchwardens' accounts]. There are drawings for this work in B.L., Add. MS. 6776, ff. 60, 61.

CAMBRIDGE, RANDALL HOUSE (now KENMARE), TRUMPINGTON STREET, for John Randall, 1768 [elevation in B.L., Add. MS. 6776, f. 89].

MILTON LODGE, CAMBS., minor alterations to house for Revd. William Cole, 1768–9 [Nichols, *Literary Illustrations* vi, 297].

WIMPOLE, CAMBS., Gothic castle in park for 2nd Earl of Hardwicke, with L. Brown, *c.*1768–70 [B.L., Add. MS. 6771, ff. 99ᵛ, 178ᵛ; M. McCarthy, *The Origins of the Gothic Revival*, 1987, 53, 188; G. Jackson-Stops, *An English Arcadia*, National Trust 1991, 86–88].

WINCHESTER COLLEGE CHAPEL, advised on repair of tower, 1772; rebuilt 1862–3 by W. Butterfield [Nichols, *Literary Anecdotes* vi, 625].

WINCHESTER CATHEDRAL, surveys of roof, 1773 and 1782 [Cocke in *Architectural Outsiders*, 218; *Hampshire Field Club Trans.* iii, 1895–8, 292–3].

DENNY ABBEY, CAMBS., alterations for Peter Standley, *c.*1773 [*V.C.H. Cambs.* ix, 241].

AMPTHILL, BEDS., Cross in memory of Catherine of Aragon, with an inscription by Horace Walpole, for 2nd Earl of Ossory, designed 1771, erected 1773 [Yale edition of Walpole's Correspondence, *Letters to Cole* i, 226, 296, 299, 322] (Camden's *Britannia*, ed. Gough, i, plate facing p. 329).

CANTERBURY CATHEDRAL. On 19 Sept. 1776, the Revd. William Cole wrote to Walpole that Essex had 'engaged himself to the Chapter there to make out a draft for a new roof for part of their cathedral' [Yale edition of Walpole's Correspondence, *Letters to Cole* ii, 26–7; cf. Add. MS. 6771, f. 271 *et seq.*].

STRAWBERRY HILL, MIDDLESEX, Gothic gateway

and the Beauclerk Tower for Horace Walpole, 1776; also designed Offices 1777, executed 1790 by James Wyatt to Essex's drawings [W. S. Lewis, 'The Genesis of Strawberry Hill', *Metropolitan Museum Studies* v (i), 1934].

ENFIELD, MIDDLESEX, GOUGH PARK, designed Gothic fireplace and window for Richard Gough's new library, 1778–80 [MS. correspondence with Gough in Bodleian Library, MS. Gough Gen. Top. 46, f. 178, etc.].

CAMBRIDGE, rebuilt the GUILDHALL, 1782–4; dem. 1933 [R.C.H.M., *Cambridge*, 310].

DEBDEN CHURCH, ESSEX, wooden spire, 1786 [an inscription, now in the vestry, records that it was erected 'from a Design of the ingenious Mr. Essex, Architect']; replaced by a spire of different design 1930.

ETHERIDGE, WILLIAM (–1776), was employed as foreman by James King, the master carpenter for the building of Westminster Bridge to the designs of Charles Labelye (*q.v.*). When King died in 1744, Etheridge took his place [R. J. B. Walker, *Old Westminster Bridge*, 1979, 82]. He invented a machine for cutting piles under water of which he published an engraving (copy in Sir John Soane's Museum). He designed the wooden bridge which was built across the Thames at Walton between 1748 and 1750 at the expense of Samuel Dicker, who obtained an Act of Parliament for the purpose in 1747. It consisted of three arches supported on stone piers, with brick abutments and approaches. The arches were formed of straight pieces of timber tangent to a circle, and it was claimed that if any of the members became decayed, they could be removed and replaced without disturbing the adjacent timbers. There is a description and an engraving of the bridge in *Gent's Mag.* 1750, 587. See also *ibid.* 1754, 116–17. In 1780, having become decayed, it was rebuilt in stone and brick to the designs of James Paine. According to some accounts, the original bridge was designed by 'White of Weybridge', but he appears only to have been the contractor. In 1749 Etheridge designed a wooden bridge of similar construction over the river Cam at Queens' College, Cambridge. It was erected by James Essex and completed in 1750 [Willis & Clark, ii, 56]. It was rebuilt to the original design in 1902. Etheridge, who afterwards became Surveyor to Ramsgate Harbour, died on 3 October 1776 [*Gent's Mag.* 1776, 483; Brayley, *History of Surrey* ii, 340].

ETTY, JOHN (*c.*1634–1708), was a leading architect-craftsman in York in the late seventeenth century. A carpenter by trade, he was the son of James Etty, a carpenter of York who died in 1674. The inscription on his monument in All Saints Church, North Street, states that 'by the strength of his own genius and application he had acquired great knowledge of mathematics, especially geometry and architecture in all its parts, far beyond any of his contemporaries in this City'. The antiquary Thoresby refers to him in 1702 as 'Mr. Etty, sen. the architect', with whom he says 'the most celebrated Gibbons wrought at York' [*Diary*, ed. Hunter, i, 1830, 366]. It was in fact in Etty's yard that Gibbons started his career as a sculptor in England in 1667 [G. Beard, *The Work of Grinling Gibbons*, 1989, 10–11]. In April 1688, when James II contemplated some works at Berwick-on-Tweed, Sir Christopher Wren wrote to 'Mr. John Etty at his house in York', thanking him for his 'description of the palace at Berwick, which was very full and satisfactory' [*Wren Soc.* xviii, 68]. Etty's competence as an architect is also illustrated by drawings attached to his contract for Strensall Manor House and by an elevation for a house signed by him (see below). Although it cannot be proved that Etty designed Sprotborough, still less Newby, their tall flat façades, with the central and/or alternate flanking bays emphasized by slight projections, sometimes with rusticated quoins, are of a type that was fashionable in Yorkshire around 1700, and it is possible that Etty was responsible for some other houses of this sort, e.g. Bell Hall, Naburn, Camblesforth Hall and Myton Hall. The Red House, Duncombe Place, York, has a façade of this kind, and as it was built (soon after 1701) by Sir William Robinson, for whom Etty had built Strensall Hall, it may very probably be attributed to him. All these houses are astylar, but in Lord Shaftesbury's archives at Wimborne St. Giles in Dorset there is a design for the elevation of a late seventeenth-century house of five bays with hipped roof and two giant pilasters supporting a central pediment, signed 'Etty Ebor. delin'. There is a similar (but unsigned) elevation among the Winn archives at Nostell Priory which may possibly be in Etty's hand.

Etty died on 28 January 1707/8 (not in 1709 as stated on his monument), leaving one surviving son William (*q.v.*). His eldest son James, a carpenter, had died the previous October, his second son Marmaduke, a painter-stainer, probably died in 1692, and his fourth son, John, a limner, also predeceased him [G. Beard, *Georgian Craftsmen*, 1966, 176; information from Dr. J. H. Harvey].

HELMSLEY CASTLE, YORKS. (N.R.), joinery for 2nd Duke of Buckingham, 1665–6; dem. [His Grace . . . desires you will take order that Etty proceed in the work according to the Patterns chosen by his Grace, and for other directions about the Roomes that are to be wainscot you are desired to write to Mr. Reynald Graham who lives . . . near Helmsely': Brian Fairfax to Sir Henry Thompson at York, 1 Jan. 1665/6: Hull University Library DD/FA/39/2].

LONDESBOROUGH HOUSE, YORKS. (E.R.), work for 1st Earl of Burlington & 2nd Earl of Cork, 1672–3; dem. 1818. On 17 Oct. 1672 Lord Burlington recorded in his diary that 'Mr. Etty, Mr. Moyser and I were designing my building' and on the following day Etty undertook to carry out some preparatory demolition on the old house [Diary at Chatsworth, *ex inf.* Dr. T. Barnard]. The 'building' may have been one of the flanking blocks added to the Elizabethan centre and seen in Kip's view of *c.*1700.

TEMPLE NEWSAM HOUSE, nr. LEEDS, rebuilt roof of central or W. wing for 2nd Viscount Irwin, 1674, after he had 'viewed the decays of the house' [*Temple Newsam House*, Leeds Corporation 1951, 41].

YORK, ST. MARTIN-CUM-GREGORY CHURCH, designed classical balustrade for top of tower, 1677; removed 1844 [R.C.H.M. *York* iii, 21].

YORK, PETERGATE, house for York Corporation, 1683–6 [York Chamberlain's Accounts, vol. 27, *ex inf.* Mr. J. A. Booth].

GOODMANHAM, YORKS. (E.R.), rebuilt house for 1st Earl of Burlington & 2nd Earl of Cork, 1683–4; dem. [contract at Chatsworth, Londesborough MSS. Box I (iv), 3, *ex inf.* Dr. T. Barnard, in which Etty, described as 'architect' of York, undertakes to rebuild the house for £1000].

NEWBY HALL, YORKS. (W.R.), payments to 'Mr. Etty', 'Mr. Etty's man' and 'Mr. Etty's son' in 1693 indicate some involvement by Etty in the completion of the house built by Sir Walter Blackett, Bart., *c.*1685–93 (not 1705), but they relate chiefly to the provision of a metal weather-vane and evidence is lacking to define Etty's role in the building of Newby [Northumberland C.R.O., Blackett papers ZBL 273/4, Household Book 1691–4, f. 25] (*C. Life*, 7 June 1979, fig. 1).

ACOMB GRANGE (a farmhouse), nr. YORK, for Henry Marwood, 1694–6; mutilated [N. Yorks. C.R.O., ZDU 82, *ex inf.* Dr. Giles Worsley].

STRENSALL HALL, YORKS. (N.R.), for Sir William Robinson, Bart., 1695 [contract in Leeds Archives, NH 2382].

SPROTBOROUGH HALL, YORKS. (W.R.). The letter-book of Sir Godfrey Copley, Bart. in Sheffield Archives contains several references to Etty which indicate that he was involved in the building of this house *c.*1696–1700. On one occasion Etty came and stayed 4 days and on another Copley wrote that when 'ill of a broken legg [Etty] desires I would send him Marrott's book', i.e. the volume of engravings published by the French architect Jean Marot.

? CANNON HALL, YORKS. (W.R.), for John Spencer, 1699; wings added 1765–7 [a payment of £1 5s. to 'Mr. Etty when the Articles was sealed' may indicate that he was the architect [Sheffield Archives, Spencer Stanhope papers, 60674 (1), *ex inf.* Mr. R. Hewlings].

ETTY, WILLIAM (*c.*1675–1734), of York, was the third son and successor of John Etty (*q.v.*). Like his father he combined the functions of carpenter, carver and architect. He acted as executant surveyor or clerk of works for Colen Campbell at Newby (now Baldersby) Park, in 1720–1 [L. O. J. Boynton in *The Country Seat*, ed. Colvin & Harris, 1970, 97–100], and for Sir John Vanbrugh first at Seaton Delaval (from 1719 onwards), and then at Castle Howard (from 1721 onwards, and subsequently for Hawksmoor's Mausoleum from 1729 to 1734) [Vanbrugh's *Letters*, ed. Webb, xxxi, 130, etc.; *Walpole Soc.* xix, *passim*]. As an architect in his own right he designed two public buildings of importance in Leeds – the Moot Hall and Holy Trinity Church, both effective essays in the English baroque style. He may also have designed the Parish Church at Sunderland, whose interior resembles that of Holy Trinity. In 1719 he was paid 2 guineas by the churchwardens of Penrith in Cumberland 'for coming over to survey the Church' preparatory to its rebuilding in 1721–2, but he does not appear to have designed the new church [Cumbria R.O., PR 110/1/57c]. It is less easy to judge Etty's status as a country-house architect, for the simple early Georgian front of Barrowby Hall is his only certain domestic work. In 1727 Etty sent George Bowes designs (now lost) for a country house (probably at Gibside, Co. Durham), complete with stables, avenues and 'bastions'. The last feature suggests a garden layout imitating Castle Howard [Glamis Castle, Bowes MSS. 8, f. 28]. Among the Bright papers there is a group of plans for country houses, some of which are endorsed as being by Etty [Sheffield Archives, WWM, Add. Deposit, Cabinet A, Drawer 7]. These plans probably represent unexecuted schemes for rebuilding either of the seats of the allied Bright and Liddell families, Badsworth in Yorkshire and Newton in Durham, both demolished. Among them is a survey plan of the old house at Newton before its rebuilding (not to any of these designs) early in the 1730s. The attribution to Etty of some drawings in the R.I.B.A. Collection for alterations to Burton Agnes Hall and Church, though probable, cannot be regarded as certain.

William Etty died in the summer of 1734, whereupon Hawksmoor wrote to Lord Carlisle to recommend the employment at Castle Howard of his son John Etty (1705–1738). John, he wrote, had been 'bread up in the way of Building under his father', and promised to be 'sober, carefull, ingenious and industrious' [*Walpole Soc.* xix, 148]. His early death in 1738, only four years after his father's, meant the end of the Etty family as builders and architects.

LEEDS, THE MOOT HALL, 1710; dem. 1825 [D. Linstrum, *West Yorkshire Architecture & Architects*, 1978, 330].

YORK, ST. MICHAEL LE BELFREY CHURCH, altarpiece, 1712 [G. Benson, 'The Church of St. Michael le Belfrey', *Associated Arch. Socs.' Reports & Papers* xxxvii, 111].

TEMPLE NEWSAM HOUSE, nr. LEEDS, laid out avenue, bridge and park for 4th Viscount Irwin, 1712 [*Temple Newsam House*, Leeds Corporation 1951, 46].

BARROWBY HALL, YORKS. (W.R.), refronted for Arthur Ingram, 1718–20 [Christopher Gilbert in *Leeds Arts Calendar*, No. 56, 1965, 9].

WHIXLEY HALL, YORKS. (W.R.), interior of hall for Charles Tancred, before Feb. 1718/9, the date of a letter from Etty to Arthur Ingram in which he stated that he had designed a hall for 'Mr. Tankred' that had been 'much commended' [Leeds District Archives, TN/Corr 12/31]; since altered: see Pevsner & Radcliffe, *Yorks. W. Riding*, 1967, 552.

?BROCKLESBY PARK, LINCS., interior of hall for Charles Pelham, before Feb. 1718/19, the date of a letter from Etty to Arthur Ingram in which he stated that he had designed a hall for 'Mr. Pellham' that had been 'much commended' [Leeds District Archives, TN/Corr 12/31]; nothing remains of the 18th-century hall at Brocklesby.

SUNDERLAND, CO. DURHAM, HOLY TRINITY CHURCH, 1719; apse added 1735: there is a payment in the building accounts to Etty for measuring stonework and as he and the York plasterer Isaac Mansfield jointly received £784 4s. 7½d., of which £368 6s. 6d. was for 'Workemen's wages per Church and Parsonage House', it is likely that he designed both buildings [parish records, *ex inf.* Mr. R. Hutchins].

LEEDS, HOLY TRINITY CHURCH, 1722–7; steeple by R. D. Chantrell 1839 [D. Linstrum, *West Yorkshire Architecture & Architects*, 1978, 186].

HOLME HALL, YORKS. (E.R.), buffet in dining room for 4th Lord Langdale, 1725 [E. Yorks. C.R.O., DDHA 14/25–6].

STAMFORD BRIDGE, YORKS. (E.R.) (R. Derwent), 1725–7 [signed plan and elevations in East Riding Quarter Sessions Rolls 1724, *ex inf.* Dr. David Neave].

SCRIVEN HALL, YORKS. (W.R.), work for Sir Henry Slingsby, Bart., 1728–9; dem. 1954: the building accounts [Yorks. Archaeological Soc., Leeds, DD 56/10, p. 21] show that Etty was responsible for the carpentry, but it is unlikely that he provided the design, which can be attributed to William Wakefield (*q.v.*).

ALDBY PARK, YORKS. (N.R.): in Nov. 1731 Etty received £64 1s. 10d. from John Brewster 'for finishing the Hall in Plaistering' and for doors, architraves and shutters [N. Yorks. C.R.O., Brewster papers, Vouchers No. 1162]. The house is dated 1726 and in the absence of full building accounts Etty's role in its building remains uncertain. A portrait of Brewster holding a plan of the house presumably indicates that he claimed to have designed it himself (*C. Life*, 13–20 Feb. 1986).

EVANS, CHARLES, of London, was a carpenter by trade. He is stated by R. Bigland, in his *History of Gloucestershire* i, 1791, 119, to have designed BADMINTON CHURCH, GLOS., for the 5th Duke of Beaufort in 1785, and this is confirmed by building accounts in the Muniment Room at Badminton [403.2:1–5], in which he is described as 'Architect'. In 1777 he supervised internal alterations to No. 30 UPPER GROSVENOR STREET, LONDON (dem. 1927–8), for Sir Thomas Cave of Stanford Hall, Leics. [Cave MSS. at Stanford]. He was presumably the Evans who rebuilt PEMBROKE HOUSE, WHITEHALL., for the 10th Earl of Pembroke, 1757; dem. 1913 [J. Harris, *Sir William Chambers*, 1970, 235] (*Survey of London* xiii, 167–75, pls. 67–88). Badminton Church has a plain exterior and a well-designed classical interior derived from Gibbs's St. Martin-in-the-Fields (*C. Life*, 25 Nov. 1939, fig. 9).

EVANS, DANIEL (*c.*1769–1846), was a builder of Oxford who was much employed in the alteration of colleges and other buildings in the University between 1820 and 1840, e.g.

at MAGDALEN, where he executed J. T. Parkinson's new north front 1822–6, and at PEMBROKE, where he refaced the master's lodgings, the front and the gateway in Gothic style in 1830, apparently to his own designs, and later, with his partner J. R. Symm, erected the New Buildings designed by C. Hayward (1845) [*V.C.H. Oxon.* iii, 292]. He carried out alterations to MERTON COLLEGE CHAPEL in 1823 and restored ST. ALDATE'S CHURCH in 1832. He also built, to the designs of W. Jenkins, the WESLEYAN METHODIST CHAPEL (1817) in New Inn Hall Street and designed parsonage houses at NUNEHAM COURTENAY, OXON., 1824 [Oxfordshire C.R.O., Oxf. Dioc. Papers c. 435, p. 449] and CHURCHAM, GLOS., 1839 [Glos. C.R.O., Diocesan Records, F 4/1]. In 1828–9 he built, and presumably designed, the terrace of houses now Nos. 34, 35 and 36 ST. GILES, OXFORD [title-deeds, *ex inf.* Miss Anne Sharpe]. Towards the end of his life he was in partnership with his son-in-law J. R. Symm, whose successors still (1992) carry on the business which he founded. Evans, who was a Wesleyan Methodist, died on 13 November 1846, aged 77 [*Jackson's Oxford Jnl.* 21 Nov. 1846].

EVANS, DANIEL (1786–1852), was the son and successor of David Evans (*q.v.*), and probably had a professional training. He practised both in Cardigan and in Fishguard. He enlarged LLANRHIAN CHURCH, PEMBROKESHIRE, 1835–6, and rebuilt the body of CILGERRAN CHURCH, PEMBROKESHIRE, 1836–7 (dem. 1853), both in a Georgian Gothick style [I.C.B.S.]. His most important recorded work was the BETHANIA BAPTIST CHURCH, WILLIAM STREET, CARDIGAN, 1845–6, with a large Greek Doric porch [*Pembrokeshire Herald*, 26 March, 29 Oct. 1847]. When Evans died in October 1852 he was described in the *Carmarthen Journal* as 'architect and landlord of The Castle Inn, Bridgend, Cardigan'. If, as is likely, he built the Inn to his own designs, he may also have designed FISHGUARD VICARAGE, which is similar in architectural character. A professional notebook and some other papers relating to Evans and his family are in the Haverfordwest Record Office [HDX/1136] [information from Mr. Thomas LLoyd].

EVANS, DAVID (–*c.*1840), was a native of the village of Eglwyswrw in Pembrokeshire. By 1810 he was established as an architect in Cardigan, where in 1825–6 he enlarged the Gaol designed by John Nash (dem.) [*Carmarthen Jnl.* 20 Jan. 1825]. In 1827 he converted part of the market-place beneath the Shire Hall into jury rooms [*ibid.*, 15 June, 1827], and in 1830 he was responsible for a development at BRIDGE END, nr. CARDIGAN, for Morris Williams of Cwmgloyn, of which only two terraces were actually built [*Carmarthen Jnl.* 4 June 1830]. He also designed THE UNION TERRACE, CHURCH LANE, CARMARTHEN, for Rees Price, 1810 (dem. 1888) [*ibid.*, 2 June 1810; signed plan in N.L.W., P 24447]; EGLWYSWRW VICARAGE, 1822 [N.L.W., St. David's Bounty, Plans 43]; CASTLE GREEN HOUSE, CARDIGAN, for Arthur Jones, 1827 [*Carmarthen Jnl.*, 6 June 1827]; and rebuilt LLANGOEDMOR CHURCH, CARDIGANSHIRE, 1829–30 [I.C.B.S.]. This was Gothicized in 1859, but retains a small classical spire. The rebuilding of EGLWYSWRW CHURCH in 1829 can be attributed to Evans: it was remodelled in 1883.

Evans had three sons who were architects or builders: John, who practised as an architect and surveyor in Cardigan in the 1830s, Thomas, a carpenter and builder, who died in London in 1825, and Daniel, who is noticed above [information from Mr. Thomas Lloyd, to whom all references are due].

EVANS, THOMAS (*c.*1784–1874), was evidently related to William Evans of Wimborne (*q.v.*), for at the time of his marriage in 1819 he was described as 'of Wimborne Minster', and unexecuted designs for rebuilding Ettington Hall, Warwicks., for E. J. Shirley in Tudor Gothic style, dated 1820–1, now in the Warwickshire Record Office (CR 229/119/3/1–8) and at Shakespeare's Birthplace, Stratford (DR 69/7/3), are signed in some cases by Thomas, in others by William, Evans. A design for Ettington was exhibited at the Royal Academy by Thomas Evans in 1821, and may be the one now in the R.I.B.A. Collection (*Catalogue: C–F*, fig. 82). In 1824 he showed a design for alterations to Crichel House, Dorset, for H. C. Sturt. Evans married the sister of William Harris (*q.v.*), and after the latter's untimely death in Sicily, he was jointly responsible with Samuel Angell for the publication of the archaeological discoveries that Harris and Angell had made there (*Sculptured Metopes . . . of Selinus*, 1826). Evans died on 22 December 1874, aged 90, and is buried at Lyminster in Sussex, where he had lived for many years [J. Challenor Smith in *Genealogist*, N.S. xxviii, 1911–12, 233].

EVANS, WILLIAM (*c.*1764–1842), was an architect and surveyor at Wimborne in Dorset. He held the post of County Surveyor from 1824 until his death on 20 January 1842 at the age of 78 [information from Dorset

C.R.O.] The portico of his Boveridge House is a fine Greek Revival design and his remodelling of Sturminster Newton church was a remarkably competent essay in Perpendicular Gothic for its date. His son George Evans (*c.*1800–1873) succeeded him as County Surveyor and designed a number of churches, including those of Holdenhurst, Hants. (1834), and Stanbridge (*alias* Hinton Parva) (*c.*1840), Melbury Abbas (1851–2), Fontmell Magna (1862–3) and Compton Abbas (1866–7) in Dorset.

GAUNT'S HOUSE, nr. WIMBORNE, DORSET, for Sir Richard Carr Glyn, Bart., 1809; much enlarged 1886–7 [plate in Hutchins, *Dorset* iii, 1868, 244, signed 'Wm. Evans Architect'].

BOURNEMOUTH, HANTS., picturesque cottage later known as PORTMAN LODGE for L. D. G. Tregonwell (of Cranborne Lodge, Dorset) and his wife Henrietta Portman, 1810 [C. H. Mate & C. Riddle, *Bournemouth 1810–1910*, Bournemouth 1910, 56]. To Evans may also be attributed the adjoining EXETER HOUSE (now part of the Royal Exeter Hotel and much enlarged in 1876 and 1888), built by Tregonwell in 1811–12.

QUEDGELEY HOUSE, GLOS., for Mrs Curtis-Hayward, 1819–21; dem. *c.*1985 [specification and contract in Glos. C.R.O., D 123/E 9; design for library signed by Evans in R.I.B.A.D.].

BOVERIDGE HOUSE, nr. CRANBORNE, DORSET, for Henry Brouncker (d. 1825); altered and enlarged 1887 and 1920 [Hutchins, *Dorset* iii, 1868, 385] (plan in R.C.H.M. *Dorset* v, 14).

STURMINSTER NEWTON CHURCH, DORSET, partly rebuilt 1825–8, Gothic [Sir Owen Morshead, *The Parish Church of Sturminster Newton*, 1971].

WIMBORNE MINSTER CHURCH, DORSET, altered W. end, inserting gallery and rebuilding W. window, shortly before 1830 [P. Hall, *Guide to the Town of Wimborne*, 1830, 28].

EVELEIGH, JOHN, was the son of John Eveleigh, 'sergeant-at-mace' of Exeter. He may have been the 'John Eveley' who was apprenticed to James Paine in 1756. In the late 1780s he established himself as an architect and builder in Bath, where he worked both independently and in conjunction with Baldwin, the City Architect. In 1790 he announced that he was prepared to execute 'Designs for Mansions, Villas, Dwellings, etc. in the Gothick or modern taste', to superintend buildings, survey estates, or collect rents. He also acted as a builder's merchant, supplying chimney-pieces and water-closets as well as architectural designs. Many speculative builders availed themselves of his services and in this way he designed CAMDEN CRESCENT, *c.*1788, for John Morgan, a carpenter and builder; a row of houses called SION ROW in Camden Road for the attorney John Jelly; BEAUFORT BUILDINGS, LONDON ROAD, for Messrs. Gunning & Tanner, 1790; and LAMBRIDGE PLACE for Richard Hewlett, 1792. His other works in Bath included SUMMER HILL PLACE, SION HILL (dem.), for Caleb Hillier Parry, 1789; ST. CATHERINE'S HERMITAGE, LANSDOWN (dem.), for Philip Thicknesse, 1791; and the pedimented central feature to SOMERSET PLACE. Elsewhere Eveleigh designed BAILBROOK LODGE, BATHEASTON, for Dr. Denham Skeet, 1789; a house at ENGLISHCOMBE, SOMERSET, for Matthew Brickdale, 1789; a row of ten houses at TROWBRIDGE, WILTS., for a Mr. Wilkins, *c.*1788; and 'a new town in America for Lewis Esq.' for which he supplied a plan on vellum in 1788 for £1 11s. 6d. In 1788–9 he made three designs for building developments at CLIFTON (BRISTOL), at least one of which was carried out. This was probably the two terraces flanking THE MALL. The others were probably ST. VINCENT'S PARADE and WINDSOR TERRACE. The latter closely resembles his Camden Crescent in Bath. In Bath he began, in 1791, in conjunction with other speculative builders, to develop the Grosvenor Gardens as a housing estate. Only GROSVENOR PLACE (including the Hotel) was completed, when the failure of the Bath City Bank led to Eveleigh's bankruptcy and to the sale of his interest in the Grosvenor project. After this disaster he left Bath and is last heard of at PLYMOUTH, where in 1800 he designed the GUILDHALL (dem. 1941) [R. N. Worth, *History of Plymouth*, 1890, 392].

Eveleigh's work at Bath shows him as an original and, for his period, somewhat unconventional designer, whose façades in Grosvenor and Somerset Places use Adamesque motifs in an almost baroque manner which is engagingly vigorous or vulgarly inelegant according to taste. The destruction of his feeble Gothic Guildhall at Plymouth need, however, cause no regrets.

[Eveleigh's ledgers in Bath Reference Library; W. Ison, *The Georgian Buildings of Bath*, 1948, 40–2, 2nd ed. 1980, 15–16; W. Ison, *The Georgian Buildings of Bristol*, 1952, 223, 226, 228; P.R.O., Apprenticeship Register IR1/21, 9 Dec. 1756; *Exeter Freemen* (Devon and Cornwall Rec. Soc. 1973), 325.]

EVELYN, JOHN (1620–1706), qualifies for inclusion in this *Dictionary* as a virtuoso whose theoretical knowledge of architecture was probably as considerable as that of Roger North or Roger Pratt, but who (unlike them) appears rarely to have put it to practical use. His life as a diarist, courtier and country gentleman is too well known to need repetition here, and a well-documented picture of him as an observer and critic of architecture has been given by Kerry Downes in *Concerning Architecture*, ed. Summerson, 1968, 28–39. His English edition of Fréart's *Parallel of the Antient Architecture with the Modern* (1664, 2nd ed. 1707), with its supplementary *Account of Architects and Architecture* dedicated to Wren, shows Evelyn's acquaintance with the principles and vocabulary of classical architecture as then understood in France and England. His scheme for the rebuilding of London after the Great Fire (apparently known only from an eighteenth-century engraving) proves that he knew something of contemporary ideas about town-planning. Drawings in the R.I.B.A. Collection show that he could make intelligible if not elegant sketches of structural and decorative details, and among his papers at Christ Church, Oxford, there is a set of designs for a large French town-house, copied by him from d'Aviler's *Cours d'architecture* of 1691. His sketch-plan (Bodleian Library, MS. Rawlinson A.195, f. 254) for a naval hospital, made in 1666, soon after his appointment as a commissioner for the sick and wounded from the Dutch War, is, however, absurdly naïve.

Although his cousin George Evelyn (1617–99) had (apparently after 1652) designed and built a Doric temple in his garden at Wotton in Surrey (as well as a 'great room' at Albury Park, Surrey, for Henry Howard, afterwards 6th Duke of Norfolk, *c.*1655),[1] there appears to be no evidence that John Evelyn built anything significant either at his house at Sayes Court, Deptford, or at Wotton itself, which he inherited in 1699, though he did much in the gardens of both houses. In 1664 he helped Hugh May to design the chapel at Cornbury House, Oxon. [J. Newman, 'Hugh May, Clarendon and Cornbury' in *English Architecture, Public and Private. Essays for Kerry Downes*, ed. Bold & Chaney, 1993]. In 1676 he undertook 'to contrive, & survey, & employ workmen' to build an apartment in Whitehall for his friend Sidney Godolphin (*Diary*, 10 Sept. 1676), but it appears from the diary of Robert Hooke (pp. 243–4, 253) that he did not fulfil his task without the latter's help. As the translator of Fréart, a Fellow of the Royal Society, Treasurer of Greenwich Hospital, and a friend of the principal English architects of his day, Evelyn's influence on English architecture may, however, have been greater than the evidence given above may suggest.

[1] For these two buildings see Evelyn's *Diary*, ed. De Beer, i. 55, and ii, 551; *C. Life*, 26 Oct. 1901, 523; and *Architectural Review*, March 1948, 124.

EVERARD, WILLIAM (1723–1792), was a Liverpool schoolmaster who commenced business as a surveyor and architect in 1759, building himself premises on the west side of John Street. He was the founder of the Liverpool Library, which is said to have been the first circulating library in the kingdom. It originated in a literary club which met at Everard's former home in St. Paul's Square. When he moved to John Street, he built a room to contain the books and became the first secretary and librarian. He was also one of the original members of the Liverpool Academy of Art, established in 1768, and subsequently delivered lectures on architecture. He was the chief promoter and architect of the LIVERPOOL OBSERVATORY, the first stone of which was laid on 9 September 1766. The building was never completed and Everard lost a considerable sum of money. Everard also designed GREAT CROSBY CHURCH, LANCS., 1769–70; dem. 1864 [*Trans. Hist. Soc. of Lancs. and Cheshire* civ, 1952, 129], and was probably the architect employed by the Revd. Mr. Bragg to design ST. MARY'S CHURCH, HARRINGTON STREET, LIVERPOOL, 1776; dem. 1809. A portrait of Everard was exhibited at a meeting of the Historic Society of Lancashire in 1869. It represented him holding the elevation of the Tuscan garden temple at INCE BLUNDELL HALL, the seat of Henry Blundell, who became president of the Liverpool Academy of Art in 1783 (see illustration of this elegant neo-classical building in *C. Life*, 17 April 1958, fig. 9). [J. A. Picton, *Memorials of Liverpool* i, 205, 208–9, ii, 20, 108; T. J. Kilpin, 'Biographical Sketch of William Everard, Architect and Surveyor', *Trans. Hist. Soc. Lancs. and Cheshire*, N.S. x, 1869–70].

EYES, CHARLES (1754–1803), was a member of a family which carried on the profession of surveyor in Liverpool for over 150 years. The first was James Eyes, a joiner who died in 1723. John Eyes, who succeeded him, was surveyor to the Corporation in the early eighteenth century, and made a number of maps of the town. He was concerned, though in what capacity is not clear, in the building of ST. THOMAS'S CHURCH in 1750. He died in 1773. A design (1761) by him for the west end of a church, with a tower copied from All Saints, Derby, is in the R.I.B.A. Collection [*Catalogue: C–F.*, fig. 86]. John and Charles

Eyes carried on the family business in the next generation. They both became members of the Liverpool Academy of Art on its foundation in 1768. Charles, who succeeded his uncle John as Town Surveyor in 1786, designed the OLD MUSIC HALL in BOLD STREET, opened in 1786, and destroyed by fire in about 1840: he also published a large-scale map of Liverpool in 1785. The business was continued by Edward, son of Charles Eyes, and finally came to an end with the death of his son, Edward Eyes, junior, in about 1860. In 1815 Thomas Rickman inspected a house being built by Edward Eyes at WALLASEY, CHESHIRE, for one Warburton, but dismissed it as 'a copy from some of the Villa Books, alter'd & showy outside but not over convenient within' [Diary, 26 Nov. 1815]. Edward Eyes also designed ST. MARY'S CHURCH, BOOTLE, LANCS., 1827, enlarged 1847, dem. after bomb-damage in 1940 [W. G. Herdman, *Pictorial Relics of Old Liverpool*, 1878, ii, 47, 53].

[R. Stewart-Brown, 'Maps and Plans of Liverpool and District by the Eyes Family of Surveyors', *Trans. Hist. Soc. Lancs. and Cheshire* lxii, 1910.]

EYKYN, ROGER (*c.*1725–1795), was an architect and builder of Wolverhampton. He was born at Worfield, Staffs., in 1724 or 1725, and established himself at Wolverhampton, where he first appears in 1760 as a master joiner, and subsequently as a nurseryman, surveyor and architect. He appears also to have been a mason, as he signs a monument at Broseley, Salop., to Elizabeth Crompton, died 1747, and another (undated) to the Weld family at Willey, Salop., and was paid £4 10s. for carving at STONE CHURCH, STAFFS., *c.*1758 [W. H. Bowers & J. W. Clough, *Researches into the History of the Parish and Church of Stone*, 1929, 58–61]. He is mentioned frequently in the diary and account-book of William Baker (*q.v.*), who paid him £1 16s. 'for 2 vases' in 1756, and £24 in 1759 for a monument in Leighton Church, Salop. Baker also notes his marriage in 1754. In 1756 Eykyn supplied plans for the rebuilding of RUSHOCK CHURCH, WORCS. in a simple Gothic style [G. K. Stanton, *Rambles and Researches among Worcestershire Churches*, 1884, 193], and he was also the architect of ST. PAUL'S CHURCH, BIRMINGHAM, 1777–9, for which he supplied designs and a model in 1776. His original design, derived from Gibbs's *Book of Architecture*, was modified in accordance with criticisms made by Samuel Wyatt, and the steeple was never completed owing to lack of funds, the present one being added by F. Goodwin in 1823 [L. D. Ettlinger & R. G. Holloway, 'St. Paul's Birmingham', *Arch. Rev.* June 1947]. He was also consulted when the galleries of ST. MARY'S, BIRMINGHAM, collapsed in 1776. In his own town Eykyn was a Commissioner and a Trustee of the Grammar School, and when he died in 1795, the *Birmingham Gazette* described him as an 'eminent architect and surveyor'.

F

FALLOWS, JOHN (*c.*1798–1861), started practice in Birmingham in the 1820s. By 1830 he was described in West's *History and Directory of Birmingham* as 'rapidly rising in his profession' and as having 'erected several elegant villas in the parish of Edgbaston'. His house and office were at 99–100 New Street, next to the Theatre. According to the same publication they had recently been modernized by Fallows 'in a singular yet not inelegant style of combined Grecian and Egyptian architecture'. The design had been exhibited by Fallows at the Birmingham Society of Artists in 1829, together with 'A villa erected at Stourbridge' and 'A hunting-box erected in Shropshire'.

In 1831 Fallows won the second prize in the competition for the new Town Hall at Birmingham, the winning design being by Messrs Hansom and Welch [Rickman's Diary, 7 June 1831]. Fallows's design is preserved in the Birmingham Central Library, but is in bad condition: a sketch based on it was reproduced in *Architecture*, 5th ser. iii, 1924–5, 228, where, however, it was wrongly attributed to Barry. In the same year a notice appeared in *Aris's Birmingham Gazette* (18 April) advertising the contract for building 'twenty houses and other Buildings near the gaol at Shrewsbury' to Fallows's design. In the mid 1830s Fallows was in partnership with an architect called Hart, in conjunction with whom he designed two buildings in SHREWSBURY, THE EBENEZER METHODIST CHAPEL, TOWN WALLS, 1834, and THE HOWARD STREET BUTTER & CHEESE MARKET, 1835, both in an unrefined classical style with Greek Revival features [*Shrewsbury Chronicle*, 27 June 1834, *ex inf.* Mr. D. C. Cox; H. Pidgeon, *Memorials of Shrewsbury*, 1851, 179, with illustration]. In 1840 he exhibited the entrance hall of FOXLYDIATE HOUSE, nr. REDDITCH, WORCS. (dem.), at the Birmingham Society of Artists.

Fallows never rivalled Charles Edge as Birmingham's leading early Victorian architect, and by 1850 he was acting as an auctioneer as well as an architect and surveyor. He died at Griffins Hill, Northfield, Birmingham, on 20 December 1861, aged 63 [*Aris's Birmingham Gazette*, 28 Dec. 1861]. F. W. Fiddian was his pupil.

FARQUHAR, COLIN, exhibited at the Royal Academy from London addresses between 1791 and 1799. His drawings included a 'Design of a house intended to be built for a gentleman near Edinburgh' (1791), 'Plans and Sections of a house now building' (1792), and a design for finishing the saloon at Thorndon Hall, Essex, the seat of Lord Petre (1799). He subscribed to Richardson's *New Vitruvius Britannicus* in 1802. He may have been connected with the Farquhars of Pitscandly in Angus, for in 1795 John Soane recommended him to a Scottish client as a young man who was anxious to be employed 'in his own country and particularly in' Angus [Sir John Soane's Museum, Letter Book 1793–5, 81–2].

FASSETT, THOMAS, is known only as the author of architectural drawings at Frampton Court, Glos., signed by him and dating from the second quarter of the eighteenth century. They represent a Doric gallery in a church, the side of a stable and a farmhouse.

FAUCONBERG, VISCOUNT, *see* Belasyse, Thomas.

FAULKNER, THOMAS, was the author of several architectural publications, including *Designs for Shop Fronts etc. also the Grecian Orders of Architecture*, 1831, and *Designs for Mural Monuments, Monumental Tombs, and Chimney-Pieces, with Useful Details*, 1835. Two other works, entitled *The Organ-Builder's Assistant* and *Select Designs for Churches*, are mentioned in Loudon's *Architectural Magazine* ii, 1835, 185, and a second edition of *The Organ-Builder's Assistant* was published in 1838. It contains 20 plates of designs for organ-cases, mostly in an elaborate Gothic style.

Faulkner exhibited at the Royal Academy in 1825, 1829 and 1833.

FEILDHOUSE, JOHN, designed the SCHOOL HOUSE at CRANBROOK, KENT, a brick building of 1727–9 [John Newman, *West Kent and the Weald*, Buildings of England 1976, 244, citing building accounts].

FELLOWS, WILLIAM (–1816), of Southwark, exhibited at the Royal Academy from 1793 to 1810, his designs including 'An elevation of a villa now building at Sydenham in Kent' (1793), the new RECTORY at WARNEFORD, HANTS. (1803), and FARLEY HILL CASTLE, nr. READING, BERKS., a castellated brick house built in 1808–9 for E. Stephenson (1810). He also designed HACKNEY TERRACE, CASLAND ROAD, LONDON E 9, an early development by a building society begun in 1792 and completed about ten years later [A. Byrne & I. Watson in *C. Life*, 12 Nov. 1987]. Fellows was an unsuccessful candidate for election as A.R.A. in 1793 [Farington's Diary, 8 Oct. 1793]. He died in Canterbury Square, Southwark, in 1816.

FENTON, JAMES (1804–1875), was born at Reading, but established himself in practice in Chelmsford, where in 1830 he married the daughter of John Copland, a wealthy Nonconformist solicitor. He specialized in the designing of chapels for Nonconformist congregations. In addition to the documented examples listed below he may also have been responsible for chapels at Beccles, Suffolk (1836), Chatteris, Cambs. (1838), and Hedingham, Essex (1842), all of which have well-designed fronts resembling those at Wingham and Marlow. In 1839–43 he and two of his Copland relations were partners in a company formed to develop a large area on the south side of Chelmsford. Besides building a cast-iron bridge to carry the principal road across the R. Can, Fenton designed several of the 'highly ornamental mansions' in the new suburb. These included his own house, 'Laurel Grove' (now the Chelmsford Club), and those of his brothers-in-law John and Edward Copland (now part of the Hospital complex). All these were built of white brick in a free classical style.

In 1850 Fenton was appointed surveyor to the newly formed Chelmsford Local Board of Health, and planned and executed a major water supply and sewerage system for the town. In 1858 he went to Croydon as Engineer and Surveyor to the Local Board of Health, but resigned in 1863 after a dispute. He died in Brixton in 1875, but was buried in the Nonconformist cemetery at Chelmsford which he had designed. [Information from Miss Hilda Grieve.]

WINGHAM, KENT, CONGREGATIONAL CHAPEL, 1835 [*Evangelical Mag.* xiv, 113].

HALESWORTH, SUFFOLK, INDEPENDENT CHAPEL, 1836 [*Evangelical Mag.* xiv, 304, 566].

OVERTON, HANTS., CONGREGATIONAL (now Wesleyan) CHAPEL, 1836, Gothic [*Evangelical Mag.*, 1837, 30].

BILLERICAY, ESSEX, INDEPENDENT CHAPEL, 1837, Gothic [H. Richman, *Billericay and its High Street,* 1963, 154–5].

MARLOW, BUCKS., CONGREGATIONAL CHAPEL, 1839–40 [H. M. Colvin in *Records of Bucks.* xv, 1947, 15].

LINCOLN, THE INDEPENDENT CHAPEL, NEWLAND, 1840, Gothic; converted into school 1874 [F. Hill, *Victorian Lincoln*, 1974, 186].

INGATESTONE, ESSEX, CONGREGATIONAL CHAPEL, 1840, Gothic [Essex Record Office, D/NC 10/49].

CHELMSFORD, ESSEX, INDEPENDENT CHAPEL, NEW LONDON ROAD, 1840; dem. 1971 [*Evangelical Mag.* xviii, 554; *Essex Standard*, 31 July 1840].

CHELMSFORD, ESSEX, development of NEW LONDON ROAD, including iron bridge over R. Can and many detached houses, *c.*1840–8 [W. White, *History and Directory of Essex*, 1848, 303–4].

DERBY, ST. MARY'S GATE, conversion of house into BAPTIST CHAPEL, 1841 [S. Glover, *History and Directory of Derby*, 1843, 31].

WIVENHOE, ESSEX, CONGREGATIONAL CHAPEL, 1847 [*Congregational Year Book*, 1847, 166].

CHELMSFORD, ESSEX, EBENEZER BAPTIST CHAPEL, NEW LONDON ROAD, 1847–8, Gothic [Minutes of the Chapel, *ex inf.* Miss Hilda Grieve].

CHELMSFORD, THE NONCONFORMIST CEMETERY, NEW LONDON ROAD, 1846 [Essex Record Office, D/Z 61].

FERGUS, JOHN, was the son of John Fergus, an Edinburgh merchant. He appears to have been as much a land surveyor as an architect, and was more than once employed by the city authorities in the former capacity. In 1759 he and Robert Robinson published a plan of lands north of the castle belonging to the City and Heriot's Hospital. In 1754 as 'John Fergus, architect', he was a member of the consortium of five (the others were Patrick Jamieson, a mason, and three wrights) who contracted to build the ROYAL EXCHANGE (now CITY CHAMBERS), EDINBURGH, to the designs of John Adam. The foundation-stone had already been laid in 1753, and the building was finally completed in 1761 [R. Miller, *The Municipal Buildings of Edinburgh*, 1895, 114–7; W. Forbes Gray, 'The Royal Exchange and the City Improvements', *Book of the Old Edinburgh Club* xxii, 1938, 12–13]. In 1755 Fergus was admitted as a burgess of Edinburgh gratis in recognition of his 'good services'. The building of the Exchange did not prove to be a profitable undertaking, and in June 1758 William Mylne, in a letter to his brother Robert about architects in Edinburgh, reported that 'Fergus that was much in vogue is reduced to shelter himself in the Abbey from his creditors. They say he might have done extremely well but ruined himself by bad company' [Mylne family letters].

FERRERS, EARL, *see* SHIRLEY, WASHINGTON.

FERRY, GEORGE, was in partnership with John Wallen (*q.v.*) until about 1826, when his name disappears from the London directories. Their office was in Spital Square, Spitalfields. In 1811 they exhibited 'additions and improvements to a villa at Leyton, Essex' at the Royal Academy, and in 1818 they designed MYDDELTON HOUSE, ENFIELD, MIDDLESEX, for H. C. Bowles [W. Robinson, *History of Enfield* i, 1823, 269–70]. Ferry became a member of the Surveyors' Club in 1806, and was its President in 1818.

FIDEL, JOHN (*c.*1733–1806), was a native of Lincolnshire, where he served his apprenticeship to a carpenter. In about 1765 he came to Berkshire in order to work on Beckett Park, nr. Shrivenham, then being enlarged by Lord Barrington to the designs of Sanderson Miller. On Lord Barrington's advice he afterwards set up in business as a builder in Faringdon. In 1800 he designed and presumably built KINGSTON BAGPUIZE CHURCH, BERKS. [B. F. L. Clarke & H. M. Colvin in *Berks. Archaeological Jnl.* 53, 1953–4, 94 and drawings in Bodleian Library, MS. Top. Berks. b. 42, f. 56].

Fidel was a Nonconformist, and 'in the pursuit of his business, would frequently converse with his workmen on the great concerns of their souls'. He allowed services to be held in his workshop at Faringdon until 1799, when he built a chapel there. He died on 30 January 1806, aged 73 [W. H. Summers, *Congregational Churches in Berks., etc.*, 1905, 230–1; obituary in *Evangelical Mag.* xiv, 1806, 557].

FIDLER, J—, was a pupil of John Yenn. He exhibited student's designs at the Royal Academy from 1784 to 1787. Two unexecuted designs by him for the KYMIN TEMPLE, nr. MONMOUTH, dated Dec. 1798, are in the National Library of Wales.

FIELD, JAMES, was a pupil of Samuel Robinson (d. 1833). He exhibited at the Royal Academy from 1819 to 1836, including a 'Design for a new front to the Sessions House, Newington, Surrey' (1824), a design for 'a literary and scientific institution, intended for the western part of Brighton' (1834), and a design, made in 1832, for the Grammar School at Stockwell, Lambeth (1835). He designed the ST. OLAVE'S GRAMMAR

SCHOOL, BERMONDSEY STREET, SOUTHWARK, 1834–5, Tudor style, dem. *c.*1850 [Brayley, *Topographical History of Surrey* v, 387, with illustrations], THE BRITISH AND FOREIGN SCHOOL SOCIETY'S SCHOOL in BOROUGH ROAD, 1841–2 [*Companion to the Almanac*, 1842, 227], and a METHODIST CHAPEL in GREAT DOVER STREET, SOUTHWARK, *c.*1835. In partnership with Robinson, he designed additional wings to ST. THOMAS'S HOSPITAL, SOUTHWARK. These were completed by Field after Robinson's death – the north wing in 1835, the south wing in 1842, both dem. 1862. [*A.P.S.D.*, *s.v.* 'Robinson, Samuel', and Brayley, *op. cit.* v, 395].

FIELD, JOHN, of Bennet Street, St. James's, is described in the London directories as 'carpenter and builder' from 1817 onwards, but as 'architect and surveyor' or 'architect and builder' from 1830 to 1853. The only building he is known to have designed was No. 6 ST. JAMES'S SQUARE (dem. 1958) which he rebuilt for the 5th Earl of Bristol in 1819–20, with Greek Revival detailing. In 1827 he was working at the Earl's country seat at ICKWORTH, SUFFOLK, where he was presumably concerned in the completion of the unfinished mansion begun by the 4th Earl [*Survey of London* xxix, 105].

FIELD, MARRIOTT (1803–*c.*1860), was admitted to the Royal Academy Schools in 1824 at the age of 21. Some porches 'in the Italian manner', illustrated in J. C. Loudon's *Encyclopaedia of Cottage, Farm and Villa Architecture*, 1833 (1846 ed., figs. 1696–8) are stated to be 'from the portfolio of Marriott Field, Esq., a young Architect, lately returned from a professional tour through Italy'. In 1832 he entered a design in the competition for the Fishmongers' Hall, exhibiting it at the Royal Academy. He subsequently emigrated to New York, of whose architecture he wrote an account which was published by Loudon in his *Architectural Magazine* v, 1839, 641–8. Field published two books on architecture in America, where he was drowned in about 1860 [information from Mr. A. Channing Downes, jr.].

FINDEN, JOHN (*c.*1782–1849), practised in London from 41 John Street, Fitzroy Square, from *c.*1805 to *c.*1840. He first exhibited at the Royal Academy in 1800, and subsequently showed 'A Cottage near the Church at Finchley, the residence of S. Staples, Esq.' (1810), 'Intended alterations to the Lower Assembly Rooms and West of England Club-House, Bath' (1811), the 'Elevation of a House now building for J. H. Hunt, Esqr. at Compton Pauncefoot' (1821), and a 'Design for the Commercial Benevolent College, intended to be erected at Barrow Hill Road, N. side of Regents Park' (1830). COMPTON CASTLE, COMPTON PAUNCEFOOT, SOMERSET, which Finden designed for J. Hussey Hunt in 1821, is a castellated house somewhat in the style of Smirke. Finden's only other recorded work appears to have been the Gothic NATIONAL SCHOOL, BATH STREET, FROME, SOMERSET, 1825, dem. 1973 [MS. diary of Thomas Bunn of Frome, *ex inf.* Mr. Michael McGarvie]. He died on 25 June 1849, aged 67 [*Gent's Mag.* 1849 (ii), 218]. Thomas Finden (*q.v.*) and the engravers William (1787–1852) and Edward Francis Finden (1791–1857) appear to have been his younger brothers.

FINDEN, THOMAS (*c.*1785–1861), appears to have been the younger brother of John Finden (*q.v.*). From about 1815 he practised as an architect and builder from 38 Upper John Street. Subsequently he moved to John Street, Adelphi, where from 1845 to 1857 he was in partnership with T. Hayter Lewis (1818–98), and later to Mitcham in Surrey. He was surveyor to Hoare's Brewery and to the Craven and other estates in London. He was elected to the Mastership of the Carpenters' Company, but died (2 Feb. 1861) before he could take office. G. W. Mayhew, A. F. Ashton and W. Snooke were his pupils [*Builder* xix, 1861, 115].

In 1825 or 1826 Finden bought Baron House in Mitcham, Surrey, and in its grounds built three semi-detached houses, of which two survive as Nos. 470/472 and 482/484 LONDON ROAD, MITCHAM [Surrey Land Tax Records, *ex inf.* Mr. Thomas Thorne]. He appears to have designed STAPLEHURST PLACE, KENT, for Henry Hoare, for in 1833 designs for this house (dem.) were exhibited at the R.A. from his address at 38 Upper John Street by 'H. Finden' (*sic*). He certainly designed the SHIP TORBAY TAVERN at GREENWICH, which was exhibited in 1839 by his pupil Mayhew as 'erected from the design of Mr. Thomas Finden'. The following works were exhibited by Finden and his partner Hayter Lewis in 1845: FARRINGDON HALL, DEVON (?), 'lately built for W. Walkin'; a house in KENSINGTON PALACE GARDENS for J. M. Blashfield (not built, see *Survey of London* xxxvii, 158); and 'intended alterations' to two houses in UPPER GEORGE STREET, PORTMAN SQUARE, 'to form an entrance to a new Presbyterian church'. They also designed ST. MARK'S CHURCH, SOUTH NORWOOD, 1852, Gothic [Port, 162], but THE ROYAL PANOPTICON OF SCIENCE AND ART (afterwards the 'Alhambra Palace') in LEICESTER

SQUARE, 1852–4, was exclusively the work of Lewis, as stated by him in *Builder* xi, 1853, 290–1.

FINDLATER, JAMES RATTRAY (*c.*1803–1873), was the son of a factor. From 1832 he practised in Dundee and Broughty Ferry, chiefly as a civil engineer. In 1833 he laid out the CONSTITUTION ROAD CEMETERY in DUNDEE, in 1834 he formed the CONSTITUTION BRAE for the Town Council, and in 1845 planned the WESTERN CEMETERY. He died at New Scone on 6 February 1873, aged 69 [information from Mr. David Walker].

FINNEY, JOSEPH (*c.*1708–1772), was a watch- and clock-maker of considerable repute at Liverpool. In Gore's *Liverpool Directory* of 1767 he is described as 'clock and watchmaker and architect'. The only building he is known to have designed was the OCTAGON CHAPEL, TEMPLE COURT, 1763; dem. 1820 [J. A. Picton, *Memorials of Liverpool* ii, 1875, 109] (illustrated in E. Meteyard, *Life of Josiah Wedgwood* i, 1865, 314). For his career as a watchmaker see Oliver Fairclough, 'Joseph Finney and the Liverpool Clock and Watch-Making Trade', unpublished M.A. thesis, Keele University 1975.

FIRMADGE, WILLIAM (1755–1836), of Leicester, was the son of William Firmadge (1726–90), slater and plasterer of Scraptoft, Leicestershire. He became a freeman of Leicester in 1778, and is variously described in directories and other sources as builder, slater, stone-mason, plasterer, architect and surveyor. He did a good deal of work as a monumental mason, and slate headstones carved by him can be seen in several Leicestershire churchyards. As a builder he appears to have been extensively employed, e.g. in constructing gaols at Leicester, Worcester and Oakham, but in 1812 he wrote to his sister that he was 'drawing affairs to a narrower compass' by disposing of his stock-in-trade as a builder and that in future he would practise only as an architect. In that capacity his only recorded works of any consequence appear to have been the enlargement of LEICESTER LUNATIC ASYLUM, 1794 [*V.C.H. Leics.* iv, 372], THE NEW MARKET, LEICESTER, 1824 [*Records of the Borough of Leicester*, ed. Chinnery, v, 464], and LUTTERWORTH HOUSE, LEICS., for Francis Burges, 1821–2; enlarged 1897, restored 1980–2 [specification in private possession].

Firmadge was a prominent member of the Corporation of Leicester, holding office as Mayor in 1809–10. His pupils included the Leicester architect William Parsons. He died at Leicester on 27 March 1836, aged 80, and was buried at Scraptoft. [J. D. Bennett, *Leicestershire Architects 1700–1850*, Leicester Museums 1968; *Gent's Mag.* 1836 (i), 566; information from family letters *ex inf.* the late Mrs. J. W. Cole; Rupert Gunnis, *Dictionary of British Sculptors*, 1968, 144.]

FISHER, —, of Bristol, is said to have designed THE SHIRE HALL, MONMOUTH, 1724. The original drawings for the building were seen in the early nineteenth century by a person who noted that 'Fisher of Bristol was the name of the Architect' [Monmouthsire County Records, C. Bu. 0004, letter from T. Phillips].

FISHER, JAMES, of Green Street, Grosvenor Square, London, variously described in directories as 'carpenter and undertaker', 'surveyor and builder' and 'architect and surveyor', was employed to alter NASH COURT, KENT, for the Hawkins family in 1801 [Lloyd's Bank archives, Pall Mall branch records, *ex inf.* Dr. J. M. L. Booker]. He was presumably the architect called Fisher who designed NORTHAW CHURCH, HERTS., for William Strode, 1809–10, Gothic; destroyed by fire 1881 [B.L., Add. MS. 36366, no. 68; cf. J. Nichols, *Literary Anecdotes* viii, 510].

FISHER, JOHN (–1852), practised in Glasgow. In 1835 or 1836 he designed a block of buildings in OXFORD STREET, GLASGOW, near the corner of Bridge Street, for Bailie Gourlay [J. Cruickshank, *Sketch of the Incorporation of Masons*, Glasgow 1879, 93]. John Baird (1816–93) was his pupil. He died on 22 Sept. 1852 [S.R.O., SC 36/48/39, p. 270].

FISHER, MONEY, a builder at Salisbury who was clerk of works to the Cathedral in the 1830s. He altered or rebuilt parsonages at TROWBRIDGE (1812) and CHILMARK (1814) in WILTSHIRE [Salisbury Diocesan Records] and at AYLESTONE in LEICESTERSHIRE (1813) [Leics. R.O., MGA]. The family business was continued by his son Frederick Richard Fisher.

FISHER, WILLIAM (–1847), of St. Ebbe's, Oxford, was a builder and auctioneer who in the latter capacity was much involved in the sale and development of property in that city [R. J. Morris in *Oxoniensia* xxxvi, 1971, 83]. In 1814–16 he rebuilt ST. EBBE'S CHURCH, OXFORD, to his own designs in a simple Gothic style [J. Ingram, *Memorials of Oxford* iii, 1837, 14], and in 1837 MARCHAM CHURCH, BERKS., Tudor Gothic [Berks.

C.R.O., D/P84/6; Trinity College Library, James Ingram's 'Scraps' naming Fisher as 'Architect and Builder'; unsigned drawings in V. & A., D.1784–7, 98]. Fisher also designed and built the ADULLAM CHAPEL, COMMERCIAL ROAD, OXFORD, for Mr. Bulteel, 1832; dem. [*The Oxford University & City Guide*, 1833, 13]. His plan for alterations to FRENCH HOUSE, THAME, OXON., dated 1826, is in the Berks. R.O. [D/EHP. 3]. Fisher died on 3 April 1847. His business was continued by his sons John and William.

FITCH, Sir THOMAS (1637–1688), was a leading master bricklayer and a prominent figure in the building world of seventeenth-century London. He was the son of William Fitch of Barkway, Herts., and elder brother of John Fitch (below). The earliest reference to his building activities so far noticed is his contract in April 1663 to perform the brickwork of Sir Ralph Bankes's new house at KINGSTON LACY, DORSET, designed by Sir Roger Pratt, in which he is described as 'Thomas Fitts of Farnham, bricklayer' [*The Architecture of Sir Roger Pratt*, ed. Gunther, 1928, 232]. His more important contracts included the work of cutting and wharfing the Fleet Ditch (1672–4), for which he received over £50,000 [T. F. Reddaway, *The Rebuilding of London after the Great Fire*, 1940, 211–16]; fortifications at PORTSMOUTH, carried out jointly with John Fitch from 1679 onwards to the designs of Sir Bernard de Gomme [B.L., Add. Charter 32751], and at HULL to those of Sir Martin Beckman, 1681–3 [*Arch. Hist.* 16, 1973, 16–17]; the GARRISON HOSPITAL at PORTSMOUTH, 1680 [C. G. T. Dean, 'Charles II's Garrison Hospital, Portsmouth', *Hampshire Field Club Papers* xiv, 1947, 280–3]; and THE GREAT STOREHOUSE at THE TOWER OF LONDON, 1688–91, a large and imposing building of considerable architectural pretensions which was destroyed by fire in 1841. The design has been attributed to Wren, but the attribution (though stylistically possible) has not been substantiated by documentary evidence [N. Blakiston, 'The Great Storehouse in the Tower', *Arch. Rev.* June 1957, 453], and it is more likely that it was designed by one of the Ordnance engineers. It is, however, possible that Fitch designed it himself, for there is evidence that he acted as an architect and surveyor on other occasions, and he was complimented on his 'great knowledge in the Art of Architecture' on two of the plates of the Orders in R. Blome's *Gentleman's Recreation* (1686). In the 1670s he was employed 'as a surveyor to order and direct' the reconstruction of the Bishop of Winchester's Palace at WOLVESEY, WINCHESTER, for Bishop Morley [P.R.O., C 10/230/32; account in B.L., Stowe MS. 541, f. 139v and duplicate in Portsmouth City Record Office]. In 1686 a kitchen was to be added to Lord Preston's house in SOHO SQUARE, LONDON, 'according to a draught' signed by the contractor, 'and the direction and satisfaction of Sir Thomas Fitch' [Graham archives at Norton Conyers, Yorks.]. According to Tighe & Davis, *Annals of Windsor* ii, 1858, 423, Fitch designed THE COURT HOUSE, WINDSOR, BERKS., *c.*1687, and supervised its erection until his death, when the Corporation ordered that it should be completed under the direction of Sir Christopher Wren. A draft contract in the Cornwall C.R.O. [DDT 1284/25] shows that in 1686 Fitch intended to employ a bricklayer called Bigg to build two four-storey houses at MOUNT EPHRAIM, TUNBRIDGE WELLS, KENT, 'according to a Plott or Designe drawen of the same and signed by the sd. Sr Thomas Fitch & Thomas Bigg', but it is doubtful whether this was proceeded with.

Fitch's efficient performance of the difficult task of constructing the Fleet Ditch earned him a gift of plate from the Corporation, and in December 1679 he was knighted. On 7 September 1688 he was created a baronet by James II, but died nine days later on 16 September. His portrait is in the possession of Mr. Marc Fitch. He had acquired an estate at North Cray in Kent, where he owned, and perhaps built, the mansion called MOUNT MASCALL (dem. *c.*1960). He married Anne, daughter and heir of Richard Comport of Eltham, and the baronetcy was inherited by his son Sir Comport Fitch (d. 1720) [Hasted, *History of Kent* i, 1778, 156–7; Hist. MSS. Comm., *7th Report*, 474 b; information from Mr. Marc Fitch].

Sir Thomas Fitch's younger brother JOHN FITCH was born at Barkway in 1642 and died early in 1706 [P.C.C. 61 EEDES]. He was a member of the London Grocers' Company. In 1679 he was associated with his brother in the important contract for fortifications at Portsmouth [B.L., Add. Charter 32751], and in 1682 he succeeded Philip Lanyon as Workmaster to the Office of Ordnance under a reversionary grant of 1678 [Pat. Roll 30 Charles II, Part 3]. He was frequently employed by Robert Hooke, e.g. at THE BETHLEHEM HOSPITAL in 1675–6, at THE COLLEGE OF PHYSICIANS in 1674–8, and at MONTAGU HOUSE in 1675–8. He also had the bricklayer's contract for ST. ANNE AND ST. AGNES CHURCH, GRESHAM STREET, 1677–80 [*Walpole Soc.* xxv, 90–6; *Wren Soc.* x, 46, 54]. In 1674 he applied for employment as chief bricklayer at St. Paul's Cathedral, but in spite of Hooke's recommendation, and a present of china to Lady Wren, he was disappointed [*Diary of Robert Hooke*, ed. Robinson & Adams, 118, 132, etc.]. In 1675 he undertook 'several works and buildings' at George, Lord Berkeley's house at CRANFORD, MIDDLESEX, in accordance with a design made by Leonard Sowersby (*q.v.*) [P.R.O., C 6/230/26], and in 1679 he contracted to finish the brick tower of HAMPTON CHURCH, MIDDLESEX (dem. 1829) [B. Garside, *The Parish Church of Hampton-on-Thames during the 16th. and 17th. Centuries*, 1937, 11]. In 1698 he was concerned in the remodelling of ALBURY PARK, SURREY, for Heneage Finch, 1st Earl of Aylesford. His 'draught' or 'moddell' is mentioned in a letter from Finch to his brother the 2nd Earl of Nottingham [Finch papers, Leicestershire Record Office, bundle 22, no. 116]. In 1700 he contracted to build the west front of CHATSWORTH HOUSE, DERBYSHIRE, for the 1st Duke of Devonshire [*Wren Soc.* xvii, 40; F. Thompson, *History of Chatsworth*, 1949, 66, 69, where he is wrongly described as a mason]. From the Chatsworth documents it appears that he had recently been at Kiveton Park, Yorkshire, and at Chatsworth there is a rejected design for the west front signed by Fitch that resembles the principal front of Kiveton as built 1698–1704. In *c.*1702 he contracted to perform all the mason's, bricklayer's, carpenter's, smith's, glazier's and sawyer's work in building BUCKINGHAM HOUSE, LONDON, for £7000 [London University MS. 533, ff. 9–11]. Here the architect was William Winde (*q.v.*).

In 1668 John Fitch married Melior, daughter of William Russell of Kingston Lacy in Dorset, and he subsequently acquired property in that county, including (in 1691) the house at High Hall, nr. Wimborne, which still belongs to his descendants, and where his portrait is preserved [Hutchins, *History of Dorset* iii, 1868, 235–6, 242; N. Luttrell, *Brief Historical Relation* iv, 1857, 481, 576, 645; information from the late Charles Gibson].

John Fitch (d. 1706) should not be confused with a master mason of the same name who died in or about 1700. He was a native of Higham Ferrers in Northamptonshire, and was made free of the Masons' Company in 1671 [D. Knoop & G. P. Jones, *The London Mason in the Seventeenth Century*, 1935, 46].

The identity of the John Fitch, described as 'Citizen and Paviour of London', who in *c.*1675 was engaged in building STOWE HOUSE, KILKHAMPTON, CORNWALL, for John Granville, 1st Earl of Bath (see agreement of 1676 between Fitch and a brickmaker cited by G. M. Trinick in *Jnl. Royal Institution of Cornwall*, N.S. x, 1986–7, 59), is not clear.

FLINT, WILLIAM (1801–1862), of Leicester, was the son of John Flint of that town. In 1812 he was apprenticed to a carpenter named Edwyn, and in 1818 to William Parsons, then the leading architect in Leicester. He began independent practice in 1826 and became architect and surveyor to the Corporation. From about 1849 to about 1855 he was in partnership with Charles Wickes, and from 1855 until his death with Henry Shenton, who carried on his practice after his death. Two years later Shenton was joined by Charles Baker, one of Flint's former pupils. Other pupils were William Millican and Isaac Barradale. Flint died on 11 January 1862, aged 60. A portrait in oils is reproduced by J. D. Bennett (see below). Flint's recorded buildings are nearly all classical and show him to have been a competent designer in the Greek Revival style. [J. D. Bennett, *Leicestershire Architects 1700–1850*, Leicester Museums 1968].

LEICESTER, NEW HALL, WELLINGTON STREET (now City Lending Library), 1831 [*V.C.H. Leics.* iv, 352–3].

KIBWORTH CHURCH, LEICS., rebuilt tower, 1832–6, Gothic [*V.C.H. Leics.* v, 174].

LOUGHBOROUGH, LEICS., ST. MARY'S CHURCH (R.C.), 1835; enlarged 1924–5 [*Orthodox Jnl.* N.S. xi, 1840, 111].

LEICESTER, NEWS ROOM AND LIBRARY, BELVOIR STREET, 1837; dem. 1901 [*Architectural Mag.* iv, 1837, 78; *Companion to the Almanac*, 1828, 228–9] (Bennett, *op. cit.*, pl. 9).

LEICESTER UNION WORKHOUSE, SPARKENHOE STREET, 1838; rebuilt 1850–1 [*V.C.H. Leics.* iv, 356].

LEICESTER, MIDLAND RAILWAY STATION, CAMPBELL STREET, 1840; dem. 1892 [Bennett, *op. cit.*, with illustration].

LEICESTER, NEW WEST BRIDGE, 1841–2; rebuilt 1890 [Bennett, *op. cit.*] (*Trans. Leics. Archaeological and Hist. Soc.* xxxvi, pl. 18).

LEICESTER, PHOENIX INSURANCE BUILDING, WELFORD PLACE, 1842 [*V.C.H. Leics.* iv, 353] (Bennett, *op. cit.*, pl. 11).

MARKET HARBOROUGH, INDEPENDENT CHAPEL HIGH STREET, 1844 [Bennett, *op. cit.*].

LEICESTER, CORAH'S WAREHOUSE, 13 GRANBY STREET, 1845; converted into G.P.O. 1865; dem. [*V.C.H. Leics.* iv, 353, n. 66].

LEICESTER, ST. MARY-DE-CASTRO CHURCH, repairs, 1845–6, severely criticized in *Ecclesiologist* vi, 1846, 195–6, vii, 1847, 35–6.

For subsequent works (mostly warehouses) by Flint and Wickes see Bennett, *op. cit.*

FLITCROFT, HENRY (1697–1769), born 30 August 1697, was grandson of Jeffery

Flitcroft of Twiss Green, Winwick, Lancs., and son of Jeffery Flitcroft, a labourer employed in the gardens at Hampton Court. He was apprenticed to Thomas Morris, citizen and joiner of London, for seven years from 6 November 1711, and was admitted to the freedom of the Joiners' Company on 3 November 1719. By 1720 he had become draughtsman and architectural assistant to Lord Burlington, a position which it is said he owed to the accident of falling from a scaffold and breaking his leg while working at Burlington House as a 'journeyman carpenter'. The Earl, hearing of his injury, 'interested himself with much humanity concerning the sufferer, and put him under proper care'. In the course of his recovery, Flitcroft was accidentally seen drawing by the Earl, who, 'noticing his more than ordinary talent', took him into his service.[1] As Burlington's assistant, he was employed in surveying the site of the new Dormitory of Westminster School in 1720 [*Memoirs of William Stukeley*, Surtees Soc. i, 1882, 67], and in drawing out designs for, and supervising the works at, Tottenham Park, Wilts., *c.*1721 [cf. a letter from Flitcroft to Stukeley, dated from Tottenham, in Bodleian, Gough Maps 229, p. 139, and drawings from Chatsworth reproduced in *Archaeological Jnl.* cii, 1945, pl. i]. He subsequently drew out for publication the drawings published by William Kent under Lord Burlington's patronage as *The Designs of Inigo Jones*, 1727; many of the original drawings for these plates are now in the R.I.B.A. Collection. Flitcroft was an accurate and elegant draughtsman, but as works of art his meticulous drawings are dull affairs compared with the lively sketches of his colleague Kent.

In May 1726, Burlington's influence procured Flitcroft the post of Clerk of the Works at Whitehall, Westminster, and St. James's,[2] and for the remainder of his life 'Burlington Harry' was an important figure in the Office of Works. In 1746 he became Master Carpenter, and in 1748 succeeded Kent as Master Mason and Deputy Surveyor. Finally, in 1758 he succeeded Ripley as Comptroller of the Works, a position which he retained until his death in 1769. Although in 1730 he had drawn out Kent's design for rebuilding the Painted Chamber at Westminster [Fiske Kimball, 'William Kent's Designs for the Houses of Parliament', *R.I.B.A. Jnl.* 6 Aug. 1932, 737], Flitcroft designed no important building in his official capacity, and his principal architectural commissions were due to private patronage. He remained faithful to the Palladian canon throughout his life, and as a careful student of Inigo Jones he showed a special aptitude for designing decorative features such as chimney-pieces in the style of the seventeenth-century master. His architecture, if not distinguished by the creative genius which marks the works of Burlington and Kent, has all the merits of a mature style in practised hands.

Like so many eighteenth-century architects, Flitcroft undertook the erection of buildings as well as their design. In 1730 he supplied marble for the base of the Column of Victory at Blenheim [D. Green, 'Blenheim Column of Victory', *Arch. Rev.* April 1950, 274], and he contracted to build both the church at Wimpole and that of St. Giles-in-the-Fields. In 1725 he took three building sites on the Harley estate in Marylebone as a speculation, and there are indications that he was involved (in association with the mason John Devall) in speculative building in Berkeley Square and elsewhere. It is as a 'builder' that he figures in Churchill's poem *The Duellist* (1764).

In 1745 Flitcroft was chosen Sheriff of London and Middlesex, but paid the fine to be excused from serving, as he also did two years later when elected a Warden of the Joiners' Company. He lived at Hampstead, where he built himself the house known as Frognal Grove. In 1744, when it was proposed to rebuild Hampstead Church, Flitcroft offered to design the new church and to supervise its erection free of charge provided that there was no competition. This offer was, however, refused by the vestry, and the present church was designed by John Sanderson, and not, as is often stated (e.g. by Ephraim Hardcastle [W. H. Pyne] in the imaginary dialogue between Flitcroft and Gainsborough which he gives in his *Wine and Walnuts* ii, 1824, 241–9), by Flitcroft [see the Vestry Minutes printed in *C. Life*, 11 Dec. 1937, 610–11]. He died at Hampstead on 25 February 1769, and was buried at Teddington, where a tablet and tombstone record his appointments as 'clerk, Master Mason and Controller' (see Lysons, *Environs of London* iii, 1795, 507, and Park, *Hampstead*, 1818, 222, 337, for the inscriptions). Kenton Couse was his assistant, and, so far as is known, his only pupil. His only son Henry (1742–1826), a barrister by profession, was educated at Corpus Christi College,

[1] I am indebted to Dr. Pamela D. Kingsbury for the information that Lord Burlington's accounts at Chatsworth show that in 1719 he did indeed pay a surgeon for the care of an unnamed workman 'that broke his leg by a fall from the scaffold' at Burlington House.

[2] From about 1728 until 1746 he was also Clerk of Works at Kew and Richmond.

Cambridge, to which he bequeathed his library. Portraits of Flitcroft and his wife are in the R.I.B.A. Library. A bound volume of his drawings of the Five Orders, with designs for a palace, a Doric pavilion, and other buildings, dedicated to the Duke of Cumberland, is in the British Library (Kings's MS. 283). From 1733 to 1737 Flitcroft had acted as the Duke's architectural tutor at a salary of £50 a year [Duke of Cumberland's accounts in B.L., Althorp papers, E 10].

[*A.P.S.D.*; *D.N.B.*; *History of the King's Works* v; *V.C.H. Middlesex* ix, 105 for Flitcroft's Hampstead property.]

CHURCHES

LONDON, ST. GILES-IN-THE-FIELDS, 1731–4, [J. Parton, *The Hospital and Parish of St. Giles-in-the-Fields*, 1822, 211–15; *Survey of London* v, 130–2 and pls. 43–51]. The original wooden model is preserved in the church, and drawings by Flitcroft, including an alternative design with a cupola instead of a spire, are in the R.I.B.A. Collection and B.L., *King's Maps* xxiii, 18.

SOUTHWARK, ST. OLAVE'S CHURCH, TOOLEY STREET, 1738–9; restored by G. Allen after a fire in 1843; dem. 1926 [Vestry Minutes, etc., printed in *Builder* ii, 1844, 252–3, 263–5, 420]. The original designs, signed by the architect and churchwardens, are in B.L., *King's Maps* xxiii, 32.

WIMPOLE, CAMBS., rebuilt for 1st Earl of Hardwicke, 1748–9; partly Gothicized 1887 [inscription in church; estimate, specification, etc., in B.L., Add. MS. 35679, ff. 13–17, 20, 28, 53–4] (R.C.H.M., *West Cambridgeshire*, 212 and pl. 126).

STOKE EDITH, HEREFS. A letter from Flitcroft to Thomas Foley dated 27 May 1740, now in the Herefordshire Record Office [Foley Papers, Portfolio 14, f. 564], shows that Flitcroft made a design 'for dressing up the recess on the North side of the Church in the Gothick manner'. This was probably an external garden seat, and there is no evidence to connect Flitcroft with the rebuilding of the nave and chancel at Foley's expense in 1740–1. The style is classical, not Gothic.

COUNTRY HOUSES, ETC.

CHICHELEY HALL, BUCKS. In Dec. 1722 Sir John Chester paid Flitcroft 5 gns. 'for drawing the designe of the Hall &c.', that is for the entrance hall completed in 1722–3. Whether Flitcroft was himself responsible for the design or whether he was acting only as a draughtsman is not clear, but the treatment of the arched screen may be compared with that of a similar screen in the Old Hall at Wentworth Woodhouse [Joan D. Tanner, 'The Building of Chicheley Hall', *Records of Bucks.* xvii (1), 1961, 46].

DITCHLEY HOUSE, OXON., employed by 2nd Earl of Lichfield from 1724 onwards, probably designing interior of hall in association with W. Kent, 1724–5, and certainly interiors of drawing and dining rooms, 1736–40 [J. Cornforth in *C. Life*, 17–24 Nov. 1988 and A. Gomme, 'Architects and Craftsmen at Ditchley', *Arch. Hist.* 32, 1989].

THORESBY HOUSE, NOTTS. The executors' accounts of Evelyn Pierrepont, 1st Duke of Kingston (d. 1726) [Nottingham University Library, Manvers papers 4352] record a payment of 14 gns. to 'Mr. Flitcroft for Drawing Two Drafts for his late Grace of some intended works at Thoresby wch. was delivered the day his Grace died and for supervising setling and adjusting Mr. Jones's bill for the marble Room at Thoresby and for some Instructions in Measuring Drawing and Architecture to Reynolds by his late Grace's special Request and Direction'.

BOREHAM HOUSE, ESSEX. The ledgers of Hoare's Bank show that in 1729 Flitcroft was paid 8 gns. by Benjamin Hoare 'for the plan of New Hall' (i.e. Boreham). The house was built in 1727–8 under the supervision of Edward Shepherd (*q.v.*), but the payment may indicate that he was following a design made by Flitcroft (*C. Life*, 11 July 1914).

THE BOWER HOUSE, HAVERING, ESSEX, for John Baynes, 1729 [inscription in house, recorded in *C. Life*, 17–24 March 1944].

AMESBURY HOUSE, WILTS., alterations for 3rd Duke of Queensberry, *c.*1730, probably including the addition of the wings; rebuilt 1834 by T. Hopper [Drummond's Bank, Duke of Queensberry's account; in 1726 Flitcroft had made a large survey of the Amesbury estate for the duke now in the Wilts. County Record Office (944/1)] (Harrison's *Views of Seats*, 1787).

WENTWORTH WOODHOUSE, YORKS. (W.R.), enlarged and rebuilt east front and added wings for Earl of Malton (later 1st Marquess of Rockingham, *c.*1735–*c.*1770, modifying a design made and already partly built by Ralph Tunnicliffe (*q.v.*); the wings were raised and given engaged Doric porticos by John Carr later in the century. Flitcroft also designed two temples and the eyecatcher known as HOOBER STAND (erected 1748). Contemporary engravings giving his name as architect of these buildings are in the Hailstone Collection in York Minster Library [A. Booth, 'The Architects of Wentworth Castle and Wentworth Woodhouse', *R.I.B.A. Jnl.* 25 Nov. 1933; Hist. MSS. Comm. *Carlisle*, 174; elevation and two plans in Estate Office inscribed 'Mr. Flitcroft 1737'] (*C. Life*, 20, 27 Sept., 4, 11 Oct. 1924).

BILL HILL, nr. READING, BERKS., unidentified work for 2nd Lord (later 1st Earl) Gower, *c.*1735–6 [payment to Flitcroft in Jan. 1736 for measuring work by Thomas Switzer worth £550: P.R.O., PRO 30/29/1/13, *ex inf.* Prof. A. Gomme].

TRENTHAM HALL, STAFFS., additions for 2nd Lord (later 1st Earl) Gower, 1737; remodelled 1838, dem. 1910 [Bodleian Library, MS. Eng. Misc. f. 556, p. 20].

SWILLINGTON HOUSE, YORKS. (W.R.), rebuilding of principal rooms for Sir William Lowther, Bart., *c.*1738; dem. *c.*1950 [Wakefield Central Library, account-book of Sir Wm. Lowther, payment to Flitcroft 'for Designing the finishing of the Dining Room, Hall, Drawing Room, and the Staircase', Sept. 1738, *ex. inf.* Mr. R. Hewlings].

MIDGHAM HOUSE, BERKS., additions for the Hon. Stephen Poyntz, 1738–9; dem. *c.*1965 [bills in B.L., Althorp Papers, E 12/2].

WIMBORNE HOUSE, WIMBORNE ST. GILES, DORSET, interiors, including Great Dining Room, Tapestry Room and probably the White Hall, for 4th Earl of Shaftesbury, 1740–4 [accounts at Wimborne House; R.C.H.M., *Dorset* v, 95–6].

attributed: STOWE HOUSE, BUCKS., interior of THE STATE GALLERY for 1st Viscount Cobham, *c.*1742 [Michael Gibbon in *The Stoic*, March 1969, 162, followed by Desmond Fitz-Gerald in *Apollo*, June 1973, 574].

WIMPOLE HALL, CAMBS., refronted and altered house for 1st Earl of Hardwicke, 1742–5 [R.C.H.M., *West Cambridgeshire*, 216 and plates].

LILFORD HALL, NORTHANTS., staircase, entrance hall and stables for Thomas Powys, *c.*1744–50 [letters and drawings in Northants. C.R.O., Lilford nos. 3800, 3803, 3805, 3806, 3832; Sir John Soane's Museum, MS. diary of William Freeman (d. 1749), p. 97, referring to stables as Flitcroft's work].

STOURHEAD, WILTS., THE TEMPLE OF CERES (now Flora), 1744–5; THE TEMPLE OF HERCULES (based on the Pantheon), 1754–6; THE TEMPLE OF APOLLO (based on the Round Temple at Baalbec), *c.*1765; ALFRED'S TOWER, designed 1765 but not completed until 1772, for Henry Hoare [K. Woodbridge, *Landscape and Antiquity*, 1970, 26–33, 56].

HAMPSTEAD, MIDDLESEX, house (later known as Montagu Grove and now as Frognal Grove) for himself, *c.*1745; altered by G. E. Street *c.*1860 and remodelled 1926 [Gordon Nares in *C. Life*, 24 June 1949].

HAMPSTEAD, BRANCH HILL LODGE, alterations for Sir Thomas Clark, Master of the Rolls, *c.*1745 [T. J. Barratt, *Annals of Hampstead* ii, 1912, 75].

SHOBDON COURT, HEREFS., internal alterations for 2nd Viscount Bateman, 1746 [Herefordshire C.R.O., Bateman papers, letter of 3 April 1746].

WOBURN ABBEY, BEDS., rebuilt for 4th Duke of Bedford, 1748–61 [G. Scott-Thompson, *Family Background*, 1949, chap. 1; *Vitruvius Britannicus* iv, 1767, pls. 21–5].

WINDSOR GREAT PARK, works for William Augustus, Duke of Cumberland, including wooden bridge over Virginia Water, and the Belvedere Tower (now the nucleus of Fort Belvedere), *c.*1750. In 1747 Flitcroft was paid £1900 on account 'for Windsor Great Park' [Duke of Cumberland's accounts, B.L. Althorp papers, E 10; W. Sandby, *Thomas and Paul Sandby*, 1892, 214; E. A. Oppé, *Sandby Drawings at Windsor Castle*, 1947, 42; drawings in Royal Library, Windsor Castle, nos. 17931A, 17927A, etc.].

MILTON HOUSE, NORTHANTS., rebuilt south front and remodelled much of interior for 3rd Earl Fitzwilliam, 1750–1 [Northants. C.R.O., estimates among Milton House drawings, nos. 88 and 90; payment of Flitcroft's 'salary for surveying the works at Milton' in 'Book of Expences relating to the New Building in 1750 and 1751' (Misc. vol. 156)] (*C. Life*, 18–25 May, 1 June 1961).

CLAPHAM, SURREY, designed house on north side of Common for Henry Hoare, 1753–4; dem. 1851 [Wilts. C.R.O., Henry Hoare's account-book, 383/6] (E. E. F. Smith, *Clapham*, 1976, 44).

REDLYNCH, nr. BRUTON, SOMERSET, alterations for 1st Earl of Ilchester, executed by Nathaniel Ireson, *c.*1755; dem. 1913–14 [B.L., Add. MS. 51373A, ff. 37–40].

STIVICHALL HALL, WARWICKS., for Arthur Gregory, 1755; dem. *c.*1930 [R. Bearman, 'A Lost Warwickshire Country House: Stivichall Hall', *Warwickshire History* i (3), 1970].

PUTNEY, SURREY, designed or altered house for Lady Bruce, 1761 [Wilts. C.R.O., Henry Hoare's account-book, 383/6].

WITLEY COURT, WORCS., porticoed lodge for 2nd Lord Foley, before 1762 [M. Williams, *The Letters of William Shenstone*, 1939, letter cccii].

LONDON HOUSES

MARYLEBONE. The sites of three houses on the Harley estate in Castle Street and Bolsover Street were taken on building leases by Flitcroft in Sept. 1725 [B.L., Add. MS. 18240, f. 14].

CRAVEN STREET, STRAND, layout for William Craven, 1728–30 [copies of plans by Flitcroft in Percy archives at Alnwick Castle, B.xv.5 a–b].

MONTAGU HOUSE, PRIVY GARDENS, WHITEHALL, for 2nd Duke of Montagu, 1731–3; dem. 1859 [referred to as Flitcroft's design by Batty Langley in his *Ancient Masonry*, 1736, 332] (*Survey of London* xiii, 217).

SACKVILLE STREET, No. 36, for Edmund Turnor, 1732–3 [*Survey of London* xxxii, 365–6].

ST. JAMES'S SQUARE, No. 10 (now Chatham House), for Sir William Heathcote, Bart., 1735–6 [*Survey of London* xxix, 122].

DOVER STREET, fitted up house for Isabella, Duchess of Manchester, at expense of Sarah, Duchess of Marlborough, 1740 [correspondence formerly at Althorp House quoted by Lord Spencer in *C. Life*, 13 March 1942, 517].

ARLINGTON STREET, house of 2nd Duke of Kingston (W. side), whose rebuilding *c.*1740–2 is probably represented by payments totalling £3934 to Flitcroft through the duke's account at Hoare's Bank in 1741–2 [Nottingham University Library, Ma. 4390, 4391, 4393]. In 1752 the duke's London account [Ma. 4416] contains a further payment of £811 'To Henry Flitcroft Architect (now and before)'; cf. Hugh Phillips, *Mid-Georgian London*, 1964, 287 and fig. 79.

GROSVENOR SQUARE, No. 4, alterations for 1st Earl of Malton, 1743; dem. *c.*1865 [*Survey of London* xl, 119–20].

UPPER GROSVENOR STREET, house (later GROSVENOR HOUSE, dem. 1927) acquired by 3rd Duke of Beaufort 1740, alterations to which may account for a payment of £1978 to Flitcroft in the duke's account at Hoare's Bank in 1743–4.

BERKELEY SQUARE, No. 16; dem. Payments by Lord Cornbury to Flitcroft, recorded in his account at Hoare's Bank in 1742–4 and 1745, may relate to this house, which Cornbury occupied from 1744 onwards.

BLOOMSBURY SQUARE, designs for two houses identifiable as Nos. 5–6, 1744 [G. Scott-Thompson, *The Russells in Bloomsbury*, 1940, 356; information from Mr. A. F. Kelsall].

ST. JAMES'S PLACE, No. 25, for Lady Hervey, 1747–50; dem. *c.*1940 [*Letters of Mary Lepel, Lady Hervey*, 1821, 111, 125, 170, 261].

BEDFORD HOUSE, BLOOMSBURY, repairs for 4th Duke of Bedford, 1758; dem. 1800 [documents at Woburn Abbey, *ex inf.* Mrs. M. P. G. Draper].

SOUTHAMPTON PLACE, layout and design of houses for 4th Duke of Bedford, probably as executed 1759–63 [A. Byrne, *Bedford Square*, 1990, 24].

UNEXECUTED DESIGNS

At Boughton House, Northants., there is a bound set of undated drawings by Flitcroft for a house in Dover Street for the 4th Earl of Cardigan. It is not certain whether this house was built.

In one of William Stukeley's notebooks in the Bodleian Library (MS. Top. Gen. d. 14, f. 59ᵛ) there is a drawing of an elevation of a house inscribed 'Flitcroft f. 7 Feb. 1726'. This was the year in which Stukeley moved to Grantham, and it is possible that the drawing represents his architect friend's sketch for a new house there that was never built.

In 1738 Flitcroft provided a design for an Anglican church to be built in Savannah, Georgia, U.S.A., which was to have been executed under the direction of an engineer whose death resulted in the abandonment of the scheme [*Colonial Records of the State of Georgia*, ed. Candler, Atlanta 1904, ii, 243, and information from Mr. Carl Lounsbury of Colonial Williamsburg].

FLOCKTON, WILLIAM (1804–1864), of Sheffield, was the son of Thomas Flockton (1772–1818), a local builder. He designed 'THE MOUNT', GLOSSOP ROAD, SHEFFIELD, a Greek Revival terrace, for James Montgomery, the poet (then editor of the *Sheffield Iris*), *c.*1835; the WESLEY PROPRIETARY GRAMMAR SCHOOL, SHEFFIELD, now THE KING EDWARD VII GRAMMAR SCHOOL, 1837–40; restored BAKEWELL CHURCH, DERBYSHIRE, 1841–52; and designed HOLY TRINITY CHURCH, WICKER, nr. SHEFFIELD, 1847–8, Gothic [W. Odom, *Memorials of Sheffield: its Cathedral and Parish Churches*, 1922, 134], and WESSINGTON CHURCH, DERBYSHIRE, 1857–9, Gothic [Sheffield Archives, AP 40/1–13, *ex inf.* Mr. N. Antram]. He also designed the consecrated part of SHEFFIELD GENERAL CEMETERY (the unconsecrated part being the responsibility of Samuel Worth), *c.*1836

[H. Schroeder, *The Annals of Yorkshire*, Leeds 1851, ii, 42–3], and laid out the FERHAM ESTATE at ROTHERHAM for James Wheat in 1840. The original plans for the latter are in the Sheffield Archives (Wheat Collection, 1858), where also are some of his designs (AP43) for the ECCLESALL UNION WORKHOUSE, 1842–3, Tudor Gothic, now part of the Nether Edge Hospital. The Sheffield Grammar School is an ambitious and imposing neo-classical building which shows that Flockton was an architect of some ability. His son, Thomas James Flockton (1823–99), designed a number of churches in and around Sheffield. [R. E. Leader, *Surveyors and Architects of the Past in Sheffield*, 1903; W. Odom, *Hallamshire Worthies*, Sheffield 1926, 148–9.]

FLOOKS, JOHN HARRIS, of Wilton, is listed in Pigot's *Directory* of 1830 as a 'building and land surveyor'. In the *Gardener's Magazine* for 1836 (pp. 506–7) J. C. Loudon describes the villa called THE MOUNT (now 'Landmark House') which Flooks had recently built for himself near Wilton, and says that he was 'very extensively employed as a land agent, surveyor, architect, landscape gardener, builder, and, in short, as an adviser in most descriptions of rural business'. In 1824 he altered or rebuilt AMESBURY PARSONAGE, WILTS. [Salisbury Diocesan Records], and in 1831 he made survey plans of Amesbury Abbey that are now in the R.I.B.A. Collection.

FOOKES, CHARLES B—, is said to have designed the MASONIC HALL, WEYMOUTH, 1834, with a Greek Revival façade based on the 'Theseion' [R.C.H.M., *Dorset* ii (2), 340]. Fookes is listed as a 'Builder' of Weymouth in Pigot's *Directory* of 1830.

FOOTE, ROBERT (–1854), of Glasgow, is known chiefly as the architect to whom the young 'Greek' Thomson was apprenticed in 1834. He was the son of a Glasgow plasterer called David Foote. According to *A.P.S.D.* he had been abroad and 'realised the beauties of Greek architecture'. By 1838 illness had obliged him to retire from practice and he died in Helensburgh in 1854 [R. MacFadzean, *Alexander Thomson*, 1979, 9]. His one known work is a severe Grecian building at the corner of Exchange Place and Buchanan Street, built in 1832 [A. Gomme & D. Walker, *Architecture of Glasgow*, 1987, 308; date formerly on parapet].

FORBES, JOHN B—, was presumably the John Forbes who was admitted to the Royal Academy Schools in 1815 at the age of 20. In 1826 he told Rickman that he had been in David Laing's office at the time the Custom House was being built, i.e. 1813–16 [Rickman's diary, 9 Jan. 1826]. He subsequently established himself in Cheltenham, where he designed THE PITTVILLE PUMP ROOM for Joseph Pitt, 1825–30 [H. Davies, *Cheltenham in its Past and Present State*, 1843, 77], and ST. PAUL'S CHURCH, 1829–31 [Port, 144]. These two handsome and prominent neo-classical buildings should have inaugurated a successful architectural practice, but Forbes's career was cut short in April 1835, when he was convicted of forgery. It appears that he had 'connected himself with a person of the name of Prosser in building speculations', had got into financial difficulties, and endeavoured to extricate himself by more or less fraudulent means. Sentence of transportation for life was passed, but appears to have been commuted to a comparatively short period of imprisonment [*The Diary of a Cotswold Parson*, ed. D. Verey, Gloucester 1986, 105–6].

FORD, WILLIAM (*c.*1790–1876), was a pupil of D. R. Roper, from whose office he exhibited student's designs at the Royal Academy in 1810 and 1813. He subsequently practised in London, but no executed architectural work by him has so far been identified. For a time (*c.*1825 onwards) he was in partnership with Samuel Paterson (*q.v.*). From 1823 to 1828 he was a member of the Surveyors' Club. He died at Coborn Lodge, Bow Road on 12 January 1876 [Principal Probate Registry, Calendar of Probates].

FORDER, GEORGE (–1864), was an architect and surveyor of Winchester until his retirement in 1861. In 1834 he became surveyor to the Dean and Chapter of Winchester in succession to William Garbett (*q.v.*). He was also surveyor to Winchester College, and in 1832 made designs for refronting the Warden's Lodgings which were rejected in favour of others by G. S. Repton [Winchester College Records, *ex inf.* Dr. J. H. Harvey]. He acted as surveyor for the rebuilding of SLAUGHTERFORD CHURCH, WILTS., in 1823 [I.C.B.S.]. He died at Winchester on 19 March 1864 [Principal Probate Registry, Calendar of Probates].

FORT, ALEXANDER (*c.*1645–1706), was well known as a master joiner in the latter part of the seventeenth century. He was probably born *c.*1645, for he was apprenticed to Henry Phillips, a leading London joiner, in May 1659. In 1678 he obtained the reversion of the post of Master Joiner in the Office of

Works, which he duly claimed on the death of Thomas Kinward in *c.*1685. Owing to royal displeasure, which he attributed to his employment on the Duke of Monmouth's house in Soho at the time of the latter's rebellion ('although he was no otherwise concerned than in doeing his work at the said house'),[1] he did not obtain full enjoyment of the position until 1689, in which year he also took the livery of the Joiners' Company. He subsequently executed joinery work at several of the royal palaces, including Windsor, Hampton Court and Kensington.

In 1671–2 Fort was engaged in 'new modelling' the furniture in the choir of SALISBURY CATHEDRAL under the direction of Sir Christopher Wren [G. J. Eltringham, 'Alexander Fort and Salisbury Cathedral', *Wiltshire Arch. Mag.* lvii, 1958]. In 1682 he was employed by Sir Stephen Fox as 'Surveyor of building the Hospitall and house' at FARLEY, WILTS., receiving £50 'for several Modells and Journeys about that Worke' [*Wren Soc.* xix, 88]. It seems clear from this evidence that Fort should be regarded as the architect of the Farley Almshouses, and he may also have been responsible for the church built there in 1688–90 (R.C.H.M., *Churches of S.E. Wiltshire*, 139), but he is not mentioned in the relevant account [Dorset C.R.O., Fox-Strangways papers, box 235]. However, in 1684 he had been paid 'for severall Journeys and severall Modalls for Farley and surveying there with a Modall for a House at Sarum (i.e. Salisbury)', and also 'For severall Modalls . . . and Surveying at Chiswick' (where Fox had just built a house) [*ibid.*, box 162].

In 1691–2 Fort received £50 for measuring and valuing the carvers' and joiners' work at Chatsworth House [accounts at Chatsworth], and he made a wooden model of the design for Sir John Lowther's new house at Lowther, Westmorland, built in 1692–5 [Pearl Finch, *Burley on the Hill*, 1901, 63–4]. In 1696 he built the Ashburnham Pew (destroyed 1877) in AMPTHILL CHURCH, BEDS., for the 1st Lord Ashburnham [Rupert Gunnis, 'A Storm about a Pew', *Bedfordshire Mag.* ii, no. 15, 1950–1, 284].

Fort died impoverished in 1706, leaving a son Thomas (*q.v.*). [*Cal. Treasury Books* viii (3), 1652; *Wren Soc.* xviii, 66, and see General Index; H. L. Phillips, *Annals of the Joiners' Company*, privately printed 1915, 112.]

[1] He had also been employed at the Duke's country house at Moor Park, Herts., where in 1682/3 he was paid £786 for joinery (S.R.O., GD 224/1059/14).

FORT, THOMAS (–1745), son of the above, applied unsuccessfully for his father's post as Master Joiner on his death in 1706. He said that he had been 'bredd up to Building in generall, and particularly to the Joyner's business, wherein hee was employed by his late Majesty as his palace at Loe [Het Loo in Holland] as Master Joyner'. The Board of Works report stated that, though well qualified as a master joiner, he lacked capital 'to carry on the works of the Crown, where often the business required is sudden, and seldom ready money' [P.R.O., WORK 6/14, ff. 114–15]. However, he was later given the post of Clerk of the Works at Hampton Court, which he held from 1714 until his death early in 1745. He held a similar post at Newmarket from 1719 onwards. A volume of early eighteenth-century survey drawings of Hampton Court and Newmarket Palaces in the library of the Property Services Agency can probably be attributed to Fort.

In his *Vitruvius Britannicus* ii, pl. 46, Colen Campbell gives the plan and elevation of a substantial but rather plain astylar house at SUNBURY, MIDDLESEX (dem.), 'designed and conducted by Mr. Fort, Anno 1712', for Roger Hudson. Like his father, Thomas Fort was employed by Sir Stephen Fox (d. 1716), among whose papers in the Dorset County Record Office (box 238) there is an undated estimate by him for the addition of a wing to Fox's house at REDLYNCH, SOMERSET.

In 1717 or 1718 Fort was employed by the 1st Earl Stanhope to add the pedimented wings to the seventeenth-century central block of CHEVENING HOUSE, KENT, and is also said in a letter of 1721 to have 'designed the Figure of a Gladiator standing upon a Pedestal in the middle of the Grass Platt and Military Trophies in the Blank Windows of the Offices' [Stanhope archives at Chevening, Old Library, Shelf C]. Two chimney-pieces in the Drawing Room and Tapestry Room, copied from ones recently designed for Hampton Court by Vanbrugh, may also be attributed to Fort (*C. Life*, 17, 24 April, 1 May 1920). Between 1720 and 1723 he was employed by the 1st Duke of Chandos at CANNONS HOUSE, MIDDLESEX, both as a joiner and as a surveyor; and in 1723 he made plans for houses on the Duke's property in CASTLE STREET, BRIDGWATER, SOMERSET [C. H. & M. I. Collins Baker, *Life and Circumstances of James Brydges, Duke of Chandos*, 1949, 146–8, 222–4]. Fort's will [P.C.C. 42 SEYMER] was proved 7 Feb. 1744/5.

FOSS, JOHN (1745–1827), was the son of James and Elizabeth Foss of Richmond in the

North Riding of Yorkshire. His father died when he was still a boy, and his mother then married a mason called Hawkins. Hawkins took his stepson into his business, and gave him a practical training as a mason. Although otherwise quite uneducated, Foss was an intelligent and enterprising man. To the trade of a mason and carver he soon added the skill of a self-taught architect, becoming in due course one of the leading men in the town and holding the office of Mayor in 1811 and 1822. From 1807 to 1816 he was also Surveyor to the North Riding, but was eventually dismissed for negligence in the performance of his duties. Foss died on 18 July 1827, aged 82, leaving a son, William Foss, to continue his practice. There is a tombstone to his memory in the parish churchyard.

Foss was an able provincial architect whose principal works appear to have been country houses in the North Riding of Yorkshire. Clifton Castle, in particular, is a well-designed house, essentially of the Palladian villa type, but with up-to-date neo-classical detailing.

[Peter Wenham, article in *Ripon and Richmond Chronicle*, 19 Nov. 1955, based on a MS. memoir of Foss by James Arrowsmith; Peter Wenham, 'John Foss of Richmond', *York Georgian Soc's Annual Report* for 1976; Peter Wenham & Jane Hatcher, 'The Buildings of John Foss', *ibid.* 1977.]

BROUGH HALL, YORKS. (N.R.), stables and bridge in park for Sir John Lawson, Bart., before 1790 [W. Angus, *Views of Seats*, pl. xxii, 1790].

SWINTON PARK, YORKS. (N.R.), works for William Danby, including north range 1791–6, south wing 1813–14 and upper part of Quarry Gill Bridge, completed 1822, all castellated [J. P. Neale, *Seats*, 2nd ser., iv, 1828; R. Lugar, *Villa Architecture*, 1828, pls. 24–5; John Cornforth in *C. Life*, 7, 14 and 21 April 1966].

SWINITHWAITE HALL, YORKS. (N.R.), works for – Anderson, 1792, including Belvedere Temple and alterations to rear of house [MS. Memoir].

SCRUTON HALL, YORKS. (N.R.), alterations for Henry Gale, 1794–6; dem. 1958 [E. Waterson & P. Meadows, *Lost Houses of the North Riding*, 1990, 54].

SEDBURY PARK, YORKS. (N.R.), rustic tower for Sir Robert Darcy Hildyard, 1795 [MS. Memoir].

THORPE PERROW, nr. BEDALE, YORKS. (N.R.), 'new modelled and in part rebuilt' for Mark Milbanke, *c.*1793 [MS. Memoir].

CLIFTON CASTLE, nr. MASHAM, YORKS. (N.R.), for Timothy Hutton, 1802–10 [MS. note-book entitled 'Records and Memoranda, Clifton' in possession of Mrs. Curzon-Howe-Herrick, 1968: 'The Architect of the house was Mr. John Foss'] (*C. Life*, 22 Sept. 1988).

RICHMOND, YORKS. (N.R.), Nos. 32 and 34 FRENCHGATE, *c.*1806 [Wenham & Hatcher, *op. cit.*, 38].

FOSTER, JAMES (*c.*1748–1823), of Bristol, was the pupil and apprentice of Thomas Paty (*q.v.*). Like Paty, he combined architectural practice with the business of a statuary mason, executing (to quote his own advertisement) 'monuments and chimney-pieces in marble with peculiar grace and elegance'. Early in the nineteenth century he was joined by his son and namesake James Foster, junior (d. 1836). From this time onwards the firm's practice appears to have become exclusively architectural in character. In 1820 James Foster & Son were at No. 10 Culver Street, while No. 24 Orchard Street was the address of Thomas Foster, architect, who had become a freeman of Bristol in 1818 on his marriage to a freeman's daughter. He was evidently another son of the elder Foster, for it was 'at the residence of his son, Orchard Street, Bristol', that James Foster died on 1 November 1823, aged 75. James Foster, junior, then joined in practice with his brother at 13 Orchard Street. By 1828 the firm was called 'Foster and Okely', James and Thomas having taken as a third partner the latter's pupil William Ignatius Okely. James Foster, junior, held office as one of the district surveyors for the City of Bristol from 1819 until his death on 5 January 1836. Soon after 1840 Okely left the firm, his place as Thomas Foster's partner being taken by the latter's son John. Thomas died on 6 July 1849, aged 56, leaving the practice to be continued by John Foster (d. 1880) and his partner John Wood.

Clifton Church, the principal independent work of the elder Foster, was designed in a thin Georgian Gothic style comparable to Paty's St. Nicholas, Bristol. Foster & Sons subsequently produced a number of routine early nineteenth-century Gothic (and a few neo-Norman) churches. Foster and Okely were responsible for the competent Greek Revival architecture of the Upper and Lower Arcades, and for the excellent terrace-houses of Clifton Vale, Caledonia Place and the New Mall. In 1835 they competed for the Houses of Parliament, submitting a design in the 'late Gothic style', with a 'castellated effect in the river front'. The works of Foster and Wood fall outside the limits of this *Dictionary*, but they included the Grammar School, the

Athenaeum, the Colston Hall, Foster's and Trinity Almshouses, and the Grand Hotel.

[*Gent's Mag.* 1824 (i), 93, 1849 (ii), 219; A. B. Beaven, *Bristol Lists*, 1899, 249; C. F. Dening, *The Eighteenth Century Architecture of Bristol*, 1923, 139; W. Ison, *The Georgian Buildings of Bristol*, 1952, 34; A. Gomme, M. Jenner & B. Little, *Bristol; an Architectural History*, 1979, 433.]

ABERGWILI PALACE, nr. CARMARTHEN, remodelled for the Bishop of St. David's, *c.*1803 onwards [A.P.S.D., *s.v.* 'David's, St.'].

MANGOTSFIELD CHURCH, GLOS., altered and repaired, 1812 [*Bath Chronicle*, 15 Oct. 1812].

BRISLINGTON CHURCH, SOMERSET, added N. aisle, 1819, Gothic [I.C.B.S.].

KINGSWOOD, nr. BRISTOL, GLOS., HOLY TRINITY CHURCH, 1819–21, Gothic: by 'J. Foster & Sons' [I.C.B.S.].

BRISTOL, ST. ANDREW'S CHURCH, CLIFTON, 1819–22, Gothic; bombed 1940 and dem. 1954 [W. Ison, *op. cit.*, 20].

STAPLETON CHURCH, GLOS., 1820–1, Gothic: by 'James Foster & Sons'; rebuilt 1856 [I.C.B.S.].

BRISTOL, MERIDIAN PLACE, 1822 [T. Mowl, *To Build the Second City: Architects and Craftsmen of Georgian Bristol*, 1991, 139].

BRISTOL, CITY MARKET, ST. NICHOLAS STREET, 1823 [A. Gomme, M. Jenner & B. Little, *Bristol*, 1979, 148, n. 10, citing drawings in City Archives, Acc. 26163, f. 4].

BRISTOL, THE UPPER AND LOWER ARCADES, 1824–5; Upper Arcade dem. 1941: by 'James and Thomas Foster' [John Evans, *Chronological History of Bristol*, 1824, 331].

SHIREHAMPTON CHURCH, GLOS., 1827, Gothic: by 'Foster & Okely'; rebuilt 1929–30 after fire [I.C.B.S.].

OLDLAND CHURCH, GLOS., 1829–30, Gothic: by 'Foster & Okely' [I.C.B.S.].

BEACHLEY CHURCH, GLOS., 1833, Gothic: by 'Foster & Okely' [I.C.B.S.].

MUCH BIRCH CHURCH, HEREFS., 1837, Gothic: by 'Foster & Okely' [I.C.B.S.].

STROUD, GLOS., HOLY TRINITY CHURCH, STROUDSHILL, 1838–9, Gothic: by Thomas Foster [brass plaque in church].

BRIMSCOMBE CHURCH, GLOS., for David Ricardo, 1839–40, neo-Norman [E. Hulbert & P. L. Smith, *Churches and Views of Stroud and its Neighbourhood*, 1889, 10].

STROUD, GLOS., ST. PAUL'S CHURCH, WHITESHILL, 1839–41, neo-Norman: by Thomas Foster [Port, 144].

BRISTOL, CLIFTON VALE, CALEDONIA PLACE and NEW MALL, CLIFTON, *c.*1840–3; by Foster & Okely [W. Ison, *op. cit.*, 237–8].

CARDIFF, ST. MARY'S CHURCH, BUTE STREET, 1841–3, neo-Norman: by Thomas Foster [Port, 172].

WHITMINSTER CHURCH, GLOS., rebuilt N. aisle, 1842 [I.C.B.S. plan in Library of Society of Antiquaries, London; churchwardens' accounts in Glos. C.R.O.].

HANHAM CHURCH, GLOS., 1842, Gothic: by 'Foster & Son' [*Gent's Mag.* 1843 (i), 75].

MINCHINHAMPTON CHURCH, GLOS., rebuilt nave and chancel, 1842, Gothic: by Thomas Foster [*Gent's Mag.* 1842 (ii), 81; H. E. Relton, *Sketches of Churches*, 1883; drawing in R.I.B.A. Coll.].

RODBOROUGH CHURCH, GLOS., rebuilt nave, 1842–3, Gothic [*V.C.H. Glos.* xi, 232].

BRISTOL, THE RED MAIDS' SCHOOL, DENMARK STREET, 1844: by 'Foster & Son'; dem. 1951 [*A.P.S.D.*, *s.v.* 'Bristol'].

BRISTOL, QUEEN ELIZABETH'S HOSPITAL SCHOOL, BERKELEY PLACE, 1845–7, Tudor: by 'Foster & Son' [*Companion to the Almanac* 1845, 240–2].

BRISTOL, ROYAL PROMENADE, VICTORIA SQUARE, *c.*1845–7: by 'Thomas Foster and Son', but probably by John Foster [A. Gomme, M. Jenner & B. Little, *Bristol*, 1979, 260, 433].

BRISTOL, THE MÜLLER ORPHANAGE, ASHLEY DOWN, 1847–9; by 'Messrs. Foster' [*Builder* v, 1847, 454]; later extended by Foster & Wood.

FOSTER, JOHN (1758–1827), was for many years a dominant figure in the architectural affairs of Liverpool. His father, John Foster (*c.*1730–1801), was a joiner and builder, and he himself continued the joinery business while also practising as an architect. In or about 1790 he took the place of Charles Eyes (*q.v.*) as surveyor to the Corporation, a post which he retained for over thirty years, receiving a salary of £500 a year, with liberty to remain in business as a builder. A contemporary described him as 'a very strong and influential character' who 'set about getting control of the Corporation affairs for himself and his family'. Another remembered him as 'the most influential as well as . . . the cleverest man of his day . . . who, although not a member of the Council himself, possessed a strange power over its decisions and judgements, and brought to his friends the aid of as much commonsense and as strong an intellect as ever was possessed by any individual'. He was surveyor to the docks as well as to the Corporation, and as his eldest son Thomas (d. 1836) became town clerk in 1832, while his second son John (*q.v.*) succeeded him as municipal architect, it can readily be appreciated that, in Picton's words, the Foster family 'managed the architectural and building affairs of the corporation' before the Municipal

Reform Act of 1835 deprived them at once of their offices and of their influence.

The elder Foster designed several public buildings in an elegant late Georgian style comparable to that of James Wyatt, with whom he came into contact over the Exchange (now the Town Hall). In 1787 he was instructed to prepare designs for its enlargement which were to be submitted to some eminent architect in London for his opinion. The architect chosen was James Wyatt, who eventually supplied new designs which were carried out by Foster. In 1795 the interior was destroyed by fire and rebuilt by Foster under Wyatt's direction. Wyatt may also have had some hand in the New Exchange, a large and important neo-classical building erected by Foster in 1803–9, but demolished in the 1860s. Few of Foster's private commissions have been recorded, but according to a writer in the *Monthly Mirror* for July 1803, it was to his 'taste and ability' that Liverpool was indebted 'for most of our well-built houses all over the town'.

Foster retired in 1824 and died at Newington (Liverpool) on 27 April 1827, in his 69th year.

[*A.P.S.D.*; J. A. Picton, *Memorials of Liverpool* i, 1875, 230; *Liverpool a Few Years since*, by an Old Stager, 1852, 33, 104–5; *Trans. Lancs. and Cheshire Hist. Soc.* lxii, 1910, 155; J. Touzeau, *The Rise and Progress of Liverpool* ii, 1910, 714; *Parliamentary Papers*, 1835, xxvi, 2708; obituary notices in Gore's *Liverpool Advertiser* and *Liverpool Mercury*; Liverpool City Library, Underhill MSS. Biography, vol. iii, 94–5 and Treasurer's accounts.] See p. 1138

LIVERPOOL

THE DISPENSARY, CHURCH STREET, 1781; dem. 1830 [Picton, *Memorials* ii, 163].

THE BOROUGH GAOL, GREAT HOWARD STREET, 1786 [*Gent's Mag.* 1813 (ii), 332].

THE EXCHANGE (now TOWN HALL), enlarged by Foster to designs of James Wyatt, 1789–92; rebuilt interior after fire of 1795, completed 1797; dome and cupola added 1802, portico 1811 [J. A. Picton, *Liverpool Municipal Records 1700–1835*, 1886, 265–72] (*C. Life*, 23 July 1927).

THE ATHENAEUM, completed 1799; dem. [G. Richardson, *New Vitruvius Britannicus* ii, 1808, pls. 43–4].

THE UNION NEWSROOM (corner of Duke and Slater Streets), 1880 [Picton, *Memorials* ii, 269–70].

THE THEATRE ROYAL, WILLIAMSON SQUARE, enlarged 1802–3; dem. *c.*1965 [*Monthly Mirror*, July 1803, commending the skill of 'Mr. Foster, the architect'].

THE NEW EXCHANGE, 1803–9; dem. *c.*1863 [Picton, *Architectural History of Liverpool*, 1858, 11, where Wyatt's share in the design is left in doubt].[1]

THE CORN EXCHANGE, 1807; rebuilt 1851 [*Lancashire Illustrated*, 1831, 15].

ST. LUKE'S CHURCH, begun for the Corporation in 1811 from designs made by Foster in 1802, but left unfinished until 1826–31, when it was completed by his son, who in 1827 proposed some alterations 'in the plans of the interior and exterior', Gothic; gutted 1940–1 [Picton, *Memorials* ii, 242–3; *Liverpool Municipal Records 1700–1835*, 396–7].[2]

ELSEWHERE

PRESTON, LANCS, ST. JOHN'S (PARISH) CHURCH, rebuilt W. tower, 1813–14; Gothic; dem. 1855 [M. Tulket, *Account of the Borough of Preston*, Preston 1821, 53].

PRESTON, LANCS., HOLY TRINITY CHURCH, 1814–16, Gothic; dem. *c.*1955 [Lancs. C.R.O., PR/2307/19, 23; 2309/7].

LEASOWE CASTLE, CHESHIRE, enlarged for Mrs. Boode, 1818 [W. W. Mortimer, *Hundred of Wirral*, 1847, 295].

FOSTER, JOHN (*c.*1787–1846), second son of the above, was a pupil of Jeffry, and also, according to some accounts, of James Wyatt. He exhibited at the Royal Academy from the former's office in Lower Brook Street in the years 1804–6. In 1809 he went abroad, and spent some time in Greece in company with Haller, Linckh and C. R. Cockerell, taking part in the excavations at Ægina and Phigaleia. Cockerell described him in his journal as 'a most amusing youth, but too idle to be anything more than a dinner companion'. He returned to England in 1816 and entered into partnership with his brother in the family building business. From this he withdrew in 1824, when he succeeded his father as architect and surveyor to the Corporation, at a salary of £1000 per annum.

[1] In 1819 a correspondent told Soane that the Exchange was 'partly by Mr. Harrison' [F. Copland to Soane, 3 Sept. 1819, incorrectly printed by Bolton, *Portrait of Soane*, 288].

[2] In his *Architectural History of Liverpool* Picton reported that although the design was 'nominally that of Mr. John Foster', the latter knew little about Gothic architecture and 'common report . . . ascribes the design to his assistant Mr. Edwards'. A drawing of the church was exhibited at the Liverpool Academy by Foster in 1813, but Thomas Rickman was told that it was 'Gandy's sent in in Foster's name' (Diary, 4 July 1813).

This post he held until 1835, when, on the reform of the Corporation, he lost his office and retired on a pension of £500 a year. He designed many important public buildings in Liverpool, mainly in a scholarly Greek Revival style comparable to Smirke's in London. His greatest work was the Custom House, an imposing Ionic building whose dome and portico were one of the architectural landmarks of Liverpool until their destruction in World War II. His St. John's Market was the first large-scale covered market in England. Few of his buildings survive, but contemporary engravings of many of them will be found in *Lancashire Illustrated* (1831) or *The Stranger in Liverpool* (11th. ed. 1837).

Foster became a member of the Liverpool Academy of Arts on its foundation in 1810, and was given the title of Professor of Ancient and Modern Architecture in 1824. He was President from 1822 to 1841. He was a Fellow of the Society of Antiquaries. In 1831 he had a house at Norris Green, West Derby, but at the time of his death he was living in Hamilton Square, Birkenhead. He died on 21 August 1846, aged 59, and was buried in the St. James's Cemetery in Liverpool which he had designed. A collection of his drawings of antique architecture in Greece and Asia Minor is in the Walker Art Gallery, Liverpool.

[*A.P.S.D.*; J. A. Picton, *Memorials of Liverpool* i, 1875, 470; Peter Fleetwood-Hesketh, *Murray's Lancashire Architectural Guide*, 1955, 88–9; Liverpool City Library, Underhill MSS. Biography, vol. iii, 94–5, and Liverpool Epitaphs, vol. vi, p. 13; copies of letters from Greece in Sir John Soane's Museum, Div. I, F. 6].

LIVERPOOL

ST. MICHAEL'S CHURCH, PITT STREET, 1816–26; dem. 1941 [*A.P.S.D.*].

ST. MARY'S CHURCH FOR THE INDIGENT BLIND, HOTHAM STREET, 1818–19; taken down in 1850 and re-erected in Hardman Street by A. H. Holme; dem. *c.*1935 [*A.P.S.D.*].

ST. GEORGE'S CHURCH, rebuilt 1819–25; dem. 1897 [*A.P.S.D.*].

ST. JOHN'S MARKET, 1820–22; dem. *c.*1965 [*A.P.S.D.*; *Architectural Mag.* ii, 129; *Gent's Mag.* 1822 (ii), 113–14].

THE ROYAL INFIRMARY, BROWNLOW STREET, 1822–4: dem. 1887 [*A.P.S.D.*].

ST. ANDREW'S SCOTTISH CHURCH, RODNEY STREET, the portico and façade, 1823–4, the body of the church being by Daniel Stewart (*q.v.*) [J. A. Picton, *Memorials of Liverpool* ii, 1875, 245; S.R.O., CH 2/245/2, memoranda in the 'Share and Transfer Book'].

THE NECROPOLIS CEMETERY, CHAPEL, ENTRANCE, etc., 1823–4 [*The Stranger in Liverpool*, 11th ed. 1837, 163; J. A. Picton, *Memorials of Liverpool* ii, 1875, 369].

LORD STREET and ST. GEORGE'S CRESCENT, street architecture, 1825–7; dem. 1940–1 [*A.P.S.D.*].

ST. MARTIN'S CHURCH, OXFORD STREET NORTH, 1825–8, Gothic; dem. [Port, 132].

ST. DAVID'S WELSH CHURCH, BROWNLOW HILL, 1826–7; dem. [J. A. Picton, *Memorials of Liverpool* ii, 1875, 214].

PUBLIC BATHS, ST. GEORGE'S DOCK, 1826–9; dem. [*A.P.S.D.*].

THE ROCK LIGHTHOUSE, 1827–30 [*Lancashire Illustrated*, 1831, 83].

THE LUNATIC ASYLYM, BROWNLOW HILL, 1828–30; dem. [*The Stranger in Liverpool*, 11th ed. 1837, 74].

THE CUSTOM HOUSE, 1828–35; bombed 1940–1 and dem. [J. H. Rideout, *The Custom House, Liverpool*, 1928; original drawings in P.R.O., WORK 30/155–7].

AINTREE RACECOURSE, THE GRANDSTAND, 1829 [*A.P.S.D., s.v.* 'Grandstand'].

ST. JAMES'S CEMETERY, CHAPEL and layout, 1827–9 [*The Stranger in Liverpool*, 11th ed. 1837, 35].

ST. CATHERINE'S CHURCH, ABERCROMBIE SQUARE, 1829–31; bombed 1940–1 and dem. *c.*1965. [*The Stranger in Liverpool*, 11th ed. 1837, 61–2].

LIVERPOOL & MANCHESTER RAILWAY, Moorish arch connecting engine-houses, 1830; dem. [H. Booth, *An Account of the Liverpool & Manchester Railway*, Liverpool 1830, 50 and frontispiece].

LIME STREET RAILWAY STATION (Liverpool & Manchester Railway), screen-wall to street, 1835–6; dem. [*A.P.S.D.*].

ST. JAMES'S CEMETERY, circular temple (with statue by John Gibson) in memory of William Huskisson, 1834 [*Architectural Mag.* iv, 77–8].

ELSEWHERE

KNOWSLEY HALL, LANCS., alterations and castellated additions for 12th Earl of Derby, *c.*1820 [J. P. Neale, *Seats*, 2nd. ser., i, 1824].

BANGOR CATHEDRAL, alterations to interior, 1825–8; removed *c.*1870 [M. L. Clarke, *Bangor Cathedral*, Cardiff 1969, 27–30].

GARSWOOD NEW HALL, ASHTON-IN-MAKERFIELD, LANCS., for Sir John Gerard Bart., *c.*1828; dem. 1921 [Twycross, *Mansions of England: Lancs.* iii, 1847, 24].

BOLLINGTON, CHESHIRE, ST. GREGORY'S CHURCH (R.C.), 1834; dem. [*Catholic Mag.* v, 1834, p. lxiv].

FOTHERGILL, RICHARD (1789–1851), amateur architect, was the son of Richard Fothergill of Lowbridge House, Selside, Westmorland, and of Caerleon, Monmouthshire [see Burke's *Landed Gentry*, 8th ed. 1894]. In 1837 he moved from Caerleon to Lowbridge, where he built a new house for himself, and in 1838 a new Gothic church was built to his designs at SELSIDE. His drawings and correspondence are in the I.C.B.S. records.

FOTHERGILL, ROBERT, a local builder, designed THE WESTMORLAND COUNTY GAOL (now the Police Station) at APPLEBY, WESTMORLAND, built in 1770–1 in a simple Georgian domestic style [B. Tyson, 'An Architectural History of the Gaols and Court Houses in Appleby', *Trans. Ancient Monuments Soc.* N.S. 32, 1988].

FOULSTON, JOHN (1772–1841), was a pupil of Thomas Hardwick. He commenced practice in 1796 from St. Alban's Place, Pall Mall, but what (if anything) was built to his designs at this stage of his career is unknown, though he may have altered some early Georgian houses in Chapel Place North (off South Audley Street) of which he was the lessee [*Survey of London* xl, 302]. In 1803 he won the second award of 150 guineas in the competition for the conversion of the Houses of Parliament at Dublin into the Bank of Ireland, and in the following year exhibited his design at the Royal Academy. In 1811 he won the competition for a group of buildings in Plymouth, comprising the Royal Hotel, Assembly Rooms, and Theatre. His design was remarkable both for the extensive use of cast iron in the 'fire-proof' theatre, and for the way in which he combined three distinct buildings into a single architectural composition. His success in obtaining this important commission established his local fame: and taking up residence in Plymouth, he remained for twenty-five years the leading architect of the neighbourhood, which he did much to transform, both by new public buildings and by well-designed street architecture. Most of his work was in the classical style of the Regency 'improvements' in London, with Greek orders accentuating stucco terraces, but at Devonport he indulged in a flight of eclectic fancy by combining in one picturesque group an 'Egyptian' library, a 'Hindoo' nonconformist chapel, a 'primitive Doric' town hall, and a street of houses dressed with an orthodox Roman Corinthian order. The influence of Soane is strongly apparent in several of his buildings, notably in the façade of St. Andrew's Chapel and the interior of the Proprietary Library, with its segmental arches supporting a circular clerestory of windows.

Towards the end of his career Foulston was for a short time in partnership with George Wightwick, who succeeded to his practice, and who wrote an amusing account of his colleague in retirement. He 'lived a pleasing amateur life for some years, decorating his pretty cottage and grounds in the suburb, and seeking to rival, in little, the famed falls of Niagara, by an artistic spreading of the Plymouth watercourse, or leet, over some yards of spa and rockwork, greatly enhancing the beauty of his shrubbery . . . The vehicle which served him as a gig . . . was built in the form of an antique *biga*, or war-chariot; with a seat furtively smuggled into the service of comfort, though he ascended it from behind with true classical orthodoxy and looked (as far as his true English face and costume allowed) like Ictinus of the Parthenon, "out for a lark" . . .' It was during his retirement that Foulston published *The Public Buildings erected in the West of England, as designed by J. Foulston, F.R.I.B.A.*, 1838, with 117 lithographic plates and a portrait. He also made a set of 19 water-colour drawings of his buildings which is now in the City Art Gallery at Plymouth. He died on 30 December 1841, aged 69, and was buried in St. Andrew's New Cemetery. M. A. Nicholson, E. W. Gribble, C. E. Lang and T. J. Ricauti were his pupils.

[*A.P.S.D.* (memoir by Wightwick); *Civil Engineer and Architect's Jnl.* v, 1842, 68; A. E. Richardson & C. L. Gill, *Regional Architecture of the West of England*, 1924, 67–73; Frank Jenkins, 'John Foulston and his Public Buildings in Plymouth, Stonehouse, and Devonport', *Jnl. Soc. Architectural Historians* (of America) xxvii, 1968; J. W. Dawe, 'John Foulston', *Procs. Plymouth Athenaeum* ii, 1971; J. Mordaunt Crook, 'Regency Architecture in the West Country', *Jnl. Royal Society of Arts* cxix, 1971, 438–51; F. G. Hall & others, *The Bank of Ireland*, 1949, 460; George Wightwick, *Nettleton's Guide to Plymouth, Stonehouse, Devonport etc.*, 1836; certificate of death, *ex inf.* Mrs. Rosamund Reid].

PUBLIC BUILDINGS, ETC., IN PLYMOUTH AND DEVONPORT

ROYAL HOTEL, ASSEMBLY ROOMS, and THEATRE, 1811–13, east wing completed 1822; dem. 1939–41 [*Public Buildings*, pls. 3–47] (Richardson & Gill, *op. cit.*, 66, 69).

THE PUBLIC or PROPRIETARY LIBRARY, 1812; enlarged and refronted by G. Wightwick as the Plymouth and Cottonian Libraries 1850; destroyed by bombing 1941 [*Public*

Buildings, pls. 54–8] (Richardson & Gill, *op. cit.*, 68–9).

THE EXCHANGE, 1813 (based on plans made by Foulston, but not carried out under his direction); dem. [*Public Buildings*, pls. 76–9].

THE ATHENAEUM, 1818–19; destroyed by bombing 1941 [*Public Buildings*, pls. 48–53].

PRINCESS SQUARE, completed 1821; destroyed by bombing 1941 [G. Wightwick, *Nettleton's Guide*, 1836, 14].

THE TOWN HALL, DEVONPORT, 1821–3 [*Public Buildings*, pls. 81–4].

ST. ANDREW'S CHAPEL (afterwards St. Catherine's Church), 1823; dem. 1958 [*Public Buildings*, pls. 59–66].

THE CIVIL AND MILITARY (or PUBLIC) LIBRARY (now Oddfellows' Hall), DEVONPORT, 1823, Egyptian style [*Public Buildings*, pls. 90–4].

MOUNT ZION BAPTIST CHAPEL, DEVONPORT, 1823–4, Indian style; dem. *c.*1925 [*Public Buildings*, pls. 95–8].

THE COLUMN, DEVONPORT, 1824 [*Public Buildings*, pls. 85–9].

ST. ANDREW'S CHURCH, altered and refitted 1826, Gothic; 'restored' by Gilbert Scott 1874–5; gutted 1941 [*Public Buildings*, pls. 67–74].

ST. PAUL'S CHAPEL, DURNFORD STREET, STONEHOUSE, 1830–1, Gothic; chancel added 1891 [*Public Buildings*, pl. 99].

OTHER WORKS

ATHENIAN COTTAGE, TOWNSEND HILL, PLYMOUTH, for himself, *c.*1813; dem. [J. C. Loudon, *Gardener's Mag.* xviii, 1842, 543] (*Proceedings of the Plymouth Athenaeum* i, 1967, 20).

BODMIN, CORNWALL COUNTY LUNATIC ASYLUM, 1818; enlarged 1842, 1847–8 and 1867 [*Public Buildings*, pls. 104–11].

SALTRAM HOUSE, DEVON, alterations, including addition of Doric porch and formation of library, for 1st Earl of Morley, 1818 [Britton & Brayley, *Devonshire Illustrated*, 1832, 52; National Trust, *Saltram*, 1981, 7] (*C. Life*, 27 April, 4, 11 May 1967).

ST. ERME CHURCH, CORNWALL, rebuilt except west tower, 1819–20, Gothic [inscription in church].

WOODBINE COTTAGE, PARK HILL, nr. TORQUAY, DEVON, for Miss Anne Johnes, *c.*1820/3; dem. [signed lithograph dated 1823].

ST. MICHAEL'S TERRACE, STOKE DAMAREL, *c.*1825 [*A.P.S.D.*; Britton & Brayley, *Devonshire Illustrated*, 1832, 84].

ALBEMARLE VILLAS, STOKE DAMAREL, *c.*1825 [Britton & Brayley, *Devonshire Illustrated*, 1832, 84].

BELMONT HOUSE, STOKE DAMAREL, for John Norman, *c.*1825 [G. Wightwick, *Nettleton's Guide*, 1836, 89] (R. Ackermann, *Views of Country Seats* ii, 1830, 123).

TAVISTOCK, DEVON, THE BEDFORD ARMS INN, *c.*1825; Gothic [Britton & Brayley, *Devonshire Illustrated*, 1832, 48; cf. *Public Buildings*, pl. 103].

WARLEIGH HOUSE, TAMERTON FOLIOT, DEVON, alterations for the Revd. Walter Radcliffe, 1825–32, Gothic [signed receipt for drawings dated 1825, at Warleigh House, *ex. inf.* Mr. Peter Reid].

TAVISTOCK, DEVON, restoration of ABBEY GATEWAY, 1829, Gothic [*Public Buildings*, pls. 101–3, showing unexecuted design for interior].

TORQUAY, THE PUBLIC BALLROOM (adjoining the Royal Hotel), 1830; dem. [*Public Buildings*, pl. 100].

TRAVERS HOUSE, STOKE DAMAREL, for R. Bromley [G. Wightwick, *Nettleton's Guide*, 1836, 89].

PARK WOOD (now NEWTON) HOUSE, nr. TAVISTOCK, DEVON [G. Wightwick, *Nettleton's Guide*, 1836, 157–8].

FOUNTAINE, Sir ANDREW (1676–1753), of Narford in Norfolk, was a well-known virtuoso and to some extent an amateur architect. He was educated at Christ Church, Oxford, under Dean Aldrich, was knighted by William III in 1699, and succeeded to the estate at Narford on his father's death in 1706. He was later Vice-chamberlain to Caroline, Princess of Wales, tutor to her son William, Duke of Cumberland, and Warden of the Mint. His collection of pictures, books, china and coins was celebrated.

In his *Essay in Defence of Ancient Architecture* (1728), Robert Morris calls Fountaine a 'practitioner of architecture' and couples his name with those of Lords Burlington and Pembroke. William Halfpenny also compliments him on his knowledge of architecture in the dedication of his *Art of Sound Building.* Narford Hall had been built by Fountaine's father in 1702, but the music room and the library were added by Sir Andrew, perhaps to his own designs. George Vertue, who visited Narford in 1739, noted that the gardens were laid out in 'the best manner, wholly I believe by his own direction' [Walpole Soc., *Vertue Note Books* v, 120]. Colen Campbell, giving a plan of the garden in *Vitruvius Britannicus* iii, 1725, pl. 95, illustrates an Ionic temple and an ornamental deer-house and states that Fountaine 'has given Marks of his good Taste and Affection for Architecture, in several Pieces lately erected there'. Horace Walpole says that he designed 'a large ugly room . . . 36 feet long, 24 high, & 24 wide' for Sir Matthew Decker at his house on Richmond Green, Surrey ['Visits to Country Seats', *Walpole Soc.* xvi, 40], and on 8 June 1728 it was reported in the *Norwich Gazette* that Fountaine was 'to direct, as 'tis said, the building of a Palace at Richmond' for King George II (a scheme in which E. L. Pearce (*q.v.*) was also involved).

[*D.N.B.*; J. Rykwert, *The First Moderns*, M.I.T. Press 1980, 256–7; A. W. Moore, *Norfolk and the Grand Tour*, Norfolk Museums 1985, chap. 2; S. Parissien *et al.*, 'Narford Hall', *Georgian Group's Report & Journal*, 1987.]

FOWLER, CHARLES (1792–1867), was born at Cullompton in Devonshire, where his family had lived for several generations. At the age of 15 he was articled to John Powning, an architect and builder of Exeter. On the completion of his apprenticeship in 1814 he left Exeter for London to work as an assistant in the office of David Laing. He began independent practice in 1818. His success in 1822 in obtaining the first premium in the competition for rebuilding London Bridge ended in disappointment, for his designs were eventually set aside in favour of Rennie's. However, by 1830 he had become well known as a result of two recent works: Covent Garden Market and the great glazed conservatory at Syon House. The former established his reputation as the leading designer of covered markets, while the latter demonstrated his mastery of construction in cast iron. The structural refinement of his Hungerford Market, London, and Lower Market, Exeter, was matched by an appropriately simplified classical style derived from French neo-classical architects such as Durand. It is these buildings which give Fowler the distinction of being one of the few nineteenth-century architects who, like the engineers Telford and Rennie, were able to handle structure and form with equal assurance. Fowler maintained his connection with his native county of Devon, where he designed several churches, and had an influential patron in the 10th Earl of Devon, for whom he remodelled the exterior of Powderham Castle. It was the Earl who was instrumental in obtaining for him the commission for the London Fever Hospital in 1848.

Fowler was closely involved in the establishment of the Institute of British Architects in 1835. For over seven years he was one of its two Honorary Secretaries and in 1850–1 was elected a Vice-President. He contributed several papers to its *Transactions*, as well as to Loudon's *Architectural Magazine*. In addition he published a *Description of the plan for the revival of Hungerford Market, with some particulars of the buildings proposed to be erected* (1829). Many of his designs were exhibited at the Royal Academy.

In 1852 Fowler gave up practice because of ill-health and retired first to Wrotham and then to Western House, Great Marlow, Bucks., where he died on 26 September 1867. His son Charles Fowler, F.R.I.B.A. (*c.*1823–1903), practised in London. Henry Roberts (*q.v.*) and J. M. Allen (1809–83) of Crewkerne were his pupils. His drawings for the Hungerford Market are in the R.I.B.A. Collection. What appears to be his winning design for London Bridge is in the Guildhall Record Office. A design in the P.R.O. (C 108/322) for a coach-house in Duke Street, Westminster, for William Courtenay, M.P., dated 1818, shows that his connection with the Earl of Devon's family went back to the early years of his practice.

[Obituaries in *Builder* xxv, 1867, 761, and *R.I.B.A. Trans.* xviii, 1867–8; Jeremy Taylor, 'Charles Fowler, Master of Markets', *Arch. Rev.*, March 1964, and 'Charles Fowler: a centenary memoir', *Arch. Hist.* xi, 1968.]

LONDON, COURTS OF BANKRUPTCY, BASINGHALL STREET, 1818–21; dem. [*Builder* xxv, 1867, 761].

GRAVESEND, KENT, THE NEW MARKET, 1818–22; dem. [R. P. Cruden, *History of Gravesend*, 1843, 490].

SCHOOL HOUSE, LATYMER'S SCHOOL, HAMMERSMITH, LONDON, 1819 [drawings and specification sold by Christie's 19 Dec. 1989, lot. 61].

YARMOUTH, NORFOLK, SILK FACTORY, THE DENES, for Messrs. Grout, Baylis & Co., 1822–3 [*Norfolk Chronicle*, 2 Feb. 1822 (advt. for tenders); cf. C. J. Palmer, *History of Great Yarmouth*, 1856, 108].

TEFFONT EVIAS CHURCH, WILTS, rebuilt 1824–6, Gothic; spire added after 1830 [I.C.B.S.].

TOTNES BRIDGE (R. Dart), DEVON, 1826–8 [signed].

LONDON, ST. PAUL'S CHURCH, KILBURN, 1826; remodelled *c.*1890, dem. 1934 [G.R.; *R.I.B.A. Trans.* xviii, 1867].

SYON HOUSE, ISLEWORTH, MIDDLESEX, conservatory for 3rd Duke of Northumberland, 1827–30 [J. C. Loudon, *Encyclopaedia of Cottage, Farm and Villa Architecture*, 2nd ed. 1846, 979].

LONDON, COVENT GARDEN MARKET, for 6th Duke of Bedford, 1828–30 [J. C. Loudon in *Gardener's Mag.* vii, 1831, 265–77, and *Architectural Mag.* v, 1838, 665–77].

EXETER, No. 14 THE CLOSE (formerly

Archdeaconry of Cornwall), for the Dean and Chapter of Exeter, 1829–30, Tudor Gothic [Exeter Diocesan Records, 1190].

LONDON, ST. JOHN'S CHURCH, SOUTHWICK (now HYDE PARK) CRESCENT, PADDINGTON, 1829–31, Gothic; altered 1888 [W. Robins, *Paddington Past and Present*, 1853, 144–5].

LONDON, HUNGERFORD MARKET, 1831–33; dem. 1862 to make way for Charing Cross Railway Station [drawings in R.I.B.A. Coll.; described in Loudon's *Architectural Mag.* i, 1834, 53–62, L. Förster's *Allgemein Bauzeitung*, 1838–9, and (by Fowler himself) in *R.I.B.A. Trans.* xiii, 1862, 54–7].

'VILLA in the Old English Manner', executed before 1833, but unidentified [J. C. Loudon, *Encyclopaedia of Cottage, Farm and Villa Architecture* ii, 1833, 846–50, 2nd ed. 1846, 846–50].

TAVISTOCK, DEVON, THE CORN MARKET, for 6th Duke of Bedford, 1835 [*Builder* xxv, 1867, 761].

EXETER, THE LOWER MARKET, 1835–7; dem. 1942 [*Builder* xxv, 1867, 761] (A. E. Richardson & C. L. Gill, *Regional Architecture of the West of England*, 1924, 39–40).

EXETER, THE HIGHER MARKET, supervised construction to the designs of George Dymond, after the latter's death, 1835–8 [J. C. Loudon, *Architectural Mag.* i. 1834, 352, and iii, 1836, 12].

CHARMOUTH CHURCH, DORSET, rebuilt 1835–6, Gothic [J. C. Loudon, *Architectural Mag.* v, 1838, 509–10].

POWDERHAM CASTLE, DEVON, castellated alterations and additions for 10th Earl of Devon, probably begun 1837 (date on rain-water-heads), but not completed until 1848, when Fowler exhibited his design for the entrance at the R.A. Loudon reported in 1842 that the castle was 'being altered by Mr. Fowler' [*Gardener's Mag.* xviii, 1842, 532] (*C. Life*, 4, 11 and 18 July 1963).

HONITON CHURCH, DEVON, 1837–8, Norman style [*Builder* xxv, 1867, 761; *Gent's Mag.* 1842 (ii), 410].

HAINES HILL, BERKS., stables and coach-house for Capt. Garth, R.N., 1838 [signed drawings at Haines Hill].

BICKLEIGH CHURCH, nr. PLYMOUTH, DEVON, rebuilt (except tower) for Sir Ralph Lopes, Bart., 1838, Gothic; altered by J. D. Sedding, 1882 [*Builder* xxv, 1867, 761].

MARISTOW HOUSE, DEVON, lodges for Sir Ralph Lopes, Bart., *c.*1839 [exhib. at R.A. 1839].

COFTON CHAPEL, nr. DAWLISH, DEVON, rebuilt 1838–9 for 10th Earl of Devon, Gothic [B. F. Cresswell, *Churches of the Deanery of Kenn*, Exeter 1912, 57].

EXETER, DEVON COUNTY LUNATIC ASYLUM, 1842–5 [*Builder* iv, 1846, 349; *Companion to the Almanac*, 1849, 239–40; plan in M. Parchappe, *Asiles d'Aliénés*, Paris, 1853, 234].

LONDON, sale-room at 16 ST. PAUL'S CHURCHYARD for Mr. Toplis, 1846; dem. [*Builder* iv, 1846, 91].

THE LONDON FEVER HOSPITAL, ISLINGTON, 1848–52 [*Builder* xxv, 1867, 761].

LONDON, WAX CHANDLERS' HALL, 13 GRESHAM STREET WEST, 1852–5; dem. 1940 [*Builder* xxv, 1867, 761] (*Builder* cxii, 1917, 413).

FOWLER, WILLIAM (1761–1832), was born at Winterton, nr. Brigg in Lincolnshire, and lived there all his life. He was 'brought up to the business of a master builder and architect', and had a considerable local practice as a builder of farmhouses, parsonages and the like. He is best known, however, as one of the greatest antiquarian artists of his time. His first drawing, a Roman pavement, was made in 1796, and three great albums of coloured engravings were published by subscription in 1804, 1809 and 1824. His principal subjects were Roman pavements and medieval glass, in whose representation he showed great skill. All the time which he could spare from his business was devoted to his antiquarian pursuits, and his children assisted him by colouring the engravings which he had learned to execute himself. He was a member of the Wesleyan connection, but remained a regular churchgoer, and had many clergymen among his patrons and clients. He spent the last years of his life in the 'Gothic Cottage' which he built for himself in West Street, Winterton, in 1827–8. Joseph Fowler (1791–1882), his eldest son, was sent to Oxford in 1812 to become a pupil of John Plowman, but did not remain owing to an illness. He took charge of the business during his father's latter years, but gradually gave it up after his marriage in 1828.

The Correspondence of William Fowler was edited and privately printed by his grandson in 1907. The works mentioned in it include repairs or alterations to the churches of MANTON, 1809, APPLEBY, 1820–3, WINTERINGHAM, 1827, and ADLINGFLEET (YORKS.), 1828; works at CLEATHAM HALL (coach-house, etc., 1802), NORMANBY PARK, 1815–17, LEADENHAM RECTORY, 1821–3, APPLEBY HALL, 1821–3 and 1827, GATE BURTON HALL, 1824–7, CAYTHORPE VICARAGE, 1827, and CAENBY HALL (billiard-room 1829); alterations for Archdeacon H. V. Bayley at the SUBDEANERY, LINCOLN, and at his VICARAGE at MESSINGHAM, 1813–18; a NATIONAL SCHOOL at NEWARK, NOTTS., 1826, and a LIBRARY and READING-ROOM in the Market Place at the same town, 1826–7.

FOX, JOHN, was a builder and architect at Hull, where in 1828–9 he was described as 'Surveyor to the Corporation'. He designed the NEW GAOL in KINGSTON STREET, 1830; dem. [T. Allen, *History of the County of York* ii, 1831, 97].

FOXHALL, EDWARD MARTIN (1793–1862), was the son of Edward Foxhall, a carver and furniture-maker who was among Sir John Soane's oldest friends. He entered Soane's office in 1812, and remained there until January 1821. He drew many of the diagrams used to illustrate Soane's lectures, and Soane left him £100 in his will, besides making him his residuary legatee. He became District Surveyor to the parish of St. George Hanover Square in 1827, and was also surveyor to the London estates of Sir John Sutton, Bart., and the Duke of Norfolk. 'His practice was principally confined to the appointments he held', and the only buildings which he is known to have designed are a Roman Catholic chapel at Southampton, another in Romney Terrace, Horseferry Road, Westminster (1853, dem. *c.*1903), R.C. schools in Great Peter Street, Westminster, 1857, and the premises at the corner of Bond and Conduit Streets (dem.). He was a member of the Institute of British Architects. [Obituary in *Builder*, 3 Jan. 1863, 8; A. T. Bolton, *The Portrait of Sir John Soane*, 55, 431–2; *The Tablet*, 25 Dec. 1853, 17 Jan. 1857, 37, 16 May 1857, 308.]

FRANKLIN, JOSEPH (*c.*1785–1855), was a native of Stroud in Gloucestershire, and probably a son of Joseph Franklin, who had a business as a monumental mason there at the end of the eighteenth century. After working in Bath he moved to Liverpool, where he was employed by Thomas Haigh, a builder with whom he eventually went into partnership. In 1837, 'having acquired an ample independence', he gave up building to become Surveyor to the Corporation of Liverpool [*Builder* xiii, 1855, 455]. He retired in 1848 and died on 12 September 1855, aged 70. He was commemorated by a tablet in the Congregational Church at Stroud.

In LIVERPOOL Franklin designed the CRESCENT CONGREGATIONAL CHAPEL, EVERTON ROW, 1835–6, THE PEMBROKE BAPTIST CHAPEL, 1839 (dem.), and the handsome GREAT GEORGE STREET CONGREGATIONAL CHAPEL, 1840–1, all in the classical style [J. A. Picton, *Memorials of Liverpool* ii, 288, 346, 442]. His honourable behaviour towards H. L. Elmes in connection with the competition for St. George's Hall deserves to be remembered [see R. P. Jones, 'The Life and Work of H. L. Elmes', *Arch. Rev.*, June 1904, 236].

FRASER, ALEXANDER (*c.*1790–1841), of Aberdeen, combined the professions of architect, landscape-painter and drawing master. He was one of the original members of the Aberdeen Artists' Society, and exhibited paintings of an architectural character at its exhibition. He appears to have died in 1841, when his office equipment was sold. [G. M. Fraser, 'Archibald Simpson and His Times', *Aberdeen Jnl.*, 14 June 1918; information from Mr. David Walker.]

WILLIAMSTON HOUSE, nr. INSCH, ABERDEENSHIRE, 1825–6 [*Aberdeen Jnl.*, 28 May 1825, 8 March 1826].

POWIS HOUSE, OLD ABERDEEN, entrance gateway for John Leslie, 1830–4, castellated [*Powis Papers*, ed. J. G. Burnett, Third Spalding Club 1951, 366].

BRAEMAR PARISH KIRK, ABERDEENSHIRE, 1832; altered 1878 [*Aberdeen Jnl.*, 19 Dec. 1832].

PORT ELPHINSTONE, ABERDEENSHIRE, warehouse and granary for the Aberdeen Lime Co., 1835 [*Aberdeen Jnl.*, 6 May 1835].

ABERDEEN, HOLBURN U.P. CHURCH, 1836; since reconstructed [*Aberdeen Jnl.*, 7 Sept. 1836].

ABERDEEN, layout of JOHN KNOX'S CHURCHYARD, 1837 [*Aberdeen Jnl.*, 31 May 1837].

FRAZER, ANDREW (–1792), was the son of George Frazer (*q.v.*). He joined the Royal Engineers in 1759 as an ensign and rose to the rank of lieutenant-colonel in 1788. He retired in about 1790, and died on his way to Geneva in the summer of 1792.

As chief engineer for Scotland Frazer was responsible in 1781 for repairing FORT CHARLOTTE at LERWICK in the SHETLANDS and for the erection of new barracks there [drawings by Frazer in N.L.S., MS. 1649, Z3, 42–44, 48]. In 1781 he won the competition for the design of the new CHURCH of ST. ANDREW in GEORGE STREET, EDINBURGH. He generously insisted on relinquishing the prize in favour of a drawing master named Robert Kay (*q.v.*), whose design had been commended. Frazer's design, for an oval church with a Corinthian portico and a small tower and cupola, was illustrated in the *Scots Magazine* for March 1781, and carried out in 1782–5. A steeple was subsequently (1787) substituted for the tower and cupola. This feature appears to have been designed by William Sibbald (*q.v.*), but as it figures in a portrait of Frazer by Zoffany now at Houghton House, Norfolk, he may have been involved in its design. In June 1781 Frazer was made a burgess of

Edinburgh in recognition of 'his services to his King and Country in general and to this city in particular in the line of his profession'.

[*D.N.B.*; *Notes on the History of St. Andrew's Church, Edinburgh*, 1884; *Scots Mag.*, 1781, 119; *Roll of Edinburgh Burgesses*, Scottish Record Soc. 1933, 60.]

FRAZER, GEORGE (*c.*1701–1774), held the office of Deputy Auditor of Excise in Scotland for more than fifty years. William Mylne mentions him in 1758 as 'another [architect] got up lately in Edinburgh' [Mylne family papers]. In 1763 he made a plan for enlarging the Excise Office in Edinburgh which 'Mr. [probably Robert] Mylne was employed to 'extend in a better form' [S.R.O., GD 150/3496, 5 & 12], and in the same year he was involved in the scheme for the North Bridge over the North Loch. A plan of the 'intended bridge' was 'to be seen in the hands of Mr. George Fraser . . . deputy auditor of the excise . . . from which any undertaker may make his calcul[ations] and proposals', and detailed plans and estimates were to be sent to him [*Scots Mag.* 25, 1763, 361–2]. The plan and elevation, drawn by James Craig (*q.v.*), presumably under Frazer's direction, were subsequently engraved [*Scots Mag.*, *ibid.*]. Although a foundation stone was laid in October 1763, nothing more was done until 1765, when the bridge was built to new designs by William Mylne (*q.v.*). In 1768–9 the MANSE at CORSTORPHINE, MIDLOTHIAN, was built 'according to a plan by Mr. George Frazer, Deputy Auditor of Excise' [S.R.O., GD 150/3288/12–13]. In 1769 he provided designs for the HIGH CHURCH at INVERNESS, completed in 1772. This was 'on the model' of the Buccleuch Church in Edinburgh, 'but . . . larger' [S.R.O., GD 44/37/50]. Frazer, who was the father of Col. Andrew Frazer (*q.v.*), died at Edinburgh on 12 Oct. 1774, aged 73 [*Scots Mag.* 1774, 559].

FREDERICK, Sir CHARLES (1709–1785), was the second son of Sir Thomas Frederick. He was educated at Westminster School and New College, Oxford, and made the Grand Tour in 1737–9. From 1741 to 1784 he was M.P., first for Shoreham and then for Queenborough. In 1746 he was appointed to a place in the Office of Ordnance and from 1750 to 1782 held the post of Surveyor-General of the Ordnance. He was created K.B. in 1761 and died on 18 December 1785. A portrait by A. Casali, painted in Rome in 1738, is in the Ashmolean Museum.

Frederick was a keen antiquary and a man of taste. A collection of drawings of monuments and ancient buildings by him and Smart Lethieullier, formerly in the possession of Horace Walpole and now in the British Library (Add. MS. 27348), shows that he was a competent draughtsman. He designed the monument in HAGLEY CHURCH, WORCS., to Lucy, Lady Lyttelton (d. 1747), which was executed by Roubiliac [Dr. Pococke, *Travels in England*, Camden Soc., i, 229; *Connoisseur*, May 1954, 256], and that in HIGHCLERE CHURCH, HANTS., to Thomas Milles, Bishop of Waterford (d. 1740), which is signed *Charles Frederick Invt. L. F. Roubiliac Sculpt.*

[Manning & Bray, *Surrey* ii, pedigree facing p. 767; Walpole Society, *Vertue Note Books* iii, 107, 134, 152–3, v. 12; R. Sedgwick, *The House of Commons 1715–54* ii, 1970, 52.]

FREEBAIRN, CHARLES, was the son of James Freebairn, a teacher of French in Edinburgh. As 'Charles Freebairn, Architect in Edinburgh', he was employed at ABERCAIRNY HOUSE, PERTHSHIRE, by James Moray to design and build a new Dining Room in 1755–9 [S.R.O., GD 24/1/624]. This was destroyed when the house was rebuilt early in the nineteenth century. In 1758–62 he designed the charming LIBRARY at INNERPEFFRAY, MUTHILL, PERTHSHIRE, founded under the will of David Lord Madderty [records at Innerpeffray, *ex inf.* Mr. David Walker]. In 1761, when he was admitted a burgess of Edinburgh, by right of his father, he was described as a wright by trade [*Roll of Edinburgh Burgesses 1761–1841*, Scottish Record Soc. 1933, 60]. In 1756 he was elected a member of the Royal Company of Archers [J. Balfour Paul, *History of the Royal Company of Archers*, 1875, 368].

FREEMAN, JOHN (*c.*1689–1752), was the owner of Fawley Court, Bucks., which he inherited on the death of his uncle in 1707. Probably under the influence of his friend Edmund Waller of Hall Barn near Beaconsfield and of the latter's stepfather, John Aislabie of Studley Royal in Yorkshire, he laid out the grounds at Fawley with plantations and a rectangular canal, and before 1732 had designed and built a Gothick folly which was intended to display classical statuary, formerly part of the Arundel Marbles, some portions of which had been acquired by Waller and himself. In building one of the earliest Gothick garden buildings in England and decorating it with ancient Greek and Roman statuary, Freeman was one of the pioneers of English romantic taste. In or shortly before 1731 he took Henley Park (in the hills above Fawley) on a long lease, and told a correspondent that he was 'planting trees, making theatres, & building castles in the air' there. Among these was the addition of a round tower to a farmhouse in order to give a Claudian aspect to the landscape.

Freeman's most important works as an amateur architect were the saloon at HONINGTON HALL, WARWICKS., and the FREEMAN MAUSOLEUM in the churchyard at Fawley. The saloon at Honington is an octagonal domed room with coffered ceiling and elaborate plaster decoration of high quality (*C. Life*, 27 Nov. 1920, 21, 28 Sept., 12 Oct. 1978; C. Hussey, *English Country Houses: Early Georgian*, 1955, 175–80). Letters and drawings show that Freeman designed it in 1751 for his friend Joseph Townsend, and that it was executed under the direction of William Jones (*q.v.*). In 1748 Freeman refitted the interior of Fawley Church at his own expense, reusing furniture from the recently demolished chapel at Cannons House, Middlesex, and in 1750 he built the mausoleum, a domed building based on one of G. B. Montano's early seventeenth-century engravings of Roman temples and mausolea. Freeman was buried in the mausoleum when he died on 9 August 1752. Some of his architectural drawings (including those for Honington and the mausoleum) and his library catalogue are among the Strickland family papers in the Gloucestershire County Record Office (D 1245, FF 38–9). Other drawings were sold at Christie's on 30 November 1983.

[D. & S. Lysons, *Magna Britannia* i, 1806, 562; Geoffrey Tyack, 'The Folly and the Mausoleum', *C. Life*, 20 April 1989; Howard Colvin, *Architecture and the After-Life*, 1991, figs. 76, 311.]

FRENCH, GEORGE RUSSELL (1803–1881), was born in London in 1803. Between 1821 and 1832 he exhibited at the Royal Academy from Wanstead in Essex, and in 1836 he was living at Leytonstone, but in the 1840s he was practising from London, where he was surveyor to the Ironmongers' Company. He had antiquarian interests, and published several genealogical works, including *The Ancestry of Queen Victoria and Prince Albert* (1841), *The Royal Descent of Nelson and Wellington* (1853) and *Shakespereana Genealogica* (1869). He was a member of the Society of Freemasons of the Church (cf. Alfred Bartholomew), a vice-president of the London and Middlesex Archaeological Society and a keen temperance reformer. He died in London on 14 October 1881, aged 78. [*Builder* xli, 1881, 586; F. Boase, *Modern English Biography* i, 1892, 1106; *D.N.B.*]

According to his obituary in the *Builder* French was 'better known by his literary labours than his professional practice', and his executed works were certainly not remarkable. They included ST. MARY'S NATIONAL SCHOOL, PLAISTOW, ESSEX, 1831, Tudor Gothic [exhib. at R.A. 1831; *V.C.H. Essex* vi, 147]; alterations to the hall at BEDDINGTON PARK, SURREY, for Admiral Sir B. H. Carew, 1832 [exhib. at R.A. 1832]; LEAVENHEATH CHURCH, SUFFOLK, 1836, Gothic, enlarged 1883 [I.C.B.S.]; WESTMARSH CHURCH, KENT, 1841, Gothic [I.C.B.S.]; and ALL SAINTS CHURCH, SHRUB END, nr. COLCHESTER, ESSEX, 1844–5, Gothic [*Builder* ii, 1844, 482]. In 1835 he entered a Tudor Gothic design for the new Houses of Parliament.

FRESON, LANCELOT (*c.*1615–), described as gentleman of Leeds, aged 50, gave evidence in 1665 in a case in the Court of Arches concerning dilapidation in the Archbishop of York's houses in Yorkshire. He stated that 'for the space of these twenty yeares last past' he had been 'employed about and undertaken the Building and reparacons of manye houses and structures for divers gentlemen and persons of quality within the County of York' [Lambeth Palace Library, Court of Arches Records Bbb 69].

FRITH, JOHN (–1856), practised in Birmingham and subsequently in Sheffield, where he died in 1856. He designed ST. MARGARET'S CHURCH, WARD END, BIRMINGHAM, 1834–5, Gothic [building accounts in Birmingham Reference Library 358858].

FRITH, RICHARD (–1695), a bricklayer by trade, was a speculative builder active in London in the reign of Charles II. In the 1670s he was much involved in transactions relating to property in the new St. James's Square, where he was himself responsible for building the Earl of St. Albans' house in the north-west corner, afterwards known as Ormonde and finally as Chandos House; dem. 1735 [*Survey of London* xxix, 119, etc.]. From 1677 onwards he was responsible for a large development in Soho, including Soho (originally 'Frith') Square and Frith Street, and he was one of the builders of Monmouth House on the south side of the Square, begun in 1681, but still unfinished at the time of the Duke of Monmouth's execution in 1685. As its principal developer, Frith was responsible for the layout of northern Soho as it exists today. Little of what he built survives in a recognizable form, but topographical drawings show that the street fronts conformed to the standard type of post-Fire London houses [*Survey of London* xxxiii, xxxiv, *passim*].

In 1687–8 Frith was concerned in a project for the rebuilding of the Royal Mews in St. James's Park, with a 'new intended street leading from Berkeley House to the new intended Mews at St. James's' [*Cal. Treasury Books* viii (iii), 1704, 1716, 1801; *History of the King's Works* v, fig. 13]. His agreement with the respective tradesmen (B.L., Add. MS. 16370, ff. 115–18) shows that 'for every £200 worth of worke wrought, or goods sold and delivered to such like Vallue', each was to receive a proportionate share in the proposed new street, 'being part of his Majesties' park neere St. James, as is set out in a draft of the same. For the terme of 99 yeares, at 18 yeares purchase' – an interesting indication of the speculative builder's methods at this date. Frith eventually got into financial difficulties, and died in debt in 1695. For a full account of his career, see B. H. Johnson, *Berkeley Square to Bond Street*, 1952; also C. L. Kingsford, *Early History of Piccadilly, Leicester Square and Soho*, 1925, 68–9.

FROME, W—, exhibited two architectural drawings at the Royal Academy in 1831. His address is not stated in the catalogue. In 1828 he designed a Gothic tower (since destroyed) for WITHAM PRIORY CHURCH, SOMERSET [I.C.B.S.].

FROST, JAMES (*c.*1774–1851), architect, builder and civil engineer, is said to have been the builder of the Martello Towers on the Essex coast. In Norwich he designed the cast-iron COSLANY BRIDGE, built in 1804 [*Norwich Mercury*, 3 March, 25 Aug. 1804, *ex inf.* Mr. David Cubitt]. He appears later to have left Norwich and may have been the James Frost who was a builder at Finchley in the 1820s and resident in Southwark in 1830. In *c.*1825–7 the latter built, presumably to his own designs, STRAWBERRY VALE HOUSE, FINCHLEY (dem.) and the adjacent HAWTHORNE DENE, 'a double cottage' with fire-resisting floors and ceilings of tiles supported by iron ribs [G.L.R.O., MLR 1827/1/124 and 1830/3/99, *ex inf.* Mr. Frank Kelsall]. The death at Brooklyn, New York, on 31 July 1851, of James Frost, aged 77, 'for many years an eminent architect in this city', was announced in the *Norwich Mercury* of 6 Sept. 1851 (*ex inf.* Mr. Cubitt).

FULCHER, THOMAS (*c.*1737–1803), was a carpenter, builder, surveyor and timber-merchant at Ipswich. In Suffolk he designed WORKHOUSES (both later Hospitals) at BULCHAMP, 1765–6 [N. Pevsner, *Suffolk*, Buildings of England, 1974, 119, citing a payment to Fulcher for plans] and STOWMARKET, 1777–81 [signed drawing in E. Suffolk C.R.O., cited by C. Brown *et al.*, *Dictionary of Architects of Suffolk Buildings 1800–1914*, 1991, 111]; a RECTORY at STRATFORD ST. MARY, 1783–4 [E. Suffolk C.R.O., FF 1/81/1]; a THEATRE and ASSEMBLY ROOMS in SMALLGATE STREET, BECCLES, 1785 [*Ipswich Jnl.* 20 Aug. 1785, advt. for tenders]; and HANDFORD BRIDGE, IPSWICH [G.R. Clarke, *History & Description of Ipswich*, 1830, 184]. He also built, and probably designed, a THEATRE at GREAT YARMOUTH, NORFOLK in 1778 [J. Preston, *History of Yarmouth*, 1819].

Fulcher died in June 1803, aged 66. His will [E. Suffolk C.R.O., IC/AAI/223/72] includes plans of his house and timber yards in Ipswich. His business was carried on by his son Robert Fulcher (d. 1815). Robert's only recorded architectural work appears to be the BRIDEWELL at WOODBRIDGE, SUFFOLK, 1804 [*Report from the Committee of Aldermen appointed to visit several Gaols in England*, 1816, 152].

Shortly before his death Fulcher patented a 'Water Proof Composition in imitation of Portland Stone, for stuccoing and colouring New and Old Brick and Stone Buildings'. According to an advertisement published in the *Ipswich Journal* (19 April 1806), 'specimens of its admired colour and lasting qualities may be seen at Major Heron's and Robert Collins, Esq. Ipswich; Richard Frank's D. D., Alderton; Rev. Samuel Kilderbee's, Campsey Ash; Sir Hyde Parker's Bart., Benhall, Suffolk; Col. Drake Garrard's, Wheathampstead, Hertfordshire; Jn. Rook's Esq. Catton, near Norwich; Thomas Needham's Esq. Dublin; and at the proprietor's Ipswich'. Some of these buildings were evidently altered by Fulcher, e.g. LAMERS, nr. WHEATHAMPSTEAD, HERTS. (dem. 1949), for in the 'Red Book' which Humphry Repton prepared for Col. Drake Garrard in 1792, he stated that he had departed somewhat from 'Mr. Fulcher's design'. The patent composition continued to be marketed by his son, who in 1813 published at St. Albans *Hints to Noblemen and Gentlemen of Landed Property*, in which he stated that the stucco was 'the same as that used by the Signor Carrabellas[1] two Italian Artists, at . . . the Earl of Bristol's Palace at Ickworth . . . which has stood fifteen years, in ornamental Panels, at a Height of eighty feet from the Ground'.

[1] Perhaps Francesco and Donato Carabelli, who decorated the façade of the Palazzo Serbelloni in Milan with a neo-classical relief *c.*1790 (C. Meeks, *Italian Architecture 1750–1914*, 80).

FULKES, THOMAS, father and son, practised in Reading until the latter's death in 1879 at the age of 78. The father was employed as surveyor by the churchwardens of UFTON NERVET, BERKS., in connection with some repairs to their church in 1809 [MS. Parish Records]. He was similarly employed at ST. MARY'S READING, in 1818 [MS. Parish Records], and in 1833 he submitted designs for enlarging and altering CHURCH OAKLEY PARSONAGE, HANTS. [Winchester Diocesan Records]. He entered a Doric design for the Royal Berkshire Infirmary competition in 1837 [*Reading Mercury*, 11 Feb. 1837].

FURNESS, RICHARD (1791–1857), born at Eyam in Derbyshire, and subsequently schoolmaster and parish clerk at Dore in the same county, was a self-educated man who is best known as a poet, though he also showed ability in several other capacities, including those of surveyor and architect. His only considerable work in an architectural capacity appears to have been the rebuilding of DORE CHURCH, DERBYSHIRE, in a simple Gothic style in 1828–9. He not only made the design, but also 'carved the ornamental figures' himself [G. C. Holland, *The Poetical Works of Richard Furness*, 1858, 45; *D.N.B.*; I.C.B.S.]

G

GADSDON, ISAAC, probably a carpenter by trade, was the author of a book entitled *Geometrical Rules Made Easy for the Use of Mechanicks concern'd in Buildings: Containing New and Infallible Methods for Striking out from proper Centres . . . the Groyns of Arches . . . the Angle Brackets of Coves, Crowns of Beaufets circular or elliptick . . . Also, an Essay, on the Nature and Properties of Arches in general. . . . The Whole design'd . . . for the Information and Use of all Building Artificers*, 1739. He was one of Robert Morris's executors and is described in the latter's will as of (High) Wycombe [Eileen Harris, *British Architectural Books and Writers 1556–1785*, 1990, 201–2].

GALILEI, ALESSANDRO (1691–1737), was a Florentine architect who came to England in 1714 at the invitation of John Molesworth, the British envoy to the Tuscan court from 1710 to 1714. Molesworth and his father (created Lord Molesworth in 1716) were men of taste who, together with Sir Thomas Hewett (*q.v.*) and Sir George Markham, formed what they called 'the new Junta for Architecture'. Their aim appears to have been to introduce a more classical and less baroque style into British architecture, and Galilei was to be their chosen architect. As members of the Whig aristocracy, they were in a position to introduce him to such influential persons as Baron Kielmansegg, Lord Stanhope and the 1st Duke of Newcastle. Although Galilei made designs for several potential patrons, including the Duke of Newcastle, few commissions resulted, and nothing came of an ambitious scheme for a royal palace to replace Whitehall. Designs offered by Galilei for some of the Fifty New Churches in London had equally little success. In May 1718 he entered into an agreement with Nicholas Dubois (*q.v.*) 'to become Copartners & Joint Dealers together in all Designs, Buildings, Architecture, Drawings, both Military and Civil' for five years. During the summer of the same year he visited Ireland, where the Molesworths had their seat (Breckdenstown, nr. Dublin). This led to a commission to design a country house for Speaker William Conolly at CASTLETOWN, CO. KILDARE. Although Castletown was not begun until about 1722, and was built under the direction of Sir Edward Lovett Pearce, its façade suggests an Italian palazzo, and may have been essentially Galilei's design [Maurice Craig & the Knight of Glin, 'Castletown, Co. Kildare', *C. Life*, 27 March, 3–10 April 1969]. In 1718–19 Galilei also designed the Doric portico on the east front of KIMBOLTON CASTLE, HUNTS., for the 1st Duke of Manchester. His original drawing is in the Record Office at Huntingdon [Arthur Oswald in *C. Life*, 26 Dec. 1968, and see also *C. Life*, 1 Feb. 1973, 270].

Despite these encouragements, and his marriage in September 1718 to an English girl, Letitia Martin, Galilei decided in the following year to return to Florence, where the Grand Duke promised him employment. He and his wife accordingly left England in August 1719. In Florence he found little more opportunity than he had in England, but eventually he became well known as the architect of the façade of St. John Lateran in Rome (1734), and of the Corsini Chapel in the same church (1731). He died in Rome on 21 December 1737. A portrait by Giuseppe Berti is at Castletown (*C. Life*, 13 Sept. 1979, 805).

A number of Galilei's unexecuted designs for English buildings are preserved in the state archives at Florence. Some of them are unexpectedly baroque in character, but they include a very neo-classical design for a church in the form of a Doric temple. In 1726 Sir Edward Gascoigne of Parlington in Yorkshire commissioned Galilei to design a monument to his parents. This was executed in Florence in coloured marbles and set up in BARWICK-IN-ELMET CHURCH in 1729, but was destroyed when the church was altered in 1858.

A design by Galilei for a large architectural greenhouse was published in Richard Bradley's *New Improvements of Planting and Gardening* (1717): see A. Tagliolini in *Jnl. Garden History* 6, 1986.

[Ilaria Toesca, 'Alessandro Galilei in Inghilterra', *English Miscellany*, ed. M. Praz, iii, 1952; Elizabeth Kieven, 'Galilei in England', *C. Life*, 25 Jan. 1973; Elizabeth Kieven, 'The Gascoigne Monument by Alessandro Galilei', *Leeds Arts Calendar* No. 77, 1975; Hist. MSS. Comm., *Various Collections* viii, 287, 307, etc.]

GALL, JOHN, of Aberdeen, described in Pigot's Directory of 1825–6 as a 'builder and cabinet-maker', was employed in 1827–8 on two works for Catholic clients: the conversion into a seminary of BLAIRS HOUSE, KINCARDINESHIRE [P. F. Anson, 'Catholic Church Building in Scotland', *Innes Review* v, 1954, 128, n. 6] and the design of TOMBAE R.C. CHAPEL at GLENLIVET, BANFFSHIRE. Owing to lack of funds this Gothic chapel was not completed until 1843–4 under the direction of Bishop James Kyle [Scottish Catholic Archives, PL 3/113, BL 5/204 and 206, *ex inf.* Mrs. E. Beaton].

GALLIER, JAMES (1798–1866), was the son of an Irish builder. He went to Liverpool in 1816 and walked to Manchester, where he worked in the building of a cotton mill. He returned to Ireland, where he improved his education and obtained some small building contracts, but was back in England in 1822, working as a builder while studying architecture in his spare time. In 1826–8 he was employed as clerk of works at Huntingdon Gaol, then being built to the designs of William Wilkins. While in Huntingdon he designed 'a small wooden bridge, of an original design, across a branch of the Ouse at Godmanchester'. This was the 'Chinese Bridge', built in 1827 and rebuilt in accordance with the original design in 1869 and again in 1960. In 1828–9 Gallier was in London, where he supervised the building of houses in Park Street to the designs of J. P. Gandy (*q.v.*), and was 'employed by several persons about that quarter of London to furnish plans for new buildings and alterations to old ones'. One of these clients was a coach-builder called John Robson for whom he designed a coach-factory and some houses in South Street, Mayfair. In 1832, having failed to establish a successful practice in London, Gallier left for America and settled in New Orleans, where he became the leading architect and 'made a signal contribution to the style of the Louisiana plantation houses'. [*The Autobiography of James Gallier, Architect*, Paris 1864, reprinted New York 1973; John Harris, *Catalogue of British Drawings for Architecture, etc. in American Collections*, 1971, 99–100; *Survey of London* xl, 251, 304, 331, 339.]

GANDON, JAMES (1742–1823), was born in London in February 1741/2, at the house of his grandfather, a Huguenot refugee. His father, Peter Gandon, was originally a man of substance, but nearly ruined himself by a passion for alchemy. Owing to his father's financial difficulties James's schooling was curtailed, but he afterwards studied at Shipley's Drawing Academy in St. Martin's Lane, and in 1758 means were found to apprentice him to Sir William Chambers. He began to practise on his own in about 1765. In 1767, in conjunction with John Woolfe of the Office of Works, he began to publish a continuation of Campbell's *Vitruvius Britannicus*. Although the second volume (1771) contained his own designs for the county hall at Nottingham, the venture seems to have been less an advertisement than a genuine attempt to provide a record of recent English architecture. A third volume was contemplated. Though stated in the list of subscribers to the second to be 'in great forwardness', it was never published. In 1767 Gandon also published a set of *Six Designs of Frizes*, followed in 1778 by *A Collection of Antique and Modern Ornaments* and *A Collection of Frizes Capitals and Grotesque Ornaments*.

Gandon exhibited at the Free Society of Artists in 1762 and 1763, at the Society of Artists from 1765 to 1773, and at the Royal Academy from 1774 to 1780. On the establishment of the Royal Academy Schools in 1769 he became a student, and won the first Gold Medal awarded for architecture. Nottingham County Hall, his first public building, was begun in 1770, and in 1776 he won the first prize of £100 for a design for St. Luke's Hospital or lunatic asylum in London (not built, but exhibited at the R.A. by Gandon in 1778).

The origins of Gandon's connection with Ireland can be traced to the years 1768–9, when he was placed second in the competition for the Royal Exchange at Dublin. In 1774 his first exhibited drawing at the Royal Academy was 'a design for a villa for a gentleman in Ireland'. As a pupil of Chambers, he had met the latter's client Lord Charlemont, the chief patron of the arts in Ireland, and his friend Paul Sandby introduced him to Lord Carlow, afterwards Earl of Portarlington, who gave him an introduction to John Beresford, later Chief Commissioner of the Irish Revenue. After refusing a tempting but uncertain offer of employment at the Russian Court, he was persuaded to go to Dublin in 1781 in order to superintend the construction of the new docks, stores and Custom House, designs for which he had made in 1780 at the instance of Lord Carlow. The building of the Custom House was attended by great difficulties, both physical and human. The site was liable to flooding, the whole project was opposed by the Corporation, and there was a serious lack of skilled workmen. But with the support of Beresford, and by his own determined conduct, Gandon successfully overcame all obstacles, and this great building, 'the Dublin counterpart to Somerset House', was completed in 1791. At the same time he was engaged on several important buildings in the Irish capital, including the Four Courts and the portico of the Parliament House, now the Bank of Ireland. The year before the rebellion of 1798 he thought it prudent to remove his family to London, but in 1799 he returned to Dublin in order to resume work. In 1808 he handed over control to his pupil H. A. Baker, and retired to the estate called Canonbrook which he had bought at Lucan, nr. Dublin, where he died of gout on 24 December 1823. He was buried in the churchyard of Drumcondra in the same grave as his friend Francis Grose the antiquary.

Although constantly subjected to hostile criticism from those who considered his buildings too pretentious and too costly, Gandon could always rely on the support of his powerful friends in the government, under whose patronage he was able to make an outstanding contribution to the architectural embellishment of the Irish capital. Like his master Sir William Chambers, he rejected what he regarded as the meretricious elegance of the current Adam style, and looked to French neo-classicism to reinvigorate the expiring tradition of English Palladianism. French influence is evident in the simplified Doric façade of his County Hall at Nottingham, and it is also apparent in many features of his public buildings in Dublin. But the dome of the Custom House and the façade of the Four Courts show that Gandon was also indebted to Wren, and this readiness to learn from a pre-Palladian architect helps to explain why Gandon's public buildings are so much more effectively monumental than Chambers's Somerset House.

Gandon became a Fellow of the Society of Artists in 1771, but failed to secure election as A.R.A. in 1776. In 1791 he was made an honorary member of the London Architects' Club on its foundation, and he was an original member of the Royal Irish Academy. A biographical memoir, based on materials arranged by his son James, was published in Dublin in 1846. It incorporates the texts of two writings by Gandon entitled 'The Progress of Architecture in Ireland' and 'Hints for erecting Testimonials'. A new edition by Maurice Craig (1969) includes a list of portraits of the architect, of which the most important is the one by Tilly Kettle and William Cuming in the National Gallery of Ireland. H. A. Baker (1753–1836) and Sir Richard Morrison (1767–1849) were Gandon's pupils.

[Obituaries in *Gent's Mag.* 1824 (i), 464–5, and *Literary Gazette*, no. 372, 6 March 1824, 156; *The Life of James Gandon*, from materials collected by his son, edited by T. Mulvany, Dublin 1846, new edition by Maurice Craig, London 1969; 'Memoirs of Thomas Jones', *Walpole Soc.* xxxii, 1946–8, 15–17, 20, 21, 23; *A.P.S.D.*; *D.N.B.*; Maurice Craig, *Dublin 1660–1860*, 1952, 2nd ed. 1992, chap. xxi; Maurice Craig, 'Burlington, Adam and Gandon', *Jnl. Warburg & Courtauld Institutes* xvii, 1954, 381–2; E. McParland, 'James Gandon and the Royal Exchange Competition, 1768–69', *Jnl. Royal Society of Antiquaries of Ireland* 102 (i), 1972; E. McParland, *James Gandon, Vitruvius Hibernicus*, 1985.]

The following list of executed works is based on Appendix I of McParland's biography, in which full references will be found.

THE WODEHOUSE, WOMBOURNE, STAFFS., temple or mausoleum to memory of Handel, 'erected in a wood belonging to Sir Samuel Hellier in Staffordshire', exhibited at Society of Artists 1768; dem. (McParland, fig. 13).

NOTTINGHAM, THE COUNTY HALL, HIGH PAVEMENT, 1770–2; extended 1876–80 (*Vitruvius Britannicus* v, pl. 72 shows the executed design, and pls. 73–77 an alternative scheme not adopted); façade altered and interior rebuilt by T. C. Hine 1877–9.

HEYWOOD, CO. LAOIS, IRELAND, for Michael Frederick Trench, *c.*1770; dem. In 1771 S. White exhibited at the Society of Artists the 'Front of Mr. Trench's house in Ireland, from a design of Mr. Gandon's'. Trench was an amateur architect and may have been partly responsible for the design of the house.

MILL HOUSE, EASTBOURNE, SUSSEX, a windmill conversion for John Hamilton Mortimer, *c.*1770; dem.

WYNNSTAY, DENBIGHSHIRE, designs for Theatre

for Sir Watkin Williams-Wynn, 1771, perhaps executed later as the Theatre (dem. 1858) bore the date 1782.

LLANGEDWYN, DENBIGHSHIRE, Mill for Sir Watkin Williams-Wynn, 1771.

LONDON, MONTAGU HOUSE, 22 PORTMAN SQUARE, assisted or collaborated with James Stuart in design of house for Mrs. Elizabeth Montagu, *c.*1780; dem. 1940.

DUBLIN, THE CUSTOM HOUSE, 1781–91; interior destroyed 1921.

WATERFORD, IRELAND, COURT HOUSE and GAOL, 1784; dem. 1837–40.

NEW GENEVA, CO. WATERFORD, IRELAND, model town for refugee Genevan craftsmen, begun 1784 but abandoned soon afterwards: see Hubert Butler, 'New Geneva in Waterford', *Jnl. Royal Society of Antiquaries of Ireland* lxxvii, 1947.

DUBLIN, THE ROTUNDA ASSEMBLY ROOMS, advice on design which appears to have resulted in the heightening of the exterior and its embellishment with a neo-classical frieze for which Gandon probably provided a drawing.

DUBLIN, THE PARLIAMENT HOUSE (now Bank of Ireland), added E. (Corinthian) portico to House of Lords and curved screen-wall, 1784–7 (the three-quarter Ionic columns were added to Gandon's astylar screen-wall in 1804–8). Gandon made designs for the W. (Ionic) portico to the House of Commons, built *c.*1787–93, but was not responsible for the executed version.

COOLBANAGHER CHURCH and MAUSOLEUM, CO. LAOIS, IRELAND, for 1st Earl of Portarlington, 1785; chancel added in 19th century.

DUBLIN, THE FOUR COURTS, 1786–1802, incorporating S. and W. sides of quadrangle designed by T. Cooley, 1776–84; interior destroyed 1922.

DUBLIN, THE MILITARY INFIRMARY (now Army Headquarters), PHOENIX PARK, 1786 (executed, with altered design for cupola, by W. Gibson, architect to the Barrack Board).

SANDYMOUNT, DUBLIN, villa (now Roslyn Park) for William Ashford, 1788–9.

DUBLIN, CHARLEMONT HOUSE, RUTLAND (now Parnell) SQUARE, THE ROCKINGHAM LIBRARY, for 1st Earl of Charlemont, 1789; dem. *c.*1930.

DUBLIN, BERESFORD PLACE, terrace of houses for J. C. Beresford, executed with modifications, 1790–3.

ABBEVILLE, nr. MALAHIDE, CO. DUBLIN, IRELAND, alterations and additions for John Beresford, 1790.

CARRICKGLAS, CO. LONGFORD, IRELAND, office court and gateway for Sir William Gleadowe Newcomen, Bart., *c.*1790–5.

EMO PARK (DAWSON COURT), CO. LAOIS, for 1st Earl of Portarlington (d. 1798), *c.*1790–8; completed later by A. & J. Williamson.

DUBLIN, CARLISLE BRIDGE (R. Liffey), 1791–4; replaced 1880 by O'Connell Bridge.

EMSWORTH, CO. DUBLIN, IRELAND, for J. Woodmason, 1794.

PORTLAOISE (originally MARYBOROUGH) CHURCH, CO. LAOIS, tower and spire, 1800.

DUBLIN, THE KING'S INNS, begun 1800, continued under Gandon's direction until *c.*1808, then completed by H. A. Baker and Francis Johnstone (who designed the cupola and the gateway to Henrietta Street).

WALWORTH, BALLYKELLY, CO. DERRY, minor works to house for John Beresford, 1804.

LUCAN CHURCH, CO. DUBLIN, IRELAND, built 1823 to designs made earlier by Gandon.

GANDY, afterwards **DEERING,** JOHN PETER (1787–1850), was the younger brother of Joseph and Michael Gandy (*q.v.*). He showed artistic leanings at an early age, and became a pupil of James Wyatt. He was admitted to the Royal Academy Schools in 1805, and was awarded the Silver Medal the following year. After leaving Wyatt's office he secured a post in the Barrack Office which he was allowed to retain when, in 1811–13, he undertook a journey to Greece and Asia Minor on behalf of the Society of Dilettanti, in company with Sir William Gell and F. Bedford. The results of their researches were published in 1817 as the *Unedited Antiquities of Attica*, and in the third volume of the *Ionian Antiquities*, issued in 1840 (see above, p. 116). With Gell, he was co-author of *Pompeiana*, 1817–19, which was for many years the standard work on the excavations then in progress at Pompeii. In 1830 he was elected a member of the Society of Dilettanti.

In 1810 Gandy was awarded the first prize in the competition for the new Bethlehem Hospital. His design, submitted under the motto *Dum spiro, spero*, was not, however, carried out. The original drawings are in St. Bartholomew's Hospital archives. The plan is illustrated in *Survey of London* xxv, pl. 38. In 1825 Gandy was the runner-up in the competition for the design of University College London, won by Wilkins, and was subsequently employed by the latter to assist in the execution of his plans. Gandy's design for a new House of Commons is among those illustrated in *Parliamentary Papers*, 1833 (487), xii, and his plan for a Public Record Office is given in *Proceedings of the Record Commissioners*, ed. C. P. Cooper, 1833, 227–9. An unexecuted design for Broomhall, Fife, made for Lord Elgin and exhibited at the

Royal Academy in 1827 and 1829, is preserved at that house. With the exception of the Tudor Gothic hospital at Stamford and the interior of the courtyard at Burleigh, most of Gandy's executed works were in an elegant and sophisticated neo-classical style of which the Greek Revival St. Mark's Church in North Audley Street is a characteristic example.

In 1828 Gandy assumed the name of Deering, on inheriting the estate known as The Lee, nr. Great Missenden, Bucks., which had been left to him by his friend Henry Deering. After this he gradually gave up the practice of his profession, and devoted himself to public life and the management of his property. He was appointed High Sheriff of Bucks. in 1840, and was elected M.P. for Aylesbury in 1847. He was elected A.R.A. in 1826, and R.A. in 1838 – an honour scarcely justified by the professional inactivity of his later life. He had, however acquired a considerable reputation both as an authority on Greek architecture and as a practising architect, before his conversion into a country gentleman cut short his professional career. [*A.P.S.D.*; *D.N.B.*; *The Times*, 6 June 1952 ('A Greek Bas-Relief').]

LONDON, THE UNITED UNIVERSITY CLUB-HOUSE, PALL MALL EAST, in collaboration with W. Wilkins, 1822–6; attic storey added 1850–1; building dem. 1906 [*A.P.S.D.*] (plan and elevation in *A New Survey of London*, J. Weale, 1853 i, 294).

LONDON, ST. MARK'S CHURCH, NORTH AUDLEY STREET, 1825–8; interior reconstructed by A. W. Blomfield, 1878 [*Gent's Mag.* 1829 (ii), 393].

LONDON, No. 28 UPPER GROSVENOR STREET, for Mrs. Curran, 1826–7; dem. [T. L. Donaldson, *Handbook of Specifications*, 1860, 670].

STAMFORD, LINCS., THE INFIRMARY, 1826–8, Tudor Gothic [exhib. at R.A. 1827; G. Burton, *Chronology of Stamford*, 1846, 201].

DUMFRIES HOUSE, AYRSHIRE, lodge for 2nd Marquess of Bute, 1827 [exhib. at R.A. 1827].

CARDIFF, GLAMORGANSHIRE, COUNTY GAOL, 1827–32 [*Carmarthen Jnl.*, 1 July 1825, *ex inf.* Mr. T. Lloyd].

LONDON, MELBOURNE (now DOVER) HOUSE, WHITEHALL, alterations for 1st Viscount Melbourne, before 1828 [payment by Lord Melbourne's executors 'for architectural services and superintending sundry works at Whitehall' in archives at Melbourne Hall, Derbyshire, *ex inf.* Mr. Edward Saunders].

BURGHLEY HOUSE, NORTHANTS., remodelled interior of courtyard, forming corridors, for 2nd Marquess of Exeter, 1828 [drawings at Burghley].

LONDON, houses in SOUTH STREET, MAYFAIR, for the Revd. John Sanford, *c.*1828–30; dem. except Nos. 15 and 24 [*Survey of London* xl, 331, 339; for Gandy's dispute with Sanford see S.R.O., GD 152/53/2/12–13].

LONDON, THE PIMLICO GRAMMAR SCHOOL (later LITERARY INSTITUTION), EBURY STREET, 1830 [*A.P.S.D.*].

LONDON, EXETER HALL, STRAND, 1830–1; dem. 1907 [exhib. at R.A. 1830] (*Survey of London* xviii, pl. 111).

SHRUBLAND PARK, SUFFOLK, alterations and additions for Sir W. F. Middleton, Bart., 1831–3; subsequently altered by Sir Charles Barry 1848–52 [exhib. at R.A. 1831] (*C. Life*, 19–26 Nov. 1953).

GANDY, JOSEPH MICHAEL (1771–1843), was the son of a man employed at White's Club, St. James's. When James Wyatt rebuilt the clubhouse in 1787–8, he was shown some of Gandy's sketches, and offered to take their author, then aged 15, into his office. In 1789 Gandy entered the Royal Academy School, winning the Silver Medal the same year, and the Gold Medal in 1790. In 1794 John Martindale, the proprietor of White's, sent him to Italy at his own expense. He travelled in company with C. H. Tatham, and achieved the distinction of being awarded a special medal by the Academy of St. Luke.[1] But Martindale's bankruptcy in 1797, combined with the advance of Napoleon's armies into Italy, put him in a serious plight, from which he was luckily rescued by a King's Messenger known to his family, who brought him home late in 1797.

Arriving in England in wartime, Gandy saw little prospect of establishing himself in practice immediately. Instead, he found employment as a draughtsman in the office of Sir John Soane, to whom he was, in one way or other, to be indebted for financial assistance for the rest of his life. He practised on his own from 1801, and in 1803 was elected A.R.A., perhaps through Soane's influence, as he had so far done little independent work. In 1808 he undertook to act as tutor to Soane's eldest son, and in 1809 he and his pupil went to Liverpool, where Gandy had entered into a short-lived partnership with the sculptor and

[1] His *prova* (a design for a triumphal arch) is in the Cooper Union Museum, New York.

modeller George Bullock (d. 1818).[1] In 1811 he returned to London, and, in the intervals of a never very extensive practice, was employed by Soane to make elaborate watercolour perspectives of his architectural designs. But with a wife and nine children to support, Gandy was constantly in financial difficulties, and in 1816, rather than declare himself a bankrupt, he allowed himself to be imprisoned in the Fleet. He is said to have been 'odd and impracticable in disposition', and it seems likely that he was temperamentally unsuited to the exacting routine of a working architect's office. In default of commissions, he devoted most of his energies to painting the architectural fantasies which he exhibited at the Royal Academy almost without a break from 1800 to 1838. It is these extraordinary compositions, highly eclectic in their stylistic sources, but all inspired by a romantic vision akin to that of Coleridge or Turner, that give Gandy a unique place in English architectural history. His independent approach to architectural aesthetics is also seen in his designs for cottages, whose studied simplicity is in pointed contrast to the picturesque artificiality of the *cottage orné*. These he published in 1805 in two separate works entitled *The Rural Architect* and *Designs for Cottages, Cottage Farms and Other Rural Buildings*, the latter being dedicated to Thomas Hope. Gandy also made drawings to illustrate topographical works such as Britton's *Architectural Antiquities*. His only other recorded publication was a paper entitled 'The Philosophy of Architecture', printed in *The Magazine of the Fine Arts* i, 1821, 289, 370.

Gandy died in December 1843. He left a son, Thomas, who became a portrait-painter. At Liverpool he had a pupil called R. Elland, of whom nothing further is known.

Many of Gandy's drawings are preserved in the collections of the Soane Museum, the R.I.B.A. and the Victoria and Albert Museum. See also J. Harris, *Catalogue of British Drawings for Architecture, etc. in American Collections*, 1971, 103. His unexecuted designs for the Government House at Quebec, exhibited at the R.A. in 1812, and now in the Public Archives at Ottawa, are described by J. F. C. Smith, 'Drawings from the Archives, Ottawa', *Jnl. Royal Architectural Institute of Canada* xv, 1938. A typescript copy of his correspondence with his father while in Italy is in the R.I.B.A. Library, together with the MS. of a projected encyclopaedic compilation on architecture.

[*A.P.S.D.*; *D.N.B.*; S. Redgrave, *Dictionary of Artists of the English School*, 1878, 166; A. T. Bolton, *The Portrait of Sir John Soane*, 1927, *passim*; John Summerson, 'The Vision of J. M. Gandy', in *Heavenly Mansions*, 1949; *Joseph Michael Gandy*, exhibition catalogue, Architectural Association 1982.]

LANCASTER CASTLE, completed COUNTY COURTS and GAOL begun by Thomas Harrison, 1802–23, and designed FEMALE PENITENTIARY, 1818–21 [drawings of Courts in Soane Museum, xxxv, 7; *The Farington Diary*, ed. J. Greig, ii, 167, vi, 227; drawings exhibited by Gandy at R.A. in 1817, 1822 and 1823; for the extent of Gandy's responsibility for the design of the interiors see J. M. Crook in *C. Life*, 15 April 1971, 878–9].

STORRS HALL, WINDERMERE, WESTMORLAND, boat-house for Sir John Legard, Bart., exhib. at R.A. 1804. In 1804 Sir J. Legard built an octagonal temple on the shore of the lake which may have been designed by Gandy (*C. Life*, 29 Nov. 1962, 1338).

LONDON, THE PHOENIX FIRE AND PELICAN LIFE INSURANCE OFFICES, CHARING CROSS, 1804–5; dem. [exhib. at R.A. 1805] (*Survey of London* xvi, pls. 89–90).

LANCASTER, PUBLIC BATH, No. 43 BATH STREET, exhib. at R.A. 1806.

BOLTON HALL, BOLTON-BY-BOWLAND, YORKS. (W.R.), rebuilt south front and other alterations in the Gothic style for John Bolton, 1806–8 [*Gent's Mag.* 1841 (i), 581].

STORRS HALL, WINDERMERE, WESTMORLAND, remodelled for John Bolton, 1808–11 [exhib. at R.A. 1808, 1811].

BATH, 'DORIC HOUSE', SION HILL, for Thomas Barker, 1818 [exhib. at R.A. 1818 as 'now building', but apparently begun some years earlier; W. Ison, *The Georgian Buildings of Bath*, 1948, 182 and pl. 107].

LEYTONSTONE, ESSEX, house near, exhibited at R.A. 1819 as 'building': possibly Wallwood House, rebuilt for William Cotton *c.*1820; dem. *c.*1905.

BIRMINGHAM, villa 'to be built near' exhib. at R.A. 1819.

CLUMBER HOUSE, NOTTS., 'proposed addition' for 4th Duke of Newcastle, exhib. at R.A. 1820, probably not carried out. The house was partly rebuilt 1879 and dem. 1938.

SWERFORD HOUSE, nr. CHIPPING NORTON, OXON., alterations and additions for Sir Robert Bolton, 1824 [exhib. at R.A. 1824 as 'now erecting'].

LONDON, LAMBETH: in 1825 Gandy exhibited at the R.A. 'Dwelling houses etc. now

[1] J. M. Gandy may have been related to a Liverpool painter named Samuel Gandy (d. *c.*1790), which would explain why several of his architectural commissions were in the north-west of England.

building in Vauxhall Road, and other places'. These probably included No. 363 KENNINGTON LANE, built in 1824 (*Survey of London* xxvi, 38) and Nos. 238–46 WANDSWORTH ROAD (dem. 1953) [John Summerson, *Georgian London*, 1945, 288–9].

LIVERPOOL, 'the subscribers' billiard-room', exhibited at R.A. 1826 as built under Gandy's superintendence and presumably to be identified with the Rotunda in Bold Street, a circular building erected 1809 for the exhibition of panoramic views, but subsequently converted into a subscribers' billard-room; dem. *c.*1864 (cf. J. A. Picton, *Memorials of Liverpool* ii, 1875, 237).

INCE BLUNDELL, LANCS., design for an entrance hall for Henry Blundell (d. 1810), exhibited at the R.A. 1832 and probably not executed.

GANDY, MICHAEL (1778–1862), was Joseph Gandy's younger brother. He was from 1793 a pupil and from October 1796, an assistant, of James Wyatt. He exhibited at the Royal Academy in 1795, 1796 and 1797 and in 1796 was admitted to the R.A. Schools. He subsequently 'accepted an appointment in the Indian naval service' and served in India and China. In 1812 he exhibited at the Royal Academy a view of the burning of Onrust and Kupers Islands, Batavia, in 1800, 'taken on the spot'. On his return, he was employed as a draughtsman by Edward Holl, civil architect to the Navy, also by Francis Goodwin, and afterwards by Sir Jeffry Wyatville, with whom he had been for thirty-three years at the time of the latter's death in 1840. In conjunction with Benjamin Baud, he published *Architectural Illustrations of Windsor Castle*, with an introduction by John Britton, fol. 1842. [*A.P.S.D.*; typescript of J. M. Gandy's correspondence with his father in R.I.B.A. Library, pp. 107, 208, 213, 226.]

GANE, JESSE (1798–1855), was a builder at Evercreech in Somerset. Between 1825 and 1835 he refitted the interior of EVERCREECH CHURCH, as recorded by an inscription on the gallery, and in 1843–4 he rebuilt the S. aisle to match the medieval N. one [I.C.B.S.]. In Somerset he also rebuilt the bodies of STOKE LANE (1838) and CHILCOMPTON (1839) CHURCHES, added a N. aisle to PENSELWOOD CHURCH (1848–9) [I.C.B.S.], remodelled LAMYATT RECTORY (1833), and designed EAST PENNARD RECTORY (1841, Tudor Gothic) [Somerset C.R.O., D/D/Bbm, 63, 81]. A tablet in Evercreech Church records his death on 18 April 1855, aged 57.

GANSEL, DAVID (1691–1753), was the son of a Huguenot refugee who had married into a prosperous Essex family of similar Huguenot origin. His father had acquired an estate at Leyton in that county, and in 1720 David, who was High Sheriff in 1716, built a house called LEYTON GRANGE (dem. 1860), which is illustrated in *Vitruvius Britannicus* iii (1725), pl. 94, where Colen Campbell states that Gansel 'designed and executed it himself'. A villa in character, it was baroque rather than Palladian in style, and its inclusion in *Vitruvius Britannicus* must presumably have been due to some personal contact between Campbell and Gansel. Gansel sold Leyton Grange some time after 1730, when he bought East Donyland Hall, where he is said to have 'made a park and greatly improved the house and gardens'. [R. Vigne, 'David Gansel of Leyton Grange and East Donyland Hall', *Proc. Huguenot Soc.* xxiii, 1977–82; P. Muilman, *History of Essex*, 6, 1772, 158; *V.C.H. Essex* vi, 186–7.]

GARBETT, EDWARD WILLIAM, was the son of William Garbett of Winchester (*q.v.*). By 1819 he was established in practice in Reading, where in that year he surveyed the tower of St. Lawrence's Church [*Berkshire Arch. Jnl.* liv, 1954–5, 80]. In 1821 he was thanked by the vestry of ST. GILES' CHURCH, READING, 'for the liberal and able manner in which he has afforded the committee [for enlarging the church] his gratuitous assistance' [MS. Vestry Minutes]. In 1820–2 he designed THEALE CHURCH, BERKS., in a remarkably precocious and accurate 'Early English' style derived from Salisbury Cathedral [*Quarterly Review* xxvii, 1822, 323]. The tower was added in 1827–8 by John Buckler, among whose drawings in the British Library is 'Mr. Garbett's original design' [Add. MS. 36357, 5–66]. The apse was added in 1892. Garbett also designed the church of HOLY TRINITY, READING, begun by him in 1825, but 'completed under the superintendence of Mr. Finlayson' [J. Doran, *History of Reading*, 1835, 167–8]. Garbett's west front was rebuilt by J. Billing in 1846 [*Ecclesiologist* vi, 1846, 196].

Garbett must subsequently have returned to Winchester, probably to assist his father, for in 1833–4 'Mr. Edward Garbett of Winchester' was consulted by the Corporation of Bath over the repair of the tower of BATH ABBEY CHURCH [Council Minutes, *ex inf.* Mr. J. Orbach]. Soon after his father's death he advertised his services in the *Hampshire Chronicle* (13 Oct. 1834), but failed to succeed to his post as surveyor to the Dean and Chapter. In 1843–5 he was living in London at 17 Fludyer Street, but no further record of him has been found thereafter.

GARBETT, WILLIAM (*c.*1770–1834), was for twenty-five years surveyor to the Dean and Chapter of Winchester, for whom he carried out extensive repairs to the Cathedral during the years 1812–28, including the reconstruction of two defective piers. The Dean and Chapter thought it necessary to take advice from John Nash as to the manner in which this should be done. Garbett resented the intervention of one who showed 'a predisposition to dictate rather than to consult', and in 1824 he published a pamphlet entitled *Observations and Correspondence occasioned by the Failure and Renovation of a Principal Pier in Winchester Cathedral.* There is a copy in Sir John Soane's Museum. Garbett's work at Winchester included the design of the episcopal throne and of a stone choir-screen, replaced by Scott in 1875 [*Gent's Mag.* 1827 (ii), 194, 411, 1828 (ii), 310–14; Winkles, *Illustrations of the Cathedral Churches of England and Wales* i, 1836, 133–4].

Other works by Garbett were: Tudor Gothic additions to HERON COURT, HANTS., for the 1st Earl of Malmesbury, 1807–15 [G. F. Prosser, *Select Illustrations of Hampshire*, 1833; *Views of the Principal Seats and Landscape Scenery in the Neighbourhood of Lymington*, drawn by L. Haghe, 1832]; the restoration in 1817 of the hall of WINCHESTER COLLEGE [T. F. Kirby, *Annals of Winchester College*, 1892, 42]; the stucco Gothic vault inserted in the nave of CHRISTCHURCH PRIORY CHURCH, HANTS., in 1819 [*Gent's Mag.* 1820 (i), 232]; UPHAM RECTORY, HANTS., 1820 [Winchester Diocesan Records]; BINFIELD RECTORY, BERKS., 1821 [Salisbury Diocesan Records]; a Greek Revival boat-house and temple combined on AWBRIDGE DANES WATER, HANTS., 1822, upper part rebuilt 1925 but see reproduction of Garbett's original design in R.I.B.A. Collection in Alistair Rowan, *Garden Buildings*, R.I.B.A. Drawings Series 1968; and the new (Gothic) buildings of ST. JOHN'S HOSPITAL in THE HIGH STREET, WINCHESTER, whose erection was in progress at the time of his death [*Hampshire Chronicle*, 8 Sept. 1834].

In 1820–2 the existing north and south blocks of the street front of MAGDALEN HALL (now HERTFORD COLLEGE), OXFORD, were built to Garbett's designs (and not, as stated in most modern works, by his son) [*Gent's Mag.* 1820 (i), 463; signed drawings in Oxford University archives UD/36/3/2 and Magdalen College archives]. In 1822 he was paid £34 13s. by St. John's College, 'for Plans of Beaumont Street'. A unified design for the street, with Greek Revival detailing, survives in the college archives, and can be attributed to Garbett (T. Hinchcliffe, *North Oxford*, 1992, fig. 6). This was not adopted, and it is not clear whether Garbett had any responsibility for the design of the street as built from 1823 onwards.

Garbett was the author of the account of Winchester in Britton's *Picturesque Antiquities of the English Cities*, 1830, and a letter from him about the history of the Cathedral was printed by Britton in his *Cathedral Antiquities.* He died on 31 August 1834, in his 65th year, and is commemorated by a tablet in the north transept of the Cathedral. He was the father of Edward William Garbett (*q.v.*), and the grandfather of Edward Lacy Garbett (d. 1900), the author of a *Treatise on the Principles of Design in Architecture* (1850) and of numerous religious tracts [will in Hants. Record Office]. O. B. Carter (*q.v.*) was his pupil.

GARDINER, JOHN BULL (1786–1867), was a pupil and afterwards a partner of Robert Chapman (*q.v.*). He was admitted to the Royal Academy Schools in 1808, and exhibited from 1803 to 1813. He became surveyor to the parish of St. Olave, Hart Street, London, and in 1823 repaired ST. OLAVE'S CHURCH, inserting Gothic tracery in the east window [G. Godwin, *The Churches of London* i, 1838; *Gent's Mag.* 1823 (i), 206–7, 315–17]. His work was destroyed by bombing in 1940–1. He was also surveyor to the Wise estate in Westminster. Gardiner, who was a Fellow of the Institute of British Architects, died at Brighton on 7 January 1867, aged 81. Three drawings by him for the decoration of the SPANISH AND PORTUGUESE SYNAGOGUE, BEVIS MARKS, LONDON, are in the R.I.B.A. Collection.

GARDNER, THOMAS (*c.*1737–1804), was an architect and builder at Uttoxeter in Staffordshire. By trade he was a carpenter, and his forbears had been carpenters and farmers in Leicestershire for at least a century. In 1764 he was still a journeyman, working on the Derby Assembly Rooms under Joseph Pickford at 2s. a day. Shortly afterwards he became Pickford's clerk and worked for him both at Etruria and at Sandon Hall. In 1772 after the death of his father he had sufficient capital to set up in partnership with Thomas Freeman, a builder of Derby. The partnership was dissolved in March 1776, and for the remainder of his life Gardner carried on an independent business as an architect and builder at Uttoxeter, where he died on 8 October 1804 and is commemorated by a tablet in the parish church. He designed several country houses in the vicinity in a plain Georgian style. [Edward Saunders in *Derbyshire Life*, Aug. 1972, 41; will, P.C.C. 345 NELSON.]

UTTOXETER, STAFFS., house overlooking churchyard for Thomas Hart, 1777 [advertisement in *Derby Mercury*, 3 Jan. 1777, announcing the recent dissolution of the partnership between Gardner and Freeman, but stating that 'the buildings now carrying on for Sir Henry Cavendish Bart. at Doveridge and Mr. Thomas Hart of Uttoxeter . . . are to be jointly carried on by the said T.G. and T.F.'].

DOVERIDGE HALL, DERBYSHIRE, works for Sir Henry Cavendish, Bart., 1777; dem. 1934 [advertisement cited above; Edward Saunders, 'Doveridge Hall', *Derbyshire Life*, Aug. 1972].

attributed: WIGGINTON CHURCH, STAFFS., 1777; chancel added 1862 [design among Faculty Papers in Lichfield Joint Record Office attributed to Gardner by Mr. Edward Saunders].

LONGTON HALL, STAFFS., extensive alterations for J. E. Heathcote, 1777; dem. 1939 [E. Meteyard, *Life of Josiah Wedgwood* ii, 1866, 373].

UTTOXETER, STAFFS., conduit in Market Place, 1780; dem. *c.*1850 [F. Redfern, *History of Uttoxeter*, 1886, 418].

FARLEY HALL, STAFFS., altered and refronted for C. Bill, 1782 [drawings and agreement in Staffs. Record Office, D554, bundle 105].

ROLLESTON HALL, STAFFS., alterations for Sir Oswald Mosley, Bart., *c.*1785; dem. 1928 [Sir O. Mosley, *Family Memoirs*, 1849, 64].

CHURCH GRESLEY CHURCH, DERBYSHIRE, repairs, 1786; restored 1872 [bill among Gresley papers in Derbyshire Record Office].

APPLEBY HALL, APPLEBY PARVA, LEICS., for Revd. Thomas Moore, 1786; dem. 1922–3 [contract in private possession, *ex inf.* Mr. Maxwell Craven].

SUDBURY HALL, DERBYSHIRE, built and presumably designed a lodge for 1st Lord Vernon, 1787 [Derbyshire C.R.O., Vernon papers, account-book D 410M.8/8].

STRELLEY HALL, NOTTS., for T. W. Edge, 1789–92 [drawings and building accounts in Notts. C.R.O., DDE 46/60].

WILLERSLEY CASTLE, DERBYSHIRE, works for Richard Arkwright, *c.*1792–5, including reconstruction after fire of 8 Aug. 1791 and design of stables and entrance gates [account-book belonging to Col. P. Arkwright].

STRATTON AUDLEY HOUSE, OXON., alterations and additions for Admiral Sir J. Borlase Warren of Stapleford Hall, Notts., 1797–8 [Derbyshire, C.R.O., Vernon papers, volume of 'Papers relating to Stapleford, Stratton Audley, etc.', ff. 264–81].

THORPE CONSTANTINE HALL, STAFFS., remodelled for William Inge, 1799 [signed drawings at Thorpe Hall, *ex inf.* Prof. Andor Gomme].

GARLAND, ROBERT (*c.*1808–1863), entered the Royal Academy Schools in December 1827 at the age of 19. He exhibited student's work at the Academy from 1826 to 1831. His name appears on the title-page of Winkles's *Cathedral Churches of England and Wales*, 1836–42, as the author of the drawings engraved in that work. In the 1840s he was in partnership with Henry Christopher (d. 1854) at 11 John Street, Adelphi. They jointly designed a new W. tower for ALL SAINTS CHURCH, UPPER NORWOOD, SURREY, in 1838–9 [I.C.B.S.], and a design for a terrace of houses on the north side of Eccleston Square, Westminster, signed 'Garland & Christopher Architects', is in the Cooper Union Museum, New York [J. Harris, *Catalogue of British Drawings for Architecture, etc. in American Collections*, 1971, 103]. Garland died in Hammersmith on 2 April 1863 [Principal Probate Registry, Calendar of Probates].

GARLING, HENRY (1789–1870), was articled to Samuel Page (*q.v.*). Immediately after the expiration of his articles, he assisted Page to carry out alterations to GRIMSTHORPE CASTLE, LINCS., for the 2nd Lord Gwydyr (afterwards 19th Lord Willoughby de Eresby). Framed drawings at Grimsthorpe are dated 1811 and endorsed 'Samuel Page Architect, Henry Garling fecit'. According to the writer of Garling's obituary, 'Mr. Page never answering any letters . . . Mr. Garling acted for him in superintending (in fact, designing and doing everything), in the remodelling of Grimsthorpe Castle'. In 1815 Garling was admitted to the Royal Academy Schools, winning the Silver Medal in 1818. He commenced practice on his own at about this time, and was extensively employed in making valuations for leases, mortgages, dilapidations, etc. In about 1821 he became surveyor to the estates of Rugby School. His principal architectural work was the CORN MARKET at GUILDFORD, erected by subscription in 1818, of which he published a print the following year. The market was closed in 1901, but the Tuscan portico survives. He also designed an entrance lodge and gates for Lord St. John at MELCHBOURNE PARK, BEDS., which he exhibited at the Royal Academy in 1833, and the HOLBORN UNION WORKHOUSE.

He carried out work for Baron Vaughan and Earl Spencer and for the Carron Iron Company of Thames Street, London. He retired in 1847 after a successful career. He was a member of the Institute of British Architects, a governor of Christ's Hospital, St. Thomas's Hospital, The Bethlehem Hospital and other institutions, and possessed a fine library. He died on 9 April 1870. His son, Henry Bayly Garling (1822–1909), succeeded to his practice. [Obituary in *Builder* xxviii, 1870, 384.]

GARRETT, DANIEL (–1753), was one of Lord Burlington's protégés, assisting him as clerk of works in many of his early building projects. In 1736, when proposing to bring Garrett to Castle Howard, in order to give advice on the completion of the Mausoleum, Sir Thomas Robinson wrote to Lord Carlisle that 'My L[d] Burlington has a much better opinion of Mr. Garret's knowledge and judgment than of Mr. Flitcroft's or any person whatever, except Mr. Kent, he lives in Burlington House and has had care and conduct of the Duke of Richmond's house [in Whitehall], my L[d] Harrington's [at Petersham] and all my L[ds] designs he ever gave.' In 1727 Garrett was given a subordinate post in the Office of Works as Labourer in Trust at Richmond New Park Lodge, where his immediate superior was Roger Morris, and subsequently in 1729 at Windsor also. In due course he might have risen to a clerkship of the works, but in 1737 he was dismissed for 'not attending his duty'. By now he had in fact begun to build up an architectural practice of his own which, being largely in the north of England, was no doubt incompatible with the performance of his duties at Windsor and Richmond. From about 1735 onwards he was engaged in remodelling Wallington Hall in Northumberland for Sir Walter Blackett; in 1736 his services were in demand at Castle Howard; and in 1737 Sir Thomas Robinson reported that he had introduced Garrett to Lord Derby, 'for whom he has drawn some plans, and who is greatly pleased with his works'. In 1741 Garrett was one of the architects consulted by Sir James Dashwood before rebuilding his house at Kirtlington in Oxfordshire, and in the course of the next few years he is known to have designed two country houses in Northumberland and various buildings at Gibside in Durham. In 1747 he published a book of engravings entitled *Designs and Estimates of farm-houses, etc. for the County of York, Northumberland, Cumberland, Westmoreland and Bishoprick of Durham.* This was the first publication ever to be devoted entirely to farmhouses, and originated 'from the great complaint of gentlemen, who have built farm-houses, that they were irregular, expensive, and frequently too large for the farms they were intended for'. At a time when many new farmhouses were required as a consequence of enclosure, the book appears to have had some success, for there were two further editions, in 1759 and 1772. Garrett died intestate early in 1753, leaving an only daughter. James Paine was his successor in so many instances (e.g. at Wallington, Gibside and Northumberland House) as to suggest that there may have been some connection between these two men, both of whom were remarkable (among London-trained architects) in having an extensive North Country clientèle.

Garrett was, as might be expected, a conscientious disciple of Lord Burlington. He does not appear to have been a very original designer, but provided his clients with handsome houses in a straightforward Palladian style. Thus the entrance to Nunwick has obvious Burlingtonian prototypes, the stairs at the Castle Howard Mausoleum are taken from Chiswick, and the pilastered front at Forcett derives presumably from Lindsey House in Lincoln's Inn Fields. In internal decoration, however, he was something of a pioneer in the use of rococo plasterwork, and he designed several Gothick buildings in the manner of William Kent. The best authenticated of these are the Banqueting House at Gibside and the additions to Kippax Park. Other Gothick buildings which may be by Garrett, including the Temple at Aske and the Culloden Tower at Richmond in Yorkshire, are discussed by Peter Leach in the article cited below.

[Peter Leach, 'The Architecture of Daniel Garrett', *C. Life*, 12, 19, 26 Sept. 1974; *History of the King's Works* v, 89; P.R.O., WORK 4/7, 11 Aug. 1737; P.R.O., PROB 6/129, f. 162; *London Evening Post*, 3–6 March 1753.]

WALLINGTON HALL, NORTHUMBERLAND, reconstructed south front, north front and interior, and probably designed service court, for Sir Walter Blackett, *c.*1735–53 [drawings by Garrett at Wallington; mid-eighteenth-century list of country houses in library at Alnwick Castle gives 'Mr. Garret' as architect of Wallington; John Cornforth in *C. Life*, 16–23 April 1970]. Garrett was also responsible for the adjoining folly known as Rothley Castle [*C. Life*, 26 Sept. 1974, 834 and fig. 3], and for Fairnley and Old Deanham Farms, 1746 [J. M. Robinson, *Georgian Model Farms*, 1983, 142].

FORCETT HALL, YORKS. (N.R.), rebuilt for Richard Shuttleworth (d. 1748), *c.*1730–

40; altered 1795 [list at Alnwick Castle (see above) gives 'Mr. Garret' as architect of 'Forcet, for Richard Shuttleworth'].

CASTLE HOWARD, YORKS. (N.R.), THE MAUSOLEUM, added balustraded steps and outer court for 3rd and 4th Earls of Carlisle, 1737–42 [G. F. Webb, 'Letters . . . relating to the building of the Mausoleum at Castle Howard', *Walpole Soc.* xix, 160–2].

STANWICK PARK, YORKS. (N.R.), probably assisted Sir Hugh Smithson, Bart. (afterwards 1st Duke of Northumberland) to rebuild the house to his own designs, *c.*1739–40; dem. 1923. In an undated diary entry Roger Gale (d. 1744) says that Smithson has 'entirely demolished the old Mansion House & given us a new Palazzo in the stile of Palladio by his own direction' [Bodleian Library, MS. Top. gen. c. 66, f. 29]. The rainwater heads were dated 1740. In July 1740 Smithson married Lady Elizabeth Seymour and her journal [Alnwick Castle, Percy Letters & Papers, vol. 24, pp. 41–9, *ex inf.* Mr. Peter Meadows] records that in Aug.–Sept. 1740 both 'Sir Hugh' and 'Mr. Garret' were making drawings for a cottage, a cold bath, etc. to be built for her use at Stanwick. As her journal makes it clear that Garret was on familiar terms with the family at Stanwick, it is probable that he had been involved in the building of the house. The dining-room ceiling was copied from Chiswick House. (*C. Life*, 17 Feb. 1900; E. Waterson & P. Meadows, *Lost Houses of York and the North Riding*, 1990, 44–46).

GILLING WOOD HALL, GILLING, YORKS. (N.R.), possible work for — Wharton, 1740, perhaps remodelling the house, destroyed by fire 1750 ['Mr. Garret left us to go to Gillingwood': journal of Lady Elizabeth Smithson as above under Stanwick, 21 Sept, 1740] (E. Waterson & P. Meadows, *op. cit.*, 47).

GIBSIDE, CO. DURHAM, works including New Laundry, 1744, Stables, 1748, and Gothic Banqueting House, 1751, for George Bowes [drawings by 'Mr. Garret' in Charter Room at Glamis Castle]. Garrett may also have been responsible for a Gothic tower built in 1743 (*C. Life*, 8 Feb. 1952, illustrates stables and banqueting house).

FENHAM HALL, NORTHUMBERLAND, for William Ord, *c.*1744–8; refronted and wings added by W. Newton *c.*1770 [list at Alnwick (see above) gives 'Mr. Garret' as architect of Fenham 'for Wm. Ord'].

TEMPLE NEWSAM HOUSE, YORKS. (W.R.), designed decoration of 'the Long Passage' executed by Thomas Perritt, plasterer, 1745 [Leeds Archives, Temple Newsam papers, EA 12/10, *ex inf.* Mr. P. Leach]. Garrett may well have been responsible for the decoration of the Long Gallery executed by Perritt in 1738–45, and perhaps also for the contemporary stables.

ALDBY PARK, YORKS. (N.R.), working drawings for 'ornaments for the Great Room' for H. B. Darby made 'by Mr. Garrett', probably *c.*1745 [N. Yorks. C.R.O., DAR MP 26].

RABY CASTLE, CO. DURHAM, internal alterations for 2nd Duke of Cleveland, including the state rooms in Clifford's Tower, *c.*1745–50 [Alistair Rowan in *Architectural History* xv, 1972, figs. 3a, 4a, and in *C. Life*, 1 Jan. 1970].

NUNWICK, NORTHUMBERLAND, for Lancelot Allgood, 1746–50; altered by I. Bonomi 1829 [payments to Daniel Garrett in Allgood's accounts: Northumberland C.R.O., ZAL 46/1, 4 June and 1 July 1746 (*C. Life*, 12–19 July 1956).

CAPHEATON, NORTHUMB., Gothic farm for Sir John Swinburne, *c.*1746 [J. M. Robinson, *Georgian Model Farms*, 1983, 120].

LONDON, No. 19 ST. JAMES'S SQUARE, internal alterations, including staircase, for the 2nd Duke of Cleveland, 1747–8; dem. 1894 [accounts at Raby Castle, *ex inf.* Mr. Peter Leach] (*Survey of London* xxix, 161–3).

WARWICK CASTLE, work for 1st Earl Brooke, 1748, probably the Gothic interior of the Chapel [Alnwick Castle, Percy Letters vol. 21, f. 189 and cf. 'The Travel Journal of Philip Yorke', ed. Godber, *Beds. Hist. Record Soc.* 47, 1968, 138].

MARDEN HILL, GODSTONE, SURREY, a proposed 'park building' for Sir Kenrick Clayton, Bart., 1748, probably the tower known as 'The Castle' (dem.) [Alnwick Castle, Percy Letters vol. 21, f. 189].

LONDON, NORTHUMBERLAND HOUSE, STRAND, extensive works for 7th Duke of Somerset, 1748–50, continued by 1st Duke of Northumberland, 1750–3, including the rebuilding of the north front to the street (of which Garrett published an engraving in 1752) and the addition of the wings extending south and containing the Ball Room and Gallery. The latter was completed by James Paine *c.*1754–7. The house was dem. 1874 [Alnwick Castle muniments, U IV 2a: Duke of Somerset's accounts with Messrs. Child and Messrs. Hoare 1748–50] (*London and its Environs described*, R. & J. Dodsley, 1761, v, 53 and 59, engravings after Samuel Wale showing Garrett's work before later alterations).

HORTON HOUSE, NORTHANTS. According to Horace Walpole ('Visits to Country Seats', *Walpole Soc.* xvi, 52) Garrett was employed by George Montagu, 1st Earl of Halifax (d. 1739), to alter and refront this house, which was subsequently further altered by Thomas Wright (*q.v.*) and dem. 1936. However, a letter from Sanderson Miller in B.L., Stowe MS. 753, f. 145, shows that Garrett was at Horton in 1750, designing 'Gothic Bridges etc.' for the 2nd Earl. Either he worked there for both Earls over a period of some years, or else Walpole's account was confused. The house is illustrated in Neale's *Views of Seats*, 1st ser., i, 1818, *V.C.H. Northants*. iv, 259–60, and *C. Life*, 26 Aug. 1971, 495.

KIPPAX PARK, YORKS. (W.R.), alterations for Sir John Bland, *c*.1750, partly Gothic [unsigned drawings among Bland papers in Leeds City Libraries, Archives Dept., identified as in Garrett's hand by Mr. Peter Leach. The house was in course of reconstruction in 1750; see Dr. Pococke's *Travels through England*, Camden Soc. 1888, i, 62] (Neale's *Views of Seats* v, 1822).

NEWCASTLE-UPON-TYNE, THE INFIRMARY, 1751–2; dem. 1954 [Margaret Wills in *C. Life*, 10 Oct. 1991].

GARRETT, JAMES, of Exeter, a joiner by trade, received an annual salary as surveyor at POWDERHAM CASTLE, DEVON, and was paid in 1754 and 1755 for 'drawings for buildings' and for 'designs and directing works' there for Sir William Courtenay. He presumably designed the great staircase, which he supplied [Mark Girouard in *C. Life*, 11 July 1963]. He was described as 'architect' in 1760, when his son John was admitted to St. John's College, Cambridge, in that year [*Admissions to St. John's College, Cambridge*, ed. R. F. Scott, iii, 1903]. In 1753 he supplied a classical altarpiece for KENN CHURCH, DEVON, removed 1862 [F. W. Vining, *Kenn*, *c*.1910, 80].

GATE, WILLIAM (1792–1839), was a builder at Carlisle. In 1824 he built DEVONSHIRE STREET, and in 1824–5 he designed and built a Gothic CATHOLIC CHAPEL in CHAPEL STREET, secularised 1906 [*Carlisle Patriot*, 28 Feb., 14 Aug. 1824]. He was the builder employed to erect the Newsroom and Library designed by Thomas Rickman, and on 31 July 1830 Rickman noted in his diary that he had seen a house (in English Street) 'built by Gate for a Mrs. Dacre'.

GATLIVE, JOHN, of Lymm, Cheshire, was Bridgemaster to the Hundred of West Derby in Lancashire from about 1736 to 1759 [*ex inf.* Dr. Janet Gnosspelius]. A person of the same name, apparently a master mason from Macclesfield, was paid 20s. in 1741 'for drawing plans and [making an] estimate' for rebuilding the tower of Rostherne Church, Cheshire, which were not adopted, although he was subsequently employed as a builder [F. H. Crossley, 'Post Reformation Church Building in Cheshire', *Jnl. Chester and N. Wales Architectural Soc.* N.S. xxv (i), 1942, 45–8; R. Richards, *Old Cheshire Churches*, 1947, 286–7]. The John 'Garlive' in accordance with whose plans KNUTSFORD CHURCH, CHESHIRE, was rebuilt in 1741–4 was presumably the same as either or both of the above [transcript of minutes of the commissioners for rebuilding the church in Cheshire C.R.O., P 7/8/2].

GAYFERE, THOMAS (1755–1827), was the son of Thomas Gayfere (*c*.1721–1812), who was appointed Master Mason to Westminster Abbey in 1766 and was Master of the London Masons' Company in 1773. The younger Gayfere exhibited a view of Norton Church, Leics.,[1] at the Society of Artists in 1774, and a drawing of the ruins of Furness Abbey in 1777. He subsequently exhibited topographical views at the Royal Academy in 1778, 1779 and 1780. In December 1802 he was appointed Master Mason to Westminster Abbey jointly with his father, and retained the post until his retirement in 1823. In 1807–8, when funds were voted by Parliament for the restoration of Henry VII's Chapel, he was commissioned to visit stone-quarries in various parts of the country to select the best stone for the purpose, and pronounced in favour of Combe Down Bath stone. The repairs were begun in 1809 and completed in 1822, at a total cost of £42,000. Although James Wyatt, as Surveyor to the Abbey, was nominally in charge, it was Gayfere who really directed as well as executed the restoration. Before starting work, he examined every part of the decaying structure and took plaster casts of such fragments of mouldings and other details as survived. From these, full-size working drawings were made at his house in Abingdon Street, and he took great pains to discover suitable masons and to instruct them in what was then an unfamiliar style of architecture. The result was an authentic restoration carried out in a manner unique in the eighteenth and early nineteenth centuries. In 1819–22 Thomas Gayfere restored the north front of Westminster Hall with Bath stone under the direction of J. W. Hiort of the Office of Works. He died at Burton-on-Trent on 20 October 1827, and was buried at Newton Solney in Derbyshire, where a tombstone

[1] Presumably King's Norton Church, then recently rebuilt to the designs of John Wing (*q.v.*).

commemorates his 'qualities as a Man' and 'his Abilities as an Architect'. [*A.P.S.D.*; obituary in *Gent's Mag.* 1828 (i), 275; P.R.O., WORK 10B/11; *Gent's Mag.* 1811 (i), 341; J. L. Chester, *Westminster Abbey Registers*, Harleian Soc. 1875, 483; J. P. Neale & E. W. Brayley, 'Henry VII's Chapel', *Abbey Church of Westminster* i, 1818, 21–7; L. N. Cottingham, *Plans, etc. of King Henry VII's Chapel at Westminster* i, 1822, 7–24; sale catalogue of Gayfere's Library (B.L., S.C.S. 138/7).]

GEARY, STEPHEN (1797–1854), entered the Royal Academy Schools in 1817 at the age (according to the Register) of 20. He exhibited a student's design in 1814, and another in 1816. In 1830 he designed KING'S CROSS, BATTLE BRIDGE, LONDON, exhibited at the R.A. that year, but not completed until 1836 [J. C. Loudon, *Architectural Mag.* iii, 41]. This consisted of a statue of George IV set on a high pedestal which was at first used as a police-station and afterwards as a public-house. The statue, caricatured by John Leech in *The Comic Latin Grammar*, 1840, 131, was removed in 1842, and the whole structure was demolished in 1845. It figures in Pugin's *Contrasts*, 1836.

In 1830 Geary was involved, with Signor Gesualdo Lanza, in a scheme for a 'Grand Panharmonium Theatre' (or music and drama centre) on an island site facing the Euston Road. Geary designed the buildings, which were to be connected by an overhead railway. Work started in 1830, but the scheme was abandoned in 1832 [*Survey of London* xxiv, 103].

Geary also designed the ST. PANCRAS COLLEGIATE SCHOOL, ARGYLL SQUARE, KING'S CROSS, of which he exhibited a view at the R.A. in 1837. He is best known, however, as the architect of HIGHGATE CEMETERY, opened in 1839 by a company of which Geary was the founder. Its architectural features, which included an 'Egyptian Avenue' and a 'Gothic Catacomb', are described by Hugh Ross Williamson in *Arch. Rev.* xcii, 1942, 87, and by J. Stevens Curl in *The Victorian Celebration of Death*, 1972, 86–102. In 1840 Geary published *Designs for Tombs and Cenotaphs*, a folding sheet with twenty-one of his characteristically crude designs for funerary monuments, of which there is a copy in the Bodleian Library. A shop-front in ISLINGTON designed by him is illustrated by N. Whittock, *On the Construction and Decoration of the Shop Fronts of London*, 1840, pl. vii.

Geary was clearly more of an entrepreneur than an artist. He is said to have designed the first gin palace in London in about 1830, and took out patents for artificial fuel, paving streets, water supply, motive power and other inventions. He died in Euston Place on 28 August 1854 and was buried in Highgate Cemetery, where a tombstone records his death in his 57th year.

[F. Boase, *Modern English Biography* i, 1892, 1133; F. T. Cansick, *The Monumental Inscriptions of Middlesex* ii, 1872, 78 (where his age at death is wrongly given as 75 instead of 57); *Gent's Mag.* 1854 (ii), 413.]

GEE, THOMAS, designed the spire which was added to the tower of ST. NICHOLAS CHURCH, LIVERPOOL, in 1746, the contractors being Messrs. Henry Sephton and William Smith. It fell in 1810, when a new steeple was designed by Thomas Harrison of Chester [J. A. Picton, *Memorials of Liverpool* ii, 58–9; *Gent's Mag.* 1814 (i), 115]. W. H. Gee, an architect practising in Liverpool in the mid-nineteenth century, may have been a descendant.

GERBIER, SIR BALTHAZAR (1592–1663), courtier, diplomatist, miniature painter and architect, figures in this *Dictionary* only in the last capacity. Born on 23 February 1591/2 at Middelburg in Zeeland, he was the son of Anthony Gerbier, a Huguenot *émigré*, but claimed a certain 'Anthony Gerbier, Baron Douvilly' as his great-grandfather, and on occasion used the title himself. Nothing is known of his upbringing, but he may have been a pupil of the artist Hendrik Goltzius. According to Sanderson he was 'a common Pen-man', and the art of calligraphy was certainly among his attainments. He himself claimed to speak 'several languages' and to have 'a good hand in writing, skill in sciences as mathematics, architecture, drawing, painting, contriving of scenes, masques, shows and entertainments for great Princes . . . as likewise for making of engines useful in war.' It was his knowledge of the 'framing of warlike machines' that brought him to the notice of Prince Maurice of Orange, who recommended him to the Dutch Ambassador in London, with whom he came to England early in 1616. He soon found a patron in George Villiers, Duke of Buckingham, who employed him to paint miniatures, embellish his houses, and collect works of art on a large scale. He was also sent on various diplomatic missions abroad, and in 1623 accompanied Buckingham and Prince Charles to Spain, where he painted a portrait of the Infanta for the royal inspection. In Paris in 1625 he met Rubens, with whom he afterwards became intimate. It was with Gerbier that Rubens lodged when he came to London in 1629, and during this visit the artist painted a portrait group of Gerbier's family, now in the Royal Collection at Windsor. After Buckingham's assassination in 1628 Gerbier was naturalized (Jan. 1629) and taken into the king's service as an 'esquire of his Majesty's body extraordinary'. In 1631 he was appointed Charles I's resident agent (a status inferior to that of ambassador) in Brussels, where he was employed on a combination of diplomatic and artistic business. Unknown to the king he betrayed state secrets to the Spanish government of the Netherlands. In 1638 he was knighted and in May 1641 he was further rewarded with the post of Master of Ceremonies in succession to Sir John Finet. According to his own account he was in addition promised the reversion of Inigo Jones's place as Surveyor of the King's Works which he had long coveted (see below). But soon afterwards a political feud with Lord Cottington led to his disgrace. In July 1641 Charles Cotterell was appointed nominally to 'assist', but in practice to supersede Gerbier as Master of Ceremonies. Gerbier's career as a courtier was now at an end, and in the course of the next few years he tried to make a living by various means, which included banking in Paris, keeping an academy at Bethnal Green, and seeking for gold in Guiana. During the Interregnum, far from regarding himself as a royalist, he dedicated a lecture on military architecture to Lord Fairfax (1650), and associated himself (*c.*1651) with a proposal to decorate the palace of Whitehall with portraits and battlepieces illustrating the 'memorable achievements' of the Parliament. When in 1660 he returned to London to claim the mastership of the ceremonies, he was promptly suspended from office, a decision afterwards confirmed by the Privy Council (*Cal. S.P. Dom. 1660–1*, 415, 522, 589; P.R.O., PC 2/56, f. 153). Excluded from the court, Gerbier decided to advertise his talents as an architect by publishing in 1662 a short tract entitled *A Brief Discourse concerning the Three Chief Principles of Magnificent Building*, and in 1663 a more substantial treatise called *Counsel and Advise to All Builders*. About this time Lord Craven (in whose regiment Gerbier's son had served as a Captain) engaged him to design or remodel a large house at Hampstead Marshall in Berkshire. It was at Hampstead Marshall that Gerbier died, apparently in 1663, leaving the unfinished house to be completed by William Winde. A tombstone in Hampstead Marshall Church commemorates 'Sr. Balthazer Gerbier, Kt. Archt. who built a stately pile of Building in the years 1662 to 1665 for the Rt. Hon. William Earl of Craven at Hampsted Marshall, the greatest part of which was destroyed by Fire in the year 1718. He died in the year 1667.' This long posthumous inscription is the only authority for stating that Gerbier died in 1667, and he must have been dead by August 1663, when his daughters were petitioning the king for relief from the starving condition in which they said they had been left by their father's death (see F. H. Cheetham in *Notes and Queries*, 11th ser., vii, 1913, 407–8). The inaccuracy of the inscription is confirmed by the fact that in 1666 Elias Ashmole noted that Gerbier was buried at Hampstead Marshall, but as yet without any monument (Bodleian Library, Ashmole MS. 850, f. 159).

Gerbier's architectural activity falls into two periods, the first in the 1620s when he was Buckingham's artistic adviser, the second in the 1660s. Letters to Buckingham in the Bodleian Library (Tanner MS. 73, ff. 491ᵛ, 510ᵛ) show that in 1624–5 he was busy with alterations both at York House in the Strand and at New Hall in Essex. For the latter house he had commissioned a wooden model for Buckingham's approval. Subsequently he reported that the 'cabinet de marbre' was being paved and that he was about to whiten the vaults. His work here appears to have been chiefly decorative in character (see *Vetusta Monumenta* ii, 1789, pls. xli–xlii and text). At York House, where the 'grande chambre' was being paved, he reported a visit from Inigo Jones in terms which make their rivalry clear. The Surveyor of the Works, he wrote, 'a esté a Jorckhouse pour veoir la Mayson et estoit comme confus et honteux, il ne me faudroit plus que la reversion de la plasse pour luy faire aveoir la gravelle car il en est fort jaloux'.

Gerbier's works at York House are also mentioned in his *Brief Discourse*, where he boasts that King Charles I was 'graciously pleased to avouch he had seen in Anno 1628 (close to the Gate of York-House, in a Roome not above 35 Foot square) as much as could be represented (as to Sceans) in the great Banquetting Room of Whitehall'. York House was pulled down in the 1670s, but the Water-Gate survives (*Survey of London* xviii, pls. 31–3). The authorship of this striking rusticated gateway is uncertain. The attribution to Gerbier by Summerson in *Architecture in Britain 1530–1830*, 1963, 351, was withdrawn in the 1991 edition and a case has been made for Inigo Jones (by John Harris in *C. Life*, 2 Nov. 1989), but a contemporary drawing (with variant features) in the Soane Museum (Fauntleroy Pennant III, f. 64) is in the hand of neither, and Charles Stoakes may have been right in claiming that his uncle Nicholas Stone (*q.v.*) both 'desined and built' the gate (*Walpole Soc.* vii, 1918–19, 137).

The case for attributing the York Water-Gate to Gerbier rests partly on its resemblance to his design for a rusticated gateway at Hampstead Marshall (Bodleian Library, MS. Gough Drawings a. 2, ff. 24–5). This dated from the 1660s and is signed by Gerbier. The mannerist cartouches on the piers may be compared with those framing Gerbier's portraits of the Prince of Orange and Frederick V of Bohemia in the British Museum (*Catalogue of British Drawings*, 1960, pls. 133–4). As Hampstead Marshall was destroyed by fire in 1718 it is now difficult to distinguish the respective shares of Gerbier and Winde in this house, but Kip's view and plans in the Bodleian Library (MS. Gough Drawings a. 2) both suggest that they were engaged in remodelling an existing Jacobean house rather than building a new one. As work on the first floor did not begin until July 1664, and as several designs for ceilings are dated in the 1670s and 1680s, it is clear that much remained to be done after Gerbier's death.

Gerbier also acted as artistic and architectural adviser to Charles I's Lord Treasurer, Richard Weston, 1st Earl of Portland, in connection with the building in *c.*1627–32 of his country house at Putney Park, Roehampton, Surrey, dem. *c.*1775. Letters from Gerbier to Weston concerning the staircase, chimney-pieces and gardens survive among the latter's papers in the Public Records [P.R.O., SP 16/153/69; SP 16/158/48,54; SP 77/21/221; SP 105/8, ff. 26–7]. Gerbier was also involved in the commissioning of Weston's tomb in Winchester Cathedral, made before his death in 1635, a sketch of which by the sculptor Isaac Besnier remains among his papers (SP 77/21, no. 69 (f. 52)).

Another influential member of Charles I's court whom Gerbier served was Archbishop Laud. In 1634, with Rubens's help, he obtained founts of type from Antwerp for Laud's Greek printing press in London, and when Laud built the Canterbury Quadrangle at St. John's College, Oxford, in 1634–6, with two frontispieces in a Flemish baroque style, it is possible that Gerbier played some part in providing or procuring designs for them, though no documentary evidence of his involvement has so far been found [H. Colvin, *The Canterbury Quadrangle*, 1988, 48–53].

One other architectural work can be attributed to Gerbier with some confidence. This was the design of the triumphal arches erected in the City of London to celebrate the coronation of Charles II in 1661. According to J. Ogilby's *Relation of His Majestie's entertainment passing through the City of London to his coronation with a description of the triumphal arches*, 1661, 2nd ed. 1662, these arches were designed jointly by Peter Mills (*q.v.*) 'and another Person, who desired to have his name conceal'd'. In Gerbier's *Brief Discourse* they are referred to in terms which suggest that he was their designer, and his banishment from court would explain his desire for anonymity at the time. There are, moreover, resemblances between the London arches and those designed by Rubens for the entry of the Cardinal Infante Ferdinand into Antwerp in 1635 and published in 1642 (*Pompa introitus*), with which Gerbier would certainly have been familiar. The original drawings for the London arches are in the R.I.B.A. Collection (see *Catalogue: G–K*, 18–19).

Gerbier's place in English architecture is difficult to assess because of the destruction, almost without record, of nearly all his known works. Despite his association with Peter Mills in 1661, and the influence of Rubens's *Palazzi di Genova* on English architectural taste in the mid seventeenth century, it is doubtful whether Gerbier had much to do with the formation of the 'artisan mannerist' style. He would, however, appear to have imported into England a florid Netherlandish baroque that might well have affected English architecture much more profoundly but for the chastening influence of his rival Inigo Jones.

[The best accounts of Gerbier's artistic activities will be found in E. Croft-Murray & Paul Hulton, *Catalogue of British Drawings in the British Museum*, 1960, 328–30, and in two articles by Lita-Rose Betcherman: 'The York House Collection and its Keeper', *Apollo*, xcii, 1970, and 'Balthazar Gerbier in Seventeenth-Century Italy', *History Today*, 1961, 325–331. For his political career see *D.N.B.* and H. Ross Williamson, *Four Stuart Portraits*, 1949. See also A. E. Richardson, 'Seventeenth-Century Buildings in Search of an Architect', *R.I.B.A. Jnl.*, 17 June 1933, E. Croft-Murray, *Decorative Painting in England* i, 1962, 202, and M. J. Power, 'Sir Balthazar Gerbier's Academy at Bethnal Green', *East London Papers* x (i), 1967, 19–33. Several of his letters to the Duke of Buckingham were printed in Godfrey Goodman's *Court of James I*, 1839. MS. sources include P.R.O., SP 105/7–18, Gerbier's entry-books as agent in Brussels, E 178/5973, which throws light on his position in Buckingham's household, and B.L., Add. MS. 32093, ff. 302–7, a protestation of his loyalty to the Commonwealth government made in 1642/3.]

GETHIN, JOHN (1757–1831), a mason of Kingsland, Herefordshire, held the office of

Surveyor of Bridges for the county from 1820 until his death at the Brick House, Kingsland, on 24 May 1831. A list of the bridges which he built or rebuilt (none of much architectural importance) is given by G. H. Jack, 'John Gethin', *Woolhope Naturalists' Field Club Trans.*, 1930–2, 86. He was presumably the ancestor of the Victorian architect John Gethin (1868–1895), who was born at Leominster in Herefordshire.

GIBBS, JAMES (1682–1754), was the younger son of Patrick Gibb(s), a merchant of Fittsmyre, on the outskirts of Aberdeen. He was educated at Marischal College, where he matriculated some time between 1696 and 1700. His family were Catholics, and in 1703, after a sojourn in Holland with relatives, Gibbs made his way to Rome to be entered at the Scots College there as a candidate for the priesthood. Within a year, he was driven out by the tyrannical régime of an over-zealous rector, and turned instead to architecture. As a boy he had 'had a great genius to drawing', and in the course of the journey to Rome (which took him through France, Switzerland and Germany) he had not been insensitive to the artistic attractions of the towns through which he had passed, especially those of northern Italy. Abandoning a clerical career, he became a pupil of Carlo Fontana, then the leading Roman architect. While in Rome he made drawings for some of the visiting English nobility and gentry, establishing contacts that were to be of service in his later career. When in 1709 he returned to Britain, he had had a professional training at the fountain-head of Italian baroque that was unique among contemporary English architects. Only his religion stood in the way of a successful career, and that was an obstacle that may have seemed less serious under Queen Anne than it was to do after the Jacobite Rising of 1715. His first important patron was, indeed, a fellow-Catholic. John, Earl of Mar (*q.v.*), himself an amateur architect, was 'very much his friend', and employed him, *inter alia*, to alter the official house in Whitehall which he shared with the Earl of Loudoun. It was through Mar's influence with Harley,[1] reinforced by a recommendation from Wren, that in 1713 Gibbs succeeded William Dickinson as one of the two surveyors to the Commissioners for building Fifty New Churches in London. The church of St. Mary-le-Strand, which he designed in this capacity, was his first public building, and 'got him great reputation in his business'. But the intended column to Queen Anne, which was to have stood in the Strand in front of the church, and for which Gibbs made designs, was abandoned after the Queen's death in 1714, and when the Commission was reconstructed in the following year, Gibbs, suspect both as a Tory and a Scot, was dismissed (Jan. 1715/16).

Although the loss of his post must have been a serious blow (made more bitter because he believed it was due to the machinations of a 'countryman' almost certainly identifiable as Colen Campbell), Gibbs was by now sufficiently well established to make his own way without the security of a salaried post. His professional training in Italy was an asset that none of his rivals had enjoyed, and if Tory patronage could not provide him with official employment, it brought him an abundance of commissions for country houses. In early Georgian England Gibbs was indeed the Tory architect *par excellence*, and most, but not all, of his clients were of that political persuasion. It was the younger Harley's patronage that gave him a stake in the profitable development of the family estate in Marylebone, where in about 1730 he built himself a substantial house on the corner of Wimpole Street and Henrietta Place. But it was the Whig Duke of Argyll who employed him to design his English seat at Sudbrooke in Surrey and who, as Master-General of the Ordnance, gave him in 1727 the post of Architect of the Ordnance. Worth £120 a year, it was 'almost if not merely a sinecure', and Gibbs was to hold it until his death twenty-seven years later.

In 1728 Gibbs advertised his success as an architect by the publication of *A Book of Architecture*, a folio containing 150 plates of his designs, both executed and otherwise. There was a second edition in 1739. This was followed in 1732 by his *Rules for Drawing the Several Parts of Architecture*, of which there were further editions in 1736, 1738 and 1753. He also published his designs for the Radcliffe Library at Oxford in a volume entitled *Bibliotheca Radcliviana*, 1747. The *Book of Architecture* served more than one purpose. By devoting a whole volume to his own works

[1] Mar and Harley were related by marriage. Harley's daughter Abigail married the 7th Earl of Kinnoull, whose sister Margaret was Mar's first wife. At Worcester College, Oxford, there is a pair of unique engravings signed 'J.G.', one for the 'Earl of Mar's lodge' (probably at Comley Bank, on Mar's Alloa estate), the other for a house for Lord Kinnoull (presumably at Dupplin Castle, Perthshire) on a plan derived from Boffrand's Malgrange and similar to the palace which Juvarra was later to build at Stupinigi (reproduced in H. M. Colvin, *Catalogue of Architectural Drawings . . . at Worcester College, Oxford*, 1964, pls. 115–16).

Gibbs more than made up for the deliberate omission of his name from Campbell's *Vitruvius Britannicus*. At the same time, by the inclusion of a number of well-conceived designs for monuments, chimney-pieces, garden buildings, urns and cartouches, he converted a personal advertisement into a general architectural pattern-book of high quality. Its success was immediate and long-lasting. In fact it was 'probably the most widely used architectural book of the century', well known to master builders both in the British Isles and in the American Colonies. It was the source of several stock features of Georgian vernacular architecture, and a host of church steeples on both sides of the Atlantic owe their form to Gibbs's engravings. Gibbs himself told George Vertue that he had made £1500 by his books, and that he afterwards sold the plates for £400 more.

In 1749, 'having been long much afflicted with the stone and gout', Gibbs visited Spa for the sake of his health. He died on 5 August 1754, aged 71, according to the tablet in St. Marylebone Church (for the inscription see Lysons, *Environs of London* ii, 1811, 554). He was unmarried, and he left £1000, three houses in Marylebone, and all his plate, to Lord Erskine, 'in gratitude for favours received from his father the late Earl of Mar'. He left his own house in London to the Scottish portrait-painter Cosmo Alexander, and another in Cavendish Square to Robert Pringle, one of his executors. To John Borlach, 'for many years my draughtsman', he left £400. He bequeathed all his books, prints and drawings to the Radcliffe Library in Oxford of which he had been the architect.[1]

Gibbs was a highly accomplished architectural designer whose work, if rarely equal in imaginative quality to that of his contemporaries Vanbrugh and Hawksmoor, always shows the practised hand of one who had been a fellow-pupil of Juvarra. His style was a successful synthesis of ideas and motifs derived partly from Italian sources (both baroque and Palladian), and partly from English ones. His steeples, in particular, show an intelligent appreciation of the work of Wren. In 1720, when he submitted his designs for the church of St. Martin-in-the-Fields, he took the committee on a tour of Wren's churches, and the steeple of St. Martin's is clearly inspired by the example of Wren's City spires. The combination of portico and steeple is not beyond criticism, but this baroque equivalent of a Gothic spire rising from the roof of a classical temple was to be the stereotype of the urban Anglican church for the next hundred years. If St. Martin's was a brilliant development of the type of church started by Wren, the Radcliffe Library at Oxford owed a good deal to Wren's pupil Hawksmoor. Both architects made several designs before the Trustees came to a decision, and although Gibbs was ultimately appointed as architect after Hawksmoor's death in 1736, it was to the latter that he owed the idea of a centrally planned domed building (his own designs were for a more utilitarian building on a rectangular plan). Having adopted the idea he transformed Hawksmoor's essentially classical conception of a stately colonnaded drum into a sophisticated piece of Italianate architecture of which Maderno or Fontana would not have disapproved. Gibbs's most conspicuously Italianate building is, however, St. Mary-le-Strand, whose elaborate external dress has echoes of Cortona and Borromini as well as of Palladio and Inigo Jones. In his later works the direct influence of Italian baroque prototypes is much less evident: in many of them, indeed, it persisted only in the elaborate plasterwork (usually executed by the Italians Artari and Bagutti) with which he decorated the halls and saloons of his country houses. For, in spite of his Italian experience, Gibbs was by no means insensitive to the change which came over English architectural taste in the 1720s, and although he never became a disciple of Lord Burlington, he tended in his later years to conform to the fashion for plain pedimented blocks which represented the common form of English Palladianism in domestic architecture.

In 1729 Gibbs was elected a Fellow of the Royal Society, and in 1749, on the opening of the Radcliffe Library, he received the honorary degree of M.A. at Oxford. A number of portraits are recorded. Gibbs presented a half-length by J. M. Williams to the Bodleian Library, and a Kit-Kat to St. Mary Hall, Oxford (now Oriel College). A duplicate of the Bodleian portrait is at the National Portrait Gallery. There is a portrait by Andrea Soldi in the Scottish National Portrait Gallery and another by Bartholomew Dandridge is in the Ionides Collection at Orleans House, Twickenham. Busts by Rysbrack can be seen in the Victoria and Albert Museum and the Radcliffe Library (both dated 1726). An engraved portrait by Hans Hysing is illustrated in Friedman's biography, together with a bookplate incorporating a profile portrait dated 1736.

Eight volumes of Gibbs's drawings are now in the Print Room of the Ashmolean Museum

[1] Many of the books were sold as duplicates in 1894, but a MS. catalogue exists (Bodleian, MS. Eng. Misc. *c*.28). For the drawings, now in the Print Room of the Ashmolean Museum, see below.

at Oxford. They include the original drawings for the *Book of Architecture*, the *Rules* and *Bibliotheca Radcliviana*, and provide many examples of his precise and elegant draughtsmanship. Seventy-two sheets of drawings, nearly all duplicates of those for the *Book of Architecture*, are in the Victoria and Albert Museum. There are also a few drawings (including that for the Strand column) in the Print Room of the British Museum, and several in the R.I.B.A. Drawings Collection (see the *Catalogue*), the Bodleian Library (Gough Collection) and the Soane Museum. At the Soane Museum there is also an important MS. memoir of the architect. This was included in the catalogue of books left to the Radcliffe Library, but marked as not received. Before its acquisition by Soane it belonged to the architect Henry Holland. It contains a fairly complete list of Gibbs's works, and a brief account of his early life and travels. There is reason to think that, despite some minor inaccuracies, it was written by Gibbs himself, or from information supplied by him, and it constitutes the principal source of information about his career. In the same volume there are some 'Cursory Remarks on some of the finest Antient and modern Buildings in Rome, and other parts of Italy', made 'by Mr. Gibbs while he was studying Architecture there' (cf. *Wren Soc.* xii, pl. xli).

Other important sources for Gibbs's life are the records of the Commissioners for Building Fifty Churches in Lambeth Palace Library; letters and references in Hist. MSS. Comm., *Egmont* ii, *Bath* iii, *Stuart Papers* ii, iv and v, and *Portland, passim*; *Vertue's Note Books*, Walpole Society iii, 17, 133; a brief memoir in *Scots Magazine*, 1760, 475–6; records of his Ordnance post in P.R.O., WO 48/68, p. 186, and WO 54/210; and Gibbs's will (P.C.C. 228 PINFOLD). The modern literature includes Marcus Whiffen, 'The Progeny of St. Martin in the Fields', *Arch. Rev.* July 1946; A. S. MacWilliam, 'James Gibbs, Architect, 1682–1754', *Innes Review* v, 1954; S. Lang, 'Gibbs: a bicentenary review of his architectural sources', *Arch. Rev.* July 1954; John Holloway, 'A James Gibbs Autobiography', *Burlington Mag.* May 1955; Bryan Little, *The Life and Works of James Gibbs*, 1955; H. E. Stutchbury, 'Palladian Gibbs', *Trans. Ancient Monuments Soc.* N.S. viii, 1960; John Field, 'Early Unknown Gibbs', *Arch. Rev.* May 1962; Arthur Oswald, 'James Gibbs and his Portraits', *Country Life Annual*, 1963; John Summerson, *Architecture in Britain 1530–1830*, 1970, chap. 21; Terry Friedman, *James Gibbs*, Yale 1984; and Eileen Harris, *British Architectural Books and Writers*, 1990, 208–13.

PUBLIC BUILDINGS

LONDON, LINCOLN'S INN, work in the Hall, 1720, evidently the insertion of plaster ceiling, removed 1924–8 [John Summerson, 'The Old Hall of Lincoln's Inn', *Trans. Ancient Monuments Soc.* N.S. 28, 1984, 14–16].

CAMBRIDGE, THE SENATE HOUSE, 1722–30. This building was intended to form the north wing of a three-sided group of university buildings, as shown in *Book of Architecture*, pl. 36. The west end, originally designed to be engaged with the central block, was not faced until 1767–8 [Willis & Clark, iii, chap. 3; T. P. Hudson, 'James Gibbs's Designs for University Buildings at Cambridge', *Burlington Mag.* Dec. 1972].

CAMBRIDGE, KING'S COLLEGE NEW BUILDING, 1724–49 [Willis & Clark, i, 560–3; *Book of Architecture*, pls. 32–5].

LONDON, THE OXFORD MARKET, MARYLEBONE, for Edward Harley, 2nd Earl of Oxford, 1726–7; dem. 1880–2 [though not specifically mentioned in the Soane MS., it can hardly be doubted that this was among the 'several buildings' there stated to have been designed for Harley by Gibbs].

LONDON, THE COURT HOUSE, MARYLEBONE, 1729–33; dem. 1803–4, was probably one of the buildings designed by Gibbs for Edward Harley, 2nd Earl of Oxford, and he certainly designed the carving of the Earl's arms that was set over the doorway [Friedman, *James Gibbs*, 306].

LONDON, ST. BARTHOLOMEW'S HOSPITAL, SMITHFIELD, 1730–52; E. block built 1758–62 to Gibbs's designs; repaired by Thomas Hardwick 1814–20 and refaced by P. Hardwick 1851. Gibbs was a governor of the Hospital and made no charge for his designs [Friedman, *James Gibbs*, 308–9, citing hospital archives].

OXFORD, THE RADCLIFFE LIBRARY, 1737–48 [J. Gibbs, *Bibliotheca Radcliviana*, 1747; *The Building Accounts of the Radcliffe Camera*, ed. S. G. Gillam, Oxford Hist. Soc., N.S. xiii, 1958, with illustrations of many of the drawings; S. Lang, 'By Hawksmoor out of Gibbs', *Arch. Rev.* April 1949; H. Colvin, *Unbuilt Oxford*, 1983, chap. v].

OXFORD, ST. JOHN'S COLLEGE, stone screen in hall, 1743 [College archives, *Computus Annuus*, 1743, f. 45].

CHURCHES

LONDON, ST. MARY-LE-STRAND, 1714–17 (consecrated Jan. 1723/4), for the Commissioners for Building Fifty New Churches. The steeple was an afterthought, designed by Gibbs when the column to Queen Anne, which was to have taken its place, was abandoned. There are two contemporary models of the church in the R.I.B.A. Drawings Collection (formerly at Westminster Abbey and at Burleigh House, Stamford). The interior was refitted by R. J. Withers in 1871 [*Book of Architecture*, pls. 16–23, 31].

LONDON, ST. CLEMENT DANES. The upper stages of the steeple were added to Gibbs's design in 1719–20, replacing Wren's wooden cupola [*Book of Architecture*, pl. 28]. Gibbs also repaired the roof, 1720.

LONDON, ST. PETER, VERE STREET, formerly known as the Oxford or Marylebone Chapel, 1721–4, for Edward Harley, later 2nd Earl of Oxford. There is a copy of the contract, dated 8 Aug. 1721, in the British Library (Add. MS. 18238, f. 37v), and a section signed by Gibbs, Harley and the contractors, in the Ashmolean collection of Gibbs's drawings, vol. i, no. 12b. The interior was altered by J. K. Colling in 1881 and by R. Potter in 1979–80 [*Book of Architecture*, pls. 24–5].

LONDON, ST. MARTIN-IN-THE-FIELDS, rebuilt 1722–6. Gibbs's designs were chosen in 1720 after the Committee had considered those submitted by John James, Sir James Thornhill, Nicholas Dubois and George Sampson [MS. Minutes of the Commissioners for Rebuilding St. Martin's Church, Westminster City Library]. Gibbs's model, showing a variant treatment of the spire, is preserved in the R.I.B.A. Drawings Collection, and there are other alternative designs in the Ashmolean Museum (see vol. vii). The interior was altered by Sir A. W. Blomfield in 1887. [*Book of Architecture*, pls. 1–15, 29, 30; *Survey of London* xx, 24–8, pls. 10–27; J. McMaster, *A Short History of St. Martin in the Fields*, 1916; K. A. Esdaile, *St. Martin in the Fields*, 1944.]

SHIPBOURNE CHURCH, KENT, rebuilt 1722 for Christopher Vane, Lord Barnard; rebuilt 1879 [Soane MS.] (M. Whiffen, *Stuart and Georgian Churches*, pl. 52).

DERBY, ALL SAINTS (now the Cathedral), rebuilt 1723–5, except the west tower. The interior was altered in 1876 by J. Young, and there was a restoration by Temple Moore in 1904–5. The E. end was extended in 1967–72. [*Book of Architecture*, pls. 26–7; J. C. Cox & W. H. St. J. Hope, *Chronicles of All Saints, Derby*, 1881, chap. iv.]

LINCOLN CATHEDRAL, strengthened west towers by building up arches at west end, *c.*1726 [Hist. MSS. Comm., *Portland* vi, 84; J. W. F. Hill, 'The Western Spires of Lincoln Cathedral and their Threatened Removal in 1726', *Lincolnshire Architectural Soc.'s Reports*, N.S. v (ii), 1954].

DULWICH COLLEGE CHAPEL, the marble font for Revd. Jas. Hume, who records in his diary that in Sept. 1729 he 'agreed with Mr. Van Spanger to make a Font of the Dimensions and form of the Draught made by Mr. Gibbs Architect' [*N. and Q.*, vol. 184, 1943, 173].

NEWCASTLE, ST. NICHOLAS (now CATHEDRAL), Library and Vestry, 1736: executed with modifications, e.g. to the window pediments, in accordance with drawings in Gibbs's hand in B.L., *King's Maps* xxxii, 57. x.

KIRKLEATHAM CHURCH, YORKS. (N.R.), mausoleum for Turner family on north side of chancel, 1740; restored 1839 [drawings in Ashmolean Museum, vol. ii, 94; A. C. Taylor, 'Kirkleatham', *Arch. Rev.* Oct. 1958].

attributed: KIRKLEATHAM, YORKS. (N.R.), THE HOSPITAL CHAPEL, for Cholmley Turner, 1741–8. As Gibbs designed the mausoleum and also made a design for a house for Turner (Ashmolean, vol. iv, 23), it is very probable that he also designed the Hospital Chapel, which has all the characteristics of his style (H. Field & M. Bunney, *English Domestic Architecture of the XVII and XVIII Centuries*, 1905, pls. xlv, xlvi; *C. Life*, 20 Jan. 1977).

PATSHULL CHURCH, STAFFS., for Sir John Astley, Bart., cons. 1743; reconstructed 1874–8 by W. C. Banks, who added a north aisle and rebuilt the upper stage of the tower to a different design [Soane MS.] (S. Shaw, *History of Staffordshire* ii, 1801, pl. xxvi*).

ABERDEEN, ST. NICHOLAS CHURCH WEST, rebuilt 1751–5. Gibbs supplied his designs gratis in 1741, but it was not until 1751 that funds permitted building [Ashmolean Museum, vol. iii, 130–2, vol. iv, 1–5; *Aberdeen Fifty Years Ago*, Aberdeen 1868, 46–7].

HOUSES

ABBOTSTONE, HANTS., see HACKWOOD.

ACTON PLACE, nr. SUDBURY, SUFFOLK. This appears to be the 'large Dwelling house with offices built by Mr. Jenings near Stowmarket (*sic*)' referred to in the Soane MS. It was begun not long before his death by Robert Jennens (d. Feb. 1725/6), whose widow and son both subscribed to Gibbs's *Book of Architecture* (1728), but it was never completed, and the central block was demolished in 1825, leaving only the wings, one of which was formed into a house. A painting of the house is reproduced by N. Pevsner, *Suffolk*, pl. 58a. [W. Copinger, *Manors of Suffolk* i, 10–12; Harrison & Willis, *The Great Jennens Case*, 1879, 85–6, 98–100, 113–14.]

ANTONY HOUSE, CORNWALL. This house, built 1720–4 for Sir William Carew, Bart., is stated to have been designed by Gibbs by D. & S. Lysons, *Magna Britannia* i, 1814, 16. Gibbs cannot have designed the main block, which is not in his style. However, the forecourt corresponds closely to the one shown in pl. 57 of Gibbs's *Book of Architecture* (to which Carew subscribed), and the width of the front of the house shown in that plate is the same (101 feet) as that of the existing house [*ex inf.* Mr. M. Trinick & Mr. H. Dalton Clifford]. The existing house may therefore have been based on a design by Gibbs which was modified by John Moyle, the master mason employed, or alternatively Gibbs may have designed the forecourt as an addition to a house already under construction. (*C. Life*, 19, 25 Aug. 1933; W. Borlase, *Natural History of Cornwall*, 1758, plate at p. 92.)

BADMINTON HOUSE, GLOS., two flanking domed pavilions for 3rd Duke of Beaufort, *c.*1730/40 [A. Gomme, 'Badminton Revisited', *Arch. Hist.* 27, 1984].

BALVENY HOUSE, nr. MORTLACH, BANFFSHIRE, for William Duff of Braco, 1724–5; wings and quadrants (shown on estate map of 1779) added to local designs dated 3 May 1725; dem. 1929 [W. Adam, *Vitruvius Scoticus*, pls. 90–1; design for wings in S.R.O., RHP 31388 and cf. RHP 31463/2 of 1779].

BANK HALL, WARRINGTON, LANCS. (now Warrington Town Hall), for Thomas Patten, 1750 [Soane MS.] (measured drawings in *Arch. Rev.* lxiv, 1928, 30–1).

BEAUMONT LODGE, OLD WINDSOR, BERKS., 'additions' to Lord Weymouth's house, 'besides other things for his Lordship' [Soane MS.]. Among the Gibbs drawings at the Ashmolean (vol. ii, 25a) there is a section of 'An Icehouse for Lord Weymouth at Old Windsor', and accounts at Longleat show that in 1743 Gibbs received £21 'for surveying of works at Longleat and Old Windsor'. The house (sold by Lord Weymouth in 1741) was rebuilt by H. Emlyn (*q.v.*) in 1785.

BELMONT HALL, GREAT BUDWORTH, CHESHIRE, appears to be the house for 'the Hon. John Smith Barry' referred to in the Soane MS., but there incorrectly identified as 'Aston Park in Cheshire'. It was built by John Smith Barry *c.*1750–1755 and has bow windows and other features for which a local executant architect was probably responsible [P. de Figueredo & J. Treuherz, *Cheshire Country Houses*, 1988, 31–4].

BYFLEET, SURREY, 'a very convenient small Hunting Box' for General Henry Cornwall *c.*1720; dem. *c.*1795 [Soane MS.; O. Manning & W. Bray, *History of Surrey* iii, 1814, 181].

CALKE ABBEY, DERBYSHIRE, designed balustraded flight of steps up to main entrance for Sir John Harpur, Bart., 1727–8; removed 1806 [accounts in Derbyshire C.R.O.] (H. Colvin, *Calke Abbey*, 1985, 103–4).

CANHAM HEATH, HANTS., see HACKWOOD.

CANNONS HOUSE, MIDDLESEX. According to the Soane MS. 'James Duke of Chandos ordered Mr. Gibbs to rebuild his House and Chapel at Cannons, which was done at a vast Expence'. Work on the new house had, in fact, begun in 1713, three years before Gibbs was consulted, but there is reason to think that he largely determined the design of the south and east elevations, and the chapel was wholly his work. He was dismissed in 1719, and the house was completed by John Price (who published the elevations with his own name as architect) and Edward Shepherd. The house was pulled down after a demolition sale in 1747. According to the memoir, 'Lord Foley bought all the pictures [in the chapel], and everything else which could be moved, and ordered Mr. Gibbs to fitt them to his Chapel' (completed 1735) at Great Witley, Worcs. These included ten windows with glass dated 1719–21, by Joshua Price after Francesco Sleter, and paintings by Bellucci which were reset in the ceiling of the chapel (*C. Life*, 8 June 1945). The pews, pulpit, etc., from the Cannons chapel are now in Fawley Church, Bucks. [C. H. and M. I. Collins Baker, *The Life and Circumstances of James Brydges, First Duke of Chandos*, 1949, 124–5, 142–4; drawings for the chapel in G.L. Record Office, CC 262/50/60–61].

CHISWICK, MIDDLESEX, 'repaired and made additions to' the dowager Duchess of Norfolk's house, afterwards known as Corney House, *c.*1748; dem. 1832 [Soane MS.; Lysons, *Environs of London* ii, 1811, 126] (*Historical Collections relating to Chiswick*, ed. W. P. W. Phillimore & W. H. Whitear, 1897, plate facing p. 29).

COMPTON VERNEY, WARWICKS., the stables, for the Hon. John Verney (d. 1741) [drawing in Ashmolean, vol. ii, 76; cf. S. Markham, *John Loveday of Caversham*, 1984, 190, 332].

DAWLEY HOUSE, nr. HARLINGTON, MIDDLESEX, 'new modelled' with 'large additions' for the 1st Viscount Bolingbroke, *c.*1725; dem. *c.*1770 [Soane MS.] (*Gent's Mag.* 1802 (ii), 725). In the Ashmolean, vol. iii, 90a, there is a design for a bridge for Lord Bolingbroke.

DITCHLEY HOUSE, OXON., for 2nd Earl of Lichfield, 1720–42. Gibbs's design appears to have incorporated a stable-wing already built by Francis Smith (*q.v.*), and may have been to some extent a modification of a design by Smith rather than a wholly independent scheme. Gibbs played little or no part in the decoration of the interior, the hall being by Kent assisted by Flitcroft, 1724–5, the drawing room and dining room by Flitcroft, 1736–40 [*Book of Architecture*, pl. 39; A. Gomme, 'Architects and Craftsmen at Ditchley', *Arch. Hist.* 32, 1989] (*C. Life*, 9–16 June 1934, 17–24 Nov. 1988; C. Hussey, *English Country Houses: Early Georgian*, 1955, 66–71).

EAST BARNET, HERTS., house known as NEW PLACE or LITTLE GROVE, for John Cotton, 1719; dem. *c.*1927 [Soane MS.; *V.C.H. Herts.* ii, 339] (F. C. Cass, *East Barnet*, 1885–92, plate).

FAIRLAWN, SHIPBOURNE, KENT, additions for Christopher Vane, Lord Barnard, *c.*1722, including 'a very handsome Room 20 ft. by 30 ft. with a fine fretwork ceiling', for which there is a drawing in the Ashmolean (vol. iv, 41) [Soane MS.; payments in Lord Barnard's account at Hoare's Bank] (*C. Life*, 30 Oct., 6 Nov. and 27 Nov. 1958, 1247).

FOXLEY, HEREFS., designed summerhouse for Robert Price, 1728, and remodelled interior of hall for Uvedale Price, 1735; dem. 1948 [MS. notes in copy of Gibbs's *Book of Architecture* formerly at Foxley, copied by the late B. Little].

GATESHEAD, DURHAM, PARK HOUSE, alterations for Henry Ellison, 1730; gutted 1891 and now part of a factory [E. Hughes, *North Country Life in the Eighteenth Century*, 1952, 29].

GUBBINS or GOBIONS, HERTS., added a large room for Jeremy Sambrook 'and did other building for that gentleman' [Soane MS.]. There are designs for a dovecote and ceiling 'for Mr. Sambrooke at Gubbins' in the Ashmolean (vol. iii, 87, iv, 40). The house was dem. soon after 1836. (Neale, *Views of Seats*, 1st ser., i, 1818; drawings by Buckler in B.L., Add. MS. 32350, ff. 143–6, and Herts. C.R.O.).

HACKWOOD PARK, HANTS., 'built a great many temples and ornamental buildings for the Duke of Bolton [Charles, 3rd Duke, succ. 1722, d. 1754] at Hackwood, and a House for him at Cannam Heath [nr. Kingsclere] about 12 miles from Hackwood, and made a great many drawings for a new House to be built there, as likewise a large design for a building to be erected at Abbotstone [nr. Alresford, Hants.], another seat belonging to his Grace', which were not executed owing to the 'finances failing' [Soane MS.]. See *Book of Architecture*, pls. 72–4, 84, for the temples, etc. at Hackwood, and Ashmolean Museum, vol. iv, 25, for design of a house 'for ye Duke of Bolton'.[1] In 1740 George Vertue mentions 'a new stone portico . . . design'd by Mr. Gibbs' on the S. front of Hackwood (*Note-Books* v, 127). This was removed *c.*1805, and of the garden buildings illustrated in Gibbs's book only the Menagerie Temple and the peristyle of the rotunda (*Book of Architecture*, pls. 72, 84) survive. The house at Cannam or Canham Heath was built *c.*1725 and dem. in 1805. There is a survey plan in Hampshire C.R.O., 11M.49/P.514–5. Abbotstone was dem. *c.*1760.

HAMPSTEAD MARSHALL, BERKS., In 1739 'he laid the foundation and carried up the walls a considerable height of a large house' for 3rd Lord Craven, to replace that burned in 1718, but work was abandoned on Lord Craven's death the same year [Soane MS.]. There is a complete set of drawings for the house in vol. v of the Gibbs Collection in the Ashmolean Museum.

HARTWELL HOUSE, BUCKS., designed 'several ornamental buildings' for Sir Thomas Lee, Bart., including the temple illustrated on the right-hand side of pl. 77 of the *Book of Architecture* [Soane MS.]. Gibbs was probably also responsible for the decoration of the hall and some of the drawings for the interior of Hartwell in Bodleian, MS. Top. Gen. b.55, appear to be in his hand (*C. Life*, 14 and 21 March 1914; 15 March 1979).

HEYTHROP HOUSE, OXON., completion of interior for 'the Earl of Shrewsbury' [Soane MS.]. The interior (destroyed by fire 1831) was said to be still unfinished in 1722 [Macky, *Journey through England* ii, 1722, 119–21] and 1735 [B.L., Add. MS. 5842, f. 130^{v}], so Gibbs's employer may have been the 14th Earl, who succeeded in 1743.

HOUGHTON HALL, NORFOLK, the four stone cupolas, for Robert Walpole, 1st Earl of Orford, 1725–8. In 1732 the 2nd Earl of Oxford noted that the roofs of the four towers 'were altered by Mr. Gibbs from the first design' (*i.e.* that published in *Vitruvius*

---

[1] See p. 953.

Britannicus) [Hist. MSS. Comm., *Portland* vi, 160]. This is confirmed by a contemporary statement that these cupolas were 'obstinately raised by the master . . . in defiance of all the virtuosi' [*Lord Hervey and his Friends*, ed. Lord Ilchester, 1950, 70]. The possibility that Gibbs's involvement in Houghton extended to the original design of the house is discussed by J. Harris in *New Light on Palladianism*, ed. C. Heath, Georgian Group Symposium, 1988, 5–9.

ISLEWORTH, MIDDLESEX, SHREWSBURY HOUSE, for George Talbot, titular Earl of Shrewsbury (d. 1733), *c.*1720; dem. *c.*1810 [Soane MS.].

ISLEWORTH, MIDDLESEX, SOMERSET HOUSE, additions for 'Sir John Chester' i.e. Chesshyre, *c.*1720; dem. 1803 [Soane MS.].

ISLEWORTH, MIDDLESEX, GUMLEY HOUSE (now Convent of Jesus), additions for John Gumley, cabinet-maker (d. 1729) [Soane MS.] (G. J. Aungier, *History of Syon . . . and the Parish of Isleworth*, 1840, 228; M. Jourdain & R. Edwards, *Georgian Cabinet-Makers*, 1944, pl. 89).

KELMARSH HALL, NORTHANTS., for William Hanbury, *c.*1728–32 [Soane MS.; *Book of Architecture*, pl. 38 (not as executed); volume of drawings in R.I.B.A. Coll. (more or less as executed)] (*C. Life*, 25 Feb. 1933).

LEIGHTON HOUSE, LEIGHTON BUZZARD, BEDS., work for the Hon. Charles Leigh; dem. *c.*1810 [Soane MS.] (Gibbs probably designed the Doric garden temple illustrated by R. Richmond, *Leighton Buzzard*, 1928, pl. 7).

LONDON, ARGYLL STREET, speculative building of houses in association with Thomas Phillips and Roger Morris, 1736–40 [T. Friedman, *James Gibbs*, 1984, 304].

LONDON, ARLINGTON STREET, No. 16 for the Dowager Duchess of Norfolk, 1734–40 [T. Friedman, *James Gibbs*, 1984, 304].

LONDON, BURLINGTON HOUSE, PICCADILLY, works for 3rd Earl of Burlington, *c.*1715. According to the Soane MS. 'the Earl of Burlington had him to build and adorn his house and offices in Piccadilly. They are all built with solid Portland stone, as is likewise the fine circular colonnade fronting the house, of the Dorick Order'. This identifies Gibbs with the unnamed architect mentioned by Colen Campbell as having rebuilt the east block in the forecourt before he (Campbell) was employed to remodel the house and build the great gateway in 1718. Gibbs's responsibility for the colonnade (dem. 1868) has, however, been questioned. For illustrations and a careful discussion of the problem see *Survey of London* xxxii, 398.

LONDON, No. 49 GREAT ORMOND STREET, library for Dr. Richard Mead, *c.*1734; dem. *c.*1872 [Soane MS.] (*C. Life*, 24 Sept. 1970, 765, for illustration of interior).

LONDON, GROSVENOR STREET, No. 52, probably designed interior for Sir Thomas Hanmer, Bart., 1727; dem. [T. Friedman, *James Gibbs*, 1984, 305].

LONDON, LEICESTER SQUARE, rebuilt No. 25 for Sir Philip Parker Long, Bart., 1733–4; dem. [Soane MS.; *Survey of London* xxxiv, 491].

LONDON, LEICESTER SQUARE, SAVILE HOUSE, added attic storey and refitted interior for Sir George Savile, Bart., 1733; dem. 1865 [*Survey of London* xxxiv, 460].

LONDON, MARYLEBONE, supervised design of houses on the Cavendish-Harley estate for Edward Harley, 2nd Earl of Oxford, and built four houses (dem.) in HENRIETTA STREET (now Henrietta Place), including one (No. 5) which he occupied himself, *c.*1727–30 [B.L., Harley estate papers, Add. MSS. 18238, ff. 40–1, 18240, ff. 16–18; John Summerson, 'Henrietta Place, Marylebone and its Associations with James Gibbs', *London Topographical Record* xxi, 1958].

LONDON, PRIVY GARDENS, WHITEHALL, divided house into two dwellings for 11th Earl of Mar and 3rd Earl of Loudoun, 1710–11; dem. [T. Friedman, *James Gibbs*, 1984, 307].

LONDON, THANET HOUSE, GREAT RUSSELL STREET, alterations for Thomas Coke (later 1st Earl of Leicester), 1718–19; dem. [T. Friedman, *James Gibbs*, 1984, 312].

PATSHULL HALL, STAFFS., rebuilt for Sir John Astley, Bart., *c.*1738–54, completed by William Baker (*q.v.*); altered by W. Burn, 1855 [Soane MS.; *V.C.H. Staffs.* xx, 165–7].

QUARRELL, STIRLINGSHIRE, designs for enlargement for John Drummond, executed with modifications 1735–6; dem. [S.R.O., GD 24/1/495, ff. 501–575 *passim*].

RAGLEY HALL, WARWICKS., works for 1st Earl of Hertford, *c.*1748–55, including completion of interior and decoration of hall [Soane MS.; plan attributed to Gibbs in B.L., Add. MS. 31323 W[3]; Warwicks. C.R.O., CR 114 A/775] (*C. Life*, 1–8 May 1958).

ROEHAMPTON, SURREY, repaired house (called Elm Grove) for Bartholomew Clarke and his brother-in-law Hitch Young and added 'a fine new room 20 ft. by 30 ft. and 20 ft. high, coved', with paintings by Amiconi and a chimney-piece by Rysbrack, *c.*1725–30; destroyed by fire *c.*1788 [Soane MS.; *Book of Architecture*, pl. 92].

STANWELL PLACE, MIDDLESEX, 'repaired and made additions' for Richard Phillips, Governor of Nova Scotia: rebuilt in 19th century [Soane MS.].

STOWE HOUSE, BUCKS., alterations to S. side of house (subsequently remodelled) for Viscount Cobham, 1731–5, and the following ornamental buildings: GIBBS'S BUILDING or THE BELVEDERE, 1726–8; dem. 1764 and re-erected elsewhere as 'The Fane of Pastoral Poetry', now a ruin; THE BOYCOTT PAVILIONS, flanking the Oxford Drive, 1726–8; altered by Borra, who substituted domes for the original pyramidal terminations, 1754; THE IMPERIAL CLOSET, 1726–8; dem.; THE TEMPLE OF FRIENDSHIP, 1739; THE GOTHIC TEMPLE or TEMPLE OF LIBERTY, 1741–44; Gothic lanterns added probably to designs of Sanderson Miller (*q.v.*), 1756; THE LADY'S TEMPLE, *c.*1744–8; remodelled *c.*1775 and renamed 'The Queen's Temple' [L. Whistler, 'The Authorship of the Stowe Temples', *C. Life* 29 Sept. 1950; M. Gibbon, 'Stowe, Bucks. The House and Garden Buildings and their Designers', *Arch. Hist.* 20, 1977].

SUDBROOK HOUSE, PETERSHAM, SURREY, rebuilt for 2nd Duke of Argyll & Greenwich, 1715–19; N. front altered *c.*1767 [*Book of Architecture*, pl. 40; T. Friedman, *James Gibbs*, 1984, 317] (measured drawings in *Arch. Rev.* xxxii, 1912, 309; *C. Life*, 19 Oct. 1918).

TRING PARK, HERTS., ornamental buildings for William Gore (d. 1739) [Soane MS.]. A pyramid and several other garden buildings are visible in Badeslade & Rocque, *Vitruvius Brittanicus* (*sic*) iv, 1734, pls. 104–5, but not the surviving obelisk and portico of an Ionic temple that are presumably by Gibbs.

TWICKENHAM, MIDDLESEX, 'new modelled' CROSS DEEP LODGE for Barnaby Backwell, banker (d. 1754) [Soane MS.; R. S. Cobbett, *Memorials of Twickenham*, 1872, 261].

TWICKENHAM, MIDDLESEX, octagon room for James Johnston, Secretary for Scotland, 1720 [*Book of Architecture*, pl. 71]. This stood in the grounds of what later became known as Orleans House. The latter was dem. 1927, but Gibbs's building survives as an art gallery (*C. Life*, 15 Sept. 1944; *Connoisseur*, Oct. 1956, 80–1).

TWICKENHAM, MIDDLESEX, added 'a fine Room' to house of Sir Chaloner Ogle (d. 1750) on N. side of Montpelier Row, known later as Chapel House or Holyrood House; dem. [Soane MS.].

TWICKENHAM, MIDDLESEX, remodelled Alexander Pope's Villa, 1719–20; dem. 1807–8 [Soane MS.; *The Correspondence of Alexander Pope*, ed. Sherborne, ii, 1956, 4, 44].

WENTWORTH CASTLE, YORKS. (W.R.), fitting up of interior of gallery (designed by Bodt) for 1st Earl of Strafford, 1734 [contract for wainscoting 'as desined by Mr. Gibbs' in B.L., Add. MS. 22329, f. 128] (*C. Life*, 25 Oct. 1924).

WHITTON PLACE, MIDDLESEX, offices and greenhouse for the Earl of Ilay (afterwards 3rd Duke of Argyll), 1725–6; *dem. c.*1935 [Soane MS.; Mary Cosh in *C. Life*, 20 July 1972].

WIMPOLE HALL, CAMBS., alterations and additions for Edward Harley, later 2nd Earl of Oxford, 1719–21, including library and chapel [Soane MS.; *Wren Soc.* xvii, 10–11; R.C.H.M., *West Cambs.* 215]. Drawings in the Soane Museum connected with this commission are reproduced in *Wren Soc.* xii, pl. xxxv, and xvii, pl. xvi. A design by Gibbs for a vase for Wimpole is in Bodleian, Gough Maps 46, nos. 266–8. (*C. Life*, 21–28 May 1927).

MONUMENTS

Gibbs was the first British architect who made a practice of designing monuments. In WESTMINSTER ABBEY he designed the monuments to John Holles, 1st Duke of Newcastle (d. 1711) [*Book of Architecture*, pl. 111; cf. alternative designs in *Wren Soc.* xii, pl. xxxiii; xvii, pl. xiii, and in vol. vi of the 'London and Westminster Prints' in the Library of the Society of the Antiquaries (f. 18)]; Sophia, Marchioness of Annandale (d. 1716), John Smith (d. 1718), Matthew Prior (d. 1721), James Craggs (d. 1721) [drawings in Ashmolean, vol. ii, 13, and V. & A. 3641–1913], Mrs. Katherine Bovey (d. 1727), Dr. John Freind (d. 1728), John Dryden (erected 1720), and Ben Jonson, all of which (with the exception of the Craggs monument) are either listed in the Soane MS. or illustrated in *Book of Architecture*, pls. 112–24.

Elsewhere he designed the monuments to Robert Stuart (d. 1714) in ST. MARGARET'S CHURCH, WESTMINSTER [*ibid.*, pl. 127], to Sir John Bridgeman (d. 1710) in ASTON CHURCH, WARWICKS. [*ibid.*, pl. 123], to Edward Colston (d. 1721) in ALL SAINTS CHURCH, BRISTOL [*ibid.*, pl. 113], to Montague Drake (d. 1698) and his wife (d. 1724) in the chancel of AMERSHAM CHURCH, BUCKS. [*ibid.*, pl. 121], to Lord and Lady Barnard (d. 1723/5) in SHIPBOURNE CHURCH, KENT [Ashmolean drawings, vol. iii, 86], to Sir Ambrose (d. 1713) and Lady Crowley (d. 1727) in MITCHAM CHURCH, SURREY [J. Physick, *Designs for English Sculpture 1680–1860*, 1969, 76–7], to

Sir Edward Seymour (d. 1708) in MAIDEN BRADLEY CHURCH, WILTS., erected 1730 under contract dated 11 June 1728 [P.R.O., C 107/126], to Robert Lovett (d. 1740) in SOULBURY CHURCH, BUCKS. [signed], to Marwood William Turner (d. 1739) in the Mausoleum attached to KIRKLEATHAM CHURCH, YORKS. (N.R.) [T. Friedman in *Burlington Mag.* Jan. 1980, 61–5], to the 4th Lord Widdrington (d. 1743) in NUNNINGTON CHURCH, YORKS. (N.R.) [signed], and to Henry, 2nd Duke of Newcastle (d. 1691) and his family in BOLSOVER CHURCH, DERBYSHIRE, 1727–8 [*Book of Architecture*, pl. 114].

UNEXECUTED

Among many unexecuted designs by Gibbs, attention may be drawn to the following: ADDERBURY HOUSE, OXON., designs for a recessed portico and for garden buildings, for 2nd Duke of Argyll and Greenwich, *c.*1725 [drawings among Buccleuch papers in S.R.O., RHP 13766–8, 13772]; ARUNDEL CASTLE, SUSSEX, designs for rebuilding for 9th Duke of Norfolk [Soane MS.]; CATTON HALL, DERBYSHIRE, design for new house for Christopher Horton, *c.*1740 [Andor Gomme, 'Catton Hall', in *The Country Seat*, ed. Colvin & Harris, 1970, 157–63]; DOWN HALL, ESSEX, designs for a house for Matthew Prior, 1720 [*Book of Architecture*, pls. 55, 68–9; drawings in Bodleian, Gough Misc. Ant. fol. 4, no. 12, Gough Maps 46, ff. 260–4, and B.L., Portland papers, Loan 29/357, set 2]; KEDLESTON HALL, DERBYSHIRE, designs for two pavilions for Sir John Curzon, Bart. (d. 1727) [*Book of Architecture*, pl. 70], probably made in 1726, when Curzon paid Gibbs 10 guineas [Kedleston archives, Day-Book 1718–50]. An elevation for a new house attributable to Gibbs is among the drawings at Kedleston; KIRKLEATHAM HALL, YORKS. (N.R.), design for a new house for Cholmley Turner [elevation in Ashmolean, vol. iv, 23; cf. *Book of Architecture*, pl. 41]; KIRTLINGTON PARK, OXON., designs for a new house for Sir James Dashwood, Bart., for which Gibbs was paid £30 in 1741 [accounts in the possession of the late Mrs. H. M. Budgett]. Gibbs's (and other) drawings for Kirklington were sold by Sotheby's in Dec. 1987; KIVETON PARK, YORKS. (W.R.), designs for additions and garden buildings, including a Gothic ruin, for 4th Duke of Leeds, 1741 [Ashmolean Museum, drawings acquired in 1953]; LONDON, THE MANSION HOUSE, designs submitted in competition in 1737 [S. Perks, *The History of the Mansion House*, 1922, 170, pls. 41–4, Ashmolean, vol. ii, 119–24]; LONDON, ST. JOHN'S CHURCH, MARYLEBONE, 1741 [drawings in Ashmolean, vol. iv, 17]; LOWTHER CASTLE, WESTMORLAND, projects for remodelling for 3rd Viscount Lonsdale, *c.*1717 and for a new mansion *c.*1728 [*Architectural Drawings from Lowther Castle*, ed. Colvin, Crook & Friedman, Society of Architectural Historians, 1980, pls. 8–9]; MILTON HOUSE NORTHANTS., designs for a new house for 2nd Earl Fitzwilliam (d. 1728) [*Book of Architecture*, pls. 48–51, Northants. Record Office, portfolio of drawings dated 1726 (nos. 59–77); RABY CASTLE, DURHAM, design for the high hall for Christopher Vane, Lord Barnard (d. 1723) [the drawings reproduced by Alistair Rowan in *Arch. Hist.* xv, 1972, figs. 5–6, are duplicated in Ashmolean, vol. ii, 48 and 50]; SACOMBE PARK, HERTS., house for Edward Rolt (d. 1722) [*Book of Architecture*, pls. 52–3]; TREWITHEN, CORNWALL, a set of designs for a new house for Philip Hawkins, probably *c.*1730, unsigned but in Gibbs's hand (Cornwall C.R.O., DDJ (2), nos. 1–8), ground-plan reproduced *C. Life*, 2 April 1953, fig. 9; WESTON UNDERWOOD, BUCKS., designs for Sir Robert Throckmorton, Bart. (d. 1720), 'which his son proposes to build' [Soane MS.]; WHITTON PLACE, MIDDLESEX, designs for a new house for Earl of Ilay (afterwards 3rd Duke of Argyll), *c.*1725 [*Book of Architecture*, pls. 59–62]; WISTON PARK, SUSSEX, designs for rebuilding for Sir Robert Fagg, Bart. [Ashmolean, vol. vi]; WITHAM PARK, SOMERSET, designs for remodelling garden front for Sir William Wyndham, Bart., *c.*1716 [Ashmolean, vol. iv, 22, *Vitruvius Britannicus* ii, 1717, pls. 91–2 (where Gibbs's authorship is not acknowledged), R.I.B.A. Drawings Coll., reproduced in John Harris, *Georgian Country Houses*, 1968, pl. 9, and discussed by T. Friedman in *R.I.B.A. Drawings Catalogue: G–K*, 24]. This house was at Witham Friary, south-west of Frome, which belonged to the Wyndhams (see Collinson, *History of Somerset* ii, 1791, 234).

GIBSON, GEORGE, was, according to James Elmes,[1] the eldest son of another architect surnamed Gibson who had been employed by Queen Caroline. The elder Gibson 'had travelled in Italy, studied architecture in Rome, collected many curiosities in Art, and deposited them in a singular Villa that he built on Loam-pit Hill, Lewisham, long known . . . by the name of the Comical House. It is now inhabited by Mr. Alderman Wire, and is called Stone House, Lewisham.' STONE HOUSE, LOAMPIT HILL, LEWISHAM, is illustrated by S. C. Ramsey & J. D. M. Harvey, *Small*

[1] In an autobiographical passage prefaced to his memoir of his son H. L. Elmes (R.I.B.A. Library).

Houses of the Late Georgian Period ii, 1923, pls. 80–2. It appears to have been built in 1771–3, and is a small, ingeniously planned and elegantly finished villa whose stylistic affinities are more French than Italian. The records of St. Paul's Church, Deptford (in whose parish the house stands), show that in 1772 Michael, son of George and Ann Gibson of Loampit Hill, was baptized, and that in 1776 George Gibson paid for two seats. Neither the burial of the elder Gibson nor the birth of the younger one is, however, recorded there.

Elmes, who was a pupil of the younger Gibson, says that, like his father, he had travelled in Italy before commencing practice. He was, however, too much a man of taste to be an effective supervisory architect. 'He would rather sip his claret, drink his Madeira, chat about Art and Music, and take snuff with a gusto, than ascend ladders, tramp scaffolds to see how Bricklayers filled in their work, or try the scantlings of wall plates and bond timbers . . . [like] the practical men of Sir Robert Taylor's working school.' Nevertheless 'he had good connections among the wealthy merchants of the City, for some of whom he designed and superintended some London residences and country mansions.' For Sir Richard Neave, Bart., he designed offices in BROAD STREET, a town-house, No. 6 ALBEMARLE STREET, and a country seat, DAGNAM PARK, PIRGO, ESSEX.[1] For Neave's son Thomas he altered BRANCH HILL LODGE, HAMPSTEAD, soon after 1799 [Elmes]. In 1774 the banker John Julius Angerstein employed him to design WOODLANDS HOUSE, GREENWICH, an elegant neo-classical villa now in Mycenae Road [*Copperplate Magazine* ii, 1794, pl. lxxx]. In LEWISHAM he designed ST. MARY'S CHURCH, with its handsome portico, in 1775–7 (damaged by fire 1830, chancel added 1881–2) [L. L. Duncan, *The Parish Church of St. Mary, Lewisham*, 1892, 12–16], and built himself a 'little box' adjoining his father's villa.

Two monuments designed by Gibson are recorded: one, to Viscountess Falkland (d. 1776), in WIDFORD CHURCHYARD, ESSEX [R. Gunnis, *Dictionary of British Sculptors*, 1968, 304], the other, a sarcophagus of black marble, in an unidentified church near Lowestoft, possibly that of L. Leathes (d. 1787) in HERRINGFLEET CHURCH, SUFFOLK [J. D. Potts, *Platt of Rotherham, Mason-Architects*, Sheffield 1959, 17].

GIBSON, GEORGE (1755–1835), a local gentleman, is stated in a monumental inscription in CROSBY RAVENSWORTH CHURCH, WESTMORLAND, to have 'supervised the reconstruction of this Church' in 1811–12, 'aiding with his own skilful hand so excellent a work'. The work which Gibson supervised is in a distinctive and somewhat naïve Gothic style also seen formerly at LITTLE STRICKLAND CHURCH, WESTMORLAND (1814), for which he may have been responsible. It is probable that he was the George Gibson to whose designs the Tuscan MARKET HOUSE or 'CLOISTER' at KIRKBY STEPHEN in the same county was built in 1810 [F. Bellasis, *Westmorland Church Notes*, Kendal 1888–9, i, 194, ii, 136].

GIBSON, JESSE (*c.*1748–1828), of Hackney in Middlesex, was the District Surveyor of the eastern division of the City of London from 1774 until his death in 1828. He was appointed Surveyor to the Saddlers' Company in 1774, to the Drapers' Company in 1797, and was employed by the Vintners' Company between 1800 and 1820.

Gibson made an estimate for alterations to MONOUX'S ALMSHOUSES, WALTHAMSTOW, ESSEX, in 1788 [S. J. Barns, *Walthamstow Vestry Minutes*, Walthamstow Antiquarian Soc. 1925–7, 79–81]; rebuilt the church of ST. PETER-LE-POER, OLD BROAD STREET, LONDON, 1788–92, dem. 1908 [minutes of Rebuilding Committee in Guildhall Library, MS. 2863; Britton & Pugin, *Public Buildings of London* ii, 1828, 72]; designed a house at WEST HILL, nr. WANDSWORTH, for J. A. Rucker in about 1790 [S. Lysons, *Environs of London* i, 1810, 390], and CLAYBURY HALL, ESSEX, for James Hatch, about the same time [*Essex Review* xxxvii, 99–108; *Gent's Mag.* 1800 (2), 990]; repaired LEYTON CHURCH, ESSEX, 1794 [J. Kennedy, *History of Leyton*, 1894, 43]; designed the VINTNERS' ALMSHOUSES, MILE END ROAD, 1802–3; dem. 1940 [Anne Crawford, *History of the Vintners' Company*, 1977, 211 and pl. 14]; and rebuilt the SADDLERS' HALL, CHEAPSIDE, LONDON, 1822–3, refronted 1865; dem. [*Record of the Saddlers' Company*, 1937, 115]. As surveyor to the Drapers' Company Gibson was responsible for most of the buildings in the small town of MONEYMORE built on their estate in Co. Londonderry, N. Ireland, in 1818–23 [J. S. Curl, *Moneymore and Draperstown*, Ulster Architectural Heritage Soc. 1979].

Gibson died on 24 June 1828, aged 80, and was buried at Wimbledon [*A.P.S.D.*]. There is a portrait at Drapers' Hall. He appears to have been a designer of only moderate ability. Despite its circular nave, St. Peter-le-Poer was not a particularly interesting example of a centrally planned church, and in Britton's opinion its tower was 'far

[1] Probably soon after 1772, when Neave purchased the estate.

from graceful, either in its general form, or in its embellishments'.

GIBSON, JOHN (–1801), 'architect' of Montrose, died in September 1801 [S.R.O., CC 3/3/73, pp. 388–9]. He was the 'undertaker' responsible for enlarging CRAIGO HOUSE, nr. MONTROSE, for the Carnegie family in 1790 [N.L.S., Dep. 267/122], and in 1791–3 he was associated with John Phair, builder of Edinburgh, in building an EPISCOPAL CHAPEL for Lord Garlies at LAURENCEKIRK, KINCARDINESHIRE. The original design was, however, superseded by one made by a Capt. Rudyerd, and after 'further changes of mind on the part of his Lordship', a lawsuit ensued [S.R.O., GD 57/1/496].

GIBSON, THOMAS, was the architect employed by the 3rd Earl of Marchmont to design MARCHMONT HOUSE, BERWICKSHIRE, 1750–4. A rare engraving of the house (illustrated by J. Macaulay, *The Classical Country House in Scotland*, 1987, 166) bears the signature 'Thos. Gibson Arch[t].', and in a letter dated 3 Dec. 1792 the Earl refers to 'late Gibson the Architect of Marchmont House', whose drawings were then in his possession [S.R.O., GD 158/2628/2]. The house was much enlarged and altered by Lorimer in 1913–16, but the originally severe character of its exterior, and some distinctive features of the interior decoration, suggest that Gibson was an able designer in a style distinguishable from that of contemporary Scottish architects such as John Adam (*C. Life*, 28 Feb., 7 March 1925). Thomas Gibson was presumably the 'Mr. Gibson' in accordance with whose sketch the arms of the Corporation of Berwick-on-Tweed were carved on the new Town Hall there in 1758 [Berwick-on-Tweed Guild Books, 22 March 1757/8].

In 1753 Henry Fielding's *Proposal for making an Effectual Provision for the Poor* was illustrated by an engraved plan and elevation of a design for a large workhouse for the County of Middlesex signed 'Thomas Gibson Arch[t].', and in 1760–5 'Mr. Gibson' was employed by the Earl of Marchmont's son-in-law Walter Scott of Harden, M.P. for Roxburghshire, whose London accounts record small payments to him 'for plans' and larger ones for marble chimney-pieces, one 'for the New Dining Room' [S.R.O., GD 157/813]. These works were probably at Scott's London house in Hertford Street rather than at Harden. If, as it appears, Thomas Gibson was a London architect, he may have been the father of George Gibson (*q.v.*), especially as Lord Marchmont's accounts record payments to George as well as to Thomas Gibson in connection with the building of Marchmont House [S.R.O., GD 648/4, p. 23].

GILBERT, THOMAS (*c.*1706–1776), designed and built ST. GEORGE'S CHURCH, REFORNE, PORTLAND, DORSET, 1754–66, a sturdy classical building of some pretensions in a style derived from the school of Wren rather than from contemporary architectural fashions. A tablet commemorates Thomas Gilbert 'of this island, Gent. Architect and Master Builder of this church', who died on 25 July 1776, aged 70 [R.C.H.M., *Dorset* ii (2), 247–9].

Gilbert was descended from a family of masons who carried on the stone-quarrying business in the Isle of Portland. Thomas Gilbert (d. *c.*1695) was 'probably the largest purveyor of Portland stone during the last quarter of the seventeenth century', and supplied stone for St. Paul's Cathedral, Winchester Palace and Hampton Court. His business was carried on by his sons, Thomas (d. 1704, aged 28) and John, both, like their father, Liverymen of the London Masons' Company. Thomas (d. 1776) was presumably the son of John. [D. Knoop & G. P. Jones, *The London Mason in the Seventeenth Century*, 1935, 28–9; *Wren Soc.*, *passim*; J. H. Bettey, *The Island and Royal Manor of Portland*, Portland, 1970; Bodleian Library, Tucker papers, will of Thomas Gilbert (d. 1704).]

GILES, ROBERT, designed a Gothic R.C. Church (dem.) at NORTH SHIELDS, NORTHUMBERLAND, in 1817–21 [B. Little, *Catholic Churches since 1623*, 1966, 61]. Nicholas Giles is listed as an architect and surveyor of Newcastle in Pigot's *Directory* of 1828–9.

GILKIE, ALEXANDER (*c.*1756–1834), was a master builder at Coldstream, Berwickshire. Between 1791 and 1795 he was employed at FORD CASTLE, NORTHUMBERLAND, by Lord Delaval. According to a confused document printed in the *Proceedings of the Society of Antiquaries of Newcastle-on-Tyne* v, 1891–2, 63, 'The great gateway, lodges and towers, amongst other buildings, were remodelled by him', but some of the these features were the work of James Nesbit (*q.v.*), who died in 1781. An estimate by Gilkie for a further addition to the east side of the castle in 1801 is in the Northumberland Record Office [2 DE 18/1/30], but is marked 'laid aside'. According to the same writer Gilkie 'was recommended by Lord Delaval to Lord Strathmore for the rebuilding of Gibside'. At GIBSIDE, CO. DURHAM, he was presumably responsible for the remodelling of the south front for the 10th

Earl of Strathmore in about 1805. This front, Jacobean in style, with Gothick details, is illustrated in *C. Life*, 8 Feb. 1952. In the R.I.B.A. Drawings Collection there is a design by Gilkie for a bridge at Blackadder House, Berwickshire, and at Kimmerghame House, Berwickshire, there are two designs by him for courts of offices for Archibald Swinton, one at Kimmerghame (1790), the other at Broadmeadows House, Hutton, Berwickshire (1807). At Manderston House, Berwicks. there is a crude design by him for a classical house, signed and dated 1789. In 1811–12 he designed EYEMOUTH CHURCH, BERWICKS., and in 1819 the SCHOOL and SCHOOLMASTER'S HOUSE there (now No. 7 High Street) [S.R.O., CH 2/516/7, 248, 351 and HR 252/2]. He also designed the MANSE at MORDINGTON, BERWICKS., in 1813–14 [S.R.O., CH 2/516/7, 358, 362–3, 370, 401].

From these recorded works it is evident that Gilkie was a provincial designer of no great ability whose works (especially at Ford Castle) nevertheless have considerable naïve charm. An inscription in Lennel churchyard, Coldstream, shows that he died on 3 May 1834, aged 78, and that his son Alexander Gilkie, 'surveyor of buildings in Edinburgh', died on 21 November 1852, aged 56.

GILKS, WILLIAM (–1727), was a builder and surveyor at Burton-on-Trent. Between 1712 and 1723 he was frequently employed by Sir John Harpur, Bart., at CALKE ABBEY, DERBYSHIRE, where in 1712 he contracted to build the handsome brick stables. In February 1719/20 he was paid £10 8s. 6d. 'for several draughts and his Directions upon several occasions', and in 1721–2 he built a school at the adjoining village of TICKNALL [accounts in Derbyshire C.R.O.; H. Colvin, *Calke Abbey, Derbyshire*, 1985, 43, 105]. In 1720–1 he was supervising alterations at MELBOURNE HALL, DERBYSHIRE, for Thomas Coke (*q.v.*) and made an estimate for a new vicarage there [account of 'my time in surveying and directing the workmen at Melbourne Hall' in the muniment room there]. Gilks died at Burton in April 1727, and was buried at the parish church on the 23rd of that month [Parish Register, *ex inf.* Mr. Edward Saunders].

GILL, ABRAHAM (?1803–1834), son of William Gill of Houghton-on-the-Hill, grazier, was apprenticed to William Parsons of Leicester (*q.v.*) in 1821, and subsequently went into partnership with him. He died young on 8 December 1834, 'greatly respected by a large circle of friends' [H. Hartopp, *Leicester Freemen*, 1927, 576; obituary in *Leicester Journal*, 12 Dec. 1834, quoted by J. D. Bennett, *Leicestershire Architects 1700–1850*, Leicester 1968].

GILL, WESTBY (1679–1746), was the eldest son of Col. John Gill of Carr-house in the parish of Rotherham, nr. Sheffield. He was christened Westby because Carr-house had come to his family through his grandmother Elizabeth Westby. He was educated at Jesus College, Cambridge, where he took his M.A. in 1702. In September 1719 he was appointed Deputy Surveyor of the Works by his neighbour Sir Thomas Hewett (*q.v.*). In 1735 he succeeded William Kent as Master Carpenter, retaining the post until his death in October 1746. After his father's death he sold the family estate and lived in London.

Little is known about Gill's architectural ability, but he is recorded to have designed one medium-sized country house and a funerary monument. The country house is BURROW HALL, LANCS., and documents in private possession show that Gill made the unsigned elevation illustrated in *C. Life*, 14 April 1960, fig. 5. The house was built by George Platt of Rotherham in accordance with a contract dated 20 January 1740 [*ex inf.* Mr. W. J. Smith]. The monument is in ABBOTS LANGLEY CHURCH, HERTS. It commemorates Chief Justice Raymond (d. 1732), was executed by Cheere, and is signed 'Westby Gill Ar. invenit'. In addition a reference in Andrews Jelfe's letter-book (B.L., Add. MS. 27587, f. 45v) points to Gill as the architect of the circular Ionic temple built by the 2nd Earl of Macclesfield in 1741 in the grounds of SHIRBURN CASTLE, OXON., for which Jelfe supplied the Portland stone. It may be noted that in 1739 Gill was elected a Fellow of the Royal Society, of which Macclesfield was a leading member.

[J. Hunter, *Hallamshire*, 1819, 234; Venn, *Alumni Cantabrigienses* i, 217; *History of the King's Works* v.]

GILLESPIE, JAMES, *see* GRAHAM, JAMES GILLESPIE.

GILLOW, RICHARD (1734–1811), was the son of Robert Gillow, a native of Great Singleton in the Fylde district of Lancashire, who became a freeman of Lancaster in 1728 and died there in 1772, having established a successful business as a joiner and cabinet-maker. Richard had an architectural training under a 'Mr. Jones', probably the London architect William Jones (*q.v.*), and the firm's books, which survive from 1731 onwards, show that he was taken into partnership by his father in 1757 and practised as an architect and surveyor as well as continuing the joinery business. Among the buildings designed by him or his father were several private houses in Lancaster and ST. THOMAS'S CHAPEL at GARSTANG, 1770. In 1762–4 he designed the carefully detailed Palladian CUSTOM HOUSE at LANCASTER, which is mentioned as his work in Pennant's *Tour in Scotland*, 1771, 220. Richard Gillow died in 1811 and was succeeded by his eldest son Richard (1772–1849), who, like his father and grandfather, was a devout Catholic and had an extensive Catholic clientèle. Richard Gillow II acquired the estate of Leighton Hall which still belongs to his descendants. The house had been built in 1759–61 for George Towneley in accordance with a design attributable to Richard Gillow I (the attribution in *C. Life*, 11–18 May 1951 to John Hird, whose design was rejected, is incorrect).

By the third quarter of the eighteenth century the Gillows were among the leading English cabinet-makers, with a branch in London and a large export business to the West Indies. The architectural side of the business was abandoned, and the subsequent history of the firm lies outside the scope of this *Dictionary*.

[J. Gillow, *Bibliographical Dictionary of the English Catholics* ii, 1885, 484–5; *Gillow's, its History and Associations*, 1901; Mary E. Burkett, *The Furniture of Gillows of Lancaster* (typescript, Lancaster Museum, 1983); Lindsay Boynton, 'Gillows' Furnishings for Catholic Chapels, 1750–1800', in *Studies in Church History* 28, 1992; Gillow records in Westminster City Library; information from Dr. L. O. J. Boynton.]

GLANVILLE, BENJAMIN (–1774), held the post of Surveyor of Works to the Victualling Office and Inspector of Repairs to the Admiralty from 1731 until his death in 1774 [J. C. Sainty, *Admiralty Officials 1660–1870*, 1975, 76]. He surveyed ST. BOTOLPH'S CHURCH, ALDGATE, LONDON, prior to its rebuilding in 1741–4 [*Commons' Jnls.* xxiii, 633], and was consulted about the completion of the steeple of ST. MARY'S CHURCH, ROTHERHITHE, in 1746 [Vestry Minutes, *ex inf.* Mrs. S. Jeffery].

GLASCODINE, SAMUEL (–*c.*1760), of Bristol, was a carpenter by trade. He was admitted to the freedom of the city in January 1737 on payment of a fine of £8. In 1741 he obtained the contract for the carpenter's work at the new Exchange, and in 1746 he was similarly employed at Clifton Hill House. For the Corporation he designed and built in 1744–5 the MARKETS (dem.) behind the Exchange, with a narrow elevation (which survives) to the High Street, and in 1746 the old POST OFFICE (now offices) in Corn Street adjoining the Exchange. He also designed the new church and vicarage of ST. GEORGE, KINGSWOOD, nr. BRISTOL, erected in 1752–6, and rebuilt after a fire in 1878. The original plans and elevations are preserved in the minute-book of the Commissioners for building the church (Bristol City Archives). The handsome house in Stokes Croft that Glascodine built for his own occupation now forms part of the former Baptist College there. Glascodine was a fairly competent imitator of John Wood's Palladian style. He must have died shortly before 1761, when the business passed to his son Joseph, who was described as a millwright and carpenter when he was admitted a free burgess in 1772. Joseph Glascodine lived at Stokes Croft until 1805, when he sold the property to the Baptists shortly after becoming one of the District Surveyors for the City of Bristol under the Act of 1788. The only building he is known to have designed is a house in Church Street, Warminster, Wilts., for William Wansey [*V.C.H. Wilts.* viii, 94]. He died in December 1817, when Richard Glascodine (presumably his son) succeeded to his surveyorship, dying on 8 May 1819 [W. Ison, *The Georgian Buildings of Bristol*, 1952, 34–5, 106–8; A Beaven, *Bristol Lists*, 1899, 248–9].

GLOVER, THOMAS (*c.*1639–1707), was formerly commemorated by the following inscription (now destroyed) in the cemetery on the north side of Salisbury Cathedral: 'In memory of Thomas Glover Architect who having erected many Stately curious and Artful edifices for others, himself is here lodged under this single Stone in full expectation however of a building with God eternal in the Heavens. ob. Dec. 2, A.D. 1707, Aetat 68' [James Harris, *Copies of the Epitaphs in Salisbury Cathedral, Cloisters and Cemetery*, 1825, 133]. The will of Thomas Glover, of the Close of New Sarum, dated 9 Nov. 1707, was proved on 2 Jan. 1707/8 [P.C.C. 8 BARRETT].

In 1682 Thomas Glover of Harnham, nr. Salisbury, contracted to build the MATRONS' COLLEGE or almshouses in SALISBURY CATHEDRAL CLOSE for Bishop Seth Ward for £1193. The work was to be under the inspection of Thomas Naish, clerk of works to the Cathedral, but there is nothing in the contract to indicate the authorship of the design [Salisbury Diocesan Records]. The building is illustrated in R.C.H.M., *Salisbury, Houses of the Close*, 1993, 152–4.

In a memorandum book of the 1st Earl of Shaftesbury (d. 1683) at WIMBORNE HOUSE,

WIMBORNE ST. GILES, DORSET, there are notes on a contract whereby Thomas Glover undertook to make substantial additions to that house for the Earl.

GODEFROY, MAXIMILIAN (1765–?1840), was a French architect of the revolutionary period who emigrated to America after he had fallen foul of the Napoleonic régime. His buildings in Baltimore (notably the Unitarian Church) are important monuments of neo-classical architecture. In 1819, hoping to achieve a European reputation, he came to England and settled in Somers Town. Although he exhibited regularly at the Royal Academy he failed to build up an English practice, and in 1827 returned to France, where he became architect to the *département* of Mayenne. In 1821 Godefroy was awarded the third premium in the competition for SALTERS' HALL, LONDON. The building, erected in 1823–7 to the designs of Henry Carr, the Company's surveyor, incorporated features from the prize-winning designs, and some elements of the façade may be attributed to Godefroy's influence. The only English building known to have been designed in its entirety by Godefroy was the CATHOLIC CHARITIES SCHOOL, CLARENDON SQUARE, LONDON, a simple astylar building in the manner of Durand, built 1825–6 and demolished *c.*1950 after war-damage. [R. L. Alexander, *The Architecture of Maximilian Godefroy*, Baltimore 1974.]

GODWIN, GEORGE (1789–1863), of Brompton, was a pupil of Thomas R. Drew, a surveyor of Kensington [P.R.O., IR 1/39, 18 Feb. 1804]. Little more is known about him beyond the fact that he was the father of George Godwin, junior (1813–88), architect, antiquary, and editor of the *Builder* from 1844 to 1883. The elder Godwin exhibited a drawing of the Théâtre Français in Paris at the Royal Academy in 1811. His designs (1834) for a gardener's lodge at Tottenham Park, Wilts., are in private possession. His younger son Henry (1831–1917) also became an architect. He died on 23 June 1863, aged 73 [*Gent's Mag.* 1863 (ii), 246; monumental inscription in Holy Trinity Church, Brompton Road, London; obituary of George Godwin, junior, in *Builder*, liv, 1888, 75].

GOFF, ELIJAH, junior, was the son of Elijah Goff, 'surveyor and coal-merchant' of Wellclose Square, London. He exhibited a 'Design for a pavilion intended to be built in North Wales' at the Royal Academy in 1792, and 'Elevations of the east fronts of two houses lately erected' in 1797. He was elected a member of the Surveyors' Club in 1799.

GOLD, JAMES, *see* GOULD, JAMES.

GOLDEN, ROBERT (*c.*1738–1809), was in 1774 appointed District Surveyor for the parishes of St. George the Martyr, St. Andrew Holborn and the Liberty of the Rolls. He was then aged 36, and was described as 'Robert Golden junior' of Lamb's Conduit Street [Middlesex County Records, General Orders, no. 10]. He became a member of the Surveyors' Club in 1795, and died on 28 September 1809, aged 72 [*Gent's Mag.* 1809, 1174]. In 1768 he made designs for 'a set of baths' at Brighton which were built the following year by Dr. Awsiter, and he also designed the Card Room of the Old Ship Tavern in the same resort [*A Description of Brighthelmstone*, 1788, 16, 17].

An architect named R. Golden, who was probably his son, exhibited at the Royal Academy from Rome in 1794, and from London in 1796. He married in 1796, but died on 6 January 1797, aged 28 [*Gent's Mag.* 1796, 81; 1797, 82].

GOLDICUTT, JOHN (1793–1842), a pupil of Henry Hakewill, was admitted to the Royal Academy Schools in 1812, gained the Silver Medal in 1814, and in 1815 that of the Society for the Encouragement of Arts. In 1815 he entered the school of A. Leclère at Paris, and competed for the monthly prizes offered by the Académie des Beaux Arts. He then visited Italy, where he spent four years collecting materials for the books which he afterwards published. In 1817–18 he made an elaborate drawing of the transverse section of St. Peter's at Rome, showing the paintings and decorations, for which he was presented with a gold medal by the Pope. The drawing was exhibited at the Royal Academy on his return in 1819. He remained in Hakewill's office until the latter's death in 1830, but appears also to have practised independently, and being by nature ambitious, rarely missed an opportunity of entering for any public competition that was advertised. In 1820 he obtained the third premium in the competition for the Post Office, London, and in 1828, in association with Henry Hakewill, a premium for the Middlesex Lunatic Asylum. He also competed for the University Observatory at Cambridge in 1821, for the new buildings for King's College, Cambridge, in 1823, for the Fishmongers' Hall in 1830, for the Royal Exchange in 1839, and for the Nelson Monument in 1841. He was an accomplished draughtsman who specialized in the production of highly finished coloured drawings. His designs were characterized by an elegant and fastidious neo-classical taste based on a close study of antique sources. Gundimore, for instance, was described by Augustus Hare as 'from a Pompeian model'. His style was probably too archaeological to be popular, and his practice appears to have been very limited.

Goldicutt was one of the first two honorary secretaries of the Institute of British Architects, and took a prominent part in the presentation of a testimonial to Sir John Soane in 1835, himself designing the decoration of Freemasons' Hall for the occasion. He was elected a member of the Academy of St. Luke at Rome, and of the Academy of Fine Arts at Naples. His publications were *Antiquities of Sicily*, fol., 1819, *Specimens of Ancient Decorations from Pompeii*, 1825, *Heriot's Hospital, Edinburgh*, 1826 (with plates etched by himself), and a pamphlet showing his designs for the Nelson Monument, 1841.[1] In 1828 he was appointed Surveyor for the combined districts of St. Clement Danes and St. Mary-le-Strand. J. H. Hakewill was his pupil. He died on 3 October 1842, aged 49, and was buried in Kensal Green Cemetery. A collection of his drawings is in the R.I.B.A. Library. A sketch-book in the Yale Center for British Art, containing drawings made in northern Italy in 1832–3, has been attributed to him because of the similarity of the draughtsmanship to the drawings at the R.I.B.A. [*A.P.S.D.*; obituary in *Civil Engineer and Architect's Jnl.* v, 372; Anon., 'John Goldicutt and his Times', *Arch. Rev.* xxxi, 1912, 321.]

GUNDIMORE, nr. CHRISTCHURCH, HANTS., for W. S. Rose, 1818–19 [R.I.B.A. drawings, no. 365; exhib. at R.A. 1819].

LONDON, PARK LANE, Nos. 98 and 99, 1823–5 [R.I.B.A. drawings, no. 376; *Survey of London* xl, 277].

WEST COWES, ISLE OF WIGHT, Marine Villa for Simon Halliday, 1827–8 [R.I.B.A. drawings, nos. 370–5; exhib. at R.A. 1828 as 'now building'].

THE DELL, nr. WINDSOR, BERKS., alterations for the Rt. Hon. H. R. Westenra, M.P., *c.*1830 [exhib. at R.A. 1830].

WORTHING, SUSSEX, CASINO on the Esplanade, 1830 [exhib. at R.A. 1830 as 'lately erected'].

DINGLEY HALL, NORTHANTS., new terrace and proposed alterations to the west front for H. H. Hungerford, 1836 [exhib. at R.A. 1836].

PADDINGTON, ST. JAMES'S CHURCH, SUSSEX GARDENS, with G. Gutch, 1841–3, Gothic, remodelled by G. E. Street 1881–2 [R.I.B.A. drawings, nos. 393–401; exhib. at R.A. 1842].

LONDON, WHITE'S CLUB-HOUSE, ST. JAMES'S STREET, alterations [*A.P.S.D.*].

Design for stables for George Watson Taylor, Esq., M.P., probably intended for STOKE PARK, WILTS. [R.I.B.A. drawings, no. 368].

[1] In 1833 he had published a lithograph showing an earlier design for a naval monument in Trafalgar Square, but with a statue of King William IV as the principal feature.

GOLDRING, GEORGE, was a pupil of William Pilkington. He exhibited student's designs at the Royal Academy between 1792 and 1802. He was President of the Surveyors' Club in 1820. In 1821 he was appointed joint surveyor of the London Orphan Asylum with William Inman (*q.v.*). In *c.*1828 he designed a workhouse for the parish of St. Anne, Limehouse [*Gent's Mag.* 1828 (ii), 297].

GOLDSMITH, ROBERT (*c.*1794–1866), practised in Manchester during the second quarter of the nineteenth century. He died at Chorlton-on-Medlock on 3 Feb. 1866 [Principal Probate Registry, Calendar of Probates]. His practice was continued by his son G. H. Goldsmith.

GOLLOP, GEORGE and WILLIAM, were carpenters and builders of Poole in Dorset. George Gollop (perhaps their father) had built a CONGREGATIONAL CHAPEL at WAREHAM in 1790. In 1837 George designed a simple CONGREGATIONAL CHAPEL at SWANAGE, and in 1841 a more pretentious one was built at LONGHAM, HAMPRESTON, to the designs of William [C. Stell, *Nonconformist Chapels and Meeting-Houses in South-West England*, R.C.H.M.E., 1991, 117, 129, 131].

GOMME, Sir BERNARD DE (1620–1685), was born in Flanders. As a young man he served in the campaigns of Frederick Henry, Prince of Orange, and afterwards accompanied Prince Rupert to England. From 1642 to 1646 he served in the royal army as engineer and quartermaster-general 'with conspicuous ability', and was knighted by Charles I. His plan of the fortifications of Liverpool, dated 1644, is in the British Library (Sloane MS. 5027 A, f. 69), and plans of the battles of Naseby, Marston Moor, etc., by him are in Add. MSS. 16370 and 16371.

After the Restoration Gomme was (March 1661) made engineer-general of all the King's fortifications and castles in England and Wales by Charles II, and in 1667 he was naturalized by Act of Parliament. According to the 'Rules and Orders for the Office of the Ordnance' drawn up in 1683, the Principal

Engineer was 'to be perfect in Architecture, civil and military', and 'to make Plots and Models of all manner of Fortifications . . . commanded by us to be erected for our service' (B.L., King's MS. 70, ff. 31v–32). In this capacity Gomme supervised the repair of Dover pier, and the construction of fortifications at Dunkirk. In August 1665 instructions were given for fortifying PORTSMOUTH according to Gomme's plans (*Cal. State Papers Domestic 1664–5*, 510), and his estimates and plans for the work are in B.L., Add. MSS. 2448, 16370 and 28088, f. 26. In 1679 Thomas and John Fitch contracted to carry out further fortifications at Portsmouth designed by Gomme (Add. Charter 32751). In November 1665 he was commissioned to build a new citadel on the Hoe at PLYMOUTH, which was built under his direction in 1666–70, the latter date appearing on the handsome baroque gateway, for whose design he was presumably responsible (*Cal. S.P.D. 1665–6*, 57, 61; *1668–9*, 371; *Addenda 1660–85*, 144; volume of accounts in National Maritime Museum). A coloured plan of the Citadel by Gomme, dated 1666/7, and a 'Plan of the King's House at Plymouth', also attributed to him, but unsigned, were sold at Sotheby's on 9 March 1948, from the Dartmouth Collection (lot 464), and there is a plan of Plymouth by him dated 1668 in B.L., Add. MS. 16371. He also designed the new fort built at TILBURY, ESSEX, in 1670–83, with a gatehouse similar to the one at Plymouth [A. D. Saunders, *Tilbury Fort*, H.M.S.O. 1960]. In 1673 he was in Ireland, where he made designs for a citadel at Ringsend, nr. Dublin. In his report he specifies that the gateway shall be of Portland stone, 'in the same forme as at Plymouth' [Sir J. Gilbert, *Calendar of Ancient Records*, Dublin, 1889–98, v, 568]. See also the 'Observations explanatory of a plan and estimate for a citadel at Dublin, designed by Sir Bernard de Gomme, Engineer-General, in the year 1673', privately printed by Charles Haliday of Dublin in 1861.

On the death of Sir Jonas Moore the younger in 1682, Gomme succeeded him as Surveyor General of Ordnance. He died on 23 November 1685, and was buried in the chapel of St. Peter within the Tower of London. There is a miniature portrait of him in a collection of plans in B.L., King's Library, cii, 21. [*D.N.B.*]

GOMME, STEPHEN (–1858), of Hammersmith, exhibited at the Society of British Artists in 1835, 1837 and 1838 and at the Royal Academy in 1839 and 1845. In 1838 he showed a BRITISH SCHOOL at HAMMERSMITH erected to his designs, and in 1839 'improvements' carried out for O. May at COCKBURN HOUSE, SHEPHERD'S BUSH, HAMMERSMITH. He died at Hammersmith on 8 July 1858 [Principal Probate Registry, Calendar of Probates].

GOOD, JOSEPH HENRY (1775–1857), was the eldest son of the Revd. Joseph Good, a clergyman with a living in Somerset. From 1795 to 1799 he was a pupil of Sir John Soane. In 1803 he entered the competition for the conversion of the Houses of Parliament at Dublin into the Bank of Ireland, and won the fourth premium (not the first two as claimed by his son). There is also some doubt about the younger Good's claim that his father was associated with W. C. Lochner in winning the Bethlehem Hospital competition of 1810, for there is no mention of Good in the Hospital's records, and in 1811 the design was exhibited at the Royal Academy under Lochner's name without any reference to Good. In about 1814 Good was appointed surveyor to the Thavie estate in Holborn and subsequently became surveyor to the parish of St. Andrew, Holborn. He succeeded W. Cresswell as surveyor to the Armourers' and Brasiers' Company in about 1819, and was surveyor to the Hope Assurance Company for many years before its dissolution in 1843. In 1826 he succeeded Edward Mawley as Surveyor to the Commissioners for Building New Churches, a post which he retained until the abolition of the Commission in January 1857. From 1829 to 1848 he also acted as Examining Architect to the Incorporated Church Building Society.

In 1830 Good obtained a post in the Office of Works as Clerk of the Works at the Tower of London, Mint, Somerset House, King's Bench, Fleet and Marshalsea Prisons, etc., and then at Kensington Palace and the Horse Guards. He lost this post in the reorganization of the Office in 1832, but was allowed by William IV (who employed him at Brighton) to retain the official residence at Kensington until his death. He was one of the original Fellows of the Institute of British Architects, and exhibited occasionally at the Royal Academy. He died on 20 November 1857. Among his pupils were Henry Ashton, Alfred Bartholomew, R. Chapman, P. F. Page and Robert Wallace. His eldest son, Joseph Henry Good, F.R.I.B.A. (d. 1885), followed his father's profession and wrote the memoir in *A.P.S.D.* which forms the basis of this entry.

Good appears to have been a competent architectural practitioner who designed nothing of any great significance. His only surviving building of any consequence, the Armourers' and Brasiers' Hall, is (to quote

Pevsner) 'a modest late neo-classical building'.

LONDON, ST. ANDREW'S CHURCH, HOLBORN, internal alterations, 1818; redecorated by S. S. Teulon 1872, interior destroyed by bombing 1941 [*A.P.S.D.*].

APPS COURT, WALTON-ON-THAMES, SURREY, for John Hambrough, 1821–2; dem. *c.*1970 [*A.P.S.D.*; working drawings by A. Bartholomew in R.I.B.A.D.].

BLENDWORTH LODGE, nr. HORNDEAN, HANTS., for Sir William Knighton, Bart., 1821–8 [*A.P.S.D.*].

LONDON, ST. ANDREW'S VESTRY HALL, HOLBORN, 1823 [*A.P.S.D.*].

AVINGTON RECTORY, HANTS., 1828–9 [John Harris, *Catalogue of British Drawings for Architecture, etc., in American Collections*, 1971, 108].

LONDON, NATIONAL SCHOOL, HOLBORN, 1830; dem. [*A.P.S.D.*].

LONDON, ST. ANDREW'S HOLBORN WORKHOUSE, SHOE LANE, 1831; dem. [*A.P.S.D.*].

BRIGHTON, ROYAL PAVILION: works for King William IV, including SOUTH LODGE, 1831, dem. 1851; DORMITORIES, 1831, dem.; STABLES, 1832, converted into Museum and Art Gallery 1872; NORTH LODGE (oriental style), 1832 [*A.P.S.D.*; *History of the King's Works* vi, 260].

LONDON, ARMOURERS' AND BRASIERS' HALL, COLEMAN STREET, 1839–41; interior altered 1872 [*A.P.S.D.*; exhib. at R.A. 1834, by his son].

GOODING, GEORGE (1764–1842), practised in Ipswich, where he designed ST. PETER'S RECTORY, 1816 [C. Brown *et al.*, *Dictionary of Architects of Suffolk Buildings 1800–1914*, 1991, 114] and THE CORN EXCHANGE, 1812; dem. 1850 [J. Wodderspoon, *Memorials of Ipswich*, 1850, 11].

GOODRIDGE, HENRY EDMUND (1797–1864), was the son of James Goodridge, a successful builder of Bath who carried out much of the later work in Bathwick. He was articled to John Lowder (*q.v.*), proved to be an able and intelligent pupil, and by the 1820s was established in independent practice in Bath. Brisk, conscientious and thoroughly professional in every way, Goodridge soon obtained numerous commissions in Somerset and Wiltshire, and his choice by the exacting Beckford as the architect of Lansdown Tower led to his later employment by Beckford's son-in-law the Duke of Hamilton at Hamilton Palace in Scotland. His earlier work was mostly in the Greek Revival style, but he also designed several Gothic churches (including Archdeacon Daubeny's bizarre chapel at Rode Hill), a neo-Norman castle at Devizes and an Italian Romanesque nonconformist chapel. Both his own house and Beckford's Lansdown Tower are eclectic compositions in which Greek, Romanesque and Italian forms are wilfully combined to create eccentric but highly picturesque architecture. His design for the Houses of Parliament (1835) envisaged an octagonal House of Commons and a House of Lords in the form of a 'baronial hall with minstrel gallery'.

Goodridge visited France in or shortly before 1818 and Italy in 1829. He exhibited occasionally at the Royal Academy. He married in 1822 and had a son, Alfred Samuel Goodridge, by whom his practice was continued after his death, which occurred on 26 October 1864. He was buried in the cemetery at Lansdown. H. L. Elmes and W. H. Campbell were his pupils.

[Memoir by A. S. Goodridge in *R.I.B.A. Sessional Papers* 1864–5, extra pagination, 3–5; *Gent's Mag.* 1822 (ii), 88; W. Ison, *The Georgian Buildings of Bath*, 1948, 45.]

BATH

ARGYLE CONGREGATIONAL CHAPEL, BATHWICK, enlarged and rebuilt façade, 1821; façade altered 1861 [*A.P.S.D.*, *s.v.* 'Bath'].

LANSDOWN TOWER, for William Beckford, 1824–7 [memoir] (E. F. English & W. Maddox, *Views of Lansdown Tower, Bath*, 1844; J. Millington, *Beckford's Tower, Lansdown, Bath*, 1973).

HIGH STREET, 'THE CORRIDOR', 1825 [memoir].

CLEVELAND BRIDGE and TOLL-HOUSES, 1827; the bridge was reconstructed in 1928–9 [inscription on bridge].

BATH, villas on BATHWICK ESTATE, including MONTEBELLO (now BATHWICK GRANGE) for himself, 1828, CASA BIANCA, and FIESOLE, 1846 [R. E. M. Peach, *Street-Lore of Bath*, 1893, 96; *Bath Chronicle*, 24 April 1915; D. Watkin, *Thomas Hope*, 1968, 142–3 and pls. 48–9].

PRIOR PARK, stone staircase leading to portico, and other works connected with the conversion of the mansion into Prior Park R.C. College, 1829–34. Goodridge was probably the architect employed to reconstruct the interior after the fire of 1836 and to design the neo-classical gymnasium in 1841–2. A large perspective by Goodridge showing an ambitious scheme for further additions is in the Yale Center for British Art.

attributed: LANSDOWN CRESCENT, No. 19, remodelled interior for William Beckford, 1837 [J. Lees-Milne, 'Beckford in Bath', *C. Life*, 29 April 1976].

JEWISH SYNAGOGUE, CORN STREET, 1841; dem. [S. D. Major, *Notabilia of Bath*, 1879, 80].

THE EASTERN DISPENSARY, CLEVELAND PLACE, 1845 [memoir] (plan in *Builder* vii, 1849, 160).

ARGYLE CHURCH SCHOOLS, GROVE STREET, 1845; dem. [S. D. Major, *Notabilia of Bath*, 1879, 97].

LANSDOWN CEMETERY, entrance archway, 1848, Romanesque style [memoir].

INDEPENDENT (now CONGREGATIONAL) CHAPEL, CHARLOTTE STREET, 1854, with A. S. Goodridge, Italian Romanesque style [*A.P.S.D.*, *s.v.* 'Bath'].

OTHER WORKS

WIDCOMBE CHURCH, SOMERSET, enlarged 1822 [I.C.B.S.].

DOWNSIDE ABBEY, SOMERSET, chapel and other buildings, 1822–3, Gothic; subsequently partly remodelled and incorporated in other buildings [B. Little, *Catholic Churches since 1623*, 1966, 62, 111, 164 and pl. 34a].

RODE HILL, SOMERSET (formerly WILTS.), CHRIST CHURCH, 1822–4, Gothic [C. Daubeny, *A Guide to the Church*, 3rd. ed. 1830, Appendix, p. lxxxvi; *Bath Chronicle*, 9 Sept. 1824; *V.C.H. Wilts*, viii, 230].

SOUTH WRAXALL CHURCH, WILTS., north aisle, 1823, Gothic [I.C.B.S.].

MALMESBURY ABBEY CHURCH, WILTS., designed west window and other alterations, 1823 [*Gent's Mag.* 1823 (ii), 170; a lithograph by Goodridge shows the alterations].

HARDENHUISH HOUSE, WILTS., alterations and additions for Thomas Clutterbuck, 1829, probably incorporating some suggestions from Sir John Soane [Sir John Soane's Museum, Journal No. 6, 1813–30, f. 161].

COTTLES HOUSE, ATWORTH, WILTS., alterations *c.*1825–30 [Gloucestershire C.R.O., D 1086, P.13].

THE HOOD MONUMENT, BUTLEIGH, SOMERSET, 1831 [memoir].

ROWDE CHURCH, WILTS., rebuilt except west tower, 1831–3, Gothic [accounts, correspondence and drawings in parish chest, 1959; drawings in R.I.B.A.D.].

ATWORTH CHURCH, WILTS., rebuilt 1832, Gothic [I.C.B.S.].

COMBE DOWN CHURCH, SOMERSET, 1832–5, Gothic; chancel added 1884 [*Gent's Mag.* 1835 (ii), 196].

POTTERNE CHURCH, WILTS., repewed 1833 [I.C.B.S.].

BRISTOL, THE R.C. PRO-CATHEDRAL OF THE TWELVE APOSTLES, PARK PLACE, CLIFTON, begun 1834 but abandoned *c.*1840 in an incomplete state; eventually completed by C. Hansom to a different design 1847–8 [B. Little, *Catholic Churches since 1623*, 1966, 102–3]. Goodridge's design is illustrated by B. Little, *The City and County of Bristol*, 1954, pl. 29, and by Pevsner, *North Somerset and Bristol* (*Buildings of England*), pl. 34a.

LYME REGIS, DORSET, ST. MICHAEL'S R.C. CHURCH, 1835–7, Gothic; tower and spire rebuilt 1937 [inscription in church].

FROME, SOMERSET, HOLY TRINITY CHURCH, 1837–9, Gothic [I.C.B.S.].

DEVIZES CASTLE, WILTS., castellated mansion on site of medieval castle for V. Leach, *c.*1840; much enlarged *c.*1860 onwards [exhib. at R.A. 1842].

HAMILTON PALACE, LANARKSHIRE, library for 10th Duke of Hamilton, *c.*1845; dem. *c.*1920 [*Builder* v, 1847, 271]; cf. the projected alterations at Hamilton Palace exhibited by Goodridge at the R.A. in 1842. Goodridge's unexecuted designs for the Hamilton Mausoleum, dated 1846, are among the Hamilton archives at Lennoxlove (photos. at N.M.R.S.).

ECCLESGREIG HOUSE, ST. CYRUS, KINCARDINESHIRE, remodelled in castellated style for Forsyth Grant, 1846 [exhib. at R.A.; memoir].

BRISTOL, CLIFTON DOWN, double house ('Avon Bank' and 'Llanfoist'), 1857, Italianate [Bristol Record Office, Building Grant plans, vol. 4, f. 109, *ex inf.* Prof. A. Gomme].

PICKWICK DISTRICT CHURCH OF ENGLAND SCHOOL, CORSHAM, WILTS., 1857, Gothic; converted into a house [Wilts. C.R.O., School Plans, *ex inf.* Mr. Alan Brooks].

GOODWIN, FRANCIS (1784–1835), was born on 23 May 1784 at King's Lynn, and became a pupil of J. Coxedge of Kensington. Later he was a pupil or assistant of John Walters, for whose Gothic church of St. Philip, Stepney (1818–20), he claimed the credit. By 1819 he was in independent practice, seeking commissions by every means in his power. Although the unsolicited designs for rebuilding Magdalen College which he submitted in 1822 merely earned him a rebuke as a 'bold speculator' (see J. C. Buckler's *Observations on the Original Architecture of Magdalen College*, 1823, 148–9), the 'inundation of pictures and promises' with which he flooded the church building committees of the Midlands had more success, and he soon had more churches in hand than the Commissioners for Building Churches thought proper. Some of these churches he contrived to pass on to others in return for a suitable consideration, but between 1820 and 1830 he designed and built nine churches paid for by the Commissioners, besides five more otherwise financed. Two of these churches (St. Leonard, Bilston, and St. Paul, Walsall) were designed in a spare neo-classical manner derived from Soane, but all the others were in the showy late Gothic style of which Goodwin was a skilful purveyor.

By the mid-1820s Goodwin had a considerable practice in the Midlands, where he was responsible for several competently designed municipal buildings, of which the Grecian Town Hall at Manchester was the most important. At the same time he was assiduously seeking national fame by entering designs for competitions. Among those for which he entered were: King's College, Cambridge (1823), the Middlesex Lunatic Asylum (1828), and King Edward's School, Birmingham (1830), for which he gained the third premium. In 1830 he made designs for a 'National Cemetery' on Primrose Hill, consisting of an outer area 'disposed somewhat after the manner of Père la Chaise' at Paris, and an inner enclosure containing temples and mausolea which were to be 'facsimiles of some of the most celebrated remains of Greek and Roman architecture' (*Gent's Mag.* 1830 (i), 351; lithograph in Soane Museum, lix, set 2, no. 29). These designs he exhibited in Parliament Street, but his proposals were not taken up by the recently formed General Cemetery Company, which eventually laid out Kensal Green Cemetery under the direction of another architect. In 1833 Goodwin was one of the architects invited to submit proposals for a new House of Commons to a Select Committee, and his designs, which are reproduced in the Report (*Parliamentary Papers* 1833 (487) xii), were 'said to have been the best of those sent in by the witnesses examined'. In 1834 Goodwin was associated with Capt. S. Browne, R.N., in a scheme for a suspension bridge over the Thames on the site of the present Lambeth Bridge, but although it was 'approved by the provisional committee' and exhibited at the Royal Academy, nothing came of the project. In the same year he was in Ireland making designs for additions to the College at Belfast, and for public baths at Dublin, neither of which were executed.

In 1835, when the competition for the new Houses of Parliament was announced, Goodwin naturally determined to compete. The task, however, proved fatal. For his concentration on the designs led first to insomnia and then to the apoplexy from which he died on 30 August 1835. Throughout his career he had been in chronic financial difficulties, and his estate was valued for probate at less than £1000. Benjamin Baud (*q.v.*) and Thomas Allom (1804–72), the architectural illustrator, were his pupils.

In 1833–4 Goodwin published *Domestic Architecture . . . A Series of Designs in the Grecian, Italian and Old English Styles*, in two volumes, with descriptive text by W. H. Leeds. In 1835 this was reissued with the alternative title of *Rural Architecture*, with additional designs for cottages, lodges, etc. There was a second edition in 1843, and a third in 1850. Goodwin also published *Plans of the New House of Commons proposed by Francis Goodwin*, fol. 1833.

[Obituaries in Loudon's *Architectural Mag.* ii, 1835, 476, and *Gent's Mag.* 1835 (ii), 659–60; *A.P.S.D.*; *D.N.B.*; Michael Port, 'Francis Goodwin: an Architect of the 1820s', *Architectural History* i, 1958; Angus Taylor, 'Francis Goodwin's *Domestic Architecture* and two Cockermouth Villas', *Arch. Hist.* 28, 1985].

Unless otherwise stated, the following list of Goodwin's works is based on the information given in his *Rural Architecture* ii, 1843, p. xiii and *passim*.

PUBLIC BUILDINGS

MANCHESTER, TOWN HALL and ASSEMBLY ROOMS, 1822–5; entrance hall and staircase by R. Lane, 1838; dem. 1912, when façade was re-erected as a screen in Heaton Park (*Lancashire Illustrated*, 1831, plate).

MACCLESFIELD, CHESHIRE, TOWN HALL and ASSEMBLY ROOMS, 1823–4; enlarged 1869–71.

DERBY, COUNTY GAOL, 1823–7; remodelled 1880; dem. except gateway (plan and elevation in S. Glover, *History of the County of Derby* ii, 1833, 450–3).

LEEDS, THE CENTRAL MARKET, 1824–7; dem. (engraving in T. Allen, *History of the County of York* ii, 1831, 536).

SALFORD, THE MARKET (at the rear of Lane's Town Hall), 1825.

BRADFORD, YORKS. (W.R.), THE PUBLIC ROOMS, 1827–9; afterwards known as EXCHANGE BUILDINGS, and from 1867 to 1887 used as the Post Office; now offices, known as 'Post Office Chambers, Piccadilly'.

CHURCHES

KING'S LYNN, NORFOLK, rebuilt TRINITY CHAPEL on north side of ST. MARGARET'S CHURCH, 1809 [H. J. Hillen, *History of Lynn* ii, 1907, 657].

SOUTHSEA (PORTSEA), HANTS., ST. PAUL, 1820–2, Gothic; dem.

WALSALL PARISH CHURCH, STAFFS., rebuilt nave, 1820–1, Gothic.

BIRMINGHAM, HOLY TRINITY, BORDESLEY, 1820–3, Gothic (*Gent's Mag.* 1827 (ii), 201).

ASHTON-UNDER-LYNE, LANCS., ST. PETER, 1821–4, Gothic.

KIDDERMINSTER, WORCS., ST. GEORGE, 1821–4, Gothic.

WEST BROMWICH, STAFFS., CHRIST CHURCH, 1821–8, Gothic; altered 1878–84; dem. 1980.

BIRMINGHAM, ST. PAUL, added steeple, 1823, classical.

BURTON-ON-TRENT, STAFFS., HOLY TRINITY, 1823–4, Gothic; rebuilt 1882 by J. O. Scott. There is a set of the architect's drawings for this church in the William Salt Library (Staffordshire Views ii, 183–9).

MANCHESTER, ST. PETER, added tower and spire, 1824, classical; dem. 1907.

BILSTON, STAFFS., ST. LEONARD, 1825–6, classical; tower rebuilt 1882–3, interior remodelled 1893. There are drawings for this church in the R.I.B.A. Collection.

WALSALL, STAFFS., ST. PAUL, 1826, classical; rebuilt by J. L. Pearson 1891–2 (plans, elevations, etc., in R. Tress, *Working Drawings of Churches*, 1841).

DERBY, ST. JOHN, 1826–8, Gothic; chancel added 1871.

MANCHESTER, ST. GEORGE, HULME, 1826–8, Gothic; altered 1884.

OLDHAM, LANCS., ST. JAMES, 1827–8, Gothic; chancel added 1883.

SOUTHAMPTON, ST. MICHAEL, rebuilt nave arcades to accommodate galleries, 1826–8. The galleries were removed in 1872.

BILSTON, STAFFS., ST. MARY, 1829–30, Gothic.

PENDLETON, LANCS., ST. THOMAS, with R. Lane, 1829–31, Gothic [Port, 148].

DOMESTIC ARCHITECTURE

BILSTON PARSONAGE, STAFFS., for Revd. William Leigh, *c.*1822 (cf. *Rural Architecture* i, pl. 23 and *Arch. Hist.* 28, 1985, 127 and pl. 2).

MEYNELL LANGLEY, DERBYSHIRE, refronted for Godfrey Meynell, 1829 [building accounts and MS. commonplace book at Meynell Langley] (R. Innes-Smith & C. H. Wood, *Notable Derbyshire Houses*, Derby 1972, 96–7).

LISSADELL COURT, CO. SLIGO, IRELAND, for Sir Robert Gore Booth, Bart., 1831–5 (*Rural Architecture* ii, pls. 31–4; *C. Life*, 6 Oct. 1977).

MARKREE, CO. SLIGO, IRELAND, castellated gatelodge to Dublin entrance, for E. J. Cooper, 1832 (*Rural Architecture* i, pl. 40).

CULLAMORE, nr. LISSADELL, CO. SLIGO, IRELAND, House for Henry Gore Booth, before 1833 (*Rural Architecture* i, pls. 30–3).

CURRAGHMORE, CO. WATERFORD, IRELAND, row of seven cottages designed for 3rd Marquess of Waterford, *c.*1834 (*Rural Architecture* ii, supplement).

DUNSTALL LODGE, nr. WOLVERHAMPTON, STAFFS., lodge to Stafford Road entrance, for Henry Hordern, before 1833 (*Rural Architecture* ii, pls. 7–8).

TEDDESLEY HALL, STAFFS., a lodge for 1st Lord Hatherton, 1835 [*A.P.S.D.*].

GORDON, WILLIAM and G—, father and son, were architects, surveyors and speculative builders in Hammersmith during the first half of the nineteenth entury. A folio of architectural drawings by them, dated between 1820 and 1838, was sold by Sotheby's in 1990. It included 'plans, elevations and sections of cottages ornés, terrace houses, villas, a prison, the Six Bells Public House at Acton, Middlesex, and properties at Hammersmith, including a pair of cottages fronting the Thames, Oak Brook Cottage, and Mr. Bursley's House in the New [now Goldhawk] Road'. [Sotheby's *Catalogue of Early British, Victorian and Architectural Drawings*, 25–6 April, 1990, lot 390].

GORHAM, JOHN (1710–1801), was described as 'an eminent surveyor and builder' when he died in 1801. He was a bricklayer by trade, and was Master of the Tylers' and Bricklayers' Company in 1755–6. He was surveyor to Gray's Inn, the Inner Temple, the Drapers' and Fishmongers' Companies, and the Duke of Bedford's London estate. His father, Thomas Gorham, had been bricklayer to Gray's Inn since 1726, and in 1738 Thomas and his son were jointly appointed 'surveyor of the new buildings in Holborn Court', i.e. Nos. 2–3 South Square (dem. 1941). In 1776 John Gorham was associated with Charles Cole (*q.v.*) in the laying out of ELY PLACE, HOLBORN, and soon after 1781 he built several houses in CHANCERY LANE on the site of the present Law Society's offices. He rebuilt the front of DRAPERS' HALL, THROGMORTON STREET, in 1778; again rebuilt 1868–9 [A. H. Johnson, *History of the Drapers' Company* iii, 1922, 286] (*C. Life*, 22 Nov. 1979). He retired in 1797, a wealthy man, but 'lived in habits of the strictest economy, though reputed to be worth upwards of £200,000'. [*Gent's Mag.* 1801, 768; *The Pension Book of Gray's Inn*, ed. R. J. Fletcher, ii, 1910, 200, 230, 378; *Trans. London and Middlesex Archl. Soc.*, N.S. vi, 1929–32, 446; D. J. Olsen, *Town Planning in London in the 18th and 19th Centuries*, Yale 1964, 183.]

GOSLING, CHARLES FLICK (–1865), exhibited at the Royal Academy from London addresses in 1836, 1838 and 1845. In 1836 he showed a 'Design for a mansion now erecting near Ipswich'. He died in London on 7 October 1865 [Principal Probate Registry, Calendar of Probates].

GOTT, JOHN (1720–1793), of Woodhouse in the parish of Calverley, nr. Leeds, was active as a bridge- and canal-builder in Yorkshire. He was resident engineer of the Aire and Calder Navigation from 1760 to 1792, and Surveyor of Bridges for the West Riding of Yorkshire from 1777 until his death in 1793, when he was succeeded by his son William (1745–1810). His younger son Benjamin (1762–1840) was a well-known woollen manufacturer in Leeds.

Among the Yorkshire bridges designed by John Gott were those at FERRYBRIDGE, 1764–5, replaced in 1797–1804 by the present bridge designed by John Carr; CASTLEFORD, 1770, replaced in 1805 by the existing bridge designed by Bernard Hartley; METHLEY, 1776–9, and HEBDEN BRIDGE, 1789 [West Riding County Records, *ex inf.* Prof. A. W. Skempton]. He also built (1760–1) the ornamental bridge at NOSTELL according to a design made by Sir George Savile [M. W. Brockwell, *The Nostell Collection*, 1915, 44–5, 385], and in 1767–70 designed HEXHAM BRIDGE, NORTHUMBERLAND, destroyed by a flood in 1771 [M. A. Richardson, *The Local Historian's Table-Book* ii, 1842, 168].

GOUD, ANTHONY, was a mason of Springfield, nr. Chelmsford in Essex. In 1726–31 he was working at Boreham House, Essex, and in 1729–41 under Leoni at Moulsham Hall in the same county [R. Gunnis, *Dictionary of British Sculptors 1660–1851*, 1968, 178]. An inscription commemorates the fact that in 1732 he rebuilt the west tower of TERLING CHURCH, ESSEX, in a vernacular classical style. In 1741 he covenanted to erect eight substantial brick houses on land he had leased in DUKE STREET, CHELMSFORD. He subsequently moved to Chatham in Kent, where he died some time before 1774 [Essex Record Office, D/DU/132/1 and 5].

GOULD, or **GOLD,** JAMES (–1734), was a surveyor in London, where in February 1722/3 he was engaged to value building materials on the Harley estate [B.L., Add. MS. 18240, f. 28]. He was very likely the 'John Gould' who in 1720 was associated with Colen Campbell as surveyor of Sir Theodore Jansen's new house at Wimbledon [*The Particulars and Inventories of the Estates of the Late . . . Directors of the South Sea Company*, 1721, 43]. In 1723 he was appointed by the South Sea Company to 'Survey and measure the works' of their new premises in Threadneedle Street, at a salary of £100 p.a. As no other architect is mentioned in the minutes, it would appear that it was to Gould's designs that SOUTH SEA HOUSE was erected in 1724–5 (dem. 1902). His salary as 'Surveyor of the new Buildings' was paid up to Christmas 1726 [B.L., Minute Books of the South Sea Company, Add. MSS. 25501, f. 76, 25502, ff. 89, 108^v, 152^v, 177^v, 257^v].

In 1725–8 ST. BOTOLPH'S CHURCH, BISHOPSGATE, was rebuilt to Gould's designs in a style derived from Wren's City churches [minutes of building committe in Guildhall Library, MS. 21,130].

In 1719 Gould's daughter Elizabeth married George Dance (senior), and Dance may have been involved in the building of GOULD or GOLD SQUARE, off Cooper's Row, undertaken by his father-in-law as a speculation in about 1730 [Dorothy Stroud, *George Dance, Architect*, 1971, 30]. The death of 'Mr. Gould, Surveyor to the South Sea Company', occurred on 31 January 1734 [*Gent's Mag.* 1734, 107].

GOVER, WILLIAM (*c.*1814–1859), an architect and surveyor of Winchester, was probably the son of William Gover, surveyor and builder of that city, and the grandson of George Gover, similarly described in 1783. He or his father enlarged HINDON CHURCH, WILTS., in 1836 [I.C.B.S.], and largely rebuilt ST. MAURICE'S CHURCH, WINCHESTER, in 1842; dem. [I.C.B.S.]. Gover died in 1859, aged 45 [Winchester Cemetery Register].

GOWAN, ALEXANDER (*c.*1710–1776), was a mason by trade, and is described as 'builder' on the tombstone in the Canongate churchyard, Edinburgh, which records his death on 8 March 1776, aged 66. From a reference in a lawsuit to 'Mr. Gowan, Architect in Edinburgh, and the tradesmen under him then building the House of Durie' [S.R.O., CS 230/R 6/4, no. 15], it appears that he built and probably designed DURIE HOUSE, FIFE, for John Gibson, *c.*1765–7, in a plain 'Palladian' style [information from Dr. Atholl Murray].

GOWAN, GEORGE (–1843), was the son of Alexander Gowan (*q.v.*). He is described as 'architect' on the family tombstone in the Canongate churchyard, which shows that he was over 80 at the time of his death on 23 October 1843. In 1791 he designed a house in GEORGE STREET, EDINBURGH, for the Countess of Balcarres [S.R.O., Edinburgh Sasines].

GOWAN, WILLIAM, then 'of Piccadilly, surveyor', was in 1769–75 employed by Charles Howard, later 10th Duke of Norfolk, to design and superintend the building of THE DEEPDENE, DORKING, SURREY, subsequently remodelled for Thomas Hope and dem. 1967 [*Surrey Archl. Colls.* lxxi, 1977, 116]. In 1782 Charles Anderson Pelham, later 1st Lord Yarborough, built a large Doric temple at BROCKLESBY PARK, LINCS., under his direction [J. Lord, 'The Building of the Mausoleum at Brocklesby', *Church Monuments* vii, 1992, 86]. Gowan was responsible for rebuilding TOTTERIDGE CHURCH, HERTS., in 1790–6 [Herts. C.R.O., 69897, 69900]. This small classical church was much altered in the nineteenth century.

GRAHAM, HENRY (1795–1819), was the third son of the Revd. John Graham, rector of St. Saviour's, York. Nothing is known of his architectural training, but at the age of 19 he undertook the restoration of the remarkable thirteenth-century church of SKELTON, YORKS. (N.R.), carried out in 1814–18 [E. Christian, *Architectural Illustrations of Skelton Church*, 1846, 4–5]. In 1818 or 1819 Graham set out for Italy, where in May 1819 he met a premature death in Naples. He is commemorated by a monument in the Protestant Cemetery at Rome, set up by 'two of his fellow students' to 'testify their friendship', and by another at Skelton which refers to 'the ardent pursuit of improvement in his profession as an Architect' which exposed him to 'the dissipating and corrupting air of foreign lands'.

GRAHAM, JAMES GILLESPIE (1776–1855), was born at Dunblane in Perthshire on 11 June 1776. His father, Malcolm Gillespie, is described as 'writer' (i.e. solicitor) in the Register of Births. James is said to have started life as a working joiner or mason, but nothing is known of his early career before the first decade of the nineteenth century, when for some years he was employed as superintendent of the 2nd Lord Macdonald's works on the Isle of Skye. These were mostly of a utilitarian character, consisting of piers, schools, inns, manses and the like, and offered relatively little scope for architectural design. Indeed at first Gillespie's status appears to have been rather that of a clerk of works than an architect. However, by 1810 he had secured several architectural commissions on the mainland, including a country house at Achnacarry in Inverness-shire and the County Buildings at Cupar in Fife. In 1815 he had the good fortune to marry an heiress. She was Margaret, daughter of William Graham, laird of Orchill in Perthshire. Gillespie now 'elongated his surname' to 'Gillespie Graham', and when his father-in-law died in 1825 he and his wife inherited the estate. She died in 1826, leaving two daughters, the elder of whom, Mrs. Graeme-Oliphant, ultimately succeeded to the property. In 1830 Gillespie Graham took a second wife, Elizabeth, the daughter of Major John Campbell of the 76th Regiment of Foot. There were no children by this marriage. He died in Edinburgh on 21 March 1855 after four years' illness, and was buried in the Greyfriars Cemetery. A portrait at Ardblair Castle, Perthshire, by Watson Gordon, shows him attired in Highland dress, and there is a caricature by Crombie in his series of *Modern Athenians*.

Gillespie Graham had an extensive practice in Scotland, specializing in Gothic churches and castellated country houses. Though basically symmetrical, the latter are generally given a picturesque outline by the addition of a large round tower at one side. The same components tend to recur in his designs, and on one occasion he even went so far as to use almost identical plans and elevations for two houses – Edmonstone and Torrisdale Castles – one in Lanarkshire, the other in Argyllshire. Only at the end of his life – at Brodick and Ayton Castles – did he graduate to the 'Scottish baronial' style of which David Bryce was the master. Though the exteriors of his earlier castles are effectively picturesque from a distance, the detailing is generally coarse and unscholarly. But the interiors often show a considerable facility in devising rich Gothic rooms of a more convincingly medieval character. Notable examples are Duns Castle and the Banner Hall at Taymouth Castle. Gillespie Graham was a prolific church architect and provided Scotland with many churches that were greatly superior to the humble and artless kirks of the early nineteenth century. Muthill, for instance, was considered in 1837 to be 'unequalled by any country church in the land'. To modern eyes his best ecclesiastical works were the steeple at Montrose (an effective version of the one at Louth in Lincolnshire) and the spire of Tolbooth St. John's in Edinburgh.

Gillespie Graham's reputation as a Gothic architect was strengthened by an intermittent association with A. W. Pugin, whom he is said to have befriended after the latter was shipwrecked on the coast near Leith. It is certain that Pugin prized a pair of compasses given him by Graham, for they appear in his portrait by Herbert, clearly inscribed 'James Gillespie Graham, architect, Edinburgh 1830'. In return Pugin helped his friend professionally, providing drawings based on authentic Gothic sources. Among the buildings whose detailing benefited from Pugin's expertise were the chapel of St. Margaret's Convent in Edinburgh, the interior of Heriot's Hospital Chapel, the Banner Hall at Taymouth Castle and Tolbooth St. John's steeple, the drawings for which, among the Dean of Guild Records in City Chambers, Edinburgh (Extracted Processes, 4 Feb. 1841) are in Pugin's hand. In 1829–30 Pugin made designs and supplied a quantity of carvings for the house at Murthly which Graham was building for Sir John Stewart in a Jacobean style apparently prescribed by the client. Pugin's most notable service to his Scottish friend was, however, to make the finished drawings for Gillespie Graham's entry in the competition for the new Houses of Parliament in 1835 [B. Ferrey, *Recollections of A. N. Welby Pugin*, 1861, 241]. Pugin's draughtsmanship was probably the best feature of this badly composed design, of which Graham published a lithograph. Perspective drawings of the interiors of the proposed Houses of Lords and Commons in elaborate Puginesque frames are preserved at Ardblair Castle. As a classical designer, Gillespie Graham is best represented by Gray's Hospital at Elgin and by his work on the Moray estate in the New Town at Edinburgh. Here, instead of continuing the grid-plan of the adjoining streets, Graham exploited the terrain to produce a masterpiece of urban planning, of which the polygonal Moray Place is the centrepiece. The elevations are boldly treated in a monumental manner derived from Robert Adam's Charlotte Square.

Gillespie Graham appears to have been ambitious, pushing and none too scrupulous. In 1818 he styled himself 'Architect in Scotland of the Prince Regent' [see S.R.O., GD 51/6/1963 and 2012], and in 1822 took advantage of the Royal visit to Scotland to convert the title to 'Architect to His Majesty for Scotland', to the justifiable annoyance of Robert Reid, who had enjoyed a similar title since 1808 [N.L.S., MS. 351, ff. 102–3]. Two years later he did his best to acquire the sinecure Mastership of the Works in Scotland, vacant by the death of James Brodie, but was defeated by Reid, who succeeded in getting that office merged with his own [N.L.S., MS. 1056, f. 141]. Graham was elected a Fellow of the Society of Antiquaries of Scotland in 1817 and became a burgess of Edinburgh in 1838 [*Roll of Edinburgh Burgesses*, Scottish Record Society, 68].

[*A.P.S.D.*; *D.N.B.*; Burke's *Landed Gentry*, 1858; James Brown, *Epitaphs and Monumental Inscriptions in Greyfriars Churchyard, Edinburgh*, Edinburgh 1867, 226–7; article on 'Edinburgh Architects' in *Builder*, 10 June 1882; *Scots Mag.* lxxvii, 1815, 556; James Macaulay, 'James Gillespie Graham in Skye', *Bull. Scottish Georgian Soc.* iii, 1974–5, *The Gothic Revival*, 1975, chap. xiii, and 'The architectural collaboration between J. Gillespie Graham and A. W. Pugin', *Arch. Hist.* 27, 1984.]

PUBLIC BUILDINGS

EDINBURGH, PICARDY PLACE, alterations to premises for Commercial Bank, 1810 [J. L. Anderson, *The Story of the Commercial Bank of Scotland*, Edinburgh 1910, 6].

CUPAR, FIFE, COUNTY BUILDINGS, ST. CATHERINE STREET, 1810; extended by W. Burn 1835–6 and again subsequently [S.R.O., B 13/18/1, f. 60].

EDINBURGH, remodelled premises (now Masonic Chapel) for THE COMMERCIAL BANK in NEW ASSEMBLY CLOSE, 142 HIGH STREET, 1813 [Edinburgh, Dean of Guild plans].

DUMFRIES, conversion of chapel in BUCCLEUCH STREET into COURT-HOUSE (later Town Hall), *c.*1813 [J. Barbour in *Trans. Dumfriesshire & Galloway . . . Archaeological Soc.* N.S. xxi, 1908–9, 88–9].

CUPAR, FIFE, COUNTY PRISON, 1813–14 [S.R.O., B 13/18/1, with plan; *Parliamentary Papers*, 1818, vi, Report on Scottish Jails, p. 17, with elevation].

ELGIN, MORAYSHIRE, GRAY'S HOSPITAL, 1815–19 [R. Young, *Annals of Elgin*, Elgin 1879, 251, 400].

DUNS, BERWICKSHIRE, THE MARKET HOUSE, 1816, Gothic; dem. 1966 [*Scots Mag.* lxxviii, 1816, 483].

INVERARAY, ARGYLLSHIRE, COURT HOUSE, 1816–20 [I. G. Lindsay & Mary Cosh, *Inveraray and the Dukes of Argyll*, 1973, 317–18].

EDINBURGH, THE DEAF AND DUMB INSTITUTE, HENDERSON ROW, 1823; extended 1893 [J. Stark, *Picture of Edinburgh*, 6th ed. 1835, 260].

DUMBARTON, COUNTY BUILDINGS, with Robert Scott, 1824; enlarged 1863 and 1895 [*Glasgow Herald*, 23 July 1824].

LEITH, THE TOLBOOTH or GAOL, 1824–7, dem. [*The Private Letter-Books of Sir Walter Scott*, ed. W. Partington, 1930, 309].

HADDINGTON, EAST LOTHIAN, addition of spire to TOWN HOUSE, 1830–1 [James Miller, *History of Haddington*, 1900, 228].

ABERDEEN, COMMERCIAL BANK OF SCOTLAND,

KING STREET, 1836 [G. M. Fraser, 'Archibald Simpson and his Times', *Aberdeen Weekly Jnl.*, 9 Aug. 1918].

EDINBURGH, VICTORIA HALL, *see* TOLBOOTH ST. JOHN'S CHURCH.

CHURCHES

SNIZORT, ISLE OF SKYE, 1800–1 [S.R.O., GD 221/15/1, 221/68/107 and 109, *ex inf.* Miss Ierne Grant].

KILMUIR, ISLE OF SKYE, 1808–10; now in ruins [J. Macaulay, 'James Gillespie Graham in Skye', *Bull. Scottish Georgian Soc.* iii, 1974–5, 8].

ARISAIG, INVERNESS-SHIRE, R. C. Chapel (now Church of Scotland Church), 1810–11 [S.R.O., GD 201/1233, 45, 48].

FALKIRK, STIRLINGSHIRE, rebuilt (except central tower), 1810–11, Gothic [S.R.O., GD 171/122; R.C.A.M., *Stirlingshire* i, 150 and pl. 35].

MONIMAIL, FIFE, modified design of steeple made by Robert Hutchinson (*q.v.*) [S.R.O., HR 432/2, pp. 2, 5, 11, 12; GD 26/10/108].

LINLITHGOW, WEST LOTHIAN, restoration of chancel, 1812–13 [J. Ferguson, *Eccelsia Antiqua, or the story of . . . St. Michael's, Linlithgow*, 1905, 105–9].

EDINBURGH, ST. MARY'S CHURCH, now CATHEDRAL (R.C.), BROUGHTON STREET, 1813–14, Gothic [*A.P.S.D.*]. Internal alterations in 1840–1 may have been designed by Pugin in collaboration with Graham [Phoebe Stanton, *Pugin*, 1971, 200]. There have been many subsequent alterations, including the addition of a new chancel in 1896.

GLASGOW, ST. ANDREW'S CHAPEL, now CATHEDRAL (R.C.), GREAT CLYDE STREET, 1814–17, Gothic; enlarged 1870 and 1890–2 [*A.P.S.D.*].

LIBERTON, MIDLOTHIAN, rebuilt 1815, Gothic [*N.S.A.* i, 11].

CLACKMANNAN, 1815, Gothic [S.R.O., HR 633/1].

KEITH, BANFFSHIRE, 1816, Gothic [S.R.O., CH 2/342/9, p. 221].

DUNOON, ARGYLLSHIRE, 1816, Gothic, enlarged by D. Hamilton 1834 [*N.S.A.* vii, 610].

CHANNELKIRK, BERWICKS., 1817, Gothic [S.R.O., HR 313/2].

ALLOA, CLACKMANNANSHIRE, 1817–19, Gothic [James Lothian, *Alloa and its Environs*, Alloa 1871, 32].

DUNBLANE CATHEDRAL, PERTHSHIRE, alterations to choir, 1817–19; Graham's work was undone in 1890 [A. B. Barty, *History of Dunblane*, Stirling 1944, 203].

STIRLING, HOLY RUDE CHURCH, restoration of West Church (nave), 1818. Graham's plaster vault was removed in 1911–14 [R.C.A.M., *Stirlingshire* i, 130].

LOGIE EASTER, ROSS & CROMARTY, 1818–19, Gothic; dem. 1988 [S.R.O., CH 2/348/13, p. 25].

ALLOA, CLACKMANNANSHIRE, Mar & Kellie mausoleum in Old Kirkyard, 1819, Gothic [S.R.O., GD 124/15/1735/77].

GLASGOW, GEORGE STREET INDEPENDENT CHURCH, 14 WEST GEORGE STREET (later offices) 1819, Doric; dem. 1975 [J. Pagan, *Sketch of the History of Glasgow*, 1847, 180].

EDINBURGH, NICOLSON STREET CHURCH (DR. JAMISON'S CHAPEL), 1819–20, Tudor Gothic; altered 1932; dem. 1979 [*A.P.S.D.*].

DUNBAR, E. LOTHIAN, 1819–20, Gothic; gutted by fire 1987 [*N.S.A.* ii, 80].

SHOTTS, LANARKS., 1819, Gothic, executed with modifications by John Brash (*q.v.*) [S.R.O., HR 739/2].

DOUNE (KILMADOCK), PERTHSHIRE, for 10th Earl of Moray, 1822, Gothic [S.R.O., HR 245/4, p. 80].

RAFFORD, MORAYSHIRE, *c.*1825–6 [*N.S.A.* xiii, 254].

INVERKEITHING, FIFE, rebuilt 1826 incorporating old tower [W. Stephen, *The Story of Inverkeithing and Rosyth*, 1938, 42].

DUNINO, FIFE, 1826, Gothic [S.R.O., HR 64/1] (G. Hay, *Architecture of Scottish Post-Reformation Churches*, 1957, pl. 19b).

MUTHILL, PERTHSHIRE, 1826–8, Gothic [S.R.O., HR 155/2].

PERTH, ST. JOHN'S CHURCH, repairs and alterations, begun in 1828 but not fully completed [*Perthshire Illustrated*, 1843, introduction by W. Hooker, 14; W. Douglas Simpson, *A History of St. John's Kirk, Perth*, 1958, 31–2].

DALGETY, FIFE, 1830, Gothic [S.R.O., HR 185/1, minute of 19 Aug. 1830].

ERROL, PERTHSHIRE, 1831–3, Romanesque [*N.S.A.* x, 386–7; L. Melville, *Errol*, Perth 1935, 117–18].

MONTROSE, ANGUS, Gothic tower and spire, 1832–4 [*N.S.A.* xi, 282].

EDINBURGH, ST. MARGARET'S CONVENT CHAPEL (R.C.), 1834–5, Romanesque [James Grant, *Old and New Edinburgh* iii, *c.*1880, 45].

EDINBURGH, GREENSIDE CHURCH, ROYAL TERRACE, 1836–8, Gothic; tower 1851–2 [*A.P.S.D.*].

EDINBURGH, HERIOT'S HOSPITAL CHAPEL, refitted interior, 1837 [*A.P.S.D.*; *Builder*, 10 June 1882, 716] (*C. Life*, 13 March 1975, fig. 8).

EDINBURGH, TOLBOOTH ST. JOHN'S CHURCH or VICTORIA HALL (Hall of Assembly for the

Church of Scotland), in association with A. W. N. Pugin, 1841–4, Gothic [*A.P.S.D.*].

MURTHLY, PERTHSHIRE, CHAPEL OF ST. ANTHONY THE EREMITE, rebuilt 1846 [*The Chapel of St. Anthony the Eremite of Murthly*, Edinburgh 1850, folio].

GASK, PERTHSHIRE, EPISCOPAL CHAPEL, 1845–6, Romanesque [*Life and Songs of the Baroness Nairne*, ed. C. Rogers, 2nd ed. 1869, 134].

KINGHORN, FIFE, alterations and repairs, 1852 [*North British Advertiser*, 3 Jan. 1852; S.R.O., CH 2/224/12, pp. 283, 289–90, *ex inf.* Mr. John Gifford].

COUNTRY HOUSES, ETC.

ACHNACARRY, INVERNESS-SHIRE, for Donald Cameron, begun 1802, but not completed internally until 1837, castle style; restored 1952 after war-damage [A. Mackenzie, *History of the Camerons*, 1884, 255; *N.S.A.* xiv, 122] (Sheila Forman, *Scottish Country Houses and Castles*, 1967, 161–5).

KILLERMONT HOUSE, DUNBARTONSHIRE, S. front for Archibald Campbell Colquhoun, 1804–7 [Campbell-Colquhoun family papers, Bdl. 28].

ALLANTON CASTLE, CAMBUSNETHAN, LANARKSHIRE, enlarged for Sir Henry Steuart, Bart., before 1809 and again *c.*1820; dem. [*N.S.A.* vi, 620, and information from Prof. A. A. Tait].

CLANSBURGH COTTAGE, ARDNAMURCHAN, INVERNESS-SHIRE, for Reginald Macdonald of Clanranald, 1809–*c.*1820; dem. [S.R.O., GD 201/5/1240].

SLEAT MANSE, ISLE OF SKYE, *c.*1810, Gothic [J. Macaulay, 'James Gillespie Graham in Skye', *Bull. Scottish Georgian Soc.* iii, 1974–5, 8–9].

CULDEES CASTLE, PERTHSHIRE, for General Andrew John Drummond, *c.*1810, castle style; restored after fire in 1887; altered by Sir R. Lorimer *c.*1910 [J. P. Neale, *Views of Seats* v, 1822].

CRAWFORD PRIORY, CULTS, FIFE, for Lady Mary Lindsay Crawford, 1811–13, succeeding David Hamilton, Gothic; enlarged *c.*1870; derelict since 1971 [inscription quoted by A. H. Millar, *Fife, Pictorial and Historical* i, 1895, 191–2] (*A Description of Craufurd Priory*, 1828).

EREDINE, LOCH AWE, ARGYLLSHIRE, completion of unfinished house, 1812 [Sale Particulars in Argyll & Bute District Archives, Poltalloch Coll. DR 4/21 and 24; *Edinburgh Evening Courant*, 11 April 1812].

ROSS PRIORY, DUNBARTONSHIRE, remodelled for Hector Macdonald Buchanan, 1812, Gothic, based on T. D. W. Dearn, *Sketches in Architecture* (1807), pl. vi [J. P. Neale, *Views of Seats* vi, 1823].

AUCHTERTOOL MANSE, FIFE, 1812, Gothic, 'in the cottage style' [*N.S.A.* ix, 258].

CAMERON HOUSE, DUNBARTONSHIRE, enlarged house and designed new offices for J. R. Smollett, 1812–14; rebuilt after fire 1865 [Smollett papers, Bdls. 14, 23].

BOWLAND, MIDLOTHIAN, remodelled for Genl. Alexander Walker, *c.*1813–15 [N.L.S., MS. 13961, ff. 300–72] (J. Small, *Castles and Mansions of the Lothians*, 1883, i).

DRUMTOCHTY CASTLE, FORDOUN, KINCARDINESHIRE, for George Harley Drummond, *c.*1815, castle style [*N.S.A.* xi, 88–9].

EDMONSTONE CASTLE, nr. BIGGAR, LANARKSHIRE, for James Brown, 1815, castle style [*N.S.A.* vi, 364] (G. V. Irving, *Upper Ward of Lanarkshire* i, 1864, 329, plate).

TORRISDALE CASTLE, KINTYRE, ARGYLLSHIRE, for Genl. Keith MacAlister, *c.*1815, castle style; wings added *c.*1900–10 [*Edinburgh Annual Register* ix, 1816, 483; R.C.A.M., *Argyll* i, 192 and pls. 84–5].

attributed: GLENBARR ABBEY (now BARR HOUSE), KINTYRE, ARGYLLSHIRE, enlarged and altered for Col. Matthew MacAlister, *c.*1815, Gothic. The owner was the brother of General K. MacAlister, who employed Graham at Torrisdale Castle, and in style the house resembles Ross Priory [R.C.A.M., *Argyll* i, 188 and pl. 78].

KILKERRAN HOUSE, DAILLY, AYRSHIRE, addition of classical wings and staircase for Sir James Fergusson, Bart., *c.*1815 [Alistair Rowan in *C. Life*, 1–8 May 1975].

ARMADALE CASTLE, ISLE OF SKYE, for 2nd Lord Macdonald, *c.*1815–20, castle style [J. P. Neale, *Views of Seats*, 2nd ser., i, 1824, illustrating a more ambitious design than the one actually executed].

PRESTONFIELD HOUSE, MIDLOTHIAN, circular stables for Sir William Cunningham, Bart., 1816 [S.R.O., SC 39/89/3, pp. 419–20].

CAMBUSNETHAN HOUSE, WISHAW, LANARKSHIRE, for Robert Lockhart, 1816–19, Gothic [J. M. Leighton, *Select Views on the Clyde*, 1830, 35; *N.S.A.* vi, 615].

BLYTHSWOOD HOUSE, RENFREWSHIRE, for Major Archibald Campbell, 1818–21, Greek Revival; dem. 1935 [J. P. Neale, *Views of Seats*, 2nd ser. iii, 1826].[1] (*The Old Country Houses of the Old Glasgow Gentry*, Glasgow 1870, no. xii).

DUNS CASTLE, BERWICKSHIRE, remodelled

[1] A contemporary reference in Sir Walter Scott's journal (ed. Andrews, 1972, 349) implies that this house was designed by Robert Smirke, but Graham's responsibility for it is amply confirmed by copies of his acrimonious correspondence with the contracting mason in S.R.O., CS 96/221.

for William Hay, 1818–22, castle style [J. P. Neale, *Views of Seats* vi, 1823] (D. MacGibbon & T. Ross, *Castellated and Domestic Architecture of Scotland* v, 1892, 265 for plan).

KINLOSS MANSE, MORAYSHIRE, 1820 [*N.S.A.* xiii, 212].

KILMARON CASTLE, CUPAR, FIFE, for Admiral Sir Frederick Maitland, *c.*1820, castle style; much altered *c.*1860; gutted 1970; finally dem. 1984 [J. M. Leighton, *History of Fife*, Glasgow 1840, ii, 35] (A. H. Millar, *Fife, Pictorial and Historical* i, 1895, 130).

MOUNT MELVILLE, FIFE, new front block for John Whyte-Melville, 1820–1, classical; dem. *c.*1900 [drawings at N.M.R.S. and National Library of Scotland, Advocates MS. 33.8.4] (J. P. Neale, *Views of Seats*, 2nd ser. ii, 1825).

LEE PLACE, LANARKSHIRE, for Sir Charles Lockhart, Bart., 1820–49, castle style [J. M. Leighton, *Select Views on the Clyde*, 1830, 25; *N.S.A.* vi, 18; J. P. Neale, *Views of Seats*, 2nd ser, iv, 1828].

EDINBURGH, CAROLINE COTTAGE (NAIRN LODGE), WILLOWBRAE ROAD, addition of wings 1822 [Diary of John Steuart of Dalguise in Blair-Oliphant papers at Ardblair Castle, *ex inf.* Dr. J. Macaulay].

MILNE GRADEN, nr. COLDSTREAM, BERWICKSHIRE, for Admiral Sir David Milne, 1822, classical [book of drawings at Milne Graden].

SPRINGWOOD PARK, KELSO, ROXBURGHSHIRE, mausoleum and entrance gate by Kelso Bridge for Sir John James Douglas, Bart., *c.*1822 [*N.S.A.* iii, 320; drawings at N.M.R.S.] (R.C.A.M., *Roxburghshire* i, fig. 206).

DUNNINALD HOUSE, CRAIG, ANGUS, for Peter Arkly, 1823–4, castle style [Alistair Rowan in *C. Life*, 14–21 Aug. 1969] (plan in J. G. Dunbar, *Historic Architecture of Scotland*, 1966, fig. 93).

DORMONT HOUSE, DALTON, DUMFRIESSHIRE, for W. T. Carruthers, 1823–6; dem. 1956 [S.R.O., SC 15/65/2, p. 224].

attributed: WESTERTOWN HOUSE, nr. ELGIN, MORAYSHIRE, for Lt.-Col. Alexander Hay, 1824, castle style [stylistic attribution].

WISHAW HOUSE, MOTHERWELL, LANARKSHIRE, enlarged and remodelled for 8th Lord Belhaven and Stenton, 1825, castle style; additions by W. Burn 1858; dem. 1953 [J. P. Neale, *Views of Seats*, 2nd ser., iv, 1828; *N.S.A.* vi, 616] (*Scottish Field*, April 1950).

MILLIKEN HOUSE, RENFREWSHIRE, for Sir William Milliken Napier, Bart., 1825; dem. *c.*1935 [B. Burke, *Visitations of Seats and Arms*, 1st ser. ii (1853), 20] (A. H. Millar, *Castles and Mansions of Renfrewshire and Buteshire*, 1890, No. 46).

MORHAM MANSE, EAST LOTHIAN, 1826–7 [D. Louden, *History of Morham*, 1889, 75].

DOUGLAS MANSE, LANARKSHIRE, 1828 [*N.S.A.* vi, 490].

MURTHLY HOUSE, nr. DUNKELD, PERTHSHIRE, for Sir John A. Drummond-Stewart, Bart., 1829–32, left unfinished, Jacobean style; dem. *c.*1950 [building accounts in S.R.O., GD 121, Box 68; *The Journal of Sir Walter Scott*, ed. Andrews, 1972, 605] (*C. Life*, 2 Oct. 1915).

BONNINGTON HOUSE, LANARKSHIRE, addition of porch for Sir Charles Lockhart-Ross, Bart., *c.*1830; destroyed by fire *c.*1900 [*N.S.A.* vi, 18].

ARDMADDY CASTLE, ARGYLLSHIRE, court of offices for 2nd Marquess of Breadalbane, 1837–9. A design by Graham for a Jacobethan addition to the house was partly carried out in 1862 by David Bryce [R.C.A.M., *Argyll* ii, 248–9].

TAYMOUTH CASTLE, PERTHSHIRE, remodelled west wing for 2nd Marquess of Breadalbane, 1838–9, castle style [Alistair Rowan in *C. Life*, 15 Oct. 1964].

BRODICK CASTLE, ARRAN, castellated addition for 10th Duke of Hamilton, 1844–6 [*Building Chronicle* i, 1855, 170; *A.P.S.D.*; *C. Life*, 10–17 Feb. 1983] (D. MacGibbon & T. Ross, *Castellated & Domestic Architecture of Scotland* iii, 1889, 285–9).

AYTON HOUSE, BERWICKSHIRE, for W. Mitchell Innes, 1846–51, 'baronial' style [*Building Chronicle* i, 1855, 170; *A.P.S.D.*; M. Hall in *C. Life*, 12 Aug. 1993].

WESTER BOGIE HOUSE, ABBOTSHALL, FIFE, for James Thomson, castle style; now in ruins [*N.S.A.* ix, 154].

EDINBURGH: DOMESTIC ARCHITECTURE

ABERCROMBY PLACE, Nos. 8–13, 1808 onwards [*Edinburgh Evening Courant*, 3 Feb. 1808, 25 Dec. 1809].

HOWARD PLACE, WARRISTON, 1809–20 [S.R.O., Edinburgh Sasines].

THE EARL OF MORAY'S ESTATE, comprising AINSLIE PLACE, ALBYN PLACE, DARNAWAY STREET, DOUNE TERRACE, FORBES STREET, GLENFILAS STREET, GREAT STUART STREET, MORAY PLACE, RANDOLPH CLIFF, CRESCENT AND PLACE, GREAT COLME STREET and WEMYSS PLACE, all designed by *c.*1822 and built by *c.*1830 [A. J. Youngson, *The Making of Classical Edinburgh*, Edinburgh 1966, 216–25].

ALVA STREET, 1823 [S.R.O., Edinburgh Sasines].

BLACKET PLACE, layout, 1825 [*Book of the Old*

Edinburgh Club xxiv, 1942, 177].

MELVILLE STREET and WALKER STREET area, general layout only for Sir Francis Walker and the Heriot Trustees, *c.*1825 [A. J. Youngson, *op. cit.*, 215–16].

QUALITY STREET, 1827 [S.R.O., Edinburgh Sasines].

QUEENSFERRY STREET, NOS. 18–20, 1830 [S.R.O., Edinburgh Sasines].

BIRKENHEAD, CHESHIRE

HAMILTON SQUARE, designed for the Scotsman William Laird in 1825 as part of a larger street plan for which Graham was also responsible. The north and east sides were begun immediately, but the south and west sides were not built until 1839–44 [*A.P.S.D.*; W. W. Mortimer, *Hundred of Wirral*, 1847, 327].

MONUMENT

DUNIRA, nr. COMRIE, PERTHSHIRE, monument to the 1st Lord Melville, 1812 [*Aberdeen Jnl.*, 23 May 1812].

GRAINGER, RICHARD (1797–1861), was a speculative builder of exceptional vision who transformed the centre of Newcastle-on-Tyne during the second quarter of the nineteenth century. He was the son of a quay porter at Newcastle who died young. After going to a charity school he was apprenticed to a carpenter and builder named Brown. Having by a fortunate marriage (to the daughter of Joseph Arundale, a wealthy tanner) acquired considerable capital, he was able not only to set up as a builder on his own account, but to embark on the extensive building projects which made him the Cubitt of the north. In 1825 he began the erection of ELDON SQUARE, and between 1829 and 1834 he built LEAZES CRESCENT and TERRACE, consisting of seventy first- and sixty second-class houses. This speculation proved so successful that in 1834 he purchased 12 acres of land in the centre of Newcastle, upon which he proceeded to build a magnificent sequence of handsome and well-planned streets reminiscent of Georgian Edinburgh and Regency London. By 1842 Grainger had built GREY STREET, GRAINGER STREET, MARKET STREET, CLAYTON STREET, NUN STREET, NELSON STREET and various lesser streets in the neighbourhood. Clayton Street was named after John Clayton, the Town Clerk, who assisted Grainger financially and did all in his power to promote his developments. Grainger's activities included the erection or rebuilding of a number of important public buildings, including the MARKETS, the THEATRE ROYAL, the EXCHANGE, the ROYAL ARCADE, the BRANCH BANK OF ENGLAND, LAMBTON'S BANK and the SALEM METHODIST CHAPEL in Hood Street.[1] In 1839 Grainger overreached himself by purchasing the Elswick estate immediately to the west of Newcastle for £114,100, but with Clayton's help he managed to extricate himself from an awkward financial predicament without resorting to bankruptcy, and although he died in debt (4 July 1861), his estate ultimately proved able to satisfy his creditors.

There can be no doubt that the new Newcastle was largely Grainger's own conception, and that he was an exceptionally able and enlightened developer and town-planner. What is doubtful is to what extent he was responsible for the design of any individual building or street. Among the architects who collaborated with him were John Dobson, Thomas Oliver, John and Benjamin Green, John Wardle and George Walker. Thus Dobson was responsible for the Market, the Greens designed the Theatre Royal, and Oliver planned Leazes Terrace. But individual responsibility for the designs of many of Grainger's other buildings remains undetermined and some of them may have been designed in his office by draughtsmen working under his immediate direction. At a time when the distinction between architect and builder was still far from absolute, and in the exceptional circumstances created by a great town-planning enterprise, the question of artistic authorship may never be satisfactorily resolved. There is, however, an obvious sense in which the Town Council was right, in 1861, to commemorate Grainger as 'one of the greatest architects of his age'.

[Obituaries in *Gent's Mag.* 1861 (ii), 216–17, and *Builder* xix, 1861, 476; Harriet Martineau, 'Self-Made Men – Richard Grainger', *Once a Week* v, 1861, 401–6; R. Welford, *Men of Mark 'twixt Tyne and Tweed* ii, 1895, 321–6; R. Turley, 'Early Victorian City Planning: the work of John Dobson and Richard Grainger at Newcastle upon Tyne', *Arch. Rev.*, May 1946; L. Wilkes & G. Dodds, *Tyneside Classical: the Newcastle of Grainger, Dobson and Clayton*, 1964; B. Allsopp, *Historic Architecture of Newcastle upon Tyne*, 1967.]

GRANTHAM, LORD, *see* ROBINSON, THOMAS.

[1] Grainger was himself a Wesleyan Methodist. His wife was 'a class-mate at chapel'. She is said to have 'kept his accounts and managed his correspondence'.

GRAVATT, WILLIAM (1806–1866), had a distinguished career as a mathematician and civil engineer. He was the son of Col. Gravatt, R.E., of the Royal Military Academy at Woolwich, was a pupil of the civil engineer Bryan Donkin, then an assistant of I. K. Brunel, and ultimately engineer to several canal and railway companies. He was a Member of the Institution of Civil Engineers and was elected a Fellow of the Royal Society in 1832. As Engineer to the Calder and Hebble Navigation in Yorkshire he designed several bridges, 'the arches of which were remarkable for their stability and cheapness'. In Somerset, where he was Surveyor and Engineer to the Parrett Navigation, the three-arched bridge at Langport was built by him in 1839–40. While in Yorkshire he had designed the LITERARY AND PHILOSOPHICAL SOCIETY'S HALL at HALIFAX. 1832. [Obituary in *Minutes of Proceedings of the Institution of Civil Engineers* xxvi, 1866–7, 565–75; J. Crabtree, *History of Halifax*, 1836, 352; drawings for Langport Bridge in Somerset River Board's offices at Bridgwater, *ex inf.* the late Bryan Little.]

GRAY, (Sir) GEORGE (1710–1773), younger son of Sir James Gray, Bart., and Colonel of the 37th Foot, was one of the original members of the Society of Dilettanti in 1734, and took a prominent part in its affairs. He acted as secretary and treasurer of the Society from 1739 to 1771, and was well known as an amateur of architecture. His portrait by Knapton is still in the possession of the Society. Gray succeeded to the baronetcy on the death of his brother in January 1773, but himself died only a few weeks later.

Gray was employed by the 1st Earl Spencer to superintend the building of SPENCER HOUSE, GREEN PARK, LONDON, in 1756–65, and that he exercised a close control over its design is shown by the existence in the Soane Museum and the R.I.B.A. Collection of several drawings for the house by Vardy with endorsements recording that they had been approved by Gray at various dates between 1755 and 1758. It was on Gray's advice that in 1758 James Stuart was brought in to design the interiors of the first floor in a more neo-classical style than Vardy was capable of [J. Friedman, *Spencer House*, 1993, 124]. Also in the R.I.B.A. Collection is a drawing for a gateway at 'Lord Cadogan's' (i.e. CAVERSHAM PARK, OXON.), 'designed by Coll. George Gray'. A design for the 'Great Door to the Armoury in the Tower [of London], by Mr. G. Gray' is in the British Library, *King's Maps* xxiv, 23 *v*.

[L. Cust & S. Colvin, *History of the Society of Dilettanti*, 1898; *D.N.B.*, supplement, *s.v.* 'Gray, Sir James'; will in P.C.C. 58 STEVENS.]

GRAY, GIDEON (–1791) was for most of his life a mason and architect in Stirling. He is first recorded at TOUCH HOUSE, STIRLINGSHIRE, which he built for Hugh Seton *c*.1750–60, and in whose design he may have played some part [MS. building accounts at Touch] (R.C.A.M. *Stirlingshire* ii, 376–9; *C. Life*, 19–26 Aug., 2 Sept. 1965). While thus engaged he married the daughter of a tenant farmer on the Touch estate, where he was later employed as a factor. Having in 1769 advised the Town Council of Stirling on the state of the Bridge and refused to take any payment, 'Mr. Gideon Gray Mason and Architect' was in February 1770 given the freedom of the town gratis. In 1785 it was to his design that the TOWN HOUSE was extended eastwards in a simple style of 'Palladian' character, and in 1788 he was paid 10 guineas 'for drawing plans and superintending erection' of the OLD GRAMMAR SCHOOL in CASTLE WYND. A gravestone in the New Churchyard of St. Ninian's, Stirling is inscribed 'Gideon Gray architek died Touch 1791. His wife died Touch House 1800 aged 73'. [R.C.A.M., *Stirlingshire* ii, 284, 293–4; A. F. Hutchinson, *History of the High School of Stirling*, Stirling 1904, 111; information from Mr. P. B. Buchanan and Mrs. C. L. Brodie, archivist of the Central Regional Council.]

GRAY, JOHN (*c*.1773–1824), 'architect in Kelso and tenant at Heriotfield', is commemorated by a monument in the churchyard at Kelso, Roxburghshire. In 1819 the name of John Gray, architect of Kelso, appears among the subscribers to Peter Nicholson's *Architectural Dictionary*.

GRAY, JOHN HOBDAY (–1843), exhibited architectural designs at the Royal Academy in 1834, 1835 and 1837, at the Society of British Artists in 1832, 1835, 1836 and 1837, and at the Liverpool Academy in 1840 and 1842. Up to 1840 he gave London addresses, but by 1841 he was at Holt Hill, Tranmere, Cheshire.

GRAY, ROBERT, practised in Edinburgh in the 1820s. ST. JOHN'S EPISCOPAL CHAPEL, PORTOBELLO, 1825, dem., appears to be his only recorded work [advt. for tenders in *Edinburgh Evening Courant*, 31 March 1825].

GRAYSON, WILLIAM, of Banner Street, Moorfields, exhibited at the Royal Academy from 1791 to 1801, including the 'Elevation of a nobleman's house intended to be built near Sedburgh in Yorkshire' (1791), a 'Design for a gentleman's seat to be built near Lancaster' (1793) and a 'Design of a gentleman's seat to be built at Kingmoor, near Carlisle' (1794). J. Grayson, junior, evidently his son, exhibited from the same address in 1800 and 1803.

GREEN, JAMES (1781–1849), was born in Birmingham, where his father was an engineer. After working under his father he found employment in 1801 with John Rennie. In 1808 he was appointed County Surveyor of Devon, a post which he retained until 1841. In 1843 he moved to London, where he died on 13 February 1849.

Green was primarily a civil engineer, whose main responsibilities were roads, bridges and canals. His most important bridges were COWLEY BRIDGE over the R. Creedy near Exeter, 1813–14, and the BEAM BRIDGE AQUEDUCT carrying the Torrington and Bideford Canal over the R. Torridge, 1824. As an architect Green's principal recorded works appear to have been BUCKLAND FILLEIGH HOUSE, DEVONSHIRE, for J. Inglett Fortescue, 1810 [R. Ackermann, *Repository of Arts*, 3rd ser., x, 1828] and ST. DAVID'S CHURCH, EXETER, 1816–17, dem. 1897 [brass foundation inscription in new church] (*Devonshire Illustrated*, 1829, 70). The church was an ambitious Greek Doric building of the type later erected in London under the 'Million Act' of 1818. The house was an essay in the same style, the interior as well as the exterior being consistently designed in the Greek Doric manner (David Watkin, 'Buckland Filleigh', in *The Country Seat*, ed. Colvin & Harris, 1970). Green was also responsible for the addition of a hexastyle Doric porch to FURSDON, DEVON, for George Fursdon, *c.*1818 [documentary evidence at Fursdon, *ex inf.* Mr. Michael Robbins]. These buildings give Green a place after Harrision of Chester as an early practitioner of the Greek Revival in the provinces.

[Obituary in *Minutes of Proceedings of the Institution of Civil Engineers* ix, 1849–50, 98–100; Charles Hadfield, 'James Green as Canal Engineer', *Journal of Transport History* i, 1953–4.]

GREEN, JOHN, 'Architect in Salisbury', edited the 8th edition of William Salmon's *Country Builder's Estimator* (1770) and the 5th edition of his *London and Country Builder's Vade Mecum* (1773).

GREEN, JOHN (–1837), was a surveyor and builder at Yarmouth. As a young man he was in the Navy, and lost an arm and an eye in the Battle of Copenhagen (1801). In 1805, when he advertised his services as an architect in the *Ipswich Journal*, he referred to his 'many years experience in the above line', and in 1816, in a similar advertisement, he stated that he had 'many years experience in the Building Line in the counties of Norfolk, Suffolk and Cambridge' and that he had 'been employed in making Designs for Building a New Street, and superintending all the Public Works lately executed at Yarmouth'. Green died on 28 January 1837 [*Bury and Norwich Post*, 1 Feb. 1837]. He may have been related to the Green who was one of the builders of the PASTON GRAMMAR SCHOOL, NORTH WALSHAM, NORFOLK, in 1764–5 [C. R. Forder, *History of the Paston Grammar School*, 1934, 84], and to the 'John Green, of Southtown, architect', who contracted to build the drawbridge at Yarmouth in 1785 [John Preston, *Picture of Yarmouth*, 1819], and whose son John Green, junior, also an architect, died at Yarmouth in 1804, aged 28 [*Norwich Mercury*, 21 April 1804]. [Information from Mr. J. Bensusan-Butt and Mr. David Cubitt.]

GREEN, JOHN (1787–1852), and his son BENJAMIN (1813–1858) had an extensive practice as architects and civil engineers in Northumberland and Durham. John Green was born on 20 June 1787 at Newton Fell House, Nafferton, where his father carried on a business as a carpenter and agricultural implement-maker. Soon after coming of age John joined his father. 'With the talent and energy which he threw into the affairs of the firm, business increased until Nafferton became too small to hold it, and the workshops were removed to Corbridge.' Here the Greens extended their activities to general building work. John Green turned his attention to the architectural side of the business, and in about 1820 left Corbridge for Newcastle, where he practised as an architect and civil engineer. He had two sons, John (*c.*1807–68) and Benjamin (1813–58), both of whom became architects. Benjamin, who was a pupil of the elder Pugin, joined his father early in the 1830s, and thereafter they practised together until the former's death in 1852. The elder Green is said to have been 'a plain practical, shrewd man of business', Benjamin 'an artistic and dashing sort of a fellow' whose style was 'ornamental, florid and costly, while the father's was plain, severe and economical'. Between them they designed a number of Gothic churches of no especial distinction and ruthlessly altered some old ones in a manner which showed that they were no antiquaries. Their abilities were better shown in the Greek Doric temple erected on Penshaw

Hill as a monument to the 1st Earl of Durham and in the handsome theatre which they designed in Newcastle. They were active as railway architects, and in 1846 George Hudson, the 'Railway King', commissioned them to design all the railway stations between Newcastle and Berwick. The elder Green specialized in the erection of bridges, and in 1841 he was awarded the Telford Medal of the Institution of Civil Engineers for a system of laminated timber arches with which he had experimented as early as 1827, and which he employed successfully in the Willington and Ouseburn railway bridges ten years later. All his wooden laminated bridges have now been replaced, but his wrought-iron suspension bridge at Whorlton in County Durham still stands as the oldest bridge of its type in the country still supported unaided by its original chains. The Greens also had a reputation as designers of farmhouses, and were much employed for this purpose on the Duke of Northumberland's estates. The elder Green died at Newcastle on 30 September 1852, his son in a mental home at Dinsdale Park, Durham, on 14 November 1858.

[Memoir in *Minutes of Proceedings of the Institution of Civil Engineers* xiii, 1853–4, 138–40; R. Welford, *Men of Mark 'twixt Tyne and Tweed* ii, 1895, 326–30; T. Fordyce, *Local Records of Northumberland and Durham* ii, 1876, 17; M. A. Richardson, *The Local Historian's Table-Book of remarkable occurrences connected with the Counties of Newcastle-upon-Tyne, Northumberland and Durham*, 8 vols., 1841–6; *Newcastle Weekly News*, 1 Jan. 1887; W. W. Tomlinson, *The North Eastern Railway*, Newcastle 1914, 323, 335, 350, 446, 483; Henry Hagger, 'The Bridges of John Green', *Northern Architect*, No. 8, April 1976.]

PUBLIC AND DOMESTIC ARCHITECTURE

STYFORD HALL, nr. BYWELL, NORTHUMBERLAND, for Charles Bacon, *c.*1820 [*Proceedings of the Inst. of Civil Engineers* xiii, 1853–4, 138].

NEWCASTLE, LITERARY AND PHILOSOPHICAL SOCIETY'S LIBRARY, WESTGATE STREET, 1822–5; added MUSEUM for the Natural History Society 1833–5 [W. Collard & M. Ross, *Architectural and Picturesque Views of Newcastle upon Tyne*, 1843, 46].

BEAUFRONT ESTATE, nr. HEXHAM, NORTHUMBERLAND, made 'twenty plans and estimates' for rebuilding or renovating the farms on this estate for J. Errington, 1824. Several of them are given by J. C. Loudon, *Encyclopaedia of Rural Architecture*, 1846, 476–7, 486–96.

SCOTSWOOD, nr. NEWCASTLE, suspension bridge over R. Tyne, 1829–31; dem. 1967 [J. Sykes, *Local Records* ii, 1866, 295–7; exhibited at R.A. 1837].

WHORLTON, nr. BARNARD CASTLE, CO. DURHAM, suspension bridge over R. Tees, 1829–31 [E. Mackenzie & M. Ross, *History of Durham* i, 1834, 193; *Table-Book* iv, 89].

CHESTERHOLME, nr. BARDON MILL, NORTHUMBERLAND, *cottage orné* for — Hedley, *c.*1830 [B. W. Richardson, *Thomas Sopwith*, 1891, 92–3].

WYNYARD PARK, CO. DURHAM, small suspension bridge in grounds, 1831 [E. Mackenzie & M. Ross, *History of Durham* i, 1834, 450].

BLACKWELL BRIDGE, nr. DARLINGTON, CO. DURHAM (R. Tees), 1832; a stone bridge widened 1961 [J. Sykes, *Local Records* ii, 1866, 362].

BELLINGHAM, NORTHUMBERLAND, stone bridge over R. Tyne, 1834–5 [inscription; see also *Table-Book* iv, 206, 252].

LINTZFORD, CO. DURHAM, stone bridge (R. Derwent), 1834–5 [H. Hagger in *Northern Architect*, no. 8, April 1976, 28].

NEWCASTLE, WESTGATE HILL CEMETERY, monument to John Bruce (d. 1834), 1835 [R. Welford, *Men of Mark 'twixt Tyne and Tweed*, 1895, i, 414; ii, 328].

NEWCASTLE, THE THEATRE, 1836–7; interior destroyed by fire 1899 [*Table-Book* iv, 342–4; original drawings now in Metropolitan Museum of Art, New York, reproduced by R. Southern in *The Georgian Playhouse*, 1948, pls. 51–4].

SOUTH SHIELDS, CO. DURHAM, UNION WORKHOUSE, 1837 [*Table-Book* iv, 390].

NORTH SHIELDS, NORTHUMBERLAND, POOR LAW GUARDIANS' HALL, 1837, Jacobethan; later incorporated in Town Hall [*Newcastle Courant*, 17 Feb. 1837, *ex inf.* Mrs. G. McCombie].

TYNEMOUTH, NORTHUMBERLAND, THE MASTER-MARINERS' ASYLUM, 1837, Tudor style [*Table-Book* iv, 395].

OUSEBURN and WILLINGTON DENE RAILWAY BRIDGES, NORTHUMBERLAND, 1837, both of laminated timber construction. The former was rebuilt in iron in 1867, the latter in 1869 [*Table-Book* iv, 337–8; *Civil Engineer and Architect's Jnl.* iv, 284, xi, 33].

BARNARD CASTLE, CO. DURHAM, WORKHOUSE, 1837–8 [*Durham Chronicle*, 24 Nov. 1837, *ex inf.* Mr. P. M. Meadows].

NEWCASTLE, THE GREY COLUMN, 1837–8, with statue by E. H. Baily [exhib. at R.A. 1837].

NEWCASTLE, THE CORN EXCHANGE, CLOTH MARKET, 1838–9; largely dem. 1854 and completely 1972 [*Table-Book* v, 42].

NETHER POPPLETON, nr. YORK, stone bridge carrying York and Newcastle Railway over R. Ouse, 1838–40 [*Procs. Inst. of Civil Engineers* xiii, 1853–4, 139].

ACKLAM HALL, YORKS. (N.R.), alterations for Thomas Hustler, 1840; remodelled by W. H. Brierly 1911–12 [Cleveland C.R.O., Diary of William Ward Jackson, 3 Oct. 1840, *ex inf.* Mr. P. Meadows] (*C. Life*, 7 March 1914).

DALKEITH, MIDLOTHIAN, colliery railway viaduct over R. Esk for 5th Duke of Buccleuch, 1840–1; dem. [*Newcastle Weekly News*, 1 Jan. 1887].

ILDERTON VICARAGE, NORTHUMBERLAND, 1841, Tudor Gothic [*Newcastle Chronicle*, 25 Sept. 1841, *ex inf.* Mrs. G. McCombie].

STREATLAM CASTLE, CO. DURHAM, added portico and three stone cupolas on roof for John Bowes, 1841–2; dem. 1927 [Durham C.R.O., St. x 81, original drawings].

WHITTINGHAM VICARAGE, NORTHUMERLAND, 1842 [Northumb. C.R.O., Q.A.B. Mortgage Papers, *ex inf.* Mr. P. M. Meadows].

PENSHAW HILL, CO. DURHAM, Doric monument to 1st Earl of Durham (d. 1840), 1844 [J. Latimer, *op. cit.*, 189–90].

EGGESCLIFFE RECTORY, CO. DURHAM, alterations and additions 1844–5 [Durham University Library (Prior's Kitchen), Q.A.B. Mortgage Papers, *ex inf.* Mr. Meadows].

BARNARD CASTLE, CO. DURHAM, THE 'WITHAM TESTIMONIAL' (MECHANICS' INSTITUTE), 1845–6 [*Durham Chronicle*, 4 April 1845, *ex inf.* Mr. Meadows].

TYNEMOUTH RAILWAY STATION, NORTHUMB., 1847 [*Durham Advertiser*, 2 July 1847, *ex inf.* Mr. Meadows].

NEWCASTLE, CORN WAREHOUSE for York, Newcastle & Berwick Railway, 1848 [*Durham Advertiser*, 12 May 1848, *ex inf.* Mr. Meadows].

PONTELAND, NORTHUMBERLAND, THE CASTLE-WARD UNION WORKHOUSE, 1848–9 [Whellan's *History and Directory of Northumberland*, 1855, 549].

SUNDERLAND, CO. DURHAM, ST. BEDE'S TOWER, RYHOPE ROAD, for A. J. Moore (Mayor of Sunderland 1845–5), Italianate [*Newcastle Weekly News*, 1 Jan. 1887].

SUNDERLAND, CO. DURHAM, NICHOLSON HOUSE, for W. Nicholson (Mayor of Sunderland 1869–71), Gothic [*Newcastle Weekly News*, 1 Jan. 1887].

CHURCHES

NEWCASTLE, SCOTCH CHURCH, BLACKETT STREET, 1821–2, Gothic; dem. [E. Mackenzie, *History of Newcastle* i, 1827, 390].

NEWCASTLE, UNITED SECESSION (PRESBYTERIAN) MEETING HOUSE, CLAVERING PLACE, 1821–2 [E. Mackenzie, *History of Newcastle* i, 1827, 395].

FALSTONE, NORTHUMBERLAND, rebuilt 1824–5, Gothic; destroyed by fire 1890 [County Record Office, ZSW 629–30].

UNSWORTH (WASHINGTON), CO. DURHAM, HOLY TRINITY, 1831–2, Gothic; chancel added 1903 [*Table-Book* iv, 86].

STELLA, CO. DURHAM, SS. MARY & THOMAS AQUINAS (R.C.), 1831–2, Gothic; enlarged by J. Dobson 1848–9 [E. Mackenzie & M. Ross, *History of Durham* i, 1834, 193].

NEWBURN, NORTHUMBERLAND, enlarged north aisle, 1832, Gothic [I.C.B.S.].

NEWCASTLE, ST. NICHOLAS, repaired west tower (with J. Dobson), 1832–3, added north-west and south-west porches or transepts, refaced north aisle, etc., 1834–44 [H. L. Honeyman & T. Wake, 'St. Nicholas, Newcastle', *Archaeologia Æliana*, 4th ser., ix, 1932, 142–4].

STOCKTON-ON-TEES, CO. DURHAM, HOLY TRINITY, 1834–5, Gothic; altered 1882–90, chancel added 1906–9; spire removed 1957; gutted by fire 1991 [W. Fordyce, *County Palatine of Durham* ii, 1857, 163–4].

NORTH SHIELDS, NORTHUMBERLAND, HOLY TRINITY, 1834–6, Gothic; dem. [*Table-Book* iv, 212–14].

ALNWICK, NORTHUMBERLAND, ST. MARY'S R.C. CHAPEL, 1836, Gothic [*Table-Book* iv, 316].

DALTON (NEWBURN), NORTHUMBERLAND, HOLY TRINITY, 1836–7, Gothic [*Table-Book* iv, 309].

SUGLEY (LEMINGTON), NORTHUMBERLAND, HOLY SAVIOUR, 1836–7, Gothic [*Table-Book* iv, 309].

EARSDON, NORTHUMBERLAND, 1836–7, Gothic; chancel 1889 [I.C.B.S.].

EGLINGHAM, NORTHUMBERLAND, altered and enlarged, 1837 [*History of Northumberland* xiv, 370].

MIDDLESBROUGH, YORKS. (N.R.), rebuilt 1838–40, Gothic; chancel 1889 [I.C.B.S.; J. Harris, *Catalogue of British Drawings for Architecture, etc. in American Collections*, 1971, 108].

TYNEMOUTH, NORTHUMBERLAND, HOLY SAVIOUR, 1839–41, Gothic; altered 1882, spire removed *c.*1955 [J. Latimer, *Historical Register of Remarkable Events in Northumberland and Durham 1832–57*, 1857, 116].

WHITTINGHAM, NORTHUMBERLAND, extensive alterations, 1840–2, Gothic; chancel 1870 [*History of Northumberland* xiv, 490].

CAMBO, NORTHUMBERLAND, 1841–2, Gothic [I.C.B.S. and drawings at Wallington Hall signed 'B. Green' 1837].

WOODHORN, NORTHUMBERLAND, restored,

refaced and refenestrated, 1843 [F. R. Wilson, *Churches in the Archdeaconry of Lindisfarne*, 1870, 181].

HORSLEY, nr. OTTERBURN, NORTHUMBERLAND, 1843–4, neo-Norman [I.C.B.S.].

SEGHILL, NORTHUMBERLAND, 1848–9, Gothic [J. Latimer, *op. cit.*, 245–6].

GREENSHIELDS, THOMAS (*c.*1800–*c.*1845), was a minor Oxford architect of the 1830s. His most important work was probably the new front of St. Peter's Hall, an ambitious Greek Revival design of which only one wing was built.

OXFORD, THE BATHS, BATH STREET, opened 1827; dem. 1877 (N. Whittock, *A Description of the Oxford Baths*, *c.*1835].

OXFORD, THE INDEPENDENT CHAPEL, GEORGE STREET, 1832, Gothic; dem. 1936 [*Congregational Magazine*, 1833, 260; *The Oxford University and City Guide*, 1833, 12].

OXFORD, ST. PETER'S HALL (now College), S. wing, 1832, as part of a new front that was never completed, but is illustrated by Ingram, *Memorials of Oxford* ii, 1837 ('New Inn Hall', 16). Greenshields's wing was remodelled in 1897 by W. K. Shirley and called 'Hannington Hall'.

LYDNEY PARK, GLOS., alterations for Charles Bathurst, 1833; dem. *c.*1877 [N. Kingsley, *The Country Houses of Gloucestershire* ii, 1992, 175].

OXFORD, boatbuilder's workshop on S.E. side of Folly Bridge, soon after 1835 [Oxford City Archives, E 5.1, Lease-book 1826–39, p. 315].

OXFORD, ST. GILES' SCHOOL, *c.*1835; dem. *c.*1955 [Bodleian, MS. Top. Oxon. d. 501, f. 86].

ASTON CHURCH, BAMPTON, OXON., 1838–9, Gothic; altered 1885–9 [*Jackson's Oxford Jnl.*, 24 June 1837].

IPING, SUSSEX, THE RECTORY (now HAMMERWOOD HOUSE) for the Revd. H. D. Clarke, 1838–9 [drawings and specification in possession of the late Hon. R. W. Morgan-Grenville].

IPING CHURCH, SUSSEX, rebuilt 1840, Gothic; rebuilt 1886 [I.C.B.S.].

MARKET LAVINGTON VICARAGE, WILTS., altered or rebuilt, 1841 [Salisbury Diocesan Records].

BLACK BOURTON VICARAGE, OXON., 1842 [Oxfordshire C.R.O., MS. Oxf. Dioc. Papers b. 102].

SWILLAND VICARAGE, SUFFOLK, 1843, Gothic: enlarged by T. Bellamy 1867 [E. Suffolk C.R.O., FF 1/85/1].

GREENWAY, FRANCIS HOWARD (1777–1837), was the youngest son of Francis Greenway, or Grinway, a mason of Mangotsfield in Gloucestershire. He went to London in order to become the pupil of John Nash, from whose office he exhibited two drawings at the Royal Academy in 1800. It was probably as a result of his connection with Nash that he came to be employed at Carmarthen, where he later claimed to have designed the 'market house' – presumably the quadrangular cheese and meat market built by the Corporation in 1801. In 1802 he exhibited at the Royal Academy a 'Chapel, Library etc., designed for the side of a quadrangle at Bristol', and a drawing of 'Thornbury Castle restored, with a canal brought from the river Severn up to Thornbury'. In about 1805 he and his elder brothers Olive and John Tripp Greenway opened a yard in Bristol, and announced their intention of doing business as 'stonemasons, architects, builders etc.' At the same time Francis took the opportunity of 'offering his services to the public in the capacity of Architect, Statuary, and Landscape-Gardener'. As the architect member of the partnership he designed in 1806 the HOTEL AND ASSEMBLY ROOMS in THE MALL at CLIFTON, which the firm contracted to build. At the same time he and his brothers were speculating by buying unfinished houses in Clifton which they completed and then sold. In May 1809 they were overtaken by bankruptcy, and the Assembly Rooms were completed by Joseph Kay. Some time after the failure Francis Greenway was accused of forgery in connection with a previous contract to complete a house in Cornwallis Crescent, pleaded guilty, and was sentenced to death at Bristol Assizes on 23 March 1812. His motive appears to have been to benefit his creditors rather than himself, and the sentence was commuted to one of transportation for life. He was sent to Australia, where he found a patron and protector in Governor Macquarie, who employed him to carry out his ambitious plans for public works in the colony. In 1816 he was appointed government architect, and in this capacity designed many of the public buildings in Sydney, including St. James's Church, the stables of Government House, the Hyde Park Barracks (now Law Courts) and the Macquarie Tower. The stables are castellated, but most of Greenway's work was designed in a bold, simple, classical manner of considerable merit. [M. H. Ellis, *Francis Greenway*, Sydney 1949; W. Ison, *The Georgian Buildings of Bristol*, 1952, 35–6; M. Herman, *The Early Australian Architects and their Work*, 2nd ed. 1970.]

Olive and John Tripp Greenway recovered from their bankruptcy and continued their business in Bristol. Olive built, and probably designed, DOWNEND CHURCH, GLOS., in a feeble Gothic style in 1831 [I.C.B.S.].

GREENWAY, THOMAS, mason and carver, had his yard at Widcombe, nr. Bath. He built the COLD BATH HOUSE, CLAVERTON STREET, WIDCOMBE, *c.*1704, 'one of the earliest buildings in Bath to show a competent use of Renaissance detail', and houses in ST. JOHN'S COURT, BATH, 1720. Other houses in Bath attributed to him on stylistic grounds are those in Trim Street, begun in 1707, and one in the Abbey Church Yard with superimposed pilasters. He and his sons acquired a considerable reputation as carvers of vases and other architectural ornaments, and were often employed by John Wood, e.g. on the Bristol Exchange. In 1730 he visited Dublin, taking with him 'a large number of Flower Potts, urns and vases' for sale. [W. Ison, *The Georgian Buildings of Bath*, 1948, 30, 116–24, 2nd ed. 1980, 4, 102, 106–11; J. Wood, *A Description of the Exchange of Bristol*, 1745; Faulkner's *Dublin Journal*, 15–19 Dec. 1730, *ex inf.* the Knight of Glin.]

GREIG, SAMUEL ALEXANDER (– 1846), was Surveyor to the County of Devon from 1841, when he succeeded James Green (*q.v.*), until his death in 1846 [County Records]. In 1839 he exhibited at the Royal Academy: a 'Villa in the old English style, lately erected near Exeter on the property of Mr. James Veitch', now 'Graslawn' in the grounds of the Princess Elizabeth Orthopaedic Hospital, and an 'Elizabethan villa' for W. B. King, identifiable as THE HENNONS, TEIGNMOUTH, DEVON. He also designed the EXETER DISPENSARY in QUEEN STREET, EXETER, 1840–3 [P. M. G. Russell, *The History of the Exeter Hospitals*, Exeter 1976, 97]. He competed for the Assize Courts at Liverpool in 1840, winning the second premium of £200.

GRELLIER, WILLIAM (1807–1852), born at Peckham, Surrey, was articled to George Smith in 1823. He was admitted to the Royal Academy Schools in 1824, winning the Silver Medal in 1826 and the Gold Medal in 1829. He became a member of the Architectural Society on its formation in 1831, contributed largely to its portfolio of measured drawings, acted as its honorary secretary for four years, and was presented with a testimonial by its members on its union with the R.I.B.A. in 1842. In 1838 he obtained the second premium of £30 for a town hall and market-place for St. John's Newfoundland [*Civil Engineer and Architect's Jnl.* i, 174], and in 1839 the first premium of £300 for a design for the Royal Exchange, London, from amongst thirty-eight competitors. The assessors did not, however, consider that it was 'practicable, advisable, or capable of being advantageously adopted', and the designs eventually executed were those of Sir William Tite. Grellier's drawings are now in the R.I.B.A. Collection. In 1834–5 he gratuitously designed and supervised the building of the Tylers' and Bricklayers' Almshouses: the Company subsequently presented him with its freedom, elected him to the court, and in 1849 to the Mastership. He was appointed District Surveyor of Whitechapel in November 1838. He exhibited at the Royal Academy from 1828 to 1848. He died on 7 January 1852, and was buried in Norwood Cemetery. There is a privately printed memoir by Dr. H. C. Barlow. [*A.P.S.D.*; *Builder* xxvii, 1869, 65].

MACCLESFIELD, CHESHIRE, ST. GEORGE'S SUNDAY SCHOOLS, 1835 [exhib. at R.A.].

TYLER'S AND BRICKLAYERS' ALMHOUSES, BALLS POND, ISLINGTON, 1834–5, north block 1838–9, Gothic [W. G. Bell, *The Tylers' and Bricklayers' Company*, 1938, 56 and plate].

LONDON, ST. ETHELBURGA'S CHURCH, BISHOPSGATE, rebuilt roof, *c.*1835 [G. Godwin, *Churches of London* ii, 1839].

LONDON, ST. ETHELBURGA SOCIETY'S CHARITY SCHOOLS, WORMWOOD STREET, BISHOPSGATE, *c.*1839; dem. [exhib. at R.A.].

ISLINGTON, THE DRY METER GAS COMPANY'S WORKS, NEW NORTH ROAD, *c.*1839 [exhib. at R.A.].

WATFORD, HERTS., NATIONAL SCHOOLS, 1841, Elizabethan style [engraving published Nov. 1841].

LIVERPOOL, ROYAL EXCHANGE INSURANCE BUILDINGS, DALE STREET, 1846–8; dem. [*Builder* vi, 1848, 619].

GREY, THOMAS PHILIP DE, EARL DE GREY (1781–1859), was the elder son of Thomas Robinson, 2nd Baron Grantham (d. 1786), by Mary, 2nd daughter of Philip Yorke, 2nd Earl of Hardwicke, and Jemima, Marchioness Grey, of Wrest Park in Bedfordshire. At the age of five he succeeded his father as 3rd Baron Grantham, inheriting with the title the family seat of Newby (now Baldersby) Park in the North Riding of Yorkshire, built by Sir William Robinson to the designs of Colen Campbell.[1] Under the will of William Weddell (a distant relative), he later inherited the latter's extensive estates in Yorkshire, including Newby Hall in the West Rid-

[1] Lord de Grey sold Newby Park in 1845.

ing, thus becoming the owner of two seats of the same name. Finally in 1833, on the death of his maternal aunt Amabel, Countess de Grey, he inherited Wrest Park together with the titles of Earl de Grey and Baron Lucas. In 1803 he had changed his surname from Robinson to Weddell, and he now changed it again to De Grey. In 1805 he married Henrietta, 5th daughter of the Earl of Enniskillen, by whom he left two daughters. He died at his London home, 4 St. James's Square, on 14 November 1859.

Lord Grantham was educated at St. John's College, Cambridge, where he took his M.A. in 1801. In 1801–2 he travelled in Russia and Italy, returning just before the resumption of the war with France in May 1803. In subsequent years his foreign travels were limited to visits to Paris. He had a brief political career as First Lord of the Admiralty in Peel's first administration (1834–5) and was sworn of the Privy Council. From 1841 to 1844 he served as Lord Lieutenant of Ireland, a position he filled with credit. On his return he was created a Knight of the Garter. But unlike his younger brother Lord Goderich, De Grey was not dedicated to a political career, preferring 'to move among men of letters and artists at the various learned societies of which he was a member'. Above all he was seriously interested in architecture. This may have been an inherited taste, for it was shared by his father, the 2nd Lord Grantham (*q.v.*). Soon after he had come into possession of Newby he added (in 1808) a dining-room on the north side, making his own designs 'with the professional assistance' of John Shaw (*q.v.*). It is a simple rectangular room with a coffered recess at each end and restrained neo-classical detailing (*C. Life*, 25 Dec. 1980). His major achievement as an amateur architect was, however, Wrest Park, which he completely rebuilt in a very competent French Louis XV style between 1834 and 1839. In a MS. account of the house (Bedfordshire Record Office, CRT 190/45/2, 1–19) he states explicitly that 'I was strictly and in every sense of the word my own architect . . . I had my French books always under my hand [and] referred to them for authority whenever I could find anything to suit me.'[1] To make the working drawings he employed 'a Mr. Brown[e], who had been Nash's clerk', and as executant architect he engaged a north-countryman called James Clephan (*q.v.*). Earl de Grey's claim to have been his own architect is confirmed by the survival of very competent architectural drawings signed G with a symbol for a coronet. The result was a *tour de force* of French eighteenth-century architectural design on English soil, carried out with consistent skill both inside and out (*C. Life*, 25 June, 2 July 1970). Earl de Grey also built (1812) a small seaside house at Cowes, Isle of Wight, to his own designs, and in 1833 carried out internal alterations to his family house in London at 4, St. James's Square, for which he 'made all [the] plans and designs' himself, employing as clerk of the works W. J. Browne and as builder George Harrison.

Other buildings for which de Grey is known to have been personally responsible are the Silsoe lodges to Wrest Park, which he designed for his aunt in 1826 (*C. Life*, 13 Aug. 1970, 405), and Silsoe Church, which was rebuilt in 1830–1 in a remarkably authentic Perpendicular Gothic style. De Grey records that he 'furnished all the designs' but that 'the detail and execution was left' to Thomas Smith of Hertford (*q.v.*). De Grey's drawings for the church are in the Bedfordshire Record Office. In addition he played an important part in the commissioning of two prominent buildings in London, the United Service Club in Pall Mall (by John Nash, 1827), and the enlargement of Buckingham Palace (by Edward Blore, 1846–50). As chairman of the building committee of the Club he refused to allow Nash to re-use Henry Holland's beautiful but too constricted staircase from Carlton House, and instead provided a sketch of a more capacious staircase of the kind that was eventually built. At Buckingham Palace he was an active member of the commission set up by Peel to superintend the erection of Blore's new entrance front, and probably exercised some influence over its design. In 1848 he was the Lords' representative on the royal commission appointed to supervise the completion of the new Houses of Parliament. In 1835 de Grey was asked to become President of the recently established Institute of British Architects, a position which he continued to hold until his death some twenty-five years later. It was an appropriate and successful choice, for de Grey brought to the new institution a combination of social distinction and political influence that was invaluable in its early years. [G.E.C., *Complete Peerage*; autobiographical memoirs (typescript copy in Beds. C.R.O., CRT/190/45/2); obituaries in *R.I.B.A. Trans.* 1860, and *Builder* xviii, 1859, 756; Simon Houfe, 'Wrest Park, Bedfordshire', *C. Life*, 25 June, 2 July 1970; *History of the King's Works* vi, 1973, 233, 289–90; 'The Earl de Grey's account of the building of

[1] The names of 'Blondel', 'Mansard' and 'Le Pautre' are inscribed on the spines of symbolical volumes over the south door of the entrance hall, and the source of the south front is to be found in Blondel's *Maisons de Plaisir* (1737).

Wrest House', ed. A. F. Cirket, *Bedfordshire Historical Record Soc.* 59, 1980.]

GRIFFIN, JOHN, of Hemel Hempstead, designed BOXMOOR CHURCH, HERTS., 1830, Gothic; dem. *c.*1870 [I.C.B.S.], and added a N. aisle to MARKYATE STREET CHURCH, HERTS., in 1842 [I.C.B.S.]. A design by him for minor alterations to DRAYTON LODGE, DRAYTON BEAUCHAMP, BUCKS., for William Jenney, dated 1837, is among the Harpur-Crewe papers in the Derbyshire C.R.O.

GRIFFITH, JAMES (1761–1821), a prebendary of Gloucester from 1816 and Master of University College, Oxford, from 1808 until his death, had some skill as an amateur artist and architect. Several of the topographical illustrations to Whitaker's *History of Craven* (1805) were supplied by him. 'Poker painting' was his speciality. His *chef d'œuvre* in this medium was a *Salvator Mundi* after Carlo Dolci which formerly hung over the altar in University College Chapel. As an architect he was responsible for redesigning the south side of the main quadrangle of the College when it was refaced in 1802. He replaced the former classical frontispiece by a gabled central feature with Gothic detailing. He also made a Gothic design for a new Master's Lodging which was not executed [*V.C.H. Oxon.* iii, 78, 80]. At Gloucester Cathedral he designed the Gothic choir-screen erected in 1820, as recorded by an inscription on the north-west pier of the crossing. [J. Britton, *History and Antiquities of Gloucester Cathedral*, 1829, 60 and Apppendix, p. 9, n. 18; G. W. Counsel, *History of Gloucester*, 1829, 98; *Memoirs of a Highland Lady*, ed. Lady Strachey, 1898, 42, 75–7, 123–4, 369–70; W. Carr, *University College*, 1902, 193–4, 212.]

GRIFFITH, JOHN WILLIAM (*c.*1790–1855), of St. John's Square, Clerkenwell, London, was surveyor to the parish of St. Botolph, Aldersgate, whose church he is said to have enlarged and decorated. He may therefore have been responsible for the design of the east front, as executed in Roman cement by Messrs. John Ward & Son, builders, in 1830 (G. Godwin, *Churches of London* ii, 1839, plate), though his name does not appear in the Vestry Minutes (now Guildhall Library, MS. 3863/2). He was also surveyor to the London estates of St. John's College, Cambridge, and to the Islington estate of James Rhodes. He designed the Islington Parochial Schools, 1815, and many villas built between 1816 and 1855 in Islington, Hornsey, Highgate and Kentish Town. He died on 27 November 1855, aged 65, and must not be confused with John Griffith of Finsbury (1796–1888), F.R.I.B.A. and Chairman of the Kensal Green Cemetery Company. His son, William Pettit Griffith (1815–84), was well known as an architect and antiquary. [obituary in *Builder* xiii, 1855, 620; W. J. Pinks, *History of Clerkenwell*, 1881, 638, 691–3].

GRIFFITHS, J—, exhibited at the Royal Academy from 27 Francis Street, Bedford Square, from 1807 to 1811. His exhibit in the latter year was a 'Mansion to be erected for E. Ruppel, Esq. opposite the Government House at Memel, in Prussia'. George Griffiths, of the same address, was a member of the Surveyors' Club from 1792 to 1810.

GRIMES, RICHARD, was among the architects who submitted designs for the Bank of England in 1731. His plan, which was criticized as too cramped, is preserved among the Bank's archives (M 61(iii)).

GRINWAY, FRANCIS HOWARD, *see* GREENWAY, F.H.

GROVES, JOHN THOMAS (*c.*1761–1811), was the son of John Grove or Groves, a London master bricklayer of repute, to whom he was apprenticed in 1775. His training was evidently that of an architect rather than a craftsman, for he exhibited views of Westminster at the Royal Academy in 1778 and 1780,[1] and visited Italy, exhibiting in 1791 a view of the Temple of the Sybil at Tivoli. In 1794 he was elected a member of the Florentine Academy *in absentia*, and in the same year he was appointed Clerk of the Works at Whitehall, Westminster and St. James's on the resignation of Sir John Soane, who is said to have 'been the means of obtaining' the post for Groves. He also held the posts of architect to the General Post Office and surveyor to the Commissioners for the Improvement of Westminster. At the Office of Works he proved to be an indolent administrator who took advantage of James Wyatt's lax regime to neglect his duties. He was Master of the Tylers' and Bricklayers' Company in 1810–11. Charles Bacon (*q.v.*) was his pupil. He died at his home in Scotland Yard on 24 August 1811 after a stroke. As an architect he designed some elegant late Georgian houses, but his most original work is the unusual pierced obelisk at Garbally in Ireland. His portrait by Francis Wheatley (not by P. Reinagle, as stated by Graves) was exhibited

[1] The view of Westminster Abbey which he exhibited in 1780 is now in the Museum of London.

at the Royal Academy in 1790. [*A.P.S.D.*; *Gent's Mag.* 1811 (ii), 287, 494; Tylers' & Bricklayers' Company Freedom Register, Guildhall Library MS. 3053/4, p. 58; *The Farington Diary*, ed. J. Greig, i, 74, iv, 149; *History of the King's Works* vi, 67–71; F. Salmon, 'British Architects and the Florentine Academy', *Mitteilungen des Kunsthistorischen Institutes in Florenz* xxxiv, 1990, 207; will (P.C.C. 411 CRICKETT).]

ELY, CAMBS., repaired BISHOP'S PALACE for Bishop James Yorke, 1795 [E. A. B. Barnard in *N. & Q.* 194, 14 May 1949, 207].

BROOMFIELD LODGE, CLAPHAM COMMON (west side), for the Hon. E. J. Eliot, *c.*1797; dem. [G. Richardson, *New Vitruvius Britannicus* i, 1810, pls. xvii, xviii].

TEWIN WATER, HERTS., rebuilt for Henry Cowper, Clerk of the House of Lords, *c.*1798; much altered. [Groves is referred to as the architect of this house in Repton's 'Red Book', now in the Herts. Record Office, C.2404] (Neale, *Views of Seats*, 1st ser., i, 1818).

MORDEN, SURREY, house for Abraham Goldsmid, *c.*1800; dem. [*A.P.S.D.*] (D. Hughson, *Circuit of London* v, 1808, 293, plate).

ELY CATHEDRAL, repaired west front in association with James Wyatt and designed a marble pulpit 'in imitation of the Norman architecture', 1800–2 [*A.P.S.D.*; G. L. Taylor, *Memoirs of an Octogenarian Architect*, 1870–2, 39; *Gent's Mag.* 1805 (i), 122]; altered W. window to accommodate painted glass for Bishop James Yorke, 1808 [E. A. B. Barnard, *op. cit.*].

TUNBRIDGE WELLS, KENT, THE BATHS, for Mrs. Shorey, *c.*1804 [P. Amsinck, *Tunbridge Wells and its Neighbourhood*, 1810, plate facing p. 34].

PORTSDOWN HILL, HANTS., monument to Lord Nelson, 1807 [exhib. at R.A. 1807].

GARBALLY PARK, CO. GALWAY, IRELAND, obelisk for the 2nd Earl of Clancarty, 1811 [inscription recording that it was 'erected from a design presented gratuitously by J. T. Groves Esq.'].

EAST GRINSTEAD CHURCH, SUSSEX, completed west tower of Gothic church designed by James Wyatt, 1811–13. His design was accepted 2 August 1811, and was carried out after his death by H. W. & W. Inwood [minutes of committee in West Sussex Record Office].

GRUMBOLD, ROBERT (1639–1720), was the best known of a family of freemasons who practised their trade in Northamptonshire and Cambridgeshire in the sixteenth, seventeenth and eighteenth centuries. They originated in the quarrying villages of Weldon and Raunds, and their names occur frequently in building records from the end of the sixteenth century. WILLIAM GRUMBOLD was a freemason much employed by Sir Thomas Tresham of Rushton, contracting with him in 1578 to build the MARKET HOUSE at ROTHWELL [Hist. MSS. Comm., *Var. Coll.* iii, pp. xxxiii–xxxiv, 2]. Later, from 1594 onwards, 'the Grumbolds' were working on Tresham's NEW BUILDING at LYVEDEN [*ibid.*, xxxv, xlix, liv, 134]. William Grumbold was employed in the construction of FOTHERINGHAY BRIDGE in 1573–4 [P.R.O., Exchequer K.R. 463/33], and may well have been the same as the 'William Grombole master workman and freemason' who, together with 'Robert Grombole our master workman freemason', was engaged in rebuilding the spire of ST. MARY THE GREAT, CAMBRIDGE, in 1593–4 [J. E. Foster, *Churchwardens' Accounts of St. Mary the Great, Cambridge*, Cambridge Antiquarian Soc. 1905, 248].[1] 'John Grombole freemason and brother of Robert Grombole' also worked at St. Mary's in 1594 [*ibid.*, 248–61].

The accounts for building HARROLD HOUSE, BEDS. (dem. 1961), in 1608–10 show that Weldon freestone for the porch, corbel-table and windows was supplied by 'old Grumbold' and Thomas Grumbold ['The Building Accounts of Harrold Hall', ed. John Weaver, *Beds. Historical Record Soc.* xlix, 1970, 79], and there are numerous references to Grumbolds in the parish registers of Weldon from their commencement in 1594. The most prominent member of the family there in the seventeenth century was ARTHUR GRUMBOLD (1603–1670), who had a lease of the Weldon quarries from Lord Hatton [Northants. Record Office, Finch-Hatton papers, 3643]. His initials and the date 1654 can still be seen on the front of a stone-built house in the main street of Weldon. In his will [Peterborough Probate Records, Liber Q, f. 73] he left 'all my workinge tooles both for hardstone and freestone and my steele two foot rule' to his younger son Thomas. All the rest of his 'Quarrye tooles plotts bookes compasses moldes' and all his 'stone at home and abroad' was to go to his elder son John (1643–1718), who was to take Thomas as apprentice 'to teach him his trade the which I taught him'.

Meanwhile other members of the family had established themselves at Cambridge.

[1] An estimate for the spire, with rough drawings, in B.L., Cotton MS. Faust. C.III, ff. 487–8, 490–1, is very likely in the hand of one of the Grumbolds.

The first to settle there appears to have been THOMAS GRUMBOLD, who was paid for work at ST. JOHN'S COLLEGE LIBRARY in 1625, at CLARE HALL in 1639–40, and at KING'S COLLEGE in 1651. He died at Cambridge in 1657. Robert Grumbold, the principal subject of this entry, was the son of Edward Grumbold of Raunds, where he was born in 1639. Whether he learned his trade in the quarries at Raunds or with Thomas Grumbold at Cambridge is not known. He must already have been a master mason of repute when, in 1667–8, He was paid £10 15s. 6d. by the Dean and Canons of Worcester 'for his journey from Cambridge to survey the [cathedral] church' of Worcester [Treasurer's account, 1677–8, *ex inf.* Mr. D. A. Whitehead]. In 1669 he and a partner named Bradwell executed the masonry of the west range of CLARE HALL. From 1674 onwards he was concerned in the building of ST. CATHARINE'S COLLEGE, where payments to him 'for surveying' may indicate that he was responsible for the architectural design. In 1676 he was appointed master mason for the building of the new LIBRARY at TRINITY COLLEGE to the designs of Sir Christopher Wren and continued working there until it was completed early in the 1690s. In 1680–2 he extended the adjoining NEVILE'S COURT to meet the Library and built 'The Tribunal', a classical feature on the east side of the Court that was almost certainly designed by Wren. In 1682–6 Grumbold designed and built the north range of CLARE HALL, containing the Hall and Buttery; in 1687 he gave a design for a new chapel for ST. JOHN'S COLLEGE, which was not, however, carried out; in 1695 he was concerned in laying out the PHYSIC GARDEN; in 1696 he designed the new printing-house in Queen's Lane, and began work on the stone bridge and gate-piers at ST. JOHN'S COLLEGE, which he completed in 1712. This bridge he appears to have designed himself, though the siting of it had been discussed in correspondence with both Wren and Hawksmoor before the work began, and there is a payment to John Longland, a London master carpenter, 'in advising about a modell for the Bridge' [*Wren Soc.* xix, 103–7]. In 1703 he built the piers at the entrance-gate of JESUS COLLEGE; in 1705–6 he finished the west front of CLARE HALL; in 1709 the north and south cloisters flanking PETERHOUSE CHAPEL were rebuilt 'according to a paper delivered by Mr. Grumbold'; in 1714 he ashlared the gatehouse and part of the west front of CHRIST'S COLLEGE; in 1715 he altered the CIVIL LAW SCHOOL, later the west room of the University Library, for the reception of Bishop Moore's books; in 1716 he rebuilt the fountain at TRINITY COLLEGE; and in 1719–20 he began the building of the WESTMORELAND BUILDING at EMMANUEL COLLEGE under the supervision of John Lumley (*q.v.*), but died before the work was completed [J.B.P., 'The College Buildings in the Eighteenth Century', in *Emmanuel College Magazine* ix (2), 1898, 87].

Outside Cambridge, Grumbold contracted in 1681 to rebuild two turrets at AUDLEY END, ESSEX, for the Board of Works [P.R.O., WORK 5/145, p. 118], and he was employed by the 1st Earl of Ailesbury at GREAT PARK HOUSE, AMPTHILL, BEDS., in 1687–9 [accounts at Tottenham Park, Wilts.], and by the 11th Earl of Kent, for whose seat at WREST PARK, BEDS., he made in 1693–5 two stone basins in the garden and a pair of gate-piers with heraldic wyverns [Beds. Record Office, L 31/288]. After the collapse of the north-west angle of the north transept of ELY CATHEDRAL in 1699, Grumbold was employed to rebuild it. He submitted a plan, but Wren was consulted, and may have been responsible for the design of the new doorway to the transept, which resembles that of St. Mary-le-Bow [W. D. Caröe, *Tom Tower*, 1923, 19; *Wren Soc.* xix, pl. 14].

Robert Grumbold died at Cambridge on 7 December 1720, aged 82, and was buried in St. Botolph's Churchyard, where his monument can be seen on the south side of the chancel (*Cambridge Antiquarian Soc.'s Procs.* xxxiv, 1934, pl. ii). His will, proved in the court of the Archdeaconry of Ely on 23 December 1720, shows that he owned a considerable amount of leasehold property in Cambridge. His house and yard stood in Trumpington Street on a site now occupied by the forecourt of St. Catharine's College.

Grumbold was the principal figure in Cambridge architecture at the end of the seventeenth century. Though he never learned the full discipline of classical architecture he achieved an attactive vernacular style compounded of artisan mannerism and baroque elements that he had picked up from Wren and others.

[Willis & Clark, iii, 533 and *passim*; D. Knoop & G. P. Jones, 'The Rise of the Mason Contractor', *R.I.B.A. Jnl.*, 17 Oct. 1936, 1069–70; G. F. Webb, 'Robert Grumbold and the Architecture of the Renaissance at Cambridge', *Burl. Mag.*, Dec. 1925 – Jan. 1926; R.C.H.M., *Cambridge, passim.*]

GUMMOW, BENJAMIN (*c.*1766–1844) practised at Ruabon in Denbighshire. He appears to have been a pupil of S. P. Cockerell, who employed him as clerk of works for the alterations to St. Margaret's Church, Westminster, in 1799–1802 [Westminster Public Library, Minutes of the committee for the repair of the church, MS. 2625]. He probably settled in North Wales as the result of his employment as supervising architect at Eaton Hall, Cheshire, then (1803–12) being rebuilt for Lord Grosvenor to the designs of William Porden. He was also employed by Sir Watkin Williams-Wynn at Wynnstay, and in 1827 he told C. R. Cockerell that he 'has always had £300 per ann. from Lord Grosvenor and Sir W. W. and is not allowed any other charge or profits – but has his lodgings and living – out of this he has saved an easy independence' [C. R. Cockerell's diary, 5 Sept. 1827]. His house at Ruabon was no doubt on the Wynnstay estate. He died there in March 1844, aged 78 [Ruabon parish register in N.L.W.]. Michael and James Reynolds Gummow, who practised in Wrexham in the mid-nineteenth century, were probably Benjamin's son and grandson, respectively. The latter was the author of *Hints on House Building*, published at Wrexham in 1874.

In 1807 Porden told Lord Grosvenor that Gummow 'speaks without thinking and is the most inconsistent man I ever met with' [Eaton Hall muniments]. Though not an architect of the first rank, his additions to Eaton Hall successfully maintained the elegant rococo Gothic of the main block designed by Porden, and at Brogyntyn his Ionic portico is a handsome addition to an existing classical house.

HALKIN MOUNTAIN, FLINTSHIRE, building (probably ornamental) for 2nd Earl Grosvenor, 1804; dem. [letter dated 20 Aug. 1804, Eaton Hall muniments].

LITTLETON, nr. CHRISTLETON, CHESHIRE, for Thomas Dixon, 1806; since much altered [E. Twycross, *Mansions of England: Cheshire* i, 1850, 43].

NERQUIS HALL, FLINTSHIRE, addition of castellated Gothic wings, stable archway, Gothic porch and Gothic orangery for Miss Gifford, 1813–20; wings dem. 1964 [drawings in Clwyd Record Office].

BROGYNTYN (PORKINGTON), SHROPSHIRE, addition of portico and other alterations for Mary Jane Ormsby and her husband William Gore, 1814–15 [P.R.O., Coade Stone Co.'s letter-book, C 111/106, ff. 123, 130, 136, 176, 191, 199, 211].

EATON HALL, CHESHIRE, added wings for 2nd Earl Grosvenor, 1823–5, Gothic; altered by William Burn 1846–51; rebuilt by Alfred Waterhouse 1870; dem. 1963 [*A.P.S.D.*, *s.v.* 'Porden, William'] (*C. Life*, 11, 18 Feb. 1971). Gummow also designed a Gothic temple to contain a Roman altar found in 1821 [R. Ackermann, *Views of Country Seats* i, 1830, 31].

HALKIN CASTLE, FLINTSHIRE, supervised construction of house designed by J. Buckler (*q.v.*) for 2nd Earl Grosvenor, 1824–7, Tudor Gothic [Eaton Hall, Grosvenor archives nos. 1147–8, building accounts initialled 'B.G.'].

WYNNSTAY, DENBIGHSHIRE, probably responsible for recasing and altering the house for Sir Watkin Williams-Wynn, Bart., *c.*1825; destroyed by fire 1858 [Peter Howell in *C. Life*, 30 March 1972].

POOL PARK, DENBIGHSHIRE, probably supervised building of house for 2nd Lord Bagot, *c.*1827–8, to the designs of John Buckler, whose designs for this 'Tudor' timber-framed building were exhibited by him at the R.A. in 1830 as executed [*Correspondence of Lady Williams Wynn*, ed. R. Leighton, 1920, 330; C. R. Cockerell's diary, 5 Sept. 1827, where Gummow tells him of a 'house built by him for Lord Bagot'].

CHIRK CASTLE, DENBIGHSHIRE, work for Robert Myddelton-Biddulph, 1831, connected with a 'porch' [National Library of Wales, Chirk E 3081].

GUNNERY, JAMES, designed a Gothic church at DELAMERE, CHESHIRE, 1816–17, altered 1878 [inscription on brass plate].

GUTCH, GEORGE (*c.*1790–1874), was the fifth and youngest son of the Revd. J. Gutch, registrar and historian of Oxford University, and for sixty-two years chaplain of All Souls College. He showed an early aptitude for drawing and at the age of 15 won a medal from the Society of Arts for a view of Wrexham Church. In 1806 he became a pupil of George Saunders. It was Saunders's recommendation that in 1825 secured him the post of District Surveyor for Paddington that he was to hold for nearly fifty years. In 1827 he succeeded S. P. Cockerell as surveyor to the Bishop of London's estate in Paddington, and it was under his direction that this important estate, lying between Hyde Park and Paddington Station, was laid out for building. His plan, published in 1838, 'fixed the architectural pattern of the whole district until the late 1930s' and created the stucco terraces characteristic of Sussex Gardens and its neighbourhood. In conjunction with J. Goldicutt, Gutch designed the Gothic church of ST. JAMES, PADDINGTON, which forms the terminal feature at the west end of Sussex Gardens. It was built in 1841–3 and rebuilt (except the steeple) by G. E. Street in 1882.

Gutch appears to have done little work outside Paddington, MELCHBOURN VICARAGE, BEDS., 1835, being his only recorded work in the country [Cambridge Univ. Library, Ely Diocesan Records, Parsonage Papers, G 3/39/2]. In 1830 he succeeded Henry Hakewill as Surveyor to the Radcliffe Trustees, but the Trustees did not commission any building of importance during his tenure of the post. In 1839 he and E. W. Trendall jointly submitted a competent but unremarkable Greek Revival design in the competition for the Ashmolean Museum at Oxford (Bodleian, MS. Top. Oxon. a. 9). He became a Fellow of the R.I.B.A. in 1835. He died in November 1874, in his 84th year, and was buried in Paddington Cemetery.

[*Builder* xxxii, 1874, 998, 1002, xxxv, 1877, 384; *Gent's Mag.* 1861 (ii), 684 n.; G. Toplis, 'The History of Tyburnia', *C. Life*, 15, 22 Nov. 1973.]

GWILT, GEORGE (1746–1807), son of Richard Gwilt, peruke-maker, was born in Southwark on 9 June 1746. At the age of 14 he was apprenticed to Moses Waite, a London mason whose yard was in Southwark. Later he was in the office of George Silverside, a surveyor with a considerable practice in London, and also worked occasionally for one of the Jupps. In about 1770 he became Surveyor to the County of Surrey, in 1771 Surveyor to the Commissioners of Sewers for Surrey, and in 1774 District Surveyor for St. George's Parish, Southwark, under the Metropolitan Building Act. He was also Surveyor to the Clink Paving Commissioners and architect to the West India Dock Company. As a young man he was employed by Henry Thrale, whose brewery was in Southwark, and through him met Samuel Johnson, though 'from a dislike to Johnson's unpleasant temper, cordiality never existed between them'. He himself is said to have been 'a person of irascible temper but easily pacified, kind hearted and an excellent father and husband'. He was the father of George and Joseph Gwilt (*qq.v.*), and his pupils included John Young (apprenticed to him 1772), Henry Ashley Keeble (1783) and John Shaw (1790). He was Master of the Masons' Company in 1790. He died in Southwark on 9 December 1807, and is commemorated by an inscription on the family monument on the south (exterior) side of Southwark Cathedral.

Gwilt was a hard-working surveyor rather than an architectural artist. When he retired in 1805 the magistrates of Surrey paid tribute to the 'integrity and ability with which as Surveyor of public works, he has served this County during the course of five and thirty years'. Nearly all his buildings were of a utilitarian character. His biggest and finest work was the great range of warehouses for the West India Dock Company which was designed by himself and his eldest son in 1800. The Company received proposals from a number of other architects, including Nash, Soane, George Dance and the two Wyatts, but the Gwilts were given the commission in preference to their more famous rivals. Within two years they had built at least six of the nine 'stacks' (i.e. blocks), each five floors high, which together made a range of warehouses nearly two-thirds of a mile long and (until their partial destruction in 1940) were the finest examples of London's dock architecture.

[Joseph Gwilt, 'Parentalia of Gwilt', MS. in Surrey County Record Office, Acc. 390; *Gent's Mag.* 1807, 1181; 1821 (ii), 380; *A.P.S.D.*; *D.N.B.*; Guildhall Library, records of the Masons' Company.]

KINGSTON-ON-THAMES, SURREY, HOUSE OF CORRECTION, 1775 [Nancy Briggs in *Arch. Hist.* 27, 1984, 301].

SOUTHWARK, ST. SAVIOUR'S WAREHOUSE (now London Fire Brigade Training Centre), 1777, since altered [Southwark Borough archives, accounts of Workhouse treasurer].

STREATHAM PLACE, STREATHAM, SURREY, alterations for Henry Thrale, 1780; dem. 1863 [*The Queeney Letters*, ed. Lord Lansdowne, 1934, 130, 135].

WEST MALLING CHURCH, KENT, rebuilt nave, 1780; again rebuilt by J. T. Micklethwaite 1900–1 [MS. Vestry Minutes].

SOUTHWARK, THE SURREY COUNTY BRIDEWELL, ST. GEORGE'S FIELDS, rebuilt 1781; dem. [*A.P.S.D.*].

COBHAM BRIDGE, SURREY, rebuilt 1782; destroyed by flood 1968 [*A.P.S.D.*].

LEATHERHEAD BRIDGE, SURREY, rebuilt 1782 [*A.P.S.D.*].

GODALMING BRIDGE, SURREY, rebuilt 1782–3 [*A.P.S.D.*].

LONDON, ST. MARY AT HILL CHURCH, rebuilt tower and west end, 1787–8 [MS. Vestry Minutes in Guildhall Library, 1240/42].

SOUTHWARK, houses on north side of UNION STREET, including No. 18 (dem. *c.*1890) as his own residence, *c.*1789 [*Survey of London* xxii, 84 and pl. 62].

SOUTHWARK, SURREY COUNTY GAOL, HORSEMONGER LANE, 1791–8; dem. 1880–92 [*A.P.S.D.*].

CAMBERWELL, THE CAMDEN CHAPEL, 1797; enlarged 1829, chancel added 1854; dem. *c.*1948 [Parish Records].

SOUTHWARK, SURREY COUNTY SESSIONS HOUSE,

NEWINGTON CAUSEWAY, 1798–9; dem. 1912 [*A.P.S.D.*].

ISLE OF DOGS, WAREHOUSES for the West India Dock Co., with George Gwilt, junior, 1800–3; all but one destroyed by bombing 1940 [exhib. at R.A. 1801; *A.P.S.D.*; S. H. Kessels, 'A Great Georgian Warehouse', *Arch. Rev.*, Sept. 1955, 191–2; Dan Cruickshank, 'Gwilt Complex', *Arch. Rev.* April 1989, 54–61].

GWILT, GEORGE (1775–1856), elder son of the above, was born in Southwark on 8 February 1775. He was apprenticed to his father in 1789, and eventually succeeded him in his practice. His inclinations 'led him rather towards the study than the active practice of architecture', and he contributed many papers to *Archaeologia* and *Vetusta Monumenta*, the publications of the Society of Antiquaries, of which he was elected a Fellow in 1815. In 1818–20 he superintended the repair of the steeple of the church of ST. MARY-LE-BOW, CHEAPSIDE, the upper part of which had to be taken down and rebuilt in consequence of the rusting and swelling of the iron cramps which held it together. The crowning obelisk was reduced in height on the grounds that its tenuity rendered it too liable to decay, and the columns beneath were renewed in Aberdeen granite. The foundations of the church were also strengthened, a work which resulted in the identification by Gwilt of the remains of the original eleventh-century structure. His account of the discovery, read to the Society of Antiquaries in June 1828, was published in *Vetusta Monumenta* v, 343–6. Between 1822 and 1825 he carried out the restoration of the choir and tower of the present SOUTHWARK CATHEDRAL at a cost of £35,000 (for details see W. Taylor, *Annals of St. Mary Overy*, 1833). In 1824 he visited Italy. On his return he rebuilt the first ten almshouses of CURE'S COLLEGE, PARK STREET, SOUTHWARK, and in 1832–3 gratuitously supervised the restoration of the LADY CHAPEL of SOUTHWARK CATHEDRAL, as described in *Gent's Mag.* 1833 (i), 254. He had made the antiquities of Southwark his particular study, and contributed two articles on the remains of Winchester Palace to the *Gent's Mag.* for 1815. He also formed a collection of local antiquities at his house in Union Street. He was Master of the Masons' Company on three occasions, in 1835, 1846 and 1854. He died on 27 June 1856, and was buried in the family vault on the south side of the choir of Southwark Cathedral. There is a lithographic portrait dated 1847 in J. S. Gwilt's *Slight Memoir of Joseph Gwilt* in the R.I.B.A. Collection. Of the four sons mentioned on his monument, only Alfred survived him, becoming Master of the Masons' Company in 1850, 1869 and 1879. George, the eldest, and Charles Edwin were both promising architects, but died young. S. T. Bull was a pupil. [*A.P.S.D.*; *D.N.B.*; obituary in *Builder* xiv, 1856, 386.]

GWILT, JOSEPH (1784–1863), younger son of George Gwilt the elder, was born in Southwark on 11 January 1784. He was educated at St. Paul's School, and in 1799 entered his father's office. He was admitted to the Royal Academy Schools in 1801, obtaining the Silver Medal in 1801. He exhibited at the Academy from 1800 onwards, and was practising as an architect before he had reached the age of 25. Between 1814 and 1818 he made a series of continental tours, visiting Paris in 1814, Flanders in 1815, Rome in 1816 (with the artist J. S. Hayward) and Paris again in 1818 and on several subsequent occasions. In or about the latter year he took up residence at No. 20 Abingdon Street, Westminster. He succeeded his father as Surveyor to the Commissioners of Sewers for Surrey, but resigned the office in 1846. He was also Surveyor to the Grocers' and Waxchandlers' Companies, and to the Imperial Fire Assurance Company. Much of his practice consisted in consultations with the Office of Woods and Forests and other official bodies, and with F. C. Penrose he assisted in drawing up a proposition for the new Metropolitan Building Act of 1855. For Sir T. Maryon Wilson he drew up a scheme for laying out his Hampstead estate for building, but it proved abortive. In 1839 he was one of the three assessors in the competition for the new Royal Exchange, and a volume containing his correspondence, etc., in this connection is now in the Guildhall Library. Though an elegant draughtsman, and the author of some accomplished neo-classical designs, he himself erected comparatively few buildings, and it is as a writer on architectural and antiquarian topics that he is best known. He was elected F.S.A. in 1815 and a Fellow of the Royal Astronomical Society in 1833. He retired to South Hill, Henley-on-Thames, where he died on 14 Sept. 1863. Among his pupils were J. L. Wolfe, G. Herron, and his younger son John Sebastian Gwilt (1811–90), who became an architect and made all the drawings for his father's *Encyclopaedia of Architecture*. In the R.I.B.A. Drawings Collection there is a volume by J. S. Gwilt entitled *Slight Memoir of Joseph Gwilt* (1882). It contains photographic portraits of Joseph Gwilt dated 1858 and a number of his drawings, with brief notes by his son. A miniature portrait by Andrew Robertson dated 1810 is in the National Portrait Gallery. The diaries he kept from 1844 to 1860 are in the Bodleian Library (MSS. Don. e. 144–150); earlier ones, recording his travels, are in the Canadian Centre for Architecture at Montreal. [*A.P.S.D.*; *D.N.B.*; obituaries in *Builder* xxi, 1863, 701; R.I.B.A. *Trans.*, 1863–4; *Gent's Mag.* 1863 (ii), 647–52; *Jnl. British Archaeological Assoc.* xx, 1864, 178–81; MS. 'Parentalia of Gwilt' by Joseph Gwilt, in Surrey County Record Office, Acc. 390.]

Gwilt's publications were: *A Treatise on the Equilibrium of Arches*, 1811, 1826 and 1838. The 2nd edition contained his design for London Bridge, placed first by the referees, but not awarded a premium. *Notitia Architectonica Italiana, or Concise Notices of the Buildings and Architects of Italy*, originally prepared for his own use when visiting Italy, and published in 1818. *A Cursory View of the Origin of Caryatides*, privately printed 1822 and reprinted in his edition of Chambers's *Treatise*. *Sciography, or Examples of Shadows, with Rules for their Projection*, 1822, 1824, 1833.[1] *The Conduct of the Corporation of London considered, in respect of the designs submitted to it for rebuilding London Bridge, in a Letter to G. H. Sumner, Esq., M.P., by an Architect*, 1823. *An Historical, Descriptive, and Critical Account of the Cathedral Church of St. Paul, London*, read to the Architects' and Antiquaries' Club, 1823, and printed in Britton & Pugin, *Public Buildings of London* i, 1825. An engraving, entitled a *Comparative View of the Four Principal Modern Churches in Europe by means of Transverse Sections to the Same Scale*, 1824. A new edition of Chambers's *Treatise on the Decorative Part of Civil Architecture*, with an introductory essay on Grecian architecture, 1825. A translation of the *Architecture of Vitruvius*, 1826. *Rudiments of Architecture, Practical and Theoretical*, 1826, 1835, 1839. The *Ordinary* to N. H. Nicolas, *A Roll of Arms*, 1829. *Observations on the Communication of Mr. Wilkins relative to the National Gallery*, 1833. The article on *Music* for the *Encyclopaedia Metropolitana*, 1835. *Rudiments of the Anglo-Saxon Tongue*, 1835. *Elements of Architectural Criticism*, 1837, 1839, in reply to articles on German architecture in the *Foreign Quarterly Review*. *A Project of a National Gallery on the Site of Trafalgar Square* (with his son), 1838. *An Encyclopaedia of Architecture, Historical, Theoretical and Practical*, 1842, 1845, 1854, 1859, 1867, 1876, 1889, the last three editions by Wyatt Papworth. All the articles relating to architecture, music, and the fine arts in Brande, *Dictionary of Science, Literature and Art*, 1842, 1853. A *Report* with I'Anson and Newman on Sewers in Surrey and Kent, 1843. A new edition of P. Nicholson's *Principles of Architecture*, 1848.

[1] For his MS. translation of a French treatise on shadows by C. Stanislas l'Eveillé, made in 1820, see J. Harris, *Catalogue of British Drawings for Architecture, etc. in American Collections*, 1971, 108.

ST. IVES VICARAGE, HUNTS., 1804 [Lincolnshire Record Office, MGA 44].

HOUGHTON COTTAGE, nr. ST. IVES, HUNTS., for John Ansley, 1807, and proposed alterations 1810 [exhibited at R.A. 1807, 1810].

HOARWITHY, HEREFS., proposed timber bridge of five spans, probably not built [exhibited at R.A. 1813; drawing in J. S. Gwilt's *Memoir*].

LEE, KENT, Tudor cottage for Thomas Brandram, 1813 [F. H. Hart, *History of Lee*, 1882, 21–2].

LEE, KENT, ST. MARGARET'S CHURCH, 1813–14, Gothic; dem. 1841 [*A.P.S.D.*; view of interior in J. S. Gwilt's *Memoir*].

SOUTHWARK, design for FLOOR CLOTH MANUFACTORY, NEWINGTON CAUSEWAY, for W. Hayward, 1814, perhaps not executed [alternative elevations in J. S. Gwilt's *Memoir*].

SOUTHWARK, planned approaches to Southwark Bridge, 1819 [*A.P.S.D.*].

LEE, KENT, conservatory at LEE GROVE (afterwards THE CEDARS) for Thomas Brandram, 1820 [F. H. Hart, *History of Lee*, 1882, 23; exhibited at R.A. 1820; drawings in J. S. Gwilt, *Memoir*].

BANBURY CHURCH, OXON., monument to Anne Brocas (d. 1824), executed by H. R. Hartley [signed].

LONDON, GROCERS' HALL, POULTRY, alterations, including interior of hall and front to Princes Street, 1838; rebuilt 1889–93 [*A.P.S.D.* (giving date 1828); engraving in J. S. Gwilt's *Memoir*, showing interior of hall as altered by Joseph Gwilt, 1838].

LONDON, ST. THOMAS (formerly STAMFORD HILL CHAPEL), CLAPTON COMMON, enlarged with addition of east tower, 1828–9 [I.C.B.S.].

MARKREE CASTLE, CO. SLIGO, IRELAND, additions for E. J. Cooper 1841–3, in conjunction with J. S. Gwilt, including interiors of Drawing Room, Boudoir, Ante-Room and Chapel executed in *carton pierre* by Wallet & Hubert of Paris to Gwilt's designs [exhib. at R.A. 1843 as 'completed by Joseph and J. S. Gwilt; Gwilt's Diary in Canadian Centre for Architecture, Montreal].

SWANSEA, GLAMORGANSHIRE, UNITARIAN CHAPEL, 1845–7 [J. Lewis, *The Swansea Guide*, 1851, 22].

CHARLTON, KENT, ST. THOMAS'S CHURCH,

MARYON ROAD, 1847–50, 'Byzantine' [*A.P.S.D.*].

OUNDLE, NORTHANTS., LAXTON'S ALMSHOUSES, CHURCH LANE, for the Grocers' Company, 1852–3 [W. G. Walker, *History of the Oundle Schools*, 1956, 341].

OUNDLE SCHOOL, NORTHANTS., rebuilt THE SCHOOLROOM, for the Grocers' Company, 1854–55, Gothic [W. G. Walker, *op. cit.*, 344–7].

GWYNN, JOHN (1713–1786), was the son of John Gwyn of Shrewsbury, where he was born in November 1713. Nothing is known of his father's occupation, or of his own early life. In 1760 he was described as 'till of late of another profession'. According to Joseph Farington he 'was originally a carpenter, and by industrious study acquired knowledge sufficient to become an Architect, in which capacity he was little employed till towards the latter part of his life'. This last statement is borne out by the list of his recorded works printed below. He had, however, been active for some time as an advocate of schemes to enhance the status of British artists and architects by the establishment of a national academy and by 'promoting the advancement of grandeur and elegance' in public building. In 1749 he published *An Essay on Design, including Proposals for erecting a Public Academy to be supported by Voluntary Subscription (till a Royal Foundation can be obtained)*[1] and two engravings, *A Plan for Rebuilding the City of London after the Great Fire in 1666, designed by that Great Architect Sir Christopher Wren* (1749), and a *Transverse Section of St. Paul's Cathedral, decorated according to the original intention of Sir Christopher Wren*, engraved by E. Rooker and dedicated to the Prince of Wales (1755). In preparing this he was assisted by Samuel Wale, who supplied the figures. While taking measurements of the dome for this plate, Gwynn missed his footing and slipped down some distance until stopped by a projecting piece of lead, where he remained in peril until rescued. The plate was reissued in 1801.

Gwynn and Wale were neighbours in Little Court, Castle Street, Leicester Fields, and are said to have given each other much mutual assistance, Gwynn providing architectural backgrounds for his friend's compositions, and receiving help from Wale in his literary work. In 1758 they published a plan of St. Paul's Cathedral, engraved by James Green, showing the dimensions. Gwynn was also aided by Dr. Johnson, who, according to Boswell, 'lent his friendly assistance to correct and improve' his next publication, entitled *Thoughts on the Coronation of George III*, 1761. Johnson also composed the dedication to the King accompanying Gwynn's last and most important work, *London and Westminster Improved, to which is Prefixed a Discourse on Publick Magnificence*, 1766. In this remarkable book, Gwynn 'urged that the map of London should be considered as a whole and future activity controlled by a general plan'. By means of coloured plans he put forward a carefully thought-out scheme of 'improvement', many features of which have since been carried out, and nearly all of which were both handsome and realistic. Nash's Regent Street, Rennie's Waterloo Bridge, the Thames Embankment and Trafalgar Square are all foreshadowed in this enlightened and prophetic work.

In 1755 Gwynn took part in the unsuccessful attempt to establish a 'Royal Academy of London for the improvement of Painting, Sculpture, and Architecture'. In 1760 he began to exhibit at the recently formed Society of Artists of Great Britain, of which he became a member, and continued to do so until the foundation of the Royal Academy in 1768, when he became one of the first Academicians. He subsequently exhibited at the Academy annually from 1769 to 1772.

In 1759 he competed for the proposed Blackfriars Bridge, and his design was one of the eight short-listed by the Committee. Mylne's design was eventually adopted, after much dispute over the relative merits of semicircular and elliptical arches, the latter being advocated by Mylne and the former by Gwynn and Smeaton.[2] Out of 'regard for his friend Mr. Gwyn', Dr. Johnson took part in the controversy, writing letters in favour of semicircular arches in the *Daily Gazetteer* of 1, 8 and 15 December 1759 (reprinted in *The Architect*, 7 Jan. 1887, 13–14; cf. Hawkins, *Life of Johnson*, 373–5). Subsequently Gwynn designed several important bridges, including that at Worcester, with its fine approaches. In December 1783 he was presented with the freedom of the city of Worcester as a token of appreciation for his services. In May 1771, he was appointed Surveyor to the Commissioners of the Oxford Paving Act at a salary of £150 per annum 'for three years certain and for one year more if necessary'. In this capacity he demolished the east and north gates of the city, and rebuilt Magdalen

[1] Other pamphlets attributed to him in *A.P.S.D.* and *D.N.B.* are now known to be by Robert Morris (*q.v.*).

[2] In 1766 it was on Smeaton's recommendation that Gwynn was employed to report on the proposed bridge over the R. Tay at Perth (see *Reports of the late John Smeaton* i, 1812, 184–7).

Bridge. He also designed the new Markets and the Workhouse, and undertook to supervise the reconstruction of the west wing of the Queen's College in accordance with the designs of Kenton Couse after the fire of December 1778 [*Letters of Radcliffe and James*, ed. Evans, Oxford Historical Society, 1888, 270–2].

Gwynn died at Worcester on 27 February 1786, and was buried in the graveyard of St. Oswald's Hospital, where tablets, now no longer legible, record his name and that of his natural son Charles, who died in 1796. He left money in trust for the latter's apprenticeship to a painter, sculptor, architect or engraver, and directed him to publish the 'most useful' of Gwynn's own drawings. In the event of Charles's own death without issue, the money was to be divided between the Royal Society and the Royal Academy for the establishment of prizes to be awarded by the former to the best essay on 'Which promotes the happiness of mankind most, . . . the establishment of societies of learning, literature, and the dead languages, or . . . societies of ingenious, honest, industry', and by the latter 'to the best die engraver, or for a bust, statue, or composition'. Both Societies appear to have refused the bequests, the Royal Society in particular considering them 'totally foreign to the purposes for which the Society is instituted'. None of Gwynn's drawings were ever published, but several of them are preserved in the King's Collection of Maps in the British Library, and there are others in the Prattinton Collection in the Society of Antiquaries' Library.

Boswell describes Gwynn as 'a fine, lively, rattling fellow', and relates an anecdote which shows that he was Dr. Johnson's match in conversation. Owen, the historian of Shrewsbury, remembered him as 'lively, quick and sarcastic, of quaint appearance and odd manners'. But the latter were not so pronounced that Shenstone could not write of him in 1757 as 'a very wellbred and ingenious man, one Mr. Gwyn from London'. There is a portrait of him by Zoffany in the Shrewsbury Museum. William Hayward, the architect of Henley Bridge and a native of Shrewsbury, was his pupil and assistant.

[Wyatt Papworth, 'John Gwynn, R.A.', *Builder* xxi, 1863, 454; 1864, 27; J. L. Hobbs, 'The Parentage and Ancestry of John Gwyn', *Notes and Queries, Jan.* 1962, 21–2; *A.P.S.D.*; *D.N.B.*; obituary in *Berrow's Worcester Jnl.*, 2 March 1786; *The Farington Diary*, ed. J. Greig, i, 180; *The Letters of William Shenstone*, ed. M. Williams, 1939, 466; Mulvany's *Life of Gandon*, 1846, 162–3; J. Chambers, *Biographical Illustrations of Worcestershire*, 1820, 504–6; J. Summerson, *Georgian London*, 1945, 103–6; Eileen Harris, *British Architectural Books and Writers 1556–1785*, 1990, 214–17; Gwynn's will (P.C.C. 220 NORFOLK).]

SHREWSBURY, THE ENGLISH BRIDGE, 1769–74. The original intention was to widen the old bridge according to a plan made by Robert Mylne, but it was eventually decided to build a new bridge designed by Gwynn. This bridge was rebuilt 1925–7, the original elevations being adapted to a flattened roadway [A. W. Ward, *The Bridges of Shrewsbury*, 1935].

ATCHAM BRIDGE, SALOP., 1769–71 (for the inscription on the foundation-stone, see Camden, *Britannia* ii, 1789, 417).

WORCESTER BRIDGE and approaches, 1771–80. The original plans are in the Prattinton Collection in the Society of Antiquaries' Library, vol. v (folio), 70, and in the B.L., *King's Maps* xliii, 67 *a.a.* [David Whitehead, 'John Gwynn and the Building of Worcester Bridge', *Trans. Worcs. Archl. Soc.* 3rd ser. 8, 1982].

OXFORD, MAGDALEN BRIDGE, 1772–90; widened 1882–3. The original plans are in the B.L., 1802 c. 17, vol. 2, and *King's Maps* xxxiv, 33 (3 *a–c*). [T. W. M. Jaine, 'The Building of Magdalen Bridge', *Oxoniensia* xxxvi, 1971].

OXFORD, THE HOUSE OF INDUSTRY or WORKHOUSE, 1772–5; dem. 1864. The original design is in the B.L., *King's Maps* xxxiv, 33 (1).

OXFORD, THE MARKETS, 1773–4. The four houses facing the High Street (Nos. 13–16) were built by the Duke of Marlborough 'in conformity with the architect's suggestion'. The Market was reconstructed in 1839 and at various subsequent dates and nothing now remains of Gwynn's building. The original design is in B.L., *King's Maps* xxxiv, 32 e, and there are plan and elevation in *New Oxford Guide*, 1783, 9 [M. Graham, 'The Building of Oxford Covered Market', *Oxoniensia* xlix, 1979].

PITCHFORD, SALOP., PARK FARMHOUSE, *c.*1774 [*V.C.H. Salop.* viii, 117].

LONDON, PICCADILLY, house for Mr. Deards, probably John Deards, of 46 Dover Street, Piccadilly [*The Farington Diary*, ed. J. Greig, i, 180].

BLEDLOW CHURCH, BUCKS., altar-piece (with painting by Samuel Wale); removed to south aisle, 1877 [C. O. Skilbeck, 'Notes on Bledlow Parish Church', *Records of Bucks.* xii, 1927–33, 145].

GYFFORD, EDWARD (1773–1856), was a pupil of J. Lewis. He was admitted to the

Royal Academy Schools in 1789 at the age of 17, was awarded the Silver Medal in 1791, and the Gold Medal in 1792 for a 'Design for a House of Lords and Commons'. He exhibited at the Academy from 1791 to 1801, and published two small volumes entitled *Designs for Elegant Cottages and Small Villas* (1806) and *Designs for Small Picturesque Cottages and Hunting Boxes* (1806–7), which together formed 'a series of Select Architecture'. The original drawings for the latter book are in the Yale Center for British Art. In 1819 he attempted without success to obtain the commission for the new church of St. Luke, Chelsea, submitting designs now in the R.I.B.A. Collection. In 1821 he obtained a church-building commission in Leeds, but was eventually dismissed as unsatisfactory [Port, 54 n.]. His only executed work so far known is BELLEVUE HOUSE, WALTHAMSTOW, ESSEX, for Charles Cooke, bookseller, dem. 1936, which is illustrated in his 1806 publication (plates 23–4) and in Hughson's *London* vi, 1809, 302. In default of commissions, Gyfford appears to have made a living as a draughtsman, making drawings for, e.g. Hughson's *London* (1805–9). Redgrave says that he was 'a rapid, clever, draughtsman, but managed only to gain a poor subsistence by his profession'. He died on 23 June 1856, aged 83, and was buried in Fulham Churchyard. His son Edward A. Gifford or Gyfford, junior, won the R.A. Gold Medal for Architecture in 1837, but gave up architecture for painting.

H

HABERSHON, MATTHEW (1789–1852), came of a family connected with Rotherham in Yorkshire, and, showing much talent for drawing, was articled to William Atkinson in 1806. He began to exhibit in 1807, and entered the Royal Academy Schools in the following year. He subsequently remained in Atkinson's office for some years as an assistant. While designing classical public buildings and Gothic churches like most of his contemporaries, Habershon became an early enthusiast for the picturesque timber-framed houses of the sixteenth and seventeenth centuries, about which he published a pioneer book, *The Ancient Half-Timbered Houses of England*, in 1836. In the text he revealed himself as an opponent of Pugin's crusade for 'Catholic architecture', subjecting the *Contrasts* to a detailed and hostile analysis. He was in fact a zealous Anglican, and was the author of *A Dissertation on the prophetic scriptures* (1834, 2nd ed. 1840) and other similar works. In 1842 he went to Jerusalem on behalf of the London Society for Promoting Christianity among the Jews, in order to give directions for the completion of the Anglican Cathedral there begun by J. W. Johns (*q.v.*), whose unsatisfactory conduct of the works had led to his dismissal. Habershon took with him a clerk of works called Critchlow whom he left in charge. On his return journey in 1843 he had an interview with the King of Prussia, who was one of the promoters of the cathedral. The King subsequently conferred on him a gold medal for his book on timber-framed houses. Habershon died in London on 5 July 1852 and was buried in Abney Park Cemetery. His sons Edward and William Gilbee Habershon both practised as architects. At first they were in partnership, but in 1863 they separated and W. G. Habershon joined A. R. Pite in a successful London practice which had an offshoot at Newport in Monmouthshire. Among Matthew Habershon's other pupils were Ewan Christian, T. C. Hine of Nottingham and C. Yoget, who practised at Cape Town. [*A.P.S.D.*; *Builder* ii, 1844, 561; Bodleian Library, minute books of the London Society for Promoting Christianity among the Jews.]

LONDON, COVENTRY STREET, ROYAL WORCESTER PORCELAIN WAREHOUSE, for Messrs. Flight & Barr, 1810; dem. [exhibited at R.A.].

BELPER, DERBYSHIRE, ST. PETER'S CHURCH, 1824, Gothic [exhibited at R.A.].

MERE HALL, nr. DROITWICH, WORCS., alterations and additions for E. H. Bearcroft, *c.*1826 [*Ancient Half-Timbered Edifices*, 17].

HADZOR HOUSE, nr. DROITWICH, WORCS., remodelled for J. H. Galton, 1827 [exhibited at R.A.].

STANMORE, MIDDLESEX, AYLMORE GROVE COTTAGE, for J. Marks, 1827 [exhibited at R.A.].

DERBY, COUNTY COURTS at rear of County Hall, 1828–9 [S. Glover, *History of the County of Derby* ii, 1833, 446–9, with plan].

DERBY, THE TOWN HALL and MARKET, 1828–30; in 1841 the interior of the Town Hall was destroyed by fire, after which the portico was removed and the front rebuilt with a clock-tower to the designs of Messrs. Duesbury & Lee [S. Glover, *History of the County of Derby* ii, 1833, 441–3, with plan].

DERBY, TRINITY SCHOOL, LIVERSAGE STREET, 1830; dem. [S. Glover, *History & Directory of Derby*, Derby 1849, 43].

HADZOR, WORCS., farmhouse for J. H. Galton, *c.*1830 [*Ancient Half-Timbered Edifices*, 10].

KINGSTON-ON-SOAR CHURCH, NOTTS., rebuilt 1832, except chancel, Gothic; reconstructed 1900 [I.C.B.S.].

THE GRANGE, SEACROFT, nr. LEEDS, YORKS. (W.R.), for John Wilson, 1834 [*Ancient Half-Timbered Edifices*, 21].

HADZOR CHURCH, WORCS., alterations 1835 [I.C.B.S.].

ASTON SANDFORD RECTORY, BUCKS., for the Revd. H. Alford, 1836–7 [*Ancient Half-Timbered Edifices*, 18; Lincolnshire Archives Office, MGA 208].

BRAMPTON, HUNTS., half-timbered cottages for Lady Olivia Sparrow, *c.*1837 [*Ancient Half-Timbered Edifices*, 13].

DERBY, CHRIST CHURCH, NORMANTON ROAD (BISHOP RYDER'S CHURCH), 1838–40, Gothic; chancel added 1865 [F. White, *History, Gazetteer and Directory of the County of Derby*, 1857, 58].

ROCKLAND ST. MARY RECTORY, NORFOLK, 1839 [Norfolk C.R.O., DN/DPL/1/3/52].

KIMBERWORTH CHURCH, YORKS. (W.R.), 1840–2, Gothic; chancel 1882 [I.C.B.S.].

WINSTER CHURCH, DERBYSHIRE, rebuilt 1842, incorporating old tower, Gothic; altered 1884–5 [*A.P.S.D.*].

BURBAGE CHURCH, LEICS., rebuilt 1842, Gothic [I.C.B.S.].

HACKER, FREDERICK, was a member of a family of builders and architects at Canterbury. He may well have been a son of James Hacker, a carpenter who in 1789 agreed to build a market-place at the Bullstake in Canterbury, 'agreeable to his plan' [Corporation Minutes]. Frederick became a pupil of John Nash and by 1825 was in independent practice in the Edgware Road. But he evidently failed to make a success of it, for Pigot's *Directory* shows that in 1827–8 he was back in Kent, giving addresses both in Canterbury and Dover. In 1832 he left England for Canada. By June of that year he was established at 14 Palace Street, Quebec. In 1834 he designed No. 43 D'Auteuil Street, a stone-fronted house with a Greek Doric doorcase. In 1838 he petitioned the Governor to be 'continued in the situation of Expert in which he has heretofore acted . . . and . . . be honoured with the appointment of architect to the Civil Government' [*Quebec Mercury*, 14 June 1832; Public Archives of Canada, MSS. R. G. 4, AL, S-401; information from the late Sir John Summerson].

HACKER, SAMUEL, was another member of the Canterbury family referred to above. He established himself at Herne Bay as an 'Architect, Builder and Estate Agent' and in 1830–1 began to lay out a new seaside resort there of which only the promenade was completed more or less in accordance with his plans [*The Watering Places of Great Britain and Fashionable Directory*, 1833, 48; John Newman, *North East and East Kent*, Buildings of England, 1969, 336].

HADFIELD, GEORGE (1763–1826), was born at Leghorn in Italy, where his father kept a hotel. In 1779, after her husband's death, his mother returned to England, and in September 1781, a few days after his eighteenth birthday, George Hadfield was admitted to the R.A. Schools as an architectural student. He was an immediate success, winning the Silver Medal in his first year and the Gold Medal in 1784. In the latter year he became a pupil of James Wyatt. On leaving Wyatt's office in 1790 he became the first recipient of the Travelling Scholarship in Architecture awarded by the Academy, and spent some time in Italy. In 1791, in conjunction with an Italian architect called Colonna, he made drawings, now in the R.I.B.A. Collection, for a restoration of the temple at Palestrina or Praeneste. In 1795 he exhibited drawings of the temples of Mars and Jupiter Tonans at the Royal Academy.

Hadfield had by now acquired a considerable reputation as a young architect of promise, but when, in January 1795, he was proposed for election to the Architects' Club by Henry Holland and James Wyatt, he was excluded by a single black ball which Wyatt attributed either to Soane or to Brettingham. It may have been this setback which induced Hadfield to accept an invitation to go to America to superintend the building of the Capitol at Washington. For this difficult task, requiring far more experience both of men and of building than he then possessed, Hadfield was by no means well equipped, and in 1798 he was dismissed after struggling in vain against 'the ignorance and the dishonesty of the commissioners and of the workmen'. Meanwhile his real abilities as an architect were largely wasted. In 1806 Benjamin Latrobe doubted whether his 'irritable pride and neglected study [will] ever permit him to take the station in the art which his elegant talent ought to have obtained'. During the last ten years of his life, however, his fortunes recovered, and he designed a number of neo-classical buildings of distinction in Washington, including the City Hall, now the District of Columbia Courthouse (1820), the wings (1803–4) and Greek Doric portico (1817) of Arlington House, the Assembly Rooms (1822), the United States Bank (1824), and Van Ness's mausoleum (1826), now in Oak Hill cemetery at Georgetown.

[*A.P.S.D.*; *D.N.B.*; Fiske Kimball in *Dictionary of American Biography*; H. F. & E.

Withey, *Biographical Dictionary of American Architects*, 1956; G. L. M. Goodfellow, 'George Hadfield', *Arch. Rev.* July 1965, 35–6; R.A. Admission Register; *The Farington Diary*, ed. J. Greig, i, 85; *The Journal of Latrobe*, ed. J. H. B. Latrobe, New York, 1905, 133–4.]

HAGUE, DANIEL (*c.*1736–*c.*1816), son of Daniel Hague, late of Corsham, yeoman, was apprenticed to Thomas Manley, mason of Bristol, in April 1750, and was admitted to the freedom of the city in August 1762 [Bristol City archives]. He developed a successful business as a builder and surveyor which was taken over by his son when he retired in about 1805. In 1784 he designed the ROYAL INFIRMARY in association with Thomas Paty. He also planned PORTLAND SQUARE in 1790, and was the architect of ST. PAUL'S CHURCH, PORTLAND SQUARE, built 1789–94 in an engagingly unscholarly Gothic style, with a tower whose receding upper stages recalled that of the Royal Exchange in London. [W. Ison, *The Georgian Buildings of Bristol*, 1952, 36–7, 76–81, 220–23].

HAKEWILL, GEORGE (1788–1836), was the third son of John Hakewill, painter and decorator, and a younger brother of Henry and James Hakewill (*qq.v.*). He exhibited at the Royal Academy from 1806 to 1810, including a 'Design for the Garden front of a Marine Villa building in Norfolk' (1808). This appears to be his only recorded work. He evidently gave up architecture for the Army, dying at the Cape of Good Hope in 1836 as 'Lieut. George Hakewill' [*Gent's Mag.* 1836 (ii), 669].

HAKEWILL, HENRY (1771–1830), was the eldest son of John Hakewill (1742–91), painter and decorator. He became a pupil of John Yenn, was admitted to the Royal Academy Schools in 1790, and won the Silver Medal the same year. He exhibited at the Academy between 1792 and 1809. In the latter year he became architect to the trustees of Rugby School, an appointment which he retained until his death. He was also architect to the Radcliffe Trustees, and to the Benchers of the Middle Temple. He wrote *An Account of the Roman Villa discovered at Northleigh, Oxfordshire, in the years 1813–14–15–16*, printed in Skelton's *Antiquities of Oxfordshire* 1823, and reissued separately in 1826. He died on 13 March 1830, aged 59, and was buried at North Cray, Kent. He was a liveryman of the Fishmongers' Company. His two sons, John Henry (1810–80) and Edward Charles (1816–72), both practised as architects. Among his other pupils were John Turner, T. M. Cook, John Winckworth and John Goldicutt, who, after his Italian tour, returned to Hakewill's office until the latter's death, and was associated with him in the competition for the Hanwell Lunatic Asylum, in which they obtained the third premium.

Hakewill's Tudor Gothic buildings are of little interest, but as a Greek Revivalist he designed two buildings of distinction: St. Peter's Church, Eaton Square, and Coed Coch, a country house whose diagonally placed portico and staircase were original and effective features. His church at Wolverton is an early example of neo-Norman.

[*A.P.S.D.*; *D.N.B.*; obituary in *Coventry Herald*, 26 March 1830; information from Mr. W. R. H. Hakewill.]

FOOTS CRAY PLACE, KENT, alterations for Benjamin Harenc, 1792; further 'improvements' for Nicholas Vansittart, Lord Bexley, 1823; dem. after a fire in 1949 [*A.P.S.D.*; exhibited at R.A. 1792, and cf. J. Dunkin, *History of Dartford*, 1844, 468].

RENDLESHAM HALL, SUFFOLK, extensive alterations for P. I. Thellusson, *c.*1801–5, Gothic; destroyed by fire 1830 [exhibited at R.A. 1801] (J. P. Neale, *Views of Seats*, 1st ser., iii, 1820).

COED COCH (now Heronwater School), DENBIGHSHIRE, for John Lloyd Wynne, 1804; portico dem. early 20th century [E. Pugh, *Cambria Depicta*, 1816, 19]; perhaps the 'villa in North Wales' exhibited by Hakewill at the R.A. in 1795.

CAVE CASTLE, YORKS. (E.R.), for H. B. Barnard, 1804, Gothic; altered 1873–5; reduced in size 1938 [exhibited at R.A. 1804] (R. A. Alec-Smith, 'Cave Castle', *E. Yorkshire Georgian Soc.* iv (2), 1956–8).

LONDON, LITTLE ARGYLL STREET, enlarged the OLD ARGYLL ROOMS for Col. H. F. Greville, 1806; dem. [plans and correspondence in Sir John Soane's Museum, 7/N/4/1–23 and 9/9–10].

WALTON HALL, WARWICKS., alterations for Sir Charles Mordaunt, Bart., *c.*1810; rebuilt 1860 [J. Britton, *Beauties of England and Wales* xv, 1814, 188].

RUGBY SCHOOL, WARWICKS, BUILDINGS 1809–15 and CHAPEL 1818–21, Gothic; chapel rebuilt 1870–98 [*A.P.S.D.*; exhibited at R.A. 1809].

WOLVERTON CHURCH, BUCKS., for the Radcliffe Trustees, 1810–15, 'Norman' style [Bodleian Library, minutes of the Radcliffe Trustees 1792–1815].

FULFORD (later SHOBROOKE) PARK, LITTLE FULFORD, DEVON, for R. Hippisley Tuckfield, 1811; refronted 1845 by T. L.

Donaldson; dem. 1947 [inscription on foundation stone, now set in terrace wall].

PACKINGTON HALL, WARWICKS., south and west terraces for 5th Earl of Aylesford, 1812. In 1828 Hakewill also designed the interiors of the billiard room and upper library [G. C. Tyack in *Archaeological Jnl.* cxxviii, 1971, 242].

BLENHEIM PALACE, OXON., the AVIARY (formerly at Shipton Court, Shipton-on-Cherwell), for 4th Duke of Marlborough, *c.*1812; dem. [J. P. Neale, *Views of Seats*, 1st ser. v, 1822]. Hakewill may also have designed the EAGLE LODGE, built by the 4th Duke *c.*1810/15.

FARNBOROUGH HALL, WARWICKS., designed stables and minor internal alterations for William Holbech, 1813–16 [drawings and accounts formerly at Farnborough Hall].

WARWICK, THE JUDGES' HOUSE, 1814–16; extended 1955 [Warwick County Records, Class 24 (36–7)].

HOLME PARK, nr. READING, BERKS., works for Robert Palmer, *c.*1815; dem. 1881 [*A.P.S.D.*] (J. P. Neale, *Views of Seats*, 2nd ser., iv, 1828).

OXFORD, ORIEL COLLEGE, remodelled PROVOST'S LODGINGS, 1815–17, Gothic [*V.C.H. Oxon*, iii, 128.]

BADBY VICARAGE, NORTHANTS., remodelled 1817 [Peterborough Diocesan records in Northants. Record Office].

NORTH CRAY CHURCH, KENT, repaired and enlarged S. side, 1819–20 [*Bexley Antiq. Soc.'s Newsletter* 6, 1979, citing Vestry Minutes in Kent Archives Office, P 102/8/1].

LAMPORT HALL, NORTHANTS., various works for Sir Justinian Isham, Bart., including rebuilding of north-west front in Tudor Gothic style (1819), entrance gates on Northampton Road (1824) and pediment on south-west front (1829). The north-west front was subsequently rebuilt by Burn [Sir Gyles Isham, 'The Architectural History of Lamport', *Reports and Papers Northants. Architectural and Archaeological Soc.* No. 106, 1951, 25–6].

BILLING HALL, NORTHANTS., alterations for R. C. Elwes, 1820; dem. 1956 [bills in Northants. Record Office].

CORNBURY PARK, OXON., alterations for Lord Churchill *c.*1820, probably unimportant and now unrecognizable [*A.P.S.D.*].

ALBURY PARK, SURREY, alterations and additions for Henry Drummond, *c.*1820, Tudor style [J. P. Neale, *Views of Seats*, 2nd ser. iii, 1826] (*C. Life*, 1 Sept. 1950).

BARFORD HILL, BARFORD, WARWICKS., for Charles Mills, *c.*1820; remodelled *c.*1845; dem. 1954 [obituary in *Coventry Herald*, 26 March 1830].

EXNING VICARAGE, SUFFOLK, 1820–1 [W. Suffolk C.R.O., 806/2/6].

LONDON, THE MIDDLE TEMPLE: designed PARLIAMENT CHAMBERS, including former library, 1822–4; restored screen, porch and louvre of Hall; designed Nos. 1–2 PLOWDEN BUILDINGS, Elizabethan style, executed after his death by J. Savage, 1831–3, enlarged 1896 and renovated 1933 [*A.P.S.D.*].

SHRUBLAND HALL, LEAMINGTON PRIORS, WARWICKS., for Matthew Wise, 1822–5; dem. 1934 [*A.P.S.D.*].

STISTED HALL, ESSEX, for C. S. Onley, 1823–5 [J. A. Rush, *Seats in Essex*, 1897, 166].

COMPTON VERNEY, WARWICKS., internal alterations for 16th Lord Willoughby de Broke, 1824 [obituary in *Coventry Herald*, 26 March 1830; drawing signed HH and dated 1824 in Victoria and Albert Museum, E 4-1937, A 231].

LEAMINGTON SPA, WARWICKS., ALL SAINTS CHURCH, enlarged N. side, 1824–5 [signed plan in Warwicks. C.R.O., DR 514/204–5].

LONDON, ST. PETER'S CHURCH, EATON SQUARE, 1824–7 [*A.P.S.D.*]. Hakewill's first design for a Gothic church was rejected. The church was gutted by fire in 1837 and reconstructed by J. H. Hakewill from the original drawings. Sir A. W. Blomfield added the chancel in 1873 and remodelled the interior of the nave in 1875. The interior was again gutted by fire in 1987 and rebuilt to a new design by the Braithwaite Partnership.

SOUTH WEALD VICARAGE, ESSEX, for the Revd. C. A. Belli, 1824–5. Belli was related to C. R. Cockerell, whom he consulted, and who revised the designs [C. R. Cockerell's diary, 12 March 1824].

DINGLEY HALL, NORTHANTS., works for H. H. Hungerford, including stable-block, probably *c.*1825 [*A.P.S.D.*].

CRAYFORD MANOR HOUSE, KENT, for Revd. Thomas Barne, *c.*1825 [A. E. Halsall, 'The Manor House, Crayford', *Procs. Crayford Manor House Hist. & Archl. Soc.* 1, 1962, 13].

STONE CASTLE, nr. GRAVESEND, KENT, alterations for Robert Talbot, probably *c.*1825, Tudor style [*A.P.S.D.*].

WORMINGTON GRANGE, GLOS., enlarged for Josiah Gist, 1826–7 [Arthur Oswald in *C. Life*, 21 Sept. 1940].

OXFORD, railings round RADCLIFFE LIBRARY, 1828; removed 1936 [I. Guest, *Dr. John Radcliffe and his Trust*, 1991, 173].

AVONBANK, STRATFORD-ON-AVON, WARWICKS., work for 6th Lord Middleton, probably including the Orangery [obituary in *Coventry Herald*, 26 March 1830]. House dem. but Orangery survives.

SANDWELL PARK, STAFFS., unidentified work for 4th Earl of Dartmouth; dem. 1928 [obituary in *Coventry Herald*, 26 March 1830].

HAKEWILL, JAMES (1778–1843), was the second son of John Hakewill, painter and decorator. On his father's death in 1791, his elder brother Henry, then a pupil in the office of John Yenn, settled the family business on James, who exhibited decorative and architectural designs at the Royal Academy from 1800 onwards. His talents, however, were literary and antiquarian rather than practical, and it is for his architectural publications that he is best known. In 1813 he published *The History of Windsor and its Neighbourhood*, illustrated from his own drawings. After the Peace of Vienna he visited Italy in 1816–17 in company with his wife, who was herself a talented artist. On his return he exhibited his drawings in Bond Street, and in 1818–20 published *A Picturesque Tour of Italy*, some of the plates of which were engraved after J. M. W. Turner's water-colours based on Hakewill's own drawings. In 1820–1 he visited Jamaica, and in 1825 published *A Picturesque Tour in the Island of Jamaica*, fol. In 1828 he published *Plans, Sections, and Elevations of the Abattoirs of Paris, with consideations for their adoption in London*, in 1831 *A Series of ten views, in the . . . Gardens of the Zoological Society in the Regent's Park, laid out from the Designs of Decimus Burton*, and in 1835 *An Attempt to determine the exact character of Elizabethan Architecture*, with plans of Dorton House, Bucks., and other Elizabethan buildings. In 1840 he was engaged on drawings for a work on the Rhine, intended to be a companion volume to his *Italy*, but it was never published. He is also said to have written a novel, *Coelebs Suited, or the Stanley Letters*, 1812.

His only recorded architectural works were a house at YARMOUTH for Thomas Penrice, *c.*1805; dem. 1844 [C. J. Palmer, *Perlustration of Great Yarmouth*, ii, 1876, 161]; the elegant domed Pump Room, at DORTON SPA, BUCKS., for C. S. Ricketts, 1834, now dem., described and illustrated by J. Knight, *History of the Dorton Chalybeate*, 1835 and in *The Mirror of Literature, Amusement and Instruction*, No. 965, 31 Aug. 1839; a Greek Doric lodge at the Rostherne entrance to TATTON PARK, CHESHIRE, for W. Egerton, 1833–4; a lodge and eating-room (dem.) at HIGH LEGH, CHESHIRE, for G. C. Legh, 1833–4; and THE CHRISTIAN UNION ALMSHOUSES, JOHN STREET, EDGWARE ROAD, 1834, remodelled 1900, for all of which he exhibited drawings at the Royal Academy. In 1835 he submitted a design for rebuilding the Houses of Parliament in a sixteenth-century classical style derived from Longleat and Hatfield. A design by him for a house for G. W. Aylmer (1829) is in the R.I.B.A. Drawings Collection. He died on 28 May 1843, and was buried in Paddington churchyard. He had four sons, Arthur William (1808–56), an architect and pupil of Decimus Burton, Frederick Charles, a portrait painter, Henry James (d. 1834, aged 20), a sculptor, and Richard Wentworth.

[*A.P.S.D.*; *D.N.B.*; obituaries in *Civil Engineer and Architect's Jnl.* vi, 1843, 324 and *Gent's Mag.* 1843 (ii), 209–10, reprinted in *Builder*, 2 Sept. 1843; Farington's Diary, 27 June 1818; Cecilia Powell, 'Topography, Imagination and Travel: Turner's Relationship with James Hakewill', *Art History* 5, 1982; T. Cabberley & L. Herrmann, *Twilight of the Grand Tour: a Catalogue of the drawings of James Hakewill in the British School at Rome Library*, Rome 1992].

HALDANE, JAMES (–1832), practised in Edinburgh, where he first appears in the directories in 1800 as a 'teacher of mathematics'. By 1804–5 he was described as 'architect'. He was responsible for the design of houses on the Morrison Estate in MAITLAND STREET WEST (Nos. 1–14), MORRISON STREET (Nos. 252–70) and TORPHICHEN STREET (Nos. 2–24), all begun in about 1825 [S.R.O., Edinburgh Sasines]. In 1806 he designed the fountain or well-head in front of the Town Hall at LINLITHGOW in an elaborate sixteenth-century style based on its decayed predecessor. It was executed by an Edinburgh mason called Robert Gray [Town Council Minutes in S.R.O., B 48/9/14, pp. 455, 460, 461, 494]. Haldane died in or before September 1832, when his testament, dated 17 December 1831, was registered in S.R.O., Register of Deeds, vol. 466, f. 786.

HALFPENNY, WILLIAM, *alias* MICHAEL HOARE (–1755), described as 'architect and carpenter' on the title-pages of several of his works, is mentioned by Batty Langley in his *Ancient Masonry*, 1736, p. 147, as 'Mr. William Halfpenny, *alias* Hoare, lately of Richmond in Surry, carpenter'. His recorded architectural works are not numerous, and he is best known as the author of a series of architectural manuals, designed to provide ordinary builders with 'easy, practical methods' of drawing the orders and other features, and of pattern-books providing designs for houses (including farm-houses and parsonages) and ornamental buildings in a variety of styles including the Chinese and Gothic. His more ambitious designs for country seats were in the Palladian vernacular of the period, but he was far from being a

Palladian purist and freely introduced Vanbrughian, baroque and rococo features into his plates. No serious attempt has so far been made to assess the use made of Halfpenny's books, but their numerous reissues suggest that they found a ready sale. Halfpenny's son John was associated with him in several of his later publications.[1]

Halfpenny's career is still somewhat obscure. As a practising architect he first appears as the author of an unexecuted design for Holy Trinity Church, Leeds. On 8 May 1723 William Halfpenny was paid £1 11s. 6d. 'for his draughts of the new Church', and the design is illustrated in his *Art of Sound Building* of 1725. It shows a building of six bays ornamented with Corinthian pilasters. The (externally Doric) design adopted and carried out in 1722–7 was, however, the work of William Etty (*q.v.*). This employment at Leeds and the dedication of *Practical Architecture* to Thomas Frankland, a Yorkshire gentleman, may suggest that Halfpenny was a native of Yorkshire, where his surname is not uncommon. By 1726 he was evidently established in Surrey, for in that year he was among those who submitted designs for a timber bridge across the river Thames at Fulham [minutes of the Fulham Bridge Commissioners, P.R.O., GD 26/12, ff. 12–13]. He is next found in Ireland, designing a HORSE BARRACKS at HILLSBOROUGH, COUNTY DOWN, for the 1st Viscount Hillsborough in 1732 [C. E. B. Brett, *Court Houses and Market Houses of the Province of Ulster*, Belfast 1973, 73]. In 1739 he was at Waterford, surveying the cathedral there and making unexecuted designs, now in the R.I.B.A. Drawings Collection, for its replacement by a modern classical church.

When Halfpenny made these Irish designs he may already have been based in Bristol, for his *Perspective Made Easy*, published in 1731, includes views of the Drawbridge, the Hotwell, the north side of Queen Square, and his own design for an Exchange. He was certainly established in Bristol by 1739–40, when he submitted several designs to the committee for building an Exchange, and also tendered unsuccessfully for the carpenter's work when the commission was given to John Wood.[2] In 1742 he was equally unsuccessful in a scheme for adding wings to the Infirmary, but the COOPERS' HALL in KING STREET was built to his designs in 1743–4. It presents a handsome though far from academically correct Palladian facade to the street (Dening, *Eighteenth-Century Architecture of Bristol*, pl. xxx).

According to Shiercliff's *Bristol and Hotwell Guide* for 1789, Halfpenny was the designer of the REDLAND CHAPEL, BRISTOL, an elegant and highly-finished building which was erected at the expense of John Cossins of Redland Court between *c.*1740 and 1743. Halfpenny's name is also connected with the Chapel by a view of it in the British Library signed 'William Halfpenny Architect delin. 1742' (*King's Maps*, Supplementary volume 24, f. 37). But the original building accounts (Bristol Record Office P/RG/T/1) show that it was not until 22 May 1742, that Halfpenny agreed with Cossins 'to Give proper Directions as is Usuall By Architects and Directors of Buildings, to all his Workmen Employ'd at his Chapple at Redland . . . and to See the Whole Compleated for the Sum of ten pounds ten shillings sterling'. It is not certain exactly when the building was begun, but it was already well advanced by 1742, when Halfpenny came on the scene, and the original estimate, which has been preserved, is not in his hand. It would appear therefore that the chapel had already been begun to the designs of another architect, and that architect was probably John Strahan, recently deceased, who had been employed by Cossins to design Redland Court a few years earlier. Halfpenny's functions would therefore have been confined to the completion of the chapel and the only specific feature which he is known to have designed is the altarpiece, which was made in 1742 by William Brooks, a London joiner, 'according to a draught drawd by William Halfpenny'. The elaborate woodcarving is stated in a contemporary account of the chapel to have been designed as well as executed by Thomas Paty of Bristol.

The only other building known to have been designed by Halfpenny was a Chinese bridge at CROOME COURT, WORCS., illustrated as his own work in *Improvements in Architecture and Carpentry* (1754). He died in debt in 1755 [P.C.C. Admon. Register].

Buildings that have been attributed to Halfpenny on stylistic grounds are No. 40 PRINCE STREET, BRISTOL, 1740–1, dem. (C. F. Dening, *The Eighteenth-Century Architecture of*

[1] The William Halfpenny who signed the monument in Isleworth Church to Mrs. Ann Dash (*alias* Tolson), who died in 1750, was a mason-sculptor apparently unrelated to the subject of this article. He was mason to Lincoln's Inn between 1752 and 1785.

[2] Several sets of alternative designs by Halfpenny are preserved in the Bristol City Archives (1024), and on 28 April 1740, Mr. Halfpenny was ordered to be paid 5 guineas in part for the trouble he had been at in drawing plans for the Exchange and Markets (Minutes of the Committee for Building the Exchange in Bristol City Archives). There are two surveys by Halfpenny, dated 1742, in Plan Book B.

Bristol, 1923, pl. xxxi) and CLIFTON COURT, CLIFTON GREEN, BRISTOL, for Martha Dandervall, *c.*1742–3 [Walter Ison, *The Georgian Buildings of Bristol*, 1952, 38]; STOUT'S HILL, ULEY, GLOS., for Timothy Gyde, *c.*1750, Gothic, and the similar Gothic garden-house or Orangery at FRAMPTON COURT, GLOS., for Richard Clutterbuck, *c.*1750 [N. Kingsley, *The Country Houses of Gloucestershire* ii, 1992, 146, 240–3]; UPTON HOUSE, TETBURY, GLOS., for Thomas Cripps, 1752 [Marcus Binney in *C. Life*, 15 Feb. 1973]; and THE ASSEMBLY ROOM, PRINCE STREET, BRISTOL, 1754–5; dem. [Ison, *op. cit.*, 108–14].

Halfpenny's publications were: *Andrea Palladio's First Book of Architecture*, 1751, *Arithmetick and Measurement Improv'd by Examples*, 1748, *c.*1783; *The Art of Sound Building*, 1725 (dedicated to Sir Andrew Fountaine); *The Builder's Pocket Companion*, 1728, 1731, 1747 (by 'Michael Hoare'); *Chinese and Gothic Architecture properly Ornamented*, 1752 (with John Halfpenny); *The Country Gentleman's Pocket Companion and Builder's Assistant*, 1753, 1756 (with John Halfpenny); *Geometry, Theoretical and Practical*, 1752; *Improvements in Architecture and Carpentry*, 1754; *Magnum in Parvo, or, the Marrow of Architecture*, 1728; *The Modern Builder's Assistant*, 1757; *A New and Compleat System of Architecture*, 1749, 1759, 1770; *New Designs for Chinese Temples*, etc., 1750, re-issued as *Rural Architecture in the Chinese Taste*, 1752, 1755; *Perspective Made Easy*, 1731, 1754; *Practical Architecture*, 1724, 1730, 1736, 1764 (?); *Rural Architecture in the Gothic Taste*, 1752 (with John Halfpenny); *Six New Designs for Convenient Farm-Houses . . . adapted more particularly to the Western Counties in England, and the whole Principality of Wales*, 1751, retitled *Useful Architecture in Twenty-one New Designs for Erecting Parsonage-Houses, Farm-Houses, and Inns*, 1752, 1755, 1760; *Twelve Beautiful Designs for Farm-Houses*, 1750, 1759, 1774; *Twenty new Designs of Chinese Lattice and other Works, for Stair-Cases, Gates, Palings, Hatches*, etc., 1750; *A Perspective View of the sunk Pier and the two Adjoining Arches at Westminster* (one folio sheet), 1748; *A Plan and Elevation of the Royal Fireworks Perform'd in St. James's Park* (one folio sheet), 1749; *Twenty-six new Designs of Geometrical Paling* (one folio sheet), 1750.

[*A.P.S.D.*; *D.N.B.*; E. Shiercliff, *Bristol and Hotwell Guide*, 1789, 42, 91; C. F. Dening, *The Eighteenth-Century Architecture of Bristol*, 1923, 95–7; K. A. Esdaile, 'The Small House and its Amenities in the Architectural Handbooks, 1749–1847', *Trans. Bibliog. Soc.* xv, 1917–19; W. Ison, *The Georgian Buildings of Bristol*, 1952, 37–8; Eileen Harris, *British Architectural Books and Writers, 1556–1785*, 1990, 218–28.]

HALL, JAMES (1769–1809), was the third son of Henry Hall, Principal Clerk to the Commissioners of Sewers for the City of London and Surveyor to the Sun Fire Office, who died in 1796. James Hall succeeded his father as Surveyor to the Sun Fire Office, and was also Surveyor to St. Bartholomew's Hospital and the Inner Temple. He died in Bloomsbury Place on 14 July 1809, in his 40th year [*Gent's Mag.* 1796, 173; 1809 (ii), 686]. In 1806 he had been consulted by the Revd. Charles Mayo about THE GREAT HOUSE, CHESHUNT, HERTS. (dem. 1965), and may have been responsible for remodelling it in a thin Gothic style [C. H. Mayo, *A Genealogical Account of the Mayo and Elton Families*, 2nd ed. 1908, 579–80].

HALL, JOHN, practised as an architect in Bangor, North Wales, during the third decade of the nineteenth century. Between 1824 and 1828 he acted as superintending surveyor for the repairs and alterations then in progress at BANGOR CATHEDRAL to the designs of Joseph Turner of Whitchurch and John Foster of Liverpool. He also designed the NATIONAL SCHOOL in DEAN STREET, 1821–2, a terrace of six houses on the Green at BEAUMARIS, 1824–5, and in 1825 carried out some alterations and repairs to BEAUMARIS CHURCH. After 1828 there is no further evidence of his architectural activities, and he appears to have attempted unsuccessfully to make a living as an inn-keeper. [M. L. Clarke, 'A Bangor Architect of the Early Nineteenth Century', *Trans. Caernarvonshire Historical Society*, 1954, 49–50].

HALL, SYLVANUS (–1792), was 'an eminent builder and carpenter' who died in Paternoster Row, London, on 23 November 1792 [*Gent's Mag.* 1792, 1062]. He had been Carpenter to the City of London since 1784. He designed CORDWAINERS' HALL, No. 7 CANNON STREET, in 1788, with interiors in the Adam style. It was demolished in 1909 [C. H. W. Mander, *History of the Guild of Cordwainers*, 1931, 113, with illustrations].

HALLAM, JOHN, became Clerk of the Works at Whitehall, Westminster, and St. James's, and Secretary to the Board of Works in 1719, in succession to Benjamin Benson, whose dismissal had followed that of his brother William, Surveyor-General from April 1718 to August 1719. Hallam was a protégé of the new Surveyor-General, Sir Thomas Hewett, and, like him, was a native of Nottinghamshire. Sir John Vanbrugh, who was hostile to Hewett, described Hallam as 'a poor mean Country Joyner who never has executed the office since he had it, not being capable', and alleged that Hewett merely 'put him in for form', taking the revenues of his office himself, and giving him 'only a small allowance out of the Income of the Place' [*The Works of Sir John Vanbrugh* iv, *The Letters*, ed. G. F. Webb, 169–70]. When Hewett died in 1726, Hallam was immediately deprived of his posts, which were given to Flitcroft and Hawksmoor respectively.

It is probable that Vanbrugh was correct in describing Hallam as a joiner, for in 1691 a joiner of that name was employed at Chatsworth [Chatsworth archives, 70.4], but the allegation that he was incapable of carrying out the duties of his office is refuted by references to his making estimates for works at St. James's Palace in 1722 [*Wren Soc.* vii, 221–2]. Moreover in 1721–3 he was employed to measure the artificers' work in connection with the new library designed by Hewett for Lord Sunderland in Piccadilly [B.L., Add. MS. 61659, ff. 143, 151], and in 1729 he designed a garden building at RUFFORD ABBEY, NOTTS., for Sir George Savile called the BATH SUMMER-HOUSE, for which some of his drawings have survived in the Nottinghamshire Record Office [DDSR/202/2, 3, 10, 15, 16, 22 and 211/58/16].

HALLETT, JOHN (–1841), of Mortimer Street, Cavendish Square, London, was President of the Surveyors' Club in 1836 and died in 1841. He exhibited at the Royal Academy between 1827 and 1835, including 'a church proposed to be built in Northamptonshire' (1827) and 'designs for cottages to be erected in Essex' (1829).

HALLEY, FRANCIS, a joiner by trade, was in business at Shiffnal in Shropshire in the 1830s as 'Architect, Builder and Surveyor'. He designed and built BADGER CHURCH, SALOP., 1834, Gothic [Shropshire C.R.O., 4480/Ch F./1–9] and enlarged BADGER RECTORY in 1838–9 [Herefordshire C.R.O., Diocesan Records, Clergy & Benefice Papers, Box 43]. In 1836 Halley built PRIOR'S LEE CHURCH, SALOP., altering designs made by Richard Ebbels (*q.v.*) which were considered too expensive. Ebbels protested that this was 'not the first time that he has vaunted in borrowed plumes by introducing my drawings as those of his own' [I.C.B.S.].

HAMILTON, DAVID (1768–1843), was for thirty years Glasgow's leading architect. Apart from the fact that he was born in Glasgow on 11 May 1768, the son of William Hamilton, mason, and admitted to the Incorporation of Masons there in 1800, very little is known about his early life. He appears, however, to have worked as a mason before becoming an architect, and his earliest recorded buildings were not designed until he was in his thirties. He must have had some contact with the Adam family, for he made many copies of Adam drawings to which he would not otherwise have had access. Hutcheson's Hospital, his first building of any consequence, is a remarkably assured neo-classical design which suggests a familiarity with the work of Wyatt and Soane as well as of Robert and James Adam. Within a few years he had assimilated the Greek Revival, using a Greek Doric order in his Town Steeple at Falkirk (1813–14) and a rich Corinthian one in the portico of the Glasgow Royal Exchange (1827–9). Never a pedantic purist, he moved on to Scots Jacobean (Dunlop House, 1831–4) and even Norman Revival (Lennox Castle, 1837–41). The Western Club (1840) has an Italianate façade, the Union Bank (1841) shows a return to complete classical purity. Whatever the style Hamilton was never its slave, but used it to produce an effective and often original design. As a Gothic Revivalist he was responsible for one symmetrical house in the Adam castle tradition (Kincaid House, *c.*1812), and another romantically asymmetrical one (Castle Toward, 1820–1) in the manner of Wyatville. His planning was resourceful and ingenious.

In 1836 Hamilton was one of the four prizewinners in the competition for the new Houses of Parliament. His designs (P.R.O., WORK 29/48–57) were in the Scottish Jacobean style he had employed at Dunlop House. Though well planned and richly detailed, his scheme lacked any tower or other dominant feature to mark it as a public building, and it reminded one critic of 'a splendid patrician mansion rather than of an edifice intended for any grand national purpose' (*Gent's Mag.* 1836 (i), 637). In 1815 he competed for the Wellington Monument in Dublin, submitting an effective design for an obelisk rising from a cluster of Doric columns (National Library of Ireland, MS. 7778), and in 1838 for Donaldson's Hospital at Edinburgh, winning the third premium. Apart from these three bids for national fame, Hamilton's practice was largely confined to Glasgow and the south-west of Scotland, where he deservedly enjoyed a high reputation, both as an architect and as an individual. In 1840 he was entertained at a public dinner at which he was presented with £500 in a gold box. He died on 5 December 1843 after a stroke.

Hamilton married in 1794 and had several sons. William, the eldest, died young. Another, John, had a stone and marble-cutter's business, known as 'David Hamilton and Son'. He emigrated to N. America in about 1839, dying in Philadelphia in 1853. James (1818–61) was in partnership with his father during the latter's last years. He was a talented designer, and his share in Hamilton's later works may have been important. After his father's death James carried on for a year or two in partnership with his brother-in-law James Smith (1808–63), but withdrew after financial troubles. Hamilton had several pupils and assistants, including John Baird (1816–93), Thomas Gildard (1822–95), J. T. Rochead (1814–78) and Charles Wilson (1810–63).

According to Gildard, Hamilton was 'a man of most impressive presence, frank and kindly in manner . . . and in social intercourse distinguished by much grace and courtesy'. He 'knew how to deport himself in the society of dukes and earls'. A marble bust by Patric Park is in the City Art Gallery at Kelvingrove. Another by William Mossman, 'considered a better likeness', belonged in the nineteenth century to Hamilton's family. An oil portrait by Sir Daniel Macnee was shown at the Old Glasgow Exhibition in 1894. Another by James Saxon is mentioned by Gildard.

Most of Hamilton's drawings were destroyed by the carelessness of an architect who got them by a misunderstanding and consigned them to a damp cellar, but three volumes of drawings, formerly the property of the Glasgow Philosophical Society, are now in the Hunterian Art Gallery of Glasgow University. Drawings from his office were often elaborately washed in colour, and the inscriptions are always written in a distinctive back-sloping script done with a quill pen.

[Glasgow birth register in New Register House, Edinburgh; *A.P.S.D.*; *D.N.B.*; *Builder* i, 1843, 537–8; Thomas Gildard, 'An Old Glasgow Architect on some Older Ones', *Trans. Philosophical Soc. of Glasgow* xxvi, 1894–5, 97–106; Glasgow City Archives, Register of the Incorporation of Masons; Andor Gomme & David Walker, *The Architecture of Glasgow*, 1987, 292; *David Hamilton, Architect*, ed. Aonghus MacKechnie, Glasgow 1993; information from Mr. A. A. Aiken.]

PUBLIC BUILDINGS

GLASGOW, HUTCHESON'S HOSPITAL, INGRAM STREET, 1802–5 [L. Hill, *Hutcheson's Hospital*, 1855, 137].

GLASGOW, THE THEATRE ROYAL, QUEEN STREET, 1803–5, destroyed by fire 1829 [R. Chapman, *Picture of Glasgow*, 1812, 130] (elevation in J. Denholm, *History of Glasgow*, 3rd ed. 1804, 214).

GLASGOW, THE NELSON MONUMENT (an obelisk), GLASGOW GREEN, 1806 [R. Chapman, *Picture of Glasgow*, 1812, 132–4].

GLASGOW, THE TRADES HOUSE, GLASSFORD STREET, extensions at rear, 1838; rebuilt 1887 [*Glasgow Ancient and Modern or Glasghu Facies*, ed. J. F. S. Gordon, Glasgow 1872, ii, 992].

GLASGOW, rebuilt THE TOLBOOTH, TRONGATE for James Cleland, 1813, Gothic; dem. *c.*1921 [J. Cleland, *Annals of Glasgow* i, 1816, 75].

FALKIRK, STIRLINGSHIRE, THE TOWN STEEPLE, 1813–14 [R.C.A.M. *Stirlingshire*, 311 and pl. 145].

IRVINE, AYRSHIRE, THE ACADEMY, 1814–16 [A. F. McJannet, *The Royal Burgh of Irvine*, Glasgow 1938, 231].

PORT GLASGOW, RENFREWSHIRE, TOWN BUILDINGS, 1815–16 [W. F. Macarthur, *History of Port Glasgow*, Glasgow 1932, 179].

GLASGOW, THE ROYAL EXCHANGE, QUEEN STREET, 1827–9, incorporating the former Cunninghame mansion [*A.P.S.D.*].

GLASGOW, NECROPOLIS, BRIDGE over Molendinar Burn at entrance, 1833–4, and GATEKEEPER'S LODGE, 1839–40 [J. M. Leighton, *Strath-Clutha, or the Beauties of Clyde*, *c.*1840, 91].

GLASGOW, THE NORMAL SCHOOL (now Dundas Vale Teachers' Centre), NEW CITY ROAD, 1836–7 [*A.P.S.D.*; Gildard, 103].

GLASGOW, HUTCHESON'S BOYS' SCHOOL, 211 CROWN STREET, 1839–41, since altered [L. Hill, *Hutcheson's Hospital*, 1855, 215; Gildard].

GLASGOW, THE WESTERN CLUB, BUCHANAN STREET, 1840; St. Vincent Street frontage subsequently enlarged by Honeyman [Gildard, 99–102] (*Art Journal*, Oct. 1889).

GLASGOW, COMMERCIAL AND URBAN ARCHITECTURE

CALTON GREEN, layout and elevations of new houses, 1812 [*Records of the Burgh of Glasgow*, ed. Renwick, x, 144].

THE CLELAND TESTIMONIAL BUILDING at corner of Buchanan and Sauchiehall Streets, 1835–6 [Gildard, 104].

THE CLYDESDALE BANK, QUEEN STREET, 1840, dem. [J. Pagan, *Sketch of the History of Glasgow*, 1847, 180–1; Gildard, 99].

THE WESTERN BANK, MILLER STREET, 1840; enlarged 1845 by W. Burn and D. Bryce;

dem. [J. Pagan, *op. cit.*, 178; Gildard, 99].

THE BRITISH LINEN COMPANY'S BANK, 110 QUEEN STREET, 1840–1; upper floors added 1903; dem. 1968 [J. Pagan, *op. cit.*, 184; Gildard, 103].

THE GLASGOW AND SHIP (later the UNION) BANK (now Lanarkshire House), INGRAM STREET, 1841; façade rebuilt 1876–9, when the columns were reused at the Royal Princess's Theatre [Gildard, 102–3].

CHURCHES

AYR, THE NEW CHURCH, 1807–12 [S.R.O., B 6/39/77, 9 and 11].

GLASGOW, GORBALS (JOHN KNOX) CHURCH, CARLTON PLACE, 1810; dem. 1973 [R. Chapman, *Picture of Glasgow*, 1812, 92–3]. Only the auditorium, west front and steeple were completed to Hamilton's design, and the spire was subsequently destroyed by lightning.

GLASGOW CATHEDRAL, alterations including restoration of west window and niche for organ in choir, 1812 [R. Chapman, *Picture of Glasgow*, 1812, 83; J. Pagan, *History of the Cathedral and See of Glasgow*, 2nd ed., Glasgow, 1856, 62].

ERSKINE, BISHOPTON, RENFREWSHIRE, 1813–14, [S.R.O., HR 135/2].

GLASGOW, ST. JOHN, BELL STREET, 1817–19, Gothic; dem. [R. Chapman, *Picture of Glasgow*, 1822, 129].

LARBERT, STIRLINGSHIRE, 1818–20, Gothic [*N.S.A.* viii, 357] (R.C.A.M. *Stirlingshire*, pl. 31*c*).

LECROPT CHURCH, PERTHSHIRE, in collaboration with William Stirling (*q.v.*), 1825–7 [S.R.O., HR 354/1, 19 Dec. 1825].

BOTHWELL, LANARKSHIRE, new church to west of ruined chancel of collegiate church, *c.*1825–33, Gothic [S.R.O., RHP 5567–8, original drawings dated 1824].

GLASGOW, ST. ENOCH, rebuilt 1827–8 incorporating steeple of 1780; dem. [J. M. Leighton, *Select Views of Glasgow*, 1829, 198].

CAMPSIE HIGH CHURCH, LENNOXTOWN, STIRLINGSHIRE, 1827–8, Gothic [J. Cameron, *The Parish of Campsie*, Kirkintilloch 1892, 15, 33–4, 36] (R.C.A.M. *Stirlingshire* 160–1 and pl. 39c).

DUNOON, ARGYLLSHIRE, enlarged church of 1816 by J. Gillespie Graham, 1834 [*N.S.A.* vii, 610].

GLASGOW, ST. PAUL, JOHN STREET, 1835; dem. [*A.P.S.D.*; Gildard, 104].

ASCOG, ISLE OF BUTE, FREE CHURCH, 1842–3 [Gildard, 99–100], probably designed by James Hamilton, as by then David was incapacitated by illness.

DOMESTIC ARCHITECTURE

SORN CASTLE, AYRSHIRE, office-court for William Somervell, 1805 [S.R.O., SC 6/72/2, *ex inf.* Miss C. Cruft].

MOORE PARK, GOVAN, LANARKSHIRE, for – Hagart, *c.*1805 [J. Guthrie Smith, *Old Country Houses of the Glasgow Gentry*, 1870, lxxiv].

KENMURE HOUSE, LANARKSHIRE, for Charles Stirling, *c.*1806 [J. Guthrie Smith, *op. cit.*, lxiii].

AIRTH CASTLE, STIRLINGSHIRE, north-west front, castellated, for T. G. Stirling, 1807–9 [J. P. Neale, *Views of Seats*, 2nd ser. iii, 1826; R.C.A.M. *Stirlingshire*, 230–6].

AUCHINRAITH, BLANTYRE, LANARKSHIRE, for — Coulter, 1809 [J. Guthrie Smith, *Old Country Houses of the Glasgow Gentry*, 1870, iii].

CRAWFORD PRIORY, CULTS, FIFE, begun for Lady Mary Lindsay Crawford, 1809; completed by J. Gillespie Graham 1811–13, Gothic; derelict since 1971 [inscription quoted by A. H. Millar, *Fife, Pictorial and Historical* i, 1895, 191–2].

RALSTON HOUSE, nr. PAISLEY, RENFREWSHIRE, for William Orr, 1810; enlarged 1864; dem. 1934 [Glasgow University, Hamilton Drawings, vol. iii, nos. 374–84] (A. H. Millar, *Castles and Mansions of Renfrewshire*, 1890).

GERMISTON HOUSE, nr. GLASGOW, enlarged for Lawrence Dinwiddie, 1810 [J. Guthrie Smith, *op. cit.*, xlix].

BARNTON CASTLE, MIDLOTHIAN, porch for William Ramsay Ramsay, *c.*1810; dem. *c.*1920 [Glasgow University, Hamilton Drawings, vol. i, no. 39] (J. Small, *Castles and Mansions of the Lothians* i, 1883).

?BROADMEADOWS HOUSE, HUTTON, BERWICKSHIRE, for John Swinton, *c.*1810; dem. *c.*1915. This was probably the house for which Hamilton's designs, dated 1811, remain among the Swinton family papers at Kimmerghame House, Berwicks.

KINCAID HOUSE, STIRLINGSHIRE, enlarged for — Kincaid, *c.*1812, Gothic [Glasgow University, Hamilton Drawings, vol. i, no. 110] (R.C.A.M. *Stirlingshire*, pl. 202).

BARSKIMMING, MAUCHLINE, AYRSHIRE, alterations and additions for Sir William Miller, Bart., *c.*1816 [*N.S.A.* v, 643].

CADDER HOUSE, LANARKSHIRE, drawing-room for Charles Stirling, *c.*1817 [*N.S.A.* vi, 407; Sir William Fraser, *The Stirlings of Keir*, 1858, 78].

LADYLAND, KILBIRNIE, AYRSHIRE, for William Cochrane, 1817–21 [drawings preserved at Ladyland].

KEIR, DUNBLANE, PERTHSHIRE, lodge and gates

for Archibald Stirling, 1820, resited 1969 [photos of signed drawings at N.M.R.S.]; enlarged house by addition of drawing-room and gallery, 1829–34 [Alistair Rowan in *C. Life*, 7 and 14 August 1975]; also Factor's House at Keir Mains, 1832 [account-book in Keir Estate Office, *ex inf.* Dr. J. M. Robinson].

LONDON, HAMILTON HOUSE, No. 12 (later 15) PORTMAN SQUARE, alterations for 10th Duke of Hamilton, *c.*1820 [*A.P.S.D.*].

GARNKIRK HOUSE, CADDER, nr. GLASGOW, rebuilt *c.*1820, retaining façade of *c.*1790, for Mark Sprott [J. Guthrie Smith, *op. cit.*, xliv].

CASTLE TOWARD, nr. ROTHESAY, ARGYLLSHIRE, for Kirkman Finlay, 1820–1, castellated; enlarged 1920–4 [*N.S.A.* vii, 610; J. P. Neale, *Views of Seats* vi, 1823] (R.C.A.M. *Argyllshire* vii, 327–9).

LARBERT HOUSE, STIRLINGSHIRE, for Sir Gilbert Stirling, 1822–5 [J. C. Gibson, *Larbert and Dunipace Parishes*, Glasgow 1908, 10].

AIKENHEAD HOUSE, KING'S PARK, GLASGOW, added wings for John Gordon, 1823 [J. Guthrie Smith, *op. cit.*, i]. Gordon had built the house in 1806, very likely to Hamilton's designs.

HAMILTON PALACE, LANARKSHIRE, rebuilt north front for 10th Duke of Hamilton, 1822–8, interpreting designs by an Italian architect, Francesco Saponieri; dem. 1919 [*N.S.A.* vi, 271–2] (*C. Life*, 7, 14 and 21 June 1919).

CASTLE HOUSE (now Public Library), DUNOON, ARGYLLSHIRE, for James Ewing, 1823–4 castellated Gothic [J. M. Leighton, *Strath-Clutha or the Beauties of Clyde, c.*1830, 208].

SCOTSTOUN, nr. RENFREW, refronted for Miss Elizabeth Oswald, 1825; dem. *c.*1960 [J. Guthrie Smith, *op. cit.*, lxxxvii].

CALLENDAR HOUSE, FALKIRK, STIRLINGSHIRE, Library for William Forbes, 1827 [drawings at Callendar, photographs at N.M.R.S.].

PRIORY LODGE (now part of Elderslie Hotel), LARGS, AYRSHIRE, for Alexander Dunlop, 1829–30 [photos. of building accounts at N.M.R.S.].

DUNLOP HOUSE, AYRSHIRE, for Sir John Dunlop, Bart, 1832–4; Scots Jacobean style [*A.P.S.D.*; Gildard, 104].

MOSESFIELD HOUSE, SPRINGBURN PARK, GLASGOW, for James Duncan, 1838, Elizabethan style [inscription].

LENNOX CASTLE, LENNOXTOWN, STIRLINGSHIRE, for J. L. Kincaid Lennox, 1838–41, 'Norman' style [*N.S.A.* viii, 244; J. Cameron, *The Parish of Campsie*, Kirkintilloch 1892, 162–4].

CAMIS ESKAN HOUSE, DUNBARTONSHIRE, additions for Colin Campbell, *c.*1840 [Gildard, 99] (J. Irving, *The Book of Dumbartonshire* iii, 1879, pl. ix).

ST. FILLAN'S VILLA (now MANOR PARK), LARGS, AYRSHIRE, for — Stewart (?), *c.*1840 [Gildard, 99–100].

STONEBYRES HOUSE, LESMAHAGOW, LANARKSHIRE, additions for James Monteath (?), *c.*1840, Jacobethan; dem. 1934 [Gildard, 99–100].

MUIRSHIEL HOUSE, LOCHWINNOCH, RENFREWSHIRE, for John Miller, *c.*1843–5; destroyed by fire [Strathclyde Regional Archives, TNJ, General Series 386, *ex inf.* Mr. Aonghus MacKechnie].

HAMILTON, GEORGE ERNEST, practised as an architect and surveyor in Staffordshire and Warwickshire. In 1831 he was living at Stone, in 1836–7 at Stratford-on-Avon, and in 1844–9 at Wolverhampton. In 1836 he published a volume of *Designs for Rural Churches*, castigated in the *Gentleman's Magazine* as exhibiting 'all the peculiar marks of the genuine "carpenters' Gothic"'. His work as a church architect was indeed not such as to commend him to the ecclesiologists. It included EARL STERNDALE CHURCH, DERBYSHIRE, 1828–9, Gothic, gutted 1940 [I.C.B.S.]; WOORE CHURCH, SALOP., 1830–1, classical, chancel added 1887 [I.C.B.S.]; CHRIST CHURCH, STAFFORD, 1838–9, Romanesque, enlarged 1863 [I.C.B.S.]; PELSALL CHURCH, STAFFS., 1843–4, Gothic [I.C.B.S.]; the addition of a N. aisle to ST. JOHN'S, BARLASTON, STAFFS., 1831, since rebuilt [I.C.B.S.]; and alterations to CHRIST CHURCH, COSELEY, STAFFS., 1847–8 [*Gent's Mag.* 1848 (i), 76]. Hamilton also designed the obelisk at LILLESHALL, SALOP., to the memory of the lst Duke of Sutherland, 1833 [*Gent's Mag.* 1833 (ii), 459], the picturesque pump-room at BISHOPTON SPA, nr. STRATFORD-ON-AVON, 1837 [printed description *c.*1840 at Shakespeare Centre, Stratford, ER 1/28, f. 45v], and SHARESHILL PARSONAGE, STAFFS., 1844–5 [Bodleian Library, records of Queen Anne's Bounty]. In 1848–9 he was in partnership with H. C. Saunders (1820–1866), with whom he jointly designed ST. MARK'S CHURCH, WEST BROMWICH, but no further record of him has been found thereafter [R. Bearman, 'Henry Caulfield Saunders', *Warwickshire History* vii, no. 3, 1988].

HAMILTON, JAMES, was in practice in Weymouth in the reign of George III. He designed the monument erected in that town in 1809 to commemorate the fiftieth year of the king's reign, which bears the signature 'J. Hamilton, Archt.' He also designed Nos. 1–4 GLOUCESTER ROW [*C. Life*, 18 Oct. 1946, correspondence], ST. MARY'S CHURCH, 1815–17 [J. Dugdale, *British Traveller* ii, 1819, 259; R.C.H.M. *Dorset* ii (2), 332 and pls. 177–8], and a monument in the Greek Revival style on the exterior of WYKE REGIS CHURCH, commemorating the wreck of the ship 'Alexander' in 1815 [*ibid.*, pl. 176]. A plan of Weymouth showing developments proposed by him is in the Bodleian Library, together with a design for an obelisk at MORETON, DORSET, to the memory of James Frampton, Esq. [Gough Maps 6, ff. 79, 105v]. This was erected in 1785–6 [*Gent's Mag.* 1787 (i), 49]. Unexecuted designs in the R.I.B.A. Drawings Collection for Langton House, Dorset, for J. J. Farquharson, dated 1810 and signed JH, are attributable to Hamilton.

HAMILTON, THOMAS (1784–1858), was one of the principal Edinburgh architects of the early nineteenth century, and a Greek Revivalist of distinction. His father, Thomas Hamilton, was a wright and builder in Edinburgh, but appears to have removed for some years to Glasgow, where Thomas was born on 11 January 1784. However the family was back in Edinburgh by 1794, when the father took up his freedom as a burgess, and in the following year Thomas entered the High School, where he received the usual classical education. After leaving school in 1801 he was apprenticed to his father and spent the next 16 years working for him and his uncle John Hamilton (also a builder). In 1813 he married, and in 1819 became a burgess of Edinburgh. The first evidence that he was proposing himself for architectural practice was the exhibition, in 1815, of an 'architectural design' at the short-lived Edinburgh Exhibition Society. Then in the following year he entered the public competition for the completion of Adam's unfinished University building. W. H. Playfair was the successful competitor, but Hamilton published a pamphlet describing his own designs (*Observations explanatory of the two designs for completing the College of Edinburgh*, 1816). He followed this with an anonymous article in the *Scots Magazine* for March 1817 proposing large-scale road-developments to open up the Old Town to the south and west. At the time this bore no fruit, but it appears to have been the first suggestion of the ideas which were eventually implemented by the Edinburgh Improvements Commissioners from 1827 onwards. The winning in 1818 of the competition for the Burns Monument at Alloway was an important success which must have done much to establish Hamilton's reputation as an architect. A free interpretation of the Choragic Monument of Lysicrates, the Monument is an elegant and effective essay in Grecian design by an architect whose only knowledge of ancient Greek architecture was derived from books. It was his 'acquaintance with all the most eminent authors [on Greek, Roman and Gothic architecture]' that Hamilton emphasized when in 1819 he applied unsuccessfully for the vacant post of Superintendent of the Edinburgh City Works. In 1825, however, the new High School gave him an opportunity to demonstrate his ability to design a major monumental building. Admirably composed, impeccably detailed, and magnificently situated, this Scottish version of the Theseion immediately took its place as one of the major monuments of the 'Modern Athens'. It was followed by the Hopetoun Rooms in Queen Street, now destroyed and inadequately recorded, but regarded by C. R. Cockerell as 'admirably disposed', and later (1844–6) by the elegant and refreshingly unconventional College of Physicians.

Although Hamilton's best-known works are Grecian, he also designed several Gothic churches and one Romanesque one (at Alyth). These are in no way outstanding, and his attempts at the domestic Jacobethan style so successfully exploited by his contemporary Burn are disappointing. At Ayr, however, he handled a traditional Scottish theme – the municipal steeple – with great success, and in the Dean Orphanage he experimented effectively with the drama of Vanbrughian towers. As a town-planner he was largely responsible for the ideas which (already adumbrated in his 1817 article, and described in detail in the *Report relative to the proposed approaches from the South and West to the Old Town of Edinburgh* which he wrote jointly with William Burn in 1824) were eventually set on foot by the Edinburgh Improvements Commission set up by Act of Parliament in 1827. Hamilton was immediately appointed architect to the Commissioners, and carried out the two major improvements for which they were responsible – the George IV and King's Bridges, together with their associated thoroughfares. Controversy and the financial difficulties which bedevilled the Commission led to his resignation in 1834.

Hamilton was a Fellow of the Institute of British Architects from 1836 to 1846. He was one of the original founders of the Royal Scottish Academy in 1826, and acted as its treasurer until 1829 and again from 1845 onwards. He took a prominent part in the projects for building galleries for the Academy on the Mound, writing in 1830 *A Report relative to Proposed Improvements on the Earthen Mound at Edinburgh* which was printed by the Improvements Commissioners. In 1850 he published *A Letter to Lord John Russell . . . on the Present Crisis relative to the Fine Arts in Scotland*, setting out his 'views of what ought to be done for the promotion of art in this city, and for the architectural adornment of the Mound', and illustrated with lithographs. There is a drawing of his design at the R.S.A. and there are water-colour sketches of his proposals in the Print Room of the National Gallery of Scotland. In 1855 he won a gold medal at the Paris International Exhibition, exhibiting drawings of the proposed galleries on the Mound and of the ill-fated 'John Knox's Church' (Flemish Gothic) which the City had commissioned him to build on Castle Hill in 1829. The foundation stone was laid in 1829, but the financial difficulties of the Town Council led it to abandon the scheme in 1831, and the site remained vacant until 1841, when Tolbooth St. John's Church was built on it to the designs of J. Gillespie Graham.

Hamilton died at 9 Howe Street, Edinburgh on 24 February 1858, after a few days' illness. He suffered from deafness in his last years and his will indicates some confusion in his financial affairs. He was buried in the Calton Cemetery near the Martyrs' Memorial, in the lair of his uncle John Hamilton (d. 1812). A bronze plaque was set up in 1929. Apart from his son Peter (d. 1861), his only recorded pupil was John Henderson (1804–62). There is a portrait by William Nicholson at the Royal Scottish Academy, and a caricature in Crombie's *Modern Athenians*. A few of Hamilton's drawings are in the Print Room of the Scottish National Gallery. A list of other surviving drawings will be found in the thesis by Ian Fisher cited below.

[*A.P.S.D.*; *D.N.B.*; *Builder* xvi, 1858, 146, xvii, 1859, 243; *Gent's Mag.* 1858 (i), 451; *Attestations referred to in a letter to the Lord Provost of Edinburgh from Thomas Hamilton relative to his qualifications for filling the Office of Superintendent of Public Works of the City of Edinburgh*, 1819 (N.L.S., 1/825(17)); F. C. Mears, 'Measured Drawings of Lawnmarket and Castlehill made by Thomas Hamilton, Architect', *Book of the Old Edinburgh Club* xii, 1923; T. H. Hughes in *Royal Inco-rporation of the Architects of Scotland Quarterly*, No. 20, 1926; A. J. Youngson, *The Making of Classical Edinburgh*, 1966; Ian Fisher, thesis entitled 'Thomas Hamilton of Edinburgh', copy at N.M.R.S.; Ian Fisher, 'Thomas Hamilton' in *Scottish Pioneers of the Greek Revival*, Scottish Georgian Soc. 1984; Joe Rock, *Thomas Hamilton Architect*, exhibition catalogue, Edinburgh 1984.]

PUBLIC BUILDINGS

EDINBURGH, NORWICH INSURANCE COMPANY'S OFFICE, 32 PRINCE'S STREET, 1820; dem. *c.*1890 [drawings in Edinburgh Dean of Guild records].

KINGHORN, FIFE, THE TOWN HOUSE, 1822, Gothic [A. Reid, *Kinghorn*, Kirkcaldy 1906, 19].

EDINBURGH, THE ROYAL HIGH SCHOOL, REGENT ROAD, 1825–9 [Edinburgh Town Council Minutes; working drawings in City Architect's Office; T. L. Donaldson, *Handbook of Specifications*, 1860, 260].

EDINBURGH, THE HOPETOUN (ASSEMBLY) ROOMS, 72 QUEEN STREET, *c.*1827; dem. 1967 [C. R. Cockerell's diary, 17 March 1828, with sketch-plan; Edinburgh Dean of Guild records 22 July 1831].

EDINBURGH, KING'S BRIDGE, carrying Johnston Terrace over King's Stables Road, 1827–31 [Edinburgh City Archives, minutes of the Improvements Commissioners; A. J. Youngson, *The Making of Classical Edinburgh*, 1966, 180–2 and pl. 51].

EDINBURGH, GEORGE IV BRIDGE and associated town planning, 1827–34 [Edinburgh City Archives, minutes of the Improvements Commissioners; A. J. Youngson, *The Making of Classical Edinburgh*, 1966, 180–7].

AYR, THE MUNICIPAL BUILDINGS AND STEEPLE, 1828–30; enlarged 1880–1 [Ayr Town Council Minutes in S.R.O., B 6/18/26–7; *N.S.A.* v, 23; preliminary design illustrated in *R.I.A.S. Quarterly*, no. 20, 1926].

KINGHORN, FIFE, THE SCHOOL, 1829 [*Edinburgh Evening Courant*, 6 Aug. 1829].

EDINBURGH, NEW GREYFRIARS SCHOOL, THE VENNEL, 1829–30 [drawings in Edinburgh Dean of Guild records, photos at N.M.R.S.; *The Scotsman*, 17 Oct. 1829].

AYR, THE WALLACE TOWER, 1831–4, Gothic [Ayr Town Council Minutes in S.R.O., B 6/18/27; contract B 6/39/101/15; drawings in Ayr Burgh Architect's Office and S.R.O., RHP 2561].

EDINBURGH, THE DEAN ORPHANAGE (now Education Centre), BELFORD ROAD, 1833–6 [*A.P.S.D.*; J. Grant, *Old and New Edinburgh*, n.d. iii, 67].

EDINBURGH, EARL GREY PAVILION, a temporay pavilion in High School Playground for dinner in honour of Earl Grey, 1834 [MS. description by Hamilton in R.I.B.A. Library, MS. SP 10/17, printed in *R.I.B.A. Trans.* 1835–6, vol. i with engraving; J. C. Loudon, *Architectural Magazine* iii, 1836, 388; *Edinburgh Evening Courant* 1–21 Sept. 1834, *passim*].

EDINBURGH, ROYAL COLLEGE OF PHYSICIANS, QUEEN STREET, 1844–6; hall enlarged by

D. Bryce, 1864 [A. J. Youngson, *The Making of Classical Edinburgh*, 1966, 279–80].

CHURCHES

ALYTH, PERTHSHIRE, 1837–9, Romanesque [*N.S.A.* x, 1119; J. Meikle, *History of Alyth Parish Church*, 1933, 268–78; account in S.R.O., GD 16/46/91].

DUNFERMLINE, FIFE, TRINITY EPISCOPAL CHAPEL, PILMUIR STREET, 1841–2, Gothic [R. Weatherley, *History of Holy Trinity Scottish Episcopal Church Dunfermline*, privately printed 1981, 3].

MUSSELBURGH FREE (now HIGH) CHURCH, MIDLOTHIAN, 1843; remodelled 1889 [*The Witness*, 8 Nov. 1843].

EDINBURGH, ST. JOHN'S ('DR. GUTHRIE'S') FREE CHURCH (now ST. COLUMBA'S FREE CHURCH), JOHNSTON TERRACE, 1843–5, Gothic [*A.P.S.D.*; D. K. & C. J. Guthrie , *Memoir of Thomas Guthrie*, 1874, 512].

LINLITHGOW, W. LOTHIAN, FREE CHURCH, 1844; dem. [*The Scotsman*, 15 May 1844].

EDINBURGH, NEW NORTH (FREE) CHURCH, FORREST ROAD (north end of George IV Bridge), 1846, Gothic [Josiah Livingston, *History of the New North Road Church, Edinburgh*, 1893, 37].

EDINBURGH, ROXBURGH FREE CHURCH, HILL SQUARE (now King Khalid Symposium Hall), 1846, Gothic [S.R.O., CH 3/1194/4, 12–36].

SOUTH LEITH, ST. MARY'S CHURCH, rebuilt 1848, Gothic [*A.P.S.D.*; J. Grant, *Old and New Edinburgh*, n.d. iii, 219–20, with illustrations; J. Campbell Irons, *Leith and its Antiquities* i, 1897, 82].

DUNBAR, E. LOTHIAN, FREE (now ABBEY) CHURCH, 1850, Gothic [James Miller, *History of Dunbar*, 1859, 210].

KENNOWAY, FIFE, 1850, Romanesque [A. H. Millar, *Fife, Pictorial and Historical*, 1891, ii, 62; S.R.O., HR 293/3].

DOMESTIC ARCHITECTURE

EDINBURGH, Nos. 1–12 CASTLE TERRACE, 1826 [S.R.O., Edinburgh Sasines].

LATHALLAN (LAURENCE PARK) HOUSE, STIRLINGSHIRE, 1826, Elizabethan style [exhib. at Royal Scottish Academy, 1828].

COMPSTONE (CUMSTOUN) HOUSE, TWYNHOLM, KIRKCUDBRIGHTSHIRE, for Adam Maitland of Dundrennan, *c.*1827–9; enlarged 1891–2, Tudor Gothic [exhib. at Royal Scottish Academy, 1828] (J. Rock, *Thomas Hamilton*, 1984, 33–7).

KIRKHILL HOUSE, nr. GOREBRIDGE, MIDLOTHIAN, for John Tod, *c.*1828 [exhib. at Royal Scottish Academy, 1828].

attributed: ARTHUR LODGE (originally SALISBURY COTTAGE), 60 DALKEITH ROAD, EDINBURGH, for David Cunningham, jeweller, *c.*1827–30 [stylistic attribution] (J. Rock, *Thomas Hamilton*, 1984, 45–7; *C. Life*, 19 Nov. 1987).

LEITH, Nos. 5, 6, 7, 10–11, CLAREMONT PARK, 1827–*c.*1830 [advt. in *Edinburgh Evening Courant*, 2 June 1827].

EDINBURGH, Nos. 43–45 GEORGE STREET, remodelled for William and Thomas Blackwood, 1829–30; No. 43 altered 1897 [J. Rock, *Thomas Hamilton*, 1984, 48–50].

COLDSTREAM, BERWICKSHIRE, THE MANSE, 1830–2 [*N.S.A.* ii, 211].

EDINBURGH, No. 93 GEORGE STREET, 1833; altered 1900, restored 1980–2 [Edingburgh Dean of Guild records, 6 Aug. 1833, *ex inf.* Mr. David Walker].

EDINBURGH, No. 7 NORTH ST. ANDREW STREET, conversion of house into shop, 1839; dem. [S.R.O., RHP 1388].

DUNBEATH CASTLE, CAITHNESS, addition for Mrs. Sinclair of Freswick, 1857–8; addition dem. [photos of drawings signed T. H. at N.M.R.S.; S.R.O., GD 136/604/40].

MONUMENTS

ALLOWAY, AYRSHIRE, THE BURNS MONUMENT, 1820–3 [J. C. Ewing, 'History of the Monument' (based on the Trustees' minutes) in the *Burns Monument Catalogue*, Ayr 1966; drawings in collection of the Royal Incorporation of Architects in Scotland].

GLASGOW NECROPOLIS, JOHN KNOX MONUMENT, 1825 [G. Blair, *Sketches of Glasgow Necropolis*, Glasgow 1857, 171].

GOGAR CHURCHYARD, MIDLOTHIAN, monument to Sir Robert & Lady Liston, 1829 [N.L.S., MS. 5683, f. 140].

PENICUIK, MIDLOTHIAN, VALLEYFIELD MILLS, monument to FRENCH PRISONERS, 1830 [*N.S.A.* i, 34].

EDINBURGH, BURNS MONUMENT, REGENT ROAD, 1830–2 [*A.P.S.D.*, *s.v.* 'Edinburgh'].

EDINBURGH, CALTON OLD BURYING GROUND, monument (obelisk) to POLITICAL MARTYRS of 1794, 1844 [*A.P.S.D.*].

HAMILTON, WILLIAM, practised in Glasgow in the reign of George III. In 1781, when he was employed to alter and enlarge the former Assembly Rooms at the Town Hall as the TONTINE HOTEL, he was described as 'an architect from London' [J. Cleland, *Annals of Glasgow* i, 1816, 74; *The Regality Club* ii, 1893, 75–6]. For the burgh of Glasgow he designed in 1785 a weigh-house and in 1786 the layout and elevation of ST. ANDREW'S SQUARE [*Extracts from the Records of the Burgh* *of Glasgow*, ed. Renwick, viii, 1913, 175, 212, 214, 215–17]. He may possibly have been the William Hamilton, 'bred a Wright or Joyner', who in 1751, being then in Edinburgh, was described as having studied drawing and architecture 'these three or four years past' and 'done business for several Architects in London' [N.L.S., MS. 17604, f. 59].

HAMPDEN, ROBERT, *see* TREVOR, ROBERT HAMPDEN.

HANCOCK, —, was employed as an architect, builder or landscape-gardener in Pembrokeshire in 1697, as appears from a letter from Sir Hugh Owen of Orielton to Sir John Philipps, Bart. of Picton (then at Westminster), dated 23 Feb. 1696/7: 'Mr Hancocke [I] suppose gives you an account of his progresse in the Alterations at Picton, which [I] believe may be convenient and will please you, he is now in his Element being full of employ for hand & head, for between yours & J. Barlows house at Haverford which new modelling, & a water follye thereabout at Landship[ing] reservs scarse eating & sleeping time' [N.L.S., Picton Castle papers, 1610]. Landshipping House has been demolished and the nature of Hancock's works at Picton Castle and Haverfordwest is not clear.

HANNAFORD, JOSEPH (*c.*1769–1847), was an architect and builder at Christchurch, Hampshire. Together with John Kent of Southampton (*q.v.*), he designed and built ST. JAMES'S CHURCH, POOLE, DORSET, in 1819–21 [R.C.H.M. *Dorset* ii (2), 192 and pl. 118]. He also designed BRANSGORE CHURCH, HANTS., in 1822 [Port, 132–3]. Both are characteristic Gothic churches of their period. Hannaford's death in 1847 at the age of 78 is recorded in Christchurch parish register.

HANSOM, JOSEPH ALOYSIUS (1803–82), *see* WELCH, EDWARD.

HARCOURT, CHARLES, *see* MASTERS, CHARLES HARCOURT.

HARDING, JAMES, practised in Farnham, Surrey, where several members of his family were in the building trade [Nigel Temple, *Farnham Buildings and People*, Farnham 1963, 183–4]. It was his father, James Harding senior (*c.*1772–1844), a mason, who in 1812 made the plans for rebuilding the nave of FROYLE CHURCH, HANTS. [MS. 'Orders of Vestry for rebuilding etc. 1812']. James Harding, junior, rebuilt the nave of BRAMSHOTT CHURCH, HANTS., in 1836 (again rebuilt 1872) [I.C.B.S.]; restored HEADLEY CHURCH, HANTS., in 1836–7, adding a new spire and porch [I.C.B.S.]; and designed WRECCLESHAM CHURCH, SURREY, 1840 (rebuilt 1877) [I.C.B.S.] and CROOKHAM CHURCH, HANTS., 1840–1 (chancel added 1876–7) [tender advertised in *Reading Mercury*, 28 Jan. 1840].

HARDWICK, PHILIP (1792–1870), younger son of Thomas Hardwick (d. 1829), was educated at Dr. Barrow's School in Soho Square. In 1808 he entered the Royal Academy Schools, and at the same time became a pupil in his father's office. He exhibited at the Academy from 1807 to 1844. In 1815 he went to Paris to see the Louvre, then filled with the pictures collected by Napoleon from all parts of Europe, and in 1818–19 he spent about twelve months in Italy. On his return he entered into partnership with his father, to whose practice he eventually succeeded. He became architect to the Bridewell and Bethlethem Hospitals in 1816, to the St. Katherine's Dock Company in 1825, to St. Bartholomew's Hospital in succession to his father in 1826, to the Goldsmiths' Company in 1828, to the Westminster Bridge Estates in 1829, and to the London and Birmingham Railway Company in 1839. He was also the London surveyor of the Portman estate, and (from 1829 to 1835) of that of the Marquess of Salisbury.

Hardwick was elected F.S.A. in 1824, F.R.S. in 1831, F.G.S. in 1837, A.R.A. in 1840, and R.A. in 1841. From 1850 to 1861 he was treasurer of the Royal Academy. He was elected a member of the Institution of Civil Engineers in 1824, and was an original member of the Institute of British Architects in 1834. He was vice-president in 1839 and 1841, and received the Royal Gold Medal in 1854. He was awarded a Gold Medal at the Paris Exhibition of 1855, at which he exhibited drawings of Goldsmiths' Hall and Lincoln's Inn. He was an efficient man of business, and was much employed as a referee, notably in connection with the Royal Exchange Competition of 1840. He was one of the examiners of candidates for district surveyorships under the Metropolitan Building Act of 1843. As an architect he is best known for his warehouses in the London docks, which showed him as a master of unadorned industrial architecture on a large scale, and for the monumental Doric gateway to Euston Station – a magnificent tribute of transport to early nineteeth-century taste that was wantonly destroyed in 1962 – but at Goldsmiths' Hall he produced a noble façade in the English baroque tradition, and at Lincoln's Inn and elsewhere he used Tudor

Gothic in an exceptionally scholarly and convincing manner.

Hardwick was described by Lord Mahon in 1842 as 'an architect of very agreeable manners and intelligent conversation'. His health broke down in 1843, when he was little more than 50 years old, and he was obliged to confine himself to such practice as could be conducted from his own room, though he continued, in spite of serious physical disabilities, to serve on the Royal Academy committee of which he was a member. From this time onwards his practice was virtually in the hands of his son, Philip Charles Hardwick (1822–92), and in 1861 he gave up all work and retired from public life. He died at his son's home, Westcombe Lodge, Wimbledon Common, on 28 December 1870, and was buried at Kensal Green. He married in 1819 a daughter of John Shaw, the architect, by whom he had two sons, Thomas and Philip Charles. T. H. Wyatt was his pupil. Several of his drawings and sketch-books are in the R.I.B.A. Collection. [*D.N.B.*; obituaries in *Builder* xxix, 1871, 24, and *Minutes of Proceedings of the Institution of Civil Engineers* xxxiii, 1871–2 (i), 215; *Notes of Conversations with the Duke of Wellington*, by Philip Henry, 5th Earl Stanhope, World's Classics 1938, 292; Hermione Hobhouse, 'Philip and Philip Charles Hardwick' in *Seven Victorian Architects*, ed. Jane Fawcett, 1976].

attributed: RICHMOND, SURREY, ST. ELIZABETH'S CHURCH (R.C.), 1822–4; enlarged 1902 [N. Hughes, *The Richmond Catholic Mission 1791–1826*, Richmond 1991, 104–5].

STRETTON CHURCH, CHESHIRE, 1826–7, Gothic; rebuilt 1807 [Port, 140; drawings in R.I.B.A. Collection].

LONDON, ST. KATHERINE'S DOCKS, WAREHOUSES and OFFICES, 1827–9; dem. 1971–81 [*Companion to the Almanac*, 1829, 219–21; exhib. at R.A. 1825 and 1830].

LAMBETH, THE HOUSE OF OCCUPATIONS (a school), WEST SQUARE, 1829–30; dem. *c.*1932 [Bethlehem Hospital archives, *ex inf.* Miss P. Allderidge].

LONDON, GOLDSMITHS' HALL, FOSTER LANE, 1829–35 [exhib. at R.A. 1831, 1839, 1842].

KNELLER HALL, WHITTON, MIDDLESEX, addition of wings for Charles Calvert, *c.*1830; remodelled by George Mair as the Kneller Hall Training School, 1849–50 [*Builder* viii, 1850, 67–8].

ENFORD CHURCH, WILTSHIRE, restoration 1830–1, after damage by lightning in 1817 [I.C.B.S.].

STOCKPORT, CHESHIRE, THE FREE GRAMMAR SCHOOL, for the Goldsmiths' Company, 1830–32, Tudor Gothic; dem. 1923 [*Companion to the Almanac*, 1833, 219].

WAINFLEET ST. MARY SCHOOL, LINCS., for the Governors of Bethlehem Hospital, 1830–2 [Bethlehem Hospital archives, *ex inf.* Miss P. Allderidge].

LONDON, THE CITY CLUB-HOUSE, No. 19 OLD BROAD STREET, 1833–4 [original drawing formerly in Sir Albert Richardson's Collection; engraved plan and elevation by Baynes & Harris].

BABRAHAM HOUSE, CAMBS., for H. J. Adeane, 1833–7, Jacobethan; enlarged 1864 [exhib. at R.A. 1840].

CHADACRE HALL, SHIMPLING, SUFFOLK, for Thomas Hallifax, *c.*1834 [letter from Benjamin De Carle, mason of Bury St. Edmunds, to Hardwick, soliciting employment at Chadacre 6 Aug. 1834, in De Carle's letter-book, W. Suffolk Record Office, Acc. 468].

DOVER, WATERLOO CRESCENT, 1834–8 [J. C. Loudon, *Architectural Mag.* i, 1834, 209–10].

LONDON, EUSTON STATION: THE EUSTON and VICTORIA HOTELS, DORIC GATEWAY and LODGES, 1836–40; dem. 1962. A building linking the two hotels was erected 1880–1. The Great Hall of the station was by P. C. Hardwick, 1846–9 [*Survey of London* xxi, 107–14; *Companion to the Almanac*, 1839, 233–5].

LONDON, GLOBE INSURANCE COMPANY'S OFFICE, CORNHILL, 1837–8 [*Companion to the Almanac*, 1838, 233].

LONDON, FREEMASONS' HALL, GREAT QUEEN STREET, alterations 1838; remodelled by F. P. Cockerell 1864–5 [*Civil Engineer & Architect's Jnl.* i, 1837–8, 204].

EVERTON CHURCH, BEDS., repairs 1838 [I.C.B.S.].

BIRMINGHAM, CURZON STREET STATION, 1838–42 [*Companion to the Almanac*, 1838, 236–7].

WESTWOOD PARK, WORCS., addition of kitchens and other alterations in Elizabethan style for J. S. Russell Pakington, *c.*1840 [*V.C.H. Worcs.* iii, 234] (*C. Life*, 14, 21 July 1928).

HEREFORD, THE BISHOP'S PALACE, alterations *c.*1840 [exhib. at R.A. 1840; drawing in Bodleian Library, MS. Top. gen. c.78, f. 21].

RHYMNEY, MONMOUTHSHIRE, ST. DAVID'S CHURCH, 1840–3 [I.C.B.S.] (J. B. Hilling, *Cardiff and the Valleys*, 1973, 115).

LONDON, ST. BARTHOLOMEW'S HOSPITAL, alterations and additions including Receiving Room and N. block, 1842 and repairs to Gibbs's building, 1851 [*Minutes . . . of the Institution of Civil Engineers, loc. cit.*; cf. *Archaeological Jnl.* viii, 1851, 103].

LONDON, LINCOLN'S INN, completion of south wing of Sir Robert Taylor's STONE BUILDINGS, 1842–5; designed new HALL, LIBRARY, etc. in conjunction with his son P. C. Hardwick, 1843–5, Tudor Gothic [published *Drawings of the Hall and Library, Lincoln's Inn,* 1842; *Companion to the Almanac,* 1844, 235–8, 1845, 241, 1846, 238–40; *Builder* iii, 1845, 521–2, 526].

LONDON, BELGRAVE SQUARE, house in south-east angle for 3rd Earl of Sefton, 1842–5; portico since removed [*Companion to the Almanac,* 1842, 205].

SUSSEX, a 'mansion to be built near Maresfield', exhib. at R.A. 1842. For possible identifications see M. A. Lower, *Compendious History of Sussex* ii, 1870, 42.

HALL, nr. BARNSTAPLE, DEVON, for Robert Chichester, 1844–7, completed by P. C. Hardwick and R. D. Gould of Barnstaple, 1847–9, Tudor Gothic [exhib. at R.A. 1844; inscription in Great Hall].

LONDON, KENSINGTON PALACE GARDENS, house (No. 10) for S. H. Sutherland, 1846–7 [*Survey of London* xxxvii, 165].

LIVERPOOL, THE DOCK TRAFFIC OFFICE, ALBERT DOCK, 1846–7 [Quentin Hughes, *Seaport,* 1964, 30].

PENGE, KENT, KING WILLIAM NAVAL ASYLUM, 1847–9, Tudor Gothic [*Illustrated London News,* 8 December 1849].

PEPER HAROW, SURREY, entrance to kitchen garden for 5th Viscount Midleton, 1847 [W. Keane, *The Beauties of Surrey,* 1849, 128].

LONDON, ST. ANNE'S CHURCH, LIMEHOUSE, restoration after fire, in collaboration with John Morris, 1850–1 [*Builder* x, 1852, 39].

WANDSWORTH, SURREY, THE ROYAL FREEMASONS' SCHOOL FOR GIRLS, 1851, Tudor Gothic [*Builder* ix, 1851, 722–3; exhib. at R.A. 1852 by P. C. Hardwick, who was no doubt the effective architect].

BIRMINGHAM, ST. MARTIN'S CHURCH, restoration of tower and spire, 1854–5, by 'Messrs. Hardwick' [*A.P.S.D., s.v.* 'Birmingham']. J. T. Bunce, *History of Old St. Martin's Birmingham,* 1875, 22, makes it clear that P. C. Hardwick was the effective architect.

LONDON, No. 7 BURLINGTON GARDENS (formerly Uxbridge House), conversion into BRANCH BANK OF ENGLAND (now Bank of Scotland), including addition of Doric porch, 1855 [*Survey of London* xxxii, 465].

LONDON, GREENWICH HOSPITAL, obelisk in memory of Thomas Bellot (d. 1857) [B.L., Add. MS. 32364, f. 12].

HARDWICK, THOMAS (1725–1798), originated in Monmouth or Herefordshire, but established himself as a master mason at New Brentford, Middlesex. In the 1760s he was the master mason for the internal remodelling of Syon House to the designs of R. and J. Adam [Percy archives, Alnwick Castle, U III 5, 21–27]. The nave of ST. LAURENCE'S CHURCH, BRENTFORD, was rebuilt to his designs in 1764 and in 1781–2 he rebuilt HANWELL CHURCH, MIDDLESEX (again rebuilt 1841) [*A.P.S.D.*]. Hardwick's will was proved on 24 Sept. 1798 [P.C.C. 600 WALPOLE].

HARDWICK, THOMAS (1752–1829), son of the above, became in 1767 a pupil of Sir William Chambers. He was admitted to the Royal Academy Schools in 1769, winning the first Silver Medal for architecture the same year. He began to exhibit at the Academy in 1772, and continued to do so almost every year until 1805. In 1776 he set out for Italy, via Paris, where he joined forces with the artist Thomas Jones. Together they reached Rome in November. In the course of the next three years Hardwick made measured drawings of many antique and some more recent buildings in Rome and its vicinity, and also visited Naples, Paestum, Pompeii and Venice. In Rome he worked for a time in collaboration with the young John Soane, but their friendship did not last. Hardwick returned to England in 1779, bringing with him a number of sketch-books filled with drawings of both ancient and later buildings. These are now in the R.I.B.A. Drawings Collection with the exception of one that is in the Fowler Collection at Baltimore, U.S.A.[1]

Soon after his return Hardwick won the competition for the best design for a female prison sponsored by the Commissioners for Penitentiary Houses established under the Penitentiary Act of 1779. This building was never erected, but Hardwick was subse-

[1] See *R.I.B.A. Drawings Catalogue: G–H,* 89–95; J. G. Dunbar, 'An English Architect at Naples', *Burlington Mag.* cx, 1968, 265–6 and J. Harris, *Catalogue of British Drawings for Architecture etc. in American Collections,* 110. Hardwick wrote a paper on the Colosseum for the Society of Antiquaries (MS. in Soane Museum, AL, Pc47 and printed version in *Archaeologia* vii, 1785, 369–73). A large cork model of the building that he had made in Rome was presented to the British Museum by Philip Hardwick in 1851 but can no longer be found and is presumed to have been destroyed. A volume of drawings by Hardwick entitled 'Sketches of Sundry Buildings already executed and Original Designs on various subjects, commencing about the year 1773' belonged in 1974 to Mr. A. P. Lyons, who kindly allowed the writer to examine it. Mr. Lyons also had the diaries kept by Hardwick on visits to Flanders in 1816 and Paris in 1822.

quently employed as the architect of the important Millbank Penitentiary begun in 1812 on marshy ground on the site of the present Tate Gallery. After building the boundary wall and gateway he resigned the post in 1813 on the ground that the remuneration of 2½ per cent offered by the commissioners was inadequate, and because 'the management of this extensive concern took up a larger portion of his time and attention than he could conveniently spare from his other business'. His place was taken by John Harvey, and ultimately by Robert Smirke, who found that, despite elaborate precautions, the foundations laid under Hardwick's direction had not been adequate.

From 1804 onwards Hardwick was surveyor to the Marquess of Salisbury's London estate. In 1809 he became surveyor to St. Bartholomew's Hospital, and in 1810 he obtained a post in the Office of Works as Clerk of the Works at Hampton Court, a position which he retained until his death. From 1815 onwards his responsibilities also included Kew Palace and its gardens. He was elected F.S.A. in 1781 and was an original member of the Architects' Club founded in 1791, but failed to secure election as A.R.A. although he was a candidate on several occasions. He died on 16 January 1829, at his house in Berners Street, and was buried in the family vault in the churchyard at Brentford, where there is a tablet to his memory. A pencil portrait by George Dance is reproduced in the latter's *Collection of Portraits sketched from the Life* (1808–14). The original drawing is in the Victoria and Albert Museum. His pupils included Samuel Angell, John Foulston, John MacDonnell, John Williams, and his younger son Philip Hardwick (*q.v.*), who eventually succeeded to his practice. His elder son John (1791–1875) was a barrister and stipendiary magistrate. J. M. W. Turner was in his office for a time, but abandoned architecture for painting on his advice. He wrote the memoir of Sir William Chambers which was first published in Gwilt's edition of Chambers's *Civil Architecture* (1825).

Hardwick was, as James Wyatt expressed it, 'a regular bred, classical architect' [Farington's Diary, 20 Jan. 1799]. He was an accomplished draughtsman and a competent designer in a conservative neo-classical manner which he inherited from Chambers. But, unlike Chambers, he never became a fashionable designer of houses for the wealthy, and he made a living chiefly as a surveyor and as a designer of churches and minor public buildings. His failure to secure election to the Royal Academy is no doubt indicative of his relatively modest standing as an architectural artist. His best surviving works are St. Marylebone Church in London, Wanstead Church in Essex and St. John's Church at Workington in Cumberland, all of which have handsome porticos.

[*A.P.S.D.; D.N.B.; Gent's Mag.* 1829(i), 92; 'Memoirs of Thomas Jones', *Walpole Soc.* xxxii, 1946–8, 40–45, 58–65, 68, 79, 89; P. de la Ruffinière du Prey, 'Soane and Hardwick in Rome: a neo-classical partnership', *Architectural History* xv, 1972.]

RUPERRA CASTLE, GLAMORGAN, rebuilt interior for Charles Morgan 1784–9, after a fire; gutted 1941 [N.L.W., Tredegar MS. 150].

WANSTEAD CHURCH, ESSEX, 1787–90 [*V.C.H. Essex* vi, 333; exhib. at R.A. 1791] (plans and elevations in C.L. Stieglitz, *Plans et Desseins tirés de la Belle Architecture*, Paris & Leipzig 1798–1800, pls. 53–4).

LONDON, ST. PAUL'S CHURCH, COVENT GARDEN, extensive repairs, including recasing of exterior in Portland stone, 1788–9. The church was gutted by fire in 1795 and restored by Hardwick 1796–8, adhering closely to Inigo Jones's original design. Hardwick's interior was altered by Butterfield in 1871–2 and his ceiling was replaced in 1887–8. [*Survey of London* xxxvi, chap. 5: pl. 17 shows the interior as designed by Hardwick].

LONDON, ST. JAMES'S CHURCH, PICCADILLY, repairs and alterations, 1789 and 1803–4 [*Survey of London* xxix, 37, 41].

LONDON, ST. BARTHOLOMEW THE GREAT, SMITHFIELD, examined and reported on the state of the church in 1790–1, and by judicious repairs saved it from demolition. Hardwick carried out further repairs in 1808 [Vestry Minutes in Guildhall Library, MS. 3990/4, pp. 8–21, 225]. He presented measured drawings of the church to the Society of Antiquaries (*Red Portfolio London*, A–B, pp. 12–16).

LONDON ST. JAMES'S CHAPEL, HAMPSTEAD ROAD, 1791–2; dem. *c.*1965 [minutes of the building committee, with plans, elevations and sections, in Westminster Public Library among the records of St. James's parish, Piccadilly, for which the chapel was built] (measured drawings in *Arch. Rev.* xli, 1917, 62–4).

BROMLEY COLLEGE, BROMLEY, KENT, the second quadrangle, 1792–4 and *c.*1800–4 [College records, *ex inf.* Mr. Roger White].

DORCHESTER, DORSET, THE SHIRE HALL, 1796–7 [Hutchins, *History of Dorset* ii, 1863, 372].

GALWAY, IRELAND, THE COUNTY GAOL, 1802–3, executed under the superintendence of R. Morrison [James Hardiman, *History of Galway*, 1820, 302; cf. the 'design for a gaol to be built in Ireland' exhibited by Hardwick at the R.A. in 1803].

HEREFORD, THE NELSON COLUMN, CASTLE GREEN, 1806–9, executed by Thomas Wood of Hereford, who modified Hardwick's design [*The Hereford Guide*, 2nd ed. 1808, 43].

QUEX PARK, BIRCHINGTON, KENT, for J. Powell Powell, 1806–13 [payments to Hardwick as 'surveyor of the New House at Quex' in Powell's accounts in possession of Mr. J. Powell Cotton].

LONDON, ST. PANCRAS WORKHOUSE, KING'S ROAD, CAMDEN TOWN, 1809; dem. [*A.P.S.D.*].

SYON HOUSE, MIDDLESEX, THE EVIDENCE ROOM (a detached building) for 2nd Duke of Northumberland, 1809 [Alnwick Castle, MS. 94, f. 49].

OXFORD, ST. JOHN'S COLLEGE, stables afterwards forming east side of North Quadrangle, 1811; dem. 1959. The stables were built 'according to a plan alter'd from Mr. Hardwick's and deliver'd by Mr. Hudson', who erected them under Hardwick's supervision [College Register viii, pp. 188–90].

LONDON, THE MILLBANK PENITENTIARY. The parts erected under Hardwick's direction in 1812–13 were the boundary wall, the lodge and gateway, the main drain, and the foundations of the first Pentagon and of the chapel. The foundations subsequently proved inadequate, and were rebuilt by R. Smirke. The prison was demolished in 1892 [G. Holford, *An Account of the Penitentiary at Millbank*, 1828, xxv–xxix].

LONDON, ST. MARYLEBONE NEW CHURCH, 1813–17. This church was begun as a chapel of ease, but completed as a parish church. To give it more consequence, the original Ionic order was altered to Corinthian when the church was half built, and the portico was enlarged from four to six columns. The apse was added in 1883–4 [Britton & Pugin, *The Public Buildings of London* i, 1825, 167–79].

LONDON, ST. JAMES'S VESTRY HALL, PICCADILLY, 1814; dem. 1861 [*Survey of London* xxix, 55 and xxx, pl. 18a].

LONDON, ST. JOHN'S CHAPEL, ST. JOHN'S WOOD, 1814 [J. Elmes, *Metropolitan Improvements*, 1829, 165 and plate].

LONDON, ST. BARTHOLOMEW'S HOSPITAL, a 'general repair', 1814–20 [*Builder* iii, 1845, 78].

BANGOR CATHEDRAL, CAERNARVONSHIRE, survey of fabric, 1820 [M. L. Clarke, *Bangor Cathedral*, Cardiff 1969, 77].

LONDON, ST. JAMES'S WORKHOUSE, POLAND STREET, 1821; dem. [*Survey of London* xxxi, 212].

KEW, SURREY, ST. ANNE'S CHURCH, extended east end, 1822 [Surrey Archdeaconry Records].

WORKINGTON, CUMBERLAND, ST. JOHN'S CHURCH, 1822–3; tower added 1847 [Port, 132].

LONDON, CHRIST CHURCH, COSWAY STREET, LISSON GROVE, MARYLEBONE, 1822–4; secularized [Port, 136]. Philip Hardwick evidently completed this church, as he exhibited a view of the interior at the R.A. in 1826.

LONDON, ST. BARNABAS CHURCH, KING SQUARE, FINSBURY, 1822–6; damaged 1941, restored 1954 [Port, 134].

LONDON, ST. BARTHOLOMEW THE LESS, SMITHFIELD, rebuilt Dance's octagonal nave in stone with iron roof, 1823–5, [G. Godwin, *The Churches of London* ii, 1839].

BOLTON, LANCS., HOLY TRINITY CHURCH, 1823–5, Gothic [Port, 132].

LONDON, ARCHBISHOP TENISON'S CHAPEL (ST. THOMAS), REGENT STREET, redecorated interior 1824; dem. 1973 [*Survey of London* xxxi, 183–4].

FARNWORTH (KEARSLEY), LANCS., ST. JOHN'S CHURCH, 1824–5, Gothic [Port, 132].

KEW PALACE, SURREY, lodges for King George IV, 1824–7; dem. [*History of the King's Works* vi, 359].

HARGRAVE, JOSEPH (*c.*1754–1802), was an architect and surveyor of Hull, where he died on 15 October 1802, aged 48 [*Gent's Mag.* 1802, 977]. He was the son of Jeremiah Hargrave, a carver who was responsible for the finely executed rococo relief in the pediment of Trinity House, Hull, in 1753 [G. Hadley, *History of Hull*, 1788, 821]. Joseph Hargrave made the drawings of buildings which illustrate Hadley's *History of Hull* (1788). The engraving of THE CHARTERHOUSE HOSPITAL, built in 1780, is the only one which he signs as 'Architect', and it may therefore be presumed that he designed it. He also designed THE SUBSCRIPTION LIBRARY in PARLIAMENT STREET, 1801 (dem.) [J. N. Crosse, *Account of . . . Subscription Library*, 1810, 5, 14; *V.C.H. Yorks. East Riding* i, 425].

HARLOW, JOHN, described as 'surveyor', designed a new altar-piece for the church of ST. MARY ABBOTS, KENSINGTON, in 1685, and in the following year supervised the enlargement of the north aisle. The church was rebuilt in 1696 and again in 1869 [J. D. G. Scott, *St. Mary Abbots, Kensington*, 1942, 33, 36, 78].

HARPER, JAMES BENJAMIN (*c.*1798–1873), was a builder and surveyor at Henley-in-Arden in Warwickshire. He rebuilt the nave of CLAVERDON CHURCH, WARWICKS., in 1828–30 [I.C.B.S., letter in Nuthurst file], designed a small Gothic church at NUTHURST, WARWICKS., 1835, rebuilt 1879 [I.C.B.S.], and another at SALTER STREET, near TANWORTH-IN-ARDEN, WARWICKS., 1840 [I.C.B.S.], to which a tower was added in 1860. Harper later moved to Great Malvern, where he combined the functions of a surveyor, agent and auctioneer. He died at Great Malvern on 16 April 1873 [Principal Probate Registry, Calendar of Probates].

HARPER, JOHN (1809–1842), was born at Dunkenhalgh Hall, near Blackburn, Lancashire. He was apparently the son of John Harper, the estate agent there. He became a pupil of Benjamin and Philip Wyatt, whom he assisted in preparing the designs for Apsley House, York House and the Duke of York's Column. He began to practise on his own in York, and was employed by the Duke of Devonshire at Bolton Abbey, by Lord Londesborough, and others. He competed for the Houses of Parliament in 1835, paying particular attention to the acoustics and ventilation of the two chambers. Most of his recorded works are in the Gothic style, and one or two of his churches (e.g. All Saints, Elton, and St. Marie's, Bury) show an ability to get away from the standard formulae of early-nineteenth-century church design.

Harper died of malaria while on a visit to Italy in 1842. He was a friend of David Roberts, Clarkson Stanfield and William Etty, who painted his portrait. He was an accomplished draughtsman, whose 'sketches of scenery, antiquity and architecture' were admired by his contemporaries. Some of them were sold in 1991 and are now in the R.I.B.A. Drawings Collection and York Museum and Art Gallery.

[S. Redgrave, *Dictionary of Artists of the English School*, 1878, 198; *D.N.B.*; Chetham Soc. vol. 85, 1926, 73.]

YORK, ST. LEONARD'S PLACE, terrace (Nos. 1–9), begun 1834 [R.C.H.M. *York* v, 205].

YORK, Gothic piazza to THEATRE ROYAL, 1834–5; dismantled 1879 and re-erected at No. 73 Fulford Road [R.C.H.M. *York* iv, 53; v, 103].

SHIBDEN HALL, nr. HALIFAX YORKS. (W.R.), addition of tower and offices for Miss Anne Lister, 1835–6 [*Castles and Country Houses in Yorkshire*, Bradford 1885] (*C. Life*, 22 Nov. 1984).

EVERINGHAM PARK, YORKS. (E.R.), CATHOLIC CHAPEL for William Constable-Maxwell, 1836–9, based on designs supplied by Agostino Giorgioli of Rome [Arthur Oswald in *C. Life*, 22 Feb. 1968].

YORK, ST. PETER'S SCHOOL, CLIFTON, 1838, Gothic [*D.N.B.*] (R.C.H.M. *York* iv, 53).

CLAYTON-LE-MOORS CHURCH, LANCS., 1838–40, Gothic; chancel rebuilt 1882 [R. Trappes-Lomax, *A History of Clayton-le-Moors*, Chetham Soc. vol. 85, 1926, 146].

BURY, LANCS., ST. PAUL'S CHURCH, 1838–41, Gothic [*Manchester Courier*, 6 Oct. 1838, *ex inf.* the Revd. T. Parry].

SELBY, YORKS. (W.R.), THE PUBLIC ROOMS, 1839 [*Leeds Intelligencer*, 28 Sept. 1839, *ex inf.* Dr. D. Linstrum].

CRAKEHALL CHURCH, YORKS. (N.R.), 1840, Gothic [I.C.B.S.].

BLACKTOFT CHURCH, YORKS. (E.R.), 1841, Gothic [I.C.B.S.].

BURY, LANCS., ST. MARIE'S CHURCH (R.C.), 1841, Gothic [*Companion to the Almanac*, 1841, 234–6].

ELTON, nr. BURY, LANCS., ALL SAINTS CHURCH, 1841–3, Romanesque [B. T. Barton, *History of Bury*, 1874, 201].

HARRIS, DANIEL (*c.*1761–1840), was an architect and builder of Oxford who also acted as Keeper of the County Gaol. This was built to the design of William Blackburn (*q.v.*) between 1785 and 1805. It was begun by Edward Edge, a mason from Gloucestershire, but was completed by Harris, who contrived that the greater part of the work should be done by the convicts themselves. He subsequently (1805–11) built the COUNTY BRIDEWELL at ABINGDON to the designs of Jeffry Wyatt(ville) [*Report from the Committee of Aldermen appointed to visit several Gaols in England*, 1816, 25; D. Linstrum, *Sir Jeffry Wyatville*, 1972, 258]. He was also employed by the Thames Commissioners to supervise the construction of locks at Oseney (1789–90), Godstow (1790) and Pinkhill (1791). [F. S. Thacker, *The Thames Highway: General History*, 1914, 151; *The Thames Highway: a History of the Locks and Weirs*, 1920, 91, 114, 135]. A mill at Eynsham that Harris had built is mentioned by J. C. Loudon in his booklet on *Paper Roofs used at Tew Lodge, Oxon.* (1811).

For some years Harris was in partnership with John Plowman (*q.v.*). The association probably dated from 1812, when Harris advertised in the *Oxford Herald* that 'his arrangements with his late foreman J. Plowman now allow him to attend to [his clients'] favours in the architectural way'. His ability as a draughtsman is shown by the fact that he made the drawings for the University Almanacks annually from 1789 to 1792, and in 1799 exhibited at the Royal Academy an elegant view of BRAZIERS, nr. IPSDEN, OXON., a Gothic house which he had built for I. G. Manley. His drawings (1797) for a small house at HEADBOURNE WORTHY, HANTS., are in the Public Record Office (MPA 89(1)). In about 1796 he was employed to examine the spire of MERTON CHURCH, OXON., and advised that it should be taken down, which was accordingly done [Oxfordshire C.R.O., Oxford Archdeaconry Papers, Oxon. b. 25, f. 238]. He made estimates for repairing or rebuilding parsonages at BAMPTON (1799), SWYNCOMBE (1803) and STOKE TALMAGE (1820) in Oxon. [Oxfordshire C.R.O., Oxford Diocesan Faculty Registers 1737–1804, 190, 227; 1804–27, 225] and at FLORE in Northants. (1816) [Peterborough Diocesan Records]. In Oxford he designed a Gothic palisade in front of WADHAM COLLEGE in 1806, replaced 1822 [T. G. Jackson, *Wadham College, Oxford*, 1893, 218] and in 1812 repaired the Warden's Lodgings at MERTON COLLEGE [*Illustrations of Oxford*, J. Ryman, 1839]. Harris died in June 1840, aged 79 [Register of St. Peter-le-Bailey, Oxford].

HARRIS, THOMAS (*c.*1688–1763), of Cublington in Bucks., was descended from a family of joiners. Both his father Thomas Harris (1654–1724), his grandfather William Harris (1616–84), and his elder brothers George (b. 1684) and John Harris (1686–1730) followed the same trade. In 1663 the churchwardens of Soulbury, Bucks., paid £2 to 'Goodman Harris of Cublington for y[e] Communion table', and his timber-framed house, with his initials and the date 1661 over the mantelpiece, still stands at the west end of Cublington village. George Harris is described as 'architect' in a Quarter Sessions record of 1713, and Thomas also had some architectural ability. From 1713 to 1726 he worked at Stowe House, Bucks., sometimes acting as a measurer of other craftsmen's work as well as a joiner [*ex inf.* Mr. G. Clarke].

In 1720 Harris was one of the two surveyors who submitted 'plans, ground plots and models' for rebuilding the PRISON and COUNTY HALL at AYLESBURY, BUCKS. The other was a 'Mr. Brandon'. Both designs were submitted to Sir John Vanbrugh, who chose the one made by Harris and charged a fee of 20 guineas for his advice. Work began in 1722–4, but was then suspended owing to lack of funds, and was not completed until 1737–40. Harris received £21 for his 'draughts and model', and £100 'for upwards of two years surveyorship'. He also performed some of the carpentry work of the building, and was presumably responsible for the handsome joinery of the Court Room. The main elevation to Market Square is Palladian in character, but is handled in a slightly clumsy manner which shows that Harris was not a complete master of the style. The Prison was demolished in 1847, but the Court Room survives [G. R. Crouch, 'The Building of the County Hall, Aylesbury', *Records of Bucks.* xii, 1927–33].

According to local tradition Harris designed or built the LOVETT SCHOOL at SOULBURY, BUCKS. (*c.*1724), but the building is so conservative in style that the attribution would be more credible if applied to his father. When Dr. Pococke visited EYTHROPE HOUSE, BUCKS., in 1751, he saw 'a handsome new front before the court, of good architecture, designed by Harris' for Sir William Stanhope [*Dr. Pococke's Travels in England*, ed. Cartwright, i, 161]. This appears to have been the screen-wall on either side of the west front of the chapel, which stood in the middle of a courtyard between the house and the stables. It was demolished in 1810–11 [H. M. Colvin, 'Eythrope House', *Records of Bucks.* xvii, 1964].

Harris died at Cublington in June 1763, and is described in the register of burials as 'Mr. Thomas Harris, Joiner and house carpenter'. His annotated copies of Vitruvius, Palladio and Gibbs remained in the possession of his descendants until the present century [information from Miss Dorothy M. Harris of Wing].

HARRIS, WILLIAM (*c.*1796–1823), was the son of William Harris, a London merchant. He became a pupil of Sir Jeffry Wyatville, was admitted to the Royal Academy Schools in 1819, and won the Silver Medal the same year. He exhibited designs at the Academy from 1815 to 1818. In 1821 he joined Samuel Angell in Paris, and with him travelled through the south of France to Rome, Naples and Sicily, where he assisted in the discovery of the sculptures at Selinus. He died of malaria in Palermo on 16 July 1823. A monument in the Protestant cemetery at Rome commemorates his 'ardor in the study of his profession' and laments the loss of 'an artist of talent and taste'. His sister married Thomas Evans (*q.v.*), who with Angell was responsible for the publication of the sculptures in 1826 [*A.P.S.D.*].

HARRIS, WILLIAM, was one of the District Surveyors for Bristol from 1840 until his resignation in 1847 [A. B. Beaven, *Bristol Lists*, 1899, 249]. He designed three Greek Revival Market Houses in Cornwall, at PENZANCE, 1836–8 [P. A. S. Pool, *History of Penzance*, 1974, 135, 189–90], HELSTON, 1837–8 [*The*

Parochial History of Cornwall ii, 1868, 177] and BODMIN, 1839 [J. Maclean, *Deanery of Trigg Minor* i, 1873, 111]. The last was based on a building on the island of Delos illustrated by Woods in the *Antiquities of Athens* (cf. J. M. Crook, *The Greek Revival*, 1972, pl. 191), and shows that Harris was a serious student of Greek architecture. In 1838 he rebuilt the INDEPENDENT CHAPEL at CLIFTON, nr. BRISTOL, and in 1838–41 the chancel and transepts of CHEPSTOW CHURCH, MONMOUTHSHIRE, the latter in Norman style [*Civil Engineer and Architect's Jnl.* i, 1837–8, 235]. Here his work was partly rebuilt by Seddon in 1890. An unexecuted design by Harris for the east front of PENROSE HOUSE, CORNWALL, dated 1837, is preserved there. He was probably a William Harris who died in Bristol in 1848.

HARRIS, WILLIAM (–1863), practised at 55 Park Street, Grosvenor Square, from about 1830 until his death on 1 April 1863. In 1840 he exhibited a design for 'A tomb in memory of the late H. Salisbury, Esq.' at the Royal Academy. His designs for a watermill at Feltham, Middlesex, dated 18 March 1839, are in the Public Record Office (LRRO 1/867). He was presumably the 'Mr. Harris' to whose designs Nos. 26–27 UPPER GROSVENOR STREET, LONDON, were remodelled as a single house in 1840–1; dem. 1927–8 [*Survey of London* xl, 231].

HARRISON, HENRY (*c.*1785–*c.*1865), was the son of John Harrison, a London surveyor and builder. He stated in 1828 that he had been 'brought up as a builder and architect', but that 'within about the last five years' he had practised solely as an architect. His brother George was, however, a builder, and had built Richmond Terrace, Whitehall, as a speculation from his designs.[1] Henry appears subsequently to have resumed business as a builder, for he was described as such when he went bankrupt in 1840. In 1856, when he was among the applicants for the post of Architect to the Metropolitan Board of Works, he furnished a long list of buildings that he had built or altered. It shows that he had a considerable practice as a designer of minor country houses and parsonages, especially in Sussex and Cornwall, and that he built or altered many town houses in the West End of London. Richmond Terrace, Bignor Park and the Lying-in-Hospital at Lambeth are typical of the somewhat tame Greek Revival style which he favoured in the 1820s, but he also designed some poorly-detailed Tudor or Jacobean houses (e.g. Swyncombe House and Hadleigh Deanery), and his Guards' Club in Pall Mall of 1848–9 had a façade of fashionably Italian character.

In the 1830s Harrison was living at 31 Park Street, Grosvenor Square, in a house of his own building, but at the time of his bankruptcy he was in Bruton Street, and later he moved to Bedford Square. He was still alive in 1861 at the age of 75, but his name disappears from the London Directories in 1864. His specification for concrete for use in foundations has been preserved (Museum of the History of Science, Oxford, MS. Gunther 9, f. 95^{v}).

[*Report from the Select Committee on the Office of Works and Public Buildings*, 1828, 86–91; G.L. Record Office, M.B.W. 213 (Harrison's letter of 1 Feb. 1856);[2] will of John Harrison in Middlesex Land Registry 1828/1/794; P.R.O., Census Returns of 1851 and 1861; *Survey of London* xxxvii, 103–4].

COUNTRY HOUSES, PARSONAGES, ETC.

ADDINGTON PARK, SURREY, added Chapel, Library and other rooms for William Howley, Archbishop of Canterbury, 1829–30 [M.B.W.; E. W. Brayley, *Topographical History of Surrey* 1841, iv, 28].

AUBERIES, BULMER, ESSEX, alterations for Col. Augustus Meyrick, *c.*1835 [M.B.W.].

AUDLEY END, ESSEX, restored house and designed 'Ice-house Lodge' for 3rd Lord Braybrooke, *c.*1825–7 [M.B.W.; Lord Braybrooke, *History of Audley End and Saffron Walden*, 1836, 132, 137].

BARMING RECTORY, KENT, alterations for the Revd. C. H. Barham [M.B.W.].

BARON HILL, ANGLESEY, extensive works for Sir Richard Williams-Bulkeley, Bart., *c.*1836 [M.B.W.]. This house was 'totally destroyed by fire' on 5 May 1836, when 'nearly completed' [*Gent's Mag.* 1836 (i), 654]. It was subsequently rebuilt in the form illustrated by T. Nicholas, *Annals of the County Families of Wales* i, 1875, 6, and is now a ruin.

BEXHILL RECTORY, SUSSEX, for the Revd. Thomas Baker [M.B.W.].

BIGNOR PARK, SUSSEX, for John Hawkins, 1826–8 [M.B.W.; Dallaway, *Rape of Arundel*, ed. Cartwright, ii (1), 1832, 249; Gordon Nares in *C. Life*, 26 April, 3 May 1956].

BLETCHLEY RECTORY, BUCKS., 1834, Gothic [Lincs. Record Office, MGA 186].

[1] George Harrison did, however, submit a design for the Houses of Parliament in his own name. He was Clerk of Works to the East India Company from *c.*1837 onwards.

[2] Cited below as 'M.B.W.'

BRAXTED PARK, ESSEX, work for Peter Du Cane (d. 1841) [M.B.W.].

CARCLEW, CORNWALL, alterations for Sir Charles Lemon, Bart., *c.*1830; gutted 1934 [M.B.W.; memoirs of Mrs. Loveday Sarah Gregor in Cornwall C.R.O].

EAST WOODHAY RECTORY, HANTS., for the Revd. T. D. Hodgson, 1828–9 [M.B.W.; Winchester Diocesan Records].

ENYS, CORNWALL, for J. S. Enys, 1833 [M.B.W.; signed drawings at Enys].

FAIRLIGHT RECTORY, SUSSEX, for the Revd. William Pearse, 1839, Tudor [M.B.W.].

FELTWELL RECTORY, NORFOLK, for the Revd. E. P. Sparke, 1832 [M.B.W.].

GOODRICH COURT, HEREFS., alterations or repairs for Col. Augustus Meyrick, *c.*1850; dem. 1950 [M.B.W.].

GREAT HAMPDEN RECTORY, BUCKS., addition of new drawing- and dining-rooms, 1820 [Lincs. Record Office, MGA 107].

HADLEIGH DEANERY (RECTORY), SUFFOLK, for the Revd. H. J. Rose, 1831, Tudor [M.B.W.].

HAM MANOR, ANGMERING, SUSSEX, for W. Gratwicke, *c.*1835 [M.B.W.].

HELIGAN, CORNWALL, alterations for J. H. Tremayne, *c.*1830 [M.B.W.; memoirs of Mrs. Loveday Sarah Gregor in Cornwall County Record Office].

?HESSENFORD CHURCH, CORNWALL, 1832–3. In June 1830 the incumbent wrote to the I.C.B.S. to say that Lord St. Germans had employed Harrison 'to inspect the plan [for rebuilding the church submitted by some local architect] and perhaps to furnish a new one'. The outcome is not known. The church was again rebuilt in 1871.

KINGSEY VICARAGE, BUCKS., remodelled 1834, Gothic [Lincs. Record Office, MGA 191].

LULLINGSTONE CASTLE, KENT, alterations or repairs for Sir Percival Hart-Dyke, probably *c.*1850 [M.B.W.] (*C. Life*, 1 Nov. 1913).

MARLBOROUGH, WILTS., ST. PETER'S RECTORY, 1832–3 [records of Queen Anne's Bounty in Bodleian Library].

NORMAN COURT, HANTS., enlarged for C. B. Wall, 1818–20; further alterations, including addition of Ionic pilasters, *c.*1910 [M.B.W.; G. F. Prosser, *Select Illustrations of Hampshire*, 1833].

OAKHAM VICARAGE, RUTLAND, for the Revd. Heneage Finch [M.B.W.].

PENDARVES, CORNWALL, alterations for E. W. W. Pendarves, 1832 [M.B.W.; memoirs of Mrs. Loveday Sarah Gregor in Cornwall County Record Office; drawing by Harrison for a lantern for Pendarves dated 1832 among drawings at Enys].

PENROSE, CORNWALL, EAST LODGE for the Revd. John Rogers, 1834, Tudor [signed drawing at Penrose, *ex inf.* Mr. Michael Trinick].

PORT ELIOT, CORNWALL, Gothic entrance hall and porch for 2nd Earl of St. Germans, 1829 [M.B.W.; C. Hussey in *C. Life*, 22–29 Oct. 1948].

PRIDEAUX, nr. LUXULYAN, CORNWALL, alterations for Sir Colman Rashleigh (d. 1847) [M.B.W.].

PUTNEY, SURREY, house in Putney Park Lane for Seymour Larpent [M.B.W.].

SAFFRON WALDEN, ESSEX, ALMSHOUSES, 1829–33, Gothic [Lord Braybrooke, *History of Audley End and Saffron Walden*, 1836, 236; drawings, specification etc., in papers of Nash, Son & Rowley in Cambs. C.R.O.].

STEEPLE ASHTON VICARAGE, WILTS., enlarged 1829–30 [Salisbury Diocesan Records].

SWYNCOMBE HOUSE, OXON., for the Revd. C. E. R. Keene, *c.*1830–40, Jacobean; dem. 1970s [M.B.W.].

TREWARTHENICK, CORNWALL, alterations and additions for C. W. F. Gregor, 1831; wings added by Harrison dem. 1925 [M.B.W.; J. Britton & E. W. Brayley, *Cornwall Illustrated*, 1831, 44; Gregor papers in Cornwall C.R.O.].

WARBOYS RECTORY, HUNTS., enlarged or rebuilt for the Revd. William Finch, 1829 [M.B.W.; Lincs. Record Office, MGA 152].[1]

WARE VICARAGE, HERTS., 1834–5 [London Diocesan Parsonage Papers in Guildhall Library, MS. 19227/30].

WARNHAM COURT, SUSSEX, for Henry Tredcroft,[2] 1829, Elizabethan [M.B.W.] (L. Jewitt & S. C. Hall, *The Stately Homes of England*, 2nd ser., n.d., 280–9).

WINWICK RECTORY, LANCS., alterations for the Revd. J. J. Hornby [M.B.W.].

WISBECH VICARAGE, CAMBS., for the Revd. H. R. Fardell, 1831 [M.B.W.; C.U.L., Ely Diocesan Records, Parsonage Papers, G 3/39/124].

LONDON HOUSES AND OTHER BUILDINGS

CAMBRIDGE SQUARE, No. 7 for Charles Harrison [M.B.W.].

THE GENERAL LYING-IN HOSPITAL, YORK ROAD, LAMBETH, 1828 [M.B.W.; *Survey of London* xxxiii (1), 42].

GROSVENOR SQUARE, No. 42 (formerly 37), in-

[1] Harrison was probably responsible for rebuilding the chancel of WARBOYS CHURCH in yellow brick in 1832, for in the same year he was employed to design new pews and galleries in the nave [I.C.B.S.].

[2] In his letter to the M.B.W. Harrison names his client at Warnham Court as Edward Tredcroft, who succeeded his father Henry in 1844. But it was Henry who built the house in 1829.

terior for the speculator Wright Ingle, who sold to 2nd Lord Wenlock, 1853; dem. [M.B.W.].

GROSVENOR STREET, No. 20, for Wright Ingle, 1852–3 [M.B.W.; *Survey of London* xl, 39].

THE GUARDS' CLUB-HOUSE, ST. JAMES'S STREET, 1828; dem. [M.B.W.; *Select Committee*, 86, 90].

THE GUARDS' CLUB-HOUSE, No. 70 PALL MALL, 1848–9; dem. 1922 [M.B.W.; *Survey of London* xxix, 380] (plan and elevation in *A New View of London*, J. Weale, 1853, i, 300–1).

OXFORD SQUARE, No. 22, for Frederick Harrison [M.B.W.].

PARK STREET, GROSVENOR SQUARE, Nos. 31 and 32 (later 54 and 56), 1825–6 (No. 31 was occupied by Harrison himself from 1828 to 1839) [M.B.W.].

PICCADILLY, No. 82, BATH HOUSE, rebuilt for Alexander Baring, cr. Lord Ashburton, 1821; interior remodelled *c.*1900; dem. 1963 [M.B.W.; *Select Committee*, 86].

RICHMOND TERRACE, WHITEHALL, 1822–5 [M.B.W.; *Select Committee*, 86].

UPPER BROOK STREET, No. 11, for Lt. Col. Sir Thomas Brotherton, 1852–3 [M.B.W.].

UPPER GROSVENOR STREET, Nos. 10 and 11 and No. 62 PARK STREET, 1843–4 [M.B.W.].

In addition, Harrison stated in 1856 that he had 'repaired or altered' the following houses: No. 51 GROSVENOR STREET, for Sir Jacob Astley and/or 11th Earl of Kinnoull, *c.*1826; No. 3 GROSVENOR SQUARE for James Balfour, 1831, dem. 1936; No. 27 BERKELEY SQUARE for Col. Meyrick; No. 61 GREEN STREET, GROSVENOR SQUARE, for 2nd Viscount Hampden (d. 1824) and for 11th Earl of Kinnoull, in or after 1833; No. 48 BERKELEY SQUARE, 'late in the occupation of Henry Baring'; No. 14 CARLTON HOUSE TERRACE for Genl. Robert Balfour, *c.*1831; Lady Glynne's house No. 36 BERKELEY SQUARE; No. 46 UPPER GROSVENOR STREET for 1st Earl of Carysfort, 1827–30, dem. 1937; THE ALFRED CLUB, No. 23 ALBEMARLE STREET; Col. Holder's house in CHARLES STREET, BERKELEY SQUARE; No. 10 CHARLES STREET, BERKELEY SQUARE, for 2nd Earl of Chatham (d. 1835), and subsequently for Lady De Dunstanville; No. 21 ST. JAMES'S SQUARE for the Bishop of Winchester, probably *c.*1830, dem. 1934; and No. 23 ST. JAMES'S SQUARE for James Angerstein.

HARRISON, JAMES, practised from addresses in Clerkenwell and Pentonville in the 1830s and 1840s. His exhibits at the Royal Academy show that he designed the following buildings: HALSON WOOD VILLA, SOUTH DEVON, for Richard Peck, 1831; THE HOLT, SOUTH DEVON, for William Jackson, 1833; DODBROOKE RECTORY, nr. KINGSBRIDGE, SOUTH DEVON, for the Revd. C. G. Owen, 1834 (exhibited 1837); a villa at TENBY, PEMBROKESHIRE, for Capt. Wells, 1839; and KENSAL HOUSE, HARROW ROAD, N.W. LONDON, for Alfred Haines, 1846. In 1844 two 'third rate' houses (dem.) were built to his designs on the E. side of HOLFORD SQUARE, PENTONVILLE [*Builder*, 20 July 1844, advt. for tenders].

HARRISON, JAMES, formerly a builder, practised as an architect in Sheffield in the second quarter of the nineteenth century. In 1828 he entered into a short-lived partnership with Samuel Worth (*q.v.*), in conjunction with whom he designed in 1829 the MEDICAL SOCIETY'S building or SURGEONS' HALL in SURREY STREET. In 1836 he designed the CIRCUS AND THEATRE. This was a building 'adapted both for dramatic performances and equestrian exercises'. It had 'a stately portico of the Ionic order'. [R. E. Leader, *Surveyors and Architects of the Past in Sheffield*, 1903; W. White, *Directory of the West Riding of Yorkshire* i, 1837, 85; S. Lewis, *Topographical Dictionary of England* iv, 1848, 62].

HARRISON, JOHN, was the nephew of the better-known Thomas Harrison (*q.v.*), whom he assisted in his practice in Chester. The relationship is made clear by correspondence between the two Chester architects and a Scottish baronet, Sir William Forbes, who in 1801 invited them to submit a design for a house to be built at Colinton near Edinburgh [Fettercairn papers, National Library of Scotland, box 27, and N.M.R.S.].

How far John Harrison practised independently is not clear, but in 1806 he was paid £20 'for planning and superintending the building of' SHERDLEY HALL, nr. ST. HELENS, LANCS. (dem.) for Michael Hughes [J. R. Harris, 'The Hughes Papers', *Trans. Hist. Soc. of Lancs. and Cheshire*, ciii, 1951, 115], and he evidently designed THE JEWISH SYNAGOGUE, SEEL STREET, LIVERPOOL, 1807, dem. 1874, for a view of it in Thomas Troughton's *History of Liverpool*, 1810, is dedicated to 'Mr. John Harrison Architect'. Sherdley Hall and the synagogue were both competently designed classical buildings.

HARRISON, JOSHUA (*c.*1772–1837), of Leicester, was a carpenter and builder who also acted as an architect and surveyor. He may have been a son of William Harrison (*q.v.*). In Leicester he built a new House of Correction for St. Mary's Parish in 1815 and was responsible for alterations to the ASSEM-

BLY ROOMS in 1817–18 [J. D. Bennett, *Leicestershire Architects 1700–1850*, 1966]. He designed a small Gothic church at ISLEY WALTON, LEICS., in 1819 [I.C.B.S.] and rebuilt HATHERN RECTORY, LEICS., in 1819–20 [drawings, etc. in Leicestershire Record Office]. He died on 24 April 1837, aged 65.

HARRISON, ROBERT, a mason, was concerned in the rebuilding of PENRITH CHURCH, CUMBERLAND, in 1721–3. He was paid £3 10s. 'for Drawing Plans for the Church', and, together with Joseph Simpson of Hawkside in the parish of Dalston, received £330 for carrying out the masonry work. It is not, however, certain that he designed the building, as William Dobson (probably a carpenter) and William Monkhouse (the clerk who kept the building accounts) were also paid for drawing plans [Cumbria Record Office, 110/1/57c].

HARRISON, THOMAS (1744–1829), the son of a joiner, was born at Richmond in Yorkshire, where he was baptized on 7 August 1744. He showed an early talent for arithmetic, mechanics and drawing, and attracted the attention of Sir Lawrence Dundas of Aske, by whose liberality he was sent to Italy in 1769 in company with his friend George Cuitt, the landscape-painter. While in Rome, he submitted to Pope Clement XIV a design for converting the Cortile del Belvedere in the Vatican into a museum which was favourably received, though not in the end adopted. In 1773 he competed for the annual architectural prize offered by the Academy of St. Luke, which carried with it eligibility for membership of the Academy. The subject (chosen by James Byres) was a town gateway decorated with columns and pilasters. The judges did not favour Harrison's design, but he appealed to the Pope against their verdict, claiming that he had been unfairly passed over, and was eventually admitted to the Academy by an exceptional exercise of the Pope's personal prerogative as patron of the institution. Harrison was subsequently commissioned to make a design for an alteration to the sacristy of St. Peter's, but the work was not carried out, probably owing to Pope Clement's death in 1774.[1]

Harrison returned to England in 1776, and in 1777 exhibited at the Royal Academy two drawings for remodelling the Piazza del Popolo in Rome. These showed that he was a master of the elegant neo-classical style fashionable on the Continent in the 1770s, though not yet aspiring to the simplified compositions which were to be characteristic of his later work as a Greek Revivalist. In 1779–80 he was back in Richmond, but in the 1780s he was living in Lancaster, and in 1795 he moved to Chester. At Lancaster he had in 1783 obtained an important commission for a bridge over the river Lune. The first stone was laid by George III, and the work was completed in 1788. This bridge was remarkable as the first large public bridge to be built in England with a level road surface from bank to bank. Its architectural treatment was highly effective, and Harrison's elliptical arches separated by pairs of Doric columns provided a formula which was afterwards employed by Rennie at Kelso Bridge, Waterloo Bridge and London Bridge. Further bridges followed at Derby and Kendal, and at Warrington and Cranage Harrison experimented successfully with a form of laminated timber construction. In 1776–8 he made designs for a triumphal bridge over the Thames on the site of the future Waterloo Bridge, but when the idea of a bridge in that position finally came to fruition in 1809 he was not employed, though his criticisms of the design made by the engineer Dodd are said to have played their part in persuading the commissioners to engage John Rennie instead. Harrison was also unsuccessful in putting forward a plan for a quay along the Thames from Westminster to the City which would have anticipated the Victorian Embankment. His biggest work as a bridge-builder was the Grosvenor Bridge at Chester, begun in 1827, and not completed until after his death. At the time of its construction its 200 foot span constituted the largest stone arch in the world. In view of Harrison's age and ill-health, its execution was entrusted to his pupil William Cole and the civil engineer Jesse Hartley, who (apart from raising the abutments one foot in height) adhered faithfully to Harrison's design.

Although Harrison designed several country houses, of which the most notable was Lord Elgin's Broomhall, it was as a civic architect that he made his reputation. The public buildings with which he adorned Manchester, Liverpool and Chester demonstrate his ability as a designer of monumental neo-classical architecture. His Chester Castle complex forms the finest group of Greek Revival buildings in Britain – the neo-classical counterpart to Greenwich Hospital – and the Anglesey Column, the Memorial Arch at Holyhead and the Jubilee Tower on Moel Fammau were among the most notable public monuments of their age. Though Harrison was best known as a classical architect, handling the Greek Doric and Ionic Orders with unfailing assurance and sensitivity, he also

[1] The Pope also gave Harrison two medals which are now in the Chester City Record Office.

used Gothic on occasion, notably at Lancaster Castle and in the highly effective steeple which he added to St. Nicholas Church in Liverpool. In either style his bold sense of mass, his concern with the quality of masonry and his capacity to design in three dimensions set his work apart from the stereotyped Gothic boxes and Grecian porticos characteristic of so much early nineteenth-century British architecture. Although his practice was limited geographically to the north-western counties, Harrison enjoyed a high reputation among contemporary architects. 'Harrison', wrote C. R. Cockerell in 1823, 'has a spark divine.' 'Almost, if not quite, the first architectural genius in the kingdom' was the verdict of his first biographer, Canon Blomfield, in 1863. Only his isolation in Chester and a natural diffidence prevented him from becoming a national figure like Soane or Smirke. The diffidence is well attested: 'a plain man in person and manners, with an embarrassed delivery in conversation; but very clear and ready in explaining with his pencil' was how Joseph Farington remembered him in 1795. 'A man of great modesty and diffidence – shy, reserved and abrupt in his manner', wrote Canon Blomfield, 'He . . . followed the profession from a mere love of the art, and not with a view to pecuniary emoluments . . . His personal qualities in some measure hindered his popularity with the world, and prevented him from becoming the public man which his genius and talents certainly entitled him to be.'

Harrison held only one public office, the county surveyorship of Cheshire, to which he was appointed in 1815 at £100 per annum. He was elected a Fellow of the Royal Society in 1804. He died at his house (St. Martin's Lodge) facing the Castle on 29 March 1829 aged 84, and was buried in St. Bridget's churchyard. He left a widow and two daughters. A portrait in oil by H. Wyatt is in the Grosvenor Museum at Chester, and another by the same artist is in the Cheshire Record Office. A portrait in chalk by John Downman, dated 1815, is in the Grosvenor Museum. An engraving of a portrait by A. R. Burt was published in 1824. There is also a lithograph by M. Gauci of one of Wyatt's portraits. The R.I.B.A. has a silhouette profile (reproduced in *C. Life*, 15 April 1971, fig. 1). A marble bust by George Caldwell, exhibited at the Liverpool Academy in 1824, appears to have been the original of the plaster busts now or formerly in the Portico Library at Manchester and the Lyceum at Liverpool, both of which are, however, dated 1839.

The most important collections of Harrison's drawings are in the Chester City Archives and the Cheshire Museums Services at Northwich. The former collection was presented to the Chester Archaeological Society by Miss Harrison in 1849. Other drawings are in the Grosvenor Museum at Chester, the County Record Office, the R.I.B.A. Drawings Collection and the Yale Center for British Art.

Harrison's principal pupils were William Cole, jr., Thomas Penson, John Hargrave of Cork and his nephew John Harrison (*q.v.*). James Harrison (1814–1866), who was in practice in Chester in the mid-nineteenth century, was apparently unrelated to Thomas.

[*A.P.S.D.*; *D.N.B.*; obituary in *Gent's Mag.* 1829 (i), 468–70; Michaud, *Biographie Universelle* xviii, 1857, 496–7; memoir by Canon Blomfield in *Builder* xxi, 1863, 203–5; J. Hemingway, *History of Chester*, 1831, i, 364–5, ii, 362–4; *The Cheshire Sheaf*, 3rd ser. i, 1896, 74 (for Harrison's will); *The Farington Diary* ed. J. Greig, i, 126, ii, 167, v, 101, vi, 227; Luigi Pirotta, 'Thomas Harrison architetto inglese accademico di San Luca per sovrano motu proprio', *Strenna dei Romanisti* xxi, 1960, 257–63; J. Mordaunt Crook, 'The Architecture of Thomas Harrison', *C. Life*, 14 & 22 April, 6 May 1971; exhibition catalogues: *The Modest Genius*, Grosvenor Museum, Chester 1977, *Thomas Harrison and Architecture of the Greek Revival*, Whitworth Art Gallery, Manchester 1981; M. A. R. Ockrim, 'The Life and Work of Thomas Harrison of Chester', unpublished Ph.D. thesis, Courtauld Institute of Art, London, 1988; information from Mr. F. R. Altmann, Prof. J. Mordaunt Crook and Mr. Peter Howell.]

PUBLIC BUILDINGS, ETC.

LANCASTER, cupola of TOWN HALL, 1782 [K. H. Docton in *Lancashire & Cheshire Historian*, Aug. 1965, 146–7].

LANCASTER, SKERTON BRIDGE (R. Lune), 1783–8 [*Historical and Descriptive Account of the Town of Lancaster*, C. Clark, Lancaster 1807, 43].

LANCASTER, ST. JOHN'S CHAPEL, tower and spire, 1784 [*op. cit.*, 39].

LANCASTER CASTLE, reconstruction, including new SHIRE HALL, GRAND JURY ROOM, GAOL, etc., 1788–99, Gothic; completed by J. M. Gandy 1802–23 [*A.P.S.D.*; J. M. Crook in *C. Life*, 15 April 1971, with illustrations].

CHESTER CASTLE, THE COUNTY COURTS, PRISON, ARMOURY, BARRACKS, EXCHEQUER and GATEWAY, 1788–1822. The Shire Hall was built 1792–1801, the flanking wings in 1804–10 and the gateway or propylaeum in 1811–13 [J. M. Crook in *C. Life*, 15 April 1971, with illustrations; Moira A. R. Ockrim, 'Thomas

Harrison and the Rebuilding of Chester Castle', *Jnl. Chester Archl. Soc.* 66, 1983].

DERBY, ST. MARY'S BRIDGE (R. Derwent), 1788–93 [*A.P.S.D.*].

HARRINGTON BRIDGE, SAWLEY, DERBYSHIRE (R. Trent), 1789–90 [contract in Harrington papers, Derbyshire C.R.O., D 518 M/Z 1–2].

KENDAL, WESTMORLAND, STRAMONGATE BRIDGE (R. Kent), 1793–4 [A. C. Taylor, 'Thomas Harrison and the Stramongate Bridge, Kendal', *Trans. Cumberland and Westmorland Arch. Soc.* N.S. lxix, 1969, 275–9].

LIVERPOOL, THE LYCEUM (Library and News-room), BOLD STREET, 1800–3 [*The Stranger in Liverpool*, 1837, 39].

MIDDLEWICH, CHESHIRE, HOUSE OF CORRECTION. enlarged 1801–2 [Ockrim, citing Cheshire Q.S. Records].

MANCHESTER, THE PORTICO LIBRARY, MOSLEY STREET (now Lloyd's Bank), 1802–6 [*A.P.S.D.*; T. Pratt, *The Portico Library, Manchester*, 1922].

CHESTER, ST. PETER'S CHURCH, refaced south side 1804 and tower 1811 [F. Simpson, *History of St. Peter's Church, Chester*, 1909, 12; *Cheshire Sheaf* xl, 1945, 120].

WHITTINGTON CHURCH, SHROPSHIRE, rebuilt nave 1805–6; tracery inserted in windows and other alterations 1894 [W. Cathrall, *History of Oswestry*, 1855, 281; D. H. S. Cranage, *Churches of Shropshire*, 1894–1901, ii, 836].

MANCHESTER, THE THEATRE ROYAL, 1806; burned 1844 [*A.P.S.D.*].

MANCHESTER, THE EXCHANGE AND COMMERCIAL BUILDINGS, 1806–9; enlarged by A. W. Mills 1847–8; dem. 1871–2 [E. Simpson, *A Sketch of the History of the Manchester Royal Exchange*, 1875; J. G. C. Parsons, *The Centenary of the Manchester Royal Exchange*, Manchester 1904].

CHESTER, CITY GAOL and HOUSE OF CORRECTION, NORTHGATE STREET, 1807–8; dem. [Ockrim, citing City Records].

CHESTER, THE NEWS-ROOM (now restaurant and City Club), NORTHGATE STREET, 1808 [*A.P.S.D.*; John Broster, *A Walk round the Walls and City of Chester*, 6th ed., 1821, 70].

CHESTER, THE NORTH GATE, for 2nd Earl Grosvenor, 1808–10 [inscription].

MOEL FAMMAU, DENBIGHSHIRE, OBELISK to commemorate King George III's Jubilee, 1810; damaged by a storm 1862 and now totally ruined [R. J. Edwards, *A History of the Jubilee Tower on Moel Vammau*, 1885; Peter Howell, 'The Jubilee Tower on Moel Fammau', *Arch. Hist.* 27, 1984].

DENBIGH, THE INFIRMARY, 1810–13 [R. Newcome, *Account of the Castle and Town of Denbigh*, 1829, 124–5].

LIVERPOOL, ST. NICHOLAS CHURCH, Gothic steeple 1811–15 [J. A. Picton, *Memorials of Liverpool* ii, 1875, 59].

CHESTER, HOLY TRINITY CHURCH, report on spire advising its demolition, 1811, printed by Hemingway, *History of Chester* ii, 1831, 93–4.

CHESTER, WESLEYAN METHODIST CHAPEL, ST. JOHN STREET, 1811; refronted 1906 [John Broster, *A Walk round the Walls and City of Chester*, 6th ed., 1821, 60].

WARRINGTON, LANCS., timber bridge (R. Mersey), 1812; replaced 1837 [*A.P.S.D.*; contract in Cheshire C.R.O., QAR 18].

SHREWSBURY, LORD HILL'S COLUMN, 1814–16, minor modifications to design by Edward Haycock (*q.v.*) [T. J. Howell, *The Stranger in Shrewsbury*, 1816, 79–80; *Gent's Mag.* 1817 (ii), 393].

HIGH LEGH, CHESHIRE, WEST HALL CHAPEL, 1814–16 (Ionic); burned 1891 and rebuilt as parish church [J. H. Hanshall, *History of Cheshire*, 1817, 398].

LLANFAIRPWLL, ANGLESEY, THE ANGLESEY COLUMN, 1816 [*A.P.S.D.*].

LIVERPOOL, ST. PAUL'S CHURCH, inserted ceiling in dome, 1818; dem. 1932 [*Gent's Mag.* 1829 (ii), 511].

CHESTER CATHEDRAL, repairs to exterior, 1818–19 [C. Hiatt, *Chester Cathedral*, 1905, 17; R. V. H. Burne, 'Chester Cathedral 1787–1837', *Jnl. Chester and N. Wales Arch. Soc.* xliii, 1956, 16–17].

HOLYHEAD, ANGLESEY, MEMORIAL ARCH to commemorate the landing in 1821 of King George IV, 1824 [*A.P.S.D.*] (R.C.H.M. *Anglesey*, pl. 128).

OXFORD, MAGDALEN COLLEGE, completed the unfinished ends of the NEW BUILDING, 1824 [*V.C.H. Oxon.* iii, 206]. Harrison also made unexecuted designs for rebuilding the College: see T. S. R. Boase, 'An Oxford College and the Gothic Revival', *Jnl. Warburg and Courtauld Institutes* xviii, 1955, 157–8.

CHESTER, widened the OLD DEE BRIDGE, 1825–6 [City Archives].

CHESTER, THE GROSVENOR BRIDGE, 1827–33, executed by James Trubshaw under the supervision of William Cole, junior, with Jesse Hartley, C.E., as clerk of works [J. W. Clarke, 'The Building of the Grosvenor Bridge', *Trans. Chester and N. Wales Arch. Soc.* xlv, 1958]. Some of Harrison's drawings are in the Yale Center for British Art.

CRANAGE, CHESHIRE, timber bridge (R. Dane) [S. Lewis, *Topographical Dictionary of England* i, 1831, 536].

CHESTER, THE EXCHANGE, NORTHGATE STREET, alterations to interior; destroyed by fire

1862 [John Broster, *A Walk round the Walls and City of Chester*, 6th ed. 1821, 72].

DOMESTIC ARCHITECTURE

LANCASTER, houses in MARKET STREET, CASTLE HILL and MEETING-HOUSE LANE, for Thomas Rawlinson, 1784 [Ockrim, citing Borough of Lancaster Minutes 1756–94, 243, 14 Dec. 1784].

KENNET HOUSE, CLACKMANNANSHIRE, for Robert Bruce, 1793–4; dem. 1967 [Sir J. Sinclair, *Statistical Account of Scotland* xiv, 1795, 616].

GOSFORD HOUSE, EAST LOTHIAN, modified Robert Adam's designs for house under construction, for which he was paid £31 10s. 6d. by 7th Earl of Wemyss in 1794 [N.M.R.S., extracts from Wemyss accounts at Gosford House].

QUERNMORE PARK HALL, LANCS., built 1795–8 for Charles Gibson, is said by Sir B. Burke, *Visitations of Seats and Arms*, 1st ser. i, 1852, 153, to have been designed by Harrison, but the drawings in the Lancs. C.R.O. are unsigned and the attribution cannot be regarded as quite certain. The neo-classical central hall is by A. W. Mills of Manchester, 1842.

BROOMHALL, FIFE, for 7th Earl of Elgin, 1796–9. The north front was left incomplete until 1865-6 when the existing porch was built to the designs of C. H. Wilson and David Thomson of Glasgow [J. M. Crook in *C. Life*, 29 Jan. 1970].

COLINTON HOUSE, MIDLOTHIAN, for Sir William Forbes, Bart., 1801, the elevation being drawn by Richard Crichton to correspond to Harrison's plan [N.L.S., Acc. 4796/47, f. 3, 48 f. 1 and 4796/222].

attributed: GLAN-YR-AFON, nr. MOLD, FLINTSHIRE, for Henry Potts, *c.*1810; enlarged 1890 [Henry Potts was Clerk of the Peace for Cheshire and as such closely involved in the building of the County Court at Chester Castle by Harrison, who later designed Watergate House, Chester, for him].

TABLEY HOUSE, CHESHIRE, formation of Picture Gallery for Sir John F. Leicester, Bart., *c.*1810 [R. Ackermann, *Repository of Arts*, 3rd ser., ii, 1823; cf. D. & S. Lysons, *Magna Britannia* ii, (2), 1810, 532].

GREDINGTON, nr. HANMER, FLINTSHIRE, for 2nd Lord Kenyon, 1810–15 [S. Lewis, *Topographical Dictionary of Wales* i, 1849, 399; unsigned drawings at Gredington].

OUGHTRINGTON HALL, LYMM, CHESHIRE, entrance-lodge and gates for Trafford Trafford, *c.*1810/20 [Mogg's edition of *Paterson's Roads*, 1826, 467].

WOODBANK, nr. STOCKPORT, CHESHIRE, for Peter Marsland, 1812 [E. Twycross, *The Mansions of England: Cheshire* ii, 1850, 127].

DEE HILLS, nr. CHESTER, for Robert Baxter, 1814 [J. Hemingway, *History of Chester* i, 1831, 429].

ALLERTON, LANCS., GROVE HOUSE for Jacob Fletcher, *c.*1815; gutted by fire 1944 [R. Stewart-Brown, *History of Allerton*, 1911, 184–5].

CHIRK CASTLE, DENBIGHSHIRE, Gothic vaulting, probably in the south-east tower, for Robert Myddelton-Biddulph, *c.*1820 [J. Parker, *The Passengers*, 1831, 6].

CHESTER, ST. MARTIN'S LODGE, for himself, *c.*1820 (*C. Life*, 22 April 1971, 944, fig. 2).

CHESTER, WATERGATE HOUSE, WATERGATE STREET, for Henry Potts, 1820 [*A.P.S.D.*].

HARDWICK GRANGE, nr. HADNALL, SHROPSHIRE, for General Lord Hill, *c.*1820, Gothic; dem. [J. P. Neale, *Views of Seats*, 2nd ser., iii, 1826].

TILSTONE LODGE, CHESHIRE, for Admiral J. R. D. Halliday, 1821–5 [P. de Figueiredo & J. Treuherz, *Cheshire Country Houses*, 1988, 179].

DORFOLD HALL, CHESHIRE, unexecuted designs for alterations and additions for the Revd. James Tomkinson, 1822, resulting in minor alterations attributable to Harrison [drawings at Dorfold, *ex inf.* Prof. A. Gomme].

HAWKSTONE, SHROPSHIRE, THE CITADEL, for Sir Rowland Hill, Bart., 1824–5, castellated [Arthur Oswald in *C. Life*, 21 Aug. 1958].

HOOLE HOUSE, CHESHIRE, added veranda, conservatory, etc. for Lady Broughton [J. C. Loudon, *Gardener's Mag.* xiv, 1838, 353–62].

RUSSIA

Harrison designed a tower or lighthouse on the Black Sea coast for Count Michael Woronzow, the Russian ambassador to Britain. He also made designs, *c.*1822, for a Greek Revival palace for Count Woronzow to be built in the Ukraine on the banks of the Dnieper, but these were never carried out [*Gent's Mag.* 1829 (i), 470]. The drawings are among those in the City Archives and Grosvenor Museum at Chester.

Note: The following ascriptions must be regarded as erroneous: Ashburton House, Piccadilly, London (by Henry Harrison, *q.v.*); the Sessions House at Knutsford, Cheshire (by George Moneypenny, *q.v.*); The Liverpool Athenaeum (by John Foster, *q.v.*); Seggieden, Perthshire (apparently by John Paterson, *q.v.*); Swarkeston Bridge, Derbyshire (by Samuel Lister, *q.v.*), Talacre Hall, Flintshire (by Thomas Jones, *q.v.*). The 'house for General Abercrombie' mentioned in *A.P.S.D.* was almost certainly not built.

HARRISON, WILLIAM (*c.*1742–1794), was an architect and surveyor of Leicester, where he died on 21 November 1794, 'after a long illness' [*Gent's Mag.* 1794, 1154]. He designed the LUNATIC ASYLUM that was added to Leicester Infirmary in 1781 and supervised the building of the COUNTY GAOL to the designs of George Moneypenny in 1790–2. His own rejected designs for the gaol, dated 1789, are among the County Records (QS 32/3/8) [J. D. Bennett, *Leicestershire Architects 1700–1850*, 1966; *V.C.H. Leics.* iv, 372]. In 1781–3 Harrison carried out minor works at the Elizabethan DALBY HALL, LEICS., for Edward Hartopp Wigley [Leics. C.R.O., LMAD/8/d/39/0205, etc. *ex inf.* Prof. A. Gomme].

HARTLEY, BERNARD, was the name of three generations of masons and architects of Pontefract in Yorkshire. Bernard Hartley I (1745–1834) was the son of Hugh Hartley, a mason active in Yorkshire in the reign of George II. In 1797 Bernard Hartley I was appointed Surveyor of Bridges to the West Riding of Yorkshire, a post which he retained until his death in 1834 at the age of 89. An inscription on FERRYBRIDGE BRIDGE shows that Hartley built it to the designs of John Carr (*q.v.*) in 1797–1804, and in 1803 the West Riding magistrates gave him a gratuity of £200 for the trouble he had taken in this work, and for inventing a pile-driving machine worked by one horse and two men 'and capable of doing the work of 40 men'. In 1805 he built CASTLEFORD BRIDGE, evidently to his own designs, for it is inscribed 'BERNARD HARTLEY ARCHITECT 1805'. In 1819 Bernard Hartley II (1779–1855) was appointed Surveyor of Bridges jointly with his father, and when he died in 1855 he was succeeded by his son Bernard Hartley III, who retired in 1882. Thus for nearly a hundred years the maintenance of the county bridges was in the hands of this family.

Bernard Hartley I designed the TOWN HALL at PONTEFRACT, built in 1785 in a style similar to that of John Carr [*The Book of Entries of the Pontefract Corporation 1653–1726*, ed. R. Holmes, Pontefract 1882, 26]. He was also responsible for rebuilding the steeple of ST. GILES CHURCH, PONTEFRACT, in 1790–1, following the existing design with its open crown [papers in W. Yorks. Archives, Wakefield]. In 1799–1800 he was engaged in alterations to WOOLLEY HALL, YORKS. (W.R.), for Godfrey Wentworth [G. Markham, *Woolley Hall*, Wakefield 1979, 38–9]. A design by him for a pair of shops, made for University College, Oxford, no doubt for their Pontefract estate, is in the archives of that college.

In 1806 Bernard Hartley II submitted designs for the Court House at Wakefield, but those of Charles Watson were preferred. According to the *Leeds Intelligencer*, 22 June 1833, 5 Sept. 1834 (*ex inf.* Dr. D. Linstrum), he, rather than James Richardby (*q.v.*), was the architect of the COURT HOUSE at BRADFORD, YORKS. (W.R.), 1833–4; dem. *c.*1960, and in 1837–8 the COURT OR SESSIONS HOUSE at KNARESBOROUGH, YORKS. (W.R.), was built to his designs [*Leeds Intelligencer*, 5 May 1838, *ex inf.* Dr. D. Linstrum]. In 1843–7 he designed the NEW PRISON at WAKEFIELD, with a handsome classical gateway in the style of Sanmichele, dem. 1980 [J. Horsfall Turner, *Annals of Wakefield House of Correction*, privately printed, Bingley 1904, 204–6]. Designs by him for LEDSHAM VICARAGE, 1821, are in the Borthwick Institute at York (MGA 1821/2 and cf. 1814/2).

Jesse Hartley (1780–1860), well known as the Surveyor to the Liverpool Dock Trustees from 1824 to 1860 and as the designer of the Albert Dock there, was the younger son of Bernard Hartley I, and was born at Pontefract in Dec. 1780. He was succeeded by his son John Bernard Hartley (1814–69).

[West Riding Quarter Sessions Order Books; Bishop's Transcripts of Pontefract Parish Registers at Borthwick Institute, York; *Gent's Mag.* 1834 (i), 342; obituary of Jesse Hartley in *Minutes of Proceedings of the Institution of Civil Engineers* xxxiii, 1871–2 (i), 219.]

HARVEY, FREDERICK (1779–1861), was an architect and builder at Ipswich. He designed HOLY TRINITY CHURCH, IPSWICH, 1836, in a simple classical style; RUSHMERE VICARAGE, SUFFOLK, 1827; ST. HELEN with ST. CLEMENT'S SCHOOL, IPSWICH, 1843, Tudor style; and repaired and partly rebuilt the ALMSHOUSES in HIGH STREET, NEEDHAM MARKET, SUFFOLK, 1836 [C. Brown *et al.*, *Dictionary of Architects of Suffolk Buildings 1800–1914*, 1991, 120]. He also built, and perhaps designed, LEVINGTON HOUSE nr. IPSWICH for Major Charles Walker shortly before 1830 [G. R. Clarke, *History & Description of Ipswich*, 1830, 377]. In 1833 he exhibited a design for a cast-iron aqueduct in the Gothic style at the Royal Academy.

HARVEY, JACOB (1783–1867), was a speculative builder who, with his sons John Tapley Harvey and William Harvey, was responsible for the developments which made Torquay a Victorian seaside resort. The initiative came from the principal landowner, Sir Lawrence Palk, but Harvey and his sons supplied the designs and did the building. Harvey came to Torquay a poor man, but when he died in January 1867 at the age of 84 he was a leading figure in the town he had so largely built. One of the earliest of Harvey's developments was HIGHER TERRACE (*c.*1811), followed by PARK PLACE, PARK CRESCENT, VAUGHAN PARADE (*c.*1830) and BEACON TERRACE. HESKETH CRESCENT, designed in a quite sophisticated style reminiscent of Brighton or Cheltenham, was the firm's most ambitious development. It was built in 1845–8 to the designs of J. T. and W. Harvey, who (unlike their builder father) described themselves as 'architects'. Their later works included THE MARKET (1852), a house called ROCKWOOD for the Hon. J. Boyle (1857) and the TORBAY HOTEL (1866). [A. C. Ellis, *An Historical Survey of Torquay*, 1930, *passim*].

HARVEY, JOHN, was the name borne by three generations of masons working in Bath during the early part of the eighteenth century. The second of the name designed and built the first PUMP ROOM in 1706, and it was probably his son, the third John Harvey, who rebuilt the church of ST. MICHAEL EXTRA MUROS in *c.*1735–42. John Wood had offered to rebuild the church partly at his own expense on conditions which were rejected by the vestry, and his displacement by Harvey explains the severe criticism to which St. Michael's is subjected in Wood's *Essay towards a Description of Bath.* It was in fact a handsome Georgian classical church ingeniously planned to fit an awkward site, but the architecture belonged to the age of Archer and Hawksmoor rather than to that of Colen Campbell and John Wood. It was demolished in 1835 to make way for the existing church by G. P. Manners. [W. Ison, *The Georgian Buildings of Bath*, 1948, 30, 60–1, 70–1, 2nd ed. 1980, 4, 38, 41, 53; plan of St. Michael's Church in I.C.B.S. records.]

HARVEY, JOHN (–*c.*1835), was probably the pupil and certainly the assistant of Samuel Wyatt, whose office he entered in or before 1785. In 1792, when he was elected to membership of the Surveyors' Club, he was described as being 'at Mr. Wyatt's, Berwick Street, Soho', and in 1794, when Wyatt's designs for Trinity House were exhibited at the Royal Academy, they were attributed to Wyatt in the text, but to Harvey in the index, of the Catalogue. Harvey continued to occupy Wyatt's house at 36 Berwick Street after the latter moved to Albion Place in 1803, and he was still living there at the time of his death in *c.*1835. He was probably related to Wyatt, for the latter's uncle William Wyatt (d. 1772) married a Mary Harvey.

Harvey's first important commission was the SHIRE HALL at STAFFORD, built in 1795–7 and illustrated as his work in Richardson's *New Vitruvius Britannicus* ii, 1808, pls. 7–10. Stafford was in the Wyatts' territory, and Harvey no doubt owed the commission to Samuel's good offices: indeed the building appears to have been a joint design, for the Quarter Sessions Order Book shows that on 14 November 1793 it was resolved 'that Mr. Wyatt's plan of the proposed New County Hall . . . with Mr. Harvey's elevation marked A be adopted subject to such alterations as have been suggested by the Magistrates respecting the Grand Jury Room'.

In 1805 Harvey succeeded James Wyatt as Deputy Surveyor to the Office of Woods and Forests, but was dismissed for incompetence after little more than a year in office [P.R.O., CREST 8/2–3]. In 1813 he took the place of Thomas Hardwick as architect in charge of the erection of the MILLBANK PENITENTIARY, but proved unable to cope with the legacy of insecure foundations left by his predecessor, and was superseded by Sir Robert Smirke [G. Holford, *An Account of the Penitentiary at Millbank*, 1828, xxix–xxxii]. His only other recorded works appear to be alterations to COMPTON PLACE, SUSSEX, for Lord George Cavendish, *c.*1808 [*R.I.B.A. Drawings Catalogue*: *C. Campbell,* 9] and the interior of the library at LITTLE GLEMHAM HALL, SUFFOLK, designed for Dudley North in 1811 [drawings in Kent Archives Office, U 471, P 6].

Harvey was President of the Surveyors' Club in 1803. He exhibited regularly at the Royal Academy from 1785 to 1810, showing *inter alia* a design for a stone bridge of 400-foot span over the Menai Straits (1787), the river front of a design for new Houses of Parliament (1790) and a design for a new London Bridge constructed of cast iron (1801) – all of which may well have been ideas suggested by Samuel Wyatt. J. L. Harvey, who entered the R.A. Schools in 1809, and exhibited an architectural drawing at the Academy the same year, was probably Harvey's son, for his address is given as '62 Berwick Street'.

HASSALL, RICHARD, *see* BAKER, RICHARD.

HASTIE, WILLIAM (*c.*1755–1832), was a Scot who had a distinguished career as an architect in Russia. Nothing is known of his early life in Scotland, but he was one of a number of Scottish artisans who went out to

Russia in 1784 in response to an advertisement placed by Charles Cameron (*q.v.*) in the *Edinburgh Evening News* (21 Jan.). He was then described as a stonemason, but by 1794 he was (perhaps as a result of Charles Cameron's tuition) making technically accomplished architectural designs, and between 1795 and 1799 he was employed as an architect in the Crimea by Prince Platon Zubov, the Governor of the Ekaterinoslav and Taurida regions. He subsequently worked in St. Petersburg, where he was the pioneer in the design and construction of cast-iron bridges and was much employed as a town-planner. The layout of Tsarskoe Selo was designed by him in 1808, and he was also concerned in town-planning projects at Kiev, Vilna, Smolensk, Ekaterinoslav, Tomsk and elsewhere. In 1813 he made a plan for rebuilding Moscow after its destruction by fire, and, although it was not accepted, many of his ideas were adopted in the plan finally approved in 1818. Hastie died at Tsarskoe Selo on 4 June 1832. [Miliza Korshunova, 'William Hastie in Russia', *Arch. Hist.* 17, 1974.]

HASWELL, GEORGE (–1784), was for many years the Duke of Argyll's chief wright at INVERARAY CASTLE, ARGYLLSHIRE, where he was responsible for the carpentry work from 1750 onwards. In 1778, as 'Mr. Haswell, architect, of Inveraray', he designed CASTLEHILL CHURCH, CAMPBELTOWN, which was built to his designs by an Inveraray mason named John Brown in 1778–80 [S.R.O., HR 67/1; R.C.A.M., *Argyll* i, 103], and in the Scottish Record Office there is a plan for seating SOUTHEND CHURCH, KINTYRE, ARGYLLSHIRE, signed by him and dated 1779 [RHP 7175]. He died at Inveraray on 24 March 1784 [I. G. Lindsay & Mary Cosh, *Inveraray and the Dukes of Argyll*, 1973, 417].

HATCHARD, CHARLES (*c.*1789–1849) was an architect and surveyor practising from Lower Belgrave Place, Pimlico. He was elected to membership of the Surveyors' Club in 1826 and was President of the Club in 1830. In 1824–5 he rebuilt EPSOM CHURCH, SURREY, in the Gothic style, retaining the medieval tower [E. W. Brayley, *Topographical History of Surrey* iv, 1850, 357]. He also designed the front of ALDRIDGE'S CATTLE AUCTION ROOMS on the west side of St. Martin's Lane, London, 1843; dem. 1955 [Hermione Hobhouse, *Lost London*, 1971, 189], and NANTCEIRO HALL, LLANBADARN FAWR, nr. ABERYSTWYTH, CARDIGANSHIRE, for John Morgan, 1847; extended 1878 [signed drawings at Nantceiro, *ex inf.* Mr. Thomas Lloyd]. Hatchard died in Ebury Street on 15 Sept. 1849, aged 60 [*Gent's Mag.* 1849 (ii), 551].

HATTON, THOMAS, was a pupil of Samuel Robinson and exhibited student's designs at the Royal Academy from his office from 1799 to 1801. In 1802 he began independent practice from 16 Dean Street, Southwark. His subsequent exhibits at the R.A. indicate that he was responsible for the following buildings: a cottage at MOUNT PLEASANT, nr. CROUCH END in north London for H. St. John, 1802; a house on DARTMOUTH HILL, BLACKHEATH, for J. Green, 1806; and the 'PUBLIC PORTER' BREWHOUSE, WESTON STREET, SOUTHWARK, 1809. He was still at Dean Street in 1825–6, but disappears from the directories soon afterwards.

HAUDUROY, S—, was a French Huguenot architect employed by William Blathwayt at DYRHAM PARK, GLOS., where he designed the west front in 1692. He is referred to in the building records as 'Mr. Hauduroy', but in his one surviving letter signs himself 'S. Hauduroy'. He may have been the Samuel Hauduroy who appears as a godfather in the records of the Huguenot church in Threadneedle Street in 1691. A drawing at Dyrham of the 'Porte de la Chambre du Conseil', offered as a pattern for a doorway, is presumably in his hand. Two other members of the family, Louis and Mark Antony Hauduroy, were painters. Louis was responsible for decorative painting (now destroyed) on the staircase at CULVERTHORPE HALL, LINCS., in 1704–5, and signs the illusionist architectural paintings in Archer's pavilion at WREST PARK BEDS., which are dated 1712 [Mark Girouard, 'Dyrham Park, Glos.', *C. Life*, 15 Feb. 1962; E. Croft-Murray, *Decorative Painting in England* i, 1962, 248, ii, 1970, 218].

HAVERFIELD, JOHN (1744–1820), was the eldest son of John Haverfield (1705–1784), chief gardener of the royal gardens at Richmond and Kew, and succeeded him in that post. Although primarily a landscape-gardener, Haverfield also practised as an architect. In 1796 he made unexecuted designs for a new classical house to be built at Ettington Hall, Warwickshire [Warwicks. C.R.O., CR 229/119/1/1–9], and from about 1806 to 1816 he was responsible for extensive improvements at ABBEY HOUSE, LITTLE WALSINGHAM, NORFOLK, for Henry Lee-Warner. A man employed there as clerk of works sent Sir John Soane in 1826 an account of 'The Mansion & stables, Bridges and gardener's house, with hot house etc., keeper's lodge, Ice House, farm house and barns with various other improvements' that he had executed to the designs of 'that ever to be respected Mr. Haverfield' [Soane Museum, 16/13/2]. Haverfield died at Kew on 19 April 1820, aged 76. He was the great-grandfather of the archaeologist Francis Haverfield (1860–1919) [pedigree in Haverfield Library, Asmolean Museum, Oxford, CXII, B 1A]. A portrait of his daughter Elizabeth by Gainsborough is in the Wallace Collection.

HAVILAND, JOHN (1792–1852), born at Gundenham Manor, nr. Taunton, Somerset, on 15 December 1792, was the son of James Haviland, a country gentleman. On his mother's side he was connected with the artist Benjamin Haydon. He became a pupil of James Elmes, who, while ill, entrusted the erection of the chapel of St. John at Chichester to him (1812). His mother's sister had married Admiral Count Mordwinoff, then minister of works to the Emperor Alexander, and at his uncle's invitation he went to Russia to enter the Imperial Corps of Engineers; but meeting there representatives of the American government, he was induced to visit America, where he landed in September 1816. He settled in Philadelphia, where he designed a number of public buildings. He became well known as a prison architect, and his Eastern State Penitentiary at Philadelphia was the first prison built in the United States in accordance with the ideas of Howard and other prison reformers. He also designed many churches and private houses, principally in the Greek revival style. A manuscript 'Description of the Halls of Justice or House of Detention, New York', with drawings, is in the R.I.B.A. Drawings Collection, and twelve volumes of his sketches, specifications, and business correspondence are in the Somerset County Record Office at Taunton.

[Fiske Kimball in *Dictionary of American Biography* viii, 1932; *A.P.S.D.*; obituaries in *Builder* x, 1852, 341; *Gent's Mag.* 1852 (i), 629–30; and *Civil Engineer and Architect's Jnl.* xv, 227.]

HAWKINS, —, 'an Englishman', is said to have designed the central portion of BARGALY, nr. NEWTON STEWART, KIRKCUDBRIGHTSHIRE, for Andrew Heron in 1694–5 [B. M. H. Rogers, 'Andrew Heron and his Kinsfolk', *Trans. Dumfriesshire & Galloway Nat. Hist. & Antiq. Soc.* 3rd ser. v, 1916–18, 214]. It is possible, though unlikely, that this was the father of the lawyer Sir John Hawkins (1719–1789), an architect and surveyor who, according to his grand-daughter, was 'fonder of making one in any convivial hall, than of measuring its proportions, or sketching its decorations' [L. M. Hawkins, *Anecdotes, etc.*, 1822, 122–3].

HAWKSMOOR, NICHOLAS (*c.*1661–1736), was a native of Nottinghamshire, and was probably born either at Ragnall or at East Drayton, both villages near Tuxford where members of the Hawksmoor or Hawksmore family were yeomen farmers in the seventeenth century. Nothing is known of his education, but according to George Vertue he was employed as a clerk by Samuel Mellish of Doncaster, a J.P. whose family had property in Hawksmoor's part of Nottinghamshire. From Mellish's service he passed to that of Sir Christopher Wren, who, hearing of his 'early skill and genius' for architecture, took him as his clerk at about the age of 18. A topographical sketch-book now in the R.I.B.A. Drawings Collection contains some of Hawksmoor's early drawings, including a view of Bath Abbey dated 1683.[1] Their somewhat amateurish draughtmanship shows that at the age of 22 Hawksmoor was still learning the techniques of his new profession. As Wren's 'domestic clerk' he was to be associated with the Surveyor-General in nearly all his architectural works from *c.*1684 onwards, either as draughtsman, measurer, or clerk of the works. Thus he is said to have been employed as 'supervisor' under Wren at Winchester Palace (begun in 1683), for which he witnessed the brickmaker's contract in 1684, and to have acted in a similar capacity at Chelsea Hospital, where, at some date between 1687 and 1692, he was paid £10 'for drawing designs for the Hospitall'. His name as Wren's 'gentleman' occurs also in connection with the City churches, and there are many payments to him for assisting Wren in making working drawings for St. Paul's Cathedral between 1691 and 1712. In 1689 Wren obtained for Hawksmoor the post of Clerk of Works at William III's newly-purchased palace of Kensington, and in 1698 that of Clerk of Works at Greenwich Hospital in succession to Henry Symonds. The latter post Hawksmoor retained until 1735, the former until 1715, when he succeeded William Dickinson as Clerk of the Works at Whitehall, Westminster and St. James's. At the same time he obtained the newly-established post of Secretary to the Board of Works which, in accordance with the new regulations of 1715, went with his Clerkship of the Works and carried with it an additional salary of £100

[1] Some pages have been cut out of this book. One of them (a drawing of the cross at Coventry) is in the Bodleian Library (Gough Maps 233, f. 33).

per annum. Hawksmoor was now a senior official of the Royal Works and a likely candidate for further promotion. But in 1718, when Wren was superseded by William Benson, Hawksmoor was deprived of his dual office in order to provide a place for Benjamin Benson, the new Surveyor's brother. Only in 1726, when Benson's successor Hewett died, was Hawksmoor restored to his secretaryship, though not to the clerkship of the Works, which was given to Flitcroft. In 1696 Hawksmoor was appointed surveyor to the Commissioners of Sewers for Westminster, but was dismissed in 1700, 'having neglected to attend the Court several days last past' [G.L. Record Office, minutes of the Commissioners of Sewers].

In 1711, on the passing of the Act imposing a duty on coals for the purpose of building fifty new churches in London, Hawksmoor was one of the two surveyors appointed by the commissioners at a salary of £200 to carry the Act into effect, and it was in this capacity that he designed the six churches which are his best-known works. This appointment came to an end in 1733 on the termination of the commission, but Hawksmoor and his colleague John James were still being paid 'for carrying on and finishing the works under their care' up to the time of the former's death. After the death of Wren in 1723, Hawksmoor succeeded him as Surveyor to Westminster Abbey, a post which carried a salary of £100 out of the money voted by Parliament for the repair and completion of the Abbey in 1698. The west towers of the Abbey were designed by Hawksmoor in the course of his duties as Wren's successor, although they were not completed until after his death.

Meanwhile Hawksmoor had come into contact with Vanbrugh, who since 1702 had held the office of Comptroller of the Works, and who in 1716 succeeded Wren as Surveyor of Greenwich Hospital. Vanbrugh, like Wren, found Hawksmoor an able assistant, and employed him both at Castle Howard and at Blenheim Palace, where he acted as assistant surveyor from 1705 onwards, and ultimately took Vanbrugh's place as architect in charge after the latter's final breach with Sarah, Duchess of Marlborough. It was to Vanbrugh that Hawksmoor owed his advancement in 1715, and it was Vanbrugh who subsequently did his best to protect Hawksmoor from the predatory Benson and his successor Hewett. In July 1721 Vanbrugh made Hawksmoor his deputy as Comptroller of the Works, a position which he retained until Vanbrugh's death in 1726.

Although never officially employed by the Board of Ordnance, Hawksmoor designed at least one building (Berwick Barracks) for the Board, almost certainly at the behest of his and Vanbrugh's friend Brigadier Richards, the Surveyor General of the Ordnance, and probably designed other buildings erected by the Board in a similar style between 1715 and 1724, e.g. at Woolwich Arsenal (1717–20), Portsmouth and Plymouth Dockyards, and at Tilbury Fort and Upnor Castle.

Hawksmoor suffered all his life from 'the vile distemper of the gout', and it was from gout in the stomach that he died at his house in Millbank, Westminster, on 25 March 1736, leaving a widow, Hester, to whom he bequeathed all his property in Westminster, Highgate, Shenley (Herts.) and East Drayton (Notts.). He was buried at Shenley, where he is commemorated by a ledger-stone with a Latin inscription cut by the mason Andrews Jelfe. The inscription is given by Downes (*Hawksmoor*, 1959, 7). Hawksmoor's only child was a daughter, Elizabeth, whose second husband, Nathaniel Blackerby, was treasurer to the Commissioners for building the Fifty New Churches. It was Blackerby who wrote the obituary of his father-in-law which appeared in *Read's Weekly Journal*, No. 603, for 27 March 1736. The only known portrait of Hawksmoor is the bust by Cheere in the buttery of All Souls College, Oxford.

As the assistant and then the colleague first of Wren and then of Vanbrugh, Hawksmoor was brought into intimate contact with two of the greatest figures in the history of English architecture. There can be no doubt that he gave to the latter the expertise that he had gained from the former, and that it was Hawksmoor's collaboration that enabled Vanbrugh's heroic designs to be translated into actuality in spite of their author's lack of previous architectural experience. What influence Hawksmoor, having worked with Vanbrugh, had on Wren's later work, is a more difficult problem that cannot be discussed here; but it is at least arguable that Wren's own architectural development owed a good deal to the persuasion and example of his former pupil, who by 1700 had emerged as a major architectural personality in his own right. In the course of the next twenty years he was to prove himself to be one of the great masters of the English baroque, more assured in his command of the classical vocabulary than the untrained Vanbrugh, more imaginative in his vision than the intellectual Wren. No one understood better than Hawksmoor the dynamic deployment of architectural form or the dramatic possibilities of light and shade. The complex forms of the London churches, whether in internal planning or in external embellishment, are as eloquent as anything by Borromini, the Italian architect with whom Hawksmoor most obviously invites comparison. Although it is the fantastic side of baroque that is apparent in so many of his unexecuted designs, he could also be gravely classical, as in the Clarendon Building, St. George's, Bloomsbury, or the Mausoleum at Castle Howard. He could also be romantically Gothic, not only in situations (as at All Souls) where collegiate or ecclesiastical associations justified the adoption of that style, but also in the ostensibly classical towers of some of his churches, which recall the silhouette of a medieval steeple crowned with a lantern. Hawksmoor was indeed a master of architectural form, for whom Antiquity, the Renaissance, the English Middle Ages and contemporary Italian baroque (studied in engravings, for he never went abroad) were all exploited and transfused into a powerful personal style that constitutes one of the highest achievements of English classical architecture.

Hawksmoor had no pupil – unless Henry Joynes, his friend and assistant, can be regarded as such – and even before his death, the romantic approach to the classical past for which he stood had begun to give way to the more rigid canons of Palladian correctitude. Both at Castle Howard, where the mausoleum which he had designed was given a staircase copied from that of Lord Burlington's villa at Chiswick, and at Blenheim, where the Column of Victory, for which he had made so many sketches, was finally 'conducted by my Lord Herbert', his work was subjected to Palladian discipline. At Oxford, his designs for the Radcliffe Library, first made in 1712, and represented by a wooden model which is still preserved, remained in abeyance for lack of funds. At Cambridge he had seen his place as architect of the new buildings at King's College taken by Gibbs. These disappointments, coupled with the loss of his offices in 1718, and the appointment of Thomas Ripley to the surveyorship of Greenwich Hospital over his head in 1729, may perhaps account for the somewhat querulous tone of some of his letters to the Duchess of Marlborough, and for the disillusionment which is so clear in his portrait bust. 'Poor Hawksmoor', wrote Vanbrugh in 1721, 'what a Barbarous Age have his fine, ingenious, parts fallen into. What wou'd Monsr. Colbert in France have given for such a man?' But something may have been due to Hawksmoor's own diffidence, for Vanbrugh thought it necessary to apply to the Duke of Marlborough on his behalf 'for some opportunity to do him good, because he does not seem very solicitous to do it for himself', and in 1734 Sir Thomas Robinson told Lord Carlisle that he 'never talk'd with a more reasonable man, nor one so little prejudiced in favour of his own performances'.

The materials for Hawksmoor's life are comparatively extensive. Over 500 of his drawings survive and have been listed by Downes (*Hawksmoor*, 1959) who also prints many of his letters. More drawings now missing are listed in the sale catalogue of Hawksmoor's collection, printed in part by Downes in *Burlington Mag.* xcv, 1953, 332–5 and in full in *Sale Catalogues of Libraries of Eminent Persons*, vol. 4, ed. D. J. Watkin, 1972, 45–106. A small notebook in Hawksmoor's hand dealing with materials and prices is in the National Maritime Museum (MS. 63/030). All previous accounts of Hawksmoor have been superseded by Kerry Downes's monograph *Hawksmoor*, 1959, 2nd ed. 1979. *Hawksmoor*, 1969, by the same author, is a shorter introductory work which supplements but does not supersede the monograph. For Hawksmoor's work for the Board of Ordnance see R. Hewlings, 'Hawksmoor's Brave Designs for the Police' in *English Architecture: Public and Private. Essays for Kerry Downes*, ed. Bold & Chaney, 1993. Attention should also be drawn to J. H. V. Davies's stylistic appraisal, 'Nicholas Hawksmoor' in *R.I.B.A. Jnl.* Oct. 1962, 368–75, to P. de la Ruffinière du Prey, 'Hawksmoor's "Basilica after the Primitive Christians", Architecture and Theology', *Jnl. Society of Architectural Historians*, xlviii, 1989; to Giles Worsley, 'Nicholas Hawksmoor: a pioneer neo-Palladian?' *Arch. Hist.* 33, 1990 and on possible sources for Hawksmoor's churches in *C. Life*, 18 Oct. 1990; and to Paul Jeffery, 'Some recently found Drawings for St. Paul's Cathedral, All Saints, Oxford, and the City Churches', *Arch. Hist.* 35, 1992.

PUBLIC AND DOMESTIC ARCHITECTURE

BROADFIELD HALL, HERTS., repairs and alterations for James Forester, 1690–93; dem. *c.*1875 [R. L. Hine, *Relics of an Un-Common Attorney*, 1951, 6–7 and endpapers].

LONDON, CHRIST'S HOSPITAL, designed SIR JOHN MOORE'S WRITING SCHOOL under Wren's direction, 1692–5; dem. 1902 [E. H. Pearce, *Annals of Christ's Hospital*, 1908, 151; cf. *Wren Soc.* xi, pls. xlviii–li].

EASTON NESTON, NORTHANTS., for Sir William Fermor, 1st Lord Leominster, *c.*1695–1702 [K. Downes, 'Hawksmoor's House at Easton Neston', *Arch. Hist.* 30, 1987]. The engravings in *Vitruvius Britannicus* i, 1715, pls. 98–100 show the house with wings, a forecourt and other additions that were never built. (*C. Life*, 7–14 Nov. 1908, 20–27 Aug. 1927; H. A. Tipping, *English Homes*, Period iv, vol. ii, 1928, 119–40; J. Kenworthy-Browne in *Connoisseur*, Oct. 1964).

GREENWICH HOSPITAL. As Clerk of the Works from 1698 to 1735 Hawksmoor was more closely associated with the building of the Hospital than any other person. At first, however, he was working to Wren's designs, and although he may well have been personally responsible for designing the east range of Queen Anne's Court, begun in 1701, and the dormitories in King William's Court, begun in 1699, it cannot be proved that he was their effective as well as their executant architect. He subsequently made many designs for enlarging the Hospital that were not carried out, including a grandiose scheme for a monumental chapel dominating the whole complex. See *Wren Soc.* vi, *passim* and his own *Remarks on the Founding and Carrying on the Buildings of the Royal Hospital at Greenwich*, 1728 (reprinted in *Wren. Soc*, vi, 17–27, in which he pleaded for the completion of the hospital on the scale originally intended).

RIPON, YORKS. (W.R.), Obelisk in Market Place for John Aislabie, 1702; rebuilt to original design 1781 [R. Hewlings, 'Ripon's Forum Populi', *Arch. Hist.* 24, 1981].

?ADDISCOMBE HOUSE, SURREY, for William Draper, 1702–3; dem. *c.*1861 (illustrations in Downes, *English Baroque Architecture*, 1966, pl. 163 and *National Views and History of London*, 1832, 118). The incomplete building accounts in B.L. Add, MS. 38480, ff. 406–12, show that the carpenter's and joiner's work was measured by Hawksmoor in 1703, but the house may have been designed by Edward Strong, the master mason employed. Draper was Treasurer to the Commissioners for Greenwich Hospital, where Hawksmoor was Clerk of Works at the time.

GREAT LODGE, WINDSOR GREAT PARK, BERKS., alterations for Sarah, Duchess of Marlborough, *c.*1702–4 [letter from Sarah referring to Hawksmoor's assistance here in Downes, 1959, 273; abstract of workmen's bills dated 16 June 1704 signed by Matthew Banckes in Blenheim Palace Muniments, Shelf G, Box 10].

KENSINGTON PALACE, THE ORANGERY was built in 1704–5 under Hawskmoor's direction as Clerk of the Works, but Wren as Surveyor General was officially responsible for the design, and a Treasury minute shows that it was revised by Vanbrugh [*History of the King's Works* v, 193–4].

Unspecified work for 6th Duke of Somerset, on whose behalf 17 letters were written to 'Mr. Hawkesmore' between March 1704 and Dec. 1706, probably in connection with alterations then in progress at SYON HOUSE, MIDDLESEX and perhaps also at NORTHUMBERLAND HOUSE, STRAND, LONDON [record of correspondence in Steward's day-book in Percy archives, Alnwick Castle, U.1.35, *passim*].

KENSINGTON CHARITY SCHOOL, 1711–12; dem. 1875 [J. D. Scott, *St. Mary Abbots Kensington*, 1942, 115–17].

LONDON, No. 3 ST. JAMES'S SQUARE, advised 3rd Lord (later 1st Earl of) Ashburnham on construction, 1712; dem. 1930 [*Survey of London* xxix, 84].

OXFORD, THE CLARENDON BUILDING, 1712–15 [*V.C.H. Oxon.* iii, 54–55] (plan in R.C.H.M. *Oxford*, 12).

OXFORD, ALL SOULS COLLEGE, North Quadrangle, Hall, Buttery and Codrington Library, 1716–35, externally Gothic [*V.C.H. Oxon.* iii, 190–3; H. M. Colvin, *Catalogue of Architectural Drawings in Worcester College Library*, 1964, pls. 59–81].

WESTMINSTER HALL, temporary Court of Judicature for trial of rebel Lords, 1716 [P.R.O., Works 4/1, 78].

ST. JAMES'S PALACE, THE BRICK ARCADE, STABLE COURT, 1716–17 [*History of the King's Works* v, 240].

BERWICK-ON-TWEED, THE BARRACKS, 1717–21 [elevation by Hawksmoor dated 1717 in drawings from Wilton House in Wilts. C.R.O., F 6/27, executed with some simplification].

WESTMINSTER, THE JEWEL TOWER, alterations 1718–19 [*History of the King's Works* v, 410].

PANTON HALL, nr. WRAGBY, LINCS., for Joseph Gace, *c.*1720; enlarged and remodelled by John Carr *c.*1775; dem. 1960 [W. Angus, *Select Views of Seats*, 1792, pl. xxx; H. M. Colvin in *Lincolnshire Historian* No. 7, 1951, but note that demolition revealed structural evidence that the centre was earlier in date than the wings].

OXFORD, WORCESTER COLLEGE. Hawksmoor assisted Dr. George Clarke to plan the new buildings that were begun in 1720, and was closely involved in the designing of the library [*V.C.H. Oxon.* iii, 307–8; H. M. Colvin, *Catalogue of Architectural Drawings in Worcester College Library*, 1964, xxiii–xxiv and pls. 8–23].

KENSINGTON, COLBY HOUSE, for Sir Thomas

Colby, *c.*1722; dem. 1873 [J. H. V. Davies, 'Colby House' in *The Country Seat*, ed. Colvin & Harris, 1970, 94–5].

BLENHEIM PALACE, OXON. First as Vanbrugh's assistant from 1705 to 1716, and later as sole architect in charge of the completion of the palace for Sarah, Duchess of Marlborough, from 1722 to 1725, Hawksmoor was closely associated with every stage in the designing and building of Blenheim. The decoration of the Long Library, with its elaborate plasterwork by Isaac Mansfield, was carried out entirely to his designs, and it has been said that while 'Blenheim as a whole is Vanbrugh's . . . yet there is not one detail of which one could say with certainty that Hawksmoor had not designed it' (L. Whistler, *Sir John Vanbrugh*, 1938, 128). He also designed the Triumphal Gateway at the Woodstock entrance to the Park, built in 1722–3, and made a number of designs for the Column of Victory, though the Doric pillar completed in 1730 was 'conducted by' Lord Herbert, afterwards Earl of Pembroke. [David Green, *Blenheim Palace*, 1951.]

CASTLE HOWARD, YORKS. (N.R.), works for 3rd Earl of Carlisle, including the PYRAMID, 1728, THE MAUSOLEUM, 1729–36, and the TEMPLE OF VENUS, 1731–5 (dem.) [G. F. Webb, 'The Letters and Drawings of Nicholas Hawksmoor relating to the Building of the Mausoleum at Castle Howard', *Walpole Soc.* xix, 1930–1; H. A. Tipping, 'The Outworks of Castle Howard', *C. Life*, 6–13 August 1927].

OCKHAM PARK, SURREY, alterations for Lord Chancellor King, 1729; altered in nineteenth century and dem. 1949 after a fire [L. Whistler, 'Ockham Park, Surrey', *C. Life*, 29 Dec. 1950; R. N. Bloxam, 'The "Big House" in Ockham Park', *Surrey Arch. Colls.* lxii, 1965; J. Harris, *Catalogue of British Drawings for Architecture etc. in American Collections*, 1971, 112–15, describing drawings now in Canadian Centre for Architecture, Montreal].

VANBRUGH CASTLE, GREENWICH, alterations for 2nd Duke of Richmond, 1733–4 [T. P. Connor in *Sussex Archl. Colls.* 117, 1979, 187].

OXFORD, THE QUEEN'S COLLEGE, screen-wall to High Street, 1733–6, executed by William Townesend with some modifications to the cupola [K. Downes, *Hawksmoor*, 1959, 107, note 14].

LONDON, No. 5 NEW BURLINGTON STREET, interior for Anne, Viscountess Irwin, 1735; dem. [*Survey of London* xxxii, 490–1].

CHURCHES

London[1]

ST. ALPHEGE, GREENWICH, 1712–14. Of the steeple designed by Hawksmoor (known from an engraving published by J. Kip in 1714) only the lower stage was built. The upper part was designed by John James in 1730. The church was gutted in 1941 and reopened in 1963 after restoration.

ST. ANNE, LIMEHOUSE, 1714–30; damaged by fire 1850 and restored by P. Hardwick and J. Morris 1851–4.

ST. GEORGE-IN-THE-EAST, WAPPING STEPNEY, 1714–29; gutted 1941, exterior restored as a shell containing a modern hall, church and rectory, 1960–4 (measured drawings in *Builder*, 28 May 1915).

CHRIST CHURCH, SPITALFIELDS, 1714–29; the spire was stripped of its original ornaments in 1822–3 and the interior was altered in 1851 and 1866 (when the galleries were removed) (*Survey of London* xxvii, chap. xii). Hawksmoor also designed the rectory in 1726.

ST. MARY WOOLNOTH, CITY, 1716–24. The interior was altered by Butterfield in 1875–6, when the galleries were removed and their fronts set back against the walls (measured drawings in *Builder*, 20 July 1901).

ST. GEORGE, BLOOMSBURY, 1716–31, refitted by G.E. Street 1871, when the lions and unicorns were removed from the steeple. Hawksmoor also designed the rectory in 1726.

ST. GEORGE, QUEEN SQUARE, alterations 1717–20, including ceiling; altered 1867.

ST. MICHAEL, CORNHILL, CITY, steeple 1718–24, Gothic. The rebuilding of the steeple was begun by Wren in 1715–17, suspended, and completed by Hawksmoor to his own designs.

ST. JOHN, HORSELYDOWN, SOUTHWARK, with John James, 1727–33; gutted 1940–1, and subsequently dem. Hawksmoor also designed the parsonage in 1733 [T. Mowl in *C. Life*, 6 Dec. 1990].

ST. LUKE, OLD STREET, FINSBURY, with John James, 1727–33; unroofed and interior dismantled 1960.

Elsewhere

attributed: CANTERBURY CATHEDRAL, archbishop's throne (now in south transept) for

[1] The authority for all Hawksmoor's London churches will be found in H. M. Colvin, 'Fifty New Churches', *Arch. Rev.* March 1950 and Kerry Downes, *Hawksmoor*, 1959.

Archbishop Tenison, *c.*1704 [Downes, *Hawksmoor*, 1959, 277].

BEVERLEY MINSTER, YORKS. Hawksmoor repaired the north transept, employing machinery devised by W. Thornton (*q.v.*), a carpenter of York, to restore it to the perpendicular, placed an ogival cupola over the crossing, and refitted the interior, introducing a stone screen (Gothic), a Corinthian baldachino over the altar, and galleries in the nave aisles, *c.*1716–20. See appeal (1716) and engravings by Hawksmoor in Bodleian, Gough Maps, 35, ff. 3–4; 44, f. 67, and descriptions in *The Diary of a Tour in 1732* (Roxburghe Club, 1890), 199–201, and by Dr. Pococke in B.L., Add. MS. 14259, f. 133. Hawksmoor's work has been largely destroyed (R. H. Whiteing, 'Georgian Restorations at Beverley Minister 1715–40', *Trans. Georgian Soc. for E. Yorks* III (i), 1951; Downes, *Hawksmoor*, 1959, 6, note 11).

ST. ALBAN'S ABBEY, HERTS.[1] Hawksmoor carried out repairs soon after 1721, when he published a plate of the Abbey in order to raise funds [B.L., *King's Maps* xv, 49, and Bodleian, MS. Rawlinson B. 376, f. 261]. There was a Brief for £5775 in 1723–4.

WESTMINSTER ABBEY. The Gothic west towers were designed by Hawksmoor in 1734, and completed by his successor, John James, *c.*1745 [*Wren. Soc.* xi, 11, 31, 33]. The gable is dated 1735. Drawings by Hawksmoor recently acquired for W.A.M. are illustrated in *C. Life*, 20 May, 1993.

UNEXECUTED DESIGNS

Hawksmoor's many unexecuted designs include schemes for INGESTRE PARK, STAFFS., 1688 [K. Downes, *Hawksmoor*, 1969, 24–5]; WINDSOR CASTLE, BERKS., 1698 [*Wren Soc.* viii, pls. xi–xv]; a MAUSOLEUM for King William III, *c.*1702 [*History of the King's Works* v, 455 and Downes, *Hawksmoor*, 1959, 66 and pl. 10b]; GREENWICH HOSPITAL, *c.*1702 onwards [*Wren Soc.* vi]; THIRKLEBY PARK, YORKS. (N.R.), 1704 [unpublished designs for stables in Yorkshire Archaeological Society's Library, Leeds and cf. the 18 drawings 'for Sir Thomas Frankland's' in Hawksmoor's Sale Catalogue]; THE QUEEN'S COLLEGE, OXFORD, 1708–9 [Downes, *Hawksmoor*, 1959, 102–7]; ALL SOULS COLLEGE, OXFORD, 1708–9 [H. M. Colvin, *Catalogue of Architectural Drawings in Worcester College Library*, 1964]; ST. PAUL'S CATHEDRAL BAPTISTERY, *c.*1710 [*Wren Soc.* iii, pls. xxiii, xxiv]; KING'S COLLEGE, CAMBRIDGE, 1712–13 [drawings at King's College and Bodleian Library, see Downes, *Hawksmoor*, 1959, 278]; THE RADCLIFFE LIBRARY, OXFORD, 1712–15 and 1733 [see S. Lang, 'By Hawksmoor out of Gibbs', *Arch. Rev.* April 1949, the plates in *The Building Accounts of the Radcliffe Library*, ed. S. G. Gillam, Oxford Historical Soc. 1958, and H. Colvin, *Unbuilt Oxford*, 1983]; OXFORD, steeple for ALL SAINTS CHURCH, *c.*1713–15 [H. M. Colvin, 'The Architects of All Saints Church, Oxford', *Oxoniensia* xix, 1954, 112–16 and cf. P. Jeffery in *Arch. Hist.* 35, 1992, 122–4]; WOTTON HOUSE, SURREY, ?1713 [*R.I.B.A. Drawings Catalogue: G–K*, 99]; BRASENOSE COLLEGE, OXFORD, 1720–34 [E. W. Allfrey, 'The Architectural History of the College', *Brasenose Quatercentenary Monograph* No. iii, 1909 and H. M. Colvin, *Catalogue of Architectural Drawings in Worcester College Library*, 1964, pls. 87–90]; MAGDALEN COLLEGE, OXFORD, 1724 [Colvin, *op. cit.*, p. xxii and Nos. 84–5]; an elaborate altar in YORK MINSTER, 1726 [drawings in York Minster archives (M/P 644 and 1021) and British Library (*King's Maps* xlv, 7 ff. 2)]; OCKHAM PARK, SURREY, 1727–9 [J. Harris, *Catalogue of British Drawings for Architecture, etc. in American Collections*, 1971, 112–15 and plates, and further drawings in Minet Library, Camberwell]; ST. GILES-IN-THE-FIELDS CHURCH, LONDON, 1730 [B.L., Add. MS. 15506]; and WESTMINSTER BRIDGE, 1736 [see Hawksmoor's publication, *A Short Historical Account of London Bridge, with a Proposition for a new Stone Bridge at Westminster*, 1736, and a drawing at the R.I.B.A.]. For Hawksmoor's town-planning schemes for Oxford and Cambridge see S. Lang, 'Cambridge and Oxford Replanned; Hawksmoor as a Town-planner', *Arch. Rev.* April 1948, *The Town of Cambridge as it ought to be Reformed, the plans of Nicholas Hawksmoor interpreted in an Essay by David Roberts and a set of eight drawings by Gordon Cullen*, privately printed, Cambridge 1955, and Howard Colvin, *Unbuilt Oxford*, 1983.

HAYCOCK, EDWARD (1790–1870), was the second son of J. H. Haycock (*q.v.*). He became a pupil of Sir Jeffry Wyatville, studied at the R.A. Schools, and exhibited student's work at the Royal Academy in 1808, 1809 and 1810. He also exhibited at the Liverpool Academy in 1812, 1813 and 1814. Returning to Shrewsbury, he joined his father in the family building firm, and continued, in conjunction with his younger brother Robert, to

[1] There is a bird's-eye view of the town of St. Albans, 'done by N. Hawksmoor Architect, anno 1721 May ye 12', in the Sutherland Collection in the Ashmolean Museum, Oxford (c. iii, 555).

combine the business of a builder with the practice of an architect until about 1845, after which he worked only as an architect. From 1834 to 1866 he was County Surveyor of Shropshire, and for many years he played an important part in the social and political life of Shrewsbury. He sat on the Council as a Conservative for 34 years, became an Alderman, and served as Mayor in 1842. He died in December 1870, and was buried in the family vault in St. Chad's churchyard. His practice was continued by his son Edward Haycock, junior (d. 1882).

Haycock had an extensive practice in Shropshire, the Border Counties and Wales. Clytha Court and Millichope Park show that he was a Greek Revivalist of some ability, and Glynliffon in Caernarvonshire is another considerable house in the same style. His numerous Gothic churches, mostly in the lancet style, are, however, routine productions of their time which do nothing to enhance his reputation.

[Obituary in *Eddowes's Shrewsbury Journal*, 28 Dec. 1870; J. L. Hobbs, 'The Haycocks', *Shropshire Magazine*, Feb. 1960.]

PUBLIC BUILDINGS

SHREWSBURY, LORD HILL'S COLUMN, 1814–16, assisted by Thomas Harrison of Chester. There was a competition, in which the first premium was won by the sculptor, (Sir) Richard Westmacott, the second by Edward Haycock, and the third by John Carline (*q.v.*). However, it was 'unanimously agreed' to adopt Haycock's design, but to 'put [it] into the hands of Mr. Harrison, of Chester, Architect, who made some alterations [chiefly to the pedestal] that were finally adopted'. Haycock exhibited his design at the Liverpool Academy in 1814. [*A Description of the Column in honour of Lord Hill erected at Shrewsbury*, J. Watten, Shrewsbury, 1818; *Gent's Mag.* 1817 (ii), 393–4, with engraving; T. J. Howell, *The Stranger in Shrewsbury*, 1816, 79–80].

SHREWSBURY, THE BUTTER MARKET, PRIDE HILL, 1819–20; dem. 1830 [Shrewsbury Public Library, Henry Pidgeon's 'Salopian Annals' 1823–30, vol. v, p. 87, *ex inf.* the late J. L. Hobbs].

DOLGELLAU, MERIONETHSHIRE, THE COUNTY HALL, 1823–5 [Gwynedd Record Office, Merionethshire Q.S. Records, 1825].

COED-CWNWR, LLANTRISANT FAWR, MONMOUTHSHIRE, ALMSHOUSES for Roger Edwards's Charity, 1825 [J. H. Clark, *The Usk Gleaner*, 1878].

PRESTEIGNE, RADNORSHIRE, THE SHIRE HALL, 1826–9 [W. K. Parker, 'Radnorshire Civic Buildings 1819–29', *Trans. Radnorshire Soc.* 50, 1980, and *ibid.* 51, 1981, 40–3].

SHREWSBURY, THE SALOP INFIRMARY, 1827–30, designed by E. Haycock, and built by Messrs. Haycock under 'the occasional inspection' of Robert Smirke [Shropshire C.R.O., minutes of the Infirmary and printed Report of the Building Committee, 3909/8/2].

MONMOUTH, SHIRE HALL, enlarged and remodelled interior, 1829–30 [Monmouthshire County Records, C. Bu. 5–11; C 7 Bu. P.S.5].

ABERAERON, CARDIGANSHIRE, probably responsible for planning of town for the Gwynne family of Monachty in the 1830s [H. V. Phythian-Adams, 'The Planning of Aberaeron', *Ceredigion* viii, 1979, 406–7].

CARDIFF, THE MARKET, ST. MARY STREET, 1835; dem. 1884 [B. L. James & P. Riden, *Cardiff Central Market 1891–1991* (Survey of Cardiff, 1991)].

NEATH, GLAMORGANSHIRE, MARKET, GREEN STREET, 1835–6; dem. [W. Glamorgan Record Office, Neath Corporation Minutes, 30 Sept. 1835, *ex inf.* Mr. Thomas Lloyd].

SHREWSBURY, SAVINGS BANK, COLLEGE HILL, 1838–9 [H. Pidgeon, *Memorials of Shrewsbury*, 1851, 168].

SHREWSBURY, THE MUSIC HALL, THE SQUARE, 1839–40 [H. Pidgeon, *Memorials of Shrewsbury*, 1851, 166].

WROCKWARDINE, SALOP., ALMSHOUSES, 1841 [*V.C.H. Salop.* xi, 323].

SHREWSBURY, THE NEW BUTTER MARKET, PRIDE HILL, 1844; dem. 1877 [H. Pidgeon, *Memorials of Shrewsbury*, 1851, 177].

DOWLAIS, GLAMORGANSHIRE, THE MARKET HALL, 1844; dem. 1971 [J. B. Hilling, *Cardiff and the Valleys*, 1973, 109].

PRESTON HOSPITAL, PRESTON-ON-THE-WEALD-MOORS, SALOP., stone bell-turret on hall, replacing wooden cupola, 1844 [contract advertised in *Builder* ii, 1844, 84] (*C. Life*, 16 April 1964, fig. 3).

LLANDOVERY, CARMARTHENSHIRE, NATIONAL SCHOOL, 1845; dem. [Carmarthenshire Record Office, Board of Education School plans].

LLANDEILO BRIDGE, CARMARTHENSHIRE (R. Tywi), 1848 [S. Lewis, *Topographical Dictionary of Wales*, 1849, i, 528].

SHREWSBURY, LANCASTERIAN SCHOOL, nr. railway station, 1851 [H. Pidgeon, *Memorials of Shrewsbury*, 1851, 194].

SHREWSBURY, ST. CHAD'S SCHOOL, BRIDGE STREET, 1859; dem. except master's house [obituary in *Eddowes's Shrewsbury Journal*, 28 Dec. 1870].

BICTON HEATH, nr. SHREWSBURY, SHROPSHIRE COUNTY LUNATIC ASYLUM, alterations [obituary in *Eddowes's Shrewsbury Journal*, 28 Dec. 1870].

CHURCHES

TETTENHALL, STAFFS., alterations 1825; dem. after fire 1950 [*V.C.H. Staffs.* xx, 41].

CAERPHILLY, GLAMORGANSHIRE, 1826; dem. [I.C.B.S.].

MACHYNLLETH, MONTGOMERYSHIRE, 1827, Gothic [I.C.B.S.].

TAI-BACH (MARGAM), GLAMORGANSHIRE, 1827, Gothic [I.C.B.S.].

SHREWSBURY, ST. GEORGE, FRANKWELL, 1829–32, Gothic [D.H.S. Cranage, *The Churches of Shropshire* ii, 1903, 914].

BARMOUTH, MERIONETHSHIRE, 1830, Gothic [I.C.B.S.].

ABERYSTWYTH, ST. MICHAEL, 1830–3, Gothic; rebuilt 1894 [N.L.W., parish records of St. Michael's Aberystwyth, 12–114].

ABERSYCHAN, MONMOUTHSHIRE, 1831–2, Gothic [*Monmouthshire Merlin*, 30 April 1831].

TREVETHIN, MONMOUTHSHIRE, ST. THOMAS, 1831–2, Gothic [Port, 172].

HAY, BRECONSHIRE, 1833–4, Gothic; chancel added 1867 [I.C.B.S.].

TILSTOCK, SALOP., rebuilt 1835 [Shropshire C.R.O., Bridgewater papers 212 (plan)].

ABERAERON, CARDIGANSHIRE, 1835; rebuilt 1875 [I.C.B.S.].

CARMARTHEN, ST. DAVID, 1835–6, Gothic [Port, 170].

WHITCHURCH, SALOP., ST. CATHERINE, DODINGTON, 1836–7, classical [Shrewsbury Public Library, Watton's cuttings].

CRUCKTON, SALOP., 1840, Gothic [I.C.B.S.; elevations in Bodleian, MS. Top. Salop. c. 2, ff. 619–20].

LLANNON, CARMARTHENSHIRE, 1841, Gothic [I.C.B.S.].

CRESSAGE, SALOP., 1841, Gothic [*Gent's Mag.* 1852 (ii), 60; elevations in Bodleian, MS. Top. Salop. c. 2, ff. 621–2].

COUND, SALOP., employed as 'surveyor' for repewing and other internal alterations carried out by the builder-architect Samuel Pountney Smith in 1842–3. It is not clear whether these works were designed by Smith or by Haycock, nor which of them designed the Gothic N. aisle simultaneously built at the expense of Mrs. Frances Thursby [Vestry Minutes in Shropshire C.R.O., 790/6].

HOPE, SALOP., 1843, Gothic [I.C.B.S.; drawings in Stackhouse Library, St. Leonard's, Bridgnorth].

CHAPEL LAWN, nr. CLUN, SALOP., 1843, Gothic [I.C.B.S.].

BAYSTONHILL, SALOP., 1843, Gothic; chancel added 1886 [I.C.B.S.].

MIDDLETON IN CHIRBURY, SALOP., 1843, Gothic [I.C.B.S.].

LLANDEVAUD, MONMOUTHSHIRE, 1843, Gothic [I.C.B.S.].

DORRINGTON, SALOP., 1843–5, Gothic [*V.C.H. Salop.* viii, 55; Bodleian, MS. Top. Salop. c. 2, f. 179].

LLANWYDDYN, MONTGOMERYSHIRE, reseating, etc., 1844–7; submerged by reservoir 1887 [I.C.B.S.].

NEWCASTLE, SALOP., 1848, Gothic [Shrewsbury Public Library, Watton's cuttings, vol. 7, p. 4; plans in Stackhouse Library, St. Leonard's, Bridgnorth].

CHURCH PULVERBATCH, SALOP., rebuilt 1852–3, Gothic [I.C.B.S.].

COUNTRY HOUSES, ETC.

HODNET RECTORY, SALOP., for Bishop Heber, 1812, Tudor Gothic [*The Cambrian Traveller's Guide*, 1840, 528].

ONSLOW HALL, SALOP., remodelled for John Wingfield, *c.*1815–20; dem. 1957 [drawings in R.I.B.A. Drawings Collection; exhib. at R.A. 1820].

LOTON PARK, SALOP., alterations for Sir Baldwin Leighton, Bart., 1819 [drawings at Loton Park, *ex inf.* Mr. John Harris and Mr. J. B. Lawson].

attributed: ASHFIELD HALL, NESFIELD, CHESHIRE, for J. H. Lyon, 1820–1; dem. 1958 [P. de Figueiredo & J. Treuherz, *Cheshire Country Houses* 1988, 213].

STANTON LACY VICARAGE, SALOP., 1823–4, Tudor Gothic [Hereford C.R.O., Diocesan Records, Clergy & Benefice papers, Box 31].

CLYTHA HOUSE, MONMOUTHSHIRE, for William Jones or Herbert, 1824–8 [*The Cambrian Traveller's Guide*, 1840, 528; R. Haslam in *C. Life*, 8–15 Dec. 1977].

CLUNGUNFORD HOUSE, SALOP., for the Revd. John Rocke, 1825–8 [family tradition as recorded in estate agent's brochure, 1990].

attributed: ALDENHAM PARK, SALOP., conversion of central courtyard into hall, for Sir Richard Acton, Bart., *c.*1826–9 [G. Jackson-Stops in *C. Life*, 7 July 1977].

ORLETON HALL, SALOP., refronted for Edward Cludde, *c.*1830 [*The Cambrian Traveller's Guide*, 1840, 528; cf. Shropshire C.R.O. 665/6040] (F. Leach, *The County Seats of Shropshire*, 1891, 305).

SHOBDON COURT, HEREFS., alterations for William Hanbury, afterwards 1st Lord Bateman, with advice from Sir Jeffry Wyatville, *c.*1830–5; dem. [D. Linstrum,

Sir Jeffry Wyatville, 1972, 248] (*C. Life*, 10 Nov. 1906).

WALFORD MANOR, SALOP., for R. A. Slaney, 1831–5 [Shropshire C.R.O., specification, 665/1223–4].

ALLTLWYD HOUSE, LLANTSANTFFRAED, CARDIGANSHIRE, for John Hughes, 1832 [N.L.W., plans by Haycock and cf. contract in MS. Alltlwyd 66, *ex inf.* Mr. Thomas Lloyd].

PLAS LLANGOEDMOR, CARDIGANSHIRE, rebuilt for Col. Herbert Vaughan, 1833 [drawings at Llangoedmor, *ex inf.* Mr. Julian Orbach].

LEATON KNOLLS, SALOP., for J. A. Lloyd, *c.*1835; dem. 1955 [obituary in *Eddowes's Shrewsbury Journal*, 28 Dec. 1870; but in his *Reminiscences of a Literary Life* i, 1836, 396, T. F. Dibdin refers to 'the mansion of Mr. Lloyd, recently erected on his own plan (for he is his own *Vitruvius*)'].[1]

MILLICHOPE PARK, SALOP., for the Revd. R. N. Pemberton, 1835–40 [obituary in *Eddowes's Shrewsbury Journal*, 28 Dec. 1870; views of the old and new houses and an elevation probably by Haycock in Bodleian, MS. Top. Salop. c. 2, ff. 377–8] (*C. Life*, 10–17 Feb. 1977).

PENLLERGARE, nr. SWANSEA, GLAMORGANSHIRE, rebuilt for J. D. Llewellyn, 1836; dem. 1961 [letters from Haycock and diaries of L. W. Dillwyn in private possession, *ex inf.* Mr. Richard Morris].

GLYNLIFFON, CAERNARVONSHIRE, mansion and stables for 3rd Lord Newborough, *c.*1836–49 [signed drawings in Caernarvon Record Office] (T. Nicholas, *Annals of the County Families of Wales* ii, 1875, 799.)

LONGNOR HALL, SALOP., alterations, including attic windows, for Panton Corbett, 1838–42 [drawings in Shropshire C.R.O., 567] (*C. Life*, 13–20 Feb. 1964).

NANTEOS, CARDIGANSHIRE, alterations and additions for W. E. Powel, *c.*1839–49, including portico and probably stables [accounts and drawings at N.L.W.].[2]

GELLIWERNAN, LLANNON, CARMARTHENSHIRE, for R. G. Thomas, begun *c.*1840 but never completed, Elizabethan style [drawings by Haycock in office of Griffiths Son & Lewis, architects of Llanelli, *ex inf.* Mr. Thomas Lloyd].

KELMARSH HALL, NORTHANTS., enlargement of morning-room for William Hanbury, 1st Lord Bateman, 1842 [Northants. C.R.O., H(K) 275, specification, estimate and account].

FARTHINGSTONE RECTORY, NORTHANTS., enlarged 1842–3 [Northants. C.R.O., Peterborough Diocesan Records].

CONDOVER VICARAGE, SALOP., 1843 [plans in Lichfield Joint Record Office, B/A/13].

SHOBDON RECTORY, HEREFS., 1844 [Hereford. C.R.O., Diocesan Records, Clergy & Benefice papers, Box 48].

STANAGE PARK, RADNORSHIRE, alterations, including Gothic dining-room, for the Revd. John Rogers, 1845 [drawings at Stanage, *ex inf.* Mr. David McLees].

CHURCHSTOKE VICARAGE, MONTGOMERYSHIRE, enlarged 1846–7 [Bodleian Library, records of Queen Anne's Bounty].

CLYNFYW, MANORDEIFI, CARDIGANSHIRE, for Thomas Lewis, *c.*1849–50, Elizabethan style [mentioned in letters from Haycock to David Lewis of Straley (below), 27 Sept. 1849 and 16 April 1850].

PENRICE CASTLE, GLAMORGANSHIRE, minor works (unspecified) for C. R. Mansel Talbot, 1849–50 [mentioned in letters from Haycock to David Lewis of Straley (below), 7, 20 Feb., 18 Sept. 1849].

BADGER HALL, SALOP., alterations or additions for Robert Cheney, *c.*1849–50; dem. 1952 [mentioned in letter from Haycock to David Lewis of Straley (below), 1 Feb. 1850].

STRADEY HOUSE (now CASTLE), LLANELLI, CARMARTHENSHIRE, for David Lewis, 1849–53, Elizabethan style; enlarged 1874 [letters from Haycock in N.L.W., Mansel-Lewis, 2086–7].

PENLYAN, LLANDYGWYDD, nr. CARDIGAN, for Morgan Jones, 1852 [*Pembrokeshire Herald*, 16 Jan., 19 March 1852: 'by Mr. Edward Haycock of Shrewsbury', *ex inf.* Mr. Thomas Lloyd].

NETLEY HALL, SALOP., for T. H. Hope-Edwardes, 1854–8 [F. Leach, *County Seats of Shropshire* i, 1891, 179: 'by the late Mr. Edward Haycock', which could mean either Edward Haycock senior (d. 1870) or his son (d. 1882)].

HAYCOCK, JOHN HIRAM (1759–1830), was the second son of William Haycock (1725–1802), a carpenter, joiner and builder of Shrewsbury. William Haycock had two other sons who were builders or architects, but William, the eldest, died in 1779 at the age of 27 and Edward, the youngest, in 1791 at the age of 23, leaving John as the only survivor. He had been apprenticed to his father in 1774, was admitted a freeman of the Shrewsbury Carpenters' and Bricklayers' Company in 1780, and became a burgess of Shrewsbury in 1796. In 1824 he was appointed County Surveyor of Shropshire. He died at Shrewsbury on 6 January 1830, aged

[1] There are unsigned drawings for this house at Wheaton College, Norton, Mass., U.S.A.

[2] See also under WILLIAM RITSON COULTHART.

70, and was buried at St. Chad's Church. He was a competent provincial architect whose most important work was probably the Shirehall, a classical building with an engaged Ionic portico. He was the father of Edward Haycock (*q.v.*) [*Gent's Mag.* 1830 (i), 380; J. L. Hobbs, 'The Haycocks', *Shropshire Magazine*, Feb. 1960, 17; Shrewsbury Public Library, 13487, register of the Shrewsbury Carpenters' and Bricklayers' Company; pedigree in *Trans. Salop. Arch. Soc.* 4th ser. ix, 1923, 29].

SHREWSBURY, THE GUILDHALL AND SHIREHALL, 1783–5; dem. 1835 [T. Minshull, *The Shrewsbury Guide*, 1786, 47; H. Owen, *Some Account of the Ancient and Present State of Shrewsbury*, 1808, 411].

OAKLY PARK, SALOP., alterations for 2nd Lord Clive (for his mother, Lady Clive, d. 1817), *c.*1784–90; subsequently remodelled by C. R. Cockerell [C. Hussey, *English Country Houses, Late Georgian*, 1958, 153].

SHREWSBURY, MILLINGTON'S HOSPITAL, FRANKWELL, remodelled central feature with portico and cupola, 1785–6 [J. B. Lawson, 'The Architect of Millington's Hospital, Shrewsbury', *Shropshire News Letter* No. 42, May 1972, 10].

SHREWSBURY, THE COUNTY GAOL, 1787–93; executed by Thomas Telford with modifications suggested by John Howard [H. Owen, *Some Account of the Ancient and Present State of Shrewsbury*, 1808, 430; A. Gibb, *The Story of Telford*, 1935, 323].

ATCHAM UNION WORK-HOUSE (now Berrington Hospital), CROSS HOUSES, SALOP., 1792–3 [Shropshire C.R.O., 13/5, minute-book 1792–1801].

MORETON CORBET CASTLE, SALOP., unexecuted designs for rebuilding for Andrew Corbet, 1796 [Shrewsbury School Library, S.IX 100, *ex inf.* Mr. J. B. Lawson].

SHREWSBURY, ALLATT'S CHARITY SCHOOL (now Health Centre), MURIVANCE, 1799–1800 [*Gent's Mag.* 1830 (i), 380].

ACTON REYNALD HALL, SALOP., enlarged for Sir Andrew Corbet, Bart., 1800 [order for chimney-pieces from Haycock in Carline's orderbook in Shropshire C.R.O., 30 Sept. 1800].

SHREWSBURY, house for Anthony Kynnersley, 1800 [in 1800 Carline supplied stone sills for 8 windows 'for Mr. Haycock to Major Kynnersley's House', *ibid.*].

BERRIEW CHURCH, MONTGOMERYSHIRE, rebuilt 1801–3; reconstructed by E. Haycock, jr. in 1876 [Vestry Minutes in N.L.W.; *Gent's Mag.* 1800 (ii), 609].

SWEENEY HALL, SALOP., for Thomas Netherton Parker, 1805 [Shropshire C.R.O., 1060/26].

THE ROVERIES, nr. LYDHAM, SALOP., house for John Oakeley, 1810 [specification and estimate in Shropshire C.R.O., 1079, Box 13].

GUNLEY HALL, MONMOUTHSHIRE, for Richard Pryce, *c.*1810 [N.L.W., Gunley papers, parcel 14, proposed plan and elevation by J. H. Haycock, similar to house as built] (T. Nicholas, *Annals of the County Families of Wales* ii, 1875, 799).

CHYKNELL, nr. CLAVERLEY, SALOP., for Farmer Taylor, 1814; Dining (now Drawing) Room added by Edward Haycock, 1858 [signed drawings at Chyknell].

OAKELEY HOUSE, nr. BISHOP'S CASTLE, SALOP., alterations and additions for the Revd. Herbert Oakeley, 1814–16; dem. [Shropshire C.R.O., 1079/13].

SHREWSBURY SCHOOL (now Public Library), remodelled Elizabethan library by removing attic storey and inserting Gothic windows and roof, 1815 [contract in Shropshire C.R.O., 3365, box lx, bdl. 2613].

PRADOE, SALOP., alterations for the Hon. Thomas Kenyon, 1818 [plan and specification in scrapbook at Pradoe, *ex inf.* Miss M. C. Hill].

SHREWSBURY, Headmaster's House in School Lane, refronted for Dr. Samuel Butler by J. H. & E. Haycock, 1818, Tudor style [Shrewsbury School Trustees' minutes 1798–1881, p. 60, *ex inf.* Mr. J. B. Lawson].

PRESTON HOSPITAL, PRESTON-ON-THE-WEALD-MOORS, SALOP., addition of curved arcades and outer blocks, 1827 [Bridgeman papers, Preston Hospital records 13/8; agreement between the trustees and J. H. & E. Haycock] (plan in *C. Life*, 16 April 1964, fig. 6).

HAYDEN, —, described as 'Surveyor at the Building of the Right Hon. the Lord Grosvenor', designed THE EASTGATE, CHESTER, 1768–9 [Chester Assembly Book 1725–85].

HAYLEY, WILLIAM (–1860), practised in Manchester from the late 1820s onwards. Until 1840 he was in partnership with Thomas Brown, in conjunction with whom he designed several Commissioners' churches. Brown died in 1840 [Port, 178], and Hayley thereafter practised on his own until he was joined by his son William Henry Hayley. He died at Broughton near Manchester on 30 June 1860. W. H. Hayley subsequently entered into partnership with

William Dawes. Richard Tattersall (*q.v.*) was a pupil of the elder Hayley.

Buildings designed by the firm of Hayley and Brown are listed below. Hayley's independent works included the Italianate tower of ST. THOMAS'S CHURCH, ARDWICK GREEN NORTH, MANCHESTER, which he built in *c.*1836 to the designs of a Mr. Frayer [Church Notes of the Revd. Richard Loxham in Manchester Central Library, ii, f. 98]; the neo-Norman ALL SOULS CHURCH, ANCOATS, MANCHESTER, 1839–40 [Port, 148–9]; the Gothic ST. MATTHEW'S CHURCH, STRETFORD, LANCS., 1841–2 [Port, 148–9] and ST. PAUL'S CHURCH, MACCLESFIELD, CHESHIRE, 1843–4 [Port, 140–1]. A design by him dated 1839 for a Post Office in Manchester is in the Public Record Office (MPD 137).

BOLLINGTON, CHESHIRE, ST. JOHN'S CHURCH, 1832–4, Gothic [Port, 140–1].

NORBURY, CHESHIRE, ST. THOMAS'S CHURCH, 1833–4, Gothic [Port, 140–1].

CHORLTON-ON-MEDLOCK, LANCS., ST. SAVIOUR'S CHURCH, cons. 1836, Gothic; dem. [C. Stewart, *The Architecture of Manchester: An Index of the Principal Buildings and their Architects*, Manchester 1956, 32, citing *Manchester Guardian*, 12 Nov. 1836].

TONG, LANCS., ST. MICHAEL'S CHURCH, 1838–9, Gothic [Port, 150–1].

NEWTON MOOR, nr. HYDE, CHESHIRE, ST. MARY'S CHURCH, 1838–9; chancel 1876–7; neo-Norman [I.C.B.S.].

WITHINGTON, nr. MANCHESTER, ST. PAUL'S CHURCH, 1840–1, neo-Norman [C. Stewart, *op. cit.*, citing *Manchester Courier*, 23 Oct. 1841].

HAYWARD, ABRAHAM (1692–1747), was a native of Whitchurch in Shropshire, but established himself as a mason and master builder in Lincoln. According to family tradition he went to Lincoln to build St. Peter at Arches Church, but as this church was in fact designed and built (1720–4) by William Smith of Warwick it is likely that Hayward was working for Smith, perhaps as his foreman. In 1735 he was one of the builders who gave evidence before the House of Commons as to the condition of Gainsborough Church [*Commons' Journals* xxii, 556–7, 619–21; xxiii, 582, 618]. The County Assembly Rooms in Lincoln were built by him in 1744 [J. W. F. Hill, *Georgian Lincoln*, 1966, 15 n.]. He built the town house of the Disney family in Disney Place, Lincoln, in 1736, and lived in a house which he had built for himself on the east side of St. Peter at Arches churchyard, on the site of the former Taylors' Hall. He died at Lincoln in 1747 and was buried at St. Peter at Arches. His younger brother John Hayward (1708–78), also a mason by trade, accompanied him to Lincoln, purchased the freedom of the city in 1753, and died there in 1778. In 1753 St. Mary's Bridge, Lincoln, was rebuilt 'pursuant to a plan and estimate made by John Hayward, mason' [Lincoln Corporation Minutes 1710–1800, pp. 341, 342]. John Hayward was the grandfather of William Hayward, surveyor to Lincoln Cathedral (*q.v.*), and the father of the architect William Hayward of Shrewsbury (*q.v.*). His daughter Ann married John Carline (*q.v.*), a Lincoln man who afterwards established himself in Shrewsbury.

[E. Venables, *Walks through the Streets of Lincoln*, 1888, 30; Society of Antiquaries, E. J. Willson's Collections, v, 74, and Thomas Sympson's MS. *Adversaria* in the same collection, p. 126; *Lincolnshire Notes and Queries* ix, 1906–7, 66; J. L. Hobbs, 'The Hayward Family of Whitchurch', *Shropshire Magazine*, Jan. 1960; information from Mr. Richard Carline].

HAYWARD, WILLIAM (*c.*1740–1782) was one of the sons of John Hayward of Lincoln (d. 1778) and grandson of Abraham Hayward (*q.v.*). He established himself in Shrewsbury, where from 1766 onwards he was employed by the Trustees for rebuilding the English Bridge, and subsequently acted as deputy surveyor under John Gwynn (*q.v.*) during the building of the new bridge in 1769–74 [MS. minutes of the Trustees in Shropshire C.R.O.]. In the 1770s he was again associated with Gwynn at Oxford, for the latter's plans for paving the city and rebuilding Magdalen Bridge are accompanied by a note that they 'were executed by William Hayward of Shrewsbury, under Mr. Gwynne Architect' [B.L., *King's Maps* xxxiv, 33, 3*a*–*c*].

Hayward himself designed at least three bridges. The first was the bridge over the river Tern at ATCHAM, SHROPSHIRE, which (in the words of the inscription on the parapet) 'was erected at the Expense of the County A.D. MDCCLXXX, and decorated at the Expense of Noel Hill, Esq. William Hayward, Architect'. It was widened in 1932. The second was the important bridge over the river Thames at HENLEY, OXON., for which Hayward made designs in 1781. He died before work had started, as a result of a 'cold and fever' contracted by 'giving up his place inside a coach to a woman on a stormy night'. He is said to have expressed a wish to be buried under the centre arch of the bridge, but was in fact interred in Henley Parish Church, where there is a tablet to his memory (now in the

THE HAYWARDS AND THE CARLINES

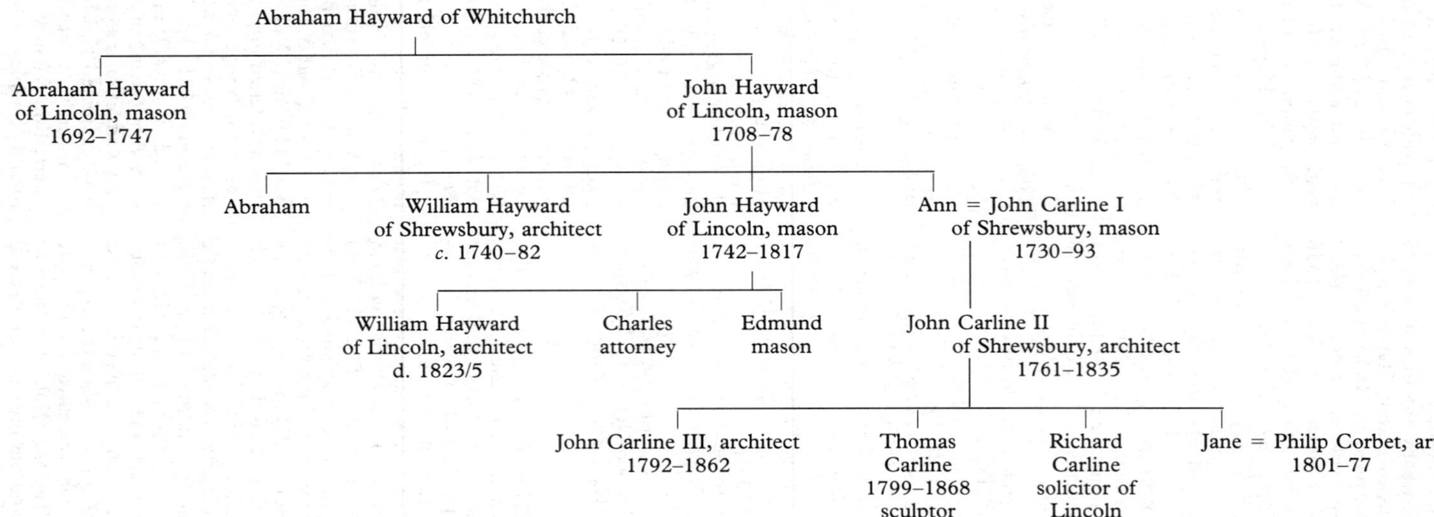

tower). The bridge was built by John Townesend of Oxford and completed in 1786 in accordance with Hayward's designs. The heads of 'Thames' and 'Isis' on the keystones were carved by Mrs. Damer, the daughter of General Conway, of Park Place nearby. Hayward's third bridge was the TERN BRIDGE over the river Tern about half a mile from his Atcham Bridge, which was built by subscription in 1782, and bears an inscription on the central arch recording that it was 'the last Edifice erected by that ingenious Architect William Hayward'.

[*A.P.S.D.*; J. S. Burn, *History of Henley*, 1861, 298; E. J. Climenson, *A Guide to Henley-on-Thames*, 1896, 28; Francis Sheppard, 'Henley Bridge and its Architect', *Arch. Hist.* 27, 1984.]

HAYWARD, WILLIAM (–1823/5), was the son of John Hayward (d. 1817) and grandson of John Hayward (d. 1778). His father, like his grandfather, was a mason by trade, and was twice Mayor of Lincoln, dying in office in 1817 at an advanced age [*Gent's Mag.* 1817 (i), 381]. William Hayward held the post of Surveyor to Lincoln Cathedral from 1799 to 1823 and is generally described as 'architect'. He had a considerable local practice, and the Judges' Lodgings at Lincoln show that he was a competent designer in the 'Regency' style. His reconstruction of Kirton-in-Holland Church in 1804 shows that he also had an understanding of Gothic architecture quite remarkable at this date, and suggests that he may have been a pupil of William Lumby, his predecessor as surveyor to the cathedral. He succeeded his father as Mayor in 1817 and appears to have died in 1823 or 1825. [J. L. Hobbs, 'The Hayward Family of Whitchurch', *Shropshire Magazine*, Jan. 1960; information from Mr. Richard Carline; Lincoln Cathedral archives, Bij.2.12, p. 403].

LINCOLN, ST. SWITHIN'S CHURCH, rebuilt 1802–3; rebuilt 1868–9 [E. Venables, 'History of St. Swithin's Church, Lincoln', *Associated Architectural Societies' Reports and Papers* xix, 1887–8, 27].

LINCOLN, SHIRE HALL, rearranged interior, 1802; dem. 1823 [Lincolnshire Record Office, Minutes of County Meetings, 1792–1823].

LINCOLN CATHEDRAL, rebuilt gable on south side of west transept, 1804 [C. Wild, *The Cathedral Church of Lincoln*, 1819, 23 note].

KIRTON-IN-HOLLAND CHURCH, LINCOLNSHIRE, demolished central tower and transepts, shortened chancel and built new west tower closely resembling and incorporating some features of the demolished central tower, 1804–5 [*Churches in the Division of Holland*, 1843, Kirton, 5; Lincolnshire Record Office, plans in Fac. 9/34] (F. J. Allen, *The Great Church Towers of England*, 1932, 129).

LINCOLN, THE CITY GAOL AND SESSIONS HOUSE (now Police Station), MONKS ROAD, 1805–9 [*The Date Book for Lincoln and Neighbourhood*, Lincoln 1866, 255, 268].

METHERINGHAM VICARAGE, LINCS., altered 1808 [Lincolnshire Record Office, MGA 58].

LINCOLN, ST. MARTIN'S CHURCH, rebuilt north aisle 1809; dem. *c.*1875 [MS. Vestry Minutes].

LINCOLN, THE JUDGES' LODGINGS, CASTLE HILL, 1810–11 [Lincolnshire Record Office, Grand Jury Minute Book, p. 282].

LINCOLN, THE GOWTS BRIDGE, 1813; since rebuilt [A.P.S.D., *s.v.* 'Lincoln'].

SILK WILLOUGHBY RECTORY, LINCS., west front, 1813 [Lincolnshire Record Office, MGA 71].

TORKSEY CHURCH, LINCS., alterations 1821–2 [accounts in parish records].

HAYWOOD, JOHN (1751–), entered the Royal Academy Schools in 1772, and gained the Silver Medal in 1774. He exhibited at the Academy between 1773 and 1794, including an 'Elevation for a market house at Bridgewater' (1780), a 'Design for a lodge to be built at Clehonger, Herefordshire' (1785),[1] and a 'Plan and Elevation for a Mausoleum to the memory of the late Mr. John Smeaton, F.R.S.' (1793), none of which are known to have been built. J. J. Haywood, junior, exhibited student's designs at the Royal Academy from 1790 to 1793 from the same address (75 Long Acre).

HEAL, SAMUEL, was the architect under whose direction the Drawing Room and Dining Room of NETTLECOMBE COURT, SOMERSET, were remodelled in Adamsian style for Sir John Trevelyan, Bart., in 1787–8 [G. U. S. Corbett, 'Nettlecombe Court: the Buildings', *Field Studies* 3 (2), 1970, 293].

HEAN, Messrs., were builders at Dundee and wrights by trade. The firm appears to have been founded by David Hean, senior, during the first quarter of the nineteenth century. Later members of the family were James (who lectured on domestic architecture at the

[1] The seat of the Aubrey family at Clehonger was destroyed by fire in 1785. The estate was bought by Col. John Matthews, who in 1788–90 built a new house called Belmont to the designs of James Wyatt (C. J. Robinson, *The Mansions of Herefordshire*, 1872, 66).

Watt Institute on 27 January 1830), Alexander (d. 1865), Peter (d. 1877) and David, junior (d. 1878). The last was a Town Councillor, Baillie and Dean of Guild. The principal architectural works for which the firm was responsible before 1840 were ST. PETER'S FREE CHURCH, DUNDEE, 1836 [*ex inf.* Mr. David Walker] and the enlargement in 1837 of the south side of ST. AIDAN'S CHURCH, BROUGHTY FERRY, DUNDEE [*Dundee Advertiser*, 1 March 1837]. [Information from Mr. David Walker.]

HEATHER, CHARLES (–1845), began his career as clerk of the works under John Nash (*q.v.*) at Ingestre Hall in Staffordshire and Garnstone Castle in Herefordshire. In 1812, following the conclusion of the works at Garnstone, he established himself as a surveyor and builder in Hereford. In 1825 he was appointed Surveyor of the County buildings and in 1831 of the County bridges also in succession to John Gethin (*q.v.*). In 1836 he added a Gothic porch to ST. PETER'S CHURCH, HEREFORD [I.C.B.S.]; in 1840–1 he rebuilt the tower of ASHPERTON CHURCH, HEREFS., at the W. end [I.C.B.S.]; and in 1840–1 he repaired MUCH COWARNE CHURCH, HEREFS., after it had been badly damaged by lightning [Vestry Minutes in Herefs. C.R.O.]. Heather died in 1845, leaving a son, William Heather, who had already established a separate business as a surveyor and builder in Eign Gate, Hereford [will in Consistory Court of Hereford, Sept. 1845; information from Mr. C. J. Pickford].

HEATON, WILLIAM, was a Georgian architect working in Cumberland and Westmorland. In 1776–82 he enlarged and remodelled UNERIGG, nr. MARYPORT, CUMBERLAND, for John Christian, adding a substantial central block with two pediments, largely dem. 1903 [B. Tyson, 'Unerigg Hall, Cumbria', *Ancient Monuments Soc's Trans.* N.S. 26, 1982]. At the same time Heaton was employed at BELLE ISLE, WINDERMERE, perhaps in fitting up the interior of the circular house designed by John Plaw (*q.v.*) for Thomas English [Tyson, *op. cit.*, 24]. In 1778–9 Heaton altered a vernacular house, THE CRAGG, TROUTBECK, WESTMORLAND, for George Otley [B. Tyson, 'The Cragg, Troutbeck, and the Otley family', *Trans. Cumberland & Westmorland Antiq. & Archl. Soc.* 78, 1978].

HEDGELAND, CHARLES, practised in Exeter during the second quarter of the nineteenth century and was a younger son of Caleb Hedgeland (d. 1839), a builder of that city. His marriage in 1823 is noted in *Gent's Mag.* 1823, 82. He designed MANATON RECTORY, DEVON, in 1825 [Exeter Diocesan Records]; enlarged the nave of SOUTH MOLTON CHURCH, DEVON, in 1825–9 [I.C.B.S.]; designed a small Greek Revival church at STARCROSS, nr. DAWLISH, DEVON, in 1826–7, remodelled in Romanesque style 1854 [Port, 142–3]; and reconstructed ST. PETROCK'S CHURCH, EXETER, in 1828 [G. Oliver, *Ecclesiastical Antiquities in Devon*, 1840, ii, 196; R. Dymond, *Calendar of Deeds and Documents belonging to the Feoffees of the Parish Property*, Exeter 1889, 38].

HEDGELAND, JOHN PIKE (1791–1873), was the son of Caleb Hedgeland (d. 1839), a builder of Exeter. He was awarded the silver medal of the Society of Arts for an architectural drawing in 1819. In the same year he was an unsuccessful competitor for the church of St. Peter, Eaton Square, Westminster. He exhibited architectural drawings at the Royal Academy in 1822 and 1823, and was the author of a work entitled *First Part of a Series of Designs for Private Dwellings*, 1821, containing 20 lithographic plates. He took up glass-painting as result of acting as executor to the enamel painter Charles Muss (d.1824), and eventually abandoned architecture for that art. In 1826–9 he supervised the careful restoration of the early sixteenth-century glass in the windows of ST. NEOT'S CHURCH, CORNWALL, subsequently publishing in 1830 *A Description, accompanied by Sixteen Coloured Plates, of the Windows of St. Neot's Church, Cornwall.* In 1841–5 he was similarly employed to repair the windows of King's College Chapel, Cambridge [Willis & Clark, i, 515].

Hedgeland died in Exeter on 2 May 1873 [Boase & Courtney, *Bibliotheca Cornubiensis*, 1874–82, i, 226, ii, 1225; *Downside Review* viii, 1889, 114]. As a glass-painter he was succeeded by his son George Hedgeland, whose major work was the west window of Norwich Cathedral [*Jnl. British Soc. of Master Glass Painters* xiii, 1959–63, 392–3].

HEDGER, WILLIAM, of South Street, West Square, Southwark, was a member of a family of speculative builders active in Southwark at the end of the eighteenth century [*Survey of London* xxv, 52–6]. In 1807–8 he supervised extensive internal alterations to ST. GEORGE'S CHURCH, SOUTHWARK, after a survey by S. P. Cockerell. They included new north and south galleries and a new ceiling with painted decoration [Surrey Archdeaconry Records]. William Hedger, junior, of the same address, exhibited a view of St. Pancras Church at the Royal Academy in 1827.

HEITON, ANDREW (*c.*1793–1858), practised in Perth, where he died on 8 August 1858 [S.R.O., SC 49/31/66]. In Perthshire he designed GARTH HOUSE for General Sir Archibald Campbell, Bart., *c.*1840, Gothic [A. H. Millar, *Castles and Mansions of Perthshire and Forfarshire*, 1890, 64]; enlarged REDGORTON CHURCH, 1840–1 [S.R.O., HR 311/2, p. 92 *et seq.*]; and rebuilt ST. MARTIN'S CHURCH, 1842–3 [S.R.O., HR 514/1]. His son Andrew Heiton, junior (1823–94), was a pupil of David Bryce. In 1848 he joined his father in practice and ultimately became City Architect. He specialized in Scottish Baronial country houses. The family practice was continued by Andrew Heiton III (born Andrew Heiton Grainger), who died in the 1920s [information from Mr. George Hay and Mr. David Walker].

HEMSLEY, HENRY (*c.*1764–1808), a pupil of Henry Holland, was admitted to the Royal Academy Schools in 1787 at the age of 23, and was awarded the Silver Medal in 1788. He exhibited student's designs at the Academy from 1785 to 1790. In 1805 he was appointed architect to the Barrack Department of the War Office in succession to James Johnson. He was presumably the Henry Hemsley of Hans Place who died on 25 May 1808 [*Gent's Mag.* 1808 (i), 405].

The Henry Hemsley who died in Vincent Square on 30 May 1825, at the age of 33, leaving a widow and six infant children, was presumably his son [*Gent's Mag.* 1825 (i), 572]. This younger Hemsley had exhibited at the Academy from Vincent Square in 1819, 1821 and 1822, and had made designs for ST. GEORGE'S CHURCH, RAMSGATE, KENT, 'but in consequence of his death, shortly after the commencement of the building, the completion of it devolved on Mr. H. E. Kendall, who made some few alterations' [*The Watering Places of Great Britain and Fashionable Directory*, 1833, 217].

HENDERSON, DAVID (–*c.*1787), was a mason from Sauchie near Alloa who established himself in Edinburgh. In February 1765, while still resident at Sauchie, he was awarded the prize of 30 guineas offered for the best design for the North Bridge, but in May the committee declared that, as he 'had failed in finding security to execute the Bridge agreeable to his estimates', the design and estimate of William Mylne (*q.v.*) would be accepted instead. However in 1769 Henderson was among those who reported on the state of Mylne's bridge after its partial collapse, and in 1784 he was employed to carry out some work on its structure. In 1781–2 AULDGIRTH BRIDGE, DUMFRIESSHIRE (R. Nith) was built to his designs [G. W. Shirley, 'The Building of Auldgirth Bridge', *Trans. Dumfriesshire & Galloway Nat. Hist. & Antiqn. Soc.* 3rd ser. 23, 1940–4], and in 1785–6 he was responsible for designing and building the important bridge of four arches which carries the main road from Edinburgh to Berwick over the Pease Dean near Cockburnspath. He was also employed to make designs and estimates for the Borrowstounness Canal Company. In Edinburgh, when the idea of rebuilding the University was first contemplated in 1767, he was paid 10 guineas for making a plan, and in 1773, as 'David Henderson, Architect', he contracted to build INVERLEITH HOUSE (now within the Edinburgh Botanic Gardens) for James Rocheid, evidently to his own designs [Edinburgh Public Library, MS. decreet referring to the contract]. Inverleith House is a small villa with quadrant wings in the Palladian tradition. It was extensively repaired after a fire in 1876.

Like most Edinburgh builder-architects, Henderson was involved in speculative developments, one of which (though abortive) is of interest because as early as 1785 it envisaged 'an assemblage of Gentlemen's Villas, bounded upon the outer line by a plantation of forest trees, and the internal boundaries of each lot by a continuation of flowering shrubs; and each Villa situated in such a manner as not to overlook another' [J. Gifford *et al.*, *Edinburgh*, Buildings of Scotland, 1984, 610].

Henderson had two sons, David and John. David was in business in Alloa as a millwright, but John was destined to be an architect, for in or about 1774 his father sent him to Rome, whence he returned in 1779. There he became friendly with Thomas Hardwick, and competed with the young Soane for the fickle patronage of the Bishop of Derry, who wanted a design for a summer dining-room at his Irish seat of Downhill [P. de la R. du Prey in *Arch. Hist.* xv, 1972, 52]. In 1785 he exhibited a 'plan, elevation and section of a temple' at the Royal Academy in London. The only buildings known to have been erected to his designs are the wings which he added to AMISFIELD HOUSE, EAST LOTHIAN in 1785 for Francis Charteris (afterwards titular Earl of Wemyss), dem. *c.*1928 [J. Miller, *History of Haddington*, 1844, 527],[1] and THE ASSEMBLY ROOMS, GEORGE STREET, EDINBURGH, 1784–7, to which the portico was added in 1818 [S.R.O., GD 15/798, minutes of the

[1] Cf. an engraving of the house from a drawing by 'that ingenious architect, Mr. John Henderson' in *Archaeologia Scotica* i, 1792, p. 46.

committee for building the Assembly Rooms]. At Amisfield the stable block and the walled garden, with four Doric porticos at the corners, dated 1783, may also be attributed to him.

John Henderson died at Edinburgh on 16 February 1786 [*Scots Mag.* xlviii, 1786, 103], and his father appears to have died within the next two years. The 'heirs and creditors' of 'the two Mr. Hendersons' are referred to in the minutes of the committee for building the Assembly Rooms in August 1788, and in June 1789 the surviving son David was claiming money due to himself as heir to both. But for John Henderson's premature death he might well have emerged as one of Edinburgh's leading Georgian architects.

In 1765 David Henderson was stated in the *Edinburgh Advertiser* to have published proposals for printing 'a book of architecture', but this evidently came to nothing. A design by him for a vine-house is among the Fairlie papers in the Scottish Record Office (GD 237/113/4).

[*A.P.S.D.*; J. Grant, *Old and New Edinburgh* i, n.d., 337; A. J. Youngson, *The Making of Classical Edinburgh*, 1966, 62–5, 124; *Scots Mag.* xxxvi, 1774, 108; S.R.O., Edinburgh Testaments, CC 8/8/128/1, 18 June 1789.]

HENDERSON, JOHN (–1786), *see* HENDERSON, DAVID.

HENDERSON, JOHN (*c.*1813–1844) was the eldest son of John Henderson, a builder of Edinburgh who died in 1860 aged 76. On the family monument in St. Cuthbert's Churchyard, Edinburgh, he is described as 'Architect', but he died in May 1844 at the early age of 31, and no building designed by him has so far been identified. His sister Margaret married Robert Brown (*q.v.*). He must be distinguished from John Henderson (1804–62), originally of Brechin, who had an extensive architectural practice in Edinburgh in the 1840s and 1850s, and is buried in the Grange Cemetery.

HENDERSON, *alias* ANDERSON, WILLIAM (*c.*1737–1824) and his son JOHN (*c.*1761–1800) were architects and builders at Loughborough in Leicestershire, where their surname usually appears in local records as 'Henderson' but sometimes as 'Anderson'. In 1768–70 William Henderson 'of Staunton' built the LEICESTER INFIRMARY under the direction of Benjamin Wyatt. He had previously submitted designs which may have been modified by Wyatt [minutes of the committee in the Leicestershire Record Office.] At this time (1762–75) he was engaged in rebuilding STAUNTON HAROLD HALL, LEICS., for Washington, 5th Earl Ferrers (*q.v.*), who, according to Throsby's *Select Views of Leicestershire* i, 1759, 126, designed the house himself [building accounts in Leicestershire Record Office]. 'Mr. Anderson' was the 'architect and undertaker' of STANFORD HALL, NOTTS., for Charles Vere Dashwood in 1771–4 [Thoroton's *History of Nottinghamshire*, ed. Throsby, 1797, i, 9] (Neale, *Views of Seats*, 1st ser., ii, 1819), and in 1781 Samuel Stretton of Nottingham built WILFORD HALL, NOTTS., for Samuel Smith, 'under the direction of Anderson of Loughborough, Architect' [*The Stretton Manuscripts*, ed. G. C. Robertson, 1910, 227]. Stanford and Wilford are substantial Georgian houses with restrained neo-classical detailing in the style of Adam. Unexecuted designs for a lunatic asylum at Leicester made by William Henderson in 1781 are in the Leicestershire Record Office. William Henderson died at Loughborough in March 1824, aged 87 [Burial Register]. His son John predeceased him, dying on 8 June 1800, aged 39. John and his mother are commemorated by a slate tombstone in All Saints churchyard, Loughborough [Edward Saunders, 'A Midlands Architect Rediscovered', *C. Life*, 10 May 1979].

HENRY, JOHN, practised in Edinburgh during the first quarter of the nineteenth century. He appears to have had some connection with William Stark (*q.v.*), and may have been his pupil. After Stark's death in 1813, Henry was appointed to oversee the execution of his plans for the Signet Library in Edinburgh, and he provided various drawings, e.g. for altering Robert Reid's staircase and for the ante-room to the new library [*History of the Society of Writers to the Signet*, 1890, 431; Iain G. Brown, *Building for Books*, Aberdeen 1989, 95]. In 1822 Henry designed WICK CHURCH, CAITHNESS, completed (after delays) in 1830. An account of the laying of the foundation stone records that 'The Church was designed and drawn by Messrs John Henry and James Cormack of Edinburgh, the latter of whom has since been appointed Contractor for completing the building' [N.M.R.S.].

HENSON, SAMUEL, was a builder and surveyor of Burlescombe, nr. Tiverton in Devon. He enlarged CULMSTOCK CHURCH, DEVON, in 1824–5 [C. Brooks in Royal Archaeological Institute, *The Exeter Area*, 1990, 91] and repewed CHURCHSTANTON CHURCH, SOMERSET, in *c.*1830 [I.C.B.S.]. Samuel Henson, jnr., of Uffculme, 'builder', repaired PLYMTREE CHURCH, DEVON, in 1827–9 [Brooks, *op. cit.*].

HENWOOD, LUKE (–1830), 'architect', was admitted to the freedom of the City of Bristol on 19 September 1789, on payment of 15 guineas [City Archives]. He was one of the District Surveyors for Bristol from 1804 until his death, which took place on 19 March 1830 [A. Beaven, *Bristol Lists*, 1899, 248; *Gent's Mag.* 1830 (i), 379]. In 1807–8 he repaired the tower of ALL SAINTS CHURCH, BRISTOL, and reconstructed the stone cupola, altering the outline of the dome. The cupola was again rebuilt in 1930 [MS. Vestry Minutes]. Among the drawings from Trewithen, Cornwall, in the Cornwall C.R.O. there are undated drawings signed by Henwood for alterations to No. 30, ARGYLL STREET, LONDON (dem.), for Christopher Hawkins, M.P. The works included a new front door with elegantly designed detail.

HEPPER, DENT (–*c.*1822), practised in Chelmsford. In 1812, when he was one of the unsuccessful candidates for the County Surveyorship of Essex, he stated that he had been in practice in the county for 25 years [Essex Record Office, Q/SO 22, pp. 40–1; advt. in *Chelmsford Chronicle*, 18 Sept. 1812]. In 1808 Hepper designed ROCHFORD RECTORY, ESSEX [Guildhall Library, London, London Diocesan Records, MS. 9532/10, Faculty Register, ff. 58–60]. In 1818 he designed a S. gallery for CHELMSFORD CHURCH, similar to an earlier design by him for a N. gallery [Essex Record Office, Chelmsford Vestry Minutes, D/P 94/8/3]. His designs for a house at Eye in Suffolk for Thomas Wythe, dated 1815, are in the Suffolk Record Office at Ipswich [S 1/2/300/69].

HERBERT, HENRY, 9TH EARL OF PEMBROKE (*c.*1689–1750), was the eldest son of Thomas, 8th Earl of Pembroke, whom he succeeded in 1733. He was educated at Christ Church, Oxford, where he matriculated in 1705 at the age of 16. His presence in Venice in 1712 is evidence that he subsequently went on the Grand Tour. On the accession of George I he was appointed a Lord of the Bedchamber to the Prince of Wales, a post which he retained on the latter's accession to the throne as George II in 1727. In 1735 he was made First Lord of the Bedchamber and Groom of the Stole. He also held various military commands, attaining the rank of Lieutenant-General in 1742. His friendship with the antiquary William Stukeley and his election to the Royal Society in 1743 are indications of his intellectual interests. He died suddenly at his house in Privy Gardens, Whitehall, on 9 January 1749/50.

Pembroke inherited his father's fondness for the arts, but architecture was his special interest. As befitted the owner of Wilton, he favoured the Palladian style which Inigo Jones had been the first to introduce into England, and which in his own time was being revived through the influence of Lord Burlington. In the absence of personal papers or correspondence, the development of his architectural taste is undocumented, but the fact that he was at Christ Church in the time of Dean Aldrich should not be overlooked.[1]

That Pembroke was more than merely an intelligent patron of architecture is clearly implied by Vertue, Walpole and other eighteenth-century writers. Walpole indeed thought him a better architect – i.e. a purer Palladian – than either Burlington or Kent, and it is true that most of the buildings with which he was associated adhere closely to Palladian prototypes – notably the bridge at Wilton and three villa-like houses reminiscent of Palladio's Villa Emo at Fanzolo, i.e. his own house in Whitehall (designed 1723), Marble Hill, Twickenham (begun 1724), and the White Lodge at Richmond (begun 1727).[2] The English prototype is Colen Campbell's Newby Park in Yorkshire, begun in 1720. Lord Herbert and Campbell had a link in their common association with the Prince of Wales (Herbert as a Lord of the Bedchamber from 1715, Campbell as the Prince's architect from 1719), and in 1723 it was Campbell who designed Herbert's house in Whitehall. He may also have had a hand in Marble Hill, but from about 1725 his place as Herbert's architectural collaborator was taken by Roger Morris, who was to be concerned in nearly all of his patron's subsequent building activities.

A list of buildings for whose design Pembroke appears to have been in some way responsible is given below. The problem is to determine whether, like Aldrich and Burlington, the 'Architect Earl' could envisage a building in detail and express his ideas on paper in a form intelligible to others, or whether he worked entirely through architectural amanuenses. No authenticated drawings by Pembroke have yet been discovered, though a plan and two elevations for the Water Tower at Houghton may be in his hand.

Apart from the buildings which he and Morris erected, Lord Pembroke's interest in

[1] As an undergraduate he subscribed £20 to the building of Peckwater Quadrangle to Aldrich's designs.

[2] For South Dalton Hall, Yorkshire, another house of this group, see W. A. Eden in *The Country Seat*, ed. Colvin & Harris, 1970.

architecture was demonstrated by the prominent part which he took in the construction of Westminster Bridge, of which he laid the first stone in 1739, and the last in 1747. He used his influence to defend the Swiss architect Labelye against the attacks of Batty Langley, Hawksmoor and others, whose designs had been rejected. Drawings and minutes connected with the bridge are preserved among the Earl's papers now in the Wiltshire County Record Office. Among these papers there are two drawings (P 6/20 for the Column of Victory at Blenheim, and H3/11 for a temple) that may possibly be in Pembroke's hand.

[G.E.C., *Complete Peerage*; *A.P.S.D.*; *D.N.B.*; Walpole, *Anecdotes of Painting*, ed. Dallaway & Wornum iii, 1862, 771–2; J. Lees-Milne, *Earls of Creation*, 1962, 59–100; R. J. B. Walker, *Old Westminster Bridge*, 1979.]

BUILDINGS ASSOCIATED WITH LORD PEMBROKE

LONDON, WHITEHALL, house (afterwards PEMBROKE HOUSE) for himself, 1724; rebuilt 1757, dem. 1913. The plate in *Vitruvius Britannicus* iii, 1725, pl. 48, is signed 'Co: Campbell Architectus'. An original elevation, dated August 1723, is in the Lister Collection in the Treasury Library, Whitehall, no. 52 b. The hand does not appear to be Campbell's. At Wilton there is another elevation signed 'Rog[r]. Morris Delt.' (reproduced by Draper & Eden, *Marble Hill House*, pl. 5). For an alternative design by William Dickinson dated 1723 see *Wren Soc.* xvii, pl. xlviii. The house is described in *Survey of London* xiii, 167–75.

MARBLE HILL, TWICKENHAM, MIDDLESEX, for Henrietta Howard, Countess of Suffolk, mistress of George II, 1724–9. Illustrated by Campbell in *Vitruvius Britannicus* iii, pl. 93, but without naming any architect. Ascribed by Walpole to Pembroke. The bills, among the Hobart papers in the Norfolk Record Office, show that Roger Morris was in charge, but that most of the money was 'Received of the Hon[ble] Mrs. Howard by the Hands of the R[t] Hon[ble] Lord Herbert'. The history of the house is fully discussed by Marie P. G. Draper and W. A. Eden, *Marble Hill House*, 1970.

THE WHITE LODGE, RICHMOND NEW PARK, begun 1727 for George I, completed 1728 for George II. Ascribed by Walpole to Pembroke, but Roger Morris was in charge of the building operations and is described as architect in *Vitruvius Britannicus* iv, 1767, pls. 1–4. The wings were added in the 1760s. See *History of the King's Works* v, 230–3 for documentation and further details.

WESTCOMBE HOUSE, BLACKHEATH, KENT, was built by Lord Herbert in 1727–8 after purchasing the property from the heirs of Capt. Galfridus Walpole, who had died in 1726. Sarah, Duchess of Marlborough, described the house in 1732 in terms which make it clear that it was designed by Herbert, and it closely resembled Whitton Place, Middlesex, designed for the Earl of Islay by Herbert's collaborator Roger Morris *c.*1732. A plan and elevation are among the Herbert papers now in the Wilts. C.R.O. It was demolished in 1854 [Larking, *Hundred of Blackheath*, ed. Drake, 1886, 53; *Letters of a Grandmother*, ed. G. Scott Thompson, 1943, 21–3, 53] (Watts, *Views of Seats*, pl. 1, 1779; Sandby, *Select Views in England etc.* i, 1781, pl. 24).

CASTLE HILL, DEVONSHIRE, remodelled for Lord Clinton (afterwards 1st Lord Fortescue) by Roger Morris under the direction of Lord Burlington and Lord Herbert, 1729 onwards [see above, p. 150 and below, p. 667].

BLENHEIM PALACE, OXON., THE COLUMN OF VICTORY, for Sarah, Duchess of Marlborough, 1730–1. Hawksmoor, who had previously made designs for the column which were not adopted, described it in 1731 as 'conducted by my Ld. Herbert' and there is evidence that Roger Morris was concerned in its construction [David Green, 'Blenheim Column of Victory', *Arch. Rev.*, April 1950; Angela Green, 'Letters of Sarah, Duchess of Marlborough, on the Column of Victory at Blenheim', *Oxoniensia* xxxi, 1966].

WIMBLEDON HOUSE, SURREY, for Sarah, Duchess of Marlborough, 1732–3; destroyed by fire 1785. Walpole, writing in the 1750s, says the house was designed 'by Henry Earl of Pembroke', but Roger Morris is given as architect in *Vitruvius Britannicus* v, 1771, pls. 20–22. A letter from the Duchess to Pembroke (then Lord Herbert), dated 25 March 1732, mentions Morris in connection with the works then in progress, but implies that he was following Herbert's directions (B.L., Add. MS. 61477, f. 34). Others published in *Letters of a Grandmother*, ed. G. Scott Thompson, 1943, 35, 70, 104, 123, indicate that Francis Smith of Warwick was employed as surveyor. There is a plan of the house at Wilton. Plans for the layout of the grounds are in Bodleian, MS. Gough Drawings a.3, f. 31 and a.4, f. 44. [M. P. G. Draper in *C. Life*, 2 August 1962].

WILTON HOUSE, WILTS., THE PALLADIAN BRIDGE,

1736–7. Vertue, writing in 1740, says 'this is the design of the present Earl of Pembroke and built by his direction' [Walpole Society, *Vertue Note Books* v, 130]. Roger Morris is, however, described as 'Architect' on the plate in *Vitruvius Britannicus* v, 1771, pl. 89, and in the Royal Library at Windsor there is a drawing of the bridge signed 'R. Morris'. Copies of the Wilton Bridge were later erected at Stowe (before 1742), Prior Park, Bath (1756), Hagley (before 1764) and Amesbury (1777).

HOUGHTON HALL, NORFOLK, THE WATER HOUSE, for Robert Walpole, 1st Earl of Orford, probably *c.*1730. Drawings in the Metropolitan Museum of Art from the grangerised manuscript of Horace Walpole's *Aedes Walpolianae* are inscribed by Walpole 'The Water-House in the Park, designed by Henry Lord Herbert, afterwards Earl of Pembroke' [John Harris, 'The Water Tower at Houghton', *Burl. Mag.* cxi, 1969, 300: John Harris, *Catalogue of British Drawings for Architecture etc. in American Collections*, 1971, 122 and pls. 88–9; R. Bowden-Smith, *The Water House, Houghton Hall, Norfolk*, 1987].

HIGHCLERE, HANTS. Pembroke's brother the Hon. Robert Herbert (1693–1769), who inherited Highclere under the will of his maternal grandfather Sir Robert Sawyer (d. 1692), may well have obtained his help in embellishing his grounds with certain garden buildings which, although undocumented and undated, appear to have been erected by him. Indeed in his *Historic Lands of England* ii, 1849, 152, Sir Bernard Burke states that Pembroke was responsible for the Palladian MILFORD LAKE HOUSE, the most important of these buildings. The Ionic Temple (remodelled by Barry) may date from the second half of the 18th century, but the Corinthian temple known as JACKDAW'S CASTLE is clearly of earlier date and was in fact built *c.*1740, incorporating columns salvaged from the ruins of Devonshire House, Piccadilly, when that house was burned in 1733 [B.L., Add. MS. 15776, ff. 272–3; letter of 1757 from Charles Lyttelton to Sanderson Miller in Warwicks. C.R.O.].

HERBERT, WILLIAM (*c.*1792–1863), was a successful London builder and surveyor who lived in Farm Street, Berkeley Square. He was one of the builders associated with Thomas Cubitt in the development of Belgravia, and established his own sawmills on a site in Pimlico. When Cubitt moved to a new house in Clapham Park in 1832 it was Herbert who took over and enlarged his former residence, Cavendish House on Clapham Common, and in 1841 Herbert's daughter married Cubitt's lawyer, James Hopgood [Hermione Hobhouse, *Thomas Cubitt*, 1971, 90, 185, 253–4; E. E. F. Smith, *Clapham*, 1975, 78].

Herbert was the builder responsible for the West Strand Improvements of 1830–2. These included the surviving stuccoed block opposite Charing Cross Station now occupied by Coutts's Bank and the Lowther Arcade demolished in 1902. In an illustrated article on 'The Improvements near Charing Cross' in the *Gentleman's Magazine* for 1831 (i), 201–6, it is stated that 'the architect and builder of the whole comprised in this triangle is Mr. William Herbert, of Farm Street, Berkeley Square', but although some details may have been left to Herbert it is clear that the whole scheme, including the elevations and the Arcade, was designed by Nash [M. V. Stokes, 'The Lowther Arcade in the Strand', *London Topographical Record* xxiii, 1972, 119–28].

For over 40 years Herbert was Surveyor of Buildings to the Excise Office. It was in this capacity that in 1829 he made plans [P.R.O., MPD 68] for internal alterations to the EXCISE OFFICE, OLD BROAD STREET, LONDON (dem. 1854) and designed the EXCISE OFFICE at BRISTOL, 1833–40 (dem.) [*A.P.S.D.*, *s.v.* 'Bristol']. He also designed a lead works at BIRMINGHAM in 1837 [B. Little, *Birmingham Buildings*, 1971, fig. 46]. He retired in 1861 and died on 18 September 1863 [*Parliamentary Papers*, 1862 (Superannuation Allowances, 260), 1864 (Increase and Diminution of Public Offices, Sessional Paper No. 169)].

HERBERTSON, JOHN (–1854), practised in Glasgow, where in 1809, as 'John Herbertson, junior, architect', he was admitted to the Incorporation of Wrights [*The Incorporation of Wrights in Glasgow*, Glasgow 1880, 55]. In early life he was in David Hamilton's office. For many years he was architect to the Lanarkshire Prison Board. John Baird (1798–1859), John Carrick (1819–90) and Alexander Munro are all stated by Gildard to have been his assistants. He reseated the OUTER HIGH CHURCH, GLASGOW, in 1812–13, designed the new COUNTY BRIDEWELL *c.*1823, submitted a design for ST. DAVID'S CHURCH in 1824 that was not accepted, and designed BALFRON CHURCH, STIRLINGSHIRE, 1832 [advt. in *Stirling Journal and Advertiser*, 5 April 1832, *ex inf.* Mr. David Walker], HAGGS CHURCH, DENNY, STIRLINGSHIRE, designed 1832, completed 1840 [*Stirling Journal and Advertiser*, 24 May

1832, *ex inf.* Mr. Walker] and ST. COLUMBA'S CHURCH, HOPE STREET, GLASGOW, 1838–9; dem. *c.*1900. He supervised the building of the Royal Exchange to David Hamilton's designs in 1827–9 [C. C. Brewsher, *The Glasgow Royal Exchange . . . Centenary*, 1927]. He died on 23 Feb. 1854 [S.R.O., SC 36/48/40, p. 418].

[Thomas Gildard, 'An Old Glasgow Architect on some Older Ones', *Trans. Royal Philosophical Soc. of Glasgow* xxvi, 1895, 108; *A.P.S.D.*, *s.v.* 'Glasgow'; *Extracts from the Records of the Burgh of Glasgow*, ed. Renwick, x, 133, 220–1, xi, 196.]

HEWETT, SIR THOMAS (1656–1726), was a Whig country gentleman and *virtuoso* who from 1719 to 1726 held the post of Surveyor-General of the King's Works. He was the great-grandson of a London merchant who had acquired the estate of Shireoaks near Worksop in Nottinghamshire, where Thomas was born on 9 September 1656. He was educated at Shrewsbury and Christ Church, Oxford, and then 'travelled about 5 years in France, Holland and Switzerland, Italy and Germany'. He is known to have visited Padua in February 1688 [*Architectural Review*, Nov. 1957, 344], and he married his wife (Frances, daughter of Sir Edward Bettinson of Scadbury in Kent) at Geneva in September 1689. He subsequently obtained some minor government posts, including the surveyorship of Woods North of Trent in 1696 and of Woods both North and South of Trent in 1715. In 1716 Walpole dismissed him from the latter in favour of another claimant, but in 1719 Walpole's rival Sunderland made him Surveyor of the Royal Works in place of the disgraced Benson. He was knighted the same year and retained the post until his death.

The surveyor-generalship was an appropriate post for Hewett to hold, for he was seriously interested in architecture. He strongly disapproved of the 'strange Bulky Buildings' of Vanbrugh and Hawksmoor, 'composed of Towers, Breaks, Rustic key stones, etc., out of all manner of proportion & reason', and was a leading member of the 'new Junta for Architecture' which was already trying to steer British architecture in a neo-classical direction before Lord Burlington's Palladian revival.[1] As Surveyor-General to George I his opportunities were limited, but he was proud of the new state rooms at Kensington Palace 'exactly done according to the Grecian tast', and George Vertue reported that in his own gardens at Shireoaks he built a 'greek Tempietto' decorated with 'pillasters of 3 greek Orders, the floors marble, ceilings painted by . . . Trench . . . [and a] Bust of Sr. Th. in Marble by [Rysbrack]'. How far he was his own architect it is difficult to say, but in his will he states that he has 'begun the building of a House in the Wood called Scratoe', and enjoins his executors to complete 'severall cutts and ornaments in and about the said wood according to a draught and design which I have made and drawn thereof'. It was under his directions – and presumably to designs prescribed if not actually drawn by him – that Lord Sunderland's celebrated library in Piccadilly was built in 1720–2 [*Survey of London* xxxii, 368; B.L., Add. MS. 61655]: described by Macky as 'the finest in Europe, both for the disposition of the Apartments, as of the Books', it was demolished in 1758.

In 1706 'Mr. Hewett' was paid £30 by the Earl of Portland at the start of his works at BULSTRODE PARK, BUCKS. [Nottingham Univ. Library, Portland Papers, Account book in Box 28]. In 1710 it was 'from a design of Sir Thomas Hewit' that HEADON HALL, NOTTS. (dem. 1796) had been built by Sir Hardolph Wastneys [Thoroton's *Antiquities of Notts.*, ed. J. Throsby, 1790–6, iii, 253], and Hewett was Lord Chancellor Macclesfield's architectural adviser in the reconstruction of SHIRBURN CASTLE, OXON., *c.*1716–25 [Shirburn Castle, N. Library, Bundle 7 and Hist. MSS. Comm., *Various Collections* viii, 371]. He acted in the same capacity in connection with the building of HURSLEY LODGE (now PARK), HANTS., for Macclesfield's son-in-law Sir William Heathcote, Bart., in 1721–4, and was responsible for the layout of the grounds as well as providing architectural advice and possibly designs [Hampshire C.R.O., 63 M 84/93, 94, 109]. For this house, whose attribution to John James by G. F. Prosser, *Select Illustrations of Hampshire*, 1833, *s.v.* 'Herriard', finds no support in the building records in the Heathcote papers in the Hampshire C.R.O., see *C. Life*. 13 Dec. 1902 (before enlargement in 1902–3) and 23–30 Oct. 1909 (after enlargement). In addition Hawksmoor (who was prejudiced against Hewett for not restoring him to his place in the Office of Works) tells us that he was responsible for the stables at THORESBY HOUSE, NOTTS., which he dismisses as 'the only piece of Building that Sr. Tho. Hewett was Guilty of, dureing his being Architect Royall. . . . and the most infamous that ever was made' [*Walpole Soc.* xix, 1931, 126]. They were built *c.*1725 and demolished in the nineteenth century.

Hewett died on 9 April 1726, and was buried at Wales Church, Yorkshire, where there

[1] See GALILEI, ALESSANDRO for further details.

is an inscription to his memory. A inventory of his possessions at Shireoaks includes several works of art, among them his own portrait by Bombelli [Arundel Castle MSS. In. 4]. Of his seat at Shireoaks there survives the basically Elizabethan house, reduced in size and much altered, and portions of the extensive and elaborate layout seen in a surviving plan in the Sheffield Archives.

[*History of the King's Works* v, 71–3; Walpole Soc., *Vertue Note Books* ii, 36 and vi, 23, 70; Ilaria Toesca, 'Alessandro Galilei in Inghilterra' in *English Miscellany*, ed. M. Praz, iii, 1952; Hist. MSS. Comm., *Various Collections* viii, 368; letters to Hugh Howard 1725–6 in National Library of Ireland, PC 227, *ex inf.* Dr. Edward McParland; J. Holland, *History of Worksop*, 1826, 175–7; P.C.C., 99 PLYMOUTH; inscription in Wales Church.]

HIDE, EDWARD, was an architect and builder at Worthing in Sussex. 'Messrs. Hides' designed the THEATRE ROYAL in ANNE STREET, 1806, closed 1855 and subsequently used as a warehouse [M. T. Odell, *The Old Theatre, Worthing*, Aylesbury 1938, 14]. In 1812 Edward Hide completed the interior of ST. PAUL'S CHURCH, WORTHING, designed by J. B. Rebecca [*The Watering-Places of Great Britain and Fashionable Directory*, 1833, 69]. In 1825–7 he enlarged and reseated BROADWATER CHURCH, SUSSEX [I.C.B.S.] and in 1828 he supervised the repewing of SOMPTING CHURCH, SUSSEX [I.C.B.S.]. Charles Hide (*c.*1810–76), for many years Town Surveyor of Worthing, was probably his son [cf. *Builder* xxxiv, 1876, 645].

HIGGINS, JAMES WHITE (1783–1854) was articled to Thomas Bush, but bought off a portion of his term of apprenticeship in order to become fully employed as a surveyor in measuring the extensive Government works then being carried out by Messrs. Holland, Copland, Rowles and others. Before he was 22 he had begun speculative building in Chelsea, on the Sloane Street estate developed by Henry Holland. In later life he was chiefly employed in valuation for dock and railway companies, the Office of Woods and Forests, the Boards of Ordnance and Admiralty, and other bodies. He was extensively employed as an arbitrator, and was one of the first referees appointed under the Metropolitan Buildings Act of 1844, but retired after holding the office for only one year, 'not liking the confinement of official life'. He usually handed over architectural commissions to others. He was a member of the Surveyors' Club, and was elected President in 1814, but did not take the Chair. He lived latterly at Hormead, Herts., and died on 13 May 1854, aged 71. His daughter Catherine married T. E. Owen of Portsmouth (*q.v.*). [*A.P.S.D.*; obituary in *Builder* xii, 1854, 293.]

HIGGINS, WILLIAM MULLINGER, was an architect and surveyor practising in London during the second quarter of the nineteenth century. He designed the LITERARY and SCIENTIFIC INSTITUTION in CLARENCE STREET, STAINES, MIDDLESEX, 1835, now the Public Library, his signature and the date being inscribed on the door-jamb. He was also the architect of the CONGREGATIONAL CHURCH, THAMES STREET, STAINES, 1836, dem. 1956, which had an inscription recording his authorship. He was presumably the architect called Higgins who designed a METHODIST CHAPEL in the NEW ROAD, LONDON [noted by C. R. Cockerell in his Diary, June 1823], and the GRANDSTAND at ASCOT RACE-COURSE in 1838–9 [G. Tattersall, *Sporting Architecture*, 1841, 92]. Higgins was the author of a work entitled *The House Painter: or, Decorator's Companion: being a complete treatise on the origin of colour . . . the manufacture of pigments, oils and varnishes; and the art of house painting, graining and marbling*, 1841, in which he is described as 'formerly professor of mechanical and experimental philosophy at Guy's Hospital'. He was a Fellow of the Geological Society and also published books about geology and music.

HIGHWAY, ISAAC, was a builder-architect of Walsall, Staffs. In 1833 he added an apsidal E. end (rebuilt 1875–7) to BLOXWICH CHURCH, STAFFS. [I.C.B.S.]. He also designed ALL SAINTS RECTORY, WALSALL, 1835, altered or rebuilt 1872–4 [Lichfield Joint Record Office, B/A/13 III]; ST. JOHN'S CHURCH, WALSALL WOOD, in a plain Gothic style in 1836–7; and ST. PETER'S CHURCH, WALSALL, in the lancet style in 1839–41 [*V.C.H. Staffs.* xvii, 237, 282].

HILL, CHARLES HAMOR (–1863), of Islington, was one of the London District Surveyors in the 1830s and 1840s. In 1837 he took a lease of Canonbury Tower, Islington, and its grounds from the Marquess of Northampton, and had built nearly fifty houses in Canonbury Place North and South and Grange Grove by 1850 [Mary Cosh, *The Squares of Islington* ii, 1993, 4]. His only other recorded architectural work appears to be the Tudor Gothic LEATHERSELLERS' ALMSHOUSES at BARNET, HERTS., 1843, of which there is an engraving naming him as the architect. He died at Canonbury Tower on 4 February

1863 [Principal Probate Registry, Calendar of Probates].

HILL, DAVID, of Arbroath, was the son of James Hill, 'an ingenious man, who spent a great deal of time in trying to invent perpetual motion'. He designed THE TRADES HALL (later THE SHERIFF COURT HOUSE), ARBROATH, ANGUS, 1814–15 [G. Hay, *History of Arbroath*, 1876, 289].

HILL or **HILLS,** DANIEL, a master bricklayer, probably of Long Melford, Suffolk, designed the timber lantern surmounting the plain brick west tower, 1712 (dem. 1903) of LONG MELFORD CHURCH, of which he was no doubt the builder [carpenter's contract for the lantern in W. Suffolk C.R.O., FL 509/5/22]. His name as 'Bricklayer' appears in the inscription commemorating the large and rather clumsily detailed brick tower of TOPPESFIELD CHURCH, ESSEX, 1699.

HILL, JAMES (–1734), of Cheltenham, was one of the two master masons employed to rebuild NEWENT CHURCH, GLOS., of which he and Francis Jones of Hasfield laid the first stone on 31 July 1675. The church was completed in 1679, the medieval steeple being retained. Externally, it is Gothic in style, but there are Ionic pilasters in the interior, and the nave was covered by a roof of exceptionally wide span designed by Edward Taylor (*q.v.*) on the model of that of the Sheldonian Theatre, Oxford [MS. account of the building of Newent Church by Walter Nourse, of Kilcot, *c.*1725]. A memorandum in the vestry minutes of CHELTENHAM PARISH CHURCH records that in 1693 'was the steeple of Cheltenham repayred from the upper hole to the top by James Hill, of Cheltenham, stonemason' ['Cheltenham Vestry Minutes', *Glos. Notes and Queries* viii (i), 1901, 38]. In 1700 Hill was employed to rebuild the central tower of BISHOP'S CLEEVE CHURCH, GLOS. The former tower had collapsed in 1696, and the churchwardens' accounts for 1699 include a payment of 16s. 'to James Hill for a draught of ye tower'. It is traditional in character, with battlements and pinnacles [MS. Churchwardens' Accounts in Gloucester County Record Office]. Hill's will, dated 19 January 1733/4, was proved at Gloucester on 11 February 1733/4.

HILLIER, WILLIAM CURRY, junior (*c.*1815–1840), of Rochester, went to Jerusalem to build a church and hospital there for the Society for promoting Christianity among the Jews, but died soon afterwards at the age of 25 [*Gent's Mag.* 1840 (ii), 676; J. W. Johns, *The Anglican Cathedral Church at Jerusalem*, 1844].

HILLYER, WILLIAM (–1782), was probably the man of this name, the son of a cooper, who was admitted to membership of the London Carpenters' Company in 1757 on the conclusion of his apprenticeship [Guildhall Library, Carpenters' Company records, MS. 4335/4]. By the 1770s he was established as an architect and surveyor in Moorfields. He designed the church of ST. ALPHEGE, LONDON WALL, LONDON, 1775–7, incorporating the old tower. The church was dem. in 1923–4, with the exception of the tower [Vestry Minutes in Guildhall Library, MS. 1431/4]. In 1772 Hillyer supervised repairs to the church of ST. SWITHIN, LONDON STONE [minutes of Committee in Guildhall Library MS. 560/2], and in 1777 to that of ST. MARY ALDERMANBURY, gutted in 1940 [P. C. Carter, *The History of St. Mary Aldermanbury*, 1913, 23].

In 1771 Hillyer stated that he had been employed as surveyor of the Assembly Room built at MARGATE, KENT, and of the buildings in the square there. This was an ambitious scheme which included a 'square of gentlemen's houses', still in part extant. Work began in 1768 but Hillyer was not the original architect and only modified the plans [Nancy Briggs, as cited below, 301; J. Nichols, *Illustrations of the Literary History of the Eighteenth Century* v, 1828, 826].

Hillyer was appointed County Surveyor of Essex in 1770, and in that capacity designed THE COUNTY GAOL at CHELMSFORD, 1773–7, subsequently much altered by his successor John Johnson. Besides several minor bridges he was also concerned in the building of HOUSES OF CORRECTION at NEWPORT and HALSTEAD, the latter completed after his death [Nancy Briggs, 'The Office of County Surveyor in Essex', *Arch. Hist.* 27, 1984]. His unexecuted designs for a County Hall at Chelmsford, dated 1770, are preserved in the County Record Office (Q/AS 1/3 and Q/SO/12, pp. 4–7). In 1779 he carried out alterations to the COUNTY GAOL at HERTFORD [Herts. County Records]. From about 1780 until his death Hillyer was also Surveyor to the Bridewell and Bethlehem Hospitals [*ex inf.* Miss P. Allderidge, Archivist to the Hospitals].

In 1847 a folio volume of drawings by Hillyer was advertised for sale by the bookseller Bohn in his catalogue (item 224). It included designs for the Gaol and County Hall at Chelmsford; for Bamber Gascoyne's house at Bifrons, nr. Barking, Essex (dem. 1815–16); and for 'Gibbs esq. at Horkesley Park', Essex (dem.).

HINSBEY, WILLIAM (–1859), was an architect and surveyor of Norwich, and was presumably the 'Builder, Carpenter and Joiner' surnamed Hinsby who advertised his ability to provide designs 'in the Castellated, Gothic, Grecian, Italian and Fancy Cottage styles' in the *Norwich Mercury* of 20 Feb. 1813. Designs by him for altering or rebuilding parsonages at TIVETSHALL (1829) and BRAMERTON, NORFOLK (1838) are in the Norfolk R.O. (DN/DPL 1/1/11 and 1/4/64). His designs for a range of cottages next to St. Martin's Church, Norwich, are in the City Archives [*ex inf.* Mr. A. P. Baggs].

HINSBY, ROBERT (–1820), an 'eminent architect and builder' of Halesworth, Suffolk, died there on 27 November 1820 [*Gent's Mag.* 1820, 571].

HIORNE, FRANCIS (1744–1789), was the elder son of William Hiorne of Warwick, and succeeded to his business as an architect and builder. His father had already executed works in the Gothic manner at Arbury and Stratford-on-Avon, and Francis became well known as an architect who specialized in that style. In 1785 the poet Mason wrote that 'Tetbury church gave me the very highest opinion of his Gothic taste', and commended Lord Harcourt for thinking of employing him as the architect of a projected 'Courtenay Castle' in the grounds of Nuneham Park, Oxon. Two years later a correspondent of Richard Gough, the antiquary, reported that 'At Greystoke Castle I found Mr. Hiorne, the gothic architect, whom the Duke of Norfolk had invited there to consult with relative to his intended repairs at Arundel Castle; and we made a party to see Alnwick Castle, etc. in Northumberland, for Mr. Hiorne's information'. 'Hiorne's Tower' still stands in the Home Park at Arundel, but his proposals for restoring and remodelling the Castle, described in Dallaway's *Western Division of the County of Sussex*, ed. Cartwright, ii (i), 1832, 188–9, were not carried out owing to his death.

Hiorne was one of the most accomplished designers of the elegant, decorative Gothic of the late eighteenth century, of which Tetbury church is an excellent example. As a classical designer he is represented by St. Anne's, Belfast, whose domed tower appears to have derived from Archer's church at Birmingham, and by Tardebigge church, whose steeple is elegantly refined in a manner which suggests that Hiorne was sensitive to neo-classical taste.

Hiorne was elected an alderman of Warwick in October 1773, and held office as Mayor for the years 1773–4, 1782–3 and 1787–8. He also acted as Treasurer to the Corporation from 1781 to 1789, and as Bridge-master to the county of Warwick during the same period. He was elected F.S.A. in 1784, and bequeathed to the Society of Antiquaries 'the ancient volume called Milles Honour[1] corrected by the hand of Sir William Dugdale', and such of his coins and medals as the Society chose to select. His other legacies included the bust of Francis Smith by Rysbrack, which he left to the Radcliffe Library at Oxford, 50 guineas to the Corporation of Warwick to buy a piece of plate, and his silver drawing instruments, which he gave to William Callow of Tardebigge 'as a token of esteem'. To his wife Elizabeth he left, *inter alia*, his newly erected house called Kyte's Nest at Beausale, near Warwick, in the occupation of himself and Richard Kyte, with instructions to his executors 'to perfect the plan by me already begun for the improvement of the said Messuage, Garden and Shrubbery'. He died on 9 December 1789, aged 45, and is commemmorated by a tablet in St. Mary's, Warwick.

[*A.P.S.D.*; Field, *History of Warwick*, 1815, 113; *Gent's Mag.* 1789 (ii), 1211; 1800 (ii), 1144–5; J. Nichols, *Literary Anecdotes* iii, 642; ix, 553, *Literary Illustrations* vi, 423; F. W. Harcourt, *The Harcourt Papers* vii, 1883, 110; *Aris's Birmingham Gazette*, 21 Oct. 1776. His will is P.C.C. 24 BISHOP, and the sale catalogue of his library (1791) is in the B.L. (129.1.19).]

WARWICK, ST. MARY'S CHURCH. In 1769 Francis Hiorne made designs for reconstructing the galleries, which are preserved among the Faculty Records now in the County Record Office, Warwick. A faculty was obtained, but nothing was done until 1777, when Edward Croft took the galleries down and rebuilt them according to Hiorne's plan. Hiorne also carried out extensive repairs to the Beauchamp Chapel in 1779, and converted the vaulted chamber under the Vestry into a burial vault for the Earl of Warwick in 1769. [T. Kemp, *History of Warwick*, 1905, 111, 125; *Notices of the Churches of Warwickshire*, 1847, i, 64; P. B. Chatwin, 'The Rebuilding of St. Mary's Church, Warwick', *Trans. Birmingham Arch. Soc.* lxvi, 1949, 33–4.]

HAGLEY CHURCH, WORCS., monument to Sir Richard Lyttelton (d. 1770) [executors' accounts in Herts. C.R.O., Bridgwater papers 1386].

BELFAST, ST. ANNE'S CHURCH, completed 1776;

[1] i.e. Thos. Milles, *The Catalogue of Honour*, 1610.

dem. 1900 [C. E. B. Brett, *Buildings of Belfast 1700–1914*, 1967, 4; cf. A. Gordon, *Historic Memorials of the First Presbyterian Church at Belfast*, 1887].

TARDEBIGGE CHURCH, WORCS., 1777; chancel rebuilt 1879–80 [M. Dickens, *A Thousand Years of Tardebigge*, 1931, 85–90].

STONY STRATFORD CHURCH, BUCKS., rebuilt, incorporating old tower, 1776–7, Gothic. The tracery in the nave windows was inserted by Street in 1876, and the present chancel is by C. G. Hare, 1928 [J. Dugdale, *British Traveller* i, 1819, 183].

attributed: BUCKINGHAM PARISH CHURCH, rebuilt 1777–81, Gothic; altered 1862 by G. G. Scott, who added the chancel. The parish records contain no information as to the architect employed, but the style is characteristic of Hiorne, and 'Mr. Hearn' is mentioned twice in a letter dated 22 April 1777 from Charles Webb to Lord Verney about the erection of the church [Verney archives at Claydon House].

TETBURY CHURCH, GLOS., rebuilt, except steeple, 1777–81, Gothic [A. T. Lee, *History of Tetbury*, 1857].

ARUNDEL CASTLE, SUSSEX, triangular tower in Home Park for 11th Duke of Norfolk, *c*.1787, Gothic [T. W. Horsfield, *History of Sussex*, 1835, ii, 128].

ALTHORP HOUSE, NORTHANTS., repairs to STABLES for 2nd Earl Spencer, 1788 [drawing and estimate in B.L., Althorp Papers, P.9].

WARWICK, rebuilt ST. PETER'S CHAPEL over the east gate, 1788, Gothic [J. Chambers, MS. *Biography of English Architects* in R.I.B.A. Library].

KYTE'S NEST, nr. BEAUSALE, WARWICKS., for himself and Richard Kyte, 1788 [referred to in Hiorne's will, P.C.C. 24 BISHOP].

HIORNE, or **HIORNS,** WILLIAM (*c*.1712–1776) and DAVID (1715–1758) were brothers who established themselves as the leading architects and master builders in Warwick in the middle of the eighteenth century. They came from Great Tew in Oxon., where members of their family had been masons since at least the early seventeenth century. They appear to have been the sons of John Hiorne of Great Tew, whose father John, described in his will as a mason, left small legacies to his grandsons William and David when he died in 1718. A specimen of their grandfather's work still survives in the village, for in the attic of a stone cottage on the east side of the Square there is an inscription recording that it was built in 1680 by John Stow and his wife, and round the tablet is cut the distich,

JOHN HIORN THAT IS MY NAME
AND WITH MY HANDS I MAD THIS SAME.

During the first half of the eighteenth century the building trade in Warwick was dominated by the family of Smith, and it was in the Smiths' employment (William as a mason, David as a carpenter) that the Hiorns became established there. When William Smith died unmarried in 1747 the Hiornes succeeded to his business. During the next twenty years they designed and built churches and country houses in many parts of the Midlands, in a style which is basically Palladian, though some of their designs for interior decoration are rococo in character, and the influence of Gibbs is also apparent.

David Hiorne predeceased his brother William, dying on 8 April 1758. He left three sons, John, Edward and David. Edward became a druggist in Coventry, and neither John nor David appears to have followed their father's trade. William died on 22 April 1776, leaving two sons by his first wife Mary Duncalfe. Francis, the elder, succeeded to the family business and became a well-known architect. William, the younger, became a merchant and perished at sea off the coast of Georgia. Their father was an alderman of Warwick at the time of his death, and held the office of Mayor in 1765–6. There is a tablet to his memory in the church of St. Mary, Warwick. He lived in a house on the north side of Warwick High Street. [notes on the family by F. R. Hiorns, published in *C. Life*, 18 Aug. 1923, 218; the wills of William and Francis (P.C.C., 271 BELLAS; 24 BISHOP), and of John Hiorn of Great Tew (Oxford Archdeaconry Court, Reg. II, vol. 15, f. 133^{v}; see also vol. 7, f. 167*b*); A. Gomme, 'William and David Hiorn' in *The Architectural Outsiders*, ed. R. Brown, 1985, where references will be found to further minor and attributed works].

COVENTRY, HOLY TRINITY CHURCH: in 1742 the spire was examined by 'Mr. Hiorn of Warwick' [T. Sharp, *Illustrations of the History of Holy Trinity Church, Coventry*, 1818, 32].

RUGBY PARISH CHURCH, WARWICKS., monument to Thomas Crossfield (d. 1744) [signed by William Hiorne].

COVENTRY, ST. MICHAEL'S CHURCH (later the CATHEDRAL). In 1747 'Mr. Hiorne of Warwick, engaged to take down the old Altarpiece, and make two wings, in stucco-work, according to his design given in, for £43: 18s.' [T. Sharp, *Illustrations of the History and Antiquities of St. Michael's Church, Coventry*, 1818, 40–41].

ARBURY HALL, WARWICKS. William Hiorne

acted as executant architect for Sir Roger Newdigate's alterations in the Gothic style from *c.*1748 onwards. Hiorne was paid 2 guineas for a 'plan of Arbury' on 23 Dec. 1748, and Sir Roger Newdigate's MS. account-book, now in the County Record Office at Warwick, contains several payments to him and his brother between 1750 and 1755. (C. Hussey, *English Country Houses: Mid Georgian*, 1956, 41–8).

GOPSALL HALL, LEICS., works for Charles Jennens (d. 1773), *c.*1750–60. According to J. Throsby, *Select Views of Leicestershire* i, 1789, 280, the house was designed by Alderman Westley of Leicester but 'the offices, through a misunderstanding, were built by Mr. Hiorn of Warwick'. A volume of designs for Gopsal in the R.I.B.A. Collection includes several designs by the Hiornes for the interiors and also for various garden buildings. Owing to the demolition of the house in 1951 it is not clear which drawings were executed , but some of the garden buildings were certainly built. [*R.I.B.A. Drawings Catalogue: G–K*, 130–2; A. Rowan, *Garden Buildings*, R.I.B.A. 1968, pls. 12, 15, 17] (L. G. G. Ramsay, 'Gopsal Hall', *Connoisseur*, 128, 1951).

EDGBASTON HALL, WARWICKS., internal alterations by W. & D. Hiorne for Sir Henry Gough, 1751–2 [account and letter in Edgbaston Estate Office, *ex inf.* Mr. D. N. Cannadine].

BIRMINGHAM, KING EDWARD'S SCHOOL, fitted up library 1752 [*Records of King Edward's School*, ed. Chatwin, Dugdale Soc. iv, pp. xxi, 101].

DAVENTRY PARISH CHURCH, NORTHANTS., 1752–8, by William and David Hiorne [*Gent's Mag.* 1826 (ii), 402; a note in William Baker's MS. diary indicates that David was concerned, but it was William who gave evidence in connection with the Faculty which was granted in Jan. 1752 [Peterborough Diocesan Records].

BIRMINGHAM, ST. BARTHOLOMEW'S CHURCH. In 1753 'Messrs. W. and D. Hiorn' gave an estimate and a design for an altar-piece in this church, which had been built in 1749–50, and may be attributed to the same architects. [*Aris's Birmingham Gazette*, 6 Aug. 1753]. It was closed in 1935 and subsequently dem.

BIRMINGHAM, ST. MARTIN'S CHURCH; the spire was repaired by William Hiorne in 1753, and the vestry and lobby at the east end of the north aisle were built by William and David Hiorne in 1760. [J. T. Bunce, 'St. Martin's Church', *Trans. Birmingham and Midland Institute*, 1870, 15–16; J. T. Bunce, *Old St. Martin's Church, Birmingham*, 1875, 19.] The spire was recased by P. C. Hardwick in 1852–5, and the whole church was reconstructed by J. A. Chatwin in 1872–5.

KYRE PARK, WORCS., was remodelled by W. & D. Hiorne for Edmund Pytts in 1753–6 [H. Avray Tipping in *C. Life*, 17 & 24 March 1917, citing accounts now in Worcestershire Record Office].

DELBURY HALL, DIDDLEBURY, SALOP., reconstructed for Frederick Cornewall, 1753–6 [A. Gomme, *op. cit.*, citing accounts at Delbury].

WARWICK, THE SHIRE HALL was built 1754–8 to the designs of Sanderson Miller by William and David Hiorn and Job Collins as contractors. An inscription on a plate fixed to the roof timbers records the names of 'MR. WILLIAM AND DAVID HIORN OF WARWICK SURVEYORS AND BUILDERS OF THIS HALL RICHARD NEWMAN MASON DAVID SANDERS CARPENTER 1754.' Estimates, bills, etc., are preserved among Sanderson Miller's papers now in the County Record Office, Warwick. Francis Hiorne afterwards published a plan and elevation of the building, but had no responsibility for its design or execution. [A. C. Wood, *The Shire Hall, Warwick*, Warwicks. Local History Soc., 1983].

GREAT HOUGHTON CHURCH, NORTHANTS., was rebuilt in 1754 in a style which suggests that the Hiornes were the architects employed and this is confirmed by an advertisement in the *Northampton Mercury* of 31 March 1755 offering for sale 'All the OLD LEAD belonging to Great-Houghton Church', and instructing prospective purchasers to apply to 'Mr. David Hiorn, or Mr. Smith, his Foreman, at Great Houghton aforesaid'. The architectural character of the church has been impaired by alterations in 1875 and 1910–11, but its original appearance is illustrated in M. Whiffen, *Stuart and Georgian Churches*, 1948, pl. 79.

DERBY COUNTY GAOL., 1755–6; rebuilt by F. Goodwin in 1823–7. By 'Mr. Irons, of Warwick' [J. C. Cox, *Three Centuries of Derbyshire Annals* ii, 10].

CHARLECOTE, WARWICKS., bridge over river Dene, designed and built by David Hiorne, 1755–7 [Mary F. Lucy, *Biography of the Lucy Family*, 1862, 82; Warwicks. C.R.O., L6/1476].

PACKINGTON HALL, WARWICKS., works for 3rd and 4th Earls of Aylesford between 1756 and 1765 [accounts cited by Gomme, *op. cit.*, 197, n. 30], including the building of the Stables in 1756–8, perhaps to the designs of Sanderson Miller (*q.v.*), who had been consulted about the proposed stables as early as 1750 [Warwicks. C.R.O., Z 489, letter from Sir E. Turner to Miller]. Sir Roger Newdigate's diary shows that he went to Packington to see the new stables on 29 Sept. 1758.

MERIDEN HALL, WARWICKS., work for the Hon. Wriothesley Digby, 1757–8, probably addition of attic storey [payments to W. & D. Hiorn in Digby's account at Hoare's Bank, 1757–8, *ex inf.* Mrs. Fiona Cowell, and estimate for addition of attic by W. & D. Hiorn in R.I.B.A. Library].

FOREMARK HALL, DERBYS., for Sir Robert Burdett, 1759–61. The architect was David Hiorne, who based his design on Isaac Ware's Wrotham Park (1754) [*Vitruvius Britannicus* v, 1771, pls. 31–5; Burdett papers in Berkshire C.R.O., accounts A1/1] (*C. Life*, 18 Aug. 1923).

NOTTINGHAM, ST. MARY'S CHURCH. The west end was rebuilt in classical style, with a pediment and Doric doorcase, in 1762, the architect being 'one Hirons of Warwick' [*The Stretton Manuscripts*, ed. G. C. Robertson, 1910, 137].

STRATFORD-ON-AVON CHURCH, WARWICKS., spire said to have been rebuilt in stone by William Hiorn, 1763–4 presumably to design of T. Lightoler (*q.v.*) [*V.C.H. Warwicks.* iii, 271, without citing source].

OVER WHITACRE CHURCH, WARWICKS., rebuilt 1766, may be attributed to William Hiorne on stylistic grounds, but there are no parish records of the period by which this attribution can be tested. The tower originally terminated in a dome, the present spire being substituted in 1850.

HIORT, JOHN WILLIAM (1772–1861), the son of a Swedish father and an English mother, was born in London on 16 April 1772. After spending a year with Peter Simon, a miniaturist and engraver, he entered the office of C. A. Craig in January 1787. Craig was the Chief Resident Clerk in the Office of Works, and in 1793 Hiort was engaged to take the place of George Horsley, an Assistant Clerk who had become insane. Hiort was recommended to the Treasury by Sir William Chambers, the Surveyor General, as 'a very intelligent young man, very industrious and attentive to business, very sober and tractable'. He was subsequently promoted to be Resident Clerk (1805) and Chief Examining Clerk (1815). He retired in 1832, when the Office of Works was merged with that of Woods and Forests. He proved to be a thoroughly capable and reliable member of the staff, and it was upon him that the main burden of administration was to fall during the negligent surveyorship of James Wyatt.

In his official capacity Hiort had few opportunities to design new buildings, but he was much employed in arranging public ceremonies, such as the funerals of William Pitt and Lord Nelson, and the coronation of George IV in 1820. For the coronation banquet in Westminster Hall he designed the Gothic triumphal arch and galleries (illustrated in *Gent's Mag.* 1821 (ii), 109). In a semi-official capacity, assisted by J. B. Papworth, he designed various ancillary buildings at CLAREMONT HOUSE, SURREY, for Princess Charlotte, including the Gothic 'Retreat' which was converted into a chapel or cenotaph after her death [Ackermann, *Repository of Arts*, 1819, 154]. His private works included DDERW, nr. RHAYADER in RADNORSHIRE, for N. S. Prickard, 1799, rebuilt *c.*1860; considerable works for Nicholas Vansittart, Lord Bexley, at FOOTS CRAY PLACE, KENT, and at his house No. 36 GREAT GEORGE STREET, WESTMINSTER; alterations for William Elliott M.P., at No. 34 OLD BURLINGTON STREET, *c.*1808; and to the London residences of Charles Arbuthnot, Secretary to the Treasury, and John Johnson, afterwards Lord Mayor of London.

Hiort invented and patented (8 Nov. 1825) bricks for building circular flues in a manner adopted at Buckingham Palace and elsewhere, and founded the London, Surrey, and Kent Safety Brick Company to carry out these and similar inventions. In 1826 he published a *Practical Treatise on the Construction of Chimneys, etc.*, and in 1847, after many years of retirement at Bath, returned to London in order to readvocate some of his ideas in a *Report of the Aeronomic Association*, 1852. He died at Bedford Place, Kensington, on 8 February 1861, and was buried in Kensal Green Cemetery. C. Hiort, who may have been a nephew, was an assistant in Soane's office, 1822–3. [Obituary in *Building News* vii, 1861, 460–61; privately printed memoir in B.L. (10826 h. 20); *A.P.S.D.*; *History of the King's Works* vi, *passim.*]

HIRD, JOHN, was an eighteenth-century Lancashire architect and a carpenter and joiner by trade. He was probably the 'John Herd, house carpenter of Kendal', who became a freeman of Lancaster in 1763–4 [*Lancs. & Cheshire Record Soc.* 87, 1935, 148], but was described as 'of Preston' when he rebuilt the nave of Preston Church in 1770–1. He was presumably the 'Mr. Hird, Joiner' who subscribed to James Paine's *Plans* of 1767, and as an unexecuted design by him for Leighton Hall, Lancs. (illustrated in *C. Life*, 11 May 1951, fig. 7) shows the influence of Paine, it has been suggested by Mr. Angus

Taylor that Hird may have been responsible for PONSONBY HALL, CUMBERLAND, built by George Edward Stanley *c.*1775 as a copy of St. Ives, Yorkshire, a house designed by Paine and illustrated in his book. Hird was certainly responsible for the rather feeble Gothick front of SIZERGH CASTLE, WESTMORLAND, for Cecilia Strickland, *c.*1770 [signed drawing at Sizergh] (*C. Life*, 21 Oct. 1949); for the plain Georgian front range of BIGLAND HALL, LANCS., for George Bigland, 1781 [drawings and estimate at Bigland, *ex inf.* Mr. Peter Leach]; for remodelling the interior of WITHERSLACK CHURCH, WESTMORLAND, in classical style in 1768 [inscription in church]; and for rebuilding the nave of PRESTON CHURCH (ST. JOHN'S), LANCS., in 1770–1 (again rebuilt 1853–8) [T. C. Smith, *Records of the Parish Church of Preston*, 1892, 249]. In 1777 he was invited to submit plans for FLOOKBURGH CHAPEL, nr. CARTMEL, LANCS., which were probably those carried out in 1776–7 (dem. 1897–1900) [J. Stockdale, *Annales Caermoelenses*, 1872, 284].

HIRST, THOMAS (*c.*1779–1842), was the son of a schoolmaster at Sheffield. From *c.*1817 to *c.*1822 he was in partnership with William Unwin (*q.v.*) [P. Eden, *Dictionary of Land Surveyors 1550–1850*, 1975–6, 133].

HISCOCK, WILLIAM (*c.*1763–1851) was a mason at Christchurch, Hants., where he carried on a business as a builder and monumental sculptor. Several well-carved tablets signed by him can be seen in Christchurch Priory Church, which he repaired in 1809 [R. Gunnis, *Dictionary of British Sculptors*, 1968, 203]. In 1825–6 he designed HAMWORTHY CHURCH, DORSET, rebuilt 1958–9 [I.C.B.S.] (Sydenham, *History of Poole*, 1839, 458), and in 1831 MILTON CHURCH, HANTS., in a weak Gothic style [I.C.B.S.] He died in January 1851, aged 88 [Christchurch Parish Register].

HITCHCOCK, JOHN THOMAS (1812–1844), was born in Amsterdam. He went to London as a youth, exhibited at the R.A. in 1827–9, became a pupil of Philip Hardwick, and entered the R.A. Schools in 1834. In the following year he made designs for the Fitzwilliam Museum at Cambridge which, although not accepted, are preserved in the museum's library. After eight years in England, he returned to Amsterdam, where he built a club-house and other houses. He migrated to the Dutch East Indies in 1841, and died at Batavia in 1844 [*A.P.S.D.*].

HOARE, —, appears to have been the architect and builder of Alderman William Beckford's magnificent Palladian house at FONTHILL, WILTSHIRE, begun *c.*1757 but not completed until *c.*1770 and demolished by his son in 1807 (*Vitruvius Britannicus* iv, 1767, pls. 82–7; John Harris, 'Fonthill, Wiltshire', *C. Life*, 24 Nov. 1966). 'Mr. Hoore' is given as the architect of Fonthill in an eighteenth-century list of country houses in the library at Alnwick Castle, and in April 1763 a correspondent of Sir Charles Farnaby wrote to him that 'there is one Hoar a Builder in the City of whom I have heard a Good character. He built Beckford the present Lord Mayor's house in Wiltshire and he is employed now in Building the new Court House at Maidstone . . .' [Hertfordshire County Record Office, DE 43213]. The employment of 'Mr. Hoare' to design the COURT HOUSE or TOWN HALL at MAIDSTONE in 1763–4 is confirmed by the Corporation Minutes, which record the decision that it should be 'new built and enlarged agreeable to the plan produced . . . by Mr. Hoare'.

HOARE, MICHAEL, *see* HALFPENNY, WILLIAM.

HOARE, WILLIAM (*c.*1770–1830), and his son HUGH DANIEL (1792–1860), were architects and builders at Lawrenny in Pembrokeshire. William Hoare worked at OLD LAWRENNY HALL in 1800–4, building and perhaps designing 'a new portico' [Pembrokeshire Record Office, D/LLW/269], and in 1816–18 carried out major internal alterations to CRESSELLY, PEMBS., for J. H. Allen, including a new staircase [account-book in private possession]. In 1827 'William Hoare and Son' made an estimate for repairs to FFYNONE, PEMBS. for John Colby [N.L.W., Spence Colby 1877]. In 1843 Hugh Hoare, 'architect and surveyor of Lawrenny', supervised the repair of MARTLETWY CHURCH, PEMBS. [I.C.B.S. and churchwardens' accounts in Pembs. R.O.] In 1850–1 he repaired and altered GUIRSHILL FARM, LYDNEY, GLOS., for Charles Mathias of Lamphey Court, Pembs. [Pembs. R.O., D/RTP/MAT/232], and in 1855 he designed RHOSMARKET RECTORY, PEMBS. [N.L.W., St. David's Diocesan Records, Parsonage plans 161]. [Information from Mr. Thomas Lloyd, to whom all references are due.]

HOBCROFT, or **HOBCRAFT,** JOHN (*c.*1720–1802), was a carpenter and builder of Titchfield Street, London, who also acted as an architect. He is first found working at STOWE HOUSE, BUCKS., where in 1755 he submitted an account which was mainly for architectural joinery supplied, but also included

10s. for 'Drawing a Plan for State Bedchamber' [Desmond Fitz-Gerald in *Apollo*, June 1973, 577, 584–5 (n. 36)]. He next appears as a builder carrying out work of high quality at various country houses designed or altered by Lancelot Brown in the 1760s, including Broadlands, Corsham, Redgrave and Newnham Paddox [Dorothy Stroud, *Capability Brown*, 1975, *passim*]. He drew out the Gothic elevations for Donnington Grove designed by John Chute which now hang framed at the Vyne,[1] and in 1768 he appears to have designed the elaborate Gothic chapel at AUDLEY END, ESSEX, for Sir John Griffin, later Lord Howard de Walden [J. D. Williams, *Audley End, The Restoration of 1762–97*, Chelmsford 1966, 31]. An album at Audley End contains two drawings signed by him, including (f. 64) a design for the chapel screen. Later, in 1778–9, he remodelled Sir John Griffin's town house at No. 10 New Burlington Street to the designs of the Adam brothers [*Survey of London* xxxii, 493]. In Berkshire Hobcroft himself designed two country seats, PADWORTH HOUSE for Christopher Griffith, 1769, for which his plans and elevations, signed and dated 1769, survive [H. Avray Tipping in *C. Life*, 16 & 23 Sept. 1922] and WASING HOUSE, nr. NEWBURY, for John Mount, 1772, destroyed by fire 1945 [Berkshire County Record Office, D/EMcA. 21]. Externally these were both plain brick buildings of no special distinction, but the interiors at Padworth are elegantly decorated in a style derived from the Adam brothers. Hobcroft probably worked for the Adams at other houses besides Sir John Griffin's. He took a building site in Mansfield Street on the Portland estate which they laid out [A. T. Bolton, *The Works of R. & J. Adam* ii, 102], and he subscribed to Robert Adam's *Spalatro* (1764). He died on 1 October 1802, aged 82 [*Gent's Mag.* 1802 (ii), 980].

Hobcroft's son John, born in 1747, entered the R.A. Schools as an architectural student in 1771, but appears to have died young, as 'Dead' is written against his name in the R.A. Register.

HOBDEN, HENRY WILLIAM, was a builder and surveyor at Warrington in Lancashire. He rebuilt the churches of LYTHAM and NEWTON-LE-FYLDE, LANCS., in 1834–5, added a N. aisle to NEWCHURCH CHURCH in WINWICK PARISH, LANCS., in 1833, and enlarged BURTONWOOD CHURCH in Warrington parish in 1834 [all I.C.B.S.].

HOBSON, WILLIAM, was brother-in-law of William Blackburn, the prison architect (*q.v.*). Writing from Southwark after Blackburn's death in 1791, Hobson told the Bedfordshire Justices that he had been 'bred up in the architectural line' and claimed to have enjoyed Blackburn's 'unbounded friendship and confidence, which has been extended to his taking my opinion for almost every plan for a gaol that he has made' [Bedfordshire County Records, QSR 17/173–4]. He was employed to complete at least one prison designed by Blackburn, the HOUSE OF CORRECTION at LEWES, SUSSEX [East Sussex Record Office, QAP/2/11 and 12/E12]. A W. Hobson exhibited a design for a museum at the Royal Academy in 1801 from Stamford Hill, and may have been the person of this name who died in Stamford Hill in May 1840, aged 87 [*Gent's Mag.* 1840 (ii), 107].

HODGE, JAMES, mason in Dundonald, Ayrshire, designed and built DUNDONALD CHURCH in 1803–4, with a thin classical steeple [S.R.O., HR 149/1].

HODGSON, CHRISTOPHER (1784–1849), was the son of Isaac Hodgson, a builder of Rosgill in the parish of Shap, Westmorland, and the brother of the Revd. John Hodgson (1789–1845), the historian of Northumberland. He practised in Carlisle, where he was Surveyor to the Dean and Chapter and held the office of Mayor in 1828. Like his nephew, John Hodgson, C. E. (1814–1857), he had antiquarian interests, and contributed several notes on local antiquities to *Archaeologia Aeliana*, the journal of the Society of Antiquaries of Newcastle-upon-Tyne, of which his brother was Secretary and of which he became an Honorary Member in 1834. He died at Carlisle on 25 Feb. 1849, aged 65 [memoir in *Archaeologia Aeliana*, 3rd ser. x, 1913, 187, 192]. He was succeeded by his son John Hodgson, who was still in practice in 1868. Most of Hodgson's buildings are in a plain Grecian style, but the otherwise simple front of Rosehill is enlivened by octagonal projections at the angles.

In CARLISLE Hodgson completed the Gaol after the death of William Nixon (*q.v.*), and designed the three houses for clergy in WEST WALLS now known as CHURCH HOUSE, 1832 [plans in Cumbria C.R.O., DRC 12/2]; THE FISH MARKET, 1834 [Pigot's *Northern Directory*, 1834, 84]; and THE LOWTHER ARCADE, LOWTHER STREET, 1844 (dem.) [*Carlisle Jnl.* 20

[1] This was presumably the 'Design for the house of a gentleman in the county of Berkshire' which Hobcroft exhibited at the Society of Artists in 1771, for Horace Walpole noted in his copy of the catalogue that it was 'designed by John Chute Esq. and executed'.

July 1844]. He also designed the ceiling (dem.) of the chancel, and probably also that of the nave (still extant) of ST. LAWRENCE'S CHURCH, APPLEBY, WESTMORLAND, 1830–1 [Church Commissioners' files, *ex inf.* the late Canon B. F. L. Clarke], and rebuilt STANWIX CHURCH, CUMBERLAND, in 1841 [I.C.B.S.]. ROSEHILL, SCOTBY, CUMBERLAND, a house built for J. S. Bond in 1833–5, can be attributed to him as the elevation (C.R.O., TL 1828/1/6) is in the same hand as the drawings for Church House.

HODKIN, DANIEL (–1839), of Chesterfield. is described as 'architect and surveyor of County bridges' in Pigot's *Directory* of 1828–9. One of the church registers records that in 1795 Daniel Hodkin made a new altar-piece for CHESTERFIELD PARISH CHURCH, and according to a MS. note in a copy of Ford's *History of Chesterfield* he designed the METHODIST CHAPEL, SALTERGATE, CHESTERFIELD, in 1822–3. He was presumably the 'David Hodkin' who according to J. C. Cox designed and built BLACKWELL CHURCH, DERBYSHIRE, in 1827–8, again rebuilt 1879 [*Churches of Derbyshire* i, 1875, 95]. He died in Jan. 1839 [Lichfield Probate Records].

HOLDEN, THOMAS, was a carpenter by trade but practised as a surveyor and architect in London in the reign of George II. He was a member of the Ironmongers' Company and in 1746 that Company chose his design for their new Hall in preference to those of Messrs. Dance, Robinson and Sampson [minutes of the Company in Guildhall Library, MS. 16967/6, 14 Jan. 1745/6 and cf. MS. 4329/17, 5 Aug. 1740]. IRONMONGERS' HALL, FENCHURCH STREET, LONDON (dem. 1917), was built in 1748–50 and Holden's name was inscribed on the façade [J. Nicoll, *Some Account of the Worshipful Company of Ironmongers*, 1866, 45]. In 1753 Holden made unexecuted designs for rebuilding Clapham Church, Surrey [B. F. L. Clarke, *The Building of the Eighteenth-Century Church*, 1963, 25]. He must be distinguished from Strickland Holden (d. 1765), a London carpenter who also acted as a building surveyor.

HOLDSWORTH, EDWARD (1684–1746), the son of a clergyman in Hampshire, was educated at Winchester and Corpus Christi College, Oxford, and became a Demy and Tutor at Magdalen College. In 1715, when he was about to be elected a Fellow, he declined to take the obligatory oath of allegiance to the Hanoverian government and had to leave Oxford, remaining, however, on the best of terms with his former colleagues at Magdalen. The rest of his life was spent acting as a travelling tutor to young men of property on the Grand Tour. He died on 30 December 1746 at Lord Digby's seat at Coleshill in Warwickshire. Holdsworth was a good classical scholar and the author, *inter alia*, of a Latin poem entitled *Muscipula* that was much admired. His friend Charles Jennens erected a small circular temple to his memory at Gopsall Hall, Leicestershire, with an inscription which praised his architectural skill.

Holdsworth's only known architectural work was the NEW BUILDING at MAGDALEN COLLEGE. This was built in 1733–4 as the first instalment of a grand Palladian design for a new quadrangle that was published in the *Oxford Almanack* for 1731, and on which Holdsworth had (with advice from James Gibbs and others) been working since the 1720s. No more was, however, built, although as late as 1744 Holdsworth sent a revised plan from Rome that has not survived, and he left £100 towards its completion in his will. [J. R. Bloxam, *Register of Magdalen College, Oxford*, vi, 1879, 164–8; H. Colvin, *Unbuilt Oxford*, 1983, 81–5.]

HOLL, EDWARD (–1824), may have been the son of Edward Holl (*c.*1751–1815), a mason at Beccles in Suffolk. Under various titles he was the official architect in charge of naval works from 1804 onwards, and in that capacity was responsible for several buildings in the Royal Dockyards, notably at Chatham and Sheerness. The large Dockyard Chapels at CHATHAM, 1808–10, and DEVONPORT, 1814–17 (dem. by bombing *c.*1941), were designed by him, as was the COMMISSIONER'S HOUSE in the DOCKYARD at BERMUDA, 1806–7 [J. Coad, *Historic Architecture of the Royal Navy*, 1983, *passim*]. At PORTSMOUTH he designed the SCHOOL OF NAVAL ARCHITECTURE, 1815–17 [H. & J. Slight, *Chronicles of Portsmouth*, 1828, 164]. According to J. Dugdale's *British Traveller* iii, 1819, 610, he was the architect of the large and monumental ROYAL NAVAL HOSPITAL (afterwards barracks and now St. Nicholas Hospital) at YARMOUTH, NORFOLK, 1809–11, though other sources say it was designed by William Pilkington (*q.v.*).

HOLLAND, HENRY (1745–1806), born on 20 July 1745, was the eldest son of Henry Holland (1712–85), a successful Georgian master builder who was Master of the Tylers' and Bricklayers' Company in 1772–3. Henry's architectural training appears to have been obtained in his father's yard in Fulham, for there is no evidence that he was the pupil of any professional architect. In 1771, however, he became the partner of Lancelot

Brown, the landscape-gardener, who was then living only a few miles away at Hampton Court, and with whom his father was acquainted. The partnership appears to have been of an informal character, and did not necessarily involve one partner in every commission that the other secured. It did, however, mean that Holland largely took over the architectural side of Brown's practice, and in this way obtained an introduction to the latter's large and influential clientèle. The alliance was strengthened in 1773 by Holland's marriage to Brown's daughter Bridget. The couple took up residence at No. 17 Hertford Street, a London house which had recently been built by Holland and his father.

Despite his lack of professional pupilage or foreign travel, Holland soon emerged as one of the leading English architects of the reign of George III. His first important work was Brooks's Club in St. James's Street, a commission which brought him into contact with those members of the Whig aristocracy who were to be his principal patrons, and which led, through them, to his employment by the Prince of Wales. The Gallic sympathies of the Whig circle into which Holland was thus introduced were reflected in the French influence which is apparent in his architecture. This was derived chiefly from the publications of French architects. For it was not until shortly before the Revolution that he actually visited France, and the French elements in his style appear to have been based less on personal observation than on a close study of French sources such as Peyre, Patte and Gondoin and on the employment of a French assistant, J. P. Trécourt, and of French craftsmen and decorative painters. In this way Holland developed a neo-classical style of his own that was as elegant and refined as that of the Adam brothers, and as valid as an alternative to the outmoded Palladianism of the mid-eighteenth century. Holland's ability in planning was demonstrated at Carlton House, where he created an elaborate sequence of rooms inside the shell of an existing building and devised a forecourt which gave consequence to the entrance in a manner very suggestive of Rousseau's Hôtel de Salm in Paris, begun in the same year. Both at Carlton House and at Berrington Hall he designed staircases of great beauty and sophistication. In his sober exteriors, his adventurous staircases and his interest in contemporary French architecture, Holland was carrying on the tradition established by Chambers. But, unlike Chambers, he did not despise the Greek Revival, using at Woburn both Doric and Ionic orders of strictly Grecian origin with more or less archaeological accuracy.

Like most eighteenth-century architects, Holland turned to speculative building to supplement the proceeds of his architectural practice, and in 1771, with the aid of capital supplied by his father, he took a lease of 89 acres of land in Chelsea from Lord Cadogan. Upon this site Holland later erected the estate known as Hans Town, comprising Sloane Street, Cadogan Place and the polygonal Hans Place, at one end of which he built himself a large detached villa known as Sloane Place.

Holland was a man of retiring disposition who did not seek public notice, and never exhibited his work at the Royal Academy. 'Pray no more public compliments to me', he admonished David Hartley in 1789. 'I began the world a very independent man and wish to hold it at arms length . . . I find myself already more the object of public notice than suits my disposition or plan of life.' Nevertheless he became a J.P. for Middlesex in 1778 and held two public offices, the one a District Surveyorship under the Act of 1774, the other the Clerkship of the Works at the Royal Mews at Charing Cross, an Office of Works appointment which he obtained in 1775 through the influence of Lord North. He lost the latter post as a result of the reforms of 1782, but it is doubtful whether a career in the Office of Works had an important place in his ambitions. In 1799 he succeeded Richard Jupp as Surveyor to the East India Company. From 1782 to 1793 he was also Surveyor to the Bridewell and Bethlehem Hospitals. He was a member of the Stationers' Company.

Holland devoted much time to methods of preventing fire, notably by means of David Hartley's 'fire-plate', which he used at Althorp and elsewhere, and was responsible for the publication of the *Resolution of the Associated Architects, with the Report of a Committee appointed to consider the causes of the frequent fires*, etc., 1793. He also contributed two papers to the *Communications of the Board of Agriculture* in 1797, one a practical essay on the construction of cottages, the other on the use of *pisé* as described by A. M. Cointereaux in his *Traité sur la construction des Manufactures et des Maisons de Campagne*, Paris 1791. According to Papworth's *Rural Residences* (1818), the use of *pisé* was 'introduced into England by the late Mr. H.'

Holland died in Sloane Place on 17 June 1806, aged 60, and was buried in the family tomb in Fulham churchyard. He left two sons, named Henry and Lancelot, and five daughters. Soane began his architectural career in 1772 as an assistant in Holland's office and C. H. Tatham became his draughtsman in about 1789. H. Hemsley, J. Jagger and

W. Plumridge were also his pupils. Marble busts by Garrard are preserved at Woburn Abbey and Southill Park, and there is an oil portrait by Opie (illustrated in Miss Stroud's biography). Holland's drawings and papers appear to have been largely destroyed by his nephew and executor Henry Rowles after his death, but two sketch-books relating to Carlton House and a volume of drawings, chiefly of interior decoration, are in the R.I.B.A. Collection (see the *Catalogue: G-K*, 134–9).

[H. B. Hodson, 'Holland, the Architect', *Builder* xiii, 1855, 437; *A.P.S.D.*; Dorothy Stroud, *Henry Holland*, 1950; Dorothy Stroud, *Henry Holland, His Life and Architecture*, 1966; David Hartley's papers in the Berkshire C.R.O.; *Stationers' Company Apprentices*, ed. D. F. McKenzie, Oxford Bibliographical Soc. 1978, 176.]

DENHAM COURT, BUCKS., work in Bow Room for Henry Wood, 1767 [bill in Boynton-Wood papers at Hollin Hall, Yorks., *ex inf.* Dr. Giles Worsley].

HALE HOUSE, HANTS., alterations for Lady Elizabeth Archer, 1770 [Stroud, 24].

HILL PARK (later VALENCE), nr. WESTERHAM, KENT, work for lst Earl of Hillsborough, *c.*1770; dem. [Stroud, 25].

BATTERSEA BRIDGE, MIDDLESEX (timber), built for 15 proprietors, 1771–2; dem. 1881 [D. Lysons, *Environs of London* i, 1810, 33].

*CLAREMONT HOUSE, nr. ESHER, SURREY, for lst Lord Clive, 1771–4 [G. Richardson, *New Vitruvius Britannicus* i, 1802, pls. 61–3].

LONDON, No. 35 UPPER GROSVENOR STREET, alterations and repairs for Sir Henry Harpur, Bart., 1772; dem. [Derbyshire C.R.O., Harpur-Crewe papers, account-book 1772–81, p. 8].

*BENHAM PLACE, BERKS., for 6th Lord Craven, 1774–5; attic storey added and pediment removed *c.*1870 [Stroud, 36–7].

*LONDON, No. 75 SOUTH AUDLEY STREET, alterations for 3rd Earl of Bute, 1775–6 [*Survey of London* xl, 312–3].

*CADLAND, nr. SOUTHAMPTON, HANTS., for the Hon. Robert Drummond, 1775–8; wing added by Holland 1782; enlarged by Wyatville 1837–8; dem. 1953 [Stroud, 39–40; Linstrum, *Wyatville*, 138–9, 233].

*TRENTHAM HALL, STAFFS., alterations for 2nd Earl Gower, 1775–8; reconstructed by Barry 1834–40 and 1840–9; dem. 1910 [Stroud, 40–1] (C. *Life*, 25 Jan. 1968, fig. 8).

LONDON, BROOKS'S CLUB-HOUSE, No. 60 ST. JAMES'S STREET, 1776–8; portico removed 1815; external and internal alterations by J. McVicar Anderson 1889–90 and A. E. Richardson 1935–8 [Stroud, 50–2; J. M. Crook in *Brooks's*, ed. Ziegler & Seward, 1991, 153–9].

*CARDIFF CASTLE, GLAMORGANSHIRE, reconstruction in Gothic style for Lord Mount Stuart, 1777–8; rebuilt 1875 [Stroud, 56–7] (*C. Life*, 6 April 1961).

LONDON, HANS TOWN, CHELSEA, comprising SLOANE STREET, SLOANE PLACE, CADOGAN PLACE and HANS PLACE, 1777 onwards [Stroud, 43–9].

BERRINGTON HALL, nr. LEOMINSTER, HEREFS., for the Hon. Thomas Harley, 1778–81 [Stroud, 52–6; Christopher Hussey in *C. Life*, 2, 9 & 16 Dec. 1954] (*C. Life*, 9 Jan. 1992).

STONE, STAFFS., THE CROWN INN, new front to street, 1779–80 [Stroud, 58].

CHART SUTTON CHURCH, KENT, rebuilt, except tower, 1779–82; remodelled 1896–8 [E. Hasted, *History of Kent* ii, 1782, 407 note; Stroud, 58].

*LONDON, No. 34 BERKELEY SQUARE, internal alterations for Lady Mary Coke, 1780; dem. 1879 [*Survey of London* xl, 318].

*NUNEHAM PARK, OXON., alterations including heightening of wings for 2nd Earl Harcourt, 1781–2 [Stroud, 58; M. L. Batey, *Nuneham Courtenay, Oxfordshire*, 1970, 11–12].

LONDON, No. 7 ST. JAMES'S SQUARE, probably refronted the house, which Holland bought in 1782 and sold to Richard Barwell in 1783 [*Survey of London* xxix, 112].

GRANGEMOUTH, STIRLINGSHIRE, layout plan for Sir Thomas Dundas, Bart., 1783 [Stroud, 59–60].

LONDON, CARLTON HOUSE, PALL MALL, works for George, Prince of Wales, 1783–96; dem. 1827–8. Holland added the Corinthian portico and the Ionic screen to Pall Mall and remodelled the interior [Stroud, 61–85; *History of the King's Works* vi, 307–12].

LONDON, SPENCER HOUSE, GREEN PARK, internal alterations for 2nd Earl Spencer, 1785–92 [*Survey of London* xxx, 521; Stroud, 103].

BRIGHTON, THE MARINE PAVILION, for George, Prince of Wales, 1786–7, enlarged by Holland 1801–4; subsequently remodelled by John Nash [G. Richardson, *New Vitruvius Britannicus* i, 1810, pls. 6–7; Stroud, 86–90].

LONDON, YORK, formerly FETHERSTONHAUGH, afterwards MELBOURNE, and now DOVER HOUSE, WHITEHALL, added portico and domed entrance hall for Frederick, Duke of York, 1787 [*Survey of London* xiv, 60–4; 92–3].

LONDON, BEDFORD HOUSE, BLOOMSBURY, re-

* In collaboration with L. Brown.

modelled eating-room for 5th Duke of Bedford, 1787; dem. 1800 [Stroud, 106].

KNIGHT'S HILL, NORWOOD, SURREY, house for lst Lord Thurlow, 1787; dem. 1810 [Stroud, 137–8; *Picturesque Views of the Principal Seats of the Nobility and Gentry*, Harrison & Co., plate dated 1788, mentioning Holland as the architect; *The World*, 18 April, 7 May, 3 July, 12 July 1787].

STANMORE HOUSE or PARK, MIDDLESEX, alterations for George Drummond, 1787; dem. 1938 [*The World*, 4, 22 Aug. 1787, *ex inf.* Mr. P. A. Bezodis; W. Keane, *Beauties of Middlesex*, 1850, 138].

WOBURN ABBEY, BEDS., remodelled south façade, added entrance portico, enlarged stables, and added the conservatory (now sculpture gallery), Chinese dairy, riding-school, tennis court and park-entrance to London Road, for 5th Duke of Bedford, 1787–1802. The portico, riding-school and tennis court were dem. 1954 [Stroud, 106–15] (C. *Life*, 1–8 Sept. 1955).

ALTHORP, NORTHANTS., recased house in white mathematical tiles and remodelled much of interior, for 2nd Earl Spencer, 1787–9 [Stroud, 97–102; B.L., Althorp Papers, L 1]. (*C. Life*, 11, 18 & 25 June, 2 July 1921, 19–26 May 1960).

LONDON, No. 105 PALL MALL, remodelled interior for Mrs. Fitzherbert, 1787; dem. 1838 [*The World*, 17 Oct., 30 Nov. 1787, *ex inf.* Mr. P. A. Bezodis] (*Survey of London* xxix, 349).

ALLERTON MAULEVERER, YORKS. (W.R.), remodelled house for Frederick, Duke of York, 1788; rebuilt 1848–51 [*The World*, 28 March 1788, *ex inf.* Mr. P. A. Bezodis].

BROADLANDS, HANTS., east Ionic portico, vestibule and interior decoration for 2nd Viscount Palmerston, 1788–92 [Stroud, 133] (*C. Life*, 31 March, 7 April 1923, 4, 11, 18 Dec. 1980).

OAKLEY HOUSE, BEDS., alterations for 5th Duke of Bedford, 1789–92 [Stroud, 113–14] (Neale, *Views of Seats* vi, 1823).

WOBURN, BEDS., THE GEORGE INN, repairs for 5th Duke of Bedford, *c.*1790 [Stroud, *Holland*, 1950, 37].

BEDFORD, THE SWAN HOTEL, for 5th Duke of Bedford, 1792 [Stroud, 114–15].

HOUGHTON CONQUEST, BEDS., unidentified inn designed for 5th Duke of Bedford, *c.*1792 [Stroud, 114].

BIRCHMORE FARM, WOBURN, BEDS., alterations for 5th Duke of Bedford, *c.*1792 [Stroud, 115].

LONDON, DRURY LANE THEATRE, rebuilt for R. B. Sheridan, 1791–4; burned 1809 [Stroud, 116–25; see also *The Georgian Playhouse*, Arts Council Exhibition 1975, Nos. 227–8].

LONDON, COVENT GARDEN THEATRE, alterations for Thomas Harris, 1792; burned 1808 [Stroud, 123–5].

OATLANDS HOUSE, WEYBRIDGE, SURREY, for Frederick, Duke of York, 1794–1800, with Gothic detailing by John Carter (*q.v.*); dem. [Stroud, 95] (*Gent's Mag.* 1808 (i), 9; *The Ambulator*, 1807, 225).

ABERDEEN, THE THEATRE, MARISCHAL STREET, 1795; dem. [W. Kennedy, *Annals of Aberdeen*, 1818, ii, 280].

DEBDEN HALL, ESSEX, for R. M. T. Chiswell, 1795; dem. 1936 [Stroud, 131–3] (Neale, *Views of Seats*, lst ser., ii, 1819).

SOUTHILL HOUSE, BEDS., remodelled for Samuel Whitbread, 1796–1800 [Stroud, 127–30] (A. E. Richardson and others, *Southill: A Regency House*, 1951).

PARK PLACE, nr. HENLEY-ON-THAMES, BERKS., alterations for lst Earl of Malmesbury, *c.*1796; remodelled 1871 [J. Britton & E. W. Brayley, *Beauties of England and Wales* i, 1801, 183; Stroud, 133].

DUNIRA, PERTHSHIRE, design for enlargement for lst Viscount Melville, 1798, carried out 1802 onwards by William Stirling (*q.v.*); rebuilt by W. Brown 1851–2 [Dundas papers at Comrie House, *ex inf.* Prof. A. A. Tait].

LONDON, EAST INDIA HOUSE, LEADENHALL STREET, completed building after death of Richard Jupp (*q.v.*), 1799–1800; dem. 1861–2. For the extent of Holland's responsibility for this building, see below, p. 567. (Britton & Pugin, *The Public Buildings of London* ii, 1828, 77–89.)

LONDON, WAREHOUSES adjacent to Middlesex Street, Harrow Place and Cutler Street for the East India Company, 1799–1800, following designs by Richard Jupp, but with a modified layout; dem. 1979 [India Office Records B/130, ff. 1092–3 and A/1/1, ff. 490, 507].

WIMBLEDON PARK HOUSE, SURREY, for 2nd Earl Spencer, 1800; dem. 1949 [Stroud, 104–5].

LONDON, ALBANY, PICCADILLY, conversion of Melbourne House into residential chambers and erection of additional buildings, 1803–4 [Stroud, 142–4; *Survey of London* xxxii, 373–85].

HERTFORD CASTLE, alterations to GATEHOUSE for temporary accommodation of the East India College, 1805 [Stroud, 142].

GLASGOW, THE ASSEMBLY ROOMS, INGRAM STREET, added terminal pavilions to building designed by R. & J. Adam, completed 1807; dem. *c.*1889 [*A.P.S.D.*].

WESTPORT, COUNTY MAYO, IRELAND, gateway at north-east end of town, for lst Marquess of

Sligo, being built 1808 'from designs of Holland'; dem. *c.*1958 [Diary of the Revd. D. A. Beaufort, Trinity College, Dublin, MS. K.6.63, f. 75].

DOUBTFUL WORKS

COLEHILL HOUSE, FULHAM, MIDDLESEX, is stated by Britton & Brayley, *Beauties of England and Wales* x (part 5), 1816, 96–7, to have been 'built in 1770 from the design of its late proprietor [James Madden] and under the direction of Mr. Holland, architect'. This was probably Henry Holland, senior. A letter from Henry Holland in the Somerset County Record Office dated Oct. 1783 refers to proposed works at KINGWESTON HOUSE, SOMERSET, for William Dickinson, but what, if anything, was done is uncertain. According to J. Stoddart, *Remarks on Local Scenery and Manners in Scotland* ii, 1801, 274, IRVINE HOUSE, LANGHOLM, DUMFRIESSHIRE, was 'a neat villa, designed by Holland'. What are probably Holland's designs for this house, signed and dated 1783, are preserved in a portfolio at Bowhill, Selkirkshire. But they were rejected as too expensive, and the modest house actually built *c.*1792 appears to have been designed by a builder in London [Buccleuch archives, S.R.O., *ex inf.* Prof. A. A. Tait]. The house still exists, enlarged in 1836–7 by William Burn (*q.v.*). The 'works at Little Willenham, Staffordshire', attributed to Holland in *A.P.S.D.*, have not been identified.

HOLLAND, JOHN J—, 'Architect and Draftsman', of 25 Warren Street, London, signs two architectural drawings in the Metropolitan Museum of Art at New York, one of them dated 1802 [J. Harris, *Catalogue of British Drawings for Architecture, etc., in American Collections*, 1971, 125]. He was probably the J. Holland, of 24 Upper Edmund Street, St. Pancras, who exhibited a design for a Military Depot at the R.A. in 1815.

HOLLAND, RICHARD (1752–1827), a cousin of Henry Holland (*q.v.*), exhibited at the Royal Academy in 1771, 1772 and 1773, having been admitted to its Schools in October 1770, at the age of 18. He was awarded the Silver Medal the same year. His subsequent career was, however, to be that of a successful builder rather than an architect. In 1786 he was employed by R. M. T. Chiswell to design a Coade stone font for Debden Church, Essex, which attracted much interest and was exhibited to the King at Buckingham Palace. It is described and illustrated in the *European Magazine* for 1786. Richard Holland is said also to have designed Debden Hall, Essex, for the same patron, but it appears in fact to have been designed by his cousin Henry. He retired in about 1804 to Madley, nr. Hereford, but moved in 1810 to Combe Royal, Kingsbridge, Devon, and ultimately to Moreton Hampstead in the same county, where he died unmarried on 28 September 1827. He was a friend of Sir John Soane, with whom he corresponded. [*A.P.S.D.*; A. T. Bolton, *Portrait of Sir John Soane*, 1927, 165–76; information from Miss Dorothy Stroud.]

HOLLINS, WILLIAM (1763–1843), architect and sculptor, was born at Shifnal on 18 March 1763, but went to Birmingham as a boy and lived there for the rest of his life. Originally a journeyman stonemason, he taught himself drawing and perspective and became a successful architect, sculptor and wax-modeller. In 1793 he assisted George Saunders of London to make the working drawings for the new Theatre Royal in New Street, and subsequently himself designed several public buildings in Birmingham in a competent Greek Revival style. He was one of the architects employed by the Earl of Shrewsbury to design the picturesque garden buildings at Alton Towers, though precisely what he did there does not appear to be recorded. He is said to have 'declined an offer to enter the service of the Empress of Russia at St. Petersburg, but made plans for the Royal Mint in that city'. The former part of this story is doubtful, but Hollins was concerned with Matthew Boulton's commission to supply minting machinery from his Soho Works at Birmingham for the new Royal Mint at St. Petersburg designed by A. Porta (1805), and some drawings by him for the mint were sold at Christie's in December 1986 and are now in Birmingham Reference Library (MS. 1381). In 1806 Hollins produced a design for the Birmingham memorial to Nelson consisting of a column 100 feet high, rising from 'an appropriate building with two fronts suitable for a dispensary and post-office', but a simpler design by Westmacott was adopted. A list of his executed buildings is given below. For his activity as a sculptor see Rupert Gunnis's *Dictionary of British Sculptors*. He was also interested in lettering, and published *The British Standard of the Capital Letters contained in the Roman Alphabet*, Birmingham 1813.

Hollins had 16 children, 'through the whole of whom was to be traced the varied genius of the original'. His eldest son Peter (1800–86) was a well-known Victorian sculptor. Hollins died on 12 January 1843, and is buried under a granite obelisk in St. Paul's churchyard at

Birmingham. He and his family are also commemorated by a glass window in the church with a sculptured surround incorporating his bust by Peter Hollins.

[H. H. Horton, *Birmingham A Poem*, 2nd ed. 1853, 285–9 (biographical notes); J. A. Langford, *Modern Birmingham* i, 1873, 31–2; *D.N.B.*; R. Gunnis, *Dictionary of British Sculptors*, 1968, 206–7; Bryan Little, *Birmingham Buildings*, 1971; I. G. Spassky, *The Russian Monetary System*, Amsterdam 1967, 222; Cornish's *Guide to Birmingham*, 1864.]

BIRMINGHAM, THE OLD LIBRARY, UNION STREET, 1798; enlarged 1845 by D. R. Hill; dem. [Langford, *Modern Birmingham* i, 31–2].

BIRMINGHAM, THE PUBLIC OFFICE and PRISON, MOOR STREET, 1805–7; enlarged 1829–30; dem. 1911 [Langford, *Modern Birmingham* i, 31–2].

BIRMINGHAM, THE GENERAL DISPENSARY, UNION STREET, 1806–8; dem. 1957 [Langford, *Modern Birmingham* i, 31–2].

BIRMINGHAM, THE BULL RING PUMP, 1807; dem. 1836 [J. A. Langford, *A Century of Birmingham Life* ii, 1871, 199].

ALTON ABBEY (later TOWERS), STAFFS., works for 15th Earl of Shrewsbury, *c.*1813–17, Gothic [papers in the Staffs. Record Office show that in Dec. 1817 it was ordered that the Hall should be 'finished agreeably to Mr. Hollins's plan', *ex inf.* Dr. J. M. Frew].

HANDSWORTH CHURCH, STAFFS., enlargement of north side 1820–1, Gothic [A. E. Everitt, 'Handsworth Church', *Trans. Birmingham Arch. Soc.* 1876, 62].

BIRMINGHAM, THE ATHENAEUM, TEMPLE ROW, for the Birmingham Institute for Promoting the Fine Arts, 1828; dem. [J. Hill & W. Midgley, *The Royal Birmingham Society of Artists*, 1928, 15, 26 and pl. 20].

HOLLIS, CHARLES, exhibited architectural designs at the Royal Academy in 1801–3. After this no further references to him have been found until 1820, when his designs for rebuilding WINDSOR PARISH CHURCH in the Gothic style were accepted, though Jeffry Wyatt was also concerned, apparently as a consultant. The church was completed in 1822 [*A.P.S.D.*; Parish Records]. Hollis also designed WINDSOR BRIDGE, consisting of three arches of iron, 1822–4 [*A.P.S.D.*], and the classical church of ALL SAINTS, POPLAR, with its parsonage house, 1821–3, illustrated in Britton & Pugin, *Public Buildings of London* ii, 1828, 202–4.[1] In the 1820s Hollis was practising from various London addresses, but his name then disappears from the London directories, and his death in or about 1830 may be presumed. He appears to have been a competent but unremarkable early nineteenth-century architect.

[1] J. J. Scoles also made designs for this church which were not accepted. He exhibited them at the R.A. in 1821.

HOLLOWAY, BENJAMIN, a local carpenter and builder, was employed by James Brydges, Duke of Chandos, in his building developments at Bridgwater in Somerset during the years 1723–8. Holloway designed at least four of the houses which he built for the Duke in New, or Castle, Street, but others may have been designed by the Duke's London surveyors, Fort and Shepherd. Holloway also built houses in Chandos Street, and one on the quay known as 'The Lions', which he occupied himself. This handsome house is illustrated in William Halfpenny's *Perspective Made Easy* (1731), with the inscription 'Benjamin Holloway invenit'. Chandos thought Holloway 'a very great knave. But being a good workman and the only one thereabouts 'tis necessary to employ him'. Stylistically he was a provincial master builder who had picked up some baroque details and made effective use of them to enliven his street-fronts. [C. H. & M. I. Collins Baker, *James Brydges, Duke of Chandos*, 1949, chap. x.]

HOLMES, WILLIAM (*c.*1761–1847), 'of Lewisham, architect', is commemorated by a tablet on the north wall of Lewisham parish church. He died on 13 August 1847, aged 86. He designed the church of ST. JOHN, CAMPHILL ROAD, SOUTH END, LEWISHAM, *c.*1823 [I.C.B.S.]. In the Public Record Office there is a 'sketch' by him for farm buildings at ELTHAM COURT FARM, KENT, dated 1828 [MPE 723].

HOLT, THOMAS (–1624), see AKROYD, JOHN.

HOOKE, ROBERT (1635–1703), was born at Freshwater in the Isle of Wight, where his father, John Hooke, was then curate of the parish. He showed an early aptitude for drawing which led to his being apprenticed to Lely, but he soon gave up painting and entered Westminster School, where he lived in the house of Dr. Busby and astonished his teachers by his progress in learning. In 1653 he went up to Oxford as a chorister or servitor at Christ Church, matriculating in 1658, and proceeding M.A. in 1663. Here he became intimate with Wren, and attended the meetings of the 'Experimental Philosophical Club' which was the precursor of the Royal Society. His flair for scientific enquiry led to his appointment as curator of experiments to the Royal Society in 1662, and his election as a fellow in the following year. In 1665 his curatorship was made perpetual, with a salary of £30 and apartments in Gresham College, Bishopsgate Street, where he lived for the rest of his life. Later in the same year he was appointed Professor of Geometry at Gresham College, where Wren had been Professor of Astronomy, and from 1677 to 1682 he acted as Secretary to the Royal Society. As a scientist, his fertility of invention and his genius for discerning the principles underlying chemical and physical processes were outstanding, and he was a pioneer in almost every branch of scientific enquiry.

Hooke's career as an architect began in September 1666, when he laid before the Common Council his plan (now lost) for rebuilding the City, and was told by the Lord Mayor that the court of aldermen 'had approved of it, and greatly preferring it to that of the city surveyor [Peter Mills] desired it might be shown to his Majesty'.[1] In October Hooke was nominated as one of the three surveyors whom the City was required to appoint under the Act for rebuilding London, the others being Peter Mills and Edward Jerman. In this capacity he was closely associated with Wren (one of the three surveyors nominated by the King) in the reconstruction of the City, surveying the sites of houses to be taken in in order to widen the streets, discussing the problems of the Fleet Ditch, agreeing with contractors, and negotiating with landowners. Both Wren and Hooke were concerned in the design and erection of the Monument on Fish Street Hill and it is not easy to decide which of them was its principal architect.[2] Hooke also collaborated with Wren in connection with the City Churches, and there are several references to him as one of the three 'Surveyors for the building of the churches in London', the third being Edward Woodroffe, Surveyor to the Dean and Chapter of Westminster. It was 'on the City Churches account' that Hooke received substantial payments from Wren, and much of his time was spent in visiting them with or without the Surveyor-General, in passing accounts, and in attending vestry meetings. Hooke's share in the designing, as distinct from the building, of the City churches, awaits further investigation. Although all of them were the product of an office of which Wren was the head, responsibility for the designing of some of them must have been delegated to Hooke, but in at least one such case (St. Edmund, Lombard Street, *Wren Soc.* ix, pl. 15) the approbatory initials 'CW' show that Wren retained ultimate control.

Although Wren as Surveyor-General was the senior officer, Hooke must not be thought of merely as his junior assistant. In the eyes of the City he was Wren's colleague, not his deputy, and his diary shows that 'he met Wren as a friend and dined with him as an equal'; indeed they were related, one of Wren's sisters having married a member of Hooke's family,[3] and in correspondence Wren addressed Hooke as 'Cousin'. Despite their kinship and their close association in both architectural and scientific matters, Hooke never took one of the Office of Works posts that were in Wren's gift. In January 1690/1, however, he was appointed Surveyor to the Dean and Chapter of Westminster at an annual salary of £20.[4] In this capacity he was consulted about repairs to the exterior of the Abbey Church in 1693. He presumably resigned in January 1696/7, when his place was taken by James Broughton.

Hooke was an active, restless little man who slept little and often worked all night, taking a short nap during the day. Estimates of his character differ, but it is clear that although as a young man he had been 'very communicative of his philosophical discoveries and inventions', as he grew older he became increasingly mistrustful and secretive. In person he was 'but despicable', being 'crooked and low in stature', 'pale faced', and as he grew older, more and more deformed. He died at Gresham College on 3 March 1702/3, at the age of 67, and was buried in the church of St. Helen Bishopsgate.

For Hooke architecture was always a secondary activity, and he never gave himself up to it in the same way as Wren did. Nor do any of his architectural works or drawings suggest that he was a designer of outstanding ability. Nevertheless he was a competent architect whose contribution to English architecture has been obscured by the destruction of his

[1] John Ward, *Lives of the Professors of Gresham College* (1740), 175. The formal entry in the Journal of the Court of Common Council (vol. 46, f. 121) is as follows: 'Mr. Hooke haveing upon the Mocion and Encouragement of this Court prepared & presented an Exquisite Modell or draught for rebuilding of this City doth declare their good Acceptance & Approbacion of the Same'.

[2] See below, p. 1090.

[3] Either Rachel or Katherine Wren married John Hooke (d. 1674), rector of Blechingdon, Oxon., and formerly Fellow of Magdalen College, Oxford. See Wood, *Life & Times*, ed. A. Clark, ii, 1892, 282. The exact relationship between Robert and John Hooke is not clear, but they appear both to have belonged to the Hampshire family of Hooke.

[4] He had previously given advice about repairing the choir (Diary, 18 July, 21 Aug., 8–10 Oct. 1676).

most important works: the domed octagonal theatre of the Royal College of Physicians, the carefully articulated blocks of the Bethlehem Hospital, and the *cour d'honneur* of Montagu House, designed (as Evelyn noted) 'after the French pavilion-way'. French planning and Dutch detailing are the most obvious characteristics of Hooke's architectural style, and his diary shows that he purchased architectural books and prints from both France and Holland. A projected visit to France is mentioned in 1676, but it did not eventuate, and if Hooke ever visited Holland the occasion is not recorded, though an elevation of the Nieuwe Kerk at The Hague is among his drawings in the British Library.

A volume of seventeenth-century architectural drawings in the British Library (Add. MS. 5238) contains a number by Hooke or his assistant Henry Hunt. A few drawings attributable to Hooke (including a section of the dome of the Physicians' College) are among the Feilding family papers in the Warwicks. C.R.O. (CR 2017/B 1–3). A design for a barracks at the R.I.B.A. and one for rebuilding the Royal Mews formerly in the Library of the Department of the Environment (Dartmouth Collection) may be in his hand.

The primary source for Hooke's life in general and for his architectural work in particular, is his diary, the surviving portions of which extend from August 1672 to May 1683 (Guildhall Library), from November 1688 to March 1690, and from December 1692 to August 1693 (B. L. Sloane MS. 4024). The Guildhall MS. was published in 1935 in *The Diary of Robert Hooke*, ed. H. W. Robinson & W. Adams, omitting the entries for 1681, 1682 and 1683, the B. L. MS. in *Early Science in Oxford*, ed. R. T. Gunther, x, 1935, 69–265.

[Aubrey's *Brief Lives*, ed. A. Clark, 1898, and O. L. Dick, 1949; *D.N.B.*; Margaret 'Espinasse, *Robert Hooke*, 1956; Geoffrey Keynes, *A Bibliography of Dr. Robert Hooke*, 1960; M. I. Batten, 'The Architecture of Dr. Robert Hooke', *Walpole Soc.* xxv, 1936–7; *Early Science in Oxford*, ed. R. T. Gunther, vols. vi, vii, viii, x, 1930–5; *Wren Society*, *passim*; T. F. Reddaway, *The Rebuilding of London after the Great Fire*, 1940; E. G. R. Taylor, 'Robert Hooke and the Cartographical Projects of the late 17th-Century', *Geographical Jnl.* 90, 1937; S. R. Pierce, 'A Drawing for a Thames Embankment by Robert Hooke', *Antiquaries' Jnl.* 44, 1964; *Sale Catalogues of Libraries of Eminent Persons*, vol. 11; *Scientists*, ed. H.A. Feisenberger, 1975, 37–116; *Robert Hooke: New Studies*, ed. M. Hunter & S. Schaffer, 1989; Westminster Abbey Muniments.]

?BUNTINGFORD, HERTS., BISHOP SETH WARD'S ALMSHOUSES, founded under a charter of December 1684, but probably not built until 1689, when Hooke's assistant Hunt 'brought designs of Sarums almes houses at Buntingford' [*Diary*, 2 April 1689].

CAMBRIDGE, MAGDALENE COLLEGE, designs 1677, probably in connection with the Pepys Building, which was under construction in 1679 [Batten, 105–6; R.C.H.M. *Cambridge* ii, 139].

CANTERBURY CATHEDRAL, panelling in choir 1676; removed *c.*1826 [*Archaeologia* lxii (2), 1911, 357; cf. *Diary*, 14 & 22 July 1676; C. E. Woodruff & W. Danks, *Memorials of Canterbury Cathedral*, 1912, plate facing p. 342].

ESCOT HOUSE, DEVONSHIRE, designs for Sir Walter Yonge, Bart., 1677–8, perhaps executed *c.*1680–8. The house illustrated in *Vitruvius Britannicus* i, pls. 78–9 as 'Sir Walter Yonge's house in Devonshire' was Escot, not Colyton: see the engraving of Escot in Polwhele's *Devon* (1793–1806). Hooke made designs for a country house for Yonge in 1677–8 [Batten, 109], but Yonge did not complete the purchase of the estate at Escot until 1680, and the new house was not finished until *c.*1688. It was subsequently altered by James Wyatt and destroyed by fire in 1808.

LONDESBOROUGH HOUSE, YORKS. (E.R.), designs for lst Earl of Burlington, including garden layout, 1676–8, and perhaps also lodges and stable-block; house dem. 1818 [Batten, 104–5; David Neave, 'Lord Burlington's park and gardens at Londesborough', *Garden History* viii, 1980, 69–73].

LONDON, ASKE'S HOSPITAL, HOXTON, for the Haberdashers' Company, *c.*1690–3; rebuilt by D. R. Roper, 1825–6 [Batten, 103–4 and pl. xl].

LONDON, BETHLEHEM HOSPITAL, MOORFIELDS, 1675–6; wings added 1733; dem. 1815–16 [Batten, 91–3; drawings in B.L., Add. MS. 5238 and Bodleian, Gough Maps 44, no. 119].

LONDON, BRIDEWELL HOSPITAL, reconstruction after fire, 1671–8; dem. 1862 [M. 'Espinasse, *Robert Hooke*, 1956, 92, 175].

LONDON, CHRIST'S HOSPITAL, NEWGATE STREET, THE WRITING SCHOOL, with John Oliver, 1675–6; dem. 1902 [Batten, 110 and *Diary*, 28 Aug. 1676] (*Wren Soc.* xi, pls. xliv, xlv).

LONDON, MERCHANT TAYLORS' HALL, THREADNEEDLE STREET, hall screen 1673, destroyed by bombing 1940–1 [Batten,

90–1 and pl. xxxvi].

LONDON, MERCHANT TAYLORS' SCHOOL, SUFFOLK LANE, 1674–5, with Lem, the bricklayer employed, 1674–5; dem. 1875 [*Diary*, 28 & 29 Jan., 3 & 11 Feb. 1674] (F. R. Nixon, *History of Merchant Taylors' School*, 1823, with lithographs).

LONDON, MONTAGU HOUSE, BLOOMSBURY, for Ralph Montagu, cr. Duke of Montagu, 1675–9; gutted Jan. 1685/6 and rebuilt 1687, apparently by the French architect Pouget (*q.v.*); sold to the British Museum Trustees 1754 and opened as Museum 1759; dem. *c.*1850 [Batten, 93–6]. The only known representation of the house before the fire of 1686 is the small-scale view in Ogilvy & Morgan's map of 1682, reproduced by K. Downes, *English Baroque Architecture*, 1966, fig. 24. A comparison between this and engravings of the house after its reconstruction suggests that, even if the walls were partially retained, the elevations were considerably altered by Pouget. Hooke's forecourt and gateway, however, survived until the nineteenth century and are illustrated, e.g. by drawings by J. C. Buckler reproduced in *C. Life*, 14 Sept. 1951.

LONDON, THE MONUMENT, FISH STREET HILL, 1671–6, in association with Wren (see p. 1090).

LONDON, THE ROYAL COLLEGE OF PHYSICIANS, WARWICK LANE, 1672–8. The domed octagonal theatre was dem. 1866 and the remainder of the buildings were destroyed by fire in 1879 [Batten, 89–90 and pls. 36–7; cf. *Wren Soc.* v, pl. xxxiii, which may be an alternative design for the elevation] (Britton & Pugin, *The Public Buildings of London* ii, 1828, 44–53).

LONDON, ST. JAMES'S SQUARE, probably supervised completion of Nos. 6–7 for John Hervey and lst Earl of Ranelagh, 1676–7; dem. [Batten, 107–8; *Survey of London* xxix, 103, 109].

LONDON, SOMERSET HOUSE, STRAND, THE STABLES for Queen Catherine of Braganza, probably *c.*1669–70; dem. *c.*1780 [*History of the King's Works* v, 258; *Wren Soc.* v, pl. xxxii].

LONDON, SPRING GARDENS, probably designed house for Sir Robert Southwell, 1684–5; dem. [a payment of 5 guineas to Hooke by Southwell on 17 June 1684, recorded in Thomas Thorpe's *Catalogue of Southwell MSS.*, 1837, 296–7, probably relates to this house, which was built by Richard Frith, B. L. Egerton MS. 1627, ff. 62v, 68].

LONDON, STRAND, designed five houses for John Hervey, 1678 [Batten, 108].

LONDON, WHITEHALL, house in Privy Gardens for 20th Earl of Oxford, 1676; dem. 1691 or 1698 [Batten, 106–7].

?LOWTHER CHURCH, WESTMORLAND, for Sir John Lowther, Bart., *c.*1686. In Jan. 1679 Hooke 'gave Sir J. Lowther a Designe of church and estimate', but this may have been Sir John Lowther of Whitehaven, F.R.S. (d. 1706), rather than his cousin of Lowther. The medieval church of Lowther was rebuilt by the latter in *c.*1686, with a dome and lantern on the central tower that Hooke could well have designed. This feature was removed in 1824, but is shown in drawings by Machell (Carlisle Cathedral Library) and Buckler (B.L., Add. MS. 36390, f. 146). The date of the reconstruction is given as 1686 in Nicholson & Burn's *History of Westmorland* (1777), but the gap in Hooke's diary between 1683 and 1688 makes it impossible to ascertain whether he made any relevant designs in that year. Among the Lonsdale papers in the Cumbria Record Office there is a large design on vellum for the façade of a house (presumably Lowther Castle) which can be attributed to Hooke. It probably dates from *c.*1690, when Sir John Lowther was about to rebuild the Castle, though not, in the event, to Hooke's design (*Architectural Drawings from Lowther Castle*, ed. Colvin *et al.*, Society of Architectural Historians, 1980, pl. 3a).

?PLYMOUTH, ROYAL DOCKYARD, HAMOAZE, THE OFFICERS' DWELLING-HOUSES, GREAT STOREHOUSE, ROPEHOUSE, etc., *c.*1690–1700. A set of the designs for these buildings, as engraved for the benefit of the Navy Commissioners, is preserved among the Hooke drawings in B.L., Add. MS. 5238, and they closely resemble the Bethlehem Hospital in style. Moreover the Deputy-Governor of the Citadel at this time was Henry Hook, who may have been a relation of Robert's. Edmund Dummer (*q.v.*) was in charge of the work, but it seems possible that Hooke was responsible for the designs, especially as he had been involved in the design of the Navy Office in London in 1674 (Batten, 85–6). There is another set of these engravings in Add. MS. 9329, ff. 156–81. The buildings were not yet finished in 1698: see the view in King's MS. 43, f. 130.

RAGLEY HALL, WARWICKS., for lst Earl of Conway, 1679–83. Hooke revised a design already made by William Hurlbutt (*q.v.*). The interior was altered by J. Gibbs *c.*1750–5 and the portico was added by J. Wyatt *c.*1780 [Batten, 97–103; P. Leach, 'Ragley Hall reconsidered', *Archaeological Jnl.* 136, 1979] (*C. Life*, 22–29 March 1924, 1–8 May 1958).

RAMSBURY MANOR, WILTS., for Sir William Jones, Attorney General, *c.*1681–6. Hooke 'drew designes' for Jones in 1673 and in 1680 designed or altered a house for him in London. It is therefore likely that Jones would have employed Hooke to design the new house which he shortly afterwards began to build at Ramsbury (*C. Life*, 2, 9 Oct. 1920, 30 Nov., 7 Dec. 1961), and the fact that in August 1682 Hooke visited Ramsbury in company with Lem (bricklayer), Avis (carpenter) and Davis (joiner), three London craftsmen regularly employed by him, makes it virtually certain that he was the architect of Ramsbury [H. Colvin, 'Robert Hooke and Ramsbury Manor', *C. Life*, 23 Jan. 1975; H. Louw, 'New Light on Ramsbury Manor', *Arch. Hist.* 30, 1987].

SHENFIELD PLACE, ESSEX for Richard Vaughan, 1689 [Batten, 111: 'House in Essex' identifiable as Shenfield Place] (R.C.H.M. *Essex* ii, 214).

attributed: WEMBURY, nr. PLYMOUTH, DEVON, remodelled for John Pollexfen, *c.*1685; dem. *c.*1800 [Bridget Cherry, 'The Devon Country House in the late 17th and early 18th centuries', *Devon Archaeological Soc's Procs.*, 46, 1988, 110–11].

WILLEN CHURCH, BUCKS., for Dr. Richard Busby, 1680 [Batten, 96–7]. The lead cupola on the tower was removed in 1814 and the apse is an addition of 1862. An alternative design is illustrated in *Wren Soc.* ix, pl. 37. An engraving in *Gent's Mag.* 1792, 1168, shows the cupola.

HOPE, JOHN (1734–1808), and SAMUEL (1737–*c.*1770), of Liverpool, must be distinguished from their contemporaries Samuel and John Hope of Manchester (*q.v.*). They were the sons of John Hope of Millington in the parish of Rostherne, architect and builder, who died in 1776. John Hope senior is said to have designed 'several residences' in Cheshire, and to have been employed by the Earl of Stamford at Dunham Massey and Enville (Staffs.). His sons succeeded to his practice, but moved to Liverpool in about 1763. In 1769 they competed jointly for the Royal Exchange in Dublin [*Builder* xxvii, 1889, 781], but Samuel's death soon afterwards left John to carry on the practice alone for over thirty years. He died in 1808 in his 73rd year, leaving his practice to be continued by his son-in-law William Byrom (*q.v.*). From 1770 onwards he kept a detailed diary of both private and professional matters whose present whereabouts is unknown, though it was still in existence in 1869 [*Builder* xxvii, 1869, 803–4, 909; will of John Hope in Lancs. C.R.O., WCW].

In 1766 John Hope designed a vaulted room in the LIVERPOOL EXCHANGE to contain the Corporation records, and in 1777, when it was proposed to build a new gaol, he was authorized to send for plans of Newgate Prison, London, 'as lately rebuilt' [J. A. Picton, *Liverpool Municipal Records 1700–1835*, 1886, 256, 264]. In 1773 he designed the W. wing of ENVILLE HALL, STAFFS. for the 5th Earl of Stamford [*V.C.H. Staffs.* xx, 98–9 and drawings in Staffs. C.R.O., Tp. 1273/55], and at about the same time made an unexecuted design for a symmetrical villa with Gothick detailing to be built at Gwydyr Castle, N. Wales, for the 3rd Duke of Ancaster [Lincs. Record Office, 5 Anc. 5/A/10/13]. He was probably the 'Mr. Hope' who designed the BLUECOAT SCHOOL at WARRINGTON, LANCS., in 1779–82 [J. Bowes, 'The Warrington Blue Coat School', *Trans. Historic Soc. of Lancs. & Cheshire* N.S. x, 1869–70, 101–2]. In 1789 the tower of ST. NICHOLAS CHURCH, LIVERPOOL, was repaired under his direction [*Gent's Mag.* 1814 (i), 116], and in 1803 he was paid £2 14s. 6d. for planning alterations to the same church [*Liverpool Vestry Books*, ed. Peet, ii, 37]. In 1790 his designs for St. John's Church, Wakefield, were rejected in favour of those of Charles Watson [J. W. Walker, *Wakefield*, 1939, 300], but in 1794 he designed HOLY TRINITY CHURCH, WAVERTREE, nr. LIVERPOOL, with a prominent classical steeple in the Wren tradition, and in 1799 a large WESLEYAN CHAPEL in LEEDS STREET, LIVERPOOL, dem. *c.*1840 [*Builder* xxvii, 1869, 803–4].

In 1789–90 Hope altered the S. front of DUNHAM MASSEY HALL, CHESHIRE, for the 5th Earl of Stamford [F. de Figueiredo & J. Treuherz, *Cheshire Country Houses*, 1988, 155–6]. The 'Mr. Hope' who measured stonework (probably of the Pantheon Gallery) at INCE BLUNDELL, LANCS., for Henry Blundell in 1802 [Lancs. C.R.O., DD/N. 53 and cf. *C. Life*, 17 April 1958] may have been either John Hope of Liverpool or one of the Hopes of Manchester.

HOPE, SAMUEL (1741–1817), and JOHN (*c.*1744–1822), of Manchester, must be distinguished from their contemporaries John and Samuel Hope of Liverpool (*q.v.*). They were the sons of Samuel Hope of Manchester, a bricklayer who died in 1781, and were both architects and statuary masons. In the latter capacity they produced a number of funerary monuments and tablets of good design that are listed by R. Gunnis, *Dictionary of British Sculptors*, 1968, 208. As architects and builders they were involved in the building of THE PIECE HALL at HALIFAX in 1775–9. Although 'Hope' was described as 'The Architect' of the building in a song commemorating its completion, it appears that Samuel and Thomas Hope acted either as contractors for some of the masonry or as surveyors supervising the execution of designs made by Thomas Bradley (*q.v.*), or possibly in both capacities [P. Smithies, *The Architecture of the Halifax Piece Hall*, 1988, 11–25]. In 1781–4 both Samuel and John were concerned in the rebuilding of HIGH LEGH HALL, CHESHIRE (dem. 1965) for Henry Cornewall Legh, Samuel as a 'bricklayer' and John as a measuring surveyor and possibly as architect. Samuel agreed to work at the same rates as he did when building a house for Egerton Legh at Twemlow, Cheshire, i.e. JODRELL HALL, 1779 [Building accounts among Legh papers in John Rylands Library, Manchester]. In 1786 Samuel Hope 'of Manchester' was paid £20 by Liverpool Corporation for his designs and elevations for rebuilding the west side of CASTLE STREET, LIVERPOOL [C. W. Chalklin, *The Provincial Towns of Georgian England*, Montreal 1974, 148].

Samuel Hope, of Manchester, 'architect', died at Altrincham on 9 May 1817, aged 76 [*Gent's Mag.*, 1817, 568]. John Hope, 'architect', died on 29 August 1822 [wills of Samuel Hope, snr. and jnr. and John Hope in Lancs. C.R.O., WCW].

HOPE, THOMAS (1769–1831), was the eldest son of John Hope, a wealthy merchant of Scottish descent whose family had been established in Amsterdam for several generations. Thomas Hope was brought up in luxurious and cultivated surroundings at his father's country house near Haarlem, and was given every opportunity to develop a natural taste for the arts. As a young man he travelled extensively in Europe and the Near East and acquired a considerable knowledge of architecture and sculpture. When the French occupation of Holland obliged him and his family to leave the country of their adoption he came to England (1795) and established himself as a connoisseur and patron of the arts. He built up a large collection of antique sculpture and vases which was augmented by the works of contemporary artists such as Flaxman, Canova, Thorwaldsen, Haydon, Westall and West. He also did his best to influence the taste of others by showing his own collections and by publishing works on architecture and furniture. In 1800 he was elected a member of the Society of Dilettanti, and in 1804 he was asked by Francis Annesley, the first Master of Downing College, Cambridge, to pronounce on James Wyatt's designs for the college buildings. Hope's report, which he published as *Observations on the Plans and Elevations designed by James Wyatt, Architect, for Downing College, Camb.; in a letter to Francis Annesley, Esq., M.P.*, 1804, was intended to discredit Wyatt's Roman Doric design and to advocate one of the most uncompromisingly Grecian character. Although pretentious and pedantic, Hope's report was not without its effect, for other architects were invited to submit plans, among them William Wilkins, whose Greek design was eventually adopted. Wyatt's defeat by Wilkins in this opening battle of the Greek Revival was an important artistic event. Although it embroiled Hope with the Royal Academy (of which Wyatt was the President), it established him – at least in the eyes of his supporters – as 'Judge Supreme of Architecture.'

Hope himself was a competent draughtsman, but as an amateur architect he confined himself to his own two houses, both of them very remarkable buildings. In 1799, in order to accommodate his collections, he bought a house in Duchess Street, Portland Place, which had been built by Robert Adam for General Robert Clerk. This house Hope enlarged and remodelled in about 1800, adding in 1819 a Picture Gallery designed by himself in order to display the collection of Flemish and Dutch pictures belonging to his brother Henry Philip Hope. The gallery was decorated in a sophisticated neo-classical style and contained furniture to match designed by its owner. There were also a Sculpture Gallery, a second Picture Gallery suggestive of a Greek temple, Indian and Egyptian rooms, a 'Flaxman Room' (enshrining the sculptor's 'Aurora and Cephalus'), and three rooms for the display of Greek vases. All these rooms were regularly open to the public, and made Hope's house (like Soane's) half-museum, half-residence. With its hard, bright colours, its uncomfortable but archaeologically correct furniture, and its esoteric symbolism, the Hope style was too uncompromising to be universally admired, but it played an important part in disseminating neo-classical ideas among contemporary architects and interior decorators. The house was demolished by Hope's son in 1850 but was recorded in Hope's *Household Furniture and Interior Decoration* (1807), in C. M. Westmacott's *British Galleries of Painting and Sculpture* (1824), and in Britton & Pugin's *Public Buildings of London* i, 1825, 308–12.

Hope's country house, the Deepdene, near Dorking in Surrey (purchased in 1807 from Sir Charles Merrick Burrell) was similarly enlarged and embellished by its owner, who employed William Atkinson (*q.v.*) to carry out his plans (apparently in two main stages, dated by Dr. Watkin 1818–19 and 1823). Here, although the architectural components were mostly classical, the planning was asymmetrical and the effect picturesque. The interior was furnished in the same style as Hope's London house, and here again there was much classical statuary and 'Egyptian' ornament, including a bed copied from a plate in Denon's *Egypte* (1802). The house was subsequently enlarged in an Italianate style by Hope's son Henry Thomas Hope. The contents were dispersed in 1917, and the fabric was demolished in 1969. Two volumes of an elaborately illustrated manuscript *History of the Deepdene* by John Britton are in the R.I.B.A. Drawings Collection and the Minet Library at Camberwell.

A complete list of Hope's publications will be found in Dr. Watkin's book. The most important were *Household Furniture and Interior Decoration executed from Designs by Thomas Hope*, fol., 1807; *Costume of the Ancients*, 2 vols. 1809; *Designs of Modern Costume*, 1812; *An Essay on the Origin and Prospects of Man*, 1831, and *An Historical Essay on Architecture by the late Thomas Hope, illustrated from Drawings made by him in Italy and Germany*, posthumously published in 2 vols. in 1835. In 1819 he published anonymously a picaresque novel entitled *Anastasius, or Memoirs of a Modern Greek, written at the Close of the Eighteenth Century*, which was at first ascribed to Byron and achieved considerable popularity.

Hope married in 1806 Louisa Beresford, daughter of William Beresford, Archbishop of Tuam. He died on 3 February 1831, leaving three sons, Henry Thomas Hope (1808–62), founder of the Art Union, Adrian John Hope (1811–63), and Alexander James Beresford Hope (1820–87), ecclesiologist and leader of the Gothic Revival, who became President of the R.I.B.A. in 1865. There is a bust of Hope by Thorvaldsen in Thorvaldsen's Museum at Copenhagen.

[*D.N.B.*; H. W. & I. Law, *The Book of the Beresford Hopes*, 1925; S. Baumgarten, *La Crépuscule Néo-Classique: Thomas Hope*, Paris 1958; David Watkin, *Thomas Hope and the Neo-Classical Idea*, 1968; David Watkin & Jill Lever, 'A Sketch-book by Thomas Hope', *Arch. Hist.* 23, 1980; Peter Thornton & David Watkin, 'New Light on the Hope Mansion in Duchess Street', *Apollo*, Sept. 1987; G. B. Waywell, *The Lever and Hope Sculptures*, Monumenta Artis Romanae, 1986.]

HOPKINS, JOHN DOUGLAS (–1869), was a pupil of J. B. Papworth. He won a premium from the Society of Arts in 1830–1, exhibited at the Royal Academy in 1831, and was admitted to the R.A. Schools in 1832. In 1835 he competed for the Houses of Parliament in conjunction with H. E. Kendall. Their design was in a Gothic style of 'a character sufficiently decorated to stand the extraordinary test of comparative richness with Henry VII's Chapel'. The only buildings erected to Hopkins' designs that have been noted are: HOLY TRINITY, WOOLWICH, KENT, a small Greek Revival church built in 1833–4 and dem. 1962 [Drake, *Blackheath Hundred*, 1886, 161n.]; the SWEDENBORG CHAPEL, ARGYLE STREET, KING'S CROSS, in the Norman style [J. Timbs, *Curiosities of London*, 1855, 176]; and THE NATIONAL SCHOOLS, ST. IVES, HUNTS., 1844–5, Gothic [*Builder* ii, 1844, 306]. Hopkins was Hon. Secretary of the Committee formed in 1834 to establish the Institute of British Architects. According to Wyatt Papworth he was 'also eminent in the engineering profession' [*J. B. Papwoth*, 1879, 96]. He had two architect sons.

HOPKINS, ROGER, of Plymouth, civil engineer and architect, designed the BRIDGE at TEIGNMOUTH, DEVONSHIRE, which was executed under his supervision between 1825 and 1827: it was 1671 feet long, and was considered at the time to be the longest bridge in the kingdom. He also designed the ROYAL UNION BATHS at PLYMOUTH, 1829 [*Devonshire Illustrated, with Historical and Descriptive Accounts by J. Britton and E. W. Brayley*, 1828, 96, 99]. He was the father of Rice Hopkins (1807–1857), civil engineer [*Minutes of Proceedings of the Institution of Civil Engineers* xviii, 1859, 192].

HOPPER, THOMAS (1776–1856), was born at Rochester, where his father was a measuring surveyor, 'clever and prominent in his business, but of intemperate habits'. Apart from the practical training which Thomas received in his father's office, his architectural knowledge was apparently self-acquired. Early in his career he carried out extensive alterations to Craven Cottage, Fulham, for Walsh Porter, converting it into the elaborate *cottage orné* described by Croker in his *Walk from London to Fulham* (1860). There were three reception-rooms. 'The centre, or principal saloon, [was] supported by large palm-trees of considerable size, exceedingly well executed, with their drooping foliage at the top, supporting the cornice and architraves of the room.' This room led to a large Gothic dining-room, and there was also a semi-circular library with an 'Egyptian' doorway. Walsh Porter's 'cottage' was much admired by his friend the Prince Regent, who commissioned Hopper to make alterations to Carlton House, including the addition of a large Gothic conservatory, *en suite* with the dining-room. This was a brilliant conceit, designed in the style of Henry VII's Chapel, but constructed of cast-iron so that the tracery of the vaulting could be pierced to admit light through coloured glass. This royal patronage brought Hopper a fashionable practice as a country-house architect, which he combined with the more mundane duties of County Surveyor of Essex, a post (worth £250 p.a.) which he obtained in 1816 and held for 40 years. He was also surveyor to the Atlas Fire Assurance Company, whose London offices he designed. From time to time Hopper competed for major public buildings such as the General Post Office (1820), the Houses of Parliament (1835), the Conservative Club (1842) and the Carlton Club (1844), but he derived more vexation than advantage from these efforts,[1] and the list of his public works contains nothing more important than two County Gaols, Arthur's Club in St. James's, St. Mary's Hospital, Paddington (for which he gave his services gratis) and a handful of country churches. Nevertheless, Hopper was among the best-known of early nineteeth-century architects, and is said to have declined a knighthood from George IV, as well as offers from the Tsar of Russia and the Duchess of Oldenburg to settle in St. Petersburg. Like all successful nineteenth-century architects he lived an active and energetic life. 'In his best days his flow of spirits was exuberant; his powers of conversation remarkable; his memory most tenacious. He never drank anything stronger than water, and could bear a marvellous amount of fatigue.' His office was first at 42 Berkeley Street, then at 40 Connaught Terrace, Edgware Road, but he had a private residence at 1 Bayswater Hill, where he died on 11 August 1856. A bust of Hopper by J. Ternouth was exhibited at the Royal Academy in 1838, and it is said that 'his form and features' can be seen in the bas relief on the east side of the base of Nelson's Column, where they were given by the same sculptor to a sailor who is supporting a wounded boy. Hopper's pupils included F. J. Francis, S. Hutchins, T. Lloyd, J. Millar, R. Papworth, G. J. Robinson and G. A. Burn, who latterly had charge of his practice. He never became a member of the R.I.B.A., but exhibited at the Royal Academy from time to time.

Hopper was an eclectic designer who held the belief that 'it is an architect's business to understand all styles, and to be prejudiced in favour of none'. He carried out his own precept, using Greek Doric at Springfield Gaol, Greek Ionic at Leigh Court, North Stoneham and Kinmel Park, Palladian classical at Arthur's Club, Boreham House and Amesbury, Tudor Gothic at Margam Abbey, Danbury Place, Rood Ashton, and Easton Lodge, Jacobethan at Llanover House and Wivenhoe Park, and Norman Revival at Gosford and Penrhyn Castles. He handled all these styles with competence, but his Grecian façades were somewhat banal and his most interesting and original works were the two Norman castles, in which he effectively combined picturesque massing with a remarkable repertoire of Romanesque detailing which owed something to his familiarity with the twelfth-century keeps of Rochester and Hedingham. A certain coarseness of touch runs through all his work, and nothing he did in later life would seem quite to have equalled the brilliant *jeu d'esprit* at Carlton House with which he began his career.

[Obituary in *Builder* xiv, 1856, 481; *A.P.S.D.*; Charlotte Fell-Smith, 'Thomas Hopper', *Essex Review* xxiii, 1914, 145–8; Robin Fedden, 'Neo-Norman', *Architectural Review* Dec. 1954; Arthur Searle, 'Thomas Hopper', *Essex Journal* v, Oct. 1970, 132–40; Neil Burton, 'Thomas Hopper' in *The Architectural Outsiders*, ed. R. Brown, 1985; Melbourne Public Library, Australia: printed testimonials in favour of Hopper's pupil John Millar include a somewhat unreliable list of buildings designed in Hopper's office during Millar's pupilage, drawn up by Hopper himself in May 1856, only three months before his death.]

PUBLIC BUILDINGS, ETC.

LONDON, THE ROYAL SOCIETY OF MUSICIANS, 11–13 LISLE STREET, 1808–9; dem. 1931 [*Survey of London* xxxiv, 474–5].

SALISBURY, WILTS., FISHERTON COUNTY GAOL (later Radnor House), 1818–22, dem. 1875 and *c.*1960 [drawings in Wilts. C.R.O.,

[1] He claimed that his design for the Post Office had been made use of by Smirke, the architect eventually employed (see his pamphlet entitled *A Letter to Lord Melbourne on the rebuilding of the Royal Exchange*, 1839), and after the Houses of Parliament competition he not only published two pamphlets, *A Letter to Lord Viscount Duncannon*, 1837, and *Hopper v. Cust, on the New Houses of Parliament*, 1837, but went to the expense of having his own entry published in a large folio volume entitled *Designs for the New Houses of Parliament*, 1840. His designs for the Carlton Club are in the R.I.B.A. Drawings Collection.

A 1/509/3].

SOUTHMINSTER CHURCH, ESSEX, new roof, apse and plaster vaulting, 1819 [I.C.B.S.].

CHELMSFORD, ESSEX, THE COUNTY GAOL, SPRINGFIELD, 1822–6, and alterations, 1845–8 [Essex County Records].

RAWRETH CHURCH, ESSEX, rebuilt except tower, 1823; rebuilt 1882 [I.C.B.S.].

CANTERBURY CATHEDRAL, report on N.W. tower, 1824 [C. E. Woodruff & W. Danks, *Memorials of Canterbury Cathedral*, 1912, 360–1].

HATFIELD PEVEREL CHURCH, ESSEX, enlarged 1826 [I.C.B.S.].

LONDON, ARTHUR'S (now THE CARLTON) CLUB, Nos. 69–70 ST. JAMES'S STREET, 1826–7 [*Survey of London* xxx, 475–7 and pls. 66–7] (C. *Life*, 1 June 1940).

ILFORD, ESSEX, THE HOUSE OF CORRECTION, 1828–31 [Essex County Records].

SALISBURY, WILTS., GUILDHALL, enlarged 1829, forming existing portico [contract in Salisbury Corporation MSS.; R.C.H.M. *Salisbury*, i, 46].

COLCHESTER, ESSEX, THE HOUSE OF CORRECTION, *c.*1832-5; dem. [Essex County Records, Q/AGb 4/2].

LONDON, THE ATLAS FIRE ASSURANCE OFFICE, No. 92 CHEAPSIDE, 1834–6 [*A.P.S.D.*].

LONDON, THE LEGAL AND GENERAL LIFE INSURANCE OFFICE, No. 10 FLEET STREET, 1838; dem. 1885 [*A.P.S.D.*].

LONDON, COUTTS'S BANK, No. 59 STRAND, alterations 1838–9; dem. 1923 [*A.P.S.D.*].

BROMLEY COMMON, KENT, HOLY TRINITY CHURCH, 1839–42; Gothic; altered 1884 [I.C.B.S.].

BRADFIELD CHURCH, ESSEX, added transepts and vestry , 1840–1 [I.C.B.S.].

SOUTHEND, ESSEX, ST. JOHN'S CHURCH, 1841–2, Gothic; aisles added 1869, chancel 1873 [I.C.B.S.].

WOODHAM MORTIMER CHURCH, ESSEX, added N. transept, 1842–4 [I.C.B.S.].

BUTTERTON CHURCH, STAFFS., 1844–5, Norman style, at the expense of Sir William Pilkington, Bart. [*Staffordshire Advertiser*, 8 Feb. 1845].

LONDON, ST. MARY'S HOSPITAL, PADDINGTON, 1845–51 [*Builder* iii, 1845, 299, 304, 321, iv, 1846, 182, 238, 245].

EPPING, ESSEX, ST. JOHN'S CHURCH, rebuilt W. end with new porch, 1849; dem. 1889 [Essex C.R.O., drawings D/Q 19/32, 33, 48].

DOMESTIC ARCHITECTURE

CRAVEN COTTAGE, FULHAM, MIDDLESEX, alterations for Walsh Porter, *c.*1806; destroyed by fire 1888 [*Builder* xiv, 481] (C. J. Fèret, *Fulham Old and New* iii, 1900, 91–2; T. C. Croker, *A Walk from London to Fulham*, 1860, 190–1).

LONDON, CARLTON HOUSE, PALL MALL, Gothic Conservatory and other works for George, Prince of Wales, 1807; dem. 1827–8 [*History of the King's Works* vi, 313, fig. 6 and pls. 12–13].

LONDON, No. 6 GRAFTON STREET, interior of library for Robert Thornton, 1811; dem. [*Journals & Correspondence of Miss Berry*, ed. Lady Theresa Lewis ii, 1865, 421, 425, 489–90].

DROMOLAND CASTLE, CO. CLARE, IRELAND, Greek Doric entrance lodge for Sir Edward O'Brien, Bart., 1812 [drawings in National Library of Ireland, *ex inf.* Mr. Nicholas Sheaff].

SLANE CASTLE, CO. MEATH, IRELAND, designs for alterations for lst Marquess Conyngham. 1812–13 [*Builder* xiv, 481; Alistair Rowan in *Bull. Irish Georgian Soc.* Jan.–March 1964, 29 n. 32; M. Odlum in *C. Life*, 31 July 1980].[1]

MELFORD HALL, LONG MELFORD, SUFFOLK, library and staircase for Sir William Parker, Bart., 1813 [G. Jackson-Stops, 'Thomas Hopper at Melford and Erddig', *National Trust Studies*, 1981].

ALTON TOWERS, STAFFS., works for 15th Earl of Shrewsbury, *c.*1813 onwards [*A.P.S.D.*; P.R.O., C 111/106, p. 12].

LEIGH COURT, nr. BRISTOL, SOMERSET, for P. J. Miles, 1814 [*Builder* xiv, 1856, 481] (Robert Cooke, *West Country Houses*, 1957, 155–8).

NORTH STONEHAM PARK, HANTS., house and 'Belvedere Lodge' for John Willis Fleming, 1818 and reconstruction after fire in 1831; dem. 1939–40 [Ackermann, *Views of Country Seats* ii, 1830; G. F. Prosser, *Select Illustrations of Hampshire*, 1833].

PURLEY HALL, BERKSHIRE, remodelled for John Wilder, 1818–20 [C. Hussey in *C. Life*, 5–12 Feb. 1970].

TERLING PLACE, ESSEX, alterations, including addition of wings, for Col. J. H. Strutt, 1818–21 [Essex C.R.O., D/Dr a, E 25/89, *ex inf.* Miss Nancy Briggs].

GOSFORD CASTLE, CO. ARMAGH, IRELAND, for 2nd Earl of Gosford, 1819–21, Norman style [*Builder* xiv, 481]. In 1859 G. A. Burn, who had been Hopper's principal assistant, designed a new entrance front, which he exhibited at the R.A.

[1] Hopper was also employed at SHANE'S CASTLE, CO. ANTRIM, to arbitrate between John Nash and Lord O'Neil, who began to rebuild the house after a fire had destroyed the old castle in 1816, but stopped the work before it was finished [information from Mr. Robin Fedden].

ALSCOT PARK, WARWICKS. (formerly Glos.), added porch for James Roberts West, shortly before 1820 [Neale's *Views of Seats* iii, 1820; original drawing in Bodleian Library, Gough Misc. Ant. fol. 4, 19] (*C. Life*, 29 May, 1958, fig. 1).

PENRHYN CASTLE, CAERNARVONSHIRE, for G. H. Dawkins Pennant, 1822–37, Norman style [exhib. at R.A. 1836 and 1838] (*C. Life*, 21, 28 July 1955, 29 Oct., 5 Nov. 1987; C. Hussey, *English Country Houses: Late Georgian*, 1958, 181–92).

WOOLVERSTONE HALL, SUFFOLK, additions for Charles Berners, 1823 [W. A. Copinger, *Manors of Suffolk* vi, 1910, 125].

ENGLEFIELD HOUSE, BERKS., alterations for Richard Benyon, *c.*1823–9 [G. Jackson-Stops in *G. Life*, 5 March 1981].

PURDYSBURN HOUSE, KNOCKBREDA, CO. DOWN, IRELAND, for Narcissus Batt, 1825, Tudor Gothic; dem. *c.*1965 [S. Lewis, *Topographical Dictionary of Ireland* ii, 1850, 200].

KENTWELL HALL, SUFFOLK, reconstructed interior for R. H. Logan, *c.*1825–6 [S. Tymms in *Proc. Suffolk Inst. Archaeology* ii, 1854, 72; Rickman's Diary, 3 July 1828; Giles Worsley in *C. Life*, 20 Feb. 1992].

SALISBURY, WILTS., No. 40 ST. ANN'S STREET, fitting up of interior for Col. Edward Baker, *c.*1825; dem. 1864 except circular dining-room [Canadian Centre for Architecture, Montreal, Joseph Gwilt's diary 12 Sept 1828: saw 'house belonging to Mr. Baker – which Hopper has fitted up for him very beautifully'].

ERDDIG PARK, DENBIGHSHIRE, remodelled dining-room for Simon Yorke, 1826–7 [G. Jackson-Stops, 'Thomas Hopper at Melford and Erddig', *National Trust Studies*, 1981].

BOREHAM HOUSE, ESSEX, added wings and flanking gateways for Sir John Tyrell, Bart., 1827–8 [Charlotte Fell-Smith in *C. Life*, 11 July 1914].

DUNKELD HOUSE, PERTHSHIRE, design for a new house for 4th Duke of Atholl, 1828. Only the foundations were laid and work was abandoned after the Duke's death in 1830. Hopper's drawings remain in the Charter Room at Blair Atholl [*Chronicles of the Atholl and Tullibardine Families*, by 7th Duke of Atholl, 1908, iv, 388, 392; exhib. at R.A. 1843].

HIGHCLERE CASTLE, HANTS., remodelled exterior in Greek Ionic style for 2nd Earl of Carnarvon, who died in 1833 leaving the work unfinished. His successor dismissed Hopper and later employed Barry to remodel the house [list in Millar testimonial; cf. Loudon, *Gardener's Mag.* 10, 1834, 247].

LLANOVER HOUSE, MONMOUTHSHIRE, for Sir Benjamin Hall, Bart., 1828–39, Elizabethan style; dem. 1935 except stables (ruined) [J. A. Bradney, *History of Monmouthshire* ii, 1906, 385].

BERWICK PLACE, HATFIELD PEVEREL, ESSEX, for A. Johnson, *c.*1830 [B. Burke, *Visitations of Seats and Arms*, 2nd. ser. i, 1854, 68].

MARGAM ABBEY, GLAMORGANSHIRE, for C. R. Mansel Talbot, 1830–5; gutted 1977, Tudor Gothic [exhib. at R.A. 1833, 1835] (*C. Life*, 5 April 1902).

CRICHEL, DORSET, alterations to entrance for H. C. Sturt, 1831 [Wiltshire Record Office, Penistone papers, letter-book, 7 and 21 Feb., 1 March 1831].

HARDWICK HOUSE, HAWSTEAD, SUFFOLK, rebuilt for Sir Thomas Cullum, Bart., probably soon after 1831; Elizabethan style; dem. 1925 [list in Millar testimonial].

WELFORD PARK, BERKSHIRE, added bow-windowed dining-room for J. A. Houblon, 1831–3 [drawings and accounts at Welford Park].

DANBURY PLACE, ESSEX, for John Round, 1832, Tudor Gothic [T. Wright, *History of Essex*, 1831–5, i, 685].

AMESBURY HOUSE, WILTS., rebuilt for Sir Edmund Antrobus, Bart., 1834–40 [exhib. at R.A. 1841] (*C. Life*, 1 March 1902).

ROOD ASHTON HOUSE, nr. TROWBRIDGE, WILTS., alterations for Walter Long, 1836, Gothic, mostly dem. 1975 [*Builder* xiv, 481].

KIRTLINGTON PARK, OXON., repairs and/or minor alterations for Sir George Dashwood, Bart., 1838 [note among drawings formerly at Kirtlington Park].

BUTTERTON HALL, STAFFS., for Sir William Pilkington, Bart., *c.*1840–50, Tudor Gothic; dem. 1921 [exhib. at R.A. 1840 as 'proposed to be built'] (a drawing by J. Buckler in the William Salt Library at Stafford, II, 211, shows the house 'now building' in 1847).

STANSTEAD HOUSE, SUSSEX, alterations for Charles Dixon, *c.*1840; destroyed by fire 1900 except lodges probably by Hopper [*Builder* xiv, 481].

KINMEL PARK, DENBIGHSHIRE, rebuilt for 1st Lord Dinorben, 1842–3; rebuilt by W. E. Nesfield 1875 [*Builder* xiv, 481] (B. Burke, *Visitations of Seats and Arms*, 2nd ser. i, 1854, frontispiece; *C. Life*, 4 Sept. 1969, fig. 2).

BIRCH HALL, ESSEX, for C. G. Round, 1843–7; dem. 1954 [J. A. Rush, *Seats in Essex*, 1897, 40].

WIVENHOE PARK, ESSEX, remodelled for J. Gurdon Rebow, 1846–9, Jacobean [*A.P.S.D.*; Rosemary Feesey, *A History of Wivenhoe Park*, Colchester, 1963].

EASTON LODGE, nr. DUNMOW, ESSEX, rebuilt for 3rd Viscount Maynard, after a fire in 1847, Tudor Gothic; reconstructed by Philip Tilden after a fire in *c.*1918 [J.A. Rush, *Seats in Essex*, 1897, 73].

LONDON, No. 17 (formerly 16), GROSVENOR SQUARE, alterations for Sir James Weir Hogg, 1847–8; dem. 1943 [*Survey of London* xl, 133].

The list of country houses where Hopper claimed in the Millar testimonial to have been responsible for unspecified work in the late 1820s or early 1830s includes BELVEDERE, ERITH, KENT, for 14th Lord Saye & Sele (whose wife had inherited this house and died there in 1834); BRAMPTON PARK, HUNTS., for Lady Olivia Sparrow; BROME HALL, SUFFOLK, for Sir Edward Kerrison, Bart.; GATTON PARK, SURREY, for Lord Monson (for which house unexecuted designs by Hopper made in 1847–8 are mentioned in *A.P.S.D.*); MERSHAM-LE-HATCH, KENT, for Sir Edward Knatchbull, Bart. (where Hopper was probably responsible for internal alterations but not for the external N. colonnade added after 1850); and POLTIMORE HOUSE, DEVON, (where he may have designed the porch and staircase).

HOPPERTON, WILLIAM (–1853), practised from Pimlico, London, from about 1810 to 1850. He competed unsuccessfully for the New Bethlehem Hospital in 1810 and exhibited his design at the Royal Academy the following year. He appears to have designed the INDEPENDENT CHAPEL, DORKING, SURREY, built in 1834–5 by William Shearburn [Brayley, *Surrey* v, 103]. He died in 1853, his will being proved in January 1854 (P.C.C.).

HOPPUS, EDWARD (–1739), was appointed surveyor to the London Assurance Corporation in 1729 in succession to John Shepherd, and retained the post until his death in April or May 1739. He is best known as the author of *Practical Measuring* (1st ed. 1736), a manual for building surveyors that was many times reissued in the course of the eighteenth, nineteenth and early twentieth centuries. The last edition was in 1942 and the book went out of print only in 1973 when it was made obsolete by metrication. Hoppus made the drawings for the engravings which illustrate the English translation of *Palladio's Architecture* published by the engraver B. Cole in 1732–4. This was an unscholarly work that was superseded a few years later by Ware's translation. Hoppus and Cole also published a collection of largely second-hand architectural designs entitled *The Gentleman's and Builder's Repository, or Architecture Displayed,* 1737, 1738, 1748, 4th ed. 1760, edited W. Salmon's *Palladio Londinensis, or London Art of Building*, 1738, and revised the same author's *Country Builder's Estimator*, 1737 [*A.P.S.D.*; S. E. Wilson, 'Hoppus through the Ages', *Timber Trades Jnl.* 6 Aug. 1955; Eileen Harris, *British Architectural Books and Writers 1556–1785*, 1990, 238–41].

HORN, R—, is known only from two exhibits at the Royal Academy: in 1812 'a Design for a museum', and in 1815 a 'Model of a design of a capital for the columns of the Caledonian Asylum', i.e. the ROYAL CALEDONIAN ASYLUM, CHALK ROAD, COPENHAGEN FIELDS, ISLINGTON, established in 1813–15; dem.

HORN, WILLIAM, was a successful Glasgow builder. He was a wright by trade, and was Deacon of the Glasgow Wrights in 1769 [*The Incorporation of Wrights of Glasgow*, Glasgow 1880, 44]. He built Horn's Court off St. Enoch's Square, Glassford Street (*c.*1792), and many of the houses in Argyle Street [Senex, *Glasgow Past and Present*, 1884, i, 100, 462, ii, 102, 239, 450, iii, 285]. In 1796 he designed the wings which were added to GLASGOW BRIDEWELL [*Records of the Burgh of Glasgow*, ed. Renwick, ix, 7, 142].

HORNE, JAMES (–1756), was probably the James Horne, joiner, who is mentioned in 1711 as the son of Thomas Horne, a citizen and joiner of London. James first appears in association with Nicholas Dubois (*q.v.*), for whom he deputised at the Office of Works on several occasions in the years 1721–4. He also acted as measurer at Stanmer Park, Sussex, a house designed by Dubois and built in 1722–7. Early in George II's reign he acted as clerk of works for the formation of the Serpentine Lake in Hyde Park. In 1740 he was one of the three arbitrators in the case between John Cordwell, the City Carpenter, and the Corporation of London, over the former's payment for making the model of the Mansion House. In 1742 he undertook to act gratuitously as surveyor to the Foundling Hospital, and supervised the erection of its buildings to the designs of the amateur architect Theodore Jacobsen. His 'ability and integrity' are praised in a letter from William Pulteney, Earl of Bath, to Zachary Pearce, Dean of Winchester, dated 1 Sept. 1742. In 1746 he succeeded John James as surveyor to the fabric of Westminster Abbey. His resignation in 1752 may have been occasioned by his appointment as surveyor of the Naval Hospital at Gosport, another building designed by Theodore Jacobsen. The death of

'Mr. Horn, surveyor of Gosport Hospital', took place on 19 Aug. 1756. Some 'Remarks and Observations on several parts of Civil Architecture, alphabetically digested, and collected by Mr. Horne', form part of an anonymous MS. formerly in the library at Ardkinglas, Argyllshire, entitled *The Architects Remembrancer, or Surveyors Pocket Companion; being a Parallel of Antient and Modern Architecture, set forth in Tables*.

As an architect Horne appears to have been employed chiefly to design churches in a handsome but rather pedestrian style which may be described as 'vernacular Palladian'. Of these Holy Trinity at Guildford is now the only surviving example.

[*A.P.S.D.*; G.L.C. Record Office, Middlesex Land Register 1711/4/20; *History of the King's Works* v, 87, 203; *Wren Soc.* vii, 68, 192–5, 205, 221–2; S. Perks, *The Mansion House*, 1922, 184; R. H. Nichols and F. A. Wray, *History of the Foundling Hospital*, 1935, 43; W.A.M. 64662; *Gent's Mag.*, 1756, 412.]

EALING, MIDDLESEX, ST. MARY'S CHURCH, 1735–40; rebuilt by S. S. Teulon, 1866–74 [MS. Vestry Minutes: there is a set of plans and elevations in B.L., *King's Maps* xxix, 9b. 1–8].

attributed: SOUTHWARK, CHRISTCHURCH, BLACKFRIARS ROAD, 1738–41; altered by C.R.B. King, 1891, gutted 1941 and subsequently dem. There is a set of plans and elevations in B.L., *King's Maps* xxvii, 50 a–g, by the same hand as those of St. Mary, Ealing, and St. Katherine Coleman, whose design Christchurch closely resembled (*Survey of London* xxii, 101).

LONDON, ST. KATHERINE COLEMAN, FENCHURCH STREET, 1739–40; dem. 1925. There is a set of plans and elevations in B.L., *King's Maps* xxiii, 22b 1–7 [MS. Minutes of Trustees for Rebuilding the church in Guildhall Library, MSS. 1133–4] (G. Godwin, *The Churches of London* ii, 1839).

WESTMINSTER, ST. JOHN'S CHURCH, reconstructed roof and interior in 1744–5 after fire of 1742, removing the twelve columns which supported the original roof designed by Archer. The interior was rearranged by W. Inwood 1824–5, gutted 1940–41 and restored 1965–8 [MS. Minutes of Committee for Repair of Church in Westminster Public Library, MS. 2626].

GUILDFORD, SURREY, HOLY TRINITY CHURCH, 1749–63 [MS. Vestry Minutes].

HORTON, JOHN (–1825), builder of Deritend, Birmingham, designed the GUNBARREL PROOF HOUSE, BIRMINGHAM, 1813, as recorded by the following inscription on a drawing preserved in the board-room: 'This building was designed and executed by John Horton Architect and Builder Bradford Street Derritend' [Mrs. Margaret Jones in *C. Life*, 24 May 1956, 1125]. Horton died on 13 March 1825 [*Aris's Birmingham Gazette*, 14 March 1825].

HOSKING, WILLIAM (1800–1861), was born at Buckfastleigh in Devon, but in 1809 his parents emigrated to New South Wales, where he was apprenticed to a builder and surveyor. Returning to England in 1819, he was in 1820 articled to William Jenkins, of Red Lion Square, for three years, and afterwards travelled in France and Italy (including Sicily), studying architecture and engineering works in company with Jenkins's son John (*q.v.*). In 1827 they jointly published *A Selection of Architectural and other Ornaments, Greek, Roman and Italian*. In 1834 Hosking became engineer to the Birmingham, Bristol and Thames Junction Railway Company, for which he designed the complicated arrangement of bridges near Kensal Green by which the Grand Junction Canal was carried over the railway and a public road over the canal. In 1840 King's College, London, made him Professor of 'the Art of Construction', and afterwards of 'the Principles and Practice of Architecture'. In 1844 he was appointed one of the referees under the Metropolitan Buildings Act. He became a Fellow of the Institute of British Architects in 1835, and served on its council in 1842–3. He was elected F.S.A. in 1830. He died on 2 August 1861.

From an early age Hosking wrote and lectured about architecture, emphasizing the importance of practical and technical considerations in a manner which earned him the reputation of being an 'anti-Vitruvianist'. Some lectures which he gave to the Western Literary and Scientific Institution led to his being invited to write the articles on 'Architecture' and 'Building' for the seventh edition of the *Encyclopaedia Britannica*. These were afterwards republished as a separate volume in 1832, 1846, 1860 and (revised by Ashpitel) in 1867. He also published an inaugural lecture entitled *The Principles and Practice of Architecture* (1842), and (with J. Hann) a standard work on *The Theory, Practice and Architecture of Bridges*, 1843. His work in connection with the Metropolitan Buildings Act led him to write *A Guide to the proper Regulation of Buildings in Towns, as a means of promoting and securing the Health, Comfort and Safety of the Inhabitants*, 1848, reissued in 1849 as *Healthy Homes*.

Hosking appears to have designed relatively few buildings. He began to exhibit designs at the Society of British Artists in Suffolk Street in 1825, and in 1827 showed a 'mansion for W. Redfern, to be erected on his estate of Campbellfield, New South Wales'. In 1839–43 he designed ABNEY PARK CEMETERY, NORTH LONDON, with a pretentious but poorly designed Gothic chapel, and in 1840–1 TRINITY INDEPENDENT CHAPEL, POPLAR (dem.), in an unusual blend of Grecian and Italian Renaissance styles [*Companion to the Almanac* 1842, 210–12, with illustrations]. Later, in the 1850s, he was responsible for some business premises for Messrs. Berens on the south side of Cannon Street. In 1849 he submitted to the Trustees of the British Museum a scheme for filling the vacant quadrangle with a circular building which he envisaged as 'a modified copy of the Pantheon in Rome'. It was illustrated in the *Builder* for 1850 (pp. 295–6), and when Panizzi's plan for the circular reading-room was adopted in 1854 Hosking regarded it as 'an obvious plagiarism', although it had nothing in common with his proposal except the circular form. In 1858, to substantiate his claim, he published a pamphlet entitled *Some Observations upon the recent Addition of the Reading-room to the British Museum.*

[*Builder* xix, 1861, 560; *D.N.B.*; application (with *curriculum vitae*) for post of architect to Metropolitan Board of Works, 1856, in G.L. Record Office, MBW 213.]

HOWELL, JAMES (*c.*1787–1866), of 1 Vincent Square, Westminster, was the nephew and pupil of William Pilkington. He was President of the Surveyors' Club in 1832 and 1849, and died on 31 July 1866, aged 79 [*A.P.S.D.*, *s.v.* 'Pilkington'; J. W. Penfold, *A Century of Surveyors*, privately printed 1892, and MS. supplement among records of the Surveyors' Club]. He designed SOUTHWICK HOUSE, HANTS., for Thomas Thistlethwayte, 1841, after the former house had been destroyed by fire. Sydney Howell, of the same address, exhibited a view of the house at the R.A. in 1841, as then erecting 'from the designs and under the superintendence of Mr. James Howell'.

HOWGILL, JOHN, was a carver and joiner of York who appears to have been William Thornton's chief assistant until the latter's death in 1721. In 1727 he supplied a cartouche for a chimney-piece in Lord Bingley's house in Cavendish Square, London [G. W. Beard. *Craftsmen and Interior Decorators in England 1660–1820*, 1981, 265], and in 1728 he was paid 10 guineas for an unexecuted plan for a new house for Thomas Yarborough at Campsmount, nr. Doncaster [Yarborough family papers, *ex inf.* Dr. T. P. Connor].

HUBERT, SAMUEL MORTON, of Mount Gardens, Lambeth, was the architect of two churches in Essex: ST. JOHN, EPPING, 1832, dem. 1889 [I.C.B.S.; Essex Record Office D/Q. 19/30] and ST. PAUL, HIGH BEECH, 1835–6, dem. 1885 [I.C.B.S.]. The latter church is included in the list of L. Vulliamy's works in *Builder* xxix, 142, but this is not supported by the I.C.B.S. records.

HUDSON, HENRY BATEMAN (*c.*1792–1865), practised in London as an architect and surveyor. In 1837 he restored THE PREBENDAL HOUSE at THAME, OXON., and converted it into a private residence for Charles Stone [lithograph in Bodleian, MS. Top. Oxon. a. 39, f. 138v]. He also 'restored' THAME CHURCH in 1843–5 [F. G. Lee, *History of Thame Church*, 1883, 179]. Hudson, who was President of the Surveyors' Club in 1837 and 1846, died on 7 May 1865, aged 73.

HUDSON, JOHN (*c.*1767–1837), of Long Wall, Oxford, held the post of surveyor of bridges to the county in the 1820s. As 'John Hudson, Clerk to James Pears', the contracting builder, his name appears on the inscription commemorating the building of the Radcliffe Observatory in 1794. Though chiefly employed as a builder, he sometimes acted as an architect. Thus in 1810–11 he designed and built a porter's lodge (dem.) at the entrance to the Observatory [Bodleian Library, Minutes of the Radcliffe Trustees 1792–1815]. The classical front of the BAPTIST CHAPEL at the corner of New Inn Hall Street and the New Road was added in 1819 to the designs of 'the architect Hudson of Oxford' [R. Lascelles, *The University and City of Oxford displayed*, 1821, 238], and in 1821–5 the Gothic tower of CHIPPING NORTON CHURCH, OXON., was rebuilt to his designs [Oxfordshire C.R.O., MS. Oxford Archdeaconry Papers Oxon. c. 61, f. 101]. He designed or altered parsonages at EAST HENDRED, BERKS., 1807 [Salisbury Diocesan Records]; CULHAM, OXON., 1816 [Oxfordshire C.R.O., Diocesan Faculty Register 1804–27, p. 87]; and FOREST HILL, OXON., 1830–1 [Oxfordshire C.R.O., MS. Oxford Diocesan Papers b. 103, no. 2d]. In 1838 he remodelled the interior of the LAUDIAN LIBRARY at ST. JOHN'S COLLEGE, probably to the designs of H. J. Underwood (*q.v.*) (St. John's College Archives, *Computus Annuus* 1838 and Munim. lxxxi, 19 (ii)].

Hudson died in June 1837, aged 70 [Burial Register of St. Peter-in-the-East, Oxford]. He was the father of John Hudson (1803–1869), a successful Oxford builder who left an estate valued at 'under £40,000' [Principal Probate Registry, Calendar of Probates, 1869].

HUÉ, WILLIAM BURNELL, was from 1801 to 1809 a pupil or assistant of William Jupp, junior. Then in 1816–19 he was living in Bloomsbury, but after that there is no trace of him in the London directories. He exhibited at the Royal Academy from 1801 to 1819, showing in 1809 a design for a 'monumental pillar' in memory of Sir John Moore, in 1816 'The grand quadrangle building before Carlton House' (i.e. Waterloo Place) and in 1819 'Annett's Crescent, now building in Lower Road, Islington' (for which see *V.C.H. Middlesex* viii, 22). J. Mullins was his pupil.

HULLS, RICHARD (1773–1841), was the son of Jonathan Hulls (1732–93), a builder of Broad Campden. Glos., and grandson of Jonathan Hulls (1699–1758), one of the inventors of steam propulsion as applied to water transport. He practised as an architect and builder at Chipping Campden for forty-seven years, as recorded on his gravestone in the parish churchyard, and left £200 to the poor of the town [P. C. Rushen, *History of Chipping Campden*, 1911, 146, 174].

Hulls was no doubt responsible for much unrecorded work in Campden. Rushen says that he built two houses on the north side of Broad Campden churchyard in 1829 and considered that the early nineteenth-century rebuilding of CHIPPING CAMPDEN TOWN HALL 'looks like' his work [Rushen, *op. cit.*, 80, 162]. Outside Campden Hulls probably designed the Gothic lodges at the entrance to ALSCOT PARK, WARWICKS., for which he tendered in 1813 [West of Alscot papers], and in 1832–4 he built the Picture Gallery at NORTHWICK PARK, GLOS., for the 2nd Lord Northwick. No evidence has been found in the Northwick Papers in the Worcestershire County Record Office to support the attribution of this building to C. H. Tatham, and the documents [5 (i) and 67] suggest that Hulls acted as architect as well as builder. In 1838 Hulls rebuilt the east wall of the chancel of the adjoining church of BLOCKLEY [Rushen, 79].

HUMFREY, CHARLES (1772–1848), was the eldest son of Charles Humfrey, a Cambridge carpenter and joiner who died in 1769. In 1789 he became a pupil of James Wyatt, was admitted to the Royal Academy Schools, and exhibited four drawings at the Academy's exhibitions in the next two years. He married in 1796 and was practising as an architect in Cambridge from *c.*1800 onwards. He designed several churches, parsonage houses, etc., and in 1820–2 a Gaol and Shire Hall at Ely, but failed to secure any major commission from the university. In 1820 his scheme for alterations at Sidney Sussex College was rejected in favour of one by Wyatville, and in 1824 his proposals for a new wing at Emmanuel College also came to nothing. His best (and also his most remunerative) works were the admirable speculative building developments which he carried out between 1815 and 1828 in the area south-east of Christ's Piece and probably elsewhere in Cambridge. By the 1840s his annual income from property was over £1000. For some years he had also been the co-proprietor of a bank in Trinity Street, and in 1829 he published an open letter to Lord Melbourne on the reform of the currency. He took an active part in local politics, was elected a Councillor after the Municipal Reform Act and served as Mayor in 1837–8. From 1819 to 1830 he was Surveyor to the Cam Conservancy Board. Early in the 1840s he got into financial difficulties which culminated in 1845 in the closure of his bank and the sale of all his Cambridge property in order to satisfy his creditors. He died in Islington in March 1848 aged 75. He left several children, one of whom (Mary Anne) became the wife of Professor Willis, the architectural historian. [Information from Mr. D. E. Chaffin].

SWAFFHAM PRIOR CHURCH (ST. CYRIAC), CAMBS., rebuilt 1806–8 incorporating old tower, Gothic [C.U.L., Ely Diocesan Records, Faculty Book 1791–1829, f. 15; MS. Churchwardens' accounts].

GRANSDEN MAGNA VICARAGE, HUNTS., altered or rebuilt 1812 [Lincolnshire Record Office, MGA 67].

CAMBRIDGE, DOLL'S CLOSE development, comprising houses in MAID'S CAUSEWAY, WILLOW WALK, SHORT STREET and FAIR STREET, 1815–26 [R.C.H.M. *Cambridge* ii, 363–4].

WILLIAN VICARAGE, HERTS., altered or rebuilt 1816 [Lincolnshire Record Office, MGA 87].

SWAFFHAM BULBECK VICARAGE, CAMBS., 1818 [C.U.L., Ely Diocesan Records, Faculty Book 1791–1829, ff. 79–84].

CHESTERTON VICARAGE, CAMBS., 1819 [C.U.L., Ely Diocesan Parsonage Papers, G3 40/99].

CAMBRIDGE, SUSSEX and SIDNEY STREETS, designed 13 houses to be built under a lease from Sidney Sussex College to Messrs. Savage and Harris dated 29 Nov. 1820: those in Sussex St. dem. 1930s, but 26–27 Sidney St. survive [*Cambridge Chronicle &*

Jnl., 21 March 1823; Sidney Sussex Coll. Muniments, MR 116/3–4, *ex inf.* Mr. Peter Salt].

CAMBRIDGE, Nos. 9–10, ST. ANDREW'S HILL, porches and railings 1818 [R.C.H.M. *Cambridge* ii, 334].

CAMBRIDGE, ST. CLEMENT'S CHURCH, new west tower, 1821–2, Gothic. The spire (known as 'Humfrey's Extinguisher') was removed in 1928 [R.C.H.M. *Cambridge* ii, 269].

ELY, CAMBS., SHIRE HALL and GAOL, 1821–2; gaol enlarged by Basevi 1845 [*A.P.S.D.*, *s.v.* 'Ely'].

CAMBRIDGE, Nos. 4–12 TENNIS COURT ROAD and (probably) No. 15 FITZWILLIAM STREET, *c.*1822–5 [R.C.H.M. *Cambridge* ii, 357].

CAMBRIDGE, ADDENBROOKE'S HOSPITAL, addition of wings and colonnade, 1823–5 [R.C.H.M. *Cambridge* ii, 312].

CAMBRIDGE, CLARENDON HOUSE (dem.) for himself and range of mews in MILLER LANE facing Christ's Piece, 1825–8 [R.C.H.M. *Cambridge* ii, 361–2].

CAMBRIDGE, ANATOMICAL LECTURE ROOM AND MUSEUM etc., DOWNING STREET, 1832–3; dem. [Willis & Clark, iii, 156].

CAMBRIDGE, PHILOSOPHICAL SOCIETY'S PREMISES, DOLPHIN LANE, 1832–3; dem. [*ex inf.* Mr. D. E. Chaffin].

CAMBRIDGE, TRINITY COLLEGE, LECTURE ROOM COURT, 1833–4, Tudor Gothic [R.C.H.M. *Cambridge* ii, 243].

HUMPHREYS, THOMAS (1747–1822), was a native of St. Ishmael's parish, Carmarthenshire, who was in business as a carpenter and builder in Carmarthen. Apart from minor alterations to municipal buildings in Carmarthen, his only recorded work as an architect is LLANDEILO TOWN HALL, which he designed and built in 1802–3 [Carmarthen R.O., Quarter Sessions Minutes, 1802–5, *ex inf.* Mr. Thomas Lloyd].

HUNT, THOMAS (1737–1816), of Wadenhoe near Oundle in Northamptonshire, appears to have been an amateur architect. He inherited Wadenhoe Manor from his father, Edward Hunt, a merchant of Oundle, and died on 12 December 1816 [*Gent's Mag.* 1816 (ii), 626]. The only evidence of his architectural interests consists of an album of drawings now in the R.I.B.A. Drawings Collection. This contains a number of plans and designs, some of existing buildings, and others apparently representing projects by Hunt for small houses and other buildings, none of which is known to have been executed. The contents of the album are fully described in the *R.I.B.A. Drawings Catalogue: G–K*, 148–51.

HUNT, THOMAS FREDERICK (*c.*1791–1831), joined the Office of Works in 1813 as Labourer in Trust at St. James's Palace, and was promoted in 1829 to Clerk of the Works at Kensington Palace, where he died on 4 January 1831, aged 40. He was well thought of both at the Office of Works and in Court circles. But he lived beyond his means, was always in debt and was constantly harassed by bailiffs. At one time he was obliged to take refuge in the gatehouse of St. James's Palace in order to escape their attentions, and could only venture out on Sundays for fear of arrest.

Hunt was an able architect who made a special study of the picturesque Tudor style, upon which he published several books listed below. He designed the elegant neo-classical BURNS MAUSOLEUM in ST. MICHAEL'S CHURCHYARD at DUMFRIES, 1815 [exhib. at R.A. 1816]. This is a domed Ionic version of James Wyatt's pyramidal Doric mausoleum at Cobham in Kent, and was originally intended to have sarcophagi standing over the columns as at Cobham [W. McDowall, *Memorials of St. Michael's Churchyard, Dumfries*, 1876, 103]. This commission, won in competition, led to his employment as architect of the OLD EPISCOPAL (now Wesleyan) CHURCH in BUCCLEUCH STREET, DUMFRIES, with a prominent Ionic portico [P. Gray, *Dumfriesshire Illustrated*, 1894, 70]. Other works, all exhibited by him at the Royal Academy, were a cottage in Hertfordshire (1825); a house 'in the old English domestic style' to be erected at SYDNEY, NEW SOUTH WALES, 'for one of the principal government officers' (1828); DANEHURST, nr. DANEHILL, SUSSEX, for – Davies (1828), illustrated in the third edition of his *Hints*; and a design for REDRICE, nr. ANDOVER, HANTS., for the Hon. William Noel Hill, afterwards 3rd Lord Berwick (1828). According to the journalist William Jerdan, who knew him well, one of Hunt's best works in the Tudor style was at BIFRONS, PATRIXBOURNE, KENT, for the dowager Marchioness Conyngham, *c.*1825.

The titles of Hunt's publications were: *Half-a-dozen Hints on Picturesque Domestic Architecture in a series of designs for Gate Lodges, Gamekeepers' Cottages, and other rural residences*, 1825, 2nd ed. 1826, 3rd ed. 1833, reprinted 1841; *Designs for Parsonage-houses, Alms house, etc., with examples of gables, and other curious remains of old English Architecture*, 1827; *Architettura Campestre, displayed in Lodges, Gardeners' Houses, etc. in the Modern or Italian Style*, 1827; *Exemplars of Tudor Architecture adapted to modern habitations, with illustrative details, selected from Ancient Edifices; and observations on the Furniture of the Tudor Period*, 1830, 1841. [*A.P.S.D.*; obituary in *Gent's*

Mag. 1831 (i) 376; *The Autobiography of William Jerdan* iv, 1853, 52–5].

HUNTER, JAMES (1755–), was a pupil of James Arrow (*q.v.*). He was admitted to the Royal Academy Schools in 1773 at the age of 17, and won the Silver Medal in 1775. He exhibited drawings at the Academy in 1776 and 1777. He may have been the James Hunter of 25 Fetter Lane, who exhibited 'A plan and elevation for a gentleman's house in Somersetshire' at the Free Society of Artists in 1774.

HUNTER, ROBERT (–1796), described as 'architect in Edinburgh', died on 20 May 1794 [S.R.O., CC 8/8/130/1]. In 1768 he made designs for an unidentified house for which his estimate is in N.L.S., Gordonstoun papers, Box 118.

HURLBATT, FRANCIS (*c.*1756–1834), was an architect and surveyor at Newington in Surrey (now Southwark), where he rebuilt ST. MARY'S CHURCH in 1791–3 (dem. 1876) [C. T. Cracklow, *The Churches of Surrey*, 1827]. In Lambeth Palace Library there is an elevation of the church which is perhaps by him [U.P. III 6b/112]. In 1807 he designed a proprietary chapel at BALHAM, SURREY (now Wandsworth), consecrated as ST. MARY'S in 1855, to which transepts were added in 1824 [G.L.R.O., P95/MRY 3/82, *ex inf.* Mr. D. Findlay], and in 1812 he enlarged the porch of HOLY TRINITY CHURCH, CLAPHAM [Cracklow, *op. cit.*].

In 1793 an Act of Parliament enabled the Dean and Chapter of Canterbury to grant building leases on their Newington property to Hurlbatt, and he subsequently laid out FRANCIS (later CRAMPTON) STREET and designed some adjacent terraces [*Survey of London* xxv, 83–4]. The area was largely redeveloped in 1979, but Nos. 140–52 WALWORTH ROAD (converted into the Labour Party Headquarters 1978) survive. In the British Library there is a plan of premises in New Road, Newington (Add. MS. 12553g), made by Francis Hurlbatt and John Leachman (*q.v.*). Hurlbatt died in 1834, aged 78, and is buried in St. Mary Newington churchyard [Parish Register in G.L. Record Office].

HURLBUTT, ROGER (–?1710), and WILLIAM (–?1698), were master carpenters in Warwickshire during the latter part of the seventeenth century. William was living at Stareton near Coventry in the 1670s, but both worked in Warwick. Roger was a freeman of the town by 1684 and was presumably the 'Roger Hulburt' who was buried at St. Mary's church in May 1710, while 'William Hurlbut alias Holbert' was buried there in September 1698 [Parish register of St. Mary's, Warwick].

In 1670 William contracted to build a MARKET HOUSE at WARWICK (now the Museum) [T. Kemp, *History of Warwick*, 1905, 190–1], and in 1676–81 he was both surveyor and contractor for the new SHIRE HALL [*Warwickshire County Records: Proceedings in Quarter Sessions* vii, 1946, pp. cxiii, cxlix, 77, 183, etc.]. The Market House is a stone building of traditional character, but the Shire Hall (again rebuilt 1753–8), had quite an ambitious classical façade with Ionic pilasters and Corinthian centre-piece. In 1669–78 the two Hurlbutts were jointly responsible for remodelling the state rooms in WARWICK CASTLE for the 4th Lord Brooke in a very handsome and fashionably up-to-date manner. The accounts show that William was sent down to Dorset to see the interiors at Kingston Lacy recently designed for Sir Ralph Bankes by Sir Roger Pratt, which were evidently the model for the new rooms at Warwick [Michael Farr in *V.C.H. Warwicks.* viii, 460–1]. The Hurlbutts were probably also responsible for the stables built at Warwick Castle in 1664–7 and demolished in 1765, but visible in the engraving of the Castle published in Rocque's *Vitruvius Brittanicus* (*sic*) iv, 1738, pls. 71–2.

One of the Hurlbutts' principal patrons was the 1st Earl of Conway, an important landowner in Warwickshire and Ireland. In 1670 William Hurlbutt designed a stable to be built on Conway's Irish estate at Portmore in Co. Antrim. It was to be oval in plan and in other respects similar to the stables at Cornbury in Oxfordshire designed by Hugh May. At Conway's insistence the oval plan was altered to 'Sex Angular as the more defensible' and on this basis it was built in 1671–2; dem. 1763 [R. Loeber, *Biographical Dictionary of Architects in Ireland 1600–1720*, 1981, 61]. In one of Conway's letters (1 July 1670), he mentioned that Hurlbutt was leaving Warwick for Gloucestershire, where he was 'upon a great peece of worke' for Lord Tracy at TODDINGTON MANOR (dem. 1819) [*ibid.*]. In 1679 'Mr. Holbert' began to rebuild Lord Conway's principal seat, RAGLEY HALL, WARWICKS. The original 'model' for this large country house appears to have been provided by Hurlbutt himself, and although the design was modified by Robert Hooke, it was Hurlbutt who was responsible for the corner pavilions which distinguish Ragley from most other contemporary houses [see letters from Hooke in *Walpole Soc.* xxv, 99–103; Arthur Oswald in *C. Life*, 1–8 May 1958; and P. Leach in *Archaeological Jnl.* 136, 1979,

265–8]. Lord Conway appears subsequently to have recommended Hurlbutt to his cousin Sir Edward Seymour, Bart. Seymour was the builder of MAIDEN BRADLEY HOUSE, WILTS., partly demolished in 1821, but illustrated in *Vitruvius Britannicus* ii, pl. 56, and in 1683 Conway, in a letter to Sir Edward Harley, reported that Seymour had taken 'Mr. Halbert' with him to Maiden Bradley [Hist. MSS. Comm., *Portland* iii, 374]. Resemblances in plan with Ragley and in architectural detail with Maiden Bradley, suggest that it was Hurlbutt who designed TREDEGAR HOUSE, MONMOUTHSHIRE, for William Morgan some time between 1664 and 1672 [H. Colvin, 'An Architect for Tredegar?' *Arch. Hist.* 25, 1982]. Furthermore, the stables at Tredegar resembled those at Warwick Castle, both having a row of oval windows between pilasters.

William Hurlbutt was employed by the trustees of the TEMPLE BALSALL HOSPITAL, WARWICKS., to build the original courtyard of the almshouses, completed in 1679, but in its present form largely an early eighteenth-century rebuilding by Francis Smith. A draft agreement specified that it was to be built 'in form of a street', each facing range to be 172 feet long, 'according to the moddell now agreed' [Hospital records in Warwicks. C.R.O., CR 112/Ba 177 (i), etc.].

In 1692 Roger Hurlbut, joiner of Warwick, contracted to remodel LANDOR HOUSE, WARWICK, for Dr. William Johnson. The contract [C.R.O., 1618/WA 6/166] is accompanied by a competent but unsigned drawing showing alternative treatments of the elevation, one of which (not adopted) incorporates heavily keystoned architraves like those in the south front of Chatsworth. In September 1694, after the great fire which devastated Warwick, Roger Hurlbutt helped to put a temporary roof on the chancel of St. Mary's Church, and he was one of the master workmen employed to estimate the losses caused by the destruction of property [*The Great Fire of Warwick*, ed. M. Farr, Dugdale Soc. 1992, 9, 117, 135].

With architectural works probably to their credit as far afield as Warwick, Gloucestershire, Wiltshire, Monmouthshire and Ireland, it is evident that the Hurlbutts were among the most important provincial builder-architects of late seventeenth-century England, and that they were capable of designing handsome and distinctive buildings whose ebullient detailing distinguishes them from the more restrained work of metropolitan architects such as May and Pratt.

HURST, AARON HENRY (1762–1799), was admitted to the Royal Academy Schools in 1788 at the age of 26, and exhibited at the Academy between 1778 and 1796. That he was an elegant draughtsman and a sophisticated neo-classical architect can be seen from the two designs for Wimbledon Lodge illustrated in John Harris, *Georgian Country Houses*, R.I.B.A. 1968, 46–7. Peterborough House, Fulham, closely resembled the alternative design on p. 47. Hurst practised in London, but died at Brighton on 23 June 1799, and was buried in the chapel at Pentonville which he had designed [*Gent's Mag.* 1799 (ii), 622].

LONDON, ST. JAMES'S CHAPEL, PENTONVILLE, 1787–8, cons. 1791; altered 1933; dem. Hurst also designed 'four houses adjoining' [exhib. at R.A. 1787] (B. F. L. Clarke, *Parish Churches of London*, 1966, fig. 35).

LONDON, WINCHESTER PLACE (on the north side of what is now Pentonville Road), ISLINGTON, 1788 [exhib. at R.A. 1788].

HAMMERSMITH, a house, 1792 [exhib. at R.A. 1792].

WIMBLEDON LODGE, WIMBLEDON COMMON (south side), SURREY, for Gerard de Visme, 1792; dem. [exhib. at R.A. 1792; elevations in R.I.B.A. Drawings Coll.] (D. Hughson, *London*, 1805–9, v, 393).

PETERBOROUGH HOUSE, PARSONS GREEN, FULHAM, MIDDLESEX, for John Meyrick, 1796; dem. *c.*1900 [exhib. at. R.A. 1796] (C. J. Fèret, *Fulham Old and New* ii, 1900, 150).

HURST, WILLIAM (1787–1844), was a native of Doncaster, and was articled to William Lindley of that town (*q.v.*). In 1811 he exhibited two drawings at the Royal Academy. He afterwards joined the firm of Lindley and Woodhead, subsequently Woodhead and Hurst, and was extensively employed in Yorkshire and the neighbouring counties. In partnership with John Woodhead, he designed a number of Gothic churches (including three for the Parliamentary Commissioners), of which the most ambitious were St. George's, Sheffield and Christ Church, Doncaster. After Woodhead's death in *c.*1838, Hurst, who had recently (1836) become a Fellow of the R.I.B.A., entered into partnership with W. L. Moffatt (1808–82), a Scottish pupil of William Burn, in conjunction with whom he was responsible for more churches, including some (e.g. Goole) of an ecclesiologically more advanced character, and various other public and private buildings in Yorkshire listed below. Hurst died on 8 December 1844, aged 57, and was buried in Doncaster churchyard. Moffatt subsequently returned to Edinburgh, where he specialized in workhouses and lunatic asylums[1]. J. G. Weightman (1801–72) and M. E. Hadfield (1812–85) were both pupils of Woodhead and Hurst [*A.P.S.D.*].

BUILDINGS DESIGNED BY WOODHEAD AND HURST

DONCASTER, YORKS. (W.R.), THE THEATRE, alterations, 1814 [*Calendar to the Records of the Borough of Doncaster* iv, Doncaster 1902, 280].

DONCASTER, YORKS. (W.R.), THE GAOL, 1819 [*op. cit.*, 284].

WAKEFIELD, YORKS. (W.R.), HOUSE OF CORRECTION, enlarged 1819 [J. H. Turner, *Wakefield House of Correction*, Bingley 1904, 150].

FIRBECK PARK, YORKS. (W.R.), alterations for Henry Gally Knight, *c.*1820 [drawing in R.I.B.A. Collection].

FIRBECK CHAPEL, YORKS. (W.R.), rebuilt for Henry Gally Knight, 1820, Gothic [I.C.B.S.].

SNEATON CASTLE, YORKS. (N.R.), for Col. James Wilson, *c.*1820, castellated [*Whitby Magazine* iii, 1829, frontispiece; signed drawing in R.I.B.A. Collection].

BARNSLEY, YORKS. (W.R.), ST. MARY'S CHURCH, rebuilt 1821–2 retaining medieval tower [E. Hoyle, *History of Barnsley Old Church*, Barnsley 1891, 35].

SNEATON CHURCH, YORKS. (N.R.), rebuilt for Col. James Wilson, 1823–5, Gothic [*Whitby Magazine* iii, 1829, frontispiece; unsigned drawings in P.R.O. MPD 113].

SHEFFIELD, ST. GEORGE'S CHURCH, 1821–5, Gothic [Port, 138–9].

SHEFFIELD, THE MUSIC HALL, SURREY STREET, 1823; dem. [R. E. Leader, *Surveyors and Architects of the Past in Sheffield*, 1903, 31] (T. Allen, *History of the County of York* iii, 1831, 70].

DONCASTER, YORKS. (W.R.), THE RACECOURSE GRANDSTAND, alterations, 1824; dem. 1969 [*A Skilful Master-Builder*, ed. H. E. C. Stapleton, York 1975, 46].

GOOLE, YORKS. (W.R.), designed new town for the Aire and Calder Navigation Company, 1824–40; largely dem. 1965–6 [J. D. Porteous, 'Goole: a pre-Victorian Company Town', *Industrial Archaeology* vi, 1969, 105–13].

SHEFFIELD, THE GRAMMAR SCHOOL, CHARLOTTE STREET, 1824–5, Gothic; dem. [Leader, *op. cit.*].

SHEFFIELD, THE BOY'S CHARITY SCHOOL, 1825–6 [report of the Charity for 1826–9 in Sheffield Archives].

SHEFFIELD, THE SHREWSBURY ALMSHOUSES, NORFOLK ROAD, 1825–7, Gothic [T. Allen, *History of the County of York* iii, 1831, 59 and plate].

PATELEY BRIDGE CHURCH, YORKS. (W.R.), 1825–7, Gothic [Port, 168–9].

ARMTHORPE CHURCH, YORKS. (W.R.), north aisle 1826; rebuilt 1885 [I.C.B.S.].

DONCASTER, YORKS. (W.R.), THE NEW BETTING ROOMS, HIGH STREET, 1826 [J. Taylor, *The Architectural Medal*, 1978, No. 85a].

THE OAKES, NORTON (nr. SHEFFIELD), DERBYSHIRE, alterations for W. J. Bagshawe, 1827, lodges 1834 [drawings at the Oakes and inscription on lead flat].

LEEDS, warehouse in Call Lane for Aire and Calder Navigation, 1827–8; destroyed by fire *c.*1965 [drawings in Inland Waterways office, *ex inf.* Dr. D. Linstrum].

DONCASTER, YORKS. (W.R.), CHRIST CHURCH, 1827–9, Gothic [*Gent's Mag.* 1830 (ii), 489, with engraving].

STANNINGTON CHURCH, YORKS. (W.R.), 1828–9, Gothic [Port, 170–1; drawings in R.I.B.A. Collection].

SHEFFIELD, THE CORN MARKET, 1830; dem. [*Sheffield Mercury*, 6 Nov. 1830].

NEW BRAMPTON, nr. CHESTERFIELD, DERBYSHIRE, ST. THOMAS'S CHURCH, 1830–1, Gothic [Port, 142–3].

DONCASTER, YORKS. (W.R.), THE MANSION HOUSE, alterations 1831 [J. Tomlinson, *Doncaster*, 1887, 226; *A Skilful Master-Builder*, ed. H. E. C. Stapleton, York 1975, 47].

DONCASTER, YORKS. (W.R.), PRIORY PLACE METHODIST CHAPEL, 1832 [C. W. Dolbey, *The Architectural Expression of Methodism*, 1964, 149].

SHEFFIELD, TOWN HALL, enlargement 1832–3; dem. [drawings in Sheffield Archives].

RIDGEWAY CHURCH, DERBYSHIRE, 1838–40, Gothic; tower added 1883–4 [I.C.B.S.].

BUILDINGS DESIGNED BY HURST IN PARTNERSHIP WITH MOFFATT

CHATSWORTH, DERBYSHIRE, unspecified work (probably on the estate) for 6th Duke of Devonshire, 1839 [G. F. Chadwick, *The Works of Sir Joseph Paxton*, 1961, 162].

[1] In 1836, before entering into partnership with Hurst, Moffatt had won the competition for the Wakefield Corn Exchange, built 1836–8, enlarged 1864, demolished 1964 [C. E. Camidge, *History of Wakefield*, 1866, 22; J. W. Walker, *Wakefield*, 1939, 521].

LEEDS, THE NEW INDEPENDENT CHAPEL, EAST PARADE, 1839–41, Greek Doric; dem. [J. Mayhall, *The Annals of Yorkshire*, 1861, 462] (D. Linstrum, *Historic Architecture of Leeds*, 1969, 48).

ROTHERHAM, YORKS. (W.R.), THE SHIP HOTEL and WESTGATE improvements, 1840 [*A.P.S.D.*].

GROSMONT CHURCH, YORKS. (N.R.), 1840, Gothic; rebuilt 1875–84 [engraving inscribed 'Hurst & Moffatt, Architects, Doncaster'].

WOODSETTS CHURCH, YORKS. (W.R.), 1841, Gothic [I.C.B.S.].

ARDSLEY, YORKS. (W.R.), CHRIST CHURCH, 1841, Gothic [I.C.B.S.].

BIRKENHEAD, CHESHIRE, ST. PETER'S CHURCH, ROCK FERRY, 1841–2, Romanesque [*A.P.S.D.*].

RAWCLIFFE CHURCH, YORKS. (W.R.), rebuilt 1842, Gothic [I.C.B.S.].

THURGOLAND CHURCH, YORKS. (W.R.), 1842–3 [I.C.B.S.].

WELBECK ABBEY, NOTTS., CLIPSTONE ARCHWAY for 4th Duke of Portland, 1842–4 [*A.P.S.D.*].

DONCASTER, YORKS. (W.R.), THE SAVINGS BANK, 16 HIGH STREET, 1843; dem. [J. M. L. Booker, *Temples of Mammon: the Architecture of Banking*, Edinburgh 1990, 303].

DONCASTER, YORKS. (W.R.), THE CORN MARKET, 1843 [*Surveyor, Engineer & Architect* iv, 1843, 197].

GOOLE CHURCH, YORKS. (W.R.), 1843–8, Gothic [*A.P.S.D.*].

HOOK CHURCH, YORKS. (W.R.), restoration 1844 [*Builder* ii, 1844, 275].

LEEDS, THE BOROUGH GAOL, 1844–7 [*Builder* ii, 1844, 643].

HUTCHENS, CHARLES (*c.*1781–1834), was born at St. Buryan in Cornwall, but practised from Torpoint in the parish of Antony near Plymouth. A tombstone in Antony churchyard records his death on 17 November 1834 at the age of 53. He designed THE CRESCENT at PLYMOUTH [G. Wightwick, *Nettleton's Guide to Plymouth, etc.*, 1836, 15] and three Commissioners' churches in Cornwall at CHASEWATER, 1826–8 (rebuilt 1892 except tower), ST. DAY, 1826–8, and ST. MARY, REDRUTH, 1827–8 [Port, 183]. He also designed MILLBROOK CHURCH, CORNWALL, 1827 (rebuilt 1893–5) [I.C.B.S.] and ST. MARY'S CHURCH, PENZANCE, CORNWALL, 1832–6 [G. B. Millet, *Penzance Past and Present*, 1880, 14].

HUTCHESON, JOHN, a land-surveyor and architect of Montrose, designed the handsome Palladian TOWN HALL, MONTROSE, ANGUS, 1763–4 [J. G. Low, *Highways and Byways of an Old Scottish Burgh*, Montrose 1938, 99].

HUTCHINSON, EDMUND, is said to have been a pupil of William Sands, architect and mason of Spalding, and to have cut the latter's epitaph in Spalding church when he died in 1751 [J. Nichols, *Literary Anecdotes* vi, 72]. He may have been the 'Mr. Hutchinson' who is reputed to have designed the Georgian church at LANGTON-BY-SPILSBY, LINCS. [E. H. R. Tatham in *Associated Architectural Societies' Reports and Papers* xxx, 1910, 363] (Jack Yates & Henry Thorold, *Lincolnshire*, Shell Guides 1965, 88–9).

HUTCHINSON, HENRY (1800–1831), born at Ingleby in Derbyshire, was the younger brother of Thomas Hutchinson, an architect who practised briefly in Birmingham before dying in his 24th year. Henry began his architectural training in his brother's office, but at the age of 18 went to Liverpool to become Thomas Rickman's first pupil. In 1820 he was transferred to the new office which Rickman had opened in Birmingham, and in the following year, on attaining his majority, was taken into partnership by him. During the next ten years the firm enjoyed an extensive practice, especially as church architects. Hutchinson's contribution to its success was probably considerable, for there is evidence that he was an able designer in his own right: the Gothic bridge at St. John's College, Cambridge, for instance, was his idea (see Rickman's diary, 10 Feb. 1827: 'Henry has made a beautiful design for the Cambridge Bridge'). A list of the buildings erected by the partnership will be found below under Rickman's name. Hutchinson fell ill in 1830, of a 'similar disease' (probably consumption) to the one that had killed his brother, and went abroad for the sake of his health. But he never fully recovered, and died at Leamington on 22 November 1831. He was buried in the church at Hampton Lucy which he and Rickman had designed. [T. M. Rickman, *Notes on the Life of Thomas Rickman*, 1901, 22, 26–7, 42, 44–5; *Gent's Mag.* 1831 (ii), 568; B.L., Add. MS. 37800, f. 96.]

HUTCHINSON, WILLIAM (*c.*1779–1869), was a builder at Hull. He was responsible for the following churches: HOLLYM, YORKS. (E.R.), 1814, rebuilt except tower 1884 [*V.C.H. Yorks. E.R.* v, 46]; CHRIST CHURCH, SCULCOATES, HULL, *c.*1815–22; dem. 1962 [*V.C.H. Yorks. E.R.* i, 305]; SPROATLEY CHURCH, YORKS. (E.R.), 1820 [*Hull Advertiser*, 18 Aug. 1820, but see p. 82 for evidence that Peter Atkinson was also involved]; DRYPOOL

CHURCH, nr. HULL, 1823–4, dem. 1941 [I.C.B.S.]; and ST. JOHN, NEWLAND, HULL, 1833 [I.C.B.S.]. The last was Romanesque in style, the others Gothic. He retired in 1860 and died on 15 December 1869 in his 91st year. His business was continued by his son Charles Hutchinson (d. 1875). [*Hull Advertiser*, 7 Jan. 1860; *Hull News*, 18 Dec. 1869; information from Mr. A. G. Chamberlain.]

HUTCHISON, JAMES (*c.*1751–1801), 'late architect in Dumfries', is commemorated by a tombstone in St. Michael's Churchyard, Dumfries. He died on 16 May 1801, aged 50.

HUTCHISON, ROBERT, was a builder and architect at Coalton of Balgonie in Fife. In 1811 he completed the steeple of MONIMAIL CHURCH, FIFE, to a design made by himself with modifications by J. Gillespie Graham [S.R.O., HR 432/2 and GD 26/10/108]. In CUPAR, FIFE, he designed the domed TOWN HALL, 1815–17, and was responsible for most of the contemporary development in the adjoining ST. CATHERINE STREET [Cupar Town Council Minutes, S.R.O., B 13/14/8, p. 261; J. Gifford, *Fife*, Buildings of Scotland, 1988, 164–5]. In 1838 he was consulted over the repair of CUPAR PARISH CHURCH [S.R.O., HR 3/15], and in 1843–4 he designed a 'Carpenter's Perp.' FREE CHURCH at MARKINCH, FIFE [*The Witness*, 17 Jan. 1844].

I

I'ANSON, EDWARD (1775–1853), was born in London, and was articled at an early age to a surveyor named Healey, who is said to have practised in the West End. He was admitted to the Royal Academy Schools in 1791, and exhibited at the Academy from 1792 to 1798. For some time he was chiefly employed as a measuring surveyor, but gave up his own business to become first the assistant, and shortly after the partner, of D. A. Alexander. On Alexander's retirement he continued their practice on his own account, acting as surveyor to large ecclesiastical and other estates in Southwark and the City of London. He was also much engaged in the compensation cases arising out of the formation of the approaches to the new London Bridge, and in superintending the erection of new houses in the streets leading to the bridge, though their external architecture was designed by Sir Robert Smirke for the Corporation of London.

I'Anson was surveyor to the Commissioners of Sewers for Surrey and Kent from 1804 until the Commission was superseded in 1846. In conjunction with Joseph Gwilt and John Newman he drained and laid out for building extensive tracts on the south side of the Thames, and with them published a *Report relating to the Sewage, etc.*, 1843. It was under his immediate supervision that large areas of Bermondsey, Walworth, Kennington and St. George's Fields were drained by sewers and outlets, whose design and construction became the model for such works elsewhere in England and abroad.

I'Anson was also much engaged in designing warehouses, chiefly in Southwark, and offices and houses in the City of London. During the latter part of his career, however, he acted chiefly as a referee, a function which he fulfilled with characteristic tact and good judgement. He became a member of the Surveyors' Club in 1815, and was elected President in 1823. In about 1842 he gave up practice and fulfilled a life-long ambition by visiting Rome. He died on 13 November 1853 at the age of 78, and was buried in Norwood Cemetery. There is a drawing of his cottage at Wandsworth in B.L., Add. MS. 36389, ff. 61–2. His eldest son, Edward I'Anson, junior (1812–88), was President of the R.I.B.A. in 1886–8. Charles Purser was his pupil [*A.P.S.D.*].

INGLEMAN, RICHARD (1777–1838), was the son of Francis Ingleman, a surveyor or builder of Southwell in Nottinghamshire, and the grandson of Richard Ingleman, a mason employed to repair Southwell Minster after damage by lightning in 1711 [P.R.O., Eccles 2/118/4463, 8/9]. From 1801 to 1808 he was paid £10 a year as Surveyor of the Fabric to the Minster, and during this period carried out a general repair of the church, which had hitherto been in a neglected state. He appears to have been responsible for the removal of the two western spires, which were then thought to be too heavy for the towers, but were replaced in 1880 without any ill effects.

Although primarily a local architect, Ingleman obtained commissions as far afield as Oxford and Devizes. The lunatic asylum which he planned at Nottingham led to his employment to design similar buildings at Lincoln and Oxford, and in 1810 he was one of the unsuccessful competitors for the New Bethlehem Hospital in London. The minutes of the Oxford Asylum testify to the trouble he took in designing what was then a relatively novel type of building. Architecturally Ingleman's asylums were classical buildings of no special distinction, but his unexecuted design for rebuilding Shelton Church. Notts. in 1819 (Borthwick Institute, York) is an essay in 'Early English' of quite creditable character for its date.

Ingleman died at Southwell on 11 January 1838 [Notts. C.R.O., DD 113/14/1–2 and will in PRSW 207/12; information from the late N. Summers.]

SOUTHWELL MINSTER, NOTTS., repairs to fabric, 1801–8 [N. Summers, *Southwell Minster*, 1972, 23].

SOUTHWELL, NOTTS., ASSEMBLY ROOMS adjoining Saracen's Head Inn, 1805 [Notts. C.R.O., minutes in DDM 71/40].

SOUTHWELL, NOTTS., THE RESIDENCE HOUSE, extensive improvements *c.*1805 [Southwell Minster records, *ex inf.* Dr. N. Summers].

SOUTHWELL, NOTTS., THE HOUSE OF CORRECTION, 1807–8; enlarged 1817 [R. P. Shilton, *A History of Southwell*, 1818].

DEVIZES, WILTS., THE COUNTY GAOL, 1810 [J. Waylen, *Chronicles of the Devizes*, 1839, 318] (plan in *V.C.H. Wilts.* v, 187).

NOTTINGHAM, THE LUNATIC ASYLUM, 1810–12 [Brenda Parry-Jones, *The Warneford Hospital, Oxford*, 1976, 8–9].

CONOCK HOUSE, nr. DEVIZES, WILTS., added Ionic porch and wings for E. Warriner, 1817 [Wiltshire Record Office, 451/74 (ix)] (*C. Life*, 29 June 1951).

ORDSALL RECTORY, NOTTS., designs for rebuilding 1819 [Borthwick Institute, MGA 1819/1].

LINCOLN, THE LUNATIC ASYLUM, 1819–20 [*A.P.S.D.*, *s.v.* 'Lincoln'].

SOUTHWELL, NOTTS., THE GRAMMAR SCHOOL, CHURCH STREET, 1820 [Southwell Chapter Decree Book, 7 Dec. 1819, *ex inf.* Dr. N. Summers].

RHYDD COURT, WORCS., work for Sir Anthony Lechmere, Bart., *c.*1820 [Ingleman's employment here is mentioned both in the Vestry Minutes of St. Clement's Church, Worcester, in the Worcs. C.R.O. and in the order-book of Messrs. Jones & Clarke, hothouse manufacturers of Birmingham, Birmingham Reference Library MS. 1056/249, no. 92].

OXFORD, THE WARNEFORD LUNATIC ASYLUM, HEADINGTON, 1821–6; enlarged 1877 [Brenda Parry-Jones, *The Warneford Hospital, Oxford*, 1976, 8–12].

INGLIS, ROBERT, a mason by trade, became a burgess of Edinburgh in January 1793 [*Roll of Edinburgh Burgesses*, Scottish Record Soc. 1933, 83]. In 1789 he was the promoter of a proposed Riding School in King Street for which he made 'a plan, section, and elevation', but it proved abortive [S.R.O., GD 1/816/1]. In 1791, when Joseph Home rejected Robert Adam's design for an addition to Ninewells House, Berwicks., he proposed to obtain one either from Alexander Laing or from Robert Inglis [N.L.S., MS. 1992, ff. 71, 91]. Inglis's name disappears from the Edinburgh directories after 1800.

INMAN, WILLIAM SOUTHCOTE (1798–1879), was the son of Captain Henry Inman, R.N., and became a pupil of Thomas Chawner [Soane Museum, Correspondence Div. VI. L]. He was admitted to the Royal Academy Schools in 1818 and exhibited at the Academy up to 1838. In 1821 he won the competition for the LONDON ORPHAN ASYLUM at CLAPTON, but because of his youth and inexperience George Goldring was appointed joint surveyor to assist in the execution of the building [Minutes of the Board of the London Orphan Asylum, *ex inf.* Mr. F. Kelsall]. This ambitious Greek Doric building, later the Salvation Army Congress Hall, was completed in 1823 and is illustrated in Shepherd's *Metropolitan Improvements* (1831). It was demolished in 1977 with the exception of the portico and colonnades. Inman subsequently competed for the new buildings at King's College, Cambridge, in 1823, obtaining the second premium with a design illustrated by A. Doig, *The Architectural Drawings Collection of King's College, Cambridge*, 1979, pls. 22–3, for the Fitzwilliam Museum and the Houses of Parliament in 1835, for the Royal Berkshire Infirmary in 1837, and for a public building at St. John's, Newfoundland, in 1838. For the last design (exhibited at the Royal Academy) he obtained the first premium of £50 [*Civil Engineer and Architect's Jnl.* i, 174].

Despite the ability he had shown in these competitions Inman appears to have obtained very few commissions, and in 1844 he secured the senior architectural post of Surveyor of Works and Buildings in the Office of Woods and Works. He retained this after the separation of Woods from Works in 1851, finally retiring in 1856. His duties were chiefly administrative, and he does not appear to have designed any building of importance in his official capacity.

Inman became a Fellow of the R.I.B.A. in 1835, and was later a Vice-President. In the R.I.B.A. Library there is a photograph of his portrait by Pickersgill. In 1836 he published, with notes, an abbreviated version of the *Report of the Committee of the House of Commons on Ventilation, Warming, and Transmission of Sound.* He also published in Weale's *Quarterly Papers on Architecture* iii, 1845, a translation of a paper on 'Symbolic Colours' by Frédéric, Baron Portal.

INWOOD, CHARLES FREDERICK (1799–1840), second son of William Inwood, entered the Royal Academy Schools in 1822. He assisted his father in some of his buildings, in particular the Westminster Hospital. He designed MARLOW PARISH CHURCH, BUCKS., 1832–5, Gothic, chancel added by J. O. Scott, 1875–6, and arcades inserted *c.*1898, of which he exhibited designs at the R.A. in 1832 and 1834; the ST. PANCRAS NATIONAL SCHOOLS, LANCING STREET, EUSTON SQUARE, 1837 (dem.), and No. 22 OLD BOND STREET (dem.) for W. Tinkler, silk and lace merchant. He died on 1 June 1840 [*A.P.S.D.*].

INWOOD, EDWARD (1802–), third son of William Inwood, entered the Royal Academy Schools in 1822. He exhibited at the Academy from 1821 to 1827. His only known work is a memorial tablet at Pangbourne, Berks., to the Revd. J. S. Breedon, D.D. (d. 1826), and his wife Elizabeth (d. 1827), which bears his signature.

INWOOD, WILLIAM (*c.*1771–1843) and HENRY WILLIAM (1794–1843). William Inwood, the father, was the son of Daniel Inwood, bailiff to Lord Mansfield at Kenwood, Highgate. He became steward to Lord Colchester and was surveyor to several other landowners. He published *Tables for the Purchasing of Estates . . . and for the Renewal of Leases held under . . . Corporation Bodies*, 1811. A second edition of this well-known work, which was based on the tables of Baily and Smart, appeared in 1820, and it reached its twenty-first edition in 1880. Inwood is said to have designed 'numerous mansions, villas, barracks, warehouses, etc.', but nearly all his known works were carried out in conjunction with his eldest son, Henry William Inwood, who contributed the Grecian scholarship so characteristic of their buildings. In his later years William Inwood was in poor circumstances and received assistance from Sir John Soane's Fund for Distressed Architects. He died in Upper Seymour Street on 16 March 1843, aged 72, and was buried in the family vault in St. Pancras New Church. Besides H. W. Inwood, he had two architect sons, Charles Frederick and Edward Inwood, who are noticed separately above. H. Lane, R. Parker, W. Railton and Thomas Taylor were among his pupils, and William Butterfield was in his office for a short time.

Henry William Inwood was born on 22 May 1794. He was trained in his father's office, and began to exhibit at the Royal Academy when he was only fifteen years old. In 1818–19 he travelled in Italy and Greece, visiting Athens in order to make a careful study of its architectural monuments.[1] His subsequent publication, *The Erechtheion at Athens: Fragments of Athenian Architecture and a few remains in Attica, Megara and Epirus*, 1827, became the standard work on the Erechtheion. The fruits of his Grecian scholarship soon became apparent in St. Pancras New Church, designed in conjunction with his father in 1819. This was a landmark in the history of the Greek Revival and the most expensive church of its day. It is a Grecian version of the type of steepled Anglican church established by Gibbs at St. Martin-in-the-Fields, all the architectural features being ingeniously adapted from authentic Greek prototypes. The result is a *tour de force* whose elegance compels admiration despite the architectural pedantry which it embodies. W. H. Inwood was also associated with his father in the design of All Saints, Camden Town, and St. Peter's, Regent Square, both in the Grecian style, and shares with him responsibility for the Somers Town Chapel, a meagre Gothic building held up to deserved ridicule by Pugin in his *Contrasts* (1836). In conjunction with his pupil E. N. Clifton (1817–89) he designed another Grecian church, St. James's, Holloway, 1837–8, and a dull Gothic one, St. Stephen's, Islington, 1837–9. Most of these buildings are named by W. H. Inwood in a letter of 1840 to John Place of Nottingham (Notts. Record Office DD 67/3/1–8). Other recent works mentioned in the same letter are a new church near Rochester (unidentified), a hotel at Windsor, and (among 'less important works'), 'Schools, Country and Town Residences'.

Inwood's career was prematurely terminated in March 1843, when a ship in which he had sailed for Spain was lost with all on board. Besides the book already mentioned he had also published in 1834 *The Resources of Design in the Architecture of Greece, Egypt, and other Countries obtained by the Studies of the Architects of those Countries from Nature*, in which he drew parallels between the fluting of Doric columns and the formation of certain shells. He was a Fellow of the Society of Antiquaries. E. N. Clifton, G. G. Place (of Nottingham), F. B. Russell and J. D. Wyatt were his pupils. There are drawings by him in the Victoria and Albert Museum and the R.I.B.A. Drawings Collection [*A.P.S.D.*; *D.N.B.*; *Builder* ix, 1851, 682, 689, xvi, 1858, 251; *Gent's Mag.* 1843 (i), 547].

---

[1] In the letter cited further on Inwood states that he was in Greece and Rome in 1818–19. He must, however, have returned very early in the latter year, for work on St. Pancras Church started on 1 May 1819.

EAST GRINSTEAD CHURCH, SUSSEX, completion of tower 1811–13 after death of J. T. Groves [minutes of committee for building church in East Sussex Record Office; exhib. at R.A. 1812 by H. W. Inwood, 1817 by W. Inwood].

RADWINTER RECTORY, ESSEX, 1812 [exhib. at R.A. 1812 by H. W. Inwood].

LONDON, ST. PANCRAS NEW CHURCH, 1819–22; redecorated by Crace 1880 but restored 1953 [exhib. at R.A. 1819 and 1821 by W. & H. W. Inwood; Britton & Pugin, *The Public Buildings of London* i, 1825, 145–66; drawings in R.I.B.A. Collection].

LONDON, CAMDEN CHAPEL, PRATT STREET, CAMDEN TOWN, 1822–4 (known at one time as St. Stephen's, but dedicated to All Saints in 1920 and in 1948 leased to the Greek Orthodox Church) [exhib. at R.A. 1823 by W. & H. W. Inwood; *Gent's Mag.* 1824 (ii), 489].

LONDON, ST. PETER'S CHAPEL, REGENT SQUARE, 1822–5; damaged by bombing and dem. 1967 [exhib. at R.A. 1823 by W. & H. W. Inwood; *Gent's Mag.* 1828 (i), 393].

LONDON, WOBURN LODGE, UPPER WOBURN PLACE, ST. PANCRAS, 1824; dem. 1930 [*Survey of London* xxi, 105] (*Architect and Building News*, Jan.–March 1930).

LONDON, ST. MARY'S CHAPEL, SOMERS TOWN, ST. PANCRAS, 1824–7, Gothic; chancel added 1878 [*Gent's Mag.* 1827 (ii), 393].

LONDON, ST. JOHN'S CHURCH, WESTMINSTER, rearranged interior (destroyed by fire 1940–1) and cut two new doorways in west towers, 1824–5 [MS. parish records in Westminster City Library].

LONDON, THE NEW WESTMINSTER HOSPITAL, BROAD SANCTUARY, 1832–4; remodelled 1923–4; dem. 1951 [exhib. R.A. 1832–3 by W. & C. Inwood].

CLANDON PARK, SURREY, Ionic temple for 3rd Earl of Onslow, 1838 [exhib. at R.A. 1838 by W. & H. W. Inwood] (*C. Life*, 24 Sept. 1927, p. 439, fig. 12).

LONDON, ST. JAMES'S CHURCH, CHILLINGWORTH ROAD, HOLLOWAY, 1837–8; subsequently much enlarged; damaged by bombing 1944; by H. W. Inwood & E. N. Clifton [S. Lewis, *History of Islington*, 1842, 373].

LONDON, ST. STEPHEN'S CHURCH, CANONBURY ROAD, ISLINGTON, 1837–9, Gothic; reconstructed 1957 after war-damage; by H. W. Inwood & E. N. Clifton [H. W. Inwood's letter cited in text; exhib. at R.A. 1839 by E. N. Clifton; S. Lewis, *op cit.*, 410].

WINDSOR, BERKS., a hotel, 1840 [H. W. Inwood's letter cited in text].

IONS, JOHN (*c.*1785–1826), of Gateshead, was a mason by trade. In 1824–5 he built the Gothic church of GATESHEAD FELL, CO. DURHAM, and when he died on 26 November 1826, at the age of 41, he was commemorated as 'architect and builder of this church'. Ions's design is, however, known to have been improved by the professional hand of Ignatius Bonomi [E. Mackenzie & M. Ross, *County Palatine of Durham* i, 1834, 107–8; Port, 132, 183].

IRELAND, JOSEPH (*c.*1780–1841), belonged to an old Roman Catholic family from Crofton near Wakefield in Yorkshire. It is possible that he was a pupil of Joseph Bonomi, for he began to exhibit at the Royal Academy from No. 12 Great Titchfield Street, London, in 1808, the year in which Bonomi died at No. 76. For the next thirty years he worked for an almost exclusively Catholic clientèle, providing them with well-designed chapels and churches in either Gothic or Grecian style. He died at Moorcroft House, Hillingdon, Middlesex, on 16 November 1841, aged 60. J. J. Scoles became his pupil in 1812. [*Catholic Directory*, 1842, 134; *Gent's Mag.* 1842 (i), 112; information from Mr. Denis Evinson.]

LONDON, R.C. CHAPEL, ROMNEY TERRACE, HORSEFERRY ROAD, WESTMINSTER, 1813; dem. [*Downside Review* viii, 1889, 115].

TRANBY PARK, HESSLE, YORKS. (E.R.), for John Todd, 1816; dem. 1950 [exhib. at R.A. 1816] (Neave & Waterson, *Lost Houses of E. Yorkshire*, 1988, 30).

HASSOP, DERBYSHIRE, R.C. CHAPEL for Francis Eyre, titular Earl of Newburgh, 1816–18, Grecian [exhib. at R.A. 1819].

LEICESTER, R.C. CHAPEL, WELLINGTON STREET, now part of HOLY CROSS CHURCH, 1817–19, Gothic [B. Little, *Catholic Churches since 1623*, 1966, 55].

CLAYTON-LE-MOORS, LANCS., ST. MARY'S R.C. CHURCH, 1819; dem. 1959 [*The Tablet*, 29 Sept. 1866, 612].

IRNHAM HALL, LINCS., R.C. CHAPEL for 6th Lord Clifford, 1822–3, Grecian; dem. 1855 [exhib. at R.A. 1822].

TIXALL HALL, STAFFS., 'restoration' for Sir Thomas Aston Constable, Bart., 1823; dem. 1930 [exhib. at R.A. 1823].

WAKEFIELD, YORKS. (W.R.), ST. AUSTIN'S R.C. CHURCH, designs made 1824 which may have formed the basis of the much simplified design executed 1828; enlarged by J. A. Hansom 1852 [drawings preserved at the church, *ex inf.* Mr. D. Evinson].

HINCKLEY, LEICS., R.C. CHAPEL (ST. PETER), 1825, Gothic; enlarged 1885; dem. 1976 [C. L. Eastlake, *History of the Gothic Revival*, 1872, 130].

WALSALL, STAFFS., ST. MARY'S R.C. CHURCH, 1825–7, Grecian [S. Lewis, *Topographical Dictionary of England* iv, 1831, 373; B. Little, *Catholic Churches since 1623*, 1966, 64].

WOLVERHAMPTON, STAFFS., GIFFORD HOUSE R.C. CHAPEL (SS. PETER & PAUL), 1827–8, Grecian; enlarged 1901 [*Catholic Magazine* v, 1834, 306–7; B. Little, *Catholic Churches since 1623*, 1966, 64–5].

HOUGHTON HALL, YORKS. (E.R.), R.C. CHAPEL for the Hon. Charles Langdale, 1827–9, Grecian; dem. 1959 [*Catholic Miscellany*, 1829, 238–9] (*Trans. Georgian Soc. for E. Yorkshire* v (ii), 1961–3, fig. 8).

TIXALL HALL, STAFFS., conversion of existing building into a domestic R.C. chapel for Sir Thomas Aston Constable, Bart., 1828; dem. [exhib. at R.A. 1830]. In 1836 Ireland exhibited at the Liverpool Academy the 'Interior of the Chapel at Tixall, Staffordshire, the seat of Sir George (*sic*) Clifford Constable, Bart.' This was presumably the Tudor Gothic R. C. chapel at Great Haywood, Staffs., which formerly stood at Tixall and was rebuilt at Haywood in 1845.

WEST BROMWICH, STAFFS., ST. MICHAEL'S R.C. CHURCH, 1830–2, Gothic; rebuilt 1877 [F. W. Hackwood, *History of West Bromwich*, 1895, 45].

BURGHFIELD, BERKSHIRE, cottage for 16th Earl of Shrewsbury, *c.*1836 [exhib. at Liverpool Academy, 1836].

TUNBRIDGE WELLS, KENT, R.C. CHURCH (ST. AUGUSTINE), GROSVENOR ROAD, 1837–8, classical; dem. 1969 [Colbran's *Guide to Tunbridge Wells*, 1840, 109] (H.-R. Hitchcock, *Early Victorian Architecture in Britain* ii, 1954, pl. III, 4).

IRESON, NATHANIEL (1686–1769), master builder, was a native of Warwickshire, but may have been related to the Iresons of Yarwell, Northants., who were master masons there in the seventeenth and eighteenth centuries. He is said to have been born in the neighbourhood of Nuneaton, probably at Ansley, but subsequently lived at Ladbrooke, where a daughter was born in 1711. He served his apprenticeship with Francis Smith of Warwick (*q.v.*), who subsequently recommended him as 'a young man . . . that understands his business very well' [N.L.W., Penrice & Margam MSS. L 945, 958]. In 1716 he may have been working for Thomas Archer at Hale in Hampshire, for 'Anne the daughter of Nathaniel Eyreson' was baptized at Hale in that year [parish register], and some years later Archer brought an action in Chancery against 'Nathaniel Ireson [then] of Hale, mason', for alleged breach of trust on the part of the latter in a transaction concerning land in Hale for which he had acted on Archer's behalf in 1719 [P.R.O., C 11/80/1, *ex inf.* Mr. Peter Wayne]. By 1720 he was established at Stourton in Wilts., where he built Stourhead House for Henry Hoare to the designs of Colen Campbell. In Stourton Church there is an inscription recording that 'This church was newly paved and seated and beautified 1722/3. Nathl. Ireson, John Butcher, Churchwardens', but it is not known whether Ireson executed the work himself. His daughter Mary died here in 1723, and was buried in the church, where Nathaniel erected a tablet to her memory the following year. In about 1726 he purchased Windmill Farm at Wincanton in Somerset, and built Ireson House, where he lived until his death on 18 April 1769, at the age of 83. In 1733 he opened a quarry on his land at Wincanton, which not only produced an excellent freestone, but also yielded an overburden of clay suitable for brickmaking and the manufacture of pottery. He made the most of these natural resources, becoming a skilled potter as well as a quarry-owner, brickmaker and master builder. As a sculptor he is represented by the signed tablet to the memory of the Revd. Robert Kingston (d. 1748) in St. Cuthbert's Church, Wells, and he is reputed to have carved the statue of himself which stands in Wincanton churchyard, 'keeping it ready to be erected after his death'.

As an architect Ireson was influenced by Archer rather than by Campbell, designing and building in a vigorous provincial baroque style that invites comparison with the work of the Smiths of Warwick in the Midlands and with that of the Bastards of Blandford in Dorset. It was doubtless from Archer that Ireson derived that fondness for the Borrominesque capitals with inturned volutes which are used at Crowcombe Court and also in an unexecuted design for the north front of Corsham Court which bears Ireson's signature (reproduced in C. Hussey, *English Country Houses: Early Georgian*, 1955, 229).

In his will, dated 24 September 1765 (P.C.C. 212 BOGG), Ireson, who describes himself as a mason, leaves Crosses or Crases House, Wincanton to his grand-daughter Mary Ireson Kittermaster, and all his books, tools and marble to John Ireson, a relation who was evidently not his son. His descendants continued to live in Wincanton until the early nineteenth century, and the quarry on Windmill Farm was not exhausted until 1900. Portraits of Ireson and his wife, painted in 1725 and 1745 respectively, were in 1896 in the possession of Mrs. William Bewsey of

Wincanton, but their present ownership is unknown.

[W. Phelps, *History of Somerset*, 1836–9, i, 162, 167; G. Sweetman, *History of Wincanton*, 1903, 209–11; H. St. George Gray, 'N. Ireson, Master-Builder and Potter', *C. Life*, 12 April 1939; H. St. George Gray, 'Nathaniel Ireson of Wincanton, Master-Builder', *Procs. Somerset Arch. Soc.* lxxxvii, 1941.]

KINGSTON DEVERILL CHURCH, WILTS., work by Ireson is recorded in the parish records in 1724 [*Procs. Somerset Arch. Soc.* lxxxvii, 1941, 82].

VEN HOUSE, MILBORNE PORT, SOMERSET, enlarged and rebuilt house for James Medlycott (d. 1731), probably *c.*1725, incorporating as west elevation the front of a smaller house built in 1698–1700 [building account in Somerset C.R.O., DD/MDL/S/947/14/9] (*C. Life*, 24 June 1911; H.A. Tipping, *English Homes* IV (i), 385–96).

MELLS PARK, SOMERSET, for Thomas Horner, 1725; canted bows added later in the 18th century; alterations by Soane 1810–24; dem. after fire in 1917 [contract in volume of drawings by Soane at Mells Manor House] (*C. Life*, 24 May 1962, p. 1254).

BERKLEY HOUSE, nr. FROME, SOMERSET, for Abigail Prowse, 1730–2 [contract in Warwickshire Record Office, Mordaunt papers CR 711, box 3].

CROWCOMBE COURT, SOMERSET, completed house begun (1724–7) by Thomas Parker (*q.v.*) for Thomas Carew, 1734–9, damaged by fire 1963. On 6 July 1734 Ireson contracted to build a house 'on foundations some time since laid and carried up by Thomas Parker Architect . . . according to Modells formes, plans and Representations of the four fronts and of the Severall Rooms . . . drawn up prepared and signed by the said N. Ireson' [contract printed *C. Life*, 15 Oct. 1938] (*C. Life*, 22–29 April 1933).

BRUTON CHURCH, SOMERSET, the chancel, for Charles Berkeley of Stratton, 1743 [Sweetman, 211].

WINCANTON CHURCH, SOMERSET, rebuilt chancel, added clerestory, re-roofed and rewindowed nave at his own expense, 1748. The altar bore an inscription that it was 'given by Nathaniel Ireson Architect 1748'. His work was destroyed by J. D. Sedding in 1887–9 [Sweetman, 45].

REDLYNCH, SOMERSET. According to Sweetman (p. 211) he built the CHAPEL in the grounds of Redlynch House in 1750. Between 1740 and 1746 he was paid £2166 for work at Redlynch, including building the stables [Dorset C.R.O., D/FSl, Box 188], and documents in B.L., Add. MS. 51373 A., ff. 37–40 show that in *c.*1755 he was carrying out alterations to the house for 1st Earl of Ilchester in conjunction with Henry Flitcroft; house dem. 1913–14.

WINCANTON, SOMERSET. According to Sweetman Ireson was responsible for the following works in Wincanton: IRESON HOUSE for himself, *c.*1726, altered *c.*1851; HILLSIDE HOUSE; the rebuilding of THE WHITE HORSE INN in 1733; and alterations to BALSAM HOUSE, RODBER HOUSE (*c.*1730), and 'THE DOGS', TOUT HILL, *c.*1745.

IVORY, THOMAS (1709–1779), was a leading architect and builder in Norwich in the eighteenth century. The place of his birth is unknown, but the fact that in September 1745 he purchased his freedom of the city as a carpenter indicates that he was neither born nor apprenticed in Norwich. In 1751 he was nominated to do all the carpenter's work for the Great Hospital 'in the room of Agabus Molden', an appointment which he held to the time of his death. He is described in his will as a builder and timber merchant, and by his son William as 'a publick spirited Man, with great activity of Mind and resolution, and great knowledge in his business as a Master builder, and employing . . . a considerable number of Workmen, and having always on his own premises, a large Assortment of Deals and Timber, being considerably employed in the profession of a Merchant in Exporting the Norwich Manufactory and other English Manufactories into the Northern Countries and Importing from thence large Quantities of Deals, Timber, Iron, etc., into this Country'. His timber yard was in Bishopsgate Street. From 1752 onwards he built as speculations a number of houses on sites leased from the Corporation and the Great Hospital, and in 1757 he not only undertook the erection of a theatre out of his own capital, but continued to be its sole proprietor until 1766, when he 'offered his whole Theatrical Estate to Publick Sale, to be divided into Thirty shares – reserving two shares to himself'. He was responsible for some excellent Georgian architecture in Norwich, his most notable building being the octagonal Nonconformist chapel in Colegate, which has quite an ambitious interior with giant Corinthian columns supporting the dome.

Thomas Ivory of Norwich is not to be confused with Thomas Ivory of Dublin (d. 1786), an architect with whom, so far as is known, he was unconnected. He died in Norwich on 28 August 1779, aged 70, as a result of an injury due to 'a large firr baulk going over his legg and thigh'. He is commemorated by a memorial tablet in the cathedral (now in the triforium), executed by his nephew John Ivory, who was a carver and monumental mason, and also by an inscription on the floor of the north transept. He left two sons, Thomas, who was employed in the Revenue Office at Fort William in Bengal, and William, who succeeded his father as an architect and builder in Norwich [S. J. Wearing, *Georgian Norwich: its Builders*, 1926, 11–36 (in which evidence will be found for the list of buildings that follows); *D.N.B.*; Norfolk Record Office, 19180, letters from William Ivory to the Earl of Buckinghamshire, 1779; Margaret C. Evans, 'The Descendants of Thomas Ivory', *Norfolk Archaeology* 39, 1985, 206–14].

NORWICH

THE METHODIST MEETING-HOUSE, BISHOPSGATE, 1751–3.

HOUSE in the entrance-court of THE GREAT HOSPITAL, for himself, 1752–3.

attributed: HOUSE in BISHOPSGATE adjoining the Meeting-House, for 'Mr. Wheatley the Methodist Preacher', 1753.

THE OCTAGON CHAPEL, COLEGATE, 1754–6 [S. J. Wearing, 'The Minute Books concerning the erection of the Octagon Chapel, Norwich', *Norfolk Archaeology* 21, 1923].

THE ASSEMBLY ROOMS, 1754. The interior was designed by Sir James Burrough (*q.v.*).

THE THEATRE, 1757–8; enlarged and altered by W. Wilkins 1800; again altered 1819; dem. 1825.

SURREY STREET, Nos. 29–35, 1761–2; Nos. 25 and 27, *c.*1770.

THE ARTILLERY BARRACKS, 1771–2.

KING STREET, No. 31, for Sir Edward Astley, *c.*1774; dem.

COLCHESTER, THE THEATRE, 1764; dem. *c.*1820.

BLICKLING HALL, NORFOLK, alterations for 2nd Earl of Buckinghamshire, 1765 onwards, including remodelling of N. and W. fronts (the former in Jacobean style), moving the Jacobean staircase and remodelling the hall as a staircase hall [J. Maddison, 'Architectural drawings at Blickling Hall,' *Arch. Hist.* 34, 1991] (National Trust, *Blickling Hall*, 1987).

IVORY, WILLIAM (*c.*1738–1801), was the elder son of Thomas Ivory of Norwich (*q.v.*). As he stated on oath in 1777 that he was then '39 years and upwards' he must have been born in the 1730s and not in 1746 as stated by Wearing. He was associated with his father in the alterations at BLICKLING HALL from about 1770 onwards, and completed them after his death. It was to his designs that the ceiling of the Peter the Great Room was decorated in Pompeian style in 1778–82. In 1770–5 he gratuitously designed and superintended the erection of THE NORFOLK AND NORWICH HOSPITAL. From evidence given by Ivory in a Chancery lawsuit in 1777 it appears that in 1770 he was consulted by John Norris (d. 1777) about a mansion which the latter was about to build at Witton in Norfolk, but whether his designs were those adopted is not clear [P.R.O., C12/2412/10, *ex inf.* Mr. David Cubitt]. Witton House was destroyed by fire in 1926.

After 1779, when he inherited his father's considerable property and married a widow (Elizabeth Sandys), Ivory appears to have done little architectural work. As his mother continued to occupy the house built by his father, he moved to St. Helen's Place, off Bishopsgate, a house possibly designed or altered by himself, and in 1780 he erected in the south transept of St. Helen's Church a Gothic pew for himself and his servants. In 1784 he and his wife left Norwich for Ipswich. She died in 1791, he on 24 June 1801. He held the rank of Captain in the East Norfolk Militia, and there is a portrait of him in military uniform in the Christchurch Mansion Museum at Ipswich.

[S. J. Wearing, *Georgian Norwich: its Builders*, 1926, 37–41; *Ipswich Journal*, June 1801; letters to the Earl of Buckinghamshire in the Norfolk C.R.O., mentioning, *inter alia*, the move to Ipswich in 1784; information from Mr. J. Bensusan-Butt; Margaret C. Evans, 'The Descendants of Thomas Ivory', *Norfolk Archaeology* 39, 1985, 206–14.]

IVORY, WILLIAM (*c.*1747–1837), carpenter and builder of Saffron Walden, carried out works at AUDLEY END, ESSEX for the 4th Lord Howard de Walden. These included repairs to the house, and a new VICARAGE in SAFFRON WALDEN, erected in 1793 [Essex C.R.O., Audley End papers, Annual Account for 1793]. His designs for the vicarage are preserved in an album of architectural drawings in the library at Audley End (f. 101). This also contains a set of plans of Audley End made by Ivory in 1787 (ff. 48–51). He died in the Edward VI Almshouses at Saffron Walden in his 91st year, and was buried in the churchyard there [J. C. Loudon, *Architectural Magazine* iv, 1837, 96; S. J. Wearing, *Georgian Norwich: its Builders*, 1926, 40–1].

J

JACKSON, —, was an otherwise unidentified surveyor employed in connection with the building of the new river front of CLARE COLLEGE, CAMBRIDGE, in 1669–71. On 24 April 1669 £1 was paid 'to Jackson for his journey hither to surveigh the building'. It is possible, but unlikely, that he was the Cambridge bricklayer called George Jackson who contracted to build Pembroke College Chapel in 1663 [Willis & Clark, i, 102, 155].

JACKSON, BENJAMIN, practised in Leeds as an architect and land-surveyor from *c.*1814 until at least 1847. He was working at DENISON HALL, nr. LEEDS, for George Rawson *c.*1823, made a plan for widening BOND STREET, LEEDS, in 1829, and designed ST. MARK'S TERRACE, LEEDS, in 1832. Elisha Backhouse was first his pupil and then from 1835 his partner until in 1839 Backhouse joined William Perkin, with whom he built up a considerable practice in Leeds [D. Linstrum, *West Yorkshire Architects and Architecture* 1978, 371, 379; *Leeds Intelligencer*, 31 May 1832, 12 Jan. 1835, 15 May 1847, *ex inf.* Dr. Linstrum].

JACKSON, GEORGE (*c.*1805–1842) was almost certainly the son of Thomas Jackson, a builder of Durham, who in 1838–40 designed SHADFORTH CHURCH, CO. DURHAM, Gothic, largely rebuilt 1889–91 and 1917 [I.C.B.S.]. Thomas Jackson died in 1840, and the certificate sent to the Incorporated Church Building Society was signed by George. George Jackson subsequently designed the following churches in County Durham, all in the 'Early English style': WINGATE, 1840–1 [J. Latimer, *Local Records*, 1857, 149]; COLLIERLY (ANNFIELD PLAIN), 1840–1 [I.C.B.S.]; PELTON, 1841–2 [J. Fordyce, *History of Durham* ii, 1855, 620]; SEATON CAREW, chancel only, 1842 [I.C.B.S.]; and SOUTHWICK-ON-WEAR, 1842–5 [I.C.B.S.]. In 1841 he made designs for a new vicarage at BLACKTOFT, YORKS. (E.R.), in the Gothic style [Borthwick Institute, MGA 1841/1]. George Jackson died on 26 August 1842, aged 37, and is commemorated by a tombstone in Durham Cathedral graveyard.

JACKSON, GEORGE, of Hull, appears to have been the son of George Jackson, a joiner of that town. He designed the HULL SAVINGS BANK, POSTERNGATE, 1828–9; dem. [*Hull Advertiser*, 6 June 1828, *ex inf.* Mr. A. G. Chamberlain], and HORNSEA VICARAGE, YORKS. (E.R.), 1831–2, in conjunction with David Thorp [Borthwick Institute, York, MGA 1831/2, *ex inf.* Dr. David Neave].

JACKSON, JOHN (*c.*1602–1663), was a master mason much employed in Oxford in the middle of the seventeenth century. He came to Oxford from London in 1634 in order to superintend the building of the CANTERBURY QUADRANGLE at ST. JOHN'S COLLEGE after the failure of the original mason-contractors. He was paid a pound a week for overseeing the work, and is always referred to in the accounts as 'Mr. Jackson'. The design had already been settled before his employment, and there is no evidence that he was called upon to make any further drawings [Howard Colvin, *The Canterbury Quadrangle, St. John's College, Oxford*, 1988, *passim*]. After the completion of the new quadrangle at St. John's in 1636 Jackson settled in Oxford, where he was employed on various jobs, such as carving the niche for Charles I's bust in the Bodleian Library, for which he received £6 in 1641, building a buttress at the north-west corner of the Schools in 1650, and 'cleansing and polishing' the antique marbles given to the University by John Selden in 1660 [Wood, *Life and Times*, Oxford Hist. Soc. i, 320, iv, 57, 62]. In 1635–6 he was paid 10s. for his advice about the new tower and gateway being built at UNIVERSITY COLLEGE, and in 1637–8 provided the 'draughts' for the wooden gates [*V.C.H. Oxon.* iii, 75, see also 76]. A more important commission was the porch of ST. MARY'S CHURCH, which he built in 1637 in a style similar to that of the Canterbury Quadrangle [for the problem of its authorship see Colvin, *op. cit.*, Appendix VI]. In 1641–2 Jackson built and doubtless designed the gabled extension of the COOK'S BUILDING over the Kitchen at ST. JOHN'S COLLEGE [St. John's College Archives, *Computus Annuus* 1642/3, f. 25; Bursar's Private Accounts 1641–3, f. 67]. In 1656 he undertook to act as 'overseer' of the new Chapel and Library at BRASENOSE COLLEGE at one pound a week, and in 1659 was paid £20 'for his modell of the Roof of the new Chapple, and his paynes taken about it' [E. W. Allfrey, 'The Architectural History of the College', *Brasenose Quatercentenary Monographs* iii, 1909, 18–28.] From this it may be concluded that Jackson was probably the designer of the whole building, in which Gothic and classical motifs are combined in a quite sophisticated manner reminiscent of St. Mary's porch. In 1663 he made a 'modell' for completing the 'great gate' (i.e. Tom Tower) at Christ Church [W. G. Hiscock, *A Christ Church Miscellany*, 1946, 202], but nothing was done for nearly twenty years, and by then Jackson was dead. He died on 22 December 1663, and was buried in St. Mary Magdalen Church, where an inscription commemorated him as 'John Jackson, stone-carver, an ingenious artist, a loyall subject, an honest man and a good neighbour' [Wood, *City of Oxford*, ed. Clark, iii, 143]. His will, dated 7 December 1663, is witnessed by John Stone (*q.v.*) and Simon White, another Oxford mason and carver [Oxfordshire C.R.O., Oxford Archdeaconry Wills 136/4/9].

One other building can probably be attributed to Jackson: WELFORD PARK, BERKS., as built *c.*1660 for Richard Jones. According to an incomplete and undated draft contract in the Berks. C.R.O. (D/EAh E.13), Robert Kymber of Hungerford was to perform the carpentry of a new house at Welford 'according to such drafte modell manner order forme and direccion as John Jackson of the Cittie of Oxford gent. hath drawne described directed or set forth'. The house was remodelled by a later owner before 1695, but features of an earlier house with shorter pilasters and panelled brickwork survive.

JACKSON, JOHN GEORGE (*c.*1799–1851), was a pupil of P. F. Robinson, and was admitted to the Royal Academy Schools in 1817. He exhibited at the Academy from 1817 onwards and at the Society of British Artists in 1824 and 1831. In 1828–9 he published a volume of *Designs for Villas . . . adapted to the vicinity of the Metropolis, or large Towns*, all classical or Italianate in style. In 1831 he established himself at Leamington in Warwickshire, where he designed the NEWBOLD or JEPHSON GARDENS for Edward Willes, 1834; the classical EPISCOPAL CHAPEL, MILVERTON, 1836, dem. 1883; the Gothic ST. MARY'S CHURCH, 1838–9; the VICTORIA BRIDGE, 1839–40; and the TENNIS COURTS in BEDFORD STREET, 1844 [T. B. Dudley, *History of Leamington*, 1896–1900, 204, 209, 223, 237; Beck's *Leamington Guide*, 1840, 102]. Jackson was the architect first employed by the Revd. John Craig to realize the latter's ambitious designs for rebuilding the parish church of ALL SAINTS, LEAMINGTON, in a Continental Gothic style, but was dismissed in 1843 in favour of another local architect named Edmund Mitchell, who continued the building on lines already laid down by Jackson. Jackson defended himself vigorously in the *Builder* (see vol. i, 1843, 305, 335, 367, 381, 388; also *Ecclesiologist* ii, 1842, 93–4), and exhibited his design at the Birmingham Society of Artists in 1844. He also designed GAVESTON'S CROSS on BLACKLOW HILL, LEEK WOOTTON, WARWICKS., 1832 [signed drawing in Society of Antiquaries' Library, BP Warwicks. P2]; a new chancel for LEEK WOOTTON CHURCH, WARWICKS., 1843; rebuilt 1899 [exhibited at Birmingham 1844]; and added a north aisle to LILLINGTON CHURCH, WARWICKS., 1847 [*Ecclesiologist* viii, 1848, 260]. He died in June 1851, aged 52 [Leamington parish register].

JACKSON, RICHARD (1703–1751), of Armitage, Staffordshire, was a master builder active in Derbyshire and Staffordshire in the second quarter of the eighteenth century. He was descended from a family of masons, and in February 1724/5 either he or his father of the same name contracted to build WALTON HALL, WALTON-ON-TRENT, DERBYSHIRE, a plain brick house with stone dressings, for William Taylor, 'as in a draught thereof signed by both parties' [Northants. C.R.O., IC 4014]. The account-book of the Mayor of Derby for 1730–4 provides evidence that THE GUILDHALL, MARKET PLACE, DERBY, was built to his designs in 1731–2 [*ex inf.* Mr. Maxwell Craven]. Drawings made before its demolition in 1828 show that it was a pedimented building with giant Doric pilasters and windows with segmental heads. The same source shows that in 1734 Jackson built ST. ALKMUND'S VICARAGE, DERBY. In 1735–6 Jackson built a new house at BETLEY HALL, STAFFS. (dem.), for the 2nd Viscount Chetwynd [William Salt Library, Stafford, Chetwynd Papers, bundle 105], and in 1739–40 he was associated with Richard Trubshaw (*q.v.*) in rebuilding BASWICH CHURCH, STAFFS. [William Salt Library, Salt MS. 436]. [Information about the Jackson family from Mr. Philip Heath and Mr. Edward Saunders].

JACOBSEN, THEODORE (–1772), was descended from a family of German origin which managed the London Steelyard on behalf of the Hanseatic merchants. After the death of his brother Sir Jacob Jacobsen in 1735, Theodore became the senior member of the family, and carried on a successful business in the Steelyard. He latterly resided in Basinghall Street, and, though actively engaged in commerce, found time to practise as an amateur architect. His first recorded work was for the East India Company, who in 1726 decided to adopt 'the ground plat and front presented by Theodore Jacobsen, Esqr.' for their new buildings in Leadenhall Street (rebuilt 1799–1800 and demolished 1861–2). On its completion in 1729 the Directors were sufficiently pleased with the result to offer Jacobsen their formal thanks, together with a piece of plate worth 200 guineas, afterwards exchanged, at his own request, for a ring of equal value. The erection of the building was, however, supervised by John James, a surveyor possessed of the technical knowledge necessarily lacking in a busy City merchant, who at the time the EAST INDIA HOUSE was being built, was prosecuting a lawsuit of long standing with the Hanse Towns.

Jacobsen's best-known work was the FOUNDLING HOSPITAL, LONDON, erected between 1742 and 1752, and demolished in 1928 (*Arch. Rev.* lviii, 1925, 127–32). Four other architects submitted plans, but the fact that Jacobsen offered his gratuitously may have influenced the Governors in his favour. The execution of his designs was entrusted to James Horne (*q.v.*) who also gave his services free of charge. Designs for the interior of the chapel are in the Yale Center for British Art. In 1745 Jacobsen made the designs for another charitable institution, the ROYAL NAVAL HOSPITAL FOR SICK SAILORS at HASLAR, GOSPORT, nr. PORTSMOUTH, HANTS., of which there is an engraving in *Gent's Mag.* 1751, 408. The building was not completed until 1761. James Horne appears again to have acted as executant architect. A third public building for which Jacobsen furnished designs was the main quadrangle of TRINITY COLLEGE, DUBLIN, as built in 1752–9. In 1755 Hugh Darley, the surveyor in charge, wrote to John (*sic*) Keene in London to say that the north range and the north-west pavilion were ready for the cornice, but that suggestions had been made for alterations to 'Mr. Jacobsen's elevation' which the College was unwilling to adopt 'without the consent and approbation of Mr. Jacobsen'.[1] The proposed modifications involved the elimination of a dome over the central pediment and of cupolas on the pavilions and an adjustment of the position of the pilasters in the main elevation. It was no doubt as a result of these suggestions that the dome and cupolas were omitted, but in other respects the elevations presumably follow Jacobsen's design, and the rôle of Henry Keene and John Sanderson in providing plans and elevations (for which they were paid £74 11s. 8d.) must have been to make detailed working drawings from Jacobsen's no doubt relatively simple ones. It may be noted that there was evidently some connection between Keene and James Horne, who had been executant architect for Jacobsen's two previous buildings, and that one of Jacobsen's few surviving architectural designs (the elevation of a house) is among Keene's drawings in the Victoria and Albert Museum (see below).

In 1731 Jacobsen offered a design for the Bank of England's new building in Threadneedle Street, but that of George Sampson (*q.v.*) was preferred. The only record of Jacobsen's design appears to be an engraving of the main elevation among the Bank's records (see *An Historical Catalogue of Engravings, Drawings and Paintings in the Bank of England*, 1928, p. 3, no. 10).

Jacobsen's three executed public buildings have in common a quadrangular layout with corner pavilions. The architectural treatment is in each case fairly simple, an order being used only at Trinity College, where it is handled in a slightly clumsy manner consistent with an amateur designer. His proposed elevation for the Bank of England was that of a conventional English Palladian villa with Ionic pedimented centre-piece.

On the strength of a portrait of Jacobsen by Hogarth, signed and dated 1742, in which he is shown holding the plan of a triangular house, it has been supposed that he was the architect employed by Sir Jacob Bouverie to remodel the interior of Longford Castle, Wilts., from 1737 onwards. The plan depicted, however, is not that of Longford Castle, but corresponds with the 'section, plan, and elevation of a design for a triangular house, by Theodore Jacobsen, Esqr.', engraved by Fourdrinier, of which there is an impression in the Bodleian, Gough Maps 30, f. 75. It is possible that the idea of designing such a house was suggested by Longford Castle, and it is certain that Bouverie, who was himself a prominent London merchant, and Vice-President of the Foundling Hospital in 1740–1, must have known Jacobsen. Moreover, the portrait itself is said to have belonged to his descendants, the Earls of Radnor. There is, however, no mention of Jacobsen in the building accounts preserved at Longford, and it can only be conjectured that Bouverie may have asked Jacobsen to advise him about the alterations to his house.

The only other building known to have been designed by Jacobsen was his own house near Dorking in Surrey, known as LONESOME LODGE or TILLINGBOURNE, which he built in 1740 and made his summer residence until 1763, when he sold the estate to Jeremiah Joyce. The house, later known as Fillbrook Lodge, was demolished early in the nineteenth century, but there is an engraving of 'Lonesome Lodge at Wootton in Surry belonging to Theodore Jacobsen Esqr., designed by himself' in the Bodleian, Gough Maps 30, f. 76. Vertue, who dined with Jacobsen here in 1747, confirms that the house was of 'his own design and building' (Walpole Society, *Vertue Note Books* v, 155).

In his will (P.C.C., 137 TAVERNER), Jacobsen refers to his books of architecture, to a portfolio containing architectural drawings

[1] For a copy of this letter I am indebted to Dr. Edward McParland of Trinity College.

by himself, and to copper-plates of his designs. Two of the latter (of the triangular house and of the Foundling Hospital) are now in the Soane Museum. There is an elevation of a house 'Design'd by T. Jacobsen' in the Victoria and Albert Museum (E. 850–1921, A. 189). He died at an advanced age on 25 April 1772, and was buried in the family vault in the churchyard of All Hallows the Great, Upper Thames Street. He was a Fellow of the Royal and Antiquarian Societies, a member of the Society of Arts, and a Governor of the Foundling Hospital, where there is a full-length portrait of him painted by Hudson in 1746 (reproduced by Nichols and Wray, *History of the Foundling Hospital*, 1935, 42). The half-length portrait by Hogarth referred to above is now in the Museum at Oberlin, Ohio, U.S.A. It is reproduced in *C. Life*, 27 March 1942. It shows a jewelled ring on Jacobsen's left hand which is doubtless the one presented to him by the East India Company in 1729. Another portrait, showing Jacobsen holding a plan titled 'Portsmouth 1761' was for sale in London in 1972.

[*A.P.S.D.*; *D.N.B.*; W. Foster, *The East India House*, 1924; R. H. Nichols and F. A. Wray, *History of the Foundling Hospital*, 1935; P. Norman, 'Notes on the later History of the Steelyard in London', *Archaeologia* lxi (ii), 1909; *C. Life*, 27 March 1942, 621; Brayley, *History of Surrey* v, 69; *V.C.H. Surrey* iii, 155.]

JAFFRAY, ALEXANDER (1677–), Laird of Kingswells near Aberdeen, came of a Quaker family well-known in that city. His wife Christian was a daughter of Robert Barclay, the Quaker apologist. Alexander was active as an agricultural improver, and was also an architect and building contractor. In 1730 he visited London in order to see 'all the fine buildings and gardens'. In the following year he became the first Surveyor of Roads and Bridges in Aberdeenshire.

At KINGSWELLS Jaffray carried out alterations commemorated by his initials over the doorway, and in 1719–20 he was consulted by Sir Archibald Grant of MONYMUSK HOUSE, ABERDEENSHIRE. Jaffray offered to design a new house, but Grant preferred to alter the old one with Jaffray's advice [*Monymusk Papers*, ed. H. Hamilton, Scottish Historical Soc. 1945, xi, xlv, 77–9; Alistair Rowan, 'House of Monymusk', *C. Life*, 19–26 Oct. 1972]. In 1721 Jaffray and James Gibbs both made designs for altering or enlarging CULTER HOUSE, ABERDEENSHIRE, for Sir Alexander Cuming. The outcome is not clear, but in 1729 Jaffray made a plan of the Culter estate for a later owner, Patrick Duff of Premnay. In 1723–5 he built BALVENY HOUSE, BANFFSHIRE (dem. 1929) for William Duff of Braco to designs by James Gibbs which he modified slightly in execution. His principal independent work appears to have been ST. PAUL'S EPISCOPAL CHAPEL, ABERDEEN, a galleried classical building which he designed and built in 1721–2; dem. 1866 ['Alexander Jaffray's Recollections of Kingswells 1755–1800', ed. G. M. Fraser, *Third Spalding Club Miscellany* i, 1935; Montcoffer papers on temporary deposit with N.R.A. Scotland 1984, A/298/5 (St. Paul's Chapel), A/309/1 (Culter and St. Paul's Chapel), A/291(2)/1 (plan of Culter), A 315/9/35, A 317/6/8–25, A 318/3 (Balveny); W. G. Rowntree Brodie, 'St. Paul's Chapel, Aberdeen', *Proc. Soc. Antiquaries of Scotland*, cviii, 1976–7; information from Mr. Tristram Clarke].

JAFFRAY, GEORGE, was a builder and architect of Aberdeen, where he designed THE TOWN HOUSE, OLD ABERDEEN, 1787–8, in a simple Palladian style. A payment to him in the accounts for building POWIS HOUSE, OLD ABERDEEN, for Hugh Leslie in 1802–4 probably indicates that he designed that house, now part of the University [*Powis Papers*, ed. J. G. Burnett, Third Spalding Club 1951, 101, 335].

JAFFREY, *or* **JEFFRAY,** JAMES, is described in the 1787 Glasgow directory as 'architect, cabinet-maker and house wright'. In 1780 he designed ST. ENOCH'S CHURCH, GLASGOW, rebuilt (except the steeple) by David Hamilton in 1827–8; dem. 1925 [R. Chapman, *Picture of Glasgow*, 1822, 125], and in 1794 he rebuilt the nave of RUTHERGLEN PARISH CHURCH, LANARKS.; rebuilt 1900–2 [E. Williamson *et al.*, *Glasgow*, Buildings of Scotland, 1990, 491]. In the Glasgow University Archives [832] there is an unexecuted design by him for the termination of College Street. His unexecuted designs for the Trades House, dated 1791, are in the City Archives [T-KF 1/1, 23]. The inscription on his tomb in the Cathedral graveyard (lair 37) describes him as 'architect and builder', but does not give the date of his death [*ex inf.* Prof. J. Stevens Curl].

JAGGER, JOSEPH, worked in the Huddersfield area in the late eighteenth century, 'probably as a mason who made designs' [D. Linstrum, *West Yorkshire Architects and Architecture*, 1978, 379]. He was paid for 'planning, surveying and measuring' at KIRKLEES HALL, YORKS. (W.R.), in 1773 [D. Nortcliffe, 'The Restyling of Kirklees Hall 1753–1790', *Trans. Halifax Antiq. Soc.* 1982]; made estimates for rebuilding HOLMFIRTH and MELTHAM

CHURCHES, YORKS. (W.R.), in 1777 and 1782, respectively [*Yorks. Archl. Jnl.* xxxii, 1935, 349, 358]; and enlarged HIPPERHOLME GRAMMAR SCHOOL, YORKS. (W.R.) in 1783–4 [P. Facer, 'Hipperholme Grammar School', *Trans. Halifax Antiq. Soc.* 1970, 52]. John Jagger, perhaps a son, was in Henry Holland's office in the 1780s and died in 1795 [D. Stroud, *Henry Holland*, 1966, 41].

JAMES, JOHN (*c.*1673–1746), is stated on his monument in Eversley Church, Hants., to have been the eldest son of the Revd. John James, master of the Holy Ghost School at Basingstoke (1673), and afterwards vicar of Basingstoke (1697–1717), and rector of Stratfield Turgis (1717–33). In a letter to the Duke of Buckingham, dated 20 October 1711, James describes himself as 'a Parson's son',[1] and there is no evidence to support the statement in *D.N.B.* that his parents were Thomas and Eleanor James, the printers. Nothing is known of his early upbringing, but in his own estimation there was 'no person pretending to Architecture among us, Sir Chr. Wren excepted, [who] has had the advantage of a better Education in the Latin, Italian, and French Tongues', besides 'a competent share of Mathematicks and ten years Instruction in all the practical parts of Building by Mr. Banks, who was well known in their Majesty's Works'.[2] Matthew Bancks was Master Carpenter to the Crown from 1683 to 1706, and James was his apprentice from Feb. 1689/90 until March 1696/7, when he was admitted to the freedom of the Carpenters' Company. In 1698 he was an unsuccessful applicant for the post of Clerk of the Works at Greenwich Hospital, but was told that the committee, 'being well satisfied with his qualifications, will, as any opportunity shall offer, be ready to prefer him accordingly'. He was, in fact, employed as Store-Keeper and assistant Clerk of the Works at Greenwich from 1705 until 1718, when he became joint Clerk of the Works with Hawksmoor, the successful candidate of 1698, and remained in charge of the buildings of the Hospital until his death. In 1711, when Richard Jennings was dismissed from the works at St. Paul's Cathedral for fraud and embezzlement, James secured his position as master carpenter to the cathedral, and in 1715 he took Thomas Bateman's place as Assistant Surveyor under Sir Christopher Wren. On Wren's death in 1723, James succeeded him as Surveyor to the Fabric. Meanwhile, he had failed to secure one of the surveyorships to the Commissioners for Building Fifty New Churches under the Act of 1711, but had obtained the carpenter's contract for four of the new churches in partnership with Robert Jeffs of Westminster. In 1716, however, when James Gibbs, one of the two surveyors appointed by the Commissioners, was dismissed, John James was given his vacant post as Hawksmoor's colleague. By this time the designs of most of the new churches had been settled, but it was left to James to design St. George's, Hanover Square, and, in conjunction with Hawksmoor, two other churches that were to be 'as cheap as possible', namely St. Luke, Old Street, and St. John Horselydown. This appointment ceased in 1733, but Hawksmoor and James were paid 'for carrying on and finishing the Works under their Care' for some time afterwards, and the Commissioners were so pleased with the latter's services that they presented him with a gratuity of £52 10s. 'for his More than Ordinary attendance upon the works and the Commissioners'. In January 1724/5, James succeeded William Dickinson as Surveyor to the Dean and Chapter of Westminster, and in 1736, on Hawksmoor's death, he became also Surveyor to the Fabric of Westminster Abbey, under the Act of 1698 providing funds for its repair. It was in this capacity that between 1736 and 1745 he completed the west towers of the Abbey, in accordance with Hawksmoor's designs. He drew a 'North-West Prospect of Westminster Abbey with the Spire as design'd by Sr Christopher Wren' which was engraved by Fourdrinier and published in 1737 (*Wren Soc.* xi, pl. vi). James was Master of the Carpenters' Company in 1734.

James was a competent architect, but he lacked inventive fancy, and his buildings are for the most part plain and unadventurous in design. The obvious exceptions are Appuldurcombe, whose elaborate decorative treatment differs so much from that of all his other works as to raise some doubt whether it can have been wholly his design, and Wricklemarsh, in its day one of the grandest of Palladian mansions. His earlier buildings are often articulated by giant orders and fall in with the English baroque tradition. In 1711, however, James made a statement which suggests some sympathy with the Palladian revival then imminent. In the letter to the Duke of Buckingham already quoted he declared

[1] Bodleian Library, MS. Rawlinson B.376, f. 8.

[2] It may be noted that at this date he does not mention foreign travel among his qualifications, and it is scarcely possible that he can have been the J. James who signed the Visitors' Book of Padua University on 4 December 1717 (*Arch. Rev.* Nov. 1957, 344), for the Minutes of the Commissioners for St. Paul's Cathedral make it clear that he was in England in June 1717 and February 1718 (*Wren Soc.* xvi, 129, 131).

that his ambition was to show 'that the Beautys of Architecture may consist with the greatest plainness of the structure', something that he claimed 'has scarce ever been hit on by the Tramontani unless by our famous Mr. Inigo Jones'. Though most of James's buildings were plain in the sense that they lacked baroque enrichments, Wricklemarsh was the only one that was consciously Palladian in the now accepted sense of the term. Its early demolition in 1787 has until recently deprived it of recognition as a pioneer Palladian mansion, almost exactly contemporary with Houghton and equally innovatory in its adoption of a format that was to be repeated at Woburn, Hagley and elsewhere.

As a surveyor James was eminently competent and trustworthy, and was much employed in this capacity, particularly by ecclesiastical patrons. In 1725, when he was a candidate for the under-surveyorship of Westminster Abbey, the subcommittee reported that 'tho' many persons well recommended both for their skill and honesty, did lately apply ... to succeed Mr. Dickenson as Surveyor of the College, yet the Dean and Chapter did unanimously chuse Mr. James into that office, who neither was recommended by any Person, nor did appear himself a Candidate for the same' (Westminster Abbey Muniment 34885), and in the same year Baron Comyns characterized him as 'a person of unquestioned skill and fidelity', in connection with a survey of Serjeants' Inn which he had carried out for the Dean and Chapter of York (Bodleian, MS. Rawl. C.441, f. 26). In 1711 he had been able to send Harley a long list of 'Persons of Quality' who would vouch for his character, and many of whom he had 'served in the business of their Buildings'. The list is as follows: 'Duke of Buckingham, Duke of Leeds, E. of Pembroke &c., Ld. Vic^{t}. Weymouth, Ld. Lempster, Mr. Benson Chancel^{r}. of the Excheq^{r}, Mr. Aislabie [and] Mr. Geo: Clark Lds. of ye Admty., Mr. John Hill, Sr. Charles Hedges, Sr. James Bateman, Sr. Willm. Gifford, Mr. James Johnston, Mr. Geo: Pitt of Hampshire &c.' (B.L., Harley Papers, xlvi).

After the death of Archbishop Tenison (Dec. 1715), James carried out a survey of the archiepiscopal palaces at Lambeth and Croydon, which was made the basis of a demand for dilapidations by his successor Archbishop Wake. This was contested by Tenison's executors, and James took part in the pamphlet warfare which ensued, publishing in 1717 *The Survey and Demand for Dilapidations in the Archiepiscopal See of Canterbury Justified against the Cavils and Misrepresentations contained in Some letters lately printed by Mr. Archdeacon Tenison.* Copies of Tenison's printed letter, which attacks James personally, and quotes from his report, are preserved in Cambridge University Library, MS. 2508, and in Bodleian, Gough Kent 16. James also engaged in the controversy over the design of Westminster Bridge, publishing *A Short Review of the several Pamphlets and Schemes that have been offered to the Publick in relation to the Building of a Bridge at Westminster*, 1736, in which he criticized those of John Price, Nicholas Hawksmoor, and Batty Langley (the last of whom published a reply in 1737). James's own design, though not accepted by the Commissioners, was stated by Ripley, the assessor, to be 'clearly and well described' (Commissioners' Minutes, vol. i, f. 83 [P.R.O., WORK 6/28]). A drawing by him for the central part of a large bridge is among Lord Burlington's drawings from Chatsworth now in the R.I.B.A. Drawings Collection (F. 14). James also made unexecuted designs for the Clarendon Building, Oxford, *c.*1710 (Colvin, *Catalogue of Architectural Drawings at Worcester College*, pl. 104), for St. Martin-in-the-Fields Church, 1720, for the Senate House at Cambridge, 1722, and for the Mansion House, London, 1734 (S. Perks, *The Mansion House*, 1922, pls. 37–40).

In 1729 James was induced to join with his brother Thomas, a typefounder, William Fenner, a stationer, and James Ged, in their unsuccessful attempt to carry out William Ged's system of block-printing or stereotyping. He is said to have been 'taken into partnership as having money, and as being universally acquainted with the nobility and dignified clergy'. His loss was proportionately severe when the venture became a total failure in 1738. He died at Greenwich, after a lingering illness, on 15 May 1746. His will (P.C.C., 155 EDMUNDS) directs that his estate at Eversley in Hants. shall be sold for the benefit of his widowed daughter-in-law, Mrs. Frances James, and that his property on Croom's Hill, Greenwich, shall be similarly disposed of for the benefit of his wife Mary. He was buried in the churchyard at Eversley, and there is an inscription to his memory in the north aisle of the church.[1] Besides the pamphlets already mentioned, he published *Rules and Examples of Perspective, proper for Painters and Architects*, translated from the Italian of Andrea Pozzo (Rome 1693), 1707, with the 'approbation' of Wren, Vanbrugh and Hawksmoor, 2nd. ed. *c.*1725; *A Treatise of the Five Orders of Columns in Architecture*, from the French of Claude Perrault (Paris

[1] Printed in *Collectanea Topographica et Genealogica* viii, 1834, 64.

1683), 1708[1]; and *The Theory and Practice of Gardening*, from the French of Dezallier d'Argenville (Paris 1709), 1712, 2nd ed. 1728, 3rd ed. 1743. James's interest in gardening is also attested by his membership of the Society of Gardeners which published a *Catalogus Plantarum or Catalogue of Trees, Shrubs, etc. for sale in the Gardens near London* in 1730.

[*A.P.S.D.*; *D.N.B.*; *Wren Soc.*, passim; Walpole, *Anecdotes of Painting*, ed. Wornum, 1862, 696; H.M. Colvin, 'Fifty New Churches', *Arch. Rev.* March 1950, reprinted as introduction to *The Queen Anne Churches*, ed. E. G. W. Bill, 1979; Willis & Clark i, 195, iii, 44, 54; Hist. MSS. Comm., *Portland* x, 120–1; *Biographical Memoir of W. Ged*, 1781 (S. Hodgson, Newcastle Reprints, 1819); K. A. Esdaile in *Times Literary Supplement*, 5 July 1941, 328; Sally Jeffery, 'John James', unpublished doctoral thesis, London University 1986; Eileen Harris, *British Architectural Books and Writers 1556–1785*, 1990, 242–5.]

ECCLESIASTICAL WORK

DEAL, KENT, ST. GEORGE'S CHURCH, surveying and advice, 1712–16. The church was built and perhaps designed by a Deal man, Samuel Simmons, in 1706, but completion was delayed by local squabbles, and a fresh contract for the carpentry of the roof was made in 1712 with James's advice [John Laker, *History of Deal*, 1917, 258–63; Kent Archives Office, Chapelwardens' accounts, De QC1, p. 32].

TWICKENHAM, MIDDLESEX, ST. MARY'S CHURCH, rebuilt, except W. tower, 1714–15 [D. Lysons, *Environs of London* ii (2), 1811, 788]. The galleries were altered in 1859.

ROTHERHITHE, SURREY (now LONDON), ST. MARY'S CHURCH, 1714–15; steeple added 1747–8; interior altered 1876 [P. & S. Jeffery in *C. Life*, 20 April 1989].

WHITCHURCH, MIDDLESEX, ST. LAWRENCE'S CHURCH, rebuilt for 1st Duke of Chandos, 1714–16 [C. H. & M. I. Collins Baker, *The Life of James Brydges, Duke of Chandos*, 1949, 116–24].

TIVERTON, DEVONSHIRE, ST. GEORGE'S CHAPEL, 1714–33; re-roofed 1841–2. There are no building records, but in 1716 a benefactor left £1000 towards the cost of construction on condition that the church was completed according to a model given by 'Mr. James, surveyor' [W. Harding, *History of Tiverton* ii, 1849, 236].

attributed: ABBOTS ANN CHURCH, HANTS., for Thomas ('Governor') Pitt, 1715–16 [Sally Jeffery, thesis as cited, 259–60].

WORCESTER CATHEDRAL, 'viewed the dilapidations' for the Dean and Chapter, 1718 [Treasurer's Book, 1718, *ex inf.* Mr. D Whitehead].

CAMBRIDGE, GONVILLE AND CAIUS COLLEGE CHAPEL, rebuilt east end and designed altarpiece 1718–26; dem. 1870 [Willis & Clark, i, 195].

LONDON, ST. GEORGE'S CHURCH, HANOVER SQUARE, 1721–5; redecorated by B. Ferrey 1871 [Lambeth Palace Library; records of the Commissioners for building Fifty New Churches; a drawing by James for the north elevation is in the R.I.B.A. Collection].

LONDON, ST. PAUL'S CATHEDRAL, High Altar, 1725; dem. 1886. No altar of an architectural character was erected until 1725, when the sculptor Francis Bird was paid £323 17s. for 'Mason's work done & Marble Work done at the Altar' [Guildhall Library, MS. 25481/8, f. 77v, receipt book for cathedral works]. John James was the Surveyor of the Cathedral at the time, and on 25 Sept. 1725 the *Norwich Gazette* recorded that 'a very curious Altar has been some Months setting up at St. Paul's Cathedral, design'd by Mr. James of Greenwich'. James also designed the font, for which he was asked to prepare a design in Feb. 1717 [*Wren Soc.* xvi, 128], but which was apparently not made until 1726–7, when Bird was paid £354 for it [MS. 25481/8, f. 83].

LINCOLN CATHEDRAL, advised on strengthening of west towers, 1726 [J. W. F. Hill, 'The western spires of Lincoln Minster and their threatened removal in 1726', *Lincolnshire Architectural Soc's Reports* N.S. v(ii) 1954].

CRANBROOK CHURCH, KENT, survey after partial collapse and recommendations for rebuilding that were rejected by the parishioners, 1726 [letter from James to Archbishop Wake in Christ Church, Oxford, Library, Wake Letters, vol. 23, no. 122].

LONDON, ST. JOHN'S CHURCH, HORSELYDOWN, SOUTHWARK, 1727–33; bombed 1940 and subsequently dem.; designed jointly with Hawksmoor [Lambeth Palace Library, Minutes of the Commissioners for Building Fifty New Churches, vol. ii, 415, 418].

LONDON, ST. LUKE'S CHURCH, OLD STREET, 1727–33; unroofed and dismantled 1960; designed jointly with N. Hawksmoor [Lambeth Palace Library, Minutes as above].

GREENWICH, KENT, ST. ALPHEGE'S CHURCH, added the steeple to Hawksmoor's church, 1730; rebuilt 1813 after damage by lightning [Lambeth Palace Library, Minutes as above, vol. iii, 34].

[1] A proof copy presented to Sir William Gifford is in Worcester College Library (B.2.2).

ROCHESTER CATHEDRAL, KENT, repaired roof of S. transept, etc., 1730–2 [G. H. Palmer, *The Cathedral Church of Rochester*, 1897, 29].

SOUTHAMPTON, ST. MICHAEL'S CHURCH, directed rebuilding of spire, 1733; heightened 9 feet 1877–8 [D. C. Cotton, *History of St. Michael's Church*, Southampton 1970, 18].

LONDON, ST. MARGARET'S CHURCH, WESTMINSTER, repaired and refaced tower with Portland stone and raised it 20 ft., adding a Gothic belfry storey, 1735 [Westminster City Library, MS. Parish records].

SALISBURY CATHEDRAL, advice about repairs, 1736–7 [Salisbury Diocesan Records, bills and accounts, 1736–7].

WESTMINSTER ABBEY, completed west towers to designs of N. Hawksmoor, 1736–45, Gothic [*Wren Soc.* xi, 11–12].

PUBLIC AND DOMESTIC ARCHITECTURE

NORTHFIELD MANOR, NORTHFIELD, WORCS. (now Birmingham University Hall of Residence), for Thomas Jervoise of Herriard Park, Hants., 1701–3; since altered at various times [S. Jeffery in *Trans. Birmingham & Warwicks. Archl. Soc.* 92, 1985].

APPULDURCOMBE HOUSE, ISLE OF WIGHT, for Sir Robert Worsley, Bart., *c.*1701–13; dismantled but preserved as an Ancient Monument. The evidence for John James's responsibility for this house is set out by L. O. J. Boynton, *Appuldurcombe House*, H.M.S.O. 1986, 26–7. It is not sufficient to prove beyond doubt that the design of this unusual house was wholly due to James, but if any other architect was involved, his identity remains unknown. (*Vitruvius Britannicus* iii, 1725, pl. 61.)

HERRIARD PARK, HANTS., for Thomas Jervoise, 1703–6; dem. 1965 [S. Jeffery, 'John James . . . at Herriard', *Arch. Hist.* 28, 1985] (*C. Life*, 1 July, 1965).

TWICKENHAM, MIDDLESEX, house (afterwards ORLEANS HOUSE), for the Hon. James Johnston, Secretary for Scotland, completed 1710, to which James Gibbs added the octagon room in 1720. The house was restored by J. B. Papworth 1837–9, but dem. 1927 except the octagon room [*Vitruvius Britannicus* i, 1715, pl. 77].

CANNONS HOUSE, MIDDLESEX. James was called in by the 1st Duke of Chandos after Talman had been dismissed in 1714. James made designs for remodelling the old house which were in part executed before James Gibbs took his place as the duke's architect in 1715 [C. H. & M. I. Collins Baker, *The Life of James Brydges, Duke of Chandos*, 1949, 116–24].

PARK HALL, CROOMS HILL, GREENWICH, built 1717–19 as his own intended residence, but never in fact occupied by him; since much altered [F. Kelsall in *Trans. Greenwich & Lewisham Antiquarian Soc.* viii, 1977, 210–33].

SWALLOWFIELD PARK, BERKS., alterations and additions (including bridge in park), for Thomas Pitt, *c.*1720–2; remodelled by W. Atkinson 1820 [accounts in P.R.O., C104/424].

WARBROOKS HOUSE, EVERSLEY, HANTS., for himself, 1724 [inscription on his monument: 'The said John James Built the House called Warbrooks in this Parish Anno 1724'] (*C. Life*, 11–18 March, 1939).

WRICKLEMARSH, BLACKHEATH, KENT, for Sir Gregory Page, Bart., *c.*1724–7; dem. 1787–1800 [*Vitruvius Britannicus* iv, 1767, pls. 58–64] (Watts's *Views of Seats*, pl. xlvii, 1782; elevation by T. Milton in B.M. Print Room). The portico and other materials were re-used by John Cator at Beckenham Place, Kent, and four chimney-pieces were removed to the First Lord's House, Whitehall (illustrated in *C. Life*, 24 Nov. 1923, 723) (John Brushe, 'Wricklemarsh and the Collections of Sir Gregory Page', *Apollo*, Nov. 1985).

LONDON, THE EAST INDIA HOUSE, LEADENHALL STREET, supervised erection to designs of Theodore Jacobsen (*q.v.*), 1726–9; rebuilt 1796–9.

attributed: MUCH HADHAM HALL, HERTS., for Revd. W. Stanley, formerly Canon of St. Paul's, 1726–9 [Gordon Nares in *C. Life*, 5 April 1956].

PICTON CASTLE, PEMBROKESHIRE, summer-house for Sir John Philipps, Bart., 1728, dem.; built according to a design 'sent from London by Mr. James, the Surveyor, [but] not entirely followed' [Journal of Erasmus Philipps, *ex inf.* Mr. Thomas Lloyd].

STANDLYNCH (now TRAFALGAR) HOUSE, WILTS., for Sir Peter Vandeput, 1731–33; portico and wings added 1766 [S. Jeffery in *C. Life*, 13 Feb. 1986] (*C. Life*, 13–20 July 1945).

LONDON, BISHOPSGATE GATE, supervised construction 1733–4; dem. 1760 [T. F. Friedman, 'The Rebuilding of Bishopsgate', *Guildhall Studies in London History* iv (2), 1980].

BAYLIES HOUSE, SLOUGH, BUCKS., altered and enlarged for Francis Godolphin, 1733–5 [accounts in Duke of Leed's papers in Bucks. C.R.O.].

LONDON, tenements off LONDON WALL known as CARPENTERS' BUILDINGS, for the Carpenters' Company, 1735–7; dem. 1876 [S. Jeffery, 'John James and Carpenters'

Buildings', *Trans. London & Middlesex Archl. Soc.* 34, 1983].

WELBECK ABBEY, NOTTS., reconstructed south wing and remodelled west front for Henrietta, Countess of Oxford, 1742–6. The west front was remodelled by Repton in 1790 and the south front was rebuilt in 1860 and again in 1901 [A. S. Turberville, *Welbeck Abbey and its Owners* i, 1938, 394–6].

JAMES, WILLIAM (1785–1880), of Stone, near Berkeley in Gloucestershire, was the son of William James (*c.*1747–1834), a carpenter of that place. As a builder-architect he designed parsonages in Gloucestershire at CROMHALL, 1817–18, SLIMBRIDGE, 1818–20, FRAMPTON-ON-SEVERN, 1838, and STANDISH, 1839; a poorhouse at ALDERLEY, 1825; National Schools at FRAMPTON-ON-SEVERN, 1842–3, and HAWKESBURY, 1845–6; and rebuilt EASTON GREY CHURCH, WILTS., 1836, and LITTLE SODBURY CHURCH, GLOS., 1859, both agreeable buildings in an unpretentious late Gothic style [Gloucestershire C.R.O., GDR/F4/1 (for parsonages), D 2186 (for schools); I.C.B.S. (for churches); Gloucester Library RF.7.9 (for poorhouse), RF. 274. 15 (for Slimbridge parsonage)]. A tombstone in Stone churchyard records his death on 23 Sept. 1880 at the age of 95.

JANSSEN, BERNARD, was one of the sons of Gerard or Garet Janssen or Johnson, a native of Amsterdam who came to England in about 1567, settled in Southwark, married an English wife, and had several sons, of whom Bernard, John, Nicholas and a younger Gerard all followed his profession. In about 1620 Bernard Janssen made a finely-carved altar-tomb in REDGRAVE CHURCH, SUFFOLK, to support the effigies of Sir Nicholas and Lady Bacon made by Nicholas Stone [*Walpole Soc.* vii, 52]. In 1619–20 he also made in London a monument to Marcel Bax, governor of Bergen-op-Zoom, which was set up in the church there but destroyed during a bombardment in 1622 [*Messager des Sciences Historiques des Arts de Belgique*, 1858, 93–4]. Stone's great-nephew Charles Stoakes told George Vertue that Janssen was the surveyor of NORTHUMBERLAND HOUSE, STRAND (*c.*1605–9, dem. 1874), AUDLEY END, ESSEX (*c.*1605–16, partly dem. 1708), 'and many other buildings' [Walpole Soc., *Vertue Note Books* ii, 49]. As the 1st Earl of Northampton, who built Northumberland House, played some part in the construction of Audley End for his nephew the 1st Earl of Suffolk, it is very probable that the same surveyor was employed for both buildings, and the same repertoire of Anglo-Flemish ornament was a prominent feature of both houses.

It is possible that a Bernard Johnson employed as a military engineer to survey the Tower of London and other royal fortifications in 1624–5 was the same person. In his claim for remuneration he stated he had been 'enforced to sett aside my former Practize and Customers' in order to work for the Crown in that capacity [*History of the King's Works* iii, 247, 275; B.L., Add. MS. 5732, f. 317].

JARMAN, EDWARD, *see* JERMAN, EDWARD.

JARRATT, THOMAS (–1785), was an Irish military engineer who was commissioned in 1760 and reached the rank of Major in 1780. In 1781, perhaps in retirement, he designed the TOWN HALL at LANCASTER, with a handsome Roman Doric façade, and was given the freedom of the corporation 'for his trouble in drawing the plan'. In the following year, however, it was concluded that the cupola shown in Jarratt's drawings would be 'inexpedient and dangerous to build', and one designed by Thomas Harrison (*q.v.*) was substituted [K. Docton, 'Lancaster Town Hall', *Lancashire & Cheshire Historian*, August 1965, 146–7]. Jarratt died on 2 December 1785 [T. W. J. Conolly, *Roll of Officers of the Corps of Royal Engineers*, Chatham 1898, 112].

JAY, WILLIAM (*c.*1793–1837), was the son of a nonconformist minister at Bath, whose father had been a stonemason. He was articled to D. R. Roper, and began to exhibit student's work at the Royal Academy in 1809. He designed the ALBION CHAPEL, MOORFIELDS, LONDON, 1815–16, dem. 1879, a building which, according to Elmes, possessed 'a character of original thinking in its design that is highly pleasing' [*Metropolitan Improvements*, 1831, 170]. In 1817 Jay emigrated to Savannah, U.S.A., where he designed several public buildings and some houses, of which the best-known example is now the Owens-Thomas House Museum. His Telfair and Scarbrough Houses are notable as being among the earliest monuments of the Greek Revival in America. In 1822 or 1823 he returned to England and worked for a time in Cheltenham. In June 1825 he offered to make designs for a new church there for the Church Building Commissioners [Church Commissioners records, C.B.C. MB. 18, 21 June 1825], and in the Gloucestershire Record Office there is a set of designs by him for a terrace [D. 1388] which closely resembles COLUMBIA PLACE, WINCHCOMBE STREET, CHELTENHAM. Another plan in the same collection marked 'Mr. Mullings' house' establishes Jay as the designer of WATERMOOR HOUSE, CIRENCESTER, GLOS., built 1825–7 for J. R. Mullings, a business associate of Joseph Pitt, of Pittville, Cheltenham. A drawing in the Cheltenham Museum dated 1826 and inscribed 'design by Mr. Jay for Pitville Parade' shows that he also began PITTVILLE PARADE, now Nos. 2–34 EVESHAM ROAD, CHELTENHAM (of which only the first two houses were built to Jay's design). In 1827 Jay married a Henley girl named Louisa Coulson, and in 1829 enlarged the CONGREGATIONAL CHURCH at HENLEY-ON-THAMES, whose minister, the Revd. Robert Bolton, had married his sister [*Berkshire Chronicle*, 6 June 1829]. After financial difficulties culminating in bankruptcy, Jay obtained a post as Assistant Chief Architect and Inspector of Works in the Colony of Mauritius, where he died on 17 April 1837.

[*The Autobiography of the Revd. William Jay*, ed. G. Redford & J. A. James, 1855, 94; B. St. J. Ravenel, *Architects of Charleston*, Charleston, U.S.A., 1945, chap. 17; G. L. M. Goodfellow, 'William Jay and the Albion Chapel', *Jnl. Society of Architectural Historians* [of America], xxii, 1963, 225; *Gent's Mag.* 1837 (ii), 660; information from Prof. Hanna Lerski, the late David Verey and the late Canon B. F. L. Clarke.]

JEANS, JOHN (*c.*1720–*c.*1800), was an architect and builder of Aberdeen, where he died in or shortly before 1800, aged 80 [S.R.O., CC 1/6/64, f. 13; Aberdeen City Library, G. M. Fraser's MS. Notes and Jottings, vol. 17, p. 73]. In Aberdeen he designed the MEAL MARKET, 1770 [Fraser, *op. cit.*, p. 75, citing Council Register vol. 63, pp. 151, 161]. In 1754 he made a plan, probably not executed, for TROUP, BANFFSHIRE, the house of Alexander Garden [S.R.O., GD 345/1173/3/27, 26 Nov. 1754]. His estimate, dated 17 Jan. 1759, for additions to BALAVIL or BELLEVILLE HOUSE, INVERNESS-SHIRE, is in the S.R.O., together with a competently drawn plan and elevations [GD 1/32/4, GD 57/1/124 and RHP 42088–9].

JEANS, THOMAS (*c.*1775–1866), was the son of Dr. T. Jeans of Christchurch, Hants. He became a pupil of Sir John Soane and subsequently held the post of architect to the Barrack Department of the War Office, in which capacity he designed a number of barracks erected during the Napoleonic Wars. He retired after the Peace of 1815 and an ample pension and a fortunate marriage made it unnecessary for him to practise thereafter. He was in Italy in 1819 and on his return became one of the original members of the Architects' and Antiquaries' Club. He was also a Fellow of the Society of Antiquaries. [A. T. Bolton, *The Works of Sir John Soane*, 1924, Appendix C, p. xli; *The Times*, 30 Nov. 1866; R.I.B.A. Archive LC/4/7/18; Principal Probate Registry, Calendar of Probates.]

JEARRAD, ROBERT WILLIAM (– 1861), practised from 260 Oxford Street, London, from about 1810 onwards. For some years he was in partnership with Charles Jearrad, who was probably his brother. He died on 14 January 1861, leaving a son, R. W. Jearrad, junior, who had assisted his father since the 1840s.

The Jearrads were both architects and builders, and in 1830 they took over an extensive speculative building development on the Lansdowne estate in CHELTENHAM from the banker Henry Thompson, dismissing his architect J. B. Papworth and managing the whole concern themselves. They completed LANSDOWNE CRESCENT on the lines indicated by Papworth, built the Italianate villas in LANSDOWNE COURT, perhaps to Papworth's designs, but more probably to their own, and built LANSDOWNE PARADE to their own designs in 1838–41. They also designed the LITERARY AND PHILOSOPHICAL INSTITUTION, with Greek Doric portico, in the Promenade in 1835–6 (dem.), the imposing QUEEN'S HOTEL, 1837–8, and the Gothic CHRIST CHURCH, MALVERN ROAD, 1838–40, of which they exhibited a model at the Royal Academy in 1838. The Jearrads must accordingly be classed with Burton and Cubitt as leading developer-architects of the early nineteenth century, and Cheltenham is as much their monument as it is Papworth's.

In 1835 R. W. Jearrad competed for the Houses of Parliament, but nothing is known about the character of his design. In 1815 C. Jearrad exhibited at the R.A. designs for alterations to a mansion in Poland for General Count Pack.

[H. Davis, *Cheltenham in its Present and Past State*, 1843, 113, 187, 190; Rowe's *Illustrated Cheltenham Guide*, 1845, 18; David Verey, *Gloucestershire*, Buildings of England, ii, 1970, 124, 141–2.]

Elsewhere R. W. Jearrad is known to have designed the following buildings:

HAMPTONS, WEST PECKHAM, KENT, for the Dalison family, exhibited at R.A. as 'now building' in 1813, but said by Greenwood, *Epitome of County History: Kent*, 1838, 140, to have been built in 1820; interior reconstructed after fire in 1883.

BADSWORTH RECTORY, YORKS (W.R.), designs

for alterations and additions, 1822 [Borthwick Institute, MGA 1822/2].

WELBECK ABBEY, NOTTS., alterations in the castellated style for 4th Duke of Portland, *c.*1826 [A. S. Turberville, *Welbeck Abbey and its Owners* ii, 1938, 392].

MALVERN WELLS, WORCS., ST. PETER'S CHURCH, 1835–6, Gothic [B. S. Smith, *History of Malvern*, 1964, 222].

HEREFORD, ST. MARTIN'S CHURCH, 1845, Gothic [I.C.B.S.; *A.P.S.D.*, *s.v.* 'Hereford'].

BIRKENHEAD, CHESHIRE, CHRIST CHURCH, CLAUGHTON, 1844–9, Gothic [*A.P.S.D.*, *s.v.* 'Birkenhead'].

LONDON, ST. MARK'S SCHOOLS, NORTH AUDLEY STREET, alterations, 1849 [*Survey of London* xl, 109].

JEFFERY, THOMAS, is known only as the designer of a fantastic Gothic villa called BELMONT CASTLE at GRAYS THURROCK in ESSEX, which he designed for Zacharias Button in 1795; dem. *c.*1945. Jeffery published two engravings of the house of which there are copies in B.L., *King's Maps* xiii, 20, a, b. One of these is reproduced in *Essex Homes* (Essex County Council, 1965), fig. 47.

JELFE, ANDREWS (–1759), master mason, was the son of William Jelfe of South Weald, Essex. His mother's maiden name was Andrews. He was made free of the London Masons' Company in 1711 by service with Edward Strong, to whom he had been apprenticed in 1704, and was subsequently in partnership with Edward Strong, junior, and Christopher Cass, until December 1728, when Strong withdrew [B.L., Stowe MS. 412, f. 98, no. 77]. His partnership with Cass continued until the latter's death in 1734. Jelfe was later in partnership with George Mercer, who succeeded Cass as Master Mason to the Board of Ordnance. He himself held a post in the Office of Works as Clerk of the Works at Newmarket from 1715 to 1718, and Clerk Itinerant from 1715 to 1728. In January 1719 he was appointed 'Architect and Clerk of the Works of all buildings erected or to be erected in the several garrisons, forts, castles, fortifications etc., belonging to the Office of Ordnance in Great Britain', and went up to Scotland to begin the erection of the barracks at Ruthven and Bernera as well as to continue those at Kiliwhimen and Inversnaid already begun by his predecessor James Smith. In the following year he was transferred to Plymouth, to supervise the construction of a new Gun Wharf or Ordnance Yard there [P.R.O., WO 47/32, ff. 21, 83, 105, 270; 47/33, ff. 16, 17, 36, 58, 158; 51/101, ff. 4, 41; 55/490]. Some of his drawings (for the Scottish fortifications) are in the National Library of Scotland (Z2/2, 2a, 10, 26a, etc.). While in Scotland he was made a burgess of Edinburgh [Edinburgh Town Council Minutes, vol. 48, p. 11].

In England Jelfe was chiefly employed as a mason-contractor. He had masonry contracts for some of the Fifty New Churches built in London under the Act of 1711, and his account and letter-book, now B.L., Add. MS. 27587, shows that he also executed monumental sculpture, chimney-pieces, and other statuary work. His biggest contract was the building of WESTMINSTER BRIDGE to the designs of Charles Labelye. For this he was in partnership with Samuel Tufnell, the Master Mason to Westminster Abbey. The contracts were signed on 22 June 1738, and the bridge was completed in 1747. Jelfe successfully overcame the structural problems caused by the sinking of the central pier by springing relieving arches across the spandrels of the adjacent arches, an expedient suggested by his friend William Stukeley, the antiquary [R. J. B. Walker, *Old Westminster Bridge*, 1979, 185 and *passim*]. Designs by Jelfe for a house (unexecuted) for Mr. Butler on Barn Hill, Stamford (1731), and for an ornamental alcove (1753), are preserved among Stukeley's collections in the Library of the Wiltshire Archaeological Society at Devizes, and in the Bodleian Library (MS. Top. Gen. d. 14, p. 59). While in Scotland in 1719, Jelfe made measured drawings of the Roman monument known as 'Arthur's O'on', which Stukeley afterwards had engraved (see Bodleian, Gough Maps 40, ff. 6[v], 7[v], and Stukeley's *Account of a Roman Temple and other Antiquities near Grahams-Dike in Scotland*, 1720). There is a portrait of Jelfe by Stukeley, dated January 1722/3, in Bodleian, MS. Eng. Misc. e. 136, f. 30. In 1744 he was fined for the office of sheriff of London and Middlesex [*Gent's Mag.* xiv, 333].

Jelfe's most important work as an architect was probably the COURT HOUSE or TOWN HALL at RYE in SUSSEX, which was built to his designs in 1743 [L. A. Vidler in *N. & Q.* 177, 1939, 11, and Add. MS. 27587, f. 106[v]]. A contemporary model is preserved in the building, and there are measured drawings in *Arch. Rev.* lx, 1926, 76–7. It is a competently designed building in what by 1743 was the somewhat outmoded style of the early eighteenth century. Jelfe's letter-book shows that he rebuilt WARESLEY CHURCH, HUNTS., in 1728 (dem. 1856), and that in 1734 he carried out works at EXNING HOUSE, SUFFOLK, where he added a stone door-case for Francis Shepherd, and at ABINGTON LODGE, CAMBS., for Col. Vachell. In 1741 he built thirteen houses 'in Two Rows adjoyning together on the North side of New Palace Yard and on the South side of Bridge Street, Westminster', of which he afterwards purchased the freehold from the Westminster Bridge Commissioners. His yard and wharf were in New Palace Yard: their position is shown on a plan in the Crowle Pennant in the British Library, ii, f. 100. In 1747 Jelfe bought for his own residence Pendrell House at Bletchingley, Surrey, where he formed the entrance courtyard and built the wall at the west end of the garden [U. Lambert, *Bletchingley* i, 1921, 316–17]. This property he left to his elder son, Captain Andrew Jelfe, R.N. He left his stone-built dwelling-house in New Palace Yard to his daughter Elizabeth, wife of Griffen Ransom, a timber merchant, together with his wharf and yard, then in occupation of his nephew William Jelfe (perhaps a son of Robert Jelfe, master carpenter), whom he had taken into partnership, and who died in 1771 (*London Magazine*, 1771, 472). He also left £10,000 to his daughter, and a similar sum to his younger son William, 'who has proved very idle and extravagant' [P.C.C., 173 ARRAN]. He desired to be buried at South Weald, where the 'surcophragus' which he had erected to the memory of his parents can still be seen on the south side of the tower. He died on 26 April 1759.

JELLY, THOMAS (–1781) was an architect and builder of Bath who made very competent designs in the Palladian manner and was probably responsible for many buildings in that town that have been ascribed to his better-known contemporary, John Wood. His best surviving buildings are KING EDWARD'S GRAMMAR SCHOOL, BROAD STREET, 1752–4, and the houses in ABBEY STREET, which he built in partnership with a mason called Henry Fisher on land leased from the Duke of Kingston in 1762 [B.L., Egerton MS. 3647, f. 113]. He also designed the adjoining KINGSTON BATHS, 1763–6, dem. *c.*1885. He was for a time in partnership with John Palmer (*q.v.*), and to either Jelly or Palmer must be attributed the design of houses such as NORTH PARADE BUILDINGS and those in MILSON STREET, in whose erection Jelly is known to have been concerned. [W. Ison, *The Georgian Buildings of Bath*, 1948, 2nd ed. 1980, *passim*]. Jelly died on 19 May 1781 [*Bath Chronicle*, 23 May 1781].

JENKINS, EDWARD, practised for a time in Cheltenham, where he designed ST. JAMES'S CHURCH, SUFFOLK SQUARE, 1825, Gothic. He got into difficulties with the enormous span of the roof, and J. B. Papworth had to be called in to help [Wyatt Papworth, *J. B. Papworth*, 1879, 74; David Verey, *Gloucestershire*, Buildings of England, ii, 1970, 128–9]. Jenkins's original designs are among Papworth's drawings in the R.I.B.A. Collection. Several of the plates in Griffith's *Description of Cheltenham* (1826) were from drawings by Jenkins, but it is not stated that he had designed any of the buildings illustrated. Pigot's *Directory* shows that by 1828 he had moved to Leamington in Warwickshire.

JENKINS, JOHN, exhibited architectural designs at the Royal Academy from 1788 to 1795, his address being 13 Hanover Square. He was employed by the 1st Earl Grosvenor to alter No. 40 (now 45) GROSVENOR SQUARE (dem. 1938) for the Earl's own residence in 1783–6 and in 1785–6 to design the unpretentious GROSVENOR MARKET, dem. 1858–60 and 1889 [*Survey of London* xl, 68–9, 159]. Joseph Salway (*q.v.*) was his pupil. He was presumably the 'J. Jenkins of London' who entered a design in the competition for the Royal Exchange at Dublin in 1769 [*Builder* xxvii, 1869, 781].

JENKINS, JOHN (–1844), appears to have been the younger son of the Revd. William Jenkins (*q.v.*). He was admitted to the Royal Academy Schools in 1821 at the age of 23, and was awarded the Silver Medal in 1823. In company with his father's pupil William Hosking (*q.v.*) he travelled in the Mediterranean in 1823–5, and subsequently exhibited drawings of temples at Rome, Pompeii, Paestum and Athens at the Academy. In 1827 he and Hosking were the joint authors of *A Selection of Architectural and other Ornaments, Greek, Roman and Italian.* At this period he was living with his father at 6, Red Lion Square.

In 1835–6 John Jenkins ('of 6 Red Lion Square, London') designed ST. GEORGE'S CHURCH, TREDEGAR, MONMOUTHSHIRE [*Monmouthshire Merlin*, 4 July 1835]. In 1841 he refronted the METHODIST CHAPEL in GREAT QUEEN STREET, LONDON, designed by his father in 1816–17 (dem. 1910), adding an Ionic portico [*Companion to the Almanac*, 1842, 213] (*Survey of London* v, pl. 32). His death was reported in *The Welshman* of 26 April 1844 [*ex inf.* Mr. Thomas Lloyd].

JENKINS, the Revd. WILLIAM (*c.*1763–1844), is said to have received an architectural training before becoming a Wesleyan Methodist minister. After some twenty years as an itinerant preacher, he retired from the ministry in 1810 for reasons of health, and set up practice as an architect in Red Lion Square, London. He specialized in designing Methodist Chapels and has been described as 'the outstanding figure in Methodist building' during the early nineteenth century. His Carver Street Chapel in Sheffield (designed while he was still a minister) was regarded at the time as 'one of the best planned, most elegant and commodious places of worship in this country' and provided an effective formula for the architectural treatment of the broad many-windowed fronts characteristic of nonconformist chapels. Jenkins died on 19 June 1844, aged 81, and was buried in Wesley's Chapel, Finsbury. William Jenkins, junior, and John Jenkins (*qq.v.*) appear to have been his sons, and William Hosking (*q.v.*), became his pupil in 1819 or 1820 [*Wesleyan Magazine*, 1844, 775; G. J. Stevenson, *City Road Chapel and its Associations*, 1872, 548–9; John Telford, *Wesley's Chapel and Wesley's House*, ?1906, 107–8; G. W. Dolbey, *The Architectural Expression of Methodism*, 1964].

SHEFFIELD, THE CARVER STREET METHODIST CHAPEL, 1804 [R. E. Leader, *Surveyors and Architects of the Past in Sheffield*, 1903].

LONDON, METHODIST CHAPEL, HINDE STREET, 1809–10; rebuilt 1886 [N. Curnock, *The Hinde Street Chapel*, 1910, 24].

ROCHESTER, KENT, METHODIST CHAPEL, 1810 [G. W. Dolbey, *op. cit.*, 161].

CANTERBURY, METHODIST CHAPEL, ST. PETER'S STREET, 1811 [J. Telford, *op. cit.*].

DARLINGTON, CO. DURHAM, METHODIST CHAPEL, BONDGATE, 1812 [W.H.D. Longstaffe, *History of Darlington*, 1854, 253].

EXETER, THE MINT METHODIST CHAPEL, FORE STREET, 1813; front rebuilt 1868; dem. 1968 [guide to chapel].

HULL, YORKS. (E.R.), WALTHAM STREET METHODIST CHAPEL, 1814; dem. [*V.C.H. Yorks. E.R.* i, 326].

LEICESTER, METHODIST CHAPEL, BISHOP STREET, 1815 [*Procs. Wesley Historical Soc.* xxv, 1945–6, 106–7].

BATH, SOMERSET, THE WALCOT METHODIST CHAPEL, 1815–16 [W. Ison, *The Georgian Buildings of Bath*, 1948, 80].

NORTHAMPTON, GOLD STREET METHODIST CHAPEL, 1816 [Chapel Account Book, 1816–1890, *ex inf.* Mr. V. A. Hatley].

LONDON, METHODIST CHAPEL, GREAT QUEEN STREET, LINCOLN'S INN FIELDS, 1816–17; refronted 1841; dem. 1910 [J. Telford, *op. cit.*] (*Survey of London* v, 86–8).

OXFORD, METHODIST CHAPEL, NEW INN HALL STREET, 1817–18; dem. 1969 [R. Lascelles, *The University and City of Oxford displayed*, 1821, 237].

LONDON, METHODIST CHAPELS in LAMBETH, KING'S CROSS, SLOANE TERRACE (1812) and SOUTHWARK [J. Telford, *op. cit.*; W. W. Pocock, *Memoir of W. F. Pocock*, 1883, 21].

JENKINS, WILLIAM WESLEY (–1864), appears to have been the elder son of the Revd. William Jenkins (*q.v.*). He was in Athens in 1820, exhibited views of buildings on the Acropolis at the Royal Academy in 1822, 1823 and 1827, and contributed to the supplementary volume of the *Antiquities of Athens* published in 1830. In 1823 he was one of the unsuccessful competitors for the new buildings at King's College, Cambridge [*Exhibition of Designs for completing King's College, Cambridge*, 1823, in Soane Museum, P.C. 55]. In 1833–4 he designed a Gothic proprietary chapel at Gravesend which later became ST. JOHN'S R.C. CHURCH [R. H. Hiscock, 'The Proprietary Chapel of St. John, Gravesend', *Archaeologia Cantiana* xciii, 1977], and was subsequently employed to design some houses there for a Building Company [*Gent's Mag.* 1836 (i), 654].

Jenkins later practised from 20 Bartlett's Buildings, winning in 1853 the second prize in the competition for the Wesleyan College in Horseferry Road, Westminster, and in 1854 exhibiting at the R.A. his executed designs for altering and enlarging GELLY DÊG, CARMARTHENSHIRE (gutted *c.*1950) for Richard Jennings. He also designed the INFIRMARY at CARMARTHEN in 1857–8 and rebuilt the ENGLISH WESLEYAN CHAPEL there (dem. 1979) in 1861–2 [W. Spurrell, *Carmarthen*, 1879, 51, 155–6]. He was probably the 'Mr. Wily Wesleyan' whose sharp practice in attempting to steal a commission from a fellow architect in Wales was the subject of a letter in the *Builder*, 21 July 1855, 348.

JENNER, JOHN (–1728), a bricklayer by trade, was active as a builder and surveyor in London in the 1720s. In 1723–5 the 2nd Earl of Tankerville had a new stable built at UPPARK, SUSSEX, according to 'a Plan or Model drawn by Mr. Jenner',[1] and in 1727 Jenner was concerned in some alterations to the Earl's London house in St. James's Square. As a speculative builder he was working in Mount Row and elsewhere on the Grosvenor estate in Westminster shortly before his death in 1728 [P.R.O., C 105/21, Montigny *v.*

[1] This was presumably one of the two outbuildings shown in the view of Uppark by Pieter Tillemans (d. 1734), which do not correspond with the ones seen in Kip's view published in 1714. The existing stables date from *c.*1750.

Jenner; *Survey of London* xxix, 79–80, xl, 36, 80, 161, 164].

JENNINGS, J—, of Hawkhurst, designed a poor Gothic church at SISSINGHURST, KENT, in 1837–8 [C. C. R. Pile, *Cranbrook*, 1955, 95–6].

JERMAN, or JARMAN, EDWARD (– 1668), belonged to a family who had been carpenters in the City of London since the reign of Queen Elizabeth. He was the elder son of Anthony Jerman (d. 1650), Master of the Carpenters' Company in 1633.[1] He was appointed City Carpenter jointly with his father in 1633 and held the post until he resigned it in October 1657. He was also Surveyor to the Fishmongers' Company from April 1654 until his death in November 1668.

Sir Robert Pratt described Jerman as 'an experienced man in buildings', and after the Great Fire of 1666 he was one of the three surveyors appointed on behalf of the Corporation to control the rebuilding of the City in conjunction with Wren, May and Pratt, the other two being Robert Hooke and Peter Mills. He declined, however, to undertake the detailed survey of the devastated area required by the Rebuilding Act, which was carried out mainly by Mills and Hooke. Together with the two latter he was also directed by the Committee for Gresham Affairs to report on the rebuilding of the Royal Exchange, and on 25 April 1667, 'the committee being very sensible of the greate burthen of businesse lying upon him [Mills] for the city at this time; and considering that Mr. Jerman is the most able known artist (besides him) that the city now hath; therefore the committee unanimously made choice of Mr. Jerman to assist the committee in the agreeing for, ordering, and directing of that worke; and haveing declared the same unto him, hee, after much reluctancy and unwillingness (objecting, it might bee thought an intrenchment upon Mr. Mills his right), at length accepted, being assured first, by the lord mayor and the committee, that itt was no intrenchment, and that this whoIle committee, at all times, would acquit him from any scandall in that behalfe'. On 9 December, the committee, 'considering that Mr. Jerman hath not yet received any gratification for his paines about drawing drafts and directing the building', ordered £50 to be paid to him on account. The last mention of Jerman occurs on 22 October 1668, and it is clear that he died soon afterwards. The appointment of a surveyor to take his place was considered, but Thomas Cartwright, the contracting mason, 'declared himself master of the wholle designe intended for that buildinge' and no appointment was made. The committee afterwards found it necessary to consult Hooke and Wren in view of 'the greatnesse of the charge given in by the workemen since Mr. *Jerman's* death, far exceeding the estimate by him', but it was substantially in accordance with Jerman's designs that the Royal Exchange was completed in 1671. The bricklayer's work was performed by John Tanner, the City Bricklayer, and the master carpenter was Edward's younger brother Roger Jerman, who held the office of City Carpenter from 1662 until his death on 24 October 1678. What were reputed to be Jerman's original drawings on vellum were in 1846 in the possession of R. W. Jupp, Clerk to the Carpenters' Company [W. Tite, 'The Old 'Changes of London', *Builder* iv, 1846, 2].

After the Great Fire Jerman was employed to make designs for rebuilding several of the City Companies' Halls, though he did not live to see most of them completed. In 1667 he provided the 'draughts' for the new Weavers' Hall, and in January 1668 the Court instructed Mr. Lewis, the master carpenter, to 'see Mr. Jerman's directions performed by all the workmen concerned'. There is similar evidence that Jerman designed new halls for the Drapers', Fishmongers', Haberdashers', Mercers' and Wax Chandlers' Companies, and supervised the repair of the Barber-Surgeons' and Goldsmiths' Halls, which had not been totally destroyed. His plans for the Mercers' Hall were carried out after his death under the superintendence of John Oliver. In the case of the Apothecaries' Hall, the accounts show that Jerman was consulted in 1667–8, but that the surveyor responsible was a Mr. Lock (*q.v.*). Jerman may also have designed the new Vintners' Hall, for which his brother Roger was master carpenter, but documentary evidence is lacking.

Jerman was essentially a City artisan who appears to have done little work outside London, though in 1666–8 there are payments to him in the Works accounts for surveying Windsor Castle (P.R.O., E 351/3280–1). The Royal Exchange was no doubt his most important work, though here, as elsewhere, some of the features may have been due to the mason Cartwright. It was elaborately detailed in the manner of the City artisans, with a

[1] In 1634 Anthony Jerman was one of those who offered designs for the Goldsmiths' Hall [J. Newman in *Arch. Hist.* xiv, 1971, 31], and in 1638 he and a Mr. Holmes were paid £1 by the churchwardens of St. Michael le Querne for making a 'modell' of their church, then about to be rebuilt with advice from Inigo Jones [Guildhall Library, MS. 2895/2].

towered entrance awkwardly related to the principal front. More sophisticated was the north front, where two systems of fenestration interpenetrated beneath a central pediment. Both here and at Mercers' and Haberdashers' Halls the prevailing taste was mannerist, but at Fishmongers' Hall the astylar front and the hipped roof showed that Jerman was not unaware of the new fashion for a simpler classical architecture associated with Hooke, May and Pratt.

[*A.P.S.D.*; T. F. Reddaway, *The Rebuilding of London after the Great Fire*, 1940, 55, 59, 108 n., 268–9; S. Perks, *The History of the Mansion House*, 1922, 148; *The Architecture of Sir R. Pratt*, ed. R. T. Gunther, 1928, 12; *Wren Soc.* xx, 112; E. B. Chancellor, *Lives of the British Architects*, 1909, 109–13; E. B. Jupp, *A History of the Carpenters' Company*, 1848; Malcolm Pinhorn, 'The Jerman Family', *Blackmansbury* i, nos. 5–6, 1965, 3–9; Guildhall Record Office, City Repertory 46, f. 440b, 48, f. 110.]

LONDON

THE ROYAL EXCHANGE, 1667–71; destroyed by fire Jan. 1838 [see above] (engraving published by the mason Cartwright in 1671, of which there is a copy in B.L., *King's Maps* xxiv, 11 a 1; *Vitruvius Britannicus* ii, 1717, pls. 23–5; Britton & Pugin, *The Public Buildings of London* i, 1825, 287–97; *The Royal Exchange*, London Topographical Soc., forthcoming).

BARBER-SURGEONS' HALL, MONKWELL STREET, repairs after Great Fire; rebuilt 1863–4 [*ex inf.* Mr. Beck].

DRAPERS' HALL, THROGMORTON STREET, rebuilt to Jerman's designs by T. Cartwright 1668–71; street front rebuilt 1778; rebuilt 1868–9 [A. H. Johnson, *History of the Drapers' Company* iii, 1922, 286].

FISHMONGERS' HALL, LONDON BRIDGE, rebuilt 1667–72; rebuilt 1831–3 [Priscilla Metcalf, *The Halls of the Fishmongers' Company*, 1977].

GOLDSMITHS' HALL, FOSTER LANE, repairs after Great Fire; rebuilt 1829–35 [J. Newman, 'Nicholas Stone's Goldsmiths' Hall', *Arch. Hist.* xiv, 1971, 34].

HABERDASHERS' HALL, GRESHAM STREET, rebuilt *c.*1667–8; damaged by fire 1864; destroyed by bombing 1940s [Court Minutes, 3 Sept. and 1 Oct. 1667, Guildhall Library MS. 15842, pp. 139, 141, 143].

MERCERS' HALL and CHAPEL, CHEAPSIDE, rebuilt to Jerman's design by John Oliver, *c.*1671–6; front to Cheapside rebuilt 1873; destroyed by bombing 1941 [Philip Norman in *Builder*, 31 March 1916, 252; Jean Imray, *Mercers' Hall*, 1991, 26–39] (plan in R.C.H.M., *London*: *The City*, 69).

WAX CHANDLERS' HALL, MAIDEN LANE, rebuilt 1668–70; rebuilt 1792–3 and again 1852–5; destroyed by bombing 1940 [J. Dummelow, *The Wax Chandlers of London*, 1973, 85].

WEAVERS' HALL, BASINGHALL STREET, rebuilt 1667–9; dem. 1856 [A. Plummer, *The London Weavers' Company 1600–1970*, 1972, 202].

ST. PAUL'S SCHOOL, ST. PAUL'S CHURCHYARD, built 1669–70 to designs made by Jerman before his death; dem. 1823 [Sir Michael McDonnell, *The Annals of St. Paul's School*, 1959, 239–40].

JERNEGAN, or **JERNINGHAM,** GEORGE (*c.*1760–1815), of London, was elected a member of the Surveyors' Club in 1805. He died on 13 December 1815, aged 55 [*Gent's Mag.* 1815 (ii), 643]. In 1793 he exhibited a drawing of 'Buildings erecting in Grosvenor Place' at the Royal Academy.

JERNEGAN, WILLIAM (*c.*1751–1836), was for many years the principal architect practising in Swansea and the first who was strictly a professional, without any interest in one of the building trades. He is said to have been a native of the Channel Islands, but had settled in Swansea by the 1780s and died there in 1836. Nothing is known about his training, but it has been plausibly suggested that he might have come to South Wales as an assistant of John Johnson, the English architect who designed Clasemont and Gnoll Castle in the 1770s. He was an elegant neoclassical architect who designed a number of villas and small country houses in the neighbourhood of Swansea. A surviving design for a copper works (in the National Library of Wales) suggests some involvement in industrial development in the area. Although bankrupted in 1811, Jernegan resumed his practice and appears to have been living in reasonable affluence at the time of his death on 12 January 1834, in his 86th year.

In SWANSEA Jernegan designed THE COUNTESS OF HUNTINGDON'S CHAPEL, 1789 (dem.) and THE ASSEMBLY ROOMS, 1805–24, and enlarged ST. JOHN'S CHURCH, 1824. He also designed WORCESTER PLACE, a mansion house and four adjacent houses, 1789 (dem.); a terrace of three houses in BANK BUILDINGS, 1809 (dem.); and laid out and designed several terraces on THE BURROWS, including UNION ROW or SOMERSET PLACE, 1779 (dem.); GLOUCESTER PLACE, 1824; ADELAIDE PLACE (dem.), where he was living at the time of his death; and probably CAMBRIAN PLACE and PROSPECT PLACE. His unexecuted design for a Town Hall, made in 1825, is illustrated in *Plans and Prospects: Architecture in Wales 1780–1914* (Welsh Arts Council Exhibition, 1975), No. 35.

Houses in the vicinity of Swansea known to have been designed by Jernegan are: MARINO, built in 1783 on an octagonal plan and later incorporated in the Vivians' mansion, Singleton Park (now part of the University College of Wales); KILVROUGH, remodelled 1785 for William Dawkins in an externally castellated style similar to Adam's Wenvoe Castle (R.C.A.M., *Glamorgan* iv (i), 1981, 287–93); STOUTHALL, REYNOLDSTON, for John Lucas, 1787–9 (*op. cit.*, 303–10); OXWICH RECTORY, 1788–9; SKETTY HALL, enlarged and remodelled for Ralph Sheldon, *c.*1790 and 1802; SKETTY PARK HOUSE for Sir John Morris, 1806 (dem. 1975); BRYNYMOR for Robert Eaton, *c.*1820; and probably the remodelling of WOODLANDS HOUSE or CLYNE CASTLE for General George Warde in 1819–20.

Elsewhere Jernegan much enlarged CARDIFF GAOL (dem.) in 1795–6, designed the MUMBLES LIGHTHOUSE in Swansea Bay, 1793, and was the first architect at MILFORD HAVEN, PEMBROKESHIRE, where the quay, Lord Nelson Hotel, Customs House and church are attributed either to him or to a refugee French shipwright called Jean-Louis Barrallier who was also involved in the design of the new town and dockyard.

[Thomas Lloyd, 'The Architects of Regency Swansea', *Gower* 41, 1990, 58–62, with references to printed and documentary sources; J. F. Rees, *The Story of Milford*, 1954, 26.]

JERNINGHAM, EDWARD (1774–1822), was the youngest son of Sir William Jerningham of Cossey (or Costessey) Hall, Norfolk. He was a barrister by profession and acted as Secretary to the General Board of British Catholics. For his brother Sir George Jerningham he designed an elaborate Perpendicular Gothic Catholic chapel (dem.) at COSSEY HALL in about 1810. He also Gothicized the CATHOLIC CHAPEL at STAFFORD, and in 1810–15 began to rebuild STAFFORD CASTLE, which was on his brother's property. This project was never completed, but Jerningham created a picturesque castellated landmark, recently demolished but illustrated in Calvert & West's *Picturesque Views in Staffordshire and Shropshire* (1830) and Mark Hughes, *The Story of Staffordshire* (1924). His interest in architecture may have been hereditary, for at Swynnerton Hall there is a portrait of his father holding an architectural plan, with a Gothic landscape tower in the background.

[*Gent's Mag.* 1822 (i), 564–5; J. P. Neale's *Views of Seats*, 2nd ser., i, 1824; J. Gillow's *Dictionary of English Catholics*, iii, 1887, 627–8; J. Gillow, *St. Thomas's Priory, Stafford*, n.d., 105–7; B.L., Add. MS. 36387, ff. 200–1.]

JERSEY, THOMAS (–1751), is an obscure figure of whom all that is at present known is that he subscribed to West and Toms' *Views of the Ancient Churches in the Cities of London and Westminster*, published in 1739, acted as Clerk of Works for the building of the Radcliffe Library in Oxford from 1737 to 1745, and was the 'man of genius' under whom James Paine 'began the study of architecture'. The date of his death is given in *D.N.B.*, *s.v.* 'Paine'.

JOHNS, JAMES WOOD (*c.*1810–1863), was admitted to the Royal Academy Schools in 1833 and exhibited a 'Design for a botanical institution' at the Academy in 1835. In 1836–7 he designed a proprietary school at HULL called HULL COLLEGE (dem.). It was near Spring Bank and had an octastyle Corinthian portico [*Hull Advertiser*, 9 Sept. 1836, *ex inf.* Mr. A. G. Chamberlain].

In 1841 Johns was engaged by the London Society for promoting Christianity among the Jews to go out to Jerusalem to design and build an Anglican Cathedral there. After work had been in progress for some months he got at cross-purposes with the committee and was dismissed in the winter of 1842–3. His place was taken by Matthew Habershon (*q.v.*), who carried the building forward to designs that, although modified in detail, appear to have been substantially those originally made by Johns. In 1844 Johns published a folio volume entitled *The Anglican Cathedral Church of St. James, Jerusalem*, in which he described the erection of the building, but made no reference to his dismissal. [Bodleian Library, minutes of the London Society for promoting Christianity among the Jews.] He died at Weymouth on 30 November 1863 [*Gent's Mag.* 1864 (i), 131].

JOHNSON, JAMES (–1807), held the post of architect to the Barrack Department of the War Office until 1805, when he retired owing to ill-health, dying two years later, in June 1807 [*Gent's Mag.* 1807 (ii), 684]. A design for a barracks to accommodate 2500 men and their officers, signed 'J. Johnson Archt. Rd. Elsam delt. June 1795', is in the British Library (*King's Maps* xxvi, 7 tt, uu). The CAVALRY BARRACKS in FULFORD ROAD, YORK, built to the designs of Johnson and his fellow surveyor James Sanders (*q.v.*) are described and illustrated in R.C.H.M. *York* iv, 46. In 1794 he became surveyor to the Mint, and shortly before his death he designed the new ROYAL MINT on TOWER HILL, LONDON. His original designs are in the R.I.B.A. Collection. The Mint was built under the direction of his successor Robert Smirke between 1807 and 1812 and was enlarged in 1881–2 [*History of the King's Works* vi, 452–60].

JOHNSON, JOEL (*c.*1721–1799), was probably a son of the builder of the same name who took several building leases on the Harley estate in Marylebone in 1719–21 [B.L., Add. MS. 18240, ff. 7–8]. He is said in his obituary notice in *Gent's Mag.* lxix (i), 1799, 358, to have designed the church of ST. JOHN, WAPPING, 1756, destroyed, except for the tower, in 1940–1: the MAGDALEN HOSPITAL, ST. GEORGE'S FIELDS, 1769–72, dem. 1869; the LONDON HOSPITAL, WHITECHAPEL ROAD, 1752–9; the 'Asylum',[1] and many chapels and other edifices. Johnson was named as 'architect' in the inscription on the foundation-stone of the Magdalen Hospital, given by D. Hughson, *London* iv, 1807, 509. He was, however, only the carpenter employed at the London Hospital under B. Mainwaring, and it may be noted that the latter was among the surveyors who gave evidence before the House of Commons on 9 March 1756, in connection with the rebuilding of St. John's Wapping, In 1774 Johnson made plans for a gallery to be built in the south aisle of WALTHAMSTOW PARISH CHURCH, ESSEX. He was a public-spirited man who was 'always usefully or innocently employed', and took 'indefatigable pains' in establishing and regulating the Walthamstow House of Industry. He was a Warden of the Carpenters' Company in 1780, 1787 and 1788, and Master in 1789. He died at Dedham Place, Essex, on 17 April 1799, at the age of 78 [*A.P.S.D.*; S. J. Barnes, *Walthamstow Vestry Minutes, etc.*, Walthamstow Antiquarian Society, 1925–7, 58].

JOHNSON, JOHN, may have been an architect of importance in the north of England in the early seventeenth century. In 1620 or 1621 John Johnson, 'surveyor', was at the head of a body of workmen who reported on the state of the CASTLE at NEWCASTLE-UPON-TYNE [P.R.O., E 178/4366]. This was presumably John Johnson, bridge master of Newcastle, who in 1621 was put in charge of the new bridge then building at Berwick-on-Tweed [*History of the King's Works* iv, 776]. In 1622 John Johnson of Little Langton, Yorkshire (N.R.), contracted to enlarge DILSTON HALL, NORTHUMBERLAND, for Sir Francis Radcliffe. The house was rebuilt in 1710–14 and demolished in 1765, but Johnson's very competently drawn plan survives and is illustrated in *History of Northumberland* x, 289–91. In the Yorkshire Archaeological Society's library at Leeds there is an elevation of a Jacobean doorway (MD 59/21) with an annotation 'this must be altered according to this line per me Johnson'.

JOHNSON, JOHN, of South Mimms in Hertfordshire, appears to have been primarily a surveyor and rent-collector. In Feb. 1723/4 he was appointed by William Pym of the Hasells in Bedfordshire to act as his steward and agent. However, litigation subsequently ensued between Johnson and his employer in the course of which the former stated that he 'drew a plan, draught and upright' of a house that Pym built in ARLINGTON STREET, LONDON, in 1724–5 [Beds. C.R.O., Pym papers 1890; cf. Herts. C.R.O., 27761].

JOHNSON, JOHN (1732–1814), was born in Southgate Street, Leicester, on 22 April 1732. Little is known of his early life. His father, John Johnson, was a joiner by trade, and he himself was probably brought up as a carpenter. At the time of his death it was stated that he 'left Leicester in early life, possessing little more than strong natural abilities, which soon found their way in the metropolis'. By 1760 he was married and established in London. In the late 1760s he was engaged in speculative building on the Berners estate in Marylebone, and by 1767 had himself taken up residence in one of the houses he had built in Berners Street. He exhibited once (1773) at the Royal Academy, and fairly regularly at the Society of Artists between 1775 and 1783. In 1782 he succeeded William Hillyer as Surveyor to the County of Essex, and it was in this capacity that he designed his most important work, the Shire Hall at Chelmsford, on whose completion he was presented with a piece of plate worth 100 guineas, 'as a public testimony of his integrity and professional abilities'. When in 1812 he retired from the county surveyorship at the age of 80, he received the formal thanks of the Justices 'for his long, active, faithful and meritorious services to this county during the space of more than thirty years'.

Johnson's private practice was considerable. He designed more than twenty country

[1] Presumably the Asylum founded in 1787 as an adjunct to the Lock Hospital in Grosvenor Place, London (dem. 1842).

houses, chiefly in Essex and the Midlands, but including some as far afield as Devon and Glamorgan. He also built several town houses for aristocratic clients, and prepared an abortive scheme for a new square in Leicester. In 1777 he attempted to patent a stucco composition similar to the one purveyed by the brothers Adam. The Adams went to law in defence of their composition and obtained a favourable judgement in the Court of King's Bench from Lord Chief Justice Mansfield. Mansfield, as a fellow-countryman and friend of the plaintiffs, was open to the charge of partiality (see *Observations on Two Trials at Law respecting Messieurs Adams's new-invented Patent-Stucco* and a *Reply* thereto, both published in 1778). In 1779 Johnson obtained another patent for 'a particular manner of securing buildings from damage by fire'. Johnson was also involved in banking. He was a partner with Sir Herbert Mackworth in a bank established in Bond Street by 1785. For a time Johnson prospered on the profits of his architectural and financial activities. In 1790 he assigned a considerable amount of leasehold property in various parts of London to his eldest son John, and in 1792–5 he was able to build and endow a small charitable foundation in Leicester for the benefit of his poor relations. This family almshouse, which he called the 'Consanguinitarium', contained five small dwellings, and was endowed with £70 a year from an estate in Lubbenham together with the rents of four adjacent houses built by Johnson. But the bank ended in bankruptcy in 1803 and towards the end of his life Johnson was in such financial straits that in 1813 the magistrates and gentlemen of the county of Essex got up a subscription for his benefit.

After the bankruptcy Johnson moved from Berners Street to Camden Town, but in 1812 he retired to his native town. He died in Leicester on 17 August 1814, and was buried in St. Martin's Church, where there is an inscription to his memory on the base of the monument (executed by Bacon) which he had erected to his parents (Nichols, *Leicestershire* i, pl. xliv). A portrait by John Russell, R.A., is in the Chelmsford and Essex Museum. Another by the same artist is in a private collection. A third portrait, of unknown authorship, was in 1974 in the possession of Mrs. Brooke-Johnson of Richmond, Surrey. His eldest son John Johnson, junior, was also a surveyor, but appears to have designed nothing of importance, and died the year before his father, on 26 February 1813, in his fifty-second year: there is a tablet to his memory in Finchley Church. His second son Charles (d. 1841) entered the Church and became a Canon of Wells. His third son, Dr. Joseph Johnson, died in 1802 in his thirty-second year.

Johnson was an able designer in a late Georgian manner somewhat akin to that of the Wyatts. Although not marked by much individuality, his work is always elegant and he was an accomplished designer of staircases. The basic authority for his architectural works is a list given in Nichols's *History of Leicestershire*. There is evidence that Nichols and Johnson were acquainted, so the list was probably based on information supplied to the historian by the architect himself.

[J. Nichols, *History of Leicestershire* i, part 2, 1815, 528; *Gent's Mag.* 1793 (ii), 1046; 1813 (i), 387; 1814 (ii), 296; *A.P.S.D.*; J. Simmons, 'Notes on a Leicester Architect; John Johnson', *Trans. Leicestershire Archl. Soc.* xxv, 1949, reprinted in *Parish and Empire*, 1952, 128–45; Nancy Briggs, *John Johnson 1732–1814*, Essex Record Office 1991.]

The following list of Johnson's executed works is based on Miss Briggs's book, where full references to sources will be found.

PUBLIC BUILDINGS, ETC.

NEWMARKET, SUFFOLK, THE NEW ROOMS (now Jockey Club), HIGH STREET, 1771–2; altered and refronted 1932–5 (*C. Life*, 1 Oct. 1932).

HALSTEAD, ESSEX, completed HOUSE OF CORRECTION designed by W. Hillyer, *c.*1782; dem. 1970s.

CHELMSFORD, ESSEX, COUNTY GAOL, alterations and additions, 1782–91; dem. 1859.

WIMBLEDON CHURCH, SURREY, rebuilt 1787–8; rebuilt 1843.

COLCHESTER, ESSEX, HOUSE OF CORRECTION in CASTLE, alterations, 1787–8.

CHELMSFORD, ESSEX, conduit in Tindal Square with Coade stone naiad, 1787–91; dem. 1814 (naiad now in foyer of Shire Hall).

CHELMSFORD, ESSEX, THE SHIRE HALL, 1789–91 (J. Johnson, *Plans, Sections and Perspective Elevations of the Essex County Hall at Chelmsford*, 1808).

BARKING, ESSEX, HOUSE OF CORRECTION, 1791–2; dem. *c.*1835.

LEICESTER, THE CONSANGUINITARIUM, SOUTHGATE STREET, with four adjacent houses (dem. *c.*1927), forming part of the endowment, 1792–3; dem. 1878, when a new building was erected at 11–19 Howe Street.

LEICESTER, THE BOROUGH GAOL, HIGHCROSS STREET, 1792–3; dem. 1837.

CHELMSFORD, ESSEX, GRAMMAR SCHOOL HOUSE, alterations, 1797–9; dem.

LEICESTER, THE COUNTY ROOMS, HOTEL STREET, 1799–1800; designed as a hotel and later used as Judges' Lodgings.

FELSTED, ESSEX, NEW SCHOOL HOUSE (now INGRAMS), 1799–1802.

LEICESTER, THE THEATRE, opened 1800; dem. 1836.

CHELMSFORD, ST. MARY'S CHURCH (now CATHEDRAL), rebuilt nave 1801–3, Gothic; since considerably enlarged.

HORNCHURCH CHURCH, ESSEX, repairs including rebuilding of S. aisle, 1802.

CHELMSFORD, ESSEX, HOUSE OF CORRECTION, 1802–7; dem. 1859.

THAXTED CHURCH, ESSEX, repairs to steeple, 1807.

GREAT HALLINGBURY CHURCH, ESSEX, repairs for J. A. Houblon, 1807.

STILTON CHURCH, HUNTS., rebuilt chancel 1808, Gothic; remodelled 1857.

LEWES, SUSSEX, THE COUNTY HALL, 1808–12.

COUNTRY HOUSES

SKREENS, ROXWELL, ESSEX, alterations including new stables for Thomas Berney Bramston, *c.*1769–71; remodelled *c.*1910; dem. *c.*1920.

NEWMARKET, SUFFOLK, stables for Lord March, *c.*1770.

CASTLE ASHBY, NORTHANTS., rebuilt Great Hall for 8th Earl of Northampton, 1771–4; altered 1884.

TERLING PLACE, ESSEX, for John Strutt, 1772–7; wings etc. added 1818–21.

SADBOROW HOUSE, THORNCOMBE, DORSET, for John Bragge, 1773–5; W. wing added 1843 (R.C.H.M. *Dorset, West*, 246–7, pls. 75, 120).

KINGSTHORPE HALL, NORTHANTS., for James Fremeaux, 1773–5 (J. A. Gotch, *Squires' Homes of Northamptonshire*, 1939, pls. 84–6).

PITSFORD HALL, NORTHANTS., for Col. James Money, *c.*1775; altered at various dates from 1887 onwards.

CLASEMONT, nr. MORRISTON, GLAMORGANSHIRE, for (Sir) John Morris, *c.*1775; dem. 1819.

HOLCOMBE HOUSE (now Missionary Institute), MILL HILL, MIDDLESEX, for Sir John Anderson, Bart., *c.*1775–8.

WOOLVERSTONE HALL, SUFFOLK (now a school), for William Berners, 1776.

GNOLL CASTLE, nr. NEATH, GLAMORGANSHIRE, remodelled for Sir Herbert Mackworth, Bart., *c.*1776–8, castellated; dem. 1956 (Neale's *Views of Seats* i, 1818).

HALSWELL PARK, SOMERSET, THE TEMPLE OF PAN, for Sir Charles Kemeys Tynte, Bart., *c.*1777 (see *C. Life* 9 Feb. 1989 for this and other buildings perhaps by Johnson).

CARLTON HALL, EAST CARLTON, NORTHANTS., for Sir John Palmer, Bart., 1777–81; enlarged 1823; rebuilt 1870 (Neale's *Views of Seats* vi, 1823).

BURLEY-ON-THE-HILL, RUTLAND, Dining Parlour for 8th Earl of Winchilsea, 1778.

KILLERTON PARK, DEVON, for Sir Thomas Acland, Bart., 1778–9: erected 'only as a temporary seat' and since much altered; stables, 1779–80 (J. Britton & E. W. Brayley, *Devonshire Illustrated*, 1829, 34–5).

FINEDON HALL, NORTHANTS., alterations for Sir William Dolben, Bart., 1780–1; dem. 1980.

BRADWELL LODGE, BRADWELL-ON-SEA, ESSEX, for the Revd. (Sir) Henry Bate-Dudley, 1781–3 (*C. Life*, 7 July 1966).

LANGFORD GROVE, LANGFORD, ESSEX, for N. Westcombe, 1782; dem. 1952.

attributed: WIMBLEDON (later BELVEDERE) HOUSE, enlarged for Sir William Beaumaris Rush, after 1783; dem. *c.*1900.

BENHALL LODGE, SUFFOLK, probably for Sir William Beaumaris Rush, *c.*1785; dem.

HATFIELD PLACE, HATFIELD PEVERELL, ESSEX, for Col. John Tyrell, 1791–5.

THE LAWN, STROUD GREEN, ROCHFORD, ESSEX, enlarged for Major G. D. Carr, after 1796.

KNIGHTON HALL, LEICS., addition for Sir Edmund Cradock Hartopp, 1799–1802.

TORRELL'S HALL, WILLINGDALE DOE, ESSEX, new front block for John Crabb, after 1800.

WHATTON HALL, LONG WHATTON, LEICS., for Edward Dawson, *c.*1802; remodelled after fire in 1876 (Neale's *Views of Seats*, 2nd ser. iii, 1826).

BOREHAM HOUSE, ESSEX, alterations for Sir John Tyrell, Bart., 1802–3 (*C. Life*, 11 July 1914).

ST. LEONARD'S LODGE, LOWER BEEDING, SUSSEX, for Charles G. Beauclerk, *c.*1803–8; dem. 1853.

BRAXTED PARK, GREAT BRAXTED, ESSEX, N. front and staircase for Peter Du Cane, 1804–6.

HALLINGBURY PLACE, ESSEX, repairs for J. A. Houblon, 1807; dem. 1924 (*C. Life*, 19 Sept. 1914).

BROOMFIELD LODGE, BROOMFIELD, ESSEX, for John Judd, *c.*1808; dem. 1964.

?FOREST HALL, HIGH ONGAR, ESSEX, *c.*1805 (dem. 1957), or WILLINGDALE DOE RECTORY, ESSEX, after 1797, for the Revd. John Bramston-Stane, for whom Johnson designed an unspecified house.

LONDON HOUSES

BERNERS ESTATE, MARYLEBONE: 49–66 NEWMAN STREET; 28–36 BERNERS STREET; 31–35 CHARLES (later MORTIMER) STREET, 1769–71.

HARLEY STREET, No. 27 (later No. 48) for the

Revd. Sir John Hotham, Bart., later Bishop of Ossory, *c.*1773; dem.

HARLEY STREET, No. 43 (later No. 63), for John Pybus, *c.*1773; dem.

CHARLES STREET, ST. JAMES'S SQUARE, No. 19 for 7th Earl of Galloway, 1775–6; dem. 1912.

NEW CAVENDISH STREET, No. 9 (now No. 63) for Sir Charles Bampfylde, Bart., *c.*1775–7.

NEW CAVENDISH STREET, No. 10 (now No. 61), for John Udney, *c.*1775–7 (*C. Life*, 20 Oct. 1917; M. Jourdain, *English Interiors in Smaller Houses*, 1923, figs. 65–73).

GROSVENOR SQUARE, No. 38 (formerly No. 33), redecoration of interior for 3rd Duke of Dorset, *c.*1776 (cf. *Survey of London* xl, 149–50).

PORTMAN SQUARE, No. 10 (later No. 13), for Hon. Henry Willoughby, later 5th Lord Middleton, 1777; dem. *c.*1965.

PORTMAN SQUARE, No. 9 (later No. 12), for Hon. Charles Greville, 1778; dem. *c.*1965.

PALL MALL, house on N. side reconstructed for Sir Hugh Palliser, Bart., after being gutted by mob 1778; dem. 1866.

PORTLAND PLACE, No. 22, for Sir Patrick Blake, Bart., *c.*1781; dem.

BRIDGES

In his capacity as County Surveyor of Essex Johnson built a number of bridges in that county. Most of them were small structures, often of timber and of little architectural interest, and very few of them are still standing. Of these the most notable is the elegantly designed MOULSHAM BRIDGE over the R. Can at CHELMSFORD, built in 1787. For a complete list of bridges by Johnson see Briggs, Appendix 2.

JOHNSON, JOHN LEES, *see under* JOHNSON, THOMAS.

JOHNSON, JOSHUA, was a carpenter of Boston, Lincs. In 1730 the Corporation resolved to rebuild the MARKET CROSS according to 'a Modell this Day presented by Mr. Joshua Johnson'. Johnson was also the contractor for the carpentry. This classical building, completed in 1732, with some advice from Robert Morris (*q.v.*), then at Culverthorpe Hall, was demolished in 1822 [Boston Corporation Minutes, vol. v, ff. 400–427, *ex inf.* Mr. Richard Hewlings].

JOHNSON, THOMAS (–1800), was an architect and builder of Warwick and later of Worcester. In Warwick he was employed in 1779 to design and build the County Gaol and St. Nicholas' Church. In recording the laying of the foundation-stone of ST. NICHOLAS' CHURCH, *Jopson's Coventry Journal* for 22 Feb. 1779 reported that 'The elevations . . . for each of which buildings were drawn and planned by a son of Mr. Thomas Johnson, an architect in Warwick (a youth not above 16 years old) under whose direction, together with that of his father, both these works are now carrying on.' Johnson's son John Lees Johnson was baptized on 5 Feb. 1762, and the statement in the newspaper is confirmed by a copy of the plan and elevation of the church among the Faculty Petitions in the County Record Office signed 'J. L. Johnson Delin., T. Johnson Archt.', and dated 'Warwick 1779' (DRO 92/28). Johnson's 'Plan Estimate and Model' had been accepted by the parish in May 1778. The wooden model, which still exists, had previously been sent up to London in a box 'to be inspected by Mr [John?] Johnson the Architect there' [Vestry Minutes in C.R.O.]. The church is in the Gothic style, the chancel being an addition of 1869.

For the COUNTY GAOL Johnson provided two models, now preserved in the County Museum, one showing how the octagonal chapel could be arranged in such a way 'that the Prisoners shall not see each other yet see and hear distinctly the Minister', the other of the proposed Doric façade to Sheep (now Northgate) Street. The contracts were signed in 1779, and the building was completed in 1782. [Warwick County Records, Class 24(671)]. The Gaol was extended on its north side in 1789 by Henry Couchman, the County Surveyor, and reconstructed as the County Council Offices in 1929–30. Johnson's façade, however, remains substantially as he left it. It is remarkable as one of the earliest attempts to adapt Greek Doric to the purposes of an English public building, and the intervention of Lord Aylesford (of Packington Hall) may perhaps be suspected.

By 1786 Johnson had removed to Worcester, where he continued to practice as an architect until his death. In 1789–92 he re-roofed the nave and rebuilt the east and west windows of WORCESTER CATHEDRAL, himself making designs for the painted glass borders of the west window; both windows have been altered in the course of subsequent restorations. Johnson's drawings for a new gallery for the church of ST. NICHOLAS, WORCESTER, dated 1790, are preserved among the parish records, and those for SHELSLEY BEAUCHAMP RECTORY, signed and dated 1791, are among the Faculty papers in the Worcester Diocesan Records.

In 1792–5 HANBURY CHURCH, WORCS., was

largely rebuilt to Johnson's designs. The Gothic tower is virtually a reproduction of the one which he had built at St. Nicholas, Warwick, in 1779–80 [*V.C.H. Worcs.* iii, 378; Society of Antiquaries, Prattinton Collections, xvii, f. 122]. In 1795 he made plans and elevations for a church at ETTINGTON in WARWICKS. for Evelyn Shirley, apparently that built *c.*1800, but demolished, except for the tower, in 1902. These drawings are in the Record Office at Warwick (CR 229/120/10). Johnson also designed the PRESBYTERIAN CHAPEL at STOURBRIDGE, WORCS., built in 1787–88 [W. Scott, *History of Stourbridge*, 1832, 471; R.C.H.M., *Nonconformist Chapels and Meeting-houses in Central England*, 1986, 253–4]; LAPWORTH RECTORY, WARWICKS., 1794, dem. 1970 [Warwicks. C.R.O., CR 290]; and ASTON SUBEDGE CHURCH, GLOS., a minute Gothic chapel built in 1797 largely at the expense of the 1st Lord Harrowby [Harrowby archives, 70].

Johnson died in Worcester in December 1800,[1] and was buried in the cathedral behind the choir. According to the obituary notice in *Berrow's Worcester Journal* for 11 December 1800, he lived in the Sidbury area of Worcester, and it was in the roof of a small building behind a house in Sidbury that the wooden models already mentioned were discovered about 1915. These were six in number: one of St. Nicholas, Warwick, two of the Gaol, one of the façade of Warwick Shire Hall as designed by Sanderson Miller in 1753, one of an unidentified classical church, and one of a circular building, possibly a prison. They are all now in the Warwick County Museum, with the exception of the classical church, which is at the Bartlett School of Architecture, University College London. Apart from the façade of the Shire Hall they all appear to represent designs by Johnson, and there is no reason to associate them with the carver Thomas White of Worcester (d. 1748), as suggested in *Trans. Worcs. Arch. Soc.* for 1943 and in *Burlington Mag.* May 1944.

As there is no mention in Johnson's will of his son John Lees Johnson, the latter had probably predeceased his father. A sheet of designs for garden temples at Bowood House is signed 'J. L. Johnson J^{r} London March 10th 1781'.

[*A.P.S.D.*; J. N. Brewer, *Introduction to the Beauties of England & Wales*, 1818, 662; copy of Johnson's will (dated 6 Nov. 1800) in Birmingham Probate Registry; J. Noake, *The Monastery and Cathedral of Worcester*, 1866, 338–40; *Aris's Birmingham Gazette*, 24 Jan. 1791; *The Register of Worcester Cathedral 1693–1811*, Worcester Parish Register Society, 1913, 86; information from Mr. R. Chamberlain-Brothers.]

[1] In his *Biographical Illustrations of Worcestershire*, 1820, p. 469, J. Chambers wrongly ascribes Johnson's death to the year 1806, and refers also to the death of an architect of the same name in Worcester in 1786. Both statements appear to be inaccurate versions of the obituary notice in the *Worcester Jnl.* for 1800.

JOHNSON, THOMAS (*c.*1762–1814), was probably the son of William Johnson (*q.v.*) of Leeds. He began practice in 1787, when he stated in the *Leeds Intelligencer* that he had been for three years 'under the inspection of James Wyatt, Esq. of London', and had 'since resided at Rome, and seen all the principal Cities of Italy', and had also made a 'tour through France'. He must have been the person of this name who was admitted to the Royal Academy Schools in 1782 at the age of 20, and was awarded the Silver Medal the same year. He was recently dead in August 1814, when L. Ingham advertised that he would complete buildings Johnson had designed. Joseph Cusworth was his pupil. Johnson was a competent classical architect whose best surviving work is Holy Trinity Church, Halifax. [D. Linstrum, *West Yorkshire Architects and Architecture*, 1978, 197, 379; F. Beckwith, *Thomas Taylor*, Thoresby Soc. 1946, 16, 89; *Leeds Intelligencer*, 5–19 June 1787, *ex inf.* Dr. Linstrum.]

LEEDS, ALBION PLACE (now Law Society's offices), ALBION STREET, 1793 [M. Beresford, *East End, West End. The Face of Leeds during Urbanisation*, Thoresby Soc. 1988, 168].

LEEDS, R. C. CHAPEL, LADY LANE, 1793–4; dem. [B. Little, *Catholic Churches since 1623*, 1966, 44].

HALIFAX, YORKS. (W.R.), HOLY TRINITY CHURCH, 1795–8 [F. Beckwith, *op. cit.*, citing *Leeds Intelligencer*, 17 Aug. 1795] (wrongly attributed to J. Oates in T. Allen, *History of the County of York* iii, 1831, 239–40).

LEEDS, Nos. 39, 40 PARK SQUARE, 1797 [M. Beresford, *op. cit.*, 149].

CAWTHORNE CHURCH, YORKS. (W.R.), added N. aisle 1805 [Sheffield Archives, Sp. S. Maps, a plan which also shows a S. aisle that was not built].

NEWLAND HALL, YORKS. (W.R.), cottages and farm-buildings for Sir Edward Smith, 1807–8 [Wakefield Central Library, Smith of Newland papers, bdl. DB].

SEWERBY HALL, YORKS. (E. R.), added bow-fronted wings and portico for John Greame, 1807–8 [*V.C.H. Yorks. E. Riding* ii, 96].

LEEDS, THE LEEDS LIBRARY, COMMERCIAL STREET, 1808; subsequently altered [F. Beckwith, *op. cit.*, 16, n. 23].

JOHNSON, WILLIAM (–1795), of Leeds, was probably the father of Thomas Johnson (*q.v.*). When he died in 1795 the *Leeds Intelligencer* described him as 'many years architect at Temple Newsham'. He was presumably the 'Mr. Johnson' who was responsible for reconstructing the S. wing of TEMPLE NEWSAM HOUSE, nr. LEEDS, for Frances, Lady Irwin, in a style approximating to that of the Jacobean mansion of which it formed part: this was completed in 1796. He may have designed the NEW WHITE CLOTH HALL at LEEDS in 1786 as in that year he was paid for valuing the old White Cloth Hall and removing its clock to the new one [D. Linstrum, *West Yorkshire Architects and Architecture*, 1978, 284, 379]. According to T. Allen's *History of the County of York* ii, 1831, 510, he designed ST. PAUL'S CHURCH, LEEDS, 1791–3; dem. 1906 (illustrated by T. D. Whitaker, *Loidis and Elmete*, 1816, 69).

JOHNSON, WILLIAM, was a surveyor at Nottingham, and was probably the William Johnson, of St. Peter's, Nottingham, described as a joiner, who married at the age of 30 in 1688. When the same William Johnson died at Nottingham in 1716, he was described in his will as 'gentleman' and left tenements in Middle Pavement called Johnson's Court [marriage licence and will proved in Notts. Archdeaconry Court, *ex inf.* Mr. Edward Saunders].

In 1690 'Mr. Johnson of Nottingham' was employed to survey works then in progress at THE RESIDENCE, SOUTHWELL [P.R.O., Eccles. 2/118]. In 1701 Sir John Harpur of CALKE ABBEY, DERBYSHIRE, paid £2 3s. 0d. to 'Mr. Johnson the Surveyor' for unspecified services in connection with the new mansion he was then building [accounts in Harpur-Crewe papers, Derbyshire C.R.O.], and in 1708 the borough of Nottingham decided that Mr. William Johnson was 'to survey part of the free School in order to rebuild it' [*Records of the Borough of Nottingham* vi, 40–1].

JOHNSTON, CORNELIUS, 'painter and architect', published in January 1754 a 'design for a British Musaeum' to contain in a quadrangular building the Cottonian Library, the Royal and Antiquarian Societies, and a Royal Academy of Painting, Sculpture and Architecture. There are impressions in the Print Room of the British Museum and in the British Library, *King's Maps* xxiv, 17a, and an illustration will be found in J. Mordaunt Crook, *The British Museum*, 1972, fig. 14. The design has a strongly rococo character unusual in English eighteenth-century architecture. No other reference to Cornelius Johnston has so far come to light.

JOHNSTON, JOHN, was an English architect who went out to Brazil in 1815 in order to superintend the erection of a replica of the gateway at Syon House, Isleworth (by Robert Adam), which the 2nd Duke of Northumberland had commissioned from the Coade Stone factory as a present to the Prince Regent of Portugal, who was then living in exile at Rio de Janeiro. Johnston established himself in Rio, where in the course of the next few a years he reconstructed the Prince's house, the QUINTA DA BOA VISTA at SAO CHRISTOVAO, and was responsible for various other buildings in a recognizably English style, notably the ENGLISH CHURCH in RIO DE JANEIRO, 1820; dem. [Michael Teague, 'An English Architect in Brazil', *C. Life*, 18 Aug. 1960].

JOHNSTON, ROBERT, of Kilmarnock, designed THE MANSE at IRVINE, AYRSHIRE, 1820 [S.R.O., HR 719/10]; TARBOLTON CHURCH, AYRSHIRE, 1820–1 [S.R.O., HR 718/1 and 2]; and THE KING STREET U.P. CHURCH at KILMARNOCK, 1832 [A. McKay, *History of Kilmarnock*, Kilmarnock 1880, 248]. The last was one of the earliest Nonconformist churches in Scotland to have a spire.

JOHNSTONE, ALEXANDER, is the name inscribed inside the cover of a quarto volume of architectural drawings on Whatman paper dated 1814 in private possession in Scotland. The drawings include plans and/or elevations of several existing country houses in Scotland, e.g. Ardgowan, Coilsfield and Langholm Lodge, and only one (an elevation of a small house) is signed by Johnstone. An unexecuted design for a portico for SPRINKELL HOUSE, KIRKPATRICK FLEMING, DUMFRIESSHIRE, and plans and elevations of the wings added to that house in *c.*1818, suggest that Johnstone may have been employed there in an architectural capacity.

JOHNSTONE, ALLAN, was a builder-architect of Stirling, where he is known to have built Nos. 13–14 MELVILLE PLACE (now TERRACE), *c.*1810 and a number of houses in QUEEN STREET. He also designed THE ERSKINE CHURCH, STIRLING, a simple but effective pedimented building of 1824–6; dem. [David Walker in *C. Life*, 28 Aug. 1969]. In 1815–16 he built THE ATHENAEUM in KING STREET to the designs of William Stirling (*q.v.*) [David Walker in *Bull. Scottish Georgian Soc.* i, 1972, 46–7].

JOINET, M—, exhibited a 'Design for a house to be built in Scotland' at the Royal Academy in 1804. His address was 6 Noel Street, Berwick Street, London. He may have been the artist named Joinet who was employed by Messrs. Eckhardt to finish by hand their printed wallpapers [E. Croft-Murray, *Decorative Painting in England* ii, 1970, 225]. A watercolour by him of Guy's Cliff House, Warwickshire, dated 1807, is in the Victoria and Albert Museum.

JONES, EDWARD, was a pupil of John Wallen. He presumably travelled in Greece, and in 1835 he published a thin folio volume entitled *Athenian or Grecian Villas, being a series of original designs for Villas or Country Residences*, dedicated to Sir Robert Smirke. He exhibited at the Royal Academy in 1819, 1826, 1831 and 1835. In 1826 he showed a drawing of the Temple of Jupiter at Athens, in 1831 a design for an ornamental temple based on the Temple on the Ilissus, 'proposed to be built' by Mrs. Powys of Berwick House, Salop., and in 1835 a 'Design for an Athenian Cottage'. In 1834 he exhibited a 'Design for a Villa in the Athenian style of Architecture' both at the Society of British Artists in Suffolk Street and at the Liverpool Academy of Arts. He was probably the 'Mr. Jones' who in 1823 made an unexecuted design for Broomhall, Fife, the seat of the 7th Earl of Elgin [J. Mordaunt Crook in *C. Life*, 29 Jan. 1970, 245–6].

JONES, EVAN, was a Flintshire master carpenter of the early seventeenth century. In 1637 it was according to 'a plott . . . drawen by Evan Jones Carpenter' that Ralph Booth, a freemason of Chester, undertook to build NERCWYS (NERQUIS) HALL, FLINTS., for John Wynne. All the architectural details were to be similar to those at RHUAL, FLINTS., recently built for Evan Edwards, and any defects noted in the work at Rhual were to be avoided at Nercwys 'accordinge to the direccion of the said Evan Jones' [Clwyd Record Office, D/NH 1007 A]. Jones must therefore be regarded as the designer of Nercwys Hall (which bears the date 1638), but his model at Rhual (1634) was inspired by English houses and may have had an English architect (see *C. Life*, 25 June 1943).

JONES, FRANCIS, of Hasfield, Glos., was one of the master masons employed to rebuild NEWENT CHURCH, GLOS., of which he and James Hill of Cheltenham laid the first stone on 31 July 1675. The roof of the Gothic nave was to have been supported by three stone columns, but the parish was persuaded by a carpenter named Edward Taylor (*q.v.*), who had worked in London after the Great Fire, to do away with the columns and erect the roof in a single span. The church was completed in 1679, the medieval steeple being retained. Soon after he had finished the church, Jones rebuilt the bridge over the Severn at OVER, nr. Gloucester; this was demolished in 1834, after the erection of the present bridge to the designs of Telford [MS. account of the building of Newent Church by Walter Nourse, of Kilcot, *c.*1725]. Francis Jones may have been the master mason employed by Uvedall and Mary Tomkins to rebuild the nave and chancel of MONNINGTON-ON-WYE CHURCH, HEREFS., in 1679–80, as the windows and finials are similar in design to those at Newent.

JONES, INIGO (1573–1652), was the son of Inigo Jones, a London clothworker of Welsh origin. He was baptised in the church of St. Bartholomew-the-Less, Smithfield, in July 1573. Very little is known about his early life, but according to George Vertue, Sir Christopher Wren had information that he was apprenticed to a joiner in St. Paul's Churchyard. It is, however, as a painter or artist that he first appears in record, for in 1603 a payment of £10 to 'Henygo Jones, a picture maker', occurs in a list of gifts and rewards in the household accounts of the 5th Earl of Rutland. In that year Jones may have accompanied the Earl on a diplomatic visit to the Danish court, but what is more important is evidence that at this period of his life Jones spent some time ('many years' according to his pupil Webb) in Italy. It is likely that he formed part of the entourage of Francis Manners, the Earl of Rutland's brother, who spent several years abroad, mainly in Italy, between 1598 and 1603. In 1605 Jones was described as 'a great traveller', and in 1606 a friend who gave him a copy of *De Rebus Gestis a Sixto V Pon: Max.* (Rome, 1588), wrote an inscription in Latin on the fly-leaf which expressed the hope that through Jones's agency, 'sculpture, modelling, architecture, painting, theatrical design and all that is praiseworthy in the elegant arts of the ancients, may one day find their way across the Alps into our England'. By the early years of James I's reign, therefore, Inigo Jones had already acquired sufficient expertise abroad to see himself as an artistic missionary capable of introducing the sophisticated arts of Italy into an England which as yet had little conception of what the Renaissance meant in terms of the visual arts.

It was in the service of Queen Anne of Denmark that Jones first enjoyed the patronage of the royal court, and it was the court masque in which he revealed his skill as an

Italian-trained designer. Between 1605 and 1640 he was responsible for staging over fifty masques, plays and other court entertainments, often in collaboration with Ben Jonson. Both poet and designer were assertive men jealous of their respective skills and reputations, and their relationship was not an easy one. More than once what Jonson saw as Jones's arrogance and pedantry were exposed to ridicule in his verses, but Jones prevailed in 1631, when Jonson retired discomfited from the court after the poor reception of his masque *Chloridia*.[1] Although nothing can now recapture the magic of these ephemeral performances to which Jones devoted so much of his time, over 450 drawings for scenery and costumes survive to demonstrate his virtuosity as a draughtsman and his familiarity with Italian stage designs, especially those of Alfonso and Giulio Parigi at Florence. All these drawings have been described and illustrated by Stephen Orgel and Roy Strong, who point out that they reveal a marked development in Jones's style between 1605 and 1609. The earliest drawings of 1605 'belong directly to an existing artistic tradition and betray no knowledge of Italian Renaissance draughtsmanship', whereas by 1609 Jones was drawing freely in an accomplished Italianate manner. This development might seem to add strength to Gotch's hypothesis of a visit to Italy in 1606, but of this there is no definite evidence, and it was not until the summer of 1609 that Jones is known to have made another foreign journey, a short visit to France, in the course of which he was able to inspect the Roman monuments of Provence.

Jones had made a name for himself as a theatrical designer some years before he became actively involved in architecture. Architectural settings are of course to be found in the early masque drawings, but they are of a romantic and insubstantial character, and do not suggest any deeper interest in architectural composition. The earliest design by Jones for a real structure that has so far been identified is for a monument to Lady Cotton (d. 1606) at Norton-in-Hales in Shropshire. A strapwork cartouche framing the inscription shows that at this date Jones had not yet wholly emancipated himself from the decorative conventions of Jacobean mannerism, but the sarcophagus supporting the effigy is classical in intention. Drawings of *circa* 1608 for the New Exchange in the Strand and for the completion of the central tower of St. Paul's Cathedral are evidence at once of a nascent architectural ambition, of an imperfect assimilation of classical themes from such sources as Serlio, Palladio and Sangallo, and of a total lack of practical architectural experience. They are, in the words of Sir John Summerson, 'obviously the work of somebody who had had little to do with architecture and nothing with building'. At Hatfield House in 1609 Jones appears in the role of an architectural consultant, apparently modifying certain features of a building already in progress, but not as an architect in general control of the whole operation.

In 1610 Jones's appointment as Surveyor to Henry, Prince of Wales, brought him a little closer to practical architecture, for besides devising a masque and a dramatic tourney for the Prince, he may have been involved in some internal alterations to St. James's Palace, where the Prince was establishing a library and picture gallery. However, the Prince's death in 1612 brought this appointment to an end, and it was not until the following year that Jones was granted the reversion of the place of Surveyor of the King's Works (27 April 1613). It may have been about this time that (perhaps through the good offices of Sir Henry Wotton) Jones acquired a number of original drawings by Andrea Palladio.

The second Italian journey which Jones made in 1613–14 was of crucial importance in his education as an architect. He went in the train of the young Earl of Arundel, destined to be one of the greatest of English patrons and collectors of art. The Earl himself was escorting Princess Elizabeth and her husband the Elector Palatine to Heidelberg after their wedding in England, but, that duty completed, he spent over a year in Italy accompanied by Jones. In 1613 they visited Milan, Padua, Parma, Siena, Florence, Bologna and Vicenza. After spending the winter of 1613–14 in Rome they visited Naples, Venice, Vicenza, Genoa and Turin before returning home via Paris. In Venice Jones met Scamozzi, on whom the mantle of the great Palladio had fallen. A surviving sketch-book shows that he was still studying the work of Italian painters such as Parmigianino, Schiavone and Guercino, on whom his own style of draughtsmanship was largely based, but his annotated copies of Palladio's *Quattro Libri* and other standard architectural works show that he was also systematically visiting the buildings illustrated in them and acquiring a critical knowledge of the theory and grammar of classical architecture. Further drawings by Palladio himself

[1] Jonson's final gibe at Jones was the character of 'Colonel Iniquo Vitruvius' in *Love's Welcome at Bolsover*, an entertainment written by Jonson for the Earl of Newcastle in 1634.

were now added to his collection, bringing the total in his possession to at least 250.

Jones's second visit to Italy gave him the necessary equipment to exploit the Surveyor's place, to which he succeeded on Simon Basil's death in September 1615. Though much routine administration fell to the Surveyor, the holder of the office had the opportunity to design whatever buildings were called for by the King, and in James I Jones had a patron whose expenditure on his palaces was lavish compared with Queen Elizabeth's careful economy. The Whitehall Banqueting House, the Queen's House at Greenwich and the queen's chapel at St. James's Palace are the surviving products of his period of office under James I. They show him not only as a careful student of Palladio and Scamozzi but also as a mature architectural designer whose skill in composition was controlled by an intellectual grasp of the principles of Renaissance architecture. Nothing like these buildings had previously been seen in England, and in a baroque Europe they were an unexpected reaffirmation of High Renaissance principle which found no contemporary parallel in France or Italy. In England they remained isolated monuments of an art which few even of Jones's own staff at the Office of Works could emulate. On contemporary English taste their influence was limited, because Jones himself designed very little outside the immediate circle of the court, and his style was too sophisticated to be easily absorbed by provincial master builders. In some designs (apparently unexecuted) for smaller private houses, made in about 1638, however, Jones did provide a prototype for the restrained astylar domestic architecture that was to be fashionable in England after the Restoration.

Between 1625 and 1640 Jones's principal architectural works were the repair and remodelling of St. Paul's Cathedral and the designing of Covent Garden for the Earl of Bedford. His work at St. Paul's provided precedents for a classical church architecture which were to be taken up by Wren in the reign of Charles II, but the outstanding feature of the building as Jones left it was the great Corinthian portico, the largest north of the Alps, in which he demonstrated the grandeur of classical architecture in a manner for which none of his other works gave an opportunity. In Covent Garden he not only designed the first wholly classical church in England, but also carried out a piece of uniform planning that was to be of immense importance in the history of English urban architecture. What might have been his greatest work was, however, never begun. This was the replacement of the old incoherent palace of Whitehall by a new architectural complex symmetrically grouped round a series of monumental courtyards, into one of which the Banqueting House was to be incorporated. This scheme, frustrated by Charles I's financial and political difficulties, is represented today by a large and confusing series of drawings, mostly in the hand of Jones's pupil and assistant John Webb, which have been ably analysed by Dr. Margaret Whinney. Of the many variant schemes distinguished by Dr. Whinney, only one can confidently be attributed to Jones himself, and even this is known only from drawings by Webb. It was, however, the starting-point of all the projects for a new Whitehall which stretch from the reign of Charles I to that of William III, and for this reason it has an importance which transcends its ephemeral character as the abortive dream of a powerless monarch.

After his appointment as Surveyor of the King's Works Jones had little time to spare for private commissions. In the 1630s, when Charles I himself was anxious to offer Jones's services to his Lord Chamberlain, the Earl of Pembroke, at Wilton House, Jones had to delegate the commission to Isaac de Caux because of pressure of work at Greenwich. Only the greatest courtiers such as the Duke of Buckingham, the Earl of Salisbury or the Earl of Bedford could normally command his services, and the attribution of undocumented private works to Jones has to be tested not only by stylistic criteria but also by the standing of the patron at court. Apart from Wilton, the only country houses that pass both these tests are Houghton and Stoke Bruern. Chevening (*c.*1630)[1] and the screen at Castle Ashby (*c.*1630)[2] both fail the stylistic test, and although Raynham (*c.*1620) was a remarkable epitome of motifs that appear in Jones's earlier drawings, it appears to be rather an intelligent reflection of his style than a personal work.[3] Apart from John Webb there were other architects such as Edward Carter, Isaac de Caux, Sir Balthazar Gerbier and Nicholas Stone whose style, though not measuring up to the exacting standards which Jones set himself, would probably have satisfied many patrons who wanted something fashionable, but could not command the services of the King's Surveyor.

For Jones, as for his royal master, the 1640s were years of distress. 'As the conductor of

[1] Illustrated in *Vitruvius Britannicus* ii, pl. 85 and *C. Life*, 17 & 24 April and 1 May 1920.

[2] For which see above, p. 227.

[3] See John Harris, 'Raynham Hall', *Archaeological Jnl.* cxviii, 1963, and above, p. 330.

ruinously expensive court entertainments, as the executor of arbitrary proclamations about London building and, most especially, as the accomplice of Archbishop Laud (in the rebuilding of St. Paul's Cathedral) he was marked out for trouble.' In December 1641 he was brought before the House of Lords to answer a charge of high-handed conduct towards the parishioners of St. Gregory's, a church whose fabric stood in inconvenient proximity to the south-west corner of St. Paul's. He was not impeached, but the Lords directed that part of the materials collected for the repair of the cathedral were to be given to the parishioners for the restoration of their church. In January 1642 the King left Whitehall, and later in the year Jones was with him in Yorkshire, no doubt to assist in the intended siege of Hull, for which his knowledge of fortification would (though hitherto untested) be useful. In July, when the court was at Beverley, the King signed a receipt for £500 lent to him by his Surveyor. In 1643 Jones was ousted from his place as Surveyor of the Royal Works by Edward Carter (*q.v.*). In 1644–5 he was among the royalists caught in Basing House, Hampshire, and was captured when Cromwell took the place by siege in October 1645. The sequestration of his estate followed, but it was restored on the payment of a fine. According to Vertue, he and Nicholas Stone had successfully hidden 'their joint store of ready money' in Lambeth Marsh, and when he made his will on 22 July 1650 Jones was able to leave a modest fortune to be divided between John Webb, who had married his 'kinswoman' Anne Jones, Richard Gammon, who married Elizabeth Jones, another kinswoman, and other legatees. He appears to have had lodgings in Somerset House, where he died unmarried on 21 June 1652. He was buried with his parents at St. Benet's, Paul's Wharf. A monument decorated with reliefs of the Banqueting House and St. Paul's Cathedral was destroyed in the Great Fire. Aubrey's sketch of it is reproduced in *The King's Arcadia* (1973), 405.

Jones had many Catholic patrons, and was said (on the authority of Sir Christopher Wren), to have died a Catholic. However, the fact that he was an M.P. (1621) and a Justice of the Peace means that he must have been a conforming Anglican during his active life. Furthermore in 1636 a papal agent in England characterized him as *puritanissimo fiero*, by which he appears to have meant that he was an irreligious person and certainly not a Catholic.

The portraits of Inigo Jones are described in the articles by C. F. Bell and Oliver Millar listed below and also in *The King's Arcadia*, Nos. 406–12. The most important are (1) a print by Francesco Villamena, made in Italy before 1624, presumably in 1613–14; (2) three self-portraits of various dates at Chatsworth; (3) the drawing by Van Dyck at Chatsworth from which Robert van Voerst made his engraving for Van Dyck's *Iconographiae* (1640); (4) an oil portrait by Van Dyck at the Hermitage, St. Petersburg; (5) an oil portrait by Dobson at Chiswick House datable *c.*1644.

Jones's drawings passed into the possession of his pupil John Webb, who bequeathed them to his son William Webb, with strict injunctions that they should not be dispersed. It appears, however, that they were sold by William's widow. In the 1680s John Aubrey noted that 'John Oliver, the City Surveyor, hath all [Jones's] papers and designs, not only of St. Paul's Cathedral, etc. and the Banquetting House, but his designe of all Whitehall.' After Oliver's death in 1701 his collection appears to have been acquired by William Talman, from whose son John (*q.v.*) it passed in the 1720s to Lord Burlington. When Burlington died in 1753 his collections passed to his daughter Charlotte, who had married the 4th Duke of Devonshire. In 1894 the 8th Duke gave the architectural drawings to the Royal Institute of British Architects (see *R.I.B.A. Drawings Catalogue: Inigo Jones & John Webb*, by John Harris, 1972), but retained the masque designs, which are the subject of a separate catalogue by Orgel and Strong. Meanwhile another collection of drawings by Jones and Webb had been acquired by Dr. George Clarke (*q.v.*) from an unknown source. These drawings were bequeathed by Clarke to Worcester College, Oxford, in 1736, and are described in the catalogue by Harris and Tait published in 1979. Many of the drawings in Lord Burlington's possession were published in William Kent's *Designs of Inigo Jones* (1727), Isaac Ware's *Designs of Inigo Jones and Others* [1731], and John Vardy's *Designs of Mr. Inigo Jones and Mr. William Kent* (1744), but without distinguishing between Jones's hand and Webb's. Scholarly analysis of the drawings in the two collections began with Gotch and Grant Keith and has been continued by Whinney, Harris, Tait and Higgott (see bibliography). A comprehensive study of all Jones's known drawings was published in 1989 (Harris & Higgott, *Inigo Jones: Complete Architectural Drawings*).

Over forty books from Jones's library are in the library of Worcester College, Oxford. Many of them contain annotations in his hand. There is a list in *The King's Arcadia*, Appendix III. Jones's annotated copy of

Serlio (1560–2) is in the library of the Queen's College, Oxford.

SELECT BIBLIOGRAPHY

A comprehensive bibliography will be found in Harris & Higgott, *Inigo Jones: Complete Architectural Drawings*, 1989, 328–30.

1. General and Biographical

W. G. Keith, 'Inigo Jones as a Collector', *R.I.B.A. Journal* xxxiii, 1925–6, 94–108.

J. A. Gotch, *Inigo Jones*, 1928.

C. F. Bell, 'Portraits of Inigo Jones', *R.I.B.A. Journal*, 11 Sept. 1937, 1007.

J. A. Gotch, 'Inigo Jones's Principal Visit to Italy in 1614: the Itinerary of his Journeys', *R.I.B.A. Journal*, 21 Nov. 1938, 85–6.

E. S. De Beer, 'Notes on Inigo Jones', *Notes and Queries*, 30 Dec. 1939, 27 April and 4 May 1940.

R. Wittkower, 'Inigo Jones, Puritanissimo Fiero', *Burlington Mag.* xc, 1948, reprinted in *Palladio and English Palladianism*, 1974: see also H. S. Ettlinger in *Burlington Mag.* Nov. 1991, 776.

D. J. Gordon, 'Poet and Architect: the Intellectual Background to the Quarrel between Ben Jonson and Inigo Jones', *Journal of the Warburg and Courtauld Institutes* xii, 1949.

Oliver Millar, 'Dobson's portrait of Inigo Jones', *Burlington Mag.* xciv, 1952, 207.

R. Wittkower, 'Inigo Jones, Architect and Man of Letters', *R.I.B.A. Journal*, 3rd ser., lx, 1953.

Lawrence Stone, 'Inigo Jones and the New Exchange', *Archaeological Jul.* cxiv, 1959.

John Summerson, 'Inigo Jones', *Proceedings of the British Academy*, 1, 1965.

John Summerson, *Inigo Jones*, 1966.

The King's Arcadia: Inigo Jones and the Stuart Court, exhibition catalogue by John Harris, Stephen Orgel and Roy Strong, 1973.

J. A. Skovgaard, *A King's Architecture*, 1973, Appendix IV: 'Inigo Jones and Christian IV [of Denmark]'.

G. K. Paster, 'Ben Johnson and Architecture', *Renaissance Quarterly* xxvii, 1974.

John Summerson, 'The Surveyorship of Inigo Jones' in *The History of the King's Works*, ed. Colvin, iii, 1975.

John Newman, 'Inigo Jones e la sua copia de "I Quattro Libri" di Palladio', *Bollettino del Centro . . . di Studi di Architettura 'Andrea Palladio'* xii, 1980.

Gordon Higgott, 'Inigo Jones in Provence', *Arch. Hist.* 26, 1983.

David Yeomans, 'Inigo Jones's Roof Structures', *Arch. Hist.* 29, 1986.

John Newman, 'Inigo Jones's Architectural Education before 1614', *Arch. Hist.* 35, 1992.

Gordon Higgott, ' "Varying with Reason": Inigo Jones's Theory of Design', *Arch. Hist.* 35, 1992.

Edward Chaney, 'Inigo Jones in Naples', in *English Architecture Public and Private: Essays for Kerry Downes*, ed. Bold & Chaney, 1993.

2. Drawings

Margaret Whinney, 'John Webb's Drawings for Whitehall Palace', *Walpole Soc.* xxxi, 1942–3.

John Harris, *Catalogue of the R.I.B.A. Drawings Collection: Inigo Jones & John Webb*, 1972.

John Harris & A. A. Tait, *Catalogue of Drawings by Inigo Jones & John Webb in the Library of Worcester College, Oxford*, 1979.

John Harris & Gordon Higgott, *Inigo Jones: Complete Architectural Drawings*, 1989.

Jeremy Wood, 'Inigo Jones, Italian Art, and the practice of Drawing', *Art Bulletin* 74, June 1992.

3. Sources and Style

Joan Sumner Smith, 'The Italian Sources of Inigo Jones's Style', *Burlington Mag.* xciv, 1952, 200–6.

John Harris, 'Inigo Jones and his French Sources', *Metropolitan Museum Bulletin*, May 1961.

John Harris, 'The Link between a Roman second-century sculptor, Van Dyck, Inigo Jones and Queen Henrietta Maria', *Burlington Mag.* cxv, 1973, 526.

4. Jones as a Theatrical Designer

Stephen Orgel & Roy Strong, *Inigo Jones, The Theatre of the Stuart Court*, 2 vols. 1973.

John Orrell, *The Theatres of Inigo Jones and John Webb*, Cambridge 1985.

FULLY AUTHENTICATED WORKS

NORTON-IN-HALES CHURCH, SALOP., monument to Lady Cotton (d. 1606), later modified to accommodate the effigy of her husband Sir Rowland Cotton (d. 1634) [John Newman, 'An early drawing by Inigo Jones and a monument in Shropshire', *Burlington Mag.* cxv, 1973, 360].

NEWMARKET PALACE, SUFFOLK, brew-house, stable, dog-house, riding-house and stables for Sir Thomas Compton and Mr. Dupper, 1615–17; the Prince's Lodging and clerk of works' house, 1619–21; dem. *c.*1650 [John

Harris, 'Inigo Jones and the Prince's Lodging at Newmarket', *Architectural History* ii, 1959; *History of the King's Works* iv].

GREENWICH PALACE, KENT, THE QUEEN'S HOUSE, begun for Queen Anne of Denmark, 1616–19, completed for Queen Henrietta Maria, 1630–5; altered 1661, when the bridges over the east and west entrances were added [G. H. Chettle, *The Queen's House, Greenwich*, London Survey monograph, 1937: *History of the King's Works* iv].

ST. JAMES'S PALACE, WESTMINSTER, the Prince's Buttery, 1617–18; dem.; the Queen's Chapel, 1623–5; Sculpture Gallery and pergola to Queen's Withdrawing Chamber, 1629; dem.; gateway in park wall, 1631; dem. [*History of the King's Works* iv].

SOMERSET HOUSE, STRAND, lantern over the hall, 1617–18; Queen's Cabinet Room, 1626; river stairs, 1628–31; the Queen's Chapel, 1630–5; refitted Cross Gallery, 1635; new cabinet room, 1637; all dem. 1776–90 [*History of the King's Works* iv]; also the fountain in the garden, with sculpture by Le Sueur, 1635–6; removed to Hampton Court 1656 and to Bushy Park 1713 [Geoffrey Fisher & John Newman, 'A fountain design by Inigo Jones', *Burlington Mag.* 127, Aug. 1985, 531–2].

OATLANDS PALACE, SURREY, great gate to park, silk-worm house and gateway to vineyard, for Queen Anne of Denmark, 1616–17; arbour in garden for Queen Henrietta Maria, 1631; balcony to Queen's lodgings, 1635; all dem. 1650 [W. G. Keith, 'The Palace of Oatlands', *Arch. Rev.* xxxix, 1916; *History of the King's Works* iv; *R.I.B.A. Drawings Cat.: Jones & Webb*, 16–17; *Inigo Jones: Complete Architectural Drawings*, 76–83].

LONDON, ARUNDEL HOUSE, STRAND, alterations for 14th Earl of Arundel, including a gateway dated 1618 and probably the addition of the sculpture gallery; dem. *c.*1678 [*R.I.B.A. Drawings Cat.: Jones & Webb*, 13; *Inigo Jones: Complete Architectural Drawings*, 126–8].

LONDON, STRAND, entrance with 'pergola' to house of Sir Edward Cecil, *c.*1618; destroyed by fire 1628 [*R.I.B.A. Drawings Cat.: Jones & Webb*, 13; *Inigo Jones: Complete Architectural Drawings*, 90–2].

WHITEHALL PALACE, lodgings for George Villiers, Marquess of Buckingham, 1619–20; lodgings for the Countess of Buckingham, 1620–1; park stairs 1624 (remodelled 1628); clock-house 1626; Cockpit reconstructed as a theatre 1629 (see below); masquing room, 1637; all dem. [*History of the King's Works* iv].

WHITEHALL PALACE, THE BANQUETING HOUSE, 1619–22; used as a Chapel Royal from 1698 to 1808, as a military chapel from 1808 to 1891 and as the Royal United Service Institution from 1891 to 1963. The exterior was progressively refaced in Portland stone in 1774, 1785 and 1828 [*History of the King's Works* iv; *Survey of London* xiii, chap. 4; Per Palme, *Triumph of Peace: a Study of the Whitehall Banqueting House*, 1957].

CHELSEA, BEAUFORT HOUSE, classical gateway for Lionel Cranfield, 1621; re-erected at Chiswick House, Middlesex, by 3rd Earl of Burlington, 1738 [*R.I.B.A. Drawings Cat.: Jones & Webb*, 13; *Inigo Jones: Complete Architectural Drawings*, 128–31].

THEOBALDS PALACE, HERTS., new stable, 1623; banqueting house, 1625; dem. *c.*1650 [*History of the King's Works* iv].

WESTMINSTER PALACE, HOUSE OF LORDS, new ceiling 1623–4; dem. 1823 [*History of the King's Works* iv].

GREENWICH PALACE, KENT, remodelling of Chapel; great gate to park, 1623–4; dem. *c.*1700 [*History of the King's Works* iv].

WHITEHALL PALACE, conversion of THE COCKPIT into a court theatre, 1629; dismantled *c.*1665 [J. Orrell, *The Theatres of Inigo Jones and John Webb*, 1985, chap. 5].

BAGSHOT PARK, SURREY, lodge, 1631–2; dem. [*History of the King's Works* iv].

LONDON, ST. PAUL'S CHURCH, COVENT GARDEN, for 4th Earl of Bedford, 1631–3; repaired and cased in Portland stone by Thomas Hardwick 1788–9; gutted by fire 1795 and rebuilt by Hardwick closely following Jones's design, 1796–8; altered internally by W. Butterfield 1871–2; refaced in brick 1887–8 [*Survey of London* xxxvi, chap. v; John Summerson, 'Inigo Jones', *Proceedings of the British Academy* 1, 1965, 170–82].

LONDON, COVENT GARDEN, THE PIAZZA, for 4th Earl of Bedford, 1631–7; for subsequent alterations and demolitions see *Survey of London*. None of the original houses now survives, but Bedford Chambers (by Henry Clutton, 1877–9) follows the character of the original design [*Survey of London* xxxvi, chap. iv].

LONDON, ST. PAUL'S CATHEDRAL, general repair, remodelled exterior of nave and transepts and added west portico, 1633–42; ruined by Great Fire of London 1666 and subsequently dem. [John Summerson, 'Inigo Jones', *Proceedings of the British Academy* 1, 1965, 182–91; *History of the King's Works* iii, 147–52].

LONDON, ST. GILES-IN-THE-FIELDS CHURCH, monument to the poet George Chapman (d. 1634), in the form of a Roman altar: inscribed 'Georgius Chapman poeta 1634. Ignatius Jones Architectus Regius ob honorem bonarum literarum familiari suo hoc mon DSPFC'. (*Survey of London* v, 136).

LONDON, HYDE PARK, lodge 1634–5; dem. [*History of the King's Works* iv; *The King's Arcadia*, 1973, 265].

LONDON, THE BARBER SURGEONS' HALL, MONKWELL STREET, ANATOMY THEATRE, 1636–7; dem. 1785 [J. Harris & A. A. Tait, *Catalogue of Drawings by Inigo Jones and John Webb in the Library of Worcester College, Oxford*, 1979, 9–10] (Isaac Ware, *Designs of Inigo Jones and Others*, 1736, pls. 8–9).

WINCHESTER CATHEDRAL, HANTS., choir-screen, 1637–8; dismantled 1820: the central portion is now in the Museum of Archaeology at Cambridge [*History of the King's Works* iii, 153; *R.I.B.A. Drawings Cat.: Jones & Webb*, 17; *Inigo Jones: Complete Architectural Drawings*, 248–9].

WIMBLEDON HOUSE, SURREY, alterations and additions for Queen Henrietta Maria, 1640–1; dem. *c.*1717 [C. S. S. Higham, *Wimbledon Manor House under the Cecils*, 1962, 31–2; *R.I.B.A. Drawings Cat.*: *Jones & Webb*, 17; *Inigo Jones: Complete Architectural Drawings*, 236–7].

DOUBTFUL OR INADEQUATELY DOCUMENTED WORKS

ASCOTT HOUSE, WING, BUCKS., apartment for 1st Earl of Carnarvon (d. 1643). According to Browne Willis (1682–1760), who lived in Buckinghamshire, 'This was a large house, and the Earl of Carnarvon, temp. Charles I, added a Noble Apartment to the old house, by the Plan of Inigo Jones: but it was never entirely finished' [B.L., Add. MS. 5840, f. 159v]. Willis says that the house was 'suffered to go to ruin' in the 1720s, but Luttrell says it was 'lately burnt down' in 1691 [*Diary of Narcissus Luttrell* ii, 233].

BYFLEET HOUSE, SURREY, as rebuilt or remodelled by Queen Anne of Denmark *c.*1617, had a classical portico in a style strongly suggestive of Inigo Jones, but known only from a sketch by John Aubrey reproduced in *Surrey Archaeological Colls.* 1, 1946–7, pl. xvi. The house was dem. *c.*1686.

COLESHILL HOUSE, BERKS. The story of Jones's involvement in the design of this house is confused and perhaps apocryphal. In the 1730s Sir Mark Pleydell, then the owner of Coleshill, recorded a local recollection that Sir George Pratt 'began a seat in the . . . Cucumber Garden and raised it one storey' before '[Sir Roger] Pratt and Jones arriving caused it to be pulled down and rebuilt where it now stands. Pratt and Jones were frequently here and Jones was also consulted about the ceilings.' There is evidence that Sir Henry Pratt, Sir George's father, had begun a house before 1645 (when he provided for its completion in his will) and there is said to have been a fire in 1647. The house ultimately built under the direction of Sir George's cousin Sir Roger Pratt (*q.v.*) was not begun until after Sir Henry's death in 1647 and was not completed until 1662: Jones may have been dead by the time work actually started and can hardly have been alive when the ceilings were executed. Three drawings by John Webb for capitals for 'Sir George Pratt at Coleshill' may help to confirm the involvement of his master Jones at some stage, but they are clearly for a house with an external order, unlike the astylar house eventually built. See further John Bold, *John Webb*, 1989, 157–8, and below, p. 778.

HALE CHURCH, HANTS., 1631–2; chancel rebuilt and transepts added by Thomas Archer, 1717; roof and cornice rebuilt in nineteenth century. Stylistic attribution [Peter Burman, 'Inigo Jones at Hale?', *C. Life*, 7 Feb. 1974].

HATFIELD HOUSE, HERTS. In 1609 Jones visited Hatfield, then being built for Robert Cecil, lst Earl of Salisbury, and was subsequently paid £10 'for drawinge of some Architecture'. It is possible that he modified the design of the arcaded south front, and probable that he designed the classical clock-tower [Lawrence Stone, 'The Building of Hatfield House', *Archaeological Jnl.* cxii, 1955].

HOUGHTON HOUSE, HOUGHTON CONQUEST, nr. AMPTHILL, BEDS., classical frontispieces for Mary, Dowager Countess of Pembroke (d. 1621), probably soon after 1615. Stylistic attribution [*The King's Arcadia*, 1973, 109–11].

LONDON, THE COCKPIT THEATRE, DRURY LANE, for Christopher Beeston, 1616–17; dem. 1649 [J. Orrell, *The Theatres of Inigo Jones and John Webb*, 1985, chap. 3, citing drawings at Worcester College]. According, however, to Higgott, *Inigo Jones: Complete Architectural Drawings*, 1989, 266, these drawings date from the 1630s and cannot therefore relate to the Drury Lane Cockpit Theatre.

LONDON, MARSHALSEA PRISON, SOUTHWARK, THE PALACE COURT, *c.*1630; dem. 1803. Stylistic attribution (*Gent's Mag.* 1803 (ii), 1205, engraving).

LONDON, advice on design of ST. MICHAEL-LE-QUERNE CHURCH, CHEAPSIDE, 1638; destroyed by fire 1666. Jones's involvement in the building of this church was an act of interference on the part of the Privy Council, who wanted the new building to be an ornament to the street. A 'modell' for a new church had already been made by Anthony Jerman and a Mr. Holmes before the Privy Council attempted to impose a new one made by Jones, and the churchwardens' accounts refer to numerous meetings between the parishioners and 'Mr. Surveyor', but the outcome is not clear [H. Colvin, 'Inigo Jones and the Church of St. Michael-le-Querne', *London Journal* 12 (1), 1986].

LONDON, house in Holborn for Sir Fulk Greville, before 1619: destroyed by fire 1666: although no design for this house survives, it had several features characteristic of surviving designs for London houses by Jones [*The King's Arcadia*, 104–5].

LONDON, YORK HOUSE, STRAND, THE WATER-GATE, for George Villiers, Duke of Buckingham, *c.*1625. It is not clear who designed this gateway, but Jones is one of the possible candidates: for discussion see p. 397.

NEW HALL, BOREHAM, ESSEX, alterations for George Villiers, Duke of Buckingham, 1622–3. Jones's involvement in New Hall is referred to in a letter from John Chamberlain to Sir Dudley Carleton dated 5 Sept. 1622, and is attested by a fragmentary memorandum dated 1622 relating to the chapel, by a design for a gateway dated 1623, and by a drawing for one bay of a coffered ceiling, probably for the closet in the chapel here rather than for the Duke's lodging in Whitehall. Jones appears to have been superseded by Sir Balthazar Gerbier (*q.v.*), who was employed here in 1624–5 [Gotch, 127; *Inigo Jones: Complete Architectural Drawings*, 132–3, 178–9].

STOKE PARK, STOKE BRUERN, NORTHANTS., for Sir Francis Crane, *c.*1630; central block destroyed by fire 1886, leaving the pavilion and quadrants. The ultimate authority for the attribution of this house to Jones is Colen Campbell, who says that 'This Building was begun by Inigo Jones; the Wings, and Collonades, and all the Foundations, were made by him; but the Front of the House was designed by another Architect, the Civil Wars having also interrupted this Work' [*Vitruvius Britannicus* iii, 1717, pl. 9]. Bridges (d. 1724), in his *History of Northamptonshire*, ed. Whalley, i, 1791, 328, says that Crane, 'brought the design from Italy, and in the execution of it received the assistance of Inigo Jones'. The pavilions are illustrated in *C. Life*, 23 July 1953.

WESTMINSTER ABBEY, monument to Isaac Casaubon, 1634. Stylistic attribution [Adam White, 'Classical Learning and the Early Stuart Renaissance', *Jnl. Church Monuments Soc.* i, 1985, 29].

WILTON HOUSE, WILTS. The evidence for Jones's involvement in the rebuilding of the south front for the 4th Earl of Pembroke in 1636 is John Aubrey's statement that 'King Charles the first did love Wilton above all places, and came thither every summer. It was he that did put Philip . . . Earle of Pembroke upon making this magnificent garden and grotto, and to new build that side of the house that fronts the garden, with two stately pavilions at each end, all *al Italiano*. His Majesty intended to have it all designed by his own architect, Mr. Inigo Jones, who being at that time . . . engaged in his Majesties buildings at Greenwich, could not attend to it: but he recommended it to an ingeniouse architect, Monsieur [Isaac] de Caus [*q.v.*], who performed it very well; but not without the advice and approbation of Mr. Jones.' When the interior was gutted in 1647 or 1648 it was rebuilt by John Webb, again 'by the advice of Inigo Jones', now too old to 'be there in person'. The existence of several designs for doorways and ceilings for Wilton by Webb, some dated 1649, and some with annotations by Jones, is evidence of his advisory role [H. M. Colvin, 'The South Front of Wilton House', *Archaeological Jnl.* cxi, 1954; A. A. Tait, 'Isaac de Caus and the South Front of Wilton House', *Burlington Mag.* 106, 1964, 74; John Bold, *Wilton House and English Palladianism*, R.C.H.M.E., 1988; John Heward, 'The restoration of the south front of Wilton House: the development of the house reconsidered', *Arch. Hist.* 35, 1992].

JONES, RICHARD, 3RD VISCOUNT and 1ST EARL OF RANELAGH (?1638–1712), was an Irish peer who as a young man enjoyed the favour of the Duke of Ormonde. Under Charles II he was Chancellor of the Irish Exchequer and manager of the Irish revenues. William III made him Paymaster of his Army (1691). A clever and plausible man, he was allowed with impunity to make large sums of money from public office. Building and gardening were his great enthusiasms, and according to Macky he 'spent more money, built more fine houses, and laid out more on household-furniture and gardening, than any other Nobleman in England'. As Treasurer of Chelsea Hospital (1685–1702) he built himself (*c.*1688–9) a handsome house (dem. 1805) immediately adjoining the hospital which, according to Bowack's *Antiquities of Middlesex* (1705), was 'Designed and built by himself'. This is supported by the fact that in 1683 Ranelagh House was taken as a model for the Earl of Rochester's new house at

Petersham, in the contract for which the Earl of Ranelagh himself is named as arbitrator in the event of any dispute between owner and builder [Surrey County Record Office, SC 13/26/102–3]. Ranelagh had, moreover, given architectural advice to Lord Conway in connection with his buildings at Newmarket and at Ragley in Warwickshire [*Cal. S.P. Dom. 1679–80*, 623; *1683* (i), 105, 128, 166, 172], and in 1704–5 it was he who supervised the enlargement of the Duke of Ormonde's house at Richmond in Surrey [Hist. MSS. Comm. *Seventh Report*, Appendix, 774–6]. The house called Cranbourn Lodge in Windsor Park, which Ranelagh bought from Lord Lexington in 1700, was of fairly recent erection, but here too his activities either as architect or as gardener are attested by a letter from Sidney Godolphin dated 18 July 1700 in which he says that 'at Cranborn . . . my Lord Ranelagh to all his usuall improvements has added more expedition than any other man could have been capable of' [Sotheby's, 6 Feb. 1973, lot 258]. An eighteenth-century view of Cranbourn Lodge by Sandby is reproduced by Oppé, *Sandby Drawings at Windsor Castle*, and there is a plan of the grounds by London and Wise (formerly Department of the Environment, 932/1155).

It was doubtless Ranelagh's reputation both for taste and for getting things done that in June 1700 led William III to make him 'Sur-intendent generall of oure Buildings & of our works in our parks' at a salary of £400 a year. This made Ranelagh in effect a minister of Works, with authority both over Wren as Surveyor-General of Works and over Talman as the officer in charge of the royal gardens. His tenure of the post lasted for less than two years before it was brought to an end by the King's death in March 1702. Ranelagh himself died on 5 January 1711/12. Among the legacies provided for in his will were two drawers of mathematical instruments, rulers and perspective glasses, which he left to his 'dear friend, John Earl of Mar' (*q.v.*), £20 each to John Churchill, Master Carpenter and Henry Wise, Master Gardener, 'to buy silver in remembrance of me who was heartily their friend', £50 to Richard, son of the joiner Sir Charles Hopson, £25 to 'honest Hugh Warren joyner', and smaller sums to his gardeners at Chelsea and Cranbourn.

[*D.N.B.*; *History of the King's Works* v, 35, 218; C. G. T. Dean, *The Royal Hospital, Chelsea*, 1950, chap. xviii; David Ascoli on Ranelagh and Chelsea Hospital in *C. Life*, 5 June 1975; *Survey of London* xxix, 67, 109–12, 299, 517; John Macky, *Memoirs of the Secret Services of John Macky*, 1733, 82; P.C.C., 99 BARNES.]

JONES, RICHARD (1703–*c.*1778), was the son of a cordwainer at Bath. He served an apprenticeship to a local mason and worked for some years at his trade before becoming in about 1730 clerk of the works to Ralph Allen, in whose service he remained until Allen's death in 1764. In 1765 he was appointed City Surveyor of Bath, but gave up the post when he was appointed Sergeant at Mace in 1772. In the City Library at Bath there is a nineteenth-century transcript of somewhat rambling reminiscences written or dictated by Jones. From these it is apparent that he had taught himself to draw and that he designed a number of buildings in and around Bath, besides building others to the designs of architects such as John Wood.

For Ralph Allen Jones began the building of PRIOR PARK to the designs of John Wood in 1735. After a disagreement between Allen and Wood in 1748 the house was completed by Jones, who altered the design of the east wing and was responsible for various outbuildings. In 1755–6 he built the Palladian Bridge in the park, but did not claim to have designed it. He does, however, state twice that the SHAM CASTLE on Claverton Down was built 'to my plan' or 'design'. Seven years earlier Sanderson Miller had been approached for a design for the eye-catcher, but there is no evidence that he was again consulted in 1762, and Jones's claim to have designed the Castle may well be correct. For Allen Jones also claimed to have built NEWTON BRIDGE at WESTON, *c.*1752–4, altered CLAVERTON HOUSE (dem. *c.*1820), and altered or repaired CLAVERTON and BATHAMPTON CHURCHES. When William Warburton, who had married Allen's favourite niece, became Dean of Bristol (1757), Jones was employed to reconstruct the DEANERY at a cost of £900, and in 1760, when Warburton was promoted to the bishopric of Gloucester, Jones dealt with the dilapidations at the BISHOP'S PALACE there. His final service to Ralph Allen was to design his elaborate pyramidal monument in CLAVERTON CHURCHYARD (1764).[1]

Among many other buildings which Jones says he was concerned with as builder or clerk of works, the only ones of which he specifically claims to have been the architect were the remodelling of the LOWER ASSEMBLY ROOMS at BATH in 1750 and the 'altering' of the OLD

[1] Jones specifically mentions his designs for Allen's monument, and relates that the latter 'sent for me to bring him the drawings of the burial place' some five days before his death, and gave him orders to have them carried out. The mason Robert Parsons, who was also consulted by Allen (cf. Gunnis, *Dictionary of British Sculptors*, 292), was probably employed to carry out Jones's design.

BRIDGE, by which he presumably meant its rebuilding in 1754. In 1766 he was one of several architects who made designs for the new Market and Guildhall, but nothing was done for several years and it was eventually built to the designs of Thomas Baldwin [W. Ison, *The Georgian Buildings of Bath*, 1948, 35]. A cryptic reference to his 'drawings of the other piece at Widcombe, done for one Squire Bennet, and his summer house in his garden', may indicate that Jones designed the delightful classical garden house at WIDCOMBE MANOR, illustrated by Ison, *op. cit.*, 30.

JONES, RICHARD (*c.*1756–1826), 'an eminent architect and surveyor', died at Worcester on 17 January 1826, aged 70. He published *The Builder's Vade-Mecum, or practice of Surveying etc., with Specifications*, 1809, and *Every Builder his own Surveyor*, 1809. He had earlier practised in Birmingham, where his son Richard (1779–1851) was born. The latter was trained as an architect, but, at the age of 18, 'an unfortunate speculation' of his father's 'caused so much embarrassment in his affairs', that, having some abilities as an actor, he decided to adopt the stage as his profession [*A.P.S.D.*; *D.N.B.*; 'Memoirs of Mr. Jones, Comedian' in *Monthly Magazine*, Aug. 1808, 68; obituary in *Gent's Mag.* 1826 (i), 94].

JONES, ROBERT, was a London tradesman who practised as a building surveyor in the reign of Queen Anne. He appears to have been a carpenter or joiner by trade, and in 1707 he told Lord Cholmondeley's agent that 'sence I left my trade of' he was 'dayly out upon vews and serveays and sumetymes in the Contry'. He said that his chief employment was fixing prices for the employment of workmen and settling their bills. The first Earl of Cholmondeley employed him at his house in Arlington Street, and in 1702 Jones was consulted about the rebuilding of CHOLMONDELEY CASTLE in CHESHIRE. Work appears to have started under his direction, but in view of the difficulty of supervising it at a distance he subsequently recommended Lord Cholmondeley to employ the Smiths of Warwick instead [Chester County Record Office, Cholmondeley archives DCH/L/29; Gervase Jackson-Stops in *C. Life*, 19 July 1973, 156].

Jones was the surveyor employed by the South Sea Company to fit up the premises in Threadneedle Street occupied by the Company before the erection of its new buildings in 1723–7. On 31 January 1711/12, the Deputy Governor reported that 'Mr. Jones the Surveyour had laid before them a Plan of the General Court in the nature of an Ampitheatre' and it was 'Resolved that a Gallary Ampitheatrewise correspondent with the lower part [of the design] be added'. In July 1712 it was ordered that Mr. Jones the carver should be paid £50 'as Rated by Mr. Robt. Jones the Surveyor of the work done for the Company's House'. No further reference to Jones occurs after this date [B.L., Minutes of the South Sea Company, vol. i, Add. MS. 25494, ff. 52v, 199].

JONES, ROBERT, was probably a joiner by trade. He appears to have succeeded Thomas Symonds (*q.v.*) as surveyor to the Dean and Chapter of Hereford. As an architect his principal recorded work was ST. ETHELBERT'S HOSPITAL, HEREFORD, a modest row of almshouses with simple Gothick detailing, built in 1804 [David Whitehead, 'St. Ethelbert's Hospital', *Trans. Woolhope Naturalists' Field Club* 45, 1986, 421–2].

JONES, THOMAS, of Exeter, *see* STOWEY, PHILIP.

JONES, THOMAS (*c.*1794–1859), had his office in Chester but practised chiefly in North Wales. He was County Surveyor of Flintshire from 1827 to 1855, when he resigned from ill-health, dying at Barmouth on 2 October 1859, aged 65. As a domestic architect he specialized in a 'Tudor' or 'Elizabethan' style comparable to that of Blore, as a church architect in a neat 'Perpendicular' Gothic, from which he never deviated into 'Early English', still less the 'Decorated' of the ecclesiologists. His most celebrated work was the Grosvenor Lodge to Eaton Hall, which was based on the gateway of St. Augustine's Abbey, Canterbury.

TALACRE HALL (now nunnery), FLINTSHIRE, for Sir Edward Mostyn, Bart., 1824–9, Tudor Gothic [J. Poole, *Gleanings of the History of Holywell, Flint*, etc., Holywell 1831, 67; J. Hemingway, *Panorama of North Wales*, 1835, 181–2]. However, Parry's *Railway Companion from Chester to Holyhead*, 1848, 62, attributes the design to Thomas Harrison (*q.v.*), and it is possible that Jones, then a young man at the start of his carerr, had taken the commission over from the aged Harrison.

ST. ASAPH, FLINTS., THE DEANERY (now Old Deanery), for Dean Charles Scott Luxmoore, 1830, Tudor Gothic [D. Pratt & A. G. Veysey, *Handlist of Topographical Prints of Clwyd*, Clwyd Record Office 1977, 80].

ST. ASAPH CATHEDRAL, FLINTS., Gothic altar-tomb to Bishop John Luxmoore (d. 1830); dem. [J. Hemingway, *op. cit.*, 4th ed. 1848, 284].

OTELEY, nr. ELLESMERE, SALOP., for C. K. Mainwaring, *c.*1830–3, Elizabethan style; enlarged 1840; dem. 1960 [J. Peake, Ellesmere 1889, 19] (F. Leach, *The County Seats of Shropshire*, 1891, 19).

LLWYNEGRIN, nr. MOLD, FLINTS., for P. Davies Cooke, 1830 [Pratt & Veysey, *op. cit.*, 70].

LOTON PARK, SALOP., additions for Sir Baldwin Leighton, Bart., 1830 and 1838 [drawings at Loton Park, *ex inf.* Mr. John Harris].

PENSAX CHURCH, WORCS., 1832–3, Gothic [I.C.B.S.].

MOLD, FLINTS., COUNTY HALL, 1833–4, 'Elizabethan' [J. Hemingway, *op. cit.*, 1835, 233].

EATON HALL, CHESHIRE, THE GROSVENOR LODGE for lst Marquess of Westminster, 1835, Gothic; dem. [J. Hemingway, *op. cit.*, 4th ed. 1848, 133].

RHYL, FLINTS., HOLY TRINITY CHURCH, 1835–6, Gothic; altered 1850–2 [D. R. Thomas, *A History of the Diocese of St. Asaph*, 1870, 304; I.C.B.S.].

WREXHAM CHURCH, DENBIGHSHIRE, Gothic monument to Sir Foster and Lady Cunliffe, *c.*1835 [J. Hemingway, *op. cit.*, 318]; altar-piece (dem.) [J. Hicklin, *Excursions in North Wales*, 1851, 211].

KINMEL, DENBIGHSHIRE, ST. GEORGE'S CHURCH, mausoleum in churchyard to Lady Dinorben (d. 1835), Gothic [J. Hemingway, *op. cit.*, 41].

TREVALYN HALL, DENBIGHSHIRE, alterations for Thomas Griffith, 1836–8 [Clwyd Record Office, Trevalyn papers 323–331] (*C. Life*, 12 July 1962).

CHESTER, CHRIST CHURCH, NEWTOWN, 1838, Gothic; dem. 1876 [*A.P.S.D.*, *s.v.* 'Chester'].

BALA UNION WORKHOUSE, 1838 [*N. Wales Chronicle*, 26 June 1838].

NORTHOP CHURCH, FLINTSHIRE, rebuilt except tower, 1839–40, Gothic; altered 1850, 1876–7, etc. [Vestry Minutes in Clwyd Record Office].

FFESTINIOG, MERIONETHSHIRE, ST. DAVID'S CHURCH, 1840, Gothic [*N. Wales Chronicle*, 4 Aug. 1840].

LLANGELYNIN CHURCH, CAERNARVONSHIRE, rebuilt 1839–40 [I.C.B.S., file 2549].

BRYN ASAPH, nr. ST. ASAPH, FLINTSHIRE, for the Misses Luxmoore, *c.*1840, Tudor Gothic; remodelled 1879 [Pratt & Veysey, *op. cit.*, 60].

LLANGELYNIN CHURCH, MERIONETHSHIRE, rebuilt 1840–2 [I.C.B.S., file 2622].

HORDLEY RECTORY, SALOP., 1840–3 [Lichfield Joint Record Office, B/A/13].

HARLECH (LLANDANWG) CHURCH, MERIONETHSHIRE, 1841, Gothic [*N. Wales Chronicle*, 12 Oct. 1841].

BARMOUTH, MERIONETHSHIRE, NATIONAL SCHOOL, 1841 [J. Hemingway, *op. cit.*, 83].

LLANFERRES CHURCH, DENBIGHSHIRE, enlarged and altered 1843 [I.C.B.S.].

LLANGWSTENYN CHURCH, CAERNARVONSHIRE, rebuilt 1843–4 [I.C.B.S.].

LLANARMON (DYFFRYN CEIRIOG) CHURCH, DENBIGHSHIRE, rebuilt 1846 [*N. Wales Chronicle*, 6 Oct. 1846; I.C.B.S.].

JONES, WILLIAM (–1757), was a minor Georgian architect best known as the designer of THE ROTUNDA in RANELAGH GARDENS, CHELSEA, a large circular building with an elegant galleried interior in which people of fashion drank tea and coffee and listened to music. It was opened in 1742 and demolished in 1805. There is an engraving in the Bodleian, Gough Maps 17, f. 36, signed 'William Jones, Architect', and various bills and contracts connected with the erection of the building are among the Chancery Masters' Exhibits in the Public Record Office (C 105/37/32).

Of Jones's earlier career all that is known is that he was the author of the 26 'Designs for Frontispieces' etc., which were appended to James Smith's *Specimen of Antient Carpentry* (1736), and which he republished in 1739 as the first part of a separate book entitled *The Gentlemen's or Builder's Companion containing Variety of usefull Designs for Doors, Gateways, Peers, Pavilions, Temples, Chimney-Pieces, etc.*, 'Printed for the Author, and sold at his house near the Chapple in King Street Golden Square'. The second part consisted of 28 designs for rococo tables, mirror-frames, chimney-pieces and ceilings, the tables being derived from Nicolas Pineau's *Nouveau Desseins de Pieds de Tables*.

Jones was the architect of SURGEONS' HALL, OLD BAILEY, LONDON, 1747–51, dem. 1803 [C. C. R. Morris, 'Surgeon's Hall, Old Bailey', *Trans. London & Middlesex Archl. Soc.* 35, 1984] and of the BERKELEY CHAPEL, BERKELEY SQUARE, *c.*1750; dem. [signed engraving in Westminster City Library, extra-illustrated Pennant, 1825 ed. iii, f. 363]. In 1752 he became Surveyor to the East India Company, and designed the Warehouses, Pay Office and Deputy Secretary's Office at EAST INDIA HOUSE, LEADENHALL STREET, in 1754; dem. 1861–2 [W. Foster, *The East India House*, 1924, 136]. In 1757 he submitted a design for NEWGATE GAOL which in layout closely followed one by the elder Dance but was treated externally in a bleak and rather amateurish castellated style [Harold Kalman in *Arch. Hist.* xii, 1969, 52–3 and fig. 28b]. An engraved view of the interior of 'the Roman Catholic Chapel in Tyburn Road as design'd by Will[m] Jones Arct.' may represent an unexecuted design by him for the Spanish Embassy Chapel.

As a country-house architect Jones is found at EDGCOTE HOUSE, NORTHANTS., where he followed William Smith as architect after the latter's death in 1747, and was largely if not wholly responsible for designing the house built by Richard Chauncey in 1747–52 [H. A. Tipping in *C. Life*, 10 Jan. 1920 and *English Homes*, Period V, vol. i, 1921, 289–300]; at ALRESFORD HOUSE, HANTS., which he rebuilt for the 1st Lord Rodney in 1749–51 [J. M. Robinson in *C. Life*, 5 Jan. 1978]; at WALLINGTON HALL, NORTHUMBERLAND, where in 1750 he made an unexecuted design, preserved in a portfolio, for a garden building; and at HONINGTON HALL, WARWICKS., where he supervised the building of the octagonal saloon (notable for its rococo decoration) for Joseph Townsend to the designs of the amateur architect John Freeman (*q.v.*) [Gloucester C.R.O., Strickland-Freeman papers, D 1245, FF 38] (*C. Life*, 27 Nov. 1920, 21, 28 Sept., 12 Oct. 1978). He was presumably the 'Jones' to whose designs Sir Sampson Gideon was building stables at BELVEDERE, KENT (dem. 1960) in 1756 [Sanderson Miller's diary in Warwicks. C.R.O., 1382/32, Sept. 1756], which raises the possibility that it was Jones whom Gideon employed to design the saloon at Belvedere, with its rococo decoration.

Though Jones was mainly a 'second-generation Palladian' of no special distinction, the Ranelagh Rotunda was an unusual building of some originality for which he deserves considerable credit, and it is likely that further works remain to be identified. William Newton became his pupil in 1750, Jacob Leroux in 1753. His death in 1757 is referred to in the minutes of the East India Company (23 Nov. 1757).

JOPLING, JOSEPH (*c.*1789–1867), was the son of Joseph Jopling of Cotherstone, near Barnard Castle. It is not known whether he was related to the J. Jopling who in 1786 submitted a design for rebuilding All Saints Church, Newcastle [T. Sopwith, *All Saints Church, Newcastle*, 1826, 47], or with John Jopling, a Newcastle marble-mason of the early nineteenth century who is said to have been 'a good sculptor' and to have had 'a fine taste for miniature painting' [E. Mackenzie, *Newcastle* ii, 1827, 589]. Nothing is known of his training, but he was probably the J. Jopling who exhibited a 'Design for a Gothic church' at the Royal Academy in 1816. He subsequently practised in London as an architect and civil engineer. His only recorded works in the former capacity appear to have been the Greek Revival PANTECHNICON (a furniture repository, latterly 'Sotheby's Belgravia') in MOTCOMB STREET, BELGRAVIA, which he designed for Seth Smith in 1830–1 [C. Hussey in *C. Life*, 31 March 1966], and the COLUMN at AMMERDOWN PARK, SOMERSET, in memory of T. S. Jolliffe, 1853–5, of which he published an elaborate account in the *Builder* xi, 1853, 633–4. He was best known as an authority on theories of proportion and the finer points of architectural draughtsmanship, on both of which subjects he wrote some abstruse treatises. The Society of Arts gave him a Gold Medal for an improvement in the construction of the ribs of groined arches. He was also the inventor of a method of drawing curves which he published as *The Septenary System of generating Curves by continued motion including sundry observations . . . on its application and utility in civil and naval architecture [and] sculpture* . . . 1823. His subsequent publications included *The Septenary System of generating lines: No. 1. Description of Jopling's Double Cranks*, 1825; *The Practice of Isometrical Perspective*, 1833, 2nd ed. 1839; *Blackfriars Bridge and Thames Navigation*, 1833; *The Septenary System of Generating Lines, No.* 2, 1844; *Letter to T. L. Donaldson . . . on the necessity of numerous correct examples of Mathematical Lines*, 1847; *Examples of Entasis*, 1848; *An Impulse to Art: or Ancient Greek Practical Principles for Volutes and Lines of Beauty* 1849; *A Key to the Proportions of the Parthenon*, 1855, and *A Key to the Proportions of the Parthenon, No.* 2, 1856. As literary executor of his uncle, Charles Waistell (d. 1825), he published in 1827 *Designs for Agricultural Buildings, Labourers' Cottages etc., by the late Charles Waistell, Esq., Chairman of the Committee of Agriculture of the Society of Arts*. He also contributed articles to the *Builder* (vol. ii, 1844, 532, 557, 585) and the *Mechanics' Magazine*. He died in Kensington on 10 May 1867 [Calendar of Probates].

JOYCE, JAMES, designed MACKRELL'S CHARITY SCHOOL, ALMER, DORSET, 1832, which bears the inscription 'James Joyce, Architect' [R.C.H.M. *Dorset* ii (2), 286]. He was probably a local builder.

JOYNES, HENRY (*c.*1684–1754), was, as stated on his monument in Hendon churchyard, 'Comptroller and Conductor of the Building of Blenheim House in Oxfordshire from 1705 to 1715'. His duties were those of a resident clerk of the works, and there are frequent references to him in Vanbrugh's letters, and in the papers relating to Blenheim in the British Library (Add. MSS. 19602–10). He also assisted Hawksmoor in connection with the erection of the Clarendon Building in Broad Street, Oxford, to the latter's designs in 1712–13 [Add. MS. 19607, ff. 14, 83, 90–100]. In 1715, when Hawksmoor became Clerk of the Works at Whitehall, Joynes succeeded him as Clerk of the Works at Kensington Palace, an appointment which he owed to the influence of Sir John Vanbrugh as Comptroller of the Works. He remained in charge of the works at Kensington until his death.

It is clear from the Blenheim papers that Joynes was a competent draughtsman, and there is evidence that he had a private practice as an architect. Letters and drawings preserved at LINLEY HALL, SALOP., show that he designed that house in 1743–6 for Robert More, M.P., F.R.S. It is an unusual house for its date, combining the strength and movement of a Vanbrughian design with the decorative conventions of the current Palladianism, and shows that Joynes was an architect of ability and originality [Arthur Oswald in *C. Life*, 7–14 Sept. 1961]. References in the letters make it clear that Joynes was also responsible for designing NORMANTON PARK, RUTLAND, for Sir John Heathcote, Bart., *c.*1735–40. This house was altered and enlarged by K. Couse in 1763–7 and demolished *c.*1920 (*C. Life*, 8 Feb. 1913). The letters also afford evidence that Joynes was, as stated by Batty Langley (*Ancient Masonry*, 1736, 227), the architect of the house in LINCOLN'S INN FIELDS (now Nos. 57–8) built by Lord Chancellor Charles Talbot in 1730. This has a Palladian elevation designed to harmonize with the adjoining Lindsey House (*Survey of London* iii, 90–1, pls. 73–5).

A payment to 'H. Joynes Surveyor' in the accounts of Sir John Fellowes, Bart., as printed in *The Particulars and Inventories of the Estates of the late . . . Directors of the South Sea Company* i, 1721, shows that Joynes was employed at CARSHALTON HOUSE, SURREY, in about 1720. Here it is possible that he designed the Water Pavilion, a markedly Vanbrughian building illustrated by Field & Bunney, *English Domestic Architecture of the Seventeenth and Eighteenth Centuries*, 1905, pl. lxviii and described in *C. Life*, 4 March 1949. In 1731 Joynes competed for the Bank of England, and his design was short-listed with that of George Sampson, the successful competitor [W. M. Acres, *The Bank of England from Within* i, 1931, 167].

From 1723 to 1748 Joynes was Surveyor to the Commissioners of Sewers in Westminster. He married Mary, daughter of Bartholomew Peisley of Oxford, a master mason whose son was employed at Blenheim. He died at Kensington on 2 July 1754, at the age of 70, leaving his house in Kensington Gore to his elder son Samuel. He desired to be buried in Hendon churchyard near the east end of the chancel, beneath a monument of Portland stone to be erected 'according to a Draught prepar'd by me'. The monument, which still exists, consists of a square pedestal with a moulded cornice.

[*A.P.S.D.*; *History of the King's Works* v, 475; *The Complete Works of Sir John Vanbrugh* iv: *The Letters, passim*, esp. 244; *Wren Soc.* xx, 116; David Green, *Blenheim Palace*, 1951, *passim*; B.L., Add. MS. 24327; P.C.C., 200 PINFOLD.]

JUPP, RICHARD (1728–1799), was the son of Richard Jupp of Clerkenwell, Master of the London Carpenters' Company in 1768, to whom he was apprenticed, being made free of the Company in 1749. Nothing is known of his architectural training, but the fact that he was one of the original members of the Architects' Club would imply that, in accordance with its rules, he had studied architecture in Italy or France.

Jupp succeeded James Steere (d. 1759) as architect to GUY'S HOSPITAL, where he supervised the building of the west wing in 1774–7 and remodelled the principal façade in 1777–8 [R. A. Cawson and T. H. E. Orde, 'The Design and Building of Mr. Guy's Hospital', *Guy's Hospital Reports* 118 (2), 1969]. He also designed DYERS' HALL, DOWGATE HILL, 1768–70, rebuilt 1839–40 [Dyers' Company minutes, Guildhall Library MS. 8164/5, pp. 216–17, 219, 221, 237].

In 1774 Jupp designed PAINS HILL HOUSE, nr. COBHAM, SURREY, for Benjamin Bond Hopkins, who had just purchased the estate from the Hon. Charles Hamilton. The 'principal front' was exhibited at the Royal Academy under his name in 1778. The house was enlarged by Decimus Burton in 1831–2, and Jupp's portico, awkwardly placed between flanking bows, was removed in the nineteenth century (*C. Life*, 2 Jan. 1958). In about 1790 Jupp altered or remodelled WILTON PARK, nr. BEACONSFIELD, BUCKS. (dem. 1967) for Josias Dupré, Governor of Madras [J. Dugdale, *The British Traveller* i, 1819, 138]. LEE MANOR-HOUSE, KENT, built in 1772 by Thomas Lucas, has been attributed to him for reasons given in E. & J. Birchenough, *The Manor House, Lee*, Lewisham 1971, 61–3.

For over thirty years (1768–99) Jupp was surveyor to the East India Company, for which he designed several warehouses in London, including the BENGAL WAREHOUSE in NEW STREET, 1796–70, those between

Houndsditch and Middlesex Street, 1792–9, and others on the south side of Crutched Friars, 1796–9 [Minutes of the Court in India Office Records, B 116, ff. 62, 772, B 125, ff. 151–2 and A/1/1, ff. 402, 490, 507]. In 1796 it was decided to rebuild the EAST INDIA HOUSE in LEADENHALL STREET, and the Company, anxious to secure a worthy design for their new building, and evidently uncertain whether their surveyor was equal to the task, decided that he should be asked to take the advice of some of the leading architects of the day. Dance, Wyatt, Holland and Soane were mentioned, but Soane's name was eventually withdrawn at Jupp's instance because he feared that this young and ambitious man, already Architect to the Bank of England, would seek to deprive him of the commission altogether. Unfortunately for Jupp, Soane was at this time the victim of some scurrilous writings which James Wyatt was unwise enough to read aloud at a meeting of the Architects' Club (of which Jupp was a member); and when the unhappy Jupp, in an endeavour to placate Soane by exposing his enemies, sent him a copy of one of these pamphlets, he merely succeeded in identifying his conduct over the East India House with the personal attack on Soane. An interview, at which, according to Soane, Jupp made himself seem 'a knave talking like an honest man', did nothing to mend matters, and in spite of Dance's counsels of moderation, Soane, while privately preparing plans for the new East India House, endeavoured unsuccessfully to bring Jupp's conduct before the General Court of Proprietors.

Meanwhile Jupp had addressed a pathetic letter to the Directors, reminding them of his twenty-nine years of faithful service, and imploring them not to deprive him of this opportunity of distinguishing himself. This had its effect. On 9 August 1796 Jupp was directed to prepare plans without any reference to other architects, and on 23 September these plans were accepted. The building was begun under Jupp's direction the following year, and was substantially complete by the time of his death on 17 April 1799. Jupp's place as Surveyor to the Company was then filled by Henry Holland, who had the task of finishing off the interior and settling the accounts. It has often been claimed that although Jupp was the nominal architect of the East India House, the design was really made for him by Holland. The basis of this allegation appears to be a note by H. B. Hodson in the *Builder* for 15 September 1855 (p. 437) recording that in 1807 he found a quantity of working drawings for the building in Holland's office. These drawings are now in the Victoria and Albert Museum (boxes A.175–6), but they relate almost exclusively to the interior, and the fact that they came from Holland's office does not prove that they were his work. Several of them are drawn on paper watermarked 1796, and one of them is a 'Section of the Lime Street Front as settled by Mr. Jupp, April 31st. 1797'. Jupp himself claimed credit for the design both by exhibiting it at the Royal Academy in 1798 and by issuing a printed description of the façade, with a key to the sculpture in the pediment. The building (demolished 1861–2) was illustrated as his work in Britton & Pugin's *Public Buildings of London* ii, 1828, 77–89, and Holland's alleged participation in its design must be regarded as unsubstantiated.

Jupp evidently designed PARK FARM PLACE, ELTHAM, KENT (now LONDON), for Sir William James, Bart., one of the Directors of the East India Company, for in 1778 the painter Rigaud was employed by Jupp to decorate one of the ceilings ['Memoir of J. F. Rigaud', ed. Pressly, *Walpole Soc.* 50, 1984, 63], and after James's death his widow commissioned Jupp to design (1784) SEVERNDROOG CASTLE, SHOOTER'S HILL, KENT, a triangular Gothic tower 'To Commemorate that Gallant Officer's Achievements in the East Indies during his Command of the Company's Forces in those Seas', and in particular his capture in 1755 of the fortress of Severndroog on the coast of Malabar [J. Dugdale, *The British Traveller* iii, 1819, 245].

[*A.P.S.D.*; *D.N.B.*; Carpenters' Company Records in Guildhall Library, London, MS. 4335/4; India Office Library, records of the East India Company, especially B 1/123, pp. 498, 642 (minutes of 9 Aug. and 23 Sept. 1796); Farington's Diary, 17 Aug. 1799; A. T. Bolton, *The Portrait of Sir John Soane*, 1927, 59–79; information from Mr. N. Kitz.]

JUPP, WILLIAM (1734–1788), was one of the sons of Richard Jupp, Master of the Carpenters' Company in 1768, to whom he was apprenticed, being made free of the Company in 1753. He exhibited two designs for gentlemen's seats at the Society of Artists in 1763 and 1764, and an unexecuted design for a country house signed by him is at the Platt Hall Art Gallery, Rusholme, Manchester. He rebuilt the LONDON TAVERN, BISHOPSGATE STREET WITHIN (dem. 1876), after its destruction by fire in 1765. The entrance hall and principal staircase of CARPENTERS' HALL, LONDON WALL, were erected to his designs, *c.*1780. The entrance hall was decorated in stucco work with figures and implements emblematic of carpentry, and with the heads of Vitruvius, Palladio, Inigo Jones and Wren, executed by Bacon. The archway forming the entrance to the street was also designed by Jupp, with a bust of Inigo Jones by Bacon on the keystone. The staircase was damaged by fire in 1849 and the Hall itself was demolished in 1876. Both at Carpenters' Hall and at the London Tavern, Jupp appears to have been assisted by William Newton, who certainly designed the Eating-Room and Ballroom of the latter building. Jupp was a warden of the Carpenters' Company in 1781. He was the father of William Jupp (d. 1839) and of Richard Webb Jupp, solicitor (1767–1852), who was Clerk to the Carpenters' Company from 1796 to 1852. The latter's son, Edward Basil Jupp, F.S.A. (1812–77), Clerk to the same Company from 1852 to 1877, was the author of an *Historical Account of the Worshipful Company of Carpenters*, 1848, 2nd ed. 1887, from which the above particulars are largely derived [*A.P.S.D.*; *D.N.B.*; C. H. L. Woodd, *Pedigrees and Memorials of the Family of Woodd and the Family of Jupp*, privately printed 1875; Carpenters' Company Records in Guildhall Library, London, MS. 4335/4].

JUPP, WILLIAM (1770–1839), was the younger son of William Jupp (d. 1788). He was Master of the Carpenters' Company in 1831. He exhibited at the Royal Academy from 1794 to 1804, including a design for a room at the 'Star and Garter' Hotel at Richmond, Surrey (1803). He was architect and surveyor to the Skinners', Merchant Taylors', Ironmongers' and Apothecaries' Companies, and was also District Surveyor for Limehouse, Blackwall, Wapping, Mile End Old Town, Poplar and Ratcliff. In 1801–3 he carried out alterations to SKINNERS' HALL, DOWGATE HILL [J. F. Wadmore, *Account of the Skinners' Company*, 1902, 133], and as surveyor to the Merchant Taylors' Company was presumably the architect of that Company's Almshouses at Lee, Kent, erected in 1826. In 1821 he designed for the Revd. John Clayton what was described as 'a neat gentleman's residence' at GREAT GAINS, UPMINSTER, ESSEX [accounts in Essex C.R.O., D/DU/651/149].

[*A.P.S.D.*; E. B. Jupp, *Historical Account of the Company of Carpenters*, 1887.]

K

KAY, JOSEPH (1775–1847), was a pupil of S. P. Cockerell. He travelled on the Continent from 1802 to 1805, for part of the time in company with Robert Smirke. The journal which he kept in Rome in 1803–4 is in the British Library (Add. MS. 45545, ff. 1–34). In 1807 he married the eldest daughter of William Porden, whom he assisted in the erection of EATON HALL, CHESHIRE [Neale, *Views of Seats* i, 1818]. In the same year he was appointed surveyor to the Foundling Hospital in succession to Cockerell, and in this capacity laid out the garden in MECKLENBURGH SQUARE and designed the block of houses on the east side, begun in 1810, but not completed until 1821. He exhibited the design at the Royal Academy in 1812. In 1811 he succeeded J. T. Groves as architect to the Post Office, and in 1818–19 designed the POST OFFICE in WATERLOO PLACE, EDINBURGH [P.R.O., WORK 1/13]. In 1814 he made preliminary designs for a new General Post Office in London, but, after much bureaucratic wavering and an indecisive competition, they were set aside in favour of plans by Robert Smirke which were executed in 1823–9. Kay's design is preserved in P.R.O., WORK 30/414–5, and in Sir John Soane's Museum (Drawer 38, 6). He keenly felt the disappointment, and from that time onward never entered into competition for any public works, confining himself to private practice and to the duties of his appointments. In 1823 he succeeded H. H. Seward as Clerk of Works to Greenwich Hospital. In this capacity he carried out extensive improvements in the town, forming NELSON STREET and the new MARKET in 1829.

Kay's private clients included the Thornhill family, for whom he supervised the development of their ISLINGTON estate from 1813 onwards [see many letters from Kay among the Thornhill papers in the Hunts. Record Office] and for whom he designed BOXWORTH RECTORY, CAMBS., in 1840 in a Tudor Gothic style [Ely Diocesan Records in C.U.L., MGA 44]; the Earl of Chichester, for whom in 1824–8 he carried out a handsome piece of town-planning at HASTINGS, consisting of PELHAM CRESCENT with the church of ST. MARY-IN-THE-CASTLE as its central feature; the Marquess Camden, who employed him on his CAMDEN TOWN estate in London; and the Earl of Radnor, for whom in 1843 he made an unexecuted scheme for housing at Folkestone which is preserved in the Radnor Estate Office there. In 1819 he made designs for large additions to Lord Radnor's seat, Longford Castle, Wilts., but these were not carried out. It is also uncertain whether the 'small library and picture gallery designed for D. W. Acraman, Esqr.', which he exhibited at the Royal Academy in 1808, was built. In 1809–11 he completed the MALL ASSEMBLY ROOMS at CLIFTON, BRISTOL, after the bankruptcy of F. H. Greenway, the original architect and builder. His designs for the decoration of the ceilings, signed and dated 1811, are in the Victoria and Albert Museum (93 H.23, nos. 3 and 20). One drawing by Kay connected with Greenwich Hospital is in the R.I.B.A. Drawings Collection, and at Rougham Hall, Norfolk, there are plans by him dated 1828 for enlarging a house at Hastings for Frederick North. He presumably designed THE CUPOLA, BELMONT ROAD, HASTINGS, a picturesque classical villa of which he was the occupant in 1840, and probably also the adjoining BELMONT HOUSE and MINNIS ROCKS.

Kay was secretary of the London Architects' Club. He also took an active part in the formation of the Institute of British Architects, and became one of its first vice-presidents. He died on 7 December 1847, aged 72, at his house, No. 6 Gower Street, and was buried in the Foundling Hospital Chapel. His eldest son, William Porden Kay, born in 1809, assisted his father for many years before going out to Australia in 1842 as Director of Public Works. His daughter Eliza married Edward Basil Jupp, grandson of William Jupp (*q.v.*). Charles Matson was a pupil.

[*A.P.S.D.*; John Summerson, *Georgian London*, 1969, 168–9; *History of the King's Works* vi, 431–2; P.R.O., Greenwich Hospital Records; F. T. Cansick, *Epitaphs of Middlesex* ii, 1872, 247.]

KAY, ROBERT (1740–1818), was an Edinburgh architect and drawing-master and a distant relative of John Kay, the Scottish caricaturist. He was born at Cairnton, nr. Penicuik, and began life as a wright or carpenter. 'But, gradually advancing himself by steady application and industry, he became a builder and architect, and attained to no small degree of respectability and professional reputation.' In 1781 he entered the competition for St. Andrew's Church in the New Town, which was won by Captain Frazer (*q.v.*) with a design for an oval church. Frazer, however, 'declined accepting the premium, desiring it might be given to Mr. Robert Kay, drawing master in Edinburgh, whose drawings and section of a square church were thought highly meritorious' [*Scots Mag.* 1781, 119].

Kay was the architect employed by the Trustees for the SOUTH BRIDGE in EDINBURGH to make plans for the Bridge built by Alexader Laing (*q.v.*) in 1785–88, and for the adjoining houses, including those in HUNTER SQUARE. A much grander architectural treatment was proposed by Robert and James Adam, and Kay's utilitarian designs were subjected to considerable criticism and modification before execution [A. G. Fraser, *The Building of Old College*, Edinburgh 1989, chap. 3].

In 1796–7 Kay designed the COLLEGE STREET RELIEF CHURCH, EDINBURGH (dem.) [*Edinburgh Evening Courant*, 22 Oct. 1796]. In the Sottish Record Office there is an unexecuted design by him for a church at Wick in Caithness, dated 1796 [RHP 12365]. For the Commissioners of Northern Lighthouses he designed lighthouses at NORTH RONALDSHAY, ORKNEY, and SCALPAY, WESTERN ISLES, in 1786–9 [R. W. Munro, *Scottish Lighthouses*, Stornoway 1979, 55].

Kay made a modest fortune by successful speculation in the South Bridge development. On his retirement in about 1806 he built a house at Wester Duddingston on the southeast outskirts of Edinburgh. When he died in 1818 he was buried in a lair in the Calton Old Burying Ground which has 'Robert Kay Architect' carved on the lintel. His fortune was mostly bequeathed to charity. A caricature portrait is given in John Kay's *Original Portraits* ii, 1838, 378, together with a short biography. See also the *Book of the Old Edinburgh Club* xxiv, 167 n.

KECK, ANTHONY (1726–1797), had a considerable practice in Gloucestershire, Worcestershire and Herefordshire between about 1760 and 1790. Nothing is known of his origins, but by 1768 he was established at King's Stanley in Gloucestershire and it was at Beech House in that village that he died in August 1797, aged 70. He had become a freeman of Worcester in 1768. Keck designed a number of medium-sized country houses, mostly with fairly plain exteriors and elegant interior decor of Adamsian derivation. A common formula for his earlier houses was a central block with lower wings, often bowed. Later he favoured a more compact three-storeyed block of the sort introduced by Sir Robert Taylor. His finest work, the great Orangery at Margam Abbey in Glamorganshire, 327 feet in length, is so much in the style of Taylor as to suggest the possibility of some involvement by the latter. Keck was also concerned in canal works, designing the Ryeford double lock on the Stroudwater Canal in 1779. Unexecuted designs by him for alterations to Allensmore Court in Herefordshire are in the R.I.B.A. Drawings Collection.

[*A.P.S.D.*; *Berrow's Worcester Jnl.*, 12 Oct. 1797; Nicholas Kingsley, 'The Work of Anthony Keck', *C. Life*, 20–27 Oct. 1988; M. Handford, *The Stroudwater Canal*, Gloucester 1979, 311.]

BEVERÉ HOUSE, NORTH CLAINES, WORCS., for Dr. T. R. Nash, *c.*1765 [*A.P.S.D.*] (illustrated on the title-page of T. R. Nash's *History of Worcestershire* i, 1781).

BOWNHAMS, STROUD, GLOS., enlarged for James

Winchcombe, 1766–70; dem. *c.*1960 [N. Kingsley, *The Country Houses of Gloucestershire* ii, 1992, 278].

WORCESTER, THE COUNTY INFIRMARY, 1767–70; altered *c.*1855 [V. Green, *History of Worcester* ii, 1796, 12; engraved plan and elevation signed by Keck in Bodleian, Gough Maps 33, f. 54].

FERNEY HILL, DURSLEY, GLOS., for W. Purnell, 1768 [N. Kingsley, *op. cit.*, 285–6].

WORCESTER, ST. MARTIN'S CHURCH, 1768–72; altered 1855–62 by W. J. Hopkins, who inserted Gothic tracery in the E. window [V. Green, *History of Worcester* ii, 1796, 62].

UPTON-ON-SEVERN CHURCH, WORCS., added cupola to W. tower, 1769–70 [MS. 'Parish Book' under date 18 July 1769] (H. Field & M. Bunney, *English Domestic Architecture of the 17th and 18th Centuries*, 1905, pl. cvii).

HAM COURT, UPTON-ON-SEVERN, WORCS., for John Martin, 1772; dem. 1925 [accounts partly reproduced in copy of 1914 sale catalogue in Birmingham Reference Library].

KENTCHURCH COURT, HEREFS., Drawing Room and other alterations for John Scudamore, 1773 [contract in Herefs. C.R.O., M 26/6/14, *ex inf.* Mr. D. Whitehead] (*C. Life*, 29 Dec. 1966, fig. 3).

PENRICE CASTLE, GLAMORGANSHIRE, for Thomas Mansel Talbot, 1773–80 [C. A. Maunsell, *The Family of Maunsell* i, 1917, 231; John Cornforth in *C. Life*, 18–25 Sept. 1975; R.C.A.M. *Glamorganshire* iv (i), 1981, 293–303].

DURSLEY, GLOS., design for WORKHOUSE, 1774 [Gloucester Public Library, MS. RF 115, 72].

MOCCAS COURT, HEREFS., for Sir George Cornewall Bart., 1776–83;[1] semicircular porch added 1792 [W. Angus, *Views of Seats*, 1787, pl. xix] (*C. Life*, 18–25 Nov. 1976).

attributed: HANBURY HALL, WORCS., alterations for Henry Cecil, later Marquess of Exeter, soon after 1776 [G. Haworth in *C. Life*, 12 Dec. 1991].

FLAXLEY ABBEY, GLOS., reconstruction after fire in 1777, for Thomas Crawley-Boevey, 1780 [N. Kingsley, *op. cit.*, 141–3] (*C. Life*, 29 March–12 April, 1973).

BATSFORD PARK, GLOS., alterations for Thomas Freeman, 1777–81; dem. 1886 [N. Kingsley, *op. cit.*, 73].

BARNSLEY PARK, GLOS., redecoration of dining-room for James Musgrave, *c.*1780 [C. Hussey in *C. Life*, 9 Sept. 1954; N. Kingsley, *op. cit.*, 62].

WORCESTER COUNTY GAOL, enlarged 1784–8 [V. Green, *History of Worcester* ii, 1796, 29].

HILL HOUSE (later RODBOROUGH MANOR), RODBOROUGH, GLOS., extensions for Sir G. O. Paul, 1784–92; burned 1906 [*V.C.H. Glos.* xi, 224; N. Kingsley, *op. cit.*, 212–14].

GLOUCESTER, inspected and altered the plans made by William Price for the EASTGATE and SOUTHGATE STREET MARKETS, which were erected by Price in 1785–6 under Keck's supervision [extracts by C. H. Dancey from Gloucester City Council Books in Gloucester Public Library, 17270].

attributed: CANON FROME COURT, HEREFS., for Richard Cope Hopton, 1786 [stylistic attribution based on resemblance to Moccas Court].

MARGAM ABBEY, GLAMORGANSHIRE, THE ORANGERY, for Thomas Mansel Talbot, 1787–90 [drawing at Penrice Castle signed 'A Keck Oct. 4 1787' and entitled 'greenhouse now building', *ex inf.* Mr. O. E. Craster, 1961; Patricia Moore, 'The Orangeries at Margam', *Glamorgan Historian* iv, 1967, 25] (R.C.A.M. *Glamorganshire* iv (i), 1981, 293–303).

FORTHAMPTON COURT, GLOS., alterations for James Yorke, Bishop of Ely, and his wife Mary, 1788; altered 1889–91 [Clive Aslet in *C. Life*, 27 Sept. 1979; N. Kingsley, *op. cit.*, 286].

LONGWORTH HALL, HEREFS., added wings for Robert Phillipps, *c.*1788 [J. P. Neale, *Views of Seats*, 2nd ser. iv].

MORETON-IN-MARSH CHURCH, GLOS., enlarged S. aisle for Thomas Freeman of Batsford Park, 1790–1; rebuilt 1858 [Glos. C.R.O., D 1447/7/4, 56: ledger of Thomas Freeman].

KEEBLE, HENRY ASHLEY (–1840), was apprenticed in 1783 to George Gwilt the elder. He exhibited at the Royal Academy from 1797 to 1806, and competed for the New Bethlehem Hospital in 1810. Under a lease dated December 1830 he designed and built Nos. 45–57 FALMOUTH ROAD, SOUTHWARK, a row of stucco-fronted houses illustrated in *Survey of London* xxv, 116. The gate and entrance-lodges of LANSDOWNE, a country house in PENNSYLVANIA, U.S.A., were erected to his designs by its owner William Bingham in 1798 [R. W. Moss, *the American Country House*, New York 1990].

[1] Alternative designs made by Robert & James Adam in 1775 were not carried out, but in 1781 they supplied some further designs for chimney-pieces and a ceiling to decorate the house designed by Keck [Soane Museum, vol. xxiii, 136–9, and information from Mr. Nicholas Thompson].

KEENE, HENRY (1726–1776), born on 15 November 1726, was the son of Henry Keene, probably the carpenter of that name who was one of the builders of Ealing Church, Middlesex, to the designs of James Horne in 1739–40. He was 'bred to the profession of architecture', and in 1746 succeeded Thomas Hinton as Surveyor to the Dean and Chapter of Westminster. In 1752 James Horne resigned his post as Surveyor to the Fabric of Westminster Abbey in favour of Keene, who thus combined both the Abbey surveyorships until his death. There are many references in the Chapter Acts to his duties in connection with the estates of the Dean and Chapter, and details of his architectural work in the Abbey are given below. A letter in which he described the opening of Edward I's tomb in 1774 is printed in Hist. MSS. Comm., *Third Report*, Appendix, 276*b*.

In 1761 Keene was taken to Ireland by Lord Halifax, the newly appointed Lord-Lieutenant, and according to a letter written by the Dean of Westminster to Lord le Despenser in the following year[1] he was 'appointed by him Architect of the Kingdom of Ireland for his Majesty's Works there'. No such office existed at this date, but from 1763 to 1766 Keene is referred to in Irish records as 'Architect to the Barrack Board' in Dublin, and it was from the Barrack Board that the Irish Board of Works later developed. Nothing is at present known of any works which Keene may have carried out in this capacity, but in the 1750s he had already been employed, in conjunction with John Sanderson, to make the working drawings for the west front of Trinity College, Dublin, designed by the amateur architect Theodore Jacobsen (*q.v.*). According to the Dean of Westminster, he also held the post of 'Gentleman of the Privy Chamber' to his patron the Lord-Lieutenant, at whose Sussex seat he and his son were afterwards to be employed.[2]

As a private architect, Keene is chiefly remarkable as one of the first to exploit the fashion for Gothic which became so characteristic a feature of English taste in the latter part of the eighteenth century. He was not a serious student of Gothic architecture in the same way as James Essex; but as Surveyor to Westminster Abbey he was in daily contact with a famous medieval building, and details from Westminster recur frequently in his Gothic work. At Arbury, for instance, the Drawing Room fireplace is copied from the tomb of Aymer de Valence, and in 1766 a joiner was taken to the Abbey to make exact copies of foliage and other Gothic details for Sir Roger Newdigate's house. The Gothicization of Arbury had begun under Sanderson Miller's direction, and it may well have been through Miller that Keene first became interested in Gothic, for as early as 1749 he was helping Miller to make drawings for Hagley,[1] and about the same time Miller records in his diary that he repaired Nelmes in Essex 'by means of Mr. Henry Keene (then a young beginner in architecture)'. The octagonal Hartwell Church (now a shell since the collapse of its plaster vaulting in 1951) was Keene's *chef d'oeuvre* in this style, but characteristic examples of his elegant rococo Gothic can still be seen at Hartlebury Castle and Harefield Church. As a classical architect, Keene is best known for the handsome Town Hall which he built for Lord Shelburne at High Wycombe, for his various works at Oxford, and for the elegant and original monument to Lord Lichfield at Spelsbury, with its cutaway perspective of urns in the base.

A conversation piece painted by Robert Pyle in 1760 (unfortunately destroyed by fire at Buxted Place in Sussex in 1940, but illustrated in *Country Life*, 30 March 1945, 556) shows Keene in company with a group of building craftsmen. According to J. G. Nichols, who owned the picture in the early nineteenth century, Keene was in the habit of dining with his favourite craftsmen and consulting them about designs he had in hand, and the picture was commissioned by some of them as a present to him. The principal figure is Keene himself, who is pointing to a plan of an unidentified building, which is laid on the table. The other persons present are Ben Carter (statuary mason), Euclid Alfray (Keene's clerk), Devereux Fox, Thomas Dryhurst (carver), Thomas Hefford (plasterer), George Mercer (mason), Edmund Rawlinson (landscape painter), Thomas Gayfere (Master Mason to Westminster Abbey), J. Pratt (bricklayer), William Cobbett (glazier), William Chapman (plumber), John Devall (mason), Jeremiah Hutchins (painter), and Thomas Collins (plasterer). Eight of the craftsmen depicted were employed by Keene in the building and decoration of Nos. 17–18 Cavendish Square in 1756–7, four in altering Sir Roger Newdigate's house in Spring Gardens in 1763, and three in building Hartwell Church in 1752–3.

[1] Bodleian Library, Oxford, MS. D. D. Dashwood (Bucks.) c. 7.

[2] For information about Keene's career in Ireland I am indebted to Mr. M. J. Craig and Dr. E. McParland.

[1] Warwick C.R.O., Sanderson Miller's correspondence, 125B/350.

Keene invested in house property in Golden Square, London, where he had a town residence (No. 13, dem. 1906). He also took a building site on the Portland estate in Harley Street at the time of its development by the Adam brothers, and possessed property in Oxford.[1] He had a country house at Drayton Green, Ealing, where he died on 8 January 1776, at the age of 50.

Keene died in mid-career, but there are indications that in Oxford at least, where a few years earlier he had been thought of as 'a very ingenious man', his reputation was declining. In 1773 it was James Wyatt who was chosen to design the Canterbury Quadrangle at Christ Church, although Keene had earlier been employed there to alter the Library, and in the same year Keene's design for the Radcliffe Observatory had been set aside in favour of 'another Elevation', almost certainly that of Wyatt, by whom the building was completed after his death. Keene was, in fact, an architect of minor stature in comparison with Wyatt, 'in whose hands the design for the Observatory acquired a distinction and an originality of treatment altogether beyond the powers' of his predecessor, and it is only in the history of the Gothic revival that he has a place of some importance.

Keene married Anne, daughter of M. Deval, a French Huguenot refugee, and had numerous children, of whom only two sons and a daughter survived him. Theodosius, who appears to have been the eldest, followed his father's profession. Thomas became the father of Henry George Keene, the Persian scholar. Elizabeth married William Parry, Welsh harper to George III. There is a small collection of drawings by Henry Keene in the Victoria and Albert Museum (A.189). It includes the design for the fireplace at University College, Oxford, and drawings for an octagonal Gothic Pavilion resembling Hartwell Church. The journal of a summer tour in the Netherlands made by Keene with his son and others in 1769 is in the British Library (Add. MS. 60356).

[*A.P.S.D.*; *D.N.B.*; H. Clifford Smith, 'A Georgian Architect', *C. Life*, 30 March 1945, and subsequent correspondence; *An Eighteenth-Century Correspondence*, ed. Dickins & Stanton, 1910, 179–80; Westminster Abbey muniments; J. G. Nichols, *The Hall of the Chancellors*, privately printed 1839; A. T. Bolton, *The Architecture of R. & J. Adam* ii, 1922, 102; T. Mowl, 'Henry Keene' in *The Architectural Outsiders*, ed. R. Brown, 1985; Keene's will is P.C.C. 22 BELLAS.]

[1] Among Keene's Oxford property was No. 65 St. Giles', whose lease he bought in 1768. The house was refronted before 1793, possibly during the period of Keene's tenancy.

WESTMINSTER, THE FLESH MARKET, *c.*1749–50; dem. 1805. Keene's designs are preserved in Westminster Abbey Muniments (P) 733, 733 A-B, see also W.A.M. (P) 734 and 24887. For a view of the Market, see *Views of Westminster by William Capon*, London Topographical Society 1923–4.

GRAY'S INN, No. 4 SOUTH SQUARE, 1750 (in conformity with Nos. 2–3, already built under the direction of Mr. Gorham, bricklayer to the Society); dem. 1941 [*Records of Gray's Inn*, ed. R. J. Fletcher, ii, 263, 268].

HARTLEBURY CASTLE, WORCS., refitted and reroofed the Castle Chapel for Bishop Maddox in Gothic style, *c.*1750 [E. H. Pearce, *Hartlebury Castle*, 1926, 243] (*C. Life*, 23 Sept. 1971).

WORCESTER CATHEDRAL. In May 1750 it was ordered 'that Mr. Kean, or some other skilful architect, be applied to for a draught of a proper ornamental Portico in the Gothick style to be erected over the great Gate of the Cathedral instead of a mean, deformed covering now over the Gate, falling into Ruins'. It is doubtful whether this was executed. [J. Noake, *The Monastery and Cathedral of Worcester*, 1866, 336.]

NELMES, HORNCHURCH, ESSEX, repairs for Godfrey Webster under the direction of Sanderson Miller, *c.*1750; dem. 1967 [Sanderson Miller's diary].

?THE MUSEUM or SUMMERHOUSE, ENVILLE HALL, STAFFS., for 4th Earl of Stamford, *c.*1750, Gothic [T. Mowl, 'The Case of the Enville Museum', *Jnl. Garden History* 3 (2), 1983].

?ALNWICK CASTLE, NORTHUMBERLAND, rebuilding in Gothic style for 2nd Earl (later 1st Duke) of Northumberland, whose Bank account records regular payments to 'Henry Keene' for unspecified services from Dec. 1750 to April 1754 and further payments in Nov. 1759 and Feb. 1770 [G. Worsley in *C. Life*, 8 Dec. 1988, 77].

TRINITY COLLEGE, DUBLIN. Although it appears from the *Journal of the House of Commons of the Kingdom of Ireland* vi, 1757–60, Appendix, p. cclxiii, no. xxxv, that £74 11s. 8d. were paid to 'Messrs. Keene and Saunderson for the Plans and Elevations' of the building erected in 1752–9, it is clear from the evidence cited above (p. 534) that they were in fact implementing designs made by the amateur architect Theodore Jacobsen.

HARTWELL CHURCH, BUCKS., for Sir William Lee, Bart., 1753–5, Gothic; reduced to a shell 1951 [W. H. Smythe, *Addenda to the Aedes Hartwellianae*, 1864, 20–1; there are some alternative designs for the church in Bodleian, MS. Top. Gen. b. 55, ff. 29–34].

HIGH WYCOMBE CHURCH, BUCKS., added Gothic parapet and pinnacles to tower, and designed Gothic pew, font-cover and west door for 1st Earl of Shelburne, 1754. Keene's drawing for the Shelburne pew is reproduced by F. Skull in *Records of Bucks.* ix, 1908. The pew itself was removed to the west end of the church in 1858 and to Wycombe Abbey School in 1891. It original position over the chancel screen is shown in Addleshaw & Etchells, *The Architectural Setting of Anglican Worship*, 1948, pl. 5 [A. T. Bolton, *Architecture of R. and J. Adam* i, 1922, 204].

EALING GROVE, MIDDLESEX, for Joseph Gulston, *c.*1755; altered by J. Yenn *c.*1780; dem. [elevation signed by Keene in Northumberland Record Office, ZBU B 5/6 (28)].

BOWOOD HOUSE, WILTSHIRE, enlarged and remodelled for 1st Earl of Shelburne, 1755–60. Keene's Doric portico was altered, the office block remodelled and the interior of the house decorated by R. Adam for 2nd Earl of Shelburne, 1761–70. The chapel by C. R. Cockerell was added in 1824 and C. Barry carried out general alterations *c.*1830–48, including the addition of the gallery between the Diocletian wing and the house. The main block designed by Keene was dem. 1956 [A. T. Bolton, *Architecture of R. & J. Adam* i, 1922, 204, 215; Earl of Kerry in *Wilts. Archl. Mag.* 41, 1920–2, 511–12; drawing of house as built by Keene in a private collection].

LONDON, Nos. 17–18 CAVENDISH SQUARE, for Thomas Bridges and William Lloyd, 1756–7 [drawings and building accounts in G.L.R.O., 85/223–64].

LOAKES MANOR, HIGH WYCOMBE, BUCKS., added E. wing for 1st Earl of Shelburne, 1757; remodelled as Wycombe Abbey by J. Wyatt *c.*1803–4 [K. A. Walpole, *From One Generation to Another*, 1966, 1–2, 9, citing accounts at Bowood].

HIGH WYCOMBE, BUCKS., THE GUILDHALL, for 1st. Earl of Shelburne, 1757 [A. T. Bolton, *The Architecture of R. & J. Adam* i, 1922, 204; *Records of Bucks.* x, 1916, 301] (meaured drawings in *Arch. Rev.* xlvii, 1920, 26–7).

CORSHAM COURT, WILTSHIRE, unexecuted designs for Peter Methuen, 1759–60 [F. Ladd, *Architects at Corsham Court*, Bradford-on-Avon 1978, chap. 1].

HARTWELL HOUSE, BUCKS., rebuilt east front, etc., for Sir William Lee, Bart., 1759–63. Keene also designed a bridge in the park, which was completed by James Wyatt in 1780, but has since been destroyed. It is illustrated in W. H. Smythe, *Addenda to the Aedes Hartwellianae*, 1864, 21. Keene's bills and estimates for his work at Hartwell were sold at Sotheby's on 8 March 1939, lot 665. Some papers connected with the house are in the Bucks. Record Office and the library of the Victoria and Albert Museum (Reserve L 4), and there are drawings in Bodleian, MS. Top. Gen. b. 55. (*C. Life*, 14–21 March 1914, 22 Nov. 1990).

ARBURY HALL, WARWICKS., assisted Sir Roger Newdigate, Bart., in connection with the remodelling of the house in Gothic style which had been in progress since *c.*1750 and was not completed until *c.*1790. Keene does not appear to have been employed at Arbury until 1761 (he was paid 15 guineas 'for drawings &c' in 1762) and after his death his place as Newdigate's architectural collaborator was taken by Henry Couchman (*q.v.*) [Warwickshire Record Office, Newdigate family papers; A. C. Wood, 'The Diaries of Sir Roger Newdigate', *Trans. Birmingham Archaeological Soc.* lxxviii, 1962, 48–53] (*C. Life*, 8, 15, 29 Oct. 1953).

LONDON, SPRING GARDENS, repairs and alterations to house for Sir Roger Newdigate, Bart., 1763; dem. *c.*1882 [Warwickshire Record Office, Newdigate family papers].

OXFORD, UNIVERSITY COLLEGE, remodelled interior of Hall in Gothic style, 1766, the chimneypiece being the gift of Sir Roger Newdigate. Keene's Gothic ceiling and woodwork were destroyed 1904 [A. Wood, *Colleges and Halls*, ed. Gutch, 1786, Appendix, 236; design for fireplace in V. and A., E 903, 1921] (Ackermann, *History of the University of Oxford*, 1814, plate).

OXFORD, CHRIST CHURCH, designed the ANATOMY SCHOOL (now Senior Common Room), 1766–7, and enclosed and fitted up ground floor of LIBRARY, 1769–72 [W. G. Hiscock, *A Christ Church Miscellany*, 1946, 70–1, 210].

OXFORD, SHELDONIAN THEATRE, inserted sash-windows, 1767–8; replaced 1959 [University Archives, Theatre Account, 1767–9].

HAREFIELD CHURCH, MIDDLESEX, new chancel arch and Gothic plasterwork in chancel, for Sir Roger Newdigate, Bart., 1768 [Warwickshire Record Office, Newdigate family papers].

attributed: ASTLEY CHURCH, WARWICKS., Gothic stalls and plasterwork in chancel, for Sir Roger Newdigate, Bart.

OXFORD, MAGDALEN COLLEGE. Keene is said to have been 'engaged at Magdalen College for about 20 years'. A plan for paving the antechapel, as 'executed by Mr. H. Keene in Octr. 1768', is preserved in a volume of drawings in the College Archives (f. 26), and the President's Lodgings are said to have been altered by him in 1769.

OXFORD, BALLIOL COLLEGE, THE FISHER BUILDING, 1768–9; north side refaced 1877 and 1963, south side refaced and altered by Waterhouse 1870 [J. Nichols, *Literary Anecdotes* viii, 1814, 248].

WESTMINSTER ABBEY. Keene remodelled the interior of the JERUSALEM CHAMBER in Gothic style, 1769 [W.A.M. 24836] (again remodelled in 19th century, but illustrated by J. T. Smith, *Antiquities of Westminster*, 1837, 38), designed Gothic gates for the entrance to the cloister from Dean's Yard, 1769 [W.A.M. 24836], and Gothic choir-stalls, pulpit, etc., 'contrived so as to be removable on public occasions', 1775 [W.A.M., Register 46, ff. 170v–172v]. The choir furniture was removed by Blore in 1848. The pulpit is now in Trottiscliffe. Church, Kent.

WESTBOURNE CHURCH, SUSSEX, Gothic spire (timber) for the Earl of Halifax, 1770. The inscription 'HENRY KEENE ARCHITECT 1770' is painted on a beam inside the spire. The crockets, quatrefoils, etc., which originally decorated the spire were removed by H. Woodyer in 1865.

SPELSBURY CHURCH, OXON., monument to 3rd Earl of Lichfield (d. 1772), signed 'H. KEENE Archs. invt. W. Tyler sculpt.' (J. Sherwood & N. Pevsner, *Oxfordshire*, Buildings of England, 1974, fig. 99).

OXFORD, THE RADCLIFFE OBSERVATORY, begun 1772 to Keene's designs, but in March 1773, after public criticisms of the design, notably by Edward Tatham in *Oxonia Explicata et Ornata* (1773), the Trustees decided to adopt 'another elevation' (by James Wyatt), which Keene carried out until his death in 1776, whereupon the Trustees ordered 'that Theodosius Keene his son be employed to finish the same under the Direction of Mr. Wyatt'. The building was completed in 1794 [Bodleian Library, MS. Minute Books of the Radcliffe Trustees] (*C. Life*, 10 May 1930).

OXFORD, WORCESTER COLLEGE, THE PROVOST'S LODGINGS, 1773–6. Keene also completed the north range of the College, of which he built the central portion and the two staircases to the west, repeating the design of the two staircases to the east erected by Dr. Clarke's trustees between 1753 and 1759 [*V.C.H. Oxfordshire* iii, 308–9; Arthur Oswald in *C. Life*, 5 Nov. 1948].

HEADINGTON HOUSE, OXFORD (now Hospital offices), remodelled for Sir Banks Jenkinson, 1773–4 [estimate and accounts in Pitchford Hall papers, N.L.W.].

HINWICK HOUSE, BEDS., offices for Richard Orlebar, designed 1774 [letter from Keene in Beds. C.R.O., OR 2071/294].

UPPARK, SUSSEX, THE VANDALIAN TOWER, for Sir Matthew Featherstonhaugh, Bart., 1774, Gothic; now a ruin [C. Hussey in *C. Life*, 21 June and 28 June 1941, 569; Margaret Meade-Featherstonhaugh & Oliver Warner, *Uppark and its People*, 1964, 46 and fig. 12].

KEENE, THEODOSIUS, was the elder son of Henry Keene, who left him all his freehold, copyhold and leasehold estates in Middlesex, Oxford and elsewhere. He exhibited an 'Elevation of a house and offices' at the Society of Artists in 1770, and in 1772 'A View of Stanstead Castle, near Emsworth'. This is the triangular Gothic folly now known as RACTON TOWER, which was built by Lord Halifax, of Stanstead Park, Sussex, who in 1770 had employed Henry Keene to design the spire of Westbourne Church. An elevation of the tower is among the Keene drawings in the Victoria and Albert Museum (E.876, 1921, reproduced in *C. Life*, 18 Sept. 1969, 682). The only other known work by Theodosius Keene is MAIDENHEAD TOWN HALL, erected to his designs in 1777, but remodelled 1879–80 and dem. *c.*1960 [J. W. Walker, *History of Maidenhead*, 1931, 75–6]. He exhibited 'A Design for a nobleman's mansion' at the Royal Academy the same year, and in 1786 Sir Roger Newdigate paid him £500 for work at his house in Spring Gardens [*Trans. Birmingham Arch. Soc.* lxxviii, 1962, 48]. In 1787 he was responsible for some 'small alterations' to Sir Charles Asgill's villa at RICHMOND, SURREY [*The World*, 16 June 1787, *ex inf.* Mr. P. A. Bezodis], but after this no further references to him have been found. An Italian sketch-book, bearing the inscription 'KEENE, Archt. 1775', is in the Victoria and Albert Museum (D.443.88).

KELSALL, CHARLES (1782–1857), eccentric, author, traveller and amateur architect, was the son of the prosperous Thomas Kelsall who was on the Council of the East India Company and whose cousin had married at Madras Clive of India. He was educated at Eton and Trinity College, Cambridge, and published many books of which the most remarkable was *Phantasm of an University*, 1814, in which he outlined an enlightened programme of educational and intellectual reform. His other publications included *A Letter from Athens addressed to a Friend in England*, 1812, *A Letter to the Society of Dilettanti on the Works in Progress at Windsor*,

1827, *Esquisse de mes travaux, de mes voyages et de mes opinions*, Frankfurt 1830, and *Horae Viaticae*, 1836. By 1841 he had purchased Knightons, a house at Hythe, nr. Southampton, which he called the Villa Amalthaea. He adorned the garden with a row of busts and a small tower which still survive. On his death he left his library to Morden College, Blackheath, where a building to house it was added to designs by P. C. Hardwick. Some of his MSS. are preserved in the library, including three drawings for a monument to Milton in the grounds of Christ's College, Cambridge, and four drawings for a new library at Morden College in the Elizabethan style. [D. J. Watkin, 'Charles Kelsall: the Quintessence of Neo-Classicism', *Arch. Rev.* cxl, 1966, 109–12, and *Thomas Hope and the Neo-Classical Idea*, 1968.]

KELSEY, RICHARD (1791–1856), was admitted to the Royal Academy Schools in 1818 at the age of 27. He was awarded Silver Medals for architectural designs by the Society of Arts in 1819 and 1820, and in 1821 gained the Gold Medal of the Royal Academy. He subsequently became David Laing's principal assistant and later practised from Finsbury [S. Redgrave, *Dictionary of Artists*, 1878, 247]. In 1829 he designed the south tower-porch of EAST BARNET CHURCH, HERTS., in a Romanesque style [I.C.B.S.], and in 1842 the circular pedestal for Samuel Nixon's statue of King William IV, now in Greenwich Park but originally in King William Street, London [*Companion to the Almanac*, 1842, 204]. He died on 7 August 1856, aged 65 [*Gent's Mag.* 1856 (ii), 394].

KEMP, CHARLES, figures in London directories of the 1830s and early 1840s as a surveyor with an office at Calvert's Brewery in Thames Street. He was presumably surveyor to the Brewery and his only recorded architectural work was for the Revd. N. R. Calvert, grandson of its founder, and Rector of Hunsdon in Hertfordshire, for whom he designed HUNSDONBURY in that parish in 1832, according to an inscription in the cellar recorded by H. C. Gibbs, *The Parish Registers of Hunsdon*, 1915, 22.

KEMP, GEORGE MEIKLE (1795–1844), was born at Hillrigs in the parish of Biggar.[1] His father was a shepherd, and George's childhood was spent in pastoral surroundings. A boyish interest in carving and model-making led to his apprenticeship to a carpenter in Peeblesshire (1809–13). Subsequently he worked as a mill-wright at Galashiels. While travelling on foot to his new job he was given a lift by Walter Scott, though he did not discover the identity of his benefactor until he had been set down at the end of the journey.

While working as a journeyman at Galashiels, Kemp developed a latent interest in architecture by studying and drawing the monastic churches at Melrose, Dryburgh and Jedburgh. Subsequent employment in Edinburgh, Lancashire and Glasgow enabled him to extend his knowledge of Gothic architecture. In 1824 he reached London and saw some of the southern cathedrals, including Canterbury. In the following year he set out on a tour of Europe, intending (though ignorant of any foreign language) to maintain himself as a mill-wright and see the principal churches abroad. After two years' travelling in northern France the news of his mother's death recalled him to Scotland. Failing to establish his own business as a carpenter in Edinburgh, he was employed as a draughtsman by William Burn (*q.v.*), and in 1831–2 made a large wooden model of Burn's design for a proposed new palace for the Duke of Buccleuch at Dalkeith. He also made drawings for a volume of Scottish ecclesiastical antiquities projected by an Edinburgh printer, but abandoned after the latter's death.

Though entirely self-taught, Kemp had by now acquired a first-hand knowledge of Gothic architecture unrivalled in Scotland, and in England equalled only by that of J. C. Buckler, Edward Blore and Thomas Rickman. In 1834 he made unsolicited drawings for the restoration of Glasgow Cathedral which were taken up by a local committee and formed the basis of a scheme for which J. Gillespie Graham (*q.v.*) unscrupulously took the sole credit, allowing the committee to publish them without acknowledgement to Kemp (*Plans and Elevations of the Proposed Restorations and Additions to the Cathedral of Glasgow, with an Explanatory Address by the Local Committee*, folio, 1836). In 1840 Kemp vindicated himself in an open letter to the committee, but the whole project fell through, and it was not until 1843 that the Cathedral was restored under the direction of Edward Blore.

In 1836 Kemp entered the competition for the Scott Monument in Edinburgh. He gained the third prize,[2] the first being awarded to Thomas Rickman and the second to Charles Fowler in collaboration with the

[1] Not at Moorfoot in Midlothian, where his father was living at a later date (see *Border Magazine* xv, 1910, 137, 156, for his birthplace).

[2] One of his original drawings for this design is in the Peebles Museum.

sculptor Sievier. However, the committee decided on a second competition, and this time Kemp was the winner. His elaborate openwork design, based on his studies of late Gothic churches on the Continent as well as in Scotland, was built in 1840–6. This much-admired work would doubtless have assured Kemp's future as an architect, but on 6 March 1844 he was accidentally drowned by falling into a canal while returning home on a foggy night. He was buried in St. Cuthbert's Cemetery, where a monument with a medallion portrait by Alexander Handyside Ritchie was erected by public subscription. A bust by Ritchie and a portrait by his brother-in-law, William Bonnar, are in the Scottish National Portrait Gallery. An attractive picture of his simple and engaging personality is given by Thomas Bonnar in his *Biographical Sketch of George Meikle Kemp*, 1892. See also James Colston, *History of the Scott Monument*, Edinburgh 1881, and Ann Martha Wrinch, 'George Kemp and the Scott Monument', *C. Life*, 5 Aug. 1971. The only other buildings which Kemp appears to have designed are MAYBOLE WEST CHURCH, AYRSHIRE, 1836–40 (see Bonnar, *op, cit.*, 81), and the south wing (dem. 1965) of WOODHOUSELEE, MIDLOTHIAN, for James Tytler, 1843 [J. Small, *Castles and Mansions of the Lothians* ii, 1883]. There are two drawings by him in the Print Room of the Scottish National Gallery. Some beautifully drawn details for the Scott Monument are in the collection of the Royal Incorporation of Architects in Scotland.

KEMPSHED, JOHN, was a carpenter who was often employed by John Johnson (*q.v.*), in one of whose houses in Berners Street, London, he was living in the early years of the nineteenth century. He had architectural ambitions, exhibiting at the Royal Academy in 1791 and again in 1825, subscribing to Elsam's *Essay on Rural Architecture* (1805), and offering himself as a candidate for the County Surveyorship of Essex in 1816 [Nancy Briggs, *John Johnson*, 1991, 58, 117–18,157]. A design by him for a castellated park entrance, dated 1808, formerly among papers at Hinton St. George, Somerset, is in the Yale Center for British Art.

KEMPSHOT, WILLIAM, of Pentonville, contributed a plan of 'an Inn in the Italian Style' to Loudon's *Encyclopaedia of Rural Architecture*, 1833, in which he is said to have built 'numerous public houses, and also some country churches, and one or two mausoleums' (1846 ed., p. 685).

KEMPSTER, CHRISTOPHER (1627–1715), master mason, was the son of William Kempster of Burford, Oxfordshire. He owned a quarry there from which stone was being sent to London as early as 1668. He was made free of the Masons' Company and of the City by redemption on 4 August 1670, and was Master of the Company in 1691 and 1700. In London, his first contract was for St. Stephen's, Walbrook, 1672–9 (jointly with Thomas Strong). He was also mason-contractor at St. James, Garlickhythe, 1674–87, St. Mary Abchurch, 1681–7, and St. Mary, Somerset, 1686–94. Elsewhere he was the mason-contractor for Abingdon Town Hall, 1678–80, and for Tom Tower at Christ Church, Oxford, 1681–2 (in partnership with Thomas Robinson). He also had contracts at Winchester Palace in about 1683. His connection with St. Paul's began in 1691 or 1692, from which time until 1707 he worked there more or less continuously in partnership with Ephraim Beauchamp, first on the legs of the Dome and then on the Dome itself. From 1707 to 1709 he was employed on his own account, chiefly in repairing the vaults. Wren had a high opinion of him and told Dean Fell in 1681 that he was 'a very able man, modest, honest and treatable . . . I have used him on good works, he is very careful to work true to his design and does strong well-banded work and I can rely upon him.'

In 1687 Kempster built the Perrot Chapel on the north side of NORTH LEIGH CHURCH, OXON., for James Perrot in a classical style reflecting that of Wren's City churches [Oxfordshire R.O., MS. Oxf. Dioc. papers *c.*455, f. 103]. In 1698 he refronted a house at UPTON, nr. BURFORD, for himself, leaving the inscription 'Christopher Kempster built this in 1698' on a window architrave. He died here on 12 August 1715, aged 88, and was buried in the parish church, where there is a monument to his memory erected by his son William (*Wren Soc.* xix, pl. lix). He left his quarry to his second son, John. His brother, William Kempster the elder, continued to work at St. Paul's after his death and was Master of the Masons' Company in 1705. Kempster's 'Day Book', found in his house in 1884 and now in St. Paul's Cathedral Library, gives some details of his business from about 1667 onwards, but adds little to what is known from other sources. Further day-books and accounts relating to Kempster's work at St. Paul's Cathedral and elsewhere are among the Chancery Masters' Exhibits in the P.R.O. (C 106/145). [D. Knoop & G. P. Jones, *The London Mason in the Seven-teenth Century*, 1935, 45–6; W. D. Caröe, *Wren and*

Tom Tower, 1923, chaps. 10–11; *Wren Soc.*, *passim*.]

KEMPTHORNE, SAMPSON (1809–1873), a native of Gloucester, became a pupil of Annesley Voysey. He was admitted to the R.A. Schools in 1833. In December of that year he was in Rome, and he exhibited drawings made in Italy at the Royal Academy in 1835 and 1836. He began practice in London, and with S. S. Teulon competed for the new town hall and market-place at Penzance in 1835. As a result of his father's friendship with the Chief Poor Law Commissioner, Kempthorne was appointed architect to the newly established Commissioners, whose *First Report* of 1835 contains designs for workhouses by him that served as models for many built in the 1830s and 1840s. He himself designed a number of workhouses in the south of England, employing as his assistant the young Gilbert Scott, then at the start of his architectural career. Kempthorne also prepared a series of designs for schoolhouses for the Committee of the Council on Education, whose *Rules to be observed in planning and fitting up Schools*, published in 1839–40, contains 23 sheets of schoolhouses provided by him. His designs for a school at Cranleigh in Surrey are in the Surrey County Record Office (264/15/1–2).

Kempthorne's father-in-law, the Revd. Josiah Pratt, was secretary of the Church Missionary Society. For the Society he made in 1836 designs for a mission church at North Waimate in New Zealand (described in *Gent's Mag.* 1836 (ii), 192) and in 1841–2 he emigrated to that country, where he continued to practise until his death in 1873. In New Zealand his connection with the Church Missionary Society provided him with several commissions, but he does not appear to have designed any building of great importance there.

[*A.P.S.D.*; G. G. Scott, *Personal and Professional Recollections*, 1879, 76–7; Anna Dickens, 'The Architect and the Workhouse', *Arch. Rev.* Dec. 1976; John Stackpoole, *William Mason, the First New Zealand Architect*, Auckland 1971, 12–13, 125, 128.]

KEMPSHOTT HOUSE, HANTS., remodelled exterior for E. W. Blunt, 1832 [G. F. Prosser, *Select Illustrations of Hampshire*, 1833].

WANTAGE, BERKS., THE TOWN HALL, 1835; dem. 1877 [A. Gibbons & E. C. Davey, *Wantage Past and Present*, 1901 53].

WORKHOUSES at ABINGDON, BERKS., 1836; BRADFIELD, BERKS., *c.*1835; BANBURY (NEITHROP), OXON., 1835; CHERTSEY, SURREY, 1836; TICEHURST, SUSSEX, 1836; EPPING, ESSEX, 1836; BISHOPS STORTFORD, HERTS., 1836; BATH, 1837–8; WINCHCOMBE, GLOS., 1837 (dem.); THORNBURY, GLOS., 1837; UPTON-ON-SEVERN, WORCS., 1836 (dem.); MARTLEY, WORCS. (dem.) [*Architectural Mag.* iii, 1836, 330, 532; *Companion to the Almanac*, 1836, 234–6; *Bath Guide*, 1853; *Gloucester Jnl.* 19 March, 19 May 1836, 4 March 1837; *Berrow's Worcester Jnl.* 26 May 1836, 27 July 1837].

HADZOR, WORCS. Italianate lodge designed for J. H. Galton [exhib. at R.A. 1837].

LONDON, alterations to BARNETT, HOARE & CO'S BANK, 62 LOMBARD STREET, 1838; dem. [exhib. at R.A. 1838].

BUCKHOLD CHURCH, BERKS., 1836, Gothic [G.R.].

ROTHERHITHE, HOLY TRINITY CHURCH, 1837–8, Gothic; dem. [*Gent's Mag.* 1837 (ii), 526].

GLOUCESTER, ST. JAMES'S CHURCH, BARTON, 1837–41; chancel rebuilt 1879 [*A.P.S.D.*].

HASELBURY PLUCKNETT CHURCH, SOMERSET, rebuilt nave, 1839 [I.C.B.S.].

ROTHERHITHE, ALL SAINTS CHURCH, 1839–40, Gothic; dem. [*British Critic* xxvii, 1840, 496].

PORTHLEVEN CHURCH, CORNWALL, 1839–41, Gothic [I.C.B.S.].

ASH CHURCH, SOMERSET, 1840–1, Gothic; chancel added 1889, tower 1920 [I.C.B.S.].

MISTERTON CHURCH, SOMERSET, rebuilt 1840 [I.C.B.S.].

HOLLOWELL CHURCH, nr. GUILSBOROUGH, NORTHANTS., 1840, Gothic [exhib. at R.A.].

KENDALL, HENRY EDWARD (1776–1875), the son of a banker, was born at York on 23 March 1776. He became a pupil of Thomas Leverton and, it is said, of John Nash. He joined the Barrack Department of the War Office, in whose employment he remained until 1823, when he became District Surveyor for the parishes of St. Martin-in-the-Fields and St. Anne, Soho, an appointment which he held for over fifty years. He was one of the founders of the Institute of British Architects, and the early meetings of the committee formed in 1834 to bring it into existence were held in his house in Suffolk Street, He exhibited at the Royal Academy from 1799 to 1843. He is described as a man of 'gentlemanly manners, noble and generous in disposition, tall and handsome in person'. He married twice, and had a son and two daughters. One of the latter married his pupil Lewis Cubitt. The son, Henry Edward Kendall, junior (1805–85), was trained in his father's office and became a successful Victorian architect.[1] Kendall died on 4 January 1875, in his 99th year. A lithographic portrait by J. B. Black dated 1852 is in the National Portrait Gallery.

Kendall was a prolific architect whose work included churches, town and country houses, gaols and workhouses, and he was equally at home with Greek Revival, Tudor Gothic or even, if the occasion demanded (as it did at Wimpole), neo-baroque. His ability in the Gothic style was shown in the designs he submitted for Kensal Green Cemetery in 1832 and subsequently published as *Sketches of the Approved Designs of a Chapel and Gateway Entrances, intended to be erected at Kensal Green, for the General Cemetery Company*. They were awarded the first prize in the competition, but were set aside by Sir John D. Paul, the chairman of the company, who wanted Grecian buildings. Kendall's proposed layout was an able essay in picturesque landscaping, and 'a scenic and picturesque effect' was what he aimed for in the design for the Houses of Parliament which he and J. D. Hopkins submitted jointly in 1835. The same qualities were shown in the town-planning schemes at Brighton and Rosherville (on the banks of the Thames near Gravesend) for which Kendall and his son were responsible. Their designs for the development of the latter place were, however, too grandiose for realization, and it eventually degenerated into an amusement park. [Obituary by T. L. Donaldson in *Builder* xxxiii, 1875, 33; *ibid*, 60; J. S. Curl, *The Victorian Celebration of Death*, 1972, 60–4; *Survey of London* xxxvii, 336–7.]

PUBLIC BUILDINGS

SPALDING, LINCS., THE HOUSE OF CORRECTION, 1824 [*Builder* xxxiii, 1875, 33].

SPILSBY, LINCS., SESSIONS HOUSE and HOUSE OF CORRECTION, 1824–6 [plans in C. Davy, *Architectural Precedents*, 1841].

RAMSGATE, KENT, ST. GEORGE'S CHURCH, 1825–7, Gothic: designed by H. Hemsley of the Barrack Department (*q.v.*), who died in 1825, and carried out by Kendall with 'some few alterations' [*The Watering-Places of Great Britain and Fashionable Directory*, 1833, 217].

KEMP TOWN, BRIGHTON, SUSSEX, Esplanade and Tunnel, 1828–30, with H. E. Kendall, junior [A. Dale, *Fashionable Brighton*, 1947, 81–92 and pls. 46–7].

LOUTH, LINCS., HOUSE OF CORRECTION, *c.*1828 [exhib. at R.A. 1829].

SLEAFORD, LINCS., THE SESSIONS HOUSE, 1828–30 [exhib. at R.A. 1831; David Brock, 'The Competition for . . . Sleaford Sessions House, 1828,' *Arch. Hist.* 27 1984].

SLEAFORD, LINCS., CARR'S HOSPITAL, east range 1830, Gothic [exhib. at R.A. 1832]. Kendall may also have designed the south range built in 1841–6.

ROSHERVILLE, NORTHFLEET, KENT, Hotel, Pier and Gardens, 1837, with H. E. Kendall, junior [*Builder* xxxiii, 1875, 33; F. W. Leakey, as cited in footnote below].

LONDON CONSERVATIVE ASSOCIATION'S BANQUET, PAVILION for, 1837 [H. E. Kendall, *Plan, etc. of the Pavilion erected for the Banquet of the London Conservative Association*, 1837].

COCKFOSTERS, MIDDLESEX, CHRIST CHURCH, 1839, Gothic [G.R.].

ST. JOHN'S WOOD, SCHOOL FOR THE BLIND, AVENUE ROAD, 1838 [E. Walford, *Old and New London* v, 250].

CLAYGATE CHURCH, SURREY, 1840, Romanesque [exhib. at R.A. 1841]. Steeples, transept and apse were added in 1860 in conformity to what may have been Kendall's original design.

SUDBURY, SUFFOLK, THE CORN EXCHANGE, 1841–2 [Suffolk Record Office, minutes of the Sudbury Market House Company, 1841].

LONDON, BEDFORD CHAPEL, BLOOMSBURY STREET, remodelled 1846; dem. [*Builder* iv, 1846, 79–80].

BANTRY, CO. CORK, IRELAND, a church [*Builder* xxxiii, 1875, 33].

WORKHOUSES at UCKFIELD, SUSSEX, and MELKSHAM, WILTS. [*Builder* xxxiii, 1875, 33].

PRIVATE WORKS

MISTERTON HOUSE, LEICS., 'intended improvements' for J. H. Franks, exhib. at R.A. 1804; perhaps not executed.

MAUSOLEUM 'to be erected' in the park of S. Forster, Esq., in Yorkshire (unidentified), exhib. at R.A. 1813.

TILLINGTON RECTORY, SUSSEX, for the Revd. J. S. Clarke, 1817–18, Tudor Gothic [exhib. at R.A. 1818; drawings in W. Sussex C.R.O., Ep.I 41/53].

MAUSOLEUM 'to be erected' in Shropshire for

[1] For H. E. Kendall, junior, see F. W. Leakey, 'Baudelaire et Kendall', *Revue de littérature comparée*, Trentième Année, no. 1, 1956, reprinted in Leakey, *Baudelaire: Text and Context. Essays 1953–1988* (Cambridge 1989), his entry in *The Architect's, Engineer's and Building Trades' Directory* (1868), and the obituary in *Builder* xlviii, 1885, 883–4. His works included the remodelling of Knebworth House, Herts. (1844), and Shuckburgh Hall, Warwicks. (1844), and the Tudor Gothic house at Twickenham known as 'Pope's Villa'.

H. Smith, Esq. (unidentified) [exhib. at R.A. 1820].

FISHTOFT RECTORY, LINCS., 1826; dem. [Lincs. Archives Office, MGA 139].

LONDON, No. 24 BELGRAVE SQUARE (later DOWNSHIRE HOUSE), for T. R. Kemp, 1827–33 [Britton & Pugin, *The Public Buildings of London* ii, 1828, 290–4].

BRIGHTON, SUSSEX, houses attributed to H. E. Kendall, jr. by A. Dale, *Fashionable Brighton*, 1947, 83, 98, 109, but more probably by his father, include Nos. 19–20 SUSSEX SQUARE for 1st Marquess of Bristol, 1829–31 and the interior of No. 14 CHICHESTER TERRACE for 6th Duke of Devonshire, 1828.

HAVERHOLME PRIORY, LINCS., remodelled for Sir Jenison Gordon, Bart., 1830, Tudor Gothic; dem. 1927 [exhib. at R.A. 1830] (*C. Life*, 24 Jan. 1903).

ASHURST LODGE (later WENTWORTH HALL), MICKLEHAM, SURREY, for William Strachan, *c.*1835 [exhib. at R.A. 1835] (Brayley, *History of Surrey* iv, 457, plate).

ASWARBY PARK, LINCS., additions for Sir Thomas Whichcote, Bart., 1836–8; dem. 1951 [exhib. at R.A. 1836–8].

CHIDDINGSTONE CASTLE, KENT, completed for Henry Streatfield, *c.*1837–8 [exhib. at R.A. as 'lately completed' 1838; Kent Archives Office, unexecuted drawings by Kendall for additions, U 908/P 94].

WIMPOLE HALL, CAMBS., works for 4th Earl of Hardwicke, including addition of wings (dem. 1952), of balustrades to house, etc., 1842; new stable-block, Arrington entrance gates and Queen's Lodge (dem.), 1849–52 [*Builder* xxxiii, 1875, 33, 60; C. Hussey in *C. Life*, 21–28 May 1927; G. Jackson-Stops, *An English Arcadia*, 1991, 126–30].

KENDALL, JOHN (1766–1829), was the son of Edward Kendall (d. 1796), a mason and monumental sculptor of Exeter. He appears to be identical with the John Kendall who became a pupil of James Paine and exhibited architectural designs at the Royal Academy in 1781–4. In 1796 he succeeded his father as stonemason to Exeter Cathedral, and retained the post until his death in September 1829, at the age of 63. Apart from his work as a monumental sculptor, his chief employment was the repair and embellishment of Exeter Cathedral, upon which he was more or less continuously engaged from *c.*1805 onwards. His works included the refacing of the chapter-house and chapel of the Holy Ghost, 1814, a new reredos (subsequently removed by Scott), 1818, the restoration of the west front, 1817–19, additions to the organ-screen, 1819, a new gallery-screen (since removed) at the west end of the chapter-house and the chimney-piece there, 1821, the refitting of the Lady Chapel, 1822, and various external repairs, 1821–7. Like a medieval master mason he himself designed all the works that he executed, and he was one of the last men of his trade in whom these two capacities were thus combined. [*A.P.S.D.*; *Gent's Mag.* 1796 (ii), 1059, 1829 (ii), 572; archives of the Dean and Chapter of Exeter.]

Kendall published *An Elucidation of the Principles of English Architecture, usually denominated Gothic*, 1818 (reissued 1842), with 23 plates of examples taken from Exeter Cathedral, and a folio print of the 'Elevation of the east end, showing the window, and the new altar-piece, stalls, etc.' (Bodleian, Douce Prints, N 8 (134)).

According to Lysons, *Magna Britannia* vi (2), 1822, 250, a new Gothic altar-piece, stone screen and stone pulpit were made in 1822 for HACCOMBE CHURCH, DEVON, at the expense of Sir Henry Carew, Bart., by 'Mr. Nicholas Kendall' – almost certainly a mistake for John Kendall.

KENT, JOHN, was apprenticed to a London surveyor named Thomas Bird in 1805 [P.R.O., Apprenticeship Registers, IR 1/40, 35]. He exhibited student's work at the Royal Academy in 1809 and 1811. He subsequently specialized in building schools and designed, among others, the PADDINGTON CHARITY SCHOOLS, the design of which is given in J. C. Loudon's *Encyclopaedia of Rural Architecture*, 1846, 740–50 (see also pp. 751–7). He was also the author of 'Instructions for choosing a dwelling-house' in Loudon's *Architectural Mag.* i, 1834, 34, 166.

KENT, JOHN, practised in Southampton from about 1800 to 1830. He rebuilt LEIGH PARK, HANTS., for William Garrett, 1802; rebuilt 1863, since dem. [G. F. Prosser, *Select Illustrations of Hampshire*, 1833], and remodelled PAULTONS, nr. ROMSEY, HANTS., for Hans Sloane-Stanley in 1805–7; dem. 1955 [Hants. Record Office, contracts in Sloane-Stanley papers, bundle 117] (*C. Life*, 17 Sept. 1938). According to A. E. Richardson and H. D. Eberlein he also designed CHESSEL HOUSE, BITTERNE, HANTS., 1802 (dem.), and a house in SOUTHAMPTON dated 1806 [*The Smaller English House of the Later Renaissance*, 1925, 34, 180]. Among J. B. Papworth's drawings in the R.I.B.A. Drawings Collection there is a plan of a house with hollow walls built by Kent 'in or near Southampton', with a note that 'it did not answer'. In collaboration with Joseph Hannaford (*q.v.*) of Christchurch he designed and built ST. JAMES'S CHURCH, POOLE, DORSET, 1819–21 [R.C.H.M. *Dorset* ii (2), 192 and pl. 118].

KENT, WILLIAM (1685–1748), was born of humble parents at Bridlington in Yorkshire, where his baptism is recorded in the parish register on 1 January 1685/6. He is said to have been apprenticed to a coach-painter in Hull, but left his master before he had served his full term. He had evidently shown promise of unusual talent, for although 'his parents' . . . circumstances [were] not in a condition to forward his practice & the expence of a profession', he 'had the good fortune to find some Gentlemen . . . to promote his studyes', who 'raised a contribution and recommended him to proper persons at London to direct him to Italy', whither he travelled in 1709 in company with John Talman and a young man named Daniel Lock.[1] Who the gentlemen were who paid for Kent to go to Italy in 1709 is not clear, but once there he attracted further patrons in the persons of Sir William Wentworth of Bretton Park in Yorkshire, Burrell Massingberd of Ormsby in Lincolnshire, and the latter's friend Sir John Chester of Chicheley in Buckinghamshire. In return for their remittances, Kent bought paintings and objects of virtu for their country houses, while he learned to paint in Rome, probably in the studio of Giuseppe Chiari (rather than that of Benedetto Luti). There 'he became acquainted with many English Noblemen', including Thomas Coke, the future Earl of Leicester, in whose company he toured northern Italy in the summer and autumn of 1714, making notes on the pictures they saw in a notebook which is now in the Bodleian Library (MS. Rawlinson D. 1162). By this time Kent's reputation as an artist was established in the eyes of his countrymen. In 1713 he had won one of the prizes awarded for painting by the Accademia di San Luca, and according to Thoresby he was admitted a member of the Tuscan Academy in Florence. In 1717 he 'gave the first proof of my painting in fresco' in the church of S. Giuliano dei Fiamminghi in Rome, whose ceiling he decorated with the apotheosis of its patron saint, St. Julian.[2]

It was as a painter that the Earl of Burlington, who had first met Kent in Rome in the winter of 1714/15, brought him back to England in 1719. At Burlington House Kent painted several ceilings for his new patron, the Duke of Chandos employed him at Cannons, and Earl Tylney at Wanstead. In 1722, with the support of Burlington, Sir Thomas Hewett (whom he had met in Italy) and Vice-Chamberlain Coke, he displaced Sir James Thornhill, the Sergeant Painter, as the decorator of the new state rooms at Kensington Palace, thereby incurring the life-long enmity of Thornhill's son-in-law William Hogarth. Burlington 'promoted him on all occasions to everything in his power, to the King, to the Court works, & Courtiers declared him the best History painter & the first that was a native of this Kingdom'.[3] As a 'history-painter' Kent was in fact second-rate, and certainly inferior to his rival Thornhill, but in the Presence Chamber at Kensington he successfully introduced the neo-antique style of 'grotesque' decoration already revived in sixteenth-century Italy by Raphael, Giulio Romano and Vasari, and in the Cube Room he provided a simulated coffered ceiling that was more in accord with the neo-classical aspirations of the room than anything in Thornhill's baroque repertoire. A number of commissions followed for interior decoration. In these Kent abandoned the overall wall and ceiling painting characteristic of the grand baroque interior for a decor in which painting was subordinated to a compartmented framework formed by pedimented wall-panels, coffered semi-domes and niches that were often filled with sculpture after the antique.

By about 1730 Kent was beginning to turn his attention from decoration to architecture. As an architect he was closely associated with Lord Burlington, who in about 1724 had given him the task of editing *The Designs of Inigo Jones . . . with some Additional Designs* (by Lord Burlington and himself) which were published in two volumes in 1727. So far Lord Burlington's architectural revolution had been confined to the country houses of his friends and to a single public building, the Dormitory of Westminster School; it still remained to bring Palladio into the Office of Works and thus to influence the design of the

[1] Vertue calls him 'William Locke', but from Kent's subsequent correspondence it is clear that he was Daniel Lock (*c.*1682–1754), a graduate of Trinity College, Cambridge, and a man of private means whose knowledge of the arts is praised on his monument (with a bust by Roubiliac) in Trinity College Chapel.

[2] Kent's drawing for this painting is illustrated in *Connoisseur*, Aug. 1954, 7. For the painting itself see E. Croft-Murray, 'William Kent in Rome', *English Miscellany*, ed. M. Praz, i, 1950.

[3] Kent appears to have painted few easel-pictures, but attention should be drawn to his 'Battle of Crécy' and 'Meeting and Marriage of Henry V and Catherine of France' in the Royal Collection at Kensington Palace, as they show Kent as probably the first English painter to attempt historical subjects drawn from the Middle Ages. The 'Marriage' is signed and dated 1729.

Royal Palaces and other buildings in its charge. That was to be the function of Kent when, in May 1726, Burlington's influence procured him a seat on the Board of Works as Master Carpenter. In 1735 he succeeded Nicholas Dubois as Master Mason and Deputy Surveyor, positions which he retained until his death in 1748. He never obtained the post of Sergeant Painter held by his rival, Thornhill, but in 1728 'Mr. Kent received as an additional favour by the interest of Lord Burlington his patron . . . a new constituted place purposely for him.' This was the post of Surveyor or Inspector of Paintings in the Royal Palaces, to which he was appointed on 24 January 1727/8, at a salary of £100 a year. It was in this capacity that he restored Rubens's painting in the Banqueting House at Whitehall – an operation that was the occasion of a flattering visit from the King and Queen, of which Kent made the following memorandum at the end of a MS. version of Ovid's *Metamorphoses*, 'istoricamente spiegate e descritte da Guglielmo Kent', which is now in the Bodleian Library (MS. Rawlinson D.540):

> The 12th day of January 1733/4 the King and Queen came to the Banquiting House at WhiteHall, and came upon the scaffold forty foot High to see the paintings of Ruben's, that I had restor'd – his Majesty was pleas'd to tell me I had done them exceeding well the Queen told me I not only deserv'd thanks from the King but to all lovers of Painting – from thence I waited on them to the Muse [*sic*] to look upon that Building of my Designe.

Finally, on the death of Charles Jervas in 1739, Kent became Portrait Painter to the King, although, according to Vertue, George II 'declared he would never sit to him for his picture'. Nevertheless, 'his true friend' the Duke of Grafton, then Lord Chamberlain, employed him to paint official portraits of the King to send abroad, and one of these, signed and dated 1741, is preserved at Rokeby, Yorkshire (*C. Life*, 19 May 1955, fig. 9).

It was as a member of the Board of Works that Kent designed his best-known works – the Horse Guards, the Royal Mews, and the Treasury Buildings, all of which were, like his project for a Royal Palace (represented by a wooden model now exhibited at Kew), and his grandiose neo-antique designs for rebuilding the Houses of Parliament with features derived from the Roman Imperial Baths, inspired by Burlington's ideals. However, in the course of his ten years' residence in Italy Kent had studied the architectural works of Raphael and Giulio Romano quite as much as those of Palladio, and his fondness for rusticated wall-surfaces, windows framed by channelled relieving arches, and other mannerist features, was derived from Rome and Mantua rather than from Venice or Vicenza. These mannerist influences were particularly apparent in the Royal Mews, with their rusticated columns and keystones breaking up into the entablature of the central archway.

Official patronage failed in the end to provide any commission more important than the Horse Guards and the Royal Mews, and most of Kent's architectural work was for private clients. The great house at Holkham in Norfolk was the most complete embodiment of the Palladian mission to recreate the glories of ancient architecture on English soil, and here Kent was working for a patron who was fully in sympathy with the aesthetic ideals of his friend Lord Burlington. At Badminton and Euston, however, the two domed pavilions that he designed for the Dukes of Beaufort and Grafton are masterpieces of a more individual kind which (in the words of David Watkin) maintain 'a perfect balance between the opposing tensions of Baroque and Palladian', while the theatrical staircase at 44 Berkeley Square suggests that in a different climate of taste Kent might have been equally successful as a professedly baroque architect. His interior decoration, always bold and architectural in character, may have lacked the elegance of the rococo or the neo-classical but has its own virtues of richness and three-dimensional solidity. The same may be said of the excellent furniture which he designed for many of his buildings, thus anticipating the later role of Robert Adam as a creator of complete interior ensembles.

Kent's pioneer Gothic designs, inspired by a characteristic sensitivity to the *genius loci* – for all of them were for the alteration or enlargement of existing buildings that were themselves Gothic, Tudor or Jacobean – show him exercising a fancy uncontrolled by Palladian constraints and establish him as the creator of an English rococo Gothick happily free from antiquarian preoccupations. His versatility extended to the illustration of books (notably Gay's *Poems*, 1720, Thomson's *Seasons*, 1730, and Spenser's *Faerie Queen*, 1751), the designing of sculpture (see below under 'Monuments'), silver, a state barge and even, it is said, of a lady's dress decorated with columns of the Five Orders, so that she seemed 'a walking Palladio in petticoats'.[1]

[1] In December 1731 Frederick, Prince of Wales, gave a masquerade in which he appeared as a

Finally, Kent has a very important place in the history of English landscape-gardening. As Horace Walpole saw it, Kent 'leaped the fence, and saw that all Nature was a Garden': in other words it was Kent who led the revolt against the formal gardening of the seventeenth century, and who first realized Addison's vision of 'a whole estate thrown into a kind of garden by frequent plantations'. Modern research has shown that the change from formality to informality was less abrupt than Walpole implied, and that others besides Kent had a hand in it. Moreover, the extensive tracts of parkland defined only by water and plantations that had by the end of the eighteenth century become the norm of the English landscape garden were rather different from Kent's reminiscences of an Italian landscape in which buildings, cascades, exedrae and the like attracted the eye at every turn. Nevertheless Kent's contribution to English landscape gardening was crucial. It was he who combined the formality of Palladian architecture with the studied informality of the surrounding park, and it was he who (as can still be seen at Rousham) set out to create on English soil a series of three-dimensional pictures comparable to (if not directly inspired by) the ideal compositions of Albano or Poussin. These were to be the essential characteristics of English landscape-gardening for the rest of the eighteenth century, and it was to Kent that its practitioners were to look back as the founder of their art.

Kent did not fail to arouse hostility in those who envied the ease with which he attracted the patronage of the great. But it is clear that the 'Signior' was an amiable and easy-going companion as well as a gifted designer, and the combination was enough to secure for him the friendship and support of one of the most influential patrons in the history of English art. For much of his life Burlington House was his home, and when he died on 12 April 1748, of 'an inflammation in his bowels and foot, which turned to a general mortification', he was buried in his patron's vault at Chiswick. He was unmarried, but kept a mistress, Elizabeth Butler of Covent Garden, by whom he had two children.

Several portraits of Kent are known or recorded (see M. Wilson, *William Kent*, Appendix I). The best-known are by Benedetto Luti at Chatsworth, painted in Rome in 1718, and by Bartholomew Dandridge in the National Portrait Gallery. A number of his architectural designs were published by John Vardy in *Some Designs of Mr. Inigo Jones and Mr. William Kent* (1744), and others by Isaac Ware in *Designs of Inigo Jones and Others* [1731]. Drawings by Kent are preserved in several places, notably at Chatsworth, the R.I.B.A. Drawings Collection (including a set of unexecuted designs for remodelling Honingham Hall, Norfolk, in the Gothic style, dated 1737), the Victoria and Albert Museum, the Public Record Office, Sir John Soane's Museum, the British Museum (Print Room) and the Ashmolean Museum at Oxford. His delightful sketches of projected landscapes, often enlivened by human and animal figures, are all reproduced by John Dixon Hunt (1987). His letters to Burrell Massingberd of Ormsby are in the library of the Society of Genealogists. They were the subject of an article by Margaret Jourdain in *C. Life*, 25 Aug. 1944. Four letters to Lord Burlington, formerly at Althorp and now in the British Library, were published in *Arch. Rev.* lxiii, 1928, 180 and 210. Seven letters to Selina, Countess of Huntingdon (who tenanted a house in Savile Row that belonged to Kent), are printed by John Willis in *Arch. Hist.* 29, 1986. Copies of the sale catalogue of Kent's library and works of art are in the Bodleian Library (Mus. Bibl. III 4[to] 17, 8° 20).

[*A.P.S.D.*; *D.N.B.*; Walpole Society, *Vertue Note Books* i, 100, iii, 139–140, vi (index), 131–2; Basil S. Long, 'Some Drawings by William Kent', *Connoisseur* lxxviii, 1927, 93–5; Trenchard Cox, 'William Kent as Painter', *Artwork* vii, 1931; Fiske Kimball, 'William Kent's Designs for the Houses of Parliament', *R.I.B.A. Jnl.* 6 Aug. and 10 Sept. 1932, see also 9 Jan. 1939; Margaret Jourdain, 'Early Life and Letters of William Kent', *C. Life*, 25 Aug. 1944; R. Wittkower, 'Lord Burlington and William Kent', *Archaeological Jnl.* cii, 1945, reprinted in *Palladio and English Palladianism*, 1974; R. Wittkower, *The Earl of Burlington and William Kent*, York Georgian Society 1948; Margaret Jourdain, *The Work of William Kent*, 1948; Hugh Honour, 'John Talman and William Kent in Italy', *Connoisseur*, cxxxiv, 1954; Boris Lossky, 'Un dessin de William Kent au Musée des Beaux-Arts de Tours', *Connoisseur* cxxxvii, 1956, 101, 'An Unpublished Drawing by William Kent', *ibid.*, 264; U. Middeldorf, 'William Kent's Roman Prize in 1713', *Burlington Mag.* April 1957, 125; J. F. Hayward, 'A "Surtoute" designed by William Kent', *Connoisseur* cxliii, 1959, 82–3; J. P. Eicholz,

shepherd attended by eighteen huntsmen 'dressed after a drawing of Kent's, in green waistcoats, leopard-skins and quivers at their backs, . . . tragedy buskins upon their legs, . . . antique gloves with pikes up to their elbows, and caps and feathers upon their heads like a Harry the 8th by Holbein' (*Lord Hervey and His Friends*, ed. Lord Ilchester, 1950, 115–16).

'William Kent's Career as Literary Illustrator'. *Bulletin of the New York Public Library* lxx, 1966, 620–46; E. Croft-Murray, *Decorative Painting in England* ii, 1970, 229–35; K. Woodbridge, 'William Kent as Landscape-Gardener: a Re-Appraisal', *Apollo*, Aug. 1974, 'William Kent's Gardening: the Rousham Letters', *Apollo*, Oct. 1974; Geoffrey Beard, 'William Kent and the Cabinet-makers', *Burlington Mag.*, Dec. 1975; *History of the King's Works* v, 1976, *passim*; John Harris, 'William Kent's Gothic', in *A Gothick Symposium*, Georgian Group 1983; Michael I. Wilson, *William Kent*, 1984; *Tercentenary Tribute to William Kent*, ed. J. Wilton-Ely, essays and exhibition catalogue, Hull and Nottingham, typescript 1985; Cinzia M. Sicca, 'On William Kent's Roman Sources', *Arch. Hist.* 29, 1986; John Dixon Hunt, *William Kent, Landscape Garden Designer*, 1987.]

PUBLIC BUILDINGS

YORK MINSTER, figured pavement, 1731–6. According to Francis Drake, *Eboracum*, 1736, 519, the 'plan was drawn by . . . Mr. Kent, under the direction of the Lord Burlington', and in 1744 Philip Yorke was told that it was 'from a design of Mr. Kent's' [Travel Journal in *Beds. Hist. Rec. Soc.* xlvii, 1968, 129]. The Dean and Chapter's archives show that the work was carried out between 1731 and 1736.

LONDON, THE ROYAL MEWS, CHARING CROSS, THE GREAT MEWS, 1731–33; dem. 1830 [*History of the King's Works* v, 212–13; A. Stratton, 'The King's Mews at Charing Cross', *Arch. Rev.* xxxix, 1916; Giles Worsley, 'Kent and the Royal Mews', *C. Life*, 12 Nov. 1987].

HAMPTON COURT PALACE, Gothic gateway in Clock Court and reconstruction of adjoining apartment for occupation by Duke of Cumberland, 1732 [*History of the King's Works* v, 181; Juliet Allan, 'New Light on William Kent at Hampton Court Palace', *Arch. Hist.* 27, 1984].

KENSINGTON PALACE, revolving garden seat on mount, 1733 (dem.); *attributed*; THE QUEEN'S TEMPLE (later part of Temple Lodge, restored 1977), 1734–5 [J. Vardy, *Designs of Jones & Kent*, 1744, pl. 38; *History of the King's Works* v, 203–4].

LONDON, THE TREASURY BUILDINGS, WHITEHALL, 1733–7 [*History of the King's Works* v, 431–3; *Survey of London* xiv, chap. 3].

LONDON, ST. JAMES'S PALACE, THE QUEEN'S LIBRARY, for Queen Caroline, 1736–7; dem. 1825 [*History of the King's Works* v, 242–3].

LONDON, WESTMINSTER HALL, Gothic screen enclosing Courts of Chancery and King's Bench, 1739; heightened 1755; dem. *c.*1825 [*History of the King's Works* v, 389–90; J. Vardy, *Designs of Jones and Kent*, 1744, pl. 48].

YORK MINSTER, Gothic pulpit and choir furniture, 1740–1; destroyed by fire 1829 [J. Vardy, *Designs of Jones and Kent*, 1744, pl. 51; drawings and contract in Dean and Chapter's archives, YM/F 90, 239, and M/P 1140/1–4].

GLOUCESTER CATHEDRAL, Gothic choir-screen, 1741; removed 1820 [J. Vardy, *Designs of Jones and Kent*, 1744, pl. 49].

LONDON, THE HORSE GUARDS, WHITEHALL, designed by Kent shortly before his death and built, 1750–9, under the direction of the Board of Works [*History of the King's Works* v, 436–40; *Survey of London* xvi, chap. 2].

PRIVATE COMMISSIONS

DITCHLEY HOUSE, OXON., probably designed interior decoration of hall for 2nd Earl of Lichfield in association with Henry Flitcroft, 1724–5 [A. Gomme in *Arch. Hist.* 32, 1989, 89].

LONDON, NEWCASTLE HOUSE, LINCOLN'S INN FIELDS, internal alterations (probably decorative) for 1st Duke of Newcastle, 1725 [*The Letters of John Gay*, ed. C. F. Burgess, 1966, 51].

LONDON, BURLINGTON HOUSE, PICCADILLY, some internal decoration for 3rd Earl of Burlington, before 1727 [Kent, *Designs of Inigo Jones* i, 1727, pls. 63, 67; *Survey of London* xxxii, 401].

HOUGHTON HALL, NORFOLK, internal decoration, *c.*1725–35, of house designed by Colen Campbell for Sir Robert Walpole. The stables built *c.*1733–5 may also have been designed by Kent. Thirteen plates of ceilings and chimney-pieces by Kent are given in Isaac Ware's *Plans, Elevations and Sections of Houghton*, 1735. A design for the interior of the Cabinet Room by Kent is in the Print Room of the Ashmolean Museum, Oxford. It is inscribed 'For Houghton W.K.' A design for a chimney-piece for Houghton signed 'W. Kent 1726' is in the Witt Collection of the Courtauld Institute of Art, London. (Tipping, *English Homes, Period V* (i), 1921, 78–110; Jourdain, *Kent*, 63–4 and figs. 57–63; Hussey, *English Country Houses: Early Georgian*, 1955, 76–86).

SHERBORNE HOUSE, GLOS. designs (probably for internal decoration and furniture) for Sir John Dutton, Bart., 1728 [Christopher Gilbert, 'James Moore the Younger and William Kent at Sherborne House',

Burlington Mag. cxi, 1969, 148–9].

RAYNHAM HALL, NORFOLK, internal alterations for 2nd Viscount Townshend, *c.*1728–9 [Jourdain, *Kent*, 65; for the date see the MS. journal at Wilton of Sir Matthew Decker, who saw the work in progress in the summer of 1728].

STOWE HOUSE, BUCKS., garden buildings for 1st Viscount Cobham, *c.*1730 onwards: THE TEMPLE OF VENUS, before 1731 (Ware, *Designs of I. Jones and Others*, 1731, pls. 46–7); THE TEMPLE OF BRITISH WORTHIES, *c.*1735; THE TEMPLE OF ANCLENT VIRTUE, *c.*1735–7 (date 1737 on capstone of dome); CONGREVE'S MONUMENT, 1736; THE OXFORD GATE; THE HERMITAGE; THE SHEPHERD'S COVE [B. Seeley, *Stowe: a Description of the House and Gardens*, 1773; L. Whistler *et al.*, *Stowe, a Guide to the Gardens*, 1968].

TWICKENHAM, MIDDLESEX, POPE'S VILLA, designs for garden buildings and ornaments for Alexander Pope, *c.*1730; dem. [James Boardman, 'Pope's Essay in the Picturesque', *C. Life*, 7 March 1968; designs for two vases for Pope in Vardy's *Designs of Jones and Kent*, pl. 25; *The Correspondence of Alexander Pope*, ed. G. Sherborne, iii, 1956, 314, 322, 329, 341].

RICHMOND GARDENS, SURREY, works for Queen Caroline, including THE HERMITAGE, 1730, dem. *c.*1775, and MERLIN'S CAVE, 1735, dem. 1766 [J. Vardy, *Designs of Jones and Kent*, 1744, pls. 32, 33; *History of the King's Works* v, 224; Judith Colton, 'Kent's Hermitage for Queen Caroline at Richmond', *Architectura*, 1974, 181–191, 'Merlin's Cave and Queen Caroline', *Eighteenth-Century Studies* 10, 1976; Cinzia Sicca, 'William Kent's "natural" architecture at Richmond', *Architectura*, 1986, 68–82].

KEW HOUSE, SURREY, for Frederick, Prince of Wales, 1731–5; dem. 1802 [*History of the King's Works* v, 227].

ESHER PLACE, SURREY, addition of wings and other alterations to 'Wolsey's Tower' for the Hon. Henry Pelham, *c.*1733, Gothic. The wings and various garden buildings have been demolished. Many of Kent's drawings are in the Victoria and Albert Museum, others in an extra-illustrated copy of Brayley's *Surrey* in Wimbledon Public Library. One is dated 1733 [J. W. Lindus Forge in *Arch. Rev.* Sept. 1949, with plans; John Harris in *C. Life*, 14 May 1959; Michael Symes, 'The Landscaping of Esher Place', *Jnl. Garden History* 8 (4), 1988].

HOLKHAM HALL, NORFOLK, for Thomas Coke, cr. Earl of Leicester (d. 1759) and his trustees, 1734–65. It is clear that the conception of the house was developed by Coke himself, in collaboration with Lord Burlington and William Kent. Kent was directly responsible only for the exterior, for the hall, and for the interior of the S. W. pavilion, the only part of the house to be completed in his lifetime. The remaining interiors were due to Matthew Brettingham, who was executant architect throughout. In 1761 Brettingham published *The Plans and Elevations of the late Earl of Leicester's House at Holkham*, without acknowledgement to Kent, but in a second edition in 1773 his son admitted Kent's responsibility for the design, and several drawings by Kent remain at Holkham to prove it, as well as an engraving of the principal elevation by Fourdrinier inscribed 'Gulielmus Kent Archit. et Pict. Invenit et Delin.' It was further stated in the 1773 edition of Brettingham's book that 'The stone Bridge at the commencement of the lake, the obelisk, the Temple-building contiguous, the Seat upon the Mount, the two Arches which enclose the pleasure garden as well as the distant building called the Triumphal Arch at the entrance of the approach, were all deduced from sketches by Mr. Kent, with considerable alterations made in the designs, long before these works were erected' [J. Schmidt, 'Holkham Hall, Norfolk', *C. Life*, 24–31 Jan., 7–14 Feb. 1980][1] (*Vitruvius Britannicus* v, 1771, pls. 64–9; Tipping, *English Homes, Period V* (i), 1921; Hussey, *English Country Houses: Early Georgian*, 1955).

LONDON, DEVONSHIRE HOUSE, PICCADILLY, for 3rd Duke of Devonshire, 1734–*c.*1740; altered by James Wyatt and Decimus Burton; dem. 1924–5 [*Vitruvius Britannicus* iv, 1767, pls. 19–20] (*C. Life*, 13–20 Nov. 1981).

EASTON NESTON, NORTHANTS., chimney-pieces in hall and 'next room' for 1st Earl of Pomfret, before 1735 [G. Baker, *History of Northants.* ii, 1822–30, 145; description of the house *c.*1735, Alnwick Castle, Percy family letters, vol. 25, f. 225; see also *C. Life*, 7 Feb. 1974, 250] (Tipping, *English Homes, Period IV* (ii), 1928, figs. 183, 192).

CHISWICK HOUSE, MIDDLESEX, interior of the Summer Parlour for 3rd Earl of Burlington, 1735 [R. Hewlings, *Chiswick House and Gardens*, English Heritage 1989, 40].

[1] Schmidt's attribution of certain drawings for Holkham to Coke himself in the catalogue of an exhibition held at Holkham in 1980 must be rejected, for reasons set out in *Country Life*, 7 and 21 Aug. 1980 (correspondence) and *Architectural Drawings from Lowther Castle*, ed. Colvin *et al.*, 1980, 29.

attributed: ASKE HALL, YORKS. (N.R.), the Gothic Temple for Sir Conyers D'Arcy, *c.*1735 [unsigned design in R.I.B.A. Collection attributed to Kent on grounds of draughtsmanship: P. Leach in *C. Life*, 26 Sept. 1974, 837].

LONDON, CARLTON HOUSE, octagonal 'saloon' in garden for Frederick, Prince of Wales, 1735; dem. [*History of the King's Works* v, 138].

CLAREMONT, SURREY, garden buildings for 1st Duke of Newcastle. Two buildings at Claremont by Kent are illustrated in Ware's *Designs of Inigo Jones and Others* [1731], pls. 40–1. One of these is identified as the BOWLING GREEN HOUSE on Rocque's engraving of the grounds at Claremont, dated 1738. In addition Rocque shows a domed temple on the island in the lake which must be attributed to Kent, who was responsible for the formation of the lake. This temple survives in ruins, but the other two have been demolished. Drawings by Kent for the gardens at Claremont are illustrated by J. Dixon Hunt (1987).

SHOTOVER PARK, OXON., octagonal garden building and obelisk for Col. James Tyrrell, before 1733 [I. Ware, *Designs of Inigo Jones and Others* [1731], pls. 38–9, 42; original drawings in Yale Center for British Art] (Tipping, *English Homes, Period IV* (ii), figs. 366, 372).

ROUSHAM HOUSE, OXON., addition of wings to north front and garden buildings for General James Dormer, 1738–41 [C. Hussey in *C. Life*, 17–24 May, 14–21 June 1946; Jourdain, *Kent*, 54–5; K. Woodbridge in *Apollo*, Oct. 1974].

GUNNERSBURY PARK, MIDDLESEX, garden layout for Henry Furnese, *c.*1740–3 [S. Lysons, *Environs of London* ii (1), 1811, 145; payment to Kent in Furnese's account at Hoare's Bank, 1743, *ex inf.* Mr. Edward Saunders; Roger White in *C. Life*, 11 Nov. 1982].

LONDON, No. 22 ARLINGTON STREET, for the Hon. Henry Pelham, 1741–50; completed by Stephen Wright after Kent's death [*A House in Town: 22 Arlington Street, its owners and builders*, ed. P. Campbell, 1984].

LONDON, No. 44 BERKELEY SQUARE, for Lady Isabella Finch, 1742–4 [building accounts in Sir John Soane's Museum, 39B] (*C. Life*, 27 Dec. 1962; *Apollo*, August 1987).

LONDON, No. 16 ST. JAMES'S PLACE, for Sir John Evelyn, Bart.; dem. 1899–1900. Evelyn built this house early in the 1740s, and on 8 July 1743 paid 'Mr. Kent architect for his directions about the house in St. James Place' [account-book among Evelyn archives at Christ Church, Oxford].

BADMINTON HOUSE, GLOS., works for 3rd Duke of Beaufort, *c.*1745, including the WORCESTER LODGE, several garden buildings no longer in existence, and the remodelling of the upper part of the N. front with pediment and twin cupolas [H. Colvin in *C. Life*, 4 April 1986; A. Gomme, 'Badminton Revisited', *Arch. Hist.* 27, 1984] (*C. Life*, 25 Nov., 1–8 Dec. 1938, 16 April 1987).

HORSEHEATH HALL, CAMBS., interior decoration for 2nd Lord Montfort, *c.*1745; dem. 1792 [C. E. Parsons, 'Horseheath Hall and its owners', *Procs. Cambridge Antiquarian Soc.* xli, 1941–7, 40]. A design by Kent for an octagonal pavilion over a grotto or cascade, inscribed 'Ld Montfort at Horseheath 1746 WK', is illustrated in *V.C.H. Cambs.* vi, 64. There is no evidence that it was built.

OATLANDS HOUSE, WEYBRIDGE, SURREY, garden building for 9th Earl of Lincoln, probably *c.*1745; dem. 'Mr. Kent's pretty building on the old Terrace' at Oatlands is referred to in a letter from Joseph Spence dated 24 March 1766 [Nottingham University Library, Newcastle Collection, Ne C], and Kent refers to a proposed visit to Oatlands in a letter to Lady Lincoln dated 6 July 1745 [*ibid.*, Ne C 3, 111].

EUSTON HALL, SUFFOLK, THE TEMPLE or BANQUETING HOUSE, for 2nd Duke of Grafton, 1746 [J. Dugdale, *British Traveller* iv, 1819, 277; Arthur Oswald in *C. Life*, 24 Jan. 1957, reproducing drawings by Kent].

WAKEFIELD LODGE, NORTHANTS., for 2nd Duke of Grafton, *c.*1748–50. [Jourdain, *Kent*, 59–60; Marcus Binney in *C. Life*, 2 Aug. 1973].

LONDON, HOLLAND HOUSE, KENSINGTON, garden terraces, etc., for Henry Fox, 1st Lord Holland, 1748 [*Horace Walpole's Correspondence*, ed. W. S. Lewis, xxx, 1961, 114].

LONDON, DOVER STREET, interior decoration for Sir William Stanhope, probably in the 1740s [*Horace Walpole's Correspondence*, ed. W. S. Lewis, xix, 485].

MONUMENTS

CHESTER CATHEDRAL, John and Thomas Wainwright (d. 1720), signed *G. Berkley S.T.P. & Gul. Kent inven.*

WESTMINSTER ABBEY, HENRY VII'S CHAPEL, George Monck, Duke of Albemarle (d. 1670), ex. Scheemakers, 1730(?) [E. W. Brayley & J. P. Neale, *History of the Abbey Church of Westminster* i, 1818, Henry VII's Chapel, 71].

YORK MINSTER, Thomas Watson Wentworth (d. 1723), ex. Guelfi, probably in 1731 [engraving in Bodleian, Gough Maps 41K, f. 37, signed *W. Kent arch.*].

WESTMINSTER ABBEY, Isaac Newton (d. 1727), ex. Rysbrack, completed 1731 [signed].

KIRKTHORPE CHURCH, YORKS. (W.R.), Thomas and Catherine Stringer, ex. Guelfi, 1731–2 [M. I. Webb in *Burlington Mag.*, May 1955, 143–4].

BLENHEIM PALACE CHAPEL, OXON., John Churchill, 1st Duke of Marlborough (d. 1722), ex. Rysbrack, designed 1730, completed 1733 [David Green, *Blenheim Palace*, 1951, 160, 274].

WESTMINSTER ABBEY, James, 1st Earl Stanhope (d. 1721), ex. Rysbrack, completed 1733 [signed].

WESTMINSTER ABBEY, William Shakespeare (d. 1616), ex. Scheemakers, 1740 [signed].

ASHBY-DE-LA-ZOUCHE CHURCH, LEICS., Theophilus Hastings, 9th Earl of Huntingdon (d. 1746), ex. Rysbrack [signed].

MISCELLANEOUS WORKS

(excluding paintings, furniture and book illustrations)

WESTMINSTER HALL, triumphal arch for coronation of King George II, 1727, of which there is a print signed *Wm. Kent invt. & delin.* (Bodleian, Gough Maps 23, f. 49v). Drawings by Kent exist in P.R.O., WORK 36/68/46, and Westminster City Library, Pennant, vol. iii, f. 48.

THE ROYAL STATE BARGE, made in 1732 for Frederick, Prince of Wales, used until 1849, now in the National Maritime Museum, Greenwich [A. E. Richardson, 'The Royal Barge, Notes on the Original Drawings by William Kent', *R.I.B.A. Jnl.* xxxviii, 1931; G. W. Beard, 'William Kent and the Royal Barge', *Burlington Mag.*, Aug. 1970].

KING'S THEATRE, HAYMARKET, designed the scenery for Nicolo Porpora's cantata *La Festa d'Imeneo*, produced in 1736 in honour of the marriage of Frederick, Prince of Wales [E. Croft-Murray in *C. Life*, 4 Sept. 1949, 269].

PLATE, CANDELABRA, etc., for various persons, illustrated by J. Vardy, *Some Designs of Mr. Inigo Jones and Mr. William Kent*, 1744, pls. 19–31, including a pair of silver chandeliers (pl. 23) made for King George II's palace at Herrenhausen in 1736, and now at Anglesey Abbey, Cambs. (see *C. Life*, 22 April 1954, 1229).

KEYS, HENRY LENT (*c.*1801–), was admitted to the Royal Academy Schools in 1823 at the age of 22. He subsequently practised as an architect from No. 6 Regent Square, London [*Survey of London* xxiv, 76]. He was elected a Fellow of the Institute of British Architects in 1835, retiring in 1848. Elevations for a Gothic rectory drawn by him in 1839 are in the National Library of Wales, Slebech MS. 3364.

KEYTE, JOHN, of Kidderminster, was the 'able architect' who in 1795 repewed and refitted TEWKESBURY ABBEY CHURCH to the designs of Edward Edgcumbe [W. Dyde, *History of Tewkesbury*, 1798, 55]. He appears to have designed ST. MARTIN'S CHURCH, TIPTON, STAFFS., in 1797 [B. F. L. Clarke, *The Building of the Eighteenth-Century Church*, 1963, 102].

KILLIGREW, WILLIAM, of Bath, was a joiner who 'laid his Apron aside about the year 1719' and thereafter practised as an architect. His few recorded buildings have all been demolished. They were vigorous examples of pre-Palladian architecture which met with the disapproval of John Wood but appear to have had considerable merit. Wood states that he added a new ballroom to the LOWER ASSEMBLY ROOMS in 1720 (remodelled 1750, gutted 1820, demolished 1933); designed THE BLUECOAT SCHOOL, UPPER BOROUGH WALLS, 1721–2 (demolished 1859–60), and the south front of the old GUILDHALL, *c.*1725 (dem. *c.*1775). WEYMOUTH HOUSE, 1720 (partially demolished 1826 and wholly in 1896), and No. 3 ST. JAMES'S STREET SOUTH (demolished 1959) have also been attributed to him. [John Wood, *Essay towards a Description of Bath*, 1749, 318, 319, 321; W. Ison, *The Georgian Buildings of Bath*, 1948, 2nd ed. 1980, *passim.*]

The Bath architect was probably not the same person as William Killigrew, described as a builder of Chippenham, who in 1740 contracted to enlarge the market house at Tetbury, Glos., and in 1742 surveyed Tetbury Church [Glos. Record Office, D 566/B12. *ex inf.* Mr. N. M. Herbert; Gloucester Public Library, MS. R.R. 300.1, p. 6].

KIMPTON, W—, of 199 Strand, London, exhibited at the Royal Academy in 1784 a plan and elevation of the seventeenth-century Lyveden New Building, nr. Thrapston in Northamptonshire. In 1785 he made a set of five measured drawings of another seventeenth-century building, Houghton House, nr. Ampthill, Beds., one of which is illustrated by H. Clifford Smith in *The Haynes Grange Room* (Victoria and Albert Museum 1935, pl. xii). He was perhaps the clerk named Kimpton who was in Robert Mylne's office until December 1781.

KING, CHARLES (1772–1856), was the son of a surgeon at Mortlake in Surrey. He became a pupil of Willey Reveley and exhibited architectural drawings at the Royal Academy between 1792 and 1807. He lived at Mortlake, where he was for many years vestry clerk, and in 1837 the chancel of MORTLAKE CHURCH was rebuilt to his designs (again rebuilt 1905). This is King's only recorded architectural work and his practice was evidently on a small scale. He also acted as a drawing-master and drew some local views which were engraved. He submitted a design for the Nelson Monument in 1839 [Richard Jeffree, *The Story of Mortlake Churchyard*, Mortlake 1983; further information from Mr. Jeffree].

KING, JAMES (–1744), of St. Martin's Lane, Westminster, a carpenter by trade, submitted in 1737 a design for building a wooden bridge at Westminster which so favourably impressed the Commissioners that they asked him to make detailed specifications for a timber bridge to be carried on stone piers designed by Charles Labelye (*q.v.*). It was eventually decided to build a bridge entirely of stone, but King was employed as carpenter to construct the centerings [R. J. B. Walker, *Old Westminster Bridge*, 1979, 79, 80–3, 147, 150, etc.].

In 1737 King, by mechanical means, saved the portico of St. Martin-in-the-Fields Church from collapse owing to shrinkage of the timbers [Parish Records in Westminster City Library]. He is said to have built the timber obelisk containing the cistern of the York Buildings Waterworks Company, which stood on the north bank of the Thames at the bottom of Villiers Street, and which forms a prominent feature in Canaletto's paintings of the river. He died in April 1744.

KING, JOHN, was a clerk or assistant of Francis Goodwin [*Arch. Hist.* i, 1958, 63]. He exhibited at the Royal Academy from a London address from 1817 to 1829. His drawings included a 'Design for a hunting seat proposed to be erected for a gentleman in Derbyshire' (1821), the new Commissioners' church at Kidderminster designed by Goodwin (1822), and a 'monumental building proposed to be erected in the County of Wicklow' (1823). He must be distinguished from the subject of the following entry, and from a mason-architect of the same name who practised in Bradford in about 1840.

KING, JOHN, practised as a surveyor in Tonbridge, Kent, in the 1820s. In 1820 he carried out repairs and alterations to TONBRIDGE CHURCH [B. Wadmore, *Some Details of the History of the Parish of Tonbridge*, 1906, 5]. By 1827 he had been joined in partnership by an architect called Brown, and in 1830 King and Brown designed SOUTH PARK HOUSE, PENSHURST, KENT, for J. W. Lloyd; altered and enlarged by A. Salvin 1848 and since largely dem. [drawings in Carmarthen Record Office, Cynghordy 1181, *ex inf.* Mr. Thomas Lloyd].

KINNARD, WILLIAM (*c.*1788–1839), the son of a magistrate, was admitted to the Royal Academy Schools in 1805 at the age of 17, and was awarded the Gold Medal the same year. In 1807 he became District Surveyor for the parishes of St. Giles-in-the-Fields and St. George, Bloomsbury, and in 1812 laid an information under the Building Act against John Soane for building a projection on to the front of his house in Lincoln's Inn Fields. The case was heard in October 1812, and was dismissed in Soane's favour. In 1817–19 Kinnard travelled in Italy and visited Greece and Turkey in company with Charles Barry and Charles Eastlake. He subsequently exhibited at the Royal Academy a number of drawings of buildings he had visited, and edited the supplementary volume of the *Antiquities of Athens* published in 1830, to which he contributed an account of buildings in Athens and Delos.

According to J. L. Wolfe Kinnard 'went mad from time to time'. Perhaps for this reason his architectural practice appears to have been small. In 1811 he exhibited at the Academy a view of a villa 'now being erected for a gentleman at Ham Frith in Essex', and in 1813 he published an engraved 'View of a Triumphal Arch, proposed to be erected at Hyde Park Corner, commemorative of the victories achieved by the British Arms during the Reign of His Majesty King George the Third', of which there are copies in the British Library (*King's Maps* xxvii *i*), and the Bodleian Library (Douce Prints N.8). He designed the monument in East Retford Church, Notts., to Sir Wharton Amcotts (d. 1807), which bears his signature. He died on 12 October 1839. His library was auctioned on 9 January 1840 (sale catalogue in B.L., S.C. Sg.53 (14)).

[*A.P.S.D.; The Farington Diary*, ed. J. Greig, vii, 283; A. T. Bolton, *The Portrait of Sir John Soane*, 181, 257.]

KINSMAN, EDMUND, was a leading London master mason of the early seventeenth century. The dates of his birth and death have not been ascertained, but he was Master of the Masons' Company in 1635. He was presumably the 'Edmund Kinsman, freemason,' who was employed at SYON HOUSE, MIDDLESEX, in 1604–5 [accounts at Alnwick Castle, U.l. 13]. In 1613–14 he was working at THE CHARTERHOUSE under Francis Carter, and presumably built the new north aisle of the Chapel there [Arthur Oswald in *C. Life*, 15 Oct. 1959]. In 1615–16 he was associated with Nicholas Stone in the contract for the monument to Thomas Sutton, the founder of the Charterhouse [*Walpole Soc.* vii, 41]. In 1618 he was again employed under Carter as master mason for the building of the SALISBURY CHAPEL at HATFIELD CHURCH, HERTS. [Hatfield House, Cecil Papers vol. 143, f. 142 *et seq.*]. Inigo Jones subsequently employed him at NEWMARKET, OATLANDS and ST. PAUL'S CATHEDRAL [*Arch. Hist.* ii, 1959, 33; *Arch. Rev.* xxxix, 1916, 76; *History of the King's Works* iii and iv]. In *c.*1630 he was concerned in some ambitious proposals, not carried out, for alterations to COPT HALL, ESSEX, for Lionel Cranfield, 1st Earl of Middlesex, and may have built the classical loggia (dem. 1748) [John Newman in *The Country Seat*, ed. Colvin & Harris, 1970, 25]. The churchwardens' accounts of ST. ALBAN'S CHURCH, WOOD STREET, show that Kinsman was (with Matthew Banckes, senior) involved in the rebuilding of the church in 1633–4, for in 1634 he was paid 50s. 'for his paynes draught & valuacon of the worke about the church' [Guildhall Library, MS. 7673/1]. In 1636 he rebuilt the 'lanthorn' on the tower of ST. MARY-LE-BOW CHURCH, which was crowned by a stone lantern supported by four flying buttresses [*Cal. State Papers Domestic 1635–6*, 149], and in 1638 he was one of the three London masons responsible for rebuilding the west tower of GOUDHURST CHURCH, KENT [*Archaeologia Cantiana* xxviii, 10–13].

The evidence at present available does not make it clear whether Kinsman was an architectural designer of any consequence or not. Although he executed strictly classical works for Inigo Jones, his church commissions suggest that he was more at home in the mixture of classical and Gothic of which the undocumented St. Katherine Cree (1628–31) is the outstanding example.

KIRBY, JOHN JOSHUA (1716–1774), born at Parham near Wickham Market in Suffolk, was the eldest son of John Kirby, author of *The Suffolk Traveller*, an early road book published in 1735, and of a *Map of the County of Suffolk*, 1736. He is said to have begun life as a coach and house painter, but achieved a modest reputation as a topographical artist, in particular making drawings to illustrate a projected history of Suffolk, twelve of which he published in 1748, together with a printed description. He was more successful in making himself an authority on perspective, upon which he lectured at the St. Martin's Lane Academy in London. In 1754 he published *Dr. Brook Taylor's Method of Perspective*, with a frontispiece by Hogarth. Despite ensuing controversies with Isaac Ware and Joseph Highmore, Kirby was, through Lord Bute's influence, appointed drawing-master to the Prince of Wales (afterwards George III), and in 1761 he and his son William were appointed joint Clerks of the Works at Richmond and Kew Palaces. Several of the drawings which Kirby exhibited at the Society of Artists during the next few years were believed to be the work of his royal pupil, and it was at the King's expense that in 1761 he published another work entitled *The Perspective of Architecture . . . deduced from the principles of Dr. Brook Taylor.* The design for a house on pl. lxiv was contributed by George III, whose original drawing is in the Royal Library at Windsor.

Kirby was secretary of the Incorporated Society of Artists, and in 1768 was elected president by a 'discontented clique', but resigned two years later on grounds of ill-health. He was elected F.R.S. in March 1767 and F.S.A. in June of the same year. He died on 21 June 1774, aged 58, and was buried in Kew churchyard. His son William, who had been sent to Italy to study architecture at the King's expense, died suddenly at Kew in 1771 at the age of 28. Some of the drawings made by him in Rome in 1767–8 are in the Royal Library at Windsor. A portrait of Kirby by Gainsborough is in the Victoria and Albert Museum, and one of himself and his wife by the same artist is in the National Portrait Gallery.

In 1744 Kirby designed an altarpiece for HADLEIGH CHURCH, SUFFOLK, which has since been removed. His drawing is attached to the contract between the Revd. David Wilkins and Josias Harris, an Ipswich joiner [Kent Archives Office, U 23, Q 3/1–3]. In 1756 he designed a workhouse (now part of Archerfield School) at NACTON in SUFFOLK [Owen, cited below, n. 38]. In 1768 KEW CHAPEL or CHURCH was enlarged by Kirby at the King's expense. In 1766 he communicated to the inhabitants 'a Most Gracious offer from His Majesty to enlarge the Chapel according to a plan now laid before them for that purpose' [Surrey Archdeaconry Records]. In the King's Collection in the British Library (*King's Maps* xl, 46 *h*) there is a 'Plan and Elevation of Kew Chapel with the proposed Alterations' signed J. K. and dated February 1768. The chapel was enlarged by adding north and south aisles and not, as shown in the plan, by an extension to the west. It was subsequently extended to the west in 1805 by R. Browne and again in 1837–8 by Sir Jeffry Wyatville. Kirby also designed ST. GEORGE'S CHAPEL, OLD BRENTFORD, MIDDLESEX, 1762, enlarged 1828, dem. 1887 [T. Faulkner, *History of Brentford*, 1845, 128, 131, 156].

[*A.P.S.D.*; *D.N.B.*; W. H. Pyne, *Wine and Walnuts* i, 1824, 175–6n; *Walpole Soc.* xxvii, 70; W. T. Whitley, *Artists and their Friends in England* i, 1928, 225; E. A. Oppé, *English Drawings of the Stuart and Georgian Periods at Windsor Castle*, 1950, 10–20; Felicity Owen, *Joshua Kirby and Thomas Gainsborough*, exhibition catalogue, Gainsborough House, Sudbury, Suffolk, 1980; Eileen Harris, *British Architectural Books and Writers 1556–1785*, 1990, 254–8.]

KIRBY, RICHARD, described as 'surveyor', supervised the building of a house on SNOW HILL, LONDON, for Paul Wickes in 1671 [P.R.O., C 107/113]. He was presumably the surveyor called 'Mr. Kirbie' whose design for Apothecaries' Hall was rejected by that Company in 1668 [Guildhall Library, MS. 8201/1, f. 109].

KIRK, WILLIAM (1749–1823), of Leicester, was born into a family long connected with the building trade, and was himself a surveyor and monumental mason. For some years he was County Surveyor of Leicestershire. In that capacity he was, with Henry Couchman (*q.v.*), jointly responsible in 1810 for the rebuilding of BENSFORD BRIDGE, on the boundary between Leicestershire and Warwickshire [Warwickshire County Records, Class 24, 28 (x)]. In 1814–15 he designed a new HOUSE OF CORRECTION at LEICESTER [Leicestershire County Records, Q.S. 32/3/12/1–6], in 1818 he added a Fever Ward to LEICESTER INFIRMARY [drawings in Leicester C.R.O.], and in 1822 he designed the bridge at MELTON MOWBRAY, LEICS. He died on 21 January 1823, aged 73 [J. D. Bennett, *Leicestershire Architects 1700–1850*, Leicester Museums 1968].

KIRSHAW, LUKE (*c.*1770–1821), practised as an architect and surveyor in Northampton. In 1792–3 he was clerk of the works in charge of the building of Northampton Infirmary to the designs of Samuel Saxon [F. F. Waddy, *History of Northampton General Hospital*, Northampton 1974]. From 1802 onwards he also acted as an auctioneer, and he was successively the proprietor of the Goat Inn in Gold Street and (from 1813) of the Peacock Inn in Market Square. He was elected Mayor in 1807 and died on 26 April 1821, in his 51st year [*Northampton Mercury*, 20 Feb. 1802, 28 April 1821, etc., *ex inf.* Mr. B. A. Bailey]. George Papworth (1781–1855) joined his office in 1804, but left 1806 in order to start practice in Dublin [*Builder* xiii, 1855, 150].

The following evidence of Kirshaw's architectural activity has been noted: plans of the GEORGE HOTEL, NORTHAMPTON, 1800 [Northants. Record Office, George Inn Tontine papers]; a payment to him by the Radcliffe Trustees for making unexecuted designs for rebuilding WOLVERTON CHURCH, BUCKS., in 1803 [Bodleian Library, Minutes of the Radcliffe Trustees, 1792–1815]; survey plans of BOUGHTON HALL, nr. NORTHAMPTON, with unexecuted proposals for alterations 1809 [Northants. Record Office, Howard-Vyse papers, Box 1, parcel 20]; a new gallery designed by him for ALL SAINTS CHURCH, NORTHAMPTON, 1815 [Peterborough Diocesan Records]; a plan and elevation of the lodges at ALTHORP HOUSE, NORTHANTS., 1818 [B.L., Althorp Papers, P. 9].

KITCHEN, HENRY (*c.*1793–1822), may have been the son of a Surrey bricklayer of the same name. He became a pupil of James Wyatt, and exhibited student's work at the Royal Academy from Wyatt's office in 1810 and 1811. By 1813 he was practising on his own at 36 St. James's Place, and in that year exhibited at the Academy his designs for EWELL HOUSE or CASTLE, SURREY, a castellated house built in 1814 by Thomas Calverley. About the same time he designed a gallery in EWELL CHURCH [Surrey Archdeaconry Records].

In 1816 Kitchen emigrated to Australia, where he died six years later at the age of 29, having failed to make a successful career for himself in the colony in competition with F. H. Greenway, the Government architect [M. Herman, *The Early Australian Architects and their Work*, 1970, 97–100].

KNIGHT, DANIEL (*c.*1784–1843), was an architect, surveyor and timber merchant at Leicester, where he died on 16 February 1843, aged 59. He also owned a public house, the 'Keck's Arms', in Archdeacon Lane. He was practising as an architect at least as early as 1816. His works included additions to GREAT GLEN VICARAGE, LEICS., 1819 [Lincolnshire Record Office, MGA 102]; repairing BARKBY CHURCH, LEICS., 1826 [specifications in Leicester C.R.O.]; and adding a north aisle to MARKFIELD CHURCH, LEICS., in 1826, altered 1865 [I.C.B.S]. His designs for a NATIONAL SCHOOL at ANSTEY, LEICS., dated 1831, are in Leicester C.R.O. [J. D. Bennett, *Leicestershire*

Architects 1700–1850, Leicester Museums, 1968.]

KNIGHT, WILLIAM (–1832), was employed in the offices both of J. B. Papworth and of Sir John Rennie. For the latter he acted as resident architect or clerk of the works for the construction of Plymouth Breakwater and of London Bridge. He exhibited at the Royal Academy from 1807 onwards, his drawings including 'the west front of Hillingdon House [Middlesex], the seat of J. D. Porcher, Esq., M.P.' (1808), the 'interior of the cathedral of Barcelona' (1819), a plan and elevation of the elder Rennie's Southwark Bridge (1822), a 'design for a nobleman's residence in the Castle style' (1823), and 'the works of the new London Bridge in progress as they appeared in August 1827' (1832). Knight was an enthusiastic antiquary, and made several communications to the Society of Antiquaries, of which he was a Fellow, on the subject of old London Bridge. The sale of his library and collections at Sotheby's in December 1832 included a number of architectural drawings and 'the Lower Jaw, and three other Bones, of Peter of Colechurch, the original Architect of London Bridge, found on removing the foundation of the Ancient Chapel'. [*Gent's Mag.* 1832 (i), 201–6, 1833 (i), 67–8; W. Papworth, *Memoir of J. B. Papworth*, 1879, 96; sale catalogue in Bodleian Library, Mus. Bibl. III.]

KNIGHT, WILLIAM (–1845), was an architect practising in Kidderminster. In 1822 he was acting as clerk of works for Francis Goodwin at St. George's Church, Kidderminster [Rickman's diary, 21 June 1822]. In 1829–30 he was paid £23 19s. 2d. for surveying in connection with the building of the new SEBRIGHT SCHOOL at WOLVERLEY, WORCS., whose striking Gothic façade (illustrated in Pevsner's *Worcestershire*) he may therefore have designed. However, at the same time a Mr. Pinches was paid 5s. a day for 10 days 'making drawings for Wolverley School' [A. L. Murray, *Sebright School, Wolverley*, Cambridge 1954, 126].

In 1830 Knight designed a new Gothic tower for EASTHAM CHURCH, WORCS. In the course of his correspondence with the Incorporated Church Building Society the incumbent described Knight as 'an Architect, whose simplicity of design and good taste the Society has been pleased to approve in more, I believe, than one instance' [I.C.B.S.]. Knight was also concerned in the rebuilding of the nave of HARTLEBURY CHURCH, WORCS., to the designs of Thomas Rickman in 1836–7. From Rickman's 'work-book' [B.L., Add. MS. 37802, f. 75^{v}] it appears that in 1834, after he had made the necessary designs, the churchwardens proposed to employ another architect, and Knight signed the drawings submitted to the Incorporated Church Building Society about this time. However, they evidently represented Rickman's design, and it was Rickman who was named as architect on the foundation-stone laid in 1836 [*Gent's Mag.* 1836 (i), 654]. Knight was later in partnership with John Nettleship, in conjunction with whom he designed a UNION WORKHOUSE at BLAKEBROOK, KIDDERMINSTER, in 1837, and an unidentified house for George Crump near Kidderminster in 1838. [*Berrow's Worcester Jnl.*, 25 May 1837, 22 March 1838, *ex inf.* Mr. A. S. Brooks]. Knight was presumably the 'William Knight of Kidderminster, gentleman', who died on 7 Sept. 1845 [will in Worcester Probate Records].

KNOWLES, GEORGE (*c.*1776–1856), was 'an able and successful civil engineer'. In that capacity he designed WHITWORTH BRIDGE over the R. Liffey in DUBLIN in 1816–17 [M. Craig, *Dublin 1660–1860*, 1952, 289]. He lived at Lucan House, Sharow, Yorkshire (W.R.), and in 1821–5 'designed and superintended the building' of SHAROW CHURCH in a competent Perpendicular Gothic style. He died at Scarborough on 23 June 1856, aged 80, and was buried at Sharow, where an inscription records his responsibility for the design of the church, which is confirmed by the I.C.B.S. records.

L

LABELYE, CHARLES (1705–?1781), was the son of François Dangeau Labelye, a French Protestant refugee living at Vevey in Switzerland. He probably came to England shortly before 1725, in which year he joined a French Masonic Lodge in London of which his friend J. T. Desaguliers was also a member.[1] This is consistent with his own statement that he 'never heard a word of English spoken till I was near twenty years of age'. His first employment in England appears to have been as a teacher of mathematics to naval personnel, for the 'Mapp of the Downes . . . together with the Soundings at

[1] Labelye contributed a paper on the laws of motion to Desaguliers' *Course of Experimental Philosophy*, 2nd ed. 1745, ii, 77–95. See also his account of the railway which conveyed stone from Ralph Allen's quarry near Bath to the R. Avon, *ibid.* i, 283–4 and pls. 21–3.

low water, Places of Anchorage and all the necessary leading marks' which he produced in 1736 was 'By Charles Labelye, Engineer, late Teacher of the Mathematics in the Royal Navy' (P.R.O., MPH 218). In 1727–8 he was in Madrid, but by November 1728 he was back in England, practising as an expert in harbours and waterways. In 1734 he supplied maps and plans of the Thames to the promoters of the project for a new bridge over the river at Westminster. In June 1737 he was one of the five persons who were 'desired to attend the Commissioners with surveys of the river', and in July his were among the many plans for a wooden bridge that were submitted to them. On 10 May 1738 he was appointed 'engineer' at a salary of £100 a year, with 10s. a day subsistence money. His commission extended only to the stone piers, as it was intended to build a bridge which could support either a timber or a stone superstructure, and the decision in favour of the latter was not taken until later. The employment of a foreigner[1] caused some jealousy among English architects, and led to the publication of a series of pamphlets in which the authors of the rejected designs gave vent to their disappointment by criticizing each other and denouncing 'the Swiss impostor' (see John James, *A Short Review of the Several Pamphlets and Schemes . . . in relation to Building a Bridge at Westminster*, 1736). Labelye had, however, a strong supporter in the Earl of Pembroke, by whom the first stone was laid on 29 January 1738/9. Richard Graham acted as 'surveyor and comptroller of the works' at £300 a year, and the contractors for the masonry were Andrews Jelfe and Samuel Tufnell.

The method of construction employed, involving the use of caissons in which to build the piers, was one not hitherto used in England. The caissons were huge timber boxes, 80 feet long and 16 feet deep, which were floated into position over the sites of the piers and sunk into excavations dug in the bed of the river to receive them. The water was then pumped out, and each pier was built inside the caisson up to water level. The sides of the caisson were then removed, leaving the flat bottom beneath the pier. In this way piling was avoided, and the piers were built of accurately laid masonry from their foundations upwards. In spite of these improved methods of construction, a subsidence occurred in one of the piers when the bridge was nearly complete, and it was not till November 1750 that it was eventually opened to the public. The accident occasioned a fresh outbreak of pamphlets, including a ballad entitled *The Downfall of Westminster Bridge, or my Lord in the Suds* (n.d.), in which Lord Pembroke, the Commissioners and Labelye were all severely handled. Batty Langley took the opportunity to publish *A Survey of Westminster Bridge, as 'tis now Sinking into Ruin*, 1748, containing a virulent attack on the Commissioners for employing 'an INSOLVENT IGNORANT, ARROGATING SWISS', and an engraved frontispiece showing his own rejected design for the bridge with a figure of Labelye hanging from a gallows in one corner. The Commissioners were, however, unimpressed by these taunts, and in February 1751 resolved to present Labelye with an honorarium of £2000 'for his great fidelity and extraordinary labour and attendances, skill and diligence'. Unfortunately for Labelye his patron the Earl of Pembroke died later that year, and he told a friend that in fact he was 'cutt off with only half the recompence promised' to him. He was now in poor health and 'voluntarily banished himself' from a country where he felt that he had been shabbily treated. In 1753 the architect Stephen Riou (*q.v.*) found him in Naples, but he appears eventually to have returned to France. The *Gentleman's Magazine* reported his death in Paris in 1762, but other sources indicate that it did not occur until 17 December 1781.

As the first major bridge to be built over an English river for more than a century, Westminster Bridge attracted much attention. Labelye himself published in 1739 *A Short Account of the Methods made use of in Laying the Foundation of the Piers of Westminster Bridge*, and *The Present State of Westminster Bridge . . . in a letter to a Friend*, published anonymously in 1743, is also believed to have been written by him. He intended to publish a full description of the bridge, and in 1744 he issued a prospectus of the proposed work, which was to have been in two volumes. *The Description of Westminster Bridge* which he published in 1751 is, however, little more than an enlarged edition of the *Short Account*, and neither work contains the promised engravings, which may have been sold loose. Copies of the original drawings made by Thomas Gayfere, Andrews Jelfe's foreman, are preserved in the Library of the Institute of Civil Engineers, bound up with a copy of Labelye's *Short Account*. There is a collection of engravings of the bridge in the Bodleian, Gough Maps 23, and also a volume of pamphlets relating to its construction (Gough Westminster 22).

Labelye's bridge was replaced by the present structure in 1854–62. It was illustrated in the *Gentleman's Magazine* for 1746, pp. 683–4, in a work entitled *Gephyralogia, an Historical Account of Bridges, ancient and*

[1] In 1746 Labelye was naturalized by Act of Parliament (19 Geo. II, cap. 26).

modern, including a . . . History and Description of the new Bridge at Westminster, 1751, and in Britton & Pugin's *Public Buildings of London* ii, 1828, 295. An authoritative account of its construction is given by R. J. B. Walker, *Old Westminster Bridge*, 1979. See also T. Ruddock, *Arch Bridges and their Builders 1735–1835*, 1979, chap. 1.

The only other English bridge for which Labelye is known to have been responsible was BRENTFORD BRIDGE, MIDDLESEX, which he rebuilt in brick and stone in 1740–2 [Middlesex Sessions Records, Orders of Court, iv, ff. 171–2, 211–12]. It was widened in 1811 and replaced in 1824.

In 1746, for the Bridgehouse committee, Labelye made drawings of London Bridge designed to show how the waterway could be doubled by reducing the size of the starlings. These were published in Maitland's *History of London* ii, 1756, 826–32. Several of his reports on harbours and waterways were published, namely: *The Result of a View of the Great Level of the Fens*, 1745; *The Result of a Particular View of the North Level of the Fens taken in August 1745*, 1748; *Abstract of Mr. C. L.'s Report, relating to the Improvement of the River Wear and Port of Sunderland in 1748*, Newcastle *c.*1748; and *The Result of a View and Survey of Yarmouth Haven, taken in the year 1747*, Norwich 1775. His plan of a projected harbour at Sandwich was engraved by Harris, *c.*1740.

[*D.N.B.; A.P.S.D.; Ars Quatuor Coronatorum* xl, 1927, 37, 244; MS. Tour in Greece by S. Riou in Yale Center for British Art; sources mentioned in text.]

LABRIÈRE, ALEXANDRE-LOUIS DE, was a French architect who came to England as a refugee during the Revolution. Before 1785 his career is difficult to distinguish from that of his relative and contemporary, Jean-Jacques de Labrière, who died in that year, but one or other of them was 'Contrôleur des bâtiments du roi' at Fontainebleau in 1772 and at Meudon in 1778, and architect both to the Comte d'Artois and to Mme. Elizabeth (sister of Louis XVI), for whom he designed the Château de Montreuil.

In England de Labrière was employed by Henry Holland at CARLTON HOUSE, LONDON, and at SOUTHILL HOUSE, BEDS., where he was responsible for the decoration of the boudoir (*c.*1796–1800) in an elegant French neo-classical style. Drawings by de Labrière formerly at BEECHWOOD, HERTS., show that he designed a chimney-piece in the library there *c.*1804, and also the interior of the library in Lord Marchmont's house in CURZON STREET, LONDON, which is stated to have been 'executed with good effect'.

[M. Gallet, *Demeures Parisiennes, l'époque de Louis XVI,* Paris 1964, 187; Dorothy Stroud, *Henry Holland*, 1966, 74, 128.]

LAING, ALEXANDER (–1823), practised in Edinburgh, first as a mason, then as an architect. He first appears in the Edinburgh directories as a mason in 1774. He was still described as a mason in 1777, when he became a member of the Royal Company of Archers, whose new Hall he had just built, and in 1782, when he was admitted as a burgess of Edinburgh [J. Balfour Paul, *History of the Royal Company of Archers*, 1875, 370; *Roll of Edinburgh Burgesses, 1761–1841*, Scottish Record Soc., vol. xc]. Thereafter, however, he described himself as an architect. His buildings are designed in a plain, masculine Georgian style without much elegance or refinement. The Edinburgh Marriage Register shows that he was married three times, first in 1772, and again in 1786 and 1789. He died at Portobello on 17 September 1823, leaving a substantial estate [*Scots Mag.* 1823, 512; testament in S.R.O., SC 70/1/29, 787–797].

EDINBURGH, THE ARCHERS' HALL, BUCCLEUCH STREET, 1776; altered and enlarged 1900 [Minutes of the Royal Company of Archers, 27 July 1776] (J. Grant, *Old and New Edinburgh* ii, 1882, 352–3).

EDINBURGH, THE HIGH SCHOOL, HIGH SCHOOL YARDS (now incorporated in Edinburgh University), 1777; reconstructed 1905 [Edinburgh Dean of Guild Records] (unsigned engraving of design in *Scots Mag.* 1777, 332–4).

? RETREAT HOUSE, ABBEY ST. BATHAN'S, BERWICKSHIRE, 1778–80, perhaps one of the buildings for which Laing made designs for Francis Charteris of Amisfield in 1778 [accounts at Gosford House].

EDINBURGH, built the SOUTH BRIDGE to the designs of Robert Kay (*q.v.*), 1785–8 [A. G. Fraser, *The Building of Old College*, Edinburgh 1989, 66–7].

DALMAHOY HOUSE, MIDLOTHIAN, bridge, offices and minor alterations to house for 16th Earl of Morton, 1787–8 [S.R.O., GD 150/2407, letters 21, 38, 41, GD 150/2466/21, 2467/14].

INVERNESS TOLBOOTH, TOWN STEEPLE, 1789 [*Old Inverness*, ed. Eveline Barron, 1967], but according to *O.S.A.* ix, 1793, 623, 'the spire was built by the architect of St. Andrew's spire in Edinburgh', which was designed by W. Sibbald (*q.v.*) and built by Alexander Stevens (*q.v.*).

DUNNIKER HOUSE, KIRKCALDY, FIFE, for James

Townsend Oswald, 1791 [contract calendared in N.R.A. (England) Report 21704, 12].

EDINBURGH, GAYFIELD SQUARE, at least one house, 1791 [advt. in *Edinburgh Evening Courant*, 4 Aug. 1791].

BRECHIN CASTLE, ANGUS, alterations for William Ramsay, 1st Lord Panmure, 1796–7 [John Dunbar & David Walker in *C. Life*, 19 Aug. 1971].

OVER RANKEILLOUR HOUSE, FIFE, supervised completion of house for Sir John Hope, *c.*1795–1800 after death of James McLeran (*q.v.*) [S.R.O., SC 20/44/1, p. 286].

SOUTH QUEENSFERRY HARBOUR, MIDLOTHIAN, piers, 1797 [advt. for tenders in *Edinburgh Evening Courant*, 2 March 1797].

EDINBURGH, No. 8 YORK PLACE, 1798 [advt. in *Edinburgh Evening Courant*, 22 Dec. 1798].

INVERMAY, nr. FORTEVIOT, PERTHSHIRE, designed or supervised alterations for Col. J. Hepburn Belshes, 1802, including stables, west lodges, game larder, dairy and gazebo [N.M.R.S., extracts from factor's letter-book at Invermay].

DYSART CHURCH, FIFE, 1802–3 [building records in S.R.O., GD 164/297/1–2].

DARNAWAY CASTLE, MORAYSHIRE, for 8th Earl of Moray, 1802–12, castellated [N.M.R.S., extracts from Moray muniments at Darnaway, vol. vi, box 18] (Sheila Forman, *Scottish Country Houses and Castles*, 1967, 141–3).

PETERHEAD OLD CHURCH, ABERDEENSHIRE, 1804–6 [J. T. Findlay, *History of Peterhead*, Aberdeen 1933, 143–4].

HUNTLY CHURCH, ABERDEENSHIRE, 1805 [S.R.O., Gordon Castle papers, GD 44/37/47].

DRUMSHEUGH HOUSE, EDINBURGH, gateway and lodge for 8th Earl of Moray, 1808–9; dem. [N.M.R.S., extracts from Moray muniments at Darnaway, vol. vi, box 18, 701].

DYSART HOUSE, FIFE, probably designed rear wings and W. extension for 2nd Earl of Rosslyn, 1808–14 [S.R.O., SC 20/44/2, p. 142].

DUNFERMLINE, FIFE, THE MANSE, MOODIE STREET, 1814 [S.R.O., CH 2/105/14, pp. 121–3, 128–9, *ex inf.* Mr. John Gifford].

GRANGE MANSE, BANFFSHIRE, 1814–15 [S.R.O., CH 2/342/9, 18 May 1814].

ABERDOUR MANSE, ABERDEENSHIRE, 1822 [*Aberdeen Jnl.*, 18 May 1822]. This was the outcome of a protracted dispute in which Laing acted initially as arbitrator, but was eventually employed to modify a plan submitted by William Robertson of Elgin: see the printed *Abstract of the Law Proceedings in the Case of the Manse of Aberdour, Aberdeenshire*, 1823 (S.R.O., GD 16/46/89).

LAING, DAVID (1774–1856), son of D. Laing, of Tower Street, London, 'cork cutter', was articled to Sir John Soane in 1790. He was still in Soane's office in 1795, when he exhibited a 'design for a saloon' at the Royal Academy, but left in 1796 to begin independent practice. In 1800 he published *Hints for Dwellings, consisting of original designs for Cottages, Farm-Houses, Villas, etc.*, which was reprinted in 1804, 1823, 1841 and 1972. This was a typical work of its kind, offering designs for villas, ornamental cottages, etc., in a style which shows the influence of his master Soane. Several of them were intended for specific patrons in England, Ireland[1] and (in one case) Germany, where Laing was later to build at least one house (at Brunswick). In 1810 Laing succeeded Pilkington as Surveyor to the Customs, and immediately designed a new Custom House at Plymouth whose elegantly accented simplicity reveals him as a student of contemporary French architecture. In 1812 he was commissioned to rebuild the London Custom House, which was completed to his designs in 1817. Here again he produced an elegant neo-classical design of considerable merit. Unfortunately he failed to supervise a delinquent contractor with sufficient care, and in 1825 part of the façade collapsed owing to the inadequacy of the beech piling employed in the foundations. Subsequent investigations revealed faulty work on a scale which indicated either gross incompetence or collusion on the part of the architect, and Sir Robert Smirke had to be called in to reconstruct the building at great expense. Laing was dismissed from his office and had difficulty in obtaining any further commissions. For some years in the 1840s he was listed among the architects practising in Brighton, but he is not known to have designed a single building there. Professionally ruined, he lived on until 1856, dependent upon the charity dispensed by the Artists General Benevolent Institution, the Fund for Distressed Architects established by Soane, and the Surveyors' Club, a society over which he had once (1821) presided.[2] He died at Brompton on 27 March 1856, aged 82.

In addition to the work already mentioned, Laing published in 1818 *Plans etc. of Buildings, Public and Private, executed in various*

[1] The 'Mansion designed for a Nobleman, and intended to be built at — in the County of Kildare, on the Banks of the Liffey', was probably for Lord Cloncurry at Lyons. It was not built, but the design is interesting as a neo-classical version of the 'Villa Rotonda'. Lord Cloncurry was among the subscribers to Laing's *Plans* in 1818.

[2] In 1815–16 he had also been Master of the Tylers' and Bricklayers' Company.

parts of England, including the Custom House. He drew many of the illustrations of public buildings for Nicholson's *Practical Builder*, 1837. In the Royal Collection at Windsor there is a design by him dated 1818 for converting Hyde Park and Kensington Gardens into the site of a royal palace. There are unexecuted designs by him for Banks Hall, nr. Lanercost, Cumberland, 1828 (Cumbria Record Office) and for a Corn Exchange at Winchester, 1835 (formerly in the collection of A. E. Richardson). A sketch-plan by him of three houses or shops for Lord Selsea in Bow Street, Westminster, is in the West Sussex Rcord Office (Westdean 3150). His pupils included T. Bellamy, Charles Fowler, R. Kelsey, T. Lee and William Tite (in conjunction with whom he designed St. Dunstan's Church). His son C. D. Laing was a wood-engraver whose work often appeared in the *Builder*.

[*A.P.S.D.; Gent's Mag.* 1856 (i), 650; *Builder* xiv, 1856, 189; A. T. Bolton, *The Works of Sir John Soane*, 1924, Appendix C, p. xli; J. M. Crook, 'The Custom House Scandal', *Arch. Hist.* vi, 1963.]

PUBLIC BUILDINGS

PLYMOUTH, DEVON, THE CUSTOM HOUSE, 1810 [G. Wightwick, *Nettleton's Guide to Plymouth*,1836, 25] (A. E. Richardson & C. L. Gill, *Regional Architecture of the West of England*, 1924, 76).

LONDON, THE CUSTOM HOUSE, THAMES STREET, 1813–17; central portion reconstructed by Sir Robert Smirke 1825–7 after collapse [*Plans* pls. 1–41; Britton & Pugin, *Public Buildings of London* i, 1825, 46–54; *History of the King's Works* vi, 1973, 422–30].

LONDON, ST. DUNSTAN-IN-THE-EAST-CHURCH, rebuilt body of church, excluding steeple, 1817–21, Gothic; destroyed by bombing 1941[exhib. at R.A. 1818, 1819 and 1822; *Plans*, pls. 54–7] (G. Godwin, *The Churches of London* i, 1838).

COLCHESTER, THE CORN EXCHANGE, HIGH STREET (now ESSEX & SUFFOLK INSURANCE SOCIETY'S FIRE OFFICE), *c.*1820; upper storey since added [T. Wright, *History of Essex* i, 1836, 307].

LONDON, THE ROYAL UNIVERSAL INFIRMARY FOR CHILDREN, WATERLOO ROAD, 1833–4; rebuilt 1903–5 [*A.P.S.D.*; lithograph signed by Laing as architect in Berkshire Record Office, D/EBy F.24].

PRIVATE HOUSES

ABBOTS LANGLEY, HERTS., house for Griffith Jones, *c.*1800 [*Hints*, pls. 15–18].

BALLYMAHON, CO. LONGFORD, IRELAND, 'design for a villa to be erected for a gentleman', *c.*1800 [*Hints*, pl. 11].

BRUNSWICK, GERMANY, 'mansion constructed for J. Retburgh, Esq.', before 1818 [*Plans*, pls. 45–6].

CASTLE TAYLOR, ARDRAHAN, CO. GALWAY, IRELAND, house 'erected' for General Sir J. Taylor, before 1818 [*Plans*, pl. 47].

COLEY PARK, nr. READING, BERKS., villa for John McConnell, before 1818; remodelled *c.*1840 [*Plans*, pl. 48].

DEDHAM, ESSEX, house for Stephen Teissier (d. 1816) [*Plans*, p. 33].

EASTHAMPSTEAD, BERKS., cottages, etc., for 3rd Marquess of Downshire, 1803 [Berkshire Record Office, D/ED. E80].

GUERNSEY, Gothic villa 'intended to be erected for Mr. Macculloch' [*Plans*, pls. 43–4].

JERSEY, villa 'erected' for J. Emery, before 1818 [*Plans*, pl. 49].

LAVENDER HILL, WANDSWORTH, SURREY, villa 'erected' before 1818, probably for Ephraim Gompertz [*Plans*, pl. 42].

LEXDEN PARK HOUSE (now Endsleigh School), ESSEX, for J. F. Mills, 1825; remodelled *c.*1850 [T. Cromwell, *History of Colchester*, 1825, 238].

THEBERTON, SUFFOLK, 'design for a lodge to be built at', *c.*1800 [*Hints*, pl.4].

LAMB, WILLIAM, was a builder-architect of Leith, where he designed 1–8 VANBURGH PLACE, 1826 [S.R.O., Edinburgh Sasines]. He also built and probably designed Nos. 1–13 BERNARD STREET and 30–34 CONSTITUTION STREET, LEITH, 1815–16 [Scottish Development Department, typescript *List of Buildings of Special Architectural or Historic Interest in Edinburgh*, Nos. 596, 2137].

LANDI, GAETANO, was a native of Bologna, and perhaps a relative of the Bolognese architect and painter, Giuseppe Antonio Landi. He described himself as 'Professor in the University of Bologna and Member of the Clementine Academy', but no record of him can be found in the archives of either institution. He was in England by 1810, when he published the first and only part of a series of aquatint plates entitled *Architectural Decorations: A Periodical Work of Original Designs invented from the Egyptian, the Greek, the Roman, the Etruscan, the Attic, the Gothic etc. for Exterior and Interior Decoration of Galleries, Halls, Apartments etc. either in Painting or Relief*, dedicated to the Marquess of Douglas, of which there is a copy in the Soane Museum. Letters in the same museum indicate that in 1810 he was in financial difficulties and about to depart for Russia. [E. Croft-

Murray, *Decorative Painting in England* ii, 1970, 236–7.]

LANDMANN, ISAAC, was a Professor at the Royal Military Academy at Woolwich from 1777 to 1815 [O. F. G. Hogg, *The Royal Arsenal* i, 1963, 191, n. 50]. He was the author of *A Course of the Five Orders of Civil Architecture with a Plan and Some Geometrical Elevations of Town Gates of Fortified Places*, 1785, 1806, and of *The Principles of Fortification reduced into Questions and Answers for the Use of the Royal Military Academy at Woolwich*, 1796. The former work was partly based on Chambers's *Civil Architecture*.

LANE, H— (*c.*1787–), a pupil of William Inwood, entered the Royal Academy Schools in 1808 at the age of 21. He exhibited at the R.A. from Inwood's office in 1808 and 1809, but by 1810 he appears to have begun independent practice, exhibiting a 'Design for a villa intended to be erected in Sussex' from 60 Berwick Street. He was presumably the Henry Lane, then of Clifton (Bristol), who designed HORTON RECTORY (now WIDDEN HILL HOUSE), GLOS., 1816 [Gloucestershire C.R.O., GDR/F4/1].

LANE, JOHN (–1753) held the combined posts of Surveyor of the Horse Guards and Clerk of the Works at Chelsea Hospital from January 1728/9 until his death in 1753. In 1732–3 he was responsible for building the new PAYMASTER-GENERAL'S OFFICE in WHITEHALL immediately to the north of the Horse Guards [*Survey of London* xvi, chap. 3]. In 1741–2 the old parish church of ST. JOHN, MARYLEBONE, LONDON (dem. 1949), was rebuilt by him to his own designs after one by James Gibbs had been rejected [T. Friedman, *James Gibbs*, 1984, 80, 310].

Lane was a joiner by trade and his employment in this capacity by Colen Campbell, Lord Burlington and others suggests that he was a craftsman of ability. A design by him for a bookcase for Lady Walpole was sold at Christie's on 19 Dec. 1989 (Shoppee album). In the same collection was a design signed 'I. Lane inve., I. S. [probably John Sanderson] D[elin].' for a Palladian building, perhaps stables, for Stamp Brooksbank at Hackney, Middlesex.

LANE, RICHARD (1795–1880), was born in London on 3 April 1795 and was presumably the R. Lane who exhibited a drawing of Southill House, Beds., at the Royal Academy in 1815 from a London address. He is said to have 'completed his architectural education in Paris in 1816–17' before returning to London in 1818. By 1821 he was in Manchester, where he was appointed Surveyor to the Police Commissioners. He was the first strictly professional architect to practise in Manchester and the first President of the Manchester Architectural Society, founded in 1837. For some years he was in partnership with P. B. Alley. He retired in 1859 and died in Ascot, Berkshire, on 25 May 1880. Alfred Darbyshire and Alfred Waterhouse were his pupils.

Lane was the leading Manchester architect of the early nineteenth century and designed many public buildings and a number of churches and chapels. His Gothic churches, marked, according to J. C. Loudon, by 'many little disagreeable negligences of style', were typical of their period. His public buildings were mostly designed in a correct, dignified and rather unenterprising Greek Revival style reminiscent of Smirke's work in London, but also influenced by the example of Thomas Harrison. It was a style that did not find favour with later Victorian architects, but there is some justice in Alfred Darbyshire's comment that Lane's practice 'was almost exclusively devoted to an attempt to force upon a commercial nineteenth-century town, with a sunless and humid climate, the refinement and beauty of the art of the Greeks in the golden age of Pericles'.

[Alfred Darbyshire, *An Architect's Experiences*, 1897, 21; Cecil Stewart, *The Stones of Manchester*, 1956, 28–30; *Art and Architecture in Victorian Manchester*, ed. J. H. G. Archer, Manchester 1985, 6, citing memoir of Lane in *Manchester Evening News* of 26 March 1898; information from Miss Clare Hartwell.]

STOCKPORT, CHESHIRE, TIVIOT DALE WESLEYAN METHODIST CHAPEL, 1825–6; dem. [H. Heginbotham, *Stockport, Ancient and Modern* ii, 1892, 70–1].

BOLTON, LANCS., EXCHANGE AND NEWS ROOM, 1825–6 [*Bolton Express*, 8, 15, 29 May 1824].

SALFORD, LANCS., THE TOWN HALL AND ASSEMBLY ROOMS, 1825–7; enlarged 1847, 1848, 1853, 1860–2 [B. Love, *Handbook to Manchester*, 1842, 250].

OLDHAM, LANCS., ST. MARY'S CHURCH, 1827–30, Gothic [*V.C.H. Lancs.* v, 104].

SWINTON CHAPEL, LANCS., alterations, 1828; rebuilt 1869 [I.C.B.S.].

MANCHESTER, THE FRIENDS' MEETING-HOUSE, MOUNT STREET, 1828–30 [plate in *Lancashire Illustrated* inscribed 'R. Lane Architect'].

OLDHAM, LANCS., THE BLUE-COAT SCHOOL, 1829–30, Gothic [G. N. Wright, *Lancashire, its History, Legends and Manufactures,* *c.*1850, 135].

PENDLETON (SALFORD), LANCS., ST. THOMAS'S CHURCH, with F. Goodwin, 1829–31, Gothic [Port, 148].

CHORLTON-ON-MEDLOCK, MANCHESTER, THE TOWN HALL, 1830 [S. Lewis, *Topographical Dictionary of England* iii, 1831, 242].

MANCHESTER, THE CONCERT HALL, PETER STREET, 1831; dem. [T. Swindells, *Manchester Streets and Manchester Men* i, 1906, 165].

STOCKPORT, CHESHIRE, THE INFIRMARY, WELLINGTON ROAD SOUTH, 1832–3 [H. Heginbotham, *Stockport, Ancient and Modern* ii, 1892, 382].

WAKEFIELD, YORKS. (W.R.), THE WEST RIDING PROPRIETARY (later Grammar) SCHOOL, NORTHGATE, 1833–4, Tudor Gothic [*Architectural Mag.* i, 1834, 142].

NEWTON-IN-MAKERFIELD, LANCS., CONSERVATIVE CLUB-HOUSE, 1835 [contemporary engraving, *ex inf.* Prof. J. M. Crook].

MANCHESTER, THE ROYAL INFIRMARY, PICCADILLY, refaced 1835, enlarged 1848–53; dem. 1909 [B. Love, *Handbook to Manchester*, 1842, 120; *A.P.S.D.*].

MANCHESTER, THE CORN EXCHANGE, HANGING DITCH, 1835–7; dem. [B. Love, *Handbook to Manchester*, 1842, 234].

MANCHESTER, THE UNION CLUB-HOUSE, MOSLEY STREET, 1836; dem [B. Love, *Handbook to Manchester*, 1842, 238].

MANCHESTER, HENSHAW'S BLIND ASYLUM AND DEAF AND DUMB SCHOOL, OLD TRAFFORD, 1836–7, Gothic; dem. [*A.P.S.D., s.v.* 'Manchester'].

SALFORD, ST. JOHN'S CHURCH, HIGHER BROUGHTON, 1836–8, Gothic; chancel by J. E. Gregan 1846 [*A.P.S.D., s.v.* 'Manchester'; drawings in Manchester Reference Library].

MANCHESTER, VICTORIA PARK ESTATE, layout and lodges (dem.), 1837 [*Architectural Mag.* iv, 487, v. 701; M. Spiers, *Victoria Park, Manchester*, Chetham Soc. 1976].

MANCHESTER TOWN HALL, KING STREET, entrance hall and staircase, 1838; dem. 1912 [G. H. Ormerod, *Selection of Sketches of Old Buildings in the Neighbourhood of Manchester*, 1877, 9].

MANCHESTER, THE MANCHESTER & SALFORD SAVINGS BANK, 84 KING STREET, 1839–42; dem. [*Builder* xxx, 1872, 200].

BOWDEN HALL, CHAPEL-EN-LE-FRITH, DERBYSHIRE, for John Slack, 1844, Tudor; partly dem. [S. Bagshaw, *History and Directory of Derbyshire*, 1846, 464].

HENBURY CHURCH, CHESHIRE, 1844–5, Gothic [I.C.B.S.].

SALFORD, LANCS., ST. SIMON'S CHURCH, 1845–9, Gothic; dem. [*Builder* iii, 1845, 187, 547].

SALFORD, LANCS., THE RICHMOND INDEPENDENT CHAPEL, BLACKFRIARS ROAD, 1845, Gothic; dem. [*Builder* iii, 1845, 547].

PENDLETON (SALFORD), LANCS., THE INDEPENDENT CHAPEL, 1846, Gothic; dem. [*Builder* iv, 1846, 452].

BOWDON, CHESHIRE, HIGH LAWN, DINGLE BANK EAST and DINGLE BANK WEST, 1840s [*Manchester Evening News*, 26 March 1898, *ex inf.* Miss Clare Hartwell].

MANCHESTER ROYAL LUNATIC ASYLUM (now Cheadle Royal Hospital), HEALD GREEN, CHEADLE, CHESHIRE, 1848–9, Elizabethan [*A.P.S.D., s.v.* 'Manchester'].

ST. JOHN'S CHURCH, PEEL, ISLE OF MAN, 1849, Gothic [L. D. Butler, *An Architectural History of the Churches of the Isle of Man*, typescript 1970, 13].

MANCHESTER, BAPTIST CHAPEL, BRIDGE STREET, STRANGEWAYS, 1851, Gothic; dem. [*Builder* ix, 1851, 296].

MANCHESTER, ARDWICK CEMETERY, THE DALTON MEMORIAL, 1854; dem. [*Builder* xii, 1854, 36].

Note: The Market Hall at Wigan, for which Lane's designs were reported to have been adopted in the *Builder* xi, 1853, 327, was not in fact built.

LANE, WILLIAM (*c.*1769–1829), was a carpenter and builder at Eton. It was to his designs that TAPLOW CHURCH, BUCKS., was rebuilt in 1826–8 (again rebuilt 1912) [parish memorandum book in Bucks. C.R.O.]. In 1829 he rebuilt the S. aisle of BISHAM CHURCH, BERKS., to his own plans [Berks. C.R.O., MS. Oxford Archdeaconry Papers, Berks., c. 160, f. 63 *et seq.*; drawings in Salisbury Diocesan Records]. He died in Sept. 1829, aged 60 [Eton parish register].

LANG, CHARLES EVANS, was a native of Devonport and a pupil of John Foulston (*q.v.*). He subsequently practised in London. In 1833 he exhibited part of a design for a royal palace at the Society of British Artists, and in 1842 he showed at the Royal Academy a design for the Assize Courts at Liverpool submitted in 1840. He became an Associate of the Institute of British Architects in 1835 and a Fellow in 1842. His membership ceased in 1853.

LANGDON, JOHN HARRIS (–1853), a London builder, appears to have designed the Greek Revival TOWN HALL at ANDOVER, HANTS. In January 1825 he submitted a plan and estimate which were accepted [Andover town records, *ex inf.* Mr. Richard Warmington]. Pigot's *Directory* shows that in

1825 Langdon was living at 14 Hadlow Street, Burton Crescent, London. He subsequently moved to NEWPORT (MON.), where he designed a NATIONAL SCHOOL, 1840, the TOWN HALL, 1842, ALMSHOUSES on STOW HILL for the Roger Williams Charity, 1845, and THE FRIARS for Octavius Morgan, *c.*1845 [*The Ancient and Modern History of Newport and Guide and Directory*, 1847; lithograph of The Friars in Newport Museum, *ex inf.* Mr. Thomas Lloyd]. He also designed a Grecian BAPTIST CHAPEL in CRANE STREET, PONTYPOOL, 1845 [A. Jones, *Welsh Chapels*, 1984, 33], and the Gothic HOLY TRINITY, PILLGWENLLY, NEWPORT, 1851–2 [I.C.B.S.]. He died in Newport in 1853.

LANGLEY, BATTY (1696–1751), was the son of Daniel and Elizabeth Langley of Twickenham, where he was baptized on 14 September 1696. His father was a gardener, and Batty appears at first to have practised as a landscape-gardener (see his *Practical Geometry*, p. 35, and several books on the subject which he published in the 1720s). For some years he lived in Twickenham, but removed to Parliament Stairs, Westminster, in or before 1735, and to Meard's Court, Dean Street, Soho, in about 1740. There he established a school or academy offering lessons in architecture and drawing, in which he was assisted by his brother Thomas, an engraver. An advertisement published in *The City and Country Builder's Treasury* (1740) indicates that Langley was prepared to make 'Designs for Buildings, Gardens, Parks, etc. in the most grand Taste', to design and build 'Grottos, Cascades, Caves, Temples, Pavillions, and other Rural Buildings of Pleasure', to survey estates, and to construct 'Engines for raising Water in any Quantity, to any height required, for the service of Noblemen's Seats, Cities, Towns, etc.' He also manufactured an artificial stone, of which he made statues, busts and architectural ornaments. He was best known, however, as the author of numerous publications designed to enable the master builder to keep abreast with current fashions, and also to minister to the growing interest in Freemasonry, of which Langley was an enthusiastic devotee.

As a practising architect Langley appears to have had little success. The extremely jejune design which he submitted in the competition for the Mansion House in 1735 (illustrated by S. Perks, *The History of the Mansion House*, 1922, pl. 49, from an engraving by Langley) suggests that his abilities as an architectural designer were small, and the only buildings actually known to have been built under his direction were an ornamental temple for Nathaniel Blackerby, whose house adjoined his own at Parliament Stairs, and a new dining-room, greenhouse and brewhouse for the Duke of Kent at Wrest Park in Bedfordshire (1735). Langley's membership of a 'Society of Artizans' which included some 'newswriters' led, much to the Duke's annoyance, to the announcement of the latter commission in the press, and it was no doubt due to the same channel of communication that in 1735 the *St. James's Evening Post* was able to publish a description of the 'curious grotesque temple in a taste entirely new, finely decorated within with busts of King William III, George I and five gentlemen of the Club of Liberty', which Langley had designed for Blackerby at Parliament Stairs [J. P. Malcolm, *Londinium Redivivum* iv, 1807, 172]. In 1736–7 Langley's were among the many projects for a bridge across the Thames which were submitted to the Westminster Bridge Commissioners, and he not only had one of his designs engraved (1736, with descriptive text) but took a prominent part in the subsequent pamphlet controvery, publishing *A Reply to Mr. John James's Review of the Several Pamphlets and Schemes . . . for the Building of a Bridge at Westminster*, 1737, and *A Survey of Westminster Bridge, as 'tis now sinking into Ruin*, 1748, reviewed in *Gent's Mag.* 1748, 96. Under the pseudonym of 'Hiram' he published in the *Grub Street Journal* (11 July 1734 *et seq.*), a 'continuation' of the well-known *Critical Review of the Publick Buildings in London and Westminster* by James Ralph, in which he attacked the Palladian dictatorship of taste established by Lord Burlington (see his admission of authorship in a letter to the Lord Mayor, printed by Perks, *op. cit.*, 165).

It was, no doubt, Langley's failure to succeed as a practising architect that induced him to make a living chiefly by his architectural publications. Most of these were manuals designed for artisans and craftsmen, but the 494 plates of *Ancient Masonry* (folio, 1733–6), derived from a wide range of sources from Vredeman de Vries to Gibbs, made it one of the largest and most comprehensive treatises in the literature of English architecture. Langley's most celebrated book, *Ancient Architecture Restored and Improved by a Great Variety of Grand and Usefull Designs, entirely new in the Gothick Mode for the ornamenting of Buildings and Gardens* (1742), reissued in 1747 as *Gothic Architecture, improved by Rules and Proportions in many Grand Designs of Columns, Doors, Windows, Chimney-Pieces . . . Temples and Pavillions etc.*, was remarkable as a pioneer attempt to make Gothic architecture intelligible to an age brought up on the classical orders. By attempting to reduce Gothic to a formula Langley incurred the ridicule of later Revivalists, but the book enjoyed considerable success in its day, and Langley's engaging but unscholarly designs for Gothic doorways and chimney-pieces found willing imitators all over the country (see examples illustrated by Rowan, of which the most striking are the Gothic Octagon at Bramham Park, Yorks. (1750), and a fireplace at Tissington Hall, Derbyshire, to which may be added a doorway at Great Fulford, Devon, and the interior of the hall at Wiston House, Sussex, described by Roger White in *Arch. Hist.* 27, 1984.

Langley died at his house in Soho on 3 March 1751, aged 55. A mezzotint portrait by J. Carwitham, who engraved the plates for several of his works, was published in 1741. It is reproduced by Harris, *British Architectural Books*, 262. He married twice, and had a large family. Several of the sons were given first names (Euclid, Vitruvius, Archimedes and Hiram) indicative both of Langley's architectural pretensions and of his interest in Freemasonry.

In addition to the works already mentioned, Langley published: *An Accurate Description of Newgate.* by B. L. of Twickenham, 1724; *Practical Geometry, applied to the Useful Arts of Building, Surveying, Gardening and Mensuration*, dedicated to Lord Paisley (a prominent Freemason), 1726, 1729; *The Builder's Chest Book, or a Compleat Key to the Five Orders of Columns in Architecture*, 1727, 1739, also published in Dublin as *The Builder's Vade Mecum*, 1729, 1735; *New Principles of Gardening; or the laying out and planting Parterres, Groves, Wildernesses, Labyrinths, Avenues, Parks, etc.*, 1728; *A Sure Method of Improving Estates by Plantations of Oak, Elm, Ash, Beech, etc.*, 1728, republished as *The Landed Gentleman's Useful Companion*, 1741; *Pomona, or the Fruit Garden Illustrated*, 1729; *A Sure Guide to Builders, or the Principles and Practice of Architecture Geometrically Demonstrated*, dedicated to Thomas Scawen of Carshalton, 1729; *The Young Builder's Rudiments, or the Principles of Geometry, Mechanicks, etc., Geometrically Demonstrated*, 1730, 1734; *The Builder's Compleat Chest Book*, 1738, reissued as *The Builder's Compleat Assistant, c.*1738, etc.; *The City and Country Builder's and Workman's Treasury of Designs*, 1740, 1745, 1750, 1756, 1770, reprint of 1745 ed. 1969; *The Builder's Jewel, or the Youth's Instructor, and Workman's Remembrancer*, 1741 and many subsequent editions, including one at Dublin 1768 and another at Edinburgh 1768, 1808; *The Measurer's Jewell*, 1742; *A Plan and Elevations of Windsor Castle*, 1743; *The Builder's Director or Bench-Mate*, 1747, 1751, 1761, 1763, 1767; *London Prices of Bricklayers' Materials and Works*, 1748, 1749, 1750; *The Workman's Golden Rule for Drawing and Working the Five Orders in Architecture*, 1750, 1756. He was also the author of the anonymous *Observations on a Pamphlet lately published entitled Remarks on the Different Construction of Bridges . . . by Charles Marquand, in which the Puerility of the Performance in considered*, 1749.

[*A.P.S.D.; D.N.B.*; Walpole Soc., *Vertue Note Books* iii, 3, 5, 51; R. Gunnis, *Dictionary of British Sculptors*, 1968, 233; Alistair Rowan, 'Batty Langley's Gothic', in *Studies in Memory of David Talbot Rice*, Edinburgh 1975; Eileen Harris, 'Batty Langley: a Tutor to Freemasons', *Burlington Mag.* May 1977; Roger White, 'The Influence of Batty Langley', in *A Gothick Symposium*, Georgian Group 1983; Eileen Harris, *British Architectural Books and Writers 1556–1785*, 1990, 262–80; Bedfordshire C.R.O., Wrest Papers, L 30/8/43/1–2, L 31/246–252 and L 28/22.]

LANGSTAFFE, or **LONGSTAFFE,** JOHN (1662–1694), was a master mason of Bishop Auckland, Co. Durham. He was the son of Thomas Langstaff, a mason of the same place. Between 1662 and 1666 he was employed by Bishop Cosin to carry out extensive alterations to BISHOP AUCKLAND CASTLE, and he was probably the mason who reconstructed the twelfth-century Great Hall as the Bishop's Chapel. Like other seventeenth-century master masons, he probably designed the buildings he executed, and a drawing by him of a scheme for the 'outward court walls of Auckland Castle', dated 1655, is preserved in Mickleton and Spearman MS. 91 in the Library of the University of Durham. In the same MS. there is a plan and elevation by Langstaffe for the School and Almshouses which Cosin built on Palace Green, Durham, in 1666. The almshouses as built do not, however, correspond to Langstaffe's 'draught', which shows a building of more classical character with pedimented doorway and rusticated coins.

Langstaffe was an active member of the Society of Friends, whose meetings were regularly held in his house at Bishop Auckland. He appears to have become a Quaker in 1654, and was repeatedly fined for refusing to take the oath of allegiance during the remainder of his life. His cattle were also distrained on for unpaid tithes by Cosin's officials, but the bishop seems to have adopted a tolerant attitude towards his mason's nonconformity, and in 1664 gave him the job of rebuilding the COUNTY HALL on Palace Green, Durham, partly (it was said) in order to reimburse him. As Langstaffe was not a freeman of Durham, it was only with the bishop's support that he was able to undertake this important contract. The 'County House' built by Langstaffe was demolished early in the nineteenth century.

Langstaffe was also employed by Cosin in connection with the LIBRARY which he founded on Palace Green in 1669. There is reason to think that the building was designed by Langstaffe, for in 1670 Cosin asked him to provide a drawing of it as a pattern for a projected library at Caius College, Cambridge, and later in the same year he got Langstaffe to make 'a handsome draught' of an addition to the Durham library which was soon afterwards built and is now known as 'Cosin's Small Room'.

Another work in Durham which Langstaffe may have carried out was the refronting of the house whose lease was bought for Cosin's son-in-law Samuel Davison in 1670. The bishop desired that 'no patcher (be employed), but that John Langstaffe should set on neat workmen to doe it'. In the following year Langstaffe was employed by Cosin to make alterations to the manor-house at BRAFFERTON, Co. Durham, which belonged to the Bishopric. They included the addition of a library and alterations to 'the kitchen-side Court'.

Langstaffe died at Middlestone, nr. Auckland, on 26 May 1694. Besides his mason's tools his possessions included 'some books' and surveying instruments. Four of his sons followed their father's trade: Thomas, of Bishop Auckland (1655–1703),[1] John, of Whitby (1649–1719), Bethwell, who appears to have migrated to Philadelphia, and Amos, of Middlestone (d. 1693). [G. B. Longstaffe, *The Longstaffs of Teesdale and Weardale*, 1923, chap. 7; *The Correspondence of John Cosin, Bishop of Durham* ii, Surtees Soc. 1870, 229, 233–4, 249, 251–2, 253, 254, 255; University of Durham Library, Mickleton and Spearman MS. 91.]

LANGWITH, JOHN (*c.*1723–1795), was a carpenter and builder of Grantham in Lincolnshire. Accounts in the Lincolnshire Record Office suggest that he designed SYSTON NEW HALL, LINCS., for Sir John Thorold, Bart. He worked on the 'new building' there between 1766 and 1775, and in the latter year a contract was made with a bricklayer for work on the north wing 'according to Mr. Langwith's plan'. The house, demolished *c.*1930, was a plain building with fenestration of 'Palladian' character. In 1785 Langwith was one of three architects who submitted designs for the Castle Gaol at Lincoln, but those of William Lumby were accepted [Lincolnshire Record Office, Quarter Sessions Records, 1785–8]. Langwith retired to Harston, nr. Grantham, where he died in January 1795 and was succeeded by his son, John Langwith, junior. He left a considerable amount of property, and according to the *Gentleman's Magazine* 'by his death the poor have lost a good benefactor' [*Gent's Mag.* 1795 (i), 355; Grantham Parish Registers, *ex inf.* the Revd. Henry Thorold].

LANGWITH, JOHN (*c.*1753–1825), son of the above, continued his father's business as a builder and surveyor at Grantham, where he held several civic offices and eventually became an alderman, despite bankruptcy in 1803. His recorded works include GRANTHAM VICARAGE, which he rebuilt in 1789 in a pleasant vernacular Georgian style; BARKSTON RECTORY, LINCS., 1801; and designs (perhaps not executed) for a prison at GRANTHAM, 1811. He died in 1825, aged 72, and was succeeded by his son Joseph Silvester Langwith (*q.v.*) [Lincolnshire Record Office, MGA 6 and 33; Grantham Borough Records; Grantham Parish Registers, *ex inf.* the Revd. Henry Thorold; Arthur Oswald, 'Grantham, Lincolnshire', *C. Life*, 17 Sept. 1964; Giles Worsley, 'Georgian Buildings in Grantham', *C. Life*, 4 June 1987].

LANGWITH, JOSEPH SILVESTER (1787–1854), son of the above, continued the family practice as an 'Architect and Surveyor', but apparently gave up the building business. In the Lincolnshire Record Office there are designs by him for enlarging or rebuilding the parsonages at NORTH and SOUTH STOKE, LINCS., 1825, GREAT PONTON, LINCS., 1826, HACEBY, LINCS., 1828, BARKSTON, LINCS., 1829, and KNIPTON, LEICS., 1830 [MGA 122, 136, 144, 150, 157]. HARSTON CHURCH, LEICS., was rebuilt to his designs in 1821–2, but was again rebuilt later in the nineteenth century [I.C.B.S.]. He died on 12 May 1854, and is commemorated by a tombstone in Grantham churchyard.

LANSDOWN, JAMES (*c.*1796–1838), was a pupil of P. F. Robinson. He was admitted to the Royal Academy Schools in 1817 at the age of 21, and exhibited student's work at the Academy in 1817 and 1818. He appears to have been involved in the building developments round Regent's Park, for in 1828 he exhibited drawings of CHESTER TERRACE,

[1] This was no doubt the mason who made the column erected at Burgh-on-Sands, Cumberland, in 1685 in memory of King Edward I. It was signed 'Tho. Langstaff Fecit 1685' (St. Edmund Hall, Oxford, MS. 7/3, f. 191).

and of STRATHERNE VILLA (i.e. 12 and 14 GLOUCESTER GATE), 'now erecting on the east side of Regent's Park'. His own address was given as Chester Terrace, and it was in Chester Place that he died on 18 October 1838 [*Gent's Mag.* 1838 (ii), 667]. Shortly before his death he had designed offices (dem.) for the Phoenix Fire Insurance Company in Lombard Street. These were completed by John Shaw [Anon., *Phoenix Assurance Company Ltd.*, privately printed 1915]. He had been elected a member of the Surveyors' Club in 1836.

LAPIDGE, EDWARD (1779–1860), was the eldest son of Samuel Lapidge of Hampton Wick (d. 1806), a former assistant of Lancelot Brown, who held the post of Chief Gardener at Hampton Court Palace.[1] Edward was appointed Surveyor to the County of Surrey in 1824, and it was in this capacity that he designed his most important work, the bridge of five elliptical arches over the Thames at Kingston. His interest in civil engineering was also shown by the design for a suspension bridge 'upon a new principle of construction, whereby oscillation and undulation will be counteracted', which he exhibited at the Royal Academy in 1850. As an architect Lapidge appears to have been a competent but fairly conventional practitioner of his day. His chief surviving works are dull Gothic churches in yellow stock brick, but he entered some more ambitious designs for public competitions. The elaborate town-planning scheme for Westminster which he submitted to the Commissioners for improving the access to the Houses of Parliament is now in the R.I.B.A. Drawings Collection. There is a contemporary description of it in the Bodleian Library (MS. Eng. lett. d. 114, f. 17). It was dismissed by the Commissioners as too 'visionary' for serious consideration. In 1823 he entered a classical design for the new buildings at King's College, Cambridge, which is illustrated in A. Doig, *The Architectural Drawings Collection of King's College, Cambridge*, 1979, pls. 24–5, and in 1835 his designs for the Fitzwilliam Museum were among the four finally considered by the Senate. He also competed for the Houses of Parliament in 1835, submitting a design described as 'collegiate, Henry VIII and Elizabethan' in style.

Lapidge was elected a Fellow of the R.I.B.A. in 1838. He had a son named Samuel who was trained as an architect, but got into financial difficulties and emigrated to New Zealand. His younger brother, William Lapidge (1793–1860), had a distinguished naval career and rose to the rank of Rear Admiral. George Wightwick and H. H. Russell were his pupils. He died in February 1860, and was buried at Hampton Wick. As a young man Lapidge was concerned in the discovery of a fine Roman pavement on the site of the East India House in Leadenhall Street, and in 1803 published a short description of it with an engraving. A volume of drawings by him belongs to Mr. Michael Darby. [*A.P.S.D.; D.N.B.*]

ESHER PLACE, SURREY, for John Spicer, *c.*1806–8; enlarged and remodelled 1895–8 [exhib. at R.A. 1808; E. W. Brayley, *History of Surrey* ii, 1841–8, 437].

HILDERSHAM HALL, CAMBS., for Thomas Fawcett or Fassett, *c.*1814 [exhib. at R.A. 1814].

WALTHAM ABBEY CHURCH, ESSEX, alterations 1818; removed 1859–60 [Essex, C.R.O., DP 75/8; *Waltham Abbey Church Monthly*, Nov. 1904, 2].

NORBITON PLACE, SURREY, works (including a dairy) for C.N. Palmer, who enlarged the house and added an Ionic portico (exhib. at R.A. 1821].

LONDON, GREEN STREET, MAYFAIR, houses on N. side, *c.*1825 [*Survey of London* xl, 186].

KINGSTON BRIDGE, SURREY (R. Thames), 1825–8; widened 1914 [exhib. at R.A. 1828; plans in Surrey C.R.O. (Q.S. Parl. Deposits, 106); *Proceedings of the Institution of Civil Engineers* ii, 1842, 184–6].

HAMMERSMITH, MIDDLESEX, ST. PETER'S CHURCH, 1827–9, Ionic [Port, 152–3].

HAMPTON WICK, MIDDLESEX, ST. JOHN'S CHURCH, 1829–31, Gothic [Port, 156–7].

HAMPTON CHURCH, MIDDLESEX, rebuilt 1830–1, Gothic; chancel 1888, tracery inserted in nave windows 1907–25 [H. Ripley, *History and Topography of Hampton*, 1885].

HAM COMMON, SURREY, ST. ANDREW'S CHAPEL, 1830–2, Gothic; chancel 1900–1 [E. W. Brayley, *History of Surrey* iii, 1841–8, 111].

KINGSWOOD CHURCH, SURREY, 1835–6, Romanesque; dem. [I.C.B.S.].

PUTNEY CHURCH, SURREY, rebuilt 1836–7, incorporating medieval west tower, nave arcades and Bishop West's Chapel; reconstructed after fire in 1973 [E. W. Brayley, *History of Surrey* iii, 1841–8, 477].

DODDINGTON CHURCH, CHESHIRE, 1836–7, Gothic [R.I.B.A. Drawings Coll., J7/33].

STEPNEY, ST. JAMES'S CHURCH, RATCLIFF, 1837–8, Gothic; dem. *c.*1950 [*A.P.S.D.*].

FULHAM CHURCH, MIDDLESEX, alterations and enlargement, 1840; rebuilt 1881 [C. J.

[1] For some information about Samuel Lapidge as a landscape-gardener see J. C. Loudon's *Gardener's Magazine* iv, 1828, 116.

Fèret, *Fulham Old and New* i, 1900, 200].

BETCHWORTH BRIDGE, SURREY (R. Mole), 1842 [Surrey C.R.O. P22/8/166–171, with drawings].

REIGATE, SURREY, POLICE STATION, 1852 [*A.P.S.D.; Builder* x, 1852, 414].

SOUTHWARK, SURREY COUNTY SESSIONS HOUSE, NEWINGTON CAUSEWAY, additions, 1853; dem. 1912 [*A.P.S.D.*].

LATHAM, GEORGE (*c.*1795–1871), of Nantwich, had a local practice in Cheshire during the second quarter of the nineteenth century. His works included WISTASTON CHURCH, in an old-fashioned Georgian style, 1827–8 [I.C.B.S.]; TILSTONE FEARNALL CHURCH, 'an aisleless box with lancet windows', 1836–7 [P. de Figueiredo & J. Treuherz, *Cheshire Country Houses*, 1988, 180]; alterations to MALPAS CHURCH in 1840 [*Jnl. Chester & N. Wales Arch. Soc.* xxxvii (2), 1949, 38–9]; and a new rectangular dome to the COURT HOUSE, PRESTON, LANCS., in 1849 [C. Hardwick, *History of Preston*, 1857, 441]. He designed two country houses in a Jacobean style; WILLINGTON HALL, CHESHIRE, for Lt. Col. William Tomkins, 1829 (E. front 1878) and ARLEY HALL, CHESHIRE, for Rowland Egerton Warburton, 1832–45 (truncated 1968) [Figueiredo & Treuherz, *op. cit.*, 23–7, 282).

In the 1840s Lord Tollemache thought of employing Latham to design Peckforton Castle before he gave the commission to Salvin, but generously paid him £2000, 'chiefly compensation for his great disappointment at another architect being appointed' [Mark Girouard in *C. Life*, 29 July 1965, 287]. In 1853 he published a *History of Stydd Chapel and Preceptory near Ribchester, Lancashire.* He died at Nantwich on 8 August 1871, leaving a son, Edwin Davenport Latham, in practice as a civil engineer and surveyor at Middlesbrough [Principal Probate Registry, Calendar of Probates].

LATHAM, JOHN (1805–), was born at Leyland in Lancashire and practised in Preston. He designed several churches in that town and its vicinity in the 1830s and 1840s, specializing in a 'Norman Revival' style of some singularity (see descriptions in Pevsner's *North Lancashire*). James Hibbert, the architect of the Harris Museum at Preston, was his pupil [information from Mr. Colin Stansfield].

ASHTON-UPON-RIBBLE, LANCS., ST. ANDREW'S CHURCH, 1835–7, Romanesque; rebuilt except tower 1876 [information from Mr. Stansfield].

PRESTON, LANCS., CHRIST CHURCH, 1836, Romanesque; dem. except W. end [C. Hardwick, *History of Preston*, 1857, 476–7 and engraving at p. 468].

PRESTON, LANCS., ST. MARY'S CHURCH, 1836–8, Romanesque [Hardwick, *op. cit.*, 477 and engraving].

PRESTON, LANCS., ST. THOMAS'S CHURCH, LANCASTER ROAD, 1837–9, Romanesque [Hardwick, *op. cit.*, 477].

CROSSENS CHURCH, LANCS., 1837; rebuilt 1883–5 [I.C.B.S.].

FRECKLETON CHURCH, LANCS., 1837–8, Romanesque [I.C.B.S.].

WARTON CHURCH, LANCS., alterations, including rebuilding of tower, 1839–40 [I.C.B.S.].

PRESTON, LANCS., THE SAVINGS BANK (now Wesleyan Lecture Hall), 7 LUNE STREET, 1842 [J.M.L. Booker, *Temples of Mammon: The Architecture of Banking*, Edinburgh 1990, 307].

PRESTON, LANCS., ALL SAINTS CHURCH, LANCASTER ROAD, 1846–7, Ionic [Hardwick, *op. cit.*, 478 and engraving].

LATROBE, BENJAMIN HENRY (1764–1820), born at Fulneck, near Leeds, was the second son of the Revd. Benjamin Latrobe, the head of the Moravian congregation in England. In 1776 he was sent to the Moravian college at Niesky in Saxony, where he received a good education. By the time he returned to England in 1784 he had evidently developed an interest in architecture, for in that year he made competent drawings for a new Moravian settlement at Fairfield, Droylesden, near Manchester. For short time he was employed in the Stamp Office, but according to family tradition he studied engineering under Smeaton at Leeds, and in 1787 he became a draughtsman in S. P. Cockerell's office in London. He left Cockerell's office in 1790, and was encouraged to begin practice on his own by a Mr. John Sperling, who in 1792 commissioned him to design HAMMERWOOD LODGE, near EAST GRINSTEAD, SUSSEX, in an advanced neo-classical style inspired by French architects of the Boullée-Ledoux school. Other works of the same period included ASHDOWN HOUSE, nr. FOREST ROW, SUSSEX, for Trayton Fuller, and alterations to BARHAM COURT, TESTON, KENT, for the 1st Lord Barham, to FRIMLEY PARK, SURREY, for James Laurell, and to SHEFFIELD PLACE, SUSSEX, for J. B. Holroyd. He also obtained a minor public post as surveyor of the London Police Offices established under the Middlesex Justices Act of 1792. Latrobe now seemed established in a successful career, but the death of his wife in 1793 led to a period of personal distress and professional confusion which resulted in his emigration to North America in 1796.

In America Latrobe was soon engaged on important works, including the Bank of Pennsylvania in Philadelphia, which has been described as 'the first monument of the Greek Revival in America'. In 1803 he became surveyor of public buildings to the Federal Government, built the south wing of the Capitol at Washington, containing the Hall of Representatives, and remodelled the whole interior after its destruction by the British in 1814. He also designed the elegant neo-classical Cathedral at Baltimore, and the important Exchange in the same town. He was concerned in various engineering projects, including the supply of water to Pennsylvania and New Orleans. He died of yellow fever on 3 September 1820, having resigned his surveyorship two years previously.

[Fiske Kimball in *Dictionary of American Biography*; Talbot Hamlin, *B. H. Latrobe*, 1955; Gillian Darley, 'The Moravians', *Arch. Rev.* April 1985; *Macmillan Encyclopaedia of Architects*, ed. Placzek, ii, 1982, 611–17, with further bibliography.]

LATTIMER, JOHN (*c.*1788–1858), was a carpenter and surveyor at Stratford-on-Avon, where he is commemorated by a tombstone in the churchyard. He designed BIDFORD-ON-AVON CHURCH, WARWICKS., 1835, in a simple sub-Gothic style more common in the seventeenth than in the nineteenth century [I.C.B.S.]. Joseph Lattimer, who was in practice in Stratford in the 1860s and 1870s, was presumably his son.

LAW, WILLIAM, was an Aberdeen architect who in 1766 carried out alterations to the GREYFRIARS CHURCH there, and designed the bridge carrying Marischal Street over Virginia Street [G. M. Fraser, *Aberdeen Street Names*, Aberdeen 1911, 48].

LAWRENCE, or **LAWRANCE,** WILLIAM, advertised in the *Leeds Mercury* on 17 January 1807 that he was offering his services as an architect. He built several houses in PARK SQUARE in 1790–7, including No. 10, where he lived. He was still practising there in 1816–17, but had moved to Harrogate by 1828–9 [M. W. Beresford, *East End, West End: The Face of Leeds during Urbanisation*, Thoresby Soc. 1988, 147, 165, 474–5; D. Linstrum, *West Yorkshire Architects and Architecture*, 1978, 380].

LAXTON, WILLIAM ROBERT (*c.*1776–), entered the Royal Academy Schools in 1797 at the age of 21 and subsequently practised from various addresses in London. He exhibited at the Royal Academy from 1796 to 1813. His exhibits included 'A Saxon gateway, designed for a place of arms, King's Mews' (1799), a 'Design for a cottage, building for Mr. E. Thomas, at Sydenham' (1799), a 'Design for a villa for R. Storey, Esq. to be built near Newcastle' (1799), presumably ARCOT HALL, CRAMLINGTON, 'Meux & Co's Brewery, Liquorpond Street' (1800), a 'Proposed improvement at the north end of Leather Lane' (1804), 'The front next the river Medway, of the Crown Inn, Rochester, now rebuilding' (1806), 'A recent improvement entering Rochester' (1809), a 'Court House now building for the parish of St. Pancras' (1810), 'The Mary Brewery, Mary Street, built for Mr. J. Raymond' (1810), 'The Union Brewery, Wapping, as rebuilt for Mr. R. Bowman' (1810), 'Stabling, now building at Mrs. Clarke's Cottage, Putney' (1810), a 'Design for rebuilding the river front of St. John's College, Cambridge' (1813). He was evidently the Mr. Laxton, described as having 'had great experience in fitting up public houses', who contributed a design for 'A Suburban Public House in the Old English Style' to Loudon's *Encyclopaedia of Cottage, Farm and Villa Architecture* (1833).

G. Colebatch, H. L. Holland and Thomas Nicholls were Laxton's pupils. He was the father of William (1802–54) and Henry Laxton, who were both in practice as architects and surveyors. William established the *Civil Engineer and Architect's Journal*, of which he and his brother were successively editors. They were also the authors of a well-known manual known as *Laxton's Builder's Price Book*. Henry Laxton was the architect responsible for designing the Castelnau estate at Barnes (1842–3). [*Builder* xii, 1854, 361; *The Architect's, Engineer's and Building Trades' Directory*, 1868, 123; *Gent's Mag.* 1854 (ii), 199–200; *D.N.B., s.v.* 'Laxton, William'.]

LEACH, JOHN (1760–1834), was the son of a coppersmith at Bedford. He was articled to Sir Robert Taylor, and while in his office is said to have made the working drawings for Stone Buildings, Lincoln's Inn. He subsequently assisted his fellow-pupil S. P. Cockerell, but decided to abandon architecture for the law, and entered himself at the Middle Temple in 1785. After a distinguished legal career he was knighted in 1818, and died Master of the Rolls in 1834. According to Foss he designed HOWLETTS, nr. BEKESBOURNE, KENT, for Isaac Baugh, but this is open to doubt, as Baugh did not acquire Howletts until 1787, two years after Leach had abandoned his architectural career. [*Gent's Mag.* 1834 (ii), 647; E. Foss, *The Judges of England* ix, 1864, 92–5; Wheatley & Cunningham, *London Past and Present* iii, 1891, 319; *A.P.S.D.; D.N.B.*].

LEACH, WILLIAM (*c.*1743–1816), spent his life in the service of the Office of Works. He was first Labourer in Trust at the Queen's House, Greenwich, then Clerk of the Works at Greenwich from 1774 to 1782, and at Greenwich, Newmarket, Winchester and the Tower of London from 1782 to 1790. In March 1790 he was appointed Clerk of Works at Windsor, a post from which he retired in 1805 [*History of the King's Works* v and vi.]. It is possible that he was the architect named Leach who largely rebuilt HUNSDON HOUSE, HERTS., for Nicolson Calvert in a Tudor Gothic style in 1805 [Mrs. W. Blake, *An Irish Beauty of the Regency*, 1911, 49–50]. He died at Turnham Green on 26 October 1816, aged 73 [*Gent's Mag.* 1816 (ii), 470].

LEACHMAN, JOHN (*c.*1795–), was a pupil of James Medland. He was admitted to the Royal Academy Schools in 1816 at the age of 21, and exhibited at the Academy from 1812 to 1834. Among his exhibits were 'Design for an entrace to the grounds of Sulby Hall, Northants., the seat of George Payne, Esq.' (1826) and the 'Entrance Gates to Warnford Park, Hants., the seat of W. Abbot, Esq.' (1829). He was responsible for two dreary Gothic churches in Wiltshire at WARMINSTER (CHRIST CHURCH), 1830–1 [Port, 164–5], and CORSLEY, 1831–3 [inscription in church].

LEADBETTER, STIFF (–1766), may have been related to Thomas Stiff, a London carpenter of the late seventeenth century, and to John Leadbetter, Master of the Joiners' Company in 1719. He was apprenticed in 1719 to Henry Leadbetter, a carpenter at Thurfield in Hampshire. He subsequently established himself as a carpenter, builder and surveyor at Eton in Buckinghamshire, where he had his yard and wharf. Although he continued in business as a builder throughout his life, he developed a considerable practice as an architect and in 1756 was appointed Surveyor of St. Paul's Cathedral in succession to Henry Flitcroft. From the same year onwards he managed the Duke of Beaufort's London property for his trustees at an annual salary of £50. Leadbetter died at Eton on 18 August 1766, leaving a son named Henry. He had a brother named John who was presumably the author of *The Gentleman and Tradesman's Compleat Assistant; or the Art of Measuring and Estimating made easy*, 'by J. Leadbetter and associates', published in 1768. John Hawks (*c.*1731–1790), the architect of Governor Tryon's 'Palace' at New Bern in North Carolina, had been 'in the service of Mr. Leadbetter' before emigrating to North America.

Leadbetter was a very competent architect who designed a number of handsome Georgian country houses that are essentially Palladian in character, but often based on the compact villa-type plan with canted bays that was simultaneously being developed by Sir Robert Taylor. His work for Francis (later 2nd Lord) Godolphin as a carpenter at Baylies House, Bucks., in the 1730s led to his employment by several of the latter's relations, including the Dukes of Portland and Marlborough. By 1759 he was complaining of 'the multiplicity of my engagements', and the list of commissions given below can be extended by others as yet unidentified that are indicated by payments in his account at Hoare's Bank from Sir Alexander Grant (£500 in 1756), William Godwin (£300 in 1760), Dr. Jeremiah Milles (£200 in 1762), Lord Chetwynd (£200 in 1762), and Thomas Coventry (£550 in 1763–6). An unexecuted design for rebuilding one of the wings of Woburn Abbey, made in 1765, the year before his death, is in the Victoria and Albert Museum (7076.11).

[Giles Worsley, 'Stiff but not Dull', *C. Life*, 25 July 1991; Guildhall Library, index to Apprenticeship Registers; will, P.C.C. 311 TYNDALL; information from Dr. Giles Worsley.]

BULSTRODE PARK, BUCKS., repairs and alterations for 2nd Duke of Portland, 1744–9; dem. 1862 [Nottingham Univ. Library, Portland London Estate papers, Box 13/5, Box 29, *ex inf.* Dr. Giles Worsley].

LONDON, BERWICK STREET (Portland estate), speculative building of three houses on E. side, 1749 and three on W. side, 1753 [Nottingham University Library, Portland London Estate Papers, Lease Book in Box 29].

MAIDENHEAD BRIDGE, BERKS., repairs to timber bridge, 1750; dem. 1772 [J. W. Walker, *History of Maidenhead*, 1931, 13–14].

DORNEY COURT, BUCKS., probably repaired or altered house for 3rd Earl of Tankerville (then the tenant of the house), 1753–4 [payment of £160 from the Earl in Leadbetter's account at Hoare's Bank, ex *inf.* Dr. Giles Worsley].

RUSSELL'S FARM, nr. WATFORD, HERTS., for Dowager Countess of Essex, *c.*1753–4; damaged by fire 1978 [letters published by C. Aspinall-Oglander, *Admiral's Wife*, 1940, 151, 160, make it clear that this house formed the model for Hatchlands (below), and was evidently designed by the same architect].

LONDON, PORTLAND HOUSE, WHITEHALL, repairs or alterations for 2nd Duke of Portland, 1753–4; dem. 1805 [Nottingham Univ. Library, Portland London Estate Papers, Box 29, *ex inf.* Dr. Giles Worsley].

LONDON, FOLEY HOUSE, PORTLAND PLACE, for 2nd Lord Foley, *c.*1754–62; dem. *c.*1815 [C.H. Smith, 'The Site of Foley House', *Builder* xxi, 1863].

LANGLEY PARK, LANGLEY MARISH, BUCKS., for 3rd Duke of Marlborough, 1756–8; balustrade and orangery added *c.*1850–60 [drawings by Leadbetter dated 1755 and 1758 in Bucks. C.R.O.; payments to Leadbetter in accounts of the Duke's trustees in B.L., Althorp Papers, D. 48, f. 25, etc.]

HATCHLANDS, SURREY, for Admiral Edward Boscawen, 1756–8, with interiors by R. Adam [G. Jackson-Stops in *C. Life*, 20 April 1989]. (*C. Life*, 17 Sept., 1 Oct. 1953).

NUNEHAM PARK, OXON., for 1st Earl Harcourt, 1756–64; alterations by L. Brown 1781–2; S. wing added by R. Smirke *c.*1834; entrance front remodelled 1904 [*Vitruvius Britannicus* v, 1771, pls. 99–100] (*C. Life*, 7–14 Nov. 1941, 3–10 Jan. 1985).

LONDON, POMFRET HOUSE, ARLINGTON STREET, built Gothic house for Countess of Pomfret to designs by Sanderson Miller and/or R. Biggs (*q.v.*), 1757–60; dem. 1920 [J. Harris in *Georgian Group Jnl.* 1991, 45].

GLOUCESTER, THE GENERAL INFIRMARY, built by Leadbetter to the designs of Luke Singleton (*q.v.*), a gentleman amateur, 1757–61 [George Whitcombe, *The General Infirmary at Gloucester*, 1903, 18].

DATCHET, BUCKS., work on house of Edmund Mason, 1758 [Leadbetter's Bank Account, cited by Worsley, 92].

SHARDELOES HOUSE, BUCKS., reconstruction for William Drake, 1758–66; begun by Leadbetter to his own designs, but completed with modifications by R. Adam, who designed the portico and the interior decoration [G. Eland, *Shardeloes Papers*, 1947, chap. ix; A. T. Bolton, *Architecture of R. & J. Adam*, 1992, chap. viii].

ELVILLS, ENGLEFIELD GREEN, SURREY, for Sir John Elvill, 1758–63, Gothic; altered [R. Ackermann, *Views of Country Seats* ii, 1830, 104] (W. Watts, *Seats of the Nobility and Gentry*, 1784, pl. lxvi; P. Sandby, *A Collection of . . . Select Views* i, 1781, pl. 61).

HARTLEBURY CASTLE, WORCS., work for James Johnson, Bishop of Worcester, 1759 [J. Lees-Milne in *C. Life*, 23 Sept. 1971, 742].

WORCESTER, BISHOP'S PALACE, repairs and addition of 'a room with a bow window to the river' for James Johnson, Bishop of Worcester, probably *c.*1759–60 [MS. 'Account of what was done at Hartlebury Castle and the Palace by Bishop Johnson' at Hartlebury Castle].

ETON COLLEGE, BUCKS., added upper storey to N. and E. sides of Cloister Court, 1759–62 [Willis & Clark i, 459].

DITCHLEY HOUSE, OXON., probably designed Temple in park for 3rd Earl of Lichfield, 1759–60, as he examined the bills [Oxfordshire C.R.O., Dil I/p/3t-v].

OXFORD, THE RADCLIFFE INFIRMARY, 1759–67; designed and built by Leadbetter and completed after his death by John Sanderson [Ivor Guest, *Dr. John Radcliffe and his Trust*, 1991, chap. 5].

STOKE PARK, STOKE POGES, BUCKS., works costing £815 for Thomas Penn, 1760–3 (dem. 1789), presumably including repair of 'Great Apartments' attributed to Leadbetter in *Historical and Descriptive Account of Stoke Park*, 1813, 45 [Vouchers in Penn Papers, Pennsylvania Historical Soc., U.S.A., *ex inf.* Mr. John Harris].

LONDON, PORTLAND (later ST. PAUL'S) CHAPEL, GREAT PORTLAND STREET, for 3rd Duke of Portland, 1760–6; dem. 1908 [C. H. Smith, 'The Site of Foley House', *Builder* xxi, 1863, 703].

NEWTON PARK, nr. BATH, SOMERSET, for Joseph Langton, *c.*1761–5 [letter from George Lucy dated 29 March 1761, referring to 'Ledbetter' as the architect [Warwicks. C.R.O., L 6/1461].

SYON HOUSE, ISLEWORTH, MIDDLESEX, work for 1st Duke of Northumberland, *c.*1762–66, to designs of, or in collaboration with, Robert Adam [Percy Archives at Alnwick, U. III.5].

FULHAM PALACE, MIDDLESEX, rebuilt S. and E. sides for Richard Terrick, Bishop of London, 1764–5, castellated Gothic; again rebuilt 1814–15 by S.P. Cockerell [Lambeth Palace Library, F.P. 453] (*C. Life*. 9 Feb. 1929. fig. 13).

STOKE PLACE, STOKE GREEN, BUCKS., work for General George Howard, 1765–6 [Leadbetter's Bank Account, cited by Worsley, 93].

LEAPER, RICHARD (1759–1838), was a member of a prosperous banking and tanning family in Derby, where he was several times Mayor. He became an amateur architect late in life, and in his history of Derby Glover describes him as 'a gentleman who has had great taste and much experience in building family mansions'. Glover specifically mentions THORNHILL HOUSE, DERBY, for Mrs. Trowell, *c.*1820, HIGHFIELDS, DERBY, for the Revd. Edward Unwin, 1827, and the remodelling of THE PASTURES, LITTLEOVER, for Cockshutt Heathcote, 1827–8 (Craven & Stanley, *The Derbyshire Country House* ii, 1984, No. 264). THE LEYLANDS, DERBY, can be attributed to Leaper as it resembles Highfields in plan and was built by his brother John Leaper Norton in 1819. WARSLOW HALL, STAFFS., built by Sir George Crewe, Bart., in 1830 (*C. Life*, 1 June 1989), is another small country house that invites attribution to Leaper on account of its resemblance to his authenticated works, which are mostly designed in a simple Regency style. [S. Glover, *History and Gazeteer of the County of Derby* ii (1), 1833, 595; Maxwell Craven in *C. Life*, 6 July 1989, correspondence; further information from Mr. Craven.]

LEE, ADAM (*c.*1772–1843), was trained as a carpenter and worked as a foreman carpenter on barracks at Bridport and at the Military Hospital at Portsmouth before joining the Office of Works in 1801 as a subordinate clerk of works at Richmond. In 1806 he was promoted to be Labourer in Trust at Whitehall and Westminster and from 1832 until his retirement in 1841 he was Clerk of Works for Whitehall and the Horse Guards.

Lee was an able and energetic man who did not always distinguish sufficiently between initiative and insubordination. He had a private business as a builder, and was a competent architectural draughtsman. In his official capacity he made plans for alterations to the Privy Council Office in Whitehall (*c.*1810), and designed a new front for the Office of the Auditors of Land Revenue in Scotland Yard. In 1833 he was among those who submitted a design for a new House of Commons (see *Parliamentary Papers*, 1833, xii, 568 and plate), and in 1835 he competed for the new Houses of Parliament. His design included a restoration of St. Stephen's Chapel, for which he made elaborate drawings, some of which are in the Museum of London, to which they were given in 1915, while others were sold at Sotheby's on 4 June 1962, lot 154. Various drawings by him connected with the Palace of Westminster are in the R.I.B.A. Drawings Collection. He exhibited a 'Design for a public building' at the Royal Academy in 1838. [*Builder* iii, 1845, 104; *History of the King's Works* vi, 119–20; M. Galinou, 'Adam Lee's Drawings of St. Stephen's Chapel, Westminster', *Trans. London & Middlesex Archaeological Soc.* 34, 1983.]

LEE, CHRISTOPHER, a carpenter and builder from London, established himself in Norwich, of which city he became a freeman in 1738. In July 1737 he advertised his services as an architect and builder and also as a drawing-master ready to teach young gentlemen to draw the Five Orders and to design 'Temples, Churches, Hermitages, Grottoes, Caves, Theatres, and other ornamental Buildings of Delight' [*Norwich Gazette*, 30 July 1737, *ex inf.* Mr. David Cubitt]. In 1753 Lee submitted designs for the Octagon Chapel and was instrumental in obtaining further designs from Robert Morris in London. In the event the designs adopted were those of Thomas Ivory, but Lee was employed as joint contractor of the building with the latter. He was declared bankrupt in July 1754 [S. J. Wearing, *Georgian Norwich: Its Builders*, Norwich 1926, 20–4].

LEE, THOMAS (1794–1834), was the son of Thomas Lee (1756–1836) of Barnstaple in Devonshire. The father was a pupil of William Rhodes and won the Royal Academy's Silver Medal in 1776, but soon after coming of age he inherited an independent fortune and went to live at Barnstaple. The son was educated at the grammar school there. He spent a short time in Sir John Soane's office in 1810, but soon transferred to that of David Laing. He was admitted to the Royal Academy Schools in 1812, and in 1816 won the Silver Medal for a drawing of Lord Burlington's villa at Chiswick. In the same year the Society of Arts awarded him a Gold Medal for a design for a British Senate House, which is now in the R.I.B.A. Drawings Collection together with two preparatory drawings of Chiswick House. Lee exhibited at the Royal Academy from 1814 to 1824, showing in 1815 a view of the cathedral at Antwerp (subsequently engraved by Woolnoth), made while staying in that town in July 1814 in order to attend his brother, Frederick Lee, R.A., who had been taken ill there; in 1817 a section of the chapel forming part of his design for a British Senate House; and in 1820 a reconstruction of Pliny's villa at Laurentinum, prepared for submission in competition for the R.A. Gold Medal. Lee was drowned on 5 September 1834, while bathing at Morthoe in Devonshire, and is commemorated by an inscription on the exterior of St. Anne's Chapel, Barnstaple.

Lee was an eclectic designer whose works included a plain classical house with Soanean interior (Arlington Court), a large Tudor

Gothic mansion (Eggesford), several Gothic churches of the Commissioners' type, and one neo-Norman one (at the early date of 1822).

[*A.P.S.D.*; A. T. Bolton, *The Works of Sir John Soane*, Appendix C, p. xlv.]

THE WELLINGTON MONUMENT, BLACKDOWN HILL, SOMERSET, 1817–18 [exhib. at R.A. 1818]. This triangular obelisk was intended to be surmounted by a cast-iron statue of the Duke of Wellington, but was left incomplete owing to lack of funds: *see R.I.B.A. Jnl.*, 24 April 1920, and *The Times*, 18 May 1960, 16.

NYNEHEAD COURT, SOMERSET, bridge in grounds for W. A. Sandford, *c.*1818 [exhib. at R.A. 1818].

LONDON, Nos. 11–12 NORTH AUDLEY STREET, alterations for Viscount Ebury, 1819 [*Survey of London* xl, 102].

ARLINGTON COURT, DEVONSHIRE, for Col. J. P. Chichester, 1820–3 [exhib. at R.A. 1822].

THE ELLOWS, nr. WOLVERHAMPTON, STAFFS., alterations for J. Fereday, 1821; dem. 1964 [*A.P.S.D.*].

EGGESFORD HOUSE, DEVONSHIRE, for the Hon. Newton Fellowes, 1822, Tudor Gothic; dismantled 1917 and now a ruin [exhib. at R.A. 1822] (F. O. Morris, *Views of Seats* vi, 17).

WORCESTER, ST. CLEMENT'S CHURCH, 1822–3, neo-Norman [I.C.B.S.; exhib. at R.A. 1824].

PRIORY HALL, DUDLEY, WORCS., for Francis Downing, *c.*1825, Tudor Gothic [Rickman's diary, 17 May 1832].

BARNSTAPLE, DEVONSHIRE, THE GUILDHALL, 1826–8 [*A.P.S.D.*].

SEDGLEY CHURCH, STAFFS., for 1st Earl of Dudley, 1826–9, Gothic [*A.P.S.D.*].

COSELEY, STAFFS., CHRIST CHURCH, 1827–9. Gothic [Port, 160].

NETHERTON CHURCH, nr. DUDLEY, WORCS., 1827–30, Gothic [Port, 138].

DISLEY CHURCH, CHESHIRE, added north and south aisles, 1828, Gothic [I.C.B.S.].

LEE, THOMAS, practised in Manchester as an 'architect and surveyor' in the 1820s and 1830s. He was no doubt the Thomas Lee, described as formerly Lewis Wyatt's clerk of works, who submitted a design for Eaton Hall (Eaton-by-Congleton), Cheshire, in 1827 [P. de Figueiredo & J. Treuherz, *Cheshire Country Houses*, 1988, 233], and the architect of the same name 'from over the Pennines' whom Anne Lister of Shibden Hall, Yorkshire, thought of consulting in 1834, but decided not to because, although 'a *very* clever man', he was 'not quite to be taken at his word' [D. Linstrum, *West Yorkshire Architects and Architecture*, 1978, 35].

LEEDS, WILLIAM HENRY (1786–1866), was an architectural critic and journalist. He was born in Norfolk, but nothing is known of his early life and it is uncertain whether he had any formal architectural training. In 1815 he showed a design for a monument at the Norwich Society of Artists and between 1829 and 1849 he exhibited several architectural drawings at the Royal Academy and at the Society of British Artists. None of them, however, represented an actual commission, and there appears to be no evidence that he was ever in regular practice as an architect. A small private income made it unnecessary for him to work for a living, and he devoted the proceeds of his literary activity to the formation of a large architectural library. He was an excellent linguist, bought many foreign books, and made it his business to communicate their contents to English architects by means of articles and reviews.He died in Charlotte Street on 1 May 1866, aged 79. The sale of his library by Puttick and Simpson lasted four days (29 April to 2 May 1867).

One of Leeds's earliest literary works was the text of the description of Sir John Soane's house in Lincoln's Inn Fields published by John Britton in 1827 as *The Union of Architecture, Sculpture and Painting.* He subsequently quarrelled with Britton, but in 1838 produced for the publisher John Weale an enlarged edition of Britton & Pugin's *Public Buildings of London*, containing descriptions of several buildings erected since the original publication in 1825–8. His other principal publications were a translation of Georg Moller's work on German Gothic architecture (1815–21) entitled *Moller's Memorials of German Gothic Architecture*, 1836; *Studies and Examples of the Modern School of English Architecture: The Travellers' Club House by Charles Barry, Architect*, 1839; *Rudimentary Architecture for the Use of Beginners: The Orders and their Aesthetic Principles*, 1848, 2nd. ed. 1852; and an edition of Chambers's *Civil Architecture*, 1862. To his friend E.B. Lamb's *Studies of Ancient Domestic Architecture*, 1846, he contributed an essay entitled 'Observations on the Application of Ancient Architecture to the Pictorial Composition of Modern Edifices'. From 1838 to 1850 he wrote the accounts of 'Public Improvements' for the *Companion to the Almanac*. Leeds is believed, with good reason, to have been the author of the articles, generally controversial in tone and hostile to the Greek Revival, which were contributed to Loudon's *Architectural Magazine* and to the *Civil Engineer and Architect's Journal* under the name of 'Candidus'. His design for a 'Villa Residence in the Tudor or Old English Style' will be found in Loudon's *Encyclopaedia of Cottage, Farm and Villa Architecture* (1846 ed.), 897–913. At the Architectural Association's first exhibition in 1849 he showed a design for a 'Victorian' capital, with a 'V' on each face, and 'a series of A's on the cresting' (*Ecclesiologist* ix, 1849, 305). Two letters from him to Soane are printed in A.T. Bolton, *The Portrait of Sir John Soane*, 1927, 416–18. [Hyde Clarke, 'W. H. Leeds, Architectural Critic', *Building News* xiv, 1867, 681–2, 697–8, 717–18; Boase, *Modern English Biography* ii, 1897, 362.]

LEES, WILLIAM, a builder-architect at Derby, made designs in 1812 for altering the office court at LOCKO PARK, DERBYSHIRE, and in 1814 for the interior of a library at DARLEY ABBEY, nr. DERBY (dem. 1960) for Mrs Holden [Nottingham University Library, Drury-Lowe papers, Dr.P.7, 92–6, 108–9].

LEES, WILLIAM, was an architect and wright living at Pittenweem in Fife. In the former capacity he was responsible for refitting the chancel of CRAIL CHURCH, FIFE, in 1828 [S.R.O., HR 242/2, pp. 56–7], for alterations to CRAIL MANSE in 1829 [*ibid.*, pp. 63–4], and for designing KINGSBARNS MANSE, FIFE, in 1835 [S.R.O., HR 184/2].

LEGG, WILLIAM DANIEL (1743–1806), was born in London and christened at St. Sepulchre, Holborn, on 11 July 1743. In 1774, as William Legg, of Coleman Street, carpenter, he applied unsuccessfully for one of the London District Surveyorships [Middlesex County Records, General Orders, No. 10]. William Legg of Coleman Street exhibited designs for 'a nobleman's seat', 'a town house', etc., at the Royal Academy in 1773, 1774 and 1775, and was doubtless the William Legg (no address given) who in 1776 exhibited at the Free Society of Artists the 'Elevation of a stable, now building at a gentleman's seat, near Wragby, in Lincolnshire'. This was probably the stable at PANTON HALL, nr. WRAGBY, LINCS., which bore the date 1777.

As William Legg was working in Lincolnshire in 1776, it is likely that he was the architect of the same name whose career in that county can be traced from 1778, when he advertised in the *St. James's Chronicle* (25–27 Aug.) that he was practising as an architect and land surveyor at Stamford. In 1796 he became a freeman on payment of £8, evidently to qualify himself for his election as a member of the Common Council the same day. He died in Stamford on 27 March 1806. His works included the attractive Gothick front of Casewick House, the entrance gate and lodge to Burghley House, competently designed in a neo-Jacobean style as early as 1799, and the handsome Tuscan portico to the Stamford markets, now incorporated in the Public Library. [Stamford Corporation Hall-Books, *sub annis* 1796 and 1804; J. Simpson, *The Obituary and Records for Lincolnshire, Rutland and Northants., 1800–1850*, 1861, 57; *Gent's Mag.* 1806 (i), 385.]

STAMFORD, THE VALE HOUSE, KING'S MILL LANE, for Joseph Robinson, *c.*1785 [R.C.H.M., *Stamford*, 108].

EXTON PARK, RUTLAND, FORT HENRY (a boat-house, etc.) for 6th Earl of Gainsborough, 1786–9, Gothic; and Gothic cow-house and dovecote, 1793–4 [Leics. C.R.O., Exton MSS (DE 3214)].

CASEWICK HOUSE, LINCS., rebuilt W. front for Sir Thomas Trollope, Bart., 1786–9, Gothic [Arthur Oswald in *C. Life*, 24–31 Dec. 1964].

KINOULTON CHURCH, NOTTS., for 6th Earl of Gainsborough, 1793 [Leics. C.R.O., Exton MSS (DE 3214)].

BURGHLEY HOUSE, NORTHANTS., lodge and gateway at west entrance, for 1st Marquess of Exeter, 1799–1801, neo-Jacobean [signed 'W. D. LEGG ARCHITECT'; exhib. at R.A. 1801].

STAMFORD, LINCS., THE BUTCHERS', FISH AND BUTTER MARKETS, 1804–7; dem. 1906 except Tuscan portico incorporated in Public Library [J. Drakard, *History of Stamford*, 1822].

BULWICK HALL, NORTHANTS., enlarged and altered house for Thomas Tryon, 1805–6 [Northants. Record Office, TB. 636].

AYSTON HALL, RUTLAND, rebuilt for George Fludyer, *c.*1806–7 [drawings at Ayston Hall, *ex inf.* the late Sir Nikolaus Pevsner].

LEMYINGE, or **LIMINGE,** ROBERT (–1628), was described as a carpenter and surveyor in 1622, when he stated in evidence that in about 1600 he had built a chimney in the Six Clerks' Office in Chancery Lane, London [*Shardeloes Papers*, ed. Eland, 1947, 2]. In 1607 he was employed as a carpenter on the almshouses at Theobalds in Hertfordshire. Then in 1607–12 he was the surveyor employed by the 1st Earl of Salisbury to design and supervise the construction of HATFIELD HOUSE, HERTS. This is proved by several references to his plots and drawings, for which he was handsomely rewarded by the Earl. Advice was, however, given by Simon Basil, the Surveyor of the

King's Works, and in 1609 Inigo Jones was also consulted and probably modified the design of the south front (see p. 560) [Lawrence Stone, *Family and Fortune*, 1973, 64–78] (H. A. Tipping, *English Homes, Period* III (ii), 1927, 305–52).

In 1616–17 Lemyinge designed another great Jacobean house, BLICKLING HALL, NORFOLK, for Sir Henry Hobart, Bart., Lord Chief Justice. His cypher RL appears in various places on the building, and the Blickling Parish Register records in 1628 that 'Robert Liminge the architect and builder of Blickling Hall was buried the 8th January' [H. A. Tipping in *C. Life*, 7 June 1930]. A design by him for a banqueting-house is preserved at Blickling.

LEONI, GIACOMO (*c.*1686–1746), described himself as a 'Venetian', and was presumably born in Venetian territory. Nothing, however, is known of his early life before 1708, when a manuscript now in McGill University Library shows that he was in Düsseldorf. Leoni's subsequent description of himself as 'Architect to the Elector Palatine', whose court was at Düsseldorf, may have been an exaggeration, but he certainly assisted the Venetian architect Count Matteo de' Alberti to build a hunting-seat for the Elector at Schloss Bensberg, nr. Cologne, where work was in progress between 1705 and 1716. The McGill manuscript is a treatise on the Five Orders based on Palladio, and shows that the idea of a revised version of Palladio had already engaged Leoni's attention in his early twenties.

At what date, and in what circumstances, Leoni arrived in England is at present unknown. The earliest evidence of his presence in England consists of the edition of Palladio which he published in 1715–20 and of a manuscript treatise entitled *Compendious Directions for Builders* which is dedicated to Henry, Duke of Kent, and contains the Duke's bookplate dated 1713.[1] The bookplate may have been affixed to the manuscript at any time after 1713, but the preparations for publishing the Palladio must have taken some months, and it is reasonable to suppose that Leoni was already in England by 1714 at the latest. The translator was Nicholas Dubois, who states in his preface that Leoni had 'spent several years in preparing the Designs from which the following cuts have been engrav'd', and that having 'seen most of the Originals of those Designs that are in the second, third and fourth Books of this Work; that is, the Houses, Palaces, Churches, and other Buildings, both publick and private, raised by Palladio himself', he had been able to add many details to the crude 'wooden cuts' by which Palladio's work had originally been illustrated. In his own preface to the second part of the second volume, Leoni states that 'after five Years' continual Labour, I have at last happily finish'd the Edition which I undertook of Palladio's Architecture', and offers his services, 'either in person or otherwise, to such of my subscribers and others, as may have occasion for me in the way of my Profession'. The book was entitled *The Architecture of A. Palladio . . . Revis'd, Design'd, and Publish'd by Giacomo Leoni, a Venetian: Architect to his most Serene Highness, the Elector Palatine*. The text was in English, French and Italian. It was published in five instalments, of which the last did not appear until 1720. Leoni's edition was not only the first adequate reprint of Palladio since 1642 but also the first to substitute large engraved plates for Palladio's woodcuts. Although he took undue liberties in redrawing some of the illustrations, the book was an immediate success, and a second edition (in English only) was published almost immediately (in 1721). A third, with the addition of 'Notes and Remarks of Inigo Jones now first taken from his original Manuscript in Worcester College, Oxford', appeared in 1742.

Leoni's *Palladio* was one of the text-books of the English Palladian revival. It remained the standard edition of Palladio until at Lord Burlington's instigation Isaac Ware produced a more scholarly one in 1738. Burlington's early approval of Leoni is indicated by the fact that he was employed to design Queensberry House immediately to the rear of Burlington House, and when, in 1726–9, Leoni published his three-volume translation of *The Architecture of L. B. Alberti* (2nd ed. 1739, 3rd ed. 1753–5), he complimented Burlington on his initiative in re-establishing Palladian architecture in England. There is, however, no evidence that Leoni was ever directly employed by Burlington, either at Burlington House or elsewhere, and his first English patron appears to have been the Duke of Kent, to whom the manuscript already mentioned is dedicated, and for whom 'Signor Leoni' was making designs as early as August 1715.

Leoni's subsequent life in England is not well documented. Apart from his publications and his architectural commissions, all that is known about him is that he lived at various

[1] In the possession of Lord Lucas and Dingwall (cf. Hist. MSS. Comm., *Second Rept.*, Appendix, p. 7, no. 48).

addresses in London.[1] As a Catholic he would have been ineligible for public employment, and he appears to have been dependent for his income entirely upon what he could make as an architect. At a time when most architectural designers were either builders or salaried officials of the Office of Works, this was inevitably a precarious means of livelihood, and it is clear that Leoni died in poor circumstances. Lord Fitzwalter of Moulsham Hall was paying him £50 a year during the last years of his life, more, as he said, out of charity than in return for services rendered, and the final entry in his account-book (in the Essex Record Office) is as follows: 'June 8, 1746. Mr. Leoni, my Italian Architect, dy'd this day, sent him during his illness, which lasted about one month pour charite £8 8s. 0d.' Leoni was buried in St. Pancras Old Churchyard, where an inscription gave his age as 60 years. He died intestate, leaving a widow, Mary, and two sons, John Philip and Joseph.[2]

Leoni was chiefly a country-house architect. Of the nineteen architectural commissions listed below, eleven were for country houses, but of these two were never completed, three were destroyed early in the nineteenth century, and only four survive today. The demolished houses are not adequately recorded, but the designs which Leoni appended to the third volume of his edition of Alberti afford some further specimens of his style.[3]

As a Venetian, Leoni would have had a first-hand knowledge of Palladio's architecture, and borrowings from both Palladio and Inigo Jones (whose drawings he presumably saw in Burlington's collection) are apparent in his own works. The plan of Carshalton House, for instance, was based on Palladio's unexecuted design for the Villa Mocenigo, and his design for a house dedicated to Lord Peterborough (*Alberti*, pls. 16–17) was conceived 'in Imitation of the Stile of Inigo Jones'. An analysis of Leoni's architectural designs has shown that they also owed a good deal to Campbell. However, he tended to avoid some of the standard clichés of English Palladianism, such as the Venetian window and the pavilion tower, and his surviving interiors at Clandon have plaster ceilings in the baroque manner of Artari and Bagutti.

[*A.P.S.D.*; *D.N.B.*; Walpole Society, *Vertue Note Books* iii, 131; R. Wittkower, 'Giacomo Leoni's Edition of Palladio's *Quattro Libri dell'Architettura'*, *Arte Veneta*, 1954, 310; P. Collins, 'The McGill Leoni', *Jnl. Royal Architectural Institute of Canada* xxxiv, 1957; P. Collins, 'New Light on Leoni', *Arch. Rev.* cxxvii, April 1960, 225–6; Timothy Hudson, 'A Venetian Architect in England', *C. Life*, 3 April 1975; Richard Hewlings, 'James Leoni' in *The Architectural Outsiders*, ed. R. Brown, 1985; Eileen Harris, *British Architectural Books and Writers 1556–1785*, 1990, *s.v.* 'Alberti' and 'Palladio'.]

LONDON, QUEENSBERRY HOUSE, No. 7 BURLINGTON GARDENS, begun 1721 for John Bligh, cr. Lord Clifton, completed 1722–3 for Charles Douglas, 3rd Duke of Queensberry; enlarged *c.*1785–9 by J. Vardy and J. Bonomi as Uxbridge House and now the Royal Bank of Scotland [Leoni's *Alberti*, pls. 14–15; *Survey of London* xxxii, 455–66 and pls. 75–9].

LONDON, ARGYLL HOUSE, KING'S ROAD, CHELSEA, for John Pierene or Perrin, 1723 [Leoni's *Alberti*, p. 4^{v} and pls. 20–2; *Survey of London* iv, 82–3 and pls. 84–99].

CARSHALTON PARK, SURREY, house for Thomas Scawen, to be built under the will of his uncle Sir Thomas Scawen (d. 1722), who left him £10,000 to build the house 'as neare to and agreeable to the Modell I now have as may be' [P.C.C. 233 MARLBOROUGH]. A letter from Leoni among the Lyme Park papers shows that preparatory work was in progress in 1725, but the house was never completed owing to financial difficulties. Leoni's designs are illustrated in his *Alberti*, pls. 3–13, which are dated 1723 and 1727.

LYME PARK, CHESHIRE, remodelled for Peter Legh, *c.*1725–35. Leoni was making designs in 1725, but major work does not seem to have begun until 1729. The roof over Leoni's portico was altered in 1817–18

[1] In 1726 he was in Charles Street, St. James's (*Survey of London* xxix, 90), between 1731 and 1742 in Vine Street, north of Piccadilly (rate-books in Westminster City Library), and in 1744–6 at 52 Poland Street, off Oxford Street (*Survey of London* xxxi, 245). In the Westminster rate-books, as in *Vitruvius Britannicus* iv, 1767, pl. 31, he is sometimes called 'Battista Leoni'.

[2] In December 1739 Joseph Leoni signed a receipt on behalf of the decorative painter Francis Sleter for a payment for work done by the latter at Mereworth Castle, Kent (Bodleian, MS. DD. Dashwood, Bucks, c. 8/10). 'Mr. Leoni my clerk' is mentioned in Matthew Brettingham's account-book (P.R.O., C 108/362) in 1748–50 in connection with Norfolk House, London.

[3] They have a separate title-page with explanatory text: *Some Designs for Buildings both Publick and Private* by James Leoni Architect, and the date 1726. However, as some of the plates are dated 1727, 1728 and 1729, the book cannot in fact have appeared before 1729. Some time in the 1740s Leoni invited subscriptions for a 'Treatise of Architecture' which was to contain 'several Noblemen's Houses & Country Seats already Built by him both in Town & Country', but this was never published.

[Lady Newton, *The House of Lyme*, 1917, 341–2, 370; John Cornforth in *C. Life*, 5, 12, 19, 26 Dec. 1974].

LOAKES MANOR, HIGH WYCOMBE, BUCKS., work for 1st Earl of Shelburne, perhaps a new house, *c.*1725; remodelled as Wycombe Abbey by James Wyatt *c.*1803–4 [R. Hewlings in *The Architectural Outsiders*, 206, citing letter in Legh Muniments].

MOULSHAM HALL, ESSEX, for 1st Earl Fitzwalter, 1728–45; dem. 1816 [accounts in the Essex R.O.; *Vitruvius Britannicus* iv, 1767, pls. 30–1] (P. Muilman, *History of Essex* i, 1770, plate).

BOLD HALL, nr. ST. HELENS, LANCS., for Peter Bold, *c.*1730–2; dem. 1901 except stable-block [E. Twycross, *Mansions of England* iii, 1847, 27–8].

CLANDON PARK, SURREY, for 2nd Lord Onslow, *c.*1730–3 [Walpole, *Visits to Country Seats*, Walpole Soc. xvi, 61; *Beauties of England and Wales* xiv, 1813, 274; Neale, *Views of Seats*, 2nd ser. iii, 1826] (*C. Life*, 10, 17, 24 Sept. 1927, 4, 11 Dec. 1969). The architectural history of this house presents some difficulty, as there is evidence that it was already being 're-edified' in the 1720s (see addenda to vol. i of Defoe's *Tour*, published in 1724), and it is possible that Leoni took over the carcase of a house begun by another architect. The rainwater leads are dated 1733, but work on the interior appears to have continued into the 1740s (see Vertue in *Walpole Soc.* xxvi, 153).

THORNDON HALL, ESSEX, partially remodelled for 8th Lord Petre, 1733–42, but left unfinished on Lord Petre's death in 1742 and demolished by his successor in 1763. The stones cut for Leoni's portico were used by James Paine to form the portico of his new house built 1764–70 on an adjoining site [drawings by Leoni dated 1733 in Essex Record Office, D/DP.P.145 A; cf. description in Defoe's *Tour*, 1738 ed., i, 124–5, and J. C. Ward, *Old Thorndon Hall*, Essex Record Office, 1972].

CLIVEDEN HOUSE, BUCKS., octagonal temple (now chapel) and 'Blenheim pavilion' for 1st Earl of Orkney, *c.*1735; also unexecuted designs for a new house dated 1727 [G. Jackson-Stops, 'The Cliveden Album: drawings by Archer, Leoni and Gibbs', *Architectural History* xix, 1976] (*C. Life*, 11 July 1931).

LONDON, No. 82 PICCADILLY, BATH HOUSE, for William Pulteney, cr. Earl of Bath, 1735; dem. 1821 [album of drawings at Cliveden House, letter from Leoni to Lord Orkney dated London, 20 June 1735, in which he says he is 'obliged to attende Mr. Pulteny and Governor Worsley in order to begin their buildings'] (A. I. Dasent, *Piccadilly*, 1920, 72).

LONDON, No. 4 NEW BURLINGTON STREET, for Henry Worsley, formerly Governor of Barbados, 1735; dem. [*ibid.*; *Survey of London* xxxii, 552–3].

ALKRINGTON HALL, LANCS., for Sir Darcy Lever, 1735–6 [P. Fleetwood-Hesketh, 'Alkrington Hall', in *The Country Seat*, ed. Colvin & Harris, 1970, 139–44].

LONDON, No. 21 ARLINGTON STREET, for 2nd Viscount Shannon, 1738; subsequently altered by Chambers (1769) and others [drawings by Leoni in R.I.B.A. Drawings Collection].

BURTON or BODECTON PARK, SUSSEX, for Richard Biddulph, 1738; destroyed by fire 1826 [Neale, *Views of Seats*, 2nd ser. i, 1824]. A view in B.L., Add. MS. 5674, f. 50, shows the date 1738 in the pediment.

LATHOM HOUSE, LANCS., for Sir Thomas Bootle, *c.*1740; altered by T. H. Wyatt 1862; central block dem. 1929, E. wing dem, *c.*1955 [*Vitruvius Britannicus* iv, 1767, pls. 94–8; R. Kerr, *The Gentleman's House*, 1864, pl. 24; for the date of building see Defoe's *Tour* iii, 1742, 225].

?LONDON, No. 4 WHITEHALL YARD, alterations for 4th Earl of Holderness, *c.*1740; dem. 1793. This may have been 'the Building' for which Leoni was paid £260 'on account' by the Earl of Holderness in 1740 [B.L., Egerton MS. 3497]. It was altered for his occupation soon after 1738 [*Survey of London* xiii, 153].

WORTLEY HALL, YORKS. (W.R.), the south front, for Edward Wortley Montagu, 1743; arms in pediment added after 1826 [Sheffield Archives, Wortley papers, Wh. M 58 (49), elevation inscribed 'Rough Draught of the Upright of Wortley by Sig[r]. Leoni, Apr. 1743'; cf. J. Hunter, *South Yorkshire* ii, 1831, 323].

STOWE HOUSE, BUCKS., two gateways flanking north front of house, for 1st Viscount Cobham, date uncertain, perhaps *c.*1740 [B. Seeley, *Stowe: A Description of the House and Gardens*, 1744].

WESTMINSTER ABBEY, monument in cloisters to Daniel Pulteney (d. 1731), executed by Rysbrack [signed 'Ia. Leoni Archs.'].

QUAINTON CHURCH, BUCKS., monument to Piggott family, after 1735 [signed].

UNEXECUTED DESIGNS

WREST PARK, BEDS., designs for rebuilding house for 1st Duke of Kent, 1715 [drawings in Bedfordshire Record Office, T. Hudson in *C. Life*, 17 Jan. 1974, T. Friedman in *Burlington Mag.* Nov. 1988, 837–40];

LONDON, HYDE PARK, TRIUMPHAL ARCH commissioned by 1st Earl Stanhope, 1719 [Leoni's *Alberti*, pls 1–2]; CLIVEDEN HOUSE, BUCKS., designs for a house for 1st Earl of Orkney, dated 1727 [drawings belonging to the National Trust]; SHARDELOES HOUSE, BUCKS., designs for remodelling the house for Montagu Garrard Drake, 1728, abandoned after his death that year [G. Eland, *Shardeloes Papers*, 1947, 129]; LONDON, THE MANSION HOUSE, designs submitted in competition, 1735 [S. Perks, *History of the Mansion House*, 1922, 166–7].

LEROUX, JACOB (–1799), architect and speculative builder, was articled in 1753 to William Jones (*q.v.*). He exhibited at the Society of Artists in 1761, and at the Royal Academy in 1771–2 and 1782–4. In 1769 he competed for the Royal Exchange at Dublin.

In 1766 Leroux was employed by Francis and William Goudge to supervise the development of part of their estate off Tottenham Court Road in London, lessees of sites in, e.g. Goudge Street, being required to build 'by direction and appointment of Jacob Leroux' [G.L. Record Office, MLR 1766/1, Nos. 140–144].

At Southampton Leroux designed the Polygon, a description of which is given in the *Southampton Guide*, 4th ed. 1787. 'This intended assemblage of elegant buildings was devised about the year 1768 by Mr. Leroux, an architect of Great Russel Street; it was to consist of twelve sides, having a house in the center of each, with the proper offices low and detached. The principal fronts were contrived to appear outwards, and the gardens to converge towards a bason of water in the center, which was to supply the several houses. . . . At the extremity a capital building was erected with two detached wings and colonades; of which the center was an elegant tavern, with assembly, and card rooms, &c. and each wing were the hotels, to accommodate the Nobility and gentry.' The 'tavern' was taken down within a few years of its erection, the wings being converted into private houses. In 1771 Leroux exhibited at the Royal Academy 'A view of part of the Polygon, now building at Southampton', and in 1772 'A design for a publick chapel and shops, forming a forum, intended to be built in the Polygon, Southampton'. The latter buildings, however, do not appear to have been erected.

In 1793 Leroux erected a second Polygon on the Somers estate in North London. He himself was the principal speculator, and the same layout was adopted as at Southampton, the houses facing outwards, with gardens converging on a central point. At first the scheme prospered, but before the Polygon was complete, 'some unforseen cause occurred which checked the fervour of building and many carcases of houses were sold for less than the value of the materials'. Leroux, however, continued to live in a house on the south side of Clarendon Square (which enclosed the Polygon) until his death, when it became the residence of the Abbé Carron. The Polygon itself was demolished in the nineteenth century.

Leroux also remodelled CAMS HALL, nr. FAREHAM, HANTS., for John Carnac, exhibiting an elevation of the front at the R.A. in 1771, and refronted BUCKDEN VICARAGE, HUNTS., in 1783 [Lincolnshire Record Office, MGA4]. In 1784, as a Justice of the Peace for Middlesex, he was a member of a committee for building a new MIDDLESEX HOUSE OF CORRECTION in COLDBATH FIELDS, CLERKENWELL, other members of which were Sir Robert Taylor and Henry Holland. Leroux was appointed architect and made plans for the prison which, after much revision by the committee, appear to have formed the basis of the design which the Justices had engraved by Charles Middleton (*q.v.*) in order to attract competitive tenders. These designs were carried out in 1788–94 under the direction of a clerk of works (first S. P. Cockerell and then Thomas Rogers). The building was demolished in 1889 [minutes of the Committee in G.L. Record Office, MA/G, CBF1].

Leroux's activities as a speculative builder are denounced by Charles Dibdin in his *Musical Tour*, published in 1788 (pp. 10–11). Dibdin claimed to have lost £290 'by building a castle in the air near Pancras, by virtue of an agreement with the famous – I had almost added another syllable – JACOB LEROUX, Esq. architect, brickmaker, and trading-justice in the district of Clerkenwell. This gentleman, with a dastardly speciousness for which a Hyena might envy him, promised me a license in the name of several magistrates *who opposed the motion*, and . . . erected the skeleton of a building which was blown down by the first high wind after the licence was refused.'

[Guildhall Library, index to Apprenticeship Registers in P.R.O.; Leroux's will, dated 11 April and proved 7 May, 1799, PCC 412 HOWE; *Gent's Mag.* 1813 (ii), 428–9; *Builder* xxvii, 1869, 781; John Summerson, *Georgian London*, 1969 ed., 314–15; *Survey of London* xxiv, 120–1; *V.C.H. Middlesex* viii, 19; R.I.B.A. Library, MS. notes on building, etc. by Leroux.]

LESLIE, ALEXANDER (1754–1835), was the son of Robert Leslie (1723–1804), a wright and cabinet-maker of Largo in Fife, and the elder brother of Sir John Leslie (1766-1832), the mathematician. His mother, Anne Carstairs, was almost certainly a sister of another local architect-builder, David Carstairs (*q.v.*). Leslie is known to have designed four churches in Fife: CERES, 1806 [S.R.O., CH/82/12, pp. 418–19]; KILRENNY, 1807 [S.R.O., HR 21/1, 5 June 1807]; NEWBURN, 1813–15, converted into a house 1970 [Heritors' minutes in S.R.O., GD 245/7/6/3–6]; and LARGO, 1816–17 [inscription in nave]. These are all simple Georgian boxes of pleasing but unpretentions character, with the exception of Largo, which Leslie reconstructed on a cruciform plan in quite creditable late Gothic style to correspond to the surviving 'chancel' of 1623. In 1815–17 Leslie was jointly responsible with Thomas Finlay, a mason, for adding rear wings to CHARLETON HOUSE, FIFE [S.R.O., SC 20/44/3, pp. 364–5, 393–415].

Leslie and his father are commemorated by a tombstone in Largo churchyard, and a silhouette portrait remains in the possession of his descendants. He was the father of James Leslie, C.E. (*q.v.*).

LESLIE, JAMES (1801–1889), was the son of Alexander Leslie (*q.v.*) of Largo in Fife, where he was born on 25 September 1801. He was educated in the local parish schools, then at Mackay's Academy in Edinburgh, and finally at Edinburgh University. In 1818 he was apprenticed to W. H. Playfair, with whom he remained for six years. Having decided to become a civil engineer rather than an architect, he went to London in 1824 to work in the office of Messrs. G. & J. Rennie. In 1828 he obtained his first post as Clerk of Works to the Leith Dock and Harbour Commissioners, and in 1832 he was appointed Resident Engineer for the Dundee Harbour Works. He subsequently had a distinguished career as a civil engineer specializing in harbour and water works, and in 1846 moved to Edinburgh as Engineer to the Edinburgh Water Company. He died in Edinburgh on 29 December 1889, in his 89th year, and is commemorated by a monument in the Dean Cemetery. His practice was continued by his only son Alexander Leslie, C.E. (1844–93), and his son-in-law R. C. Reid. His grandson Alexander Leslie (1881–1921) and his great-grandson of the same name (1910–82) were also civil engineers. [Obituary in *Minutes of Proceedings of the Institution of Civil Engineers*, vol. c, 1889–90, part ii; information from the late Alexander Leslie.]

Though James Leslie did not follow the profession of an architect, his early training enabled him to furnish designs for buildings from time to time. Of these the most important were WOOD'S HOSPITAL at his native village of LARGO, which he designed in a competent Jacobean style in 1830 [J. M. Leighton, *History of Fife* iii, 1840, 140], and the handsome classical CUSTOM HOUSE at DUNDEE, which he designed in 1839–40 in conjunction with John Taylor (*q.v.*), Surveyor to H.M. Customs [London Custom House Records, MS. 160]. In 1843 he designed a bridge and new approach to AULDBAR CASTLE, ANGUS, for Patrick Chalmers [N.L.S., MS. 15436, f. 29]. A number of plans and drawings in the Scottish Record Office illustrate his activities as a harbour and railway engineer from 1831 onwards.

LETHBRIDGE, JOHN (–*c.*1830), practised in Exeter, where he designed the Greek Revival BATHS in SOUTHERNHAY, opened in 1821; dem. [J. Britton & E. W. Brayley, *Devonshire Illustrated*, 1832, 67, where he is described as 'the late Mr. Lethbridge'], and NORTHERNHAY TERRACE, begun in 1821 by a builder who went bankrupt [*Middle Class Housing in Britain*, ed. Simpson & Lloyd, Newton Abbot 1977, 32]. Lethbridge was also the architect of the Grecian ST. JOHN'S CHURCH, TORQUAY, 1822–3, rebuilt *c.*1870 [R. J. E. Boggis, *History of St. John's Church, Torquay*, 1930, 7], and of the Gothic HOLY TRINITY CHURCH, EXMOUTH, 1824, reconstructed 1909–10 [G.R.].

LEVERTON, THOMAS (1743–1824), was the son of Lancelot Leverton, a builder, and was born at Waltham Abbey in Essex. After learning his father's business, he 'was subsequently enabled, by influential patrons, among whom were Mr. Kendall, a banker, to perfect himself in architecture'. Nothing, however, is known of his architectural training or career before 1771, when he began to exhibit his works at the Royal Academy. He designed a number of town and country houses, and (according to his own account) 'had a principal concern in promoting the finishing of Bedford Square'. For the external form of the square he almost certainly had no responsibility, but he designed the interiors of at least four of the houses, including one (No. 13) in which he took up residence, and the elegant doorway of No. 1 was probably also his work.

Leverton was Surveyor to the Grocers' Company and to the Phoenix Fire Insurance Company, for whom he designed both their offices in Lombard Street and a striking fire-engine house at Charing Cross. For some years he appears to have assisted John Marquand at the Land Revenue Office, and when Marquand retired in 1809 Leverton and Thomas Chawner succeeded him as joint architects to that department. In 1811 they submitted a scheme for the development of Marylebone (afterwards Regent's) Park. Their plan, which would have involved extensive building in the form of new streets and squares, was rejected in favour of Nash's more imaginative idea of a park surrounded by terraces and occupied only by a small number of villas designed like miniature country houses. It is illustrated in the *First Report* of the Commissioners of Woods, Forests and Land Revenue, 1812.

Leverton's architectural style was at first closely modelled on that of the Adam brothers. Watton Wood Hall and Plaistow Lodge, for instance, both have exquisite interiors in a neo-classical style akin to that of the Adams. The subsequent development of Leverton's style is obscured by the destruction of most of his buildings, but at Scampston Hall the domed exterior probably reflects a favourite motif of the Wyatts, while the interior is designed in a style of refined simplicity without decorative elaboration.

Leverton, who had a country residence at Woodlands, Sewardstone, Essex, as well as his London house in Bedford Square, was a J.P. for Westminster, Middlesex, Surrey and Kent. He died on 23 September 1824, in his 81st year, and was buried in Waltham Abbey Church, where there is a tablet to his memory. He left a considerable fortune, of which about £50,000 went to his relations and friends, and £12,000 to various charitable purposes. He left no children, his only son having died in boyhood, but his nephew William Leverton (q.v.) practised as a surveyor, while his niece Jane married his pupil James Donaldson (*q.v.*) and was the mother of Thomas Leverton Donaldson, Professor of Architecture at London University. Other pupils were Benjamin Birkhead, H. E. Kendall, J. Lotan and R. Walker.

A portrait of Leverton is in the church of St. Giles-in-the-Fields, London, whose charities benefited largely under his will. Another, by John Russell, R.A., belongs to the Phoenix Assurance Company, which also possesses a silver salver presented to Leverton on his retirement from the Company's service in 1811. Many surveys and other drawings by him are among the Land Revenue Records in the Public Record Office. His designs for a new Exchequer Office are to be found in P.R.O., WORK 30/317, and Sir John Soane's Museum (Drawer 38, 5). The R.I.B.A. Drawings Collection has some designs for lodges at Culford Hall, Suffolk, dated 1803.

[*A.P.S.D.*; *D.N.B.*; *V.C.H. Essex* vi, 268 n.; *Gent's Mag.* 1784 (i), 237, 1789 (i), 182, 1793 (i), 424, 1802(ii), 879, 1824(ii), 469; P.C.C. 558 ERSKINE; D. J. Olsen, *Town Planning in London*, Yale 1964, 48, n. 21; A. Byrne, *Bedford Square*, 1990; information from Mr. Frank Kelsall and Mr. K. N. Bascombe.]

WOODFORD HALL, ESSEX, for William Hunt, 1771; dem. *c.*1900 [exhib. at R.A. 1771].

LONDON, No. 65 LINCOLN'S INN FIELDS, for Henry Kendall, 1772 [*A.P.S.D.*; *Survey of London* iii, 108, pls. 86, 97].

KENT, an unidentified villa exhibited at the R.A. as 'now building' in 1773.

LONDON, ST. MILDRED'S COURT, POULTRY, house and warehouse for Matthew Bloxam, 1775–6; dem. [P.R.O., C 12/1658/18, *ex inf.* Mr. Frank Kelsall].

ESSEX, unidentified stables and offices exhibited at R.A. as 'erected' in 1775.

BOYLES COURT, GREAT WARLEY, ESSEX, exhibited at R.A. 1776.

An unidentified chapel exhibited as 'now building' in 1777.

WATTON WOOD HALL (now WOODHALL PARK), HERTS., for Sir Thomas Rumbold, Bart., 1777–82; wings enlarged after 1791 [G. Richardson, *New Vitruvius Britannicus* i, 1810, pls. 27–8] (*C. Life*, 31 Jan., 7 Feb. 1925, 6 Oct. 1977).

LONDON, BEDFORD SQUARE, No. 1 for Sir Lionel Lyde, Bart., 1778–82; No. 6, interior for Alexander Wedderburn, 1st Lord Loughborough, *c.*1782; No. 10, interior for Samuel Lyde, *c.*1782; No. 13, interior for himself, 1782 onwards [A. Byrne, *Bedford Square*, 1990].

PLAISTOW LODGE (now Quernmore School), BROMLEY, KENT, for Peter Thellusson, 1780: almost certainly the 'gentleman's seat building in Kent' which Leverton exhibited at the R.A. in 1780, as it closely resembles Watton Wood Hall [J. Newman, *West Kent and the Weald*, Buildings of England, 1969, 182].

PARLINGTON HOUSE, YORKS. (W.R.), triumphal arch in park to commemorate the War of American Independence, for Sir Thomas Gascoigne, Bart., exhibited at R.A. as 'now building' in 1781. The arch bears the inscription 'LIBERTY IN N. AMERICA TRIUMPHANT MDCCLXXXIII'. Leverton's original drawing is among the Gascoigne papers in Leeds Archives Dept., together with an unexecuted design by him for a single-storey quadrangular house dated 1782 (T. F. Friedman in *Leeds Arts Calendar*, No. 66, 1970, figs. 1 and 5).

LONDON, THE PHOENIX FIRE OFFICE, LOMBARD STREET, *c.*1787; dem. [*exhib.* at R.A. 1787].

ENFIELD CHURCH, MIDDLESEX, extensive repairs, 1789 [Bodleian Library, MS. Gough Middlesex 8, ff. 44–6].

RIDDLESWORTH HALL, NORFOLK, for Silvanus Bevan, 1792; rebuilt 1900 after fire in 1892 [exhib. at R.A. 1792] (J. P. Neale, *Views of Seats* vi, 1823).

TOWN HILL PARK, SOUTH STONEHAM, HANTS., for Nathaniel Middleton, 1792; since reconstructed [exhib. at R.A. 1792].

LONDON, THE PHOENIX FIRE-ENGINE HOUSE, CHARING CROSS, 1794; dem. *c.*1830 [exhib. at R.A. 1794; drawings in P.R.O., MPE 380] (*Arch. Rev.* xxix, 1916, 118).

LONDON, No. 15 LOMBARD STREET, BANK for Messrs. Robarts & Curtis, 1796; dem. 1861 [exhib. at R.A. 1796].

LONDON, HAYMARKET OPERA HOUSE, design for façade, partially executed 1796, never completed [*Survey of London* xxix, 237–8].

LONDON, GROCERS' HALL, POULTRY, 1798–1802; altered by Joseph Gwilt 1838; rebuilt 1889–93 [G. Richardson, *New Vitruvius Britannicus* ii, 1808, pls. 5–6].

LONDON, No. 23 ST JAMES'S PLACE, for Sir John Lubbock, Bart., 1801–2; dem. [*A.P.S.D.*].

SCAMPSTON HALL, YORKS. (E.R.), remodelled for W. T. St. Quintin, 1801–3 [exhib. at R.A. 1803] (*C. Life*, 1–8 April 1954).

attributed: LONDON, THE SCOTCH PRESBYTERIAN CHAPEL, SWALLOW STREET, with J. Marquand, 1801–4; dem. 1915 [*Survey of London* xxxi, 63–4].

NEW YORK, U.S.A., a sugar-house, exhibited as 'now building' in 1803.

LISLEE, CO. CORK, IRELAND, 'marine villa' for the Revd. Dr. Synge, 1803. Although exhibited at the R.A. in 1803. as 'now building' and illustrated in G. Richardson's *New Vitruvius Britannicus* ii, 1808, pls. 45–50, it is doubtful whether this house was ever completed and no trace of it now remains.

HERRINGSTON, WINTERBORNE HERRINGSTON, DORSET, remodelled for Edward Williams, soon after 1803, Gothic [Arthur Oswald, *Country Houses of Dorset*, 1959, 88; R.C.H.M., *Dorset*, ii (2), 388–9].

LONDON, HAMILTON PLACE, PICCADILLY, layout for the Crown, 1806 [*Third Report of the Surveyor-General of Woods, Forests and Land Revenues*, 113; P.R.O., CREST 2/1729]. The Earl of Lucan's papers, formerly at Althorp House, Northants., show that he and the 4th Earl of Buckinghamshire both built houses in Hamilton Place to Leverton's designs in 1807.

LONDON, No. 1, WHITEHALL GARDENS, for 12th Earl of Cassilis, 1806–7; dem. 1938 [letter from Leverton's clerk of works to Sir John Soane, 1826, Sir John Soane's Museum, 16/13/2] (*Survey of London* xiii, 211–13).

LONDON, CHELSEA HOSPITAL, house for General J. W. Gordon, 1812; altered 1825 and 1931–2 [C. G. T. Dean, *The Royal Hospital, Chelsea*, 1950, 258].

LONDON, WHITEHALL PLACE, SCOTLAND YARD, *c.*1810–20, in conjunction with T. Chawner; dem. [*Survey of London* xvi, 220; *History of the King's Works* vi, 541].

LEVERTON, WILLIAM (*c.*1758–1849), was the son of Thomas Leverton's younger brother Andrew. He became a pupil of his uncle, from whose address he exhibited at the Royal Academy in 1780–2. He continued to exhibit up to 1807, showing designs for unspecified lodges, theatres, baths., etc., from his office in Gate Street, Lincoln's Inn Fields, but no executed works, and it appears that he was chiefly employed as a builder and surveyor. The firm of 'Leverton and Moore', builders and surveyors, was still in business in Gate Street in the 1820s. Leverton was elected a member of the Surveyors' Club in 1797 and was its President in 1809.

LEWIS, JAMES (*c.*1751–1820), was probably born at Brecon in South Wales. He went to Italy in 1770, at the age of 19, returning in December 1772. A volume of drawings of friezes, urns, classical ornaments, etc., which he made in Rome is in the Yale Center for British Art. He told Farington that he got to know Piranesi well, and that he kept a journal which he subsequently destroyed because he was ashamed of the bad Italian in which it was written. From 1774 to 1778 he exhibited at the Society of Artists, and in 1779–80 he published a volume of *Original Designs in Architecture, Consisting of Plans, etc. for Villas, Mansions, Town Houses, etc.*, which was evidently intended to advertise his talents, since it contained very few executed buildings. In preparing this work Lewis was apparently assisted by an Italian draughtsman called Vincenzo Berrarese,[1] who told Milizia in a letter that he had been responsible for the drawings although his name did not appear in the book. A second volume was published in 1797.

In 1792 Lewis succeeded R. Norris as surveyor to Christ's Hospital, and in November 1793 he received a gratuity of 100 guineas 'for his great attention during the building of the new grammar schools', as he had charged only $2\frac{1}{2}$ per cent, instead of the usual 5 per cent. In 1793 he made a design for many additions to the Hospital to cost about £15,400, and in 1794 a model was made of a

[1] Probably the 'V. Ferrarese' who exhibited a design for a workhouse at the R.A. in 1780.

design he had prepared 'for the uniform and gradual rebuilding of the hospital'. This model, which is probably identical with one now preserved at Christ's Hospital, Horsham, comprised a three-storied edifice, 360 feet by 285 feet, round a colonnaded court 264 feet by 190 feet. He also made a smaller design in 1795, but neither was carried out, though drawings were exhibited at the Royal Academy in 1799 and 1800. One of these schemes is represented by a drawing in the R.I.B.A. Collection.

In 1793 Lewis was appointed surveyor to the Bridewell and Bethlehem Hospitals. In 1810 a competition was held for designs for a new Bethlehem Hospital for lunatics in St. George's Fields, Southwark. The first premium was awarded to W. C. Lochner,[1] the second to J. A. and G. S. Repton, and the third to John Dotchen. None of these designs was adopted, but instead Lewis was instructed to incorporate their best features in a new design of his own, which was approved in 1811 and carried out between 1812 and 1815 at a cost of about £100,000. The result was a well-planned but somewhat barrack-like building whose chief architectural ornaments were a large portico and a low saucer-dome rising behind it. The present more lofty dome was substituted by Sydney Smirke in 1844–6.

Ill-health led Lewis to resign his office at Christ's Hospital in January 1816, and the surveyorship of the Bethlehem Hospital the following year. From 1784 to 1814 he was also Surveyor to the Mercers' Company. He died in Powis Place on 16 July 1820, aged 69, leaving a considerable fortune to his two sons and two daughters. He had a house at Totteridge in Hertfordshire, to which his elder son John retired. His portrait by George Dance was in 1899 in the possession of E. E. Wellesley (N. *and Q.*, 9th ser. iv, 1899, 2). E. Gyfford, W. C. Lochner and A. P. Moore were his pupils, and George Hawkins was in his office as a clerk.

Lewis was an elegant neo-classical architect whose best works were country houses such as Bletchingdon, Eydon, Hackthorn and Lavington. These are neo-classical versions of the Palladian villa with interiors treated in a restrained style of Adamsian character. His unexecuted designs included a country house for R. P. Thelwall (*Original Designs* i, pls. 12, 13), a villa and temple at Lodore, nr. Keswick, Cumberland, for Edward and Rowland Stephenson (ii, pls. 9 and 25–6), a park entrance and stable courtyard (1799) at Longleat House, Wilts. (ii, pl. 35 shows the former), a market house and a theatre at Limerick in Ireland, 1788 (ii, pls. 1, 2 and 21–4) and a design for Coole House, Co. Galway, for Robert Gregory (ii, pls. 29–30).

[*A.P.S.D.*; *The Farington Diary*, ed. J. Greig, iv, 192; P.C.C. 481 KENT.]

LONDON, GREAT ORMOND STREET, three houses with a uniform façade, before 1780; dem. [*Original Designs* i, pl. 7].

BLETCHINGDON HOUSE, OXON., remodelled for Arthur Annesley, 1782 [*Original Designs* ii, pls. 3–8].

HAWNES OR HAYNES, BEDS., a greenhouse for 1st Lord Carteret, 1782 [*Original Designs* ii, pl. 15]. The rebuilding of the south front of the house for Lord Carteret in 1790 may also be attributed to Lewis. A view of it was exhibited at the R.A. in 1797 by his pupil A. P. Moore, who regularly exhibited drawings of his master's recent works. The original designs are (or were) preserved in the house, but are not signed (*C. Life*, 29 Dec. 1934).

SUTTON PARK, BEDS., alterations for Sir Montagu Burgoyne, Bart., *c.*1786, and a proposed temple for Lady Burgoyne, *c.*1795 [*Original Designs* ii, pls. 19–20].

EYDON LODGE, NORTHANTS., for the Revd. Francis Annesley, 1788–9 [*Original Designs* ii, pls. 16–18] (*C. Life*, 21 Jan. 1971).

LAVINGTON HOUSE, SUSSEX, for John Sargent, 1790–4; enlarged 1903 and 1912–13 [*Original Designs* ii, pl. 12*] (*C. Life*, 25 July 1925).

LONDON, CHRIST'S HOSPITAL, the Grammar Schools, 1793; dem. 1903 [*A.P.S.D.*].

LONDON, CLEVELAND HOUSE, ST. JAMES'S, remodelled south front and interior for 3rd Duke of Bridgwater, 1795–7; dem. 1840 [*Survey of London* xxx, 494 and pl. 233].

NAZEING PARK, ESSEX, alterations for William Palmer, *c.*1797 [*Original Designs* ii, pls. 27–8].

HACKTHORN HOUSE, LINCS., for J. Cracroft, *c.*1798 [exhibited at R.A. 1798 by A. P. Moore as 'designed and built under the direction of Mr. J. Lewis, architect'].

WELWYN RECTORY, HERTS., 1798 [Huntingdon Archdeaconry papers in Herts. C.R.O.].

HERTFORD, CHRIST'S HOSPITAL SCHOOL FOR GIRLS, Dining Hall and Infirmary, 1800 [*A.P.S.D.*].

WOOLMERS, HERTINGFORDBURY, HERTS., alterations for 3rd Duke of Bridgwater, 1802 [Bridgwater papers in Herts. C.R.O.].

LONDON, BRIDEWELL HOSPITAL, BLACKFRIARS, pedimented entrance to New Bridge Street (now Life Association of Scotland), *c.*1802 [E. G. O'Donoghue, *Bridewell Hospital*, 1929, 244].

[1] Not to J. M. Gandy, as stated in *Survey of London* xxv, 76–80.

DELAFORD PARK, IVER, BUCKS., remodelled for Charles Clowes, *c.*1802; burned 1845, dem. 1959 [*The Ambulator*, 1811, 270; J. N. Brewer, *The Beauties of England and Wales* x (iv), 1816, 539–40 and plate].

LONDON, THE ROYAL COLLEGE OF SURGEONS, LINCOLN'S INN FIELDS, in collaboration with George Dance, 1806–13; rebuilt 1835–7 by Sir Charles Barry [Dorothy Stroud, *George Dance Architect*, 1971, 193–5].

LONDON, THE BETHLEHEM HOSPITAL, SOUTHWARK (now the Imperial War Museum), 1812–15; new dome, addition of chapel, etc., by Sydney Smirke 1838–46; wings truncated 1930 [Britton & Pugin, *The Public Buildings of London* i, 1825, 298–304; original designs in P.R.O., MR 76; *Survey of London* xxv, 76–80].

CLAVERING VICARAGE, ESSEX, rebuilt under a faculty granted in 1822, of which a copy is preserved among the Leicester Archdeaconry Records (Faculties 230 j). The designs are stated to have been made by James Lewis, presumably shortly before his death in 1820.

LEWIS, THOMAS, was surveyor to the Harpur Trust Estate in Holborn. In 1765–7 he made plans for redeveloping property in Lambs Conduit Street, Theobalds Road and the surrounding area, but in 1767 he was dismissed because his charges were too high [Harpur Trust Minutes at Bedford]. In 1782 the 1st Earl of Mansfield's house in BLOOMSBURY SQUARE (dem.) was being rebuilt under his direction after its destruction in the riots of 1780 [G.L.R.O., HFCS 18, p. 417]. He designed the WELSH CHARITY SCHOOL in GRAYS INN LANE, LONDON, built in 1771–2; dem. He was a trustee of the school, and gave his services gratis. His portrait, showing him with a plan of the school, now hangs in the Welsh Girls' School at Ashford, Middlesex [Rachel Leighton, *Rise and Progress: the Story of the Welsh Girls' School*, 1950, with illustration of the portrait].

LEWIS, THOMAS, of Bath, is described as 'Builder and Surveyor' in Pigot's *Directory* of 1830. In his *Rambles Round Bath*, 1848, 287, J. Tunstall records that Lewis designed a new tower for BATHFORD CHURCH, SOMERSET. The existing tower dates from 1879.

LIDDELL, THOMAS (1800–1856), was the second son of Sir Thomas Henry Liddell, 1st Lord Ravensworth. In 1808 his father began to rebuild RAVENSWORTH CASTLE, CO. DURHAM, to the designs of John Nash, but the work went on for over twenty years, and in its later stages was superintended by Thomas. According to Britton [*Illustrations of Toddington*, 1840, 26], 'The Honourable Thomas Liddell . . . has devoted some years to the pleasing and arduous task of superintending these works, and, I am well informed, has manifested both architectural skill and taste in the different parts of the mansion, which have been raised from his designs.' This elaborate castellated mansion, demolished in 1952–3, is illustrated in Morris's *Views of Seats* v. For Nash's original drawings see *R.I.B.A. Drawings Catalogue: L–N*, 107–9, and note the inscription 'Plan suggested by Thomas' on No. 10, a sketch elevation of the south front dating probably from the 1820s. A Gothic gate-lodge at Ravensworth designed by Liddell is described and illustrated in Loudon's *Encyclopaedia of Cottage, Farm and Villa Architecture*, 1846, 1152–3.

In 1823 Liddell's sister married the 6th Viscount Barrington and in 1843 Liddell himself married Lord Barrington's sister. According to E. Churton, *The Railroad Book of England*, 1851, BECKETT PARK, BERKSHIRE, Lord Barrington's seat, was built in 1831 'from designs of the Hon. Thomas Liddell, and under his superintendence'. This is confirmed by Earl de Grey (*q.v.*), who in a MS. in the Bedfordshire Record Office [CRT 190/45/2, pp. 1–19] records that in 1834 he took over his clerk of works James Clephan (*q.v.*) from Lord Barrington, 'whose house was built by an amateur architect, his brother [-in-law], Tom Liddell'. William Atkinson (*q.v.*) had been commissioned to make designs for rebuilding Beckett Park for the 5th Lord Barrington as early as 1805 [Lysons, *Magna Britannia* i, 1806, 366], and further designs were made by him in 1814 [British Library, MS. Deposit 9389], but nothing appears to have been done until Shute Barrington, Bishop of Durham, who died in 1826, left £10,000 for a mansion to be built for Lord Barrington at Beckett 'according to the plan delivered by Mr. Atkinson, architect' [J. B. Nichols, *Literary Illustrations* v, 1828, 628]. As the 5th Viscount died in 1829, it was left to his successor to erect the new Gothic house with the help of his brother-in-law. How far the design was Atkinson's or Liddell's requires further investigation.

Liddell's reputation as a Gothic expert was such that in 1835 he was one of the members of the committee appointed to select the design for the new Houses of Parliament [*History of the King's Works* vi, 576]. In 1836 he made designs that were not carried out for remodelling BRIDGWATER HOUSE, GREEN PARK, LONDON, for Lord Francis Leveson-Gower [N.L.S., Dep. 313/764]. Early in the 1850s he designed the interior and furnishings of the great dining-room at GLAMIS CASTLE, ANGUS, for the 12th Earl of Strathmore [archives at Glamis, *ex inf.* Mr. H. Gordon Slade]. Shortly before his death he designed a classical 'memorial room' at WYNYARD PARK, CO. DURHAM, to commemorate the 3rd Marquess of Londonderry (d. 1854). This was decorated with marble Corinthian pilasters, between which were niches containing military trophies of the Peninsular War, etc. [W. Fordyce, *County Palatine of Durham* ii, 1855, 321]. A sketch by Liddell for remodelling the front of WIMPOLE HALL, CAMBS., in a neo-classical style is preserved at Wimpole.

LIDSTONE, JOSEPH (–1865), of Dartmouth, was probably a son of Thomas Lidstone, a carpenter and builder of that place who designed ALL SAINTS CHURCH, LOWER BRIXHAM, DEVON, *c.*1819–24, Gothic; rebuilt 1885–1900 [Port, 132–3]. Joseph designed SOUTH POOL RECTORY, DEVON, 1828 [Exeter Diocesan Records], ST. PETROCK'S CHAPEL, HIGHER STREET, DARTMOUTH, 1831–3 [I. C. B. S.] and STRETE CHURCH, DEVON, 1836, Gothic [I. C. B. S.]. By the 1850s the family business had been taken over by Lidstone's son Thomas. Joseph died on 14 Feb. 1865 [Principal Probate Registry, Calendar of Probates].

LIGHTFOOT, JOHN JACKSON (1795–1843), was a Liverpool accountant who made the acquaintance of Thomas Rickman (*q.v.*) at the time when the latter was similarly employed in the same town. Encouraged by Rickman he became a keen amateur architect, entering for several competitions and exhibiting from time to time at the Liverpool Academy. Among the drawings which he showed were a design for the General Post Office in London (1822), 'a Grecian Temple . . . being one of the unsuccessful designs for the Assize Courts, Liverpool' (1840), 'a Gothic interior' (1842), and an elevation of the north front of 'The Wray, Windermere, . . . designed by J. Lightfoot' (1842), presumably WRAY CASTLE, nr. HAWKSHEAD, LANCS., which was built by Dr. James Dawson in 1840–7, it is said to the designs of H. P. Horner of Liverpool. He was the father of Joseph Barber Lightfoot, Bishop of Durham (1828–1889) [*D. N. B., s. v.* 'Lightfoot, J. B.'; Rickman's diaries, *passim*, esp. 29 May 1816].

LIGHTOLER, TIMOTHY (1727–1769), was one of the sons of Thomas Lightoler or Lightowler, a joiner of Walton-le-Dale in Lancashire. He and his brother Thomas were brought up as carvers and joiners, and in about 1750 came to Warwick to work on the interior of the castle, where the chapel was then being remodelled to the designs of Daniel Garrett. Thomas Lightoler subsequently turned his hand to coining, and fled the country after escaping from prison. Timothy remained at Warwick, where he married (1752) and settled down as a carver of doorframes, ornamental chimney-pieces and the like, particularly in the rococo manner. In 1762 he patented a machine for cutting files. Sanderson Miller's correspondence shows that in 1758 he gave an estimate for carving the tympanum in the pediment of the newly built Shire Hall at Warwick, and that in 1759 he was making moulds for decorative work at Belhus in Essex. In about 1760 he designed a Gothic altar-piece for the Beauchamp Chapel at Warwick that was executed by the sculptor William Collins, and he and Collins were also associated in the redecoration of some of the principal rooms at Burton Constable in Yorkshire. Some of his work here is remarkable for the introduction of neo-Jacobean motifs.

In 1757 Lightoler was employed by the publisher Robert Sayer to complete *The Modern Builder's Assistant* after the deaths of its authors, William Halfpenny and Robert Morris, adding some further plates chiefly of a decorative character but including plans and elevations for a country house. In 1762, with Sayer as publisher, Lightoler produced *The Gentleman and Farmer's Architect*, a collection of designs for parsonages, farmhouses and farm-buildings both practical and ornamental. The former included hothouses, cowsheds and Dutch barns, the latter a Chinese farmhouse and 'Facades to place before disagreable objects', such as artificial ruins in the manner of Sanderson Miller. In 1761 a prospectus was issued announcing that 'Mr. Lightoler is at this Time making a Tour of England, to take Perspective Views and Plans of the Chief Seats of all the Peers.' Some of his drawings were subsequently engraved, with elegant rococo frames, as illustrations to William Guthrie's *Complete History of the English Peerage* (1763).

During the 1760s Lightoler developed a considerable practice as an architect. His most important works in this capacity were Platt Hall, a substantial country house in the manner of John Carr, the church of St. Paul at Liverpool and the Octagon Chapel at Bath. The two last were both domed buildings of considerable merit. St. Paul's was built under an Act of Parliament of 1762 which authorized the Corporation to build two churches. The building of the second one was postponed until 1775, when St. John's was begun to Gothic designs which had probably been made by Lightoler before his death, but no contemporary evidence has so far been found to confirm Picton's attribution of the church to him. In 1766 Lightoler made designs for a new town hall at Bath that were not adopted [W. Ison, *The Georgian Buildings of Bath*, 1948, 35] and in 1769 he was among the unsuccessful competitors for the Exchange at Dublin [*Builder* xxvii, 1869, 781]. The death at Lancaster of 'Mr. Lightholder of Warwick, Architect' was announced in the *Coventry Mercury* of 31 July 1769.

[*The Registers of the Parish of Walton-le-Dale*, ed. G. E. C. Clayton, Lancashire Parish Register Soc. 1910, 56, 414; *The Proceedings of J. Hewitt, Alderman and . . . J. P. . . . for Coventry in . . . 1756, being a particular account of the Gang of Coiners . . . pursued by the Author . . .*, Birmingham 1783; B. Woodcroft, *Alphabetical Index to Patentees of Inventions*, 1854, 339; Joan Lane, 'Timothy Lightoler of Warwick', *C. Life*, 19 March 1987; Eileen Harris, *British Architectural Books and Writers 1556–1785*, 1990, 296–7; information from Mr. R. J. Chamberlain-Brothers and the late S. A. Harris of Liverpool].

BURTON CONSTABLE, YORKS. (E.R.), designed quadrangular stable-block and interiors of Great Hall, staircase hall and dining-room for William Constable, *c.*1757–68 [W. Watts, *Seats of the Nobility etc.*, pl. 12, 1779; C. Hussey in *C. Life*, 27 Aug., 3 Sept. 1932; Ivan Hall in *C. Life*, 22, 29 April, 6, 13 May 1982].

WARWICK, ST. MARY'S CHURCH, designed Gothic altar-piece in Beauchamp Chapel executed by William Collins, *c.*1760 [*Notices of the Churches of Warwickshire* i, 1847, 71, where the date is wrongly given as 1735].

THE SOHO MANUFACTORY, HANDSWORTH, nr. BIRMINGHAM, began construction for Matthew Boulton 1761, but was superseded by Benjamin Wyatt & Co., probably in 1763. In 1766 William Wyatt described Lightoler as 'the greatest lyar I have yet met' [Birmingham Assay Office, Tew MSS., W. Wyatt to Boulton, 22 Jan. 1766].

MANCHESTER, ST. MARY'S CHURCH, addition of spire to classical church, 1762; dem. 1854 [*Lancs. & Cheshire Antiquarian Soc's Trans.* x, 1892, 135].

STONELEIGH ABBEY, WARWICKS., internal alterations for 5th Lord Leigh, 1763–5 [Shakespeare's Birthplace Trust Records Office, Stratford, Stoneleigh Papers DR 61/33 and drawings in volume DR671/33, including one signed by Lightoler].

BIDSTON HILL, CHESHIRE, signal house for shipping, 1763; dem. [Minutes of the Liverpool Common Council, 11 May 1763, *ex inf.* the late S. A. Harris].

LIVERPOOL, ST. PAUL'S CHURCH, 1763–9; dem. 1932 [J. A. Picton, *Memorials of Liverpool* ii, 1875, 39–40, where the architect's Christian name is wrongly given as 'Thomas'].

PLATT HALL, RUSHOLME, LANCS., for John Worsley, *c.*1763. A set of designs for the interiors of the principal rooms signed 'T. Lightoler' is preserved at Platt Hall (now a Museum of Costume). Only one room in Lightoler's style survives, but there is an unsigned plan and elevation in the same hand for the house as executed.

STRATFORD-ON-AVON CHURCH, WARWICKS., designs for spire, probably as executed 1763–4 [*Correspondence of the Revd. Joseph Greene*, ed. L. Fox, Hist. MSS. Comm. 1965, 100; see above, p. 498].

WARWICK CASTLE, new dining-room and other alterations for 1st Earl of Warwick, 1763–9 [*V. C. H. Warwicks.* viii, 462].

TEDDESLEY HALL, STAFFS., designs for chimney-pieces for Sir Edward Littleton, Bart., 1766; dem. 1954 [Staffs. C. R. O., Hatherton papers D 260/M/E/116].

BATH, THE OCTAGON CHAPEL, MILSOM STREET, 1766–7 [engraving signed 'T. Lightoler' reproduced by W. Ison, *The Georgian Buildings of Bath*, 1948, p1. 23].

STRATFORD-ON-AVON, WARWICKS., a payment of £10 in 1770 in connection with the recent (1767–8) rebuilding of the TOWN HALL may indicate that Lightoler designed it, but the contract with Robert Newman, 'Builder and Mason' of Whittington, Glos., does not name the architect [*Correspondence of the Revd. Joseph Greene*, ed. L. Fox, Hist MSS. Comm. 1965, 100n.; M. Macdonald, *The Town Hall Stratford-upon-Avon*, 1986].

LIVERPOOL, ST. JOHN'S CHURCH, built 1775–83 to Gothic designs probably made by Lightoler before his death; dem. 1898 [J. A. Picton, *Memorials of Liverpool* ii, 1875, 188, where the architect's Christian name is wrongly given as 'Thomas'].

LIMINGE, ROBERT, *see* LEMYINGE, ROBERT.

LINDLEY, WILLIAM (*c.*1739–1818), of Doncaster, may have been related to Joseph Lindley (1710–91) of Heath, nr. Wakefield, whose son Joseph (1756–1808) was a surveyor and cartographer. William Lindley began his professional career as John Carr's draughtsman and assistant. In September 1774, when advertising his services as an architect in the *York Courant*, he stated that he had been 'an Assistant to Mr. Carr of York upwards of 20 years'. In October 1774 the Corporation of Doncaster applied to 'Mr. Lyndley of York to draw a plan for a play-house', and the theatre was built to his designs in the following year. In 1783 he became a freeman of Doncaster, where he lived for the rest of his life. The house which he built for himself in South Parade was sufficiently large and important for the Prince of Wales to be lodged in it in 1806. In the 1790s Lindley was in partnership with Charles Watson (*q.v.*), who had been his pupil, and from about 1810 with John Woodhead (*q.v.*). William Hurst (*q.v.*), afterwards Woodhead's partner, was also his pupil. Lindley died in February 1818, aged 79, and was buried in Doncaster Church.

Lindley was a competent but unadventurous architect who never deviated far from the basically Adamsian style that he had learned from John Carr, though some of his favourite motifs, e.g. open-based pediments and floating cornices over windows, can be traced to the influence of James Paine. Most of his clients were men of 'conservative tastes and limited means' (Taylor), and Lindley's simplified classical façades, usually astylar and often with the minimum of conventional ornament, no doubt suited relatively modest purses and minds unattuned to the more sophisticated neo-classical architecture of Holland or Soane. Lindley worked chiefly for a nexus of interrelated gentry families in the West Riding of Yorkshire, and further country houses in that area such as Bawtry Hall, Hooton Pagnell Hall (S. range) and Ackworth House can be attributed to him on grounds of style or patronage or both. For these and other attributions see Angus Taylor; 'William Lindley of Doncaster', *Georgian Group Journal*, 1994.

Lindley occasionally made drawings for engraving, e.g. of Carr's stables at Harewood, of Kirby Hall, Yorks. (n.d., engraved by Basire) and of a Roman altar found at Doncaster (*Gentleman's Magazine* 1781, 361), for which the original drawing is in the Bodleian Library (Gough Maps 36, f. 49).

[J. Hunter, *South Yorkshire* i, 1828, 46; MS. History of the Lindley family in Yorkshire Archaeological Soc's Library, MS. MD 280 (22); *Calendar of the Records of the Borough of Doncaster*, Doncaster 1902, iv, *passim*; R. B. Wragg, 'Two Architects of York', *York Georgian Soc's Report* 1957–8, 38–40; letters to Bryan Cooke of Owston, 1785–1796 in Doncaster Archives, DD.DC/H 1/1/2, cited below as 'Owston letters'; information from Mr. Angus Taylor.]

PUBLIC BUILDINGS

DONCASTER, YORKS. (W.R.), THE THEATRE, 1775–6; altered 1814; dem. [John Tomlinson, *Doncaster*, 1887, 238].

DONCASTER, YORKS. (W.R.), GAOL and KEEPER'S HOUSE, 1779; dem. [Doncaster Corporation Records, Credit Book 1772–178, p. 107, *ex inf.* Mr. Angus Taylor].

ACKWORTH SCHOOL, YORKS. (W.R.), THE OLD MEETING HOUSE, 1779 [H. Thompson, *History of Ackworth School*, 1879, 32]. Lindley's design for a Cold Bath House here is in the Hailstone Collection in York Minster Library.

DONCASTER, YORKS. (W.R.), TOWN HALL, rebuilt Common Council room and façade, 1784–6 [Wragg, *op. cit.*, citing Order Books of the Corporation].

SHEFFIELD, YORKS. (W.R.), THE MARKET PLACE, for the Earl of Surrey, 1784–6; dem. 1851 [Sheffield Archives, Arundel MS. P425329, *ex inf.* Mr. Angus Taylor].

ECCLESALL, nr. SHEFFIELD, YORKS. (W.R.), COURT HOUSE and GAOL for 4th Earl Fitzwilliam, 1791; dem. [Sheffield Archives, Fitzwilliam Papers, MP 36].

WAKEFIELD, YORKS. (W.R.), ST. JOHN'S CHURCH, with Charles Watson, 1791–5; tower taken down 1880 and rebuilt 1885–95; chancel added 1904–5 [engraving by Malton in Soane Museum, Drawer lix, inscribed 'Lindley & Watson Archts.'].

SHEFFIELD, YORKS. (W.R.), ST. PETER'S CHURCH (now Cathedral), alterations 1791–1802 [Sheffield Archives, R. E. Leader's Notes, 141, p. 39].

DONCASTER, YORKS. (W.R.), THE DISPENSARY, FRENCH GATE, 1793–4; dem. 1969 [G. Swann, *The Doncaster Royal Infirmary, 1792–1972*, 1973, 13–15].

DONCASTER, YORKS. (W.R.), THE MANSION HOUSE, added attic storey, 1800–1; new dining-room, 1806 [J. Tomlinson, *Doncaster*, 1887, 225; *A Skilful Master-Builder*, ed. H. E. C. Stapleton, York 1975, 37, 44].

DONCASTER, YORKS, (W.R.), RACECOURSE GRANDSTAND, alterations, 1804; dem. 1969 [*A Skilful Master-Builder*, ed. H. E. C. Stapleton, York 1975, 40–1].

DOMESTIC ARCHITECTURE

KIRKLEES HALL, YORKS. (W.R.), remodelled drawing-room, etc. for Sir George Armytage, Bart., 1777 [D. Nortcliffe, 'The Re-Styling of Kirklees Hall, 1753–1790', *Halifax Antiquarian Soc's Trans.* 1982] (*C. Life*, 22 Aug. 1908).

attributed: MARKHAM HALL, EAST MARKHAM,

NOTTS., partial rebuilding for Edmund Cartwright of Doncaster, *c.*1777 [stylistic attribution by Mr. Taylor, based on resemblance to other works by Lindley, notably the drawing-room at Ferham House].

LEEDS, YORKS. (W.R.), Nos. 5, 6 and 7 PARK PLACE, for John Arthington, 1777–8 [Owston Letters, 20 Aug. 1787; Leeds City Archives, Acc. 3249, *ex inf.* Mr. A. Taylor].

THORPE HALL, RUDSTON, YORKS. (E.R.), added wings (one containing gallery) for Godfrey Bosville, 1778–9 [Hull University Library, DDBM/32/7, *ex inf.* Dr. David Neave].

DONCASTER, YORKS. (W.R.), HALLCROSS HOUSE, altered for Bryan Cooke, *c.*1780; dem. [Sheffield Archives, Baxter Papers 65161, *ex inf.* Mr. A. Taylor].

attributed: DONCASTER, YORKS. (W.R.), ST. SEPULCHRE GATE, house for J. J. Jarratt, 1781–2; dem. [stylistic attribution by Mr. A. Taylor, supported by drawing by Lindley of Roman altar found in digging the foundations, published in *Gent's Mag.* 1781, 361].

FERHAM HOUSE, ROTHERHAM, for Jonathan Walker, 1783 [Owston letters, 16 June 1785].

NEWHILL HALL, WATH-ON-DEARNE, YORKS. (W.R.), for John Payne, 1784–5; dem. [Owston letters, 16 June 1785].

DONCASTER, YORKS. (W.R.), THE VICARAGE, enlarged for the Revd. George Hay Drummond, 1785; dem. [Owston letters, 21 July 1785; plan and elevation in Yorkshire Archaeological Soc.'s Library, MS. 387].

BECCA HALL, YORKS. (W.R.), for William Markham, *c.*1785 [signed elevation in Hailstone Collection, York Minster Library].

DENISON HALL, LITTLE WOODHOUSE, LEEDS, YORKS. (W.R.), for John Denison, 1786–8 [A. Taylor in *Yorks. Archl. Jnl.* 63, 1991, 220–1] (R. Hewlings, 'Denison Hall', *ibid.* 61, 1989).

OSSINGTON HALL, NOTTS., alterations and additions for John Denison, 1788–90 and 1805–6; dem. 1963 [H. A. Johnson, 'The Architecture of Ossington Hall', *Trans. Thoroton Soc.* 84, 1980].

DARFIELD NEW HALL, YORKS. (W.R.), remodelled for William Bosville, 1787; largely dem. [Owston letters, 12 Aug. 1787; plan at Bretton Hall, BEA/C2/MP0 17/2, *ex inf.* Mr. A. Taylor].

WISETON HALL, NOTTS., new wing for Jonathan Aclom or Acklom, *c.*1787; dem. 1960 [Owston letters, 15 Sept. 1787].

?POTTERTON HALL, YORKS, (W.R.), new wing for Thomas Wilkinson (brother of John Denison, formerly Wilkinson), *c.*1787–8 [*Yorks. Archl. Jnl.* 61, 1989, 174].

STORTHES HALL, nr. KIRKBURTON, YORKS. (W.R.), for Horsfall/Bill family, 1787–90 [accounts among Goodchild Loan MSS in Wakefield Archives].

WATH-ON-DEARNE VICARAGE, YORKS. (W.R.), with Charles Watson, 1793; dem. 1910 [Borthwick Institute, York, MGA 1793/1].

GROVE HALL, NOTTS., lodges for Anthony H. Eyre, 1794 [H. A. Johnson & A. Cox, 'The Architecture of Grove Hall', *Trans. Thoroton Soc.* 89, 1985, 83].

OWSTON HALL, YORKS. (W.R.), for Bryan Cooke, 1794–5 [G. A. Usher, *Gwysaney and Owston*, 1964, 191; Owston letters, *passim*]. Lindley had previously altered the old house for Cooke.

GRANGE HALL (THUNDERCLIFFE GRANGE), nr. ECCLESFIELD, YORKS. (W.R.), work for 4th Earl of Effingham, 1794–5 [Owston letters, 6 Aug. 1796).

OGSTON HALL, DERBYSHIRE, proposed alterations for William Turbutt, 1795, rejected with possible minor exceptions [G. Turbutt, *History of Ogston*, Ogston 1975, 86–7].

DONCASTER, YORKS. (W.R.), several houses, including Nos. 19, 20 and 21 SOUTH PARADE (PILLAR HOUSE), for himself, 1797 [Sheffield Archives, Baxter papers, 61926, *ex inf.* Mr. A. Taylor].

STANTON HALL, STANTON-IN-THE-PEAK, DERBYSHIRE, enlarged on S. side for Bache Thornhill, 1799 [family papers, *ex inf.* Mrs. Thornhill].

attributed: OSBERTON HALL, NOTTS., THE STABLES, for F. F. Foljambe, *c.*1800 [H. A. Johnson, 'Osberton Hall', *Trans. Thoroton Soc.* 65, 1983].

BRETTON HALL, YORKS. (W.R.), office wing for Mrs. Beaumont, *c.*1800 [Allendale papers at Bretton, BEA/C2/B40/5, 160, etc., *ex inf.* Mr. Angus Taylor].

CAMPSMOUNT, CAMPSALL, YORKS. (W.R.), minor alterations for George Cooke Yarborough, 1802; dem. 1940 [T. Connor, 'The Building of Campsmount', *Yorks. Archl. Jnl.* xlvii, 1975, 129].

CANTLEY HALL, YORKS. (W.R.), remodelled for J. W. Childers, 1802; altered 1930 [drawing in Hailstone Collection, York Minster Library].

PARLINGTON HALL, YORKS. (W.R.), circular Gothic cattle-shed for Sir Thomas Gascoigne, Bart., 1802 [T. F. Friedman in *Leeds Arts Galendar* 66, 1970, 24, n. 24].

ROSSINGTON RECTORY, YORKS. (W.R.), for the Corporation of Doncaster, 1804 [*Records of the Borough of Doncaster* iv, 1902, 268–9].

CANTLEY VICARAGE, YORKS. (W.R.), with J. Woodhead, rebuilt 1812 [Borthwick Institute, York, MGA 1812/1].

SERLBY HALL, NOTTS., with J. Woodhead remodelled house for 5th Viscount Galway, 1812 [Arthur Oswald in *C. Life*, 26 March, 2 and 9 April 1959; basement plan with proposed alterations by Lindley & Woodhead dated 1810 in Nottingham University Library, Galway papers 12788].

LISTER, SAMUEL, was a master mason of Bramley, nr. Leeds. In 1795 the County of Derby advertised for designs and estimates for rebuilding SWARKESTON BRIDGE near Derby. Lister's plan and estimate were accepted, and the existing five-arch bridge was built by him in 1795–7 [Derbyshire Record Office, Quarter Sessions Order Book and draft contract]. In a letter dated 25 December 1795 Lister says that he has four brothers who are all masons, and the John Lister of Rotherham to whose designs the nave of WICKERSLEY CHURCH, YORKS. (W.R.), was rebuilt in 1835 [I.C.B.S.] was no doubt a relation.

LITCHFIELD, WILLIAM, a mason by trade, was a builder-architect at Daventry in Northamptonshire during the first half of the nineteenth century. In about 1820 he was responsible for alterations to EVERDON CHURCH, NORTHANTS. [I.C.B.S.], and in 1829 he made unexecuted designs for alterations to CANONS ASHBY HOUSE, NORTHANTS. in the Tudor Gothic style [Northants. C.R.O., Dryden (Canons Ashby), 420].

LLOYD, JOHN (*c.*1793–1867), practised in Caernarvon, where he altered ST. MARY'S CHURCH in 1828 [I.C.B.S. plan at Society of Antiquaries] and designed the WESLEYAN CHAPEL, 1829 [Leigh's *Guide to Wales*, 3rd. ed. 1835, 99], WILLIAMS & CO'S BANK, BANK QUAY, 1830 [R. Chambers Jones, *Arian, the Story of Banking in Wales*, Swansea 1978, 78], and the MARKET HALL, 1831–2, which bears his signature. He also rebuilt BRYNGWRAN CHURCH, ANGLESEY, in 1840–2 [I.C.B.S.] and designed bridges at PONT NEWYDD (R. Gwyrfai), 1840, and PONT BEBLIG (R. Seiont), 1844, both in Caernarvonshire [E. Jervoise, *Ancient Bridges of Wales and Western England*, 1936, 48–9]. Jones died at Twthill, Caernarvon, on 24 October 1867 [Principal Probate Registry, Calendar of Probates].

LLOYD, JOHN, practised in Mold, Flintshire. He designed CHRIST CHURCH, PONTBLYDDYN, FLINTSHIRE, 1836, reconstructed 1865 [D. R. Thomas, *History of the Diocese of St. Asaph*, 1870, 597]; ST. MARK'S, CONNAH'S QUAY, nr. NORTHOP, FLINTSHIRE, 1836–7 [I.C.B.S.]; ST. CATHERINE'S, OLD COLWYN, DENBIGHSHIRE, 1837–8 [I.C.B.S.]; HOLY TRINITY, GWERNAFIELD, FLINTSHIRE, 1838, rebuilt 1870 [drawings in R.I.B.A. Coll.]; ST. MARY, BRYMBO, DENBIGHSHIRE, 1838, dem. *c.*1870 [Port, 172–3]; EMMANUEL CHURCH, BISTRE (BUCKLEY), FLINTSHIRE, 1841–2, remodelled 1881 [Port, 172–3]; and CHRIST CHURCH, LLANFYNYDD, FLINTSHIRE, 1842–3, altered 1868 [Thomas, *op. cit.*, 597]. These were mostly cheap churches of poor design and (as proved to be the case at Brymbo, Gwernafield and Pontblyddyn) bad construction as well. Thomas states that the one at Bistre was copied from Casterton Church in Westmorland, a model illustrated by its builder, the Revd. W. Carus Wilson, in *Helps to the Building of Churches, Parsonage Houses and Schools* (*c.*1838). Lloyd also enlarged NERQUIS CHURCH, FLINTS., in 1847–8 [I.C.B.S.].

LLOYD, LEONARD WILD (*c.*1802–1868), was a pupil of William Brooks. He exhibited at the Royal Academy from 1821 to 1830, at the Norwich Society of Artists in 1823 and at the Society of British Artists in 1825. He practised in London, dying at 29 Gilbert Street, Grosvenor Square, on 10 January 1868 [Principal Probate Registry, Calendar of Probates]. G. T. Bower, J. M. Clark and H. B. Parry were his pupils.

Lloyd designed a MASONIC LODGE at PETERSFIELD, HANTS., 1826 [exhibited at R.A.]; the Greek Revival ASYLUM FOR FEMALE ORPHANS, LAMBETH, 1827, dem. 1866 [exhibited at R.A. 1827] (J. Elmes, *Metropolitan Improvements*, 1831, 170 and plate); three villas near Richmond Bridge for George Topham, 1828, of which one survives as BUTE LODGE [exhibited at R.A.]; and TWICKENHAM PARK, MIDDLESEX, for Joseph Todd, 1828, dem. 1929 [exhibited at R.A.]. His designs for Butterton Hall, Staffs., exhibited as 'about to be built' in 1830, were not in fact carried out.

LOAT, SAMUEL (*c.*1802–1876), was the son of a London builder. He was admitted to the Royal Academy Schools in 1823 at the age of 21. In 1825 he was awarded a premium by the Society of Arts and a Silver Medal by the Royal Academy, and in 1827 he gained the Academy's Gold Medal. In the following year he was given a Travelling Scholarship, and in 1832 he exhibited a 'Section of the Corsini Chapel in the church of S. Giovanni in Laterano, Rome'. He subsequently emigrated to Canada, dying at Kingston, Ontario, on 12 October 1876 [Principal Probate Registry, Calendar of Probates]. His only recorded work in England is a tablet in East Retford

Church, Notts., to the memory of Beaumont Marshall (d. 1826), which bears the signature 'S. Loat Archt. London'.

LOBAN, JOHN, was a builder-architect at Stornoway in the Western Isles of Scotland. In 1794 he built ST. COLUMBA'S (OLD PARISH) CHURCH, STORNOWAY, remodelled 1884–5 [S.R.O., GD 46/17/3]. He also built manses at CUITHIR (BARRA) (now CUITHIR HOUSE), 1814–16 and SCARISTA (HARRIS), 1825–6 [S.R.O., CH/2/361/1, pp. 426–7, 2, p. 51].

LOCHNER, WILLIAM CONRAD (*c.*1780–1861), was a pupil of James Lewis. He was admitted to the Royal Academy Schools in 1800 at the age of 20. He won the Silver Medal in 1800 and the Gold Medal in 1805. He exhibited at the Academy from 1798 onwards. In 1810 he obtained the first premium in the competition for the new Bethlehem Hospital, but his design was not carried out (see p. 615). He rebuilt the south aisle of ENFIELD PARISH CHURCH in 1824 [*V.C.H. Middlesex* v, 247], and designed the churches of ST. JAMES, ENFIELD HIGHWAY, MIDDLESEX, 1829–31 [Port, 156–7], and ST. PETER, DE BEAUVOIR TOWN, HACKNEY, 1840–1 [W. Robinson, *History of Hackney* i, 1842, 180], both in the thin, starved Gothic of the period. He may also have designed the houses in DE BEAUVOIR SQUARE, HACKNEY, for the De Beauvoir Estate records in the G.L. Record Office show that he was the lessee of Nos. 1 and 2. Lochner, who was a Fellow of the R.I.B.A., died at Haxted, nr. Edenbridge in Kent, in September 1861 [Pricipal Probate Registry, Calendar of Probates]. He had been Surveyor to the Royal Exchange Assurance Company.

LOCK, THOMAS, was a carpenter by trade and a member of the Fishmongers' Company. As a master carpenter he was employed by Wren in rebuilding the London City churches of St. Magnus Martyr, St. Mary at Hill and St. Mildred, Poultry, and by Sir Roger Pratt at Horseheath Hall, Cambs., in 1665. He was also the master carpenter for the rebuilding of FISHMONGERS' HALL in 1667–72 under Edward Jerman, and when Jerman died in 1668 Lock took his place as the surveyor in charge, for there is a payment to him in 1672 for surveying and drawing draughts for the Hall. He was evidently the 'Mr. Locke' who in April 1668 similarly succeeded Jerman as surveyor of the new APOTHECARIES' HALL, completed in 1670. [*Wren Soc.* xx, 127; *The Architecture of Sir Roger Pratt*, ed. R. T. Gunther, 1928, 118, 129; Priscilla Metcalf, *The Halls of the Fishmongers' Company*, 1977; Arthur Oswald, 'The Hall of the Worshipful Company of Apothecaries', *C. Life*, 10 Oct. 1947; Guildhall Library, Minutes of the Apothecaries' Company, MS. 8201, f. 109.]

LOGAN, DAVID, practised in Montrose, where in 1791 he designed THE PARISH CHURCH [J. G. Low, *Memorials of the Parish Church of Montrose*, Montrose 1891, 138, 142]. His design for a steeple, dated 1811, is preserved among the burgh records: it was not carried out, the existing Gothic steeple being erected to the designs of J. Gillespie Graham in 1834. Logan's most distinguished work is the MONTROSE ACADEMY, 1815, with a Greek Ionic façade of some originality and much charm [drawings at the Academy]. At FORFAR ACADEMY in 1815 he used the same formula of an engaged order (here Greek Doric) recessed between slightly projecting wings [contracts advertised in *Dundee Advertiser*, 28 April 1815]. He also designed the TOWN HALL (now SHERIFF COURT), ARBROATH, ANGUS, 1808, altered 1844 [G. Hay, *History of Arbroath*, 1876, 365]. A set of drawings for farm buildings signed 'David Logan' is in the Yale Center for British Art.

Other members of the Logan family were civil engineers. David Logan (d. *c.*1839) and his father Peter Logan were both concerned in the building of Robert Stevenson's Bell Rock Lighthouse in 1807–10, the former as clerk of works at the yard in Arbroath where the stone was prepared, the latter as foreman builder at the lighthouse itself [Robert Stevenson, *Account of the Bell Rock Lighthouse*, 1824]. David became resident engineer at Dundee Harbour under Telford (1816–20), and was subsequently responsible for the construction of harbours at Donaghadee and Ardglass in Northern Ireland under Sir John Rennie [E. R. R. Green, *Industrial Archaeology of County Down*, 1963, 76, 79]. In 1834 he was appointed engineer to the River Clyde Trustees. His death was reported in *Minutes of Proceedings of the Institution of Civil Engineers* for 1840 (i, 12). At Dundee he had been succeeded by his cousin Peter Logan, who subsequently worked at St. Catherine's Dock in London under Telford. It seems likely that David Logan of Montrose and Peter Logan the foreman were brothers, and that David Logan, junior, was therefore the architect's nephew. [Information from Prof. A. W. Skempton.]

LONG, FREDERICK, of Liverpool, exhibited two designs at the Royal Academy in 1834 in conjunction with R. J. Barrow: 'an elevation for a cathedral' and a design for Fishmongers' Hall, London. He subsequently left Liverpool and designed the Greek Revival ROYAL INSTITUTION OF SOUTH WALES at SWANSEA, 1838–40 [*Companion to the Almanac*, 1840, 241–2].

LOUDON, JOHN CLAUDIUS (1783–1843), was the eldest son of a Scottish farmer at Gogar, nr. Edinburgh. As a child he showed a fondness for gardening, and after a schooling in Edinburgh he was apprenticed to a nurseryman and landscape-gardener at Easter Dalry. In 1803 he left Scotland for London, where he began a successful practice as a landscape-pardener. The Duchess of Brunswick employed him at Brunswick House, Blackheath, and Lord Mansfield engaged him to improve the grounds at Scone Palace in Perthshire. In 1804 he exhibited three drawings at the Royal Academy and published his first book, entitled *Observations on the Formation and Management of Useful and Ornamental Plantations, on the Theory and Practice of Landscape Gardening and on Gaining and Embanking Land from Rivers or the Sea.* For the rest of his life he was to combine his practice as a landscape-gardener with incessant literary activity. In 1806 he published a two-volume *Treatise on forming, improving and managing Country Residences*, in 1812 *Observations on laying out Farms in the Scotch Style, adapted to England*, and *Hints on the Formation of Gardens and Pleasure Grounds*, in 1822 an *Encyclopaedia of Gardening*, in 1825 an *Encyclopaedia of Agriculture*, in 1829 an *Encyclopaedia of Plants*, in 1833 an *Encyclopaedia of Cottage, Farm and Villa Architecture and Furniture*, in 1836 *The Suburban Gardener and Villa Companion*, in 1838 an encyclopaedia of British trees and shrubs entitled *Arboretum et Fruticetum Britannicum*, and in 1843 a work *On the Laying Out, Planting and Management of Cemeteries*. These were merely his principal publications. In addition he conducted three periodicals: *The Gardener's Magazine* (1826–42), *The Magazine of Natural History* (1829–36) and *The Architectural Magazine* (5 Vols., 1834–8), all replete with information assembled by their indefatigable editor, who frequently worked all night in order to get his copy to the printer in time.

In 1809 Loudon rented a farm at Great Tew in Oxfordshire, where he took pupils in agriculture, and by 1812 he had made a profit of £15,000. He then gave up the farm and went on a tour of northern Europe , studying foreign methods of farming and gardening. On his return he found that his investments had failed, and further financial difficulties followed the publication of the costly eight-volume *Arboretum* in 1838. His health had been poor since an attack of rheumatic fever in 1806, and he was disabled both by a stiff leg and, more seriously, by the amputation of his right arm in 1825. Nevertheless, with the help of his wife Jane, whom he married in 1830, he remained active as a writer, botanist and landscape-gardener up to the time of his death in December 1843.

As a landscape-gardener Loudon was a follower of Payne Knight and Uvedale Price, whose belief in irregularity and picturesque grouping he shared. Though at first critical of Repton, he eventually recognized that Repton's ideas combined 'all that was excellent in the former schools [of landscape gardening]', and in 1840 he gave fresh currency to Repton's theories by reprinting all his works on the subject in one volume. In the introduction he recognized the emergence of a new approach to landscape-gardening which he called 'the Gardenesque'. The object of the Gardenesque was to combine the picturesque grouping of the past with the display of individual trees and shrubs for their botanical interest. In applying these principles to the smaller scale of the suburban villa and the public park, Loudon helped to establish the characteristics of the Victorian garden. The arboretum perfectly embodied his ideas, and his Derby Arboretum (1839–41) was a pioneer example of its kind. Ornamental buildings figured prominently in such layouts, and it was no doubt as a picturesque adjunct to gardening that Loudon first approached architecture. It would, however, have been uncharacteristic of him not to make himself the master of any subject that he chose to take up, and in 1831 he wrote that 'though we are not a practising architect, yet we pretend to as thorough a knowledge of the principles of architecture, as of those of landscape-gardening' (*Gardener's Magazine* vii, 404–5). The result was *The Encyclopaedia of Cottage, Farm and Villa Architecture* (1833, 2nd ed. by Mrs. Loudon 1846) and *The Architectural Magazine.* Both had the same object – 'to diffuse among general readers a taste for architectural beauties and comforts, and to improve the dwellings of the great mass of Society in all countries'. Unlike most previous architectural publications (including the numerous slim volumes offering elegant designs for picturesque cottages) the *Encyclopaedia* and the *Magazine* were addressed to the middle classes rather than to the aristocracy. Comfort and convenience were studied in detail and it is the farmhouse and the suburban villa rather than the country seat whose siting, planning, construction and embellishment form the main theme of the *Encyclopaedia.* In fulfilling his task Loudon had the help of a number of contributors, who provided him with plans, elevations and descriptions of appropriate buildings. One of his most faithful assistants was Edward Buckton Lamb, a young architect then in his twenties upon whom he relied particularly for Gothic designs. At the end of the *Encyclopaedia* Loudon summarized his architectural theory in terms largely derived from the tradition of Scottish rationalist philosophy as set out in Alison's *Essays on the Nature and Principles of Taste* (1790). Guided by Alison, Loudon rejected the niceties of the orders for fitness of purpose and the appropriate expression of function. The latter did not necessarily mean functionalism in the modern sense. But it did mean that architectural forms – whether Gothic or classical – had to be chosen because they were actually or symbolically expressive of the building's function. Having discovered 'the beauty of truth' (*Encyclopaedia*, 1846 ed., 1113), Loudon was on the same road as Pugin and the ecclesiologists, though stylistically he accepted a degree of eclecticism which to them was anathema. With its numerous illustrations Loudon's *Encyclopaedia* therefore has an important place in the formation of Victorian architectural taste, especially at the suburban level with which loftier theorists such as Ruskin or Pugin scarcely condescended to concern themselves.

Although he did not regard himself as a practising architect, there is evidence that in his early days as a landscape-gardener Loudon did occasionally act in that capacity. In 1804 he exhibited at the Royal Academy an 'Elevation of a house proposed to be built at Balliad in Perthshire for P. Campbell, Esq.', and in 1806 he altered the exterior of BARNBARROW (BARNBARROCH), WIGTOWNSHIRE (burned 1942), whose grounds he landscaped for R. V. Agnew (see original drawings by Loudon in the Yale Center for British Art and his *Treatise on forming . . . Country Residences*, pls. xiii-xiv and one opposite p. 613). His principal architectural work appears to have been GARTH, nr. WELSHPOOL, MONTGOMERYSHIRE (dem. 1947), which he designed for R. Mytton in 1809–10. This crudely detailed Gothic house is described and illustrated in his *Observations on laying out Farms in the Scotch Style, adapted to England*, 1812. In the same work he states that 'extensive improvements to house and grounds are now executing from my designs' at HOPE END, nr. LEDBURY, HEREFS., for E. M. Barrett. Hope End (mostly demolished 1873) was a most eccentric building coarsely designed in a pseudo-Moorish Style, presumably at the owner's behest, but certain resemblances to Garth confirm Loudon's responsibility for the architecture (cf. Sandra Blutman in *C. Life*, 19 Sept. 1968). Later in life Loudon designed Nos. 3 and 5 PORCHESTER TERRACE, LONDON, a 'double detached villa' which he built in 1823–4, occupying No. 3 himself, and was responsible for the singular monument, consisting of a sarcophagus projecting from an obelisk, which he erected in PINNER CHURCHYARD, MIDDLESEX, to the memory of his parents.

[Jane Loudon, 'A Short Account of the life and Writings of John Claudius Loudon', in *Self-Instruction for Young Gardeners*, 1844; *D.N.B.*; Geoffrey Taylor, *Some Nineteenth Century Gardeners*, 1951, chap. 2; John Gloag, *Mr. Loudon's England*, 1970; G. L. Hersey, 'J. C. Loudon and Architectural Asso–ciationism', *Arch. Rev.* Aug. 1968; L. Fricker, 'John Claudius Loudon: the Plane Truth', in *Furor Hortensis: Essays on the History of the English Landscape Garden in Memory of H. F. Clark*, ed. P. Willis, Edinburgh 1974; *John Claudius Loudon and the Early Nineteenth Century in Great Britain*, ed. Elisabeth Macdougall, Dumbarton Oaks 1980; Melanie L. Simo, *Loudon and the Landscape: from Country Seat to Metropolis*, Yale 1989. All Loudon's papers were destroyed during the Second World War.]

LOVELL, WILLIAM, practised as a surveyor in Pentonville. In 1828 he designed the CLERKENWELL PAROCHIAL SUNDAY SCHOOL, altered by W. P. Griffith in 1858 [W. J. Pinks, *History of Clerkenwell*, 1881, 178]. He appears to have been the father of a District Sureyor named William Lovell who died in 1874.

LOVEN, or **LOVIN,** JOHN (–1679), was a master mason of Peterborough. In February 1660/1 he contracted to build THORNEY ABBEY HOUSE, CAMBS., for the 5th Earl of Bedford 'according to the draught and order of works designed for the same and now delivered in to the said Earl under the hand of the said John Lovin' [G. Scott Thompson, *Family Background*, 1949, 180–4]. The house, which has features recalling Thorpe Hall, is illustrated in *C. Life*, 27 Sept. 1919. Loven repaired the BISHOP'S PALACE at PETERBOROUGH after damage done during the Commonwealth, and in 1671 built the arcaded MARKET HOUSE there [W. T. Mellows, *History of Peterborough's Public Buildings*, 1934; B.L., Lansdowne MS. 1027, f. 200]. Loven's will, dated 11 May 1679, was proved at Peterborough on 7 June the same year [Northants. Record Office]. He left sons named Thomas and John.

LOWDER, JOHN (1781–1829), was a member of a banking family at Bath. He exhibited a design for the interior of a mausoleum at the Royal Academy in 1803. In January 1817 he was appointed Surveyor to the City of Bath at a salary of £100 p.a., but resigned in July 1823. He designed the BATH AND DISTRICT NATIONAL SCHOOL, 1816, dem. 1896, which was built on a circular plan, with wedge-shaped classrooms. He also designed the Gothic HOLY TRINITY CHURCH, JAMES STREET, BATH, 1819–22, dem. 1957, and the simple but elegant BISHOPSTONE RECTORY (now HOUSE), WILTS., for the Revd. Thomas Bromley, *c.*1816–20 [Salisbury Diocesan Records; C. Hussey in *C. Life*, 12 Nov. 1959]. His original designs for Holy Trinity, Bath, were in the Grecian style, but in deference to the wishes of the building committee he substituted the Gothic design which was carried out at a greatly increased cost. The ensuing difficulties are said to have hastened his death. H. E. Goodridge was his pupil. [W. Ison, *The Georgian Buildings of Bath*, 1948, 82, 101, 2nd ed. 1980, 67, 90; Bath City Archives.]

LUCY, EDWARD and JAMES, were carpenters and surveyors of Worcester. James Lucy was admitted a freeman of the city in 1809. In the *Worcester Journal* for 11 June 1816 he offered himself to the public as a builder who was prepared to act as a surveyor or architect. It appears that he also owned a verandah factory in Sidbury. In 1821 he was responsible for laying out a new street which became known as Carden Street [*Berrow's Worcester Jnl.* 24 May 1821]. For the Parliamentary Commissioners he designed the small Gothic chapel of ST. GEORGE at CLAINES, nr. WORCESTER, 1829–30, dem. 1894, which was completed by Lewis Belling after Lucy's bankruptcy (3 December 1829) and death [Port, 164–5; *Berrow's Worcester Jnl.*]. HALLOW CHURCH, WORCS., 1829–30, dem. 1867, was apparently designed by James Lucy but completed by Edward Lucy [*Berrow's Worcester Jnl.* 2 April 1829; I.C.B.S. information from Mr. D. Whitehead.]

LUGAR, ROBERT (*c.*1773–1855), was the son of Edward Lugar, a carpenter of Colchester. He may have had some early association with John Nash, for in 1796 the name of 'Mr. Lugar, Carmarthen', appears with that of 'John Nash, Esq. Carmarthen', in the list of subscribers to *Dynevor Castle with other Poems* by J. T. Hughes. From about 1799 he was practising independently in London, and exhibited regularly at the Royal Academy for the next twenty years. In 1812 he succeeded John Johnson as County Surveyor of Essex, but resigned four years later. He retired from practice some years before his death in Pembroke Square, Kensington, on 23 June 1855, at the age of 82 [*A.P.S.D.*]. Archibald Simpson of Aberdeen was his pupil.

Lugar was a skilful practitioner of the picturesque, exploiting the fashion for *cottages ornés* and castellated Gothic mansions in the manner of John Nash. His two Dunbartonshire castles were among the first to introduce the picturesque formula into Scotland (where the symmetrical Adam castle style was still in vogue), and at Shoreham in Kent he designed an early example of an Italianate villa in 1806. Though effective in mass, his Gothic Castles are apt to be coarsely detailed.

Lugar published *Architectural Sketches for Cottages, Rural Dwellings, and Villas*, 1805, dedicated to George Ward, reprinted 1815 and 1823; *The Country Gentleman's Architect; Designs for Farm Houses and Yards*, 1807; *Plans and Views of Buildings executed in England and Scotland in the Castellated and Other Styles*, 1811, 2nd ed. 1823; and *Villa Architecture, a Collection of Views, with Plans, of Buildings executed in England, Scotland, etc.*, 1828, with a dedication to William Crawshay. In 1835 he entered a design for the new Houses of Parliament jointly with J. Burrell (*q.v.*). It was in the Gothic style, based on 'the best examples of its date' in England and on the Continent, 'and so disposed as to unite (in connection with Westminster Hall, the Abbey towers, &c.) in forming a dignified and characteristic composition' [*Catalogue of the Designs for the New Houses of Parliament*, 1836, 12–13].

BALLOCH (now ARDOCH) CASTLE, DUNBARTONSHIRE, additions for John Buchanan, 1809, castellated [*Plans and Views*, 1823, pls. 10–13; Neale, *seats* vi, 1823; exhib. at R.A. 1809] (J. Irving, *Book of Dumbartonshire* iii, 1879, pl. vii).

BETTESHANGER HOUSE, KENT, for F. E. Morrice, before 1828, Tudor style; rebuilt by George Devey 1856 onwards [*Villa Architecture*, 1828, pls. 17–19].

BOTURICH CASTLE, DUNBARTONSHIRE, repaired for John Buchanan, *c.*1830; burnt [J. B. Burke, *Visitations of Seats* ii, 1853, 249].

BRANDON COTTAGE or LODGE (now Brandon Hall Hotel), nr. WOLSTON, WARWICKS., for 19th Lord Grey de Ruthyn (d. 1810) [*Plans and Views*, 1823, pls. 14–16].

CHEPSTOW, MONMOUTHSHIRE, WYELANDS ESTATE, advertised in 1846 as 'lately erected from the designs of Lugar' [*Monmouthshire Merlin*, 18 July 1846].

attributed: COLCHESTER, ESSEX, THE TURRETS, LEXDEN ROAD, for Francis Smythies, 1818,

Gothic [stylistic attribution supported by the fact that Lugar became a freeman of Colchester during Smythies' mayoralty in 1812].

CROSBY HALL, LANCS., bailiff's cottage for William Blundell, before 1828 [*Villa Architecture*, 1828, pl. 4].

CULZEAN CASTLE, AYRSHIRE, cottage and pheasantry for 12th Earl of Cassilis, before 1823 [*Plans and Views*, 1823, pl. 31; cf. design for a lodge attributable to Lugar in portfolio at Culzean Castle, no. 39].

CYFARTHFA CASTLE, GLAMORGANSHIRE, for William Crawshay, 1825; since enlarged, castellated [*Villa Architecture*, 1828, pls. 41–2] (T. Nicholas, *Annals of the County Families of Wales* i, 1875, 474].

DEDHAM, ESSEX, a cottage 'to be built', exhibited at the R.A. 1803.

DENHAM MOUNT, DENHAM, BUCKS., for Nathaniel Snell, before 1823 [*Plans and Views*, pls. 24–5].

DUDDESTONE HOUSE, WARWICKS., designs, perhaps unexecuted, for a fishing lodge, etc., for Samuel Galton, 1818–19 [Warwickshire Record Office, CR 1198/85, 92].

EASTWOOD, CO. TIPPERARY, IRELAND, a cottage 'to be built', exhibited at the R.A. 1802.

FINGRINGHOE BRIDGE, ESSEX, 1814; a wooden bridge dem. 1923 [G. M. Burton, 'Fingringhoe Bridge', *Essex Arch. Soc. Trans.*, N.S. xx, 1933].

GLANUSK PARK, BRECONSHIRE, for Joseph Bailey, 1825–35, Elizabethan style; dem. 1952 [MS. copy of Burke's *Visitation of Seats*, *ex inf.* Mr. Peter Reid] (J. B. Burke, *Visitations of Seats* i, 1852, 209–11, plates).

GLENLEE, nr. NEW GALLOWAY, KIRKCUDBRIGHTSHIRE, enlarged for Lady Ashburton, 1823 [*Villa Architecture*, 1828, pls. 30–1].

GLIFFAES, BRECONSHIRE, house 'to be built' for William West, exhibited at R.A. 1841.

GOLD HILL (now DUNSTALL PRIORY), SHOREHAM, KENT, 1806, Italianate [exhib. at R.A. 1806].

GREENMEADOW, TONGWYNLAIS, nr. CARDIFF, GLAMORGANSHIRE, remodelled in Gothic style for Wyndham Lewis, *c.*1825; remodelled *c.*1865; dem. 1938/9 [N.L.W., Vivian papers, vol. 1, letters A 207, 217, *ex inf.* Mr. Thomas Lloyd].

HENSOL, nr. CASTLE DOUGLAS, KIRKCUDBRIGHTSHIRE, for John Cunningham, *c.*1825 [*Villa Architecture*, 1828, pls. 26–9].

HOLDERS HILL COTTAGE, nr. HENDON, MIDDLESEX, alterations and additions for William McInerheny, before 1823; dem. [*Plans and Views*, 1823, pls. 26–7].

HORSLEY PLACE (TOWERS), SURREY, lodge for William Currie, before 1828 [*Villa Architecture*, 1828, pl. 2].

KIRBY HALL, OUSEBURN, YORKS. (W.R.), lodge for R. J. Thompson, *c.*1814 [*Villa Architecture*, 1828, pl. 6].

LEE HALL, GATEACRE, LANCS., lodge for John Okill, before 1828 [*Villa Architecture*, 1828, pl. 1].

MAESLWCH CASTLE, RADNORSHIRE, for Walter Wilkins, 1828–39, castellated; partly dem. *c.*1965 [exhib. at R.A. 1841] (T. Nicholas, *Annals of the County Families of Wales* ii, 1875, 913).

MARKYATE CELL, HERTS., remodelled for D. G. Adey, 1825–6, Elizabethan style [*Villa Architecture*, 1828, pls. 39–40].

NEWLAITHES HALL, HORSFORTH, YORKS. (W.R.), for Charles Greenwood, before 1828, Tudor Gothic [*Villa Architecture*, 1828, pls. 22–3].

OXNEY PARK, KENT, enlarged for John May, 1816, Gothic; now in ruins [*Villa Architecture*, 1828, pls. 20–1] (Neale, *Seats*, 2nd ser. ii, 1825).

PUCKASTER COTTAGE, nr. NITON, ISLE OF WIGHT, for James Vine, probably *c.*1815 [*Villa Architecture*, 1828, pls. 11–12].

THE ROOKERY, WOODFORD, ESSEX, picturesque cottages for John Hanson, before 1823 [*Plans and Views*, 1823, pl. 32].

ROSE HILL COTTAGE, WARGRAVE, BERKS., for J. F. Nicholas [signed drawing in Bodleian Library, MS. Top. Oxon. b. 91, f. 193, no. 298].

THE RYES LODGE, LITTLE HENNY, ESSEX, for N. Barnardiston, 1809 [*Plans and Views*, 1823, pls. 7–9; exhib. at R.A. 1809].

ST. MARGARET'S, ISLEWORTH, MIDDLESEX, lodge for 12th Earl of Cassilis, before 1828 [Villa *Architecture*, 1828, pl. 3; see above under Culzean Castle].

STANFORD (?STAMFORD) HILL, house 'to be built' for Mr. Bayley, exhibited at the R.A. 1806.

SWINTON PARK, YORKS. (N.R.), remodelled in castellated style for William Danby, 1821–4; tower heightened 1889 [*Villa Architecture*, 1828, pls. 24–5; John Cornforth in *C. Life*, 7, 14, 21 April 1966].

TULLICHEWAN CASTLE, DUNBARTONSHIRE, for John Stirling, 1808, castellated; dem. 1954 [*Plans and Views*, 1823, pls. 1–6; exhib. at R.A. 1808; drawing in R.I.B.A. Coll.] (J. Irving, *Book of Dumbartonshire* iii, 1879, pl. xx).

WARLEY HALL, WORCS., for Hubert Galton, *c.*1820, Gothic; dem. *c.*1956 [*Villa Architecture*, 1828, pls. 32–5].

WEDDINGTON HALL, WARWICKS., for Lionel Place, before 1823, castellated; dem. *c.*1928 [*Plans and Views*, 1823, pls. 28–30].

? THE WHITE HALL, WINESTEAD, YORKS. (E.R.),

for Col. Arthur Maister, 1814–15[1] [letter from Lugar dated 13 Sept. 1814 directing correspondence to be sent to him at 'Col. Maister's, Winestead', Essex C.R.O., Q/AB p 9] (*C. Life*, 11 Sept. 1980).

YAXHAM RECTORY, NORFOLK, for the Revd. J. Johnson, 1820–2, classical [*Villa Architecture*, 1828, pls. 13–14].

LUMBY, THOMAS and his son WILLIAM (–1804), were master carpenters at Lincoln. Thomas Lumby 'did a great deal of business in that line of building', but went bankrupt in 1775. He rebuilt the roof of the Chapter House of Lincoln Cathedral under the direction of James Essex, who told the Bishop in 1775 that 'I am well satisfied no one in Lincoln knows better the business of a Carpenter in general, and I much doubt if there is a man in the County of Lincoln who is so good a judge of the work that is wanting in the Cathedral.' William Lumby was brought up to his father's business, but succeeded William Jepson as clerk of the works to the cathedral in about 1775, and thereafter practised as an architect. He was closely associated with James Essex in the refitting of the cathedral in 1777–9, and several of his designs for Gothic screens intended to conceal the beams over the lateral gateways to the choir are in a volume of designs and estimates made by himself and Essex and now among the Dean and Chapter's records (A4, 15). According to an account of his work in the cathedral, preserved by E. J. Willson, he designed 'the ornaments upon the beams over the choir-side-gates', and 'the tabernacles opposite to the bishop's throne in the choir. The antient stained glass was removed into the transepts, and to the two eastern windows in the aisles of the presbytery under him. The iron rails before the altar were removed from the steps on which the table stands, and put across in a straight line by him.' When the cathedral was repaved, he made a plan of the old pavement, showing all the gravestones, which was engraved by Gough in his *British Topography*. The original drawing is in the Bodleian Library, Gough Maps 16, f. 10. He also drew the plan and elevation of the cathedral published in *Vetusta Monumenta* iii, 1791, pls. 10, 11.

E. J. Willson described William Lumby as being 'of a very ingenious turn of mind, mild and gentle'. He died at Greatford, nr. Stamford, on 18 August 1804, 'before the age of 50, after falling into a low and nervous state of health, which almost rendered him incapable of attending to business'.

As a secular architect William Lumby was competent but unremarkable. But his drawings for the interior of Lincoln Cathedral show that he was a pioneer Gothic Revivalist of the same sort as James Essex. The church at Doddington which Thomas Lumby reconstructed in 1770–5 is also notable for its Gothic detailing. It is natural to suppose that it was designed by the son, but if E. J. Willson was correct about his age at the time of his death this would hardly be feasible. The possibility that Essex himself helped cannot be excluded.

A design by William Lumby for a Palladian lodge on the Dashwood estate at Dunston, Lincolnshire, is preserved at West Wycombe Park.

[*Gent's Mag.* 1775, 47, 1804 (ii), 795, 983; E. J. Willson's MS. Lincolnshire Collections in the Library of the Society of Antiquaries of London, v, f. 71, vii, f. 99, xiii, f. 54, and Folder Q; Records of the Dean and Chapter of Lincoln, A4, 13 and 15; B. L., Add. MS. 6772, f. 281 (letter from T. Lumby to Essex).]

DODDINGTON HALL, LINCS., internal alterations for Sir John Hussey Delaval, Bart., carried out by Thomas Lumby in 1761–2. They included a new staircase and the refitting of the principal rooms [Bodleian, MS. Top. Lincs. c. 14, and R. E. G. Cole, *History of Doddington*, 1897, 149, where, however, the elder Lumby is confused with his son].

CAENBY HALL, LINCS., built by Thomas Lumby for Lawrence Monck, 1763–4; dem. [Northumberland C.R.O., Monck-Middleton papers, ZMI/B48/1: letters of 28 April and 27 Aug. 1763, *ex inf.* Mr. R. Hewlings].

BOSTON, LINCS., CORPORATION (now EXCHANGE) BUILDINGS, MARKET PLACE, designed by Thomas Lumby, 1770–2 [Boston Corporation Minutes vi, ff. 133, 135, 238 and Chamberlain's Accounts 1773–4, *ex inf.* Mr. R. Hewlings].

DODDINGTON CHURCH, LINCS., reconstructed by Thomas Lumby for Sir John Hussey Delaval, Bart., 1770–5, Gothic [building accounts in Bodleian, MSS. Top. Lincs. c. 23, 24, 25, 26, 29; letters from the steward at Doddington in Northumberland C.R.O., 2 DE 20/6/1–27].

REDBOURNE CHURCH, LINCS., partially rebuilt by 'Mr. Lumby' for the Revd. Robert

[1] If Lugar designed The White Hall, then he, rather than John Nash, may have been the 'eminent architect from London' who (according to a sale advertisement of the house in the *Hull Advertiser* of 19 May 1820) simultaneously designed WOODHALL, nr. SWINE, YORKS. (E.R.), for Col. Maister's brother H. W. Maister, in a style closely resembling Nash's Cronkhill.

Carter, 1772–4, Gothic; subsequently altered [Lincolnshire Record Office, Red. 3/1/4/6, 1772].

STAMFORD, LINCS., surveyor's work by Thomas Lumby for 9th Earl of Exeter in connection with building work on the Earl's estate in the town, and in 1781 at Burghley House, probably in connection with the Grand Staircase [Burghley archives, *ex inf.* Dr. E. R. Till].

LINCOLN, THE BLUE COAT SCHOOL, designed by William Lumby, 1784–5 [Society of Antiquaries, E. J. Willson's Collections v, f. 71].

LINCOLN, THE COUNTY GAOL, designed by William Lumby, 1786–8. According to E. J. Willson this was designed by John Carr of York, but the Grand Jury Minute Book shows that although Carr did make a design in 1774 nothing was done for over ten years. No reference was made to Carr's plan in 1785, when Messrs. Legg, Langwith and Lumby submitted designs and Lumby's were adopted [Lincolnshire Record Office, Q.S. Records 1785–88].

SOUTHWELL, NOTTS., THE RESIDENCE HOUSE, refronted by William Lumby, 1786 [M. Summers, *A Prospect of Southwell*, 1974, 67 and pl. xlvii].

LINCOLN, house opposite St. Mary's Church designed by William Lumby for Alderman Gibbeson [Society of Antiquaries, E. J. Willson's Collections, xiii, f. 54].

GRIMSBY, LINCS., WAREHOUSES for George Tennyson, before 1799 [E. Gillett, *History of Grimsby*, 1970, 165].

LUMLEY, JOHN (1654–1721), was the only son of John Lumley of Harlestone, Northants., where his family had been masons since the Middle Ages. In 1686 he was made free of the London Masons' Company as a 'Foreign Member', and in 1703 he became a freeman of Northampton gratis in repayment of a debt owed to him by the Corporation. He established a yard in Northampton and carried on business as a surveyor and master mason there until his death in November 1721. In his will he left half his marble and alabaster and all his working tools to his apprentice William Swan and the other half to the stone-carver Samuel Cox, whom he describes as 'my loving kinsman' [L. G. Horton-Smith, 'The Later Lumleys of Harlestone', *Trans. Northants. Natural History and Field Club* xxx, 1943, 103; Shelagh M. Lewis, 'The Coxes of Northamptonshire', *Northamptonshire Past and Present* i, 1953, 21–2].

In 1697 Lumley took the place of Henry Dormer (*q.v.*) as the surveyor employed by the 2nd Earl of Nottingham to supervise the building of his mansion at BURLEY-ON-THE-HILL, RUTLAND. The foundations had been laid in 1694, and the main features of the design had already been determined by the time Lumley took charge.[1] There are, however, several references to moulds, draughts, etc., made by Lumley, and some of the architectural details may have been determined by him. The house was structurally complete by 1700, but Lumley was still in correspondence with Lord Nottingham in connection with the stables as late as 1705 [H. J. Habakkuk, 'Daniel Finch, 2nd Earl of Nottingham: his House and Estate', in *Studies in Social History*, ed. J. H. Plumb, 1955; Pearl Finch, *Burley on the Hill*, 1901, 30, 64–5, 73, 110].

It was by Lord Nottingham's advice that his friend the 1st Lord Ashburnham employed Lumley as surveyor at GREAT PARK HOUSE, AMPTHILL, BEDS., in 1704–7. Hawksmoor had previously been consulted, but letter-books formerly at Ashburnham Park, Sussex, show that Lumley was making plans, elevations and estimates for rebuilding the house in the winter of 1704–5, and that he remained in control of the works for the next two years. In 1706–7 Lord Ashburnham was consulting William Winde about the decoration of the interior and the employment of 'Tissue the french iron worker', but Winde's name does not occur until the house was structurally complete, and it seems clear that Lumley was the principal architect of this typical house of the 1700s.

In 1719 Lumley was employed to 'draw the plan' for rebuilding the south range of the Front Court of EMMANUEL COLLEGE, CAMBRIDGE, and superintended the work until his death two years later [J.B.P., 'The College Buildings in the Eighteenth Century', *Emmanuel College Magazine* ix (2), 1898]. The principal benefactor of the work was the 6th Earl of Westmorland (after whom the new range was named 'The Westmorland Building') and as Lumley is described in the accounts as the Earl's 'overseer' at Apethorpe, it is evident that his employment at Cambridge was due to Westmorland's patronage. At APETHORPE, NORTHANTS., he may have been responsible for the orangery forming the south side of the second court, which was built in 1718 (cf. *V.C.H. Northants.* ii, 545). The Westmorland Building is a three-storied range somewhat clumsily dignified by a pair of giant Ionic pilasters and a swept-up balustrade.

Other references to Lumley show him surveying the house at AYNHO PARK, NORTHANTS., in 1698 (a date when no structural work was carried out) [account-book among Cartwright

[1] Above, p. 319, n. 1.

family papers in Northants. C.R.O.], helping in some unspecified capacity to build COTTESBROOKE HALL, NORTHANTS., to the designs of Francis Smith of Warwick from 1702 onwards [Sir John Langham's account-book in Northants. C.R.O., L(C) 2597], and examining the defective spire of GREENS NORTON CHURCH, NORTHANTS., in 1718 [Peterborough Diocesan Records].

LUSH, EDMUND (*c.*1722–1795), was Clerk of the Works of Salisbury Cathedral for nearly forty years prior to his retirement in 1792 [Cathedral archives, *ex inf.* Miss Suzanne Edwards]. He died at Salisbury on 7 January 1795 [*Gent's Mag.* 1795 (i), 168].

Drawings and documents at Longford Castle (Box 38) show that in 1778–9 Edmund and his son William were employed by the 2nd Earl of Radnor to convert the former HUNGERFORD CHAPEL in SALISBURY CATHEDRAL into a family pew, and that the new Gothic cornice and other details were designed by him. William Lush succeeded his father as a builder in Salisbury, but not as Clerk of Works to the Cathedral.

M

MABERLEY, WILLIAM (*c.*1798–), was admitted to the Royal Academy Schools in 1817 as an architectural student at the age of 19. Pigot's *Directory* shows that ten years later he was practising as an architect in Davies Street near Berkeley Square.

McBRIDE, JAMES (*c.*1785–1845), a carpenter by trade, practised as a builder-architect at Elgin. Designs by him for enlarging ALTYRE HOUSE, MORAYSHIRE, for Sir William Gordon Cumming, Bart., 1818, are in N.L.S. Dep. 175/61/file 2. In 1832–5 alterations and additions to BALNAGOWAN CASTLE, ROSS-SHIRE, including a new entrance-hall and portico, were made for Sir Charles Lockhart Ross, 'according to a Plan and Specifications made by James McBride, Elgin' [S.R.O., SC 34/23/4, p. 109]. McBride died on 7 October 1846, aged 60, and is commemorated by a tombstone in the churchyard of Elgin Cathedral.

McCANDLISH, WILLIAM (*c.*1779–1855), was a builder-architect of New Galloway in Kirkcudbrightshire. He designed Gothic churches in KIRKCUDBRIGHTSHIRE at KELLS, 1822 [inscription] and DALRY, 1830–2 [S.R.O., HR 377/1, 20 Dec. 1830] and in DUMFRIESSHIRE at GLENCAIRN, 1836 [S.R.O., HR 116/1], and was responsible for alterations to KENMURE CASTLE, KIRKCUDBRIGHTSHIRE, for the 7th Viscount Kenmure in 1841 [S.R.O., SC 16/64/10, p. 135]. At Dalry and Glencairn his rather elementary Gothic architecture is enlivened by a dramatic arch in the end wall of the transept. McCandlish's death on 12 December 1855 at the age of 76 is recorded on a large tombstone in Kells churchyard.

McCRACKEN, JOHN, a mason in Dumfries, designed very simple churches at KIRKPATRICK JUXTA, 1798–1800 [S.R.O., HR 19/1, 1 May 1799] and KIRKMICHAEL, 1813–15 [S.R.O., CH 2/247/14, p. 107] and a manse at CUMMERTREES, 1802–3 [S.R.O., CH 2/13/4, pp. 52–3, 113], all in DUMFRIESSHIRE; also ST. ANDREW'S R.C. CHURCH, DUMFRIES, 1814; largely destroyed by fire 1961 [W. Dillon, *The Story of St. Andrew's*, 1964, 8]. [Information from Mr. J. Gifford, to whom all references are due.]

MACDONNELL, JOHN (1770–), son of J. MacDonnell, of Mount Street, Berkeley Square, carpenter, was a pupil of Sir John Soane from 1786 to 1791, and afterwards of Thomas Hardwick from 1792 to 1794. He entered the Royal Academy Schools in 1793, and exhibited at the Academy from 1788 to 1804. His exhibited designs included 'a theatre intended to be built at Lewes, Sussex' (1789) and a 'Design for a government house for the island of Antigua' (1804) [A. T. Bolton, *The Works of Sir John Soane*, Appendix C, p. xl, where his name is wrongly given as 'McDowell'].

MacDOUGALD, DONALD, 'architect in Craignish', Argyllshire, made an estimate for repairing KILCHRENAN CHURCH, ARGYLLSHIRE, in 1807 and designed the very simple classical CRAIGNISH CHURCH built at Ardfern in Argyllshire in 1826 [R.C.A.M. *Argyllshire* ii, 147, vii, 61–2].

MACFARLANE, JAMES (–1857), was a mason-architect at Doune in Perthshire, where he lived at Woodside Cottage. He was a prominent elder of the parish church, and was several times Master of the local Freemasons' Lodge [M.S. Mackay, *The Parish of Kilmadock and Borough of Doune*, typescript 1952, 111]. In 1834–5 he designed and built a simple church at COWDENBEATH, FIFE [S.R.O., HR 56/1, pp. 3–6]. He signs a design dated 1838 for enlarging a lodge to REDNOCK HOUSE, PERTHSHIRE [drawing at Rednock]. He died on 12 May 1857, and was succeeded by his son of the same name, who died in 1863 [S.R.O., SC 49/31].

McGILL, ALEXANDER (–1734), was the son of George McGill, minister of Arbirlot in Angus. Owing to a gap in the Arbirlot parish registers the date of his birth cannot be ascertained, but in June 1697 he was apprenticed to Alexander Nisbet, mason of Edinburgh. In 1710 he was admitted to the Edinburgh masons' lodge gratis as 'architector'. He became one of the leading Scottish architects of the early eighteenth century, and in November 1720 was appointed to the newly constituted post of City Architect of Edinburgh, with a salary of £50 a year. In December 1725 this salary was discontinued as a measure of economy at a time when 'no publick work of importance' was in progress, but McGill continued to be employed from time to time on an *ad hoc* basis. From the business correspondence of the 2nd Earl of Bute (for whom McGill designed Mount Stuart), we learn that he had the reputation of 'knowing his business very well', and that he was in London in December 1717.

Early in his career McGill was associated with James Smith, for Yester House is stated in *Vitruvius Scoticus* to have been their joint work, and among the Seafield papers in the Scottish Record Office [RHP 2541] there is an unexecuted design for Cullen House, Banffshire, endorsed as 'Mrs. Smith & McGill's 3rd design of Cullen House 1709'. The connection between the two architects appears to have continued up to the time of Smith's death in 1731, for in 1727 McGill appears as Smith's assignee in a lawsuit brought by the latter against the Earl of Leven for non-payment of money due for the building of Melville House, and in the same year he witnessed an agreement concerning a pumping-engine which Smith had installed in a coalmine on his estate at Whitehill. In 1729 McGill and Smith were employed jointly by the City of Edinburgh to inspect a defect in the quay at Leith [Edinburgh City Records; Sederunt Book of the Sub-Committee for managing the Ale Duty, 2 Sept. 1729]. Yester is, however, the only executed building for which Smith and McGill are at present known to have been jointly responsible.

To judge by his independent work McGill favoured a simple, dignified style of country-house architecture probably derived largely from Sir William Bruce. Indeed at Nairne he appears to have been involved in the completion of a house begun to Bruce's design, and at Kellie Castle he had dealings with Bruce's associate Alexander Edward. Although he provided his houses with extensive subsidiary buildings, the main block was usually rectangular, with hipped roof and regular fenestration without any of the baroque ornamentation favoured by William Adam. In one of his last works, Donibristle Chapel, he used blocked architraves and other features characteristic of James Gibbs.

McGill died in Edinburgh in May 1734.

[Hew Scott, *Fasti Ecclesiae Scoticanae* v, 1925, 421; *Edinburgh Register of Apprentices 1666–1700*, Scottish Record Soc. 1929–59; Edinburgh Town Council Minutes, vol. 48, pp. 282, 288, and Sederunt Book of the Sub-Committee for managing the Ale Duty, 6 Dec. 1725; Ale Duty accounts 1718–68, *passim*; J. G. Dunbar, 'The Building of Yester House', *Trans. of the E. Lothian Antiquarian and Field Naturalists' Soc.* xiii, 1972, 23–4; extracts from letters to 2nd Earl of Bute at N.M.R.S.; S.R.O., Edinburgh Testaments, 28 Feb. 1737, 28 May 1756.]

DOMESTIC ARCHITECTURE

KELLIE CASTLE, ANGUS, alterations for Henry Maule, in association with Alexander Edward, 1699–1705 [S.R.O., GD 45/18/1233, 1236; GD 45/14/332].

YESTER HOUSE, EAST LOTHIAN, for 2nd Marquess of Tweeddale, in partnership with James Smith, *c.*1700–15; altered by W. Adam 1730 and by Robert Adam 1788 [*Vitruvius Scoticus*, pls. 28–9; J. G. Dunbar, 'The Building of Yester House', *Trans. of the E. Lothian Antiquarian and Field Naturalists' Soc.* xiii, 1972] (*C. Life*, 23–30 July 1932, 9, 16 and 23 Aug. 1973).

CRAIGIEHALL HOUSE, WEST LOTHIAN, ornamental gates for 1st Marquess of Annandale, in association with the Earl of Mar (*q.v.*), 1708 [letters from McGill to the Earl of Mar, S.R.O., GD 124/15/752/1–2].

HOUSE OF NAIRNE, PERTHSHIRE, advice or designs for completion of house in March 1710 after death of Sir William Bruce, who appears to have designed it for 2nd Lord Nairn [J. G. Dunbar, *Sir William Bruce, (exhibition catalogue)*, 1970, 20].

BLAIR DRUMMOND, PERTHSHIRE, for George Drummond, 1715–17; dem. 1870 [*Vitruvius Scoticus*, pls. 83–5].

LOUDOUN CASTLE, AYRSHIRE, landscape gardening for 3rd Earl of Loudoun, 1716 (?) [S.R.O., GD 220/5/703/2].

GLASGOW, partial reconstruction of house in Dry Gate for 1st Duke of Montrose, 1718–19; dem. *c.*1855 [designs by McGill in S.R.O., RHP 6285]. The Duke's accounts in S.R.O., GD 220/6, vol. 11, show that the house cost £28,481 (presumably Scots). Macky, *Journey through Scotland*, 1723, 296, implies that it was unfinished.

MOUNT STUART, ISLE OF BUTE, for 2nd Earl of

Bute, 1718–22; main block destroyed by fire 1877, leaving McGill's pavilions [drawings at Mount Stuart, *ex inf.* Prof. A. A. Tait and Mr. J. G. Dunbar].

DONIBRISTLE HOUSE, nr. ABERDOUR, FIFE, for 6th Earl of Moray, 1719–23; main block destroyed by fire 1858 [*Vitruvius Scoticus*, pls. 92–4; N.M.R.S., extracts from Moray muniments, vol. vi, box 16].

INVERARAY CASTLE, ARGYLLSHIRE, temporary 'pavilion' or lodging for 2nd Duke of Argyll, 1720–2; dem. 1745 [I. G. Lindsay & Mary Cosh, *Inveraray and the Dukes of Argyll*, 1973, 25–6, 350–1, n. 62].

BRUNSTANE HOUSE, MIDLOTHIAN, plan for alterations, perhaps not executed, for Andrew Fletcher, Lord Milton, 1730 [letters in National Library of Scotland, MS. 16544, ff. 1, 3].

PICARDY VILLAGE, BROUGHTON, EDINBURGH, layout of village for Picardy weavers, 1730; dem. *c.*1800 [John Mason, 'The Weavers of Picardy', *Book of the Old Edinburgh Club* xxv, 1945, 9].

CHURCHES

EDINBURGH, GREYFRIARS WEST CHURCH, 1719–22 [G. Hay, *The Kirk of the Greyfriars, Edinburgh*, 1959, 9].

DUMFRIES NEW CHURCH, 1724–7; dem. 1866 [W. McDowall, *History of Dumfries*, Edinburgh 1867, 616].

NEWBATTLE CHURCH, MIDLOTHIAN, 1727–8 [Dalkeith Presbytery Records, S.R.O., CH2/424/11, pp. 411–14, 420].

DONIBRISTLE CHAPEL, FIFE, for 6th Earl of Moray, 1729–32 [inscription in gallery and N.M.R.S., extracts from Moray muniments, vol. vi, box 16].

PUBLIC BUILDING

STIRLING, alterations to the 'court place' in the TOLBOOTH, 1710 [*Extracts from the Records of the Royal Burgh of Stirling 1667–1752*, ed. Renwick, 1889, 122, and cf. 188 and 194 for his advice about a ford in 1726].

UNEXECUTED DESIGNS

The following unexecuted designs have been noted: for rebuilding ALLOA CHURCH, CLACKMANNANSHIRE, 1709 [S.R.O., RHP 13258, no. 29, unsigned but in McGill's hand]; for CULLEN HOUSE, BANFFSHIRE, 1709 [S.R.O., RHP 2541, in McGill's hand and endorsed as 'Mrs. Smith & McGill's 3rd design of Cullen House']; for alterations to ALLOA HOUSE, CLACKMANNANSHIRE, for 11th Earl of Mar, 1710 [S.R.O., RHP 13258, no. 5, unsigned but in McGill's hand]; for refronting MAKERSTOUN HOUSE, ROXBURGHSHIRE, 1714 [in private hands, photos at N.M.R.S.]; and for adding wings to the old castle at INVERARAY, ARGYLLSHIRE, in 1720 [I. G. Lindsay & Mary Cosh, *Inveraray and the Dukes of Argyll*, 1973].

McGOWAN, WILLIAM (–1858), was a mason who became a burgess of Dumfries in 1825. He designed a small and unpretentious church at WAMPHRAY, DUMFRIESSHIRE, in 1834 [S.R.O., HR 562/1, pp. 58–62]. He died at Dumfries on 5 July 1858 [S.R.O., SC 15/41/11]. Alexander Fraser of Dumfries was his pupil.

MACHELL, the Revd. THOMAS (1647–1698), was the second son of Lancelot Machell of Crackenthorpe Hall, Westmorland, where he was born in 1647. He was probably educated at Appleby Grammar School before going up to The Queen's College, Oxford, where he graduated B.A. in 1668, proceeded to M.A. in 1672, and became a Fellow of the College the same year. Five years later he was presented by the 3rd Earl of Thanet to the well-endowed rectory of Kirkby Thore in Westmorland, and for the rest of his life he remained the parson of this remote parish, where he died in November 1698.

In Oxford Machell had become acquainted with some of the leading intellectuals of the time, notably with Sir Joseph Williamson, a fellow-Cumbrian at whose expense the Williamson Building at Queen's was built to Wren's designs in 1671–4, and with the antiquaries Dugdale and Wood. He shared their interests and in 1684 was elected a member of the Oxford Philosophical Society. Far away in Westmorland he saw himself as a lone representative of the new historical and aesthetic attitudes that he had learned in Oxford. Emulating Dugdale, he set about making collections for a history of the two Cumbrian counties, copying deeds, drawing Roman inscriptions and making sketches of notable buildings. At the same time, being interested in 'the most Beautifull Art of Architecture', he determined to promote classical architecture in an area where nearly every manor-house was still a fortified tower and the influence of London had scarcely penetrated. In one of his manuscripts he claims that he and the master mason Edward Addison (*q.v.*) were 'the first introducers of Regular building into these Parts; Hutton Hall in the County of Cumberland was Altered by Addison; Rose Castle in Cumberland, Caesar's Tower,

Howgill Castle & Crackenthorp Hall in the County of Westmorland by Mr. Machell.'

Machell's claim to have been the first to introduce 'Regular architecture' into Cumbria was not strictly correct, for it ignored some classical houses recently built by William Thackeray (*q.v.*). Nevertheless, the houses which Machell and Addison designed were among the earliest of their kind in the area. At CRACKENTHORPE HALL he designed in 1685 a pedimented front for his brother Hugh, 'exactly uniforme & of such a surprising symetry, that it semeth greater by far than it is'. On the roof he built two cupolas, 'one being designed for pleasure only, the other for a stack of chimneys'. For William Sandford he regularized HOWGILL CASTLE '(with much art and small cost) from an old & irregular piece of Building to a very elligent & uniform structure', but the 'Ionic Bellcony' and 'double transom windows curiously carved' with which he embellished the front have been removed, as have the 'railes & Ballisters' which he substituted for the medieval battlements. At ROSE CASTLE he probably rebuilt the north-west corner for Bishop Thomas Smith (1684–1702), with pedimented windows to match the new north front built by Thackeray in the 1670s [B. Tyson in *Trans. Ancient Monuments Soc.* N.S. 27, 1983, 73–4]. At APPLEBY CASTLE he was presumably responsible for the east range built by the 6th Earl of Thanet in 1686–8 in a handsome classical style (*C. Life*, 13–20 April 1940). In 1694–5 Bishop Smith employed him to design an arcaded market building in APPLEBY, consisting of a 'cloister' with a shop at each end on a site adjoining the churchyard [Cumbria C.R.O., Bishop Smith's Register, 1695; *Diary of Ralph Thoresby*, ed. Hunter, i, 1830, 276]. Inside the church the Tudor organ-case was remodelled by Machell in such a way that 'the Guttae & Triglyphy' were 'rendered Musicall, & the fluting turn'd into Organ pipes' (cf. *Antiquaries' Jnl.* lviii (2), 1978, 321, 325).

Six volumes of Machell's Cumbrian collections are preserved in Carlisle Cathedral Library. Among Francis Douce's MSS. in the Bodleian Library there are notes by him on a note-book of Machell's then in the possession of James Bindley (d. 1818), which contained drawings of various buildings, including Crackenthorpe Hall, the library of Queen's College, Oxford, and the Sheldonian Theatre, 'taken immediately after the front was finished'. A letter from Machell to Dugdale, describing an ancient well at Kirkby Thore, was printed in *Philosophical Transactions of the Royal Society* xiii, 1683–4, 559–63.

[Machell MSS. in Carlisle Cathedral Library; T. Rogan & Eric Birley, 'Thomas Machell the Antiquary', *Trans. Cumberland and Westmorland Antiquarian Soc.*, N.S. lv, 1955; Jane M. Ewbank, *Antiquary on Horseback*, 1963; Bodleian Library, MSS. Tanner 22, ff. 97, 112, 134, Douce e.64, ff. 101–110.]

McINNES, ALEXANDER, drew out for engraving a design made by Sir John Sinclair, Bart., of Thurso Castle, Caithness, for a model village consisting of circular cottages arranged round a circular green, that was published in *Annals of Agriculture* 34, 1800, 360–94. In the British Library (*King's Maps*, xlix, 47.2) there is an engraved design for a 'Washington Monument' to be built 'on a natural mound opposite the New Town of Thurso'. It is in the form of a circular castellated tower and is signed 'Edinburgh, A. McInnes delt. 1801'. In 1807 A. McInnes exhibited two drawings at the Royal Academy from 7 Salisbury Street, Strand. One was a 'View of the altars in the chapel at Roslin, near Edinburgh', the other a design for alterations at TAPLOW LODGE, BUCKS., for P. C. Bruce, an M.P. of Scottish birth.

MACKENZIE, DAVID, was the second son of Alexander Mackenzie (d. 1827), and younger brother of W. M. Mackenzie (*q.v.*). By 1830 he was established at Dundee, where in 1831 he entered unsuccessfully for the Seminaries competition and in 1833 for the Courthouse and Bridewell competitions. However, in June 1833 his scheme for the layout of the Chapelshade grounds for building was accepted in preference to that of his principal rival George Angus (*q.v.*). In or shortly after 1842 Mackenzie died or left Dundee. His place was subsequently taken by his nephew David Mackenzie (1832–75), the son of W. M. Mackenzie of Perth [information from Mr. David Walker].

MONIFIETH MANSE, ANGUS, 1830 [*Dundee Advertiser*, 6 May 1830].

BALDOVAN HOUSE, ANGUS, stables for Sir John Ogilvy, Bart., 1832 [*Dundee Advertiser*, 19 Jan. 1832].

FORFAR, ANGUS, 20–26 HIGH STREET, 1832 [*Dundee Advertiser*, 19 April 1832].

DUNDEE, feued FLEUCHAR CRAIG, LOGIE, for villas, 1833 [*Dundee Advertiser*, 12 Dec. 1833].

DUNDEE, TAY SQUARE U.P. CHURCH (now Halls), 1833 [G. Jamieson, *Tay Square Church, Dundee: A Centenary Retrospect*, 1932, 22–3].

INVERGOWRIE, ANGUS, West Toll House, 1834 [*Dundee Advertiser*, 4 July 1834].

INCHTURE CHURCH, PERTHSHIRE, 1835, Gothic

[N.S.A. x, 833].

MONIFIETH, ANGUS, SCHOOLHOUSE, 1836 [*Dundee Advertiser*, 13 May 1836].

KINGOLDRUM CHURCH, ANGUS, 1840 [drawings in S.R.O., RHP 7874–5].

MACKENZIE, WILLIAM MACDONALD (1797–1856), was the eldest son of Alexander Mackenzie, architect of Scone (d. 1827), the founder of a dynasty of Scottish architects. W. M. Mackenzie practised in Perth, where he held the post of City Architect for some thirty years, dying there on 15 February 1856. According to the obituary in the *Builder*, he designed 'forty to fifty churches', most of which have yet to be identified, and had a considerable reputation as a designer of farm-buildings, which was recognized by the award of a medal by the Highland Society of Scotland.

William Macdonald's younger brother Thomas Mackenzie (1814–54) was apprenticed to him before becoming assistant to Archibald Simpson of Aberdeen. Thomas practised in Elgin from 1841 onwards in partnership with James Matthews (1820–98), and was the father of A. Marshall Mackenzie of Aberdeen (1848–1933). W. M. Mackenzie was the father of David Mackenzie II of Dundee (1832–75). [*Builder* xii, 1854, 593, xiv, 1856, 174; information from Mr. David Walker.]

PUBLIC BUILDINGS

KINFAUNS, PERTHSHIRE, Schoolhouse, 1832 [S.R.O., HR 323/1, pp. 29–35].

KINNAIRD, PERTHSHIRE, Schoolhouse, 1834 [S.R.O., HR 418/1, pp. 32–3].

PERTH, THE CITY AND COUNTY INFIRMARY, YORK PLACE (now County Council Offices), 1836: wing added later [*N.S.A.* x, 129].

PERTH, THE EXCHANGE COFFEE ROOMS, 26–32 GEORGE STREET, 1836 [D. Peacock, *Perth*, 1849, 501].

PERTH, Triumphal Arch for Queen Victoria's visit, 1842 [D. Peacock, *Perth*, 1849, 406].

PERTH, THE CITY HALL, 1845; dem. 1877 [D. Peacock, *Perth*, 1849, 506].

CHURCHES

METHVEN, PERTHSHIRE, enlarged 1825–6 [S.R.O., HR 315/1].

CARGILL, PERTHSHIRE, 1831 [S.R.O., HR 453/1].

PERTH, ST. LEONARD, 1834 [*N.S.A.* x, 86].

LIFF AND BENVIE CHURCH, ANGUS, 1838–9 [*N.S.A.* xi, 586; A. B. Dalgety, *The Church and Parish of Liff*, Dundee 1940, 42].

KINFAUNS OLD PARISH CHURCH, PERTHSHIRE, enlargement, 1838; dem. [S.R.O., HR 323/1, pp. 47, 59].

CLUNIE, PERTHSHIRE, 1839–40, Gothic [S.R.O., HR 334/1].

DOMESTIC ARCHITECTURE

MEGGINCH CASTLE, PERTHSHIRE, additions for Admiral Sir Adam Drummond, 1817–20 [drawings at Megginch, *ex inf.* Mr. David Walker].

Manses at ARNGASK, PERTHSHIRE, 1828–9 [S.R.O., HR 457/2]; KINNAIRD, PERTHSHIRE (now 'MANSFIELD'), 1831 [S.R.O., HR 418/1]; DRON, PERTHSHIRE, 1838 [S.R.O., HR 320/1, pp. 33–5]; KINFAUNS, PERTHSHIRE (enlargement), 1840 [S.R.O., HR 323/1, pp. 65–76].

ELCHO CASTLE, PERTHSHIRE, farmhouse [J. C. Loudon, *Encyclopaedia*, 1846, 537–44].

MACKIE, WILLIAM, was a pupil of Samuel Robinson. He exhibited student's work at the Royal Academy in 1810–13, and Pigot's *Directory* shows that he was practising from Charles Street, Blackfriars Road, London, in 1827–8.

MACKINTOSH, THOMAS, was a pupil of Robert Abraham. He exhibited student's work at the Royal Academy in 1818 and 1820. In 1840 he was practising from 106 Fenchurch Street, London.

MACKLINE, —, an otherwise unknown architect, is recorded by a payment of £1 made by Sir John Wittewronge, Bart., in Sept. 1664 to 'Mr. Mackline for drawing plot of my intended building' [Herts. C.R.O., D/ELW/F20]. This was probably at STANTONBURY, nr. WOLVERTON, BUCKS., a house (dem. 1791) belonging to Wittewronge, but possibly at Rothamsted, his Hertfordshire seat.

MacKNIGHT, ALEXANDER, was an architect and builder at Whitehaven in Cumberland in the 1820s. In 1825 he made designs for a parsonage at PONSONBY, CUMBERLAND [Cumbria Record Office, DRC/12/10].

McLERAN, JAMES (–*c.*1795), was a minor Scottish architect who was responsible for some plain late Georgian country houses. He was practising in Edinburgh at the time of his death in or about 1795. McLeran's responsibility for the design of OCHTERTYRE HOUSE, PERTHSHIRE, 1784–90, for Sir William Murray, Bart., and his recent death are mentioned in a letter dated 25 April 1796 from Sir Patrick Murray to Sir John Hope [S.R.O., GD 364]. The Hope of Lufness papers show that Sir John Hope employed McLeran to design OVER RANKEILLOUR HOUSE, MONIMAIL, FIFE, in 1792, and that after his death the building of the house was superintended (1795–1800) by Alexander Laing (*q.v.*) [S.R.O., GD 364/1/92 and 95].

In 1787–9 McLeran (described as 'McLaren') was in charge of alterations to BRAHAN CASTLE, ROSS-SHIRE (dem. 1965) for Francis Humberston Mackenzie [S.R.O., GD 46/1/417], and in 1789–90 large sums were being paid to 'Mr. M'Laren and his son' for works at DUNROBIN CASTLE, SUTHERLAND, for the Countess of Sutherland [W. Fraser, *The Sutherland Book* i, 1894, 470, n. 2]. McLeran is mentioned in the contract (1790) for building NETHERURD HOUSE, PEEBLESSHIRE, for William Lawson. He was to superintend the work failing 'Mr. Burns' [S.R.O., GD 120/415]. He was the author of some drawings for TARBAT HOUSE, ROSS-SHIRE, *c.*1790, now at Castle Leod, which are signed 'J. McLeran Archt.'

McNIVEN, CHARLES (*c.*1746–1815) and his brother Peter were Scots who had by the late 1770s established themselves in Manchester as 'surveyors and nurserymen'. By 1788 Charles was described in a directory as 'architect and designer', but later in life he became a partner in an iron foundry, and when he died in May 1815 he was said to have 'arrived at a state of opulent competency'. Apart from some speculative building on the Byrom estate in Manchester, NcNiven's only recorded work as an architect is WOODFOLD HALL, nr. BLACKBURN, LANCS., for Henry Sudell, 1796–9. When tenders for building this house were advertised in the *Blackburn Mail* in 1796, the plans could be seen by applying to McNiven in Manchester. The house (now a ruin) was elegantly designed in the style of James Wyatt. In 1800 McNiven submitted proposals for the continuation of the works at Lancaster Castle after the dismissal of Thomas Harrison, but they were not accepted. [*Gent's Mag.* 1815 (i), 569; *Manchester Mercury*, 16 May 1815; information from Mr. Colin Stansfield.]

MACPACKE, JOSE, *see* PEACOCK, JAMES.

McPHERSON, JAMES, described as 'architect at the Dean' (Edinburgh), and a mason by trade, was responsible for building houses in NICOLSON STREET, EDINBURGH, in the 1760s and 1770s [*Edinburgh Evening Courant*, 9 Sept. 1769, 4 Feb. 1771]. They included a plain five-bay house for Thomas Carnegie of Craigo, for which McPherson's drawings survive in N.L.S., Dep. 267/122. An architect of the same name practised in Edinburgh in the second quarter of the nineteenth century until his death in about 1847.

McTAVISH, PETER, a mason of Fortwilliam, built and probably designed KINLOCHMOIDART HOUSE, INVERNESS-SHIRE, for Col. Alexander Macdonald in 1781–2; dem. 1885 [N.L.S., MS. 3945, ff. 74–92].

McWILLIAM, ROBERT, exhibited at the Royal Academy from 5 Furnival's Inn, London, in 1818, 1821 and 1823. He showed in 1818 a 'View of a Gothic mansion, with the late alterations and improvements', in 1821 a 'View of Weeting Hall, Norfolk, the residence of Sir R. Sutton, Bt.' and in 1823 a 'View of a Gothic mansion in the county of Southampton'. In 1818 he published *An Essay on the Origin and Operation of the Dry Rot, with a View to its Prevention and Cure, to which are annexed, Suggestions on the Cultivation of Forest Trees, and an Abstract of the Several Forest Laws*, with a dedication to the Duke of Gordon. In 1837 he wrote several controversial pamphlets about the proposed London Grand Junction Railway.

MADDOX, GEORGE (1760–1843), was the son of a builder of Monmouth, to whom he was apprenticed. Having served his term, he went to London, became for a time an assistant in the office of Sir John Soane, but soon found the latter's régime intolerable and left in disgust. In 1789 he was employed to make designs for a new opera house on the north side of Leicester Square to replace the burnt-out King's Theatre in the Haymarket. This came to nothing, but Maddox's design is said to have been adopted for the Grand Theatre at Moscow, which was completed in 1796, but destroyed by fire in 1812. Instead of building in Leicester Square the promoters of the opera house proceeded to convert the Pantheon in Oxford Street for the purpose, with James Wyatt as architect. Maddox appears to have been one of the shareholders who suffered serious loss when the building was destroyed by fire in 1792. This may have contributed to his subsequent failure to establish himself in regular architectural practice, though for this he appears in any case to have been temperamentally unfitted. In 1796 he was assisting S. P. Cockerell in his office in Savile Row, and for the rest of his life he made a living chiefly by tuition and by designing and drawing for other architects. He died on 7 October 1843, in his 83rd year.

In the 1820s Maddox had a connection with the London builders, Messrs. G.

Woolcott and B. Browning (*q.v.*), and according to the memoir in *A.P.S.D.* he was employed by them to assist with their contracts to build Strensham Court, Worcs. (1824) for the banker John Taylor and York (now Lancaster) House, St. James's (1825–7), for the Duke of York. Lancaster House was designed by Benjamin Wyatt, but at Strensham Maddox presumably provided the designs for this Greek Revival house (dem. 1974), to which a large Ionic portico was added later.

In London Maddox designed a number of shop-fronts: one for a chemist in the Strand opposite St. Mary's Church, one for Messrs. Godfrey & Cooke in Southampton Street, another in Tavistock Place, Woburn Square (exhibited at Society of British Artists, 1827), and a long front in High Holborn for a glazier named Tucker. The fronts which he designed for Hammersley's Bank at 69 Pall Mall and for Jones & Loyd's Bank in Lothbury are praised in the *Monthly Magazine* for June 1817, p. 399. In 1819 he exhibited a 'design for a church to be built at Greenock' at the Royal Academy, but it is doubtful whether it was erected.

Maddox was chiefly celebrated as an architectural drawing-master and among his many pupils were W. J. Booth, W. M. Brooks, Decimus Burton, John Davies, Edward Browning, W. Hosking, Edwin Nash, Charles Parker and Gilbert Scott. In his *Recollections* Scott pays a tribute to Maddox's 'wonderful power of drawing', but describes him as an 'infidel', whose 'conversation on such subjects was truly appalling'. He exhibited occasionally at the Royal Academy, but more often at the Society of British Artists, showing architectural compositions, in oils as well as water-colours, which are said to have been 'as interesting as those of Gandy'. An album of his sketches of classical compositions, etc., is in the R.I.B.A. Drawings Collection, to which it was presented by Decimus Burton in 1869. At the time of his death Maddox is said to have been engaged on a series of about forty etchings of 'architectural groups and fragments'.

[*A.P.S.D.*; *Civil Engineer and Architect's Jnl.* vii, 1844, 6, 118; *Building News* xii, 1865, 659.]

MADDOX, GEORGE VAUGHAN (1802–1864), was the only son of James Maddox, a builder of Monmouth, and was no doubt related to George Maddox (*q.v.*). He had a local practice as an architect and builder. In Monmouth his principal work was THE NEW MARKET, PRIORY STREET, opened in 1839, damaged by fire 1964. This formed part of a new street built on arches, and Maddox was presumably responsible for the whole scheme, which formed a handsome new entrance to the town from the north [*Monmouthshire Merlin*, 29 Nov. 1834, 28 Dec. 1839].

In 1826 a theatre (dem.) was built to Maddox's designs in CROCKHERBTOWN, a suburb of CARDIFF [Cecil Price, *The English Theatre in Wales*, Cardiff 1948, 113]. He also designed CLEARWELL CHURCH, GLOS., 1829, rebuilt 1866 [I.C.B.S.]; a small house near Monmouth called THE HENDRE, built as a shooting-lodge for John Rolls in 1829–30, and altered and enlarged in 1833–4 for J. E. W. Rolls, who subsequently employed T. H. Wyatt to enlarge it still further in 1837–40 and 1858 [Monmouthshire Record Office, FIF. 32, 35, 36]; alterations to PENTWYN HOUSE, ROCKFIELD, MONMOUTHSHIRE, which he owned, *c.*1834 [*Monmouthshire Merlin*, 25 March 1837]; and two houses and shops in PONTYPOOL, MONMOUTHSHIRE, 1840 [*Monmouthshire Merlin*, 30 May 1840]. He died at Hempsted Rectory, Glos., the home of his brother-in-law, the Revd. Thomas Jones, on 27 February 1864, aged 62, and is commemorated by a tablet in Hempsted Church. Designs by him for a house for Thomas Dyke of Monmouth are in the National Library of Wales (Aberpergwn papers). [References to *Monmouthshire Merlin ex inf.* Mr. A. G. Chamberlain.]

MAINWARING, BOULTON (1702–1778), was the son of Henry Mainwaring, a surgeon of Talke in the parish of Audley, Staffs. In or about 1715 he was apprenticed to John Beech of Barthomley in Cheshire, a joiner [Guildhall Library, index to Apprenticeship Registers in P.R.O.]. By the 1750s he was practising as a surveyor in Bedford Row, London. He was a J.P. for Middlesex, and between 1750 and 1764 carried out some surveying for the county for which, in 1774, he claimed remuneration at the rate of 5 per cent. This was refused, on the grounds that his services had been voluntary [Middlesex County Records, General Order Book No. 10, ff. 4, 7, 11]. He passed carpenters' bills for work done at OSTERLEY PARK, MIDDLESEX, in 1756–9 [accounts at Victoria and Albert Museum], and in 1770 examined the plasterers' bills at BENHAM PLACE, BERKS., then being built to the designs of Lancelot Brown [Berkshire C.R.O., Craven Papers, D/DEC. A.9].

Mainwaring was surveyor to the LONDON HOSPITAL, WHITECHAPEL ROAD, built in stages between 1752 and 1771. The hospital is stated to have been 'Designed by Boulton Mainwaring' on an engraving published in 1753 and reproduced by N. Brett-James, *The Growth of Stuart London*, 1935, 286, and this is confirmed by the minutes of the Building Committee quoted in E. W. Morris, *A History of the London Hospital*, 1910, 83–7. The plan is given in *Gentleman's Magazine*, 1752, 103. Mainwaring also rebuilt part of the FRENCH PROTESTANT HOSPITAL in OLD STREET in 1753–4; dem. 1865 [*Huguenot Soc.* Quarto Series, 56, 1983, 61].

Mainwaring resigned from the surveyorship of the London Hospital on 4 December 1771, on account of age and ill-health. His will (P.C.C. 120 HAY) shows that he died early in 1778. Andrew Thornthwaite was a pupil. [*A.P.S.D.*; information from Mr. Hugh Torrens.]

MALIPHANT, GEORGE (*c.*1788–1865), was probably related to a monumental sculptor called Maliphant who lived at Kidwelly in South Wales,[1] and perhaps to Richard Maliphant, a London builder or surveyor who carried out some alterations and repairs to GATTON PARK, SURREY, for Sir Henry Harpur-Crewe, Bart., when the latter rented that house in 1809 [letter in Harpur-Crewe papers, Derbyshire C.R.O.]. George Maliphant became a pupil of Charles Beazley. He was admitted to the Royal Academy Schools in 1809 at the age of 21, and exhibited at the Academy between 1806 and 1829. He also exhibited at the Society of British Artists from 1824 to 1833. He practised in London until the 1840s and died in Camberwell on 30 August 1865 [Principal Probate Registry, Calendar of Probates]. He was the author of a volume of *Designs for Sepulchral Monuments*. Unexecuted designs by him for Gothic alterations to HORNBY CASTLE, YORKS. (N.R.), dated 1815, are preserved there. Other works by Maliphant were a conservatory 'proposed to be erected for Sir R. Levinge, Bart., in Ireland', presumably at KNOCKDRIN CASTLE, CO. WESTMEATH [exhib. at R.A. 1812]; the EPISCOPAL JEWS' CHAPEL, BETHNAL GREEN, in collaboration with C. A. Busby, 1813–14, dem. 1895 [exhib. at R.A. 1814 and see p. 201 above]; a villa 'designed to be erected in the Highlands for R. Douglas, Esq.' [exhib. at R.A. 1815]; WORLINGTON RECTORY, SUFFOLK, 1819–20 [W. Suffolk Record Office, 806/2/23]; HAVERSTOCK LODGE, HAMPSTEAD, for J. Lund [exhib. at R.A. 1821 as 'erected']; some cottages at EMBERTON, BUCKS., for John Osmond [exhib. at R.A. 1829 as 'erected']; a design for a proposed 'Gallery of Arts' at Bolton, Lancs. [exhib. at Soc. of British Artists 1831]; and a villa at WEST HILL, WANDSWORTH, SURREY, for W. Newton [exhib. at Soc. of British Artists as 'erected', 1833].

[1] A cottage at Kidwelly was the subject of a drawing exhibited by George Maliphant at the Society of British Artists in 1826.

MALPAS, HENRY, stated in 1850 that he was a clerk of works of twenty-five years' standing who had been employed by Rickman and Hutchinson and Sampson Kempthorne, under whom he had spent seven years building workhouses in various parts of the country [Birmingham Reference Library, Bateman & Drury papers, MS. 1542/Box 31, bundle 3]. In 1837 he was appointed clerk of works to build GILLINGHAM CHURCH, DORSET, to the designs of William Walker of Shaftesbury, but these were eventually set aside in favour of designs made by Malpas and carried out in 1838–9. [*Somerset & Dorset Notes & Queries* xv, 1917, 33; I.C.B.S.] He was presumably the 'pretended architect' of the same name, who, having recently built a workhouse at Frome, was employed to restore BECKINGTON CHURCH, SOMERSET, in 1844 [*ex inf.* Mr. Michael McGarvie]. He may have been related to T. Malpas, who exhibited architectural designs at the Royal Academy between 1796 and 1806.

MALTON, JAMES (1765–1803), was the younger son of Thomas Malton (*q.v.*), architectural draughtsman and writer on perspective. He was born in England, but accompanied his father to Dublin when financial difficulties obliged the latter to live in Ireland. For some time he was employed as a draughtsman in James Gandon's office, but 'he so frequently betrayed all official confidence, and was guilty of so many irregularities, that it became quite necessary to dismiss him from the employment.' He returned to London in the 1790s, and made a living, chiefly as a topographical artist, publishing in 1797 *A Descriptive View of Dublin*. However, his numerous exhibits at the Royal Academy included architectural designs, and he published two early works on picturesque cottages, *An Essay on British Cottage Architecture: being an attempt to perpetuate on Principle, that peculiar mode of building, which was originally the effect of Chance* (1798, 2nd ed. 1804), and a *Collection of Designs for Rural Retreats . . . principally in the Gothic and Castle styles of architecture* (1802). These two books establish Malton as a pioneer of the *cottage orné*. Attention should also be drawn to the 'Elevation of a country mansion in the Norman style of architecture' which he exhibited at the Royal Academy in 1801, as it represents one of the earliest attempts to design a modern building in the 'Norman' style. Malton died in Marylebone of brain fever on 28 July 1803. Two designs by him for *cottages ornés,* dated 1798, are in the Victoria and Albert Museum, and a design for a hunting lodge in the castle style dated 1803 now in the Yale Center for British Art is reproduced in B. Weinreb's *Catalogue* No. 2, 1963, item 84. [*D.N.B.*; J. Gandon, *The Life of James Gandon*, ed. Mulvany, 1846, 67; *Gent's Mag.* 1803 (ii), 791.]

MALTON, THOMAS (1726–1801), born in London in 1726, is said originally to have kept an upholsterer's shop in the Strand. In 1766 he exhibited at the Society of Artists a view of St. Stephen's Church, Walbrook, the first of a number of architectural and perspective drawings which he showed at London exhibitions. He never practised as an architect but appears to have taught perspective at his house in Poland Street, Soho. In 1776 he published *The Royal Road to Geometry* and in 1775 *A Compleat Treatise on Perspective.* Financial difficulties are said to have led to his removal to Dublin, where he lived for many years and died on 18 February 1801. He was the father of Thomas Malton, junior, and James Malton (*qq.v.*). [S. Redgrave, *Dictionary of Artists*, 1878, 284; *Gent's Mag.* 1801 (i), 277; *D.N.B.*]

MALTON, THOMAS (1752–1804), was the elder son of Thomas Malton (*q.v.*), architectural draughtsman and writer on perspective. Having been admitted to the Royal Academy Schools in 1773 as an architectural student, he gained in 1774 the Silver and in 1782 the Gold Medal. From 1773 onwards he was a regular exhibitor at the Academy, showing an occasional architectural design for a bath, a temple or a theatre, but chiefly appearing as a topographical artist of considerable skill. He was one of the first to make use of the newly invented process of aquatinta, and in 1792–1801 published the work by which he is now best known, *A Picturesque Tour through the Cities of London and Westminster*, containing 100 aquatint plates which form a valuable topographical record of Georgian London. At the time of his death he was engaged upon a similar series of views of Oxford, some of which appeared in parts in 1802 and were reissued in 1810. He was also responsible for the series of aquatint views of buildings by Sir Robert Taylor which were made after the latter's death. Several of the original drawings for this series are in the Ashmolean Museum, Oxford. Other drawings attributed to him are in the R.I.B.A. Collection.

Although he never practised as an architect, Malton attempted in 1795 to secure election as an Associate of the Royal Academy, but was rejected on the ground that he was 'only a draughtsman of buildings, but no architect'. From 1783 to 1787 he lived in Conduit Street, where he held evening classes in perspective which were attended by Thomas Girtin and J. M. W. Turner as young men. He died on 7 March 1804, leaving a widow and six children. One of his sons, Charles Malton, became a pupil of Sir John Soane, and won the Royal Academy's Silver Medal in 1807, but does not appear ever to have practised as an architect. [*D.N.B.*; *The Farington Diary*, ed. J. Greig, i, 74, 107, 124, ii, 208; R.A. Admission Register, giving the date of his 21st birthday as 22 Aug. 1773; A. T. Bolton, *The Works of Sir John Soane*, 1924, Appendix C, p. xliii.]

MAN, THOMAS, *see* MANN, THOMAS.

MANDEY, VENTERUS (1645–1701), held the post of bricklayer to Lincoln's Inn from 1667 to the time of his death. He was buried at Iver, Bucks., where in the north aisle of the church there is a tablet with the following inscription:

> Beneath this place lyes interred the Body of VENTERUS MANDEY of the Parish of St. Giles in the Fields, in the County of Middlesex, Bricklayer; son of MICHAEL MANDEY, Bricklayer, & Grandson to VENTERUS MANDEY, of this parish, Bricklayer, Who had y[e] honour of being Bricklayer to the Hon[ble] Society of Lincoln's Inn from the year of our Lord 1667 to the day of his Death, He was studious in the Mathematicks & wrote & published three Books for Publick Good: one Entituled Mellificium Mensionis or ye Marrow of Measuring; Another of Mechanic powers or the Mystery of Nature & Art Unvayled: the third An Universal Mathematical Synopsis. He also translated into English Directorum Generale Vranometricum and Trigonometria Plana & Sphærica Linearis & Logarithmica: Auctore Fr. Bonaventura Cavalerio Mediolanesi: & some other tracts which he designed to have Printed if Death had not prevented him. He Dyed the 26th day of July *Anno Domini* 1701 aged 56 years & upwards.

The Marrow of Measuring (1682) proved to be a successful manual. It went through four editions, the last in 1727, when it was superseded by Hawney's *Compleat Measurer*. It contains a portrait of the author at the age of 37. *Mechanick Powers; or the Mistery of Nature and Art Unvail'd* was written by Mandey in collaboration with James (not Joseph) Moxon and published as their joint work in 1696. There were later editions in 1699, 1702 and 1709. *The Synopsis Mathematica Universalis* was a translation from the Latin of John James Heinlin. It was dedicated to the Benchers of Lincoln's Inn, who, in 1701, acknowledged the gift of a copy by making the author a present of £8 [*The Black Book of Lincoln's Inn* iii, 1899, 100, 147, 209]. Several payments to 'Mr. Mandey the measurer' are recorded in the accounts for building a house at BARN ELMS, SURREY, for Thomas Cartwright of Aynho in 1694–5 [Northants. C.R.O., Cartwright papers]. Mandey's library was sold by auction on 15 March, 1713/14. There is a copy of the sale catalogue in the B.L. (S.C. 301(2)). His will is P.C.C. 99 DYER.

[F. M. L. Thompson, *The Chartered Surveyor*, 1968, 67–70; Eileen Harris, *British Architectural Books and Writers, 1556–1785*, 1990, 311–12.]

MANN, THOMAS, of York, was a surveyor and perhaps an instrument-maker. His knowledge of instruments for surveying and astronomy is shown by a letter to Richard Beaumont in which he refers to a 'waywiser' and to a quadrant for measuring altitudes which he had supplied. A brass inscription in Rudston Church, Yorks. (E.R.) to Katherine Constable (d. 1677), signed 'Tho: Mann Eboraci sculp' also indicates skill in metalwork.

As a builder or architect Mann was paid £93 4s. 2d. in 1672 'for rebuilding the Cross on the Pavement' at York, presumably the Ionic Market Cross illustrated in Drake's *Eboracum* (1735), 293 [D. Linstrum, *West Yorkshire Architects and Architecture*, 1978, 381]. Robert Hooke's diary contains several references to Mann, whom he met in London in the winter of 1676/7 and who appears to have been engaged to supervise or execute alterations to the house and garden at Londesborough House, Yorks. (E.R.), for which Hooke had made designs for the Countess of Burlington [*Diary of Robert Hooke*, ed. Robinson & Adams, 1935, 254, 266, 268, 270]. In 1680 Mann made competently drawn plans for partly remodelling the Elizabethan Whitley Beaumont House, Yorks. (W.R.) (dem. 1952) for Richard Beaumont. They are in the W. Yorks. Archives at Huddersfield (WBM 5–6). Alternative schemes show a classical façade with an internal colonnade to the courtyard and an open court with a balustrade joining the wings.

MANNERS, GEORGE PHILLIPS (*c.*1789–1866), practised in Bath, where he held the post of City architect from 1823 until he retired in 1862. Early in his career he was working with C. Harcourt Masters (*q.v.*) and from about 1845 onwards he was in partnership with C. E. Gill (d. 1874). He was a prolific architect who appears to have designed nothing of great distinction. His earlier churches were usually 'Perpendicular' or 'Norman' in style, with wide naves and shallow chancels, but after the arrival of Gill they conformed better to ecclesiological principles. Manners died at Send Lodge, Ripley, Surrey, on 28 November 1866, aged 77 [Principal Probate Registry, Calendar of Probates; *Gent's Mag.* 1867 (i), 120].

THE MOOR, CLIFFORD, HEREFS., alterations for F.R.B.S. Penoyre (d. 1827) of The Moor and Batheaston Villa, Bath, and his executors, 1827–9; dem. 1952 [executors' accounts in Herefs. C.R.O., ff. 105, 195, 196, 203].

BATH, ST. CATHERINE'S HOSPITAL, 1829, Tudor style [*A.P.S.D.*, *s.v.* 'Bath'].

BATH, reconstructed HOT BATH and added TEPID SWIMMING BATH (dem. 1923) to designs of Decimus Burton, 1830 [W. Ison, *Georgian Buildings of Bath*, 1948, 64].

COLEFORD CHURCH, SOMERSET, 1830–1, Gothic [Somerest C.R.O., D/P Coleford, 8/3/2, *ex inf.* Mr. Michael McGarvie].

BATH, ST. MARK'S CHURCH, LYNCOMBE, 1830–2, Gothic; chancel 1883 [*A.P.S.D.*, *s.v.* 'Bath'].

CHARLCOMBE RECTORY, SOMERSET, 1834, Tudor Gothic [Somerset C.R.O., D/D/Bbm, 64].

BATH ABBEY CHURCH, restored exterior and repaired interior, 1835 [*Companion to the Almanac*, 1837, 229–31].

BATH, ST. MICHAEL'S CHURCH, 1835–6, Gothic [*Architectural Mag.* iii, 483; iv, 78–9].

BATH, ROYAL VICTORIA PARK, obelisk, 1837 [*A.P.S.D.*, *s.v.* 'Bath'].

WESTON, nr. BATH, SOMERSET, ST. JOHN'S CHURCH, 1838, Gothic; enlarged 1869 by C. E. Davis [I.C.B.S.].

TWERTON CHURCH, SOMERSET, rebuilt 1839; rebuilt 1885–6 [*I.C.B.S.*].

GODNEY CHURCH, SOMERSET, 1839–40, 'Norman'; chancel 1902 [I.C.B.S.].

EAST HUNTSPILL CHURCH, SOMERSET, 1839, 'Norman' [I.C.B.S.].

CLEEVE CHURCH, nr. YATTON, SOMERSET, 1840, 'Norman' [I.C.B.S.].

BATH, THE CATHOLIC APOSTOLIC CHURCH, VINEYARDS, 1841, 'Norman' [*A.P.S.D.*, *s.v.* 'Bath'].

BRADFORD-ON-AVON, WILTS., CHRIST CHURCH, BEARFIELD, 1841, Gothic; chancel 1878 [I.C.B.S.].

SHEPTON MALLET, SOMERSET, rebuilt upper

part of Market Cross, 1841 [note by F. J. Allen accompanying photograph in National Monuments Record].

BATH, THE COUNTESS OF HUNTINGDON'S SCHOOLS, VINEYARDS, 1842 [S. D. Major, *Notabilia of Bath*, 1879, 98].

SOUTH BRENT CHURCH, SOMERSET, organ gallery, 1843 [*Builder* i, 1843, 360].

BATH, THE NEW PRISON, TWERTON, 1843 [*A.P.S.D.*, *s.v.* 'Bath'].

BROMHAM CHURCH, WILTS., restoration of interior, 1843–4 [Salisbury Diocesan Records].

BATH, THE ABBEY CEMETERY CHAPEL, 1843–4, 'Norman' [*A.P.S.D.*, *s.v.* 'Bath'].

SOUTH STOKE CHURCH, SOMERSET, repaired and enlarged, 1845, Gothic [J. Tunstall, *Rambles round Bath*, 1848, 135].

TWERTON VICARAGE, SOMERSET, 1845 [Bath Reference Library, R. Naish's MS. collections for a history of Twerton, *ex. inf.* Mr. J. Orbach].

MANNERS & GILL

The principal works of the partnership from *c.*1845 to 1862 were Gothic churches at WIDCOMBE, BATH, ST. MATTHEW, 1846–7 [G. N. Wright, *Historic Guide to Bath*, 1864, 244]; WESTON-SUPER-MARE, EMMANUEL, 1846–8 [*Builder* iv, 1846, 140; *Gent's Mag.* 1848 (i), 76] and CHRIST CHURCH, 1855 [G.R.]; KINGSTON DEVERILL, WILTS., 1847 [*Gent's Mag.* 1847 (ii), 417]; CLANDOWN, SOMERSET, 1847 [*Gent's Mag.* 1848 (i), 75]; BATH, ST. JAMES, rebuilding of tower and remodelling of nave in Italianate style, 1848; dem. 1957 [G. N. Wright, *Historic Guide to Bath*, 1864, 216; W. Ison, *Georgian Buildings of Bath*, 1948, 74]; CLIFTON (BRISTOL), ST. PAUL, 1853; dem. 1867 [A. Gomme *et al.*, *Bristol, an Architectural History*, 1979, 300]; COMPTON BISHOP, SOMERSET, N. aisle, 1851–2 [I.C.B.S.]; CLAVERTON, SOMERSET, enlarged 1858 [*The Church Rambler* i, 1876, 254]; alterations to HINTON HOUSE, HINTON CHARTERHOUSE, SOMERSET, 1847 [drawings at Hinton]; THE CORN MARKET, WALCOT STREET, BATH, 1855 [*Bath Express*, 10 Nov. 1855, *ex inf.* Mr. J. Orbach]; the enlargement of AMMERDOWN PARK, SOMERSET, for Sir William Hylton Jolliffe, 1856–7 [B. Little & A. Aldrich, *Ammerdown*, Ammerdown 1977, 15]; and the BLUECOAT SCHOOL, BATH, 1859–60, Jacobean style [R.E.M. Peach, *Bath Old & New*, 1888, 139].

MANOCCHI, GIUSEPPE, was an Italian architectural draughtsman employed by the Adam brothers in the 1760s. He may have been engaged by James Adam during his Italian tour in 1760–3, for dated drawings and payments in the Adam bank accounts show that he was in their employment in London by 1765. Manocchi was an accomplished draughtsman of the neo-classical and arabesque ornament that was an important feature of the decorative style created by the Adam brothers. How much he contributed to the Adam repertoire is difficult to say. Some of his drawings are inscribed 'di Mia invenzione', but according to Prof. Stillman 'none of Manocchi's renderings appear to have served as sources for specific Adam decorations.' Manocchi himself considered that he had been 'treated very ungenerously by the Adamses'. In October 1774 Lord Arundell was told by a correspondent in Rome that Manocchi 'has been above a year out of England, and is by no means disposed to return'. A number of his drawings are to be found in the Soane Museum, R.I.B.A. Drawings Collection, Victoria and Albert Museum, Royal Library at Windsor, and Metropolitan Museum of Art, New York. [D. Stillman, *The Decorative Work of Robert Adam*, 1966, 42–3; John Harris, *Catalogue of British Drawings for Architecture, etc. in American Collections*, 1971, 136–7; *R.I.B.A. Drawings Catalogue: L–N*, 63; letter from Fr. Thorpe, S.J., to Lord Arundell, 22 Oct. 1774, at Ugbrooke Park, Devonshire.]

MANSFIELD, GEORGE, *see* WIGG, JOSEPH.

MAR, EARL OF, *see* ERSKINE, JOHN.

MARDELL, CHARLES, signs three competently drawn elevations for a Georgian mansion among the Bromley-Davenport papers in the John Rylands Library at Manchester. They appear to be connected with Capesthorne Hall, Cheshire, and probably date from about 1730. One of them is reproduced by A. H. and S. M. Gomme in *Trans. Historic. Soc. of Lancs. and Cheshire* cxxi, 1969, 36. No other reference to Mardell has so far been found, and the character of his handwriting suggests that he may have been trained on the Continent.

MARKS, J—, exhibited at the Society of Artists in 1791 and at the Royal Academy from 1790 to 1799. Most of his exhibits were of a topographical character, but they included a 'Design for a town hall and assembly rooms' (1794) and a 'Design for a villa' (1796). He may have been the John Marks who signs two sheets of plans for a house for Lord Suffield in Albemarle Street, London [Soane Museum, lvii, 7].

MARQUAND, CHARLES (–1767), was a civil engineer who, according to Batty Langley, was a native of Guernsey. In 1737 he submitted a design for Westminster Bridge that was not accepted, but he had been to Paris to confer with French engineers and in 1749 published a pamphlet entitled *Remarks on the Different Construction of Bridges* in which he proposed a method of repairing the notorious 'sinking pier' in Labelye's bridge. In 1741 he was one of the contractors for rebuilding Brentford Bridge to Labelye's designs [Middlesex Sessions Records, Orders of Court iv, ff. 200, 211]. In the same year he designed a bridge over The Haven at Boston, Lincs. (dem. 1804) [Boston Corporation Minutes v, ff. 493–501, *ex inf.* Mr. R. Hewlings]. He had also been involved in repairing breaches at Lymington in Hampshire and in draining fens in Lincolnshire. [Eileen Harris, *British Architectural Books and Writers 1556–1785*, 1990, 312–13; R. J. B. Walker, *Westminster Bridge*, 1979, 184].

MARQUAND, JOHN (*c.*1727–1810), son of the above, was employed as a surveyor by the Navy Board in the 1780s, and in that capacity appears to have designed the CHAPEL OF ST. ANNE in PORTSMOUTH DOCKYARD, HAMPSHIRE, in 1785–7 [J. G. Coad, *Historic Architecture of the Royal Navy*, 1983, 109]. For many years he was also a surveyor in the Land Revenue Office. He retired in 1809 and died in Brixton on 24 April 1810, aged 87 [*Gent's Mag.* 1810 (i), 498; P.C.C. 260 COLLINGWOOD]. He was a member of the Smeatonian Society of Civil Engineers. The attribution to him of Gwydyr House, Whitehall, by Wheatley & Cunningham, *London Past & Present* ii, 1891, 176, appears to be without foundation.

MARSH, SAMUEL, is stated by George Vertue to have been the architect employed by the 1st Duke of Newcastle at Nottingham Castle in the 1670s, and at Bolsover Castle, Derbyshire, 'about the same time' [Walpole Soc., *Vertue Note Books* ii, 33]. His employment at BOLSOVER CASTLE in the 1660s is confirmed by documents in the Portland papers at Nottingham University (Pwl 624, a–c), but these appear to relate to repairs and alterations rather than to new construction. It is probable, however, that Marsh was responsible for the façade and interior of the Hall on the west side of the Great Court. The date of this is disputed (cf. M. Girouard, *Robert Smythson and the Elizabethan Country House*, 1983, 302, fig. 20, and P. A. Faulkner, *Bolsover Castle*, H.M.S.O. 1972), but the stylistic resemblance to Nottingham Castle is unmistakable and confirms Vertue's statement.

NOTTINGHAM CASTLE was begun by the Duke of Newcastle in 1674 and completed after his death in 1676. According to Charles Deering's *Historical Account of the Ancient and Present State of Nottingham*, 1751, 186–7, 'the Architect was one March, a Lincolnshire man, who with [others] was made Joint Trustee for finishing the work.' There is, however, no mention of Marsh in the Duke's will, which provides for an expenditure of £2000 a year out of his personal estate on finishing the building 'according to the fforme and modell thereof by me laid and designed' [P.C.C. 22 HALE]. An inscription recorded that the Castle was completed in 1679 in accordance with the Duke's will, 'and by the model he left' [Deering, *op. cit.*]. The building was gutted by fire in 1831 but restored as a Museum and Art Gallery in 1878. A wooden model, still known in 1925 as 'Mr. Marsh's model' (*R.I.B.A. Jnl.* 3rd ser. xxxii, 1925, 520), is preserved in the Museum. The elevations are designed in an elaborate Italian mannerist style with ornament reminiscent of Alessi (some of whose works were illustrated in Rubens's *Palazzi di Genova* of 1622): see photograph and measured drawings in Belcher & Macartney, *Later Renaissance Architecture in England*, 1901.

Marsh was also employed by the Duke of Newcastle at WELBECK ABBEY, NOTTS., for a letter exists in which the Duke directs an agent to 'gett Mr. Marshe to come to Welbeck, – & make a draughte, for the makinge of a good stare to my Ridinge house Chamber' [S. A. Strong, *Catalogue of Letters and other Historical Documents exhibited in the Library at Welbeck*, 1903, 56].

Deering states that Marsh was a Lincolnshire man, and records connect him with the quarries at Haydor and Culverthorpe, nr. Grantham. A rental of Haydor and Culverthorpe in the British Library shows that Samuel Marsh paid £3 a year for 'Haydor pitts' from 1678 to 1695 [Add. MS. 28647, ff. 3, 157]. Samuel Marsh 'the elder', described as 'gentleman', was living at Culverthorpe in 1666, and Samuel Marsh 'the younger', variously described as 'freemason', 'stonecutter' and 'architect', is found there between 1670 and 1697 [Lincolnshire Record Office, Welby of Denton deeds and BRA 866/5/1]. The elder Marsh was doubtless the 'Mr. Marsh' who supplied stone for building Belton House from a quarry at Haydor in 1684–6 and died in 1686 or the following year [accounts in Lincs. C.R.O.].

Samuel Marsh was clearly an important architect of the mid-seventeenth century with a distinctive style derived from sources different from those which formed the origin of the more restrained manner of Pratt and May which dominated English architecture from 1660 to 1700. In 1654–5 and 1667 he is known to have been carrying out masonry at BELVOIR CASTLE, LEICS. [Belvoir Castle archives, Account 461 and Misc. MS. 67], but here the controlling architect was John Webb (*q.v.*). There was, however, one other important house which may have reflected Marsh's Italian mannerist style. This was THORESBY HOUSE, NOTTS., now known to have been built by William Pierrepont before 1660, though subsequently remodelled in the 1680s (below, p. 951). The ornamentation of the lower windows as illustrated in *Vitruvius Britannicus* i, pl. 91, is similar to that of Marsh's work at Nottingham Castle, and if these windows formed part of the house built *c.*1650, then it would be logical to attribute them to Marsh.

MARSHALL, EDWARD (*c.*1598–1675), was a prominent London master mason in the seventeenth century. He was apprenticed to John Clarke (probably the mason of that name who built Lincoln's Inn Chapel), was made free of the Masons' Company in January 1626/7, was admitted to the Livery in 1630/1, was Warden in 1643, and Master in 1650. He carried on business as a stonemason in Fetter Lane, and was much employed as a monumental mason. In June 1660, despite the claims of John Stone to the post, he was appointed Master Mason to the Crown: in his petition he professed to have 'constantly endeavoured to promote His Majesty's interest in the late Common Council', though according to his rival he was 'a Pretender . . . who in no kind served Your Majestie' [*Cal. State Papers Domestic 1660–1*, 13; *Walpole Soc.* vii, 28]. He resigned in 1673 in favour of his son Joshua, and died on 10 December 1675, at the age of 77 years, as recorded on the family monument in the church of St. Dunstan-in-the-West.

As a mason-contractor Marshall worked under John Webb at THE VYNE, HANTS., where in 1654 he built the portico, NORTHUMBERLAND HOUSE, STRAND, where in 1655–7 he carried out work valued at nearly £900, and GUNNERSBURY HOUSE, MIDDLESEX, 1658 [W. G. Keith in *R.I.B.A. Jnl.*, 22 July 1933, 733; accounts at Alnwick Castle, U.III.3].

Marshall also acted as an architect. In 1661–2 the church of ST. DUNSTAN-IN-THE-WEST, LONDON, of which he was a parishioner, was extensively repaired and partly rebuilt under his direction and to his designs [C.U.L., Add. MS. 4144, minutes and accounts of the repairs]. In 1662 he was one of those consulted by the vestry of St. Martin-in-the-Fields about rebuilding the tower of their church [MS. Vestry Minutes in Westminster City Library, vol. iii]. He seems to have been employed by John Cartwright of Aynho, Northants., to supervise the rebuilding of AYNHO PARK after the Restoration, for in several of the surviving contracts (e.g. for the staircase and the piers in the garden) it is stated that the work shall be carried out 'according to Mr. Marshall's direction' or 'according to Mr. Edward Marshall's draught' [Northants. Record Office, Aynho papers, book of 'Agreements with the Workmen'] (*C. Life*, 2, 9 and 16 July 1953). He also provided a design for a gallery in Aynho Church, and when John Cartwright advertised his house at BARN ELMS, SURREY, to be let in 1659, prospective tenants were directed to 'enquire further of Mr. Edward Marshall, stone cutter' (*Mercurius Politicus*, 5 May 1659).

Joshua Marshall (1629–78), Edward's eldest son, had, like his father, an extensive business as a monumental sculptor and mason-contractor. He was Master of the Masons' Company in 1670 and again in 1677, and in 1673 succeeded his father as Master Mason to the King. He was one of the mason-contractors for St. Paul's Cathedral, and built the Monument, Temple Bar (in conjunction with Thomas Knight, the City Mason) and six of the City churches. He died in April 1678, and was buried with his father in the church of St. Dunstan-in-the-West.

[*A.P.S.D.*; *D.N.B.*; D. Knoop & G. P. Jones, *The London Mason in the Seventeenth Century*, 1935, 34–5; K. A. Esdaile, *English Monumental Sculpture since the Renaissance*, 1927, 136–7; R. Gunnis, *Dictionary of British Sculptors*, 1968, 254–6; *Wren Soc.* xx, 139; *History of the King's Works* v.]

MARSHALL, WILLIAM (– *c.*1793), designed the church of BOURTON-ON-THE-WATER, GLOS., 1784 [D. Royce, *A History of the Church of Bourton-on-the-Water*, 1874, 12]. The nave was rebuilt by T. G. Jackson in 1873–8 and 1891–2, but the domed west tower remains. In 1787 the church of LONGDON, WORCS., was rebuilt to Marshall's designs, incorporating the medieval tower and spire [MS. Vestry Minutes and churchwardens' accounts]. The original drawings, signed 'Wm M.', are in the Worcester Diocesan Records. A new chancel was added in 1868. Marshall appears to have lived at Bourton-on-the-Water. His will, dated 19 July 1789, was proved at Gloucester on 6 May 1793.

MARSHALL, WILLIAM, was an architect and surveyor of Northallerton in the second quarter of the nineteenth century. He designed INGLEBY ARNCLIFFE CHURCH, YORKS. (N.R.), as rebuilt 1821–2 [churchwardens' accounts in N. Yorks. R.O., *ex inf.* Mr. D. Findlay] (*Yorks. Archl. Jnl.* xxi, 1901, 133).

MARTIN, THOMAS, was in business as a builder and surveyor in London in the early nineteenth century, first in George Street, Portman Square, and then in Osnaburgh Street. In 1814–16 he was employed by the 4th Viscount Grimston to rebuild No. 47 (formerly 42) GROSVENOR SQUARE (dem. 1938), apparently to his own designs, though at the same time he was working at GORHAMBURY, HERTS., Lord Grimston's country seat, under the direction of William Atkinson (*q.v.*) [*Survey of London* xl, 160; *C. Life*, 25 Nov. 1933, 560]. By 1825 Thomas Martin was in partnership with George Martin (d. 1856), who was presumably his son, at 67 Mortimer Street. Their clientele appears to have been largely Catholic, for in 1828–31 Thomas Martin was employed by Michael Henry Blount to repair and restore the front of the Elizabethan MAPLEDURHAM HOUSE, OXON., discreetly reinstating the mullioned windows and adding a Gothic porch and a pinnacled gable [Blount papers, c. 46, c. 150] (*C. Life*, 13–20 May 1971), while in 1834 George Martin was working at STONOR PARK, OXON., where he designed a new drawing-room with a screen of Ionic columns for Thomas Stonor [Stonor papers, 152/15/10, *ex inf.* Lord Camoys] (*C. Life*, 20 Oct. 1950, where his surname is wrongly given as 'Masters'). In 1848–51 George designed a spectacular but coarsely detailed Gothic mansion at ALLERTON MAULEVERER, YORKS. (W.R.), for another Catholic client, the 18th Lord Stourton [box of drawings in Leeds Archives] (*C. Life*, 24 Dec. 1987). He lived at 85 Baker Street, where he died in 1856 [P.C.C., 1856 Register, f. 569].

MARTIN, WILLIAM, was an architect and builder of Bretby, Derbyshire. A farm at Bretby designed by him is illustrated by John Farey, *General View of the Agriculture of Derbyshire* ii, 1813, pl. 1. Henry Isaac Stevens (1807–1873), architect of Derby, was his son-in-law and perhaps his pupil. In 1831 Martin made designs for enlarging CONGERSTONE CHURCH, LEICS., that were carried out in 1834 under Stevens's direction [I.C.B.S.].

MARTYR, THOMAS (*c.*1777–1852), was the son of a builder. He became a pupil of S.P. Cockerell, and exhibited student's work at the Royal Academy from 1794 to 1799. He subsequently made a continental tour in company with his fellow-pupil, Joseph Kay, and on his return to England commenced practice in about 1805. But on his marriage he entered into partnership with his father, then established 'with a good government connection' at Greenwich. He died on 2 January 1852, aged about 75 years. His son, Richard Smirke Martyr (1811–54), became a pupil of his godfather, Robert Smirke, and after a short continental tour established himself in practice in Greenwich. He was much engaged in surveys and valuations of property in connection with the building of railways in south-east London and Kent. He was surveyor to several local charities and trusts, to the Burney estate, and to the newly created district of Deptford. He was a member of the Architectural Society, and in 1842 became a fellow of the Institute of British Architects on its union with that body. He died at Greenwich on 10 October 1854, aged 43 [*A.P.S.D.*].

MARVIN, JOSEPH, exhibited architectural and topographical drawings at the Royal Academy from 1815 to 1819. He subsequently practised as an architect and surveyor in the Edgware Road. In 1819 he had a pupil named B. May, who exhibited a design for a mausoleum at the Royal Academy from his office.

MASON, GEORGE (1782–1865), architect and builder, was born at Wickham Market in Suffolk. After a period in London, he returned to Suffolk and settled at Ipswich, where he became Borough Surveyor and one of the Dock Commissioners under an Act of 1837. The RECTORIES that he designed at SHOTTISHAM and CHELMONDISTON in SUFFOLK in 1847 and 1848, respectively, are in a 'vernacular Georgian' style [C. Brown *et al.*, *Dictionary of Architects of Suffolk Buildings, 1800–1914*, 1991, 143].

Mason was the father of William Mason (1810–97), who became a pupil of Edward Blore and practised for a few years in Ipswich before emigrating first to New South Wales (1838) and then to New Zealand, where he had a successful career and ranks as the colony's pioneer architect. His principal works in England were the churches of ST. JAMES, BRIGHTLINGSEA, ESSEX, 1837, Gothic [*Architectural Mag.* iv, 1837, 79–80], ST. BOTOLPH, COLCHESTER, 1837–8, in the 'Norman style' [H.E. von Stürmer, *Historical Guide to Colchester*, 1852, 25], for which the original drawings are in the Colchester Museum, and

EAST DONYLAND, ESSEX, 1837–8, Gothic, on an octagonal plan said to be based on the Chapter House at York [G. M. Benton, 'The Destroyed Church of . . . East Donyland', *Essex Arch. Soc's Trans.*, N.S. xix, 1930, 99]. He also designed several parsonage houses and workhouses, and a R.C. convent chapel in Woodbridge Road, Ipswich, has been attributed to him because of similarities to his church at East Donyland [J. Stackpoole, *William Mason, the First New Zealand Architect*, 1971].

MASON, JOHN, was a London mason who began as an assistant to William Stanton (*q.v.*), and was, through him, employed at Stonyhurst in Lancashire, where he worked as a stone-carver between 1702 and 1713. He later had a yard in the parish of St. Sepulchre's, Holborn [R. Gunnis, *Dictionary of British Sculptors*, 1968, 258]. In 1707 Mason designed the SHIREBURN ALMSHOUSES at STONYHURST. The contract between Sir Nicholas Shireburn, Bart., and Richard Rideing of Waddington, Yorkshire, mason, dated 17 October 1707, specifies that the almshouses are to be built 'according to Mr. John Mason's draught', and Rideing's workmanship was afterwards measured by Mason [contract and account-book among archives of Weld of Lulworth]. These very handsome almshouses, originally built on a remote site, were re-erected at Hurst Green, Stonyhurst, in 1946. They are illustrated in *C. Life*, 22 Oct. 1910, 582–3.

MASON, JOHN (1794–1847), was the son of a carpenter of Derby of the same name. He acted as clerk of the works under Francis Goodwin at the County Gaol in 1826–7 and in the same capacity under Matthew Habershon at the Guildhall in 1828. On the completion of the gaol the committee formally recorded their 'approbation of his conduct in the discharge of every part of his duty'. Thereafter Mason practised as an architect. In 1836 he was appointed surveyor of bridges for the southern part of Derbyshire, a post which he retained until his death in 1847 [Derbyshire Q.S. Records]. After the Derby riots of 1831 he designed eight 'martello towers' to defend the perimeter wall of the County Gaol against attack [S. Glover, *History of the County of Derby* ii (1), 1833, 455]. He designed the Gothic LIVERSAGE ALMSHOUSES, LONDON ROAD, DERBY, 1835–6 [S. Glover, *History and Directory of Derby*, 1843, 41], and the UNION WORKHOUSE, OSMASTON ROAD (now Derby China factory), 1839 [*Derby Mercury, ex inf.* Mr. Maxwell Craven]. He built as a speculation three 'Tudor' villas, Nos. 112–116 GREEN LANE, DERBY, 1832–5 [title deeds, *ex inf.* Mr. Craven] and may have been responsible for LONDON TERRACE, LONDON ROAD, as he occupied No. 1 in 1827. APPLEBY MAGNA CHURCH, LEICS., was restored by Mason in 1829–32 [G. K. Brandwood, 'Leicestershire Churches 1825–50', in *The Adaptation of Change*, Leicester Museum 1980, 46], and he enlarged the S. side of OCKBROOK CHURCH, DERBYSHIRE, in 1835 [I.C.B.S.]. He also designed undistinguished Gothic churches at HULLAND, DERBYSHIRE, 1837–8 [I.C.B.S.] and TANSLEY, DERBYSHIRE, 1839–40 [I.C.B.S.] and rebuilt the W. end of ST. MARY'S CHURCH, BOULTON, DERBY, 1840; altered 1871 [Vestry Minutes *ex inf.* Mr. Craven].

MASON, WILLIAM, made three drawings of gateways among the Fitzwilliam papers from Milton House, Northants., in the Northants. Record Office (Nos. 37, 38, 39). One is signed 'William Mason June 28 [16] 75', another is described as 'A Patterne of ye L. Berkeley's Gate drawen by Wm. Masonne'.

MASON, WILLIAM, was the surveyor responsible for rebuilding DAGENHAM CHURCH, ESSEX, in an unsophisticated Gothic style in 1801–5. His name appears on the west porch [Vestry Minutes in Essex Record Office; *V.C.H. Essex* v, 296 and plate].

MASON, WILLIAM (1810–1897), *see* MASON, GEORGE.

MASSEY, EDWARD, *see* SCOLTOCK, SAMUEL.

MASSIE, JAMES (–1811), was a builder-architect of Aberdeen, where he had a yard on Castlehill. In 1790–1 he was employed by William Fraser to carry out an overhaul of the roofs of CASTLE FRASER, ABERDEENSHIRE [H. Gordon Slade, 'Castle Fraser', *Proc. Soc. Antiquaries of Scotland* 109, 1977–8, 257], and in 1803–4 he designed the Gothic ST. PETER'S CHURCH, ABERDEEN (R.C.) [minute-book at church, *ex inf.* Mr. David Walker]. Massie died on 11 June 1811 [*Scots Mag.* 1811, 559]. Archibald Simpson (*q.v.*) was in his office for a time.

MASTERS, CHARLES HARCOURT (1759–), the son of Benedict Masters, a goldsmith of Bath, practised there as an architect and surveyor. In 1786–7 he made a fine set of maps of the roads managed by the Bath Turnpike Trust which are now in the Somerset Record Office. In 1789 he constructed a model of Bath to the scale of 30 feet to 1 inch, which he exhibited at his house, and afterwards in London. It was based on a survey of the city which he published in 1794. Masters was much employed as a land surveyor, and was concerned in the development of property in Widcombe and Lyncombe, where he designed several small houses, including those in Cottage (now Bloomfield) Crescent. His most important work was the SYDNEY HOTEL, built in 1796–7 at one end of the hexagonal SYDNEY GARDENS, for whose layout Masters was also responsible. The house, heightened by J. Pinch in 1836, and remodelled by Reginald Blomfield in 1913–5, is now the Holburne of Menstrie Museum. According to Bryan Little, *The Buildings of Bath*, 1947, 129, Masters also remodelled BATTLEFIELD HOUSE at LANSDOWN, nr. BATH, in Gothic style in 1802. At DYRHAM PARK, GLOS., he altered the planting and re-routed the drive for William Blathwayt in 1798–9 [Anthony Mitchell, *The Park and Garden at Dyrham*, 1977, 9], and a plan for the layout of the grounds of HARPTREE COURT, SOMERSET, made by him *c.*1802, is in private hands.

Towards the end of his life, Masters 'practised under the name of Harcourt, at first on his own account and later in partnership with George P. Manners'. It was in conjunction with the latter that in 1817–18 he designed the neo-classical COTHELSTONE HOUSE, SOMERSET (dem. 1968), for E. J. Esdaile [Somerset Record Office, DD/ES, Box 15] (J.P. Neale, *Views of Seats*, 2nd ser.iv, 1828).

[W. Ison, *The Georgian Buildings of Bath*, 1948, 43, 95–8, 2nd ed. 1980, 17, 20, 84, 181; information from Mr. I. P. Collis and Mr. J. Orbach.]

MATHEWS, CHARLES JAMES (1803–1878), was the son of Charles Mathews (1776–1835), a well-known actor. In 1819 he became a pupil of Augustus Pugin. On the expiry of his articles in 1823 he went over to Ireland to build a house for Lord Blessington at Mountjoy Forest, Co. Tyrone. No progress was made with the house, but Mathews became intimate with Lord Blessington, who invited him to spend some time in Naples with a party of aristocratic friends, whom he delighted by his humour and vivacity. In 1824 he became architect to an iron and coal company at Coed Talwyn in North Wales, and while in this employment designed an inn, a bridge, some cottages and a house for the director called HARTSHEATH HALL, nr. MOLD in FLINTSHIRE, 1825. Two years later he returned to London, where for a short time he worked in Nash's office. An allowance from his father allowed him to make another visit to Italy in 1827 in company with James D'Egville. In 1832 he became District Surveyor for Bow and Bethnal Green, but in 1835 he finally abandoned architecture for the stage, where he achieved some celebrity. A sketch of a vase made by Mathews in Rome is in the R.I.B.A. Drawings Collection. [*The Life of C. J. Mathews*, ed. C. Dickens, 1879; *Builder* xxxvi, 1878, 695; *D.N.B.*; Dudley Harbron, 'Charles Mathews', *Arch. Rev.* lxxx, 1936, 77–80.]

MATHEWSON, GEORGE, practised in Dundee from 1832 or 1833 until about 1853, the date of his death or retirement. His unexecuted designs for the Watt Institute at Dundee are in Dundee Public Library [information from Mr. David Walker, to whom all references to the *Dundee Advertiser* are due].

? CUNMONT HOUSE, NEWBIGGING, nr. DUNDEE, 1834 [probably the house whose contract was advertised in *Dundee Advertiser*, 27 Jan. 1834].

DUNDEE, ST., ANDREW'S R.C. CHURCH, NETHERGATE, 1836, Gothic [C. Mackie, *Historical Description of Dundee*, 1836, 129].

DUNDEE, ELM LODGE and houses in MAGDALEN PLACE, 1836–40 [*Dundee Advertiser*, 12 Feb. 1836].

DUNDEE, new street on the CROFT OF BLAIRGOWRIE, 1836 [*Dundee Advertiser*, 16 Sept. 1836].

TOMINTOUL, BANFFSHIRE, R.C. CHAPEL OF OUR LADY & ST. MICHAEL, 1837, Gothic; altered internally 1939 [Scottish Catholic Archives, BL 6/175/9 and IM 29/4/4, *ex inf.* Mrs. E. Beaton].

BEACH COTTAGE, 23 DOUGLAS TERRACE, WEST FERRY, DUNDEE, for himself, *c.*1838.

DUNDEE LUNATIC ASYLUM, additions, 1838 [*Dundee Advertiser*, 23 March 1838].

DUNDEE, north-east corner of UNION STREET, 1839 [*Dundee Advertiser*, 14 Aug. 1840].

DUNDEE, DUDHOPE CHURCH (now Repertory Theatre), LOCHEE ROAD, 1839, Romanesque [*Dundee Advertiser*, 7 Oct. 1839].

DUNDEE, WALLACETOWN CHURCH, 1840, Romanesque; altered 1876 [*Forfarshire Illustrated*, Dundee, 1843, 23].

INVERARITY, ANGUS, SCHOOL, 1840 [*Dundee Advertiser*, 20 March 1840].

DUNDEE, MAINS SCHOOL (now private house called 'St. Malo'), 1841 [*Dundee Advertiser*, 22 Jan. 1841].

MONIFIETH, ANGUS, LINLATHEN SCHOOL, 1841 [*Dundee Advertiser*, 26 Feb. 1841].

DUNDEE, ST. DAVID'S PARISH SCHOOL, LARCH STREET, 1842; dem. [*Dundee Advertiser*, 7 Jan. 1842].

DUNDEE, ST. DAVID'S FREE CHURCH, 1843

[*Dundee Advertiser*, 28 July 1843].

ARBROATH, ANGUS, ST. THOMAS'S R.C. CHURCH, 1846–8 [article in *Dundee Advertiser*, 9 Sept. 1899].

DUNDEE, ST. MARY'S R.C. CHURCH, FOREBANK, 1850; towers added 1900–1 [*Dundee Advertiser*, 18 Oct. 1850].

MATSON, CHARLES (*c.*1797–), was a pupil of Joseph Kay. He entered the Royal Academy Schools in 1815, aged 18, and exhibited at the Academy from 1816 to 1819, his last exhibit being a 'View of Heath Lodge, Hampstead, the seat of C. King Esq.'

MATSON, JOHN (1760–1826), the son of a builder, was in business as a master builder at Bridlington from about 1790 until 1823, when he removed to London. As a young man he was trepanned into the Indian Army, and underwent a series of adventures which earned him some celebrity. He had received instruction in draughtsmanship, and may have designed some of the buildings which he erected in Bridlington, which included the Baths and 'several good houses'. In 1806 he built the lighthouse on Flamborough Head to the designs of Samuel Wyatt. His son John moved to London in 1817, and presumably built Matson Terrace, Kingsland Road, Shoreditch, where his father died on 23 February 1826. [*Indian Warfare; or the Extraordinary Adventures of John Matson, the Kidnapped Youth late of Kingsland Road, London, and formerly of Bridlington Quay in the county of York, Architect and Builder*, 1842; information from Mr. Francis Johnson, F.R.I.B.A.]

MATTHEWS, JAMES TILLY (–1814) was a London tea merchant who was a self-appointed intermediary between France and England at the time of the outbreak of war in 1793 [*English Historical Review* liii, 1938, 661–8]. In 1797 he was pronounced insane and was sent to the Bethlehem Hospital. While in confinement he amused himself with drawing and engraving, and was the author of a publication entitled *Useful Architecture*, in which he proposed to give designs for buildings 'from the £50 Cot to the £200,000 Mansion, mostly grounded on the Grecian, Roman, Gothic, and Plain Styles of Architecture'. The first and only part was published in 1812.

MATTHEWS, WILLIAM (*c.*1780–1847), was a builder and surveyor of Ashby-de-la-Zouche in Leicestershire, where he died on 18 June 1847, aged 67. In 1825 he was the surveyor who supervised the rebuilding of the nave of SWANNINGTON CHURCH, LEICS. (not necessarily to his own designs) [I.C.B.S.], and in 1831 he altered STONEY STANTON RECTORY, LEICS. (rebuilt 1844) [J. D. Bennett, *Leicestershire Architects 1700–1850*, Leicester 1968].

MATTHEWS, WILLIAM LAUGHER (*c.*1798–1827), was the son of W. Matthews of Birmingham. He died at Penzance on 10 May 1827, aged 29 [*Aris's Birmingham Gazette*, 21 May 1827]. He exhibited architectural designs at the Royal Academy in 1822–6 and at the Birmingham Society of Artists in 1827.

MAUND, ANDREW (*c.*1722–1803), 'architect of this town and county', died at Brecon on 24 March 1803, aged 81, and is commemorated by a monument in the cathedral. He was doubtless the father of Andrew Maund who was in business as a builder at Bromyard in Herefordshire in the 1790s and who in 1802–8 was responsible for alterations to HANLEY COURT, WORCS. (dem. 1931) for Col. Wakeman Newport, including the insertion of a gallery in the hall and enlarging the stables [Birmingham Reference Library Archives, Hanbury Court 666, *ex inf.* Mr. N. Kingsley]. The Andrew Maund who was in practice as an architect in Worcester in 1828–9 may have represented a third generation, while John Maund of Brecon, who estimated for fitting up a library at PENPONT, BRECONSHIRE, in 1801 [N.L.W., Penpont MSS. II, 1303, *ex inf.* Mr. Thomas Lloyd] was presumably another son of Andrew (d. 1803).

See p. 1138

MAWLEY, EDWARD (–1826), was an architect of whose career little is known before 1821, when he was appointed architect to the Commissioners for Building New Churches. He was a member of the Painter-Stainers' Company and an original member of the Surveyors' Club, of which he was President in 1799. In 1807 he exhibited at the Royal Academy a 'Design for a gentleman's house, now building in Oxfordshire'. BITTESWELL CHURCH, LEICS., was restored under his direction in 1822 [Parish records in Leics. C.R.O. DE 759/2, *ex inf.* Mr. G. K. Brandwood]. In 1824 he was staying at STANFORD HALL, LEICS., in order to give Mrs. Otway Cave advice about some proposed alterations there [Church Commissioners, file 21744, part 5]. He died on 30 January 1826, as the result of a carriage accident, and was succeeded as the Commissioners' architect by J. H. Good.

Henry Mawley (d. 1871), Edward's son, followed the same profession and was in turn succeeded by his son Septimus Mawley. His works included HOLY TRINITY CHURCH,

HOUNSLOW, MIDDLESEX, Gothic, 1828–9 [G. J. Aungier, *History of Syon Monastery and Isleworth*, 1840, 508–9]; some chambers in DEVEREUX COURT, MIDDLE TEMPLE [exhibited at R.A. 1841]; and TWINING'S COFFEE HOUSE, 215 STRAND [exhibited at R.A. 1841].

MAY, HUGH (1621–1684), was the seventh son of John May, a Sussex gentleman with an estate at Rawmere in the parish of Mid Lavant, three miles north of Chichester.[1] He was baptized at Mid Lavant on 2 October 1621. Nothing is known of his early life, but in 1669 he told Pepys that he had served the Duke of Buckingham 'for twenty years together, in all his wants and dangers'. This statement is confirmed by the account-book of Sir Charles Cotterell, the Duke's steward, which in 1650–1 records 'My charges to Rotterdam and the Hagh, going to meet Mr. May when he came out of Scotland', and indicates that the latter was engaged in effecting the transfer of works of art from York House to Holland, where they were to be sold for the Duke's benefit.[2] Letters from May to Cottrell, written in London during this period, show that he was living with 'my friend Mr. Lely' in Covent Garden, and in 1656, when Lely had a pass to go to Holland, May was allowed to accompany him as his 'servant'. This was presumably an expedient designed to get May out of the country without attracting unwelcome attention, for the object of his journey was to join the exiled Court, and the favour shown to May after the Restoration shows that he must have rendered not inconsiderable services to the Royalist cause. On 29 June 1660 he was appointed Paymaster of the Works and in that capacity dealt with the financial side of the great overhaul of the royal palaces which occupied the years immediately after 1660. In April 1666 he received a warrant to act as Surveyor of the Works during the illness of Sir John Denham, and when the latter died in 1669 he hoped to be his successor. But he was (as he told Pepys) 'put by' in favour of Wren, and had to be content with the comptrollership, to which he had been promoted in June 1668. This gave him an income of less than £200 a year, whereas Wren as Surveyor was receiving nearly £400, besides the many incidental perquisites of his office. In conversation with Pepys, May attributed this disappointment to the ingratitude of the Duke of Buckingham. 'But he tells me', Pepys noted, 'the King is kind to him, and hath promised him a pension of £300 a year out of the Works' – an increment which was, in fact, granted to him on 24 March 1669, 'as a mark of the King's gracious acceptance of his loyal and faithfull service'. Moreover in the following year he succeeded his brother Adrian both as Clerk of the Recognizances in the Courts of Common Pleas and King's Bench and as inspector of French and English gardeners at Whitehall, St. James's, Greenwich and Hampton Court. The latter post was worth £200 a year, while the former entitled him to a fee of 3s. 4d. for each recognizance. Finally, in November 1673, within a few days of Wren's appointment as architect to St. Paul's, May succeeded Hartgill Baron as Comptroller of the Works at Windsor, and took charge of the reconstruction of the Castle for Charles II.

May's ability as a practising architect had already been shown at Eltham Lodge and Cornbury House, and as Pepys's Diary shows, he had the reputation of being 'a very ingenious man'. He does not seem to have shared Wren's scientific interests, but both John Evelyn and Roger North were his friends, and it was with his help that in 1664 the former published his translation of Fréart's *Parallel of Architecture*, 'perhaps the most influential work of its kind in English'. In 1665–6 he was involved, with Pratt, Webb and Wren, in the problem of how best to repair the decrepit fabric of old St. Paul's Cathedral. After the Great Fire he was one of the three surveyors nominated by the King to supervise the rebuilding of the City in conjunction with three representatives chosen by the Lord Mayor and Corporation. As a public official with experience of the finance of building, he was well qualified to act in this capacity, and although he did not himself design any of the new churches and public buildings, his duties as a commissioner took up so much of his time that in March 1667 he was allowed to have a deputy at the Office of Works on account of his 'extraordinary business'.

As Comptroller of the Works, and architect to Windsor Castle, May was a well-known figure in the Court of Charles II, and it was for Court acquaintances that most of his recorded works were erected. The houses which he designed for them are remarkable for the

[1] Pedigrees of the family are printed in Dallaway's *Western Division of Sussex*, 1815, 114, Nichols's *Leicestershire* iv (2), 548, and *Harleian Soc.* viii, 229–30.

[2] I am indebted to the late Mr. T. Cottrell-Dormer for allowing me to examine his ancestor's account-book, preserved at Rousham Park, Oxon. There is a story that May fought at the Battle of Worcester under the Duke of Buckingham, and was entrusted with the latter's 'George', which he preserved through all dangers and eventually restored to his master in Holland (Collins's *Peerage* iii, 1812, 783).

introduction of what has been described as 'a mature baroque style of interior treatment', which he achieved with the aid of Verrio, the painter, and Grinling Gibbons, who owed his first important commissions to May. Unfortunately, few of his works survive, and his career has been overshadowed by that of his rival, Wren. But of his importance as one of the two or three men who determined the character of English domestic architecture after the Restoration there can be no doubt, and his work at Windsor is of the greatest interest in the history of English baroque architecture. Of his ability as a draughtsman, nothing is known, for no drawings by his hand have so far been identified.[1] But that he understood the technicalities of architecture is shown by an observation of John Aubrey that 'twas Mr. Hugh May that brought in the Staff-moulding on solid right Angles, after the Restauration of the King. The fashion has taken much' (*Chronologia Architectonica*, 1671 – Bodleian, MS. Top. Gen. c. 25, f. 179).

May's association with Lely – first recorded during the Commonwealth – was to be one of long standing, for in later years May asked Lely's advice when designing Cassiobury Park, and they were both consulted by Sir Ralph Verney about the value of a monument executed by Grinling Gibbons. At Audley End there is a portrait of May by Lely which shows him in company with the painter, and when Lely died in 1680 May was one of his executors. May himself died on 21 February 1683/4, aged 62, and was buried in the family vault in Mid Lavant Church. When the vault collapsed in 1829, May's coffin-plate was removed to the chancel. The inscription on it is as follows:

> Hugh May Esqr Comptroller of the Works to King Charles the Second. Comptroller to the Castle of Windsor and by his Maj.^{tie} appointed to be Sole Architect in Contriving and Governing the Works in the Great Alterations made by his Maj.^{tie} in that Castle Dyed the 21th day of February 168$\frac{3}{4}$ in the Sixty Second yeare of his Age.

By his will [P.C.C. 32 HARE], dated 19 January 1683/4, and witnessed by, among others, Nicholas Hawksmoor, May left to his nephew Thomas, son of his elder brother John, £1000, all the silver plate given to him by the Earl of Essex, and the leases of certain properties which he had purchased 'for the greater conveniency they are to Rawmeare estate'. He also left £100 towards the repair of Mid Lavant Church, 'in case I doe not see and procure it to bee repaired in my Lifetime', and a similar sum to the fabric of Chichester Cathedral. His executors were Sir Henry Capell, Thomas May and Nathaniel Cole, the King's Chaplain. A miniature portrait of May painted by Samuel Cooper in 1653 was acquired for the Royal Library at Windsor in 1958. It is reproduced in *The History of the King's Works* v, pl. 2.

[*A.P.S.D.*; *Wren Soc.* xx, 141–2; *Cal. State Papers Domestic: Charles II, passim; Cal. Treas. Books 1667–8* ii, pp. xxx–xxxiii; *Builder* xi, 645; C. H. Collins Baker, *Lely and the Stuart Portrait Painers*, 1912, i, 142, 149, ii, 132–3; the *Diaries* of Evelyn and Pepys; *Sussex Arch. Colls.* cvii, 1969, 1–3, cxx, 1982, 231; T. F. Reddaway, *The Rebuilding of London after the Great Fire*, 1940, 57; G. F. Webb, *Wren* (Great Lives series); G. F. Webb, 'The Architectural Antecedents of Sir Christopher Wren', *R.I.B.A. Jnl.*, 27 May 1933, 582; G. F. Webb, 'Baroque Art', *Proceedings of the British Academy* xxxiii, 1947; Kerry Downes, *English Baroque Architecture*, 1966, *passim; History of the King's Works* v, 1976, *passim*.]

CORNBURY HOUSE, OXON., rebuilt east front and designed stables and chapel for 1st Earl of Clarendon, 1663–8; interior completely altered at various times [J. Newman, 'Hugh May, Clarendon and Cornbury', in *English Architecture Public and Private: Essays for Kerry Downes*, ed. Bold & Chaney, 1993].

ELTHAM LODGE, KENT, for Sir John Shaw, Bart., 1664 [*The Architecture of Sir Roger Pratt*, ed. R. T. Gunther, 1928, 232] (*C. Life*, 9–16 Aug. 1919; H. A. Tipping, *English Homes, Period IV* (i), 1929, 93–110).

LONDON, BERKELEY HOUSE, PICCADILLY, for 1st Lord Berkeley of Stratton, 1665; dem. 1733 [Evelyn's *Diary*, 25 Sept. 1672; *The Architecture of Sir Roger Pratt*, ed. R. T. Gunther, 1928, 139, 261].

CHILTON LODGE, nr. HUNGERFORD, BERKS., 'advised' his cousin Bulstrode Whitelock about an addition built in 1666; rebuilt 1789–90 [*The Diary of Bulstrode Whitelock*, ed. R. Spalding, 1990, 714, 716–7].

LONDON, BURLINGTON HOUSE, PICCADILLY, supervised completion of house, 1667–8, for 1st Earl of Burlington after the latter had bought it in an unfinished state from Sir John Denham; completely remodelled in the eighteenth and nineteenth centuries. It is possible that May had also been Denham's architect, but evidence is lacking

[1] He may have relied to some extent on draughtsmen, for the Cornbury accounts (Bodleian, MS. Clarendon 78) contain two payments 'For Drawing the first Draft of Cornbury for Mr. May' and 'For Drawing the 2nd. Draft of Cornbury for Mr. May'.

[*Survey of London* xxxii, 391–2 and illustrations].

HOLME LACY HOUSE, HEREFS., was built by Anthony Deane of Uffington for 1st Viscount Scudamore, by a contract dated 16 Feb. 1673/4, in which it is stated that many of the details were to be copied from those of Sir John Duncombe's house at Battlesden, Beds. It was agreed that in the event of any dispute both parties should submit to the 'finall Arbitrament and determination of Hugh May Esqr,', who may possibly have made the designs [P.R.O., Chancery Masters' Exhibits, 'Duchess of Norfolk Deeds', Box M, bundle 24, no. 7789] (*C. Life*, 12–19 June 1909).

WINDSOR CASTLE, remodelling of the Upper Ward, including St. George's Hall and the King's Chapel, 1675–84 [W. H. St. J. Hope, *Windsor Castle*, 1913, 312 *et seq.*; *History of the King's Works* v, 315–28]. Nearly all May's work has since been destroyed or altered.

CASSIOBURY PARK, HERTS., for 1st Earl of Essex, *c.*1677–80; remodelled by James Wyatt *c.*1800; dem. 1922 [Evelyn's *Diary*, 18 April 1680; a letter from May to the Earl of Essex about 'severall meettings and consultations concerning the frontis's peece on the courteside at Caishobury' which he had had with Lely is printed in part by C. H. Collins Baker, *Lely and the Stuart Portrait Painters* ii, 1912, 133; what appear to be some of the original working drawings for the plasterwork are in Bodleian, MS. Gough Drawings a.3] (J. Britton, *Cassiobury Park*, 1837, gives plans and views; *C. Life*, 17 Sept. 1910).

MOOR PARK, HERTS., for James, Duke of Monmouth, and his wife Anne Scott, *suo jure* Duchess of Buccleuch, 1679–84; remodelled 1725–8. The house was built by a team of Office of Works craftsmen whose names are given in S.R.O., GD 224/1059/14. The mason's and carpenter's contracts both name May as arbitrator, and all artificers' work was to be 'certified' to May by Matthew Bancks, who acted as site supervisor. The cornice was to be copied from Cassiobury (above), a house recently begun to May's designs. [Dorset C.R.O., Fox-Strangways papers, Box 238 and B.L., Add. MS 51326, ff. 4–5]. For plans of the house as built see *Arch. Hist.* 35, 1992, fig. 36.

attributed: FROGMORE HOUSE, BERKS., for Thomas May (Hugh May's nephew), 1680; remodelled by James Wyatt 1793–5 [Nicola Smith, 'Frogmore House before James Wyatt', *Antiquaries' Jnl.* lxv, 1985].

KILKENNY CASTLE, CO. KILKENNY, IRELAND, was altered and embellished, *c.*1682, for 1st Duke of Ormonde. Sir William Robinson, the Surveyor-General of Ireland, was probably the architect [cf. Bodleian, Carte MS. 54, f. 74], but in December 1681 the Earl of Longford wrote to the Duke of Ormonde from England to say that he had gone 'immediately to Mr. May to consult with him about the Proportion of the Peeres [presumably of a gateway] in which as yett he is not of opinion to make any alteration from the draught he sent & your Grace returned' [National Library of Ireland, Ormonde papers, MS. 2417, f. 237, misquoted in Hist. MSS. Comm., *Ormonde*, N.S. vi, 282–3, *ex inf.* Dr. Loeber]. For a water-house here attributed to May by Dr. Loeber see *Arch. Hist.* 22, 1979, 57 and pl. 9a.

CHISWICK, MIDDLESEX, house (later Morton House) for Sir Stephen Fox, 1682–4; dem. 1812 [Evelyn's *Diary*, 30 Oct. 1682; T. Faulkner, *History of Brentford, Ealing and Chiswick*, 1845, 372–3]. The building accounts in the Fox-Strangways papers in Dorset C.R.O. (Box 162) show that the house was built by a team of Office of Works craftsmen.

MAY, MARTIN (1639–1707), of Kidlington, Oxfordshire, was a member of a family established in that parish since the sixteenth century, and is described as 'gentleman' (*generosus*) on his tombstone in Kidlington churchyard. When the S.E. and N.E. blocks of the GARDEN QUADRANGLE of NEW COLLEGE, OXFORD, were built in 1700 and 1706, respectively, the structural timberwork was to be 'such as Mr. Martin May of Kidlington . . . shall approve' and he was to act as arbitrator in the event of any dispute. He received a present of £10 14s. from the College in 1704 [New College archives; M. H. A. Stapleton, *History of Kidlington*, Oxford Hist. Soc. 1893, 134–5, 143].

MAYHEW, JAMES GRAY (1771–1845), was born on 8 February 1771. He exhibited architectural designs at the Royal Academy from 1792 to 1796. In 1798 he became Surveyor to the Westminster Fire Office and in 1823 District Surveyor of the Parish of St. James, Westminster. Mayhew's practice consisted chiefly in surveying and repairing buildings for the Fire Office. In 1808–10 he was responsible for converting premises in King Street, Covent Garden, as offices for its use [Westminster Fire Office Records, *ex inf.* Mr. G. F. Osborn]. Mayhew died on 24 March 1845, aged 75, leaving a son, Charles Mayhew, who succeeded him in both his surveyorships. Several notebooks and sketch-books belonging to J. G. Mayhew and his son were sold at Sotheby's on 27 October 1970. [*A.P.S.D.*]

MEAD, JOHN CLEMENT (1798–1839), born 3 April 1798, was the son by his second wife of Clement Mead, a London surveyor who in 1794 designed BRYNBELLA, DENBIGHSHIRE, for Gabriel Piozzi [exhib. at R.A. 1794; letters from Mead to Piozzi in John Rylands Library, Manchester, English MS. 607]. Mead was trained in his father's office, and was admitted to the Royal Academy Schools in 1815. In 1820 he obtained the second premium in the competition for the new General Post Office in London, drawings of which he exhibited at the Academy in 1824 and 1826. In 1821 he won the competition for the new hall of the Salters' Company, but the designs executed were by the Company's surveyor H. Carr. In 1823 he competed for the completion of King's College, Cambridge, and in the following year made designs (reproduced in *Arch. Rev.* July 1946, p. lxii), which were not adopted, for a new court at St. John's College, Cambridge. In 1822–4 he designed and erected the CAMBRIDGE OBSERVATORY, which is described and illustrated in Weale's *New Survey of London* ii, 1853, 670–2: see also Willis & Clark, iii, 195. His other works included the premises of Messrs. Rundell, Bridge & Rundell on Ludgate Hill, built 1825, dem. *c.*1895, the designs for which (sold at Sotheby's 4 Feb. 1988) he exhibited in 1827. He visited France, where he was professionally employed, and became much interested in the system of abattoirs as well as the casting of works of art in bronze. He died, after a long illness, on 15 January 1839, at the age of 41, and was buried at Piddletrenthide, Dorset, to which place he had retired. He left a widow and three sons. [*A.P.S.D.*; *The Farington Diary*, ed. J. Greig, viii, 42, 114, 115.]

MEADOWS, JOHN (*c.*1732–1791), practised as an architect and surveyor in New Peter Street, Westminster. Most of his recorded works were, however, in Devonshire. In 1770–2 he was engaged in altering EGGESFORD HOUSE (rebuilt 1822) for H. A. Fellowes [accounts in Portsmouth papers in Hants. C.R.O., Box 31, *ex inf.* Mr. J. Rothwell]; in 1779 he remodelled HARTLAND ABBEY for Paul Orchard in a Gothic style [R. P. Chope, *The Book of Hartland*, 1940, 65] (*C. Life*, 8–15 Sept. 1983); and in *c.*1790 he rebuilt ARLINGTON COURT for J.P. Chichester in a plain Georgian style [R. Polwhele, *History of Devonshire* iii, 1797, 401]. The last house was again rebuilt in 1820–3, owing it is said to the defective construction of Meadows's building. He also repaired EGGESFORD RECTORY in 1782 [Exeter Diocesan Records]. In about 1780–5 Meadows supervised the rebuilding of HURSTBOURNE PARK, HANTS. (destroyed by fire 1870) for Fellowes's brother-in-law, the 2nd Earl of Portsmouth, to the designs of James Wyatt [Harrison's *Views of Seats*, 1787]. It was at Hurstbourne that Meadows made his will on 15 November 1786 [P.C.C. 583 BEVOR]. He died at Arlington on 26 September 1791, aged 59, and is commemorated by a tablet on the south wall of the church there. His daughter Jane married as her second husband the Devonshire surveyor James Rendle or Rendel, and was the mother of the civil engineer James Meadows Rendel (1799–1856).

MEAR, STEPHEN (*c.*1752–1827), and his son WILLIAM (1796–1866), were architects and builders in Norwich. Stephen died on 15 August 1827 in his 76th year, and is commemorated by a tablet in the church of St. John de Sepulchre. He had been for many years surveyor to the Great Hospital [*Norwich Mercury*, 18 Aug. 1827]. In 1820 he altered MOUSEHOLD HALL, nr. NORWICH, for Sir Robert J. Harvey in such a way as to make it 'fit for the residence of a Gentleman's family' [contract in Norfolk C.R.O., HAR 1, 165 x 3]. His business was continued by his sons William and Stephen, who were declared bankrupt in 1837 [*Norfolk Chronicle*, 27 Jan. 1838, 8 Feb. 1840, 5 June 1841]. William Mear designed the CORN EXCHANGE and the adjoining EXHIBITION ROOM for the Norwich artists, 1826–8, dem. [Chambers, *Norfolk Tour* iii, 1829, 1109–10]. He also made designs for vicarages in NORFOLK at LITTLE MELTON, 1833 and WOODBASTWICK, 1838 [Norfolk C.R.O., DN/DPL 1/3/39 and 4/72], restored ST. JULIAN'S CHURCH, NORWICH in 1846 [*Norfolk Chronicle*, 17 Jan. 1846], and designed 'THE ITALIAN VILLA' in UNTHANK ROAD, NORWICH in 1853 [*Norfolk Chronicle*, 8 Oct., 1853]. He died in May 1866 and is commemorated by an inscription in the Rosary Cemetery, Norwich. [references to *Norfolk Chronicle* provided by Mr. David Cubitt].

MECLUER, JOHN, of Carnaby Street, was appointed District Surveyor of St. Clement Danes and adjoining parishes under the Act of 1774. He was described as 'architect' in 1778 when he was granted a lease of a large plot in Bedford Square, on which No. 6 was built [A. Byrne, *Bedford Square*, 1990, 29–30, 91].

MEDLAND, JAMES, was a pupil in 1789 of Charles Beazley, and in 1790 of Samuel Robinson. He exhibited at the Royal Academy from 1789 to 1828, and at the Society of British Artists in 1826 and 1827. He practised first in Newington Butts and later (in the 1820s) in the New Kent Road. J. Leachman and J. P. Pritchett were his pupils. In 1805 he erected a terrace of five houses, now Nos. 17–25 CLAPHAM ROAD, BRIXTON [*Survey of London* xxvi, 107]. In 1813–14 he altered BEDDINGTON HOUSE, SURREY, for Henry Bridges [exhib. at R.A.]. His last exhibit at the Royal Academy (1828) was a 'Design for a villa intended to be erected in Kerry'. He was the father of James Medland of Gloucester (1808–94).

MEDWORTH, JOSEPH (*c.*1754–1827), was a native of Wisbech, Cambs. He began life as a bricklayer, and became a builder in Bermondsey. By 1793 he had acquired sufficient capital to be able to buy the seventeenth-century house known as Wisbech Castle, which was then being offered for sale by the Bishop of Ely. He developed its grounds by building the Crescent 'according to a design which he had previously drawn'. Subsequently he built further houses to form a circus, and began to lay out approach roads to the bridge, the market and the churchyard. In 1811 he offered the Castle itself to the Corporation for £2000 for use as a grammar school. The offer was refused, whereupon Medworth pulled the house down and on its site erected the present low, two-storied building as his own residence. When the Corn Exchange (now the Exchange Hall) was built in 1811, Medworth was asked to oversee the work, though it is not certain that he made the designs. He was Bailiff of Wisbech in 1819. He died on 17 October 1827, aged 73. There is a monument to his memory in Wisbech churchyard.

[N. Walker & T. Craddock, *History of Wisbech and the Fens*, 1849, 278–9; F. J. Gardiner, *History of Wisbech and Neighbourhood 1848–98*, 1898, 15, 473 ff.; anonymous article on 'The Five Castles of Wisbech' in *The Isle of Ely and Wisbech Advertiser*, 28 Dec. 1932; F. J. Rudsdale, 'Wisbech Castle', Wisbech Society's *Annual Report* for 1946; Arthur Oswald, 'Wisbech, Cambridgeshire', *C. Life*, 23–30 May 1947.]

MEE, ARTHUR PATRICK (1802–1868), son of Joseph Mee, of Upper Berkeley Street, London, was a pupil of Sir John Soane from 1818 to 1823. He was admitted to the Royal Academy Schools in 1822, and subsequently travelled in Italy and France. He began to exhibit at the Academy in 1824. In 1838–9 he was associated with Alexis de Châteauneuf of Hamburg in competing for the new Royal Exchange in London; they obtained the second premium of £200 for a design whose principal features appear to have been due to Châteauneuf [*Civil Engineer and Architect's Jnl.* ii, 1839, 437; *Arch. Rev.* cxl, 1966, 366–7, figs. 4–5]. Mee was a Fellow of the R.I.B.A. and in 1849–56 a member of its Council. He died on 19 September 1868 [*A.P.S.D.*; A. T. Bolton, *The Works of Sir John Soane*, Appendix C, p. xlvi].

HARE PARK, nr. NEWMARKET, CAMBS., additions for General Thomas Grosvenor, 1834 [exhib. at R.A. 1834].

GRAVESEND, KENT, a proprietary school, 1835, 'Elizabethan' style [*Gent's Mag.* 1836 (i), 654].

HAMBURG, GERMANY, villa, In de Bost 39/40, Hamburg-Nienstedten, for R. Godeffroy, 1836 [exhibited at R.A. 1837; cf. G. Dehio, *Handbuch der Deutschen Kunstdenkmäler, Hamburg, Schleswig-Holstein,* ed. Johannes Habich, 1971, 68].

WOOD GREEN, MIDDLESEX, FISHMONGERS' AND POULTERERS' ALMSHOUSES, in association with W. Webbe, 1847–8, 'Elizabethan' style; dem. *c.*1955 [*A.P.S.D.*].

LONDON, ST. GEORGE'S HOSPITAL (now Lanesborough Hotel), GROSVENOR PLACE, extensive alterations, 1850, addition of upper storey, 1859, addition of new wing, 1868 [*A.P.S.D.*].

MEIKLEHAM, ROBERT STUART (1786–1871), began life as an architect, but became better known as a civil engineer and writer on steam engines. He was admitted to the Royal Academy Schools in 1813, and in 1814–15 designed the ISABELLA BATHS at RAMSGATE, KENT (dem.). These were heated by steam, and much of Meikleham's work was concerned with heating and ventilation. By 1826 he was engaged in the manufacture of steam engines, on which he wrote several books. As 'Robert Stuart, Architect and Civil Engineer' he was the author of a *Dictionary of Architecture* in three volumes that was published in 1832 by Jones & Co. at the Temple of the Muses in Finsbury Square. He died at Kingston-on-Thames on 1 September 1871 in his 85th year. [H. W. Dickinson & A. A. Gomme, 'Robert Stuart Meikleham', *Trans. Newcomen Soc.* xxii, 1941–2, 161–7.]

MENELAWS, ADAM (*c.*1749–1831), was an architect of Scottish origin who, like William Hastie (*q.v.*), found employment in Russia. A mason by trade, he was one of a number of Scottish building craftsmen who in

1784 responded to an invitation from Charles Cameron (*q.v.*) to work on the new buildings he had designed for the Empress Catherine at Tsarskoe Seloe near St. Petersburg. As an experienced mason Menelaws was almost immediately sent south to build a cathedral at Mogilev, between Minsk and Smolensk, to the designs of Nikolai Lvov. Although described as 'architect' and highly regarded for his 'competence and diligence', Menelaws was employed in a subordinate capacity until 1798, when he began to work for the School of Practical Agriculture, where he demonstrated the working of a steam-engine and other machinery imported from England. He now began to receive private architectural commissions, e.g. for the Razumovskys' Gorenki mansion near Moscow and for the same family's palace at Baturin in the Ukraine. He was also responsible for the reconstruction (including the existing façade) of the large Razumovsky town house (later the Museum of the Revolution) at 21 Gorky Street, which had been destroyed in the burning of Moscow in 1812. By 1818 Menelaws had effectively taken Cameron's place as the leading Court architect and soon after his accession in 1825 Nicholas I employed him to design an informal country residence at Alexandria on the Gulf of Finland. This is a large *cottage orné* with elaborate Gothic interiors (illustrated in *House & Garden*, Jan. 1993). Menelaws is also credited with the design of various ornamental buildings in the Alexander Park at Tsarskoe Seloe, including a ruined chapel (1827), a Turkish elephant house (1828) and the Egyptian Gate, consisting of two cast-iron pylons covered with Egyptian decoration. In the last year of his life he acted as executant architect for the Gothic chapel at Alexandria designed by C. F. Schinkel. [information from Mr. Dmitri Shvidkovski and Mr. Vladimir Chekmarev].

MEREDITH, GEORGE (1762–1831), was articled to John Yenn in 1780 and was admitted to the Royal Academy Schools the same year. He remained in Yenn's office until 1795 and exhibited at the Academy from 1782 to 1799. Many of his exhibits were measured drawings of medieval architecture, and he was elected a Fellow of the Society of Antiquaries in 1799. His marriage in that year may have given him an independent income and in later life he inherited a large estate from his brother and lived at Berrington Court in Worcestershire. He was probably the architect called Meredith who wrote a life of Sir William Chambers for C. G. Dyer's *Biographical Sketches of . . . Eminent Men* (1819). He was a friend of George Basevi and his son William George Meredith, who also died in 1831, was a close friend of Benjamin Disraeli [*Gent's Mag.* 1799 (ii), 1189, 1831 (i), 477, 570; *Letters of Benjamin Disraeli*, ed. Gunn, Toronto 1982, i, 108; information from Mr. Hugh Pagan].

MEREDITH, JAMES, was paid £78 10s. for 'drawing and attendance' in connection with the building of HOLY TRINITY CHURCH, WARRINGTON, LANCS., in 1758–60. No other architect is mentioned in the detailed building accounts [W. Beamont, *Warrington Church Notes*, 1878, 140–1].

MEREDITH, MICHAEL (–1865), was admitted to the Royal Academy Schools in 1809. He subsequently practised in London, dying at 99 Guilford Street on 16 June 1865 [Principal Probate Registry, Calendar of Probates]. In 1827 he altered or rebuilt the VICARAGE at OLD WINDSOR, BERKS. [Salisbury Diocesan Records], and in 1828–30 he designed ALL SAINTS CHURCH, SKINNER STREET, BISHOPSGATE, Gothic; dem. 1869 [*Architectural Mag.* iii, 1836, 498].

MEW, HENRY, was an architect and builder at Brighton, where he designed the classical church of ALL SOULS, EASTERN ROAD, 1833–4, remodelled by E. Scott in 1879; dem. 1968 [*V.C.H. Sussex* vii, 260]. In 1830, in conjunction with – Stroud, he built a Gothic school in CHURCH STREET [A. Dale, *Fashionable Brighton*, 1947, 62]. He was still in practice in 1853.

MEYMOTT, WILLIAM GURR (*c.*1761–1842), was the eldest son of William Meymott (*c.*1732–1819), a surveyor of Southwark, whose 'large handsome house' on the south side of St. George's Road is mentioned by James Edwards, *A Companion from London to Brighthelmston* (published 1801, but compiled *c.*1789). He was admitted to the Royal Academy Schools in 1787 and exhibited at the Academy in 1784 and 1788. He and his younger brother Joseph (*c.*1770–1819) both became District Surveyors. The latter married Elizabeth, daughter of the artist J. F. Rigaud [*Gent's Mag.* 1818 (i), 469, 1819 (ii), 569, 572, 1821 (i), 467, 1842 (i), 336; 'Memoir of J. F. Rigaud', *Walpole Soc.* 1, 1984, 110].

MICHELL, JOHN, contracted in 1691 to recase the walls of the nave of ST. THOMAS'S CHURCH, PORTSMOUTH, but abandoned the undertaking [H. J. Lilley & A. J. Everitt, *Portsmouth Parish Church*, Portsmouth 1921, 91]. He is probably to be identified with the 'Mr. Michell' who in 1670 was paid £389 5s. 4d.

for building the tower of LYMINGTON CHURCH, HANTS. [C. Bostock, *History of Lymington Parish Church*, 1912].

MIDDLETON, CHARLES (1756–), was a pupil of James Paine, from whose office he exhibited at the Society of Artists in 1778 a 'section of the Great Staircase at Wardour Castle, built by James Paine, Esq.' He was admitted to the Royal Academy Schools in 1779 at the age of 22, and was awarded the Silver Medal the same year. He exhibited architectural designs at the Royal Academy from 1779 to 1793, but none of them represented executed buildings, and for some years he appears to have been employed in Henry Holland's office. In one of his publications he refers to 'my having had the superintendence of the building of Carlton House', and in the G.L. Collection there is a perspective by him of Holland's design for that house. Moreover, among drawings from Holland's office in the Victoria and Albert Museum there are several drawings of classical ornament signed by Middleton (Box 176, D. 1752–1773–98). In 1786 a committee of Middlesex Justices of the Peace, of whom Holland was one, commissioned Middleton to produce a set of engravings of their designs for a new prison in Coldbath Fields, Clerkenwell, in order to attract tenders. This appeared in 1788 as *Plans, Elevations and Sections of the House of Correction for the County of Middlesex to be erected in Cold-Bath Fields, London*, engraved . . . from the original drawings, with the authority of the Magistrates, by Charles Middleton, Architect, 1788. Middleton had no other connection with this building, which appears to have been chiefly designed by Jacob Leroux (*q.v.*), and was erected in 1788–94 under the direction of S. P. Cockerell and Thomas Rogers [G.L. Record Office, Minutes of the Committee, MA/G. CBF/1]. He must not be confused (as he is in *A.P.S.D.* and earlier editions of this *Dictionary*) with John Middleton (d. 1833/4), the partner of James Bailey (*q.v.*).

Middleton was the author of *Picturesque and Architectural Views for Cottages, Farm Houses, and Country Villas*, engraved by himself, 1793, 1795; *The Architect and Builders Miscellany, or Pocket Library*, containing a series of small-scale designs 'through all the gradation of Buildings, from the Primitive Hutt, to the superb Mansion', 1799 (for later editions see J. Archer, *The Literature of British Domestic Architecture 1715–1842*, MIT Press 1985, 562–3); *Designs for Gates and Rails suitable to Parks, Pleasure Grounds, Balconys, etc.*, n.d.; and *An Abstract of the Building Act* (of 1774), 1810. The anonymous book entitled *Decorations for Parks and Gardens* that was formerly attributed to Middleton is now known to have been the work of Thomas Elison (*q.v.*). Middleton's name appears on two large plates of carefully measured elevations of the north and west fronts of Westminster Abbey, published in 1808.

MIDDLETON, SIR CHARLES (1799–1867), *see* MONCK, SIR CHARLES.

MIDDLETON, WILLIAM (1730–1815), was the leading builder in Beverley during the reign of George III. He was a joiner by trade, but did considerable business as a builder's merchant besides acting as an architect. His excellent reputation as a builder is referred to in a letter of 1769 from Charles Hotham of South Dalton [Hull University Library, DD Ho/13/5]. He became an Alderman in 1778 and served as Mayor in 1779, 1789, 1794 and 1802. His portrait hangs in the Guildhall. Middleton's most important works in Beverley were the remodelling of the GUILDHALL in 1762–5 and the reconstruction of the BEVERLEY ARMS HOTEL in NORTH BAR in 1794. He was also responsible for No. 39 NORTH BAR WITHOUT, 1769, No. 40 NORTH BAR WITHIN, 1793–4, Nos. 72–74 LAIRGATE, and for a number of other attractive examples of Georgian vernacular architecture in the town. [K. A. MacMahon, 'William Middleton', *Trans. Georgian Soc. for East Yorkshire* iv (1), 1953–55, 68–82; Ivan & Elizabeth Hall, *Historic Beverley*, 1973, *passim.*]

MILLARD, DANIEL, 'Surveyor, Carpenter, Joiner, Sworn-Appraiser, and Auctioneer' at Bedford, offered his services as an architect in the *Northampton Mercury*, 6 May 1771, *ex. inf.* Mr. V. A. Hatley. He designed the HOWARD CONGREGATIONAL CHAPEL in MILL STREET, BEDFORD, in 1774–5, as recorded by a MS. inscription [Beds. C.R.O., X 420/1/1].

MILLER, J—, 'Architect', was the author of *The Country Gentleman's Architect*, 1787, a collection of designs for cottages, farmhouses, villas and lodges, of which there were several later editions up to 1810. Nothing else is known about Miller, who has been confused with other people of the same name in *D.N.B.* and elsewhere (see Eileen Harris, *British Architectural Books and Writers, 1556–1785*, 1990, 316).

MILLER, JAMES, 'a local architect', carried out internal alterations to the East Church of HOLY RUDE CHURCH, STIRLING, in 1803 [R.C.A.M., *Stirlingshire*, 130].

MILLER, SANDERSON (1716–1780), was the son of Sanderson Miller, a wealthy merchant of Banbury. He was born at Radway Grange, a Tudor house near Edgehill which his father had recently acquired. He matriculated at St. Mary Hall, Oxford, in 1734, and studied there for the next two or three years, but did not take a degree. His father's death in 1737 made him master of an independent fortune at the age of 21, and he settled down to the life of a country gentleman with a taste for literature, landscape-gardening and architecture. His first experiments in building were at Radway itself. In 1744 he built a picturesque thatched cottage on Edgehill and proceeded to give a more pronouncedly Gothic character to his Cotswold manor-house by rebuilding the south-east front with pointed arches and by setting small crocketed pinnacles on the angles. Shortly afterwards he built an octagonal Gothic tower on the summit of Edgehill and decorated it with stained-glass windows and heraldic shields. These were pioneer buildings of their kind, more effectively picturesque than anything by Kent, and making a strong appeal to an enthusiastic if somewhat uncritical antiquarianism. For others besides Horace Walpole, Miller's ruined tower at Hagley had 'the true rust of the Barons' War', and an ever-widening circle of aristocratic friends and neighbours was soon demanding the services of the squire of Radway in the embellishment of their houses and parks. As a Gothic architect Miller had two highly successful formulae. One was the two-storied bay window, with cusped panelling, which he used at Radway, Arbury, Adlestrop and Rockingham Hall. The other was the half-ruined tower or castle, of which he furnished much-admired examples for Hagley and Ingestre. Elsewhere – notably at Hagley Hall and the Shire Hall, Warwick – Miller showed that he was also competent in orthodox classical architecture, but it was as a purveyor of Gothic that he was chiefly in demand.

Miller was essentially a gentleman architect whose architectural activities formed part of an active social life. Like other amateur architects he had professional assistants. His plans for Hagley – based, as Horace Walpole was at pains to point out, on those of Houghton – were drawn out by John Sanderson before they were given to the workmen, and his other major work, the Shire Hall at Warwick, was executed by William and David Hiorn of Warwick, master masons who were themselves competent architects, and who described themselves as 'surveyors' as well as 'builders' of the Hall. Miller often operated in conjunction with a mason called William Hitchcox whom Sir Edward Turner aptly called his 'mason *a latere*'. Very few drawings by Miller survive. There are some sketches for Arbury among the Newdigate papers in the Warwickshire Record Office (CR 764) and the R.I.B.A. Collection has two drawings attributed to him (see *Catalogue: L–N*, 71 and fig. 45).

Miller married in 1746 Susannah, daughter of Edward Trotman of Shelswell in Oxfordshire, by whom he had several children. From 1759 onwards he became subject to fits of insanity, which recurred four or five times before his death on 23 April 1780, at the age of 63. He is commemorated by a monument in Radway Church. There is a portrait at Lacock Abbey. Another, now in private hands in Canada, forms the frontispiece to the book by Dickins and Stanton cited below. A large collection of letters from Miller's friends is preserved in the Warwickshire Record Office. It formed the basis of *An Eighteenth-Century Correspondence*, ed. Lilian Dickins & M. Stanton, 1910.

[Dickins & Stanton, *op. cit.*; references in the *Letters of William Shenstone*, ed. M. Williams, 1939, and in Horace Walpole's Correspondence; letters and two diaries (CR 1382/1 and 32) in Warwicks. C.R.O.; A.C. Wood & W. Hawkes, *Sanderson Miller of Radway*, Banbury Hist. Soc. 1969; W. Hawkes, 'The Gothic Architectural Work of Sanderson Miller' in *A Gothick Symposium*, Georgian Group 1983; information from Mr. W. Hawkes, Prof. Michael McCarthy and the late A. C. Wood.]

Unless otherwise stated, the following list of Miller's principal executed works is based on his correspondence in the Warwickshire Record Office. For a fuller list, including uncertain, unexecuted and attributed works, see Wood & Hawkes, *op. cit.*, 108–10.

EDGEHILL, WARWICKS., thatched cottage, 1743–4 (*C. Life*, 13 Sept. 1946, figs. 6 and 8).

RADWAY GRANGE, WARWICKS., rebuilt south and east fronts, 1744–6, Gothic (*C. Life*, 6 Sept. 1946).

AMBROSDEN HOUSE, OXON., assisted Sir Edward Turner, Bart., with the completion of his new house, 1745 onwards. The house had been begun *c.*1739 to the designs of an unknown architect (possibly Miller himself), was not completed until the 1760s, and was demolished soon after Turner's death in 1766. Miller designed a Gothic front to a barn (1747) and new offices (1761) [Sir Edward Turner's accounts among Leigh papers at Shakespeare's

Birthplace Records Office, Stratford-on-Avon; J. Dunkin, *Bullington & Ploughley Hundreds* i, 1823, 3n.].

EDGEHILL, WARWICKS., octagonal Gothic castellated tower, 1745–7 (*C. Life*, 13 Sept. 1946).

WROXTON ABBEY, OXON., advised 1st Earl of Guilford about Gothic window in E. wall of Chapel, 1747; designed octagonal Gothic temple (dem.), and pendant in Hall ceiling in Jacobean style [Wood & Hawkes, *op. cit.*, 99–106] (*C. Life*, 10–24 Sept. 1981).

WROXTON CHURCH, OXON., Gothic tower surmounted by an 'octagon of stone' for 1st Earl of Guilford, 1747–8. The octagon 'fell down the first winter' and was not rebuilt [Bodleian Library, MS. North b. 29, ff. 175–7; cf. Walpole to Chute, 4 Aug. 1754] (Wood & Hawkes, *op. cit.*, fig. 11).

HAGLEY PARK, WORCS., Gothic castle for 1st Lord Lyttelton, 1747–8 (*C. Life*, 16 Oct. 1915).

HONINGTON HALL, WARWICKS., advised Joseph Townsend on layout of grounds and designed grotto, 1749.

WALTON HALL, WARWICKS., BATH HOUSE in park for Sir Charles Mordaunt, Bart., 1749 [Miller's diary, Oct. 1749] (*C. Life*, 26 Dec. 1991).

MIDDLETON PARK, OXON., designs for 3rd Earl of Jersey, 1749, probably for the Gothic gate lodge at the south-east corner of the park, on the road from Middleton to Weston.

INGESTRE HALL, STAFFS., Gothic tower for 2nd Viscount Chetwynd, *c.*1750; dem. *c.*1850.

ENVILLE HALL, STAFFS., Gothic greenhouse or summerhouse for 4th Earl of Stamford, 1750 [*Letters of William Shenstone*, ed. Williams, 1939, 262; *The Travels through England of Dr. R. Pococke*, ed. Cartwright, Camden Soc. 1888–9, ii, 231; see also T. Mowl, 'The Case of the Enville Museum', *Jnl. Garden History* 3 (2), 1980].

HANWORTH HOUSE, MIDDLESEX, designs for stables for Lord Vere Beauclerk, 1750, evidently for the existing eighteenth-century Gothic stables [diary, 1749–50] (W. H. Tapp, *The Royal Manor of Hanworth*, n.d., pl. 1).

OXFORD, ALL SOULS COLLEGE, fitted up Old Library in Gothic style to serve as rooms for Robert Vansittart, 1750–1; partitions since removed but panelling, etc., remains.

FRANKLEY CHURCH, WORCS., advice or designs for alterations and new tower, 1750–1; rebuilt 1873 [Miller's diary, 24 Oct. 1749 and letter from Sir G. Lyttelton, CR 125B/626; *Gent's Mag.* 1813 (ii), 417].

ARBURY HALL, WARWICKS., advice and designs for Sir Roger Newdigate, Bart., *c.*1750–2, including Gothic dressing-room for Lady Newdigate, 1750, and bay window of library, 1750–2 [Newdigate archives, including drawing for dressing-room, CR 764/214; C. Hussey, *English Country Houses: Mid Georgian*, 1956, 43].

ADLESTROP PARK, GLOS., remodelled for James Leigh, 1750–4 and 1759–62, including rebuilding of S.W. front in Gothic style [Leigh papers in Shakespeare's Birthplace Records Office, Stratford-on-Avon, DR 18/8/7, DR 18/25/Bn.1, DR 18/31/843 and 882] (Neale, *Views of Seats* vi, 1823).

HAGLEY, WORCS., reconstructed house known as ROCKINGHAM HALL for Admiral Thomas Smith (half-brother of 1st Lord Lyttelton), 1751, Gothic.

CHART PARK, SURREY, designs for a Gothic greenhouse for Henry Talbot, 1751 [*Eighteenth-Century Correspondence*, 179–80; Bodleian Library, MS. North d. 19, ff. 68–9].

CROOME COURT, WORCS., built for 6th Earl of Coventry in 1751–2 by the landscape-gardener Brown, may have owed something to Miller's advice, for it closely resembles Hagley, and when both house and garden were finished Lord Coventry wrote to Miller to say that 'whatever merits it [Croome] may in future time boast it will be ungrateful not to acknowledge you the primary Author.' Miller's surviving diary for 1749–50 shows that in 1750 he 'drew stables' for Lord Deerhurst, who succeeded as 6th Earl of Coventry in the following year.

DURHAM CASTLE, internal alterations, including dining-room (now Senior Common Room), for Joseph Butler, Bishop of Durham, 1751–2.

BELHUS, ESSEX, advised Thomas Barrett Lennard, afterwards 17th Lord Dacre, on alterations to interior, 1752–7, and perhaps also on the rebuilding of the south and west fronts in Tudor Gothic style, 1745–7; dem. 1956 (*C. Life*, 15, 22 May 1920).

WARWICK, THE SHIRE HALL, 1754–8 [A. C. Wood, *The Shire Hall, Warwick*, Warwicks. Local Hist. Soc. 1983].

LACOCK ABBEY, WILTS., Great Hall and Gothic gateway for John Ivory Talbot, 1754–5 (*C. Life*, 17 March 1923; for the statuary by V. A. Sederbach in the Hall see N. Pevsner in *Arch. Rev.* May 1958).

HAGLEY CHURCH, WORCS., rebuilt chancel for 1st Lord Lyttelton, 1754–6, Gothic; rebuilt 1858. Miller also designed the monument to Sir Thomas Lyttelton (d. 1751), destroyed 1858. See R. Pococke, *Travels through England*, Camden Soc. 1889, ii, 235–6, for a description of Miller's work, written in 1756.

HAGLEY HALL, WORCS., for 1st Lord Lyttelton, 1754–60, assisted by Thomas Prowse and John Sanderson [Michael McCarthy, 'The Building of Hagley Hall', *Burlington Mag.*, April 1976] (*Vitruvius Britannicus* v, 1771, pls. 14–15; *C. Life*, 19–26 Sept. 1957). Miller had previously designed the stables for Sir Thomas Lyttelton in 1750–1 [Miller's diary, July 1750].

GOSFIELD HALL, ESSEX, addition to west front for 1st Lord Nugent, 1755.

BATH, SOMERSET, design for a sham castle on Claverton Down for Ralph Allen, 1755. The sham castle built here by Allen in 1762 may have been based on Miller's design, but Richard Jones (*q.v.*) claimed to have designed it himself.

KINETON CHURCH, WARWICKS., rebuilding of nave and transepts in Gothic style for the Revd. William Talbot, 1755–6; remodelled 1873–80 [Miller's diary, 1756–7, contains several references to his supervision of this work].

STOWE HOUSE, BUCKS., Miller's diary shows that on 15 July 1756 he was at Stowe 'contriving a finishing to Gibbs building', which suggests that he may have designed the two Gothic lanterns which surmount the two lower towers of Gibbs's Gothic temple. These are not shown on Gibbs's original drawing (cf. illustrations in *C. Life*, 29 Sept. 1950, figs. 6–7).

KILKENNY CATHEDRAL, IRELAND, advice and designs for restoration of Gothic choir, etc. for Bishop Richard Pococke, 1756–7. As subsequently executed the choir may have incorporated some features suggested by Miller. Bishop Pococke's work was removed in the 19th century [Michael McCarthy, 'Correspondence relating to St. Canice's Cathedral, Kilkenny' in *Studies*, Dublin, Winter 1976, Spring 1977].

PARK PLACE, nr. HENLEY, BERKS., library for General Henry Seymour Conway, 1757; destroyed by fire 1768 [Miller's diary, 1756–7; for the fire see P. Noble, *Anne Seymour Damer*, 1908, 48].

WOTTON HOUSE, WOTTON UNDERWOOD, BUCKS., bridge for George Grenville, 1758.

ADLESTROP CHURCH, GLOS., alterations including building of south transept (containing Leigh family pew), 1758–9, Gothic, since altered [Shakespeare's Birthplace Records Office, Stratford-on-Avon, Leigh papers, DR 18/8/9].

LONDON, POMFRET HOUSE, ARLINGTON STREET, for Lady Pomfret, 1758–60, Gothic; dem. 1920. According to Horace Walpole, who was living in Arlington Street at the time, the house was 'designed by Mr. Miller of Radway' [Walpole, *Anecdotes of Painting* v, ed. Hilles & Daghlian, 1937, 161], but see above (p. 125) for evidence that Richard Biggs was involved, perhaps as executant architect (photographs in *C. Life Annual*, 1970, 138–9).

BARROWBY RECTORY, LINCS., stables and coach-house for the Revd. J. Stuart Monteith, 1759; dem. [memoir of Monteith by Miller in Warwicks. C.R.O., CR 1382/2, pp. 127–8].

SISTON, GLOS., design for a classical almshouse, 1759, apparently not built. Miller may, however, have designed the octagonal entrance-lodges to Siston Court for his Trotman relations (*C. Life*, 7 Oct. 1905).

BECKETT PARK, BERKS., stables and alterations to house for 2nd Viscount Barrington, 1766–9; house dem. 1834.

BROUGHTON CASTLE, OXON.: for the possibility that Miller was responsible for the internal redecoration of the hall, long gallery, etc. in Gothic style for 13th Lord Saye and Sele, *c.*1768, see H. Gordon Slade in *Archl. Jnl.* 135, 1978, 168–71.

MILLS, JOHN (–1841), of Worcester, rebuilt ST. PETER'S CHURCH, WORCESTER, in a poor Gothic style in 1838–9; dem. 1976 [I.C.B.S.]. In 1839–40 the nave and chancel of ELMLEY LOVETT CHURCH, WORCS., were rebuilt in accordance with his designs. The Vestry Minutes show that he was instructed to 'keep in view the utmost economy consistent with durability'.

MILLS, PETER (1598–1670), was the son of John Mills, a tailor of East Dean in Sussex, where he was baptized on 12 February 1597/8. On 30 November 1613 he was apprenticed to John Williams, a tyler and bricklayer of London. Mills took his first apprentice in 1629, and on 17 October 1643 he was appointed Bricklayer to the City of London. He was Master of the Tylers' and Bricklayers' Company in 1649–50 and 1659–60. He ceased to be City Bricklayer at about the time of the Restoration, perhaps because by then he had come to be increasingly employed as a surveyor and architect. In 1661 he and 'another person' (probably Sir Balthazar Gerbier, *q.v.*) were commissioned by the City to design the triumphal arches erected to celebrate Charles II's coronation. In 1664 he acted as the City's surveyor in negotiations with the Dean and Chapter of St. Paul's, and after the Great Fire of 1666 he was one of the four surveyors appointed by the City to supervise the rebuilding of London in conjunction with Wren, May and Pratt. He was himself the author of a plan for the City of which nothing is known except that it was thought inferior to the one submitted by Hooke. Together with Hooke and Oliver he was responsible for making a detailed survey of the destroyed areas and for directing the staking out of the new and widened streets. Mills also played an active part in rebuilding the property of St. Bartholomew's Hospital, of which he had been a Governor since December 1644. In 1667–8 he was acting as surveyor to Christ's Hospital, and the Gresham Trustees would have employed him to rebuild the Royal Exchange, but for 'the great burthen of businesse lying upon him for the city att this time', which induced them instead to appoint Edward Jerman as 'the most able knowne artist (besides him) that the city now hath'. Mills's own losses in the Fire included the destruction of three tenements in Budge Row which he held under the Master and Fellows of Pembroke College, Cambridge, by a lease dated 10 April 1662. This was to have expired in 1702, but in July 1668 the College, 'in consideration of his (Mills's) great 'losse susteyned by the Fire', agreed to extend it for a further period of thirty-four years on condition that he rebuilt the houses 'with all convenient speed', and in accordance with the 'Act of Parliament lately made for the Rebuilding the City of London'. The tenements in question occupied the site of No. 26 Budge Row. Mills himself lived in a house in Bartholomew Close which he rented from St. Bartholomew's Hospital, and when he made his will in July 1670 he left 10s. apiece to the twenty Governors 'that most frequently meet at the Compting House about the affairs of the Hospital whom I desire may be at my Funerall . . . to buy each of them a Ring'. He left money for the same purpose to 'every person of the Kindred meeting att the Greene Dragon whereof I am a member'. He died in the following month and was buried in the middle aisle of the church of St. Bartholomew the Less on 25 August.

Mills's activity as a surveyor and architect can be traced at least as far back as 1638, when he and a mason called Llewellyn made a plan of the church of St. Michael-le-Querne and were involved on behalf of the churchwardens in subsequent negotiations with Inigo Jones over the design of a new church to replace it [H. Colvin in *London Jnl.* 12 (1), 1986]. In about 1640 he probably designed the houses in Great Queen Street that were an early example of uniformity in London street architecture, their elevations defined by Corinthian pilasters and decorated with carved panels of mannerist derivation. By far the most important of his known works was Thorpe Hall, nr. Peterborough, which he designed for Oliver St. John in 1653–4. Though internally fitted up in what has been called the 'artisan mannerist' style, the exterior of Thorpe Hall is a sophisticated essay in astylar classical architecture whose south front has been compared with certain (perhaps unexecuted) designs by Inigo Jones for lesser domestic buildings in the City of London. Other comparable houses are Cromwell House, Highgate (for Robert Sprignell, *c.*1637–8), Tyttenhanger, Herts. (for Sir Henry Blount, *c.*1655), and Wisbech Castle, Cambs. (for John Thurloe, *c.*1658, dem. 1815). Tyttenhanger (*C. Life*, 4–11 Oct. 1919) is a brick house which Mills may well have built, and the resemblances between Wisbech Castle and Thorpe Hall are so striking as to suggest that he was probably Thurloe's architect. As Cromwell's Secretary of State and Chief Justice, respectively, Thurloe and St. John must have been well known to each other, and in 1642 Thurloe had actually witnessed an agreement whereby Mills had undertaken to build houses on land in Holborn leased to him by St. John [Huntingdonshire Record Office, dd. M 69/4/1]. It may be added that Mills's own sympathies evidently lay with the Parliamentary party, for in May 1648 he was appointed a member of the Committee for the City of London Militia, an office which he still held in Feb. 1659/60 [*Acts and Ordinances of the Interregnum*, ed. Firth & Rait, i, 1138; *The Diurnall of Thomas Rugg*, ed. Sachse, Camden Ser., 1961, 45].

Whatever Parliamentary connections Mills may have had, they did not prevent his employment at the Restoration both to design the triumphal arches to celebrate Charles II's coronation, and to organize the 'shews and pageants' on the Thames with which the City welcomed Charles and his Queen to Whitehall on 23 August 1662 [John Tatham, *Aqua Triumphalis*, 1662]. Nor did the royalist Duke of Lennox scruple to employ Mills to rebuild the centre of his house at Cobham in Kent in the 1660s. At Cobham Hall, moreover, Mills showed that he had largely assimilated the new domestic style associated with architects such as May and Pratt: only in the main doorway are some traces of 'artisan mannerism' still perceptible. The interior was handsomely fitted up by the same team of London craftsmen whom Mills had employed to construct and decorate the coronation arches.

[*A.P.S.D.*, *s.v.* 'Mills' and 'Jerman'; Malcolm Pinhorn, note on date of Mills's birth in *Blackmansbury* i (3), 1964, 21; Guildhall Library, records of the Tylers' and Bricklayers' Company; Guildhall Record

Office, City Repertories; T. F. Reddaway, *The Rebuilding of London after the Great Fire*, 1940, *passim*; S. Perks, *The History of the Mansion House*, 1922, 143–52; *The Survey of Building Sites in the City of London after the Great Fire of 1666*, ed. W. H. Godfrey, London Topographical Soc. 1946, 1956; Gweneth Whitteridge, 'The Fire of London and St. Bartholomew's Hospital', *London Topographical Record* xx, 1952; R. A. Beddard, 'Church and State in Old St. Paul's', *Guildhall Miscellany* iv (3), 1972; *Wren Soc.* xi, 63–4 (Christ's Hospital); P.C.C. 147 PENN.]

LONDON, houses on the south side of GREAT QUEEN STREET, LINCOLN'S INN FIELDS, *c.*1640; dem. George Vertue states that it was Mills who 'design'd & built the great houses in Great Queen Street', *Vertue Note Books*, Walpole Soc. i, 130. This is partly confirmed by the lease of the site of Nos. 66–68 to Mills on 15 Sept. 1639. The whole south side of the street was rebuilt at approximately the same time to a uniform pattern for which Mills may have been responsible [*Survey of London* v, 42–5, 56 and pls. 16–22, cf. J. Parton, *Some Account of the Hospital and Parish of St. Giles in the Fields*, 1817, 290, and R. W. Paul, *Vanishing London*, 1894, pl. xxvii].

LONDON, houses in CASTLE (now FURNIVAL) STREET, HOLBORN, on the site of a 'great garden' leased to Mills by Oliver St. John in Feb. 1642. The houses were to be of brick, three storeys high, and were to be 'in the same uniformitie and beauty' as the adjoining houses to be built under a royal licence to St. John dated 5 Aug. 1641. [Huntingdonshire Record Office, dd. M 69/4/1].

THORPE HALL, NORTHANTS., for Oliver St. John, 1654–6 [B.L., Add. MS. 25302, f. 153, contract dated 8 Feb. 1653/4 (printed in *Fenland Notes and Queries* iv, 1898–1900, 272–3), whereby John Ashley and Sampson Frisbey of Ketton, freemasons, undertake to execute the windows of the north and south fronts 'as is expressed & sett forth in a Draught or map of the said intended House made by Peter Mills of London Surveyor']. The date 1656 is carved on the stable-block. The house was restored by F. Ruddle of Peterborough in 1850–1, and in 1852 A. W. Hakewill published a *General Plan and External Details of Thorpe Hall.* The panelling in the library was removed to Leeds Castle, Kent, *c.*1929. [H. M. Colvin, 'The Architect of Thorpe Hall', *C. Life*, 6 June 1952; Sir Gyles Isham, 'Thorpe Hall', *Northants. Antiquarian Soc.'s Report* for 1958–9, 37–45] (J. Belcher & M. E. Macartney, *Later Renaissance Architecture in England* ii, 1901, 97–9 and plates; Oliver Hill & John Cornforth, *English Country Houses: Caroline*, 1966, 102–10; Giles Worsley, 'Thorpe Hall in Context', *Georgian Group Jnl.* 1993).

attributed: WISBECH CASTLE, CAMBS., for John Thurloe, *c.*1658; dem. 1815 [Arthur Oswald in *C. Life*, 23 May 1947, 955–6; H. M. Colvin in *C. Life*, 6 June 1952, 1733–4].

LONDON, TRIUMPHAL ARCHES to celebrate coronation of King Charles II, 1661, in association with 'another Person, who desired to have his name conceal'd', who can probably be identified as Sir Balthazar Gerbier (*q.v.*) [J. Ogilby, *Relation of His Majestie's Entertainment passing through the City of London to his Coronation with a Description of the Triumphal Arches*, 2nd ed. 1662]. For the original drawings see *R.I.B.A. Drawings Catalogue: G-K*, 18–19. See also E. Halfpenny, 'The Citie's Loyalty Display'd', *Guildhall Miscellany*, No. 10, 1959.

CAMBRIDGE, PEMBROKE COLLEGE, THE HITCHAM BUILDING, 1659–61, was measured by Mills on its completion in 1661, and he may probably be regarded as its designer [A. Attwater, *Pembroke College, Cambridge*, 1936, 76] (R.C.H.M., *Cambridge* ii, pl. 212).

COBHAM HALL, KENT, remodelled central block (or 'Cross Wing') for Charles Stuart, 3rd Duke of Richmond and 6th Duke of Lennox, 1661–3; attic storey altered *c.*1767–70 [H. M. Colvin, 'Peter Mills and Cobham Hall', in *The Country Seat*, ed. Colvin & Harris, 1970].

LEWISHAM, KENT, COLFE'S ALMSHOUSES for the Leathersellers' Company, 1664–5; dem. *c.*1955 after bomb-damage [L. Duncan, *History of the Borough of Lewisham*, 1908, 126].

LONDON, five warehouses on BREWERS' QUAY, THAMES STREET, 1667–8; dem. [Northants. Record Office, B(D)282, item 3, a Fire Court case which suggests that Mills had designed the warehouses].

LONDON, CHRIST'S HOSPITAL, designed in 1667–8 a 'Compting House, Court Roome, and Schoole, with a house for the Treasurer, and houses for other Officers of this Hospital', which were built, at least in part, before his death in 1670 [*Wren Soc.* xi, 63–4].

LONDON, BUDGE ROW, houses on site leased from Pembroke College, Cambridge, 1668–9; dem. ['A Copie of the agremt. between ye College & Mr. Mills about Rebuilding the Wrastlers, Budgrow', as confirmed by the Fire Court on 26 June

1668, among the title deeds of No. 26 Budge Row, formerly in the muniment room of St. John's College, Oxford].

MILLWARD, JOHN, is described in Pigot's *Directory* (1830) as a 'carpenter, joiner and stone-cutter' at Hay-on-Wye. In 1806–8 he remodelled RIDGEBOURNE, nr. KINGTON, HEREFS., for Edmund Cheese [Parry's *History of Kington*, 1845, 224].

MILNE, JAMES, is listed among the architects practising in Edinburgh from 1809 to 1834, after which he appears to have moved to Newcastle. He was doubtless the James Milne, mason, who was admitted as a burgess of Edinburgh in 1809 [*Roll of Edinburgh Burgesses*, Scottish Record Soc., 112], but must be distinguished from the 'James Milne, Builder' (d. 3 Jan. 1826) who is commemorated on a tombstone in Leith churchyard, and also from the James Miln or Milne (*c.*1792–1863) who was County Surveyor of Northamptonshire from 1826 to 1863. Milne was the author of *The Elements of Architecture*, Edinburgh 1812, a little-known work of which only the first volume was published. In addition to the buildings in Edinburgh listed below, he designed ST. COLUMBA'S CHURCH, LERWICK, SHETLAND, 1826–9 [advt. for tenders in *Edinburgh Evening Courant*, 1 June 1826].

EDINBURGH

NORTHUMBERLAND PLACE, Nos. 3–5, before 1818 [title deeds, *ex inf.* Mr. Douglas Hall].
LYNEDOCH PLACE, Nos. 3–22, 1820–3 [S.R.O., Edinburgh Sasines].
SAXE COBURG PLACE, Nos. 1–8 and 25–32, 1822–30 [S.R.O., Edinburgh Sasines].
ST. BERNARD'S CHURCH (originally CLAREMONT STREET CHAPEL), SAXE COBURG STREET, 1823; apse, etc., added 1888 [J. Stark, *Picture of Edinburgh*, 6th ed. 1835, 226].
CARLTON STREET, 1824 [S.R.O., Edinburgh Sasines].
DANUBE STREET, 1824 [S.R.O., Edinburgh Sasines].
DEAN TERRACE, 1824 [S.R.O., Edinburgh Sasines].
DEANHAUGH STREET, 1824–5 [S.R.O., Edinburgh Sasines].
ST. BERNARD'S CRESCENT, 1824 [S.R.O., Edinburgh Sasines].

MILNE, JOHN, practised in Edinburgh in the 1830s, appearing in the directories as 'civil engineer and teacher of architecture'. He appears to have been an expert on ventilation, for he contributed two articles on the subject to Loudon's *Architectural Magazine* i (1834), 64–70, and ii (1835), 27–31. He designed a house in RANDOLPH CRESCENT, EDINBURGH, for Sir John Robison which incorporated an elaborate ventilation system [J. C. Loudon, *Cottage, Farm and Villa Architecture*, 1846, 1197–1205].

In 1842 he applied unsuccessfully for the vacant post of Master of the School of Architecture run by the Royal Dublin Society [*Proceedings*, 78, 128, *ex inf.* Dr. E. McParland], but evidently obtained some other employment as his name disappears from the Edinburgh directories in the same year. He must not be confused with John Milne (1823–1904), a pupil of John Henderson who practised in St. Andrews from about 1850 onwards.

MILNER, THOMAS, is stated in Campbell's *Vitruvius Britannicus* ii, 1717, pl. 47, to have designed GREGORIES, nr. BEACONSFIELD, BUCKS., for John Waller in 1712. Nothing else is known about Milner except that he is described as 'esquire' and subscribed to volumes ii and iii of *Vitruvius Britannicus*. Gregories was destroyed by fire in 1813. A late eighteenth-century elevation of the house is preserved in the Aylesbury Museum (V. G. Garvin, 'Gregories, Bucks.', *Arch.Rev.* lxvii, 1930, 169–74).

MINDHAM, WILLIAM (*c.*1772–1843), was a builder-architect at Holt in Norfolk. Although in announcing his death in his 72nd year, the *Norfolk Chronicle* of 23 Sept. 1843 described him as 'for many years an eminent architect at Holt', no building designed by him has so far been identified.

MITCHELL, ROBERT, is said to have been born in Aberdeen, but his exhibits at the Royal Academy show that he was practising in London from 1782 onwards. In 1801 he published *Plans, etc. of Buildings erected in England and Scotland; with An Essay to elucidate the Grecian, Roman, and Gothic Architecture.* He was presumably also the author of a work advertised in an early nineteenth-century bookseller's catalogue as 'Mitchell's Designs for Rural Villas on Economical Principles, 8°, 25 plates, 1785', of which no copy has so far been found. Mitchell designed mainly in the manner of James Wyatt, but his larger houses combine the neo-classical detail of the late eighteenth century with a liking for the large Palladian porticos and attached office blocks characteristic of the earlier Georgian period. His book includes a design for a country house in the form of a Greek Doric temple, anticipating Wilkins's Grange Park.

Mitchell probably had a son or younger relative named George Mitchell, for in June 1796 a person of this name wrote from Tobago to Mr. T. Webster (*q.v.*) at Robert Mitchell's office in Newman Street to say that he had given up architecture and become a planter. He was probably the George Mitchell who had been admitted to the Royal Academy Schools as an architectural student in 1795 at the age of 20 [*R.I.B.A. Drawings Catalogue: L–N*, 72].

COTTESBROOKE HALL, NORTHANTS., alterations for Sir James Langham, Bart., *c.*1770–80, probably including the bridges and entrance lodges [*Plans*, pls. 7–8] (*C. Life*, 17–24 March 1955, 19 Feb. 1970).

MOORE PLACE, MUCH HADHAM, HERTS., for James Gordon, 1777–9 [*Plans*, pls. 7–8] (*C. Life*, 26 Jan, 2 Feb. 1956).

PRESTON HALL, MIDLOTHIAN, for Alexander Callender (d. 1792) and his brother Sir John Callender, Bart., 1791 onwards [*Plans*, pls. 9–13; exhib. at R.A. 1794] (*C. Life*, 24–31 Aug. 1961).

LONDON, THE ROTUNDA, LEICESTER SQUARE, for Mr. Barker, 1793–4; reconstructed 1865–8 as the R.C. Church of Notre Dame [*Plans*, pl. 14].

SILWOOD PARK, BERKS., for Sir James Sibbald, Bart., 1796; rebuilt 1876 [*Plans*, pls. 1–4; exhib. at R.A. 1796–7] (Neale's *Views of Seats*, 1st ser., iv, 1821).

TWICKENHAM, MIDDLESEX, HEATH LANE LODGE, for Isaac Swainson, before 1801; dem. [*Plans*, pls. 5–6].

MONTREAL, CANADA, THE NELSON COLUMN, 1808–9 [Elizabeth Collard in *C. Life*, 24 July 1969, 210–11].

MITCHELL, ROBERT, was a builder-architect of Peterhead, Aberdeenshire. In 1804–6 he and his brother John appear to have built PETERHEAD OLD CHURCH to the design of Alexander Laing of Edinburgh (*q.v.*). Robert subsequently designed ST. PETER'S EPISCOPAL CHURCH, PETERHEAD, 1813–14, Gothic [J. T. Findlay, *History of Peterhead*, Aberdeen 1933, 143–4, 171].

MOFFAT, JOHN (–1708), a 'master builder' then resident in Liverpool, was in 1704 employed to go to Dumfries and furnish a 'modall' for a new Town Hall and steeple there. His design, which was based on the steeple of the College at Glasgow, appears to have been the one carried out in the following year by Tobias Bachop (*q.v.*) [W. McDowall, *History of Dumfries*, Edinburgh 1867, 539–42]. At Liverpool Moffat was probably responsible for the new ST. PETER'S CHURCH, built in 1700–4 to a design based on Wren's St. Andrew's Holborn, and demolished in 1922 [Janet Gnosspelius & Stanley Harris, 'John Moffat and St. Peter's Church, Liverpool', *Trans. Hist. Soc. of Lancs. & Cheshire*, 130, 1981]. He died at Liverpool in 1708, having established a dynasty of local masons which, under the name of Moffatt, Moffitt or Morfitt, was active in Lancashire and Cheshire throughout the eighteenth century.

MOFFATT, WILLIAM LAMBIE (1808–1882), *see* HURST, WILLIAM.

MONCK, Sir CHARLES (1779–1867), was the third but only surviving son of Sir William Middleton, Bart., of Belsay Castle, Northumberland, whom he succeeded in 1795. His mother was Jane Monck, only child and heiress of Lawrence Monck of Caenby Hall, Lincolnshire. On Lawrence Monck's death in 1798 he inherited the Caenby estate and took the name of Monck in accordance with his grandfather's will.

Monck received a good classical education at Rugby School. He was prevented by the Napoleonic War from making the usual Grand Tour, but immediately after his marriage in 1804 he and his wife made an extended visit to Greece, where he studied the temples in company with his friend Sir William Gell. Soon after his return in 1806 he decided to build a new house at BELSAY in the Grecian style. The foundations were laid in 1807 and the house was first inhabited ten years later. Monck was entirely his own architect, making his own drawings and supervising the work himself. Surviving drawings show that he was a neat and accurate draughtsman, and it was only when confronted with such difficult tasks as drawing the volutes of an Ionic capital that he was obliged to seek the professional assistance of John Dobson of Newcastle. He demanded exceptionally high standards from his craftsmen, and according to Dobson he did much to raise the standard of masonry in the North of England. Belsay is one of the outstanding monuments of the Greek Revival. It represents a personal and exceptionally uncompromising approach to the problem of adapting ancient Greek architecture to domestic purposes. Planned round a peristyle, it recalls internally the layout of a Graeco-Roman villa. Externally every detail from the stylobate to the cornice has classical authority, but archaeological nicety is subordinated to a noble simplicity which redeems the house from being no more than a monument of architectural pedantry.

Monck designed one other country house

in Northumberland. This was LINDEN HOUSE, nr. MORPETH, which he planned for his friend Charles William Bigge in 1812–13. Here the design is more conventional, and the Doric order is confined to a portico. Monck's designs are among the family papers in the County Record Office (5/223–6). The house is illustrated by B. Allsopp & Ursula Clark, *Historic Architecture of Northumberland*, 1970, 70 (where it is wrongly ascribed to Dobson).

At Belsay Monck also designed the stables (with a belfry based on the 'Tower of the Winds'), a row of houses with an arcaded lower storey probably inspired by a visit to Italy and Sicily in 1830–1, and a school (1842). He was an improving landlord who took a keen interest in farming, and created a remarkable romantic garden from the quarry out of which the house was built.

Monck, who was a prominent figure in the public life of Northumberland, and represented the county in Parliament from 1812 to 1820, died on 20 July 1867. His diaries and other papers are deposited in the Northumberland Record Office, together with a MS. memoir by his son Sir Arthur Middleton.

[MS. memoir by Sir Arthur Middleton; R. Welford, *Men of Mark twixt Tyne and Tweed* iii, 1895, 206–12; J. Dobson in *Building News* vi, 1859, 404; *C. Life*, 5, 12 Oct. 1940; C. Hussey, *English Country Houses: Late Georgian*, 1958, 83–90; J. M. Crook, *The Greek Revival*, 1972, 126–7.]

MONEYPENNY, GEORGE (1768–*c.*1830), was the son of George Moneypenny, a sculptor and carver of Derby, who died in 1807. He was baptized at St. Werburgh's Church on 21 July 1768. Prisons were his speciality, and he appears to have succeeded William Blackburn (d. 1790) as the leading designer of such buildings. He could express their purpose effectively. Pevsner describes his Winchester Gaol as 'among the most impressive in the country', and at Leicester he showed a 'knowledge of grand design' which, according to a contemporary critic, 'bordered on the terrific'. His Sessions House at Knutsford (often supposed to be the work of Harrison of Chester) has a polite Ionic portico flanked by two frowning Vanbrughian doorways. At Leicester, where he was the contractor as well as the architect, Moneypenny got into financial difficulties, and was one of the first to be imprisoned for debt in his own building. He eventually moved to London, where he was still in practice in the 1820s.

Moneypenny also designed bridges: in 1799 Northam Bridge at Southampton and in 1821 one at Weymouth. In 1813 the *Gentleman's Magazine* published a letter from him criticizing the centering designed for the construction of Waterloo Bridge. In 1823 he was employed to design a bridge over the R. Severn near Tewkesbury consisting of three cast-iron arches. Of this he laid the first stone on 8 September [*Carmarthen Jnl.* 19 Sept. 1823]. But 'misunderstandings' having arisen between himself and the trustees, Thomas Telford (*q.v.*) was called in to report on the case and recommended the abandonment of Moneypenny's design in favour of the single-arched iron bridge which was built under Telford's direction in 1824–6 [W. Mackenzie, 'Account of the Bridge over the Severn, near . . . Tewkesbury', *Trans. Institution of Civil Engineers* ii, 1838].

[*A.P.S.D.*; register of St. Werburgh's and St. Alkmund's churches, Derby, *ex inf.* Mr. Edward Saunders; J. Dugdale, *The British Traveller* iii, 1819, 570; N. Pevsner & D. Lloyd, *Hampshire*, Buildings of England, 1967, 54; *Gent's Mag.* 1809 (ii), 1019, 1813 (i), 124–6, 225, 411–12, 1813 (ii), 221–3.]

LEICESTER, THE COUNTY GAOL, 1790–2; dem. *c.*1880 [J. Dugdale, *The British Traveller* iii, 1819, 570; J. Flower, *Views of Ancient Buildings in the Town and County of Leicester*, *c.*1826, 4].

SOUTHAMPTON, HANTS., NORTHAM BRIDGE, 1799 [P. Brannon, *Picture of Southampton*, 1850, 59].

WINCHESTER, THE COUNTY GAOL, JEWRY STREET, 1805; largely dem. [J. Dugdale, *The British Traveller* ii, 1819, 556; *Gent's Mag.* 1808 (i), 204].

TILSHEAD LODGE, WILTS., for George Lowther, 1806 [engraved map of Tilshead dedicated to Lowther and incorporating a view of the house which names Moneypenny as the architect: copy in Wilts. Archl. Soc's Museum at Devizes].

EXETER, THE COUNTY HOUSE OF CORRECTION, 1807–9; dem. 1848–50 [J. Dugdale, *The British Traveller* ii, 1819, 136–7; *Gent's Mag.* 1810 (i), 121].

PETWORTH, SUSSEX, THE COUNTY PRISON, alterations, 1816; dem. 1835 [*A.P.S.D.*, *s.v.* 'Wyatt, James'].

KNUTSFORD, CHESHIRE, THE SESSIONS HOUSE AND HOUSE OF CORRECTION, 1817–19 [J. H. Hanshall, *History of Cheshire*, 1817, 389; G. Ormerod, *History of Cheshire* i, 1819, 380].

TABLEY HOUSE, CHESHIRE, reinstatement of east wing for Sir John Leicester, Bart., after damage by fire, 1819–20 [Cheshire Record Office, Leicester-Warren papers, uncatalogued 1976].

WEYMOUTH, DORSET, BRIDGE (R. Wey), 1821–4; reconstructed 1885 [G. A. Ellis, *History of Weymouth*, 1829, 93].

MONTAGU, JOHN, 2ND DUKE OF MONTAGU (1690–1749), was the son of Ralph, 1st Duke of Montagu, and succeeded him in 1709 as the owner of Boughton House, Northants., Clitheroe Castle, Lancs., Palace House, Beaulieu, Hants., and Montagu House, Bloomsbury. He was a Knight of the Garter and a Fellow of the Royal Society, and his status as a great nobleman brought him various offices, including those of Master-General of the Ordnance (1740–1 and 1743–9). In private he was a Man of Feeling before his time, and shared with his friend William Stukeley many unfashionable enthusiasms, including a precocious taste for medieval architecture. It was to him that Batty Langley dedicated his *Ancient Architecture Restored* in 1742, and it was for him that Stukeley designed (1744) a Gothic bridge to be erected in the park at Boughton, and a Gothic mausoleum to be added to Weekley Church. Neither was built (though a wooden model of the bridge survives at Boughton), but the Duke himself was something of an amateur architect in his own right. Stukeley records that he had 'a very good knack of drawing and designing'. Among a list of drawings formerly in the Ordnance Office (P.R.O., WO 55/2281) there appears a 'Plan and elevation for building Barracks at Woolwich by His Grace the Duke of Montagu 1741', and at Boughton there are two drawings which show him as an early designer of buildings in the castle style. One (marked 'Box, 3, No. 32') is a scheme (superimposed on a surveyor's plan) for some castellated farm-buildings to be built on an ancient moated site on his Northamptonshire estate. This does not seem to have been carried out, but is remarkable for the deliberately irregular layout which the Duke envisaged, giving the impression of a picturesque fortified manor-house, at a time when such follies were invariably conceived in strictly symmetrical terms. The other drawing (marked 'Box 3, No. 49') is for a house to be built within the walls of CLITHEROE CASTLE, LANCS., and is inscribed 'Plan for a New House at Clithero drawn by the Duke in 1740, and since built'. Though the draughtsmanship is crude, the annotations show that the Duke knew exactly what he wanted–a building in 'comon ordinary plane stone work the same as comon farm houses are built of', without plinth, cornice, architraves or other ornaments. There were to be no sash windows, but only 'plane comon iron casements', and none of the rooms were to be wainscoted, but only plastered and whitewashed. These were architectural precepts of which Pugin might have approved. For 1740 they were astonishingly precocious. The existing building corresponds closely to the Duke's drawing, and although the windows have since been sashed, the rubble stonework is so convincing that it is difficult to decide what is medieval and what is Georgian.

Earlier in his life, probably in about 1714, Montagu had altered PALACE HOUSE, BEAULIEU, HANTS., in such a way as to turn this former monastic gatehouse into a small castle-like house, complete with moat, drawbridges, a surrounding curtain wall and corner towers with conical roofs.

[*D.N.B.*; G.E.C., *Complete Peerage; The Family Memoirs of the Revd. William Stukeley*, Surtees Soc. i, 1880, 114–15; T. D. Whitaker, *History of the Parish of Whalley and the Honor of Clitheroe*, 1872, i, 253–4, ii, 69 n. 2; Stuart Piggott, *William Stukeley*, 1950, 144–6, 150–1, 153; John Cornforth, 'Castles for a Georgian Duke', *C. Life*, 8 Oct. 1992.]

MONTGOMERY, JOHN, was a mason of Old Rayne, Aberdeenshire. In 1685 he was made an honorary burgess of Old Aberdeen for 'the good service' he had done in making Bishop Scougal's monument in ST. MACHAR'S CATHEDRAL CHURCH [*Records of Old Aberdeen*, New Spalding Club, i, 277]. In 1686 he built the MERCAT CROSS at ABERDEEN for £100 sterling in accordance with 'ane moddell and frame therof of timber and pasteboard' which he had 'formed and given in'. It is a polygonal structure with an elaborately decorated parapet supported by an Ionic order and was extensively repaired in 1821. [*Extracts from the Council Register of the Burgh of Aberdeen 1643–1747*, Scottish Burgh Record Society 1872, 306–7; D. MacGibbon & T. Ross, *The Castellated and Domestic Architecture of Scotland* v, 1892, 212–13; G. M. Fraser, 'The Market Cross of Aberdeen', *Scottish Historical Review* v, 1907–8, 178–9.]

MONTIER, JOHN, senior and junior, were builders and architects of Tunbridge Wells in the early nineteenth century. Their works included rebuilding the chancel of BRENCHLEY CHURCH, KENT, in 1814 [archives of Lord Courthope, *ex inf.* the late Rupert Gunnis], rebuilding FRANT CHURCH, SUSSEX, 1819–22 [H. S. Eeles, *Frant, a Parish History*, 1947, 194], and a number of picturesque lodges and cottages on the ERIDGE ESTATE, nr. Tunbridge Wells [K. Clark, *The Gothic Revival*, 1947, 194, n. 1]. A farm-house 'in the style of a yeoman's house of the Tudor times . . . built by Messrs. Montier and Douch from their own designs' is illustrated in Colbran's *New Guide to Tunbridge Wells*, 1840, 144. Edward Douch was another local builder, with whom the younger Montier was perhaps in partnership after his father's death. He himself probably died in 1844.

MOOR, THOMAS, was a Leicestershire master builder of the 1720s. Among the Herrick papers in the Leicestershire Record Office (DG/9/2134) there is an estimate submitted by Moor in about 1725 for building a mansion at Beaumanor to a design drawn by himself. It was not adopted, the accepted design being by John Westley (*q.v.*). In 1725–6 Moor rebuilt the nave and tower of Sibson Church to the designs of Francis Smith (*q.v.*).

MOORE, ALEXANDER POOLE (*c.*1777–1806), was a pupil of James Lewis. He was admitted to the Royal Academy Schools in 1792 at the age of 15, and was awarded the Silver Medal in 1794. He was subsequently employed in the Surveyor's office at Christ's Hospital. He died on 11 July 1806 at the age of 28, after a short illness, leaving a father who had long depended upon him for support. He is described as 'a young man of very eccentric habits but a clever Artist'. He exhibited regularly at the Royal Academy, showing views and drawings of various buildings, including St. Paul's Cathedral, St. Stephen's, Walbrook, and St. Mary's, Taunton. [*Gent's Mag.* 1806 (ii), 686; J. Chambers, MS. *Collections for a Biography of British Architects* in R.I.B.A. Library; S. Redgrave, *Dictionary of Artists*, 1878, 296.]

MOORE, FRANCIS, rebuilt the tower and reroofed the nave of EAST BRIDGFORD CHURCH, NOTTS., in 1778, as recorded by a tablet on the south wall of the tower giving the name of 'Moore, archt.' [A. Du Boulay Hill, *East Bridgford, Notts.*, 1932, 119, 158]. He was no doubt the Francis Moore, carpenter, who received nearly £100 in 1776 for repairs to CHESTERFIELD CHURCH, DERBYSHIRE [Churchwardens' accounts].

MOORE, GABRIEL, was the surveyor employed by Sir John Strode to design his house, CHANTMARLE, DORSET, in 1612. In a surviving notebook Strode describes Moore as 'a skilfull architect', and says that he was 'born about Chinnock' and 'had of me 20s. monethly, with his dyet, for his paines only, to survey and direct the building to the forme I conceived and plotted it' [Dorset Record Office, MW/M4, f. 24v]. The house, designed in a rather conservative style for its date, is described in Arthur Oswald, *Country Houses of Dorset* (2nd ed. 1959), 97–9, and R.C.H.M., *Dorset* (*West*), 71–2.

MOORE, GEORGE (*c.*1777–1859), began his career in partnership with William Leverton, the builder, and afterwards established himself as an architect in Lincoln's Inn Fields. He exhibited at the Royal Academy between 1797 and 1810. He was surveyor to the Skinners' Company, a member of the Society of Arts, a Fellow of the Royal Society, and an original member of the Institute of British Architects. He was President of the Surveyors' Club in 1817. He died in Grenville Street, Brunswick Square, in November 1859, in his 83rd year [*Builder* xvii, 1859, 765]. In *c.*1825 he designed a Gothic addition (dem.) to TONBRIDGE SCHOOL, KENT [J. F. Wadmore, *History of the Skinners' Company*, 1902, 230].

MOORE, GEORGE, (*c.*1810–), was a pupil of Edward Blore. He was admitted to the Royal Academy Schools in 1830, at the age of 20, and exhibited at the Academy from 1831 to 1840. He was an able architectural draughtsman and artist, and in that capacity accompanied Henry Gally Knight on his tour of Norman architecture in Sicily. In 1835–6 he travelled extensively in eastern Europe, reaching Moscow. A volume of fine topographical sketches, mostly from this tour, and including buildings in Copenhagen, Stockholm, Novgorod, Gdansk, Lübeck, Potsdam, Nürnberg, Bamberg, Zwickau and Regensburg, is in the R.I.B.A. Drawings Collection. On his return he exhibited a view of Prague at the Royal Academy. Other drawings exhibited by him at the Academy show that he designed the following buildings: THE ARCHERS' LODGE in REGENT'S PARK, LONDON, 1833; a new Tudor Gothic front to LITCHBOROUGH HOUSE, NORTHANTS., for William Grant, 1838; some (half-timbered) houses at MUCH HADHAM, HERTS., for N. G. Times, 1840; and a cottage at WALLINGTON, SURREY, for T. F. Reynolds, 1840. He, rather than his elderly namesake (*q.v.*), was presumably the George Moore who designed YAZOR CHURCH, HEREFS., in 1843 [*Hereford Times*, 1 April 1843, 539]. The R.I.B.A. Collection has designs by Moore for a Gothic cathedral and a neo-Grecian villa, and a view of a room in Exeter Hall, Strand, as arranged for a conversazione of the Architectural Society [*Catalogue: L–N*, 91 and figs. 53–4]. Moore's career ended in 1846, when he became an imbecile. A fund for his support was raised by subscription through the *Builder* [*Builder* iv, 1846, 80, 345].

MORGAN, DAVID (*c.*1774–1851), stated in 1836 that he had been in business for 46 years as a builder and surveyor in Lammas Street, Carmarthen, and had 'built many houses' during that time [N.L.W., Slebech 3964, p. 24]. He presumably designed the newly built house in Picton Terrace that he advertised in 1834 [*Carmarthen Jnl.* 21 March 1834]. The simple chapel-like CHURCH of TRELECH at BETTWS was designed by him in 1834–5 [I.C.B.S.], and in 1843 he was probably responsible for enlarging CARMARTHEN COUNTY GAOL [*Carmarthen Jnl.* 3 March, 19 May 1843]. In 1848 he repaired LLANDEILO TOWN HALL [Carmarthen Q.S. Records]. A gravestone in Carmarthen Cemetery records Morgan's death in 1851 at the age of 77 [information from Mr. Thomas LLoyd, to whom all references are due].

MORGAN, JAMES (*c.*1773–1856), was a Welshman who spent most of his career in the office of John Nash, whose principal assistant he was for some forty years. From 1806 to 1815 he was officially Nash's partner as architect to the Department of Woods and Forests. In this capacity he was responsible for the routine work of repairs to the buildings in the royal parks and forests [John Summerson, *The Life and Work of John Nash*, 1980, 25, 63, 198]. Through Nash's influence Morgan was in 1812 appointed engineer to the Regent's Canal Company, for which he designed the MACCLESFIELD BRIDGE, REGENT'S PARK, built in 1815–16 to carry a road over the canal [J. Elmes, *Metropolitan Improvements*, 1831, 57–8]. In REGENT STREET he built No. 326, and in PARK PLACE he collaborated with Nash and the elder Pugin in the design of the DIORAMA (1823), an ingenious revolving spectacle for which he devised the machinery [Elmes, *op. cit.*, 81]. In 1828–30 he designed ST. GEORGE'S CHURCH, WOLVERHAMPTON, for the Church Building Commissioners in a classical style [Port, 162], and in 1834 he rebuilt the south side of BUSHBURY CHURCH, STAFFS. [I.C.B.S.]. Morgan exhibited occasionally at the Royal Academy, showing in 1802 a 'Design for a Gothic mansion,' in 1807 his executed design for rebuilding SHOLEBROKE LODGE, WHITTLEBURY FOREST, NORTHANTS., and in 1819 and 1821 designs for mausolea. Morgan died in Hammersmith in February 1856, aged 83 [*Gent's Mag.* 1856 (i), 435].

MORGAN, JAMES DAVIES (1811–1846), exhibited at the Royal Academy in 1830 (a view of part of the crypt of Kirkstall Abbey, Yorkshire) and 1831 (a lodge for D. Cheetham, Esq., of Stalybridge, Cheshire, 'now erecting under the direction of Mr. T. W. Atkinson'). In 1835 he competed for the Houses of Parliament with a 'Perpendicular' Gothic design, and in 1839 for the Ashmolean Museum at Oxford [Bodleian Library, MS. Top. Oxon. c. 202]. He was then living at Castle Hedingham in Essex. In 1840, when he designed ST. JOHN'S CHURCH, CORNISH HALL END, ESSEX, in the 'Early English' style, his address was given as Chelmsford [I.C.B.S.]. He became an Associate of the Institute of British Architects in 1837, retiring in 1844, and dying at Hedingham in 1846, aged 34.

MORISON, DAVID, was Secretary of the Literary and Antiquarian Society at Perth, and not a professional architect. In 1822 he designed a building in George Street, originally known as THE MONUMENT, in order to accommodate the Society and the Public Library. It was remodelled in 1854 as the Perth Art Gallery [D. Peacock, *Perth*, 1849, 505].

MORISON, ROBERT (–1825), appears to have begun his professional life as a draughtsman in the office of Robert and James Adam. Writing to Lord Buchan in 1807, Joseph Bonomi described him as 'a clever architect' who had been in the Adams' office for over fourteen years before leaving [N.L.S., MS. 14835, f. 127; Bodleian Library, MS. Eng. Misc. c. 40, f. 56]. In July 1791 he was engaged by Sir John Soane as an assistant at a salary of £100 per annum [A. T. Bolton, Th*e Works of Sir John Soane*, 1924, Appendix C, xli]. In the same year he exhibited a design for a villa at the Royal Academy, and in 1794 he published the first part of a little-known work, entitled *Designs in Perspective for Villas in the Ancient Castle and Grecian Styles*, with a dedication to the Duchess of Gordon. The Edinburgh directories show that he was practising there from 1807 until his death.

In 1789 Morison submitted a design for the new Edinburgh University of which the original section is preserved in the Scottish National Monuments Record (EDD/220/1), and in 1815 he was one of the selected architects who competed for the completion of Adam's building [A. G. Fraser, *The Building of Old College*, Edinburgh 1989, 133–5, 145, 152]. Alternative designs by him for a toll-house (1798) are in the Scottish Record Office (RHP 10318–9). The only architectural work at present known to have been carried out to his design is Nos. 26, 28 and 30 HOWE STREET, EDINBURGH, 1807, which originally formed a symmetrical group [Edinburgh Dean of Guild plans, 26 June 1807].

Morison died at Raeburn Place, Stockbridge, Edinburgh, on 9 August 1825 [*Scots Mag.* xvii, 1825, 384].

MORLIDGE, JOHN, acted as clerk of the works at Longleat House, Wilts., under Jeffry Wyatville from 1807 to 1813 [D. Linstrum, *Sir Jeffry Wyatville*, 1972, 26]. According to *Gentleman's Magazine*, 1814 (ii), 491, and J. Dugdale's *British Traveller* iv, 1819, 463, he designed EVERLEIGH CHURCH, WILTS., built in the Gothic style in 1813–14 at the expense of Francis Dugdale Astley. Pigot's *Directory* of 1825–6 lists John Morlidge as a builder in Horseferry Road, Westminster, and Samuel Morlidge as a carpenter at the same address.

MORRIS, JOHN (*c.*1716–1792), was the successor, and almost certainly the son, of Arthur Morris (d. 1744), the principal stonemason in Lewes in the first half of the eighteenth century. From 1750 onwards he did a great deal of work at GLYNDE PLACE, SUSSEX, for Richard Trevor, Bishop of Durham. Between 1753 and 1756 he built the stable range, perhaps to the designs of Sir Thomas Robinson (*q.v.*), and in 1758–9 he remodelled the interior of the hall. In 1763–5 he built GLYNDE CHURCH to Robinson's designs [*Sussex Archl. Colls.* xx, 1868, 78–9]. Morris's craftsmanship at Glynde is of a very high standard, and his use of dressed stone, flint and brick shows a subtle appreciation of their contrasting effects of colour and texture [Trevor archives in East Sussex Record Office and *C. Life*, 14–28 April 1955]. Morris was also employed in the rebuilding of ASHBURNHAM PLACE, SUSSEX, between 1757 and 1761 [*C. Life*, 23 April 1953]. In 1761–3 he designed and built the TOWN HALL or SESSIONS HOUSE at LEWES, dem. 1810 [E. Sussex County Records, QAF/2/1/E1; letter among the Trevor archives dated 24 Aug. 1760, referring to his plans for the Sessions House], and a ground plan of the west gate at Lewes made by him in 1777 is in the British Library [Add. MS. 5677, f. 8]. In 1776–8 he built the stables and pigeon-house at COOMBE PLACE, HAMSEY, SUSSEX, for Sir John Bridger, apparently to the designs of John Robinson, Clerk of the Works at Greenwich (for whom see p. 832) [E. Suffolk R.O., Shiffner MS. 1379, etc.].

Morris was one of the constables of Lewes in 1751 and 1765, and died there in 1792, aged 76 [Register of All Saints, Lewes]. In his will he is described as 'Surveyor and Stone Mason' [E. Sussex Record Office: Wills of the Archdeaconry of Lewes, A 66, f. 423]. His business was continued by the firm of Parsons (afterwards Bridgeman) of Eastgate Street, Lewes.

MORRIS, ROBERT (1703–1754), was born at Twickenham in February 1702/3, the son of Thomas Morris, a joiner. He was related to Roger Morris (*q.v.*), for the second part of his *Lectures* is dedicated to the latter, and in the dedication he refers to him as his 'kinsman', and acknowledges the 'erudition' he has received 'in your service'. He practised as an architect and surveyor, but is chiefly notable as the author of several architectural publications. Their titles were: *An Essay in Defence of Ancient Architecture or, A Parallel of the Ancient Buildings with the Modern: showing the Beauty and Harmony of the Former, and the Irregularity of the Latter*, 1728; *Lectures on Architecture, consisting of Rules founded upon Harmonick and Arithmetical Proportions in Building*, 1734, 2nd. ed. 1759; *An Essay upon Harmony, as it relates to Situation and Building*, published anonymously, 1739; *The Art of Architecture, A Poem in imitation of Horace's Art of Poetry*, published anonymously, 1742; *Rural Architecture*, 1750, reissued as *Select Architecture*, 1755, 2nd. ed. 1757 (reprint New York 1973); *The Architectural Remembrancer: being a Collection of New and Useful Designs, of Ornamental Buildings and Decorations for Parks, Gardens, Woods, etc., to which are added, A variety of Chimney-Pieces, after the Manner of Inigo Jones and Mr. Kent*, 1751; reissued as *Architecture Improved*, 1755, 1757; *The Qualifications and Duty of a Surveyor, Explained in a Letter to the Earl of —*, published anonymously, 1752; and *A Second Letter to the Rt. Hon. the Earl of — concerning the Qualifications and Duty of a Surveyor*, published anonymously, 1752. The last work contains a list of 'some tracts wrote by the author of this letter' which includes the *Essay upon Harmony, The Art of Architecture*, and two poetical effusions entitled *Rupert to Maria. An Heroic Epistle* (1748) and *An Inquiry after Virtue* [1740]. These latter works have been attributed (e.g. in *A.P.S.D.* and *D.N.B.*) to John Gwynn (*q.v.*), but internal evidence makes it clear that the *Essay upon Harmony, The Art of Architecture* and *Rupert to Maria* are in fact by Morris, who must therefore have been the author of the two essays on *The Qualifications of a Surveyor.* In addition Morris is stated by D. E. Baker, *Biographica Dramatica* ii, 1812, 230, to have been the author of *Fatal Necessity: or, Liberty Regain'd*, a political play published in Dublin in 1742, soon after the general election of that year, and dedicated by the author, under the character of 'An Independent Elector', to Charles Edwin, one of the M.P.s elected for the City of Westminster. The *Lectures* are stated to have been 'Read to a Society Establish'd for the improvement of Arts and Sciences'. No other reference to this society has been found, but it was evidently more than a literary fiction, for Morris gives the date upon which each lecture was read (starting on 22 October 1730).

Morris's publications – especially his *Essay in Defence of Ancient Architecture* and his *Lectures* – establish him as the most important British writer on architectural theory of the first half of the eighteenth century. Although he was not a member of Lord Burlington's circle, his ideas (for a précis of which see Eileen Harris, *British Architectural Books and Writers, 1556–1785*, 1990, 317–22), were generally in conformity with those of the English neo-Palladians. His advocacy of a rational simplicity based on the Orders was, however, tempered by respect for Wren and Gibbs (though not for Vanbrugh or Hawksmoor) and he was neither a primitivist nor a 'Bigot to Antiquity'. His belief in a strict adherence to the canon of the Orders and in the virtues of a classical simplicity was exemplified in the designs that he published in *The Architectural Remembrancer* and *Select Architecture*.

Morris's published designs are competent but somewhat pedestrian. They hardly suggest that he was an architect of much distinction, and no building of any importance can be attributed to him. There is, however, evidence to connect him with the building of the south front of CULVERTHORPE HALL, LINCOLNSHIRE, for Sir Michael Newton (*c.*1730–5). It was to Newton that his *Lectures* (1734) were dedicated, and plate 23 of his *Select Architecture* (1755) is a variation on the design of Culverthorpe. The building accounts (among the Halliwell-Phillipps MSS. in the Library of Congress in Washington) show that he was in control of the work, charging in 1731 'Board wages 37 weeks at 4s. per week', and passing the craftsmen's bills. But as Sir Michael Newton was simultaneously employing Roger Morris to alter his London house, it is likely that the latter was also involved at Culverthorpe, which has several features found in his documented works elsewhere (see plan and measured drawings in H. Field & M. Bunney, *English Domestic Architecture of the XVII and XVIII Centuries*, 1905, 46–7 and pl. xlix; *C. Life*, 15–22 Sept. 1923). In 1753–4, at the behest of Christopher Lee, a carpenter of Norwich (*q.v.*), Morris supplied alternative plans and elevations for the Octagon Chapel in that city, for which he was paid 8 guineas by the Committee, though in the event another design was adopted. His drawings are in the Norfolk Record Office, FC 13/1 (minutes) and 13/80, drawings at end (nos. 1 and 4). Some drawings for chimney-pieces in the R.I.B.A. Drawings Collection are attributed to Morris on the strength of their resemblance to plates in his *Architecture Improved*.

Morris probably made his living more as a surveyor than as an architect. Thus in 1740 he was called in to value the model of George Dance's design for the Mansion House made by John Cordwell, the City Carpenter [City of London records; S. Perks, *History of the Mansion House*, 1922, 184], in 1743 he was paid £1 6s. for 'surveying or measuring' some brickwork at Twickenham for the banker George Middleton [Coutts Bank, P/L 1735–55, f. 135], and in 1753 or 1754 he measured plasterer's work done for Sir William Beauchamp Proctor in his house in Bruton Street, London [Norfolk Record Office, BEA 339, 438 x 7].

In 1728 Morris described himself as 'of Twickenham', but by 1740 he was living in Hyde Park Street, near Grosvenor Square, and in his will [P.C.C. 334 PINFOLD] he is described as 'of St. George's, Hanover Square, Surveyor'. According to a contemporary note in a copy of his *Essay in Defence of Ancient Architecture* in the R.I.B.A. Library he died on 12 November 1754. He directed that all his 'real and personal estate, goods, books, copper plates, copyright to Books wrote printed and published by me, my drawings, manuscripts, etc.' were to be sold for the benefit of his children Thomas, Mary, James and Hannah, with the exception of 'the silver tankard, the silver cup and salver given me by John Cope, which I would have preserved in my family'. According to the *Public Advertiser* of 8 April 1755, the sale of Morris's possessions included '2 new Books of Drawings intended to be published this Summer'.

[*A.P.S.D.*; *D.N.B.*; Steven Parissien, *The Careers of Roger and Robert Morris*, unpublished D. Phil. thesis, Oxford 1989.]

MORRIS, ROGER (1695–1749), was born in London on 19 April 1695 and baptized in the church of St. Martin-in-the-Fields. Nothing is known of his father, Owen Morris, or of his own early life, though he is said to have been involved, as a foreman bricklayer, in the building of Hanover and Grosvenor Squares. The first certain record of his activities as a builder occurs in 1724, when he took a lease of a plot on the Harley estate in Oxford Street, and built a house for his own occupation. He was then described as a bricklayer. By 1730, when he moved to a larger house which he had built in Green Street, he was described by the rate collector as 'gentleman'. Later he was to be concerned in extensive speculative building developments in Argyll Street (1736) and on the approaches to Westminster Bridge (1740–2), and it may be presumed that speculative building formed the basis of his prosperity.

As an architect, Morris's career appears to have been closely linked with two persons: Colen Campbell and Henry Herbert, the 'Architect Earl' of Pembroke. On loan to the R.I.B.A. Drawings Collection there is a set of drawings for rebuilding Goodwood House. These drawings correspond to the designs for Goodwood by Colen Campbell which he published in the third volume of *Vitruvius Britannicus* (1725). But the draughtsmanship is certainly not Campbell's and may be Morris's. Among the Wilton papers there is an elevation signed by Morris which represents a variant version of Campbell's design for Pembroke House, Whitehall (built in 1724), and in 1729, shortly before Campbell's death, Morris was acting on his behalf in connection with the building of the stables at Studley Royal in Yorkshire. Campbell (as Morris explained in a letter to John Aislabie, the owner of the estate) had been taken ill in Norfolk and was got back to London only with 'grate difficulty'. In a letter written a fortnight later from his sick-bed Campbell dismisses two drawings by Morris as 'very ugly' and says that he has 'ordered him to correct' a third.

It would appear, therefore, that as a young man Morris acted, at least on occasion, as Campbell's assistant, and it may have been through Campbell that he came into contact with the future Earl of Pembroke, whose architectural collaborator he was to be at Marble Hill (1724–9), the White (New Park) Lodge at Richmond (1727–8), the Column of Victory at Blenheim (1730–1), Wimbledon House (1732–3), the Palladian Bridge at Wilton (1736–7) and probably at Westcombe House, Blackheath. Lord Pembroke evidently valued Morris's services highly, for in 1734 he presented him with a large silver cup as a token of his regard. Still preserved by Morris's descendants, it bears the inscription: 'Given by my Noble Patron Henry, Earl of Pembroke, By whose favour alone I am Enabled to fill it. R. Morris 1734.' Above there is a portrait of Inigo Jones framed in a cartouche of architectural instruments (see illustration in *C. Life*, 31 Oct. 1952, 1409).

As the former assistant of Colen Campbell and the acknowledged collaborator of the Architect Earl, Morris was now well placed to attract a wider patronage. The accuracy of the estimates provided by 'the noted architect Mr. Morris' had already been commended by Edward Laurence in *The Duty of a Steward to his Lord* (1727), and in 1731–2 Morris gave himself the benefit of foreign travel, for between June 1731 and November 1732 he was reported to be 'absent from the Kingdom and beyond the seas'.[1] In 1727 he had been given the newly created Office of Works post of Clerk of the Works at Richmond New Park Lodge, and in 1734 he succeeded Sir William Ogbourne as Master Carpenter to the Office of Ordnance – a post which he undoubtedly owed to the 2nd Duke of Argyll, who was Master-General of the Ordnance from 1725 to 1740, for whom he had recently enlarged Adderbury House, and with whom he is said to have 'stood high in favour and on terms of great friendship'. It was a valuable appointment which brought him work at Woolwich and elsewhere that was worth £2000 or £3000 a year. At the time of his death he was also Surveyor to the Mint, an appointment which he may have owed to Sir Andrew Fountaine, Warden of the Mint since 1727.

Despite his association with Campbell and Herbert, Morris was by no means a tamely orthodox Palladian. Marble Hill and the lodge at Richmond were, of course, Palladian villas *par excellence*. But elsewhere, notably at Combe Bank and Whitton Place, Morris developed a villa style of his own which, if it had basically Palladian antecedents, had some markedly individual features, notably the pyramidal roof, the *œil-de-bœuf* windows, and the distinctive porch. The arcaded wings which he added to Adderbury House are his most obvious, but not his only, borrowing from Vanbrugh, while for the stables at Althorp he designed a Tuscan portico which followed the lead of Inigo Jones's St. Paul's, Covent Garden, in a manner which has no obvious parallel in contemporary Georgian architecture. Most remarkable of all are his two castellated houses, Clearwell (*c.*1728) and Inveraray (1745). In its appreciation of the simple massing of genuine medieval domestic architecture Clearwell is unique, having no affinity with either Vanbrugh's castellated villas or Hawksmoor's transvestite Gothic churches and colleges. Inveraray, on the other hand, was to be the progenitor of a whole sequence of symmetrical Georgian castles, and must itself be related to a sketch in Vanbrugh's Elton album which shows that he had envisaged just such a castle-like house as Morris designed for the Duke of Argyll at Inveraray. Though Morris had little understanding of Gothic detail, he therefore emerges as a figure of some importance in the long and

[1] A drawing exists of the front of Palladio's house in Vicenza, 'taken from a scetch of Mr. R. Morris who took it on the spot'. For other references to Morris's visit to Italy see *Survey of London* xxxv, 73 and the Earl of March, *A Duke and his Friends* i, 1911, 251–2.

complex history of neo-medieval architecture in Britain.

Morris died on 31 January 1749. He had been twice married. His first wife, Mary, died in 1729, and in 1731 Roger married Elizabeth, daughter of Sir Philip Jackson of Richmond, Surrey. She died in 1744. By his first marriage he had two sons, James and Roger, and by his second, one son and four daughters. All the daughters appear to have married well, and the eldest son, who succeeded to his post as Master Carpenter to the Ordnance, lived the life of a gentleman in Surrey, of which county he was High Sheriff in 1764. The second son, Col. Roger Morris, married Mary Philipse and became the ancestor both of the family of Morris of New York and of an English family of Morris which figures in Burke's *Landed Gentry*.

[Wyatt Papworth in *Builder* xxxiii, 1875, 881–2; correspondence in *C. Life*, 25 Feb., 17, 24 March, 7 April 1944; Marie P. G. Draper, *Marble Hill House*, 1970, 17–19; O. F. G. Hogg, *The Royal Arsenal* i, 1963, 285; *Survey of London* xxxi, 284, 290; G. L. M. Goodfellow, 'Colen Campbell's Last Years', *Burlington Mag.* cxi, 1969, 189–90; Burke's *Landed Gentry* under 'Morris of York' or 'Morris of Netherby'; P.C.C. 49 LISLE; Steven Parissien, *The Careers of Roger and Robert Morris*, unpublished D.Phil. thesis, Oxford 1989.]

MARBLE HILL, TWICKENHAM, MIDDLESEX, for Henrietta Howard, Countess of Suffolk, mistress of George II, 1724–9 [see above, p. 490].

COMBE BANK, nr. SUNDRIDGE, KENT, for Col. John Campbell, later 4th Duke of Argyll, *c.*1725; subsequently much altered by D. A. Alexander, G. Legg (1835–9) and others [*Vitruvius Britannicus* iv, 1767, pls. 75–7; Mary Cosh in *C. Life*, 13 July 1972, 80, and 28 Sept. 1972, 723].

THE WHITE LODGE, RICHMOND NEW PARK, begun 1727 for George I, completed 1728 for George II [see above, p. 490].

CLEARWELL CASTLE, GLOS., for Thomas Wyndham, *c.*1728, castellated Gothic [National Library of Wales, Dunraven papers 347, an estimate by Roger Morris dated 29 Dec. 1727 and 1 Jan. 1728, corresponding to the building as erected] (Alistair Rowan, 'Clearwell Castle', in *The Country Seat*, ed. Colvin & Harris, 1970, 145–9).

LONDON, No. 30 OLD BURLINGTON STREET, interior decoration for Sir Michael Newton, Bart., 1729–32; dem. 1935 ['Mr. Matthew Lamb's Accounts with Sir Michael Newton 1728–40' at Welford Park, Berks., record payments to Roger Morris and a number of London craftsmen (including Isaac Mansfield, plasterer, James Richards, carver, and James Morris, painter) in the years 1731–2. See also Library of Congress, Halliwell-Phillipps MSS., vols. xvii, xviii, xix. The building is not specified, but was evidently 30 Old Burlington Street, whose interior Newton embellished after acquiring the lease in 1725: see *Survey of London* xxxii, 505 and plates].

CASTLE HILL, DEVONSHIRE, remodelled for Lord Clinton (afterwards 1st Lord Fortescue) under the direction of Lord Burlington and Lord Herbert, 1729–*c.*1740. Morris's contract for the Portland stonework of the exterior, dated 22 Feb. 1728–9, specifies that the proportions of the entablature 'shall be made as the Earl of Burlington or Lord Herbert shall direct and the carving of . . . all other parts of the said cornice [shall be] according to the plan or drawing thereof signed by the said Roger Morris' [Devon C.R.O., Fortescue papers, E1/93]. For further evidence of Lord Burlington's participation in the design, see above, p. 150. The centre was gutted by fire in 1934, and subsequently restored (*C. Life*, 17, 24 March 1934, 29 Oct. 1938).

attributed: BEECHWOOD PARK, HERTS., library for Sir Thomas Sebright, Bart., *c.*1730; internally remodelled by Thomas Cundy 1804 [drawings formerly preserved at Beechwood included designs by Roger Morris for a new west front. These were not carried out, but are similar to the existing library] (*C. Life*, 12 Nov. 1938, fig. 4).

LONDON, GREEN STREET, house (now No. 61) for himself, *c.*1730 [*Survey of London* xl, 190–4].

*WESTCOMBE HOUSE, BLACKHEATH, KENT, rebuilt for Lord Herbert, *c.*1730; dem. 1854 [above, p. 490].

*BLENHEIM PALACE, OXON., THE COLUMN OF VICTORY, for Sarah, Duchess of Marlborough, 1730–1 [above, p. 490].

attributed: CULVERTHORPE HALL, LINCS., rebuilding of south front for Sir Michael Newton, Bart., *c.*1730–5 [above, p. 665].

LONDON, No. 6 ST. JAMES'S SQUARE, repairs or alterations for 1st Earl of Bristol, 1731; dem. 1819 [*Survey of London* xxix, 104].

CHICHESTER, SUSSEX, THE COUNCIL HOUSE, 1731 [Walpole Soc., *Vertue Note Books* v, 144; for Lord Burlington's involvement see above, pp. 151–2].

ADDERBURY HOUSE, OXON., added arcaded wings, including gallery, for 2nd Duke of Argyll, 1731; south wing and gallery dem.

* Buildings designed in conjunction with Henry, Lord Herbert, afterwards 9th Earl of Pembroke.

1808 [signed drawings among Duke of Buccleuch's papers in S.R.O., RHP 13735, etc.] (plan in *V.C.H. Oxfordshire* ix, 8; *C. Life*, 7 Jan. 1949).

*LONDON, PEMBROKE HOUSE, WHITEHALL, addition of outbuildings for Henry, Lord Herbert, 1731–2; house rebuilt 1757, dem. 1913 [accounts in Wilton papers, *ex inf.* Dr. T. P. Connor; cf. Ralph's *Critical Review of the Publick Buldings in London and Westminster*, 1734, 45].

LONDON, PALL MALL, house for George Bubb Dodington, later Lord Melcombe, 1731–3; incorporated in Carlton House *c.*1763–9, dem. 1827–8 [record of smith's work done 'for Mr. Morris at Esq. Doddington's in Pall Mall', 1733, P.R.O., C 109/25/7; T. P. Connor, 'Bubo's House', *Arch. Hist.* 27, 1984].

WHITTON PLACE (or PARK), MIDDLESEX, for the Earl of Ilay (afterwards 3rd Duke of Argyll), *c.*1732–9; dem. *c.*1847 [Mary Cosh in *C. Life*, 20 July 1972; cf. related designs, not necessarily for Whitton, reproduced by John Harris, *Catalogue of British Drawings for Architecture, etc. in American Collections*, 1971, pls. 98–104].

*WIMBLEDON HOUSE, SURREY, for Sarah, Duchess of Marlborough, 1732–3; destroyed by fire 1785 [above, p. 490].

ALTHORP HOUSE, NORTHANTS., THE STABLES, for 5th Earl of Sunderland and 3rd Duke of Marlborough, *c.*1732–3 [Woburn Abbey archives, letter from Sarah, Duchess of Marlborough, to the Duchess of Bedford, 11 Sept. 1733, referring to Morris as the architect of the stables and of some other buildings in the park, no doubt including the Palladian Gardener's House: *ex inf.* the late Lord Spencer and Mr. David Green].

EASTBURY PARK, DORSET, completed interior of house for George Bubb Dodington, later Lord Melcombe, after death of Sir John Vanbrugh, *c.*1733–8; dem. 1775 [F.J.B. Watson in *C. Life*, 11 Feb. 1949, 317; L. Whistler, *The Imagination of Vanbrugh*, 1954, 174–5 and fig. 76].

MONKEY ISLAND, on R. Thames nr. BRAY, BERKS., BANQUETING PAVILION and FISHING LODGE for 3rd Duke of Marlborough, *c.*1735 [Gervase Jackson-Stops in *Georgian Group Jnl.* 1994, 20–4].

*WILTON HOUSE, WILTS., THE PALLADIAN BRIDGE, for 9th Earl of Pembroke, 1736–7 [above, pp. 490–1].

LONDON, PARK STREET, stables and riding-house for the Second Troop of Horse Guards, 1738; dem. 1914–15 [*Survey of London* xl, 185–6].

LONDON, GREAT GEORGE STREET, repairs to seven houses belonging to the trustees of the late Col. Francis Charteris (d. 1732), 1738–41 [N.L.S., SCA 10, account of the trustees].

LONDON, No. 59 STRAND, for George Middleton and George Campbell, bankers, 1739–40; dem. 1923 [Coutts & Co. P/L 1735–55, ff. 95, 102, *ex inf.* Miss Mary Cosh; drawings in doc. no. 838] (*Survey of London* xviii, pl. 62).

attributed: LANGLEY PARK, nr. SLOUGH, BUCKS., domed temple for 3rd. Duke of Marlborough, *c.*1740; dem. [Gervase Jackson-Stops in *Georgian Group Jnl.* 1994, 26–7].

LONDON, WESTMINSTER, houses on north side of NEW PALACE YARD, 1740–2; dem. [P.R.O., Works, records of the Westminster Bridge Commissioners] (*Arch. Hist.* ix, 1966, fig. 51).

LONGFORD CASTLE, WILTS., unidentified building for 1st Viscount Folkestone, perhaps not executed, 1742. Accounts at Longford show that on 31 May 1742 Lord Folkestone paid 'Mr. Morris for drawing a design of the building at Longford'. In 1745 he paid him a further 5 gns. 'for drawing designs of the cupola to the building'.

attributed: GOODWOOD HOUSE, SUSSEX, CARNÉ'S SEAT, for 2nd Duke of Richmond, 1743. Vertue states that the Duke of Richmond was the 'greatest promoter' of the Council House at Chichester, which Morris designed, and a letter in B. L., Add. MS. 27587, f. 83, shows that Morris was obtaining Portland stone for building operations at Goodwood in the autumn of 1742: see also C. Hussey in *C. Life*, 17 March 1944, correspondence (*C. Life*, 16 July 1932).

INVERARAY CASTLE, ARGYLLSHIRE, for 3rd Duke of Argyll, 1745–60, castellated Gothic; centre damaged by fire 1877, restored 1878–9 [Ian G. Lindsay & Mary Cosh, *Inveraray and the Dukes of Argyll*, 1973].

INVERARAY, ARGYLLSHIRE, THE GARRON BRIDGE, 1747–9 [W. Adam, *Vitruvius Scoticus*, pl. 74; Ian G. Lindsay & Mary Cosh, *Inveraray and the Dukes of Argyll*, 1973, 125].

KIRBY HALL, OUSEBURN, YORKS. (W.R.), elevation for Stephen Thompson, in association with 3rd Earl of Burlington, 1747–*c.*1755; dem. 1920 [above, p. 151].

LONDON, No. 19 ST. JAMES'S SQUARE, alterations for 2nd Duke of Cleveland, 1746–7; dem. 1894. In 1747 Morris's place was taken by Daniel Garrett after a disagreement between himself and the Duke [accounts at Raby Castle, *ex inf.* Mr. Peter Leach] (*Survey of London* xxix, 161–3).

* Buildings designed in conjunction with Henry, Lord Herbert, afterwards 9th Earl of Pembroke.

BRANDENBURG HOUSE, HAMMERSMITH, MIDDLESEX, rebuilt for George Bubb Dodington, later Lord Melcombe, who bought the house in 1748; gallery added by J. N. Servandoni; dem. 1822 [*Vitruvius Britannicus* iv, 1767, pls. 26–7].

Note: Further buildings which may prove to have been designed by Roger Morris include three commissioned by the 7th Earl of Westmorland: the remodelling of the inner quadrangle of APETHORPE, NORTHANTS., *c.*1740–2 (cf. plan in *V.C.H. Northants.* ii, 544), the wings which he added to MEREWORTH CASTLE, KENT, about the same time, and the remarkably neo-classical church which he built at MEREWORTH in 1744–6. These suggestions are prompted by stylistic considerations too complex to set out in this *Dictionary* and too tentative to justify a firm attribution. The possibility that Morris designed ARGYLL HOUSE, ARGYLL STREET, LONDON, for the Earl of Ilay (afterwards 3rd Duke of Argyll) and No. 12 GROSVENOR SQUARE, for John Aislabie, *c.*1729, is discussed in *Survey of London* xxxi, 296 and xl, 127–8, respectively.

Unexecuted designs by Morris include a bound volume of drawings for a new house at MILTON, NORTHANTS., (Northants. C.R.O., Milton Drawings 99–111); designs for a coach-house, stable, etc., dated 1742 at Blair Atholl, Perthshire; drawings probably by him for remodelling ROSNEATH CASTLE, DUNBARTONSHIRE, dated 1744 and 1747 (N.L.S., MS. 17878); and drawings in the Yale Center for British Art for a house supposed to be WHITTON PLACE, MIDDLESEX.

MORTON, RICHARD (–1814), was apprenticed to a carpenter and cabinet-maker of Worcester in 1768. He subsequently became a carpenter and builder in that city, and held various offices in the Corporation, including that of Mayor in 1797. As an architect his works included the MARKET HALL in HIGH STREET, WORCESTER, 1804, dem. 1954, which is illustrated as a vignette on the title-page of T. Eaton's *Concise History of Worcester* (1816) [Worcester City Chamber Order Book, 16 July 1801], and extensions to NASH'S HOSPITAL in NEW STREET, 1809 [Chamber Order Book, 1809]. [information from Alderman B. Brotherton and Mr. D. Whitehead].

MORTON, SELBY, of Tweedmouth, rebuilt LOWICK CHURCH, NORTHUMBERLAND, in 1794, in conjunction with Henry Perry, a carpenter of Berwick-on-Tweed [Vestry Minutes, *ex inf.* Mr. D. Findlay]. Their names are inscribed on the tower as joint architects. The church was remodelled in the nineteenth century. In 1810 the foundation of a Masonic lodge at Tweedmouth was laid by 'brother Selby Morton, acting master' [J. Sykes, *Local Records* ii, 1866, 60].

MOSELEY, WILLIAM (*c.*1799–1880), was a pupil of George Julian. He practised in London from the late 1820s until his death on 29 July 1880, in his 82nd year [*Times*, 31 July 1880]. He held the post of County Surveyor of Middlesex from 1829 to 1846, and that of District Surveyor for West Islington from 1853 onwards. Latterly he was in partnership with his brother Andrew Moseley. Charles Henman (d. 1884) was his pupil.

Moseley designed the following churches in Sussex: HOLTYE COMMON, cons. 1836, dem. 1892 [I.C.B.S.]; FOREST ROW, cons. 1836, enlarged 1879 [I.C.B.S.]; HADLOW DOWN, 1836, rebuilt 1913 [I.C.B.S.]; UCKFIELD, incorporating old tower and chancel, 1839 [I.C.B.S.; *Civil Engineer and Architect's Jnl.* ii, 1839, 316]; and ST. MARK'S, HORSHAM, 1840–1, remodelled 1870 [exhib. at R.A. 1841]. None of them satisfied nineteenth-century ecclesiological standards. In 1843–4 he designed ST. THOMAS'S CHURCH, RED BANK, MANCHESTER, Gothic [W. E. A. Axon, *The Annals of Manchester*, 1886, 221], but his ambitious designs for St. Mary's Church, Kingston, Portsea, Hants., were rejected in favour of less expensive ones by T. E. Owen (*q.v.*).

Moseley's public works included the enlargement of the MIDDLESEX HOUSE OF CORRECTION in COLDBATH FIELDS, CLERKENWELL, 1830, dem. [exhib. at R.A. 1833]; the addition of wings to the COUNTY LUNATIC ASYLUM at HANWELL, MIDDLESEX, 1838 [exhib. at R.A. 1838]; the COUNTY LUNATIC ASYLUM FOR SURREY at WANDSWORTH, 1839–41 [exhib. at R.A. 1839; Brayley, *Surrey* ii, 498]; the MIDDLESEX HOUSE OF DETENTION at CLERKENWELL, 1845–6; dem. [*Builder* iv, 1846, 277, 282–3; W. G. Pinks, *History of Clerkenwell*, 1881, 185]; and the completion of the COUNTY LUNATIC ASYLUM at RAINHILL, LANCS., after the death of H. L. Elmes, 1847–51 [exhib. at R.A. 1853]. He also designed a GIRLS' SCHOOL at NEW BRENTFORD, MIDDLESEX, 1840 [exhib at R.A.], and a house called SUTTON HURST at BARCOMBE in SUSSEX for Capt. Thomas Richardson, 1838 [exhib. at R.A.]. In conjunction with Andrew Moseley he designed THE CITY BANK in THREADNEEDLE STREET, LONDON, 1856 [exhib. at R.A.], a branch bank in BROAD STREET, and THE WESTMINSTER PALACE HOTEL, VICTORIA STREET, 1859–61, said to have been the first hotel in London to be equipped with lifts [*Builder* xx, 1862, 165–7].

[*The Architect's, Engineer's and Building Trades' Directory*, 1868, 127; *Builder* xxxix, 1880, 171.]

MOSS, WILLIAM (1754–), was admitted to the Royal Academy Schools in 1774 at the age of 20. He was awarded the Silver Medal in 1775, and the Gold Medal in 1778. He exhibited at the Academy from 1775 to 1782. According to Redgrave's *Dictionary of Artists* (1878), he 'painted some landscapes and both drew and etched'. An architect of this name was employed to rebuild the tower and part of the nave and chancel of LUDDENHAM CHURCH, KENT, after they had collapsed in 1807 [C. E. Woodruff, *An Inventory of Parish Registers and Records in the Diocese of Canterbury*, 1922, 114].

MOUNTAGUE, JAMES (*c.*1776–1853), was the younger brother of William Mountague, and, like him, began his architectural career as a clerk in the office of George Dance. In 1821 he became District Surveyor for the North Division of the City of London. He was also Surveyor to the Port of London (1806–28) and of Blackfriars Bridge. He designed, in *c.*1820, the SCHOOLS of the Benevolent Society of St. Patrick in STAMFORD STREET, SOUTHWARK, now the London Nautical School [*Survey of London* xxiii, 18; *Gent's Mag.* 1822 (i), 497]. He died on 24 April 1853, aged 77 [*A.P.S.D.*; *Gent's Mag.* 1853 (i), 675].

MOUNTAGUE, WILLIAM (1773–1843), was the son of William Mountague (d. 1791), a minor City official who was for a time a clerk in the office of George Dance, the Surveyor to the City of London. After being employed by Dance in a similar capacity for some years, the younger Mountague succeeded James Peacock as Assistant Clerk of the City Works in 1814, and in 1816 succeeded Dance himself as City Surveyor. He had, in 1812, been appointed surveyor to the City Improvement Committee, and in this capacity was responsible for the formation of Finsbury Circus, planned by Dance in 1802, but not carried out until the demolition of the Bethlehem Hospital in 1815. Among the buildings which he designed were the DEBTORS' PRISON in WHITECROSS STREET, 1813–15, dem. 1873; the COURTS of KING'S BENCH and COMMON PLEAS at GUILDHALL, 1823, dem.; THE CITY LIBRARY, 1828, dem. 1871; FARRINGDON MARKET, 1828–9, dem. 1873 and 1892; the Gothic panelling under the window at the east end of GUILDHALL, 1838, removed 1866; and the lobbies and committee rooms at GUILDHALL, 1842. He was also responsible in 1842 for the removal of the attic storey over the Ballroom of the MANSION HOUSE, and for designing the existing new coffered ceiling to take its place.

Besides these works, he made the valuations for purchasing the property required for various improvements in the City, including the widening of St. Martin's le Grand and the erection of the new Post Office in 1824, the formation of King William Street and of Wellington Street in the Borough, as north and south approaches to London Bridge; and for the formation of Moorfields Pavement, Sir Robert Smirke being employed as architect of the new houses in each case. He was similarly employed in clearing the site for the new Royal Exchange, begun in 1841, and in valuations preparatory to the construction of Moorgate Street, Prince's Street and Gresham Street. The enlargement of Smithfield Market was also carried out under his direction. He was District Surveyor for the West Division of the City from 1808, and was surveyor to the estates of Sir Charles Morgan, the Sons of the Clergy, Baroness von Zandt, and the Thames Tunnel Company. He died on 12 April 1843, aged 70, and was interred in the Bunhill Fields Burial Ground. His only son and chief assistant, Frederick William Mountague (*c.*1801–41), was a successful surveyor with a considerable practice, but predeceased his father, dying on 2 December 1841, aged 40, after being thrown from his gig. [*A.P.S.D.*; *D.N.B.*; S. Redgrave, *A Dictionary of Artists of the English School*, 1878, 301; Dorothy Stroud, *George Dance*, 1971, 137, 155–6, 221–2, 246; *The Farington Diary*, ed. J. Greig, vi, 63.]

MOUNTAIN, CHARLES (*c.*1743–1805), was prominent as an architect and builder in Hull during the last quarter of the eighteenth century. He was much employed by the wealthy merchant J. R. Pease, for whom he designed a country house at HESSLE called HESSLEWOOD, and probably a town house at 12 CHARLOTTE STREET, HULL (dem. 1969). He also designed a house in MOSLEY STREET, MANCHESTER, for Pease's Robinson connections, the TRINITY HOUSE NAVIGATION SCHOOL, HULL, 1786–7, dem. 1844, and a plain row of houses in MYTON PLACE, HULL. From about 1781 onwards he was involved in the development of the Hull Dock Company's estate on the north side of the Queen's Dock, and probably designed most of the handsome houses in GEORGE STREET, CHARLOTTE STREET, NORTH STREET and CARROLL PLACE (formerly PARADISE ROW), some of which survive. RIMSWELL CHURCH, YORKS. (E.R), 1801, was also his work [*V.C.H. Yorks. E.R.* v, 96].

Mountain's style was late Palladian in

character, with internal detailing influenced by the Adam brothers. He died on 7 August 1805, aged 62, leaving his practice to be continued by his son Charles Mountain, junior (*q.v.*). [A. G. Chamberlain & I. Hall in *V.C.H. Yorks.: E. Riding* i, 349, 445, 447–8, 451–2; I. & E. Hall, *Georgian Hull*, 1978–9; *Gent's Mag.* 1805 (ii), 781.]

MOUNTAIN, CHARLES (*c.*1773–1839), only son of the above, appears to have practised in Lincoln until his father's death in 1805, when he returned to Hull. Under the terms of his father's will he inherited his architectural books, papers, etc., the materials of his building business, and his copyhold property in the manor of Myton. He was declared bankrupt in 1812, whereupon his assets were offered for sale, one of them being an estate of twenty-one houses and tenements lately crected at Brigg in Lincolnshire. His affairs soon recovered, and in 1820, while continuing to practise as an architect, he started a new business as a slater and slate merchant. In or shortly before 1835 he moved to Malton, and subsequently to Wakefield, where he died on 23 April 1839, aged 66.

Mountain was Hull's first neo-classical architect. His work was nearly all in a competent Greek Revival style which he sometimes handled with considerable elegance (*e.g.* at Goodmanham Rectory).

[A. G. Chamberlain, 'Mountain of Hull', *Arch. Rev.*, Oct. 1968, 299; J. Greenwood, *Picture of Hull*, 1835, 126 n.]

HULL, THE MEAT MARKET or SHAMBLES, 1806; dem. [*Monthly Magazine*, 1806 (i), 575].

HULL, THE THEATRE ROYAL, HUMBER STREET, 1809–10; destroyed by fire 1859 [J. Greenwood, *Picture of Hull*, 1835, 136].

BRIGG, LINCS., twenty-one houses and tenements, 'lately erected' in 1812 [*Hull Advertiser*, 4 Sept., 27 Nov. 1812].

WAKEFIELD PARISH CHURCH (now Cathedral), rebuilt upper 15 feet of spire, 1823 [J. L. Sisson, *Historic Sketch of the Parish Church of Wakefield*, 1824, 10].

GOODMANHAM RECTORY (now HALL GARTH), YORKS. (E.R.), 1823–4 [Borthwick Institute, York, MGA 1822/1; Arthur Oswald in *C. Life*, 23 Feb., 2 March 1961].

HULL, THE TRINITY ALMSHOUSE, POSTERNGATE (now offices), 1828; portico destroyed 1941 [J. Greenwood, *Picture of Hull*, 1835, 95].

HULL, WHITEFRIAR GATE, rebuilt south side, including Smith's Bank (now Woolworth's stores), for Trinity House, 1829–31 [*V.C.H. Yorks.: E. Riding* i, 449].

HULL, THE MECHANICS' INSTITUTE, CHARLOTTE STREET, 1830; dem. [J. Greenwood, *Picture of Hull*, 1835, 126].

HULL, THE PUBLIC ROOMS, KINGSTON SQUARE, 1830–4; completed by H. R. Abraham after Mountain had moved to Malton [J. Greenwood, *Picture of Hull*, 1835, 134; I. & E. Hall, *Georgian Hull*, 1978/9, 88].

BEVERLEY, YORKS. (E.R.), added portico to GUILDHALL, 1832 [R. H. Whiteing, 'The Guildhall, Beverley', *Trans. Georgian Soc. for E. Yorkshire* ii, part iv, 1948–9].

HULL, THE MASTER MARINERS' ALMSHOUSES, CARR LANE, for Trinity House, 1834; dem. 1941 [J. Greenwood, *Picture of Hull*, 1835, 95].

WAKEFIELD, YORKS. (W.R.), THE SAVINGS BANK, 1834 [*Architectural Mag.* i, 1834, 142].

MOXSON, JOHN (1700–1782), held the office of Surveyor of Highways at Leeds, where he designed the MIXED CLOTH HALL, 1756–8; dem. 1889. An engraving records that the building was 'Design'd, delineated and superintended by John Moxson'. In 1765 he made plans for additional galleries in ST. JOHN'S CHURCH. It was probably his son John who in 1792–3 was employed by Joseph Gott as surveyor for the erection of BEAN ING MILL [D. Linstrum, *West Yorkshire Architects and Architecture*, 1978, 382].

MOYLE, JOHN, of Exeter, was a master builder of some importance in the south-western counties in the reign of George I, and was probably capable of making his own architectural designs, although no direct evidence of this has so far been found. In 1713, as 'John Moyle of the Citty of Exeter, Bricklayer', he contracted to build a garden wall at Antony in Cornwall for Sir William Carew, Bart., and in 1718 to build the shell of ANTONY HOUSE 'according to a draught agreed upon' [Carew papers at Antony, CE/E/22] (*C. Life*, 19, 25 Aug. 1933, 9–16 June 1988). Between 1710 and 1727 'Mr. Moyle the Builder' carried out considerable works at POWDERHAM CASTLE, DEVON, for Sir William Courtenay, Bart. [Mark Girouard in *C. Life*, 4 July 1963], and in 1721 he was working for Thomas ('Governor') Pitt in Cornwall, presumably at BOCONNOC HOUSE, which Pitt had recently bought, and to which he added an east wing that was demolished in 1834 [P.R.O., C 108/424, Pitt's Letter-Book No. 14, no. 513, 1721].

MOYSER, JAMES (*c.*1688–1751), was the eldest son of John Moyser (*c.*1660–1738) of Beverley, M.P. for that town in 1705–8, by his first wife Mary Eyre. His early life was spent in the Army, first as an officer in Sir

Charles Hotham's regiment of foot, and subsequently as a Colonel in the lst Regiment of Foot Guards. He saw active service in Spain, where in 1710 he was Stanhope's Adjutant. The rest of his life was spent in Beverley, where he died in November 1751.

The elder Moyser had taken a leading part in raising money for the repair of Beverley Minster in the reign of Queen Anne, but although he subscribed to the third volume of *Vitruvius Britannicus* (1725), there is no evidence that he had any architectural skill. In the 1730s and 1740s, however, his son was active as an amateur architect. Both the Moysers were on friendly terms with Lord Burlington, and the Colonel appears to have been one of his provincial disciples. The first building with which he can be connected is BRETTON HALL, YORKS. (W.R.), which was built by Sir William Wentworth in about 1730 in a plain style of Palladian character (*C. Life*, 21–28 May 1938; D. Linstrum in *Leeds Arts Calendar*, No. 68, 1971). According to a list of houses found by Dr. Eileen Harris in a copy of the *Builder's Dictionary* (1734) in the Metropolitan Museum at New York, Bretton was designed 'by Sir Wm. and Col. Moyser'. This is confirmed by a note added to a letter of Moyser's to Godfrey Bosvile of Gunthwaite in which he is identified as the person 'who gave Sr. William Wentworth the plan of Britton House, and was his most intimate friend' [Hull University Library, Bosvile-Macdonald papers, DD BM/32/8].

The list already cited also names 'Col. Moyser' as the architect of NOSTELL PRIORY, YORKS. (W.R.), built by Sir Rowland Winn *c.*1737 onwards.[1] A plan at Nostell [C3/1/1/2] shows that the basic design, with four wings connected to the main block by quadrants in the manner of Palladio's Villa Mocenigo, had been envisaged as early as 1731. It is related to a similar design for a large country house by Colen Campbell (now in the R.I.B.A. Drawings Collection) which Moyser may have seen. The supervision of the work was entrusted to the young James Paine, who was responsible for a good deal of the detailed designing as the work proceeded. He did not, however, claim to have been the architect of the house, stating quite correctly in the preface to his *Plans* (1767) that 'at the age of nineteen (he) was entrusted to conduct a building of consequence in the West Riding of Yorkshire'. Nostell is illustrated in *Vitruvius Britannicus* iv, 1767, pls. 70–3, and in *C. Life*, 16–30 May 1952.

In 1746 Moyser made a design for a new house at Gunthwaite, nr. Penistone, Yorks. (W.R.), for Godfrey Bosvile, but it was not built, although Moyser assured him that it would be 'the most convenient, the hansomest & the cheapest of any House in Yorkshire' [Hull University Library, Bosvile-Macdonald papers, DD BM/32/8]. In 1746 Moyser was one of the architectural experts consulted by Stephen Thompson before he began to build KIRBY HALL, nr. Ouseburn. He provided Thompson with a plan which the latter admired and described as 'a perfect Model of Ld. Orford's at Houghton'. In the event Thompson progressively altered the plan until it no longer met with Moyser's approval. But he took the Colonel's advice in consulting Roger Morris, who was persuaded to call at Kirby on his way to Scotland in the summer of 1747. Lord Burlington also helped, and the final outcome was a house planned by the owner, with elevations by Burlington and Morris (p. 151) [E. Yorks. Record Office, Grimston papers, DD GR/41/3–7].

Moyser also designed ANNE ROUTH'S HOSPITAL in KELDGATE, BEVERLEY, which was built in 1749 'pursuant to a plan drawn by Mr. Moyser' [*Beverley Corporation Minute Books*, ed. K. A. MacMahon, Yorks. Arch. Soc. Record Series, 1958, p. xvii].

Family connections and stylistic similarities suggest that Moyser may have designed ORMESBY HALL, YORKS. (N.R.), for James Pennyman, *c.*1740–5 [L. F. Pearson, 'Ormesby Hall, Cleveland', *Yorks. Arch. Jnl.* 61, 1989] (*C. Life*, 26 Feb. 1959).

No drawings of Moyser's have so far been identified, and his ability as an architect is difficult to assess on the strength of the few buildings for which he is known to have been responsible. Bretton is merely a rectangular block dressed up with 'Palladian' windows. Though Nostell is a large and ambitious mansion there is a certain stolidity about the main elevations which shows that Moyser was not an architect of the same calibre as his friend Lord Burlington. In short, although James Moyser was evidently a competent amateur, there is no reason to suppose that he made a contribution of any importance to English Palladian architecture.

[J. W. Clay, 'Dugdale's Visitation of Yorkshire, with Additions', *Genealogist*, N.S. xxv, 1909, 111, corrected by documents U 245 333 and AK 265 345 in Northallerton Deeds Registry; G. Poulson, *Beverlac* ii, 1829, 678; G. Oliver, *History of Beverley*, 1829, 241, 326;

[1] A contemporary note in a book of plans of Kirtlington Park, Oxon., in the Oxfordshire County Record Office (Dash. III/xlix/1) records that 'The idea of the House is taken from Sr Rowland Winn's which was originally planned by Col. Moyser of Beverley.'

Yorkshire Diaries, Surtees Soc. 1875, 349; Dalton, *English Army Lists and Commission Registers i*, 172, v, 19, vi, 169; *Beverley Corporation Minute Books*, ed. K. A. MacMahon, Yorks. Arch. Soc. Record Series 1958, pp. xiii, 7, 13; Chatsworth House, Lord Burlington's Correspondence, 127/9 and 10 (1735); Borthwick Institute of Historical Research, York Probate Register vol. 86, f. 252 (will of John Moyser); P.C.C. 146 SEARLE (will of James Moyser); information from Mr. Jeremy Moiser.]

MUIRSON, THOMAS, described as 'architect' or 'builder', designed and executed additions to ERCHLESS CASTLE, INVERNESS-SHIRE, for William Chisholm in 1814–15, including a 'new wing and colonnade', a 'portico' and a 'bridge on east approach' [account in S.R.O., SC29/64/6, p. 183, *ex inf.* Miss Ierne Grant]. He also designed and built a MANSE (now HILL HOUSE) at AVOCH, ROSS & CROMARTY, 1820–2 [S.R.O., CH2/66/6, P. 327].

MULLINS JOHN (*c.*1795–1880), was in 1816–17 a pupil of W. B. Hué. In the 1820s he was practising from Fenchurch Street. He exhibited at the Royal Academy between 1814 and 1827. He designed the IMPERIAL PLATE GLASS MANUFACTORY on the north bank of the Thames opposite Greenwich, of which he exhibited a drawing in 1826. A monument in ORPINGTON CHURCH, KENT, to William Dredge (d. 1820) is signed 'J. Holder Sculp. John Mullins Arch.' Mullins was District Surveyor for Streatham and Brixton from 1844 until his death on 22 November 1880 [*Builder* xxxix, 1880, 683; Principal Probate Registry, Calendar of Probates].

MUNRO, DONALD, was a builder-architect in Tain, Ross & Cromarty, from the 1820s to the 1840s. His only recorded work of any consequence was EDDERTON CHURCH, ROSS & CROMARTY, 1842, a sturdy essay in late Georgian Gothic with a steepled façade [S.R.O., CH2/348/13, pp. 523–6] (J. Gifford, *Highlands & Islands*, Buildings of Scotland, fig. 34).

MÜNTZ, JOHANN HEINRICH (1727–1798), was an artist of German–Swiss origin born at Mülhausen. As a young man he travelled in Spain as well as in France, Germany and Italy. He arrived in England in 1755 via the Channel Islands, where he was discovered by Richard Bentley (*q.v.*). 'I have a painter in the house', wrote Horace Walpole to Sir Horace Mann in 1758, 'who is an engraver too, a mechanic, an everything. He was a Swiss engineer in the French service, but, his regiment being broken at the peace, Mr. Bentley found him in the Isle of Jersey, and fixed him with me. He has astonishing genius for landscape, and added to that all the patience and industry of a German.' For four years he worked for Walpole before being dismissed 'for some amorous misdemeanour' with one of Walpole's female servants. At STRAWBERRY HILL he painted the ceiling of the China Closet with 'convolvulus's on poles' in a manner suggested by a ceiling in the Borghese Villa at Frascati, and designed several Gothic features, including probably the doorway of the Gallery and the niches in the Chapel or Cabinet. For Richard Bateman's 'half Gothick, half Attic, half Chinese and completely fribble house' at OLD WINDSOR, BERKS., he designed in 1761–2 an octagonal Gothic room with a pyramidal roof like a chapter-house, which still survives although the rest of the house has been rebuilt. For the Earl of Charlemont he designed in 1762 an 'Egiptian Room' (really a Gothic room with Egyptian figures) for his house at MARINO, nr. DUBLIN, which does not appear to have been built, but in 1768 he was making further designs for Lord Charlemont which may have been carried out. And at KEW GARDENS he not only designed the 'Gothic Cathedral' in about 1759 (see W. Chambers, *Plans etc. of the Gardens and Buildings at Kew in Surrey*, 1763, pl. 29), but may have provided the original drawing from which the Moorish 'Alhambra' was developed.

Müntz's interest in Gothic architecture is shown not only by the measured drawings which he made of doorways in St. Albans Abbey Church in 1759 and 1762, but also by his proposals for publishing by subscription *A Course of Gothic Architecture*, of which there is a prospectus, dated 12 April 1760, among James Essex's MSS. in the British Library (Add. MS. 6771, f. 215). Had it been published, it would have been one of the pioneer works on Gothic architecture.[1] Müntz was also interested in the process of encaustic painting, upon which he published a treatise in 1760 entitled *Encaustic: or, Count Caylus's Method of Painting in the Manner of the Ancients.* The five drawings which he exhibited at the Society of Artists in 1762 included a landscape painted in encaustic as well as his

[1] Richard Gough was, however, sceptical of Müntz's pretensions as an architectural historian. In a MS. note in his own copy of his *British Topography* in the Bodleian Library he wrote that 'Munz was totally incapable of executing this work; nor knew what Gothic Architecture was, but by living 4 years with Mr. Walpole, and drawing some Antiquities for him while Strawberry Hill was building.' I owe this reference to Dr. J. M. Frew.

designs for Richard Bateman's Gothic room and for Lord Charlemont's Egyptian one.

In 1763 Müntz went to Holland. From 1780 to 1783 he was in Poland, where he designed a villa for Prince Poniatowski. He eventually died in Kassel in 1798. Drawings by Müntz exist in several European collections. The W. S. Lewis collection at Farmington, U.S.A., contains a number of his English drawings, including those made for Richard Bateman, Lord Charlemont and Horace Walpole, and also an album of drawings of vases 'entrepris et commencé à Rome en 1751 et réduit à ce terme à Amsterdam 1772 par J. H. Muntz, Ingénieur et Architecte' (see John Harris, *Catalogue of British Drawings for Architecture, etc. in American Collections*, 1971, 143–8 and pls. 105–8.

[Thieme & Becker, *Allgemeines Lexikon der Bildenden Künstler* xxv, 253; Walpole's *Letters*, especially 9 Sept. 1758, to Sir Horace Mann; Hist. MSS. Comm., *Charlemont* i, 286; A. Graves, *The Society of Artists and The Free Society of Artists*, 1907, 180; John Harris, *Sir William Chambers*, 1970; J. M. Crook, 'Strawberry Hill Revisited', *C. Life*, 14 June 1973, 1728–9; M. J. McCarthy, 'Johann Heinrich Müntz: the Roman Drawings (1749–76)', *Burlington. Mag.* May 1977.]

MURRAY, GEORGE (–1841), practised in Glasgow, where he added the FEVER HOSPITAL to the ROYAL INFIRMARY in 1825–32 and designed the CITY HALL, CANDLERIGGS, 1840–1, and the OBSERVATORY, VICTORIA CRESCENT, 1840, Tudor, dem. [*A.P.S.D.*, *s.v.* 'Glasgow']. The City Hall was built on arches over the Bazaar, and originally had no façade to the street. The existing front dates from 1882–6, when the building was altered and enlarged by John Carrick. Murray died on 30 May 1841 [S.R.O., SC 36/48/28, p. 570].

MURRAY, JAMES (–1634), was the son of James Murray (d. 1615), a master wright who had been appointed overseer of the King's works in Scotland in 1601. The son was appointed Master Wright in 1601, and in 1605 his father surrendered the office of overseer in his favour. In 1607 he succeeded David Cunningham of Robertland as 'principal master of all his majesties works in Scotland', with a yearly fee of 500 merks. In 1611 he was reported to be the 'surveyor and builder' of a great house (never finished) which George Home, Earl of Dunbar, had been building at BERWICK-ON-TWEED before his death in January that year. In 1612 he was granted an estate at Baberton (or Kilbaberton), nr. Currie in Midlothian, where in 1622–3 he proceeded to build a house which still exists. Though traditional in character, it is decorated with classical detail reminiscent of Heriot's Hospital. Further evidence of Murray's ability as an architect is afforded by the Edinburgh Town Council Minutes, which record that in 1633 he was paid £1000 (Scots) for past services in the town's works, 'and for drawing up of the modell of the workes of the Parliament and Counsel hous presentlie intendit'. This was the PARLIAMENT HOUSE begun in 1633 and completed in 1640, whose structure still exists, though embedded in later buildings by Robert Reid and others. Engravings show an L-shaped building decorated with small turrets and mannerist detail akin to that at Baberton House.

Murray was knighted in 1633 and died in December 1634.

[R. S. Mylne, 'The Masters of Work to the Crown of Scotland', *Proceedings of the Society of Antiquaries of Scotland*, 3rd ser. vi, 1895–6; *History of the King's Works*, ed. Colvin, v, 1982, 771 (for Berwick); D. MacGibbon & T. Ross, *The Castellated and Domestic Architecture of Scotland* iv, 1892, 67–8 (for Baberton House), v, 547; R. K. Hanney, 'The Building of the Parliament House', *Book of the Old Edinburgh Club* xiii, 1924; *Accounts of the Masters of Works*, vol. i, ed. H. M. Paton, 1957, xxix, vol. ii, ed. Imrie & Dunbar, 1982, lviii–lix; testament in S.R.O., CC8/8/57, ff. 269v–271v.]

MYLNE, JOHN (–1621), is the first of his family to come within the chronological limits of this *Dictionary*. Traditionally he was the second John Mylne to be a leading Scottish master mason, the first having 'come from the North Country' some time in the sixteenth century. However, if the conjectures of the family historian can be accepted, the first John Mylne practised his craft in the reigns of James III and IV (1460–1513), and the second John Mylne was the son of Thomas Mylne, a Dundee master mason who may have been a native of Elgin. Certainly the John Mylne who is the subject of this entry was established in Dundee during the last decade of the sixteenth century. According to a document drawn up by the masons' lodge at Perth in 1658 he and his father successively held the post of King's Master Mason. Although no official or contemporary record appears to confirm this statement, it may be noted that John Mylne is also referred to as royal master mason in the memoirs of James, Lord Somerville (d. 1690). Writing in 1679, Lord Somerville recalled that in 1584–5 the 7th Lord Somerville employed 'John Millne, the king's master meassone', to build the family seat called THE DRUM, MIDLOTHIAN (rebuilt

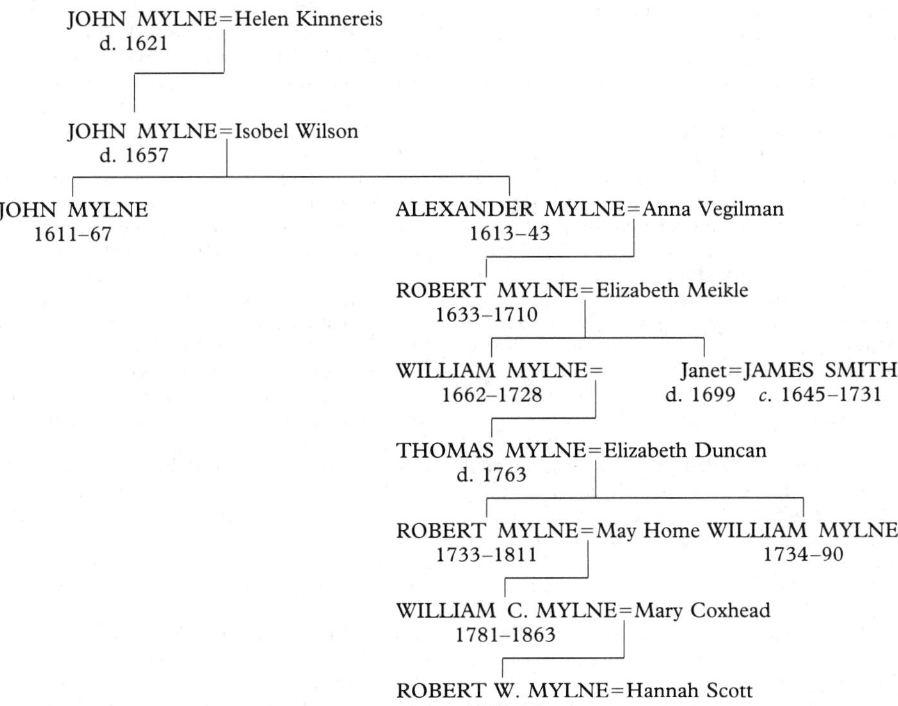

by William Adam *c.*1725) [*Memorie of the Somervilles*, ed. Walter Scott, Edinburgh 1815, i, 460].

During the 1580s John Mylne was engaged in various works at Dundee, where in September 1587 he was admitted a burgess 'for services done and to be done' in the burgh, 'and especially for repairing the whole harbour' [R. S. Mylne, *Master Masons*, 66]. He erected in 1586 the market cross in the High Street, a polygonal shaft surmounted by a heraldic unicorn [Alexander Maxwell, *The History of Old Dundee*, Dundee 1884, 245] (R. S. Mylne, *op. cit.*, plate at p. 65). In February 1589/90 he and another Dundee mason named George Thomson contracted to build a gallery and other additions for Thomas Bannatyne at BANNATYNE HOUSE, NEWTYLE, ANGUS [R. S. Mylne, *op. cit.*, 66–9]. In 1604 he undertook the major task of building a new bridge of eleven arches over the R. Tay at Perth [R. S. Mylne, *op. cit.*, 93]. This bridge was eventually completed in 1617, but was destroyed by a great flood in October 1621.

In 1607 Mylne was admitted to the freedom of Perth gratis. As Master of the Lodge of Scone he entered King James VI by his own desire as 'frieman Meason and Fellow Craft' [R. S. Mylne, *op. cit.*, 128]. Mylne died early in 1621 and was buried in the Greyfriars burial ground at Perth, where there is a stone (originally the top of a table-tomb, restored in 1849 and again in 1913) with a quaint epitaph in verse to his memory. The architect Robert Mylne added a mural tablet in 1774. By his wife Helen Kinnereis John Mylne had a son John (d. 1657) (*q.v.*).

[R. S. Mylne, *The Master Masons to the Crown of Scotland*, Edinburgh 1893; *A.P.S.D.*; *D.N.B.*]

MYLNE, JOHN (–1657), was the son of John Mylne (d. 1621), and assisted him for some years in the erection of the Tay Bridge at Perth. In 1616 he left Perth for Edinburgh, in response to an invitation from the town council to complete a statue of King James I and VI for the Netherbow Port after the sudden death of the original sculptor, a Frenchman named Benjamin Lambert [R. S. Mylne, *Master Masons*, 105–6]. In conjunction with a mason called Tailefer he was subsequently employed to take down and re-erect the Market Cross, and in June 1617 he was made a burgess of Edinburgh [*op. cit.*, 106–7]. In 1618 he appears to have returned to the north (whether to Perth or Dundee is not clear), and in January 1620 he contracted with David Murray, Lord Scone, to rebuild FALKLAND CHURCH, FIFE (again rebuilt 1850) [*op. cit.*, 110–11]. His next engagement was in Aberdeen, where he executed the masonry of the new Tolbooth steeple in 1622–3 [*Aberdeen Burgh Records*, Spalding Club 1848, ii, 379]. In consequence he was in May 1622 made a burgess of the city *ex gratia* [R. S. Mylne, *Master Masons*, 113]. In 1627 he became a burgess of Dundee in right of his late father [*op. cit.*, 113]. In 1629–30 he carried out some works at DRUMMOND CASTLE, PERTHSHIRE, for the 2nd Earl of Perth [*op. cit.*, 114]. These included the elaborate faceted sundial in the garden, which is dated 1630 (D. MacGibbon & T. Ross, *The Castellated and Domestic Architecture of Scotland* v, 1892, 417–18).

By 1629 John Mylne was back in Edinburgh constructing a pond at Holyroodhouse for King Charles I, and in 1631 he succeeded William Wallace (*q.v.*) as Master Mason to the Crown [R. S. Mylne, *Master Masons*, 114–15]. The principal memorial to his tenure of this office is the sundial in the gardens of Holyroodhouse, which he constructed in 1633 with the aid of his sons John and Alexander [D. MacGibbon & T. Ross, *op. cit.* v, 441–2]. In 1636 he resigned his office in favour of his elder son John, and returned to Dundee, where between 1643 and 1651 he was employed upon various works, including the repair of the church steeple and the fortification of the town [Alexander Maxwell, *The History of Old Dundee*, Dundee, 1884, 151, 213–14, 492; R. S. Mylne, *op. cit.*, 127]. His admission in 1643 as a burgess of Kirkcaldy was no doubt connected with the repair and enlargement of the church there: his recent involvement in 'the building of the Ile of the kirk of Kirkcaldie' is mentioned in a letter of 2 Jan. 1650 [S.R.O., GD 26/13/329].

Like his father, John Mylne was Master of the Masons' Lodge at Scone. He married Isobel Wilson of Perth in 1610, and died in 1657. A portrait is reproduced by R. S. Mylne in his *Master Masons*, 104. His elder son John (d. 1667) is noticed below. His younger son Alexander (1613–43), commemorated by a monument in Holyrood Abbey, was a sculptor and carver.

[R. S. Mylne, *The Master Masons to the Crown of Scotland*, Edinburgh 1893; *A.P.S.D.*; *D.N.B.*]

MYLNE, JOHN (1611–1667), son of John Mylne (d. 1657), was born in Perth in 1611. On 9 October 1633 he was admitted a burgess of Edinburgh by right of patrimony, and on the same day was made 'fellow of craft' in the Edinburgh Masonic Lodge. In February 1636, at the age of 25, he succeeded his father as Master Mason to the Crown, and in 1646 he was appointed Captain of Pioneers and Master Gunner of Scotland. For over thirty years he was a prominent figure in the Scottish capital. He repeatedly served as Deacon of the Edinburgh masons, and was for several years a member of the town council. In 1652 he was sent to London as one of the Scottish Commissioners to negotiate a Treaty of Union with the English Parliament, and from 1655 to 1659 represented Edinburgh at the convention of royal burghs. In 1662 he was elected M.P. for Edinburgh in the Scottish Parliament, and attended the second and third sessions of Charles II's first parliament in Edinburgh.

John Mylne was married three times, but his only son died in infancy, and it was his nephew Robert (1633–1710) who succeeded him as Master Mason to the Scottish Crown. John died in Edinburgh on 24 December 1667, and was buried in the Greyfriars Cemetery, where he is commemorated by a handsome monument erected by Robert. Another inscription to his memory was erected over the door of St. Mary's Chapel (the masons' meeting-place) by the Incorporated Trades of Scotland, in which he was described as

> . . . . the Fourth John
> And by descent from Father unto Son
> Sixth Master Mason to a Royal Race
> of seven successive Kings . . .
> Rare man he was, who could unite in one
> Highest and lowest occupation.
> To sit with Statesmen, Councillors to Kings
> To work with Tradesmen, in Mechanick things.

His portrait, now in the Scottish National Portrait Gallery, shows him with a bust and an architectural plan. Another is in the possession of his descendants.

Early in his career Mylne was commissioned to make designs for the two new churches required to house the congregations displaced by Charles I's decision (1633) to erect St. Giles' Church into a cathedral. One church was begun on Castle Hill, but later abandoned; the other was THE TRON CHURCH in the High Street, begun in 1637 but not completed until 1647. Though truncated in 1788 and partly rebuilt after a fire in 1824, the Tron Church is a striking example of Scoto-

Flemish mannerism and as such indicative of Mylne's style [see *Extracts from the Records of the City of Edinburgh 1626–41*, ed. M. Wood, 307–11 for the estimate, and *op. cit. 1642–55*, 40; also R.C.A.M., *Edinburgh*, 35, *Book of the Old Edinburgh Club* xxix, 1956, 99–103, and plan in G. Hay, *The Architecture of Scottish Post-Reformation Churches*, 1957, fig. 15]. His next recorded work was COWANE'S HOSPITAL, STIRLING, built to his designs by a Stirling mason in 1637–48. Though the E-shaped plan was unusual for Scotland, the architectural character of the building was traditional, with restrained mannerist detailing [R.C.A.M., *Stirlingshire*, 289–92]. In 1642 Mylne reported on the dangerous state of the fabric of the ABBEY CHURCH at JEDBURGH, ROXBURGHSHIRE [R. S. Mylne, *Master Masons*, 138–9]. In 1643 he succeeded William Aytoun (*q.v.*) as master mason to HERIOT'S HOSPITAL, begun in 1628, but still incomplete owing to the political and financial troubles of the time. In 1648 he was instructed to take down the upper part of the south-west tower and rebuild it uniform with the others [*Extracts, etc. 1642–55*, 142]. He was still employed at the Hospital as late as 1659 [R. S. Mylne, *op. cit.*, 139–40]. In 1648 he also repaired the openwork crown of ST. GILES'CATHEDRAL, then in a dangerous state [R. S. Mylne, *op. cit.*, 144]. In 1649–50 he fortified Leith [*Extracts etc. 1642–55*, 41, 130, 204, 226, 228, 249, 293] and in February 1650 made an estimate for adding a frontispiece, etc., to NEWBATTLE ABBEY, MIDLOTHIAN, for the 1st Earl of Lothian, 'in a perfect manner off gudlie Architect[ure]' [S.R.O., GD 40/2/xviii /1/82]. In 1655–6 he was employed to divide the GREYFRIARS CHURCH, EDINBURGH, to accommodate two congregations [*Extracts from the Records of the City of Edinburgh 1642–55*, ed. M. Wood, 391–2]. In 1656 he undertook to build a professor's house and six chambers at the COLLEGE in EDINBURGH [*Extracts etc. 1655–65*, 34, 109; *Book of the Old Edinburgh Club* iv, 1911, 148]. These were demolished in 1790 to make way for the new College designed by R. & J. Adam, but the monument to Bartholomew Somervell (d. 1640) which ornamented the building survives at Craighall Rattray in Perthshire.

After the Restoration Mylne was confirmed in his office of Master Mason to the Crown, and in October 1663 made a survey of the second floor of HOLYROODHOUSE showing how 'it is intendet to be finished' [Bodleian Library, Gough Maps 39, f. 1^{v}, reproduced by R. S. Mylne, *op. cit.*, 148–9]. Nothing, however, was done until after his death, when Sir William Bruce and Robert Mylne reconstructed the palace in its existing form.

In 1661 the repair and partial rebuilding of COLDINGHAM CHURCH, BERWICKSHIRE, was to be carried out 'by the sight of John Milne master mason or any other they shall bring to visite the same after finishing thereof' [S.R.O., Register of Deeds, Dal. 7, 223, Warrant No. 1930 (1662)]. The draft of a contract exists whereby in November 1661 Mylne was to execute the masonry of a 'great addition' to ADDISTON HOUSE, RATHO, MIDLOTHIAN, for Sir John Gibson, but it is not known whether this was carried out [S.R.O., GD 45/17/299]. In 1665–6 he was employed to build, and apparently to design, FORT CHARLOTTE in SHETLAND [R. G. Bell, 'The Shetland Garrison 1665–1666', *Jnl. Society for Army Historical Research*, 43, 1965, 5–26; R.C.A.M., *Shetland*, 63].

In 1666 Mylne was employed by the 7th Earl (1st Duke) of Rothes, acting as guardian of the infant Margaret, Countess of Leven, to add a large 'scale-and-platt' staircase to BALGONIE CASTLE, FIFE [account in S.R.O., GD 26/6/134]. In the same year he contracted to build PANMURE HOUSE, ANGUS, for the 2nd Earl of Panmure, 'according to the maner forme and dimensions of the said structure and edifice designed and set down by the said John Mylne in draughts' [R. S. Mylne, *op. cit.*, 153–4]. On his death in the following year the work was completed by Alexander Nesbit, mason of Edinburgh, 'according to the maner, forme and dimensions already begun' [S.R.O., GD 45/18/565]. With its quadrangular plan and picturesque silhouette of cupola'd towers the house (dem. 1955, illustrated in *Vitruvius Scoticus*, pls. 129–31) bore a certain resemblance to Heriot's Hospital. Like Drumlanrig Castle it looked backwards to the early seventeenth century, and showed little evidence that John Mylne was participating in the new architectural ideas already current in England and soon to be introduced into Scotland by Sir William Bruce. The unexecuted design which he made for LINLITHGOW TOLBOOTH just before his death in 1667 [Mylne, *op. cit.*, 240–1] was also somewhat old-fashioned.[1] In the same year he was engaged by the Earl of Rothes to enlarge and remodel LESLIE HOUSE, FIFE, but here Bruce's advice was sought, and the house as completed by Robert Mylne in 1672 was rather more up to date in style. John Mylne must

[1] The minutes of the Linlithgow Town Council show that after Mylne's death they found a new master mason (John Smith), and it was to his design that the existing Tolbooth was built in 1668–73 [S.R.O., B 48/9/3].

therefore be seen as the leading master of the last phase of Scottish mannerism.

[R. S. Mylne, *The Master Masons to the Crown of Scotland*, Edinburgh 1893; *A.P.S.D.*, *D.N.B.*; *Extracts from the Records of the City of Edinburgh*, ed. M. Wood, *1642–55* and *1655–65*, *passim*; information from Mr. J. G. Dunbar.]

MYLNE, ROBERT (1633–1710), was the eldest son of Alexander Mylne (1613–43), younger son of John Mylne (d. 1657). He was apprenticed to his uncle John Mylne (d. 1667), and in 1668 succeeded him as Master Mason to the Scottish Crown.

His earliest recorded work appears to be WOOD'S HOSPITAL at LARGO, FIFE, which he built in 1665: it was rebuilt in 1830 [*The Chronicles of Fife, being the diary of John Lamont of Newton 1649–1672*, 1810, 223–4]. In 1668 he built a MARKET CROSS at PERTH to replace one destroyed by Cromwell's army in 1652: it was completed in 1669 and stood in the High Street until 1765, when it was demolished [R. S. Mylne, *Master Masons*, 214–16]. At the same time he was completing LESLIE HOUSE, FIFE, which had been begun by his uncle for the 7th Earl (lst Duke) of Rothes shortly before his death [J. G. Dunbar, *Sir William Bruce* (exhibition catalogue, 1970), citing Rothes papers in Kirkcaldy Museum]. In 1669 he contracted with the 2nd Earl of Wemyss to build an addition to WEMYSS CASTLE, FIFE, which was completed in 1672 [Sir William Fraser, *Memorials of the Family of Wemyss of Wemyss* i, 1888, 284; *Scottish Diaries and Memoirs 1550–1746*, ed. J. G. Fyfe, Stirling 1927, 129–30]. In 1671 he began work on the rebuilding of HOLYROODHOUSE under the direction of Sir William Bruce. His name and the date July 1671 are cut on the north-west pillar of the quadrangle. Although Bruce was responsible for the design, much of the practical planning must have fallen to Mylne as master mason, and a set of drawings formerly in the possession of the Mylne family and now in the British Library (Egerton MSS. 2870–1) appears to be in his hand. The palace was completed in 1679. Another work which he carried out at that period under Bruce's direction was the remodelling of THIRLESTANE CASTLE, BERWICKSHIRE, for the Duke of Lauderdale, *c.*1670–80. He also made gate-piers to Bruce's designs for the Duke's English seat of HAM HOUSE, SURREY [J. G. Dunbar, 'The Building-activities of the Duke and Duchess of Lauderdale, 1670–82', *Archaeological Jnl.* 132, 1975]. In 1662 and again in 1677 and 1685 Mylne was employed in repairing the fortifications of EDINBURGH CASTLE, where a battery on the north side formerly bore his name [R. S. Mylne, *op. cit.*, 203–5, 233; R.C.A.M., *Edinburgh*, 8; J. Grant, *Old and New Edinburgh* i, 75].

Between 1674 and 1681 Robert Mylne, under the direction of Sir William Bruce, constructed cisterns in various parts of Edinburgh in connection with the new water-supply from Comiston [*Extracts from the Records of the City of Edinburgh 1665–80*, ed. M. Wood, 426–31]. In 1674 he built the west tower of SOUTH LEITH PARISH CHURCH (taken down 1836) [D. Robertson, *South Leith Records*, 1911, 128–9] (view in J. Grant, *Old and New Edinburgh* iii, 217). In 1682 he contracted to build a bridge of one arch over the R. Clyde at Ramelwell Crags or Ram's Horn Pool, 29 miles above Lanark. This no longer exists, but the site is shown on a map in R. S. Mylne's *Master Masons*, 226 [for the contract, etc., see 221–5]. In 1693, having undertaken to complete the steeple of HERIOT'S HOSPITAL in accordance with a drawing which he had submitted, he built the existing octagonal stone cupola [R. S. Mylne, *op. cit.*, 232]. In 1703 he made a draught for NEWHALL HOUSE, nr. PENICUIK, but one by Sir John Clerk was preferred [S.R.O., GD 18/5188, no. 17]. In 1709 he began the burial place of the Trotter family of Mortonhall in the GREYFRIARS CHURCHYARD, but it was unfinished at the time of his death and was completed by his son William [MS. notes on the history of the family by Robert Mylne, d. 1811].

Robert Mylne engaged in a considerable amount of speculative building. In 1678 he built a block of ten dwellings on waste land which he had acquired on the Shore of Leith [cf. *Extracts etc. 1665–80*, 339]. The date and his initials appeared in the pediment [survey drawings from Mylne family archives in N.M.R.S.]. In Edinburgh he built MYLNE'S SQUARE opposite the Tron Church in 1684–6 (dem. 18—) [I. A. Stirling, 'Mylne Square', *Book of the Old Edinburgh Club* xiv, 1925, and contract for completion of a flat in Scottish Hist. Soc. *Miscellany* xi, 1990, 316–21], MILNE'S COURT in the High Street opposite the West Bow (1690), and MILNE'S LAND outside the Potter-Row Gate. Contracts in the S.R.O. show that he also built tenements for others in HART CLOSE, HIGH STREET, 1687 [Register of Deeds, Dal. 74.44], SIMPSON'S CLOSE, 1689 [Dal. 70, 497 (1689)], WRITER'S COURT, HIGH STREET, *c.*1695–6 [*Book of the Old Edinburgh Club* xii, 1923, 28, xxix, 1956, 125–7], and WEIR'S LAND, ST. JOHN STREET, 1705 [Register of Deeds 1709, Dur. Warrant No. 710].

The profits of his trade and his rents were sufficient to enable Mylne to acquire two estates, one at Balfargie in Fife, the other at Inveresk, nr. Edinburgh, 'where he generally retired to live free from the hurry of business'. In 1672 he had registered a coat of arms [R. S. Mylne, *op. cit.*, 213]. He died at Inveresk on 10 December 1710, aged 77, and was buried in the family vault in the Greyfriars Churchyard. He is commemorated on the monument he had erected to his uncle John. A portrait by Roderick Chalmers is reproduced by R. S. Mylne, *op. cit.*, 217.

Robert Mylne married in 1661 Elizabeth Meikle, by whom he had eight sons and six daughters. His eldest daughter Janet married the architect James Smith (*q.v.*). He was succeeded as head of the family by his eldest son William. William Mylne (1662–1728) did not play as important a part in Scottish architecture as his father, and does not require a separate biography. He was admitted a burgess of Edinburgh in 1687 and was a prominent member of the Edinburgh masonic lodge. In 1711 he sold the Balfargie estate to George Balfour of Balbirnie, and lived at Leith in one of the houses built by his father. He died on 9 March 1728, aged 66, and was buried at South Leith. He is commemorated by an inscription cut on the left-hand column of the family monument in the Greyfriars Cemetery. The only building for which he is known to have been wholly responsible was a land of houses in HALKERSTON'S WYND, EDINBURGH, which bore the inscription 'BUILT BY WILLIAM MYLNE MASON 1715'. It was partially destroyed by fire in 1756. He was succeeded by his son Thomas Mylne (*q.v.*).

[R. S. Mylne, *The Master Masons to the Crown of Scotland*, Edinburgh 1893; *A.P.S.D.*; *D.N.B.*; S.R.O., Mylne papers (GD 1/51); *Extracts from the Records of the City of Edinburgh*, ed. Wood & Armet, *1665–80, 1681–9, 1689–1701, 1701–18, passim.*]

MYLNE, ROBERT (1733–1811), was descended from the long line of Scottish master masons whose genealogy is set out on page 675. His father Thomas Mylne (*q.v.*) was one of the leading Edinburgh masons in the reign of George II. Robert, his eldest surviving son, was born in Edinburgh on 4 January 1733. In 1747 he was apprenticed to Daniel Wright, a carpenter, for six years, and the Edinburgh Lodge of Freemasons of which he became an honorary member in 1754 was by now a 'speculative' fraternity only tenuously connected with the masons' craft. After working for a time as a woodcarver at Blair Atholl he determined to qualify himself as an architect and persuaded his father to allow him to go abroad, first to Paris, where he joined his brother William (Oct. 1754), and then to Rome (Dec. 1754). Robert Adam was making the same journey at the same time, but the two Mylne brothers lacked his financial resources and travelled as cheaply as they could, even 'footing a good deal of it'. Nevertheless Robert was sure that 'a little studye will make more than one family of Architects in Scotland', and made the most of his opportunities. In 1758 he had the satisfaction of winning the Silver Medal for architecture in the *Concorso Clementino* at St. Luke's Academy, a distinction never before achieved by a Briton. The subject was a palatial public building, which Mylne treated in an elaborate neo-classical manner. In the following year he was elected a member of the Academy, and, through the good offices of Prince Altieri, obtained the necessary dispensation to take his seat. He was also made a member of the academies of Florence and of Bologna. In Rome he became friendly with Piranesi and made useful contacts with several members of the British aristocracy to whom he was later to be indebted for employment, including Lord Garlies, Sir Wyndham Knatchbull and William Fermor of Tusmore. In 1757 a connoisseur named Richard Phelps took him to Sicily, where he made drawings of the Greek temples with the intention of publishing a volume on the 'Antiquities of Sicily'. This was never completed, but Piranesi and Winckelmann were both indebted to Mylne for information about the Sicilian temples. After travelling through northern Italy and the Rhineland to Holland he reached London in July 1759, bringing with him an introduction to Lord Charlemont which had been given to him by the Abbé Grant in Rome.

Mylne's arrival coincided with the scheme to build a bridge over the Thames at Blackfriars. This was one of the major public works of the eighteenth century, and the competition attracted sixty-nine entries. Eight of these were short-listed (Barnard, Chambers, Dance, Gwynn, Mylne, Phillips, Smeaton and Ware). All except Mylne's were adversely criticized in a pamphlet entitled *Observations on Bridge-Building, and the several Plans offered for a New Bridge*, which there is reason to believe was written by Mylne himself. When, in February 1760, Robert Mylne was adjudged the winner, it was nevertheless an astonishing triumph for a young and totally untried man. 'The English nation' (he wrote to his father) 'holds up their hands–and my countrymen stare. Nay I cannot account for it myself–[that] a young man just arrived in a great city, where he knew nobody, should, against the cabballing interests of city factions, contrary to the interests of the Prince of Wales's court [which no doubt supported Chambers], and in spite of the specious plausibility of the Royal Society, step at once into the head of his profession, and several hundreds a year.' Mylne's design was both handsome and efficient. It spanned the river in only nine arches (Westminster Bridge needed twelve), the masonry was beautifully detailed, and the pair of Ionic columns which adorned each pier was a nicely calculated concession to contemporary architectural taste. A feature which gave rise to much discussion at the time was the use of elliptical arches, an innovation which Dr. Johnson was induced to criticize in print (*Daily Gazetteer*, 1, 8 and 15 Dec. 1759) on behalf of his friend John Gwynn, who had been among the unsuccessful competitors. Further attacks on Mylne were made during the construction of the bridge, and popular feeling against the employment of an unknown Scot was exploited by Charles Churchill in his poem *The Ghost* (1763). The bridge was opened on 19 November 1769, and cost £152,840, which was £163 less than the original estimate. A view of Mylne's design was engraved in 1760, and in 1766 a plan and elevation were published by his assistant R. Baldwin.[1] In the same year Mylne himself published a fine oblique view showing the centering, which he had had engraved in Rome by Piranesi. Mylne was also responsible for planning the approaches to the bridge on both sides of the river, and for designing the obelisk erected in 1771 to mark the junction of the roads which radiated from St. George's Circus. The bridge itself was taken down in 1868 and replaced by the present iron structure.

Blackfriars Bridge proved Mylne's ability as civil engineer as well as architect, and bridges and canal-works formed an important part of his practice throughout his life: indeed, in the 1790s most of his time was taken up by business connected with waterways, including many appearances before parliamentary committees considering canal bills. His most important engineering works were the planning of the Gloucester and Berkeley Ship Canal and the improvement of the fen drainage by means of the Eau Brink Cut above King's Lynn. The latter project, though authorized by Act of Parliament, was delayed by opposition until 1817, when it was carried out by Rennie. After the destruction of the old Tyne bridge at Newcastle in 1772, Mylne was involved in the siting and design of it successor; in 1775 he surveyed the harbour at Yarmouth, and in 1781 that at Wells-next-the-Sea in Norfolk. In 1783 he reported on the disaster to Smeaton's bridge at Hexham; in 1784 on the Severn navigation; in 1789 on the state of the mills and waterworks of the city of Norwich; in 1790 on the Worcester Canal; in 1791–4 on the Thames navigation;[1] in 1800 on the problems connected with the Port of London and the proposed reconstruction of London Bridge;[2] in 1807 on the East London Waterworks; and in 1808 on Woolwich Dockyard. In 1800 both he and George Dance submitted designs for a new London Bridge, but neither was proceeded with.

As an architect Mylne had to compete with Robert Adam and James Wyatt, and he never rivalled their celebrity as fashionable designers. However, in Shropshire he obtained a number of country-house commissions from a group of interrelated county families, and at Inveraray he had the opportunity of carrying out extensive works for the Duke of Argyll, who also employed him at Rosneath. Outside Shropshire his principal country houses were Cally, Kirkcudbrightshire (1763–5), Tusmore, Oxon. (1766–70), Wormleybury, Herts. (1767–70), Addington, Surrey (1773–9), and Bickley Place, Kent (*c.*1780). The exteriors of his houses are characterized by a fastidious restraint that is prophetic of the neo-classical simplicity of the 1790s, while the portico at Woodhouse (Salop.) and the obelisk at Woolverstone (Suffolk) show that occasionally he could design something as strikingly original as anything by Dance or Soane. In his interiors he developed a decorative style very similar to Adam's. How far this was the result of his own studies in Rome, how far it derived from Adam, and how far it was dependent on the help of George Richardson (whom he paid for drawings from time to time) it is not easy to say. He rarely Gothicized, but deserves to be remembered as the designer of Blaise Castle, a well-known castellated folly near Bristol.

In 1764 Mylne applied for the vacant post of Master of the Works in Scotland, but this was a political sinecure which he could hardly hope to secure. In 1767, however, he obtained the congenial post of surveyor to the New River Company (the precursor of the Metropolitan Water Board). At first this was a joint appointment with his aged predecessor

[1] Baldwin was also responsible for seven plates entitled *Plans, Elevations and Sections of the Machines and Centering used in erecting Black-Friars Bridge, drawn and engraved by R. Baldwin, Clerk of the Work*, which was published by Taylor in 1787.

[1] His report on the navigation between Lechlade and Abingdon was printed by the Thames Commissioners in 1791. They also printed his *Report on a Survey of the River Thames from Boulter's Lock to the City Stone near Staines* in 1793.

[2] See *Parliamentary Papers* xiv, 1793–1802, 550–4.

Henry Mill, who died in 1770. The salary was £200 per annum, and a house was provided at Islington. Mylne was assiduous in his attention to his duties, and in 1806 the Company expressed its appreciation by the gift of a silver-gilt cup. In 1770 he had rebuilt its offices in Clerkenwell, and in 1800 he commemorated Sir Hugh Myddelton, the founder of the Company, by placing an elegant urn near the source of the New River at Great Amwell in Hertfordshire.

Other appointments which Mylne held were the surveyorships of St. Paul's (Oct. 1766) and Canterbury (Oct. 1767) Cathedrals and the Clerkship of the Works at Greenwich Hospital (Nov. 1775). He was also Surveyor to the Stationers' Company. Though he performed his duties at the two cathedrals with credit, a dispute with James Stuart over the rebuilding of the chapel at Greenwich Hospital led to his dismissal by the governors in September 1782.

Mylne's aspirations were scientific rather than artistic. He never exhibited at the Royal Academy and never sought election to that body. But he became a Fellow of the Royal Society in 1767 and was a member of the group of literary and scientific men which met at Slaughter's Coffee House in St. Martin's Lane. He was a prominent member of the Society of Civil Engineers founded in 1771 and one of the original members of the Architects' Club founded in 1791. He is described by Elmes as 'a man of austere manners, (and) of violent temper, (who) appeared to have a contempt for every art but his own, and for every person but himself'. One of his workmen said that 'Mr. Mylne was a rare jintleman, but as hot as pepper and as proud as Lucifer.' He was, however, punctilious in the performance of his duties, and Farington describes him as a sociable man, 'much addicted to conversation', as well as one who was 'extremely exact in all his affairs'. His principal pupils and assistants were Robert Baldwin, Thomas Cooley, R. W. Douthwaite and James Donaldson. His son W. C. Mylne succeeded to his practice.

Mylne married in 1770 May, daughter of Robert Home, a surgeon, by whom he had ten children, five of whom survived him. He died on 5 May 1811, in his 79th year, and was, at his own request, buried in the crypt of St. Paul's Cathedral near the remains of Sir Christopher Wren. The rest of his family were buried at Great Amwell in Hertfordshire, where he built himself a small country house in 1794–7, and where he erected a plain brick mausoleum in the churchyard. His portrait, drawn by Brompton in Rome in 1757, was engraved in Paris by Vangeliste in 1783 (see reproductions in Nichols, *Literary Anecdotes* ix, 233, and R. S. Mylne, *Master Masons*). A pencil portrait by Dance in the National Portrait Gallery shows him in later life: it was published in W. Daniell's *Collection of Portraits*, 1808–14.

Mylne's professional diaries and his early letters were placed on permanent loan in the R.I.B.A. Library in 1986. A grossly inaccurate transcript of the diaries was published by A. E. Richardson in 1955 in his *Robert Mylne*. Brief notes made on a visit to Edinburgh in 1781 are among the Mylne papers in the Scottish Record Office (GD 1/51/37). A volume of architectural drawings by Mylne formerly in the collection of A. E. Richardson was sold and broken up in 1983. Others are in the R.I.B.A. Drawings Collection. Mylne's unexecuted drawings for Mersham-le-Hatch, Kent, made for Sir Wyndham Knatchbull in 1761, are among the Arundell of Wardour papers in the Wiltshire C.R.O.

[*A.P.S.D.*; *D.N.B.*; *Gent's Mag.* 1811 (i), 499–500; J. Nichols, *Literary Anecdotes* ix, 1815, 231–3; *Builder* xxii, 1864, 8; J. Elmes in *Civil Engineer and Architect's Jnl.* x, 1847, 340; Cussans, *Hertfordshire* ii, 1870, 126–7; R. S. Mylne, *The Master Masons to the Crown of Scotland*, Edinburgh 1893, chap. xiii; Hist. MSS. Comm., *12th Report* x, 252 (Abbé Grant's letter); Bodleian Library, Gough Norfolk 1(4), a printed exchange of letters between Mylne and George Hardinge following the latter's allegations at the Wells Harbour case at Norwich in 1782–3; *The Farington Diary*, ed. Greig, vi, 271–2; *Memoirs of R. L. Edgeworth* i, 1821, 183; *The Whitefoord Papers*, ed. W. A. S. Hewins, 1898, 176, 184; K. A. Esdaile, 'A Forgotten Episode in the History of Robert Mylne', *R.I.B.A. Jnl.* Feb. 1944; Lesley Lewis, 'The Architects of the Chapel at Greenwich Hospital', *Art Bulletin* xxix, 1947; C. Gotch, 'The Missing Years of Robert Mylne', *Arch. Rev.* Sept. 1951; C. Gotch, 'Mylne and Adam', *Arch. Rev.* Feb. 1956; C. Lloyd on Mylne as Clerk of Works to Greenwich Hospital in *Trans. Greenwich & Lewisham Antiq. Soc.* v (1), 1954–6, 14–20; A. E. Richardson, *Robert Mylne, Architect and Engineer*, 1955; J. Harris, 'Robert Mylne and the Academy of St. Luke', *Arch. Rev.* Nov. 1961; D. Wiebenson, *Sources of Greek Revival Architecture*, 1969, 124–5 (for Mylne's Sicilian expedition); Damie Stillman, 'British Architects and Italian Architectural Competitions, 1758–1780', *Jnl. Society of Architectural Historians* (of America), xxxii, 1973, 45–50; *I disegni di architettura dell' Archivio storico dell' Accademia di San Luca*, 1974, Nos. 535–6; *Numismatic Chronicle*, 4th ser. iv, 1904 (for Mylne's medals); A. W.

Skempton, *The Smeatonian Society of Civil Engineers*, 1971; Eileen Harris, *British Architectural Books and Writers 1556–1785*, 1990, 328–31.]

BRIDGES

BLACKFRIARS BRIDGE, LONDON (R. Thames), 1760–9; dem. 1868. A parapet was substituted for the original balustrading in 1839, in the course of repairs by Walker and Burgess (cf. A. T. Bolton, *The Portrait of Sir John Soane*, 524). For Mylne's own account of the building of this bridge, see *Parliamentary Papers* xiv, 1793–1802, 580–5. His design was illustrated in the *London Magazine* for 1760.

WELBECK ABBEY, NOTTS., bridge in park for 3rd Duke of Portland, 1765–7; collapsed soon after completion [Diary, April and June 1765; Nottingham University Library, Portland papers, PwF. 7087–7130].

WARWICK, LEAFIELD BRIDGE in the Park (R. Avon) for lst Earl of Warwick, 1772–6 [*V.C.H. Warwicks*. viii, 472]. In 1773–4 Mylne was asked to survey the GREAT BRIDGE over the R. Avon by the corporation. He condemned it and recommended the building of a new bridge on a different site. This advice was followed in 1789–93, when the existing bridge was built by W. Eboral to a design closely resembling the Leafield Bridge. There appears, however, to be no evidence that Mylne furnished the drawing or gave further advice (cf. *V.C.H. Warwicks*. viii, 463).

GLASGOW, THE NEW (JAMAICA) or BROOMIELAW BRIDGE (R. Clyde), 1768–72 [*The Picture of Glasgow,* Glasgow 1812, 132]. Designed in conjunction with his brother William Mylne and built by John Adam (*q.v.*); cf. drawing in R.I.B.A.D.

NEWCASTLE, NORTHUMBERLAND (R. Tyne), 1774–81, in association with John Wooler; dem. 1873. The Bishop of Durham and the Corporation of Newcastle were each responsible for half the bridge: Mylne was the Bishop's engineer, Wooler the Corporation's [J. Sykes, *Local Records*, Newcastle 1865, i, 294; C. Gotch, 'Robert Mylne and Tyne Bridges', *Archaeologia Æliana*, 4th ser. xxxiii, 1955, 88–91].

GLASGOW, widened the OLD BRIDGE (R. Clyde), 1774–5 [Diary, 12 Sept., 26 Oct. 1774, 5 Feb., 30 Aug. 1775; R. S. Mylne, *Master Masons*, 270–3].

INVERARAY, ARGYLLSHIRE, ARAY BRIDGE, 1774–6, and DUBH LOCH (DOWLOCH) BRIDGE, 1786–7, for the 5th Duke of Argyll [I. G. Lindsay & Mary Cosh, *Inveraray and the Dukes of Argyll*, 1973, 234–5, 243].

TONBRIDGE, KENT (R. Medway), 1775–6; dem. 1888 [Diary, Nov. 1773, July, Aug. 1775; J. Dugdale, *British Traveller* iii, 1819, 259].

ROMSEY, HANTS., MIDDLE BRIDGE (R. Test), 1782–3; rebuilt to modified version of original design 1930–1 [Diary, 1 Oct. 1782, etc.; A.W. Mason, 'Middle Bridge, Romsey', *Hants. Field Club. Trans*. xxxii, 1975].

HEXHAM BRIDGE (R. Tyne), NORTHUMBERLAND, surveyed ruins of Smeaton's bridge, 1783, and advised Northumberland magistrates about the rebuilding of the bridge (following Smeaton's original design) by their Bridge Surveyors, *c*.1790–5 [J. Sykes, *Local Records*, Newcastle 1865, i, 301; E. Mackenzie, *Northumberland* ii, 1825, 295; E.C. Ruddock, 'The Foundations of Hexham Bridge', *Geotechnique* 27, no. 3, 1977].

RIDLEY HALL BRIDGE (R. Tyne), NORTHUMBERLAND, 1787–92 [Diary, 8–9 Oct. 1785, 16 Oct. 1786, 30 July 1788; Northumberland Q.S. Order Books 1786–93, p. 36].

CLACHAN BRIDGE, SEIL, ARGYLLSHIRE, probably revised design made by John Stevenson of Oban and executed by the latter in 1791 [R.C.A.M., *Argyll* ii, 294–5].

PUBLIC BUILDINGS

EDINBURGH, ST. CECILIA'S HALL, NIDDRIE STREET, for the Musical Society of Edinburgh, 1761–3; restored 1966 [Diary, 10 March 1763; *Book of the Old Edinburgh Club* xix, 1933, 225] (*C. Life*, 15 Aug. 1968).

LONDON, ALMACK'S CLUB (afterwards WILLIS'S ROOMS), KING STREET, ST. JAMES'S, 1764–5; destroyed by bombing 1939/45 [*Survey of London* xxix, 304–6 and plates].

LONDON, rebuilt NEW RIVER COMPANY'S OFFICES, CLERKENWELL, 1770; dem. [R. S. Mylne, *Master Masons*, 268] (W. Maitland, *History of London*, ed. Entick, ii, 1775, pl. 128).

LONDON, THE CITY OF LONDON LYING-IN HOSPITAL, CITY ROAD, 1770–3; dem. *c*.1903 [Diary, 7 April 1770; R. S. Mylne, *Master Masons*, 269; W. Maitland, *History of London*, ed. Entick, ii, 1775, pl. 127: 'Mylne Architect'].

ROCHESTER CATHEDRAL, surveyed building 1776–7 and subsequently [Diary, 1776–82, *passim*].

ST. PAUL'S CATHEDRAL, repairs to south transept, 1781; designed new pulpit 1805 ['The Fabric of St. Paul's 1760–1810', *R.I.B.A. Jnl.* 3rd ser. xxiii, 1916; Lambeth Palace Library MS. 1489, Mylne's report on the fabric dated 1781; see also MS. 2027].

TOBERMORY, ISLE OF MULL, ARGYLLSHIRE, Inn for the British Fisheries Society, 1790 [R.C.A.M., *Argyllshire* 3, 237 and pl. 85].

INVERARAY, ARGYLLSHIRE, CHURCH for 5th Duke of Argyll, 1795–1800 [I. G. Lindsay & Mary Cosh, *Inveraray and the Dukes of Argyll*, 1973, chap. viii].

LONDON, STATIONERS' HALL, LUDGATE HILL, rebuilt east front, 1800–1 [R. S. Mylne, *Master Masons*, 280; Diary].

DOMESTIC ARCHITECTURE

LONDON, No. 1 STRATTON STREET (No. 79 PICCADILLY), for 10th Earl of Eglinton, 1763 [Diary, 16, 22 Dec. 1763, recording the passing of bills totalling £3195 on Lord Eglinton's behalf]. In 1771 an attic storey was added by Sir W. Chambers for Lord Fitzwilliam. In 1795 Mylne surveyed the house for a new owner, Thomas Coutts [Diary, 20 Oct. 1795; A. I. Dasent, *Piccadilly*, 1920, 68–9]; dem. 1929 (A. E. Richardson & C. L. Gill, *London Houses from 1660 to 1820*, 1911, pls. lxxv, lxxvi, where the attribution to R. F. Brettingham should be disregarded.)

CHISWICK, MIDDLESEX, alterations to house for 16th Earl of Morton, 1763 [Diary, 1763, esp. 7 Dec.]

LONDON, No. 47 BROOK STREET, alterations or repairs for 16th Earl of Morton, 1763 [Diary, 1 Sept. 7 Dec. 1763].

CALLY HOUSE, KIRKCUDBRIGHTSHIRE, for James Murray, 1763–5 [*N.S.A.* iv, 297; Diary; S.R.O., GD 10/142/287, 288A (earlier plan and elevation)]. The wings were raised in 1794 by Thomas Boyd (*q.v.*), and the house was extensively altered in 1833–7 by J. B. Papworth.

KINGS WESTON, GLOS., stables and alterations to interior (including saloon) for Edward Southwell, Lord de Clifford, 1763–8 [Diary; accounts of Lord de Clifford's executors at Badminton House, Glos.; Christopher Gotch, 'Mylne and Kings Weston', *C. Life*, 23 Jan. 1953].

LONDON, ARGYLL HOUSE, No. 7 ARGYLL STREET, alterations for the Marquess of Lorne (afterwards 5th Duke of Argyll), 1764–5; dem. 1864–5 [Diary, 9, 28 Feb. 1764, etc.]. At Inverary Castle there is an engraved survey plan of the house, probably the 'printed plan' referred to in Mylne's Diary on 10 Feb. 1774.

TWICKENHAM, MIDDLESEX, CROSS DEEP HOUSE, alterations, including new hall and portico, for Stafford Briscoe, 1764 [Diary, 5 May, 22 Sept. 1764].

GALLOWAY HOUSE, GARLIESTOWN, WIGTOWNSHIRE, alterations for Lord Garlies, 1764 [Diary, 10 April 1764; *A.P.S.D.*].

NORWICH, house in SURREY STREET (now Norwich Union Fire Office) for T. Patterson, 1764 [Diary, 29 Jan., 21 Aug. 1764, etc.; drawings formerly in Richardson Collection; *A.P.S.D.*].

LONDON, house in HIGHGATE ROAD, KENTISH TOWN, for H. S. Woodfall, 1766 [contract drawings formerly in Richardson Collection].

BLAISE CASTLE, nr. BRISTOL, GLOS., a castellated tower for Thomas Farr, 1766 [Diary, Jan. 1766: 'Sent finished Drawings of . . . a Castle to Mr. Farr'; drawing of a variant design formerly in Richardson Collection].

AMISFIELD HOUSE, EAST LOTHIAN, alterations for Francis Charteris, 1766 [Diary, 12, 14 Aug. 1766]. The house was dem. *c.*1928, but the 'castle' mentioned in Mylne's diary may be the surviving castellated folly by the main road.

CONDOVER HALL, SALOP., designs for internal alterations for Miss Anna Maria Leighton, 1766 [Diary, 22 May, 10, 26 June 1766]. T. F. Pritchard (*q.v.*) also made designs for Condover at the same time. As the Georgian interiors have been destroyed it is not certain what was done.

HALSTON HALL, SALOP., alterations for John Mytton, 1766–8, including interior of saloon [Diary, 1766–8, *passim*].

TUSMORE HOUSE, OXON., for William Fermor, 1766–70; altered by W. Burn 1858; dem. 1961 [G. Richardson, *New Vitruvius Britannicus* i, 1802, pls. 3–5; Diary, 1766–70, *passim*] (*C. Life*, 30 July, 6 Aug. 1938; *V.C.H. Oxon.* vi, 334–5 and plate).

CAVERSHAM GROVE, OXON., alterations for — Bindley, 1767 [Diary, 2 April, 14 and 16 May, 6 June 1767].

LONDON, No. 16 GREAT WINDMILL STREET, for Dr. William Hunter, 1767; remodlled 1887 and later [*Survey of London* xxxi, 48–50 and pl. 135].

WORMLEYBURY, WORMLEY, HERTS., for Sir Abraham Hume, 1767–70. The principal rooms were decorated by Robert Adam, 1777–9 [Diary, 19 May 1767, etc.; drawings by Mylne in R.I.B.A. Drawings Coll.] (*C. Life*, 30 Jan. 1915).

HANWELL, MIDDLESEX, house for Henry Berners, 1768–9 [Diary, 16 April 1768, etc.; drawings formerly in Richardson Collection] (A. E. Richardson, *Robert Mylne*, pl. 31).

ARDINCAPLE CASTLE, DUNBARTONSHIRE, alterations (?) for Lord Frederick Campbell, 1769; dem. 1958 [*A.P.S.D.*] The Diary records a visit to Ardincaple on 11 Sept. 1769, but it is doubtful what, if anything, was done here to Mylne's design.

EDINBURGH, WHITEFOORD HOUSE, 53 CANONGATE, for Sir John Whitefoord, 1769–70 [Diary, 18 Sept. 1769: 'Sent Sir John Whitefoord plans elevations and sections of a house to be built at Edinburgh'].

GOODNESTONE PARK, KENT, alterations for Sir Brook Bridges, Bart., probably including the decoration of the two bow-ended rooms on the east front, 1770 [Diary, 4 March 1770, etc.].

LONDON, NEW BRIDGE STREET, CHATHAM PLACE and ALBION PLACE, forming the approaches to Blackfriars Bridge, 1772–*c.*1790; dem. [C. Gotch, 'Blackfriars Bridge', *Arch. Rev.* Oct. 1952].

ADDINGTON LODGE, SURREY, for Barlow Trecothick, 1773–9; enlarged 1829–30 by H. Harrison (*q.v.*) [G. Richardson, *New Vitruvius Britannicus* i, 1802, pls. 32–3].

LOTON PARK, SALOP., alterations for Sir Charlton Leighton, Bart., 1773–4 [Diary, 27 Jan.–9 April 1773, 24–25 June 1774].

TERN HALL, ATTINGHAM, SALOP., proposed alterations and additions for Noel Hill (d. 1782), 1773–4, probably not carried out; dem. *c.*1785 [Diary, 16 Feb., 26 March 1773, 18–19, 26 June 1774; design for semicircular stables 'for Mr. Hills Shropshire' formerly in Richardson Collection].

WOODHOUSE, nr. WHITTINGTON, SALOP., for William Mostyn-Owen, 1773–4 [Diary, 14 April 1773, 22–23 June 1774]

BRYNGWYN HALL, MONTGOMERYSHIRE, works for William Mostyn-Owen, 1773–4; damaged by fire 1802 and largely rebuilt [Diary, 22 Sept. 1771, 26 Jan., 10 Feb., 23 Dec. 1773, 20 and 30 April, 24 June, 20 and 23 Oct. 1774].

SUNDORN HALL, SALOP., alterations to offices for John Corbet, 1774 [Diary, 19–20 June, 1 Nov. 1774].

ONSLOW HALL, SALOP., additions for Richard Morhall, 1774; rebuilt 1780 by G. Steuart for Rowland Wingfield [Diary, 20 June, 8 Oct. 1774].

THE WICK, RICHMOND HILL, SURREY, for Lady St. Aubyn, 1775 [Diary, 10 Dec. 1774, 3 June 1775; contract drawings formerly in Richardson Collection] (*C. Life*, 1 Feb. 1941).

CLOWANCE, nr. CROWAN, CORNWALL, advised on rebuilding of defective front for Lady St. Aubyn, 1775–6 [Diary, 28 March, 17 May, 28 June 1775, 10 May 1776]: cf. p. 794 below.

INVERARAY CASTLE, ARGYLLSHIRE, alterations to windows on main floor, 1777, and redecoration of principal rooms, 1782–9, for 5th Duke of Argyll [I. G. Lindsay & Mary Cosh, *Inveraray and the Dukes of Argyll*, 1973, 200, 208–16, etc.].

INVERARAY ESTATE, ARGYLLSHIRE, works for 5th Duke of Argyll, including FISHERLAND BARN, 1774–5, parts of MALTLAND COURT or SQUARE (barns, etc.), 1774–82, GARRON LODGE, 1783–4, and a semicircular court of farm-buildings at MAAM STEADING, GLENSHIRA, 1787–9. In Inveraray town Mylne was responsible for two rows of tenements called ARKLAND and RELIEF LAND, 1774–6, as well as for the arched screen-wall which forms the façade to Loch Fyne, 1787 [I. G. Lindsay & Mary Cosh, *op. cit.*, *passim*].

LONDON, No. 17 HILL STREET, alterations for Sir Abraham Hume, *c.*1777 [Diary, 31 May 1777, payments in March 1781 and April 1782].

BOLESWORTH CASTLE, CHESHIRE, alterations to dining-room for John Crewe, 1777 [Diary, 15 May, 30 Oct. 1777]. The house was rebuilt in 1829.

BICKLEY PLACE, KENT, for John Wells (d. 1805), *c.*1780; dem. 1963 [drawings formerly in Richardson Collection] (J. P. Neale, *Views of Seats*, lst ser. iii, 1820). As this commission is not mentioned in Mylne's diaries it is just possible that the drawings were copied by Mylne from those of another architect, but as the house had all the characteristics of his style this is unlikely.

EDGMOND RECTORY, SALOP., enlarged for the Revd. William Pigott, 1780 [Diary 14 April, 25 July 1780].

BERWICK HOUSE, SALOP., alterations and additions (since removed) for Thomas Jelf Powys, 1780 [Diary, 17 July, 4 Sept. 1780].

SOUTHWARK, house on east side of GREAT SURREY (now Blackfriars) STREET (afterwards the YORK HOTEL) for himself, 1780; dem. 1864 [*Survey of London* xxii, 115].

EDINBURGH, WEST BOW, shop and tenement, his own property, 1782; dem. 1830 [Edinburgh Dean of Guild plans].

POWDERHALL, nr. EDINBURGH (his own property, on lease to a tenant), new lodge and gate, *c.*1782–4 [sketch in S.R.O., GD 1/51/37 (1781); payments in Diary, Sept.–Oct. 1785].

PITLOUR HOUSE, STRATHMIGLO, FIFE, for General Robert Skene, 1783–4 [N.L.S., Advocates' Charter B 2225, contract dated 10 June 1783, with drawings] (A. E. Richardson, *Robert Mylne*, pls. 48–9).

ROSNEATH, DUNBARTONSHIRE, castellated alterations for 5th Duke of Argyll, 1784–6; destroyed by fire 1802 [Diary, especially 24 April, 15 May and 2 June 1784; I. G. Lindsay & Mary Cosh, *Inveraray and the Dukes of Argyll*, 1973, 382, n. 51].

LITTLE WOODCOTE, CARSHALTON, SURREY, additions to house and offices for — Durand, 1790 [Diary, 29 May, 19 June, 24 July 1790].

THE GROVE, GREAT AMWELL, HERTS., for himself, 1794–7; since enlarged [Diary, 4 Aug. 1794, etc.; drawings preserved in house].

SYON HOUSE, MIDDLESEX, domed Ionic BOATHOUSE for 2nd Duke of Northumberland, 1803 [Diary, 19 July, 6 Aug., 8 and 31 Oct. 1803] (measured drawings in S. C. Ramsey & J. D. M. Harvey, *Small Houses of the Late Georgian Period* ii, 1923, pls. 72–3).

BUTE HOUSE, PETERSHAM, SURREY, alterations for lst Marquess of Bute, 1805–6; dem. [Diary, 1804–6, *passim*].

MAUSOLEA AND MONUMENTS

ASKHAM RICHARD CHURCHYARD, YORKS. (W.R.), monument (urn on column) to Elizabeth Berry (d. 1767), erected 1770, signed 'MYLNE FECIT 1770'.

ADDINGTON CHURCH, SURREY, monument (urn) to Barlow Trecothick (d. 1770), erected 1776 [Diary, 3 Jan. 1776].

CLOWANCE, CORNWALL, St. Aubyn family mausoleum, 1778 [Diary, 16 Nov. 1777, 26 March 1778].

LUNDIE CHURCHYARD, ANGUS, mausoleum in memory of Sir William Duncan, Bart. (d. 1774), built 1787–9 for Lady Mary Duncan [Diary, 6 Oct. 1786, 31 Jan., 3 Feb. 1787].

DUBLIN, ST. CATHERINE'S CHURCH, tablet to his brother William Mylne (d. 1790) [R. S. Mylne, *Master Masons*, 260].

WOOLVERSTONE HALL, SUFFOLK, obelisk in memory of William Berners, erected by Charles Berners, 1791–3; dem. 1945 [Diary, 14 Feb., 18 Sept. 1791] (H. R. Barker, *East Suffolk Illustrated*, 1908–9, 539).

GREAT AMWELL, HERTS., Mylne family mausoleum in churchyard, 1800; urn in memory of Sir Hugh Myddelton on island in New River, 1800.

FAREHAM, HANTS., HOLY TRINITY CHURCH, monument (originally in parish church) to Admiral Sir Charles Thompson (d. 1799), 1802, Flaxman sculptor [Diary, 25 Oct. 1802].

ST. PAUL'S CATHEDRAL, monument in crypt to Sir Christopher Wren, 1807 [Diary, 21 May, 20 June 1807, 12 March 1808].

MYLNE, THOMAS (–1763), was the son and successor of William Mylne (d. 1728). In 1729 he was admitted a burgess of Edinburgh and a member of the Edinburgh Masonic Lodge, of which he was subsequently (1735–6) Master. Although in origin an association of working masons, this lodge was by now assuming the social and 'speculative' character associated with modern Freemasonry. In 1736 the Grand Lodge of Edinburgh was established, and Thomas Mylne appears to have been a prominent member of this purely 'speculative' society, of which he was Grand Treasurer from 1737 to 1755.

In 1743 Thomas Mylne was one of the witnesses in William Adam's lawsuit against Lord Braco. His evidence shows that he was active as a mason-contractor in Edinburgh and its neighbourhood, but that (unlike the more enterprising Adam) he 'never built a House of his own undertaking above three miles from Edinburgh'. However, he stated that he sometimes provided plans for houses which he did not himself build, for instance at Fisherrow and Inveresk, both near Musselburgh, Midlothian. The only other buildings whose design can at present be attributed to him are a 'land' near the cross on the north side of High Street, Edinburgh, which bore the Mylne mark[1] and the date 1744 on the lintel, and his own house at Powderhall on the north-east outskirts of the city (illustrated by J. Grant, *Old and New Edinburgh* iii, 93 (6)).

Thomas Mylne died on 5 March 1763, and is commemorated on the family monument in the Greyfriars Churchyard. A portrait by Mossman, painted in 1752, remains in the possession of his descendants, and is illustrated by R. S. Mylne, *Master Masons*, 251. By his wife Elizabeth Duncan he had seven children, of whom Robert (1733–1811) and William (1734–90) are the subjects of separate entries [R. S. Mylne, *The Master Masons to the Crown of Scotland* Edinburgh 1893; *A.P.S.D.; D.N.B.*].

MYLNE, WILLIAM (1734–1790), was the second son of Thomas Mylne of Edinburgh (*q.v.*). After a period of apprenticeship as a mason he went (1754) to France, where he studied under J.F. Blondel, and then to Italy with his elder brother Robert. He returned in 1758 and took over his father's business as a mason. In 1759 he designed a bridge over the Tweed at FAIRNILIE, SELKIRKSHIRE, which he appears to have built the following year [letter to Robert Mylne, 27 Feb. 1759], and in 1768–72 he was jointly responsible with his brother Robert for the design of the NEW (JAMAICA) BRIDGE (dem. 1833) over the Clyde at GLASGOW, for which the Glasgow mason John Adam (*q.v.*) was the contractor [R. S.

[1] ⋈⋈

Mylne, *Master Masons*, 258–9; *N.S.A.* vi, 219; *The Picture of Glasgow*, Glasgow 1812, 132; Robert Mylne's Diary, 11 Sept. 1772, 11 Sept. 1774]. In 1770–2 he was employed by the 5th Duke of Argyll at INVERARAY CASTLE, ARGYLLSHIRE, where he was responsible for rearranging the interior, though not for the subsequent redecoration to the designs of his brother Robert [I. G. Lindsay & Mary Cosh, *Inveraray and the Dukes of Argyll*, 1973, 196–7]. Meanwhile in 1765 he had submitted a design for the NORTH BRIDGE linking the New and Old Towns of Edinburgh. The design was pedestrian, but Mylne (unlike his principal competitor, David Henderson) was able to find security to execute the bridge according to his proposals, and contracted to build it for £10,140. In 1769, when it was almost finished, part of the southern abutment gave way, burying five people in the ruins. Mylne made good the damage, but he was now in serious financial difficulties, and in 1772 he decided to leave Scotland and settle in America. At first he tried the life of a planter in South Carolina, but in 1774 he moved to New York in the hope of obtaining employment as an architect. Finding, however, that there was little prospect of success unless he 'turned undertaker' again, he migrated to Ireland, where he became engineer to the Dublin Water Works. His success in this capacity is tesified by a silver salver which was presented to him by the Lord Mayor and Aldermen of Dublin in 1786 to record 'their entire approbation of the laudable exertion of his great abilities in rescuing those important works from the very bad condition they were in, and bringing them to a state of perfection'. Mylne died at Dublin in March 1790, aged 56. His brother erected a tablet in St. Catherine's Church 'to inform Posterity of the uncommon Zeal, Integrity and Skill with which he formed, enlarged, and established on a perfect system the water works of Dublin'.

[A. J. Youngson, Th*e Making of Classical Edinburgh*, 1966, 60–5; R. S. Mylne, *The Master Masons to the Crown of Scotland*, Edinburgh 1893, 235–60; *Reports of the late John Smeaton* iii, 1812, 218 (report on failure of North Bridge); E. C. Ruddock, 'The Building of the North Bridge, Edinburgh', *Newcomen Soc's Trans.* 47, 1974–6; Mylne family papers.]

MYLNE, WILLIAM CHADWELL (1781–1863), second son of Robert Mylne, was born in London on 5 or 6 April 1781. As early as 1797 he was assisting his father to stake out the lands purchased for the Eau Brink Cut, and he was also employed on the Gloucester and Berkeley Ship Canal. In 1804 he was appointed assistant engineer to the New River Company, and on his father's death in 1811 succeeded him in control of the works. He held this appointment for fifty years, retiring only two years before his death. He also succeeded his father as surveyor to the Stationers' Company in 1811, and held the post until 1861.

Although mainly engaged in engineering works connected with water-supply and drainage, Mylne also practised as an architect, and is said to have altered or enlarged several country houses. He was also much employed as a surveyor and valuer. As surveyor to the New River Company he laid out their property at Clerkenwell for building purposes. The new streets, including MYDDELTON SQUARE, AMWELL, INGLEBERT and RIVER STREETS, were begun in 1819. Mylne also designed ST. MARK'S CHURCH, MYDDELTON SQUARE, 1826–8, Gothic [*Gent's Mag.* 1829, 579–81], and the CLERKENWELL PAROCHIAL CHARITY SCHOOLS in AMWELL STREET, 1828, Gothic [W. J. Pinks, *History of Clerkenwell*, 1881, 577]. His work in Clerkenwell is described and illustrated in *C. Life*, 28 Jan. 1939.

In 1815 he supervised the repair of CAVERSHAM BRIDGE, nr. READING, for Lord Cadogan [Treacher papers in Reading Public Library], and he designed GARRET HOSTEL BRIDGE over the R. Cam at Cambridge, 1835–7; dem. 1960 [R.C.H.M., *Cambridge*, 309]. It was a single iron arch, with Gothic detailing, and is illustrated in Hann & Hosking, *Bridges*, 1843. In 1827 he was one of the unsuccessful competitors for Clifton Bridge, Bristol. For the Stationers' Company he designed an octagonal card-room at STATIONERS' HALL in 1825 [C. Blagden, *The Stationers' Company*, 1960, 225–6].

Mylne designed HARPOLE RECTORY, NORTHANTS., in 1816 [Northants. Record Office, Peterborough Diocesan Records], and in 1842–4 built THE FLINT HOUSE, AMWELL, HERTS., for himself to take the place of his father's house (The Grove), whose situation near the river he regarded as unhealthy.

Mylne was elected a Fellow of the Royal Society in 1826, and of the Institute of British Architects on its foundation in 1834. He was Treasurer of the Smeatonian Society of Civil Engineers for forty-two years, and in 1842 became a member of the Institution of Civil Engineers. He retired from his profession in 1861, and died at Amwell on 25 December 1863, in his 83rd year. His portrait by H. W. Phillips is given in R. S. Mylne's *Master Masons*. His son, Robert William Mylne (1817–90), architect, engineer and geologist, was the last of the family to practise architecture.

[*A.P.S.D.*; *D.N.B.*; *Builder* xxii, 1864, 7;

Minutes of Proceedings of the Institution of Civil Engineers xxx, 1869–70, 448–51; R. S. Mylne, *The Master Masons to the Crown of Scotland*, 1893, chap. xiv.]

N

NASH, JOHN (1752–1835), was probably born in London. His father, a Welsh millwright working in Lambeth, died when John was still a boy. He was employed in the office of Sir Robert Taylor, at first 'in a subordinate capacity', but later as a draughtsman. By 1775 he had left Taylor to establish himself as an architect and speculative builder in London. But in 1783 he was declared bankrupt, and removed to Carmarthen, where he contrived to mix freely with the local gentry. He maintained an association with the London architect Samuel Saxon (*q.v.*). Together they reroofed the parish church and carried out other works of minor importance. In 1788 Nash designed his first public building, the County Gaol at Carmarthen. Other commissions followed, and by 1793 he was employing the refugee Augustus Charles Pugin as a draughtsman. In 1796 he was able to return to London as an architect with an established practice and a distinctive style.

Nash's Welsh exile had not been fruitless, for it was there that he emerged as the leading architect of the Picturesque. Nash's initiation into the Picturesque can probably be traced to his contacts with Thomas Johnes, the creator of the romantic landscape of Hafod, and with Uvedale Price, the author of a celebrated *Essay on the Picturesque* (1796), for whom he designed a triangular castellated house on the shore of Cardigan Bay at Aberystwyth. Through Price he may also have met Payne Knight, whose 'Castle' at Downton in Herefordshire was the prototype of the picturequely asymmetrical country house of which Nash was soon to be the acknowledged master. Many of Nash's country houses were, like Downton, to affect a castle air externally, but he offered his clients an alternative formula in which a simple Italianate architecture, almost vernacular in character, was used to form picturesque houses composed like buildings in a landscape by Claude. A few suburban villas (notably Southgate Grove) showed that he could also design in a sophisticated neo-classical style which owed something to recent French architecture (studied of course in engravings, for France was enemy territory from 1793 onwards, and Nash's first recorded visit to that country took place in 1814).[1]

It was another Herefordshire squire, Edward Foley of Stoke Edith, who introduced Nash to Humphry Repton. As a fashionable landscape-gardener Repton had many opportunities to obtain architectural commissions. A partnership was formed, and between them Nash and Repton transformed many old-fashioned houses into elegant seats with grounds carefully landscaped to enhance their picturesque character. By 1802, when the partnership was dissolved, in circumstances not very creditable to Nash, he had executed commissions in many parts of the country. At the Royal Academy that year he showed designs for four houses – one in Surrey, one in Shropshire, one in Wales and one in Scotland. He could also claim royal patronage, for in 1798 he had designed a conservatory for the Prince of Wales, presumably at Brighton, where Repton was engaged in landscaping the grounds of the Pavilion.

In 1806 Nash was appointed architect to the Department of Woods and Forests, with James Morgan (*q.v.*), one of his early assistants, as his colleague. In this capacity he prepared a plan for the layout of Marylebone Park, an estate on the northern outskirts of London which in January 1811 reverted to the Crown on the expiration of the lease. This, as laid out by Nash with the approval of his royal patron, became the Regent's Park, a carefully landscaped open space containing a small number of private villas and surrounded by palatial 'terraces', most of which were designed by Nash himself. In this way the amenities of a park were combined with the development of the estate as a fashionable residential area. In order to connect the park with the West End and the seat of government at Westminster, Nash designed a new street running north to south in such a way as to provide 'a boundary and complete separation between the Streets and Squares occupied by the Nobility and Gentry' to the west, and the 'narrow Streets and meaner Houses occupied by mechanics and the trading part of the community' on the east. It was also intended to form a royal route from Carlton House to a villa or pavilion which was to be erected for the Prince Regent in the new park: though, as the villa was not built, and as Carlton House itself was demolished in 1827, this idea was

---

[1] In the Coade Stone firm's letter-book there is a letter to Nash's assistant James Morgan dated 25 Oct. 1814, which begins, 'If Mr. Nash is returned from France' (*Arch. Hist.* xi, 1968, 46, n. 20). He visited Paris again in January 1818 (*The Farington Diary*, ed. J. Greig, viii, 159).

never realized. The Bill authorizing the building of Regent Street was passed in 1813. Nash himself designed many of the buildings along its route, including the colonnaded Quadrant and the church of All Souls, Langham Place, which were its most striking architectural features. In Lower Regent Street he built an ingeniously planned double residence for his own occupation and that of his relative, John Edwards, a successful lawyer with whom he was closely associated in business. Like an Italian *palazzo*, it occupied the upper parts of a block whose ground floor was divided into shops.

On the sudden death of James Wyatt in 1813, Nash was the Prince Regent's choice for his place as Surveyor-General of the Works. He was in fact given responsibility for the maintenance of the royal palaces until a successor should be formally appointed. But Wyatt's inefficiency resulted in the suppression of his office and a reorganization of the Works with three 'attached architects' under an administrative head who enjoyed the title of Surveyor-General. With Soane and Smirke, Nash was one of the triumvirate. As a working arrangement the three architects divided the royal palaces between them. Carlton House, Kensington, St. James's and the royal lodges in Windsor Great Park fell to Nash. It was, however, as the Regent's personal architect that he remodelled the Royal Pavilion at Brighton in 1815–22, and when the Prince became King in 1820 it was by his personal direction that Nash received orders to reconstruct Buckingham House on a palatial scale, regardless of the claims of Sir John Soane as the architect officially responsible for that building. At a time when the King himself had forfeited the affections of his subjects, such partiality was not calculated to make his architect a popular figure, and when the extravagant expenditure on Buckingham Palace became a national scandal, Nash had to undergo the ordeal of being interrogated by a Select Committee of the House of Commons (1828). Although its findings were scarcely to his credit, there was 'no actual reflection on his professional ability or his integrity'. But in the following year he was accused by Colonel Davies, the Member for Worcester, of malversation and fraud in connection with his building activities in Regent Street. Once more he was exonerated on every charge, but the committee added a rider to the effect that 'it was undesirable for official architects to acquire a financial interest in property for which they might be called upon to give a valuation', and Baring voiced the general feeling when he declared that although 'from what he had heard of Mr. Nash, he should be inclined to think that he was incapable of dishonesty; . . . he must say that, as a manager of public money and as an exhibitor of taste, he was sorry the public ever had anything to do with him'. Nash himself issued a printed *Statement* in which he declared that while 'claiming no greater dislike for fair emolument' than any other architect, he had been induced to assume the role of a speculator solely by the desire to see his own designs carried out. The King, who regarded the attack on Nash as a personal affront, would have vindicated both his own injured dignity and the reputation of his architect by making Nash a baronet, but the Duke of Wellington dissuaded him from conferring the honour until the completion of Buckingham Palace – an event which George IV did not live to see. When the King died in 1830, Nash's career as a public architect was virtually at an end. The direction of Buckingham Palace was taken out of his hands and he was dismissed from the Office of Works. A third Select Committee enquired into the expenditure on the Palace and employed a committee of architects to investigate its alleged structural weaknesses. Once more nothing positively discreditable to Nash was found, but the design of the Palace was universally criticized, and both the building and its architect shared in the odium which the name of George IV inspired. When Nash himself died in 1835, his reputation as an architect was at its lowest ebb, and Victorian taste did nothing to vindicate the name of one who showed so marked a predilection for the 'fatal facility of stucco'. His picturesque castles were far removed in style and intention from the earnest Gothic of Pugin or Scott, while his use of the orders was too slipshod to commend itself to an age in which scholarship was the first requisite of the classical architect. Though he had little interest in the finer points of architectural design, he had a remarkable gift for composition on a large scale which was the secret of his success both as a country-house architect and as a town-planner. In London he brilliantly applied the principles of the Picturesque to the problems of urban development presented by Regent's Park and Regent Street; and he alone had the enthusiasm and the organizing ability to carry through the great schemes of metropolitan improvement which were his major contribution to English architecture.

Nash died at his country house, East Cowes Castle, on 13 May 1835, and was buried in East Cowes churchyard, where a tomb marks his grave. He had a putative son by his first wife Jane Kerr (from whom he subsequently sought to be divorced), but none by his second wife, Mary Anne Bradley. However, the latter helped to bring up the children of some relations of hers named Pennethorne. One of these, James Pennethorne (1801–71), was trained in Nash's office, assisted him in his later years, and succeeded to his practice. He carried out many public works in London and was knighted in 1870. Nash's other principal assistants were Augustus Pugin, James Morgan and John Foulon. George Stanley and John Adey Repton, F. H. Greenway and the brothers Henry, James and George Pain were among his pupils. The last two established themselves in Ireland, where they designed a number of country houses in a picturesque castle style derived directly from that of their master. Anthony Salvin is also said to have been in his office.

The finest portrait of Nash is one by Lawrence painted in 1824–5 and now in the possession of Major Allan J. Cameron of Lochiel. Another portrait by Lawrence is at Jesus College, Oxford. A wax miniature by J. A. Couriguer is in the National Portrait Gallery. A marble bust by J. C. F. Rossi was exhibited at the R.A. in 1823. A marble bust by Behnes (exhibited at the R.A. in 1831) is in private possession. There is a plaster cast in the R.I.B.A. Drawings Collection, and a modern copy in the portico of All Souls Church, Langham Place.

[John Summerson, *John Nash: Architect to George IV*, 1935, 2nd ed. 1949; Terence Davis, *The Architecture of John Nash*, introduced with a critical essay by John Summerson, 1960; Terence Davis, *John Nash*, 1966. All the above were superseded by John Summerson, *The Life and Works of John Nash*, 1980. Michael Mansbridge, *John Nash: a Complete Catalogue*, 1991, illustrates virtually every building known to be by Nash, but uncritically includes a number of dubious attributions. See also R. Liscombe in *Arch. Hist.* xiii, 1970, on Nash's specimen designs for the 1818 Church Building Commission; *Catalogue of the R.I.B.A. Drawings Collection: L – N*, 1973; *History of the King's Works* vi, 1973, *passim*; John Summerson, 'John Nash's Statement', *Arch. Hist.* 34, 1991; Geoffrey Tyack, *Sir James Pennethorne*, 1992.]

The following list of Nash's executed works does not include a number of small Picturesque cottages, lodges, etc., attributable to him, for which see Nigel Temple, *John Nash and the Village Picturesque*, Gloucester 1979, and *George Repton's Pavilion Notebook*, 1993.

PUBLIC BUILDINGS, ETC.

CARMARTHEN CHURCH, new roof and ceiling, 1785; destroyed 1860 [W. Spurrell, *Carmarthen*, 1879, 32, 129].

CARMARTHEN, THE 'SIX BELLS' INN, *c.*1785; dem. [W. Spurrell, op. cit., 51 n.].

CARMARTHEN, THE COUNTY GAOL, 1789–92; dem. [W. Spurrell, op. cit., 51].

ST. DAVID'S CATHEDRAL, PEMBROKESHIRE, rebuilt west front and designed new Chapter-House, 1791–3. The west front was again rebuilt by Scott in 1862, and the Chapter-House was demolished in 1829 [I. Wyn Jones, 'John Nash at St. David's', *Arch. Rev.* Oct. 1952].

TRE-CEFEL BRIDGE, CARDIGANSHIRE (R. Teifi), 1792–3; dem. [National Library of Wales, Cardiganshire Q.S. Order Book, 17 July 1793].

CARDIGAN, THE COUNTY GAOL, 1792–3; dem. [S. Lewis, *Topographical Dictionary of Wales* i, 1849, 161].

HEREFORD, THE COUNTY GAOL, 1793–6; dem. 1928 [J. Duncumb, *History of the County of Hereford* i, 1804, 425].

ABERGAVENNY, MONMOUTHSHIRE, THE MARKET HOUSE, 1794–5; altered by J. Westcott 1825; dem. [Summerson].

ABERYSTWYTH, CARDIGANSHIRE, bridge over R. Rheidol, *c.*1797–1800; destroyed by flood 1886 [National Library of Wales, Cardiganshire Q. S. Order Book, 13 Oct. 1792, 8 Oct. 1794].

STANFORD-ON-TEME, WORCS., iron bridge over R. Teme for Sir Edward Winnington, Bart., 1797; dem. 1905 after collapse [Summerson]. Nash patented an iron bridge in 1797 (Patent No. 2165).

WHIPPINGHAM CHURCH, ISLE OF WIGHT, remodelled 1804, Gothic; rebuilt 1855–61 [Nigel Temple in *Isle of Wight Nat. Hist. & Archl. Soc.* viii, 1988, 92–4].

CHICHESTER, SUSSEX, THE MARKET HOUSE, NORTH STREET, 1807–8; top storey added 1900 [T. W. Horsfield, *History of Sussex* ii, 1835, 11].

NEWPORT, ISLE OF WIGHT, THE ISLE OF WIGHT INSTITUTION (library and news-room), 1811 [Summerson].

BRISTOL, MILES & HARFORD'S BANK, CORN STREET, for J. S. Harford, *c.*1811; façade altered 1877 [*A.P.S.D.*, *s.v.* 'Bristol'].

HIGHGATE, LONDON, THE ARCHWAY, 1812; dem. 1901 [Summerson].

LONDON, ST. JAMES'S PARK, bridge, pagoda, polygonal ballroom and other temporary buildings for fête in honour of the allied sovereigns, 1814. The ballroom was re-erected at Woolwich Arsenal as a military museum in 1819 [Summerson, 147–51; *History of the King's Works* vi, 317–19].

NEWPORT, ISLE OF WIGHT, MARKET HOUSE AND GUILDHALL, 1814–16 [Summerson].

WEST COWES CHURCH, ISLE OF WIGHT, tower,

incorporating a mausoleum, for George Ward, 1816 [Summerson].

LONDON, THE ROYAL OPERA HOUSE, HAYMARKET, remodelled in collaboration with G. S. Repton, 1816–18; interior destroyed by fire 1867 and rebuilt in 1868–9; dem., except the Arcade, *c.*1895 [Britton & Pugin, *The Public Buildings of London* i, 1825, 72–9].

OXFORD, JESUS COLLEGE, advice on altering roofs, battlements, etc., of both quadrangles, 1815–18 [*V.C.H. Oxfordshire* iii, 275; J. Ingram, *Memorials of Oxford* iii, 1837, 15].

CAHIR CHURCH, CO. TIPPERARY, IRELAND, 1817–20, Gothic [S. Lewis, *Topographical Dictionary of Ireland*, 1850, i, 229].

OXFORD, EXETER COLLEGE, the hall was repaired in 1818 'from the designs of Mr. Nash, under the superintendence of Mr. Repton' [J. Ingram, *Memorials of Oxford* i, 1837, 12–13].

LONDON, THE OPHTHALMIA HOSPITAL, ALBANY STREET, 1818; dem. *c.*1960 [Summerson].

LONDON, THE ARGYLL ROOMS, REGENT STREET, in collaboration with G. S. Repton, 1819–20; destroyed by fire 1830 [Summerson; drawing by Repton in the Yale Center for British Art].

LONDON, NEWMAN STREET, PICTURE-GALLERY for Benjamin West's sons, 1820–1; dem. [Summerson; *The Farington Dirary*, ed. J. Greig, viii, 300].

LONDON, THE HAYMARKET THEATRE, 1820–1 [Britton & Pugin, *The Public Buildings of London* i, 1825, 262–72].

ASCOT RACECOURSE, ROYAL STAND, 1822; dem. [*History of the King's Works* vi, 257].

COOKSTOWN, CO. TYRONE, IRELAND, DERRYLORAN PARISH CHURCH, *c.*1822, Gothic [S. Lewis, *Topographical Dictionary of Ireland*, 1850, i, 381].

LONDON, ST. JAMES'S SQUARE, Ionic garden seat, 1822 [*Survey of London* xxix, 69–70].

LONDON, THE ROYAL MEWS, PIMLICO, 1822–4 [*History of the King's Works* iv, 303–7].

LONDON, ALL SOULS CHURCH, LANGHAM PLACE, 1822–5 [Britton & Pugin, *the Public Buildings of London* ii, 1825, 99–101].

LONDON, SUFFOLK STREET, GALLERY for the Society of British Artists, in collaboration with James Elmes, 1823 [Summerson].

LONDON, THE ADULT ORPHAN ASYLUM, ST. ANDREW'S PLACE, REGENT'S PARK (later Someries House), 1823–4; dem. *c.*1960 [H. B. Wheatley, *London Past & Present* i, 1891, 9].

CARMARTHEN, THE PICTON MONUMENT, 1825–7; dem. 1846 [W. Spurrell, *Carmarthen*, 1879, 53–6].

BUCKINGHAM PALACE, LONDON, 1825–30; completed by Edward Blore, 1832–7; east front to Mall rebuilt to Blore's designs 1847–50 and again rebuilt by Sir Aston Webb 1913. The Marble Arch designed by Nash to stand in front of the Palace was removed in 1851 and re-erected at Cumberland Gate. [Britton & Pugin, *The Public Buildings of London, Supplement* by W. H. Leeds, 1838, 103–23; H. Clifford Smith, *Buckingham Palace*, 1931; John Harris, G. de Bellaigue & O. Millar, *Buckingham Palace*, 1968; *History of the King's Works* vi, 263–302.]

LONDON, CLARENCE HOUSE, ST. JAMES'S, rebuilt for the Duke of Clarence, 1825–8; altered 1874–5 [C. Hussey, *Clarence House*, 1949; *History of the King's Works* vi, 323–6].

LONDON, ST. MARY'S CHURCH, HAGGERSTON, 1826–7, Gothic; remodelled by James Brooks 1861–2; dem. 1940/1 [Summerson].

LONDON, THE UNITED SERVICE CLUB, PALL MALL, 1826–8; altered and enlarged by D. Burton 1858–9 [*Survey of London* xxix, 386–94].

BEMBRIDGE CHURCH, ISLE OF WIGHT, 1827; built under the supervision of Jacob Owen of Portsmouth to a plan and estimate supplied gratuitously by Nash; rebuilt 1845 [I.C.B.S.].

WINCHESTER, HOSPITAL OF ST. CROSS, completed restoration begun by S. P. Cockerell, 1827–9 [Summerson].

LONDON, THE WEST STRAND INPROVEMENTS, 1830–2, including THE LOWTHER ARCADE (dem. 1902), executed by W. Herbert (*q.v.*) [M. V. Stokes, 'The Lowther Arcade in the Strand', *London Topographical Record* xxiii, 1972, 119–28].

LONDON, ST. MARTIN'S VICARAGE, VESTRY HALL and NATIONAL SCHOOLS, ST. MARTIN'S PLACE, *c.*1830 [P.R.O., CREST 26/32, ff. 59, 268; Vestry Minutes in Westminster City Library, and file at the National School Society, *ex inf.* Mr. A. F. Kelsall] (*Survey of London* xx, 55, pl. 34).

EAST COWES CHURCH, ISLE OF WIGHT, 1831–3, Gothic; rebuilt, except tower, by T. Hellyer, 1868 [I.C.B.S.].

DOMESTIC ARCHITECTURE

LONDON, built Nos. 66–71 GREAT RUSSELL STREET for Sir John Rushout, Bart., 1777–8 [Summerson].

LONDON, Nos. 16–17 BLOOMSBURY SQUARE (now combined as offices), 1777–8 [Summerson].

GOLDEN GROVE, nr. CARMARTHEN, bathroom for John Vaughan, *c.*1787, dem. 1829 [*The Farington Diary*, ed. J. Greig, viii, 301].

CLYTHA HOUSE, MONMOUTHSHIRE: a payment of £10 by William Jones in 1790 for a 'plan' may represent a rejected design for 'Clytha

Castle', a folly built in that year and almost certainly designed by John Davenport (*q.v.*) rather than by Nash [Monmouthshire C.R.O., M 413/2114]. However, according to Sir Richard Colt Hoare, Nash designed a Gothic gateway here that was built in 1797 [*Journeys of Sir Richard Colt Hoare*, ed. M. W. Thompson, 1983, 96; R. Warner, *Walks through Wales in 1797*, 1798, 26].

EMLYN COTTAGE, NEWCASTLE EMLYN, CARMARTHENSHIRE, for William Brigstocke, 1792; dem. 1880s [N.L.W., letter from Nash to Mrs. Brigstocke, 8 Sept. 1792 in Cilgwyn Additional papers and plan in Fitzwilliam papers inscribed 'Emlyn Cottage by Nash', *ex inf.* Mr. Thomas Lloyd].

FFYNONE, PEMBROKESHIRE, for John Colby, 1792–6; remodelled 1904 [Summerson; bills in N.L.W., Owen & Colby papers, 1139–1267].

STOKE EDITH, HEREFS., restoration of part of interior for the Hon. Edward Foley after fire, 1793–6; gutted by fire 1927 and since dem. [Herefs. C.R.O., E 12 FIII, *ex inf.* Mr. D. Whitehead].

HAFOD HOUSE, CARDIGANSHIRE, work for Thomas Johnes, probably including the octagonal library, built in 1794; destroyed by fire 1807 [Summerson; D. Watkin, *C.R. Cockerell*, 1974, 5].

HAVERFORDWEST, PEMBROKESHIRE, FOLEY HOUSE, GOAT STREET, for Richard Foley, 1794 [sale advt. in *Cambrian*, July 1821].

LLANAERON, CARDIGANSHIRE, for Major William Lewis, *c.*1794 [James Baker, *Guide through Wales* ii, 1795, 200].

WHITSON COURT, MONMOUTHSHIRE, 'finished' for William Phillips, *c.*1794 [James Baker, *Guide through Wales* i, 1795, 47].

LLYSNEWYDD, HENLLAN BRIDGE, CARDIGANSHIRE, for Col. Lewes, *c.*1795; remodelled in nineteenth century, dem. *c.*1970 [Summerson].

TEMPLE DRUID, MAENCLOCHOG, PEMBROKESHIRE, for Henry Bulkeley, *c.*1795; dem. 1824 except one wing [sale advt. in *Cambrian*, 8 Sept. 1821].

DOLAUCOTHI, CARMARTHENSHIRE, remodelled for John Johnes, 1795; dem. *c.*1955 [N.L.W., Dolaucothi papers].

TENBY, PEMBROKESHIRE, SION HOUSE (later WOOFFERTON GRANGE), for William Routh, *c.*1795; subsequently enlarged; destroyed by fire 1937 [Summerson].

CARDIGAN, CARDIGAN PRIORY, for Thomas Johnes, senior, *c.*1795; since remodelled as a hospital [E. M. Pritchard, *Cardigan Priory in the Olden Days*, 1904, 121; Summerson].

ABERYSTWYTH, CARDIGANSHIRE, THE CASTLE HOUSE, for Sir Uvedale Price, Bart., *c.*1795; dem. 1895 [*Cambrian Directory*, 1800, 65] (*C. Life*, 4 July 1952, 33).

KENTCHURCH COURT, HEREFS., partly remodelled E. range for John Scudamore, *c.*1795, Gothic [J. P. Neale, *Views of Seats*, 2nd ser., iv, 1828] (*C. Life*, 15, 22, 29 Dec. 1966).

HOME FARM, BURLEY-ON-THE-HILL, RUTLAND, for 9th Earl of Winchilsea, *c.*1795–6 [drawings marked 'Mr. Nash' in Leics. C.R.O., DG7/4/32].

HARROW-ON-THE-HILL, MIDDLESEX, FLAMBARDS (now THE PARK), for Richard Page, *c.*1795–1803; since altered [letters in wallpaper-maker's letter-book in G. L. Record Office, B/TRL/9, pp. 20–1, 25–6; E. D. Laborde, *Harrow School*, 1948, 184].

TOWNELEY HALL, LANCS., lodges (dem.) for Charles Towneley, 1796 [letter from Nash to Towneley, 11 Sept. 1796 among Towneley papers in British Museum Archives].

MERLY HOUSE, DORSET, stables for J. Willett Willett, *c.*1796 [R.I.B.A.D. and letter of 11 Sept. 1796 to J. Towneley cited above in which Nash says he has recently been to Merly].

CORSHAM COURT, WILTS., alterations including remodelling of north front, for P. C. Methuen, in collaboration with J. A. Repton, 1797–8, Gothic; with the exception of the library nearly all Nash's work was destroyed by T. Bellamy in 1844–9 [exhib. at R.A. 1797; J. P. Neale, *Views of Seats*, 2nd ser. ii, 1825; J. Britton, *Historical Account of Corsham House*, 1806; F. J. Ladd *Architects at Corsham Court*, 1978, ch. 3].

HIGH LEGH HALL, CHESHIRE, alterations and additions for G. J. Legh, 1797–1818; dem. *c.*1963 [correspondence among Legh papers in John Rylands Library, Manchester].

SOUTHGATE GROVE, MIDDLESEX, for Walker Gray, 1797 [exhib. at R.A. 1797; G. Richardson, *New Vitruvius Britannicus* i, 1802, pls. 29–31].

CASINO, DENMARK HILL, DULWICH, SURREY (now LONDON), for Richard Shaw, 1797; dem. 1906 [exhib. at R.A. 1797].

BANK FARM or POINT PLEASANT, KINGSTON-ON-THAMES, SURREY, for Major-General St. John, 1797; burnt 1907 [Summerson].

EAST COWES CASTLE, ISLE OF WIGHT, for himself, 1798 onwards, castellated; dem. 1950 [exhib. at R.A. 1800; Summerson] (*Builder*, 1 Sept. 1950, 270–3).

LONDON, No. 29 DOVER STREET, for himself, *c.*1798; mutilated 1934, dem. 1940/1 [Summerson].

SUNDRIDGE PARK, nr. BROMLEY, KENT, for Sir Claude Scott, Bart., in association with Humphry Repton, 1799. Samuel Wyatt (*q.v*) was responsible for the interior, and also for the stables [exhib. at R.A. 1799; W. Angus, *Seats of the Nobility and Gentry*, pl. lvi, 1804; J. P. Neale, *Views of Seats*, 2nd ser. v, 1829; John Newman, *West Kent and the Weald*, Buildings of England, 1969, 182–3].

HELMINGHAM HALL, SUFFOLK, alterations for 6th Earl of Dysart, 1800, Tudor Gothic style [exhib. at R.A. 1800; Arthur Oswald in *C. Life*, 23 Aug. 1956].

BARR HALL, GREAT BARR, STAFFS., Gothic gateway from grounds to churchyard, for Joseph Scott, *c.*1801; dem. [S. Shaw, *History of Staffordshire* ii, 1801, 106 and engraving p. 103].

CHALFONT HOUSE, BUCKS., remodelled exterior for Thomas Hibbert, *c.*1800; again remodelled by A. Salvin 1836 [*The Gardener's Magazine*, ed. J. C. Loudon, iv, 1828, 119–20; for Salvin's alterations see *Builder* xli, 1881, 810].

LUSCOMBE CASTLE, DAWLISH, DEVON, for Charles Hoare, 1800–4 [exhib. at R.A. 1800] (*C. Life*, 9, 16 and 23 Feb. 1956; C. Hussey, *English Country Houses: Late Georgian*, 1958, 55–65).

KILLYMOON CASTLE, CO. TYRONE, IRELAND, for Col. William Stewart, *c.*1801–3, castellated [exhib. at R.A. 1803].

THE WARRENS, BRAMSHAW, HANTS., for George Eyre, 1801–5 [N. Temple in *Hants. Field Club Trans.* 44, 1988].

CRONKHILL, nr. CROSS HOUSES, SHREWSBURY, for Francis Walford, *c.*1802 [exhib. at R.A. as 'house near Shrewsbury', 1802; Summerson].

HOLLYCOMBE, nr. LINCH, SUSSEX, for Sir Charles Taylor, Bart., *c.*1805; rebuilt *c.*1895 [T. W. Horsfield, *History of Sussex* ii, 1835, 103].

MOCCAS, HEREFS., 'BRIDGE LODGE' and 'DAW'S LODGE' for Sir George Cornewall, Bart., *c.*1805 [Summerson].

HARPTON COURT, RADNORSHIRE, additions for Thomas Frankland Lewis, *c.*1805; dem. 1956 [Summerson].

LONGNER HALL, SALOP., for Robert Burton, *c.*1805, Gothic [Summerson].

WITLEY COURT, WORCS., alterations including addition of Ionic portico on west side for 3rd Lord Foley, *c.*1805; altered *c.*1860, now ruinous [Summerson; *R.I.B.A. Drawings Catalogue: L–N*, 109] (sketch-plan by C. R. Cockerell reproduced in *Arch. Hist.* xiv, 1971, fig. 24; *C. Life*, 8, 15 June 1945).

SANDRIDGE PARK, STOKE GABRIEL, DEVON, for Lady Ashburton, *c.*1805 [exhib. at R.A. 1805].

HALE HALL, LANCS., south front, etc., for John Blackburne, 1806; dem. [Summerson].

GARNSTONE CASTLE, HEREFS., for Samuel Peploe, *c.*1806–10, castellated; dem. 1958 [J. P. Neale, *Views of Seats*, 2nd ser. iv, 1828].

BRAMPTON PARK, HUNTS., new offices and alterations to house for Lady Olivia Sparrow, 1806–7; house rebuilt by T. S. Whitwell 1821–2 and destroyed by fire 1907 [Hunts. C.R.O., DDM 16 J/5, contract and litigation with Nash, *ex inf.* Mr. N. Temple].

AQUALATE HALL, STAFFS., rebuilt for John Fletcher Boughey, 1806–9, Gothic; destroyed by fire 1910 [Summerson].

BARNSLEY PARK, GLOS., lodge, conservatory and interior of library for Sir James Musgrave, Bart., 1806–10 [Bodleian Library, Wykeham-Musgrave papers, c. 53; C. Hussey in *C. Life*, 2–9 Sept. 1954].

CHILDWALL HALL, LANCS., for Bamber Gascoyne, 1806–13, castellated; dem. 1949 [J. P. Neale, *Views of Seats*, 2nd ser. ii, 1825].

HAMSTEAD FARM, nr. NEWTOWN, ISLE OF WIGHT, for himself, *c.*1806; since rebuilt [Summerson].

WEST GRINSTEAD PARK, SUSSEX, for Walter Burrell, *c.*1806–9, Gothic; enlarged *c.*1865; dem. 1964 [Summerson; D. G. C. Elwes & C. J. Robinson, *Castles & Mansions of West Sussex*, 1867, 108].

LISSAN RECTORY, CO. DERRY, IRELAND, for the Revd. John Staples, 1807 [Summerson; E. M. Jope, 'Lissan Rectory . . . and the Buildings in the North of Ireland designed by John Nash', *Ulster Jnl. of Archaeology* xix, 1956].

KILWAUGHTER CASTLE, CO. ANTRIM, IRELAND, for E. J. Agnew, 1807, castellated; dismantled 1951 [E. M. Jope, *op. cit.*].

NUNWELL HOUSE, ISLE OF WIGHT, repairs for Sir William Oglander, Bart., 1807, evidently after rejection of Nash's design for a new house (illustrated *C. Life*, 26 Feb. 1976, fig. 5 and Mansbridge, 117) [estimate among Oglander papers in Isle of Wight Record Office, *ex inf.* Mr. N. Temple].

PARNHAM HALL, DORSET, additions for Sir William Oglander, Bart., 1807–11, Gothic [Dorset County Record Office, MW/M8] (*C. Life*, 29 Aug. 1908; Arthur Oswald, *The Country Houses of Dorset*, 2nd ed. 1959, 58–9).

ATTINGHAM HALL, SALOP., picture gallery and staircase for 2nd Lord Berwick, 1807–10 [Summerson; Michael Rix in *C. Life*, 21 Oct. 1954] (C. Hussey, *English Country Houses: Mid Georgian*, 1956, 195–202). Nash also appears to have planned a model village at Atcham, which was at least partly built, and of which there are some traces opposite the park gates [Nigel Temple, 'A

Recent Discovery at Attingham', *Arch. Rev.* Aug. 1976].

SOUTHBOROUGH PLACE, ASHCOMBE AVENUE, SURBITON, SURREY, for Thomas Langley, 1808 [Summerson].

CAERHAYS CASTLE, ST. MICHAEL CAERHAYS, CORNWALL, for J. B. Trevanion, *c.*1808, castellated [E. Twycross, *The Mansions of England and Wales: Cornwall*, 1846, 52].

CALEDON, CO. TYRONE, IRELAND, alterations and additions for 2nd Earl of Caledon, 1808–10; portico added 1833 by Thomas Duff of Newry [Summerson and information from Prof. Alistair Rowan] (*C. Life*, 27 Feb., 6 March 1937).

INGESTRE HALL, STAFFS., alterations including reconstruction of north front for 2nd Earl Talbot, 1808–13; Nash's work was destroyed by fire in 1882 [Summerson] (*C. Life*, 17, 24 and 31 Oct. 1957).

RAVENSWORTH CASTLE, CO. DURHAM, for 1st Lord Ravensworth, begun 1808 to Nash's designs, but still in progress 1824, and eventually completed under the direction of the Hon. Thomas Liddell (*q.v.*), the owner's son; dem. 1952–3 [Summerson; drawings in R.I.B.A. Coll., including one (E 4/3 (16)) by Nash dated 1824].

KNEPP CASTLE, WEST GRINSTEAD, SUSSEX, for Sir Charles Burrell, Bart., *c.*1808, castellated; damaged by fire 1904 [signed drawings formerly at Knepp; cf. J. Harris, *Catalogue of British Drawings for Architecture etc. in American Collections*, 1971, 150].

BETLEY COURT, STAFFS., alterations to drawing-room for Sir Thomas Fletcher, Bart., 1809–10 [T. R. Twelmlow, *The Twelmlows*, 1910, 218].

ROCKINGHAM HOUSE, CO. ROSCOMMON, IRELAND, for 1st Viscount Lorton, 1809–10; altered 1822; destroyed by fire 1957 [Summerson; building accounts in National Library of Ireland, MS. 3755; James Bettley in *C. Life*, 17 Nov. 1988].

PRESHAW HOUSE, HANTS., additions for Walter Long, 1810 [G.F. Prosser, *Select Illustrations of Hampshire*, 1833].

CHARBOROUGH PARK, DORSET, alterations for Richard Erle Drax Grosvenor, *c.*1810 [J. B. Burke, *A Visitation of Seats and Arms* ii, 1853, 166] (R.C.H.M., *Dorset* ii, 163–8).

NORTHERWOOD, nr. LYNDHURST, HANTS., 'improved . . . at the suggestion of . . . Mr. Nash', probably by the addition of pavilions and veranda, for Capt. Charles William Mitchell, *c.*1810; later enlarged by Thomas Cubitt [G. F. Prosser, *Select Illustrations of Hampshire*, 1833; *R.I.B.A. Drawings Catalogue: L–N*, 110].

BLAISE CASTLE, HENBURY, GLOS., group of picturesque cottages forming BLAISE HAMLET for J. S. Harford, 1810–11. Nash also designed a conservatory in 1806 [Summerson] (*C. Life*, 28 Dec. 1901, with plan, 14 Oct. 1939, 3 Sept. 1943, 429).

LOUGH CUTRA CASTLE, CO. GALWAY, IRELAND, for the Hon. Charles Vereker, 1811, castellated; enlarged 1856, restored 1967 [Summerson; D. Guinness & W. Ryan, *Irish Houses and Castles*, 1971, 177–80].

HOPTON COURT, SALOP., added portico and additional storey for Thomas Botfield, 1811–13 [J. B. Burke. *A Visitation of Seats and Arms* i, 1852, 268; B. Botfield, *Stemmata Botevilliana*, 1858, p. ccxxi].

RHEOLA, nr. NEATH, GLAMORGANSHIRE, enlarged for John Edwards, *c.*1812 [Summerson]; also designed Steward's House *c.*1818 [R.I.B.A.D., K1/18/1, 2 (wrongly captioned as 'Blaise'), *ex inf.* Mr. Nigel Temple].

LONDON, No. 14 GROSVENOR SQUARE, alterations, including new staircase, for 2nd Lord Berwick, *c.*1812–13; dem. *c.*1935 [Sir John Soane's Museum, 7/B/4].

STREATHAM MANOR HOUSE (COVENTRY HOUSE), SURREY, rebuilt for 7th Earl of Coventry, 1812–14, retaining existing offices; refronted 1877; dem. 1982 [Coventry Estate papers at Croome Court, Worcs., F68/3/3, 7; F 18, 7].

WINDSOR, ROYAL LODGE in THE GREAT PARK, for the Prince Regent, 1813–16; dem. 1830 [O. Morshead, *George IV and Royal Lodge*, 1965; *History of the King's Works* vi, 399–401].

LONDON, CARLTON HOUSE, PALL MALL, remodelled basement storey for the Prince Regent, 1813; dem. 1827–8 [*Survey of London* xx, 74–5].

LONDON, LANGHAM HOUSE, PORTLAND PLACE, for Sir James Langham, Bart., 1813–15; dem. *c.*1864 [Summerson].

LONDON, LANGHAM PLACE, houses on west side, 1813; dem. [Summerson].

WESTOVER HOUSE, ISLE OF WIGHT, alterations for Sir Leonard Holmes, Bart., *c.*1815 [letter from Nash dated 9 Dec. 1813 in Isle of Wight Record Office, JER/HBY/160, *ex inf.* Mr. Nigel Temple].

BRIGHTON, THE ROYAL PAVILION, remodelled for the Prince Regent, 1815–22 [John Nash, *The Royal Pavilion at Brighton*, 1826, 2nd ed. 1838; H. D. Roberts, *History of the Royal Pavilion, Brighton*, 1939; John Dinkel, *The Royal Pavilion, Brighton*, 1983; John Morley, *The Making of the Royal Pavilion, Brighton*, 1984].

SHANE'S CASTLE, CO. ANTRIM, IRELAND, designs for a new house for 2nd Viscount O'Neil, to replace one destroyed by fire in 1816, and partially executed before work was stopped by Lord O'Neil. Thomas Hopper (*q.v.*) was then employed to arbitrate between Nash and Lord O'Neil [account-book in Estate Office at Gosford Castle, *ex inf.* Mr. Robin Fedden]. Nash's design is illustrated by Davis, *John Nash*, pl. 29, and the unfinished walls in *C. Life*, 18 Aug. 1955, 344. It is doubtful whether (as has been supposed) Nash made any designs for Shane's Castle before the fire of 1816.

GRACEFIELD LODGE, CO. KILDARE, IRELAND, for Mrs. Kavanagh, 1817, executed by William Robertson of Kilkenny [J. N. Brewer, *The Beauties of Ireland* ii, 1826, 105].

SHANBALLY CASTLE, CO. TIPPERARY, IRELAND, for 1st Viscount Lismore, completed 1819, castellated; dem. 1960 [Summerson].

attributed: TYNAN ABBEY, CO. ARMAGH, IRELAND, enlarged for Sir James Stronge, Bart., *c.*1820, Gothic; gutted by fire *c.*1980 [photographs of destroyed drawings in Nash's hand in Architectural Survey of N. Ireland, *ex inf.* Prof. A. Rowan].

WEST COWES, ISLE OF WIGHT, Gothic villa for Sir J. Coxe Hippisley, Bart., *c.*1825; now incorporated in premises of Royal Corinthian Yacht Club [R. Ackermann, *Views of Country Seats* i, 1830, 112].

NORTHWOOD HOUSE, WEST COWES, ISLE OF WIGHT, two classical lodges (one dem.) for George Ward, date uncertain [Summerson].

WORCESTER PARK, nr. EWELL, SURREY, enlarged for William Taylor, date uncertain; dem. [G. F. Prosser, *Select Illustrations of Surrey*, 1828].

LONDON: REGENT STREET, REGENT'S PARK, ETC.

Besides planning REGENT STREET and REGENT'S PARK as a whole, Nash himself designed THE QUADRANT, 1818–20 (colonnades removed 1848, Quadrant as a whole rebuilt by R. N. Shaw and Sir R. Blomfield 1906–23); No. 15 REGENT STREET for C. T. Blicke, 1819 (dem. *c.*1838); Nos. 14–16 REGENT STREET as a double mansion for himself and John Edwards, 1822–4 (dem., illustrated in Britton & Pugin, *Public Buildings of London* ii, 1828, 287–9); and CARLTON HOUSE TERRACE, 1827–33 (described in *Survey of London* xx, 77–87).

In REGENT'S PARK Nash was responsible for the terrace façades generally, for the siting of the villas, and for the planting. The façades of CORNWALL TERRACE and CLARENCE TERRACE were, however, delegated to Decimus Burton, and elsewhere the executant architects employed by the builders sometimes modified Nash's designs, notably in the case of GLOUCESTER GATE (see 'Scoles, J. J.'). For CUMBERLAND GATE and CUMBERLAND TERRACE the executant architect was James Thomson. The other terraces with façades by Nash are ULSTER TERRACE, YORK TERRACE (E. and W.), YORK GATE, SUSSEX PLACE, HANOVER TERRACE, KENT TERRACE, CHESTER TERRACE, CAMBRIDGE TERRACE, ST. ANDREWS TERRACE and PARK SQUARE (E. and W.), all of which were building during the period 1821–30. PARK CRESCENT, built 1812–22, was rebuilt to the original elevations, but with new interiors, in 1963–5. The PARK VILLAGES, forming a satellite model suburb, were completed by James Pennethorne.

Nash's first plan for Regent's Park (1811), showing the proposed building sites planted as nurseries, is in the Public Record Office (MPEE 58), together with two panoramic drawings of the whole design (MR 1045 and 1047). For these and other plans and drawings connected with Nash's metropolitan improvements see *Maps and Plans in the Public Record office* i, 1967. See also Ann Saunders, *Regent's Park*, Newton Abbot 1969, and John Summerson, 'The Beginnings of Regent's Park', *Arch. Hist.* 20, 1967.

LEAMINGTON, WARWICKSHIRE

A 'Plan of Newbold Comyn at Leamington Priors the Estate of Edw. Willes Esq. as now laid out for building on by Jno. Nash & Jas. Morgan Architects 1827' [Warwickshire Record Office, CR 1247/8 and 9] shows that Nash was involved in the planning of Leamington Spa. But other architects were employed, and little of the existing town can be regarded as Nash's design. The WILLES ROAD BRIDGE is, however, stated to have been designed by Nash and Morgan in *The Warwick Advertiser*, 23 July 1827. See Robin Chaplin, 'the Rise of Royal Leamington Spa', *Warwickshire History* ii (2), 1972, and L. F. Cave, *Royal Leamington Spa*, 1988.

NASH, WILLIAM THOMAS (1799–1867), was a pupil of Wallen and Ferry (*q.v.*). From 1821 onwards he was a partner in the firm of Cockett and Nash (subsequently Nash, Son & Rowley), auctioneers and land surveyors of Royston, Herts. During the following quarter of a century the firm undertook a number of minor architectural commissions in Royston and neighbourhood. Among these were UPTON HOUSE, BALDOCK STREET, ROYSTON, 1829; ROYSTON MARKET HOUSE, 1829–30; ICKLETON VICARAGE, CAMBS., *c.*1832; WYDDIAL RECTORY, HERTS., 1838 [London Diocesan Records, Guildhall Library, MS. 19227/12]; WESTMILL RECTORY, HERTS., 1841 [Lincs. C.R.O., MGA 268]; HINXTON GRANGE,

CAMBS., for Charles Nash, *c.*1840; and several WORKHOUSES built under the Act of 1834, including those at BISHOPS STORTFORD and BRAINTREE in ESSEX, BUNTINGFORD in HERTS. and ST. IVES in HUNTINGDONSHIRE. After Nash's death in 1867 his architectural practice was continued by his son Edward. The firm's records, including many architectural drawings, are in the County Record Office at Cambridge.

[Information from Mr. J. L. Corfield.]

NASMITH, ROBERT (–1793), was an architect of whom little is known except that he designed STOKE PARK, STOKE POGES, BUCKS., for John Penn in 1789. He died in Upper Norton Street, Marylebone, on 30 August 1793, leaving the house to be completed by James Wyatt. At the time of his death he was also carrying out alterations to KENWOOD HOUSE, HIGHGATE, LONDON, for the 2nd Earl of Mansfield. These were completed by George Saunders (*q.v.*). At HACKWOOD PARK, HANTS., there is an undated drawing endorsed 'Nasmith' showing 'the alteration proposed in [the] Withdrawing room'. Owing to subsequent alterations it is impossible to say whether this was carried out. [J. Penn, *An Historical and Descriptive Account of Stoke Park*, 1813, 60–1; J. P. Neale, *Views of Seats* i, 1818; R. Ackermann, *Repository of Arts*, 3rd ser. iii, 1824, 313; Earl of Mansfield's archives at Scone Palace, TD 80/137; *Gent's Mag.* 1793 (ii), 866; *Scots Mag.* lv, 1793, 467; will, P.C.C. 517 DODWELL.]

NASMYTH, ALEXANDER (1758–1840), was descended from a family of Scottish masons. His father, Michael Nasmyth (d. 1803), was a successful Edinburgh builder in the Grassmarket.[1] Alexander was educated at the High School and apprenticed to a house-painter and decorator, but attracted the attention of the portrait-painter Allan Ramsay, who employed him in his London studio. In 1778 he returned to Edinburgh and established himself as a portrait-painter, and in 1782–4 visited Italy. Although he enjoyed considerable success as an artist, his liberal political views alienated some of his aristocratic clients, and during the latter part of his life his work was increasingly confined to landscape subjects.

Nasymth's involvement in architecture was largely a by-product of his activities as a landscape consultant. Sir Uvedale Price had 'always been of the opinion that the two professions [of] landscape gardening and landscape painting' ought to be combined, and Nasmyth had a considerable practice as a landscape consultant who could envisage a park or a garden as a romantic composition on literally picturesque principles. He acted in this capacity at e.g., Inveraray and Rosneath for the 5th Duke of Argyll (1801–4), at Dunglass for Sir James Hall (1806–10), at Taymouth Castle for the 4th Earl of Breadalbane (1806), at Loudoun Castle for the 2nd Earl of Moira (1803–6), and at Kinfauns Castle for the 14th Lord Gray (1809). Nasmyth's involvement often included suggesting not only the siting of the house in relation to the landscape, but also an indication of its architectural character, to be worked out in detail by a professional architect – Richard Crichton at Dunglass, the Elliots at Taymouth and Loudoun Castles. At Elleray, Westmorland, he actually designed (*c.*1820) a small and picturesquely sited house (dem. 1871) for his friend John Wilson.

In Edinburgh Nasmyth was responsible for the elegant circular temple which was built over St. Bernard's Well, romantically situated in the Dean Valley (1789), and for a design (1806) for the Nelson Monument on Calton Hill (illustrated in his *Autobiography*, p. 45), which proved to be too expensive for the limited funds available, and was set aside in favour of an inferior design by Robert Burn (*q.v.*). In 1813 he was one of the prize-winners in the competition for the layout of the area to the north of Calton Hill, submitting a scheme in which the emphasis was on the views to be created.

In addition Nasmyth designed two bridges: one with a battlemented parapet at Almondell, West Lothian, for Henry Erskine, *c.*1810, and a large one over the R. Dee at Tongueland, Kirkcudbrightshire, built by Telford to a modified design 1805–6. He also made designs for 'bow-and-string' bridges and roofs, a form of construction of which he appears to have been one of the theoretical pioneers.

Nasmyth died in Edinburgh on 10 April 1840. He was the father of Patrick Nasmyth (1787–1831), landscape-painter, and of James Nasmyth (1808–90), engineer.

[*The Autobiography of James Nasmyth*, 1883; *D.N.B.*; National Gallery of Scotland, *Catalogue of Scottish Drawings*, 1960, 145–9; A. A. Tait, *The Landscape Garden in Scotland 1735–1835*, Edinburgh 1980; J. C. B. Cooksey, *Alexander Nasmyth*, Whittinghame 1991.]

NAYLOR, WILLIAM RIGBY (–1773), then of London, in 1769 submitted two de-

[1] Michael Nasmyth built and probably designed BARNS HOUSE, PEEBLESSHIRE, for James Burnet, *c.*1773–80 [R.C.A.M. *Peeblesshire* ii, 280].

signs in the competition for the Royal Exchange at Dublin [*Builder* xxvii, 1869, 781]. He subsequently emigrated to North America, practising as an architect and surveyor in Charleston, South Carolina, until his death in October 1773. [Beatrice St. J. Ravenal, *Architects of Charleston*, Charleston 1945, 33–4.]

NEALE, WILLIAM (–1822), and his son William (*c*.1794–1838), were architects and builders at Melton Mowbray in Leicestershire. The father was responsible for alterations and additions to EASTWELL RECTORY, LEICS., in 1814. The son was Surveyor to the Oakham Canal Company, and died suddenly at the house of the Company's treasurer on 12 October 1838, aged 44 [J. D. Bennett, *Leicestershire Architects*, Leicester Museums 1968].

NEAVE, DAVID (1773–1841), was the son of Thomas Neave, a mason of Forfar, where he was born on 17 March 1773. He practised in Dundee, where he succeeded Samuel Bell (d. 1813) as the leading architect. No formal appointment has been traced, but in June 1833 he resigned the post of Town's Architect which he appears to have held for some twenty years. He died at Dundee on 23 January 1841.

Neave was a competent architect whose best work is in the Greek Revival style, sometimes with Soanean mannerisms. A large volume of his architectural drawings belongs to the Royal Incorporation of Architects in Scotland. Two MS. plans of parts of Dundee made by Neave in 1813 are in the S.R.O. (RHP 37 and 64). [David Walker, *Architects and Architecture in Dundee*, Abertay Historical Society's Publications No. 2, 1955, 6–8; information from Mr. David Walker.]

PUBLIC BUILDINGS

MONIKIE CHURCH, ANGUS, 1811–12, Gothic [drawings in S.R.O., RHP 35162].

EDZELL CHURCH, ANGUS, 1818 [vol. of drawings].

KILSPINDIE CHURCH, PERTHSHIRE, 1821 [S.R.O., HR 417/1].

DUNDEE, reconstructed THE TABERNACLE, N. TAY STREET, as ST. DAVID'S CHURCH, 1822–4 [Dundee Town Council Minutes, 6 April 1822].

HIGH or WEST LIGHTHOUSE at SOUTH FERRY, nr. TAYPORT, FIFE, 1823, apparently in collaboration with Robert Stevenson; since heightened [vol. of drawings].

FORFAR, THE COUNTY BUILDINGS, 1823–4 [signed drawings and specifications preserved in the building 1972; also in vol. of drawings].

DUNDEE LUNATIC ASYLUM, additions, 1824–5 [*Dundee Advertiser*, 2 Dec. 1824].

DUNDEE INFIRMARY (later Victoria Road School), completion of John Paterson's original designs of 1793–8, 1824–6; dem. [*Dundee Advertiser*, 12 Sept. 1824, 6 Mar. 1826].

DUNDEE, THISTLE HALL, UNION STREET, 1826–9; largely rebuilt, but façade survives as part of Royal Hotel [David Walker, *op. cit.*, 8, with illustration].

LIFF AND BENVIE SCHOOL, ANGUS, 1828 [*Dundee Advertiser*, 29 May 1828].

ABERNYTE SCHOOL, PERTHSHIRE, 1829; dem. [*Dundee Advertiser*, 2 July 1829].

LOCHEE, ANGUS, ST. NINIAN'S CHAPEL, 1829–30; remodelled 1880 [*Dundee Advertiser*, 21 May 1829].

DUNDEE, CHAPELSHADE CHURCH, reconstructed 1830–1 [David Walker, *op. cit.*, 81 from Kirk Session Minutes].

DOMESTIC ARCHITECTURE

Most of Neave's private commissions were for villas and small houses in and around Dundee. BALRUDDERY HOUSE, LIFF, ANGUS, for James Webster, for which there are drawings in the Neave volume, appears to have been his only country house; it was rebuilt in 1889 after a fire, but there is a small engraving in *Forfarshire Illustrated*, Dundee 1843, plate at end. In 1823–4 he designed LONGFORGAN MANSE, PERTHSHIRE [S.R.O., HR 441/1].

In DUNDEE Neave was responsible for the layout of UNION, DOCK and EXCHANGE STREETS, 1828 [Town Council Minutes, 17 Jan. and 20 March 1828, *ex inf.* Mr. David Walker], and designed a terrace of houses comprising Nos. 1–27 SOUTH TAY STREET, *c*.1818–20, one of which he occupied himself [David Walker, *op. cit.*, 7].

The drawings in the volume mentioned above include the following: a cottage at STRATHMARTINE, ANGUS, for the heirs of Admiral Laird; a cottage at IDVIES, ANGUS, for John Baxter (dem.); a villa (dem.) at CHAPELSHADE for James Soot; a lodge at LOGIE HOUSE, DUNDEE, for Isaac Watt, 1817 (dem.); a house at BINROCK, DUNDEE, for Mr. Clayhills; a house in PERTH ROAD, DUNDEE, for Thomas Miller, brewer; a house for James Davidson in SEAGATE, DUNDEE; a small house at MILNBANK, DUNDEE, for James Reid; a large house in PERTH ROAD called UNION MOUNT for Mr. Alison; remodelling a house at ROSEANGLE for the Revd. P. McVicar, 1819; a house at ROSEANGLE for David Martin; a house (dem.) at BONNYBANK, DUNDEE, for William Straton; a house (166 NETHERGATE) for Mr. Gray, 1817; a house (dem.) in PARK PLACE for James Ogilvie, 1820; a villa in FERRY ROAD for William Small, Town Clerk of Dundee, 1818; houses in MAGDALEN YARD ROAD for Capt. Shaw and Mr. Watt; a villa (dem.) at ANNFIELD for Capt. Black, 1818; a villa at ROSEANGLE for Robert Adie, 1819; a house (dem.) in FERRY ROAD for James Souter; refronting THE NEW BANK, 65 MURRAYGATE, for William Roberts (dem.); and a house at ROSEANGLE (now LAING'S HOTEL) for Mr. Calman.

NEILL, JOHN (1781–1837), 'Architect', is commemorated by a monument in the Calton Old Burial Ground at Edinburgh. He was probably the John Neill, 'builder', who was admitted a burgess in June 1809 in right of his father, Andrew Neill, builder [*Roll of Burgesses of the City of Edinburgh, 1761–1841*, Scottish Record Soc. 1933, 119].

NEILL, THOMAS, was an architect of St. Marylebone, London. In 1790 he exhibited a design for a villa at the Society of Artists and in 1793 he was elected a member of the Surveyors' Club. He designed the MARKET HOUSE at UXBRIDGE in MIDDLESEX in 1788–9 [K. R. Pearce, 'Uxbridge Market House', *The Uxbridge Record* 17, 1972, 8], and in 1817–18 directed minor alterations to No. 20 GROSVENOR SQUARE for Lord Whitworth [*Survey of London* xl, 138].

NEILSON, SAMUEL (–1753), was an Edinburgh master mason. He was the son of William Neilson, a merchant who was Lord Provost of the City in 1717, and himself became a burgess in 1733 in right of his father [*Roll of Edinburgh Burgesses 1701–60*, Scottish Record Soc. 1929, 152]. In 1743 he gave evidence in William Adam's lawsuit against Lord Braco. He stated that besides carrying on his business as a mason he sometimes made designs for country houses. As an example he mentioned MONKTON HOUSE, AYRSHIRE, for Hugh Baillie, *c.*1740. He had also advised Mr. Blair of ADAMTON, nr. MONKTON, 'about repairing an old House' [*Depositions in the Cause William Adams v. Lord Braco*, 1743, 14–15]. In 1748–9 he designed and built the stone steeple of BURNTISLAND CHURCH, FIFE [S.R.O., B9/12/17, pp. 424, 429, 436]. In 1750–3 he built the ROYAL BANK OF SCOTLAND in the Old Town of Edinburgh, following (with some modifications) the designs made by William Adam some years previously [John Fleming, *Robert Adam and his Circle*, 1962, 336]. His death in 1753 is recorded in S.R.O., CC/8/8/114/2.

NELSON, SAMUEL (–1803), was a pupil of Joseph Bonomi, from whose address he exhibited at the Royal Academy from 1790 to 1795. By 1800 he was in independent practice at 9 Pratt Street, Hampstead Road. A 'design for a gentleman's villa', circular in plan and neo-classical in style, which he exhibited in 1790, is now in the Metropolitan Museum at New York and is illustrated by John Harris, *Catalogue of British Drawings for Architecture, etc. in American Collections*, 1971, pl. 109. In 1800 Nelson exhibited 'a design for a pavilion to be erected at the Mote, the seat of Lord Romney', evidently the circular Greek temple or 'pavilion' at MOTE PARK, nr. MAIDSTONE, KENT, erected in 1801 by the Volunteers of Kent as a tribute to the Lord Lieutenant, Lord Romney (*Gent's Mag.* 1801 (ii), 1046; *C. Life*, 7 Sept. 1951, 737). The death on 15 March 1803 of 'my beloved scholar Samuel Nelson' is recorded in Bonomi's will [P.C.C. 174 ELY].

NEVIS, ROBERT, practised as an architect and surveyor in Hull in the 1820s. In 1829 he designed a house – apparently EAGLE HOUSE – at BARTON-ON-HUMBER, LINCS., for R. Hall of Hull. His designs are in the Lincolnshire Record Office [B.H. 12].

NEWALL, WALTER (1780–1863), was the leading architect in Dumfries from about 1820 until his retirement a few years before his death in 1863. He was the son of a farmer at New Abbey in Kirkcudbrightshire. Nothing is known of his training, but he must have been in the office of an architect of standing, as his buildings show an up-to-date knowledge of both the Greek Revival and the Picturesque Gothic styles of the day, and he appears to have travelled in Italy and Germany. His subsequent professional career is fully documented by a large collection of his drawings and office papers that was acquired by the Dumfries Archives Centre in 1991.

Newall's practice was almost exclusively confined to Dumfriesshire and Galloway, where he designed several churches, a number of minor country houses and villas, and many farmsteads, especially on the estates of the Duke of Buccleuch. In Dumfries he was responsible for a modest urban development in and around George Street and for the conversion of a windmill into a neo-classical observatory (now the Museum) that became one of the town's landmarks.

Newall designed nothing of special distinction, but his Greek Revival bungalow villas are attractive buildings of a distinctively Scottish kind, and J. C. Loudon thought well enough of one of them to give an account of it in his *Encyclopaedia of Cottage, Farm and Villa Architecture*, in which he also illustrated six of Newall's farmsteads. By the 1840s Newall had abandoned the Greek Revival for the picturesque domestic style, partly 'Tudor' and partly Scottish vernacular, made fashionable by Burn and others. Kirkmahoe is the best of his simple Gothic churches. Designs for a number of churchyard monuments, both Gothic and classical, are among Newall's drawings, and two examples in St. Michael's churchyard in Dumfries are illustrated in Loudon's *Gardener's Magazine*, 1831, 529. George Corson (1829–1910) of Leeds was his pupil.

[Dumfries Archives Centre, Newall Collection (GD 130–1); A. Mackechnie, 'Walter Newall, Architect in Dumfries', *Trans. Dumfriesshire & Galloway Nat. Hist. & Antiq. Soc.* 3rd. ser. lxiii, 1988; information from Mr. W. J. Woolfe and Miss M. M. Stewart.]

The list of Newall's principal works that follows will in due course be extended as his drawings are more fully catalogued and identified. D. = Dumfriesshire, K. = Kirkcudbrightshire, DAC = Dumfries Archives Centre.

PUBLIC BUILDINGS

DUMFRIES, conversion of Windmill into OBSERVATORY (now MUSEUM) for the Dumfries and Maxwelltown Astronomical Society, 1835–6 [MS. Minute-book at Museum].

DUMFRIES, BRITISH LINEN BANK, 1839 [Bank of Scotland, Minutes of Directors of British Linen Bank, 6/8/16, p. 166, 16 Nov. 1839, *ex inf.* Mrs. E. Beaton].

CHURCHES

BUITTLE, K., 1818–19, Gothic [S.R.O., HR 376/1, pp. 2, 12, 13].

KIRKMAHOE, D., 1822–3, Gothic [S.R.O., HR 148/1].

NEW ABBEY (R.C.), K., 1824, Gothic with integral priest's house [DAC, GD 131/N7/27–34; S.R.O., RHP 3545].

ANWOTH, K., 1826–7, Gothic [S.R.O., HR 136/1, pp. 17, 18, etc.].

PARTON, K., 1833–4, Gothic [S.R.O., HR 381/1, p. 12].

KIRKBEAN, K., upper part of tower, 1835, Gothic [S.R.O., HR 759/1, p. 23].

LOCHMABEN FREE CHURCH, D., 1843, Gothic [S.R.O., CH3/595/3, p. 82].

KIRKPATRICK DURHAM, K., 1849–50, Gothic [S.R.O., HR 380/1, 12 March, 11 April 1850].

MANSES (all in DUMFRIESSHIRE)

CAERLAVEROCK [DAC, GD 131/N4/157]; GLENCAIRN, 1840 [J. Corrie, *Glencairn*, 1911, 50]; LOCHMABEN, 1838–40 [S.R.O., HR 624/1, 4 Feb, 1839; CH2/247/17, p. 216]; MOUSWALD [DAC, GD 131/N2/83–7]; TINWALD, 1837 [DAC, GD 131/N2/121–5].

DOMESTIC ARCHITECTURE

BLACKET HOUSE, EAGLESFIELD, MIDDLEBIE, D., Tudor [DAC, GD 131/B1/44–51].

CARDONESS, GATEHOUSE OF FLEET, K., Tudor, for Sir David Maxwell, Bart., 1828 [DAC, GD 131/N4/133, N14/95–100];

CASTLE DYKES, nr. DUMFRIES, for J. B. Hepburn; dem. [DAC, GD 131/N8].

CONHEATH, nr. DUMFRIES, for James Connell [DAC, GD 131/N8 and N1/199 (for farmyard)].

DALLAWOODIE, HOLYWOOD, D., for H. Simpson [DAC, GD 131/131/98, etc.].

DILDAWN or DALDAWN, KELTON, K., for Capt. A. McDougall (d. 1823/4); porch added probably in 1852 [DAC, GD 131/N13/16].

DUMFRIES, MOAT BRAE, 101 GEORGE STREET, 1823 [DAC, GD 131/N16].

FRIARS CARSE, DUNSCORE, D., additions for Dr. James Crichton [DAC, GD 131/N2/61].

GILLESBIE, BORELAND, D., greatly enlarged for William Rogerson, *c.*1843–4 [DAC, GD 130/2/51 and 131/B2/41].

GLENLAIR, KIRKPATRICK DURHAM, K., for J. Clerk Maxwell, 1830, castle style ('a border tower'); remodelled 1884 [DAC, GD 131/N1/69–75].

GRIBTON, HOLLYWOOD, D., for Francis Maxwell, soon after 1827 [DAC, GD 131/N29, etc.].

HANNAYFIELD (now 'Ladyfield West House'), nr. DUMFRIES, for John Hannay, *c.*1828 [J. C. Loudon, *Encyclopaedia of Cottage, Farm and Villa Architecture*, 1846, 850–1].

MAVISGROVE, nr. DUMFRIES, for — McMurdo [DAC, GD 131/N8].

MOFFAT, D., GLASSMOUNT (now 'Hunters Croft'), WELL STREET, 1850 [DAC, GD 131/N 18].

MOFFAT, D., GRANTON HOUSE, probably for Thomas Jardine, *c.*1840 [DAC, GD 131/N2/15–33].

MOFFAT, D., SIDMOUNT COTTAGE, SIDMOUNT AVENUE, for — Maxwell, 1832 [DAC, GD 131/N4/95–99].

MOUNT ANNAN COTTAGE, ANNAN, D., for Capt. Alexander Dirom [DAC, GD 131/N4/111–115].

MUNCHES, DALBEATTIE, K., for — Maxwell [DAC, GD 131/N2/159–65].

MURRAYTHWAITE, DALTON, D., for — Murray

[DAC, GD 131/N32/2–6].

ORCHARDTON, AUCHENCAIRN, K., for Col. Maxwell [DAC, GD 131/N1/73 and 195].

UNDERWOOD HOUSE, DRYFESDALE, nr. LOCKERBIE, D., for — Johnstone, 1825, Tudor Gothic [DAC, GD 131/N3/51–55].

YOUNGFIELD (later Lincluden House), DUMFRIES, for – Young, Gothic; destroyed by fire 1875 and rebuilt by D. Bryce; dem. *c.*1945 [DAC, GD 131/N8/13, 15–31].

NEWBOROUGH, LORD, *see* WYNN, THOMAS.

NEWCOURT, RICHARD (–1679), was a gentleman with a small estate at Somerton in Somerset. He is best known as a surveyor and topographical draughtsman. For his friend Sir William Dugdale he made a number of drawings of cathedrals, etc., in the south-west of England to illustrate the *Monasticon Anglicanum* (1655–73). These were subsequently reused by Daniel King in his *Cathedrall and Conventuall Churches of England and Wales orthographically delineated* (1656, 2nd ed. 1672). In 1658 Newcourt published an important map of London which was engraved by Faithorne, and after the Great Fire he was the author of an ambitious but impracticable plan for rebuilding the city on a rectilinear grid of streets with fifty-five arcaded piazzas each containing a parish church in the centre [Guildhall Library, MS. 3441]. In the accompanying text he refers to a design he had made for rebuilding Whitehall Palace. The only other evidence of Newcourt's activity as an architect so far noted is a design by him for a Gothic chapel, dated 29 July 1670, which survives among the Longleat archives (Box xxx, vol. lxxvii, f. 19).

Newcourt died in 1679 and was buried at Somerton. He was the father of Richard Newcourt (d. 1716), registrar of the diocese of London and author of *Repertorium Ecclesiasticum Parochiale Londinense* (1708–10).

[*D.N.B.*; T. F. Reddaway in *Town Planning Review* xviii, 1939, 155 *et seq.*; will, P.C.C. 89 KING.]

NEWDIGATE, Sir ROGER (1719–1806), was a wealthy landowner whose architectural activities at Arbury Hall, Warwicks., Harefield Church, Middlesex, and elsewhere, give him a place of some importance in the history of the Gothic Revival. The 7th son of Sir Richard Newdigate, 3rd Bart., he was educated at Westminster School and University College, Oxford, and made the Grand Tour in 1738–40. He succeeded his brother as 5th Bart. in 1734, and sat in the House of Commons from 1742 to 1747 as M.P. for Middlesex and from 1751 to 1780 as M.P. for Oxford University. He visited Italy again in 1774–5 after the death of his first wife.

Sir Roger was a man of taste who is more important as a patron than as an architectural designer in his own right. At Arbury, Sanderson Miller, the Hiornes, Henry Keene and Henry Couchman successively helped him to make his family seat the Strawberry Hill of the Midlands, and elsewhere (e.g. at University College, Oxford, and Harefield Church) Henry Keene was much employed by him or through his influence. Nevertheless, he was himself a sufficiently competent draughtsman to make a drawing of the Roman arch at Aosta which served as the basis for an engraving by Piranesi (1774), and besides many preliminary drawings for Arbury he made designs in the 1740s for a new Palladian house at Copt Hall in Essex for his brother-in-law John Conyers. These were not carried out, and Arbury remains the principal monument to Newdigate's architectural enthusiasm.[1] At Oxford he is remembered by the Newdigate Prize for Poetry which he endowed and by the two candelabra constructed by Piranesi from antique fragments which he presented to the University in 1776.

[*D.N.B.*; L. B. Namier & J. Brooke, *The House of Commons 1754–1790*, 1964, 196–9; A. C. Wood, 'The Diaries of Sir Roger Newdigate', *Trans. Birmingham Arch. Soc.* lxxviii, 1962; C. Hussey, *English Country Houses: Mid Georgian*, 1956; Michael McCarthy, 'Sir Roger Newdigate and Piranesi', *Burlington Mag.*, July 1962, 466–72; Michael McCarthy, 'Sir Roger Newdigate: Drawings for Copt Hall, Essex and Arbury Hall, Warwickshire', *Arch. Hist.* xvi, 1973; Michael McCarthy, 'Sir Roger Newdigate: some Piranesian Drawings', *Burlington Mag.*, Oct. 1978, 671–2.]

NEWEY, ISAAC (*c.*1810–1861), practised at Birmingham. For a time he appears to have been in partnership with F. W. Fiddian, for in 1834 Messrs. Fiddian & Newey exhibited at the Birmingham Society of Artists a 'villa erecting at Edgbaston' and in 1835 a 'villa now erecting in Wellington Road for James Kimberley, Esq.' The WORCESTERSHIRE NATURAL HISTORY SOCIETY'S MUSEUM (dem.) in FOREGATE STREET, WORCESTER, was erected

[1] Mr. Keith Goodway informs me that among the Sneyd MSS. at Keele University (S. 1458) there is evidence that Sir Roger Newdigate made designs for Gothick alterations to Keele Hall, Staffs., that were carried out by William Baker, either in 1757–9 (see p. 95) or later.

to their joint design in 1835 [drawing in Commandery Museum, Worcester, *ex* inf. Mr. Alan Brooks]. Thereafter, however, they exhibited separately. In 1838 Newey designed ST. MICHAEL'S CHURCH, BARTLEY GREEN, nr. BIRMINGHAM, a simple Gothic building consecrated in 1840 [I.C.B.S.]. He died on 16 February 1861, aged 51 [*Aris's Birmingham Gazette*, 23 Feb. 1861]. Christopher Isaac Newey, who was in practice in Birmingham in 1868, was no doubt his son.

NEWHAM, WILLIAM (*c*.1776–1858), was the son of Samuel Newham (1749–1816), a Methodist builder-architect of King's Lynn who built the WESLEYAN CHAPEL, TOWER STREET, KING'S LYNN, in 1813 [H. J. Hillen, *History of King's Lynn* ii, 1907, 549]. He became a pupil of James Wyatt, from whose office he exhibited two architectural designs at the Royal Academy in 1796–7. An advertisement in the *Norwich Mercury* for 14 July 1798 shows that he joined his father's business in that year. Thereafter he practised as an architect and builder in King's Lynn until his death on 28 January 1858, in his 83rd year [*Lynn Advertiser*, 30 Jan. 1858]. He was succeeded by his son William Newham, junior. His few recorded works include THE THEATRE ROYAL, KING'S LYNN, 1815, dem. *c*.1910/20 [J. Burley, *Playhouses . . . of East Anglia*, 1928, 128], improvements to the ASSEMBLY ROOMS at SWAFFHAM, NORFOLK, 1827 [*Norfolk Chronicle* 17 Nov. 1827], the enlargement of STOKE FERRY CHURCH, NORFOLK, in 1832–3 [I.C.B.S.], and re-roofing and repairing RUNCTON HOLME CHURCH, NORFOLK, in 1841–2 [I.C.B.S.]. [information from Dr. John Stable].

NEWMAN, JOHN (1786–1859), was born in London and baptized in St. Sepulchre's Church on 8 July 1786. His father, John Newman, was a wholesale dealer in leather in Skinner Street, Snow Hill, and a common councillor of the ward of Farringdon Without. His grandfather was Sheriff of London in 1789–90.

Nothing is known of Newman's architectural training, but he evidently visited Italy, for in 1807 he exhibited at the Royal Academy a drawing of the remains of the Temple of Jupiter Tonans in Rome. He was employed under Sir Robert Smirke in the erection of Covent Garden Theatre in 1809, and at the General Post Office in 1823–9. Early in life he obtained an appointment in the office of the Bridge House estates, and eventually succeeded to the clerkship, which he held for more than thirty years. From about 1815 he was one of the surveyors to the Commission of Sewers for Surrey and Kent, and in conjunction with his colleagues (Joseph Gwilt and Edward I'Anson) published a *Report relating to the Sewage, etc.*, in 1843. He held several other surveyorships, including that to the commissioners of pavements and improvements for the west division of Southwark, and to Earl Somers's estate at Somers Town, St. Pancras. He exhibited at the Royal Academy between 1807 and 1838. As an architect he was responsible for one outstanding building, the ambitious and cleverly designed Catholic Church in Moorfields. Here, for the first time in nineteenth-century London, the Mass was given a dramatic setting comparable to that in continental churches. At the east end concealed lighting, contrived in a manner which Newman had observed in France, illuminated a panorama of Calvary painted by Agostino Aglio and viewed through a screen of marble columns.

In the course of his professional work Newman was able to form a valuable collection of antiquities found in London and the neighbourhood. Some bronzes in his possession from the bed of the Thames were described by C. Roach Smith in a paper read to the Society of Antiquaries in June 1837 (*Archaeologia* xxviii). His antiquities were sold by auction at Sotheby's in 1848. Among them was the bronze head of Hadrian now in the British Museum. He was a Fellow of the Society of Antiquaries from 1830 to 1849, and an original Fellow of the Institute of British Architects, whose travelling fund he originated. He retired in 1851, and died at the home of his son-in-law, Dr. Alexander Spiers, at Passy, nr. Paris, on 3 January 1859, aged 72. He had married in 1819 a daughter of the Revd. B. Middleton, Sub-Dean of Chichester, and left a son, Arthur Shean Newman (1828–73), who succeeded to some of his father's appointments, and in 1858 entered into partnership with Arthur Billing [*A.P.S.D.*; *D.N.B.*].

LONDON, ST. MARY'S R. C. CHURCH, BLOMFIELD STREET, MOORFIELDS, 1817–20; dem. 1899 [Britton & Pugin, *Public Buildings of London* ii, 1828, 5–10].

SOUTHWARK, terrace of houses in DUKE (now UNION) STREET, with wharves and warehouses at the back, facing the river, erected when the line for the new London Bridge was settled in 1824 [*A.P.S.D.*].

ISLINGTON, THE PROPRIETARY SCHOOL, BARNSBURY STREET, 1830, 'Elizabethan' [*A.P.S.D.*].

SOUTHWARK, SCHOOL FOR THE INDIGENT BLIND, ST. GEORGE'S FIELDS, 1834–8, Tudor Gothic; dem. 1901 [*Civil Engineer and*

Architect's Jnl. i, 1838, 207–12; *Companion to the Almanac*, 1836, 220–1].

SOUTHWARK, ST. OLAVE'S GIRLS' SCHOOL, MAZE POND, 1839–40; dem. [plans, elevations, and sections in C. Davy, *Architectural Precedents*, 1841].

NEWMAN, W— S—, exhibited at the Royal Academy in 1792, 1794 and 1798, giving his address in 1792 as 'At Mr. Smith's, Knightsbridge'. In 1794 he showed a 'Design for the floor cloth manufactory building at Knightsbridge'. He does not appear to have been the same person as William Newman, who was admitted to the Royal Academy Schools in 1778 at the age of 22 and won the Silver Medal in 1780.

NEWNHAM, WILLIAM HENRY (*c.*1802–1843), was a pupil or assistant of Joseph Walker (*q.v.*), from whose office at 21 Earl Street, Blackfriars, he exhibited at the Royal Academy in 1822. He subsequently visited Egypt, returning in August 1829, and in 1830 exhibited at the Royal Academy an 'Interior View of a tomb near the Pyramids of Saccara the scite of ancient Memphis, taken on the spot in 1828'. In association with G. B. Webb he designed the UNION BANK, ARGYLE PLACE, REGENT STREET, LONDON, 1840; dem. [*Civil Engineer & Architect's Jnl.* iii, 1840, 183]. He died in Sussex on 2 July 1843, aged 41 [*Gent's Mag.* 1843 (ii), 217; will, P.R.O., PROB. 11/1983, f. 504].

NEWTON, WILLIAM (1730–1798), christened at St. Andrew's Church, Newcastle, on 20 December 1730, was the son of Robert Newton, a shipwright who turned his attention to architecture and practised as a builder-architect in Newcastle-upon-Tyne. In 1762 Robert and William Newton were both concerned in repairs and alterations to Simonburn Church, Northumberland, whose aisles were rebuilt under their direction in the following year [*History of Northumberland* xv, 179]. Newton spent the whole of his life in Newcastle and had a considerable local practice. He was a competent but conventional Georgian architect whose work is sometimes elegant, always pleasing, but never remarkable. In 1763 he married Dorothy Bell of Gateshead, by whom he had six sons and six daughters. In 1769 he obtained a lease of land from the Corporation upon which he built Charlotte Square, the first development of its kind in the city. He occupied one of the houses himself for the next twenty years. He died at Newcastle on 29 April 1798, aged 68, and was buried in St. Andrew's Church. His tombstone is now covered by the organ. Some drawings by Newton for a garden house, etc., are preserved in a portfolio at Wallington Hall, Northumberland. [*Proceedings of the Society of Antiquaries of Newcastle-on-Tyne*, 3rd ser. vi, 1913–14, 28–9; Terence Scott, *William Newton, Architect and Builder*, 1971, unpublished dissertation, Architecture Seminar Library, Newcastle University.]

PUBLIC BUILDINGS IN NEWCASTLE-UPON-TYNE AND VICINITY

ST. ANNE'S CHAPEL, CITY ROAD, 1764–8 [J. Dugdale, *The British Traveller* iii, 1819, 721] (B. Allsopp, *Historic Architecture of Newcastle*, 1967, 36–7].

THE LUNATIC ASYLUM, 1765–7; reconstructed by J. Dobson 1824; dem. *c.*1866 [E. Mackenzie, *Account of Newcastle* ii, 1827, 525].

CHARLOTTE SQUARE, *c.*1770 [*Proc. Soc. Antiq. Newcastle-on-Tyne*, 3rd ser. vi, 1913–14, 28].

THE ASSEMBLY ROOMS, WESTGATE, 1774–6 [E. Mackenzie, *Account of Newcastle* i, 1827, 231] (B. Allsopp, *Historic Architecture of Newcastle*, 1967, 38–9).

attributed: ST. ANDREW'S CHURCH, refitting of interior, *c.*1780 [H. L. Honeyman, 'The Church of St. Andrew, Newcastle', *Archaeologia Æliana*, 4th ser. xix, 1941].

THE ROYAL FREE GRAMMAR SCHOOL, added the porch, 1782; dem. [E. Mackenzie, *Account of Newcastle* ii, 1827, 443].

ST. NICHOLAS CHURCH, refitted interior in conjunction with David Stephenson, 1783–5 [M. A. Richardson, *The Local Historian's Table Book* ii, 1842, 284–8].

LONGBENTON CHURCH, NORTHUMB., rebuilt nave and W. tower, 1790–1, Gothic [G. W. D. Briggs in *Archaeologia Aeliana*, 5th ser. 13, 1985, 217].

TRINITY HOUSE, internal alterations, 1791 [G. McCombie, 'The Buildings of Trinity House, Newcastle', *Archaeologia Aeliana*, 5th ser. 13, 1985, 217].

THE EXCHANGE AND GUILDHALL, rebuilt N. front, 1795–6, in collaboration with David Stephenson [E. Mackenzie, *Account of Newcastle* i, 1827, 216].

COUNTRY HOUSES, ETC.

CASTLE EDEN, CO. DURHAM, for Rowland Burdon, *c.*1760 [*Proc. Soc. Antiq. Newcastle-on-Tyne*, 3rd ser. vi, 1913–14, 28; E. Mackenzie & C. Ross, *County Palatine of Durham* i, 1834, 403].

FENHAM HALL, NORTHUMBERLAND, addition of wings and new front for William Ord, *c.*1770 [E. Mackenzie, *History of Northumberland* ii, 1825, 410].

HEATON HALL, NORTHUMBERLAND, remodelled for Sir Matthew Ridley, Bart., *c.*1770–80; dem. *c.*1932 [E. Mackenzie, *History of Northumberland* ii, 1825, 478].

KIELDER CASTLE, NORTHUMBERLAND, for the 1st Duke of Northumberland and Earl Percy, 1772–5, Gothic [memorandum in Kielder Castle Game Book in Alnwick Castle Library, shelf 49/3] (Watts's *Views of Seats*, pl. 58, 1783).

BACKWORTH HALL, NORTHUMBERLAND, for R. W. Grey, 1778–80 [estimate, etc., in Northumberland Record Office, ZBU B7; *Proc. Soc. Antiq. Newcastle-on-Tyne*, 3rd ser. vi, 1913–14, 28].

HOWICK HALL, NORTHUMBERLAND, for Sir Henry Grey, Bart., 1781–2; north front rebuilt 1808–9 to designs of George Wyatt; remodelled internally 1928 after a fire [M. A. Richardson, *The Local Historian's Table Book* ii, 1842, 269] (F. O. Morris, *Views of Seats* vi, 1880, 63).

WHITFIELD HALL, NORTHUMBERLAND, for William Ord of Fenham, 1785; storey added 1856 [J. Hodgson, *History of Northumberland*, part ii, vol. iii, 1840, 105].

CAPHEATON HALL, NORTHUMBERLAND, rebuilt north front for Sir John Swinburne, Bart., 1789–90 [Northumberland Record Office, Capheaton papers ZSw 452] (*C. Life*, 12 Aug. 1965).

DISSINGTON HALL, NORTHUMBERLAND, for Edward Collingwood, *c.*1795–7 [signed drawings dated 1794 on sale in London 1977, now at Dissington; rainwater-head dated 1797].

HESLEYSIDE, NORTHUMBERLAND, rebuilt east front for William Charlton, 1796–1800 [*History of Northumberland* xv, 253] (*C. Life*, 18 May 1989).

HEXHAM ABBEY HOUSE, NORTHUMBERLAND, work for Col. Beaumont, interrupted by illness, 1797; altered by J. Dobson after fire in 1818 [Northumberland Record Office, ZBL 226/2].

LEMMINGTON HALL, NORTHUMBERLAND, altered for Nicholas Fenwick (?), date uncertain; restored 1913 after being in ruins, now a convent [*Proc. Soc. Antiq. Newcastle-on-Tyne*, 3rd ser. vi, 1913–14, 29].

ALNWICK, NORTHUMBERLAND, house at foot of Clayport occupied successively by families of Farquhar, Dawson and Drysdale, date uncertain [*Proc. Soc. Antiq. Newcastle-on-Tyne*, 3rd ser. vi, 1913–14, 29].

NEWTON, WILLIAM (1735–1790), born on 27 October 1735, was the eldest son of James Newton, a cabinet-maker of Holborn, who claimed to be related to Sir Isaac Newton. His mother was the daughter of a clergyman who was mathematical master at Christ's Hospital. William was admitted to Christ's Hospital in November 1743, and on leaving the school in December 1750 was apprenticed to the architect William Jones (*q.v.*). He was afterwards in the London office of Matthew Brettingham. He began to exhibit at the Society of Artists in 1760, and was practising on his own by 1764. He also exhibited at the Free Society of Artists in 1761 and 1783, and at the Royal Academy in 1776. In 1766 he visited Rome, returning to England early in the following year. Newton's drawings in the R.I.B.A. Collection indicate a fairly extensive practice in and around London, but major commissions eluded him. In 1769 he competed unsuccessfully for the Royal Exchange at Dublin, in 1774 for the church of St. Alphege, London Wall, and in 1775 for that of St. Mary, Battersea. From time to time he appears to have acted as 'ghost' to William Jupp the elder, for whom he designed the Ballroom and Eating-Room of the London Tavern (1768), and probably also the entrance to Carpenters' Hall (1779), for which there is a design among his drawings. His drawings suggest that he was trained in the Palladian tradition, but developed a neo-classical style for which his visit to Rome was no doubt a preparation. For Battersea Church he produced a competent neo-classical design in 1775, and his interiors were decorated in an elegant 'antique' style comparable to that of the Adam brothers.

In 1771 Newton published the earliest English translation of the first five books of Vitruvius, under the title *The Architecture of M. Vitruvius Pollio: translated from the original Latin by W. Newton, Architect.* He was also the author of *Commentaires sur Vitruve*, written in French but published in London in 1780, and helped to edit and complete the second volume of Stuart's *Antiquities of Athens*, which, though dated 1787, was not published until after its author's death in 1788. After Newton's death a complete edition of Vitruvius, including a translation of the remaining five books, was published (1791) by his brother and executor James Newton 'from a correct manuscript prepared by himself'.

In September 1782 Newton succeeded Robert Mylne as Clerk of the Works at Greenwich Hospital. Mylne had been dismissed by the Governors after a disagreement with their Surveyor, James Stuart, who was then engaged in rebuilding the Chapel after its destruction by fire in 1779. Newton had already been acting as Stuart's assistant since the previous February, and as Clerk of the

Works he was closely involved in the design as well as the execution of the Chapel, whose rebuilding was not completed until 1790. When Stuart died in February 1788, Newton not unnaturally hoped to succeed him as Surveyor, but was passed over in favour of Sir Robert Taylor. The latter died within a year, but Newton's claims were again set aside by the appointment of John Yenn. Newton now thought of resigning, 'as it will be displeasing to me to be placed under a younger man and perhaps I may say less eminent in the profession than myself'. In the event he did not do so, but endeavoured to obtain from the Governors an admission that, as the effective architect of their Chapel, he was entitled to professional remuneration in addition to his salary as Clerk of the Works. Whatever truth there may have been in Newton's claim, the Governors did not admit that it involved them in any additional financial obligation towards him.

In February 1790, Newton, whose health was failing through overwork, obtained three months' leave of absence from Greenwich in order to take a course of sea-bathing. He died at Sidford, nr. Sidmouth, on 6 July 1790. A portrait, engraved by James Newton after R. Smirke, R.A., is given in the 1791 edition of his *Vitruvius*, and there is a self-portrait (*aetat.* 26) in the Print Room of the British Museum. A collection of over one hundred drawings by Newton was presented to the R.I.B.A. in 1891, together with some of his papers.

[Wyatt Papworth, 'W. Newton and the Chapel of Greenwich Hospital', *R.I.B.A. Jnl.* 1891, 417–20; *D.N.B.*; Lesley Lewis, 'The Architects of the Chapel at Greenwich Hospital', *Art Bulletin* xxix, 1947; *R.I.B.A. Drawings Catalogue: L–N*, 128–44; Eileen Harris, *British Architectural Books and Writers 1556–1785*, 1990, 464–66.]

DURDANS, nr. EPSOM, SURREY, rebuilt for Charles Dalbiac, 1764–8; altered by George Devey 1878 and recently by Claude Phillimore. [A tablet over the entrance is inscribed 'Chas. Dalbiac Rest./1764/Wm. Newton Ar^t.' and there are drawings in the R.I.B.A. Collection dated 1764 and 1768].

LONDON, THE LONDON TAVERN, BISHOPSGATE STREET WITHIN, assisted William Jupp, senior, in designing, 1765–8; dem. 1876 [drawings in R.I.B.A. Coll.].

HIGHAMS, WOODFORD GREEN, WALTHAMSTOW, ESSEX (now Woodford County High School for Girls), for Anthony Bacon, 1768 [drawings in R.I.B.A. Coll.].

HUNGERFORD PARK, BERKS., for Charles Dalbiac, 1768; altered 1934, dem. [drawings in R.I.B.A. Coll.].

ISLEWORTH, MIDDLESEX, house at SMALLBERRY GREEN for Lewis Chauvett, 1769; dem. 1795 [drawings in R.I.B.A. Coll.; D. Lysons, *Environs of London* ii (2), 1811, 457].

LONDON, QUEEN SQUARE, BLOOMSBURY, rebuilt house for —Kingston, 1779 [R.I.B.A., MS. New 1/9/5].

Unidentified house exhibited at R.A. in 1780 as 'now building in Berkshire'.

GREENWICH HOSPITAL, assisted James Stuart in rebuilding the CHAPEL, 1782–88, and completed the building after Stuart's death in 1788 [Lesley Lewis, 'The Architects of the Chapel at Greenwich Hospital', *Art Bulletin* xxix, 1947, and 'Greece and Rome at Greenwich', *Arch. Rev.* cix, 1951, 17–24].

GREENWICH HOSPITAL, THE BOYS' SCHOOL, KING STREET, 1782–3; incorporated in Nurses' Home 1929 [*R.I.B.A. Drawings Catalogue: L–N*, 131–2].

GREENWICH, MARKET HOUSE, *c.*1786–9; dem. [R.I.B.A., MS. New/1/3/1].

The list above comprises all the buildings certainly known to have been built to Newton's designs. In addition the drawings in the R.I.B.A. Collection include designs by Newton for the following buildings, some of which may have been executed, others not: a house for Mr. Fellows, 1763; a house for Mr. Lewis at CHESHUNT, HERTS., 1765; a house at EWELL, SURREY, for Philip Rowden, the builder of BOURNE or GARBRAND HALL, EWELL, *c.*1765, dem. 1962; a house at SPITALFIELDS for Mr. Ouvry, 1765; a house 'building in the country' for a Mr. Vilion, 1768; an addition to a house for Mr. Nouailles, 1768; a house at WALTHAMSTOW, ESSEX, for Mr. Fullager (*i.e.* Fulger), 1769; a villa at TWICKENHAM for Daniel Giles, the builder of the house known as SPENCER GROVE or TWICKENHAM MEADOWS, *c.*1775; a villa at LITTLE MARLOW, BUCKS., for Sir John Borlase Warren; a house in Yorkshire for the Lascelles family; a building for the Society of Dilettanti, probably *c.*1764; an Assembly Room at SNOW HILL, HOLBORN, for Mr. Warford, 1767; THE ORPHAN SCHOOL, CITY ROAD, ISLINGTON, 1772 (probably built to Newton's designs, but dem.); ST. ALPHEGE CHURCH, LONDON WALL, 1774–5 (rejected); and ST. MARY'S CHURCH, BATTERSEA, 1775 (rejected).

Drawings by Newton for a villa on LUNDY ISLAND for Sir John Borlase Warren, made *c.*1775, were in 1973 in the custody of the Curator of the Lundy Museum. The designs which he submitted for the Dublin Royal Exchange competition in 1769 are in the Murray Collection at the National Library of Ireland

(Portfolio I). Another drawing for the Exchange is in the Print Room of the British Museum, together with a section through the east end of Newton's design for Battersea Church.

NICHOL, JOHN (*c.*1781–1846) of Wellesbourne, 'Civil Engineer', held the office of Surveyor of Bridges to the County of Warwick. He designed bridges at WHITLEY, nr. COVENTRY, over the R. Avon, 1831, at NUNEATON, over the Hinch Brook, 1835, and at BARSTON, over the R. Thame, 1838 [Warwickshire County Records, Class 24, No. 28, *passim*]. COMBROKE CHURCH, WARWICKS., was rebuilt to his designs in 1831; it was again rebuilt 1866–7 [I.C.B.S.]. He died at Wellesbourne in October 1846, aged 65 [Parish Register].

NICHOLLS, THOMAS, was a pupil of W. R. Laxton (*q.v.*), from whose office in Tottenham Court Road he exhibited at the Royal Academy in 1810 and 1811. He subsequently practised as an architect and surveyor from various London addresses. The Thomas Nicholls who exhibited architectural designs at the Royal Academy in 1832 and 1836 and at the Society of British Artists in the latter year was probably his son, for in the British Artists' Catalogue he appears as 'Thomas Nicholls, junior'.

NICHOLSON, GEORGE (–1793), a mason by trade, was surveyor to the Dean and Chapter of Durham until his death in 1793, when he was succeeded by William Morpeth. In 1772–7, with some advice from Robert Mylne, he designed and built the PREBENDS' BRIDGE over the R. Wear for the Dean and Chapter. From about 1773 onwards he carried out repairs to DURHAM CATHEDRAL which included an unfortunate attempt to restore the west and north fronts by paring off the decayed surface of the stone. The present parapets of the two western towers, the upper parts of the north transept and the twin turrets of the north face of the Chapel of the Nine Altars were his work, and he also rebuilt the north porch. His unexecuted design for rebuilding the church of St. Mary the Less, Durham, is described and illustrated by C. W. Gibby in *Transactions of the Architectural and Archaeological Society of Durham and Northumberland* x (iii), 1950. [Durham Cathedral Chapter Act Books; W. Hutchison, *History of the County Palatine of Durham* ii, 1787, 226, 317; correspondence in *R.I.B.A. Jnl.*, Oct., Nov. 1955, Jan., March 1956.]

NICHOLSON, MICHAEL ANGELO (*c.*1796–1841), was the son of Peter Nicholson (*q.v.*), by his first wife. He studied architectural drawing at the school of Richard Brown (*q.v.*), and then became a pupil of John Foulston (*q.v.*). He was admitted to the Royal Academy Schools in 1814 at the age of 18, and exhibited occasionally at the Academy between 1812 and 1828. He engraved plates for his father's works, and collaborated with him in the publication of *The Practical Cabinet Maker*, 1826. He drew the frontispiece for Richard Elsam's *Practical Builder's Perpetual Price Book*, 1825, and lithographed the plates for Inwood's *Erechtheion*, 1826. His own publications were: *The Carpenter and Joiner's Companion*, 1826; *The Five Orders, Geometrical and in Perspective* 1834; and *The Carpenter's and Joiner's New Practical Work on Hand-Railing*, 1836. He kept a school for architectural drawing in Melton Place, Euston Square, and rarely, if ever, practised as an architect. He claimed some responsibility for CARSTAIRS HOUSE, LANARKSHIRE, for he exhibited a view of it at the Royal Academy in 1823, and a plan and elevation of the house, 'Designed by M. A. Nicholson, Architect', appear in his father's *Practical Builder.*

Nicholson died on 11 November 1841, leaving two daughters, one of whom married Alexander ('Greek') Thomson of Glasgow, and the other Thomson's partner John Baird. [*A.P.S.D.*; *D.N.D.*; R. McFadzean, *Alexander Thomson*, 1979, 17–18.]

NICHOLSON, PETER (1765–1844), born on 20 July 1765, at Prestonkirk, East Lothian, was the son of a stonemason. Disliking his father's trade, he was apprenticed to a cabinet-maker at Linton, Haddingtonshire. On the conclusion of his apprenticeship, he worked as a journeyman in Edinburgh, and at the age of 23 went to London, where he taught in an evening school for mechanics as well as pursuing his craft. In this way he acquired sufficient capital to finance his first publication, *The New Carpenter's Guide*, 1792, for which he engraved his own plates. In it he described an original method of constructing groins and niches of complex forms. This was followed by *The Principles of Architecture*, 1795–8, 2nd ed. 1809, and *The Carpenter's and Joiner's Assistant*, 1797. In 1800 he returned to Scotland and went to Glasgow, where he practised as an architect until 1808. During this period he designed several buildings listed below, and laid out the town of Ardrossan in Ayrshire for the 12th Earl of Eglinton. The harbour at Ardrossan was constructed under the direction of Thomas

Telford, whose recommendation is said to have been instrumental in obtaining for Nicholson the post of Surveyor to the County of Cumberland in 1808 on the death of John Chisholme. In this capacity Nicholson supervised the building of the new Courts of Justice at Carlisle to Telford's designs until 1810, when he returned to London, leaving the courts to be completed by Sir Robert Smirke.

In 1812–19 Nicholson produced *The Architectural Dictionary*, 2 vols., which contains plates of many of his executed works. A second edition, largely rewritten, was published by Lomax & Gunyon in 1852–4. In 1827 he began the publication of a work entitled *The School of Architecture and Engineering*, intended to have been completed in twelve numbers, but abandoned after the fifth number owing to the bankruptcy of the publishers. Nicholson lost heavily, and probably for this reason went in 1829 to live at Morpeth on a small property left him by a relative. In 1832 he moved to Newcastle-upon-Tyne, where he opened a school. It does not appear to have been a financial success, for in July 1834 he was presented with £320 by public subscription. In the following year he was elected president of the Newcastle Society for the Promotion of the Fine Arts, and received many other honours locally. During his last years he was supported by the generosity of Thomas Jamieson of Newton, Northumberland. He died at Carlisle on 18 June 1844, and was buried in the Christ Church graveyard. A monument to his memory, curiously designed by R. W. Billings in the form of two interpenetrating obelisks, was erected in the Carlisle Cemetery in 1856 (see illustration in the Edinburgh *Building Chronicle* i, 1855, 175). His portrait is given in several of his own works, e.g. the *Builder and Workman's New Director* and the *Guide to Railway Masonry* (edition of 1846). He was twice married, and had two sons and a daughter. His elder son, Michael Angelo (*q.v.*), shared his father's interests and engraved the plates for some of his books.

Nicholson was one of the leading intellects behind nineteenth-century building technology. He used his great ability as a mathematician to simplify many old formulae used by architectural draughtsmen as well as to devise new ones. His improvements in the construction of hand-railing were recognized by the award of the Gold Medal of the Society of Arts in 1814, and although he never derived financial advantage from his inventions, his contribution to the mechanics of building was very considerable. He was the first author to write on the construction of hinges and the hanging of doors, and was also the first to notice that Grecian mouldings were conic sections. His invention of the 'centrolinead', an instrument for drawing lines which are required to converge towards an inaccessible point, brought him a gift of £20 from the Society of Arts in 1814, and a silver medal for its improvement later in the same year.

His principal publications, apart from those already mentioned, were: *The Student's Instructor in drawing and working the Five Orders of Architecture*, 1795; *Mechanical Exercises, or the Elements and Practice of Carpentry, Joinery, etc.*, 1811; *A Treatise on Practical Perspective*, 1815; *An Introduction to the Methods of Increments*, 1817; *Essays on the Combinatorial Analysis*, 1818; *The Rudiments of Algebra*, 1819; *Essay on Involution and Evolution*, 1820; *A Treatise on the Construction of Staircases and Handrails*, 1820; *Analytical and Arithmetical Essays*, 1820; *Popular Course of Pure and Mixed Mathematics*, 1822; *The Rudiments of Practical Perspective*, 1822; *The New Practical Builder and Workman's Companion*, 1823; *The Builder and Workman's New Director*, 1824; *The Carpenter and Builder's Complete Measurer*, 1827; *Popular and Practical Treatise on Masonry and Stone-Cutting*, 1827; *Practical Masonry, Bricklaying, and Plastering*, 1830; *A Treatise on Dialling*, Newcastle 1833; *A Treatise on Projection, with a Complete System of Isometrical Drawing*, Newcastle 1837; *The Guide to Railway Masonry, containing a Complete Treatise on the Oblique Arch*, Newcastle 1839; *The Carpenter, Joiner, and Builder's Companion*, 1846; *Carpentry*, ed. Ashpitel, 1849; *Carpentry, Joining and Building*, 1851; with John Rowbotham Nicholson, published *A Practical System of Algebra*, 1824; and with his son, Michael Angelo Nicholson, *The Practical Cabinet Maker, Upholsterer, and Complete Decorator*, 1826. Further editions of nearly all Nicholson's books were published, only the first edition being listed above in each case.

[*A.P.S.D.*; *D.N.B.*; *Architectural Mag.* i, 1834, 140–1; *Civil Engineer and Architect's Jnl.*, iii, 1840, 152–3, vii, 1844, 425–7; memoir in *Builder and Workman's New Director* (reprinted in *Mechanic's Magazine*, 1825); *Builder* iv, 1846, 514, vii, 1849, 615–16.]

GLASGOW, CARLTON PLACE, LAURIESTON, for James Laurie, 1802–18 [*Architectural Dictionary* ii, 1819, 912] (*Architects' Jnl.* 27 Nov. 1991, 40–3).

GLASGOW, timber foot-bridge over R. Clyde, 1803; dem. *c.*1829 [*A.P.S.D.*].

GLASGOW, timber bridge over R. Clyde, *c.*1805; dem. [*A.P.S.D.*].

CRUXTON, nr. GLASGOW, cottage for Mr. Buchanan, *c.*1805 [*Architectural Dictionary* i, 1819, 102–3].

GLASGOW, house for Mr. Grey, jeweller, *c.*1805 [*Architectural Dictionary* i, 1819, 102–3].

PAISLEY, RENFREWSHIRE, Coffee House (? executed), *c.*1805 [*Architectural Dictionary* i, 1819, 102–3].

PARTICK, LANARKSHIRE, YORKHILL HOUSE for Fulton Alexander, 1806; dem. [*Architectural Dictionary* i, 1819, 102–3; frontispiece to *Practical Builder*, 1825; two drawings in N.M.R.S.]

CASTLETOWN HOUSE, ROCKLIFFE, CUMBERLAND, for Robert Mounsey, 1809–11, in conjunction with William Reid, *q.v.* (*C. Life*, 7 Sept. 1989).

HOUGHTON HOUSE, HOUGHTON, CUMBERLAND, for William Hodgson, Clerk of the Peace, *c.*1810 [*Architectural Dictionary* ii, 1819, 908].

GLASGOW, OLD COLLEGE, THE HAMILTON BUILDING, executed 1811–13 to a modified design by John Brash, *q.v.*

CORBY CASTLE, CUMBERLAND, enlarged and remodelled for Henry Howard, who was to some extent his own architect, 1812–14 [*Architectural Dictionary* i, 1819, 102–3; Catherine Howard, *Reminiscences for my Children*, privately printed 1836] (*C. Life*, 7–14 Jan. 1954).

CLIVEDEN, BUCKS., Tea Room at the Spring, 1813 [*Architectural Dictionary* ii, 1819, 913]. In 1816 Nicholson published an engraved design for rebuilding Cliveden House for the Countess of Orkney in the castellated style.

TAPLOW, BUCKS., house for a country baker [*Architectural Dictionary* i, 1819, 102–3].

NISBET, DAVID (1790–1853), is described as 'Architect' on his monument in the Calton Old Burial Ground in Edinburgh. He died on 4 October 1853 and his testament is in S.R.O., SC 70/1/83, 440. He figures in the Edinburgh directories from 1811/12 onwards as 'builder' or 'architect'.

NISBET, JAMES (–1781), of Kelso, was a mason by trade. He may have been the James, son of James Nisbet, who was born at Kelso on 2 December 1746 [Register in New Register House, Edinburgh], and his recent death is mentioned in the Wedderburn papers in November 1781 [S.R.O., GD 267/1/3]. His first recorded work appears to be EDNAM HOUSE, KELSO, built for James Dickson in 1761, and described in the *New Statistical Account of Scotland* iii, 1845, 320, as 'one of the most elegant private mansions that Nisbet ever designed' (for description see R.C.A.M., *Roxburghshire*, 248–9, where Nisbet is wrongly stated to have been of Berners Street, London).

From 1771 onwards Nisbet was at work remodelling FORD CASTLE, NORTHUMBERLAND, for Sir John Hussey Delaval, afterwards 1st Lord Delaval, in the Gothick style [Northumberland Record Office, Hussey Delaval papers, M 17/29 and 2 DE 18/1] (for plans and illustrations see *History of Northumberland* xi, 420–2 and *C. Life*, 11–18 Jan. 1941). From one of Sir John Delaval's letters to Nisbet [2 DE 18/1/7] it appears that in 1771 the latter was being employed by Mr. (later Sir) Francis Blake, presumably at TWIZEL CASTLE, NORTHUMBERLAND, which Blake was then engaged in building. Twizel was a fantastic Gothick building in a romantic situation on the Tweed: it was never finished and is now a ruin. There are survey drawings in the Northumberland Record Office [2BU B 5/6]. It is possible that Nesbit was also employed by Sir Francis Blake when he remodelled FOWBERRY TOWER, NORTHUMBERLAND, in the Gothick style in 1776–8, but documentary evidence is lacking.

In 1771–5 Nisbet superintended the building of WEDDERBURN CASTLE, DUNS, BERWICKSHIRE, to the designs of Robert Adam [drawings at Paxton House, *ex inf.* Prof. A. Rowan]. In 1771 he designed the octagonal church at KELSO in conjunction with two fellow-builders, John Laidlaw (a mason) and John Purves (a carpenter): it was completed in 1773. In 1823 a flat ceiling was substituted for the original domed one [S.R.O., HR 651/3 and 4: cf. RHP 8462 and 8466] (for illustrations see R.C.A.M., *Roxburghshire*, figs. 105, 304).

In December 1774 Nisbet made a report, now in the Charter Room at Floors Castle, on the state of BROXMOUTH HOUSE, EAST LOTHIAN.

The subject of this entry should not be confused with James Nisbet, an Edinburgh plasterer who was active from about 1780 to 1810 and is occasionally referred to as an architect. It was the latter who in 1790 made designs for the façades of Charlotte Square in Edinburgh that were rejected in favour of those of Robert Adam. In 1791 John Paterson reported to Adam that Nisbet 'is so much flattered by his abilitys in Architecture that he has given up the most of his plaistering business after this his favourite study' [N.L.S., MS. 19992, ff. 27, 66].

NISBET, ROBERT (–1831), was a mason in Newbiggin, Musselburgh, Midlothian. In 1802 his design for a new church at INVERESK, MIDLOTHIAN, was chosen from five submitted, and the building was erected under his supervision in 1803–5. The handsome classical steeple was added to his designs in 1805–10 [S.R.O., HR 6/1, pp. 17, 22, 41, 94, 97–8]. He died on 11 February 1831 [S.R.O., SC 70/1/49, p. 555].

NIXON, ROBERT FEAKE (*c.*1761–1836), was a builder and surveyor at Woburn in Bedfordshire. He rebuilt LIDLINGTON CHURCH, BEDS., in 1809–10, dem. [*Gent's Mag.* 1849 (ii), 481], remodelled RIDGMONT (SEGENHOE) CHURCH, BEDS., in 1818–20 [I.C.B.S.], and probably rebuilt HEATH AND REACH CHURCH, BEDS., in 1829, as he reported on its condition in 1828 [I.C.B.S.]. None was a building of any architectural merit. Nixon's destructive alterations to MARSTON MORETAINE CHURCH, BEDS., were complained of by the Revd. G. Boissier in 1827 [B.L., Add. MS. 48977, ff. 413–14].

NIXON, WILLIAM (1760–1824), was one of the bridge-masters for the County of Cumberland from 1816 until his death on 2 March 1824, aged 64. Although described as 'Architect' in the Carlisle probate records, he appears to have been mainly a builder and surveyor. He lived at Chalk Lodge, Dalston, and was a member of the Nixon family of masons of Cumdivock, nr. Dalston.

A reference in Margaret Lady Vane's notebook at Hutton-in-the-Forest to 'Mr. Nixon of Carlisle' (who had recently clumsily Gothicized some windows in the south front of Hutton) as 'a man of no taste but much employed by the Duke of Norfolk' points to Nixon as the executant architect employed by the 11th Duke of Norfolk to carry out his alterations to GREYSTOKE CASTLE, CUMBERLAND, from *c.*1790 onwards [*ex inf.* Mr. J. M. Robinson]. At Carlisle he was responsible for completing the County Buildings designed by Smirke [Soane Museum, Corresp. xv. 18], and in 1822, when the County accepted the designs of J. Orridge (*q.v.*) for a new gaol, the drawings were made by Nixon under the latter's instructions, and directions were given that the building should be supervised by Christopher Hodgson five days a week and by Nixon one day [Cumbria Record Office, Q.S. Order Books 1816–24 and Gaol Committee's Second Report AG/4]. It was completed in 1827 by Hodgson, remodelled in the 1860s and demolished 1932–7.

NIXON, WILLIAM (*c.*1810–1848), may have been the elder son of William Nixon (d. 1826), Nash's clerk of works at Brighton and elsewhere. Like the elder Nixon, he was employed in the public service as a Clerk of Works, and was in April 1840 transferred from Phoenix Park, Dublin, to head the small establishment of the Office of Works at Edinburgh. In this capacity he was responsible for the maintenance of Holyroodhouse and the law courts in Parliament Square, and for the repair of several cathedrals (Glasgow, Elgin, Kirkwall, etc.) which were Crown property. It was to his designs that the interior of Gillespie Graham's TOLBOOTH ST. JOHN'S CHURCH was furnished in 1842–5 [S.R.O., RHP 6501]. The POLICE OFFICE at 192 HIGH STREET was designed by him in 1845 in conformity with the architecture of the adjoining buildings in Parliament Square [Edinburgh Dean of Guild plans]. In 1845 he undertook the completion of the buildings of the UNITED COLLEGE at ST. ANDREWS begun by Robert Reid in 1829–31. The north wing and the 'cloister' behind the church were built to his designs between 1845 and 1849. At ST. ANDREWS he also designed the MARTYRS' MONUMENT (an obelisk with neo-classical detailing) in 1842 and the (WEST) INFANT SCHOOL (Romanesque) in 1844. He died on 24 March 1848, aged 38, and was succeeded by his assistant Robert Matheson. [*History of the King's Works* vi, 1973, 253–4; R. G. Cant, 'St. Andrews Architects', *St. Andrews Preservation Trust Year Book*, 1966–7, 12; C. Roger, *History of St. Andrews*, 1849, 54; information from Mr. L. Russell Muirhead.]

NIXSON, PAUL (1768–1850), of Carlisle, was a builder, statuary mason and architect See p. 1138 who had an extensive business until he and his partner and son-in-law William Denton went bankrupt in 1837. He owned quarries of black marble near Dent in Yorkshire and imported white Carrara marble from Italy. In the 1820s he built a church in Carlisle to the designs of Rickman and another in Whitehaven to those of Hardwick. Monuments signed by him are to be seen in many Cumbrian churches and in 1825 he supplied chimney-pieces for the Council House at Bristol. His portrait (in private possession) shows him with dividers and plans. As an architect his principal work was THE ACADEMY OF FINE ARTS at CARLISLE, 1823, dem. 1929. This was an exhibition room whose classical façade, adorned with busts of Wren, West and Chantrey, was also the entrance to his own yard in Finkle Street. The houses at Nos. 26, 28 and 30 CASTLE STREET can be attributed to him as he is known to have acquired their site. A simple design for St. Cuthbert's Vicarage, Carlisle, made in 1814, is in the Cumbria Record Office (DRC 12/18). Nixson died in January 1850, aged 82. [D. R. Perriam, 'The Carlisle Academy of Fine Art', *Connoisseur*, Aug. 1975; R. Gunnis, *Dictionary of British*

Sculptors, 1968, 273; information from Mr. Angus Taylor.]

NOBLE, JAMES (*c*.1795–1875), was the nephew of Charles Noble (died 1827, aged 72), who had for many years been a trusted clerk in S. P. Cockerell's office, and who received a legacy of £500 under the latter's will in recognition of his 'long attachment to me through life . . . and faithful and constant service'. James Noble became principal assistant to C. R. Cockerell, but was dissatisfied with his subordinate status, and eventually established himself in independent practice. He was an original member of the Institute of British Architects in 1834, and exhibited designs for churches at the Royal Academy in 1837 and 1838, but, apart from some portions of Cockerell's Seckford Hospital at Woodbridge in Suffolk, no building designed by him has been identified, and he is best known as the author of the first book on architectural practice, entitled *The Professional Practice of Architects, and that of Measuring Surveyors . . . from the time of the celebrated Earl of Burlington*, 1836. He died at Florence Villa, Warwick Gardens, Kensington, on 14 April 1875 [Principal Probate Registry, Calendar of Probates].

NOLLORTH, SAMUEL, of East Dereham, Norfolk, announced in the *Norfolk Chronicle* of 29 June 1771 that he was in practice as an architect, having had '3 years regular instruction under Ward of Bury St. Edmunds and many years of his own experience'. He was presumably the Mr. Nolloth who was paid for making a plan of Kimberley Hall, Norfolk, in 1755 [Kimberley accounts, *ex inf.* Mr. T. P. Connor].

NORRIS, JOHN, was active in South Lancashire and Cheshire in the reign of George II. According to Lysons, *Magna Britannia* ii, 1810, 513, he was the architect from whose designs DUNHAM MASSEY HALL, CHESHIRE, was rebuilt by the 2nd Earl of Warrington between 1732 and 1740. An account-book records several payments to 'Mr. Norris about the New Building' [J. Swarbrick, 'Dunham Massey Hall', *Trans. Lancs. & Cheshire Antiq. Soc.* xlii, 1927]. In 1742 a chimney-piece for ADLINGTON HALL, CHESHIRE, was carved 'according to Mr. Norris' design' [P. de Figueiredo & J. Treuherz, *Cheshire Country Houses*, 1988, 19], and in 1753 'Mr. Norris Architector' was paid 6 guineas by Richard Atherton in connection with the building of a Georgian wing (since dem.) at BEWSEY HALL, nr. WARRINGTON, LANCS. [Lancs. C.R.O., DDLi, Cash Book 1742–64, *ex inf.* Mr. John Jenkins]. He was presumably the John Norris who subscribed to Gibbs's *Book of Architecture* (1728).

NORRIS, RICHARD (*c*.1750–1792), was the eldest son of Richard Norris (*c*.1719–79), a builder and surveyor who lived at Hampstead but had premises in Holborn. In 1767 the elder Norris was among those who submitted designs for the Shire Hall at Hertford, but although they were at first accepted, they were ultimately set aside in favour of drawings by James Adam [Hertfordshire Quarter Sessions records]. In 1773–5 he remodelled BROKE HALL, NACTON, SUFFOLK, for Philip Broke in a banal late Georgian style, but the house was rebuilt to the designs of James Wyatt less than twenty years later [Suffolk C.R.O., HA 93/12/27–8 (drawings) and 3/222–4 (specifications)]. The elder Norris lived in Pond Street, Hampstead, where he was probably the builder of Nos. 23 and 25 (before 1764) and of Nos. 19 and 21 (between 1764 and 1774). He died on 24 May 1779 at the age of 60, and was buried at Finchley.

In 1766 the younger Norris exhibited a drawing at the Free Society of Artists representing 'a Triumphal Arch, proposed for the reception of her Majesty on her intended landing at Greenwich, from a design of Mr. Stuart'. This suggests that he may have been Stuart's pupil. Two volumes of sketches (V. & A., 95 A. 17–18) show that he travelled in Italy, and in 1791 he was one of the original members of the Architects' Club. He became surveyor to Christ's Hospital, the Apothecaries' Company, the Clothworkers' Company, the Charterhouse estates, the London Assurance Corporation, the Sun Fire Insurance Office and (from October 1790) the Corporation of Trinity House. He died suddenly on 7 January 1792, aged 42, 'oppressed with overweight of business, the loss of a beloved consort about 15 months ago, and of a useful foreman and clerk lately', and was buried at Finchley, where he is commemorated on the family monument. His only recorded architectural works appear to be a design for a new dining-room at WANLIP HALL, LEICS. (dem.), for Charles Grave Hudson, *c*.1780 [drawings in Leics. Record Office], and some alterations to FETCHAM PARK, SURREY, for Thomas Hankey in 1789–91 [Surrey County Record Office, S.C. 19/175/2]. As surveyor to the Clothworkers' Company he was succeeded by his younger brother Philip Norris, who retired in 1797 and died in 1806, aged 52. Philip Norris was the nominal architect of RAY LODGE, WOODFORD, ESSEX, which was built in 1796–7 for Sir James Wright, Bart., with the young J. B. Papworth (*q.v.*) as clerk of works. Papworth made the drawings under Norris's general direction and supervised the work.

[*A.P.S.D.*; *Gent's Mag.* 1792 (i), 485; Wyatt Papworth, *John B. Papworth*, 1879, 11–12; information from Miss P. G. Mann and Mr. Roger White.]

NORTH, ROGER (?1653–1734), was the sixth and youngest son of Dudley, 4th Lord North. Like his brother Francis, afterwards Lord Chancellor Guilford, Roger was educated for the law, and partly by his own abilities, partly through his brother's influence, he had a not unsuccessful career. He was called to the Bar in 1675, and became in due course a Bencher of the Middle Temple, steward to Archbishop Sancroft, and Solicitor-General to the Duke of York. But although the law provided North with a profession, it by no means monopolized his mind, and in the course of a long life he found time to study optics and mathematics, to listen to and to theorize about music, to collect pictures, to plant, and to build. Although never a member of the Royal Society, North was nevertheless in touch with the intellectual and scientific ideas of his time. He had read Descartes at Cambridge at a time when 'the new philosophy was a sort of heresy'; he had attempted to arrive 'at a system of nature, upon the Cartesian or rather mechanical principles'. He was an expert at dialling, and as a 'dabbler in mathematics . . . fell into that disease that all tyros in that art do, a conceit of having found a perpetual motion'. For a person of these tastes, the transition from science to architecture was an easy one, as it had been for Robert Hooke and Sir Christopher Wren before him.

It was the fire that destroyed the Temple in January 1678/9 which first led Roger North to number building among his 'mechanical entertainments'. He played a prominent part in the negotiations with Nicholas Barbon, the 'undertaker' of the new buildings, and it was in 'drawing the model of my little chamber and making patterns for the wainscot' that he learned the use of a scale and tasted for the first time 'the joys of designing and executing known only to such as practise or have practised it'. This, however, was 'but a beginning'. Soon he was buying the architectural text-books of the day, Palladio, Scamozzi, and Evelyn's *Parallel of the Orders*. He learned the principles of perspective, and spent many happy hours in drawing 'which might have been better and more profitably employed'. Architecture, in fact, became for him a passion second only to that for music, and North's active mind delighted in the technicalities of building just as it did in the niceties of draughtsmanship.

In 1683–4 the building of the Great Gateway leading from the Temple into Fleet Street gave him an opportunity to display his talents as an architect. The gateway has traditionally been ascribed to Wren, but a passage in North's essay on building (B.L., Add. MS. 32540, f. 37v) makes it clear that it was he and not Wren who made the designs.

> When I built the Temple gate, I designed 4 pilaster columes, and a frontoon.[1] But it being necessary for preserving the dignity of such a fabrick, between very high houses to rais the frontoon eves, above the Cornish of the houses, . . . I raised the first story with Rustick stone, & made a flatt arch for the coaches to pass, whereby I gained the Greatest passage height I could: & compass ones for the shopps, lower so as to lay the thrust of the other upon the solid, clear of the void, and set balconys over these compass arches. Then a fillett of stone, and above that a deep plane, which served as Stylobate, or foundation for the Columnes, being more in height than ordinary, & upon that sett the bases, by which means the Columnes were brought into due proportion to the height, and altogether hath no ill aspect. I could not compass the Midle Arch, & flatt the side ones, because the Story above must be preserved, but that bin much more proper.

Wren did indeed offer his advice, suggesting that it might save expense if the pediment and entablature were made of wood and plaster, 'but' (North tells us) 'out of a proud high spirit I declined it, and made the whole intablature & frontoon of stone, & it is as lusty, as most are'. He was, however, on excellent terms with the Surveyor-General, for he records several conversations of great interest which passed between them, and he and his brother made regular visits to St. Paul's to inspect the progress of the works. He was also a friend of Hugh May, the Comptroller of the Works, and his essay 'Of Building' shows that he was familiar with all the most important architectural works of his time, whose design and construction he criticizes freely.

Roger North's own contribution to English architecture was not large, for unlike Sir Roger Pratt, he never became a 'profest architect', and did not 'pretend either to great publick designes, nor new models of great howses'. There are, however, some highly competent designs by him in the British

[1] i.e. a pediment.

Library (Add. MS. 23005), and between 1680 and 1685 he assisted his brother, Lord Guilford, to make considerable alterations to the latter's country seat, Wroxton Abbey in Oxfordshire [*V.C.H. Oxon.* ix, 172–3; B.L., Add. MS. 32510, ff. 136–9]. In 1690–1 he bought a large but old-fashioned house at Rougham in Norfolk, which he remodelled gradually, as his purse allowed, adding a gallery at the back and an Ionic portico in front. He also built a library on the north side of Rougham Church, to which he proposed to leave his large collection of books. But before the end of the eighteenth century 'not one stone was left upon another' of the house which he had reconstructed, the library too had been destroyed and the books dispersed. Fortunately his papers survived. Most of them were acquired by the British Library in 1885, and some others (including a variant version of the treatise on building) are still at Rougham. Also at Rougham are some drawings in North's hand, including two plans of Wroxton Abbey, and an elevation of the Temple Gateway. Roger North died at Rougham on 1 March 1733/4, and is commemorated by a monument in the church. His portrait by Lely hangs in the present Rougham Hall, formed in the nineteenth century from the outbuildings of Roger's house.

[*D.N.B.*; *The Autobiography of the Hon. Roger North*, ed. A. Jessopp, 1887; *The Lives of the Norths*, ed. A. Jessopp, 1890; H. M. Colvin, 'Roger North and Sir Christopher Wren', *Arch. Rev.* Oct. 1951; *Of Building. Roger North's Writings on Architecture*, ed. H. Colvin & J. Newman, 1981].

NORTON, CHARLES (*c.*1748–1833) was a builder and surveyor of Birmingham. In 1793–4 he was jointly employed with George Saunders to rebuild the THEATRE ROYAL in NEW STREET after the fire of 1792, and acted as 'superintendent in the erecting and finishing the Theatre and Buildings adjoining' [MS. Minutes of the Proprietors in Birmingham Reference Library, Archives, Lee Crowder 387]. In 1795, having obtained plans from the architect Charles Rawstorne, he issued *Proposals with the Plan and Specification for Building the Crescent at Birmingham*, of which there is a copy in the Birmingham Reference Library, 63066. The Crescent was to have consisted of a 'superb range of twenty-three stone houses, elevated upon a terrace 1182 feet long and 17 feet wide', but only the wings were built. There is an engraving of the original project in the British Library (*King's Maps* xlii, 82m).

In 1786–8 Norton rebuilt ALL SAINTS CHURCH, WEST BROMWICH, STAFFS. (again rebuilt 1870–2) [agreement among parish records, *ex inf.* Mr. D. A. Johnson], and it was to designs made by him jointly with an engineering manufacturer named William Whitmore that CHRIST CHURCH, BIRMINGHAM (dem. 1899) was begun in 1806. In 1810 they were superseded by Benjamin Wyatt (*q.v.*), who carried on the building until his death in 1813, when it was completed under the direction of William Stock, 'Builder and Surveyor of Bristol' [Birmingham Reference Library Archives, Minutes of the Trustees, 660234 and one drawing in 446844].

The death on 5 September 1833 of Charles Norton 'of the Crescent' at the age of 85 is recorded in *Aris's Birmingham Gazette* of 9 September 1833. His son Charles, a builder, died at Camp Hill Cottage on 5 May 1827 (*ibid.*, 7 May 1827).

NOSWORTHY, MATTHEW (1750–1831), a speculative builder of Exeter, was responsible for much of the excellent late eighteenth-century domestic architecture of that city. He was born at Widecombe-in-the-Moor, but came to Exeter at an early age and proved to be a man of 'great industry and perseverance' in his business as a builder. He died in Exeter on 14 March 1831, aged 81.

The Exeter City accounts show that in 1789 Nosworthy was paid 8 guineas 'for drawing plans of the buildings on Southernhay' – that is for the terraces of brick houses built in SOUTHERNHAY during the next few years. In 1792 he contracted to build BARNFIELD CRESCENT [*Flying Post*, 24 May 1792], and he subsequently designed and built DIX'S FIELD, begun 1806, and probably COLLETON CRESCENT, 1802–5. He also designed THE NEW LONDON INN, HIGH STREET, EXETER, 1793–4 (dem.). [A. E. Richardson & C. L. Gill, *Regional Architecture of the West of England*, 1924, 26–31; *Devon and Cornwall Illustrated*, with text by J. Britton & E. W. Brayley, 1832, 67; information from the late Prof. W. G. Hoskins.]

NOVOSIELSKI, MICHAEL (1750–1795), was born in Rome of Polish parents and is said to have come to London as a young man in order to assist James Wyatt at the time when he was building the Pantheon (1770–2). In 1772 he was living at the house of the artist Bartoli in Golden Square.

In 1785 Novosielski leased some 14 acres of land on the south side of Brompton Road, Kensington, on which he proceeded to build, as a speculation, MICHAEL'S PLACE (forty-two houses), MICHAEL'S GROVE (ten houses), BROMPTON CRESCENT (twenty-five houses) and a large detached house (dem. 1843) for his own occupation. Some of these houses remained in an unfinished state for many years, and the whole development was demolished in 1886 to make way for Egerton Gardens and Egerton Place [T. C. Croker, *A Walk from London to Fulham*, 1860, 43, 50; Dorothy Stroud, *The South Kensington Estate of Henry Smith's Charity*, 1975, 16–17]. Three houses built by Novosielski 'opposite Lord William Gordon's' in PICCADILLY are mentioned in *The World* for 22 May, 30 June and 3 August 1787, where it is stated that he had also begun to build in GROSVENOR PLACE.

After the fire of 27 June 1789, Novosielski reconstructed the OPERA HOUSE in the HAYMARKET in 1790–1, exhibiting his designs at the Royal Academy in 1794. This was then the largest theatre in Europe, except La Scala at Milan. It was reconstructed by J. Nash and G. Repton in 1816–18, incorporating Novosielski's auditorium, and the interior was redecorated in 1846. The interior was destroyed by fire in 1867, rebuilt in 1868–9, and finally demolished in the 1890s [Britton & Pugin, *Public Buildings of London* i, 1825, 72–9]. Novosielski was also concerned with Francis Pasquali in fitting up the CONCERT ROOM in the TOTTENHAM COURT ROAD for the 'Concerts of Ancient Music' which were held here from 1786 onwards. This building, later known as the Queen's Theatre, was demolished in 1882 [*Survey of London* xxi, 36–9]. Novosielski was a scene-painter as well as an architect, and it was probably his theatrical connections which led to his employment by the 7th Earl of Barrymore to design a house for him in Piccadilly (No. 105, at the corner of Brick Street). In 1850–1 it was reconstructed as Hertford House [*Builder* ix, 1851, 227]. An engraving of the original front is reproduced by A. I. Dasent, *Piccadilly*, 1920, 117.

Novosielski died at Ramsgate on 8 April 1795, aged 45. At the time of his death he was engaged in a new speculative building venture at SIDMOUTH, then beginning to be a fashionable seaside resort. In a letter from C. H. Tatham to Henry Holland dated 10 July 1795, he writes: 'Mr. Jenkins . . . informed me of Mr. Novosielski's death, by which he is a sufferer on account of a Crescent of considerable magnitude contracted for by the deceased and now erecting near the sea at Sidmouth in Devonshire, the property of Mr. Jenkins' [Victoria and Albert Museum, 92.D.28, f. 16]. 'Mr. Jenkins' was the 'antiquary' and archaeologist Thomas Jenkins who, though long resident in Rome, was a native of Devon and lord of the manor of Sidmouth. The terrace is identifiable as FORTFIELD TERRACE, begun in about 1790, and still existing in the incomplete state in which it was left by Novosielski [cf. Anna Sutton, *A Story of Sidmouth*, 1959, 23].

A portrait of Novosielski by Angelica Kauffmann is in the National Gallery of Scotland and is reproduced in *Survey of London* xxx, pl. 30. It shows him holding a plan of the Opera House, and in the background is the projected Crescent at Sidmouth.

[*A.P.S.D.*; *Gent's Mag.* 1795 (ii), 616; J. Boaden, *Life of Kemble* ii, 1825, 141; Horace Walpole, *Anecdotes of Painting* v, ed. F. W. Hilles & P. B. Daghlian, 1937, 189–90; will, P.C.C. 269 NEWCASTLE.]

NURSEY, PERRY (1771–1840), was a surgeon who as the result of an advantageous marriage was able to give up his practice and devote himself to gardening, painting and other arts, including architecture. He lived in Suffolk, at first at The Grove, Little Bealings, and later at Foxhall, nr. Ipswich, and was a friend of Edward Fitzgerald and an acquaintance of John Constable [*Letters of Edward Fitzgerald*, ed. Terhune, Princeton 1980, i, 55–6]. In 1830–4 he remodelled THEBERTON HOUSE, SUFFOLK, for T. W. Wooton, with stuccoed elevations in an idiosyncratic classical style [*Pewsey's Ladies Directory*, 1839, 4, cited by C. Brown *et al.*, *Dictionary of Architects of Suffolk Buildings 1800–1914*, 150]. THE GROVE, LITTLE BEALINGS, has a similar façade, and Nursey evidently designed this house for James Colvin, who had purchased it from him in 1824 and rebuilt it in 1830 [White's *Gazetteer of Suffolk*, 1844, 130].

O

OAKLEY, EDWARD, stated in 1730 that he had been in government service abroad (in what capacity is not stated), where he had 'long contemplated a famous republic', perhaps Venice. He had connections with Carmarthen, where in 1726 he was the senior warden of a recently founded Freemasons' lodge. But in 1725 he was also senior warden of a lodge meeting at the 'Three Compasses' in Silver Street, London, where in 1728 he delivered a speech mainly concerned with architecture that was published in *The Ancient Constitution of the Free and Accepted Masons*, London 1731. In 1721 Oakley applied unsuccessfully for the post of clerk of works at St. Martin-in-the-Fields, then about to be rebuilt to the designs of James Gibbs, and in 1730 he was living in St. Martin's Lane and advertising as follows:

Estates Survey'd, Designs made, and Estimates calculated, for Building or repairs; Articles and Contracts for Agreements with Workmen fairly drawn; Artificers' works measured, and Bills adjusted; And all Affairs relating to Building carefully managed By Edward Oakley.

In 1725 'Oakley the Builder' was paid 3 guineas for 'viewing the old house' at Wrest Park, Beds. [Beds. C.R.O., L 31/198, p. 7]. He designed the greenhouses and hothouses for the PHYSIC GARDEN at CHELSEA, the first stone of which was laid by Sir Hans Sloane on 12 August 1732. They were completed in 1734. Plans and elevations of these buildings, drawn by Oakley and engraved by B. Cole, are in the British Library (*King's Maps* xxviii, 4 g). In 1735 he made three designs for a bridge across the Thames at Westiminster, of which he published an engraving. In 1756 he reissued the same engraving as a design for Blackfriars Bridge, merely altering the date and lettering. In the latter form it appears in W. Maitland's *London*, 1756, 1387.

Oakley published in 1730 a substantial but derivative architectural treatise entitled *The Magazine of Architecture, Perspective and Sculpture*, with a dedication to Sir Robert Walpole, a second edition of which was appearing in parts in 1732–3. The plates were copied from seventeenth-century works by Abraham Brosse. He was also the author of another compilation, *Every Man a Compleat Builder; or Easy Rules and Proportions for Drawing and Working the several Parts of Architecture*, 1766, 2nd ed. 1774. This was basically the text and plates of Robinson's *Proportional Architecture* (1733) with additions. In 1750 Oakley published an engraved plan of Calais (B.L., *King's Maps* lxix, 40). The date of his death is not known, but it occurred between 1756 and 1766. [*A.P.S.D.*; *D.N.B.*; *Ars Quatuor Coronatorum* xxvii, 1914, and xl, 1927, 134; T. Friedman, *James Gibbs*, 1984, 310; Eileen Harris, *British Architectural Books and Writers 1556–1785*, 1990, 334–6.]

OATES, JOHN (1793–1831), was the eldest son of John Oates, a quarry owner at Salter Hebble, Halifax, and a member of a family long resident in that area. He may have become a pupil of a Manchester architect, for in 1813 he gave a Manchester address when exhibiting a design for a villa at the Liverpool Academy. He subsequently practised in Halifax until his death in 1831 at the early age of 37. Oates designed a number of Commissioners' churches, which are often more picturesquely composed and more carefully detailed than most of their kind. His Infirmary at Halifax is dignified by a handsome Greek Doric portico. J. A. Hansom and Edward Welch were both in his office.

In 1831 John and his younger brother Matthew Oates (1795–1861) entered into partnership with Thomas Pickersgill (*q.v.*) in York. John died on 16 May of that year, probably in the cholera epidemic, but Matthew continued to practise in partnership with Pickersgill until 1840. He subsequently took his eldest son John Edwin Oates (1820–1869) into a partnership which lasted until 1850. His youngest son James Daniel Oates (1833–1908) was also an architect [family information from Miss E. M. Alty; D. Linstrum, *West Yorkshire Architects and Architecture*, 1978, 213].

PUBLIC BUILDINGS

HALIFAX, YORKS. (W.R.), ASSEMBLY ROOMS, etc. 1828; dem. *c.*1900 [J. Crabtree, *History of Halifax*, 1836, 347].

RISHWORTH GRAMMAR SCHOOL, YORKS. (W.R.), 1827–8 [J. H. Priestley, *History of Rishworth School*, Halifax n.d., 51].

HUDDERSFIELD, YORKS. (W.R.), THE INFIRMARY (now part of Huddersfield University), 1829–31 [W. White, *History, Gazeteer and Directory of the West Riding of Yorkshire* i, 1837, 365].

CHURCHES

SOWERBY BRIDGE, YORKS. (W.R.), CHRIST CHURCH, 1819, Gothic; chancel 1873–89 [I.C.B.S.].

*BUCKLEY, FLINTSHIRE, 1821–2, Gothic; rebuilt [Port, 138–9].

WINKSLEY, YORKS. (W.R.), 1822–4; dem. 1917 [I.C.B.S.].

BROUGHTON, FLINTSHIRE, 1823–4, Gothic; chancel added 1876–7 [I.C.B.S.].

*WILSDEN, YORKS. (W.R.), 1823–5, Gothic; dem. [Port, 138–9].

BIRDSALL, YORKS. (E.R.), 1824, Gothic, for 6th Lord Middleton; chancel 1879–81 [design exhibited by Oates at Northern Society for the Encouragement of the Arts, Leeds, 1823].

BISHOP THORNTON, YORKS. (W.R.), rebuilt 1825; dem. 1888 except tower [I.C.B.S.].

*SHIPLEY, YORKS. (W.R.), ST. PAUL, 1823–5, Gothic [Port, 138–9].

*LINDLEY, YORKS. (W.R.), ST. STEPHEN, 1828–9, Gothic [Port, 168–9].

*PADDOCK, YORKS. (W.R.), ALL SAINTS, 1828–9, Gothic [Port, 168–9].

*Designed for the Commissioners for building New Churches.

*HUDDERSFIELD, YORKS. (W.R.), ST. PAUL, 1828–30, Gothic [Port, 168–9].
*IDLE, YORKS. (W.R.), HOLY TRINITY, 1828–30, Gothic [Port, 168–9].
HARROGATE, YORKS. (W.R.), CHRIST CHURCH, 1830–1, Gothic; chancel and transepts 1862 [W. Grainge, *History of Harrogate*, 1882, 159].
*HALIFAX, YORKS. (W.R.), ST. JAMES, 1830–1, Gothic; dem. 1955 [Port, 166–7].
*SHELTON, nr. HANLEY, STAFFS., ST. MARK, 1831–3, Gothic, completed by M. Oates & T. Pickersgill [Port, 160–1].
*HEBDEN BRIDGE (MYTHOLM), YORKS. (W.R.), ST. JAMES, 1832–3, Gothic, erected by M. Oates & T. Pickersgill [Port, 166–7].

OGBOURNE, Sir WILLIAM (*c.*1662–1734), was a prominent London master carpenter. After an apprenticeship to John Olley (*q.v.*) he was admitted a freeman of the Carpenters' Company on 20 October 1693. For many years he was Master Carpenter to the Board of Ordnance. He was Master of the Carpenters' Company in 1724 and 1726, and was knighted in 1727 after serving as Sheriff of London the previous year. He died on 13 October 1734, aged 72, and was buried in St. Olave's Church, Hart Street, where there is a monument to his memory. From time to time Ogbourne is found acting as a surveyor in contemporary records, and his 'draught' for alterations to two houses in St. James's Place is mentioned in 1699. In 1694–7 he built the TRINITY ALMSHOUSES, MILE END, STEPNEY, for the Corporation of Trinity House, who also employed him in 1704 to erect a sea-mark in the Isle of Wight. Documents in Streatham Public Library show that he certified the bills for building STREATHAM HOUSE for Mrs. Howland in 1706. [Guildhall Library, Carpenters' Company records, MSS. 4329/11 and 15; A. Povah, *Annals of St. Olave Hart Street and All Hallows Staining*, 1894, 31, 115; *Survey of London* xxx, 514–15; Corporation of Trinity House Cash Books.]

OGILVY, JAMES (*c.*1700–   ), was a Scottish master mason from a place in Morayshire called Pittensair in the parish of St. Andrews Lhanbryde near Elgin, where a small but well detailed house is inscribed with his name and the date 1735. In 1743, in the course of giving evidence in William Adam's lawsuit against Lord Braco, Ogilvy stated that as a young man he had worked at Mereworth Castle, Kent, Sir Gregory Page's house at Blackheath, and the church of St. Martin-in-the-Fields. He said that 'the works he has performed in the North-country consisted of repairing of Kirks and building one Kirk, also building and repairing Ministers' Manses, and putting up Ministers' Monuments'. The church he had built was at SPEYMOUTH, MORAYSHIRE (1732), and here he was 'Architect and Undertaker for the mason-work', though he and the minister had 'contrived' the building between them [*Depositions of the witnesses adduced by William Lord Braco*, 1743, 14–15].

*Designed for the Commissioners for building New Churches.

OGILVY, JAMES, 7th Earl of Findlater and Seafield (1750–1811), was the son of the 6th Earl and in 1770 inherited his titles and extensive estates at Cullen and elsewhere in N.E. Scotland. Believed to be a homosexual, he was separated from his wife, and lived abroad in self-imposed exile, dying at Dresden in 1811. Here he sponsored the volume of engravings entitled *Les Plans et Desseins tirés de la Belle Architecture*, published in Paris and Leipsig in 1798, with an introduction by C. L. Stieglitz. A number of the neo-classical architectural designs that it contains are stated to have been contributed by Findlater ('de sa propre invention'). At Cullen he built nothing, and the only buildings he is known to have designed are an office-court at PENIG, SAXONY, for Count Schoenburg, 1796, and alterations to his own house in Dresden. [A. A. Tait, 'Lord Findlater, Architect', *Burlington Mag.* 128, 1986, 738–41].

OGLE, JOHN, of High Ongar, Essex, was an unsuccessful candidate for the office of County Surveyor of Essex in 1812 and again in 1816 [Essex County Records, Q/So 24]. He designed ASHWELL VICARAGE, HERTS., in 1814 [Lincolnshire Record Office, MGA 73].

OLDFIELD, HENRY GEORGE, was the son of John Oldfield (d. 1788), a bricklayer of Wingham in Kent. He practised as an architect in Great Scotland Yard, Westminster, exhibiting architectural designs at the Royal Academy in 1787 and 1788 and at the Society of Artists in 1790. In 1788 he was described as 'architect to the late Princess Amelia'. His only recorded work appears to be the rebuilding of the parish church of CHATHAM, KENT, after a fire. In 1786 plans were made by 'Mr. Oldfield of Scotland Yard' [Vestry Minutes in Kent Archives Office, P85/18/1]. The church, completed in 1788, was again rebuilt 1884–1903. Oldfield had antiquarian interests, collaborating with R. R. Dyson in writing a *History of the Parish of Tottenham High Cross* (1790), and publishing in 1791 *Anecdotes of*

Archery, Ancient and Modern. In the 1790s he made a precarious living by selling his own topographical drawings, a collection of which is in the Herts. Record Office [*Trans. E. Herts. Archl. Soc.* xi, 1942, 212–4; *D.N.B.*; *Gent's Mag.* 1788 (i), 271].

OLDHAM, WILLIAM (*c*.1740–1814), was an architect and builder of Leicester. He was a prominent member of the corporation, serving as Mayor in 1783–4. He was married three times, his third wife, Ann, being the daughter of Alderman John Westley (*q.v.*). Oldham died at his house in Leicester High Street on 25 March 1814, aged 74, and was buried in St. Martin's Church. His son, Thomas Westley Oldham of Atherstone, was High Sheriff of Leicestershire in 1826 [J. D. Bennett, *Leicestershire Architects 1700–1850*, Leicester Museums 1968].

LEICESTER RACECOURSE, GRANDSTAND, 1770 [Bennett, *op. cit.*].

BRAUNSTONE HALL, LEICS., for Clement Winstanley, 1776 [J. Throsby, *Select Views in Leicestershire* i, 1789, 257].

LEICESTER, RECORDER'S HOUSE (BOWLING GREEN HOUSE), addition of attic storey, 1785 [Bennett, *op. cit.*].

LEICESTER, ALDERMAN NEWTON'S SCHOOL, Master's House, 1789 [Bennett, *op. cit.*].

LEICESTER, COUNTY GAOL, HIGHCROSS STREET, alterations 1803; dem. *c*.1880 [Bennett, *op. cit.*].

LEICESTER, NEW HOUSE OF CORRECTION, FREE SCHOOL LANE, 1803 [Bennett, *op. cit.*].

OLIVER, JOHN (*c*.1616–1701), was a glazier by trade, a surveyor by profession, and a master mason by virtue of office. He stated in 1687 that he had practised surveying for forty years, and from January 1685/6 until his death he held the office of Master Mason to the Crown, with a seat on the Board of Works. He was not, however, a mason by trade, and his will contains a small legacy to the Glaziers' Company. Payments to him in the St. Paul's Cathedral accounts for glazing confirm that this was his trade, and it follows that he must have been the John Oliver who gave a painted glass window to Oxford Cathedral which bore the inscription 'John Oliver aetatis suae lxxxiv, A° 1700 pinxit deditque'. This establishes his birth as having occurred *c*.1616 and his age at the time of his death in 1701 as 85.

After the Great Fire of London Oliver was one of the four surveyors appointed by the corporation to supervise the rebuilding of the City in conjunction with Wren, May and Pratt. Like Jerman, he at first declined to assist in carrying out the detailed survey of the devastated area provided for by the Rebuilding Act, but offered to act without pay when Mills was ill during the summer of 1667. He was ultimately prevailed upon to accept the post, and was sworn on 27 January 1667/8. His surveys were more careful and detailed than those of either Hooke or Jerman, and many more of them contain plans of the site concerned. Oliver's name is frequently mentioned in connection with the rebuilding of the City churches, and, like Wren, he was the recipient of gratuities from more than one parish 'for his help in forwarding the building of the Church', or for 'coming to direct the building (of) the Steeple'. In 1679–82 he was closely involved in the rebuilding of St. Mary Aldermary at the expense of a private benefactor [*Arch. Hist.* 24, 1981, 27–9]. He appears to have been a parishioner of St. Michael's Queenhithe, a church in whose records he is often mentioned, and to which he presented a bell in 1685. He also assisted in supervising the building of the Monument, and in January 1676 he succeeded Edward Woodroffe as assistant surveyor of St. Paul's Cathedral, a post which he retained for over twenty-five years.

Little is known of his architectural works, but the records of the Mercers' Company show that it was he who supervised the erection of their new hall and chapel in Cheapside after the death of Edward Jerman in November 1668. He was also appointed surveyor to the Skinners' Company, and designed their Hall on Dowgate Hill which was completed *c*.1670 [*Builder*, 14 July 1916, 26]. In 1673 he and Hooke prepared designs for the new Boys' and Girls' Wards at Christ's Hospital, which were built at the expense of Erasmus Smith. They also designed the Writing School in 1675–6. In 1683 Oliver was thanked for 'the great paines' he had taken in the erection of the new Mathematical School built in 1682–3 and attributed to Wren (*Wren Soc.* xi, 60 ff.). He also supervised the building of the Christ's Hospital Girls' School at Hertford in 1691–5, and presumably made the designs for this attractive work (*Wren Soc.* xi, 81–3). He was himself a Governor of Christ's Hospital and left money in his will for an annual dinner of roast meat for the boys. In 1676 he and Edward Pierce made designs for the woodwork of the Chapel of Emmanuel College, Cambridge, which were executed by Cornelius Austin [Willis & Clark, ii, 707], and in 1700 he designed the screen and other woodwork in the hall of Corpus Christi College, Oxford, executed in 1700–1 by Arthur Frogley, with carving by Jonathan Maine [Corpus College archives, H/1/43, ff. 8, 9].

Oliver was a cartographer as well as a building surveyor. He was the author of *A Mapp of the Cityes of London & Westminster & Burrough of Southwark, with their suburbs as it is now rebuilt since the late dreadfull Fire*, published in or about 1680, of engraved maps of the counties of Hertford (1695) and Essex (1696), and of the town plan of St. Albans in Chauncy's *History of Hertfordshire* (1700).

Oliver's will was proved on 18 November 1701 (P.C.C., 157 DYER). He left property in Ironmonger Lane and elsewhere in the City to his wife Susanna. He desired to be buried in the vault under the choir of St. Paul's Cathedral. His portrait in crayons was the last done by W. Faithorne, who died in 1691 (Walpole Soc. *Vertue Note Books* i, 140). Aubrey, writing between 1681 and 1691 (*Brief Lives*, ed. Clark, ii, 10), recorded that all Inigo Jones's 'papers and designes, not only of St. Paul's Cathedral etc., and the Banquetting House, but his designe of all Whitehall . . .' were then in Oliver's possession. These appear to have been the drawings subsequently in the possession of William Talman, and later of Lord Burlington. A copy of Palladio's *Quattro Libri* (1570), with a MS. translation and Oliver's name on the title-page, was sold at Sotheby's on 29 November 1972.

[*A.P.S.D.*; *D.N.B.*; Walpole Soc. *Vertue Note Books* ii, 60; D. Knoop & G. P. Jones, *The London Mason in the Seventeenth Century*, 1935, 6; T. F. Reddaway, *The Rebuilding of London after the Great Fire*, 1940, 108 n.; *Wren Soc.* xx, 152–3.]

OLIVER, THOMAS (1791–1857), the son of a weaver, was born at Crailing, near Jedburgh, on 14 January 1791, and was educated at Jedburgh School. As a youth he went to Newcastle, where he is said to have been for some time in John Dobson's office. In 1814 he married Margaret Lorrimer, the daughter of a Kelso mason, and in 1821 he began independent practice as a 'land surveyor and architect'. Although best known in the former capacity, Oliver shares with Dobson the credit for much of the early nineteenth-century development of the city. In 1824 he designed for Dr. John Baird two houses at the junction of Northumberland Street and Elswick Court, which he claimed were the first stone-fronted dwelling-houses to be built in Newcastle for over a century. At the same time he was consulted by the Common Council in connection with the laying out of the new streets between Newgate and the Fickett Tower, and he made the original plans for BLACKETT STREET, subsequently built to modified designs by Dobson. For Richard Grainger (*q.v.*) he designed LEAZES CRESCENT and the adjoining houses and the handsome block known as LEAZES TERRACE, built 1829–34. He also designed the triangular VICTORIA BAZAAR, 1836–7, dem. *c.*1965 [*The Topographical Conductor*, 1851, 65], warehouses on the banks of the River Tyne at HILLGATE, GATESHEAD, for Messrs. Bertram and Spencer, 1843–4, destroyed by fire 1854 [drawings in Gateshead Public Library], and the INDEPENDENT CHAPEL in WEST CLAYTON STREET, NEWCASTLE, 1850 [J. Latimer, *Local Records*, 1857, 277].

In addition to the excellent engraved plans of Newcastle which he issued in 1830, 1844, 1849, 1851 and (posthumously) in 1858, Oliver was the author of *The New Picture of Newcastle upon Tyne*, 1831, and of *The Topographical Conductor, or descriptive Guide to Newcastle and Gateshead*, 1851. On the title-page of the former work he is described as the author of *The Geographical Synopsis of the World* and of a *Topographical View of Great Britain and Ireland*. Neither of these works is, however, to be found in the British or Bodleian Libraries.

Oliver died at Newcastle in December 1857, leaving four sons, one of whom, Thomas (1824–1902), practised as an architect in Sunderland until his father's death, when he returned to Newcastle, afterwards becoming the founder of the firm of Oliver, Leeson and Wood. Among his works was the Greek Revival LONDONDERRY INSTITUTE at SEAHAM HARBOUR, DURHAM, 1853–5 [J. Latimer, *Local Records*, 1857, 327–8]. Adam and James both became civil engineers.

[M. E. Jones and H. L. Honeyman, 'Thomas Oliver and his Plans for Central Newcastle', *Archaeologia Aeliana*, 4th ser. xxix, 1951; L. Wilkes & G. Dodds, *Tyneside Classical*, 1964, *passim*; John Noddings, 'Thomas Oliver 1791–1857', unpublished dissertation, School of Architecture, University of Newcastle, 1971.]

OLLEY, JOHN, was appointed Clerk of the Works to the City of London on 14 December 1693, and resigned on 29 September 1711. He was succeeded by his son, Isaac Olley, a carpenter by trade, who retained the post until his death early in 1724. John Olley designed the EMANUEL ALMSHOUSES in TOTHILL FIELDS, WESTMINSTER, which were built in 1699–1701. His plans are preserved in the Guildhall Record Office [Rep. 106, f. 119]. These handsome almshouses were demolished in 1893. They are illustrated by R. W. Paul, *Vanishing London*, 1894, pls. i–ii. In *c.*1700 John Olley and a bricklayer named Richard Smith built WATERSTOCK HOUSE, OXON., for Sir Henry Ashurst, Bart., dem.

1787 [Bodleian Library, MS. Top. Oxon. d. 385, f. 28 and MS. d. d. Ashurst d. 8].

ORAM, WILLIAM (–1777), held the post of Master Carpenter in the Office of Works from 1748 until his death in 1777. Horace Walpole says that he 'was bred an architect, but taking to landscape painting arrived at great merit in that branch. He was made Master Carpenter to H. M. Board of Works, by the interest of Sir Edward Walpole, who has several of his pictures and drawings' (*Anecdotes of Painting*, ed. Wornum, 1862, 711). He designed the Triumphal Arch erected in Westminster Hall for the coronation of George III in 1761, of which he published a print (B.L., Crowle Collection, iii, 172, and Bodleian, Gough Maps 23, f. 49^{v}). According to his posthumously published *Precepts on the Art of Colouring in Landscape Painting*, 1810, viii n., 'a single building of his only is remembered, a house in Lancashire at the instance of his friend counsellor Lucas.' He was known as 'Old' Oram in order to distinguish him from his son Edward, who assisted de Loutherbourg as scene-painter to the Drury Lane Theatre [J. T. Smith, *A Book for a Rainy Day*, ed. W. Whitten, 1905, 98]. He was elected a member of the Florentine Academy *in absentia* in 1765 [*Burlington Mag.* Aug. 1990, 537]. His will is P.C.C. 124 COLLIER. For his work as a decorative painter see E. Croft-Murray, *Decorative Painting in England* ii, 1970, 251–2.

ORME JOHN, advertised in the *Chester Chronicle* of 16 January 1778 that he had been a pupil or assistant of John Carr of York (*q.v.*) and was setting up in practice as an architect in Liverpool.

ORRIDGE, JOHN (1773–1844), was for forty-seven years the governor of the County Gaol at Bury St. Edmunds in Suffolk. As a young man he studied the law, but found it uncongenial and became a prison governor while still in his twenties. In 1819–20 Bury Gaol was enlarged by William Wilkins (*q.v.*) on lines indicated by Orridge, who published the plan in his *Description of the Gaol at Bury St. Edmunds*, 1819. This work also contains plans of a prison made by him for the Emperor of Russia at the request of T. F. Buxton, M.P. In 1822 Orridge and John Dobson (*q.v.*) competed for the design of the new County Gaol at Carlisle. Orridge's plans were preferred as those of 'a man of long experience' in the management of gaols and were carried out under the direction of two local surveyors, Christopher Hodgson and William Nixon (*qq.v.*) [Cumbria R.O., Gaol Committee's Second Report, QAG/4]. Orridge died on 29 June 1844, aged 71 [*Gent's Mag.* 1844 (ii), 332].

OSBORNE, ROBERT (*c.*1798–), was admitted to the Royal Academy Schools in 1816 at the age of 18, and was awarded the Silver Medal in 1821. He was a pupil of H. H. Seward, and exhibited architectural drawings at the Royal Academy between 1817 and 1822.

OVER, CHARLES, published in 1758 a work entitled *Ornamental Architecture in the Gothic, Chinese and Modern Taste, being above fifty entire new designs . . . (Many of which may be executed with roots of trees) for gardens, parks, forests, woods, canals, etc., containing paling of several sorts, gates, garden-seats both close and open, umbrellos, alcoves, grottoes and grotesque seats, hermitages, triumphal arches, temples, banqueting houses and rooms, rotundos, observatories, ice-houses, bridges, boats and cascades . . . from the designs of Charles Over.* Nothing is known about Over, but his book was an elegant collection of designs for ornamental buildings, including the earliest use of the umbrella as a functional shelter [Eileen Harris, *British Architectural Books and Writers 1556–1785*, 1990, 336–7].

OVERTON, THOMAS COLLINS, exhibited architectural drawings at the Free Society of Artists in 1764, 1765 and 1766. They included a design for a Gothic pavilion, an elevation of St. Peter's, Rome, and designs for a large country house. In 1766 he published fifty plates of designs for garden temples, etc., entitled *Original Designs of Temples, and other ornamental Buildings for Parks and Gardens, in the Greek, Roman and Gothic taste*. This was reissued later the same year as *The Temple Builder's Most Useful Companion*. Plate 30 shows a Gothic temple 'built for Mr. Richards at Spittle Croft near Devizes', plate 34 a rustic cottage 'designed for Edward Goddard to be built near Cliffhill Copse, Wiltshire', and plate 41 a triangular building 'built for Mr. Maynard near Devizes'. Overton was no doubt a member of a family of land surveyors of that name practising in Devizes in the eighteenth century (for whom see P. Eden, *Dictionary of Land Surveyors and Cartographers 1550–1850*, 1975–6, 196).

OWEN, JACOB (1778–1870), was born in North Wales on 28 July 1778, and received his training under William Underhill, a civil engineer much engaged in canal works, principally in South Staffordshire. Having in 1804 joined the Royal Engineers Department of the

Ordnance, he became in 1820 Clerk of the Works at Portsmouth. In 1832 he was transferred to Dublin as architect and engineer to the Irish Board of Works, and remained there until 1856, when he retired. He died at Tipton in Staffordshire on 26 October 1870.

In England Owen designed two Gothic Commissioners' churches, ALL SAINTS, LANDPORT, PORTSMOUTH, 1825–7, and ST. JOHN, FORTON, nr. GOSPORT, HANTS., 1829–30, the latter in conjunction with his son T. E. Owen [Port, 132–3, 144–5]. In 1827 he acted as executant architect for a church at BEMBRIDGE, ISLE OF WIGHT, designed by John Nash [I.C.B.S.]. It became unsafe and was replaced in 1845. In Ireland he was responsible for MOUNTJOY PRISON, 1850, the CRIMINAL LUNATIC ASYLUM at DUNDRUM, 1848, additions to the FOUR COURTS and to the KING'S INNS in DUBLIN, and for several model schools and other government buildings in various parts of the country.

Owen married the daughter of his master Underhill, and by her had seventeen children. Five of the sons followed their father's profession: Thomas Ellis Owen (d. 1862) is the subject of the next entry. David Price Owen was in the Royal Engineers' Department. William Henshaw Owen practised as an architect and civil engineer at Limerick, Henry Owen at Waterford, while James Higgins Owen (d. 1891) succeeded his father as architect to the Irish Board of Works. One of the daughters married Sir Charles Lanyon, architect and civil engineer of Belfast, who was her father's pupil [*A.P.S.D.*, memoir by J. H. Owen; *D.N.B.*].

OWEN, THOMAS ELLIS (1804–1862), was one of the sons of Jacob Owen, clerk of the works at Portsmouth (*q.v.*). He became the pupil of an 'eminent' (but unidentified) 'architect and civil engineer' in London, and then went to Italy to complete his professional education. The 'architect' in question may have been the surveyor J. W. Higgins (*q.v.*), whose daughter Owen married soon after his return from Italy. Surveying and land valuation were certainly skills in which Owen was proficient, and they formed the basis of his later success as a developer in Southsea. His earliest architectural works were Gothic churches, some of which he designed in collaboration with his father. These were characteristic works of their period, but in his later churches (notably St. Jude's, Southsea) Owen endeavoured to develop a more 'ecclesiological' style, and his Greek Orthodox church in London was an essay in the Byzantine style.

Owen also designed one or two public buildings in Portsmouth, and was involved in railway and civil engineering works (e.g. in the Camber Docks), but he was chiefly notable as an enterprising and successful speculative builder who was responsible for some extensive and attractive residential development in Southsea, first (*c.*1835–51) in the form of stuccoed brick terraces and Italianate villas in the area to the west of Grove and Palmerston roads, and later (*c.*1851–60) of informal layouts of detached villas in various styles to the east of those roads.

By the 1830s Owen was a prominent figure in Portsmouth. In 1831 he became a member of the unreformed corporation, and after the Municipal Reform Act he was first a councillor, then an alderman and Mayor (1847–8 and again in 1862). He died suddenly on 11 December 1862 aged 58, and was buried at Milton in the same grave as his father-in-law J. W. Higgins. His practice was continued by George Rake, who had been his partner since the 1850s. In the 1870s Rake joined forces with A. E. Cogswell, whose practice is now in its third generation [Tony Preedy & Ian Stewart, 'Thomas Ellis Owen 1804–1862', unpublished dissertation, Portsmouth Polytechnic School of Architecture, 1972).

CHURCHES AND OTHER PUBLIC BUILDINGS

EAST STOKE CHURCH, DORSET, 1828–9, Gothic; chancel 1885 [I.C.B.S.].

FORTON, HANTS., ST. JOHN'S CHURCH, in collaboration with Jacob Owen, 1829–30, Gothic; rebuilt 1905 [Port, 144–5].

GOSPORT, HANTS., HOLY TRINITY CHURCH, galleries, etc., in collaboration with Jacob Owen, 1829–30; removed 1887–8 [I.C.B.S.].

WATERLOOVILLE CHURCH, HANTS., 1830–1, Gothic; remodelled 1969 [I.C.B.S.].

PORTSEA ISLAND CEMETERY, Greek Doric entrance screen, 1831; dem. [Preedy & Stewart, 16–18].

PORTSMOUTH, THEATRE ROYAL, HIGH STREET, alterations 1831 [Preedy & Stewart, 34–5].

HORDLE CHURCH, HANTS., rebuilt 1831, Gothic; rebuilt 1872 [I.C.B.S.].

HAVANT CHURCH, HANTS., rebuilt west end of nave, 1831–2; rebuilt 1874 [I.C.B.S.].

ALVERSTOKE CHURCH, HANTS., repairs and alterations, 1832 [I.C.B.S.].

FAREHAM, HANTS., HOLY TRINITY CHURCH, 1834–6, Gothic; chancel 1911 [*Southern Daily Mail*, 31 Oct. 1896].

REDHILL, nr. HAVANT, HANTS., ST. JOHN'S CHURCH, 1838, Gothic; chancel rebuilt 1853 [I.C.B.S.].

PORTSMOUTH, ST. MARY'S CHURCH, HIGHBURY

STREET, 1839, Gothic; dem. 1921 [I.C.B.S.].

LONDON, FRENCH PROTESTANT CHURCH, ST. MARTIN-LE-GRAND, 1842–3, Gothic; dem. 1888 [exhib. at R.A. 1843, H. B. Wheatley & P. Cunningham, *London Past and Present* ii, 1891, 78].

PORTSMOUTH, ST. THOMAS'S CHURCH (now Cathedral), restoration of chancel in collaboration with Jacob Herbert, surveyor to Winchester College, 1843 [*Builder* i, 1843, 187].

PORTSEA, HANTS., ST. MARY'S CHURCH, KINGSTON, 1843–4; Gothic; rebuilt 1887–9 [R. Hubbuck, *Portsea Island Churches*, Portsmouth 1969, 9–10].

PORTSMOUTH, THE PORTSEA ISLAND UNION WORKHOUSE (now St. Mary's Hospital), with A. F. Livesay, 1843–5 [Preedy & Stewart, 133].

PORTSEA, BAPTIST CHAPEL, off KENT STREET, 1846; dem. [Preedy & Stewart, 134].

PREES VICARAGE, SHROPSHIRE, 1846–8 [Lichfield Joint Record Office, B/A/13].

LONDON, THE GREEK CHURCH, LONDON WALL, 1850, Byzantine style; dem. [J. Timbs, *The Curiosities of London*, 1867, 227].

SOUTHSEA, HANTS., ST. JUDE'S CHURCH, KENT ROAD, 1850–1, Gothic; galleries, Bishop Ingham's Chapel and south transept added later by Owen [R. Hubbuck, *Portsea Island Churches*, Portsmouth 1969, 23].

MARTLETWY, PEMBROKESHIRE, CHURCH OF ENGLAND SCHOOL, 1852 [Haverfordwest Record Office, TSE/1/14].

HADLEY CHURCH, SHROPSHIRE, 1856, Gothic [I.C.B.S.].

RESIDENTIAL DEVELOPMENT

The first phase of Owen's activity as a speculative builder began in 1834–5 with the development of the area north of Kent Road. Here he was responsible for QUEEN'S TERRACE, 1834–7, a terrace (dem.) in SUSSEX PLACE, 1835–7, SUSSEX TERRACE, 1837–8, etc. Later terraces to the south of Kent Road included NETLEY TERRACE, RICHMOND TERRACE and CLIFTON TERRACE, all completed in the 1840s. The largest was PORTLAND TERRACE, built 1845–6. The detached villas built by Owen in the neighbourhood of Elm Grove, Grove Road South, Albany Road, Merton Road, Nelson Road, Clarendon Road and The Circle are too numerous to particularize, but special mention must be made of his own house, DOVER COURT, PORTLAND ROAD, a Gothic mansion built in 1848–50 and now a school. For Robert Cruickshank he designed a grand development near GOSPORT called ALVERSTOKE CRESCENT, 1828–31 [*Hampshire Telegraph*, 11 Aug. 1828, 5 Oct. 1829].

OWEN, WILLIAM (1791–1879), was the son of William Owen (d. 1831), a cabinet-maker and builder of Haverfordwest. In partnership with his brother James, Owen carried on his father's business, while developing a considerable practice as an architect and becoming a leading figure in Pembrokeshire. In 1832 he had been appointed County Surveyor and he was a member of many local boards and charities. He was four times Mayor of Haverfordwest and in 1859 High Sheriff of Pembrokeshire. In 1832 he was the leading promoter of a radical improvement of the layout of Haverfordwest, forming a new thoroughfare leading into the town over a bridge which he designed and built at his own expense, recouping his outlay from tolls. He also designed a handsome new Shire Hall, a Corn Market and other buildings to embellish the town, and appears to have designed several minor country houses, of which Scolton Manor (now a Country Museum) is the only documented example, though several others (e.g. Avallenau, near Haverfordwest, and Pantsaison, Pembrokeshire) can be attributed to him. Owen died in January 1879, leaving four sons, of whom the most notable was the Welsh historian Dr. Henry Owen [information from Mr. Thomas Lloyd, to whom all the following references are due].

HAVERFORDWEST, PEMBS., NEW MARKET, 1824; dem. [signed elevation in Haverfordwest R.O., Borough Records 1443].

CARMARTHEN, HEOL AWST CHAPEL, 1827 [Carmarthen R.O., Heol Awst 69; *Carmarthen Jnl.* 6 April 1827].

MATHRI RECTORY, PEMBS., 1826 [N.L.W., St. David's Bounty plans 138].

HAVERFORDWEST, PEMBS., BRIDGE (R. Cleddau), 1833–6 [letter from Owen in *Haverfordwest & Milford Haven Telegraph*, 24 Jan. 1855].

HAVERFORDWEST, PEMBS., SHIRE HALL, 1835–7 [*Carmarthen Jnl.* 10 April 1835; Haverfordwest R.O., PQ/F/7/1].

HAVERFORDWEST, PEMBS., ALBANY CHAPEL, 1839; remodelled 1890 [*Welshman*, 29 Oct. 1839, where James Owen is said to be architect and builder].

MANORDEIFI RECTORY, PEMBS., 1839 [N.L.W., St. David's Bounty plans 136].

SCOLTON MANOR, SPITTAL, PEMBS., for James Higgon, 1840–2 [Haverfordwest R.O., Scolton 2].

BEGELLY RECTORY, PEMBS., 1842–4 [N.L.W., St. David's Bounty plans 4].

HAVERFORDWEST, PEMBS., CORN MARKET (now a cinema), 1847–9 [*Welshman*, 3, 17 Dec. 1847; *Pembrokeshire Herald*, 13 Nov. 1863].

P

PACE, RICHARD (*c.*1760–1838), was a builder and architect of Lechlade in Gloucestershire. Little would be known about him but for the large trade-card issued by him and his son in 1830. This gives small engraved views of twenty-seven buildings, described as 'a part of their designs which they have executed'. It shows that they designed and built a number of parsonages and small country houses in the neighbourhood of Lechlade, and a few further afield. These are mostly in a simple late Georgian style, sometimes with fashionable Grecian or Gothic detailing. The information given on the trade card is not wholly to be trusted, for one of the buildings illustrated, Dancers Hill, South Mimms, Middlesex (not 'Herts.') seems never to have been enlarged in the manner indicated, while at Broadwell Grove, Oxfordshire, the Paces were merely carrying out designs by William Atkinson. Richard Pace died on 28 April 1838, aged 78, and is commemorated by a monument in the churchyard at Lechlade. The business was continued by his son Richard Pace, junior. A lithographic copy of the trade card is preserved in the Bodleian Library, together with some of Pace's business correspondence [MS. Eng. Hist. *c.*298]. A portrait of Pace in the uniform of the Life Guards, in which he served from 1784 to 1788, is in the possession of his descendants.

LONDON, remodelled premises in LEICESTER SQUARE* for Messrs. Gedges, 1788; dem. 1936.

LONDON, house in SOHO SQUARE* for Robert Hervey Gage or Gedge, 1791 or 1794; dem. 1937.

LUSHILL HOUSE,* nr. HIGHWORTH, WILTS., for William Peek, 1795.

BIBURY RACE STAND,* GLOS., 'for H. R. Highness the Prince of Wales, Noblemen etc. of Bibury Club', 1800; dem.

BOWDENDALE,* WILTS., for R. Broome, 1803.

WOODHILL PARK,* CLYFFE PYPARD, WILTS., added S. E. range for B. Pinneger, 1804.

BROADWELL,* OXON., house for William Hervey, occupied by Mr. Large, 1804.

SHRIVENHAM VICARAGE,* BERKS., for Revd. Edward Berens, 1805.

LECHLADE RECTORY,* GLOS., for Revd. J. L. Bennet, 1805; façade since altered.

BROADLEASE,* BUSCOT, BERKS., for E. Loveden Loveden, 1808.

BROUGHTON POGGS RECTORY,* OXON., for Revd. Samuel Goodenough, 1808.

FILKINS HALL,* OXON., stables for E. Colston, 1809.

COLN ST. DENNIS RECTORY,* GLOS., for Revd. William Price, 1810.

LITTLE HINTON RECTORY,* WILTS., for Revd. Charles Moysey, 1810.

KINGSTON LISLE,* BERKS., addition of wings, etc., for A. E. M. Atkins, 1812 (*C. Life*, 17 June 1971).

CHINNOR RECTORY,* OXON., for Sir James Musgrave, Bart., 1813.

COXWELL RECTORY,* BERKS., for Revd. J. F. Cleaver, 1816.

SALPERTON PARK,* nr. NORTHLEACH, GLOS., added wings for J. Brown, 1817.

SHIPTON-UNDER-WYCHWOOD VICARAGE,* OXON., for Revd. Robert Phillimore, 1818 (cf. Oxon. C.R.O., Oxford Diocesan Papers, Faculty Register 1804–27, pp. 113–14).

SHERBORNE, GLOS., STONE FARM HOUSE* for 1st Lord Sherborne, 1819.

ODDINGTON RECTORY,* GLOS., for Hon. and Revd. Dr. Edward Rice, 1820.

WILLIAMSTRIP PARK,* NR. FAIRFORD, GLOS., Gothic lodge for M. Hicks Beach, 1822.

LITTLECOTE PARK,* WILTS., stables and Gothic lodge for General E. W. Popham, 1822.

LECHLADE CHURCH, GLOS., repairing and refitting, including Gothic altar-piece and insertion of N. and S. galleries, 1823, all removed 1882 [A. Williams, *Lechlade*, 1888, 85].

COBERLEY RECTORY,* GLOS., for Revd. W. Hicks, 1826.

FAIRFORD,* GLOS., house (probably CROFT HOUSE) for J. Wane, 1826.

BURFORD CHURCH, OXON., refitted interior 1826–7; altered by G. E. Street 1870–2 [I.C.B.S.; cf. W. J. Monk, *History of Burford*, 1891, 38–9].

BROADWELL CHURCH, OXON., gallery and other fittings, 1829 [I.C.B.S.].

LANGFORD CHURCH, OXON., repewing 1829 [I.C.B.S.].

HATHEROP RECTORY (now SEVERALLS), GLOS., 1833 [Glos. Diocesan Records F4/1].

PACEY, JEPTHA, was an architect and builder at Boston in Lincolnshire, where the ASSEMBLY ROOMS were built under his direction in 1820–2, perhaps adapting designs made by William Atkinson (*q.v.*) in 1813 [Boston Corporation Records, *ex inf.* Mr. R. Hewlings]. At Boston he also designed an EPISCOPAL CHAPEL, HIGH STREET, *c.*1828; dem.

* Buildings shown on the trade card.

[T. Allen, *History of the County of Lincoln* i, 1834, 253]. In 1821 he designed WHAPLODE DROVE CHURCH, LINCS., in a classical style in conjunction with W. Swansborough of Wisbech [I.C.B.S.] and in 1826–7 a chapel (dem. 1888) at CHAPEL HILL, nr. TATTERSHALL [I.C.B.S.]. Five of the six small churches in the Fens built under an Act of Parliament of 1812 are attributed to him by Pevsner and Harris, *Lincolnshire*, Buildings of England, 1989, 65. His plans for altering or rebuilding WIGTOFT VICARAGE, LINCS., in 1817 are in the Lincs. C.R.O. (MGA 90). Pacey is said to have moved to Manchester later in life [*Boston Independent*, 31 Oct. 1891].

PAGE, JOHN, was a builder-architect at Lossiemouth in Morayshire. His name appears on designs for THE YORK TOWER, KNOCK OF ALVES, MORAYSHIRE, an octagonal castellated tower built in 1827 by Alexander Forteath of Newton to commemorate the Duke of York [photos of drawings in N.M.R.S.]. Page's name also occurs in connection with repairs to Milton Brodie House, Morayshire, in 1829 and to Gray's Hospital, Elgin, in 1833–4 [information from Mrs. E. Beaton].

PAGE, JOSEPH (*c.*1718–1776), born at Barton-on-Humber in Lincolnshire, was the son of a brickmaker and was himself trained as a bricklayer and plasterer. He became one of the leading architects and master builders of Georgian Hull. For Henry Maister he designed MAISTERS HOUSE, No. 160 HIGH STREET, in 1743. Lord Burlington's advice was sought and given, and may well have affected the design of the staircase. Palladian influence is also apparent in other Hull mansions, notably ETHERINGTON HOUSE (*c.*1750, dem. 1947), for which Page may have been responsible. Nos. 9–12 KING STREET, including the archway to Prince Street, were designed by him *c.*1771. His last recorded work was the redecoration of the court room suite at TRINITY HOUSE in 1773–4. He died on 23 April 1776, aged 58, and is commemorated by a gravestone in St. Peter's churchyard, Barton-on-Humber [*V.C.H. Yorkshire: E. Riding* i, 445–7; I. & E. Hall, *Georgian Hull*, York 1978/9, figs. 170, 171, 194; National Trust Guide to Maisters House].

PAGE, SAMUEL (1771–1852), was a builder, surveyor and architect with an office at 14 King's Road, Gray's Inn. In 1803 he exhibited a 'design for a gentleman in Kent' at the Royal Academy. In the same year he altered HAREWOOD HOUSE, HANOVER SQUARE, LONDON, for the 1st Earl of Harewood [Harewood archives]. In 1806–9 he rebuilt SAVILE HOUSE, Nos. 5–6 LEICESTER SQUARE, LONDON, as premises for Mary Linwood, an artist in needlework, in association with a surveyor called George Boyd. A Chancery suit which ensued over the payments due to Page became a *cause célèbre* which is said to have gone on for forty years, and involved an appeal to the House of Lords in 1841. Savile House was destroyed by fire in 1865 [J. Timbs, *The Curiosities of London*, 1868, 512; *Survey of London* xxxiv, 462–3]. In 1811 Page was responsible for alterations to GRIMSTHORPE CASTLE, LINCS., for the 2nd Lord Gwydyr (afterwards 19th Lord Willoughby de Eresby), assisted by his pupil Henry Garling (*q.v.*). He died at Dulwich on 2 April 1852, aged 80 [A. P. Burke, *Family Records*, 1897, 462–3; *Gent's Mag.* 1852 (i), 535; Foster, *Alumni Cantabrigienses, 1752–1900* v, 5].

Page was married three times, and had nine children. His two eldest sons by his first wife, Mary Flood, were Samuel Flood Page (1796–1854) and Philip Flood Page (b. 1798). Samuel began his career as an architect, but was subsequently ordained. Philip became a pupil of J. H. Good, from whose office he exhibited student's work at the Royal Academy in 1814, 1816 and 1817. In 1825–7 Samuel Flood Page and his brother jointly designed the Greek Revival PARTIS' COLLEGE at WESTON, nr. BATH [*A.P.S.D.*, *s.v.* 'Bath'; lithograph in Baker Collection, Bath Reference Library, vol. xviii, 29]. Samuel Flood Page also designed ST. PAUL'S CHURCH, MILL HILL, MIDDLESEX, 1829–36, in a cheap Gothic style with cement-rendered walls [*V.C.H. Middlesex* v, 35].

PAGETT, HENRY (–1718), of Bridgnorth, Shropshire, came from a family of master masons connected with that town, earlier members of which built a Market House at Newport (Salop.) in 1662 [E. C. Peele & R. S. Clease, *Shropshire Parish Documents*, 1903, 247] and rebuilt two arches of Bridgnorth Bridge in 1670 [*Trans. Salop. Archl. Soc.* 49, 1937–8, 206]. In 1697 Henry Pagett contracted to build NANTCRIBBA, FORDEN, MONTGOMERYSHIRE (destroyed by fire 1899: T. Lloyd, *Lost Houses of Wales*, 1986, 36) for Arthur Devereux, 'according to a draught or plott drawne & produced at the ensealing of these Articles', and by a subsequent agreement he undertook to construct a wooden staircase like one recently made in John Edwards's new house at Maesmawr, Meiford, Montgomeryshire [N.L.W., Glensevern, 11602, 11622]. Both Nantcribba and Maesmawr were up-to-date houses of their period, with regular fenestration and hipped roofs. In *c.*1700 William Pagett assisted the Worcester mason Charles Green to repair WORCESTER BRIDGE [*Trans. Worcs. Archl. Soc.* 3rd ser. 8, 1982, 33], and in 1714 Henry Pagett the elder, freemason of Bridgnorth, and William Higgins of Pitchford, freemason, rebuilt the nave and west tower of QUATFORD CHURCH, SALOP., in traditional Gothic style [contract in parish records]. The churchwardens' accounts of RYTON, nr. SHIFNAL, SALOP., record a payment of 12s. in 1710 to 'the two Patchetts for Measuring the Steeple' after it had been built by Roland Richards, mason. Several building leases in Bridgnorth obtained by Henry Pagett at the end of the seventeenth century are in Shrewsbury Public Library (8863–5). The burial of 'Henry Pagett Mason' on 11 October 1718 is recorded in the register of St. Mary's Bridgnorth. A monument in St. Alkmund's Church, Shrewsbury, by James Paget (1702) is recorded by Pevsner, *Shropshire*, Buildings of England, 1958, 257.

PAIN, WILLIAM, called in his publications 'architect and joiner', or 'architect and carpenter', was the author of numerous architectural pattern-books published during the second half of the eighteenth century. They were as successful in popularizing the 'Adam style' as the earlier books of William Halfpenny had been in disseminating Palladian and rococo motifs, and nearly all of them went into several editions. Their titles, with the date of the first edition in each case, were: *The Builder's Companion and Workman's General Assistant*, 1758; *The Builder's Pocket Treasure; or, Palladio delineated and explained*, 1763; *The Practical Builder*, 1774; *The Carpenter's and Joiner's Repository; or, a new System of lines, etc. for Doors, etc., Staircases, Soffits, etc.*, 1778; *The Builder's Golden Rule; or, Youth's sure Guide in Architecture and Carpentering*, 1781; *A Supplement to the Builder's Golden Rule*, 1782; *The Carpenter's Pocket Directory*, 1781; *The Practical Measurer*, 1783; *The Practical House Carpenter*, date of 1st ed. uncertain, 2nd ed. 1788; *The British Palladio; or, Builder's General Assistant*, 1786; *The Builder's Sketch Book*, 1793; and *List of Prices of Materials*, 1793. A selection of plates from his works was published in 1946 as *Decorative Details of the Eighteenth Century by William and James Pain*, with an introduction by A. E. Richardson.

Apart from his publications, nothing is known of Pain's career, unless he is to be identified with the William Paine of Bellyard, Temple Bar, carpenter and builder, who was one of the unsuccessful candidates for a District Surveyorship in 1774, when he was 56 years of age [Middlesex County Records, General Orders, No. 10]. In *The British Palladio* Pain was assisted by his son James, 'builder and surveyor'. This James Pain was the father of James, George Richard, Henry and Thomas Pain. All except the last became pupils of John Nash, who was instrumental in establishing James (*c.*1779–1877) and George Richard (*c.*1793–1838) as architects and builders in Ireland, where they had an extensive practice as designers of churches and castellated houses. Henry Pain practised as an architect and surveyor in London until the 1840s. William Pain, who exhibited architectural designs at the Royal Academy in 1802–9 from the same address (1 Diana Place, Fitzroy Square) as G. R. Pain, was presumably another of James Pain's sons. [*A.P.S.D.*; *D.N.B.*, *s.v.* 'Pain, James'; James Wicks, 'Narrative Pedigree of the Pain Family', *Blackmansbury* ix, 1972, 79–80; Eileen Harris, *British Architectural Books and Writers 1556–1795*, 1990, 338–46.]

PAINE, JAMES (1717–1789), was born in Hampshire and was probably the son of John Pain, a carpenter at Andover. The baptism of 'James, son of John Pain' took place there on 9 October 1717. Very little is known about Paine's early life, but in the preface to the first volume of his *Plans*, published in 1767, he stated that he 'began the study of architecture in the early part of his life, under the tuition of a man of genius', identified in a footnote as 'the late Mr. Thomas Jersey'. Jersey (*q.v.*) is in fact an obscure figure, and a more significant influence on Paine's early life may have been the St. Martin's Lane Academy, where he is believed to have been a student, and where he would have come into contact with some of the leading artistic personalities of the time, including the architect Isaac Ware. Paine's first commission suggests that he had found favour in Lord Burlington's circle, for it was to act as clerk of the works or superintending architect at Nostell Priory, a large Palladian house in Yorkshire about to be built to the designs of Col. James Moyser (*q.v.*), a friend and disciple of Burlington's. The building of Nostell occupied Paine for some seven years. It established him in architectural practice in Yorkshire, and led, in 1741, to his marriage to Sarah, the daughter of a gentleman of Pontefract named Jennings. In the course of the 1750s Paine appears to have taken over the north-country practice of Daniel Garrett (*q.v.*), and between 1745 and 1770 he designed or altered some thirty country houses in the northern counties, including Alnwick, Chatsworth, Kedleston, Sandbeck and Worksop. His practice was never, however, confined exclusively to the north. From 1746 onwards he was again resident in London, and it was commissions such as Melbourne House, Whitehall (1754–8), Brocket Hall, Herts. (*c.*1760–75), Thorndon Hall, Essex (1764–70), and Wardour Castle, Wilts. (1770–6), as well as his numerous northern houses, that prompted Hardwick's well-known remark that Paine and Sir Robert Taylor 'nearly divided the practice of the profession between them, for they had few competitors till Mr. Robert Adam entered the lists'.[1]

Like many other Georgian architects, Paine aspired to a place in the Office of Works. In January 1745 he was appointed Clerk of the Works at the Queen's House at Greenwich, a post which he is said to have owed to the patronage of a former Surveyor-General, the Hon. Richard Arundell. In December 1746 he was promoted to be Clerk of the Works at the Mews at Charing Cross, but in 1750 exchanged this post with Kenton Couse for the almost sinecure clerkship of the works at Newmarket, which he retained until 1780. From 1758 onwards he was also Clerk of the Works at Richmond New Park Lodge. Paine's acceptance of these offices must have been due more to the hope of promotion to a senior post than to the small salaries which they commanded. With Arundell's help he did in fact aspire to succeed Ripley as Comptroller in 1758, but it was Flitcroft who got the job, and it was not until 1780 that Paine obtained a seat on the Board of Works as one of the two Architects of the Works, only to lose it two years later as a result of Burke's reform of the Civil Service.

In July 1755 Paine obtained a year's leave from the Board of Works in order 'to make the Tour of Italy'. Very little is known about this journey, and it does not appear to have played an important part in Paine's artistic development. Indeed, in the preface to his *Plans* (1767), he writes deprecatingly about the value of foreign travel to an architect, emphasizing the importance of practical experience rather than the pursuit of 'inconsistent antiquated modes' abroad. For him the publications of Palmyra and Baalbek were 'curious' rather than 'useful' works which 'furnish no new lights in the great parts of architecture, and are only valuable for the ornaments'. As for the ancient Greek architecture studied by Stuart and Revett, he dismissed it as 'despicable ruins'. As these passages make clear, Paine was no neo-classicist. His architecture is basically Palladian in character, but he was by no means a slavish imitator of Kent and Burlington, and his work is distinguished by several characteristic features that give it a strong individuality. Prominent among these were tripartite grouping (derived from the wings at Holkham, but frequently used by Paine for the principal blocks of his houses), very wide pediments (e.g. at Serlby Hall and originally at South Ormsby Hall), 'open' pediments with a vestigial strip of cornice at the base, and the hollowing of solid surfaces by niches. Like his rivals Taylor and Chambers he was one of the pioneers of the country house designed as a compact, centrally planned villa, and he was an accomplished designer of staircases, of which the finest surviving example is at Wardour Castle. In interior decoration he was from the first attracted towards lighter rococo forms, and eventually devised a type of compartmented ceiling elegantly patterned into coiling festoons which was offered as an alternative to Adam's neo-classical repertoire. Though charming enough (as can be seen in the Ballroom at Sandbeck or the Temple of Diana at Weston Park), it failed to hold its own against Adam's brilliant decorative schemes, and at Kedleston, Nostell and Alnwick Paine had the mortification of seeing Adam supersede him as the interior decorator.

Paine was for some years a prominent member of the Society of Artists of Great Britain, and many of his designs were shown at the Society's exhibitions between 1761 and 1772. In 1770, at time when the Society was shaken by the recent defection of a group led by Chambers, Paine was elected President, and shortly afterwards he designed for the Society the academy or exhibition-room in the Strand, of which he laid the first stone on 16 July 1771. The first exhibition was held in the new premises in May 1772, but the Society was heavily in debt and losing ground rapidly to the newly established Royal Academy headed by Reynolds and Chambers. Paine resigned the Presidency in October 1772, leaving the Society to its fate. The traditional story that it was rivalry between himself and Chambers that led to the break-up of the Society appears to be unfounded, but Paine's loyalty to the older Society in 1768 may help to explain why he never became a Royal Academician. The only occasion when he exhibited at the Academy was in 1783, when he showed the designs for the three bridges that he built across the Thames. In 1767 he published a folio volume of *Plans, Elevations and Sections of Noblemen and Gentlemen's Houses . . . executed in the Counties of Derby, Durham, Middlesex, Northumberland, Nottingham and York* as the first instalment of

[1] In his introduction to Gwilt's 1825 edition of Chambers's *Treatise on Civil Architecture*.

his collected works. The second volume, illustrating a number of further buildings, was published in 1783. A second edition of the former volume was issued at the same time. A reprint of both was published by the Gregg Press in 1967.

In 1754 Paine built a new house for himself in St. Martin's Lane. At the end of the garden, facing onto Little Court, Castle Street, were three smaller houses, in one of which he established his friends John Gwynn and Samuel Wale. He removed in 1766 to Salisbury Street, Strand, which he was building as a private speculation on land leased from the Earl of Salisbury, and in 1773 acquired a country retreat at Sayes Court near Chertsey in Surrey. Here he assumed the status of a country gentleman, serving as J. P. for Middlesex and Surrey and in 1785 as High Sheriff for the latter county. His death took place in France in the autumn of 1789, in circumstances which have never been satisfactorily explained. According to the obituary in the *Gentleman's Magazine*, 'some months preceding his decease, finding the infirmities of age steal fast upon him, and a family occurrence of a singular nature preying upon his spirits', he 'retired' to the Continent, where he died at the age of 72.

Paine's first wife died after only a few years of marriage, and in 1748 he made a second, and socially superior, marriage to Charlotte, youngest sister of Richard Beaumont of Whitley Beaumont near Huddersfield. By his first wife he had a son James (*q.v.*) and by the second two daughters, the younger of whom married Tilly Kettle the painter. Paine's principal pupils were R. W. Douthwaite, Christopher Ebdon, John Kendall and John Sanderson.

A portrait of Paine by P. Falconet, intended as one of a 'set of artists', was engraved by D. Pariset in 1769; Grignion's engraving of another, by Paine's friend Francis Hayman, is prefixed to his volume of designs for the Mansion House at Doncaster, published in 1751. The finest portrait, however, is that of Paine and his son by Sir Joshua Reynolds, which was painted in 1764. It was bequeathed to Oxford University by the younger Paine in 1829 and now hangs in the Ashmolean Museum. There is a companion portrait of the second Mrs. Paine and her two daughters in the Lady Lever Art Gallery at Port Sunlight. Several drawings by Paine are in the Victoria and Albert Museum, and there are others in the R.I.B.A. Drawings Collection, the Soane Museum (xlvi, 9 no. 14, a design for a country house), and among the Fitzwilliam papers in Sheffield Archives (unexecuted design for a grandstand on Knavesmire race-course, 1754).

[*A.P.S.D.*; *D.N.B.*; will (P.C.C. 260 BISHOP); sale catalogue of library (B.L., S.C.S. 24 (6)); obituary in *Gent's Mag.* 1789 (ii), 1153; Marcus Binney, 'The Villas of James Paine', *C. Life*, 20, 27 Feb., 6 March 1969; Peter Leach, *James Paine*, 1988; Eileen Harris, *British Architectural Books and Writers 1556–1785*, 1990, 346–8.]

The following list of works is based on the catalogue in Leach's biography, where full references will be found to the relevant sources for each commission. References are given, as usual, in round brackets to illustrations or descriptions of the individual buildings.

PUBLIC BUILDINGS

DONCASTER, YORKS (W.R.), THE MANSION HOUSE, 1745–8; attic storey added by W. Lindley 1800–1 (J. Paine, *Plans, Elevations, Sections, and other ornaments of the Mansion House of Doncaster*, 1751).

LONDON, THE MIDDLESEX HOSPITAL, MARYLEBONE, 1755–78; remodelled in nineteenth century; dem. 1928.

NORWICH, ROMAN CATHOLIC PRIEST'S HOUSE and CHAPEL, MUSEUM COURT, for 9th Duke of Norfolk, 1764; dem.

LONDON, ST. ANNE'S, SOHO, WORKHOUSE, No. 14 MANETTE STREET, 1770–1; heightened 1804 (*Survey of London* xxxiii, 190–1).

LONDON, ACADEMY or EXHIBITION ROOMS in STRAND for Incorporated Society of Artists, 1771–2; converted into Lyceum Theatre 1790, reconstructed as the English Opera House 1809; dem. 1815.

BRIDGES (PUBLIC)

WALLINGTON BRIDGE, NORTHUMBERLAND, for Sir Walter Blackett, 1755.

CAVENDISH BRIDGE, SHARDLOW, DERBYSHIRE (R. Trent), 1758–61; collapsed 1947 (Paine, *Plans* i, pls. 10–11, where it is called 'Welden Bridge').

RICHMOND BRIDGE, SURREY (R. Thames), in collaboration with Kenton Couse, 1774–7; widened 1937 (Paine, *Plans* ii, pls. 82, 83).

CHERTSEY BRIDGE, SURREY (R. Thames), 1780–5; partly rebuilt 1894.

WALTON BRIDGE, SURREY (R. Thames), 1783; rebuilt 1863–4.

KEW BRIDGE, SURREY (R. Thames), for Robert Tunstall, 1783–9; rebuilt 1903.

LONDON: DOMESTIC ARCHITECTURE

NORTHUMBERLAND HOUSE, STRAND, completion of gallery begun by Daniel Garrett, for 1st Duke of Northumberland, *c.*1753–7; dem. 1874.

ST. MARTIN'S LANE, No. 76, and three small houses in LITTLE COURT, CASTLE STREET, the former for himself, the others as speculations, 1754; dem. 1843.

WHITEHALL, house for Sir Matthew Fetherstonhaugh, Bart, afterwards MELBOURNE and now DOVER HOUSE, 1754–8. The portico and entrance were added by Henry Holland, who also rebuilt the west front (*Plans* i, pls. 26–32; *Survey of London* xiv, 60–4 and pls. 38–56).

ST. JAMES'S SQUARE, No. 19, completed remodelling of house for 2nd Duke of Cleveland, 1754–60, succeeding Daniel Garrett; dem. 1894 (*Survey of London* xxix, 161–3).

NORFOLK HOUSE, ST. JAMES'S SQUARE, alterations for 9th Duke of Norfolk, 1756–69, including Catholic chapel (1768); dem. 1938 (*Survey of London* xxix, 187–202).

LEICESTER SQUARE, No. 47, chimney-piece for Sir Joshua Reynolds, *c.*1760; dem. 1937 (*Plans* ii, pl. 97). Paine may have designed the gallery and painting-room built by Reynolds in 1760–1 (*Survey of London* xxxiv, 508–9).

SALISBURY STREET, STRAND, 1765–73. This was a personal speculation by Paine on land leased to him by 6th Earl of Salisbury in 1765. The two end houses facing the Strand, illustrated in Tallis's *London Street Views*, 1838–40, pl. 19, were demolished in 1888, the remainder in *c.*1923.

SOUTH AUDLEY STREET, LUMLEY HOUSE, alterations and repairs for 4th Earl of Scarbrough, 1766.

ST. JAMES'S SQUARE, No. 17, chimney-piece for Sir Henry Bridgeman, Bart., 1766; dem. 1865.

PARK LANE, house (later BREADALBANE HOUSE) for 9th Lord Petre, 1766–70; dem. 1876–7 (*Plans* ii, pls. 72–5, 89, 98).

PALL MALL, No. 79, for Dr. William Heberden, 1769–71; dem. 1866 (*Plans* ii, pls. 76–8; *Survey of London* xxix, 378).

SACKVILLE STREET, No. 28, chimney-piece for 1st Lord Melbourne, *c.*1770; dem. (*Plans* ii, pl. 100).

STRAND, No. 59, COUTTS'S BANK, alterations for James Coutts, 1770–1, and for Thomas Coutts, 1780–3; dem. 1923.

MELBOURNE HOUSE (now ALBANY), PICCADILLY, chimney-pieces for 1st Lord Melbourne, 1773; one removed 1803 and now at Renishaw Hall, Derbyshire (*Plans* ii, pls. 99, 100).

attributed: KING STREET, COVENT GARDEN, No. 37, for John Lane, 1773–4 (*Survey of London* xxxvi, 160–5 and pls. 69b, 82).

PALL MALL, No. 105, alterations for Hon. Thomas Fitzmaurice, 1779–80; dem. 1838 (*Plans* ii, pls. 79–81; *Survey of London* xxix, 349).

COUNTRY HOUSES

NOSTELL PRIORY, YORKS. (W.R.), acted as executant architect for house designed by the amateur architect James Moyser (*q.v.*), for Sir Rowland Winn, Bart., *c.*1737–*c.*1750. Paine was left to make his own designs for the interior decoration, but this was never completed under his direction, and the principal rooms were designed by Robert Adam between 1765 and 1775 (*Vitruvius Britannicus* iv, 1767, pls. 70–3; *C. Life*, 16–30 May 1952).

HEATH HOUSE, nr. WAKEFIELD, YORKS. (W.R.), enlarged for Robert Hopkinson, 1744–5 (*Plans* i, pls. 61–2).

HICKLETON HALL, YORKS. (W.R.), completion of new house for Godfrey Wentworth, 1745–8; enlarged *c.*1775 and altered 1857–60.

WILSFORD HALL, LINCS., east end enlarged for Matthew Lamb, 1749–51; dem. 1918.

CUSWORTH HALL, YORKS. (W.R.), alterations, including addition of wings containing chapel and library for William Wrightson, 1749–53 (*Vitruvius Britannicus* iv, 1767, pls. 88–9; W. Angus, *Select Views of Seats*, pl. xvi, 1788).

WADWORTH HALL, YORKS. (W.R.), for Josias Wordsworth, *c.*1750 (*C. Life*, 1 Sept. 1966).

SPROTBOROUGH HALL, YORKS. (W.R.), unidentified work for Godfrey Copley *c.*1750; dem. 1926.

YORK, work for the Revd. John Fountayne, Dean of York, *c.*1750 (presumably at the Old Deanery, dem. 1831).

attributed: MILNSBRIDGE HOUSE, nr. HUDDERSFIELD, YORKS. (W.R.), for William Radcliffe, *c.*1750; altered 1795–6 (J. P. Neale, *Views of Seats*, 1st ser. iv, 1821).

BRAMHAM, YORKS. (W.R.), THE BIGGIN, remodelled for Mr. Allison, *c.*1750–6.

FELBRIGG HALL, NORFOLK, built quadrangular service-wing, fitted up Gothic library, designed staircase, added bow window at north end of west block, and decorated several rooms, including the dining-room, for William Windham, 1751–6 (*C. Life*, 22 Dec. 1934).

ORMSBY HALL, SOUTH ORMSBY, LINCS., for William Burrell Massingberd, 1751–6 (*C. Life*, 26 March, 2 April 1959).

attributed: DINNINGTON HALL, YORKS. (W.R.),

alterations and additions for Henry Athorpe, 1752.

attributed: THE GRANGE (now Beckett Park College), HEADINGLEY, nr. LEEDS, YORKS. (W.R.), for Walter Wade, 1752.

BLAGDON HALL, NORTHUMBERLAND, new south range for Sir Matthew White, Bart., 1752–6.

COWICK HALL, YORKS. (W.R.), alterations for 3rd Viscount Downe, 1752–60, including remodelling of north front and internal alterations (the latter since largely destroyed) (*Plans* i, pls. 12–14; J. Killeen, *A Short History of Cowick Hall*, 1967).

RABY CASTLE, CO. DURHAM, alterations and repairs for 1st Earl of Darlington, including suite of rooms of west range, Raby Hill House (Gothic) and the Home Farm, *c.*1752–8 (Alistair Rowan in *C. Life*, 1 Jan. 1970 and *Arch Hist.* xv, 1972).

WHITLEY BEAUMONT, YORKS. (W.R.), redecoration of Great Hall for his brother-in-law Richard Beaumont, *c.*1752–4; dem. 1953–5.

GLENTWORTH HOUSE, LINCS., east front for 4th Earl of Scarbrough, 1753; façade mutilated *c.*1950. This was a fragment of a grandiose scheme for rebuilding the house, for which Paine's drawings, dated 1753, remain at Sandbeck Park, Yorks. Two of them are illustrated in *C. Life*, 7 Oct. 1965, p. 883, figs. 8–9; cf. *Plans* i, p. 12.

attributed: COXHOE HALL, CO. DURHAM, alterations for John Burdon, *c.*1754; dem. *c.*1955.

HARDWICK, nr. SEDGEFIELD, CO. DURHAM, the Temple, Banqueting House, Bath House, Gothic Ruin and other ornamental buildings for John Burdon, 1754–7. Designs by Paine for a Banqueting House and a large mansion (never built) are in the County Record Office (D/Br.). The latter is illustrated in *C. Life*, 20 Feb. 1969, p. 406, fig. 1.

ALNWICK CASTLE, NORTHUMBERLAND, reconstruction of keep as residence for 1st Duke of Northumberland, *c.*1754–68, Gothic; destroyed *c.*1854. Paine's work included the dining-room, the great staircase and the state bedrooms. Robert Adam, who succeeded him, was responsible for the saloon, drawing-room and library. For the possible involvement of Henry Keene, see above, p. 572. (plans in *Castles of Alnwick and Warkworth &c.* from sketches by C[harlotte] F[lorentia], Duchess of Northumberland, privately printed 1823, and *R.I.B.A. Sessional Papers* 1856–7, 14).

SERLBY HALL, NOTTS., for 2nd Viscount Galway, 1754–73; remodelled by Lindley & Woodhead 1812 (*Plans* i, pls. 37–40; *C. Life*, 26 March, 2 April 1959).

GOSFORTH HOUSE, NORTHUMBERLAND, for Charles Brandling, *c.*1755–64 (*Plans* i, pls. 15–25). In 1880 the house was converted into a club and grandstand for the Newcastle Races, with a hotel in one wing and stables in the other. It was gutted by fire in 1914 and reconstructed internally in 1921.

BELFORD HALL, NORTHUMBERLAND, for Abraham Dixon, 1754–6; altered and enlarged by J. Dobson 1817; restored and converted into flats 1983–7 (*Plans* i, pls. 33–6; *C. Life*, 28 Jan. 1988).

CHATSWORTH, DERBYSHIRE, works for 4th Duke of Devonshire, including the office wing, 1756–60 (dem. *c.*1820), the stables 1758–63, the bridge in the park over the river Derwent, 1760–4 and the bridge at Beeley, 1759–60 (*Plans* i, pls. 1–9; Francis Thompson, *A History of Chatsworth*, 1949, 90–1; *C. Life*, 18 July 1968; *Derbyshire Archl. Jnl.* c, 1980, for stables).

attributed: HIGH MELTON HALL, YORKS (W.R.), rebuilt for John Fountayne, Dean of York, 1757.

AXWELL PARK, CO. DURHAM, for Sir Thomas Clavering, Bart. 1758; altered and enlarged by J. Dobson 1817–18 (*Plans* i, pls. 56–60).

STOCKELD PARK, nr. WETHERBY, YORKS. (W.R.), for William Middleton, 1758–63; enlarged 1895 (*Plans* i, pls. 41–6).

RAVENSWORTH CASTLE, CO. DURHAM, alterations for 1st Lord Ravensworth, before 1759; rebuilt 1808 onwards.

ST. IVES, nr. BINGLEY, YORKS. (W.R.), for Benjamin Ferrand, 1759; dem. 1859 (*Plans* i, pls. 63–6).

SYON HOUSE, ISLEWORTH, MIDDLESEX, Gothic bridge for 1st Duke of Northumberland, 1760; dem.

BYWELL HALL, NORTHUMBERLAND, enlarged for William Fenwick, *c.*1760; west wing added 1817 (*Plans* i, pls. 53–5).

BRAMHAM PARK, YORKS. (W.R.), temple, now chapel, for George Fox, Lord Bingley, *c.*1760 (*Plans* i, pl. 73); *attributed*: the pavilions at either end of the stables (*C. Life*, 1 Oct. 1921, figs. 5 and 7).

GIBSIDE, CO. DURHAM, chapel and mausoleum for George Bowes, 1760–6 (*Plans* i, pls. 67–9; *C. Life*, 15 Feb. 1952); also interior decoration in house, *c.*1756–60; now a ruin.

BROCKET HALL, HERTS., rebuilt for Sir Matthew Lamb, Bart., and his son Sir Peniston Lamb, *c.*1760–75; also bridge in park 1772–4, and entrance screen and lodges, *c.*1770–5 (*Plans* ii, pls. 53–9, 84–5, 90–2; *C. Life*, 4, 11, 18 July 1925).

KEDLESTON HALL, DERBYSHIRE, for Sir Nathaniel Curzon, Bart. (cr. Lord Scarsdale), 1759–60. Paine superseded

Matthew Brettingham, who had already built the north-east wing, and was himself superseded by R. & J. Adam after he had built the north-west wing and started work on the central block and quadrants. Paine's design, evidently conditioned by Brettingham's, was exhibited at the Society of Artists in 1759 and is illustrated in his *Plans* ii, pls. 42–52.

FORCETT HALL, YORKS. (N.R.), banqueting house for James Shuttleworth, 1762; dem. (*Plans* i, pls. 70–2).

WORKSOP MANOR, NOTTS., for 9th Duke of Norfolk, 1763–7, never completed and dem. 1843 apart from triumphal arch, screen-wall and basement of north front. Paine had also been responsible for internal decorations in the old house, burnt down in 1761 (*Plans* ii, pls. 1–16, 96, 101; *C. Life*, 15–22 March 1973).

SANDBECK PARK, YORKS. (W.R.), remodelled for 4th Earl of Scarbrough, *c.*1763–8 (*Plans* i, pls. 47–52; *C. Life*, 7, 14, 21 Oct. 1965).

GOPSALL HALL, LEICS., garden temple for Charles Jennens, *c.*1764; collapsed 1835 (*Plans* i, pl. 74). Drawings in R.I.B.A. Collection for internal decoration in the house (dem. 1951) were probably not carried out.

TOWN HILL HOUSE, BRADFORD, YORKS. (W.R.), for John Buck, 1764–8 [drawings inscribed as 'J. Buck's house by Paine' published by R. Hewlings in *Burlington Mag.* 133, Aug. 1991, 552–3].

THORNDON HALL, ESSEX, for 9th Lord Petre, 1764–70; gutted 1878 (*Plans* ii, pls. 17–29, 88). Though on a different site, Paine's house incorporated the portico designed by Leoni for the house begun by 8th Lord Petre in 1733, but never completed owing to the latter's death in 1742.

WESTON PARK, WESTON-UNDER-LIZARD, STAFFS., TEMPLE OF DIANA, 'ROMAN BRIDGE', and chimney-pieces, for Sir Henry Bridgeman, Bart., *c.*1765–70 (*Plans* ii, pls. 68–71, 86, 95, 97; *C. Life*, 23 Nov. 1945, 26 April 1946, p. 760).

BAGSHOT PARK, SURREY, remodelled for 3rd Earl of Albemarle, 1766–72; dem. 1877 (Paul Sandby, *Select Views in England, Wales etc.*, pl. 66 (1777); G. F. Prosser, *Select Illustrations of the County of Surrey*, 1828).

HAMPSTEAD, MIDDLESEX (now LONDON), NORTH END (later PITT) HOUSE, alterations and additions for Charles Dingley, 1767; dem.

attributed: ST. PAUL'S WALDEN BURY, HERTS., north range for Mrs. Bowes, widow of George Bowes of Gibside, 1767 (*C. Life*, 15–22 March 1956).

BURTON HALL, LINCS., addition of new south range for 2nd Lord Monson, 1767–71. Paine's range was retained when the remainder of the house was demolished in 1959.

HARE HALL, ROMFORD, ESSEX, for J. A. Wallinger, 1769–70 (*Plans* ii, pls. 60–3).

CHILLINGTON HALL, STAFFS., bridge in park for Thomas Giffard, *c.*1770 (*Plans* ii, pl. 87; *C. Life*, 13 Feb. 1948, p. 328, fig. 7).

SHRUBLAND PARK, SUFFOLK, for the Revd. John Bacon, 1770–2; remodelled by J. P. Gandy Deering 1831–3 and Sir Charles Barry 1848–52 (*Plans* ii, pls. 64–7; *C. Life*, 19–26 Nov. 1953).

attributed: MOOR PARK, nr. FARNHAM, SURREY, remodelling for Basil Bacon, *c.*1770–5 (*C. Life*, 25 Nov. 1949).

WARDOUR CASTLE, WILTS., for 8th Lord Arundell, 1770–6 (*Plans* ii, pls. 30–41, 93–4; *C. Life*, 22–9 Nov. 1930).

GAYNES PARK, UPMINSTER, ESSEX, for Sir James Esdaile, 1771–6; dem. 1820.

SAYES COURT, ADDLESTONE, SURREY, alterations for himself *c.*1773; dem. 1925 (*Blackmansbury* viii, 1971, 83).

HAMPTON, MIDDLESEX, alterations to a house for James Coutts, 1774–5.

PONSONBY HALL, CUMBERLAND, built by Edward Stanley *c.*1775, is virtually a duplicate of Paine's St. Ives, built in 1759, and was probably copied from Paine's published designs without his knowledge, perhaps by J. Hird (*q.v.*).

PAINE, JAMES (1745–1829), the only son of James Paine (*q.v.*), was born at Pontefract in August 1745. His father brought him up as an architect, employing him as clerk of the works at Thorndon Hall. But he vacillated between architecture, painting and sculpture, exhibiting a mixture of paintings, watercolour drawings and sculptures at the Society of Artists between 1761 and 1773, and in the list of subscribers to his father's first volume of *Plans* he is described as 'Sculptor'. So far as architecture was concerned, a serious and prolonged breach with his father, healed only in 1783, must have had an adverse effect on his prospects, and apart from some employment as surveyor to the 1st Marquess of Salisbury's London estate, he appears by the 1790s to have largely abandoned architecture for a modest career as a water-colourist.

On attaining his majority Paine immediately set out for Italy, and was in Rome from 1767 to 1769. He was there again in 1773–5, following his marriage in August 1773 to the daughter of a land-surveyor sometimes employed by his father. He was elected a Fellow of the Society of Antiquaries in 1771, and of the Architects' Club in 1791. He died at Sunninghill, Berks., in May 1829, aged 83.

His pictures, casts and architectural books were sold at Christie's on 12 March 1830 (copy of catalogue in Soane Museum). The nineteen volumes of 'Architectural Drawings and Memoranda by Mr. Paine of Ascot Heath' sold by Puttick and Simpson on 12 November 1863, lot 1413, may have been James Paine's, as Ascot Heath is close to Sunninghill, where he lived. Surviving drawings by Paine in the Victoria and Albert Museum include some made in Rome in 1774 (93 E. 26), and there are others in the British Library (Add. MS. 31,323). The joint portrait of the two Paines painted by Reynolds in 1764 is referred to above (p. 723). A half-length portrait of himself by Romney, described as 'a shew performance' of the latter's ability, is mentioned in the younger Paine's will. He left three daughters, his son James Thomas Paine, born in Rome in 1774, having died in boyhood[1].

The only building known to have been erected to the younger Paine's designs is a villa called BELMONT at MILL HILL, MIDDLESEX, for which the elevation, inscribed 'villa erected at Mill Hill for Peter Hammond, Esq.', is in the British Library (Add. MS. 31,323, A[3]), but he may also have designed a house in Bond Street for his brother-in-law Tilly Kettle. According to a marginal note in the Bodleian copy of his father's *Works* ii, 17, the chimney-piece in the saloon at Brocket Hall, Herts., was 'the Design and Performance of Ja. Paine Junr. A. D. 1771'. The drawings in the Victoria and Albert Museum include several designs for monuments, and the following monuments signed by Paine have been noted: to William Powell the actor (d. 1769) in Bristol Cathedral; to Lady Sondes (d. 1777) in Rockingham Church, Northants. (for which there is a drawing in the V. & A.); and to Mrs. Sarah Proby (d. 1783) in Chatham parish church. Paine's architectural designs (several of which are illustrated by Leach, see below) show an interest in the Greek Revival of which his father would not have approved, but as executed his villa at Mill Hill is an interesting variation on his father's style of domestic architecture without any of the Grecian features shown in his original drawing. At Hatfield House there is a large perspective by Paine of an ambitious scheme for laying out the Marquess of Salisbury's land on Millbank for building, made in 1787.

[*A.P.S.D.*; *D.N.B.*; R. Gunnis, *Dictionary of British Sculptors*, 1968, 286–7; *The Farington Diary*, ed J. Greig, ii, 123, 286; iii, 210; v, 155, 190; viii, 26; will, P.C.C. 438 LIVERPOOL; Peter Leach, 'James Paine junior: an unbuilt architect', *Arch. Hist.* 27, 1984.]

PAINE, JOHN DAVIS (*c.*1807–1869), was admitted to the Royal Academy Schools in 1824 at the age of 17. He was awarded the Gold Medal in 1833, and exhibited at the Academy from 1828 to 1843. From 1828 to 1832 he worked for Jeffry Wyatville at Windsor Castle, and then he was in the office of Benjamin Dean Wyatt [*C. Life*, 14 Nov. 1968, 1257]. He appears to have started independent practice from 57 Lincoln's Inn Fields in 1836. He designed a London terminus for the Westminster and Greenwich Railway Company (not executed), and a bridge across the Water of Leith for the Edinburgh, Leith and Newhaven Railway Company. He also designed the terminus of the St. Petersburg and Tsarskoe Selo Railway in Russia. His other works included CHRIST CHURCH, NEWARK-ON-TRENT, NOTTS., 1836, an unidentified church in Hampshire, 1839, the GRAMMAR SCHOOL at DAGENHAM in ESSEX, 1840, POPLAR HOUSE, BATTERSEA, for Henry Fownes, 1840, and the LIGHTHOUSE on GOODWIN SANDS, 1842, for all of which he exhibited designs at the Royal Academy. A scheme for building villas in Osterley Park, Middlesex, for the 5th Earl of Jersey, exhibited by Paine at the R. A. in 1841 and 1843, was not carried out. A volume of his engraved *Plans and Sections of the Proposed Westminster Bridge, Deptford and Greenwich Railway* is in the Bodleian Library (Gough Adds., fol. D. 28). The design which he submitted for the Royal Exchange competition in 1839 was engraved, and is illustrated in *London as it might have been* (Guildhall Library exhibition catalogue, 1975). He died in Holborn, London, in 1869, aged 61 [St. Catherine's House Index of Births, Marriages and Deaths].

PAINTER, JOHN, junior, was the son of a builder at Emsworth in Hampshire, where he was born in about 1791. He exhibited at the Royal Academy in 1807–8, showing in 1807 'a villa now building near Portsmouth' and in 1808 a 'villa now building at Widley, near Portsmouth', and a design for the 'improvement of an old building near Chichester'.

PALMER, HENRY (1805–1830), was the son of Robert Palmer of Reading. He was admitted to the Royal Academy Schools in 1825 at the age of 20, and won the Silver Medal in 1827. He exhibited views of buildings in Reading at the Academy in 1828 and

[1] A portrait of 'Master James Thomas Paine' was painted by Romney in 1776 and engraved by John Dean in 1780 (H. Ward & W. Roberts, *Rommey* ii, 1904, 115).

1829. He died at Paris in 1830 'on his return from Italy, where he had been completing his education as an architect' [*Gent's Mag.* 1830 (ii), 574].

PALMER, JOHN (*c.*1738–1817), was the son of Thomas Palmer, a successful glazier of Bath, who had been associated with the architect and builder Thomas Jelly (*q.v.*). John Palmer was taken into partnership by Jelly in about 1765, and was associated with him in offering to build a new Guildhall in return for a ninety-nine years' lease of the shops and houses which were to be included in the layout. The rejection of their proposal by the Corporation in 1775 occasioned a violent controversy between Palmer and Atwood, the city's architect, which was terminated only by the latter's death.

In September 1792 Palmer was elected Supervisor of Bounds, and soon afterwards he succeeded Thomas Baldwin as city architect. In this capacity he enlarged the Pump Room and built the Theatre Royal in Beauford Square, largely from designs by George Dance the younger, though it appears that Palmer did his best to take the whole credit for the building.

Palmer died on 19 July 1817, at the age of 79, and was buried in St. Swithin's Church, where there is a memorial tablet. Although not an architect of the first stature, his works maintain the high standards of design and craftsmanship characteristic of eighteenth-century Bath [W. Ison, *The Georgian Buildings of Bath*, 1948, 2nd ed. 1980, *passim*].

BATH

ST. JAMES'S CHURCH, rebuilt nave 1768–9, with Thomas Jelly, Gothic; interior altered by Manners & Gill, 1848, gutted 1942, dem. 1957 [Ison]; plan in B.L., Egerton MS. 3647, f. 158].

ST. SWITHIN'S CHURCH, WALCOT, 1777–80; tower and spire 1789–90 [Vestry Minutes and drawings in Somerset C.R.O.].

ORCHARD STREET THEATRE, remodelled auditorium 1775; closed 1805; since dem. [Ison].

LANSDOWN CRESCENT, for Charles Spackman, 1789–93 [Ison].

ST. JAMES'S SQUARE, for Richard Hewlett & James Broom, 1791–4 [Ison].

attributed: SEYMOUR STREET and part of GREEN PARK BUILDINGS, 1792–6; partly dem. at various dates [Ison].

THE ROYAL MINERAL WATER HOSPITAL, addition of attic storey, *c.*1793 [Ison].

ALL SAINTS CHAPEL, LANSDOWN, 1794, Gothic; altered 1878, dem. 1942 [Ison].

KENSINGTON CHAPEL, LONDON ROAD, and adjacent houses, for John Jelly, 1795 [Ison].

CHRIST CHURCH, MONTPELIER ROW, 1798, Gothic; chancel added 1866 [Ison].

THE THEATRE ROYAL, BEAUFORD SQUARE, 1804–5, built by Palmer largely to the designs of G. Dance, junior; rebuilt internally after fire of 1862 [Ison].

NEW BOND STREET, 1805–7 [Bath Council Minutes, 2 Jan. 1801, 4 Jan. 1803, 27 Feb. 1805, *ex inf.* Mr. J. Orbach].

COTTLES HOUSE, ATWORTH, WILTS., for Robert Hale, in association with Thomas Jelly, 1775 [Glos. C.R.O., D 1086, E 191, F 91].

SHOCKERWICK HOUSE, nr. BOX, SOMERSET, for Walter Wiltshire, *c.*1785 [James Tunstall, *Rambles about Bath*, 2nd ed. 1848, 288 and elevation inscribed 'Palmer Architect' in Bath Reference Library, Chapman Coll., vol. 2, p. 89].

PALMER, JOHN (1785–1846), was the fourth son of a humble family at Bishop Middleham, Co. Durham, where he was born on 28 January 1785. At the age of sixteen he was apprenticed to his uncle, a mason at Durham, and it was as a mason that in 1804 he obtained employment at Scone Palace in Perthshire, then being built to the designs of William Atkinson (*q.v.*). By now he had taught himself to read and write, and, with Atkinson's help, he 'learned the rudiments of architecture'. After two years in London (1806–8) he went to Yarmouth in order to assist in the building of the Naval Hospital, and while there married. In 1811 he returned to London, but in August 1813 he removed to Manchester, where he established a successful practice as an ecclesiastical architect. Himself a Catholic, he designed at least two churches for his co-religionists as well as several for the Church of England. His most notable work was the Catholic Church at Pleasington, a remarkably ambitious Gothic design of 1816–19 with a large traceried rose window and other elaborate decorative features.

Palmer had antiquarian interests which found expression in a book entitled *The History of The Siege of Manchester by the King's Forces* (1822) and in his *Guide to the Collegiate Church of Manchester* (Manchester 1829). With Dr. S. Hibbert-Ware and W. R. Whatton he collaborated in writing a *History of the Foundations in Manchester* (1834), to which he contributed the detailed description of the Collegiate Church in volume ii. Some of his papers and antiquarian collections are in the Chetham Library and Manchester Central Library. Towards the end of his life he lived in Chorlton-on-Medlock, where he died on 23 August 1846, aged 61. [R. W. Procter, *Memorials of Manchester Streets*, 1874, 191–2; J. Gillow, *Bibliographical Dictionary of English Catholics*, 1885, v, 238–9.]

MANCHESTER, COLLEGIATE CHURCH (now CATHEDRAL), alterations and restorations, 1814–15 [Joseph Aston, *A Picture of Manchester*, 1816, 45 n., 56].

PLEASINGTON, LANCS., SS. MARY AND JOHN (R.C.), 1816–18, Gothic, for J. F. Butler [*Catholic Gentleman's Magazine* 1818, 146, 241–2].

BLACKBURN, LANCS., ST. PETER'S CHAPEL, 1819–21, Gothic [W. A. Abram, *History of Blackburn*, 1877, 352].

MANCHESTER, ST. AUGUSTINE'S CHAPEL, GRANBY ROW (R.C.), 1820, Gothic [S. Lewis, *Topographical Dictionary of England* iii, 1831, 244].

BLACKBURN, LANCS., ST. MARY (formerly Parish Church, now CATHEDRAL), 1820–6, Gothic; damaged by fire 1831 and restored by Thomas Stones, clerk of works, with advice from T. Rickman [W. A. Abram, *History of Blackburn*, 1877, 306; I.C.B.S.].

ABRAM, LANCS., ST. JOHN'S CHURCH, 1837–8, Gothic; rebuilt 1936–7 [I.C.B.S.].

ASHTON-IN-MAKERFIELD, LANCS., HOLY TRINITY CHURCH, NORTH ASHTON, 1837–8, Gothic; chancel 1914, top of tower 1938 [I.C.B.S.].

PALMER, ROBERT (–1776), was a surveyor practising in Westminster in the latter part of the eighteenth century. In 1771 he was employed by the Hertfordshire justices to survey the new Shire Hall at Hertford designed by R. & J. Adam, and in 1774–6 he supervised the building of a new County Gaol there [L. Turner, *History of Hertford*, 1830, 293; Hertfordshire Quarter Sessions Records]. He was employed as a surveyor by the Bedford Estate and was involved in the layout of BEDFORD SQUARE at the time of his death in September 1776 [A. Byrne, *Bedford Square*, 1990, 29].

PALMER, T—, junior, exhibited at the Royal Academy from 17 Abchurch Lane, London, between 1798 and 1804. In the latter year he exhibited 'Tolworth Farm, nr. Kingston, Surrey, the property of T. Stanton, Esqr.', presumably TOLWORTH COURT HOUSE, on the road from Kingston to Ewell, which was occupied as a farmhouse in the nineteenth century.

PANCHARD, R—, of Bath, exhibited a design for a cathedral at the Royal Academy in 1804. In 1811 he was one of the architects who submitted plans for rebuilding the tower of Hungerford Church, Berks. They were not accepted [MS. minutes of trustees for rebuilding Hungerford Church].

PAPENDIEK, CHARLES EDWARD (1801–1835), was the youngest son of Christopher Papendiek, a member of the royal household staff at Kew. He was a pupil of Sir John Soane from 1818 to 1824, and exhibited at the Royal Academy between 1823 and 1831. At the time of his death in 1835 he had a post in the Office of Works as a writing clerk. He was the author of a series of twenty-four coloured lithographs of Kew Gardens, published by Ackermann in about 1820, and of *A Synopsis of Architecutre, for the information of the Student and Amateur*, 1826. [A. T. Bolton, *The Works of Sir John Soane*, 1924, Appendix C, p. xlvi; *History of the King's Works* vi, 185.]

PAPILLON, DAVID (1581–1659), was a Huguenot refugee who was brought to England as a child in 1588. He became an architect and military engineer and is said to have 'built houses in the city and suburbs of London'. During the Civil War he fortified Leicester and Gloucester for the Parliamentary forces. He established himself near Lubenham in Leicestershire, where he built an octagonal house called PAPILLON HALL, rebuilt by Lutyens in 1903 and demolished *c.*1950 (see eighteenth-century drawing reproduced in *C. Life*, 15 Aug. 1957, fig. 13). In the 1650s Sir Justinian Isham sought his advice about rebuilding Lamport Hall in Northamptonshire, which Papillon condemned as a 'structure si fort repugnant aux reigles de l'art'. His plans for replacing it were not, however, adopted. He was the author of *A Practicall Abstract of the Arts of Fortification and Assailing*, dedicated to Fairfax (1645). [A. F. W. Papillon, *Memoirs of Thomas Papillon*, 1887; J. Nichols, *History of Leicestershire* ii, 1798, 708; Sir Gyles Isham, 'The Architectural History of Lamport', *Reports and Papers of the Northants. Architectural and Archaeological Soc.* lvii, 1953, 17.]

PAPWORTH, JOHN BUONAROTTI (1775–1847), born in Marylebone, London, on 24 January 1775, was the second son of John Papworth (1750–99), the leading stuccoist of his day, who was much employed by the Office of Works in the time of Sir William Chambers. John was intended by his father for a medical career, but he showed an early talent for drawing which attracted the attention of Chambers, by whose advice it was decided to give him an architectural training. He received instruction in drawing from John Deare, the sculptor, and acquired the rudiments of a knowledge of perspective from Thomas Malton. On Chambers's advice he spent two years in the office of John Plaw, and in November 1789 he was apprenticed for three years to Thomas Wapshott, a builder, in order to learn the practical side of his profession. Subsequently he worked for a year at Sheringham's, a well-known firm of decorators in Great Marlborough Street, and he also assisted Michael Novosielski for a time. He exhibited at the Royal Academy from 1794 onwards, and was admitted to its Schools in December 1798. Owing to the outbreak of war with France, he was unable to complete his training in the usual way by a foreign tour, and it was not until much later in life that he went abroad, and then only to Paris (1824) and other places in northern Europe.

In 1796–7 he supervised the building of a house at Woodford in Essex for Sir James Wright. The nominal architect was Philip Norris, then upon the point of retirement, who introduced Papworth to his client as clerk of the works and allowed him to take complete charge of the building. This employment continued until 1799, and brought him other commissions in the neighbourhood. By the time he was 25, Papworth was well established in practice, and in 1803 he took up the freedom of the Clothworkers' Company and accepted his first pupil, Samuel Benwell, a nephew of John Plaw.

Papworth was a prolific architect, who was much employed in the alteration and decoration of country houses, in which he showed considerable skill. But his interests were not confined to his professional work, and he acted as honorary secretary to the Associated Artists in Watercolours from 1808 to 1810, himself exhibiting a work entitled 'The Hall of Hela', which had been shown at the Royal Academy the previous year, and was bought by Lord Tankerville. His 'Sketch for an Altarpiece in the private chapel at the Seat of a Nobleman, intended to combine in its structure architecture, painting, and sculpture', exhibited at the Academy in 1815, is now in the R.I.B.A. Drawings Collection. He was a member of the Society of Arts, and joined the Graphic Society on its foundation in 1833. His facility in drawing figure subjects as well as those of an architectural character is shown by the nine volumes of his drawings now in the R.I.B.A. Collection. His friends included John Varley, Henry Pickersgill, W. H. Pyne, James Ward, who painted his portrait, T. C. Hofland, for whom he designed the architectural part of the latter's picture of Jerusalem, and M. C. Wyatt, after whom he named his younger son. He contributed four illustrations (the breakfast-room, the dressing-room, the dining-room, and the architectural part of 'the carriage at the portico') to Peter Coxe's poem *The Social Day*, 1823, and he was a regular contributor to Ackermann's *Repository of Arts*, 1809–28. In it appeared *Select Views in London*, consisting of seventy-six coloured plates, reprinted under his name in 1816: in 1813 and 1814 a series of papers entitled *Architectural Hints*, and in 1816 and 1817 a second series of *Architectural Hints*, which were republished as *Rural Residences, consisting of a Series of Designs for Cottages, small villas, and other ornamental Buildings*, 1818, 2nd ed. 1832. This was followed by a series of designs for garden buildings, which appeared between 1819 and 1820, and was reprinted under the title of *Hints on Ornamental Gardening* in 1823. Of the *Poetical Sketches of Scarborough*, 1813, illustrated by the drawings of James Green, he wrote fourteen of the twenty-one chapters, and he was also the author of an unpublished farce entitled *The Artist, or Man of Two Masters*, and of some verses. In 1818–19 he assisted W. H. Pyne in the descriptions of Marlborough House, St. James's, and Kensington Palace for his *Royal Residences*, 1820, and in 1823 he wrote for Pyne's *Somerset House Gazette* the article on 'Antony Pasquin and Somerset House', which was reprinted by Gwilt in the preface to his edition of Chambers's *Civil Architecture* in 1825. He also wrote several descriptions of buildings for Britton and Pugin's *Public Buildings of London*, 1825–8, and edited in 1826 the fourth edition of Chambers's *Treatise on the Decorative Part of Civil Architecture*, adding copious notes, and *An Essay on the Principles of Design in Architecture, with nine plates, illustrative of Grecian Architecture*. In 1803 he had published a pioneer *Essay on the Causes of Dry Rot in Timber*. His 'Explanation of the method adopted in 1820, to confine the lateral walls, then inclining outwards, of Trinity Church, on Clapham Common', was printed in *The Architect, Engineer and Surveyor* iv, 1843, 187, and his paper on 'The Benefits resulting to the Manufactures of a Country from a well-directed cultivation of architecture, and of the art of ornamental Design', read at the R.I.B.A. in 1835, was published in the first volume of its *Transactions*.

Papworth's skill as a designer procured him many commissions to make 'artistic designs' for furniture, manufactured articles, silverwork, ornamental glassware, etc., as well as for testimonials, such as the salver given to Arthur Onslow, M.P., in 1816 for his parliamentary services. He designed the glass throne made by John Blades for the Shah of Persia, and an elaborate sherbet service for the Pasha of Egypt; the figurehead and other decorations of the 'London Engineer' paddle-steamer, the first of its kind to ply on the Thames below London Bridge; the covers of the *Forget-me-not Annual* from 1825 to 1830; three blinds with Greek ornamentation for the Phoenix Bank at New York, 1827; and a Gothic lantern for Eaton Hall, Cheshire. The monument which he erected to Colonel Gordon on the field of Waterloo was the first to be made in the form of a 'broken column', and other features regarded as characteristic of nineteenth-century taste could probably be traced to his designs. At a time when the improvement in the manufacture of glass permitted larger windows, Papworth was much in demand as a designer of shop-fronts, and he also built a number of warehouses, in which he made an early use of iron-framed construction. He was extensively employed as a landscape-gardener and townplanner. In the latter capacity he was responsible for Lansdowne Place and Crescent at Cheltenham, for the layout of the Brockwell estate at Dulwich and for the formation of St. Bride's Avenue in Fleet Street. Between 1825 and 1830 he planned and surveyed a proposed 'London Central Street' in continuation northwards of the Fleet Market, and a 'Greshambury New Street' from Cheapside to Queen Street – schemes which, although not carried out at that time, have since been largely effected. For William Bullock, the former owner of the Egyptian Hall, Piccadilly, he made a design for laying out an estate on the river Ohio opposite Cincinnati, upon which it was proposed to build a town called 'Hygeia', but this was not carried out (for a description of the estate, see W. Bullock, *Sketch of a Journey through the Western States of North America*, 1827).

Between 1817 and 1820 he was commissioned to make three sets of designs for a palace to be erected at Cannstatt for Wilhelm I, King of Württemberg, who had expressed the 'intention to anglicize some of the Royal Domains'. Drawings of the entrance and south fronts of one of these designs were exhibited at the Royal Academy in 1823, and those of the east and west fronts in 1827. None, however, were carried out, but Papworth's design for laying out the park at Cannstatt in the English fashion was partly executed, and in 1820 he received a diploma conferring upon him the title of 'architect to the King of Württemberg'. One of his designs for the palace, now at Broomhall, Fife, is illustrated in *Country Life*, 29 Jan. 1970, p. 245, fig. 11.

Papworth's versatility was recognized by his contemporaries, and when in 1815 he produced a design for a 'Tropheum' to commemorate the victory of Waterloo, his friends hailed him as a second Michelangelo. He was thereupon induced to add 'Buonarotti' to his name. The drawing was, however, rejected by the Royal Academy.

In 1835 he gave evidence to William Ewart's select committee on arts and manufactures, and in the following year he was appointed director of the Government School of Design, which occupied the rooms vacated by the Royal Academy on its removal to the west wing of the National Gallery. The detailed organization of the school was left in his hands, and he was assisted by his son John as secretary. The school was opened in May 1837, but a reduction in the government grant after it had been in existence only fifteen months necessitated his retirement in the interests of economy.

Papworth was one of the twelve architects who, on 2 July 1834, signed the resolution which led to the foundation of the Institute of British Architects. He was several times vice-president, and was made an honorary member on his retirement in December 1846. In January 1847 he was presented with a salver inscribed by a number of his pupils and other architects 'as a tribute of their respect and esteem for his talents as a distinguished architect, and for his worth as a man'.

Failing health led to Papworth's retirement from professional life at the end of 1846, and in February 1847 he left London to take up residence at Little Paxton, near St. Neots in Hunts., in a house designed by him many years before for his aunt Mary Papworth. Here he died on 16 June 1847. His portrait was painted by James Ward, R.A., in 1813; another was painted in the following year by James Green, and engraved in mezzotint by William Say. A third was painted in 1833 by F. R. Say.

Papworth was twice married: first, in 1801, to Jane, daughter of Thomas Wapshott, his former master; she died in 1809; and secondly, in 1817, to Mary Anne, the eldest daughter of William Say, mezzotint engraver, by whom he had two sons and one daughter. The elder son, John Woody Papworth (1820–70), architect and antiquary, is best known as the author of Papworth's *Ordinary of British Armorials*, a standard work of heraldic reference. His brother, Wyatt Angelicus Van Sandau Papworth (1822–94),[1] was the

[1] Andrew Van Sandau, of 34 Dowgate Hill, was one of J. B. Papworth's clients in the 1820s. Was he Wyatt Papworth's godfather?

founder of the Architectural Publication Society and the editor of its *Dictionary of Architecture*.

Papworth's pupils included his brother George (1781–1855), who had a successful career as an architect in Ireland, Samuel Benwell, James Thomson, W. A. Nicholson, J. D. Hopkins, Samuel West, who became a portrait-painter, and Charles Edwards, who also gave up architecture. William Knight, George Guillaume, G. H. Stokes, and Thomas Latter were in his office.

[Wyatt Papworth, *John B. Papworth, A Brief Record of his Life and Works*, privately printed, 1879; abstract of his diaries by Wyatt Papworth, typescript in R.I.B.A. library; *A.P.S.D.*; *D.N.B.*; R. P. Ross Williamson, 'John Buonarotti Papworth', *Arch. Rev.* lxxix, 1936; G. McHardy, *The Office of J.B. Papworth* (R.I.B.A. Drawings Catalogue), 1977.]

The following list of architectural works is based on Wyatt Papworth's privately printed memoir of his father, supplemented by reference to his abstract of the latter's diaries and to the R.I.B.A. Drawings Catalogue.

RAY LODGE, WOODFORD, ESSEX, for Sir James Wright, Bart. (as a residence for his son George), 1796–7; dem. Papworth was executant architect on behalf of Philip Norris (*q.v.*).

CHIGWELL, ESSEX, minor works for Mr. Wilkins, Mr. Noble, Mr. Hodgson, Mr. Richmond, Mr. St. Albans, and Miss Harrison, *c.*1798–1802.

DENNE HILL, BARHAM DOWNS, nr. CANTERBURY, KENT, additions for John Harrison, 1802; replaced *c.*1870 by a new house by George Devey.

COBHAM LODGE, COBHAM, SURREY, for Col. Joseph Hardy, 1803–4.

LALEHAM PARK, MIDDLESEX, for 2nd Earl of Lucan, 1803–6, with additions 1827–30, and further alterations in 1839 for 3rd Earl, including the model farm, stables, etc.

WANDSWORTH, SURREY, additions to residence of George Tritton, 1805–8.

CHIGWELL ROW, ESSEX, alterations to house for Sir David Wedderburn, Bart., 1807–10; dem.

WOOLWICH RECTORY, KENT, for the Revd. H. Fraser, 1807–11; dem.

YEADING BRIDGE, HILLINGDON, MIDDLESEX, 1812.

WHITE KNIGHTS, BERKS., rustic seats, etc., for the Marquess of Blandford, 1815–16 (Mrs. Hofland, *A Descriptive Account of the Mansion and Gardens of White-Knights*, 1819).

FYFIELD HOUSE, ESSEX, additions, including farmyard, for George Dorrien, 1815–17.

WATERLOO, BELGIUM, monument to Col. Sir Alexander Gordon, 1815.

KNEBWORTH, HERTS., mausoleum for Mrs. Bulwer Lytton, 1817 (executed by Whitelaw).

GWYNNE HOUSE, WOODFORD BRIDGE, ESSEX (now Dr. Barnardo's Home), large additions for H. Burmester, 1816.

CLAREMONT, SURREY, assisted J. W. Hiort in designing (1816) many of the works for Prince Leopold and Princess Charlotte, including the conservatories, entrance gates, cottages, coach-houses, stabling, etc., and the Gothic summerhouse which was eventually remodelled as a memorial to the Princess after her death in Nov. 1817.

FYFIELD CHURCH, ESSEX, repairs and wooden steeple, 1817.

HARESFOOT, nr BERKHAMSTED, HERTS., alterations for Thos. Dorrien, 1817–19; dem. *c.*1965.

ST. JULIAN'S, nr. SEVENOAKS, KENT, for Robert Herries, 1818–20, Gothic; enlarged by Sir James Pennethorne, 1836–7.

ALTON TOWERS, STAFFS., bridge of seven arches, Grecian and Gothic temples, park entrance, garden seats, etc., for 16th Earl of Shrewsbury, 1818–22.

TAMWORTH, STAFFS, additions to Dr. Woody's Lunatic Asylum, 1819.

NORTH END, HAMMERSMITH, MIDDLESEX, remodelled for Wm. Jones, 1819–30.

LEIGHAM COURT, STREATHAM, for J. G. Fuller, 1820–2, and added to it a second and larger house in 1823–44; dem. 1908.

GRANADA, SPAIN, monument to Mrs. Duncan, wife of Thomas Duncan, *c.*1829.

BALHAM HILL., SURREY, redecorated residence of James Morrison, 1821–3.

KEW PRIORY, SURREY, additions and landscape-gardening for Miss Elizabeth Doughty, 1823–5; dem.

BRAMPTON PARK, HUNTS., decoration of library and dining-room for Lady Olivia Sparrow, 1825; largely destroyed by fire 1907 (*V.C.H. Hunts.* iii, 12–13).

BRAMPTON SCHOOLS, HUNTS., for Lady Olivia Sparrow, *c.*1825.

GRAFHAM SCHOOL, HUNTS., for Lady Olivia Sparrow, *c.*1825; enlarged 1870.

HOLLY LODGE, HIGHGATE, MIDDLESEX, landscape-gardening, including a conservatory and new room, for Mrs. Coutts, afterwards Duchess of St. Albans, 1825; dem.

DULWICH, laid out Brockwell estate for John Blades, 1825–30; built two houses in Brockwell Terrace for John Blades, 1828–30; dem. 1908; altered or repaired Brockwell Hall for John Blades, 1824–9; designed Brockwell (later Clarence) Lodge for Mrs. Emma Murray, 1825–6; dem. *c.*1908 [*Survey of London* xxvi, 161–4].

CHELTENHAM, GLOS., designed MONTPELLIER PUMP ROOM (ROTUNDA) and laid out MONTPELLIER GARDENS, for Pearson Thompson, 1825–6.

CHELTENHAM, GLOS., designed LANSDOWNE PLACE and CRESCENT for R. W. & C. Jearrad (*q.v.*), 1825–9.

CHELTENHAM, GLOS., a 'large detached house' for Dr. John Shoolbred, *c.*1824; a terrace for Robert Morris, probably on the north side of Suffolk Square, 1825; Charlton House for Capt. F. Cregoe, 1825; a house near St. John's Chapel for Capt. Daniel Capel, 1828.

CHELTENHAM, GLOS., completed ST. JAMES'S CHURCH, SUFFOLK SQUARE (begun by E. Jenkins), 1826–32, Gothic.

CHELTENHAM, GLOS., ST. JOHN'S CHURCH or BERKELEY STREET CHAPEL, for the Revd. W. Spencer Phillips, 1827–9; dem. 1967.

DENFORD HOUSE, BERKS., drawing-room, offices, lodge, entrance gates, dairy, etc., for G. H. Cherry, 1827–8.

PRICKLER'S HILL, BARNET, HERTS., additions for Thos. Wyatt, 1828–32; dem. *c.*1890.

LITTLE GROVE, EAST BARNET, HERTS., extensive alterations and farm buildings for Frederick Cass, 1828–46; dem. 1932.

HENBURY COURT, GLOS., additions for Thomas Stock, 1829; dem. 1953.

CLAPHAM, SURREY, SOUTH SIDE, added picture gallery, saloon, and stables for John Allnutt, 1829–33; dem. *c.*1863 (E. E. F. Smith, *Clapham*, 1975, 71–2).

NEVILL HOLT, LEICS., alterations for Charles Nevill, 1829–32, Tudor Gothic.

TWICKENHAM PARK, MIDDLESEX, landscape-gardening, with conservatory, aviary, etc., for Thos. Todd, 1829; dem.

FONTHILL HOUSE, WILTS., lodges, entrance gateway, and other alterations for James Morrison, 1829–42; dem. 1921.

PARK HILL, STREATHAM, SURREY, billiard-room, conservatories, lodge and garden buildings, etc., for William Leaf, 1830–41.

HOLY TRINITY CHURCH, CLAPHAM COMMON, repairs, 1829, including new foundations and screwing up lateral walls to upright, as described in *Architect, Engineer and Surveyor* iv, 1843, p. 187.

CRANBURY PARK, HANTS., interior of library, fountain and other works for Thomas Chamberlayne, *c.*1830 (*C. Life*, 15 Nov. 1956).

DENFORD CHURCH, BERKS., for G. H. Cherry, 1830–2, Gothic; dem. *c.*1957.

ST. JOHN'S WOOD, house and cottage for Edward May, *c.*1830.

FROGNAL, HAMPSTEAD, large additions to two houses for C. P. Sullivan, *c.*1830.

CHICKLADE CHURCH, WILTS., 1832.

DULWICH, SURREY, stables and landscape-gardening for James Hannen, 1832.

CROUCH END, nr. HORNSEY, pavilion for J. G. Booth, 1832; dem.

KIRBY HALL, YORKS. (W.R.), landscape-gardening and conservatory for R. J. Thompson, 1833.

CALLY HOUSE, KIRKCUDBRIGHTSHIRE, remodelled house for Alexander Murray, 1833–7.

HILFIELD, YATELEY, HANTS., alterations and additions for Capt. H. B. Mason, R. N., 1834; destroyed by fire 1900.

KILLYBEGS, CO. DONEGAL, IRELAND, chapel, stables, and alterations to house for Alexander Murray, 1834–9.

ORNHAMS HALL, nr. BOROUGHBRIDGE, YORKS., house and farm buildings for Geo. Crow, 1835–6.

CLAPHAM COMMON, SURREY, landscape-gardening and conservatory for J. T. Betts, 1835–9.

HERNE HILL, alterations to house for Mrs. Simpson, 1835.

ALEXANDRIA, EGYPT, monument to Thomas Galloway Bey, 1837.

GLASSERTON CHURCH, WIGTOWNSHIRE, tower 1836 [B. Burke, *Visitation of Seats*, ser, i, vol. ii, 1853, 91; S.R.O., RHP 7697, no. 2, drawing probably by J.B.P.].

ORLEANS HOUSE, TWICKENHAM, MIDDLESEX, restored for Alexander Murray, 1837–9; dem. 1927.

BASILDON PARK, BERKS., completion of interior, including the principal ceilings, etc., and the cottages, octagonal lodges, entrance gates, park farm, etc., for James Morrison, 1839–44.

PENSHURST, KENT, 'THE BIRCHES', added attic storey for Mrs. Yates, *c.*1840.

FONTHILL BISHOP, WILTS., SCHOOL, Gothic, *c.*1840.

CASTLEBAR, CO. MAYO, IRELAND, farmyard, bailiff's cottage etc. for 3rd Earl of Lucan, *c.*1840–4.

MORDEN, SURREY, stabling, etc., for the Revd. R. Garth, 1841; dem.

HYLANDS, ESSEX, alterations for John Attwood, 1842–8, including *porte-cochère* (E. Abraham, *Hylands, an Architectural History*, Chelmsford 1988).

CHOBHAM LODGE, SURREY, repairs for Sir Denis le Marchant, 1842.

CLAPHAM PARK, house in King's Road for J. E. B. Stevenson, 1844–6.

FIR GROVE, WEYBRIDGE, SURREY, lodges and other buildings for Sir John Easthope, 1844.

HENDON, MIDDLESEX, alterations to house for George Morant.

LONDON

STRAND, No. 101, showroom for R. Ackermann, 1812, and new premises at No. 96, 1826; dem. (*Repository of Arts*, 3rd ser. ix, 363).

NEW BOND STREET, No. 88, shop-front for George Morant, 1817–19; dem.

PICCADILLY, EGYPTIAN HALL, gallery for William Bullock, 1819; dem. 1905 (Ackermann, *Repository of Arts*, 2nd ser. viii, 153).

MARYLEBONE, porch and verandah of house at corner of Brook Street for John Braithwaite, *c.*1820–9; dem.

BOODLE'S CLUB, ST. JAMES'S, Reading Room and other alterations, 1821; Dining Room (now kitchen), 1833–4 [*Survey of London* xxx, 443].

WEST STREET, W. SMITHFIELD, factory for Alexander Galloway, 1821–2, enlarged 1835 and 1840; dem.

BERKELEY SQUARE, No. 24, repairs for Wm. Snell, 1822–3.

LUDGATE HILL, No. 8, façade to Messrs. F. & R. Sparrow's Tea Warehouse, 1822–3, Chinese style; dem.

COVENTRY STREET, No. 17, shop-front for Messrs. Clarkson & Turner, 1822–7.

RICHMOND GARDENS, WHITEHALL, house for J. Irvine, 1824; dem.

LUDGATE HILL, No. 5, shop-front for John Blades, 1824–30.

MILTON STREET, warehouses, etc. for Messrs. Morrison & Co., 1824–35; dem. 194–.

LEICESTER SQUARE, No. 47, interior arrangement and addition of lecture theatre for the Western Literary and Scientific Institution, 1826; dem. 1937 (cf. *Survey of London* xxxiv, 510–11).

ST. BRIDE'S AVENUE, FLEET STREET, 1825–30 (J. Elmes, *Metropolitan Improvements*, 1831, 149 and plate).

FORE STREET, Nos. 103–7, alterations, etc., to premises of Messrs. Morrison & Co., 1829–30; dem.

GREAT CORAM STREET, No. 57, shop-front for William Dutton, 1829.

HOLBORN HILL, No. 94, 'gin-palace' for Messrs. Thompson & Fearon & Co., 1829–32; dem.

CHARLES STREET, ST. JAMES'S, No. 10, reconstructed façade for John Howell, 1833–8.

GRAY'S INN ROAD, workshops for Messrs. G. & T. Seddon, cabinet-makers, 1830–2; afterwards used as a hospital; dem.

BELGRAVE ROAD, workshop for Messrs. Wm. & Edward Snell, 1831–5; dem. 1860–2.

HARLEY STREET, No. 57, redecorated interior, including library, for James Morrison, 1831–3.

ACADEMY COURT, CHANCERY LANE, two houses for Alexander Galloway, 1832; dem. *c.*1865.

FRITH STREET, SOHO, shop-front for Messrs. Sewell & Cross, linen drapers, 1832; dem.

CHEAPSIDE, No. 26, shop-front for Messrs. Collard & Co., 1834; dem.

No. 2 SEAMORE PLACE, PARK LANE, alterations, including iron verandahs, for 1st Earl of Ducie, 1835; dem. *c.*1910.

GLOUCESTER LODGE (12, GLOUCESTER GATE), REGENT'S PARK, additions for J. Cryder, 1836.

YORK HOUSE, CHURCH STREET, KENSINGTON, alterations and repairs for Princess Sophia of Gloucester, 1838; dem. 1904.

KENSAL GREEN CEMETERY, Galloway family monument, 1838, and monument to Sir Charles Grey, Bart., 1839.

OXFORD STREET, No. 314, shop-front for Messrs. Duppa & Collins, *c.*1840; dem.

WHITE'S CLUB HOUSE, ST. JAMES'S, repairs and decorations for Henry Raggett, 1842–3.

PORTLAND PLACE, No. 56, repairs and alterations for Sir Roger Palmer, Bart., 1843.

WEYMOUTH STREET, No. 41, work for George Dorrien; dem.

PORTMAN SQUARE, No. 1, work for Thomas Dorrien.

FINCH LANE, premises for Messrs. Dorrien, Magens & Co.

WESTMINSTER BRIDGE ROAD, shop-front for Messrs. Collinge.

HOLBORN, No. 69, factory for Alexander Galloway; dem.

PICCADILLY, shop-fronts to Nos. 29 and 115; dem.

FLEET STREET, No. 43, alterations for Joseph Butterworth.

GLOUCESTER TERRACE, REGENT'S PARK, No. 4, conservatory for Mrs. T. Wyatt.

PARKE, HENRY (?1792–1835), was the son of John Parke, an eminent oboist. He was intended for the Bar, and studied for a time under a special pleader. But owing to an impediment in his speech he decided to give up the law, and after taking up several subjects without pursuing them, he developed a strong interest in architecture and was apprenticed to Sir John Soane in 1814. He became proficient in mathematics, geometry, mechanics and drawing, and some of the finest of the diagrams which were used by Soane to illustrate his lectures were made by Parke. These are still preserved in Sir John Soane's Museum, together with other drawings made by him at this time. He was awarded five Silver Medals by the Society of Arts, and in 1812 received their Gold Medal for a sea-piece.

Between 1820 and 1824 he travelled in

Italy, Sicily and Egypt, ascending the Nile in 1824 with his fellow-student J. J. Scoles. In 1829 he published a 'Map of Nubia, comprising the country between the first and second cataracts of the Nile', showing the positions of all the temples, rock-cut tombs, and other ancient monuments on the banks of the river. At Rome and elsewhere in Italy, he worked with Catherwood, T. L. Donaldson, and others, laboriously measuring the buildings of antiquity as well as those of the Renaissance. On returning to England he worked up his sketches and made a large number of fine architectural drawings, many of which were presented to the R.I.B.A. Library by his widow. Some drawings of Pompeii by Parke are in the Victoria and Albert Museum. He frequently exhibited at the Royal Academy from 1815 onwards, but most of his exhibits were of a topographical character, and he appears never to have practised as an architect. 'Diffident and retiring', he was 'ill fitted for the jarring warfare of life, and consequently was little known beyond the immediate circle of his friends'. He was a member of the committee of architects who, in 1835, presented a Gold Medal to Sir John Soane, and was largely responsible for the design of the medal, from the die of which the Soane medallion awarded annually by the R.I.B.A. was reproduced. He built a house in Queen Square, Westminster, facing St. James's Park, where he died on 5 May 1835, aged about 43. Many of Parke's works in oil and water-colour were sold at Sotheby's in May 1836. In 1838 a bust of Parke was presented to the R.I.B.A. by J. J. Scoles.

[*A.P.S.D.*; *D.N.B.*; *Gent's Mag.* 1835 (ii), 325, 670, 1838 (i), 528; A. T. Bolton, *Portrait of Sir John Soane*, 1927, 289–93; S. Rowland Pierce, 'Some Early R.I.B.A. Travellers', *R.I.B.A. Jnl.* Nov. 1962, 412.]

PARKER, CHARLES (1799–1881), was a pupil of Sir Jeffry Wyatville, and attended the drawing school run by George Maddox. He subsequently spent several years in Italy. He began practice in London in about 1830, and became a Fellow of the Institute of British Architects on its foundation in 1834. He contributed a number of papers to its sessional meetings until his retirement in 1869. In 1834 he was elected a Fellow of the Society of Antiquaries, but resigned in 1844. He was steward and surveyor to the Bedford Estate in London from 1859 to 1869. Towards the end of his life his sight failed and he became totally blind. He died on 9 February 1881, aged 81, and was buried at St. Thomas's Church, Fulham, where a tombstone gives the date of his birth as 1799 (not 1800 as stated in *D.N.B.*).

Parker published in monthly parts an influential work entitled *Villa Rustica*, containing 93 lithographic plates 'selected from Buildings and Scenes in the Vicinity of Rome and Florence, and arranged for Lodges and Domestic Dwellings, with Plans and Details', 1832–41, 2nd ed. 1848. It showed how Italian domestic architecture could be adapted to English needs, and was one of the principal sources for the Italianate architecture of the early Victorian period.

Parker designed MESSRS. HOARE'S BANK in FLEET STREET, 1829–32 [C. Hussey in *C. Life*, 6 March 1958] and in about 1840 was employed by Sir Hugh Hoare to add the portico to STOURHEAD HOUSE, WILTS., in accordance with the original design, and to make other alterations [R. Colt Hoare, *Modern Wiltshire* v, 1837, Addenda, 15]. He also designed the west tower of KIMPTON CHURCH, HANTS., 1837–8, in flint and brick in a distinctive 'lancet' style [I.C.B.S.]; the R.C. CHURCH OF ST. RAPHAEL, SURBITON, in a neo-Lombardic style for Alexander Raphael, M.P. for St. Albans, 1846–7 [*Builder* v, 1847, 602–3]; and presumably CHRIST CHURCH, ST. ALBANS, which was built by the same patron in a similar style in 1850–1, but sold to the Church of England in about 1860. He altered the R.C. SPANISH CHAPEL in MANCHESTER SQUARE, in 1846, heightening the campanile [H. B. Wheatley & P. Cunningham, *London Past and Present* iii, 1891, 290]. His designs for an Italianate R. C. Church in Hastings, illustrated in the *Catholic Magazine* v, 1834, 673 and vi, 1835, cxiv, cxv, were not executed.

PARKER, THOMAS (–1745), of Gittisham, Devon, was a joiner by trade. In March 1723/4 he undertook to build CROWCOMBE COURT, SOMERSET, for Thomas Carew, but abandoned the contract in 1727, leaving the house to be completed by Nathaniel Ireson (*q.v.*) in 1734–9 'on foundations sometime since laid and carried up by Thomas Parker, Architect'. It was subsequently discovered that Parker had stolen old coins worth £900 which he found hidden in the old house while demolishing it. In the course of the legal proceedings that followed, it was stated that Parker had made designs for the house that he refused to hand over to Ireson [Somerset C.R.O., DD/TB, Box 29; *V.C.H. Somerset* v, 58]. In 1729 Parker was paid £73 10s. 'for making the screens, flooring and wainscotting the Altar' of CROWCOMBE CHURCH. His screen survived alterations to the church in 1856 [*Proc. Somerset Archl. Soc.* liv, 1908, 61]. Parker was buried at

Gittisham on 3 March 1744/5 [Gittisham Parish Register].

PARKER, WILLIAM (–*c.*1805), was a builder of Hereford who owned a stone quarry at Lugwardine. In the 1790s he was one of the undertakers of the County Gaol designed by John Nash (*q.v.*). As an architect he designed the GENERAL INFIRMARY, 1781. [engraving of that date with Parker's name as architect]; the THEATRE in BROAD STREET, 1785 [*Hereford Jnl.* 16 June 1785]; and the SWAN INN [*Hereford Jnl.* 2 March 1791]. He acted as surveyor to the Hereford Improvement Commissioners, making plans for houses in WIDEMARSH STREET after the demolition of the medieval gate in 1799, one of which is in Hereford Record Office, GH1/550. He went bankrupt in 1799 [*Hereford Jnl.* 24 July 1799], and died in about 1805 [information from Mr. D. Whitehead].

PARKINSON, JAMES T—, was probably related to John Parkinson (d. 1840) a well-known dentist, whose address in Racquet Court, Fleet Street, he sometimes used. As a young man he was a member of James Burton's volunteer force, 'The Loyal British Artificers', and one of his earliest commissions was to design a country house for Burton's own occupation. He practised in London from various addresses (32 Ely Place in 1811, 9 Upper Montagu Street in 1825–6, 1 Wyndham Place in 1827–8, and 6 Melcombe Street in 1831) and exhibited at the Royal Academy in 1810, 1811, 1818 and 1831. As surveyor to the Portman Estate he was responsible for the stuccoed façades of Montagu and Bryanston Squares, but his country houses were designed in a picturesque Gothic style reminiscent of Nash. Early in the 1830s he left London for Jersey, where he was still in practice ten years later. G. L. Taylor and Edward Cresy were his pupils, and the architect Rawlinson Parkinson (d. 1885) appears to have been his son [G. L. Taylor, *Autobiography of an Octogenarian Architect* i, 1870, 1; *Dorset County Chronicle*, 31 Jan. 1839, referring to him as resident in Jersey].

MABLEDON PARK, QUARRY HILL, TONBRIDGE, KENT, for James Burton (*q.v.*), *c.*1803–5, castellated; enlarged by Decimus Burton 1829 [exhib. at R.A. 1810] (E. W. Brayley, *Beauties of England and Wales* viii, 1808, 1295).

HAMPSTEAD, LONDON, BELSIZE HOUSE, HAVERSTOCK HILL., for George Todd, 1810; dem. *c.*1865 [exhib. at R.A. 1810].

TOOTING, SURREY, BEDFORD COTTAGE, TOOTING COMMON, 1810 [exhib. at R.A. 1810].

LONDON, BRYANSTON SQUARE, MONTAGU SQUARE, and adjacent streets on the Portman estate, *c.*1811 [exhib. at R.A. 1811; G. L. Taylor, *op. cit.*].

ROTHERFIELD PARK, HANTS., for James Scott, 1818–21, Tudor Gothic; refaced in stone *c.*1885 [exhib. at R.A. 1818, 1831; G. F. Prosser, *Select Illustrations of Hampshire*, 1833] (*C. Life*, 23, 30 April, 7 May 1948).

BAGSHOT, SURREY, ST. ANNE'S CHAPEL, 1819–21; dem. 1882 [I.C.B.S.].

FRIMLEY CHURCH, SURREY, 1825, Gothic; chancel etc. 1882–4 [I.C.B.S.].

STREATHAM CHURCH, SURREY, rebuilt nave and Gothicised tower and spire, 1830–1; spire rebuilt 1841, apse rebuilt 1863–4, church altered by B. Ferrey in 1870s [*D.N.B.*].

ST. HELIER, JERSEY, ALL SAINTS' CHURCH, 1835, classical [I.C.B.S.; C.E.B. Brett, *Buildings in . . . St. Helier*, National Trust for Jersey 1977, 22, 63].

ST. HELIER, JERSEY, ST. MARK'S CHURCH, begun 1842 to Parkinson's designs, but collapsed in course of construction and was completed 1845 to designs of John Hayward [C. E. B. Brett, *op. cit.*, 22, 51].

PARKINSON, JOSEPH (1783–1855), was one of the two sons of James Parkinson (d. 1813), a successful land agent. Joseph was articled to William Pilkington (*q.v.*) and subsequently practised in London, at first from his father's house in Newman Street, and later from 41 Sackville Street. As a young man he acted as secretary to the Emigrant Office for refugees from Revolutionary France. In about 1811 he became surveyor to the Union Fire Office, a post which he retained for over forty years, resigning it about two years before his death. Parkinson became a liveryman of the Fishmongers' Company in 1821. His pupils included John Haies, afterwards a stockbroker, Joseph Jennings, Raphael Brandon, Prof. T. Hayter Lewis, and his nephew Frederick Claudius Parkinson. He died in May 1855, and was buried in Kensal Green Cemetery [*A.P.S.D.*; *D.N.B.*].

Parkinson exhibited at the Royal Academy in 1806, 1807, 1809 and 1824. In 1809 he showed his designs for adapting the Leverian Museum in Blackfriars Road (built by his father in the 1780s to exhibit the collections of Sir Ashton Lever, which he had acquired in a lottery) in order to house the library and lecture-room of the SURREY INSTITUTION (*Survey of London* xxii, 115–17, and pl. 81b). Between 1822 and 1828 Parkinson was employed to rebuild the north and east sides of the Quadrangle of MAGDALEN COLLEGE, OXFORD, and to reconstruct the cloisters, all in a somewhat coarse Gothic style that was criticized by J. C. Buckler in a contemporary pamphlet. Parkinson also refitted the College Library, giving it a plaster Gothic ceiling that was destroyed in 1940 [T. S. R. Boase, 'An Oxford College and the Gothic Revival', *Jnl. Warburg & Courtauld Institutes* xviii, 1955, 158–68]. His only other recorded work appears to have been HARROW WEALD PARK, GREAT STANMORE, MIDDLESEX, built for William Windle soon after 1805 [*A.P.S.D.*].

PARKYNS, SIR THOMAS (1662–1741), was the son and heir of Sir Thomas Parkyns, first baronet, of Bunny in Nottinghamshire. He was educated at Westminster School and Trinity College, Cambridge, and in 1684 succeeded his father as the squire of Bunny. For the rest of his life he was active as a landowner and magistrate, but his less conventional activities included wrestling and architecture. Not only did he practice the former sport himself, but he also wrote an entertaining work on the subject entitled *The Inn-Play: or, The Cornish Hugg-Wrestler* (1713), and designed a monument for himself in Bunny Church which shows him 'in the primary posture of wrestling'. The inscription records, *inter alia*, that he 'Built the Schoolhouse and Hospital . . . the Mannor Houses in Bunney and East Leake . . . the Vicaridge House & most of the Farm Houses in Bunney and Bradmore. He . . . had a Competent knowledge of most part of the Mathematicks, especially Architecture & Hydraulics, & Contriving & Drawing all his Planns without an Architect.'

BUNNY HALL (dated 1723) is a highly eccentric building dominated by a castellated tower which interpenetrates with a huge segmental pediment. On the face of the tower beneath the pediment there is a colossal achievement of the Parkyns arms. All this is at one end of a rectangular house clasped by four giant Ionic pilasters. EAST LEAKE MANOR HOUSE (1704, dem. *c.*1785) has not survived, but at Bunny Parkyns's SCHOOL AND ALMSHOUSES (1700) still stand, as do several of the farm-buildings which he built for his tenants, notably HIGHFIELDS FARM, COSTOCK (1729), and RANCLIFFE FARM, BRADMORE (1736). These are relatively conventional buildings of traditional character, but Bunny Hall belongs to the lunatic fringe of the Baroque.

[Ellis Flack, 'Sir Thomas Parkyns of Bunny Hall', *Trans. Thoroton Soc.* xlix, 1945; B. Twelvetrees, *Sir Thomas Parkyns of Bunny*, Nottingham, 1973.]

PARSONS, WILLIAM (1796–1857), was one of the leading Leicester architects of the early nineteenth century. He was born at Scraptoft, educated at Billesdon School, and apprenticed to William Firmadge (*q.v.*) in 1809. In 1819 he succeeded his father as Surveyor to the Harborough-Loughborough Turnpike Trust, and in 1823 he was appointed County Surveyor of Leicestershire. He was active both as a road-builder and as a railway architect, and had a considerable private practice. His most important works were Caythorpe Hall, the County Lunatic Asylum and the County Gaol. His pupils included William Flint (1818), Henry Webb (1823), Frederick Plant (1826), James Ray (1833), and Abraham Gill (1821), with whom he went into partnership for a time. In about 1845 he took M. J. Dain into partnership, and Dain took over his practice after his death. Parsons died at his house, No. 21 St. Martin's, on 4 January 1857, aged 60, and was buried in Scraptoft churchyard. He was an amateur artist, and three of his drawings appeared in a volume of lithographic views entitled *Sketches in Leicestershire* which was published at Leicester in 1846. [*A.P.S.D.*; J. D. Bennett, *Leicestershire Architects 1700–1850*, Leicester Museums 1968; W. Hartopp, *Leicester Freeman*, 1927.]

HINCKLEY, LEICS., THE NATIONAL SCHOOL, 1820 [*Leicester Journal*, 26 May 1820, cited by Bennett, *op. cit.*].

LEICESTER, ST. GEORGE'S CHURCH, 1823–7, Gothic; burnt 1911 and reconstructed 1913 minus the spire [J. Curtis, *Topographical History of Leicestershire*, 1831, 106].

BIRSTALL CHURCH, LEICS., rebuilt nave 1826; remodelled 1869 [I.C.B.S.].

CAYTHORPE HALL, LINCS., for Col. G. H. Packe, 1824–7 [*The Correspondence of William Fowler of Winterton*, ed. J. T. Fowler, 1907, 475 ff.; building accounts in Packe papers, Leicestershire C.R.O., 700 (xxiv)].

LEICESTER, THE NEW COUNTY GAOL, WELFORD ROAD, 1825–8 and additions 1844–6, castellated [J. Curtis, *Topographical History of Leicestershire*, 1831, 111].

STONEY STANTON, LEICS., STONEY BRIDGE, 1826 [plan and specification in C.R.O., cited by Bennett, *op. cit.*].

GALBY RECTORY, LEICS., remodelled W. Wing 1829 [Lincolnshire Record Office, MGA 153].

LOUNT LODGE, LEICS., work for Mr. Burton, 1831 [papers cited by Bennett, *op. cit.*].

KEYHAM BRIDGE, LEICS., 1832 [*Leicester Journal*, 6 April 1832, cited by Bennett, *op. cit.*].

DISEWORTH VICARAGE, LEICS., enlarged 1833 [Lincolnshire Record Office, MGA 182].

BELGRAVE BRIDGE, LEICS., 1834; since enlarged [*V.C.H. Leics*. iv, 424].

MARKET BOSWORTH, LEICS., WRITING-MASTER'S HOUSE and farm-buildings for trustees of the Grammar School, 1834, Tudor Gothic [drawings in P.R.O., MPA/21, *ex inf.* the Revd. T. Parry].

BURY HOUSE, COTTINGHAM, NORTHANTS., alterations, including new staircase, for the Hon. Mrs. Cockayne Medlycott, 1835 [plans etc. in Northants. C.R.O., Map 639 a, b, c].

LEICESTER, THE LEICESTERSHIRE AND RUTLAND LUNATIC ASYLUM (now part of Leicester University), 1837 and additions 1844 [*V.C.H. Leics*. iv, 374].

HINCKLEY, LEICS., HOLY TRINITY CHURCH, 1837–9; altered 1883; dem. [G. K. Brandwood, 'Leicestershire Churches 1825–50', in *The Adaptation of Change*, Leicestershire Museums 1980, 36].

THURMASTON VICARAGE, LEICS., rebuilt 1838 [Lincolnshire Record Office, MGA 220].

LEICESTER, ST. MARGARET'S VICARAGE, additions and repairs, 1838; dem. 1964 [Lincolnshire Record Office, MGA 227].

LEICESTER, CHRIST CHURCH, 1838–9, Gothic; dem. 1957 [*V.C.H. Leics*. iv, 359].

EVINGTON VICARAGE, LEICS., rebuilt 1839 [Lincolnshire Record Office, MGA 237].

AYLESTONE RECTORY, LEICS., rebuilt 1839 [Lincolnshire Record Office, MGA 225].

BARKESTONE CHURCH, LEICS., added S. aisle, 1840, Gothic [G. K. Brandwood, *op. cit.*, 49].

BOTTESFORD, LEICS., Bridge over Winter Beck, 1841 [plan in C.R.O. cited by Bennett, *op. cit.*].

QUORNDON CHURCH, LEICS., enlarged north aisle 1841–2, Gothic [I.C.B.S.].

HATTON PARSONAGE, WARWICKS., alterations *c.*1845 [Bodleian Library, MS. Top. gen. b. 80, ff. 18–19].

RAILWAY STATIONS at REARSBY, BROOKSBY, FRISBY, ASFORDBY, MELTON MOWBRAY and SAXBY, for the Midland Railway Co., 1846–8 [Bennett, *op. cit.*, citing Minute Book of the Syston-Peterborough Committee of the Midland Railway].

BITTESWELL, LEICS., ALMSHOUSES, 1847 [*A Reply to the Question: 'Where and What is Bitteswell?'*, Lutterworth 1848, 23].

LEICESTER, STAMFORD STREET, warehouse for Mr. Jacques, 1851 [plan cited by Bennett].

LEICESTER, THE CASTLE HALL, altered interior, 1856 [*V.C.H. Leics*. iv, 345].

LEICESTER, a pair of semi-detached Greek villas designed by Messrs. Parsons and Gill 'for a particular situation in the suburbs of Leicester' are described and illustrated in Loudon's *Encyclopaedia of Rural Architecture*, 1846, pp. 870–7, but have not been identified.

PASCOE, JOSEPH (–1863), 'architect and surveyor' of Bodmin, new seated ST. NEOT'S CHURCH, CORNWALL, in 1832 [I.C.B.S.], and designed the JUDGES' LODGINGS at BODMIN, *c.*1840 [J. Maclean, *Deanery of Trigg Minor* i, 1870, 109]. He died at Bodmin on 11 July 1863 [Principal Probate Registry, Calendar of Probates].

PATCH, JOHN (*c.*1794–1871), of Crewkerne, variously described as 'carpenter, builder and surveyor' and as 'surveyor and auctioneer', rebuilt LOPEN CHURCH, SOMERSET, in 1834, Gothic [I.C.B.S.]. William Patch, 'surveyor and builder' of Ilminster (d. 1863), remodelled ASHILL VICARAGE, SOMERSET, in an elegant *cottage orné* style in 1841 [Somerset C.R.O., D/D/Bbm, 84].

PATERSON, DAVID, was a local Scottish architect living at Newton of Airlie in Angus. In 1828–9 he designed CORTACHY CHURCH, ANGUS, Gothic, for the 8th Earl of Airlie [S.R.O., GD 16/46/97 and drawings in RHP 5160 and 5165]. In the Scottish Record Office there are designs by him for BOTTOM STEADING, LINTRATHEN, ANGUS, 1833 [RHP 5023], and for additions to CRAIG HOUSE, ANGUS, 1833, dem. [RHP 5127].

PATERSON, GEORGE (–1789), practised as an architect in Edinburgh, but was at the same time the owner of a small estate at Monimail in Fife called Cunnochie. In 1793, in the course of legal proceedings, he was described as 'the deceased George Paterson Architect in Edinburgh, father of George Paterson of Cunochy', and the death of 'George Paterson of Cunoquhy, Esq.' on 26 February 1789 is recorded in the *Scots Magazine* for that year. He appears to have had a connection with Robert Mylne (*q.v.*), for whom in 1761–3 he superintended the building of St. Cecilia's Hall, Edinburgh [*Book of the Old Edinburgh Club* xix, 1933, 227], and in 1766 some alterations to Amisfield House, E. Lothian, for Francis Charteris [Robert Mylne's diary, 12 & 14 Aug. 1766]. In 1758 he was elected a member of the Royal Company of Archers, and in 1776 was a member of the Committee for building Archers' Hall, Edinburgh [J. Balfour Paul, *History of the Royal Company of Archers*, 1875, 368; minutes of the Royal Company of Archers, 27 July 1776]. According to a letter of 1770 he was 'looked upon to be the most reasonable and least expensive architect in this country' [S.R.O., GD 220/5/1757/13].

ROSSIE HOUSE, FIFE, design for addition of wings for Henry Cheape, 1753, probably not built [St. Andrews University Library, Rossie papers 7/305].

MARLEFIELD HOUSE, nr. ECKFORD, ROXBURGHSHIRE, repairs and alterations for William Nisbet, 1754 onwards; reconstructed 1891 [S.R.O., GD 6/1649, lawsuit 1793].

DUNFERMLINE ABBEY CHURCH, FIFE, repairs 1755 and 1770 [S.R.O., CH 2/105/8, pp. 289–96 and HR 159/1, 9 May 1770].

DYSART HOUSE, FIFE, apparently designed new house for James Sinclair (d. 1762), 1756–8 [vouchers in S.R.O., GD/723].

BOTHWELL CASTLE, LANARKS., alterations for Duke of Douglas, 1759–60; remodelled by J. Playfair, 1788 [papers in Douglas Estate Office, *ex inf.* Prof. A. A. Tait].

ST. ANDREWS, FIFE, ST. SALVATOR'S CHURCH (thereafter ST. LEONARD'S), alterations 1759–61 [R. G. Cant, 'St. Andrews Architects', *St. Andrews Preservation Trust Year Book*, 1966–7, 15].

KINGSBARNS MANSE, FIFE, 1765; dem. [S.R.O., HR 184/1, p. 5].

CUPAR, FIFE, some houses 'built ten years before to plans by George Paterson', i.e. 1769 [advt. in *Ruddiman's Weekly Mercury*, 13 Jan. 1779].

DYSART MANSE, FIFE, 1779–80 [S.R.O., GD 164/1218].

MOUNT STUART, BUTE, repairs for 3rd Earl of Bute, 1780 [N.R.A. Scotland, Report 631 on Bute archives, p. 756].

DALHOUSIE CASTLE, MIDLOTHIAN, repairs for 8th Earl of Dalhousie, 1778–9 [S.R.O., GD 45/19/123].

SCONE PALACE, PERTHSHIRE, alterations for 7th Viscount Stormont, *c.*1780–3 [J. Cornforth in *C. Life*, 11 Aug. 1981].

PATERSON, JAMES (–1838), came to Dundee with George Angus (*q.v.*) to superintend the building of the seminaries. In July 1832 he opened a class for architectural drawing at 22 Union Street. In 1837 he advertised for contractors for additions to the DUNDEE ASYLUM. He began building the WATT INSTITUTION to Angus's designs, but died on 18 February 1838 before the building was finished and was buried in the Constitution Road cemetery. His place was taken by his brother William. [information from Mr. David Walker].

PATERSON, JOHN (–1832) was probably the son of George Paterson (*q.v.*), whom he succeeds in the Edinburgh directories as the occupant of a house in St. John's Street. He was living at this address from 1777 to 1784, but then or soon afterwards moved to Elgin, where he practised until July 1789, when (as 'Mr. John Paterson, late Architect and Builder at Elgin') he was appointed clerk of works for the University buildings in Edinburgh. This appointment he owed to their architect Robert Adam, whose Scottish practice he simultaneously helped to manage until 1791, when (for reasons that are not clear) Adam dismissed him from both employments. Thereafter he practised as an independent architect in Edinburgh for over thirty years, first from 2 North Bridge Street and later from 24 Buccleuch Place. He died on 19 November 1832 at what must have been a fairly advanced age [Edinburgh City Records, College Trust Minute Book, 18 Nov. 1789 and 15 Dec. 1791; letters from Paterson to Adam in S.R.O., MS. 19992; testament in S.R.O., SC 70/1/48, p. 412].[1]

Paterson had a considerable practice in Scotland and the north of England. After the death of the Adam brothers he became the leading practitioner of the 'Castle style' that they had developed. He was also an accomplished designer of elegant classical interiors, with a special predilection for oval and circular rooms. Statements by Paterson of his terms of employment as an architect (1 per cent for designs and 4 per cent for superintendence) will be found in the Abercairny and Breadalbane papers in the S.R.O. (GD 112/16/7 and GD 24/1/624).

The following unexecuted designs by Paterson may be noted: the addition of wings to GRANT LODGE, ELGIN, MORAYSHIRE, for Sir James Grant, 1789 [S.R.O., RHP 9064–6]; an oval drawing-room at ABERCAIRNY, PERTHSHIRE, 1797 [letter in S.R.O., GD 24/1/624]; a tontine inn and assembly room at AYR, 1802 [drawings at Culzean Castle]; a new house at 'Putachie', i.e. CASTLE FORBES, ABERDEENSHIRE, 1807 and 1811 [drawings in S.R.O., RHP 24365–6]; a house at DALGUISE, PERTHSHIRE, for Charles Stewart, 1794 [specification in Paterson's hand in S.R.O., GD 38/1/1143] and alterations to PITFIRRANE HOUSE, FIFE, 1811 [N.L.S., MSS. 6509 and 6511].

Houses which might be attributed to

[1] John Paterson the architect must be dis tinguished from John Paterson, civil engineer in charge of Leith Docks from *c.*1803 until his death on 4 January 1823 (*Scots Magazine*, 1823, 256). It was John Paterson of Leith who briefly held the post of Superintendent of Public Works in Edinburgh from May to December 1809 (Edinburgh Town Council Minutes, 24 May 1809). In June 1809 he was also appointed Surveyor or Superintendent of Works to the Heriot Trustees, but resigned in July of the following year (Minutes of the Heriot Trust, vol. 18, pp. 199, 438).

Paterson on stylistic grounds include: ST. BRYCEDALE HOUSE in KIRKCALDY, FIFE, for George Heggie, 1786 (oval rooms); HARVIESTOUN CASTLE, CLACKMANNANSHIRE, remodelled for Crawfurd Tait, 1804, dem. 1965; FASQUE CASTLE, KINCARDINESHIRE, for Sir Alexander Ramsay, Bart., and his son, 1807–10 (*C. Life*, 9–16 Aug. 1979); and the stables at PINKIE HOUSE, MUSSELBURGH, MIDLOTHIAN, *c*.1800. SEGGIEDEN, PERTHSHIRE (dem. *c*.1975), was said in the *Scots Mag.* for June 1808, 403, to have been built 'fourteen or fifteen years ago, upon a plan by Paterson'. Although the oval saloon and drawing-room suggested Paterson, building accounts now in the Sandeman Library at Perth appear to indicate that it was built in 1772–5, several years before any other recorded work of Paterson's.

PUBLIC BUILDINGS

DUNDEE, THE INFIRMARY (later Victoria Road School), 1794–8; completed by D. Neave 1824–6; dem. [C. Mackie, *Historical Description of Dundee*, 1836, 156].

GLASGOW, THE BRIDEWELL, 1795; dem. [*Extracts from the Records of the Burgh of Glasgow*, ed. Renwick, viii, 1913, 595].

PERTH, ST. PAUL'S CHURCH, *c*.1800–7, Gothic (octagonal plan) [Perth Town Council Minutes, 5 March 1799].

EDINBURGH, MAGDALEN ASYLUM, CANONGATE, 1805–7; dem. [*Edinburgh Evening Courant*, 8 and 24 June 1805].

attributed: LEITH, THE LEITH BANK, BERNARD STREET, 1805–6 [façade almost identical with that of Coilsfield House, Ayrshire, listed below].

FETTERESSO CHURCH, STONEHAVEN, KINCARDINESHIRE, 1810–12, Gothic [S.R.O., GD 105/781].

LEITH, THE SEAFIELD BATHS, SEAFIELD PLACE, 1810–13 [signed engraving in *Edinburgh Almanac*, 1812].

DOMESTIC ARCHITECTURE

KEITH HALL, ABERDEENSHIRE, repairs and alterations for 5th Earl of Kintore, 1788 [Giles Worsley in *C. Life*, 28 May, 1987].

CASTLE FRASER, ABERDEENSHIRE, hexagonal stable court for Elyza Fraser, *c*.1794 [H. Gordon Slade, 'Castle Fraser', *Proc. Soc. Antiquaries of Scotland* 109, 1977–8, 258; variant plans by Paterson dated 1794].

MONZIE, PERTHSHIRE, for General Alexander Campbell, *c*.1795–1800, castellated; interior reconstructed by R. S. Lorimer after a fire in 1908 [J. C. Nattes, *Scotia Depicta*, 1804, pl. 15] (*Neale's Seats* vi, 1823).

COILSFIELD (or MONTGOMERIE) HOUSE, nr. TARBOLTON, AYRSHIRE, for 12th Earl of Eglinton, 1798; dem. 1971 [B. Burke, *Visitations of Seats*, 2nd. ser. i, 1854, 187] (M. C. Davis, *Castles & Mansions of Ayrshire*, 1991, 333–4).

EGLINTON CASTLE, AYRSHIRE, rebuilt for 12th Earl of Eglinton, 1798–1803; castellated; altered by W. Railton of Kilmarnock 1857–60; dem. 1925 [J. C. Nattes, *Scotia Depicta*, 1804, pl. 22: for the alterations of 1857–60 see S.R.O., RHP 2058] (M. C. Davis, *op. cit.*, 253–55).

BARMOOR CASTLE, NORTHUMBERLAND, for Francis Sitwell, 1801, castellated [signed drawings formerly at Barmoor, sold at Christie's, 24 March 1982].

TAYMOUTH CASTLE, PERTHSHIRE, began to rebuild for 4th Earl (1st Marquess) of Breadalbane, 1801, but was dismissed 1805 before the building was complete: it was then demolished by A. & J. Elliot, who designed a new house on a different site [Alistair Rowan in *C. Life*, 8 Oct. 1964].

GREENOCK, LANARKSHIRE, TONTINE INN, 1802 [advt. for tenders in *Edinburgh Evening Courant*, 2 Oct. 1802].

CANAAN LODGE, MORNINGSIDE, EDINBURGH, for himself, *c*.1802; dem. 1907 [S.R.O., RHP 38141; cf. RHP 24365–7 for drawings dated by Paterson at Canaan Lodge].

CHILLINGHAM CASTLE, NORTHUMBERLAND, rebuilt E. side for 4th Earl of Tankerville after a fire, 1803, castellated [*History of Northumberland* xiv, 336].

WINTON HOUSE, EAST LOTHIAN, castellated addition for Col. John Hamilton, 1805 [payment in S.R.O., RH15/119/98].

MILBOURNE HALL, NORTHUMBERLAND, for Ralph Bates, 1807–10 [B. Burke, *Visitation of Seats*, 2nd. ser. i, 1854, 187; *History of Northumberland* xii, 542].

FETTERESSO CASTLE, KINCARDINESHIRE, alterations and additions for Col. Robert William Duff, 1808; gutted 1954 [tracing of plan at N.M.R.S.].

ERROL HOUSE, PERTHSHIRE, court of stables for John Lee Allen, 1811 [engraving in Dumfries Archive Centre, GD 131/B2/21, 'Designed by Paterson Edr. Published 1813'].

LEITH, EDINBURGH, feu-plan and elevations for development of SEAFIELD ESTATE, 1813–18 [*Edinburgh Evening Courant, ex inf.* Mr. J. Gifford].

KINRARA HOUSE, INVERNESS-SHIRE, enlarged wings for 4th Duke of Gordon, *c*.1814; since much altered [S.R.O., GD 44/48/70].

KINGHORN MANSE, FIFE, 1816 [*Edinburgh Evening Courant*, 16 March 1816].

BRANCEPETH CASTLE, CO. DURHAM, alterations

including addition of Russell Tower, for Matthew Russell, 1818–19, castellated [M. A. Richardson, *The Local Historian's Table-Book* iii, 1843, 194; A. T. Bolton, *Portrait of Sir John Soane*, 1927, 306].

LENNEL HOUSE, COLDSTREAM, BERWICKSHIRE, for 8th Earl of Haddington, *c.*1820 [N.R.A. Scotland, Report 1454, Sect. 2, Bdl. 197, letter of 1818 in Blairadam papers mentioning Paterson's design for Lennel, whose unusual plan closely resembles an unexecuted design by Paterson for Castle Forbes].

EDINKILLIE MANSE (now HOUSE), MORAYSHIRE, 1823 [drawings at Dunphail House, *ex inf.* Mrs. E. Beaton].

PATERSON, ROBERT (*c.*1790–1846), 'architect and surveyor' of Edinburgh, who died on 6 July 1846, aged 56, is commemorated in the Warriston Cemetery there. A latter from him dated 1837 is in N.L.S., MS. 3441, f. 234.

PATERSON, SAMUEL (*c.*1788–), a pupil of James Elmes, was admitted to the Royal Academy Schools in 1809 at the age of 21. He was awarded the Silver Medal in 1817. In 1820 he went to Rome with John Davies (*q.v.*), and subsequently exhibited drawings of St. Peter's and the church at Loreto at the Royal Academy. Northing is known of his subsequent career.

PATEY, ANDREW (–1834), is said to have begun life as a mason in Yorkshire before establishing himself as an architect in Exeter [*A.P.S.D.*, *s.v.* 'Paty']. His best work was the Fire Assurance Office in the High Street, whose façade derived from Soane's Bank of England. Patey died at Teignmouth on 2 September 1834, having gone there for the sake of his health [*Gent's Mag.* 1834 (ii), 443].

EAST TEIGNMOUTH, DEVON, ST. MICHAEL'S CHURCH, 1822–3, 'Norman' style; chancel added 1875, steeple 1887–9 [I.C.B.S.].

DAWLISH CHURCH, DEVON, rebuilt (except tower), 1824; chancel and transepts added 1874 [J. Britton & E. W. Brayley, *Devonshire and Cornwall Illustrated*, 1832, 90].

EAST TEIGNMOUTH, THE PUBLIC ROOMS (later Riviera Cinema), forming the central feature of Den Crescent, 1826 [J. Britton & E. W. Brayley, *Devonshire and Cornwall Illustrated*, 1832, 76].

EXETER, ST. THOMAS'S CHURCH, rebuilt chancel 1829–30, Gothic [Vestry Minutes in Devon C.R.O.].

EXETER, ST. LEONARD'S CHURCH, 1831–3; dem. 1876, 'in the Grecian style' [Davidson's Church Notes in Exeter City Library].

EXETER, THE WEST OF ENGLAND FIRE ASSURANCE OFFICE (afterwards the Commercial Union), HIGH STREET, 1833, destroyed by bombing 1942 [*The Exeter Guide*, 1836, 53, with illustration].

PATIENCE, JOHN THOMAS (*c.*1774–1843), stated in 1822 that he had spent twelve years in London and the remainder in Essex and Suffolk [advt. in *Norfolk Chronicle*, 17 Aug. 1822, *ex inf.* Mr. David Cubitt]. During the first decade of the nineteenth century he was working as a mason in Colchester and Bury St. Edmunds, but in 1812 he went bankrupt, leaving an unfinished mansion in Westgate, Bury St. Edmunds, to be sold by his assignees [*Ipswich Jnl.*, 7 Nov. 1812]. By 1820 he was practising in Norwich as an 'Architect, Surveyor and House Agent' and in 1836 he became City Surveyor. He exhibited at the Norwich Society of Artists from 1820 to 1830, and made several designs for public buildings which are preserved in the City Archives. He died on 10 April 1843, aged 69 [*Gent's Mag.* 1843 (ii), 107; information from Mr. J. Bensusan-Butt and Mr. A. P. Baggs].

NORWICH, ST. PETER'S METHODIST CHAPEL, LADY'S LANE, 1824 [John Chambers, *Norfolk Tour* iii, 1829, 1151, 1260].

NORWICH, THE FRIENDS' MEETING-HOUSE, UPPER GOAT LANE, 1825 [John Chambers, *Norfolk Tour* iii, 1829, 1151, 1169–70].

NORWICH, THE CATHOLIC CHAPEL, WILLOW LANE, 1828–9, converted into a Catholic school 1894 [John Chambers, *Norfolk Tour* iii, 1829, 1151–2].

BELAUGH RECTORY, NORFOLK, 1831 [Norfolk C.R.O., DN/DPL 1/6].

RAVENINGHAM, NORFOLK, cast-iron milestone for Sir Edmund Bacon, 1831, signed 'Patience Archt. 1831'.

NORWICH, THE NORFOLK AND NORWICH SUBSCRIPTION LIBRARY, GUILDHALL HILL, 1835; rebuilt 1898–9 after fire, retaining Doric portico [*Norfolk Chronicle*, 24 Oct. 1835].

NORWICH, NEW DISTRICT SCHOOLS, ST. AUGUSTINE'S GATES, 1837–8, Gothic; dem. [*Norwich Mercury*, 30 Sept. 1837, 13 June 1838, *ex inf.* Mr. David Cubitt].

PATIENCE, JOSEPH (*c.*1739–1797), of Wormwood Street, Bishopsgate, London, was an unsuccessful candidate for a District Surveyorship in 1774 [Middlesex County Records, General Orders, No. 10]. He was elected a member of the Surveyors' Club in 1793 and died on 27 September 1797, aged 58. He is commemorated by a monument in

All Hallows Church, London Wall. He was the father of Joseph Patience, junior (*q.v.*). A design for an organ-gallery in St. Michael Bassishaw Church by 'the late Jos. Patience', 1780, was in the collection of the late Sir Albert Richardson.

PATIENCE, JOSEPH (*c.*1767–1825), son of the above, practised from the same address in Wormwood Street, Bishopsgate, until his death in May 1835, aged 58. He was elected a member of the Surveyors' Club in 1797 and was its President in 1817. He exhibited at the Royal Academy from 1786 onwards. He designed new offices at BEAVER HALL, SOUTHGATE, MIDDLESEX (dem. 1870), exhibited 1793 and 1806; completed GREAT SAXHAM HALL, SUFFOLK, for T. Mills, by adding an upper floor to the former stable-block, already partly converted into a house after the destruction of the former mansion by fire in 1779 [exhib. at R.A. 1797 and 1808 and cf. N. Scarfe, 'Great Saxham Hall', *Proc. Suffolk Inst. Archaeology* xxvi, 1954, 230–1 and *ibid.*, xxxiv, 1980, 300–1 and *C. Life*, 27 Nov. 1986]; and designed a villa at DULWICH for J. Willes, exhibited in 1804. He was consulted about repairs to HANWORTH CHURCH, MIDDLESEX, in 1807 [Vestry Minutes], and in 1822 repaired and altered the church of ST. STEPHEN, COLEMAN STREET, LONDON [Vestry Minutes in Guildhall Library, MS. 4458/5]. He made plans for rebuilding FRINGFORD and ODDINGTON RECTORIES, OXON., in 1818 and 1821 [Oxfordshire C.R.O., Oxford Diocesan Faculty Register 1804–27, pp. 97, 241]. A drawing by him for alterations to premises in COVENT GARDEN, LONDON, is in the R.I.B.A. Collection. He is commemorated on the monument to his father in the church of All Hallows, London Wall. This is signed by 'T. Patience', who appears to have been a sculptor member of the family (see R. Gunnis, *Dictionary of British Sculptors*, 293, where he is confused with Joseph Patience).

PATON, DAVID (1801–1882), was the son of John Paton (d. 1842), a successful speculative builder in Edinburgh. David was educated at Edinburgh University and afterwards joined his father's business before setting up in practice as an architect. Buildings in Edinburgh designed by him include SUMMERFIELD HOUSE, S. TRINITY ROAD (dem.) for George Fulton and his nephew George Knight, *c.*1824–5 and a block at the corner of YORK PLACE and N. ST. ANDREW STREET with a distinctive pilastered corner tower, 1824. In 1825 he appears to have been in Paris, for several plans of buildings in the French capital, signed by him and dated 1825, were among the drawings from the Signet Library sold in 1960. In November 1829 he joined the office of Sir John Soane, but left the following May. Following the death of his wife in February 1833 he emigrated to New York, where he was employed first to execute and then considerably to modify Ithiel Town's designs for THE STATE CAPITOL at RALEIGH, N. CAROLINA, 1833–4. Dissatisfied with his remuneration, Paton returned to Edinburgh in 1840. Here his practice seems to have been on a modest scale, chiefly surveying work, and in 1849 he went back to New York, where he died in 1882 [Mary Jane Scott, 'David Paton', *Jnl. Architectural Heritage Soc. Scotland*, 13, 1986].

PATTERSON, WILLIAM (*c.*1793–1875), was a builder at Nottingham, where he designed a Gothic INDEPENDENT CHAPEL in FRIAR LANE, 1828 (dem.) [J. Orange, *History of Nottingham* ii, 1840, 812], and the semi-detached houses, Nos. 1–12 PARK TERRACE [Brand, as cited below]. From 1834 to 1849 he was in partnership with the architect T. C. Hine (1813–99), in conjunction with whom he designed and built a school and parsonage at STAPLEFORD, NOTTS., 1836 [Northants. C.R.O., Map 734], a rectory at AVERHAM, NOTTS. 1838 [Borthwick Institute, York, MGA 1838/1] and a Grammar School at CHESTERFIELD, DERBYSHIRE, 1846, and reroofed and reseated OXTON CHURCH, NOTTS., 1840–1 [I.C.B.S.]. [K. Brand, *Thomas Chambers Hine*, Nottingham Civic Society, n.d.]. Patterson died on 3 March 1875 [Principal Probate Registry, Calendar of Probates].

PATY, THOMAS (*c.*1713–1789), was a member of a large and complex family of masons, carvers and architects who were active in Bristol throughout the eighteenth century. He was the elder son of James Paty, a statuary mason who died in 1746 or 1747 and the brother of James Paty the younger, who died in 1779. Thomas was an accomplished carver. Between 1741 and 1743 he executed the wood- and stone-carving in the Redland Chapel and later supplied the font. All his work here is of the finest quality, and a contemporary note on the chapel, preserved with the original bills in the Bristol Record Office, observes that Paty 'is generally esteemed one of the best Carvers in England, either in Wood or Stone', and that 'all the Ornaments in the Chapel were designed and carved' by him. In 1741–2 he was employed by John Wood to carve the architectural ornamentation of the Bristol Exchange. He was responsible for the dressed masonry and carving at Clifton Hill House, designed by Isaac

Ware, in 1746, and at the Royal Fort, *c.*1758–60 [S.R.O., GD 152/6, bdl. 9/7, quoting the Royal Fort building accounts]. He and his sons John and William Paty had an extensive business as monumental masons, and tablets signed by them are to be found in many churches in Bristol and the neighbouring counties.

Paty played a large part in the development of Georgian Bristol. Clare, High, Bridge, Union and Bath Streets were laid out by him, and there is evidence that he and his sons provided the elevations not only for the buildings lining these streets, but also for many of those in College, Park, Great George, Charlotte and Lodge Streets, and in Berkeley Square and Crescent and Upper Berkeley Place. Between 1763 and 1769 he carried out James Bridges's plans for rebuilding Bristol Bridge and the adjoining church of St. Nicholas. Bridges had intended to retain the steeple of the old church, but it proved to be insecure, and Paty replaced it with a Gothic tower and spire of his own designing.

As an architect Paty was no more than a competent provincial. His house elevations were consistently designed with repetitive Gibbsian surrounds to doorways and five-stepped voussoirs over every window, without much attempt to unify street or terrace. The steeple which he designed for St. Nicholas Church is an effective piece of Georgian Gothic, but his St. Martin's Church is 'an illiterate compromise between the classical and the barely Gothic' (Mowl).

Paty died on 4 May 1789 in his 77th year, leaving, besides his two sons, a daughter Elizabeth, who had married Thomas King, a statuary of Bath. His business was continued by his sons, but their partnership was cut short by John Paty's premature death on 10 June 1789, leaving William to continue on his own.

[W. Ison, *The Georgian Buildings of Bristol*, 1952, 40–3; R. Gunnis, *Dictionary of British Sculptors*, 1968, 294–5; A. H. Gomme, M. Jenner & B. Little, *Bristol: an Architectural History*, 1979, 439–40; T. Mowl, *To Build the Second City: Architects and Craftsmen of Georgian Bristol*, 1991, chap. 4.]

BRISTOL

ST. NICHOLAS' CHURCH, completed to designs of James Bridges, himself designing the Gothic tower and spire; gutted 1940; repaired for museum use 1974 [Ison].

THE THEATRE ROYAL, 1764–6 [Gomme *et al.*, 173].

ST. MICHAEL'S CHURCH, 1775–7, Gothic, retaining medieval tower [Ison].

ST. JAMES'S MARKET, UNION STREET, c.1775; dem. [Ison].

ALL SAINTS CHURCH, repaired cupola, 1781 [Vestry Minutes].

THE MERCHANT'S HALL, remodelled 1783; destroyed by bombing 1940 [Ison].

THE ROYAL INFIRMARY, central portion, with Daniel Hague, 1784–8 [Ison].

WELLS, SOMERSET, THE CEDARS, NORTH LIBERTY, for Charles Tudway, 1758–60 [L. S. Colchester *et al.*, *History of Wells Cathedral School*, Wells 1985, 67–8].

FONMON CASTLE, GLAMORGANSHIRE, alterations and internal decoration for Robert Jones, 1762 [Patricia Moore, *Fonmon Castle*, Glamorgan Archives Committee 1976].

WELLS, SOMERSET, THE TOWN HALL, 1776–80, since rebuilt. According to *Felix Farley's Journal* of 17 Aug. 1776, 'The Corporation of Wells have agreed to rebuild the assize hall and market house, after a plan of the Revd. Dr. Camplin's, to be completed under the direction of Mr. Paty of this city.'

PATY, WILLIAM (1758–1800), of Bristol, the son of Thomas Paty (*q.v.*), was the only member of his family to be trained in the Royal Academy Schools (to which he was admitted in December 1775), and perhaps in the office of a London architect. He was back in Bristol by 1777 and after the death of his father and elder brother in 1789 he carried on the family business as a statuary mason and executed many monumental tablets. He was one of the three city surveyors appointed under the Act of 1788 and was admitted a freeman in December 1790.

As his father's partner and assistant Paty played an important part in the Georgian development of Bristol and appears to have designed many of the terraces built in Clifton during the last decade of the eighteenth century. He was also the architect of houses in Great George Street, including No. 7, now THE GEORGIAN HOUSE MUSEUM, for John Pretor Pinney, a West India merchant, 1789–91. In designing BLAISE CASTLE HOUSE, nr. BRISTOL, for J. S. Harford, 1795–6, he is said to have been assisted by John Nash, who later designed the well-known picturesque 'Hamlet' on the same estate [J. & H.S. Storer, *Delineations of the County of Gloucester*, 1824, 105]. His best building was CHRIST CHURCH, BRISTOL, 1786–9, which has an elegant classical interior derived from Taylor's Transfer Office at the Bank of England.

Paty died on 11 December 1800, aged 43, leaving a son, George William Paty, who did not follow his father's profession. He is commemorated by a tablet in the S. aisle of St.

Augustine's Church. James Foster (*q.v.*) was his pupil and assistant, but his business and yard were bought by Henry Wood, a London mason. A volume of his designs for monumental tablets is in Bristol University Library. Drawings in the R.I.B.A. Collection for rebuilding Butleigh Court, Somerset, initialled 'WP', are attributed to him.

[*A.P.S.D.*; C. F. Dening, *The Eighteenth-Century Architecture of Bristol*, 1923, 132–4, 138–9; J. Evans, *History of Bristol* ii, 1816, 169; W. Ison, *The Georgian Buildings of Bristol*, 1952, 43; R. Gunnis, *Dictionary of British Sculptors*, 1968, 295; A. Gomme, M. Jenner & B. Little, *Bristol: an Architectural History*, 1979, 440; T. Mowl, *To Build the Second City: Architects and Craftsmen of Georgian Bristol*, 1991; A. B. Beaven, *Bristol Lists*, 1899; will, P.C.C. 54 ABERCROMBIE.]

PAUL, ROWLAND (–1850), practised in Cheltenham from before 1820 until his death on 20 November 1850. He was latterly in partnership with his two sons Andrew and Charles Paul. Charles, who had been secretary to the Cheltenham and Oxford Railway Company, died at Charlton Kings on 10 April 1854, aged 44 [Gloucester Probate Act Book 1842–52, p. 183; *Gent's Mag.* 1854 (i), 666]. The firm's works included the Greek Doric ST. MARY'S CEMETERY CHAPEL in LOWER HIGH STREET, CHELTENHAM, 1831 [J. Goding, *History of Cheltenham*, 1863, 550], EASTINGTON RECTORY (now 'Oldbury'), GLOS., 1832 [drawings in Gloucester Diocesan Faculty Register (GDR 350a), f. 34], and DOWDESWELL COURT, GLOS., for Mrs. Hester Rogers, 1833–5 [Glos. Record Office, D. 269 A/F 9]. This house, designed in the style of the early 18th century, is illustrated in Burke's *Visitation of Seats*, ser. I (i), 247. The interior of the hall was remodelled by Samuel Onley, junior, in 1848, and the attic storey was removed in the present century.

PEACOCK, ALEXANDER (*c.*1733–1818), who died at Burdiehouse Mains, nr. Edinburgh, on 11 May 1818, aged 85, is described as 'architect' in his obituary notice in the *Edinburgh Magazine* ii, 1818, 598. He was doubtless the 'Mr. Peacock' of Edinburgh who appears to have designed LEUCHIE HOUSE, NORTH BERWICK, EAST LOTHIAN, for Sir Hew Darlrymple in 1779–85, with elaborate decoration in the Adam style [Mark Girouard in *C. Life*, 12 Oct. 1961; S.R.O., GD 110/783, letters to Dalrymple from his factor].

PEACOCK, JAMES (?1738–1814), was for over forty years assistant Clerk of the Works to the City of London. In 1771 George Dance the younger, who had succeeded his father as Clerk of the Works in 1768, asked for the appointment of an assistant, as he found that his duties often required his presence in two places at the same time. The City Lands Committee agreed, provided that the arrangement involved no charge to the City, and in December 1771 Peacock was appointed on Dance's recommendation, and presumably at his expense [Lands Committee Jnl., vol. 105, f. 156.[v]]. Nothing is known of Peacock's origins or early life, though according to Sir John Soane he had become acquainted with Dance soon after the latter's return from Italy in 1765 (*Memoirs of Professional Life*, 1835, 11). He became Dance's lifelong assistant, and remained in his office until his death in 1814. He took up the livery of the Joiners' Company in 1774, and appears at one time to have held a post in the Ordnance Office, whose loss in 1780 he attributed to the machinations of James Wyatt, then Surveyor of the Ordnance.

Peacock's only independent work of importance was the STOCK EXCHANGE in CAPEL COURT, which was built to his design in 1801–2, but rebuilt by Thomas Allason in 1853–4. A minor work was the PHILANTHROPIC SOCIETY'S CHAPEL, ST. GEORGE'S ROAD, SOUTHWARK, 1803–6, an unpretentious Gothic building demolished in 1898 except for a fragment incorporated in St. Jude's Church, which occupies its site [Philanthropic Society's records in Surrey C.R.O., *ex inf.* Mr. A. Saint] (*Survey of London* xxv, 68–9). Peacock also carried out repairs to ST. ANNE & ST. AGNES CHURCH, GRESHAM STREET, in 1781–2 [W. McMurray, *A City Church Chronicle*, 1914, 63], and to ST. STEPHEN'S CHURCH, WALBROOK, in 1803–4 [*A.P.S.D.*]. A drawing of the elevation of the Mines Royal, Dowgate Hill, by him and a plan of proposed quays between London Bridge and the Tower (1795) are in the British Library (*King's Maps* xxi, 28 and xxv, 16).

Peacock published several works on architectural subjects. The most important of these was entitled Οἰκίδια or *Nutshells*, and was published under the anagrammatic pseudonym of 'Jose Mac Packe, bricklayer's labourer', in 1785. It contains 'ichnographic distributions' (i.e. plans) for small villas, together with some satirical directions for prospective builders.

Peacock's 'Account of Three Simple Instruments for Drawing Architecture and Machinery in Perspective' was printed in the *Philosophical Transactions of the Royal Society* for 1785, and he also published *A New*

Method of Filtration by Ascent, 1793,[1] and *Subordinates in Architecture*, 1814. A MS. volume compiled by him, on 'Terms of Contracts for Bricklayers', Slaters' and Joiners' Works, on the Peace Establishment, for the Service of the Board of Ordnance', is in Sir John Soane's Museum.

Peacock was also interested in social and economic questions, and published several small treatises on these subjects which are of considerable interest in the history of social welfare. His *Outlines of a Scheme for the General Relief, Instruction, Employment, and Maintenance of the Poor*, was published in 1777, and is described by its author as 'an imperfect and crude performance' in the *Proposals for a Magnificent and Interesting Establishment for the Employment of the Poor*, which he issued in 1790. He also published *Superior Politics*, 1789, and *The Outlines of a Plan for establishing a United Company of British Manufacturers*. His object in all these projects was to give 'protection and suitable incitement, encouragement, and employ to every class of the destitute, ignorant, and idle poor, who shall be healthy, able to work, and willing to conform . . . to such . . . regulations as the company shall exact, and which are intended to be of mutual benefit and advantage to the company and the work-people, and eventually so to society at large'.

Peacock died on 22 February 1814, 'in the 76th year of his age', as stated on the headstone formerly in the cemetery of St. Luke's Church, Old Street. Little is known of his personality, but he was friendly with Sir John Soane as well as with George Dance, and in his edition of Chambers's *Civil Architecture*, Gwilt paid a tribute to his 'virtues and moral excellence', which 'will be honoured as long as the memory of his surviving friends remains sound'.

[*A.P.S.D.*; *D.N.B.*; A. T. Bolton, *The Portrait of Sir John Soane*, 1927, 59, 96–8; Dorothy Stroud, *George Dance, Architect*, 1971, *passim*.]

PEARCE, EDWARD, *see* PIERCE, EDWARD.

PEARCE, SIR EDWARD LOVETT (– 1733), was the son of General Edward Pearce and his wife Frances, daughter of Christopher Lovett, a prominent Dublin merchant. His connections were chiefly with Ireland, but his family had a property at Whitlingham in Norfolk, and he may have been brought up in England. He may have been intended for a military career and as early as 1707 (when he was still a boy) he was given a commission (presumably bought for him by his father) as a Captain in Neville's regiment of dragoons. Nothing more is known of his life before 1723–4, when he was in Italy studying architecture. By 1726 he was established in Dublin. In the following year he was elected a Member of the Irish Parliament, and in January 1731 he succeeded Thomas Burgh as Surveyor of Works and Fortifications in Ireland. He was knighted in 1732 and died on 7 December 1733 while still in his thirties.

Nothing certain is known about Pearce's architectural education, but it is evident from the fact that his drawings and Vanbrugh's form a single collection (once at Stillorgan House near Dublin, later at Elton Hall in Huntingdonshire and now in the Victoria and Albert Museum) that there was some connection between the latter and himself. They were in fact second cousins, and Pearce probably acquired Vanbrugh's drawings after his death. Whether he was in any sense a pupil of Vanbrugh's is less certain and in any case he soon developed a classical style more akin to (though quite independent of) Lord Burlington's Palladianism than to Vanbrugh's baroque. By 1731 he had become the leading Palladian architect of his day in Ireland, and as the designer of Bellamont Forest, Cashel Palace, the Parliament House and the Christ Church Deanery (dem.) in Dublin, a major figure in the history of Irish architecture and one of the pioneers of European neo-classicism.

It is unlikely that in the course of his brief but brilliant career Pearce had time or opportunity to do much architectural work in England. However his drawings show that he made a survey of the seat of the Earle family at HEYDON HALL, NORFOLK, and that he made designs (perhaps not executed) for a service wing to be added to ASHLEY PARK, nr. WALTON-ON-THAMES, SURREY (dem. *c.*1925) for Richard Boyle, 2nd Viscount Shannon. Here he was probably involved in more extensive alterations to the house, including the formation of the gallery illustrated in Oliver Brackett's *Encyclopaedia of English Furniture* (1927), 195 [John Harris, 'Ashley Park, Surrey', in *Decantations. A Tribute to Maurice Craig*, ed. Agnes Bernelle, Dublin 1992]. In about 1725 he helped John Buxton (*q.v.*) to design his new house at SHADWELL PARK, NORFOLK, providing him with 'the first design for the front', but how far this was followed is uncertain [Mark Girouard in *C. Life*, 2 July 1964]. The possibility that he designed No. 12 NORTH AUDLEY STREET, LONDON, for Col. Edward Ligonier in *c.*1728–30 is discussed in *Survey*

[1] In 1791 he patented a machine for purifying water by filtration.

of London xl, 101. Among the drawings in the Victoria and Albert Museum there is a set of unexecuted designs by Pearce for a large Palladian 'lodge' at Richmond, probably made for George II soon after his accession. In the R.I.B.A. Drawings Collection there are several drawings from the Papworth collection that are attributable to Pearce.

[T.W.J. Conolly, *Roll of Officers of the Corps of Royal Engineers*, 1898, 112; T.U. Sadleir, *Sir Edward Lovett Pearce*, Dublin 1927; H. Colvin & M. Craig, *Architectural Drawings in the Library of Elton Hall by Sir John Vanbrugh and Sir Edward Lovett Pearce*, Roxburghe Club 1964; *History of the King's Works*, v, 220; Maurice Craig & the Knight of Glin, 'Castletown, Co. Kildare', *C. Life*, 27 March, 3–10 April 1969; J. Cornforth, 'Dublin Castle', *C. Life*, 6 Aug. 1970; Maurice Craig, 'Sir Edward Lovett Pearce', *Bull. Irish Georgian Soc.* Jan.–June 1974; Edward McParland, 'Edward Lovett Pearce and the Parliament House in Dublin', *Burlington Mag.* 131, 1989, 'Edward Lovett Pearce and the Deanery of Christ Church, Dublin', in *Decantations. A Tribute to Maurice Craig*, ed. Agnes Bernelle, Dublin 1992.]

PEARCE, MATTHEW (–1775), a bricklayer by trade, was described as 'Architect' of WHITFIELD'S TABERNACLE, TOTTENHAM COURT ROAD, LONDON, of which he was also the builder. It was erected in 1756, enlarged in 1759–60, damaged by fire in 1857, and entirely rebuilt in 1890–2. Pearce is commemorated by a tablet in the chapel [*Survey of London* xxi, 67, 71; will in P.C.C., PROB 11/1291, f. 245]. He may well have built WHITFIELD'S TABERNACLE (dem.) in LEONARD STREET, ISLINGTON, 1752–3, which was of similar design, a square with a high pyramidal roof [P. Temple, *Islington Chapels*, R.C.H.M. 1992, 126].

PEARS, JAMES (*c.*1740–1804), of Oxford and a carpenter by trade, was a builder much employed by James Wyatt from his earliest Oxford commission, the Canterbury Quadrangle at Christ Church (1775–8), onwards. Wyatt relied on him to interpret designs that had not always been fully worked out in his office, and where necessary to supplement them with his own drawings. He was the builder of the Radcliffe Observatory, which was completed by him to Wyatt's designs in 1794, and his name is inscribed on the copper ball which surmounts its roof. In 1783 he repaired and improved the President's Lodgings at CORPUS CHRISTI COLLEGE [College archives]. In 1790 he was employed to carry out alterations to the interior of ST. JOHN'S COLLEGE CHAPEL, and in 1795 he built the HOLMES BUILDING at the same college, apparently to his own designs, though in a Gothic style very like Wyatt's. He also designed and built a secondary staircase in the PRESIDENT'S LODGINGS at ST. JOHN'S in 1797 [St. John's College archives, Bills and Receipts and Registers VII, 636, VIII, 32, 44]. A design by Pears for a proposed screen wall at WORCESTER COLLEGE is among drawings preserved there (No. 491B). He became a freeman of Oxford in 1776, was for many years a member of the Council, and served as Mayor in 1793. He died at Woodperry House on 1 January 1804, aged 64, and is commemorated by a brass inscription on the floor of Iffley Church. [G. Jackson-Stops in *New College, Oxford*, ed. Buxton & Williams, 1979, 238–9; *Oxford Council Acts 1752–1801*, ed. Hobson, Oxford Historical Soc. 1962, 120, 219 etc.]

PEISLEY, BARTHOLOMEW, was the name of three generations of Oxford master masons. Bartholomew Peisley and partners supplied Headington stone for the building of St. Paul's Cathedral in 1686 and in 1697 [*Wren Soc.* xiv, 19–21; xv, 28, 30, 35], and it is safe to assume that, like the Strongs of Taynton, they were quarry-owners as well as master builders.

In 1673–6 the elder Peisley (1620–1692) built the SENIOR COMMON ROOM of ST. JOHN'S COLLEGE [College Archives, *Computus Annuus*, 1673–8, f. 150v], and in 1685–6 he completed the LIBRARY and CHAPEL of ST. EDMUND HALL, which had been begun by William Byrd in 1680–2 [A. B. Emden, *An Account of the Chapel and Library Building, St. Edmund Hall, Oxford*, 1932, 22]. In November 1681, when giving evidence in a lawsuit, he stated that he was 61 years of age, and that he had built a stone house in ST. GILES' (No. 62, now demolished) 'wherein Esqr. Bateman lately lived' [Oxford University Archives, Vice-Chancellor's Court, 1681 M]. He died in December 1692, dividing his property in St. Giles' and St. Ebbe's between his two sons, Bartholomew and Charles, and his daughter Miriam. He was buried at St. Giles' Church [Bodleian Library, Oxford Consistory Court Register, f. 209; St. Giles' Parish Register, 1692].

Bartholomew Peisley II (*c.*1654–1715), who had been apprenticed to his father in 1669, stated in 1689 that he had 'severall times been chief contriver of buildings of about £200 and 300 value' [Oxford University Archives, Vice-Chancellor's Court, 1689 Easter, bundle 54]. He was the master mason who built TRINITY COLLEGE CHAPEL in 1691–4 [Wood, *Life & Times* iii, 314], and the New

Building at the S.W. corner of WADHAM COLLEGE facing the Parks Road in 1693–4 [Wadham College archives]. In 1695 Sir William Trumbull intended to employ him to build a proposed gallery at EASTHAMPSTEAD PARK, BERKSHIRE [Hist. MSS. Comm., *Downshire* I (ii), 501, 507, 655]. In 1697 he contracted to build STONE'S ALMHOUSES, ST. CLEMENT'S, OXFORD [Strickland Gibson, 'Stone's Hospital', *Bodleian Quarterly Record* viii, 1935]. It may have been Bartholomew II who built ST. GILES' HOUSE, OXFORD, for Thomas Rowney in 1702 (date on leadwork of roof) for a note among St. John's College Muniments records that 'Bath. Piesly's 2 tenements were pull'd down when the New House was built', and in 1709 Peisley is referred to in a letter of Sir John Vanbrugh as bringing him 'Mr. Rowney's Draught' in London [*The Complete Works of Sir J. Vanbrugh* iv, *The Letters*, ed. G. F. Webb, 227]. There are measured drawings of the house in *Arch. Rev.* 57, 1925, 122–5. Peisley was one of the principal contractors at BLENHEIM PALACE, where he built the great arch of the Grand Bridge. When he died in 1715 his will referred to a 'debt of £1200 due to me for worke done at Blenheim House' [copy in B.L., Add. MS. 24327, f. 12]. His daughter married Henry Joynes (*q.v.*), the Comptroller at Blenheim, to whom he left £300. His business was continued by his eldest son, Bartholomew Peisley III (*c.*1683–1727), who had been apprenticed to him in July 1698.

The third Bartholomew appears to have entered into partnership with William Townesend, for they are found in association in several important contracts, and Hearne wrote of Peisley that 'he and one Townsend carried (as it were) all the business in masonry before them, both in Oxford and all the Parts about it.' It was Townesend and Peisley who built the RADCLIFFE QUADRANGLE at UNIVERSITY COLLEGE between 1717 and 1719 [Bodleian Library, Minutes of the Radcliffe Trustees, 1717–20], and the CODRINGTON LIBRARY at ALL SOULS from 1715 onwards [College Archives], and it was with the same two master masons that Sir John Stonehouse contracted for the erection of RADLEY HALL, BERKSHIRE, in June 1721 [V. Hope, 'the Architect of Radley Hall', *C. Life*, 27 Jan. 1950]. Like his father Peisley worked at Blenheim, where he and Townesend built the WOODSTOCK GATE to Hawksmoor's designs in 1722–3 [W. J. Churchill, 'Some Unpublished Letters of Sarah, Duchess of Marlborough, relating to the Building of Blenheim Palace', *Trans. Birmingham and Midland Institute*, 1884–5].

Peisley died on 29 August 1727, aged 44, and was buried in St. Giles' churchyard. He is described on the monument erected to his memory in the south aisle of the church, as 'in Re Architectonica Peritus Artifex', and the ungracious Hearne, who had no love for his partner Townesend, admitted that Peisley 'was looked upon as a very courteous well behaved man'. He left a widow, described by Hearne as 'a very pretty woman', who afterwards married President Hudsford of Trinity [*Hearne's Collections* ix, Oxford Historical Society, 1914, 343], and a son, Bartholomew (1722–81), who became a Fellow of the same college.

The Peisleys lived in a house in St. Michael's Street (until 1899 part of New Inn Hall Street) now known as 'VANBRUGH HOUSE', which they refronted *c.*1721 with a façade in the style of Vanbrugh [E. Hibbert, *Vanbrugh House, Oxford*, 1982].

Like other master builders of their time, the Peisleys must have been capable of designing buildings in the current style that they had learned from the London architects for whom they worked as masons. Thus Stone's Almshouses are a vernacular version of the domestic architecture of the late seventeenth century, and 'Vanbrugh House' is an obvious derivation from Blenheim. But at University College the vaulting of the Radcliffe Gate shows that they were skilled in the technicalities of Gothic masonry as well as in the classical detail that they executed at Blenheim and Radley.

PEMBROKE, EARL OF, *see* HERBERT, HENRY.

PENISTON, JOHN (*c.*1779–1848) established himself as an architect and surveyor in Salisbury, where he lived in the Close, first at No. 27 (which he refronted) and then from *c.*1830 in De Vaux Place. Farmhouses, cottages and other utilitarian buildings formed the bulk of his practice, but, being a Catholic, he was also employed to design several chapels for members of the same faith. He held the post of County Surveyor from 1822 onwards. After his death on 22 June 1848 at the age of 69 his practice was continued by his son John Michael Peniston (1807–58) and his grandson Henry Peniston (1832–1911), who succeeded him in turn as County Surveyor. A large collection of the firm's drawings, letter-books and other records is preserved in the Wiltshire County Record Office and is the principal source of the list of works given below. For biographical details see Michael Cowan, 'The Penistons', *Wilts. Archl. Mag.* 80, 1986.

POULSHOT RECTORY, WILTS., altered or rebuilt, 1823 [Salisbury Diocesan Records].

BROADLANDS, HANTS., enlarged service wing for 3rd Viscount Palmerston, 1825 [G. Jackson-Stops in *C. Life*, 18 Dec. 1980].

WYLYE RECTORY, WILTS., altered or rebuilt, 1827 [Salisbury Diocesan Records].

CLARENDON PARK, WILTS., additions and alterations (including stuccoing of exterior) for Sir Frederick Hervey Bathurst, 1828 [Letter-book, 6 Oct. 1828 etc.].

BRAMSHAW CHURCH, HANTS., repaired and enlarged, 1829 [I.C.B.S.].

SPETTISBURY, DORSET, Catholic Chapel, 1829–32, Gothic [Wilts. R.O. 451/200].

CANNINGTON COURT (now Somerset Farm Institute), SOMERSET, octagonal Catholic Chapel, 1830 [Wilts. R.O. 451/74 (ix); B. Little, *Catholic Churches since 1623*, 1966, 110] (plan in *V.C.H. Somerset* vi, 77).

UPTON HOUSE, DORSET, enlarged (Kitchen, Conservatory and Chapel), 1830 [Wilts., R.O. 451/72 (iii)].

SALISBURY, DE VAUX PLACE (terrace of six houses), *c.*1830 [R.C.H.M., *Salisbury* i, 131].

LANDFORD HOUSE, WILTS., drawing-room for – Bolton, 1831 [Wilts. R.O. 451/74 (xxiiiA)].

IBSLEY CHURCH, HANTS., 1832, Gothic [inscription in church].

DEVIZES, ST. JAMES'S CHURCH, SOUTHBROOM, rebuilt (except tower) 1833–4, Gothic, following designs made by Benoni White of Devizes (d. 1833) [Wilts. R.O. 451/72 (xii)].

WESTMEAD HOUSE, BRECON ROAD, WESTBURY-ON-TRIM, GLOS., Catholic Chapel (now library) 1834–5 [Wilts. R.O. 451/74 (vii) & 231].

WINCANTON, SOMERSET, house for E. Yalden Cooper, 1835 [Wilts. R.O. 451/72 (xxii)].

SOMERLEY PARK, HANTS., proposed alterations for 2nd Earl of Normanton, *c.*1830–40 [Wilts. R.O. 451/73 (xxxiv)].

FRYERN COURT, HANTS., alterations 1845 [Wilts. R.O. 451/73 (xxiv)].

THORNHILL HOUSE, DORSET, altered interior of entrance hall for W. Boucher [Wilts. R.O. 451/73 (xxii)].

PENNEL, MARMADUKE (– *c.*1732), was a successful bricklayer and alderman of Nottingham in the early eighteenth century, holding the office of Mayor in 1718–19 and 1724–5. He built ST. MARY'S WORKHOUSE in 1714, and during his second mayoralty he paved St. Peter's Square, established a Monday Market there for butter, fruit, and vegetables, and erected a MARKET CROSS, consisting of a tiled roof supported by four Tuscan columns. 'Pennel's Cross', as it was called, was converted into a fire-engine house in 1733, and demolished in 1787. In 1724–5 Pennel built (and presumably designed) the front rooms of the NEW EXCHANGE (illustrated in C. Deering, *Nottinghamia Vetus et Nova*, 1751, 8) and on 19 March 1724/5, he was appointed surveyor to design and build a new County Hall in the city. He visited Worcester in order to make drawings of the new Guildhall there, but nothing came of the scheme, as it was eventually decided to repair the old County Hall. [*The Stretton Manuscripts*, ed. G. C. Robertson, 1910, 156, 159, 165; *Records of the Borough of Nottingham* vi, 99, 140; *Nottinghamshire County Records of the Eighteenth Century*, ed. K. T. Meaby, 1947, 47–9; will proved in Notts. Archdeaconry Court, 12 Jan. 1732/3.]

PENRICE, JOHN, practised in Colchester. In 1823–5 he supervised the building of STISTED HALL, ESSEX, for C. S. Onley to the designs of Henry Hakewill [*Ipswich Journal*, 7 May 1825]. On 26 December 1834 the *Essex Standard* reported that the BAPTIST MEETING HOUSE in ELD LANE, COLCHESTER, had recently been erected 'under the superintendence of Mr. Penrice, architect', and on 19 September 1845 the same journal advertised building plots in new roads in Colchester (Osborn, Forster, Cross and Arthur Streets) for which Penrice was the superintending architect. He was still in practice in 1847, when he designed public baths in the town [*Builder* v, 1847, 277], but was dead by 1860.

Penrice was the principal architect involved in the development of WALTON-ON-THE-NAZE, ESSEX, as a seaside resort in the 1830s. In his *Descriptive Account of Walton on the Naze*, Colchester 1860, Thomas Wilmshurst states that Penrice built the wooden pier in 1830, and that he also designed Kent's Hotel (1832), while Pigot's *Directory* of *c.*1835 says 'Many of the dwellings present peculiar neatness and taste, particularly those erected by Mr. Penrice, architect, of Colchester.' Another hotel at Walton designed by him is illustrated in *An Historical Account of Walton-on-the-Naze*, published at Colchester in 1829. [Information from Mr. J. Bensusan-Butt.]

PENSON, THOMAS (*c.*1760–1824), was the founder of a dynasty of architects practising in Chester and North Wales. He himself lived at Wrexham, where he combined the function of architect, auctioneer and County Surveyor of Flintshire from 1810 to 1814, when he was dismissed following the collapse of a bridge he was building at Overton. In

1799 he bought a large house in Charles Street, Wrexham, which he subsequently rebuilt before moving in about 1818 to a house which he built for himself in Theatre Lane behind the THEATRE which he erected in Beast Market. In 1784 he designed THE COUNTY GAOL at CAERNARVON (dem.), whose design was an almost literal copy of Joseph Turner's recently erected gaol at Ruthin [W. H. Jones, *Old Karnarvon*, 1889, 115]. He also designed a small country house near Wrexham called BRYNMALLY HALL (dem.) for Richard Kirk [A. N. Palmer, *History of the Country Townships of the Old Parish of Wrexham*, 1903, 104]. Penson died on 30 March 1824, aged 64, and was buried in the Old Cemetery at Wrexham [A. N. Palmer, *History of Wrexham*, 1893, 123, 128, 215; *History of the Parish Church of Wrexham*, 1886, 172n.].

Thomas Penson had two sons. The younger, John William Todd Penson, was an artist and died at the age of 36 in 1826. The elder, Thomas Penson (*c.*1790–1859), became a pupil of Thomas Harrison of Chester and established himself in practice at Oswestry in Shropshire. He was County Surveyor of Denbighshire and Montgomeryshire for over thirty years, a Fellow of the R.I.B.A. and a member of the Institution of Civil Engineers. He revolutionized the road system of Montgomershire, and designed many bridges, including NEW BRIDGE over the River Dee near Wynnstay and one at LLANYMYNECH over the River Vyrnwy. He also designed the FLANNEL MARKET HALL at NEWTOWN, MONTGOM., 1832 [*Carmarthen Jnl.* 27 Jan. 1832, *ex inf.* Mr. T. Lloyd], the NEWTOWN & LLANIDLOES UNION WORKHOUSE (now a Hospital) at CAERSWS, MONTGOM., 1838–40 [B. Owen in *Montgom. Colls.* 78, 1990] and several buildings in Oswestry. He was responsible for rebuilding or altering three country houses in the 'Elizabethan' syle: PENTREHEYLIN, MONTGOM., for John James Turner, *c.*1830; dem. 1955 [*Montgom. Colls.* 32, 1902, 242], VAYNOR PARK, MONTGOM., for J. Lyon Winder, 1840–53 [*A.P.S.D.*], and LLANRHAIADR HALL, DENBIGHS., for W. Price, 1842 [*A.P.S.D.*]. Churches by him included HOLY TRINITY, OSWESTRY, 1836–7, with the unusual feature for its date of a vaulted apse [I.C.B.S.]; ST. DAVID'S, DENBIGH, 1838–40, rebuilt 1894; CHRIST CHURCH, WELSHPOOL, MONTGOM., 1839–44, neo-Norman; ST. DAVID'S, NEWTOWN, MONTGOM., 1843–7; LLANYMYNECH, SALOP., 1845, neo-Norman; HOLY TRINITY, GWERSYLLT, DENBIGHS., 1850–1; and RHOS LLANERCHRUGOG, DENBIGHS., 1852–3, cruciform neo-Norman.

The younger Thomas Penson had two sons, Thomas Mainwaring Penson and Richard Kyrke Penson, both of whom practised in Chester, the former until his death in 1864 and the latter thereafter until his death in 1885.

[*A.P.S.D.*; *Minutes of Procs. of the Institution of Civil Engineers* xx, 1860–1, 156; D. R. Thomas, *History of the Diocese of St. Asaph*, 1870, 340, 365, 634, 660, 812, 841; Peter Howell in *Arch. Hist.* 27, 1984, 335–6; I. Watkin, *Oswestry*, 1920, 143; letters to W. Owen of Glansevern in N.L.W.]

PEPPER, JOHN (1751–1811), was a builder and architect of Newcastle-under-Lyme in Staffordshire, where he built the THEATRE ROYAL in 1787 [Newcastle Borough *Reporter*, May 1992, 6]. PEPPER STREET, which he presumably built as a speculation, commemorates his name. In 1796 he patented an improvement in the structure of kilns for firing china, etc. (Patent no. 2140). In 1802–3, with advice from J. H. Haycock (*q.v.*), he altered and improved MAER HALL, STAFFS., for Josiah Wedgwood [Eliza Meteyard, *A Group of Englishmen*, 1871, 306–7]. A tombstone in the churchyard of St. Nicholas, Newcastle-under-Lyme, records the dates of his birth and death [*ex inf.* Mr. Maxwell Craven].

PEPPER, WILLIAM, may have been the son of George Pepper, a surveyor practising in Westminster who was President of the Surveyors' Club in 1801. In 1808 William Pepper exhibited at the Royal Academy a design for a monumental building in memory of Admirals Howe, Duncan, Vincent and Nelson, giving his address as Park Prospect, Westminster. He subsequently established himself in Kingston-on-Thames, where in 1823 he was responsible for altering the galleries in the parish church [Surrey Archdeaconry Records]. In 1826 COBHAM CHURCH, SURREY, was enlarged on the N. side to his designs [contract in Guildford Record Office, PSH/COB/5/3/1–2].

PERCY, EDWARD THOMAS, was practising as an architect and surveyor in Sherborne in the early nineteenth century. In 1830 he repaired the central tower of SHERBORNE ABBEY CHURCH (see his report, of which there is a copy in Sir John Soane's Museum, Soane Case, 'Misc. MSS. relating to Architecture', I, and Vestry Minutes in Dorset C.R.O.).

PERCY, JOHN, was a pupil of James Wyatt, from whose office in London he exhibited drawings of two of Wyatt's buildings at the R.A. in 1793 and 1795. He also studied drawing under James Malton. He subsequently moved to Norwich, where he practised as a land-surveyor [*Norfolk Chronicle*, 17 March 1804]. In 1806 he exhibited a design for a monument to Lord Nelson at the Norwich Society of Artists (see also *Norfolk Chronicle* 19 April 1806).

PERRY, EBENEZER (–1850), practised in London from the 1820s onwards. In 1825–7 FOLLY BRIDGE, OXFORD, was built to his designs [J. M. Davenport, *Oxfordshire Bridges*, Oxford, 1869, 11]. In 1832 he was employed by Messrs. Dunston, Robinson and Flanders to lay out their Battle Bridge estate in St. Pancras [*Survey of London* xxiv, 106]. A design by him for 'a house of the fourth rate' in Hackney was sold at Sotheby's on 30 April 1987, lot 519.

PERRY, GEORGE, practised at Bewdley in Worcestershire. In 1773 he rebuilt one arch of BRIDGNORTH BRIDGE at a cost of £1300 [*Trans. Salop. Archaeological Soc.* xlix, 1937, 208]. He was the author of some designs for Gothic almshouses, 'proposed to be built in Park Lane' Bewdley in 1802, which are in the Prattinton Collection in the Library of the Society of Antiquaries (Portfolio v, 72/2 and 3(i)). Another drawing in the same collection shows that he designed the Gothic monument in the churchyard at Hartlebury to Bishop Hurd (d. 1808).

PERRY, JOHN, was an architect and surveyor of Godalming, Surrey, where in 1814 he designed the attractive TOWN HALL. [Brayley, *Topographical History of Surrey* v, 201]. Several of his executed works are illustrated in Loudon's *Encyclopaedia of Rural Architecture*, 1846, including a 'Bailiff's Cottage, in the Old English Style', built at BURY HILL, nr. DORKING, for Charles Barclay in 1831, a farm at the same place, and a stable nr. GODALMING. In 1839 he reported on the condition of GODALMING CHURCH, and in the following year carried out a number of alterations, all of which were swept away by Gilbert Scott in 1879 [S. Welman, *The Parish and Church of Godalming*, 1900, 45–6]. His designs for rectories at PUTTENHAM, SURREY, 1823, and GUILDFORD, ST. NICHOLAS, 1838, are in the G.L.R.O. He also 'enlarged and rearranged' LEA (later WITLEY) PARK, SURREY (dem.), for John Leech [Brayley, *op. cit.* v, 255]. R. Varden was his pupil.

PETTIT, C— A—, exhibited 'A Ceiling for Stuco ornaments and painted pannels' at the Free Society of Artists in 1771, and a 'Design for a Prison' at the Royal Academy in 1814.

PHILLIPS, AMBROSE (1707–1737), was the owner of GARENDON PARK, LEICS., which he inherited from his father William Phillips in 1729. He travelled extensively in Italy, making drawings of Roman antiquities that are now in the R.I.B.A. Collection, and on his return was probably one of the original members of the Society of Dilettanti. He was quite a competent architectural draughtsman, and the drawings at the R.I.B.A. include several designs by him of a Palladian character. At Garendon he designed and built a Triumphal Arch, a Temple of Venus, and an Obelisk, and had begun to rebuild the house before his early death in 1737 at the age of 30. The Triumphal Arch is based on the Arch of Titus in Rome, of which only the central portion then remained, embedded in medieval fortifications. The Garendon Arch is therefore an essay in archaeological reconstruction which shows that Phillips was a serious student of Roman architecture. The Temple of Venus is inspired by the Temple of Vesta in Rome and the coffered ceiling of the portico of the new house derived from the barrel-vault of the so-called Temple of the Sun at Rome. The façade was moreover flanked by two gateways based on the well-known archway by Inigo Jones which Lord Burlington re-erected at Chiswick. The house, completed by Ambrose Phillips's successor, was remodelled in the French château style in 1866 and demolished in 1964, but the Arch, Temple and Obelisk remain as monuments to their builder's taste. On his monument in Shepshed church his architectural enthusiasm is commemorated by an inscription which claims that *Ex Italia reversus/ Inspectis antiquorum aedificiorum Reliquijs Artes Romanas in Patriam transtulit,/Et inter Principes viros qui jam Architecturam/in Anglia restituere et perpolire coeperant/Enituit pene Primus.*

[Mark Girouard, 'Ambrose Phillips of Garendon', *Arch. Hist.* viii, 1965; *Catalogue of the R.I.B.A. Drawings Collection: O–R*, 52.]

PHILLIPS, HENRY (*c.*1796–1851), of Bermondsey, Surrey, exhibited a design for a public library to be erected in Dublin at the Royal Academy in 1820. He was elected to membership of the Surveyors' Club in 1829, and was President in 1834. His death in 1851, aged 55, is recorded in Bermondsey parish register. BERMONDSEY RECTORY was built to his designs in 1828 [G.L.R.O., WD/OP/ 1828/6]. The R.I.B.A. Drawings Collection has an unexecuted design probably by him for the Public News Room at Leicester, dated 1837.

PHILLIPS, JOHN (*c.*1709–1775), was a London master carpenter of considerable repute in the reigns of George II and George III. He was the son of Matthew Phillips, of East Hagbourne in Berkshire, and grandson of another Matthew Phillips, a mason or bricklayer of the same place. His uncle Thomas Phillips (*c.*1689–1736) was another well-known London master carpenter of the early eighteenth century, whose 'skill and diligence in his profession' are commemorated on his monument in East Hagbourne churchyard. The latter (who had been apprenticed to Jeremiah Franklin of Oxford, carpenter, in 1705) was active as a speculative builder in London, e.g. on the Harley estate between 1723 and 1730 [B.L., Add. MS. 18240] and in Sackville Street in 1730 [*Survey of London* xxxii, 345]. He had the carpenter's contract for two churches designed by Gibbs, St. Martin-in-the-Fields and St. Peter's, Vere Street, and for several buildings erected by the Office of Works, including Kent's Treasury Buildings [*Gent's Mag.* 1736, 488]. In 1729–30 he built the wooden bridge across the Thames between Fulham and Putney 'according to a scheme and principles laid down by' Dr. William Cheselden of St. Thomas's Hospital [G.L. Record Office, Commissioners' Minutes, 2 July 1730, etc.].

John Phillips appears to have succeeded to his uncle's business in London, and to have been in partnership with George Shakespear (*q.v.*). In, London he was responsible for the development of CHARLES STREET, MAYFAIR (1750), and of a block of land with frontages to KING STREET, WESTMINSTER, and PALL MALL (1759) [B. H. Johnson, *Berkeley Square to Bond Street*, 1952, 179; *Survey of London* xxix, 328–9]. In Oxford he built the wooden dome of the RADCLIFFE LIBRARY to the designs of James Gibbs and made the fine joinery for the interior of the building (1742–50) [*Building Accounts of the Radcliffe Camera*, ed. Gillam, Oxford Historical Soc. 1958, *passim*]. Together with Shakespear he was responsible for the even finer joinery in CHRIST CHURCH LIBRARY (1752–62) [W. G. Hiscock, *A Christ Church Miscellany*, 1946, 69]. It was also in partnership with Shakespear that he demolished the east wing of AUDLEY END, ESSEX, for Lady Portsmouth in 1749 [Lord Braybrooke, *History of Audley End*, 1836, 93–4] and between 1750 and 1764 rebuilt ALSCOT HOUSE, WARWICKS., for James West in a Gothick style akin to that of Batty Langley [accounts at Alscot; Mark Girouard in *C. Life*, 15, 22, 29 May 1958]. In 1767–9 he carried out alterations to AUBREY HOUSE, NOTTING HILL, for Lady Mary Coke [*Letters and Journals of Lady Mary Coke* ii, 1889, 45, 221, 388–9, iii, 1892, 15, 24, 38, 54, 114], in 1769–70 he built a large house (dem. 1915) at the north end of PARK LANE for the 2nd Viscount Bateman [*Survey of London* xl, 285–6], and in 1771–2 he built the wooden bridge (dem. 1881) at BATTERSEA under the direction of Henry Holland [Dorothy Stroud, *Henry Holland*, 18, 25, 97]. In 1772–4 he acted as surveyor on behalf of the Society of Arts during the building of their premises in the Adelphi by the brothers Adam [A. T. Bolton, *The Architecture of R. & J. Adam* ii, 42–3]. Though more notable as a master builder than as an architect, Phillips was undoubtedly capable of making his own designs, and he was presumably the 'Phillips' who in 1760 was short-listed by the committee for the selection of a design for Blackfriars Bridge. According to the anonymous *Observations on Bridge Building and the several Plans offered for a New Bridge* (1760), he 'submitted 11 different designs'.

Phillips lived in Brook Street[1] and died, a wealthy man, on 28 December 1775, aged 66. He was the lord of the manor of Blewbury in Berkshire, and since 1763 had been the lessee of the rectorial manor of Culham, near Abingdon, where he occupied and rebuilt CULHAM HOUSE (OXON.). When he died childless in 1775 he left his property first to his father (who died two years later) and then to his brother William (d. 1782), whose descendants continued to live at Culham until 1935.

[Oxford City Records (apprenticeship of Thomas Phillips); Oxfordshire C.R.O., MS. Wills Berks. 21, f. 127v (will of Matthew Phillips the elder), MS. Oxf. Dioc. Papers *c.*2115, nos. 4–15 (lease of Culham); P.R.O. PROB 6/112, f. 34 (administration of Thomas Phillips); P.C.C. 87 BELLAS (will of John Phillips); *Passages from the Diary of Mrs. Lybbe Powys*, ed. Climenson, 1899, 153; *V.C.H. Berkshire* iii, 281; *V.C.H. Oxon.* vii, 29, 36; monumental inscriptions at East Hagbourne and Sutton Courtenay.]

PHILLIPS, JOHN (1771–1843), a pupil of George Byfield, was admitted to the Royal Academy Schools in 1791 and gained the Silver Medal in 1793. He exhibited at the Academy from Byfield's office in 1790–3 and thereafter from various London addresses. He died in Kennington, S. London, on 6 January 1843, aged 72 [*Gent's Mag.* 1843 (i), 218].

Phillips's first exhibit at the Academy, a

[1] His house, now 39 Lower Brook Street, was built by Thomas Phillips, who lived there from 1724 until his death in 1736 (*ex inf.* Survey of London). A later occupant was Sir Jeffry Wyatville, who remodelled it.

'Perspective view of the two new fronts intended for the seat of Thomas Bund, Esqr.', i.e. WICK HOUSE, ST. JOHN IN BEDWARDINE, WORCESTER, probably represented a building designed by Byfield. But subsequent exhibits indicate that he designed THE ROYAL NAVAL HOSPITAL at DEAL in KENT (1799); an unidentified house for a gentleman in East Kent (1804); UPTON HOUSE, WORTH, KENT, for Robert Small (1809); and 'improvements' to GREAT DOODS, nr. REIGATE, SURREY (1810).

PHILLIPS, MATTHEW (*c.*1781–1825), of York, was in partnership with Peter Atkinson II until 1819, when he set up office in New Bridge Street [York Public Library, Knowles MSS.]. He died in February 1825 in his 45th year, and is commemorated by a tomb in the churchyard at Acomb, nr. York. J. A. Hansom (1803–82) was his pupil.

PHIPPS, JOHN (*c.*1796–1868), spent his life in the service of the Office of Works. He entered the Office in 1819 as a temporary clerk, became an Examining and Measuring Clerk in 1822, and in 1832 was promoted to the new post of Assistant Surveyor of Works and Buildings. He was regarded as 'an excellent draughtsman' and an 'active, zealous and intelligent' member of the staff. His architectural opportunities were confined to minor works at Windsor, Frogmore and elsewhere. [*History of the King's Works* vi, 185 and *passim; Builder* xxvi, 1868, 117.]

PICKERNELL, JONATHAN (*c.*1738–1812), was sent from London[1] to assist John Wooler in investigating the site for Hexham Bridge, Northumberland, in 1775, and subsequently supervised the building of the bridge (destroyed by a flood in 1782) to the designs of John Smeaton [Samuel Smiles, *Lives of the Engineers* ii, 1861, 62]. In 1776 he was appointed Surveyor of Bridges in the County of Northumberland, and held the post until his resignation in January 1781 [Northumberland Record Office, QS Order Books 11, p. 306 and 12, p. 99]. In that year he became Harbour Engineer at Whitby, where he remained until his death in August 1812 at the age of 74. At WHITBY he built the west pier of the harbour and designed in 1788 the TOWN HALL in an attractive but somewhat old-fashioned classical style. His name is recorded on an oval plaque. His son, of the same name, was harbour engineer at Sunderland from 1795 to 1804 and built the lighthouse on the north pier there. A design by the younger Pickernell for centering to support the single arch of the great iron bridge over the river Wear at Sunderland during its construction in 1793–6 is preserved in Sir John Soane's Museum (Portfolio 3, no. 56). Francis Pickernell, Harbour Engineer at Whitby from 1822, was probably the grandson of Jonathan Pickernell senior. [G. Young, *History of Whitby* ii, 1817, 526; *Parliamentary Reports* xiv, 1803, 334; information from Prof. A. W. Skempton.]

[1] He probably came from Hampshire, for in 1769 Jonathan Pickernell of 'East Wasdy', Southampton, carpenter, took William Pickernell as an apprentice (P.R.O., Apprenticeship Registers).

PICKERSGILL, THOMAS (*c.*1807–1869), started practice in York in 1829. From 1831 to 1840 he was in partnership with Matthew Oates (*q.v.*). He held the post of Surveyor to the Corporation from 1854 until his death on 5 May 1869, aged 62. His earliest recorded works were the WESLEYAN METHODIST CHAPEL in LADY PECKITT'S YARD, built in 1829 and demolished in 1874–5 [*New Guide to York*, 1838, 162], and a tannery in BLAKE STREET, built in the same year [R.C.H.M. *York* v, 107]. In 1831 he was employed to restore the portion of the City wall between Micklegate Bar and North Postern [R.C.H.M. *York* ii, 32]. He designed SEATON CAREW CHURCH, CO. DURHAM, in 1831 [I.C.B.S.], rebuilt the tower and arcades of ST. DENYS CHURCH, YORK, in 1846–7 [I.C.B.S.], and largely rebuilt ST. MARGARET'S CHURCH, YORK, in 1851–2 [I.C.B.S.].

PICKFORD, JOSEPH (1734–1782), was the leading architect in Derbyshire in the reign of George III. He was the son of William Pickford, a mason of Ashow near Warwick, and the nephew of Joseph Pickford, a sculptor and monumental mason with a yard at Hyde Park Corner in London. His father died soon after his birth, and in 1748 he was sent to London to be trained in his uncle's yard. He remained in London for about ten years, gaining experience by working on buildings designed by leading architects such as Stephen Wright and Sir William Chambers. At the same time he became a competent architectural draughtsman. In 1759 he went to Derbyshire to supervise the building of Foremark Hall on behalf of the Warwick architects David and William Hiorne. Subsequent work at Longford Hall led to his marriage to the daughter of the owner's agent, and to his own establishment as an architect and builder in Derby. During the next twenty years Pickford designed and built several small country houses and some town mansions in a competent late Palladian style that owed something to James Paine. Among the buildings which he erected to the designs of others was

James Gandon's County Hall at Nottingham, which no doubt explains the inclusion of one of his own houses (Sandon Hall) in Woolfe and Gandon's *Vitruvius Britannicus* (vol. 5, 1771).

In Derby Pickford built a handsome house for himself in Friargate, became a member of the corporation, and was a close friend both of the artist Joseph Wright, who painted a portrait of his two sons as children, and of John Whitehurst, an intellectual clockmaker who was the author of an *Inquiry into the Original State and Formation of the Earth* (1778). Pickford died in July 1782, aged 47, leaving a widow and two sons, the elder of whom became a Fellow of Oriel College, Oxford. His business was not continued by his family, but he had two pupils, Thomas Gardner and James Pollard (*qq.v.*), the former of whom established a provincial practice as an architect at Uttoxeter. [Edward Saunders, *Joseph Pickford*, 1993, where the works listed below are documented and illustrated, and where further stylistic attributions will be found.]

LONGFORD HALL, DERBYS., remodelled for Wenman Coke, 1762.

DERBY, THE ASSEMBLY ROOMS, built under Pickford's supervision 1762–5, probably to the designs of Washington Shirley, Earl Ferrers (*q.v.*); interior completed, probably by Robert Adam, 1774; gutted by fire 1963 and dem. 1971; façade re-erected at Crich Tramway Museum (*C. Life*, 16 Aug. 1930, 215).

attributed: ASHBOURNE, THE GREY HOUSE, 61 CHURCH STREET, refronted and remodelled for Brian Hodgson, 1763.

attributed: ASHBOURNE, THE MANSION, refronted and remodelled for Dr. John Taylor, *c.*1764–5 (*C. Life*, 28 March 1968).

attributed: DERBY, QUEEN STREET, house for John Whitehurst, 1764; dem. 1926.

attributed: ASHBOURNE, COMPTON HOUSE (now a bank) for Francis Beresford, *c.*1766 This house is almost a duplicate of No. 44 Friar Gate, Derby (see below).

DERBY, ST. HELEN'S HOUSE, for John Gisborne, 1766–7.

OGSTON HALL, DERBYSHIRE, design for remodelling house for William Turbutt, 1767, executed with modifications by E. Stanley of Chesterfield (*q.v.*), 1768–9; altered *c.*1840–50 and remodelled 1864.

ETRURIA HALL, nr. BURSLEM, STAFFS., for Josiah Wedgwood, 1768–9.

BANK HOUSE, ETRURIA, nr. BURSLEM, STAFFS., for Thomas Bentley (Wedgwood's partner), 1768–9; dem. 1819.

THE ETRURIA WORKS, nr. BURSLEM. STAFFS., for Josiah Wedgwood, 1768–70; dem.

HAMS HALL, nr. COLESHILL, WARWICKS., work for C.B. Adderley, 1768. A letter from Josiah Wedgwood to Bentley, 15 Sept. 1768, mentions Pickford's employment at Hams. He may have designed this house which, according to Neale's *Seats* iii, 1820, was built in 1760, and according to Burke, *Visitation of Seats* ii, 1853, 67, in 1764. It was reconstructed internally after a fire in 1890 and dem. *c.*1920, when the upper part of the façade was rebuilt at Coates, Glos., as part of what is now Bledisloe Lodge.

attributed: SHARDLOW HALL, DERBYS., addition of wings for Leonard Fosbrooke, *c.*1768.

CALKE ABBEY, DERBYSHIRE, THE RIDING SCHOOL, for Sir Henry Harpur, Bart., 1768.

DERBY, FRIAR GATE, Nos. 41, 44 and 45, on plots acquired by Pickford in 1768. No. 41, his own house (now the Pickford House Museum), was built by 1770, Nos. 44 and 45 by 1771, the latter originally as a warehouse.

SANDON HALL, STAFFS., for Lord Archibald Hamilton, 1769–71; destroyed by fire 1848 (*Vitruvius Britannicus* v, pls. 90–3).

NOTTINGHAM, ST. MARY'S CHURCH, design for restoration of Gothic windows, 1770 (Nottingham University Library, MAB 115).

attributed: SWANWICK HALL, nr. ALFRETON, DERBYS., for Hugh Wood, *c.*1771.

MELBOURNE HALL, DERBYS., reroofing and redecoration for 1st Viscount Melbourne, 1772.

DERBY, THE SHIRE HALL, designed GRAND JURY ROOM, 1772; room dem. 1828.

WIRKSWORTH, DERBYS., THE MOOT HALL, for the Duchy of Lancaster, 1772–3; dem. 1814 and rebuilt on new site.

BIRMINGHAM, ST. MARY'S CHURCH, 1773–4, on an octagonal plan; dem. 1925.

EDENSOR, DERBYSHIRE, THE INN for 5th Duke of Devonshire, 1776–7.

EDENSOR, DERBYSHIRE, VICARAGE for Revd. John Wood, 1777–9; dem. 1838.

DERBY, THE DEVONSHIRE HOSPITAL (almshouses), FULL STREET for 5th Duke of Devonshire, 1777; dem. 1894.

attributed: CHATSWORTH, DERBYSHIRE, THE LODGE GATE HOUSE, BASLOW ROAD, for 5th Duke of Devonshire, 1779.

COVENTRY, HOLY TRINITY CHURCH, rebuilt three windows at E. end and all windows on S. side, 1774–5.

SOLIHULL CHURCH, WARWICKS., rebuilt spire 1774–5.

DARLEY ABBEY, DERBYS., alterations for Robert Holden, 1775–8; dem. 1962.

LEICESTER, TRINITY HOSPITAL, NEWARKE, reconstructed for the Duchy of Lancaster, 1776; dem. 1898 except medieval chapel.

attributed: ASHFORD HALL, ASHFORD-IN-THE-WATER, DERBYS., for John Barker, *c.*1776.

attributed: LONG EATON HALL, DERBYS., for John Howitt, *c.*1778.

PIERCE, or PEARCE, EDWARD (*c.*1630–1695), was the son of Edward Pierce (d. 1658), a member of the London Painter-Stainers' Company. The elder Pierce was, in Vertue's words, 'a good History and Landskip Painter, in the Reigns of King Charles the First and II. He also drew Architecture, Perspective, etc; and was much esteem'd in his time.' The exact date of his son's birth is not known, and the first recorded event in his career is his admission to the freedom of the Painter-Stainers' Company by patrimony in 1656. He was 'chosen of the Livery' in 1668, and was Master of the Company in 1693. Of his early life and training nothing is known, but he married in 1661, and he was working as a mason under Sir Roger Pratt at Horseheath, Cambs., in 1665 [R. T. Gunther, *The Architecture of Sir Roger Pratt*, 1928, 130]. He became well known as a sculptor, and, as Vertue observes, 'was much employed by S[r] Chr. Wren in his Carvings and Designs'. After the Great Fire he had masonry contracts in connection with several of the London City churches. He also worked on the GUILDHALL between 1671 and 1673, and held masons' contracts for the building of ST. PAUL'S CATHEDRAL. As a sculptor, Pierce is best known for his fine portrait-busts of Oliver Cromwell and Sir Christopher Wren, now in the Ashmolean Museum at Oxford. He worked with equal facility in either stone or wood, and much of his best carving in the latter material has been erroneously attributed to Grinling Gibbons. In 1680 he carved the wooden model for the copper dragon which forms the weathervane on the steeple of St. Mary-le-Bow, and he executed carving in several other churches, including the fonts at St. Andrew, Holborn, and St. Matthew, Friday Street.

In 1676 Pierce was associated with John Oliver in designing the fittings of EMMANUEL COLLEGE CHAPEL, CAMBRIDGE, in whose erection Archbishop Sancroft was closely concerned [Willis & Clark, ii, 707]. It was to Sancroft that Pierce owed what was probably his most important architectural commission, the BISHOP'S PALACE at LICHFIELD, which was built under his supervision and to his designs in 1686–7 [H. Colvin & A. Oswald in *C. Life*, 30 Dec. 1954]. The palace was rebuilt under the archbishop's direction during a sequestration of the see, and its erection is described in a series of letters from Dean Addison to Sancroft which are preserved in the Bodleian Library [Tanner MS. 131, ff. 170–88]. In addition to his remuneration as architect, Pierce received £14 for carving, probably in the pediment [Church Commissioners, Muniment 123828]. In Staffordshire, Pierce was also employed at WOLSELEY HALL (dem. 1966), where he executed the woodwork in the dining-room for Sir Charles Wolseley, Bart. [R. Plot, *Natural History of Staffordshire*, 1686, 383] (*C. Life*, 12 Feb. 1910), and he carved the staircase at SUDBURY HALL, DERBYSHIRE, in 1676–7 [C. Hussey in *C. Life*, 15, 22, 29 June, 1935]. In 1680–1 he probably designed the screen and panelling in WINCHESTER COLLEGE CHAPEL, subsequently removed to Hursley Park, but now reinstalled in the New Hall at Winchester [J. H. Harvey, 'Winchester College', *Jnl. British Archaeological Assn.* 3rd ser. xxviii, 1965, 126; John Cornforth in *C. Life*, 11 May 1961 and 26 March 1964].

In 1682–3 Pierce was employed by William Winde to design and carve the pediment of COMBE ABBEY, WARWICKS., for the 1st Earl of Craven [Bodleian Library, MS. Gough Warwicks. 1, ff. 14, 31, 45, 47], and he also worked at the house at HAMPSTEAD MARSHALL, BERKSHIRE, which Winde built for the same nobleman in the years following the Restoration. A design for a gate-pier at Hampstead Marshall, inscribed 'E. Peirce F[ct]', is in the Bodleian Library [MS. Gough Drawings a.2, f. 36]. In 1694 Pierce was employed to design the pillar at Seven Dials in the parish of St. Giles-in-the-Fields, London. His original drawing is in the Print Room of the British Museum. The pillar was removed in 1773, and is now at Weybridge, Surrey (*Survey of London* v, pl. 40; *C. Life*, 9 June 1986).

In 1676 Pierce was involved in the development of the site of Norfolk House in the Strand. He made a 'draft' for one of the fronts of the new mansion that was to have been built on part of the site (but was abandoned), and himself leased 45 feet of frontage on the east side of Surrey Street [Arundel Castle, MS. MD 1514, 19 Oct. 1676].

Pierce died at his house in Surrey Street in March 1695, and was buried at St. Clement Danes. He left a curious memorandum of his 'Dues Debts and Disposalls' which on 20 April 1695 was proved as his will in the Archdeaconry Court of Middlesex. In it he states that he 'may justly be supposed to be worth 2516 pounds'. This sum was to be shared between his son John Pierce, his son-in-law John Killingworth, and his widow. In addition there was his 'Clositt of Books, prints and drawings', of which his 'very good freind'

William Talman was 'to have the choise and picking of what therein shall seeme to make up the worthy colection he intends'. The 'sirpluce' was to be divided between his son and son-in-law, and evidently supplied the material for the 'curious collection of Books, Drawings, Prints, Models, and Plaster Figures' that was sold by auction in February 1696, together with that of the landscape-painter Thomas Manby, who had died in November 1695. Anne Pierce, his widow, died in 1703. A portrait of Pierce by Isaac Fuller at Sudeley Castle is reproduced in *Walpole Society* xi, pl. 24. The sculptor William Kidwell (d. 1736) was his pupil [H. Potterton in *Burlington Mag.* Dec. 1972, 864].

Talman evidently availed himself of the opportunity to select drawings from Pierce's 'closet', for several drawings by Pierce formerly in Talman's collection are in the Print Room of the British Museum,[1] and others bearing indications of Talman's ownership are in the Victoria and Albert,[2] Soane and Ashmolean[3] Museums, the R.I.B.A. Drawings Collection and the Art Institute at Chicago.[4] Some of these drawings are reproduced in *Wren Soc.* xvii, pls. 22, 23, 24 and 26, where they are wrongly ascribed to Talman. In addition there is a design by Pierce for a monument to Archbishop Matthew Parker at the end of Bodleian, Tanner MS. 89. This was made for Archbishop Sancroft but was not executed.

[Rachel Poole, 'Edward Pierce, the Sculptor', *Walpole Soc.* xi, 1922–3; D. Knoop & G. P. Jones, *The London Mason in the Seventeenth Century*, 1935, 25–6; K. A. Esdaile in *The Architect*, 2 Sept. 1921; June Seymour, 'Edward Pearce: Baroque Sculptor of London', *Guildhall Miscellany*, No. 1, 1952; R. Gunnis, *Dictionary of British Sculptors*, 1968, 296–7; Walpole Soc. *Vertue Note Books, passim; Wren Soc.* xx, 160; abstract of will published by J. H. Harvey in *Jnl. British Archaeological Assn.* 3rd ser. xxviii, 1965, 127.]

[1] See E. Croft-Murray & P. Hilton, *Catalogue of British Drawings* i, 1960, 451–5 and plates.

[2] Numbered 3436, 318–20, 421, 432, 433, 441. No. 421 is reproduced by John Physick, *Designs for English Sculpture*, 1969, 46–7.

[3] Gibbs Collection iii, 99 and 110, and Talman album, f. 87 (sketch for a bust identified by Dr. Margaret Whinney as that of Baldwin Hamey at the Royal College of Physicians, which is known to have been executed by Pierce in 1675).

[4] John Harris, *Catalogue of British Drawings for Architecture, etc. in American Collections*, 1971, 160–1.

PIERCE, THOMAS, was an architect and surveyor of Stamford, Lincs. A new GAOL behind the Town Hall at STAMFORD was built to his designs in 1821 [advt. in *Lincoln, Rutland and Stamford Mercury*, 23 Feb. 1821], and he also designed the Tudor Gothic SNOWDEN'S HOSPITAL in the same town, as rebuilt in 1822–3 by Robert Goodwin, mason [Stamford Corporation Records, Mayor's Accounts for 1823–4].

PILKINGTON, REDMOND WILLIAM (1789–1844), the younger son of William Pilkington (*q.v.*), followed his father's profession, succeeding him in 1824 as surveyor to the Charterhouse, in 1826 as architect to the Earl of Radnor, and in 1838 as Surveyor to the Sun Fire Assurance Office. At the CHARTERHOUSE he rebuilt PREACHER'S and PENSIONERS' COURTS in 1825–30, apparently to designs provided by Edward Blore (*q.v.*), though in 1827 he exhibited at the Royal Academy under his own name a 'view of one of the quadrangles now erecting' at the Charterhouse. He died suddenly on 22 May 1844, aged 54. He had purchased an estate called Ash Hill near his father's property in Yorkshire. In London, where he was a magistrate, he lived in Hyde Park Gate, Kensington Gore. His son Lionel Scott Pilkington, *alias* Jack Hawley, was well known as a sportsman and eccentric. [*A.P.S.D.; D.N.B.*]

PILKINGTON, WILLIAM (1758–1848), born on 7 September 1758, at Hatfield, near Doncaster, was the elder son of William Pilkington of that place. He became a pupil of Sir Robert Taylor, whom he assisted until the latter's death in 1788 and whom he succeeded as Surveyor to the Grafton estate in London. In 1781 he was appointed Surveyor to the Board of Customs, resigning in 1810. He also became District Surveyor to the parishes of St. Margaret and St. John, Westminster (1784), and was surveyor to the Sun Fire Assurance Office (1792) and to the Charterhouse (1792). He was employed as surveyor and architect by the Earl of Radnor, for whom he built the Council House at Salisbury to the designs of Sir Robert Taylor in 1788–95. He exhibited occasionally at the Royal Academy between 1780 and 1790. He retired in about 1842 to his estate at Hatfield, where he died in 1848. He married in 1785 Sarah, daughter and co-heiress of John Andrews of Knaresborough, Yorks., by whom he had two sons. The elder, Henry, was called to the Bar; the younger, Redmond William (*q.v.*), followed his father's profession, and succeeded to several of his posts. His pupils included Joseph Parkinson, G. Goldring, and his nephew, James Howell. A volume of sketch-plans of premises made by Pilkington for the Sun Fire Office is in the Guildhall Library (MS. 11936 D). [*A.P.S.D.; D.N.B.*; H. Walpole, *Anecdotes of Painting* v, ed. F. W. Hilles & P. B. Daghlian, 1937, 199.]

PORTSMOUTH, THE CUSTOM HOUSE, 1785; dem. [*A.P.S.D.*].

LIVERPOOL, THE CUSTOM HOUSE, enlargement of accommodation 1786; dem. 1828 [E. H. Rideout, *The Custom House, Liverpool*, Liverpool 1928, 46].

BRENTFORD, MIDDLESEX, LONDON STYLE HOUSE, for Luke Wetten, 1790–1; dem. [*A.P.S.D.*].

LONDON, DOVER STREET, No. 38, for the Hon. W. H. Bouverie, 1791 [*A.P.S.D.*].

LONDON, HALF MOON STREET, house for 3rd Duke of Grafton (who himself lived in Clarges Street), 1798 [*A.P.S.D.*].

CHILTON LODGE, nr. HUNGERFORD, BERKSHIRE, rebuilt for John Pearse, 1800; altered by Sir A. W. Blomfield [J. Britton, *Beauties of Wiltshire* iii, 1825, 266–7]. Pilkington also designed the PEARSE MONUMENT in CHILTON FOLIAT CHURCHYARD [*ibid.*].

FOLKESTONE, KENT, gaol for 2nd Earl of Radnor, 1801; dem. [*A.P.S.D.*].

OTTERDEN PLACE, KENT, rebuilt for Granville Hastings Wheler, 1802, Tudor style [J. Lees-Milne in *C. Life*, 27 Aug. 1970].

LONDON, THE CHARTERHOUSE, THE 'BIG SCHOOL', 1803; dem. *c.*1872 [*Chronicles of Charter House*, by a Carthusian, 1847, 175].

YARMOUTH, NORFOLK, THE ROYAL NAVAL HOSPITAL (later barracks and now St. Nicholas Hospital), 1809–11, is said to have been designed by Pilkington by J. Preston, *Picture of Yarmouth*, 1819, 7 and J. H. Druery, *Great Yarmouth*, 1826, 89, but according to J. Dugdale's *British Traveller* iii, 1819, 610, it was designed by Edward Holl, the official Architect to the Navy (*q.v.*).

BATSFORD PARK, GLOS., alterations, including new entrance front, for 1st Lord Redesdale, 1809–16; dem. 1890 [references to 'Pilkington' as Lord Redesdale's architect in a letter dated 10 Dec. 1811, Glos. C.R.O., D 2002/3/1/25: N. Kingsley, *Country Houses of Gloucestershire*, 2, 1992, 73].

CLERMONT LODGE (now HALL), LITTLE CRESSINGHAM, NORFOLK, remodelled for 2nd Viscount Clermont, 1812 [*A.P.S.D.*; R. Garnier in *C. Life*, 23 Sept. 1993].

WYCK HILL HOUSE, nr. STOW-ON-THE-WOLD, GLOS., alterations for Charles Pole, 1812 and 1815; enlarged and remodelled *c.*1880–90; restored 1962 after fire in 1958 [*A.P.S.D.*].

WESTMINSTER, THE TRANSPORT OFFICE (afterwards the India Board of Control), CANNON ROW, WHITEHALL, 1816; dem. [*A.P.S.D.*].

POLSTEAD HALL, SUFFOLK, improvements for Thomas Cooke, 1816–19 [*A.P.S.D.*].

NORK HOUSE, BANSTEAD, SURREY, alterations, including addition of wings, for 2nd Lord Arden, 1812 onwards; dem. *c.*1930 [*A.P.S.D.*].

CALVERTON HOUSE, nr. STONY STRATFORD, BUCKS., alterations for 2nd Lord Arden, 1819 onwards. [*A.P.S.D.*].

CALVERTON CHURCH, BUCKS., for 2nd Lord Arden, 1818–24, Gothic, with neo-Norman tower [contract in Bucks. Record Office].

LONDON, THE TEMPLE PRINTING OFFICE, No. 13 BOUVERIE STREET, for James Moyes, 1824 [drawings by 'Mr. Pilkington' in St. Bride Printing Library, Bride Lane, Fleet Street, cf. Iain Bain, 'James Moyes and his Temple Printing Office', *Jnl. Printing Historical Soc.* iv, 1968].

An unexecuted design by Pilkington for PARLINGTON HALL, YORKS. (W.R.) 1810, is illustrated by Angus Taylor in *Leeds Arts Calendar*, No. 77, 1975, 27.

PINCH, JOHN (*c.*1770–1827), of Bath, was a builder-architect who went bankrupt soon after 1800, and thereafter practised only as an architect and surveyor. In about 1793 he succeeded Thomas Baldwin as surveyor to the Pulteney Estate, and in that capacity was responsible for the building of Northampton Street. He also acted as surveyor to the Earl of Darlington's estate in Bathwick. His terraces are marked by great elegance and refinement, and represent the final phase of Georgian building in Bath. His churches are also attractive examples of Georgian Gothic. Pinch died at his house in Duke Street on 11 May 1827, aged 57. His practice was continued by his son John Pinch, junior (*q.v.*). [W. Ison, *The Georgian Buildings of Bath*, 1948, 2nd ed. 1980, *passim*; J. M. Hunt, 'A little-known Architect of Bath', *C. Life*, 14 June 1962; Francis Kelly, 'Threatened Houses in Bath', *C. Life*, 6 Nov. 1980.]

BATH, NORTHAMPTON STREET, *c.*1793–4 [Kelly, *op. cit.*].

BATH, terraces on Darlington estate in BATHWICK, including NEW SYDNEY PLACE, 1807–8, DANIEL STREET, 1810, and RABY PLACE, 1825 [Ison].

BATH, terraces on Lansdowne slopes, including CAVENDISH PLACE, 1808–15, CAVENDISH CRESCENT, 1817–30, and SION HILL PLACE, 1817–20 [Ison].

HUNGERFORD CHURCH, BERKSHIRE, 1814–16; Gothic [*V.C.H. Berks*, iv, 197].

BISHOPSTROW HOUSE, WILTS., for William Temple, 1817–21 [*V.C.H. Wilts.* viii, 7].

BATH, ST. MARY'S CHURCH, BATHWICK, 1817–20, Gothic; chancel 1873 [G. N. Wright, *Historic Guide to Bath*, 1864, 248].

STOURTON CHURCH, WILTS., Gothic mausoleum in churchyard for Sir Richard Colt Hoare, Bart., 1819 [*Journal of a Somerset Rector 1803–34*, ed. Coombs, 1971, 121].

BATH, SPA VILLA, No. 9 BATHWICK HILL, 1820 (originally octagonal) [signed plan among title deeds cited in estate agent's brochure, 1982].

TWERTON CHURCH, SOMERSET, enlarged 1824; rebuilt by G. P. Manners 1839 [I.C.B.S.].

BATH, THE ROYAL UNITED HOSPITAL (now Technical College), BEAU STREET, 1824–6; Albert Wing added by J. E. Gill, 1864 [S. D. Major, *Notabilia of Bath*, 1879, 40].

An unexecuted design by Pinch for an Assembly Room, etc. at FROME, SOMERSET, is in the Frome Museum.

PINCH, JOHN, junior (–1849), was the son of John Pinch of Bath, to whose practice he succeeded. In 1823, when he was employed by General Alexander Goldie to design his new house in the Isle of Man, the general's wife described him in her diary as 'a very intelligent young man . . . a very clever Architect in the Gothic style especially – the Father and Son built two beautiful new Churches, the Houses in New Sidney Place and some Gentlemen's Seats'. His Gothic churches are mostly in an early nineteenth-century rendering of the 'Perpendicular' style, but his domestic work in Bath shows the influence of the Greek Revival. He died at Bath on 23 December 1849 [W. Ison, *The Georgian Buildings of Bath*, 1948, 2nd ed. 1980; *Gent's Mag.* 1850 (i), 229].

THE NUNNERY, ISLE OF MAN, for General Goldie, 1823, Gothic [family papers, *ex inf.* Capt. J. W. L. Fry-Goldie-Taubman].

BATH, ST. SAVIOUR'S CHURCH, WALCOT, 1829–31, Gothic; chancel 1882 [Port, 158–9].

BATH, QUEEN SQUARE, central block on west side, 1830 [Ison, 1948, 132].

MIDSOMER NORTON CHURCH, SOMERSET, rebuilt (except tower), 1830–1, Gothic [I.C.B.S.].

WESTON CHURCH, SOMERSET, rebuilt (except tower), 1832, Gothic [I.C.B.S.].

BATHEASTON CHURCH, SOMERSET, added N. aisle, 1834, Gothic [B. M. W. Dobbie, *An English Rural Community*, Bath 1969, 40].

BATH, SYDNEY HOTEL, addition of attic storey, 1836 [Ison, 1948, 95].

GRITTLETON CHURCH, WILTS., added south aisle and porch, 1836, Gothic [J. E. Jackson, *History of Grittleton*, Wilts. Topographical Soc. 1843].

DOWNSIDE, SOMERSET, CHRIST CHURCH, 1837–8, Gothic [I.C.B.S.].

PAULTON CHURCH, SOMERSET, rebuilt (except tower), 1839, Gothic [I.C.B.S.].

COMPTON HOUSE, OVER COMPTON, DORSET, for John Gooden, *c.*1840. Tudor Gothic [signed lithograph].

BATH, ST. MARY'S SCHOOLS, HENRIETTA ROAD, 1840, Gothic [S. D. Major, *Notabilia of Bath*, 1879, 103].

FARRINGTON GURNEY CHURCH, SOMERSET, 1843–4, Norman style [I.C.B.S.].

PITT, JOHN (*c.*1706–1787), of Encombe in Dorset, was the second son of George Pitt of Stratfield Saye and a distant cousin of Thomas Pitt, Lord Camelford (*q.v.*). His public career as M.P., Lord of Trade and Surveyor General of Woods and Forests will be found in the *History of Parliament.* His activities as an amateur architect are less well documented. He appears, however, to have designed two garden buildings, an Ionic rotunda and a half-octagon seat, at HAGLEY, WORCS., for the 1st Lord Lyttelton in 1748–9, and his architectural skill is praised in an ode addressed to him by a clerical relation, the Revd. Christopher Pitt. It may be concluded that Pitt was his own architect at ENCOMBE, DORSET, a small country house that he gradually enlarged and rebuilt from 1734 onwards in an individual style that owes something to Vanbrugh (*C. Life*, 24, 31 Jan. 1963 and R.C.H.M., *Dorset* ii (1), 78–80).[1] Family connections and stylistic affinities suggest that Pitt may also have designed WEST LODGE, nr. IWERNE MINSTER, DORSET (R.C.H.M., *Dorset* iv, 38) and GREY'S BRIDGE, DORCHESTER (built at his mother's expense in 1748); remodelled BINFIELD LODGE, BERKSHIRE, for his elder brother William soon after 1754; altered STRATFIELD SAYE HOUSE, HANTS., for his nephew George Pitt, 1st Lord Rivers, in 1755 (*C. Life*, 10–17 April 1975); and designed STRATFIELD SAYE CHURCH (*C. Life*, 15 June 1967) and RECTORY for the same nephew soon afterwards.[2] In these buildings conventional Palladian elements have been invigorated by ideas of Vanbrughian origin to produce a distinctive personal style of considerable interest and merit. Pitt, who was a member of the Society of Dilettanti, died in February 1787.

---

[1] The interior of Encombe was largely remodelled by J. & J. Belcher in the 1860s, and by A. Salvin in 1871–4.

[2] The church was dedicated by the Bishop of Salisbury on 1 Sept. 1758.

[Edward Marsden, 'John Pitt of Encombe: an 18th Century Dilettante Architect', *C. Life*, 9 Sept. 1976.]

PITT, THOMAS, 1st BARON CAMELFORD (1737–1793), was the only son of Thomas Pitt of Boconnoc in Cornwall, elder brother of William Pitt, first Earl of Chatham. His mother was Christian, daughter of Sir Thomas Lyttelton, Bart., of Hagley. He was admitted to Clare College, Cambridge, as a fellow-commoner in January 1754, and took the degree of M.A. in 1759.

Pitt suffered from ill health from an early age, and it was for the sake of his health that he accompanied Lord Kinnoull on his embassy to Lisbon in 1760.[1] From Lisbon he passed through Spain to Barcelona, sailed thence to Genoa, and spent some time in Italy. He was staying at Florence with his uncle, Sir Richard Lyttelton, when news reached him of his father's death. Besides the family estate of Boconnoc, Pitt now inherited the rotten borough of Old Sarum, and a considerable interest in that of Okehampton in Devonshire. As member for the former he entered Parliament in December 1761, and continued to sit for one or the other until he was raised to the peerage in 1784 as Baron Camelford, through the influence of his cousin, the younger Pitt.

In March 1762, Pitt took a small house at Twickenham which he referred to facetiously as the 'Palazzo Pitti'. Horace Walpole welcomed him as a neighbour, and described him in a letter to Montagu as 'very amiable and very sensible, and one of the very few that I reckon quite worthy of being at home at Strawberry'. He was, in fact, privileged to advise on the internal decoration of Walpole's Gothic villa, and himself designed the 'ornaments' of the Gallery and Chapel. From this time onwards there is considerable evidence of Pitt's activities as an amateur architect. In 1763 he appears to have designed the Gothic cottage, the bridge of rocks and a conservatory, at PARK PLACE, nr. HENLEY-ON-THAMES, for Walpole's friend General Conway. In 1764 Dr. Richard Pococke noted that the PALLADIAN BRIDGE at HAGLEY, WORCS. (dem., illustrated in *Arch. Hist.* 25, 1982, pl. 15a), was built 'after young Mr. Pitt's design [B. L., Add. MS. 14260, f. 178]. At STOWE HOUSE, BUCKS. he not only designed the CORINTHIAN ARCH (erected in 1765–6) for his near relative Richard Grenville, Lord Temple, but appears also to have been responsible for the final form of the south front, as rebuilt between 1772 and 1777 [M. J. McCarthy, 'The Rebuilding of Stowe House, 1770–7', *Huntington Library Quarterly* xxxvi, 1973].

At BOCONNOC Pitt added in 1772 a new south wing (mostly dem. 1975) containing a library and picture-gallery (built by Charles Rawlinson, *q.v.*), and in the previous year he erected an obelisk in the park to the memory of his uncle, Sir Richard Lyttelton (d. 1770). After his marriage in 1771 he built CAMELFORD HOUSE (dem. 1913) at the Oxford Street end of Park Lane, presumably to his own designs (*Survey of London* xl, 287–8).

For his uncle, Bishop Charles Lyttelton, Pitt made designs, executed in 1765, for refurnishing the choir of CARLISLE CATHEDRAL in the Gothic style. His woodwork was ejected in 1856, but the reredos went to Featherstone Castle, Northumberland, and the pulpit is in Thursby Church, Cumberland. He also had a hand in some similar alterations to the choir of NORWICH CATHEDRAL in 1766–7 [B.L., Stowe MS. 754, f. 235]. In 1784 he was called in by Lord Harcourt to help to give an authentic Gothic character to HOLYWELL HOUSE, ST. ALBANS (dem. 1837), then being remodelled by George Shakespear (*q.v.*) for the Dowager Countess Spencer [Frances Harris in *British Library Jnl.* 12, 1986].

In 1763 Pitt was elected a member of the Society of Dilettanti, and he proposed in 1785 that the shell of two adjoining houses built on his property in Hereford Street should be converted into a museum by the Society: but the project was not carried out on grounds of expense.

Pitt was one of John Soane's earliest patrons, employing him in 1781–2 to repair Petersham Lodge, Surrey, of which he had taken a lease, in 1783 to alter and enlarge Westgate House, Burnham Market, Norfolk, which he had inherited through his wife, in 1785 to design the proposed museum for the Society of Dilettanti, and in 1786 to carry out some repairs at Boconnoc [Dorothy Stroud, *The Architecture of Sir John Soane*, 1961, 14, 24, 33, 157, 158]. Soane not only paid tribute in his *Memoirs* to Pitt's 'classical taste and profound architectural knowledge', but in one of his lectures coupled his name with those of Burlington and Pembroke as leaders of English architectural taste. If Pitt was not quite a neo-classical Burlington, he was certainly an able and influential amateur, and at Stowe he had an important share in creating one of the major monuments of Georgian architecture.

[1] Lord Strathmore was his travelling companion, and B.L., Add MS. 5845, ff. 111–46 is a transcript by William Cole of 'Observations in a Tour to Portugal and Spain 1760 by John Earl of Strathmore and Thos. Pitt Esq.' It contains some interesting passages on Gothic and Moorish architecture.

Pitt married in 1771 Anne, daughter and coheiress of Pinckney Wilkinson, a wealthy London merchant, by whom he had one son, Thomas, whose misspent life ended in his death in a duel in 1804. He himself died at Florence in 1793, and was buried at Boconnoc. His portrait by Reynolds (formerly at Boconnoc) is now in the Plymouth City Art Gallery.

[*D.N.B.*; Horace Walpole's *Letters, passim*; J. Nichols, *Literary Illustrations* vi, 1831, 67–119; *An Eighteenth-Century Correspondence*, ed. Dickins & Stanton, 1910, 369, 444; J. Soane, *Lectures on Architecture*, ed. Bolton, 1929, 56; A. T. Bolton, *The Portrait of Sir John Soane*, 1927, 16, 21–5; Tresham Lever, *The House of Pitt*, 1947; L. Namier & J. Brooke, *The House of Commons 1754–1790* iii, 1964, 269–90; J. Frew & C. Wallace, 'Thomas Pitt, Portugal and the Gothic cult of Batalha', *Burlington Mag.* Aug. 1986, 582–4; Michael McCarthy, 'Thomas Pitt, Piranesi and John Soane', *Apollo* 134, Dec. 1991.]

PLATT, a family of mason-architects who originated at Lyme Park in the parish of Disley in Cheshire in the seventeenth century, and were the leading architects and builders at Rotherham in Yorkshire in the eighteenth century. As early as 1680 a mason called John Platt was employed to build the New Parlour at LYME PARK for Richard Legh, and between 1727 and 1730 several members of the family were engaged in rebuilding the house for Peter Legh to the designs of Giacomo Leoni [John Cornforth in *C. Life*, 19 Dec. 1974]. Those principally concerned were Edmund, John and George Platt, the sons of Edmund Platt (d. 1715).

JOHN PLATT, whose death in 1730 is noted in the Lyme Steward's book now in Stockport Public Library, appears to have designed ST. PAUL'S CHURCH, SHEFFIELD, a handsome baroque building in the style of Thomas Archer, built in 1720–1, but not wholly finished until 1772. In his *History of Hallamshire* (1819, p. 158), Joseph Hunter states that the church was built by 'Platts of Rotherham', whom he describes elsewhere as 'an architect of no slender merit', and in 1769 John Platt II recorded in his journal that he made drawings for 'finishing the steeple of St. Paul's Church in Sheffield, which was built [by] Mr. Tunnicliffe [*q.v.*] and my uncle John Platt . . . but never finished'. For measured drawings etc., of the church, which was demolished in 1937, see *Building News*, c, 23 June 1911, 876.

GEORGE PLATT (1700–1743), the third son of Edmund Platt, left Lyme in about 1730 and established himself in the neighbourhood of Rotherham. He lived at the Red House, Woodlaithes, and owned a quarry at Thrybergh. In 1731–3 he partly rebuilt the church of CHAPEL-EN-LE-FRITH, DERBYSHIRE, whose steeple had been taken down by his brother John in 1729 [W. M. Bunting, *The Parish Church of Chapel-en-le-Frith*, 1925, 157], and in 1738 he took down and rebuilt the top of the spire of HATHERSAGE CHURCH, DERBYSHIRE, as recorded by a memorandum in the parish records. In 1740 he contracted to build BURROW HALL, LANCS., for Robert Fenwick to the designs of Westby Gill (*q.v.*). His most important recorded work was CUSWORTH HALL, YORKS. (W.R.), a house of Palladian character which he designed and built for William Wrightson, M.P., in 1740–1. An engraving dated 1743 is inscribed '*Geo: Platt Architecto*', and there are payments to Platt in the building accounts in the Leeds Archives (BW/Ma 5, A 22, 32 etc.). The wings containing the chapel and library were added to the designs of James Paine in 1750–3 (see *Vitruvius Britannicus* iv, pls. 88–9, which also shows modifications to the main elevation by Paine). George Platt contracted consumption, and died at Bristol Hot Wells on 9 November 1743, aged 43. He was buried in Rotherham churchyard, where a monument (destroyed in 1950) described him as 'Architect and Builder' and as 'a Man of great abilities in his profession and of the strictest integrity in his dealings'. His widow carried on the business until her eldest son John was able to take charge of it.

JOHN PLATT (1728–1810) was only 15 when his father died, but took charge of the business at Rotherham as soon as he was old enough, and had a very successful career as an architect, builder and statuary mason. Later he took over the quarries of black marble at Ashford nr. Bakewell, together with the works for sawing and polishing the marble established by Henry Watson of Bakewell earlier in the century. He also worked the quarries of grey marble at Richlow Dale, nr. Monyash. In 1765 he established pottery works, which (after a period of partnership) he eventually sold to the ironmaster Samuel Walker.

Platt's journal, which extends from 1763 to 1796, throws considerable light on his activities as an architect and builder. As a contracting mason he was employed at Wentworth Castle (where in 1762 he carved the pediment of the portico), Wentworth Woodhouse, and elsewhere. He made numerous monuments and chimneypieces, and was responsible for the marble staircases at Aston Hall (1776–7) and Clifton Hall (1783–4).

Surviving drawings[1] show that he was quite a competent draughtsman, and it is clear from his journal that he designed several minor country houses and other buildings in the neighbourhood of Sheffield and Rotherham, an incomplete list of which is given below.

In 1757 John Platt married Anne Fitzgerald, the illegitimate daughter of a member of the locally influential family of Buck. They had ten children, none of whom chose to follow their father's trade. John (1763–1832) was sent to York to become a pupil of Thomas Atkinson (*q.v.*), but after running away he was allowed by his father to enter the Navy and eventually rose to the rank of Captain. Charles (1770–1817) was apprenticed to Westmacott, the sculptor, but in 1794 joined the Army and fought in the Napoleonic Wars. George Edmund (1779–1850) was articled to the architect John Rawstorne, but like his brothers he preferred a military career and took part in the Peninsular Campaign. William (1775–1811) became an engraver, but lost his sight and committed suicide at the age of 36. John Platt himself died at Halifax on 14 December 1810, aged 85, and was buried in Rotherham churchyard.

[J. H. Cockburn, 'A Rotherham Architect and his Family', *Rotherham Advertiser*, 8 Feb. 1936; J. D. Potts, *Platt of Rotherham, Mason-Architects 1700–1810*, Sheffield, 1959; C. M. Ross, *John Platt Mason Architect*, Rotherham Musem 1984; A. J. B. Kiddell, 'John Platt of Rotherham, Potter and Mason-Architect', *Trans. English Ceramic Circle* v (iii), 1961, 172–5; Rupert Gunnis, *Dictionary of British Sculptors*, 1968, 308; J. Dugdale, *The British Traveller* ii, 1819, 21; J. Guest, *Historic Notices of Rotherham*, 1879, 410–11; B. L., Strafford Papers, Add. MS. 22241, ff. 130–3, 140 *et seq.*]

DOMESTIC ARCHITECTURE

WORTLEY HALL, YORKS. (W.R.), is stated by Hunter, *South Yorkshire* ii, 1831, 323, to have been rebuilt by Edward Wortley Montagu in stages, beginning in 1743, 'with the assistance of Platts of Rotherham'. The Platts built the south front designed by G. Leoni (*q.v.*) in 1743, and surviving accounts show that John Platt was employed more or less continuously from 1749 to 1789. In 1757–9 he built the east wing, probably to the designs of Matthew Brettingham (*q.v.*), but the house was still unfinished when Montagu died in 1761, and in the 1780s Platt built a new west wing and offices for Montagu's daughter Lady Bute. Further work was done (not apparently by Platt) when Lady Bute's grandson James Archibald Stuart Wortley (later 1st Lord Wharncliffe) came to live at Wortley *c.*1800 [Wortley papers in Sheffield Archives; R. Hewlings, 'Wortley Hall', *Archaeological Jnl.* 137, 1980, 397–9].

GATE BURTON HALL, LINCS., temple or summerhouse for Thomas Hutton, 1747–8 [drawing in Sheffield Archives, AP 508 (1) inscribed 'Built for T. Hutton at Burton nr. Gainsbro' per J. Platt 1747 & 1748'] (B. Howlett, *Views in the County of Lincoln*, 1797).

MOORGATE HALL, nr. ROTHERHAM, YORKS. (W.R.), office buildings for Samuel Tooker, 1764 [Potts, 11].

CANKLOW HOUSE, nr. ROTHERHAM, YORKS. (W.R.), for J. Taylor, 1767 [Potts, 12].

MASBROUGH HALL, nr. ROTHERHAM, YORKS. (W.R.), for Samuel Walker, 1768; dem. except stables [Potts, 12].

TONG HALL, YORKS. (W.R.), gateway (1773) and alterations to house for Major John Tempest [Potts, 13]. These alterations must have included the addition of the top floor and of the bow windows to the north front.

PAGE HALL, nr. ECCLESFIELD, YORKS (W.R.), for Thomas Broadbent, 1774–6 [Potts, 13; Ross, 9].

WORSBROUGH HALL, YORKS. (W.R.), drawing-room for Francis Edmunds, 1775 [Potts, 14].

ROTHERHAM, house in WESTGATE for Dr. James Wilkinson, 1777 [MS. Journal, 1777].

MOUNT PLEASANT, nr. SHEFFIELD, YORKS. (W.R.), for Francis Hurt Sitwell, 1777–8 [Potts, 15; Ross, 8–9].

GRANGE HALL (THUNDERCLIFFE GRANGE), ECCLESFIELD, YORKS. (W.R.), for 3rd Earl of Effingham, 1777–8 [Potts, 15].

ROTHERHAM, FERHAM HOUSE, KIMBERWORTH ROAD, for Jonathan Walker, 1787 [MS. Journal, 4 Sept. 1787].

ROTHERHAM, house in WESTGATE for himself, 1794; dem. [Potts, 19].

OTHER BUILDINGS

WORTLEY CHURCH, YORKS. (W.R.), rebuilt steeple and chancel for Edward Wortley Montagu, 1753–4; rebuilt 1815 [Sheffield Archives, Wortley papers M. 58 (1–9)].

[1] Of which there is a small collection in Sheffield Archives (AP 508). Others in private ownership are illustrated in Mr. J. D. Potts's booklet cited below. Platt may have helped Lord Strafford to design the south front of Wentworth Castle (see the drawing illustrated by Potts, and another at Temple Newsam House signed 'Per John Platt' which shows the front as completed in 1764).

DONCASTER, YORKS. (W.R.), THE MARKET CROSS AND SHAMBLES, 1756; dem. [engraving in Hailstone Collection, York Minster Library, signed 'Platt Archt.'; Potts, 8].

ECKINGTON CHURCH, DERBYSHIRE, rebuilt south aisle, 1763 [Potts, 10].

PENISTONE, YORKS. (W.R.), THE CLOTH HALL AND SHAMBLES, designed 1763, erected 1768? [Potts, 10].

BARNSLEY, YORKS. (W.R.), THE SHAMBLES, 1768; dem. [Potts, 12].

ROTHERHAM, FEOFFEES' CHARITY SCHOOL and HOUSE in THE CROFTS, 1776 [Potts, 14].

SHEFFIELD, built and probably designed THE THEATRE, 1777–8; rebuilt 1855 [Potts, 15; Ross, 9].

DONCASTER, THE GREEN DRAGON INN, FRENCHGATE, 1778; dem. 1961 [MS. Journal, Jan. 1778].

ROTHERHAM, THE MARKET HOUSE, 1780–1; dem. [Potts, 16].

SHEFFIELD, THE TONTINE HOTEL, HAY MARKET, 1782–3 [MS. Journal, 1782–3].

ROTHERHAM, BREWERY (later Mappin's), 1791 [MS. Journal, April 1791].

PLAW, JOHN (1746–1820), was presumably the John Plaw who in 1759 was apprenticed to Thomas Kaygill, a member of the Tylers' and Bricklayers Company. He was described as an 'architect and master builder in Westminster' when in 1763 he was awarded a premium by the Society of Arts for a drawing of the Banqueting House in Whitehall (*Register of Premiums*, p. 39). He was a member of the Incorporated Society of Artists, and was the last president elected before its dissolution in 1791. He exhibited with the Society in 1773, 1790 and 1791, and at the Royal Academy from 1775 onwards. In about 1795 he moved to Southampton, where he prepared ambitious plans for residential development at Albion Place and Brunswick Place of which little or none was carried out, and is said to have designed the Barracks on the site of the present Ordnance Survey Office. In 1807 he emigrated to Canada, settling in Charlottetown, Prince Edward Island. Here he designed several buildings before his death at the age of 75, on 24 May 1820. There is an illustration of his tombstone in *Arch. Rev.* xlv, 1919, 130. George Byfield, J. Taylor and J.B. Papworth were his pupils, and Samuel Benwell was his nephew.

Plaw had a son John, who was apprenticed to him in 1780 and was admitted to the freedom of the Tylers' and Bricklayers' Company in 1787, but must have either died young or abandoned architecture. A Miss Plaw, who appears to have been his daughter, exhibited drawings of architectural subjects at the Society of Artists in 1791.

Plaw published *Rural Architecture; or Designs from the Simple Cottage to the Decorative Villa*, 1785, 1794, 1796, 1800, 1802 and 1804, in which many of his executed designs were illustrated; *Ferme Ornée or Rural Improvements,* 1785, 1813; and *Sketches for Country Houses, Villas ad Rural Dwellings*, 1800, 1803. These were among the earliest of the cottage and villa books which became so popular during the first quarter of the nineteenth century. Plaw's best-known architectural works are the romantically sited and unusually planned circular house on an island in Lake Windermere and the neatly geometrical church at Paddington.

[*A.P.S.D.*; *D.N.B.*; *Gent's Mag.* 1820 (ii), 376; records of the Tylers' & Bricklayers' Company, Guildhall Library MSS. 3053/3, under 1768, 3053/4, p. 77.]

BELLE ISLE, LAKE WINDERMERE, WESTMORLAND, for Thomas English, 1774–5 [exhib. at R.A. 1775; *Rural Architecture*, pls. 25–30] (*C. Life*, 3–10 Aug. 1940).

LONDON, an unidentified villa at VAUXHALL, 1781 [*Rural Architecture*, pls. 14–15].

WOOTTON COURT, nr. CANTERBURY, KENT, refronted for the Revd. E. T. Bridges, 1781; dem. [*Rural Architecture*, pl. 33; *Topographical Miscellanies* i, 1792, p. xviii].

LONDON, CHRIST CHURCH, NEWGATE STREET, monument to Peter Dore (d. 1781), executed by Robert Chambers [K. A. Esdaile, *English Monumental Sculpture since the Renaissance*, 1927, 99].

SELSDON FARMHOUSE, nr. CROYDON, SURREY, additions for Thomas Lane, before 1785 [*Rural Architecture*, pls. 8–9].

LONDON, GREEN PARK LODGE, a 'hermitage' in the garden, before 1785 [*Rural Architecture*, pl. 1*; original design in B.L., *King's Maps* xxvi, 7–*n*–2].

PHILADELPHIA, U.S.A., design for a house in Third Street, exhib. at the Society of Artists in 1790: identified by R. W. Moss, *The American Country House*, New York 1990, 101, as one (dem.) built in South Third Street by William Bingham in 1786.

BELMONT, nr. THROWLEY, KENT, pair of cottages 'in the American style' (now house named 'New York') for Col. John Montresor, *c.*1780/90 [*Ferme Ornée*, pl. 17; J. Poesch in *C. Life*, 27 April 1978].

HARESFOOT, nr. BERKHAMSTED, HERTS., 1787; rebuilt by J. B. Papworth 1817–19; dem. *c.*1965 [exhib. at R.A. 1787].

LONDON, ST. MARY'S CHURCH, PADDINGTON, 1788–91 [exhib. at Society of Artists 1791; C.L. Stieglitz, *Plans et Desseins tirés de la*

Belle Architecture, Paris & Leipsig, 1798–1800, pls. 45–6; working drawings in R.I.B.A.D.] (*C. Life,* 1 Nov. 1973).

THORNVILLE ROYAL (i.e. ALLERTON MAULEVERER), YORKS. (W.R.), farm-buildings, etc. for Col. Thomas Thornton, *c.*1790 [*Ferme Ornée,* pls. 1, 24, 25] (*C. Life,* 26 Jan. 1989).

BROCKENHURST HOUSE, HANTS., domed bath-house and fishing-lodge for John Morant, before 1795 [*Ferme Ornée,* pls. 1, 14–15].

SEACLIFF, EAST LOTHIAN, for Robert Colt, M.P., *c.*1795; rebuilt by William Burn 1841 [*Rural Architecture,* pls. 42–3].

LYMINGTON, HANTS., *cottage orné* near, before 1800 [*Sketches,* pls. 16, 17].

UNEXECUTED

Among the designs in Plaw's *Rural Architecture,* and apparently not executed, are a 'Design made for —Scott Esqr. of Ireland' (pls. 44–5), 'Designs made for Glenfiddoch in Scotland for the Duke of Gordon' (pls. 52–3), and a 'Design for a House for Humberston Mackenzie Esq. intended to be built in Scotland' (pl. 56). Plaw's bill for making this design, dated 1786, is in S.R.O. GD 46/1/413. Humberston Mackenzie later became Lord Seaforth, and the design may have been for the Seaforth seat, Brahan Castle, Ross-shire.

Sketches for Country Houses includes a shooting-box for the Marquess of Huntly (pl. 25) and a design for Wodehouse, Wombourne, Staffs., for the Revd. Shaw Hellier (pls. 29–31), neither of which was carried out.

Plaw's exhibited designs included a 'Design for a bridge over the River Suir from the city of Waterford to the County of Kilkenny in Ireland' (1779), a 'Design for a bridge across the Thames at Fulham' (1780), and a 'Design for an assembly room, intended to be built at Harrogate' (1790).

At Penicuik House, Midlothian, there is a set of drawings for an unexecuted park entrance, signed 'J. Plaw Arch[t]', and his plans and elevations for an 'Admiral's House, Halifax, Nova Scotia', signed and dated 1813, are in the Public Record Office (MPI/166).

PLAYFAIR, JAMES (1755–1794), born on 5 August 1755, was the fourth son of the Revd. James Playfair, minister of Liff and Benvie in Angus. His elder brother John (1748–1819) became a distinguished mathematician and geologist, while his younger brother William (1759–1823) gained a precarious living and some notoriety as an inventor and pamphleteer. Nothing is known about James's early life or training as an architect, but the last ten years of his life are well documented owing to the survival of his professional journal for the years 1783–93 (National Library of Scotland, Advocates MS. 33.5.25) and many of his drawings are preserved in Sir John Soane's Museum and the R.I.B.A. Drawings Collection. By 1783 he was established in London, with an office in Bloomsbury, and began to exhibit regularly at the Royal Academy. His practice was largely in Scotland (where he had the good fortune to secure Henry Dundas as a patron), but no doubt he hoped to acquire an English clientèle in the course of time, and the commission (though abortive) to design a picture-gallery in London for Sir George Beaumont must have been encouraging. In 1783 he had published *A Method of Constructing Vapour Baths.*

Playfair made at least two visits to the Continent. A drawing in the R.I.B.A. Collection shows that he was in Paris in August 1787, probably on a visit to his brother William, who was the Paris agent of the Scioto Land Company of Ohio. The drawing is of the Baths of the Emperor Julian in the Rue de la Harpe, but Playfair no doubt inspected the latest French architecture besides this Roman antiquity. In 1792–3 he made an Italian tour. In October 1791 he obtained an introduction to Canova from the painter Henry Tresham [Canova archive, Bassano, 5188], and a set of drawings for Townley Hall in the National Library of Ireland was dated by him at 'Rome, April 13, 1792'. A design for a 'Casina' in the R.I.B.A. Collection is dated at Rome on 24 April 1793. On his return Playfair exhibited at the Royal Academy views of the Appian Way near Capua and of one of the Greek temples at Paestum.

Playfair's career was terminated prematurely by his death at Edinburgh on 23 February 1794 at the age of 39. According to Joseph Farington he 'died of a broken heart in consequence of the death of his eldest boy' [Diary, 18 April 1794]. Soane and Farington helped his widow to dispose of his books and drawings, which were sold at Christie's on 10 January 1795 (catalogue in Soane Museum). It was then that Soane acquired the portfolio of drawings now in his Museum. Playfair was the father of James George Playfair, M.D. (1786–1857), who practised medicine in Florence, and of the architect W. H. Playfair (*q.v.*), who was only three at the time of his death.

Playfair was an elegant architectural designer with a strong predilection for a refined neo-classical simplicity. The simplicity is already apparent in Forfar Town Hall and Kirriemuir Church (both begun in 1786), but in later buildings a more sophisticated taste appears which shows an evident interest in the works of both Soane and Ledoux. This is most manifest in the remarkable mausoleum at Methven in Perthshire (1793), which takes the form of a Greek temple embedded in rusticated masonry, in his unexecuted designs for a house at Ardkinglas in Argyllshire (1790), and in the clear-cut geometrical forms of Cairness, with its hemicycle of offices, bold semi-circular arches, primitivist Doric columns and Egyptian billiard-room. Most of these features have parallels or prototypes in the works of Boullée or Ledoux, and were no doubt the first-fruits of the French visit of 1787. Playfair's interest in neo-classical architecture in general and French architecture in particular is confirmed by the sale catalogue of his library, which includes such items as Winckelmann's *Histoire des Arts Anciens*, 'Ruines de Pestum', '4 French books on building' and 'A portfolio with architectural designs and the Halles aux Grains'. But for his premature death he would probably have emerged as an important figure in the neo-classical movement. As it is, the remote and in some respects immature Cairness remains as a remarkable testimony to his advanced architectural ideas. None of his other classical houses was of comparable significance. The exteriors of Kinnaird and Melville Castles were perfunctory and ineffective essays in castellation which compared poorly with the contemporary works of Robert Adam, but at Farnell in Angus Playfair designed a small Gothic church of unusual and precocious character. The designs for 'an American City' which he made in 1790, apparently at the behest of his brother William, are not known to have survived, but might well show further evidence of French neo-classical influence.

[*A.P.S.D.*; A. G. Playfair, *Notes on the Scottish Family of Playfair*, 1932; W. W. Robertson, 'The Journal of James Playfair', *Trans. Edinburgh Architectural Assn.* iii, 1894; David Walker & Colin McWilliam in *C. Life*, 28 Jan. 1971; letters to Robert Graham of Fintry in S.R.O., GD 151/11/32.]

PUBLIC BUILDINGS, ETC.

FORFAR, TOWN AND COUNTY HALL, 1786–8 [W. S. McCulloch, *Forfar Town and County Hall*, 1968].

KIRRIEMUIR CHURCH, ANGUS, 1786–90. The heritors employed Playfair in preference to a local builder because they wanted the church to be 'an ornament to the village', but some serious deficiencies in the internal accommodation made them regret their choice [drawings in Soane portfolio and set of engraved plans etc. in S.R.O., RHP. 176 and 8086–93; legal proceedings against Playfair in S.R.O., HR 479/4/1].

FARNELL OF FARNWALL CHURCH, ANGUS, Gothic, exhibited by Playfair at R.A. as 'now building' in 1789, but said in *N.S.A.* xi, 112 to have been built in 1806. His diary shows that he made the working drawings in 1788 and the specification in 1789.

METHVEN, PERTHSHIRE, mausoleum in churchyard for Thomas Graham, cr. Lord Lynedoch (whose wife had died in 1792), 1793 [Diary].

EDINBURGH, ST. PETER'S EPISCOPAL CHAPEL, ROXBURGH PLACE, 1790–1 [*Scots Mag.* 1790, 359, recording inscription on foundation stone as 'ARCHITECTO JOANNE PLAYFAIR' (*sic*)].

DOMESTIC ARCHITECTURE

HAWKHEAD PARK, RENFREWSHIRE, repairs and alterations for the Countess of Glasgow, 1784–6; dem. 1952 [exhib. at R.A. 1785 and cf. his letters to Lord Findlater in S.R.O., GD 248/589/2].

KINNAIRD CASTLE, ANGUS, remodelled for Sir David Carnegie, Bart., 1785–93, castellated; enlarged and remodelled by D. Bryce 1855–62 [drawings in Soane portfolio; exhib. at R.A. 1791] (*Forfarshire Illustrated*, Dundee 1843, 86).

ANNISTON HOUSE, ANGUS, for John Rait, 1785–6; dem. [drawings in Soane portfolio].

RAITH PARK, FIFE, gateway and lodge for William Ferguson, 1786 [drawings in Soane portfolio, and cf. letter to Lord Findlater, S.R.O., GD 248/591/2].

CLAPHAM, SURREY, house for David Webster, 1786 [Diary; drawings in Soane portfolio].

LANGHOLM LODGE, DUMFRIESSHIRE, additions for 3rd Duke of Buccleuch, 1786–7; rebuilt after fire in *c.*1790; dem. 1953 [drawings in Soane portfolio].

DALKEITH HOUSE, MIDLOTHIAN, added bow window to library for 3rd Duke of Buccleuch, 1786 [drawings in Soane portfolio]. Playfair also made unexecuted designs for an entrance gate and lodges.

PETERSHAM, SURREY, DOUGLAS HOUSE, greenhouse for Archibald Douglas, 1786 [drawings in Soane portfolio].

MELVILLE CASTLE, MIDLOTHIAN, for Henry Dundas, 1st Viscount Melville, 1786–91, castellated [Diary; letters to Lord Findlater; working drawings in S.R.O., RHP 6699].

MOLESEY HURST, SURREY, alterations to house for 9th Earl of Winchilsea (who had it on a lease), 1787–8 [drawings in Soane portfolio].

BOTHWELL CASTLE, LANARKS., remodelled

house for Archibald Douglas, 1787–8; dem. 1926 [Diary: exhib. at R.A. 1787].

BURLEY-ON-THE-HILL, RUTLAND, 'farm offices', etc. for 9th Earl of Winchilsea, 1788–9 [Diary; letters to Lord Findlater; drawings in Soane portfolio; J. M. Robinson, *Georgian Model Farms*, 1983, 119].

BROOKSBY HALL, LEICS., minor alterations for Thomas Graham (cr. Lord Lynedoch), 1788–9 [Diary].

DUPPLIN CASTLE, PERTHSHIRE, works for 9th Earl of Kinnoull, including a 'Temple of Virtue and Honour', 1789 (dem.); the house was destroyed by fire 1827 and rebuilt by W. Burn [Diary].

BUCHANAN HOUSE, STIRLINGSHIRE, enlarged for Lord Graham, afterwards 3rd Duke of Montrose, 1789 [Neale, *Seats*, 1st ser. i, 1818; letter to Earl of Findlater, S.R.O., GD 248/588].

WESTER OGLE (GLENOGIL), ANGUS, design for house for William Lyon, 1788, probably not built [Diary, f. 50].

LYNEDOCH LODGE, PERTHSHIRE, offices, etc. for Thomas Graham, cr. Lord Lynedoch, 1789 [Diary].

INCHMURRIN, LOCH LOMOND, design for tower for Lord Graham, afterwards 3rd Duke of Montrose, 1789 [letter to Earl of Findlater, S.R.O., GD 248/588]. It contained a dining-room and drawing-room, and appears to have been intended as a hunting-lodge, disguised as an old 'Gothic tower of strength'.

SKENE HOUSE, ABERDEENSHIRE, additions for George Skene, 1790; remodelled 1847–50 [Diary].

LONDON, house and premises in LONG ACRE for Mr. O'Keefe, coach-maker, 1791 [drawings in Soane portfolio].

CAIRNESS HOUSE, ABERDEENSHIRE, for Charles Gordon, 1791–7 [drawings in Soane portfolio and Aberdeen University Library: David Walker & Colin McWilliam in *C. Life*, 28 Jan.-4 Feb. 1971].

UNEXECUTED DESIGNS

The following unexecuted designs have been noted: alterations to BLACKADDER HOUSE, BERWICKS., 1782 [R.I.B.A.D.]; a small house at BALDOVIE, KINGOLDRUM, ANGUS, for Alexander Anderson, 1785 [Soane portfolio]; house, village and market for David Scott at DUNNINALD, ANGUS, 1787 [Soane portfolio and separate folio of drawings]; remodelling URIE, KINCARDINESHIRE, for Robert Barclay, 1789 [Soane portfolio]; additions to MURIE, PERTHSHIRE, for James Yeoman, 1789 [Soane portfolio]; alterations and additions to KIPPENROSS, PERTHSHIRE, for John Stirling, 1789 [Soane portfolio]; numerous designs for 7th Earl of Findlater, *c.*1788–9, including a Temple of Pomona at CULLEN HOUSE, BANFFSHIRE, and a house at EASTER ELCHIES, MORAYSHIRE [S.R.O., RHP 2545–7 and Soane portfolio]; a picture-gallery for Sir George Beaumont at his house in Grosvenor Square, London, 1790 [F. Owen & D. B. Brown, *Collector of Genius*, 1988, 77]; a house at ARDKINGLAS, ARGYLLSHIRE, for Sir Alexander Campbell, Bart., 1790 [Colin McWilliam in *The Country Seat*, ed. Colvin & Harris, 1970, 193–8]; additions to DOUGLAS CASTLE, LANARKS., 1791 [drawings at The Hirsel, Berwicks.]; and a design for TOWNLEY HALL, CO. LOUTH, IRELAND, for B. T. Balfour, 1792 [National Library of Ireland, Portfolio 23, nos. 67–71, N.M.R.S. (a duplicate set), and R.I.B.A.D., G 6/5].

PLAYFAIR, WILLIAM HENRY (1790–1857), was a younger son of James Playfair (*q.v.*). He was born in Russell Place (Fitzroy Square), London, on 15 July 1790 and baptized in the Fitzroy Chapel. In 1804, at the age of 14, he went to live with his uncle, Professor John Playfair, in Edinburgh. In due course he became a pupil of William Stark (*q.v.*). After Stark's death in 1813, he is said to have gone to London to work in the offices of 'Wyatt and Smirke'. In the summer of 1816 he made a short visit to France in the company of his uncle before returning to Edinburgh. Later that year he won the first prize in the competition for the completion of Adam's University building. In 1818 he was entrusted with the planning of the important Calton Hill estate on the northern outskirts of the city. These early successes suggest that Playfair may have been regarded as the architectural heir of the brilliant Stark, and in the Calton Hill scheme he certainly adhered closely to the principles of town-planning previously advocated by Stark.

For the next thirty years Playfair was, with his rivals Burn and Gillespie Graham, at the top of the Scottish architectural profession. Quantitatively, his practice never equalled theirs. Fastidious and scholarly, he had no desire to emulate their mass-production of country houses and churches. Of the former, he could show a mere score to put beside Burn's hundreds, of the latter only two to compete with Graham's large ecclesiastical output. But as a designer of public buildings in the Scottish capital he was pre-eminent. The Royal Institution, the Surgeons' Hall, the National Gallery, Donaldson's Hospital and the Free Church College were among the most prominent and important buildings in nineteenth-century Edinburgh. The first three, like the monumental Dollar Academy, were academic exercises in the classical tradition of the 'Modern Athens'. But the Gothic towers of the Free Church College, and the Jacobethan cupolas of Donaldson's Hospital showed that Playfair could master other styles besides the Grecian, while St. Stephen's Church has all the dramatic power – as well as the stylistic ambivalence – of a church by Hawksmoor. His early houses were conceived as picturesque Italianate villas, but by 1830 he was following Burn and Blore in the revival of the Scottish and English vernacular styles of the sixteenth and seventeenth centuries. The remodelling of Floors Castle was his biggest work in this manner. Though undeniably picturesque at a distance, at close quarters its coarse and overcrowded detailing repels. Lurgan, Bonaly and Islay were serious and relatively successful attempts to recapture the Elizabethan or Stuart past.

In his practice Playfair was very much a professional. All his designs were worked out with immense care. 'Nothing good in Architecture', he wrote, 'can be effected without a monstrous expenditure of patience and Indian Rubber.' A perfectionist himself, he expected the highest standards from his builders, relentlessly insisting on precise conformity to his specifications. To his pupils and staff he was equally exacting, and David Cousin (who was one of them) 'used to tell with great glee many stories of the strictness and rigour of Mr. Playfair's rule, and the devices to which his assistants had to resort to escape detection if at fault'.

Playfair never visited Rome or Greece. His early visit to France has already been mentioned. In 1842, after a long period of increasing ill-health, he went to Florence in order to obtain the advice of his elder brother James, who practised medicine there. Architecturally this journey was of little or no significance, for in Florence he found 'little to admire and a great deal to shudder at'. Back in Edinburgh, despite increasing deafness, crippling rheumatism and chronic bronchitis, he managed to struggle on for another decade, but illness compelled him to refuse a number of commissions during the last years of his life. He died at Edinburgh on 19 March 1857, and was buried in the Dean Cemetery next to his great friends Andrew and Sophia Rutherford. He was unmarried. There is a water-colour portrait of Playfair as a young man in the R.I.B.A. Drawings Collection. A portrait by John Watson Gordon, P.R.S.A., hangs in the Board Room of Donaldson's Hospital, Edinburgh.

A large collection of Playfair's drawings is preserved in Edinburgh University Library, and there are others in the collection of the Royal Incorporation of Architects in Scotland. In the same library are a diary for the year 1817 with accounts for 1817–22, and two surviving volumes of an elaborate series of letter-books (vol. 4, covering the years 1830–3, and vol. 7 for 1840–5). A brief journal of a visit to the island of Arran in 1811 is in Cambridge University Library (Add. MS. 6305). Many letters to Andrew Rutherford and his family from 1834 onwards are in the National Library of Scotland (MS. 9704). The sale catalogue of his library (National Library of Scotland KR. 16, f. 5 (1)) shows that he owned a large number of views of Athens by his friend H. W. ('Grecian') Williams.

[*A.P.S.D.*; *D.N.B.*; G.L.R.O., Register of Fitzroy Chapel; obituaries in *Builder* xv, 1857, 208; xviii, 1860, 140; *Building News*, 10 April 1857, 359–60; and Edinburgh *Building Chronicle* ii, 1857, 181–2; J. M. Graham, 'Notice of the Life and Works of W. H. Playfair', *Trans. Architectural Institute of Scotland* v, part iv, 1859–61, 13–28; T. H. Hughes, 'W. H. Playfair', *Quarterly of the Incorporation of Architects in Scotland*, Nos. 17–18, 1926; Ian Gow, 'William Henry Playfair', in *Scottish Pioneers of the Greek Revival*, Scottish Georgian Soc. 1984, 'Playfair: A Northern Athenian', *R.I.B.A. Jnl.* May 1990; see also *Builder* 10 June 1882, 717 for David Cousins's recollections of Playfair's office.]

In the following list, drawings in Edinburgh University Library are referred to by the letter U.

EDINBURGH, THE UNIVERSITY, completion 1817–26 of the buildings commenced by R. & J. Adam in 1798–93; dome added by Sir Rowand Anderson 1887 [A.G. Fraser, *The Building of Old College*, Edinburgh 1989, chaps. 6–8; U 10 and 15].

EDINBURGH, THE CITY OBSERVATORY, CALTON HILL, 1818; boundary wall and Playfair Monument, 1825–7 [U 45].

DOLLAR, CLACKMANNANSHIRE, THE ACADEMY, 1818–20; enlarged 1867 [U 16].

EDINBURGH, THE ROYAL INSTITUTION (now the ROYAL SCOTTISH ACADEMY), 1822–6; enlarged and altered by Playfair, 1832–5 [U 29].

EDINBURGH, premises in ALBYN PLACE for the Highland Society, 1823–41 [U 28].

EDINBURGH, THE NATIONAL MONUMENT, CALTON HILL, in collaboration with C. R. Cockerell, 1824–9 (unfinished) [U 43; N.L.S., MS. 352, ff. 164–87 and correspondence with Cockerell in MS. 639].

INNERLEITHEN, PEEBLESSHIRE, PUMP-ROOM,

1826; rebuilt *c.*1890 [drawings in R.I.A.S. Collection, N.M.R.S.].

EDINBURGH, ST. STEPHEN'S CHURCH, 1827–8; refurnished 1880, interior reconstructed 1956 [U 50].

EDINBURGH, HERIOT'S HOSPITAL, gateway and terraces, Jacobean style, 1828–30 [U 26].

EDINBURGH, THE ADVOCATES' (now SIGNET) LIBRARY, staircase for the Faculty of Advocates, 1819–20; remodelled by William Burn for the Writers to the Signet, 1833. The Corinthian columns at the top are by Playfair, the Ionic columns below and the stairs themselves by Burn. [U 1 and Portfolio 6; *History of the Society of Writers to the Signet*, 1890, 439: cf. Letter-Book 4, pp. 57–60.]

EDINBURGH, THE ADVOCATES' LIBRARY, 1829–30 [U 1 and Portfolio 6; I. G. Brown, *Building for Books: The Architectural Evolution of the Advocates' Library*, Aberdeen 1989].

EDINBURGH, THE SURGEONS' HALL, NICOLSON STREET, 1830–2; remodelled internally 1908–9 [U 13].

MINTO CHURCH, ROXBURGHSHIRE, 1830–1, Gothic [U 39].

DALCRUE BRIDGE, REDGORTON, PERTHSHIRE (R. Almond), 1832–6, at the expense of Thomas Graham, Lord Lynedoch [U 19].

EDINBURGH, DONALDSON'S HOSPITAL, 1842–54, Jacobethan style [U 20]. Won in a limited competition with Gillespie Graham and David Hamilton [David Walker, 'The Donaldson's Hospital competition and the Palace of Westminster', *Arch. Hist.* 27, 1984].

EDINBURGH, THE FREE CHURCH COLLEGE, 1846–50; Gothic. The Assembly Hall was added by D. Bryce 1858–9 [U, Supplementary].

EDINBURGH, THE NATIONAL GALLERY OF SCOTLAND, 1850–7 [U 44].

EDINBURGH: DOMESTIC ARCHITECTURE

In 1818 Playfair was appointed architect for the development of the area to the north of Calton Hill, and in 1819 produced a printed *Report to the Lord Provost, Magistrates and Council of the City of Edinburgh on a Plan for laying out the new Town between Edinburgh and Leith.* In this he followed the ideas of his master William Stark (*q.v.*) in paying 'the strictest attention to the nature of the ground, and none whatever to the neatness of the plan, as it appears on paper'. As a result the following streets were laid out under Playfair's direction, and in most cases built to his designs, from 1821 onwards: BLENHEIM PLACE, BRUNSWICK STREET, BRUNTON PLACE, CARLTON TERRACE, ELM ROW, HILLSIDE CRESCENT, LEOPOLD PLACE, MONTGOMERY STREET, REGENT TERRACE, ROYAL TERRACE, WINDSOR STREET [A. J. Youngson, *The Making of Classical Edinburgh*, 1966, 152–6; drawings in U 2, 3, 4, 6, 12, 21, 27, 31, 37, 48, 51].

In 1820 Playfair designed ROYAL CIRCUS for the Trustees of Heriot's Hospital. With CIRCUS PLACE and CIRCUS GARDENS it was built in 1821–3 [Youngson, *op. cit.*, 206–8; drawings in U 49]. In 1824 he designed No. 8, INVERLEITH ROW for Daniel Ellis [drawings in U 22], and in 1825 No. 20 INVERLEITH PLACE [minutes of the Caledonian Horticultural Soc., Oct. 1825].

COUNTRY HOUSES, ETC.

GLEN HOUSE, PEEBLESSHIRE, additions for William Allan, 1821; dem. *c.*1853 and rebuilt by D. Bryce [U 24; W. Chambers, *History of Peeblesshire*, 1864, 389–90].

DUDDINGSTON MANSE, MIDLOTHIAN, octagonal curling-house and studio, for the Duddingston Curling Society and the Revd. John Thomson, 1823–4 [David B. Smith, *Curling: An Illustrated History*, Edinburgh 1981, 33].

MINTO MANSE, ROXBURGHSHIRE, 1827; 'a Tuscan villa' [U 38].

DUNPHAIL HOUSE, MORAYSHIRE, for C. L. Cumming Bruce, 1828–9; enlarged 1833; remodelled 1965; Italianate [U 17].

BELMONT, MURRAYFIELD, CORSTORPHINE, MIDLOTHIAN, for Thomas Mackenzie, Lord Mackenzie, 1828–30, Italianate [U 7].

DRUMBANAGHER HOUSE, CO. ARMAGH, IRELAND, for Maxwell Close, 1829; Italianate; dem. [U 18].

PRESTON GRANGE, PRESTONPANS, EAST LOTHIAN, enlarged for E. Grant Suttie, 1830; stables for Sir George Grant Suttie, 1845; additions for same 1850; Scottish vernacular style [U 46] (J. Small, *Castles and Mansions of the Lothians*, 1883).

GRANGE HOUSE, GRANGE LOAN, nr. EDINBURGH, alterations for Sir Thomas Dick Lauder, 1830–1, Scottish vernacular style; dem. *c.*1936 [U 25] (J. Small, *Castles and Mansions of the Lothians*, 1883; T. Hannan, *Famous Scottish Houses: The Lowlands*, 1928, 165–8].

LYNEDOCH LODGE, PERTHSHIRE, drawing-room for Thomas Graham, Lord Lynedoch, 1832; dem. *c.*1870 [U 32].

DALCRUE, PERTHSHIRE, Italianate farm-house for Thomas Graham, Lord Lynedoch, 1832 [U 19].

LURGAN, or BROWNLOW HOUSE, CO. ARMAGH, IRELAND, for the Right Hon. Charles Brownlow, 1833–5, 'Elizabethan' style [U 33; see also Ian Gow in *Architectural Heritage* ii, 1991, 79–83].

MEADOWBANK HOUSE, KIRKNEWTON, MIDLOTHIAN, additions for Alexander Maconochie, Lord Meadowbank, 1835; reduced in size *c.*1950 [U 40] (J. Small, *Castles and Mansions of the Lothians*, 1883).

CRAIGCROOK CASTLE, CRAMOND, MIDLOTHIAN, enlarged for Francis Jeffrey, Lord Jeffrey, 1835; further additions 1891; Scottish vernacular style [U 14] (J. Small, *Castles and Mansions of the Lothians*, 1883; T. Hannan, *Famous Scottish Houses: the Lowlands*, 1928, 69–72; J. Taylor, *Lord Jeffrey and Craigcrook*, Edinburgh 1892].

BONALY TOWER, MIDLOTHIAN, for Henry Thomas Cockburn, Lord Cockburn, 1836–8; wings added 1874 and 1886–9; Scottish vernacular style [U 9] (J. Small, *Castles and Mansions of the Lothians*, 1883; T. Hannan, *Famous Scottish Houses: the Lowlands*, 1928, 33–6).

BARMORE (now STONEFIELD CASTLE), LOCH FYNE, ARGYLLSHIRE, for John Cambell, 1836–40, Scottish vernacular style [U 8] (R.C.A.M., *Argyllshire* vii, 354–8).

MINTO HOUSE, ROXBURGHSHIRE, alterations for 2nd Earl of Minto, 1837–8; dismantled 1973, dem. 1992–3 [N.L.S., MS. 13217, f. 185; Letter Book 7, p. 85].

FLOORS CASTLE, ROXBURGHSHIRE, remodelled for 6th Duke of Roxburghe, 1837–45, Jacobethan style [U 23] (*C. Life*, 11–18 May, 1978).

ISLAY HOUSE, ISLAY, INNER HEBRIDES, offices, etc. for W. F. Campbell, 1841–5, Scottish vernacular style [U 30].

COLINTON HOUSE (now Merchiston Castle School), MIDLOTHIAN, kitchen offices for James Abercromby, Lord Dunfermline, 1840–2 [Letter Book 7, *passim*].

LAURISTON CASTLE, MIDLOTHIAN, alterations and additions, including staircase and two porches, for Andrew Rutherfurd, 1845 [Letter Book 7, *passim*].

MONUMENTS

ST. QUIVOX, AYRSHIRE, Doric mausoleum in churchyard for James Campbell, 1822 [U 35, portfolio 10].

EDINBURGH, HERIOT'S HOSPITAL, monument to James Denholm, 1824 [U, portfolio 11].

EDINBURGH, CALTON HILL, monument to Professor John Playfair (d. 1819), 1825–6 [U 45].

EDINBURGH, CALTON HILL, monument to Dugald Stewart, 1831 [U 42].

DUTHIL, INVERNESS-SHIRE, mausoleum for Seafield family, 1837 [*N.S.A.* xiii, 132].

KENSAL GREEN CEMETERY, MIDDLESEX, monument to Robert Ferguson of Raith, 1842 [Letter Book 7, pp. 217–19, 383].

EDINBURGH, DEAN CEMETERY, monument to Francis Jeffrey, Lord Jeffrey, 1851 [N.L.S., MS. 9704, f. 179v].

EDINBURGH, DEAN CEMETERY, pyramidal monument to Sophia Rutherfurd (d. 1852) [N.L.S., MS. 9704, ff. 193, 197].

EDINBURGH, DEAN CEMETERY, monument to himself (d. 1857) [U, portfolio 39].

PLEVINS, JOSEPH (–1846), was a builder in Birmingham. According to Francis White's *History, Gazetteer and Directory of Warwickshire*, 1850, 612, he designed the Greek Revival BATHS in BATH STREET, LEAMINGTON, WARWICKS., 1836, dem. 1867. His death at Edgbaston is recorded in *Aris's Birmingham Gazette*, 27 July 1846. He was the father of the Birmingham architect Thomson Plevins (1825–97).

PLOWMAN, JOHN (*c.*1773–1843), was an architect and builder of Oxford. After working for some time as foreman to Daniel Harris (*q.v.*), he was from 1812 to 1837 the latter's partner in business. His most ambitious works were the demolished St. Martin's Church at Carfax, Oxford, and the church at Churchill, with a tower copied, on a smaller scale, from that of Magdalen College. Plowman died in Oxford on 12 August 1843, aged 70. He was the father of Thomas and John Plowman. Thomas, who predeceased his father, is noticed below. John, who was born on 2 April 1807, and died on 1 October 1871, began to practise in Oxford in the 1830s, and assisted his father during the last years of the latter's life. In 1839 he won the second prize in the competition for the Ashmolean Museum. Sir Robert Smirke, the assessor, considered his design 'more like a distinguished residence than a collegiate establishment'. His principal work was the Shire Hall on the site of Oxford Castle, for which he provided a 'Norman' façade guarded by fasces of cast-iron battle-axes.

[*Oxford Herald*, 2 May 1812; *Jackson's Oxford Jnl.*, 19 Aug. 1843; *Oxford Chronicle*, 14 Oct. 1871; Oxon. C.R.O., MSS. Wills Oxon. 103, f. 283, 109, f. 160; St. Michael's, Oxford, baptism register for 1807.]

The following list contains works by both John Plowmans. All buildings before *c.*1835 must be the father's, and those known to be by the son are indicated.

OXFORD, ST. MARTIN'S CHURCH, rebuilt (except tower), 1820–2, Gothic, in collaboration with D. Harris; dem. 1896 [J. Ingram, *Memorials of Oxford* iii, 1837, 2].

CHURCHILL CHURCH, OXON., 1826–8, Gothic [Oxon. C.R.O., MS. Oxford diocesan papers *c.*2166].

BAVERSTOCK RECTORY, WILTS., altered or rebuilt 1826 [Salisbury Diocesan Records].

LONG WITTENHAM VICARAGE, BERKSHIRE, altered or rebuilt 1827 [Salisbury Diocesan Records].

ADDERBURY CHURCH, OXON., west gallery (removed 1866) and font, 1831–2 [*V.C.H. Oxon.* ix, 35–6].

OXFORD, ST. MICHAEL'S CHURCH, rebuilt North Chapel, 1833 [J. Ingram, *Memorials of Oxford* iii, 1837, 5].

RAVENSTHORPE VICARAGE, NORTHANTS., enlarged and refronted 1835 [Northants. Record Office, Peterborough Diocesan Records].

OXFORD, ST. PETER'S-IN-THE-EAST CHURCH, repaired and reseated, 1836 [Vestry Minutes 1769–1842, f. 129; *Gent's Mag.* 1836 (ii), 637].

BICESTER, OXON., THE UNION WORKHOUSE, 1835–6, *by J. P. junior* [*V.C.H. Oxon.* vi, 40].

CIRENCESTER, GLOS., THE WORKHOUSE (now Council Offices), 1836 [*Gloucester Jnl.* 29 Oct. 1836, *ex inf.* Mr. Alan Brooks].

EVESHAM, WORCS., THE WORKHOUSE, 1836–7; dem. [*Berrow's Worcester Jnl.* 22 Sept. 1836, *ex inf.* Mr. Alan Brooks].

CUBLINGTON RECTORY, BUCKS., remodelled 1837 [Lincolnshire Record Office, MGA 210].

ROSS-ON-WYE, HEREFS, THE ROYAL HOTEL, 1837, *by J.P. junior* [*Jackson's Oxford Jnl.* 30 Sept. 1837].

LAUNTON RECTORY, OXON., enlarged 1838 [*V.C.H. Oxon.* vi, 233].

OXFORD, THE FLOATING CHAPEL for BOATMEN, 1839; foundered *c.*1868 [Bodleian Library, MS. Top. Oxon. d. 505, f. 272].

BISHOPSWOOD CHURCH, HEREFS., 1839–41, *by J.P. junior* [G.R.].

OXFORD, THE SHIRE HALL, 1839–41 *by J.P. junior* [*A.P.S.D., s.v.* 'Oxford'].

BECKLEY RECTORY, SUSSEX, *c.*1840 [I.C.B.S., file 2683, f. 1].

BENSON CHURCH, OXON., repaired and reroofed south aisle 1841 [Oxfordshire C.R.O., MS. D. D. Par. Benson c. 9/28].

WARBOROUGH CHURCH, OXON., alterations 1842 [*Oxford Herald*, 2 April 1842].

STEEPLE ASTON CHURCH, OXON., restoration 1842 [W. Wing, *History of Steeple Aston*, 1845, 61–2].

STANTON ST. JOHN RECTORY, OXON., *c.*1842, *by J. P. junior* [plans in parish chest].

BODICOTE CHURCH, OXON., rebuilt 1843–4, Gothic [*V.C.H. Oxon.* ix, 38].

PLOWMAN, THOMAS (*c.*1805–1828), elder son of John Plowman of Oxford, was awarded medals for architectural designs by the Society of Arts in 1822 and 1824. After spending some time in the office of Sir Jeffry Wyatville he returned to Oxford in order to assist his father. He had already, in 1823, submitted a Gothic design in the competition for the completion of King's College, Cambridge, and in 1826 his designs for refitting ST. MARY'S CHURCH, OXFORD, with Gothic pews and galleries, were approved by Convocation. The drawings (one of which is now in the Bodleian Library) were exhibited at the Royal Academy in 1826. Plowman died on 19 February 1828, aged 22 or 23, a few days before the completion of the work (some of which was removed in 1900).

[*A.P.S.D; Jackson's Oxford Jnl.*, 23 Feb. 1828; *Oxford Herald*, 23 Feb. 1828; *Gent's Mag.* 1828 (i), 380; T. G. Jackson, *The Church of St. Mary the Virgin, Oxford*, 1897, 139–43.]

POCKLINGTON, JOSEPH (1736–1817), was the younger son of a Newark banker whose inherited wealth enabled him to live as a gentleman and to indulge in a taste for building. He claimed to be 'Surveyor to his own Board of Works', and altogether built five small country houses, all of which (with one exception) he appears to have designed himself. In 1765 he built CARLTON HALL, CARLTON-ON-TRENT, NOTTS., and in 1793 MUSKHAM HOUSE (dem.). His elder brother Roger lived nearby at Winthorpe Hall, and Joseph may have provided the design for the tower of WINTHORPE CHURCH (dem. 1886) which was rebuilt at Roger's expense in 1779, as formerly recorded by an inscription. In 1776 Joseph visited the Lake District, where he first built a house on Pocklington's Island in Derwent Water and then another called FINKLE STREET HOUSE at PORTINSCALE and finally a third called BARROW CASCADE HOUSE. The first was somewhat in the style of James Paine and may have been designed by a professional architect, but the others were evidently Pocklington's own work. Apart from showing an early appreciation of the picturesque scenery of the Lakes (which he embellished with several follies), Pocklington was one of the least innovative of Georgian amateur architects, his façades being similar to those of many Midland builder-architects of his day [Angus Taylor, 'Joseph Pocklington', *C. Life*, 5 Sept. 1985, 'The Pocklington Brothers and their Buildings', *C. Life*, 1 May 1986].

POCOCK, WILLIAM FULLER (1779–1849), was the eldest son of William Pocock, a carpenter, joiner and maker of patent extensible furniture, then resident in the City of London, but subsequently at Leyton in Essex.[1] He was at first apprenticed to his father, who wished him to follow the same trade as himself. Pocock, however, had made up his mind to be an architect, and eventually persuaded his father to cancel his articles and allow him to enter the office of Charles Beazley as a pupil. In 1799 he began to exhibit at the Royal Academy, and in 1801 he was admitted to the Academy Schools. After leaving Beazley's office he acted for some years as an assistant to Thomas Hardwick. By 1802 or 1803 he was beginning independent practice, and in 1804 secured a commission from a London business firm (Messrs. Warner of Rood Lane) to which he was to be indebted for much subsequent employment. In 1811 he leased some land in Knightsbridge from Lord Dungannon, and began to build houses in Trevor Place as a speculation. One of these, No. 5, was reserved for his own occupation.[2] Pocock was now well established as an architect and surveyor, with a number of City clients, and several estates to administer, including those of Lord Dungannon and the Brewers' Company. He was an early member of the Institute of British Architects, and was Master of the Carpenters' Company in 1840. He died on 29 October 1849, aged 69, leaving a son, William Willmer Pocock (1813–99), who succeeded to his practice and designed the Metropolitan Tabernacle for the celebrated Baptist minister Charles Spurgeon. W. W. Pocock's son Maurice Henry Pocock (1854–1921) was also an architect. F. Wehnert (1801–71) was a pupil of W. F. Pocock.

Pocock, who was an active member of the Wesleyan Church, was a meticulous, hard-working man, reserved in manner and 'scrupulously clean and neat' in appearance. His probity and business efficiency do much to explain his extensive practice as a surveyor. As an architect he was competent but unremarkable, his best work being in the Greek Doric style. In 1835 he made a somewhat pedestrian design for the Houses of Parliament competition, of which there is a lithograph made by his son, under whose name it is described in the *Catalogue* of designs exhibited in 1836. He published the following works: *Architectural Designs for Rustic Cottages, Picturesque Dwellings, Villas, etc. with appropriate scenery*, dedicated to Sir J. Courtenay Honywood, Bart., 1807, 1819, 1823 (reprinted 1971); *Modern Finishings for Rooms: a series of designs for vestibules, staircases, boudoirs, libraries, etc., to which are added some designs for villas and porticos*, 1811, 1823, 1837; *Designs for Churches and Chapels*, 1819, 3rd ed. 1835 (savagely reviewed in *The British Critic* xxviii, 1840, 471 *et seq.*); and *Observations on Bond in Brickwork*, 1839. An album of prints and drawings collected by him is in the R.I.B.A. Drawings Collection.

[*A.P.S.D.*; MS. Memoir by W. W. Pocock in R.I.B.A. Library; W. W. Pocock, *William Fuller Pocock, F.R.I.B.A.*, privately printed 1883, reprinted in *Blackmansbury* ix, 1972; E. T. Joy, 'Pocock's – the ingenious inventors', *Connoisseur* clxxiii, Feb. 1970, 88–92; C. Binfield, 'Architects in Connexion: Four Methodist Generations' in *Revival and Religion since 1700: Essays for John Walsh*, ed. J. Garnett and C. Matthew, 1993; information from the late Miss M. A. Powel.]

[1] George Pocock, the builder of Cornwall Place, George's Place, and other streets on the Marquess of Northampton's estate in Islington (*c.*1800), and of Nos. 120–2 Maida Vale (1819), was perhaps a member of the same family: see S. Lewis, *History of Islington*, 1842, 370 and *C. Life*, 25 Jan. 1936, 103.

[2] In 1827 he moved to No. 10, where he continued to live until his death.

Unless otherwise stated, the following list is based on the privately printed memoir by W. W. Pocock.

LEYTON, ESSEX, house for Mr. Banks, 1802.

LEYTON CHURCH, ESSEX, monument to Wildman family [exhib. at R.A. 1802].

HAFOD, WALES, obelisk to memory of 5th Duke of Bedford, for Thomas Johnes, 1803 [exhib. at R.A.].

ESSEX, villa, probably at WHIPS CROSS, WALTHAMSTOW, for E. Warner, 1804 [exhib. at R.A.].

EVINGTON PLACE, KENT, work (unspecified), for Sir John Honywood, 1806; dem. 1938.

BLACKHEATH, cottage orné for Sir John Eamer [exhib. at R.A. 1811].

KNIGHTSBRIDGE, TREVOR TERRACE, Nos. 5–8, 1811, Nos. 9–10, 1826.

MONTREAL, CANADA, MANSION HOUSE HOTEL, ballroom for Mr. Molson, 1817 [exhib. at R.A. 1819].

RANELAGH CHAPEL, GEORGE STREET, SLOANE SQUARE, 1818; dem. 1887 (illustrated in *Belgrave Presbyterian Church, Jubilee Memorial*, 1896, 13, 17, 30).

FAN GROVE (now COURT), nr. CHERTSEY, SURREY, for Genl. Sir Herbert Taylor, 1818–20: since enlarged and remodelled.

LONDON, LEATHERSELLERS' COMPANY'S HALL GREAT ST. HELEN'S PLACE, BISHOPSGATE, 1820–2 (used as offices from 1878); dem. *c.*1930.

KNIGHTSBRIDGE, Messrs. Smith & Baber's Floorcloth Manufactory, 1822.

HORNSEY PRIORY, MUSWELL HILL, for Henry Warner, 1823–5, Tudor Gothic; dem. 1902 [exhib. at R.A. 1825–7].

THE 'CLOCK CASE' TOWER, VIRGINIA WATER, SURREY, alterations for his brother-in-law Henry Willmer, 1824 (this building, named in W. W. Pocock's Memoir, had been built by the Duke of Cumberland in the 18th century, and must be the 'Cumberland Tower' exhibited by Pocock at the R.A. in 1824. It was later sold to George IV, as it overlooked Virginia Water).

GLENRIDGE, CALLOW HILL, VIRGINIA WATER, SURREY, for himself, 1825, *cottage orné* style.

ALDENHAM GRAMMAR SCHOOL, HERTS., for the Brewers' Company, 1825 [exhib. at R.A. 1828; drawings in R.I.B.A. Collection].

HIGHGATE, MIDDLESEX, THE LITTLE PRIORY, for his brother-in-law Henry Willmer, 1826.

LONDON, restored BREWERS' HALL, ADDLE STREET, 1828 [*A.P.S.D.*].

LONDON, HEADQUARTERS OF THE LONDON MILITIA, BUNHILL ROW, 1828 [*A.P.S.D.*].

COWES, ISLE OF WIGHT, buildings for Mr. Broster, junior, 1829.

LONDON, No. 66 PATERNOSTER ROW, 1833, 'ostensibly for Revd. J. Mason'; dem.

CLIMPING VICARAGE, SUSSEX, for the Revd. Owen Marden, *c.*1833.

CHELSEA DISPENSARY, 1835.

THE WESTERN GRAMMAR SCHOOL (now ALEXANDER HOUSE), No. 7 NORTH TERRACE, SOUTH KENSINGTON, 1835–6; interior rebuilt *c.*1928.

DOWN COTTAGE, HARTING, SUSSEX, for his brother-in-law Henry Willmer, *c.*1835; subsequently enlarged by W. W. Pocock and known thereafter as DOWN PLACE.

KENSINGTON, WESLEYAN CHAPEL, 1836.

ANTIGUA, W. INDIES, a chapel, 1837.

VIRGINIA WATER, SURREY, CHRIST CHURCH, 1837, Gothic.

GUNNERSBURY HOUSE, MIDDLESEX, entrance gates and lodges for Thomas Farmer, probably 1838–40; alterations to stables, 1844.

LONDON, WESLEYAN CENTENARY HALL, BISHOPSGATE, 1840; dem. 1969 [exhib. at R.A.] (*Companion to the Almanac*, 1841, 246–7).

TWICKENHAM, CARPENTERS' COMPANY'S ALMSHOUSES, 1841, Gothic; dem. *c.*1951 [*A.P.S.D.*].

VIRGINIA WATER, SURREY, SCHOOLS, 1843.

POGMIRE, ALEXANDER, was the 'excellent and skillful mayson and carver' employed by Sir John Lowther, 1st Bart., to 'beautify the hall porch' at LOWTHER HALL, WESTMORLAND, 'with pilasters and other cuttwork' in 1642, and to build the gallery on the east side of the forecourt in 1655–6 ['Memorable observations' by Lowther in Cumbria Record Office, D/Lons./L/A1/1, ff. 273, 276]. This gallery, demolished *c.*1805, is illustrated in Kip's *Britannia Illustrata* i, 1714, pl. 41. It so closely resembled the gallery still remaining on the north side of the forecourt of HUTTON-IN-THE-FOREST, CUMBERLAND, and built by Sir Henry Fletcher, Bart., some time between 1641 and 1645 (*C. Life*, 4 Feb. 1965), as to make it virtually certain that the latter was also Pogmire's work. In 1653–5 he was employed at ROSE CASTLE, CUMBERLAND, by its Parliamentary owner, William Heveningham [B. Tyson in *Trans. Ancient Monuments Soc.* N.S. 27, 1983, 61].

POLLARD, JAMES, was a pupil of Joseph Pickford of Derby. He was awarded premiums for architectural designs by the Society of Arts in 1764 and 1765. He is described as being under 18 years of age on both occasions [*Register of Premiums*, 1778]. He was still in Pickford's office in 1771 [University of Keele, Sneyd papers 10095–11.]

PONDER, NATHANIEL, was a builder-architect in Fenchurch Street, London, from about 1815 to about 1835. He designed LANCING VICARAGE, SUSSEX, in 1817 [W. Sussex C.R.O., Ep. I. 41/27]. He was the son of Stephen Ponder, a London carpenter who had exhibited architectural drawings at the Royal Academy in 1794, 1795 and 1796. Nathaniel was in partnership with his father until the latter retired or died soon after 1810.

PONSFORD, THOMAS, was a builder at Totnes in Devon in the 1820s and 1830s. He designed SOUTH ALLINGTON HOUSE, CHIVELSTONE, DEVON, for the Pitts family, *c.*1840 [drawings in Devon C.R.O., 1399 M/17/2].

POOL, JOHN LIDBURY (1783–), practised in London during the early nineteenth century. He exhibited at the Royal Academy from 1802 onwards, showing in 1804 a 'Design for a mausoleum to the memory of the late unfortunate Lord Camelford', who had been killed in a duel, in 1810 a 'Design for a Theatre', and in 1817 a 'design for a villa, now building for a gentleman, in the Coburg road, near Peckham'. In 1811 his designs for rebuilding Hungerford Church, Berkshire, were selected in a competition, but he was dismissed the following year, apparently because his estimates were considered excessive. His place was taken by John Pinch of Bath. [MS. Minutes of the Trustees.] An elevation of his design for the tower, signed and dated 1812, is among the Treacher papers in the Berkshire R.O.

POOLE, the Revd. HENRY (*c.*1785–1857), appears to have had some architectural training before being ordained in 1811 at the age of 26. After a curacy at Ossett, nr. Wakefield, he moved to Corsham in Wiltshire, and then in 1818 to the living of Coleford and Bream in the Forest of Dean. Here he was able to gratify a long-felt desire to design and build a church, first at COLEFORD (1820–1; dem. except the tower in 1880), then at PARK END (cons. 1822), and finally at BREAM (1823). He also designed a new tower for BERRY HILL CHURCH in 1822. His drawings for Coleford and Bream churches (the latter signed 'Henry Poole, Minister and Surveyor') are among the I.C.B.S. records now in Lambeth Palace Library. His Gothic detailing was typical of its date, but his churches at Coleford and Park End were unconventional in having octagonal plans. Poole died on 22 December 1857, aged 72, and was buried in the churchyard at Park End, which he had 'long endeavoured to render as attractive as possible, by regulating the character of the tomb-stones erected in it'. [H. G. Nicholls, *The Forest of Dean*, 1858, 166, 169; H. G. Nicholls, *The Personalities of the Forest of Dean*, 1863, 152–60; *Something about Coleford and the old Chapel*, 1877.]

POPE, RICHARD SHACKLETON (*c.*1793–1884), was the son of a clerk of works employed by Sir Robert Smirke, and as a young man was himself employed in the same capacity by both Smirke and C. R. Cockerell. In 1821–3 Cockerell sent him to Bristol to supervise the building of the Philosophical Institution, and he decided to settle in that city, where he remained for the rest of his life. He had a large practice, designing many commercial buildings, and holding the office of District Surveyor with monopolistic tenacity for forty years from 1831 to 1872. His principal works in Bristol were the Guildhall, the earliest Gothic Revival town hall in the country, and the church of St. Mary-on-the-Quay, dignified by a handsome Corinthian portico. His unexecuted designs for a new Mansion House are in the Bristol Record Office. From 1849 onwards he was in partnership with John Bindon and J. A. Clark, and from the 1860s with his son Thomas Shackleton Pope. He died at Shirehampton on 10 February 1884, in his ninety-second year [*Builder* xlvi, 1884, 426; Principal Probate Registry, Calendar of Probates; A. Gomme *et al.*, *Bristol: an Architectural History* 1979, 440–1].

WORKS PRIOR TO 1849

BRISTOL, COURT OF JUSTICE adjoining the Council House in Corn Street, in collaboration with George Dymond, 1827–8 [City Archives].

BRISTOL, THE CATTLE MARKET, TEMPLE MEADS, 1828–9; dem. [minutes of the Committee for the Cattle Market and Wool Hall in Bristol Record Office].

BRISTOL, THE WOOL HALL, ST. THOMAS'S STREET, 1830–1 [minutes as above].

BRISTOL, THE GAOL, CUMBERLAND ROAD, repairs 1831–2; dem. 1895 [*A.P.S.D.*].

BRISTOL, THE BRIDEWELL, BRIDEWELL LANE, 1832; dem. 1865 [*A.P.S.D.*].

BRISTOL CATHEDRAL, restoration of CHAPTER-HOUSE, 1833 [*A.P.S.D.*].

HOLT CHURCH, WILTS., added N. aisle, 1836–7; rebuilt 1891 [I.C.B.S.].

BRISTOL, THE ROYAL WESTERN HOTEL (now Brunel House), COLLEGE PLACE (St. George's Road), 1837–8 [*Builder* xlvi, 1884, 426].

OKEFORD CHURCH, DEVON, 1838, Gothic [I.C.B.S.].

BRISTOL, ST. MARY-ON-THE-QUAY CHURCH, 1839–40, built originally for the Irvingites, but purchased by the Roman Catholics in 1843 [*A.P.S.D.*].

BRADFORD-ON-AVON VICARAGE, WILTS., altered or rebuilt 1840 [Salisbury Diocesan Records].

WINSLEY CHURCH, WILTS., 1841, Gothic [I.C.B.S.].

BRISTOL, THE GUILDHALL, 1843–6, Gothic [*Companion to the Almanac*, 1845, 248–50].

BRISTOL, THE CENTRAL POLICE STATION, BRIDEWELL ST., 1844; dem. *c.*1927 [*A.P.S.D.*].

BRISTOL, THE BUCKINGHAM BAPTIST CHURCH, CLIFTON, 1844–7, Gothic [*A.P.S.D.*].

BRISTOL, with S. C. Fripp planned VICTORIA STREET, 1845 (carried out 1870) [*Builder* iii, 1845, 399].

BRISTOL, THE MEAT MARKET, ST. NICHOLAS STREET, 1848–9 [J. Latimer, *Annals of Bristol*, 1887, 307].

POPE, THOMAS (–1805), was an architect and builder of Bristol, where he held the office of District Surveyor from 1801 until his death in 1805 [A. Beavan, *Bristol Lists*, 1899, 248]. In the City Archives (Plan Book B, nos. 111b, 119a) there are designs by him for two houses for John Wadham at the corner of Bell Lane and Broad Street (1802), and for additions to a house in Lower Park Row (1804).

POPE, WILLIAM (–1678), was a Warden of the Carpenters' Company in 1670, 1673 and 1674, and its Master in 1675. In 1664 he was among those who made designs for the Company's new Court Room, but the Committee (of which he was a member) preferred those of John Wildgos. In May 1671, however, when it was resolved 'that the ceiling of the Hall be handsomely done', it was decided to leave this 'to the discretion of Warden Pope'. Carpenters' Hall was demolished in 1876 [E. B. Jupp and W. W. Pocock, *Historical Account of the Carpenters' Company*, 1887, 229, 232]. After the Great Fire, Pope was one of the carpenters employed in the rebuilding of the Guildhall [Guildhall Library, MS. 184/41]. In 1674 he and Thomas Clarke contracted to enlarge the Synagogue in Cree Church Lane, London, for some £760 [L. D. Barnett, *Bevis Marks Records* i, 1940, 10]. The translation by Godfrey Richards of Palladio's *First Book of Architecture*, 1663, contains an appendix on the framing of Roofs 'By that ingenious Architect Mr. William Pope of London'. At his death in 1678, Pope left a rent charge of £3 10s., to be paid out of some property in Coleman Street to seven poor members of the Carpenters' Company or their widows. He was then living in Whitehorse Lane, Stepney. His will is P.C.C., 9 KING.

PORDEN, CHARLES FERDINAND (1790–1863), was the son of Isaac Porden, an obscure architect who is said to have practised in Birmingham. He was articled to his uncle, William Porden, and was also in the office of George Wyatt. In 1806 he gained a gold medal for architectural design offered by the Society of Arts, and in 1809, having been admitted to the Royal Academy School, he was awarded the Silver Medal of the Academy. He exhibited at the Academy between 1810 and 1825 and provided drawings for some of the plates in Rutter's *Delineations of Fonthill* (1823). He supervised the building of ST. PANCRAS CHURCH for Messrs. Inwood between 1819 and 1822, and designed the fine Greek Doric church of ST. MATTHEW, BRIXTON, 1822–4, skilfully solving the problem of combining a steeple with a porticoed temple by placing the tower at the east end [*Survey of London* xxvi, 132–4 and plates]. He was for ten years in the office of Sir William Tite, whom he assisted in the erection of the Royal Exchange, London. He died on 6 March 1863, aged 73 years, and was buried in Highgate Cemetery, where a tombstone states that he was 'nephew of William Porden, architect to King George the 4th, and grandson of Roger Pourden [*sic*] of York, architect'. [*A.P.S.D.*]

PORDEN, WILLIAM (1755–1822), was baptized at St. Mary's Church, Hull, on 29 January 1755. His father, Thomas Purden or Porden, was described as 'Labourer'. In 1774 he became a pupil of James Wyatt, to whom he had been introduced by the poet Mason. He was in Wyatt's office in 1778, when he exhibited at the Royal Academy for the first time, and in 1779, when he was responsible, with the elder Smirke and a young painter called Watson, for an amusing skit on the Royal Academy entitled *The Exhibition, or a second Anticipation:*[1] *being Remarks on the principal works to be exhibited next month at the Royal Academy: by Roger Shanhagan, Gent.* Porden was presumably responsible for the architectural portion of the text, in which Chambers, Sandby, Paine and other members of the architectural establishment were criticized or ridiculed, while Wyatt was praised. According to Redgrave he was 'afterwards the pupil of S. P. Cockerell' (though he and Cockerell were almost the same age), 'then became secretary to Lord Sheffield, who appointed him paymaster to the 22nd Dragoons, a regiment raised by his Lordship', and eventually 'turned again to architecture after the reduction of this regiment'. As Sheffield's regiment was raised in 1779 (not 1770 as stated by Redgrave) and disbanded by 1783, Porden would have returned to architecture about the latter year. It may be noted that although he exhibited at the Royal Academy in 1778 he did not do so again until 1784. There is some evidence that for a time Porden returned to Wyatt's office as a senior assistant,[2] but his appointment as Lord Grosvenor's surveyor appears to date from *c.*1785, and he must by then have been in independent practice.

Porden obtained several commissions for country houses, and enjoyed a considerable reputation as a Gothic architect in the manner of his master Wyatt. The Prince of Wales employed him at Brighton, and at Eaton Hall he designed 'the most extravagant Gothic house of the Regency period'. But he failed to secure election as A.R.A. in 1797, and in

[1] The first *Anticipation* was a well-known political satire published by Richard Tickell in 1778.

[2] See the letter from Samuel Wyatt cited at the end of this biography. It was presumably as Wyatt's assistant that, as Redgrave records, Porden made the arrangements for the Handel Commemoration in Westminster Abbey in 1785, for Wyatt was the Surveyor to the Abbey, and had been responsible for the arrangements for the first Commemoration in 1784.

1805 he was unsuccessful in the competition for Downing College, Cambridge (his designs for which are in the R.I.B.A. Collection). His connection with Lord Grosvenor was also to end unhappily, for in 1821 his retirement from the surveyorship of the Grosvenor Estate in London was hastened by the failure of a scheme, for which he had been responsible, to rebuild the north side of Berkeley Square on a speculative basis. According to Redgrave, 'this preyed upon his spirits' and he died 'two years after', on 14 September 1822, aged 67. He was then living at 59 Berners Street, and was buried in St. John's Wood Chapel. He had a large family, all of whom died young, except two daughters. The elder married Joseph Kay (*q.v.*), the younger (Eleanor) married Sir John Franklin, and became a well-known figure in literary circles. Henry Rhodes, P. F. Robinson, J. Temple and John Young were Porden's pupils. His portrait by W. Stavely, exhibited at the Royal Academy in 1795, is at the Brighton Pavilion. Another by Beechey, formerly at Hopton Hall, was sold at Sotheby's 5–6 September 1989. His younger brother Charles (born 1762) had an architectural training under James Wyatt, but does not seem to have practised independently. In 1785 he was engaged as a draughtsman by the engineer James Watt on the recommendation of Samuel Wyatt.

[*A.P.S.D.*; F. T. Cansick, *Epitaphs of Middlesex* ii, 1872, 85; will P.C.C. 35 RICHARDS; S. Redgrave, *Dictionary of Artists of the English School*, 1878, 338–9; *D.N.B.*; *The Farington Diary*, ed. J. Greig, i. 165, ii, 270, iii, 230, vii, 137; A. T. Bolton, *The Portrait of Sir John Soane*, 1927, 155, 217, 288; W. T. Whitley, *Artists and their Friends in England 1700–1799*, 1928, i, 343–4, ii, 216; Hermione Hobhouse, *Thomas Cubitt*, 1971, 53, 88–9; Birmingham Reference Library, Boulton & Watt Collection, S. Wyatt to J. Watt, 31 Jan. 1785.]

LONDON, PHILLIMORE PLACE, KENSINGTON, 1787–9; dem. *c.*1935 [exhib. at R.A. 1788; J. Summerson, *Georgian London*, 1945, 263].

LONDON, THE EBURY CHAPEL, FIVE FIELDS, CHELSEA, 1790 [cutting recording laying of foundation stone in Westminster Public Library, 'Cuttings relating to the Dukes of Westminster'].

ALDWARK HALL, nr. ROTHERHAM, YORKS. (W.R.), stables, dairy and farmyard, for Francis F. Foljambe, *c.*1790; dem. [exhib. at R.A. 1790 and 1792].

DOVER HOUSE, ROEHAMPTON, SURREY, enlarged and remodelled for Beilby Thompson, 1794; dem. 1930s [exhib. at R.A. 1794: G. Richardson, *New Vitruvius Britannicus* i, 1810, pls. 19–21].

SOUTH KELSEY CHURCH, LINCS., rebuilt (except tower) 1795–6, Gothic; remodelled by Butterfield 1853 [exhib. at R.A. 1797].

'A house in the Gothic style of the fourteenth century', exhibited at R.A. 1796, and said by Graves (*The Royal Academy of Arts, Dictionary of Contributors* vi, 1906, 183), to have been 'for R. T. Gordon Esq.'

An unidentified 'house in Sussex for W. Breton, Esq.', exhibited at R.A. 1796 and perhaps not built.

OSBORNE HOUSE, ISLE OF WIGHT, 'design for the West front' for B. P. Blachford (?), exhibited at R.A. 1797; rebuilt for Queen Victoria 1845–8.

SWAINSTON HOUSE, CALBOURNE, ISLE OF WIGHT, rebuilt principal front for Sir John Barrington, Bart. 1798; damaged by bombing 1941 but subsequently restored [exhib. at R.A. 1798] (W. Cooke, *New Picture of the Isle of Wight*, 1808, 75).

EATON HALL, CHESHIRE, rebuilt for 2nd Earl Grosvenor, 1804–12, Gothic; wings added by B. Gummow, 1823–5; altered by W. Burn, 1846–51; rebuilt by A. Waterhouse, 1870; dem. 1963 [exhib. at R.A. 1804, 1805, 1807, 1810, 1812; drawings etc. in Cheshire County Record Office; J. & J. C. Buckler, *Views of Eaton Hall*, 1826; G. Aclocque & J. Cornforth in *C. Life*, 11–18 Feb. 1971].

BRIGHTON, THE PAVILION, stables, riding-house, tennis-court and other alterations for George, Prince of Wales, 1804–8. The stables (now known as The Dome) were converted into an Assembly Room in 1867 and remodelled internally as a Concert Hall in 1934–5; the riding-house was later used as a Corn Exchange [H. D. Roberts, *History of the Royal Pavilion, Brighton*, 1939].

BRIGHTON, house on the Steine (now Y.M.C.A.) for Mrs. Fitzherbert, 1804 [exhib. at R.A. 1805].

HARE PARK, DULLINGHAM, CAMBS., alterations for 2nd Earl Grosvenor, 1805–6 [Grosvenor archives, *ex inf.* Survey of London].

LONDON, GROSVENOR HOUSE, UPPER GROSVENOR STREET, alterations and extensive redecoration for 2nd Earl Grosvenor, 1806–8; addition of picture-gallery *c.*1817–19; dem. 1927 [*Survey of London* xl, 240–3].

ECCLESTON CHURCH, CHESHIRE, for 2nd Earl Grosvenor, *c.*1806–9, Gothic; dem. 1899 [exhib. at R.A. 1809, 1813].

SHOTTESBROOKE PARK, BERKSHIRE, enlarged and remodelled for Arthur Vansittart, 1807, Gothic [drawings at Shottesbrooke] (*C. Life*, 1 Feb. 1913).

LONDON, No. 49 BROOK STREET, alterations for Sir Joseph Copley, Bart., 1807 [letter from

Joseph Kay to Porden, Royal Academy, Jupp catalogue 8/241].

BROOMHALL, FIFE, proposed north front for 7th Earl of Elgin, exhibited at R.A. in 1808 as 'now building', but not in fact executed (design illustrated by J. M. Crook in *C. Life*, 29 Jan. 1970, fig. 7).

PORTER, GEORGE (*c.*1796–1856), was a pupil of Thomas Chawner. He was admitted to the Royal Academy Schools in 1816 at the age of 20, and exhibited at the Academy from 1815 onwards. He subsequently practised from Fort Place, Bermondsey, and is said to have laid out part of the West estate in that neighbourhood. From 1824 onwards he was District Surveyor for Newington and North Lambeth. He was a Fellow of the Institute of British Architects and a member of the Surveyors' Club, of which he was President in 1839. He died in October 1856. S. S. Teulon was his pupil.

GUILDFORD BRIDGE, SURREY, widened 1825 by 'Mr. Porter, engineer and architect', presumably George Porter [Brayley, *Topographical History of Surrey* i, 1841, 384].

BERMONDSEY, ST. MARY MAGDALEN'S CHURCH, remodelled W. front 1830, Gothic [G. W. Phillips, *History of Bermondsey*, 1841, 54].

SURREY, a villa 'now erecting for a gentleman', exhibited at R.A. 1834.

BERMONDSEY, premises for London Leather Company, *c.*1837 [exhibited at R.A.]

FINSBURY, LONDON, DUTCH ALMSHOUSES, CROWN STREET, *c.*1837 [exhibited at R.A.]

BERMONDSEY, ST. JAMES'S SCHOOLS, *c.*1840 [Brayley, *Topographical History of Surrey* iii, 195].

PENGE, KENT, WATERMEN'S COMPANY'S ALMSHOUSES, 1840–1 [H. Humpherus, *History of the Watermen's Company*, n.d. iii, 349].

CLEWER, WINDSOR, BERKS., ST. ANNE'S SCHOOL, *c.*1855; dem. [Berks. C.R.O., D/EX 268/56].

PORTWOOD, GEORGE (–1742), of Stamford, was probably the most prominent of the master masons who had their yards in that town in the first half of the eighteenth century. He was Chamberlain of Stamford in 1736, and held office as Mayor at the time of his death on 3 May 1742. The Chamberlains' accounts record many payments to him for minor repairs to the Corporation's buildings between 1711 and 1741, and he did a good deal of repair work at BURGHLEY HOUSE in the 1720s for the 8th Earl of Exeter, who also employed him to take down the steeple of the ruinous church of PICKWORTH, RUTLAND, in 1723, and to refront the GEORGE HOTEL, STAMFORD, in 1724 [Exeter Archives 51/21/23, *ex inf.* Mr. P. I. King]. In 1722 he rebuilt the bridge over the River Nene at FOTHERINGHAY, NORTHANTS. [H. K. Bonney, *Historic Notices relating to Fotheringhay*, 1821, 2], and in 1735 designed another bridge (dem.) at WOODNEWTON, NORTHANTS. [R.C.H.M., *North Northants.*, 166]. In 1727–9 he was concerned in the rebuilding to its original design of the medieval tower of BRAUNSTON CHURCH, RUTLAND [Leics. C.R.O., Exton MSS (DE 3214)], and in 1737 he was paid 5 guineas by the churchwardens of WITHAM-ON-THE-HILL, LINCS., 'for Drawing Several designs for the rebuilding of there Church Steeple', which were carried out in the following year in Ketton stone by Messrs. Jackson and Chaplin for £318 [bill and accounts in parish records]. In 1741 he made a design for rebuilding the front of Dr. William Stukeley's house on BARN HILL, STAMFORD, which has been preserved among Stukeley's papers in the Bodleian Library [Gough Maps 16, f. 52]. It was not executed, but similar elevations, with blocked architraves and prominent keystones, are to be seen on other eighteenth-century houses in Stamford, some of which were probably designed and built by Portwood.

POTTER, JOHN, a carpenter by trade, was the builder and proprietor, and no doubt also the architect, of the LITTLE THEATRE, HAYMARKET, LONDON, which was erected in 1720 and replaced by Nash's Haymarket Theatre in 1820 [*Survey of London* xx, 98–9]. He is presumably to be identified with 'J. Potter Archt.', who signed the monument to James Cart (d. 1706) formerly in St. Mary-le-Bow Church, which was executed by Samuel Tufnell [K. A. Esdaile, *English Monumental Sculpture since the Renaissance*, 1927, 98], and may have been the Potter who was associated with Thomas Edwards of Greenwich (*q.v.*), in some of his building activities in Cornwall.

POTTER, JOSEPH (*c.*1756–1842),was an architect and builder of Lichfield with a considerable practice in Staffordshire and the neighbouring counties in the early nineteenth century. Early in his career he was employed by James Wyatt to supervise the latter's alterations to the cathedrals at Lichfield (1788–93) and Hereford (1790–3). He was also associated with Wyatt in the repair of St. Michael's Church, Coventry (1794), and the rebuilding of Plas Newydd for the first Marquess of Anglesey. At Lichfield he became the established Cathedral architect, carrying out further works after Wyatt's employment had ceased, including the repair of the south-west spire (1794), the restoration of the vaults of the north transept (1795–7) and of the west front (1820–2). By the standards of the early nineteenth century he was a competent Gothic architect, but he designed nothing of great distinction. He was County Surveyor of Staffordshire for forty-five years, and also Engineer to the 'Grand Trunk' (i.e. Trent & Mersey) Canal Company. He died at Lichfield on 18 August 1842, in his 87th year. His three sons all followed their father's profession in one of its branches. Robert (*c.*1795–1854), the eldest, is noticed separately below. Joseph (*c.*1797–1875) took over his father's office, and had an extensive local practice in the mid-nineteenth century. James (1801–1857), the youngest, became a civil engineer working chiefly for canal and railway companies. Thomas Johnson of Lichfield (1794–1865) was a pupil of the elder Potter, and James Fowler of Louth (1828–1892) was in the office of his son. A number of Potter's drawings (including those for Oscott College) are among the portfolios of his son's drawings in Sheffield Archives.

[*Gent's Mag.* 1842, 556; J. Hewitt, *Handbook to Lichfield Cathedral*, 1875, 49; *Proceedings of the Institution of Civil Engineers* xvii, 1858, 94; R.B. Lockett, 'Joseph Potter: Cathedral Architect at Lichfield 1794–1842', *Trans. S. Staffs. Archl. & Hist. Soc.* xxi, 1974–80.]

As it is not always possible to distinguish between the later works of Joseph Potter senior and the earlier works of his son, the following list contains all the recorded products of the Potter office up to the former's death in 1842.

HANBURY VICARAGE, STAFFS., 1792–3 [P.R.O., MPC 203, designs dated 1791].

COVENTRY, ST. MICHAEL'S CHURCH, repaired tower 1794, after a joint survey with James Wyatt; further repairs 1818 [T. Sharp, *Illustrations of the History of St. Michael's Church, Coventry*, 1818, 48–9].

LICHFIELD, NEWTON'S COLLEGE, THE CLOSE, 1800–2 [building contract, *ex inf.* Lichfield Joint Record Office].

HANDSWORTH CHURCH, STAFFS., rebuilt W. end *c.*1800 [A. E. Everitt, 'Handsworth Church', *Trans. Birmingham Arch. Soc.* 1876, 52].

STAFFORD, THE JUDGES' LODGINGS, 1802 [*V.C.H. Staffs.* vi, 202].

LICHFIELD, STAFFS., THE BISHOP'S PALACE, alterations and repairs for Bishop James Cornwallis, 1804–5 [*Journals & Correspondence of T.S. Whalley*, ed. H. Wickham, 1863, ii, 252–3, 260–1, 274].

OKEOVER HALL, STAFFS., demolition of W. wing for H. F. Okeover, *c.*1810 [Arthur Oswald in *C. Life*, 12 March 1964].

COLTON RECTORY, STAFFS., 1811 [Lichfield Joint Record Office, B/A/13].

ALREWAS VICARAGE, STAFFS., 1813–14; enlarged 1853 [Lichfield Joint Record Office, D 30/9/1/10/2–3].

HATHERTON HALL, STAFFS., for Moreton Walhouse, *c.*1815–17, Tudor Gothic [drawings from Potter's office in Staffs. C.R.O., D 260/M/E/374–6].

POLESWORTH SCHOOLS, WARWICKS., 1817–18, Tudor Gothic [Warwicks. C.R.O., DRB 16/262–9].

POLESWORTH VICARAGE, WARWICKS., alterations 1817–19 [Warwicks. C.R.O., DRB 16/271–8].

STAFFORD, THE LUNATIC ASYLUM, 1818 [*V.C.H. Staffs.* vi, 235].

BURNTWOOD CHURCH, STAFFS., 1819–20, Gothic [I.C.B.S.].

CAERNARVON, BATHS and ASSEMBLY ROOMS for 1st Marquess of Anglesey, *c.*1822–8, subsequently converted into training college [Bangor Univ. Coll. Library, Plas Newydd MSS. ii, 1392–1549, *ex inf.* Prof. M. L. Clarke].

CHETWYND BRIDGE, ALREWAS, STAFFS. (cast-iron), 1823–4 [*N. Staffs. Jnl. Field Studies*, ii, 1962, 97].

PLAS NEWYDD, ANGLESEY, works for 1st Marquess of Anglesey, 1823–6. Potter had already been employed here from 1796 onwards as executant architect under Wyatt, and appears to have been solely responsible for the Gothic chapel (dem.) built in 1805–9 [drawings in R.I.B.A. Collection: G. Jackson-Stops in *C. Life*, 1 July 1976].

GRENDON HALL, WARWICKS., rebuilt for Sir George Chetwynd, Bart., 1824–5, Elizabethan style; dem. 1932 [W. White, *Directory of Warwicks.* 1874, 1359; designs for chimney-pieces by Potter dated 1825 in Victoria & Albert and Metropolitan Museums].

GRENDON CHURCH, WARWICKS., alterations and repairs, 1824–5 [account loose in Vestry Minutes 1845–1906].

BEAUDESERT, STAFFS., remodelled Great Hall for 1st Marquess of Anglesey, 1826; interior destroyed by fire 1909; dem. 1935 [H. Colvin, 'Beaudesert, Staffs.', *Trans. Ancient Monts. Soc.* 29, 1985].

FREEFORD HALL, STAFFS., enlarged for General William Dyott, 1826–7 [Staffs. C.R.O., D 661/8/1/2/6].

SHEFFIELD, ST. MARY'S CHURCH, 1826–9, Gothic; reconstructed 1957 after bomb-damage [Port, 138–9; W. Odom, *Memorials of Sheffield*, 1922, 111]. An inscription on the roof recorded the names of 'Jos. Potter architect' and 'R. Potter resident architect'.

ARMITAGE, STAFFS., HIGH BRIDGE (cast-iron), 1829–30 [*N. Staffs. Jnl. Field Studies* ii, 1962, 97].

TAMWORTH, STAFFS., ST. JOHN BAPTIST CHURCH (R.C.) 1829–30, classical; enlarged 1929 and 1954–6 [*Catholic Mag.* i, 1831, 512 and v, 1834, 324 with illustration at p. 301].

NEWPORT, SALOP., STS. PETER & PAUL CHURCH (R.C.), 1832, Gothic [*Catholic Record Soc.* xiii, 1913, 338].

STAFFORD, HOUSE OF CORRECTION in COUNTY GAOL, 1832–3 [*V.C.H. Staffs.* vi, 204].

WADSLEY CHURCH, YORKS. (W.R.), 1833–4, Gothic [plans in Sheffield Archives].

LICHFIELD, HOLY CROSS CHURCH (R.C.), addition of sanctuary 1835, neo-Norman [*Catholic Mag.* v, 1834, 322 and frontispiece].

ST. MARY'S R.C.COLLEGE, NEW OSCOTT, SUTTON COLDFIELD, WARWICKS., 1835–8, with some alterations by A. W. N. Pugin, especially to the Chapel [*Companion to the Almanac*, 1839, 222; drawings by Potter in Sheffield Archives; B. Little, *Catholic Churches since 1623*, 1966, 77–8].

GENTLESHAW CHAPEL, STAFFS., enlarged for 1st Marquess of Anglesey, 1839; enlarged 1903 [account in Paget papers in Staffs. C.R.O., D 603/N/9/2].

POTTER, ROBERT (*c.*1795–1854), was the eldest son of Joseph Potter of Lichfield (*q.v.*). In 1826–9 he acted as 'resident architect' in charge of the building of St. Mary's Church, Sheffield, to the designs of his father, as recorded by an inscription on the roof. He subsequently established himself in Sheffield, where he designed CHRIST CHURCH, FULWOOD, 1837–9, Gothic, enlarged by G. G. Pace 1953–5 [printed record of the laying of the foundation stone in Sheffield Archives]. In Sheffield Archives there is a collection of his drawings, which includes designs for several schools, the SAVINGS BANK in SURREY STREET, SHEFFIELD (1831–2), alterations to ST. PETER'S CHURCH (now the Cathedral), including screen, singers' gallery and altar-piece (1841), and Tudor Gothic stables for STUMPERLOWE HALL, FULWOOD (1844). Potter died on 26 July 1854, aged 59, and was buried in the churchyard of St. Chad's Church at Lichfield.

POUGET, —, was a French architect said to have been employed by Ralph, 1st Duke of Montagu, at MONTAGU HOUSE, BLOOMSBURY. Montagu was Charles II's ambassador at the Court of Louis XIV in 1676–7 and became a great admirer of French art and artists. In 1675–9 he built Montagu House 'after the French pavilion way', employing Robert Hooke as his architect. The house designed by Hooke was destroyed by fire in Jan. 1685/6 and rebuilt by Montagu the following year. It was sold to the British Museum Trustees in 1754 and demolished *c.*1850 to make way for the existing Museum. Illustrating the rebuilt house in *Vitruvius Britannicus* i, 1715, pls. 34–6, Colen Campbell stated that 'the Architecture was conducted by Monsieur Pouget, 1678'. George Vertue, who says that the house was designed 'by an architect brought over on purpose', adds that the decorative painter Jacques Rousseau (1630–93) acted as 'assistant surveyor and designer for the building of (the) house' [*Note Books*, Walpole Soc. ii, 85, iii, 24]. As the 1678 house was in fact designed by Hooke, it has generally been supposed that what Pouget and Rousseau were employed to do was to rebuild it after the fire. No other reference to Pouget's presence in England has, however, been found, and his identity remains uncertain: he may possibly have been François Puget (1651–1707), a member of a family of sculptors and archi-tects from Marseilles. A painting in a French collection purporting to show 'le Duc et la Duchesse de Montaigu arrètant le Plan de Montaigu-house qui leur est presenté par un Architecte français' appears at first sight to lend support to Campbell's statement, but it was probably not painted until early in the eighteenth century, and the duke depicted wears the insignia of the Garter, an Order of which Montagu was not a member [Tessa Murdoch in *Antiques*, June 1986, 1244–51].

POUGET, FRANCIS (1794–1867), was admitted to the Royal Academy Schools in 1818 at the age of 24. He subsequently practised as an architect and surveyor from Trinity Square, Southwark. In 1821 he won the second premium in the competition for Salters' Hall, exhibiting his design at the Royal Academy in 1823. Later works included a house called MOUNT HILL at SPRINGFIELD, nr. CHELMSFORD, ESSEX, for A. R. Chalk [exhib. at R.A. 1844]; a house at OATLANDS, SURREY, for R. Mathews [exhib. at R.A. 1849]; the CONGREGATIONAL CHURCH, SNELL'S PARK, EDMONTON, MIDDLESEX, 1849, dem. 1955 [F. Fisk, *History of Edmonton*, 1914, 86]; and an Italianate hotel near the Crystal Palace in Upper Norwood, 1853 [*Civil Engineer and Architect's Jnl.* xvi, 1853, 361]. Pouget died at Grove Lodge, Tottenham on 14 January 1867. [Principal Probate Registry, Calendar of Probates; information from Mr. P. J. Seaman.]

POULTON, CHARLES (–1822), was a cabinet-maker at Reading, of which town he was Mayor in 1798 and again in 1809. The TOWN HALL was rebuilt to his designs in 1786 [J. Man, *History of Reading*, 1816, 77]. It is a plain brick structure which still exists behind the present municipal buildings by Alfred Waterhouse. In 1799 Poulton was paid £60 by Michael Eyston for 'attending' the repairs and alterations to MAPLEDURHAM HOUSE, OXON., carried out between 1794 and 1797. These included the Gothic R.C. chapel [Blount archives, c. 92]. Poulton's will, proved in May 1822, is in the Archdeaconry of Berks. wills in the Berks. C.R.O. William Ford Poulton (*c.*1820–1900), architect of Reading, may have been a relation.

POWELL, WILLIAM, was a builder and architect at Swansea in the early nineteenth century. By 1830 he was Surveyor to the Swansea Paving and Lighting Commissioners and was living at Cae Bailey House in Mount Pleasant. He appears to have done a certain amount of speculative building, and in 1817 was employed by the Corporation to lay out The Parade for building houses and warehouses [Swansea Corporation Hall Books]. In 1822 he designed a new SLAUGHTER HOUSE for which his engraved design is preserved and in 1825–6 he enlarged the WESLEYAN METHODIST CHAPEL in GOAT STREET [*Carmarthen Jnl.* 3 March 1826]. Outside Swansea he added a service wing to PENRICE CASTLE, GLAM., for Thomas Mansel Talbot and his widow, 1812–17 [R.C.A.M. *Glamorgan* iv (i), *The Greater Houses*, 1981, 295]. [Information from Mr. Thomas Lloyd, to whom all references are due.]

POWER, JOSEPH, was a builder and architect of Colyton in Devon. He designed WISCOMBE PARK, nr. SOUTH LEIGH, DEVON, for C. Gordon in an unsophisticated Gothic style in 1826 [J. R. W. Coxhead, *Honiton and the Vale of the Otter*, 1949, 74]. The I.C.B.S. records show that in 1820 he made an unexecuted design for enlarging SOUTH LEIGH CHURCH.

POWNING, JOHN (1763–1832), was an architect and builder of Exeter. His designs for STOWFORD RECTORY, DEVON, are among the Exeter Diocesan Records. A tablet in St. Mary the Great Church recorded his birth on 6 June 1763 and his death on 16 July 1832. Charles Fowler (1792–1867) was his pupil.

POWSEY, JOHN (*c.*1731–1800), was a builder and surveyor of Poplar. In 1770 he supervised alterations to the premises of John Steinmetz, gingerbread and biscuit-maker of Limehouse [contract in R.I.B.A. Library, MS. 728.3 (42.13)]. In 1774, at the age of 40, he was appointed District Surveyor for Wapping and Limehouse [Middlesex County Records, General Orders No. 10]. In 1789–90 he acted as engineer for the construction of BRUNSWICK DOCK at Blackwall for the famous shipwright John Perry [*ex inf.* Prof. A. W. Skempton]. In 1794 he made a plan for docks at Wapping [*East London Papers* x, 1967, 77]. His death on 10 May 1800, in his 70th year, is recorded in *Gent's Mag.* 1800 (i), 491.

PRATT, Sir ROGER (1620-1685), was descended from a family of country gentlemen who had their seat at Ryston, nr. Downham in Norfolk. His father, Gregory, was the younger brother of Francis Pratt, the owner of Ryston, and a lawyer by profession. Roger Pratt matriculated at Magdalen College, Oxford, on 12 May 1637, at the age of 19, and entered the Inner Temple in 1639. His father died in 1640, leaving him an income which enabled him in 1643 to set out on a six years' tour of France, Italy, Flanders and Holland, in order to avoid the Civil War and 'to give myself some convenient education'. In January 1645 he matriculated in the faculty of law at Padua, and about the same time he was 'cohabitant' with John Evelyn in Rome. It is evident from his notebooks that architecture was already a major interest, and although he resided in the Inner Temple for some time after his return to England in 1649, he seems to have had no desire to resume his legal studies. Within a year or two he had entered on the architectural career which was to give him congenial employment and eventually a knighthood. He had a fine collection of architectural books, and his notebooks display more than a merely amateur interest in architecture, with their eminently practical 'Rules for the Guidance of Architects' and 'Notes on the Building of Country Houses'. In these, the new rôle of the gentleman architect is made clear: the prospective builder is advised to 'get some ingenious gentleman who has seen much of that kind abroad and been somewhat versed in the best authors of Architecture: viz. Palladio, Scamozzi, Serlio etc. to do it for you, and to give you a design of it in paper.' In this capacity Pratt himself was to become one of the leaders of architectural taste in Restoration England. Although his output was limited (so far as is known) to four large houses, they were all of considerable importance in establishing the type of astylar 'double-pile' house (already adumbrated by Inigo Jones) that was to be the norm until the reign of Queen Anne. The one which he built in

Piccadilly for Lord Clarendon was, indeed, to be one of the most influential buildings in the history of English domestic architecture. Evelyn considered it 'the best contrived, the most usefull, gracefull and magnificent house in England', and, although demolished in 1683, only sixteen years after its completion, it was the model upon which gentlemen's seats all over the country were being erected in the reigns of Charles II and James II.

After the Restoration Pratt was, with Webb, May, Hooke, Evelyn and Wren, one of the few educated Englishmen with any serious interest in architecture. Together with May and Wren he was called in to advise the commissioners for the repair of St. Paul's Cathedral shortly before the Great Fire of 1666, and after the Fire he was one of the three commissioners appointed by the King to supervise the rebuilding of the City. His notebooks show how seriously he took his duties in this capacity, and in 1668 his services were rewarded by knighthood. In the same year he married Anne, daughter and coheiress of Sir Edmond Monins, Bart. of Waldershare in Kent, and set about rebuilding the house at Ryston which he had recently inherited under the will of his cousin, Edward Pratt (d. 1664). This appears to have been his last architectural work, and his later years were spent in leading the life of a country gentleman. But some notes, made probably in 1672, concerning a projected palace on the Thames for 'the Prince' – probably the Duke of York, who had married Lord Clarendon's eldest daughter, and had since 1664 been in possession of the site of the old royal palace of Richmond-on-Thames – show that he still maintained his architectural interests. Pratt died at Ryston on 20 February 1684/5, and was buried in the parish church which stands in the park. His portrait by Lely is preserved at Ryston, together with his library and the elaborate manuscript notebooks in which he set down his architectural experience. His intention was probably to publish a systematic architectural treatise. This was never completed, but in 1928 the notes were edited by R. T. Gunther as *The Architecture of Sir Roger Pratt*, which constitutes the principal source of information about Pratt's architectural career.

[R. T. Gunther, *The Architecture of Sir Roger Pratt*, 1928; *D.N.B.*; Francis Blomefield, *History of Norfolk* vii, 1807, 393; *Students admitted to the Inner Temple*, ed. Cooke, 1877, 302; *The Diary of John Evelyn*, ed. de Beer, 1959, 360, 493, 494, 541; *Wren Soc.* xiii, 4, 14–15, 18; J. W. Stoye, *English Travellers Abroad*, 1989, 143–4; Jane Lang, *Rebuilding St. Paul's*, 1956; John Summerson, *Architecture in Britain 1530–1830*, 1963, 85–88; N. Silcox-Crowe, 'Sir Roger Pratt' in *The Architectural Outsiders*, ed. R. Brown, 1985.]

COLESHILL HOUSE, BERKSHIRE, for Sir George Pratt, Bart., begun after 1649, completed 1662; repaired 1744–5 'by the Direction of the Earls of Burlington and Leicester' (as recorded by a brass plate), again repaired 1814–16 by D. A. Alexander; demolished after a fire in 1952.

The circumstances of the building of this house are confused. The will of Sir Henry Pratt, Sir George Pratt's father, dated 1645, nearly 4 years before his death in 1649, shows that he was then building a house at Coleshill, for he directed his executors to finish it. This may explain a story recorded by Sir Mark Pleydell (1692–1768), a later owner of Coleshill, to the effect that Sir George Pratt was persuaded by his distant 'cousin', (Sir) Roger Pratt, to abandon a house that had been begun on a different site ('in the cucumber garden'). According to this story, Pratt was supported by Inigo Jones, who 'was also consulted about the ceilings' (see above, p. 560). Though Jones's involvement in the design of the house is problematical, the possibility that the astylar format was suggested by him and worked out by Pratt with his help cannot be excluded. [H. A. Tipping in *C. Life*, 26 July, 2 Aug. 1919; R. T. Gunther, *The Architecture of Sir Roger Pratt*, 1928, 4, 5, 92–7; W. Grant Keith in *R.I.B.A. Jnl.* 22 July 1933, 732–3; M. Pinhorn, 'A Note on the date of construction of Coleshill, Berks.', *Blackmansbury* i (1), 1964, 5–7; John Harris, *Catalogue of the R.I.B.A. Drawings Collection: Inigo Jones and John Webb*, 1972, 23] (*Vitruvius Britannicus* v, 1771, pls. 86–7).

KINGSTON LACY, DORSET, for Sir Ralph Bankes, 1663–5; cased in stone and altered by Sir C. Barry 1835–41 [R. T. Gunther, *op. cit.*, 98–116; *Kingston Lacy, Dorset*, National Trust, 1990] (*C. Life*, 17, 24 April, 5, 12 June, 1986).

HORSEHEATH HALL, CAMBS., for William, Lord Alington, 1663–5; enlarged *c.*1700 by John Bromley and dem. 1792 [R. T. Gunther, *op. cit.*, 117–31; Miss C. Parsons in *Proceedings of the Cambridge Antiquarian Society* xli, 1941–7] (*Vitruvius Britannicus* iii, 1725, pls. 91–2).

CLARENDON HOUSE, PICCADILLY, for Edward Hyde, 1st Earl of Clarendon, 1664–7; dem. 1683 [R. T. Gunther, *op. cit.*, 9–11, 135–66]. For plan see *Burlington Mag.* cxxviii, Oct. 1986, fig. 24.

RYSTON HALL, NORFOLK, for himself, 1669–72; remodelled by Sir John Soane 1787–8 [R. T. Gunther, *op. cit.*, 167–93].

PRICE, FRANCIS (*c.*1704–1753), held the post of Surveyor or Clerk of the Works to Salisbury Cathedral from 1737 until his death. He made a general survey of the cathedral soon after his appointment, and carried out considerable repairs in the following years. In 1736–8 he also altered and repaired the BISHOP'S PALACE for Bishop Sherlock [drawings and estimates in Diocesan Records]. He appears to have designed the west end of ELLINGHAM CHURCH, HANTS., as rebuilt in brick in 1747, for in October he was paid one guinea by the churchwardens for his 'Estimate and advice' [churchwardens' accounts]. If so, it is possible that he was also the architect of HEMINGSBY HOUSE, No. 56 THE CLOSE, SALISBURY, as its design resembles the contemporary work at Ellingham. In 1753 he was consulted by Ivory Talbot concerning the alterations which the latter was about to make to LACOCK ABBEY, WILTS., but his suggestions for a Gothic front with bow windows were not adopted [*An Eighteenth-Century Corre-spondence*, ed. Dickins and Stanton, 1910, 304]. He appears to have been well thought of, for in William Hanbury's directions for the management of his projected collegiate foundation at Church Langton, Leics. (*c.*1760), he stated that the 'diligence of Mr. Price, of Salisbury, affords a laudable pattern for him (the Resident Surveyor) to copy after' [J. H. Hill, *History of Langton*, 1867, 137–9].

In 1733 Price published *The British Carpenter, or a Treatise on Carpentry*, dedicated to Algernon Seymour, Earl of Hertford, afterwards 7th Duke of Somerset, a work recommended by Nicholas Hawksmoor, John James and James Gibbs, as 'a very Usefull and Instructive Piece'. Later editions appeared in 1735, 1753, 1759, 1765 and 1768, and the book was long regarded as one of the best of its kind. It contains a description of a trammel for describing an ellipse, which, as 'Price's Trammel', was still in current use in builders' workshops in the nineteenth century. He was also the author of *A Series of particular and useful Observations . . . upon . . . the Cathedral Church of Salisbury*,, published in 1753. This is notable as the first serious attempt to describe and analyse the structure of a major Gothic building. It originated in a survey undertaken at the request of Bishop Sherlock, and formed the basis of many subsequent accounts of the cathedral. The anonymous *Description of . . . the Cathedral Church of Salisbury* published in 1774 was in effect a second edition, with additional material derived from Price's manuscripts.

Price died on 20 March 1753, in his 50th year, and was buried in the cloisters at Salisbury, where a monument was erected to his memory. His portrait by George Beare, dated 1747, is in the National Portrait Gallery. [*A.P.S.D.; D.N.B.; Gent's Mag.* 1789 (ii), 875; James Harris, *Copies of the Epitaphs in Salisbury Cathedral*, 1825, 127; *Builder* xxxi, 1873, 765; Peter Ferriday, 'Francis Price, Carpenter', *Arch. Rev.* Nov. 1953; Eileen Harris, *British Architectural Books and Writers 1556–1785*, 1990, 374–77.]

PRICE, JOHN (–1736), 'of London', was the architect and builder of the church of ST. MARY-AT-THE-WALLS, COLCHESTER, 1713–14. With the exception of the tower, the church was rebuilt by A. W. Blomfield in 1871–2 [G. O. Rickword, 'The Rebuilding of the Church of St. Mary-at-the-Walls, Colchester, 1713–14', *Essex Arch. Soc.'s Trans.* N.S. xxiii (2), 1945]. There can be no doubt that he was the same as the John Price 'of Richmond', who designed ISLEWORTH CHURCH, MIDDLESEX, 1705–7, gutted 1943 [Bodleian, MS. Rawlinson B. 389c, ff. 111–26; M. Robbins in *The London and Middlesex Historian* i, 1965, 4], and who, in conjunction with his son John Price, junior (also of Richmond), designed and built ST. GEORGE'S CHAPEL, YARMOUTH, in 1714–16. In 1715 Messrs. Price and Son also contracted to build a new TOWN HALL and ASSEMBLY ROOM at YARMOUTH, 'according to a draft and plans delivered . . . by the said Messrs. Price' [J. Preston, *Picture of Yarmouth*, 1819, 23–4, 191–2]. The latter building was enlarged in 1772 and 1842 and demolished in 1882 (A. W. Yallop, *Ancient Yarmouth*, 1905, pl. 80). John Price subsequently designed the church of ST. GEORGE, SOUTHWARK, whose foundation stone was laid on 23 April 1734, by the deputy of King George II, *adjuvante Johanne Price armiger, architecto*. It was completed in 1736, and refitted internally in 1808. The present ceiling, designed by Basil Champneys in 1897, replaces one of 1808. [Manning & Bray, *History of Surrey* iii, 1814, 637; *Survey of London* xxv, chap. 4].

The evidence set out above establishes Price as a designer of early Georgian churches in a pleasant but rather unsophisticated vernacular style derived from Wren. In 1720 he was responsible for a remarkable project for residential development at HEADLEY in SURREY, not far from Epsom, then a fashionable watering place. This is known from an engraving (found separately, and as plates 96–7 of Badeslade and Rocque's *Vitruvius*

Brittanicus iv of 1739) inscribed 'the Elevation or West Prospect of Part of a Design of Building already began to be Erected on the Lawne at Headly in Surrey/Design'd by John Price, Architect, 1720'. It shows a grand central building with portico and mansard roofs (presumably some sort of Assembly Rooms) flanked by two identical ranges each of nine houses treated as a uniform composition. Though poorly composed, this design is remarkable as 'the earliest English essay in urban terrace composition' since Inigo Jones's Covent Garden, anticipating Colen Campbell's designs for Grosvenor Square by five years (C. Hussey in *C. Life*, 6 June 1968, 1539). It was never completed, but Manning and Bray record that some traces of Price's unfinished buildings were still to be seen at Headley in the early nineteenth century (*History of Surrey* ii, 1814, 637, and cf. the printed 'Proposals for Building in the Parishes of Headly and Walton on the Hill in the County of Surrey' in Bodleian, MS. North b. 1, f. 15). Price had already had some experience of speculative building in London, having in 1718 taken several leases on the Harley estate in Holles, Oxford, Margaret and Prince's Streets [B.L., Add. MS. 18240, f. 7].

The elder Price was the fourth architect employed by the Duke of Chandos at CANNONS HOUSE, MIDDLESEX, in 1720–1. By this time the structure was largely complete, and Price's contribution, so far as original designs were concerned, was probably small. However, the elevations of Cannons published by Hulsbergh at this time are inscribed 'John Price Architect, Built Anno 1720', although what they show was largely the work of his predecessors in the Duke's service. The engraved elevation of the Duke's projected mansion in Cavendish Square is similarly described as 'Design'd by John Price, architect 1720'. Its design obviously owed much to Cannons. It was never built, and by 1723 Price's place as the Duke's surveyor had been taken by Edward Shepherd [C. H. & M. I. Collins Baker, *James Brydges, Duke of Chandos*, 1949, *passim*].

In 1726–8 Price was among those who made designs for a bridge to be built across the Thames between Fulham and Putney. He published *Some considerations humbly offer'd to the Commissioners . . . for building a Bridge over the Thames from Fulham to Putney,* and *Mr. Price's Second Letter to one of the Commissioners for Building a Bridge over the Thames from Fulham to Putney, together with some Proposals for building a Wooden Bridge.* Neither design was, however, accepted by the Commissioners [G.L. Record Office, Commissioners' Minutes]. In 1735 Price took part in the Westminster Bridge controversy by publishing *Some Considerations humbly offered to the House of Commons, for building a Stone-Bridge over the River Thames from Westminster to Lambeth,* with an engraved design. This was criticized by John James in his *Short Review of the Several Pamphlets and Schemes . . . in relation to Building a Bridge at Westminster*, 1736.

John Price the elder died in November 1736 [*Historical Register*, 1736, 60], where he is described as 'Architect of St. George's Church in Southwark'.[1] It is doubtful whether he is to be identified with the 'Mr. Price of Wandsworth' whose design for a stable at King's Weston, nr. Bristol, dated 1720, is among drawings connected with that house reproduced in *Architectural History* x, 1967 (fig. 24) and who as John Price of Wandsworth Hill, 'architect', subscribed in 1735 to Eleazar Albin's *Natural History of English Insects*, or with the 'Mr. Price of York Buildings, Surveyor and Architect', to whose designs the tower of LALEHAM CHURCH, MIDDLESEX, was rebuilt in 1730–1 [Vestry Minutes]. In both cases there is a Vanbrughian character about the designs which does not altogether accord with John Price's recorded works. In the John Johnson Collection in the Bodleian Library there is a MS. prospectus by John Price of Wandsworth announcing his intention to publish a book entitled *Vignola Revived, being a Translation of Daviller's Architecture,* a proposal endorsed by Wren, Vanbrugh and Talman as 'highly usefull and deserving encouragement'.

Not much is known of the career of John Price, junior. In 1737 he was one of the several surveyors who reported on the state of the City church of St. Katherine Coleman before its rebuilding [churchwardens' accounts in Guildhall Library], and it is possible that he was the same as 'John Price of Hounsditch' who submitted estimates for enlarging the church of St. John Hackney in 1756 [R. Simpson, *Memorials of St. John at Hackney*, 1881, 156–7]. He was a Warden of the Carpenters' Company in 1751–2, and was elected Master in 1753. He acted as Surveyor to the Fishmongers' Company, and his drawings, signed and dated 1 December 1760, for rebuilding two houses on Aldgate Hill belonging to the Company, are in the Guildhall Print Collection (10/ALD). His death on 17 October 1765 is recorded in the Company's records [Guildhall Library, MS. 5573/3, p. 344].

[1] Reference to the parish registers of Richmond and Wandsworth shows that he was buried in neither place.

PRICE, JOHN (1795–1859), was the son of a joiner at Derby and was himself a carpenter, joiner, builder, and ultimately architect. He exhibited architectural designs at the Derby Mechanics' Institute in 1839. One of these was for a house at LEA GREEN, nr. DETHICK, for Joseph Wass, built in Jacobethan style in that year. HADDON HOUSE, nr. BAKEWELL, built in 1840 for the Duke of Rutland's Agent, and CHURCHDALE HALL, nr. ASHFORD-IN-THE-WATER, built in 1842 for Sydney Smithers, the Duke of Devonshire's Agent, resemble Lea Green and may also have been Price's work. In Derby Price was probably the builder of WILMOT STREET. He eventually moved to Littleover, where he died on 20 May 1859 [information from Mr. Maxwell Craven].

PRICE, WILLIAM, was an architect and builder of Gloucester. In 1785–6 he built the new MARKETS (dem.) in EASTGATE and SOUTHGATE STREETS, in accordance with plans and estimates made by himself and altered by Anthony Keck, who was employed by the Corporation to inspect them, and to act as surveyor during their execution; and in 1788–9 he built the Gothic almshouses known as ST. BARTHOLOMEW'S HOSPITAL, in accordance with his own designs, and without the supervision of a surveyor. [Extract from Gloucester Corporation Records by C. H. Dancey in Gloucester Public Library, Ref. 17270.]

PRICE, WILLIAM LAKE (*c.*1809–1896), described as 'Architect and Painter', exhibited at the Royal Academy between 1828 and 1841, and at the Society of British Artists in 1830. His exhibits included designs for a mausoleum (1828), a palace and gardens (1829), 'the square of a city with a triumphal bridge and arch' (1830), views of buildings in Rouen (1831–2), and a 'design for a marine residence for a nobleman, suggested by the Palace of the King of Naples' (1841). He died at Lee in Kent on 9 December 1896, aged 87 [Principal Probate Registry, Calendar of Probates].

PRIDDEN, Revd. JOHN (1758–1825), was a clergyman of antiquarian tastes who also had 'a considerable knowledge and natural taste for architecture and civil engineering'. He was one of the founders of the Sea-Bathing Infirmary at Margate, Kent, whose buildings were erected to his designs in 1796 (see engravings in *Gent's Mag.* lxvii (ii), 841 and lxxxvi (i), 17). He shortly afterwards became vicar of Caddington in Beds., where in 1812 he rebuilt the vicarage (dem. 1970), acting as his own architect and surveyor. He made an elaborate design for uniting the summits of Snow Hill and Holborn Hill by means of a bridge, 'under which the road from Black Friars to the great North road might conveniently have been carried', for which he received the thanks of the Corporation of London. The project was considered too expensive at the time, but eventually found realization in the modern Holborn Viaduct. For a full account of Pridden's many-sided career, see *Gent's Mag.* 1825 (i), 467–8; Nichols, *Literary Illustrations* viii, 676–7; and *D.N.B.* His MS. journal of a tour in Wales in 1780, with sketches, is in the National Library of Wales (MS. 15172 D), and two volumes of 'Topographical Collections' by him (1783–97) are in the Essex Record Office.

PRINCE, JOHN, acted as agent and surveyor to Edward Harley in connection with the laying out of the Harley estate in Marylebone. He was responsible for the planning of the new streets, including Cavendish Square, and a plan signed by him was engraved in 1719,[1] although alterations were subsequently made in execution. There are several references to him in an inventory of Harley estate documents in the British Library (Add. MS. 18240, ff. 30–6), including 'Draughts for rebuilding Marybone Church and an Estimate of the Charge thereof by John Prince', 'A Plan of the Building Ground set out in Marybone Fields on Vellum by Mr. John Prince, 1720', and 'A Plan of Coll° Guise's House by Mr. J. Prince, 1723'.

Prince appears to have been a bricklayer by trade, and was himself one of the principal speculators who built on the estate. He appears to have given his name to Prince's Street, and was in the habit of calling himself the 'Prince of Surveyors'–a boast which brought on him a violent attack in the *Weekly Medley* for September 1719 [T. Smith, *St. Marylebone*, 1833, 157].

It was presumably the same John Prince who designed COUND HALL, SALOP., for Edward Cressett in 1703–4. An elevation for this house, signed 'John Prince Inv^{t}. et Delineavit', was seen by Tipping in 1918 and is reproduced in his *English Homes, Period IV*, i, 1929, 420.[2] The house is remarkable for the

[1] It is entitled 'A Design of Buildings already begun to be built in the Parish of St. Mary la Bonne Belonging to the Rt. Honble Edward Ld. Harley and ye Rt. Honble Lady Henrietta Cavendish Holles Harley, AD. 1719', 'Design'd and Delineated by John Prince' and is reproduced by Baker, *James Brydges, Duke of Chandos*, 1949, 272.

[2] On p. 418 Tipping quotes the words 'Prince, architect, Salop' as if they were inscribed on the drawing, which is not the case. The inscription is clearly legible on a print kindly provided by *Country*

ambitious but inept use of a giant Corinthian order applied to the main elevations in a manner perhaps suggested by the King William block at Greenwich Hospital.

There is evidence that Prince also designed BUNTINGSDALE HALL, SALOP., for Bulkeley Mackworth, *c.*1719–21. References in the surviving fragments of the building accounts to workmen's wages to be paid 'as Mr. Prince shall appoint', and to 'Mr. John Prince at his house in Henrietta Street, Covent Garden' (? a mistake for Henrietta Street, Cavendish Square) permit the conclusion that it was he rather than Francis Smith who designed this idiosyncratic house, which differs in several respects from the norm of Smith's architectural work [Shropshire C.R.O., 3887/Box 39][1] (Tipping, *English Homes, Period V*, i, 1921, 193–8).

The name of 'Mr. John Prince' appears among the subscribers to James Gibbs's *Book of Architecture*, published in 1728.

PRITCHARD, EDWARD (*c.*1783–1863), of Tarrington in Herefordshire, designed the north aisle that was added to TARRINGTON CHURCH in 1835 in a late Gothic style [I.C.B.S.]. As 'Edward Pritchard, surveyor', he was concerned in repairs to WESTON BEGGARD CHURCH, HEREFS., in 1826 [I.C.B.S.]. A monument in Tarrington churchyard praises his 'integrity and uprightness' and records that he died on 23 March 1863, aged 83, having been for 'upwards of sixty years Head Builder for the Foley family Stoke Edith'.

PRITCHARD, THOMAS FARNOLLS (1723–1777), was baptized at St. Julian's Church, Shrewsbury, on 11 May 1723. Like his father he was a joiner by trade, but developed a considerable practice as an architect in Shropshire and the neighbouring counties. An album of drawings by Pritchard in the library of the American Institute of Architects at Washington shows that he was a competent designer of decorative features in the rococo style and that he also made Gothic designs in the manner of Batty Langley.

Pritchard's houses and churches are no more than good examples of mid-Georgian provincial architecture, but in the history of bridge-building he has a place of national importance. In 1767 he made a design for rebuilding the English Bridge at Shrewsbury that was not accepted, but ten years later he was the key figure in the building of the cast-iron bridge over the R. Severn in Coalbrookdale – the first of its kind in the world. In 1773 he had made designs for a timber bridge with stone abutments to span the same river at Stourport, and the contract to build such a bridge under his direction was advertised in *Berrow's Worcester Journal* on 15 December 1773. But being dissatisfied with this method of construction he designed a single-arch brick bridge on an iron centre, with circular perforations in the haunches of the arch to allow for the passage of flood-water. The bridge actually built in 1775 (and destroyed by a flood in 1794) was of three stone arches, but Pritchard continued to explore the possibility of employing iron in the construction of bridges, and in 1775 he made the designs for a bridge of completely iron construction which (with some modifications) were executed by Abraham Darby in Coalbrookdale in 1777–9. Pritchard's designs both for this bridge and for the one at Stourport are described and illustrated in a note by his grandson John White published in *The Philosophical Magazine and Annals of Philosophy* N.S. xi, 1832, 81–2, and also printed separately in White's booklet *On Cementitious Architecture as applicable to the Construction of Bridges, with a prefatory notice of the first introduction of iron as the constituent material for arches of large span, by Thomas Farnolls Pritchard in 1773*, 1832.

Pritchard did not live to see his iron bridge constructed, dying on 23 December 1777. Since about 1770 he had been living at Eyton-on-Severn, in a Jacobean garden-building converted into a house known as 'Eyton Turret'. He was buried at St. Julian's Church, Shrewsbury, where there is a tablet to his memory. His wife Eleanor had died in 1768. Three of their children died young, but their surviving daughter became the wife of John White (*q.v.*), whose son published the account of Pritchard's bridge-building activities already referred to. Portraits of Pritchard and his wife are in the Ironbridge Gorge Museum. Drawings by Pritchard for a house for a Mr. Good (unidentified) are in the R.I.B.A. collection.

[*A.P.S.D.*; J. L. Hobbs, 'Thomas Farnolls Pritchard', *Shropshire Magazine*, Aug.–Sept. 1959; John Harris, 'Pritchard Redivivus', *Architectural History* xi, 1968; Robin Chaplin, 'New Light on T. F. Pritchard', *Shropshire News Letter*, No. 34, 1968; John Harris, *Catalogue of British Drawings for Architecture etc. in American Collections*, 1971, 162–8; Rupert Gunnis, *Dictionary of British Sculptors*, 1968, 311; A. W. Ward, *The Bridges of Shrewsbury*,

Life, and reads 'John Prince Inv[t]. et Delineavit', without any reference to 'Salop.'

[1] I am grateful to Prof. Andor Gomme for drawing my attention to this document.

Shrewsbury, 1935, 40–1; information from Mr. J. B. Lawson.]

HILL COURT, ROSS-ON-WYE, HEREFS., unexecuted design for addition of wings, etc., which indicates that Pritchard was probably responsible for the enlargement carried out for the Clarke family, *c.*1745–50 [J. Harris in *Arch. Hist.* xi, 1968, 19] (*C. Life*, 27 Jan., 3 Feb. 1966).

SHREWSBURY, three shops in CARRIERS INN (now SHOPLATCH) for the Shrewsbury Drapers' Company, 1749; dem. [Salop. Record Office, estimate and contract in records of Shrewsbury Drapers' Co.].

SHREWSBURY, ST. JULIAN'S CHURCH, rebuilt, incorporating medieval tower, 1749–50 [D. H. S. Cranage, *The Churches of Shropshire*, 1894–1912, ii, 921].

WOLVERHAMPTON, STAFFS., ST. JOHN'S CHURCH, 1756–8; refitted 1881–2, exterior refaced 1964–83 [H. Owen, *Account of the Ancient and Present State of Shrewsbury*, 1808, 300].

LUDLOW, HOSYER'S ALMSHOUSES, 1758–9 [*V.C.H. Salop.* ii, 109].

SHREWSBURY, CANN OFFICE (now Kingsland Bank) for the Shrewsbury Drapers' Co., 1759 [Salop. Record Office, accounts of Drapers' Co.].

TERN HALL, ATTINGHAM, SALOP., remodelled for Thomas Hill, 1759–61; replaced by Attingham Hall 1783–5 [B. Coulton, 'Tern Hall', *Shropshire History & Archaeology* 66, 1989] (*C. Life*, 5 Feb. 1921, p. 162, fig. 6).

TATTON PARK, CHESHIRE, dining-room for Samuel Egerton, *c.*1760 [P. de Figueiredo & J. Treuherz, *Cheshire Country Houses*, 1988, 167].

SHREWSBURY, THE FOUNDLING HOSPITAL (now Shrewsbury School), 1760–5; remodelled by Sir Arthur Blomfield 1878–82 [*ex inf.* Mr. J. B. Lawson, Librarian of Shrewsbury School].

LUDFORD HOUSE, nr. LUDLOW, SALOP., remodelled E. front for Sir Francis Charlton, Bart., 1761 [estimate and specification in Salop. Record Office, 783/box 25].

SHREWSBURY, SWAN HILL COURT HOUSE for the trustee (the Earl of Bath) of John Newport, 1761–2 [P.R.O., C110/6 and C110/4].

WOLVERHAMPTON, STAFFS., enlarged and largely rebuilt the RED LION INN for the trustee of John Newport, 1764–5; dem. [P.R.O., C110/6; designs for picture-frame and chimney-piece in Pritchard album].

LUDLOW, SALOP., perhaps designed or supervised building of GAOLFORD TOWER 1764–5 (dem.), as he was paid 2 gns. by the Bailiff of Ludlow in 1765 [Bailiff's account in Salop. Record Office, 441/1].

WOLVERHAMPTON, STAFFS., THE DEANERY, additions and repairs for the trustee of John Newport, 1764–5; dem. [P.R.O., C110/6].

HATTON GRANGE, SALOP., for Plowden Slaney, 1764–8 [John Cornforth in *C. Life*, 29 Feb. 1968].

LUDLOW CASTLE, SALOP., survey plan and elevation for 1st Earl of Powis, 1765 [Salop. Record Office, 552/8/1000–1007].

CROFT CASTLE, HEREFS., internal decorations, including Gothic staircase, for Thomas Johnes, 1765 [J. Harris in *Arch. Hist.* xi, 1968, 21; National Trust guidebook] (*C. Life*, 5 May 1960, 31 Dec. 1987).

GAINES, WHITBOURNE, HEREFS., internal alterations, including a Gothic saloon, for John Freeman, probably *c.*1765 [J. Harris in *Arch. Hist.* xi, 1968, 21].

attributed: BROCKHAMPTON HALL, nr. BROMYARD, HEREFS., for Bartholomew Barneby, *c.*1765 [John Cornforth, letter in *C. Life*, 4 April 1968, 815; Michael Hall in *C. Life*, 4 Jan. 1990].

SHREWSBURY, Nos. 10–11 HIGH STREET, for John Ashby, 1766 [designs for chimneypieces in Pritchard album; cf. Salop. Record Office, 3460/5/1].

EYTON TURRET, EYTON-ON-SEVERN, SALOP., conversion of one of two Jacobean turrets in the garden of the demolished seat of the Newport Earls of Bradford into a dwelling-house for his own occupation, 1767–9 [P.R.O., C 110/6] (Mrs. S. Acton, *The Castles and Old Mansions of Shropshire*, 1868, 45).

WYNNSTAY, DENBIGHSHIRE, work for Sir Watkin Williams-Wynn, Bart., 1768–73, probably including 'Great Room'; dem. [N. L. W., Wynnstay Estate Rentals 1768–73, *ex inf.* Mr. J. B. Lawson; lost drawing by Pritchard listed *ibid.*, 115/28; P. Howell & T. W. Pritchard in *C. Life*, 23 March 1972, 689].

RUABON CHURCH, DENBIGHSHIRE, repairs and alterations to chancel for Sir Watkin Williams-Wynn, Bart., 1769–70 [P. Howell & T. W. Pritchard in *C. Life*, 23 March 1972, 688].

BITTERLEY COURT, SHROPSHIRE, alterations, probably including south front, for Charles Walcot, 1769 [J. Harris in *Arch. Hist.* xi, 1968, 20].

SHREWSBURY, THE ABBEY, internal alterations, probably including the drawing room, for Henry Powys, *c.*1769; dem. [J. Harris in *Arch. Hist.* xi, 1968, 23].

DOWNTON CASTLE, HEREFS., made designs and assisted Payne Knight in initial stages of building, 1772 [Alistair Rowan, 'Downton Castle' in *The Country Seat*, ed. Colvin & Harris, 1970].

KINNERLEY CHURCH, SHROPSHIRE, rebuilt 1773–4, perhaps in accordance with a plan made by Pritchard in 1768–9 [D. H. S. Cranage, *The Churches of Shropshire*, 1894–1912, ii, 794–5].

LUDLOW, SALOP., THE GUILDHALL, MILL STREET, rebuilt exterior 1774–6, with Gothic doorway [Salop. Record Office, 356/box 461, No. 9676 and vouchers in box 462, nos. 1774, 1776].

SUDBOROUGH MANOR, NORTHANTS., proposed repairs and additions for the trustee of John Newport, 1775–6; dem. [plan, estimate etc. in P.R.O., C 110/6].

POWIS CASTLE, MONTGOMERYSHIRE, works including conversion of Long Gallery into Ballroom, for 2nd Earl of Powis, 1775–7 [J. Lawson & M. Waterson, 'Pritchard as Architect and Antiquary at Powis', *National Trust Year Book 1975–6*].

KYRE PARK, WORCS., proposed alterations for Jonathan Pytts, rejected as too ambitious, 1776 [H. A. Tipping in *C. Life*, 24 March 1917, citing report now in Worcestershire C.R.O., BA 4707/4].

SHIPTON HALL, SHROPSHIRE, redecoration of hall etc., for Henry or Thomas Mytton [design for chimney-piece in Pritchard album: see Harris, 23] (*C. Life*, 19 March 1910).

attributed: COTON HALL, SALOP., the Gothic chapel for Lancelot Lee [a design for a frame for Lancelot Lee in the Pritchard album connects Pritchard with this house].

THE IRON BRIDGE, COALBROOKDALE, SALOP., 1777–9 [J. White, *On Cementitious Architecture*, etc., 1832; R. Maguire & P. Matthews, 'The Iron-bridge at Coalbrookdale', *Architectural Assoc. Jnl.* July–Aug. 1958, 31–45].

MONUMENTS AND CHIMNEY-PIECES

The following monuments designed by Pritchard are recorded: ACTON ROUND, SALOP., Gothic monument to Sir Whitmore Acton (d. 1732), erected 1763 [signed]; ALBERBURY SALOP., Richard Lyster (d. 1766) [Harris, 20]; LUDFORD, SALOP., Dr. Samuel Sprott, 1759 [signed]; MAMBLE, WORCS., Sir Edward Blount, Bart. (d. 1765) [Harris, 22]; MORETON CORBET, SALOP., Richard Corbet (d. 1770) [Gunnis]; PONTESBURY, SALOP., R. W. Offley, 1769 [Harris, 22]; SHREWSBURY, ST. MARY'S CHURCH, Revd. John Lloyd (d. 1758) and Mary Morhall (d. 1765) [Gunnis]; SHREWSBURY, OLD ST. CHAD'S, Richard Hollings [signed]; WREXHAM, DENBIGHSHIRE, Ann Wilkinson (d. 1756) [signed].

Designs by Pritchard exist for chimney-pieces, etc., in the following houses: BROSELEY, SALOP., THE LAWNS; CONDOVER HALL, SALOP.; HIGH HATTON, SALOP.; KINSHAM COURT, HEREFS.; LONGNER HALL, SALOP.; LOTON PARK, SALOP.; LUDLOW, No. 27 BROAD STREET; PENDLEFORD HALL, STAFFS.; SHAWBURY PARK, SALOP.; several houses in SHREWSBURY [Harris, 20–4].

PRITCHETT, JAMES PIGOTT (1789–1868), born at St. Petrox, Pembrokeshire, on 14 October 1789, was the fourth son of Charles Pigott Pritchett, rector of St. Petrox and Stackpole Elidyr, prebendary of St. David's and private chaplain to Lord Cawdor of Stackpole Court. He was articled to James Medland of Southwark (*q.v.*) and afterwards spent two years in the office of D. A. Alexander (*q.v.*). He became a student at the Royal Academy in 1808, and exhibited there in 1808 and 1809. After a short period in the Barrack Office, he began practice in London in 1812 but soon afterwards removed to York, where from January 1813 he was in partnership with Charles Watson (*q.v.*). The partnership was dissolved on 1 January 1831, when Pritchett opened his own office at 13 Lendal. He had an extensive practice in Yorkshire, especially as an ecclesiastical architect, and was for over fifty years architect and surveyor to Earl Fitzwilliam at Wentworth Woodhouse, where he was responsible for various buildings on the estate.[1] Pritchett was a prominent Congregationalist, and took part in many philanthropic and religious activities at York. He died there on 23 May 1868.

Pritchett married twice. By his first wife, Peggy Terry, he had three sons and one daughter. The eldest son became a Congregational minister, the second, Charles Pigott Pritchett (1818–91), an architect. The daughter married her father's pupil, the architect John Middleton (1846–96), who later practised in Cheltenham. By his second wife, Caroline Benson, Pritchett had three sons and two daughters. The eldest son, James Pigott Pritchett, junior (1830–1911), worked in his father's office before setting up practice in Darlington in 1854. Another architect member of the family, George Edward Pritchett (1824-1912), was the son of James's elder brother the Revd. C. R. Pritchett. He practised in London. Pritchett's pupils were Walter Blackett, S. W. Daukes, James Medland of Gloucester, John Middleton and J. C. Gilbert of Nottingham.

Pritchett was a competent but never a brilliant designer. His favourite style was Perpendicular or Tudor Gothic. His earlier churches were preaching houses scarcely distinguishable from his nonconformist chapels (at

[1] His unexecuted designs for a library at the Fitzwilliams' Northamptonshire seat at Milton, nr. Peterborough, are in the Northamptonshire Record Office. The most ambitious scheme is dated 1837 and 1854.

Norton in 1816 he and Watson even used the Scottish T-shaped plan for an Anglican church), and it was only in his later works that he made some attempt to conform to Camdenian ideas. His classical buildings included the dignified portico of the York Assembly Rooms, the elegant Greek Revival cemetery chapel, the handsome railway station at Huddersfield, and the Soaneic façade of the Savings Bank in St. Helen's Square, York. In such matters as heating and ventilation his buildings were among the best equipped of their day.

[*A.P.S.D.; D.N.B.; Builder* xvi, 1868, 406; G. H. Broadbent, 'The Life and Work of Pritchett of York', in *Studies in Architectural History*, ed. Singleton ii, 1956; W. Ellerby & J. P. Pritchett, *A History of the Nonconformist Churches of York*, ed. E. Royle, York 1993.]

CHURCHES, CHAPELS AND PUBLIC BUILDINGS

*YORK, LENDAL INDEPENDENT CHAPEL, 1816; now a shop [*A.P.S.D.*].

*NORTON CHURCH, YORKS. (E.R.), rebuilt 1816; dem. 1899; classical (T-shaped plan) [Borthwick Institute, York, Fac. 1814/2].

*WAKEFIELD, THE WEST RIDING LUNATIC ASYLUM, 1816–18 [*Plans etc. of the Pauper Lunatic Asylum lately erected at Wakefield*, York, 1819].

*YORK, THE FRIENDS' MEETING HOUSE, CLIFFORD STREET, 1816–19 [plans, etc., in W. Alexander, *Observations on the Construction of Meeting Houses*, York, 1820].

*BISHOP BURTON CHURCH, YORKS. (E.R.), rebuilt nave 1820; altered 1864–5 [Borthwick Institute, York, Fac. 1820/2 and churchwardens' accounts in E. Yorks. Record Office, *ex inf.* Dr. David Neave].

*WAKEFIELD, YORKS. (W.R.), library and newsroom (later Mechanics' Institution, now Museum), 1820–1 [Yorkshire Archaeological Society's Library, MS. 1142, *ex inf.* Dr. D. Linstrum].

*HUDDERSFIELD, YORKS. (W.R.), THE RAMSDEN STREET NONCONFORMIST CHAPEL, 1824; dem. 1936 [Broadbent, 110, citing Sykes, *History of the Ramsden St. Chapel*].

*GREASBROUGH CHURCH, YORKS. (W.R.), rebuilt 1826–8, Gothic [Port, 166–7].

*SHEFFIELD, NETHER CHAPEL (INDEPENDENT), 1827; altered 1878; dem. 1970 [R. E. Leader, *Surveyors and Architects of the Past in Sheffield*, 1903].

*YORK, ASSEMBLY ROOMS, new façade and portico, 1828 [*A.P.S.D.*].

*YORK, THE SAVINGS BANK, ST. HELEN'S SQUARE, 1829–30 [W. Camidge, *History of the York Savings Bank*, 1886, 49–51].

*NETHER HOYLAND CHURCH, YORKS. (W.R.), 1830, Gothic [Port, 168–9].

*YORK, ST. PETER'S SCHOOL (now Choir School), MINSTER YARD, 1829, Tudor Gothic [R.C.H.M. *York* v, 104].

BRAFFERTON CHURCH, YORKS. (N.R.), rebuilt nave 1831, Gothic [I.C.B.S.].

OAKAMOOR CHURCH, STAFFS., 1832, Gothic [I.C.B.S.].

HUDDERSFIELD, YORKS, (W.R.), ST. PETER'S CHURCH, rebuilt 1834–6, Gothic [I.C.B.S.; Borthwick Institute, York, Fac. 1834/1].

YORK, CEMETERY CHAPEL, 1836–7, Greek Revival [Broadbent, 114].

MELTHAM CHURCH, YORKS. (W.R.), west tower and north aisle, 1835, classical to match existing church of 1787 [I.C.B.S.].

BREARTON CHURCH, YORKS. (W.R.), 1836, Gothic [I.C.B.S.].

BRADFORD, YORKS. (W.R.), COLLEGE CHAPEL, HIGH STREET, 1837–9; partly dem. [*Bradford Observer, ex inf.* Mr. David Griffiths].

CHEADLE CHURCH, STAFFS., 1837–9, Gothic [I.C.B.S.].

BROTHERTON, YORKS. (W.R.), INDEPENDENT CHAPEL, 1838, Gothic [*Evangelical Mag.* 1839, 79].

WORSBOROUGH CHURCH, YORKS. (W.R.), remodelled aisles, 1838, Gothic [I.C.B.S.].

MELTHAM MILLS CHURCH, YORKS. (W.R.), 1838, Gothic, rebuilt by Pritchett on a larger scale 1845–6 [*Civil Engineer and Architect's Jnl.* ii, 1839, 28; *Gent's Mag.* 1846 (i), 84].

TINSLEY CHURCH, YORKS. (W.R.), enlarged 1838 [I.C.B.S.].

YORK, SALEM CHAPEL, ST. SAVIOURGATE, 1838–9; dem. 1964 [*A.P.S.D.*] (R.C.H.M. *York* v, 54–5).

RAWMARSH CHURCH, YORKS. (W.R.), 1839, Gothic; tower added 1855, chancel 1898 [I.C.B.S.].

HUDDERSFIELD, YORKS. (W.R.), HUDDERSFIELD COLLEGE, NEW NORTH ROAD, 1839–40, Gothic [*Bradford Observer*, 4 April 1839, *ex inf.* Mr. David Griffiths].

BURLEY-IN-WHARFEDALE, YORKS. (W.R.), INDEPENDENT CHAPEL, 1839–40, Gothic [*Bradford Observer*, 17 Oct. 1839, *ex inf.* Mr. David Griffiths].

BRADFORD, YORKS. (W.R.), WESTGATE CHAPEL, remodelled 1840 [*Bradford Observer*, 6 Feb. 1840, *ex inf.* Mr. David Griffiths].

YORK, LADY HEWLEY'S HOSPITAL, ST. SAVIOURGATE, 1840, Gothic [*A.P.S.D.*].

GATE HELMSLEY, YORKS. (N.R.), THE RETREAT (a private Mental Asylum), enlarged and altered for James Martin, *c.*1840 [advt. at end of Pigot's *National and Commercial Directory of York, Leicester, Rutland etc.*, 1841].

BROTHERTON CHURCH, YORKS. (W.R.), rebuilt

*Designed in partnership with Charles Watson.

1842–3, Gothic [I.C.B.S.].

ACKWORTH, YORKS, (W.R.), THE FRIENDS' MEETING HOUSE, 1846 [Leeds Archives, Nettleton papers, *ex inf.* Dr. D. Linstrum].

ACKWORTH, YORKS. (W.R.), THE FLOUNDERS INSTITUTE, 1847–8 [*ibid.*].

HUDDERSFIELD, YORKS. (W.R.), THE RAILWAY STATION, 1846–7 [C. Barman, *An Introduction to Railway Architecture*, 1950, 100].

YORK, THE EBENEZER CHAPEL, LITTLE STONEGATE (now printing works), 1851 [*V.C.H. York*, 414].

HUDDERSFIELD, THE LION ARCADE, 1852–4 [*Huddersfield Chronicle*, 14 Jan. 1854, cited by Broadbent, 123–4].

BRAMPTON BIERLOW CHURCH, YORKS. (W.R.), 1854–5, Gothic [Port, 166–7].

LEEDS, SHEEPSCAR WESLEYAN CHAPEL, 1861; dem. [D. Linstrum, *West Yorkshire Architects & Architecture*, 1978, 383].

DOMESTIC ARCHITECTURE

*BURGHWALLIS RECTORY, YORKS. (W.R.), rebuilt 1815 [Borthwick Institute, York, MGA 1815/2].

**attributed*: RISE PARK, YORKS. (E.R.), for Richard Bethell, 1815–20 [design for Doric lodge at Rise in album formerly at Stoneleigh Park, Warwicks., signed 'Watson & Pritchett 1818'].

*BRAFFERTON VICARAGE, YORKS. (N.R.), enlarged 1818 [Borthwick Institute, Yorks, MGA 1818/3].

*SLEDMERE HOUSE, YORKS. (E.R.), gates to main road for Sir Mark Sykes, Bart., 1818 [drawings at Sledmere].

*COPGROVE HALL, YORKS. (W.R.), remodelled for Thomas Duncombe, *c.*1820 [Doncaster Archives, DZ Ros. p. 87, *ex inf.* Mr. Angus Taylor].

LEEDS, HANOVER SQUARE layout, 1823–4 [D. Linstrum, *West Yorkshire Architects & Architecture*, 1978, 105].

*SALTMARSHE HALL, YORKS. (E.R.), for Philip Saltmarshe, 1825–8, stables 1842 [drawings in the possession of Mr. J. E. Scott of Huyton, 1971].

*YORK, THE DEANERY, 1827–31, Gothic; dem. 1938 [drawings in Minster Library signed 'Watson, Pritchett & Watson'].

*LOTHERTON HALL, YORKS. (W.R.), probably designed interior of drawing-room for R. O. Gascoigne, *c.*1828 [Angus Taylor in *Leeds Arts Calendar*, No. 77, 1975, 28].[1]

*NOSTELL PRIORY, YORKS. (W.R.), N. and E. sides of stable block for C. W. Winn, 1828–9, adopting Robert Adam's design of 1776 for the cupola [drawings at Nostell].

attributed: WHITWELL HALL, WHITWELL-ON-THE-HILL, YORKS. (N.R.), for Joseph Haigh, *c.*1833, Gothic [closely resembles the Deanery, York, in plan, elevation and detailing].

YORK, Nos. 8–9 MINSTER YARD and 48–50 LOW PETERGATE, 1837–8, Gothic [*R.C.H.M. York* v, 165, 187].

YORK, Nos. 24–36 HIGH PETERGATE, 1838 [R.C.H.M. *York* v, 181].

BOSSALL VICARAGE, YORKS. (N.R.), 1838 [Borthwick Institute, York, MGA 1838/2].

NEW MALTON VICARAGE, YORKS. (N.R.), 1840 [Borthwick Institute, York, MGA 1840/2].

BURLEY GRANGE, BURLEY-IN-WHARFEDALE, YORKS. (W.R.), for J. P. Clapham, 1840 [*Leeds Mercury*, 23 June 1840, *ex inf.* Dr. D. Linstrum].

THORNTON DALE RECTORY, YORKS. (N.R.), altered or rebuilt 1841–2 [Borthwick Institute, York, MGA 1841/4].

NUNBURNHOLME RECTORY, YORKS. (E.R.), 1853 [Borthwick Institute, York, MGA 1853/2].

*Designed in partnership with Charles Watson.

[1] Unexecuted designs for Gascoigne's family seat at Parlington Hall, Yorks. (W.R.) are illustrated in the same article.

PROSSER, HENRY, was in the 1820s in partnership with John Staff of Croydon (*q.v.*). In 1825 SUTTON CHURCH, SURREY, was enlarged to their designs [I.C.B.S]. In 1828 Prosser exhibited at the Royal Academy his designs for 'a college proposed to be erected by the Honourable Artillery Company for widows and orphans of deceased members'. This does not appear to have been built. In the same year he exhibited a drawing of All Saints, Beulah Hill, Upper Norwood, 'executing under the direction of His Majesty's Commissioners for building new churches', although this church is known to have been designed by James Savage. A number of topographical drawings by Prosser are in an extra-illustrated copy of Brayley's *Surrey* in Wimbledon Public Library. He may have been related to George Frederick Prosser, the author of *Select Illustrations of the County of Surrey* (1828) and of *Select Illustrations of Hampshire* (1833).

PROSSER, THOMAS, exhibited a design for a villa at the Royal Academy in 1819, giving a London address. He was presumably the architect of the same name who was practising in Worcester in 1828–9, in Hereford in 1830, and again in Worcester up to about 1836 (Pigot's *Directories*). In 1836 he designed alterations and additions to WHEATFIELD, POWICK, WORCS. for William Wall [*Berrow's Worcester Jnl.* 11 Feb. 1836, *ex inf.* Mr. A. S. Brooks]. He must be distinguished from Thomas Prosser (d. 1842) of Seaham Harbour, Co. Durham, who designed SEAHAM HARBOUR CHURCH, 1835–7 [I.C.B.S.], and was the father of Thomas Prosser (d. 1888), architect of Newcastle [Principal Probate Registry, Calendar of Probates, 1887, 1888].

PROWSE, THOMAS (*c.*1708–1767), was a country gentleman and an amateur architect. He was the son of John Prowse of Compton Bishop and Berkley in Somerset. In 1731 he married Elizabeth Sharp, through whom he inherited the estate of Wicken in Northamptonshire, and on his mother's death in 1763 he inherited Berkley House nr. Frome in Somerset. He represented Somerset in Parliament continuously from 1740 to 1767, and declined the Speakership in 1761 because of ill-health.

Prowse was on friendly terms with Sanderson Miller (*q.v.*), and helped him in his designs for Hagley Hall and the Shire Hall at Warwick. He was also involved in the projects for rebuilding Copt Hall in Essex for John Conyers in the 1740s. The principal buildings for which he was himself responsible (usually with John Sanderson as executant architect) are listed below. Both at Hatch Court and at Kimberley Hall he used Palladian pavilion towers like those at Hagley, but Hatch Court has the attractive and unusual feature of an arcade across the main front between the flanking towers. His work at Wicken Church is in a Gothick style similar to that of his friend Sanderson Miller. It is possible that he also designed the simple classical church at Berkley, as rebuilt in 1749–53, but the Berkley property then belonged to his mother, and there is no evidence of his involvement.

Prowse died on 1 January 1767, aged 59, and was buried at Axbridge. A portrait of him attributed to Gainsborough belongs to Mr. Derek Sherborne. Another portrait, still at Berkley House, is illustrated in *C. Life*, 19 May 1988, fig. 6.

[R. Sedgwick, *The House of Commons 1715–1754*, 1970, 371; E. F. Wade, 'Notes on the Family of Prowse', *Miscellanea Genealogica et Heraldica* N.S. iii, 1880, 162, 165; J. Collinson, *History of Somerset* iii, 1791, 562–3; *An Eighteenth-Century Correspondence*, ed. Dickins & Stanton, 1910, 286, 289, 290, 314; *Arch. Hist.* xvi, 1973, 28; *Gent's Mag.* 1763, 565, 1767, 47; *London Magazine*, March 1760 (letter from Prowse about the use of elliptical arches in bridges); will (P.C.C., 24 LEGARD).]

WICKEN CHURCH, NORTHANTS., rebuilt except tower 1753–67, Gothic; windows altered and transepts added 1897 [An inscription records that 'This Church was designed and built by Thomas Prowse Esq[r]. in the year 1758 and finished after his Death'. However it appears from the Peterborough Faculty Register that the chancel was already being rebuilt under Prowse's direction in 1753, and Mr. Sanderson's plan for the chancel is mentioned in a letter from Thomas Prowse written in that year (Prowse papers in Northants. Record Office). In a letter from John Sanderson to John Conyers dated 10 June 1758 (Essex Record Office D/D W.E. 36/7), he states that he intends to go to Wicken 'to give directions for finishing the groyned ceiling of Esq[r]. Prowse's Church there, the carcase of which has been built and used for service these 4 years past'. The diary of Prowse's daughter-in-law Elizabeth Prowse records that the church was 'new paved' in 1770, when 'Mr. Sanderson came down to give directions'.

HATCH COURT, SOMERSET, for John Collins, 1755 [described by Edward Knight of Wolverley in 1761 as 'built by Prowse': Kidderminster Public Library MS. 294] (*C. Life*, 22–9 Oct. 1964).

KIMBERLEY HALL, NORFOLK, remodelled for Sir Armine Wodehouse, Bart., *c.*1755–7 [*Kymber: a Monody*, by the Revd. Robert Potter, 1759, contains the following lines about Kimberley: '. . . fix'd by Prowse's just palladian hand / its towred honours stand', and Sir Armine's 'cautions about Gentlemen-Architects' in general and Prowse in particular are referred to in a letter in the Mordaunt of Walton MSS. in the Warwicks. Record Office, letter-book v, opp. f. 57]. John Sanderson's employment here in 1757 is documented by family accounts seen by Mr. T. P. Connor, and there are drawings by him for this house in the R.I.B.A. Collection.

SWINDON HOUSE ('THE LAWN'), WILTS., advice about refronting house for Thomas Goddard, 1757; dem. 1952 [Warwicks. Record Office, Mordaunt of Walton MSS., letter-book v, f. 57].

HALSWELL PARK, SOMERSET, THE TEMPLE OF HARMONY, for Sir Charles Kemeys Tynte, 1764–5, with interior feature added by R. Adam 1767 [G. Jackson-Stops in *C. Life*, 9 Feb. 1989, 86].

WICKEN HOUSE, NORTHANTS., enlarged and altered for himself, 1765–6 [diary of Elizabeth Sharpe *penes* Col. Lloyd-Baker of Hardwicke Court, Glos.] (J. P. Neale, *Views of Seats* 1st ser. i, 1818).

PUGIN, AUGUSTUS CHARLES (1769–1832), came to this country as a refugee from

Revolutionary France. He claimed to be of aristocratic birth, but little is known about his ancestry. The circumstances in which he arrived in England 'a penniless foreigner' are not clear, and the dramatic story of his escape from death in Paris told by Benjamin Ferrey may or may not be literally true. The first record of his presence in England is in March 1792, when he was admitted to study in the Royal Academy Schools as a painter. He was soon engaged as a draughtsman by John Nash, then an architect with a considerable practice in Wales, and some drawings connected with Nash's rebuilding of the west front of St. David's Cathedral are signed by Pugin as draughtsman. After Nash's move to London in 1796 Pugin must have followed him, and he was still working for Nash as late as 1819–24, when he was drawing the plates for the latter's book on the Brighton Pavilion, published in 1826. Long before this Pugin had, however, formed connections with topographical writers and publishers such as Ackermann, Britton and Brayley, for whose works he drew and etched many plates. In this antiquarian company he developed an interest in medieval architecture which made him something of an authority on the subject. His publications were among the first to provide accurate drawings of medieval architectural detail at a time when many architects were beginning to work in the Gothic style. In London he established a flourishing school of architectural drawing and colouring, and among his many pupils were J. Amos, Francis Arundale, Benjamin Green, Talbot Bury, T. Cramer, J. D'Egville, F. T. Dollman, Benjamin Ferrey, R. Grantham, C. E., C. J. Mathews, G. B. Moore, Joseph Nash, James Pennethorne, W. Lake Price, W. Shoubridge, T. L. Walker and F. Whitaker. In 1808 he was elected an associate of the Old Water Colour Society, and was a frequent exhibitor at its annual exhibitions.

Pugin was a draughtsman and drawing-master rather than a practising architect. His exhibits at the Royal Academy were mostly of a topographical character, but in 1826–7 he showed three designs for cemeteries, and early in 1830 he was concerned in the layout of the cemetery at Kensal Green. He may also have helped J. B. Papworth (*q.v.*) to remodel a Gothic summerhouse at Claremont as a mausoleum for Princess Charlotte in 1817 [Wedgwood, *op. cit.* below, 11]. In 1823 he designed the interior of the Diorama in Regent's Park in conjunction with James Morgan [J. Elmes, *Metropolitan Improvements*, 1831, 81], and the Vicarage at Portbury in Somerset appears to have been his work, for in 1832 Thomas Rickman went to see 'Pugin's Parsonage at Portbury [which] looks well outside but is miserable within' [diary, 1 Feb. 1832]. Pugin may also have designed the Picture Gallery which his friend Charles Mathews, the actor, added to Ivy Cottage, his house in Kentish Town [J. T. Smith, *A Book for a Rainy Day*, ed. Whitten, 1905, 85 n. 2], and according to the obituary in *Arnold's Magazine of the Fine Arts* N.S. i, 1833, 326, he was employed as an architect by the Earl of Essex and the Marquess of Downshire.

As well as being an accomplished artist, Pugin was an agreeable companion whose social talents no doubt contributed to his success. They may also account for his marriage, while still a far from affluent refugee, to Catherine, the daughter of William Welby of Islington, a barrister-at-law and member of an old Lincolnshire family. Their only child, born in 1812 at their house in Stone Street, Bedford Square, was Augustus Welby Northmore Pugin. Pugin died on 19 December 1832, at No. 106 Great Russell Street, Bloomsbury. The sale catalogue of his library is in the Bodleian Library (Mus. Bibl. III, 80, 413). His portrait is given in Ferrey's *Recollections of A. W. N. Pugin*, 1861, facing page 26.

The following is a list of the principal publications with which he was associated: R. Ackermann, *The Microcosm of London* (with plates by Pugin & Rowlandson), 1808–10; with F. Mackenzie, *Specimens of Gothic Architecture . . . Selected from ancient buildings at Oxford* [1816]; with E. W. Brayley, *A Series of Views in Islington and Pentonville*, 1819; *Specimens of Gothic Architecture*, 2 vols. 1821–3, with descriptions by E. J. Willson; with J. Britton, *Illustrations of the Public Buildings of London*, 2 vols. 1825–8, 2nd ed. by W. H. Leeds, 1838; *Gothic Furniture*, 1827, consisting of plates previously published in Ackermann's *Repository of Arts* in 1825–7;[1] with J. Britton and J. & H. Le Keux, *Specimens of the Architectural Antiquities of Normandy*, 1827–8; *Examples of Gothic Architecture*, vol. i, 1828–30, vol. ii, 1831–4 with text by E. J. Willson, vol. iii with text by Pugin's executor T. L. Walker, 1836; translated Normand, *New Parallel of the Orders of Architecture*, with 2 extra plates, 1829; with C. Heath, *Paris and its Environs*, 1829–31; *Gothic Ornaments from Ancient Buildings in England and France*, 1828–31; *A Series of Ornamental Timber Gables, from existing examples in England*

[1] This was not, as is sometimes said, the first edition of the younger Pugin's *Gothic Furniture in the style of the 15 Century* (1835), which is an entirely different book.

and Wales, 1831, drawn by B. Ferrey under Pugin's direction, with text by E. J. Willson.

[*A.P.S.D.*; *D.N.B.*; *Gent's Mag.* 1833 (i), 278–9; B. Ferrey, *Recollections of A. W. N. Pugin*, 1861; M. Trappes-Lomax, *Pugin*, 1933; John Summerson, *The Life and Work of John Nash*, 1980, 24–5; Alexandra Wedgwood, *The Pugin Family*, R.I.B.A. Drawings Catalogue, 1977, 9–37.]

PURSER, CHARLES (1803–), was a younger brother of William Purser (*q.v.*). He was a pupil of Edward I'Anson, became a student at the Royal Academy in 1820, and was awarded the Silver Medal in 1822. He exhibited at the Academy in 1821 and 1824. In 1833 he published a pamphlet entitled *The Prospects of the Nation in regard to the National Gallery*, in which he severely criticized the designs of William Wilkins.

PURSER, WILLIAM, junior (1788–), was the son of William Purser, of whom little is known except that he was one of the original members of the Surveyors' Club in 1792. The younger Purser was admitted to the Royal Academy Schools in 1807, and began to exhibit architectural designs in 1805. From 1817 to 1820 he travelled in Italy and Greece with John Sanders (*q.v.*), acting as his draughtsman, and taking part in the discovery of the Lion of Chaeroneia. On his return to England he exhibited at the Royal Academy from 1820 to 1834 as 'architect and painter'. Among his exhibits was a 'Design for a villa, proposed to be erected on the banks of the Ouse near Bedford' (1820), but it is not known whether this was built. He appears to have made a living chiefly as an illustrator of books such as Finden's *Landscape Illustrations to the Bible* [information from Mr. R. G. Searight].

PYCOCK, GEORGE (*c.*1749–1799), was the principal architect and builder in Hull in the latter part of the eighteenth century. Among his works in that town were the GENERAL INFIRMARY, 1784, façade altered by H. F. Lockwood 1840–2, dem. *c.*1970; the NEW GAOL at MYTON GATE, 1786 (dem.); and THE NEPTUNE INN, WHITEFRIARGATE (later known as Custom House Buildings), 1794–6 [G. Hadley, *History of Hull*, 1788, 837–9 and plates facing pp. 349, 356; *V.C.H. Yorks. E. Riding* i, 383, 449]. Some houses he had built in HANOVER SQUARE *c.*1785 were advertised for sale in the *Hull Advertiser*, 3 May 1800. In 1793 he designed MARFLEET PARISH CHURCH, YORKS. (E.R.), rebuilt 1884 [Borthwick Institute, York, Fac. 1793/2]. His design for a small house at Tealby, Lincs., for George Tennyson (1797) is among the Tennyson d'Eyncourt papers in the Lincolnshire Record Office (T.D.E.H. 169).

Pycock died at Hull on 27 March 1799, aged 50 [*Gent's Mag.* 1799, 349]. His business was carried on by his son Marmaduke Ward Pycock, who died on 8 August 1815, aged 35 [*Hull Advertiser*, 12 Aug. 1815, *ex inf.* Mr. A. G. Chamberlain]. A plan and elevation for an 'intended New House' for D. Sykes at EPPLEWORTH, nr. HULL, signed by M. W. Pycock and dated 1803, are in the Gott Collection at Wakefield Museum (vol. 6, p. 98).

Q

QUICK, SAMUEL (–1842), was a surveyor and builder of Marylebone, London, and probably a native of Newton Bushell in Devon. In 1826 he enlarged NEWTON BUSHELL CHAPEL (now St. Mary's Hall), giving his services free [I.C.B.S.]. A few of Quick's papers were sold at Sotheby's on 6 June 1978, lot 397.

QUINCEY, JAMES (–1716), was Town's Surveyor of Newcastle-upon-Tyne from 1691 to 1716 and as such would have been responsible for building the MANSION HOUSE in 1692, but whether he designed this large classical town house (dem.) is not known.

R

RAEBURN, JAMES (1787–1851), was born at Boyndie, nr. Banff, on 20 February 1787. From 1827 to 1839 he held the post of First Clerk in the Scottish Office of Works at Edinburgh. On the abolition of the Office in 1839 he retired with a pension. He died in Edinburgh on 30 September 1851, and is commemorated by a monument in St. Cuthbert's churchyard. His practice was continued by his son Robert R. Raeburn (1819–88). In the Register House there is a copy of a sheet of lithographs, 'drawn and presented by Robert R. Raeburn' 1845, representing designs for Free Churches, manses and schools by James Raeburn [RHP 970/20]. The buildings illustrated include THE TRINITY AND ALVAH FREE CHURCH at BANFF, designed by James Raeburn in 1843, and a 'Design of a Church proposed to be built in Montreal'. The Trinity and Alvah Church presents a competently designed Ionic portico to the street. Raeburn also designed the obelisk erected near RUTHWELL, DUMFRIESSHIRE, to the memory of the Revd. Henry Duncan (d. 1846), the founder of savings banks, which bears his signature.

RAFFIELD, JOHN, was the son of George Raffield, a Northumbrian joiner who was largely responsible for alterations to FORD CASTLE, NORTHUMBERLAND, which were carried out by Sir John Hussey Delaval in the 1760s 'without the aid of any architect'. A reference in Richard Pococke's northern tour of 1760 (B.L., Add. MS. 14259, f. 82) suggests that George Raffield was also employed at SEATON DELAVAL, NORTHUMBERLAND, by Sir John's brother Sir Francis Blake Delaval. The son appears first as a joiner working at Ford Castle under James Nisbet in the early 1770s, and subsequently as an assistant of the Adam brothers in their London office. By 1797 he was in independent practice in Great Portland Street, exhibiting a design for a castle in Scotland at the Royal Academy. In 1792 he showed a design for a cast-iron bridge over the Thames 'from the Strand, in the vicinity of the Adelphi, to Lambeth', and in 1805 a design for a suspension bridge over the Danube at Vienna. In 1818 or 1819 he was declared bankrupt, and during the next few years he was acting as a clerk of works under Atkinson at Tulliallan Castle and under Wilkins at Dunmore Park, both in Scotland; in 1825 he exhibited at the Royal Academy for the last time. Adam influence is apparent in his work, notably in the 'Chain Gate' at Easton Neston, which is based on the screen at Sion House. [*Proceedings of the Society of Antiquaries of Newcastle-on-Tyne* v, 1891–2, 62–3; Northumberland Record Office, Delaval papers, M 17/29, 2 DE, *passim*; R. M. Howard, *The Longs of Jamaica and Hampton Lodge*, 1925, ii, 450; *Letters to and from Charles Kirkpatrick Sharpe*, ed. Allardyce ii, 1888, 238.]

NEW CROSS, OLD KENT ROAD, KENT, villa for John Rolls, 1804–5; dem. [exhib. at R.A. 1805; Monmouthshire Record Office, Rolls papers, E4. A2–3; cf. D. Hughson, *London* v, 1808, 59, for a view of the house based on a drawing by Raffield].

LONDON, ST. JOHN'S LODGE, REGENT'S PARK, for C. A. Tulk, 1818–19; enlarged 1844–7 [exhib. at R.A. 1818–19] (J. Elmes, *Metropolitan Improvements*, 1831, 79–80).

EASTON NESTON, NORTHANTS., THE 'CHAIN' GATE and LODGES for 3rd Earl of Pomfret, 1822–3 [exhib. at R.A. 1825]. The decorative features are of Coade stone, dated 1822 (*C. Life*, 7 Nov. 1908, 635).

RAILTON, WILLIAM (*c.*1801–1877), was a pupil of William Inwood. He became a student at the Royal Academy in 1823 at the age of 22, and travelled abroad in the years 1825–7, visiting Greece, Corfu and Egypt. His 'Account of the newly-discovered Temple at Cadachio, in Corfu' was published in 1830 in the supplementary volume of Stuart's *Antiquities of Athens*. He exhibited regularly at the Royal Academy from 1829 onwards. From 1838 to 1848 he was architect to the Ecclesiastical Commissioners, for whom he designed a number of parsonage houses in an economical style of vaguely Italianate character which was strongly disapproved of by the *Ecclesiologist*. His Gothic churches, mostly in the Early English style, do not reward the architecturally minded visitor. Railton did, however, secure the approval of his contemporaries on two occasions. The first was in 1835, when his design for rebuilding the Houses of Parliament was awarded the fourth premium on the ground that it was well planned, and in other respects 'inferior to none in attention to the instructions and specifications delivered to the competitors'. The other was in 1839, when he won the competition for the Nelson Memorial in Trafalgar Square with the conventional but unexceptionable idea of a column surmounted by a statue. Railton died on a visit to Brighton on 13 October 1877. He should not be confused with William A. Railton (1820–1902), an architect practising at Kilmarnock to whom he appears to have been unrelated. [*A.P.S.D.*; *D.N.B.*; *Ecclesiologist* ii, 1843, 145–7; A. Savidge, *The Parsonage in England*, 1964, 135, 145, 151; *R.I.B.A. Drawings Catalogue: O–R*, 111.]

RANDALLS, nr. LEATHERHEAD, SURREY, for N. Bland, *c.*1830, Gothic; dem. *c.*1935 [exhib. at R.A. 1830] (Brayley, *History of Surrey* iv, 433, engraving).

GRACE-DIEU MANOR, LEICS, house and R.C. chapel for Ambrose Lisle March-Phillipps, 1833–4, Gothic; enlarged by A. W. Pugin and others [exhib. at R.A. 1834].

DUDDON CHURCH, CHESHIRE, 1835, Gothic [I.C.B.S., under 'Tarvin'].

COPT OAK (CHARLEY) CHURCH, LEICS., 1836–7, Gothic, chancel 1889 [*Gent's Mag.* 1836 (ii), 648].

WOODHOUSE EAVES CHURCH, LEICS., 1836–7, Gothic, altered 1880 [*Gent's Mag.* 1836 (ii), 648].

WILDEN CHURCH, BEDS., repaired and repewed, 1837 [I.C.B.S.].

GARENDON PARK, LEICS., lodges at Dishley and Hathern entrances for Charles March-

Phillipps, 1838, Gothic [exhib. at R.A. 1838].

RIPON, YORKS. (N.R), residence (now Spring Hill Schools) for the Bishop of Ripon, 1838–9, and the chapel, 1848, Gothic [exhib. at R.A. 1839, 1849].

LAUNDE ABBEY, LEICS., repaired and altered medieval chapel for E. Dawson, 1839 [exhib. at Society of British Artists 1839].

ANSTEY PASTURES HALL, LEICS., alterations for the Revd. R. Martin, *c.*1839–40 [Leics. C.R.O., DG6/C/25–28].

GROBY CHURCH, LEICS., 1840, Gothic [G. K. Brandwood, 'Leicestershire Churches 1825–1850', in *The Adaptation of Change*, ed. D. Williams, Leicester Museums 1980, 57].

LONDON, NELSON'S COLUMN, TRAFALGAR SQUARE, 1840–3 [exhib. at R.A. 1846]. The statue is by E. H. Baily; the lions were added in 1867.

RISEHOLME HALL, LINCS., enlarged and altered as residence for the Bishop of Lincoln, 1840–5 [exhib. at R.A. 1846].

TETTENHALL CHURCH, STAFFS., repaired and reroofed 1841–3; rebuilt 1955 after fire [I.C.B.S.].

WOLVERHAMPTON, STAFFS., ST. MARY'S CHURCH, 1842–3, Gothic; dem. 1950 [*Gent's Mag.* 1843 (i), 75].

SHEPSHED CHURCH, LEICS., new galleries, etc., 1843–4 [I.C.B.S.].

RIPON MINSTER, YORKS. (W.R.), repair of south-west tower and gable of west front and insertion of sham Romanesque vaulting in north and south transepts, 1843–4 [*A.P.S.D.*; *Gent's Mag.* 1844 (i), 182–3]. Railton's plaster and papier-mâché vaulting was removed by Scott in *c.*1865.

LONDON, ST. MARY'S CHURCH, BROMLEY ST. LEONARD'S, rebuilt 1843, Romanesque; destroyed by bombing 1941/3 [exhib. at R.A. 1844, 1851].

LONDON, ST. BARTHOLOMEW'S CHURCH and SCHOOLS, BETHNAL GREEN, 1843–4, Gothic [exhib. at R.A. 1844].

THORPE ACRE CHURCH, LOUGHBOROUGH, LEICS., 1844–5, Gothic [I.C.B.S.].

BEAUMANOR PARK, LEICS., for W. P. Herrick, 1843–6, Jacobean style [exhib. at R.A. 1845; Herrick papers in Leics. C.R.O.].

LONDON, HOLY TRINITY CHURCH, HOXTON, 1846–8, Gothic [exhib. at R.A. 1849].

MEANWOOD, nr. LEEDS, YORKS. (W.R.), HOLY TRINITY CHURCH, 1849, Gothic [exhib. at R.A. 1849–50; *Ecclesiologist* x, 1850, 237–40].

PARSONAGE HOUSES

The many parsonage houses designed by Railton for the Ecclesiastical Commissioners in the 1840s included those of ST. BARNABAS, BRISTOL; ST. JOHN, CARISBROOKE, ISLE OF WIGHT; CHURCHSTOW, DEVON; CORRINGHAM, LINCS.; ST. JAMES, MUSWELL HILL, MIDDLX.; HOLY TRINITY, ROTHERHITHE, SURREY; UPLEADON, GLOS and CILGERRAN, PEMBS. His designs for all but the last two are in the R.I.B.A. Collection.

RAINEY, EDWARD (1797–1860), was a builder and architect of Spilsby in Lincolnshire. In 1838 he designed and built CANDLESBY CHURCH, LINCS. in a poor Gothic style [I.C.B.S.]. He died at Spilsby on 11 January 1860 [Principal Probate Registry, Calendar of Probates].

RALPHS, JOHN, was an architect of Warminster. He designed the new Gothic tower which was built on the north side of the nave of WALTON CHURCH, SOMERSET, in 1836, in place of a former central tower [I.C.B.S.]. In the correspondence with the I.C.B.S. he is mentioned as being seriously ill.

RAMPLING, CLARK (1793–1875), born at Brandon in Suffolk, was in C. H. Tatham's office in London in 1818–19. He was also a pupil of Richard Brown (*q.v.*) [*Builder* vii, 1849, 615]. He went first to Manchester (where he was living in 1825–9), and then to Birkenhead and Liverpool. He was still practising in Birkenhead in 1866, but by 1868 had retired to Quarry Bank, Tranmere, Cheshire, where he died on 7 March 1875. He exhibited at the Royal Academy in 1815–19 and at the Liverpool Academy in 1831, 1832 and 1834. His principal work was the Greek Revival Medical Institution at Liverpool, ingeniously planned to make the most of a triangular site. R. B. Rampling, who practised from Preston in the 1850s, appears to have been his younger brother.

BRANDON, SUFFOLK, design for parsonage house, exhibited at R.A. 1818.

BIRCH, nr. MIDDLETON, LANCS, ST. MARY'S CHURCH, 1827–8, Gothic; dem. [Port, 146–7].

MILL BANK, nr. WEST DERBY, LANCS., villas 'now erecting', exhib. at Liverpool Academy 1832.

WEST DERBY, LANCS., house for Spencer Jones, *c.*1834 [exhib. at Liverpool Academy 1834].

LIVERPOOL, THE MEDICAL INSTITUTION at angle of HOPE and MOUNT STREETS, 1836–7 [*Architectural Mag.* iv, 1837, 383; *Companion to the Almanac*, 1838, 229–31].

LIVERPOOL, THE FISH HALL, MURRAY STREET,

for the Liverpool Fish Company, 1837 [*Architectural Mag.* iv, 402–3].

BIRKENHEAD, THE MAGISTRATES' OFFICES, 1840 [*A.P.S.D., s.v.* 'Birkenhead'].

BUGLAWTON CHURCH, CHESHIRE, 1840, Norman [I.C.B.S.].

BIRKENHEAD, THE TOWN HALL, MARKET, etc., 1845; dem. [W. W. Mortimer, *Hundred of Wirral*, 1847, 362].

RAMSAY, ALEXANDER (*c.*1777–1847), was a builder in Edinburgh. He became a burgess in 1829 [*Roll of Edinburgh Burgesses*, Scottish Record Soc., 129]. A stone in the Warriston Cemetery records his death on 18 May 1847 in his 71st year. He rebuilt CRAIGEND CASTLE, STIRLINGSHIRE, for James Smith of Craigend. At first it was intended only to enlarge the existing house to the designs of Smith's cousin James Smith of Jordanhill (*q.v.*), but 'after the erection had gone some length, it was found more suitable to pull down the old house entirely, and the present building was completed according to plans furnished by Mr. Alexander Ramsay, architect and builder, Edinburgh, preserving as much as possible the internal arrangement as designed by Mr. Smith' [Jones's *Views of Scottish Seats*, n.d.]. This castellated house, completed in 1812 and demolished in 1968, is illustrated in *The Old Country Houses of the Glasgow Gentry*, Glasgow 1870, xxvi.

RAMSAY, JAMES (–1800), was a Scottish architect and landscape-gardener. According to J. C. Loudon [*Encyclopaedia of Gardening*, 1828, 82], he began life as a mason and was employed in that capacity by Robert Robinson (*q.v.*), 'but soon displayed a taste for disposing of verdant scenery, and afterwards became a landscape-gardener of considerable repute. He gave ground-plans and drawings in perspective, both of the buildings and . . . scenery. Leith Head, a small place near Edinburgh, is entirely his creation. His style was that of Brown. . . . He died at Edinburgh in 1794.' Ramsay's activities as a landscape-gardener are documented at Cally House, Kirkcudbrightshire, Gosford House, East Lothian, and elsewhere [*ex inf.* Prof. A. A. Tait]. Loudon was, however, mistaken in the date of his death, for the *Scots Magazine* records that he died on 22 May 1800 [*Scots Mag.*, 1800, 432]. As an architect he is represented by a plan dated 1782 for an 'Intended New Street' at STEWARTON, AYRSHIRE [S.R.O., RHP 1202], by designs at REDNOCK HOUSE, PERTHSHIRE, for a stable-block there dated January 1797, and by CATHKIN, CARMUNNOCK, LANARKSHIRE, an agreeably unpretentious and rather old-fashioned house illustrated in *The Old Houses of the Glasgow Gentry*, Glasgow 1870, xxi, where is stated to have been built by Walter Ewing Macrae in 1799, 'from designs of James Ramsay of Edinburgh'. Ramsay must be distinguished from a man of the same name who figures in the Edinburgh directories from 1774/5 to 1796/7 as a 'slater and builder', and was one of the 'ordained measurers' for the City [cf. S.R.O., RHP 591).

RAMSHAW, WILLIAM, was a joiner and builder at Bishop Auckland, Co. Durham. He designed churches at SADBERGE (1831) and ETHERLEY (1832), CO. DURHAM, both altered later in the nineteenth century [I.C.B.S.].

RANDALL, JAMES (1778–1820), was the son of John Randall, an Oxford mason. He published *Designs for Mansions, Casinos, Villas, Lodges and Cottages in the Grecian, Gothic and Castle Styles*, 1806, and *A Philosophical Enquiry on the Cause, with Directions to Cure, the Dry Rot in Buildings*, 1807. His exhibits at the Royal Academy between 1798 and 1814 provide almost the only record of his activity as an architect. They included a 'design for an entrance to Merton Grove' (or Place), Surrey, then the property of a Mr. Graves (1798); a 'design for a casino intended to be erected in Oxfordshire' (1801); a 'lodge and gateway as executed for Lord Hobart at Roehampton' (1803); a 'design for a villa for J. S. Collenguin, Esq. in Dorset' (1807); a 'design for a conservatory for Col. E. Agar, M.P.' (1809); 'a bath, now erecting for J. Collingridge, Esq.' at Sunbury Villa, Middlesex (1810); and 'A gallery, as it was intended to have been erected in the garden of Leicester Square by B. West, P.R.A.' (1814). His front to the ESSEX STREET UNITARIAN CHAPEL, STRAND, is praised in the *Monthly Magazine*, June 1817, 399. He practised from various addresses in London, and died on 27 October 1820, aged 42 [*Gent's Mag.* 1820 (ii), 474].

RANELAGH, EARL OF, *see* JONES, RICHARD.

RANGER, WILLIAM (*c.*1800–1863), was the son of a builder and surveyor of the same name at Brighton (see the list of subscribers to Horsfield's *History of Sussex* ii, 1835). He practised in London, chiefly as a civil engineer, and in that capacity was much employed by the Board of Health in enforcing the Public Health Act. He was also known as the patentee of an 'artificial stone' or cement composition (1832), and of a concrete block designed to be used as a substitute for masonry (1834). The latter was used by Barry in the College of Surgeons in Lincoln's Inn Fields, and the former by Ranger himself at WESTLEY CHURCH, SUFFOLK, which he built in 1835–6 in an elementary Gothic style with a spire which had to be demolished *c.*1960 [I.C.B.S.]. He also designed ST. JOHN'S CHURCH, BURY ST. EDMUNDS, SUFFOLK, 1839–40 [I.C.B.S.], which was built entirely of brick, including the spire and a full vocabulary of 'Early English' detail. Ranger's 'Patent Stone Manufactory' was in Lambeth, and he died in St. George's Square, Southwark, on 12 September 1863, aged 63 [*Builder* xxi, 1863, 672].

RATHBONE, THOMAS (–1722), sometimes called 'Captain Rathbone', is referred to as a building surveyor in London records of the early eighteenth century. In 1694 he built a watch-house for the parish of St. Giles in the Fields and in 1703 made a survey of houses in Portugal Row [J. Parton, *Some Account of the Hospital and Parish of St. Giles-in-the-Fields*, 1822, 229, 292]. He was also employed by Gray's Inn and by Lord Scudamore on his estate at Battle Bridge [P.R.O., Chancery Masters' Exhibits, Duchess of Norfolk Deeds, Box C, bundle 10, nos. 1178, 1180, 1182 and N9/8891]. He is best known, however, as the speculative builder of Rathbone Place, 1718, where he died in 1722 [P.R.O., PCC 81 MARLBRO].

RAWLINS, THOMAS (–1646?), described as 'gentleman', was employed to supervise the erection of a new royal lodging in TUTBURY CASTLE, STAFFS., in 1634–6. This was demolished in 1751 with the exception of its south wall. It was of some interest as a provincial essay in classical architecture. Whether Rawlins designed it himself is not clear. He may have been a Thomas Rawlins of Alton who died in 1646. [*History of the King's Works* iii, 297.]

RAWLINS, THOMAS (*c.*1727–1789), was the son of Thomas Rawlins, a worsted weaver of Norwich. He appears to have been apprenticed to a statuary mason in London, for in an advertisement he claimed to have 'worked at the most eminent Carvers in London'. Returning to Norwich, he ran a successful business as a monumental mason from about 1743 to 1780, specializing in tablets incorporating coloured marbles. He also practised as an architect, exhibiting designs at the Society of Artists in London in 1767, 1769 and 1770, and at the Royal Academy in 1773, 1774 and 1776. Some of these were of quite an ambitious character, e.g. a 'design for a palace' (1769), a 'section of a rotunda' (1773) and 'three designs for a Forum, for the Four Courts of Judicature, designed to be built in Lincoln's Inn Fields' (1774). In 1769 he competed for the Royal Exchange at Dublin. In 1765 the *Ipswich Journal* contained an advertisement for a proposed work on architecture by Rawlins, and in 1768 he published *Familiar Architecture; or Original Designs of Houses for Gentlemen and Tradesmen; Parsonages; Summer Retreats; Banqueting-Rooms; and Churches*, with an excursus on the masonry of semicircular and elliptical arches. There was a second edition in 1789 and a third in 1795. The character of the designs is Palladian, with some affinity to the works of James Paine. Plate xlvi shows the unexecuted design which he submitted in 1753 for the Octagon Chapel at Norwich. His only documented architectural works are the entrance to ST. ANDREWS HALL, NORWICH, 1774, since rebuilt [Chambers, *Norfolk Tour* iii, 1829, 1193], and WESTON HOUSE, WESTON LONGVILLE, NORFOLK, for John Custance, 1781, dem. 1926 [*Woodforde's Diary*, ed. Beresford, i, 1924, 317, 323], but several buildings in Norwich can be attributed to him on stylistic grounds, notably No. 94 ST. GILES and Nos. 10–12 THE CLOSE. In 1772 his reinforcement of the S. aisle of ST. JOHN MADDERMARKET CHURCH with ironwork was the subject of some satirical verses in the *Norfolk Chronicle* (8 August). Rawlins died on 18 March 1789, in his 63rd year, and is commemorated by a stone in the floor of St. John Maddermarket Church.

[S. J. Wearing, *Georgian Norwich: its Builders*, Norwich 1926, 53–5; C. L. S. Linnell & S. J. Wearing, *Norfolk Church Monuments*, Norwich 1952, 25–6, 30–1; R. Gunnis, *Dictionary of British Sculptors*, 1968, 315; information from Mr. A. P. Baggs.]

RAWLINSON, CHARLES (1729–1786), was a carpenter and joiner at Lostwithiel in Cornwall, where he is buried in the parish church. He signs the design for rebuilding REDRUTH CHURCH, CORNWALL, completed *c.*1768, among the Faculty papers in the Exeter Record Office, and the minutes of the committee for building ST. AUBYN'S CHAPEL, DEVONPORT, 1770–1, show that he was probably the designer and certainly the surveyor in charge [W. Devon R.O., 358/1/4]. In 1772 Thomas Pitt (*q.v.*) employed him to build the new south wing of BOCONNOC, CORNWALL, containing a library and picture-gallery. This (mostly dem. 1975) was probably designed by Pitt himself [B.L., Add. MS. 59489, ff. 115–127, 132, 134, 147]. In 1775–6 Rawlinson rebuilt or rectified the leaning front of

CLOWANCE HOUSE, CORNWALL, for Lady St. Aubyn after consultation with Robert Mylne [Mylne's *Diary*, ed. Richardson, 102–3, 109], and in about 1780 he partly rebuilt CATCHFRENCH, nr. LISKEARD, CORNWALL, for Mrs. Glanville [memoirs of Sarah Loveday Gregor in Cornwall C.R.O.]. From the same source it appears that he had designed a long gallery at PORT ELIOT for Edward (afterwards 1st Lord) Eliot. This was demolished in 1829, but is illustrated in *C. Life*, 22 Oct. 1948, fig. 4. Mrs. Gregor thought Rawlinson 'a very dull architect', a verdict which his surviving works do nothing to upset.

RAWLINSON, GEORGE (1734–1823), described as 'Architect' on a monumental inscription in All Saints, Derby, was a builder at Matlock, where he is believed to have built Walker's Hotel, among other buildings. He died on 26 October 1823, aged 89, at Belle Vue, Matlock Bath, a house designed and built by himself on a site acquired in 1799. He was the father of the artist James Rawlinson (1769–1848) [*Derby Mercury*, 5 Nov. 1823; information from Mr. Maxwell Craven].

RAWSTORNE, JOHN (1761–1832), was the son of the Revd. William Rawstorne, rector of Badsworth, nr. Doncaster, and his wife Elizabeth, daughter of Samuel Walker of Stapleton Park. He became a pupil of James Wyatt, and subsequently practised in Birmingham, Doncaster and York. In 1787 he exhibited two architectural designs at the Royal Academy from Wyatt's office, but soon afterwards he moved to Birmingham, where he designed the BLUE COAT SCHOOL in ST. PHILIP'S CHURCHYARD, 1792–4, dem. 1935 (measured drawings in *Architect and Building News*, 1 May 1936), and the CAVALRY BARRACKS in GREAT BROOK STREET. For a speculative builder called Charles Norton (*q.v.*) he designed in 1790 THE CRESCENT, a large terrace of twenty-three stone houses, of which only the extremities were ever built. An engraving, of which there is a copy in B.L., *King's Maps* xlii, 82 *m*, shows the complete design [B. Walker, 'Some Eighteenth-Century Birmingham Houses', *Trans. Birmingham Arch. Soc.* lvi, 1932, 27; *V.C.H. Warwickshire* vii, 48]. His unexecuted designs for rebuilding MOSELEY HALL, destroyed in the Birmingham riots of 1791, are in the Birmingham Central Library Archives (634730). His elegant trade card, inscribed 'RAWSTORNE Architect BIRMINGHAM. Estates Surveyed, Pleasure Grounds Laid out &c.', is illustrated in *C. Life*, 13 Sept. 1956, 539.

In 1793 Rawstorne designed THE ROYAL INFIRMARY at SHEFFIELD, opened in 1797 [*Aris's Birmingham Gazette*, 9 Sept. 1793; J. Hunter, *History of Hallamshire*, 1869, 323–4]. Soon afterwards he moved to Doncaster. His designs, in the Adam style, for redecorating the drawing-room at CUSWORTH HALL, nr. DONCASTER, are among the Battie-Wrightson papers in Leeds Archives (BW/Ma3). From Doncaster he exhibited at the Royal Academy in 1798 his design for the Sheffield Infirmary, in 1800 an elevation of 'Bilham Belvedere, Yorkshire', a building (now ruinous) in the grounds of BILHAM HALL, nr. HICKLETON, YORKSHIRE (W.R.) for W. N. W. Hewett, and in the same year a design for proposed additions to CHEVET HALL, nr. WAKEFIELD (dem. 1955), for his nephew Sir Thomas Pilkington.[1] An advertisement in the *Doncaster, Nottingham & Lincoln Gazette* for 31 July 1801 shows that he had recently designed a house identifiable as No. 2, SOUTH PARADE, DONCASTER [*ex inf.* Miss A. Sheppard].

Soon afterwards Rawsthorne appears to have moved again, for in 1802 the *Monthly Magazine* reported (p. 434) that 'Mr. Rawsthorne, the architect, who resides near York, has lately invented a new kind of bricks, dove-tailed into each other, for constructing arches for the cieling of rooms, &c. in lieu of timber', and in 1805 the *York Chronicle* reported the opening of the NEW STREET METHODIST CHAPEL (dem. 1966) 'after a design of Mr. Rawstorne, architect in this city' [R. Willis, *Nonconformist Chapels of York*, York Georgian Soc. 1964, 22]. In 1809 he was awarded the second prize in the competition for the Ouse Bridge [*York Courant*, 25 Sept. 1809]. Later he moved to Sheffield (see a design by him for houses to be built on Little Sheffield Moor, dated 1819, in Sheffield Archives, F. Maps 37), but after this his practice appears to have collapsed, and during his latter years he was in serious financial straits. In 1821 he was reduced to begging for money to enable him to move from Sheffield 'to another part of Yorkshire' [Farington's Diary, 3 April 1821 and Soane Museum Archives 16/13/33]. It was from Manchester that in 1822 he issued the prospectus of a proposed book of *Designs in Architecture* that was never published [prospectus in Sheffield Archives, F66/108]. Eventually he died in Liverpool on 24 August 1832, aged 71 [*Gent's Mag.* 1832 (ii), 286]. He appears to have had at least three architect sons, George, who was apprenticed to John Platt of Rotherham in 1793

[1] Rawstorne's sister Isabella married Sir Michael Pilkington (d. 1788) and was mother of Sir Thomas Pilkington (d. 1811). A design for lodges at Chevet Hall by Rawstorne (1797) is among the Pilkington papers in the Central Library at Wakefield.

[J. D. Potts, *Platt of Rotherham*, 1959, 19], Walker (*q.v.*) who practised in Bradford, and William, born in about 1798, who was looking for work in London in 1821 [Farington's Diary, 3 and 20 April, 30 Nov. 1821] and who subsequently practised in Liverpool [Pigot's *National Commercial Directory* ii, 1828–9, 292].

RAWSTORNE, WALKER (*c.*1807–1867), was one of the sons of John Rawstorne (*q.v.*), whose mother's maiden name had been Walker. He practised in Bradford from about 1835 to 1854. He designed a number of churches in the lancet or Norman styles. He died at Headingley, nr. Leeds, on 21 June 1867 [Principal Probate Registry, Calendar of Probates; information from Mr. D. Griffiths].

BINGLEY CHURCH, YORKS. (W.R.), north chapel for Walker Ferrand, 1834, Gothic [Borthwick Institute, York, Fac. 1834/4].

BRADFORD, YORKS. (W.R.), ST. JAMES'S CHURCH, 1836–8, Gothic; dem. 1966 [J. James, *History of Bradford*, 1841, 222].

BUTTERSHAW CHURCH, YORKS. (W.R.), 1838, Gothic [*Bradford Observer*, 22 March 1838].

STOCKTON-ON-TEES, CO. DURHAM, EXCHANGE BUILDINGS, later Mechanics' Institute and now Literary and Philosophical Society's Institute, 1839–40 [*Bradford Observer*, 7 June 1838].

BRADFORD, YORKS. (W.R.), THE INFIRMARY, WESTGATE, 1840–3, Tudor Gothic; heightened 1864, dem. 1936 [John James, *Continuation and Additions to the History of Bradford*, 1866, 212].

MANNINGHAM, YORKS. (W.R.), ST. JUDE'S CHURCH, 1840–3, Norman; dem. 1966 [*Bradford Observer*, 19 March 1840].

BURLEY-IN-WHARFEDALE CHURCH, YORKS. (W.R.), 1841–3, Gothic [R. V. Taylor, *Churches of Leeds*, 1875, 233].

YEADON CHURCH, YORKS. (W.R.), 1841–4, Gothic [Port, 170–1; *Leeds Intelligencer*, 19 Oct. 1841].

INGROW CHURCH, YORKS. (W.R.),[1] 1841–2, Norman [Port, 168–9].

ECCLESHILL CHURCH, YORKS. (W.R.), 1846–8, Gothic [Port, 166–7].

BURNLEY, LANCS., ST. PAUL'S CHURCH, 1852–3, Norman [Port, 146–7].

READ, JOHN, 'surveyor', made a specification and estimate for a mansion to be built at Hursley, Hants., for Sir William Heathcote, Bart., in about 1720 [Hants. C.R.O., 63 M 84/89, 90, 92]. This appears not to have been the design executed 1721–4 (for which see above, under 'Sir Thomas Hewitt'), as the Order was to be Ionic, not Doric. Read may possibly have been the John Read who died at Low Leyton, Essex, in November 1741 [Parish Register], who was described in his will [P.R.O., PROB 11/714, f. 361] as 'gentleman' and in the *London Daily Post* of 27 Nov. 1741 as 'a very eminent Architect'.

[1] Otherwise known as St. John, Paper Mill Bridge, nr. Keighley.

READ, THOMAS, of Deal, enlarged ST. LEONARD'S CHURCH, DEAL, in 1819 [I.C.B.S.], and reseated ST. GEORGE'S CHURCH, DEAL, in 1822 [I.C.B.S.]. He designed the BAPTIST (now the UNITARIAN) CHAPEL, ADRIAN STREET, DOVER, in 1819-20 [*The Watering-Places of Great Britain and Fashionable Directory*, J. Robins, 1833, 178], and was probably the 'Mr. Read' who won the first prize in the competition for the esplanade at Brighton in 1828, though in the event his design was not carried out [Hermione Hobhouse, *Thomas Cubitt*, 1971, 367].

REBECCA, JOHN BIAGIO (–1847), was the son of Biagio Rebecca (1735–1808), a decorative painter who worked in England from 1761 onwards and was elected A.R.A. in 1771. J. B. Rebecca appears to have practised partly from London and partly from Worthing in Sussex. His works included an aggressively Greek Doric church, Tudor Gothic alterations to two country houses, and the extraordinary fantasy of Castle Goring, suavely neo-classical on one side and romantically castellated on the other. Rebecca died in London on 3 June 1847 [*Gent's Mag.* 1847 (ii), 105; will, P.R.O., PROB 11/2058, f. 144].

CASTLE GORING, nr. ARUNDEL, SUSSEX, for Sir Bysshe Shelley, Bart., *c.*1795–1815 [J. Evans, *Picture of Worthing*, 1805, 96; Sandra Blutman, 'Castle Goring', in *The Country Seat*, ed. Colvin & Harris, 1970].

WORTHING, SUSSEX, ST. PAUL'S CHURCH, 1812; reconstructed 1893 [*The Watering Places of Great Britain and Fashionable Directory*, J. Robins, 1833, 69].

KNEBWORTH HOUSE, HERTS., partly rebuilt for Mrs. Bulwer Lytton, 1813–16, Tudor Gothic; reconstructed by H. E. Kendall jr., 1844–5 [contract at Knebworth dated 18 Sept. 1813] (J. P. Neale, *Views of Seats*, 2nd ser. i, 1824; *C. Life*, 31 Jan., 7, 14 Feb. 1985).

PENSHURST PLACE, KENT, alterations and additions for Sir John Shelley Sidney, *c.*1818 onwards, Tudor Gothic [exhib. at R.A. 1818 and 1820; *The Farington Diary*, ed.

J. Greig, viii, 206] (*C. Life*, 9, 16 March, 4 May 1972).

attributed: PENSHURST CHURCH, KENT, rebuilding of SIDNEY CHAPEL for Sir John Shelley Sidney, 1820, Gothic.

BUCKINGHAM PLACE, SHOREHAM, SUSSEX, for H. Bridger, 1820; now preserved as a shell at Woodville, The Drive, Shoreham [exhib. at R.A. 1820].

WORTHING, SUSSEX, BEACH HOUSE, for — Helmes, 1820 [David Watkin, *Thomas Hope*, 1968, 192] (*C. Life*, 29 Jan. 1921).

CROWELL RECTORY, OXON., 1822 [Oxfordshire C.R.O., Oxford Diocesan Faculty Register, 1804–27, p. 351].

WORTHING, SUSSEX, THE SEA (later ROYAL) HOTEL, THE ESPLANADE, *c.*1826; dem. 1901 [exhib. at R.A. 1827].

REDGRAVE, JOHN, of Harleston (presumably Suffolk), is shown by the building accounts (now at Welford Park, Berks.) to have been the architect or surveyor responsible for rebuilding HALLINGBURY PLACE, ESSEX, for Jacob Houblon in 1771–3; dem. 1924 (*C. Life*, 19 Sept. 1914). In 1763–4 he had carried out alterations to COOPERSALE, ESSEX, for John Archer, Houblon's father-in-law [Dorothy Stroud, *Capability Brown*, 1950, 165]. THE ANGEL HOTEL, BURY ST. EDMUNDS, SUFFOLK, was rebuilt to his designs in 1776 [minutes of the Guildhall Feoffees, Suffolk C.R.O.(B.), H 2/6/2/1, *ex inf.* Mrs. M. Statham]. He was presumably the 'Redgrave' who was paid 5 guineas in 1788/9 by the churchwardens of St. Peter's Church, Thetford, for a plan and estimate for rebuilding the tower of their church that was apparently rejected in favour of one 'bought in by Mr. Richard Todd' [churchwardens' accounts in Norfolk C.R.O.].

REED, BENJAMIN (*c.*1780–1853), practised in Old Broad Street, London, from about 1826 until his death on 11 December 1853, aged 73 [*Gent's Mag.* 1853 (i), 110]. He was succeeded by his son William Candler Reed.

REID, JAMES, a wright by trade, designed the simple TOWN HOUSE at BANFF in 1796–7 [W. Cramond, *Annals of Banff* i, 1891, 348].

REID, ROBERT (1774–1856), was the principal government architect in Scotland during the first half of the nineteenth century. He was born in Edinburgh on 8 November 1774 (not 1776 as stated in *A.P.S.D.* and *D.N.B.*) and was the son of Alexander Reid, a mason in the Tron Kirk parish [inscription on monument in Dean Cemetery; New Register House, Edinburgh, Baptism Register No. 35]. Nothing is at present known of his early life or architectural training. His long career as a public architect began in 1803 when he was commissioned by the Trustees for Public Buildings to design the new Law Courts in Parliament Square, Edinburgh. In 1808, on the strength of this important public work, he obtained a warrant authorizing him to use the title of 'King's Architect and Surveyor in Scotland'. This was purely honorary and conferred no emoluments on its holder, but when the titular Master of Works to the Scottish Crown, James Brodie of Brodie, died in 1824, Reid succeeded in getting that office merged with his own. As 'Master of Works and Architect' to the King in Scotland he was to receive a salary of £200 a year. His next move was to persuade the government to establish a properly constituted Scottish Office of Works, with himself at its head, an office in Parliament Square and a salary of £500 a year (1827). In 1839, as a measure of economy, Reid's office and title were abolished, and the Scottish Works were henceforth administered from London. Reid was retired on full pay, and went to live at a house called Lowood which he had acquired near Melrose.[1] He died in Edinburgh on 20 March 1856, and was buried in the Dean Cemetery, where he is commemorated by a monument with a bronze portrait medallion.

In his exteriors Reid adhered closely to the style of the brothers Adam. Their Edinburgh University was the source of his Parliament Square façade, and most of his public buildings are designed in a slightly coarsened version of the Adams' monumental manner. This did not command universal approval, and both the Faculty of Advocates and the Writers to the Signet insisted on employing a different architect (William Stark) for the interiors of their respective libraries, which formed part of the Parliament Square complex. St. George's Church and the Custom House at Leith (a pedestrian essay in Greek Doric) were also the subjects of adverse criticism, and an Aberdeen professor regarded it as a deliverance when Archibald Simpson was employed to design the new Marischal College there instead of 'the King's Architect . . . a dull, staid personage who had acquired much discredit by the plans for the new Custom House at Leith and his repairs at St. Andrews'. To modern eyes Reid's slightly ponderous public buildings make a by no means contemptible contribution to the fabric

[1] This house was rebuilt in 1914, but an old photograph shows a small early nineteenth-century villa which Reid had enlarged for himself.

of Edinburgh, and his sector of the New Town forms a distinctive and well-planned portion of the whole. His finest work, however, is the picture-gallery at Paxton House, Berwickshire, whose interior is an ambitious neo-classical composition of considerable merit. So far as is known this was Reid's only major country-house commission, for (as he informed the Barons of the Exchequer in 1837) his official duties obliged him first 'to restrict my private practice, and ultimately to relinquish it altogether' [S.R.O., T 1/4381].

[*A.P.S.D.*; *D.N.B.*; *History of the King's Works* vi, 1973, 251–3; G. M. Fraser, 'Archibald Simpson, Architect', *Aberdeen Weekly Jnl.* 26 July 1918; *Gent's Mag.* xlv, 1856, 547.]

PUBLIC BUILDINGS

PERTH, THE ACADEMY, ROSE TERRACE, 1803–7 [E. Smart, *History of Perth Academy*, Perth 1932, 87, 93; photographs of original drawings in N.M.R.S.] (*C. Life*, 10 Oct. 1968, 916, fig. 1).

EDINBURGH, THE BANK OF SCOTLAND ON THE MOUND, jointly with Richard Crichton, 1802–6 [Bank of Scotland Minutes, 29 Oct. 1800: 'Resolved to employ Robert Reid and Richard Chrichton, Architects in Edinburgh, jointly']; remodelled by D. Bryce 1865–70 (T. H. Shepherd, *Modern Athens*, 1829, 74).

EDINBURGH, NEW LAW COURTS, PARLIAMENT SQUARE, including façade to square, 1804–10, and eastern extensions, 1825–40 [S.R.O., E343/1–5, minutes of the Trustees for Public Buildings; drawings in RHP 6525/13–15 and P.R.O., MPD 103].

EDINBURGH, THE LUNATIC ASYLUM (EAST HOUSE), MORNINGSIDE, 1809–10; dem. 1896 [*A.P.S.D.*] (plan and elevation in *Scots Mag.* March 1808). In 1809 Reid published *Observations on the Structure of Hospitals for the Treatment of Lunatics . . . to which is annexed an account of the intended establishment of a Lunatic Asylum at Edinburgh.*

EDINBURGH, external shell of THE SIGNET AND ADVOCATES' LIBRARIES (now the UPPER AND LOWER SIGNET LIBRARY), PARLIAMENT SQUARE, 1810–12. Reid originally designed interiors for these libraries, which form two storeys of the same building, but both the Writers to the Signet and the Faculty of Advocates commissioned William Stark (*q.v.*) to design the interiors. Reid as the government architect supervised the execution of Stark's designs in 1812–16. The staircase to the Advocates' Library on the upper floor was designed by W. H. Playfair in 1819–20, but altered by W. Burn for the Writers to the Signet after they had acquired the upper library from the Advocates in 1826. [Iain G. Brown, *Building for Books: The Architectural Evolution of the Advocates' Library*, Aberdeen, 1989].

PERTH, THE PRISON, EDINBURGH ROAD, 1810–12, originally designed as a military prison but remodelled in 1841–2 as the General Prison for Scotland [J. Morison, *A Guide to the City of Perth*, 1812, 6].

EDINBURGH, ST. GEORGE'S CHURCH, CHARLOTTE SQUARE, 1811-14; converted into WEST REGISTER HOUSE 1968–70 [T. H. Shepherd, *Modern Athens*, 1829, 43 and plate].

LEITH, THE CUSTOM HOUSE, 1811–12; altered by W. Burn 1824–5 [*A.P.S.D.*]

EDINBURGH, THE ORPHANS' HOSPITAL, additional buildings 1812; dem. 1845 [*Edinburgh Evening Courant*, 9 Jan. 1812].

EDINBURGH, completed THE REGISTER HOUSE, designing the north wing, 1822–30 [*Book of the Old Edinburgh Club* xvii, 167–8].

DOWNPATRICK GAOL. CO. DOWN, IRELAND, 1824–30 [Dublin Castle, S.P.O., Chief Secretary's Office, RP 1823/6726 and 1827/1956, *ex inf.* Dr. E. McParland].

ST. ANDREWS, FIFE, THE UNITED COLLEGE, begun 1829–31, when the east wing only was built. The buildings were eventually completed 1845–9 by William Nixon in a simplified version of Reid's Jacobethan design [R. G. Cant, 'St. Andrews Architects', *St. Andrews Preservation Trust Year Book* for 1966–7, part ii, 12].

ST. ANDREWS, FIFE, remodelled ST. MARY'S COLLEGE, 1829–30 [R. G. Cant, *op. cit.*].

ST. ANDREWS, FIFE, extended THE UNIVERSITY LIBRARY, 1829 [R. G. Cant, *op. cit.*].

EDINBURGH, HOLYROODHOUSE, general repair, 1824–35. Reid rebuilt the south-east quarter which had been damaged by subsidence and refaced the south front, originally built of rubble, in ashlar. He also took down and rebuilt the sixteenth-century Abbey Court House [S.R.O., General Report on Works executed at Holyroodhouse by Reid, 1836].

DOMESTIC ARCHITECTURE

PERTH, Nos. 1–28 MARSHALL PLACE, 1801 [S.R.O., Perth Sasines].

LUFFNESS HOUSE, E. LOTHIAN, addition for General Sir Alexander Hope, 1803 [S.R.O., SC 40/67/3, f. 192].

PAXTON HOUSE, BERWICKSHIRE, east wing containing Library and Picture Gallery for George Home, 1812–13 [Alistair Rowan in *C. Life*, 31 Aug. 1967].

EDINBURGH, NEW TOWN. In conjunction with William Sibbald (*q.v.*), Reid was responsible for the layout of the northern extension of the New Town comprising ABERCROMBY PLACE, CUMBERLAND STREET, DUNDAS STREET, DUBLIN STREET, DUNDONALD STREET, DRUMMOND PLACE, FETTES ROW, GREAT KING STREET, HERIOT ROW, INDIA STREET, MANSFIELD PLACE, NELSON STREET, NORTHUMBERLAND STREET, ROYAL CRESCENT and SCOTLAND STREET. The plan was drawn up in 1802, and building was in progress from 1803 onwards. Reid designed the principal elevations, including those of Heriot Row (1803–8) [A. J. Youngson, *The Making of Classical Edinburgh*, 1966, 206–11].

EDINBURGH, QUEENSFERRY STREET, houses on E. side, 1807 onwards [*Edinburgh Evening Courant*, 26 Feb. 1807].

EDINBURGH, Nos. 33–46 CHARLOTTE SQUARE, 1807–15 [*Book of the Old Edinburgh Club* xxiii, 25–28].

UNEXECUTED DESIGNS

These include a project for a new town at DUNKELD, PERTHSHIRE, 1806 [drawings at Blair Castle, D.1. 27–8]; a COURT HOUSE at INVERARAY, ARGYLLSHIRE, 1807–8 [I. G. Lindsay & Mary Cosh, *Inveraray and the Dukes of Argyll*, 1973, 316–17]; a design for rebuilding GOSFORD HOUSE, EAST LOTHIAN, for the Earl of Wemyss, *c.*1810 [*C. Life*, 21 Oct. 1971, 1050]; a design for the MERCHANT MAIDEN HOSPITAL, EDINBURGH, 1810–12 [*Book of the Old Edinburgh Club* xxix, 21–2]; the COUNTY BUILDINGS at PERTH, 1812–14 [drawings in Perth Art Gallery]; a design for a new building for Edinburgh University on the south side of Leith walk, exhibited at the R.A. in 1818; and a design for 'a National Monumental Church for Scotland, in the style of the Parthenon at Athens, to perpetuate the memory of the great Naval and Military Achievements of the late war', designed to be built on the Mound in Edinburgh, and exhibited at the R.A. in 1819.

REID, WILLIAM (1772–1849), was a quarry-owner, builder and architect at Lochee on the outskirts of Dundee. In all three capacities he was largely employed in assisting the expansion of Dundee in the early nineteenth century. In Lochee itself he was a prominent figure, known popularly as 'the Baron'. Most of the buildings erected in Lochee during the early nineteenth century are said to have been designed and built by him, including THE WEAVERS' HALL, 1824, and ST. LUKE'S U.P. CHURCH (afterwards Church of Scotland), 1826–7, remodelled 1856. An elaborate monument in Mains Churchyard records his death on 19 September 1849 at the age of 77 [Alexander Elliot, *Lochee*, Dundee 1911, 61, 185–6].

REID, WILLIAM (–1849), practised in Glasgow in the early nineteenth century. He was probably the 'Mr. Reid' referred to by Joseph Bonomi in 1807as a 'young architect of Glasgow' who was friendly with his sons [letter to Duke of Argyll's factor among papers at Inveraray]. In 1813 he was one of the prize-winners in the competition for laying out the Calton Hill area of Edinburgh [A. J. Youngson, *The Making of Classical Edinburgh*, 1966, 307]. He designed some bonded warehouses in Howard Street, Glasgow, 1818 [Chapman's *Picture of Glasgow*, 1820, 193], and a 'villa in the old Scotch style' at SPRINGFIELD, BISHOPBRIGGS, LANARKSHIRE, for D. S. Cleland, 1831, described and illustrated in Loudon's *Encyclopaedia*, 1846, 879–84. At PAISLEY he designed ST. GEORGE'S CHURCH, an able classical work of 1819–20 [Town Council Minutes, 9 Sept. 1816, *ex inf.* Mr. David Walker]. He may also have designed the castellated COUNTY (now MUNICIPAL) BUILDINGS at PAISLEY, 1818–20, but in his *Abbey and Town of Paisley*, 1835, 148, C. Mackie states confusingly that 'The plan of the building was drawn by William Reid, Esq. The architect was Archibald Elliot, Esqr., Edinburgh.' Some drawings by Reid are in the R.I.B.A. Collection. They comprise two designs (1795) for steeples in a manner derived from Gibbs, a plan and elevation of a villa at LARGS, AYRSHIRE, for Dr. Brown, 1811, probably to be identified as BROOMFIELD HOUSE, dem. 1963, and a perspective of CASTLETOWN HOUSE, ROCKLIFFE, CUMBERLAND, a Greek Revival mansion as built 'by Reid & Nicholson architects' for Robert Mounsey, 1811. A set of drawings preserved in the house is signed by 'Nicholson & Reid Archt' and dated 1809. This house is illustrated in Peter Nicholson's *Architectural Dictionary* ii, 1819, 102–3, where, however, it is stated that 'This design was made from a sketch by Thomas Telford, Esqr., but the working drawings were made, and the work was superintended, by the Author.' In 1833 Reid read a paper on the acoustics of public buildings to the Edinburgh Society of Arts [Loudon's *Architectural Mag.* i, 1834, 212]. His unexecuted design for a gaol at Carlisle (1822) is in the Cumbria Record Office (Q.AG/5). He died on 10 December 1849 [S.R.O., SC 36/48/36, p. 526].

RENDLE, JOHN, was a builder and surveyor at Teignmouth in Devon. His only known work was KINGSTEIGNTON VICARAGE (now 'The Chantry'), which he designed in 1815 for Thomas Whipham, D.D., in the form of a thatched *cottage orné*, with oval rooms arranged in a plan of some sophistication [Exeter Diocesan Records]. Rendle was probably a relation, and perhaps the uncle, of James Meadows Rendel (1799–1856), a celebrated civil engineer who was the son of James Rendle, a land surveyor at Okehampton who married Jane, daughter of the architect John Meadows (*q.v.*). J. M. Rendel's third son Stuart, also a civil engineer, entered politics and was raised to the peerage in 1895 as Lord Rendel. The latter's grandson was Harry Stuart Goodhart-Rendel (1887–1959), architect and architectural critic [genealogical information from Mr. Vincent Rendel; *D.N.B.*, *s.v.* 'Rendel, James Meadows'].

RENNIE, JOHN (1761–1821), the younger son of a Scottish farmer, was born at Phantassie in East Lothian on 7 June 1761. As a child he showed a remarkable aptitude for mechanical pursuits, and he afterwards found congenial employment with a millwright. His earnings enabled him to study at Edinburgh University for three years before establishing himself as a millwright and general engineer. In 1784 he went to Birmingham in order to assist Boulton and Watt in designing and executing the machinery for the Albion Flour Mills at Southwark. Although destroyed by fire in 1791, these power-driven mills had attracted great interest, and Rennie's connection with them established his reputation as a mechanical engineer. It was, however, as a planner of docks and harbours, as a drainer of fens, and as a builder of bridges that Rennie eventually became famous, and it is chiefly in the last capacity that he figures in this *Dictionary*.

Rennie began his career as a bridge-builder at the age of 22 and in the course of his life he designed many minor bridges over canals, etc., as well as major ones over rivers such as the Thames and the Tweed. All of them are admirable as architecture as well as engineering, and Rennie ranks as one of the great British bridge-builders of the nineteenth century. His first major bridge was the one over the Tweed at Kelso, which, with its semi-elliptical arches separated by pairs of Doric columns, its boldly defined masonry and its level roadway, anticipates the chief characteristics of his later bridges across the Thames at London.

In 1809 he and William Jessop were asked to report on the plans for a new bridge across the Thames at Somerset House which had been prepared by the engineer George Dodd with the assistance of J. L. Bond. As a result of their unfavourable criticism, Rennie himself was asked to prepare the designs which were adopted, and in June 1810 he undertook to supervise the construction of the bridge at a salary of £1000 a year. Foreseeing that the eventual removal of Old London Bridge would result in an increased scour higher up the river, Rennie laid the foundations of the piers in coffer dams instead of in the caissons advocated by Dodd, thus securing an absolutely firm basis for his bridge. The Strand Bridge, as the Waterloo Bridge was at first called, was opened by the Prince Regent in 1817. Rennie was then offered a knighthood, which he refused.

In 1813 a company was formed to provide a bridge across the Thames between Blackfriars and London Bridge, of which Rennie was appointed Engineer. This (Southwark) bridge consisted of three cast-iron arches designed to allow the largest possible waterway. It was completed in 1819 and replaced in 1920–1.

Rennie's last great work was to design a new bridge to take the place of the medieval London Bridge, with its narrow roadway, decrepit arches and battered starlings. The Corporation had already taken the advice of its surveyor, George Dance, in consultation with Messrs. Chapman, Alexander and Mountague. They recommended that eight of the arches should be removed and replaced by four larger ones: but Rennie, in a report which he submitted on 12 March 1821, showed convincingly that it would be better in the end to build a new bridge rather than to spend large sums of money in altering the old one. An Act of Parliament was accordingly obtained, but Rennie died in October 1821, and in 1823 a competition was held in which about one hundred designs were submitted. The assessors were Messrs. Soane, Smirke and Nash, of the Office of Works, with whom was associated Mountague, the City Architect. Prizes of £250, £150 and £100 were awarded to the authors of the three best designs (Charles Fowler, John Boorer and Charles Busby), but as none of these was considered to be entirely satisfactory, the competition was set aside, and it was Rennie's original design which was eventually executed under the direction of his son, Sir John Rennie, and completed in 1831. The original specification is in the Library of London University (MS. 158).

Rennie died on 4 October 1821, and was buried in the crypt of St. Paul's Cathedral. His practice as a civil engineer was continued by his younger son John (1794–1874), who was knighted in 1831 on the completion of

London Bridge. As engineer to the Admiralty, a post in which he succeeded his father, Sir John Rennie completed various works in the royal dockyards, including the great breakwater across Plymouth Sound which had been begun by his father in 1811, of which he published an *Account* in 1848. He also planned and designed the ROYAL WILLIAM VICTUALLING YARD at STONEHOUSE nr. PLYMOUTH, built between 1824 and 1832, a group of buildings, monumental in scale and massive in construction, which is amongst the finest works of the engineer-architect in England [Jonathan Coad, *Historic Architecture of the Royal Navy*, 1983, 120–22]. This, however, was his only important architectural work,[1] and his achievements as an engineer fall outside the scope, as well as the chronological limits, of this book. Sir John Rennie retired in about 1862 and died on 3 September 1874.

[S. Smiles, *Lives of the Engineers* ii, 1861, part vii; Edward Cresy, *Encyclopaedia of Civil Engineering*, 1847; *The Autobiography of Sir John Rennie*, 1875; *A.P.S.D.*; *D.N.B.*; C. T. G. Boucher, *John Rennie*, Manchester 1963; T. Ruddock, *Arch Bridges and their Builders*, 1979; Rennie papers in the Library of the Institution of Civil Engineers; letters in the National Library of Scotland, MS. 2909].

PRINCIPAL BRIDGES DESIGNED BY JOHN (1761–1821)

Bridge over Water of Leith, nr. Stevenhouse Mill, Midlothian, 1784; dem. (Smiles, ii, 131).

LUNE AQUEDUCT, nr. LANCASTER, carrying the Lancaster Canal over the R. Lune, 1794–8.

DUNDAS AQUEDUCT, LIMPLEY STOKE, WILTS., carrying the Kennet and Avon Canal over R. Avon, *c.*1796–9.

WOLSELEY BRIDGE, nr. COLWICH, STAFFS., 1798–1800.

KELSO BRIDGE, ROXBURGHSHIRE (R. Tweed), 1800–3 (Cresy, 434).

WHITEADDER BRIDGE, BERWICKSHIRE, 1800.

BOSTON BRIDGE, LINCS.* (R. Witham), 1804–7; dem. 1913 (Smiles, ii, 176).

VIRGINIA WATER, SURREY, bridge on Great West Road, 1805.

DARLASTON BRIDGE, STAFFS. (R. Trent), 1805.

MUSSELBURGH BRIDGE, MIDLOTHIAN (R. Esk), 1806–7; widened 1924 (Cresy, 435).

LONDON, bridge* over R. Lea at East India Dock Road, 1809; dem.

FOSDYKE BRIDGE,* LINCS. (R. Welland), 1810; dem.

LONDON, WATERLOO BRIDGE (R. Thames), 1811–17; dem. 1938 (Cresy, 436–41).

NEWTON STEWART BRIDGE, WIGTOWNSHIRE (R. Cree), 1812–13 (Cresy, 435).

LUCKNOW, INDIA,* bridge over R. Goomtee, 1814.

STONELEIGH ABBEY, WARWICKS., NEW BRIDGE, GRECIAN DRIVE, for J. H. Leigh, 1814–15 [Shakespeare's Birthplace, Stratford, Leigh MSS. Ser. D. Warwicks., bundles 17 and 37–8] (Cresy, 436).

LONDON, SOUTHWARK BRIDGE* (R. Thames), 1815–19; dem. 1920 (Smiles, ii, 190).

LEEDS, YORKS. (W.R.), WELLINGTON BRIDGE (R. Aire), 1817–19.

BRIDGE OF EARN, PERTHSHIRE, 1819–21.

CRAMOND BRIDGE, MIDLOTHIAN (R. Almond), 1819–23.

KEN BRIDGE, NEW GALLOWAY, KIRKCUDBRIGHTSHIRE, 1820–1.

CHEPSTOW BRIDGE,* MONMOUTHSHIRE (R. Wye), 1815–16.

LONDON BRIDGE (R. Thames), designed by John Rennie, but carried out by his son, 1824–31; dem. 1967 and rebuilt at Lake Havasu City, Arizona, U.S.A., 1970–1 (Cresy, 442–58).

RENNY, WILLIAM, was paid £2 3s. in 1699 for drawing the 'draught' for the TOWN HALL at SHEFFIELD, and £200 for building it in the following year. It was demolished in 1810 [J. D. Leader, *Extracts from the Earliest Book of Accounts of the Town Trustees of Sheffield*, Sheffield 1879, 139–41; R. E. Leader, *Surveyors and Architects of the Past in Sheffield*, 1903, 32].

REPTON, GEORGE STANLEY (1786–1858), the fourth and youngest son of Humphry Repton, was born on 30 January 1786. He exhibited his first drawing at the Royal Academy at the age of 15,[1] and soon afterwards became a pupil of John Nash, in whose office he remained long enough to become his chief assistant. In 1817 he married Lady Elizabeth Scott, the daughter of Lord Chancellor Eldon, secretly, and in defiance of her father's wishes. Lord Eldon was at first furious, but relented after the birth of his daughter's first child in 1820, and in his will

[1] According to J. Britton, *The Original Picture of London*, 26th ed. *c.*1828, 122, the STAMFORD STREET UNITARIAN CHAPEL in BLACKFRIARS was 'built in 1823 by Mr. Rennie'. When it was demolished in 1964 the Greek Doric portico was preserved as an adjunct to the London Nautical College.

* Iron bridges.

[1] He subsequently exhibited sometimes as 'G. Stanley Repton' and sometimes as 'G.S.R.'. In Graves's *Royal Academy Exhibitors* the latter exhibits will be found in the 'Anonymous' section.

her children were placed on the same footing as those of his other daughter. As a young man, Repton assisted his father and elder brother in their designs for the Pavilion at Brighton, and in conjunction with John Nash he remodelled the Royal Opera House in the Haymarket. After about 1820 he practised on his own, and achieved a considerable reputation as a designer of country houses, especially in the west of England. A number of his architectural designs are in the R.I.B.A. Collection. They show that he was an excellent draughtsman and a versatile architect, whose classical work forms part of the brief Palladian revival which preceded the introduction of the Italianate style by Barry. His picturesquely composed Tudor Gothic country houses owed much to his early training in Nash's office.

Repton appears to have retired from practice in about 1845. He died on 29 June 1858, and was buried at Kensal Green. His only son, George William Repton, was for many years M.P. for St. Albans and afterwards for Warwick.

Two sketch-books used by G. S. Repton while in Nash's office survive, one in the R.I.B.A. Drawings Collection, the other in the Royal Pavilion Art Gallery, Brighton. The former is described in the *Catalogue of the R.I.B.A. Drawings Collection: O-R*, 1976, the latter in Nigel Temple, *George Repton's Pavilion Notebook: a catalogue raisonné*, Scolar Press 1993.

[*A.P.S.D.*; *D.N.B.*; *The Farington Diary*, ed. J. Greig, viii, 159; John Summerson, 'A Repton Portfolio', *R.I.B.A. Jnl.*, 25 Feb. 1933; Dorothy Stroud, *Humphry Repton*, 1962; John Summerson, *The Life and Work of John Nash, Architect*, 1980.]

THE RIDGE, WOTTON-UNDER-EDGE, GLOS., for Edward Sheppard, *c.*1815–17; dem. 1934 [T. & H.S. Storer, *Delineations of the County of Gloucester*, 1840, 142; R.I.B.A.D.; N. Kingsley, *The Country Houses of Gloucestershire* ii, 1992, 209–10].

LONDON, ROYAL OPERA HOUSE, HAYMARKET, remodelled in collaboration with John Nash, 1816–18; interior destroyed by fire 1867 and rebuilt 1868–9; dem. except the Arcade *c.*1895 [Britton & Pugin, *The Public Buildings of London* i, 1825, 72–9].

COBHAM HALL, KENT, the library for 4th Earl of Darnley, 1817–20 [J. P. Neale, *Views of Seats* vi, 1823, where the library is stated to have been 'lately fitted up' by G. S. Repton; R.I.B.A.D.].

OXFORD, EXETER COLLEGE, the hall was repaired in 1818 'from the designs of Mr. Nash, under the superintendence of Mr. Repton' [J. Ingram, *Memorials of Oxford* i, 1837, 12–13].

SARSDEN RECTORY (now SARSDEN GLEBE), OXON., 1818 [N. Temple, *Jnl. Garden History* 6 (2), 1986, 99–100].

LONDON, HOPKINSON & CO'S BANK, No. 3 REGENT STREET, completed 1819; dem. [R.I.B.A.D.].

LONDON, ST. PHILIP'S CHAPEL, REGENT STREET, for his brother, the Revd. Edward Repton, 1819–20; dem. 1904 [Britton & Pugin, *The Public Buildings of London* i, 1825, 102–6].

ABERYSTWYTH, CARDIGANSHIRE, THE ASSEMBLY ROOMS, 1820 [Nicholson's *Cambrian Traveller's Guide*, 1840, 25; J. Hemingway, *Panorama of North Wales*, 1835, 41; R.I.B.A.D.].

KITLEY HOUSE, DEVONSHIRE, remodelled for E. P. Bastard, *c.*1820–5, Elizabethan [R. Ackermann, *Views of Seats* ii, 1830; R.I.B.A.D.; building accounts in W. Devon R.O., Acc 74/625] (*C. Life*, 7 Oct. 1939; C. Hussey, *English Country Houses: Late Georgian*, 1958, 168–74).

SANDGATE CHAPEL, KENT, for 4th Earl of Darnley, 1822; dem. 1849 or later [R.I.B.A.D.].

SARSDEN HOUSE, OXON., added portico, colonnade and conservatory for J. H. Langston, *c.*1823–5 [R.I.B.A.D.]. The domed hall appears to have been built earlier by Humphry or perhaps J. A. Repton. Humphry submitted a 'Red Book' for landscaping the park in 1795, and he says in his book (ed. Loudon, 270) that he 'advised covering the inner court entirely, and converting it into a hall of communication'.

SARSDEN CHURCH, OXON., reconstructed *c.*1823–5 [Oxfordshire C.R.O., Oxford Diocesan Faculty Register 1804–27, 408].

FOLLATON HOUSE (now Council Offices), nr. TOTNES, DEVONSHIRE, rebuilt for S. Cary, *c.*1826–7 [R. Ackermann, *Views of Seats* ii, 1830; R.I.B.A.D.].

WOLTERTON HOUSE, NORFOLK, added E. wing and perron to S. front for 3rd Earl of Orford, 1828–9 [drawings at Wolterton dated 1828; R.I.B.A.D.; Gordon Nares in *C. Life*, 18–25 July 1957]. An intended W. wing was not built and a terminal tower was later added to the E. wing to the designs of P. Hardwick or J. Stannard (*q.v.*).

WIDWORTHY COURT, nr. HONITON, DEVONSHIRE, for Sir Edward Marwood Elton, 1830 [R.I.B.A.D., showing portico, etc., not built].

DUMBLETON HALL, nr. EVESHAM, GLOS., for Edward Holland, *c.*1830, Tudor Gothic [R.I.B.A.D.].

SARSGROVE COTTAGE (now HOUSE), OXON., remodelled for J. H. Langston, *c.*1830 [R.I.B.A.D.; *Connoisseur* cxxxviii, 1956, 222–5].

PEAMORE HOUSE, EXMINSTER, DEVONSHIRE, remodelled for S. T. Kekewich, *c.*1825–30, Tudor Gothic [*A.P.S.D.*; R.I.B.A.D.].

WINCHESTER COLLEGE, HAMPSHIRE, refronted Outer Court of Warden's Lodgings, 1832–3, and designed New Commoners, 1837–9, and Headmaster's House, 1839–41 [College Archives, *ex inf.* Dr. J. H. Harvey].

KINGSTON CHAPEL (now Church Hall), nr. CORFE, DORSET, for his father-in-law, Lord Eldon, 1833, Gothic [R.I.B.A.D.].

HURSLEY PARK, HANTS., addition of porch for Sir William Heathcote, Bart., 1834; porch dem. *c.*1905 [J. Harris, *Catalogue of British Drawings for Architecture, etc., in American Collections*, 1971, 171; R.I.B.A.D.] (*C. Life*, 13 Dec. 1902).

HURSLEY CHURCH, HANTS., alterations to tower, 1834 [J. Harris, *Catalogue of British Drawings for Architecture, etc., in American Collections*, 1971, 171].

CAMERTON COURT, SOMERSET, for John Jarrett, 1838–40 [R.I.B.A.D.].

? SHIRLEY RECTORY, HANTS., for the Revd. William Orger, 1839 [R.I.B.A.D., inscribed 'Parsonage-Shirley-Surrey' (*sic*)].

CHIPPING NORTON TOWN HALL, OXON., 1842, largely at the expense of J. H. Langston of Sarsden House; damaged by fire 1950 ['First Design' in R.I.B.A.D., design as executed in Town Hall].

MEDMENHAM CHURCH, BUCKS., restored chancel, 1844–5, including new stone altar (removed 1846), reredos (removed 1906), aumbry and font [R.I.B.A.D.].

SOUTHAMPTON, HANTS., BECKFORD HOUSE, conservatory for F. L. Beckford [R.I.B.A.D.].

BURGH HALL, nr. AYLSHAM, NORFOLK, design (perhaps not executed) for addition of porch, etc., for J. H. Holley, probably *c.*1830 [R.I.B.A.D.]. Holley built a new house in the 1840s.

REPTON, HUMPHRY (1752–1818), was born at Bury St. Edmunds on 21 April 1752. His father had for many years held 'the honourable and lucrative situation of a Collector of Excise', and designed a mercantile career for his son. It was, in fact, as a general merchant in Norwich that Repton began his career in about 1773, but his business soon failed, and he decided to retire to Sustead, nr. Aylsham, where his sister had married a solicitor named John Adey. Here he followed his natural inclinations by studying botany and gardening, and living the life of a country gentleman. One of his neighbours was William Windham of Felbrigg, whom he accompanied to Ireland as private secretary on the latter's appointment as Chief Secretary in 1783. On his return to England, he removed to a cottage at Hare Street in Essex, where he lived for the rest of his life. Having lost more money in a project for establishing mail-coaches, he was obliged to find some way of supporting his family. All his life he had been keenly interested in gardening, and now at the age of 36 he resolved to 'turn his hobby into a profession' and become a 'landscape gardener'. The death of Lancelot Brown in 1783 had made way not only for new men but for new ideas, and Repton exploited and systematized the current desire for something at once more natural and more picturesque than Brown's Arcadian landscapes. Repton had both the theoretical knowledge and the practical ability to make a success of his art, and his facility as a water-colourist enabled him to illustrate his proposed 'improvements' by means of charming perspective views furnished with flaps designed to allow the prospective client to make a direct comparison between his park in its improved and unimproved condition. In the case of his more important commissions Repton was in the habit of presenting his client with an elaborately illustrated report bound in red morocco and known as a 'Red Book'. Very soon he became famous; he was mentioned by name in Jane Austen's *Mansfield Park*, and as 'Mr. Milestone' he figures in T. L. Peacock's *Headlong Hall*. By the time of his death in March 1818, at the age of 65, Repton had established himself as one of the great figures in the history of English landscape-gardening. Over seventy 'Red Books' are recorded,[1] and

[1] Those now in public collections include: Armley, Yorks. (Yale Center for British Art), Beaudesert, Staffs. (Princeton Univ. Library), Blaise Castle, Glos. (Blaise Castle Museum), Bracondale, Norfolk (Norfolk County Library), Brandesbury, Middlesex (Dumbarton Oaks Garden Library, Washington), Claybury, Essex (G.L. Record Office), Ferney Hall, Salop. (Pierpont Morgan Library, New York), Hatchlands, Surrey (*ibid.*), Hill Hall, Essex (Essex C.R.O.), Holme Park, Berks. (C.U.L.), Hooton Hall, Cheshire (Architectural Association Library), Langley Park, Kent (R.I.B.A.), Leigh Court, Somerset (Bristol Univ. Library), Little Green, Sussex (W. Sussex C.R.O.), Oulton Hall, Yorks. (Leeds Archives), Owston Hall, Yorks. (Doncaster Museum), Rose Hill, Sussex (Bodleian Library), Royal Fort, Bristol (Yale Univ. Library), Stonelands, Sussex (*ibid.*), Tewin Water, Herts. (Herts. C.R.O.), Trewarthenick, Cornwall (Cornwall C.R.O.), Waresley Park, Hunts. (Lindley Library, Royal Horticultural Society). Facsimiles of the Antony, Attingham and Sheringham Red Books were published in a limited edition by the Basilisk Press in 1976, with commentary by Edward Malins.

a total of nearly two hundred commissions has been listed by Miss Stroud.

Repton was not trained as an architect, but architecture was, as he himself put it, 'an inseparable and indispensable auxiliary' to the art of landscape-gardening. In planning a park, he could never ignore the architectural character of its mansion: he might, and did, recommend alterations that he thought essential to his proposals: and his opinion might be asked by a gentleman who intended to build and plant at the same time. Brown had found the ideal solution for this problem in his partnership with Henry Holland, and Repton established a somewhat similar but short-lived relationship with John Nash, to whom he undertook to turn over the architectural commissions that came his way in return for $2\frac{1}{2}$ per cent on the cost of the work executed. Nash proved, however, to be an unscrupulous partner who failed to honour his part of the bargain and the partnership came to an end in 1800. Repton's eldest son, John Adey Repton (*q.v.*), now became his architectural adjutant and in later years he was also assisted from time to time by his younger son, George Stanley Repton (*q.v.*). Repton's most ambitious architectural schemes – those for remodelling Brighton Pavilion in the Hindu, and Magdalen College, Oxford, in the Gothic style – were both prepared in collaboration with his sons, but neither was executed, though the designs for both are still in existence, the former in the volume dedicated to the Prince Regent which Repton published in 1808, the latter in Magdalen College Library. The assistance of his eldest son 'in the architectural department' was specifically acknowledged by Repton in the cases of 'Brenty Hill, Cotham Bank, Organ Hall, Stapleton, Stratton Park, Scarisbrick, Panshanger, Bayham, &c.', and can be documented in several other instances.

Only in a few early commissions does it appear that Humphry Repton was indebted neither to Nash nor to his sons for architectural assistance. At WELBECK ABBEY, NOTTS., it was he who dictated the remodelling of the east and west fronts in 1790 [A. S. Turberville, *Welbeck Abbey and its Owners* ii, 1938, 312–16].[1] In 1792 he advised certain minor alterations to HONING HALL, NORFOLK, for Mrs. Cubitt [R. W. Ketton-Cremer, *A Norfolk Gallery*, 1948, 205], in 1793–4 he added an iron balcony, etc., to HIGHAM HILLS, nr. WALTHAMSTOW, ESSEX, for John Harman [*V.C.H. Essex* vi, 260], in 1795 he advised the conversion of the central courtyard of SARSDEN HOUSE, OXON., into a domed 'hall of communication' [Loudon, 270], and the 'Red Book' for WARLEY HALL, WORCS., dated 1795 (now in Warley Public Library), includes a design for a Doric temple which existed until about 1940. In 1805 he designed a new entrance to UPPARK, SUSSEX, for Sir Harry Fetherstonhaugh, Bart. [C. Hussey in *C. Life*, 14, 21, 28 June 1941; C. Hussey, *English Country Houses: Mid Georgian*, 1956, 30, fig. 34 (plan)]. More significant than these minor architectural works was the 'lodge of a new and singular description' illustrated as Repton's work by William Cooke in his *New Picture of the Isle of Wight*, 1808, 90. It consisted of two thatched cottages, one on either side of the drive, and was evidently one of the first of its kind. In 1791 the Hon. John Byng had already commented on the thatched roof of a Lincolnshire rectory (at Scrivelsby) 'repair'd upon Mr. Repton's plan' [*The Torrington Diaries*, ed. C. B. Andrews, ii, 1935, 377], and it is evident that Repton was, with his associate Nash, one of the pioneers of the picturesque cottage style so successfully exploited by the latter in the early years of the nineteenth century.

Repton's principal publications on the subject of landscape-gardening – which include his observations on architectural design – were reprinted with a memoir by J. C. Loudon in 1840 as *The Landscape Gardening and Landscape Architecture of the late Humphry Repton*. Between 1789 and 1809 Repton contributed vignettes of country seats, etc., to the almanack called *Peacock's Polite Repository*. In the Yale Center for British Art there is a set of some forty of these small engravings, mounted on a decorated sheet and inscribed 'Proof Impressions of Plates engraved from Drawings by H. REPTON of Scenery improving under his directions'. Other sources for Repton's career are a MS. autobiography acquired by the British Library in 1981 (Add. MS. 62112), the obituary notices in *Gent's Mag.* 1818 (i), 372, 648, and (ii), 102, and a list of views of Norfolk drawn by him printed in *Collectanea Topographica et Genealogica* viii, 1843. The standard modern biography is Dorothy Stroud, *Humphry Repton*, 1962. A comprehensive list of commissions and a full bibliography will be found in George Carter *et al.*, *Humphry Repton, Landscape Gardener*, Victoria & Albert Museum, 1983. See also K. Laurie, 'Humphry Repton: new discoveries', *The Garden* 108 (9), Sept. 1983, 361–6, and S. Daniels, 'Troubles in the later career of Humphry Repton', *Jnl. Garden History* 6 (2), 1986.

[1] For Repton's Welbeck 'Red Books', which include designs for a completely new house, see John Steegmann in *C. Life*, 30 Sept. 1933.

REPTON, JOHN ADEY (1775–1860), eldest son of Humphry Repton, was born at Norwich on 29 March 1775. He became a pupil of William Wilkins of Norwich (the father of William Wilkins, R.A.), for whom he made complete measured drawings of Norwich Cathedral which are now in the Library of the Society of Antiquaries.[1] In 1796 he entered the office of his father's associate John Nash, as an assistant. Nash found his knowledge of Gothic a useful asset, and Repton afterwards claimed the credit for the alterations to Corsham Court which were carried out by Nash in 1797–8. Repton's partial responsibility for this and other buildings was, however, never publicly acknowledged by Nash, and rather than act as a 'ghost' he joined his father at Hare Street, in order to collaborate with him in his publications and in the architectural side of his practice. From 1800 (the date he left Nash's office) until 1818, J. A. Repton was concerned in the alteration of many country houses whose gardens his father was improving. After his father's death in the latter year, he practised from Springfield in Essex. He was stone-deaf from infancy and for this reason lived a very retired existence, though his handicap did not prevent him from visiting the Continent in 1821–2, in order to advise on the improvement of various estates in Holland and Germany, including those of Prince Pückler-Muskau at Muskau in Silesia (cf. Ackermann, *Repository of Arts*, 3rd ser. xi, 1828, 313–14) and of the latter's father-in-law Prince Hardenberg at Neu-Hardenberg, nr. Frankfurt-on-Oder, and at Glienicke, nr. Potsdam.

Repton specialized in the enlargement and restoration of country houses in an Elizabethan style that owed something to East Anglian manor-houses. He also designed some classical houses, of which Sheringham Hall is the most attractive example, and one neo-Romanesque church. In 1809 he and his brother shared with C. Bacon the first prize for the design of public buildings then intended to be built in Westminster [P.R.O., WORK 8/10B, 24], and in 1810 they gained the second prize in the competition for the Bethlehem Hospital. Repton also competed for the Houses of Parliament. He exhibited at the Royal Academy between 1798 and 1804.

Repton's inclinations were antiquarian, and in later years he took a strong interest in the Camdenian movement, even contributing a paper on Gothic mouldings to the *Ecclesiologist*. He was elected F.S.A. in 1803, and was a frequent contributor to *Archaeologia* (see vols. xv, xvi, xix, xxi, xxiv and xxvii). Many articles by him appeared in the *Gentleman's Magazine* from 1795 onwards, and in the *Journal of the British Archaeological Association* (cf. xvii, 175–80). In 1820 he printed eighty copies of an 'oldentyme romance', entitled *A Trew Hystorie of the Prince Radapanthus*, and in 1839 a paper on beards and moustaches which he had read to the Society of Antiquaries. The drawings of Norwich Cathedral in Britton's *Cathedral Antiquities* (vol. ii, 1816) were his work. He died unmarried at Springfield on 26 November 1860. Frederick Mackenzie was a pupil.

[*A.P.S.D.*; *D.N.B.*; obituaries in *Gent's Mag.* x, 1861, 107–10, and *Jnl. British Archaeological Assn.* xvii, 1861, 175–80; J. Summerson, 'A Repton Portfolio', *R.I.B.A. Jnl.*, 25 Feb. 1933; *Catalogue of the R.I.B.A. Drawings Coll*; M. Uhlitz, 'Prince Pückler and John Adey Repton's visit to Prussia', *Jnl. Garden History* 9 (4), 1989].

CORSHAM COURT, WILTS., assisted John Nash in alterations, including remodelling of north front for P. C. Methuen, 1797–8, Gothic; destroyed 1844–9 [above, p. 691; drawing for north front in Yale Center for British Art attributed to Repton].

*BRENTRY HILL, nr. BRISTOL, GLOS., for William Payne, *c.*1802; now nucleus of Royal Victoria Hospital [exhib. at R.A. 1802; Loudon, 282–3].

*COTE or COTHAM BANK, OLVESTON, GLOS., for William Broderip, before 1803; dem. [Loudon, 130, 284 n.].

*ORGAN HALL, ALDENHAM, HERTS., designs (? executed) for William Towgood, before 1803; dem. [Loudon, 131, 284 n.].

*STAPLETON, nr. BRISTOL, GLOS., designs (? executed) for Dr. Lovell, M.D., before 1803 [Loudon, 131, 284 n.].

*STANAGE PARK, RADNORSHIRE, enlarged for Charles Rogers, 1803–7; further additions by E. Haycock 1845 ['Red Book' at Stanage; J. Williams, *History of the County of Radnor*, 1905 (written *c.*1810), 241].

*LAXTON HALL, NORTHANTS., enlarged and remodelled entrance-front for George Freke Evans, 1806–9, with hall by George Dance, jr., and designed stables [J. P. Neale, *Views of Seats*, 2nd. ser. i, 1824: Loudon, 506–7 and fig. 207; Stroud, 148; Sir Gyles Isham, 'Laxton Hall', *Northants. Antiq. Soc.* lxvi, 1969, 18–21; plans in R.C.H.M., *North Northants.*, 1984, 109–13].

*LAXTON VICARAGE, NORTHANTS., 1806

[1] These were published by the Gregg Press in 1965 as J. A. Repton, *Norwich Cathedral at the End of the Eighteenth Century*, with an introduction by S. Rowland Pierce.

* In association with his father.

[R.C.H.M., *North Northants.*, 1984, 114].

*BARNINGHAM HALL, NORFOLK, alterations for John Thruston Mott, 1807, Elizabethan style [Loudon, 435–9; drawings at Barningham dated 1807].

*?HOVETON HALL, NORFOLK, for Mrs. Burroughs, *c.*1809. There is an unexecuted design for this house in the Colman Collection, Norfolk City Library, marked 'Plan B' and signed 'H. Repton and Sons', 1809. It is possible that the house was built to Plan A, which has not survived [K. Laurie in *The Garden* 108 (9), Sept. 1983, 365].

*HARLESTONE HOUSE, NORTHANTS., remodelled house for Robert Andrew and designed stables, 1809–11; house dem. 1939 [Loudon, 428–9; photos of drawings by Repton in Northants. C.R.O., P. 1280/1/2 and P. 5572] (J. A. Gotch, *Squires' Homes of Northants.*, 1939, figs. 94–6).

*UPPARK, SUSSEX, alterations, including remodelling of dining-room, for Sir Harry Fetherstonhaugh, 1810–13 [C. Hussey in *C. Life*, 14, 21, 28 June 1941].

*SHERINGHAM HALL, NORFOLK, for Abbot Upcher, 1813–19 [C. Hussey in *C. Life*, 31 Jan., 7 Feb. 1957].

*COBHAM HALL, KENT, alterations and additions for 4th Earl of Darnley, *c.*1813–31, including ceiling of Queen Elizabeth's Room (1817), and Brewer's Gate and Shepherd's Gate lodges, Elizabethan style [Loudon, 418–19, 564; Stroud, 52; drawings in Yale Center for British Art and R.I.B.A.D.].

*BOURN HALL, CAMBS., reconstructed for 5th Earl De La Warr, 1817–19, Elizabethan [J. P. Neale, *Views of Seats*, 1st ser., vi, 1823].

BLICKLING HALL, NORFOLK, alterations and additions for Dowager Lady Suffield, including restoration of W. front, new arcades to wings, clock-tower, and estate cottages, *c.*1823–30 [John Maddison, 'Architectural Drawings at Blickling Hall', *Arch. Hist.* 34, 1991, 81–3].

BLICKLING CHURCH, NORFOLK, Gothic screen, *c.*1825 [John Maddison, *op. cit.*, 82].

SPRING (WOODCHESTER) PARK, nr. STROUD, GLOS., alterations, including library and dining-room, for 1st Earl of Ducie, *c.*1825; dem. 1846 [J. & H. S. Storer, *Delineations of the County of Gloucester*, 1828, 40; cf. drawings in R.I.B.A.D.].

BUCKHURST (formerly STONELANDS) PARK, WITHYHAM, SUSSEX, remodelled for 5th Earl De La Warr, *c.*1830–5, Elizabethan [Colbran's *New Guide for Tunbridge Wells*, 1840, 284; B. Burke, *Visitation of Seats and Arms* ii, 1853, 162; cf. J. Harris, *Catalogue of British Drawings for Architecture, etc., in American Collections*, 1971, 178].

SPRINGFIELD, nr. CHELMSFORD, ESSEX, HOLY TRINITY CHURCH, 1842–3, Romanesque [*Gent's Mag.* 1843 (ii), 421].

ATTINGHAM PARK, SALOP., Tern Lodge for 2nd Lord Berwick, date uncertain [R.I.B.A.D.].

Note: J. A. Repton's designs for BAILBROOK HOUSE, BATHEASTON, SOMERSET (*c.*1805), BAYHAM ABBEY, SUSSEX (*c.*1800), GREAT TEW PARK, OXON. (1803), PANSHANGER, HERTS. (1800), and SCARISBRICK HALL, LANCS (1802), were not carried out.

* In association with his father.

REVELEY, WILLEY (1760–1799), born on 14 March 1760, was the son of William Reveley (d. 1806), a member of a North Country family which had inherited the estate of Newby Wiske in Yorkshire by the marriage of William Reveley (d. 1725 and probably the architect's grandfather) to Margery, daughter and heiress of Robert Willey. Willey became a pupil of Sir William Chambers in 1777 and was admitted to the Royal Academy Schools the same year. From July 1781 to December 1782 he was employed by Chambers as assistant clerk of works at Somerset House. In 1785 he accompanied Sir Richard Worsley as 'architect and draughtsman' on his tour through Italy, Greece and Egypt, in the course of which he spent some time in Athens studying the temples made famous by Stuart and Revett. The journal describing his journey from Rome to Malta, Crete and Greece is in the R.I.B.A. Library (ff. 165–188 of a MS. Architectural Dictionary, etc.).

On his return to England, Reveley appeared to have every prospect of a successful career. He had already begun to exhibit at the Royal Academy, and he had acquired a considerable reputation as an authority on Greek architecture. He was a friend of Thomas Holcroft and William Godwin, and assisted Jeremy Bentham in preparing the plans for a panopticon prison which were published by the latter in 1791. In 1792–5 the church of ALL SAINTS, SOUTHAMPTON, was erected to his designs by a builder named John Hookey: it was an interesting essay in neo-classical design with an Ionic portico and a segmental, coffered ceiling 61 feet wide. It was destroyed by bombing in 1940. For plan and elevation see C. L. Stieglitz, *Plans et Desseins tirés de la Belle Architecture*, Paris & Leipsig, 1798–1800, pls. 23–4. Reveley also designed a mansion at WINDMILL HILL, SUSSEX, for W. H. Pigou, completed in 1798, and illustrated in G. Richardson, *New Vitruvius Britannicus* i, 1810, pls. 24–6: and he was the architect of the lodges at PARHAM in SUSSEX, the seat of Sir

Cecil Bisshopp, Bart. (1789), and of those at STOURHEAD, WILTS. (1793), designs for which he exhibited at the Royal Academy in those years. References in Sir John Soane's journal suggest that in 1798 Reveley may also have made designs for a house for W. Moffat at WESTON, nr. SOUTHAMPTON (dem.).

In 1794 he was chosen to edit the third volume of Stuart's *Antiquities of Athens*, and in the introduction showed himself an enthusiastic champion of the use of the Greek orders in contemporary architecture. Indeed, he did not hesitate to take Sir William Chambers himself to task for his strictures on the 'gusto Greco'. 'Sir William', he wrote, 'seems to insinuate that the Parthenon would gain considerably with respect to beauty by the addition of a steeple. A judicious observer of the fine arts would scarcely be more surprised were he to propose to effect this improvement by adding to it a Chinese pagoda.' This was not in the best of taste, nor was it prudent in a young architect to make fun of the Surveyor-General of His Majesty's Works. 'But Mr. Reveley had rather an awkward way of letting loose his opinions; and had habituated himself to a sarcastic mode of delivering them.' It had already, in 1786, been responsible for his separation from Worsley, who finished his tour alone, and if it alienated even those who could appreciate his talents, it was fatal with the less enlightened clientèle of aldermen and churchwardens. At Canterbury it was exasperating to learn that his plans for the County Infirmary were to be executed under the supervision of a 'common Carpenter', 'in order to save the expense of an architect'; but his annoyance was so unconcealed that it cost him the commission altogether. Some such incident may have led to the rejection of his designs for the new Pump Room at Bath, which were said to be 'of great beauty and elegance, replete with convenience, . . . , and disposed in an original style of accommodation', and a similar lack of success attended the plans for wet docks on the Thames which he submitted to Parliament in 1796 (see *Parliamentary Reports* xiv, 1803, 342b, 422, 424, etc., *Monthly Magazine*, 1799, 147, and Sir Joseph Broodbank, *History of the Port of London* i, 1921, 87). Even at Southampton, his plans for the new church had to be 'modified somewhat drastically to suit the prejudice of the mayor and aldermen of that city'.

Reveley died, 'after a few hours illness, in the prime of life', on 6 July 1799. His widow married John Gisborne and became intimate with the poet Shelley in Italy. A portrait of Reveley was in the possession of the late C. E. Kenney. Some of his drawings of buildings in Egypt and Greece are in the Victoria and Albert Museum. A folio volume of his 'Tracings and Drawings of Architectural Ornaments' and the sale catalogue of his drawings, designs and books (Christie's, 11–12 May 1801) are in Sir John Soane's Museum. Another copy of the sale catalogue is in the R.I.B.A. Library. An album of architectural designs made by Reveley as a young man was sold at Sotheby's in November 1979 and June 1982 and again at Christie's in December 1982. Drawings by him of the Pyramids, formerly in the Library of New College, Oxford, cannot now be found.

Reveley's son Henry Willey Reveley (*c.*1789–1875) practised first in Cape Town, where in 1826 he obtained the post of Civil Engineer and Superintendent of Buildings, and then in Australia. At Cape Town his work included St. Andrew's Presbyterian Church (Doric) and St. George's Church (Ionic). He returned to England and died at Reading in 1875, aged 86. He and his wife Cleobulina are buried in Reading Cemetery.

[*A.P.S.D.*; *D.N.B.*; J. Nichols, *Literary Anecdotes of the Eighteenth Century* ix, 1815, 148–50; *Gent's Mag.* 1799 (ii), 627, 1801 (i), 419–20, 1806 (i), 587; A. T. Bolton, *The Portrait of Sir John Soane*, 1927, 25, 60; *The Works of Jeremy Bentham*, ed. J. Bowring, x, 1843, 251–2; F. L. Jones, *Maria Gisborne and Edward E. Williams: their Journals and Letters*, Oklahoma 1951, 3 *et seq.*; *C. Life*, 19 June 1958, 1382; *Catalogue of the R.I.B.A. Drawings Coll.*]

REVETT, NICHOLAS (1720–1804), was the second son of John Revett of Brandeston Hall, nr. Framlingham in Suffolk, where he was born. He left England for Italy in September 1742, and studied painting in Rome under Cavaliere Benefiale. Here he became friendly with James Stuart, Matthew Brettingham, junior, and Gavin Hamilton, the painter. In April 1748 he accompanied them on an expedition to Naples, in the course of which they decided to visit Athens in order to measure the Greek antiquities there. This proposal was encouraged by many of the English dilettanti in Rome and money was raised to finance the expedition. Hamilton and Brettingham both withdrew, but Stuart and Revett left Rome for Venice in March 1750. At Venice they made the most of an enforced delay by visiting the antiquities at Pola in Istria. They became acquainted with Sir James Gray, the British resident in Venice, through whose agency they were elected members of the Society of Dilettanti in 1751. Reaching Athens in the spring of 1751, they remained there, with some intervals, for nearly three years. In spite of the difficulties caused by the disturbed state of the city's government and an outbreak of plague, they measured and drew nearly all the principal monuments of antiquity in Athens. Revett was responsible for the architectural part of the drawings and it was from him that, according to a writer in the *Gentleman's Magazine* of March 1788, 'Mr. Stuart first caught the ideas of that science, in which (quitting the painter's art) he afterwards made so conspicuous a figure.' On their return to England in 1755, they obtained support from the Society of Dilettanti for the publication of their discoveries, and the first volume of *The Antiquities of Athens, measured and delineated by James Stuart, F.R.S. and F.S.A., and Nicholas Revett, Painters and Architects,* eventually appeared in 1762.

The book was an immediate success, but all the profits, as well as most of the credit, went to Stuart, who had bought out Revett's interest before the publication of the first volume. Revett, however, remained an active member of the Society of Dilettanti, and was chosen by them to go on an expedition to the coast of Asia Minor with Richard Chandler (a Fellow of Magdalen College, Oxford, and author of *Marmora Oxoniensia,* 1763) and William Pars ('a young painter of promising talents'). They left England in June 1764, returning in September 1766. Revett undertook the measuring of the architectural antiquities, and a selection of the drawings was afterwards published by the Society of Dilettanti under his editorship as *The Antiquities of Ionia* (2 vols. 1769–97). His original drawings are now in the R.I.B.A. Drawings Collection and the British Library (Add. MSS. 21152–3). Thus Revett was the leading figure in the production of two books which were to be of great importance both in disseminating a knowledge of Greek architecture in Europe, and in providing sources for the later Greek Revival in England.

Revett, having private means, did not practise extensively as an architect, and his chief works were undertaken for friends like Henry Dawkins, for whom soon after 1766 he added a portico to STANDLYNCH (now TRAFALGAR HOUSE), WILTS., and designed the ceilings, chimney-pieces, and many internal decorations [*Vitruvius Britannicus* v, 1771, pls. 78–81; drawings in Bodleian, Gough Misc. Ant. fol. 4, ff. 55, 57, 151, 153, etc.; C. Hussey in *C. Life*, 13, 20 July 1945]. For Sir Francis Dashwood (afterwards Lord Le Despenser), a member of the Dilettanti Society, he added the Ionic portico to the west front of WEST WYCOMBE PARK, BUCKS. This was based on the Temple of Bacchus at Teos which Revett had measured in 1764–6. According to a MS. note in the copy of Langley's *Hundred of Desborough* in the Library of the Society of Antiquaries, it was completed in 1771. The Dashwood papers (now in the Bodleian Library, Oxford) show that Revett was still working at West Wycombe in 1778, 1779 and 1780, presumably in connection with the Temple of Flora (dem.) and the 'Music Room' or Island Temple, both of which he is stated to have designed in a letter from James Dawkins, junior, to the publisher of the fourth volume of the *Antiquities of Athens.* Some of his drawings for the temples and other buildings at West Wycombe are in the Bodleian Library (Gough Misc. Ant. fol. 4). There is no documentary evidence that he designed the church at West Wycombe, which was rebuilt by Lord Le Despenser in the years 1761–3, and Dawkins specifically told Joseph Taylor in 1809 that Revett was not its architect. Dawkins's claim that Revett designed the east (Doric) portico of the house is incorrect, as it was built in 1754–5, long before he had any connection with West Wycombe.

The only other building of importance of which Revett is known to have been the architect is the church at AYOT ST. LAWRENCE, HERTS., which he designed for Sir Lionel Lyde in 1778. It was consecrated on 28 July 1779 (*Gent's Mag.* 1779, 374; 1789 (ii), 972). As at Standlynch, he employed the Order of the Temple of Apollo at Delos, whose shafts were fluted at the extremities only.

From a letter in the Bodleian Library (Gough Misc. Ant. fol. 4, no. 174), it appears that in 1757 Revett designed an ornamental 'portico' which was built in the garden of his brother's house at Brandeston in Suffolk. This, if Grecian in character, would have been one of the earliest recorded buildings in that style. He also designed the memorial tablet to Alexander Ballantyne, M.D., in Salisbury Cathedral (erected 1783), and the monument to James Dawkins (d. 1766) in Chipping Norton Church, Oxon.

In 1791 Revett was made an Honorary Member of the Architects' Club on its foundation. Towards the end of his life he is said to have been in financial difficulties. He died on 3 June 1804, aged 84, and was buried in Brandeston churchyard. There is an inscription to his memory in the north aedicule of Ayot St. Lawrence Church. His library was sold at Christie's on 26–27 June 1804. There is a copy of the catalogue in Sir John Soane's Museum. A portrait of Revett in old age by G. Dance, R.A., is engraved in W. Daniell's *Collection of Portraits* (1808–14). There is an engraving of a portrait by Allan Ramsay at the R.I.B.A., and E. B. Jupp, in his *Catalogue of Original Drawings, illustrating the Catalogues of the Society of Artists*, 1871, 7, notes an engraving by William Woollett of a 'Portrait of Revett sketching Ruins' by James Stuart (1765).

A large volume containing some drawings by Revett and a number of proof engravings (chiefly for the *Ionian Antiquities*) is in the Bodleian Library (Gough Misc. Ant. fol. 4). Other drawings by him are at West Wycombe Park. His copies of Chandler's *Travels in Asia Minor*, 1775, and *Travels in Greece*, 1776, with MS. notes, were bought at his sale by George Saunders, who presented them to the British Museum (now Library): they were republished in 1825 with the notes.

[*A.P.S.D.*; *D.N.B.*; Lesley Lawrence, 'Stuart and Revett; their Literary and Architectural Careers', *Jnl. Warburg Institute* ii, 1938–9; memoirs in Wood, *Antiquities of Athens*, vol. iv, 1816, pp. xxviii-xxxi; *Gent's Mag.* lxxiv (ii), 1804, 690, 860; lxxix (ii), 1809, 596–7; xci (ii), 1821, 423; letter from James Dawkins, junior, in B. L., Add. MS. 22152, f. 35, describing his architectural works; Dora Wiebenson, *Sources of Greek Revival Architecture*, 1969; J. Mordaunt Crook, *The Greek Revival*, 1972; Gervase Jackson-Stops, *West Wycombe Park*, National Trust 1973; Giles Worsley, 'The First Greek Revival architecture', *Burlington Mag.* April 1985, 226–7; Eileen Harris, *British Architectural Books and Writers, 1556–1785*, 1990, 439–448.]

REYNOLDS, ESAU (1725–1778), was the son of Jonathan Reynolds, a prosperous carpenter and joiner at Trowbridge in Wiltshire. Esau followed his father into the family business, but, with the advantage of a better education, also practised as an architect. He designed the TOWN BRIDGE at TROWBRIDGE in 1777, altered the BRIDEWELL at DEVIZES in 1775, and was responsible for repairs and alterations to several local churches, notably at RODE, where he rebuilt the clerestory in 1773, replacing the original window by 'segmental-headed substitutes' which were in turn removed in 1872. His principal work was the almshouses known as HEYTESBURY HOSPITAL, which were built to his designs in 1766–8. In the R.I.B.A. Drawings Collection there is a design for a Palladian gateway signed 'Esau Reynols Delin. 1748'. On 29 September 1778 Reynolds was returning from a visit to Bath when his horse bolted, he 'struggled to stop him for above two miles' but eventually fell and was killed on the spot. He left a number of books, pictures, busts, statues and medals. [K. H. Rogers, *Esau Reynolds of Trowbridge*, Trowbridge 1967.]

REYNOLDS, SAMUEL WILLIAM (1773–1835), is best known as an artist and engraver (see *D.N.B.*). In about 1805 he began to practice as a landscape-gardener, though his lack of training as a surveyor proved a serious obstacle, and frustrated the realization of his plan for laying out the grounds at Coleorton for Sir George Beaumont [Beds. C.R.O., W1/4066, 4073–4]. There is evidence that he also acted as an architect. In 1810–11 Lee Antonie of Colworth, to whom Reynolds had been introduced by their mutual friend Samuel Whitbread, employed him to supervise various alterations to the offices and grounds at COLWORTH HOUSE, BEDS. [Beds. C.R.O., UN 370, 457, 509, etc.] In 1813 he fitted up a house in STRATFORD PLACE, LONDON, for Lord Henry Fitzgerald [*ibid.*, 384, 387], and in 1815 he designed FOSTON RECTORY (now HOUSE), LEICS. [Leics. C.R.O., Faculty papers]. Reynolds exhibited regularly at the Royal Academy, but none of his exhibits were of an architectural character.

REYNOLDS, THOMAS, of London, contracted in 1759 to build WIVENHOE PARK, ESSEX, for Isaac Rebow, apparently to his own designs [Rosemary Feesey, *Wivenhoe Park*, 1963, 10–14]. A person of this name signs an elevation of the Pantheon in Rome among drawings collected by William Stukeley and now in the Bodleian Library (Gough Maps 230, p. 373). In 1774 Thomas Reynolds of Islington, surveyor, then aged 39, was appointed District Surveyor for the parishes of St. Mary, Islington, and St Sepulchre, Holborn [Middlesex County Records, General Orders No. 10].

RHODES, HENRY (–1846), was the son of William Rhodes (*q.v.*), and was articled at an early age to William Porden. In about 1808 he entered the Land Revenue Office as a clerk. He subsequently succeeded Thomas Leverton as one of the two surveyors to the Office of Woods, Forests and Land Revenue (amalgamated in 1832 with the Office of Works). Owing to ill-health he retired on a pension in 1840 and was succeeded by James Pennethorne. He exhibited occasionally at the Royal Academy, and was one of the first members of the Council of the Institute of British Architects. He had antiquarian interests, and was a member of the Royal Archaeological Institute. As an architect he has to be judged chiefly by Egham Church, a somewhat clumsy essay in the style of Sir John Soane. Rhodes died at his house in Margaret Street, Cavendish Square, on 27 January 1846. His library and collection were sold by Christie's on 24 March and the following days. [*Gent's Mag.* 1846 (i), 329; *Builder* iv, 1846, 58; *A.P.S.D.*]

CHEQUERS, BUCKS., alterations for Sir George Russell, Bart., 1802, Gothic [L. Fleming, *Memoir and Select Letters of Samuel Lysons*, 1934, 35–6; exhib. at R.A. 1805].

FIRLE PLACE, SUSSEX, proposed alterations for 3rd Viscount Gage, 1807 [drawings at Firle].

HALTON CHURCH, BUCKS., 1813, Gothic; reconstructed 1886–7 [*Builder* v, 1846, 58].

EGHAM CHURCH, SURREY, 1818–20 [exhib. at R.A. 1817].

DOWNLEY FARMHOUSE, WEST WYCOMBE, BUCKS., for Sir John Dashwood, Bart., 1819 [drawings at West Wycombe Park].

LONDON, No. 31 HAYMARKET, shop-front for Messrs. Brecknell & Turner, tallow-chandlers, 1821; dem. [order-book of Messrs. Jones & Clarke, metal window manufacturers of Birmingham, Birmingham Reference Library MS. 1056/249, no. 221].

LONDON, premises at corner of PALL MALL EAST and COCKSPUR STREET for Messrs. Hancock & Rixon, glass manufacturers, *c.*1830; dem. [J. Elmes, *Metropolitan Improvements*, 1831, 155] (N. Whittock, *On the Construction and Decoration of the Shop Fronts of London*, 1840, pl. ix).

BARRINGTON HALL, ESSEX, unexecuted designs for extensive alterations for Sir William Barrington, Bart., 1833 [Essex Record Office].

LONDON, ST. JAMES'S PARK, entrance from Duke Street, Whitehall, in conjunction with T. Chawner, 1834; dem. [*Architectual Mag.* i, 1834, 316].

LONDON, COX'S HOTEL Nos. 53–55 JERMYN STREET, in conjunction with T. Chawner, 1836–7; dem. 1923–4 [*A.P.S.D.*; *Survey of London* xxix, 275].

LONDON, stabling at corner of HAYMARKET and COVENTRY STREET, in conjunction with T. Chawner: dem. [*A.P.S.D.*].

RHODES, WILLIAM, was an obscure London architect of the eighteenth century. In 1772, as 'William Rhodes of St. James's Westminster, architect and surveyor', he took an apprentice named Robert Greening [P.R.O., Apprenticeship Registers], and in 1774 and 1776 Thomas Lee (*q.v.*) exhibited architectural designs at the Royal Academy from 'Mr. Rhodes', Great Marlborough Street'. Rhodes subscribed to George Richardson's *Book of Ceilings* (1776), and was presumably the plasterer called William Rhodes who in 1771–4 redecorated the drawing-room and dining-room at DRAYTON HOUSE, NORTHANTS., for Viscount Sackville [*Associated Architectural Societies' Reports and Papers* xxxiii, 1915–16, 78–80] (*C. Life*, 3 June 1965).

RIBBANS, WILLIAM PARKES (*c.*1810–1871), practised in Ipswich, where he died on 15 January 1871 [Principal Probate Registry, Calendar of Probates]. In 1835 he won the competition for the EAST SUFFOLK HOSPITAL at IPSWICH, which was erected to his designs in 1835–6. It has a striking but awkwardly composed façade [J. Wodderspoon, *Memorials of Ipswich*, 1850, 10; *Ipswich Jnl.*, 13 June 1835, 6 August 1836]. He also designed the TOWN HALL at HADLEIGH, SUFFOLK, in 1851 in an attractively old-fashioned classical style of Palladian derivation [archives of the Hadleigh Market Feoffees, *ex inf.* Mr. R. Hewlings]. F. B. Ribbans, a schoolmaster who in 1843 published *An Essay on Perspective . . . intended for Architectural Students and Civil Engineers*, was presumably a relation.

RICAUTI, THOMAS JAMES (–1842), was a pupil of John Foulston. He published two books, entitled *Rustic Architecture*, 1840, containing 42 plates of designs for picturesque cottages, etc., and *Sketches for Rustic Work including Bridges, Park and Garden Buildings, Seats and Furniture*, 1842, 2nd ed. 1848. The latter was dedicated to Sir Robert Howland of Orwell Park, Suffolk, whom the author acknowledged as his first patron. Both were intended to demonstrate 'the picturesque and pleasing appearance of rough wood, thatch etc., when applied as the only decorations of rural buildings'. A design for a half-timbered cottage by Ricauti is given by Loudon, *Encyclopaedia of Rural Architecture, Supplement* 1842, 1155. He died in London in 1842.

RICE, WILLIAM (*c.*1734–1789), was successively Clerk of Works at Richmond from 1751 to 1758, and at Hampton Court from 1758 until his death in 1789. He was also Surveyor of the Horse Guards, and from 1768 to 1780 Surveyor of Buildings to H. M. Customs. For Henry Bankes, a Commissioner of the Customs, he designed in the 1770s the laundry and other offices in the Kitchen Yard at KINGSTON LACY, DORSET [drawings at Kingston Lacy]. As Surveyor of the Horse Guards he was succeeded by his nephew Thomas Rice, who also held his uncle's former post at Hampton Court from 1808 until his death in 1810. A portrait of William Rice at the age of 10, painted by R. Scadder in 1744, is in the possession of the proprietors of Lord's Cricket Ground.

RICH, JAMES, 'surveyor now residing at Cromarty', reconstructed FEARN ABBEY CHURCH, ROSS-SHIRE, in 1771–2, after it had been in a state of ruin since 1742 [S.R.O., GD 71/305/1].

RICHARDBY, JAMES (*c.*1776–1846), practised in Bradford for many years until his death on 6 August 1846 at the age of 70. He was a prominent Liberal and in 1838 received a presentation silver cup in recognition of forty years' service to the Liberal cause. His works in Bradford included a MARKET HOUSE built at HALL INGS in 1823, but demolished two years later because it infringed the manorial market rights [John James, *Continuation to the History of Bradford*, 1866, 98]; warehouses in PICCADILLY, 1830–4 [D. Linstrum, *West Yorkshire Architects and Architecture*, 1978, 383]; and FIELD HOUSE, SMITH LANE (now part of the Royal Infirmary), for Mrs. S. Ward, 1835–6 [W. Cudworth, *History of Manningham, Heaton and Allerton*, 1896, 55]. W. Cudworth, *History of Bradford Corporation*, 1881, 72, gives his name as 'architect' in connection with the BRADFORD COURT HOUSE (dem. *c.*1960), but see under 'Bernard Hartley', above, p. 470.

RICHARDS, GEORGE, of Truro, was in 1792 appointed 'inspector' of the building of THE ROYAL CORNWALL INFIRMARY there to the designs of W. Wood (*q.v.*) [C. T. Andrews, *The First Cornish Hospital*, Penzance 1975, 11]. Some designs for stables signed by him and dated 1826 are noticed by J. Harris, *Catalogue of British Designs for Architecture, etc. in American Collections*, 1971, 178. In 1822 he took out a patent for grates and stoves.

RICHARDS, GEORGE, of Rotherhithe, submitted a design for rebuilding London Bridge in 1823 [*Catalogue of the Exhibition of Designs for rebuilding London Bridge*, 1823, Soane Museum, P.C. 55].

RICHARDS, JOHN (1690–1778), was born at Mariansleigh, N. Devon, and received 'some little instruction at a Grammar School'. As 'his Genius chiefly inclined him to Mathematical studies', he was apprenticed to a joiner in Exeter named Abraham Voysey 'who also made and sold Gunther's scales and Sea-Quadrants'. Voysey died in 1710 and in the following year Richards, then only 20, married his widow and carried on his business. Eventually he gave up joinery and building and was chiefly employed as a valuer, accountant and surveyor of land and buildings. He was the author of two tracts on Life Annuities, etc. (1730, 1739), and of another on Cask Gauging (1740). In 1741–3 he gratuitously designed THE DEVON AND EXETER HOSPITAL in SOUTHERNHAY, EXETER, enlarged in 1772, 1856, 1896, etc. Towards the end of his life he became insane, dying in January 1778 at the age of 87. [W. G. Hoskins, *Two Thousand Years in Exeter*, 1960, 89; obituary in *Exeter Flying Post* of Jan. 1778, *ex inf.* the late Prof. W. G. Hoskins; *Trans. Devonshire Association* civ, 1972, 176.]

RICHARDS, WILLIAM (–*c.*1827), of Penzance, designed the COINAGE HALL at HELSTON, CORNWALL, in 1807 [Cornwall Record Office, 37A/BAR/33, signed drawings]. He was presumably the architect called Richards who designed SAUNDERS HILL, nr. PADSTOW, CORNWALL, for Thomas Rawlings in about 1810 [J. P. Neale, *Views of Seats*, 2nd ser. ii, 1825; S. Lysons, *Magna Britannia* iii, 253]. As the latter is somewhat Soanean in character it is possible that its author was the William Richards who was a clerk in Sir John Soane's office from 1789 to 1803 [A. T. Bolton, *The Works of Sir John Soane*, 1924, p. xl].

RICHARDSON, GEORGE (–*c.*1813), began life as a draughtsman in the office of Robert and James Adam. He may have been apprenticed to their elder brother John Adam, for on 10 March 1759 he was described as 'apprentice' when witnessing the latter's will in Edinburgh. From 1760 to 1763 he accompanied James Adam on his Grand Tour, gaining in this way a first-hand knowledge of the antique sources that formed the basis of the Adam style. He was not, however, treated at all generously by his master, and complained in a letter to a friend that he was obliged to conceal such sketches as he had made for his own use, as Adam would be very angry if he discovered them, although they were made in Richardson's own time. On his return to Britain he had, however, little prospect of establishing an independent practice, 'well knowing my own incapacity, small fortune, want of books, and little hopes of interest'. For some years he continued to be employed as a draughtsman in the Adams' London office. Exactly when he left their service is not known. The fact that in 1765 he obtained a premium from the Society of Arts for an architectural design may indicate his emancipation, and from 1766 onwards he exhibited at the Society of Artists under his own name. According to the Society of Arts register he was under 30 in 1765, and in 1774 he stated that he had been 'draughtsman and designer' to the Adam brothers for 'upwards of eighteen years'.

Although he was an accomplished

draughtsman and designer of internal decoration in the Adam style, Richardson appears to have designed few complete buildings, and to have made a living chiefly by his publications and by acting as a drawing-master (see advertisement in his *New Designs in Architecture*). Towards the end of his life he was in seriously reduced circumstances. Joseph Nollekens is known to have helped him financially, and Joseph Farington records that he received 30 guineas out of the Royal Academy Charity Fund in 1807. The exact date of his death is not known, but news of it reached Joseph Farington on 16 May 1814, and in March of the same year the *Gentleman's Magazine* reported that the drawings and prints of 'the late Mr. George Richardson' had been sold on 29 November 1813.

Richardson competed for the Royal Exchange at Dublin in 1769. In 1783 he exhibited at the Royal Academy the 'Elevation of a church building at Stapleford, in Leicestershire, for the Earl of Harborough'. This elaborately Gothic church was one of three built by the 4th Earl of Harborough, the others being Teigh, Rutland (1782, Gothic), and Saxby, Leics. (1789, classical). It is likely that the same architect was responsible for all three. According to J. Throsby's *Select Views in Leicestershire* i, 1790, 153, the 'architect' of Stapleford Church was Christopher Staveley of Melton Mowbray (*q.v.*), but he was probably only the builder.

As a decorative designer Richardson appears to have played an important part at KEDLESTON HALL, DERBYSHIRE, in the late 1760s, for there are a number of drawings for ceilings, etc., signed by him both at Kedleston and in the Soane Museum, and in 1776 he exhibited at the Royal Academy 'The Ceiling executed in the Grecian Hall at Keddlestone'. Ceilings designed by him at Kedleston, Drapers' Hall, London, and Sir Lawrence Dundas's house in Edinburgh are illustrated in his *Book of Ceilings*. He was also employed at BROCKENHURST PARK, HAMPSHIRE, in 1775 [*Antique Collector*, Aug. 1954, 134], and a design by him for a ceiling at BENTON HOUSE, NORTHUMBERLAND, is illustrated by John Harris, *Catalogue of British Drawings for Architecture, etc., in American Collections*, 1971, 180–1.

Richardson's publications were, in order of date: *A Book of Ceilings composed in the Stile of the Antique Grotesque*, dedicated to Lord Scarsdale, 1774–6, 1793; *Iconology, or a Collection of Emblematical Figures*, 2 vols. 1779–80 (an English version of Cesare Ripa's *Iconologia* of 1593); *A New Collection of Chimney Pieces*, dedicated to Sir Lawrence Dundas, 1781; *A Treatise on the Five Orders of Architecture* (with observations on antiquities in Rome, Pola and Southern France, made in 1760–3), dedicated to Thomas Sandby, 1787; *New Designs in Architecture* (dedicated to Henry, Earl of Gainsborough), 1792; *New Designs of Vases, Tripods, etc.*, 1793; *Capitals of Columns and Friezes measured from the Antique*, 1793; *Original Designs for Country Seats or Villas*, 1795; *A New Book of Ornaments in the Antique Style*, 1796, reissued in 1816 as *A Collection of Ornaments in the Antique Style*; *The New Vitruvius Britannicus*, 2 vols. 1802–8 and 1808–10. The most ambitious of these works was the *New Vitruvius Britannicus*, which attempted to do for English architecture of the late eighteenth century what Colen Campbell and Woolfe and Gandon had done for earlier decades. Except in the case of *Iconology* Richardson engraved in aquatint all the plates for his books. In his later works he was assisted by his son William, who himself exhibited decorative designs at the Royal Academy in 1783, 1784, 1793 and 1794.

[*A.P.S.D.*; *D.N.B.*; *Gent's Mag.* 1814 (i), 210; Joseph Farington's diary, 12 July 1807, 12 July 1812, 16 May 1814; J. T. Smith, *Nollekens and his Times* i, 1829, 110–12; *Builder* xxvii, 781; John Fleming, *Robert Adam and his Circle*, 1962, 368–9, 377, etc.; Eileen Harris, *British Architectural Books and Writers 1556–1785*, 1990, 387–90; I. G. Brown, 'George Richardson in Rome', *Architectural Heritage* ii, 1991.]

RICHARDSON, JOHN (1774–1864/5), practised in Kendal, where he designed the NEW THEATRE, 1828–9, an INFANTS' SCHOOL, 1829, the WHITE HART HOTEL, *c.*1830, and 'TOWN VIEW' for William Wilson, 1831–3 [C. Nicholson, *Annals of Kendal*, 1861, 297–8; drawings for Hotel in C.R.O., Kendal].

RICHMOND, JOHN, appears to have designed RICCARTON CHURCH, AYRSHIRE, 1823, as his name appears on a set of drawings preserved in the church [G. Hay, *The Architecture of Scottish Post-Reformation Churches*, 1957, 135]. The façade of this otherwise unremarkable Georgian church is enlivened by two pediments with an unusual concave profile.

RICKETTS, JOHN, was one of a family of masons and carvers who were active in Gloucester throughout the eighteenth century (see Rupert Gunnis, *Dictionary of British Sculptors*, 1968, 321–2). He was probably a grandson of John Ricketts (d. 1734), the founder of the firm. In addition to designing and carving a number of elegant monuments, he appears to have designed the triumphal arch erected in Gloucester in 1777 in honour of William Bromley Chester, M.P. for that city. An engraving of the arch in Bishop Hooper's Museum is signed 'John Ricketts, Statuary at Gloucester'. In 1784 Ricketts was among those who surveyed the tower of St. Nicholas Church, Gloucester, receiving £1 11s. 6d. for his plan [Gloucester Public Library, extracts from Vestry Minutes]. Documents in private hands are said to show that he built and presumably designed EASTGATE HOUSE, GLOUCESTER, *c.*1780.

RICKMAN, THOMAS (1776–1841), born on 8 June 1776, was the eldest son of Joseph Rickman, an apothecary at Maidenhead. The Rickmans were a large, close-knit, Quaker family of long standing. Thomas was destined by his father for a medical career, but he found medicine uncongenial, and after various vicissitudes gave it up in favour of commerce. In 1804 he started business in London as a corn-factor and married his first cousin Lucy Rickman. Both actions proved to be disastrous. The marriage was not sanctioned by the Friends, who proceeded to disown Thomas and his wife,[1] and in 1807 the business failed and left him heavily in debt. He found employment in the office of a Liverpool insurance-broker, but the death a few weeks later of his wife, coupled with his other misfortunes, reduced him to a state of near despair from which he recovered only gradually. It was during this period of acute depression that he began to take the long country walks in the course of which he developed a latent interest in medieval architecture. Being 'very minute in his observation on any subject which he selected', he began to classify the window-tracery and other architectural details which he noted and to arrange them in a typological sequence which he labelled 'Norman', 'Early English', 'Decorated English' and 'Perpendicular English' (terms which he was already using in his diary as early as 1811). Soon afterwards he joined a small Philosophical Society in Liverpool in which scientific subjects were discussed, and it was to this society that in September 1811 he gave the first of a series of lectures on medieval architecture. In 1812, with the encouragement of George Harrison, an iron-founder of Chester with whom he became friendly, he wrote an account of the architectural history of Chester Cathedral (eventually printed in the *Journal of the Architectural, Archaeological and Historic Society of Chester*, 1864, 277–8). He also wrote a long article on Gothic architecture for *Smith's Panorama of Arts and Sciences* (Liverpool 1812–15), which was reprinted separately in 1817 as *An Attempt to discriminate the Styles of English Architecture from the Conquest to the Reformation.* This, the first systematic treatise on Gothic architecture in England, soon became well known, and Rickman's nomenclature was followed by all subsequent writers on the subject. The book was reprinted, with additions, several times during its author's lifetime. A seventh edition, edited by J. H. Parker, appeared in 1881.

In addition to the works already mentioned, Rickman published 'A Tour in Normandy and Picardy in 1832' (*Archaeologia* xxv, 1833), 'Four Letters on the Ecclesiastical Architecture of France and England' (*ibid.*) and an important paper on pre-Conquest architecture (*Archaeologia* xxvi, 1836, 26–46). He contributed the 'architectural observations' to J. S. Cotman's *Specimens of Architectural Remains*, 1838. He was elected a Fellow of the Society of Antiquaries in 1829, and was an early member of the British Association for the Advancement of Science. His achievement as an architectural scholar lay in the application of elementary scientific method to a subject that hitherto had been the preserve either of antiquaries like Britton who lacked his analytic powers, or of topographical artists whose approach was picturesque rather than historical. Rickman's acute observation of architectural detail, coupled with his grasp of evolutionary principle, enabled him to demonstrate once and for all the essential stylistic sequence to which all English medieval architecture conforms.

As an architect Rickman was self-taught. As early as 1794–7 he is said to have drawn and coloured several thousand figures wearing army uniforms, which he cut out and arranged against an architectural background of military buildings. But draughtsmanship did not come easily to him, and it was not until 1810–11 that he developed a thoroughly professional technique. In 1812 he began to show his drawings at the annual exhibitions of the Liverpool Academy, and in the same year he met John Cragg, a wealthy ironmaster with an interest in church-building. In 1813–14 he assisted Cragg to build a Gothic church at Everton, nr. Liverpool, in whose construction iron entered largely, and two more churches designed jointly by Rickman and Cragg were built at the latter's expense in 1814–16. At the same time Rickman was helping the Liverpool builder-architect John Slater to remodel Scarisbrick Hall in Lancashire in the Gothic style. These and other such tasks gave Rickman valuable practical experience, and in

[1] The marriage of first cousins was contrary to Quaker rules. Rickman was readmitted in 1813, shortly before his second marriage to Christiana Hornor.

December 1817 he gave up his job and opened an architect's office in Liverpool. During the next few years Rickman assiduously sought commissions. He entered for every architectural competition that was announced, and having persuaded the Church Building Commissioners of his competence, gained a large share of their patronage in the West Midlands. By 1820 he was beginning to be well known as a church architect, and for the next fifteen years he was one of the busiest architects in England. In 1820 he started a second office in Birmingham, to which his pupil Henry Hutchinson was transferred, becoming in December 1821 Rickman's partner. Hutchinson died in 1831, after much illness. Meanwhile a brother, Edwin Swan Rickman, had become an assistant in the Liverpool office, and was for a short time (1831–3) Rickman's partner in Birmingham (to which town the entire practice had by then been transferred). By 1833 Edwin was already showing sings of the mental illness which was later to incapacitate him. His place was taken by R. C. Hussey (1802–87), who became Rickman's partner in 1835. Failing health now began increasingly to interfere with Rickman's practice. In the spring of 1838 he handed over the office entirely to Hussey, and he died on 4 January 1841, in his 64th year. He was buried in the churchyard of St. George's, Birmingham, where a monument was erected in 1845 by several of his friends. Though for the greater part of his life he had been a conscientious member of the Society of Friends, he joined the Irvingites a few years before his death. His first wife, Lucy Rickman, had died in 1807. His second wife, Christiana Hornor, sister of Thomas Hornor, the proprietor of the Colosseum in Regent's Park, died in childbirth in 1813. In 1825 he married his third wife, Elizabeth Miller of Edinburgh, by whom he had several children, one of whom, Thomas Miller Rickman (1827–1912), became a pupil of R. C. Hussey and followed his father's profession.[1] Rickman's pupils included J. A. Bell of Edinburgh, John Broadbent of Liverpool, S. C. Fripp of Bristol, Thomas Fulljames of Gloucester, A. H. Holme of Liverpool, John Smith of Cambridge, G. Vose and L. Zeugheer of Zurich. A. E. Perkins of Worcester was also in his office for some years.

In 1823 Rickman & Hutchinson competed unsuccessfully for the new buildings at King's College, Cambridge, and in 1829 were placed third in the limited competition for the new University Library. In the course of the subsequent controversy they published an *Answer to Observations* [by G. Peacock] *on the Plans for the New Library*, Birmingham 1831. In 1831 they won the third prize in the competition for Birmingham Town Hall. In conjunction with Hussey Rickman also competed in 1835 for the Fitzwilliam Museum at Cambridge and for the Houses of Parliament at Westminster. For the former building they submitted three designs, one Gothic, one Roman and one Grecian in the manner of Schinkel [Ann James, 'Rickman and the Fitzwilliam Competition', *Arch. Rev.* April 1957; John Cornforth in *C. Life*, 22 Nov. 1962]. For the latter they proposed a building 'in the decorated style, as it prevailed in the time of King Edward III' [*Catalogue of the Designs for the New Houses of Parliament*, 1836, 8]. In 1836 they won the first prize in the competition for the Scott Monument in Edinburgh, but the committee eventually set their design aside in favour of one submitted by G. M. Kemp (*q.v.*) [T. Bonnar, *G. M. Kemp*, 1892, 83].

Rickman's considerable success as an architect rested partly on his enormous capacity for work ('he could', Hussey wrote, 'without material inconvenience, pass two nights of three in travelling'), and partly on his reputation as an expert on Gothic architecture. He and his friend Edward Blore (whom he first met in 1811 sketching at Doncaster) were probably the first English architects since James Essex who had a thorough knowledge of medieval architectural detail. Not only could Rickman date an ancient building correctly: he could reproduce its characteristic mouldings and enrichments accurately in a new one. But he was no ecclesiologist. If the detailing of his buildings was unusually scholarly, the planning remained Georgian, and the total effect of most of his churches is thin and brittle, if by no means unattractive. Many of them are in the Perpendicular style disliked by later revivalists, and Rickman did not scruple to make use of cast-iron tracery and to admit galleries and other features that were anathema to the next generation of church-builders. Many of his churches were economical jobs for the Church Building Commissioners, but Hampton Lucy, Ombersley, Oulton and Stretton-on-Dunsmore show what he could do if funds permitted. Rickman's most ambitious secular buildings were the classical Exhibition Room for the Birmingham Society of Artists (demol-

[1] Another architect member of the Rickman family was Thomas Rickman, who died at Harting in Sussex in 1849 at the age of 23. He is said to have been a cousin of the subject of this entry, and to have made designs for refitting Harting Church in 1845 [M. C. W. Hunter, *The Restorations of Harting Church, 1796–1876*, Harting 1970]. Some drawings by him are in the R.I.B.A. Collection.

ished in 1928) and the Gothic New Court at St. John's College, Cambridge, which exploits to the full the picturesque possibilities of Gothic architecture. The most brilliant feature of the latter building – the Bridge of Sighs – was designed by his partner Hutchinson, who must share the credit for everything built by the firm between 1821 and 1831.

Fifty-seven of Rickman's diaries, covering the years 1807 to 1834, are in the R.I.B.A. Library, together with a number of drawings. His 'work books' or professional journals for the years 1821–37 are in the British Library (Add. MSS. 37793–37802). Besides constituting a day-by-day record of Rickman's architectural practice they contain many notes on and sketches of medieval churches made by him in the course of his professional journeys. With them is a volume (Add. MS. 37803) of drawings of churches made by Rickman, chiefly in the years 1809–12. The first draft of the *Attempt* forms part of a notebook in the possession of Mr. John Baily, R.I.B.A. Notes and sketches for the 3rd edition (1825) are in the Bodleian Library (MSS. Top. eccles. c. 3–4). A large collection of Rickman's sketches of medieval architecture was purchased by the Oxford Architectural Society in 1842 and is described in the Society's *Report* for 1846, pp. 37–56. It is now in the Bodleian Library (MS. Dep. b. 140). A number of Rickman's architectural designs are in the R.I.B.A. Collection.

[*A.P.S.D.* (with list of works contributed by T. M. Rickman); T. M. Rickman, *Notes on the Life of Thomas Rickman*, 1901 (based on the diaries); *Gent's Mag.* 1841 (i), 322, 1861 (i), 523; *D.N.B.*; A. T. Brown, *How Gothic came back to Liverpool*, Liverpool 1937; M. H. Port, *Six Hundred New Churches*, 1961, chap. 6; *R.I.B.A. Drawings Catalogue*; Megan Aldrich, 'Gothic architecture illustrated: the Drawings of Thomas Rickman in New York', *Antiquaries' Jnl.* lxv, 1985; information from Mr. John Baily.]

The principal sources for Rickman's architectural work are his diaries and work-books (see above), which together provide an almost complete record of his working life. In addition there is the list of buildings contributed to the *A.P.S. Dictionary* by his son T. M. Rickman, and a list of churches left by Rickman himself in one of his workbooks (Add. MS. 37802, f. 290v). Many of the minor commissions present problems of identification, and the following list attempts only to give Rickman's principal executed works.

Buildings designed in partnership with H. Hutchinson are marked by an asterisk (*), those designed in partnership with R. C. Hussey by a dagger (†).

CHURCHES[1]

LIVERPOOL, ST. GEORGE, EVERTON, in conjunction with John Cragg, 1813–14; altar 1817.

LIVERPOOL, ST. MICHAEL, TOXTETH, in conjunction with John Cragg, 1814–15; N. aisle enlarged 1900.

LIVERPOOL, ST. PHILIP, HARDMAN STREET, in conjunction with John Cragg, 1815–16; dem. 1882.

BIRKENHEAD, CHESHIRE, ST. MARY, for Francis Price, 1819–21; transepts added 1832–5; dem. 1976 [see also R.I.B.A.D.].

BIRMINGHAM, ST. GEORGE, 1819–22; enlarged 1883–4; dem. 1960.

WARRINGTON, LANCS., HOLY TRINITY, rebuilt classical tower, 1820–1; rebuilt 1862.

*BARNSLEY, YORKS. (W.R.), ST. GEORGE, 1821–2; dem. 1992.

*ERDINGTON, WARWICKS., ST. BARNABAS, 1822–3; enlarged 1883; reroofed 1893.

*GLOUCESTER, CHRIST CHURCH, BRUNSWICK SQUARE, 1822–3, classical; remodelled in Romanesque style 1899–1900.

*CHORLEY, LANCS., ST. GEORGE, 1822–5.

*PRESTON, LANCS., ST. PETER, 1822–5; spire added 1851–2.

*HAMPTON LUCY, WARWICKS., for the Revd. John Lucy, 1822–6; apse added by Scott 1856.

*CHILDWALL, LANCS., alterations, 1823–4, probably including north aisle (rebuilt 1906).

*HANBURY, STAFFS., rebuilt north aisle, 1823–4; rebuilt 1869–70 [see also I.C.B.S.]

*MOSELEY, WORCS., rebuilt 1823–4; rebuilt 1886, 1897, 1909–11 and 1940 [see also I.C.B.S.].

*PRESTON, LANCS., ST. PAUL, 1823–5; chancel 1882.

*GLASGOW, ST. DAVID, INGRAM STREET (RAMSHORN CHURCH), 1824–6; interior remodelled 1886-7.

*BEVERLEY MINSTER, YORKS. (E.R.), alterations to choir and removal of galleries in nave, 1825 [cf. G. Poulson, *Beverlac*, 1829, 683].

*BIRMINGHAM, ST. PETER, DALE END, 1825–7, classical; reconstructed 1834–7 by C. Edge after fire in 1831; dem. 1899.

*OMBERSLEY, WORCS., for the Marchioness of Downshire, 1825–9.

*HANDSWORTH, STAFFS., ST. MARY, THE WATT CHAPEL, 1826.

*COVENTRY, WARWICKS., HOLY TRINITY, recased tower, etc., 1826 onwards [cf. B. Poole, *History of Coventry*, 1870, 202].

[1] All Gothic unless otherwise stated.

*GREAT TEW, OXON., repaired and repewed, 1826–7 [see also I.C.B.S.].

*BIRMINGHAM, ST. THOMAS, 1826–9, classical; refitted 1893; damaged by bombing 1940/1 and dem. except tower [see also R.I.B.A.D.].

*HAGLEY, WORCS., added north aisle, 1827–7; dem. 1858. [see also I.C.B.S.].

*DARWEN, LANCS., ST. JAMES, LOWER DARWEN, 1827–8.

*DARWEN, LANCS., HOLY TRINITY, OVER DARWEN, 1827–9.

*MELLOR, LANCS., 1827–9; altered 1899.

*OULTON, YORKS. (W.R.), for John Blayds, 1827–9.

*HARBORNE, WARWICKS., rebuilt 1827–9 retaining medieval tower; rebuilt 1867 [see also I.C.B.S.].

*CLITHEROE, LANCS., ST. MARY MAGDALENE, rebuilt 1828–9 retaining medieval tower, etc. [see also I.C.B.S.].

*CARLISLE, CUMBERLAND, CHRIST CHURCH, 1828–30; dem. 1952.

*CARLISLE, CUMBERLAND, HOLY TRINITY, 1828–30; dem. 1981.

*WHITTLE-LE-WOODS, LANCS., 1828–30; dem. 1880.

CANTERBURY CATHEDRAL, survey of north-west tower, etc., 1828–31.

*BRISTOL, HOLY TRINITY, 1829–31; enlarged 1889. [see also R.I.B.A.D.].

*RUGBY, WARWICKS., ST. ANDREW, added south aisle, *c.*1830; rebuilt 1877–9.

*HAIGH WITH ASPULL, LANCS., ST. DAVID, 1830; chancel 1886–7.

*PEMBERTON, nr. WIGAN, LANCS., ST. JOHN, 1830–2.

*COVENTRY, WARWICKS., CHRIST CHURCH, 1830–2, incorporating medieval steeple; dem. after bombing in 1941, except steeple.

*LIVERPOOL, ST. JUDE, LOW HILL, 1830–1; altered 1882; dem. 1966.

BLACKBURN, LANCS., ST. MARY (now Cathedral), survey after fire of 1831 and advice about subsequent restoration conducted by Thomas Stones as 'clerk of works' [cf. I.C.B.S.].

*SAFFRON WALDEN, ESSEX, rebuilt belfry and spire, 1831–2.

*TOCKHOLES, LANCS., ST. STEPHEN, 1831–3; dem. 1965.

LOWER HARDRES, KENT, rebuilt 1831–2.

WORCESTER CATHEDRAL, repairs, 1832.

BIRMINGHAM, ALL SAINTS, WINSON GREEN, 1832–3; chancel 1881; dem. *c.*1977.

REDDITCH, WORCS., OUR LADY (R.C.), BEOLEY ROAD, 1833–4.

BAVERSTOCK, WILTS., alterations, 1833; much altered by Butterfield 1880–2.

BRISTOL, ST. MATTHEW, KINGSDOWN, 1833–5 [see also R.I.B.A.D.].

MELLOR BROOK CHAPEL, MELLOR, LANCS., remodelled Independent Chapel for use by Established Church, 1834.

HENBURY, GLOS., repairs and alterations, 1834–5; altered by G. E. Street 1875–7 [see also *Trans. Bristol and Glos. Arch. Soc.* xxviii, 1915, 182–3].

STRETTON-ON-DUNSMORE, WARWICKS., rebuilt 1835–7.

LOUGHBOROUGH, LEICS., EMMANUEL CHURCH, FOREST ROAD, 1835–7.

HARTLEBURY, WORCS., rebuilt nave, 1836–7 [for inscription on foundation-stone see *Gent's Mag.* 1836 (i), 654].

SETTLE, YORKS (W.R.), 1836–8.

CLEVEDON, SOMERSET, CHRIST CHURCH, 1838–9.

†BIRMINGHAM, BISHOP RYDER'S MEMORIAL CHURCH, 1838; chancel 1894; dem. 1960.

†HALESOWEN, WORCS., internal alterations, 1838–9 [see also I.C.B.S.].

†SNEINTON, NOTTS., 1838–9; dem. 1912.

†HORSLEY, GLOS., rebuilt 1838–9 retaining medieval tower.

†GOODNESTONE, KENT, rebuilt nave and chancel, 1838–41 [S. Lewis, *Topographical Dictionary of England* ii, 1848, 315].

†ROCHESTER, ST. MARGARET, rebuilt chancel, 1839–40 [I.C.B.S.].

PUBLIC BUILDINGS, ETC.

LIVERPOOL, PARADISE STREET, premises for Messrs. Cropper, Benson & Co., merchants, 1816; later the 'Museum of Anatomy'; dem. 1941.

LIVERPOOL, CHARLOTTE STREET, Riding School for the Liverpool Light Horse Volunteers (later Lucas's Repository for Horses and Carriages), 1817.

CLITHEROE, LANCS., THE TOWN HALL, 1820–1, Gothic.

*PRESTON, LANCS., THE COURT HOUSE, STANLEY STREET, 1825; dome removed 1849.

*GLOUCESTER, THE INFIRMARY, south wing, 1826–7 [cf. G. W. Counsel, *History of Gloucester*, 1829, 176; G. Whitcombe, *The General Infirmary at Gloucester*, 1903, 18].

*CAMBRIDGE, ST. JOHN'S COLLEGE, THE NEW COURT, 1827–31, Gothic [cf. Willis & Clark, ii, 278; Marcus Whiffen in *Arch. Rev.* Dec. 1945, 160–5].

*BIRMINGHAM, PUBLIC NEWS ROOM, additions, 1828; dem.

*BIRMINGHAM, EXHIBITION ROOM in NEW STREET for the Birmingham Society of Artists, 1829; dem. 1928 [see also J. Hill & W. Midgley, *History of the Royal Birmingham Society of Artists*, 1928, 16].

*EDGBASTON, BIRMINGHAM, DEAF AND DUMB

ASYLUM, designed Master's House, 1829.

*COVENTRY, WARWICKS., THE DRAPERS' HALL, 1829–32.

*CARLISLE, CUMBERLAND, NEWSROOM AND LIBRARY (later Barclay's Bank), ENGLISH STREET, 1830–1, Gothic; dem. 1970 (S. Jefferson, *History of Carlisle*, 1838, frontispiece).

*BIRMINGHAM, THE BIRMINGHAM BANKING COMPANY'S OFFICE (now Midland Bank), BENNETT'S HILL, 1830–1.

*BORDESLEY, NR. BIRMINGHAM, HOLY TRINITY SCHOOL, 1831; dem. 1854.

*COVENTRY, BOND'S HOSPITAL, partial reconstruction, 1832, timber-framed Tudor style [cf. B. Poole, *History of Coventry*, 1870, 295].

*COVENTRY, THE BABLAKE BOYS' SCHOOL, 1832–3, Tudor Gothic; dem. 1890 [cf. *V.C.H. Warwicks*, viii, 141].

WHITEHAVEN, CUMBERLAND, THE TRUSTEE SAVINGS BANK, LOWTHER STREET, 1832–3.

†BRISTOL, ASYLUM FOR THE BLIND, PARK STREET, 1835–7, Gothic; dem. *c.*1914.

DOMESTIC ARCHITECTURE

SCARISBRICK HALL, LANCS., alterations for Thomas Scarisbrick in conjunction with John Slater (*q.v.*), 1812–16, Gothic; remodelled by A. W. N. Pugin 1837 onwards.

RHIWLAS, nr. BALA, MERIONETHSHIRE, Gothic gateway for R. Thelwall Price, 1813; house dem. 1951.

LEE HALL, GATEACRE, LANCS., stables for John Okill, 1815, castellated; dem. 1956.

EVERTON, nr. LIVERPOOL, stables, etc., for Colin Campbell, 1815; dem.

GATEACRE, LANCS., house for John Bibby, 1816.

GWRYCH CASTLE, DENBIGHSHIRE, Gothic designs for L. B. Hesketh, 1816 onwards. Some of Rickman's drawings are in the National Library of Wales. Hesketh designed the house himself with help from C. A. Busby, Rickman and others. The foundation-stone was not laid until 1819 (J. P. Neale, *Views of Seats*, 2nd ser. ii, 1825).

GREAT TEW, OXON., work for M. R. Boulton, 1820–1. Rickman appears to have been responsible for some elements of the picturesque village created by Boulton, for a farmhouse (with carefully designed chimneys) and an ornamental well are both mentioned in his diary (*C. Life*, 29 July 1949).

*THE DOWN HOUSE, nr. REDMARLEY, GLOS., for George Dowdeswell, 1822–3.

*SANDWELL PARK, STAFFS., minor works for 4th Earl of Dartmouth, 1822 onwards, including alterations to stables; dem. 1928.

*ETTINGTON PARK, WARWICKS., alterations for E. J. Shirley, 1824–6; rebuilt by John Prichard of Llandaff 1862 [cf. E. P. Shirley, *Lower Ettington*, 1880, and drawings in Warwicks. C.R.O., CR 229/119/5–8].

*LOUGH FEA HOUSE, CO. MONAGHAN, IRELAND, for E. J. Shirley, begun 1825, Elizabethan [cf. E. P. Shirley, *Lough Fea*, 1869].

*CASTLE BROMWICH HALL, WARWICKS., added kitchen-block 1826 and remodelled hall and drawing-room 1837–8 for 2nd Earl of Bradford [cf. Bradford archives 8/5 and *C. Life*, 17 Aug. 1912].

*BADGEWORTH COURT, GLOS., for J. Ellis Viner, 1827–8, Gothic; rebuilt 1896–7.

*BRUNSTOCK HOUSE, nr. CARLISLE, CUMBERLAND, for George Saul, 1828–30, Gothic.

*BURFIELD LODGE, nr. BRISTOL, SOMERSET, for E. B. Fripp, 1827–8.

*HARBORNE, nr. BIRMINGHAM, WARWICKS., house for George Simcox, 1828–9.

*BURY, HUNTS., house for John Julian, 1828–9.

*ROSE CASTLE, CUMBERLAND, alterations and additions for Hugh Percy, Bishop of Carlisle, 1828–9 (*C. Life*, 23 Nov. 1989).

*LAUNDE ABBEY, LEICS., new offices, etc., for E. Dawson, 1829.

*BIRMINGHAM, No. 12 ISLINGTON ROW, house for himself, 1830.

*WESTON HALL, WESTON-UNDER-LIZARD, STAFFS., alterations for 2nd Earl of Bradford, 1830–1 [cf. Bradford archives 3/32] (*C. Life*, 9, 16, 23 Nov. 1945).

STANWICK, YORKS. (N.R.), works on estate for Lord Prudhoe, 1830–1, including farmhouses at ALDBOROUGH, MELSONBY and probably at STANWICK [cf. drawings for further unexecuted works among Percy archives at Alnwick Castle].

TETTENHALL WOOD HOUSE, nr. WOLVERHAMPTON, STAFFS., for Miss Hinckes, 1831–6, Gothic; dem. 1969.

MATFEN HALL, NORTHUMBERLAND, for Sir Edward Blackett, Bart., 1832–5. Blackett was a difficult client who insisted on the 'Elizabethan' style for the exterior. He was to some extent his own architect, made many changes as the work progressed, and eventually dismissed Rickman in 1835, when the house was nearly finished.

RUGBY, WARWICKS., BROOKSIDE, DUNCHURCH ROAD, for H. S. Gibbs, 1833; dem.

SOHAM VICARAGE, CAMBS., for the Revd. H. Tasker, 1833–4.

THE GROVE, KIRKPATRICK-IRONGRAY, DUMFRIESSHIRE, for Wellwood Maxwell (of Liverpool), 1833–5 [cf. *N.S.A.* iv, 270].

BAYNARDS PARK, CRANLEIGH, SURREY, additions for the Revd. Thomas Thurlow, 1833–41,

Tudor Gothic; further alterations and additions by B. Ferrey after 1841; dem. 1980.

GREAT OAKLEY RECTORY, ESSEX, for the Revd. W. Tatham, 1834–5.

AUDLEY END, ESSEX, THE MAIN GATE LODGE, for 3rd Lord Braybrooke, 1834 [cf. Lord Braybrooke, *History of Audley End*, 1836, 137].

†OUSDEN HALL, SUFFOLK, alterations, including north and west porticoes, for T. J. Ireland, 1835–6; dem. 1955.

MONUMENTS

Monuments (nearly all Gothic) designed by Rickman were erected in the following churches: ASHTON-BY-SUTTON, CHESHIRE (Catherine Harrison, 1813); BUCKDEN, HUNTS. (Robert Whitworth, d. 1831); DURHAM CATHEDRAL; EVERTON, ST. GEORGE, nr. LIVERPOOL (R. P. Buddicum); GLOUCESTER CATHEDRAL (the Revd. Richard Raikes, d. 1823); HAMPTON LUCY, WARWICKS. (Henry Hutchinson, d. 1831); HINDLEY CHAPEL, WIGAN, LANCS. (John Layland, 1813); KINGS NORTON, WORCS.; LISMORE CATHEDRAL, IRELAND (J. H. Lovett); PRESTON PARISH CHURCH, LANCS. (three monuments); WALTON, LANCS.; WARRINGTON, LANCS.; WHITFORD, FLINTS. (Caroline Pennant).

RIDDELL, THOMAS, of Hull, is recorded to have designed the MERCHANT SEAMEN'S HOSPITAL there in 1781 in conjunction with one Hammond, and also No. 8 CHARLOTTE STREET, HULL, *c.*1796–9 [*V.C.H. Yorks. E.R.* i, 407, 447, 451].

RIDE, WILLIAM (*c.*1723–1778), was employed by several eighteenth-century noblemen to supervise their works. Described as 'surveyor' in his will, he was probably a native of Haslemere in Surrey, where he was living towards the end of his life [P.R.O., PROB 11/1042, f. 217]. He appears, however, to have operated from London, and was living in Westminster in 1763, when he took an apprentice named John Ride, who may have been his son [P.R.O., IR1/23, p. 155]. John Ride subsequently exhibited architectural designs at the Royal Academy from addresses in Westminster in 1773 and 1781.

One of William Ride's principal employers was the Duke of Richmond, whose seat was at Goodwood near Chichester. Ride corresponded with George Vertue on the subject of some ancient paintings in Chichester Cathedral [Walpole Soc., *Vertue Note Books* v, 74], and in a volume of prints in the Library of the Society of Antiquaries there is an engraving of the recently repaired Market Cross at Chichester, dedicated to the 2nd Duke and inscribed 'Wm Ride delin. A° 1749 G. Vertue sculpsit'. In 1749 a group of subscribers (one of whom was the Duke of Richmond) appointed Ride to be 'surveyor and inspector' for the rebuilding of ST. PANCRAS CHURCH, CHICHESTER, 'according to the plan already settled and agreed on' [W. Sussex R.O., PAR/42/4/1]. In 1775 'Mr. Ride' was paid £21 for his set of plans for the new SUSSEX COUNTY GAOL at HORSHAM (dem. *c.*1845). They were produced at Quarter Sessions by the 3rd Duke of Richmond, and executed between 1778 and 1779 [W. Albery, *A Horsham and Sussex Millennium of Facts*, 1947, 392–3].

Between 1756 and 1778 Ride was regularly employed by Lord Temple both at his London house in Pall Mall and at STOWE HOUSE, BUCKS., and in 1771 he spent a week at Eastbury, Dorset, surveying that house (then empty) for him [M. McCarthy, 'The Rebuilding of Stowe House, 1770–1777', *Huntington Library Quarterly* xxxvi, 1973, 274]. When Ride died Lord Temple provided for an annuity of £20 to be paid to his widow [*ex inf.* Mr. George Clarke]. Ride was also employed by the 6th Lord Digby at his London house in 1763 and at SHERBORNE CASTLE, DORSET, where he was responsible for remodelling the library in Gothick style in 1757–8, possibly to his own designs [Digby account-book 1757–63 in Dorset C.R.O., D/SHC 1262]. His death in May 1778 at the age of 55 is recorded in Haslemere parish register.

RIDER, RICHARD, *see* RYDER, RICHARD.

RIDER. On 15 June 1688, it was agreed by the Society of Gray's Inn that Mr. Rider should be 'chiefe surveyor to this Society, and to supervise and direct the buildings of the Gate . . . and all publique structures belonging to this Society'. The gatehouse was rebuilt that year [*The Pension Book of Gray's Inn: Records of the Honourable Society, 1669–1800* ii, 1910, 97]. This may have been Richard Rider, who in 1705 directed the building of a Rectory and Watch House for the parish of St. Anne's, Soho [Vestry Minutes in Westminster City Library]. The latter was probably the elder son of Richard Ryder (d. 1683), *q.v.*

RIOU, STEPHEN (1720–1780), was the son of Stephen Riou, a London merchant of Huguenot origin who had become naturalized in 1702. Stephen was therefore 'born a subject of Britain', and served in Flanders in the war of 1741 as a Captain in the 2nd troop of Horse Grenadier Guards. He eventually retired on half pay and studied architecture 'in a foreign protestant academy'. This was the University of Geneva, where Riou in 1743 wrote in French a MS. treatise on civil architecture based on Vignola, Daviler, etc., that is now in the Yale Center for British Art. In 1746 he published the first volume of *The Elements of Fortification, translated and collected from the works of the most celebrated authors*, but it was almost immediately superseded by a similar work by John Muller, the professor of fortification at the Royal Military Academy at Woolwich, and Riou then abandoned the intended second volume. Another MS. in the Yale Center shows that he subsequently travelled in Italy and Greece, acting as *cicerone* to a Mr. Barton. It is entitled 'Itineral Remarks from Italy to the Archipelago and Constantinople by Sea and thence by land thro' Romelia, Bulgaria, Servia & Hungary to Vienna in the years 1753 & 1754'. In Smyrna he met Stuart and Revett on their way to Athens and spent some time in their company. After returning to England Riou (who had met Charles Labelye, *q.v.*, in Naples) rather belatedly contributed to the controversy over the design of Blackfriars Bridge by publishing *Short Principles for the Architecture of Stone Bridges*, 1760. In 1768 he published *The Grecian Orders of Architecture delineated and explained from the Antiquities of Athens*, with a dedication to James Stuart. This was intended to give wider currency to the discoveries of Stuart and Revett, and included a number of plates drawn by the author to show how Grecian features could be incorporated in buildings of basically Palladian character.

No executed building by Riou is known, but a volume of architectural designs made by him in Rome in 1752 is in the Yale Center, and in the Metropolitan Museum at New York there is a sketch by him for an elevation of Palladian character described as 'a Museum or Repository to preserve Works of Sculpture, Painting, etc.' (J. Harris, *Catalogue of British Drawings for Architecture, etc., in American Collections*, 1971, pl. 132). A design by him for an Academy of Painting, Sculpture and Architecture, dated 1753, is in the R.I.B.A. Drawings Collection (see James Bettey in *Burlington Mag.* Aug. 1986, 581–2). In the Royal Library at Windsor there is a volume of designs by Riou for a royal palace, begun at Rome in 1751–3 and completed in London in 1754. A design by him for a villa, dated 1758, is in a copy of Du Cerceau's *Livre d'Architecture* in the Library of the Queen's University, Ontario. He competed for the Royal Exchange at Dublin in 1769, and in the same year was an exhibitor at the Free Society of Artists, showing his designs both for the palace and for the exchange. In 1760 he was living at Herne Hill in Kent, and in 1769 at Canterbury. He died in Bentinck Street, Cavendish Square, on 12 March 1780, and was buried in Marylebone churchyard. He left two sons, Col. Philip and Capt. Edward Riou. The latter's gallantry as one of Nelson's commanders earned him a monument in St. Paul's Cathedral. Stephen Riou's granddaughter Charlotte married Moses George Benson of Lutwyche Hall, Salop., where his portrait was formerly preserved.

[*A.P.S.D.*; *Gent's Mag.* 1780, 153; S. Lysons, *Environs of London* ii (2), 1811, 558; *Builder* xxvii, 1869, 781; H. Wagner, 'Pedigree of Riou', *Miscellanea Genealogica et Heraldica*, 3rd ser. iv, 1900–1, 190; P. H. Ditchfield, 'The Family of Riou', *Proceedings of the Huguenot Society of London* x (2), 1913, 236–64; Eileen Harris, *British Architectural Books and Writers 1556–1785*, 1990, 390–3.]

RIPLEY, THOMAS (*c.*1683–1758), rose from humble origins to the status of a senior officer of the Board of Works. He was born in Yorkshire and is said to have walked to London to seek his fortune. He was admitted to the Carpenters' Company on 14 March 1705, and at first he combined the trade of a carpenter with keeping a coffee-shop in Wood Street, off Cheapside. His subsequent career was due to the patronage of Sir Robert Walpole, one of whose servants he married. In April 1715 he was appointed Labourer in Trust at the Savoy and in February 1716 Clerk of the Works at the Mews. In September 1721 he succeeded Grinling Gibbons as Master Carpenter, and on the death of Sir John Vanbrugh in 1726 he became Comptroller of the Works. In 1729 Walpole obtained for him the further appointment of Surveyor of Greenwich Hospital, and he also held the sinecure post of Surveyor of the King's Private Roads from 1737 until his death in 1758. In 1742 he obtained a grant of arms from the College of Heralds, and in 1744 was fined for the office of Sheriff of London and Middlesex. He was a Warden of the Carpenters' Company in 1740 and 1741, and Master in 1742.

As an architect Ripley has not been much esteemed either by his contemporaries or by posterity. Certainly the ill-proportioned portico of the Admiralty was a poor advertisement of his abilities as a designer, and none of his other works quite atones for this notorious failure. The porticoed Blatherwycke and the astylar Wolterton were, however, handsome enough houses. Many other second-rate Georgian architects did no better without incurring public censure, but it was Ripley's misfortune that his inferior professional ability, combined with his dependence on Walpole, earned him the contempt both of Vanbrugh and of Burlington. When, in 1721, the former 'met with his name (and Esquire to it) in the Newspaper; such a Laugh came upon me, I had like to Beshit my Self'; while the latter's disapproval found its echo more than once in Pope's scathing couplets:

> Heav'n visits with a taste the wealthy fool,
> And needs no rod but Ripley with a rule.
> *Epistle to the Earl of Burlington*, ll. 17–18 (1731)

> Who builds a bridge that never drove a pile?
> (Should Ripley venture, all the world would smile).
> *Imitations of Horace*, Bk. II, Ep. 1, ll. 185–6 (1737)

> See under Ripley rise a new White-hall,
> While Jones' and Boyle's united labours fall.
> *Dunciad*, Bk. III, ll. 327–8 (1743)

That Ripley did, in fact, aspire to build bridges is shown by the Minutes of the Commissioners appointed in 1726 to erect a bridge across the Thames from Fulham to Putney. He attended the first meeting in person, was subsequently employed to survey the river, and produced a design for a timber bridge which was accepted by the Commissioners on 22 August. But for some unexplained reason it was not executed, and in 1728, when further plans were invited, Ripley again submitted one for a timber bridge, this time with stone piers. The timber bridge that was finally built in 1729 was, however, constructed 'according to a scheme and principles' laid down not by Ripley but by William Cheselden, a surgeon at St. Thomas's Hospital [G.L. Record Office, Fulham Bridge Minutes]. In 1737 Ripley was employed as an assessor by the Commissioners for building a bridge at Westminster, and his report on the plans submitted is preserved among the minutes now in the Public Record Office [WORK 6/28, f. 83]. He himself submitted a design for a bridge of fifteen arches, but that of Charles Labelye (*q.v.*) was eventually adopted.

Like most eighteenth-century architects, Ripley engaged in speculative building. In 1724 he was the original building lessee of the west side of Grosvenor Square, but in the end his only involvement in the development of the Grosvenor estate was one large house in Grosvenor Street. In 1732 the Duke of Chandos was endeavouring to persuade him to build in St. James's Square on the site of Chandos House, and wrote that he 'is very rich and though he is in good employments continues still this sort of business' [Baker, *Life and Circumstances of James Brydges, Duke of Chandos*, 1949, 216]. He also engaged, with Richard Holt, in the manufacture of 'a compound liquid metall, by which artificiall stone and marble is made by casting the same into moulds of any form, as statues, columns, capitalls', for which they took out a patent in 1722. A manuscript in the British Library (Add. MS. 11394, ff. 45–6) shows that the chief ingredients of Holt's 'secret formula' were powdered glass and clay. In 1730 Holt published *A Short Treatise of Artificial Stone* in which he alleged that the composition had been pirated by Batty Langley [Alison Kelly, *Mrs Coade's Stone*, 1990, 31–2; Eileen Harris, *British Architectural Books and Writers*, 1990, 237–8].

Ripley's first wife died in November 1737. On 22 April 1742 he married a Miss Bucknall of Hampton, Middlesex, who is said to have had a fortune of £40,000. She died in September 1752, aged 48, and Ripley himself died at Hampton on 10 February 1758, aged 75. He is commemorated by a ledger-stone, formerly in the chancel, but now in the tower of Hampton Church. A Kit-Kat portrait by Joseph Highmore dated 1746 is in the National Portrait Gallery. A bust by Rysbrack was sold at the latter's sale in 1765 (lot 28).

Ripley left three sons, named Richard, Thomas and Horatio. Richard is said to have been called to the Bar, but did not pursue a legal career. Through his father's influence he was appointed Chief Clerk of the King's Works in April 1756, and on the reorganization of the Office of Works in 1782 became Resident Clerk. He died in 1786. Richard Ripley, junior, who was apprenticed to Sir William Chambers in 1771, admitted to the Royal Academy Schools in 1776 at the age of 21, and exhibited a design for a casino at the Academy in 1779, was presumably his son.

[*A.P.S.D.*; *D.N.B.*; H. Walpole, *Anecdotes of Painting*, ed. Dallaway & Wornum, iii, 1862, 769–70; *Gent's Mag.* 1737, 702; 1742, 274; 1744, 333; 1758, 94; *Builder* ix, 1851, 2–3; xx, 1862, 563; *Walpole Soc.* xix, 145; *The Works of Sir John Vanbrugh* iv: *The Letters*, ed. G. F. Webb, 1928, 138; Sir J. Hawkins, *Life of Samuel Johnson*, 1787, 375–6; *History of the King's Works* v; *Survey of London* xxxix, 22; will (P.C.C. 53 HUTTON).]

LONDON, THE CUSTOM HOUSE, reconstruction after fire, 1718–25, and additional buildings on north side, 1738–40; destroyed by fire 1814 [T. F. Reddaway, 'The London Custom House 1660–1740', *London Topographical Record* xxi, 1958; *History of the King's Works* v, 347–8].

LIVERPOOL, THE CUSTOM HOUSE, 1719–21;

dem. 1828 [E. H. Rideout, *The Custom House, Liverpool*, Liverpool 1928, 5–8; *Customs Letter-Books of the Port of Liverpool 1711–1812*, ed. R. C. Jarvis, Chetham Soc. 1957, 13–14]. See also S. A. Harris, 'The Old Blue Coat Hospital, Liverpool: was it designed by Thomas Ripley?' *Trans. Historic Soc. Lancs. and Cheshire* cix, 1957.

BLATHERWYCKE HALL, NORTHANTS., for Henry O'Brien, 1720–4; dem. 1948 [Northants. Record Office, OBB/12, contract dated 26 July 1720 to build the house 'according to the plan and designe thereof made by Thomas Ripley of London Gent'] (J. A. Gotch, *Squires' Homes of Northamptonshire*, 1939, pl. 5).

LONDON, No. 16 GROSVENOR STREET, *c.*1720–4 [*Survey of London* xl, 36].

HOUGHTON HALL, NORFOLK, supervised erection of house for Sir Robert Walpole to designs of Colen Campbell and William Kent, 1722–35 [Isaac Ware, *The Plans, Elevations and Sections of Houghton in Norfolk*, 1735; H. A. Tipping in *C. Life*, 1 Jan. 1921, 21–2].

LONDON, THE ADMIRALTY, WHITEHALL, 1723–6; entrance screen by R. Adam, 1760 [*Builder* ix, 1851, 3; *Survey of London* xvi, 57–64] (*C. Life*, 17–24 Nov. 1923).

WOLTERTON HALL, NORFOLK, for 1st Lord Walpole, 1727–41; east wing, stone stairs and perron added by G. S. Repton 1828 [H. Walpole, *Anecdotes of Painting* ii, 1862, 769–70; Gordon Nares in *C. Life*, 18–25 July 1957].

KINGSTON-ON-THAMES CHURCH, SURREY, alterations 1731; restored 1862–6 and 1883 [*Daily Courant*, 2 June 1731].

GREENWICH HOSPITAL: Ripley was responsible for the completion of the QUEEN MARY BLOCK *c.*1735. The central pediment, popularly known as 'Ripley's Saddle', was removed and replaced by a balustraded attic in 1777 (see drawing in Westminster City Library). Ripley was also responsible for the roof and interior of the CHAPEL 1735–9, destroyed by fire 1779 [*A.P.S.D.*].

LONDON, PALL MALL, No. 71 for Sir Edward Walpole, *c.*1737–8; dem. *c.*1830 [*Survey of London* xxix, 378–9].

ROBERTS, HENRY (1803–1876), was the second son of Josiah Roberts, an English merchant with business interests in America, and was born at Philadelphia on 16 April 1803. In 1818 he became a pupil of Charles Fowler and in 1824 was awarded two medals by the Society of Arts. In 1825 he was admitted to the Royal Academy Schools and joined the office of Sir Robert Smirke, 'whose tastes, habits, modes of construction, and method of making working drawings, he thoroughly imbibed'. A continental tour followed, in the course of which he visited Naples (1829). On his return, he set up in practice in Suffolk Street. In 1832 he won the competition for Fishmongers' Hall with an elegant Greek Revival design in the manner of Smirke. Escot House is in a similar style, but many of Roberts's subsequent works were Gothic designs of no special distinction. Nearly all his commissions were for members of the Evangelical establishment, and the discovery in 1852 or 1853 that he had formed an adulterous liaison 'with a member of the lower orders' proved fatal to his position in society. Having independent means, he was able to retire from practice, and in 1853 went to live in Italy, where he spent the last twenty years of his life. He died in Florence on 9 March 1876. Gilbert Scott, who entered his office in 1832, describes him as 'a gentlemanly, religious, precise, and quiet man'.

Roberts is best known as a pioneer of working-class housing. From the 1840s onwards he devoted most of his energies to improving the appalling housing conditions of the Victorian working classes, and even after his retirement to Italy he continued to be active in this cause. He was a founder-member and honorary architect to Lord Shaftesbury's Society for Improving the Conditions of the Labouring Classes, formed in 1844, and also acted as honorary architect to the society founded by Prince Albert to improve working-class housing in Windsor. His designs for model houses for the working classes were widely disseminated and were influential in many parts of Europe as well as in the British Isles: in fact Roberts was one of the key figures in the history of rural and industrial housing. On this and allied subjects he published a number of works, of which the principal were *The Dwellings of the Labouring Classes*, 1850 (revised edition 1867), of which a translation was published in France the same year; *House Reform; or, what the Working Classes may do to improve their dwellings* [1852]; *The Improvement of the Dwellings of the Labouring Classes*, 1859; *The Essentials of a Healthy Dwelling, and the extension of its benefits to the Labouring Population*, 1862; *The Physical Condition of the Labouring Classes, resulting from the State of their Dwellings*, 1866; and *Efforts on the Continent for improving the Dwellings of the Labouring Classes*, Florence 1874.

[*A.P.S.D.*; *D.N.B.*; *Builder* viii, 1850, 37; G. G. Scott, *Personal and Professional Recollections*, 1879, 73–5; N. Pevsner, 'Model Houses for the Labouring Classes', *Arch. Rev.* May 1943; J. N. Tarn, *Five Per Cent Philanthropy: an account of housing in urban areas between*

1840 and 1914, Cambridge 1973; J. Stevens Curl, *The Life and Work of Henry Roberts*, 1983.]

LONDON, FISHMONGERS' HALL, LONDON BRIDGE, 1832–5 [W. H. Leeds, *Supplement* to Britton & Pugin's *Public Buildings of London*, 1838, 21–32; Priscilla Metcalf, *The Halls of the Fishmongers' Company*, 1977] (*C. Life*, 19 Jan. 1939).

CAMBERWELL, SURREY, THE COLLEGIATE SCHOOL, 1834–5, Tudor Gothic; dem. 1867 [*Companion to the Almanac*, 1836, 219–20; W. H. Blanch, *Ye Parish of Camberwell*, 1875, 307].

LONDON, THE DESTITUTE SAILORS' ASYLUM, WELL STREET, LONDON DOCKS, 1835 [*A New Survey of London*, John Weale, i, 1853, 268].

SOUTHBOROUGH, KENT, THE GLEBE HOUSE, 1836 [drawings and contract in R.I.B.A.D.].

YOXFORD CHURCH, SUFFOLK, added north aisle, 1837, Gothic [I.C.B.S.].

MANCHESTER, GROSVENOR SQUARE PRESBYTERIAN CHAPEL, 1838; dem. [exhib. at R.A. 1838].

ESCOT HOUSE, DEVON, rebuilt for Sir John Kennaway, Bart., 1838 [exhib. at R.A. 1838; drawings in Devon C.R.O., 961 M/E29].

ESCOT CHURCH, DEVON, for Sir John Kennaway, Bart., 1839–40, Gothic [W. Spreat, *Picturesque Sketches of the Churches of Devon*, 1842, no. 69].

CLAYDON HOUSE, BUCKS., minor alterations for Sir Harry Verney, Bart., 1839–40 [plans at Claydon House].

ELVETHAM CHURCH, HANTS., rebuilt for 3rd Lord Calthorpe, 1840–1, Norman [exhib. at R.A. 1841, specifically mentioning 'new towers and porch'].

LONDON, LONDON BRIDGE RAILWAY STATION, in conjunction with George Smith & Thomas Turner, *c.*1841–44; rebuilt 1851, dem. 1969 [*Companion to the Almanac*, 1843, 248–9; 1844, 239–41].

NORTON MANOR, NORTON FITZWARREN, SOMERSET, for C. Noel Welman, *c.*1842, Tudor Gothic [exhib. at R.A. 1843].

LONDON, ST. PAUL'S CHURCH FOR SEAMEN, DOCK STREET, WHITECHAPEL, 1846–7, Gothic [*Builder* iv, 1846, 241; *Illustrated London News* viii, 321; *Ecclesiologist* vi, 1846, 34–5].

NORBITON, SURREY, ST. PETER'S PARSONAGE, 1846–7, Tudor [Surrey C.R.O., Acc. 1056/441].

SIDMOUTH, DEVON, ALL SAINTS SCHOOL, 1846–8, Tudor Gothic [drawings in Devon C.R.O., 961 M/E 40].

LONDON, NATIONAL SCOTCH CHURCH, CROWN COURT, COVENT GARDEN, enlarged 1848, with two schools adjoining; rebuilt 1905 [*A.P.S.D.*].

AYLESBURY, BUCKS., TRINITY CHURCH, WALTON, added in 1849 N. transept to church built 1845, Gothic [I.C.B.S.].

TOFT HALL, CHESHIRE, additions for Ralph G. Leycester, 1850–1 [*The Architect's, Engineer's and Building Trades' Directory*, 1868, 133].

KIMBOLTON CASTLE, HUNTS., works for 6th Duke of Manchester, *c.*1850 [*ibid.*].

NORBITON, SURREY, NATIONAL SCHOOL, 1851 [Surrey C.R.O., 264/51/1–5].

EXTON HALL, RUTLAND, rebuilt centre for 1st Earl of Gainsborough, 1851–2, Elizabethan [*The Architect's, Engineer's and Building Trades' Directory*, 1863, 133].

SAXMUNDHAM CHURCH, SUFFOLK, new N. aisle, etc., 1851–2, Gothic [I.C.B.S.].

WIGTOWN CHURCH, WIGTOWNSHIRE, 1851–3, Gothic [S.R.O., HR 355/1 and 4].

BRAMPTON VICARAGE, HUNTS., for the Revd. T. J. Mackee, 1853 [C.U.L., Ely Diocesan Records, Parsonage papers, G3/39/77 and 40/6].

NOTTINGHAM, ST. MATTHEW'S CHURCH, 1853–4, Gothic; dem. *c.*1955 [*Ecclesiologist* xv, 1854, 142].

MODEL DWELLINGS

As architect to the Society for Improving the Conditions of the Labouring Classes, etc., Roberts designed houses in LOWER ROAD, PENTONVILLE, 1844, dem. [*Builder* ii, 1844, 630, iii, 1845, 1]; GEORGE STREET, BLOOMSBURY, 1846–7 [*Builder* v, 1847, 286–7]; NEWCOMEN ROAD, TUNBRIDGE WELLS, 1847 [J. S. Curl, 108–9]; STREATHAM STREET, BLOOMSBURY, 1849–50 [*Builder* vii, 1849, 325–6, viii, 1850, 49, 250]; THANKSGIVING BUILDINGS, PORTPOOL LANE, GRAY'S INN ROAD, 1850 [*Builder* viii, 1850, 369]; model houses exhibited at the Great Exhibition of 1851 and subsequently re-erected as lodges in Kennington Park [*Builder* ix, 1851, 311–12]; and houses in ALEXANDRA ROAD, WINDSOR, BERKS., 1852 [*Builder* x, 1852, 468–9]. Many other model houses and cottages were built to designs by Roberts published by the Society.

ROBERTS, JOHN and WILLIAM, were builders at Nottingham in the second half of the eighteenth century. They built the GREYHOUND YARD at NOTTINGHAM in 1754 [*The Stretton Manuscripts*, ed. G. C. Robertson, 1910, 216]. In 1768 'Mr. Roberts' made designs (which were not adopted) for the new COUNTY HALL, and in 1770–2 William Roberts acted as clerk of the works during its erection to the designs of James Gandon

[*Nottinghamshire County Records of the Eighteenth Century*, ed. K. T. Meaby, 49, 55]. He also made estimates for enlarging BULWELL CHURCH in 1767 and (jointly with John White and Samuel Stretton) for repairing EAST BRIDGFORD CHURCH in 1769 [*ibid.*, 160–1].

ROBERTS, WILLIAM, a carpenter, designed and built the TOLSEY or COUNCIL HOUSE at GLOUCESTER in 1750–1 [extracts by C. H. Dancey from Gloucester Council Books in Public Library, Book B, p. 108]. It was demolished in 1893–4. There is an illustration in *Trans. Bristol and Gloucester Arch. Soc.* xix, facing p. 185. Roberts's will, dated 20 January 1754, was proved at Gloucester on 27 October 1773.

ROBERTSON, DANIEL, appears to have been related to the family of Robert and James Adam, whose mother was a Robertson of Gladney. He was probably their pupil, for among some Adam drawings in the Victoria and Albert Museum there is one (3436–52) signed 'Daniel Robertson fecit'. He certainly had connections with their younger brother William Adam. At Blair Adam there are several drawings for lodges and cottages in the park signed 'Daniel Robertson *delt.*', and for a time Daniel and his brother Alexander were in partnership with Adam as builders and timber merchants. In 1800 the firm contracted to build the six large warehouses (designed by George Gwilt) in the West India Docks, completed in 1803, and in 1801–2 they also built the dock walls and the locks [C. Hadfield & A. W. Skempton, *William Jessop, Engineer*, 1979, 210]. However, the Robertsons eventually got into financial difficulties and went bankrupt in 1817 [S.R.O., GD 18/4977–4991/23, ff. 56–68]. This contributed to William Adam's own difficulties, and in January 1821 he formally undertook, 'at the express desire of my nearest and best friends', to 'give up all connection with Alexander and Daniel Robertson' [S.R.O., GD 18/4996].

Speculative building may have been the trouble, for in 1812 Daniel Robertson exhibited at the Royal Academy an elaborate project for a new square between Covent Garden and Drury Lane theatres, and in 1813 he and his brother were involved in an abortive scheme for speculative building in Belgravia [Hermione Hobhouse, *Thomas Cubitt*, 1971, 89]. In 1817 (at a time when his father-in-law, Dr. Thomas Clarke of Greenwich, was trying to persuade him to take a post in Dublin – see S.R.O., GD 18/4992), Daniel was preparing a design (now in the Royal Library at Windsor) for a vast building in Whitehall to accommodate 'all the offices which form the Executive Departments of the Government of the United Kingdom'.

Robertson's first recorded architectural commission was the alteration of premises in Pall Mall for the Travellers' Club in 1821. Between 1825 and 1828 he obtained several commissions in Oxford, notably the design of the new University Press building in Walton Street, for whose handsome Graeco-Roman façade he was responsible. He also restored the Gothic front of All Souls College and designed two local churches in a starved Romanesque style which earned one of them the nickname of 'the Boiled Rabbit'.

In 1829 Robertson left Oxford for Ireland. That something discreditable had occurred is evident from a remark in a contemporary periodical that 'We regret the loss of Mr. Robertson to Oxford; but the reason for his departure is no subject for public discussion' (*The Crypt* iii, 1829, 200). In Ireland he had several commissions for country houses, particularly in Co. Wexford, and on his drawings he described himself as of 'Dublin and Gorey'.[1] In 1843 he was working at Powerscourt, where he designed the Upper Terrace. Improvident as ever, he was on one occasion hidden in the dome of the house when sheriff's officers came to arrest him for debt. 'He was' (Lord Powerscourt recalled) 'given to drink, and always drew best when he was excited with sherry. He suffered from gout, and used to be driven about in a wheelbarrow with a bottle of sherry; while that lasted he was always ready to direct the workmen, but when it was finished he was incapable of working any more' (Lord Powerscourt, *Description and History of Powerscourt*, 1903, 77).

Unexecuted designs by Robertson are illustrated in Colvin, *Architectural Drawings in the Library of Worcester College, Oxford*, 1964, pl. 36 (new front for Worcester College), and Harris, *British Drawings for Architecture, etc., in American Collections*, 1971, pls. 133–6 (Burton Park, Lincs.).

LONDON, No. 49 PALL MALL, alterations for the Travellers' Club, 1821; dem. [*Survey of London* xxix, 400, but see above, p. 259].

OXFORD, THE UNIVERSITY PRESS, WALTON STREET 1826–7; north wing completed by E. Blore 1829–30 [J. Ingram, *Memorials of Oxford* iii, 1837, 16].

OXFORD, WADHAM COLLEGE, fireplace in Hall and Warden's stables, 1826 [T. G. Jackson, *Wadham College, Oxford*, 1893, 130 n., 178].

[1] He must not be confused with the Irish architect William Robertson of Kilkenny (1770–1850).

OXFORD, ORIEL COLLEGE, rebuilt west side of north (St. Mary Hall) quadrangle, *c.*1826 [*V.C.H. Oxon.* iii, 131].

OXFORD, ST. JOHN'S COLLEGE, the inner Senior Common Room, 1826–7 [the College Register viii, 325–6, refers to the architect as 'Mr. Robinson', but in the accounts (*Computus Annuus*, 1826) he is 'Mr. Roberson'].

OXFORD, ALL SOULS COLLEGE, restored High Street front and refronted Warden's house, 1827 [exhib. at R.A. 1828; original designs in Sir John Soane's Museum, Drawer xv, 4].

OXFORD, ST. CLEMENT'S CHURCH, 1827–8, 'Norman' style; altered internally by E. G. Bruton 1874 [*A.P.S.D.*; Thomas Rickman's diary, 8 June 1826].

attributed: KENNINGTON CHURCH, BERKS., 1828, 'Norman' style [stylistic attribution].

CRICK RECTORY, NORTHANTS., 1829; dem. *c.*1960 [Northants. Record Office, drawings in Peterborough Diocesan Records].

JOHNSTOWN CASTLE, CO. WEXFORD, alterations and additions for Hamilton Knox Grogan Morgan, *c.*1833–6, castellated [*Connoisseur* clxvii, 1961, 282–3].

CARRICKGLAS, CO. LONGFORD, IRELAND, for Anthony Lefroy, 1837–8, Tudor style [The Knight of Glin in *The Country Seat*, ed. Colvin & Harris, 1970, 192, n. 10].

DUBLIN, ST. MATHIAS CHAPEL, WELLINGTON SQUARE, 1840 [drawings in National Library of Ireland, Portfolio 1, *ex inf.* Dr. E. McParland].

WELLS HOUSE, CO. WEXFORD, for Robert Doyne, *c.*1840, Jacobethan [drawings formerly at Wells, *ex inf.* Mr. J. O'Callaghan].

BALLINKEEL HOUSE, CO. WEXFORD, for John Maher, *c.*1840–3 [drawings at Ballinkeel, *ex inf.* Messrs. E. McParland & J. O'Callaghan].

KILRUDDERY HOUSE, CO. WICKLOW, garden layout for 10th Earl of Meath, *c.*1840 [drawings at Kilruddery, *ex inf.* Dr. E. McParland].

CASTLEBORO HOUSE, CO. WEXFORD, for 1st Lord Carew, soon after 1840; now a ruin [C. L. Adams, *Castles of Ireland*, 1904, 102] (*C. Life*, 30 May 1974, 1357, fig. 3).

POWERSCOURT, CO. WICKLOW, IRELAND, the Upper Terrace for 6th Viscount Powerscourt, 1843 [inscription: 'The Upper Terrace was designed by Daniel Robertson Archt. after the Villa Butera in Sicily'].

ROBERTSON, JAMES, of Edinburgh, designed REDHALL HOUSE, COLINTON, MIDLOTHIAN (now a suburb of Edinburgh), for George Inglis in 1758 [James Steuart, *Notes for a History of Colinton Parish*, 1938]. In 1770 he and Alexander Gowan were the 'architects' by whose advice COLINTON CHURCH was condemned as beyond repair [S.R.O., HR 728/1].

ROBERTSON, JOHN, was a nephew of Robert and James Adam. He practised in Glasgow, where in 1798–1800 he built the BARONY CHURCH to the designs of James Adam [*Glasgow Delineated*, 1826, 73]. In the Scottish Record Office there are designs by him for various public buildings in Ayr, including a Market (1799), Assembly Rooms (1802) and Church (1804–6) [RHP 2554–5, 2558, 2563, 2582, 2585]. None of these appears to have been built, but Robertson did design the AYR ACADEMY in 1800. This elegant astylar building was rebuilt in 1895 [*Air Academy and Burgh Scule 1233–1895*, Ayr 1895, 100, with illustration]. Robertson appears to have been a competent late Georgian architect.

ROBERTSON, JOHN, of Bayswater, was employed as a draughtsman in the office of J. C. Loudon from 1829 onwards, and was responsible for many of the figures which illustrate the latter's *Encyclopaedia of Cottage, Farm and Villa Architecture*, 1833 (2nd ed. 1846). In 1833 he published under his own name a *Supplement to Loudon's Manual of Cottage Gardening, Husbandry and Architecture containing Thirty Designs for Dwellings in the Cottage Style*. Robertson subsequently became architectural assistant to Sir Joseph Paxton, and in this capacity helped to design the picturesque village of EDENSOR, nr. Chatsworth in Derbyshire, for the 6th Duke of Devonshire, *c.*1839–45. Robertson may also have been concerned in some other of Paxton's works, such as the Cemetery at Coventry and the Park at Birkenhead, but in 1846 or 1847 he appears to have left Paxton's office, his place being taken by G. H. Stokes [G. F. Chadwick, *The Works of Sir Joseph Paxton*, 1961, 160–6, 186–8, 198–9].

ROBERTSON, WILLIAM, was the author of books entitled *A Collection of various forms of Stoves, used for forcing pine plants, fruit trees, and preserving tender exotics*, 1798, and *Designs in Architecture for Garden Chairs, Small Gates for Villas, Park Entrances, Aviarys, Temples, Boat Houses, Mausoleums, and Bridges*, 1800. Nothing else appears to be known about him, and it is unlikely that he was the Irish architect William Robertson of Kilkenny (1770–1850).

ROBERTSON, WILLIAM, of Leven in Fife, was active in Dundee as a designer of industrial buildings in the middle of the eighteenth century and is described as 'architect' in contemporary records. In 1752 he reconstructed and refitted the TOWN'S MILLS, in 1755 he contracted to build the PACKHOUSES (or Public Warehouse) on a well-designed symmetrical plan, and in 1757 he designed a large WINDMILL of novel construction described by Dr. Pococke in his *Tours in Scotland* (Scottish History Soc. 1887, 224). He took a lease of the Town's Mills in 1766 [Dundee Town Council Minutes, 10 May, 13 Nov. 1752, 29 March 1755, 4 April 1757, and 1766, *ex inf.* Mr. David Walker].

ROBERTSON, WILLIAM (1786–1841), was the leading architect in Morayshire from the early 1820s until his death in 1841. He was born in the parish of Lonmay in north-east Aberdeenshire and nothing is known of his training or early career before he established himself in Elgin in or about 1823. But his highly professional draughtsmanship and up-to-date knowledge of both Greek and Gothic Revival styles suggest that he must have been in the office of some leading architect in Aberdeen or Edinburgh, possibly John Paterson, who had been in Elgin before returning to Edinburgh in 1789. Robertson provided Elgin, Forres and Banff with some dignified public buildings, designed churches for both Established, Episcopal and Roman Catholic congregations, and built or altered a number of country houses, of which the austere Aberlour is the most notable. Robertson died at Elgin on 12 June 1841, aged 55, and is commemorated by a tombstone in the Cathedral churchyard. His practice was continued by his nephews and pupils Alexander and William Reid, who later moved to Inverness. In 1826 *A Series of Views of the Ruins of Elgin Cathedral . . . with ground plan and table of measurements by Mr. Robertson, architect*, had been published in Elgin. [Elizabeth Beaton, *William Robertson*, Elgin 1984, and further information from Mrs. Beaton.]

In the following list of Robertson's principal executed works, references marked 'EB' and 'DW' have been provided by Mrs. Beaton and Mr. David Walker respectively.

PUBLIC BUILDINGS

CULLEN, BANFFSHIRE, TOWN HALL, POST OFFICE, HOTEL ('SEAFIELD ARMS') and STABLES, for Col. F. W. Grant, 1822–3 [S.R.O., GD 248/784/5].

FORRES, MORAYSHIRE, ANDERSON'S INSTITUTION (School), 1823 [Moray District Record Office, ZBFo SUAn 632/826: EB].

BOHARM SCHOOL (now house), BANFFSHIRE, 1828 [*Aberdeen Jnl.* 2 July 1828: DW].

BOAT OF BRIGG TOLLHOUSE, BOHARM, BANFFSHIRE, 1830 [S.R.O., GD 248/1564/80: EB].

FOCHABERS, MORAYSHIRE, MR. DEWAR'S SCHOOL (now part of White Lodge), for Duchess of Gordon, *c.*1830 [S.R.O., RHP 2375, 31773: EB].

DINGWALL, ROSS & CROMARTY, NATIONAL BANK (now Hydro Board Offices), 1836 [*Aberdeen Jnl.* 27 July 1836].

BANFF ACADEMY, 1836–8 [*N.S.A.* xiii, 55].

STORNOWAY, ISLE OF LEWIS, GAOL and COURTHOUSE, 1836–9 [*Inverness Courier*, 29 June 1836; S.R.O., RHP 21754–6, 21758–61: EB].

ELGIN, MORAYSHIRE, COURTHOUSE, etc., 1837–8; dem. 1930 [*Aberdeen Jnl.* 22 Nov. 1837].

FORRES, MORAYSHIRE, TOLBOOTH and COURTHOUSE, 1838 [R. Douglas, *Annals of Forres*, Elgin 1934, 285].

INVERNESS, UNION (later GROSVENOR) HOTEL, 39 HIGH STREET, 1838–9 [*Aberdeen Jnl.* 1 Aug. 1838].

ELGIN, MORAYSHIRE, BRITISH LINEN BANK, 115 HIGH STREET, refronted, etc., 1839 [Minutes of the Directors of the British Linen Bank, 6/6/16, p. 125, in Bank of Scotland Papers: EB].

INVERNESS, DR. BELL'S ACADEMY, FARRALINE PARK (now Public Library), 1839 [*Inverness Courier*, 2 Oct. 1839; 'Record of Bell's Trust' in Public Library, 5/7A1/153: EB].

AULDEARN INFANT SCHOOL and SCHOOLHOUSE (now 'Innesmount'), NAIRNSHIRE, 1841 [*Inverness Courier*, 17 Feb. 1841: EB].

CHURCHES AND CHAPELS

ELGIN, MORAYSHIRE, EPISCOPAL CHURCH and PARSONAGE, NORTH STREET, 1825, Gothic [*Aberdeen Jnl.* 13 April 1825: DW].

DUFFTOWN, BANFFSHIRE (R.C.), 1825, in consultation with the Revd. James Kyle, 1825, Gothic [Scottish Catholic Archives, PL 3/100/2, BL 5/188/13, 5/168: EB].

DUTHIL, INVERNESS-SHIRE, for Col. F. W. Grant, who specified 'a neat plain church', 1826 [S.R.O., GD 248/1558, Grant & Seafield Estate Letter-Book, pp. 510–11].

CHAPELTOWN, GLENLIVET, BANFFSHIRE (R.C.), 1827–8; dem. *c.*1895 [Scottish Catholic Archives, BL/213: EB].

KEITH, BANFFSHIRE (R.C.), 1828–31, classical [Scottish Catholic Archives, IM 21/2: EB].

BANFF PARISH CHURCH, design for spire *c.*1830, executed under direction of Thomas Mackenzie, 1849 [*N.S.A.* xiii, 34; S.R.O., HR 721/1].

GAMRIE, BANFFSHIRE, 1829–30 [S.R.O., CH2/

1120/7/107: EB].

HUNTLY, ABERDEENSHIRE (R.C.), in collaboration with Bishop James Kyle, 1833–4, classical [Scottish Catholic Archives, IM 18/2, BL/6/102/5: EB].

WICK, CAITHNESS, ST. JOACHIM (R.C.), 1833–6, classical [Scottish Catholic Archives, PL3/ 228/12, 3/257/7–8: EB].

BUCKIE, BANFFSHIRE, 1835–6; dem. *c.*1880 [*Aberdeen Jnl.* 22 July 1835].

DRUMNADROCHIT, INVERNESS-SHIRE, URQUHART PARISH CHURCH, 1836–8 [S.R.O., GD 248/ 3375/3 and RHP 82194–98: EB].

INVERNESS, ST. MARY (R.C.), HUNTLY STREET, 1836–7, Gothic [Scottish Catholic Archives, BL 6/178/9/i: EB].

INVERNESS, EPISCOPAL CHAPEL (ST. JOHN), 1837–8, Gothic; dem. 1903 [*Scottish Episcopal Church Year Book*, 1973–4, 249].

ABERLOUR, BANFFSHIRE, tower, 'Saxon', 1838 [*Aberdeen Jnl.* 28 Nov. 1838].

PORTNOCKIE, BANFFSHIRE, (now 'Kirk House') 1838, Tudor Gothic [*Aberdeen Jnl.* 8 Aug. 1838].

MAUSOLEA, ETC.

BELLIE BURIAL GROUND, FOCHABERS, MORAYSHIRE, Greek Revival tomb of Jane, Duchess of Gordon (d. 1824), for 4th Duke of Gordon, 1824–5 [S.R.O., GD 44/52/ 215, 216 and 44/51/391/103: EB].

INVERAVON BURIAL GROUND, BANFFSHIRE, MACPHERSON-GRANT MAUSOLEUM, 1829, Gothic [Macpherson-Grant papers at Ballindalloch Castle: EB, *ex inf.* Mr. A. Kerr].

MANSES

ST. ANDREWS LHANBRYDE (now 'Kilcluan'), MORAYS., 1825–6 [Moray District Record Office, XPE1 A2/12/262: EB]; KEITH, BANFFSHIRE, 1826–7 [S.R.O., CH2/342/9/ 434, 438: EB]; CULLEN, BANFFSHIRE (No. 3, SEAFIELD PLACE), 1830 [S.R.O., GD 248/ 3349: EB]; ARRADOUL, Episcopal (now Arradoul House), BANFFSHIRE, 1833–4 [NRA(S), 2490, bdls. 117, 214: EB]; INVERAVON, BANFFSHIRE (now Inveravon House), enlarged 1834 [*Aberdeen Jnl.* 5 March 1834: EB]; ABERLOUR, BANFFSHIRE, 1837–8 [S.R.O., CH2/65/206, 237: EB]; ROTHES, MORAYS. (now 'The Grange'), 1839 [*Aberdeen Jnl.* 23 Oct. 1839]; SPYNIE, MORAYS. (now 'Kirk House'), 1840–1 [Moray District Record Office, XPEI A/13/205, 271: EB].

DOMESTIC ARCHITECTURE

CULLEN HOUSE, BANFFSHIRE, Temple ('of Pomona') and Tea-room for Col. F. W. Grant, 1822 [S.R.O., CS 96/2374, f. 260; GD 248/3340/28, 35, 54, 65 etc].

CULLEN, BANFFSHIRE, 6, 8, 10, 12 and probably 1, 3, 7, 9 and 16 THE SQUARE, 1823 [S.R.O., GD 248/784/5: EB].

CULLEN, BANFFSHIRE, 18, 20, 22, 24, 26 SOUTH DESKFORD STREET, 1824 [records of Lowtie's Mortification Trust: EB].

BURNSIDE HOUSE, FOCHABERS, MORAYS., remodelled for 4th Duke of Gordon, 1824–5; dem. [S.R.O., GD 44/51/391/103 and RHP 2462–37: EB].

GORDON CASTLE, MORAYS., QUARRY GARDENS LODGE for 4th Duke of Gordon, 1825 [S.R.O., GD 44/51/39/103 and 53/215: EB].

AUCHLUNKART HOUSE, BANFFSHIRE, additions for P. Steuart, 1824–5 [N.R.A.(S.), 2940, Gordon of Cairnfield papers, bdl. 211, letter from Robertson referring to Auchlunkart: EB].

CULLEN, BANFFSHIRE, probably designed villas in SEAFIELD PLACE, 1825–30 [EB].

ORTON HOUSE, ROTHES, MORAYS., added wings for Richard Wharton Duff, 1826 [*Aberdeen Jnl.* 20 Sept. 1826: DW].

ARNDILLY HOUSE, BANFFSHIRE, additions for William MacDowall Grant, 1826; remodelled *c.*1850 [*Aberdeen Jnl.* 11 Oct. 1826; DW].

FINDRASSIE HOUSE, MORAYS., additions for Col. Alexander Grant, 1826 [Moray District Record Office, ZBE1 A 71/826, 52, 328, 375: EB].

WESTER ELCHIES HOUSE, MORAYS., addition for Charles Grant, 1828; dem. 1970 [*Aberdeen Jnl.* 9 Jan. 1828: DW].

EDEN COTTAGE (now HOUSE), by TURRIFF, ABERDEENSHIRE, additions 1828 [Elgin library, DAW P629: *Aberdeen Jnl.* 15 Oct. 1828: EB].

GLENGUNNERY or CLUNE COTTAGE (a shooting lodge), KNOCKANDO, MORAYS., for Charles Grant, 1828: dem. *c.*1939 [*Aberdeen Jnl.* 16 Jan. 1828: DW; cf. *N.S.A.* xiii, 70].

attributed: ALDROUGHTY HOUSE, ELGIN, MORAYS., for George Taylor, 1829–30: probably the house designed by Robertson for which tenders were advertised in *Elgin Courier*, 25 Dec. 1829 [*Aberdeen Univ. Review* 176, 1986)].

attributed: ELGIN, MORAYS., SOUTH VILLA, MOSS STREET, for Mrs Grant, 1830 [EB].

attributed: TOCHIENEAL HOUSE, LINTMILL, CULLEN, BANFFSHIRE, remodelled for John Wilson, Factor to Seafield Estate, *c.*1830 [EB].

COULMONY HOUSE, NAIRNSHIRE, additions for James Campbell Brodie, *c.*1830; dem. [Elgin Library, Wittet Collection, DAW P 2167/1–3: EB].

attributed: INVERESHIE HOUSE, KINCRAIG, INVERNESS-SHIRE, additions for Sir John Macpherson-Grant, *c.*1830 [EB].

ELGIN, MORAYS., GALA COTTAGE (now 'Strath Donan'), HIGH STREET, for himself, *c.*1830 [EB].

PRESHOME, BANFFSHIRE, house for Bishop James Kyle, based on a design made by the bishop, 1830 [Scottish Catholic Archives, IM 28/5/10: EB].

INNES HOUSE, MORAYS., stables for 4th Earl of Fife, 1830; altered 1912 [*Elgin Courier*, 19 Feb. 1830: EB].

ELGIN, MORAYS., WINCHESTER HOUSE, KING STREET, 1831–2 [*Elgin Courier*, 30 Dec. 1831, 5 Jan. 1832: EB].

UDOLL HOUSE, nr. CROMARTY, 1832; dem. [*Inverness Jnl.* 3 March 1832, *ex inf.* Mr J. Gifford].

DUFFUS HOUSE, MORAYS., large additions for Sir Archibald Dunbar, Bart., 1835 [*Aberdeen Jnl.* 26 Aug. 1835].

BRAEMORISTON HOUSE, ELGIN, MORAYS., remodelled for Admiral Archibald Duff, 1837 [Elgin Library, Wittet Collection, DAW P 3060/1–5: EB].

REELIG (formerly Easter Moniack) HOUSE, INVERNESS-SHIRE, refronted, etc. for James Baillie Fraser, 1837–8 [NSA(S), 240, bdls. 15, 16, 31: EB].

BLACKHILLS HOUSE, nr. ELGIN, MORAYS., 'cottage' for 4th Earl of Fife, 1837–8 [Elgin Library, Wittet Collection, DAW P 241: EB].

ABERLOUR HOUSE, BANFFSHIRE (now Gordonstoun Prep. School), for Alexander Grant, 1838; also the square of offices and a Tuscan column [*Aberdeen Jnl.* 8 Aug. 1838].

DOCHFOUR HOUSE, INVERNESS-SHIRE, large additions and new Factor's House (DOCHGARROCH HOUSE), for Evan Baillie, 1839–40 [*Aberdeen Jnl.* 12 June 1839].

CRAIGDARROCH HOUSE (now hotel), CONTIN, ROSS & CROMARTY, alterations for Horatio Ross, 1840 [*Inverness Courier*, 2 Dec. 1840, *ex inf.* Mr. J. Gifford].

KININVIE HOUSE, BANFFSHIRE, addition and square of offices (dem.) for Archibald Young Leslie, 1840 [*Aberdeen Jnl.* 16 Dec. 1840].

KINLOCHLUICHART LODGE, ROSS & CROMARTY, additions 1840 [*Inverness Courier*, 14 Oct. 1840, *ex inf.* Mr. J. Gifford].

TOMINTOUL (formerly BRIN COTTAGE), CROACHY, INVERNESS-SHIRE, 1841 [*Inverness Courier*, 17 April 1841, *ex inf.* Mr. J. Gifford].

ROBINS, GREENWAY (–1853), of Crosby Row, Walworth, designed EDEN PARK, BECKENHAM, KENT, for John Woolley, exhibiting a drawing of the house at the Royal Academy in 1827 as 'lately erected'. The house (dem.) is illustrated by C. Greenwood, *Epitome of County History: Kent*, 1838, 32. Robins also designed ST. JAMES'S CHURCH, RYDE, ISLE OF WIGHT, 1827–8, Gothic [Stephen Green, *St. James's Church, Ryde*, Ryde 1975, 3]. He was elected a member of the Surveyors' Club in 1827 and was its President in 1831. His will was proved in the Prerogative Court of Canterbury in June 1853.

ROBINSON, LAWRENCE (–1797), was employed as clerk of the works at Heaton Hall, nr. Manchester under James Wyatt early in the 1770s and subsequently practised as an architect from Middleton in Lancashire. A framed drawing at WINSTANLEY HALL, LANCS., associates him with the reconstruction of the interior of that house in the Wyatt style for Thomas Bankes in 1785 [J. M. Robinson, *Country Houses of the North-West*, 1991, 252]. In 1795–6 he made designs, formerly at Rudding Park, for minor alterations to MILNSBRIDGE HOUSE, YORKS. (W.R.), and he is stated by J. P. Neale, *Views of Seats*, 2nd. ser. v, 1829, to have enlarged SOMERFORD HALL, CHESHIRE (dem. 1926) for C. W. S. Shakerley in a style that was derived from Wyatt (cf. Robinson, *op. cit.*, 63–4). Robinson died in 1797, when administration of his estate was granted to his son John Robinson, also described as 'architect' [*ex inf.* Mr. W. John Smith]. John Robinson estimated the cost of rebuilding GRINDLETON CHURCH, YORKS. (W.R.), and may have designed the new church completed in 1809 and rebuilt, except the tower, in 1898 [*Yorks. Archl. Jnl.* xxx, 1931, 299].

ROBINSON, PETER FREDERICK (1776–1858), was apprenticed to William Porden in 1790 [P.R.O., IR 1/34, p. 188]. He subsequently became an assistant of Henry Holland, and in 1801–4 supervised the execution of the latter's works at the Royal Pavilion, Brighton. He was a prolific designer of country mansions and picturesque cottages. His published works show that he was prepared to provide his clients with residences in either the 'Old English', 'Edwardian', 'Tudor', 'Elizabethan' or half-timber styles, and he even proposed to build a 'Norman' villa in Hampshire with a tower copied from Christchurch Priory, windows derived from Barfreston Church, and a hall like the nave of a Romanesque cathedral. His most exotic work was the 'Egyptian Hall' in Piccadilly, designed as a museum for William Bullock, naturalist and antiquarian. This was a famous architectural novelty in its day, and represented the first attempt to graft Egyptian features on to an English building.

In 1816 Robinson travelled on the Continent, visiting Rome, and returning by way of Switzerland, thus enabling him to add the 'Swiss chalet' to his architectural repertoire. He became an F.S.A. in 1826 and was one of the first vice-presidents of the Institute of British Architects. He exhibited at the Royal Academy from 1795 to 1833. James Lansdown, H. F. Lockwood and J. G. Jackson of Leamington were his pupils. Financial difficulties obliged him to live at Boulogne from about 1840 onwards, and he died there on 24 June 1858, aged 82.

Robinson was employed by E. Willes of Leamington to make plans for the development of his property there in 1823–6. Several of his plans are in the Warwickshire Record Office, and the layout which he proposed is illustrated by H. G. Clarke, *Royal Leamington Spa*, 1947, 88–9. The streets round Beauchamp Square were developed under his direction in 1825–6. In 1825 he was employed by the 4th Duke of Newcastle to make a plan for the development of the Park Estate on the outskirts of Nottingham which was published in 1827. None of Robinson's proposal for a rigid grid of streets was realized, but a few villas were built to his designs in Park Terrace.

Robinson's designs (1827) for re-erecting the portico of Carlton House as a memorial to the Duke of York are preserved in the Royal Library at Windsor. In 1831 he made designs, now in the Library of the Society of Antiquaries (pressmark 64, I), for a building on the north side of Trafalgar Square to accommodate the Royal and Antiquarian Societies. In 1835 he competed for the Houses of Parliament, submitting a Tudor Gothic design (now among the Hadfield drawings in Sheffield Archives) whose detailing was derived from Hengrave Hall, Suffolk. In the Monmouthshire Record Office there are unexecuted designs by him dated 1838 for a castle-style house for Pryse Powell.

Robinson projected a continuation of *Vitruvius Britannicus*, publishing plates of *Woburn Abbey*, 1827; *Hatfield House*, 1833; *Hardwicke Hall*, 1835; *Castle Ashby*, 1841; and *Warwick Castle*, ?1842. He also published *Rural Architecture; or a Series of Designs for Ornamental Cottages*, 1823, 5th ed. 1850, with landscapes redrawn by J. D. Harding; *Designs for Ornamental Villas*, 1827, 1836, 4th ed. 1853; *Village Architecture, being a Series of Designs . . . illustrative of the Observations contained in the Essay on the Picturesque by Sir Uvedale Price*, 1830, 4th ed. 1837; *Designs for Farm Buildings*, 1830, 3rd ed. 1837; *Designs for Lodges and Park Entrances*, 1833, 3rd ed. 1837; *Domestic Architecture in the Tudor Style*, 1837; *A New Series of Designs for Ornamental Cottages and Villas*, 1838. He was also the author of *An Attempt to ascertain the Age of Mickleham Church in Surrey*, 1824, and read papers to the Institute of British Architects on 'The Newly Discovered Crypt at York Minster' (6 July 1835), 'Observations relating to the proposal for removing the choir screen', and 'Oblique arches' (5 Dec. 1836).

[*A.P.S.D.*; *D.N.B.*; *Builder* xvi, 1858, 458.]

LONDON, THE HANS TOWN ASSEMBLY ROOMS, CADOGAN PLACE, 1807; dem. [exhib. at R.A.].

HUTTON BUSHELL, nr. SCARBOROUGH, YORKS. (N.R.), stabling for G. Osbaldeston, *c.*1807–8; dem. [exhib. at R.A.]. The house was largely destroyed by fire about this time, and not rebuilt. Robinson exhibited designs for 'alterations and additions' in 1808, and for a 'banqueting-seat' at Yedmandale, on the same estate, in 1809, but it is unlikely that these were built. After the fire Osbaldeston went to live at Ebberston Lodge (see p. 211), and in 1823 Robinson exhibited another abortive design for a new house for Osbaldeston there.

WESTPORT, CO. MAYO, IRELAND, Marine Bath for 1st Marquess of Sligo, 1807 [exhib. at R.A].

SANDGATE, KENT, 'Seaman's Cottage' for Capt. Waller, R.N., 1808 [exhib. at R.A.].

CAMPDEN HILL, KENSINGTON, villa for W. Phillimore, 1808 [exhib. at R.A.].

KEW CHURCHYARD, SURREY, monument to Luke Wetten (d. 1807) [exhib. at R.A. 1808].

LONDON, THE EGYPTIAN HALL, PICCADILLY, for W. Bullock, 1811–12; dem. 1905 [exhib. at R.A. 1811; Wyatt Papworth in *Notes and Queries*, 5th ser. iii, 1875, 284–5; *Survey of London* xxix, 266–70].

LAMPETER, CARDIGANSHIRE, TOWN HALL AND MARKET PLACE for R. H. Davis, 1813; dem. 1879 [exhib. at R.A.].

MILLFIELD COTTAGE, BOOKHAM, SURREY, for Major-General Bayley Wallis, 1814; enlarged 1863 [exhib. at R.A.].

FERNACRES, nr. FULMER, BUCKS., for J. Woodcock, 1815 [exhib. at R.A.].

KIPLIN HALL, nr. CATTERICK, YORKS. (N.R.), drawing-room for 4th Earl of Tyrconnel, 1819; remodelled *c.*1879 [exhib. at R.A.].

SHINFIELD, BERKS., remodelled east front of house for E. Willes, 1820, and further alterations *c.*1826 [Warwickshire C.R.O., Willes drawings 58–60, etc.].

NORBURY PARK, nr. DORKING, SURREY, additions

for F. Maitland, including castellated lodge, 1821–3; front remodelled *c.*1860 and again by Mewès and Davis 1920 [exhib. at R.A. 1820–3] (*Arch. Rev.*, 1, 1921, 40–2; engraving of lodge in Brayley, *Surrey* iv, 453).

MICKLEHAM CHURCH, SURREY, alterations in Norman style, including rebuilding of south arcade to support a new gallery and refitting of interior, 1822–3 [exhib. at R.A. 1821–4]. All Robinson's work was removed in 1891.

LEAMINGTON, WARWICKS., YORK TERRACE (now Upper Parade), 1823–30 [Lyndon F. Cave, 'The Architectural Development of Royal Leamington Spa', unpublished M. Phil. thesis, University of Warwick, 1990].

CHESHUNT, HERTS., cottage for E. Clarke, 1824 [exhib. at R.A.].

TRELISSICK HOUSE, nr. TRURO, CORNWALL, for Thomas Daniell, 1824 [R. Ackermann, *Repository of Arts*, 3rd ser. ix, 1827, 64; cf. *Ornamental Villas*, no. 3].

LEAMINGTON, WARWICKS., BINSWOOD (now 'Magnolia') COTTAGE, CLARENDON SQUARE, for E. Willes, 1824 [*New Series of Designs*, 1838, part 2, pls. 1–4].

LEAMINGTON, WARWICKS., CHRIST CHURCH, BEAUCHAMP SQUARE, for E. Willes, 1825, Norman; dem. 1961 [T. B. Dudley, *History of Leamington*, 1896–1900, 180, 272].

THE QUERNS, nr. CIRENCESTER, GLOS., for Charles Laurence, 1825–7 [*Ornamental Villas*, no. 5].

YORK, CASTLE GAOL, rebuilt Prison, Governor's House, Gatehouse, etc., 1826–35, castellated; dem. 1935 [*Companion to the Almanac*, 1834, 219–22; T. P. Cooper, *History of the Castle of York*, 1911, 236–41].

LEAMINGTON, WARWICKS., COPP'S ROYAL HOTEL, 1826–7; dem. 1847 [exhib. at R.A. 1828; T. B. Dudley, *History of Leamington*, 1896–1900, 187].

THE HOLMWOOD, nr. DORKING, SURREY., for Miss Arnold, 1827 [*Ornamental Villas*, no. 7].

WOOLMER LODGE, BRAMSHOTT, HANTS., for Sir James Macdonald, Bart., 1827–8 [exhib. at R.A. 1830; *Ornamental Villas*, 1836 ed., p. 28].

SAMPFORD HOUSE, LITTLE SAMPFORD, ESSEX., for John Hinxman, 1828; destroyed by fire 1836 [exhib. at R.A. 1832; *New Series of Designs*, 1838, part 2, pls. 13–16].

LONDON, SWISS COTTAGE, in the grounds of THE COLOSSEUM, REGENT'S PARK, for Thomas Hornor, *c.*1828; dem. [*A.P.S.D.*; Thomas Rickman's diary, 26 June 1828] (*The Mirror* xx, 1832, 257–9).

WARTER HALL, YORKS. (E.R.), additions for 3rd Lord Muncaster, *c.*1830; dem. *c.*1973 [*Ornamental Villas*, 1836 ed., 16].

HEVER CASTLE, KENT, drawing-room for Mrs. Waldo, *c.*1830 [exhib. at R.A. 1831; *Colbran's New Guide for Tunbridge Wells*, 1840, 261].

SINGLETON HOUSE (now UNIVERSITY COLLEGE), SWANSEA, remodelled for J. H. Vivian, 1831 [*Domestic Architecture in the Tudor Style*, 1837].

BLAIR DRUMMOND, PERTHSIRE, toll-house for H. H. Drummond, 1831 [signed drawing: photograph at N.M.R.S.].

NOTTINGHAM, PARK TERRACE, villas, *c.*1831–2 [*New Series of Designs*, 1838, pt. 2, pls. 8–12; K. Brand, *The Park Estate, Nottingham*, Nottingham Civic Soc., n.d., 8, 11–13].

BRIDEHEAD, LITTLE BREDY, DORSET, remodelled for Robert Williams, 1831–3, Tudor [exhib. at R.A. 1831, 1833].

COOLHURST, nr. HORSHAM, SUSSEX, for Dowager Marchioness of Northampton, 1831–3, Elizabethan [exhib. at R.A. 1831; T. W. Horsfield, *History of Sussex* ii, 1835, 265, with engraving].

STORA SUNDBY, SÖDERMANLAND, SWEDEN, remodelled castle in 'Anglo-Norman' style, for Carl de Geer, 1831–48 [exhib. at R.A. 1830; information from Mr. R. Tatchell].

SEAFORDE HOUSE, CO. DOWN, IRELAND, Front Gate, Lodge and Almshouses for Mathew Forde, 1833 [drawings by Robinson, *ex inf.* Messsrs. T. Connor and J. A. K. Dean].

YORK, BOOTHAM BAR, rebuilt inner face, replacing Georgian elevation, 1834 [R.C.H.M., *York* ii, 117, pl. 33].

YORK, CITY AND COUNTY (now MIDLAND) BANK, 13 PARLIAMENT STREET, in collaboration with G. T. Andrews, 1835 [R.C.H.M. *York* v, 174].

YORK, DE GREY HOUSE, ST. LEONARD'S PLACE, for William Blanshard, in collaboration with G. T. Andrews, 1835 [R.C.H.M., *York* v, 204].

KEMBLE HOUSE, GLOS., THE GARDEN HOUSE for Robert Gordon, 1835 [*Ornamental Villas*, 1836 ed., 37].

?TICKTON GRANGE, nr. BEVERLEY, YORKS. (E.R.), for Smith Wormald, 1836, dem.: apparently the house stated on p. 40 of *Ornamental Villas*, 1836 ed., to be 'now erecting near Beverley for Smyth Wyndham, Esq.'

DUNSLEY MANOR HOUSE, nr. STOURBRIDGE, STAFFS., for H. H. Foley, *c.*1838 [*New Series of Designs*, 1838, part 2, pls. 17–20].

MAESGWYN, GLYN NEATH, GLAMORGANSHIRE, remodelled for Rees Williams, *c.*1840; dem. *c.*1970 [N.L.W., Aberpergwn MSS. 1387–1400, *ex inf.* Mr. Thomas Lloyd].

PRESTWOOD, nr. STOURBRIDGE, STAFFS., farmhouse for H. H. Foley [*New Series of Designs*, 1838, part 2, pls. 5–8].

CASSIOBURY PARK, HERTS., conservatory for 5th Earl of Essex [*Ornamental Villas*, 1836 ed., 10].

LANCYCH, BONCATH, PEMBROKESHIRE, closely resembles Design No. 20 (pl. 96) in *Rural Architecture*, 1823, there said to have been 'erected a few years since in Surrey'.

OYSTERMOUTH, GLAMORGANSHIRE, seaside villa [*New Series of Designs*, 1838, part 2, pls. 21–4].

Note: The design claimed (*Ornamental Villas*, 1836 ed., 43), to have been 'partially adopted' by Sir Charles Long, cr. Lord Farnborough, at Bromley Hill House, Kent, shows no specific resemblance to that house as recorded by Buckler in B.L., Add. MS. 36367, ff. 181–92.

ROBINSON, ROBERT (1734–1794), son of William Robinson (d. 1757), a gardener of Durham, and a younger brother of William Robinson (*q.v.*), became a leading landscape gardener in Scotland. He described himself as 'late Draughtsman and Executor of the Designs of Lancelot Brown, Esq.', and, like Brown, was prepared to act as an architect as well as a landscape gardener. In 1757 he proposed to open a school in Edinburgh to teach architecture and perspective, and in 1760, in announcing that he had entered into partnership with William Boutcher 'for designing, drawing and executing all kinds of policy and gardening', he stated that he would continue to 'give Designs, and carry on buildings, as formerly'. In 1773 he was described as 'architect' when he was made a burgess of Edinburgh *gratis* 'for good services'. While Robinson's career as a landscape gardener is well documented, little evidence has been found of his architectural activities. He married the daughter of a Berwickshire gentleman and was the father of Alexander Ramsay Robinson (d. 1824), superintendent of the royal farms at Windsor and Kew. [*Edinburgh Evening Courant*, 5 Nov. 1757; *Caledonian Mercury*, 8 March 1760; *Roll of Edinburgh Burgesses 1761–1841*, Scottish Rec. Soc., 136; A. A. Tait, *The Landscape Garden in Scotland*, Edinburgh 1980, 73–4, 85 n. 105; Burke's *Landed Gentry*, 1894, *s.v.* 'Robinson of Poston Court'.]

ROBINSON, SAMUEL (1752–1833), was admitted to the Royal Academy Schools in 1775 at the age of 23, and exhibited at the Academy between 1775 and 1821. He was surveyor to the estates of St. Thomas's Hospital, and to those of St. Olave's Schools, the Cordwainers' Company, and the parishes of St. Magnus Martyr and St. Margaret Lothbury. He specialized in the design of warehouses and similar buildings, and was much employed in valuations, particularly those connected with the formation of the new Regent Street, which he carried out in conjunction with his former pupil D. R. Roper. D. A. Alexander, V. Davis, T. Hatton, W. Mackie, J. Medland, Edwin Nash and W. Strutt were also his pupils. He died on 4 September 1833, aged 82, and was buried in front of the almshouses at Hackney which he had built and endowed [*A.P.S.D.*].

A brewhouse for Edmund Dawson [exhib. at R.A. 1783].

WOODFORD CHURCHYARD, ESSEX, monument to Edward Keepe (d. 1781), executed in Coade stone [exhib. at R.A. 1784] (*Architect and Building News*, 26 Jan. 1940, 114).

LONDON, 'Buildings now erecting on the bank of the River, where the late great fire happened opposite the Tower', exhib. at R.A. 1786.

HACKNEY, THE WIDOWS' RETREAT ALMSHOUSES, 1812, Gothic [W. Robinson, *History of Hackney* ii, 1842, 320].

ST. THOMAS'S HOSPITAL, SOUTHWARK, anatomical theatre, 1814–15. In about 1833, in partnership with J. Field, he designed N. and S. wings, entrance gates and lodges as part of a general plan of rebuilding that was never completed. The N. wing was built under Field's direction in 1833–5, the S. wing in 1840–2. The whole hospital was dem. 1862.

SOUTHWARK, premises of BRITISH AND FOREIGN SCHOOL SOCIETY, BOROUGH ROAD, 1817 [*A.P.S.D.*].

THE PROTESTANT DISSENTERS' COLLEGE, HOMERTON, 1823; dem. [W. Robinson, *History of Hackney* ii, 1843, 282].

SOUTHWARK, ST. OLAVE'S GRAMMAR SCHOOL, MAGDALEN STREET, 1824; dem. [*A.P.S.D.*].

ROBINSON, Sir THOMAS (*c.*1701–1777), was the eldest son and heir of William Robinson of Rokeby, Yorks. As a young man he travelled widely on the Continent and acquired the taste for architecture which was to be his dominant interest in later life. In 1727 he was returned to Parliament as Member for Morpeth through the influence of George Bowes. In the following year he married Elizabeth, the eldest daughter of Charles Howard, 3rd Earl of Carlisle, and widow of Nicholas, Lord Lechmere. He was created a baronet in 1731, and was a commissioner of excise from 1735 to 1742. Both in London, where he 'gave balls to all the men and women in power and in fashion', and at Rokeby, where he rebuilt the mansion and enclosed the park, his expenditure was extravagant, and it was chiefly in order to relieve his finances that in 1741 he accepted the post of Governor of Barbados. Here his love of building led him into further difficulties, for he ordered extensive alterations to his official residence at Pilgrim without consulting the assembly, and also undertook to build an armoury and arsenal. The assembly refused to vote sufficient money, and in the end he had to pay most of the building expenses himself. After further troubles over the command of the armed forces in the island, he was recalled in 1747. His first wife had died in 1739, and while in Barbados he married the widow of a rich ironmonger who brought him a considerable fortune but refused to accompany him back to England.

On his return Robinson acquired shares in Ranelagh Gardens and undertook the congenial duties of master of ceremonies. Under his management the Gardens reached the height of their celebrity, and the tall figure of 'Long Sir Thomas' figures largely in the social satires of the time. He built a house called Prospect Place on a site adjoining the Gardens, and once more gave the magnificent entertainments for which he had been famous as a young man. But renewed extravagance brought a return of his financial troubles, and in 1769 he was obliged to sell Rokeby, which had been in the possession of his family since 1610. He died at his house in Chelsea on 3 March 1777, at the age of 76, and was buried in the chancel of Merton Church, Surrey, where a monument was erected to his memory. A second monument, with busts of himself and his wife by John Walsh, was erected in Westminster Abbey in accordance with his will. He was succeeded in the baronetcy by his brother William. His portrait by Frans van de Mijn is in the National Portrait Gallery.

It is as a man of fashion that Sir Thomas Robinson is chiefly celebrated: but in the eighteenth century building was a fashionable occupation, and Sir Thomas counted architecture among his polite accomplishments. He was on friendly terms with Lord Burlington, whose Palladian principles he did his best to follow. It was in the Palladian manner that he rebuilt ROKEBY between 1725 and 1730. A design had been made by the Yorkshire architect Wakefield in 1724 and was published in *Vitruvius Britannicus* iii, 1725, pl. 90. But Robinson rejected Wakefield's design in favour of one for which he claimed the credit himself, issuing in *c.*1735–41 a set of engravings signed 'T. Robinson Bar. architectus'.[1] His new house was a villa, perhaps intended to recall Pliny's villa at Tusculum, which occupied a somewhat similar site. Its basic form, a compact rectangle with a pyramidal roof, was probably suggested by Marble Hill, but the twin towers were an unusual addition authorized both by Pliny and by Palladio's design for a villa at Bagnolo. Another remarkable feature is the porch or portico of baseless Doric columns, which replaced the balustraded stairs shown in the published engravings, almost certainly during Robinson's ownership. Out of the park Robinson created the romantic landscape which, nearly a hundred years later, was to form the setting for Sir Walter Scott's poem *Rokeby* (*C. Life*, 22–29 Sept. 1917, 19 May 1955, 19, 26 March, 2 April 1957; H. A. Tipping, *English Homes*, *Period V* (i), 1921).

In 1749 Robinson acquired the lease of a house in Whitehall overlooking the river which, despite its restricted site, he proceeded to rebuild, presumably to his own designs, giving its north side (overlooking his neighbours' gardens) a blind classical elevation [*Survey of London* xiii, 157; Giles Worsley in *C. Life*, 6 Oct. 1988]. It was demolished *c.*1896.

Sir Thomas maintained a long correspondence on architectural and other matters with his father-in-law, Lord Carlisle, and criticized Hawksmoor's designs for the mausoleum which the latter was building at CASTLE HOWARD. After Hawksmoor's death in 1736, it was by his advice that Daniel Garrett was employed to complete the dual stairway and the surrounding wall in a manner which, although it may have been more 'Palladian', accorded ill with Hawksmoor's intentions [G. F. Webb, 'The Letters and Drawings . . . relating to . . . the Mausoleum at Castle Howard', *Walpole Soc.* xix, 1931]. Later on, between 1753 and 1759, Robinson was allowed to carry out alterations to the mansion itself. The western court had been left unfinished on Vanbrugh's death in 1726, and Robinson, instead of completing it in accordance with the published designs, built a new wing in an orthodox Palladian style inspired by William Kent which, however excellent of its kind, gave the house an unfortunately lop-sided appearance (mitigated by the removal in the nineteenth century of the attic storeys above Robinson's terminal pavilions). Robinson no doubt hoped to remodel the

[1] Sets of these engravings can be seen in B.L. (*King's Maps* xlv, 26), Bodleian Library (Gough Yorks. 52) and York Minster Library, Hailstone Collection.

eastern court to correspond, but this he was not permitted to do [L. Whistler, *The Imagination of Vanbrugh*, 1954, 48–50; Giles Worsley in *C. Life*, 30 Jan. 1986].

For Ralph, 2nd Lord Verney, one of the proprietors of Ranelagh Gardens, Robinson designed new state rooms at CLAYDON HOUSE, BUCKS, with a central rotunda and a large ballroom occupying one wing. The work proceeded slowly, and was still incomplete at the time of Robinson's death in 1777. The ballroom and rotunda were pulled down after Lord Verney's death in 1791, but one wing remains, built before the rotunda and ballroom, and perhaps not designed by Robinson. The latter's correspondence with Lord Verney was published by Margaret Lady Verney and Patrick Abercrombie as 'Letters of an Eighteenth Century Architect', *Arch. Rev.*, June–September 1926. See also Christopher Hussey in *C. Life*, 24, 31 Oct., 7 Nov. 1952, and in *English Country Houses: Early Georgian 1715–1760*, 1955, 242–50.

For Richard Trevor, Bishop of Durham, Robinson designed in 1760 the Gothic gateway at BISHOP AUCKLAND CASTLE, CO. DURHAM [W. Fordyce, *History of Durham* i, 1857, 549, confirmed by a contemporary drawing of the gateway preserved at the Palace, on which Robinson is named as the architect, illustrated *C. Life*, 24 Feb. 1972, 462], and in 1763–5 the classical church at GLYNDE, SUSSEX [T. W. Horsfield, *History of Lewes* ii, 1827, 125; W. de St. Croix, 'Parochial History of Glynde', *Sussex Arch. Colls.* xx, 1868, 78–9]. He may also have designed the stable block built at Glynde in 1753–6 by John Morris of Lewes and illustrated in *C. Life*, 28 April 1955. For the Rt. Hon. Arthur Onslow, Robinson designed an addition to EMBER COURT, SURREY, of which there is a signed engraving (B.L., *King's Maps* xl, 20, 2a, and Bodleian, Gough Maps 30, f. 51v), but it is not known whether this was built.

According to Surtees [*History of Durham* iv, 1840, 35], Robinson designed the bridge over the R. Tees at WINSTON, CO. DURHAM, in 1762–3, but the attribution to him of Greta Bridge near Rokeby is incorrect, as it was designed and built by John Carr of York in 1773, four years after Robinson had parted with the Yorkshire estate. He does, however, appear to have designed ROKEBY CHURCH, which although not completed until 1776, was built in accordance with drawings made under his direction, probably by Isaac Ware, whose name as draughtsman appears on several of the Rokeby engravings, and who seems to have acted as Robinson's architectural amanuensis.

Robinson's personal papers were destroyed after his death, but a portfolio of his architectural designs remains at Rokeby.

[*A.P.S.D.*; *D.N.B.*; R. Sedgwick, *The House of Commons* ii, 1970, 388–9; R. Blunt, *Mrs. Montagu* ii, 1923, 28; Hist. MSS. Comm., *Carlisle, passim*; J. H. Round, 'Family History from Private Manuscripts', *The Ancestor* ix, 1904, 6–19; Dudley Harbron, 'The Modern Proteus', *Arch. Rev.* lxxx, 1936, 167–70; Michael McCarthy, 'Sir Thomas Robinson: An Original English Palladian', *Architectura* 10, 1980; Giles Worsley, 'The baseless Roman Doric column in mid-eighteenth-century English architecture', *Burlington Mag.* May 1986 and 'Archaeological Neoclassicism in mid-18th century Britain' in *New Light on English Palladianism*, ed. C. Hind, Georgian Group Symposium, 1988.]

ROBINSON, THOMAS, BARON GRANTHAM (1738–1786), was the son of Sir Thomas Robinson of Newby Hall, Yorks., whom he succeeded as 2nd Baron Grantham in 1770. He was the nephew, on his mother's side, of Thomas Worsley of Hovingham (*q.v.*), and the father of Earl de Grey (*q.v.*). A few drawings by him, preserved at Newby Hall, show that he had some ability as an amateur architect. Among them are designs for a 'Triumphal arch to be erected across the Great Western Road near St. George's Hospital between Hyde Park & the Green Park, 1761', for offices and stables for Newby (now Baldersby) Park, and for an octagonal tower for Saltram House, Devonshire, the seat of his brother-in-law John Parker, cr. Lord Boringdon (cf. the National Trust guide-book to Saltram, 7 and 27). For Robinson's political career see *D.N.B.* and Namier & Brooke, *The House of Commons 1754–1790* iii, 1964, 367.

ROBINSON, WILLIAM, 'of Bow Lane', London, is known only as the author of a small volume consisting of 32 pages of engraved plates and text entitled *Proportional Architecture, or the Five Orders regulated by Equal Parts*, 1733, 2nd. ed. 1736. Robinson was presumably dead by 1766, when the entire book was reissued as part of Edward Oakley's *Every Man a Compleat Builder* [Eileen Harris, *British Architectural Books and Writers 1556–1785*, 1990, 395–6].

ROBINSON, WILLIAM (–1767), Surveyor to the Gresham Trustees, was responsible for the extensive repair of the Royal Exchange for which the House of Commons voted £10,000 in 1767. According to Britton & Pugin, *Public Buildings of London* i, 1825,

292, 'almost the whole of the western side was rebuilt' under his direction. He also held the surveyorship of the Mercers' Company from 1745 and of the East India Company from 1747. He died on 25 December 1767, leaving large sums of money to London charities. He was a carpenter by trade [*Gent's Mag.* 1767, 611; *A.P.S.D.*].

ROBINSON, WILLIAM (*c.*1720–1775), was the eldest son of William Robinson of Durham (d. 1757), described as 'gardener' in his will. He came to London at an early age, served under Thomas Ripley, the Surveyor of Greenwich Hospital, and in 1746 was appointed Clerk of the Works at the Hospital, retaining the post until his death. From about 1752 to 1767 he was Surveyor of Buildings to the Board of Customs, and in 1754 he was appointed to the Office of Works post of Clerk of the Works at Whitehall, Westminster and St. James's. In 1762 he was promoted to be Secretary to the Board of Works and Clerk Itinerant. From 1762 onwards he was also Clerk of the Works at the Queen's (Buckingham) House.

Robinson was chiefly an official architect. In 1750–9 he and John Vardy supervised the building of the Horse Guards building in Whitehall to the designs of William Kent (d. 1748), and at Greenwich he supervised the erection of the Infirmary to the designs of James Stuart in 1763. His most important work was the EXCISE OFFICE in OLD BROAD STREET, built in a competent but conservative Palladian style in 1769–75 and demolished in 1854. His death in 1775 deprived him of the commission for the new public offices on the site of Somerset House which then fell to Sir William Chambers.

In a private capacity Robinson was employed by Horace Walpole to make the first alterations to STRAWBERRY HILL, TWICKENHAM, in 1748, but this was 'before there was any design of further improvements to the house', and they were not 'truly Gothic' – that is, they were in the kind of Gothic devised by William Kent which no longer satisfied Walpole's antiquarian tastes. It was in the same sort of Gothic that in 1753 Robinson designed a church for the parish of STONE in STAFFORDSHIRE, which was built in 1754–8 under the direction of William Baker (*q.v.*) [W. H. Bowers & J. W. Clough, *Researches into the History of the Parish of Stone*, 1929, 58–61].

Robinson died suddenly of gout on 10 October 1775, and was buried in the Chapel at Greenwich Hospital. He was the father of George Robinson (d. 1822), Governor of Senegal, and of John Robinson (d. 1774), Clerk of the Works at the Queen's House, Greenwich. His brother Thomas (1727–1810) was a master-gardener at Kensington, while another brother, Robert (*q.v.*), practised as an architect and landscape-gardener in Edinburgh.

[*A.P.S.D.*; P.R.O., ADM. 65/106; *History of the King's Works* v; Horace Walpole, *Works* ii, 1798, 421; Burke's *Landed Gentry*, 1894, *s.v.* 'Robinson of Poston Court'.]

ROBINSON, WILLIAM (*c.*1744–   ), of Hackney, architect and surveyor, was, in 1774, a candidate for a District Surveyorship. He was then aged 30 [Middlesex County Records, General Orders No. 10]. In the same year he published *The Gentleman and Builder's Director*, which contains a commentary on the regulations laid down in the Building Act of 1774 and 'Directions to build Chimneys to prevent them Smoking'.

ROBINSON, WILLIAM (1762–1820), was the son of William Robinson, a builder of Saffron Walden in Essex. He followed his father in the business and died in April 1820, aged 58. On his tombstone in Saffron Walden churchyard he is styled 'Architect and Builder'. Apart from the house called 'The Grove' which he built for himself, no buildings designed by Robinson appear to be recorded, but in 1784 a view of Saffron Walden Church by him was engraved, and in 1818 he published *The Sawyer's Ready Reckoner, an entire new work formed on equitable principles.* In 1816 he was a candidate for the County Surveyorship of Essex [Essex Record Office, Q/SO 24, p. 194]. [R. Heffer, 'William Robinson, Architect and Engraver of Saffron Walden', *Essex Review* xxx, 1921, 20–3.]

ROBSON, JOHN (*c.*1773–1844), practised in Great Marlborough Street, London. He exhibited at the Royal Academy between 1797 and 1833. His exhibits included a 'Design for a cottage intended to be built in Hunts.' (1803), a 'Design for a cottage to be built in Northumberland' (1806), a 'Design for a Cottage for Mr. Keats, to be built at Paddington' (1810), a 'Design for a castellated mansion for A. Bonelli, Esq.' (1815), a 'Design for the west end of the church at Norwood' (1819), a 'Design for a ball-room executed in Harley Street' (1820). Some unexecuted designs by him for additions to Littlecote House, Wilts., are described in a letter in *C. Life*, 27 Jan. 1966. He was one of the architects who submitted designs for rebuilding Hungerford Church, Berks., in 1811, and he competed for the University Observatory at Cambridge in 1821 and for the Middlesex Lunatic Asylum in 1827. He died on 28 April 1844, aged 71 [*Gent's Mag.* 1844 (i), 663].

ROCHE, PETER DE LA, see DE LA ROCHE, PETER.

ROGERS, THOMAS (*c.*1744–1821), was Surveyor to the County of Middlesex from *c.*1773 to 1802, and District Surveyor of the parish of St. Marylebone from 1774 onwards. He exhibited at the Society of Artists (of which he was elected Director in 1774) from 1766 to 1790, and at the Royal Academy in 1786 and 1787. Among his exhibits was (1776) the 'Elevation of a new Front, erected to an old villa at Chigwell, Essex'. He was the successful competitor for the MIDDLESEX COUNTY SESSIONS HOUSE at CLERKENWELL GREEN, built in 1779–82. John Carter, however, claimed quite unjustifiably that Rogers had merely copied a design published by himself in the *Builder's Magazine* (pls. xc, xci). The building is illustrated in G. Richardson, *New Vitruvius Britannicus* i, 1802–8, pls. xxxiv–xxxv, and the original drawings and contracts are in the Middlesex County records. Rogers was President of the Surveyors' Club in 1795. He died at Hampstead on 20 March 1821, aged 77 [*A.P.S.D.*; *Gent's Mag.* 1821 (i), 379].

ROLFE, WILLIAM EDWARD (– *c.*1827), son of W. Rolfe of East Ham, Essex, a builder, was a pupil of Sir John Soane from 1801 to 1804 [A. T. Bolton, *The Works of Sir John Soane*, 1924, Appendix C, p. xliii]. He exhibited at the Royal Academy from London addresses between 1802 and 1820, showing in 1808–10 his designs for KEMPTON PARK, nr. HAMPTON, MIDDLESEX (dem.), with its lodges and entrance-gates, as built for J. Fish. He also designed two buildings in WEST TEIGNMOUTH, DEVON: a PUBLIC LIBRARY, 1815, and the octagonal Gothic ST. JAMES'S CHURCH built by Andrew Patey in 1821 [*Teignmouth, Dawlish and Torquay Guide*, 1830, 24, 28, where he is described as 'late']. In about 1823 he published *Miscellaneous Sketches of Designs in Architecture*, printed by Boosey & Co.

ROMER, JOHN LAMBERTUS (1680–?1754), was the son of Wolfgang William Romer (1640–1713), a military engineer in the service of William III. In 1708 he was appointed assistant engineer to his father at Portsmouth, and in 1715 he became engineer at Sheerness, with charge of the defences of the Thames and Medway. In July 1719, he took part in the expedition to Vigo under Lord Cobham, and on his return was (Jan. 1720) appointed surveyor in charge of the northern district and Scotland in succession to Andrews Jelfe. In Scotland he was responsible for the completion of barracks at Inversnaid, Ruthven, Bernera and Kiliwhimen, as well as for important defence works at Forts Augustus, William and George. In 1723 he was promoted engineer-in-ordinary, and went to the Board of Ordnance in London as officer in charge of the administration of Scotland and the northern engineer districts. In 1745–6 he served under the Duke of Cumberland, and was wounded at Culloden. He retired in 1751 [*D.N.B.*; P.R.O., Ordnance Office records].

In the British Library there is a 'Plan and Section of a Cistern built at Sheerness in the year 1716 by John Romer Engineer' (*King's Maps* xvii, 19k), and in the Public Record Office there is a copy made by Isaac Swan in 1781 of the 'Plans and Sections of a Market House and stables built at Sheerness in the year 1718', signed 'Romer' (MPH 15). Drawings connected with his Scottish works are in the National Library of Scotland (MS. 1648).

ROOKS, JOHN (*c.*1760–1833), practised as an architect and surveyor in Norwich, where he was Surveyor to the Paving Commissioners, the Commissioners of Sewers and the Trustees of the Great Hospital. He died on 24 June 1833, and was commemorated by a tombstone in St. Stephen's churchyard.

ROPER, DAVID RIDDALL (*c.*1774–1855), was a pupil of Samuel Robinson, to whom he was articled for three and a half years from June 1792 [P.R.O., IR 1/35, p. 160]. He became well known as a surveyor and, in conjunction with Robinson, made the valuations of property in connection with the formation of Regent Street. He exhibited at the Royal Academy between 1797 and 1822, and was President of the Surveyors' Club in 1813. He died on 11 April 1855 in his 82nd year. W. Ford, W. Jay and T. Ruck were among his pupils. Joshua and David Roper, who exhibited architectural designs from his Blackfriars office at the Royal Academy in 1815–17 and 1820, respectively, were his sons. A. B. Clayton (*q.v.*) was an assistant in his office, and is said to have been the effective designer of two of his principal buildings, St. Mark's Church, Kennington, and the Shot Tower at Lambeth. [*A.P.S.D.*; letter from H. C. Barlow in *Builder* xxvii, 1869, 65; *The Times*, 14 April 1855.]

LONDON, ALBION FIRE OFFICE, NEW BRIDGE STREET, BLACKFRIARS, *c.*1805 [*A.P.S.D.*].

ACTON, MIDDLESEX, a villa in Horn Lane for

N. Selby, *c.*1807 [exhib. 1807].

BROCKWELL HALL, nr. DULWICH, for John Blades, 1811–13, repaired by J. B. Papworth 1824–9 [Brayley, *Topographical History of Surrey* iii, 379; *Survey of London* xxvi, 161].

SOUTHWARK, SURREY CHAPEL ALMSHOUSES, 1812 [exhib. at R.A. 1814].

CAMBERWELL, SURREY, GROVE CHAPEL, 1819 [Brayley, *Topographical History of Surrey* iii, 275].

LONDON, ST. MARK'S CHURCH, KENNINGTON, 1822–4; reconstructed internally by S. S. Teulon 1873–6; damaged by bombing 1941 [exhib. at R.A. 1822].

LONDON, HABERDASHERS' (ASKE'S) ALMSHOUSES, HOXTON, 1825–6, now the City and East London College [*A.P.S.D.*] (J. Elmes, *Metropolitan Improvements*, 1831, 143 and plate).

LAMBETH, THE SHOT TOWER, for Messrs. Maltby, 1826; dem. [*Survey of London* xxiii (i), 47].

GRAVESEND, KENT, improvement of Town Quay, 1828–9 [R. P. Cruden, *History of Gravesend*, 1843, 496].

ROPER, ROBERT (1757–1838), practised in Preston. He was the son of William Roper, a local mason who died in the 1790s, and succeeded to his business. In 1816 Lewis Wyatt wrote that 'he has the character of doing his work well and is considered to be a good general builder' [Lancs. C.R.O., DDX 1564]. He developed an architectural practice, in which the patronage of fellow Roman Catholics played a part (e.g. at Leagram, Thurnham and Leighton Halls). His churches are in the lancet style of the 1820s and his two Gothic houses were designed in the symmetrical late Georgian manner. [Information from Mr. Colin Stansfield].

LEAGRAM HALL, LANCS., rebuilt E. front for George Weld, 1822; dem. [J. Weld, *History of Leagram*, Chetham Soc. 1913, 81].

KIRKHAM CHURCH, LANCS., rebuilt 1822, retaining medieval tower [R. Cunliffe Shaw, *Kirkham in Amounderness*, 1949, 137].

HOGHTON, LANCS., HOLY TRINITY CHURCH, for the Church Building Commissioners, 1822–3, Gothic [Port, 132–3].

THURNHAM HALL, LANCS., refronted for John Dalton, 1823, Gothic [payments in Dalton family papers in Lancs. C.R.O., *ex inf.* Mr. C. Stansfield].

LUND CHAPEL, NEWTON-WITH-CLIFTON, LANCS., 1824; since rebuilt [I.C.B.S.].

attributed: LEIGHTON HALL, LANCS., remodelled for Richard Gillow, 1825, Gothic; enlarged 1870 by Paley & Austin [stylistic attribution based on resemblance to Thurnham Hall] (*C. Life*, 11 May 1951).

BROUGHTON CHURCH, nr. PRESTON, LANCS., retaining the Tudor tower, 1826 [I.C.B.S.].

ROSE, HENRY (1755–1826), of Sevenoaks, Kent, is described as 'architect' in Burke's *Landed Gentry, s.v.* 'Rose of Worth Court' and as 'surveyor' in his will (P.R.O., PROB 11/1710).

ROSE, HENRY (–?1853), practised in Southwark. His principal work was THE LICENSED VICTUALLERS' ASYLUM, ASYLUM ROAD, CAMBERWELL, 1827–8, an ambitious classical building with a pedimented portico, now known as 'Caroline Gardens'. According to *A.P.S.D.* he was also responsible for the subsequent addition of the north and south wings, 1831–3, the ladies' wing, 1849, and the chapel, board room, court house and four additional houses, 1850, but a medal commemorating the laying of the foundation-stone of the ladies' wing in 1849 gives the name of C. J. Kemp as architect. He also designed a simple terrace of houses in PARK STREET, SOUTHWARK, 1831, on which plaques name him as architect, THE LICENSED VICTUALLERS' SCHOOL, KENNINGTON LANE, 1835–6, renamed 'Imperial Court' [*Architectural Mag.* iii, 1836, 140], and the BOROUGH MARKET, SOUTHWARK, 1851, rebuilt 1863–4. In 1839–40 he rebuilt the nave of ST. SAVIOUR'S CHURCH, SOUTHWARK (now the CATHEDRAL), in a feeble Gothic style caricatured by Pugin in his *Contrasts*, pl. 18. It was again rebuilt by Sir A. W. Blomfield in 1890–7. The church of ST. MARK, ROSHERVILLE, KENT, which Rose designed in 1851–3 in conjunction with Edward Rose (presumably his son) was better calculated to satisfy Camdenian critics [*Builder* xii, 1854, 175]. [*A.P.S.D.*]

ROSE, JAMES (1731–1796), was a mason and architect-builder at Bewdley in Worcestershire, where he was established from the 1770s onwards, but he was a native of Chaddesley Corbett, where a family tomb records his death on 9 May 1796 at the age of 65. He designed and built STANFORD-ON-TEME CHURCH, WORCS., in 1768–9 for Sir Edward Winnington, Bart., and in 1778–82 rebuilt the tower and spire of CHADDESLEY CORBETT CHURCH, WORCS., both in quite a creditable Gothic style [J. Noake, *The Rambler in Worcestershire* ii, 1854, 172, iii, 1854, 227; J. S. Roper, *History of St. Cassian's Church, Chaddesley Corbett*, 1969]. LOWER MITTON CHAPEL, STOURPORT, WORCS., was rebuilt to Rose's designs in 1790–1; dem. *c.*1920 [W.

A. Trippas, *The Church of St. Michael, Stourport*, 1946, 10–11].

'Mr. Rose's first plan for New Rooms at Besford Court' was among architectural drawings formerly at Beechwood Park, Herts., and a drawing in private possession shows a dining parlour at 'Arely', 'alter'd by Rose'. His contract for building a farmhouse at Shorncote, Somerford Keynes, Glos., in 1774–7 is among the Lloyd-Baker family papers.

ROSS, CHARLES (–1770/5), was a London carpenter and joiner who sometimes acted as an architect or surveyor. As a carpenter and joiner he is recorded to have worked under Matthew Brettingham at the 2nd Earl of Strafford's house in St. James's Square in 1748–9 [*Survey of London* xxix, 100] and at Marble Hill, Twickenham, in 1750–1 [M. P. G. Draper, *Marble Hill House*, 1970, 43–4]; to have been employed at St. James's Church, Piccadilly, under James Horn in 1756 [*Survey of London* xxix, 37]; and to have made furniture for the Royal Society of Arts in 1760 [*Jnl. Royal Society of Arts* cxiv, 1966, 431–2]. As an architect Ross (described as 'of Piccadilly, carpenter') undertook on 30 August 1748 to rebuild the west front of KIRTLING HALL, CAMBS. (dem. 1801), for the 1st Earl of Guilford, 'according to a plan given by him' [Bodleian Library, MS. North adds. b. 1, ff. 1–2]. He may have been the 'Mr. Ross' who seems to have finished off the works at BLAIR CASTLE, PERTHSHIRE, after the death of Roger Morris in 1749 [Blair Castle archives D.2.13 (38)], and in 1759 he undertook 'to superintend' the building of the Palladian south-east wing of WENTWORTH CASTLE, YORKS. (W.R.), for the 2nd Earl of Strafford. He was 'to provide a clever man that understands drawing and the several branches of building' and 'to anser all letters and draw what planes is relating to the building' [agreement printed in *R.I.B.A. Jnl.*, 25 Nov. 1933, 70, from B.L., Add. MS. 22241, f. 137]. Receipts show that Ross continued to superintend the new building until its completion in 1764. As contemporary writers are unanimous in stating that Lord Strafford (*q.v.*) designed the new building himself, it is clear that Ross's function was to act as his draughtsman and executant architect. In 1770 Ross was responsible for building or rebuilding a house in Mortimer Street, London, for Lord Robert Bertie. The relevant documents show that he was dead by 1775 [Berkshire C.R.O., D/ED. F. 29A].

ROSS, CHARLES (1722–1806), of Greenlaw, nr. Paisley, was a land surveyor much employed in Scotland during the second half of the eighteenth century. In 1773 he published an engraved map of Lanarkshire, and numerous estate plans signed by him are in the Scottish Record Office. He was also the author of a *Traveller's Guide to Lochlomond* (Paisley 1792), in which he illustrates an eccentric Gothic gateway at GARSCADDEN HOUSE, DUNBARTONSHIRE (dem.), which he says was 'designed and executed by the author of this work' for James Colquhoun, the owner of the house. The Campbell-Colquhoun family papers (bdl. 1) show that in 1779 he had added a wing to Garscadden House for William Colquhoun (d. 1784), and the surviving battlemented coach-house (now the garage of No. 38 Mansion House Drive) can be attributed to him on stylistic grounds. On p. 120 of the *Traveller's Guide* he mentions a Gothic farm-house that he had designed on the Ardoch estate near Dumbarton. This is now Nos. 20, 22 Cardross Road, Dumbarton.

ROSS, WILLIAM, of Bristol, contributed designs for farm-buildings and for a 'Tudor' public-house and ale-house to Loudon's *Encyclopaedia of Cottage, Farm and Villa Architecture* (1833). He was a native of Ross-shire and one of the farms illustrated had been built in the parish of Tarbat in that county in accordance with his designs. In or about 1834 he emigrated to New York, where he was employed to revise the designs for the interior of the Customs House (now Sub-Treasury), as described in Loudon's *Architectural Mag.* ii, 1835, 525–33.

ROUCHEAD, ALEXANDER (–1776), was a mason by trade. He became free of the London Masons' Company by redemption on 27 May 1728 [Guildhall Library, MS. 5308], but was already active as a builder, e.g. on the Harley estate in Oxford Street, where he took a plot in 1726 [B.L., Add. MS. 18240, f. 15; see also *Survey of London* xxix, 90–1, Addendum]. He appears to have been identical with the 'Alexander Rovehead' of London who apparently designed, and certainly superintended the erection of, the NAVAL HOSPITAL at STONEHOUSE, PLYMOUTH, in 1758–64 [*A.P.S.D.*]. This building, designed on what was then a novel plan of insulated but linked blocks, marked an important step forward in the planning of hospitals, and was commended by J. R. Tenon in his *Mémoires sur les hôpitaux de Paris*, 1788, 385–6, and illustrated in plate 29 of Durand's *Recueil et parallèle des édifices anciens et modernes*, 1800. A contemporary plan, perhaps drawn by Rouchead, is in the Public Record Office (ADM 140/321). Rouchead lived in a house of his own building in North Audley Street until his death in 1776 [*Survey of London* xl, 99; P.R.O., PCC 472 BELLAS].

ROUMIEU, ABRAHAM (1734–1780), son of John Roumieu of London, refiner, was a member of a Huguenot family. He was apprenticed first to Isaac Ware (1748) and then to Thomas Reynolds before being admitted a freeman of the Carpenters' Company in 1756 [Guildhall Library, Records of the Carpenters' Company, MSS. 4329/17 and 4335/4]. An architectural book seen in the sale-room in 1972 was inscribed 'Abraham Roumieu Architect 1756'. No building designed by Roumieu appears to be known, but in the 1760s he was in the service of the 4th Duke of Gordon, for whom he made unexecuted designs for Gordon Castle, Morayshire, that are now in the Register House, Edinburgh (Gordon Castle Plans 1072–4, dated 1766–7). According to *A.P.S.D.* he was the grandfather of the Victorian architect Robert Lewis Roumieu, F.R.I.B.A. (1814–77).

ROWE, HENRY (1787–1859), practised in Worcester, where he designed the METHODIST CHAPEL, PUMP STREET, 1813; dem. [*Worcester Jnl.*, 16 July 1812]; THE CITY GAOL, 1823–5; dem. [Worcester Corporation Archives, Gaol Ledger 1823–31]; and ST. GEORGE'S (R.C.) CHURCH, SANSOME PLACE, 1829; façade rebuilt 1887 [B. W. Kelly, *Historical Notes on English Catholic Missions*, 1907, 449]. His plans for a new vicarage for St. Swithin's Church are among the Worcester Diocesan Records. In 1829 he was appointed City Surveyor, an office in which he was succeeded by his son Henry Rowe, junior. He died on 6 June 1859, aged 72 [information from Mr. D. Whitehead].

ROWE, ISAAC, was a seventeenth-century architect who appears to have been based in London, but to have had some connection with Northamptonshire. No coherent account of his career can at present be given, but he following evidences of his architectural activity have been noted:

1663–6 payments in the accounts of Sir Thomas Proby of Elton Hall, Hunts., two totalling £50 'to Mr. Roe' or 'Rowe' in 1663, and one of 10s. 'To Roe for drawing a Chymney peice' in 1666. These payments relate to the building of the west wing of ELTON HALL in 1664–6 (see *C. Life*, 21 Feb. 1957, fig. 3, and plan in R.C.H.M., *Huntingdonshire*, 79) [Proby MSS. at Elton Hall], but a further payment of £1 1s.6d. was 'To him for my house in Pel Mel [Pall Mall, Westminster] to end all disputes for his drawing designs for the joyner'.

1667 an elegantly drawn design for a large cupboard or wardrobe among the Isham papers from Lamport Hall, Northants., signed 'Isaac Rowe 1667'.

1672 a plan and elevation of a small house with pedimented central feature, signed 'Isaac Rowe November 25, 1672' [Hampshire Record Office, Cope papers in Mildmay Collection].

?1674 a drawing in the R.I.B.A. Collection (G1/4) signed 'I Rowe' in a monogram with a date which may be 1674. It consists of three alternative plans of a small house, roughly drawn.

1676 a contract dated 1 May between the 2nd Earl of Peterborough and Richard Warner of Weldon, stone-mason, to erect a building 'on either side of the New Gate' at DRAYTON HOUSE, NORTHANTS., 'According to a Draught Designed by Isaac Rowe now servant to the said Earle of Peterborough' [Stopford-Sackville papers at Drayton]. The buildings in question are presumably those on either side of the seventeenth-century outer gateway (*C. Life*, 13 May 1965).

1676 an elevation of a doorway signed 'I. Rowe 1676' in a monogram [Northants. Record Office, Fitzwilliam papers from Milton Hall].

1680 a design for a hexagonal pedestal signed 'I. Rowe Aprill ye 28 1680' in a monogram [among drawings by Robert Hooke in B.L., Add. MS. 5238, f. 85].

1683 two leases (perhaps fictitious) on Nicholas Barbon's Wellclose development near the Tower of London [*Guildhall Miscellany* iv, 1972, 107].

1686 drew a 'platform' for a square of thirty houses (later reduced to twenty-eight) in the parish of St. Margaret, Westminster, for Bevis Lloyd, staked out 1687 and largely built by 1688 [P.R.O., C7/210/8, *ex inf.* Mr. Frank Kelsall].

ROWE, JOSEPH, a joiner by trade, was a builder and surveyor of Exeter. He designed KENTISBURY RECTORY, DEVON, in 1779, and enlarged and refronted CORNWORTHY VICARAGE, DEVON, in 1784 [Exeter Diocesan Records]. He was probably the father of Joseph Rowe, who built (and no doubt designed) the elegant Regency houses in PENNSYLVANIA PARK, EXETER, in 1822–3 [W. G. Hoskins, *A Thousand Years in Exeter*, 1960, 146], and who reroofed and remodelled ST. STEPHEN'S CHURCH, EXETER, in 1826 [Vestry Minutes in Devon C.R.O.]. A third generation of the family is represented by Joseph's son Joseph Coplestone Rowe, who took up his freedom in 1828 [*Exeter Freemen*, Devon and Cornwall Rec. Soc. 1973, 359].

ROWLAND, SAMUEL (–1844), was the nephew and successor of William Byrom of Liverpool (*q.v.*). He had a considerable practice and is said to have 'accumulated a large fortune'. In Liverpool he designed some excellent Greek Revival buildings, notably the Ionic portico of St. Bride's Church and the former Royal Bank in Dale Street. He left no successor to his practice when he died childless in December 1844 [*Builder* iv, 1846, 530, xxvii, 1869, 803–4; will in Lancs. C.R.O., *ex inf.* Dr. Janet Gnosspelius].

LIVERPOOL, THE NORTHERN DISPENSARY, VAUXHALL ROAD, *c.*1826; dem. [J. A. Picton, *Architectural History of Liverpool*, 1858, 69].

LIVERPOOL, THE SCOTCH PRESBYTERIAN CHAPEL, MOUNT PLEASANT, 1827; dem. [J. A. Picton, *Memorials of Liverpool* ii, 1875, 212].

WARRINGTON, LANCS., ST. JAMES'S CHURCH, WILDERSPOOL CAUSEWAY, 1829–30, Gothic [I.C.B.S.].

LIVERPOOL, ST. BRIDE'S CHURCH, PERCY STREET, 1830–1 [J. A. Picton,*Memorials of Liverpool* ii, 1875, 261].

LIVERPOOL, THE ROYAL BANK (later Queen Insurance Buildings), DALE STREET, 1837–8 [J. A. Picton, *Memorials of Liverpool* ii, 1875, 106].

ROWLAND, THOMAS (*c.*1696–1748), held the post of Clerk of the Works at Windsor Castle from 1715 until 1729, when he was dismissed. He was a carpenter by training, and had previously been foreman to John Churchill, the Master Carpenter at Windsor. A 'plan and upright of the Engine House at Windsor with the Dimensions of Measurement of the Severall Artificers' Works', drawn up by himself and Thomas Fort in 1718, is in the Bodleian Library (Gough Maps 1, f. 23).

As an architect, Rowland's most important recorded work was the LIBRARY at ETON COLLEGE. In 1719–20 the Hall at Eton was repaired 'according to Mr. Rowland's model', and in December 1725 the Provost and Fellows agreed 'to proceed to the building of a new Library According to Mr. Rowland's Plan'. He received £50 for 'surveying' in 1726, and a like sum in 1729 for 'surveying the Inside Works of the Library' [Willis & Clark, i, 452, 455]. In 1726 Dr. Godolphin, the Provost of Eton, employed Rowland to design a new attic storey which he added to his residence, BAYLIES HOUSE, nr. SLOUGH. The house was considerably altered a few years later by John James [R. A. Austen-Legh in *The Times*, 22 July 1938, citing documents among the Godolphin family papers now in the Bucks. C.R.O.]. In 1727–8 Rowland was employed by Charles Aldworth to make an estimate for repairs to FROGMORE HOUSE, nr. WINDSOR, of which Aldworth was then the lessee [Berkshire, C.R.O., Account Book of Charles Aldworth, D/EN F.30].

In 1730, no doubt in the hope of establishing himself in private architectural practice, Rowland issued proposals for *A General Treatise of Architecture*, based largely on Perrault and other French textbooks. The title-page is dated 1732, but of the remainder of the book only six parts were eventually published in 1743. The somewhat incoherent text was accompanied by some irregularly arranged plates, including some from his own designs. Rowlands was also the author of two sets of tables entitled *Mensuration of Superfices and Solids, by Tables of Feet, Inches and Parts, chiefly applied to the several Artificers' Works in Building*, 1739, and *Compleat Tables for Measuring Round and Square Timber*, 1745.

Rowland, who was Mayor of Windsor in 1736–7, died in 1748, aged 52.

[*History of the King's Works* v, 121, 477; J. Langton, 'The Second Hall Book of the Borough of New Windsor', *Windsor Borough Historical Record Publications*, ii, 1973, 163; Eileen Harris, *British Architectural Books and Writers 1556–1785*, 1990, 397–9.]

ROWLANDS, THOMAS (*c.*1803–1883), was the son of William Rowlands (d. 1850), a successful builder of Haverfordwest in Pembrokeshire. After a period of 'education' in London (presumably in the office of an architect) he joined his father's business and soon obtained an important commission to remodel the front entrance of PICTON CASTLE, PEMBS., for Richard Philipps in the 'Norman' style, 1826–8, and to add other subsidiary buildings, including the stable block and a Romanesque conservatory (dem.) [*Cambrian*, 6 Jan. 1827 and 2 Feb. 1828]. Subsequent works, for which he was often both architect and contractor, were ST. MICHAEL'S CHURCH, PEMBROKE, 1829–33, Gothic, partly remodelled 1886 [I.C.B.S.]; a MARKET HALL at NARBERTH, PEMBS., 1832–6 (dem.), based on Haverfordwest Market by W. Owen (*q.v.*) [N.L.W., Slebech 3962–5]; the DE RUTZEN ARMS HOTEL and five adjoining houses at NARBERTH, 1834–6 [*ibid.*]; CASTLE HOUSE, PICTON TERRACE, CARMARTHEN, 1836 [*Carmarthen Jnl.* 4 Aug. 1837]; and LETTERSTON CHURCH, PEMBS., 1844, Gothic, remodelled 1881 [I.C.B.S.].

Professional incompetence in estimating

and valuation got Rowlands into serious difficulties on several occasions and by the 1830s he was losing ground to William Owen (*q.v.*). After his father's death in 1850 he effectively retired from practice, becoming a local councillor and J.P. and living at Glenover, a house on the edge of the town which he had probably built for himself. His younger son, William Bowen Rowlands, M.P., had a distinguished legal career. [obituary in *Haverfordwest & Milford Haven Telegraph*, 4 April 1883; information from Mr. Thomas Lloyd, to whom all references are due].

ROWSON, JOHN, of Macclesfield, mason, designed and built the tower of ROSTHERNE CHURCH, CHESHIRE, in 1742–3, after the fall of its predecessor in 1741. He was paid £3 'for drawing plans and estimates' in the latter year. [F. H. Crossley, 'Post-Reformation Church Building in Cheshire', *Jnl. Chester and N. Wales Architectural Society*, N.S. xxxv (i), 1942, 45–8 and plate.]

ROYLE, THOMAS (–1830), appears in Manchester directories of the 1820s as an architect and land-agent. He was for a time in partnership with Robert Unwin, and in W. Westall & T. Moule's *Great Britain Illustrated* (1830), there is an engraving of the Greek Revival façade of Messrs. Cunliffe's & Brooks's Bank (dem.) in Market Street, Manchester, as built in 1827 to the designs of 'Messrs. Royle and Unwin architects'. Royle's will was proved in February 1830 [*Lancs. & Cheshire Rec. Soc.* 113, 1972, 108].

RUDD, JOHN (1754–), was apprenticed to Sir William Chambers in 1770 or 1771 [P.R.O., Apprenticeship Registers], and was admitted to the Royal Academy Schools in 1772, winning the Silver Medal in the same year. He exhibited a design for a villa at the Academy in 1774. Measured drawings of the Banqueting House, Whitehall, by him are in the R.I.B.A. Collection.

RUDHALL, WILLIAM (*c.*1660–1733), was a mason living at Henley-in-Arden in Warwickshire. In *c.*1700 he was one of three architects or master builders who submitted designs for Hanbury Hall, Worcs. It is not clear which of them was eventually employed, but Rudhall supplied a chimney-piece for the house *c.*1718 [J. Lees-Milne in *C. Life*, 4 Jan. 1968, where Rudhall's drawing is reproduced; Worcs. R.O., BA 7335/65 (v) for chimney-piece; genealogical information about the Rudhall family from Mr. William Hawkes].

RUNDLE, ABRAHAM (–1750), was a joiner by trade and lived at Tavistock, where he died in November 1750 [parish register]. He designed KELLY HOUSE, DEVONSHIRE, for Arthur Kelly, 1743–5, in a competent Georgian style with handsome interiors. Documents at Kelly show that he provided an estimate for the new house in December 1742, and that £340 was paid to 'Mr. Rundle, Architect, Joiner, etc.' [Kelly family archives, E 4/7–9]. A design for a Tudor Gothic fireplace signed 'John Rundle Arct.' is in the collection of the Hon. Christopher Lennox-Boyd.

RUSSELL, HENRY HEATHCOTE, is said to have been a nephew of Admiral Sir Henry Heathcote (1777–1851). He became a pupil of Edward Lapidge, exhibited designs at the Royal Academy in 1829 and 1845, and competed for the Ashmolean Museum at Oxford in 1839. He was still in practice in the 1850s.

RUSSELL, JOHN (*c.*1791–1840), practised in Leamington, Warwicks., where he was for a time in partnership with E. Mitchell. He designed STOCKINGFORD CHURCH, WARWICKS., for the Church Building Commissioners in a simple classical style in 1822–3 [Port, 138–9]; ST. PETER'S (R.C.) CHURCH, LEAMINGTON, 1828, Greek Ionic, dem. 1863 [T. B. Dudley, *History of Leamington*, 1896–1900, 189]; and the CONGREGATIONAL CHURCH, SPENCER STREET, LEAMINGTON, 1836, with an Ionic portico [Dudley, *op. cit.*, 23]. He also enlarged ST. CHARLES' (R.C.) CHURCH, HAMPTON-ON-THE-HILL, WARWICKS., in 1830, Gothic [Warwicks. C.R.O., 895/85/4], and made alterations and additions to RUGBY RECTORY, WARWICKS., in 1827 [Lichfield Joint Record Office, B/A/13 III]. A design by him for a veranda at Newbold Comyn House, Warwicks, dated 1821, is in the Warwicks. C.R.O. [CR 1247/38]. Russell died in February 1840, aged 49 [Leamington Parish Register].

RUSSELL, W—, exhibited at the Royal Academy in 1834 and 1837, and competed unsuccessfully for the Houses of Parliament in 1835.

RYDER, RICHARD (–1683), was a master carpenter by trade, and in 1668 succeeded John Davenport as Master Carpenter in the Office of Works. He frequently acted as an architect and surveyor, and was also active as a speculative builder in London. He is first referred to in 1647–50 in connection with the repairs and alterations to CRANBORNE MANOR

HOUSE in DORSET for William Cecil, 2nd Earl of Salisbury. This house had recently been damaged by the Royalist army, and Ryder was employed to carry out repairs and to rebuild the west wing in a style that was quite advanced for its date (H. Field & M. Bunney, *English Domestic Architecture of the XVII and XVIII Centuries*, 1905, 16, *C. Life*, 7 June 1924, 3–10 May 1973; R.C.H.M., *Dorset* v, 9–10, pl. 44). The plans are described as 'Captain Ryder's plott', and a letter has been preserved in which Thomas Fort, the mason employed, refers to Ryder's design for the roof and asks his employer 'to lett Capt. Rider draw a platt for the gate and for the tarrasse to his Lordshipp's liking' [Hatfield Muniments, General 74/11]. That Ryder was at this time in touch with John Webb may be inferred from the fact that, in addition to his bill for 'a design for the new building at Cranborne', he charged for coming over on two occasions to Cranborne from Wilton, where Webb was then engaged in restoring the Earl of Pembroke's house after a fire [Hatfield Muniments, Bills 239].

After the Restoration Ryder is found repairing BEDFORD HOUSE in Bloomsbury for the 5th Earl of Bedford, 1660 [accounts at Woburn Abbey], surveying with John Davenport the decayed tower of ST. MARTIN-IN-THE-FIELDS, and eventually reconstructing it, 1662–8 [Vestry Minutes in Westminster City Library] (*Survey of London* xx, pls. 8–9), valuing houses to be pulled down in connection with the repair of ST. PAUL'S CATHEDRAL, 1665 [minute-book of Commissioners for repair of St. Paul's Cathedral in Guildhall Library, p. 7], estimating, with Davenport, for carpenter's and joiner's work at CLARENDON HOUSE, 1666/7 [*The Architecture of Sir Roger Pratt*, ed. Gunther, 153–5], playing some part in the completion of BURLINGTON HOUSE, PICCADILLY, 1667 [*Survey of London* xxxii, 392], surveying SYON and NORTHUMBERLAND HOUSES for the Earl of Northumberland, 1667 [Alnwick Castle, Percy archives U.I. 43], surveying, with Edward Jerman, the site of APOTHECARIES' HALL, 1667 [Apothecaries' Company minutes, Guildhall Library, MS. 8201/1, f. 102], acting as surveyor for (and presumably therefore designing) BROMLEY COLLEGE, KENT, for the executors of John Warner, Bishop of Rochester, *c.*1670–2 [payment of £240 to 'Capt. Rider the Surveigher for his paines & care' in the executors' accounts, Bodleian Library, MS. Eng. hist. b. 205, f. 34ᵛ; Roger White in *C. Life*, 12–19 Nov. 1981], designing a window in the chapel at GORHAMBURY HOUSE, HERTFORDSHIRE, 1673 [J. C. Rogers, 'The Manor and Houses of Gorhambury', *Trans. St. Albans and Herts. Arch. Soc.* 1933, 41], and supervising repairs at GREAT PARK HOUSE, AMPTHILL, BEDS., for the 1st Earl of Ailesbury, 1676 [accounts among Ailesbury archives formerly at Tottenham Park, Wilts.].

In his official capacity as King's Master Carpenter Ryder was responsible in 1675 for constructing the elaborate scenery designed by Robert Streeter for the production in the Whitehall Theatre of the play *Calisto* [E. Boswell, *The Restoration Court Stage*, 1932, 208]. In 1662–3 he built THE THEATRE ROYAL in Brydges Street (destroyed by fire in 1672) for a contract price of £2100 ['The New Theatre Account' in Sir Robert Clayton's ledger No. 6, Surrey Record Office, Guildford, 84/1/3, f. 207, and cf. *Survey of London* xxxv, 41–2].

One of Ryder's principal building speculations was on land in Newport Street leased from the Earl of Salisbury in 1653. On 2 April of that year he undertook that within the next seven years he would lay out at least £500 in erecting and new building two fair new brick houses in Newport Street 'answerable to any twentie foot howse built in Covent Garden' and in rebuilding four other tenements in the street 'towards Newport House'. A further indenture dated 18 December 1657 states that he has pulled down all but one of the old houses in Newport Street and has built in their stead nine fair messuages, five of which face on to Newport Street on the south, the rest on to St. Martin's Lane on the east [Hatfield Muniments, Leases 1649–57, ff. 46ᵛ, 47ᵛ, 48, 140, 142]. Ryder's will shows that in 1683 he owned houses in Newport Street in the occupation of Sir Christopher Musgrave, Lady Hewitt, Charles Bertie and Lady Exeter, and others in Suffolk Street and Russell Street, leased from the Earls of Suffolk and Bedford. In 1664 he was himself resident in Newport Street, but at the time of his death he was living in Swan Close off Leicester Fields, and he appears to have given his name to Ryder's Court at the north-east corner of Leicester Square, described by Strype in 1720 as 'newly built and neat' [C. L. Kingsford, *Piccadilly, Leicester Square and Soho*, 1925, 55, 63]. Ryder Street, St. James's, laid out in the 1670s, may also owe its name to Captain Ryder, but his connection with the street has not been established [*Survey of London* xxix, 317].

Ryder died in the early months of 1683, leaving a widow Joan and sons named Richard and George [P.C.C. 61 DRAX]. It is possible that one of these sons was the 'Mr. Rider' whose employment as surveyor to Gray's Inn is noted above (p. 817).

S

SALISBURY, JAMES, was brought from London in about 1774 in order to supervise the building of the Register House in Edinburgh to the designs of R. & J. Adam. When he was made a burgess of Edinburgh in 1778 he was described alternatively as 'carpenter' or 'architect' [*Roll of Edinburgh Burgesses 1761–1841*, 139]. In the same year he was consulted by the Writers to the Signet about a new library which they then thought of building [*History of the Society of Writers to the Signet*, 1890, 409]. In 1783, when he was employed as mediator in a dispute between the Duke of Gordon and John Baxter (*q.v.*), he was stated to be employed by the Duke of Roxburghe and to have 'a job of consequence' at Lawers for Mr. Drummond [S.R.O., GD 44/49/16, letter of 10 July 1783]. In 1789 he was employed by Charles Watson of Saughton to design a stair and cellar under the terrace at NEW SAUGHTON or CAMMO HOUSE, MIDLOTHIAN (dem. after a fire in 1977) [S.R.O., GD 150/3199/10–12]. In 1796 he was employed by Sir William Forbes to make plans for a new house at BANTASKINE, STIRLINGSHIRE (probably built, but dem.), for which Forbes's wife had made a sketch [N.L.S., Acc. 4796/47/2, letter of 13 June 1796, *ex inf.* Mr. J. Gifford]. In EDINBURGH he is recorded to have made 'a new elevation, plain and unornamented', for LEITH TERRACE, LEITH STREET, in 1786 and in 1793 to have completed No. 53 PRINCES STREET [*Edinburgh Evening Courant*, 18 Feb. 1786, 2 Sept. 1793]. In 1798–1800 he was responsible for altering and refitting the interior of HOLY TRINITY CHURCH, ST. ANDREWS, FIFE [*The Parish Church of Holy Trinity, St. Andrews*, 1920, 5]. By the 3rd Earl of Rosebery, who employed him to carry out repairs and alterations to BARNBOUGLE CASTLE, WEST LOTHIAN, in 1789–91, Salisbury was described as 'a lying, ill tempered vulgar builder' [MS. accounts at Dalmeny House].

SALMON, ROBERT (1763–1821), was the youngest son of William Salmon, a carpenter and builder of Stratford-on-Avon, where he was born. He was employed by Henry Holland as a clerk of works at Carlton House and subsequently at Woburn Abbey. Here he attracted the notice of the 5th Duke of Bedford, who in 1794 gave him employment as resident estate surveyor and agricultural manager. It was in the latter capacity that he showed the remarkable ability as an inventor that won him considerable celebrity and several medals from the Society of Arts. The haymaking machine which he patented in 1814 was only the best known of his many inventions. As an architect he was chiefly employed in designing model farms on the Woburn estate in Bedfordshire, but he is also credited with the rebuilding in 1800, at the Duke's expense, of the body of SOULDROP CHURCH, BEDS., again rebuilt in 1860–1. His unexecuted design for a circular prison is in the Bedfordshire Record Office (PP2/3). He was the author of *An Analysis of the General Construction of Trusses*, 1807. [*D.N.B.*; Kelly's *Directory of Bedfordshire*, 1914, *s.v.* 'Souldrop'.]

SALMON, WILLIAM (*c.*1703–1779), was the son of a carpenter and joiner at Colchester and followed the same trade himself. He died at Colchester in March 1779, in his 77th year [*Ipswich Jnl.* 3 April 1779, and will in Essex C.R.O., D/ABR 27/82, *ex inf.* Mr. J. Bensusan Butt].

Salmon was the author of a number of modestly priced and eminently practical builders' manuals whose success may be judged from the number of editions through which they passed. Their titles were *The Country Builder's Estimator: or, the Architect's Companion*, 1733, 2nd ed. revised by E. Hoppus, 1737, 3rd ed. 1740, 4th ed. 1752, 7th. ed. 1759, 8th ed. by John Green of Salisbury, 1770; *Palladio Londinensis, or the London Art of Building*, 1734, 2nd ed. by E. Hoppus, 1738, 3rd ed. 1748, 4th ed. 1752, 6th ed. 1762, 8th ed. 1773; *The Builder's Guide*, 1736; *The London and Country Builder's Vade Mecum: or, the Compleat and Universal Estimator*, 1741, 2nd ed. 1748, 3rd ed. 1755, 4th ed. 1760, 5th ed. by John Green of Salisbury, 1773. The manuscript of an unpublished work by Salmon entitled *The Vitruvian Principles of Architecture Practically Demonstrated*, with a title-page dated 1737, is in the Yale Center for British Art [Eileen Harris, *British Architectural Books and Writers, 1556–1785*, 1990, 404–8].

SALWAY, JOSEPH, was a pupil of J. Jenkins of London and exhibited drawings at the Royal Academy from his office in 1785–9. He was among the subscribers to George Richardson's *New Vitruvius Britannicus*, published in 1802.

SAMBELL, PHILIP (1798–1874), was born at Devonport on 15 August 1798. He was deaf and dumb from birth, but appears nevertheless to have had a successful architectural practice in Cornwall. In the 1830s he was living in Truro, but he moved later to Falmouth, and died at Stonehouse, nr. Plymouth, on 5 December 1874. In 1840

Caroline Fox attended a lecture at Falmouth 'written by Sambell, the deaf and dumb architect, and read by young Ellis. It was a good lecture, and beautifully illustrated, principally by subjects of Egyptian architecture.' Sambell was the author of an 'Essay on Architecture' published in the *Journal of the Royal Institute of Cornwall* for 1840, and of a letter on the construction of chapels which was printed in *The Baptist Magazine* xxxiii, 1841, 355. He competed for the Houses of Parliament in 1835.

[G. C. Boase & W. P. Courtney, *Bibliotheca Cornubiensis* ii, 1878, 619; *The Journals and Letters of Caroline Fox*, ed. H. N. Pym, 1882, 58.]

TRURO, CORNWALL, ST. JOHN'S CHURCH, 1827–8, Grecian [Port, 142–3].

TRURO, CORNWALL, DORIC COLUMN in LEMON STREET to commemorate the explorer Richard Lander, 1835 [*Architectural Mag.* ii, 1835, 137–8].

PENZANCE, THE BAPTIST CHAPEL, CLARENCE STREET, 1835–6, Norman [J. S. Courtney, *Guide to Penzance*, 1845, 42].

HELSTON, CORNWALL, THE BAPTIST CHAPEL (later a cinema), 1836–7, Norman [*Baptist Mag.* 30, 1838, 29].

CAMBORNE, CORNWALL, THE LITERARY INSTITUTE (now Community Centre), 1842 [*West Briton*, 28 Oct. 1842, *ex inf.* Mr. R. Douch].

TRURO, CORNWALL, THE SAVINGS BANK (now Royal Institution of Cornwall), FRANCES (now River) STREET, 1845–7 [*West Briton*, 12 Sept. 1845; *Royal Cornwall Gazette*, 21 Feb., 26 Sept. 1845, *ex inf.* Mr. J. M. L. Booker].

TRURO, CORNWALL, BAPTIST CHAPEL, RIVER STREET, 1849–50, baroque [*Baptist Mag.* 42, 1850, 225].

SAMPSON, GEORGE (–?1759) was given the posts of Clerk of the Works at the Tower of London and Somerset House by William Benson in 1718, his predecessor, Thomas Kynaston, being deprived to make way for him. After Benson's dismissal in 1719, he was himself deprived and Kynaston was restored through the influence of Sir John Vanbrugh, then Comptroller of the Works (cf. *The Letters of Sir John Vanbrugh*, ed. G. F. Webb, 118).

Sampson subsequently became surveyor to the Bank of England, and was the architect of the central portion of the old Bank, erected in 1732–4, altered by Sir John Soane, and demolished in 1925 [H. R. Steel & F. R. Yerbury, *The Old Bank of England*, 1930, pp. 3–5, pl. xi]. It was described by Soane as being 'in a grand style of Palladian simplicity' [*Works*, 32]. What appear to be contemporary copies of Sampson's original designs are in Sir John Soane's Museum (Drawings 1, 1). He was also employed as a surveyor by the Fishmongers' Company, St. Thomas's Hospital and Guy's Hospital. The inclusion in a book-sale held on 15 February 1762 of '151 Drawings in architecture, plans, elevations, sections by Sampson' [B.L., 128 i ii(1)], suggests that he may have been the George Sampson of St. Giles-in-the-Fields, 'gentleman', whose will was proved on 15 November 1759 [P.R.O., PROB 11/550, f. 378].

Sampson's only other known works are a former Dissenting Chapel in CARTER LANE, LONDON, built 1732–3 [C. Titford, *Unity Chapel, Islington*, 1912, 26–7], and the monument in HURSLEY CHURCH, HANTS., to Mrs. Elizabeth Cromwell (*d.* 1731), which is signed 'G. Sampson architect. John Huntington fecit.' In 1720 he was among those who submitted designs for rebuilding the church of St. Martin-in-the-Fields [MS. Minutes of the Commissioners for rebuilding the church, f. 16]. In 1726–7 he appears to have supervised the building of the stables at THORESBY HOUSE, NOTTS., to the designs of Sir Thomas Hewett (*q.v.*) [Manvers papers, Nottingham University Library 4352]. In 1739 Sir Hans Sloane consulted him about the cost of repairing BEAUFORT HOUSE, CHELSEA, which he had recently purchased. Sampson said it would cost £500, but Sloane did nothing, and Sampson eventually persuaded him to pull it down and sell the materials to two acquaintances of his, one a master bricklayer, the other a master carpenter [R. Davies, *The Greatest House at Chelsey*, 1914, 230–4]. In 1746 Sampson's design for Ironmongers' Hall in the City of London was rejected in favour of one by Thomas Holden [Guildhall Library, minutes of the Company, MS. 16967/6, 14 Jan. 1745/6].

SAMWELL, WILLIAM (1628–1676), was the eldest son of Anthony Samwell, of Dean's Yard, Westminster, who was the fourth son of Sir William Samwell of Upton Hall, Northants., Auditor of the Exchequer in the reign of Queen Elizabeth. He was admitted to the Middle Temple in 1648 and lived in chambers there until 1656 (the year of his father's death), but was never called to the Bar.

Aubrey describes Samwell as 'an excellent architect, that has built severall delicate houses (Sir Robert Henley's, Sir Thomas Grosvenor's in Cheshire)', and Evelyn mentions him as the architect of Charles II's 'new building' at Newmarket. He was, in fact, a gentleman architect of the same sort as Hugh

May and Roger Pratt, and his houses are excellent examples of the type which became fashionable in England immediately after the Restoration. Nearly all his works have been mutilated or destroyed, but the planning of Grange Park and Eaton Hall shows considerable sophistication, and suggests that Samwell was an able designer whose contribution to English seventeenth-century architecture may have been under-estimated. In 1668 a 'Mr. Samuel' was among the six applicants for the post of surveyor to the new Royal Exchange in succession to Edward Jerman. It is probable, however, that this was not Samwell but a master bricklayer of that name who is mentioned more than once in Hooke's diary. The design of Euston Hall, Suffolk, built *c.*1670 by Henry Bennet, 1st Earl of Arlington, has been attributed to Samwell (cf. *Wren Soc.* xix, p. xiii), but upon what evidence is not clear. Some connection (not necessarily of an architectural nature) between Arlington and Samwell is, however, indicated by a document among the Shaftesbury papers in the Public Record Office (P.R.O., 30/24/VI B, no. 394).

Samwell purchased the manor of Watton in Norfolk some time after 1660, and remained its owner until his death in 1676. He married Anne, daughter of Sir Denner Strutt of Little Warley in Essex, by whom he had two daughters, Anne and Mary. Anne married William Henry Fleming of Suffield, High Sheriff of Norfolk in 1736. By his will, dated 25 April 1676, and proved on 26 June, Samwell directed that his body should be buried at Upton in Northants. 'in a private manner and without Funerall Pompe'. There are monuments at Watton to his daughter and widow.

[Aubrey's *Brief Lives*, ed. A. Clark, i, 288, 293; Burke's *Extinct Baronetcies*, 1838, 465; Blomfield's *History of Norfolk* iii, 315–17; Baker's *History of Northants.* i, 225; *Middle Temple Records*, ed. C. H. Hopwood, 1904–5, ii, 968, 982, iii, 1071, 1099; P.C.C. 71 BENCE.]

attributed: LOWER LODGE (now BUSHY HOUSE), BUSHY PARK, MIDDLESEX, for Edward Proger, 1664–5; altered and enlarged in eighteenth century [Peter Foster & Edward Pyatt, *Bushy House*, National Physical Laboratory, 1976].

NEWMARKET, SUFFOLK, THE KING'S HOUSE, for King Charles II, 1668–71; partly dem. after 1814 (south-east block survives as 'Palace House Mansion') [*History of the King's Works* v, 214–16].

GRANGE PARK, nr. ALRESFORD, HANTS., for Sir Robert Henley, *c.*1670; remodelled by W. Wilkins, 1809 [E. Mercer, 'William Samwell and the Grange', in *The Country Seat*, ed. Colvin & Harris, 1970, 48–54; J. Redmill in *C. Life*, 8 May 1975; Jane Geddes, 'The Grange, Northington', *Arch. Hist.* 26, 1983].

HAM HOUSE, PETERSHAM, SURREY, remodelled for 1st Duke and Duchess of Lauderdale, 1672–4 [J. G. Dunbar, 'The Building-activities of the Duke and Duchess of Lauderdale, 1670–82', *Archaeological Jnl.* cxxxii, 1975].

LONDON, THE ROYAL MEWS, CHARING CROSS, coach-house, etc., 1673–4; dem. [*History of the King's Works* v, 208].

FELBRIGG HALL, NORFOLK, added the west wing for William Windham, completed 1686. Samwell's designs, signed and dated 1674, are preserved at Felbrigg [*C. Life*, 22 Dec. 1934; R. W. Ketton-Cremer, *Felbrigg*, 1962].

EATON HALL, CHESHIRE, for Sir Thomas Grosvenor, Bart., 1675–82; rebuilt by W. Porden, 1804–12 [Aubrey's *Brief Lives*, ed. A. Clark, i, 293; C. T. Gatty, *Mary Davies and the Manor of Ebury* i, 1921, 210–11, citing accounts in Eaton Hall MS. 68] (*Vitruvius Britannicus* ii, 1717, pls. 35–6).

SANDBY, THOMAS (1721–1798), was the elder son of Thomas Sandby, a gentleman with property at Babworth in Nottinghamshire. He was born in Nottingham, where he and his brother Paul appear to have been apprenticed to Thomas Peat, of Messrs. Peat & Badder, land surveyors. The drawings which decorate the margins of the map of Nottingham published by Peat & Badder in 1744 were made by Thomas Sandby during his apprenticeship. In 1741 or 1742 the brothers left Nottingham in order to take up situations in the military drawing office in the Tower of London which had been procured for them by John Plumptre, the Member for Nottingham, who held the office of Treasurer of the Ordnance. From 1743 onwards Thomas was attached to the Commander-in-Chief, William Augustus, Duke of Cumberland. He was present at the Battle of Dettingen in 1743, and was with the Duke on the Culloden campaign in 1745–6. He made a sketch of the latter battle which is now in the Royal Library at Windsor Castle, together with views of Fort Augustus and other military scenes. He afterwards accompanied the Duke on his campaigns in the Netherlands, and probably remained there until the Peace of Aix-la-Chapelle in 1748. In 1750 he was appointed Draughtsman to the Duke at a salary of £100, and in 1764 he became his Steward and Clerk of the Stables at Windsor. In 1746 the Duke had become Ranger of

Windsor Great Park, and appointed Sandby his Deputy, a post which he held for the rest of his life.

As Deputy Ranger Sandby enjoyed financial independence and was provided with a residence in Lower Lodge (afterwards rebuilt by John Nash). Here he was joined by his brother Paul, who assisted him in the landscape-gardening activities which became his principal occupation at Windsor. Chief among these was the formation of Virginia Water, then the largest artificial lake in the kingdom. The original dam, constructed only of sand and clay, gave way as a result of a storm in 1768, earning for its engineer the nickname of 'Tommy Sandbank'. It was reconstructed in more enduring materials with the assistance of Charles Cole (*q.v.*), and Sandby constructed a series of grottoes and artificial ruins at the head of the Water which were completed in 1785. He also designed the stone bridge over the northern arm of the Water, replacing a wooden one erected by Flitcroft in the reign of George II. A number of plans and drawings connected with these works are preserved in the Royal Library at Windsor Castle, Sir John Soane's Museum, the Bodleian Library (Gough Maps 41 A, ff. 4–23), the Victoria and Albert Museum (3436, 172–9), and the Achenbach Foundation at San Francisco.

Another project with which Sandby was associated at this time was for the re-erection in Windsor Great Park of the 'Holbein' Gateway at Whitehall, which had been taken down in 1759. His design for its reconstruction, with Gothic additions on either side, is given in J. T. Smith's *Antiquities of Westminster*, 1807, facing p. 21. This was never carried out, but two of the terracotta busts with which the gateway was decorated were incorporated by Sandby in a keeper's lodge at Virginia Water, whence they were removed in the nineteenth century to Hampton Court. In 1754 he published a set of eight folio plates, engraved on copper by his brother Paul, illustrating the works at Virginia Water. They were reissued by Boydell in 1772.

Sandby enjoyed the favour not only of William Augustus, Duke of Cumberland, and of his successor Henry Frederick, Duke of Cumberland, but also of George III, who retained him as Deputy Ranger when he took the management of the Park into his own hands on Frederick's death in 1790. In April 1777 he was appointed Architect of the King's Works in succession to Sir Robert Taylor, and in November 1780 he was promoted to the titular office of Master Carpenter, which carried with it a seat on the Board of Works. The latter office was, however, abolished two years later as a result of Burke's Act. He was one of the committee of artists which was formed in 1753 with the object of establishing an Academy of Art, and in 1759 he became a member of the committee of the newly formed Society of Artists. But he exhibited only once with the Society (in 1767), and after his nomination as one of the original Royal Academicians in 1768 he exhibited at the Academy. He was chosen to be the first Professor of Architecture, and in 1770 delivered the first of six lectures which he repeated annually until the last two years of his life, when they were read for him. The sixth was illustrated by about forty drawings and designs, including one for a 'Bridge of Magnificence' across the Thames at Somerset House, based on a similar idea of Piranesi's. It was shown at the Academy's exhibition in 1781 and attracted much attention. Several versions of this design are in existence (at Windsor, the R.I.B.A. and the National Gallery of Scotland). The manuscript of Sandby's lectures is in the R.I.B.A. Library, but the illustrations were sold with his other drawings after his death. There is another copy of the lectures in Sir John Soane's Museum. Sandby was elected an honorary member of the Architects' Club on its foundation in 1791.

In February 1769 Sandby competed for the Royal Exchange at Dublin, obtaining the third premium [*Builder* xxvii, 1869, 781]. His drawings for this building are in the R.I.B.A. Collection and the library of Vassar College, U.S.A. His most important executed work was the FREEMASONS' HALL in QUEEN STREET, LINCOLN'S INN FIELDS, which was built in 1775–6, reconstructed by F. P. Cockerell in 1864–6 (preserving Sandby's Great Hall), damaged by fire in 1883, and finally demolished in 1932. The fine interior is illustrated by Britton & Pugin, *Public Buildings of London* i, 1825, 321–33, and there are two sections in the British Museum (Crowle Pennant, vii, 36–7).

Sandby also designed the Gothic wainscoting round the altar in ST. GEORGE'S CHAPEL, WINDSOR, carved with emblems of the Order of the Garter, which was executed by Henry Emlyn in 1782 [W. H. St. J. Hope, *Windsor Castle*, 398–95]; the BLEACH-WORKS at LLEWENNI in the VALE OF CLWYD, nr. DENBIGH, *c.*1785 [plate 9 of Colt Hoare's *Views of Seats, etc., in North and South Wales*, shows this building as originally designed by Sandby for the Hon. Thomas Fitzmaurice]; and a stone bridge over the R. Thames at STAINES which was built in 1792–7 but failed in 1799 and was replaced by an iron bridge in 1801–3. For the Duke of Cumberland Sandby enlarged and refronted the GREAT LODGE in WINDSOR PARK in *c.*1757. The house was largely rebuilt in 1869 (after a fire) and in 1912, and is now known as Cumberland Lodge [Oppé, no. 103 and pl. 144]. He also designed a few private houses, including ST. LEONARD'S HILL, nr. WINDSOR, for the Dowager Countess Waldegrave, afterwards Duchess of Gloucester, remodelled in French Renaissance style in the nineteenth century [J. P. Neale, *Views of Seats*, 1st ser. iii, 1820, with distant view: see a closer view by Neale in Bodleian, MS. Top. Berks. d. 13, f. 21]; and HOLLY GROVE, OLD WINDSOR, for Col. Deacon [*D.N.B.*]. A drawing at Vassar College, U.S.A., shows that he designed the Gothic tower known as LUTTRELL'S FOLLY at EAGLEHURST, HANTS., for T. S. Luttrell, *c.*1780.

Sandby was an accomplished topographical artist, whose water-colour drawings cannot easily be distinguished from those of his brother Paul. As an architect he is less easy to evaluate, because his restricted practice and the destruction of virtually all his executed works leave only his drawings for the architectural historian to study. It is clear, however, that he was an able designer in a neo-classical style closely akin to that of Chambers, and the influence that he exerted through his lectures at the Royal Academy should not be under-estimated.

Sandby died at the Deputy Ranger's Lodge on 25 June 1798, and was buried in the churchyard at Old Windsor. There is no monument, but a memorial brass was put up in 1883. There are several portraits of Sandby, of which the most accessible is the one by Beechey in the National Portrait Gallery. Many of Sandby's drawings were sold with his library in 1799 (catalogue in B.L., S.C.5.34 (14)). Another sale of drawings (from the collection of William Sandby, author of *Thomas and Paul Sandby*, 1902) took place at Christie's in 1959. Two volumes of architectural drawings are in Sir John Soane's Museum, and there are others at Windsor Castle, the British and Victoria and Albert Museums, the R.I.B.A. Collection, and in various American collections (see John Harris, *Catalogue of British Drawings for Architecture, etc., in American Collections*, 1971).

[*A.P.S.D.*; *D.N.B.*; W. H. Stevenson's articles on Badder & Peat's map of Nottingham in *Nottinghamshire Weekly Express*, 25 Sept.–23 Oct. 1896; T. Mulvany, *Life of James Gandon*, 1846, 189, 296; J. T. Smith, *A Book for a Rainy Day*, ed. W. Whitten, 1905, 92, 102–3, 303; *The Farington Diary*, ed. J. Greig, i, 233, iv, 106; W. Sandby, *Thomas and Paul Sandby*, 1902; F. H. Ramsden, 'The Sandby Brothers in London', *Burl. Mag.* lxxxix, 1947; E. A. Oppé, *Sandby Drawings at Windsor Castle*, 1947; Johnson Ball, *Paul and Thomas Sandby, Royal Academicians*, Cheddar 1985; Luke Herrmann, *Paul and Thomas Sandby*, 1986.]

SANDERS, JOHN (1768–1826), born on 27 April 1768, was the son of Thomas Sanders, a tallow-chandler of the parish of St. Dunstan-in-the-East, London. In 1784 he became Sir John Soane's first pupil, and at the end of the following year he was admitted to the Royal Academy School. In 1786 he began to exhibit his designs, and in 1788 he was awarded the Gold Medal of the Academy. After leaving Soane's office in 1790, he began to practise on his own, and from 1794 onwards was architect to the Barrack Department of the War Office with James Johnson. His principal works were the ROYAL MILITARY ASYLUM (now the Duke of York's Barracks) at CHELSEA, 1801–3 [G. Richardson, *New Vitruvius Britannicus* ii, 1808, pls. 39–42], and the ROYAL MILITARY COLLEGE at SANDHURST, BERKS., 1808–12, the designs for which he exhibited at the Royal Academy in 1811 and 1813. At Sandhurst he was, however, executing what was essentially a design by James Wyatt. Wyatt had characteristically failed to get the building started, and had to be superseded by Sanders, who in 1822 told Joseph Farington that 'he was employed by government in building the military college . . . designed by Wyatt' [Farington's diary, 3 Feb. 1811, 4 Feb. 1812]. The result was a long plain building dignified by an impressive Greek Doric portico (*C. Life*, 26 June 1969). Sanders also made additions to BEOLEY HALL, WORCS., for Thomas Holmes, 1791 [exhib. at R.A.]; restored HOLLAND HOUSE, KENSINGTON, for the 3rd Lord Holland in 1796–7 [*A.P.S.D.*]; designed a drawing-room for the 1st Marquess of Headfort, probably for his London house at 13 STANHOPE STREET, MAYFAIR [exhib. at R.A. 1804]; was employed by the Duchess of Gordon in 1805 in connection with her 'cottage' at KINRARA in INVERNESS-SHIRE [S.R.O., GD 44/51/279 and RHP 2498]; and altered the unfinished WINCHESTER PALACE, HANTS., for use as a barracks in 1810 [exhib. at R.A. 1812]. In 1808 he issued a printed *Letter to the Lords Commissioners of His Majesty's Treasury* replying to criticisms of the Barrack Department made in the *Fourth Report of the Commissioners of Military Inquiry*. There is a copy in Sir John Soane's Museum.

In later life Sanders was very well off. He was able to retire early from practice, and travelled on the Continent from 1817 to about 1820. He employed William Purser as a draughtsman, and was joined in Rome by G.L. Taylor and Edward Cresy, two young architects (*qqv.*) who were similarly engaged in investigating the architectural antiquities of Italy. Together they explored the Mediterranean, drawing and sketching wherever they went. 'They measure every thing; even the Gothic buildings in Sicily have not escaped them', wrote John Soane, junior, to his father. At Chaeronea in Boeotia they discovered the lion commemorating the Thebans who fell in the battle of 338 B.C. [*Builder* xx, 1862, 908; and W. S. W. Vaux, 'On the Discovery of the Lion at Chaerona, by a Party of English Travellers in 1818', *Trans. Royal Society of Literature*, 2nd ser. viii, 1866]. On his return, Sanders became the first president of the Architects' and Antiquaries' Club, founded by ten gentlemen who had seen the value of architectural academies abroad, and were resolved to establish one in their own country. He himself had a fine library and collection of antiquities at his house at Reigate, where he died early in 1826. His collection of architectural casts was bought by Sir Thomas Lawrence, who offered them in his will to the Royal Academy for £250.

[*A.P.S.D.*; A. T. Bolton, *The Portrait of Sir John Soane*, 1927, 129–30, 252–70, 276, 281–2; A. T. Bolton, *The Works of Sir John Soane*, 1924, Appendix C, p. xl; G. L. Taylor, *Memoirs of an Octogenarian Architect*, 1870–2; *The Farington Diary*, ed. J. Greig, vii, 26, 96, 135, 200, 230, viii, 67; will P.C.C. 181 SWABEY.]

SANDERSON, JAMES (1790–1835), born at East Grinstead, Sussex, was the son of a local builder of the same name. He was a pupil of Jeffry Wyatville from 1813 to 1816. He afterwards practised from Cork Street, London, where he died on 1 March 1835, in his 45th year [*Gent's Mag.* 1835 (i), 443; P.C.C. 452 GLOSTER]. His exhibits at the Royal Academy included 'Stanmore Cottage [at Great Stanmore, Middlesex], now building for Dr. Hooper' (1817), a 'House erected at St. Clare, near Ryde, for E. V. Utterson, Esq[r].' (1824), the 'garden front of St. Leonard's near Stanmore, now erecting for Henry Stone, Esq[r].' (1825), a 'Gothic House proposed to be built near Ryde' (1826), and extensive alterations to Ryde Church, Isle of Wight, carried out at the expense of George Player in 1827 (1828). For John Hambrough Sanderson designed STEEPHILL CASTLE, nr. Ryde, which is described as newly built in 1833 [G. Brannon, *The Pleasure Visitor's Companion to the Isle of Wight*, 1833, 71–2]. It was demolished in 1964, but is illustrated by Brannon, and by J. B. Marsh, *Steephill Castle*, privately printed 1907. According to a later edition of Brannon's *Companion*, Sanderson 'gave the designs for nearly all the principal buildings of Ryde', including BRIGSTOCK TERRACE, and the Ionic TOWN HALL is mentioned as his work in W. B. Cooke's *Bonchurch, Shanklin and the Undercliff*, 1849, 109. He was probably the author of some unexecuted designs for a library at KIDBROOKE PARK, SUSSEX, for the 1st Lord Colchester, signed 'Sanderson' and dated 1813 [P.R.O., Colchester papers 9/10, pt. 2, no. 19].

SANDERSON, JAMES WRIGHT (– 1813), was a pupil of James Wyatt, from whose office he exhibited at the Royal Academy in 1790 and 1791. He was admitted to the Royal Academy Schools in 1789 and won the Silver Medal in 1790. He was an unsuccessful candidate for election as A.R.A. in 1797 [W. T. Whitley, *Artists and their Friends in England 1700–1799* ii, 1928, 216]. He practised in Reading, where he died in 1813 [*Gent's Mag.* 1813 (i), 393; P.C.C. 218 HEATHFIELD].[1] His trade card is illustrated in Sotheby's Belgravia catalogue, 13 April 1976, lot 80.

Sanderson's exhibits at the Royal Academy show that he designed COOMBE LODGE, nr. WHITCHURCH, OXON., for Samuel Gardiner, 1794–5, dem. *c.*1950; extensive additions to PROSPECT HILL, nr. READING, for J. E. Liebenrood, 1800; 'peasants' cottages' at WOODLEY, BERKS., for the Rt. Hon. Henry Addington, 1801; and a Gothic lodge at BILLINGBEAR, BERKS., for the 2nd Lord Braybrooke, 1801. He also appears to have designed a house at BEARWOOD, nr. WOKINGHAM, BERKS., for John Walter II, though it was not built until after his death and was demolished in 1865 [Mark Girouard in *C. Life*, 17 Oct. 1968, 964 and fig. 9].

SANDERSON, JOHN (–1774), was a Georgian architect who practised in London. In 1725 he was living in Covent Garden, later at Parkgate, Hampstead. Nothing is known of his early life, but the bookplate in his copy of Leoni's *Palladio* (1721) indicates that he claimed to be a member of an armigerous family from Headley Hope, Co. Durham. He died in 1774, leaving, *inter alia*, 'two terra

[1] J. W. Sanderson should not be confused with James Sanderson of Reading (d. *c.*1787), a land surveyor who laid out the grounds of Claydon House, Bucks., between 1768 and 1776 [bills at Claydon House], and partly rebuilt Chalfont St. Peter parsonage in 1780, dem. 1966 [Muniments of St. John's College, Oxford, xli, 16].

cotta figures of the Crouching Venus and Roman Charity done by Delvaux' to John Wodehouse of East Lexham in Norfolk. To 'John Sanderson, late Chamberlain of Lynn Co. Norfolk, Gent., but now residing with Mr. Johnson in Berners St., Builder' he left £10. Neither wife nor children are mentioned in the will, the principal legatees being Anne Lejolivet, of Laval in France, and Beaumont, son of George Stubbs. According to J. J. Park's *History of Hampstead* (1818), 'the articles disposed of at his sale' included 'the model of a very large seat, his own design; with a capital, said to have been brought from the ruins of Herculaneum; [and] some of the better authors on architecture'.

Sanderson was a competent 'second-generation Palladian' who designed several handsome country houses of what by then was a conventional Georgian type. At Stratton Park the interior decoration, as illustrated in *Vitruvius Britannicus*, was also of a standard Palladian character, but at Kirtlington and Kimberley, and perhaps also at Hagley, he showed himself to be an accomplished designer of rococo decoration. At Hagley he had helped the amateur architect, Sanderson Miller, to draw out the plans for the main structure 'properly figured for the direction of the workmen', and he assisted Theodore Jacobsen and Thomas Prowse in a similar fashion at Trinity College, Dublin, and Wicken Church, respectively. His unexecuted designs for a large Palladian mansion at Woburn for the 4th Duke of Bedford, dated 1733, are preserved in Woburn Abbey MS. 151. Drawings by, or attributed to, him are described in the *Catalogue of the R.I.B.A. Drawings Collection* and in John Harris's *Catalogue of British Drawings for Architecture, etc., in American Collections*, 1971. Further drawings by him were sold at Christie's on 19 December 1989.

KELHAM HALL, NOTTS., for the executors of 2nd Lord Lexington, *c.*1730; destroyed by fire 1857 [Belvoir Castle Muniments, Account No. 377] (J. P. Neale, *Views of Seats*, 1st ser., iv, 1821).

STRATTON PARK, HANTS., for 3rd Duke of Bedford, 1731; said to have been partly demolished by 4th Duke (1732–71) for fear his successors should prefer it to Woburn; remodelled by George Dance, junior, for Sir Francis Baring, 1803–6; dem. 1960 [*Vitruvius Britannicus* iv, 1767, pls. 52–5].

BARRINGTON HALL, HATFIELD BROADOAK, ESSEX, for John Barrington, *c.*1735–40; remodelled in Jacobean style by Edward Browning 1867 [elevation inscribed 'Built by Mr. John Sanderson, Joseph Sanderson Delin.' in Shoppee Album sold at Christie's 19 Dec. 1989; smith's work done here 1738 'by order of Mr. Sanderson', P.R.O., C 109/25/7; *V.C.H. Essex* viii, 167].

CHEAM CHURCH, SURREY, design and estimate for rebuilding, 1741, possibly the one carried out in 1746; rebuilt 1862–4 [Surrey County Record Office, Q.S. Roll 1741, *ex inf.* Miss Mary Jackson].

ELY CATHEDRAL, monument to Humphry Smith (d. 1743), erected 'by John Sanderson of London Architect' [inscription].

HAMPSTEAD, MIDDLESEX, ST. JOHN'S CHURCH, 1745–7 [Vestry Minutes printed by C. H. Collins Baker in *C. Life*, 11 Dec. 1937, 610–11; cf. J. J. Park, *History of Hampstead*, 1818, 222–3]. The small copper spire was added in 1784. In 1843–4 the church was lengthened and transepts were added, and in 1878 an apsidal chancel designed by F. P. Cockerell was added at the west end.

KIRTLINGTON PARK, OXON., completed house for Sir James Dashwood, Bart., 1747–8, succeeding William Smith (d. 1747). Sanderson designed the interiors and probably the wings [drawings and accounts formerly at Kirtlington; *Vitruvius Britannicus* iv, 1767, pls. 32–6; Ingrid Roscoe, 'The Decoration and Furnishing of Kirtlington Park', *Apollo*, Jan. 1980] (*C. Life*, 13 April 1912). The dining-room was dismantled and sold in 1931 and has since been re-erected in the Metropolitan Museum of Art at New York: see P. Remington in *Metropolitan Museum Bulletin* xiv, no. 7 (March 1956), and *C. Life*, 1 Oct. 1970, 823, fig. 3.

PUSEY HOUSE, BERKS., for John Allen Pusey, *c.*1750 [in 1754 Sanderson proposed to show his next client, John Conyers, two large framed drawings of 'Mr. Pusey's house in Berkshire', which he had evidently designed: Essex Record Office, D/DW. E 36/6]; attic storey added 1834 to designs of W. & L. Cubitt (*C. Life*, 23–30 Dec. 1976).

TRINITY COLLEGE, DUBLIN. Although it appears from the *Journal of the House of Commons of the Kingdom of Ireland* vi (1757–60), Appendix, p. cclxiii, that £74 11s. 8d. were paid to 'Messrs. Keene and Sanderson for the Plans and Elevations' of the building erected in 1752–9, it is clear from the evidence cited above (p. 534) that they were in fact implementing designs made by the amateur architect Theodore Jacobsen.

LANGLEY PARK, NORFOLK, work for Sir William Beauchamp Proctor, Bart., probably *c.*1750–5 [Norfolk C.R.O., BEA 340, letter from Sanderson, 10 Dec. 1757, referring to a Mr. Smith as formerly his servant working at Langley]. It is likely that Sanderson was responsible for the rococo interiors, and possibly for exterior features, including the four towers (*C. Life*, 2 July 1927).

COPPED HALL, ESSEX, rebuilt for John Conyers, 1753–8, under the amateur direction of Sir Roger Newdigate and Thomas Prowse; altered internally by James Wyatt 1775–7; enlarged *c.*1895; damaged by fire 1917 [letters from Sanderson in Essex Record Office, D/DW E. 29–36; drawings in R.I.B.A. Coll.] (T. Muilman, *History of Essex* 1770–2, iv, 152; *C. Life*, 29 Oct., 5 Nov. 1910).

WICKEN CHURCH, NORTHANTS., assisted Thomas Prowse (*q.v.*) to rebuild church, 1753 onwards, and completed it after his death in 1767 [above, p. 787].

KIMBERLEY HALL, NORFOLK, assisted Thomas Prowse (*q.v.*) to remodel the house for Sir Armine Wodehouse, Bart., *c.*1755–7, as shown by accounts seen by Dr. T. P. Connor. Drawings in the R.I.B.A. Collection show that Sanderson was designing interiors here as late as 1770.

HAGLEY HALL, WORCS., assisted Sanderson Miller (*q.v.*) by drawing out his plans 'properly figured for the direction of the workmen' in 1754 [*An Eighteenth-Century Correspondence*, ed. Dickins & Stanton, 1910, 290], and may, as Mr. Michael McCarthy has suggested, have been responsible for the interior decoration as completed in 1760 (*C. Life*, 16 Oct. 1915, 19, 26 Sept. 1957; C. Hussey, *English Country Houses: Early Georgian*, 1955, 195–9).

OXFORD, THE RADCLIFFE INFIRMARY, completed building, 1766–70, after death of Stiff Leadbetter (*q.v.*) [Bodleian Library, Minutes of the Radcliffe Trustees, 1752–91].

HAMPTON, MIDDLESEX: presumably the 'Sanderson' who carried out alterations to David Garrick's villa in 1767 [*The Letters of David Garrick*, ed. D. M. Little & G. M. Kahrl, 1963, No. 454].

SANDERSON, JOSEPH (–1747), was a carpenter and joiner by trade, and a cousin of John Sanderson (*q.v.*). He lived in Little Queen Street, Bloomsbury. The Okeover family papers show that in 1745–7 he enlarged OKEOVER HALL, STAFFS., for Leak Okeover to his own designs in a style akin to that of Gibbs [Arthur Oswald in *C. Life*, 23–30 Jan. 1964]. In February 1744/5 he made an unexecuted design for another Staffordshire house, Ashenhurst Hall, Bradnop, nr. Leek [signed drawing in B.L., Add MS. 36663, f. 564]. From his letters to Leak Okeover it appears that in 1745 he was also working at GARENDON PARK, LEICS., and a design for a triumphal arch that may be connected with the one at Garendon was among drawings by him sold at Christie's on 19 December 1989. In 1746 he was building BASSINGBOURNE HALL, TAKELEY, ESSEX, for Francis Bernard. On 22 November he wrote to say that he hoped 'to keep at home pretty much from Essex having near compleated the Parsonage and quite covered in Mr. Bernard's house' [Arthur Oswald in *C. Life*, 2 April 1964, correspondence].

In 1745 Sanderson refers to a quarrel with 'Mr. Jno. Sanderson (my cozen)', but in his will he left the latter 'my gold ring of Inigo Jones's head and a small book of my own drawings of the five Orders . . . as a token of our former friendship'. Leak Okeover was to receive 'two pictures of fish and fowls painted by Ross and six of my principal Books of Architecture'. Other legatees were his 'much honoured master John Barrington Esquire' of Barrington Hall, Essex (a house designed by his cousin), and John Silvester, to whom he left his silver drawing instruments and his remaining books of architecture. He died on 17 August 1747 [P.C.C. 214 POTTER].

SANDS, JAMES, was a pupil of Lewis Wyatt. He exhibited at the Royal Academy from Wyatt's office in 1813 and 1816, and from Warwick Street, Golden Square, in 1819 and 1820. In 1813–16 he showed designs for intended alterations to TORRIE HOUSE, TORRYBURN, FIFE, for Sir William Erskine, Bart. (d. 1813), and his successor Sir John Erskine. In 1824 he was among the unsuccessful competitors for St. David's Church, Glasgow [R. Renwick, *Extracts from Glasgow Records* xi, 196], but he had more success in Ireland, where in 1824, as 'James Sands of London, architect', he agreed, in conjunction with Thomas Alfred Cobden of Carlow, to build RUSSELLSTOWN HOUSE, CO. CARLOW, for William Duckett [National Library of Ireland, Sir John Ainsworth's Report — private MSS. No. 259]. He is subsequently found in County Down, making a plan of HILLSBOROUGH HOUSE for the 3rd Marquess of Downshire in 1844, and designing a terrace at ROSEMOUNT, GREYABBEY, in 1846 [P.R.O. N. Ireland, D 671/C173/C, P 8/15A and P 13/5, *ex inf.* Dr. E. McParland].

SANDS, WILLIAM (–1751), was an architect and mason of Spalding, Lincs., where he was Master of the local Freemasons' Lodge and a member of the Gentlemen's Society. His estimate for 'Ceiling the Town Hall in Spalding in a Circular Arch to the upper Beames' was laid before the Society on 26 February 1740/41, and among the Society's records is a design for a Triumphal Archway to be erected in Spalding Market Place to celebrate the peace of 1749 which bears the signatures 'M. J[ohnson][1] designavit, W. S[ands] Architectus', and 'J. Newstead del'. According to J. Nichols, Sands 'drew three plans and designs of stages and uprights for a new mansion-house at Burton Pedwardine, near Sleaford, in Lincs., for Thomas Orby Hunter, esq., Lord of that manor: who was himself a curious dranghtsman, and designed the house himself, but altered his mind and added to his house at Croyland'. In 1722 Sands designed the octagonal MOULTON CHAPEL, nr. SPALDING, for Maurice Johnson [J. R. Jackson, 'Moulton Chapel', *Fenland Notes and Queries* iii, 1897, 172–4]; and Robert Harmstone records in his *Notices of Remarkable Events and Curious Facts connected with the History of Spalding*, 1846, 8, that 'Towns End Manor House was pulled down in 1746 and the materials sold to Mr. William Sands, Architect, and Mr. John Heals, Builder, who built two houses, one occupied by Mr. Byford, Boot Maker, Bridge-Street, and the other [now No. 12 High Street] by Mr. Capps, Builder.' In 1729 John Proudlove of Kirton-in-Holland, carpenter, undertook to rebuilt MONKS HALL, GOSBERTON, LINCS., 'according to a Plan or Form drawn by Mr. William Sands' [contract printed by M. W. Barley, *The English Farmhouse and Cottage*, 1961, Appendix C].

Sands executed monumental sculpture, examples of which, bearing his signature, can be seen in the churches of Weston (nr. Spalding) and Crowland. He died on 2 October 1751, and was buried in Spalding Church, where a tablet (which no longer exists) cut by his pupil Edmund Hutchinson was erected to his memory. He left a son, William Sands, junior, who built HOLLAND HOUSE, HIGH STREET, for John Richards in 1768, and the two houses on either side of the brewery in Cowbit Road known as WESTBOURNE HOUSE (now the brewery offices) and LANGTON HOUSE. [J. Nichols, *Literary Anecdotes of the Eighteenth Century* vi, 111; E. H. Gooch, *A History of Spalding*, 1940, 357; records of the Spalding Gentlemen's Society.]

SANDYS, FRANCIS, was a native of Ireland, and is described as 'of Kilrea' (Co. Londonderry) in the entries in the parish register of Ickworth, Suffolk, which record the baptism of his children. He may have been a son of the Irish architect of the same name who designed Sallymount, Co. Kildare, and a Gothic 'dining-room' in the grounds of Bellevue, Co. Wicklow, in 1788 [J. N. Brewer, *The Beauties of Ireland* ii, 1826, 53; J. Ferrar, *Ancient and Modern Dublin*, 1796, 111]. His brother Joseph was domestic chaplain to Frederick Hervey, 4th Earl of Bristol and Bishop of Derry, and it was probably at Hervey's expense, and certainly with his encouragement, that Francis went to Italy in 1791, taking with him a letter of introduction to Canova [Canova archive, Bassano, 2433]. He was in Rome in 1793 [B.L., Add. MS. 39790], and did not return until 1796, when Flaxman called on Joseph Farington in company with 'Mr. Sandys an Architect; a young man who left Rome at the beginning of April, and is now employed, as he says, in beginning to build a Palace at Ickworth for Lord Bristol' [*The Farington Diary*, ed. J. Greig, i, 152].

The 'palace' which Sandys began to build at Ickworth in 1796 (and of which he exhibited a design at the Royal Academy in the following year) was an eccentric building consisting of an oval domed rotunda connected to wings by quadrants. Lord Bristol had already (1787) begun a similar house at Ballyscullion, Co. Londonderry, which is said to have been inspired by John Plaw's circular house on an island in Lake Windermere. Ickworth House was a neo-classical version of Ballyscullion, apparently worked out in Rome by the Italian architect Mario Asprucci (whose responsibility for the design, first mentioned in print in the *Civil Engineer and Architect's Jnl.* for 1846, has been confirmed by two drawings discovered by Mr. John Harris and published in *C. Life*, 17 May 1973) and executed, with modifications, in Suffolk by Sandys.

Sandys settled in Bury St. Edmunds, and besides supervising the building of Ickworth, enjoyed for the next few years a modestly successful practice, chiefly in Suffolk. He continued to exhibit at the Royal Academy, and became a Fellow of the Society of Antiquaries. But in 1809 he contracted to design and build a new court house and goal at Durham. The work was carried out by local builders in a fraudulent manner and much of it had to be taken down and rebuilt. Sandys was superseded, first by George Moneypenny and ultimately by Ignatius Bonomi, to whose design the building was completed in 1811. Public controversy ensued, in the course of which Moneypenny attacked Sandys in print. Sandys brought an action for libel against Moneypenny which was heard in the Court of King's Bench and resulted in a verdict of £100 in Sandys's favour. But he lost the

[1] The founder of the Society.

much more serious action which was brought against him by the Durham magistrates, who were awarded £20,000 damages against their architect. According to Sir Robert Smirke, Sandys was the victim of 'a juggling trick' by the Durham workmen, but whether his own conduct was fraudulent or merely negligent, he was legally responsible, and must have been financially as well as professionally ruined. No further record of him has been found, and for practical purposes his career terminates in 1814 [*Annual Register*, 1814, 298–9; W. Fordyce, *History of Durham* i, 1857, 292–3].

ICKWORTH HOUSE, nr. BURY ST. EDMUNDS, SUFFOLK, begun 1796 for 4th Earl of Bristol and Bishop of Derry, on the basis of a design by Mario Asprucci, left unfinished on the Earl's death in 1803, completed by the 1st Marquess of Bristol *c.*1825–30 [*Civil Engineer and Architect's Jnl.* ix, 1846, 60–1; Pamela Tudor-Craig 'The Evolution of Ickworth', *C. Life*, 17 May 1973] (*C. Life*, 31 Oct., 7 Nov. 1925; C. Hussey, *English Country Houses: Mid Georgian*, 1956, 239–46).

FINBOROUGH HALL, GREAT FINBOROUGH, SUFFOLK, for Roger Pettiward, 1795 [Britton & Brayley, *Beauties of England and Wales* xiv, 1813, 207; exhib. at R.A. 1800].

WORLINGHAM HALL, SUFFOLK, remodelled for Robert Sparrow, *c.*1800 [exhib. at R.A. 1800] (*C. Life*, 12 March 1970).

CHIPPENHAM PARK, CAMBS., entrance lodges for John Tharp, *c.*1800 [J. Dugdale, *The British Traveller* i, 1819, 245; exhib. at R.A. 1802]. In 1797 Sandys had made unexecuted designs for a new house that are preserved at Chippenham [*ex inf.* Dr. David Watkin and cf. Cambs. C.R.O., R.55.7. 14/1].

BURY ST. EDMUNDS, SUFFOLK, THE ASSEMBLY ROOMS (now the Athenaeum), 1804 [exhib. at R.A. 1806].

AYSTON HALL, RUTLAND, unexecuted design for alterations and additions for George Fludyer, 1808 [drawings at Ayston Hall, *ex inf.* the late Sir Nikolaus Pevsner].

WEST DEAN PARK, SUSSEX, design for 2nd Lord Selsey for completion of house begun by James Wyatt for his father (d. 1808); rebuilt 1893 [exhib. at R.A. 1809].

WORCESTER, THE COUNTY PRISON, 1809–13; enlarged 1845; dem. Plans had been made by George Byfield, but he disagreed with the Justices over his charges, and was superseded by Sandys, who is named as architect of the prison both in the *Report from the Committee of Aldermen appointed to visit Several Gaols in England*, 1816, 155, and by J. Chambers, *History of Worcester*, 1819, 350. Sandys's specification is among the County Records.

DURHAM, THE COUNTY COURTS AND GAOL, begun 1809 to the designs of Sandys but completed by George Moneypenny and Ignatius Bonomi after the failure of part of the building and Sandys's dismissal [W. Fordyce, *History of Durham* i, 1857, 292–3].

DORCHESTER BRIDGE, OXON. (R. Thames), 1813–15 [*Gent's Mag.* 1816 (ii), 297; J. M. Davenport, *Oxfordshire Bridges*, 1869, 3].

SAUL, THOMAS (–1776), was an architect or surveyor in Birmingham. In 1773 he was employed to inspect the building of St. Mary's Chapel to the designs of Joseph Pickford (*q.v.*). He designed THE THEATRE ROYAL, 1773–4, given a new façade by Samuel Wyatt in 1780–2 and rebuilt 1793–4 [J. E. Cunningham, *Theatre Royal*, 1950, 21]. His death intestate in 1776 is recorded in the Lichfield Probate Records.

SAUL, WILLIAM (1792–1853), of Norwich, was the son of a builder of the same name who died in 1825. He exhibited a design for a Catholic Chapel at the Norfolk and Norwich Society of Artists in 1818, and his design for a new gaol at St. Giles, Norwich, is in the City archives [*ex inf.* Mr. A. P. Baggs]. In 1815 he was responsible for alterations to STANFIELD HALL, NORFOLK, for the Revd. George Preston [*Norfolk Chronicle*, 8 Aug. 1818] (Neale's *Views of Seats*, 1st ser. ii, 1819). He died in June 1853, aged 61 [*Norwich Mercury*, 18 June 1853, *ex inf.* Mr. David Cubitt].

SAUNDERS, GEORGE (1762–1839), was the son of Joseph or Joshua Saunders, a carpenter. He practised from a house in Oxford Street (No. 252) built by his father. He was an intellectual who reviewed books on architecture for the *Monthly Review* from 1795 to 1815 and had contacts with Quatremère de Quincy in France and with Sir Joseph Banks in England. To judge from a letter which he wrote to the latter in 1803, he was an architectural rationalist, believing that 'architectural forms were more properly founded on convenience, construction, and economy' than on 'the imitative or the ideal', and that 'permanently pleasing compositions could only result from those principles' [B.L., Add. MS. 33981, f. 92]. He was particularly interested in improved methods of construction such as fireproof floors made of hollow earthenware pots, whose use he had studied in Paris in such buildings as the Théâtre du Palais Royal (1789–90). On the subject of theatres he wrote a systematic work (*A Treatise on Theatres*, 1790), describing the principal European theatres and discussing scientifically the optical, acoustic and other problems connected with theatre design. He was a Fellow of the Royal Society (1812) and of the Society of Antiquaries, and published papers on 'The Origin of Gothic Architecture' and 'The Situation and Extent of London at Various Periods' in *Archaeologia* xvii, 1814 and xxvi, 1836. The former was an important contribution to the study of vaulting and the first clear exposition of the connection between vaulting and the Gothic arch. His 'Observations on Brick Bond as practised at various periods' were printed in the *Civil Engineer and Architect's Jnl.* i, 1838.

Although his practice does not appear to have been large, Saunders had a reputation for administrative efficiency which led to his employment by the Treasury to investigate the accounts of the Office of Works at a time (1809–12) when it was suffering from the incompetent management of James Wyatt. He was a magistrate for the County of Middlesex and for twenty-eight years chairman of the Commission of Sewers for that county. In 1826 he was a member of the committee of three magistrates appointed to report on the county bridges, and was joint author of the printed *Report*. He died at his house in Oxford Street in the summer of 1839, aged 77. A bust in ivory by B. Cheverton after Sir Francis Chantrey is in the collection of the R.I.B.A. His brother Thomas Saunders, who died on 11 May 1798, is said to have been an architect in the notice of his death in *Gent's Mag.* 1798 (i), 448.

[*A.P.S.D.*; *Gent's Mag.* 1839 (ii), 321; *Survey of London* xl, 171; R. S. Fitton & A. P. Wadsworth, *The Strutts and the Arkwrights*, Manchester 1958, 201–3; Paul Frankl, *The Gothic*, Princeton 1960, 499-502; *History of the King's Works* vi, 79–81, 84, etc.]

BIRMINGHAM, rebuilt THE THEATRE ROYAL, NEW STREET, and adjoining ASSEMBLY ROOMS, etc., 1793–4, retaining the façade by Samuel Wyatt (1780); executed under the direction of Samuel Norton (*q.v.*); destroyed by fire 1820 [MS. Minutes of the Proprietors in Birmingham Reference Library Archives, Lee Crowder 387].

KEN (CAEN) WOOD HOUSE, HIGHGATE, MIDDLESEX, alterations for 2nd Earl of Mansfield, 1793–6, continuing works started by Robert Nasmith (*q.v.*) [*A.P.S.D.*; *The Farington Diary*, ed. J. Greig, i, 17; A. T. Bolton, *The Architecture of R. & J. Adam* i, 1922, 304].

LONDON, THE STAG BREWERY, PIMLICO, for John Elliott, 1797–1802; internally reconstructed 1860; dem. *c.*1960 [B. Spiller, 'The Georgian Brewery', *Arch. Rev.*, Nov. 1957, 322].

LONDON, THE ROYAL INSTITUTION, ALBEMARLE STREET, revised design of Lecture Theatre, *c.*1800 [A. D. R. Caroe, *The House of the Royal Institution*, 1963, 17].

OXFORD, THE SHELDONIAN THEATRE, reconstruction of roof, 1801–2 [*V.C.H. Oxon*, iii, 53].

OXFORD, BODLEIAN LIBRARY, designed the 'Antiquaries' Closet' for the reception of the MSS. of Dodsworth, Tanner, Browne Willis, etc., *c.*1805 [J. Nichols, *Literary Illustrations* v, 553–5]. There is a sketch of the 'Closet' in Bodleian, MS. Top. Oxon. a. 36, f. 79.

LONDON, BRITISH MUSEUM, THE TOWNLEY GALLERY, 1804–8; dem. *c.*1850 [J. Mordaunt Crook, *The British Museum*, 1972, 68–70 and figs. 21–4].

DARTINGTON HALL, DEVON, survey of medieval house for Arthur Champernowne, 1805 [A. Emery, *Dartington Hall*, 1970, 85 and plates, pp. 162–3].

SAVAGE, JAMES (1779–1852), born at Hackney on 10 April 1779, was articled to D. A. Alexander, under whom he served for several years as clerk of the works. In 1798 he became a student at the Royal Academy, and subsequently exhibited at the Academy between 1799 and 1832. In 1800 his design for improving the city of Aberdeen obtained the second premium of £150. In 1805 he was the successful competitor for a design for rebuilding Ormonde Bridge over the R. Liffey at Dublin. This was not carried out, but in 1808 his designs for Richmond Bridge in the same city were accepted, and subsequently executed. In 1806 he read a paper on 'Bridge-building' to the London Architectural Society (of which he was a member), which was printed in the second volume of the Society's *Essays*, 1810, 119–67. In 1823 he made a design for rebuilding London Bridge which was highly thought of; but the chairman of the committee of the House of Commons gave his casting vote in favour of that submitted by Sir John Rennie. Savage thereupon published a pamphlet entitled *Observations on the proposed new London Bridge*, in which he criticized Rennie's design, and claimed that his proposed centering was deficient in construction, 'implicating stability and security'. In 1825 he published a plan for improving the south bank of the R. Thames by forming a 'Surrey Quay' to extend from London Bridge to Bishop's Walk, Lambeth. He competed for the Houses of Parliament in 1835, submitting a design in 'the castle style of Gothic'.

The interest in construction which made Savage a successful bridge-builder is also apparent in the church of St. Luke at Chelsea, which was built to his plans in 1820–4. Over forty designs were submitted, and Savage's, although pronounced by the Attached Architects to the Board of Works to be of 'extremely difficult construction', was accepted, though he was not allowed to carry into execution his plans for a stone spire constructed like that of St. Dunstan-in-the-East. With its flying buttresses supporting a genuine stone vault, St. Luke's is remarkable as one of the first serious attempts to revive medieval forms of construction, and it was recognized at the time as a landmark in the history of the Gothic revival. None of Savage's other Gothic churches has the same interest or importance as St. Luke's, but his one classical church, St. James, Bermondsey, has the merit of demonstrating an original and effective solution to the problem of combining a Grecian portico with a steeple.

Savage was much employed as an adviser in legal cases concerning architecture or engineering, and in 1827–30 he gave evidence on behalf of Henry Peto, the builder, in the action consequent upon the failure of the foundations of the Custom House.

In about 1830 he succeeded Henry Hakewill as architect to the Society of the Middle Temple, for whom he designed Plowden Buildings and other works noted below. In 1840 he began the restoration of the Temple Church for the Societies of the Inner and Middle Temples, but was superseded by Sydney Smirke and Decimus Burton after grossly exceeding his estimates. This affair no doubt had an adverse effect on his practice, and he appears to have had relatively few commissions between 1842 and his death ten years later.

Savage was President of the Surveyors' Club in 1825, and was a vice-president of the London Architectural Society. He was also chairman of the Committee of Fine Arts of the Society for the Promotion of Arts, Manufactures and Commerce, a member of the Institution of Civil Engineers, a member of the Graphic Society from its foundation in 1831 and, for a short time, a Fellow of the Institute of British Architects, from which he resigned after a 'difference of views upon some matters of regulation'. He was a freeman of the City of London, and a member of the Skinners' Company.

He died at North Place, Hampstead Road, London, on 7 May 1852 in his 74th year, and was buried at St. Luke's Church, Chelsea. His books and drawings were sold on 9 December 1853. Several of the latter were presented to the R.I.B.A. Library in 1854. His designs (1841) for a new Armoury at the Tower of London are in the British Library (Add. MS. 16368, A–B).

In addition to the work already mentioned, Savage published, with L. N. Cottingham, *St. Saviour's Church, reasons against pulling down the Lady Chapel*, 1832; and *Observations on Style in Architecture, with suggestions on the best mode of procuring Designs for Public Buildings, and promoting the improvement of Architecture, especially in reference to a Recommendation in the Report of the Commissioners on the Designs for the New Houses of Parliament*, 1836, in which he took exception to the proposal that the architect's drawings should 'be submitted from time to time to competent judges of their effect, lest from over-confidence, negligence, or inattention . . . we fail to obtain that result to which our just expectations have been raised'. He is also believed to have been the author of *Observations on the Varieties of Architecture used in the Structure of Parish Churches*, 1812.

[*A.P.S.D.*; *D.N.B.*; obituaries in *Builder* x, 1852, 377, *Civil Engineer and Architect's Jnl.* xv, 1852, 226, *Gent's Mag.* 1852 (ii), 206–7.]

CHURCHES

LONDON, ST. LUKE, CHELSEA, 1820–4, Gothic [*Gent's Mag.* 1826 (ii), 201–5; Britton & Pugin, *Public Buildings of London* ii, 1828, 205–18].

LONDON, ST. MARY-AT-HILL, repairs, 1827–8, and refitting of interior, 1848–9, after a fire [*Gent's Mag.* 1852 (ii), 207].

UPPER NORWOOD, SURREY, ALL SAINTS, BEULAH HILL, 1827–9, Gothic; chapel added 1861 [Port, 162–3].

LONDON, ST. JAMES, BERMONDSEY, assisted by George Allen, 1827–9 [Port, 134–5; *A.P.S.D.*].

LONDON, HOLY TRINITY, SLOANE STREET, CHELSEA, 1828–30, Gothic; dem. 1890 [*Gent's Mag.* 1831 (i), 298–300, with engraving].

TOTTENHAM GREEN, MIDDLESEX, HOLY TRINITY, 1828–9, Gothic [Port, 158–9].

ILFORD, ESSEX, ST. MARY, 1829–31, Gothic; tower 1866, chancel 1920 [Port, 144–5].

SPEENHAMLAND, BERKS., 1829–31, Gothic; chancel by G. E. Street 1879; nave rebuilt by A. E. Street 1911 [*Gent's Mag.* 1852 (ii), 207; exhib. at R.A. 1830].

NEWPORT PAGNELL, BUCKS., rebuilt south aisle and added pinnacles and battlements to tower, 1830 [I.C.B.S].

GREAT MARLOW, BUCKS., reported on old

church and made unexecuted designs for a new one [*Records of Bucks*. xv, 1947, 14].

LONDON, ST. MICHAEL, BURLEIGH STREET, STRAND, 1832–3, Gothic; dem. *c*.1906 [*Gent's Mag*. 1852 (ii), 207]. The fittings are in St. Michael's Church, Sutton Court, Chiswick.

BRENTWOOD, ESSEX, ST. THOMAS, 1835, Gothic; chancel rebuilt by J. Clarke 1856, the remainder by E. C. Lee 1883–6 [*Gent's Mag*. 1852 (ii), 207].

LONDON, ST. MARY-LE-BOW, CHEAPSIDE, repaired belfry floor and bell-frame, 1835 [minutes of parish bell-committee in Guildhall Library, MS. 5051]; repairs and repewing, 1838 [I.C.B.S.].

ADDLESTONE, SURREY, ST. PAUL, 1836–8, Gothic; subsequently altered at various dates [*Gent's Mag*. 1852 (ii), 207].

LINCOLN CATHEDRAL, new floor and bell-frame in central tower for 'Great Tom', 1836 [*Gent's Mag*. 1852 (ii), 207].

SOUTH WEALD CHURCH, ESSEX, repairs and repewing, 1838 [I.C.B.S.].

LONDON, TEMPLE CHURCH, commenced restoration 1840–1, was superseded by Sydney Smirke and Decimus Burton [J. Mordaunt Crook, 'The Restoration of the Temple Church: Ecclesiology and Recrimination', *Arch. Hist*. viii, 1965].

OTHER WORKS

DUBLIN, RICHMOND BRIDGE (R. Liffey), 1813–16 [*Gent's Mag*. 1852 (ii), 207].

TEMPSFORD BRIDGE, BEDS. (R. Ouse), 1815–20 [R.I.B.A.D.; *Gent's Mag*. 1852 (ii), 207].

BROXBOURNE VICARAGE, HERTS., 1822–3 [London Diocesan Papers, Guildhall Library, MS. 19227/7].

LONDON, PAROCHIAL SCHOOLS, CHELSEA, 1824–6, Gothic [T. Faulkner, *Chelsea*, 1829, i, 98–101; ii, 92, engraving].

READING, BERKS., two bridges on road made through Crown lands, *c*.1825 [R.I.B.A.D.; *Gent's Mag*. 1852 (ii), 207].

LONDON, BAPTIST COLLEGE, STEPNEY GREEN, 1830; mostly dem. [*Gent's Mag*. 1852 (ii), 207].

LONDON, 'BULL AND MOUTH' INN (later Queen's Hotel), ST. MARTIN'S-LE-GRAND, 1830–1; dem. 1887 [*A.P.S.D.*].

LONDON, THE MIDDLE TEMPLE, built domed louvre (destroyed 1944) and north entrance to Hall to designs of Henry Hakewill, 1830; designed Clock Tower 1830–1, and completed Plowden Buildings (begun by Hakewill) 1831–3 [*A.P.S.D.*].

ILFORD, ESSEX, CHURCH SCHOOLS, 1831 [*A.P.S.D.*].

LONDON, ST. MARY-AT-HILL RECTORY, 1834 [*A.P.S.D.*].

BRENTWOOD, ESSEX, CHURCH SCHOOLS, *c*.1835, Gothic [*A.P.S.D.*].

DARTFORD UNION WORKHOUSE (now West Hill Hospital), DARTFORD, KENT, 1836 [*A.P.S.D.*].

TENTERDEN UNION WORKHOUSE, KENT, 1843–7 [*Gent's Mag*. 1852 (ii), 207].

BROMLEY UNION WORKHOUSE, LOCK'S BOTTOM, FARNBOROUGH, KENT [*Gent's Mag*. 1852 (ii), 207].

HAMPSTEAD, LONDON, house for – Husband [*A.P.S.D.*].

LUTON, BEDS., HOLLY LODGE for R. Vyse [*A.P.S.D.*].

'House for Sir J. Shaw' [*A.P.S.D.*], probably STAPLEFIELD PLACE, SUSSEX, since completely rebuilt.

House (unidentified) for Samuel Cartwright [*A.P.S.D.*].

SAXON, SAMUEL SIMON (1757–1831), born on 30 June 1757, became a pupil of Sir William Chambers. He was admitted a student at the Royal Academy in November 1776, and exhibited at the Academy between 1778 and 1782. He was appointed a Labourer in Trust at Whitehall in 1780, and would no doubt have been promoted to a clerkship of the works but for the reforms which abolished many Office of Works posts in 1782. For a few years in the 1780s he was in partnership with John Nash (*q.v.*).

Saxon designed the GENERAL INFIRMARY at NORTHAMPTON, 1791–3, enlarged 1840 and 1887 [F. F. Waddy, *History of the Northampton General Hospital*, Northampton 1974]; and two elegant country houses: COURTEENHALL, NORTHANTS., for Sir William Wake, Bart., 1791–4 (*C. Life*, 12–19 Aug. 1939), and BUCKMINSTER PARK, LEICS., for Sir William Manners, Bart., *c*.1795–8, dem. 1950, both illustrated in G. Richardson's *New Vitruvius Britannicus* i, 1810, pls. 67–72. In 1810–11 he was employed to repair the tower of WALTHAM ABBEY CHURCH, ESSEX, a commission which he no doubt owed to the Wake family, who were lords of the manor [*Waltham Abbey Church Monthly*, Aug. 1904, 2–3]. He died at Evercreech in Somerset on 28 September 1831, aged 75 [*Gent's Mag*. 1831 (ii), 381]. His will [P.R.O., PROB 11/1795, f. 52] shows that he owned property in London and Somerset.

SCAMP, WILLIAM (1801–1872), was born on 5 June 1801, at Georgeham, nr. Barnstaple, where his father was a prosperous maltster and shipowner. He showed an early aptitude for geometry and surveying, and but for his father's early death he would doubtless have received a regular professional training. As it was, he was largely self-taught, and it was his success in winning the competition for the ASSEMBLY ROOMS at ILFRACOMBE which brought him to the notice of Sir Jeffry Wyatville. For thirteen years he served Wyatville as a clerk of the works during the rebuilding of Windsor Castle, proving himself a man of untiring energy with 'an iron frame and a good constitution'. During this period, he designed the parish church at UPTON-CUM-CHALVEY, nr. SLOUGH, BUCKS., a building in the Lombardic style, which was completed in 1837 and rebuilt by J. O. Scott between 1876 and 1918 [P. W. Phipps, *Records of Upton-cum-Chalvey*, 1886, 24]. On the completion of the work at Windsor, Scamp was appointed assistant engineer to the Works Department at Woolwich Dockyard, and in 1841 he accompanied Capt. Brandreth, Director of Engineering Works to the Admiralty, on a visit to Malta in order to report on the naval accommodation there. It was he who supervised the construction of the first dry dock in 1841–8, and he subsequently remodelled the Dockyard by designing a new bakery, coal stores, officers' quarters, and other buildings. The NAVAL BAKERY, now the Maritime Museum, is an accomplished building with windows copied from Hugh May's at Windsor Castle and striking vaulted interiors. Scamp was also put in charge of the dockyard at Gibraltar, where the new Mole and other works were completed under his direction, largely by convict labour.

Shortly after his arrival in Malta, Scamp was asked to report on the half-finished Anglican CATHEDRAL OF ST. PAUL which had been founded by Queen Adelaide in 1839. Its architect, Richard Lankesher, the English Director of Public Works, had failed to understand the peculiar properties of the local stone, and certain 'cracks, splits and crushings began to appear' which caused the Building Committee to seek the professional advice of the Admiralty architects. Their report showed that the Ionic portico was in danger of collapse and that the whole building must be condemned as insecure. The incompetence of the Director of Public Works gave unwelcome force to a campaign against the English monopoly of Government posts which then occupied the Maltese press: and when the unfortunate Lankesher died in 1841 at the age of 38, the completion of Queen Adelaide's church became a matter involving the prestige of the British Government in Malta. It was in these circumstances that the Committee turned to Scamp as the only competent representative of his profession available. He proved equal to the occasion and not only saved the church from collapse, but designed and built the handsome tower and spire which form one of the principal landmarks of Valletta. Scamp also enlarged a building at St. Julian's Bay for use as THE MALTA PROTESTANT COLLEGE. On his return to England in 1845, Queen Adelaide presented him with a silver candelabrum 'in grateful remembrance of his services in completing the Collegiate Church of St. Paul, at Malta'. He was now promoted to be Chief Assistant to the Admiralty Director of Engineering and Architectural Works, and in 1852 he became Deputy Director under G. T. Greene, with whom he shares the credit for designing some of the important iron-framed structures built by the Admiralty in the 1850s. Between 1845 and 1867 he was engaged in re-equipping British naval bases in all parts of the world for the new fleet of ironclads, and in 1860 the Director of Admiralty Works wrote that 'The present Admiralty establishments at Malta, Gibraltar, and Bermuda, are almost entirely projected by him. Deptford, Woolwich, Sheerness, Portsmouth and Pembroke, owe many of their best buildings to his professional talent. Keyham is almost entirely his own, from first to last.' Scamp died on 13 January 1872, five years after his retirement in 1867. He was a member of the Institution of Civil Engineers. [Obituary in *Proceedings of the Institution of Civil Engineers* xxxvi, 1872–3, 273–8; H. M. Colvin, 'Victorian Malta', *Arch. Rev.*, June 1946, 179–80; *The First Annual Report of the Malta Protestant College*, London 1847; A. W. Skempton, 'The Boat Store, Sheerness (1858–60) and its Place in Structural History', *Trans. Newcomen Soc.* xxxii, 1959–60, 63–4; *Gent's Mag.* 1844 (ii), 632–3.]

SCAMPION, JOHN, was employed in the construction of a new building in MONTGOMERY CASTLE for the 1st Lord Herbert of Chirbury in the 1620s. Between 1622 and 1625 the parish register of Montgomery records the baptisms of two of his children and the burial of his wife, and refers to him as *Johannes Scampion, artificiossimus jam architectus novi operis in Castello de Mountgomeri*. He appears to have been a master carpenter by trade, to have lived previously in Whitechapel, London, and to have been a native of Great Hormead in Essex [J. D. K. Lloyd, 'The New Building at Montgomery Castle', *Archaeologia Cambrensis* cxiv, 1965, 60–8].

SCARBOROUGH, JOHN (–1696), was Clerk of the Works at Greenwich Palace from 1681 until his death in November 1696.

In May 1696, on the commencement of the new Hospital at Greenwich, he was appointed Clerk of the Works there, still retaining his former post. He was also appointed Clerk of the Works at Winchester soon after the commencement of the new Palace there in 1682, and was Surveyor to the Westminster Commissioners for Sewers from 1691 to 1696. He was frequently employed by Sir Christopher Wren as a measuring clerk – e.g. at St. Paul's from 1687, at Hampton Court from 1689, and in connection with several of the new City churches. He also assisted Robert Hooke in a similar capacity [*Wren Soc.* xx, 204; *Walpole Soc.* xxv, 93]. In 1680 he was the measurer employed at ABINGDON TOWN HALL [Arthur Oswald in *C. Life*, 21 Sept. 1929, 394, referring to B.L., Add. MS. 28666, ff. 338–9], and in 1690 he spent a week at PETWORTH HOUSE, SUSSEX, measuring work carried out on the Duke of Somerset's great new mansion, a task for which he received £10 15s. [*Sussex Arch. Colls.* xcvi, 1958, 98].

SCHOFIELD, JOHN, of Jewin Street, London, exhibited a 'Design for a mausoleum for the interment of warlike heroes' at the Royal Academy in 1802. Pigot's *Directory* shows that he was practising as an architect from the same address in 1827–8.

SCOLES, JOSEPH JOHN (1798–1863), born in London on 27 June 1798, was the son of Matthew Scoles, a joiner. His parents were Roman Catholics, and Scoles was apprenticed in 1812 to Joseph Ireland, the leading Roman Catholic architect of the time, to whom he was related through his mother. While in his office Scoles came into contact with John Carter, who corrected his drawings of medieval detail and encouraged his interest in ecclesiastical architecture. In 1820 he was admitted to the Royal Academy Schools, and began to exhibit his designs.

In 1822 Scoles left England in company with Joseph Bonomi, junior, and travelled extensively on the Continent and in Sicily, Greece, Egypt and Syria, devoting himself to architectural and archaeological research. In Sicily he assisted Angell and Harris in their explorations, and in Syria and Egypt he was the companion of Henry Parke and Frederick Catherwood. In 1829 he and Parke published an engraved Map of Nubia, based on a survey made by them in 1824. The illustrations to the article 'Catacomb' in the Architectural Publication Society's Dictionary include plans of a catacomb in Alexandria drawn by Scoles, Parke and Catherwood in 1823 and his plan of the Church of the Holy Sepulchre at Jerusalem was utilized by Professor Willis in his monograph on that building (1849).

On returning to England in 1826 Scoles was employed to plan Gloucester Terrace, Regent's Park, for which John Nash supplied a characteristic elevation. The internal arrangement of the houses forming the terrace was entirely Scoles's work, and he attempted to improve Nash's façade by enlarging the scale of the mouldings. Nash is said to have 'passed the work with the observation that the parts looked larger than he expected'. It was, however, as a designer of churches (nearly all Roman Catholic) that Scoles made his reputation. These were chiefly in a Gothic style which satisfied everyone except Pugin (who criticized St. Mary's Islington in his *Present State of Ecclesiastical Architecture in England*, 1843), but some were 'Norman' and a few, notably at Prior Park College and Ince Blundell Hall, were handsome classical buildings.

Scoles was one of the original fellows of the Institute of British Architects in 1835, acted as its honorary secretary from 1846 to 1856, and was vice-president in 1857–8. At its meetings he read a number of papers, principally on the monuments of Egypt and the Holy Land. He died on 29 December 1863, at his residence, Crofton Lodge, Hammersmith, leaving four sons and eight daughters by his wife Harriott, daughter of Robert Cory of Great Yarmouth. Two of his sons, Ignatius and Alexander Joseph, received an architectural training, but subsequently entered the church, and practised only in a clerical capacity. S. J. Nicholl and T. J. Willson were his pupils. [*A.P.S.D.*; *D.N.B.*; *Builder* xxii, 1864, 41; S. J. Nicholl's reminiscences in *Downside Review* viii, 1889, 114–17; J. Gillow, *Bibliographical Dictionary of the English Catholics*, 1885; list of works in *Catholic Annual Register*, 1850, 106–7, cited below as *C.A.R.*; B. Little, *Catholic Churches since 1623*, 1966.]

ESHER, SURREY, WEST END LODGE, for Thomas Roberts, *c.*1820 [*A.P.S.D.*].

KNOWSLEY, LANCS., conservatory 'proposed to be erected' for 12th Earl of Derby, exhib. at R.A. 1820.

LONDON, interior of GLOUCESTER TERRACE, REGENT'S PARK, and houses in GLOUCESTER GATE, 1827–8 [*D.N.B.*].

YARMOUTH, NORFOLK, suspension bridge over R. Bure, 1828–9, failed 1845 [*Builder* iii, 1845, 253–4].

YARMOUTH, NORFOLK, ST. PETER'S CHURCH, 1831–3, Gothic [Port, 158–9].

YARMOUTH, NORFOLK, ST. MARY'S CHAPEL, SOUTH TOWN, 1831–2, Gothic; enlarged 1893 [*A.P.S.D.*].

HOLYWELL, FLINTSHIRE, ST. WINIFRIDE'S CHURCH (R.C.), 1832–3, classical; enlarged 1895–8 [*C.A.R.*].

STONYHURST COLLEGE, LANCS., ST. PETER'S CHURCH (R.C.), 1832–5, Gothic [*C.A.R.*].

LONDON, OUR LADY'S CHAPEL (R.C.), LISSON GROVE, ST. JOHN'S WOOD, 1833–6, Gothic [*C.A.R.*].

PRESTON, LANCS., ST. IGNATIUS' CHURCH (R.C.), 1833–6, Gothic; chancel by J. A. Hansom 1858 [*C.A.R.*].

YARMOUTH, NORFOLK, ST. NICHOLAS' CHURCH, repaired tower, 1834 [*Norfolk Chronicle*, 8 March 1834, *ex inf.* Mr. D. C. Young].

BANGOR, CAERNARVONSHIRE, ST. MARY'S CHURCH (R.C.), 1834–44, Gothic [*C.A.R.*].

HULL, YORKS. (E.R.), ST. CHARLES' CHURCH, JARRATT STREET (R.C.), alterations, 1835, classical [*C.A.R.*].

WOOLTON, nr. LIVERPOOL, LANCS., THE MAGDALEN ASYLUM (R.C.), 1835 [*C.A.R.*].

BIRMINGHAM, ST. GEORGE'S CHURCH, EDGBASTON, 1836–8, Gothic; chancel by C. Edge, 1856; rebuilt 1884–5 by J. A. Chatwin [*A.P.S.D.*].

COLCHESTER, ST. JAMES'S CHURCH (R.C.), 1837, Norman; enlarged 1904–10 [*C.A.R.*].

NEWPORT, MONMOUTHSHIRE, ST. MARY'S CHURCH (R.C.), 1838–40, Gothic [*C.A.R.*].

CARDIFF, GLAMORGANSHIRE, ST. DAVID'S CHURCH (R.C.), 1841–2, Norman; rebuilt 1884–7 [*C.A.R.*].

LONDON, ST. JOHN'S CHURCH, DUNCAN TERRACE, ISLINGTON (R.C.), 1841–3, Norman; towers added 1873–7 [*C.A.R.*; *Builder* i, 1843, 98–9].

INCE BLUNDELL, LANCS., school (R.C.), 1843 [*Builder* i, 1843, 487].

PRESTON, LANCS., ST. WILFRID'S CHURCH (R.C.), added Lady Chapel, 1844; retained when church was rebuilt 1879–80 and now called St. Joseph's Chapel [*C.A.R.*].

DOWLAIS, GLAMORGANSHIRE, ST. ILLTYD'S CHURCH (R.C.), 1844–6, Gothic; enlarged 1894 [*C.A.R.*].

PONTYPOOL, MONMOUTHSHIRE, ST. ALBAN'S CHURCH (R.C.), 1844–6, Norman [*C.A.R.*].

PRIOR PARK COLLEGE, BATH, SOMERSET, CHURCH (R.C.), begun 1844, not completed until after 1863, classical [exhib. at R.A. 1844].

LIVERPOOL, ST. FRANCIS XAVIER'S CHURCH, EVERTON (R.C.), 1845–9, Gothic; Lady Chapel 1888 [*C.A.R.*].

LONDON, CHURCH OF THE IMMACULATE CONCEPTION, FARM STREET (R.C.), 1846–9, Gothic [*C.A.R.*] (*Builder* vii, 1849, 258).

CHELMSFORD, ESSEX, CHURCH OF THE IMMACULATE CONCEPTION (R.C.), 1847, Gothic [*C.A.R.*; *Builder* v, 1847, 545].

BURGH CASTLE CHURCH, SUFFOLK, N. aisle and refitting, 1846–7 [I.C.B.S.]. In 1847 Scoles read a paper on the 'Construction of the Roof of St. Peter's Church, Burgh, Suffolk' to the R.I.B.A.

YARMOUTH, NORFOLK, ST. MARY'S CHURCH (R.C.), 1848–50, Gothic [*C.A.R.*].

LONDON, THE ORATORY, BROMPTON, KENSINGTON, for the Oratorians, 1849–53 [*C.A.R.*]. Scoles's residential building remains, but his temporary church was replaced in 1878.

LYDIATE, LANCS., OUR LADY'S CHURCH (R.C.), 1854–5, Gothic [*A.P.S.D.*].

INCE BLUNDELL HALL, LANCS., CHAPEL (R.C.) for Thomas Weld Blundell, 1858–9, classical [*D.N.B.*]. Scoles may also have been responsible for the redecoration of the Drawing Room, Gallery, etc., as he exhibited 'intended alterations to Ince Blundell Hall' at the R.A. in 1854 (cf. *C. Life*, 10, 17, 24 April 1958).

LONDON, R.C. SCHOOLS in CHARLES (now MACKLIN) STREET, DRURY LANE, *c.*1860, Gothic [*A.P.S.D.*].

ST. HELEN'S, LANCS., HOLY CROSS CHURCH (R.C.), 1860–2, Gothic [*A.P.S.D.*; *D.N.B.*].

NEW HALL CONVENT, BOREHAM, ESSEX, fitted up hall as chapel [*C.A.R.*].

SCOLTOCK, SAMUEL (*c.*1739–1819), is described as 'architect' on a tablet to his memory in Shrewsbury Abbey Church. He died on 18 March 1819, aged 80. He was a bricklayer by trade and was no doubt the successor of Richard Scoltock, a bricklayer who, with Edward Massey, a carpenter, jointly designed and built MILLINGTON'S HOSPITAL, FRANKWELL, SHREWSBURY, in 1747–8 (central feature altered by J. H. Haycock in 1785–6). In an affidavit to the estimate Massey stated that he and Scoltock had 'for several years . . . been very much employed in making plans of Publick and other great Buildings and making calculations of the expences of the building thereof' [J. B. Lawson, 'The Architect of Millington's Hospital, Shrewsbury', *Shropshire News Letter*, No. 42, May 1972, 10]. So far Samuel's only identified architectural work is the Gothic SHAM CASTLE or LODGE at ACTON BURNELL HALL, SALOP., designed for Sir Edward Smythe, Bart., in 1779–80, with plasterwork by Joseph Bromfield [Shropshire C.R.O., 1514/2/452]. Jonathan Scoltock, variously described as 'Builder' or 'Architect' of Sutton, near Shrewsbury, is mentioned in the 1790s.

SCOTT, —, from London, was employed by Horatio, Lord Townshend, in 1661 to supervise the fitting up of the interior of RAYNHAM HALL, NORFOLK, which had probably been left at least partially incomplete after Sir Roger

Townshend's death in 1637. Scott gave directions for both joiner's, painter's and ornamental plasterer's work in the dining-room, gallery, etc., and incurred expenditure in excess of £1500 [B.L., Add. MS. 41655, f. 130]. Most of his work was destroyed in the eighteenth century.

SCOTT, ARCHIBALD (*c.*1798–1871), practised in Edinburgh for many years. Shepherd's *Modern Athens* (p. 77) records that he designed the STOCKBRIDGE MARKET, ST. STEPHEN PLACE, 1825, of which only the entrance archway now remains. In Edinburgh he also designed the modest PORTSBURGH CHURCH in THE VENNEL, 1828 [S.R.O., CH 3/1152/10] and (gratuitously) the Gothic LAURISTON PLACE U.P. CHURCH, 1857–9 [S.R.O., CH 3/1152/11]; elsewhere, HOWMORE CHURCH, SOUTH UIST, OUTER HEBRIDES, 1837 [S.R.O., GD 201/3/91] and the spire of NEWCASTLETON CHURCH, ROXBURGHSHIRE, 1835 [G. Hay, *The Architecture of Scottish Post-Reformation Churches*, 1957, 274]. He died on 3 July 1871, aged 73 [S.R.O., SC70/1/154, p. 386].

SCOTT, G—, of Furnival's Inn, exhibited a 'Design for a house at Demerary, for R. Fernier Esq.' at the Royal Academy in 1802. He also exhibited a drawing of Louth Church, Lincs., in 1832. A person of this name was appointed District Surveyor of the Western District of the City of London in 1774.

SCOTT, JOHN (–1666), was a leading master wright in Edinburgh, where he became a burgess in 1636 and was a member of the town council in 1653. He was appointed master wheelwright at Edinburgh Castle in 1636, master wright to the burgh of Edinburgh in 1637 and the king's master wright for life in 1641. Apart from routine work in Edinburgh Castle, he built and presumably designed the striking hammerbeam roofs of the PARLIAMENT HOUSE, 1634–9 and of the TRON CHURCH, 1636–47. In 1645–6 he was the 'surveyor' who was sent for from Edinburgh to consider a site for the new church at Berwick-on-Tweed designed and built by John Young (*q.v.*). As master wright he was succeeded by his eldest son James Scott. [*Accounts of the Masters of Works* ii, ed. Imrie & Dunbar 1982, lxii; *Book of the Old Edinburgh Club* xiii, 53–4, xxix, 103–9; Berwick-on-Tweed, Guild Minute-Book No. 12.]

SCOTT, JOSEPH, junior, advertised in the *Leicester Journal* (23 Nov. 1810) and the *Northampton Mercury* (15 Dec. 1810) that having been 'many years in the employ of James Wyatt, Esq.' he was established in Market Harborough, where he 'engages to design and execute in a masterly and workmanlike manner, MODERN, GOTHIC, and GROTESQUE Architecture, on the most reasonable terms'. Joseph Scott figures as a 'builder and surveyor' under Market Harborough in Pigot's *Directory* of 1828–9 and subsequently as a 'builder' up to the 1840s.

SCOTT, ROBERT (–1839), was presumably the Robert Scott of the 'Architectural Academy, Glasgow', who appears among the subscribers to Peter Nicholson's *Architectural Dictionary* (1819). In 1830 he was in partnership with — Wilson and in 1834 he was a member of the firm of 'Scott, Stephen and Gale'. He died in April 1839 [S.R.O., SC 36/48/27, p. 499].

DUMBARTON, THE COUNTY BUILDINGS, in collaboration with J. Gillespie (Graham), 1824; enlarged 1863 and 1895 [*Glasgow Herald*, 23 July 1824].

GLASGOW, THE POLICE OFFICES, ALBION STREET, 1824–5; dem. [Thomas Rickman's Diary, 16 Feb. 1824].

GLASGOW, ST. MARY'S EPISCOPAL CHAPEL, RENFIELD STREET, 1835, Gothic [J. Pagan, *Sketch of the History of Glasgow*, 1847, 182].

CAMERON HOUSE, DUNBARTONSHIRE, alterations for Capt. J. R. Smollett, 1827 [Smollett papers, bdl. 43].

GLASGOW, Nos. 176–86, WEST REGENT STREET, 1830–2 [A. Gomme & D. Walker, *Architecture of Glasgow*, 1987, 324].

BOTURICH CASTLE, DUNBARTONSHIRE, work for John Buchanan, 1834 [*Glasgow Herald*, 29 Aug. 1834].

SEABROOKE, WILLIAM, apparently a bricklayer by trade, also acted as a surveyor. In 1698, in conjunction with Robert Jeffs, a carpenter, he was engaged in reconstructing SCHOMBERG HOUSE, PALL MALL, for the 3rd Duke of Schomberg [*Survey of London* xxix, 369]. In 1723 and 1729/30 he was remunerated for making drawings, plans and estimates, etc. for buildings in CLEMENTS INN, STRAND (dem. 1868) [*The Pension Book of Clements Inn*, ed. C. Carr, Selden Soc. lxxviii, 1960, 107, 152–3].

SEARLES, MICHAEL (1751–1813), was the son of Michael Searles (d. 1799), a carpenter and surveyor of Greenwich who was the author of several surveyors' manuals. Michael was brought up by his father as a surveyor. He married in 1771 and in 1776 established himself in Bermondsey, where from 1783 onwards he was employed as surveyor to the Rolls Estate. By 1784 he had designed a terrace of houses in the Old Kent Road, and he subsequently developed a considerable architectural practice, chiefly as a designer of residential property in South London. In 1784 a fortunate legacy provided him with the capital to engage in speculative building on his own account, but in 1795 he got into financial difficulties and had to abandon building. A large collection of his drawings in the R.I.B.A. collection shows that he was an able designer of domestic architecture in an elegant late Georgian style, but much of his time was spent building small houses and shops and in repairs to existing buildings. His ability can, however, still be appreciated at the Paragon in Blackheath, a crescent of semi-detached houses attractively linked by colonnades, and at Clare House, East Malling, Kent, a skilfully composed sequence of geometrically planned rooms, circular, oval and octagonal.

Searles died at Lee in Kent on 20 October 1813, after a road accident in which his chaise was overturned. As surveyor to the Rolls Estate he was succeeded first by his elder son Richard and then by his younger son Robert Thomas Searles (d. 1863). [*Gent's Mag.* 1813 (ii), 507; P.C.C. 582 BRIDPORT; *R.I.B.A. Drawings Catalogue: S.*; W. Bonwitt, *Michael Searles, a Georgian Architect and Surveyor*, Society of Architectural Historians, Monograph No. 2, 1987; Eileen Harris, *British Architectural Books and Writers 1556–1785*, 1990, 412.]

The sources for the following list of Searles' principal executed works will be found in Bonwit, *op. cit.* and the *R.I.B.A. Drawings Catalogue*.

LONDON, SURREY PLACE, OLD KENT ROAD, SOUTHWARK, 1786; dem.

LONDON, UNION PLACE, DEPTFORD, 1786; dem.

STREATHAM, SURREY, THE ROOKERY, STREATHAM COMMON SOUTH, for William Wilkinson, 1786; dem.

LONDON, MARLBOROUGH HOUSE, 317 KENNINGTON ROAD, for William Edridge, 1787.

STREATHAM, SURREY, house for John Smith, 1787; dem.

LONDON, PRINCES PLACE, KENNINGTON PARK ROAD, 1787–8.

LONDON, THE PARAGON, NEW KENT ROAD, 1789–90; dem. 1898 except end houses.

STREATHAM, SURREY, THE WORKHOUSE, 1790–1; dem.

LONDON, THE CIRCUS, GREENWICH, begun 1790–3 as one side of a double crescent, of which the other half was built in the 1820s to the designs of George Gwilt.

CLARE HOUSE, EAST MALLING, KENT, for John Larking, 1793 (*C. Life*, 16–23 Sept. 1949).

CHERRY TREE COTTAGES, SOUTHGATE, MIDDLESEX, 1792.

DARTFORD CHURCH, KENT, repairs, 1792.

LONDON, SURREY SQUARE, SOUTHWARK, 1792–3 (*Survey of London* xxv, 89–90).

LONDON, BLACKHEATH, THE PARAGON, PARAGON HOUSE, BRYAN HOUSE and COLONNADE HOUSE, *c.*1793–1807.

LONDON, No. 155 OLD KENT ROAD (later the Rolls Estate office) for himself, 1795.

REIGATE PRIORY, SURREY, alterations to W. front for George Mowbray, 1802 (*C. Life*, 6–13 April 1918).

SEPHTON, HENRY (*c.*1686–1756), was the leading mason and architect in Liverpool during the second quarter of the eighteenth century. His most important work was Ince Blundell Hall, for which an original drawing bearing his signature survives. This is a handsome Georgian house with a façade derived, with variations, from that of Buckingham House, London. He also designed the Court House at Halton in Cheshire in a vernacular baroque style and was the architect or builder of several churches in both Gothic and classical styles. In *c.*1726 he made plans for St. George's Church, Liverpool, which were not adopted, those of Thomas Steers being preferred [J. A. Picton, *Liverpool Municipal Records* ii, 1886, 70–1], and his alternative Gothic and classical designs, both unexecuted, for St. Mary's Church, Rochdale, 1740, are in the Lancs. R.O., DDX 1423, acc. 5336. In 1746 'Messrs. Sephton and Smith' contracted to build the spire of St. Nicholas Church, Liverpool, in accordance with designs made by Thomas Gee (*q.v.*). As a master mason Sephton was also employed at Knowsley Hall, at Gisburn Park, Yorkshire, and at the Exchange in Liverpool.

Sephton died on 2 June 1756, aged 70, and was buried at Walton, nr. Liverpool, where a tablet (destroyed by bombing during the Second World War) also commemorated his wife Esther (d. 1759) and his son Daniel, 'late of Manchester, Eminent in Carving', who died on 11 January 1759, aged 45. A fine example of the latter's work is the monument to William Wright (d. 1753) at Stockport, Cheshire.

BILLINGE CHURCH, LANCS., rebuilt 1717–18; enlarged 1907 [contract and drawings in Wigan Archives, D/DZA 13/8, *ex inf.* Mr. D. Findlay]

INCE BLUNDELL HALL, LANCS., for Robert Blundell, probably *c.*1720; enlarged 1800

See p. 1138 and 1847–50 [elevation among Everingham papers in Hull University Library, with damaged signature 'Hen[ry] S[ep]hton Invenit & Delin', ref. DDEv/13(j)] (*C. Life*, 10 April 1958).

PRESCOT CHURCH, LANCS., rebuilt tower and spire, 1729 [MS. parish books].

HALTON COURT HOUSE (now Hotel), CHESHIRE, for the Duchy of Lancaster, 1737–8 [A. Gomme, 'Four eighteenth-century buildings at Halton', *Trans. Lancs. & Cheshire Hist. Soc.* 135, 1986, 43–4].

LIVERPOOL, ST. THOMAS'S CHURCH, built 1748–50; spire removed after damage in 1822; dem. *c.*1907 [obituary of Sephton's widow in *Williamson's Liverpool Advertiser*, 12 Jan. 1759, which stated that he was 'an eminent architect and mason, who built St. Thomas's Church'].

LANCASTER, ST. MARY'S CHURCH, designed new Gothic west tower, built by William Kirkby of Lancaster, mason, 1753–4 [*V.C.H. Lancs.* viii, 24, n. 229].

SERJEANSON, THOMAS (–1656/7) was a master mason at Coventry in the early seventeenth century. In 1611 Sir Edward Pytts of Kyre Park in Worcestershire invited 'Sergianson of Coventry' to make a 'platt' for extending his house, but the latter 'did nothing' [Mrs. Baldwyn-Childe, 'The Building of Kyre Park', *The Antiquary* xxii, 1890, 26]. Subsequently Thomas Serjeanson is found repairing the spire of HOLY TRINITY CHURCH, COVENTRY, in 1623 [T. Sharp, *Illustrations of the History of Holy Trinity, Coventry*, 1818, 30]; measuring mason's work at JOYCE POOL HOUSE, WARWICK, for William Fetherston in 1634 [Warwickshire Record Office, calendar of Fetherston-Dilke papers, pp. 97–100, no. 42] (for a view of the house see B.L., Add. MS. 29264, ff. 77–8); building fortifications for Richard Greville in 1645 at either Coventry or Warwick [P.R.O., E 101/634/32]; and supervising the building of LAMPORT HALL, NORTHANTS., to the designs of John Webb in 1655 [see letters from him in Northants. C.R.O., I.C. 4968–4979]. His burial on 3 Jan. 1656/7 is recorded in the register of Holy Trinity Church, Coventry.

SERVANDONI, GIOVANNI NICCOLO (1695–1766), was born in Florence, became a pupil of the painter Pannini in Rome, and later studied architecture under G. I. Rossi. He was primarily a theatrical scene-painter, and as such worked in Portugal, France and England. He first came to London in about 1722 and was employed as scene-painter to the Italian Opera at the King's Theatre in the Haymarket. In 1724 he removed to Paris, where in 1732 he designed the façade of S. Sulpice in a manner perhaps influenced by the west front of St. Paul's Cathedral, but returned to London early in 1747 and provided the scenery for a number of productions at Covent Garden Theatre. In 1749 he designed the structure of the elaborate firework display staged in the Green Park to celebrate the Peace of Aix-la-Chapelle. This took the form of a Doric temple with flanking pavilions, ornamented with 'Frets, Gilding, Lustres, Artificial Flowers, Inscriptions, Statues, Allegorical Pictures &c', and was constructed by the Office of Ordnance. During the performance the left-hand pavilion caught fire and the agitated architect (who was notoriously irascible) so far forgot himself as to draw his sword and affront Charles Frederick (*q.v.*), then Comptroller and later Surveyor of the Ordnance, for which he was 'disarmed and taken into custody, but discharg'd the next day on asking pardon before the Duke of Cumberland'.

According to J. F. Blondel's *Architecture Françoise* ii, 1752, 37, n. *a*, Servandoni was employed by Frederick, Prince of Wales, and this is confirmed by a document in the Hartwell Sale at Sotheby's on 8 March 1939 (lot 667) which included a payment of £100 by way of 'Cash Advanced to Mr. Salvadoni (*sic*) in consideration of his pains & expences in making & drawing Designs at Kew & for his attendances thereon' (1751). His principal architectural work in England was the lavish interior of the sculpture gallery at George Bubb Dodington's house at Hammersmith (then known as 'La Trappe' but later as Brandenburg House, demolished in 1822), which is illustrated as his design in *Vitruvius Britannicus* iv, 1767, pls. 28–9. He may also have been employed by Dodington's close friend Sir Francis Dashwood at West Wycombe Park, Bucks. He returned to Paris in May 1751 and, after visits to Lisbon, Dresden, Vienna and Poland, died there on 19 January 1766.

[J. Bouché, 'Servandoni', *Gazette des Beaux-Arts*, 1910, 121–46; E. Croft-Murray, *Decorative Painting in England* ii, 1970, 274–6; Walpole Soc., *Vertue Note Books* iii, 134; letters from Servandoni to Dodington in Paul Grinke's *Catalogue of Autograph Letters of Artists and Architects*, Spring 1976, No. 145; *Description of the Machine for the Fireworks*, published by the order of the Board of Ordnance, 1749; account of fireworks in *Gent's Mag.* 1749, 187, and engraving in Bodleian, Gough Maps 22, f. 34^{v}, B.L., Crace Collection, etc., reproduced in E. Walford, *Old and New London* iv, 181; L. Hautecœur, *Histoire de l'architecture classique en France* iii, 1950,

266–9; Clare Hornsby, 'Antiquarian Extravagance at Hammersmith: Sculpture Gallery of George Bubb Dodington', *Apollo*, Dec. 1991; G. Jackson-Stops, *An English Arcadia*, National Trust 1991, 93–4, for designs for buildings at W. Wycombe Park attributed to Servandoni.]

SEWARD, HENRY HAKE (1778–1848), was articled to Sir John Soane in May 1794. He remained in Soane's office for some time after the expiration of his articles, leaving in 1808 to become District Surveyor of the parishes of St. Martin-in-the-Fields and St. Anne Soho. In 1810 he entered into partnership with George Byfield (*q.v.*), in consequence of whose ill-health he was appointed joint surveyor with him of the estates of the Dean and Chapter of Westminster. In the same year he was appointed Clerk of the Works at Greenwich Hospital, and in 1821 succeeded John Yenn as Surveyor to the Hospital. It was in this capacity that he designed four new churches in the parish of Simonburn in Northumberland on its division in 1811, the Governors of Greenwich Hospital being the patrons and lords of the manor. On the death of George Byfield in 1813, he took Francis Edwards as his assistant. In 1823, on the retirement of Robert Browne, he was appointed Assistant Surveyor-General and Cashier of the Office of Works, following which he resigned the surveyorship of Greenwich Hospital and relinquished general practice. On the amalgamation of the Works with the Department of Woods and Forests in 1832, Seward became first Surveyor of Works and Buildings. He resigned on account of ill-health in 1844, and died on 19 January 1848, aged 70. He exhibited at the Royal Academy between 1797 and 1823. George Aitchison, R. Osborne and H. J. Underwood were pupils. Seward's career was largely devoted to his official duties, and he had neither the opportunity nor perhaps the ability to design a building of distinction. His four Northumbrian churches are small Gothic buildings of the simplest kind.

[*A.P.S.D.*; A. T. Bolton, *The Works of Sir John Soane*, 1924, Appendix C, p. xlii; *History of the King's Works* vi; MS. Memoir by Francis Edwards in R.I.B.A. Library.]

NEW COURT, LUGWARDINE, HEREFS., reconstructed for the Revd. J. Lilly, 1808–10, Gothic [exhib. at R.A. 1810; drawings in R.I.B.A. Coll.].

EAST WITTON CHURCH, YORKS. (N.R.), 1809–12, Gothic; altered 1872 [exhib. at R.A. 1812].

GREENWICH HOSPITAL, KENT, rebuilt west façade of King Charles Block, in association with John Yenn, 1811–14 [Hasted's *History of Kent: Hundred of Blackheath*, ed. Drake, 1886, 69].

TINGRITH MANOR, BEDS., additions and alterations for Robert Trevor, 1814; dem. [Beds. C.R.O., Z 133/7].

STEVENTON VICARAGE, BERKS., design for the Dean and Chapter of Westminster, 1815 [W.A.M., P. 743].

WARK-ON-TYNE CHURCH and parsonage, NORTHUMBERLAND, 1815–17, Gothic [exhib. at R.A. 1816] (E. Mackenzie, *Northumberland* i, 1825, 244).

GREYSTEAD CHURCH and parsonage, NORTHUMBERLAND, 1815–17, Gothic [exhib. at R.A. 1816].

HUMSHAUGH CHURCH and parsonage, NORTHUMBERLAND, 1815–17, Gothic [exhib. at R.A. 1816].

THORNEYBURN CHURCH and parsonage, NORTHUMBERLAND, 1815–17, Gothic [one of the four new churches built for the Governors of Greenwich Hospital].

attributed: BELLINGHAM RECTORY, NORTHUMBERLAND, for the Governors of Greenwich Hospital, 1818 [stylistic attribution].

LONDON, ST. MARTIN'S ALMSHOUSES, BAYHAM STREET, CAMDEN TOWN, 1818 [J. McMaster, *St. Martin-in-the-Fields*, 1916, 282].

LEDBURY PARK, HEREFS., improvements for J. Biddulph, 1818–20 [exhib. at R.A. 1820; drawings in Herefs. C.R.O., D 51/1–97].

BRISTOL, THE COUNTY GAOL, CUMBERLAND ROAD, 1819–20; dem. 1898 [exhib. at R.A. 1817, 1819].

BRISTOL, THE PUBLIC BATHS AND READING ROOM, CLIFTON HOT WELLS, 1820–2; dem. 1867 [exhib. at R.A. 1820].

SHAKESPEAR, GEORGE (–1797), was a master carpenter who also acted on occasion as an architect. He was the son of George Shakespear, a leatherseller of the parish of St. George, Hanover Square, and was apprenticed to Isaac Ware in September 1739. As a pupil of Ware he would have received an architectural training, but it is chiefly as a carpenter and builder that he figures in contemporary records. He was much employed by the Office of Works, and was for some time in partnership with John Phillips (*q.v.*). He died at his house in Ranelagh Street, Pimlico, on 28 March 1797 [*Gent's Mag.* 1797(i), 355–6; records of the Carpenters' Company, Guildhall Library MS. 4329/17].

One of Shakespear's first jobs was to act as Clerk of the Works at the Radcliffe Library in Oxford from 1745 to 1747 [*The Building Accounts of the Radcliffe Library*, ed. S. G. Gillam, Oxford Historical Soc. 1958, xv]. An annotated copy of the sale catalogue of Cannons House, Middlesex, in the Yale Center for British Art shows that in 1747 Shakespear was the purchaser of the fittings of the Chapel. As in the following year these were reused at FAWLEY CHURCH, BUCKS., it is probable that Shakespear was the builder employed to remodel the church under the direction of the amateur architect John Freeman (*q.v.*), who was the patron of the living. Together with John Phillips Shakespear was responsible for the splendid joinery in the library of CHRIST CHURCH, OXFORD (1752–62), and for rebuilding ALSCOT HOUSE, WARWICKS., for James West in the Gothic style, apparently to their own designs (above, p. 751). Between 1770 and 1781 he was responsible for designing and executing considerable alterations to the interior of COBHAM HALL, KENT, for the 3rd Earl of Darnley, including the redecoration in neo-classical style of the Gilt Hall [John Cornforth in *C. Life*, 3–10 March 1983, citing documents in Kent Archives Office]. In 1776 he wrote to Lord Darnley to say that he would be behindhand with his work because he was engaged on 'business' for the Earl of Thanet, Lord Hardwicke, the Earl of Plymouth, Lord Beauchamp, 'Mr. Heron's office building', the Bishop of Bath and Wells, Lord Shelburne, Mrs. Cornwallis and Messrs. Brookes & Co. of St. James's Street (for whom he was presumably building Brooks's Club to the designs of Henry Holland). In 1779 he undertook to execute Kenton Couse's plans for restoring the west wing of THE QUEEN'S COLLEGE, OXFORD, after it had been gutted by fire [*Letters of Radcliffe and James*, ed. Evans, Oxford Historical Soc. 1888, 270–2]. In the course of the same year he was asked to give a plan and estimate for rebuilding the nave of WEST MALLING CHURCH. KENT, but declined [MS. Vestry Minutes]. In 1784 he was employed by the Dowager Countess Spencer to remodel HOLYWELL HOUSE, ST. ALBANS, HERTS., under the direction of Lords Harcourt and Camelford, giving it a new Gothick E. front [Frances Harris, 'Holywell House: a Gothic villa at St. Albans', *British Library Jnl.* 12, 1986]. The house was demolished in 1837, but the Gothic front is illustrated in Britton & Brayley's *Beauties of England and Wales* vii, 1808, 108.

SHARMAN, JOHN, was a builder in the Peterborough area in the mid-eighteenth century. In 1757 the Corporation of Wisbech, Camb., resolved to build a stone bridge to a design submitted by George Swaine and John Sharman provided that James Burrough (*q.v.*) was satisfied that it was 'likely to stand and answer the purposes of a bridge' [N. Walker & T. Craddock, *History of Wisbech and the Fens*, 1849, 419]. The bridge was erected in 1758–9, but demolished in 1855. An engraving of it was published in 1761, with the inscription 'J. Sharman, Archt. and G. Swain, Builders' (B.L., *King's Maps* viii, 79*d*). Among the papers from Milton House, nr. Peterborough, in the Northamptonshire Record Office, are estimates by J. Sharman submitted in 1747 for building a new house to the alternative designs of Henry Flitcroft and Matthew Brettingham. Edward Sharman of Peterborough, 'statuary and mason', who died on 9 July 1805, aged 32, was probably his son [*Gent's Mag.* 1805 (ii), 686].

SHARP, RICHARD HEY (1793–1853), was the eldest son of Richard Sharp, a member of a Yorkshire family with property at Gildersome, nr. Bradford. He became a pupil of Peter Atkinson, junior, at York. In 1816–19 he travelled through France to Rome, Naples and Greece. In Paris he met Joseph Woods (*q.v.*), who was to be his travelling companion for much of the journey. On his return he exhibited two drawings of Roman antiquities at the Royal Academy. His former master Atkinson now took him into partnership, and together they designed and built several Gothic churches for the Church Building Commissioners (listed at p. 82). In addition Sharp collaborated with William Wilkins in the erection of the Greek Revival York Museum in 1827–30. According to the *Library of the Fine Arts* 'the exterior design was made by Mr. Wilkins, but most of the internal arrangements were adopted from plans prepared in 1825 by Mr. Sharp, though subsequently much enlarged and improved'. In 1827 Sharp left Atkinson's office to start practice on his own at 18 St. Saviour Gate, assisted by his younger brother Samuel Sharp, whom he took into partnership in 1831. In about 1830 they were commissioned to prepare a scheme for the development of the Valley at Scarborough, of which a print was published in 1832 (*C. Life*, 18 April 1974, 942, fig. 5). Some features of this, including the Crescent, were carried out during the next twenty years. Sharp had already designed the Museum in the form of a small domed rotunda in 1828. Another notable building was the 'Norman' church at Roecliffe, whose nave is vaulted in stone in a remarkably authentic manner.

Sharp died at Heyworth Moor on 25 February 1853, aged 59. His unexecuted designs for the Public Assembly Rooms in Kingston Square, Hull (1827) are in the Gott Collection in Wakefield Museum (vol. 7, ff. 1–7).

[*A.P.S.D.*; John James, *History of Bradford*, 1841, 421; *York Chronicle*, 29 July 1831; J. Woods, *Letters of an Architect*, 1828, i, 137, ii, 211, 287, 294; *Gent's Mag.* 1853 (i), 452.]

YORK, THE MUSEUM, in collaboration with William Wilkins, 1827–30 [*Gent's Mag.* 1827 (ii), 457; *Library of the Fine Arts* i, 1831, 172–3].

SCARBOROUGH, YORKS. (N.R.), THE ROTUNDA MUSEUM, 1828–30; wings added 1860 [*Theakston's Guide to Scarborough*, 1845, 71; F. D. Klingender, 'Scarborough Museum', *Arch. Rev.* Dec. 1951].

SCARBOROUGH, YORKS. (N.R.), TRINITY HOUSE, ST. SEPULCHRE STREET, 1832–3 [*Theakston's Guide to Scarborough*, 1845, 74].

CRAMBE VICARAGE, YORKS. (N.R.), rebuilt 1836 [Borthwick Institute, York, MGA 1836/3].

BRADFORD, YORKS, (W.R.), HOLY TRINITY CHURCH, rebuilt 1836–7, Gothic; chancel added 1883 [John Ayers, *Architecture in Bradford*, 1973, 74].

BRADFORD, YORKS. (W.R.), ST. JOHN'S CHURCH, MANCHESTER ROAD, 1838–9, Gothic; dem. *c.*1873 [*Bradford Observer*, 13 Sept. 1838, *ex inf.* Mr. D. Griffiths].

HOWDEN CHURCH, YORKS. (E.R.), repairs after damage by storm, 1839 [*Bradford Observer*, 28 Feb. 1839, *ex inf.* Mr. D. Griffiths].

BOWLING CHURCH, YORKS. (W.R.), 1840–2, Gothic [W. Cudworth, *Bolton and Bowling*, 1891, 274].

KIRBY UNDERDALE RECTORY, YORKS. (E.R.), alterations, 1843 [Borthwick Institute, York, MGA 1843/4].

ROECLIFFE CHURCH, YORKS. (W.R.), 1843–4, Norman [*Builder* ii, 1844, 598].

YORK, ST. SAVIOUR'S CHURCH, largely rebuilt 1844–5, Gothic [*Yorkshire Gazette*, 3 and 31 May 1845; drawings in Diocesan Faculty Register 1816–58, pp. 485–90, *ex inf.* Dr. E. A. Gee].

HORBURY NATIONAL SCHOOL, YORKS. (W.R.), 1845, Gothic [*Civil Engineer and Architect's Jnl.* viii, 1845, 307].

YORK, ST. SAVIOUR'S CHURCH, monument to the Revd. John Graham, 1846 [*Builder* iv, 1846, 212].

SHARP, SAMUEL (1808–1874), was a younger brother of Richard Hey Sharp and, like him, began his architectural career in the office of Peter Atkinson, junior, at York. In 1831 he was taken into partnership by his brother, but later practised in Leeds, where he died in 1874, aged 66. In 1838 he was awarded the Soane Medal of the R.I.B.A. for a restoration drawing of St. Mary's Abbey at York, and in 1839 another with a gold rim for drawings of Sheriff Hutton Castle (now in the R.I.B.A. Drawings Collection). His only independent architectural work appears to have been the classical church of ST. JAMES at THORNES, nr. WAKEFIELD, 1829–31. [*A.P.S.D.*; John James, *History of Bradford*, 1841, 421; W. Cudworth, *Rambles round Horton*, Bradford 1886, 132; Port, 170–1; *York Chronicle*, 29 July 1831; *Gent's Mag.* 1838 (i), 299, 528–9, 1839 (i), 193, 296.]

SHAW, JOHN (1776–1832), was born at Bexley, Kent, on 10 March 1776. He was apprenticed to George Gwilt the elder in 1790 and commenced practice in 1798. He exhibited at the Royal Academy from 1799 onwards.

In 1803 Shaw was appointed surveyor to the Eyre estate in St. John's Wood and in 1803 he exhibited at the Academy an ambitious town-planning project for its development by the construction of a 'British Circus' consisting of detached and semi-detached houses with gardens, arranged in two circles on either side of a circular road one mile in circumference. This scheme, of which Shaw was not the originator (a version of it had already been engraved in 1794, when he was still in his pupilage) was not carried out, but Shaw and his son were to be pioneers in the development of suburbs of semi-detached houses set in irregularly aligned roads rather than of terraced houses in grids of streets.

In 1816 Shaw succeeded James Lewis as architect and surveyor of Christ's Hospital, London, to which he made extensive additions costing about £30,000. They were in the Gothic style which Shaw also used with picturesque effect in the church of St. Dunstan, Fleet Street, at Ilam Hall and in his alterations to Newstead Abbey for Col. Wildman.[1]

Shaw was also architect to the trustees of Ramsgate harbour, where he designed the clockhouse and the obelisk to commemorate the visit of King George IV in 1821. He was extensively employed in the valuation of property in London for street improvements, and was architect to the Phoenix Assurance Company. He was a member of the Architects' Club, a Fellow of the Royal and Linnean Societies and of the Society of Antiquaries. He died suddenly at Ramsgate on 30 July 1832, and was buried at Bexley. He left

[1] It is natural to suppose that Shaw was the 'modern Goth . . . call'd an architect' whose 'restoration' of a country house called the Abbey was so savagely satirized by Byron (the former owner of Newstead) in *Don Juan*, canto xvi, 58, but Dr. Rosalys Coope tells me that this is unlikely, as the reports of Col. Wildman's alterations that reached Byron were favourable.

six sons and two daughters. His practice was continued by his eldest son, John Shaw (*q.v.*). His youngest son, Thomas Budge Shaw, became professor of English literature at St. Petersburg. T. Johnson of Lichfield (1794–1865) was in his office after leaving that of Joseph Potter. [*A.P.S.D.*; *D.N.B.*; John Summerson, *Georgian London*, 1945, 158–9; F. M. L. Thompson, *Hampstead*, 1974, 66.]

?LITTLE BARFORD RECTORY, BEDS., 1799 [Lincs. R.O., MGA 24, drawings made in 1799 by John Shaw of Bunhill Row, whereas from 1799 onwards the architect was living at 25, Great James Street, Bedford Row].

Villa 'intended to be built in Surrey for G. Whitfield', exhibited at R.A. 1799.

PUTNEY HILL, SURREY, 'a suite of rooms lately erected', exhibited at R.A. 1801.

PUTNEY HILL, SURREY, villa for William Leader, 1804 [exhib. at R.A. 1804].

FLAMBARDS, HARROW, MIDDLESEX, 'proposed alterations' for 1st Lord Northwick, exhibited at R.A. 1806.

LONDON, THE RUSSELL INSTITUTION, GREAT CORAM STREET, reroofed *c.*1812; dem. [*Builder* xiv, 1856, 72].

LAMORBEY PARK, SIDCUP, KENT, alterations for John Malcolm, after 1812 [*A.P.S.D.*].

BEAUDESERT, STAFFS., lodge at Lichfield entrance to park for 2nd Earl of Uxbridge, 1814 [exhib. at R.A. 1814].

BLENDON HALL, nr. BEXLEY, KENT, remodelled for John Smith, *c.*1815, Gothic; dem. 1934 [exhib. at R.A. 1815].

RAMSGATE, KENT, CLOCK-HOUSE, and steps called 'Jacob's ladder', *c.*1815; obelisk to commemorate visit of King George IV, 1821–2 [*A.P.S.D.*].

HEATH HOUSE, TEAN, STAFFS., lodge for John Philips, *c.*1816 [exhib, at R.A. 1816].

SPURN HEAD LIGHTHOUSE, YORKS. (E.R.), 1816; dem. *c.*1830 [G. de Boer, *A History of the Spurn Lighthouses*, E. Yorks. Local History Soc. 1968, 63].

CHILHAM CASTLE, KENT, alterations for James B. Wildman, after 1816 [*A.P.S.D.*].

NEWSTEAD ABBEY, NOTTS., remodelled for Col. Thomas Wildman, 1818–*c.*1830, Gothic [exhib. at R.A. 1820; R.I.B.A.D.; Gervase Jackson-Stops in *C. Life*, 9, 16 May 1974].

ROOKSNEST (now Croome House), nr. GODSTONE, SURREY, for C.H. Turner, *c.*1818 [*A.P.S.D.*].

LONDON, UXBRIDGE HOUSE, stables in Boyle Street for 1st Marquess of Anglesey, 1819 [Hermione Hobhouse, *Thomas Cubitt*, 1971, 25].

CRESSWELL HALL, NORTHUMBERLAND, for A. J. Baker Cresswell, 1820–4; dem. 1931 [*A.P.S.D.*]. Mackenzie, *Northumberland* ii, 1825, 127, says the house was erected 'under the superintendence of Mr. Green of Newcastle', but Shaw's name was cut in the masonry (N. Lloyd, *The English House*, 1931, 270, fig. 294).

LONDON, CHRIST'S HOSPITAL, NEWGATE STREET, the Infirmary and west side of quadrangle, 1820–2; the Great Hall (Gothic), 1825–9; the Mathematical and Grammar Schools, 1832; all dem. 1902 [*A.P.S.D.*] (Britton & Pugin, *The Public Buildings of London* ii, 1828, 187–92, for plan and elevation of Hall, for the interior see *London Interiors*, 1841–4).

ILAM HALL, STAFFS., for J. Watts Russell, 1821–6, Gothic; partly dem. *c.*1935 [R.I.B.A.D.; *A.P.S.D.*] (F. O. Morris, *Picturesque Views of Seats* i, 1880, 41).

ILAM CHURCH, STAFFS., octagonal Gothic funerary chapel for J. Watts Russell, built under a Faculty dated 19 Oct. 1819 [signed drawing dated 1819 in Lichfield Diocesan Records, Lichfield Joint Record Office].

DUNHAM MASSEY HALL, CHESHIRE, alterations for 6th Earl of Stamford, 1822 [*A.P.S.D.*].

LEYTON CHURCH, ESSEX, addition of south aisle and vestry, 1822 [J. Kennedy, *History of the Parish of Leyton*, 1894, 62].

THRUMPTON HALL, NOTTS., work (probably including library and Gothic gateways) for John Emerton Wescomb, *c.*1825 [letter in Manchester Central Library (M6/A1, p. 51) dated 19 April 1825 from the builder James Trubshaw, mentioning an appointment with Shaw at Thrumpton].

DUNSTON VICARAGE, LINCS., 1827–8 [Bodleian Library, records of Queen Anne's Bounty].

PARKHURST, BEXLEY, KENT, alterations for himself, 1831, Elizabethan style; dem. 1955 [C. Greenwood, *Epitome of County History: Kent*, 1838, 47].

LONDON, ST. DUNSTAN'S CHURCH, FLEET STREET, 1831–3, Gothic; completed by his son [Britton & Pugin, *The Public Buildings of London*, ed. Leeds, i, 1838, 187–93].

SHAW, JOHN (1803–1870), born in London on 17 May 1803, was the son and pupil of John Shaw (*q.v.*), whom he succeeded in 1832 as architect of Christ's Hospital. In about 1825 he also became surveyor to Eton College, for whom he designed the Tudor Gothic buildings in Weston's Yard at Eton and developed their Chalcots estate near Chalk Farm in Hampstead with semi-detached villas.

Shaw's employment by the Church Building Commissioners to design a new church in London led him to write *A Letter on Ecclesiastical Architecture as applicable to Modern Churches: addressed to the Lord Bishop of*

London, 1839, in which he advocated the use of the Romanesque style as most practical and economical for the purpose. It was, however, as a designer of buildings in a revived 'Renaissance' style that Shaw was most successful and original. His reputation as a designer in the manner of Wren was remarked on by the *Builder* as early as 1843, and his Wellington College was a *tour de force* of revived Anglo-French baroque. Like his father, the younger Shaw was much engaged in valuations, and was one of the official referees under the Metropolitan Buildings Act of 1844. He was a fellow of the R.I.B.A. He died on 9 July 1870, and was buried at Kensal Green. [*A.P.S.D.*; *D.N.B.*]

BOGNOR REGIS, SUSSEX, SUDLEY LODGE, 1827, exhibited at the R.A. as the 'first of a series of detached houses to be built on the property of the Earl of Arran'.

LONDON, CHRIST'S HOSPITAL, NEWGATE STREET, completed the Grammar Schools to his father's design, 1832, and designed the east range of dormitories, 1836, the entrance from Newgate Street, 1836, and the baths, 1868–9; all dem. 1902 [*A.P.S.D.*].

LONDON, LAW LIFE ASSURANCE OFFICE, No. 187 FLEET STREET, 1834, Jacobean [exhib. at R.A. 1833].

LONDON, HOLY TRINITY CHURCH, GOUGH SQUARE, 1837–8, Romanesque; altered 1873; dem. 1913 [G. Godwin, *The Churches of London* ii, 1839, with plate].

LONDON, CHRIST CHURCH, WATNEY STREET, STEPNEY, 1840–1, Romanesque; apse 1870; dem. after war damage 1940–1 [Port, 156].

HILMARTON CHURCH, WILTS., rebuilt west tower, 1840, Gothic [*Wiltshire Arch. Mag.* xxxvii, 1911–12, 431].

WALTHAMSTOW, ESSEX, ST. PETER'S CHURCH, 1840, Romanesque; much altered [*Christian Guardian*, 1840, 477; *V.C.H. Essex* vi, 292].

LONDON, CHALCOTS ESTATE, CHALK FARM, HAMPSTEAD, laid out Adelaide Road, Provost Road, and Eton College Road, etc., for Eton College, 1840–50 [D. J. Olsen in *The Victorian City*, ed. H. J. Dyos & M. Wolff, 1973, i, 348–52 and pls. 285–6].

ETON COLLEGE, BUCKS., altar, altar-rails and pulpit in Chapel, 1842; new buildings in Weston's Yard, 1844–6, Tudor Gothic [Willis & Clark, i, 450, 463; Eton College archives; R.I.B.A.D.].

DEPTFORD, KENT, ROYAL NAVAL COLLEGE (now Goldsmiths' College), 1843–4, Renaissance style; CHAPEL, 1853 [*Builder* i, 1843, 218–19; *A.P.S.D.*].

STOKE POGES CHURCH, BUCKS., alterations (including rebuilding of chancel arch), 1844–5 [parish records].

BOURNE PARK, KENT, repairs and internal alterations for Matthew Bell, 1848–9 [H. A. Tipping in *C. Life*, 6, 13 May 1922] (*C. Life*, 10, 17 Nov. 1944).

LONDON, ST. DUNSTAN'S PAROCHIAL SCHOOL, FETTER LANE, 1849, Jacobean [*A.P.S.D.*].

LONDON, ST. BRIDE'S CHURCH, FLEET STREET, 'repaired, painted, marbled and gilded' the interior, 1852; gutted 1940 [*Builder* x, 1852, 397].

COWBRIDGE HOUSE, nr. MALMESBURY, WILTS., for S. B. Brooke, 1852–3, French Renaissance style; dem. 1980 [signed lithograph dated 1853].

LONDON, LONDON AND PROVINCIAL LAW LIFE ASSURANCE OFFICE, No. 21 FLEET STREET, 1853–5, 'Renaissance' style [*Builder* xiii, 1855, 474].

WELLINGTON COLLEGE, SANDHURST, BERKS., 1855–9, 'Renaissance' style [*Builder* xiv, 1856, 86–7; T. L. Donaldson, *Handbook of Specifications*, 1860, 549–636] (*C. Life*, 18 June 1959).

SHELTON, THEOPHILUS (–1717), is said to have been 'the son of a clergyman in one of the eastern counties', but established himself at Wakefield in Yorkshire and lived, or owned property, in the neighbouring villages of Heath and Darrington.[1] He appears to have been a lawyer by profession, for he was Clerk of the Peace for the West Riding and in 1704 became the first Registrar of Deeds for the same County. He married Margaret, daughter of the Revd. Joshua Witton, rector of Thornhill, and died at Nottingham in November 1717 [J. W. Walker, *Wakefield, its History and People* ii, 1939, 497–8; *Surtees Soc.* lxxvii, 1883, 127–8; will at Borthwick Institute, York]. His son Theophilus was a Fellow of Magdalene College, Cambridge, and in 1715 a successful applicant for the post of chaplain to the Duke of Chandos [Venn, *Alumni Cantabrigienses*, part I, iv, 1927, 58; C. H. & M. I. Baker, *James Brydges, Duke of Chandos*, 1949, 126].

Shelton's skill as an architect is attested by several contemporary records. In 1699 he gave Richard Beaumont a design for a garden-house to be built at WHITLEY BEAUMONT, YORKS. (W.R.) [W. Yorks. Archives, Kirklees, WBM/8]. When Sir George Tempest rebuilt

[1] He bought Heath (formerly Eshald) Hall in 1694, and he probably built and designed the house that forms the nucleus of the existing Hall (cf. Ivan & Elizabeth Hall, *Heath*, 1975, 14). He may also have designed Lupset Hall, nr. Wakefield, for his brother-in-law Richard Witton.

TONG HALL, YORKS. (W.R.), in 1700–2 he recorded in an inscription that it was erected 'Domini Theophili Sheltoni de Heath Ingenio Prudentiaque vere Architectonica' [Thoresby's *Ducatus Leodiensis*, ed. Whitaker, 1816, 204]. An original elevation of the house, perhaps in Shelton's hand, is in the muniment room at Nostell Priory. In about 1710 the Corporation of Pontefract proposed to build a cupola on the newly built tower of ST. GILES' CHURCH 'pursuant to such a modell thereof as Theophilus Shelton, Esq. shall draw for that purpose'. It is not, however, certain that it was carried out, and the tower itself was rebuilt in its present form in *c.*1789 [*The Book of Entries of the Pontefract Corporation 1653–1726*, ed. R. Holmes, Pontefract 1882, 283].

Shelton also designed the existing MARKET CROSS at BEVERLEY, a polygonal building supported by four pairs of Doric columns and surmounted by a dome and lantern, and probably designed the similar MARKET CROSS at WAKEFIELD, built in 1707 but demolished in 1866 (illustrated Walker, *op. cit.*, 475, and *C. Life*, 9 Nov. 1945, 828). In 1710 Shelton had already designed a CHARITY SCHOOL in HIGHGATE, BEVERLEY, and in July 1711 the Chamber of Beverley sent a carpenter over to Wakefield 'to consult and advice with Mr. Shelton' about building the proposed Cross. 'The draught of a new cross drawn by Mr. Shelton' was approved in September, and it was completed in 1714 [K. A. MacMahon, 'The Building of the Beverley Market Cross', *Trans. Georgian Soc. for East Yorkshire* iii (3), 1952–3].

SHEPHERD, EDWARD (–1747), was one of the most successful builder-architects of his time. According to Vertue, he began his career as a plasterer, and ornamental plasterwork is a prominent feature of his houses. He is first found in the service of James Brydges, 1st Duke of Chandos, who employed him to supervise the completion of his mansion at Cannons in 1723–5, and for whom he soon afterwards built two houses on the north side of Cavendish Square in place of the mansion which the Duke originally intended to erect on that site. He was also in charge of the Duke's building operations at Bridgwater and Bath, though, except in one or two cases, he does not seem to have been responsible for the designs executed by the local master builders; and he carried out repairs to the duke's property in Scotland Yard and at Shaw House in Berkshire. In 1730, when he was, with Gibbs and Flitcroft, one of the candidates for rebuilding the church of St. Giles-in-the-Fields, the *Daily Post* described him as 'that ingenious architect Edward Shepherd Esq., who built the Duke of Kent's fine house in St. James's Square, the Earls of Thanet's and Albemarle's in Grosvenor Square, and many other magnificent Buildings for his Grace the Duke of Chandos and other Persons of Quality and Distinction'.

In 1735 Shepherd engaged in a successful speculation of his own by building Shepherd's Market and the adjoining streets on the site of the ancient fairground in Mayfair. The Market House consisted of two stories, the lower containing butchers' shops, while the upper was used as a theatre in fairtime. In March 1738 Shepherd obtained permission to hold a market for live cattle here, and at the time of his death he was stated to be the owner both of the market itself and of 'many other buildings about Mayfair'. He lived first in Brook Street and then in a small house in Curzon Street on the site of the present Crewe House. Shepherd died in October 1747. In his will, dated 13 December 1746, he left the Shepherd's Market estate to his wife Elizabeth, who, as his executrix, was instructed to spend £300 in building an almshouse for ten poor decayed housekeepers of the parish of St. George, Hanover Square. It was to be built 'upon the ground that the Lease belongs to Shepherd's Market', in accordance with a 'Plan and Elevation drawn and signed by me'. He also left his silver watch and an annuity of £50 to his brother, John Shepherd.

[*A.P.S.D.*; Walpole Society, *Vertue Note Books* iii, 51; C. H. & M. I. Collins Baker, *James Brydges, Duke of Chandos*, 1949, *passim; Gent's Mag.* viii, 164, xvii, 497, xx, 40, lxxxvi, 228; *Daily Post*, 31 Dec. 1730, 4 Feb. 1731; E. B. Chancellor, *The Private Palaces of London*, 1908, 222; P.R.O., C 105/32, bundle 1; P.C.C. 266 POTTER.]

LONDON

CAVENDISH SQUARE, designed and built the two end houses on the north side for the Duke of Chandos, 1724–8; dem. [Baker, *Duke of Chandos*, 1949, 276–7; J. Summerson, *Georgian London*, 1945, 92, pl. xvi].

BROOK STREET, No. 66, built as a speculation *c.*1725 and fitted up for Sir Nathaniel Curzon, Bart., 1730–1; reduced in size 1823–4 [*Survey of London* xl, 4–13].

BROOK STREET, No. 72 (formerly No. 25), 1725, occupied by himself 1725–9 [*Survey of London* xl, 14–15].

ST. JAMES'S SQUARE, No. 4, for the Duke of Kent, 1726–8 [*Daily Post*, 31 Dec. 1730; copy of the joiner's contract in Notts. C.R.O., DDR 215/60, in which he is 'to be directed by Edward Shepherd surveyor'; *Survey of London* xxix, 90–1, addendum] (*Survey of London* xxx, pls. 134–9).

GROSVENOR SQUARE, Nos. 18–21 on north side, *c*.1728–30; dem. 1933–4 [*Survey of London* xl, 132–9].

GOODMAN'S FIELDS THEATRE, GREAT ALIE STREET, GOODMAN'S FIELDS, *c*.1730; dem. *c*.1746 [H. B. Wheatley & P. Cunningham, *London Past and Present* ii, 1891, 127].

COVENT GARDEN THEATRE, for John Rich, 1731–2; destroyed by fire 1808 [*Survey of London* xxxv, 71–2, 86–7].

SHEPHERD'S MARKET and adjoining streets, Mayfair, *c*.1735; dem. [*Gent's Mag*. 1747, 497].

SOUTH AUDLEY STREET, Nos. 71–75, 1736–7 [*Survey of London* xl, 304–15].

attributed: BRUTON STREET, No. 17, built by his brother as a speculation 1736–41; dem. 1937 [V. Belcher in *London Topographical Record* xxiv, 1980, 81–92].

ELSEWHERE

CANNONS HOUSE, MIDDLESEX, supervised completion for 1st Duke of Chandos, 1723–5; dem. 1747 [Baker, *Duke of Chandos*, 1949, 146, 148–9].

GREAT STANMORE RECTORY, MIDDLESEX, for 1st Duke of Chandos, 1725 [Baker, *Duke of Chandos*, 1949, 280].

BOREHAM HOUSE, ESSEX, supervised building for Benjamin Hoare, 1727–8, probably executing designs by Henry Flitcroft (*q.v.*) (*C. Life*, 11 July 1914).

SHAW HOUSE, NEWBURY, BERKS., repairs and internal decorations for 1st Duke of Chandos, 1730 [Baker, *Duke of Chandos*, 1949, 369–70].

GREAT (WEST) LODGE, ENFIELD CHASE, MIDDLESEX, remodelled for 1st Duke of Chandos, 1730–2; dem. 1832 [Baker, *Duke of Chandos*, 1949, 387–9].

FLITTON CHURCH, BEDS., monuments to Lady Amabel de Grey (d. 1727), wife of John Campbell, afterwards 3rd Earl of Breadalbane, and to Henry de Grey, Duke of Kent (d. 1740). The Breadalbane papers [S.R.O., GD 112/21/77] show that the former monument was designed by Shepherd and set up in 1739. The latter is signed 'Edwd. Shepherd Arch[t].'.

HAMPDEN HOUSE, GREAT HAMPDEN, BUCKS., surveyed works for John Hampden, 1743–6, in particular the curved screen-walls at each end of the garden front [Bucks. Record Office, Hampden papers, day-books 1743–6].

PETERSHAM LODGE, SURREY, added wings with octagonal terminations for 1st Earl of Harrington, *c*.1740; dem. *c*.1835 [Walpole, *Anecdotes of Painting*, ed. Wornum, iii, 1862, 776].

SHEPERD, JOHN, architect of York, was among the subscribers to Peter Nicholson's *Architectural Dictionary* in 1819. He was presumably the 'J. Shepherd' who in 1816 provided Capt. John Campbell with plans and specifications for CARSE HOUSE, ARGYLLSHIRE, a 'two storied house of suburban character' that was eventually built, with modifications, in 1828 [R.C.A.M., *Argyllshire* 7, 326].

SHEPHERD, or **SHEPPERD,** RICHARD (–1673), belonged to a family of masons in South Derbyshire, members of which lived at Ingleby and Hartshorne, two villages near Repton. There was a quarry at Hartshorne which they presumably worked. In 1629–31 part of MELBOURNE HALL was rebuilt by Richard Shepherd for Sir John Coke with stone from Hartshorne [accounts at Melbourne, *ex inf*. Mr. Philip Heath], and in 1630–2 'Richard Shepperd the mason' was paid £111 12s. 4d. by the executors of Sir John Harpur for building a 'Bowl-alley house' at SWARKESTON HOUSE which can probably be identified as the existing Banqueting House [Harpur-Crewe accounts in Derbyshire C.R.O.]. In 1632 he was employed to build a stone bridge on Swinfin Moor near Derby [*ibid*.]. A mason of the same name built the remarkable Gothic church which Sir Robert Shirley began at STAUNTON HAROLD, LEICS., in 1653, for a volume of Shirley accounts in the Warwickshire Record Office shows that he was paid £60 'for finishing the battlements' in 1662, and his name RICHARD SHEPHEARD ARTIFEX is prominently carved on the inside of the parapet at the east end [J. Simmons & H. M. Colvin in *Archaeological Jnl*. cxii, 1955, 173–6]. Although it cannot be proved that the mason or masons in question designed any of these buildings, it would be normal practice at this date for the master mason employed to be responsible for the design. Two masons named Richard Shepherd died in 1673, one at Ingleby, the other at Hartshorne [wills in Lichfield Joint Record Office; information from Mr. Philip Heath].

SHEPHERD, VINCENT (*c*.1750–1812), was probably the son of Thomas Shepherd, a carpenter of Alnwick in Northumberland who died in 1790 [*Surtees Soc*. 118, 314]. He was apprenticed to George Thompson of Alnwick, carpenter, in 1764 [P.R.O., Apprenticeship Registers]. He spent the greater part of his life working for the Duke of Northumberland at ALNWICK CASTLE, where he appears to have acted as resident architect. He is said to have 'united the powers of execution with those of design', and in Gothic design to have been 'without a rival in the county of Northumberland'. Although the principal Gothic rooms in the Castle were designed by Robert & James Adam, Shepherd was no doubt responsible for their execution. In 1781 he reconstructed the chancel of ALNWICK CHURCH in the Gothic style, giving it a 'fan-vaulted' plaster ceiling and a screen of Gothic 'trellis-work' (all destroyed by Salvin in 1863, but illustrated in *Proceedings of the Society of Antiquaries of Newcastle* iii, 1867, 74), and in 1796 he designed a castellated building called 'Mount Athelstan' in the park at RODDAM HALL, NORTHUMBERLAND [drawing at Roddam]. This has been demolished, but the castellated stables may well be Shepherd's design. Shepherd died at Alnwick in May 1812, aged 62 [*Gent's Mag.* 1812 (i), 601].

SHEPPERD, RICHARD, see SHEPHERD, RICHARD.

SHERLOCK, JOHN, junior, was a carpenter of Boston in Lincolnshire. In 1715 he and his father were among the 'able and experienced workmen' who estimated the value of the damage caused by a fire in Spalding [E. H. Gooch, *History of Spalding*, 1940, 264]. The 'Geometrical Plan & South prospect of St. Botolph's att Boston Taken and Drawn by John Sherlock Junr. Carpenter of Boston 1711' is in the Bodleian Library, Gough Maps 16, f. 26, and drawings by him after Scamozzi and Palladio are in Gough Maps 230, ff. 105, 340.

SHIRLEY, THOMAS, apparently a joiner by trade, appears to have acted as architect or surveyor of works carried out simultaneously in 1718–19 at two houses in Co. Durham, RAVENSWORTH CASTLE, which was partly rebuilt for Sir Henry Riddell, Bart., and NEWTON HALL, which was rebuilt for his son John, who had taken the surname of Bright [letters in Sheffield Archives, WWM/Br 173(7) and 174(2,4), *ex inf.* Mr. R. Hewlings] (Ravensworth was rebuilt from 1808 onwards and dem. in 1952–3, Newton Hall in 1926). In 1720–6 'Mr. Shirley' received payments from the Bowes family in connection with the remodelling of STREATLAM CASTLE, CO. DURHAM (dem. 1927; *C. Life*, 18 Dec. 1915), which suggests that he may have been the person responsible for its transformation into a grand baroque mansion [Durham C.R.O., Strathmore Papers, Box 311, D/St 279/9, 263/152(iii), 263/957, *ex inf.* Mr. Hewlings]. He may have been the Thomas Shirley who, in conjunction with Kenton Couse (*q.v.*), surveyed the Bishop of Durham's castles in 1750 and supervised the subsequent repairs [B.L., Add. MS. 9815].

SHIRLEY, WASHINGTON, 5TH EARL FERRERS (1722–1778), was a nephew of the 3rd Earl Ferrers and in 1760 succeeded his brother as 5th Earl. He was in the Navy and rose to the rank of Vice-Admiral. His interests included astronomy and shipbuilding. In 1761 he was elected a Fellow of the Royal Society, and in 1775 he was an honorary exhibitor at the Royal Academy, showing three sectional drawings of different vessels designed by himself.

Both Throsby [*Select Views in Leicestershire*, 1789, 126] and Nichols [*History of Leicestershire* iii (2), 1804, 717] state that it was to his own designs that Ferrers rebuilt STAUNTON HAROLD HALL, LEICS., in 1762–75 in what by then was a somewhat old-fashioned Palladian style (*C. Life*, 5, 12 April 1913, 24 Feb. 1950). It is probable that he also designed the ASSEMBLY ROOMS at DERBY, for he laid the first stone in March 1775, and Joseph Pickford (*q.v.*), who superintended the building (1763–5), was paid £100 for his 'time and trouble' by Ferrers' order [E. Saunders in *C. Life*, 9 Nov. 1972, 1207]. The interior was completed by Robert Adam in 1774. The building was demolished in 1971 after damage by fire, but the Palladian façade (again distinctly old-fashioned for its date) was re-erected as part of the Tramway Museum at Crich, nr. Matlock.

SHORT, WILLIAM (–1753), 'An Architect or Builder at Cirencester', was among those who, in 1751, submitted designs for building the new church of St. George at Kingswood, nr. Bristol. They were not adopted, but Short was paid 25 guineas for his trouble [Commissioners' Minutes in Bristol City Archives]. His will, proved at Gloucester on 18 June 1753, shows that he was a carpenter by trade.

SHORTESS, J—, 'Gentleman', was the author of a work entitled *Harmonic Architecture, exemplified in a Plan etc. of a Building, with four different fronts, upon an Harmonic Form or Cube, now made Octangular, Being designed for a Museum, in a retired situation of a Park or Garden*, which was published in 1741 by the 'Society of Booksellers for promoting learning'. It contains plans and elevations of a garden building externally square but internally octagonal, designed on 'harmonic' principles. There is in the Bodleian Library an engraved 'Draught of a Building erected for an Apiary in the Garden of Thomas Hayley Esq., near Erith (now Lord Baltimore's)', which bears the signature 'J. Shortis inv[t] & fecit' (Gough Maps 14, f. 10*b*).

SHOUT, ROBERT (1702–1774), of Helmsley in Yorkshire, was the founder of a large family of North Country masons and civil engineers. He was Surveyor of Bridges in the North Riding of Yorkshire east of the Hambleton Hills from 1757 to 1765 and designed and built several fine bridges, including those at Newsham, nr. Malton, 1752–3, Scawton, nr. Rievaulx, 1755–7, and Egton, in Eskdale, 1760–1. In 1749–53 he designed and built ELEMORE HALL, CO. DURHAM, for George Baker in an individual and rather old-fashioned blend of baroque and Palladian [J. Gosden, 'Elemore Hall transformed 1749–53', *Trans. Architectural & Archaeological Soc. of Durham & Northumberland*, N.S. 6, 1982].

Robert's son Robert Shout, jr. (1743–97), of Helmsley, also designed and built bridges, e.g. at Whitby, 1765–8, Welburn, 1768–9, and Sinnington, 1768–9. From 1781 to 1795 he was harbour engineer of Sunderland, Co. Durham, where he died in March 1797, aged 64. In 1788 he made a design for a stone bridge of large span over the River Wear at Sunderland. It was not built, but Shout's design is in Sir John Soane's Museum (Portfolio 3, nos. 60–2) [*A.P.S.D.*; *Antiquities of Sunderland* xiii, 1913, 113].

John Shout (1738–81), a younger son of Robert Shout, sr., worked at Stockton-on-Tees, where he died on 13 June 1781, aged 42. From 1780 to 1781 he was harbour engineer of Sunderland. In 1768 he built the Tuscan column in the Market Place at Stockton [T. Richmond, *Local Records of Stockton*, 1868, 74]. Matthew Shout (1774–1817), son of the younger Robert Shout, was harbour engineer at Scarborough from 1801 to 1804, and at Sunderland from 1804 to 1817 [A. W. Skempton, 'The Engineers of Sunderland Harbour', *Industrial Archaeology Review* i (2), 1977; information from Prof. Skempton and Dr. J. H. Harvey].

The relationship of William Shout (*c.*1750–1826), for many years master mason to York Minster, to the above is uncertain, but Robert Shout (*c.*1763–1843) appears to have been the son of John Shout (1738–81), a mason of Stockton-on-Tees who was a younger son of Robert Shout of Helmsley (d. 1774). Together with his brother Benjamin he moved to London, where they kept a mason's yard in Holborn in which they made funerary monuments and plaster casts. As manufacturers of the latter they were evidently well known, for in *A Letter to Maria Gisborne* (1820) the poet Shelley described Leigh Hunt's study as 'adorned with many a cast from Shout'. An album of designs by Robert Shout for monuments, chimney-pieces etc. is in the Victoria and Albert Museum. Robert, who was Master of the London Masons' Company in 1822, handed over to his son Charles Lutwyche Shout in about 1825 and died at Treherne House, Hampstead, in September 1843, aged 80. Charles Lutwyche, who died in 1855, aged 61, was the father of the architect Robert Howard Shout (1823–82), a pupil of Lewis Vulliamy whose practice, though run from London, was chiefly in the west of England [*A.P.S.D.*; *Gent's Mag.* 1843 (ii), 552, 1855 (i), 663; *Builder* xlii, 1882, 385; R. Gunnis, *Dictionary of British Sculptors*, 1968, 350–1].

SHURMUR, THOMAS MOLARD (*c.*1804–1872), of Andover, designed APPLESHAW CHURCH, HANTS., 1830–1, Gothic [I.C.B.S. and inscription in church], and altered or rebuilt BOSCOMBE RECTORY, WILTS., in 1836 [Salisbury Diocesan Records]. He subsequently lived at Hackney, and died at Prospect House, Lower Clapton, on 11 April 1872 [Principal Probate Registry, Calendar of Probates].

SIBBALD, WILLIAM (–1809), was an architect and builder of Edinburgh who held the post of Superintendent of Public Works in that city from January 1790 until his death on 29 March 1809 [Edinburgh Town Council Minutes; *Scots Mag.* lxxi, 1809, 319]. He appears to have come from Inverness, for in 1793 the Heritors of St. Cuthbert's Church, Edinburgh, chose the plan for a new manse submitted by 'William Sibbald Surveyor & Builder late of Inverness' [S.R.O., HR 152/2]. He was presumably the 'William Sibbald, mason', who became a burgess of Edinburgh in August 1794 [*Roll of Edinburgh Burgesses, 1761–1841*, Scottish Record Soc., 144]. In 1802 Sibbald was associated with Robert Reid (*q.v.*) in settling the layout of the first extension of the New Town [A. J. Youngson, *The Making of Classical Edinburgh*, 1966, 206–7]. He acted as surveyor or overseer of works for the Heriot Trust who owned the land, and was active in making surveys, laying out the new streets, etc. Though Reid was responsible for the principal elevations, Sibbald must share the credit for the successful planning of the second New Town.

In 1785 Sibbald received the premium of 10 guineas offered by the Town Council for the best design for a steeple to be added to ST. ANDREW'S CHURCH in the New Town, recently erected to the designs of the military engineer Andrew Frazer (*q.v.*). However, this steeple, as eventually built by Alexander Stevens (*q.v.*) in 1787, closely resembles one shown in the background of Zoffany's portrait of Frazer, so the latter may have had the last word in its design [*Notes on the History of St. Andrew's Church, Edinburgh*, 1884, 5; Edinburgh City Archives, Town Council Minutes 1785–7 and account of Hugh Buchan, City Chamberlain, for building the church]. The attribution to Sibbald of the steeple of Inveresk Church appears to be unfounded despite its resemblance to that of St. Andrew's (see pp. 706–7).

Sibbald designed LADY YESTER'S CHURCH, EDINBURGH, in a neo-Jacobean style at the remarkably early date of 1803 [Edinburgh Town Council Minutes, vol. 138, pp. 419–20, 24 Aug. 1803] (see contemporary illustrations in *Scots Mag.* 1805, 571 and T. H. Shepherd, *Modern Athens*, 1829, pl. 87). He also designed the flanking pavilions containing shops [*Edinburgh Evening Courant*, 2 July 1803]. In PORTOBELLO he designed the BATHS, 1805–6 [signed drawings in S.R.O., RHP 4997], and the OLD CHURCH, 1809 [*Report on the Burgh of Portobello*, 1832]. BEECHWOOD, nr. CORSTORPHINE, MIDLOTHIAN (now part of Murrayfield Hospital), was enlarged by him for Robert Dundas (afterwards 1st Baronet), *c.*1799 [Dundas papers at Comrie House, Perthshire, *ex inf.* Prof. A. A. Tait]. From his testament in the Scottish Record Office it appears that he had been in partnership with a builder named William Lumley who died in 1808 [CC 8/8/138, f. 487].

William Sibbald is often referred to as 'senior' to distinguish him from William Sibbald, junior, who was also an architect and builder, and died on 12 November 1823 [*Edinburgh Mag.* xiii, 1823, 768]. The younger Sibbald built the Bank of Scotland on the Mound to the designs of Reid & Crichton in 1802–6 [Minutes of the Bank of Scotland]. In 1805 either he or his father was associated with John Thin (*q.v.*) in an abortive design for rebuilding Falkirk Church [S.R.O., HR 139/1].

SIBLEY, ROBERT (1789–1849), was the son of a builder and surveyor (probably James Sibley of Wapping). He became a pupil of S. P. Cockerell and subsequently practised from Great Ormond Street. In 1818 he was appointed County Surveyor of Middlesex, resigning in 1828 to become District Surveyor of Clerkenwell. From 1839 onwards he was also surveyor to the Ironmongers' Company. He was a friend and admirer of Telford, and a member of the Institution of Civil Engineers, on whose Council he served. As County Surveyor he built a number of roads and bridges in Middlesex and supervised the erection of Hanwell Lunatic Asylum to the designs of William Alderson (*q.v.*). A list of buildings designed by himself which he drew up in 1828 shows that he remodelled the chapel of the MIDDLESEX HOUSE OF CORRECTION (dem. 1889) in 1825, designed BRENTFORD BRIDGE (R. Brent), 1828, and rebuilt the cheeks of CHERTSEY BRIDGE (R. Thames) in 1821; designed THE SUN BREWERY and WHARF at WAPPING, a warehouse in the London Docks and a house at 26 CITY ROAD for George Oliver, tinplate manufacturer, and several private houses, including THE FIRS, HAMPSTEAD, for Charles Bosanquet, 9 STAFFORD ROW, PIMLICO, for Grosvenor Bedford, and 10 MONTAGUE PLACE, BLOOMSBURY, for Robert Ray.

During the latter part of his life Sibley was chiefly engaged in valuation and arbitration. He died on 31 March 1849, aged 59, leaving a son, Robert Lacon Sibley, to continue his practice. [*Minutes of Proceedings of the Institution of Civil Engineers* ix, 1849–50, 101; *Builder* vii, 1849, 160; G.L. Record Office, MRO MA/AJ/1, list of buildings supplied by Sibley to the Committee of Visiting Justices of the Hanwell Lunatic Asylum in 1828.]

SIDNELL, MICHAEL, was a statuary mason working at Bristol during the second quarter of the eighteenth century. A list of monuments signed by him will be found in R. Gunnis's *Dictionary of British Sculptors*, 1968, 351. Among them is the monument to Edward Colston (d. 1721) in All Saints Church, which was designed by James Gibbs, and is illustrated in his *Book of Architecture* (1728), to which Sidnell subscribed. The figure of Colston is by Rysbrack.

Bankruptcy in 1742 [*London Magazine*, 1742, 518] may have put Sidnell out of business as a mason, but in 1742–5 he acted as surveyor of a new house at WESTBURY COURT, WESTBURY-ON-SEVERN, GLOS., for Maynard Colchester, at 3s. a day. That he made the designs is shown by his receipt for £13 9s. 'in full for surveying Drawing and attending the Building', and by his description of himself as 'Master Workeman and Architect' [account-book formerly in possession of the late Sir Francis Colchester-Wemyss]. The house was demolished soon after 1800.

SIM, CHARLES, a Perthshire builder, designed and built the very simple church at STRUAN, PERTHSHIRE, in 1828–9 [S.R.O., CH 2/430/8]. He was also responsible for WEEM MANSE, PERTHSHIRE, 1829–30 [S.R.O., HR 405/1]. In the Weem records he is said to be 'presently residing at Pitnacree' (in Logierait parish). He was probably the same person as a mason from Stanley called Charles Syme who in 1819 repaired DULL CHURCH, PERTHSHIRE, after submitting a design for a new church which was not carried out [S.R.O., HR 658/1].

SIMMONS, JOHN (–1738), a carpenter by trade, was the son of a London cooper and was a freeman of the Merchant Taylors' Company. He had a house and workshop on the Grosvenor estate at Millbank, and was one of the speculative builders who developed the Grosvenor estate in Mayfair. Between 1724 and 1725 he built the houses forming the east side of GROSVENOR SQUARE to an approximately symmetrical design for which he may have been himself responsible. He also built houses in Brook Street, Grosvenor Street and Upper Brook Street. After his death in 1738 his widow, Elizabeth, continued his business until her own death in 1755 [*Survey of London* xxxix, 23, 31, xl, *passim*]. In 1737 Simmons submitted a design for building a wooden bridge across the Thames at Westminster [P.R.O., Minutes of the Westminster Bridge Commissioners, i, f. 69].

SIMMONS, SAMUEL, of Deal, was the builder and apparently the designer of the church of ST. GEORGE at DEAL, KENT, of which he laid the foundation-stone on 21 July 1707. In 1712 John James of Greenwich was consulted as to the desirability of a parapet. He recommended 'plain mondillion eaves' instead, and the design was altered accordingly. Owing to difficulties over the carpenter's contract, due to local politics, the church was not completed until 1716 [J. Laker, *History of Deal*, 1917, 258–63].

SIMPSON, ARCHIBALD (1790–1847), was the leading architect in Aberdeen during the early nineteenth century, and the designer of many of its principal public buildings. He was the fifth and youngest son of William Simpson, a prosperous clothier of Aberdeen, where he was born in May 1790. After an education at the Grammar School he was at first placed with James Massie (*q.v.*), a local architect-builder, but in 1810 transferred to the more professional London office of Robert Lugar (*q.v.*). By April 1811 he was working for David Laing (*q.v.*), but this appears to have been only a temporary situation, and soon afterwards he made a visit to Italy of which no details are known. On his return in 1813 Simpson set up in practice in Aberdeen, a town then entering upon a period of prosperity and expansion which offered many opportunities to an able architect. John Smith (*q.v.*) was already established as the City Architect, and for the next thirty years almost every architectural commission of importance in Aberdeen went to one or the other of these two men, who often found themselves in competition. Though Smith had the advantage of his official post, Simpson was the abler designer, and contributed more to the city's architecture. He made excellent use of the local granite, and it is to the intelligent exploitation of its monumental qualities (hitherto largely neglected) that many of his buildings owe their special distinction. This is most obvious in his Greek Revival designs such as the Aberdeen Music Hall and the country house of Crimonmogate, whose faultless masonry gives them a dignity unattainable in brick or stucco. Simpson's Gothic and castellated buildings are in general less notable, but the group of Free Churches which he built in Aberdeen in 1843–4 is remarkable for the octagonal brick spire of north German derivation – an alien but architecturally effective importation into the 'granite city'. Towards the end of his life Simpson experimented with a simplified classical style of which the most interesting examples are Thainston House and Woodside Church.

Though Simpson was one of the ablest architects of his day, he appears never to have competed for public buildings in Edinburgh and elsewhere. Content with his extensive local practice, he spent the whole of a busy and prosperous professional career in Aberdeen, where he died on 23 March 1847, in his 57th year. He was unmarried and died intestate. He is said to have been a man of 'strong and indeed eccentric character', whose main recreation was music. He was a member, and in 1844 the president, of a local dining club known as the Maryculter Club. At least three portraits exist, all by his friend James Giles, R.S.A. One is in the Aberdeen Art Gallery and two are the property of Aberdeen University. There is no major collection of his drawings, many of which were in any case burned in a fire which destroyed his office in February 1826, but some are in Aberdeen Public Library. His principal pupils were Thomas Mackenzie (1814–54) and James Matthews (1820–98), who subsequently practised jointly in Elgin and Aberdeen.

The principal sources for Simpson's life and works are the obituary in *Builder* v, 1847, 217, and a series of scholarly and well-informed articles by G. M. Fraser, entitled 'Archibald Simpson, Architect, and his Times', which appeared in the *Aberdeen Weekly Journal* from 5 April to 11 Oct. 1918. See also *A.P.S.D.*, the catalogue of an exhibition of Simpson's works held in Aberdeen in 1908 (*Aberdeen Journal Notes and Queries* i, 1908, 168–9), *The Archibald Simpson Centen-*

ary Celebrations, with a memoir by W. Douglas Simpson, reprinted (with amplifications) from the *Quarterly Journal of the Royal Incorporation of Architects in Scotland*, 1947, *Archibald Simpson*, Aberdeen Civic Soc. 1978, and Malcolm Higgs, 'Archibald Simpson' in *Scottish Pioneers of the Greek Revival*, Scottish Georgian Soc. 1984.

PUBLIC BUILDINGS

ABERDEEN, THE MEDICO-CHIRURGICAL SOCIETY'S HALL (now Customs & Excise), KING STREET, 1818–20 [Fraser, v].

ABERDEEN, THE LUNATIC ASYLUM, 1819–22 (dem.), and additions, 1845–6 [Fraser, viii, xxvi].

ABERDEEN, THE COUNTY ASSEMBLY ROOMS (MUSIC HALL), 1820–2 [Fraser, vii].

ABERDEEN, THE ATHENAEUM READING ROOM, UNION STREET, 1822–3; gutted 1973 [Fraser, vi].

ABERDEEN, THE TOWN AND COUNTY BANK, 91–93 UNION STREET, 1826; dem. [plans at Clydesdale Bank, Aberdeen].

FORRES, MORAYSHIRE, ST. LAWRENCE MASONIC LODGE AND ASSEMBLY ROOMS, 1829; refronted 1899–1901 [Fraser, xi; *N.S.A.* xiii, 165].

ELGIN, MORAYSHIRE, THE ELGIN or ANDERSON INSTITUTION, 1830–3 [*N.S.A.* xiii, 9].

ABERDEEN, INFANT SCHOOL, PRINCES STREET, 1831; dem. [*Aberdeen Jnl.* 2 Feb. 1831].

FOCHABERS BRIDGE, MORAYSHIRE, timber arch to replace central spans of stone bridge over R. Spey destroyed by floods, for 5th Duke of Gordon, 1831–2; replaced by an iron bridge 1852 [Fraser, xiv; accounts in S.R.O., GD 44/53/Box 1].

ABERDEEN, THE ROYAL INFIRMARY, 1832–40, and additions, 1844 [Fraser, xv, xxiii].

ELGIN, MORAYSHIRE, THE ELGIN DISTRICT LUNATIC ASYLUM, BILBOHALL, 1833–5; enlarged 1865; dem. 1992 [minutes of the Elgin Lunacy Board, Grampian Health Board, Aberdeen, GHRB 46/1/1, *ex inf.* Mrs. E. Beaton].

ABERDEEN, DR. BELL'S SCHOOL, FREDERICK STREET, 1834–5; dem. [Fraser, xvii].

ABERDEEN, MARISCHAL COLLEGE, 1837–44, Tudor Gothic; new front, etc., by Marshall Mackenzie 1903–6 [Fraser, xvii–xviii].

ABERDEEN, MRS. ELMSLIE'S INSTITUTION (later GIRLS' HIGH SCHOOL), ALBYN PLACE, 1838–40 [Fraser, xix; drawings in Aberdeen Public Library].

HUNTLY, ABERDEENSHIRE, THE GORDON SCHOOLS, for the Duchess of Gordon, 1839, Tudor Gothic; wings added to north 1888 [Fraser, xxi].

ABERDEEN, NORTHERN ASSURANCE CO.'S premises, KING STREET, 1840 [Fraser, xx].

ABERDEEN, NORTH OF SCOTLAND BANK, CASTLE STREET, 1840–2 [Fraser, xx] (*C. Life*, 19 Aug. 1965, fig. 3).

HUNTLY, ABERDEENSHIRE, NORTH OF SCOTLAND BANK, *c.*1840 [Fraser, xxi].

ABERDEEN, THE NEW MARKET (dem.) and layout of MARKET STREET, 1840–2 [Fraser, xxi] (*C. Life*, 19 Aug. 1965, fig. 7).

ABERDEEN, THE POST OFFICE, MARKET STREET, 1841–2 [Fraser, xxii].

ABERDEEN, THE MECHANICS' INSTITUTE, MARKET STREET, 1845–6 [Fraser, xxv].

ABERDEEN, WEST PARISH CHURCH SCHOOL (subsequently part of Training College), GEORGE STREET, 1846; dem. [Fraser, xxvi].

LERWICK, SHETLANDS, UNION BANK OF SCOTLAND, 1846 [Fraser, xxvi].

attributed: EDINBURGH, DUCHESS OF GORDON'S FREE CHURCH SCHOOL (now chauffeurs' quarters), PALACE YARD, HOLYROODHOUSE, 1846, Jacobethan [attribution based on stylistic grounds and Simpson's employment elsewhere by the Duchess].

CHURCHES

ABERDEEN, ST. ANDREW'S EPISCOPAL CHURCH (now CATHEDRAL), KING STREET, 1816–17, Gothic; chancel by G. E. Street 1880, choir fittings, etc., by N. Comper 1941 [Fraser, iv].

KINTORE PARISH CHURCH AND MANSE, ABERDEENSHIRE, 1819, Gothic [Fraser, vi].

ELGIN, MORAYSHIRE, ST. GILES, 1827–8, Greek Revival [Fraser, x; *N.S.A.* xiii, 9].

INVERBROTHOCK CHAPEL, ARBROATH, ANGUS, 1828 [*Aberdeen Jnl. N. and Q.* i, 1908, 168–9].

WOODSIDE CHAPEL (afterwards Free Church), nr. ABERDEEN, 1829–30, Gothic [P. Morgan, *Annals of Woodside and Newhills*, Aberdeen 1886, 82–3].

BANFF, ST. ANDREW'S EPISCOPAL CHURCH, 1833–4, Gothic [Fraser, xvii].

FOCHABERS, MORAYSHIRE, EPISCOPAL CHAPEL AND SCHOOL for the Duchess of Gordon, 1833–4, Gothic [Fraser, xvii].

FOCHABERS, MORAYSHIRE, BELLIE CHURCH, repairs and alterations, 1835 [*Aberdeen Jnl.* 15 April 1835].

DRUMOAK PARISH CHURCH, ABERDEENSHIRE, 1835–6, Gothic [Fraser, xvii; *N.S.A.* xii, 895].

ABERDEEN, ST. NICHOLAS EAST, 1835–7; gutted 1874 and rebuilt to original design by William Smith [Fraser, xvi].

ABERDEEN, UNITED FREE CHURCHES, BELMONT STREET, 1843–4, Gothic; partly dem. 1990 [Fraser, xxiv].

ROTHESAY FREE CHURCH, BUTESHIRE, 1844 [*Builder* v, 217].

ABERDEEN, OLD ABERDEEN FREE CHURCH, 1845–6, Gothic, 'simplified greatly from what he intended' [Fraser, xxiv].

WOODSIDE CHURCH, nr. ABERDEEN, Gothic, 1846 [Fraser, xxiv].

ABERDEEN: DOMESTIC ARCHITECTURE

The following list includes only Simpson's principal domestic commissions in Aberdeen:

UNION BUILDINGS, UNION AND CASTLE STREETS, 1819–22; gutted 1973 [Fraser, v].

House at corner of Union Street and Shiprow for Alexander Galen, 1819 [Fraser, v].

BON-ACCORD SQUARE AND CRESCENT, 1823–6 [Fraser, viii] (*C. Life*, 19 Aug. 1965, fig. 6).

MARINE TERRACE, FERRYHILL, designed 1831, Nos. 9–10 built 1837–8, others later [Fraser, xiii].

ALBYN PLACE, Nos. 2–16, begun to Simpson's designs *c.*1836, but only 2 and 4 built by 1849 and the remainder built thereafter to modified design [*Aberdeen Jnl.* 11 Nov. 1835].

WESTBURN HOUSE (now public park) for David Chalmers, 1839 [Fraser, xix].

COUNTRY HOUSES

CASTLE FORBES (formerly PUTACHIE), ABERDEENSHIRE, for 17th Lord Forbes, 1814–15, castellated [*Builder* v, 1847, 217; S.R.O., GD 52/349] (J. P. Neale, *Seats*, 1st ser. i, 1818; F. O. Morris, *Picturesque Views of Seats* v, 61).

PARK HOUSE, ABERDEENSHIRE, for William Moir, 1822 [*Builder* v, 1847, 217].

HEATHCOT, BANCHORY DEVENICK, KINCARDINESHIRE, 1822; dem. [*Builder* v, 1847, 217].

HADDO HOUSE, ABERDEENSHIRE, alterations for 4th Earl of Aberdeen, 1822 [*Builder* v, 1847, 217] (*C. Life*, 18–25 Aug. 1966).

MURTLE HOUSE (now Rudolph Steiner School), ABERDEENSHIRE, for John Thurburn, 1823 [*Builder* v, 1847, 217; Fraser, x].

DURRIS HOUSE, KINCARDINESHIRE, additions for John Innes, 1824 [*Builder* v, 1847, 217].

CRIMONMOGATE, LONMAY, ABERDEENSHIRE, for Sir Alexander Bannerman (?), *c.*1825; mansard roof added 1875 [*Builder* v, 1847, 217; Fraser, xi].

LETHAM GRANGE, nr. ARBROATH, ANGUS, for John Hay, *c.*1825–30 [*Builder* v, 1847, 217; Fraser, x] (*Forfarshire Illustrated*, Dundee 1843, 71).

PITLURG (formerly LEASK) HOUSE, SLAINS, ABERDEENSHIRE, for General William Cumming Skene Gordon, 1826–7; burned 1927 [Fraser, x].

GORDON CASTLE, MORAYSHIRE, alterations and repairs to east wing after fire, for trustees of 4th Duke of Gordon, 1827 [S.R.O., GD 44/49/16], and Castle Farm, 1828–9 [drawings attributed to Simpson in S.R.O., RHP 2393-2404].

TILLERY HOUSE, FOVERAN, ABERDEENSHIRE, for — Hunter, *c.*1827; gutted [Fraser, x].

STRACATHRO HOUSE, ANGUS, for Alexander Cruickshanks, 1828 [*Builder* v, 1847, 217; Fraser, x] (*Forfarshire Illustrated*, Dundee 1843, 137).

CASTLE NEWE, ABERDEENSHIRE, rebuilt for Sir Charles Forbes, Bart., 1831; dem. [*N.S.A.* xii, 546; Fraser, xii] (*Castles of Aberdeenshire*, Aberdeen 1887, 130).

BOATH HOUSE, NAIRNSHIRE, for Sir James Dunbar, *c.*1830 [*Builder* v, 1847, 217; photostats at N.M.R.S. of signed drawings].

CRAIG CASTLE, AUCHINDOIR, ABERDEENSHIRE, altered or enlarged for — Gordon, 1832; burned 1942 [*Builder* v, 1847, 217].

LINTON HOUSE, CLUNY, ABERDEENSHIRE, for— Craigie (?), *c.*1835 [elevation exhibited in 1908, *Aberdeen Jnl. Notes and Queries* i, 1908, 169, no. 65].

MELDRUM HOUSE, ABERDEENSHIRE, rebuilt for B. C. Urquhart, *c.*1835/40, castellated; altered 1934–7 [*Builder* v, 1847, 217; Fraser, xix] (*Castles of Aberdeenshire*, Aberdeen 1887, 120).

CARNOUSIE NEW HOUSE, BANFFSHIRE, for Capt. Alexander Grant, *c.*1835/40; dem. *c.*1930 [*Builder* v, 1847, 217; Fraser, xxi; W. Douglas Simpson in *Banffshire Field Club's Trans.*, 1966].

LESSENDRUM HOUSE, DRUMBLADE, ABERDEENSHIRE, altered and enlarged for William Bisset, 1840, Scottish vernacular style; destroyed by fire *c.*1925 [*Builder* v, 1847, 217].

PITTODRIE HOUSE, ABERDEENSHIRE, additions for Allan C. Dunlop, 1840; canted bay added 1926 [*Builder* v, 1847, 217].

GLASSAUGH HOUSE, PORTSOY, BANFFSHIRE, remodelled for Arthur Abercromby, 1840 [Fraser, xi].

DRUMINNOR HOUSE, AUCHINDOIR, ABERDEENSHIRE, enlarged for Alexander Grant, 1841–3; Simpson's additions dem. *c.*1965 [*Builder* v, 1847, 217].

GLENFERNESS HOUSE, NAIRNSHIRE, for John Dougal, 1844–5 [*Builder* v, 1847, 217; Fraser, xxiii].

MORKEU, BANCHORY DEVENICK, KINCARDINESHIRE, *c.*1845; porch added 1910 [Fraser, xxv].

SCOTSTON HOUSE, nr. OLD ABERDEEN, for Sir

Michael Bruce, Bart.; dem. [*Builder* v, 1847, 217].

THAINSTON, nr. KINTORE, ABERDEENSHIRE, remodelled for Duncan Forbes-Mitchell [*Builder* v, 1847, 217] (Colin McWilliam in *Scotland's Magazine*, July 1955, 47).

SKENE HOUSE, ABERDEENSHIRE, designed additions for trustees of late George Skene, *c.*1847, carried out after Simpson's death by — Ramage, who published a lithograph of the house [trustees' minutes in S.R.O., CS 96/485, pp. 193–4; *Builder* v, 1847, 217].

SIMPSON, JAMES (1791–1864), was the son of a labourer at Aberford, Yorkshire. By 1822 he had moved to Leeds, where he was initially a joiner, and as such contracted for the joinery of the Brunswick Chapel designed by Joseph Botham (*q.v.*). He was still working as a joiner in the 1830s, but by 1839 was described as an architect. Strong family links with the Wesleyan community in LEEDS helped to bring him a number of commissions for chapels in that city, including ST. PETER'S STREET WESLEYAN CHAPEL, 1834, dem. [*Kelly's Directory of Leeds*, 1886, ix]; OXFORD PLACE WESLEYAN CHAPEL, 1835, remodelled 1896–1903 [B. L. Austwick and H. B. Jobbings, *A Century Not Out! The Story of . . . Oxford Place Chapel, Leeds*, 1935, 12]; HUNSLET WESLEYAN CENTENARY CHAPEL, 1839; dem. 1972 [*Wesleyan Methodist Mag.* 1840, 325]; WOODHOUSE METHODIST CHAPEL, 1840, dem. *c.*1972 [Trust accounts]; LADY LANE WESLEYAN METHODIST ASSOCIATION CHAPEL, 1840, rebuilt as offices [Kelly, *op. cit.*]; HEADINGLEY WESLEYAN CHAPEL, 1844–5, Gothic [Trust records]; HUNSLET METHODIST NEW CONNEXION CHAPEL, 1846, rebuilt as offices [*Methodist New Connexion Mag.*, 1853, 230]. In YORK he designed the CENTENARY METHODIST CHAPEL in ST. SAVIOURGATE, with a prominent Ionic portico, 1839–40 [R.C.H.M., *York* v, 52].

By the 1840s Simpson had become a leading Nonconformist architect in the north of England, at a time when large chapels were being built in every industrial town. Chapels by him with well-designed classical façades are or were formerly to be seen in Barnsley, Bradford, Burnley, Derby, Hull, Keighley, Morley, Newark, Oldham, Rawtenstall, Ripon, Scarborough and Warrington. The most notable of his few Gothic chapels was the demolished ROWLANDS METHODIST CHAPEL at SUMMERSEAT, BURY, LANCS., 1845–7 [signed drawings]. Towards the end of his life Simpson was joined in practice by his son John (b. 1831), who subsequently designed a number of chapels on his own. Simpson died at Leeds on 13 March 1864 [Principal Probate Registry, Calendar of Probates]. [Information from Mr. D. Colin Dews, to whom all the Leeds references are due.]

SIMPSON, JAMES CHARNOCK (– 1876), practised at Brighton, where in 1830 he designed the COUNTESS OF HUNTINGDON'S CHAPEL in ANN STREET, LONDON ROAD; dem. 1976. [*The Watering Places of Great Britain and Fashionable Directory*, J. Robins, London 1833, 33]. He died in Jersey on 2 July 1876 [Principal Probate Registry, Calendar of Probates].

SIMPSON, JOHN, 'of Budby', made a design for the new County Hall at Nottingham in 1768 which was not accepted, but in the following year John Simpson 'of Thoresby' was paid £43 7s. 6d. for drawing plans and attending Parliament in connection with the Act to build the new County Hall designed by James Gandon. The change of address is explained by the fact that Simpson was then engaged in supervising the building of Thoresby House to the designs of John Carr of York. He was presumably the John Simpson who in 1781–2 designed the GENERAL HOSPITAL at NOTTINGHAM, of which he published a print (Bodleian Library, Gough Maps 26, ff. 21^{v}–22), and who was concerned in rebuilding the LEEN BRIDGE at NOTTINGHAM in 1764, GAINSBOROUGH BRIDGE in 1787, and RETFORD BRIDGE in 1794. In 1787–9 lodges at the 'Worksop Corner' and 'Blyth Corner' of CLUMBER PARK, NOTTS., were built by the 2nd Duke of Newcastle to his designs.

[*A.P.S.D.*; *Nottinghamshire County Records of the Eighteenth Century*, ed. K. T. Meaby, 1947, 49, 55, 106; J. Blackner, *History of Nottingham*, 1815, 160; T. Whitehead, *Original Anecdotes of the late Duke of Kingston*, 1792, 106; J. F. Sutton, *The Date Book for Nottingham*, 1852, 144; Nottingham University Library, Ne C4, 339, 359, Minutes of the Committee for Gainsborough Bridge; J. S. Piercy, *History of Retford*, 1828, 150; D. J. Bradbury, *Clumber*, 1988, 34.]

SIMPSON, JOHN (1755–1815), born at Stenhouse in Midlothian, was probably a mason by trade. He was regularly employed by Telford, who described him as 'a treasure of talents and integrity'. Under Telford's direction he built bridges at Bewdley, Dunkeld, Craigellachie and Bonar, the Chirk and Pont-y-Cysyllte aqueducts, and the locks and basins of the Caledonian Canal. He eventually settled in Shrewsbury, where he superintended the erection of New St. Chad's Church to the designs of George Steuart in

1790–2. Although primarily a builder and clerk of works, he was sometimes described as an architect, and he may have been the 'Sympson' who, according to the antiquary Thomas Prattinton, designed the TOWN HALL at BEWDLEY, WORCS., in 1808 [original drawings in Library of the Society of Antiquaries of London, Prattinton Collection, vol. v, 25/5, inscribed 'Sympson, Architect']. He died at Shrewsbury on 16 June 1815, and is commemorated by a monument in New St. Chad's Church, with a bust by Chantrey. His business was taken over by his nephew, John Straphen (d. 1826), the builder of Lord Hill's Column. [A. Gibb, *The Story of Telford*, 1935, 39; *Gent's Mag.* 1815 (i), 572, 1820 (ii), 303; C. Hulbert, *Memoirs*, Shrewsbury 1852, 191.]

SINCLAIR, JOHN (*c.*1789–1863), of Hartshill, Warwicks., was for 'upwards of 42 years resident engineer to the Coventry Canal Company', according to the inscription on his tombstone at Mancetter. He died on 17 March 1863, aged 74. An iron bridge at HAWKESBURY, WARWICKS., dated 1837, bears his signature, and in 1847 the west tower of GRENDON CHURCH, WARWICKS., was rebuilt to his (Perpendicular Gothic) design [Vestry Minutes in County Record Office]. The 'John Sinclair, junior' of Coventry who competed for the Ashmolean Museum at Oxford in 1839 was no doubt a relation, and Robert Cooper Sinclair, who practised from Hartshill in the 1870s as 'engineer and architect', was presumably his son.

SINGLETON, LUKE (1720–1768), of Gloucester, is known only as the designer of the GENERAL INFIRMARY in that city. The minutes of the committee for building the Infirmary show that Singleton's plan was approved in 1755 after consultation with John Wood of Bath. The building (dem. 1984) was erected by Stiff Leadbetter (*q.v.*) and completed in 1761. When Singleton died in 1768 he was described as 'gentleman' in the probate records and as 'esquire' in the *London Magazine*. [G. W. Counsel, *History of Gloucester*, 1829, 176; George Whitcombe, *The General Infirmary at Gloucester*, 1903, 18; *London Magazine*, 1768, 501; notes from committee book *ex inf.* the late Bryan Little.]

SISSON, JEREMIAH (1720–1783/4), was, like his father Jonathan (d. 1747), a well-known mathematical instrument-maker in London [*D.N.B., Missing Persons*, 1993, 607]. As a youth he may have had some training as an architect, for he signs a very competent elevation of a house dated 1735 (Bodleian Library, Gough Maps 230, f. 415).

SKAE, DAVID (–1818), was a builder in Edinburgh. The only building he is known to have designed is THE ALBANY STREET INDEPENDENT CHAPEL, EDINBURGH (now an office), 1816 [J. & H. Storer, *Views in Edinburgh* i, 1820]. The façades were designed to conform to the domestic architecture of Broughton and Albany Streets. Skae, who died young, was the father of David Skae (1814–73), a distinguished physician (see *D.N.B.*).

SKAIFE, THOMAS, advertised himself in *Aris's Birmingham Gazette* of 17 August 1789 as a 'Surveyor and Builder from London (No. 9 Fleet Street,)' who 'proposes drawing Plans, Elevations and Sections, and to measure and value the different Artificers' Works in Buildings upon the most reasonable Terms'. He was also prepared to 'Estimate and undertake all Sorts of Building By Contract'. He was a carpenter and joiner by trade and was the author of *A Key to Civil Architecture, or the Universal British Builder*, 1774, 2nd ed. 1776, 3rd ed. 1788, an unillustrated treatise on building practice. The names of numerous workmen from York among the subscribers suggest that this was Skaife's native city [Eileen Harris, *British Architectural Books and Writers 1556–1785*, 1990, 423–4].

SKINNER, WILLIAM (1700–1780), was a military engineer who was appointed Chief Engineer of Great Britain in 1757, and rose to the rank of lieutenant-general. His activities as a military engineer fall largely outside the scope of this *Dictionary*, but he may be mentioned here as the designer of FORT GEORGE at ARDERSIER, nr. INVERNESS (1748–69), a major monument of Georgian military architecture. See Iain MacIvor, *Fort George*, H.M.S.O. 1970, and *D.N.B.* for a full account of Skinner's career. A portrait of him hangs at Firle Place, Sussex.

SLATER, JOHN, was a joiner in Seel Street, Liverpool, who also practised as an architect. At the Liverpool Academy's exhibition in 1812 he showed a 'Design for an altarpiece for a Catholic Chapel'. Between 1812 and 1816 he was employed by the Catholic Thomas Scarisbrick to carry out extensive alterations to SCARISBRICK HALL, LANCS. These were in the Gothic style and in making the designs Slater was assisted by Thomas Rickman (*q.v.*), then at the outset of his career as an architect. From 1837 onwards the house was again remodelled in a more advanced Gothic style to the designs of A. W. N. Pugin, but some traces of Rickman and Slater's work can still be seen [Rickman's diaries, 1812–16, *passim*; information from

Mr. John Baily]. Slater later designed the classical R.C. church of ST. PATRICK, PARK PLACE, LIVERPOOL, 1821–3 [*Liverpool Mercury*, 23 March 1821], and according to *Gent's Mag.* 1839 (ii), 532, the Gothic parish church of HURDSFIELD, CHESHIRE, but drawings for the latter preserved in the church are reported to be signed by William Hayley of Manchester.

SLOANE, CHARLES (1690–1764), was a native of Dartford, but established himself as a carpenter and builder in Gravesend. In 1731–3 he designed and rebuilt the parish church of ST. GEORGE, GRAVESEND, after its destruction by fire in 1727. He also designed the TOWN HALL, which, before its refronting in 1836 by A. H. Wilds, bore on a stone fascia an inscription recording that it was 'ERECTED IN THE YEAR 1764, JOHN DELAP, ESQ., MAYOR; C. SLOANE ARCHITECT' [R. P. Cruden, *History of Gravesend*, 1843, 408, 425]. In 1746 he designed the COUNTY GAOL, MAIDSTONE, which likewise bore the inscription 'C. SLOANE, ARCHITECT' [*Gent's Mag.* 1809 (ii), 813]; it was enlarged by William Tyler in 1784 and entirely rebuilt in 1810. In 1742–3 he repaired and refitted the choir of ROCHESTER CATHEDRAL, and in 1749 rebuilt the central spire [G. H. Palmer, *The Cathedral Church of Rochester*, 1897, 29–30]. In 1751 two large brick buttresses were erected against the south-east transept in accordance with his advice [*Archaeologia Cantiana* xxiii, 1898, 283]. In 1754 he supplied plans for rebuilding DARTFORD BRIDGE which were carried out in the following year [Kent Record Office, QS. County Bridges]. The bridge was rebuilt in 1790–1 and again in 1922–3.

In 1754 a letter from Sloane concerning Dartford Bridge was written from Calehill, Little Chart, the seat of the Darell family. As CALEHILL HOUSE (dem. 1951) was rebuilt in 1753–4 [Kent Record Office, U386, E1–3], Sloane was probably the architect employed. It was a well-proportioned plain brick house with flanking wings.

Sloane died at Gravesend in 1764 and is commemorated by an inscription in St. George's churchyard.

SMALLWOOD, JOHN, 'the Duke [of Buccleuch]'s architect' at Drumlanrig, is mentioned as making designs (apparently unexecuted) for Eskdalemuir Church, Dumfriesshire, in 1825 [S.R.O., CH2/235/4, p. 455] and as enlarging and repairing KEIR MANSE, DUMFRIESSHIRE, in 1827 [S.R.O., CH2/298/10, p. 359].

SMALLWOOD, WILLIAM FROME (1806–1834), born at Peasemarsh in Sussex, was the son of the proprietor of the Grand Hotel, Covent Garden. He became a pupil of L. N. Cottingham, but never practised as an architect, preferring the profession of an artist. He specialized in architectural subjects, and exhibited a number of drawings of cathedrals, etc., in northern France and Belgium at the Royal Academy in 1830–4. Drawings made by him at Amiens and Rouen in 1831–3 are in the Avery Library of Columbia University, New York, and one of Notre Dame at St. Omer, dated 1833, is in the Victoria and Albert Museum. A number of his drawings were engraved for the *Penny Magazine*. According to *Gent's Mag.* 1834 (i), 661, his early death at the age of 27 was due to brain fever, brought on by the 'great exertions made to support a young and increasing family'. Loudon, in reporting his death in the *Architectural Magazine* i, 1834, 184, gave his age as 34.

SMALMAN, JOHN (*c.*1783–1852), was a builder and architect of Quatford, nr. Bridgnorth in Shropshire. He had pretensions to gentility, and claimed descent from the Smalmans of Wilderhope, but it is likely that he was more closely related to the 'J. Smallman' who signs a monumental tablet in Much Wenlock Church to Thomas and Mary Smyth (d. 1780). He made a fortune as a builder in the Bridgnorth area, but his known architectural works are neither numerous nor distinguished. In about 1816 he enlarged STANLEY HALL, SALOP., for Sir John Tyrwhitt Jones, Bart., after designs by Thomas Cundy had been rejected [J. P. Neale, *Views of Seats*, 1st ser. iii, 1820]. In 1823 he widened the two middle arches of BRIDGNORTH BRIDGE by the insertion of iron girders [*Trans. Salop. Arch. Soc.* xlix, 1937, 209]; in 1823–4 he designed and built the BRIDGNORTH THEATRE (dem. *c.*1855), for which some of his designs survive among the Corporation archives; in 1828 he designed DITTON PRIORS VICARAGE, SALOP. [Bodleian Library, records of Queen Anne's Bounty]; and in 1829 he rebuilt the west tower of CHETTON CHURCH, SALOP., in a somewhat perfunctory Gothic style [I.C.B.S.]. A plan of the dining-room at DUDMASTON HALL, SALOP., by Smalman, dated 1826, shows that he was concerned in the early nineteenth-century alterations to that house for W. W. Whitmore, and was very likely responsible for the new attic storey that was added at that time. At Quatford he built himself in 1829–30 a castellated mansion called QUATFORD CASTLE which is somewhat in the style of Wyatville's work at Windsor, and largely rebuilt the village (see George Griffith's poem *The*

English Village, 1847, which is dedicated to Smalman).

Smalman, who appears to have been a Whig in politics, was elected an alderman of Bridgnorth immediately after the Municipal Reform Act of 1835, and served as Mayor in 1837–8. He died unmarried on 11 March 1852, aged 69, and is buried at Quatford, where a eulogistic epitaph refers to the 'vigorous will . . . simplicity of life, sound judgment and indomitable perseverance' which enabled him to rise to 'Honour and Fortune'. The epitaph also refers to his literary interests, of which evidence survives in the form of several long manuscript poems of a somewhat eccentric character. Among them are 'Lines addressed to Mrs. Farmer [of] Ludstone Hall on her judicious attention to the preservation of the character and state of that ancient mansion'. A portrait of Smalman hangs in the Mayor's Parlour at Bridgnorth. The architect S. Pountney Smith of Shrewsbury (1812–83) was his nephew and pupil.

[Bridgnorth Corporation Archives; National Library of Wales, Bridgnorth Peculiar records (will); information from Dr. J. F. A. Mason.]

SMART, ALFRED RAWDON (*c.*1804–1842), was in practice as an architect and surveyor in Leicester by 1827. His career, however, was a short one, for he died of epilepsy in the County Lunatic Asylum on 2 September 1842, aged 38 [J. D. Bennett, *Leicestershire Architects 1700–1850*, Leicester Museums 1968].

SMART, ANDREW (*c.*1676–1736), is described as 'mason and architect' on his monument (No. 978) in the Howff Cemetery at Dundee. He owned a quarry at Dundee, and according to the inscription 'built the Town House of Dundee [to the designs of William Adam], and many other public and private buildings'. He died on 3 October 1736, aged 60 [James Thomson, *History of Dundee*, Dundee 1847, 149]. The monument was erected by his son Thomas, who may have been the father of Thomas Smart, 'mason and architect' of Dundee, whose death in 1801 in his 76th year is recorded in *Gent's Mag.* 1801, 377. ABERNYTE CHURCH, PERTHSHIRE, was built in 1736 by David Smart, mason in Dundee [S.R.O., HR 499/1, f. 4^{v}].

SMART, HENRY (*c.*1676–1760), a mason of Chichester, was the son of Robert Smart, a bricklayer. He served as Mayor of Chichester in 1751–2 and was buried in the Cathedral cloister in August 1760. A Chancery lawsuit shows that in about 1711 he made a design for Pallant House, Chichester, for Henry and Elizabeth Peckham, but the Peckhams went to London and obtained an alternative design, described as 'the London Modell', which they proceeded to build in 1712–13 [Sibylla J. Flower in *Pallant House*, Chichester 1993, 32–4].

SMIRKE, Sir ROBERT (1780–1867), second son of the artist Robert Smirke, R.A., was born in London on 1 October 1780. He was educated at a well-known private school at Aspley Guise in Bedfordshire, where he showed 'an inclination towards drawing'. In May 1796 he entered the office of Sir John Soane, but left a few months later owing to a mutual antipathy between master and pupil. For his subsequent training he was indebted to George Dance, junior, and to the surveyor Thomas Bush (*q.v.*). He had begun to study at the Royal Academy Schools in July 1796, gaining the Silver Medal in that year and the Gold Medal in 1799. In 1801 he went abroad with his elder brother Richard. Abandoning the risky idea of visiting Paris disguised as Americans, they eventually went there after the Peace of Amiens, and subsequently travelled extensively in Italy and Sicily. Robert also visited Greece, then a wild and bandit-ridden country, and with considerable intrepidity succeeded in drawing most of the ancient buildings in the Morea. He returned to England in 1805, and in the following year published the first and only part of a projected work entitled *Specimens of Continental Architecture*.[1]

As a practising architect in London Smirke enjoyed an immediate success. His father's connections helped to bring him clients, and he soon became the favoured architect of the Tory establishment. It was to Tory patronage that he was indebted for all his official posts and for most of his commissions. George Dance and Sir George Beaumont recommended him to Lord Lonsdale, a Tory magnate who gave him his first major commission as a country-house architect. Earl Bathurst, another Tory, employed him at Cirencester Park and made him architect to the Royal Mint (1807). The painter Sir Thomas Lawrence introduced him to the future Prime Minister, Sir Robert Peel, who employed him to design a town house in Whitehall and a country seat in Staffordshire. In fact Smirke became such a favourite of Peel that the Radical press made fun of the 'two Sir Roberts' and wrote derisively of 'the Prime Minister and his pet'.

[1] He also published a paper on 'Gothic Architecture' in Italy and Sicily in *Archaeologia* xv.

In 1813, at the age of 33, Smirke rose to the top of his profession by being nominated as one of the three architects attached to the Office of Works, the others being Soane and Nash, both many years his seniors. This appointment brought him several major commissions, notably the British Museum, the General Post Office, the Custom House and King's College in the Strand. In 1819 he became surveyor to the Inner Temple, where he carried out extensive works. From 1820 he was also Surveyor-General for the South Parts of the Duchy of Lancaster, and as such was responsible for the development of the Savoy estate in London. His private commissions were numerous. Outside London he built or enlarged some thirty country houses and designed eight county halls: at Carlisle, Gloucester, Hereford, Bristol, Shrewsbury, Lincoln, Maidstone and Perth. Inside London he was responsible for Covent Garden Theatre, the Royal College of Physicians, four clubs and several churches. His was in fact one of the biggest and most successful architectural practices of the nineteenth century. At the height of his career he was rumoured to have declined commissions for work costing less than £10,000, and he died worth £90,000.

Smirke was elected A.R.A. in 1808, R.A. in 1811, and held the office of Treasurer of the Royal Academy from 1820 to 1850. In 1832, when the Office of Works was reorganized without the three 'attached architects', he received a knighthood in recognition of his services. He was a Fellow of the Royal Society and of the Society of Antiquaries, and an Honorary Fellow of the R.I.B.A., whose Gold Medal was awarded to him in 1853. He retired from practice in 1845, when Peel made him a member of the Commission for London Improvements. At the same time he was presented by his former pupils and assistants with a bust of himself by Thomas Campbell which is now at the R.I.B.A. In 1859 he resigned from the Royal Academy and retired to Cheltenham, where he died on 18 April 1867, at the age of 87.

Smirke's professional success owed more to a reputation for reliability than it did to brilliance in design. His meticulous and businesslike methods commended themselves to a generation that had suffered from the mismanagement first of Wyatt and then of Nash. He rarely exceeded his estimates, and sound construction was his speciality. The frequency with which he was called in to remedy the defective work of others led Croker to call him 'the Dr. Baillie of architects', alluding to the author of a well-known work on morbid anatomy. The Carlisle County Courts, the Millbank Penitentiary and the London Custom House were the most celebrated architectural casualties to benefit from his skill. Technically he was thoroughly up to date. Indeed he was something of a structural innovator, being the first British architect to use load-bearing foundations of lime concrete in measured quantities, and one of the first to make regular use of load-bearing cast-iron beams in public and domestic (as opposed to industrial) architecture.

Aesthetically Smirke was a dedicated Greek Revivalist. His Covent Garden Theatre was London's first building in the pure Doric style, the British Museum its greatest neoclassical monument. It was not, however, the archaeological niceties of Greek architecture that Smirke admired so much as its rational simplicity. Once having found one or two Grecian formulae (notably the Order of the Temple on the Ilissus) which satisfied him, he adhered to them with tedious fidelity, repeating them again and again in his churches and public buildings. His public works, though invariably dignified, are in consequence frequently dull. Only in the front of the British Museum did grandeur of scale and the novel combination of a portico with a colonnade enable him to transcend his usual urbane banality and produce a masterpiece of classical dignity. As a country-house architect he was less inhibited by Grecian precept. Indeed, with the exception of Armley, none of his country houses is dominated by the conventional Doric or Ionic portico. Several, like Lowther and Eastnor, are castellated Gothic, a few, like Drayton and Cultoquhey, are Tudor or Jacobean. But others represent a serious attempt to evolve a simplified classical style whose lack of elegance should not be allowed to detract from its originality. Such are Eden Hall, the Homend, Kinmount, Normanby, Whittinghame and Worthy House: cubical compositions which represent Smirke's most interesting contribution to British architecture. But what Pugin called 'the New Square Style of Mr. Smirke' did not save him from the reputation of being in general a conventional and unenterprising designer. Already in 1831 a writer in *The Library of the Fine Arts* described him as an architect who (in the words of Pope) was 'content to dwell in decencies for ever', and in 1842 he was the object of a scathing attack in the *Surveyor, Engineer and Architect*. Long before his death in 1867 he had been repudiated by contemporary taste, and modern scholarship has emphasized his constructive virtues without doing much to vindicate his reputation as an artist.

Smirke married in 1819 Laura, the fifth

daughter of the Revd. Anthony Freston, a nephew of Matthew Brettingham (*q.v.*) by whom he had one daughter. His extensive practice demanded a large and well-organized office, and his many pupils included William Burn, C. R. Cockerell, William Doull, C. C. Nelson, John Newman, Henry Roberts, Lewis Vulliamy, and his younger brother Sydney Smirke (1797–1877).

There is a large collection of Smirke's drawings in the R.I.B.A. Drawings Collection. Many of his continental drawings (1802–4) are in the Yale Center for British Art. His correspondence with Sir Robert Peel is in the British Library (Add. MS. 40605). Busts by E. H. Baily (1828) and Thomas Campbell (1845) are in the British Museum and the R.I.B.A. respectively. There is a portrait by George Dance at the Royal Academy.

[*A.P.S.D.*; *D.N.B.*; obituary by Sir E. Smirke in *R.I.B.A. Jnl.*, 1866–7, reprinted in *Builder* xxv, 1867, 604; *Building News* xiv, 567–8; *The Farington Diary, passim*; J. Mordaunt Crook, 'The Career of Sir Robert Smirke', Oxford D. Phil. thesis, 1961, and the following articles: 'Sir Robert Smirke: A Pioneer of Concrete Construction', *Trans. Newcomen Soc.* xxxviii, 1965–6; 'Architect of the Rectangular: a Reassessment of Sir Robert Smirke', *C. Life*, 13 April 1967; 'Sir Robert Smirke: a Centenary Florilegium', *Arch. Rev.* Sept. 1967; 'Sir Robert Smirke: A Regency Architect in London', *Jnl. of the London Society*, March 1968; *History of the King's Works* vi, 1973, *passim*.]

PUBLIC BUILDINGS IN LONDON

SOMERSET HOUSE, STRAND, alterations to the Library of the Society of Antiquaries, 1807–8 [Joan Evans, *History of the Society of Antiquaries*, 1956, 216].

COVENT GARDEN THEATRE, 1808–9; altered 1846–7 and rebuilt by E. M. Barry 1856–8 after a fire [Britton & Pugin, *Public Buildings of London* i, 1825, 193–226; *Survey of London* xxxv, 93–7].

THE ROYAL MINT, TOWER HILL, completion of building begun by James Johnson, 1809–11, and repairs after fire in 1815 [*History of the King's Works* vi, 453–8].

THE BRITISH MUSEUM, MONTAGU HOUSE, BLOOMSBURY, repairs and additions, 1815–16, and temporary rooms for the Elgin Marbles, 1816; dem. *c.*1840 [*History of the King's Works* vi, 405; J. Mordaunt Crook, *The British Museum*, 1972].

THE MILLBANK PENITENTIARY, completion of building designed by Thomas Hardwick (*q.v.*) after failure of foundations, 1816–19; and further alterations 1824 and 1828; dem. 1892 [G. Holford, *An Account of the Penitentiary at Millbank*, 1828, pp. xxxi–xxxii; *Builder* lxiii, 1892, 474].

THE INNER TEMPLE, alterations to HALL, 1816–17, 1827 and 1837, rebuilt by Sydney Smirke 1867–70, destroyed by bombing 1940–1; LIBRARY and PARLIAMENT CHAMBERS, 1819 and 1827–8, destroyed by bombing 1940–1; refaced CROWN OFFICE ROW, 1827; alterations to Nos. 4 and 5 HARE COURT, 1827 and 1832; repairs and alterations to MASTER'S HOUSE, 1827 and 1831; Nos. 12 and 13 KING'S BENCH WALK, 1829–30; No. 9 KING'S BENCH WALK, 1836–7; TANFIELD COURT, 1832–3, rebuilt 1896; HARCOURT BUILDINGS, 1832–4, destroyed by bombing 1940–1; PAPER BUILDINGS, rebuilt north front after fire in 1838, south front rebuilt by Sydney Smirke 1847–8, damaged by bombing 1940–1 [J. M. Crook, 'Career of Sir Robert Smirke', 174–181].

SOMERSET HOUSE, STRAND, THE LEGACY DUTY OFFICE in north-west corner, 1817–19 and 1821–33 [*History of the King's Works* vi, 481].

THE UNITED SERVICE CLUB, CHARLES STREET, ST. JAMES'S, 1817–19; altered by Decimus Burton for the Junior United Service Club 1830; rebuilt 1855–7 [*Survey of London* xxix, 289–91, and xxx, pl. 64].

LANCASTER PLACE, STRAND, and DUCHY OF LANCASTER OFFICES, *c.*1817–23; dem. [R. Somerville, *The Savoy*, 1960, 111–13; *A.P.S.D.*].

WHITMORE'S BANK, No. 24 LOMBARD STREET, *c.*1820; burnt before 1867 [Crook, 'Career of Sir Robert Smirke', 375, n. 7].

THE LONDON OPHTHALMIC INFIRMARY, MOORFIELDS, 1821–2; rebuilt 1898 [*A.P.S.D.*] (J. Elmes, *Metropolitan Improvements*, 1831, plate).

THE MILITARY DEPOT, TOOLEY STREET, SOUTHWARK, 1821–3; dem. [*History of the King's Works* vi, 451–2].

THE ROYAL COLLEGE OF PHYSICIANS (now CANADA HOUSE), TRAFALGAR SQUARE, 1822–5; remodelled 1925, when new south portico was added [Britton & Pugin, *Public Buildings of London* ii, 1828, 219–23].

THE UNION CLUB (now CANADA HOUSE), TRAFALGAR SQUARE, 1822–7; attic storey added by D. Burton 1841–50; remodelled 1925 [Britton & Pugin, *Public Buildings of London* ii, 1828, 219–23].

attributed: THE WESTERN NATIONAL SCHOOL, BRYANSTON SQUARE, 1824; dem. [erected 'in a corresponding style with the church': T. Smith, *Parish of St. Mary-le-bone*, 1833, 107].

THE BRITISH MUSEUM, 1823–46, completed under direction of Sydney Smirke, 1846–

52. The domed reading-room was built to Sydney Smirke's design in 1854–7 [Britton & Pugin, *Public Buildings of London*, ed. Leeds, ii, 1838; *History of the King's Works* vi, 403–21; J. Mordaunt Crook, *The British Museum*, 1972].

THE GENERAL POST OFFICE, ST. MARTIN'S LE GRAND, 1824–9; attic storey added 1892; dem. 1912 [Britton & Pugin, *Public Buildings of London*, ed. Leeds, ii, 1838; *History of the King's Works* vi, 430–7].

THE CUSTOM HOUSE, rebuilding after failure of foundations, 1825–7 [J. Mordaunt Crook, 'The Custom House Scandal', *Arch. Hist.* vi, 1963; *History of the King's Works* vi, 422–30].

THE EQUITABLE ASSURANCE COMPANY'S OFFICE, BRIDGE STREET, BLACKFRIARS, 1829; dem. [*A.P.S.D.*].

LONDON BRIDGE APPROACHES, street façades to KING WILLIAM STREET, BOROUGH HIGH STREET, etc., 1829–35, including BRIDGE HOUSE HOTEL (No. 4 BOROUGH HIGH STREET), ST. MAGNUS MARTYR RECTORY, 1833–5, and ST. MARY WOOLNOTH RECTORY, 1834–9 (dem.) [*A.P.S.D.*].

KING'S COLLEGE, STRAND, forming the east wing of Somerset House, 1830–5; chapel remodelled by Scott 1861–62; attic storey added 1886–8 [*History of the King's Works* vi, 483].

THE CARLTON CLUB, PALL MALL, 1833–6; rebuilt by Sydney Smirke 1854–6; dem. 1940 [*Survey of London* xxix, 354–5].

WESTMINSTER PALACE, refaced interior of WESTMINSTER HALL, 1834–7; temporary HOUSE OF LORDS in former Painted Chamber and temporary HOUSE OF COMMONS in former House of Lords, 1834–5 [*History of the King's Works* vi, 503, 573–5].

MOORGATE STREET, façades, 1835–9 [*A.P.S.D.*].

THE MANSION HOUSE, alteration of steps to portico, 1836 [*A.P.S.D.*].

THE OXFORD AND CAMBRIDGE CLUB, PALL MALL, 1836–8; staircase altered 1907 [*Survey of London* xxix, 419–22].

SERJEANTS' INN, CHANCERY LANE, largely rebuilt, 1836–9; dem. 1910 [*A.P.S.D.*; R.I.B.A.D.].

ST. JAMES'S PALACE, new lodge at entrance to park from stable yard, 1838 [*History of the King's Works* vi, 370].

PUBLIC BUILDINGS ELSEWHERE

CARLISLE, CUMBERLAND, COUNTY COURTS, completion, after failure of foundations, of buildings begun by Telford, Chisholme and Nicholson, 1810–12, castellated [*A.P.S.D.*; R.I.B.A.D.].

APPLEBY, WESTMORLAND, THE MARKET HOUSE, 1811, Gothic [S. Lewis, *Topographical Dictionary of England* i, 1831, 42].

CARLISLE, CUMBERLAND, THE EDEN BRIDGE, 1812–15; widened 1932 [*A.P.S.D.*].

WHITEHAVEN, CUMBERLAND, THE FISH MARKET, 1813, dem. *c.*1852; THE BUTTER MARKET, 1813, dem. 1880 [S. Lewis, *Topographical Dictionary of England* iv, 1831, 458].

GLOUCESTER, THE SHIRE HALL, 1814–16; enlarged 1909–11 [*A.P.S.D.*; R.I.B.A.D.].

GLOUCESTER, WESTGATE BRIDGE (R. Severn), 1814–17 [*A.P.S.D.*].

BOLTON, WESTMORLAND, iron chain bridge over R. Eden, 1815–16; collapsed 1822 [J. F. Curwen, *The Later Records relating to N. Westmorland*, Kendal 1932, 345].

HEREFORD, THE SHIRE HALL, 1815–17 [*A.P.S.D.*].

PERTH, THE COUNTY BUILDINGS, 1815–19; enlarged 1866–7 [*N.S.A.* x, 86].

DUBLIN, THE WELLINGTON TESTIMONIAL, PHOENIX PARK, 1817–22, unfinished [*A.P.S.D.*, *s.v.* 'Dublin'; R.I.B.A.D.].

MAIDSTONE, KENT, THE COUNTY GAOL, completion of building designed by D. A. Alexander, 1817–19 [*A.P.S.D.*].

LEDBURY, HEREFS., ST. KATHERINE'S HOSPITAL, 1822–5, Gothic [*A.P.S.D.*].

LINCOLN, THE COUNTY COURTS in THE CASTLE, with repairs and additions to gaol, watch-tower, battlements, etc., 1823–30, Gothic [J. Mordaunt Crook, 'The Building of Lincoln County Hall', *Lincolnshire Arch. Soc. Reports* ix, 1962].

BRISTOL, THE COUNCIL HOUSE and adjoining shops in BROAD STREET, 1824–7 [*A.P.S.D.*].

MAIDSTONE, KENT, THE SESSIONS HOUSE, 1826–7; enlarged 1850, 1862 and 1914 [*A.P.S.D.*].

OXFORD, THE SCHOOLS QUADRANGLE, repairs to roof, including new ceiling of present Upper Reading Room, 1830 [*Bodleian Library Record* iii, 1951, 89–91].

OXFORD, CLARENDON BUILDING, fitted up interior as university offices, etc., 1831 [*V.C.H. Oxon.* iii, 55].

ST. JOHN'S, NEWFOUNDLAND, GAOL, *c.*1831 [*A.P.S.D.*].

SHREWSBURY, SHIRE HALL, 1834–7; interior reconstructed after fire in 1880; dem. 1971 [*A.P.S.D.*].

CHURCHES

GLOUCESTER CATHEDRAL, Gothic screen behind altar, 1807; removed 1873 [J. Britton, *History and Antiquities of Gloucester Cathedral*, 1829, 62–3, pl. xvii; R.I.B.A.D.].

CARLISLE CATHEDRAL, repairs and alterations

to Fratry, 1809–11; restored 1880 [J. M. Crook, 'The Career of Sir Robert Smirke', 324].

STROOD CHURCH, KENT, incorporating medieval tower, 1812 [*A.P.S.D.*; H. Smetham, *History of Strood*, 1899, 55–75].

LONDON, THE BELGRAVE CHAPEL, HALKIN STREET, 1812; dem. *c.*1910 [J. Elmes, *Metropolitan Improvements*, 1831, 153–4 and plate].

LONDON, THE SAVOY CHAPEL, rebuilt south wall and added west tower, 1820–1, Gothic [R. Somerville, *The Savoy*, 1960, 128–9].

LUTON HOO PARK CHAPEL, BEDS., 1816, Gothic [H. Shaw, *The History and Antiquities of the Chapel at Luton Park*, 1829].

MILTON BRYANT CHURCH, BEDS., added N. transept *c.*1820, Gothic [note by the Revd. G. Boissier in B.L., Add. MS. 48977, f. 389].

WANDSWORTH, SURREY, ST. ANNE, 1820–2; chancel 1896 [Port, 136–7].

CHATHAM, KENT, ST. JOHN, 1821–2; altered 1869 [Port, 132–3; R.I.B.A.D.].

BRISTOL, ST. GEORGE, BRANDON HILL, 1821–3; altered 1871–6 [Port, 132–3].

LONDON, ST. JAMES, WEST HACKNEY, 1821–3; altered 1859 by W. White and 1879 by G. F. Bodley; dem. 1958 [Port, 134–5] (J. Elmes, *Metropolitan Improvements*, 1831, plate).

LONDON, ST. MARY, WYNDHAM PLACE, BRYANSTON SQUARE, 1821–3; altered internally 1874 [Port, 136–7].

TYLDESLEY, LANCS., ST. GEORGE, 1821–4, Gothic [Port, 134–5; R.I.B.A.D.].

SALFORD, LANCS., ST. PHILIP, 1822–4; altered 1895 [Port, 134–5].

LONDON, GROSVENOR CHAPEL, CHAPEL STREET, GROSVENOR PLACE, *c.*1825 [*A.P.S.D.*].

LONDON, THE TEMPLE CHURCH, repairs and alterations, 1825–30 [J. Mordaunt Crook, 'The Restoration of the Temple Church', *Architectural History* viii, 1965, 40].

YORK MINSTER, restoration of choir roof after fire, 1830–2. Smirke also made a report after the fire which destroyed the roof of the nave in 1840, but the subsequent repairs were entrusted to Sydney Smirke [E. Wylson, 'York Minster; its Fires and Restorations', *Builder* iii, 1845, 158, 175].

MARKHAM CLINTON, NOTTS., church and mausoleum for 4th Duke of Newcastle, 1831–2 [W. White, *History and Directory of Nottinghamshire*, 1832, 383].

ASKHAM CHURCH, WESTMORLAND, 1832, Tudor Gothic [I.C.B.S.].

LONDON, CHAPEL ROYAL (*i.e.* BANQUETING HOUSE), WHITEHALL, repairs and internal alterations, 1835–8 [*History of the King's Works* vi, 548–9].

LONDON, CHAPEL ROYAL, ST. JAMES'S PALACE, refitted interior, 1836–7 [*History of the King's Works* vi, 370].

LONDON, ST. JAMES'S CHURCH, PICCADILLY, repair of roof, 1836 [*Survey of London* xxix, 39].

DOMESTIC ARCHITECTURE

EYWOOD, HEREFS., additions for 5th Earl of Oxford, 1806–7; dem. *c.*1955 [R.I.B.A.D.].

OFFLEY PLACE, HERTS., for the Revd. Lynch Burroughs, 1806–10, Gothic [J. P. Neale, *Views of Seats*, 2nd ser. v, 1829].

LOWTHER CASTLE, WESTMORLAND, for lst Earl of Lonsdale, 1806–11, castellated; interior gutted 1957 [J. P. Neale, *Views of Seats* ii, 1819].

OFFLEY RECTORY, HERTS., for the Revd. Thelwall Salusbury, 1810 [Farington's Diary, 13 July 1810].

WILTON CASTLE, YORKS. (N.R.), for Sir John Lowther, Bart., *c.*1807, castellated; enlarged 1887 [J. P. Neale, *Views of Seats*, 2nd ser. iv, 1828].

SHERWOOD LODGE, BATTERSEA, statue gallery for Jens Wolff, Danish consul, 1807–8; dem. [*The Farington Diary*, ed. J. Greig, iii, 97 n.; v, 34].

UPLEATHAM HALL, YORKS. (N.R.), enlarged for Lawrence Dundas, cr. lst Earl of Zetland, *c.*1810; dem. 1897 [*V.C.H. Yorks. N.R.* ii, 411] (*Apollo*, Sept. 1967, 175, fig. 14).

BICKLEY PLACE, KENT, added library wing for John Wells, M.P., 1810; dem. 1963 [Farington's Diary, 6 March 1810, 31 Jan. 1811].

LONDON, MORTIMER HOUSE, HALKIN STREET, for 5th Earl of Oxford, *c.*1810; remodelled *c.*1860 [*A.P.S.D.*].

CIRENCESTER PARK, GLOS., added north wing and rebuilt east front for 3rd Earl Bathurst, 1810–11 and 1830 [*A.P.S.D.*; C. Hussey in *C. Life*, 16 June 1950].

ROSE HILL (now BRIGHTLING) PARK, nr. ROBERTSBRIDGE, SUSSEX, works for John Fuller, including additional wing to house (dem. 1955), temple and observatory, *c.*1810–12. Smirke also designed in 1810–11 the pyramidal mausoleum in Brightling churchyard in which Fuller (d. 1834) is buried [T. W. Horsfield, *History of Sussex* i, 1835, 564–5, 567; *A.P.S.D.*; R.I.B.A.D.].

KINMOUNT, DUMFRIESSHIRE, for 5th Marquess of Queensberry, 1812 [J. P. Neale, *Views of Seats* ii, 1819; R.I.B.A.D.].

BOULTIBROOKE, RADNORSHIRE, for Sir Harford Jones-Brydges, 1812–15 [signed drawing at Kentchurch Court, Herefs., *ex inf.* Mr. Derek Sherborne].

EASTNOR CASTLE, HEREFS., for 2nd Lord Somers, 1812–20, castellated [J. P. Neale, *Views of Seats* ii, 1819; Alistair Rowan in *C. Life*, 7, 14 and 21 March 1968].

THE HOMEND, STRETTON GRANDISON, HEREFS., enlarged for Edward Poole, 1814–21; altered 1973 [letters in Herefordshire County Record Office, C95].

BENTLEY PRIORY, STANMORE, MIDDLESEX, enlarged for 1st Marquess of Abercorn, 1815–18 [*A.P.S.D.*].

NEWTON DON, nr. KELSO, ROXBURGHSHIRE, for Sir Alexander Don, Bart., *c.*1815 [*A.P.S.D.*; design for lodge in R.I.B.A.D.].

POWIS CASTLE, MONTGOMERYSHIRE, repairs and alterations for 1st Earl of Powis, 1815–18 [J.M. Crook, 'The Career of Sir Robert Smirke', citing Powis accounts].

LONDON, No. 45 BERKELEY SQUARE, additions for 1st Earl of Powis, *c.*1816 (?) [*A.P.S.D.*].

LONDON, LANSDOWNE HOUSE, BERKELEY SQUARE, remodelled library as a picture-gallery for 3rd Marquess of Lansdowne, 1816–19 [*A.P.S.D.*; J.M. Crook, 'The Career of Sir Robert Smirke', 361] (*C. Life*, 11 May 1935 and D. Stillman in *Art Bulletin* lii, 1970, 75–80).

GLOUCESTER, SOMERSET HOUSE (now JUDGE'S LODGINGS), for John Phillpotts, *c.*1816 [G. W. Counsel, *History of Gloucester*, 1829, 188].

WORTHY HOUSE, HANTS., for Sir Charles Ogle, Bart., 1816, and addition of *porte-cochère* for Charles Wall, 1825 [G. F. Prosser, *Select Illustrations of Hampshire*, 1833].

STRATHALLAN CASTLE, PERTHSHIRE, additions for James Drummond, cr. Lord Strathallan, 1817–18 [*A.P.S.D.*].

BOWOOD HOUSE, WILTS., designed upper terrace for 3rd Marquess of Lansdowne, 1817–18 [John Cornforth in *C. Life*, 8–22 June 1972].

WALBERTON HOUSE, SUSSEX, for Richard Prime, 1817–18 [*A.P.S.D.*].

HAFFIELD HOUSE, nr. LEDBURY, HEREFS., for William Gordon, 1817–18 [*A.P.S.D.*].

HARDWICKE COURT, GLOS., for T. J. Lloyd Baker, 1817–19 [*V.C.H. Gloucestershire* x, 182; J. Lees-Milne in *C. Life*, 5 July 1973].

WHITTINGHAME HOUSE, EAST LOTHIAN, for James Balfour, 1817–18; altered 1827 by W. Burn [*A.P.S.D.*; R.I.B.A.D.].

LUDLOW CASTLE, SHROPSHIRE, repairs for 1st Earl of Powis, 1818 [J.M. Crook, 'The Career of Sir Robert Smirke', citing Powis accounts].

CARDIFF CASTLE, GLAMORGANSHIRE, additions for 2nd Marquess of Bute, *c.*1818 [*A.P.S.D.*].

GRANGE PARK, HANTS., additions (dem.) for Alexander Baring, *c.*1818 [J. Mordaunt Crook in *The Country Seat*, ed. Colvin & Harris, 1970, 223].

ARMLEY HOUSE, nr. LEEDS, YORKS (W.R.), remodelled for Benjamin Gott, *c.*1818; wings dem. [J.P. Neale, *Views of Seats*, iv, 1821].

CULTOQUHEY HOUSE, PERTHSHIRE, for Anthony Maxtone, *c.*1820, Tudor [*N.S.A.* x, 257].

KINFAUNS CASTLE, PERTHSHIRE, for 15th Lord Gray, 1820–2, castellated [J. P. Neale, *Views of Seats*, 2nd ser. iv, 1828; R.I.B.A.D.].

EDEN HALL, CUMBERLAND, for Sir Philip Musgrave, Bart., 1821; dem. 1934 [*A.P.S.D.*] (F. O. Morris, *Picturesque Views of Seats* ii, 1880, 63).

OULTON HALL, nr. LEEDS, YORKS. (W.R.), for John Blayds, *c.*1822; reconstructed by Sydney Smirke after fire in 1850 [*A.P.S.D.*].

LONDON, No. 4 WHITEHALL GARDENS, for Sir Robert Peel, Bart., 1823–4; dem. 1938 [*A.P.S.D.*; *Survey of London* xiii, 198–200, pls. 89–90].

LONDON, Nos. 5 and 6 WHITEHALL GARDENS, for Sir Alexander Grant and Sir Charles Long, 1823–4; dem. 1938 [J. M. Crook, 'The Career of Sir Robert Smirke', 355–6] (*Survey of London* xiii, 193–7).

WARREN HOUSE, STANMORE, MIDDLESEX, additions for himself, 1824, Jacobean; dem. *c.*1957 [J. M. Crook, 'The Career of Sir Robert Smirke', 274].

EDMOND CASTLE, CUMBERLAND, enlarged and remodelled for Thomas Graham, 1824–6 Tudor; enlarged by S. Smirke 1844–6 [*A.P.S.D.*; drawings in Cumbria Record Office].

LONDON, BARRYMORE HOUSE, No. 105 PICCADILLY, addition of Doric porch, etc., for 3rd Marquess of Hertford, *c.*1824; rebuilt 1850–1 [*A.P.S.D.*].

HEREFORD, POOL COTTAGE (now THE FOSSE), CASTLE GREEN, for Capt. Pendegrass, 1825 [J. M. Crook, 'Career of Sir Robert Smirke', 275].

NORMANBY PARK, LINCS., for Sir Robert Sheffield, Bart., 1825–30; enlarged 1906 [*A.P.S.D.*; John Cornforth in *C. Life*, 17 Aug. 1961].

LUTON HOO, BEDS., additions for 2nd Marquess of Bute, *c.*1825–30; reconstructed by Sydney Smirke after fire in 1843; remodelled by Mewès & Davis 1903 [*A.P.S.D.*].

SEDBURY PARK nr. CHEPSTOW, GLOS., remodelled for George Ormerod, 1826–30; altered 1896–8 [*A.P.S.D.*] (G. Ormerod, *Strigulensia*, 1861, frontispiece).

LONDON, No. 13 PORTMAN SQUARE, alterations for 2nd Earl Manvers, *c.*1827 [*A.P.S.D.*; B.L., Egerton MS. 3527, f. 144].

LONDON, Nos. 5 and 6 CARLTON GARDENS, for

J. W. Croker and Henry Baring, 1827–30 [*A.P.S.D.*].

DRAYTON HOUSE, NORTHANTS., structural survey for 5th Duke of Dorset, 1828 [Stopford Sackville archives].

ERSKINE HOUSE, RENFREWSHIRE, for 11th Lord Blantyre, 1828, Gothic [*N.S.A.* vii, 515] (A. H. Millar, *Castles and Mansions of Renfrewshire*, 1898).

PUTNEY HILL HOUSE, SURREY, for the dowager Countess of Guilford, 1828; dem. 1933 [*A.P.S.D.*] (plans in Bodleian Library, MS. North a. 17 (R)).

CHOLMONDELEY CASTLE, CHESHIRE, addition of towers for 2nd Marquess of Cholmondeley 'under the advice of Sir Robert Smirke', *c.*1829 [G. Ormerod, *History of Cheshire*, ed. Helsby, ii, 1875, 636; Gervase Jackson-Stops in *C. Life*, 26 July 1973].

DRAYTON MANOR, nr. TAMWORTH, STAFFS., for Sir Robert Peel, 1831–5, Elizabethan; gallery added by Sydney Smirke 1846; dem. 1919 [*A.P.S.D.*] (*C. Life*, 28 March 1908).

NUNEHAM PARK, NUNEHAM COURTENAY, OXON., alterations for Edward Vernon Harcourt, Archbishop of York, including addition of south wing, 1832 [*A.P.S.D.*; M. Batey, *Nuneham Courtenay, Oxfordshire*, 1970, 14–15] (*C. Life* 7–14 Nov. 1941).

MARKHAM CLINTON VICARAGE, NOTTS., for 4th Duke of Newcastle, 1832–3 [J. Curtis, *Topographical History of Nottinghamshire*, 1843, 179].

WARFIELD HALL (now WINKFIELD PLACE), BERKS., enlarged for General Sir John Malcolm, 1832–3 [*Seats and Mansions of Berkshire*, Beard & Co., Twyford, *c.*1880].

LONDON, No. 12 BELGRAVE SQUARE, for 1st Earl Brownlow, *c.*1833 [*A.P.S.D.*].

SHILLINGTHORPE HALL, LINCS., additions for Dr. John Willis, 1833; dem. *c.*1950 [*A.P.S.D.*].

STOURTON CASTLE, KINVER, STAFFS., alterations for James Foster, *c.*1835 [*A.P.S.D.*; G. & R. M. Grazebrook, *History of Stourton Castle*, 1919, 46–7].

LONDON, STAFFORD (now LANCASTER) HOUSE, ST. JAMES'S, acted as supervisory architect for completion of house by Benjamin Wyatt for 2nd Duke of Sutherland, 1833–8 [Howard Colvin, 'The Architects of Stafford House', *Arch. Hist.* i, 1958; John Cornforth in *C. Life*, 7–14 Nov. 1968].

LONDON, No. 2 HAMILTON PLACE, repairs for Duchess-Countess of Sutherland, 1835 [N.L.S., Dep. 313/763, letters of 2 and 5 Jan., 28 July, 22 and 24 Dec. 1835, etc., *ex inf.* Mr. J. Gifford].

SMITH, CHARLES HARRIOTT (1792–1864), was the son of Joseph Smith, a monumental sculptor of Portland Road, Marylebone. He was intended by his father to follow the same trade, but, with the encouragement of Joseph Bonomi, he decided to study architecture, and was admitted to the Royal Academy Schools in 1814. Here he showed unusual skill in drawing the human figure, and was awarded the Gold Medal for Architecture in 1817. It was, however, as a sculptor that he made his career, and the Corinthian capitals and other architectural enrichments of University College London, the National Gallery and the Royal Exchange were executed by him. He also carved the cornice and frieze of Dorchester House, London, in 1851–3, and the ornamental stonework of Bridgewater House.

He was an occasional competitor for architectural works, including the Nelson Column and the South Kensington Museum, and his exhibits at the Royal Academy included designs for a villa, a church, etc., as well as works of sculpture. His drawing of the 'interior of a pagan temple', exhibited in 1821, was in the possession of the late Sir Leonard Woolley, and a design for a classical church attributed to him is illustrated in *London Topographical Record* xxiii, 1972, 104–5. He also lectured and wrote many articles (notably in the *Builder*) on architectural and aesthetic topics, and was, in his own words, 'a strange mongrel of art, science, literature, and business'. He had a considerable knowledge of geology and mineralogy, and in 1838 he was one of the four Commissioners appointed to examine and select the most suitable stone for the new Houses of Parliament (see their *Report*, published in 1839 and reprinted 1845). He was a member of the Society of Arts, and in 1855 was elected an honorary member of the Institute of British Architects, a distinction of which he was very proud. He died on 27 October 1864, leaving one son, Percy Gordon Smith, who was for many years architect to the Local Government Board. [*Builder* xxii, 1864, 802; *A.P.S.D.*; *D.N.B.*; R. Gunnis, *Dictionary of British Sculptors*, 1968, 354–5.]

SMITH, CHARLES SAMUEL (*c.*1790–), was born in Birmingham and became a pupil of Sir Jeffry Wyatville. He was admitted to the Royal Academy Schools in 1808 at the age of 18 and exhibited at the Academy between 1808[1] and 1816 and again in 1828. In the 1830s and 1840s he was practising in

[1] He was probably the 'S. Smith' who exhibited at the Academy from Wyatville's office in 1807.

Warwick, but by 1850 he had moved to Birmingham. The date of his death has not been ascertained, but he appears to given up practice by about 1855. His buildings, especially those in the Gothic style, show the influence of his training in Wyatville's office.

LEAMINGTON SPA, WARWICKS., THE UPPER ASSEMBLY ROOMS, UNION PARADE, 1811–13; dem. 1878 [Moncrieff's *Guide to Leamington Spa*, 1833, 56].

LEAMINGTON SPA, WARWICKS., THE ROYAL BATHS and PUMP ROOM, 1813–14; largely rebuilt 1885, 1926 and 1948 [Moncrieff's *Guide to Leamington Spa*, 1833, 17].

STONELEIGH ABBEY, WARWICKS., works for J. H. Leigh, including castellated stables, 1815–19 [drawings formerly at Stoneleigh]; alterations for 1st Lord Leigh, including Gothic entrance-hall, etc., 1837–9 [G. H. Parks, 'Stoneleigh Abbey', *Trans. Birmingham Archl. Soc.* lxxix, 1964, 83–4].

STANK HILL (later BUDBROOKE HOUSE), nr. WARWICK, for J. Edwards, *c.*1815; dem. *c.*1925 [exhib. at R.A., 1815].

LEAMINGTON SPA, WARWICKS., THE REGENT HOTEL, 1819 [Moncrieff's *Guide to Leamington Spa*, 1833, 41].

STONELEIGH CHURCH, WARWICKS., LEIGH CHAPEL or MAUSOLEUM, forming N. transept, for J. H. Leigh, *c.*1820, Gothic [drawings in Smith's hand in Leigh papers in Shakespeare's Birthplace Records Office, Stratford, DR 18/25/61].

ADDERBURY, OXON., repairs and additions to unidentified house for Mrs. Holford Cotton, 1823–4 [*V.C.H.Oxon.* ix, 12].

CORLEY VICARAGE, WARWICKS., 1824 [Lichfield Joint Record Office, B/A/ 13/III].

LEAMINGTON SPA, WARWICKS., DENBY VILLA, a Gothic 'cottage' near the Regent Hotel, for J. Williams, 1828; dem. *c.*1882 [exhib. at R.A. as 'now building' in 1828; *Leamington Spa Courier*, 11 Oct. 1828].

CHARLECOTE HOUSE, WARWICKS., designs (not all executed) for alterations for George Lucy, *c.*1830–8 [Alice Fairfax-Lucy, *Charlecote and the Lucys*, 1958, 277; Clive Wainwright in *C. Life*, 21 Feb. 1985, 448].

GROVE PARK, WARWICKS., for 11th Lord Dormer, 1833–4, Gothic; dem. 1976 [drawings, etc. in Warwicks. C.R.O., 895/87].

TEMPLE BALSALL HOSPITAL, WARWICKS., rebuilt MASTER'S HOUSE, 1835–6, Tudor Gothic [Eileen Gooden, *Temple Balsall*, n.d.].

FOLESHILL VICARAGE, WARWICKS., alterations or repairs, 1852 [Worcestershire C.R.O., 2755/2].

SMITH, EDWARD BLAKEWAY (1804–1875), was a builder and surveyor of Stanton Lacy, Shropshire, and later of Ludlow, where he died on 7 February 1875 [Principal Probate Registry, Calendar of Probates]. He designed the W. tower of EARLS CROOME CHURCH, WORCS., in a Romanesque style in 1832 [Vestry Minutes in Worcs. C.R.O., 8706/4], and probably designed the similar tower of HOPTON WAFERS CHURCH, SALOP., in 1827. He designed or altered several parsonages, including those of BRAMPTON BRYAN, HEREFS., 1832–4, STOKESAY, SALOP., 1839, TENBURY, WORCS., 1843–4, and WHEATHILL, SALOP., 1852 [Herefs. C.R.O., Diocesan Records, Clergy & Benefice Papers].

SMITH, FRANCIS (1672–1738) and WILLIAM (1661–1724), were sons of Francis Smith, a bricklayer of The Wergs, nr. Tettenhall in Staffordshire. William, his second son, was baptized on 1 April 1661, Francis, his youngest son, on 4 January 1671/2. Like their elder brother Richard (1658–1726), they were both brought up in the building trade, William apparently as a bricklayer, Francis as a mason. They often worked in partnership, and by the time of William's death they had become the leading master builders in the Midland counties of England. William died on 21 August 1724, in his 64th year, and was buried at Tettenhall, where Francis erected a monument to his memory on which he was described as an 'Architect Eminent in his profession'.

William Smith lived and died at The Wergs, but it was at Warwick that Francis was based for over thirty years, and as 'Smith of Warwick' he is celebrated as one of the most successful master builders in English architectural history. The town had been devastated by fire in September 1694, and in July 1695 William was appointed one of the two surveyors who were to regulate its rebuilding under the direction of Commissioners appointed by Act of Parliament. Then in 1697 he and his brother contracted to rebuild the parish church of St. Mary in accordance with designs made by Sir William Wilson (*q.v.*). It is likely that the Smiths owed their employment at Warwick to Andrew Archer, a Warwickshire gentleman who was one of the Commissioners and whose house at Umberslade in the parish of Tanworth they were then engaged in rebuilding. It was at Tanworth that in January 1694/5 Francis married his first wife Mary Morteboys, but she must have died within a few years, for in 1702 he married a Warwick girl called Anne Lea and settled in the town.

Although it was the rebuilding of Warwick that gave Smith an opportunity of which he no doubt took full advantage, his subsequent career was based on the patronage of the Midland gentry, many of whom employed him to build their country houses. A list of the country houses with which he was concerned either as architect or as builder (and usually in both capacities) will be found below. If this list is analysed topographically and chronologically, it will be seen that he or his brother built houses in all the Midland counties except (apparently) Nottinghamshire, that nearly all of them fall within a fifty-mile radius of Warwick, and that there must have been years when he had three, four or even more houses in progress at once.

Of the business methods which enabled Smith to maintain this remarkable output there is, unfortunately, too little evidence. None of his personal accounts or papers are known to have survived, and the documentation of many of his houses is incomplete. By trade a mason, he maintained a yard at the 'Marble House' in Warwick from which he supplied chimney-pieces and statuary marble-work such as the monument to Sir Justinian Isham in Lamport Church, for which he was paid £87 in 1732. There are indications that the Smiths dealt in timber as well as in stone and marble. In 1712 William Smith was buying timber from Lord Cholmondeley's woods in Cheshire to roof the church he was building at Whitchurch, and a reference in Francis Smith's will (1736) to 'all my stock of Marble and Timber' implies some involvement in the raw material of carpentry, if not in its actual workmanship. Like other enterprising Georgian master builders, the Smiths were prepared to undertake the construction of an entire building on behalf of the owner, though Francis appears to have preferred to contract on a 'cost plus' basis rather than 'by the great', providing his client with a detailed estimate of the cost of workmanship and materials and charging a 5 per cent commission on the actual outlay. 'One shilling in the Pound' was, he told Sir Justinian Isham, 'my usuall Pay from other Gentlemen', and at Ditchley he asked 'five pounds for every Hundred I have paid, & for my own trouble, Journeys, proffits out of my workmen, & measuring the work'. Whether as builder or as surveyor he enjoyed a reputation for honesty which does much to explain his popularity among the Midland gentry. In 1707 a London surveyor called Robert Jones considered that it would be greatly to Lord Cholmondeley's advantage to employ 'one Smith that does great deal of busness in the Contry and they have done a great deal of worke thearabout & in Warwick you may easy hear of them for [they] are brothers both masters and very good Workmen'. When the redoubtable Sarah, Duchess of Marlborough, was building a house at Wimbledon in Surrey she insisted 'that Mr. Smith of Warwickshire the Builder may be employed to make Contracts and to Measure the Work and to doe every thing in his Way that is necessary to Compleat the Work as far as the Distance he is at will give him Leave to do'. Francis Smith was almost certainly the unnamed builder whom Sir Roger Cave recommended to Sir John Langham of Cottesbrooke as 'as honest a dealor as the Kingdom has and as retionable', and when he died in 1738 Sir Edmund Isham was not alone in lamenting the loss of 'our honest Builder Mr. Smith of Warwick'.

Honesty and reliability were the qualities which stood Francis Smith in good stead rather than any great distinction as an architectural designer. One eighteenth-century critic who had seen several of his houses noted that although 'all of them (are) convenient and handsome . . . there is a great sameness in the plans, which proves he had but little invention'.[1] The typical Smith house is, indeed, easily recognizable. It is three storeys in height, and the centre is emphasized by slight projection or recession. The fenestration is uniform throughout, and there is little external ornamentation other than that provided by keystones, architraves, aprons, quoins and a balustraded parapet. On the ground floor the centre contains only two rooms – a hall and a saloon – and the staircase is set to one side in one of the flanks. Superb plasterwork and joinery – there is marquetry too at Davenport and Mawley – may create some splendid interiors, but the spatial effects are simple and unenterprising. Essentially it is the standard late seventeenth-century country house, typified by Belton (Lincs.), brought up to date by the substitution of a balustraded parapet for a hipped roof (at William Smith's Stanford even this concession to modernity is dispensed with). Such are Umberslade, Alfreton, Kinlet, Meriden, Newbold Revel, Wingerworth and Wynnstay. Of the same family, but with variations such as the substitution of pilasters for quoins, are Davenport, Mawley, Shenstone, Swynnerton and Berwick. In the first quarter of the century the trimmings are generally of a vernacular baroque character, derived in some instances from engravings in Rossi's *Studio d'Architettura Civile* (1702–21), but thereafter they become progressively more conven-

[1] In a letter from the Hon. Daines Barrington, F.S.A., to the Revd. Mr. Norris, dated 22 December 1784, and read before the Society of Antiquaries on 20 January 1785.

tional under the influence of Gibbs and the Palladians.

The list given below does, however, include four exceptional houses which do not conform to the standard Smith pattern: Kedleston, Chicheley, Stoneleigh and Sutton Scarsdale. Smith's Kedleston (pulled down to make way for the existing house by Paine and Adam) was based on a rectangular plan with projecting corner pavilions and seems to have derived from Ragley in Warwickshire (1679–83), a house with which Robert Hooke was concerned, though the basic design was due to the Warwick master carpenter Roger Hurlbut (*q.v.*). The special characteristics of Chicheley, with its illusionistic baroque front and Borrominesque doorways, are probably best seen as evidence of the personal taste of its owner, Sir John Chester, and his connoisseur friends, rather than of Francis Smith's unaided invention. Stoneleigh represents a somewhat inept attempt to use a giant order in the grand baroque manner, but at Sutton Scarsdale Smith produced a notable façade in which a giant Corinthian order is used with an assurance that is quite unexpected. Gibbs's engraved design for the University buildings at Cambridge of 1721 could have suggested several of the essential elements of this front, including the three-quarter Corinthian columns and the channelled masonry. Indeed, the contrast between the confident grandeur of Sutton Scarsdale and Stoneleigh's gauche assemblage of over-crowded windows and leggy pilasters is so striking that one cannot help suspecting a helping hand from Gibbs himself. However, it is Francis Smith who alone appears as 'gentleman architect' on the lead plate (now lost) which also recorded the names of Edward Poynton of Nottingham, carver, Thomas Eboral of Warwick, joiner, Francis Butcher of Duckmanton, carpenter, Joshua Reading of Derby, painter, Joshua Needham of Derby, plasterer, and other craftsmen employed in the building and adorning of this magnificent house, now an empty shell since its interiors were dismantled in 1920. As Reading and Needham were employed at Ditchley, and as Poynton and Eboral worked at both Ditchley and Chicheley, it looks as if we have here a list of Smith's regular associates, and their names recur in a manuscript notebook in the Bodleian Library giving the rates of work done in the 1730s under Smith's direction at Badminton, Netheravon and elsewhere (MS. Eng. misc. f. 556).

The only public building of any consequence designed by Francis Smith was the Court House at Warwick, a building of some sophistication whose façades are dignified by channelled masonry and an order of Doric pilasters. The earlier churches with which he or his brother were concerned (Lichfield, Burton-on-Trent, Newcastle-under-Lyme and Lincoln) were evidently designed by the latter on the model of the one which he had built at Whitchurch in Shropshire to the designs of John Barker (*q.v.*), who was himself following precedents afforded by Wren's churches in London, and at Monmouth Francis continued this simple and unadventurous formula after his brother's death. However in 1723–5 he had built All Saints, Derby, to Gibbs's designs, and Gainsborough church (which he probably designed) is externally an essay in the manner of Gibbs.

In his later years Smith put on the weight that is all too apparent in an unflattering portrait painted by Winstanley. But his energies appear to have been undiminished. 'It is unlucky', wrote Dr. George Clarke of All Souls College in February 1730, 'that Mr. Smith is grown so unweildy and engaged in so much business.' When he died in April 1738 at the age of 66, he left a flourishing business and an estate at Knowle in Warwickshire that he had bought from Sir Fulk Greville for £10,000. He had twice been Mayor of Warwick (in 1713–14 and 1728–9). He was buried in St. Mary's Church, but there is no record of any monument to his memory. Several portraits are, however, preserved. One in the Court House at Warwick is reproduced in *Birmingham Arch. Soc.'s Trans.* lix, 1935, pl. iv, and by Christopher Hussey, *English Country Houses: Early Georgian*, 1955, 36. Another, from Stoneleigh Abbey, is now on loan to the Warwick Museum; it is reproduced in *Connoisseur* cxviii, Dec. 1946, 73. A third, by W. Winstanley, formerly at Abington Hall, Northants., is now in the Bodleian Library, Oxford. There is an engraving of it by A. Vanhacken, with a dedication to J. H. Thursby, the builder of Abington Hall (A. Gomme in *Bodleian Library Record* xi (5), 1984, 277–9). The Bodleian also owns a terracotta bust of Smith by Rysbrack, which was bequeathed to the Radcliffe Trustees by Francis Hiorne in 1789, and is now in the Radcliffe Library. It is dated 1741 (three years after Smith's death), and appears to be based on the Abington Hall portrait. It was intended by Hiorne to occupy a vacant niche in the Library, of which Smith had been one of the mason-contractors in 1737, although he did not live to see its completion (see E. G. Tibbits, 'A Bust by Rysbrack', *Bodleian Library Record* i, 1941, 230–4). A marble version of it was sold at Sotheby's on 7 July 1988.

Francis Smith had four sons and one daughter, but only two of the sons survived their father. William, the elder, to whom he left 'all my stock of Marble and Timber . . . in my Marble Yard in Warwick', continued his father's business and is separately noticed below. Richard died in 1753, aged 39. Neither had any children. Elizabeth, the daughter, married John Stokes of Dippens, and it was her son, Francis Stokes, who eventually inherited Smith's property.

Among some Stokes family papers formerly (1947) in the possession of Mrs. Calcott Stokes there is a memoir of Mrs. Nancy Stokes (d. 1838), whose husband was Francis Stokes's second son and eventual heir.[1] In this document Francis Smith is described as 'the architect . . . from whose plans the church of St. Philip in Birmingham, the great mansions of Ombersley Court, Kinlet, Patshull, Davenport House etc. arose'. This evidently represents the account of Francis Smith's works handed down in the Stokes family, and although it is demonstrably incorrect in connecting him with St. Philip's, Birmingham, his responsibility for Ombersley, Davenport and Kinlet is confirmed by other sources. A letter at Ombersley written in 1861 by G. W. L. Childe, then the owner of Kinlet, records an independent tradition that Kinlet, Ombersley, Mawley and Buntingsdale were designed by Francis Smith, and a MS. history of the Fitzherbert family, compiled in 1828 and preserved at Swynnerton, ascribes Swynnerton, Wingerworth and Mawley to the same architect, but wrongly names him as Carr of York. Apart from these somewhat doubtful family traditions, the list of Smith's works has to be pieced together from the various sources cited below.

[*Tettenhall Parish Register*, ed. P. W. L. Adams, Staffordshire Parish Register Soc. 1930; Warwick County Records, vii: *Quarter Sessions Records 1674–1682*, 1946, cxii; Francis Smith's will, P.C.C. 162 BRODREPP; B.L., Add. MS. 29265, ff. 227–9 (for Smith's Knowle estate); H. M. Colvin, 'Francis Smith of Warwick 1672–1738', *Warwickshire History* ii (2), 1972/3; A. Gomme, 'Smith and Rossi', *Arch. Hist.* 35, 1992; *The Great Fire of Warwick. The Record of the Commissioners appointed under an Act of Parliament for rebuilding the Town of Warwick*, ed. M. Farr, Dugdale Soc. 1992; information from Prof. Andor Gomme.]

[1] A version of this document was printed by John Randall, *A Guide to Worfield*, Madeley 1887, 102.

CHURCHES DESIGNED OR BUILT BY WILLIAM AND FRANCIS SMITH

WARWICK, ST. MARY'S CHURCH, rebuilt (except chancel and Beauchamp Chapel) by William & Francis Smith to designs of Sir William Wilson, 1698–1704 [*The Great Fire of Warwick*, ed. Farr, 1992, xxiv-xxix; cf. P.B. Chatwin, 'The Rebuilding of St. Mary's Church, Warwick', *Trans. Birmingham & Midland Institute* lxv, 1943–4].

HALL GREEN CHAPEL, YARDLEY, WORCS., built to designs of Sir William Wilson, cons. 1704 [D. Whitehead, 'Job Marston's Chapel', *Georgian Group Jnl.* 1992].

WHITCHURCH CHURCH, SALOP., rebuilt by William Smith to designs of John Barker, 1712–13; interior refaced 1902 [MS. churchwardens' accounts].

COLESHILL CHURCH, WARWICKS., repair of tower supervised by Francis Smith, 1714 [agreement among parish records in Warwicks. C.R.O.].

LICHFIELD, STAFFS., ST. MARY'S CHURCH, built by William Smith 1717–21; rebuilt 1868–70 [letter from John Kent to John Ward dated 16 Sept. 1727 in John Rylands Library, Manchester, Bromley-Davenport papers, Box 19, referring to Lichfield church as a work undertaken by the late William Smith. The churchwardens' accounts show that he had been consulted when the spire threatened to fall in 1715] (drawings by Buckler in B.L., Add. MS. 36386, ff. 219, 251).

BURTON-ON-TRENT CHURCH, STAFFS., rebuilt by William and Richard Smith, 1719–26, completed by Francis Smith after William's death in 1724; restored 1886–1904 [W. Molyneux, *Burton-on-Trent*, 1869; MS. Vestry Minutes].

NEWCASTLE-UNDER-LYME CHURCH, STAFFS., rebuilt by William Smith except west tower, 1720–1; rebuilt 1873–6 [R. Fenton, *St. Giles Parish Church, Newcastle-under-Lyme*, reprinted from the *Staffordshire Times*, June 1876].

LINCOLN, ST. PETER-AT-ARCHES CHURCH, *c.*1720–4; taken down 1932, and rebuilt in the suburbs of Lincoln as St. Giles, 1936. The original church was of Roche Abbey stone: it was rebuilt in brick with the old stone dressings. The urns and balustrades had been renewed in the 1820s, and there were alterations by S. S. Teulon in 1853–4. A plan of the church by Teulon is in the Diocesan Records (Fac. 11/44). The Corporation Minute Book shows (29 Oct. 1723) that the contractor was a 'Mr. Smith' and a visitor noted in 1725 that 'the mason and architect was Smith of Warwick' [Hist. MSS. Comm., *Portland* vi, 84].

DERBY, ALL SAINTS CHURCH, nave and chancel rebuilt by William and Francis Smith to the designs of James Gibbs, 1723–5. In 1719 'Mr. Smith of Warwick' made a design and estimate, but objections were raised, and in 1723 a new plan 'contrived by Mr. Gibbs and Mr. Smiths' was adopted. William and Francis Smith were the joint contractors, but owing to William's death in 1724, only his brother's name appears in the accounts after that date. [J. C. Cox and W. H. St. J. Hope, *Chronicles of All Saints Derby*, 1881, 63–80].

WORCESTER CATHEDRAL, 'plan and directions' for repairing S. Transept given by 'Mr. Smith', then working at Ombersley Court [Dean & Chapter's records, Treasurer's accounts, 1725, *ex inf.* Mr. David Whitehead].

SIBSON CHURCH, LEICS., nave and W. tower rebuilt by Thomas Moor (*q.v.*) 'according to a draught given in by Francis Smith', 1725–6 [contract in Leicestershire C.R.O., DE 373/3].

HEREFORD CATHEDRAL, W. window rebuilt under the direction of Francis Smith, 1736; destroyed 1786 [D. Whitehead, 'Hereford Cathedral in the 18th Century', *Friends of Hereford Cathedral 57th Annual Report*, 1991, 30–1].

MONMOUTH, ST. MARY'S CHURCH, rebuilt except steeple, 1736–7; remodelled by G.E. Street 1881–2 [A. Gomme, 'St. Mary's Monmouth: the Building of the 18th Century Church', *Monmouthshire Antiquary* v (3), 1985–8].

GAINSBOROUGH CHURCH, LINCS., nave and chancel rebuilt, 1736–44. The 'Report of the Committee for Rebuilding Gainsborough Church' in the Lincoln Diocesan Records (Fac. 9/68) shows that Francis Smith made a plan and estimate in 1734, and this is confirmed by the evidence given in 1735 before the House of Commons (*Commons' Jnls.* xxii, 556–7, 619–21; xxiii, 582, 618). There is no mention of Gibbs, who is said to have been the architect of the new church by the Lincolnshire antiquary, E. J. Willson (1787–1854) and by T. Mozley (b. in Gainsborough 1806) in his *Reminiscences* (1855). The parish records of this period have been lost or destroyed.

SECULAR BUILDINGS DESIGNED OR BUILT BY WILLIAM AND FRANCIS SMITH

UMBERSLADE HALL, TANWORTH, WARWICKS., for Andrew Archer, *c.*1693–1700; altered in 19th century [W. Field, *History of Warwick*, 1815, 374, where the house is said to have been built 'by John Smith', referred to elsewhere in the book as the builder of St. Mary's Warwick. Francis Smith was presumably working here in Jan. 1694/5, when he was married in Tanworth Church. For evidence that work started in 1693 see Archer Papers in Shakespeare's Birthplace Records Office, Stratford, ER 24/26.2]. (*Vitruvius Britannicus* iii, 1731, pl. 101; *Wren Soc.* xvii, pl. xlii).

WROTTESLEY HALL, STAFFS., for Sir Walter Wrottesley, Bart., *c.*1696; dem. after fire in 1897 [payments to William and Richard Smith for building work in fragmentary accounts 1694–7, Staffs. C.R.O., Tp. 1226, folder 17] (*V.C.H. Staffs.* xx, 27 and ill. p. 32).

STANFORD HALL, LEICS., designed and built by William Smith for Sir Francis Cave, Bart., 1697–1700. The stables (completed 1737) were added by Sir Verney Cave to the designs of Francis Smith, to whom the remodelling of the east front *c.*1735 may also be attributed. The interior of the great hall was altered by William Smith, jr. (*q.v.*), in 1745 [estimates and contracts in Leics. R.O.; drawings and letter among Verney archives at Claydon House, Bucks.] (*C. Life*, 4, 11 and 18 Dec. 1958).

KEDLESTON HALL, DERBYSHIRE, for Sir Nathaniel Curzon, *c.*1700; rebuilt 1758 onwards [plan at Kedleston inscribed 'Kedleston built by Smith', reproduced in *Warwickshire History* ii (2), 1972–3, 9].

SUTTON COLDFIELD RECTORY, WARWICKS., built by William Smith for the Revd. John Riland, 1701; dem. 1936 [W. K. R. Bedford, *History of the Rilands of Sutton Coldfield*, 1889, 19–20].

STRATFORD-ON-AVON, WARWICKS., THE VICARAGE (now the Headmaster's House) built by 'Mr. Smith', 1702–3 [Stratford Chamberlains' Accounts, 1702–3].

COTTESBROOKE HALL, NORTHANTS., for Sir John Langham, Bart., 1703–13 [payments to Francis Smith in Langham's account-book in Northants. C.R.O., L(C) 2597, under dates 14 Feb. 1701/2 and 7 Dec. 1713, and cf. Sir Gyles Isham and Bruce Bailey in *C. Life*, 19 Feb. 1970] (*C. Life*, 15–22 Feb. 1936, 17–24 March 1955).

CHOLMONDELEY HALL, CHESHIRE, remodelled by William Smith for 1st Earl of Cholmondeley, 1704–13; dem. *c.*1805 [Gervase Jackson-Stops in *C. Life*, 19 July 1973] (*Vitruvius Britannicus* ii, 1715, pls. 31–4, iii, 1725, pls. 79–80).

SANDWELL PARK, STAFFS., rebuilt by William Smith for 1st Earl of Dartmouth, 1705–11;

dem. 1928 [*V.C.H. Staffs.* xvii, 19, with plan] (S. Shaw, *History of Staffordshire* ii, 1801, 128, plate).

HEYTHROP HOUSE, OXON., built 'by Smith' to the designs of Thomas Archer (*q.v.*) for the Duke of Shrewsbury, *c.*1705–8 [notebook (1759–61) of Edward Knight in Kidderminster Public Library].

TRENTHAM HALL, STAFFS., built by William Smith for lst Lord Gower, *c.*1707–10 [Staffordshire Record Office, D 868/9/52, 53, 55]; additions by Francis Smith 1736–7 [*ibid.*, D 593/P/16/2/4/20 and accounts for 1736–7]; altered 1764–78, remodelled 1838; dem. 1910 (*C. Life*, 25 Jan. 1968).

DUNCHURCH SCHOOL, WARWICKS., built by Francis Smith, 1708–9 [Trustees' minutes in Warwickshire C.R.O., CR 786/1].

CLIFTON CAMPVILLE HALL, STAFFS., for Sir Charles Pye, Bart., 'who built the wings before the centre, and was unable to finish it according to his plans'. The wings are said to have been built in 1708. A plan in Francis Smith's hand showing both the existing wings and the projected main building is among Pye papers in Sheffield City Library (Elmhirst 1337). For an alternative design for the main building by William Dickinson dated 1710, see above, p. 303.

BAGINTON HALL, WARWICKS., built by Francis Smith for William Bromley, *c.*1708–14 (dated 1714 on the front); destroyed by fire 1889 [F. L. Colvile, *Worthies of Warwickshire*, 1869, 61, note, citing building accounts now lost].

WOLVERHAMPTON, STAFFS., THE GRAMMAR SCHOOL, JOHN STREET, built by William Smith, 1712–14; converted into shops 1877; dem. *c.*1970 [G. P. Mander, *History of Wolverhampton Grammar School*, 1913, 179] (*V.C.H. Staffs.* vi, 145, plate).

ETWALL HALL, DERBYSHIRE, centre refronted and other alterations by William & Francis Smith for Rowland Cotton, *c.*1713–14; dem. 1954–5 [accounts in Derbyshire C.R.O., 286 M/E 1–3] (*C. Life*, 27 May 1899).

COMPTON VERNEY, WARWICKS., probably built by the Smiths to the designs of an unknown architect for 12th Lord Willoughby de Broke and Dean of Windsor, *c.*1714 (1714 being the date recorded by George Vertue, *Notebooks* vi, 75), for two payments of £200 were made to 'Mr. Smith by order' from Lord Willoughby's Staffordshire estate in 1714–15 [Shakespeare's Birthplace Records Office, DR 98/1811], the Warwickshire accounts for those years being lost (*Vitruvius Britannicus* v, 1771, pls. 43–4).

CHETTLE HOUSE, DORSET, built by the Smiths for George Chafin to designs attributed to Thomas Archer (*q.v.*), *c.*1715–20. According to a Wynnstay letter of 1718 [N.L.W., Williams-Wynn papers C. 69] 'Mr. Chaffin's' house 'was built by [Francis] Smith's Brother', and in Sept. 1721 Francis wrote that he had set out 'to conclude some busines that I had in Dorsettshire' [N.L.W., Penrice & Margam MSS., L 958].

STONELEIGH, WARWICKS., STONE FARM HOUSE, built by Francis Smith for 3rd Lord Leigh, 1716 [Shakespeare's Birthplace Trust Record Office, Stratford, Leigh papers, DR 18/3/47/38].

CROOME COURT, WORCS., stables built by 'Mr. Smith' for 4th Earl of Coventry, 1716–19 [account-book of Gilbert, Earl of Coventry, at Antony House, Cornwall, CVA/H3/22].

CHARLECOTE HOUSE, WARWICKS., repairs and alterations by Francis Smith for George Lucy, 1718–19 [accounts in John Rylands Library, Manchester, Bromley-Davenport papers 114 and cf. Alice Fairfax-Lucy, *Charlecote & the Lucys*, 1958, 22].

CHICHELEY HALL, BUCKS., built by Francis Smith for Sir John Chester, Bart., 1719–21; stables 1723–5 [Joan D. Tanner, 'The Building of Chicheley Hall', *Records of Bucks.* xvii, 1961; see also Arthur Oswald in *C. Life*, 9, 16, 23 May 1936, and Marcus Binney in *C. Life*, 13, 20 Feb. 1975] (J. Lees-Milne, *English Country Houses: Baroque*, 1970, 227–35).

CAPESTHORNE HALL, CHESHIRE, wings built by William Smith for John Ward, 1720; house rebuilt by Francis Smith for John Ward, 1732–3; enlarged by E. Blore 1839–42; rebuilt by A. Salvin after a fire in 1861 [contract of Jan. 1719/20 and estimate of Feb. 1731/2 among Bromley-Davenport papers in John Rylands Library, Manchester; A. H. & S. M. Gomme, 'Who Designed Capesthorne Hall?' *Trans. Historic Soc. of Lancs. and Cheshire* cxxi, 1969].

STONELEIGH ABBEY, WARWICKS., largely rebuilt by Francis Smith for 3rd Lord Leigh, 1720–26 [G. H. Parks, 'Stoneleigh Abbey', *Trans. Birmingham Arch. Soc.* lxxix, 1964, 78; Andor Gomme in *Archaeological Jnl.* cxxviii, 1971, 246–51] (C. Hussey, *English Country Houses: Early Georgian*, 1955, 37–9).

MERIDEN HALL, WARWICKS., built by Francis Smith for Martin Baldwin, *c.*1720; attic storey added later [Birmingham Reference Library, Digby deposit, 7313L/19–21, 98].

DITCHLEY HOUSE, OXON., built by Francis Smith for 2nd Earl of Lichfield to the designs of James Gibbs, 1720–42. Smith submitted a design of his own and Gibbs's design may have been to some extent a modified version of it. The stable-block appears to have been built by Smith to his own design before Gibbs was employed [A. Gomme, 'Architects and Craftsmen at Ditchley', *Arch. Hist.* 32, 1989] (J. Gibbs, *Book of Architecture*, 1728, pl. 39).

BUNTINGSDALE HALL, SALOP., built (or building supervised) by 'Smith of Warwick' to designs made by John Prince (*q.v.*) for Bulkeley Mackworth, completed 1721; enlarged 1857 [S. Leighton, *Shropshire Houses*, 1901, 30; H. A. Tipping in *C. Life*, 3 Nov. 1917, citing accounts now lost, including an agreement to provide Smith with 'a pad nag to ride hither from Warwick' in order to inspect the works; H. A. Tipping, *English Homes, Period V* (i), 1921, 193–8].

WILTON, HEREFS., unexecuted project by Francis Smith for mansion for the Duke of Chandos, 1723 [C. H. C. & M. I. Baker, *James Brydges, Duke of Chandos*, 1949, 213, 276].

OMBERSLEY COURT, WORCS., built by William & Francis Smith for Samuel Sandys, 1723–6; exterior remodelled by John Webb 1812–14 [bills at Ombersley; the first receipt for £400, dated 4 Dec. 1723, is signed by both William and Francis Smith. William died in 1724 and all the other payments, amounting to some £1500, are to Francis] (*C. Life*, 2, 9, 16 Jan, 1953).

STANWAY MANOR, GLOS., alterations for John Tracy, 1724 [Anne Tracy's diary, 10 Feb. 1723/4, *ex inf.* Prof. A. Gomme].

SUTTON SCARSDALE, DERBYSHIRE, built by Francis Smith for 4th Earl of Scarsdale, begun 1724; unroofed 1920, now a ruin; three rooms are in Philadelphia Museum of Art. An inscription on a lead plate, now lost, recorded that:

This house was begun to be rebuilt in the year 1724 by the order of the Right Honourable Nicholas Earl of Scarsdale. Francis Smith of Warwick Gent. architect. Ed[d]. Poynton of Nottingham Gent. Carver. Tho. Eboral of Warwick Joyner. Francis Butcher of Duckmanton carpenter. Albert Arteri Gent. and Francis Vossali Gent. Italians who did the stuke work. Joshua Reading of Derby Gent. Painter. Joshua Needham of Derby Plaisterer. Willm. Jeffery of Chesterfield Plummer. Tho[s] How of Westminster upholsterer. John Wilks of Birmingham Gent. Locksmith. John Lillyman Gent. Steward. Jn[o] Christian Gent. Gardener. John Mott Gent. Keeper. [B.L., Add. MS. 6674, f. 179].

(H. A. Tipping in *C. Life*, 15 Feb. 1919 and *English Homes*, Period V (i), 1921, 199–206; *C. Life*, 16 April 1970; A. Gomme, 'The Genesis of Sutton Scarsdale', *Arch. Hist.* 24, 1981).

ALFRETON HALL, DERBYSHIRE, for Rowland Morewood, 1724–5; dem. 1968 [Derbyshire C.R.O., D 1763, Morewood account-book no. 3]. The only reference to Smith is a payment 'for going to Mansfield Post-House to put in a Letter for Mr. Smith', but this, coupled with the architectural character of the house, makes Smith's responsibility for the design almost, if not quite, certain.

TEMPLE BALSALL HOSPITAL, WARWICKS., rebuilt by Francis Smith except Master's House, *c.*1724–6 [Warwicks. C.R.O., Minutes of the Trustees, CR 112/180 and Vouchers, CR112/173, 1724–6].

SHARDELOES HOUSE, BUCKS., stables and offices built by Francis Smith for Montague Garrard Drake, 1724–7; much altered 1960–5 [Drake's account at Hoare's Bank and accounts in Bucks. C.R.O., Drake papers, *ex inf.* Prof. A. Gomme].

MELBOURNE HALL, DERBYSHIRE, W. wing rebuilt by Francis Smith for Thomas Coke, 1725–6 [Philip Heath, 'Melbourne Hall Reconsidered', *Georgian Group's Report & Jnl.* 1988].

WARWICK, THE COURT HOUSE, designed and built by Francis Smith, 1725–30 [*Trans. Birmingham Archl. Soc.* lix, 1935, 72–3].

DAVENPORT HALL, SALOP., designed and built by Francis Smith for Henry Davenport, *c.*1726 [F. Calvert & W. West, *Picturesque Views and Descriptions of . . . Staffordshire and Shropshire*, 1831, 124] (*C. Life*, 27 June, 4, 11 July 1952).

FOXLEY, HEREFS., stables for Robert Price, 1726; dem. [MS. note in copy of Gibbs's *Book of Architecture* formerly at Foxley, copied by the late B. Little: 'stables built 1726 by Francis Smith of Warwick after designs of his own']. Smith may well have built the house (dem. 1948) which was begun in 1719 according to a plan 'invented by Uvedale Price' (the owner's son), as Prof. Gomme reports payments to the Smiths in Robert Price's bank account from 1720 onwards.

KINLET HALL, SALOP., designed and built by Francis Smith for William Lacon Childe, 1727–9; library added 1827 [S. Leighton, *Shropshire Houses*, 1901, 42; Stokes memoir cited above].

CALKE ABBEY, DERBYSHIRE, new flight of steps up to front door built by Francis Smith to designs of James Gibbs, 1727–8; removed 1806 [H. Colvin, *Calke Abbey*, 1985, 104].

LAMPORT RECTORY, NORTHANTS., designed and built by Francis Smith for Sir Justinian Isham, Bart., 1727–30 [Northants. C.R.O., Isham papers, correspondence 2826 and I.L. 3959, estimate].

BADMINTON HOUSE, GLOS., altered exterior and remodelled interior for 3rd Duke of Beaufort, 1729 onwards, probably to Smith's own designs, except for the pavilions designed by Gibbs [A. Gomme, 'Badminton Revisited', *Arch. Hist.* 27, 1984].

ALMINGTON HALL, STAFFS., for Edward Sneyd, 1730–4; altered in 19th century [Keele University Library, Sneyd papers S. 1917, 1924, *ex inf.* Prof. A. Gomme].

CAPESTHORNE HALL, CHESHIRE, house rebuilt by Francis Smith for John Ward, 1732–3 [see above, p. 887].

WIMBLEDON HOUSE, SURREY, Francis Smith called in by Sarah, Duchess of Marlborough, in 1732–3 to act as surveyor of house being built to designs of Lord Pembroke and Roger Morris; destroyed by fire 1785 [Frances Harris, 'The Building of Wimbledon House, 1730–42', *Georgian Group Jnl.* 1992].

LAMPORT HALL, NORTHANTS., alterations and additions by Francis Smith for Sir Justinian Isham, Bart., including the addition of the wings, 1732–8, completed by William Smith, jr. [Sir Gyles Isham, 'The Architectural History of Lamport', *Reports & Papers Northants. Arch. & Archl. Soc.* lvii, 1951] (*C. Life*, 26 Sept., 3 Oct. 1952).

BROGYNTYN, SALOP., built by Francis Smith for William Owen, 1735–6; portico added 1814–15 [N.L.W., Owen papers 1582, 1852, 2008].

NETHERAVON HOUSE, WILTS., built by Francis Smith for 3rd Duke of Beaufort, 1735–6; altered 1791 and later [Badminton archives, *ex inf.* Prof. A. Gomme; rates of work in Bodleian, MS. Eng. Misc. f. 556, pp. 1, 11].

ST. ALBANS, HERTS., THE MARLBOROUGH ALMSHOUSES, for Sarah, Duchess of Marlborough, 1735–6 [Northants. C.R.O., Spencer papers, Bd. 23/2].

ASTROP PARK, NORTHANTS., built by Francis Smith for Sir John Willes, 1735–8; altered 1805 and 1961 [Smith's and Willes's accounts in Hoare's Bank, *ex inf.* Prof. A. Gomme; rates of mason's work in Bodleian, MS. Eng. Misc. f. 556, p. 17].

WYNNSTAY, DENBIGHSHIRE, built by Francis and his son William Smith for Sir Watkin Williams-Wynn, Bart., 1736–9; remodelled by James Wyatt 1785; destroyed by fire 1858 [Peter Howell in *C. Life*, 23–30 March, 1972; Bodleian Library, MS. Eng. Misc. f. 556, p. 21].

TEMPLE BALSALL HOUSE, WARWICKS., rebuilt for the Trustees of Temple Balsall Hospital 1738–9 after Francis Smith had been asked to provide an estimate [Minutes of the Trustees in Warwicks. C.R.O., CR 112/180].

PATSHULL HOUSE, STAFFS., built to designs of James Gibbs by Francis and his son William Smith, for Sir John Astley, *c.*1738 onwards, completed by William Baker (*q.v.*); altered by W. Burn, 1855 [*V.C.H. Staffs.* xx, 165–66].

STYLISTIC ATTRIBUTIONS

A considerable number of buildings can plausibly be attributed to Francis Smith on stylistic grounds. There were, however, other Midland master builders who were capable of designing in a style similar to Smith's, and the following list is confined to those buildings for whose attribution to Smith the case seems particularly strong.

ABINGTON HALL, NORTHANTS., refronted for J.H. Thursby, *c.*1738–43 [attribution supported by the fact that the Thursby portrait of Smith came from Abington] (J. A. Gotch, *Squires' Homes of Northamptonshire*, 1939, 34–5).

BERWICK HOUSE, SALOP., for Thomas Powys, 1731; altered by R. Mylne 1780; S.W. front rebuilt 1878 (F. Leach, *The County Seats of Shropshire*, Shrewsbury 1891, 1).

CALDWELL HALL, DERBYSHIRE, remodelled for Thomas Sanders, 1729 (M. Craven & M. Stanley, *The Derbyshire Country House* ii, 1984, 24).

DALLINGTON HALL, NORTHANTS., for Sir Joseph Jekyll, *c.*1725–30 (J. P. Neale, *Views of Seats*, 1st ser. i, 1818; J. A. Gotch, *Squires' Homes of Northamptonshire*, 1939, 34).

DOWNTON HALL, SALOP., has a S. front in the style of William and Francis Smith of *c.*1700, representing a house probably built by Serjeant William Hall (d. 1721). Rainwater heads dated 1738 may record an enlargement by Wrendenhall Pearce, who inherited the house by marriage to Hall's niece (*C. Life*, 21 July 1917).

DUDMASTON HALL, nr. BRIDGNORTH, SALOP., for Sir Thomas Wolryche, Bart., *c.*1695; attic storey and other alterations *c.*1820 [attribution based on close resemblance to Stanford Hall, supported by a letter dated 10 April 1695 from George Weld of Willey asking Andrew Archer of Umberslade to lend a plan or model of his house to his son-in-law Sir Thomas Wolryche (Shropshire

C.R.O., uncatalogued Forester papers)] (*C. Life*, 8, 15, 22 March 1979).

FAWSLEY HALL, NORTHANTS., N. block for Lucy Knightley, 1732; remodelled in 19th century. The monument to Richard Knightley (d. 1728) in Fawsley Church can also be attributed to Smith as the word 'Warwick' appears on a gun butt in the achievement. (engraving showing N. block in *Gent's Mag.* 1794 (ii), 977).

HALTON, CHESHIRE, PARISH LIBRARY, for Sir John Chesshyre, 1730–3 [A. H. Gomme in *Trans. Lancs. & Cheshire Hist. Soc.* 135, 1986, 55–6].

HAMPTON LUCY RECTORY, WARWICKS., *c.*1725: built with a legacy of £500 from the Revd. George Lucy (d. 1724), who had employed Francis Smith in a dilapidations case against the previous incumbent.

HEWELL GRANGE, WORCS., for 2nd Earl of Plymouth, 1712; portico added 1815; a ruin since *c.*1890 (T. Nash, *History of Worcs.* ii, 1782, 403; J.P. Neale, *Views of Seats* vi, 1823).

KISLINGBURY RECTORY, NORTHANTS., *c.*1710–20, for the Revd. John Perkins, Rector 1709–28. The house contains a chimney-piece identical to one at Lamport Rectory.

LOCKO PARK, DERBYSHIRE, for Robert Ferne, *c.*1725–30; enlarged by H. I. Stevens 1853–64 (*C. Life*, 5, 12, 19 June 1969).

LOTON PARK, SALOP., enlarged probably for Sir Edward Leighton, Bart., *c.*1712; altered and enlarged in 19th century (*C. Life*, 12 Aug. 1939, 160).

MAWLEY HALL, SALOP., for Sir Edward Blount, Bart., 1730 [H.A. Tipping in *C. Life*, 2 July 1910 and *English Homes, Period V* (i), 217–18; Mary Parry, 'Mawley Hall', *Archaeological Jnl.* cxiii, 1956, 194–5].

NEWBOLD REVEL HALL, WARWICKS., for Sir Fulwar Skipwith, Bart., 1716 (*Vitruvius Britannicus* ii, 1717, pl. 94; S.M. Stanislaus, *Newbold Revel*, 1949).

SANDYWELL PARK, GLOS., addition of wings for 1st Lord Conway, *c.*1720/30 (N. Kingsley, *The Country Houses of Gloucestershire* ii, 1992, 219–20).

SWYNNERTON HALL, STAFFS., for Thomas Fitzherbert, 1725–9; hall altered 1811–12 and 1974; new entrance 1949–50 [attribution supported by a confused tradition current in the early nineteenth century that the house was designed by the architect of Ince Blundell (*sic*), Wingerworth and Mawley; see MS. history of the Fitzherbert family at Swynnerton by Michael Jones, 1828, 160]. (J. P. Neale, *Views of Seats*, 1st ser. iii, 1820).

WARWICK, house in Market Place known as 'ABBOTSFORD', for Francis Smith's father- or brother-in-law, Job Lea, 1714; restored 1963.

WINGERWORTH HALL, DERBYSHIRE, for Sir Thomas Winsor Hunloke, Bart., 1726–9; dem. 1924 [H. A. Tipping in *C. Life*, 29 Jan. 1910 and *English Homes, Period V* (i), 1921, 207–16].

WYCHNOR OR WICHNOR PARK, STAFFS., for Crewe Offley (*c.*1685–1739), after 1708, when he inherited Wychnor from his mother; cf. S. Shaw, *History of Staffordshire* i, 1798, 124, and R. Sedgwick, *History of Parliament: The House of Commons 1715–54*, 1970, 304.

SMITH, GEORGE, was Clerk of Works to the City of London from 1724 to 1734, when he was dismissed following the partial collapse of the new BISHOPSGATE GATE (dem. 1760) which he had designed [T. Friedman, 'The Rebuilding of Bishopsgate', *Guildhall Studies in London History* iv (2), 1980].

SMITH, GEORGE (1782–1869), was born at Aldenham, Herts., on 28 September 1782. He was articled to R. F. Brettingham in October 1797, leaving his office in 1802 to become clerk to James Wyatt, D. A. Alexander and C. Beazley in turn. He frequently exhibited at the Royal Academy between 1801 and 1849. In 1810 he was appointed District Surveyor of the Southern Division of the City of London, and in 1814 surveyor to the Mercers' Company, retaining both posts until his death. He was for a time surveyor to the Coopers' Company, of which he was a member and twice Master. He was also surveyor to the Cator estate in Blackheath, and from 1830 onwards to the Morden College estate in Greenwich. From 1836 to 1842 he was in partnership with his pupil W. Barnes (1807–68) and subsequently with G. B. Williams, also a pupil, who took over much of the responsibility for the Morden College estate from the 1850s onwards.

Smith was a careful and meticulous man whose office was a model of orderliness. He exercised a close control over the development of the Morden College property in Greenwich, carefully approving, rejecting and sometimes modifying plans submitted by speculative builders. His own designs for buildings on the Morden estate, which included surviving houses in, e.g. Brand and Pelton Streets, show a progression from a plain late Georgian style to restrained Italianate or Jacobethan detailing. His most important works were Whittington's Almshouses at Highgate (Gothic), St. Paul's School (Greek Corinthian), the Corn Exchange in Mark Lane (Greek Doric) and St.

Albans Town Hall (Greek Ionic). These were all handsome civic buildings, and were favourably received by contemporary critics.

Smith was a Fellow of the Society of Antiquaries, a member of the Surveyors' Club from 1807, and a Fellow of the Institute of British Architects, of which he was Vice-President in 1844–5. His pupils included H. C. Barlow, W. Barnes, James Barr, David Brandon, W. Grellier, George Low, Arthur Scrivenor and G. B. Williams. T. Nichols and A. B. Clayton were assistants. Smith died at Copthorne, Sussex, on 5 January 1869, aged 87. He should not be confused with George Smith, the author of *A Collection of Designs for Household Furniture*, 1808, etc. [*A.P.S.D.*; *Builder* xxvii, 1869, 42, 65, 92; Michael Kerney, 'The Development of an early Victorian artisan estate in East Greenwich', *Trans Greenwich & Lewisham Antiq. Soc.* ix (6), 1984, 'The Architectural Work of George Smith in Greenwich & Blackheath', *London Topographical Record* 25, 1985.]

ALDENHAM LODGE, HERTS., design (perhaps not executed) for the entrance to the grounds of the late G. Mason, exhibited at R.A. 1807.

COLNEY LODGE, HERTS., south front exhibited at R.A. 1810.

CLAY HALL, HERTS., proposed alterations and additions for J. Gosling, exhibited at R.A. 1810.

HORTON KIRBY CHURCH, KENT, rebuilt tower and chancel and other alterations, 1816–17, Gothic [Edward Cresy's notebook in Kent Archives Office, f. 9].

MITCHAM CHURCH, SURREY, rebuilt 1819–22, Gothic [Brayley, *History of Surrey* iv, 92].

LONDON, THE ROYAL EXCHANGE, rebuilt entrance-front and tower, 1820–6; destroyed by fire 1838 [Britton & Pugin, *Public Buildings of London* i, 1825, 292–7].

LONDON, WHITTINGTON'S ALMSHOUSES, HIGHGATE, for the Mercers' Company, 1822, Gothic; dem. 1966 [J. Elmes, *Metropolitan Improvements*, 1831, 141–2 and plate].

LONDON, ST. MICHAEL'S CHURCH, QUEENHITHE, altar-piece, 1823; dem. 1876 [G. Godwin, *The Churches of London* ii, 1839].

LONDON, ST. PAUL'S SCHOOL, ST. PAUL'S CHURCHYARD, for the Mercers' Company, 1823–4; dem. 1884 [J. Elmes, *Metropolitan Improvements*, 1831, 126 and plate].

LONDON COLNEY CHURCH, HERTS., 1825–6, Romanesque [I.C.B.S.].

BLACKHEATH, BROOKLANDS, BLACKHEATH PARK, for himself, 1825 [*A.P.S.D.*].

LONDON, MERCERS' HALL, entrance to Architect's Office, *c.*1826 [exhib. at R.A.].

LONDON, THE CORN EXCHANGE, MARK LANE, assisted by A. B. Clayton, 1827–8; dem. 1941 [*A.P.S.D.*; J. Elmes, *Metropolitan Improvements*, 1831, 146–7 and plate; W. H. Leeds, *Supplement* to Britton & Pugin's *Public Buildings of London*, 1838, 9–20].

FINCHLEY, MIDDLESEX, villa 'lately erected' for R. Hughes, exhibited at R.A. 1827.

LONDON, MERCERS' SCHOOL, COLLEGE HILL, DOWGATE, 1829–32 [Sir John Watney, 'Mercers' School', *Trans. London and Middlesex Arch. Soc.*, N.S. i, 1898, 135].

ST. ALBANS, HERTS., COURT-HOUSE AND TOWN HALL, 1829–33 [*Sessions Records of the Liberty of St. Albans 1770–1840* iv, 1923, pp. xxix–xxxiv; *V.C.H. Herts.* ii, 472; drawings in Victoria and Albert Museum].

BLACKHEATH, ST. MICHAEL AND ALL ANGELS CHAPEL, 1828–30, Gothic [*A.P.S.D.*].

BROMLEY CHURCH, KENT, rebuilt 1820 except tower; enlarged 1883–4; destroyed by bombing 1940–1 [I.C.B.S.].

HORNSEY CHURCH, MIDDLESEX, rebuilt 1830–3 except tower, Gothic; dem. 1927 [*A.P.S.D.*].

BLACKHEATH, PROPRIETARY SCHOOL at corner of LEE TERRACE and TRANQUIL VALE, 1831; dem. 1936 [Kerney, 1985].

GREENWICH, CROWN & SCEPTRE TAVERN, new hall, in conjunction with W. Barnes, 1836; dem. 1934 [exhib. at R.A. 1837].

LONDON, ST. THOMAS'S CHURCH, ARBOUR STREET, STEPNEY, in collaboration with W. Barnes, 1838, Gothic; dem. 1955 [exhib. at R.A. 1838].

GREENWICH RAILWAY STATION, 1840; reconstructed 1878 [Kerney, 1985].

HORSHAM, SUSSEX, THE GRAMMAR SCHOOL, 1840–1 [*A.P.S.D.*].

LONDON, ST. GEORGE'S WESLEYAN CHAPEL, BACK ROAD, STEPNEY, 1840 [*A.P.S.D.*].

NOAK HILL, ESSEX, ST. THOMAS'S CHURCH, 1841, Tudor [Port, 144–5].

KILREA CHURCH, CO. LONDONDERRY, IRELAND, rebuilt for the Mercers' Company, 1841–2 [*A.P.S.D.*].

LONDON, LONDON BRIDGE RAILWAY STATION, in collaboration with Henry Roberts, 1841–4; rebuilt 1851; dem. 1969 [*Companion to the Almanac*, 1843, 248–9].

LONDON, GRESHAM COLLEGE, BASINGHALL STREET, 1842–3; rebuilt 1912 [*A.P.S.D.*].

GREENWICH, Hall of the Society for the Diffusion of Useful Knowledge, Royal Hill, 1842–3; dem. 1937 [Kerney, 1985].

LONDON, CHRIST CHURCH SCHOOLS, JOHNSON STREET, MILE END, STEPNEY, 1848–9 [exhib. at R.A. 1849].

NEWLANDS, COPTHORNE, SUSSEX, for himself, 1848–9 [*A.P.S.D.*].

GREENWICH, JUBILEE ALMSHOUSES, pair of additional almshouses, 1854–5, dem. 1974 [Kerney, 1985].

LONDON, PRINTING OFFICES, PILGRIM STREET, LUDGATE, in collaboration with G. B. Williams, 1860 [*A.P.S.D., s.v.*. 'Williams, G. B.'].

WOODBASTWICK HALL, NORFOLK, altered or rebuilt for John Cator, date uncertain; destroyed by fire 1882 [*A.P.S.D.*].

SMITH, GEORGE (1793–1877), was born at Aberdeen, where in 1818 he endeavoured to establish himself as an architect. But making no headway against John Smith and Archibald Simpson, he moved to Edinburgh, where he became an assistant of William Burn. Finding him 'ignorant and useless', Burn sacked him after three years, and from about 1827 he practised independently, obtaining in 1834 a salaried post as architect to the Edinburgh Improvement Commissioners. In the same year he won the competition sponsored by the Highland Society for the design of 'Cottages for the Labouring Classes' [J. C. Loudon, *Architectural Mag.* i, 1834, 93]. He published his designs in a small book entitled *Essay on the Construction of Cottages suited for the Dwellings of the Labouring Classes, illustrated by Working Plans* (Glasgow 1834). Smith was also the author of a manual on the *Elements of Architecture*, intended for the use of students attending the architectural lectures at the Edinburgh School of Arts (1827). In Glasgow on Woodlands Hill he designed several handsome terraces of houses for the well-to-do. Latterly he was in partnership with Henry Hardy (1831–1908). He died in Edinburgh in October 1877, and was buried in the Warriston Cemetery. David Rhind was his pupil. [Information from Mr. David Walker; Ian Gow, 'David Rhind' in *The Architectural Outsiders*, ed. R. Brown, 1985, 154.]

EDINBURGH, ST. MARY'S PARISH SCHOOL, CANONMILLS, 1828–9 [S.R.O., RHP 35291, printed plan and elevation].

DUNDEE, EXCHANGE COFFEE ROOM, now 8–11 EXCHANGE STREET, 1828–30 [C. Mackie, *Historical Description of Dundee*, 1836, 140].

TAYFIELD HOUSE, FORGAN, FIFE, enlarged and remodelled for William Berry, 1829–31, Jacobethan [drawings at Tayfield] (A. H. Millar, *Fife, Pictorial and Historical* ii, 1895).

GLASGOW, WOODLANDS HILL, the following terraces, etc.: WOODSIDE CRESCENT, 1831; WOODSIDE TERRACE, 1835–42; WOODSIDE PLACE, 1838; LYNEDOCH CRESCENT and LYNEDOCH STREET, 1845 [J. Pagan, *Sketch of the History of Glasgow*, 1847, 181; A. Gomme & D. Walker, *Architecture of Glasgow*, 1968, 279].

KIMMERGHAME, BERWICKSHIRE, lodge for James Bonar, 1835 [drawings at Kimmerghame].

EDINBURGH, ST. STEPHEN'S SCHOOL, ST. STEPHEN STREET, 1835–6 [S.R.O., CH2/607/1, pp. 60–2, 66, *ex inf.* Mr. John Gifford].

EDINBURGH, 1–12 MELBOURNE PLACE, 1837 [Edinburgh City Archives, Minutes of City Improvement Trust].

GLASGOW, NEWTON PLACE, SAUCHIEHALL STREET, 1837 [A. Gomme & D. Walker, *Architecture of Glasgow*, 1968, 279].

EDINBURGH, ST. JOHN'S CHURCH, VICTORIA STREET (now furniture store), 1838–40, 'in a mixed style of architecture, with a Saxon doorway' [*A.P.S.D., s.v.* 'Edinburgh'].

EDINBURGH, BUCCLEUCH SCHOOL, NORTH MEADOW WALK, 1839 [S.R.O., CH2/718/281, *ex inf.* Mr. John Gifford].

EDINBURGH, VICTORIA STREET, shops, Mechanics' Library, etc., *c.*1840–6 [Edinburgh City Archives, Minutes of City Improvement Trust].

EDINBURGH, NORMAL SCHOOL (now Public Health Chambers), JOHNSTON TERRACE, 1844–5, Jacobethan [A. Morgan, *Two Famous Old Edinburgh Colleges*, 1935, 13].

EDINBURGH, Nos. 37–65 LOTHIAN ROAD, designed 1848, not completed until the 1860s [S.R.O., Edinburgh Sasines].

EDINBURGH, No. 87 WEST BOW, 1850 [Edinburgh City Archives, Minutes of City Improvement Trust].

EDINBURGH, No. 22 QUEEN STREET, reconstructed in Jacobethan style, 1852; altered 1892 [Edinburgh Dean of Guild records, 7 May 1852, *ex inf.* Mr. David Walker].

SMITH, GEORGE H— (*c.*1805 –), was a pupil of T. F. Hunt and was admitted to the Royal Academy Schools in 1824 at the age of 19. He exhibited at the R.A. from London addresses between 1825 and 1837, but no trace of him has been found thereafter. His exhibited drawings included STOBARS HALL, nr. KIRKBY STEPHEN, WESTMORLAND, shown as 'now erecting' in 1825; 'a roadside inn designed for Chenies, Bucks.' (1830); 'a park lodge designed for Sir William Somerville, Bart.' (1833), probably at SOMERVILLE, NAVAN, CO. MEATH, IRELAND; a cottage designed for the antiquary Nicholas Carlisle, 'to be built in Sussex' (1835); CULVERHOUSE, HOLCOMBE BURNELL, nr. EXETER, 'now erecting' in Tudor Gothic style for the Revd. Richard Stephens (1835); alterations and additions carried out to BIFRONS HOUSE, PATRIXBOURNE, KENT (dem. 1948), for the Dowager Marchioness Conyngham (1835); and the west front of ORTON HOUSE, HUNTS., as remodelled in Tudor Gothic style for Lord Strathavon (1836) (*V.C.H. Hunts.* iii, 190).

SMITH, JAMES (*c.*1645–1731), was a figure of considerable importance in the history of Scottish, and perhaps indirectly of English, architecture. In Scotland his reputation is well attested. 'Our first architect' was how a Scottish laird described him in 1719 [Hist. MSS. Comm., *Xth Report*, Appendix 1, p. 197], and in 1693 it was 'Mr. Smith' whom the Earl of Lothian wanted to consult about his house at Newbattle because 'he hath really the best skill of them all' [S.R.O., GD 40/viii/58]. To Colen Campbell he was 'the most experienc'd Architect of that kingdom' (*Vitruvius Britannicus* ii, 1717, 3), and in the reign of George III the Scottish-born Robert Mylne (d. 1811) was aware that Smith had been 'a remarkable man'.

Smith was the son of a master mason of the same name who died in 1684 or early in 1685. The elder Smith was living at Tarbat in Ross-shire in 1656, but became a burgess of Forres (Morayshire) in 1659 [S.R.O., Deeds Mackiness 58.609 and Forres Burgh Records, *ex inf.* Mr. J. G. Dunbar]. According to Robert Mylne's notes, Smith 'was bred to the Church, but afterwards took to building', to which he adds the crucial information that 'He went abroad to Italy and studied his Art.' It is probable that he went to Italy as a candidate for the Catholic priesthood, and that he was the 'James Smith of Morayshire' who in May 1671 was admitted to the Scots College in Rome, where he studied rhetoric, philosophy and theology for four years. In October 1675, however, he 'left with permission and promising to return, but became an apostate' [*Records of the Scots Colleges in Douai, Rome, etc.*, New Spalding Club, 1906, i, 118]. He was undoubtedly an educated man, whose knowledge of Latin is attested by a surviving letter written in that language in 1714 [N.L.S., MS. 1103, f. 171]. In 1715, when offering himself as a candidate for election to Parliament as representative for Edinburgh, he claimed to have had a 'liberall education at schools and Colledges at home and abroad and occasion to know the world by traveling abroad'. One journey is documented by a receipt dated December 1677 acknowledging a contribution of 20s. towards 'my . . . necessare expenses on my voyage upon the account of Sr. William Bruce . . .' [S.R.O., GD 29/263], but the destination is not stated, and the document is chiefly of interest because it shows that by 1677 Smith was already in touch with the leading figure in the Scottish architectural scene.

In 1715 Smith stated that he had 'lived with a fair character' in Edinburgh 'for many years'. He had in fact become a burgess of Edinburgh in December 1679 by right of his recent marriage to the eldest daughter of Robert Mylne (d. 1710), Master Mason to the Scottish Crown, and a prominent figure in the Scottish capital. At the time Mylne was engaged in rebuilding Holyroodhouse under the direction of Sir William Bruce, and the accounts show that James Smith had undertaken some of the masonry [R. S. Mylne, *The Master Masons to the Crown of Scotland*, 1893, 200]. He was soon to have a closer connection with the King's Works in Scotland, for the dismissal of Sir William Bruce in 1678 had left them without a superior officer, and in February 1683, on the recommendation of the Duke of Queensberry (for whom he was then working at Drumlanrig), James Smith was appointed Surveyor or Overseer of the Royal Works, with a salary of £100 p.a.[1] His chief responsibility in this capacity was the maintenance of Holyroodhouse, and in 1688 he was engaged in fitting up the former abbey church as a Chapel Royal for King James II. His tenure of the post was not affected by the Revolution, and it was renewed by Queen Anne's government in 1707. But payment of his salary ceased after the Union, and although he subsequently acted as surveyor of the Highland forts erected by the Board of Ordnance early in the reign of George I, this employment was terminated in 1719 by the appointment of Andrews Jelfe as 'Architect and Clerk of the Works' for all fortifications under the Board's jurisdiction. A visit to London failed to recover either his lapsed salary or his lost employment, and in a long petition to the Barons of the Scottish Exchequer, as well as in a private letter to Sir John Clerk of Penicuik, Smith complained bitterly of the way in which he had been 'disgracefully turn'd out of His Majesty's service in the 73^{d} year of his age' [S.R.O., E 307/2 and GD 18/5004].

In his letter to Sir John Clerk, Smith wrote that he was forced to 'hunt for my living elsewhere'. From about 1700 he appears to have had some sort of professional association with Alexander McGill (*q.v.*), but after about 1710 he is not known to have received any private architectural commission of consequence, and it was evidently during these years that (as Robert Mylne records), 'he ruined himself by a Drowned Colliery near Musselburgh', eventually obliging himself to part with the estate at Whitehill in the parish of Inveresk that he had purchased in 1686, and from

[1] Though less than Bruce's exceptional salary of £300 p.a., Smith's £100 corresponded to the salary of earlier Masters of the King's Works in Scotland.

whose possession he was generally known as 'Mr. Smith of Whitehill'.[1]

So far as firm evidence goes, the last ten years of Smith's life are almost a blank, but there is some reason to think that he may have formed a connection with Colen Campbell, then emerging as the publicist of the new Palladianism that was soon to transform English architecture. The evidence consists of a number of drawings, now in the R.I.B.A. Collection, which belonged to Campbell but are not in his hand. One of them is a plan of Dalkeith House, as remodelled by Smith in 1702–10, another is a design for a mansion with a façade stylistically similar to Dalkeith, and a third is virtually a duplicate (both in content and in draughtsmanship) of Smith's surviving plans (S.R.O., RHP 4093) for Melville House, the mansion which Campbell illustrates as Smith's work in *Vitruvius Britannicus*. Moreover there are certain mannerisms which these drawings share with an unexecuted design made by Smith and McGill for Cullen House, Banffshire, in 1709 (S.R.O., RHP 2541).[2] The bulk of the drawings, however, consists of studies on Palladian themes. There are numerous designs for villas with centralized plans related to Palladio's Villa Rotonda, one with a façade based on the Palazzo Iseppo Porto in Vicenza, and one which formed the starting-point of Campbell's design for a house 'in the theatrical style' (*Vitruvius Britannicus* ii, 1717, pl. 90). The existence of the last drawing, and of another related to the engraving of Somerset House in vol. i (pl. 16), makes it clear that the drawings in question must have been known to Campbell at least sixteen years before Smith's death in 1731. Whether Campbell was Smith's pupil, or whether he acquired the drawings from Smith at a time when the latter was in financial difficulties, must be a matter for conjecture. It does, however, seem probable that, just as Campbell's Palladianism preceded Burlington's, so Smith's Palladianism preceded Campbell's and it is tempting to go further and suggest that Smith's interest in Palladian architecture went back to his sojourn in Italy in the 1660s or 1670s. If so, it is to James Smith's Italian travels that the origins of British Palladianism must ultimately be traced.

Smith's executed buildings, on the other hand, show little evidence of any Palladian intentions. Though (as Mr. Dunbar had observed) the plan of the Canongate Church 'is more reminiscent of Continental Catholicism than of Scottish Presbyterianism', its façade appears to be of baroque rather than of Palladian extraction. Apart from Drumlanrig Castle, whose romantic design (derived from Heriot's Hospital) may to some extent have been determined by previous plans, Smith's country houses follow the direction indicated by Sir William Bruce. With their hipped roofs and pedimented fronts they are plain, handsome and for the most part undemonstrative houses which hardly betray the classical aspirations revealed by the drawings. Smith was, it seems, a Palladian only on paper.

The death at Edinburgh on 6 November 1731, of 'Mr. James Smith of Whitehill, a famous Architect in that Country', was announced in *The Political State of Great Britain* xlii, 552, and in *The Caledonian Mercury* of 8 November 1731. He was 86 years old, and left a family of patriarchal size. In 1720, in his petition to the Barons of the Exchequer, he mentioned the needs of 'his numerous family of 32 children'. This is corroborated by Robert Mylne, who in his notes on the history of his family records that Smith's first wife, Janet Mylne, 'had 18 children, and died of twins at the age of 37 years in 1699. Her husband [then] married a second wife, named [Anna] Smith, by whom he had 14 children'. Janet was 'a good Drawer and very Clever'. Smith was evidently proud of her, for after her death he had her portrait by Faithorne engraved, with an inscription in Latin recording her death and the number of her children. The names of all thirty-two children are not known, but Robert Mylne noted that one of Smith's sons by his second wife was christened 'Climacterick Smith, because born in his father's 70th. year'. One of his daughters married Gilbert Smith (d. 1726), an Edinburgh mason who was appointed Master Mason to the Crown in 1715. Gilbert appears to have been James Smith's first cousin, and had been apprenticed to him in 1694, as was Gilbert's elder brother James (d. 1705) in 1680. In contemporary documents the subject of this entry is often distinguished from his cousin and namesake by the title 'Mr. James Smith'.

James Smith's activities were by no means confined to architecture. He was a justice of the peace and in 1704 one of the Commissioners of Supply for the County of Edinburgh [*Acts of Parliament of Scotland* xi, 139]. When offering himself for election as Member of Parliament for the City of Edin-

[1] According to R. S. Mylne, *Master Masons*, 245–6, he sold part of it in 1706, and in 1726 assigned the remainder to his son-in-law Gilbert Smith as security for a debt of £365 sterling.

[2] Two more drawings by the same hand are among the Adam drawings in Sir John Soane's Museum (Drawer 68, Set 3, 6–7).

burgh in 1715 he claimed to have 'had the honour to be a representative in Scots parliaments and [to] acquit himself to the satisfaction of his constitutents'. Although unsuccessful in 1715, there is no reason to doubt the truth of his statement, and it is likely that he was the James Smith who represented Forres in the Scottish Parliament of 1685–6. According to Robert Mylne he was 'no contemptible sculptor'. Although he supplied the lead statue of King Charles II which stands in Parliament Square, Edinburgh, for £2580 Scots in 1685 (see *Book of the Old Edinburgh Club* xvii, 1930, 83), it is not clear that he made it himself, since £38 was paid for 'shipping it' either from London or from Holland. But in 1683 'Mr. James Smith statuary' was among those paid for recent works at Holyroodhouse [S.R.O., E 26/11/4, p. 317], and the list of his works includes at least one monument.[1]

That Smith was also an engineer is demonstrated by the employment of 'Mr. Smith, Architectour', as arbitrator in a dispute over the construction of a harbour at Cockenzie, East Lothian, because 'he had the repute to be very well skilled in works of this nature' [*Register of the Privy Council of Scotland* vi, 385], by his involvement in 1696 in a scheme to supply Scottish towns with water, and by his obtaining in 1701 the Scottish rights to operate an engine to raise water invented by Thomas Savery [*Acts of Parliament of Scotland* x, 80, 267]. Early in the eighteenth century, with William Adair, Alexander McGill and George Sorocold, he carried out a survey to investigate the possibility of a Forth-Clyde Canal [J. Crawford, *Memorials of Alloa*, 1874, 91].

[*Extracts from the Records of the Burgh of Edinburgh, 1681–9*, ed. M. Wood & H. Armet, *passim; 1689–1701, passim; 1701–18*, 282–3; *Roll of Edinburgh Burgesses 1406–1700*, Scottish Rec. Soc., 456; *Cal. Treasury Books* xxii, 469, xxiv, 257, xxv, 52; *Cal. Treasury Papers 1708–14*, 194; R. S. Mylne, *The Master Masons to the Crown of Scotland*, 1893, 245–6; letters from Smith to the Earl of Mar in S.R.O., GD 124/15 and to John Mackenzie of Delvine in N.L.S., MS. 1103; H.M. Colvin, 'A Scottish Origin for English Palladianism?', *Arch. Hist.* xvii, 1974; *Catalogue of the R.I.B.A. Drawings Collection: S*, 1976, 86–7; A. Mackechnie, 'James Smith's Smaller Country Houses', in *Aspects of Scottish Classicism*, ed. J. Frew & David Jones, St. Andrews 1988.]

[1] The James Smith who contracted to erect the monument in Holyrood Abbey Church to the 15th Earl of Sutherland (d. 1703) was probably the younger Smith (d. 1705). He was associated with 'Mr. James Smith' in the contract for the Hamilton monument now in Bothwell Church. The contract for the Sutherland movement is printed in *Book of the Old Edinburgh Club* xxv, 1945, 210.

INVERNESS BRIDGE, 1681–4; destroyed by flood 1849 [*Register of the Privy Council of Scotland* xi, 528–30; cf. *Letters of two Centuries*, ed. C. Fraser-Mackintosh, Inverness 1890, 114–16].

DRUMLANRIG CASTLE, DUMFRIESSHIRE, rebuilt for 1st Duke of Queensberry, *c.*1680–90, perhaps on the basis of designs made by Robert Mylne, Smith's father-in-law. The ogee-roofed pavilions were added by Smith in 1697–8 [Mark Girouard in *C. Life*, 25 Aug. 1960].

ST. ANDREWS, ST. SALVATOR'S COLLEGE, advice on repair, 1683 [*Proc. Soc. Antiquaries of Scotland* liv, 1919–20, 237].

EDINBURGH, QUEENSBERRY HOUSE, 64 CANONGATE, advice on completion for 1st Duke of Queensberry of house bought incomplete from Lord Hatton, 1686 [N.R.A.(S), 1275, Bdl. 497] (R.C.A.M., *Edinburgh*, 160–1).

WHITEHILL (now NEWHAILES) HOUSE, MUSSELBURGH, MIDLOTHIAN, for himself, *c.*1686; enlarged in 18th century (T. Hannan, *Famous Scottish Houses: the Lothians*, 1928, 133–6; *C. Life*, 15 Sept. 1917, 29 Jan.–5 Feb. 1987).

EDINBURGH, THE CANONGATE CHURCH, 1688–90 [*Register of the Privy Council of Scotland* xiii, p. xlviii, xiv, 22; *Extracts from the Records of the Burgh of Edinburgh 1681–9*, ed. H. Armet, xxxi; *1689–1701*, xxxvi] (plan in G. Hay, *Architecture of Scottish Post-Reformation Churches*, 1957, fig. 22).

EDINBURGH, HOLYROODHOUSE, fitted up Abbey Church as Chapel Royal for King James II, 1688; destroyed by mob later same year. The accounts [S.R.O., E 26/12/3, pp. 187, 190, 288] show that Smith was in charge as Surveyor of the Royal Works, and was presumably responsible for the designs, though this cannot be proved. In December 1687, after a visit to James II in Whitehall, he was paid an extra £120 as an expression of the King's satisfaction with 'the performance of his duty' [S.R.O., E 28/369/54]. The interior of the Chapel is illustrated in *Vitruvius Scoticus*, pl. 5. William Morgan, recently employed at Chelsea Hospital, was the Master Carver [S.R.O., E 28/477/2] and 'three image-peeces for the high Altar' were carved by Grinling Gibbons [S.R.O., SP 57/13, p. 181].

EDINBURGH, GREYFRIARS CEMETERY, domed mausoleum for Sir George Mackenzie of Rosehaugh (d. 1691), *c.*1690–2 [bills for building the mausoleum in S.R.O., GD 121/469, Box 83].

EDINBURGH, repaired house in TWEEDDALE COURT, HIGH STREET, for 1st Marquess of Tweeddale, 1692–3 [National Library of Scotland, Yester papers, MS. 14637, f. 140] (J. Grant, *Old and New Edinburgh* i, 277).

NEWBATTLE ABBEY, MIDLOTHIAN, alterations were carried out by 4th Earl of Lothian in 1693 onwards. Smith's advice was sought, but it is not clear whether he was the effective architect or not [S.R.O., GD 40/2/viii/53, 58, 76, 108, xviii/1, 77] (*C. Life,* 13 Sept. 1902, 22 Feb. 1941).

HAMILTON PALACE, LANARKSHIRE, for 3rd Duke and Duchess of Hamilton, 1693–1701; new north front by D. Hamilton 1822–5; dem. *c.*1920 [*Vitruvius Scoticus*, pl. 8; Rosalind K. Marshall, *The Days of Duchess Anne*, 1973, chap. 9] (*C. Life*, 7, 14 and 21 June 1919).

TRAQUAIR HOUSE, PEEBLESSHIRE, alterations for 4th Earl of Traquair, including the forecourt and gate-piers, *c.*1695–9 [R.C.A.M., *Peeblesshire* ii, 313 and pls. 89, 90, 116].

DURISDEER, DUMFRIESSHIRE, 'aisle' or mausoleum for 1st Duke of Queensberry, 1695–1708. The mausoleum forms the N. transept of the parish church, rebuilt in 1716–20, probably to Smith's designs [A. Mackechnie, 'Durisdeer Church', *Procs. Soc. of Antiquaries of Scotland* 115, 1985].

BOTHWELL CHURCH, LANARKSHIRE, monument to 3rd Duke of Hamilton (d. 1694), originally in Hamilton Collegiate Church [contract and drawing dated Feb. 1696 in Hamilton MSS., Box 463/10/2].

EDINBURGH, SURGEONS' HALL and ANATOMICAL THEATRE, SURGEONS' SQUARE, 1696–7; now incorporated, much altered, in the High School Yards Building of the University of Edinburgh [G. H. Creswell, *The Royal College of Surgeons of Edinburgh*, 1926, 51].

MELVILLE HOUSE, FIFE, for 1st Earl of Melville, 1697–1700 [C. Campbell, *Vitruvius Britannicus* ii, 1717, pl. 50; original drawings in S.R.O., RHP 4093; plumber's contract witnessed by Smith in S.R.O., GD 26/6/158; lawsuit over contract in S.R.O., GD 26/6/164]. For the possible involvement of Sir William Bruce, see above, p. 176.

YESTER HOUSE, EAST LOTHIAN, for 2nd Marquess of Tweeddale, in partnership with Alexander McGill, *c.*1700–15; altered by W. Adam 1730 and by Robert Adam 1788 [*Vitruvius Scoticus*, pls. 28–9; J. G. Dunbar, 'The Building of Yester House', *Trans. E. Lothian Antiquarian and Field Naturalists' Soc.* xiii, 1972] (*C. Life*, 23–30 July 1932, 9, 16 and 23 Aug. 1973).

DALKEITH HOUSE, MIDLOTHIAN, remodelled for Anne, Duchess of Buccleuch, 1702–10 (*Vitruvius Scoticus*, pls. 23–4; building accounts in S.R.O., GD 224/625/1] (*C. Life*, 7 Oct. 1911, 19, 26 April, 3 May 1984).

GIFFORD CHURCH, EAST LOTHIAN, was built in 1710 at the expense of 2nd Marquess of Tweeddale, and many of the craftsmen engaged at Yester House were employed. It may therefore have been designed by Smith and McGill, the architects of Yester [J. G. Dunbar, 'The Building of Yester House', *Trans. E. Lothian Antiquarian and Field Naturalists' Soc.* xiii, 1972, 40, n. 24].

DELVINE, CAPUTH, PERTHSHIRE, architectural advice for William Mackenzie, 1714 [N.L.S., MS. 1103, f. 172]. The evidence is insufficient to determine what role Smith played in the building or altering of this house, dem. 1961.

DUPPLIN CASTLE, PERTHSHIRE, office-wings for 7th Earl of Kinnoull, *c.*1720–5; destroyed by fire 1827 [J. Macky, *Journey through Scotland*, 1723, 153–4, where he states that 'Mr. Smith, the Architect, lives there till he finishes it']. Smith may have been responsible for earlier works here, for in Oct. 1707 he says in a letter to the Earl of Mar that he has been detained at Dupplin by Lord Dupplin, afterwards 6th Earl of Kinnoull (d. 1719) [S.R.O., GD 124/15/663/2].

EDINBURGH, SMITH'S LAND or CLOSE, later known as Paisley's Close, on the north side of the High Street, built by Smith as an investment [*Book of the Old Edinburgh Club* xii, 1923, 45].

SMITH, JAMES, a carpenter by trade, is known only as the author of two books, one entitled *The Carpenters Companion: Being an Accurate and Compleat Treatise of Carpenters Works,* together with the Five Orders of Architecture 'in a more easy and concise Method than any yet Published', dedicated to George Fox, 1733, the other *A Specimen of Antient Carpentry, consisting of Variety of Designs for Roofs, exemplefy'd in common circular mixt spiral & such which have been fram'd in Publick & Private Antique Buildings,* Collected by James Smith, Carpenter. *To which are added, Designs of Frontispieces to Doors, Gateways, Piers, Pavillions, Temples, Chimney Pieces etc.* by William Jones, 66 copper plates, 1736. A second edition of the latter work, consisting of 36 plates only, and omitting Jones's designs, was published in 1787 as *Specimens of Ancient Carpentry, consisting of Framed Roofs, selected from various Ancient Buildings, Public & Private, Also some Specimens of Mouldings for*

Cornices, Doors & Windows, by the late Mr. James Smith. There was a reprint by Taylor of Holborn in *c.*1820. *The Specimens of Antient Carpentry* is devoid of text, but the plates constitute the earliest antiquarian study of English medieval carpentry, and are still valuable as a record of some roofs that were destroyed in the eighteenth century.[1] The plates of Gothic mouldings, taken from 'several churches &c. in Town & Country', are likewise the earliest of their kind. [Eileen Harris, *British Architectural Books and Writers 1556–1785*, 1990, 425–7].

SMITH, JAMES (1734–1807), of the Coppice Green, nr. Shifnal in Shropshire, was a member of a family of minor architects and surveyors practising in that county. In 1776 he acted as arbitrator in a dispute over the contract for building the English Bridge at Shrewsbury [A. W. Ward, *The Bridges of Shrewsbury*, Shrewsbury 1935, 68]. In 1781–2 he was employed by Bishop Hurd to design the library at HARTLEBURY CASTLE, WORCS., in an Adam style: his original drawing is illustrated in *C. Life*, 7 Feb. 1931 and 23 Sept. 1971. In 1783 he submitted three alternative designs for the Shirehall at Shrewsbury [Shropshire C.R.O., 348/10]. He also made designs for minor alterations to PITCHFORD HALL, SALOP., some of which appear to have been executed [*C. Life*, 25 June 1992].

Smith died at Coppice Green on 15 January 1807, aged 72 [Shifnal Parish Register in Shropshire C.R.O.]. James Smith, who designed a large pew projecting from the N. side of DONINGTON CHURCH, SALOP. for Thomas Bishton in 1819 [Faculty in Lichfield Joint Record Office], and John Smith (d. 1813), who was employed on the Trentham estate as a builder and surveyor, were presumably his sons.

SMITH, JAMES (–1845), a native of Banffshire, was an architect and builder at Inverness. His principal works in the former capacity were the 'simple and stylistically rather old-fashioned' ACADEMY at TAIN, ROSS & CROMARTY, 1810–13, and the former PARISH CHURCH, 1811–14, now the Duthac Centre [R. W. & Jean Munro, *Tain through the Centuries*, Tain 1966, 104, 106]. He also designed the MANSE at TAIN, 1822–4 [S.R.O., CH2/348/13], stables at ERCHLESS CASTLE, INVERNESS-SHIRE, 1805, added battlements and bartizans to the tower of MONIACK CASTLE, INVERNESS-SHIRE, in 1804, and in 1824 was appointed one of the two surveyors of the Highland churches built under the direction of Thomas Telford (*q.v.*). [J. Gifford in *Bull. Scottish Georgian Soc.* 1980, 36].

SMITH, JAMES (1779–1862), the eldest son of John Smith of Darnick (see below, under 'John and Thomas Smith'), was an architect and builder in Edinburgh. He enjoyed the title of 'H.M. Master Mason for Scotland', conferred on him in 1819, perhaps through the good offices of Robert Reid, 'King's Architect in Scotland' (*q.v.*) [R. S. Mylne, *The Master Masons to the Crown of Scotland*, Edinburgh 1893, 247]. He designed ROSSKEEN CHURCH, ROSS & CROMARTY, 1828–32, effectively composed with a tower-cum-vestry as a central feature [S.R.O., CH2/348/13, p. 220]. Smith was also responsible for farm offices at TORRISDALE CASTLE, ARGYLLSHIRE, 1841–5 [S.R.O., SC 51/60/3, p. 367], and for the reconstruction of the GREYFRIARS CHURCH, EDINBURGH, after the fire of 1845 [*Builder* iii, 1845, 305].

SMITH, JAMES (1782–1867), F.R.S., of Jordanhill, nr. Glasgow, is best known as a geologist and man of letters, but also had some reputation as an amateur architect. He was the son of a prosperous Glasgow merchant and enjoyed a private income which allowed him to devote his life to science, literature and the arts. According to the author of *The Old Country Houses of the Glasgow Gentry* (Glasgow 1870), 'he had a great taste for architecture, and furnished plans for many of his friends' houses'. Among these was CRAIGEND CASTLE, STIRLINGSHIRE, the seat of his cousin James Smith, which was rebuilt by Alexander Ramsay of Edinburgh in 1812, partly in accordance with Smith's plans (see under 'Ramsay'). In 1824 he remodelled his own house at JORDANHILL (dem. *c.*1960) in a plain style (*see Old Country Houses of the Glasgow Gentry*, pl. lix), and in 1826 designed a Gothic church, since rebuilt, at GOVAN, LANARKS., with a steeple said to have been based on Stratford-on-Avon Parish Church [*N.S.A.* vi, 711] (W. Fraser, *The Kirk and the Manse*, 1857, plate). For the ANDERSONIAN INSTITUTION, GLASGOW, of which he was president from 1830 to 1839, he designed a circular museum and lecture theatre which were added at the back of the Institution's premises (dem.) in George Street [A.H. Sexton, *The First Technical College, the History of the Andersonian Institution*, 1894, 33–4,

[1] The roofs illustrated include those of Netley Abbey, Westminster School, Burleigh House, Northants., the Savoy Hospital, Staple Inn, Holborn, Gray's Inn, the London Guildhall, Pinners' Hall, London, the Middle Temple, Westminster Hall, Lambeth Palace, Eltham Palace, Hampton Court, Jesus and St. John's Colleges, Cambridge, and eight of the Oxford Colleges.

with illustration]. For further biographical details see *D.N.B.*

SMITH, JOHN, was a master mason working in Linlithgow in the reign of Charles II. In 1667 John Mylne, the King's Master Mason, designed a new Tolbooth for the Town Council of Linlithgow which would doubtless have been built but for his death in December of that year. In January 1668 the Council approved 'the concording with John Smith maister meason for edifeing our Tolbuth in all respects conforme to the draught thereof drawn up be him', and it was completed in 1669 or 1670. It was repaired after a fire in 1847, when Smith's classical façade was carefully reproduced, and the existing external stone stairs were added in 1906. In 1670 Smith built a Grammar School for the town [S.R.O., Linlithgow Town Council Minutes, B48/9/3, 1667–70, *passim*].

SMITH, JOHN, was Clerk of the Works first at Richmond and Kew Palaces (1758–61) and then at Kensington (1761–82), retiring on a pension in 1782 [*History of the King's Works* v, 475, vi, 24]. Like other members of the Office of Works he evidently had a small private practice, for his designs for a new dining-room for the 1st Earl of Hardwicke, dated 1763, are in the Bedfordshire Record Office (L 31/260–272).

SMITH, JOHN (1781–1852), was the son of William Smith (d. 1812), a builder and architect of Aberdeen. After learning his father's trade he went to London, where he is said to have become a pupil of James Playfair (who died, however, in 1794, when Smith was only 13). In 1804 or the following year he returned to Aberdeen, where he established himself in practice. At that date he was virtually the only professional architect in Aberdeen, and soon developed an extensive local practice. He was appointed Master of Work or City Architect in 1824, and for some thirty years directed the public works of a rapidly expanding town in an able and conscientious manner. From about 1820 his virtual monopoly of architectural practice in Aberdeen was challenged by Archibald Simpson (*q.v.*), whose superior ability as a designer was probably a salutary stimulus. Smith's best works were Greek Revival designs such as the North Church and the small but monumental Schools in Little Belmont Street, but his numerous works in the vernacular styles of the sixteenth and seventeenth centuries earned him the nickname of 'Tudor Johnny'. Like Simpson he knew how to make the most of granite, and, with Simpson, he must be regarded as the principal creator of the 'granite city' of the nineteenth century. In 1810 he published an engraved plan of Aberdeen City and harbour.

Smith is said to have been personally 'a shy, retiring man, as well as an able and diligent official'. From 1845 he was in partnership with his son William Smith (1817–91), the architect of Queen Victoria's Balmoral Castle. He died at Rosebank, Hardgate, on 22 July 1852, aged 71. Robert Kerr of London, Alexander Ellis of Aberdeen and Thomas Mackenzie of Elgin were his pupils. A number of his professional account-books for the years 1807–32 are in the National Monuments Record of Scotland. At the end of vol. viii there is a list of drawings which provides evidence for a number of Smith's commissions. Some of his drawings are in Aberdeen Art Gallery. [Obituary in *Builder* x, 1852, 506; *A.P.S.D.*; G. M. Fraser's articles on Archibald Simpson in *Aberdeen Weekly Jnl.*, 1918; information from Mr. David Walker.]

PUBLIC BUILDINGS IN ABERDEEN

THE COURT HOUSE, LODGE WALK, 1818–20; dem. 1865 [*Builder* x, 506; *N.S.A.* xii, 104].

THE TOWN HOUSE or TOLBOOTH, new front, Gothic, 1820; dem. 1865 [*Builder* x, 506].

KING'S COLLEGE, rebuilt street front and other alterations, 1825–6 [*Builder* x, 506].

THE BRIDGE OF DON, in association with Thomas Telford, 1827–30 [G. M. Fraser in *Aberdeen Weekly Jnl.*, 14 June 1918].

THE EAST PRISON, LODGE WALK, 1829–31; dem. 1865 [*Builder* x, 506; *A.P.S.D.*, *s.v.* 'Aberdeen'].

ST. NICHOLAS CHURCHYARD, Ionic screen to Union Street, based on a rejected design by Decimus Burton, 1830 [G. M. Fraser in *Aberdeen Weekly Jnl.* 21 June 1918]; monument to Dr. Robert Hamilton, 1833 [G. M. Fraser in *Aberdeen Weekly Jnl.*, 28 June 1918].

ROBERT GORDON'S HOSPITAL, addition of wings, 1830–4 [*Builder* x, 506].

THE RECORD OFFICE, KING STREET, 1832 [*Builder* x, 506].

THE ADVOCATES' HALL, Nos. 116–120 UNION STREET, 1837–8 [*Builder* x, 506].

THE TOWN'S SCHOOLS, LITTLE BELMONT STREET, 1841 [*Builder* x, 506].

THE BRIDGE OF DEE, widened on west side in association with James Walker, C.E., 1841–2 [G. M. Fraser, *The Bridge of Dee*, Aberdeen 1913, 95–103].

ASYLUM FOR BLIND, HUNTLY STREET, 1841–3 [G. M. Fraser *in Aberdeen Weekly Jnl.* 30 Aug. 1918].

TRINITY HALL, UNION STREET, for the Incorporated Trades, 1845–6, Tudor Gothic [G. M. Fraser in *Aberdeen Weekly Jnl.* 20 Sept. 1918].

PUBLIC BUILDINGS ELSEWHERE

STRICHEN, ABERDEENSHIRE, THE TOWN HOUSE for Mrs. Fraser of Strichen, 1816, Gothic [List of Drawings, no. 130].

STONEHAVEN, KINCARDINESHIRE, COUNTY HOUSE AND GAOL, alterations and additions, 1822 [*Aberdeen Jnl.* 1 Jan. 1822].

MONYMUSK, ABERDEENSHIRE, PAROCHIAL SCHOOL, 1826 [*Aberdeen Jnl.* 28 June 1826].

CULTS, ABERDEENSHIRE, SUSPENSION FOOTBRIDGE over R. Dee to Banchory Devenick, for the Revd. George Morison, 1837 [*N.S.A.* xi, 185].

PITSLIGO, ABERDEENSHIRE, SCHOOL, 1839 [*N.S.A.* xii, 404].

DYCE, ABERDEENSHIRE, SCHOOL, 1841 [*Aberdeen Jnl.* 26 May 1841].

NEW DEER, ABERDEENSHIRE, SCHOOL, 1845 [*Aberdeen Jnl.* 26 Feb. 1845].

CLUNY, ABERDEENSHIRE, SCHOOL, 1847 [*Aberdeen Jnl.* 10 March 1847].

CRUDEN, ABERDEENSHIRE, SCHOOL, 1847 [*Aberdeen Jnl.* 14 July 1847].

CHURCHES

UDNY, ABERDEENSHIRE, 1821, Gothic [List of Drawings, no. 266; Account-Book, i].

FINTRAY, ABERDEENSHIRE, 1821, Gothic [List of Drawings, no. 180].

ABERDEEN, UNION UNITED FREE CHURCH, SHIPROW, *c.*1822; dem. [plans in Aberdeen Public Library].

BANCHORY-TERNAN, KINCARDINESHIRE, 1824 [S.R.O., GD 44/37/9].

FORDOUN, KINCARDINESHIRE, 1828–9, Gothic [*N.S.A.* xi, 104].

ABERDEEN, ST. CLEMENT, FOOTDEE, 1828–9, Gothic [G. M. Fraser in *Aberdeen Weekly Jnl.* 14 June 1918].

NIGG, KINCARDINESHIRE, 1828–9, Gothic [contract in S.R.O., HR 487/6].

NEWHILLS, ABERDEENSHIRE, 1829–30, Gothic [*Aberdeen Jnl.* 29 April 1829].

ABERDEEN, NORTH CHURCH (now Arts Centre), 1830–1 [G. M. Fraser in *Aberdeen Weekly Jnl.* 14 June 1918].

ABERDEEN, SOUTH CHURCH, 1830–1, Gothic [G. M. Fraser, *op. cit.*].

CRUDEN, ABERDEENSHIRE, additions and alterations, 1833–4 [*Aberdeen Jnl.* 9 Oct. 1833].

KEIG, ABERDEENSHIRE, 1834, Gothic [*Aberdeen Jnl.* 27 Dec. 1834].

LONGSIDE, ABERDEENSHIRE, 1836 [*Aberdeen Jnl.* 8 April 1835].

TOUGH, ABERDEENSHIRE, 1837–8 [*Aberdeen Jnl.* 29 March 1837].

NEW DEER, ABERDEENSHIRE, 1838–9; tower completed 1865 [S.R.O., HR 403/1, minute of 21 June 1864 referring to the completion of the tower 'either on the original plan by the late John Smith, or on a modified plan submitted to the meeting'].

ABOYNE, ABERDEENSHIRE, 1842 [*Aberdeen Jnl.* 21 April 1841].

INVERURIE, ABERDEENSHIRE, 1841–2, Gothic [*Aberdeen Jnl.* 14 April 1841].

ELLON, ABERDEENSHIRE, a church – probably the new church at Savoch of Deer completed 1834; altered 1897 [List of Drawings, nos. 157–60].

DOMESTIC ARCHITECTURE

ABERDEEN, CRIMONMOGATE HOUSE, UNION STREET (later Northern Club), for Patrick Milne of Crimonmogate, *c.*1810; dem. 1964 [*Builder* x, 506; design for 'finishing hall for Patrick Milne' in Aberdeen Art Gallery].

KEITH HALL, ABERDEENSHIRE, stables for 6th Earl of Kintore, *c.*1810 [List of Drawings, nos. 226–8, 252] (*C. Life*, 28 May 1987).

PHESDO, FORDOUN, KINCARDINESHIRE, for Alexander Crombie, *c.*1810–15 [*Builder* x, 506].

BRUCKLAY CASTLE, NEW DEER, ABERDEENSHIRE, addition of entrance-hall, etc., for John Dingwall, 1814; remodelled by James Matthews 1849; dem. 1953 [drawings in Aberdeen Art Gallery; J. B. Pratt, *Buchan*, 1901, 179–80].

RAEMOIR, BANCHORY, KINCARDINESHIRE, for William Innes, 1817 [*Builder* x, 506], and addition, 1844 [N.R.A.S. Report 1186, p. 17].

STRICHEN HOUSE, ABERDEENSHIRE, for Thomas Fraser, cr. Lord Lovat, 1818–21; gutted 1954 [*Builder* x, 506].

DUNECHT HOUSE, ECHT, ABERDEENSHIRE, for William Forbes, 1820; enlarged by William Smith 1859–63 and by G.E. Street 1870 onwards [*Builder* x, 506].

CLUNY CASTLE, ABERDEENSHIRE, for Lt. Col. John Gordon, *c.*1820–40, castellated [H. Gordon Slade, 'Cluny Castle', *Proc. Soc. Antiquaries of Scotland* 111, 1981].

ABERDEEN, Nos. 7–8 CASTLE STREET and 2–10 KING STREET, 1822 [*Aberdeen Jnl.* 15 Jan. 1823].

INCHMARLO, KINCARDINESHIRE, reconstructed for W. S. Davidson (?), 1823 [account-book].

KIRKVILLE (now KIRKTON) HOUSE, SKENE, ABERDEENSHIRE, for James Knowles, 1826 [*Builder* x, 506].

TONLEY HOUSE, ABERDEENSHIRE, alterations and additions for General Patrick Byres, 1829; dem. [*Aberdeen Jnl.* 3 March 1829].

FINTRAY HOUSE, ABERDEENSHIRE, for Sir John Forbes, Bart., 1829–31, Tudor Gothic; rebuilt 1880, dem. 1952 [*Builder* x, 506; S.R.O., GD 250, Box 41].

CASTLE FRASER, ABERDEENSHIRE, alterations, including interior of library, for Col. Charles Mackenzie Fraser, *c.*1830–8 [H. Gordon Slade, 'Castle Fraser', *Proc. Soc. Antiquaries of Scotland* 109, 1977–8, 246, 260–1].

EASTER SKENE, ABERDEENSHIRE, for William McCombie, 1832, Elizabethan [*Builder* x, 506].

ADEN HOUSE, OLD DEER, ABERDEENSHIRE, altered and enlarged for James Russell, 1832–3; gutted [*Builder* x, 506].

KEMNAY HOUSE, KINTORE, ABERDEENSHIRE, alterations and additions, including porch, for John Burnett, 1833 [*Builder* x, 506].

AUCHMACOY HOUSE, LOGIE BUCHAN, ABERDEENSHIRE, completed house begun by W. Burn (*q.v.*) for James Buchan, 1833, Jacobethan [*Builder* x, 506].

BALMORAL, ABERDEENSHIRE, additions for Sir Robert Gordon, 1834–9, Jacobethan; dem. and replaced by a new house for Queen Victoria designed by William Smith, 1853–6 [*Builder* x, 506]. At Haddo House there is a set of unexecuted designs by John & William Smith for remodelling the house for Queen Victoria, dated 1848.

MONTBLAIRY, ALVAH, BANFFSHIRE, stables for Alexander Morison, 1835 [*Aberdeen Jnl.* 10 June 1835].

CANDACRAIG, STRATHDON, ABERDEENSHIRE, for Robert Anderson, 1835; burned *c.*1900 [*Builder* x, 506; *N.S.A.* xii, 546–7].

MANAR HOUSE, INVERURIE, ABERDEENSHIRE, for James Gordon, probably *c.*1835 [*Builder* x, 506].

HAZELHEAD HOUSE, ABERDEENSHIRE, offices for — Robertson, 1836 [*Aberdeen Jnl.* 30 March 1836].

MENIE, nr. ABERDEEN, for Col. George Turner, *c.*1836, Jacobethan [*Builder* x, 506].

SLAINS CASTLE, ABERDEENSHIRE, rebuilt for 17th Earl of Erroll, 1836–7 [*Builder* x, 506].

CRAIGSTON CASTLE, ABERDEENSHIRE, porch for William Pollard-Urquhart, 1838 [drawings at Craigston] (*C. Life*, 17–24 Oct. 1963).

LEARNEY HOUSE, ABERDEENSHIRE, rebuilt for Mrs. E. Brebner, after fire, 1838 [*Builder* x, 506; *Aberdeen Jnl.* 3 Jan. 1838].

WHITEHAUGH, KEITH HALL, ABERDEENSHIRE, added wings for Col. J. J. F. Leith, *c.*1838–40 [*Builder* x, 506; cf. *N.S.A.* xii, 447–8].

BANCHORY HOUSE, KINCARDINESHIRE, for Alexander Thomson, 1839 [*Builder* x, 506: drawings in house].

CRAIGELLIE HOUSE, MINTLAW, ABERDEENSHIRE, for William Shand, 1840 [*Builder* x, 506].

CORSINDAE HOUSE, nr. MONYMUSK, ABERDEENSHIRE, reconstructed 1840 [accounts in house].

FORGLEN HOUSE, TURRIFF, BANFFSHIRE, for Sir Ralph Abercromby, Bart., *c.*1840, Tudor [*Builder* x, 506].

WILLOWBANK, nr. ABERDEEN, enlarged for his son-in-law Alexander Gibb, *c.*1843 [L. M. Rae, *The Story of the Gibbs*, privately printed Edinburgh 1961, 86].

BADENTOY HOUSE, BANCHORY, KINCARDINESHIRE, for — Nicol, 1849 [*Aberdeen Jnl.* 6 June 1849].

BUCHANNESS LODGE, PETERHEAD, ABERDEENSHIRE, enlarged for 4th Earl of Aberdeen [*Builder* x, 506].

DUNLUGAS, ALVAH, BANFFSHIRE, work for — Leslie [*Builder* x, 506].

PITFOUR HOUSE, OLD DEER, ABERDEENSHIRE, works for Capt. George Ferguson, probably including the Greek Doric temple; house dem. 1927 [*Builder* x, 506].

SMITH, JOHN (1782–1864) and THOMAS (1785–1857), were the younger sons of John Smith (*c.*1748–1815), a mason and builder of Darnick, nr. Melrose in Roxburghshire, whose business they continued after his death. They were intelligent and enterprising men. The first volume of the *R.I.B.A. Transactions* (part i, 1837, 52–60) contains a paper by them on the subject of building bridges in whinstone rubble without the use of ashlar, an economical method of construction which they employed with success on several occasions. The chain suspension bridge which they built at Dryburgh was one of the first of its kind.

As architects the Smiths' practice consisted chiefly in designing and enlarging small houses, rural churches, schools and manses. Local landowners who employed them included Sir Walter Scott, for whom they enlarged ABBOTSFORD to the designs of William Atkinson (*q.v.*), and for whom they built CHIEFSWOOD, ROXBURGHSHIRE, to their own designs in 1820–1; James Ballantyne, for whom they designed and built HOLYLEE, WALKERBURN, PEEBLESSHIRE, in 1825–7; the 5th Duke of Buccleuch, for whom they worked at BOWHILL, SELKIRKSHIRE; and the 16th Lord Somerville, to whose house called PAVILION, nr. MELROSE, they added a wing with cavity walls described in their paper to the R.I.B.A.

Bridges built by the two Smiths (evidently to their own designs) included: THE CHAIN BRIDGE, DRYBURGH, BERWICKSHIRE, 1817, blown down 1818, successfully re-erected 1818, but since demolished (original drawing in R.I.B.A. Collection); the two bridges over the Rivers Tweed and Ettrick between Selkirk and Galashiels, 1831;[1] one over the Hermitage Water in Liddesdale for the 5th Duke of Buccleuch, 1832; YARROW BRIDGE, SELKIRKSHIRE, 1833; the bridge carrying the drive to Bowhill over the Ettrick at FAULDSHOPE, SELKIRKSHIRE, 1834; and LOW PEEL BRIDGE, over the Tweed at ASHIESTEEL, SELKIRKSHIRE, completed 1848 after an initial failure [T. Craig-Brown, *History of Selkirkshire* i, 1886, 388]. In 1834 they widened the TWEED BRIDGE at PEEBLES [R.C.A.M., *Peeblesshire* ii, 341].

Other buildings designed by the Smiths included: churches at MELROSE, 1809–10 [S.R.O. HR 233/3], GALASHIELS, 1812–13 [R. Hall, *History of Galashiels*, 1898, 208–9]; ETTRICK, SELKIRKSHIRE, 1824, Gothic [S.R.O., HR 1/1, pp. 96–106, 114, 117]; YETHOLM, ROXBURGHSHIRE, 1836 [N.L.S., MS. 8499] and WESTRUTHER, BERWICKS., 1839–40, Gothic [S.R.O., HR 86/1]; GATTONSIDE HOUSE, nr. MELROSE, 1826 [N.L.S., MS. 8499]; the ETTRICK MILLS, SELKIRK, 1850 [*ibid.*]; and John Smith's own house, DARNLEE, DARNICK, nr. MELROSE, 1816.

John Smith was also an occasional sculptor, his best-known work in this capacity being the colossal statue of William Wallace at Dryburgh, carved in 1814.

[Monumental inscriptions in Melrose churchyard; family papers in S.R.O., GD 241/250; typescript extracts from John Smith's diary 1812–54 in N.L.S., MS. 8499; architectural drawings in S.R.O., RHP 5525, 7190–6, 7196, 8220–1, 8429–44; N.L.S., MS. 3899, f. 199, letter to Scott, 1824; *The Journal of Sir Walter Scott*, ed. Tait, 1950, 732.]

SMITH, ROBERT, junior, figures in Jones's *Glasgow Directory* of 1787 as 'architect, cabinetmaker and house-wright'. J. Cleland, *Annals of Glasgow* i, 1816, 99, records that he was responsible for fitting up the interior of ANDERSON'S INSTITUTION in JOHN STREET, GLASGOW, *c.*1796.

SMITH, SAMUEL (1766–1851), was a builder-architect at Madeley in Shropshire. His plans for alterations to SHADWELL HALL, SALOP. (perhaps not executed), and for farmhouses at Shadwell and Llanhedrick, made in 1809 for William Botfield, are in the Garnett-Botfield Collection in the Shropshire Record Office. In 1829 he completed the rebuilding of PONTESBURY CHURCH, SALOP., after the death of John Turner (*q.v.*) [I.C.B.S.; *V.C.H. Salop.* viii, 288], and in 1833 he and his son Thomas were jointly responsible for designing the classical HOLY TRINITY CHURCH, WROCKWARDINE WOOD, SALOP. [D.H.S. Cranage, *Churches of Shropshire*, 1903, ii, 650]. Thomas Smith, who is described in the 1851 Shropshire directory as 'architect, builder and surveyor', designed several minor Shropshire churches, including those of ST. LUKE, IRONBRIDGE, 1835–6, CHRIST CHURCH, WELLINGTON, 1838, and EATON CONSTANTINE, 1847–9, all Gothic [Cranage, *op. cit.*, i, 200, ii, 634; I.C.B.S.]. Samuel died at Madeley in February 1851, aged 84 [parish register in Shropshire C.R.O.].

SMITH, THOMAS (1798–1875), was the son of John Smith (1775–1833), Surveyor of Bridges to the County of Kent from 1810 to 1825, and grandson of Thomas Smith, described as an architect of Lambeth. By the 1820s he was in practice as an architect in Hertford, where he lived at North End House from 1838/9 until 1870. He was County Surveyor of Hertfordshire from 1837 onwards and held a similar appointment in Bedfordshire from 1847 to 1855. He was Mayor of Hertford in 1868 and died on 1 October 1875, aged 76.

In Hertfordshire Smith designed the County Hospital, several churches and various other buildings. In Bedfordshire he was employed by Earl de Grey as executant architect for Silsoe Church and the Silsoe lodges to Wrest Park. In London he was surveyor to two Hertfordshire landowners, the Marquess of Salisbury (from 1851 onwards) and Baron Dimsdale, and is said to have erected a number of buildings on the latter's property. In Ireland he acted for Lord Ranfurly and Sir Patrick (afterwards Lord) Bellew, and designed or remodelled several country seats in County Louth. In conjunction with his son Thomas Tayler Smith (1834–1910) he designed Radlett Church, Herts. (1864), the English Hotel at Nice, the Protestant chapels at Nice, Cannes, Stuttgart and Naples, and the Château Ste-Ursule at Cannes for Lord Londesborough [*A.P.S.D.; Builder* xxxiii, 1875, 904, 995; information from Mr. T. Stafford-Smith].

HERTFORD, ALL SAINTS CHURCH, N. aisle and porch, 1824, Gothic; destroyed by fire 1891 [I.C.B.S.].

BARMEATH, CO. LOUTH, IRELAND, remodelled

[1] The foundation-stone of the Tweed bridge was laid by Sir Walter Scott, who records in his diary that 'Mr. Smith gave a proper repast to the workmen'.

for Sir Patrick Bellew, Bart., *c.*1830 [J. Leslie, *History of Kilsaran*, Dundalk 1908, 125].

CASTLE BELLINGHAM, CO. LOUTH, IRELAND, for Sir Alan Edward Bellingham, Bart., *c.*1830 [J. Leslie, *History of Kilsaran*, Dundalk 1908, 125].

BRAGANSTOWN HOUSE, CO. LOUTH, IRELAND, remodelled for the Revd. Anthony Garstin, *c.*1830, Elizabethan [J. Leslie, *History of Kilsaran*, Dundalk 1908, 125].

HERTFORD, THE GENERAL INFIRMARY or COUNTY HOSPITAL, NORTH ROAD., 1832–3 [reports in local newspaper, *ex inf.* Mr. P. Walne].

HARLOW, ESSEX, ST. MARY MAGDALENE'S CHURCH, 1833–4, Gothic; dem. 1888 [drawings in Essex Record Office, D/P 533/6/1].

HODDESDON, HERTS., THE CLOCK TOWER, 1835 [J. A. Tregelles, *History of Hoddesdon*, 1908, 283].

STEVENAGE RECTORY, HERTS., altered or rebuilt, 1835 [Lincs. Record Office, MGA 184].

LOUTH COUNTY INFIRMARY, DUNDALK, IRELAND, 1835 [*Builder* xxxiii, 1875, 994].

LECKHAMSTEAD RECTORY, BUCKS., altered or rebuilt, 1836 [Lincs. Record Office, MGA 205].

NEWNHAM VICARAGE, HERTS., 1837–8 [Bodleian Library, records of Queen Anne's Bounty].

WESTON VICARAGE, HERTS., altered or rebuilt, 1838 [Lincs. Record Office, MGA 221].

LETCHWORTH RECTORY, HERTS., altered or rebuilt, 1839 [Lincs. Record Office, MGA 238].

GREAT AMWELL VICARAGE, HERTS., 1839, Tudor Gothic [London Diocesan Records, Guildhall Library, MS. 19227/16].

GILSTON RECTORY, HERTS., alterations and additions, 1839 [*ibid.* MS. 19227/26].

ST. ALBANS, HERTS., GAOL AND HOUSE OF CORRECTION (ABBEY GATEWAY), alterations, 1840 [Hertfordshire County Records, *Sessions Records of the Liberty of St. Albans* iv, 1923, 319–22].

WESTON CHURCH, HERTS., rebuilt chancel, 1840, Norman [A. H. Bradbeer, 'Weston Church', *Trans. E. Herts. Arch. Soc.* iv (1), 1908–9, 68].

ENGLISH HALL CHURCH, nr. WARE, HERTS., 1840–1. [I.C.B.S.].

STEVENAGE CHURCH, HERTS., south transept, 1841, Gothic [I.C.B.S.].

WARESIDE, HERTS., HOLY TRINITY CHURCH, 1841, Norman [I.C.B.S.].

HERTFORD, THE COUNTY GAOL, alterations and additions, 1842 [*Builder* i, 1843, 267–8, xxxiii, 1875, 994; *Hertfordshire County Records: Sessions Books* x, 1957, 387–8].

HIGHNAM COURT, GLOS., terrace on S. side of house for Thomas Gambier Parry, 1843–4 [E. Gambier Parry, 'Highnam Memoranda' in Glos. C.R.O., D 2586, 61].

ORSETT RECTORY, ESSEX, 1843–4 [Bodleian Library, records of Queen Anne's Bounty].

WEST HYDE CHURCH, HERTS., 1844–5, Norman [I.C.B.S.].

KILNWICK PERCY VICARAGE, YORKS., rebuilt 1848 [Borthwick Institute, York, MGA 1848/1].

CLOPHILL CHURCH, BEDS., 1848–9, Gothic [I.C.B.S.].

HUNTINGDON COUNTY GAOL, altered 1850 [Cassey's *History, Topography and Directory of Beds., Hunts and Herts.*, 1863, 240].

HUNTINGDON INFIRMARY AND DISPENSARY, 1853 [Cassey's *History, Topography and Directory of Beds., Hunts. and Herts.*, 1863, 242].

SMITH, WILLIAM (1661–1724), *see* SMITH, FRANCIS.

SMITH, WILLIAM (1705–1747), was the eldest surviving son of Francis Smith of Warwick (*q.v.*), and succeeded him in his business as an architect and master builder. After his father's death in 1738 he took over the contract for the masonry of the Radcliffe Library at Oxford which (in conjunction with the Oxford mason John Townesend) he completed shortly before his own death in April 1747. William and David Hiorne appear to have succeeded to his business.

As an architect Smith was a competent provincial Palladian with some indebtedness to Gibbs. One of his earlier independent works, Catton Hall, retains the tall proportions and absence of central emphasis characteristic of his father's country houses, but at Radburne he adopted the current fashion for a two-storied block (with or without a rusticated basement) with a central pediment that he subsequently used at Kirtlington, Melbourne, Thame and perhaps Edgcote.

RADBURNE HALL, DERBYSHIRE, for German Pole, 1739–54 [a MS. account of the family written by Sacheverell Pole, who inherited Radbourne in 1780, says the house was built by 'Smith of Warwick'].

CATTON HALL, DERBYSHIRE, for Christopher Horton, *c.*1742–5 [Andor Gomme, 'Catton Hall', in *The Country Seat*, ed. Colvin & Harris, 1970, 157–63] (*C. Life*, 17, 24 March 1960).

STANWICK HALL, NORTHANTS., for James Lambe, 1742–3 [payment of £750 by Lambe to Smith in his account at Hoare's Bank, *ex inf.* Prof. A. Gomme].

KIRTLINGTON PARK, OXON., for Sir James

Dashwood, Bart., 1742–7, completed by John Sanderson (*q.v.*) [drawings and accounts formerly at Kirtlington; *Vitruvius Britannicus* iv, 1767, pls. 32–6] (*C. Life*, 13 April 1912).

LAMPORT CHURCH, NORTHANTS., rebuilt chancel, outer walls of nave and south porch, 1743 [Sir Gyles Isham, *All Saints Church, Lamport*, 1950].

BRIXWORTH HOUSE, NORTHANTS., work for John Nicolls Rainsford, 1743–5; dem. 1954. Smith's employment here is mentioned in a letter from the Revd. Euseby Isham dated 14 Dec. 1743 among the Isham Correspondence (no. 2508). He probably rebuilt or at least refronted the house. (J. P. Neale, *Views of Seats*, 1st ser. iii, 1820).

STANFORD HALL, LEICS., work for Sir Thomas Cave, Bart., *c.*1743–5. Smith was here in 1743 (Isham Correspondence, no. 2508), and documents in Leics. R.O. show that the 'improvements' referred to in 1746 (Hist. MSS. Comm., *13th Report*, Appendix IV, 478) were carried out by him during the previous year. They included remodelling the hall by 'removing entirely the upper row of windows and sinking the ceiling by a cove'. The plasterwork is by John Wright of Worcester (*C. Life*, 4, 11, 18 Dec. 1958).

MELBOURNE HALL, DERBYSHIRE, regularized S. front and rebuilt E. front for G. L. Coke, 1743–4 [accounts at Melbourne] (*C. Life*, 7, 14 April 1928).

THAME PARK, OXON., is said by F. G. Lee, *History of Thame*, 1883, 393, to have been designed for 6th Viscount Wenman by 'Mr. Smith, an architect of Coventry', *c.*1745. This is presumably a mistake for 'Smith of Warwick' [Arthur Oswald in *C. Life*, 28 Nov. 1957].

EDGCOTE HOUSE, NORTHANTS. The stables were built by Richard Chauncey in 1745–7, and there is a payment of £40 6s. to William Smith for 'surveying the building'. The house itself was rebuilt between 1747 and 1752 under the direction of William Jones, who was perhaps carrying out a design by Smith [MS. abstract of building accounts at Edgecote; H. A. Tipping in *C. Life*, 10 Jan. 1920, and *English Homes, Period V* (i), 1921, 289–300].

SMITH, WILLIAM, an architect and builder of Montrose, designed the upper storey which was added to MONTROSE TOWN HALL in 1818 [J. G. Low, *Highways and Byways of an Old Scottish Burgh*, Montrose 1938, 99]. He is also said to have designed ST. JOHN'S FREE CHURCH, MONTROSE, 1829, a Greek Revival building with an Ionic portico and a well-designed cupola [G. Hay, *The Architecture of Scottish Post-Reformation Churches*, 1957, 138].

SMITH, WILLIAM (*c.*1790–1848), practised in Alnwick from the 1820s until his death in March 1848 at the age of 58 [Register of St. Michael's, Alnwick, *ex inf.* Mrs. G. McCombie]. In ALNWICK he designed the MECHANICS' INSTITUTE off GREEN BATT, a nicely detailed Greek Revival building of 1831–2, and the former SAVINGS BANK at the junction of NARROWGATE and FENKLE STREET, a surprisingly early essay in fifteenth-century French domestic Gothic of 1835 [G. Tate, *History of Alnwick*, 1868–9, 2, 210, 219]. He also designed EDLINGHAM VICARAGE, NORTHUMBERLAND, 1840 [*Newcastle Jnl.* 25 April 1840].

SMYTHSON, JOHN (–1634), was the son of Robert Smythson (*c.*1535–1614), a celebrated Elizabethan architect whose works included Wollaton Hall, Notts. (1580–8), Worksop Manor, Notts. (*c.*1585), and Hardwick Hall, Derbyshire (1591–7). Like his father, John Smythson was by trade a mason, and he is first found working as a freemason at Wollaton in 1588. But by the 1590s he was probably helping his father in an architectural capacity, and in 1600, when he married, he was described in the register of St. Peter's Church, Nottingham, as 'gentleman'. In his will he called himself 'Architecter'.

John Smythson's principal patrons were members of the Cavendish family, for whom he worked at Bolsover Castle in Derbyshire, Welbeck Abbey in Nottinghamshire, and Slingsby Castle in Yorkshire. In 1615 Sir Charles Cavendish gave him the lease for life, at a nominal rent, of a farm at Kirkby-in-Ashfield (Notts.), 'in consideration of the just and faithful service to him heretofore done and hereafter to be done'. The service which Smythson gave in return appears to have included estate management as well as architectural supervision. In 1618–19 he visited London and made a number of drawings of recent buildings by Inigo Jones and others. His own architecture, as seen at Bolsover, was baroque rather than Jonesian in intention, and he delighted in rustication, fractured pediments, exaggerated mouldings and the like. The result is a highly personal style, mannered almost to the point of eccentricity, but unexpectedly attractive as well as whimsical. The drawings made by himself and his father are now in the R.I.B.A. Collection, and constitute a unique record of architectural practice in Elizabethan and Jacobean England.

John Smythson died in November or

December 1634, leaving a house in Bolsover and considerable property in Nottinghamshire to his widow and his sons Huntingdon and John Smythson. Huntingdon Smythson (d. 1648), who called himself 'Practioner of the Mathematiqs', appears, like his father, to have been partly a land surveyor and partly an architect. Of the 'skill in architecture' with which he is credited in his epitaph in Bolsover Church there is little evidence, though he probably assisted his father at Bolsover Castle, and may have designed some of the buildings erected by Sir William Cavendish, whose exact dating is in doubt. He died on 27 September 1648, leaving property valued at £960, including unspecified books and mathematical instruments in his study.

['The Smythson Collection of the R.I.B.A.', ed. Mark Girouard, *Arch. Hist.* v, 1962; Mark Girouard, *Robert Smythson and the Elizabethan Country House*, 1983.

BOLSOVER CASTLE, DERBYSHIRE, works for Sir Charles Cavendish (d. 1617) and his son Sir William Cavendish (later 1st Duke of Newcastle), *c.*1612–34, including the interior of the 'Little Castle' or keep (completed *c.*1621), and the gallery, either 1617–20 (Faulkner) or *c.*1631–4 (Girouard) [D. Knoop & G. P. Jones, 'The Bolsover Castle Building Account, 1613', *Ars Quatuor Coronatorum* xlix (1), 1936; Girouard, *Robert Smythson*, chaps. 6–7 and Appendix II; P. A. Faulkner, *Bolsover Castle*, H.M.S.O. 1972].

WELBECK ABBEY, NOTTS., RIDING SCHOOL for Sir William Cavendish, 1622–3; remodelled 1889; STABLES 1625, dem. [Girouard, *Robert Smythson*, 251–2].

AULT HUCKNALL CHURCH, DERBYSHIRE, monument to Anne Cavendish, Countess of Devonshire, 1627 [Girouard, *Robert Smythson*, 270].

attributed: SLINGSBY CASTLE, YORKS. (N.R.), for Sir Charles Cavendish (d. 1654), *c.*1630; now in ruins [Girouard, *Robert Smythson*, 257–60].

CLIFTON HALL, NOTTS., stables and probably other works for Sir Gervase Clifton, 1632; dem. [Girouard, *Robert Smythson*, 269–70].

SOANE, SIR JOHN (1753–1837), born on 10 September, 1753, was the son of John Soan, or Soane, a bricklayer at Goring-on-Thames, nr. Reading. Nothing is known of his early upbringing, but in 1768 he entered the office of George Dance, junior, the City Surveyor, through the good offices of the latter's assistant James Peacock, to whom he had been introduced by 'a near relative'. In October 1771 he was admitted to the Royal Academy Schools, and in the following year he exhibited a design for the 'Front of a Nobleman's Town House', and was awarded the Silver Medal for a measured drawing of the façade of the Banqueting House in Whitehall. He competed unsuccessfully for the Gold Medal in 1774, but won it in 1776 with a design for a triumphal bridge.[1] Meanwhile, in 1772 he had been taken on as an assistant at a salary of £60 a year by Henry Holland, then newly established in practice in Mayfair. Holland was at that time engaged in completing Claremont House for Lord Clive, and Soane afterwards claimed to have been responsible for the design of the entrance hall. His engagement with Holland came to an end in 1778, when, having attracted the attention of Sir William Chambers, he was awarded the King's Travelling Studentship and set out for Italy in company with R. F. Brettingham. In Rome, besides studying the architectural monuments, he made the acquaintance of Thomas Pitt, Lord Camelford, and of Frederick Hervey, Bishop of Derry (afterwards Earl of Bristol). The latter, whose passion for building was well known, offered Soane employment in designing country houses for him at Ickworth in Suffolk and at Downhill in Ireland. Soane, dazzled by 'the magnificent promises and splendid delusions of the Lord Bishop of Derry', cut short his tour in order to follow his patron to Ireland, but after remaining at Downhill for six weeks 'without any prospect of professional employment' he returned to England in June 1780, depressed in spirits and uncertain of the future. A further disappointment awaited him when the prospect of various works at Allanbank, nr. Berwick, for John Stuart also came to nothing. But a series of more modest commissions, chiefly in East Anglia, established him in practice, and in 1784 he was able to marry. His bride was Elizabeth Smith, a niece of George Wyatt, a wealthy builder to whose property he succeeded in 1790.

In 1788 Soane applied unsuccessfully for the vacant surveyorship of Greenwich Hospital, but gained a greater prize in that of the Bank of England, to which he was appointed in October 1788, through the influence of William Pitt. His competitors included James Wyatt, Henry Holland, S. P. Cockerell and Charles Beazley, who had 'transacted the whole of the Bank business' for Sir Robert Taylor during the last years of his life, and who was believed to 'stand well with the governors'. The surveyorship of the Bank gave Soane financial security, professional status

[1] Cf. Dorothy Stroud, 'Soane's Design for a Triumphal Bridge', *Arch. Rev.* April 1957.

and the most important commission of his life, besides introducing him to some of his wealthiest clients. From 1788 onwards he had an established place among the leading English architects, and enjoyed a professional practice second only to that of Wyatt. In 1791 he secured his first government appointment – that of Clerk of the Works at Whitehall, Westminster, and St. James's (£300 a year); in 1795 he became Deputy-Surveyor of H. M. Woods and Forests (£200 a year);[1] and in 1807 Clerk of the Works to Chelsea Hospital. In 1814, on the reorganization of the Board of Works, he was appointed one of the three 'Attached Architects', with personal responsibility for the public buildings in Whitehall, Westminster, Richmond Park, Kew Gardens and Hampton Court Palace. This appointment lasted until 1832, when Soane retired from the Office of Works with a knighthood.

Soane was elected A.R.A. in 1795, and R.A. in 1802. In 1806 he succeeded George Dance as Professor of Architecture at the Royal Academy, and in 1809 began to deliver the elaborately illustrated lectures which he continued to repeat until the year before his death.[2] In 1810–11 they were temporarily suspended in consequence of a vote of censure passed upon him by the Academy for criticizing the work of a 'living artist' in the person of Robert Smirke, whose Covent Garden Theatre had figured in the fourth lecture as an example of the misuse of the Greek Doric Order. The care which he took in the preparation and presentation of his R.A. lectures was characteristic of Soane's interest in architectural education, and both in this way and by his personal influence over his many pupils he did much to raise the standards of architectural practice. He was outspoken in condemnation of what he regarded as unprofessional conduct, and although he was debarred by the rules of the R.A. from accepting the Presidency of the Institute of British Architects which was offered to him on its foundation in 1834, his position as the father of his profession was recognized in the following year by the presentation to him of a Gold Medal on behalf of 350 subscribers. To acknowledge the honour then showed to him Soane gave £5000 as a fund for distressed architects and their dependants. Later in the same year he presented the sum of £750 to the Institute and £250 to the Architectural Society, expressing the hope that they would before long be united. The former gift was commemorated by the foundation of the Soane Medal, which became the principal award offered by the Institute to architectural students.

In 1833, Soane, then in his 80th year, was compelled by failing eyesight to resign the surveyorship of the Bank of England which had been 'the pride and boast' of his life. His connection with the Office of Works had already been terminated in 1832 upon its amalgamation with the Department of Woods, Forests, and Land Revenues. He spent his last years in writing a *Description* of the house in Lincoln's Inn Fields which had been his home since 1812, and which he left to the nation as a museum for 'the study of Architecture and the Allied Arts', obtaining an Act of Parliament to that effect in 1833. Throughout his life Soane had collected architectural drawings, models and casts, besides paintings, sculpture and miscellaneous antiquities of all kinds. The house had gradually been extended and adapted for their reception until every available space was occupied by a bust or an antique vase, a painting by Hogarth or a drawing by Piranesi, all disposed in accordance with their collector's declared purpose of demonstrating 'the unity of the arts'. The result was a kind of personal Academy of the Arts, contained within the walls of a private residence, but intended for public display; and what had been a museum in its builder's lifetime retains after his death the atmosphere of a private house.

Soane was a man of difficult temperament, austere, exacting, touchy and neurotic. His private life was strained by difficulties with his sons, whose failure to follow their father's profession caused him life-long regret: and the sudden death of Mrs. Soane in 1815 was a tragedy which he never allowed himself to forget. He was punctilious in his relations with his clients, and spared neither himself nor his staff in accomplishing what he admitted to be 'the ruling passion of my life', namely 'to be distinguished as an architect'.

Although a master of the established conventions of classical architecture, which he expounded in his lectures and used himself in appropriate contexts, Soane also developed a highly individual architectural style based on an elegantly mannered – it might almost be said 'mannerist' – interpretation of the neo-classical vocabulary. Structurally, the Soane style is marked by a fondness for shallow domes associated with clerestory lighting, by

[1] This proved too small a salary to secure Soane's attention to the duties of his office, and he resigned in 1799 after complaints about his negligence. He had already, in 1793, resigned his Clerkship of the Works at Whitehall after a disagreement about his duties.

[2] They were published in 1929 under the editorship of A. T. Bolton as *Lectures in Architecture by Sir John Soane* (Soane Museum Publications, No. 14). A new edition by Dr. David Watkin is in preparation.

the extensive use of segmental arches, and by great ingenuity in planning, particularly in cases where the site was circumscribed by existing buildings. In the field of decoration its distinguishing feature was the elimination of the classical column and entablature, together with their appropriate mouldings, and their replacement by a system of linear ornamentation, incised more often than raised, and eked out by the use of antique motifs such as *paterae* and *acroteria*. These characteristic features first appear fully developed in Soane's work at the Bank (from 1792 onwards),[1] and he also used them to good effect in the Dulwich Picture Gallery, where financial stringency forbad a more conventional architectural programme. In its earlier form this personal style owed much to the work of Soane's 'revered master', George Dance, junior, whose Guildhall Council Chamber (1777) anticipated its essential features; later, it reflected both Gothic and Pompeian forms in the endeavour to achieve what Soane called 'the poetry of Architecture'. To deviate from the accepted canons of classical architecture was inevitably to invite attack, and Soane had his share of abuse in the shape of a facetious article on 'The Sixth or Boeotian Order of Architecture', which appeared in *Knight's Quarterly Magazine* in 1824, and led him to institute an unsuccessful libel action. Although not without influence on his contemporaries, Soane's style found no serious imitator, and his death meant the end of the attempt to develop a new kind of classical architecture that was not a revival of any historical style, either Greek, Roman or Italian, but a distillation of all three into forms of great beauty and originality.

Apart from controversial pamphlets, Soane's published works were *Designs in Architecture, consisting of Plans, Elevations and Sections for Temples, Baths, Cassines, Pavilions, Garden-Seats, Obelisks, and other Buildings*, 1778 (commissioned by the publisher Isaac Taylor and reissued by him in 1789, 1790 and 1797); *Plans, Elevations and Sections of Buildings erected in the Counties of Norfolk, Suffolk*, etc., 1788 (actually 1789);[2] *Sketches in Architecture, containing Plans and Elevations of Cottages, Villas and other Useful Buildings*, 1793, 2nd ed. 1798; and *Designs for Public Improvements* (1827, 25 copies only),[1] reprinted with additions as *Designs for Public and Private Buildings*, 1828. His *Description of the House and Museum on the North Side of Lincoln's Inn Fields*, 1832, of which an enlarged version was printed in 1835–6, and his *Memoirs of the Professional Life of an Architect*, 1835, were both privately printed.

The Soane Museum contains many portraits of its founder (notably that by Sir Thomas Lawrence), and all his private and professional papers, besides a large collection of his architectural drawings and lecture-diagrams. Several portraits of Soane and some of his drawings are preserved at the Bank of England (see *An Historical Catalogue of Engravings, Drawings and Paintings in the Bank of England*, 1928, 57–8, 69–73). There are also a few drawings by Soane in the R.I.B.A. Collection and a number in the Victoria and Albert Museum (Catalogue by P. de la Ruffinière du Prey, 1985).

In the course of his long career Soane had many pupils and assistants. The former included J. Adams, George Bailey (who remained with Soane until his death, and was appointed first Curator of the Museum under his will), George Basevi, S. Burchell, H. Burges, J. Buxton, R. D. Chantrell, Thomas Chawner, F. Copland, E. Davis, E. M. Foxhall, J. H. Good, Thomas Jeans, David Laing, C. Malton, John McDonnell, A. P. Mee, David Mocatta, C. E. Papendiek, Henry Parke, C. J. Richardson, W. E. Rolfe, John Sanders, H. H. Seward and Charles Tyrrell. Chief among Soane's assistants was J. M. Gandy, A.R.A., who spent most of his life as Soane's chief draughtsman and illustrator. Others were Christopher Ebdon, J. W. Hiort, G. E. Ives, William Lodder, R. Morrison, D. Paton and G. A. Underwood. George Wightwick was his secretary for about eight months in 1826–7, and wrote a brilliant and amusing account of his eccentric employer.

[*A.P.S.D.*; *D.N.B.*; T. L. Donaldson, *A Review of the Professional Life of Sir John Soane*, 1837; list of works by G. Bailey in *Builder* iv, 1846, 577, 590; A. T. Bolton, *The Works of Sir John Soane, R.A.*, 1924; A. T. Bolton, *The Portrait of Sir John Soane, R.A.*, 1927; H. J. Birnstingl, *Sir John Soane*, 1925; John Summerson, *Sir John Soane*, 1952; Dorothy Stroud, 'The Early Work of Soane', *Arch. Rev.* Feb. 1957; Dorothy Stroud, *The Architecture of Sir John Soane*, 1961; *History of the King's Works* vi, 1973, *passim*; John Summerson, 'Sir John Soane and the Furni-

[1] A comparison between his published designs for the saloon at Chillington, which shows a domed hall in the manner of Wyatt or Holland, and those actually executed in 1785–9 shows that the characteristic Soaneic Hall had already been conceived and executed before the Bank gave its author an opportunity of employing it on a large scale.

[2] The original drawings for pls. 28–32 are in the Hailstone Collection in York Minster Library.

[1] The copy presented by Soane to the Royal Library at Windsor contains a number of original drawings.

ture of Death', *Arch. Rev.* March 1978; P. de la Ruffinière du Prey, *John Soane: The Making of an Architect*, 1982; *John Soane*, Academy Editions 1983; Dorothy Stroud, *Sir John Soane Architect*, 1984; Eileen Harris, *British Architectural Books and Writers 1556–1785*, 1990, 427–31; *Apollo*, April 1990 (articles on Soane's library, drawings and papers).]

The following list of Soane's executed works is (unless otherwise stated) based on his publications (referred to as *Plans*, *Sketches* and *Designs*, respectively), on the list of his buildings printed in *A.P.S.D.* and reprinted by A. T. Bolton in *The Works of Sir John Soane*, and on the comprehensive list of commissions compiled by Miss Dorothy Stroud from the journals, account-books and drawings in Sir John Soane's Museum and printed at the end of her book entitled *Sir John Soane, Architect*, 1984.

PUBLIC BUILDINGS, ETC.

NORWICH, BLACKFRIARS BRIDGE (R. Wensum), 1783–4; since widened (*Plans*; Stroud, *Architecture*, pl. 7).

WALTHAMSTOW CHURCH, ESSEX, alterations, 1784 (cf. *V.C.H. Essex* vi, 289).

NAYLAND CHURCH, SUFFOLK, pewing, etc., 1785.

HINGHAM CHURCH, NORFOLK, alterations to chancel, including Gothic reredos since removed, 1785.

LONDON, THE BANK OF ENGLAND, rebuilt 1788–1833; rebuilt 1924–40 (*Designs*; Bolton, *Works*; H. R. Steele & F. R. Yerbury, *The Old Bank of England*, 1930; Stroud, *Architecture*, pls. 65–92; John Summerson, 'The evolution of Soane's Bank Stock Office at the Bank of England', *Arch. Hist.* 27, 1984; Eva Schumann-Bacia, *John Soane and the Bank of England*, 1991).

NORWICH CASTLE, rebuilt COUNTY GAOL, 1789–94, castellated; dem. 1825 (*Designs*; Stroud, *Architecture*, pl. 46).

CAMBRIDGE, rearranged area round SENATE HOUSE, 1792 [Willis & Clark iii, 73].

CAMBRIDGE, CAIUS COLLEGE, remodelled interior of Hall, 1792; remodelled as rooms (now library), 1853 [Willis & Clark i, 197].

CAMBRIDGE, ST. JOHN'S COLLEGE, repairs to First and probably Second Court, 1792 [A. C. Crook, *From the Foundation to Gilbert Scott: A History of the Buildings of St. John's College, Cambridge*, Cambridge 1990, 71–2].

LONDON, HYDE PARK, CUMBERLAND GATE and lodge, 1797; dem. (Stroud, *Architecture*, pl. 109).

LONDON, CONSTITUTION HILL, lodge and gateway, 1797; dem.

BRAMLEY CHURCH, HANTS., added BROCAS CHAPEL for Mrs. Brocas, 1802, Gothic.

WAKEFIELD, ALL SAINTS CHURCH (now Cathedral), report on repair of spire, 1802 [J. W. Walker, *Wakefield*, 1939].

READING, BERKS., obelisk in Market Place for Edward Simeon, 1804 (*Arch. Rev.* xlvii, 1920, 110–11, measured drawings).

OXFORD, BRASENOSE COLLEGE, converted cloister into rooms, 1807.

BELFAST, IRELAND, THE ACADEMICAL INSTITUTION, COLLEGE SQUARE, 1809–14, representing a much simplified version of his original designs (C. F. B. Brett, *Buildings of Belfast*, 1967, pls. 14, 15).

CHELSEA HOSPITAL, LONDON, the INFIRMARY, STABLES and additions to Clerk of the Works' House, 1809–17. The house was dem. 1858 and the Infirmary was destroyed by bombing in 1941 (Stroud, *Architecture*, pls. 145–53).

DULWICH COLLEGE, THE PICTURE GALLERY and MAUSOLEUM, 1811–14; restored after bomb damage in 1944 (*Designs*; Bolton, *Works*, 76–82; Stroud, *Architecture*, pls. 156–63; Giles Waterfield, *Soane and After: The Architecture of Dulwich Picture Gallery*, 1987).

LONDON, THE NATIONAL DEBT REDEMPTION AND LIFE ANNUITIES OFFICE, OLD JEWRY, 1818–19; dem. *c.*1900 (*Designs*; Bolton, *Works*, 83–6; Stroud, *Architecture*, pls. 176–7).

WESTMINSTER, THE LAW COURTS, 1822–5; dem. 1883. The exterior was Gothicized against Soane's wishes, in accordance with a design which he disowned. [*History of the King's Works* vi, 1973, 504–12] (*Designs*; Bolton, *Works*, chap. 9; Stroud, *Architecture*, pls. 205–13).

WESTMINSTER, THE HOUSE OF LORDS: royal entrance, royal gallery, library and committee rooms, 1822–7; partly destroyed by fire 1834, remainder dem. 1851 [*History of the King's Works* vi, 1973, 520–5] (*Designs*; Bolton, *Works*, 103–14).

LONDON, ST. PETER'S CHURCH, WALWORTH, 1823–4 (Stroud, *Architecture*, pl. 189).

LONDON, THE INSOLVENT DEBTORS' COURT, PORTUGAL STREET, LINCOLN'S INN FIELDS, 1823–4; dem. 1911 [*History of the King's Works* vi, 438–40] (Stroud, *Architecture*, pls. 196–7).

LONDON, BOARD OF TRADE AND PRIVY COUNCIL OFFICES, WHITEHALL, 1824–6; remodelled by Barry 1845–6 [*History of the King's Works* vi, 1973, 551–62] (*Designs*).

WESTMINSTER, THE HOUSE OF COMMONS: LIBRARY and COMMITTEE ROOMS, 1826–7, Gothic; destroyed by fire 1834 [*History of the King's Works* vi, 527–9].

LONDON, HOLY TRINITY CHURCH, MARYLEBONE, 1826–7; chancel 1878; converted into S.P.C.K. offices 1955–6 (Stroud, *Architecture*, pls. 186–7).

LONDON, ST. JOHN'S CHURCH, BETHNAL GREEN, 1826–8; interior remodelled after fire in 1870 and chancel extended 1888 (Stroud, *Architecture*, pl. 188).

LONDON, FREEMASONS' HALL, GREAT QUEEN STREET, the new COUNCIL CHAMBER, 1828; dem. 1864 (*Designs*; Bolton, *Works*, 116, 119; Stroud, *Architecture*, pl. 221).

LONDON, THE BANQUETING HOUSE, WHITEHALL, restoration of exterior, 1829–33 [*History of the King's Works* vi, 547–8].

WESTMINSTER, THE STATE PAPER OFFICE, DUKE STREET, 1830–4; dem. 1862 [*History of the King's Works* vi, 1973, 567–70] (*Designs*; Bolton, *Works*, 128–31; Stroud, *Architecture*, pls. 222–4).

COUNTRY HOUSES, ETC.

PETERSHAM LODGE, SURREY, repairs and decorations for Thomas Pitt, later 1st Lord Camelford, 1781–2; dem. *c.*1835.

WALTHAMSTOW, ESSEX, new room for James Neave, 1781, perhaps at CLEVELANDS, dem. 1960.

HAMELS (later Crofton Grange), nr. BUNTINGFORD, HERTS., alterations, entrance lodges and dairy (dem.) for the Hon. Philip Yorke, 1781–3; house remodelled *c.*1830/40 (Stroud, *Architecture*, pl. 8).

COOMBE HOUSE, nr. KINGSTON, SURREY, repairs and alterations for the Hon. Wilbraham Tollemache, 1782–5; dem. 1933.

BURN HALL, CO. DURHAM, neo-classical cowhouse for George Smith, 1783 [P. de la R. du Prey in *C. Life*, 8 Jan. 1976, 84] (*Plans*).

WALTHAMSTOW RECTORY MANOR, ESSEX, enlarged for William Cooke, 1783–4; dem. *c.*1897.

BURNHAM WESTGATE HALL, NORFOLK, alterations and additions for Thomas Pitt, later 1st Lord Camelford, 1783–5.

TYTTENHANGER, HERTS., repairs for the Hon. Mrs. Yorke, 1783 and 1789.

MALVERN HALL, SOLIHULL, WARWICKS., added wings, etc., for Henry Greswold Lewis, 1783–6; wings dem. 1899 (*Plans*; cf. *Constable's Correspondence*, ed. R. B. Beckett, iv, 62); Doric barn (now No. 936 Warwick Road), 1798 (Stroud, *Architecture*, pl. 107).

LETTON HALL, NORFOLK, for B. G. Dillingham, 1783–9 (*Plans*; Stroud, *Architecture*, pls. 1–6).

SAXLINGHAM RECTORY, NORFOLK, for the Revd. J. Gooch, 1784–7 (*Plans*; Stroud, *Architecture*, pls. 9–10).

COSTESSEY HALL, NORFOLK, stable and dovecote for Sir William Jerningham, Bart., 1784; dem.

TAVERHAM HALL, NORFOLK, alterations for M. S. Branthwayt, 1784–8; rebuilt by D. Brandon, 1858–9.

EARSHAM HALL, nr. BUNGAY, NORFOLK, Music Room for William Wyndham, 1784–5 (*Plans*; Stroud, *Architecture*, pls. 17–19).

TENDRING HALL, SUFFOLK, for Sir Joshua Rowley, Bart., 1784–6; dem. 1955 (Stroud, *Architecture*, pls. 11–16).

LANGLEY PARK, NORFOLK, two pairs of lodges for Sir Thomas Beauchamp-Proctor, Bart., 1784 onwards, and roof repairs, etc., 1788 (*Plans*; Stroud, *Architecture*, pls. 20–22).

SHOTESHAM PARK, NORFOLK, for R. Fellowes, 1785–8 (*C. Life*, 10 Aug. 1967; Stroud, *Architecture*, pls. 23–7). There are drawings by Soane in the Norfolk C.R.O., FEL 1115, P 157C.

BLUNDESTON HOUSE, SUFFOLK, for Nathaniel Rix, 1785–6 (*Plans*, where it appears under the name of 'Oulton'; Stroud, *Architecture*, pl. 36).

CHILLINGTON HALL, STAFFS., remodelled for Thomas Giffard, 1785–9 (*Plans*; *C. Life*, 27 Feb. 1948). There are drawings by Soane in the William Salt Library at Stafford: 'Staffordshire Views' iii, ff. 95–107.

PIERCEFIELD, nr. CHEPSTOW, MONMOUTHSHIRE, rebuilt for George Smith, 1785–93; now in ruins (Stroud, *Architecture*, pls. 44, 45).

LEES COURT, KENT, alterations to house and new stables for L. T. Watson, 1786 (Stroud, *Architecture*, pls. 30–2).

CRICKET LODGE, CRICKET ST. THOMAS, SOMERSET, alterations and additions, including farmhouse, etc., for Admiral Hood, 1st Viscount Bridport, 1786 and 1801–7; since much altered (Stroud, *Architecture*, pl. 134).

BOCONNOC, CORNWALL, repairs for 1st Lord Camelford, 1786–88.

MULGRAVE HALL, YORKS. (N.R.), alterations and additions for 2nd Lord Mulgrave, 1786 (*Plans*); remodelled by William Atkinson as Mulgrave Castle, *c.*1804–11.

HOCKERILL, nr. BISHOPS STORTFORD, HERTS., house for R. Winter, 1786 (*Plans*).

CASTLE HILL, DEVON, alterations for 1st. Earl Fortescue, *c.*1786–90; central block gutted by fire 1934 and rebuilt (*C. Life*, 17–24 March 1934).

NACKINGTON HOUSE, KENT, alterations for R. Milles, 1786; dem.

HOLWOOD HOUSE, KENT, alterations and additions for William Pitt, 1786 and 1795; dem. 1823 (*Designs*; Stroud, *Architecture*, pl. 35).

SKELTON CASTLE, YORKS. (N.R.), alterations

and additions, including stables, for John Hall (later Wharton), 1787 (*Plans*).

FONTHILL HOUSE, WILTS., picture gallery for Alderman William Beckford, 1787; dem. 1807 (Stroud, *Architecture*, pls. 37–8).

RYSTON HALL, NORFOLK, remodelled for Edward Pratt, 1787–8 (*Plans*; Stroud, *Architecture*, pls. 33–4).

KELSHALL RECTORY, HERTS., designs for alterations for the Revd. Thomas Waddington, 1788.

BENTLEY PRIORY, STANMORE, MIDDLESEX, alterations and additions for 1st Marquess of Abercorn, 1788–98; enlarged by W. Wilkins and R. Smirke *c.*1810–18; subsequently much altered (Stroud, *Architecture*, pls. 40–3).

WARDOUR CASTLE, WILTS., enlarged CHAPEL (R.C.) for 8th Lord Arundell of Wardour, 1788 (*C. Life*, 10 Oct. 1968).

BEMERTON RECTORY, WILTS., designs for alterations for Dr. William Coxe, 1788.

RICHMOND PARK, SURREY, HILL or PEMBROKE LODGE, alterations for the Countess of Pembroke, 1788 and 1796.

GAWDY HALL, nr. HARLESTON, NORFOLK, alterations for the Revd. Gervase Holmes, 1788; dem. 1939.

HONING HALL, NORFOLK, alterations for Thomas Cubitt, 1788; altered in nineteenth century.

WOKEFIELD PARK, BERKS., alterations and new gateway for Mrs. Brocas, 1788–9; altered *c.*1845.

TAWSTOCK COURT, DEVON, alterations to exterior (castellated) and new staircase for Sir Bourchier Wrey, Bart., 1789 (*Gent's Mag.* 1817 (i), 489; Stroud, *Architecture*, pls. 50–1).

FAIRFORD PARK, GLOS., alterations for J. R. Barker, 1789; dem. 1957.

GUNTHORPE HALL, NORFOLK, for Charles Collyer, 1789; altered 1880 and 1900.

HALSNEAD HALL, WHISTON, LANCS., south front for Richard Willis, 1789; dem. 1932 (S. A. Harris in *Trans. Historic Soc. of Lancs. and Cheshire* cvi, 1954, 153–8).

CHILTON LODGE, nr. HUNGERFORD, BERKS., for William Morland, 1789–90; rebuilt by W. Pilkington 1800 (*Sketches*; Stroud, *Architecture*, pl. 53).

WOOD EATON MANOR, OXON., new porch and kitchen wing for John Weyland, 1790.

WILLIAMSTRIP PARK, GLOS., alterations, including library, for Michael Hicks Beach, 1791; library removed 1946.

WISTON HALL, WISSINGTON, SUFFOLK, for Samuel Beachcroft, 1791.

WHICHCOTES, HENDON, MIDDLESEX, repairs for John Cornwall, 1791.

NETHERAVON HOUSE, WILTS., enlarged for Michael Hicks Beach, 1791; since much altered.

WIMPOLE HALL, CAMBS., alterations and additions to house, including Yellow Drawing Room and Book Room; also *Castello d'Aqua* (dem.), Arrington lodges (dem.) and Home Farm, for 3rd Earl of Hardwicke, 1791–4 (*C. Life*, 21–28 May, 1927; R.C.H.M. *W. Cambs.*, 217; Stroud, *Architecture*, pls. 58–62; D. Souden, *Wimpole Hall*, National Trust 1991).

BARON'S COURT, CO. TYRONE, IRELAND, remodelled for 1st Marquess of Abercorn, 1791–5; centre gutted by fire 1796 and rebuilt in 1837–41 (Stroud, *Architecture*, pls. 63–4).

TAPLOW, BUCKS., additions to house for Lady Wynn, 1792.

SULBY HALL, NORTHANTS., rebuilt for René Payne, 1792–5; remodelled *c.*1825; dem. *c.*1949 [stated to be by Soane in J. P. Neale, *Views of Seats*, 1st ser. vi, 1823, and confirmed by Soane's ledgers] (J. A. Gotch, *Squires' Homes of Northants.*, 1939, 23–4; illustrating the house after 1830).

TYRINGHAM HALL, BUCKS., including lodge and bridge, for William Praed, 1793–*c.*1800; interior altered, dome a modern addition (*Designs*; Bolton, *Works*, 12–20; Stroud, *Architecture*, pls. 93–9).

SYDNEY LODGE, HAMBLE, HANTS., for the Hon. Mrs. Yorke, 1793–5 (G. Richardson, *New Vitruvius Britannicus* i, 1810, pl. 10; Stroud, *Architecture*, pls. 47–9).

SOUTHGATE, MIDDLESEX, alterations to house for Thomas Lewis, 1793.

CAIRNESS HOUSE, ABERDEENSHIRE, completion, 1794–7, of house designed by James Playfair (*q.v.*) for Charles Gordon.

CUFFNELLS, nr. LYNDHURST, HANTS., south front, etc., for George Rose, 1794–5; dem. *c.*1950 (G. F. Prosser, *Select Illustrations of Hampshire*, 1833).

PITSHILL, nr. TILLINGTON, SUSSEX, designs for north front for William Mitford, executed in modified form, 1794.

SUNBURY HOUSE, MIDDLESEX, designs for alterations for Roger Boehm, 1794; dem.

SOUTHGATE, MIDDLESEX, alterations to house at Palmer's Green for Samuel Boddington, 1795.

BAGDEN or SAVERNAKE LODGE, SAVERNAKE FOREST, WILTS., enlarged for 1st Earl of Ailesbury as a residence for his son Lord Bruce, 1795; destroyed by fire 1861.

WESTON, nr. SOUTHAMPTON, HANTS., alterations for W. Moffat, 1797; dem. Although Soane made designs for alterations to this house in 1797, subsequent references in Soane's journal suggest that he may have been superseded by Willey Reveley (*q.v.*).

NORTH MIMMS PARK, HERTS., repairs and new

dairy and greenhouse, etc., for 5th Duke of Leeds, 1797.

CLAPHAM, WANDSWORTH, SURREY, alterations to house for T. A. Green, 1798.

BAGSHOT PARK, SURREY, alterations for Prince William (afterwards Duke of Gloucester), 1798; dem. 1878 (G. F. Prosser, *Select Illustrations of* Surrey, 1828; Stroud, *Architecture*, pl. 108).

BETCHWORTH CASTLE, SURREY, alterations to house and new stables, etc., for Henry Peters, 1798–9 (Stroud, *Architecture*, pls. 110–14).

HEATHFIELD LODGE, ACTON, MIDDLESEX, alterations for John Winter, 1798.

RICHMOND PARK, SURREY, THATCHED HOUSE LODGE, alterations to dining-room, etc., for General Sir Charles Stuart, 1798.

DOWN AMPNEY HOUSE, GLOS., alterations for the Hon. John Eliot, 1799.

AYNHO PARK, NORTHANTS., remodelled interior and altered exterior for W. R. Cartwright, 1799–1804 (*C. Life*, 2, 9, 16 July 1953).

MICKLEFIELD HALL, nr. RICKMANSWORTH, HERTS., remodelled entrance hall and staircase for Elisha Biscoe, 1800 [P. Guillery in *Arch. Hist.* 30, 1987, 181–9].

ALBURY PARK, SURREY, north front and internal alterations for Samuel Thornton, 1800–2; exterior remodelled by A. W. & E. W. Pugin 1842 onwards (*C. Life*, 25 Aug., 1 Sept. 1950).

PITZHANGER PLACE or MANOR, EALING, MIDDLESEX, largely rebuilt for himself, 1800–3 (G. Richardson, *New Vitruvius Britannicus* ii, 1808, pls. 57–9; Stroud, *Architecture*, pls. 122–30).

SOUTH HILL PARK, BRACKNELL, BERKS., alterations for George Canning, 1801.

NORWOOD HALL, NORWOOD GREEN, MIDDLESEX, for John Robins, 1801–2; much altered in late 19th century [P. Guillery in *Arch. Hist.* 30, 1987, 181–9].

COOMBE HOUSE, nr. KINGSTON, SURREY, alterations, including addition of library, for Lord Hawkesbury, later 2nd Earl of Liverpool, 1801–9; dem. 1933.

GREENWICH, KENT, MACARTNEY HOUSE, alterations for the Hon. G. F. Lyttelton, 1802.

HAMPSTEAD, LONDON, new entrance and other alterations to house for Daniel Bayley, 1803.

PORT ELIOT, ST. GERMAN'S, CORNWALL, remodelled house and designed new stables for 2nd Lord Eliot, 1804–6, castellated; entrance hall and porch by H. Harrison 1829 (*C. Life*, 15, 22, 29 Oct. 1948; Stroud, *Architecture*, pls. 136–8).

RAMSEY ABBEY, HUNTS., remodelled for W. H. Fellowes, 1804–7; remodelled by E. Blore 1838–9 (Stroud, *Architecture*, pl. 139).

ROEHAMPTON, SURREY, CEDAR COURT, enlarged for John Thomson, 1804–7; dem. 1910–13.

STOWE HOUSE, BUCKS., Gothic library for 1st Marquess of Buckingham, 1805–6 (Michael McCarthy, 'Soane's "Saxon" Room at Stowe', *Jnl. Society of Architectural Historians* xliv, 1985).

ASTROP PARK, NORTHANTS., additions for the Revd. W. S. Willes, 1805; reduced in size 1961.

ENGLEFIELD HOUSE, BERKS., repairs for Richard Benyon, 1806 [drawings in Berks. County Record Office, D/EBY 23 and C14].

WHITLEY ABBEY, WARWICKS., alterations for 1st Viscount Hood, 1810; dem. 1953 (J. P. Neale, *Views of Seats*, 1st ser. iii, 1820).

MOGGERHANGER HOUSE, BEDS., rebuilt for Stephen Thornton, 1809–11 (Stroud, *Architecture*, pls. 143–4).

MELLS PARK, SOMERSET, alterations, including entrance and library, for Col. Thomas Horner, 1810–24; dem. after fire in 1917 (*C. Life*, 24 May 1962, 1254; Stroud, *Architecture*, pls. 154–5).

EVERTON HOUSE, BEDS., alterations for William Astell, 1811–12; dem.

WALMER COTTAGE, KENT, additions for Capt. Lee, 1812.

RINGWOULD HOUSE, KENT, for the Revd. John Monins, 1813 (C. Greenwood, *Epitome of County History: Kent*, 1838, 433; Stroud, *Architecture*, pl. 172).

BUTTERTON, STAFFS., BUTTERTON GRANGE FARMHOUSE, for Thomas Swinnerton, 1815 (Stroud, *Architecture*, pl. 174).

MARDEN HILL, TEWIN, HERTS., new porch and other alterations for C. G. Thornton, 1818–19 (*C. Life*, 22 Aug. 1941; Stroud, *Architecture*, pls. 178–9).

WOTTON HOUSE, BUCKS., reconstructed interior after fire for 2nd Marquess of Buckingham, 1821–2 (*C. Life*, 15 July 1949; Stroud, *Architecture*, pls. 180–2).

PELLWALL HOUSE, nr. MARKET DRAYTON, STAFFS., for Purney Sillitoe, 1822–8; enlarged and internally remodelled 1861; gutted 1986 (*C. Life*, 7 April 1988).

LONDON HOUSES, ETC.

PICCADILLY, No. 148, completion and decoration for the Hon. Wilbraham Tollemache, 1781–8; dem.

ADAMS PLACE, SOUTHWARK, shops and tenements for Francis Adams, 1781–4; dem.

BERKELEY SQUARE, alterations for the Hon. Mrs. Perry, 1782–3.

NEW CAVENDISH STREET, No. 7 (later 63), alterations for the Hon. Philip Yorke, 1782–4.

WIMPOLE STREET, No. 42, repairs for Sir John

Stuart of Allanbank, 1783.

SAVILE ROW, No. 18, alterations to drawing-room for Lady Banks, 1784; dem.

PALL MALL, No. 103, shop-front for Mr. Crooke, 1790; dem. 1836–7 [*Survey of London* xxix, 350].

HILL STREET, No. 23, alterations for 1st Earl Fortescue, 1791.

PALL MALL, No. 56, alterations for Messrs. Ransom, Morland & Hammersley, bankers, 1791.

PHILPOT LANE, No. 15, repairs and decorations for Peter Thellusson, 1792; dem.

FENCHURCH STREET, No. 27, repairs and decorations for Charles Thellusson, 1792.

MARK LANE, No. 17, repairs and alterations for Samuel Boddington, 1792.

UPPER GROSVENOR STREET, No. 1, repairs for Mrs. Brocas, 1792 and 1819; dem 1957.

BUCKINGHAM HOUSE, No. 91 PALL MALL, rebuilt for 1st Marquess of Buckingham, 1792–5; further alterations and repairs 1813–14; dem. 1908 (*Designs*; *Survey of London* xxix, 360–3 and pls. 224–7).

LINCOLN'S INN FIELDS, No. 12, for himself, 1792–4 (Stroud, *Architecture*, pls. 100–4).

OLD PALACE YARD, Nos. 6–7, alterations to basement and ground floor, with interior decoration, for George Rose and Henry Compton, Clerks of the Parliament, 1793 [P.R.O., WORK 5/82 and Soane Museum, Soane's Journal no. 1, f. 26, *ex inf.* Mr. R. Hewlings].

PALL MALL, No. 104, alterations for Lady Louisa Manners, 1793–4; dem. *c.*1837 [*Survey of London* xxix, 350].

LINCOLN'S INN FIELDS, No. 51, alterations for John Pearse, 1794; dem. 1904 (*Survey of London* iii, pls. 61–5).

STRATTON STREET, No, 12, for Col. Thomas Graham, 1795–7; dem.

SOUTH AUDLEY STREET, No. 56, repairs and decorations for Miss Anguish, 1795.

LINCOLN'S INN FIELDS, Nos. 57–8, divided into two houses, with new porch, 1795 (*Survey of London* iii, pls. 73–5).

PORTLAND PLACE, No. 25 (later 70), repairs and alterations for Sir Alan, later 1st Lord Gardner, 1795 and 1810.

ST. JAMES'S SQUARE, No. 21, completion of house designed by R. F. Brettingham for 5th Duke of Leeds, 1795; dem. 1934 [*Survey of London* xxix, 175–80, pls. 191–3].

PARK LANE, alterations and repairs to house for 2nd Earl of Mornington, 1796.

LOWER GOWER STREET, No. 34, alterations for Mrs. Peters, 1798.

ST. JAMES'S SQUARE, No. 22, internal alterations for Samuel Thornton, 1799, and repairs, 1805 and 1811; dem. 1847 (*Survey of London* xxix, 180–1).

MANSFIELD STREET, No. 12, alterations for Charles Mills, 1799.

GEORGE STREET, HANOVER SQUARE, No. 24, alterations for Dr. Pemberton, 1799.

GROSVENOR SQUARE, No. 22 (later 25), alterations for 1st Marquess of Abercorn, 1799; dem. 1957.

OLD BROAD STREET, No. 54, alterations for Stephen Thornton, 1800.

PARK STREET, MAYFAIR, No. 50, repairs for Henry Peters, 1800; dem.

NEW NORFOLK (now DUNRAVEN) STREET, No. 22 (131 PARK LANE), alterations for J. Hammet, 1801, completed by James Spiller.

FLEET STREET, No. 189, Bank for William Praed, 1801; dem. 1923 (Stroud, *Architecture*, pls. 131–2).

FOUNTAIN COURT, ALDERMANBURY, new premises for W. A. Jackson, Peters & Co., 1802–5; dem.

GROSVENOR SQUARE, No. 44 (later 49), alterations for Robert Knight (of Barrells), 1802–3 and later; dem. 1925–6 (Stroud, *Architecture*, pl. 135; *Survey of London* xl, fig. 40).

PARK LANE, BREADALBANE HOUSE, alterations to windows for 4th Earl of Breadalbane, 1803; dem. 1876–7.

UPPER GROSVENOR STREET, No. 14, alterations for Thomas Raikes, 1803–4; dem. 1908.

CURZON STREET, No. 19, alterations for Sir John Sebright, Bart., 1803.

ST. JAMES'S SQUARE, No. 33, alterations for 2nd Lord Eliot, 1805–7 [*Survey of London* xxix, 207–10].

SOUTH AUDLEY STREET, No. 6, decorations for Richard Benyon, 1805.

FREDERICK'S PLACE, No. 4, alterations for Thomas Lewis, 1806.

DEAN STREET, MAYFAIR, No. 4, alterations for Robert Knight (barrister), 1807.

NEW BANK BUILDINGS, PRINCES STREET, LOTHBURY, 1807–10; dem. 1891 (*Designs*; Stroud, *Architecture*, pl. 140).

GROSVENOR SQUARE, No. 34 (later 39), alterations for Mrs. Benyon, 1807–8; dem. 1962–5.

WHITEHALL, FIFE HOUSE, repairs and alterations for 2nd Earl of Liverpool, 1809; dem. 1869.

PARK LANE, No. 22 (later 18), for John Robins, 1812; dem.

LINCOLN'S INN FIELDS, No. 13, for himself, 1812–13 (J. Britton, *The Union of Architecture, Sculpture and Painting*, 1827; John Summerson, *A New Description of Sir John Soane's Museum*, 1977).

WHITEHALL, CARRINGTON HOUSE, stables and minor alterations to house for 1st Lord

Carrington, 1816–18; dem. 1886 (*Survey of London* xvi, pls. 94–5).

GROSVENOR SQUARE, No. 13, alterations for 2nd Lord Berwick, 1816.

ST. ALBAN'S STREET, ST. JAMES'S, stabling for 1st Earl of St. Germans, 1816–18; dem. [*Survey of London* xxix, 208].

THREADNEEDLE STREET, No. 62, alterations to Bank for Grote, Prescott & Grote, 1818.

ST. JAMES'S SQUARE, No. 3, alterations and additions for 4th Earl of Hardwicke, 1818–19; dem. 1930 [*Survey of London* xxix, 85–6].

MONTAGUE PLACE, BLOOMSBURY, No. 16, alterations for Henry Hase, 1820.

REGENT STREET, Nos. 156–170 on E. side, houses and shops for J. Robins and others, 1820–1; dem. (Stroud, *Architecture*, pls. 183–4).

LINCOLN'S INN FIELDS, No. 14, for himself, 1823–4.

DOWNING STREET, Nos. 10–11, internal alterations, 1825–6 [*History of the King's Works* vi, 565–6] (Stroud, *Architecture*, pls. 217–20).

BELGRAVE PLACE, No. 30, ante-room to sculpture gallery for Sir Francis Chantrey, 1830–1; dem. [*Designs*; Bolton, *Works*, 120–22].

MISCELLANEOUS WORKS

BURY ST. EDMUNDS, SUFFOLK, No. 81 GUILDHALL STREET, enlarged for James Oakes, banker, 1789–90.

READING, BERKS., SIMONDS' BREWERY, new house and brewery buildings on east side of Bridge Street, 1789–91; dem. 1900 (Stroud, *Architecture*, pl. 52).

NORWICH, SURREY STREET, additions to house (now Norwich Union Fire Office) for John Patteson, 1790 (Stroud, *Architecture*, pls. 56–7).

WINCHESTER, HANTS., school (now drill-hall) for the Revd. Charles Richards, 1795 (Stroud, *Architecture*, pls. 105–6).

LONDON, No. 38 CHARLOTTE (now HALLAM) STREET, mausoleum for Sir Francis Bourgeois, 1807; dem.

MONUMENTS

KENSINGTON, ST. MARY ABBOTS CHURCHYARD, monument to Miss Elizabeth Johnston for the Earl of Bellamont, 1784 (*C. Life*, 8 Oct. 1953, 1135).

FELBRIDGE PLACE, SURREY, column in memory of his parents for James Evelyn, 1785–6, moved to Lemmington, Northumberland, 1928 [B.L., Add. MS. 38480, ff. 372–4].

LONDON, ST. STEPHEN'S CHURCH, COLEMAN STREET, monument to Claude Bosanquet, 1786; destroyed by bombing 1940.

COLNE PARK, COLNE ENGAINE, ESSEX, Ionic column in memory of Michael Robert Hills, for Philip Hills, 1790–1.

LEYTON CHURCHYARD, ESSEX, monument to Samuel Bosanquet, 1806; dem. 1957–8.

SOUTHWARK CATHEDRAL, tablet in S. choir aisle to Abraham Newland, 1808.

HAGLEY CHURCH, WORCS., monument to 1st Lord Lyttelton, 1808; mutilated 1858.

CHISWICK CHURCHYARD, MIDDLESEX, monument to P. J. de Loutherbourg, R.A., 1812.

CRICKET ST. THOMAS CHURCH, SOMERSET, monument to 1st Viscount Bridport, 1814 (Stroud, *Architecture*, pl. 173).

ST. GILES' BURIAL GROUND (now St. Pancras Gardens), monument to Mrs. Soane, 1816 (Stroud, *Architecture*, pl. 175; John Summerson in *Revue de l'Art*, No. 30, 1975, 51–4).

LAMBETH PARISH CHURCH, monument to Anna Storace, 1817; mutilated.

SOWERSBY, LEONARD (–1694), was employed by Sir Christopher Wren as a measurer of works at several of the London City Churches, and at the Sheldonian Theatre, Oxford, in 1669 [*Wren Soc.* xx, 212–3]. In 1675 it was 'according to a designe mencioned and expressed in a letter then lately written by Leonard Sowersby gentleman to . . . Lady Berkeley' that the master bricklayer John Fitch (*q.v.*) undertook to build a large addition to CRANFORD PARK, MIDDLESEX (dem. 1944) [P.R.O., C6/230/26]. Sowersby's will shows that he owned a considerable amount of property in the form of houses, wharves, and vaults in London and Westminster, including the Strand and King Street, Westminster, where he was living at the time of his death in May or June 1694 [P.R.O., PROB 11/418, f. 44].

SPEDDING, CARLISLE (1695–1755), principal colliery steward to Sir William Lowther of Whitehaven, was an able and inventive mining engineer. In 1752–3 he designed ST. JAMES'S CHURCH, WHITEHAVEN, CUMBERLAND, with an excellent galleried nave and apsidal chancel. This is his only certain architectural work [J. V. Beckett, 'Carlisle Spedding, Engineer, Inventor and Architect', *Trans. Cumberland & Westmorland Antiq. & Archl. Soc.* lxxxiii, 1983, 134–5].

SPEED, JOHN, a mason of Newburgh in Fife, designed the TOWN HOUSE there with its octagonal steeple in 1808 [Newburgh Town Council Minutes, *ex inf.* Mr. David Walker].

SPILLER, JAMES (–1829), was the son of John Spiller, a speculative builder of Christ

Church, Southwark, who built Highbury Place, Islington, in 1774–7. James became a pupil of James Wyatt, and was in his office in 1780, the year in which he exhibited his first drawing at the Royal Academy. He began practice soon afterwards and became surveyor to the Royal Exchange Assurance Company in about 1790. He resigned this post in 1799 and subsequently became Surveyor to the British Fire Office. He was a temperamental architect, who was rarely satisfied with his work and frequently disagreed with his clients. He corresponded for many years with Sir John Soane, who occasionally employed him to survey or supervise works in his care, and took over at least one commission – for Mells Park – which Spiller had abandoned. In 1807 he and Thomas Spencer were employed to survey the houses then in course of erection on the Foundling Hospital estate in London, and in their report strongly criticized both the architect, S. P. Cockerell, and the principal builder, James Burton. Despite this, Cockerell succeeded in regaining the confidence of the Governors, and the services of Messrs. Spiller and Spencer were dispensed with. They thereupon printed an *Address to the Governors and Guardians of the Foundling Hospital . . . intended as a Justification of their Reports and Proceedings* (1807), of which there is a copy in Sir John Soane's Museum, together with a second version dated 1808. Spiller was also the author of a pamphlet entitled *A Letter to John Soane, Esq. on the subject of the New Churches*, 1822, and of *A Second Letter* dated 1823, in which he complained of the inferior design of the churches erected under the Act of 1818. Spiller's own church of St. John, Hackney, is a striking neo-classical building which suggests that he was an architect of considerable originality, though of very limited performance. He died at his house in Guilford Street (No. 35) in April or May 1829, after a long illness. The MS. 'Observations' on the reorganization of the Office of Works in 1814–15 which he prepared on Soane's behalf are in the Soane Museum, together with some church designs related to St. John's, Hackney, and nearly a hundred of his letters. His brothers John (d. 1794) and Robert were both in business as masons and sculptors.

[*A.P.S.D.*; A. T. Bolton, *The Portrait of Sir John Soane*, 1927, *passim*; R. Gunnis, *Dictionary of British Sculptors*, 1968 (for John and Robert Spiller); information about John Spiller, senior, from Mr. Frank Kelsall.]

LONDON, THE LONDON HOSPITAL, WHITECHAPEL ROAD, additional buildings, 1781–3 [*A.P.S.D.*].

LONDON, THE GREAT SYNAGOGUE, DUKE'S PLACE, ALDGATE, 1788–90; destroyed 1941 [T. Pennant, *London*, 1793, 278].

LONDON, ST. JOHN'S CHURCH, HACKNEY, 1792–7; steeple and porches 1812–13; damaged by fire 1955 [exhib. at R.A. 1792; J. N. Brewer, *Beauties of England and Wales* x (iv), 265; W. Robinson, *History of Hackney* ii, 1843, 113] (Elizabeth & Wayland Young, *Old London Churches*, 1956, pls. 48A, 49).

ROEHAMPTON, SURREY, ELM GROVE for Benjamin Goldsmid, *c.*1797; bombed 1940, dem. 1957 [exhib. at R.A. 1801; sketch for decoration of one of the rooms in Soane Museum (F.14)].

LONDON, THE ROYAL INSTITUTION, Nos. 20–21 ALBEMARLE STREET, revised designs of Thomas Webster for the Lecture Theatre, Library and Repository, 1800–1; altered 1928–30 [exhib. at R.A. 1801; cf. drawings reproduced in *Architects' Jnl.* 23 Oct. 1941, 269–70].

WOODFORD, ESSEX, a 'design for a gentleman', exhibited at R.A. 1801.

TOLMERS, or TOLLIMORE, NEWGATE STREET, nr. HATFIELD, HERTS., for Robert Taylor, 1805–6 [exhib. at R.A. 1805; *A.P.S.D.*].

LONDON, WOODBRIDGE HOUSE, ST. JAMES'S WALK, CLERKENWELL, for William Cook, *c.*1808 ['Recollections of the Vice Chancellor Sir James Bacon (1798–1895)', ed. Lesley Lewis, 1983, typescript in London Library, 11–12].

MELLS PARK, SOMERSET, began additions for Thomas Horner, but gave up the commission after a disagreement with his client, who employed John Soane to complete the work to his own designs between 1810 and 1824 [A. T. Bolton, *Works of Sir John Soane*, 101].

SQUAIR, ALEXANDER, a builder-architect, supervised repairs to the offices at BRAHAN CASTLE, ROSS-SHIRE, for J. A. Stewart Mackenzie in 1819 [S.R.O., GD 46/1/433] and remodelled ARDGOUR HOUSE, ARGYLLSHIRE, for Alexander Maclean after a fire in 1825, adding wings [R.C.A.M., *Argyllshire* iii, 228]. As he dated a letter to Stewart Mackenzie from Teaninch, nr. Alness in Ross-shire, in 1819, he may also have been responsible for alterations to TEANINCH HOUSE.

SQUIRE, RICHARD (1700–1786), was a mason and monumental sculptor of Worcester, of which city he became a freeman in 1733. On his ledger-stone in All Saints Church he is described as 'one of the Master-Builders of this Church; which, with many Memorial-works here, and throughout this

County will be lasting Monuments of his Skill and Abilities'. ALL SAINTS CHURCH was built between 1738 and 1742. Squire's name and that of his brother-in-law William Davis, the master carpenter, were inscribed on the tower, but are now no longer legible. In 1737 Squire gave evidence before the House of Commons about the condition of the old church [*Commons' Jnls.* xxiii, 48], and it is likely that he designed as well as built the new one [D. Whitehead, 'The Georgian Churches of Worcester', *Trans. Worcs. Archl. Soc.*, 3rd ser. 13, 1992, 218–20]. At UPTON-ON-SEVERN CHURCH in 1755–7 Squire acted as a building surveyor, inspecting the workmanship of John Willoughby in rebuilding it, besides himself supplying the marble altar-table and font [MS. 'Parish Book']. Many monuments bearing his signature are to be seen in Worcestershire churches.

SQUIRHILL, CHARLES, practised as an architect and surveyor in Northampton in the 1820s and 1830s. He had previously been in the office of Francis Goodwin [Thomas Rickman's Diary, 15 May 1821]. His works included rebuilding ABINGTON CHURCH, NORTHANTS., in 1824–6 [churchwardens' accounts]; rebuilding the spire of RAUNDS CHURCH, NORTHANTS., in 1826 after it had been struck by lightning [minute-book among parish records]; reconstructing the interior of DENTON CHURCH, NORTHANTS., in 1828 [I.C.B.S.]; and designing a new gallery in ALL SAINTS CHURCH, NORTHAMPTON, in the same year [parish records, no. 166]. His work at Abington and Denton reveals him as a purveyor of the feeblest sort of early nineteenth-century Gothic. Daniel Goodman Squirhill (1809–63), who practised at Leamington in the 1840s, may have been his son.

STAFF, JOHN (*c.*1751–1833), practised in Croydon, where he died in December 1833, aged 82, and was buried in the parish churchyard. He is stated in James Edwards' *Companion from London to Brighthelmston*, 1801, part 2, 48, to have designed JUNIPER HILL, MICKLEHAM, SURREY, for Mr. Jenkinson in about 1780. In 1789–90 BETCHWORTH CHURCH, SURREY, was repaired and repewed under his direction [MS. Vestry Minutes]. The minutes of the Croydon Waste Lands Trustees show that the COURT HOUSE at CROYDON, built in 1807–9 and dem. 1894, was designed by Staff after plans by S. P. Cockerell had been rejected.[1] Towards the end of his life Staff evidently took Henry Prosser (*q.v.*) into partnership, for they appear as 'Staff & Prosser, Surveyors and Architects', in Pigot's *Directory* of 1827–8, and in 1825 they were jointly responsible for the enlargement of SUTTON CHURCH, SURREY (rebuilt 1862–4) [I.C.B.S.].

STANDBRIDGE, JOHN, described in the Warwick Castle records in 1777 as 'an architect of skill in this place', later moved to Birmingham, where he is listed as 'surveyor' in Holden's directory of 1805–7. Between 1765 and 1771 he carried out internal alterations to CHARLECOTE HOUSE, WARWICKS. for George Lucy [Warwicks. C.R.O., Lucy of Charlecote papers, L6/1476 at end], and in 1768 he designed a wooden bridge in the park [*ibid.*, L6/1110]. His design for a stone bridge at Alscot Park, Warwicks., is among the West papers there. In 1776–7 he made an unexecuted design for rebuilding the chancel of St. Nicholas Church, Warwick [MS. Churchwardens' accounts], and in 1781 ELMDON CHURCH, WARWICKS. was rebuilt to his designs in a simple Gothic style [signed plan and elevation in Lichfield Joint Record Office]. After the destruction of MOSELEY HALL, WORCS., in the Birmingham Riots of 1791 John Taylor employed Standbridge to design a new house built 1792–6 in a classical style reminiscent of the Wyatts [drawings in Birmingham Reference Library Archives, 634730] (Neale's *Views of Seats*, 1st ser. ii, 1819). In 1804 Standbridge was among those who submitted designs for Christ Church, Birmingham [minute-book in Birmingham Reference Library Archives, 660234].

STANDEN, THOMAS, of Lancaster, designed the COUNTY LUNATIC ASYLUM (now known as the Moor Hospital) at LANCASTER, built 1812–16. Though he is described as 'architect' no other work by him has been noted [T. Baines, *History and Gazeteer of Lancashire* ii, 1825, 17; Lancashire County Records, Q.A.M.1/1].

STANLEY, EDMUND, of Chesterfield, was employed by William Turbutt to design a new front to OGSTON HALL, DERBYSHIRE, in 1768–9, modifying a proposal by Joseph Pickford of Derby [drawings, letters, etc., in Derbyshire C.R.O.]. In 1768 he submitted designs for the County Hall at Nottingham that were not carried out [*Nottinghamshire County Records of the Eighteenth Century*, ed. K. T. Meaby, 1947, 49].

[1] This accounts for the erroneous attribution to S. P. Cockerell in Brayley's *History of Surrey* iv, 22, and other topographical works. For extracts from the MS. minute-book of the Trustees I am indebted to Mr. K. Ryde of the Central Library, Croydon.

STANLEY, IGNATIUS (–1771), of Holbeck Woodhouse in Nottinghamshire, was the son of John Stanley (*q.v.*) and, like him, a carpenter by trade. He was employed by the 2nd Duke of Portland at WELBECK ABBEY, NOTTS., from 1757 to 1761. Payments to him 'for joiner's work and for drawing plans and overseeing all the building work' are recorded in the accounts, now in Nottingham University Library. A list of plans at Welbeck drawn up in 1764 [PwF 10.052] includes designs by Stanley for a bridge and a pavilion in the garden. Stanley's will was proved at Nottingham on 11 May 1771 [*ex inf.* Mr. Edward Saunders].

STANLEY, JOHN (–1728), of Holbeck Woodhouse, nr. Worksop, Notts., was described as 'Mr. Stanley the Surveyor & Carpenter' in 1710, when he was paid £2 3s. 0d. 'for drawing 2 or 3 designs at severall times' for a 'new intended house' for the Duke of Norfolk at Sheffield. At the same time he was employed to view defects in the chancel of Sheffield Parish Church [R. E. Leader's notes in Sheffield Archives, 141, p. 37]. In the same year he was employed by the Nottinghamshire magistrates to consider a draught for a new County Hall made by a Mr. Twell and to make 'two new Draughts in Plans and Perspective for the new County Hall' (which was not proceeded with) [*Nottinghamshire County Records of the Eighteenth Century*, ed. K. T. Meaby, 1947, 46]. His will was proved at Nottingham on 28 August 1728 [*ex inf.* Mr. Edward Saunders].

STANNARD, JOSEPH, senior (1771–1855), was the son of Joseph Stannard (1748–1831), a carpenter and joiner of Norwich, and the father of Joseph Stannard, junior (1795–1850). He and his son practised as architects and builders in Norwich during the first half of the nineteenth century. Their business in the latter capacity was evidently on a considerable scale, for in 1824 they contracted to build the new court at King's College, Cambridge, to the designs of William Wilkins for £73,000 [Willis & Clark i, 565]. In 1807 the firm had been employed to carry out J.A. Repton's alterations to Barningham Hall, Norfolk [contract at Barningham], and from 1827 onwards they and G. S. Repton were both concerned in alterations to Wolterton Hall, Norfolk, where they (rather than P. Hardwick) may have designed the tower added to Repton's east wing *c.*1849 [Walpole archive at Wolterton, *ex inf.* Mr. David Cubitt].

Drawings at HEYDON HALL, NORFOLK, show that in the 1830s the Stannards were employed by William Earle Lytton Bulwer to make alterations and additions to that house in the Jacobean style, including the staircase and the ceiling of the adjoining Drawing Room (*C. Life*, 29 July, 5 Aug. 1982). In 1835–6 the younger Stannard was responsible for replacing the brick south wall of NORWICH GUILDHALL by flint and stone more in keeping with the rest of the building [*Norfolk Chronicle*, 20 Feb. 1836]. His principal architectural works in the city appear to have been the ROYAL HOTEL in the Market Place, *c.*1840, of which part of the façade only remains as the entrance to the Royal Arcade [G. K. Blyth, *Directory & Guide to Norwich*, 1843, 192], and the NEW SAVINGS BANK in HAYMARKET, 1843–4, dem. 1899 [*Norfolk Chronicle*, 29 June 1844]. Both were classical in style.

Other buildings designed by the Stannards included STRUMPSHAW HALL, NORFOLK, for Thomas Gilbert Tuck, 1837 [report of lawsuit, Tuck *v.* Norwich & Yarmouth Railway Co. in *Norwich Mercury*, 20 May 1843]; LAVENHAM RECTORY, SUFFOLK, alterations and additions, 1826–30 [W. Suffolk C.R.O., 806/2/14]; HARDINGHAM RECTORY, NORFOLK, 1833 [Norfolk C.R.O., DN/DPL 1/2, 29]; and SUTTON VICARAGE, CAMBS., 1840 [C.U.L., EDR G 3/39/11]. They restored and reseated the churches of ST. PAUL and ST. JAMES, NORWICH, 1841–2 [I.C.B.S.]., and repaired the church of REEPHAM ST. MARY, NORFOLK, in *c.*1845, giving it a new E. window based on one in the Slipper Chapel at Houghton St. Giles [C. Thomas, *Sketches for an Ecclesiology of the Deaneries of Sparham, Taverham and Ingworth*, 2nd ed. Norwich 1846].

Father and son were both commemorated by a monument in the churchyard of St. George, Colegate, Norwich. Their practice was continued by the elder Stannard's youngest son Richard Stannard (1815–1881). [Information from Mr. David Cubitt.]

STANTON was the name of a family prominent as masons and sculptors throughout the greater part of the seventeenth century. Though chiefly famous for their monumental sculpture, they also took important masonry contracts. Their yard was in Holborn, close to St. Andrew's Church, in whose graveyard the family tomb once stood.[1] The earliest recorded member of the family was THOMAS STANTON (1610–74), who was made free of the Masons' Company in February 1630/1.

[1] In 1735 William Stanton was stated to have his 'house and shop' in Shoe Lane, which joins Holborn close to St. Andrew's Church. Stonecutter Street on the east side of Shoe Lane may perhaps mark the exact site of the Stantons' yard.

He served as Warden in 1658 and as Master in 1660. He is known to have been established in Holborn by 1635. His son Thomas having predeceased him, he was succeeded in his business by his nephew, WILLIAM STANTON (1639–1705), who, as his apprentice, had been made free of the Masons' Company in 1663. William was Warden in 1681 and 1684 and Master in 1688 and 1689. He erected numerous monuments, many of which are recorded by Le Neve in his *Monumenta Anglicana* (1717–19), from information supplied by his son Edward. In 1684 he was associated with Edward Pierce in the mason's contract for rebuilding ST. ANDREW'S, HOLBORN, to the designs of Wren [*Wren Soc.* x, 95–8]. In 1685 he contracted to build BELTON HOUSE, nr. GRANTHAM, LINCS., receiving over £5000 for his work [P.R.O., C8/527/2 and building accounts in Lincs. C.R.O.]. The house was completed in 1688. It is not known who supplied the design, which is based on Pratt's Clarendon House, but it may well have been William Winde (*q.v.*). In 1688 Stanton began to build another large country house for Sir Roger Hill at DENHAM PLACE, BUCKS. It was completed in 1701 and bears an obvious resemblance to Belton. The identity of the designer is again unknown, but in this case it is possible that it was Stanton himself [John Harris, 'The Building of Denham Place', *Records of Bucks.* xvi, 1957–8] (Hill & Cornforth, *op. cit.*, 203–10). In 1704–5 Stanton and his son Edward were working at CULVERTHORPE HALL, LINCS., then being remodelled for Sir John Newton, Bart., and were presumably responsible for the existing garden front [Newton's banking accounts at Welford Park, Berks.] (*C. Life*, 15, 22 Sept. 1923).

William Stanton died on 30 May 1705, leaving two sons, Thomas and Edward. The elder brother went abroad, leaving EDWARD STANTON (*c.*1681–1734) to carry on the family business. He had been apprenticed to his father in 1694, and was made free of the Masons' Company in June 1702. He was a Warden in 1713 and 1716 and Master in 1719. It was probably in the latter year that he became Master Mason to Westminster Abbey, a post which brought him work in connection with the repairs to the Abbey and the building of the new Dormitory of Westminster School in 1722–6. He was for many years in partnership with Christopher Horsenaile, whose signature is found with Edward's on many monuments after 1718, and to whom, as 'my honest and industrious copartner', he left £40 in his will. He was a Captain in the Train Bands, and it is as 'Captain Edward Stanton' that he usually figures in contemporary documents. The list of works which he supplied to Le Neve shows that during the ten years after his father's death over 140 monuments were made in his yard in Holborn, and he ranks as one of the greatest of the eighteenth-century sculptor-masons. He died in 1734, leaving two sons, William and Edward. His will shows that he had a well-furnished house at Highgate, and the library of 'that ingenious Architect Capt. Edward Stanton' was sold with two others as 'Bibliotheca Splendidissima' on 17 November 1735. His elder son William was appointed Master Mason to the Mint and the Navy shortly before 1727, when he entered into a limited

THE STANTON FAMILY

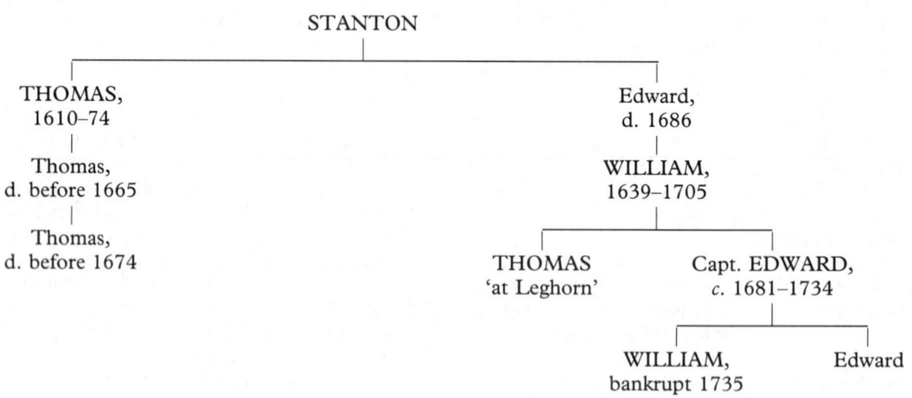

partnership with John Churchill, Master Mason to the Board of Ordnance [B.L., Stowe MS. 412, no. 75]. He continued 'to get his living by buying selling and working of severall sorts of Marble Stone Free Stones and divers other work of Stones . . . as is usual for Persons of that Employ to do' until 1735, when, falling into debt, he absconded and was declared bankrupt [Stowe MS. 412, no. 80]. His property was sold by auction at Hodgson's Coffee-House in Chancery Lane on 18 May 1736 (*ibid.*, no. 37). [K. A. Esdaile, 'The Stantons of Holborn', *Archaeological Jnl.* lxxxv, 1929; K. A. Esdaile, 'Some Annotations on John Le Neve's *Monumenta Anglicana*', *Antiquaries' Jnl.* xxii, 1942; D. Knoop & G. P. Jones, *The London Mason in the Seventeenth Century*, 1935, 21; R. Gunnis, *Dictionary of British Sculptors*, 1968.]

STANTON, CHARLEY, of St. Olave's, Southwark, was a carpenter by trade, and was Master of the London Carpenters' Company in 1693. In about 1670 he made designs for houses to be built by the Tallow Chandlers' Company on Dowgate Hill [*Builder*, 10 Aug. 1917], and in 1674 he was paid 10s. by the Corporation of Trinity House 'for a draft of three houses to be built at Southwark'. In 1680 the same Corporation paid him £704 for building eighteen almshouses forming part of TRINITY HOSPITAL, DEPTFORD (dem. 1877), and a further £42 for timber and workmanship in connection with their lighthouse at Scilly [archives of Trinity House Corporation]. He also built, and perhaps designed, two churches: ST. MARY MAGDALENE, BERMONDSEY, 1676–9, and ST. NICHOLAS, DEPTFORD, 1697–8, gutted 1940/1 [B. F. L. Clarke, *Parish Churches of London*, 1966, 199, 218]. Both are artisan's versions of a cross-in-rectangle plan.

STAPLES, SAMUEL (–1860), exhibited at the Royal Academy from 1 Staple Inn, Holborn, between 1824 and 1837. In the latter year he submitted what the *Reading Mercury* described as 'a commonplace design' in the competition for the Royal Berks. Infirmary. He designed a Gothic chapel at SHENLEY, HERTS., illustrated in *The Surveyor, Engineer and Architect*, 1841, 172, and the NATIONAL SCHOOLS, ST. THOMAS'S DISTRICT, STEPNEY, 1841–2 [*ibid.*, 305]. He was President of the Surveyors' Club in 1842, and died in October 1860.

STARK, WILLIAM (1770–1813), was the son of Mark Stark, a manufacturer of Dunfermline, where he was born on 25 May 1770. An elder sister married in 1787 the Glasgow architect John Craig [*q.v.*], and it may have been in his brother-in-law's office that William received his professional training. In 1798 he was in St. Petersburg, apparently in connection with an abortive architectural commission. He practised at first in Glasgow, but shortly before his death moved to Edinburgh for the sake of his health. He was only 43 when, on 9 October 1813, he died at Drumsheugh on the western outskirts of Edinburgh. His wife Catherine was a daughter of George Thomson, the musical scholar, and by her he had a daughter of the same name.

Contemporaries were agreed that Stark was an architect of unusual ability. In 1811 Sir Walter Scott wrote of him as 'a young man of exquisite taste who must rise very high in his profession if the bad health under which he suffers does not keep him down or cut him short', and when he heard of Stark's death he lamented that with him 'more genius has died than is left behind among the collected universality of Scottish architects'. The *Scots Magazine* said that 'his reputation, deservedly high in Scotland, was spreading rapidly in England at the time of his death'. Lord Cockburn thought him 'the best modern architect that Scotland has produced'. Stark was undoubtedly a very able and versatile architect, whose short list of works contains several buildings of distinction. His Glasgow Court House of 1810 disputes with Smirke's Covent Garden Theatre the distinction of being the first public building in Britain to be ornamented with a Greek Doric portico.[1] For St. George's Church he took a Wren steeple and transformed it into an original and effective neo-baroque composition perfectly adapted to its situation at a focal point in the city. In Edinburgh his Advocates' (now Upper Signet) Library triumphantly overcame the difficulty of making architectural sense of a long narrow room. At Glasgow his Lunatic Asylum was a pioneer attempt to achieve that segregation by sex, social background and mental condition which was considered desirable by contemporary medical opinion (see his *Remarks on the Construction of Public Hospitals for the Cure of Mental Derangement*, Glasgow 1810). Even his two rural churches represent a serious if slightly crude attempt to recapture the sturdy quality of medieval

[1] See A. Gomme & D. Walker, *Architecture of Glasgow*, 1987, 70. But it appears from the Glasgow Burgh Records that the Court House was not designed until 1809, whereas Smirke's theatre was designed in 1808 and completed in 1810. Another contender is John Sanders's Royal Military Academy at Sandhurst, built 1808–12 to designs made earlier by James Wyatt.

masonry so lacking in the stereotyped Gothic boxes of the early nineteenth century.

Stark also made his mark as a town-planner. His posthumously printed *Report to the Lord Provost, Magistrates and Council of Edinburgh on the Plans for Laying out the Grounds for Buildings between Edinburgh and Leith* (1814: also published in *Scots Mag.* lxxvii, 1815, 576–82) is a remarkably enlightened appreciation of the potentialities of the Edinburgh townscape, and his principles (variety in layout rather than a rigid grid of streets, careful attention to contours, the attraction of oblique views, the picturesque value of trees, etc.) were largely embodied in the plan ultimately carried out by his pupil W. H. Playfair (*q.v.*).

[S.R.O., Dunfermline Register; S.R.O., CC8/8/142, f. 315, testament of William Stark; sale catalogue of his library (1815) in N.L.S., KP 14 e.l (11); E. Henderson, *Annals of Dunfermline*, 1879, 569; *A.P.S.D.*; *Scots Mag.* 1813, 879; *The Letters of Sir Walter Scott*, ed. Grierson, *1811–14*, 34, 65, 368; Henry Cockburn, *Memorials of his Time*, 1910, 278–9; T. Harold Hughes, 'Edinburgh: An Early Nineteenth Century Town Planning Scheme', *Town Planning Review* xiii, 1928, 69–71; A. J. Youngson, *The Making of Classical* Edinburgh, 1966, 149–52; Andor Gomme & David Walker, *Architecture of Glasgow*, 1987, 69–71, 300; memoir by R. Gordon Stark in N.L.S., MS. 1758; *D.N.B. Missing Persons*, 1993.]

GLASGOW CATHEDRAL, alterations to E. end of chancel, 1802–3; since removed [J. Durkan, *The Precinct of Glasgow Cathedral*, Glasgow 1986, 7]; refitted the Inner High Church, 1805; Stark's fittings removed *c.*1890 [*The Picture of Glasgow*, 1813, 84–5].

GLASGOW, THE HUNTERIAN MUSEUM, 1804–5; dem. 1870 [*The Picture of Glasgow*, 1813, 101–3; signed drawings in S.R.O., RHP 1997].

GLASGOW, ST. GEORGE'S CHURCH, BUCHANAN STREET, 1807–8 [*The Picture of Glasgow*, 1813, 90–1].

BROOMHALL, FIFE, designed friezes, etc. in State Rooms for 7th Earl of Elgin, 1808, and made unexecuted designs for Greek Revival portico, etc. [drawings at Broomhall].

SALINE CHURCH, FIFE, 1809–10 [S.R.O., HR 411/2, p. 63].

GLASGOW, COURT HOUSE, GAOL and PUBLIC OFFICES, SALTMARKET, 1810–11; remodelled 1845 and 1859 and rebuilt 1910–13, retaining portico [*Extracts from the Records of the Burgh of Glasgow*, ed. Marwick, x, 43; *The Picture of Glasgow*, 1813, 139–47] (A. Gomme & D. Walker, *Architecture of Glasgow*, 1987, fig. 46).

GLASGOW, THE LUNATIC ASYLUM (later used as workhouse), 1810–11; dem. 1908 [*The Picture of Glasgow*, 1813, 135–6].

DUNFERMLINE ABBEY CHURCH, FIFE, rebuilt south-west tower after collapse (1807), 1810–11 [E. Henderson, *Annals of Dunfermline*, 1879, 569].

DUNDEE, THE LUNATIC ASYLUM, 1812–20; altered and enlarged by W. Burn 1830 and 1839 [James Thomson, *History of Dundee*, 1847, 190; *Dundee Delineated*, 1822, 117, with plan].

MUIRKIRK, AYRSHIRE, THE OLD CHURCH, 1812–13, Gothic [S.R.O., HR 287/3, pp. 12, 20, 22, 26; RHP 7651 (plan dated 1810)].

BOWHILL, SELKIRKSHIRE, centre block of S. front for 4th Duke of Buccleuch, 1812–14, continued by W. Atkinson (*q.v.*) [letter dated 21 April 1812 and drawing in S.R.O., GD 224/Box 29] (R.C.A.M., *Selkirkshire*, 65–6; *C. Life*, 5 June 1975, fig. 3).

EDINBURGH, interior of THE SIGNET LIBRARY (now Lower Signet Library), PARLIAMENT SQUARE, for the Society of Writers to the Signet, 1812–15 [Iain G. Brown, *Building for Books: The Architectural Evolution of the Advocates' Library*, Aberdeen 1989, chap. 6].

EDINBURGH, interior of THE ADVOCATES' LIBRARY, (now Upper Signet Library), for the Faculty of Advocates, 1812–16 [Iain G. Brown, *op. cit.*].

GLOUCESTER, THE LUNATIC ASYLUM, built 1813–23 by J. Collingwood, the County Surveyor, was based on a plan provided by Stark [Ann Bailey, 'The Founding of the Gloucestershire County Asylum', *Trans. Bristol and Glos. Arch. Soc., etc.*, 1971, 184].

GREENOCK, RENFREWSHIRE, MIDDLE CHURCH, monument to Lt.-Col. Henry Crawfurd (d. 1813) [G. Williamson, *Old Greenock*, 1886, 311].

For unexecuted designs for a school at Greenock (1805 and 1808) with a Greek Doric façade, see Strathclyde Regional Archives, T-ARD/1/5/5 and G. Williamson, *Old Greenock*, 2nd ser., 1888, 250. In a letter of 24 Oct. 1813 (N.L.S., MS. 578, f. 163), Lord Elgin mentions Stark's 'beautiful designs for an Observatory on Calton Hill' in Edinburgh, which may have influenced W. H. Playfair's executed design of 1818.

STARLING, RICHARD (1632–1723), was the son and apprentice of Richard Starling, a carpenter of Norwich, where he lived all his life. According to the inscription beneath a wash portrait of him, inserted into a copy of *The True Effigies of the most eminent Painters and other Famous Artists* (1694), formerly in the library at Melton Constable, Norfolk, Starling was 'not only the famousest carpenter in Norwich but a good Mathemat[ic]ion, a good Archytect, Surveyer and well skiild in Arethmetick' [information from Mr. Hugh Pagan]. No evidence of Starling's activity as an architect has so far been noted. He died on 1 November 1723, aged 92, and is commemorated by a monument in St. Peter Mancroft Church, Norwich.

STARTIN, WILLIAM, practised in Leamington, where his wife kept a boarding-house. In 1832 he designed BEECH LAWN, LEAMINGTON, a house and consulting rooms (dem. 1946) for Dr. Henry Jephson, of which a medal was struck in 1856 [J. Taylor, *The Architectural Medal*, 1987, 98; information from Mr. R. Lyndon Cave].

STAVELEY, CHRISTOPHER (1726–1801), was a member of a Leicestershire family which produced four generations of monumental masons and surveyors. He was the son of Stephen Staveley (1705–75) of Melton Mowbray, and was the father of Christopher Staveley (1759–1827) and perhaps also of Edward Staveley (*q.v.*). Good examples of his work as a mason and carver can be seen in Grantham Church and churchyard. A tomb in Melton churchyard records his death on 31 January 1801, in his 75th year. In the *Monthly Magazine* for that year he was described as an 'eminent architect', and according to Throsby's *Select Views in Leicestershire* i, 1790, 153, he was the 'architect' of STAPLEFORD CHURCH, LEICS., built in 1783 by the 4th Earl of Harborough. But as the design was exhibited at the R.A. by George Richardson (*q.v.*), Staveley was probably only the builder. He had, however, supervised repairs and alterations to STAPLEFORD HALL for the trustees of the 3rd Lord Harborough in 1768–9 [Bray archives, Leicester C.R.O.]. [J. D. Bennett, *Leicestershire Architects 1700–1850*, Leicester Museums 1968.]

STAVELEY, CHRISTOPHER (1759–1827), the eldest son of the above, practised as an architect, surveyor and engineer, first at Melton Mowbray, then at Loughborough, and ultimately (from 1819) at Leicester. He was surveyor to several canal companies and also acted as a land agent. As an architect he is recorded to have repaired the tower and spire of ST. MARY'S CHURCH, STAMFORD, in 1787 [Vestry Minutes, churchwardens' accounts, and framed drawings in Vestry]; designed LEADENHAM HOUSE, LINCS., for William Reeve, in 1790–6 [Arthur Oswald in *C. Life*, 17, 24 June 1965]; repaired LOUGHBOROUGH RECTORY, LEICS., in 1799–1800 (dem. 1962) [Lincs. Record Office, MGA 23]; altered THURCASTON RECTORY, LEICS., in 1803 [*ibid.*, MGA 40]; rebuilt SUTTON BONINGTON RECTORY, NOTTS., in 1811 [Borthwick Institute, York, MGA 1811/1]; and altered the interior of LOUGHBOROUGH CHURCH, LEICS., in 1815 [Faculty, etc., in Leics. Record Office]. After his death in 1827 his practice was at first carried on by his elder son Edward (1795–1872). But in 1833 the latter absconded with nearly £1700 of the funds of the Leicester Navigation Company. His brother Christopher, who was involved in the scandal, appears to have committed suicide, but Edward made good his escape to North America, where he worked as a canal and railway engineer, first in Baltimore, and later in Canada. He died in Quebec in 1872. [F. Burgess, *English Churchyard Memorials*, 1963, 269–70; J. D. Bennett, *Leicestershire Architects 1700–1850*, Leicester Museums 1968.]

STAVELEY, EDWARD (–1837), was a member of the Staveley family of Melton Mowbray. In 1796 he was appointed Surveyor to the Corporation of Nottingham at a salary of £20 [*Records of the Borough of Nottingham* vii, 1947, 336]. He remodelled the NEW EXCHANGE in that city in 1814–15 (dem. 1920) [J. Blackner, *History of Nottingham*, 1815, 410] and designed the GEORGE STREET BAPTIST CHAPEL, 1815 [W. H. Wylie, *Old and New Nottingham*, 1853, 122], and the PLUMPTRE HOSPITAL (almshouses), 1823 [J. F. Sutton, *The Date-Book of Events connected with Nottingham*, 1852, 378]. He died in 1837 [Sutton, *op. cit.*, 454].

STEAD, JOHN, practised in Wakefield in the 1820s. In 1823 he advertised for tenders for the PRIMITIVE METHODIST CHAPEL, and in 1827 he designed the WESLEYAN METHODIST CHAPEL at WESTGATE END. In 1823 he also advertised for tenders for a large house to be built seven miles from Wakefield. In 1827 he was surveyor to the abortive Wakefield and Ferrybridge Canal. In December of that year he went bankrupt, and by 1830 he had left Wakefield for good [information from Mr. J. Goodchild of Wakefield Library]. In 1830 he exhibited at the Liverpool Academy an elevation of a Gothic church 'intended for Askrigg, Yorkshire'. He may have been the John Stead who was appointed surveyor to the Brighton Commissioners in 1837 [*Builder* v, 1847, 161].

STEAD, SAMUEL (1804–1861), of Ludlow, was a member of a family of masons who were active as statuaries and builders in Shropshire in the early nineteenth century. He signs tablets in local churches and designed THE ASSEMBLY ROOMS, LUDLOW, 1840 [R. Morriss & K. Hoverd, *The Buildings of Ludlow,* 1993, 61–2]. He died on 20 January 1861 [Principal Probate Registry, Calendar of Probates, 1866]. In 1827 Matthew Stead of Ludlow designed offices and stables to be added to STOKE ST. MILBOROUGH VICARAGE, SALOP., and made plans for landscaping the garden [Herefs. C.R.O., Diocesan Records, Clergy & Benefice Papers, Box 31]. In 1832 the W. tower added to LLANSILIN CHURCH, DENBIGHSHIRE, was designed by 'Mr. Stead, architect of Llanymynech' [*British Mag.* i, 1832, 308].

STEAD, THOMAS, (*c.*1775–1850), was probably starting practice when he exhibited architectural designs at the Royal Academy in 1797 and 1801. He subsequently had an office in Bloomsbury, where he acted as surveyor to the Bedford estate. He died at Hampstead on 8 August 1850, aged 75 [*Gent's Mag.* 1850 (ii), 340]. His only recorded architectural work appears to be the BEDFORD ESTATE OFFICE in MONTAGUE STREET, built in 1841–3 [Bedford Estate records, *ex inf.* Mrs. M. P. G. Draper].

STEDMAN, JAMES, made designs for, and superintended the execution of, extensive alterations to POLESDEN LACEY HOUSE, GREAT BOOKHAM, SURREY, for Thomas Moore between 1735 and 1748, as shown by the accounts in the Bodleian Library, MS. North *c.*62, f. 28. The house is illustrated in J. P. Neale, *Views of Seats*, 2nd ser. i, 1824, and *C. Life*, 5–12 March 1948, 12–19 Feb. 1981. Stedman was one of the bridge-surveyors for the County of Surrey in the 1740s [Surrey County Records, QS 5/7, 7–9, 59, 61, 67, etc.].

STEEL, THOMAS, of Chichester, a carpenter, appears to have been the architect of SHILLINGLEE PARK, SUSSEX, for Edward Turnour. On 18 October 1734, he agreed 'to survey or carry on a Building or Dwelling house at Shillingly Park According to a Draught signed by the above mencioned partys', for a fee of £100. The house, gutted by fire *c.*1943, bears the date 1735 [Arthur Oswald in *C. Life*, 8 Aug. 1936]. The names of several boys apprenticed to Steel between 1711 and 1742 are given in *Sussex Apprentices and Masters*, Sussex Rec. Soc., xxviii.

STEER, JAMES (–1759), was by trade a carpenter and joiner. He was made free of the London Carpenters' Company in 1729 after a five years' apprenticeship, and subsequently rose to be a Warden of the Company in 1758. But for his death in the following year he would probably have been elected Master. In 1736 he was appointed Town Surveyor by the Hand in Hand Fire Office, and in the same year he became Surveyor to St. Thomas's Hospital. He died on 28 January 1759. Though chiefly employed in surveying property for his two principal employers, Steer occasionally acted as an architect, designing in 1738 the WELSH CHARITY SCHOOL (now the Marx Memorial Library), 37–8 CLERKENWELL GREEN, and in 1738–9 the east wing of GUY'S HOSPITAL (destroyed by bombing in the 1940s). The latter was a building of conventional 'Palladian' character (*Survey of London* xxii, pls. 32, 34). Steer was an officer of the city's Train Bands, and evidently a staunch Protestant, for in 1746 he published an engraved design for an obelisk to be erected in Smithfield, in order to 'Perpetuate the Memory of the Cruel Triumph of Popery, and to instruct Protestants what may again be expected, If the British Crown should ever be plac'd on a Popish Head' (Bodleian Library, Gough Maps 19, f. 41^{v}).

[Andrew Rothstein, 'Mr. Steere the Surveyor', *Builder*, 27 March 1964; *London Magazine*, 1759, 107.]

STEERS, THOMAS (*c.*1670–1750), engineer and architect, was a pioneer of dock construction whose works at Liverpool laid the foundation of the town's greatness as a seaport. The place and date of his birth are unknown, but as a young man he held a Commission in the 4th Regiment of Foot, which was partially disbanded in 1697 after three years' service in the Netherlands. Thereafter Steers is found living at Rotherhithe at the time when the Howland Great Dock – the first of its kind in England – was under construction. There can be little doubt that Steers was in some way concerned in this work, but in what capacity is at present unknown. In 1710 he went to Liverpool in order to supervise the construction of a wet dock similar to that at Rotherhithe, and for the remainder of his life he played a leading part in the affairs and development of the town. The dock was constructed on land reclaimed from the sea, and was surrounded by new streets laid out by Steers. In 1717 he was appointed Dock Master, and from 1724 combined the offices of Dock Master and Water Bailiff of Liverpool. In 1717–18 he constructed a Dry Dock (now the Canning

Dock) adjoining the Old Dock, and he also planned the South (now Salthouse) Dock, which was completed in 1753 after his death. Apart from these and other engineering works, which took him to Ireland in 1736–41 to advise the Newry Navigation Commission, Steers established a lucrative anchor-smithy in Liverpool, and engaged in a good deal of speculative building in that town. In 1740 he built the OLD ROPERY THEATRE as a personal speculation, and the house in PARADISE STREET in which he lived was one of a pair which he had erected on the reclaimed land in the Pool. He designed a large house in HANOVER STREET (damaged by fire 1867 and destroyed by bombing 1941) for Thomas Seel in 1740, but his principal architectural work was ST. GEORGE'S CHURCH, LIVERPOOL, which was erected to his designs between 1726 and 1734. Externally it was liberally decorated with engaged Doric columns, and had a classical tower and spire. Unfortunately, the tower was built on the edge of the filled-in Castle Ditch, and subsidences led to the removal of the spire in 1809, and to the subsequent reconstruction of the whole church by John Foster between 1819 and 1825. It was finally demolished in 1897. Its architect was elected Mayor of Liverpool in 1739, and was buried there on 2 November 1750.

[H. Peet, 'Thomas Steers, A Memoir', *Trans. Historic Soc. of Lancs. and Cheshire* lxxxii, 1930; J. A. Picton, *Municipal Records of Liverpool* ii, 1886, 70–1, 398; S. A. Harris, 'Paradise Street, Liverpool: the Derivation of the Name,' *Trans. Historic Soc. of Lancs. and Cheshire* civ, 1952, 143–4; *D.N.B. Missing Persons*, 1993, 632–3.]

STEGGLES, WILLIAM (*c*.1777–1859), was the son of William Steggles (*c*.1752–1834), a bricklayer of Bury St. Edmunds, Suffolk, where he and his father were responsible for a good deal of building in the early nineteenth century, including the BARNABY ALMSHOUSES in COLLEGE STREET, 1826, and the BAPTIST CHAPEL in GARLAND STREET, 1834, both of which they probably designed. The younger Steggles, who was County Surveyor for West Suffolk, designed, *inter alia*, GREAT THURLOW VICARAGE, SUFFOLK, 1837 [C. Brown *et al.*, *Dictionary of Architects of Suffolk Buildings 1800–1914*, 1991, 185; M. Statham, *Yesterday's Town, Bury St. Edmunds*, 1992, 99–101, and further information from Mrs. Statham].

STEPHEN, JOHN (*c*.1807–1850), practised in Glasgow, where in the 1830s he was a partner in the firm of 'Scott, Stephen and Gale'. He died in November 1850, aged 43, and is buried in the Necropolis [Necropolis records, *ex inf.* Prof. J. Stevens Curl]. Stephen's works in Glasgow included the gateway and chapel of the SIGHTHILL CEMETERY, 1839 [*A.P.S.D.*, *s.v.* 'Glasgow']; ST. JUDE'S EPISCOPAL CHURCH (now St. Jude's House), WEST GEORGE STREET, 1840, Greek Revival [J. Pagan, *Sketch of the History of Glasgow*, 1847, 181]; a large tea warehouse (mostly dem.) in YORK STREET, 1843 [J. R. Hume, *The Industrial Archaeology of Glasgow*, 1974, 231 and pl. 1]; the monument in THE NECROPOLIS to the Revd. Robert Muter (d. 1842), 1844 [G. Blair, *Sketches of Glasgow Necropolis*, 1857, 233]; and THE FREE TRON CHURCH, NORTH DUNDAS STREET, dem. [David Thomson in *Trans. Glasgow Philosophical Soc.* 1882, 2].

STEPHENSON, DAVID (1757–1819), was born on 31 October 1757. His father, John Stephenson (d. 1796), was a master carpenter in Newcastle-on-Tyne who was well known in his day for the construction of a temporary timber bridge across the Tyne after the old one had been destroyed by a flood in 1771. At the age of 24 David went to London to study in the Royal Academy Schools, to which he was admitted in January 1782. If at the same time he became the pupil of a London architect, the fact is not recorded, and early in 1783 he returned to Newcastle to start practice as an architect. He immediately obtained several civic commissions, for some of which he was indebted to the favour of Sir Matthew White Ridley of Blagdon, and in 1786 he won the competition for the new church of All Saints with a bold design for an elliptical building with transverse seating. This was his most important work, and ranks as one of the most striking and original churches built in England in the eighteenth century.

Stephenson appears to have received no country-house commissions, but in 1805 he was appointed surveyor and architect to the Duke of Northumberland, and in that capacity designed several farmhouses on the Duke's estate and some minor buildings at Alnwick Castle. He died at Alnwick on 29 August 1819, aged 63, and is commemorated by a tablet in the vestibule of All Saints Church at Newcastle. Although his practice had doubtless been curtailed by the Napoleonic War, he had been sufficiently prosperous to be able to purchase an estate called Waldridge, nr. Chester-le-Street in County Durham. His widow was still living there in the 1830s. John Dobson was his pupil.

[*A.P.S.D.*; R. Welford, *Men of Mark 'twixt Tyne and Tweed* iii, 1895, 434–7; F. Mackenzie & M. Ross, *County Palatine of*

Durham i, 1834, 146; D. W. Johnson, 'A Study of the Life and Works of David Stephenson 1757–1819', unpublished dissertation, School of Architecture, University of Newcastle-upon-Tyne, 1972.]

NEWCASTLE

THE SCALE or KALE CROSS, erected 1783 at the expense of Sir Matthew Ridley, Bart. but taken down in 1807 and presented by the Corporation to its original donor, who re-erected it in his grounds at Blagdon, Northumberland [M. A. Richardson, *The Local Historian's Table Book* ii, 1842, 280; iii, 1843, 66].

THE NEW WHITE CROSS, NEWGATE STREET, erected 1784, removed to the Butcher Market in 1808, Gothic; dem. [E. Mackenzie, *Newcastle* i, 1827, 173].

ST. NICHOLAS CHURCH (now the CATHEDRAL) was repaired and repewed under the joint direction of John Dodds and David Stephenson in 1783–5 [Richardson, *op. cit.* ii, 284–8]. Stephenson repaired the church in 1792, and the steeple in 1795 [E. Mackenzie, *Newcastle* i, 1827, 255].

ALL SAINTS CHURCH, 1786–9, spire completed 1796 [T. Sopwith, *An Historical and Descriptive Account of All Saints Church, Newcastle*, 1826].

THE THEATRE ROYAL, MOSLEY STREET, 1787–8; dem. 1836 [E. Mackenzie, *Newcastle* i, 1827, 229].

THE CIRCUS or AMPHITHEATRE (a riding-house), 1789; dem. [E. Mackenzie, *Newcastle* ii, 1827, 594; *Civil Engineer and Architect's Jnl.* vi, 1843, 147].

THE EXCHANGE, rebuilt the north front, with W. Newton, 1795–6 [E. Mackenzie, *Newcastle* i, 1827, 216].

TYNE BRIDGE, widening, 1801; dem. 1873 [E. Mackenzie, *Newcastle* i, 1827, 214].

NORTHUMBERLAND AND DURHAM

NORTH SHIELDS, NORTHUMBERLAND, the NEW QUAY AND MARKET PLACE, 1806–17 [Richardson, *op. cit.* iii, 58].

ALNWICK, NORTHUMBERLAND, farm-houses at LONGDYKE, DENWICK WATERSIDE and BRISLEY WEST, 1807 [D. W. Johnson, *op. cit.*], and iron bridge in Hulne Park, *c.*1813 [Alnwick Castle Library, Sir David Smith's Atlas of Northumberland, vol. iii].

ALNWICK, NORTHUMBERLAND, column erected by the Duke of Northumberland's tenantry to commemorate his munificence, 1816 [Richardson, *op. cit.* iii, 166–7; Alnwick Castle Library, MS. 187A/27].

WALDRIDGE, CO. DURHAM, *attributed*: THE HALL and THE COTTAGE, after 1794 [B. I. Bagnall, 'David Stephenson at Waldridge', *Durham Archl. Jnl.* i, 1984].

STEUART, GEORGE (*c.*1730–1806), was a Highland Scot from Atholl in Perthshire. He and his brother Charles are said both to have been Gaelic speakers. Charles was a topographical painter who exhibited at the Royal Academy between 1764 and 1790. Some of his pictures can still be seen at Blair Atholl. George appears to have started his career as a house-painter, but from 1770 onwards he was practising as an architect in London, first in Berners and afterwards in Harley Street. His first recorded work was a town house for the 3rd Duke of Atholl, and the patronage of the 3rd and 4th Dukes evidently played an important part in his career. Some of his most important works were, however, in Shropshire, where he had a number of commissions from the local gentry. Towards the end of his life he lived at Douglas in the Isle of Man, where the Dukes of Atholl were the Governors and principal landowners. Steuart died at the Lough House, Douglas, on 20 December 1806, leaving a substantial estate to his son Major Robert Steuart (who subsequently built the Villa Marina overlooking Douglas Bay). His will mentions his intention to be buried 'in the vault of the mausoleum intended to be built upon the summit of his land near Douglas', but in fact he was interred in Kirk Braddan churchyard, where a simple tombstone records his death at the age of 76.

Nothing is known about Steuart's architectural training, but his buildings show a markedly neo-classical taste. Mr. Lees-Milne has noted his fondness for 'a uniform severity of wall surface broken occasionally by slightly recessed arches containing a window (after the fashion set by J. Wyatt) and a tenuousness of pilaster and column'. These characteristics are found in all his country houses, whose elegant restraint verges on bleakness. At St. Chad's, Shrewsbury, he achieved a bolder and more original composition by the juxtaposition of a circular nave and a massive steeple of three clearly defined stages, one square, one octagonal and one circular. This was probably his most important work and is certainly one of the most striking and original of English Georgian churches. Unexecuted designs by Steuart for rebuilding Onslow Hall, Shropshire, are in the R.I.B.A. Drawings Collection.

[*A.P.S.D.*; *Chronicles of the Atholl and Tullibardine Families*, compiled by the 7th Duke of Atholl, iv, 1908, *passim*; M. M. Rix & W. R. Serjeant, 'George Steuart, Architect, in the Isle of Man', *Jnl. Manx Museum* vi, 1962–3, 177–9; information from Mr. B. R. S. Megaw and Mr. M. M. Rix.]

LONDON, GROSVENOR PLACE, house for 3rd Duke of Atholl, 1770; dem. [C. T. Gatty, *Mary Davies and the Manor of Ebury* i, 1921, 181].

MILLICHOPE PARK, SALOP., Ionic temple or cenotaph for More family on rock facing the house, 1770 [J. B. Blakeway, *The Sheriffs of Shropshire*, Shrewsbury 1831, 208].

BLAIR CASTLE and DUNKELD HOUSE, PERTHSHIRE, various subsidiary buildings (lodges, greenhouses, etc.) for 4th Duke of Atholl, 1777, etc. [drawings at Blair Castle].

BARONS COURT, CO. TYRONE, IRELAND, for 8th Earl of Abercorn, 1779–82; remodelled by Sir John Soane 1791–5 and again in 1837–41 [G. Jackson-Stops in *C. Life*, 12–19 July 1979].

PAISLEY, RENFREWSHIRE, inn in Gauze Street, for 8th Earl of Abercorn, 1780–2 [G. Crawford and W. Semple, *History of the Shire of Renfrew*, Paisley 1782, part 2, 290].

ATTINGHAM HALL, SALOP., for Noel Hill, cr. 1st Lord Berwick, 1783–5 [G. Richardson, *New Vitruvius Britannicus* ii, 1808, pls. 25–30; drawings preserved in house and in John White volume in R.I.B.A. Drawings Coll.] (*C. Life*, 5–12 Feb. 1921, 21 Oct. 1954; C. Hussey, *English Country Houses: Mid Georgian*, 1956, 195–202; J. Lees-Milne, *Guide to Attingham*, National Trust 1949).

LYTHWOOD HALL, SALOP., for Joshua Blakeway, *c.*1785; converted into flats 1950, destroying portico and other architectural features [H. Owen & J. B. Blakeway, *History of Shrewsbury* ii, 1825, 248; drawings in Shropshire C.R.O., 4068/1–5].

STOKE PARK, EARL STOKE, WILTS., for Joshua Smith, 1786–91; gutted 1950 and dem. except wings [G. Richardson, *New Vitruvius Britannicus* i, 1810, pls. 36–8; original drawings in R.I.B.A. Coll.].

WELLINGTON CHURCH, SALOP., 1788–90 [plans and elevations signed 'G. Steuart Archt. 1787' in Lichfield Joint Record Office and cf. B.L., *King's Maps* xxv, 19–1].

SHREWSBURY, NEW ST. CHAD'S CHURCH, 1790–2 [H. Owen & J. B. Blakeway, *History of Shrewsbury* ii, 1825, 248–50].

MIDDLETON, LANCS., MARKET HOUSE for 1st Lord Suffield, 1791; dem. [volume of signed drawings in Greater Manchester R.O., E7/28/2].

DOUGLAS, ISLE OF MAN, THE COURTHOUSE, RED PIER and LIGHTHOUSE, 1793–9; courthouse dem. *c.*1860, lighthouse 1936, when the pier was remodelled [drawings and accounts in Manx Museum Library, see *Jnl. Manx Museum* vi, 1962–3, pls. 264–5].

RAMSEY, ISLE OF MAN, THE COURT HOUSE, 1798 [drawings in Manx Museum Library] (*Jnl. Manx Museum* vi, 1962–3, pl. 266).

CASTLE MONA, DOUGLAS, ISLE OF MAN, for 4th Duke of Atholl, 1801–6 [drawings in Manx Museum Library] (*Jnl. Manx Museum* vi, 1962–3, pl. 266).

attributed: KIRK BRADDAN CHURCHYARD, ISLE OF MAN, obelisk in memory of Lord Henry Murray, 5th son of the 3rd Duke of Atholl (d. 1805).

STEVENS, ALEXANDER (*c.*1730–1796), was a Scottish architect and civil engineer who specialized in bridge-building. A mason by trade, he contracted to build many of the bridges that he designed. He lived at Prestonhall in the parish of Cranston in Midlothian, about 10 miles S.E. of Edinburgh, where he tenanted a farm. According to his obituary in the *Gentleman's Magazine*, he had, 'in the course of the last forty years, erected more stone bridges, and other buildings in water, than any man in these kingdoms. . . . The North of England and Scotland exhibit numberless works of his execution.' His bridges are handsomely designed and, although presumably self-taught, he 'was conversant with the most up-to-date structural techniques'. The following bridges have been identified as his work:

HYNDFORD BRIDGE, nr. LANARK (R. Clyde), *c.*1773 [*Statistical Account of Scotland* xv, 1795, 26].

DRYGRANGE or LEADERFOOT BRIDGE, nr. MELROSE, ROXBURGHSHIRE (R. Tweed), 1779–80 [signed 'Alexander Stevens, architect'; contract in S.R.O., GD 244, box 19].

attributed: OXENFOORD CASTLE, MIDLOTHIAN, castellated bridge in grounds, *c.*1783 [Alistair Rowan in *C. Life*, 15 Aug. 1974].

ANCRUM BRIDGE, ROXBURGHSHIRE (R. Teviot), 1784 [T. Ruddock, *Arch Bridges and their Builders 1735–1835*, 1979, 121].

BRIDGE OF DUN, nr. MONTROSE (R. South Esk), 1785–7 [contract in S.R.O., GD 244, box 19].

AYR BRIDGE (R. Ayr), 1786–9; dem. 1878 [S.R.O., B6/29/7, minutes of the trustees].

DUBLIN, SARAH BRIDGE (R. Liffey), 1791–3 [*Edinburgh Encyclopaedia* iv, 1830, 487].

MONTROSE, ANGUS, timber bridge (R. South Esk), 1793–6; dem. 1828 [D. Mitchell, *History of Montrose*, Montrose 1866, 70].

THE TEVIOT BRIDGE, KELSO, ROXBURGHSHIRE (R. Teviot), built by W. Elliot 1794–5, was probably designed by Stevens [T.

Ruddock, *Arch Bridges and their Builders 1735–1835*, 1979, 121].

Stevens was also responsible for the locks on the 'grand canal of Ireland', and for the major task of building John Rennie's aqueduct over the R. Lune at Lancaster. In the R.I.B.A. Drawings Collection there is a design by him for a one-arch bridge at Blackadder House, Berwickshire.

Stevens died at Lancaster on 29 January 1796, while supervising the construction of the Lune aqueduct. He was aged 66. He is commemorated by a tablet on the external south wall of Lancaster Parish Church. His practice was continued by his son Alexander (*q.v.*). In 1783–4 he had built a handsome double-fronted Gothic house close to the Bridge of Ayr. This house he subsequently gave to his daughter on her marriage in 1794 to James Fyfe, Agent to Lord Mountjoy [Ayr Town Council Minutes and titles, *ex inf.* Mr. David Walker].

[*Gent's Mag.* lxvi (i), 1796, 169; *A.P.S.D.*; T. Ruddock, *Arch Bridges and their Builders 1735–1835*, 1979, 120–3.]

STEVENS, ALEXANDER, junior, was the son of the above, and, like him, was a civil engineer as well as an architect. He was concerned in his father's engineering works at Montrose and Lancaster, and completed the Lune Aqueduct after the latter's death in 1796. A surviving notebook shows that he tendered for Rennie's Wolseley Bridge (Staffs.) in 1797 and for his Kelso Bridge (Roxburghshire) in 1799. He was also concerned in harbour works at Leith, where he designed the Upper Drawbridge (1788), and at Starleyburn, Burntisland, Fife (1789), and he designed Wamphray Bridge, Dumfriesshire, in 1795.

As an architect Stevens's principal recorded work was RAEHILLS, nr. MOFFAT, DUMFRIESSHIRE, for the 3rd Earl of Hopetoun, 1786, in imitation of the Adam castle style, subsequently enlarged by W. Burn [building accounts at Hopetoun, *ex inf.* Mr. Basil Skinner]. He built, and probably designed, MONREITH HOUSE, MOCHRUM, WIGTOWNSHIRE, for Sir William Maxwell, Bart., 1791 [S.R.O., SC 19/65/1]. In a portfolio at Raehills there is a design by Stevens for a small castellated house on paper watermarked 1807. At Culzean Castle there is a plan by him for a projected square on the site of the Citadel at Ayr, together with an elevation of the proposed houses dated 1799.

Stevens designed the classical porch and steeple that were added to MOFFAT CHURCH, DUMFRIESSHIRE (dem. 1887) in 1795 [S.R.O. CS 96/3842 and signed elevation in RHP 8018]. He was also the builder, and perhaps the designer, of the steeple of ST. CUTHBERT'S CHURCH, EDINBURGH. In April 1789 the Heritors decided to build the steeple by subscription according to a plan 'marked by the Praeses as relative hereto' [S.R.O. HR 152/2], and on 8 July 1790 the *Caledonian Mercury* reported that 'The steeple of St. Cuthbert's Church is now finished . . . Mr. Stephen, the builder of this elegant structure, was also the builder of St. Andrew's Church steeple;[1] and the drawbridge at Leith, the masterly execution of all which does him great honour as an architect.' In 1792 'Alexander Steven Architect' was one of the three architects who were asked to survey St. Cuthbert's Manse [S.R.O., HR 152/2, 28 Dec. 1792].

Stevens lived in Edinburgh, where he continues to appear in the directories up to 1811/12.

[S.R.O., CS 96/3842 (notebook); CS 229/ G.8/6 (Bridge of Montrose); GD 150/2407 (Starleyburn Harbour); information from Miss C. Cruft, Mr. John Gifford and Miss Ierne Grant.]

STEVENS, EDWARD (*c.*1744–1775), was a pupil of Sir William Chambers from 1760 [P.R.O., IR1/22] until 1766. He gained premiums offered by the Society for the Encouragement of Arts, Manufactures, and Commerce in 1762 and 1763, and exhibited at the Free Society of Artists in 1762–3, at the Society of Artists in 1765–8, and at the Royal Academy in 1770–3, giving his address as Charles Street, Cavendish Square. In 1769 he competed for the Royal Exchange at Dublin, exhibiting his design at the Royal Academy the following year. He was elected A.R.A. in 1770. He went abroad in 1774, and was made a member of the Florentine Academy.[2] He was taken ill soon after his arrival in Rome, and died there on 27 June 1775 at the age of 31, leaving a widow and daughter. He is commemorated by a monument in the Protestant cemetery.

Stevens's principal executed works were a new front to SPYE PARK, WILTS., for Sir Edward Baynton, Bart., which he exhibited at the Society of Artists in 1767 (demolished 1868); and DOVERIDGE HALL, DERBYSHIRE, for Sir Henry Cavendish, Bart., begun in 1769, which he exhibited at the R.A. in 1771 (demolished 1934, described by E. Saunders in *Derbyshire Life*, Aug. 1972). The latter house was in a conservative Palladian style with rusticated basement, pedimented façade and

[1] Designed by W. Sibbald and built 1786–7.

[2] His diploma is in the R.I.B.A. Collection (E4/ 20A).

narrow, pavilion-like wings. Stevens was also employed at WREST PARK, BEDS., by the 2nd Earl of Hardwicke, for whom in 1770 he designed a Bridge and a classical Cold Bath [Bedfordshire Record Office, abstract of bills in L 31/318]. Among the Wrest drawings in the same Record Office there is an unexecuted design for a 'Theatre or Colonnade designed for the Gardens at Wrest', signed 'Edw. Stevens Arct. 1769'.

The R.I.B.A. Drawings Collection possesses an album of drawings (mostly of a 'theoretical' character) made by Stevens in Chambers's office, a design for a large town house (probably 'the London House, fit for a person of distinction', which he exhibited at the Free Society of Artists in 1763), and a design for a ceiling for Thomas Collins, who was Chambers's partner in a building speculation in Berners Street in 1770 [*R.I.B.A. Drawings Catalogue*].

The Apprenticeship Registers in the Public Record Office show that Stevens had two pupils, William Wickham (1767) and William Grantham (1769 or 1770).

STEVENS, JOHN, of Wantage, was the surveyor employed in connection with the erection of the COUNCIL CHAMBER at ABINGDON in 1731–3. According to the agreement made between the Corporation and Samuel Westbrook, mason, and Charles Etty, carpenter, on 13 August 1731, the 'ornaments' were 'to be made with the best Heddington Freestone well wrought according to the draught of Mr. John Stevens of Wantage'. Subsequently there are payments to Stevens for unspecified services which probably included surveying [contract in Abingdon Corporation records, *ex inf.* the late Miss A. C. Baker].

STEVENS, JOHN (–1857), practised as an architect and surveyor from 54 Green Street, Grosvenor Square, during the period 1810–30, and later from 6 Clements Inn. From 1843 until his death in 1857 he was Surveyor of the Western District of the City. In 1813 he supervised repairs and alterations to BEACHBOROUGH HOUSE, HYTHE, KENT (destroyed by fire *c.*1965), for James Drake-Brockman [accounts in B.L., Add. MS. 42673, ff. 254–5, 269–70, 280] (C. Greenwood, *Epitome of County History: Kent*, 1838, 305). He appears to have been the father of John Hargrave Stevens (d. 1875), District Surveyor of Bethnal Green.

STEWART, DANIEL (–1842), was a Scot from Ayrshire who established himself in Liverpool, at first as a builder, and from about 1810 as an architect and surveyor. J. A. Picton (1805–89) became his assistant in 1826 and eventually took over his practice when he retired at the end of 1834 [J. A. Picton, *Sir James A. Picton*, 1891, 54–61]. Stewart designed several churches: ST. ANDREW'S SCOTTISH CHURCH, RODNEY STREET, LIVERPOOL, 1823–4, with a portico designed by John Foster, jr. (*q.v.*) [S.R.O., CH2/245/2, memoranda in 'share and transfer book']; ST. PETER, WOOLTON, LANCS., 1835–6, 'Grecian'; dem. *c.*1886 [*Liverpool Mercury*, 22 Sept. 1826, *ex inf.* Miss Joan Borrowscale]; ST. JOHN, BURSCOUGH BRIDGE, LANCS., 1829–31, Gothic [Port, 146–7]; ST. ANNE, STANLEY (OLD SWAN), nr. LIVERPOOL, 1831; rebuilt 1890–1 [I.C.B.S.]; and (in partnership with Picton), ST. MATTHIAS, LIVERPOOL, 1832–33, Ionic; dem. 1848 to make way for a railway. He died in 1842, aged over 80.

Stewart's son John Stewart (1791–1871), at first his father's assistant, left in about 1824 in order to enter into partnership with the Foster family as building contractors (and occasionally as architects, e.g. for NORLEY CHURCH, CHESHIRE, 1832, dem. 1878, for which plans among the I.C.B.S. records are signed 'Foster & Stewart architects, Liverpool'). He was 'long and intimately connected with the public affairs of the town', and served as Mayor in 1855–6 [J. A. Picton, *Memorials of Liverpool*, 1875, i, 464, ii, 210].

STEWART, JOHN, was an architect and carpenter of Dunkeld in Perthshire. In about 1804 he appears to have moved to Perth, but by 1811 he was back in Dunkeld. He designed the following Perthshire churches: LITTLE DUNKELD, 1798 [S.R.O., HR 470/1, p. 63]; LOGIERAIT, 1804–6 [S.R.O., HR 38/1, p. 23]; COMRIE, 1805 [S.R.O., copies of Heritors' minutes in GD 16/20]; and AUCHTERGAVEN, 1811–13 [S.R.O., HR 663/1, p. 5].

STIBBS, THOMAS (–1759), was a carpenter in London. He was probably the brother of Joseph Stibbs, who was one of the surveyors considered for rebuilding the church of St. Katherine Coleman in 1739. James Horne was the successful applicant, but Thomas Stibbs, of the parish of St. Giles, Cripplegate, was the contracting carpenter [Guildhall Library, MSS. 1133, 1134]. In 1732–5 he designed and built the ARMOURY HOUSE, ARTILLERY GROUND, FINSBURY, for the Honourable Artillery Company [A. Highmore, *History of the Honourable Artillery Company*, 1804, 198, 201–2], and in 1743 he built the JEWISH SCHOOL (now the Talmud Torah Classes) in Bride Lane, Stepney [*Sur-*

vey of London xxvii, 221]. He was Surveyor to the London Assurance Company, and in 1749–50 built its office in Birchin Lane, Cornhill, to the designs of one Joseph Manning. When he died in 1759 he was succeeded by his son William Stibbs. [Guildhall Library, Minutes of the London Assurance Company, MSS. 8728/6, p. 152, 8728/7, p. 196.]

STICKELLS, ROBERT (–1620), appears to have been a mason by trade, but the surviving records of his career show him acting as an architect, clerk of works and naval engineer. In the 1580s he was one of the 'masters of the work' then in progress at Dover harbour, his main task being raising rocks by barrels and chains and floating them to a jetty in process of construction. Stow's *Chronicle* records that in 1595 'master Stickles, the excellent Artichect of our time', constructed in Leadenhall a small pinnace that could be taken to pieces and reassembled. This was launched in Tower Dock, 'but there came no good of it'. In the Lansdowne MSS. there is a paper by Stickells proposing to build a ship that would be 'shot free and fire free' and a boat that could be propelled 'without sails or oars'. As an architect Stickells is known to have been employed by Sir Thomas Tresham of Rushton in Northants, and a surviving drawing by him has been identified as a design for an elaborate classical lantern surmounting the cruciform LYVEDEN NEW BUILDING which Tresham started to build in about 1594 but never completed. In 1613 he was paid by Sir Edward Pytts of Kyre in Worcestershire for 'drawing the platt of my house [probably in London] anewe', and two papers survive in which Stickells discusses, in esoteric terms, the proposition whether the 'Antique' or the 'Modern' was the more valid way of building.

In 1595 the Earl of Derby recommended Stickells as a candidate for the Surveyorship of the Queen's Works. In fact he had to be content with a subordinate clerkship of the works, which he held from 1597/8 until his death. From 1598/9 he was stationed at Richmond, where in 1605–6 he designed a new lodge in the park of which there are drawings in the Thorpe MS. in Sir John Soane's Museum. Stickells died in May 1620. In his will he describes himself as a 'citizen and freemason of London' living in the parish of St. Olave, Southwark.

[John Summerson, 'Three Elizabethan Architects', *Bulletin of the John Rylands Library* xl, 1957, 216–21, 225–8; *History of the King's Works* iii, 134–5.]

STIRLING, WILLIAM (1772–1838), was the principal member of a family of builder-architects established at Dunblane in Perthshire. He was the eldest son of James Stirling, a wright and cabinet-maker, and continued his business besides acting as an architect. His marriage in 1803 to Jean, daughter of David Erskine, W.S., allied him to the closely related families of Erskine, Graham, Stirling and Masterton who were among the principal Perthshire landowners, and brought him many commissions on their estates. The bulk of his work consisted of stables, offices, manses, farm-houses and country churches, and he never designed any building of the first rank. His designs reflect the styles current in early nineteenth-century Scotland — Adamesque or Grecian for domestic purposes, simplified Gothic for churches, 'Tudor' for manses, etc. The profits of a highly successful business enabled him to build up a small estate in Dunblane upon which in 1826 he built himself a house (Holmehill) of some pretensions. He died on 5 February 1838, and was succeeded in his practice by William Stirling II (*c.*1789–1876), who may have been a cousin and had been his 'chief assistant and superintendent' for some years. William Stirling II retired long before his death in 1876 at the age of 87, and handed the business on to his son William Stirling III (born *c.*1819), who predeceased his father, dying in 1867.

[A. B. Barty, *History of Dunblane*, 1944, 219, 231–2; David Walker, 'The Stirlings of Dunblane and Falkirk', *Bull. Scottish Georgian Soc.* i, 1972.]

The following list of work is (unless otherwise stated) based on Mr. Walker's article, where full references will be found.

CHURCHES AND OTHER PUBLIC BUILDINGS

LOGIE CHURCH, STIRLINGSHIRE, 1805; reconstructed 1901.

PORT OF MENTEITH CHURCHYARD, PERTHSHIRE, mausoleum for Graham of Gartmore family, *c.*1810.

STIRLING, THE ATHENAEUM, 1814–16 (R.C.A.M., *Stirlingshire* ii, pl. 134 B).

AIRTH, STIRLINGSHIRE, NORTH CHURCH, 1818–20, Gothic [R.C.A.M., *Stirlingshire* i, 142 and plates].

RATTRAY CHURCH, PERTHSHIRE, 1820, Italianate.

KIPPEN CHURCH, STIRLINGSHIRE, 1823; altered 1928; Gothic.

LECROPT CHURCH, PERTHSHIRE, 1825–7, Gothic, executing a design that appears to have been basically by David Hamilton (*q.v.*).

LECROPT SCHOOL, PERTHSHIRE, 1826.

DRON CHURCH, PERTHSHIRE, *c.*1825, Gothic [signed drawings among Fettercairn papers in N.L.S.].

CRIEFF CHURCH, PERTHSHIRE, completion of church built 1786–7 but left unfinished, 1826.

TILLICOULTRY CHURCH, CLACKMANNANSHIRE, 1827–9, Gothic.

MONZIE CHURCH, PERTHSHIRE, 1830–1, Gothic [*N.S.A.* x, 278].

CREICH CHURCH, FIFE, 1830–3 [S.R.O., HR 273/1].

DUNIPACE CHURCH, STIRLINGSHIRE, 1832–4, Gothic.

TOM A CHAISTEL, STROWAN, PERTHSHIRE, obelisk in memory of Sir David Baird, 1832.

PLEAN HOSPITAL (almshouses), STIRLINGSHIRE, *c.*1835–7.

DOMESTIC ARCHITECTURE

DUNIRA, PERTHSHIRE, works for 1st and 2nd Viscounts Melville, 1802–16, based on designs by Henry Holland; rebuilt by W. Burn 1851–2 [Dundas papers, Comrie House, *ex inf.* Prof. A. A. Tait].

COMRIE LODGE, PERTHSHIRE, works for 4th Earl of Aberdeen, 1803 and *c.*1820.

TULLIBODY HOUSE, CLACKMANNANSHIRE, repairs for 2nd Lord Abercromby, *c.*1803; dem.

CARDROSS HOUSE, PERTHSHIRE, alterations for David Erskine, 1803.

STROWAN, CRIEFF, PERTHSHIRE, for Sir Thomas Stirling, 1804–8; since rebuilt.

ALVA HOUSE, CLACKMANNANSHIRE, stables for James Johnstone, 1805–9.

DOUNE LODGE, KILMADOCK, PERTHSHIRE, stables for the 8th Earl of Moray, 1807–9 (*C. Life*, 10 Sept. 1987, 135).

KINNAIRD HOUSE, nr. LARBERT, STIRLINGSHIRE, repairs for James Bruce, 1808–11; rebuilt 1895.

KIPPENROSS, PERTHSHIRE, alterations for John Stirling, 1809; since modified.

AIRTHREY CASTLE, STIRLINGSHIRE, lodges for Sir Robert Abercromby, 1809; one demolished.

METHVEN CASTLE, PERTHSHIRE, work on offices (dem. 1954) for Robert Smythe, 1810–12.

KEAVIL HOUSE, DUNFERMLINE, FIFE, work for J. R. Barclay, 1810–12.

ALVA MANSE, CLACKMANNANSHIRE, 1810–12.

MONZIE, PERTHSHIRE, lodge to east gate for General Alexander Campbell, 1812.

LECROPT MANSE, PERTHSHIRE, 1812.

AIRTH MANSE, STIRLINGSHIRE, 1813–14 [S.R.O., HR 244/1, 20 & 29 May 1813].

DUPPLIN CASTLE, PERTHSHIRE, south-west wing for 10th Earl of Kinnoull, 1814–15; remodelled by W. Burn 1828–32; dem.

COMRIE MANSE (now TULLICHETTLE HOUSE), PERTHSHIRE, new front block, 1818–20.

KINCARDINE-IN-MENTEITH MANSE, PERTHSHIRE, 1821–3.

LINLATHEN HOUSE, nr. DUNDEE, ANGUS, enlarged for Thomas Erskine, *c.*1820–6; partly dem. 1958 (excluding Stirling's work).

MONCREIFFE HOUSE, PERTHSHIRE, enlarged stable-block for Sir David Moncreiffe, Bart., 1821.

MONCREIFFE, PERTHSHIRE, enlarged the Inn, 1821.

TIBBERMORE MANSE, PERTHSHIRE, 1824.

FORTEVIOT MANSE, PERTHSHIRE, 1825–6.

ARDOCH HOUSE, PERTHSHIRE, addition to offices, etc., for William Moray Stirling, 1826.

HOLMEHILL HOUSE, DUNBLANE, PERTHSHIRE, for himself, 1826, Tudor style.

COLQUHALZIE, CRIEFF, PERTHSHIRE, wing for John Hepburn, 1826.

DUNBLANE MANSE, PERTHSHIRE, 1829; dem.

BRIDGE OF ALLAN, STIRLINGSHIRE, an inn, probably the 'Westerton Arms', 1831.

FALKIRK, STIRLINGSHIRE, RED LION INN (now shop), 148–154 HIGH STREET, 1828.

GARDEN HOUSE, STIRLINGSHIRE, east block for James Stirling, 1830 [R.C.A.M., *Stirlingshire*, 370–1 and pl. 200].

MUCKHART MANSE, PERTHSHIRE, 1832.

STOAKES, CHARLES, was the great-nephew of Nicholas Stone (*q.v.*), and ultimately inherited his business as a mason and architect from his sons. He had in his possession the Stone account-books, which are now in Sir John Soane's Museum, and gave George Vertue information about sculptors of his generation. In 1712 he repaired and partly rebuilt the south side of MERE CHURCH, WILTS., as recorded by two circular tablets in the spandrels of the arcade stating that the work was 'performed by Mr. Charles Stoakes of London Surveyor of Buildings' [*Wilts. Arch. Mag.* xxix, 1896–7, 51–2]. A 'Plan of Stafford House and Grounds taken in the year 1725 by Chas. Stokes senior' is in the Library of the Society of Antiquaries (Harley Collection of Topographical Drawings, vi, f. 57).

STODDART, CHARLES (*c.*1770–1840), was an architect at Lichfield, where he died in August 1840, aged 70 [*Lichfield Advertiser*, 29 Aug. 1840]. In 1829 he gave expert advice in connection with Joseph Potter's dispute with Sir George Chetwynd over his work at

Grendon Hall [William Salt Library, Stafford, Hand Morgan, uncatalogued 47/7(a)].

STOKES, GEORGE (1804–1870), was an architect whose career is difficult to reconstruct. He exhibited at the Royal Academy from 1827 onwards, showing in 1831 a 'Design for a Town Hall and Assembly Rooms proposed to be built at Halifax', in 1843 'a Portion of Westbourne Terrace, now completing on the Bishop of London's estate at Paddington', and in 1844 a 'Sketch of a proposed new church' on the same estate. Thereafter he showed only topographical drawings. From 1843 until his death his address was Porchester Gardens, where he is believed to have acted as developer as well as architect. Sir Charles Barry's son Charles received 'instruction' from him that was acknowledged by the gift of a silver tray in 1842. He appears to have retired relatively early, and died at Ryde on 27 August 1870 [Principal Probate Registry, Calendar of Probates; family information in R.I.B.A. file].

STOKES, ROBERT, exhibited student's work at the Royal Academy in 1828 and 1829. He was admitted to the Royal Academy Schools in 1830, and won the Silver Medal the same year. By 1831 he had moved to Cheltenham, where he designed the Tudor Gothic FEMALE ORPHAN ASYLUM, 1833–4 [H. Davies, *Cheltenham in its Past and Present State*, 1843, 148]. His only other recorded works are AMBERLEY CHURCH, GLOS., 1836, Gothic [*V.C.H. Glos.* xi, 204] and OAKRIDGE CHURCH, GLOS., 1836–7, Gothic [I.C.B.S.]. He subsequently emigrated to New Zealand, where he was employed in the Survey Department and designed a Wesleyan Chapel at Wellington in 1844 [J. Stackpoole & P. Beaven, *New Zealand Art: Architecture 1820–1970*, 1972, 10].

STOKOE, JOHN (1756–1836), was the son and successor of William Stokoe, a master builder of Newcastle-upon-Tyne who died in 1802, aged 79 [*Newcastle Chronicle*, 18 Dec. 1802], and the father of William Stokoe (*q.v.*). In the 1790s he was involved in alterations to TRINITY HOUSE, NEWCASTLE [G. McCombie, 'The Buildings of Trinity House', *Archaeologia Aeliana*, 4th ser. xiii, 1985, 176–8] and in 1807 he was responsible for 'repairing and casing' the S. front of THE EXCHANGE [*Newcastle Chronicle*, 20 July 1807]. In conjunction with his father he designed ELSWICK HALL, NORTHUMBERLAND, for John Hodgson, completed 1803; dem. 1977 [J. Dobson in *Building News* v, 1859, 403; Margaret Dobson, *Memoir of John Dobson*, 1885, 11]. He, rather than his teen-age son, must have been the 'Mr. Stokoe' who designed HARTFORD HALL, NORTHUMBERLAND, for William Burdon, 1807 [E. Mackenzie, *Northumberland* i, 1825, 348], and he certainly designed HEWORTH CHURCH, CO. DURHAM, in a simple Gothic style in 1821–2 [I.C.B.S.]. Advertisements in the *Newcastle Chronicle* show that he was responsible for building developments in the city at SCOTCH ARMS, NEWGATE STREET, 1814, BALLS COURT, PILGRIM STREET, 1817, and RYE HILL, 1829 [*ex inf.* Mr. R. Hewlings]. He died in Newcastle on 23 August 1836, aged 80 [*Newcastle Courant*, 27 Aug. 1836; All Saints Burial Register, *ex inf.* Mr. Terry Scott].

STOKOE, WILLIAM (*c.*1786–1855), was the son of the above. In 1808 he exhibited two designs for villas at the Royal Academy, but without giving any address. By 1810 he had designed THE MOOT HALL, NEWCASTLE-UPON-TYNE, a remarkably competent Greek Revival building which suggests that he must have had a training in London or Edinburgh [inscription: 'William Stokoe, Architect' on foundation plate recorded in *Newcastle Chronicle*, 26 July 1810, p. 3]. He subsequently practised in Newcastle, where his works are sometimes difficult to distinguish from his father's. However, he is specifically stated in the *Newcastle Courant* to have designed the tunnel through the Mound at TYNEMOUTH DEAN, 1810; the PANDON DEAN BRIDGE, 1810–12; and the EXCHANGE and TOWN HALL at SUNDERLAND, 1812–14; dem. [*Newcastle Courant*, 23 June, 7 July 1810, 11 July 1812]. Subsequent advertisements in the Newcastle newspapers show that he became an active speculative developer, building houses in ELLISON PLACE, 1813; WESTGATE STREET and COLLINGWOOD STREET, 1818; a house and shop in THE SIDE, 1819; a house near ELSWICK VILLAS, 1847, and a house in GRAINGERVILLE, 1852. He died in Argyle Street on 1 April 1855, aged 69 [*Newcastle Chronicle*, 6 April 1855]. [References to newspapers *ex inf.* Mr. S. Chamberlain *via* Mr. R. Hewlings.]

STONE, FRANCIS (1770–1835), practised in Norwich, where he held the post of County Surveyor from 1806 until his death. He was a founder member of the Norwich Society of Artists in 1805, and served as President in 1812 and 1822. He exhibited drawings at the Society's exhibitions from 1805 onwards, and was the author of a set of lithographs entitled *Picturesque Views of all the Bridges belonging to the County of Norfolk*, 1830–1. A manuscript account of the county bridges, with water-colour drawings by Stone, is described in Weinreb's Catalogue No. 9, *Bridges*, of 1965.

Stone died on 23 August 1835, aged 65, and is commemorated by a monument in the church of St. George Tombland in Norwich. His son, Francis Henry Stone, exhibited architectural designs at the Norwich Society of Artists from 1815 to 1825, but no further evidence of his architectural activity has been found [*A.P.S.D.*; *Architectural Mag.* iii, 1836, 48; information from Mr. A. P. Baggs and Mr. K. S. Mills].

WILBY RECTORY, NORFOLK, designs, presumably executed, 1805 [Norfolk C.R.O., DN/DPL 1/4/68].

BLOFIELD RECTORY, NORFOLK, 1806 [Norfolk C.R.O., DN/DPL 1/1/10].

NORWICH, ST. MARY'S BAPTIST MEETING HOUSE, SOUTERGATE, 1811–12; enlarged 1838; dem. 1942 [accounts, *ex inf.* Mr. C. B. Jewson].

NORWICH, THE NORFOLK LUNATIC ASYLUM (now St. Andrew's Hospital), THORPE, 1811–14 [exhib. at Norwich Society of Artists].

THORPE ST. ANDREW RECTORY, NORFOLK, 1814 [Norfolk C.R.O., DN/DPL 1/4/63].

NORWICH CATHEDRAL, repaired W. front, 1815 [*A.P.S.D.*]

GREAT YARMOUTH, NORFOLK, THE GAOL, 1818 [J. H. Druery, *Great Yarmouth*, 1826, 76].

NORWICH CASTLE, repairs and alterations to County Courts, etc., 1807 [*Norfolk Chronicle*, 21 Feb., 25 July 1807]; repaired and largely refaced E. face of keep, *c.*1829 [*A.P.S.D.*]; began refacing of S. and W. faces, 1834–5, continued by A. Salvin after his death [J. Allibone, *Anthony Salvin*, 1988, 95–7].

BRIDGES in NORFOLK at BABURGH, 1815; BARNEY, 1814; BRANDON CREEK; CROSTWICK, 1809; FAKENHAM, 1833; GREAT CRESSINGHAM, 1810–11; HILGAY, 1809 (timber); HONINGHAM, 1810; LUDHAM, 1811; MODNEY CREEK; NORWICH, FYE BRIDGE, 1829 (iron); ROXHAM DRAIN; SEDGE FEN DRAIN; THETFORD, 1829 (iron) [*A.P.S.D.*; *Norfolk Chronicle*, Jan. 1829; *Norwich Mercury*, 11 May 1811, 30 Nov.1833].

STONE, JOHN (1620–1667), was the third and youngest son of Nicholas Stone (*q.v.*). According to his near relation Charles Stoakes, he 'was bred a scoller by Docttor Busby'. George Vertue says that he was 'brought up at Oxford, design'd for a clergyman', and if so he was probably the John Stone who was Bible Clerk and Librarian at University College from 1644 until 1648, when he was expelled by the Parliamentary Visitors. According to Vertue he was the author of a book entitled *Enchiridion of Fortification, or a handfull of knowledge in Martiall affairs*, published anonymously in London in 1645. On leaving Oxford he 'went out to serve the King', and subsequently became a fugitive from the Parliamentary forces, living for a whole year concealed in London before escaping to France. He returned to England some time after his father's death and helped to carry on the family business, which devolved on him after his brother Henry's death in 1653. Stoakes says that he was 'an excelent architect', and like his father he evidently combined the practice of architecture with that of sculpture, though it may be doubted whether he actually carved with his own hands. Caius Gabriel Cibber (*q.v.*) acted as his foreman, and was probably the actual sculptor of most of the monuments which are recorded to have been made in Stone's workshop between 1650 and 1657 (listed in Spiers, 138–42). Stone's principal recorded work as an architect was CHESTERTON HOUSE, WARWICKS., a classical building of considerable pretensions which he probably designed for the royalist Sir Edward Peyto before the latter's death in 1658, and for which he was supplying capitals and other architectural details in 1660. The house was demolished in 1802, but two monuments from the Stone workshop remain in the parish church [H. M. Colvin, 'Chesterton, Warwickshire', *Arch. Rev.* Aug. 1955].

At the Restoration John Stone went over to Breda to petition the King for the office of Master Mason held by his father. He was given the Windsor office, but not that of Master Mason of the King's Works, which went to Edward Marshall. While at Breda he was stricken with paralysis. Cibber brought him home, but he never recovered sufficiently to resume the management of his affairs, and eventually died an inmate of the Hospital of St. Cross at Winchester in 1667.

[*The Note-Book and Account-Book of Nicholas Stone*, ed. W. L. Spiers, *Walpole Soc.* vii, 1918–19, 26–30, 138–42, etc.; *Vertue Note Books*, Walpole Soc. i, 89–93; D. Knoop & G. P. Jones, *The London Mason in the Seventeenth Century*, 1935, 24; *History of the King's Works* v, 3–4].

STONE, NICHOLAS (1587–1647), sculptor and master mason, was born in Devonshire, where his father was a quarryman. At the age of 16 or 17 he was apprenticed to Isaac James, a sculptor of Dutch origin working in Southwark. When Hendrik de Keyser, master mason to the City of Amsterdam, visited London in 1606, Stone was introduced to him and engaged to work for him in

Holland. He eventually married de Keyser's daughter and in 1613 returned to London, where he established himself in Long Acre. He immediately obtained important commissions for monuments and soon became the leading English monumental sculptor. His large output is documented by a notebook in which he recorded his commissions and by an account-book covering the years 1631–42. He was a sculptor of considerable ability, whose monuments are often novel and inventive in design, and responsive to new influences such as the antique sculptures acquired by Charles I from Mantua.

Stone's activities were by no means limited to tomb-making. He also acted as a master mason and was employed in this capacity by Inigo Jones at the building of the Banqueting House in Whitehall in 1619–22, William Cure, the King's Master Mason, having declined the task. In April 1626 Stone was formally brought into the royal works by his appointment as 'master mason and architect' to Windsor Castle, and in October 1632 he succeeded Cure as Master Mason to the Crown, while retaining the parallel office at Windsor. At Windsor he designed a banqueting house which was not built, but carried out other works for whose design his responsibility is less certain. Other recorded architectural commissions are listed below. They show Stone as a designer who had partly absorbed the new classicism of Inigo Jones, but without accepting its full discipline and without rejecting some of the mannerist or baroque features that he had learned in London and Amsterdam. The result was a vernacular classical architecture of considerable merit, of which regrettably little remains extant today.

Nicholas Stone was a member of the London Masons' Company. He was Warden in 1627 and 1630, and served as Master in 1633 and 1634. His career, like that of Inigo Jones, was no doubt disrupted by the Civil War, and according to Vertue he and Jones joined together to bury their joint stock of ready money, first in Scotland Yard and later in Lambeth Marsh. Stone died on 24 August 1647, and was buried in the church of St. Martin-in-the-Fields, where a monument (now destroyed, but illustrated in Bodleian, Gough Maps 22, f. 70[v]) commemorated his 'knowledge in Sculpture and Architecture'. His business was continued by his sons Henry and John (*q.v.*), his second son Nicholas having died in the same year as his father.

The two manuscripts already mentioned, an office notebook kept by Stone from 1614 to 1641 and an account-book for the years 1631 to 1642, are in Sir John Soane's Museum, together with sketch-books belonging to his sons Nicholas and Henry. A diary kept by the younger Nicholas on a visit to Italy in 1638–42 is in the British Library (Harleian MS. 4049, printed by Spiers, *op. cit. subt.*). For this visit see further D. Howarth, 'Samuel Boothouse and English Artistic Enterprise in Seventeenth-century Italy', *Italian Studies* xxxii, 1977.

[*The Note-Book and Account-Book of Nicholas Stone*, ed. W. L. Spiers, *Walpole Soc.* vii, 1918–19; D. Knoop & G. P. Jones, *The London Mason in the Seventeenth Century*, 1935, 22–4; Margaret Whinney, *Sculpture in Britain 1530–1830*, 1964, 24–31; *History of the King's Works* iii, 1975, 132–3, 330–1.]

CHILHAM CHURCH, KENT, chapel on south side of chancel, for Sir Dudley Digges, to contain monument by Stone to Lady Digges, 1631–2; dem. 1863 [*Note-Book*, 86].

CORNBURY HOUSE, OXON.; partly rebuilt for 1st Earl of Danby, 1632–3; west front rebuilt by Hugh May 1663–8; interior altered at various dates [*Note-Book*, 70] (*C. Life*, 22 Sept. 1950).

OXFORD, THE BOTANIC GARDEN, built and probably designed three gateways at expense of 1st Earl of Danby, 1632–33 [*Note–Book*, 70, 137; *V.C.H. Oxon.* iii, 49].

LONDON, GOLDSMITHS' HALL, FOSTER LANE, 1635–8; damaged in the Great Fire of 1666 and restored; dem. 1829 [John Newman, 'Nicholas Stone's Goldsmiths' Hall, *Arch. Hist.* xiv, 1971].

WINDSOR CASTLE, BERKS., built and perhaps designed gateway to park at E. end of terrace, 1636; dem. [*History of the King's Works* iii, 330–1]. Stone may well have designed Crane's Building in the Lower Ward, begun *c.*1636, completed 1658; dem. 1847 [*ibid.*, 332–3].

COPT HALL, ESSEX, work for 1st Earl of Middlesex, including new windows in the gallery, 1638–9; dem. 1748 [*Note-Book*, 120; John Newman, 'Copthall', in *The Country Seat*, ed. Colvin & Harris, 1970, 25–6].

MILCOTE HOUSE, WESTON-ON-AVON, WARWICKS., a 'plot' made for 1st Earl of Middlesex, 1638, whether executed or not unknown; house destroyed by fire 1644 [letter from Stone among Cranfield papers, Sackville MSS., Kent Record Office, *ex inf.* Mr. John Newman].

LONDON, TART HALL, WESTMINSTER, surveyor for enlargement of the house for Countess of Arundel, 1638–9; dem. 1720 [*Note-Book*, 125–6]. The Catholic priest George Gage (see *D.N.B.*) is described as 'the Architect of Tart-hall' in a letter from the painter Nicholas Herman to Lionel Cranfield cited by D. Howarth, *Lord*

Arundel and his Circle, 1985, 245 n. 38. The work may have been begun in 1636.

KIRBY HALL, NORTHANTS., remodelled N. front for Sir Christopher, later 1st Lord Hatton, 1638–40 [*Note-Book*, 119, 125, 128—9] (G. H. Chettle, *Kirby Hall*, revised by P. Leach, English Heritage 1984).

ATTRIBUTIONS

John Stoakes, who was related to Nicholas Stone, left a list of 'the most Eminentt Workes' that the latter 'did in England . . . Holland and Scotland' [*Note-Book*, 136–7]. This list of architectural works includes some, like the Banqueting House, where Stone was merely the executant, others, like Cornbury House and the Goldsmiths' Hall, that are confirmed by documentary evidence, and a residue, whose authenticity can be neither proved nor disproved. These last include the WATER-GATE at YORK HOUSE, LONDON (1626), which Stoakes says Stone both 'desined & built'; 'many curious pavements and other workes' within HOLYROODHOUSE, EDINBURGH, which according to Stoakes he 'desined & built' for King James I (cf. *Note-Book*, 43–4); and the 'Virgin Porch' at ST. MARY'S CHURCH, OXFORD (1637), which Stoakes claims Stone 'desind & built', although in fact it is known to have been built by John Jackson (*q.v.*).

Stoakes does not mention LINDSEY HOUSE, LINCOLN'S INN FIELDS, which Stone may well have designed, since it was built *c.*1640 by Sir David Cunningham, whom Stone described as his 'noble friend', and who in 1639 had commissioned him to make the monument to Sir Thomas Puckering in St. Mary's Church, Warwick (*Note-Book*, 76). Nor does he mention BALLS PARK, HERTS., built by Sir John Harrison in 1638–40 (*C. Life*, 20 April 1912), which shares several distinctive features with Stone's Goldsmiths' Hall, notably the irregularly spaced brackets supporting the cornice and the unusual rusticated basement windows on either side of the front doorway. Harrison, like most of Stone's clients, was a royalist.

STOWEY, JAMES, was, in partnership with Thomas Jones, active as a builder-architect in Exeter in the 1770s. In 1771–3 they were responsible for various improvements for Henry Fownes Luttrell at DUNSTER CASTLE, SOMERSET, and elsewhere, and James Stowey charged for 22 visits to supervise the work [Dunster (Luttrell) papers, Shelf 22/8]. Messrs. Stowey and Jones built THE GENERAL HOSPITAL at TAUNTON, SOMERSET, in 1772–5 [J. Toulmin, *History of Taunton*, 1791, 42]; THE SESSIONS HOUSE (now the Crown Court) in the CASTLE at EXETER, 1773–5 [Devon County Order Book, 1759–1776]; and a house (dem.) for the Master of the Exeter Grammar School in 1776 [Parliamentary Papers, *Report of the Charity Commissioners* vi, 1821, 86]. The designs for the Sessions House were submitted to James Wyatt in February 1773 and he made criticisms of the elevations which were adopted.

In 1775 plans and elevations both of the Sessions House and of the Hospital were exhibited at the Society of Artists in London by Philip Stowey of Exeter, who was presumably James Stowey's son or younger brother. He subsequently went out to Madras. Here he evidently made a sufficient fortune to retire to Devonshire, where he was living in the 1790s as a country gentleman and serving as a J. P. and Deputy Lieutenant of the County. Kenbury House, Exminster, which he built, presumably to his own designs, has been demolished, but its unusual plan is paralleled at Ashley House, nr. Tiverton, of which he may also have been the architect. Philip Stowey died at Kenbury on 3 September 1804, aged 62 [*Gent's Mag.* 1789, 577, 1793, 189, 1804, 889; will, P.C.C., 794 HESELTINE; information from Mr. Alastair Forsyth].

STOWEY, PHILIP, *see* STOWEY, JAMES.

STRACHAN, ROBERT, 'architect of Dundee', was, together with Alexander McGill of Edinburgh (*q.v.*), consulted by the Town Council of Aberdeen about the repair of the Bridge of Dee in 1717 [G. M. Fraser, *The Bridge of Dee*, Aberdeen 1913, 62]. C. Maclean and D. Walker state in *Dundee: An Illustrated Introduction*, 1984, 129, that Strachan and McGill were both involved in the design of THE HOUSE OF GRAY, nr. DUNDEE, in 1716.

STRAFFORD, EARL of, *see* WENTWORTH, WILLIAM.

STRAFFORD, GEORGE, of Wakefield, a carpenter by trade, was by 1814 referred to as an architect. He designed two small late Georgian churches in the West Riding at HIGH HOYLAND, 1803 and OSSETT, 1806, both later rebuilt [D. Linstrum, *West Yorkshire Architects and Architecture*, 1978, 385; Borthwick Institute, York, Faculty papers, for plan of High Hoyland church signed 'Geo. Strafford & Son, Wakefield'].

STRAHAN, JOHN (–*c.*1740), was an architect of Bristol. According to the first edition of John Wood's *Description of Bath*, 1749, 242, it was in 1725 that Strahan 'came to Bristol and by printed Bills, [offered] his services to the Publick as a land surveyor and Architect', but in the 1765 edition the date 1725 was omitted and there is reason to think that Strahan had been working in Bristol some years earlier. In 1727 he was employed by John Hobbs, a Bristol timber merchant who had interests in Bath, to lay out 'Some Meadow and Garden Ground on the West Side of the Body of the City of Bath into Streets for Building'. This new quarter consisted of Kingsmead and Beauford Squares, with Kingsmead, Monmouth and Avon Streets, and the New Quay. John Wood, who resented the intrusion of a Bristol architect, referred scathingly in his book (p. 341) to what he called 'the Piratical Architecture of . . . Mr. Strahan', and contrasted the lack of uniformity in the two new squares with the rigid control which he had himself imposed on the builders of Queen Square. Nevertheless, he admitted that 'Beaufort Buildings [i.e. Beauford Square] have a sort of Regularity to recommend them', and the surviving portions of the Kingsmead layout show that Strahan was by no means so negligent a surveyor as Wood made out.

According to Shiercliff's *Bristol and Hotwell Guide* of 1789, Strahan was 'the architect who built Redland-Court House, and many other capital mansions in and near Bristol'. REDLAND COURT was erected by John Cossins in about 1735, and Shiercliff's statement is confirmed by a contemporary elevation of the garden front in the British Library (*King's Maps* xiii, 77. 3*b*) which bears the inscription 'Delin. H. de Wilstar. Invented and Executed by I. Strahan Archit.' None of the 'other capital mansions' designed by Strahan has so far been identified by documentary evidence, but it was probably he who designed Nos. 68 and 70 PRINCE STREET for John Hobbs (his patron at Bath), and it is possible that he was the architect of FRAMPTON COURT, GLOS., for Richard Clutterbuck in 1731–3. Clutterbuck was an official of the Bristol Customs House, and there are similarities between the architecture of his house and that of Redland Court (*C. Life*, 8–15 Oct. 1927; N. Kingsley, *The Country Houses of Gloucestershire* ii, 1992, 144–8). Both exhibit a free mixture of baroque and Palladian elements in a manner that was characteristic of Bristol's early Georgian architecture. Another building in Strahan's style is the garden house (*c.*1730), originally at WOODCHESTER, GLOS., but rebuilt at BODNANT, DENBIGHSHIRE, in 1938 (*C. Life*, 14 Sept. 1961, 554), and a case has been made for the attribution to him of EARNSHILL, nr. HAMBRIDGE, SOMERSET, built for a Bristol merchant named Henry Combe and completed in 1731 [C. Hussey in *C. Life*, 13, 20 Oct. 1960].

In Bristol Strahan's only other recorded work appears to be the former organ gallery and case in ST. MARY REDCLIFFE CHURCH (1717), which is mentioned as his by Shiercliff. It is possible, however, that he was the architect of the REDLAND CHAPEL, which was built by John Cossins between 1740 and 1743 (measured drawings in *Details*, ed. R. R. Phillips, i, 1909, 193–6). William Halfpenny, under whose direction the chapel was completed, did not undertake the supervision of the building until May 1742, when the structure was already finished, and as Wood refers to Strahan as 'deceas'd' in the 1742 edition of his *Essay*, it is natural to suppose that it was his death in or about that year which led to Halfpenny's employment. The building accounts (Bristol Record Office, P/RG/T/1) do not refer to Halfpenny's predecessor by name, but accompanying them is the original 'Roff Computation what Expences the Materials and Workmanship (of) the Chappel will amount to', which may be in Strahan's hand. In the British Library there is an original design for the gallery and Cossins monuments, and a contemporary view of the interior dedicated to Cossins (*King's Maps* xiii, 95. *a–d*).

A bust of 'Mr. John Straughan Surveyor of Bristol' is included in a list of Rysbrack's works compiled by George Vertue in 1732.

[C. F. Dening, *The Eighteenth-Century Architecture of Bristol*, 1923; W. Ison, *The Georgian Buildings of Bath*, 1948, 33, 133–4, 2nd ed. 1980, 6, 121–4; W. Ison, *The Georgian Buildings of Bristol*, 1952, 45–6; C. H. & M. I. Collins Baker, *Life of James Brydges, Duke of Chandos*, 1949, 301; J. Charlton & D. M. Milton, *Redland 791 to 1800*, 1951; Walpole Soc., *Vertue Note Books* iii, 57; Michael Jenner in *Bristol: An Architectural History*, 1979, 125–40.]

STRAITON, GEORGE, 'architect', is said by A. Laing, *The Donean Tourist*, 1828, 47, to have built INVERERNAN, STRATHDON, ABERDEENSHIRE, for Alexander Forbes in 1762. The date 1764 appears on the E. elevation. BELLABEG is a similar house in the same parish dated 1765.

STRATFORD, FERDINANDO (1719–1766), was a civil engineer and surveyor who appears to have lived at Gloucester before moving to Bristol in about 1760. Before coming to Bristol he had been responsible for a highly commended scheme to make the R. Avon navigable from Bath to Chippenham. He died at Tidenham in Gloucestershire in April 1766, from ague contracted while investigating the possibility of making the R. Chelmer navigable from Chelmsford to Maldon in Essex. At Bristol he was one of the engineers who made designs for rebuilding the bridge and was involved in the ensuing controversy, publishing in 1760 *A Short Account of the Manner proposed for Rebuilding Bristol Bridge* (see also *Reports of the Late John Smeaton* i, 1812, 99–102). As an architect he is known to have made designs for BROMSBERROW HOUSE, GLOS. (dem.), for Robert Dobyns Yate in 1758–62 [estimate and account among Yate-Allen papers, Glos. Record Office], and to have designed the handsome classical MARKET HOUSE (now TOWN HALL) at NEWTOWNARDS in CO. DOWN, IRELAND, in 1765 [C. E. B. Brett, *Court Houses and Market Houses of the Province of Ulster*, Belfast 1973, 72–5]. There are estate maps and surveys by Stratford in the Public Record Office, Gloucestershire Record Office and National Library of Wales. [I. E. Gray, 'Ferdinando Stratford of Gloucestershire', *Trans. Bristol and Glos. Archaeological Soc.* lxvii, 1946–8, 412–15; W. Ison, *The Georgian Buildings of Bristol*, 1952, 46–7, 114–123; P. Eden, *Dictionary of Land Surveyors 1550–1850*, 1975–6; will, P.C.C. 246 TYNDALL.]

STRETTON, SAMUEL (1731–1811) and WILLIAM (1755–1828), were the principal builder-architects in Nottingham in the second half of the eighteenth century. They were descended from a family of minor gentry with property at Longdon in Staffordshire, but Samuel's father had 'dissipated' the estate, and in 1750 he was obliged to leave Longdon and establish himself as a builder at Lenton, on the outskirts of Nottingham. He married in 1754, and had two sons, William and Samuel. The elder son was for many years in partnership with his father and succeeded to his business on the latter's death in 1811. He had his yard in Cow Lane (now Clumber Street) and did a good deal of surveying for the Corporation. In 1790 he brought the first Welsh slates to Nottinghamshire by canal from Lord Penrhyn's quarries at Llandegai in North Wales.

The Strettons erected many industrial and commercial buildings in Nottingham, including Richard Arkwright's pioneer cotton-mill at Hockley (Goosegate) in 1769; the Navigation Inn, Wilford Street, 1787; Dawson's (later Beardmore's and Fellows's) silk-mill, High Pavement; Alderman Green's cotton-mill in Broad Marsh, 1792–3; and Green and Killingley's bleach-yard at Lenton, 1797, all or most of which have been demolished. They also designed the TOWN HALL and PRISON, 1789–91 (dem. 1894–5); and designed and built the CAVALRY BARRACKS in Castle Park, 1792–3 (dem. *c.*1870); the SEVEN ARCH BRIDGE on the Flood (now London) Road, 1796–7, and a RIDING SCHOOL in Castle Road for the Nottingham Troop of Yeomanry, 1798 (dem. 1926), and laid out RICKS GARDEN for building, drawing 'an elevation of houses proper to be built' there in 1791. In 1808–9 William Stretton designed ST. JAMES'S CHURCH, STANDARD HILL, Gothic (dem. 1935), and in 1811–12 he inserted the existing stucco vaulting into the tower of ST. MARY'S CHURCH. Elsewhere, Samuel Stretton built WILFORD HALL, NOTTS., to the designs of William Henderson (*q.v.*) in 1781, while William Stretton was responsible for the main park gateway of WOLLATON HALL in 1790, for partly rebuilding a house at REMPSTONE, NOTTS., for Gregory Williams in 1792, and for enlarging COLWICK RECTORY, NOTTS., in 1819 [Borthwick Institute, York, MGA 1819/2]. He also designed the castellated LENTON HALL, NOTTS. (now part of Hugh Stewart Hall, Nottingham University) for John Wright in 1804 [M. W. Barley & R. Cullen, *Nottingham Now*, Nottingham 1975, 38].

William Stretton was an able surveyor and cartographer who made a large-scale map of Nottingham which is now in the County Record Office (M 8630). He had antiquarian interests and made extensive notes on local antiquities which were privately printed by G. C. Robertson in 1910. He carried out excavations on the site of the Cluniac priory of Lenton, whose site he had acquired, and built the house known as 'Lenton Priory' (now enveloped by Nazareth House), where he died in 1828. He married in 1778 and called his children Stella, Sempronius, Salacia, Sabrina and Severus. [*The Stretton Manuscripts*, ed. G. C. Robertson, Nottingham 1910, with list of buildings built by the Strettons on pp. 180–1; *Records of the Corporation of Nottingham* vii, 1947; information from Mr. K. Brand.]

STRIBLING, ROBERT, was a builder at Exeter. He was apprenticed to a carpenter and joiner in 1727. He had a son Robert who was apprenticed to him in 1761. From 1765 onwards he held the post of carpenter and joiner to Exeter Cathedral. In 1773–5 he built the north side of BEDFORD CIRCUS, EXETER, as a speculation. The south side was not completed until 1826, and the whole was destroyed by bombing in 1942. [*Exeter Freemen*, ed. Rowe & Jackson, Devon and Cornwall Record Soc. 1973, 241, 290; A. Jenkins, *History of Exeter*, 1806, 323–4; information from the late W. G. Hoskins; A. E. Richardson &

C. L. Gill, *The Regional Architecture of the West of England*, 1924, 26–7.]

STRONACH, ALEXANDER, the name of at least three generations of master masons living in the parish of Tarbat, Easter Ross, and active from the mid-seventeenth century to the end of the eighteenth. They shared a conservative style, continental rather than Scottish in its affinities, characterized by strongly expressed turrets surmounted by stone cones or domes separated only by a slight string-course from the vertical wall. The Tolbooth at Tain is their most notable extant building. Documented works by them include the existing girnel on the quay at PORTMAHOMACK, ROSS & CROMARTY, 1699 [Cromartie papers in S.R.O., GD 305/1]; the rebuilding of the TOLBOOTH, TAIN, ROSS & CROMARTY, after its collapse in 1703, 'nearly completed' 1708 [W. Macgill, *Old Ross-shire and Scotland*, Inverness 1911, 130–2]; TARBAT MANSE, 1709, and a survey of TARBAT CHURCH, 1739, prior to repairs [A. Fraser & F. Munro, *Tarbat: Easter Ross*, 1988, 34, 36]; repairs to DORNOCH CASTLE, SUTHERLAND, 1720 [Macgill, *op. cit.*, 132]; the belfry of the LOVAT MAUSOLEUM at WARDLAW, KIRKHILL, INVERNESS-SHIRE, 1722 [inscription]; work at NEW TARBAT HOUSE, 1728; dem. 1795 [references in S.R.O., GD 305]; and the supervision of the repair of the roof of the great hall of DARNAWAY CASTLE, MORAYSHIRE, 1795 [Moray muniments, box 18, vol. 6, no. 701]. The upper part of the round tower of KILMUIR EASTER CHURCH, ROSS & CROMARTY, dated 1634, is an early example of the type of turret associated with the Stronachs. [Monica Clough, *Two Houses*, Aberdeen 1990, 73, 75, 79, 90, 96, and further information from Mrs. Clough, to whom all references are due.]

STRONG was the name of a family of master masons active throughout the seventeenth and early eighteenth centuries, and well known for the important buildings which they executed to the designs of Wren, Vanbrugh, Hawksmoor and other architects. The foundation of the family fortunes was laid in the freestone quarries at Little Barrington in Gloucestershire and Taynton in Oxfordshire, which were acquired by TIMOTHY STRONG early in the seventeenth century. He came from Wiltshire but settled at Little Barrington, where, according to his grandson's account of the family, printed by Clutterbuck in his *History of Hertfordshire*, 'he had several apprentices, and kept several masons and labourers employed in those quarries, to serve the Country with what they wanted in the way of trade.' In 1632–3 he largely rebuilt CORNBURY HOUSE, OXON., for Henry Danvers, Earl of Danby, to the designs of Nicholas Stone. In 1634 he and his sons were working on the CANTERBURY QUADRANGLE at ST. JOHN'S COLLEGE, OXFORD, having been 'fecht out of my Lord Danvers's work' by the promise of 'extraordinary rates' which the College 'yeilded to give them but concealed from the other workemen' [St. John's College Muniments lxii, 13]. Timothy Strong died in 1635 or 1636, leaving the quarries to his only son, Valentine Strong, who soon afterwards moved to Taynton.

According to Clutterbuck's manuscript, VALENTINE STRONG (d. 1662) enlarged SHERBORNE HOUSE, GLOS., for John Dutton in 1651–3 (cf. letter from Mark Girouard in *C. Life*, 25 Oct. 1956, 954); and in 1656 he contracted to build LOWER SLAUGHTER MANOR-HOUSE, GLOS., for Richard Whitmore, 'according to one moddell or plattforme by him lately received from the said Mr. Whitmore and according to such moulds as hee hath given to the said Mr. Whitmore concerning the same' [Whitmore papers in Gloucestershire C.R.O., 8 (4/1)]. His last work was at FAIRFORD, where he began to build a new manor-house for Andrew Barker in 1661, but died in 1662 before it was finished.[1] He was buried at Fairford, where he is commemorated by a rhyming epitaph.

Valentine Strong married Anne Margetts of Charlbury in 1633. By her he had six sons and five daughters. All his sons were bred to the mason's trade and THOMAS STRONG (*c.*1634–81), the eldest, carried on the family business as a mason and quarry-owner. At the time of his father's death he had been working at LONGLEAT HOUSE, WILTS., where various alterations and improvements were being carried out by Sir James Thynne,[2] and he completed the unfinished house at Fairford for Andrew Barker. In about 1663 he built the stables at CORNBURY HOUSE, OXON., which had been designed by Hugh May for the Earl of Clarendon, and in 1665–6 he built the east

[1] His will, dated 3 Oct. 1661, and proved 5 Nov. 1662, is P.C.C. 148 LAUD. But according to the inscription on his tomb in Fairford churchyard he died on 26 Dec. 1662.

[2] According to a MS. account of Longleat written by the 1st Lord Weymouth (Longleat archives, Box 179B), Sir James Thynne 'made the Stone Terras from the outward Gate to the Hall Door, and made the Door by the direction of Sr. Chr. Wren, now taken away and placed at the School House in Warminster. He also new made the Great Stairs, paved the Hall and passages with stone . . . finished the Blew Parlor and Drawing roome ioyning to it . . . walled and planted the old Kitchin Garden and made the door out of the Hall into the Greate Parlor.'

THE STRONG FAMILY

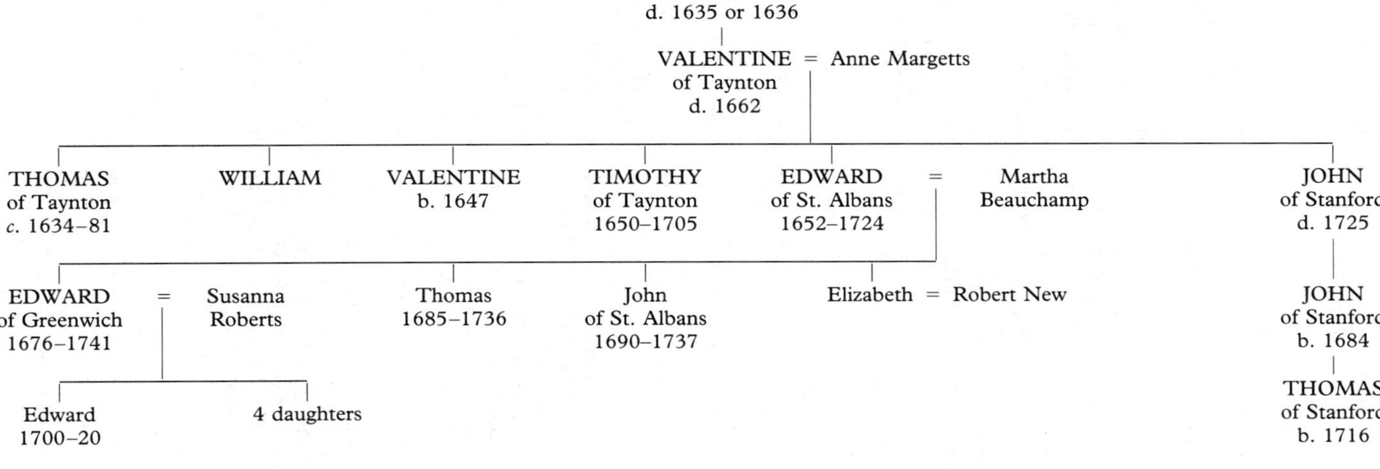

front to the designs of the same architect. At the same time he was engaged in building the first part of the new quadrangle at TRINITY COLLEGE, OXFORD, designed by Wren and completed in 1668.

Meanwhile, the Great Fire of London had attracted him to the capital, where he not only obtained several important contracts but also sold large quantities of stone to other masons. In 1670, taking advantage of the Act for rebuilding the City, which permitted 'foreign' artificers to take up their freedom, Strong was made free of the Masons' Company and of the City by redemption. Besides undertaking to build three of the City churches, he became one of the principal contractors for St. Paul's Cathedral when work began in 1675, laying the foundation-stone 'with his own hands' on 21 June. In 1678 he was employing thirty-five men on the site. At the same time he was building 'a front of stone betwixt the wings of Lord Craven's house at Hampstead Marshall, in Berkshire'. He died unmarried in the summer of 1681, leaving everything to his younger brother Edward, whom he made his sole executor [P.C.C. 99 NORTH].

EDWARD STRONG (1652–1724), who now took over his brother's contracts, had probably learned the mason's trade in the family quarries at Taynton and Little Barrington. He had been apprenticed to his brother on 2 January 1671/2, and no doubt came to London in order to assist him. He was made free of the Masons' Company in April 1680, became a Warden in 1694, and Master in 1696. He completed the churches which his brother had begun and was himself responsible for the masonry of several more, representing contracts amounting to over £11,000. At the same time he was working at WINCHESTER PALACE, where, according to his own account, he 'had all the designs of all the masons' work committed to his care, by Sir Christopher Wren, the surveyor'. But the main work of his London career was the building of ST. PAUL'S CATHEDRAL, in which he took a prominent part, supplying large quantities of 'Burford' stone, and contracting for the east end, the north portico, the north side of the nave, and the north-west quarter of the dome. In 1695 he was employing sixty-five masons at St. Paul's, more than twice the number employed by his fellow-contractors, Kempster and Beauchamp. In 1694 he 'performed all the stone work of Sir John Morden's Hospital on Blackheath', i.e. MORDEN COLLEGE, and in 1696 he took the first mason's contract for the building of GREENWICH HOSPITAL. For this he was in partnership with Thomas Hill, but in the performance of succeeding contracts he was associated first with Ephraim Beauchamp, and afterwards with his son, Edward Strong, junior. Their MS. Day Book for this work, covering the years 1699 to 1708, is in the Guildhall Library (MS. 233). In 1705 Edward Strong and his son took the chief mason's contract at BLENHEIM PALACE, OXON., where they erected the whole of the main pile. After the dispute between Vanbrugh and the Duchess of Marlborough had brought the works to a standstill in 1712, the Strongs had recourse to litigation in order to recover the considerable sums of money owing to them (see David Green, *Blenheim Palace*, 1951, and *Cal. Treas. Papers 1714–19*, 15, 63, 323).

Edward Strong made the most of his opportunities as a master mason and quarry-owner at a time when unprecedented building activity offered great rewards to the master builder with capital and experience. With the fortune which he had made in London, he established himself as a landowner, not in his native Cotswolds, but in the neighbourhood of St. Albans. In 1714 he bought the manor of Hyde at Abbot's Langley, and in 1716 that of Herons at Wheathampstead. He lived at St. Albans in the house known as New Barnes, where he died on 8 February 1723/4, aged 71. He was buried in St. Peter's Church, where there is a monument with a portrait bust. The epitaph is given in Cussans's *Hertfordshire*, 1881, 299–301, and in *Builder* xxii, 1864, 700. His will is P.C.C. 45 BOLTON. A portrait of Strong, formerly at Shaloch, Aberdeenshire (*N. and Q.* 7th ser. i, 1886, 228), was exhibited at the Wren Tercentenary Exhibition at St. Paul's Cathedral in 1932. It now belongs to the United Grand Lodge of England. Ivy House, No. 107 St. Peter's Street and a house in the Market Place on the site of the former north gateway to the abbey precinct are said to have been built by Strong, the former as his own residence [*V.C.H. Herts.* ii, 473; J. C. & C. A. Buckler, *History of the Abbey Church of St. Albans*, 1847, 165]. He married Martha, sister of Ephraim Beauchamp, and left three sons, Edward Strong, junior, who carried on the business, Thomas, who died in 1736, and John, who sold the Wheathampstead estate in 1726 and died at St. Albans in 1737.

EDWARD STRONG, junior (1676–1741), was apprenticed to his father in 1691, and made free of the Masons' Company in October 1698. He was Warden in 1712 and 1715, and Master in 1718. He lived at Greenwich, where he was engaged in building the Hospital for many years. In 1702 he contracted to build the NORTH GATE of ST. BARTHOLOMEW'S HOSPITAL, SMITHFIELD, 'according to the model drawn by the said Edward Strong and approved of by the

Governors . . . of this Hospital for the sum of £550'. This, the existing gateway to Smithfield, was completed in 1703 [Gweneth Whitteridge, 'The Henry VIII Gateway into Smithfield', *St. Bartholomew's Hospital Jnl.* 1949]. At ST. PAUL'S Strong assisted his father in building the lantern in 1706–8, and subsequently laid the marble pavement beneath the dome and transepts. He also built the 'lanterns' or spires of CHRISTCHURCH, NEWGATE STREET, ST. VEDAST, FOSTER LANE, ST. STEPHEN, WALBROOK, ST. MICHAEL, COLLEGE HILL, and ST. JAMES, GARLICKHYTHE, and the steeple of ST. MICHAEL, CORNHILL (completed 1722). With Edward Tufnell as partner, he built the churches of ST. JOHN, WESTMINSTER (1713–28), ST. PAUL, DEPTFORD (1713–30), ST. GEORGE IN THE EAST (1714–23), ST. ANNE, LIMEHOUSE (1714–24), and ST. GEORGE, BLOOMSBURY (1716–30). The 'Book of Entry for Masons work' kept by Strong and Tufnell while engaged on these five churches is preserved in the R.I.B.A. Library. Strong was also for a time in partnership with Christopher Cass and Andrews Jelfe, an arrangement which was terminated on 31 December 1728, at Strong's desire (B. L., Stowe MS. 412, no. 77).

Private houses with which Strong is known to have been concerned were William Draper's house at ADDISCOMBE in SURREY, which he built to the designs of an unknown architect in 1702–3; MARLBOROUGH HOUSE, LONDON; and CANNONS HOUSE, MIDDLESEX, of which he built the north front in 1715. In the summer of 1711 he accompanied Sir James Thornhill and his brother Thomas on a visit to Holland. The diary kept by Thornhill is now in the British Library (Add. MS. 34788).[1]

In 1699 he married Susanna, daughter of Joseph Roberts, Serjeant Plumber, by whom he had a son Edward, who died of smallpox at the age of 20, and four daughters, the eldest of whom married Sir John Strange, Master of the Rolls. Strong died on 10 October 1741, leaving his property in Hertfordshire and elsewhere[2] to be divided among his daughters [P.C.C. 284 SPURWAY]. A group portrait of Strong and his family by Charles Philips, signed and dated 1732, is in the Metropolitan Museum at New York.

In about 1720 a Thomas Strong, presumably Edward's younger brother, was involved in the building of ARDINGTON HOUSE, BERKS., for Edward Clarke, and either he or his brother presumably designed this substantial baroque mansion [G. Jackson-Stops in *C. Life*, 15 Oct. 1981]. Other members of the family were by this time established in Berkshire at Stanton-in-the-Vale, where Valentine Strong's fourth and sixth sons, Timothy and John, are mentioned as masons in some late seventeenth-century documents formerly belonging to the Aston family, who were lords of a moiety of the manor at that time.[1] John, like his father, had many children, and the family continued to live and work in Stanford throughout the eighteenth century. As late as 1866, it was remembered that some of the best of the tombstones in the churchyard were 'the workmanship of a family of the name of Strong, who for many years were masons at Stanford, and who were famous in the country round' [L. G. Maine, *A Berkshire Village, its History and Antiquities*, 1866, 54]. John Strong lived in the neighbouring village of Shellingford, but was buried at Stanford when he died in August 1725 [Archdeaconry Court of Berkshire, Register 21, f. 285].

John Strong's eldest son John was baptized at Stanford on 26 October 1684. In January 1733 he was consulted in connection with the building of the new COUNCIL CHAMBER at ABINGDON, for there is a payment of 6 guineas 'to Mr. John Stevens and Mr. John Strong per Bill', and the former is known to have made designs for the 'ornaments' which are referred to in the builders' contract. Either John or his father rebuilt the tower of LONGCOT CHURCH, BERKS., in 1722, as appears by a note on the flyleaf of the Shrivenham Parish Register[2] to the effect that after the old tower had fallen in 1721 it was result by 'Strong of Standford, who not only finished the Tower . . . , but added the flower pots. He was a reputable Mason, and built Wadley House for Mr. Charles Pye.' The churchwardens' accounts of UFFINGTON, BERKS., show that 'Mr. Strong' also rebuilt the octagonal central tower of that church after its destruction by lightning in December 1740. The present battlements and pinnacles were substituted in the nineteenth century for Strong's parapet with classical ornaments at the angles. The house at WADLEY, nr. SHRIVENHAM, mentioned above, was rebuilt by Charles Pye in 1768, and must have been the work of a later member of the family, perhaps of Thomas, son of John Strong, junior, who was born on 19 March

[1] Some extracts from it were printed in the *Proceedings of the Suffolk Institute of Archaeology* xiii, 1907–9, 33–43.

[2] His London property included six houses in Bartlett's Buildings (parish of St. Andrew's, Holborn) and others in Wellclose Square. Some papers relating to his estate are in the Bodleian library, MS. Top. Herts. c. 2.

[1] I owe this information to Dr. J. H. Harvey.

[2] Based on 'the books containing the accounts of the Churchwardens of Longcote since the year 1721'. These no longer exist.

1715/16, and repaired Stanford Church more than once between 1750 and 1775. In 1766 'Mr. Strong' was working at BECKETT PARK, BERKS., for Lord Barrington under Sanderson Miller's direction [Sanderson Miller's correspondence in Warwick Record Office, Letters 777, 842–3]. The baptisms and burials of members of the family continue to occur in the parish registers until the end of the century, and as late as 1814–16 a Thomas Strong was employed to carry out repairs to COLESHILL HOUSE, BERKS., under D. A. Alexander.

Other branches of the family were established at Box in Wiltshire, where a Thomas Strong owned one of the quarries in the early nineteenth century, and at Warminster in the same county, where three generations of the family were in business as masons from 1830 until the death of Egerton Strong at the age of 83 in August 1964.

[R. Clutterbuck, *History of Hertfordshire* i, 1815, 167; D. Knoop & G. P. Jones, *The London Mason in the Seventeenth Century*, 1935, 43–5; transcript of Taynton Parish Registers in Bodleian Library, MS. Top. Oxon. c. 526; *V.C.H. Herts.* ii, 302, 324, 412, 420, 473; W. H. Blacker, *Gloucestershire Notes and Queries* ii, 1884, 262–4, iii, 1885–7, 365; *Wren Soc.* xx, 218–20; *A.P.S.D.*; *Warminster Jnl.* 21 Aug. 1964 (obituary of Egerton Strong); B. J. Smith, 'A Cotswold Quarrying Agreement', *Post-Medieval Archaeology* viii, 1974, 101–4.]

STUART, CHARLES, an architect of Darnaway, nr. Forres, designed the castellated NELSON MONUMENT at FORRES, MORAYSHIRE, 1806. A rival design by Richard Crichton was rejected [R. Douglas, *Annals of Forres*, Elgin 1934, 313, 318).

STUART, JAMES (1713–1788), the son of a Scottish mariner, was born in Creed Lane, Ludgate Street, in 1713. As a boy he displayed a considerable talent for drawing, and when his father died, leaving his mother and the other children without means of support, Stuart obtained employment with Lewis Goupy, the well-known fan-painter. It may have been Goupy who first aroused Stuart's interest in classical antiquity, for George Vertue says that Lord Burlington engaged Goupy to accompany him on his Grand Tour, and many of his fans were decorated with views of classical buildings. While working for Goupy, Stuart studied mathematics, geometry and anatomy to good effect, becoming a skilful draughtsman as well as a competent painter in gouache and water-colours. He also taught himself Latin and Greek, being led to study the former language 'by the desire of understanding what was written under prints published after pictures of the ancient masters'. After his mother's death, his brother and sister being by now in employment, Stuart was able to realize a long-cherished plan to visit Rome, in order to pursue his studies in art. He set out in 1742, travelling most of the way on foot, and earning money as opportunity offered.[1] Having arrived in Rome, he appears to have acquired a considerable reputation as a judge of pictures, and it is very probable that he supported himself by acting as *cicerone* to English visitors. In 1748 he accompanied Gavin Hamilton, Matthew Brettingham and Nicholas Revett on an expedition to Naples, in the course of which the project of visiting Athens was first discussed. He also occupied himself by making drawings of the obelisk found in the Campus Martius, which were published by Bandini in his treatise *De Obelisco Caesaris Augusti* (Rome 1750). Appended to the book was an account of the obelisk in the form of a letter addressed by Stuart to Charles Wentworth, Earl of Malton (afterwards Marquess of Rockingham).

It was in 1748 that Stuart and Revett issued their 'Proposals for publishing an Accurate Description of the Antiquities of Athens'. Their scheme was well received by the English dilettanti then in Rome, some of whom, including the Earl of Malton, the Earl of Charlemont, James Dawkins and Robert Wood, agreed to finance their projected expedition. They left Rome in 1750, but were delayed for some months in Venice. The British Resident there was Sir James Gray, a prominent member of the Society of Dilettanti, who procured their election to that body in 1751. His brother, Colonel George Gray, secretary and treasurer to the Society, published the *Proposals* in London, while Consul Smith issued a further version in Venice in 1753. On 19 January 1751 Stuart and Revett embarked for Greece, arriving at Athens on 18 March. Here they enjoyed the protection of Sir James Porter, Ambassador at Constantinople, who was a member of the Dilettanti Society, and experienced comparatively little difficulty in making their survey of the antiquities, one person even pulling down a house to enable them to get a better view of the Tower of the Winds. There was, however, an awkward occasion when Stuart was 'provoked' to knock down the British consul, a Greek who was also his landlord, and he narrowly avoided murder at the hands of some Turks when in the autumn of 1753 he set out

[1] He apparently acted as an 'itinerant Fan-painter' (see 'Memoirs of Thomas Jones', *Walpole Soc.* xxxii, 1946–8, 74).

for Constantinople to obtain a renewal of the firman granted by the Sultan. Escaping with difficulty he made his way to the coast and rejoined Revett at Salonika. After visiting the Greek archipelago, they returned to England early in 1755, in order to prepare their drawings for publication. For various reasons they had left the major buildings on the Acropolis to the last, and in the end left Athens without having properly surveyed them. They were consequently obliged to alter the advertised table of contents, which had given priority to the Acropolis, and to illustrate smaller buildings, such as the Temple of the Winds, in the first volume, reserving the major temples for a second volume which was not in fact to be published until 1789. The first volume appeared in 1762 as *The Antiquities of Athens measured and delineated by James Stuart, F.R.S. and F.S.A., and Nicholas Revett, Painters and Architects*, with a dedication to the King. It constituted the first accurate survey of Greek classical remains and was later to be the principal source-book of the Greek Revival in Britain. Though immediately recognized as a major work of architectural scholarship, its effect on contemporary architecture was limited, for neither Stuart nor Revett saw themselves as leaders of an architectural revolution, and in so far as they were employed as architects, it was as designers of garden buildings and elegant interiors rather than of public buildings or major country houses.

The delay over the publication of the first volume was due partly to Stuart's natural dilatoriness and partly to his decision to revise the text at the last moment in order to expose the errors in Le Roy's rival publication, *Les Ruines des plus beaux Monuments de la Grèce*, published in 1758. This contributed to disagreements between Stuart and his fellow-author, which resulted in Stuart buying out Revett's financial interest in the book before its publication, although his name still appeared on the title-page. It was Revett, however, who had been responsible for all the measured drawings which gave the *Antiquities* its unique importance as the first accurate survey of the Athenian buildings, and made its publication a major event in the history of classical archaeology. Stuart's contribution was limited to the text and to the general topographical views which were engraved from his original gouache drawings, many of which are now in the R.I.B.A. Collection.

But it was Stuart whom the *Antiquities* of Athens made famous, and for the rest of his life he had as much employment as a painter and architect as he chose to accept. He was elected a Fellow of the Royal Society and of the Society of Antiquaries, and remained a prominent member of the Society of Dilettanti. In 1763 he was appointed painter to the Society in succession to George Knapton, but, failing to fulfil his statutory duties by painting portraits of its members, he was superseded by Reynolds in 1768. In 1758 he became surveyor of Greenwich Hospital, a post worth £200 a year which he owed to the influence of his patron Lord Anson, and in 1764 he succeeded Hogarth as Sergeant Painter in the Office of Works. The latter post was abolished in 1782, but he retained the former until his death in 1788.

Stuart exhibited for some years with the Free Society of Artists, showing mainly the watercolour drawings of Athens in which he seems to have done something of a trade. He also executed a certain amount of decorative painting in the houses of his patrons (e.g. the 'Zephyrs and Zephirettes' in Mrs. Montagu's bedroom at Sandleford Priory) and 'was frequently applied to when anything particularly elegant was required', such as a commemorative medal or a monument.[1] He was constantly consulted by Josiah Wedgwood and was regarded as an arbiter of taste by all except those who shared Sir William Chambers's contempt for the 'Gusto Greco'.

As an architect Stuart failed to make the most of his opportunities. The commissions which he received seem (as Miss Lawrence has said) 'to have been executed with reluctance, and, in some cases, to have been completed by other hands'. Mrs. Montagu, who employed him to build 22 Portman Square, 'on account of his disinterestedness and contempt of money', complained bitterly of his failure to deliver designs to the workmen, of his unreliability, and of his carelessness over accounts. Sir Sampson Gideon, she said, had been 'obliged to take many precautions to prevent being imposed on by the workmen whose bills he assented to', and at Greenwich it is clear from surviving correspondence that his conduct was equally unsatisfactory. His architectural practice was, in consequence, very limited, and he owed his principal com-

[1] The latter were chiefly executed by Peter Scheemakers and his son Thomas, who exhibited several 'models from the designs of Mr. Stuart' at the Free Society of Artists between 1765 and 1783. Among the medals designed by Stuart was one to celebrate the birth of the Prince of Wales in 1762 [Walpole, *Anecdotes of Painting* v, ed. Hilles & Daghlian, 1937, 109], and the medal awarded by the Royal Society of Arts from 1757 until 1805 [H. T. Wood, *A History of the Royal Society of Arts*, 1913, 316]. He also designed the frontispieces to James Harris's *Hermes* (2nd ed. 1765) and *Philosophical Arrangements* (1775).

missions almost entirely to members of the Dilettanti Society and their friends. Comfortably circumstanced (at least in his latter days),[1] he preferred an easy and convivial life to the exacting routine of a busy architect's office. The success of the brothers Adam in popularizing their architectural innovations is the measure of Stuart and Revett's failure to do the same, and suggests that what they lacked was 'the capacity rather than the opportunity to be leaders of fashion'. Nevertheless, Stuart has an important place in the history of architectural taste. The temples which he designed at Hagley in 1758 and at Shugborough in the 1760s were the first buildings in Europe in which the Greek orders were used. Features of Greek derivation also appeared in his designs for interior decoration and furniture, but his vocabulary 'was eclectic, including Greek and Palmyran ornament, as well as Ancient and Renaissance Roman elements. Accurate archaeological details from different periods were often combined in a single room to create interiors strong in Antique overtones but avoiding any feeling of pedantic reconstruction' (Worsley).

It was largely Stuart's own indolence which delayed for twenty-six years the appearance of the second volume of the *Antiquities*. It was almost ready for the press when its appearance was further postponed by its author's sudden death at his house in Leicester Square on 2 February 1788. He was buried in the crypt of the church of St. Martin-in-the-Fields. Stuart was twice married, his first wife being his house-keeper, by whom he had a son who died in infancy. By his second wife, whom he married late in life, he had five children, three of whom survived him.

The second volume of the *Antiquities of Athens* was published by Stuart's widow with the help of William Newton, his assistant and former Clerk of Works at Greenwich Hospital. It bore the date 1787 but was not actually published until 1789. The third volume, for which he left the completed drawings, appeared in 1795 under the editorship of Willey Reveley. In 1816 a further volume of miscellaneous papers and drawings by Stuart and Revett was issued by Josiah Taylor, the architectural publisher, with a memoir of its authors by Joseph Woods. A supplementary volume was published by C. R. Cockerell and others in 1830. An edition of the first three volumes on a reduced scale was published in 1825–7, and there were others in 1837, 1841, 1849 and 1858. Stuart was long believed to have been the author of a well-known pamphlet entitled *Critical Observations on the Buildings and Improvements of London*, published anonymously in 1771, but an inscribed copy suggests that it was in fact written by 'John Stewart', probably John Stewart, F.R.S., M.P. (d. 1781).

Miniature portraits of Stuart and his second wife were presented to the National Portrait Gallery in 1858 by his son. An engraved portrait serves as the title-page of an anonymous work entitled *Rudiments of Ancient Architecture*, published by I. & J. Taylor (2nd ed. 1794). A self-portrait of Stuart as a youth is among his drawings in the R.I.B.A. Collection and is illustrated by Watkin. Portraits by J. Basire, Sir J. Reynolds (etched by S. W. Reynolds) and Probon (engraved by W. C. Edwards) are mentioned by E. B. Jupp in his *Catalogue of Drawings illustrating the Catalogues of the Society of Artists*, 1871, 7. A Wedgwood portrait medallion is reproduced by Eliza Meteyard in her *Life of Josiah Wedgwood* ii, 1866, 220.

Twenty of Stuart's gouache drawings for the *Antiquities of Athens* are in the R.I.B.A. Collection, together with a sketch-book containing notes on Italian painters and sketches of buildings in Venice, Verona, etc. (see the *Catalogue*), and further drawings were acquired in 1977 (described by John Harris in *Arch. Hist.* 22, 1979). Some fine decorative designs in the Pierpont Morgan Library are illustrated by John Harris in his *Catalogue of British Drawings for Architecture, etc., in American Collections*, 1971, 227–31. A sketch-book (of coins, etc.) kept in Greece in 1751–3 was sold at Sotheby's on 17 December 1981, lot 158. Stuart's original drawings of monuments in Lydia were Phillipps MS. 16099.

[Obituaries in *Gent's Mag.* 1788 (i), 95–6, 181, 216–8, 1809 (ii), 596–7; and in *European Mag.* xiii, 1788, 68, 143, 284; A. Caldwell, *An Account of the Extraordinary Escape of James Stuart*, 1804 (a broadsheet, also printed in *European Mag.* xlvi, 1804, 369); memoir prefixed to vol. iv of the *Antiquities of Athens*, 1816; J. Mulvany, *Life of James Gandon*, 1846, 195–9; Eliza Meteyard, *Life of Josiah Wedgwood* ii, 1866, 219–26; J. T. Smith, *Nollekens and his Times* (World's Classics ed.), 15–16, 27; *Original Letters of Eminent Literary Men*, ed. Ellis, Camden Soc. 1843, 379–89 (for the 'Prospectus' of 1751); B.L., Add. MSS. 22152 (papers used in the preparation of vol. iv of the *Antiquities*), 27576 (memoir written by his son, James Stuart, R.N.); *A.P.S.D.*; *D.N.B.*; *Notes and Queries*, 2nd ser. ii, 80, 100, xi, 163, 3rd ser. ii, 275; Lesley

[1] 'Athens Stuart, unexpectedly to most people, has died possessed of much property, chiefly on mortgage on new buildings in Marybone' reported *The World* newspaper (22 Feb. 1788).

Lawrence, 'Stuart and Revett: their Literary and Architectural Careers', *Jnl. Warburg Institute* ii, 1938–9; John Harris, 'Early Neo-Classical Furniture', *Jnl. Furniture History Soc.* ii, 1966; Dora Wiebenson, *Sources of Greek Revival Architecture*, 1969; E. Croft-Murray, *Decorative Painting in England* ii, 1970, 283–5; Nicholas Goodison, 'Mr. Stuart's Tripod', *Burlington Mag.* cxiv, 1972, 695–704; David Watkin, *Athenian Stuart*, 1982; Eileen Harris, *British Architectural Books and Writers, 1556—1785*, 1990, 439–50; Martin Hopkinson, 'A Portrait by James 'Athenian' Stuart', *Burlington Mag.* Nov. 1990; Giles Worsley in *C. Life*, 14 May 1992.]

WENTWORTH WOODHOUSE, YORKS. (W.R.), internal decoration for 2nd Marquess of Rockingham, *c.*1755 onwards. A letter from Stuart to the Marquess [Sheffield City Library, Wentworth Woodhouse Muniments R1.70, 28 Sept. 1755] shows that he was employed here as early as 1755. Arthur Young [*Six Months Tour through the North of England* i, 1770, 281] mentions the panels over the niches in the hall as Stuart's work, and Horace Walpole ['Visits to Country Seats', *Walpole Soc.* xvi, 71] saw a chimney-piece by Stuart in 1772 (*C. Life*, 4 Oct. 1924).

WESTMINSTER SCHOOL, designed the scenery for the Latin play 1758, last used 1808 [*A Naval Career: the Life of Admiral John Markham*, 1883, 14].

HAGLEY PARK, WORCS., Greek Doric temple for the 1st Lord Lyttelton, 1759 [Stuart's design is mentioned by Lord Lyttelton in a letter to Mrs. Montagu dated Oct. 1758, quoted by A. T. Bolton in *C. Life*, 16 Oct. 1915, 528]

LONDON, SPENCER HOUSE, GREEN PARK, designed interiors of rooms on first floor for 1st Earl Spencer, 1759–65 [Earl Spencer in *C. Life*, 30 Oct., 6 Nov. 1926; M. Jourdain, 'Furniture designed by James Stuart at Althorp', *C. Life*, 24 Aug. 1935; E. Croft-Murray, 'A Drawing by Athenian Stuart for the Painted Room at Spencer House', *British Museum Quarterly* xxi, 1957, 14–15].

LONDON, HOLDERNESSE (later LONDONDERRY) HOUSE, HERTFORD STREET, was 'largely decorated and perhaps completely designed' by Stuart for 4th Earl of Holdernesse, *c.*1760–5; reconstructed by Benjamin Wyatt 1825–8; dem. *c.*1964 [Arthur Oswald in *C. Life*, 10 July 1937; Lesley Lawrence, *Jnl. of Warburg Institute* ii, 1938–9, 134, 139]. The possibility that Stuart also worked for the Earl of Holdernesse at HORNBY CASTLE, YORKS. (N.R.) is discussed by G. Worsley in *C. Life*, 29 June, 1989.

SION HILL, ISLEWORTH, MIDDLESEX, chimney-piece in drawing-room and probably other internal work for 4th Earl of Holdernesse, *c.*1760 [G. Worsley in *C. Life*, 4 Oct. 1990, correspondence].

NUNEHAM PARK, OXON., chimney-piece in dining-room and ceiling of drawing-room for 1st Earl Harcourt, *c.*1760–4. The church, which forms an important feature in the landscaped park, was built in 1764, 'at the expense of Simon, Earl Harcourt, after a design of his own, slightly corrected by Stuart' [J. N. Brewer, *Beauties of England & Wales* xii (2), 1813, 273, 275, 278–9] (*C. Life*, 7–14 Nov. 1941, 3–10 Jan. 1985).

GREENWICH HOSPITAL, THE INFIRMARY (now Dreadnought Hospital), 1763–4; damaged by fire 1811 [drawings in National Maritime Museum Library]; alterations to GOVERNOR'S APARTMENT, 1765–9 [G. Worsley in *C. Life*, 14 May 1992, 101–2].

LONDON, LICHFIELD HOUSE, No. 15 ST. JAMES'S SQUARE, for Thomas Anson, 1764–6; alterations by Samuel Wyatt 1791–4 [*Survey of London* xxix, 142–53 and plates].

SHUGBOROUGH, STAFFS., buildings in the park for Thomas Anson, including the TRIUMPHAL ARCH (a copy of the 'Arch of Hadrian' at Athens), *c.*1761–5; the TOWER OF THE WINDS, *c.*1764–5; the GREENHOUSE, *c.*1763–4, dem. *c.*1800; the LANTHORN OF DEMOSTHENES (i.e. a copy of the 'Monument of Lysicrates'), 1764–71. The last was surmounted by a tripod and bowl, the former made at Soho and the latter at Etruria. Stuart appears also to have been responsible for some internal alterations to the house, now no longer recognizable [J. P. Neale, *Views of Seats*, 1st ser. iii, 1820; E. Meteyard, *Life of Wedgwood* ii, 1866, 222–3; Philip Yorke's Journal (1763) in *Beds. Hist. Rec. Soc.* xlvii, 1968, 161; C. Hussey in *C. Life*, 25 Feb., 4–11 March, 15–22 April 1954; J. M. Robinson, *Shugborough*, National Trust 1989].

attributed: RATHFARNHAM CASTLE, CO. DUBLIN, IRELAND, internal decoration, including lower gallery, for Henry Loftus, 1st Earl of Ely, 1769 [E. McParland in *C. Life*, 9 Sept. 1982, 737].

WINDSOR CASTLE, BERKSHIRE, ST. GEORGE'S CHAPEL, altar-piece 'of Grecian architecture', 1771; removed 1786 [W.H. St. J. Hope, *Windsor Castle* ii, 1913, 426]. An alternative Gothic design by Stuart is preserved (D. Watkin, *Athenian Stuart*, fig. 80).

BELVEDERE, nr. ERITH, KENT, rebuilt for Sir Sampson Gideon, cr. Lord Eardley, *c.*1775; dem. *c.*1960 [Lesley Lawrence, *Jnl. Warburg Institute* ii, 1938–9, 142].

WIMPOLE HALL, CAMBS., the 'PROSPECT HOUSE' for 2nd Earl of Hardwicke, 1775; remodelled by H. Repton *c.*1802; dem. [engraving in B.L., *King's Maps* viii, 83g, published 1778, inscribed 'Stuart Architect'] (G. Jackson-Stops, *An English Arcadia*, National Trust 1992, 88).

WARFIELD PARK, BERKS., alterations for John Walsh, *c.*1775–80 [J. Hakewill, *History of Windsor and its Neighbourhood*, 1813, 291].

LONDON, MONTAGU (later PORTMAN) HOUSE, PORTMAN SQUARE, for Mrs. Elizabeth Montagu, *c.*1775–82; Great Room by J. Bonomi 1789–90, portico a later addition; destroyed by bombing 1941 [R. Blunt, *Mrs. Montagu* ii, 1923, 13, 18, 82–3, 101].

GREENWICH HOSPITAL, rebuilt the CHAPEL after a fire, 1780–8, assisted by William Newton, who completed the building after Stuart's death [Lesley Lewis, 'The Architects of the Chapel at Greenwich Hospital', *Art Bulletin* xxix, 1947, and 'Greece and Rome at Greenwich', *Arch. Rev.* cix, 1951, 17–24].

PARK PLACE, nr. HENLEY, BERKS., artificial classical ruin for General H. S. Conway, *c.*1780; dem. [P. Noble, *Park Place, Berkshire*, privately printed 1905, 41].

MOUNT STEWART, CO. DOWN, IRELAND, the 'TEMPLE OF THE WINDS', for Robert Stewart, cr. Marquis of Londonderry, 1782–3 [S. Lewis, *Topographical Dictionary of Ireland* i, 1837, 674; the Knight of Glin, *The Temple of the Winds, Mount Stewart*, National Trust 1966; G. Jackson-Stops in *C. Life*, 6 March 1980].

WIMBLEDON HOUSE, SURREY, decorative work for 1st Earl Spencer, date uncertain; destroyed by fire 1785 [Horace Walpole, *Jnl. of Visits to Country Seats* in *Walpole Soc.* xvi, 1927–8, 15, and Lesley Lawrence, *op. cit.*, 132.

BLITHFIELD HOUSE, STAFFS., conservatory for 1st Lord Bagot, built by Samuel Wyatt 'from designs and under the immediate supervision of Athenian Stuart' [William, 2nd Lord Bagot, *Memorials of the Bagot Family*, 1824, 146] (*C. Life*, 28 Oct. 1954, fig. 3).

MONUMENTS

ASHLEY CHURCH, STAFFS., William, Visct. Chetwynd (d. 1770), 1772 [E. Meteyard, *Life of Wedgwood* ii, 1866, 225].

BRAUGHING CHURCH, HERTS., Ralph Freeman (d. 1772), executed by Thomas Scheemakers [signed by Stuart].

BRISTOL CATHEDRAL, Mary Mason (d. 1767), wife of the poet William Mason, executed by J. F. Moore [B.L. Add. MS. 29926, f. 111].

CHISWICK CHURCH, MIDDLESEX, Thomas Bentley, Wedgwood's partner (d. 1780), executed by Thomas Scheemakers, 1781 [E. Meteyard, *Life of Wedgwood* ii, 1866, 460].

EASTNOR CHURCH, HEREFS., monuments to Joseph Cocks (d. 1775), erected 1778, and Mrs. Mary Cocks (d. 1779), executed by Thomas Scheemakers [signed 'J. Stuart inv.'].

EDINBURGH, GREYFRIARS CHURCHYARD, Lady Catherine Drummond (*née* Powlet) (d. 1774), 1776 [*Scots Magazine* xxxviii, 1776, 496].

PRESTON-ON-STOUR CHURCH, WARWICKS., Thomas Steavens (d. 1759), executed by Thomas Scheemakers, *c.*1780 [signed 'J. Stuart inv.'] (J. Physick, *Designs for English Sculpture*, 1969, fig. 99).

attributed: SUDBURY CHURCH, DERBYSHIRE, the Hon. Catherine Venables Vernon (d. 1775), daughter of George Venables Vernon and Martha, daughter of the Hon. Simon (later Earl) Harcourt, with epitaph by William Whitehead.

WESTMINSTER ABBEY, 3rd Viscount Howe (d. 1758), executed by P. Scheemakers [J. P. Neale & E. W. Brayley, *Westminster Abbey* ii, 1823, 237].

WESTMINSTER ABBEY, Admiral Charles Watson (d. 1757), executed by P. Scheemakers [J. P. Neale & E. W. Brayley, *Westminster Abbey* ii, 1823, 214].

WIMPOLE CHURCH, CAMBS., monuments to 1st Earl of Hardwicke (d. 1764), erected 1766, and Catherine, wife of the Hon. Charles Yorke (d. 1759, erected 1761), executed by Peter Scheemakers [signed 'J. Stuart inv.'; R.C.H.M., *West Cambridgeshire*, 213 and pl. 127].

STUART, ROBERT, *see* MEIKLEHAM, ROBERT STUART.

STUDHOLME, ROBERT (1786–1836), is listed as a 'stone mason' of Sutton Coldfield, Warwicks., in Pigot's *Directory* of 1828–9. He was presumably the 'Mr. Studholme of Sutton Coldfield' who is described as the architect of ST. JOHN'S CHURCH, PERRY BAR, BIRMINGHAM, 1831–3, Gothic, in *Gent's Mag.* 1833 (ii), 172. He died in 1836, aged 49 [Sutton Coldfield Parish Register].

STURGES, JOHN, was an architect or surreyor active in the East Midlands in the late seventeenth century. LYNDON HALL, RUTLAND, a house built in 1671–3 in a style reminiscent of Thorpe Hall, nr. Peterborough, appears to have been designed by an architect of this name. A notebook kept by the owner, Sir Abel Barker, lists 'varianda de Modello nuper facto per Johannem Sturges', and records that 'Sturges dit the pitch of the roof must be 4–5 pts. of the wideness from outside of wall plate'. [information from Mr. James Lees-Milne; John Cornforth in *C. Life*, 10 Nov. 1966]. There are references to 'Mr. John Sturges' in the accounts for building BELTON HOUSE, LINCS. (1684–8), which indicate that he was employed as a measurer. Accounts at Chatsworth show that in 1686–7 'Mr. Sturgess & Jacson . . . came to give directions for the new hall dore' at HARDWICK HALL, DERBYSHIRE, and in 1685 'Mr. Sturgesse the Surveyour' was paid 5 guineas for a 'designe for altering the east side of' CHATSWORTH HOUSE for the 4th Earl of Devonshire. It was not carried out, and Sturges's place as the Earl's architect was taken by William Talman [Francis Thompson, *A History of Chatsworth*, 1949, 34]. Sturges may, however, have had some connection with the latter, for, in August 1688, Talman told Lord Fitzwilliam's steward that the siting of the new office buildings at MILTON HOUSE, NORTHANTS., 'should be according to Mr. Sturges his draughts' [Fitzwilliam papers in North-amptonshire Record Office]. They were built under the direction of Robert Wright (*q.v.*) and bear the date 1690. The 'Mr. Samuel Sturgis' who is several times mentioned in the building accounts of THORESBY HOUSE, NOTTS. (1684–5), appears to have been a steward or estate official rather than a building surveyor [B.L., Egerton MS. 3539, ff. 153–63].

STURGES, JOHN (–1770), was a carpenter of the parish of St. George, Bloomsbury, London, who died early in 1770 [P.R.O., PCC 120 JENNER]. He appears to have been the owner of a substantial collection of pictures, prints and other things, including surveying instruments, that was sold in London on 4 April 1770, as the property of 'John Sturges, Architect, lately deceased' [Bodleian, Vet. A 5 e. 5565].

SUMSION, THOMAS (*c.*1672–1744), of Colerne in Wiltshire, was one of the last English master masons to carry on authentic medieval traditions of design into the early eighteenth century. His earliest recorded work of this kind was the west tower of DURSLEY CHURCH, GLOS. Its predecessor fell on 7 January 1698/9, and it was rebuilt with the aid of a brief in 1708–9. The contractors were 'Barker and Sumsion', who received £500 'for building the Tower'. Its design is based on that of the existing fifteenth-century tower of Colerne, with the addition of openwork battlements and pinnacles in the style of the 'Gloucester coronet'. In 1730 Sumsion provided the very similar design in accordance with which the central tower of SHERSTON CHURCH, WILTS., was rebuilt by Thomas West, mason. He received £1 15s. for his 'draught', and there is a payment in the churchwardens' accounts 'to Moses Rice for his sons goeing to Cullourn to give notice to Thom[s]. Sumption to come the second time'.

Although it is these two Gothic towers for which Sumsion is chiefly remarkable, he could also design secular works in a contemporary classical style. It is not known whether the design which he made for the old COUNCIL HOUSE at BRISTOL in 1699 was the one carried out in 1701–4, but it would certainly have been classical, not Gothic, in character [W. Ison, *The Georgian Buildings of Bristol*, 1952, 90–1], and in 1717 he designed and executed two urns on the north front of KING'S WESTON HOUSE, GLOS. [Kerry Downes, 'The Kings Weston Book of Drawings', *Arch. Hist.* x, 1967, figs. 13–14]. Another classical building was the lower part of the tower of ALL SAINTS CHURCH, BRISTOL, which Sumsion and another mason called William Paul built in 1712. The work was then suspended until 1716, when 'Sumsion and his man' gave in an estimate for completing it. This was apparently not accepted, as the masons employed were George Townesend and William Paul [MS. churchwardens' accounts].

Sumsion died at Colerne on 21 October 1744. His will, proved on 11 October 1745 by his widow, Joan Sumsion, is enrolled on the court roll of the manor of Colerne for that date, preserved among the muniments of New College, Oxford. He left goods worth £329, including 'working Tools' in the 'Shop', and a writing-desk in the kitchen. His monument in the churchyard bears the inscription 'Thomas Sumsion of this Parish Freemason who died October the 21, 1744, aged 72 years'. Members of the family continued to follow the masons' trade in Colerne until the war of 1939–46 [H. M. Colvin, 'Gothic Survival and Gothick Revival', *Arch. Rev.* March 1948].

SURPLICE, WILLIAM, was the eldest son of William Surplice (1771–1831), a builder established at Beeston, nr. Nottingham, and the grandson of Thomas Surplice, a builder of Lenton in the same neighbourhood. The younger William Surplice, who was probably born soon after his father's marriage in 1796, appears to have taken over the goodwill of the building firm established by the Strettons (*q.v.*). He also practised as an architect and surveyor until 1848, when he emigrated to

Australia. His only recorded architectural work appears to be ST. JOHN'S CHURCH, CARRINGTON, nr. NOTTINGHAM, built in the lancet style in 1843 [*Builder* i, 1843, 504], but a town-planning project in which he was concerned is described in *Builder* v, 1847, 88. William had two younger brothers who both practised as architects and surveyors, William at Manchester and Samuel at Beeston [information from Mr. M. A. L. Cooke].

SUTER, RICHARD (1797–1883), began his architectural career as a pupil of D. A. Alexander, whom he succeeded both as Surveyor to Trinity House Corporation and (1822) as Surveyor to the Fishmongers' Company. For the former body he designed some houses that were built by Thomas Cubitt in 1821–3 on sites adjoining Trinity House [Hermione Hobhouse, *Thomas Cubitt*, 1971, 50–2]. For the Fishmongers' Company he designed two classical churches at BANAGHER and BALLYKELLY on their estate in CO. DERRY, exhibiting the designs at the Royal Academy in 1827. He was probably responsible for some other buildings erected by the Company in Ballykelly about the same time, including the Model Farm (1824), the Lancasterian School (1828) and the Dispensary (1829). For the same Company he designed ST. PETER'S HOSPITAL, WANDSWORTH, SURREY, 1849–51 [exhib. at R.A. 1851], and THE OLD SCHOOLHOUSE, GRESHAM'S SCHOOL, HOLT, NORFOLK, in the Elizabethan style [*An Account of the Reopening of the Gresham Free School*, Holt 1859]. His designs for COOKHAM SCHOOL, BERKS., 1858, are in the Berkshire C.R.O., D/Ex 268/13.

Suter retired in 1867 and died on 1 February 1883. In the 1830s he was in partnership with Annesley Voysey (*q.v.*). He married Ruth, daughter of Major-General Andrew Burn, and was the father of Andrew Burn Suter (1830–1895), Bishop of Nelson, New Zealand, and of Richard George Suter, A.R.I.B.A., later minister of the Catholic Apostolic Church in Australia.

SUTTON, THOMAS (1746–), was apprenticed to Jacob Leroux in 1762, and gained an award from the Society of Arts in 1764. He was admitted to the Royal Academy Schools in 1770, and exhibited architectural designs at the Academy in 1771, 1772 and 1773. In 1774 he was appointed District Surveyor of Clerkenwell. He may have been the Thomas Sutton who was later Surveyor to the Corporation of Great Yarmouth and died shortly before 1819. [P.R.O., IR1/23, Jan. 1762; Society of Arts, *Register of Premiums*; Middlesex County Records, General Orders, No. 10; John Preston, *Picture of Yarmouth*, Yarmouth 1819, 42.]

SWAN, ABRAHAM, was a carpenter and joiner who published several books of architectural designs from 1745 onwards. Though his external elevations were more or less Palladian in character, his interior designs reflected the contemporary taste for rococo decoration. His books enjoyed considerable popularity in America, and the Philadelphia edition of his *British Architect* was the first architectural book to be printed in that country.

The titles of Swan's publications were: *The British Architect: or The Builder's Treasury of Stair-Cases*, 1745, 1750, 1758, etc., Philadelphia 1775, Boston 1794; *A Collection of Designs in Architecture, containing New Plans and Elevations of Houses, etc.*, 2 vols. 1757 (two editions, the second with 5 extra plates), 1765(?), 1768(?), Philadelphia 1775 (pt. 1 only); *Designs for Chimnies*, 1765, second ed. 1768 entitled *One Hundred and Fifty New Designs for Chimney Pieces*; *Designs in Carpentry*, 1759, second ed. 1768 entitled *The Carpenters Complete Instructor* [Eileen Harris, *British Architectural Books and Writers 1556–1785*, 1990, 450–4].

Very little is known about Swan's career, but in the preface to his *Designs in Architecture* he stated that he had had 'more than thirty years application, and experience in, the Theory and Practice of Architecture'. Four of the engravings in the second volume of his *Collection of Designs in Architecture* represent the front staircase at BLAIR CASTLE, PERTHSHIRE, which he designed for the 2nd Duke of Atholl in 1757 [Arthur Oswald in *C. Life*, 11 Nov. 1949]. The same volume also includes two designs for Chinese bridges constructed in the grounds at Blair, and one for a large timber bridge, 'intended to cross the River Tay at Dunkeld'. Swan also executed the interior fittings at EDGCOTE HOUSE, NORTHANTS., for Richard Chauncey in *c.*1750, a total of £1990 10*s.* being paid to 'Abraham Swan and Co. joiners' [H. A. Tipping in *C. Life*, 10 Jan. 1920]. He was subsequently employed at KEDLESTON HALL, DERBYSHIRE, under James Paine, for when Paine was superseded by Robert Adam in 1760, the latter wrote that 'Mr. Swan the great is dismissed and Mr. Wyatt the carpenter now fills his place' [J. Fleming, *Robert Adam and his Circle*, 1962, 368].

SWANSBOROUGH, WILLIAM, an architect and builder of Wisbech, Cambs., designed the OCTAGON CHAPEL at WISBECH, 1826–30; dem. 1953. The original octagonal lantern was replaced in 1846 by a corona of battlements and pinnacles designed by J. C. Buckler [N. Walker & T. Craddock, *History of Wisbech*, 1849, 383–4]. In 1821 J. Pacey and William Swansborough completed WHAPLODE DROVE CHURCH, LINCS., after the original architect, J. Cunnington of Spalding, had proved incompetent [I.C.B.S.]. The chancel was altered in 1907–8.

SWERDFEGER, or **SWORDFEGGER,** THEODORE, may have been the German architect of that name who was working in St. Petersburg *c.*1720–30 [Thieme-Becker, *Künstler-Lexikon* xxx, 383]. A design by him for a triumphal arch dated 29 January 1746/7 is in the Bodleian Library (Gough Maps 44, f. 18), and Vertue says that he drew a perspective view of St. Paul's Cathedral that was engraved by Fourdrinier [*Note Books*, Walpole Soc., iii, 117]. In 1765, when the Board of Works recommended him for the royal charity on Maundy Thursday, he was described as 'a distressed artist now living in the Parish of St. Martin's in the Fields . . . greatly advanced in years', and nearly blind [P.R.O., Works 1/4, p. 42]. In 1769 Sir William Chambers described him as an architect when recommending him for charity to the Royal Academy [Royal Academy, Minutes of Council, vol. i, 15 June 1769]. He must be the 'T. Schwerdfeyer' who signs the plate of Wentworth Woodhouse in the 1770 edition of Kent's *Designs of Inigo Jones* (ii, pl. 64).

SWETLAND, JOHN (–1776) and TIMOTHY, of Ringwood, Hampshire, designed and built the brick tower of MINSTEAD CHURCH, HANTS., in 1774 [MS. Vestry Minutes]. A Payment of £2 2s. to Timothy Swetland occurs in the churchwardens' accounts of ELLINGHAM, HANTS., in 1752. [date of death from Ringwood parish register].

SWINGLER, JAMES (–1712), of Penrith, was a carpenter by trade. He was in 1679 in partnership with William Thackeray (*q.v.*) and was responsible for considerable carpentry and joinery work for the Lowther family at Whitehaven and Lowther Hall [B. Tyson, 'The Work of William Thackeray and James Swingler at Flatt Hall (Whitehaven Castle) and other Cumberland Buildings 1676–1684', *Trans Ancient Monuments Soc.* N.S. 28, 1984]. In 1709–11 he rebuilt COCKERMOUTH CHURCH, CUMBERLAND (again rebuilt 1852) to his own designs [parish records, *ex inf.* Mr. D. Findlay].

SWINTON, JOHN, of Haddington, was a wright by trade. In 1825 he was responsible for an extension of MYRES CASTLE, FIFE [S.R.O., GD152/218/5/3]. He designed DIRLETON MANSE, E. LOTHIAN, in 1825 and in 1832 DIRLETON CHURCH was repaired in accordance with his estimate [S.R.O., HR 42/2].

SWITHIN, THOMAS (–1814), practised in Southwark, where he designed the ASYLUM FOR DEAF AND DUMB CHILDREN, OLD KENT ROAD, 1807–9; dem. 1886 (*Survey of London* xxv, pl. 91) [*Gent's Mag.* 1807 (ii), 678, 1814 (ii), 503].

SYKES, THOMAS, of Chesterfield, was Surveyor of Bridges to the County of Derby from 1786 to 1816. During his tenure of office he widened or rebuilt many bridges in the county. The specification for the new bridge built under his direction at BELPER in 1796–8 is printed in *Derbyshire Archl. Jnl.* xii, 1890, 8–10. His notebook, covering the period 1791–1813, is preserved among the Derbyshire Quarter Sessions Records [J. C. Cox, *Three Centuries of Derbyshire Annals* ii, 1890, 224].

SYMONDS, THOMAS (–1791), was an architect and monumental mason who became a freeman of Hereford in 1753, and worked there until his death in 1791. He was responsible for some excellent monuments, examples of which can be seen in many local churches. He was for many years surveyor to the dean and chapter of Hereford, and endeavoured without success to get them to take effectual steps to prevent the collapse of the W. end of Hereford Cathedral, which finally occurred in 1786 [D. Whitehead in *C. Life*, 23 Nov. 1989, correspondence].

Symonds probably designed EVESBATCH COURT, HEREFS. (rebuilt *c.*1898) for Robert Dobyns in 1757, for he witnessed the building contract [Yate Allen family papers], and in 1784–5 he refronted ALLENSMORE COURT, HEREFS., for Edmund Patteshall [N. Kingsley in *C. Life*, 12 Jan. 1989, correspondence]. According to F. Calvert and W. West, *Picturesque Views of . . . Shropshire*, 1831, 125, he carried out extensive alterations to THE LODGE, nr. LUDLOW, SALOP., for Theophilus Richard Salwey (1757–1837), giving it 'the air . . . of an Italian villa'.[1] After Symonds's death in March 1791 his business was carried on by his widow, who announced in the local press that she had 'engaged a Person of acknowledged abilities . . . from London' to

[1] For an alternative attribution to Sir Robert Taylor see R. Garnier and R. Hewlings in *C. Life*, 21 Sept. 1989.

assist her [*Hereford Jnl.* 16 March and 20 April 1791].

SYMPSON, —, *see* SIMPSON, JOHN (1755–1815).

T

TAIT, JAMES (*c.*1762–1854), is described as 'Architect' on his monument in St. Cuthbert's churchyard, Edinburgh. It is known from other sources that he was from Glencorse, Midlothian, and afterwards lived at Belwood and Portobello. He was the father of William Tait, publisher (1793–1864) and his daughter Isabella married the publisher Adam Black (1784–1874) [notes at N.M.R.S.]. He designed SHANDWICK PLACE, EDINBURGH, 1807–8, largely rebuilt [information from Mr. David Walker; *Edinburgh Evening Courant*, 21 Dec. 1807].

TAIT, JOHN (*c.*1787–1856), is buried in the Dean Cemetery at Edinburgh, where an inscription commemorates his death on 3 November 1856 at the age of 69. In 1830–1 he made additions to KERSE HOUSE, STIRLINGSHIRE (dem. *c.*1958), for the 1st Earl of Zetland, and in 1837 designed the neighbouring church of GRANGEMOUTH (WEST) for the Earl [drawings in Kerse Estate Office, photos at N.M.R.S.]. He also designed a school at DUNBOG, FIFE, 1840 [S.R.O., HR 254/1] and another at FALKIRK, STIRLINGSHIRE, 1845–6 [J. Love, *Schools and Schoolmasters of Falkirk*, Falkirk 1898, 91] and POLMONT CHURCH, STIRLINGSHIRE, 1844–5 [S.R.O., HR 8/2, pp. 236–7, 243].

In Edinburgh Tait was employed in 1830–40 to carry out Archibald Elliot's designs of 1819 for RUTLAND PLACE, STREET and SQUARE, modifying them considerably in execution [Edinburgh Sasines]. He also made the feuing plan for INVERLEITH TERRACE in 1830 and presumably designed at least the elevations of the houses built by 1835 [*Edinburgh Evening Courant*, 3 April 1830, 8 Oct. 1835]. For the Heriot Trustees he designed CLARENDON CRESCENT, 1850–3, ETON TERRACE, 1855, and OXFORD TERRACE, 1858–9 [Heriot Trust records].

TALMAN, JOHN (1677–1726), eldest son of William Talman (*q.v.*), was educated at Eton College. In June 1697 he was admitted to Leiden University as a student of law, and from Leiden visited other parts of Holland and Germany in 1698, making topographical drawings that are now in the R.I.B.A. Collection. He subsequently spent much of his life in foreign travel, partly, as stated in his father's petition to Harley in 1713, 'to view the most famous buildings', and partly to form a remarkable collection of prints and drawings. According to the inscription on his grave-slab he spent 'near 20 years in travels through France, Germany and Italy in which he made a fine collection of the most curious paintings and drawings of the noblest buildings and Curiosities in those Countrys'. According to a note in a MS. volume (xiii) in the Marquess of Ailesbury's archives he was in Italy in 1699. By 1702 he was back in England, but his letter-book for the years 1708–12 (Bodleian Library, MS. Eng. Letters e. 34) shows that he made another expedition to Italy in 1709, travelling by sea in company with William Kent. A volume of 'Plans &c taken by Mr. Talman in Italy' in the course of this visit is in the Witt Collection at the Courtauld Institute. The letter-book shows that while in Italy Talman obtained large numbers of drawings for his own and other English collections, and corresponded with connoisseurs such as Richard Topham and Dean Aldrich of Christ Church, Oxford. A letter to his father describes an elaborate entertainment which he gave in Rome in 1711. Those invited were 'all the top virtuosi in Rome both for learning and arts'. The 'best music' was composed for the occasion, and the dinner was held in a room decorated with festoons of myrtle and flowers and painted with twelve heads 'representing Vitruvius, Fabius the painter, Glycon the sculptor; Palladio, Rafael and Bonarota; on another side Inigo Jones, Fuller and Pierce; [and] at the upper part . . . Horace the poet, Rossius the comedian and Ismenia a singer, with abundance of mottos in Latin and Italian &c.' While Talman was in Italy he was employed by the Commissioners for Building Fifty New Churches to have a statue of Queen Anne made to surmount the proposed column in the Strand. This was never erected, and although the commissioners paid Sir Edward Gould £340 in 1715, 'in order to his remitting the same to Mr. John Talman at Florence towards defraying the charge of making a statue of her late Ma[ty] Queen Anne in Braswork', it is not known whether the figure ever reached this country [*Arch. Rev.* March 1950, 191].

Talman returned to England in or about 1716, but he was apparently in Italy again in 1719, for in the Cottonian Collection in Plymouth City Art Gallery there is a drawing of the font in St. Mark's at Venice signed 'I. Talman 1719'. In 1717 he was chosen to be the first Director of the Society of Antiquaries, in which capacity he was responsible for the publication of prints of antiquarian subjects. He himself was a competent draughtsman and made architectural designs as well as drawings of antiquities, etc. His projects show his familiarity with Italian baroque architecture and his fondness for opulent interior decoration, but some of them have a somewhat bizarre character which is particularly evident in his scheme for remodelling All Souls Chapel in Italian Gothic. A design for paving the area beneath the dome of St. Paul's Cathedral, initialled 'March 26, 1708 JT', is illustrated in *Wren Society* xiii, pl. 30, and there is a similar pavement design, evidently by Talman, in a volume of engravings in the Gibbs Collection in the Ashmolean Museum. In December 1725 he supplied the Spalding Gentlemen's Society with a design for a Museum 'in the proportion of a double cube'. It was not carried out, but the drawing is still preserved among the Society's archives. No building is known actually to have been built to the younger Talman's designs, and it was not as a practising architect, but as one of the greatest English collectors of his time, 'the most unwearied conservator of all that can be called curious, both of the present and past ages', that he was known to his contemporaries. His taste was in fact remarkably catholic, embracing mosaics and thirteenth-century sculpture as well as most aspects of Italian art and architecture since the Renaissance. In January 1724/5 his collections were described as follows by a member of the Spalding Gentlemen's Society:

> At Hinxworth in Hertfordsh^r the Seat of my learned & most Ingenious F^rd John Tallman Esqr. I had the pleasure of seeing his Noble & Sumptuous Collection. It is of the greatest Value & Beauty I ever beheld. The drawings are not black & white but every thing in proper Colours & beautyfully Limned by himself, Seignior Grisoni a Florentine & other Eminent & accurate hands, upon the Largest paper as strong as past-board & most things in their full & exact proportion except his Drawing[s] of Buildings wch are done by a Scale but so large that the Vast Volums in wch they are conteined are Four feet high & require 2 men to open & shutt them. This Treasure consists of ab^t 200 volls. distinguished into Different Subjects the Chiefest of wch are
>
> 1. Churches, Pallaces, Castles, Monum^ts. & Publick Edifices wth the Alterpieces & Processions in them.
> 2. Statues, Alto Releivo & Basso Releivo Sculpture.
> 3. Vases. Utensils.
> 4. The Exact Dimentions Weights Shape & Colour of all the most Valuable & pretious Jewels in the known World. Cameos & Intaglios.
> 5. The Crowns, Coronetts, Scepters &c of all Sovereigns Princes & States.
> 6. All parts of the Habitts of the Emperors, Kings, Doges, Popes, ArchBp^s., Cardinals.
>
> Besides all these aboundance of Fine Paintings, & peices of Antiquity, Porphery.

In 1718 John Talman married Frances Cokayne of Hinxworth, Herts., and it was there that he died on 3 November 1726, at the age of 49. By his will, dated 7 March 1719, he had left the greater part of his collection to the Library of Trinity College, Cambridge. But by a codicil, dated 4 August 1726, he directed that all his books, drawings, paintings, and pictures should be sold for the benefit of his children. The sale appears to have taken place in April 1727 and lasted six days, in the course of which over 1600 architectural drawings alone were dispersed. Some of them have since found their way into public collections, where they are in most cases easily distinguished by their elaborate gilt borders and 'triple T' mark.

[*A.P.S.D.*; *D.N.B.*; *Wren Soc.* xvii, 1–6, 19–22, 48; Sir E. B. Brabrook, 'On the Fellows of the Society of Antiquaries who have held the office of Director', *Archaeologia* lxii (i), 1910; J. Nichols, *Literary Anecdotes* vi, 1812, 159–60; J. Nichols, *Literary Illustrations* iv, 1822, 496; Sir H. Ellis, *Original Letters of Eminent Literary Men*, Camden Soc. 1843, 100–2; Madox, *History of the Exchequer*, 1711, supplementary treatise, 63–4 (for a drawing of the Pipe Office at Westminster made by Talman for the author); Minutes of the Spalding Gentlemen's Society; Walpole Society, *Vertue Note Books*, Index vol., 256; *The Diary of Humphrey Wanley*, ed. C. E. & R. Wright, 1966, 16, 17–18, 22, 25, 123; Poll Tax List for Eton College, 1694 in Bucks. C.R.O., *ex inf.* Dr. T.P. Connor; journals of Talman's continental tours in Beds. C.R.O., D.D.HY. 926/940–2; Hugh Honour, 'John Talman and William Kent in Italy', *Connoisseur*, Aug. 1954; John Harris on a sketch by John Talman for the decoration of a room in *Burlington Mag.* cii, 1960, 535–6 and fig. 33; H. M. Colvin, *Catalogue of Architectural Drawings of the Eighteenth and Nineteenth Centuries in the Library of Worcester College, Oxford*, 1964; S. Rowland Pierce, 'Turris Fortissima: A Baroque Design and Drawing by John Talman', *Antiquaries' Jnl.* xliv, 1964; T. Friedman, 'The English Appreciation of

Italian Decoration', *Burlington Mag.* Dec. 1975; Iain Pears, 'John Talman in Italy 1709–12', *Oxford Art Jnl.* 5 (1), 1982; *Catalogue of the R.I.B.A. Drawings Collection: T–Z*, 1984, 9–10; C. D. van Strien, 'John Talman en andere Britse Toeristen in Leiden en Omstreken rond 1700', *Leids Jaarboekje*, Leiden 1990.]

DRAWINGS FORMERLY IN JOHN TALMAN'S COLLECTION

Ashmolean Museum

(1) A volume of cartouches entitled *Cartels Prints and Drawings*: from the collection of James Gibbs.
(2) A volume of prints and drawings entitled *The Five Orders and Ornaments Relating Thereto*: with the bookplate of Christopher Turnor.
(3) A volume of *Architectural Drawings* consisting largely of plans and elevations of churches in Rome.
(4) A volume containing drawings of fountains, bound up with a set of Le Brun's *Recueil de divers Desseins de Fontaines*, etc.: from the collection of James Gibbs.

Victoria and Albert Museum

(1) An album of architectural drawings with a note that it was bought by Francis St. John 'at Mr. Talman's Sale February 2nd 1725/6 [*sic*] cost £7–10' (92 D.46).
(2) A bound volume containing many rough sketches of architectural details and some of mitres and other ecclesiastical subjects (E 79–185. 1940). On the fly-leaf are the following notes: '25 Different Designs by Mr. Hawkesmoor No. 27. 3d. Night Lot 1, A Portefolio with about 300 drawings of Churches etc. in Italy by Mr. Tahlman'. The latter was bought by George Vertue and sold when his collection was dispersed on 18 March 1757.
(3) A portfolio of loose drawings (E 186–360. 1940).

Society of Antiquaries

A volume of antiquarian drawings including some of monuments in Norfolk churches made by John Talman in 1705–8, and a design by him for a tower in North Italian baroque style dated 1704.

Royal Institute of British Architects

A collection of architectural designs by William Talman, with some topographical drawings made by John Talman on the Lower Rhine (one dated 13 August 1698): presented by J. W. Hiort in 1835.

Sir John Soane's Museum

Some designs for monuments by Edward Pierce (in a folio volume, now disbound, containing designs by Wren, William Talman and other architects).

British Museum (Print Room)

(1) A large folio containing coloured drawings of papal and other Italian vestments, etc., by Grisoni and Talman.
(2) A small folio containing drawings of chalices, pectorals, crosses, etc., by Grisoni and Francesco Bartoli, with annotations by Talman: from the Sloane Collection.
(3) Designs for monuments attributed to Edward Pierce: formerly in the collection of Richard Bull of Ongar.

Courtauld Institute of Art (Witt Collection)

A volume of 'Plans &c. taken by Mr. Talman in Italy', with the bookplate of Richard Bull of Ongar.

Westminster Abbey Library

Fifty-four drawings of architecture, sculpture, ecclesiastical jewellery, etc., mostly made in Italy (some dated 1709), but including St. Edward's Crown (Randall Davies gift, 1939).

Private Collection

Two volumes entitled *Insignia Auguralia, Sacralia et Sacerdotalia*, consisting of coloured drawings of ecclesiastical ornaments, etc., sold at Sotheby's, 2 April 1993.

TALMAN, WILLIAM (1650–1719), born at West Lavington, Wilts, in 1650, was the second son of William Talman, a gentleman with a small estate in the neighbouring hamlet of Eastcott. When William Talman, senior, died in 1663, he left the Wiltshire property in trust for his elder son Christopher, but William inherited three houses in King Street, Westminster, which his father held on lease from the Dean and Chapter of Westminster. Nothing is known of his early life or of his training as an architect. It would be surprising if so sophisticated an architectural designer had not travelled on the Continent but, when he was petitioning Harley for reinstatement in the Office of Works in 1713, he mentioned only his son's travels, not his own.

In 1678 Talman obtained the office of King's Waiter in the Port of London, worth £52 per annum, which he subsequently served by deputy.[1] For this he must have been indebted to a patron. Dr. Whinney has drawn attention to some indications that that patron might have been the 2nd Earl of Clarendon, who was influential at Court during the 1670s. Talman appears to have shared the customs post with his uncle Thomas Apprice, who was a member of Clarendon's household; he was involved with Clarendon financially, for in 1685 judgement was given against Clarendon for a debt of £800 owing to Talman;[2] and in 1689 he designed the Earl's country seat at Swallowfield in Berkshire. It can hardly, however, have been Clarendon who was instrumental in getting Talman appointed Comptroller of Works to King William III in May 1689, for he had withdrawn from Court on James II's deposition in 1688. The post had been vacant since Hugh May's death in 1684, and might not have been filled at all had not someone begged it for Talman. The courtier most likely to have intervened in his favour was the Earl of Portland, who at the same time made him his own deputy as Superintendent of the Royal Gardens, a post newly created by the King for Portland's benefit. As Portland's deputy Talman was now in effective charge of a department which was laying out very large sums of money on the King's behalf, chiefly at Hampton Court. At the same time he was, as Comptroller, a senior officer of the Royal Works, with a seat on the Board and an official house in Whitehall. His double appointment gave him a degree of independence which he used to undermine Wren's position as Surveyor of the Works. In 1689, when part of the new buildings at Hampton Court collapsed, killing two workmen and injuring eleven others, Talman went out of his way to throw the blame on Wren; in 1699 he not only accused Wren of nepotism in the appointment of a clerk of the works but went so far as to petition the Treasury for the Comptrollership of the Works at Windsor which Wren had held without interruption since 1684. His attitude, in short, was that of a rival rather than a colleague. As an administrator the Surveyor-General was by no means faultless, and these tactics might in the end have brought Talman some preferment at Wren's expense. But it was not only at the Office of Works that he made enemies. One after another he quarrelled with nearly all his private clients. His employment at Chatsworth came to an abrupt end in 1696, when the Duke of Devonshire also dismissed his favourite mason Benjamin Jackson:[1] in 1703 he demanded such stiff terms from the Duke of Newcastle for building at Welbeck that the Duke abandoned the idea altogether; in the same year he failed in a lawsuit against the Earl of Carlisle, who had refused to pay him more than £40 for visiting Castle Howard and making designs for a new house there; and in 1714 the Duke of Chandos was complaining of his 'ridiculous and extravagant' charges for designing the offices at Cannons. In 1703 Vanbrugh was able to send the Duke of Newcastle an even longer list of those whose employment of Talman had ended in 'vexation and disappointment'. Besides the Duke of Devonshire and Lord Carlisle, it included Lord Normanby, Sir John Germain, Lady Falkland, Lord Coningsby, Lord Portmore and the Earl of Kingston. Private intransigence led in the end to public disgrace, for when King William died in 1702 it was Carlisle who became Queen Anne's first Lord Treasurer, and in that capacity he made it his business to see that Talman's patent was not renewed. On 20 May Talman was dismissed from the Works, and Vanbrugh was appointed Comptroller in his place. When Vanbrugh was dismissed in turn in 1713, Talman made an attempt to regain the Comptrollership, but it was in vain, and in 1715 Vanbrugh was reinstated.

Despite his loss of office Talman cannot have been in serious financial difficulties, for he was able to pay for the prolonged and expensive travels of his son John (*q.v.*), and in 1718 he purchased the manor of Felmingham in Norfolk, where he died on 22 November 1719, aged 69. He left £1500 to his son John 'to clear off the incumberances upon his wife's estate and have likewise given him my chambers in Grays' Inn and also the use of all my collection of drawings prints and books for his life'. He provided annuities for his wife

[1] He surrendered the office in 1711 in favour of his brother-in-law James Tate (*Cal. Treasury Papers 1708–14*, 305).

[2] This appears from some deeds which in 1908 were in the hands of H. F. Johnson, solicitor to Mr. John Dutton of Oakhanger. Their present whereabouts are unknown, and for information about them I am indebted to Mr. John Harris.

[1] Benjamin Jackson, who was Master Mason of the King's Works from 1701 until his death in 1719, was often employed in works with which Talman was concerned, e.g. at Chatsworth (1687–96), Dyrham (1699, inspecting work with Talman) and Drayton (1702).

Hannah and his younger children, James, Hannah and Henry. His grave was marked by a black marble slab with a now illegible inscription (given in *Wren. Soc.* xvii, 7) and the device of three interlaced T's which he and his son used as a collector's mark.

It is evident that, before his eclipse by Vanbrugh, Talman enjoyed a considerable reputation as a country-house architect. In fact he was probably the leading Whig architect of the 1680s and 1690s. The evidence for his commissions is unfortunately confined to a small number of drawings (chiefly in the R.I.B.A. Collection) and to scattered references in private archives, supplemented by Vanbrugh's enumeration of his disappointed clients. Though the list of his fully authenticated works is confined to some eight or nine buildings,[1] several more can be assigned to him with some confidence, and there are others which have been attributed to him on stylistic grounds (notably Hackwood Park, Hants, 1683–8, Blyth Hall, Notts., 1684–5, and Waldershare Park, Kent, *c.*1705). Both the buildings listed below and the drawings reveal Talman as a disconcertingly eclectic designer whose work shows no consistency of style, nor any clearly discernible chronological development. Thus the documented Holywell House, St. Albans (*c.*1686), the undocumented Stanstead (*c.*1686–90) and Uppark (*c.*1690), which are attributed to Talman by the county historian Dallaway in the early nineteenth century, and an unexecuted design for a London house for the Earl of Devonshire (before 1694) all follow the astylar convention established by Sir Roger Pratt after the Restoration. French channelled masonry and ornaments from Rubens's *Palazzi di Genova* embellish the façade of Dyrham Park (1698–1704), while in many unexecuted designs a fondness for baroque enrichment is apparent. At the same time an interest in Palladian motifs can be detected both in Talman's sketches and perhaps in some executed buildings.

In the history of English architecture the most important works with which Talman has been associated are Thoresby and Chatsworth, the two houses in which the splendours of Stuart palace architecture were first employed to dignify the residence of a Whig nobleman. In the light of the evidence set out below Talman's responsibility for Thoresby must be questioned, but his authorship of the south and east ranges of Chatsworth is indisputable. Here the new grandeur is clearly seen in the monumental south front and in the sumptuous interior, in which all the resources of craftsmanship at the disposal of the Crown were employed for the benefit of a subject. Nowhere else did Talman find so lavish a patron as at Chatsworth, but at Burghley House he probably directed a similar, though purely internal transformation, and but for his arrogance towards his noble clients he might also have been the architect of great new houses at Castle Howard and Welbeck Abbey. Vanbrugh's reference to Lord Normanby (later Duke of Buckingham) as one of those whose patronage of Talman had ended in vexation has led to the suggestion that he may have played some part in the design of Buckingham House, another highly influential building, of which William Winde was the effective (though possibly not the original) architect. At Hampton Court Talman was largely responsible for the interior of William III's new building as well as for the gardens, on which over £80,000 were spent between 1689 and 1702. William III's death in the latter year meant the end of Talman's career as an official architect, and Vanbrugh's ascendancy as the leading Whig architect of the reign of Queen Anne was largely achieved at Talman's expense. After 1702 very few commissions are known to have come Talman's way, and the latter part of his life is almost as obscure as its beginning.

Talman was, as his will indicates, a collector and connoisseur as well as a practising architect, and in the petition which he addressed to Harley in 1713 he stated that he had made 'and is still collecting by his son abroad, the most valuable Collection of Books, Prints, Drawings &c., as is in any one person's hands in Europe, as all the artists in Towne well know'. A fuller account of this collection will be found in the notice of John Talman above. Besides many drawings by Italian masters, it appears to have included the architectural drawings by Inigo Jones and John Webb that afterwards passed to Lord Burlington. In addition, Talman's probate inventory lists a large and impressive collection of pictures, busts, statues, vases, marble tables and the like, which at the time of his death was in Dr. Desaguliers's house in Channel Row, Westminster. In 1700 Talman was elected Steward of the Society of Virtuosi of St. Luke, a body of artists and connoisseurs which met on St. Luke's Day to enjoy an annual feast.

A bust of Talman by John Bushnell was in the latter's studio at the time of his death, but it is not known whether it is still extant. A small painting of Talman, his son John, and their wives, attributed to Grisoni, was

[1] Chatsworth, Swallowfield, Dyrham, Hampton Court Palace, Fetcham, Drayton, Holywell House and the offices at Cannons.

acquired by the National Portrait Gallery in 1984. A small and inferior woodcut in Wornum's edition (1862) of Walpole's *Anecdotes of Painting* purports to represent Talman but is more probably a portrait of his son. At Freemasons' Hall there is a portrait of an unnamed architect whose unamiable features may well be those of the man who quarrelled with so many of his contemporaries.

[*A.P.S.D.*; *D.N.B.*; *Wren Soc.* xvii, 1–8, 20–43, and xx, 222–3; *History of the King's Works* v; Walpole Society, *Vertue Note Books* i, 129, ii, 8; W. T. Whitley, *Artists and their Friends in England* ii, 1928, 243; *R.I.B.A. Drawings Catalogue: Inigo Jones and John Webb*, 7, and *T–Z*; L. Whistler, *The Imagination of Vanbrugh and his Fellow Artists*, 1954, 35–8; *Cal. Treasury Books* v, 161, 1458; P.C.C. 44 SHALLER (will); P.R.O., PROB 3/19/45 (inventory); M. D. Whinney, 'William Talman', *Jnl. Warburg and Courtauld Institutes* xviii, 1955; John Harris, *William Talman*, 1982; Giles Worsley, 'William Talman: some stylistic suggestions', *Georgian Group Jnl.* 1992.]

The following is a chronological list of buildings in whose design William Talman is known to have been involved and includes abortive as well as executed designs.

THORESBY HOUSE, NOTTS., is stated by Campbell (*Vitruvius Britannicus* i, 1715, 6) to have been 'built *Anno* 1671', the front being 'performed by the same hand that afterwards built Chatsworth'. It has been assumed that by this Campbell meant that William Talman was the architect of Thoresby as well as of Chatsworth. But the date 1671 is certainly wrong, as a large house had already been built at Thoresby in the reign of Charles I, and the Hearth-Tax returns show that there was no change in its assessment of 43 hearths between 1661 and 1678. The accounts of the 4th Earl of Kingston, who succeeded in 1682 and died in 1690, show that in 1685–7 the house was being remodelled (but not rebuilt) by a team of craftsmen that included Benjamin Jackson (master mason), Edward Goudge (plasterer), John Nost and C. G. Cibber (carvers), Antonio Verrio and Louis Laguerre (painters), and René Cousin (gilder) [B.L., Egerton MSS. 3256 and 3539; Nottingham University Library, Pierrepont papers, 4205, 4206, 4210]. There is no mention of Talman, and the only reference to architectural supervision is a payment of 5 guineas to 'Sr. Christopher Wren's man' (presumably Hawksmoor) in June 1686. The existence among Wren's drawings at All Souls of an alternative elevation for Thoresby (*Wren Soc.* vii, pl. 2) is further evidence of the involvement of Wren's office. As for the front being 'performed by the same hand that afterwards built Chatsworth', the word 'performed' is one that Campbell uses elsewhere of masons, not architects,[1] and it would fit Benjamin Jackson, who was master mason both at Thoresby and at Chatsworth. The possibility that Talman was concerned in Thoresby, perhaps at a later date, cannot, however, be ruled out, for Vanbrugh includes 'my Lord Kingston' (i.e. the 5th Earl, who succeeded in 1690) in his list of those who had employed Talman and regretted it.

Hawksmoor, writing in 1731, says that Thoresby 'was burnt down as soon as finished', and that the attic storey shown in Campbell's plate 'was added at the refitting the house after the fire, but all the walls remained as the fire had left them' [*Walpole Soc.* xix, 126; cf. *Vertue* vi, 24, 73]. This fire is not mentioned in the accounts, but the attic existed by 1690, for it is visible in a miniature drawing of the house on a map made in that year (Nottingham University Library). Other early views of the house were reproduced by John Harris in *Architectural History* iv, 1961, fig. 4, and vi, 1963, 105. It was finally destroyed by fire in 1745.

LONDON, ST. ANNE'S CHURCH, SOHO: Talman was, with Wren, concerned in the completion of this church in 1685, and provided a design for the steeple in 1714. It is not clear whether he or Wren was responsible for the design of the church (reconstructed 1830–1 and dem. 1953 after war-damage), nor whether the steeple built in 1714 (dem. 1800) was in accordance with his 'draught' [*Survey of London* xxxiii, 256–62].

STANSTEAD PARK, STOUGHTON, SUSSEX, was designed by Talman for 1st Earl of Scarbrough in 1686, according to J. Dallaway, *Western Division of Sussex* i, 1815, 158–9, but a visitor in 1689 found only the shell complete (N.L.S., Wod. folio xxvi). The house was remodelled by Joseph Bonomi and James Wyatt in 1786–9 and destroyed by fire in 1900 (J. Kip, *Britannia Illustrata* i, 1714, pl. 26).

HOLYWELL HOUSE, ST. ALBANS, HERTS., for John

[1] Thus St. Paul's Cathedral is 'performed in stone, by those excellent and judicious Artists, Mr. Edward Strong, senior and junior', and Chatsworth itself is 'performed in the best stone'. For pointing out the significance of this word in Campbell's vocabulary I am indebted to Dr. T. P. Connor.

and Sarah Churchill (afterwards Duke and Duchess of Marlborough), *c.*1686; altered by George Shakespear in 1786; dem. 1837: attributed to Talman on the evidence of a payment to Talman in 1686 [Frances Harris, 'Holywell House, St. Albans: an early work by William Talman?' *Arch. Hist.* 28, 1985].

CHATSWORTH HOUSE, DERBYSHIRE, rebuilt south and east fronts for 4th Earl, cr. 1694 1st Duke of Devonshire, 1687–96. Talman was dismissed in 1696, and the authorship of the west front, built in 1700–3, is uncertain. The north front (1705–7) is by Archer [Francis Thompson, *A History of Chatsworth*, 1949, chaps. 2–4; contract, etc., printed in *Wren Soc.* xvii, 22–42] (*Vitruvius Britannicus* i, 1715, pls. 72–6; *C. Life*, 5–26 Jan. 1918, 11–25 April, 2 May 1968).

MILTON HOUSE, NORTHANTS., advice about building of offices and proposed rebuilding of house for 1st Earl Fitzwilliam, 1688. The house was not rebuilt and there is no evidence that the offices (dated 1690) were designed by Talman, though he advised about their siting [Northants. Record Office, Fitzwilliam papers F (M) C 651, 652, and letters from J. Pendleton dated 14 Aug. and 11 Sept. 1688].

BURGHLEY HOUSE, NORTHANTS., probably directed redecoration of interior for 5th Earl of Exeter, *c.*1688–90 [several visits by Talman to Burghley in August and Sept. 1688 are mentioned incidentally in correspondence among the Fitzwilliam papers in the Northants. Record Office, e.g. F (M) C 651, 652]. The Earl's trustees paid him £200 in 1704, probably for services rendered in the 1680s [accounts at Burghley, *ex inf.* Dr. E. R. Till] (*C. Life*, 17 Dec. 1953).

SWALLOWFIELD HOUSE, BERKS., for 2nd Earl of Clarendon, 1689–91; altered by John James 1720–2, remodelled by W. Atkinson 1820 [*Correspondence of Henry Hyde, Earl of Clarendon*, ed. S. W. Singer, ii, 1828, 273, 285, 288, 309; Constance, Lady Russell, *Swallowfield and its Owners*, 1901] (J. Lees-Milne, *English Country Houses: Baroque 1685–1715*, 1970, fig. 7, reproduces a late eighteenth-century drawing of the front from B.L., *King's Maps* vii, 49*a*).

UPPARK, SUSSEX, was designed by Talman for Forde, Lord Grey, cr. 1st Earl of Tankerville, *c.*1690, according to J. Dallaway, *Western Division of Sussex* i, 1815, 193. The detached wings are a later addition, and the entrance was remodelled by H. Repton in 1805. The house was gutted by fire in 1989 and restored in 1990–3 (*C. Life*, 14–28 June 1941).

LONG DITTON, SURREY, unexecuted design for a house and garden, probably for himself and not a royal 'Trianon', *c.*1699; site later sold to George London, whose small square lodge may have been designed by Talman [R. G. M. Baker, 'William Talman and a supposed project to improve Hampton Court', *Surrey Archl. Colls.* 75, 1984, with references to earlier literature].

FETCHAM PARK, SURREY, for Arthur Moore, *c.*1700; remodelled *c.*1870 [described as 'from the Design of the late Mr. Tallmann' in Bodleian Library, MS. North b. 24, f. 196; cf. MS. Eng. Letters e. 34, p. 83].

DORCHESTER HOUSE, WEYBRIDGE, SURREY, alterations for 1st Earl of Portmore, *c.*1700; dem. *c.*1830 [John Harris, 'Dorchester House, Surrey', in *The Country Seat*, ed. Colvin & Harris, 1970, 72–4].

HERRIARD PARK, HANTS., unexecuted designs for Thomas Jervoise, *c.*1700 [F. H. J. Jervoise, 'The Jervoises', *The Ancestor* iii, 1902, 7].

KIMBERLEY HALL, NORFOLK, designs for Sir John Wodehouse, Bart., *c.*1700, probably executed soon afterwards; stables built 1720; house altered by T. Prowse and J. Sanderson *c.*1755–7; quadrants by A. Salvin 1835 [payment of £50 to Talman in Sir John Wodehouse's bank account, *ex inf.* Dr. T.P. Connor; plan by Talman for Kimberley in R.I.B.A. Coll. resembling house as built].

DRAYTON HOUSE, NORTHANTS., rebuilt south front of the hall facing the courtyard, for Sir John Germain, Bart., 1702, and probably designed the cupolas on the two towers [contract printed by Margaret Whinney in *Archaeological Jnl.* cx, 1953, 189] (*C. Life*, 27 May 1965).

WITHAM PARK, SOMERSET: Talman made designs for remodelling the front of the house for Sir William Wyndham, Bart. *c.*1702. His proposal for a columnar screen or transparent portico was not carried out, but the idea was taken over by Gibbs in an unexecuted design illustrated by Campbell in *Vitruvius Britannicus* (see p. 407). See also the drawings by Dr. Clarke and others illustrated by H. M. Colvin, *Catalogue of Architectural Drawings . . . in the Library of Worcester College, Oxford*, 1964, pls. 119, 120, 121, which are evidently for Witham, and not for Eastbury as there suggested, p. 45 [J. Harris, 'The Transparent Portico', *Arch. Rev*, cxxviii, 1958, 108–9; *R.I.B.A. Drawings Catalogue: G–K*, 24].

WELBECK ABBEY, NOTTS., unexecuted design for a new house for 1st Duke of Newcastle, 1703 [*Wren Soc.* xii, pls. 39–40, and xvii, pls. 11–13; letter from Talman to Newcastle printed in *Wren Soc.* xvii, 8; L. Whistler, *The Imagination of Vanbrugh*, 1954, 34–9; Margaret Whinney, *Jnl. Warburg and Courtauld Institutes* xviii, 1955, 134].

LOWTHER HALL, WESTMORLAND, as rebuilt by Edward Addison (*q.v.*) for Sir John Lowther, Bart., in 1692–5, may have been derived from a design supplied by Talman, for in a MS. in the Cumbria Record Office (D/Lons.L, Sir John Lowther's MS. Book 1690–7) Lowther wrote that 'for my Hous. after I had directed Mr. Talman the King's Comptroller off his Works to draw me a design such as I thought convenient for me, I had the Correction and approbation off Sir Samuel Morland'. One surviving drawing (D/Lons./L/L1), a design for a double flight of external stairs, can be attributed to Talman, but was not carried out. The house was destroyed by fire in 1718.

CAMBRIDGE, ST. CATHARINE'S COLLEGE; in 1694–5 the College paid 'Mr. Talman Controwler of the King's Works' £1 10s., probably for advice in connection with the building of the Chapel, then in progress [Arthur Oswald in *C. Life*, 29 Oct. 1932, 493]. In 1696 Talman was paid a further £2 4s. 'for advice about the Chappell' [College accounts, *ex inf.* Mr. R. Luckett].

KIVETON or KEITON PARK, YORKS. (W.R.), was built for 1st Duke of Leeds, 1698–1704; dem. 1811. A plan 'For ye D. of Leeds at Keiton in Yorkshire' is among Talman's drawings at the R.I.B.A. but does not correspond to the house as built. No architect is mentioned in the contract dated 3 March 1697–8 whereby Daniel Brand of the Minories, London, a carpenter, undertook to erect the main body of the house for the Duke, but see above under 'Fitch', p. 365 [Yorks. Archl. Soc., Duke of Leeds papers, DD5, Box 3; cf. G. Beard, *Georgian Craftsmen*, 1966, 184–5] (Badeslade & Rocque, *Vitruvius Brittanicus* (*sic*) iv, 1739, pls. 11–12).

CASTLE ASHBY, NORTHANTS: in 1695 Talman made an estimate for remodelling the north wing of the house for 4th Earl of Northampton, but nothing was done [Castle Ashby archives 1084/34]. He may, however, have designed the Greenhouse which was erected on the south side of the churchyard in 1695 and demolished *c.*1868.

DYRHAM PARK, GLOS., east front, etc., for William Blathwayt, Secretary of State, 1698–1704 [*Vitruvius Britannicus* ii, 1717, pls. 91, 93; letter from Talman printed in *Wren Soc.* iv, 59–60; Mark Girouard in *C. Life*, 15, 22 Feb. 1962].

CASTLE HOWARD, YORKS (N.R.), unexecuted design for 3rd Earl of Carlisle, *c.*1698 [plan in R.I.B.A. Coll.; L. Whistler, *The Imagination of Vanbrugh*, 1954, 31–5].

HAMPTON COURT PALACE, MIDDLESEX, completion of interior of state apartments for King William III, 1699–1702, and layout of gardens, 1689–1702 [*History of the King's Works* v, 163–74].

RAYNHAM HALL, NORFOLK, unexecuted design for remodelling E. and W. fronts for 2nd Viscount Townshend, *c.*1703. The alterations to the fenestration which took place about this time may have been directed by Talman [Giles Worsley in *Georgian Group Jnl.* 1992, 11–12].

CANNONS HOUSE, MIDDLESEX, added offices (dem.) for 1st Duke of Chandos, 1713–14, and made unexecuted plans for rebuilding the house [C. H. & M. I. Collins Baker, *The Life of James Brydges, Duke of Chandos*, 1949, 114–15].

ABBOTSTONE, nr. ALRESFORD, HANTS., designs for a house for 1st Duke of Bolton (d. 1699) perhaps by Talman, and represented by drawings in Bodleian, Gough Maps 10, f. 37, and Ashmolean Museum, Gibbs Collection II, 28, the latter with the name 'Talman' crossed out. A house was built at Abbotstone *c.*1685 and dem. *c.*1760. Talman may be regarded as a possible candidate for the design of HACKWOOD PARK, HANTS., built by the 1st Duke in 1683–8. A portico was added by Gibbs, but removed *c.*1805, when the house was remodelled by Samuel & Lewis Wyatt (*C. Life*, 17, 24 May 1913, with plan; eighteenth-century view by Sandby in Bodleian, Gough Maps 10, f. 52).

BULSTRODE PARK, BUCKS., was acquired by the 1st Earl of Portland (whose Deputy Talman then was as Superintendent of the Royal Gardens to William III) after the death of Judge Jeffreys in 1689 and was extensively altered in 1706–7, when George London was employed as landscape-gardener [Nottingham University Library, Portland Papers, Box 28, unlisted]. The only documentary evidence of Talman's employment as an architect at Bulstrode so far discovered dates from the time of the 2nd Earl (1st Duke) of Portland, and consists of 'Particulars of the charges in making bricks at Bullstrode given by Mr. Tallman Feb. 9 1715' [*ibid.*, Box 41, *ex inf.* Mr. John Harris].

TAPPEN, GEORGE (*c.*1771–1830), was probably related to J. Tappen, who was a Warden of the Carpenters' Company in 1793.

Nothing is known of his early life beyond the fact that he travelled on the Continent in 1802–3, publishing on his return a *Short Description of a Tour*, 1804, afterwards enlarged as *Professional Observations on the Architecture of the Principal Ancient and Modern Buildings in France and Italy*, 1806. He subsequently practised from London, exhibiting at the Royal Academy from 1802 onwards, and held the office of Surveyor to Dulwich College. His executed works included a house called GLENLEA at DULWICH for C. Druce, 1803–4 [exhibited 1803] (*C. Life*, 29 Nov. 1962, 1349); a Gothic house at SYDENHAM for R. Shute, exhibited 1806; EASTCOMBE HOUSE, nr. CHARLTON, KENT, for D. Hunter, exhibited 1807; THE WILLOWS and NORTHCROFT, DULWICH, for William Price and Robert Grafton, respectively, 1810–11 [Dulwich College archives, *ex inf.* Mr. Roger White]; the SCHOOL FOR THE INDIGENT BLIND, ST. GEORGE'S FIELDS, SOUTHWARK, 1811–12, subsequently rebuilt in Gothic style by John Newman [exhibited 1812] (J. Elmes, *Metropolitan Improvements*, 1831, plate); alterations and/or additions to HENBURY HOUSE, DORSET, for W.G. Paxton, before 1825 [letter from Paxton in Sir John Soane's Museum, Correspondence Div. VI L, Clerks of Works, f. 9]; and the Greek Revival ROYAL CALEDONIAN ASYLUM, ISLINGTON, with a portico based on that of Philip of Macedon at Delos, 1827–8, dem. [exhibited 1827; S. Lewis, *History of Islington*, 1842, 345] (J. Elmes, *Metropolitan Improvements*, 1831, plate). His unexecuted designs included one for a 'mansion in the style of an old Norman Castle', exhibited at the R.A. in 1819. In conjunction with J. Narrien he was the author of *A New and More Effectual Method of building Groined Arches in Brickwork*, 1808, and published an article on the same subject in the *Monthly Magazine* xxiv, 1807, 140–3. He died on 1 March 1830, aged 59 [*Gent's Mag.* 1830 (i), 282; *A.P.S.D.*].

TASKER, EDWARD, described himself in 1670 as 'a skilful surveyor and contriver of buildings'. In that year there was litigation between himself and Elizabeth Tyther about the rebuilding of three houses in Love Lane, London, of which Tasker had undertaken the 'surveying, ordering and contrivance'. Other buildings of which he claimed to be the surveyor were a house at Hampton Court and a building in the Inner Temple for Francis Phillips [P.R.O., C6/289/21 and 34, *ex inf.* Mr. Frank Kelsall]. Tasker had been admitted to the freedom of the Salters' Company by redemption on 1 July 1649, and from 1661 to 1668 held the office of Collector of dues from Leadenhall Market, together with custody of the City's building store-yard in the Greenyard at Leadenhall [*ex inf.* Guildhall Record Office].

TASKER, JOHN (*c.*1738–1816), was an architect and builder who belonged to the Catholic Church and who worked chiefly for Catholic clients. He practised in Mortimer Street, Cavendish Square, and exhibited at the Royal Academy in 1782, 1784 and 1814. He retired in 1814 or 1815 to a house that he had designed and built at 8 Baker Street, where he died on 6 March 1816, aged 78. The building side of his business was continued by his nephew, John Tasker II (*c.*1769–1817), who was the grandfather of the Catholic architect Francis William Tasker (1848–1904) [*Gent's Mag.* 1816 (i), 373; *Catholic Record Soc.* xii, 1913, 134, 140; information from Mr. D. Evinson].

Tasker was much employed by Thomas Weld, of Lulworth, Dorset, for whom he redecorated the interior of LULWORTH CASTLE in 'Adam' style in 1780–2 [J. Manco & F. Kelly, 'Lulworth Castle from 1700', *Arch. Hist.* 34, 1991]. His work here was destroyed by fire in 1929, but is illustrated in *C. Life*, 9 Jan. 1926. In 1786–7 a domed ROMAN CATHOLIC CHAPEL was built at LULWORTH to Tasker's designs. It is a building of considerable architectural merit in an elegant neo-classical style reminiscent of Wyatt [R.C.H.M. *Dorset* ii (1), 145]. For Thomas Weld Tasker also designed in about 1798 a house at ASTON, nr. STONE, STAFFS., as a residence for his son Joseph [S. Shaw, *History of Staffordshire* i, 1798, 355; drawings in Weld archives, 1955]. For John Wright, another Catholic client, Tasker presumably designed the chapel within KELVEDON HALL, ESSEX, *c.*1780, for a plan of the house signed by him is preserved at Kelvedon [*ex inf.* Dr. David Watkin] (*C. Life*, 10 May 1941).

In 1811 Tasker designed SPETCHLEY PARK, WORCS., for Robert Berkeley [J. P. Neale, *Views of Seats*, 1st ser. ii, 1819] (*C. Life*, 8 July 1916), and in 1814 he refronted ACTON BURNELL HALL, SALOP., for Sir Joseph Edward Smythe, Bart. [*V.C.H. Salop.* viii, 8; drawing by Tasker in Shropshire C.R.O., 1514/2/1222] (J. P. Neale, *Views of Seats*, 2nd ser. ii, 1825). Spetchley and Acton Burnell both have competently designed Greek Revival façades with Ionic porticoes, showing that Tasker was able to adapt his style to changing taste right up to the end of his life.

To Tasker may also be attributed the Greek Revival R.C. Chapel which was built at WOOTTON WAWEN HALL, WARWICKS., in 1813 by the Dowager Lady Smythe, Sir Joseph Smythe's mother.

In London Tasker repaired and altered No.

17 PORTMAN SQUARE and designed new stables, coach-house, etc., for John Tharp, 1796–7 [account in Tharp papers, Cambs. C.R.O., R.55.101/1], and in 1808–17 he designed and built seven houses on the Phillimore estate at CAMPDEN HILL, all dem. except Thorpe Lodge [*Survey of London* xxxvii, 62, 68–71]. A book of survey plans made by Tasker of houses on the Portman estate in George Street, Gloucester Place, Lower Berkeley Street and Bedford Street is in the R.I.B.A. Drawings Collection, together with sections of a Gothic chapel. Drawings for Downside Abbey made in 1814 are referred to in *Downside Review* xxiii, 1914, 143 and *Burlington Mag.*, April 1981, 231 n.

TATHAM, CHARLES HEATHCOTE (1772–1842), was born in Duke Street, Westminster, on 8 February 1772. He was the youngest of the five sons of Ralph Tatham, a native of Stockton in Durham, who married the daughter of a wealthy London tradesman. His father, after attempting unsuccessfully to establish himself as a gentleman farmer in Essex, became private secretary to Admiral Rodney, but died suddenly at the age of 50. Tatham was educated in the grammar school at Louth in Lincolnshire. At the age of 16 he was engaged as a clerk by S. P. Cockerell in his London office, but resented the menial duties he was expected to perform and ran away. For a time he lived with his mother, teaching himself to draw with the help of Chambers's *Treatise*, until he fortunately attracted the attention of Henry Holland, who gave him employment as a draughtsman and eventually helped him to visit Italy. Tatham arrived in Rome in July 1794, and remained there for two years. During this period he made numerous drawings of architectural details and acquired for Holland a large number of antique Roman fragments (subsequently bought by Sir John Soane, and now in his Museum). In Italy he became friendly with Antonio Canova, Angelica Kauffmann, Sir William Hamilton, Abate Carlo Bonomi (brother of Joseph Bonomi, R.A.), the Italian architect Mario Asprucci, and the Spanish architect Isidoro Velasquez, afterwards the designer of the Casa del Labrador at Aranjuez. In Rome he also met the eccentric Earl-Bishop of Derry, who talked of employing him at Ickworth, and the 5th Earl of Carlisle, who was to be one of his principal English patrons. Tatham left Rome in 1796, when Napoleon's first attack on the Papal States was imminent, reluctantly declining the opportunity to buy the Altieri Claudes from their owner, Prince Altieri, who was convinced that if they remained in Rome they would fall into the hands of the French.[1] He returned to England through Venice, Dresden, Prague and Berlin, making architectural drawings on the way.

In England Tatham began practise as an architect, exhibiting frequently at the Royal Academy, and entering for such competitions as the proposed naval monument (1799). His unwillingness to compromise and his severe neo-classical taste did not, however, invite extensive employment, and picture-galleries, mausolea and the like formed a large part of his practice. Of these, the most important were the Sculpture Gallery which he designed for Lord Carlisle at Castle Howard, and the mausoleum for Lord Stafford at Trentham. The latter is a formidable statement of neo-classical principle, almost brutalist in its exaggeratedly simple forms. His other works are listed below. To these should be added two important projects that were never executed: a palace for the Duke of Wellington at Stratfield Saye, Hants. (illustrated in *C. Life*, 26 Nov. 1948, 1107, and 25 May 1972, 1322), and a design for the Fitzwilliam Museum at Cambridge, made in 1827 (before the competition had been announced) and based on the Library of Hadrian at Athens (illustrated in *C. Life*, 13/20 April 1972, 921).

As Holland's agent in Rome Tatham made an important contribution to the development of the former's style. His publications were equally important in providing exemplars for neo-classical decoration and furniture. *His Etchings of Ancient Ornamental Architecture drawn from the Originals in Rome and other Parts of Italy during the years 1794, 1795 and 1796* was published in 1799–1800. It was a major source-book, based on the results of the excavations at Pompeii, Herculaneum, Tivoli and Rome, and enjoyed immediate success. There was a second edition in 1803, a third in 1810, and a German translation was published in Weimar in 1805. Tatham's linear etchings followed the style established by Flaxman and Tischbein (whom he had met in Italy), and the technique was copied in turn by Hope in his *Household Furniture* of 1807 (which drew extensively on Tatham's book) and by Percier and Fontaine in their *Recueil de décorations intérieures* of 1812. Tatham himself designed candelabra and other ornamental metalwork of high quality, and through his relation John Linnell and his brother Thomas Tatham, both leading cabinet-makers of their day, he probably had a direct influence on the design of contemporary furniture. A mah-

[1] Tatham wrote an account of this incident which was published in *Gent's Mag.* 1799 (ii), 647–8, and in *Monthly Mag.* viii (1799), 536–7.

ogany copy of the Barberini candelabrum at Kenwood is a case in point.

In 1806 Tatham published a further work of the same kind entitled *Etchings representing Fragments of Grecian and Roman Architectural Ornaments*. In 1826 this and the earlier book were republished in one volume as *Etchings representing the Best Examples of Grecian and Roman Architectural Ornament drawn from the Originals, and chiefly collected in Italy, before the late Revolutions in that Country*. He also published *Three Designs for the National Monument proposed to be erected in commemoration of the late glorious victories of the British Navy*, 1802; *Designs for Ornamental Plate*, 1806; *The Gallery at Castle Howard*, 1811; *The Gallery at Brocklesby*, 1811; *Representations of a Greek Vase in the Possession of C. H. Tatham*, 1811, and a description of *The Mausoleum at Castle Howard* designed by Nicholas Hawksmoor, 1812. He also wrote the descriptions for Coney's *Cathedrals* (1829–31), and for some other works. A proposed *Collection of Designs*, illustrating his executed works, was projected by Tatham, but is represented only by an 'Advertisement' bound into some copies of his book on *Ornamental Plate*. This lists eighteen buildings which were to have been illustrated.

Tatham married in 1801 and built a house for himself in Alpha Road, St. John's Wood. This became a centre of artistic society, for Tatham had many artist friends, including Benjamin Robert Haydon, William Blake and Samuel Palmer. But in the 1830s his practice declined and ill-advised litigation with more than one of his clients got him into financial difficulties. In 1831 he was given a clerkship in the Office of Works, only to lose it in the reorganization of the following year. As a result the house had to be sold, together with Tatham's collections (Christie's, 10 July 1833). From this predicament he was eventually rescued by Thomas Grenville, the Duchess of Sutherland and other friends, who in 1837 obtained for him the place of Master of Holy Trinity Hospital, Greenwich. Here 'he ended his days happily and usefully', dying on 10 April 1842, aged 71.

Tatham had four sons and six daughters. His eldest son Frederick (1805–78) became a sculptor and painter. His second daughter, Julia, married George Richmond, R.A., the portrait-painter. A crayon portrait of Tatham by B. R. Haydon is in the Print Room of the British Museum. Another by Haydon dated 1823 is in the possession of Mr. John Harris. A bust by his son is in the Holy Trinity Hospital at Greenwich. A portrait by Thomas Kearsley was, in 1965, in the possession of his great-grandson Sir John Richmond.

Tatham left a MS. autobiography written in 1826. This is believed to have been destroyed by his daughter Julia, and all that survives is a transcript of the first 31 pages, describing his early life and his residence in Rome. A collection of original letters written by Tatham in Rome to Henry Holland, accompanied by drawings, is in the Print Room of the Victoria and Albert Museum (D 1479–1551, 1898). Copies of these letters, together with a number of original drawings, are in Sir John Soane's Museum. Several drawings, including a sketch of himself on a horse, were among the Fetherstonhaugh papers destroyed by fire at Uppark in 1989. A design by him for a hunting pavilion dated 1796 is at the Academy of St. Luke at Rome (*I disegni di architettura dell'Archivio storico dell' Accademia di San Luca*, 1974, Nos. 2148–9). Six alternative versions of his design for the Naval Monument are in the Yale Center for British Art. His design for the Court House at Perth (1802) is S.R.O., RHP 44864–5.

[*A.P.S.D.*; *D.N.B.*; *The Farington Diary*, ed. J. Greig, viii, 43; W. T. Whitley, *Artists and their Friends in England* ii, 1928, 225–6; A. M. W. Stirling, *The Richmond Papers*, 1926, 24, 32, 98–9; W. S. Childe-Pemberton, *The Earl Bishop*, ii, 1924, 465; *Gent's Mag.* 1842 (ii), 436; D. Udy, 'The Neo-Classicism of C. H. Tatham', *Connoisseur* clxxvii, 1971; C. Proudfoot & D. Watkin, 'A pioneer of English Neo-classicism', *C. Life*, 13/20 April 1972, and 'The Furniture of C. H. Tatham', *C. Life*, 8 June 1972; *Catalogue of the R.I.B.A. Drawings Collection: T–Z*, 17–18; R. Riddell, 'Neo-Classical Designs for Medals by C. H. Tatham', *Apollo* cxxiii, Feb. 1986.]

In the following list of works 'Advertisement' refers to the printed list of contents of a proposed Collection of Tatham's designs, issued *c.*1808 and bound up with some copies of his book on *Ornamental Plate*.

COWDRAY LODGE (now COWDRAY PARK), EASEBOURNE, SUSSEX, for W. S. Poyntz, *c.*1800; rebuilt 1876 [exhib. at R.A. 1801].

CASTLE HOWARD, YORKS. (N.R.), THE SCULPTURE GALLERY AND MUSEUM for 5th Earl of Carlisle, 1800–2 [exhib. at R.A. 1802; C. H. Tatham, *The Gallery at Castle Howard*, 1811].

STOKE EDITH, HEREFS., drawing-room, park gate and cottage for the Hon. Edward Foley, *c.*1800; house gutted 1927 and since demolished ['Advertisement'] (*C. Life*, 25 Sept. 1909, 430).

ALPHA ROAD, ST. JOHN'S WOOD, house (No. 34) for himself soon after 1801; dem. [A. M. W. Stirling, *The Richmond Papers*,

1926, 98–9].

GREAT MALVERN PRIORY CHURCH, WORCS., survey and estimate for repairs, 1802 [printed *Report of a Survey of the Parish Church of Great Malvern, made by the direction of the Hon. Edward Foley*, May 1802, of which there is a copy in the Bodleian Library, Gough Worcester 1].

CHESHUNT NUNNERY, HERTS., works for William Butt, *c.*1802 onwards, including an 'American cottage', 'designed to be built' in 1802 [exhib. at R.A.], entrance lodge, Fisherman's Hut, and improvements to house and offices ['Advertisement'].

STOKE EDITH CHURCH, HEREFS., monument to the Hon. Edward Foley (d. 1803), executed by R. Blore [*Gent's Mag.* 1805 (i), 278].

WILTON PARK, nr. BEACONSFIELD, BUCKS., alterations to house, new dairy and greenhouse for James Dupré, 1803–5; dem. 1967 [exhib. at R.A. 1809; 'Advertisement'].

LONDON, CLEVELAND HOUSE, ST. JAMES'S, additions for 2nd Marquess of Stafford, including Doric portico, park elevation and Picture Gallery, 1803–6; dem. 1840 ['Advertisement'; C. M. Westmacott, *British Galleries of Painting and Sculpture*, 1824, 177].

LONDON, No. 12 GROSVENOR PLACE, library for 5th Earl of Carlisle, *c.*1805 ['Advertisement'].

ROCHE COURT, nr. WINTERSLOW, WILTS., for Francis T. Egerton, *c.*1805 [J. Britton, *Beauties of England and Wales* xv, 1814, 201].

TRENTHAM PARK, STAFFS., fountain, greenhouse, park bridges and new lodge for 2nd Marquess of Stafford, 1805–8 [exhib. at R.A. 1807, 1809; 'Advertisement'].

DROPMORE, BUCKS., greenhouse, dairy, gardener's house 'and other works' for Lady Grenville, *c.*1806–9 ['Advertisement']. As Lord Grenville's bank account [B.L., Add. MS. 59454] shows that he paid Tatham over £10,000 between 1806 and 1809, the 'other works' may well have included the enlargement of the house itself (*C. Life*, 11–18 Oct. 1956).

BALGOWAN, nr. METHVEN, PERTHSHIRE, lodges for Col. Thomas Graham, cr. Lord Lynedoch, before 1807 ['Advertisement'].

BROCKLESBY PARK, LINCS., the PICTURE GALLERY for 1st Lord Yarborough, 1807; since remodelled [exhib. at R.A. 1807; 'Advertisement'; C. H. Tatham, *The Gallery at Brocklesby*, 1811].[1]

TRENTHAM, STAFFS., mausoleum for 2nd Marquess of Stafford, 1807–8 [exhib. at R.A. 1807; 'Advertisement'; engraving in B.L., *King's Maps* xxxviii, 57 *b*] (*C. Life*, 15 Jan. 1968, 180, figs. 11–12).

LYNEDOCH LODGE, PERTHSHIRE, for Col. Thomas Graham, cr. Lord Lynedoch, 1807–9; dem. 1870 [exhib. at R.A. 1807; 'Advertisement'].

OCHTERTYRE, PERTHSHIRE, park gates and Gothic mausoleum in park for Sir Patrick Murray, Bart., 1809 [exhib. at R.A. 1807; 'Advertisement'] (*C. Life*, 13/20 April 1970, figs. 9–10).

ALTHORP, NORTHANTS., park entrance for 2nd Earl Spencer, exhibited at R.A. as 'now building' in 1809, but never completed [original drawing at Althorp].

BROXMORE HOUSE, WHITEPARISH, WILTS., for R. Bristow, *c.*1810; dem. [J. Britton, *Beauties of England and Wales* xv, 1814, 218; exhib. at R.A. 1809, 1818].

COWSFIELD HOUSE, WILTS., enlarged for Sir Arthur Paget, 1814; dem. [J. Britton, *Beauties of England and Wales* xv, 1814, 216–17].

HENNERTON HOUSE, nr. WARGRAVE, BERKS., for C. F. Johnson, *c.*1817 [exhib. at R.A. 1817].

QUIDENHAM HALL, NORFOLK, decorated interior for 4th Earl of Albemarle, *c.*1820 [A. E. Garnier, *Chronicles of the Garniers*, 1900].

ROOKESBURY, nr. WICKHAM, HANTS., for the Revd. W. Garnier, 1820–5 [exhib. at R.A. 1825; G. F. Prosser, *Select Illustrations of Hampshire*, 1833].

MONREPOS, VIBURG, KARELIA, RUSSIA, 'Saxon Gothic tower' for Baron Paul Nicolay, 1822 [design by Tatham in archives of Finnish Museums Board, Helsinki, *ex inf.* Dr. Eeva Ruoff], and monument in memory of Nicolay's brothers-in-law, Auguste and Carl de Broglie [exhib. at R.A. 1829].

ROOKESBURY, HANTS., Gothic tower on HOLLY HILL for the Revd. W. Garnier, 1826; dem. 1973 [exhib. at R.A. 1826].

PAULTONS, nr. ROMSEY, HANTS., alterations, addition of office wing, and bridge for William Sloane-Stanley, 1826–8; dem. 1955 [G. F. Prosser, *Select Illustrations of Hampshire*, 1833; drawings in R.I.B.A. Coll.] (*C. Life*, 17 Sept., 1938, 276].

MORESTEAD RECTORY, HANTS., 1835–6 [Bodleian Library, records of Queen Anne's Bounty; Winchester Diocesan Records].

NAWORTH CASTLE, CUMBERLAND, work for 5th Earl of Carlisle [*D.N.B.*].

[1] The monument in Godshill Church, Isle of Wight, to Sir Richard Worsley (d. 1805), erected by Lord Yarborough's son, the Hon. Charles Pelham, may well have been designed by Tatham.

TATTERSALL, GEORGE (1817–1849), was the younger son of Richard Tattersall (d. 1859), the proprietor of the well-known auction mart for horses. Having shown an early talent for drawing, he was placed in an architect's office and eventually established himself in practice at 52 Pall Mall. Besides working as an architect he had some reputation as a topographical and sporting artist, publishing in 1836 a small illustrated guide-book to the Lakes, and subsequently, under the pseudonym of 'Wildrake', several sets of sporting engravings. His experience in designing stables, including Messrs. Tattersall's at Willesden, led him to publish in 1841 an illustrated treatise entitled *Sporting Architecture*, dealing with stables, stud-farms, kennels and racestands. In 1847 he won the first competition for the Army and Navy Club in Pall Mall, but was not successful when the acquisition of a larger site necessitated a second competition. His winning design of 1847 is in the Museum of London. He was surveyor to the Brewers' Company and exhibited at the Royal Academy in 1840, 1846 and 1848. His early death in August 1849 was due to brain-fever [*A.P.S.D.*; *D.N.B.*].

WILLESDEN, MIDDLESEX, MESSRS. TATTERSALL'S STABLES, *c.*1840 [*Sporting Architecture*, 1841, plates facing pp. 10, 18, 23].

ISLINGTON, LADY OWEN'S ALMSHOUSES and SCHOOL, for the Brewers' Company, 1840–1, Elizabethan style; dem. [W. J. Pinks, *History of Clerkenwell*, 1881, 477; exhib. at R.A. 1840, 1846].

WYNNSTAY, DENBIGHSHIRE, Kennels and Kennel Lodge for Sir Watkin Williams-Wynn, Bart., 1843 [exhib. at R.A. 1846; Peter Howell & T. W. Pritchard in *C. Life*, 6 April 1972, 853].

LADYKIRK HOUSE, BERWICKSHIRE, stables for David Robertson, *c.*1846 [exhib. at R.A. 1846].

TATTERSALL, RICHARD (1802–1844), was born in May 1802 at Burnley in Lancashire and articled to William Hayley (*q.v.*) of Manchester, in whose office he remained until about 1830, when he commenced practice on his own. Having won the competition for the County Infirmary at Carlisle, he designed the existing building, which has a fine Greek Doric portico. According to the Architectural Publication Society's *Dictionary*, his Gothic designs were considered 'far in advance' of their time. He designed many cotton-mills, notably those for Peter Dixon & Sons at Carlisle, at that time the largest in the country: they were fireproof and had a chimney 300 feet high.

Tattersall became stone deaf in 1835. His last work, the 'moral and industrial training schools' at Swinton, proved too great a strain, and he died 'in confinement' in 1844. Shortly before his death he had taken T. Dickson as a partner. Dickson subsequently took W. H. Brakspear into partnership and they finished the schools. J. S. Crowther of Manchester was a pupil until 1843 [*A.P.S.D.*].

CHASELY, nr. PENDLETON, LANCS., for R. Gardner (his first work), *c.*1830; dem. *c.*1950 [*A.P.S.D.*].

CARLISLE, CUMBERLAND, THE COUNTY INFIRMARY, 1830–2 [*A.P.S.D.*].

ASHTON-ON-MERSEY CHURCH, CHESHIRE, restoration, 1835 [*A.P.S.D.*].

CARLISLE, CUMBERLAND, cotton-mills (now the Shaddon Works) for Peter Dixon & Sons, 1835–6 [*A.P.S.D.*].

MANCHESTER, THE MANCHESTER & SALFORD BANK (now Bradford & Bingley Building Society), MOSLEY STREET, 1838 [*Civil Engineer & Architect's Jnl.* i, 235].

MANCHESTER, ST. ANN'S CHURCH, rearranged interior 1838–9 [I.C.B.S.].

STALYBRIDGE, CHESHIRE, ST. PAUL'S CHURCH, 1839, Gothic [*Companion to the Almanac*, 1839, 221].

GOLBORNE, LANCS., cotton-mill for Samuel Brewis, 1839 [*A.P.S.D.*].

DUKINFIELD, CHESHIRE, OLD (UNITARIAN) CHAPEL, 1840–1, Gothic [*Companion to the Almanac*, 1840, 235–7].

STOCKPORT, CHESHIRE, UNITARIAN CHAPEL, ST. PETER'S GATE, 1841–2, Gothic [*A.P.S.D.*].

MANCHESTER, ST. BARNABAS CHURCH, RODNEY STREET, OLDHAM ROAD, 1842–4; dem. [*Civil Engineer and Architect's Jnl* v, 211].

SWINTON, nr. MANCHESTER, THE MORAL AND INDUSTRIAL TRAINING SCHOOLS, 1842–5, Elizabethan; completed by T. Dickson & W. H. Brakspear [*Civil Engineer and Architect's Jnl.* viii, 129].

MANCHESTER COLLEGIATE CHURCH (now CATHEDRAL), restored DERBY CHAPEL [*A.P.S.D.*].

MANCHESTER, warehouse behind the Royal Infirmary, for George Faulkner [*A.P.S.D.*].

HIGHER BROUGHTON, LANCS., houses for Dr. Radford and Mr. Armstrong [*A.P.S.D.*].

BIRCH, LANCS., parish schools [*A.P.S.D.*].

CHEETHAM, LANCS., ST. LUKE'S RECTORY [*A.P.S.D.*].

TAWNEY, RICHARD (1774–1832), was a member of a family of Oxford carpenters. He was Surveyor to the Oxford Canal Company and in 1827–8 designed the Greek Revival offices of the Company, now the Master's Lodging of St. Peter's College [P.R.O., Minutes of the Oxford Canal Co., RAIL 855/16, p. 61]. He died on 31 January 1832, aged 58, and was buried at Dunchurch, Warwicks.

TAYLOR, ALEXANDER (–1846), practised for a time in Edinburgh, and later in Glasgow, where he died on 21 June 1846 [S.R.O., SC 36/48/32, p. 766]. Gildard states that he designed CLARENDON PLACE, GLASGOW and the somewhat idiosyncratic ROYAL CRESCENT, SAUCHIEHALL STREET, 1839–49 [T. Gildard, 'An Old Glasgow Architect on some Older Ones', *Trans. Royal Philosophical Soc. of Glasgow* xxvi, 1895, 116; J. Pagan, *Sketch of the History of Glasgow*, 1847, 181; A. Gomme & D. Walker, *Architecture of Glasgow*, 1987, 89].

TAYLOR, BENJAMIN BROOMHEAD (–1848), of Sheffield, designed the classical entrance to the SHEFFIELD BOTANICAL GARDENS in 1836. In 1832 he was the runner-up in the competition for the design of the CUTLERS' HALL, SHEFFIELD, the winner being Samuel Worth (*q.v.*). In the event the building was erected to designs made jointly by Worth and Taylor [R. E. Leader, *Surveyors and Architects of the Past in Sheffield*, 1903; R. E. Leader, *History of the Company of Cutlers in Hallamshire*, Sheffield 1905, i, 191–2]. Taylor also designed DODWORTH CHURCH, YORKS. (W.R.), in the neo-Norman style in 1844 [Port, 166–7].

TAYLOR, EDWARD (*c*.1635–1722), of Newent, Glos., was, as stated on his table-tomb in Newent Churchyard, 'Head Workman in contriving and rebuilding the roof of this Church in the year 1679'. He was a carpenter by trade, and had worked in London under Sir Christopher Wren before retiring to his native town. His part in rebuilding Newent Church is described in a manuscript written by Walter Nourse early in the eighteenth century:[1]

> The old church of Newent fell down January 18th. 1673, which was built up again in six years time. . . . The first stone [was] laid in the foundation July 31st. 1675 by Francis Jones of Hasfield who was the head workman,[2] likewise three pillars of Freestone were being built answering to the three pilasters. Francis Jones and another were to have for the pillars 25£ each (into 75£). When the pillars were built about halfway some Gentlemen coming in to take a view of the Building (I think Mr. Kyrle of Ross was one) they mightily disliked these pillars and would have them taken down by all means. They said the pillars would take up much room in the church which they thought was too little for so large a parish. Edward Taylor Carpenter of Newent, [now] in the 85th. year of his age 1719, hearing of this came to the Gentlemen and proferred to build the rest of the church and they should take down the pillars. They asked him how he could do it, he told them that when he was at work in London after the Fire he saw at Saint Bride's and at some other places such Blades[1] as would soon run up this Building. The Gentlemen desired to see a draft of it which he drew and they liked it well enough but thought they had better shew it to somebody that understood it. Old Edward desired to send it to his old Master in London who was accounted the best carpenter there.[2] Capt. Woodward when he went to London carried the draft to Edward's master who liked it very well and told Captn. Woodward that he need not fear the building and sent a letter to Edward Taylor to put a double buttiment in every pair of blades and then it would be a firm piece of work. When the walls were built up some way it was time to look after the timber, which they considered must be the best the country could afford and likewise a large quantity. This made a great many repent that they had let the pillars be taken down, [but] the timber was soon found in the Lea Bailey which is the King's Wood. This put the parish in hopes of having it for nothing, to obtain which they made friends to acquaint the King of it. The case was fully drawn out for His Majesty to know that the parish had been at so great an [expense] and was not able to buy the timber. . . . The King readily acquiesced in their demand and gave them the timber . . . Edward Taylor went to look it out and being felled was hauled home with great strength of cattle, he and his workmen got it up that summer. The Blades 7 in number they hauled up with a great cable containing 4 Tons in timber which is accounted 6 Tons in weight. Mr. Greenbank of Worcester was the plumber, the church being leaded with 2 sorts of lead Mendip and Derbyshire.

[1] Printed from a copy of the original made by Edward Conder in 1898.

[2] Elsewhere in the MS. it is stated that the 'head workmen' were Francis Jones of Hasfield and James Hill of Cheltenham, masons, some account of whom will be found in this *Dictionary* under their respective names.

[1] i.e. beams.

[2] Perhaps John Longland, master carpenter at St. Paul's, who built the roof of St. Bride's.

Thomas Careless of this town was Glazier. Jno. Wall made the Iron Work, Nathaniel Seny of Tewkesbury was the joiner, the timbers that made the seats came from that place. Mrs. Elizabeth Rogers gave the pulpit value 5£. Edward Taylor laid the flooring of the seats 2 feet [apart] which saved the parish a great deal of expense.

Taylor's roof appears to have been constructed on the same principle as that of the Sheldonian Theatre at Oxford. It has since been rebuilt. Taylor died on 11 February 1721/2, aged 87, and was buried in Newent Churchyard.

TAYLOR, GEORGE LEDWELL (1788–1873), was born in London on 31 March 1788 and educated at Rawes's Academy at Bromley. In 1804 he was articled to J. T. Parkinson (*q.v.*), under whom he supervised the building of Montagu and Bryanston Squares and the neighbouring streets on the Portman estate. In 1816 he undertook a walking tour of England in company with his fellow-pupil, Edward Cresy, and in 1817–19 they travelled, largely on foot, in France, Italy, Greece, Malta and Sicily. In Rome they met John Sanders and his draughtsman, W. Purser, in whose company they discovered the Theban lion at Chaeronea in June 1818 (see Taylor's account of the discovery in *Builder* xx, 1862, 908). On their return, they published *The Architectural Antiquities of Rome, measured and delineated by G. L. Taylor and E. Cresy*, 2 vols., 1821–2, of which a second edition appeared in 1874. Their interests were not confined to classical architecture, and in 1829 they published *The Architecture of the Middle Ages in Italy illustrated by views . . . of the Cathedral, etc. of Pisa*, 1829. They intended a third work on the architecture of the Renaissance, but it was abandoned after the publication of a section dealing with the *Palaces of Genoa* in 1822. Taylor shared an office in Furnival's Inn with Cresy, and lived in London (first at 52 Bedford Square, afterwards in Spring Gardens and later at various addresses in Bayswater). In February 1824 he was appointed Civil Architect to the Navy as successor to Edward Holl. In this capacity he carried out important works in the dockyards at Sheerness, Chatham and Woolwich, and in 1828–32 built the new Clarence Victualling Yard at Gosport. He came into contact with William IV, and claimed that it was his tact which led the King in 1830 to accept 'Trafalgar Square' instead of 'King William IV Square' as the name of the new open space on the site of the King's Mews.

In 1837 Taylor lost his post as a result of a reorganization at the Admiralty and was obliged to take up general practice. In 1843–8 he laid out much of the Bishop of London's estate in Paddington, including Chester Place and parts of Hyde Park Square and Gloucester Square. In 1848 he succeeded J. T. Parkinson as District Surveyor of Westminster. In 1849 he undertook the extension of the North Kent Railway from Strood through Chatham and Canterbury to Dover, but the project fell through, at a personal loss to Taylor of £3000. After this he appears to have given up professional work and devoted himself to archaeological pursuits. In 1856 he made a second visit to Italy with his wife, in order to collect material for his *Stones of Etruria and Marbles of Ancient Rome*, 1859. He finally returned to England in 1868 and settled at Broadstairs, where he died on 1 May 1873. His last years were spent in writing *The Auto-Biography of an Octogenarian Architect*, 2 vols., 1870–2, a diffuse and incoherent work which consists mainly of sketches and descriptions of places visited during his travels.

Taylor was a member of the Architects' Club founded in 1791, and also of the Architects' and Antiquaries' Club founded in 1819, of which he was President in 1822–3. He was a Fellow of the Society of Antiquaries, of the Institute of Civil Engineers, and of the Royal Institute of British Architects. He read several papers to the last body, one of which, an 'Account of the Methods used in Underpinning at Chatham Dockyard in 1834', was printed in the *Transactions* i, 40, in *Professional Papers of the Corps of Royal Engineers*, ed. Denison, 1844 (i), and also in his *Auto-Biography*. Another on *Gas Works*, read on 7 February 1848, was printed separately. In 1855 he published a *Programme and Plan of the Metropolitan General Junction Railways and Roads*, advocating, *inter alia*, the construction of a new bridge over the Thames to the east of Blackfriars Bridge. As an architect he achieved nothing of great distinction, but in London he was responsible for some agreeable stuccoed architecture in the Nash tradition. Elsewhere his most remarkable work was the 170 foot high Gothic tower of Hadlow Castle — an early Victorian folly rivalling Beckford's Fonthill in vertiginous drama.

Taylor was married three (according to some accounts four) times. By his first wife, Bella Neufville, he had eleven children. The sketchbook of his tour in Italy and Greece in 1817–18 is in the Victoria and Albert Museum (E 4087–1918) and thirty-one further drawings are in the Brighton Art Gallery. A survey which he made of all the naval dockyards is in the National Maritime Museum (LAD/11). [*D.N.B.*; *A.P.S.D.*; Taylor's *Auto-Biography*, 1870–2; A. T. Bolton, *The Portrait of Sir John Soane*, 270–1; Patrick Connor, 'George Ledwell Taylor and the Lion of Chaeronea', *Apollo*, Aug. 1979.]

SHEERNESS DOCKYARD, KENT, completed works begun by E. Holl (including the Quadrangle, dated 1829), and designed the DOCKYARD CHAPEL, 1828 (damaged by fire 1881) [*Auto-Biography*, 163; *The Watering Places of Great Britain*, 1833, ii, 26–7].

LONDON, SUFFOLK STREET, Nos. 4 and 5, *c.*1826 [*Survey of London* xx, 92].

LONDON, THE ADMIRALTY, WHITEHALL, cut openings through the Adam screen, 1827–8; restored 1923 [*Auto-Biography*, 165–6].

CHATHAM, KENT, THE MELVILLE HOSPITAL, 1827; dem. [*Auto-Biography*, 173].

GOSPORT, HANTS., THE CLARENCE VICTUALLING YARD, 1828–32 [*Auto-Biography*, 172].

WANDSWORTH VICARAGE, SURREY, 1829 [G.L.R.O., DW/OP/1829/9].

LONDON, TRAFALGAR SQUARE, block (afterwards Morley's Hotel) on east side, 1830; dem. 1936 [*Auto-Biography*, 177] (*Survey of London* xx, pl. 38).

LEE, KENT, BELMONT HOUSE for himself, 1830 [*Auto-Biography*, 162; F. H. Hart, *History of Lee*, 1882, 20, 33].

PEMBROKE DOCK, PEMBROKESHIRE, DOCKYARD CHAPEL, 1830–1 [P.R.O., ADM/140/467, 471, *ex inf.* Mr. Julian Orbach].

BROUGHTON RECTORY, nr. BRIGG, LINCS., for the Revd. Henry de Brett (of Linton, Kent), 1831 [Lincolnshire Record Office, MGA 164].

WOOLWICH, KENT, THE RIVER WALL, 1831 [*A.P.S.D.*; *D.N.B.*].

SHEERNESS, KENT, HOLY TRINITY CHURCH, 1835–6, Gothic [Port, 146–7].

LEE, KENT, THE PROPRIETARY SCHOOL (built of concrete and based on the Propylaea at Athens), 1836 [*Auto-Biography*, 171].

HORSHAM VICARAGE, SUSSEX, 1840, Tudor Gothic [W. Sussex C.R.O., Ep. I 41/24].

HADLOW CASTLE, KENT, the tower for W. B. May, *c.*1840, Gothic [cf. lithograph of the 'projected tower' by G. L. Taylor in Greenwood's *Epitome of County History: Kent*, 1838, 129].[1]

LONDON, PADDINGTON: HYDE PARK SQUARE, the west end and the south side, with the exception of three houses; CHESTER PLACE; GLOUCESTER SQUARE, the south side consisting of thirty houses, 1843–8 [*Auto-Biography*, 180–1].

LONDON, WESTBOURNE TERRACE, No. 140 for himself, 1850 [*Auto-Biography*, 181].

HUTTON JOHN, CUMBERLAND, entrance hall, etc. for his son-in-law William Hudleston, 1866 [F. Hudleston, 'A Short Description of Hutton John', *Trans. Cumberland & Westmorland Archl. Soc.* N.S. xxiv, 1924, 170] (*C. Life*, 26 Jan. 1929).

BROADSTAIRS, KENT, THE MAISONETTE, *c.*1870, 271; *Auto-Biography*, 162].

ERIDGE CASTLE, SUSSEX, enlarged *c.*1820/30, dem. 1939, is stated in *Notes and Queries*, 10th ser. vi, 1906, 371, to have been designed by an architect called Taylor who lived in Bayswater, presumably to be identified as G. L. T. (*C. Life*, 23, 30 Sept. 1965).

TAYLOR, JAMES (*c.*1765–1846), was a Roman Catholic architect and builder who lived from 1791 in Greenwich and from 1820 at Weybridge, but operated from an office at 2 York Place, City Road, Islington. Deeds in the Middlesex Land Registry show that in ISLINGTON he developed and presumably designed NEW TERRACE (now Nos. 46–58 DUNCAN TERRACE), 1791–4, and CHARLTON PLACE, 1790–5. In GREENWICH he appears to have built PARK PLACE, dated 1791, which in 1820 he presented to the Greenwich R.C. Mission for the use of the priest [letter of 30 June 1820 in Southwark Diocesan Archives, *ex inf.* Mr. D. Evinson]. He also designed Roman Catholic chapels at GREENWICH (East Street), 1792; SOUTHWARK (London Road, superseded by Pugin's cathedral in 1848), 1793; CHATHAM, 1793 (dem. 1804); and WEYBRIDGE (now the sacristy of the church of St. Charles Borromeo), 1836. His most important works for the Catholic Church were ST. EDMUND'S COLLEGE, OLD HALL GREEN, nr. STANDON, HERTS., 1795–9, and the original (classical) buildings of ST. CUTHBERT'S COLLEGE, USHAW CO. DURHAM, 1804–8. [B. W. Kelly, *Historical Notes on English Catholic Missions*, 1907, 365, 404, 428; Bernard Ward, *History of St. Edmund's College, Old Hall*, 1893, 147–8, 177; B. Little, *Catholic Churches since 1623*, 1966, 45, 46, 48, 54; information from Mr. D. Evinson and Mr. F. Kelsall.]

TAYLOR, JOHN (–*c.*1841), received his architectural training in the Dublin Society's Schools [J. D. Herbert, *Irish Varieties*, 1836, 56]. In 1791 and 1792 he was awarded premiums for architectural drawing [*Procs. Royal Dublin Soc.* vol. 27, 7 April 1791, vol. 28, 26 April 1792]. By 1815 he was estab-

[1] The castle itself appears to have been designed by J. B. Bunning, who exhibited his design for the south front at the R.A. in 1821. But see J. Dugdale, above, p. 325.

lished as an architect in Dublin, where he designed the churches of STS. MICHAEL AND JOHN (R.C.) and ST. MICHAEL AND ALL ANGELS (C. of I.) [Maurice Craig, *Dublin 1660–1860*, 1952, 291], and supervised the erection of the neo-classical Roman Catholic Pro-Cathedral in Marlborough Street, designed 'by an amateur artist residing in Paris' [G. N. Wright, *Historical Guide to Dublin* 1821, 175; E. McParland, 'Who was P?', *Arch. Rev.* Feb. 1975, 72]. In about 1820 he became Chief Clerk to J. E. Davis, Surveyor of Revenue Buildings in Ireland, and subsequently succeeded Davis as Surveyor. In that capacity he made designs [P.R.O., MPD 28 and 33] for the CUSTOM HOUSE at WATERFORD (1825, a very unpretentious building, dem. 1874) and for a symmetrical row of Revenue Houses at BALTIMORE, CO CORK.

In 1830 Taylor was transferred from Dublin to London to fill the post of Surveyor of Buildings to H.M. Customs, vacant since the dismissal of David Laing in 1825 [P.R.O., CUST 29/9]. In 1839–40 he designed the Greek Revival CUSTOM HOUSE in CLYDE STREET GLASGOW [P.R.O., T1/3783; J. M. Leighton, *Strath-Clutha, or the beauties of Clyde*, n.d., 113]. In 1839–40 he collaborated with James Leslie, the local Harbour Engineer, in designing a new CUSTOM HOUSE at DUNDEE. The plan was Leslie's work, but the façade was chiefly Taylor's [London Custom House Records, MS. 160; J. Thomson & J. Maclaren, *History of Dundee*, 1874, 280].

Taylor appears to have died soon after 1840.

TAYLOR, JOHN, was practising as an architect in Southampton in 1830 [Pigot's *Directory* iii, 1830, 468]. He was presumably the J. Taylor who was an honorary exhibitor at the Royal Academy between 1797 and 1800, giving 'At Mr. Plaw's, Southampton' as his address. His exhibits included (1798) the north front of CHESSEL HOUSE, HANTS (dem.), a view (1798) of BANNISTER LODGE, HANTS., and a design (1799) for a bridge over the R. Itchen at Northam, Hants. He is stated in Brayley & Britton, *Beauties of England and Wales* vi, 1805, 121, to have added a portico to PORTSWOOD HOUSE, HANTS. (dem. *c.*1850). He may have been related to the 'TAYLOR Mason SOUTHAMPTON', whose name appears on the Heathcote Mausoleum in HURSLEY CHURCHYARD, HANTS., or to the Taylor family of Southampton who were well known as makers of mechanical equipment for the Navy during the Napoleonic Wars.

TAYLOR, JOHN HENRY (*c.*1792–1867), practised from 22 Parliament Street, London. He exhibited at the Royal Academy between 1827 and 1841. He was President of the Surveyors' Club in 1838 and was one of the founding members of the R.I.B.A. in 1834. In 1825 he repaired the interior of ST. MARGARET'S CHURCH, WESTMINSTER [*A.P.S.D.*] and in 1830–1, in collaboration with Alfred Ainger, repaired the City church of ST. AUGUSTINE, OLD CHANGE [Guildhall Library, MSS. 8881, 8898]. He designed ST. JOHN'S CHURCH, WALHAM GREEN, FULHAM, 1827–8, Gothic [*Gent's Mag.* 1830 (i), 577–8; C. J. Fèret, *Fulham Old and New* ii, 1900, 235–7]; ST. ANNE'S SOCIETY SCHOOLS, BRIXTON HILL, 1829 [*A.P.S.D.*]; THE ALBANY (DISSENTERS') CHAPEL, FREDERICK STREET, HAMPSTEAD ROAD, 1835 [exhib. at R.A. 1837]; ALL SAINTS CHURCH, SIDMOUTH, DEVON, 1838–40, Gothic [exhib. at R.A. 1835 and 1838]; premises at 9 LUDGATE HILL for Messrs. John Harvey & Co., linen-drapers, 1841 [exhib. at R.A. 1841 by Taylor's son]; and the INFIRMARY of the INFANT ORPHAN ASYLUM at WANSTEAD, ESSEX, 1854 [*A.P.S.D.*]. He restored LINDFIELD CHURCH, SUSSEX, in 1849–50 [I.C.B.S.]. In 1841 he laid out an estate in the neighbourhood of HACKNEY for J. B. Nichols, designing NICHOLS SQUARE (dem.) as its principal feature [exhib. at R.A. 1841]. Two sets of unexecuted designs for rebuilding Escot House, Devonshire, in a conventional Grecian style labelled as by 'Mr. Taylor' are probably his work [Devon C.R.O., 961 M/E 29].

Taylor died on 22 March 1867, aged 75. He was the father of John Taylor, junior, who also practised as an architect and who in 1834 published an engraved 'View of the Remains of St. Stephen's Chapel, on the Morning after the Fire of 16 October 1834'. One of the latter's principal works was St. Mary's Church, Spring Grove, Hounslow. [*A.P.S.D.*; *Architectural Mag.* ii, 1835, 186–7; *Builder* xiv, 1856, 691–2.]

TAYLOR, Sir ROBERT (1714–1788), was the son of Robert Taylor, a successful master mason and monumental sculptor who was Master of the London Masons' Company in 1733. The elder Taylor settled at Woodford in Essex, where he built himself a villa and lived beyond his means. His son, Robert Taylor, junior, was born at Woodford in 1714, and at the age of 18 was apprenticed to the sculptor Henry Cheere. When his apprenticeship was over his father, whose wealth was already somewhat depleted, managed to give him 'just money enough to travel on a plan of frugal study to Rome'. While Robert was in Rome news reached him of his father's death, and he decided to return home at once. Lacking the passports which were necessary to cross Europe in wartime, Taylor is said to have disguised himself as a Franciscan friar. Having thus 'passed unmolested through the enemy's camp', he found on reaching England that his father had died a bankrupt. In this crisis he received generous aid from his father's friends, the Godfrey family of Woodford,[1] which enabled him to set up in business as a sculptor. His father's death had taken place in 1742, and by 1744 he was sufficiently well known to be commissioned by Parliament to design and erect the monument to Captain Cornewall in Westminster Abbey. That to General Guest (d. 1747) is also his work. In 1744 he was chosen to carve the pediment of the Mansion House in preference to Roubiliac, a commission which he owed to his City connection (like his father he was a member of the Masons' Company) and also perhaps to the fact that his father had been one of the mason-contractors for the building. The composition, intended to typify London's commercial prosperity, is trivial in conception and undistinguished in execution. Though generally competent enough as a sculptor, Taylor was undoubtedly inferior in talent to his principal rivals, Roubiliac, Rysbrack and Scheemakers, and by the time he was 40 he had embarked on a more distinguished career as an architect.

Taylor's success as an architect was due partly to ability as a designer and partly to an exceptional capacity for hard work. It was said that he never remained in bed after 4 o'clock in the morning and that he made a point of travelling by night in order to save time by sleeping in the coach. Certainly he was an extremely active and business-like man. George Byfield told Joseph Farington that 'Sir Robert Taylor had three rules for growing rich viz: rising early, keeping appointments and regular accounts.' The result was that extensive practice which led Thomas Hardwick, in his *Memoir* of Sir William Chambers, to observe that Taylor and James Paine 'nearly divided the practice of the profession between them till Mr. Robert Adam entered the lists'. City merchants formed the basis of Taylor's clientèle, and for them he designed offices in London and villas in the country. As surveyor to the Bank of England from about 1764 onwards he held one of the principal architectural posts in their gift. In March 1769 he joined the Office of Works as one of the two Architects of the Works; in 1777 he became a member of the Board of Works with the title of Master Carpenter and in 1780 was promoted to be Master Mason and Deputy Surveyor. Both these posts were, however, abolished as a result of the reforms of 1782.

In February 1788 Taylor was appointed Surveyor of Greenwich Hospital, and at the time of his death he was also surveyor to the Foundling Hospital and Lincoln's Inn. Other estates for which he acted as surveyor were those of the Duke of Grafton and General Pulteney. The tradition that he and George Dance, junior, drafted the London Building Act of 1774 cannot be substantiated, but in February of that year it was Taylor and James Adam (then Joint Architects of the Royal Works) who, on behalf of the builders of London, successfully petitioned the House of Commons for new regulatory legislation (*Commons Jnls*. 34, 452, 667, 731, 751, 763).

Taylor was knighted in 1782 on his election as Sheriff of London. He died on 27 September 1788, from a chill caught at the funeral of his friend Sir Charles Asgill, and was buried in the church of St. Martin-in-the-Fields. There is a monument to his memory in the south transept of Westminster Abbey, on which the date of his death is incorrectly given as 26 September and his age as 70 instead of 74. He left an only son, Michael Angelo Taylor, who was called to the Bar and was well known as a Member of Parliament. The bulk of his fortune of £180,000 was left to the University of Oxford 'for establishing a foundation for the teaching and improving the European languages'. The will was, however, contested by his son, and it was only after the latter's death in 1834 that the bequest took effect. The result was the Taylorian Institution, designed by C. R. Cockerell, which still forms the centre of modern language studies in Oxford. Two similar half-length portraits of Taylor exist, one at the Taylorian Institution, the other at the R.I.B.A. Neither is signed, but both appear, on the evidence of an engraving in the British Museum, to be by William Miller. There is also an anonymous stipple portrait in the 'Crowle Pennant' in the British Museum (vol. xii, 93).

As one of the most successful architects of his time Taylor attracted a number of pupils, some of whom were to be among the leading members of the profession in the next generation. They included Charles Beazley, T. Burnell, S. P. Cockerell, C. A. Craig, John Leach, John Nash and William Pilkington.

Taylor was an architect of considerable originality who was by no means content merely to follow established Palladian prototypes. His villas, with their ingeniously varied plans, represented a new departure in

[1] On Peter Godfrey's death Taylor erected a monument to his memory costing £1500. It stands in Woodford Churchyard and consists of a marble column surmounted by an urn.

country-house architecture that was calculated to appeal to his clientèle of rich merchants and bankers, building relatively compact yet handsome houses on new sites without large estates to support them. At Purbrook House he gave himself a place in the history of the neo-classical revival by designing what was almost certainly the first re-creation of a Roman atrium in England. At the Bank of England the side-lit domes and segmental arches of his Reduced Annuities Office formed one of the starting-points of Soane's distinctive style. In the interiors of his earlier works he showed a fondness for features of a rococo character, including rich plasterwork and octagonal patterns in doors, shutters and glazing, but at Purbrook, the Bank of England and elsewhere he developed an elegant decorative style based on antique sources in a manner comparable to that of Robert Adam. With Chambers and Paine he must therefore be ranked as one of the outstanding English architects of the generation between the Palladians and the school of Adam. But for the unfortunate destruction of nearly all his work at the Bank of England he would be better known as a major English classical architect. As it is his skill as an architectural designer can still be appreciated in his surviving country houses (notably Sharpham) and in the 32 aquatint plates of his executed designs by Thomas Malton, junior, that were commissioned by his son and distributed privately in 1792.[1]

A large volume of Taylor's designs for monuments is in the library of the Taylorian Institution, together with a smaller one containing 12 designs for rococo chimney-pieces and overmantels and a third consisting of 'Problems in Geometry and Mensuration with Diagrams'. The same Institution contains some seventy architectural books from Taylor's library (see *Books from the Library of Sir Robert Taylor in the Library of the Taylor Institution Oxford*, a checklist compiled by D. J. Gilson, 1973).

[*A.P.S.D.*; *D.N.B.*; obituaries in *Gent's Mag.* 1788 (ii), 842, 930, 1070, and *London Mag.* lxiv, 1788, 27–30 Sept., 319; Walpole, *Anecdotes of Painting* v, ed. Hilles & Daghlian, 1937, 190–200 (mostly copied from the *Gent's Mag.* obituary); *The Farington Diary*, 20 May 1797, 20 Aug. 1807, 5 Nov. 1821; S. Perks, *The History of the Mansion House*, 1992, 185; Walpole Soc., *Vertue Note Books* iii, 161; Marcus Binney, 'The Villas of Sir Robert Taylor', *C. Life*, 6–13 July 1967; Marcus Binney, *Sir Robert Taylor*, 1984; information from Mr. Richard Garnier.]

[1] A set of these plates can be found in the Ashmolean Museum, Oxford, together with some of Malton's original drawings. There are other sets at the Courtauld Institute of Art and Sir John Soane's Museum.

PUBLIC BUILDINGS, ETC.

LONDON BRIDGE, removal of houses, replacement of two central arches by a single arch, and erection of balustrades and parapets, in collaboration with George Dance, senior, 1756–66; dem. 1831 [Dorothy Stroud, *George Dance, Architect*, 1971, 52].

LONDON, No. 70 LOMBARD STREET, BANKING HOUSE for Sir Charles Asgill, *c.*1756, afterwards the Pelican Life Assurance Co.'s offices; dem. *c.*1920 [Malton].

LONDON, THE LORD MAYOR'S COACH, 1757 (in the mayoralty of Sir Charles Asgill) [Marcus Binney in *C. Life*, 16 Nov. 1978].

LONDON, BANK BUILDINGS, consisting of two facing blocks in Threadneedle Street opposite the Bank of England, 1764–6; dem. 1844 [Marcus Binney in *C. Life*, 13 Nov. 1969, 1247 and figs. 1, 10]

LONDON, THE BANK OF ENGLAND, extensive additions, including the wings on either side of Sampson's original façade, the Reduced Annuity Office, the Transfer and other offices, the Court and Committee rooms, etc., 1766–88. Some of Taylor's work was replaced by his successor, Sir John Soane: the remainder was destroyed or mutilated in 1921–37, but the Court Room (*c.*1767–70) survives in reconstructed form [Malton; H. R. Steele & F. R. Yerbury, *The Old Bank of England*, 1930; Marcus Binney, 'Sir Robert Taylor's Bank of England', *C. Life*, 13–20 Nov. 1969; drawings in Bank archives].

OXFORD, six minor bridges on the Botley Road, of which Osney Bridge is a survivor, 1767 [*Jackson's Oxford Jnl.* 13 June 1767].

MAIDENHEAD BRIDGE, BERKS (R. Thames), 1772–7 [Malton; drawings in Berkshire County Record Office, MAB 4].

LONDON, LINCOLN'S INN, STONE BUILDINGS, begun 1774–80; south wing completed by P. Hardwick 1842–5. For Robert Adam's rival design, see A. T. Bolton in *Arch. Rev.* June 1917. Those by Brettingham and Paine, long lost, are now in Lincoln's Inn Library. A plan in the Ashmolean Museum (Print Room) shows Taylor's original scheme extending the whole length of the Chancery Lane frontage of the Inn [*Records of the Society of Lincoln's Inn: The Black Books* iii, 407, 410, 412, 423 *et seq.*; iv, 5–9, 17, 219, 226].

LONDON, THE SIX CLERKS' AND ENROLMENT OFFICES, CHANCERY LANE, 1775–7 [*A.P.S.D.*;

cf. *Records of the Society of Lincoln's Inn: The Black Books* iii, 423–4, etc.].

BELFAST, IRELAND, ASSEMBLY ROOM in OLD EXCHANGE, 1776; exterior altered by C. Lanyon 1845, interior by W. H. Lynn 1895; now offices of Belfast Banking Co. [Malton].

WALLINGFORD, BERKS., ST. PETER'S CHURCH, the Gothic spire, 1776–7. Taylor was also employed to fit up the interior of the church on its completion in 1767, but there is no evidence that he designed the church as a whole [MS. Vestry Minutes; documents in Berks. C.R.O., D/P. 139/6/2–3].

LONG DITTON CHURCH, SURREY, 1778–9; dem. 1880 [Malton, who shows an alternative Gothic design with a spire resembling the one at Wallingford; drawings in Surrey Archdeaconry Records, now G.L. Record Office, DWOP/1778/5].

SALISBURY, WILTS., THE GUILDHALL, 1788–95, executed 'with some alterations' by Taylor's pupil W. Pilkington after his death; enlarged by T. Hopper 1829, forming existing portico [Malton; J. Britton, *Beauties of Wiltshire* i, 1801, 86–9; R.C.H.M., *Salisbury* i, 46–7].

COUNTRY HOUSES, ETC

BRAXTED PARK, ESSEX, rebuilt for Peter Du Cane, 1753–6; north front rebuilt by J. Johnson 1804–6 [Nancy Briggs in *Essex Jnl.* v, 1970, 98].

THE GROVE, nr. WATFORD, HERTS., alterations for Thomas Villiers, 1st Earl of Clarendon, 1754–6 [*Gent's Mag.* 1788 (ii), 930; *A.P.S.D.*; J. T. Smith, *Hertfordshire Houses*, R.C.H.M. 1933, 166].

CHESTER, THE BISHOP'S PALACE, remodelled for Edmund Keene, Bishop of Chester, 1754–7; dem. 1874 [B. C. Redwood in *Chester Observer*, 9 Dec. 1966, citing payment to Taylor in Cheshire Record Office, EEB 99487, 61, 62; cf. J. H. E. Bennett, 'The Old Bishop's Palace, Chester', in *Jnl. Chester and N. Wales Architectural . . . Soc.*, N.S. xxxvii, 1948].

HARLEYFORD MANOR, nr. MARLOW, BUCKS., for Sir William Clayton, Bart., 1755 [T. Langley, *Hundred of Desborough*, 1797, 100].

ARNO'S GROVE, SOUTHGATE, MIDDLESEX, library and dining-room for Sir George Colebrooke, Bart., who owned the house from 1752 to 1762 [Watts's *Views of Seats*, pl. 63, 1784].

COPTFOLD HALL, MARGARETTING, ESSEX, extensive alterations for Richard Holden, soon after 1755; dem. 1850 [Malton].

ASGILL HOUSE, RICHMOND, SURREY, for Sir Charles Asgill, Bart., 1761–4 [*Vitruvius Britannicus* iv, 1767, pl. 74; Malton] (*C. Life*, 9 June 1944).

OTTERSHAW PARK, nr. CHERTSEY, SURREY, for Sir Thomas Sewell, soon after 1761; rebuilt 1908 [*The World*, 7 Dec. 1787, *ex inf.* Mr. P. A. Bezodis] (*C. Life*, 5 Aug. 1965, 349).

DANSON HILL, BEXLEYHEATH, KENT, for (Sir) John Boyd, *c.*1762–5; interior completed by Sir W. Chambers [Malton] (*C. Life*, 6 July 1967, figs. 3–6; Roger White, 'Danson Park', *Archaeologia Cantiana* xcviii, 1982).

LONGFORD CASTLE, WILTS., unspecified 'additions' for 2nd Viscount Folkestone, presumably in 1763, when he received a fee and expenses for a professional visit [*Gent's Mag.* 1788 (ii), 930; account-book at Longford, *sub anno* 1763].

TREWITHEN, nr. TRURO, CORNWALL, dining-room, drawing-room, etc., for Thomas Hawkins, 1763–4 [Cornwall C.R.O., Hawkins papers, letter from James Heywood to Hawkins, 9 April 1764, mentioning Taylor as architect, and drawings attributable to Taylor] (*C. Life*, 2–9 April 1953).

KEVINGTON, ST. MARY CRAY, KENT, enlarged for Herman Berens, 1767–9; dem. [photocopy in R.I.B.A. Library of account-book in the possession of Mr. H.C.B. Berens].

CLUMBER, NOTTS., unspecified rooms for 1st Duke of Newcastle (d. 1768); destroyed by fire 1879 [*Builder* iv, 1846, 505 n.; C.R. Cockerell quoted by D. Watkin, *C.R. Cockerell*, 1974, 61; Binney, 1984, 28–9].

CHUTE LODGE, nr. LUDGERSHALL, WILTS., for John Freeman, *c.*1768 [Binney, 1984, 51] (*C. Life*, 13 July 1967, 81–2, figs. 8–11).

PURBROOK HOUSE, PORTSDOWN HILL, HANTS., for Peter Taylor, 1770; dem. 1829 [Malton].

SHARPHAM HOUSE, DEVON, for Capt. Philemon Pownall, *c.*1770 [Marcus Binney in *C. Life*, 17–24 April 1969].

MOUNT CLARE, ROEHAMPTON, SURREY, for George Clive, *c.*1771–2; portico added by P. Columbani *c.*1780 [Anne Riches, 'Mount Clare, Roehampton', *Arch. Hist.* 27, 1984].

ELY, CAMBS., works for Bishop Edmund Keene, who carried out extensive alterations to the Bishop's Palace on his appointment to the see in 1771 [*A.P.S.D.*].

ALTHORP, NORTHANTS., repairs for 1st Earl Spencer after the fall of part of the roof in 1772 [*A Short History of Althorp and the Spencer Family*, 1949].

THORNCROFT, LEATHERHEAD, SURREY, for Henry Crabb Boulton, 1772 [Brayley, *Topographical History of Surrey* iv, 1841, 431].

PORTERS LODGE, SHENLEY, HERTS. (now part of Shenley Mental Hospital), for 1st Earl Howe, soon after 1772; altered in 1903 [*Gent's Mag.* 1788 (ii), 930; Howe letters in B.L., Althorp Papers, F 42–3].

GORHAMBURY, HERTS., for 3rd Viscount Grimston, 1777–90; alterations by W. Atkinson 1816–17 and 1826–8 and by W. Burn 1847 [Malton; J. C. Rogers, 'The Manor and Houses of Gorhambury', *Trans. St. Albans and Herts. Archaeological Soc.*, 1933] (*C. Life*, 25 Nov. 1933).

HEVENINGHAM HALL, SUFFOLK, for Sir Gerard Vanneck, Bart., 1778–*c.*1780; completed by James Wyatt [Malton] (*C. Life*, 19–26 Sept. 1925; C. Hussey, *English Country Houses: Mid Georgian*, 1956, 165–76).

SALISBURY, WILTS., THE BISHOP'S PALACE, alterations, including Gothic porch, and doors, windows and chimney-piece of great room, for Bishop Shute Barrington, 1783–5 [*The Farington Diary*, ed. J. Greig, v, 228; J. Nichols, *Literary Illustrations* v, 1828, 610 n.; R.C.H.M., *The Houses of the Close*, 1993, 70].

LONDON HOUSES

CHARING CROSS, No. 66, for himself, after 1745; dem. [*Survey of London* xvi, 140].

BISHOPSGATE STREET, No. 112, for John Gore, *c.*1750; dem. [*Gent's Mag.* 1788 (ii), 930, 1070].

LINCOLN'S INN FIELDS, Nos. 35 and 36, 1754–5. No. 35 was destroyed by bombing in 1941, No. 36 was rebuilt in 1859 [*Survey of London* iii, 36–47 and pls. 24–41].

GRAFTON HOUSE, PICCADILLY, for 3rd Duke of Grafton, *c.*1760; afterwards the Turf Club; façade and interior altered 1876; dem. 1966 [*Gent's Mag.* 1788 (ii), 930].

SPRING GARDENS, No. 34, for himself, date uncertain but before 1767; dem. 1885 [*London Chronicle*, 27–30 Sept. 1788, 319] (*Survey of London* xx, pl. 45).

ARLINGTON STREET, No. 4, alterations for George Clive, 1767 [payment of £1060 to Taylor on 3 Feb. 1768 in Clive's account at Gosling's (now Barclay's) Bank, *ex inf.* Mr. R. Garnier].

UPPER BROOK STREET, No. 33, for (Sir) John Boyd, 1767–8 [Binney, 1984, 59–60].

GRAFTON STRRET, 14 houses on N. and W. sides for 3rd Duke of Grafton, 1768–75; dem. except Nos. 3–6 and part of 7 [Binney, 1984, 60–1].

SPENCER HOUSE, ST. JAMES'S PLACE: some involvement by Taylor in the decoration of the ceiling of the staircase for 1st Earl Spencer in 1772 is indicated by a letter of that date quoted by *Survey of London* xxx, 521.

ELY HOUSE, No. 37 DOVER STREET, for Edmund Keene, Bishop of Ely, 1772–6; interior remodelled 1909 and 1993 [Malton; *Gent's Mag.* 1788 (ii), 930; drawings in Ely Diocesan Records, C.U.L., EDR/D9/2] (C. Hussey, *The Story of Ely House*, 1956).

DOWNING STREET, No. 10, repairs and alterations, including new kitchen, 1781–2 [*Survey of London* xiv, 122; *History of the King's Works* v, 442, n. 8].

WHITEHALL YARD, No. 4 (later No. 1 HORSE GUARDS AVENUE), built by Taylor's son M.A. Taylor 'according to a plan of Sir Robert's' immediately after his death, according to *The World* 24 Oct. 1788, but not begun until 1793 according to *Survey of London* xiii, 153; dem. *c.*1938.

PHILPOT LANE, No. 15, date uncertain; dem. [*A.P.S.D.*].

MAUSOLEUM

CHILHAM CHURCH, KENT, domed mausoleum on N. side of chancel for Robert Colebrooke, 1755; dem. 1862 [*Gent's Mag.* 1800 (ii), 825, with engraving].

ATTRIBUTIONS

Unlike his contemporaries Chambers and Paine, Taylor left no published or manuscript record of his practice which would enable a definitive list of buildings designed by him to be compiled, and he apparently never signed his drawings. In an active career of some 35 years, he must have had considerably more than the 49 commissions listed above, and a number of further buildings can be attributed to him on stylistic or other grounds. Some of the most probable of these are listed below. 'R.G.' indicates those due to Mr. Richard Garnier.

ABINGDON, BERKS., TWICKENHAM HOUSE, EAST ST. HELEN'S STREET, for Thomas Tomkins, *c.*1760 [R.G.] (*C. Life*, 28 Sept. 1929, supplement).

ALBYNS, STAPLEFORD ABBOTS, ESSEX, refenestration 1754 for Sir John Abdy, Bart. (d. 1759), first occupant of 36 Lincoln's Inn Fields, a house designed by Taylor; mostly dem. 1945 [R.G.].

BARLASTON HALL, STAFFS., for Thomas Mills, 1756–8 [A. Gomme in *C. Life*, 18 April 1968].

BAYFORDBURY, HERTS. An estate survey of 1758 (Herts. C.R.O. D/Ex 33. P 1[3]34) shows in a vignette a farmhouse on the estate, evidently of recent erection, which has a pediment with eaves like those of

Asgill House, which at this date points strongly to Taylor as the architect. Lateral doorways under segmental arches resemble the attic windows of Bayfordbury House, built by Sir William Baker, alderman of London, in 1759–62, suggesting that Taylor may have been the architect employed for the house too [R.G.]. The Doric portico was added in 1809–12 (see p. 69) (*C. Life*, 17–24 Jan. 1925).

CARSHALTON HOUSE, SURREY, Hall and Blue Parlour for Sir George Amyand, Bart. (d. 1766), or his successor the Hon. Thomas Walpole (d. 1782) (*C. Life*, 4 March 1949).

CLERMONT LODGE (now HALL), NORFOLK, for 1st Earl of Clermont, 1777–8; remodelled 1812 by W. Pilkington [R. Garnier in *C. Life*, 23 Sept. 1993].

COMARQUES, THORPE-LE-SOKEN, ESSEX, staircase, ceiling, glazing, etc., *c.*1750/60 [R.G.] (*C. Life*, 5 Feb. 1916, Supplement, 2*–4*).

DELAPRÉ ABBEY, NORTHANTS., internal alterations, probably for Edward Bouverie soon after 1764; altered in 19th century [drawings in Northants. C.R.O., 1179 a, b, c, d and 1229, attributable to Taylor on grounds of similarity to unexecuted 'Plan for a New Farm from Mr. Robert Taylor 1769' in same collection, B (D) 618; R.G.].

ELTHAM LODGE, KENT, internal alterations for Sir John Shaw, Bart. (d. 1779), *c.*1750/60 [R.G.] (*C. Life*, 9–16 Aug. 1919).

LONDON, Nos. 56, 58 ARTILLERY LANE (formerly 3–4 Raven Row), SPITALFIELDS, for Nicholas Jourdain, 1756–7 [R.G.] (*Survey of London* xxvii, 227–36).

LONDON, JOHN STREET, HOLBORN, block of 18 houses and adjoining houses in THEOBALDS ROAD, 1759–61 [R.G.].

LONDON, No. 7 SOHO SQUARE, for George Weston, 1745–8; dem. 1929 [*Survey of London* xxxiii, 60].

LONDON, No. 32 SOHO SQUARE, for Sir George Colebrooke, Bart., 1773–5; dem. 1937 [*Survey of London* xxxiii, 118].

LONDON, TRUMAN'S BREWERY, BRICK LANE, SPITALFIELDS, Dining Room and corridor in DIRECTOR'S HOUSE, for Sir Benjamin Truman, *c.*1775 [stylistic attribution based on characteristic vaulted corridor and chimney-piece similar to one in Bank of England: R.G.].

THE OAKS, CARSHALTON, SURREY, dining- or ball-room for General John Burgoyne, *c.*1770; dem. 1957–60 [Binney, 1984, 37, 96].

RICHMOND, SURREY, No. 3 THE TERRACE, for Christopher Blanchard, playing-card manufacturer, 1769 (cf. Ely House, London).

SOUTHGATE, MIDDLESEX, unidentified house belonging to 'Mr. Bearing', whose plan, sketched in 1765 by William Newton (d. 1790) (R.I.B.A.D.) was characteristic of Taylor [R.G.].

SWINFORD BRIDGE, EYNSHAM, OXON. (R. Thames), for 4th Earl of Abingdon, 1767–9 (cf. H. C. D. Cooper in E. de Villiers, *Swynford Bridge*, Eynsham 1969, 27–30).

TENDRING HALL, STOKE-BY-NAYLAND, SUFFOLK, fishing pavilion, *c.*1750/60 [R. White, *Georgian Arcadia*, Georgian Group Exhibition, 1987, No. 242].

WATLINGTON PARK, OXON., for John Tilson, *c.*1760 [R.G.] (*C. Life*, 1–8 Jan, 1959).

WORTHING, SUSSEX, house (later WARWICK HOUSE) for John Luther, *c.*1770 (?); dem. (view dated 1790 in B.L., Add. MS. 5678, f. 19; John Evans, *Picture of Worthing*, 1814, frontispiece and plan at pp. 42–3).

TAYLOR, SAMUEL, of Stoke Ferry, Norfolk, appears to have been a gentleman farmer with literary and architectural interests. He was a friend of J. C. Loudon, who published several of his designs in his *Encyclopaedia of Rural Architecture* (1833). These include a farmyard built for the British Iron Company at ABERYSCHAN, MONMOUTHSHIRE (pp. 511–12 and cf. pp. 238–9), a farmhouse and farm at STARSTON PLACE, nr. HARLESTON, NORFOLK, for his uncle, Meadows Taylor (pp. 516–19), and a design for a country inn in the Italian style, with an elevation supplied by John Robertson (pp. 678–80).

TAYLOR, THOMAS (*c.*1778–1826), was the leading architect practising in Leeds during the Regency and designed many churches in the industrial towns of the West Riding. According to his own statement, made in the *Leeds Mercury* of 9 September 1811, he had had 'Five Years Practice under Mr. Andrews, a builder of eminence in London', followed by a period of eight years in the office of James Wyatt, for whom 'he was in the Habit of making Plans, Elevations, and Sections, for executing some of the most distinguished Buildings in the Kingdon.' It was from James Wyatt's office that he exhibited his first drawings at the Royal Academy in 1792–3, and he continued to send topographical drawings and architectural designs to the Academy annually until 1811. By then he was established in Yorkshire and was employed to make the drawings to illustrate Whitaker's *Loidis and Elmete* and the same author's new edition of Thoresby's *Ducatus Leodiensis*, both of which were published in 1816. In 1811 he obtained his first important architectural commission, the Leeds Court House, and in the following year he built his first church, Christ Church, Liversedge, for the Revd. Hammond Roberson. This was, for its date, a serious essay in the Gothic style. It had, as Whitaker put it, 'every constituent part of a church of the fifteenth century, tower, nave columns, pointed arches, side aisles, clerestory and choir', and as such it established Taylor's reputation as an ecclesiastical architect at a time when church-building was beginning to be affected by antiquarian influence. The Act for building new churches which was passed in 1818 gave Taylor extensive employment, and in 1825 he stated that he was so preoccupied with ecclesiastical work that he had no time even to compete for a secular building. He died on 25 March 1826, aged 48, after catching cold in the new church of Quarry Hill, and was buried in the crypt of Christ Church, Liversedge.

[Frank Beckwith, *Thomas Taylor, Regency Architect, Leeds*, Thoresby Society's Publications, 1949, upon which the following list of buildings is based.]

SECULAR BUILDINGS

LEEDS, THE COURT HOUSE, PARK ROW, 1811–13; altered by R.D. Chantrell 1834; dem. 1901.

LEEDS, THE LANCASTERIAN SCHOOL, ALFRED STREET, 1811–12; dem. 1975.

LEEDS, THE NATIONAL SCHOOL, KIRKGATE, 1812–13; dem.

LEEDS, THE UNION BANK, COMMERCIAL STREET, 1812–13; since rebuilt.

LEEDS, THE CHARITY SCHOOL (for Girls), in St. John's churchyard, 1815–16; dem.

SHEFFIELD, THE NATIONAL SCHOOL FOR GIRLS, 1823–4.

CHURCHES (all Gothic)

LEEDS, ST. PETER, repaired S. side, 1808–12 [E. Parsons, *The History of Leeds, Halifax, Huddersfield, Bradford, Wakefield, etc.*, 1834, 420].

LIVERSEDGE, YORKS. (W.R.), CHRIST CHURCH, 1812–16.

BRADFORD, YORKS. (W.R.), CHRIST CHURCH, 1813–15; dem. 1878.

COLNE PARISH CHURCH, LANCS., repairs, 1815.

ROCHDALE PARISH CHURCH, LANCS., repairs, 1815–16; obliterated by later restorations.

LUDDENDEN, YORKS. (W.R.), ST. MARY, 1816–17; altered 1866.

SOUTHOWRAM, YORKS. (W.R.), ST. ANNE, 1816–19; chancel 1869.

HUDDERSFIELD, YORKS. (W.R.), HOLY TRINITY, 1816–19.

LITTLEBOROUGH, LANCS., HOLY TRINITY, 1818–20, galleries 1823; chancel 1889.

OSSETT PARISH CHURCH, YORKS. (W.R.), addition of a semi-transept on south side, 1821; rebuilt 1865.

PUDSEY, YORKS. (W.R.), ST. LAWRENCE,* 1821–4.

SHEFFIELD, YORKS. (W.R.), ST. PHILIP,* 1822–8; dem. 1952.

ATTERCLIFFE (SHEFFIELD), YORKS. (W.R.), CHRIST CHURCH,* 1822–6; altered by W. Fawcett 1867, and destroyed by bombing 1940. The original plans are in the Sheffield Archives.

LEEDS, ST. MARY'S,* QUARRY HILL, 1823–6; altered 1862; dem. 1978.

WOODHOUSE HILL, nr. HUDDERSFIELD, YORKS. (W.R.), CHRIST CHURCH, 1823–4; chancel 1901.

DEWSBURY MOOR, YORKS. (W.R.), ST. JOHN,* 1823–7.

HANGING HEATON, YORKS. (W.R.), ST. PAUL,* 1823–5; east end altered 1894; rebuilt after a fire in 1917.

ROUNDHAY, nr. LEEDS, YORKS. (W.R.), ST. JOHN, 1824–6; altered 1885.

EARLS HEATON, YORKS. (W.R.), ST. PETER,* 1825–7; dem.

RIPON, YORKS. (W.R.), HOLY TRINITY, 1826–7; altered 1876 and 1884.

TAYLOR, THOMAS FISH, was practising from Salisbury Street, Strand, in the late 1820s. He appears to have been the 'J. F. Taylor' of 7 Salisbury Street, whose design for a suspension bridge on the site of the future Holborn Viaduct was exhibited at the Royal Academy in 1830.

TAYLOR, WILLIAM, was a London surveyor active in the reigns of Charles II and James II. In 1668–70 he was employed to make a design for the rebuilding of PEWTERERS' HALL in Lime Street. For this John Wildgos (*q.v.*) made three draughts, but 'Mr. Taylor' was paid 'for a later draught' [C. Welch, *History of the Pewterers' Company* ii, 1902, 137]. In 1671–2 'Mr. William Taylor the Surveyor' was paid for surveying by Sir Robert Clayton in connection with his new house in THE OLD JEWRY, LONDON [Guildhall Library, MS. 6428/1, ff. 237–241]. In March 1673/4 he was in Dorset supervising industrial work for Clayton at BROWNSEA, and in August of the same year he wrote to Clayton's partner Alderman John Morris about the need to rebuild a farmhouse at ROSSALL, nr. SHREWSBURY [Sotheby's, 14 Dec. 1993, lot 523]. His letter was dated from 'Weston in Staford sheer', raising the possibility that Taylor had been involved in the building of

* Commissioners' church.

WESTON HALL, recently completed by Sir John and Lady Wilbraham.

In 1678 Sir John Banks paid 'Wm. Taylor Surveyor' £10 in connection with the remodelling of his house, THE FRIARS, at AYLESFORD, KENT [Kent Record Office, U. 234. A. 24, Dec. 1678]. Most of Banks's work was destroyed by fire in 1930: see Arthur Oswald, *Country Houses of Kent*, 1933, 18–19. The 1st Viscount Weymouth employed Taylor to carry out alterations to LONGLEAT HOUSE, WILTS., soon after he succeeded to the property in 1682. They included the fitting up of the chapel in the west wing, the formation of the gallery in the east wing, and extensive works in the office-buildings. In March 1682/3 Lord Weymouth wrote to his brother to say that he was 'pulling all downe in the Country, but desiring a little better advice than either my owne, or Mr. Tayler's', he would be grateful for 'Sir Christopher Wren's opinion' [Longleat archives, Thynne papers, xxxiv, ff. 103, 109]. A year latter Taylor wrote to Lord Weymouth, then in London, to report on the progress of the work [*ibid.*, xxii, f. 75]. In the same letter he refers to an intended visit to Shropshire, and adds that he will not be in London for some weeks, 'as I must be att Sir William Portment's and Sir Haswell's before I come to London'. His engagements in Shropshire included visits to 'Sir Edward Acton's place', i.e. ALDENHAM PARK, where he may have been responsible for the north-west wing dated 1691 (*C. Life*, 23–30 June, 1977), and MINSTERLEY, where a new church was about to be built at Lord Weymouth's expense (it was completed in 1689). A design for it is preserved in the library at Longleat, and as Taylor was paid £14 in 1688 'in part of £40 for the Chapell at Minsterley' [Longleat account-book 176], he was presumably the architect of this curious semi-baroque building.

Sir William Portman's seat was ORCHARD PORTMAN, SOMERSET (dem., but illustrated by Kip as a building probably altered in the late seventeenth century) and 'Sir Haswell' was Sir Halswell Tynte, whose house, HALSWELL PARK, SOMERSET, was then about to be rebuilt, for the date 1689 is carved on the north front (*C. Life*, 21 Nov. 1908). Halswell is quite a sophisticated building, with a fashionable parapeted roof, whose attribution to Taylor would, if substantiated, establish him as a Stuart architect of some importance. A further letter at Longleat [MS. 4036, *ex inf.* Mr. James Lawson] shows that in March 1687/8 Taylor was to be at KEDLESTON HALL, DERBYSHIRE, where any work for which he may have been responsible would have been demolished when that house was rebuilt *c.*1700.

TAYLOR, WILLIAM ALEXANDER (–1839), was articled to J. B. Papworth in 1835 and died on 5 August 1839 [R.I.B.A. Library, list of J.B.P.'s pupils by Wyatt Papworth]. He exhibited a design for a museum at the Royal Academy in 1838 and competed for the Ashmolean Museum at Oxford in 1839. There are two drawings by him in the R.I.B.A. Collection.

TEANBY, WILLIAM, was a bricklayer of Old Street, London. For Francis Cobb, junior, he designed and built COBB'S BREWERY, MARGATE, KENT (dem.), in 1807–8, as commemorated by a plaque beneath the pediment.

TEASDALE, JAMES, was born at Greystoke in Cumberland, on the estates of the 11th Duke of Norfolk, and was one of the local artificers who were trained as architects and sculptors at the Duke's expense with the intention of employing them at Arundel Castle. He established himself in Arundel as a builder-architect and assisted the Duke, who was largely his own architect, in remodelling the Castle in Gothic style (*C. Life*, 7 July 1983). Teasdale's name appeared as 'architect' on the foundation-stone of the Barons' Hall, built between 1806 and 1815 [*Gent's Mag.* 1816 (ii), 32]. RUSTINGTON VICARAGE, SUSSEX, was enlarged by him in 1820 [W. Sussex C.R.O., Ep. I 41/41]. For his brother John, who executed much of the sculpture, see Rupert Gunnis, *Dictionary of British Sculptors* [J. Dallaway, *West Sussex* ii (i), 1832, 188].

TELFORD, THOMAS (1757–1834), born at Glendinning in the parish of Westerkirk in Dumfriesshire, was the son of a shepherd. After being apprenticed to a country mason, he worked for some time on the building of the New Town at Edinburgh, before going to London in 1782 to find employment as a journeyman mason at Somerset House. He had by now acquired a considerable knowledge of architecture and surveying, and was employed by William Pulteney, the brother and heir of Sir James Johnstone, Bart., of Westerhall, to make plans for alterations to that house and to the vicarage of a living, of which Pulteney was the patron. In 1784–6 he was engaged in supervising the building of the Commissioner's House at Portsmouth Dockyard to the designs of Samuel Wyatt. Soon afterwards he removed to Shrewsbury in order to fit up the Castle as a residence for Pulteney, who was one of the two M.Ps. for that town. Here his abilities received a considerable advertisement as a result of the dramatic collapse of the church of St. Chad, soon after he had warned the incredulous churchwardens that it was about to fall; and with Pulteney behind him, he was busy making plans for improvements in the town, rebuilding the County Gaol in accordance with the principles of John Howard, and even designing a country house for a Shopshire gentleman. As an architect Telford's most important work was the neo-classical church at Bridgnorth, designed in a spirit of rational simplicity that is even more evident in his bleak octagonal church at Madeley.

In 1788 Telford was appointed Surveyor of Bridges to the County of Shropshire. As a bridge-builder he was not slow to realize the possibilities of iron, already demonstrated by T. F. Pritchard at Coalbrookdale, and his iron bridge at Buildwas was one of the pioneer structures of its kind. The Menai and Conway Suspension Bridges in Wales and the Craigellachie Bridge over the R. Spey in Scotland are the best known of his later iron bridges. Altogether Telford was responsible for well over a thousand bridges of one arch or more, a selection of which is listed below. In 1793 he was appointed surveyor, engineer and architect to the Ellesmere Canal, and from this time onwards his engineering activities left little time for architectural works other than bridges. His achievements as a road-builder and canal-maker, his successes as a drainer of fens and an improver of harbours, fall outside the scope of this *Dictionary*. In 1820 he became the first president of the Institution of Civil Engineers, and the death of John Rennie in the following year left Telford the unchallenged head of a new profession. When he himself died in 1834 architecture and civil engineering were recognized as distinct occupations, and the time had passed when the practice of both could be united in one person.

[*The Life of Thomas Telford, Civil Engineer, written by himself; containing a descriptive narrative of his professional labours*, ed. J. Rickman, 1839; *Atlas to the Life of Thomas Telford, Civil Engineer, containing eighty-three copper plates illustrative of his professional Labours*, 1838; biography by James Cleland, *Enumeration of the Inhabitants of Glasgow*, Glasgow 1832, 278–80; obituary by J. C. Loudon, *Architectural Mag.* i, 1834, 320; Samuel Smiles, *Lives of the Engineers* ii, 1861; Sir A. Gibb, *The Story of Telford*, 1935; L. T. C. Rolt, *Thomas Telford*, 1958; A.R.B. Haldane, *New Ways through the Glens*, 1962; A. E. Penfold, 'A guide to the sources for a study of the life and works of Thomas Telford', *Business Archives* 43, 1977; T. Ruddock, *Arch Bridges and their Builders*, 1979.]

The following list comprises Telford's early architectural works, together with a selection of his bridges. For a complete list of the canals, docks, bridges, harbours, piers, waterworks, etc., executed under his supervision, see Sir A. Gibb, *The Story of Telford.*

SHREWSBURY CASTLE, alterations for William Pulteney, 1787.

SHREWSBURY COUNTY GAOL, designed by J. H. Haycock, but executed by Telford, with modifications designed to make the building conform to the principles advocated by John Howard, 1787–93.

BOREATTON HALL, SALOP., alterations for Rowland Hunt, 1791; dem. [Shropshire R.O., P 41/B/11/5, f. 4, *ex inf.* Dr. T. Friedman].

BRIDGNORTH, ST. MARY'S CHURCH, 1792–4; chancel by Blomfield 1876; refitted 1889 (*Atlas*, pl. 9; *Edinburgh Encyclopaedia* vi, 1830, pl. clxxvi).

CLEOBURY MORTIMER CHURCH, SALOP., emergency buttressing, etc., 1793.

MADELEY CHURCH, SALOP., 1794–6, octagonal; chancel formed 1910 (*Edinburgh Encyclopaedia* vi, 1830, pl. clxxvi).

DAWLEY CHURCH, SALOP., 1805 [*Edinburgh Encyclopaedia* vi, 1830, 644].

CARLISLE, THE COUNTY COURTS were begun by Telford with the assistance of John Chisholme, who was in actual charge of the building. On Chisholme's death in 1808 the work was continued by Peter Nicholson until 1811, when the foundations were found to be defective, and Robert Smirke completed the buildings largely to his own designs.

PULTENEYTOWN, nr. WICK, CAITHNESS, model fishing-town for the British Fisheries Society, 1808 [A. J. Youngson, *After the Forty-five*, 1973, 132].

LONDON, warehouses at ST. KATHERINE'S DOCKS, 1827–8; dem. (plan in *Atlas*, pl. 40).

HIGHLAND CHURCHES

Over thirty churches and manses were built in the Highlands between 1825 and 1834 by a Parliamentary Commission under Telford's general supervision. They were economically built to uniform designs at a total cost of £54,442. The plans and specifications were delegated to two subordinate surveyors, James Smith (*q.v.*) and William Thomson [A. Maclean, *Telford's Highland Churches*, Society of W. Highland Historical Research, 1989].

Argyllshire: ACHARACLE, ARDGOUR, DUROR, KINLOCHSPELVIE, LOCHGILPHEAD (dem.), OA, PORTNAHAVEN, STRONTIAN, TOBERMORY

(dem.), ULVA.
Banffshire: TOMINTOUL.
Caithness: BERRIEDALE, KEISS.
Hebrides: CROSS (Lewis), IONA, KNOCK (UIE) (Lewis), STEINSCHOLL and WATERNISH (Skye).
Inverness-shire: NORTH BALLACHULISH.
Ross-shire: CROICK, KINLOCHLUICHART, PLOCKTON, POOLEWE, SHIELDAIG, STRATHCONON (CARNOCH), ULLAPOOL.
Shetland: QUARFF.
Sutherland: KINLOCHBERVIE, STOER, STRATHY.
Western Isles: BERNERAY, TRUMISGARRY (N. Uist).

SELECT LIST OF BRIDGES

MONTFORD BRIDGE, SALOP. (R. Severn), 1790–2 (*Atlas*, pl. 5).
TERN AQUEDUCT, LONGDON, SALOP., carrying the Shropshire Union Canal over the R. Tern, 1793–4.
BUILDWAS BRIDGE, SALOP. (R. Severn), 1795–6; dem. 1905 (*Atlas*, pl. 6).
PONT-Y-CYSYLLTE AQUEDUCT, carrying the Ellesmere Canal over the R. Dee, 1795–1805 (*Atlas*, pl. 14).
CHIRK AQUEDUCT, DENBIGHSHIRE, carrying the Ellesmere Canal over the R. Ceiriog, 1796–1801 (*Atlas*, pl. 13).
BEWDLEY BRIDGE, WORCS. (R. Severn), 1797–9 (*Atlas*, pl. 7).
WICK BRIDGE, CAITHNESS (Water of Wick), 1805–7 (*Atlas*, pl. 51).
TONGLAND BRIDGE, KIRKCUDBRIGHTSHIRE (R. Dee), 1805–6 (*Atlas*, pl. 8).
DUNKELD BRIDGE, PERTHSHIRE (R. Tay), 1806–9 (*Atlas*, pl. 46).
CONON BRIDGE, ROSS-SHIRE (R. Conon), 1806–9; dem. (*Atlas*, pl. 49).
BALLATER BRIDGE, ABERDEENSHIRE (R. Dee), 1807–9 (*Atlas*, pl. 51).
ALFORD BRIDGE, ABERDEENSHIRE (R. Don), 1810–11 (*Atlas*, p. 51).
HELMSDALE BRIDGE, SUTHERLAND (R. Helmsdale), 1811–12 (*Atlas*, pl. 48).
LOVAT BRIDGE, INVERNESS-SHIRE (R. Beauly), 1811–14 (*Atlas*, pl. 51).
POTARCH BRIDGE, ABERDEENSHIRE (R. Dee), 1811–15 (*Atlas*, pl. 49).
CRAIGELLACHIE BRIDGE, BANFFSHIRE (R. Spey), 1814–15 (*Atlas*, pl. 47).
BETTWS-Y-COED, CAERNARVONSHIRE, WATERLOO BRIDGE (R. Conway), 1815 (*Atlas*, pl. 69).
BEATTOCK BRIDGE, DUMFRIESSHIRE (Evan Water), 1819; widened 1951 [inscription].
MENAI SUSPENSION BRIDGE, MENAI STRAITS, CAERNARVONSHIRE, 1819–26 (*Atlas*, pls. 70–5).
CARTLAND CRAGS BRIDGE, LANARKSHIRE (Mouse Water), 1821–2 (*Atlas*, pls. 55–7).
CONWAY SUSPENSION BRIDGE, CAERNARVONSHIRE (R. Conway), 1821–6 (*Atlas*, pl. 78).
TEWKESBURY, GLOS., MYTHE BRIDGE (R. Severn), 1824–6 (*Atlas*, pl. 81).
HAMILTON, LANARKS., bridge over R. Avon, 1825 (*Atlas*, pl. 54).
OVER BRIDGE, nr. GLOUCESTER (R. Severn), 1825–8 (*Atlas*, pls. 63, 82).
DON BRIDGE, nr. ABERDEEN (R. Don), 1826–9.
PATHHEAD BRIDGE, MIDLOTHIAN (Tyne Water), 1827–31 (*Atlas*, pl. 64).
EDINBURGH, DEAN BRIDGE (Water of Leith), 1829–31 (*Atlas*, pl. 62).
GLASGOW, BROOMIELAW BRIDGE (R. Clyde), 1833–5; dem. 1899 (*Atlas*, pl. 61).
CHIRK BRIDGE, DENBIGHSHIRE (R. Ceiriog), 1831.
MORPETH BRIDGE, NORTHUMBERLAND (R. Wansbeck), 1831 (*Atlas*, pl. 65).

THACKERAY, WILLIAM, of Torpenhow in Cumberland, was a leading mason-architect in that county in the reign of Charles II. His recorded works include the repairing and remodelling of ROSE CASTLE, CUMBERLAND, in 1673–5 for Edward Rainbow, Bishop of Carlisle; the refronting of DRAWDYKES CASTLE, CUMBERLAND, for John Aglionby in 1676; the alteration and enlargement of FLATT HALL (now WHITEHAVEN CASTLE), CUMBERLAND, for Sir John Lowther, Bart., 1676–8; and unspecified work at MUNCASTER CASTLE, CUMBERLAND, for Sir William Pennington, Bart., in 1677–8. At Rose Castle he was referred to as 'Architect' and was paid for 'Journeys and 'Advice' and for making a 'Modell in Paistboard' as well as for workmanship. At Rose Castle the north front (Gothicized in 1829–31), and at Drawdykes the existing façade, had regular fenestration with pedimented windows, etc., and it is likely that Thackeray was also responsible for some other early classical houses in Cumberland, in particular for RIBTON HALL, nr. Camerton (dem. 1923), formerly the seat of the Lamplugh family, where the window pediments were similar to those at Drawdykes, and perhaps also for the somewhat similar MORESBY HALL, nr. Whitehaven.

The Revd. Thomas Machell (*q.v.*) claimed that he and the mason Edward Addison (*q.v.*) were 'the first introducers of Regular [i.e. classical] building into these parts', but Machell did not arrive in Westmorland until 1677, and it was not until the 1680s that he was active as an amateur architect. Thackeray's status as the pioneer of classical architecture in Cumbria seems therefore to be clearly established. [Blake Tyson, 'William Thackeray's rebuilding of Rose Castle Chapel, Cumbria, 1673–75', *Trans. Ancient*

Monuments Soc. N.S. 27, 1983, 'William Thackeray and James Swingler at Flatt Hall', *ibid.*, N.S. 28, 1984.]

THIN, JOHN (*c.*1765–1827), is described as 'Builder and Architect' on the monument in the Calton Hill New Cemetery at Edinburgh which records his death on 10 January 1827 at the age of 62. At Culzean Castle there are two designs for a gateway by him dated 1796 and a design for an octagonal lodge and gateway endorsed 'Mr. Thin's plans 1801' is among the Saltoun Hall plans in the National Library of Scotland (No. 97). In 1805 he was associated with William Sibbald, senior or junior (*q.v.*), in an abortive design for rebuilding Falkirk Church [S.R.O., HR 139/11]. In 1810 he made a feuing plan for 32 villas on the lands of STEWARTFIELD, off the Newhaven Road, Edinburgh [*Edinburgh Evening Courant*, 5 July 1810]. In 1814–15 a house at KINGSTON, EAST LOTHIAN, was built to his designs for John Burn [S.R.O., GD 152/53/6, bd. 13].

Towards the end of his life Thin was in 'indifferent circumstances' and was employed by W. H. Playfair as a draughtsman [Edinburgh University Library, Playfair's letter-book No. 4, p. 239].

THOM, ALEXANDER, 'architectour', was on 9 October 1678 given licence to reside in the burgh of Glasgow, 'and to exerce his imployment and calling in architectorie or in measonrie' until Candlemas 1680. He may have been Alexander Thom, a mason and burgess of Dumfries, who took an apprentice in 1675 [S.R.O., Deeds, Dal. 61, 749, *ex inf.* Mr. J. G. Dunbar]. He was still working in Glasgow in 1684, when he submitted an account for various tasks which he had performed for the city authorities. They included 'cutting the king's armes upon stone', 'cutting the king's arms in timber for the king's seat in the High Kirk, contriving the modells of the frontespiece of the lofts thereof . . . taking down and putting up the said lofts' and supplying eight cedar tables [*Extracts from the Records of the Burgh of Glasgow 1663–90*, 259, 363].

THOM, JOHN, was an architect-builder of Oban. He designed a substantial manse (now KILMORE HOUSE) at Kilmore in Argyllshire in 1828, and a simple Gothic church at ARDCHATTAN, completed in 1836 [R.C.A.M., *Argyll* ii, 99, 260].

THOMAS, DANIEL (–*c.*1658), was (according to his will) a native of Wainfleet in Lincolnshire. He appears to have died in or about 1658 at Ballymoe, Co. Galway, Ireland, where he was building a fort. In 1657 he offered his services to Henry Cromwell, who became Lord Deputy of Ireland in November of that year, and in the British Library there is a letter from him to Cromwell dated 14 October 1657, in which he gives the following account of his career as a master builder:

> My education and practice from my youth untill this warr hath binn with the best of undertakers for Buildinges in London and cann make knowne my former performances before I cam thence. As the buildings of the Inn of Chancery called Furnifall's Inn, Holborne, South Hampton house behinde Gray's Inn, the Lord Grey of Warke in the Charter house yard. The Charter house itself for 20 years together untill the warre and severall other good Buildings of my owne undertaking and performinge . . . I have built within 2 yeares space: the Castle of Termonbury: this of Belamor. Coll. Rich. Cootes & Castle Coote: & all at greate distances . . . [B.L., Lansdowne MS. 822, ff. 212, 218].

Of the London buildings mentioned in Thomas's letter, FURNIVAL'S INN, HOLBORN (dem. 1818) had been built in 1640 in a striking 'artisan mannerist' style (see illustration in Thornbury, *Old and New London* ii, 570), while SOUTHAMPTON, later BEDFORD, HOUSE (dem. 1800) was an important mansion begun in the 1640s for Thomas Wriothesley, 4th Earl of Southampton, but not completed until after the Restoration. Its astylar classical façade, with alternating segmental and triangular pediments, was very much in the manner of Inigo Jones and John Webb, and may not have been Thomas's unaided work (for the history of the house see Rosemary Weinstein, 'Southampton House and the Civil War', in *Collectanea Londiniensia: Studies in London Archaeology and History presented to Ralph Merrifield*, London & Middlesex Archl. Soc. 1978, and for a view of the façade G. Scott Thompson, *The Russells in Bloomsbury*, 1940, 340). What Thomas did at THE CHARTERHOUSE is not clear, and nothing significant remains of his works in Ireland, for which see R. Loeber, *Biographical Dictionary of Architects in Ireland 1600–1720*, 1981, 107–8. But as the builder and perhaps the designer of Furnival's Inn and Southampton House, he may have been one of the leading architect-builders of London in the reign of Charles I.

THOMAS, MATTHEW EVAN (1788–1830), became a student at the Royal Academy in 1812 and was awarded the Academy's Gold Medal in 1815. In the following year he went to Italy, where he became a member of the academies of Florence and Rome. He returned to England in 1819, and exhibited drawings of buildings in Italy at the Royal Academy from 1820 to 1822. He died at Hackney on 12 July 1830, aged 42, and was buried in St. John's Wood Chapel. His executed works, if any, appear to be unrecorded [*Gent's Mag.* 1830 (ii), 91; *A.P.S.D.; D.N.B*].

THOMAS, WILLIAM (–1800), was the son of William Thomas of Pembroke, in whose obituary (*Gent's Mag.* 1800 (i), 87), he is described as 'architect to his Royal Highness the Duke of Clarence'. He practised in Marylebone and exhibited at the Royal Academy from 1780 onwards. From 1781 to 1792 he was a member of the Smeatonian Society of Civil Engineers. In 1783 he published a volume entitled *Original Designs in Architecture*, containing designs for villas, temples, a grotto, etc., as well as some executed works. These were all in an elegant neo-classical style derived from Robert Adam. Thomas died on 25 October 1800. His library and architectural drawings were sold by auction in February 1801 (catalogue in Ashmolean Museum, Oxford, Sutherland Coll. 55 (5)). At the R.I.B.A. Drawings Collection there is a portrait of Thomas holding a drawing of Willersley Castle [*A.P.S.D.; D.N.B.*; Marylebone Parish Register]. T. D. W. Dearn (*q.v.*) was his pupil.

Thomas's principal executed works are listed below. Designs illustrated in his book, but apparently not carried out, include a Gothic garden temple for Lord Shelburne[1] and 'the garden front of the west wing of Stackpole Court, Pembrokeshire, for John Campbell' (also exhibited at the R.A. in 1782). In 1794 he exhibited 'the garden front of Eaton Hall, Cheshire, the seat of Lord Grosvenor', at the Royal Academy, and among the drawings sold after his death was a set of designs for Eaton Hall, described as 'highly finished, in colours'. Another unexecuted design was represented by the 'elevation of a villa at Upton, Pembrokeshire', exhibited at the Academy in 1795. His sale included a design for a column at Runnymede 'to the immortal memory of King William III'. For his design for a naval obelisk to be erected on Portsdown Hill, nr. Portsmouth, exhibited at the R.A. in 1799, see *The Banks Letters*, ed. W. R. Dawson, 1958, 808. Among the Ferrers papers in the Leicestershire Record Office there is an undated design by him for a temple at Chartley Park, Staffs., 'to be dedicated to the Deities that preside over learning, music and oratory'.

[1] Two unexecuted designs for temples by Thomas are preserved at Bowood, one Gothic, one classic, both dated 1780.

LONDON, THE SURREY CHAPEL, BLACKFRIARS ROAD, SOUTHWARK, for the Revd. Rowland Hill, 1782–3; subsequetly used as a boxing ring, destroyed by bombing 1940 [*Original Designs*, pls. 20–1] (*Survey of London* xxii, pl. 85).

BROWNSLADE HOUSE, CASTLEMARTIN, PEMBROKESHIRE, for John Mirehouse, before 1783; built to a reduced design, without wings, which were added later to a different design; dem. [*Original Designs*, pls. 22–3].

LONDON, GROSVENOR HOUSE, MILLBANK, alterations for 1st Earl Grosvenor, *c.*1785; dem. 1809 [design for ceiling in R.I.B.A.D.].

WILLERSLEY CASTLE, nr. MATLOCK, DERBYSHIRE, for Sir Richard Arkwright, 1789–90; interior restored after fire on 8 Aug. 1791 [drawings in Bodleian Library, Gough Maps 41 A, ff. 53–81].

MOUNTSORREL, LEICS., THE MARKET HOUSE, for Sir John Danvers, Bart., 1793 [J. Nichols, *History of Leicestershire* iii (1), 1800, 85 (engraving, for which the original drawing by Thomas is in an extra-illustrated copy in Leicester City Library); *The Copper Plate Magazine* iv, *c.*1800, text to pl. clxxi] (*C. Life*, 10 Oct 1947; Pevsner, *Leicestershire*, Buildings of England, pl. 56).

THOMAS, WILLIAM (1799–1860), was the elder brother of John Thomas (1813–62), a well-known sculptor, and like him was a native of Chalford, nr. Stroud in Gloucestershire. He began his architectural career at Birmingham as a pupil of Richard Tutin (*q.v.*), with whom he was briefly in partnership before establishing an independent practice in Leamington Spa in 1831. Here he was active as an architect and property developer, but suffered bankruptcy as a result of the failure of the Leamington Bank in 1837 [information from Mr. Lyndon F. Cave]. In 1843 he emigrated to Canada, where he died in 1860 after a successful career, in the course of which he designed 'some thirty churches, several town halls, gaols, and other public buildings, besides numerous mansions and villas in all the principal cities and towns of the Western Province' [*Illustrated London News*, 30 Aug. 1862, 231]. Among his Canadian works were St. Paul's Anglican Cathedral at London, Ontario, and St. Michael's Roman Catholic Cathedral at Toronto. Thomas exhibited at the Birmingham Society of Artists in 1827, 1834, 1838 and 1839, and published a book of rather commonplace *Designs for Monuments and Chimney Pieces* in 1843.

BEDWORTH CHURCH, WARWICKS., rebuilt S. side of nave, 1827; rebuilt 1888–9 [I.C.B.S.].

LEAMINGTON SPA, WARWICKS., numerous villas and houses, including No. 31 CLARENDON SQUARE and No. 1 BEAUCHAMP AVENUE for William Phipson, 1831–3; GRAFTON VILLA, WARWICK NEW ROAD, 1834–6; Nos. 34–40 WARWICK PLACE, 1834–6; 'THE CEDARS', No. 42 WARWICK PLACE, 1834–6; villas in HOLLY WALK and ELIZABETHAN PLACE (where No. 19 was Thomas's own house), 1835–9; No. 42 WARWICK STREET for A. S. Field, solicitor, 1839; LANSDOWNE CRESCENT and CIRCUS, 1835–8 [*ex inf.* Mr. Lyndon F. Cave].

LEAMINGTON SPA, WARWICKS., BAPTIST CHAPEL, WARWICK STREET, 1833–4 [R.C.A.M., *Nonconformist Chapels & Meeting Houses in Central England*, 1986, 235].

LEAMINGTON SPA, WARWICKS., VICTORIA TERRACE, PUMP ROOM AND BATHS, 1837 [exhib. at Birmingham Soc. of Artists, 1838].

RADFORD SEMELE HALL, WARWICKS., restored and improved for H. Greswold, *c.*1835–7 [exhib. at Birmingham Soc. of Artists, 1839].

RADFORD SEMELE CHURCH, WARWICKS., alterations, including addition of N. aisle incorporating materials from demolished church of Stretton-on-Dunsmore, 1837–8; rebuilt 1889 [Warwicks, C.R.O., accounts in DR 295/56].

HENWOOD COURT, HANDSWORTH, nr. BIRMINGHAM, for J. Russell, 1839, Gothic [exhib. at Birmingham Soc. of Artists 1839].

BIRMINGHAM, WARWICK HOUSE, NEW STREET, for W. Holliday, a draper, 1839 [exhib. at Birmingham Soc. of Artists 1839; watercolour by Thomas dated 1840 in Birmingham Art Gallery].

BIRMINGHAM, ST. MATTHEW'S CHURCH, DUDDESTON, 1839–40, Gothic [*Gent's Mag.* 1839 (ii), 641].

THOMPSON, GEORGE (1777–1862), was a native of Woodbridge, Suffolk, where he was in business as a builder and surveyor [C. Brown *et al., Dictionary of Architects of Suffolk Buildings 1800–1914*, 1991, 188]. In *c.*1805 he designed and built for William Lockwood a castellated house in WOODBRIDGE called THE CASTLE (dem. *c.*1962) which was intended for use as a club for officers and as a Freemasons' Lodge [W. Lockwood, *Woodbridge in the Olden Times*, privately printed 1889, 12–13]. He refitted the interiors of SAXMUNDHAM and BAWDSEY CHURCHES, SUFFOLK, in 1824–6 and 1841–2 respectively [I.C.B.S.]. He was the father of the architect Francis Thompson (1808–1895).

THOMPSON, JAMES ROBERT (*c.*1799–), was a pupil or assistant of John Britton, the architectural topographer, from whose address he first began to exhibit drawings of ancient buildings at the Royal Academy in 1808. In 1807–8 he was one of those employed to survey Henry VII's Chapel at Westminster in connection with its proposed restoration, and subsequently crossed pens with John Carter in the pages of the *Gentleman's Magazine* (1811 (i), 232, 327, 424). He continued to exhibit at the Royal Academy up to 1843, showing an occasional architectural design (e.g. a 'design for a Doric column to the memory of Sir Walter Scott', 1841), but chiefly topographical drawings. In the 1840s he was probably working as an assistant in the office of Lewis Vulliamy, for he exhibited views of buildings designed by the latter in 1841 and 1842.

THOMPSON, JOHN (–1792), was 'an eminent architect' of Wakefield, where in 1791 the terrace of houses known as ST. JOHN'S NORTH was begun to a uniform elevation specified by him [J. Goodchild, *Wakefield Town Trail*, 1975, 2].

THOMPSON, MARK GRAYSTONE (1783–1852), born at Woodbridge, Suffolk, was the brother of George Thompson (*q.v.*). He was a carpenter by trade and described himself as such in 1806 when he advertised in the *Ipswich Jnl.* (10 May) that he had taken premises near the Wharf at Dedham in Essex. He remained at Dedham until about 1825, when he moved elsewhere, dying at Beccles in 1852 [C. Brown *et al., Dictionary of Architects of Suffolk Buildings 1800–1914*, 1991, 189].

ORMESBY HOUSE, NORFOLK, for Sir Edmund Lacon, Bart., *c.*1810, Gothic; dem. *c.*1970 [J. P. Neale, *Views of Seats* vi, 1823].

LOUND RECTORY, SUFFOLK, 1818 [Norfolk C.R.O., DN/DPL 1/3, 38].

BOXFORD RECTORY (now 'House'), SUFFOLK, *c.*1818 [W. Suffolk C.R.O., 806/2/3].

COLCHESTER, ESSEX, ESSEX COUNTY HOSPITAL, 1819 [Hospital Minute Books, *ex inf.* Dr. Paul Thompson].

BURES VICARAGE, SUFFOLK, partial rebuilding, 1820 [W. Suffolk C.R.O., 806/2/4].

HARTEST RECTORY, SUFFOLK, rebuilding 1821 [W. Suffolk C.R.O., 806/2/9].

LEXDEN CHURCH, ESSEX, rebuilt 1820–1, lancet style (cemented), 1820–1 [MS. Vestry Minutes].

HARWICH, ESSEX, ST. NICHOLAS CHURCH, 1820–1, 'Perp.' Gothic (brick) [accounts in Essex C.R.O.]

MANNINGTREE CHURCH, ESSEX, enlarged and repewed, 1821; dem. *c.*1968 [I.C.B.S.].

THORPE HALL, THORPE-LE-SOKEN, ESSEX, rebuilt for John Martin Leake, 1822–5 [Essex C.R.O., D/DHf. T92/77, 1–2, plan and perspective signed by Thompson; cf. F.A. Wood, 'Three Georgian Houses', *Essex Archl. Soc's Trans.* 3rd ser. ii, 1967, 125–9].

THE CHANTRY, SPROUGHTON, SUFFOLK, the Doric lodge by 'Thompson' mentioned by J. P. Neale, *Views of Seats* ii, 1819, was presumably designed by M. G. Thompson rather than by his brother George.

DEDHAM VICARAGE, ESSEX, rebuilt 1825 [Bodleian Library, records of Queen Anne's Bounty].

THOMPSON, PETER (*c.*1800–1874), was an ingenious but dubious character who made a precarious living on the fringes of early Victorian architectural practice. He was born in Norwich and exhibited designs for a mansion and the interior of a palace at the Norwich Society of Artists in 1817. By 1828 he was established in London as a carpenter and builder. He appears to have designed THE ROYAL BAZAAR, ST. ANDREW'S STREET, NORWICH, 1831, dem. [see advt. for tenders in *Norfolk Chronicle*, 20 Aug. 1831], and his design for SUTTON RECTORY, NORFOLK, is in the Norfolk C.R.O. [DN/DPL/1/4/58]. In 1835 he competed for the new Houses of Parliament, publishing his very indifferent Gothic design (copy in Soane Museum). In the 1840s he turned his attention to prefabricated buildings, erecting several temporary churches in London and manufacturing 'portable houses' for export to the colonies. In the 1850s he was active as an antiquarian forger, producing a number of topographical drawings purporting to be the work of Wenceslas Hollar and of a certain 'Captain John Eyre'. When these were exposed as fraudulent he started a shortlived trade journal, *The Oil and Colourman* (1863), and issued a series of pamphlets about working-class housing. He died in Barnet in 1874 [Ida Darlington, 'Thompson Fecit', *Arch. Rev.* cxxiv, 1958, 187–8].

THOMSON, ALEXANDER, was the author of an unexecuted design for a new Town and County Hall at Forfar in about 1785 [photo at N.M.R.S. of drawing at Forfar]. No other reference to him has so far been found.

THOMSON, JAMES (–1814), a mason of Leith, died in 1814 [S.R.O., CC8/8/140]. In 1785 he designed and built CURRIE CHURCH, MIDLOTHIAN, in an attractive mixture of classical and Gothic styles [S.R.O., CH2/83/7, pp. 24–5], and he was presumably 'the late Mr. James Thompson of Leith' who designed the classical ST. JAMES'S EPISCOPAL CHAPEL, CONSTITUTION ST., LEITH, in 1804–5; rebuilt 1862–3 [J. & S. Storer, *Views in Edinburgh and Vicinity* ii, 1822].

THOMSON, JAMES (*c.*1784–1832), a native of Edinburgh, practised in Dumfries. He first came to Dumfries in 1815 in order to convert a chapel in Buccleuch Street into a court-house, settled there, and eventually became Convener of the Trades. He designed unsophisticated Gothic churches at LOCHMABEN, 1818–20 [S.R.O., CH 2/247/15, pp. 89–90, 110 and 16, p. 61, *ex inf.* Mr. John Gifford] and DUNSCORE, 1823–4 [contract in S.R.O., GD 165, Box 39]. In 1832 he fell victim to a cholera epidemic which, as a member of the newly formed Board of Health, he was engaged in combating. His son George Thomson, engineer, died at Poona in 1842, aged 27 [W. McDowall, *Memorials of St. Michael's Churchyard, Dumfries*, Edinburgh 1876, 125].

THORNHILL, SIR JAMES (1675–1734), came of an old Dorsetshire family seated at Thornhill and Woolland in that county. James was the youngest son of Walter Thornhull (as the name was then spelled), himself the youngest (and impoverished) son of George Thornhull of Thornhill. At the age of 14 James was sent to London to be apprenticed to Thomas Highmore, the King's Sergeant Painter, who was a distant kinsman. He eventually became the leading English decorative painter of his day, working with great success in the baroque style established by Verrio and Laguerre. In 1718 he was appointed History Painter in Ordinary to George I, and on Highmore's death in 1720 he succeeded him as Sergeant Painter. He was knighted at the same time through the influence of Lord Sunderland, but the latter's death two years later deprived him of his chief patron and protector, and in March 1722 the decoration of the new apartments at Kensington Palace was entrusted to William Kent, although by his patent as Sergeant Painter Thornhill was entitled to expect the commission. Kent's employment was due to the influence of his patron, Lord Burlington, but Vertue believed that the latter was exploiting differences which already existed between Thornhill and the Board of Works. According to Vertue, the 'original cause' of Thornhill's loss of favour was his declared intention of setting himself up as an architect in competition with the existing officers of the King's Works:

> Everybody may remember some years ago . . . when Sr. James Thornhill declar'd he would practice as an Architect, and certainly had skill and knowledge enough in that branch to practice it. Yet what a clamour! What outcries of invasion! What blending of parties together – against him in all his affairs of painting also, that to this Time [1731] he sensibly feels it and has long been unimployed even in his own way of history painting.

Vertue's account is confirmed by a letter written by Sir John Vanbrugh to the Duke of Newcastle in August 1719, in which he reported that Thornhill was actually seeking to secure the vacant Surveyorship of the King's Works, and that there was a 'great struggle' between him and Hewitt for the post. He thought it 'a Monstruous project' that 'such a Volatile Gentleman as Thornhill, shou'd turn his thoughts & Application to the duty of a Surveyor's business' (*Works* iv, ed. G. F. Webb, 116–17). But Vanbrugh himself had successfully abandoned play-writing for architecture, and Kent, as 'volatile' as Thornhill in character and immeasurably his inferior as a painter, was similarly embarking upon an architectural career with Lord Burlington's assistance. At a time when rigid professional barriers did not exist there was, in fact, nothing to prevent a versatile artist such as Thornhill from turning his attention to architecture, and Vertue stated that 'he had much studied architecture and has executed some designs in building and made infinitely more.'

That Vertue was not alone in taking Thornhill's architectural pretensions seriously is shown by the fact that in 1720 both the Radcliffe Trustees and the Commissioners for the rebuilding of St. Martin-in-the-Fields should have applied to him for designs along with other well-known architects. There is no evidence to show that he accepted the former invitation, but on 20 July he attended the St. Martin's Committee 'about his plans and Estimate and left several others with the Committee'. His original design for the west front of St. Martin's Church is preserved in the R.I.B.A. Drawings Collection. It shows an Ionic portico flanked by two towers, and there is an estimate for £20,000 on the back. Several other architectural drawings by Thornhill are in existence, and according to the French virtuoso Dezallier d'Argenville, who met him in 1728, he practised architecture 'like a professional' ('comme un homme de métier') and had 'built several houses'. The earliest documentary evidence of Thornhill's architectural activities seems to be an unexecuted design for remodelling the screen in the CHAPEL of ALL SOULS COLLEGE, OXFORD, which he was then engaged in redecorating. This is in the Clarke Collection in Worcester College Library and is inscribed 'Half the Skreen of All Souls Chappell as it was first proposd to be alterd, by Mr. Thornhill, 1715'. In the same collection there are several designs by Thornhill for a 'Banquetting Room' or garden house for 'Mr. Berkeley's Terrace' which can be connected with STOKE GIFFORD HOUSE, GLOS., where a banqueting house was built by John Symes Berkeley about this time [H. M. Colvin, *Catalogue of Architectural Drawings in the Library of Worcester College, Oxford*, 1964, pls. 82, 114]. In the Victoria and Albert Museum there is a somewhat similar design by Thornhill for a 'Pleasure room' (D. 126–1891, illustrated by E. de N. Mayhew, *Sketches by Thornhill*, 1967, pl. 40), and in the same Museum there are designs by Thornhill for the façade of a small house dated 1721 (D. 129A–1891) and for a small town house, endorsed 'Mr. Tho. Carr over against ye Crown & P . . . in Chancery Lane' (D. 91, 92–1891).

A more ambitious design is represented by an elevation in Thornhill's hand for a large country house dated 15 January 1716/17. This is among the Cannons House drawings in the G.L. Record Office (Acc 262/71/5) and was reproduced (without identification of its authorship) in *C. Life*, 30 Dec. 1949, fig. 11. There is evidence that Thornhill designed one, and probably two, country houses. One is MOOR PARK, HERTS., a mansion often but erroneously attributed to Leoni, despite the fact that 'Sir James Thornhill Arch.' appears beneath the plates in *Vitruvius Britannicus* v, 1771, pls. 50–5. The house was rebuilt *c.*1720–8 for the South Sea Company profiteer Benjamin Styles, and Thornhill's responsibility for the architectural design (as well as for the internal decoration) is confirmed by the record of a lawsuit, in which Thornhill claimed remuneration not only for painting, but also for acting 'as Chiefe Architect for several years before the undertaking [of] the said Painting as well as during the time of the said Painting in directing the workmen in the building done and performed about the said house'. After a long hearing, in the course of which evidence was given by several architects and builders, it was 'proved that Sr. James Thornhill was imployd as Surveyor & designer of that building', and Styles was ordered to pay him £500 and costs [T. P. Hudson, 'Moor Park, Leoni and Sir James Thornhill', *Burlington Mag.*, Nov. 1971]. The house is described in *C. Life*, 6–13 Jan. 1912, Tipping, *English Homes, Period V* (i), 1921, and Hussey, *English Country Houses: Early Georgian*, 1955. The wings (shown in

Vertue's sketch-plan of 1730) were removed in 1785.

LUXBOROUGH HOUSE, CHIGWELL, ESSEX (dem. *c.*1800), was built *c.*1716–20 by another beneficiary of the South Sea Company, its Cashier, Richard Knight. It had a large recessed portico (see painting illustrated in *C. Life*, 19 July 1973, 147). When Sir John Evelyn visited Luxborough on 14 July 1721 in Thornhill's company, he noted in his diary (Christ Church Library, Oxford) that the exterior had been 'adorn'd with a [portico] & plaister'd in imitation of stone' by Thornhill's direction, and that the interior had been 'painted by Sir James'. Designs by Thornhill for chimney-pieces, etc. for this house exist in a private collection.

In 1721 Thornhill again appeared in an architectural role when he gave evidence to a committee of the House of Commons that was considering the building of a bridge across the Thames at Westminster. He said he had measured and bored the river, that the ground was firm and capable of providing a good foundation, and that it would be practicable to build a bridge there [*Commons' Jnls.* xix, 1718–21, 708]. His design for a bridge of nine arches in this position is in the R.I.B.A. Collection. In 1723 the interior of the chapel at DUNSTER CASTLE, SOMERSET (remodelled *c.*1865) was designed by Thornhill for Margaret Luttrell [Somerset C.R.O., DD/L MR.2/43.1], and at some date before 1729 Thornhill was giving advice to Lord Chancellor King in connection with proposed alterations to his house at OCKHAM in SURREY, for in February of that year Hawksmoor noted that one of the designs 'was proposed when Sr. James Thornhill was at Occham', and on the back of a design for wainscoting the hall is written what appears to be the signature 'Jacobus T.' [L. Whistler in *C. Life*, 29 Dec. 1950, 2221]. In an album at Hovingham Hall, Yorks., there is a set of plans and a corresponding elevation by Thornhill for an institutional building, perhaps a school.

In 1720 Thornhill bought back the family estate at Thornhill, and built a new house there (THORNHILL HOUSE) in which he died on 13 May 1734. In the grounds he erected in 1727 an obelisk in honour of George II's accession. There is a drawing of it by himself in B.L., *King's Maps*, Supplementary volume 124, f. 31. From 1722 to 1734 he sat in Parliament as Member for Weymouth and Melcombe Regis, and in 1732 he was one of the Commissioners appointed under the Act for rebuilding the town of Blandford, which had been destroyed by fire on 4 June 1731. This explains how he came to make a plan and elevation of a 'Town Hall, or Genll. Assembly, Market House, etc.' for Blandford, which is now in Sir John Soane's Museum. It is signed and dated 'J. Th. 1733' (*Archaeological Jnl.* civ, 1948, pl. xxiv).

The buildings and designs mentioned above are sufficiently numerous to justify Thornhill's claim to be taken seriously as an architect, but it is unlikely that they tell the full story of his architectural activity, and they scarcely afford enough evidence for a full assessment of his ability as an architectural designer. Moor Park and the Cannons design belong to the English baroque tradition, but Thornhill House and some of the unexecuted drawings (notably the one for Blandford Town Hall) show a degree of Palladian influence that is unexpected in one who as an artist was so consistently baroque in style.

[*A.P.S.D.*; *D.N.B.*; Walpole Society, *Vertue Note Books* i, 100–1, iii, 35, 46, 55, 70, 114, v, 94; Ralph Edwards, 'Sir James Thornhill as an Architect', *C. Life*, 9 Feb. 1935, correspondence; Arthur Oswald, 'Sir James Thornhill and Dorset', *C. Life*, 27 April 1935, correspondence; Minutes of the Radcliffe Trustees (Bodleian Library); Minutes of the Commissioners for building St. Martin's Church (Westminster Library); J. S. Corder, 'Extracts from the Diary of Sir James Thornhill May 16–June 7, 1711', *Procs. Suffolk Institute of Archaeology* xiii, 1909, 33–43;[1] Hutchins, *History of Dorset* ii, 1774, 245–6, 451; *Builder* i, 1843, 414–15; 'Sir James Thornhill's Collection', *Burlington Mag.* lxxxii, June 1943; C. Lloyd, 'The Decoration of the Royal Hospital, Greenwich', *Trans. Greenwich & Lewisham Antiquarian Soc.* v. (i), 1954–6; Catalogue of *An Exhibition of Paintings & Drawings by Sir James Thornhill* at the Guildhall Art Gallery, 1958; E. Croft-Murray, *Decorative Painting in England* i, 1962, chap. vii; H. M. Colvin, *Catalogue of Architectural Drawings of the Eighteenth and Nineteenth Centuries in the Library of Worcester College, Oxford*, 1964; John Harthan, 'Two Travel Diaries by Sir James Thornhill', *Victoria and Albert Museum Bulletin*, ii, no. 3, 1966; E. de N. Mayhew, *Sketches by Thornhill*, H.M.S.O. 1967; John Harris, *Catalogue of British Drawings for Architecture, etc., in American Collections*, 1971; Joan Brocklebank, 'James Thornhill', *Notes and Queries for Somerset and Dorset* xxx, March 1975, 73–82; *History of the King's Works* v, 1976; Brian Allen, 'Thornhill at Wimpole', *Apollo*, Sept. 1985.]

[1] There are transcripts of this diary in the British Library (Add. MS. 34788, formerly Phillipps MS. 1777), and the Library of the Society of Antiquaries (187 D., formerly Phillipps MS. 17479).

THORNTHWAITE, ANDREW, was no doubt related to the engraver J. Thornthwaite. He began life as an architectural draughtsman but subsequently entered the Army. He was awarded premiums by the Society of Arts in 1763, 1764 and 1765. In 1763 he was described as a pupil of the artist Pars, in 1765 of the architect Boulton Mainwaring [R. Dossie, *Memoirs of Agriculture* iii, 1782, 421]. In 1771 he exhibited at the Society of Artists an elevation of the east end of Henry VII's Chapel at Westminster. He designed the frontispiece to the second edition of William Wrighte's *Grotesque Architecture*, published in 1790.

THORNTON, WILLIAM (*c.*1670–1721), of York, was a carpenter and joiner by trade. In his *Eboracum*, 1736, p. 260, Francis Drake describes him as a 'Joyner and architect', and says that 'by the ablest judges in the former kind of work, he was look'd upon as the best artist in *England*; and, for architecture, his reparation of Beverley-minster ought to give him a lasting memorial.' At BEVERLEY MINSTER he had, in 1716–20, restored the leaning north face of the north transept to the perpendicular under the direction of Nicholas Hawksmoor. The elaborate timber framing employed in this operation is shown in an engraving published in 1739 (reproduced by C. Hiatt, *Beverley Minster*, 1898, 35). An inscription refers to the framing as being of Thornton's invention, and according to John Loveday, who visited Beverley in 1732, 'Hawksmoor . . . and He had concerted of the Affair between 'em' [*The Diary of a Tour in 1732*, Roxburghe Club 1890, 199–201].

Thornton's employment as a carpenter or joiner is documented at several Yorkshire country houses, including CANNON HALL, CAWTHORNE, 1700–4 [Sheffield Archives, Sp. St. 60674/1 (ii, iv, viii), *ex inf.* Mr. R. Hewlings]; CASTLE HOWARD, from 1706 onwards [G. Beard, *Craftsmen and Interior Decorators in England 1660–1820*, 1981, 287]; WENTWORTH CASTLE, 1714 [Strafford Papers, B.L., Add. MS. 22238, f. 10]; Sir Charles Hotham's house at BEVERLEY, 1720 [accounts in East Yorks. R.O., DD Ho/15/4]; and WHITLEY BEAUMONT, 1721 [Kirklees District Archives, WBL/107/21].

Thornton's activity as an architect is less well documented, but in 1700 'Wm. Thornton's Model for a summer-house at SWINTON PARK, YORKS. (N.R.), was approved by Sir Abstrupus Danby [J. Cornforth in *C. Life*, 7 April 1966], and there is reason to think that he was responsible for alterations to LEDSTON HALL, YORKS. (W.R.), for Lady Elizabeth Hastings after she had inherited that house in 1701 [D. Linstrum, *West Yorkshire Architects and Architecture*, 1978, 61]. According to an eighteenth-century list of Yorkshire houses in a copy of *The Builder's Dictionary* (1734) in the Metropolitan Museum at New York, Thornton was the architect of 'Mr. Bourchier's', i.e. BENINGBROUGH HALL, YORKS. (N.R.), built by John Bourchier and completed in 1716 in a style which shows a familiarity with Roman baroque architecture as illustrated in Rossi's *Studio d'architettura civile* (1702–21) (*C. Life*, 26 Nov., 3 Dec. 1927, 3, 10 Dec. 1981; H.A. Tipping, *English Homes, Period IV* (ii), 1928, 221–46). Independent evidence of Thornton's responsibility for the joinery at Beningbrough is afforded by a letter from him to the Earl of Strafford suggesting the use of glazing-bars at Wentworth Castle 'of the same thickness I have done for Mr. Bourchier' [B.L., Add. MS. 22238, f. 10]. If Thornton designed Beningbrough, then he could well have designed other important baroque houses in Yorkshire whose architects are unrecorded, and he was no doubt responsible for many staircases such as the one at BANKS HALL near CAWTHORNE which is known to have been made by his assistant John Godier or Goodyear [G. W. Beard, *op. cit.*, 261].

A tablet in St. Olave's Church, York, records the death of William Thornton, 'Joyner & Architect', on 23 September 1721, at the age of 51 (R.C.H.M., *York* iv, pl. 51). His will indicates that he lived in Marygate and that he left seven children. Nothing is at present known of his origins or training, but it may be noted that a Thomas Thornton was Master of the London Joiner's Company in 1691. William Thornton's eldest son Robert died in 1724 and his business was carried on by his widow and second son William, who in 1728 subscribed to Gibbs's *Book of Architecture* and in 1732 provided a design for rebuilding the cupola on the roof of BURTON CONSTABLE HOUSE, YORKS. (E.R.) [letter dated from York 16 Sept. 1732 in letterbook in E. Yorks. Record Office].

THOROLD, WILLIAM (1798–1878), of Norwich, was well known in East Anglia as a farmer, millwright, engineer and surveyor. He also practised as an architect. In 1824 he exhibited a design for a County Hall and Corn Exchange at the Norwich Society of Artists, and in 1835 he submitted plans for the Houses of Parliament (presumably those described in the *Catalogue of Designs* as by 'J. Thorold'). The church of ST. MARTIN-AT-OAK, NORWICH, was reseated under his direction in 1837 [I.C.B.S.]. Designs by him for a Norfolk farm-house incorporating a windmill were published by J. C. Loudon in his *En-*

cyclopaedia of Rural Architecture (1846, ed., 471–3, 544–5), and his executed buildings appear mostly to have been farm-buildings and Union Workhouses. Six of the latter were erected to his designs in Norfolk in 1836–7 at THETFORD, PULHAM MARKET, KENNINGHALL, ROCKLAND ALL SAINTS, HINDRINGHAM and GREAT SNORING, and another at CHELMSFORD in ESSEX in 1838.

[*Minutes of Proceedings of the Institution of Civil Engineers* lv, 1878–9, 321–2; *Norfolk Chronicle*, 19 March, 23 and 30 April, 14 May, 25 June 1836, 4 Feb. 1837, *ex inf.* the late D. C. Young; Essex C.R.O., G/Ch M2, pp. 38, 56–309 *passim*.]

THORP, JAMES (–*c.*1811), of Princes (now Wardour) Street, Soho, was described as 'Ornament and Composition-maker' in *The Universal British Directory* of 1791. In 1796–1800 the interior of the medieval chapel at STONOR PARK, OXON., was remodelled with a plaster vault, etc., to his designs [Arthur Oswald in *C. Life*, 13 Oct. 1950; *V.C.H. Oxon.* viii, 176].

THORPE, JOHN (*c.*1565–1655?), born at Kingscliffe in Northamptonshire, was the second son of Thomas Thorpe, a master mason of that parish. As a child he laid the first stone of Kirby Hall, a house of which his father was presumably the principal mason, but he does not appear to have been brought up to the mason's trade. Instead he joined the Office of Works, serving as a clerk at Richmond, Greenwich, Whitehall and other palaces from 1583 to 1601. In the latter year he left the Office of Works and practised as a land and building surveyor, at first independently, and from 1611 onwards as assistant to Robert Treswell, the Surveyor-General of Woods South of Trent. In this capacity he surveyed numerous royal estates in various parts of the country. He appears to have retired in the 1630s, but to have lived on to an advanced age, dying probably in 1655. For most of his working life he lived in Little Church Street near St. Martin-in-the-Fields, of which he was a vestryman.

Thorpe was primarily an eminent land surveyor of the same sort as John Norden. But a serious interest in architecture is attested by his book of plans preserved in Sir John Soane's Museum. This contains over 150 plans, mostly of country houses. Some of these are projects for new houses, some are surveys of existing buildings, and others are probably copies of designs by other surveyors. At present only a few can be identified as designs by Thorpe himself for specific buildings, notably THORNTON COLLEGE, LINCS., for Sir Vincent Skinner, *c.*1607–10 [David L. Roberts in *Lincs. History & Archaeology* 19, 1984]; AUDLEY END, ESSEX, where he probably designed the outer court for Thomas Howard, 1st Earl of Suffolk, *c.*1615 [P. J. Drury in *Arch. Hist.* 23, 1980, 16–17, 22]; ASTON HALL, WARWICKS., for Sir Thomas Holte, 1618–35 [O. Fairclough in *Arch. Hist.* 32, 1989]; and perhaps DOWSBY HALL, LINCS., for Richard Burrell, soon after 1610 [David L. Roberts in *Lincs. History & Archaeology* 8, 1973] and SOMERHILL, nr. TONBRIDGE, KENT, for 4th Earl of Clanricarde, *c.*1610–13 [cf. *Book of Architecture*, 99–100]. These are typical examples of prestigious Jacobean architecture, sometimes (as at Somerhill) with a plan of Palladian origin, sometimes (as at Audley End) with features derived from French sources, particularly Du Cerceau, and always with that witty and ingenious manipulation of plan and silhouette that is so characteristic of English country-house architecture in the reign of James I. In addition Thorpe may have designed a gallery between the Rosse and Stanton Towers on the south front of BELVOIR CASTLE, LEICS, for which a drawing is preserved in the muniment-room at Belvoir (Map no. 164). As 'surveir of the contractinge' he was paid £5 by command of the 6th Earl of Rutland for superintending the work in the years 1625–7 [Belvoir Castle MSS., Accounts nos. 144–5]. The drawing shows a symmetrical facade of eight bays (3-2-3) with a large balcony linking the two central windows.

In his *Gentleman's Exercise* (1612 edition) Henry Peacham pays a compliment to the learning of his 'especial friend Master John Thorpe', whom he describes as an 'excellent Geometrician and Surveyor'. It is probable that one of the fruits of Thorpe's learning was the English translation of Hans Blum's Latin treatise on the orders (Zurich 1550) as *The Booke of Five Collumnes of Architecture*, translated by I T, 1601 (copy at Worcester College, Oxford), 1608. He certainly prepared for publication an English version of Du Cerceau, *Leçons de Perspective positive* (Paris 1576), his copy of which, complete with his translation, is in the Bodleian Library (LL 23* Art. Seld.): see K. J. Höltgen, 'An Unknown Manuscript Translation by John Thorpe of du Cerceau's *Perspective*', in *England and the Continental Renaissance: Essays in Honour of J. B. Trapp*, ed. Chaney & Mack, Woodbridge 1990.

[John Summerson, 'John Thorpe and the Thorpes of Kingscliffe', *Arch. Rev.* Nov. 1949; *The Book of Architecture of John Thorpe*, ed. John Summerson, Walpole Soc. xl, 1966.]

TILLETT, ABEL TOWLER (–1844), practised in Yarmouth. He designed parsonage houses at HOPTON, nr. LOWESTOFT, SUFFOLK, 1842 [C. Brown *et al.*, *Dictionary of Architects of Suffolk Buildings 1800–1914*, 1991, 189] and HADDISCOE, NORFOLK, 1843 [*Norfolk Chronicle*, 10 June 1843], and a UNITARIAN CHAPEL in GAOL STREET, YARMOUTH, designed just before his death in 1844 and built in 1845 [*Norwich Mercury*, 16 Nov. 1844, *ex inf.* Mr. David Cubitt].

TIMBRELL, BENJAMIN (–1754), was one of the leading carpenters and master builders in Georgian London. He was probably the most prominent speculative builder in London between 1720 and 1750, especially in the Mayfair area. He built on the Earl of Scarbrough's land near Hanover Square, on the City of London's Conduit Mead estate, and on the Berkeley and Grosvenor estates [information from Mr. Frank Kelsall]. Between 1723 and 1730 he took three building leases on the Harley estate in Marylebone [B.L., Add. MS. 18240, ff. 10–18]. In 1735 he bought Chandos House in St. James's Square, pulled it down, and built three houses on the site [*Survey of London* xxix, 122–3]. His last scheme, the redevelopment of the site of Stafford House, Buckingham Gate, was completed by his executors [deeds in Middlesex Land Register]. For some time Timbrell appears to have been in partnership with another well-known London carpenter, Thomas Phillips (d. 1736),[1] in conjunction with whom he executed the structural woodwork of the church of St. Martin-in-the-Fields in 1722–6 [J. McMaster, *St. Martin-in-the-Fields*, 1916, 79] and built the church of St. Peter, Vere Street, in 1721–4 [B.L., Add. MS. 18238, ff. 37–9]. Though he often built to the designs of others, Timbrell was no doubt capable of being his own architect. In February 1727/8 it was 'according to the scheme or plann . . . delivered by the said Benjamin Timbrell' that he undertook to build a riding-house and stables in ADAMS MEWS (now Adams Road) to the south of Grosvenor Square for the Earl of Hertford (later 7th Duke of Somerset) [Percy archives, Alnwick Castle, X.ll.1], and it appears that in 1737/8 he designed as well as built Nos. 1–3 CROWN OFFICE ROW, INNER TEMPLE, altered by S. Smirke in 1863–4 and destroyed by bombing in 1941 [*Calendar of Inner Temple Records* iv, 1933, 348, 353, 365, 366–9, 371–2, 373, 391]. In 1743 he was paid 'for supervising the Repairing and fitting up' of LEICESTER HOUSE, LEICESTER SQUARE, for the Prince of Wales [*Survey of London* xxxiv, 447]. In 1730 he was the principal member of the group of 'undertakers' who contracted to build the GROSVENOR CHAPEL in SOUTH AUDLEY STREET, and may well have made the design, although there is no direct evidence that this was the case [*Survey of London* xl, 298–302]. In the same way he was very likely the designer, as well as the principal builder, of HUNTINGDON TOWN HALL, a modest brick building erected in 1745 [Huntingdon R.O., Common Council Order Book 1732–85, p. 82, *ex inf.* Mr. R. Hewlings].

Timbrell, who lived from 1729 to 1751 in Upper Grosvenor Street (No. 12), was a vestryman of St. George's Hanover Square. He died in or about January 1754. His will, dated December 1750 [P.C.C. 28 PINFOLD], refers to his purchase of a house in Fulham 'which I have pulled down and am rebuilding'. A codicil shows that he had sold it by November 1753.

[1] See above, p. 751.

TINLEY, —, made designs for rebuilding DITCHLEY HOUSE, OXON., for the 2nd Earl of Lichfield in 1720. They were criticized by Francis Smith of Warwick in a letter to the Earl dated 4 May 1720, and were not adopted. What appears to be Tinley's plan is preserved among the Ditchley papers in the County Record Office at Oxford. It is crudely drawn and bears a note, 'This Plane drawn in imitation of Mr. Wallop's House. But not at all like it.' Mr. Wallop's house was at Hurstbourne Priors, Hants.

TITE, SIR WILLIAM (1798–1873), was the son of Arthur Tite, a wealthy London merchant. He became a pupil of David Laing and assisted him (1817–20) in rebuilding the body of the church of St. Dunstan-in-the-East (of which, according to Eastlake, he was the effective architect). He was admitted to the Royal Academy Schools in 1818, and exhibited at the Academy in 1817 and the following years.[1] After failing in several competitions he obtained the commission to design Mill Hill School in 1825, followed by the National Scotch Church in Regent Square in 1827–8. His most important work was the Royal Exchange. Tite was not among the thirty-eight architects who entered designs for the original competition in 1839, but when the three best designs were set aside on the ground that they could not be built within the

[1] In 1854, after a long absence from the Academy, he showed 'a composition of the works of Inigo Jones' which was evidently intended to be a companion to Cockerell's well-known 'Tribute to Wren of 1838. This drawing, now in the R.I.B.A. Collection, is illustrated in *R.I.B.A. Jnl.* July 1965, 342–3.

prescribed sum, Tite was brought in, first as an adviser and then as a competitor. Ultimately only he and Cockerell were left in the field, and Tite's design was chosen by 13 votes to 7. In the circumstances the propriety of his conduct was questionable, and in the eyes of everyone but the committee his design was markedly inferior to Cockerell's. The building was completed at a cost of £150,000, and was opened by Queen Victoria on 28 October 1844.

Tite's practice was largely concerned with railways. In the 1840s he was extensively engaged in the valuation, purchase and sale of land for railways, and designed a number of railway stations, notably the termini of the London and South-Western Railway Company at Vauxhall (Nine Elms) and Southampton (both illustrated in *Surveyor, Engineer & Architect* i, 1840, 49), the Citadel Station at Carlisle, most of the stations on the Caledonian and Scottish Central Railways, those on the Exeter and Yeovil Railway, and on the line from Havre to Paris; and the station at Windsor (1850).

After a serious illness, followed by a journey to Italy in 1851–2, Tite gradually withdrew from practice, but his wealth ('I inherited a fortune, I married a fortune, and I have made a fortune', he is reported to have told the Prince of Wales) enabled him to remain active in other capacities. In 1838 he was elected President of the Architectural Society, which was merged with the R.I.B.A. in 1842. He was President of the Institute from 1861 to 1863 and from 1867 to 1870. He was Liberal M.P. for Bath from 1855 until his death, a member of the Metropolitan Board of Works, and chairman of several companies. He was a member of numerous committees, and in 1860 headed a deputation to Lord Palmerston opposing Scott's Italianate Gothic design for the Foreign Office. He was knighted in 1869, and in 1870 was made a Companion of the Bath. Tite was also well known as an antiquary and collector of books, manuscripts and works of art. He was elected a Fellow of the Royal Society in 1835, of the Society of Antiquaries in 1839, and was President of the Cambridge Camden Society in 1866. From 1824 to 1869 he was honorary secretary of the London Institution.

As an architect Tite was eclectic, his works ranging stylistically from Greek Revival (Mill Hill School) and Durandesque neo-classical (Nine Elms Station) to Perpendicular Gothic (the Scotch Church) and neo-Byzantine (church at Gerrards Cross). His most famous building, the Royal Exchange, is a somewhat coarse amalgam of classical sources, chiefly Italian Renaissance and Baroque in origin. Though it inevitably compares unfavourably with the elegant sophistication of C. R. Cockerell's contemporary work, it was by no means inappropriate as the temple of Victorian finance. As a Gothicist Tite is better represented by his railway stations at Carlisle (1847) and Perth (1848) than by the reduced version of York Minster which he built in Regent Square, London (1826–8).

Tite married in 1832 Emily, daughter of John Curtis, of Herne Hill, Surrey. He died without issue at Torquay on 20 April 1873, and was buried in Norwood Cemetery. His estate was valued for probate at 'under £400,000'. A portrait of Tite by J. P. Knight is at the R.I.B.A. and there is a bust by Theed (1869) at the Guildhall. Ebenezer Trotman and Charles Ferdinand Porden were his principal assistants, and Arthur Baker, Charles Bailey and J. H. Steinmetz were also in his office in various capacities. His nephew Arthur John Green (d. 1855, aged 34) and T. Hayter Lewis were his pupils. E. N. Clifton was for some years his partner.

[*A.P.S.D.*; *D.N.B.*; *Builder* xxxi, 1873, 337–9; *R.I.B.A. Proceedings*, 1873–4, 209–12; S. Redgrave, *Dictionary of Artists of the British School*, 1878, 432; M. S. Briggs, 'Sir William Tite, M.P.', *Builder*, 13–20 Jan. 1950.]

MILL HILL SCHOOL, MIDDLESEX, 1825–7 [N. G. Brett-James, *The History of Mill Hill School*, 1924, 60, 65, 66, 89 (plate)].

LONDON, THE NATIONAL SCOTCH CHURCH, SIDMOUTH STREET, REGENT SQUARE, 1826–8, Gothic; dem. *c.*1955 [J. Elmes, *Metropolitan Improvements*, 1829, 151–2 and plate].

LONDON, THE GOLDEN CROSS HOTEL, STRAND, 1832; dem. 1936 [*A.P.S.D.*] *(Survey of London* xx, pl. 36*b*).

LONDON, THE KING'S WEIGH-HOUSE CHURCH, FISH STREET HILL, 1833–4; dem. 1883 [Elaine Kaye, *The King's Weigh-House Church*, 1968, 66].

LONDON, THE LONDON AND WESTMINSTER BANK, LOTHBURY, in collaboration with C. R. Cockerell, who designed the exterior, 1837–9; dem. 1928 [see Tite's account of the partnership in *R.I.B.A. Trans.*, 1863–4, 24] (measured drawings in *Architect and Building News*, 1 March 1935).

LONDON, THE SOUTH METROPOLITAN CEMETERY, NORWOOD, 1838; Gothic; chapels dem. 1955–60 [*A.P.S.D*].

DOLLAR PARISH CHURCH, CLACKMANNANSHIRE, 1841, Gothic; enlarged 1921 [*N.S.A.* viii, 109].

LONDON, THE ROYAL EXCHANGE, THREADNEEDLE STREET, 1842–4; external attic storey added and courtyard heightened by addition of Corinthian order 1988 [*Proceedings con-*

nected with the rebuilding of the Royal Exchange, 1838–44, 1845; T. L. Donaldson, *Handbook of Specifications*, 1860, 277–379].

BROOKWOOD, SURREY, THE LONDON METROPOLIS CEMETERY, 1853–4 [*A.P.S.D.*].

LONDON, GRESHAM HOUSE, OLD BROAD STREET, 1854–6, with E. N. Clifton; dem. [*A.P.S.D.*].

LONDON, warehouse for Messrs. Tapling & Co., 1–8 GRESHAM STREET, 1857; dem. 1940 [*A.P.S.D.*].

GERRARDS CROSS, BUCKS., ST. JAMES'S CHURCH, 1858–9, in memory of Major-General Reid [*Builder* xvii, 1859, 588, 616].

TOD, A—, was employed by Robert Mylne as a clerk from 1801 onwards. He exhibited at the Royal Academy from 1800 to 1805, showing a drawing of the west front of Gosford House, East Lothian (1800), 'a mausoleum near Edinburgh' (1801), a 'Villa at Norwood, in Surrey' (1803), and the 'west front of a house intended to be built in Shropshire' (1805). An elevation of 'Mr. Tassie's House, Leicester Square', signed 'A. Tod, architect 1806', exists in a private collection. The house in question was No. 20 Leicester Square, which was occupied by William Tassie, the modeller, from 1799 to 1837 [*Survey of London* xxxiv, 489].

TOWNESEND, GEORGE (1681–1719), was one of the sons of John Townesend of Oxford (d. 1728), and a brother of William Townesend (*q.v.*). He established himself as a mason and carver in Bristol, and was made free of the city on 8 July 1706, on his marriage to Margaret, the widow of Malachi Harford, a former burgess. There are one or two payments to him in connection with the building of the new TOLSEY OF COUNCIL HOUSE (rebuilt 1824) in 1701–4, though the principal contractor was a carpenter named Joseph Jones. Townesend received 9s. 'for a stone chimney piece in the lower room' in 1704, and in January 1709/10 he was paid £12 'for the frontispiece at the Council House' [Bristol City Archives; cf. W. Ison, *The Georgian Buildings of Bristol*, 1952, 90]. In 1716 he contracted to complete the tower of ALL SAINTS CHURCH, BRISTOL, and was presumably responsible for the design of the cupola[1] by which it is surmounted. He was associated in this work with William Paul, a mason who had been concerned in rebuilding the lower part of the tower in 1711–12 [MS. churchwardens' accounts].

George Townesend is probably to be identified with the 'Mr. Townesend' who is referred to by Sir John Vanbrugh in one of his letters as the mason 'who did Mr. Southwell's masonry' at KINGS WESTON, nr. BRISTOL. Kings Weston was built by the Hon. Edward Southwell to Vanbrugh's designs in 1711–19, but there exists a 'Book of Designs' made for Southwell by various architects, and in it there is a design for a terminal feature signed by George Townesend and dated 21 May 1717, together with an undertakihng to 'do the same for Forty Pounds and twelve pence per Perch for the inside wall' [H.A. Tipping, *English Homes, School of Vanbrugh*, fig. 153; *Arch. Hist.* x, 1967, fig. 23]. Another of the designs in the book is for a fireplace similar to one in Kingston Bagpuize House, Berks., which may have been built by one of the Townesends (*C. Life*, 6–13 Nov. 1942).

There are two monuments in LONG ASHTON CHURCH, SOMERSET, which bear the signature 'Townesend of Bristol'. They commemorate Sir Hugh Smyth (d. 1680, monument erected 1697) and Lady Smyth (d. 1715).

George Townesend appears to have left no children, and by his will, proved on 14 May 1719, he left all his plate to his nephew John Townesend, son of his brother William Townesend of Oxford [P.C.C. 92 BROWNING].

TOWNESEND, JOHN (1678–1742), was one of the sons of John Townesend of Oxford (d. 1728). Having in 1693 been apprenticed to Samuel Fulkes, a well-known London mason who was a member of the Haberdashers' Company, he was in due course admitted to membership of that, rather than of the Masons' Company. He became one of London's leading master masons, being in 1732–4 one of the contractors for building the Bank of England, and in 1739–42 the Mansion House [*Ars Quatuor Coronatorum* xli, 1928, 160 ff.; Sally Jeffery, *The Mansion House*, 1993, Appendix 3]. Although from time to time employed to inspect buildings in need of repair, e.g. St. George's Church, Southwark, [*Commons Jnls.* xxii, 43, Feb. 1732/3], no evidence has been found that he made architectural designs. The death of 'Mr. John Townesend, Mason, one of the Common Council men for Castle-Baynard Ward, and Brother to the late Mr. Townesend of Oxford', was announced in the *London Magazine* for 1742, p. 205.

TOWNESEND, JOHN (1709–1746), was the son and successor of William Townesend of Oxford (d. 1739). He figures as 'stone-

[1] This was rebuilt in 1807–8 when the tower was repaired by Luke Henwood. A survey drawing made in April 1807 shows that it originally had a different profile in the form of an inverted *cyma recta*, the lower (concave) portion being separated from the upper (convex) by a bold torus moulding.

THE TOWNESEND FAMILY

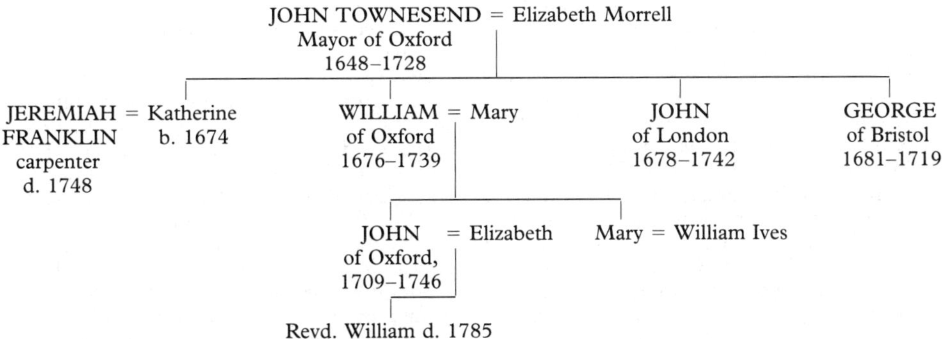

carver' in the list of workmen employed on the Radcliffe Library given by Gibbs in his *Bibliotheca Radcliviana*, and succeeded his father as one of the principal mason-contractors for that building in 1739. He also took his place as mason to the Dean and Chapter of Christ Church. In 1742, when James Gibbs went to Tetbury, Glos., in order to report on the state of the church, he took with him Mr. John Townesend, 'an eminent master builder from Oxford' [A. T. Lee, *History of Tetbury*, 1857, 104]. He was at that time engaged in building the stone screen in St. John's College Hall to the designs of James Gibbs, and himself submitted alternative schemes for raising the front of the college which were not carried out [St. John's College Archives]. Shortly before his death, he refronted the north side of Corpus Christi College, and in 1748 William Robinson produced an estimate of £335 which 'his late Master, Mr. John Townesend, had made for the mason's work in making the west front of Corpus Christi College in all things agreeable to the north side of the building already done' [Corpus Christi College Archives]. He died in 1746, leaving a son named William. He owned a 'large handsome House' in Oxford and considerable other property [P.C.C. 25 POTTER; *Jackson's Oxford Jnl.* 12 Oct. 1754].

TOWNESEND, JOHN (–1784), succeeded to the family business after the death of John Townesend II in 1746, although his precise relationship to the latter is at present uncertain. He was a mason-contractor of considerable importance but appears to have had few opportunities to act as an independent architect. After John Townesend's death he finished off the masonry of the RADCLIFFE LIBRARY, making in 1751 the fourteen obelisks of Burford stone which surrounded the Library until their removal in the nineteenth century [*Building Accounts of the Radcliffe Camera*, ed. S. G. Gillam, Oxford Hist. Soc. 1958, xxix, etc.]. In 1751 he contracted, with Richard Piddington and Robert Tawney, to build the new OXFORD TOWN HALL to the designs of Isaac Ware [Bodleian, MS. Top. Oxon. c. 300, f. 154]. In 1757, in conjunction with his partner Edward King, he submitted an 'Estimate for an additional building at Queen's (the benefaction of Mr. Mitchell) joined to that already done on the East side of the South Quadrangle to consist of 3 sets of Rooms on each floor and a staircase' [Bodleian, MS. Rawlinson D.912, f. 534]. This was built between 1757 and 1759, and comprises the greater part of the east side of the front quadrangle of THE QUEEN'S COLLEGE [Queen's College Archives 5 L 11, a–b]. In 1758–9 Townesend built in stone the Gothic fan vault over the CONVOCATION HOUSE beneath the Selden End of the Bodleian Library. This reproduced the pattern of the seventeenth-century plaster vault, which was found to be insecure [I. G. Philip in *Bodleian Library Record* vi, 1958, 416–27]. In 1779 he designed and built the classical library of EXETER COLLEGE under the supervision of the Revd. William Crowe of New College (*q.v.*): it was destroyed in 1859 to make way for a new building designed by Sir Gilbert Scott [J. Ingram, *Memorials of Oxford* i, 1837, 14]. An elevation of 'St. Mary's spire in Oxford measured by Jno. Townesend 1757' is preserved among the Buckler drawings in the British Library [Add. MS. 36402, f. 23; see also Add. MS. 36979, f. 71], and in 1758 he rebuilt the spire of SHOTTESBROOKE CHURCH, BERKS., at the expense of Arthur Vansittart. A note in the register made by Vansittart's son William records that 'My Father advertised the steeple to be repaired. A Stone Mason from London engaged to repair it at £900. One from Bath at six hundred. Mr. Townshend from Oxford at £300. His offer was accepted.' The spire was again altered in the course of a restoration by G. E. Street in 1852, but its previous appearance is shown in W. Butterfield's *Elevations, Sections and Details of Shottesbrooke Church, Berks.*, published by the Oxford Architectural Society in 1844. In 1767 Townesend was employed by the Earl of Abingdon to build an inn near Swinford Bridge. Litigation over the value of the work performed was still in progress at the time of Townesend's death in 1784 [Bodleian, MS. Top. Oxon. c. 388]. One of Townsend's most important contracts was the building of MAIDENHEAD BRIDGE to the designs of Sir Robert Taylor (*q.v.*) in 1772–7. The contract price (with extras) was £15,523 [Berks. C.R.O., M/AB4/12]. In 1782 he contracted to build HENLEY-ON-THAMES BRIDGE to the designs of William Hayward (*q.v.*) for £9452. [F. Sheppard, 'Henley Bridge', *Arch. Hist.* 27, 1984, 325]. It was not completed until 1786, two years after his death on 4 Sept. 1784 [*Jackson's Oxford Jnl.* 11 Sept 1784]. He left a widow, Mary, and a son, Stephen (*q.v.*), who carried on the business.

In 1771–2 Townesend had bought two large tenements on the north side of Oxford High Street immediately to the west of its junction with Longwall, and including what is now Longwall Place [*Oxford City Properties*, Oxford Historical Society, 311–12]. Here he presumably had his working premises, and here he built a new house which is indicated as such on a plan of the approaches to Magdalen Bridge made soon after his purchase (B.L., *King's Maps* xxxiv, 33, 3(b), reproduced in *Surveys and Tokens*, Oxford Hist. Soc., lxxv, 1920).

Townesend signs monuments in St. Mary's, Oxford, to the Countess of Pomfret (d. 1762), in New College Chapel to Henry Bowles (d. 1765), and in Swalcliffe Church, Oxon., to Richard Wykeham and wife (d. 1751, 1768).

TOWNESEND, STEPHEN (1755–1800), was the son of John Townesend (d. 1784), and is probably to be identified with the Stephen, son of John Townesend, mason, and Elizabeth his wife, who was baptized in St. Michael's Church on 23 September 1755.[1] In 1780–1 he completed the tower of BENSON CHURCH, OXON., in a plain classical style with battlemented parapet and pinnacles. The original decision to build a new tower had been taken in 1765, but the work was stopped for lack of funds in 1771. The mason employed was called Hart, but a surveyor named Townesend (probably Stephen's father John) was paid a guinea in 1772. In 1780 Stephen Townesend contracted to complete it in Headington stone for £264 [Vestry Minutes in Oxfordshire C.R.O., MS. D.D.Par. Benson c.9/6–8]. In 1785 he rebuilt the tower of WOODSTOCK CHURCH, OXON., in accordance with designs he had submitted to the vestry [H. M. Colvin, 'The Rebuilding of Woodstock Church Tower 1770–1786', *Oxfordshire Archaeological Society's Report* no. 87, 1949].

In 1793–5 WHEATLEY CHURCH, OXON., was rebuilt by Stephen Townesend and Henry Tawney of Oxford, the latter being a carpenter by trade. An original elevation for this church is preserved in the Bodleian Library (MS. Top. Oxon. b. 220, f. 254). It was probably made by Townesend, as the tower resembled that of Woodstock Church. The church was demolished in 1857 [MS. parish records].

At MAGDALEN COLLEGE Townesend was the builder of the Gothic 'necessary house' known as West's Building, which was erected in 1782 [T. S. R. Boase, 'An Oxford College and the Gothic Revival', *Jnl. Warburg & Courtauld Institutes* xviii, 1955, 148]. Between 1782 and 1785 he acquired and rebuilt No. 64 (formerly 63) HIGH STREET, OXFORD, for whose elegant façade he was presumably responsible [deeds at Magdalen College].

Townesend lived at Iffley towards the end of his life, apparently in Court Place, the large house near the church. He died on 6 October 1800, aged about 45, according to a memorandum in a notebook kept by Thomas Knowles, who seems to have been Townesend's foreman. His will is P.C.C. 903 ADDERLEY. On 15 March 1799 Knowles announced that, having for 'many years conducted the business of Mr. S. Townsend', he had 'opened a yard near the bottom of Holywell Street where he means to carry on the above business in its various branches'. The site of his yard (seen in the Oxford Almanack for 1844) is now occupied by the New College Memorial Library, but the firm which he founded is still in business and has in its possession the ledger which he opened in 1799.

TOWNESEND, WILLIAM (1676–1739), was the most successful member of a family of master masons who lived and worked in Oxford throughout the eighteenth century and have an important place in its architectural history. He was the son of John Townesend I

[1] If so, his father married twice, for he left a widow Mary at his death in 1784 [Bodleian, MS. Top. Oxon. c. 388].

(1648–1728), who served his apprenticeship under Bartholomew Peisley and became an alderman of Oxford, holding office as Mayor in 1682–3 and 1720–1. Hearne, who disliked both father and son, records that 'This old Townesend is commonly called old Pincher, from his pinching his workmen.' He died of dropsy on 23 May 1728 and was buried in St. Giles' Churchyard, where there is a handsome monument to his memory erected by his son. According to the inscription, he was 'in [re] architectonica magister peritissimus, exactis demum pluribus et ad scientiam et ad universitatis hujusce ornamentum aedificiis'. Little, however, is known of his building activities, except that he was employed at Queen's College from 1688 onwards, at Pembroke College from 1691, and at Blenheim Palace from 'about the latter end of the year 1705 until some time in or about the year 1711' [B.L., Add. MS. 19617, f. 79].

William Townesend was baptized in St. Giles' Church on 17 December 1676. By the second decade of the eighteenth century he was beginning to take his father's place as the leading master mason in Oxford, and it is clear that, like other men of his kind, he was competent to design as well as to build. In the Queen's accounts he is referred to as 'architecto Townesend', whereas the payments to his father were credited to 'Lapicidae Townesend', and it would appear that he was largely responsible for the design of the main quadrangle of that college as well as for its execution. In particular, he modified Hawksmoor's design for the cupola over the entrance-screen. At Christ Church it was Townesend whose practical knowledge gave actuality to the schemes of the learned Doctors Aldrich and Clarke, and at Magdalen he was instrumental in working out Edward Holdsworth's designs for the New Building. From the list given below it will be apparent that Hearne was not exaggerating when he stated that Townesend 'hath a hand in all the Buildings in Oxford, and gets a vast deal of Money that way', for it includes nearly every important building erected in the University between 1720 and 1740. That they should differ widely in style is scarcely surprising, for, while some represented the designs of a competent architect of which Townesend was merely the executant (e.g. the Clarendon Building and the Radcliffe Library), others were conceived in the academic minds of Aldrich and Clarke, and only a minority were entirely of his own invention. A design for All Souls in the Clarke Collection at Worcester College, dated 30 June 1709, and endorsed as 'Young Mr. Townesend's draft', shows the influence of Vanbrugh, under whom he and his father were working at Blenheim; but Palladian motifs appear in the design for Christ Church Library which he prepared under Dr. Clarke's direction, and at Oriel and University Colleges he erected buildings in a traditional Jacobean style scarcely distinguishable from that of their older neighbours.

Like most eighteenth-century master masons, Townesend was a sculptor as well as a mason, and much carved work, both for decorative and for monumental purposes, must have been executed in his yard. He does not, however, appear to have signed his monuments, and the list of documented examples given below cannot represent more than a small fraction of his total output. That he was also a quarry-owner is shown by a letter among the archives of All Souls in which Hawksmoor writes to Dr. Clarke that 'you are in some measure, ty'd by his haveing all the best quarry's of stone in his owne hands.'

Townesend's wife (wrongly identified by Hiscock) was named Mary, and by her he had a son John (*q.v.*), who succeeded to his business, and a daughter Mary, who married William Ives, a wealthy mercer of Oxford. He died in September 1739 and was buried in St. Giles' churchyard on the 22nd of that month. His will is P.C.C. 219 HENCHMAN. His apprentices included William King (1704), John Osborne (1706) and Daniel Bowdon (1714).

[W. G. Hiscock, 'William Townesend, mason and architect of Oxford', *Arch. Rev.* Oct. 1946, reprinted in *A Christ Church Miscellany*, 1946; H. M. Colvin, *Catalogue of Architectural Drawings . . . in the Library of Worcester College, Oxford*, 1964, *Unbuilt Oxford*, 1983; parish registers of St. Giles and St. Michael-at-the-Northgate, Oxford; information from Mr. David Sturdy.]

OXFORD

EXETER COLLEGE, *executed* vaulting and carving of new gateway to Turl Street, 1702–3 [College Archives].

CORPUS CHRISTI COLLEGE, *built, and perhaps designed*, THE FELLOWS' BUILDING and CLOISTER, 1706–12, and the GENTLEMEN COMMONERS' BUILDING, 1737 [Hiscock, *A Christ Church Miscellany*, 1946, 41–2; *V.C.H. Oxon.* iii, 227].

CHRIST CHURCH, *built* PECKWATER QUADRANGLE to the designs of Dean Aldrich, 1706–14 [Hiscock, *A Christ Church Miscellany*, 1946, 40].

NEW COLLEGE, *built* the north-east block of THE GARDEN QUADRANGLE in 1707 to match the south-east block built by Richard Piddington in 1700 [Willis and Clark, iii, 280 n.].

THE QUEEN'S COLLEGE, *built* THE FRONT QUADRANGLE, including HALL and CHAPEL, under the direction of Dr. George Clarke, 1710–21: in 1733–6 he built the entrance-screen and cupola, for which Hawksmoor had made designs which were modified by Townesend [Hiscock, *A Christ Church Miscellany*, 1946, 42–4; Kerry Downes, *Hawksmoor*, 1959, 107, n. 14; H. M. Colvin, *Catalogue of Architectural Drawings in . . . Worcester College*, 1964, xviii–xix; building account in Bodleian, MS. Rawlinson D.912, f. 528; letter from Townesend about the cupola in Queen's College MS. 475, ff. 188–9].

THE CLARENDON BUILDING, *built* to the designs of Nicholas Hawksmoor, 1712–15 [*V.C.H. Oxon.* iii, 54–5].

BALLIOL COLLEGE, *built* THE BRISTOL BUILDINGS, 1716–20; refaced 1826 and since heightened; and *built* the south-east portion of the FRONT QUADRANGLE, 1738–9 (completed 1743); dem. 1866 [extracts from bursars' accounts in Bodleian, MS. Top. Oxon. e. 124/12, ff. 13[v], 15–16].

ALL SOULS COLLEGE, *built* (with B. Peisley) THE NORTH QUADRANGLE, HALL, BUTTERY and CODRINGTON LIBRARY to the designs of Nicholas Hawksmoor, 1716–35 [*V.C.H. Oxon.* iii, 190–3]. For Townsend's own rejected design see Colvin, *Catalogue of Architectural Drawings in . . . Worcester College*, 1964, pl. 51.

UNIVERSITY COLLEGE, *built* (with B. Peisley) THE RADCLIFFE QUADRANGLE under the direction of Dr. George Clarke, 1717–19 [*V.C.H. Oxon.* iii, 77–8; Colvin, *Catalogue of Architectural Drawings in . . . Worcester College*, 1964, xx].

CHRIST CHURCH, *built* THE LIBRARY to the designs of Dr. George Clarke, 1717–38 [Hiscock, *A Christ Church Miscellany*, 1946, 49–53].

ALL SAINTS CHURCH, *completed* (with B. Peisley) the steeple, 1718–20, to a design which represents a compromise between Aldrich's original proposal and an alternative one submitted by Hawksmoor [H. M. Colvin, 'The Architects of All Saints Church, Oxford', *Oxoniensia* xix, 1954].

ORIEL COLLEGE, *designed and built* THE ROBINSON BUILDINGS, 1719–20, the mouldings and ornaments being 'answerable to the rest of the college' [Hiscock, *A Christ Church Miscellany*, 1946, 52].

CHRIST CHURCH, *wainscoted* the east end of the Hall (removed 1799) and *designed and built* THE BUTTERY, 1722 [Hiscock, *op. cit.*, 54].

NEW COLLEGE, *paved* THE HALL, 1722 [Hiscock, *op. cit.*, 54].

BOTANIC GARDEN, *built* GREENHOUSES, 1726–7 and 1734–5; dem. 1774 [Oxford University Archives, Vice-Chancellor's Accounts 1726–7 and 1734–5 and estimates in WP α60(3)].

TRINITY COLLEGE, *rebuilt* north range of DURHAM QUADRANGLE, 1728, to correspond with the north range of the Garden Quadrangle, built to Wren's designs in 1668 [Hiscock, *op. cit.*, 55].

attributed: PEMBROKE COLLEGE CHAPEL, 1728–32; interior decorated by C. E. Kempe 1884 [Hiscock, *op. cit.*, 55].

ST. JOHN'S COLLEGE, *erected* marble chimney-piece in Hall, 1731 [College Archives].

Completed building of ST. PETER LE BAILEY CHURCH after the death of William Chipps, the original master mason, 1732–40 (the foundation-stone had been laid in Jan. 1728); dem. 1874 [Hearne, *Collections* xi, 114].

MAGDALEN COLLEGE, *drew designs* for the NEW BUILDINGS on lines prescribed by Edward Holdsworth (*q.v.*). These were carried out by the Oxford masons William King and Richard Piddington in 1733–4. Only the northern range of what was to have been a new quadrangle was completed, and the returns remained incomplete until 1826, when they were faced in ashlar by Thomas Harrison (*q.v.*) [Magdalen College archives; H. Colvin, *Unbuilt Oxford*, 1983, 81–5].

WORCESTER COLLEGE, submitted an estimate for completion of Hall, Chapel and Library to designs of Nicholas Hawksmoor and Dr. George Clarke, Jan. 1734/5; he was probably the contracting mason from the commencement of the new buildings in 1720 [Hiscock, *A Christ Church Miscellany*, 1946, 59].

THE RADCLIFFE LIBRARY, *contracted* (with Francis Smith) to execute the masonry to the designs of James Gibbs, 1737. John Townesend completed the contract after his father's death in 1739 [*The Building Accounts of the Radcliffe Camera*, ed. S. G. Gillam, Oxford Historical Soc. 1958, xiii–xvi].

OTHER WORKS

ABINGDON, ST. HELEN'S CHURCH. In 1706 Thomas Fletcher, carpenter, agreed to build a gallery in Read's Isle, 'the Front to be done with Spanish Oake according to a designe to be given by Mr. Townsend' [MS. Vestry Minutes]. This may, however, have been John Townesend I.

RADLEY HALL, BERKS., *built, and probably designed*, for Sir John Stonehouse, in partnership with Bartholomew Peisley, 1721–4 [V.

Hope, 'The Architect of Radley Hall, *C. Life*, 27 Jan. 1950].

BLENHEIM PALACE, OXON., masonry contracts in partnership with Bartholomew Peisley, *c.*1720–39, including the erection of the Woodstock Gate (1722–3) and the Column of Victory (1727–30) [W. J. Churchill, 'Some Unpublished Letters of Sarah, Duchess of Marlborough, relating to the Building of Blenheim Palace', *Trans. Birmingham and Midland Institute*, 1884–5; Angela Green, 'Letters of Sarah Churchill, Duchess of Marlborough, on the Column of Victory at Blenheim', *Oxoniensia* xxxi, 1966; David Green, *Blenheim Palace*, 1951].

THORNHILL MANOR FARM-HOUSE, CLYFFE PYPARD, WILTS., *enlarged* for Brasenose College, 1723–4 [*V.C.H. Wilts.* ix, 31].

attributed: WOODPERRY HOUSE, OXON., for John Morse, 1728–30; wings added by F. Codd 1879–80 [John Cornforth in *C. Life*, 5–12 Jan. 1961].

EAST STANDEN, ISLE OF WIGHT, *designed* a farm-house for the Dean and Chapter of Christ Church, 1737 [Hiscock, *A Christ Church Miscellany*, 1946, 60].

ROUSHAM HOUSE, OXON., *designed and built* 'Townesend's Temple' for Lieut.-Gen. James Dormer, 1738–9 [M. Jourdain, *The Work of William Kent*, 1948, 80, fig. 114].

MONUMENTS

LLANBADARN CHURCH, ABERYSTWYTH, Sir Thomas Powell, 1706 [R. T. Gunther, *Life and Letters of Edward Lhwyd, Early Science in Oxford* xiv, 508–9].

OXFORD CATHEDRAL, James Narborough (d. 1707), for the Dean and Chapter of Christ Church [Hiscock, *A Christ Church Miscellany*, 1946, 59.].

OXFORD, ST. MARY'S CHURCH, David Gregory (d. 1708) [Bodleian, Ballard MS. xxxv, f. 158, cited by Hiscock, *op. cit.*, 60].

attributed: OXFORD, ST. MARY'S CHURCH, John Wallis (d. 1703) [Hiscock, *op. cit.*, 60].

OXFORD CATHEDRAL, Lord Charles Somerset, erected 1713 [Hiscock, *op. cit.*, 60].

OXFORD, ST. GILES' CHURCHYARD, tomb of his father, John Townesend (d. 1728).

TOWSEY, JOSEPH, of Blandford, was primarily a builder, but an inscription on the three-arched bridge over the R. Stour at DURWESTON, DORSET (nr. Blandford), records that it 'was Built by Henry Portman Esq. Anno Domini 1795. Joseph Towsey Architect.' In 1780 Towsey was working at LULWORTH CASTLE, DORSET, where he rebuilt the staircase in Portland stone for Thomas Weld, and where in 1792–3 he built the lodges [contract and bills in Dorset County Record Office]. In 1788 he built AMMERDOWN PARK, SOMERSET, to the designs of James Wyatt [C. Hussey in *C. Life*, 16 Feb. 1929, 216].

TRACY, CHARLES HANBURY, cr. BARON SUDELEY (1778–1858), was the third son of John Hanbury of Pontypool Park, Monmouthshire, the wealthy owner of the Pontypool Ironworks. He was educated at Rugby and Christ Church, Oxford. In 1798 he married his cousin Henrietta, daughter and heiress of Henry, 8th and last Viscount Tracy, the owner of the mansions and estates of Toddington in Gloucestershire and Gregynog in Montgomeryshire. He thereupon added the name of Tracy to that of Hanbury. He took an active part in public life, serving as High Sheriff of Gloucestershire in 1801 and of Montgomeryshire in 1804, and entering Parliament in 1807 as Whig Member for Tewkesbury. In 1835 he became chairman of the Commissioners appointed to judge the designs submitted for the new Houses of Parliament, and subsequently showed much pertinacity in defending the choice of Charles Barry as architect. His interest in architecture had earlier been manifested in the rebuilding of Toddington, carried out entirely to his own designs between 1820 and 1835 at a cost of £150,000. With details derived (*via* Pugin's *Specimens*, etc.) from Magdalen College Tower, Christ Church cloister, the roof of Crosby Hall, and other well-known medieval buildings, the house represents a serious attempt to adapt Gothic architecture to domestic purposes, and achieves considerable effect as a picturesque composition. In 1834 Hanbury Tracy offered his services to John Arkwright, the owner of the medieval mansion of Hampton Court in Herefordshire, who contemplated extensive alterations there. Though begged by the architect John Atkinson (*q.v.*) not to 'make Hampton Court a cell to the Abbey of Toddington', Arkwright was induced to adopt Hanbury Tracy's plans, and the south front and other parts of the house were rebuilt under his direction during the years 1835–41.

Toddington and Hampton Court appear to have been Hanbury Tracy's only architectural works, but they are sufficiently remarkable to give him a place in the history of the Gothic Revival alongside the professionals who by then were monopolizing the style. He died at Toddington in February 1858, aged 79, leaving £5000 for the erection of a monument to himself and his wife in the parish church.

[M. J. McCarthy, 'Tracy of Toddington', *Trans. Bristol & Glos. Archl. Soc.* 83, 1964, and typescript catalogue of drawings by Hanbury Tracy in Lord Sudeley's possession, 1991; J. Britton, *Toddington, Graphic Illustrations with Historical and Descriptive Accounts*, 1841; *Country Life*, 9 Oct. 1937 (Toddington), 22 Feb., 1, 8 March 1973 (Hampton Court); Arkwright papers in Hereford C.R.O., A 63; C. Hussey, *English Country Houses: Late Georgian 1800–1840*, 1958, 161–7.]

TRACY, JOHN, was one of the architects who submitted designs for the Bank of England in 1731. Two plans by him and a printed sheet of dimensions, etc. are preserved among the Bank's archives (M 61, i–ii).

TREACHER, JOHN (*c.*1735–1802), a carpenter of Sonning on Thames, was the founder of a firm of builders and surveyors who specialized in work connected with the river. He was surveyor to the Thames Commissioners from 1787 until his death, when his son John Treacher, junior, succeeded to the post. The latter died in about 1835, in which year his son, George Treacher, took over the surveyorship. George died in 1862 at the age of 71, just before the Commissioners were superseded by the Thames Conservancy Board (1866). John Treacher, senior, was responsible for the building of the first pound-locks between 1770 and 1773. Several new locks were constructed by his son in the 1820s, and it was John Treacher, junior, who designed the charming 'Pound Houses' or lock-keeper's cottages, which in many cases still remain. His designs for those at CLIFTON HAMPDEN, SANDFORD, BOULTERS, RAY MILL, ST. JOHN'S BRIDGE, COOKHAM, CLEEVE and MARLOW are preserved in the Treacher Collection in the Berkshire R.O. John Treacher the younger also held the post of Surveyor of Bridges to the county of Berkshire, and was concerned in the repair or construction of a number of small bridges in that county. In 1810–13 he and his son rebuilt the principal arches of WALLINGFORD BRIDGE, reducing their number from four to three and widening the roadway. They also carried out extensive repairs to CAVERSHAM BRIDGE in 1815 under the direction of W. C. Mylne. The Treacher family papers, covering the period 1773–1862, and containing many plans and drawings connected with the Thames navigation, were bequeathed to the Reading Public Library by Llewellyn, grandson of George Treacher. Some account of the family will be found in F. S. Thacker, *The Thames Highway: A History of the Locks and Weirs*, 1920, 249–50.

TRENDALL, EDWARD WILLIAM (– 1852), practised from various London addresses, exhibiting at the Royal Academy from 1816 to 1836 and at the Society of British Artists in 1827 and 1831. His exhibits included a 'Design for a Public Library and Baths proposed to be built on the East Cliff, Brighton' (1830), and a 'Design for a residence about to be erected on the coast of Normandy' (1836). The only buildings actually known to have been erected to his designs are the GRANDSTAND on EPSOM RACE-COURSE, 1829–30 [Brayley, *Topographical History of Surrey* iv, 370] and the ULVERSTON UNION WORKHOUSE (now a hospital), LANCS., 1837 [advt. for tenders in *Westmorland Gazette*, 5 Aug. 1837, *ex inf.* Mr. Angus Taylor].

Trendall published several books of designs under the following titles: *Original Designs for Cottages and Villas, in the Grecian, Gothic and Italian styles of Architecture*, 1831; *Examples for Interior Finishings*, consisting of 24 plates of folding doors, staircases, cornices, french windows, chimney-pieces, etc., 1833; *Examples for Roofs for Stables, Cottages, Schools, etc.*, 1843; *Examples for Exterior and Interior Finishings*, 1848; and *Monuments, Cenotaphs, Tombs, and Tablets*, 1850, 1858.

TREVOR, ROBERT HAMPDEN, 1ST VISCOUNT HAMPDEN and 4TH BARON TREVOR (1706–1783), was the third son of Thomas, Lord Trevor of Bromham. He was educated at Queen's College, Oxford, and became a Fellow of All Souls in 1725. In 1734 he was appointed secretary to the British legation at The Hague, and rose to be minister plenipotentiary before his recall in 1746. From 1759 to 1765 he was joint postmaster-general. In 1754, on succeeding to the Hampden estates at Great Hampden in Buckinghamshire, he took the additonal name of Hampden, and in 1764 he succeeded his elder brother as Lord Trevor and owner of Bromham in Bedfordshire. He died at Bromham on 22 August 1783 [*D.N.B.*]. A portrait of him and his family painted in Italy by David Allen is in the Cheltenham Museum & Art Gallery.

Trevor was a man of scholarly tastes whose collection of drawings and prints was regarded as 'one of the choicest in England'. He was the author of Latin poems entitled *Britannia, Lathmon* and *Villa Bromhamensis*, and a number of surviving drawings show that he was an amateur architect of some ability. One is a proposal for the Radcliffe Library in Oxford based on the Roman Pantheon [*The Building Accounts of the Radcliffe Camera*, ed. S. G. Gillam, Oxford Historical Soc. 1958, pl. 17]. Others in the R.I.B.A. Collection include an exchange, a house, an obelisk (reproduced by A. Rowan, *Garden Buildings*, 1968, 20), a building in Spring Gardens, London, apparently intended for a society, and an ingenious design for Glynde Church, Sussex (evidently made for his brother, Richard Trevor, Bishop of Durham and owner of Glynde), in the form of interlocking hexagons. Drawings attributable to him among the Hampden papers in the Buckinghamshire Record Office include a design for a Gothic alcove, and for a rotunda for Lord Foley. At West Wycombe Park there is a 'Plan of an Hospitable Nobleman's Kitchen' in Trevor's hand. So far no building erected to his designs has been identified, though he was probably responsible for alterations to Hampden House in the 1750s.

TRISTRAM, JOHN, a builder of Ross-on-Wye, Herefordshire, designed MORASTON HOUSE, nr. BRIDSTOW, HEREFS., for Guy's Hospital in 1810 as a residence for the Hospital's Agent, Whaley Armitage [Herefordshire C.R.O., *Herefordshire Houses, Parks and Gardens*, typescript 1964, 23–4, citing plans (ref. C99)].

TROLLOPE, or **TROLLAP,** ROBERT (–1686), is said to have been 'descended from a line of stone-masons'. He is first found at York, where in 1647, as 'Robert Trollop, freemason', he obtained the freedom of the city by redemption. When, in 1655, the Corporation of Newcastle-on-Tyne decided to build a new Exchange and Guildhall, a committee was appointed for the purpose, and in May of that year received instructions to 'confer further with the surveyor that came from Yorke about it'. That this surveyor was Trollope is clear from a subsequent minute resolving 'to write to Mr. Trolop to bee surveyor and to intreate him to come, for that the Towne is desireous that the worke may be forthwith taken in hand'. In October the committee reported that 'they conceive that the first modell presented in pastboard is the fittest Modell to be observed', and a contract was made by which Trollope agreed to erect the building for £2000 and to perform the work 'according to the best Authors now in English'. Various modifications were, however, made to the design before it was completed in 1658 at considerably greater cost. The new Exchange, whose original appearance is known from a seventeenth-century painting in the Mayor's Parlour, was an exuberant classical building with paired superimposed orders, pedimented windows, a balustraded parapet and a bulbous cupola 'which could have strayed from the Kremlin' (J. Cornforth in *C. Life*, 12 Aug. 1993). The principal front was rebuilt by Messrs. Newton and Stevenson in 1791–3, and the south front was 'new fronted in a corresponding style' in 1809. [Newcastle Corporation Archives, Common Council Book 1649–59, pp. 260 *et seq.*; E. Mackenzie, *History of Newcastle* i, 1827, 215–16.]

On 25 September 1657 Trollope was admitted a freeman of Newcastle, and he subsequently established himself at Redheugh, in the parish of Gateshead on the other side of the Tyne. In 1663 he undertook to complete the building of CHRISTCHURCH, TYNEMOUTH, to raise and ceil the roof, and to plaster the walls. The church had been begun in 1658 and was eventually consecrated in July 1668. It was reconstructed in 1792 [*History of Northumberland* viii, 1907, 359]. In 1667 Trollope contracted to build CAPHEATON HALL, NORTHUMBERLAND, for Sir John Swinburne, and according to John Hodgson he also designed NETHER WITTON HALL, NORTHUMBERLAND, built in 1672 by Sir John's son-in-law Nicholas Thornton [J. Hodgson, *History of Northumberland* ii (1), 1827, 218, 220–1 (where the Capheaton contract is printed in full), 323] (*C. Life*, 12 Aug. 1965, article on Capheaton). These buildings establish Trollope as the author of a vigorous and individual style of vernacular baroque, 'totally free of academic inhibitions', but engagingly inventive. Other Northumbrian buildings in a similar style which may have been designed by Trollope are BOCKENFIELD MANOR HOUSE, nr. Morpeth, *c.*1670 (*History of Northumberland* vii, 364); the south front of CALLALY CASTLE, dated 1676 (*C. Life*, 12–19 Feb. 1959); and alterations to WIDDRINGTON CASTLE (dem. *c.*1775) as shown in an engraving by Samuel and Nathaniel Buck. His only other documented works appear, however, to be a small fort built on LINDISFARNE ISLAND in 1675, of which there is a plan in the William Salt Library at Stafford (Dartmouth Collection D 1778/III 03) [J. Raine, *North Durham*, 1852, 151; *Proc. Soc. Antiquaries of Newcastle on Tyne*, 3rd ser. ii, 1907, 42–4; Peter Orde, *Lindisfarne Castle*, National Trust Guide, 1975], and the font (a gadrooned bowl standing on a twisted column) which he made for SOUTH SHIELDS CHURCH, CO. DURHAM, in the same year [G. B. Hobson, *The Borough of South Shields*, 1903, 241].

In September 1671 Robert Trollop and his son Henry gave evidence on behalf of the Bishop of Carlisle in his suit against Archbishop Sterne of York for the cost of dilapidations at ROSE CASTLE, CUMBERLAND. Their submission was accompanied by 'a platforme for a new building under their hands', but this was not adopted in the subsequent partial reconstruction of the castle [J. Wilson, *Rose Castle*, 1912, 239; cf. B. Tyson in *Trans. Ancient Monuments Soc.* N.S. 27, 1983, 64–5].

In 1671 Robert Trollope played an important part in obtaining from the Bishop of Durham a charter incorporating the freemasons, carvers, stone-cutters, sculptors, brickmakers, tilers, bricklayers and other building craftsmen of Gateshead. He died in 1686, and was buried on 11 December in Gateshead churchyard, where he is supposed to have erected the square mausoleum afterwards used by the Green family, by whom it was repaired in 1855–60. No trace now remains of the statue and doggerel inscription (beginning 'Here lies Robert Trollop/who made yon stones roll up') which are said to have formed part of the monument, but of whose existence there appears to be no authentic record.

A contract whereby in Feb. 1675/6 Henry Trollope undertook to build the walls of a small house in NORTH SHIELDS, NORTHUMB., for a master mariner is in the Northumberland C.R.O., Blackett/Ord W3/17.

[R. Surtees, *History of Durham* ii, 1820, 112 n. (d), 120; E. Mackenzie, *History of Newcastle* ii, 1827, 752; *Freemen of York* ii (Surtees Soc. 1899), 106, 136; *Notes and Queries*, 6th ser. xi, 1885, 14; Bruce Allsopp & Ursula Clark, *Historic Architecture of Northumberland*, 1970, 54, 58–9.]

TROTMAN, EBENEZER (*c.*1810–1865), was the son of a Baptist minister at Tewkesbury. He was educated at Mill Hill School and was subsequently articled to William Wallen. He entered the office of William Tite as a junior clerk and eventually became his principal assistant. All his working life was spent in Tite's office, and his only independent work appears to have been HOLY TRINITY CHURCH, TEWKESBURY, 1837, Gothic [*Tewkesbury Yearly Register* i, 1840, 244, 283]. He was the author of two well-written articles, one on Tudor architecture in Loudon's *Encyclopaedia of Cottage, Farm and Villa Architecture* (1833), the other on 'the Extent to which the elementary forms of Classic Architecture are fixed or arbitrary' in the first volume of Loudon's *Architectural Magazine* (1834). Failing health obliged him to give up his post in Tite's office, and he died at his house in Park Village East on 1 January 1865, in his 56th year [*Builder* xxiii, 1865, 31].

TROUGHT, JOSEPH, exhibited architectural designs at the Free Society of Artists between 1765 and 1769. They included a 'Plan, elevation, and section for an assembly room intended to be built in Chelsea' (1766), a 'Design for a gentleman's villa, intended to be built in the North Riding of Yorkshire' (1767), and a 'Design calculated for a military gentleman, with regular bastions, in the angles of a square' (1767). A house of the latter description was actually built at Sidcup, Kent, by an officer of the Royal Engineers in 1743: it now forms the nucleus of the Council Offices. Another, known as 'The Fort', was built on Hampton Common by a military gentleman, but was burned down in 1845 [Brayley, *Surrey* iv, 438].

TRUBSHAW, CHARLES, COPE (1715–1772), born at Haywood, Staffs., was the eldest and only surviving son of Richard Trubshaw (*q.v.*). He was sent to London to learn carving under Peter Scheemakers, and afterwards carried on an extensive business as a sculptor and master mason. His ledgers (now lost) showed that chimney-pieces and monumental sculpture were carved in his yard at Haywood from marble supplied by an agent at Westminster. He executed monuments to various persons, including Christopher Horton (d. 1764) in Croxall Church, Staffs., the husband of Mrs. Talbot of Hoar Cross (1767), and a Mr. Lucas (1770). He made chimney-pieces for Keele Hall, Himley Hall, Tixall Hall, Hoar Cross (Mr. Talbot), and the Raven Inn at Shrewsbury: and he did carving of a decorative character for Sir Lynch Cotton, Madame Boswell (1759) and others, including Mr. Corbet of Sundorn Hall, Salop., whom he supplied with a marble sideboard. He continued the works at TIXALL HALL begun by his father, and built BELLAMOUR HOUSE, nr. RUGELEY; dem. *c.*1920. He also 'built, or added to, and altered, Acton Chapel [i.e. Acton Church, Cheshire], Newborough Chapel (near Lord Bagot's), Darfold Chapel, Gayton Church, Trentham Church, Ellenhall, Sidway Hall, and others'. He rebuilt STONE CHURCH to the designs of William Robinson (*q.v.*) in 1754–8, and he was presumably the 'Mr. Trubshaw' under whose direction BARLASTON and FRADSWELL CHURCHES, STAFFS, were rebuilt in a plain Gothic style in 1762 and 1764–5, respectively [Staffs, C.R.O., D 3538/9 and D 3033/3/3]. He also built SWYNNERTON RECTORY in 1760 and TRENTHAM BRIDGE in 1766.

Miss Trubshaw gives the following list of persons for whom he executed work at various times: Hon. Thomas Anson (of Shugborough, where in 1764 he built the Temple of the Winds to the designs of James Stuart); Hon. J. Barry, Esq., Sir Thomas Broughton, Hon. Mr. Clifford, Sir Brian Broughton Delves, Lord Kilmorey, Hon. Mrs. Talbot (of Hoar Cross), George

THE TRUBSHAW FAMILY

Showing the relationship of the principal members engaged in architecture and civil engineering

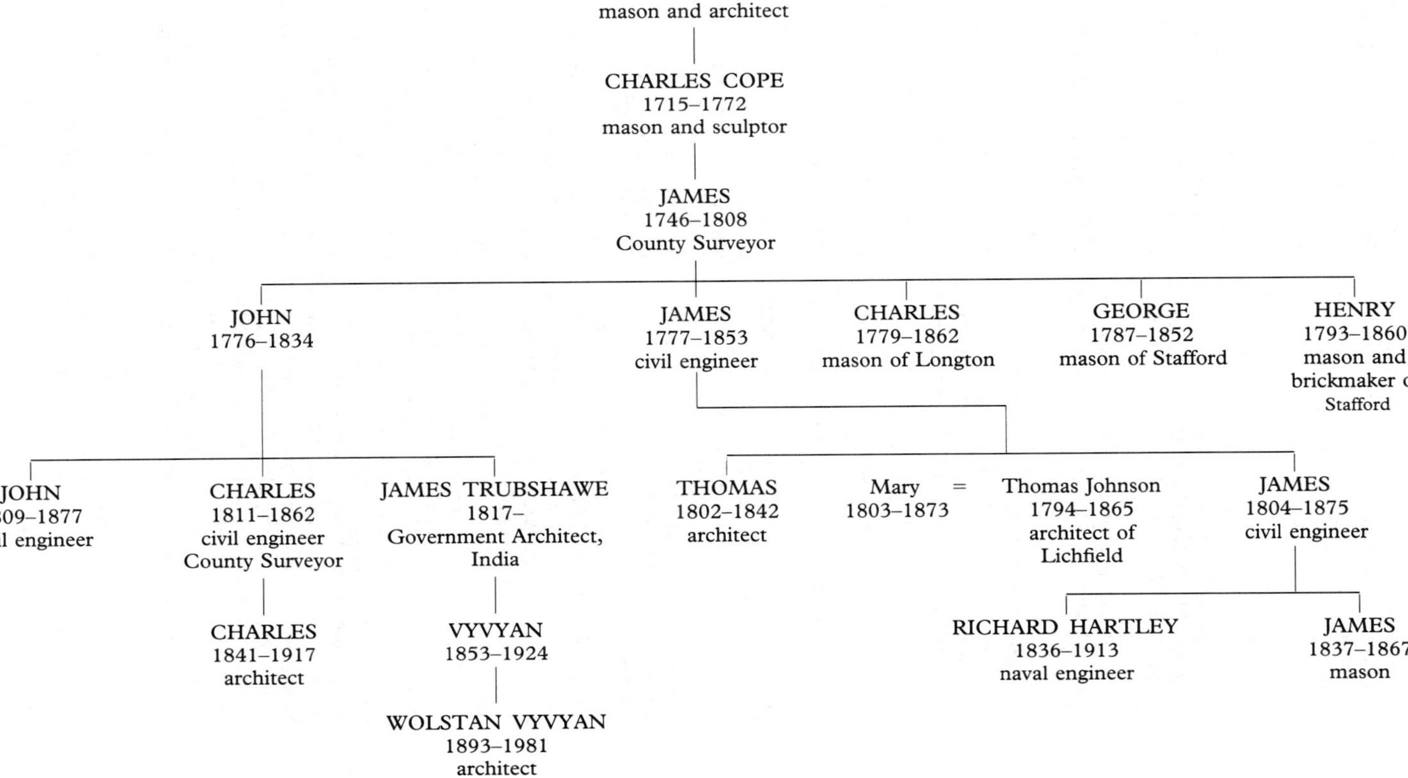

Venables Vernon, George Adams, Revd. Mr. Bagot, Sir Wm. Bagot (of Blithfield), Viscount Chetwynd (of Ingestre), Thos. Fitzherbert (of Swynnerton), Sir Edward Littleton (of Teddesley), Mainwaring, Esq., of Whitmore, Mr. Whitby.

Trubshaw died at Haywood on 22 December 1772, at the age of 56, and is commemorated by a tablet in Colwich Church, of which he was a warden. His pocket-book for the years 1754–5 is in the National Library of Wales (MS. 16635 B). He left a son James (1746–1808), who carried on the family business. [Susanna Trubshaw, *Family Records*, 1876; 'Stafforda', *Guide and History of Haywood*, 1924, and *Supplement*, 1930.]

TRUBSHAW, JAMES (1746–1808), the son and successor of Charles Cope Trubshaw, was appointed County Surveyor of Staffordshire in January 1793, at a salary of £52 12s. He was 'required to attend two days a week to the work under hand, and also to deliver a report of necessary repairs wanting at every Quarter Sessions'. He lived at first at Mount Pleasant, now Colwich Priory, but getting into difficulties, sold it in 1791 and moved to a smaller house in Haywood village, In 1788 he carried out some alterations to SANDON HALL for Lord Harrowby, but little else is known of his activities as a builder and architect. He died on 13 April 1808, aged 61, leaving seven sons, of whom James, his successor, is noticed below.

His eldest son John (1776–1834) had three sons, John (1809–1877), Charles (1811–1862) and James (b. 1817), all of whom were in practice as architects or civil engineers. John and Charles appear to have been in partnership in Newcastle-under-Lyme in the 1840s and were responsible for several churches in that neighbourhood, some of which, however, are also said in contemporary sources to have been designed by their cousin James Trubshaw (1804–1875), then in practice in the same town.[1] John subsequently practised as a civil engineer at Isigny in Normandy, but retired to his native county, dying at Uttoxeter in 1877. Charles, also a civil engineer, was County Surveyor of Staffordshire from 1850 until his death in 1862, and was the father of Charles Trubshaw of Derby (1841–1917), A.R.I.B.A. and architect to the Midland Railway Company. The third son James went out to India as Government Architect there and was responsible for alterations to Bombay Cathedral in the 1860s. He and his descendants (who included his grandson Wolstan Vyvyan Trubshawe, A.R.I.B.A., 1893–1981) added a terminal 'e' to the family name.

[Susanna Trubshaw, *Family Records*, Stafford 1896; information from Staffordshire County Record Office; genealogical information from Mr. T. A. Trubshaw of Queensland, Australia.]

TRUBSHAW, JAMES (1777–1853), born on 13 February 1777, was the son of James Trubshaw of Haywood (d. 1808) by his second wife Elizabeth. He attended a school at Rugeley and learned the mason's trade in his father's yard. At the age of 16 he went to London to seek employment through his father's friend, Richard Westmacott (father of Sir Richard). Westmacott sent him to Fonthill Abbey, then in course of erection for William Beckford, and afterwards to Buckingham Palace and Windsor Castle. He married in 1800 and settled in Haywood, but, failing to prosper, set up business on his own at Stone with very slender resources. He was fortunate enough to attract the attention of Mrs. Sneyd, then about to build Ashcombe Hall. 'Struck by his integrity and business-like habits', she insisted on employing him as builder, despite his lack of capital, and helped by timely advances of money. He afterwards said that he 'never built a better house than this, his first formidable undertaking'. On his father's death in 1808, he returned to Haywood to take charge of the family business, which he managed with considerable success. Among the buildings which he erected were Ilam Hall, nr. Ashbourne, to the designs of John Shaw, Weston House, Warwicks., to those of Edward Blore, and Trentham Park, Staffs., to those of Charles Barry. Although he designed several churches and other buildings Trubshaw regarded himself primarily as a builder and civil engineer, and 'as far as possible avoided that which he considered as interfering with the professional Architect'. As a builder his most celebrated achievement was the construction of the Grosvenor Bridge at Chester to the designs of Thomas Harrison. This consisted of a single arch of 200 feet span, and competent engineers, Telford included, were doubtful whether it could be built. Harrison died in 1829, but the bridge was successfully completed by Trubshaw in 1833 under the direction of Jesse Hartley, C.E.. Models of the bridge, showing the method of construction

[1] The churches in question are BROWN EDGE, STAFFS., 1843–4; HOLY TRINITY, CONGLETON, CHESHIRE, 1844–5; SMALLWOOD, CHESHIRE, 1845; NORTH RODE, CHESHIRE, 1845–6; ASTON, STAFFS., 1846; ST. JAMES, CONGLETON, CHESHIRE, 1847–8, NORTHWOOD, nr. STOKE-ON-TRENT, STAFFS., 1847–8, and ST. PETER, MACCLESFIELD, CHESHIRE, 1848–9.

employed, were afterwards presented by Trubshaw to the Institution of Civil Engineers, of which he became a member in 1827. He also built the Exeter Bridge over the R. Derwent at Derby (opened in Oct. 1850), a work of great difficulty owing to sudden floods and quicksands. Another of Trubshaw's engineering achievements was to restore the tower of Wybunbury Church, in Cheshire, to the perpendicular, from which it had declined more than 5 feet. He accomplished this by means of specially constructed gouges, with which he removed the soil from beneath the higher side (see *Architectural Mag.* i, 1834, 209, for an account of the operation). He was for some time engineer to the Trent and Mersey Canal Company, whose works he directed with characteristic competence.

Trubshaw's success as a practical engineer was remarkable in view of his very limited education. He 'seemed to be gifted with an instinctive perception of all great mechanical principles', and a combination of intelligence, integrity and hard work enabled him to surmount problems that to others seemed insuperable. As an architect he does not appear to have designed anything remarkable, his Gothic churches being typical products of their time.

Like his great-grandfather Richard, Trubshaw was a man of exceptional stature and strength. His daughter records that when he was building Ilam Hall he was invited to run against the Watts Russells' family tutor, who was held in repute for swiftness of foot. Trubshaw 'eyeing his man and knowing his own powers, offered to compete with Chantrey[1] on his back, and came off victorious'. He died on 28 October 1853, aged 76, and was buried in Colwich Churchyard. There is a monument to his memory in the church. A posthumous bust was exhibited at the Royal Academy by E. W. Wyon in 1857. Trubshaw had three sons and three daughters. The eldest son, Thomas (1802–42), is noticed below. One of the daughters married Thomas Johnson (1794–1865), the Lichfield architect, with whom her father appears to have been for a time in partnership.[2] Another daughter, Susanna, who died unmarried, was the author of a volume of *Poems* (1863) and of the *Family Records* (1876) upon which this account of her father is largely based. Several drawings by Trubshaw are in the R.I.B.A. Collection.

[Susanna Trubshaw, *Family Records*, 1876; obituaries in *Gent's Mag.* 1854 (i), 97–100, and *Minutes of Proceedings of the Institution of Civil Engineers* xiv, 1854–5, 142–6; *D.N.B.*; 'Stafforda', *Guide and History of Haywood*, 1924; Anne Bayliss, *The Life and Works of James Trubshaw*, Stockport 1978.]

[1] The sculptor, who was then at work on the Pike-Watts monument in Ilam Church.

[2] The I.C.B.S. certificate for St. Mary's Church, Uttoxeter (1828), is signed by 'James Trubshaw and Thomas Johnson, surveyors', and Messrs. Trubshaw & Johnson were the contractors for Barry's Royal Manchester Institution in 1829 [Whiffen, *The Architecture of Sir Charles Barry in Manchester*, 1950, 9].

ASHCOMBE PARK, nr. LEEK, STAFFS., for Mrs. Sneyd, *c.*1808–10 [S. Trubshaw, *Family Records*, 17] (F. O. Morris, *Picturesque Views of Seats* iv, 75). It is not certain that Trubshaw designed as well as built this house.

SWYNNERTON HALL, STAFFS., alterations for Thomas Fitzherbert, including new staircase and columnar screen in hall, 1810–11 ['Stafforda', *Haywood*, 86; letters in Staffs. C.R.O., D641/5/E(C)/7].

KINGSLEY CHURCH, STAFFS., rebuilt (retaining old tower), 1821, Gothic [I.C.B.S.].

WOLSELEY HALL, STAFFS., reconstructed for Sir Charles Wolseley, Bart., 1821, Tudor Gothic; dem. *c.*1965 ['Stafforda', *Haywood*, 45; P. W. Montague-Smith, letter in *C. Life*, 15 Sept. 1966, 641–2] (J. P. Neale, *Views of Seats* iv, 1821).

ILAM VICARAGE (now 'Dovedale House'), STAFFS., 1824; altered 1925 [*R.I.B.A. Drawings Catalogue: T–Z*, 80].

WALKERINGHAM VICARAGE, NOTTS., 1825 [Borthwick Institute, York, MGA 1823/5].

CHAPEL CHORLTON CHURCH, STAFFS., rebuilt 1826–7 on the basis of a plan by Trubshaw that was considerably modified in execution, Gothic [I.C.B.S.].

UTTOXETER CHURCH, STAFFS., rebuilt in conjunction with Thomas Johnson (retaining old tower), 1828, Gothic [I.C.B.S.].

GREAT WOLFORD CHURCH, WARWICKS., rebuilt 1833–5, Gothic [I.C.B.S.].

WYBUNBURY CHURCH, CHESHIRE, rebuilt church and restored tower to perpendicular, 1833–4; rebuilt (except tower) 1893 [I.C.B.S.; *Architectural Mag.* i, 1834, 209].

WILLINGTON BRIDGE, DERBYSHIRE (R. Trent), 1836–9 [*Companion to the Almanac*, 1840, 249].

KETLEY CHURCH, SALOP., 1838–9, Gothic [*V.C.H. Salop.* xi, 274].

PIPE RIDWARE CHURCH, STAFFS., 1840–2; chancel added 1899, Romanesque [A. Williams, *Sketches in and around Lichfield*, 1892, 280].

DERBY, EXETER BRIDGE (R. Derwent), 1848–50; rebuilt 1931 [*Gent's Mag.* 1854 (i), 99].

TRUBSHAW, RICHARD (1689–1745), of Haywood, Staffs., was a mason and quarry-owner who established a considerable business as a master builder in the west Midlands in the early eighteenth century. He came of a family of Staffordshire masons,[1] but spent some time in Oxford as a young man, and may perhaps have been employed in the building of Blenheim Palace, for he records that it was at Woodstock that he 'kept company' with his future wife, whom he married in Merton College Chapel on 6 January 1714. Like other members of his family, Trubshaw was a man of fine physique and great strength. His fame as a wrestler is celebrated in a contemporary ballad which relates how he defeated Richard Allen, or Green, of Hucknall, who had 'reign'd Champion of Nottinghamshire, and the Neighbouring Counties for twenty years at least', until he was thrown by Trubshaw in a wrestling-match at Repton. Trubshaw's account-books, which remained until the 1940s in the possession of his descendants, showed that while in Oxford he bought books on architecture, including *Vitruvius Britannicus*. These ledgers (now lost) contained architectural sketches as well as details of Trubshaw's building activities. Some extracts from them were printed by Susanna Trubshaw in her *Family Records* (1876), and they were also made use of by 'Stafforda' (Miss Whitehouse) in writing her *Guide and History of Haywood* (1924) and *Supplement* thereto (1930). It is from these works that the following imperfect list of Trubshaw's works is (unless otherwise stated) taken. In the absence of the original accounts it is difficult in many cases to determine the exact nature of Trubshaw's various commissions, and still more to assess his ability as an architectural designer. However, the demolished Emral Hall, with a reversed Borrominesque pediment over the main doorway, establishes its architect as the author of a vernacular baroque style comparable to that of Francis Smith of Warwick, and both family connections and architectural resemblances suggest that Trubshaw was also the designer of Pickhill House, Denbighshire, built by John Puleston *c.*1720–30. Emral and Pickhill both share distinctive features with Hilton Hall, Staffs. (*c.*1720–30), the seat of the Vernon family, for whom Trubshaw is known to have worked, both at Sudbury in 1734 and at Hilton itself in 1743. A case can therefore be made for attributing to Trubshaw an interesting group of provincial baroque houses, but without further evidence in the form of drawings or documents this cannot be regarded as more than tentative.

Trubshaw died at Haywood on 28 April 1745, aged 56, and is commemorated by a tombstone in Colwich Churchyard. He left a son, Charles Trubshaw (*q.v.*), to succeed to his business.

TIXALL HALL, STAFFS., much work for 4th Lord Aston from 1721 onwards, including the erection of a lodge (1721), the repair of the Elizabethan gatehouse, and the rebuilding of the east front (8 April 1729: 'Then began to pluck down the East front of Tixall'). The house was dem. *c.*1925.

EMRAL HALL, FLINTS., work for Thomas Puleston in conjunction with Joseph Evans, including addition of wings, 1724–6, and refronting of central block, 1727; damaged by fire 1904, dem. 1936 [National Library of Wales, Puleston papers, no. 776] (*C. Life*, 19 Feb. 1910).

WOLSELEY BRIDGE, STAFFS., repaired or rebuilt 1725; destroyed by a flood 1795.

ASTON HOUSE, nr. STONE, STAFFS., work for Sir Edward Simeon, Bart., 1725; dem. *c.*1800. A survey plan of this house in Trubshaw's hand is in the Bodleian Library (MS. d.d. Weld a.1).

GRENDON HALL, WARWICKS., work for Walter Chetwynd, 1725; rebuilt *c.*1825; dem. 1932.

BANGOR ISCOED CHURCH, FLINTS., rebuilt tower and south side of church, 1726.

COLWICH CHURCH, STAFFS., repairs and alterations, 1730–3.

KEELE HALL, STAFFS., works for Ralph Sneyd, 1731.

SWYNNERTON, STAFFS., work (perhaps to dower house) for Mrs. Fitzherbert, 1731.

SUDBURY HALL, DERBYSHIRE, work for George Vernon, 1734.

WORTHENBURY CHURCH, FLINTS., 1736–9 [T. H. G. Puleston, *The Story of a Quiet Country Parish*, *c.*1895, 174–7].

STAFFORD, work for 'Lord Falconbridge' at his house, 1737.

NORTON-IN-THE-MOORS CHURCH, STAFFS., rebuilt 1737–8; enlarged 1914.

BLITHFIELD HOUSE, STAFFS., work for Sir Walter Bagot, Bart., 1738. A survey plan of the house in Trubshaw's hand is reproduced in *C. Life*, 4 Nov. 1954, fig. 9.

HAUNCH HALL, nr. LICHFIELD, STAFFS., work for 'Esqr. Parkhurst', 1739.

BASWICH CHURCH, STAFFS., rebuilt 1739–40 by

[1] The name of 'Edward Trubshaw, Mason, 1655' is carved on the gable of the south-east chapel of Sandon Church, Staffs., and that of 'Thomas Trubshaw' appears on the tower of Armitage Church in the same county, which is dated 1632 [Shaw, *History of Staffordshire* i, 210].

Richard Trubshaw and Richard Jackson, masons [William Salt Library, Stafford, Salt MS. 436, pp. 167–8].

LICHFIELD, STAFFS., ST. MICHAEL'S CHURCH, rebuilt spire, 1742.

Work for Sir Theophilus Biddulph, Bart., probably the stables at BIRDINGBURY HALL, WARWICKS., 1742.

Work for 'Esqr. Congreve', presumably at STRETTON HALL, STAFFS., 1742.

Work for 'Esqr. Arblaster', presumably at LYSWAYES HALL, LONGDON, STAFFS., 1742.

STAFFORD, ST. CHAD'S CHURCH, repairs including casing exterior in brick, 1743; since restored [William Salt Library, Stafford, Hickin papers 319/40].

HILTON HALL, STAFFS., work for Henry Vernon, 1743.

MARCHINGTON CHURCH, STAFFS., rebuilt by Trubshaw 1743, according to a design 'to be drawn by William Wyatt gentleman' [agreement in parish records, *ex inf.* Mr. Donald Findlay; cf. variant design attributed to Trubshaw in Wm. Salt Library, Stafford, Staffs. Views vii, f. 63v].

TRUBSHAW, THOMAS (1802–1842), born on 4 April 1802, was the eldest son of James Trubshaw (d. 1853). His early death on 7 June 1842 cut short a successful practice as an architect and landscape-gardener. Some of his churches – notably Knightley and Salt – display a perverse originality criticized by Professor Pevsner in the Staffordshire volume of his 'Buildings of England'. He was elected a Fellow of the Society of Antiquaries in 1836. A collection of architectural drawings by Trubshaw in the William Salt Library at Stafford includes some for Manley Hall and for Brereton, Moreton, Knightley and Walton churches. [S. Trubshaw, *Family Records*, 1876, 25; *Architectural Mag.* i, 1834, 47.]

HILDERSTONE CHURCH, STAFFS., 1827–9, Gothic ['Thomas Trubshaw Architect, 1829' carved on a corbel on south side of nave].

WESTON-ON-TRENT CHURCH, STAFFS., rebuilt upper part of tower and spire, 1830 [A. Scrivener, 'Weston-upon-Trent Church', *Trans. North Staffs. Field Club* xxxix, 1905, 150].

HEATH HOUSE, TEAN, STAFFS., orangery and layout of flower-garden for John Philips, 1830–1 [*Architectural Mag.* i, 1834, 47, but the drawings for the garden are reported to be signed by his father James Trubshaw] (*C. Life*, 10 Jan. 1963).

MANLEY HALL, nr. LICHFIELD, STAFFS., for J. S. Manley, 1831–6, Tudor style[1] [B. Burke, *Visitation of Seats and Arms*, 2nd ser. ii, 1855, 70, with illustration].

KEELE HALL, STAFFS., three lodges for Ralph Sneyd, 1832 [steward's letters at Keele University, *ex inf.* Mr. Keith Goodway].

BIDDULPH CHURCH, STAFFS., largely rebuilt 1833, Gothic [I.C.B.S.].

BRERETON CHURCH, STAFFS., 1837, Gothic; enlarged 1877–8 [I.C.B.S.].

MORETON CHURCH, STAFFS., 1837–8, neo-Norman [I.C.B.S.].

STAFFORD UNION WORKHOUSE (Fernleigh Hospital), 1837–8; dem. 1971 [*N. Staffs. Jnl. of Field Studies* ii, 1962, 97].

UTTOXETER UNION WORKHOUSE, STAFFS., 1838–9, Tudor style [R.I.B.A.D.].

BAGOTS PARK, STAFFS., woodman's lodge for 2nd Lord Bagot, 1839 [S. Trubshaw, *Family Records*, 25; *Historical Collections for Staffs: Staffordshire Views*, 1942–3, 24; B.L., Add. MS. 36385, f. 152].

SANDON CHURCH, STAFFS., repaired nave and aisles, 1839 ['TRUBSHAW F.S.A. 1839' carved on west gable of nave; F. E. Coplestone, *Sandon Church Restorations*, 1929].

WOOTTON HALL, ELLASTONE, STAFFS., alterations for Revd. W. D. Davenport, *c.*1839 [sash-windows ordered for this house by Thomas Trubshaw, 1839: order-book of Messrs Jones & Clarke of Birmingham, Birmingham Reference Library, MS. 1056/249, Nos. 1486, 1493].

KNIGHTLEY CHURCH, STAFFS., 1840–1, Gothic [B.L., Add. MS. 36386, f. 146; drawings by Trubshaw in Wm. Salt Library, Stafford, 177/71/6].

SALT CHURCH, STAFFS., 1840–2, Gothic [S. Trubshaw, *Family Records*, 25].

WALTON CHURCH, nr. BASWICH, STAFFS., 1842, Gothic; the stone spire designed by Trubshaw was destroyed by lightning in 1845 and replaced by a wooden spire, of different design [B.L., Add. MS. 36388, ff. 81–3].

GREAT HAYWOOD, STAFFS., ST. STEPHEN'S CHAPEL, *c.*1842–5, designed by Trubshaw before his death but altered in execution and subsequently enlarged by H. I. Stevens [S. Trubshaw, *Family Records*, 25; G.R.].

TUCK, WILLIAM (–1805), of King's Lynn, was a carpenter by trade, and was probably the William Tuck of Denver, Norfolk, who in 1741 was apprenticed to John Green of West Dereham, carpenter [P.R.O., Ap-

[1] Burke says that 'The interior of the mansion was arranged on Mr. Manley's own plan, and the external architecture was designed by Mr. Thomas Trubshaw, architect, of Great Haywood.'

prenticeship Registers]. He was one of the two Town Chamberlains from 1772 to 1804, and by 1775 was described as 'gentleman' [information from Dr. John Stabler]. In 1766–8 the NEW ASSEMBLY ROOMS in the rear of the Guildhall at KING'S LYNN were built in accordance with plans produced by himself and Thomas King, a bricklayer, and in July 1784 it was agreed that the GAOL should be rebuilt agreeable to his plans [Corporation Minute Book, ff. 118v, 153, 394v]. This building (now a police-station) has a central feature ornamented with an iron grille and festooned shackles evidently derived from Dance's Newgate Prison in London.

TULLOCH, JOHN, was a builder-architect of Poole in Dorset (though twice in the 1830s described as of the neighbouring town of Wimborne). He designed several local churches in a spiritless Gothic style.

STRADBROKE VICARAGE, SUFFOLK, 1824 [E. Suffolk C.R.O., FF1/80/1].

PARKSTONE CHURCH, DORSET, 1833–5, Gothic; rebuilt 1876–1892 [I.C.B.S., East Boldre file].

LYTCHETT MINSTER CHURCH, DORSET, rebuilt 1833–4, except tower; Gothic [*British Magazine*, Sept. 1833; I.C.B.S.].

HOLT CHURCH, DORSET, 1834, Gothic; chancel 1889 [I.C.B.S.].

BLANDFORD CHURCH, DORSET, inserted galleries in nave, 1836–7; removed 1970 [I.C.B.S.].

POOLE, DORSET, POOLE UNION WORKHOUSE (now St. Mary's Hospital), 1838–9 [R.C.H.M., *Dorset* ii (2), 205–6].

SWAY CHURCH, HANTS, 1838–9, Gothic [Hants. R.O., 6 M 86/PW 5].

EAST BOLDRE CHURCH, HANTS., 1839, Gothic; chancel 1891 [I.C.B.S.].

BOURNEMOUTH, HANTS., ST. PETER'S CHURCH, 1841–3, Gothic; south aisle added 1851, remainder rebuilt 1854–79 [E. W. Leachman, *St. Peter's Bournemouth*, Bournemouth 1915, 9].

PENNINGTON CHURCH, HANTS., 1843, Gothic; rebuilt *c.*1865 [I.C.B.S.].

TULLY, GEORGE (–1770), was a carpenter and surveyor at Bristol. A native of Surrey, he was apprenticed at Bristol, first to John Stibbs, a carpenter, and then, on the latter's death, to John Price. Having completed his apprenticeship he was admitted a free burgess of Bristol on 17 May 1715. Soon after 1720 he laid out DOWRY SQUARE and CHAPEL ROW on ground leased to him jointly with Thomas Oldfield. KING SQUARE, laid out shortly before 1740, was probably planned by Tully, who built houses there, one for his own occupation and others for letting. His last important development was the laying out of BRUNSWICK SQUARE and the adjoining streets in 1766.

Tully designed DOWRY CHAPEL, 1746 (dem. 1871), the FRIENDS' MEETING HOUSE in THE FRIARS, 1747–9, at least part of THE INFIRMARY, 1749 (dem. 1784), and probably WESLEY'S CHAPEL in BROADMEAD, as enlarged in 1748. In 1741 he was among those who were invited to submit designs for the Bristol Exchange, but those of John Wood were eventually adopted. He may have been the author of a design for a Palladian country house in the collection of the late W. S. Lewis at Farmington, Connecticut, which is signed with the initials GT and the date [17]40. Tully died in 1770, leaving considerable property in Bristol. His son William, a Quaker, had predeceased him in 1763. Little is known about William Tully except that he 'delivered several ingenious plans for rebuilding Bristol Bridge' and was regarded by the builder-architect John Wallis as one 'whose Knowledge and Experience exceed that of all Mankind'. [W. Ison, *The Georgian Buildings of Bristol*, 1952, 47–9; Michael Jenner in A. Gomme, M. Jenner & B. Little, *Bristol: An Architectural History*, 1979, 141.]

TUNNICLIFFE, RALPH (*c.*1688–1736), of Dalton, nr. Rotherham, was an architect and builder who practised chiefly in Derbyshire and South Yorkshire. He is described as 'architect' in his will, and as 'gentleman' on his memorial brass in Rotherham Church. At the time of his death in 1736 he was employed at WENTWORTH WOODHOUSE, YORKS. (W.R.), by the Earl of Malton, later 1st Marquess of Rockingham. An engraving signed 'R. Tunniclif, *architectus*' and dedicated to Baron Malton (the Earl's title before 1734) shows a Palladian design for the new east front derived from Campbell's Wanstead House as published in *Vitruvius Britannicus*. Building began under Tunnicliffe's direction in the 1730s. By 1735, however, the Earl was consulting higher authority in the persons of Lord Burlington and William Kent, and Henry Flitcroft was brought in to advise and in the event to complete the building after Tunnicliffe's death. He made minor adjustments to the elevation, including raising the columns of the portico on pedestals and altering the shape of the attic windows, but the east front of Wentworth Woodhouse is essentially Tunnicliffe's design rather than Flitcroft's [Juliet Allan in *Archl. Jnl.* 137, 1980, 394].

Most if not all the following references presumably relate to the same person. In 1716

'Mr. Tunicliff' was paid £12 in part for taking down the tower of ST. MARY'S CHURCH, LICHFIELD [MS. churchwardens' accounts, 1683–1726]. In 1720–1 the steeple of ST. PAUL'S CHURCH, SHEFFIELD, was begun by 'Mr. Tunnicliffe' and John Platt, but left unfinished [J. D. Potts, *Platt of Rotherham*, Sheffield 1959, 3]. In 1722 'Mr. Tunnicliffe' was paid £3 3s. by the churchwardens of ALL SAINTS CHURCH, DERBY, 'for drawing a draught of the church and other expenses' [MS. churchwardens' accounts, *ex inf.* Mr. Edward Saunders]. In 1723 'Mr. Tuniclif' was paid 10s. 6d. for making a 'draft' for steps at CALKE ABBEY, DERBYSHIRE [accounts in Harpur-Crewe papers in Derbyshire C.R.O.]. In 1731 'Mrs. Tonycliffe' was paid £20 'for her husband in part' towards the cost of supplying a marble slab to be placed in MORLEY CHURCH, DERBYSHIRE, in memory of Henry Sitwell (d. 1726) and his brother [Sir George Sitwell, *Letters of Sitwells and Sacheverells*, Scarborough 1901, ii, 53], and between 1731 and 1734 Ralph Tunnicliffe was involved in alterations at WORTLEY HALL, YORKS. (W.R.) for Edward Wortley Montagu [R. Hewlings in *Archl. Jnl.* 137, 1980, 397].

The will of 'Ralph Tunnicliffe of Dalton in the County of York Architect' dated 14 April 1738, was proved in July of the same year. He left a wife and three children, Ralph, Mary and Dorothy [Borthwick Institute, York, York Prerogative Wills, July 1736]. The inscription on the brass in Rotherham Church is given by Hunter, *Hallamshire* ii, 1831, 21.

TURNBULL, ADAM OGILVIE (– *c.*1834), was a builder-architect of Edinburgh, where he was responsible for designing and building SAXE COBURG PLACE and SAXE COBURG (formerly WEST CLAREMONT) STREET for James Rose's Trustees, *c.*1825–30 [Edinburgh Sasines].

TURNER, JOHN, was paid 30 guineas in 1739 as a gratuity 'for his care and trouble in surveying and directing the work of the new Town Hall' at Portsmouth, Hants. (dem. 1837) [R. East, *Extracts from the Portsmouth Records*, 1891, 808]. He is said to have assisted in the construction of the NAVAL HOSPITAL at HASLAR in 1745.

TURNER, JOHN (–1827), was one of a family of architects from Whitchurch in Shropshire. When part of the Exchange at Chester was in danger of collapse in 1756, 'Mr. Turner, an architect, was sent for from Whitchurch, to survey it' [J. Hemingway, *History of Chester* ii, 1831, 17]. This Mr. Turner was probably the Samuel Turner, of Whitchurch, builder, who was employed at HAWARDEN CASTLE, FLINTS., in 1750–5, and received a gratuity of £87 'for his inspection and honest dealing' [John Cornforth in *C. Life*, 15 June 1967, 1519]. He was no doubt the father of the William Turner, also an architect of Whitchurch, who married in 1782 [Shropshire C.R.O., 665], and whose will, made in 1784, shows that he had a brother Samuel living at Whitchurch and a cousin Joseph (*q.v.*) who was in practice as an architect in Chester [Shrewsbury Public Library, 12332–3]. In the 1790s William Turner made a number of preliminary surveys for the Ellesmere Canal, and subsequently assisted Telford in its construction [L. T. C. Rolt, *Thomas Telford*, 1958, 40–6]. In 1801–4 he was employed by the 1st Marquess of Cholmondeley to design and build a new castellated house at CHOLMONDELEY CASTLE, CHESHIRE, subsequently given a more convincingly medieval profile by the addition of towers designed by Sir Robert Smirke [historical display by County Archivist in Cholmondeley Chapel and Gervase Jackson-Stops in *C. Life*, 19–26 July 1973], and in 1811 he was the architect and builder of OVER PEOVER CHURCH, CHESHIRE, a poorly designed brick building [R. Richards, *Old Cheshire Churches*, 1947, 271].

John Turner was probably the son either of the younger Samuel Turner or of the latter's brother William. In 1814 he was awarded the Silver Medal of the Society of Arts for a design for a church. He held the post of County Surveyor of Flintshire from 1815 until his death in 1827 [M. Bevan-Evans, *Guide to the Flintshire Record Office*, 1955, 23]. He was presumably the 'Mr. Turner' who was employed to furnish the choir of ST. ASAPH CATHEDRAL in 1809–10 [D. R. Thomas, *History of the Diocese of St. Asaph*, 1870, 207]. In 1816 the Dean and Chapter of BANGOR CATHEDRAL employed him to make estimates for the repair of their church and for the enlargement of the choir. Owing to a Chancery suit the work was not carried out until 1824–7, and then under the direction of a different architect, John Hall of Bangor [M. L. Clarke, 'Bangor Cathedral 1700–1828', *Caernarvonshire Historical Soc.'s Trans.* xiii, 1952, 32]. In 1819 John Turner carried out some alterations (since obliterated) to LLANDEGAI CHURCH, CAERNARVONSHIRE [*North Wales Gazette*, 7 Jan. 1819]; in 1822 he made designs for altering or rebuilding BENINGTON RECTORY, LINCS. [Lincolnshire Archives Office, MGA 115]; and shortly before his death in 1827 he made plans for rebuilding PONTESBURY CHURCH, SALOP., which were completed in 1829 by Samuel Smith of Madeley [*V.C.H.*

Salop. viii, 288]. This church is built in an 'Early English' style of unusual competence for its date.

TURNER, JOSEPH (*c.*1729–1807), was the cousin of William Turner of Whitchurch and therefore probably the uncle of John Turner of the same place (*q.v.*). In the 1760s and early 1770s he was living at Hawarden in Flintshire, but in October 1774 he became a freeman of Chester, and evidently took up residence there, for he subsequently became an alderman of the city and was always referred to as 'Mr. Turner of Chester'. During the last quarter of the eighteenth century he was the leading architect practising in Cheshire and Flintshire, and appears to have been a competent designer in an orthodox late Georgian style. He died in 1807 at the age of 78, and was buried at Hawarden, where there is a tablet to his memory in the parish church. The inscription claims that 'the many Splendid & Publick Works in which he was concern'd in the Counties of Flint, Denbigh, and Chester, will be a lasting Memorial of his Taste and Abilities as an Architect'.

CHIRK CASTLE, DENBIGHSHIRE, internal alterations, including new staircase, for Richard Myddelton, 1766–73 [Steward's MS. commonplace book at Chirk Castle, recording the employment of 'Mr. Turner from Hawarden'; C. Hussey in *C. Life*, 12 Oct. 1951].

GARTHEWIN, DENBIGHSHIRE, remodelled for Robert Wynne, 1767–72 [C. Hussey in *C. Life*, 13 Feb. 1958].

ERDDIG HALL, DENBIGHSHIRE, employed by Philip Yorke, 1772–4, probably to implement designs for alterations by James Wyatt [letters and accounts at Erddig, *ex inf.* Mr. G. Jackson-Stops].

MOLD CHURCH, FLINTS., rebuilt west tower, 1773, Gothic [W. Bell-Jones, *The Story of the Parish Church of St. Mary Mold*, 7].

LLANFERRES CHURCH, DENBIGHSHIRE, largely rebuilt 1774; altered by T. Jones 1843 [building account in Clwyd Record Office, PD 57/1/36].

RUTHIN, DENBIGHSHIRE, THE GAOL, 1775 [inscribed 'J. TURNER, ARCHITECT'].

OULTON HALL, CHESHIRE, entrance lodge for Philip Egerton, *c.*1775 [*Jnl. Chester Archaeological Soc.*, N.S. xxxvii, 1948–9, 216].

DYFFRYN ALED, DENBIGHSHIRE, main body of house for Mrs. Meyrick, 1777; wings and interior by J. Woolfe; dem. *c.*1920 [W. Angus, *Select Views of Seats*, pl. xlviii, 1797].

CHESTER, THE BRIDGE GATE, 1782 [J. Hemingway, *History of Chester* i, 1839, 369].

FLINT, THE COUNTY GAOL, 1785; dem. *c.*1965 [inscribed 'J. TURNER, ARCHITECT'].

PENTRE, nr. MOLD, FLINTS., bridge over R. Alyn, 1786 [M. Bevan-Evans, *Guide to the Flintshire Record Office*, 1955, 22].

TURNER, WILLIAM (1789–1862), of Oxford, well known as an artist in watercolours, is known to have designed one building: SHIPTON-ON-CHERWELL CHURCH, OXON., which was rebuilt in 1831–2 at the expense of his uncle, William Turner, who in 1804 had bought the Shipton estate together with the patronage of the living. Correspondence with the elder Turner in the I.C.B.S. records confirms the tradition that his nephew acted as architect for the church, which is competently designed in an early fourteenth-century style. A north-west view of the church by Turner is in the R.I.B.A. Collection. When Turner died in 1862 he was buried at Shipton, where a new screen was erected to his memory in 1896. For his career as an artist, see Luke Herrmann, 'William Turner of Oxford', *Oxoniensia* xxvi–xxvii, 1961–2.

TUTIN, RICHARD, practised as an architect and surveyor in Birmingham from before 1820 until after 1840. William Thomas (d. 1860) (*q.v.*) was his pupil or partner *c.*1830, and they are credited in a contemporary Directory with the design of the AMPHITHEATRE, BRADFORD STREET, BIRMINGHAM, converted into a chapel in 1849 [*ex inf.* Mr. R. Stanley-Morgan].

TWADDELL, THOMAS (*c.*1707–1762), 'late Deacon of the Squaremen of Dumfries', is commemorated by a tombstone in St. Michael's Churchyard, Dumfries. He was a mason by trade, and in 1744–5 he was, with Alexander Fleck or Affleck, another Dumfries mason, and James Harley, wright, responsible for rebuilding ST. MICHAEL'S CHURCH in a plain classical style. A plan submitted by William Adam was rejected as too expensive, and the design adopted was submitted by the contracting builders themselves [John Paton, *The Book of St. Michael's Church, Dumfries*, Dumfries 1904, 13, 37–8, 60–3]. Alexander Twaddell (*c.*1735–87), likewise Deacon of the Squaremen, appears to have been Thomas's son.

TYERMAN, THOMAS (–1862), was a pupil of Messrs. Bailey & Willshire of Lambeth. He exhibited a design for a museum at the Royal Academy in 1821, competed for the Houses of Parliament in 1835, and for the Royal Berkshire Infirmary at Reading in 1837. He subsequently practised from various London addresses. W. J. Gardiner (d. 1896) was his pupil and latterly his partner. His designs for PRESTON BISSETT RECTORY, BUCKS., dated 1839, are in the Lincolnshire Archives Office [MGA 244]. He designed schools (both dem.) at UPTON-CUM-CHALVEY, SLOUGH, BUCKS., 1840 [Bucks. C.R.O., AR 39/65/57] and WINDSOR, BERKS., 1842 [Berks. C.R.O., D/EX268/55a].

TYLER, WILLIAM (–1801), was known chiefly as a sculptor, but practised also as an architect. As he told a City committee in 1762, he was 'the son and grandson of a citizen [of London] and many years student under the late Mr. Roubiliac'. He exhibited with the Society of Artists from its foundation in 1760, becoming one of its directors in 1765. On the foundation of the Royal Academy in 1768 Tyler was one of the original forty members. At a later date he would hardly have been considered eligible for election, and Benjamin West afterwards explained his inclusion on the ground that 'there was not a choice of Artists as at present, and some indifferent artists were admitted.' However, he proved useful as an auditor of the Academy's accounts, and in 1799 was presented with a silver cup in recognition of his services in drawing up a report on the financial position of the Academy in conjunction with George Dance. He exhibited annually at the Academy from 1769 to 1786, and again in 1800. As an architect he enjoyed the patronage of the Duke of Gloucester, who employed him to alter his house at Hampton Court, and to design a villa at Kensington for the Duchess.

As a sculptor Tyler is represented by some thirty-five monuments (listed by Gunnis), which illustrate his progression from a baroque manner derived from Roubiliac to the neo-classical style of the late eighteenth century. His best architectural work, the short-lived Ordnance Office in Westminster, had an elegant façade in the style of Sir William Chambers.

Tyler died at his house in Caroline Street, Bedford Square, on 6 September 1801. There is a portrait by George Dance in the Royal Academy Library.

[*A.P.S.D.*; *D.N.B.*; *The Farington Diary*, ed. J. Greig, ii, 179; R. Gunnis, *Dictionary of British Sculptors*, 1968, 403–4; M. Whinney, *Sculpture in Britain 1530–1830*, 1964, 142.]

WESTMINSTER, ORDNANCE OFFICE, OLD PALACE YARD, 1779–80; dem. 1805 [T. Malton, *Picturesque Tour through the Cities of London and Westminster*, 1792–1801, 7].

MAIDSTONE, KENT, COUNTY GAOL, addition of wing, 1784; dem. in nineteenth century [Kent Record Office, QS Gaol Plans S.1 and QS Papers 213].

DORCHESTER, DORSET, COUNTY GAOL, 1784–5; superseded by new gaol designed by William Blackburn 1789–95 [exhib. at R.A. 1784; Hutchins, *History of Dorset* ii, 1863, 372].

LONDON, THE FREEMASONS' TAVERN, GREAT QUEEN STREET, 1786; dem. 1863 [Britton & Pugin, *The Public Buildings of London* i, 1825, 331 n.; *Survey of London* v, 61–2 and pl. 23].

BRIDPORT, DORSET, TOWN HALL, 1786–7 [exhib. at R.A. 1786].

HAMPTON COURT, MIDDLESEX, enlarged THE PAVILIONS for the Duke of Gloucester, 1792–3 [*History of the King's Works* vi, 332 and pl. 14 A].

LONDON, THE VILLA MARIA, KENSINGTON, for the Duchess of Gloucester, *c.*1800; dem. [exhib. at R.A. 1800; cf. *Beauties of England and Wales* x (5), 1816, 157].

TYRRELL, CHARLES (1795–1832), was the fifth son of Timothy Tyrrell, a solicitor who was an old friend of Sir John Soane. He was articled to Soane in January 1811, and remained in his office for six years [A. T. Bolton, *The Works of Sir John Soane*, 1924, Appendix C, p. xlv]. Tyrrell became a student at the Royal Academy in 1814, and was awarded the Silver Medal in 1815. He was in practice by 1820, when he was commissioned to carry out repairs to ST. ANNE AND ST. AGNES CHURCH, GRESHAM STREET, LONDON [W. McMurray, *A City Church Chronicle*, 1914, 66]. In 1821–2 he travelled in Italy and Sicily, where he made measured drawings in company with a fellow-pupil of Soane, Henry Parke (*q.v.*). Immediately after his return he published (1823), in conjunction with an engineer named William Anderson, a design for rebuilding London Bridge on the old foundations. There is a copy in Sir John Soane's Museum (P.C. 52). In 1828 he was appointed Surveyor for the Eastern District of London. In 1830 he repaired ST. MARY ALDERMANBURY CHURCH in the City [P. C. Carter, *History of St. Mary Aldermanbury*, 1913, 24]. In the same year he made unexecuted designs for enlarging ST. ANNE'S CHURCH, KEW, that are preserved among the Surrey Archdeaconry Records. He died on 23 September 1832, aged 37, and is commemorated by a tablet in Kew Church. His library was sold by Southgate & Co. on 6–11 August 1833 (*Catalogue of a miscellaneous collection of books including the library of an architect deceased*). Some of the drawings that he made in Italy are now in the R.I.B.A. Collection.

U

UNDERWOOD, CHARLES (*c.*1791–1883), was originally a builder at Cheltenham, but was bankrupted in 1821 [I.C.B.S., Rugeley file]. Having moved to Bristol he became a leading neo-classical architect there and in 1851 was elected the first chairman of the Bristol Society of Architects. He designed a number of villas and terraces in Clifton, including Nos. 1–4 KENSINGTON TERRACE, 1842, WORCESTER TERRACE, 1851, STONELEIGH HOUSE, 1853, and houses in CLIFTON PARK, including Nos. 10–11, *c.*1853 [A. Gomme, M. Jenner & B. Little, *Bristol: An Architectural History*, 1979, 442]. He also designed the Greek Revival buildings of the ARNO'S VALE CEMETERY, 1836 [*A.P.S.D.*, *s.v.* 'Bristol'] and the ROYAL WEST OF ENGLAND ACADEMY, QUEEN'S ROAD, CLIFTON, with a façade by J. H. Hirst, 1857 [*Builder* xv, 1857, 531]. BURLEY CHURCH, HANTS., was built to his designs in the lancet style in 1838–9 [I.C.B.S.]. He died in Clifton on 5 March 1883, aged 92 [Principal Probate Registry, Calendar of Probates].

UNDERWOOD, GEORGE ALLEN (*c.*1793–1829), was the brother of Charles and Henry Underwood. After a period (1807–15) in the office of Sir John Soane, he started practice on his own in Cheltenham. His first patron was Sir John Coxe Hippisley, a Somerset landowner from whose seat at Ston Easton he wrote to Soane in 1816, and who recommended him in 1819 to the Catholic community at Downside. Exactly what Underwood did for Hippisley is uncertain, but he appears to have been concerned in the villa which the latter was about to build at Cowes to the designs of John Nash. He became Surveyor to the Counties of Somerset and Dorset and to the Dean and Chapter of Wells. In the 1820s he moved to Bath, where he died unmarried on 1 November 1829, aged 36. He designed several minor public buildings in Cheltenham, Bath and the south-western counties in a style that sometimes shows the characteristic influence of Soane. Among the architectural drawings at Kingston Lacy, Dorset, there is an unexecuted design by Underwood dated 1822 for remodelling the Dining Room at that house. [A. T. Bolton, *The Works of Sir John Soane*, 1929, Appendix C, xliv, *The Portrait of Sir John Soane*, 1927, 130–1, 216; *Gent's Mag.* 1829 (ii), 476; P. C. C. Admon. Register, 1830.]

CHELTENHAM, GLOS., THE MONTPELLIER SPA (now Lloyd's Bank) for Henry Thompson, 1817; Rotunda or Pump Room added by J. B. Papworth 1825–6 [*The New Guide to Cheltenham*, 1824, engraving inscribed 'G. A. Underwood Archt.'].

CHELTENHAM, THE SHERBORNE SPA, 1818; dem. 1938 [*The New Guide to Cheltenham*, 1824, engraving signed 'G. A. Underwood Archt.'].

CHELTENHAM, GLOS., THE MASONIC HALL, PORTLAND STREET, 1818–23 [Hugh Casson, 'Masonic Temple, Cheltenham', *Arch. Rev.* June 1941].

FROME, SOMERSET, CHRIST CHURCH, 1818, Gothic; altered by Manners & Gill at various dates [I.C.B.S.].

CHELTENHAM, GLOS., HOLY TRINITY CHURCH, 1820–2, Gothic; interior altered 1875–8 [correspondence in Sir John Soane's Museum, Cupboard 2, Div. XV, A 14].

BEAMINSTER MANOR HOUSE, DORSET, enlarged 1822 [R.C.H.M., *Dorset* i, *West*, 23].

MARNHULL, DORSET, KINGS MILL BRIDGE, 1823 [R.C.H.M., *Dorset* iii (2), 156].

BATH, rebuilt the burnt-out LOWER ASSEMBLY ROOMS as the ROYAL LITERARY INSTITUTION, 1823–5, retaining the portico added by Wilkins in 1808–9; dem. 1933 [lithographic plan signed by Underwood in Sir John Soane's Museum, private correspondence XVA, 14].

ASHWICK CHURCH, SOMERSET, rebuilt (except tower) 1825; remodelled 1876 [I.C.B.S.].

TIMSBURY CHURCH, SOMERSET, rebuilt 1826; chancel and transepts added 1852 [I.C.B.S.].

CHELTENHAM, GLOS., THE PLOUGH HOTEL, HIGH STREET, before 1826 [Griffith's *New Historical Description of Cheltenham* i, 1826, engraving 'drawn by G. A. Underwood Esq. Architect'].

UNDERWOOD, HENRY (*c.*1787–1868), was the brother of Charles and George Allen Underwood. He worked for a time in Cheltenham, where he took over the contracts relinquished by his bankrupt brother Charles, but moved to Bath in about 1830 and remained there until his death on 8 March 1868 [Principal Probate Registry, Calendar of Probates]. In 1829 he was responsible for alterations to PENPONT, BRECONSHIRE, for Penry Williams that included the addition of a colonnade and a conservatory and internal alterations to the dining-room [R. Haslam in *C. Life*, 18 June 1992]. In Bath his most important work was the Greek Revival

SWEDENBORGIAN CHURCH in HENRY STREET, 1843–4 [*A.P.S.D.*, *s.v.* 'Bath'].

UNDERWOOD, HENRY JONES (1804–1852), was a native of Bristol. He became a pupil of H. H. Seward in London, attended the Royal Academy Schools, and exhibited at the Academy in 1822 and 1823. He subsequently joined the office of Sir Robert Smirke. In 1830 Smirke sent Underwood to Oxford to supervise the alterations to the interior of the Bodleian Library, and he decided to settle there. Since the death of Thomas Plowman and the departure of Daniel Robertson there had been no London-trained architect in practice in Oxford, and Underwood soon received numerous commissions, especially for ecclesiastical work. Although St. Paul's Church and the Library at the Botanic Garden showed that he could design in an orthodox Greek Revival style, it was as a Gothic Revivalist that he made a modest reputation. His authentically 'Early English' design for Newman's church at Littlemore was much admired, and the plans were published by the Oxford Architectural Society in 1845 as a model to be imitated elsewhere.[1] Underwood's career was cut short on 22 March 1852, when a nervous breakdown or an attack of insanity culminated in his suicide at the White Hart Hotel in Bath. E. G. Bruton, who was then his assistant, took over his practice. W. J. Hopkins was also a pupil.

[*A.P.S.D.*; *Jackson's Oxford Jnl.*, 27 March 1852].

OXFORD, ST. JOHN'S CHURCH, SUMMERTOWN, 1831–3, Gothic; chancel added 1854; dem. 1924 [*A.P.S.D.*] (*Oxoniensia* xi–xii, 1946–7, pl. xvi).

OXFORD, EXETER COLLEGE, section of Broad Street front next to Old Ashmolean, 1833–4; remodelled Turl Street front 1834–5, Gothic [*V.C.H. Oxon.* iii, 117].

OXFORD, WOLSEY'S ALMSHOUSES, ST. ALDATE'S (now part of Pembroke College), restoration, 1834 [*V.C.H. Oxon.* iii, 292; Bodleian Library, MS. Top. Oxon. c. 77, f. 79].

OXFORD, BOTANIC GARDEN, LIBRARY AND LECTURE ROOM (now Magdalen College Bursary), 1835 [*A.P.S.D.*].

LITTLEMORE CHURCH, OXON., for J. H. Newman, 1835–6, Gothic; chancel and tower added by Joseph Clarke 1848 [H. J. Underwood, *Elevations, Sections and Details of Littlemore Church*, 1845; *V.C.H. Oxon.* v, 213; E. A. Greening Lamborn, 'Newman's Church at Littlemore', *Notes & Queries* cxc, 1946, 46–9; Peter Howell, 'Newman's Church at Littlemore', *Oxford Art Jnl.* 6 (i), 1983].

OXFORD, ST. PAUL'S CHURCH, WALTON STREET, 1836; apse added by E. G. Bruton 1853–4 [J. Ingram, *Memorials of Oxford* iii, 1837, 'Parish of St. Thomas', 4].

BUSHEY HEATH CHURCH, HERTS., 1836–7, Gothic; chancel added *c.* 1891, nave rebuilt 1911 [I.C.B.S.; *Gent's Mag.* 1837 (ii), 187].

BOOTLE CHURCH, CUMBERLAND, enlarged 1837 [I.C.B.S.].

LOWER SWELL VICARAGE, GLOS., 1837, Tudor Gothic [Gloucester Diocesan Records, F4/1].

OXFORD, ST. JOHN'S COLLEGE, refitted LAUDIAN LIBRARY in Gothic style, 1838–9 [H. Colvin, *The Canterbury Quadrangle, St. John's College, Oxford*, 1988, 76].

LITTLEWORTH CHURCH, BERKS., 1838–9, Gothic; chancel added 1876 [*Gent's Mag.* 1839 (ii), 303].

OXFORD, ST. GILES' CHURCH, repairs and internal alterations, 1838–9 [Bodleian Library, MS. Top. Oxon. b. 111].

LATHBURY VICARAGE, BUCKS., alterations and additions, 1839 [Lincolnshire Archives Office, MGA 236].

BRAUNSTON RECTORY, NORTHANTS., 1839 [plans and specifications formerly in the Rectory, *ex inf.* the late Sir Gyles Isham, Bart.].

LOWER BEEDING CHURCH, SUSSEX, 1840, Gothic; enlarged 1864 [I.C.B.S.].

SIBFORD GOWER CHURCH, OXON., 1840, Gothic [Oxfordshire C.R.O., MS. Oxf. dioc. papers c. 2172].

GARSINGTON SCHOOL, OXON., 1840, Tudor Gothic [drawings in archives of Trinity College, Oxford].

KINGSTHORPE, NORTHANTS., THE NATIONAL SCHOOL, 1840, Tudor Gothic [Northants. C.R.O., School Plans 33].

LLANGORWEN CHURCH, CARDIGANSHIRE, 1841–2, Gothic; bell-turret and porch added by Butterfield 1848 [building accounts in N.L.W.].

BROUGHTON RECTORY, OXON., new kitchens, offices and upper coach-house, 1842 [MS. notes in parish chest by C. F. Wyatt, rector].

WHAPLODE VICARAGE, LINCS., altered or rebuilt, 1842 [Lincolnshire Archives Office, MGA 274].

OXFORD, HOLY TRINITY CHURCH, 1844–5, Gothic; dem. 1957 [*V.C.H. Oxon.* iv, 407].

HOOK NORTON CHURCH, OXON., repaired roof, 1845, and probably refitted interior, 1848–

[1] Withyham Church, Sussex, built in 1839 by a surveyor named W. L. Blaker, junior, was stated by the incumbent to be 'an exact copy of Littlemore' (I.C.B.S. file).

9 [Margaret Dickins, *History of Hook Norton*, Banbury 1928, 151–2].

WOODCOTE CHURCH, OXON., rebuilt 1845–6, Norman style [*V.C.H. Oxon.* vii, 109].

SWERFORD CHURCH, OXON., added north aisle, etc., 1846 [I.C.B.S.].

OXFORD, OSENEY, HOLYWELL and ST. SEPULCHRE CEMETERY CHAPELS, 1848, Norman and Gothic; all dem. [H. J. Underwood, *Oxford Parish Burial Ground Chapels*, 1849].

LOWER HEYFORD CHURCH, OXON., reroofed nave and north aisle, 1848 [*V.C.H. Oxon.* vi, 194].

BANBURY, CHRIST CHURCH (UNITARIAN), 1849–50, Gothic [*Gardner's Gazetteer of Oxfordshire*, 1852, 418].

OXFORD, COUNTY GAOL, enlarged 1850–2 [*A.P.S.D., s.v.* 'Oxford'].

DIDCOT RECTORY, BERKS., 1852 (completed by E. G. Bruton) [*A.P.S.D.*].

HORSPATH CHURCH, OXON., rebuilt north wall of nave, added north transept, etc., 1852 (completed by E. G. Bruton) [*V.C.H. Oxon.* v, 187].

UNWIN, ROBERT, *see* ROYLE, THOMAS.

UNWIN, WILLIAM (–1843), practised in Sheffield as an architect and surveyor from before 1820 onwards. From *c.*1817 to *c.*1822 he was in partnership with Thomas Hirst (*q.v.*), and he was no doubt the father of Charles Unwin, who took his place in the 1840s and was still in practice in Sheffield in 1868.

UPSDELL, PETER, practised in Soho, London, from 1786 to 1797 [*Survey of London* xxxiv, 393] and later in Westminster. In 1792 he exhibited a 'Sketch of a section of an intended church' at the Royal Academy. He became a member of the Surveyors' Club in 1792 and was still in practice in 1817.

UPWARD, J— WILLIAM, *see* CHAPMAN, ROBERT.

V

VALDRÈ (VALDRATI), VINCENZO (*c.*1742–1814), was an Italian painter-architect who came to England in the 1770s and subsequently established himself in Ireland. He was born in Faenza and studied painting at Parma and Rome. By 1774 he was in London, where he designed scenery for the Italian operas at the King's Theatre in the Haymarket. Soon afterwards he was employed by the 1st Marquess of Buckingham at STOWE HOUSE, BUCKS., where his works included the Pompeian decoration of the Music Room and at least the sculptured frieze of the oval Saloon. In the park the small lodges flanking the Oxford Gate and the base of Lord Cobham's pillar were designed by him, and the Menagerie may also have been his work. While at Stowe he attended a wedding in the neighbourhood and, when the bridegroom failed to appear, chivalrously offered himself as a substitute – and was accepted. In 1787 he accompanied his patron to Ireland when the latter was appointed Lord Lieutenant and eventually settled in Dublin, where he decorated the ceiling of St. Patrick's Hall in the Castle (*C. Life*, 6 Aug. 1970, fig. 7). In 1792 he succeeded Thomas Penrose as architect to the Irish Board of Works, and in that capacity was responsible for reconstructing the House of Commons in the Parliament House after its destruction by fire in February of that year. His circular chamber, completed in 1796, was destroyed in 1804–6 when the building was remodelled for use by the Bank of Ireland. Valdre, who in Ireland was usually known as Waldre, died in Dublin in August 1814, aged 72.

[Edward Croft-Murray, 'Un Decoratore Faentino in Inghilterra: Vincenzo Valdrati o Valdrè', *Studi Romagnoli* viii, 1957; Michael Gibbon, 'A Forgotten Italian at Stowe', *C. Life*, 4 Aug. 1966; E. Croft-Murray, *Decorative Painting in England* ii, 1970, 288–9; Michael McCarthy, 'The Rebuilding of Stowe House, 1770–1777', *Huntington Library Quarterly* xxxvi, 1973, 275–6; Desmond Fitz-Gerald, 'A History of the Interior of Stowe', *Apollo*, June 1973, 577–8; T. J. Mulvany, *Life of James Gandon*, 1846, 143–8; F. G. Hall, *The Bank of Ireland*, 1949, 450.]

VALENTINE, JOHN, was an Italian architect who specialized in the building of public baths. The *London Gazette* No. 2906 for 14–18 Sept. 1693 contains the following advertisement: 'John Valentine, our Italian, living in the Venetian Coffee-House in the Pall Mall, who built the Royal Bagnio in Newgate Street, and that in Long Acre, is ready to Build any Bagnio, or Hummums, after the best manner, for Persons of Quality, and others, who are desirous to build the same.' The two baths referred to were the one (sometimes known as 'Charles II's Bath') in BATH STREET, NEWGATE STREET, which was built by some Turkey merchants in about 1679, and the KING'S BAGNIO in LONG ACRE, built by Sir William Jennens in 1682. Both were architecturally buildings of some sophistication. The Newgate Street bath was octagonal in plan with a circular brick dome ornamented with plaster coffering and lit by a central oculus. The King's Bagnio was oval in plan. A crude broad-sheet issued by Jennens in 1686 shows a cupola 40 feet high supported by a continuous arcade concentric with the walls and enclosing an oval or circular central bath. The Newgate Street bath was demolished in 1876, but an illustrated account of it by A. W. Hakewill was published in *The Architect and Building Gazette* ii, 1850, 483–4. See also *A.P.S.D., s.v.* 'Bath-House', and Wheatley & Cunningham, *London Past and Present* i, 1891, 89–90.

VANBRUGH, Sir JOHN (1664–1726), was born in January 1664. His father, Giles Vanbrugh, was the son of Giles van Brugg, a merchant from Haarlem whose parents had left Flanders as Protestant refugees. His mother was Elizabeth, the youngest daughter of Sir Dudley Carleton of Imber Court in Surrey. John Vanbrugh, the fourth of their nineteen children, was born in London, but before he was three years old the family moved to Chester, perhaps as a result of the Great Plague of 1665. Here Vanbrugh may have been educated, but nothing is known of his early life until 1681, when he was working for his cousin William Matthews in the wine trade in London. In January 1686 he received a commission in the regiment of foot commanded by the Earl of Huntingdon, to whom he was distantly related, but resigned six months later for reasons that are not clear. Instead, he went abroad with Robert, Lord Willoughby (another distant relation), and succeeded in getting himself arrested in France in September 1688, 'accus'd of speaking something in favour of [William of Orange]'. For over four years he was imprisoned, first at Calais, then at Vincennes, and finally in the Bastille in Paris. This unfortunate episode may not have been wholly disastrous for Vanbrugh, for to it he probably owed his taste for French plays, and a period of freedom in Paris before his final release would have given him the opportunity to familiarize himself with French architecture. After his return he served as a volunteer in the marines and took part in an attempted raid on the French coast near Brest. He subsequently resumed his connection with the Earl of Huntingdon's regiment, resigning a new commission in 1702 on his appointment as Comptroller of the Works. In 1702 he also relinquished a sinecure auditorship in the Duchy of Lancaster whose profits he had enjoyed since 1689.

In the meantime 'Captain Vanbrugh' had abandoned the profession of soldiering for that of playwriting. The production of Cibber's *Love's Last Shift* at the Theatre Royal in January 1695/6 inspired Vanbrugh with the idea of writing a sequel: the result was *The Relapse, or Virtue in Danger*, a comedy 'Got, Conceiv'd, and Born (according to the Prologue) in six weeks' space'. Its performance on Boxing Day 1696 was an unqualified success, which Vanbrugh followed up by *Aesop*, a free translation of a French play by Boursault. This, containing as it did:

> No Hero, no Romance, no Plot, no Show,
> No Rape, no Bawdy, no Intrigue, no Beau,

did little to enhance Vanbrugh's reputation as a dramatist. But almost all these ingredients of a popular play were present in *The Provok'd Wife*, which was performed at Lincoln's Inn Fields in May 1697, with Betterton as Sir John Brute. Its indecencies did not escape the notice of Jeremy Collier, and both *The Relapse* and *The Provok'd Wife* figured prominently in his *Short View of the Immorality and Profaneness of the English Stage*, published in March 1698. Vanbrugh replied in June with *A Short Vindication of The Relapse and The Provok'd Wife from Immorality and Profaneness*. But puritanism prevailed, and Vanbrugh's witty but improper comedies were to be among the last of their type. None of his subsequent plays achieved quite the success of the first two, perhaps because he never again offered the public a comedy entirely of his own invention. For *The Pilgrim*, which was performed at Drury Lane early in 1700 to celebrate the advent of 'a new century', was a prose adaptation of Beaumont and Fletcher's play of the same name, while *The Country House* (1698), *The False Friend* (1702), *The Confederacy* (1705), and *The Mistake* (1705), were all based on French comedies. Nevertheless, Vanbrugh's plays maintained their popularity throughout the eighteenth century, and his unfinished *Journey to London*, completed by Cibber and produced by him as *The Provok'd Husband* in 1728, long remained a favourite with the play-going public.

In 1704 Vanbrugh involved himself more closely in the dramatic world by building his own theatre. The Queen's Theatre or Italian Opera House in the Haymarket enjoyed only a moderate degree of success. The enterprise was supported by thirty shareholders at £100 each, but Vanbrugh was the legal proprietor, and although he disposed of the management to Owen Swiney in 1708 it is doubtful whether he ever recovered all the capital that he had invested in this theatrical speculation.

Meanwhile playwriting had been superseded by architecture as Vanbrugh's ruling interest. How and when the ambition to be an architect first entered his mind will probably never be known: but the transformation was sufficiently abrupt for even a contemporary (Swift) to remark how

> Van's genius, without thought or lecture,
> is hugely turn'd to architecture.

All that is certainly known is that in 1699 he made designs for Castle Howard, the Earl of Carlisle's great house in Yorkshire, which began to be carried into effect in the following year with the assistance of Nicholas Hawksmoor. Whatever indications of immaturity may be detected in Castle Howard, and however considerable may have been Hawksmoor's contribution as assistant architect and draughtsman, the conception of this great design remains a remarkable achievement for one whose architectural experience was as slight as Vanbrugh's appears to have been. Moreover, in thus becoming Lord Carlisle's architect Vanbrugh had superseded no less a person than William Talman, the Comptroller of His Majesty's Works, who had made designs for Castle Howard for which he charged more than Lord Carlisle thought reasonable. Talman's discredit was Vanbrugh's opportunity, for Lord Carlisle was First Lord of the Treasury and in a position to make and unmake the officers of the King's Works. Thus it came about that, in June 1702, Vanbrugh displaced Talman as Comptroller and so became Wren's principal colleague on the Board of Works. Having secured Talman's post, Vanbrugh succeeded in the course of the next few years in supplanting him as the architect chiefly employed by the Whig aristocracy: and a letter from the new Comptroller to the Duke of Newcastle shows that he lost no opportunity of calling attention to the 'vexations and disappointments' which were the lot of those who were so ill-advised as to employ his rival.

For ten years Vanbrugh enjoyed the authority and perquisites of a Comptroller of Her Majesty's Works: but in 1713 an indiscreet letter to the Mayor of Woodstock provided the pretext for his dismissal at the hands of a Tory government, and on 16 April his patent was revoked. But no successor was appointed, and when Queen Anne died and the Whigs returned to power in the following year, Vanbrugh was first knighted (19 Sept. 1714), and then restored to the comptrollership (24 Jan. 1714/15). In the following June, he became the first holder of the newly created surveyorship of Gardens and Waters, which brought him an additional salary of £400 a year, and for the next few years he was the dominant figure in the Office of Works. According to his own account, the Surveyor's post itself was within his grasp, but – as he afterwards told Jacob Tonson – he refused it, 'out of Tenderness to Sir Chr. Wren'. It was an act of self-denial which he had reason to regret when, in 1718, Wren was superseded by William Benson, and Vanbrugh saw Hawksmoor dismissed from his post as Secretary to the Board to make way for the new Surveyor's brother. He himself contrived to retain his post as Comptroller until his death. But during his last years the Office of Works became increasingly influenced by the Palladian protégés of Lord Burlington, and by the time of his death his own highly individual baroque style was already outmoded. In 1703 Vanbrugh was appointed a member of the Board of Directors of Greenwich Hospital, and the minutes of its meetings show that he played an increasingly important part in the affairs of the hospital until in 1716 he took Wren's place as the surveyor in charge. By then the general plan of the Hospital had already been determined, and his own contribution to its design appears to have been small, though he may have encouraged Hawksmoor in some of the grandiose schemes for its further embellishment for which the latter was responsible.

Already a soldier, a playwright and an architect, Vanbrugh became in 1704 a herald, being created Clarenceux King of Arms in March of that year. He owed this profitable appointment to his friend the Earl of Carlisle, who was acting as Earl Marshal during the incapacity of the Duke of Norfolk. The choice of one who was 'totally ignorant of the profession of heraldry and genealogy', who had, moreover, ridiculed it in public in his plays, caused great indignation in the College of Heralds, above all to Gregory King, the senior pursuivant, who had hoped for the office himself. He 'persuaded some other heralds to join with him in a petition against the Lord Marshall's power', but their objections were overruled by the Council, and Vanbrugh was installed on 29 March 1704, having previously been appointed Carlisle Herald Extraordinary in order to satisfy a rule of the College that a King of Arms should have passed through the grade of herald. In later years there was further rivalry and recrimination over the office of Garter King of Arms, for which both Vanbrugh and John Anstis were angling. Anstis finally secured the reversion when Vanbrugh fell into disfavour with the Queen in 1714. But when the office was vacant in the following year, Anstis found himself in prison as a Jacobite, and it was granted to Vanbrugh for the time being. In 1717, however, Anstis renewed his claim, and in April 1718 a decision was reached in his favour.

It was in the winter of 1704–5 that Vanbrugh obtained what was to be his greatest architectural commission – the designing of Blenheim Palace, near Woodstock. This vast mansion was intended as a mark of royal gratitude to the Duke of Marlborough for his victories over Louis XIV. For Vanbrugh it was a unique opportunity to build on a heroic scale, uninhibited by considerations of economy. Unfortunately, there was no written agreement between the Duke and his Queen: even Vanbrugh's position as architect depended upon an ambiguous document in the name of Lord Treasurer Godolphin declaring that whereas the Duke had 'resolv'd to erect a large Fabrick . . . at Woodstock', he, Godolphin, had, 'at the request and desire of the said Duke', appointed 'John Vanbrugh, Esq., to be Surveyor of all the Works and Buildings so intended to be erected . . .', and had authorized him to make contracts and to engage labourers as required. A model was made for the Queen's approval, Wren estimated the cost at £100,000, and building started in 1705 with the aid of liberal grants from the Treasury. Their continuance depended entirely upon royal favour, and when that was diverted from the Duchess to Mrs. Masham, Treasury payments for the building of Blenheim began to dwindle and finally ceased. The masons and others whose wages were in arrears sued the Duke, who understandably 'resented and resisted the notion of having to pay for his own reward'. For four years all work at Blenheim was at a standstill, but with the accession of George I in 1714 the Duke and Duchess were restored to favour, and in the summer of 1716 work on the unfinished palace was resumed. By this time, however, the masterful Duchess and her ever-sanguine architect were already confirmed in opposition to one another: 'I made Mr. Vanbrugh my enemy by the constant disputes I had with him to prevent his extravagance', wrote the Duchess, and now that money was short, and the Duke approaching his end, their disagreements became continually more bitter. The final breach came in November 1716, when the Duchess formally accused him of mismanagement in such terms that, as he wrote, he

> shou'd put a very great affront upon your understanding if I suppos'd it possible you cou'd mean any thing in earnest by them; but to put a Stop to my troubling you any more. You have your end Madam, for I will never trouble you more Unless the Duke of Marlborough recovers so far, to shelter me from such intolerable Treatment.
>
> I shall in the mean time have only this Concern on his account (for whom I shall ever retain the greatest Veneration) That your Grace having like the Queen thought fit to get rid of a faithfull servant, the Torys will have the pleasure to see your Glassmaker, Moor, make just such an end of the Dukes Building as her Minister Harley did of his Victories for which it was erected.

It was, in fact, under the direction of the cabinet-maker James Moore that work proceeded during the next five years, and it was not until after the Duke's death in 1722 that Hawksmoor was recalled to design the Woodstock Gateway and other outworks. Vanbrugh himself remained 'in permanent and irretrievable disgrace', and in 1725, when, with the Earl of Carlisle and his party, he and Lady Vanbrugh came to see the finished palace, they were refused admittance even to the park.

Though Vanbrugh could communicate architectural ideas by means of eloquent free-hand sketches, there is no evidence that he ever troubled to learn the tedious discipline of formal architectural draughtsmanship. For that he had recourse sometimes to an unidentified draughtsman whom he called 'Arthur', and more often to Nicholas Hawksmoor, upon whose professional expertise he relied for the realization of all his major buildings from Castle Howard onwards. But Hawksmoor, a distinguished designer in his own right, was never merely Vanbrugh's architectural amanuensis, and his collaboration helped to create the architectural style that Vanbrugh made his own. It was a style that had no exact parallel in the history of European architecture, though it drew on French, English and Italian sources. Its character was baroque in the sense that it aimed at effects of 'movement', but it achieved them by the grouping of masses and the skilful handling of recession and projection rather than by the mere manipulation of the conventional apparatus of classical architecture. In achieving these effects Vanbrugh drew inspiration from the medieval and Elizabethan past as well as from the English baroque of Talman and Wren. But his evocation of medieval towers or Elizabethan turrets was no more deferential to the past than his use of the classical orders. The desire to give his buildings 'something of the Castle Air' was achieved without the actual use of Gothic forms, but is none the less apparent in the composition of such houses as Eastbury and Seaton Delaval. The result was the 'heroic architecture' with which, at Blenheim, Vanbrugh so well expressed a nation's gratitude to its victorious general, and which, on a smaller scale, found so appropriate an outlet in the buildings which Hawksmoor designed for the Board of Ordnance. His 'massive and masculine style' was most successful when deployed on the largest scale, and it was Vanbrugh's good fortune to live in an age when great men had both the desire and the means to house themselves with appropriate magnificence. Despite their formal settings and strictly symmetrical ground-plans,[1] Vanbrugh's mansions show a strong sense of the picturesque. The 'painter-like' quality of his architectural composition was indeed recognized by Sir Joshua Reynolds, and Vanbrugh's attempt to preserve the remains of Woodstock Manor is evidence that he was fully conscious of the value of ruins in a landscape. Though never himself a professed landscape-gardener, Vanbrugh was involved in the planning of two famous gardens at Stowe and Castle Howard, and must be regarded as one of the pioneers of the Picturesque landscape.

In 1711 Vanbrugh was put on the Commission for building Fifty New Churches in the suburbs of London. The designs which he submitted to his fellow-Commissioners for St. Mary-le-Strand (1714) and St. George, Bloomsbury (1715) were not carried out, but the memorandum on church-building which he drew up in 1712 was not without its influence. Like Wren, he emphasized the importance of open or detached sites, condemned intramural burial, and deprecated the internal clutter of too many pews. But unlike Wren he urged that the new churches should be envisaged as 'monuments to posterity . . . ornaments to the Town, and a credit to the Nation'. His plea for architectural grandeur, though coming from a Whig, coincided with the inclination of the predominantly Tory commissioners, and most of the new churches were in fact designed in a manner which fully satisfied the spirit of Vanbrugh's 'Proposals'.

In private life Vanbrugh was a witty and convivial companion, the friend of Tonson and Congreve, and one of the forty-eight members of the Kit-Cat Club which met at the former's house at Barn Elms. He lived on terms of easy familiarity with the great men who were his clients, and he was a close friend of the Earl of Carlisle to whose patronage he owed so much.

The author of *The Provok'd Wife* did not escape insinuations of personal immorality: but there is nothing to suggest that he was a rake, and his married life appears to have been entirely happy, though short. For it was not until January 1719, that, at the age of 54, Vanbrugh married Henrietta Maria, the daughter of Colonel Yarburgh of Heslington Hall in Yorkshire. By her he had two sons, of whom the younger died in infancy. Charles, the survivor (b. 1720), obtained an ensigncy in the Coldstream Guards and was killed at the Battle of Fontenoy in 1745. Vanbrugh himself died at his house in Whitehall on 26 March 1726, and was buried in the Vanbrugh vault in the north aisle of the church of St. Stephen, Walbrook. He had previously disposed of his place as Clarenceux King of Arms to Knox Ward for £2500. His will (P.C.C. 84 PLYMOUTH) was proved on 22 April. Lady Vanbrugh lived to the age of 82, dying at Greenwich on 26 April 1776.

The best-known portrait of Vanbrugh is the Kit-Cat by Kneller, painted when he was about 40, and now in the National Portrait Gallery. There is another in the same Gallery, formerly attributed to Closterman and now to Murray. A third, painted by J. Richardson in 1725, is at the College of Heralds.

The first collected edition of Vanbrugh's plays was published in 1719: the best is the Nonesuch edition of 1927–8, in four volumes, of which the fourth contains Vanbrugh's letters, edited by G. F. Webb. These and further letters published by Whistler (1954), Rosenberg (1966) and Downes are listed by Downes (1987, Appendix B). To these may be added an unpublished letter of 26 July 1698 to Lord Wharton (Bodleian, Carte MS. 79, f. 483). A 'Journal of Receipts and Payments' kept by Vanbrugh from Jan. 1715 until his death, and continued by Lady Vanbrugh, is in the Borthwick Institute of Historical Research at York and was published by Downes (1977). The principal collection of Vanbrugh's drawings is in the Victoria and Albert Museum. It includes those, formerly at Elton Hall, edited by H. Colvin & M. Craig for the Roxburghe Club in 1964 as *Architectural Drawings in the Library of Elton Hall by Sir John Vanbrugh and Sir Edward Lovett Pearce*. Other drawings, from various sources, are reproduced in the Wren Society's volumes and by Whistler (1954).

[*A.P.S.D.*; *D.N.B.*; *Wren Soc.*, *passim*; H. A. Tipping, *English Homes, Period IV* (ii), *The Works of Sir John Vanbrugh and his School, 1699–1736,* 1928; Laurence Whistler, *Sir John Vanbrugh*, 1938, *The Imagination of*

[1] Vanbrugh Castle became asymmetrical by accretion, but it was originally symmetrical, and only the eastern extension appears to have been of Vanbrugh's own building (see the plan published by G. F. Webb in *Burlington Mag.* xlvii, 1925, 226). In the album of Vanbrugh's drawings from Elton Hall there is, however, one sketch for a small house in which he has allowed himself to envisage a deliberately asymmetrical building.

Vanbrugh and his Fellow Artists, 1954; *History of the King's Works*, v, 1976, *passim*; Kerry Downes, *Vanbrugh*, 1977, *Sir John Vanbrugh*, 1987; Geoffrey Beard, *The Work of Sir John Vanbrugh*, 1986; F. McCormick, *Sir John Vanbrugh. The Playwright as Architect*, Pennsylvania 1991.]

AUTHENTICATED WORKS

CASTLE HOWARD, YORKS. (N. R.), for 3rd Earl of Carlisle, 1700–26. The original design engraved in *Vitruvius Britannicus* i, 1715, pls. 63–71, and iii, 1725, pls. 5–6, was never completed, and the west wing is the work of Sir Thomas Robinson, 1753–9. The centre and east wing were seriously damaged by fire in 1940. Vanbrugh also designed the Obelisk, 1714, the Pyramid Gate, 1719, and the Belvedere Temple, 1725–8 [H. A. Tipping, *English Homes*, IV (ii), 1928, 1–62; Whistler, *Imagination*, 1954, 26–82; Downes, 1977, 26–39; C. Saumarez Smith, *The Building of Castle Howard*, 1990].

LONDON, 'GOOSE-PIE HOUSE', WHITEHALL, for himself, 1700–1; wings added 1719; dem. 1898 [*Wren Soc.* iv, 74–5; *Survey of London* xvi, 168–71; Whistler, *Imagination*, 1954, 197–9; Downes, 1977, 12–14].

KENSINGTON PALACE, revised the design for the ORANGERY, probably basically the work of Hawksmoor [*History of the King's Works* v, 193–4].

LONDON, THE QUEEN'S THEATRE, HAYMARKET, 1704–5; refitted 1778; destroyed by fire 1789 [Downes, 1977, 40–44, pl. 25].

BLENHEIM PALACE, OXON., for 1st Duke of Marlborough, 1705–16, completed by Hawksmoor 1722–5 [David Green, *Blenheim Palace*, 1951; Whistler, *Imagination*, 1954, 83–123; Downes, 1977, 55–75; F. Harris, 'Parliament and Blenheim Palace', *Parliamentary History* 8, 1989]; also THE GRAND BRIDGE, 1706–24 [H. Colvin & A. Rowan, 'The Grand Bridge in Blenheim Park', in *English Architecture, Public & Private*, ed. Bold & Chaney, 1993].

KIMBOLTON CASTLE, HUNTS., remodelled for 1st Duke of Manchester, 1707–10. The Doric portico on the E. front is by Alessandro Galilei, 1718–19 [Tipping, *English Homes* IV (ii), 113–18; Whistler, *Imagination*, 1954, 131–43; Arthur Oswald in *C. Life*, 5, 12, 19, 26 Dec. 1968; Downes, 1977, 48–50].

AUDLEY END, ESSEX, alterations for the Earl of Bindon, afterwards 6th Earl of Suffolk, 1708, involving the demolition of the N. and S. sides of the decayed outer court. The attribution to Vanbrugh of the staircase and screen in the Hall is doubtful [P. Drury, 'The Evolution of Audley End', *Arch. Hist.* 23, 1980].

ESHER, SURREY, house (known as CHARGATE) for himself, 1709–10; subsequently incorporated in Claremont (see below).

ROBIN HOOD'S WELL, SKELBROOKE, nr. DONCASTER, YORKS. (W.R.), for 3rd Earl of Carlisle, *c.*1710 [Hist. MSS. Comm., *Portland* vi, 90; *Stukeley's Memoirs*, Surtees Soc. iii, 1887, 373] (Downes, 1977, pl. 147).

KINGS WESTON, nr. BRISTOL, GLOS., for Edward Southwell, *c.*1710–19; interior altered by R. Mylne, who also designed the stables, 1763–8; staircase hall altered *c.*1835 [*Vitruvius Britannicus* i, 1715, pls. 47–8; Tipping, *English Homes* IV (ii), 141–56; 'The Kings Weston Book of Drawings', ed. Downes, *Arch. Hist.* x, 1967; Michael Jenner in A. Gomme, M. Jenner & B. Little, *Bristol, An Architectural History*, 1979, 107–114].

MORPETH, NORTHUMBERLAND, THE TOWN HALL, for 3rd Earl of Carlisle, 1714; reconstructed to the original design after a fire *c.*1875 [stated by Sir John Clerk of Penicuik to be 'of the architecture of Sir John Vanbrook' in 1724: S.R.O., GD 18/2106; S. Lewis, *Topographical Dictionary of England* iii, 1848, 347] (measured drawings by B. Ferrey in R.I.B.A. Coll.).

LONDON, NEWCASTLE HOUSE, Nos. 66–67 LINCOLN'S INN FIELDS, internal alterations for 1st Duke of Newcastle, 1714–17; rebuilt 1930–1 [*Letters*, 61, 88; joiner's account in B.L., Add. MS. 33442] (*Survey of London* iii, 110–13).

CLAREMONT, ESHER, SURREY, for 1st Duke of Newcastle, 1715–20, incorporating the house previously built by Vanbrugh for himself, which he sold to the duke in 1714; dem. *c.*1763 except the Belvedere tower and the White Cottage [Tipping, *English Homes*, IV (ii), 167–74; Whistler, *Imagination*, 144–55; joiner's account in B.L., Add. MS. 33442; inscription on obelisk in *Notes and Queries* clxxvii, 1939, 279].

WALPOLE HOUSE, CHELSEA HOSPITAL, alterations for Sir Robert Walpole, cr. 1st Earl of Orford, 1715–16; converted into infirmary 1809; dem. 1941 [C. G. T. Dean, *The Royal Hospital Chelsea*, 1950, 202–3; Walpole (Cholmondeley) papers, letter 759].

HAMPTON COURT PALACE, completion of interiors of Prince's (now Queen's) Guard Chamber, Presence Chamber, etc., at north end of east front, for George, Prince of Wales, 1716–18 [*History of the King's Works* v, 176–8].

GREENWICH, VANBRUGH CASTLE, MINCE-PIE

HOUSE, THE NUNNERY (later Sherwood), two WHITE TOWERS, etc., for himself and his brothers and sisters, 1718 onwards; all dem. except Vanbrugh Castle [H. G. Lovegrove in *London Topographical Record* iv, 1907; *Trans. Greenwich Antiquarian Soc.* i(3), 1910–11; Tipping, *English Homes*, IV (ii), 187–92; Whistler, *Imagination*, 200–6; *Architectural Drawings at Elton Hall*, pls. xvii, xxv, xxvi].

EASTBURY PARK, DORSET, begun 1718 for George Dodington (d. 1720), and continued for his nephew George Bubb Dodington, cr. Lord Melcombe; completed by Roger Morris *c.*1733–8; dem. 1775 except one wing and gateway [*Vitruvius Britannicus* ii, 1717, pls. 52–3, iii, 1725, pls. 15–17; Tipping, *English Homes*, IV (ii), 175–186; Whistler, *Imagination*, 156–77].

NOTTINGHAM CASTLE, internal alterations for 1st Duke of Newcastle, 1719; interior destroyed by fire 1831 and rebuilt as a museum 1878 [*Letters*, 105–6, 110, 112; joiner's account in B.L., Add. MS. 33442].

STOWE, BUCKS., additions to house, perhaps including north portico, and garden buildings for 1st Viscount Cobham, *c.*1719–24. The principal garden buildings designed by Vanbrugh were THE LAKE PAVILIONS (altered), THE ROTONDO (altered), THE TEMPLE OF BACCHUS (dem.), THE TEMPLE OF SLEEP (dem.), NELSON'S SEAT (dem.), THE COLD BATH (dem.) and THE PYRAMID (dem.) [L. Whistler, 'The Authorship of the Stowe Temples', *C. Life*, 29 Sept. 1950 and 12 Jan. 1951, 119; *Imagination*, 178–93; 'Stowe in the Making', *C. Life*, 11 July 1957].

SEATON DELAVAL, NORTHUMBERLAND, for Admiral George Delaval, 1720–8; interior of centre block destroyed by fire 1822 [*Vitruvius Britannicus* iii, 1725, 20–1; Tipping, *English Homes*, IV (ii), 271–90].

LUMLEY CASTLE, CO. DURHAM, remodelled entrance front and altered interior for 2nd Earl of Scarbrough, 1722 [*Letters*, 137, 138, 142; Tipping, *English Homes*, IV (ii), 291–4].

KENSINGTON PALACE, THE WATER TOWER on THE PALACE GREEN, 1722–4; dem. [*History of the King's Works* v, 195 n. 2 and pl. 19 A].

GRIMSTHORPE CASTLE, LINCS., rebuilt N. front for 1st Duke of Ancaster, 1722–6; forecourt completed 1729–30 [*Vitruvius Britannicus* iii, 1725, pls. 11–14, showing the unexecuted design for the S. front; Tipping, *English Homes* IV (ii), 295–322; H. Colvin, 'Grimsthorpe Castle, the North Front', in *The Country Seat*, ed. Colvin & Harris, 1970; T. P. Connor, note with dated plan in *Archl. Jnl.* 131, 1974, 330–3; J. Lord, 'Sir John Vanbrugh and the 1st Duke of Ancaster', *Arch. Hist.* 34, 1991].

ESHER CHURCH, SURREY, THE NEWCASTLE PEW, for 1st Duke of Newcastle, 1723–5 [*Letters*, 83, No. 69, dated 1723 by an endorsement] (Downes, 1977, pl. 152).

DOUBTFUL AND ATTRIBUTED WORKS

BARN ELMS, SURREY, alterations for Jacob Tonson, 1703; dem. [*Letters*, 7, refers to alterations here which were apparently under Vanbrugh's direction].

CHOLMONDELEY HALL, CHESHIRE, advice about the remodelling of the house for 1st Earl of Cholmondeley, 1713 [letter printed by Whistler, *Imagination*, 242]. This house had been in process of reconstruction by Francis Smith since 1704. Vanbrugh's advice probably related to the north front, and the engravings in *Vitruvius Britannicus* ii, 1717, pls. 31–2, may represent his proposal. A drawing made before the demolition of the house in 1801 shows that it was not carried out [Gervase Jackson-Stops in *C. Life*, 19 July 1973].

KENSINGTON, Henry Wise's house, on the site of the Victoria and Albert Museum, was a small house in the Vanbrugh manner [*Survey of London* xxxviii, 6–7].

KINGSTON, SURREY, a house formerly standing 'near the Free Grammar School' on the Wandsworth Road, and described as 'a residence of peculiar character (formerly inhabited by Massy Dawson, Esq., M.P. for Clonmel), one of the latest productions of Sir John Vanbrugh. It is of brick, and strongly built. Its stack of chimneys forms a turret in the centre of the roof' [Brayley, *Surrey*, ed. Walford, ii, 1878, 237].

LONDON, ST. JAMES'S PALACE, the kitchen built in 1716–19 may be attributed to Vanbrugh [*History of the King's Works* v, 240–1].

MIDDLETON PARK, MIDDLETON STONEY, OXON., alterations probably for Henry Boyle, cr. Lord Carleton, *c.*1715; destroyed by fire 1755. In a letter of 3 Sept. 1734 (at Woburn Abbey) to her grand-daughter Diana, Duchess of Bedford, Sarah, Duchess of Marlborough, says the house was 'fancifi'd in a very whimsical rediculous manner by Sir John Vanbrugh', and an estate map of 1736 in the Oxon. C.R.O. (J. 1a/24) shows a house with a plan of Vanbrughian character.

PECKHAM, SURREY, HANOVER HOUSE, may confidently be attributed to Vanbrugh on stylistic grounds: see *Architectural Drawings at Elton Hall*, p. xxxvi and pl. xxxi.

SACOMBE PARK, HERTS., belonged to Edward Rolt (d. 1722), who laid out the gardens and intended to build a house. The walling of the Kitchen Garden is described by Salmon in his *History of Hertfordshire* (1728), 225, as 'equal to that of Blenheim, with Houses of Pleasure at the Corners', and by Sir Matthew Decker as 'so strongly built by Van Brock, as if they were to defend a Citty' (MS. journal at Wilton, 1728). A plan of the estate in the Bodleian Library (MS. Gough Drawings a. 4, f. 64) shows the bastioned garden together with the outline of a Vanbrughian house that was never built. For Gibbs's unexecuted design see p. 407).

SOMERSBY HALL, LINCS., built by Robert Burton in 1722, is a small house which could unhesitatingly be ascribed to Vanbrugh on stylistic grounds, but see p. 73 for evidence that it was designed by Robert Alfray.

SWINSTEAD, LINCS., on the Ancaster estate, has a Summer House attributed to Vanbrugh by J. Harris, *Arch. Rev.* Feb. 1961. Cf. a sketch by Buck in Bodleian, Gough Maps 16, f. 53^{v}. See also J. Lord in *Arch. Hist.* 34, 1991, 140–3.

THE VINE, SEVENOAKS, KENT, is said to have been designed by Vanbrugh for Col. Lambert in the diary of William Freeman in Sir John Soane's Museum (p. 97, under the year 1743). Designs for this house exist in the Elton Album and the Victoria and Albert Museum. Photographs show a simpler building (dem.) which may have been designed by Vanbrugh [*Architectural Drawings at Elton Hall*, 23–4 and pl. xxx].

WINDSOR PARK, PUMP HOUSE, 1718, probably designed by Vanbrugh: see *History of the King's Works* v, 335.

VARDEN, RICHARD (1812–1873), of Godalming, contributed designs for country cottages, villas, lodges, etc., to Loudon's *Encyclopaedia of Cottage, Farm and Villa Architecture* (1833). In 1835 he purchased the practice of a retiring architect in Worcester and was recommended by Loudon both as an architect and as a garden designer [*Arch. Mag.* ii, 1835, 282]. In 1836 he was about to build a villa at MALVERN for Edward Foley [*Arch. Mag.* iii, 1836, 141]. In 1837 he designed the colonnaded conservatory behind the west quadrant wall of DITCHLEY HOUSE, OXON., for the 14th Viscount Dillon [*Arch. Mag.* iv, 1837, 548–9], and in 1843–4 he and J. Varden (perhaps a brother) enlarged and remodelled ARLEY CASTLE, UPPER ARLEY, WORCS. (dem. *c.*1960), for the Earl of Mountnorris, exhibiting their designs at the Royal Academy in 1843. Richard Varden died at Seaford Grange, Peopleton, Worcs. on 5 May 1873, and is buried in Peopleton churchyard.

VARDY, JOHN (1718–1765), was a native of Durham, where he was born in February 1717/18. His father was a labourer, and nothing is known about his early life. His long career in the Office of Works began in May 1736, when he was appointed Clerk of the Works at Greenwich. He was subsequently Clerk of the Works at Hampton Court (Jan. 1745–1746), at Whitehall, Westminster and St. James's (Dec. 1746–1754) and at Kensington (July 1754–1761). In 1756 he was in addition appointed Clerk of the Works at Chelsea Hospital, and from 1749 to 1763 he was also Surveyor to the Royal Mint.

Vardy had close connections with William Kent, who was his senior colleague at the Office of Works, and whose style he imitated. If not actually a pupil of Kent in the strict sense, he was certainly one of his most faithful disciples. It was he who in 1744 published the volume of engravings entitled *Some Designs of Mr. Inigo Jones and Mr. William Kent*, and he also drew and engraved Kent's design for the pulpit erected in York Minster in 1741 and a view of the interior of the Great Hall at Hampton Court, based on a drawing by Kent (1749). After Kent's death in 1748 Vardy and William Robinson were the clerks of works jointly responsible for building the Horse Guards in Whitehall to his designs, and in 1751–3 Vardy published plans and elevations of the building. Many of the drawings for the projected Houses of Parliament were made by Vardy under Kent's direction, and it was he who was chiefly responsible for the 'New Stone Building' in St. Margaret's Lane for the records of the Court of King's Bench whose erection in 1755–8 represented a fragmentary realization of the great scheme.

Vardy spent most of his life as an official architect, and relatively few private commissions came his way. Of these the most important was Spencer House, London, built to his designs by the 1st Earl Spencer in 1756–65. Col. George Gray, a member of the Society of Dilettanti, acted in a supervisory capacity, and several of Vardy's drawings for interior features of the house bear endorsements recording Gray's approval. Spencer House as designed by Vardy was a Palladian house, and he was not responsible for the neo-classical interiors on the upper floor, which were designed by James Stuart at Gray's behest from 1759 onwards. Although essentially an orthodox Anglo-Palladian, Vardy designed at least one Gothick house (Milton Abbey) and showed a certain liking for the rococo in his designs for furniture and garden buildings.

Vardy exhibited a number of drawings at the Society of Artists in 1761–4. They included a design for a royal palace, made in 1748, for a building for the Society of Dilettanti, made in 1751, and for a British Museum, made in 1754. The last design, now in the British Museum Print Room, is a Palladian composition consisting of a central block flanked by two vast octagonal domed galleries with screened exedrae on alternate sides. Other unexecuted designs by Vardy were for a large Palladian country house for the 2nd Viscount Midleton (Guildford Record Office, Midleton 145/91/4–6), and for another country house endorsed 'J.V. 1746 for Mr. Arundell', presumably Lord Burlington's friend Richard Arundell of Allerton Mauleverer, Yorkshire (Victoria and Albert Museum). An elaborate map of Windsor Great Park by Vardy, with elevations of the buildings, dated 1750, is in the Public Record Office (MR 280).

Vardy died on 17 May 1765. His will, dated 13 April 1762, mentions his brother Thomas, a carver of Park Street, Grosvenor Square, and his son John (*q.v.*), to whom he left 'all my books, drawings, instruments and matters relating to architecture' [P.R.O., PROB 11/909, f. 239]. [*A.P.S.D.*; *D.N.B.*; Roger White, 'John Vardy' in *The Architectural Outsiders*, ed. R. Brown, 1985.]

LONDON, ST. JAMES'S PALACE, rebuilt N.E. corner, 1748; heightened and bow window added 1768 [*History of the King's Works* v, 244].

LONDON, DORCHESTER HOUSE, PARK LANE, probably designed house begun 1751–2 for 1st Lord Milton (later Earl of Dorchester) and certainly designed stable, terrace and probably interiors, *c.*1764; dem. 1849 [exhib. Soc. of Artists 1764, cf. *Walpole Soc.* xxvii, 80; R.I.B.A.D.; White, *op. cit.*, 71].

LONDON, WHITEHALL, house at N. end of island block between Parliament and King Streets, for Col. George Wade, 1753; dem. 1875 [exhib. at Soc. of Artists, 1764; White, *op. cit.*, 70].

LONDON, RUTLAND HOUSE, KNIGHTSBRIDGE, for 3rd Duke of Rutland, 1753; dem. *c.*1835 [plan and elevation in V. & A. 6821/4 signed 'John Vardy 1763', but building accounts at Belvoir Castle (n. 633) show that the house was built in 1753: cf. view of house corresponding to drawings in W. E. Manners, *The Marquis of Granby*, 1899, 55].

LEES COURT, KENT, designs (R.I.B.A.D.) for internal alterations for Lewis Watson, cr. Lord Sondes, 1754; gutted by fire *c.*1913 and reconstructed.

MILTON ABBEY, DORSET, remodelled for 1st Lord Milton in Gothick style, *c.*1754–5 but never completed and superseded by house by Sir W. Chambers, 1771–[R.I.B.A.D.; White, *op. cit.*, 72].

?WOODCOTE PARK, EPSOM, SURREY, for 6th Lord Baltimore, *c.*1755; reconstructed after fire in 1934; Drawing Room removed to Boston Museum of Fine Arts 1911 [stylistic attribution based on resemblance to Col. Wade's house in Whitehall of 1753: White, *op. cit.*, 70; for previous attribution to Isaac Ware see J. Harris in *Connoisseur*, May 1961].

LONDON, WESTMINSTER PALACE, probably designed the 'NEW STONE BUILDING', ST. MARGARET'S LANE, begun 1755–8, continued 1768–9; dem. 1883 [*History of the King's Works* v, 428–30].

LONDON, SPENCER HOUSE, GREEN PARK, for 1st Earl Spencer, 1756–65; decoration of upper floor by James Stuart (*q.v.*) [*Vitruvius Britannicus* iv, 1767, pls. 37–40; drawings in R.I.B.A. and Soane and V. & A. Museums; J. Friedman, *Spencer House*, 1993].

FULHAM CHURCHYARD, MIDDLESEX, monument to Bishop Thomas Sherlock (d. 1761) [signed].

HACKWOOD PARK, HANTS., remodelled S. front for 5th Duke of Bolton, 1761–3; again remodelled 1805–13, and designed lodges; dem. [Vardy's account in Hants. C.R.O., 11.M.49; drawings at Hackwood] (P. Sandby, *Select Views* i, 1783, pl. xix).[1]

LONDON, No. 37 (formerly 32) GROSVENOR SQUARE, for 5th Duke of Bolton. *c.*1761–5; dem. 1934 [*Survey of London* xl, 149].

LONDON, DURHAM YARD, STRAND, 'plans and planning' for 3rd Duke of St. Albans, 1763 [Duke's account at Drummond's Bank].

STANMORE HOUSE or PARK, MIDDLESEX, for Andrew Drummond, 1763–4, completed by Sir William Chambers; dem. 1938 [J. Harris, *Chambers*, 1970, 247] (*Beauties of England & Wales* x (4), 1816, 630).

VARDY, JOHN, junior, was the son of John Vardy (*q.v.*), and was presumably the architect's son of this name who was admitted to Westminster School in April 1752 at the age of 7 [*The Record of Old Westminsters* ii, 1928, 944]. He succeeded his father as Surveyor to the Royal Mint, retiring in 1793. His only recorded architectural work appears to be the alteration and enlargement of Leoni's Queensberry House, Burlington Gardens, London, for the 1st Earl of Uxbridge in 1785–

[1] See also A. Coleridge, 'John Vardy and the Hackwood Suite', *Connoisseur* cxlix, 1962, 12–17, for furniture at Hackwood designed by Vardy.

9. His skilful adaptation of what thereafter became known as UXBRIDGE HOUSE (now the Royal Bank of Scotland) is fully described and illustrated in *Survey of London* xxxii, 461–4. The G. Vardy who exhibited architectural designs at the Royal Academy from an address in Knightsbridge in 1800 and 1818 may perhaps have been his son.

VARNHAM, HENRY (*c.*1781–1823), practised as an architect and surveyor in Tooley Street, Southwark, and was Surveyor to the Grocers' Company at the time of his death on 2 October 1823, aged 42 [*Gent's Mag.* 1823 (ii), 380]. He was responsible for taking down the steeple of ST. MARY MAGDALENE CHURCH, BERMONDSEY, in 1811 [Vestry Minutes, *ex inf.* Canon B. F. L. Clarke].

VASS, NICHOLAS, of Portsea, Hampshire, was a carpenter by trade [deed of 1744 in Portsmouth Record Office, 95A/1/1/12]. In 1753–4 he was employed to 'oversee the workmanship and materials' for the building of ST. GEORGE'S CHURCH, PORTSEA [Vestry Minutes in Portsmouth Record Office, f. 7], and in 1787–9 ST. JOHN'S CHAPEL, PORTSEA (dem. 1941), was built under his inspection [B. F. L. Clarke, *The Building of the Eighteenth-Century Church*, 1963, 105]. Both churches were attractive examples of Georgian vernacular architecture which Vass may well have designed himself [R. Hubbuck, *Portsea Island Churches*, 1969, 6–7].

VEZY, —, is at present known only from two payments by James Master, the builder *c.*1656–8 of YOTES COURT, MEREWORTH, KENT, one in 1656 of £1 to 'Mr. Vezy when I carried him to survey Yotes', and another in 1658 of £2 'for drawing a plot for an house' [S. Robertson, 'The Expense Book of James Master', *Archaeologia Cantiana* xvi, 1886, 254]. Yotes Court is a precursor of the type of gentry house that became fashionable after the Restoration (*C. Life*, 18–25 June 1964).

VILET, or **VILETT,** J—, signs a design for an entrance archway dated 1763 in the Yorkshire Archaeological Society's Library (MD 290/9). It is competently drawn in a style resembling that of James Paine. At Syon House, Middlesex, there is a design by him for a Gothic 'necessary house' dated 1771.

VINER, CHARLES, was a member of a family of builders at Bath, of whom Gabriel was a mason and Richard a carpenter and joiner. In 1821–2 he competed for the Cambridge Observatory and in 1838 he exhibited a design for a triumphal monument at the Royal Academy. In the Hunt Collection in the Reference Library at Bath there is an unexecuted design by him for a colonnade through Gay Street to Gravel Walks.

VINING, ROBERT, described in Pigot's *Directory* (1830) as a builder of Weymouth, designed the octagonal NOTTINGTON SPA at BROADWEY, nr. WEYMOUTH, DORSET, in 1830 [R.C.H.M., *Dorset* ii (2), 360].

VOKINS, CHARLES, of Wilton Road, Pimlico, was a pupil or assistant of Charles Bacon (*q.v.*). He completed OAKLANDS, nr. OKEHAMPTON, DEVON, for Albany Savile after Bacon's death in 1818. There is a plan of this Greek Revival mansion in Loudon's *Encyclopaedia of Rural Architecture*, 1846, 915, and a view of it, dated 1831, is given in *Devonshire illustrated from Original Drawings by Thomas Allom and W. H. Bartlett.* Loudon also gives (p. 919) a design by Vokins for a castellated villa. In the 1840s Vokins appears to have given up practice and become a coal-merchant in Pimlico.

VOYSEY, ANNESLEY (*c.*1794–1839), practised as an architect and surveyor in London in the early nineteenth century. In 1811 he exhibited a design for a bridge over the Thames at Vauxhall at the Royal Academy. According to Edward I'Anson he was responsible for the first building in London to be designed exclusively for use as offices. It stood at the Lombard Street end of Clement's Lane and was built in about 1823 [*R.I.B.A. Trans.* 1864–5,25]. In the early 1830s Voysey was in partnership with Richard Suter (*q.v.*), but he subsequently emigrated to Jamaica, where he died of fever on 5 August 1839, aged 45 [*Gent's Mag.* 1839 (ii), 667]. His son, the Revd. Charles Voysey, was the father of the well-known architect Charles Francis Annesley Voysey (1857–1941). Sampson Kempthorne was his pupil.

VULLIAMY, LEWIS (1791–1871), born on 15 March 1791, was the son of Benjamin Vulliamy, the celebrated clockmaker. He was articled to Sir Robert Smirke and became a student at the Royal Academy in 1809, winning the Silver Medal in 1810 and the Gold Medal in 1813. In 1818 he was awarded the Academy's travelling scholarship, which enabled him to spend four years abroad, chiefly in Italy. On his return he began to exhibit at the Royal Academy and soon obtained a considerable practice, especially for churches of the Commissioners' sort. In London he designed the Greek Revival Law Institution in Chancery Lane, gave the Royal Institution in

Albemarle Street a handsome new Corinthian front, and provided urbane elevations for speculative builders in Bloomsbury. His principal patron was R. S. Holford, a millionaire who employed him to design a prestigious town house in Park Lane and a large country house at Westonbirt in Gloucestershire. The former was in the Italianate, the latter in the Elizabethan, style; but Vulliamy could also design Grecian façades in the manner of his master (e.g. the Law Institution) and his churches show equal facility in Romanesque and Gothic. He was in fact an eclectic designer who could turn his hand to any style that early Victorian taste might demand. To his contemporaries he was not quite in the first rank of metropolitan architects, and posterity has not sought to alter his standing as a highly competent practitioner of the second rank. His churches were mostly routine productions of their time, but his houses were buildings of greater pretensions. Dorchester House was a dexterous synthesis of motifs from the Italian Renaissance rendered splendid by the sculpture of Alfred Stevens. Westonbirt is externally a magnificent amalgam of Wollaton and Bramshill with a sumptuous Renaissance interior and elaborate formal gardens. Technically Vulliamy was a thoroughly professional architect who prided himself on the accuracy of his estimates and the efficiency of his office. He was, however, 'known to be peculiar in his notions' and his eccentricities are said to have occasioned 'many odd anecdotes'.

Vulliamy remained in practice until the day of his death, and left a considerable fortune. He died at his house on Clapham Common on 4 January 1871. In 1838 he had married Elizabeth Papendiek, only daughter of the Revd. Frederick Papendiek, vicar of Morden in Surrey. They had four sons, with all of whom Vulliamy quarrelled. He published two works early in life: *The Bridge of the Sta. Trinita at Florence*, 1822, and *Examples of Ornamental Sculpture in Architecture, drawn from the originals in Greece, Asia Minor, and Italy in the years 1818, 1819, 1820, 1821,* 1823, 2nd ed. 1828(?). He also made the drawings of the Castle at Newcastle which were published in *Vetusta Monumenta* v, 1835, pls. 10–18. His pupils included Owen Jones, C. F. Maltby, F. W. Porter, R. H. Shout, J. Williams and W. Wright. Talbot Bury, John Johnson and Edward Walters were assistants. His nephew George John Vulliamy (1817–86) was in his office for some years, but left in 1861, 'being dissatisfied with his uncle's treatment' of him, and became Superintending Architect to the Metropolitan Board of Works. A quantity of drawings from Vulliamy's office remained in the possession of his family until about 1950, when they were dispersed. A number of drawings and letters, etc., including those relating to Westonbirt House, are in the R.I.B.A. Collection. An elaborate list of his works, drawn up by himself, is printed in *Builder* xxix, 1871, together with a short memoir.

[*A.P.S.D.*; *D.N.B.*; *Builder* xxix, 1871, 142; private information.]

Unless otherwise stated, the following list is based on the one printed in *Builder* xxix, 1871.

PUBLIC BUILDINGS, INCLUDING CHURCHES

ST. BARTHOLOMEW'S CHURCH, WEST HILL, SYDENHAM, KENT, 1826–31, Gothic; chancel by E. Nash 1857.

WOLVERHAMPTON, STAFFS., THE RACECOURSE GRANDSTAND, 1828.

BISHOP'S STORTFORD, HERTS., THE CORN EXCHANGE, 1828.

LONDON, ST. BARNABAS CHURCH, ADDISON ROAD, KENSINGTON, 1828–9, Gothic; chancel 1861 and 1909.

LONDON, ST. JAMES'S CHURCH, PARK HILL, CLAPHAM COMMON, 1828–9; enlarged 1870–1; destroyed by bombing 1940 (E. E. F. Smith, *Clapham*, 1975, 86–7).

BURSLEM, STAFFS., ST. PAUL'S CHURCH, 1828–30, Gothic; dem. *c.*1975.

LONDON, THE LAW SOCIETY'S HALL, CHANCERY LANE, 1828–32, completed 1849 and 1857; enlarged by P. C. Hardwick 1864–70 [P. W. Chandler, 'The Site of the Law Society's Hall', *Trans. London and Middlesex Arch. Soc.*, N.S. vi, 1929–32].

WOLVERHAMPTON, STAFFS., THE ASSEMBLY ROOMS, QUEEN STREET, addition of upper (Ionic) storey to façade, 1829 (J. S. Roper, *Historic Buildings of Wolverhampton*, 1957, 44).

WORDSLEY, STAFFS., HOLY TRINITY CHURCH, 1830–1, Gothic; chancel 1887.

RICHMOND, SURREY, ST. JOHN'S CHURCH, 1830–1, Gothic; chancel 1905.

TODMORDEN, YORKS. (W.R.), CHRIST CHURCH, 1830–1, Gothic; chancel 1885.

LONDON, ST. MICHAEL'S CHURCH, HIGHGATE, 1830–2, Gothic; chancel 1881.

LONDON, CHRIST CHURCH, WOBURN SQUARE, 1831–3, Gothic; dem. 1974.

WARDLE (SMALLBRIDGE), LANCS., ST. JOHN'S CHURCH, 1831–3, Gothic.

SPOTLAND, LANCS., ST. CLEMENT'S CHURCH, 1832–4, Gothic.

RICHMOND, SURREY, HICKEY'S ALMSHOUSES, SHEEN ROAD, 1834, Tudor.

WORSTHORNE, LANCS., ST. JOHN'S CHURCH,

1834–5, Gothic; chancel 1894, tower 1903.

BURNLEY, LANCS, HOLY TRINITY CHURCH, ACCRINGTON ROAD, 1835–6, Gothic; gutted 1990.

HABERGHAM EAVES, LANCS., HOLY TRINITY CHURCH, 1835–6, Gothic.

BRIERLY HILL CHAPEL, nr. STOURBRIDGE, STAFFS., enlargement at east end, 1836–7 [I.C.B.S.].

GLASBURY CHURCH, BRECONSHIRE, 1836–7, Norman.

EPPING UNION WORKHOUSE (now St. Margaret's Hospital), ESSEX, 1837 [Essex C.R.O., G/EM1 pp. 228, 231; G/EZ 2/1–4].

STURMINSTER UNION WORKHOUSE (now Stour View House), STURMINSTER NEWTON, DORSET, 1838.

BRENTFORD UNION WORKHOUSE, MIDDLESEX, 1838; dem.

LONDON, ST. JAMES'S CHURCH, CURTAIN ROAD, SHOREDITCH, 1838–9, Gothic; altered 1872; dem. 1937.

LONDON, THE ROYAL INSTITUTION, ALBEMARLE STREET, refronted with façade of Corinthian half-columns, 1838.

STONEGATE CHAPEL, TICEHURST, SUSSEX, for Mrs. Courthope, 1838; Gothic; rebuilt 1904.

LONDON, CHRIST CHURCH, JAMAICA ROAD, ROTHERHITHE, 1838–9, Gothic.

COBRIDGE, nr. BURSLEM, STAFFS., CHRIST CHURCH, 1838–41, Gothic; chancel 1899.

WINTERBORNE CLENSTON CHURCH, DORSET, 1839–40, Gothic.

ROSEDALE CHURCH, YORKS. (N.R.), 1839–40, Gothic.

RAYNE CHURCH, ESSEX, rebuilt (except Tudor tower), 1840.

ROYDON CHURCH, nr. DISS, NORFOLK, south porch, 1840, Gothic; removed to different position 1864.

LONDON, ST. PETER'S CHURCH, BETHNAL GREEN, 1840–1, Norman; also the Rectory.

LONDON, ST. JAMES THE LESS CHURCH, BETHNAL GREEN, 1840–2, Norman; reconstructed after war-damage in 1940; also the Rectory.

LONDON, THE SMALLPOX HOSPITAL, UPPER HOLLOWAY, HIGHGATE, alterations, 1841.

WING RECTORY, NORTHANTS., alterations, 1841 [Northants. Record Office, Peterborough Diocesan Records].

ROCHESTER, KENT, KING'S SCHOOL, 1842, Tudor; enlarged 1911.

LONDON, THE LOCK HOSPITAL, CHAPEL and ASYLUM, HARROW ROAD, PADDINGTON, 1842–3 and 1845–9; chapel and W. wing dem. 1953.

HAWKESBURY UPTON, GLOS., MONUMENTAL TOWER in memory of Lord Edward Somerset, 1843–8 (drawings in Yale Center for British Art).

CHINGFORD, ESSEX, ST. PETER AND ST. PAUL CHURCH, 1844, Gothic; enlarged 1903.

BEVERSTON CHURCH, GLOS., rebuilt south aisle and porch for R. S. Holford, 1844, Gothic.

LONDON, THE LONDON AND WESTMINSTER BANK (WEST END BRANCH), No. 1 ST. JAMES'S SQUARE, conversion of mansion for bank premises, 1844–5, and subsequent alterations in 1858, 1864 and 1867; dem. 1955–6 (*Survey of London* xxix, 81–2).

LONDON, ST. JAMES'S CHURCH, NORLANDS, ST. JAMES'S CARDENS, KENSINGTON, 1844–5, Gothic; enlarged 1876.

ROCHESTER CATHEDRAL, KENT, alterations, 1845.

LONDON, ALL SAINTS (now Greek Orthodox) CHURCH, ENNISMORE GARDENS, WESTMINSTER, 1848–9, Italianate; W. front remodelled 1892.

LONDON, ST. THOMAS'S CHURCH, BETHNAL GREEN, 1849–50; dem. 1954.

THORLEY CHURCH, HERTS., restoration, 1855 [J. E. Cussans, *History of Hertfordshire* i, 1870–3, 104].

LASBOROUGH CHURCH, GLOS., rebuilt for R. S. Holford, 1861–2, Gothic [Kelly's *Directory of Gloucestershire*].

DOMESTIC ARCHITECTURE

SYSTON NEW HALL, LINCS., library and other additions and alterations for Sir J. H. Thorold, Bart., 1822–4; dem. *c.*1935.

LONDON, LIMEHOUSE, alterations to house for T. Thornwaite, 1823.

BOOTHBY PAGNELL HALL, LINCS., for J. Litchford, 1825, Tudor.

LONDON, TAVISTOCK SQUARE, houses on north and west sides for the speculative builders G. Anstey and J. A. Frampton, 1827 (Hermione Hobhouse, *Thomas Cubitt*, 1971, pl. 12).

LONDON, GORDON (now ENDSLEIGH) PLACE, BLOOMSBURY, houses for James Humphries, builder, 1827 (Humphries, like Anstey and Frampton, must have been a 'taker' under Cubitt: see Hermione Hobhouse, *Thomas Cubitt*, 1971, 71).

LEADENHAM HOUSE, LINCS., alterations for General John Reeve, probably including porch and stables, 1829 (*C. Life*, 17–24 June 1965).

ASHBURNHAM PLACE, SUSSEX, alterations for 3rd Earl of Ashburnham, 1829.[1]

NORTON PLACE, LINCS., alterations for Sir Montague Cholmeley, Bart., 1830.

EDITH WESTON HALL, RUTLAND, for the Revd.

---

[1] This is the date given in Vulliamy's list of his commissions, but cf. *The Ashburnham Archives*, ed. F. W. Steer, Lewes 1958, 45–6.

R. Lucas, 1830, Tudor; dem. 1954.

BLOXHOLM HALL, LINCS., alterations for G. Manners, 1830–6; dem. 1954.

ROCKHILL HOUSE, SYDENHAM, KENT, alterations for — Nix, 1832.

LEIGH PARK, HAVANT, HANTS., lodges, octagonal Gothic Library, etc., for Sir G. T. Staunton, Bart., 1832–3; dem. (G. F. Prosser, *Select Illustrations of Hampshire*, 1833, plate and description).

CARLTON LODGE, GREAT CARLTON, LINCS., for S. Forster, 1833–6, Elizabethan; dem.

RICHMOND, SURREY, UNDER-THE-HILL, alterations to house for Samuel Painter, 1834.

CLYDACH HOUSE. CO. GALWAY, IRELAND, 'proposed alterations' for Sir G. T. Staunton, Bart., exhib. at R.A. 1834, of which at least the porch was built.

EMO PARK, CO. LEIX, IRELAND, alterations for 2nd Earl of Portarlington, 1834–6 (*C. Life*, 23, 30 May 1974).

TWICKENHAM, MIDDLESEX, CAMBRIDGE HOUSE, alterations for Henry Bevan, 1835.

RICHMOND, SURREY, QUEENSBERRY VILLA, alterations for Sir William Dundas, Bart., 1835; dem.

TWYFORD HOUSE, HOCKERILL, HERTS., stables, etc., for G. Frere, 1835.

WHILIGH HOUSE, TICEHURST, SUSSEX, alterations for G. Courthope, 1836.

TWICKENHAM, MIDDLESEX, HEATH LANE, alterations to villa for J. Weld, 1836.

RICHMOND GREEN, SURREY, alterations to house for J. Ward, 1836.

DOWNHAM HALL, SANTON DOWNHAM, SUFFOLK, alterations for Lord William Powlett, 1836; dem.

MEREWORTH CASTLE, KENT, alterations for Lady le Despencer, 1836.

LONDON, No. 51 GROSVENOR STREET, alterations for John Mansfield, 1836.

WORDSLEY RECTORY, STAFFS., for the Revd. William Penfold, 1837.

LONDON, HIGHGATE, house for — Snow, 1838.

SOUTHEND, LEWISHAM, KENT, alterations for S. Forster, 1839; dem.

WINDHILL HOUSE, BISHOP'S STORTFORD, HERTS., for J. Fairman, 1839.

WESTONBIRT HOUSE, TETBURY, GLOS., extensive alterations and additions to the old house for R. S. Holford, 1839; subsequently rebuilt by Vulliamy (see below).

HILL PARK, WESTERHAM, KENT, cottages, conservatory, stables, etc., for David Baillie, 1839; house dem.

BURSTON RECTORY, NORFOLK, for the Revd. Temple Frere, 1840; enlarged 1862.

BALSHAM RECTORY, CAMBS., for the Revd. W. H. Chapman, 1840 [C.U.L., Ely Diocesan Records, G3/39/19 *bis*].

FRIDAY HILL HOUSE, CHINGFORD, ESSEX, for the Revd. R. B. Heathcote, 1839–40, Tudor.

DULLINGHAM, CAMBS., farm buildings, 1841.

TREGOTHNAN HOUSE, CORNWALL, enlarged house and designed Nansawn Lodge for 2nd Earl of Falmouth, 1842–8 (*C. Life*, 17, 24 May 1956).

LONDON, No. 26 ST. JAMES'S PLACE, alterations for Dowager Lady Arden, 1843; destroyed by bombing 1939–45 (*Survey of London* xxx, 518).

LONDON, No. 15 CHARLES STREET, alterations for General J. Humphry, 1843.

NORK HOUSE, BANSTEAD, SURREY, alterations for Dowager Lady Arden 1844; dem. *c.*1930.

ROCHESTER, KENT, CANON'S HOUSE, for the Revd. John Griffith, 1844.

BEVERSTON, GLOS., estate cottages and alterations to Nesley Farm (1844), for R. S. Holford.

COTTENHAM RECTORY, CAMBS., alterations for the Revd. John Frere, 1845.

SEWARDSTONE MANOR HOUSE, HIGH BEECH, ESSEX, alterations for Admiral Charles Sotheby, 1845.

DINGESTOW COURT, MONMOUTHSHIRE, rebuilt south front for S. Bosanquet, 1845–6, Elizabethan.

NEWTON HOUSE, nr. BEDALE, YORKS. (N.R.), alterations for Dowager Duchess of Cleveland, 1846; dem. 1956.

WESTONBIRT, GLOS., BABDOWN, DOWN and ELMSTREE FARMS, for R.S. Holford, 1846–8.

CHESTAL HOUSE, DURSLEY, GLOS., for James Phelps, 1848, Jacobethan.

WOOLHAMPTON HOUSE, BERKS., alterations for 2nd Earl of Falmouth, 1848.

LAMORRAN RECTORY, CORNWALL, for 2nd Earl of Falmouth, 1848.

WANLIP HALL, LEICS., alterations and conservatory for Sir Geoffrey Palmer, Bart., 1849; dem. 1938.

TETBURY, GLOS., THE WHITE HART INN., for R. S. Holford, 1849, Jacobean.

WOOTTON, ISLE OF WIGHT, PALMER'S FARM, for R. S. Holford, 1849.

LONDON, DORCHESTER HOUSE, PARK LANE, for R. S. Holford, 1850–63; dem. 1929 (*Builder* x 1852, 550–1; *C. Life*, 5–12 May 1928; *R.I.B.A. Jnl.*, 3rd ser. xxxv, 1928, 623, 667; measured drawings in *Architect and Building News*, 4 July, 1 Aug., 5 Sept., 3 Oct. 1930; D. J. Watkin, 'Holford, Vulliamy and the Sources for Dorchester House', in *Influences in Victorian Art & Architecture*, ed. Macready & Thompson, 1985).

ISLEWORTH, MIDDLESEX, ST. MARGARET'S HOUSE (afterwards the Royal Naval Female School) for 2nd Earl of Kilmorey, 1852; dem. 1945 (*Builder* x, 1852, 424–5).

SHERNFOLD PARK, FRANT, SUSSEX, for the Hon. P. Ashburnham, 1853.

HIGHNAM COURT, GLOS., W. wing for Thomas Gambier Parry, 1855 and other earlier alterations [N. Kingsley, *Country Houses of Gloucestershire* ii, 1992, 166] (*C. Life*, 12–19 May 1950).

BRAMSHOTT GRANGE, HANTS., for Sir William Erle, 1855.

LONDON, Nos. 20–21 BERKELEY SQUARE, alterations for Lord Lindsay, 1856.

ALDERLEY HOUSE (now Rosehill School), nr. WOTTON-UNDER-EDGE, GLOS., for R. B. Hale, 1859–63 [N. Kingsley, *Country Houses of Gloucestershire* iii, forthcoming].

WESTONBIRT HOUSE, GLOS., for R.S. Holford, 1863–70, Elizabethan (*C. Life*, 18–25 May 1972).

W

WADMAN, WILLIAM (*c.*1792–1857), 'Surveyor and Architect' of Martock, Somerset, designed the Tudor Gothic south aisle that was added to WEST COKER CHURCH, SOMERSET, in 1834 [I.C.B.S.]. He died at Martock in October 1857, aged 65 [Martock Parish Register].

WAGSTAFF, JOHN (–1784), was a carpenter and joiner at Daventry in Northamptonshire. In the 1730s he sometimes worked under Francis Smith, e.g. at Brogyntyn and Wynnstay. An 'Elevation of a House design'd for Thos. Langton Esqr. at Teeton per Jno. Wagstaff', shows that he designed TEETON HALL, NORTHANTS., a small Georgian mansion of *c.*1750, remodelled 1879 [Langton-Lockton papers]. In 1772 or 1773 he refitted the chapel in ALTHORP HOUSE, NORTHANTS., for the 1st Earl Spencer [B.L., Althorp Papers, F 43, letter of 13 March 1773]. Either he or his son John Wagstaff (d. 1802) built EAST HADDON HALL, NORTHANTS., for Henry Sawbridge in 1780–3, probably to his own designs, though possibly to those of John Johnson (*q.v.*) [G. Isham in *Reports & Papers of the Northants. Antiqn. Soc.* lxiv, 1962–3, 37; Nancy Briggs, *John Johnson*, 1991, 45]. In 1790–1 the younger Wagstaff was responsible for building the new east front of BOSWORTH HALL, HUSBANDS BOSWORTH, LEICS., for E. F. Turville, making designs which appear to have superseded some previously made by Joseph Bonomi [Leics. C.R.O., DG 39]. The elder Wagstaff was bailiff (i.e. mayor) of Daventry in 1764, the younger in 1781 and 1799 [information from the late Sir Gyles Isham].

WAINWRIGHT, JOHN (1762–1828), was apprenticed to Charles Rawlinson of Lostwithiel (*q.v.*) in 1774, and was described as 'architect' in 1790 when he married Elizabeth Westlake of Lostwithiel. He subsequently moved to Bruton in Somerset and later to Shepton Mallet, where he died in 1828. His business as an architect and builder was continued by his elder son Charles Rawlinson Wainwright (1790–1852), who became surveyor to the Dean and Chapter of Wells. The latter's architectural work included DINDER RECTORY, SOMERSET, 1827 [Somerset C.R.O., D/D/Bbm, 54]; additional pewing in CROSCOMBE CHURCH, SOMERSET, 1830–1 [I.C.B.S.]; and rebuilding the aisles of SHEPTON MALLET CHURCH in 1837 [J. E. Farbrother, *Shepton Mallet*, 1859, 54]. He died at Christon Court in 1852, leaving a son Charles Rawlinson Wainwright II (1823–92), who was a pupil of G. P. Manners of Bath and practised as an architect and surveyor at Shepton Mallet. John Wainwright's younger son John Westlake Wainwright (born 1793) enlarged CHILTON POLDEN CHURCH, SOMERSET, in 1829 [I.C.B.S.]. Other buildings for which the family were responsible were PYLLE RECTORY, the north front of CROSCOMBE RECTORY, Union Workhouses at WELLS and SHEPTON MALLET and the POLICE STATION at SHEPTON MALLET. [Information from Mr. David Wainwright, A.R.I.C.S.]

WAKEFIELD, WILLIAM (–1730), of Huby Hall, nr. Easingwold in Yorkshire, was a gentleman who enjoyed a considerable reputation as an architect in his native county. Francis Drake, noting in 1736 that he was buried ('as yet without any memorial') in the church of St. Michael-le-Belfry at York, speaks of him as 'that worthy gentleman William Wakefield esquire, whose great skill in architecture will always be commended, as long as the houses of Duncombe Park and Gilling Castle shall stand'. Sir Thomas Robinson, writing to Lord Carlisle in December 1730, thought it 'but doing a justice to my late dear friend Mr. Wakefield' to believe that had he lived he would have made plans for the York Assembly Rooms 'full as convenient as' Lord Burlington's, and certainly cheaper, 'tho' perhaps [with] not so many Palladian strokes in 'em'. He would, he said, make 'this distinction between them', that he would 'chuse to follow the plan of a house from the one and that for a publick building from the other, for examine all Mr. Wakefield's designs and the many alterations he has made in the old houses of his friends, we shall always find state [and] conveniency with good economy inseparable companions . . .'

What little is known of Wakefield's architectural activities is set out below. The massing of Duncombe, and above all the external expression of its twin staircase towers, shows that he was strongly influenced by Vanbrugh, and his other designs confirm his status as a provincial member of the English baroque school. Of the many old houses that he is said to have altered, Gilling and Holme are the only ones so far definitely identified, but SCRIVEN PARK, nr. KNARESBOROUGH, YORKS. (W.R.) (dem. 1954), as remodelled *c.*1728–30 for Sir Henry Slingsby, Bart., whose sister had married Thomas Duncombe, son of the builder of Duncombe Park, may well have been designed by Wakefield, as suggested by Giles Worsley in *C. Life*, 21 June 1990, Correspondence. At Newburgh Priory there is a pulvinated gateway closely resembling one at Gilling, and it has more than once been noted that the undocumented Debtors' prison at York (1701–5) is a building that might have been designed by Wakefield.

Wakefield died in April 1730, and was buried at St. Michael-le-Belfry on 28 April of that year. [F. Drake, *Eboracum*, 1736, 341 n. *c.*; T. Gill, *Vallis Eboracensis*, 1852, 410–11; *Walpole Soc.* xix, 132; *Registers of St. Michael le Belfry, York*, York Parish Register Soc. 1901, 236, 245; Kerry Downes, *English Baroque Architecture*, 1966, 92, 111.]

DUNCOMBE PARK, YORKS. (N.R.), for Thomas Duncombe, 1713; wings added by Sir Charles Barry 1843–6; gutted by fire 1879 and reconstructed in the 1890s with modifications to east front, etc. [*Vitruvius Britannicus* iii, pls. 85–6] (H. A. Tipping, *English Homes, Period IV* (ii), 193–200).

HOLME HALL, YORKS. (E.R.), enlarged for the 4th Lord Langdale, 1720–3; remodelled *c.*1840 [E. Yorks. Record Office, DD HA 14/25–6; letter from Lord Langdale's agent 6 July 1720: 'Mr. Wakefield hath been here att Hoome setting out the Foundation for the New Building and giving his Directions to the Bricklayers and Carpanders . . .'].

ATHERTON HALL, LANCS., for Richard Atherton, 1723–43; dem. 1825 [*Vitruvius Britannicus* iii, pl. 89; J. Rose, *Leigh in the Eighteenth Century*, 1882, 78, records the inscription on the foundation-stone as 'Marcij 28 1723, Rics. Atherton Ar[miger], W. W: Ar[miger] Arch[itectu]s'].

ROKEBY HALL, YORKS. (N.R.), unexecuted design for Sir Thomas Robinson, Bart., 1724, illustated in *Vitruvius Britannicus* iii, pl. 90.

GILLING CASTLE, YORKS. (N.R.), design attributed to Wakefield by F. Drake, *Eboracum*, 1736, 341. The remodelling of Gilling was probably begun by the 8th Viscount Fairfax soon after his succession in 1719 and completed by the 9th Viscount after his death in 1738, for Fairfax documents in Yorks. Archaeological Society's library show that the 'new building' was still in progress in 1738 and that the gallery was not complete until *c.*1740 [*ex inf.* the late Fr. James Forbes] (H. A. Tipping, *English Homes, Period IV* (ii), 201–10). The arched features on coupled columns in the hall resemble the main doorway in Wakefield's design for Rokeby, and the plan of the wings should be compared with Vanbrugh's unexecuted scheme for Hampton Court Palace of *c.*1716 (*History of the King's Works* v, pl. 14 and fig. 6).

WALFORD, WILLIAM, probably a local builder, designed the MECHANICS' INSTITUTE (now Recruiting Office), QUEEN STREET, WOLVERHAMPTON, in *c.*1835–6 [J. S. Roper, *Historic Buildings of Wolverhampton*, 1957, 61]. Obadiah Walford was a builder in Wolverhampton in 1802 [J. S. Roper, *Trades and Professions in Wolverhampton in 1802*, Wolverhampton 1969, 10], and William Walford was a timber merchant in 1851 [W. White's *Directory of Staffordshire*, 1851, 135].

WALKER, JOHN (–1626), of West Hanningfield, Essex, was primarily a land surveyor, but also described himself as 'architector' or as 'architect and surveyor' [E. G. R. Taylor, *Mathematical Practitioners of Tudor and Stuart England 1485–1714*, 1967, 188].

WALKER, JOSEPH, practised from 21 Earl Street, Blackfriars, in the 1820s. In 1821 he made designs for the IRISH CHAMBER, GUILDHALL YARD, LONDON, that were carried out in 1824–5 [Guildhall Record Office, Minutes of the Irish Society, *ex inf.* London Division, English Heritage]. He may have been the J. Walker who exhibited a design for an academy at the Royal Academy in 1834 from 105 Stamford Street, Blackfriars. W. H. Newnham was his pupil or assistant.

WALKER, RICHARD, exhibited at the Royal Academy from 1802 to 1813, giving as his address 20 Bentinck Street, then the office of William Atkinson, whose pupil or assistant he must have been. His exhibits included 'Chedburgh Hall' (1813), perhaps an unexecuted design for a house at Chedburgh in Suffolk, and 'the seat of the Earl of Harrington' (1813), i.e. ELVASTON CASTLE,

DERBYSHIRE, which, according to Neale's *Seats* vi, 1823, was rebuilt by the 3rd Earl 'from designs by the late James Wyatt, by Mr. Walker, architect'. In 1816 a local correspondent informed Daniel Lysons that 'Mr. Richard Walker is the Architect of Lord Harrington's building' and added that 'he was an assistant of Mr. [B. D.] Whyatt's in the building [of] Drury Lane [Theatre'] [B.L., Add. MS. 9425, f. 200]. Richard Walker must be distinguished from Robert Walker, a pupil of Thomas Leverton who was admitted to the Royal Academy Schools in 1792 at the age of 21 and exhibited at the Academy in 1793 and 1795.

WALKER, WILLIAM (*c.*1765–1837), was a builder and surveyor of Chertsey, Surrey, where he is commemorated by a gravestone in the churchyard [*ex inf.* Mr. B. F. J. Pardoe]. The churches at ASHFORD and FELTHAM in MIDDLESEX were rebuilt to his designs in 1796 and 1801–2, respectively [Guildhall Library, London Diocesan Faculty Register, MS. 9532/9, ff. 6–9, 129–32].

WALKER, WILLIAM, of Stratford-on-Avon, designed undistinguished Gothic churches in Warwickshire at NEWBOLD-ON-STOUR, 1835 [I.C.B.S.], ALVESTON, 1839 [I.C.B.S.], and LONG LAWFORD, 1839 [G.R.], and enlarged GREAT ALNE CHURCH in 1837 [I.C.B.S.].

WALKER, WILLIAM (*c.*1789–1843), of Shaftesbury, rebuilt the chancel and extended the nave of DONHEAD ST. ANDREW CHURCH, WILTS., in 1838; designed an unconvincing neo-Norman church with twin west towers at CHARLTON, nr. DONHEAD ST. MARY, WILTS., 1839; rebuilt CANN CHURCH, DORSET, in the lancet style in 1840; and rebuilt NORTON BAVANT CHURCH, WILTS. (except the tower) in 1840 [all I.C.B.S.]. He also designed ST. MARY'S R.C. CHURCH, POOLE, DORSET, 1839 [*British Critic* xxviii, 1840, 494]. He died at Shaftesbury in May 1843, aged 54 [Parish Register].

WALLACE, LEWIS ALEXANDER (*c.*1789–1861), was the son of William Wallace, an Edinburgh builder who was active in the northern part of the New Town. He was admitted a burgess of Edinburgh in 1815 [*Roll of Edinburgh Burgesses 1761–1841*, 164], and died on 23 November 1861, aged 72 [H.M. New Register House, Edinburgh Death Register]. *The Report on the Burgh of Portobello* of 1832 shows that in 1815–16 he had been responsible for the layout of REGENT STREET, WELLINGTON (now MARLBOROUGH) STREET, and STRAITON PLACE, PORTOBELLO. A plan and elevation by him for a small house at HYVOT'S MILL, EDINBURGH 1818, are in S.R.O., RHP 6012.

WALLACE, ROBERT (*c.*1790–1874), was evidently of Scottish origin, but lived and practised in London. He became a pupil of J. H. Good, was admitted to the Royal Academy Schools in 1813 at the age of 23, and exhibited at the Academy between 1809 and 1838. In 1824 his designs for the National Scotch Church in Regent Square, London, were selected in competition, but were eventually turned down in favour of those of William Tite. Wallace published *A Letter* protesting against his treatment. In 1823 he competed unsuccessfully for the new buildings at King's College, Cambridge, and in 1835 for the Houses of Parliament; but in 1837 he won the competition for the new Athenaeum and adjoining public buildings at Derby. This was a comprehensive development comparable to Foulston's at Plymouth. Besides the Athenaeum it included a hotel, a Post Office and a bank, treated as a single architectural composition. The whole scheme cost the then considerable sum of £20,000, and constituted Wallace's most important work. His Romanesque remodelling of the Scotch Church in Crown Court (1842) was praised in the *Builder*, and showed considerable ingenuity.

Wallace retired in about 1849, and went to live at Tunbridge Wells, where he died on 11 February 1874 [*A.P.S.D.*; Principal Probate Registry, Calendar of Probates]. His unexecuted design of 1824 for enlarging the Castle Prison at York in the Romanesque style is described in R.C.H.M., *York* ii, 65. At Blairquhan, Ayrshire, there are unexecuted designs by him for that house, made in 1818. John Blore was a pupil.

AYR, THE COUNTY BUILDINGS, WELLINGTON SQUARE, 1818–20 [*N.S.A.* v, 22].

CLONCAIRD CASTLE, nr. MAYBOLE, AYRSHIRE, entrance gateway and lodge for Robert Cunynghame, 1819 [exhib. at R.A. as 'erecting' 1819].

AUCHANS, AYRSHIRE, designs for a mansion 'proposed to be erected' for C. Monteaulieu Burgess Esq. of Colesfield, exhibited at R.A. 1819, perhaps not built.

ORE PLACE, SUSSEX, designs for a 'residence in the villa style', proposed to be erected for Sir Howard Elphinstone, Bart., exhibited at R.A. 1827.

CROYDON, SURREY, ST. JAMES'S CHURCH, 1827–9, Gothic; chancel 1881 [exhib. at R.A.].

SOUTHWARK, ST. SAVIOUR'S CHURCH (now CATHEDRAL), restored transepts and stone reredos, 1829–30 [W. Taylor, *Annals of St. Mary Overy*, 1833, 50–1, 58–60].

EMBLETON VICARAGE, NORTHUMBERLAND, alterations 1832 [Northumberland C.R.O., Queen Anne's Bounty Papers, Ser. 1, 8].

PENTON MEWSEY RECTORY, HANTS., 1833 [Winchester Diocesan Records].

STOTTESDEN VICARAGE, SALOP., 1835, Gothic [Hereford Diocesan Records, Clergy & Benefice Papers, Box 42].

DERBY, THE ATHENAEUM, ROYAL HOTEL, POST OFFICE and DERBY AND DERBYSHIRE BANK, 1837–9. The bank was altered by James Thomson in 1850 [*Companion to the Almanac*, 1839, 240–3; *Civil Engineer and Architect's Jnl.* ii, 1839, 31–2].

LONDON, remodelled the NATIONAL SCOTCH CHURCH, CROWN COURT, COVENT GARDEN, 1842, Romanesque; enlarged by H. Roberts 1848; rebuilt 1905 [*Builder* i, 1843, 267; *Civil Engineer and Architect's Jnl.* v, 1842, 33].

GLASGOW NECROPOLIS, Gothic monument to his sister, Mrs. Mary Anne Lockhart (d. 1842) [G. Blair, *Sketches of Glasgow Necropolis*, 1857, 57].

WALLACE, WILLIAM (–1631), held the post of Master Mason to the Scottish Crown from 18 April 1617 until his death in October 1631. Shortly before this appointment he was employed as a carver at Edinburgh Castle, where he stood first in the list of masons and was in addition paid for making moulds for the plasterers. He appears to have lived at Musselburgh, for in 1618–19 there are payments for his travelling expenses from there to the royal works then in progress at Linlithgow and Stirling. In 1621 Wallace was admitted a burgess of Edinburgh, and was subsequently Deacon of the masons' lodge there. From 1628 until his death he was engaged in building HERIOT'S HOSPITAL, EDINBURGH. After his death his widow, in petitioning the governors for help for herself and her 'small bairns', drew attention to the 'extraordinar panes and cair my said umquhile spous paid and tuik upone the said wark thir divers yeiris bygane, and at the begynning thairof upone the modell and fram thairof'. The governors agreed to assist her, and asked her to let them have the 'haill muildis and drauchtis' which her husband had left. There can therefore be no doubt that Wallace was the effective designer of this important building, and in particular of its exuberant Anglo-Flemish mannerist decoration. As he was responsible for work of a similar character in the KING'S LODGING at EDINBURGH CASTLE (1615–17) and at LINLITHGOW PALACE, WEST LOTHIAN (the 'new wark' on the north side, 1618–20), it is clear that Wallace was 'a key figure in the popularisation of the Anglo-Flemish style' in Scotland (Dunbar). Though there are several buildings (e.g. Pinkie House, Midlothian, and the original design for Drumlanrig Castle, Dumfriesshire) which have been attributed to Wallace on stylistic grounds, only two others can at present be connected with him by documentary evidence: Wintoun Castle and Moray House, Edinburgh. WINTOUN CASTLE, EAST LOTHIAN, was rebuilt by the 3rd Earl of Wintoun *c.*1620 onwards. After Wallace's death 500 merks were found to be due to his estate 'in acknowledgment of his panes in his Lordship's works'. Though traditional in plan, Wintoun Castle is stylistically akin to Heriot's Hospital and the royal works with which Wallace was associated. £100 was similarly due from 'the Lady Home', i.e. Mary, Dowager Countess of Home, who early in the reign of Charles I had built MORAY HOUSE, CANONGATE, EDINBURGH, perhaps to Wallace's designs.

Wallace's testament shows that he was also responsible for making the monument to John Byres of Coates (d. 1629) in the Greyfriars Cemetery at Edinburgh, for which 500 merks were still owed by Byres's widow. This large monument, plentifully decorated with strapwork, is illustrated by James Brown, *Epitaphs . . . in Greyfriars Churchyard*, Edinburgh 1867, 81. Another monument made by Wallace was that (apparently no longer extant) of his colleague Arthur Hamilton, Master Wright to Charles I. The epitaph was composed by the Principal of Edinburgh College, 'at the desire of William Wallace, Master Mason, Cutter of the Stone' [*The Works of Alexander Pennecuick*, Leith 1815, 366].

[*Builder* ix, 1851, 770; R. S. Mylne, *The Master Masons to the Crown of Scotland*, 1893, 70–8; D. MacGibbon & T. Ross, *The Castellated and Domestic Architecture of Scotland*, 1887–92, ii, 520–9, iv, 144, v, 559–60; J. G. Dunbar, *The Historic Architecture of Scotland*, 1966, 54–5; Alistair Rowan, 'George Heriot's Hospital, Edinburgh', *C. Life*, 6 March 1975; testament in S.R.O., CC 8/8/56, ff. 39v–40v.]

WALLEN, JOHN (1785–1865), was a pupil of D. A. Alexander. Until about 1826 he was in partnership with George Ferry (*q.v.*) in Spitalfields. In 1818 they designed MYDDELTON HOUSE, ENFIELD, MIDDLESEX, for H. C. Bowles [W. Robinson, *History of Enfield* i, 1823, 269–70]. Though largely employed as a quantity surveyor, Wallen also designed several warehouses in the City of London, such as one in Milton Street, Cripplegate, for Messrs. Morrison. His later works included a block of buildings in Cateaton (later

Gresham) Street for Morley & Co., destroyed by bombing in 1940/1; a warehouse in Wood Street for Dent & Co., 1850, and ST. MARK'S HOSPITAL, CITY ROAD, 1852. He repaired the UNITARIAN CHAPEL, SOUTH PLACE, FINSBURY CIRCUS, in 1843, the CHURCH OF ST. ANNE AND ST. AGNES, GRESHAM STREET, in 1847–50, and the GREAT SYNAGOGUE, DUKE'S PLACE, ALDGATE, in 1852. Sir Horace Jones was among his many pupils. He died on 13 February 1865, aged 80 [*A.P.S.D.*]. His elder brother, William Wallen (d. 1853), practised in Finsbury, London, until 1838, when he moved to Huddersfield [*Leeds Intelligencer*, 27 Oct. 1838, *ex inf.* Dr. D. Linstrum]. He designed Nonconformist chapels in NEWBURY, BERKS., 1822 [plans and specifications among Nash, Son & Rowley's papers in Cambs. C.R.O.] and NEWARK, NOTTS., 1822–3 [R.C.H.M. England, *Nonconformist Chapels in Central England*, 1986, 159–60]. His works in Yorkshire included several churches in the lancet style, e.g. FARNLEY, 1843, and OAKWORTH, 1845–6 [D. Linstrum, *West Yorkshire Architects and Architecture*, 1978, 386].

WALLIS, CHARLES, of Dorchester, designed the following churches in Dorset: DORCHESTER, HOLY TRINITY, 1824, Gothic, rebuilt 1876; ALLINGTON, nr. BRIDPORT, with Tuscan portico and cupola, 1826–7; and LANGTON MATRAVERS, 1828, rebuilt 1876 [all I.C.B.S.]. In 1825 he designed BATHS at SWANAGE, now converted into houses called 'Marine Villas' [R.C.H.M., *Dorset* ii (2), 294], and in 1836–8 the UNION WORKHOUSE at CERNE ABBAS [E. Cockburn, 'The Cerne Abbas Workhouse', *Dorset Nat. Hist and Archl. Soc's Procs.* xciv, 1972]. He was presumably the builder-architect of the same name who had previously practised in SWANSEA, where he designed the THEATRE in GOAT STREET, 1806, and the INDEPENDENT CHAPEL, CASTLE STREET, 1814 [*The New Swansea Guide*, 1823], and who was 'of Bristol' in 1832, when he made a design for a tontine hotel to be built in Caswell Bay, nr. Swansea [*The Cambrian*, 23 June, 1832]. C. Wallis of Swansea had previously remodelled PENPONT, BRECONSHIRE, for Penry Williams in 1802–4 [C. Haslam in *C. Life*, 18 June 1992].

WALLIS, JAMES (*c.*1748–1824), was apprenticed to Christopher Staveley of Melton Mowbray in 1761 [P.R.O., IR1/22, p. 203]. He subsequently established himself as a builder and monumental mason in Newark, where he is said to have designed several houses. He died on 6 January 1824, aged 76, and is described as 'Architect' in a monumental inscription now in the north transept of Newark Church. For his work as a monumental mason see Gunnis, *Dictionary of British Sculptors*.

WALLIS, JOHN (–1777), was apprenticed to Samuel Sage of Bristol, carpenter, in 1724 [P.R.O., IR1/48, p. 135]. He was described as 'late an eminent architect of this city' when he died on 30 October 1777. He erected 'Wallis's Wall' along the edge of the great ravine on Durdham Down, and in about 1758 designed and built a large building known as 'The Circular Stables' which was situated between Stokes Croft and Wilder Street. He was one of the principal opponents of James Bridges in the Bristol Bridge controversy, and 'appears to have held considerable influence in civic affairs' [W. Ison, *The Georgian Buildings of Bristol*, 1952, 49].

WALLIS, JOHN, exhibited at the Royal Academy in 1808–10 and again in 1825. His exhibits included the 'elevation of a villa erected for Mr. Robinson' (1808), and the 'elevation for a villa at Ingress near Gravesend for the late Sir H. D. Roebuck, Bt.' (1810). Ingress was the property which afterwards passed to James Harmer, who in the 1830s employed Charles Moreing to design a new house for him known as Ingress Abbey or Park [*Architectural Mag.* i, 1834, 47].

WALLIS, N —, 'architect', was the author of three pattern-books – *A Book of Ornaments in the Palmyrene Taste, containing upwards of Sixty New Designs for Ceilings, Pannels, Pateras and Mouldings*, 1771; *The Complete Modern Joiner, or a Collection of Original Designs in the Present Taste, for Chimney-Pieces and Door-Cases*, 1772; and *The Carpenter's Treasure, a Collection of Designs for Temples, etc., in the Gothic Taste*, 1773. Though both the *Modern Joiner* and the *Carpenter's Treasure* were twice reissued, the standard of Wallis's designs was not high, and they were not among the more influential patternbooks of their time.

WALMSLEY, JOHN (*c.*1765–1812), was the son of Isaac Walmsley, a mason of Liverpool. He had a considerable business as a builder and statuary mason, owning his own quarries of stone and marble at Toxteth Park, nr. Liverpool, and at Kilkenny in Ireland. Picton says the he was 'a man of considerable taste' and records that in 1798 he designed and built handsome new premises for himself in Berry Street. 'The wings were faced with pediments and pilasters, and the centre set back, with an open quadrangle, in which the business was carried on'. He also designed an octagonal Unitarian Chapel in Paradise

Street, built in 1791 (engraving in *Lancashire Illustrated*, 1831). He was the father of Sir Joshua Walmsley, M.P. [J. A. Picton, *Memorials of Liverpool* ii, 1875, 280; information from Mr. S. A. Harris and Mr. Andrew Wells].

WALTER, JAMES, was a minor architect practising in CAMBRIDGE, where he superintended the execution of William Wilkins's new buildings at CORPUS CHRISTI COLLEGE in 1825, enlarged the UNIVERSITY PRESS in 1826–7, added two wards to ADDENBROOKE'S HOSPITAL in 1833, and designed Nos. 21–22 BRIDGE STREET in 1835. He competed unsuccessfully for the Fitzwilliam Museum in 1835 [Willis & Clark, iii, 135, 204; R.C.H.M., *Cambridge*, 24, 57, 312, 337]. The records of the Incorporated Church Building Society show that he repewed BARRINGTON CHURCH, CAMBS, in 1840, MELDRETH CHURCH, CAMBS., in 1841–2, and GREAT WILBRAHAM CHURCH, CAMBS., in 1846. He was still in practice in 1852.

WALTERS, JOHN (1782–1821), was educated at the Grammar School at Bishop's Waltham, Hants., of which two of his relations were successively headmasters. For his architectural education he was indebted to D. A. Alexander. He lived and practised in Fenchurch Buildings, London. He was an able architect whose principal works were the Palladian AUCTION MART, BARTHOLOMEW LANE, LONDON, 1808–9, dem. 1865 [R. Ackermann, *Repository of Arts* vi, 1811, 93–6, and *Beauties of England and Wales* x (3), 1815, 235]; the Perpendicular Gothic ST. PHILIP'S CHAPEL, TURNER STREET, STEPNEY, 1818–20, dem. 1888 [specification in Soane Museum, P.C. 93, description in *Gent's Mag.* 1823 (i), 7, and engraving in Shepherd, *Metropolitan Improvements*, 1831]; and the classical ST. PAUL'S CHURCH, SHADWELL, 1820–1, with a steeple rising from a Greek Revival body [*Gent's Mag.* 1823 (i), 201 and lithograph]. In 1808 the porch of BROWNE'S HOSPITAL, STAMFORD, was rebuilt under Walters' direction [R.C.H.M., *Stamford*, 37]. In 1811 his plans for enlarging LEYTON PARISH CHURCH, ESSEX, were accepted, but not executed [J. Kennedy, *History of Leyton*, 1894, 53–4].

Walters was much interested in naval architecture and invented a diagonal truss with metal braces, of which he published a description in the *Philosophical Magazine* xlv, 1815, 280. 'Enthusiastically devoted to his profession, he pursued with indefatigable ardour the various studies connected with it', and it was to the consequences of over-work that his early death was attributed. He died at Brighton on 4 October 1821, aged 39. He married the sister of Edward I'Anson, senior, and left a son Edward (1808–72) who had a successful practice in Manchester. [*A.P.S.D.*; *Gent's Mag.* 1821 (ii), 374; *Civil Engineer and Architect's Jnl.* x, 1847, 381; *Builder* xxx, 1872, 199.]

WARD, JOHN, was a pupil of James Paine, to whom he was apprenticed in 1767 [P.R.O., Apprenticeship Registers]. He was among the District Surveyors for London appointed under the Act of 1774. As 'John Ward, Architect', he subscribed to George Richardson's *Five Orders*, 1787, and to his *New Designs in Architecture*, 1792.

WARDE, THOMAS, was the surveyor under whose direction THE KING'S HOUSE at LYNDHURST, HANTS., was built as a hunting-lodge for King Charles I in 1634–5 [*History of the King's Works* iv, 1982, 162].

WARDLE, JOHN (–1860), was an architect who played an important part in designing the new streets and other buildings erected in Newcastle-on-Tyne by Thomas Grainger (*q.v.*) in the 1830s. In the *Newcastle Journal* of 3 June 1837, it was stated that the central three ranges on the west side of Grey Street, the western half of Market Street, and Grainger Street were 'entirely designed in Mr. Grainger's office by Mr. Wardle under Mr. Grainger's immediate directions'. In addition Wardle is said in the same article to have designed the south side of Shakespeare Street, and according to a letter published in the *Newcastle Daily Chronicle* in 1868, the Central Exchange 'was not Mr. Dobson's design but Mr. Wardle's assisted by Mr. George Walker'. Wardle appears in fact to have been Grainger's principal architectural designer, but of his earlier or subsequent career nothing is at present known. He died on 11 May 1860, leaving a son of the same name in practice as an architect in Newcastle. [L. Wilkes and Gordon Dodds, *Tyneside Classical*, 1964, 97, 99–101; Principal Probate Registry, Calendar of Probates, 1873.]

WARE, ISAAC (1704–1766), was the son of Isaac Ware, a London cordwainer, and was baptised in the church of St. Giles, Cripplegate, on 6 March 1703/4 [parish register, Guildhall Library MS. 6419/13]. On 1 August 1721 he was apprenticed to Thomas Ripley (*q.v.*) for seven years. Ripley was an official of the Royal Works, and was no doubt instrumental in obtaining for his pupil the post of Clerk Itinerant and Draughtsman (April 1728). Later in the same year Ware was appointed Purveyor, holding the post in trust for the two sons of his predecessor, Robert Hardy. What this meant was that a deduction was made from Ware's salary for the support of the Hardy children. A year later, on 14 October 1729, he was given the Clerkship of the Works at Windsor Castle. In 1733 he moved to the equivalent post at Greenwich. Finally, on 24 May 1736, he was apointed Secretary to the Board, retaining his posts at Purveyor and Clerk Itinerant, but resigning the Clerk's place at Greenwich. For over thirty years Ware was thus a senior official of the Works, though never a member of the Board, which he attended only in the capacity of Secretary.

The recorded facts of Ware's early life throw some doubt on the well-known story that he began life as a chimney-sweeper's boy, and owed his career as an architect to a benevolent gentleman who, walking down Whitehall, found him sketching an elevation of the Banqueting House with a piece of chalk. This unknown benefactor, reputed to have been Lord Burlington himself, is said to have given him 'an excellent education; then sent him to Italy; and upon his return, employed him and introduced him to his friends as an architect'. This story, said to have been told by Ware himself to Roubiliac while sitting for his bust, can hardly be true as it stands. But as a young man Ware did undoubtedly have close connections with Lord Burlington's circle, and his career may well have benefited in some way from Burlington's patronage. In 1727 his name appears among the subscribers to Kent's *Designs of Inigo Jones*, whose publication was sponsored by Burlington, and his own translation of Palladio (1738) is dedicated to the Earl, whose assistance is acknowledged in the preface. The ability to translate Palladio was, moreover, something that Ware could not have learned from Ripley, and references to ancient Roman buildings in Ware's publications suggest that he had visited Italy in person. Burlington's benevolence would hardly have led to the boy's apprenticeship to the unscholarly Ripley, but it might well have made it possible for him to make an all-important visit to Italy as a young man.

By 1733 Ware had obtained (very likely through Burlington's influence) his first recorded commission, the conversion of a London mansion into a hospital, and in 1731 he published a small volume entitled *Designs of Inigo Jones and Others*, containing designs for chimney-pieces, etc., by Inigo Jones, Lord Burlington and William Kent. There was a second edition in 1743. The original drawings are in Sir John Soane's Museum. This was followed in 1735 by *The Plans, Elevations and Sections of Houghton in Norfolk* (the great house designed by Campbell and Kent whose erection had been superintended by Ripley), and in 1738 by the translation of Palladio's *Four Books of Architecture*. In 1741 Ware drew and engraved two views of Rokeby House, Yorks., the seat of Sir Thomas Robinson (*q.v.*), and in 1756–7 he published, in weekly parts, *A Complete Body of Architecture* and a translation of Sirigatti's *La Prattica di Prospettiva* (Venice 1596), entitled *The Practice of Perspective, from the Original Italian of Lorenzo Sirigatti, with the figures engraved by Isaac Ware, Esq.* The *Palladio* was a careful and scholarly work in which 'particular care' was taken 'to preserve the Proportions and Measures from the Original, all the plates being Engraved by the Author's own hand'. It was in fact (and still remains) the best and most reliable English translation of Palladio. The *Complete Body* was commissioned by its publishers (Osborne and Shipton) as a companion to similar treatises on Husbandry and Gardening. It was a comprehensive statement of Georgian architectural theory and practice which sought to strike a balance between adherence to Palladian rules and the exercise of judgement and imagination in design. Like Ware's translation of Sirigatti, it was attacked by Joshua Kirby, 'between whom and Mr. Ware there subsisted a settled animosity'. More serious was the publication in 1759 of Chambers's shorter and more authoritative *Treatise on Civil Architecture*. Nevertheless there was a second edition in 1767, reissued in 1768.

As a practising architect Ware's principal works were Lord Chesterfield's town house in South Audley Street, the former Town Hall at Oxford, and a small mumber of country houses listed below. Like many other Georgian architects he engaged in speculative building. In 1738 he was involved in the development of Long Alley on the north side of the Strand, and in 1736–7 of some property in Kensington [*Survey of London* xxxvi, 264; xxxvii, 39]. In 1739 he was co-lessee with John Phillips (*q.v.*) of No. 23 Bruton Street, a house subsequently occupied by the Mr. Pitt whose chimney-piece is illustrated in plate 90 of the *Complete Body*; and other houses in this area can probably be attributed to him on the strength of chimney-pieces designed for Earl Poulett and Admiral Byng, who occupied adjoining houses on the west side of Berkeley Square.

In 1742 Ware purchased a small estate at Westbourne Green, Paddington, upon which he built himself a house that was later occupied by S. P. Cockerell. It is said to have been built partly of materials taken from the old house in South Audley Street which Ware rebuilt for Lord Chesterfield in 1748–9. In 1764 he sold Westbourne House to Sir William Yorke, and moved to Frognall Hall, Hampstead, where he died on 6 January 1766. He was buried in the chancel of the old church at Paddington. According to J. T. Smith he also occupied the house on the west side of Bloomsbury Square which was afterwards the house of Isaac Disraeli, but W. L. Rutton showed that there is no evidence to support Smith's statement. Park, in his *Topography of Hampstead*, states erroneously that Ware's death occurred 'at his house in Kensington Gravel Pits' and that he was in depressed circumstances at the time. There is no suggestion that this was the case in Ware's will (P.C.C. 41 TYNDALE), but it is true that after his death his younger daughter Mary received some financial assistance from the Royal Academy [W. T. Whitley, *Artists and their Friends in England* i, 1928, 318]. Ware married twice. His first wife was Elizabeth, the daughter of James Richards, Master Carver in the Office of Works. By her he had a son, Walter James Ware. By his second wife Mary Bolton he had two daughters. A portrait of Ware by Andrea Soldi is in the R.I.B.A. Collection. He is depicted with a drawing of Wrotham Park, the most important of his country houses. A bust of Ware by Roubiliac, formerly at Buckland House, Berks., is now in the National Portrait Gallery. Another (probably the primary) version of this bust, formerly at Ripley Castle, Yorks., is in the Detroit Institute of Arts, U.S.A.

Ware was a Warden of the Carpenters' Company in 1761–2 and served as Master in 1763. The Company's records show that the following were his apprentices: George Shakespear (*q.v.*) (1739), Thomas (son of Leonard) Phillips (1745), Abraham Roumieu (*q.v.*) (1748), Thomas Fulling (1755) and William Fisum (1763). Charles Cameron (*q.v.*) was also his pupil.

Although Ware was probably a protégé and certainly an associate of Lord Burlington, his conformity to Palladian orthodoxy was by no means complete, Externally his houses were, like his Mansion House design of 1735 (S. Perks, *The Mansion House*, Cambridge 1922, pls. 33–6), conformist enough, but Chesterfield House contained several rooms decorated in an elaborate French rococo style, and Ware illustrated a ceiling of this sort in the *Complete Body* (pls. 81–2). He is known, moreover, to have been a prominent member of the St. Martin's Lane Academy, where Hogarth, Roubiliac, Hayman and others were busy undermining the Palladian establishment to which Ware nominally belonged. The extent of Ware's deviation from strict Palladian principle is apparent from a careful reading of the *Complete Body*, which allows a considerable degree of latitude in the interpretation of the Palladian canon. Ware was, therefore, more than a mere disciple of Lord Burlington. Having thoroughly assimilated Palladian theory, he looked beyond it, and in the 1740s himself helped to dissolve the dictatorship of taste that Burlington imposed in the 1720s.

[*A.P.S.D.*; *D.N.B.*; records of the Carpenters' Company in Guildhall Library; Walpole Soc., *Vertue Note Books* vi, 170; J. T. Smith, *Nollekens and his Times* ii, 1828, 206–8; W. L. Rutton, 'Bloomsbury Square: Isaac Ware and Isaac D'Israeli, Residents', *Home Counties Mag.* iv, 1902; B. H. Johnson, *Berkeley Square to Bond Street*, 1952, 178–80; H. M. Colvin, 'Roubiliac's Bust of Isaac Ware', *Burlington Mag.* May 1955, 151; Mark Girouard, 'English Art and the Rococo', *C. Life*, 13 Jan. 1966; R. Wittkower, *Palladio and English Palladianism*, 1974, 88–9; Eileen Harris, *British Architectural Books and Writers 1556–1785*, 1990, 468–76; information from Mr. Frank Kelsall and Mr. Roger White.]

AUTHENTICATED WORKS

LONDON, conversion of Lanesborough House into ST. GEORGE'S HOSPITAL, HYDE PARK CORNER, 1733; rebuilt by W. Wilkins 1828–9 [B.M., Crace Views, portfolio x, 29, engraving signed by Ware as architect].

CHICKSANDS PRIORY, BEDS., remodelled S. and E. ranges for Sir Danvers Osborn, Bart., *c.*1740–50, Gothic; further altered by J. Wyatt 1813–14 [Lysons, *Magna Britannia* i, 1806, 68; I. D. Parry, *Select Illustrations of Bedfordshire*, 1827, 116; Emily Osborn, *Political and Social Letters of a Lady of the Eighteenth Century*, 1890, 49, 95, where the letter referring to Ware's engagement at Chicksands should be dated 1739 rather than 1733] (W. Watts, *Seats of the Nobility and Gentry*, engraving dated 1781).

BRISTOL, CLIFTON HILL HOUSE, for Paul Fisher, 1746–50 [Ware, *Complete Body*, pl. 40; W. Ison, *The Georgian Buildings of Bristol*, 1952, 177–81].

LONDON, CHESTERFIELD HOUSE, SOUTH AUDLEY STREET, for 4th Earl of Chesterfield, 1748–9; dem. 1937; staircase balustrade now in Metropolitan Museum, New York [Ware, *Complete Body*, pls. 60, 61, 81–3, 85, 88; *Vitruvius Britannicus* iv, pl. 46; original drawings in Soane Museum, xliii, 2] (*C. Life*, 25 Feb., 4 March 1922; R. White, 'Isaac Ware and Chesterfield House' in *The*

Rococo in England, ed. C. Hind, Victoria & Albert Museum, 1986).

LONDON, WESTBOURNE HOUSE, WESTBOURNE GREEN, PADDINGTON, for himself, *c.*1750; dem. 1846 (plan by C. R. Cockerell in *Arch. Hist.* xiv, 1971, fig. 14b, views in B.M., Crace Views, portfolio xxx, 23–4).

OXFORD, THE TOWN HALL, 1751–2; dem. 1893 [Ware, *Complete Body*, pl. 48; what appear to be Ware's original drawings are in B.L., *King's Maps* xxxiv, 32 *b,c*]. (J. Ingram, *Memorials of Oxford* iii, 1837, plate.)

WROTHAM PARK, MIDDLESEX, for Admiral John Byng, 1754; wings raised 1811 [Ware, *Complete Body*, pls. 52–3; *Vitruvius Britannicus* v, pls. 45–6] (*C. Life*, 9, 23 Nov. 1918).

EYTHROP HOUSE, BUCKS., stables and garden buildings for Sir William Stanhope, *c.*1750; house and stables dem. 1810–11; Gothic eye-catcher known as 'Winchendon Castle' dem. 1916 [Ware, *Complete Body*, pls. 104, 105, 107; H. M. Colvin, 'Eythrop House and its Demolition in 1810–11', *Records of Bucks.* xvii, 1964].

AMISFIELD HOUSE, EAST LOTHIAN, SCOTLAND, for Francis Charteris, 1756–9; wings added by J. Henderson 1785; dem. *c.*1928 [*Ware, Complete Body*, pls. 39, 45] (engraving by Henderson in *Archaeologia Scotica*, i, 1792, 46; photo in J. Small, *Castles and Mansions of the Lothians* i, 1883).

DANBURY PLACE, ESSEX, chimney-piece for Thomas Ffytche; house rebuilt 1832 [Ware, *Complete Body*, pl. 94].

CALDECOTE, nr. BIGGLESWADE, BEDS., farmhouse [Ware, *Complete Body*, pl. 36].

LONDON, houses in which Ware illustrates chimney-pieces, etc., presumably designed by himself: James Lumley in SOUTH AUDLEY STREET (pl. 86); Mr. Pitt at 23 BRUTON STREET (pl. 90); John de Pesters in HANOVER SQUARE (pl. 91); Henry Fox, afterwards Lord Holland, in ALBEMARLE STREET (pl. 95); William Bristow in DOVER STREET (pl. 95); Admiral John Byng at 41 BERKELEY SQUARE (pl. 96); 2nd Earl Poulett at 40 BERKELEY SQUARE (pl. 65); Richard Chandler at 3 BURLINGTON GARDENS (pl. 69); Sir William Stanhope in DOVER STREET (staircase, pl. 74); and 1st Earl Cornwallis in DOVER STREET (pl. 7 b).

DOUBTFUL AND ATTRIBUTED WORKS

BELVEDERE HOUSE, nr. ERITH, KENT, addition of Great Room for Sampson Gideon (d. 1762), after 1751; dem. 1960 [stylistic attribution, based on the combination of Palladian exterior and rococo interior] (*London and its Environs Described*, R. & J. Dodsley, i, 1761, 270, engraving).

BLACKHEATH, KENT, RANGER'S (formerly CHESTERFIELD) HOUSE, addition of gallery for 4th Earl of Chesterfield, 1749–51 [Ware was simultaneously building Chesterfield House, London, for the same nobleman].

CARNSALLOCH, KIRKMAHOE, DUMFRIESSHIRE, for Alexander Johnstone, *c.*1754 [in his *Complete Body*, pls. 54–5, Ware illustrates a 'House built for Alexander Johnston, Esq., in Scotland'. The design does not correspond to any house known to have been built in Scotland at this date, but Alexander Johnstone was the builder of Carnsalloch, a Palladian mansion with features for which Ware might well have been responsible] (*Scottish Field*, April 1957).

FOOTS CRAY PLACE, KENT, is said to have been designed by Ware for Bourchier Cleeve, *c.*1754, in a 'Chronological Lists of Works of Architects who died in the 18th and 19th centuries', published by W. H. Leeds in *Civil Engineer and Architect's Jnl.*, 1840. There seems to be no evidence that this Palladian villa was designed by Ware, but the attribution is acceptable on stylistic grounds. Drawings of the house in a copy of Ware's *Palladio* in the British Library do not appear to be by Ware. The house was dem. after a fire in 1949 (*Vitruvius Britannicus* iv, pls. 8–10).

WARE, SAMUEL (1781–1860), was the son of a prosperous London leather-merchant. He was articled to James Carr (*q.v.*), became a student at the Royal Academy in 1800, and exhibited there between 1799 and 1814. According to James Elmes he was 'architect to many excellent buildings in Ireland' and was responsible for 'the splendid alterations at Chatsworth, at Northumberland House, and other places for the Dukes of Devonshire and Northumberland'. He is known to have been employed at Chatsworth in 1813, and he appears to have designed the Conservatory at CHISWICK HOUSE, MIDDLESEX, for the 6th Duke of Devonshire in 1812–13 [Donald Insall in *C. Life*, 1 Sept. 1983]. In 1814 he exhibited at the Academy a 'view of Lismore Castle, Ireland, a seat of the Duke of Devonshire' (then recently altered and repaired by William Atkinson, *q.v.*). For Lord George Cavendish he altered the interior of BURLINGTON HOUSE, PICCADILLY, between 1815 and 1818, and remodelled the north elevation [*Survey of London* xxxii, 407–12 and plates]. At the same time he designed the BURLINGTON ARCADE, PICCADILLY, containing some seventy shops. The Piccadilly entrance was rebuilt in 1911 to the designs of Beresford Pite, but Ware's original elevation is illustrated in *Metropolitan Improvements*, 1831 [*Survey of London* xxxii, chap. xxiv]. For the 3rd Duke of Northumberland he is said to have carried out alterations to NORTHUMBERLAND HOUSE, STRAND (dem. 1874), and for the 4th Duke of Portland (whose London estate he managed) he designed (*c*.1825) stabling in the rear of HARCOURT HOUSE, CAVENDISH SQUARE (dem. 1906). He also designed the MIDDLESEX HOUSE OF DETENTION at CLERKENWELL, 1816–18, rebuilt by William Moseley, 1845–6 [Parliamentary Papers, *Report on the Police of the Metropolis*, 5 June 1818, 423] and the RECTORY of HOLY TRINITY AND ST. MARY, GUILDFORD, SURREY, 1826 [Surrey Record Office, Q.A.B. Records 1056/869].

Ware published *Remarks on Theatres, and on the propriety of vaulting them with brick and stone, with an Appendix on the construction of Gothic vaulting*, 1809, 1822; a *Treatise on the Properties of Arches*, 1809; and *Tracts on Vaults and Bridges*, 1822. He was elected a Fellow of the Society of Antiquaries in 1816, and contributed papers to *Archaeologia*, e.g. on vaults (xvii, 1814). His collection of drawings and engravings of bridges, British and foreign, is in the British Library (1802 *c*.17, 2 vols).

Ware was a good businessman, and by industry and skilful investment accumulated a large fortune. By the 1840s, when he retired, he had a town house in Portland Place and a country seat at Hendon Hall in Middlesex (which he appears largely to have rebuilt). His practice was continued by his nephew C. N. Cumberlege, to whom he bequeathed the bulk of his property when he died in December 1860. Henry Baker, F.R.I.B.A., was a pupil.

[*A.P.S.D.*; James Elmes, *Metropolitan Improvements*, 1831, 141; *Builder* i, 1843, 24, xxiii, 1865, 372, xxviii, 1870, 1024; W. J. Pinks, *History of Clerkenwell*, 1881, 268; William Keane, *The Beauties of Middlesex*, 1850, 237–8; Sotheby & Co., *Catalogue of MSS.*, 6 June 1966, lot 2294.]

WARREN, HUGH (–1728), was Surveyor of Chelsea Hospital and of the Horse Guards building in Whitehall from 1710 until his death in 1728. In 1719 he was concerned in the building of the BURLINGTON SCHOOL FOR GIRLS IN BOYLE STREET, WESTMINSTER [*Survey of London* xxxii, 541].

WATKINS, GRIFFITH (*c*.1745–1822), was a builder and architect of Haverfordwest. In the latter capacity he was concerned in the addition of aisles to STEYNTON CHURCH, nr. MILFORD HAVEN, in 1799 [Haverfordwest Record Office, HPR 3/55], and in 1809–10 he designed a house (dem.) for Lord Milford at TENBY, PEMBS. [N.L.W., Picton Castle, no. 1822]. In 1783 he subscribed to William Thomas's *Original Designs in Architecture* [information from Mr. Thomas Lloyd, to whom both references are due].

WATSON, CHARLES (*c*.1770–1836), practised in Yorkshire from *c*.1790, first in Wakefield and later in York. He was probably the son of John Watson (d. 1771) and the grandson of John Watson (d. 1757), who both lived in Wakefield and were successively surveyors of bridges to the West Riding of Yorkshire from 1743 onwards.[1] Architectural activity by Charles Watson's father or grandfather included making survey plans of KIRKLEES HALL, YORKS. (W.R.), 'for Mr. Paine's perusal' in 1753–4 [D. Nortcliffe in *Halifax Antiqn. Soc's Trans*, 1982]; designing RETFORD TOWN HALL, NOTTS., 1755–6; dem. 1866 [J. S. Piercy, *History of Retford*, Retford 1828, 144]; designing the Foundling Hospital (later Quaker) SCHOOL at ACKWORTH, YORKS. (W.R.), in 1759–63 [H. Thompson, *Ackworth School*, 1879, 2–3]; and altering HORSFORTH HALL, YORKS. (W.R.) (dem.) for John Stanhope in 1767 [Bradford Central Library, Spencer-Stanhope papers, 952/37]. Among the plans for Campsall House, Yorks. (W.R.), in the R.I.B.A. Collection there is one 'drawn by John Watson Junr.' in 1752, and another described as 'Mr. Paine's Plan, as proposed to be altered per Mr. Watson 1752'.

Charles Watson was a pupil and from 1792 to 1800 the partner of William Lindley of Doncaster (*q.v.*). He lived in Wakefield until 1807, when he moved to York, perhaps with the idea of succeeding to John Carr's practice. Here from 1813 to 1831 he was in partnership with J. P. Pritchett (*q.v.*). In about 1825 Watson's son William joined the partnership, which then became 'Watson, Pritchett and Watson', but William died in 1829 in his 25th year, and in 1831 Charles retired, dying five years later at the age of 66.

During the first decade of the nineteenth century Watson was the leading architect in Yorkshire. His two partnerships make it difficult to isolate his personal style, but the Court Houses at Beverley, Wakefield, Pontefract and Sheffield were his independent work, and show him as a competent purveyor of public buildings in the Grecian style of the period.

[1] The West Riding Quarter Sessions Records show that John Watson the elder was appointed jointly with Robert Carr in 1743. In 1757 John Watson, junior, succeeded his late father, and in 1761 Robert Carr (d. 1760) was replaced by his son John. When John Watson died in 1771 his place was taken by J. Billington.

All his Gothic buildings were designed in partnership with Pritchett.

[R.C.H.M., *York* iii, 64; *Yorkshire Gazette*, 5 Dec. 1829, 3 Dec. 1836; D. Linstrum, *West Yorkshire Architects and Architecture*, 1978, 386; P.R.O., IR1/33, p. 198, apprenticeship to Lindley, 1788; information from Mr. Angus Taylor.]

†WAKEFIELD, YORKS. (W.R.), ST. JOHN'S CHURCH, 1791–5 [engraving by Malton in Soane Museum, Drawer lix, inscribed 'Lindley & Watson Archts.'].

†WATH-UPON-DEARNE VICARAGE, YORKS. (W.R.), 1793 [Borthwick Institute, York, MGA 1793/1].

†WAKEFIELD, YORKS. (W.R.), ALL SAINTS CHURCH (now Cathedral), surveyed spire 1796 [J. W. Walker, *Wakefield*, 1939, 260].

SHEFFIELD, YORKS. (W.R.), ST. PETER'S CHURCH (now Cathedral), alterations 1802 onwards [R. E. Leader, *Surveyors and Architects of the Past in Sheffield*, 1903, 31].

BEVERLEY, YORKS. (E.R.), THE COURT HOUSE and GAOL, 1804–14 [G. Poulson, *Beverlac* i, 1829, 426].

WILLOW HALL, nr. HALIFAX, YORKS. (W.R.), for Mr. Dyson, 1805 [letter from Watson in archives at Nostell Priory, C 3/2/4/5].

OUSLETHWAITE HALL, nr. BARNSLEY, YORKS. (W.R.), farm buildings for William Elmhirst, 1805 [drawing in Sheffield Archives, EM 1753].

WOOLLEY HALL, YORKS. (W.R.), repairs and alterations after fire for Godfrey Wentworth, 1807; probably designed Lodge and Gateway, 1814 [G. Markham, *Woolley Hall*, Wakefield 1979, 40, 45].

WAKEFIELD, YORKS. (W.R.), THE COURT HOUSE, 1807–10; enlarged 1849–50 [J. W. Walker, *Wakefield*, 1939, 555].

PONTEFRACT, YORKS. (W.R.), THE COURT HOUSE, 1807–8 [West Riding Quarter Sessions Order Book 1807–9, p. 51].

SHEFFIELD, YORKS. (W.R.), THE TOWN HALL (later Court House), 1807–8 [J. D. Leader, *Burgery of Sheffield*, 1897, 405, 411, 413, 418].

CASTLEFORD RECTORY, YORKS. (W.R.), repairs, 1810 [Borthwick Institute, York, MGA 1810/1].

HOLLIN HALL, YORKS. (W.R.), remodelled for Richard Wood, 1810–13 [Giles Worsley in *C. Life*, 14 July 1988].

PARLINGTON HALL, YORKS. (W.R.), alterations for R. O. Gascoigne, 1811–12; dem. [Angus Taylor in *Leeds Arts Calendar*, No. 77, 1975, 25].

*BURGHWALLIS RECTORY, YORKS. (W.R.), rebuilt 1815 [Borthwick Institute, York, MGA 1815/2].

**attributed*: RISE PARK, YORKS. (E.R.), for Richard Bethell, 1815–20 [design for Doric lodge at Rise in album formerly at Stoneleigh Park, Warwicks., signed 'Watson & Pritchett 1818'].

*YORK, LENDAL INDEPENDENT CHAPEL, 1816; now a department store [*A.P.S.D.*; *s.v.* 'Pritchett'].

*NORTON CHURCH, YORKS. (E.R.), rebuilt 1816; dem. 1899; classical (T-shaped plan) [Borthwick Institute, York, Fac. 1814/2].

*WAKEFIELD, THE WEST RIDING LUNATIC ASYLUM, 1816–18 [see p. 785].

*YORK, THE FRIENDS' MEETING HOUSE, 1816–19 [plans, etc., in W. Alexander, *Observations on the Construction of Meeting Houses*, York 1820].

*BRAFFERTON VICARAGE, YORKS. (N.R.), enlarged 1818 [Borthwick Institute, York, MGA 1818/3].

*SLEDMERE HOUSE, YORKS. (E.R.), gates to main road for Sir Mark Sykes, Bart., 1818 [drawings at Sledmere].

*COPGROVE HALL, YORKS. (W.R.), remodelled for Thomas Duncombe, *c.*1820 [Doncaster Archives, DZ Ros. p. 87, *ex inf.* Mr. Angus Taylor].

*BISHOP BURTON CHURCH, YORKS. (E.R.), rebuilt nave 1820; altered 1864–5 [see p. 785].

*WAKEFIELD, YORKS. (W.R.), library etc. (now Museum), 1820–1 [Yorkshire Archl. Soc. MS. 1142, *ex inf.* Dr. D. Linstrum].

*LEEDS, HANOVER SQUARE, layout, 1823 [see p. 786].

*HUDDERSFIELD, YORKS. (W.R.), THE RAMSDEN STREET NONCONFORMIST CHAPEL, 1824; dem. 1936 [see p. 785].

*SALTMARSHE HALL, YORKS. (E.R.), for Philip Saltmarshe, 1825–8 [drawings in the possession of Mr. J. E. Scott of Huyton, 1971].

*GREASBROUGH CHURCH, YORKS. (W.R.), rebuilt 1826–8, Gothic [Port, 166–7].

*SHEFFIELD, NETHER CHAPEL (INDEPENDENT), 1827; altered 1878 [R. E. Leader, *Surveyors and Architects of the Past in Sheffield*, 1903].

*YORK, THE DEANERY, 1827–31, Gothic; dem. 1938 [see p. 786].

*YORK, ASSEMBLY ROOMS, new facade and portico, 1828 [*A.P.S.D.*, *s.v.* 'Pritchett'].

*LOTHERTON HALL, YORKS. (W.R.), alterations, probably including drawing-room, for R. O. Gascoigne, *c.*1828 [Angus Taylor in *Leeds Arts Calendar*, No. 77, 1975, 28].

*NOSTELL PRIORY, YORKS. (W.R.), north and east sides of stable block for C. W. Winn, 1828–9, adopting Robert Adam's design

† Designed in partnership with William Lindley.
* Designed in partnership with J. P. Pritchett.

(1776) for the cupola [drawings at Nostell].

*YORK, THE SAVINGS BANK, ST. HELEN'S SQUARE, 1829–30 [W. Camidge, *History of the York Savings Bank*, 1886, 49–51].

*NETHER HOYLAND CHURCH, YORKS. (W.R.), 1830, Gothic [Port, 168–9; contract drawings in R.I.B.A.D.].

*YORK, ST. PETER'S SCHOOL (now Song School), MINSTER YARD, 1830–3, Tudor Gothic [*A.P.S.D.*, *s.v.* 'Pritchett'].

WATSON, JOHN (–1707), is described as 'architect of Glashampton' on his tombstone in Astley Church, Worcs. GLASHAMPTON HOUSE, ASTLEY, was built by a member of the Winford family (probably Thomas Cookes Winford) *c.*1705, and was destroyed by fire in 1810. An engraving in Nash's *History of Worcestershire* shows a large rectangular mansion of the sort associated with the Smiths of Warwick. Watson died intestate on 26 October 1707 and was buried at Astley on 28 October [P.C.C., Admon. Act Book 1707; Astley Parish Register].

It is possible, but by no means certain, that this John Watson is to be identified with an architect or architects of this surname who were employed at WROXTON ABBEY, OXON., in 1680–5 and at MELBURY HOUSE, DORSET, in 1692. A portrait inscribed 'Mr. Watson, architect to Thos. Strangways senr. esqr. who enlarged & adorned this house 1692' is preserved at Melbury. Horace Walpole refers to these alterations in his *Journal of Visits to Country Seats* (Walpole Soc. xvi, 47), but ascribes them to 'Thomas Sutton, styling himself Architect to Thomas Strangways esq.' – a statement which must have been due to a faulty recollection of the inscription on Watson's portrait. The house is described in R.C.H.M., *Dorset* i, 164–7 and Watson's employment as architect is confirmed by references to 'Mr. Watson' in the building accounts (Dorset C.R.O., D/FSI, Box 190).

The alterations at Wroxton were due to Francis North, 1st Lord Guilford (d. 1685). Roger North (*q.v.*) wrote that his brother 'had a plain man to put out his work, and see to the executory part, one Watson, very fitt for the business, . . . but I took upon me the honor of being prime architect' [B.L., Add. MS. 32510, ff. 137–9; cf. *V.C.H. Oxon.* ix, 172–3.]

WATSON, JOHN (–1771), *see* WATSON, CHARLES.

WATSON, JOHN BURGES (1803–1881), was the son of Joseph Burges Watson of Surbiton Hill House, nr. Kingston, Surrey. He was a pupil of William Atkinson, became a student at the Royal Academy Schools in 1823 and gained medals at the Society of Arts in 1824 for a perspective drawing of a crane and for a design for houses in Grecian architecture. In 1824 he also obtained a premium in public competition for his design for a cast-iron bridge at Kingston-on-Thames, Surrey, of which he published a perspective view. He exhibited at the Royal Academy from 1824 to 1838, and competed for the Houses of Parliament (1835), the Royal Berkshire Infirmary (1837), and the Surrey Lunatic Asylum (1839). He was for forty years surveyor to the Pentonville Estate. Having considerable knowledge of trees, he also practised as a landscape-gardener. T. W. Fletcher, who was his pupil in the 1850s, describes him as a bald, florid man with a fondness for music and a fund of smutty stories. He was three times Master of the Farriers' Company. He died at Carondolet, Hornsey, on 10 April 1881, aged 78. One of his sons, Thomas Henry Watson, also practised as an architect. [*A.P.S.D.*; *The Architect's, Engineer's and Building Trades' Directory*, 1868, 142; 'The Auto-biography of Thomas Wayland Fletcher', ed. M. H. Port, *East London Papers* xi, 1968, 27.]

CHURCHES, PARSONAGES AND SCHOOLS

STAINES CHURCH, MIDDLESEX, rebuilt 1828–9, Gothic; chancel extended 1885 [*Gent's Mag.* 1828 (ii), 393, with engraving].

EAST BEDFONT CHURCH, MIDDLESEX, added north transept, 1828–9 [I.C.B.S.].

NORTON VICARAGE, HERTS., for the Revd. Joseph Burges Watson, 1831 [exhib. at R.A. 1831].

HOLMWOOD CHURCH, SURREY, 1837–8, Norman; rebuilt at various dates [*Architectural Mag.* iv, 499]; also PARSONAGE, 1839 [Surrey County Record Office, 1079/3].

HOOK CHURCH, SURREY, 1837–8, Gothic; rebuilt 1881 [*Architectural Mag.* iv, 499; exhib. at R.A. 1838]; also PARSONAGE [*The Architect's . . . Directory*].

HAM PARSONAGE, SURREY, 1838–9 [Surrey County Record Office, 1079/1].

MESSING CHURCH, ESSEX, enlarged by addition of transepts, 1840 [I.C.B.S.].

LAYER BRETON RECTORY, ESSEX, *c.*1840 [*The Architect's . . . Directory*].

LAPLEY VICARAGE, STAFFS., *c.*1840 [*The Architect's . . . Directory*].

BRANSGORE PARSONAGE, HANTS., 1843–4 [*The Architect's . . . Directory*].

SCHOOLS at HAM, KINGSTON and SYDENHAM [*The Architect's . . . Directory*].

* Designed in partnership with J. P. Pritchett.

OTHER WORKS

LONDON, houses in HYDE PARK GARDENS and SUSSEX SQUARE, PADDINGTON, *c.*1837 onwards [*The Architect's . . . Directory*].

LONDON, No. 21 PARK LANE, alterations for 2nd Marquess of Breadalbane; dem. 1876–7 [*The Architect's . . . Directory*].

LONDON, ST. JAMES'S PARK, cottage for the Ornithological Society, 1840 [*A.P.S.D.*].

LONDON, THE NATIONAL PROVINCIAL BANK, No. 112 BISHOPSGATE, added Greek Revival lodges, *c.*1840; rebuilt 1864 [*A.P.S.D.*].

ASHLEY PARK, SURREY, alterations for Sir Henry Fletcher, Bart.; dem. *c.*1925 [*The Architect's . . . Directory*].

RAYMEAD, COOKHAM, BERKS., additions for Albert Ricardo, 1858 [*A.P.S.D.*].

WATT, JAMES (–1832), was an architect practising in Glasgow, where he was a member of the Philosophical and Dilettante Societies [T. Gildard, 'An Old Glasgow Architect on Some Older Ones', *Trans. Royal Philosophical Soc. of Glasgow* xxvi, 1895, 121]. He died on 12 Sept. 1832 [*Glasgow Courier*, 1832, *ex inf.* Prof. J. Stevens Curl].

WEBB, JOHN (1611–1672), was born in London in 1611, and educated at Merchant Taylors' School, where he remained three years (1625–8). He came of a Somerset family, but nothing is known of his parentage, or of the circumstances in which, in 1628, he became a pupil of Inigo Jones. According to his own statement, made in 1660, he was 'brought up by his Unckle Mr. Inigo Jones upon his late Maiestyes command in the study of Architecture, as well that wch relates to building as for masques Tryumphs and the like'. Webb was Jones's 'nephew' by marriage, his wife, Anne Jones, being a 'near relation' (apparently a second cousin) of Inigo. As Jones's pupil, Webb received a thorough training in classical architecture based on a careful study of the works of Serlio, Palladio, Scamozzi and other Italian masters. There is no evidence that he ever visited Italy,[1] but his drawings show 'a high degree of technical competence' and 'an exact knowledge of Italian detail'. His earliest datable drawings belong to the 1630s, when he was assisting Jones in the repair of St. Paul's Cathedral and the building of the Barber-Surgeons' Theatre. Drawings for a lodge or villa at Hale in Hampshire and for a stable for a Mr. Fetherstone (probably at Hassenbrook in Essex), both dated 1638, may represent Webb's first wholly independent commissions, though neither is known to have been carried out. It was probably at this period too that under Jones's supervision he made the first of the many surviving drawings for a new Whitehall Palace in the Palladian style already exemplified by the Banqueting House; and in 1638, again under Jones's direction, he made designs of similar character for a proposed extension of Somerset House for the Queen.

With the outbreak of the Civil War in 1642 these projects had to be laid aside together with the masques to whose production Jones and his pupil had devoted so much of their time. Jones himself went north with the King, leaving Webb as his deputy in charge of the Royal Works until in 1643 they were both displaced by Edward Carter (*q.v.*). Thus deprived of his official employment, Webb appears to have acted as a royal agent, for, according to his own account, he 'sent to the King at Oxford the designs of all the fortifications about London, their proportions, the number of guns mounted on them, how many soldiers would man them, how they might be attempted and carried and all particulars relating thereto in writing'. Moreover, he carried £500 to the King 'sew'd up in his waistcoat through all the enemy's quarters unto Beverley in Yorkshire, which being afterwards discovered, Mr. Webb was plundered to the purpose, and a long time kept in prison being close prisoner for a month'. But apart from this confinement, Webb appears to have suffered little for his royalist sympathies, and he was even allowed to 'attend his Majesty . . . at Hampton Court and at the Isle of Wight, where he received his majesty's command to design a palace for Whitehall,[1] which he did until his majesty's unfortunate calamity caused him to desist'. The Kings' death in 1649 did not, however, prevent Webb from practising as an architect, for during that year he was engaged in reconstructing the interior of Wilton House for the Earl of Pembroke after a fire, and in designing a proposed new house for him in the Strand. When Jones made his will in 1650 he named Webb as his executor, and his 'kinswoman Anne Jones', Webb's wife, was his principal legatee.

Jones's death in 1652 left his pupil almost without a rival in the field of architectural design, and during the next few years 'Inigo Jones's man' had no lack of employment. He was working for the Earl of Rutland at Belvoir, for the Earl of Peterborough at

[1] He may, however, have visited France, for in July 1656 the Protector granted a warrant for a John Webb (not necessarily the architect) to have a pass to go to that country (*Cal. State Papers Domestic 1656–7*, 58).

[1] This refers to the 'taken' design of 1647 which Webb submitted to Charles II at the Restoration.

Drayton, for Lord Dacre at Chevening in Kent, and for Sir Justinian Isham at Lamport in Northants. The fortunate survival of his letters to the last show, moreover, that he was still living in Scotland Yard, where the officers of the Works had their quarters,[1] though there appears to be no evidence that he was in official employment.[2] For this, he must wait for the restoration of King Charles II, when, as Jones's pupil and deputy, he hoped to take his rightful place as Surveyor of His Majesty's Works. With that object, he petitioned the King in May 1660. But there were others – including Hugh May and John Denham – who claimed the post, and it was in vain that Webb represented that he 'was by the especiall command of y^{r} Maties Royall Father of ever blessed memory, brought up by Inigo Jones Esqr., Y^{r} Maties late Surveyor of the Works in ye study of Architecture, for enabling him to do y^{or} Royall Father and y^{r} Matie service in ye said office', that there were arrears of salary due to him, both on his own account and as Jones's executor, that 'Mr. Denham may possibly, as most gentry in England at this day, have some knowledge in the Theory of Architecture; but nothing of ye practique soe that he must of necessity have another at his Maties charges to doe his business; whereas Mr. Webb himself designes, orders, and directs . . . without any other man's assistance. His Matie may please to grant some other place more proper for Mr. Denham's abilityes and confirme unto Mr. Webb the Surveyor's place wherein he hath consumed 30 years study, there being scarce any of the greate Nobility or eminent gentry of England but he hath done service for in matter of building, ordering of medalls, statues and the like.' Denham was appointed Surveyor in June 1660, and Webb had to content himself with a promise of the reversion of the surveyorship, for which he obtained a warrant in June 1660. But even this proved abortive, for Denham, fearing that it would prevent him from selling his place at some future date, stopped it from passing the Great Seal.[1]

But Webb's services were too valuable to be dispensed with altogether and in 1663 he was recalled in order to design the King Charles block at Greenwich Palace, to superintend the fortification of Woolwich Dockyard, and to initiate others in the mysteries of 'the Scenicall Art, which to others than himself was before muche unknowne'. It was, in fact, Webb who designed the setting for *The Tragedy of Mustapha*, given by D'Avenant's company at Whitehall in October 1666, and W. Grant Keith has shown how Webb 'carried on the traditions of stagecraft of Inigo Jones, as it had been left to him to carry on the traditions of his architecture'. In November 1666 he was formally placed in charge of the works at Greenwich, 'to execute, act and proceed there, according to your best skill and judgment in Architecture, as our Surveyor Assistant unto Sir John Denham'. The salary was £200 a year, with travelling expenses, and was to be paid as from January 1664. But even this belated remuneration was allowed to fall into arrears, and in 1669, when Denham lay dying, a new rival appeared in the person of Dr. Christopher Wren. Webb now made a last effort to gain office, reminding the King of his past services, of his promised reversion of the Surveyorship, and of his inadequate remuneration. He had, he said, 'acted under Sr. John Denham, a person of Honour', but he 'conceived it much beneath him, to doe ye like under one, who in whatever respects is his inferior by farr. May Y^{or} Majestie please if not to confirm y^{or} Petitioner's Grant as in the honor of a King you appear to bee obliged, then to Joyne him in Patent with Mr. Wren and he shalbee ready to instruct him in the course of the office of y^{or} works, whereof hee professeth to bee wholy ignorant, and y^{or} Petitioner, if you vouchsafe, may take care of your Majesties works at Greenwich, or elsewhere as hitherto hee hath done.' But once more Webb's claims were passed over, and it was Wren who took Denham's place as Surveyor-General. Webb himself had only three more years to live; he died at Butleigh on 30 October 1672, and was buried in the aisle of the parish church. He left three sons and four daughters. One of the latter married Dr. John Westley (d. *c.*1687), a

[1] Webb appears as the occupant of Jones's house in Whitehall in a survey made in 1650, but Jones himself reappears in 1651 and presumably remained in occupation until his death in 1652 (E. S. de Beer, 'Notes on Inigo Jones', *Notes and Queries*, 178, 27 April 1940, 292.).

[2] But he was not prepared to refuse it if the opportunity arose, for, in April 1657, he wrote to Sir Christopher Hatton to say that his name had been put forward for nomination as a Commissioner under the Act for regulating building in London, and that although he 'would not seeme to seeke after so troublous emploiment yett I think it improper to neglect so faire opportunity whereby I may bee further enabled to expresse my selfe' (B.L., Add. MS. 29550, f. 297). For this: 'Act for preventing multiplicity of Buildings in and about the Suburbs of London', which was passed on 26 June 1657, see *Acts and Ordinances of the Interregnum*, ed. Firth and Rait, i, 1223–34.

[1] The original document, lacking only the Great Seal, is among the Butleigh deeds in the Somerset County Record Office.

lawyer practising in Ireland who was also an architect.[1]

By his will (P.C.C. 145 EURE), dated 24 October 1672, Webb left his library and all his 'Prints and Cutts and drawings of Architecture of what nature or kind soever' to his son William, with instructions to 'keepe them intire together without selling or imbezzling any of them'. But William Webb did not long survive his father, and his widow disregarded her father-in-law's last wishes. Some of Webb's books were already on sale in London in 1675 (see Hooke's *Diary*, 2 April and 22 June), and by the 1680s many of the drawings had already passed into the possession of John Oliver (*q.v.*). Their subsequent acquisition by Lord Burlington and Dr. George Clarke, and their ultimate division between the R.I.B.A. Drawings Collection and Worcester College, Oxford, is described above (p. 557). Many of the drawings in Lord Burlington's collection were published by William Kent in 1727 as *The Designs of Inigo Jones*, though the selection was in fact almost entirely from Webb's drawings, and it was not until 1911 that J. A. Gotch demonstrated that these and other drawings hitherto attributed to Inigo Jones were in reality from the hand of his pupil. Apart from the two collections already mentioned, the only other drawings known to be by Webb are several in the Isham papers, one at Belvoir, another at Alnwick, and two in the Victoria and Albert Museum. Webb's somewhat hard and meticulous hand is, in fact, easily distinguishable from that of his master, which has a spontaneous quality lacking in the more studied work of the pupil. Webb was nevertheless an accomplished draughtsman, and some of his later drawings (e.g. for Lamport) show something of the ease and freedom which are lacking in his earlier studies.

Webb's achievement as a practising architect was curtailed by war and misfortune. Many of the buildings for which he made designs never materialized, and the list given below contains less than a dozen works of any consequence. Some of these, however, were buildings of crucial importance in the history of English architecture; the famous interiors at Wilton, the first country-house portico at The Vyne, one of the outstanding houses of the Restoration period at Amesbury, and the King Charles Block of Greenwich Palace. The last demonstrates, moreover, that Webb was something more than just a faithful disciple of Inigo Jones, who never deviated from the manner that he had learned from his master. For it shows that in the ten years after Inigo Jones's death, Webb had learned to handle such baroque devices as the giant order and the impendent keystone, while the Whitehall drawings, as analysed by Dr. Whinney, can now be seen to 'bridge the gap, in style as well as in time, between the school of Inigo Jones and that of Wren'.

In 1655 Webb published an account of *The Most Notable Antiquity called Stone-Heng*, based on notes left by Inigo Jones, in which he endeavoured to show that it was of Roman origin. Dr. William Charleton, in his *Chorea Gigantum* (1663), was equally emphatic in attributing the monument to the Danes, and in 1665 Webb replied in *A Vindication of Stone-Heng Restored* (2nd ed. 1725). He also published in 1669 a curious work entitled *An Historical Essay endeavouring a Probability that the Language of the Empire of China is the Primitive Language*, with a dedication to Charles II. An intended treatise on architecture is represented only by many drawings at Worcester College that were evidently prepared with such a publication in mind. Among Webb's drawings there is his design for the architectural title-page of B. Walton's *Biblia Polyglotta*, engraved by Hollar and published in 1657.

[*A.P.S.D.*; *D.N.B.*; Wood, *Athenae Oxonienses*, ed. Bliss, iv, 1820, 754; *Register of Merchant Taylors' School*, ed. C. J. Robinson, i, 1882, 114; Walpole Soc., *Vertue Note Books* i, 49; Hist. MSS. Comm., *Seventh Report*, 88a (note); *Wren Soc.* xviii, 154–7; will, P.C.C. 145 EURE; W. G. Keith, 'John Webb and the Court Theatre of Charles II', *Arch. Rev.* lvii, Feb. 1925; W. G. Keith, 'John Webb and the Marshalls', *R.I.B.A. Jnl.*, 3rd ser., xl, 1933, 732; Margaret Whinney, 'Some Church Designs by John Webb', *Jnl. of the Warburg and Courtauld Institutes* vi, 1943; Margaret Whinney, 'John Webb's Drawings for Whitehall Palace', *Walpole Soc.* xxxi for 1942–3, 1946; *Catalogue of the R.I.B.A. Drawings Collection: Inigo Jones & John Webb*, by John Harris, 1972; *History of the King's Works* v, 1976, *passim*; John Harris & A. A. Tait, *Catalogue of the Drawings by Inigo Jones, John Webb & Isaac De Caus at Worcester College*, Oxford, 1979; A. Pritchard, 'A Source for the Lives of Inigo Jones and John Webb', *Arch. Hist.* 28, 1985; Esther Eisenthal, 'John Webb's Reconstruction of the Ancient House', *Arch. Hist.* 28, 1985; John Bold, *John Webb*, 1989.]

HALE PARK, HANTS., design, apparently unexecuted, for a 'lodge' or villa for John Penruddock, 1638 [R.I.B.A.D.].

HASSENBROOK HALL, ESSEX, design, probably

[1] For Westley see R. Loeber, *Biographical Dictionary of Architects in Ireland 1600–1720*, 1981.

unexecuted, for a stable for Henry Fetherstone, 1638 [R.I.B.A.D.].

NEW MEAD, MAIDEN BRADLEY, WILTS., design for a house for 'Colonel Ludlow at Mayden Bradley, Wiltshire' (Worcester Coll.), presumably before 1650, when Col. Edmund Ludlow was promoted to the rank of Lieut. General by Cromwell. It is very doubtful whether this was built, as Aubrey says (1671) 'there was a handsome well-built house, built by Sir Henry Ludlowe [Edmund's father] or his ancestors, now dilapidated since the late warres' (*Wiltshire Collections*, ed. J. E. Jackson, 1862, 383–4). A farmhouse was built on the site *c.*1881.

WILTON HOUSE, WILTS., reconstruction of interior and upper parts of towers after fire of 1647/8, for 4th Earl of Pembroke, 1648–50 [H. M. Colvin, 'The South Front of Wilton House', *Archl. Jnl.* 111, 1955, 187–9; J. Heward, 'The Restoration of the South Front of Wilton House: the Development of the House Reconsidered', *Arch. Hist.* 35, 1992] (Oliver Hill & John Cornforth, *English Country Houses: Caroline*, 1966, 75–87)

LONDON, DURHAM HOUSE, STRAND, unexecuted designs for a new house for 4th Earl of Pembroke, 1649 [Worcester Coll.].

COLESHILL HOUSE, BERKS., designs for chimney-piece, etc., for Sir George Pratt, Bart., *c.*1650 [R.I.B.A.D. and 'Book of Capitals']. For this house see above, p. 778.

?NUN APPLETON HOUSE, YORKS. (W.R.), works for Thomas, 3rd Lord Fairfax, *c.*1650; remodelled 1711–12 and enlarged 1862 and 1920. The attribution of works here to Webb depends on the appearance in his 'Book of Capitals' (f. 7) of designs for capitals for the front, hall, great parlour, great chamber and withdrawing room of a house, faintly inscribed in pencil 'Lo. ffay.', and on the incorporation in the capital of military symbols and a lion (the Fairfax crest) [Bold, *John Webb*, 164–5].

LONDON, THE ROYAL COLLEGE OF PHYSICIANS, library and repository, 1651–3; destroyed by fire 1666 [Worcester Coll. and 'Book of Capitals'; see C. E. Newman, 'The First Library of the Royal College of Physicians', *Jnl. Royal College of Physicians* iii (3), 1969].

DRAYTON HOUSE, NORTHANTS., designs for chimney-pieces for 2nd Earl of Peterborough, 1653 [R.I.B.A.D.]. One of Webb's chimney-pieces still exists in the State Bedchamber (H. A. Tipping, *English Homes, Period IV* (i), 1929, figs. 343–4).

THE VYNE, HANTS., altered the interior and designed the portico for Chaloner Chute, 1654–6 [there are two designs for capitals by Webb for 'Mr. Chute at the Vine', one dated 1654, in the 'Book of Capitals': for other evidence pointing to Webb as the architect see W. G. Keith in *R.I.B.A. Jnl.* 3rd ser. xl, 1933, 732; Edward Marshall's contract to build the portico, dated 4 March 1654, is now in the Hants. Record Office] (*C. Life*, 14–21 May 1921, 3 Jan. 1957).

CHEVENING HOUSE, KENT, work for 14th Lord Dacre, 1655. On 16 April 1655 Webb wrote to Sir Justinian Isham of Lamport that he was designing 'ornaments of wainscott for a roome in Kent for my Lo: Dacres wch is 31 fo: long 22 broad & 24 fo: high', and in the 'Book of Capitals' there is a drawing of a capital by Webb which is inscribed 'Lo. Dacre's at Chevening'. The room in question may have been the existing Saloon, but the dimensions do not correspond with those given by Webb. See *Vitruvius Britannicus* ii, 1717, pl. 85, for plans and elevation of the house as existing in 1717, and Oliver Hill & John Cornforth, *English Country Houses: Caroline*, 1966, 25–6, and John Newman, *West Kent and the Weald*, Buildings of England, 1976, for the problems connected with its architectural history.

LUDLOW, SALOP., corresponded with Col. Edward Harley about a projected building there, 1655 [*Wren Soc.* xviii, 154–5].

LAMPORT HALL, NORTHANTS., for Sir Justinian Isham, Bart., 1655–7; wings added by Francis and William Smith 1732–40, ceiling of Music Hall remodelled 1738 [J. A. Gotch, 'Some Newly-found Drawings and Letters of John Webb', *R.I.B.A. Jnl.* 3rd ser. xxviii, 1921; Sir Gyles Isham, 'The Architectural History of Lamport', *Reports of the Northants. Architectural and Archaeological Soc.* lvii, 1951] (*C. Life*, 26 Sept., 3, 10 Oct. 1952).

BELVOIR CASTLE, LEICS., reconstruction after 'slighting' by Parliamentary forces in 1649, for 8th Earl of Rutland, 1655–68; remodelled 1800 onwards. Webb visited Belvoir in 1654 [letter of 20 July 1654 to Sir Justinian Isham of Lamport], and a working drawing in his hand for 'The Architrave freese and cornice that goes about the roome 1667' is preserved in the Belvoir archives [Map 127]. A summary of the building accounts [Belvoir archives, Misc. MS. 67] shows that £11,730 was spent between 1655 and 1668. Unexecuted designs by Webb for a much grander house are in R.I.B.A.D. The castle as rebuilt in 1655–68 is shown in an engraving by Badeslade & Rocque in *Vitruvius Brittanicus* (*sic*) iv, 1739, and by a model made in 1799 and preserved at Belvoir.

LONDON, NORTHUMBERLAND HOUSE, STRAND, external stairs to S. front and internal alterations for 10th Earl of Northumberland, *c.*1655–9; stairs removed 1818, house dem. 1874 [J. Wood, 'The Architectural Patronage of the 10th Earl of Northumberland' in *English Architecture Public and Private: Essays for Kerry Downes*, 1993, 72–3].

SYON HOUSE, ISLEWORTH, MIDDLESEX, extensive repairs and alterations for 10th Earl of Northumberland, 1656–60 [J. Wood, *op. cit.*, 74–9], but note that Webb's design for a modillion cornice (fig. 32) does not correspond to that seen on three sides of the courtyard in fig. 33, whose modillions appear to be identical with those beneath the pedimented windows, themselves closely resembling those in the sixteenth-century Strand front of Somerset House.

GUNNERSBURY HOUSE, MIDDLESEX, for Sir John Maynard, *c.*1658–63; dem. 1801 [R.I.B.A.D., design by Webb for chimney-piece in 'the little Parlor, Gunnersbury', and designs for capitals 'for Serjeant Maynard Gunnersbury' in the 'Book of Capitals'. In a letter at Chatsworth printed by W. G. Keith in *R.I.B.A. Jnl.* 3rd ser. xl, 1933, 733, Webb writes to tell Edward Marshall that he is about to 'measure off the worke at Gunnersbury', 17 Oct. 1658; the date 1663 is that given by Campbell (plan and elevation in *Vitruvius Britannicus* i, 1715, pls. 18–19; engraving in Dodsley's *London and its Environs* iii, 1761, 110).

AMESBURY HOUSE, WILTS., for William Seymour, 1st Marquess of Hertford (1640) and 2nd Duke of Somerset (1660), begun before 1660, perhaps completed 1661 (the date given by Campbell); rebuilt 1834–40 [drawing by Webb at Chatsworth (vol. 24, no. 13) for a capital inscribed 'Ambresbury for Marquesse Hertford'; cf. Walpole Soc., *Vertue Note Books* ii, 32] (*Vitruvius Britannicus* iii, 1725, pl. 7; W. Kent, *Designs of Inigo Jones* ii, 1727, pls. 8–9; sketches by C. R. Cockerell in *Architectural History* xiv, 1971, fig. 1A; measured drawings by Wyatt Papworth in R.I.B.A.D.; detail of staircase in *Builder* ii, 1844, 563).

attributed: LONDON, SOMERSET HOUSE, STRAND, THE GALLERY for the Queen Mother Henrietta Maria, 1662–3; dem. 1776 [*History of the King's Works* v, 255–6 and pl. 32] (inaccurate engraving in *Vitruvius Britannicus* i, 1715, pl. 16).

GREENWICH PALACE (now HOSPITAL), THE KING CHARLES II BLOCK, 1664–9, designed as part of a new palace that was not completed [*History of the King's Works* v, 147–51; for the complete plan see figs. 2 and 3] (*Vitruvius Britannicus* i, 1715, pls. 88–9).

LONDON, WHITEHALL PALACE, probably remodelled the COCKPIT THEATRE for King Charles II, *c.*1665; dem. [W. G. Keith, 'John Webb and the Court Theatre of Charles II', *Arch. Rev.* lvii, 1925].

attributed: LONDON, ASHBURNHAM HOUSE, WESTMINSTER, which was apparently built by William Ashburnham *c.*1662. His descendant John, 1st Earl of Ashburnham, told Batty Langley that Webb was the architect employed [B. Langley, *Ancient Masonry* i, 1736, 391] (H. Sirr, 'Ashburnham House', *R.I.B.A. Jnl.* 3rd ser. xvii, 1910; *C. Life*, 3 Sept. 1943; plan and section of staircase in Isaac Ware's *Designs of Inigo Jones*, pls. 6–7).

WEBB, JOHN (*c.*1754–1828), was an architect and landscape-gardener who lived at Lee Hall in the village of Armitage, nr. Lichfield. By 1805 his practice as a landscape-gardener was reported to be 'all over England', and in the course of that year he is known to have been consulted at Eaton Hall, Cheshire, Sandon Hall, Staffs., Ashridge Park, Herts., and Cassiobury Park, Herts. [correspondence in Harrowby and Grosvenor archives]. In Cheshire he laid out the grounds at Cholmondeley Hall, Bradwell Manor (Sandbach), Poole Hall (Nantwich), Oulton Park, Somerford Park and Tatton Park [see Ormerod, *History of Cheshire*, ed. Helsby, i, 444, ii, 219, iii, 114, 352, 560, and Loudon's *Encyclopaedia of Gardening*, 1828, 1081]. Elsewhere he is known to have been consulted about landscaping at Astley Hall, Lancs., Campsmount (Campsall), Yorks. (1802), Grove Park, Warwicks. (1804), Holkham Hall, Norfolk (1801–3), Lowther Castle, Westmorland (1807), Quernmore Park, Lancs., Serlby Hall, Notts., Shugborough, Staffs. (1804), Weston Hall, Staffs. (1827–8), and Woolley Park, Yorks. (1811). According to Ormerod he was a pupil of William Eames (d. 1803), a landscape-gardener himself said to have been 'an élève of the great Brown'.

In Neale's *Seats* (2nd ser. iii, 1826) it is stated that Webb designed WANSTEAD GROVE, ESSEX, for the Hon. Anne Rushout, and he no doubt laid out the 'extensive Pleasure Grounds'. The house, which was built in 1821–3, was demolished later in the nineteenth century. In her diaries (in private possession) Miss Rushout refers on several occasions to 'my friend Mr. Webbe', and mentions his employment as an architect at APLEY PARK, SALOP., a castellated Gothic mansion built by Thomas Whitmore *c.*1811–20 [building accounts in Essex C.R.O. D/Dwt A3] (F. Calvert & W. West, *Picturesque Views in Staffs & Salop.* ii, 1831, 131; *C. Life*, 25 May 1907, 738), and at THRYBERGH PARK, YORKS. (W.R.), which he rebuilt for Col. J.

Fullerton in *c.*1820. He also designed WARLEIGH HOUSE, SOMERSET, for Henry Skrine in the Tudor Gothic style in 1814, as recorded in Neale's *Seats*, 2nd ser. i, 1824, and carried out alterations to SOMERFORD BOOTHS HALL, CHESHIRE, for Clement Swetenham in 1817 [Ormerod, iii, 560] (Neale, 2nd ser. i, 1824). He was doubtless the 'Mr. Webb' who remodelled the exterior of OMBERSLEY COURT, WORCS., for the Marchioness of Downshire in 1812–14 and designed the stables [Arthur Oswald in *C. Life*, 16 Jan. 1953].

Unexecuted designs by Webb include an alternative plan dated 1801 for Leck Hall, nr. Kirkby Lonsdale, Lancs., a house (*C. Life*, 4 Aug. 1988) of which he may nevertheless have been the architect; a Gothic lodge for Alscot Park, Warwicks. (1810); a Gothic scheme for the reconstruction of Ettington Park, Warwicks. (1814), among the Shirley papers in the Warwicks. C.R.O.; and Gothic fittings for the chapel at Locko Park, Derbyshire [Nottingham Univ. Library, Dr. P. 115–119].

Webb died at Lee Hall on 25 May 1828, aged 74, and was buried in Armitage Churchyard [*Gent's Mag.* 1828 (i), 573; P.C.C. 565 SUTTON].

WEBB, THOMAS (–1699), of Middlewich in Cheshire, 'freemason', designed ERDDIG PARK, DENBIGHSHIRE, for Joshua Edisbury in 1683. In November of that year he agreed to 'undertake and performe the care and oversight of the contriveing building and finishing of a case or body of a new house for the said Joshua Edsbury att Erthigg aforesaid . . . according to the designes, compasse, manner and methodde of draughts already given by the said Thomas Webb'. Contracts were made in March 1684 with Edward Price, mason, Philip Rogers, carpenter, and William Carter of Chester, bricklayer, and the house was completed in about three years [Clwyd Record Office, D/E/269–72] (*C. Life*, 16–23 Aug. 1930, 6, 13, 20 April 1978).

In 1696 Webb is named as measurer in a contract between Sir Willoughby Aston and Edward Nixon of Chester, mason, for building the chancel of the church of ASTON-BY-SUTTON, CHESHIRE [B.L., Add. MS. 36919, ff. 249–50]. The Middlewich parish register shows that he was buried on 28 March 1699.

WEBSTER, FRANCIS (1767–1827), was the son of a mason at Quarry Flat, nr. Cartmel. As a young man he moved to Kendal, where he entered into partnership with a mason called William Holme. Here he developed a highly successful business as a builder, specializing in the production of monuments and marble chimney-pieces. In 1788 he was the first to polish Kendal Fell limestone for making into chimney-pieces, and in 1800 he devised water-powered machinery for sawing and polishing marble, and eventually for accurately cutting both classical and Gothic mouldings. Although primarily a builder and marble-mason, Francis Webster also acted as an architect, designing such buildings as workhouses, mills, bridges and the firm's own offices and showrooms at Bridge House in Kendal. Between 1796 and 1802 he was responsible for an abortive scheme to rehabilitate the gutted Lowther Hall for the 1st Earl of Lonsdale, who eventually employed Robert Smirke to design an entirely new house. In about 1820 he took his son George into partnership, and began to extend the architectural side of the firm of 'Francis Webster and Sons'. Although some highly finished sets of drawings of this period bear Francis's name he was probably not their author but signed as the senior partner. By 1818 he was sufficiently prosperous to buy an estate at Eller How, nr. Lindale, where he enlarged a cottage into a small country house. He was a prominent figure in the public life of Kendal, and served as Mayor in 1823–4. He died at Eller How on 10 October 1827, and is commemorated both by a tombstone in Kendal churchyard and by a tablet at Lindale. [Jeffrey Haworth & Angus Taylor, *The Websters of Kendal*, catalogue of exhibition at Abbot Hall, Kendal, 1973; information from Mr. Taylor, to whom all documentary references in the following list are due.]

KENDAL, WESTMORLAND, obelisk on Castle Howe to commemorate the Glorious Revolution, 1788 [J. F. Curwen, *Kirkbie Kendal*, 1900, 85–6].

HAWKSHEAD, LANCS., MARKET HOUSE, built and perhaps designed by Francis Webster, 1790–1 [B. Tyson, 'Francis Webster and the Market House at Hawkshead', *Abbot Hall Quarto* xxxi (3), Oct. 1993].

SHAW END, PATTON, WESTMORLAND, for Arthur Shepherd, 1796–1801 [Dr. Fahy's papers, C.R.O., Kendal].

HAVERTHWAITE, LANCS, LOW WOOD GUNPOWDER WORKS, 1798 [A. Palmer, 'The Low Wood Gunpowder Works', unpublished thesis, 1970].

FINSTHWAITE HOUSE, LANCS., castellated tower commemorating naval victories, for James King, 1799 [A. Palmer, *op. cit.*].

WHITESTOCK HOUSE, COLTON, LANCS., for William Strickland, 1800 [C.R.O. Barrow-in-Furness, Z.62].

KENDAL, WESTMORLAND, HOUSE OF CORRECTION, enlarged 1801, 1817, 1819, 1824–6

[C.R.O., Kendal, Q.S. Books].

LEVENS HALL, WESTMORLAND, alterations and additions, including Howard Tower, for Sir Charles Bagot (d. 1818) and his heir Col. Fulke Greville Howard, 1805 onwards [Levens account-book in C.R.O., Kendal].

KIRKBY LONSDALE CHURCH, WESTMORLAND, repairs and alterations, including new roof, 1807 [Lancs. C.R.O., ARR 13/5/108].

KENDAL, WESTMORLAND, FRIENDS' MEETING HOUSE, 1815–16 [D.M. Butler, *Quaker Meeting Houses of the Lake Counties*, 1978, 99].

MILNTHORPE, WESTMORLAND, WORKHOUSE, 1813–15 [C.R.O., Kendal, Q.S. Books].

KENDAL, WESTMORLAND, DOCKWRAY MILLS, for James Gandy, 1816–17; rebuilt after fire, 1824, castellated [C. Nicholson, *Annals of Kendal*, 1861, 293].

APPLEBY, WESTMORLAND, added HOUSE OF CORRECTION and JURY ROOM to GAOL, 1818–20, and further alterations 1824 [B. Tyson, 'Architectural History of the Gaols and Court-Houses at Appleby', *Trans. Ancient Monuments Soc.* N.S. 32, 1988].

SOULBY, WESTMORLAND, BRIDGE (Scandal Beck), 1818 [C.R.O., Kendal, drawings and specification].

KENDAL, WESTMORLAND, MILLER BRIDGE (R. Kent), 1818 [C.R.O., Kendal, drawings and specification].

HELME LODGE, nr. KENDAL, WESTMORLAND, for W. D. Crewdson, 1824; altered 1990 [C. Nicholson, *Annals of Kendal*, 1861, 295; *The Websters of Kendal*, no. 9].

KENDAL, WESTMORLAND, ASSEMBLY ROOMS (now TOWN HALL), HIGHGATE, 1825–7; converted into Town Hall 1859, when Clock Tower was added by George Webster; enlarged 1893 [*The Websters of Kendal*, no. 64].

AMBLESIDE, WESTMORLAND, SALUTATION INN, 1821–2 [*Westmorland Advertiser & Kendal Chronicle*, 2 June 1821, *ex inf.* Mr. Taylor].

WEBSTER, GEORGE (1797–1864), of Kendal in Westmorland, was the son and successor of Francis Webster (*q.v.*). Unlike his father, he must have had a professional training in an architect's office. As he did not attend the Royal Academy Schools in London it seems likely that he was apprenticed to some northern architect such as Harrison of Chester or Foster of Liverpool, or perhaps William Atkinson, who had an office in Manchester in 1812–16. After his father's death in 1827 George devoted his time entirely to architecture, leaving the management of the marble works to his brother Francis. In 1845 Miles Thompson, who had been employed as a draughtsman since the 1820s, was taken into partnership, and the firm became 'Webster and Thompson'. Webster was Mayor of Kendal in 1829–30. He visited Italy more than once in middle life, and made a collection of Roman coins, medals and other antiquities. He died on 16 April 1864, and was buried in a vault which he had built in Lindale churchyard.

George Webster had a considerable practice in north-west England in the 1820s and 1830s. His classical public buildings and Gothic churches were standard products of their time, but at Eshton and Underley he designed two of the earliest country houses in the revived Jacobean style which became his speciality. These were contemporary with William Burn's experiments with the same style in Scotland, and were (with Salvin's Moreby and Harlaxton) singled out for praise in the preface to Henry Shaw's *Details of Elizabethan Architecture* (1839). Other houses in the same style that may have been designed by Webster are Netherside Hall, Threshfield, Yorks. (N.R.), *c.*1822, for Alexander Nowell, for whom Webster was later to design Underley Hall; Whelprigg, Barbon, Westmorland, 1834; Mozergh House, Selside, Westmorland, 1835; Grimes Hill, Middleton, Westmorland, remodelled *c.*1836 (dem. 1938); Aireville, Skipton, Yorks. (W.R.), 1836; Aynsome, Cartmel, Lancs., remodelled 1842; Summerlands, Preston Richard, Westmorland, 1846; and Merlewood, Grange-over-Sands, Lancs., 1853.

[Jeffrey Haworth & Angus Taylor, *The Websters of Kendal*, catalogue of exhibition at Abbot Hall, Kendal, 1973; C. Nicholson, *Annals of Kendal*, 1861; Angus Taylor on Webster's architectural training in *Abbot Hall Quarto* xxxi, April 1992; monumental inscriptions at Cartmel, Kendal and Lindale.]

PUBLIC BUILDINGS, ETC.

SETTLE, YORKS. (W.R.), PUBLIC ROOMS (now TOWN HALL), MARKET PLACE, 1832, Jacobean [*The Websters of Kendal*, no. 65].

KENDAL, WESTMORLAND, DOWKER'S HOSPITAL, HIGHGATE, 1833, Tudor; dem. 1965 [C. Nicholson, *Annals of Kendal*, 1861, 228].

KENDAL, WESTMORLAND, THE BANK OF WESTMORLAND (now Midland Bank), HIGHGATE, 1834–5 [C. Nicholson, *Annals of Kendal*, 1861, 153].

BOWNESS-ON-WINDERMERE SCHOOL, WESTMORLAND, 1836, Tudor; dem. 1973 [signed tablet formerly on school].

ULVERSTON, LANCS., THE TRUSTEE SAVINGS BANK, 1837–8; clock-tower added 1844; interior of ground floor rebuilt 1850 [Angus Taylor, 'Ulverston Trustee Savings Bank', *Trans. Cumberland & Westmorland A. and A. Soc.* lxxiv, 1974].

BOWNESS-ON-WINDERMERE, WESTMORLAND, THE ROYAL HOTEL, *c.*1839, Italianate [engraving endorsed by Webster as built 'under my direction', *ex inf.* Mr. Angus Taylor].

RIGGS (now WINDERMERE) HOTEL, WINDERMERE, WESTMORLAND, 1845 [*Westmorland Gazette*, 8 Nov. 1845, *ex inf.* Mr. Angus Taylor].

KENDAL, WESTMORLAND, THE MARKET HALL, 1855; converted into public library 1892, when façade was re-erected in Sandes Avenue [C. Nicholson, *Annals of Kendal*, 1861, 157–8].

EAGLEY VILLAGE, nr. BOLTON, LANCS., 1854 [advt. for tenders, *Bolton Chronicle*, 28 Jan. 1854, *ex inf.* Mr. Angus Taylor].

CHURCHES

RYDAL, WESTMORLAND, 1822–4, Gothic [specification in C.R.O., Kendal, *ex inf.* Mr. Angus Taylor].

BURNESIDE, WESTMORLAND, rebuilt 1823–6, Gothic; rebuilt 1880 [I.C.B.S.].

NATLAND, WESTMORLAND, rebuilt 1825–6, Gothic; rebuilt 1909 [I.C.B.S.]

LINDALE, LANCS., 1828–9, Gothic; north aisle 1912 [I.C.B.S.].

NEW HUTTON, WESTMORLAND, rebuilt 1828–9, Gothic [I.C.B.S.].

MANSERGH, WESTMORLAND, enlarged 1829; rebuilt 1880 [plan, etc. in Leeds Archives, DR/AF/2/3/10, *ex inf.* Mr. Angus Taylor].

KENDAL, WESTMORLAND, HOLY TRINITY (R.C.), 1835–7, Gothic [*Civil Engineer and Architect's Jnl.* i, 1837–8, 57].

attributed: MILNTHORPE, WESTMORLAND, rebuilt 1835–7, Gothic; remodelled 1882–3 [stylistic attribution].

KENDAL, WESTMORLAND, ST. THOMAS, 1835–7, Gothic [C. Nicholson, *Annals of Kendal*, 1861, 76–7].

GRAYRIGG, WESTMORLAND, rebuilt 1838, Gothic; west tower 1869 [I.C.B.S.].

HOLME, WESTMORLAND, 1839, Gothic [plans in C.R.O., Kendal, *ex inf.* Mr. Angus Taylor].[1]

KENDAL, WESTMORLAND, ST. GEORGE, 1839–41, Gothic; chancel 1910–11; west towers truncated 1940 and 1979 [C. Nicholson, *Annals of Kendal*, 1861, 77].

GRASMERE, WESTMORLAND, alterations, 1840 [*The Websters of Kendal*, no. 96].

CLEATOR, CUMBERLAND, 1841–2, Gothic [I.C.B.S.].

BARDSEA, LANCS., 1843–53, Gothic [*Westmorland Gazette*, 9 Sept. 1843, *ex inf.* Mr. Angus Taylor].

attributed: CONISTON COLD, YORKS. (W.R.), 1846 [a simpler version of Bardsea church].

DOMESTIC ARCHITECTURE

READ HALL, nr. WHALLEY, LANCS., for John Fort, 1818–25 [T. D. Whitaker, *History of Whalley* ii, 1876, 40].

KENDAL, WESTMORLAND, houses on THORNY HILLS, including No. 4 for himself, 1823 onwards [*The Websters of Kendal*, no. 44].

RIGMADEN, nr. KIRKBY LONSDALE, WESTMORLAND, for Christopher Wilson, 1825; interior reconstructed 1991–2 [*The Websters of Kendal*, no. 10].

ESHTON HALL, GARGRAVE, YORKS. (W.R.), for Matthew Wilson, 1825–7 and later, Jacobean [J. P. Neale, *Views of Seats*, 2nd ser. v, 1829].

UNDERLEY HALL, nr. KIRKBY LONSDALE, WESTMORLAND, for Alexander Nowell, 1825–8, Jacobean; tower, etc., added 1872 [exhib. at R.A. 1826; *Local Chronology, being notes of the Principal Events published in the Kendal Newspapers*, 1865, 61] (*The Websters of Kendal*, plate showing original design and house before alteration).

DALLAM TOWER, BEETHAM, WESTMORLAND, remodelled for George Wilson, 1826 [*The Websters of Kendal*, no. 13].

HUTTON-IN-THE-FOREST, CUMBERLAND, south-east tower for Francis Vane, 1826; further alterations by A. Salvin 1862–7 [John Cornforth in *C. Life*, 4, 11 and 18 Feb. 1965; *The Websters of Kendal*, no. 14].

THURLAND CASTLE, TUNSTALL, LANCS., new drawing-room, etc., for R. T. North, *c.*1827–9; altered after fire in 1879 [*V.C.H. Lancs.* viii, 236; cf. D. Linstrum, *Wyatville*, 249].

ELLER HOW, LINDALE, LANCS., enlarged first by Francis Webster, *c.*1818, and then by G. Webster, 1828, *cottage orné* style [Twycross, *Mansions of England and Wales: Lancashire* ii, 1847, 31].

MORETON HALL, WHALLEY, LANCS., for John Taylor, 1829, Jacobethan; dem. 1955 [T. D. Whitaker, *History of Whalley* ii, 1876, 41] (E. Baines, *History of Lancashire* iii, 1836, 192 engraving).

CLIFFE HALL (now CASTLE), nr. KEIGHLEY, YORKS. (W.R.), for Christopher Netherwood, *c.*1830, Elizabethan; enlarged 1875–6 [Slater's *Directory of the Northern Counties*, 1848, Yorkshire section, 228].

ORMEROD HOUSE, nr. BURNLEY, LANCS., porch, etc., for Col. John Hargreaves, 1833–4,

[1] The I.C.B.S. file shows that this church was based on the Revd. W. Carus Wilson's model church at Casterton.

dem. *c.*1950 [T. D. Whitaker, *History of Whalley*, 4th ed., ii, 1876, 221, n. 1].

BIRKLANDS, KENDAL, WESTMORLAND, for E. W. Wakefield, 1831, Tudor [C. Nicholson, *Annals of Kendal*, 1861, 298].

WHITTINGTON HALL, LANCS., rebuilt for Thomas Greene, 1831–5, Jacobean [B. M. Copeland, *Whittington*, Leeds 1981, 18–21].

PENWORTHAM PRIORY, nr. PRESTON, LANCS., remodelled for Lt. Col. Lawrence Rawstorne, 1832, Jacobethan; dem. *c.*1922 [*The Websters of Kendal*, no. 22].

DOWNHAM HALL, CLITHEROE, LANCS., remodelled for William Assheton, 1834–5 [*The Websters of Kendal*, no. 25] (*C. Life*, 5 Oct. 1989).

RYDAL HALL, WESTMORLAND, alterations for Lady le Fleming, 1835–6 [bills in C.R.O. Kendal, *ex inf.* Mr. Angus Taylor].

BROUGHTON HALL, nr. SKIPTON, YORKS. (W.R.), alterations and additions, including refacing of north front, addition of portico and clock-tower, and lodges, for Sir Charles Tempest, Bart., 1838–41 [C. Hussey in *C. Life*, 31 March-14 April 1950; *The Websters of Kendal*, no. 30].

HOLKER HALL, nr. CARTMEL, LANCS., remodelled for 2nd Earl of Burlington (d. 1891), 1838–42, Elizabethan; partly rebuilt after a fire in 1871 [*V.C.H. Lancs.* viii, 272, n. 33] (*C. Life*, 26 June, 3 July 1980).

CONISHEAD PRIORY, LANCS., completed 1838–44 for T.R.G. Braddyll to Webster's designs after dismissal of P. Wyatt in 1829 [drawings in C.R.O., Barrow, *ex inf.* Mr. Angus Taylor].

HEYSHAM HALL, LANCS., for Thomas Rawstorne, *c.*1840; mutilated [letter from Rawstorne in C.R.O., Kendal, 6 July 1840, *ex inf.* Mr. Angus Taylor].

BLACK ROCK VILLA, GRANGE-OVER-SANDS, LANCS., for himself, 1840–1, Italianate, and alterations, 1851; mutilated [*The Websters of Kendal*, no. 47].

INGFIELD (now Falcon Manor Hotel), SETTLE, YORKS. (W.R.), for Revd. H. Swale, 1841, Jacobethan [specification at hotel referring to 'Mr. Webster the architect', *ex inf.* Mr. Angus Taylor'].

CONISTON COLD HALL, YORKS. (W.R.), for J. B. Garforth, 1841–9; dem. except portico [drawings at modern house, *ex inf.* Mr. Angus Taylor].

HEVERSHAM VICARAGE, WESTMORLAND, 1843 [C.R.O. Kendal, Log Book of Heversham School, *ex inf.* Mr. Angus Taylor].

EDEN GROVE, BOLTON, WESTMORLAND, for Richard Tinkler, 1844, Tudor [stated to be 'by the late Mr. Webster of Kendal' in sale catalogue of 1872 in Kendal Library].

WEBSTER, THOMAS (1773–1844), was a native of the Orkneys. He was admitted to the Royal Academy Schools as an architectural student in 1793, and appears to have been a pupil of Robert Mitchell (*q.v.*), at whose address in Newman Street he was living in 1796. His professional card in the R.I.B.A. Collection (E4/114) shows that he subsequently described himself as a 'Teacher of Architecture, Perspective, etc.', and offered to give instruction in 'Geometry, Mensuration, Land Surveying, Architecture, The doctrine of Light & Shadow, Perspective, Landscape & the Elements of Natural Philosophy'. In 1800 he assisted Count Rumford in the design of the Lecture Theatre, Library and Repository of the ROYAL INSTITUTION in ALBEMARLE STREET, LONDON, though their plans were subsequently revised by James Spiller (*q.v.*) [*Architects' Jnl.*, 23 Oct. 1941, 269–70]. His only recorded work as an architect appears to be THE OBSERVATORY at GLASGOW, built in 1810 to the designs of 'Mr. Webster of London' [R. Chapman, *Picture of Glasgow*, 1822, 166]. By 1814 he had abandoned architecture and embarked on a distinguished career as a geologist, ending with a chair at University College, London. He died in London on 26 December 1844, aged 72 [*D.N.B.*]. Eight volumes of drawings by him are in the Canadian Centre for Architecture at Montreal and those for the Royal Institution are in the R.I.B.A. Collection.

WEIR, JAMES, of Tolcross, Edinburgh, variously described as 'wright' and 'architect', contracted in October 1773 to complete the structure of ST. CUTHBERT'S CHURCH, EDINBURGH, on foundations already laid, but to modified designs whose authorship is unknown [S.R.O., GD 69/210]. The attribution to Weir of the steeple added in 1789 is without authority: its authorship is not mentioned in the Heritors' minutes [S.R.O., HR 152/2], but it may have been designed by Alexander Stevens (*q.v.*).

WEIR, JOHN, was described as 'architect' when he was admitted to the Incorporation of Wrights of Glasgow in 1814 [*The Incorporation of Wrights in Glasgow*, 1880, 68]. His only known work appears to be the façades of LONDON STREET, GLASGOW, 1824; dem. [T. Gildard in *Trans. Royal Philosophical Soc. of Glasgow* xxvi, 1895, 122; A. Gomme & D. Walker, *Architecture of Glasgow*, 1987, 72]. James Wylson (1811–70) was his pupil [*A.P.S.D.*, *s.v.* 'Wylson, James'].

WELCH, EDWARD (1806–1868), was born at Overton in Flintshire in 1806. He became a pupil or assistant of John Oates of Halifax and in 1828 entered into partnership with Joseph Aloysius Hansom (1803–82), who was also in Oates's office. They established themselves first in York and then in Liverpool, and designed several churches and other buildings in Yorkshire, Lancashire and North Wales. In 1830 they won the important competition for the Town Hall at Birmingham, defeating, among others, Barry, Beazley, Goodwin and Rickman. The successful design was Hansom's, but a modification of the clients' requirements led ultimately to the adoption of a different design for which Welch claimed some share of credit. The result was a large peripteral temple of the Corinthian order standing on a high rusticated basement and enlosing a spacious galleried hall. As an architectural concept it was simple and dignified, though much less sophisticated than H. L. Elmes's Liverpool hall of ten years later. The building was to be faced with a hard stone from Anglesey recommended by the architects. Doubts were expressed about the contractors' ability to perform the work for the agreed sum, and the architects unwisely stood surety for the builders. The cost of quarrying, transporting and working the Anglesey stone proved to be far greater than the two young architects had supposed: all their financial resources were soon exhausted, and bankruptcy ensued in 1834. John Foster of Liverpool was then brought in to supervise the work, but the building was eventually completed in 1849 under the direction of Charles Edge (*q.v.*).

After this catastrophe the two architects parted company. Hansom took up business management (incidentally founding the *Builder* and inventing the 'Hansom cab') before resuming an architectural practice which lasted until 1879.[1] Welch returned to Liverpool, where he practised from 1837 to 1849. Of the latter years of his life little is known, but he appears to have devoted his attention chiefly to the heating and ventilation of houses, for which he took out patents in 1850 and 1865. He died in Southampton Row, London, on 3 August 1868. According to the *Builder* he was 'a man of liberal and expansive ideas, and generously open to the merits and abilities of others, while modestly undervaluing his own'.

[*Builder* xxvi, 1868, 863, xliii, 1882, 43–4; *D.N.B.*, *s.v.* 'Hansom, J. A.'; *Architectural Mag.* ii, 1835, 16–27, 237–9, 325–6.]

[1] Among Hansom's early architectural works were THE TOWN HALL at LUTTERWORTH, LEICS., 1836 [*Architectural Mag.* iii, 1836, 569–73, iv, 405–7]; the DOMINICAN CONVENT at ATHERSTONE, WARWICKS., 1837–41 [*Gent's Mag.* 1837 (ii), 644]; parts of the BENEDICTINE PRIORY at PRINCETHORPE, WARWICKS., 1837–50 [*Catholic Annual Register*, 1850, 116]; and the NONCONFORMIST PROPRIETARY SCHOOL, now THE MUSEUM, LEICESTER, 1837 [*V.C.H. Leics.* iv, 335].

BUILDINGS BY HANSOM & WELCH

COLLINGHAM VICARAGE, YORKS. (W.R.), enlarged 1828 [Borthwick Institute, York, MGA 1828/3].

BEAUMARIS GAOL, ANGLESEY, 1828–9 [*Builder* xxvi, 1868, 863; *N. Wales Chronicle*, 17 Jan. 1828].

MIDDLEHAM, YORKS. (N.R.), SUSPENSION BRIDGE (R. Ure), 1829 [inscription].

YORK, THE DISPENSARY, NEW STREET, 1829; dem. 1899 [*V.C.H. Yorks., City of York*, 470–1].

HULL, YORKS. (E.R.), ST. JAMES'S CHURCH, MYTON, 1829–31; dem. 1957, Gothic [*V.C.H. Yorks., E.R.* i, 293].

ACOMB CHURCH, YORKS. (W.R.), rebuilt 1830–1, Gothic [I.C.B.S.].

LIVERPOOL, ST. JOHN'S CHURCH, TOXTETH PARK, 1830–2, Gothic [*Builder* xxvi, 1868, 863].

KING WILLIAM'S COLLEGE, ISLE OF MAN, 1830–3, Gothic; gutted by fire 1844 and rebuilt [*Builder* ii, 1844, 41].

BEAUMARIS, ANGLESEY, VICTORIA TERRACE, 1830–5 [*Builder* xxvi, 1868, 863] (*Shell Guide to North Wales*, 1971, 68).

BEAUMARIS, ANGLESEY, THE BULKELEY ARMS HOTEL, 1831–5 [*Builder* xxvi, 1868, 863].

BODELWYDDAN HALL, FLINTS., for Sir John Williams, Bart., *c.*1830–40, castellated [*Builder* xliii, 1882, 43–4; cf. Lewis's *Topographical Dictionary of Wales* i, 1842, *s.v.* 'St. Asaph'] (*C. Life*, 23 Oct. 1986, 21 July 1988).

DOUGLAS, ISLE OF MAN, ST. BARNABAS'S CHURCH, 1832, Gothic; dem. *c.*1975 [L. D. Butler, *An Architectural History of the Churches in the Isle of Man*, typescript 1970, 9].

NEW BALLAUGH CHURCH, ISLE OF MAN, 1832, Gothic; altered 1893 [L. D. Butler, *op. cit.*, 10].

BIRMINGHAM, THE TOWN HALL, 1832–4, completed by Charles Edge (*q.v.*) [*Architectural Mag.* ii, 1835, 16–27, 237–9, 325–6; iii, 1836, 430–4].

ONCHAN CHURCH, ISLE OF MAN, 1833, Gothic; altered 1885 and 1933 [L. D. Butler, *op. cit.*, 10].

BIRMINGHAM, THE OPERATIVE BUILDERS' GUILDHALL, SHADWELL STREET, 1833–4; dem. [*The Pioneer; or Trades Union Magazine*, 7 Dec. 1833, 107].

BUILDINGS BY EDWARD WELCH

LIVERPOOL, THE NORTHERN HOSPITAL, GREAT HOWARD STREET, 1834, Tudor; rebuilt [*Builder* xxvi, 1868, 863].

RHOS-Y-MEDRE CHURCH, nr. RUABON, DENBIGHSHIRE, 1836–7, Gothic [I.C.B.S.].

YSGEIVIOG CHURCH, FLINTS., 1836–7, Gothic [D. R. Thomas, *History of the Diocess of St. Asaph*, 1870, 495].

WREXHAM, DENBIGHSHIRE, SAVINGS BANK, HOPE STREET, 1837 [*Welshman*, 27 Jan. 1837, *ex inf.* Mr. T. Lloyd].

BOLTON, LANCS., EMMANUEL CHURCH, CANNON STREET, 1837–9; chancel 1848; Gothic [G.R.].

ADLINGTON, LANCS., CHRIST CHURCH, 1838, neo-Norman [Port, 146–7].

HARPURHEY, nr. MANCHESTER, LANCS., CHRIST CHURCH, 1838–41, Gothic [*Christ Church Harpurhey, Centenary Souvenir*, 1938, 10, engraving with Welch's name].

SOWERBY, YORKS. (W.R.), ST. GEORGE'S CHURCH, QUARRY HILL, 1839–40, neo-Norman [account in Sowerby Parish Records, Leeds Archives].

BARTON-UPON-IRWELL, LANCS., ST. CATHERINE'S CHURCH, 1843; chancel 1893; Gothic [G.R.].

RAINHILL CHURCH, LANCS., enlarged 1843; reconstructed 1869 [I.C.B.S.].

WEST DERBY, LANCS., ST. JAMES'S CHURCH, for Mrs. Thornton, 1845–6; chancel 1876–9, Gothic [G.R.].

BIRKENHEAD, CHESHIRE, THE MONKS' FERRY HOTEL, *c.*1845; dem. [*Builder* xxvi, 1868, 863].

BIRKENHEAD, CHESHIRE, ASSEMBLY ROOMS, MARKET STREET, 1846 [*Builder* iv, 1846, 200].

WELCH, JOHN (1810–1855), was Edward Welch's younger brother, and was born at Overton in Flintshire on 7 May 1810. Nothing certain is known about his early life, and his career as an architect appears to have begun when he arrived in the Isle of Man in about 1830. Here he was for a short time in partnership with a builder's merchant called John Moore, and may have superintended the erection of the buildings designed by his brother and Joseph Hansom. He was certainly involved in their financial disaster in 1834–5, but escaped bankruptcy and in 1836 advertised his services as 'architect, civil engineer and general surveyor'. By 1838, however, he had migrated to North Wales, where from 1839 he was established in St. Asaph. Later he moved to Preston in Lancashire, where he died in 1855. He designed a number of churches and other buildings in the Isle of Man, North Wales and Preston, some of which display a somewhat crude individuality (notably the twin west towers of Bettwys yn Ros church). According to W. Cubbon's *Bibliography of the Isle of Man*, 1939, he was the author of the anonymous *Six Days' Tour through the Isle of Man* published in 1836. [L. D. Butler, *An Architectural History of the Churches of the Isle of Man*, typescript 1970, 8–9.]

DOUGLAS, ISLE OF MAN, THE TOWER OF REFUGE, 1832, castellated [Butler, *op. cit.*].

MICHAEL CHURCH, ISLE OF MAN, 1835, Gothic [Butler, *op. cit.*].

LEZAYRE CHURCH, ISLE OF MAN, 1835, Gothic [Butler, *op. cit.*].

CASTLETOWN, ISLE OF MAN, THE SMELT COLUMN, 1836 [Butler, *op. cit.*].

FLINT TOWN HALL, 1837–9 [N.L.W., MSS. 6277–8].

BAGILLT CHURCH, FLINTS., 1837–9, Gothic [N.L.W., MS. 2590 E].

HOLYWELL, FLINTS., unexecuted design for Baths, 1837 [N.L.W., MS. 6293 E].

HOLYWELL, FLINTS., SAVINGS BANK, 1838 [Butler, *op. cit.*].

LLANBEDROG RECTORY, CAERNARVONSHIRE, alterations, 1838 [Butler, *op. cit.*].

ST. ASAPH UNION WORKHOUSE, FLINTS., 1838 [Butler, *op. cit.*].

BETTWS YN ROS CHURCH, DENBIGHSHIRE, 1838, Gothic [D. R. Thomas, *History of the Diocese of St. Asaph*, 1870, 356] (*Shell Guide to N. Wales*, 1971, 100).

LLANSANTFFRAID GLAN CONWAY CHURCH, DENBIGHSHIRE, rebuilt 1839, Romanesque [I.C.B.S.].

LLANDUDNO CHURCH, CAERNARVONSHIRE, 1840, Gothic [I.C.B.S.].

LLANDEGWNING CHURCH, CAERNARVONSHIRE, 1840, Gothic [I.C.B.S.].

ABERDARON NEW CHURCH, CAERNARVONSHIRE, 1840–1, Romanesque [I.C.B.S.].

LLANFFINAN CHURCH, ANGLESEY, 1841, Romanesque [I.C.B.S.].

LLANIDAN NEW CHURCH, ANGLESEY, 1843, Gothic [I.C.B.S.].

PRESTON, LANCS., THE LITERARY AND PHILOSOPHICAL INSTITUTION, 1844–5, Gothic [C. Hardwick, *History of Preston*, 1857, 451–2].

PRESTON, LANCS., ST. JAMES'S CHURCH, added chancel 1845–6, Gothic [I.C.B.S.].

PRESTON, LANCS., THE INSTITUTION FOR THE DIFFUSION OF USEFUL KNOWLEDGE, Grecian, 1846–9 [C. Hardwick, *History of Preston*, 1857, 449–50].

WELLS, JOHN (*c.*1790–1864), was a leading architect in Montreal, where he designed several important neo-classical buildings, including the Dominion Theatre, 1844 (dem.) and the Bank of Montreal, 1846–8. He arrived in Canada in 1830, and was described in an obituary notice as 'a native of the county of Norfolk, England'. He is probably to be identified as John Wells, a carpenter by trade, who became a freeman of Norwich in 1820 and who exhibited architectural drawings at the Norwich Society of Artists: 'Three Cottages and a Dwelling House at Mile End' in 1824, and a 'Design for a Gothic Mansion in the style of the Fourteenth Century' in 1825. The 1824 exhibit probably related to a speculative development off the Newmarket Road on the S.W. outskirts of Norwich, for which Wells was responsible according to the *Norwich Mercury* of 8 May 1824. His name does not appear under Norwich in Pigot's *Directory* of 1830, making it probable that he was the John Wells who had emigrated to Canada. [Information from Mr. A. P. Baggs, Mr. David Cubitt and Mr. Robert Hill of Toronto.]

WENTWORTH, WILLIAM, 2ND EARL OF STRAFFORD (1722–1791), who succeeded his father in 1739, had some skill as an amateur architect. At his Yorkshire seat, WENTWORTH CASTLE, he built the Palladian south-east wing to his own designs in 1759–64, with John Platt (*q.v.*) as master mason, and Charles Ross (*q.v.*) as executant architect. Lord Verulam wrote in 1768 that 'Lord Strafford himself is his own architect and contriver in everything', and this is confirmed both by Horace Walpole and by William Bray. Lord Strafford employed Matthew Brettingham (*q.v.*) to design his London house, No. 5 ST. JAMES'S SQUARE, in 1748–9, but Horace Walpole tells us that he 'chose all the ornaments himself'. His only other recorded architectural work appears to have been an obelisk on his estate at BOUGHTON, nr. NORTHAMPTON, erected soon after 1764. [G.E.C., *Complete Peerage*; Horace Walpole, 'Journals of Visits to Country Seats', *Walpole Soc.* xvi, 65; Walpole, *Anecdotes of Painting* v, ed. Hilles & Daghlian, 161; Hist. MSS. Comm., *Verulam*, 239; W. Bray, *Sketch of a Tour into Derbyshire and Yorkshire*, 2nd ed. 1783, 249; *Letters and Journals of Lady Mary Coke*, ed. J. A. Home, 1889–96, i, 36, ii, 276, 326, 339, iii, 2.]

WEST, ROBERT, received payment in March 1738/9 'for plans and Elevations for the building a house at Garn' [*Chirk Castle Accounts 1666–1753*, ed. W. M. Myddelton, 1931, 502]. Garn, in the parish of Henllan, Denbighshire, was the house of John Griffith, chief steward of the lordship of Chirk, and had recently been burned down. It was rebuilt in 1739, presumably to West's designs.

WEST, THOMAS, was an architect of Wisbech, Cambs., where he designed the SESSION HOUSE erected in 1807 [N. Walker & T. Craddock, *History of Wisbech and the Fens*, 1849, 426]. His designs for stables, a gardener's house, and other buildings on the estate at WIMPOLE, CAMBS., made in 1805, are among the Hardwicke papers in the British Library (Add. MS. 36278, K.1–4, M.2).

WESTCOTT, JAMES, 'Architect, Builder, sworn Timber Measurer, Appraiser, and Auctioneer', issued a printed circular in November 1819, announcing that he had removed from Lydney to Ailburton in Gloucestershire, where he would continue to practise those professions [Monmouthshire County Records, C. Bu. 0003]. In 1825 he altered the MARKET HOUSE at ABERGAVENNY designed by John Nash in 1794–5 and since demolished [John Summerson, *John Nash*, 1935, 43].

WESTLEY, JOHN (–1644), was a master builder of some standing at Cambridge in the reign of Charles I. He first appears as the contractor for the BRICK BUILDING erected at EMMANUEL COLLEGE in 1633–4. In 1637 he extended the CHAPEL of GONVILLE AND CAIUS COLLEGE eastwards, and in 1638 he began the rebuilding of CLARE COLLEGE, of which he erected the east and south ranges before work was suspended in 1642 owing to the outbreak of the Civil War. He himself died in December 1644 and was buried in St. Benedict's Church. Although there is no evidence that Westley designed any of the buildings that he erected, it is very likely that he did so. [Willis & Clark, i, 34, 94, 193, 531 n., 620; ii, 695; iii, 531.]

WESTLEY, JOHN (1702–1769), of Leicester, was a carpenter and joiner by trade, and described himself as 'master builder' in his will. He is believed to have been a native of Mountsorrel or Woodhouse, and was admitted a freeman of Leicester in 1723. He was elected Chamberlain in 1746, and held office as Mayor in 1760–1 and 1768–9. He died on 4 February 1769, and was buried in St. Martin's Church, where there is a tablet to his memory. [Hartopp, *Leicester Freemen* i, 312, 539; J. D. Bennett, *Leicestershire Architects 1700–1850*, 1968; will in Leicestershire C.R.O.].

As an architect Westley is recorded to have designed BEAUMANOR PARK, LEICS., for William Herrick, 1725–7, rebuilt 1845–6 [J. Nichols, *History of Leicestershire* iii (1), 1800, 147 and pl. xxvi; contract, with Westley's drawing attached, in Leicestershire C.R.O., DG9/2135]; THE SHAMBLES, LEICESTER, 1726 [*Records of the Borough of Leicester* v, 106]; THE CORN EXCHANGE, MARKET PLACE, LEICESTER, 1747–8, rebuilt 1851 [*V.C.H. Leics.* iv, 364]; GOPSALL HALL, LEICS., for Charles Jennens, *c.*1750, but after a 'misunderstanding' between the owner and his architect the stables and probably the interior were completed by William and David Hiorn (*q.v.*); dem. 1951 [J. Throsby, *Select Views in Leicestershire* i, 1789, 280] (L. G. G. Ramsay, 'Gopsal Hall', *Connoisseur*, vol. 128, 1951); and an altarpiece in CARLTON CURLIEU CHURCH, LEICS., *c.*1767 [Throsby, *op. cit.* ii, 48]. Beaumanor was a compact rectangular house with an order of pilasters, Gopsall a more pretentious one with a large portico awkwardly related to a pedimented centre. In 1737 Westley was one of those who submitted designs for a timber bridge over the Thames at Westminster [J. Hann, *Theory, Practice & Architecture of Bridges*, ed. Hosking, ii, 1843, xcvi].

WESTLEY, WILLIAM, a builder and surveyor of Birmingham, was the son of another William Westley, a carpenter and builder of the same town who died in about 1730. Both he and his father engaged in speculative building in Birmingham, where Westley's Row (near the Square) bore their name. As a surveyor Westley was responsible for an engraved plan of Birmingham, published in 1732, and for two engraved views, one of the town and one of St. Philip's Church. As an architect he probably designed, and certainly supervised the building of ST. THOMAS'S CHURCH, STOURBRIDGE, WORCS., 1728–36, with a striking baroque tower and an interior arranged like Wren's St. James's Piccadilly [R. L. Chambers, *St. Thomas's Church, Stourbridge*, typescript, Dudley 1979].

WESTMACOTT, JOHN, *see* WESTMACOTT, WILLIAM BERNERS.

WESTMACOTT, THOMAS, *see* WESTMACOTT, WILLIAM BERNERS.

WESTMACOTT, WILLIAM BERNERS (*c.*1793–1880), was the youngest son of Richard Westmacott the elder (1748–1808), sculptor and statuary mason. Richard Westmacott and his wife Sarah (the daughter of the carver Thomas Vardy, and not, as often stated, of his brother John, the architect) had a large family. Their eldest son Richard (1775–1856) had a very successful career as a sculptor and was knighted in 1837. Three of his brothers, Thomas, John and William, were brought up as architects. Thomas and John both became pupils of James Wyatt, an architect with whom their father was often associated professionally. But Thomas died in 1798 at the age of 19, two weeks after winning the Royal Academy's Silver Medal, while John, who won the same medal in 1802, became an officer in the Royal Staff Corps and was murdered at Halifax, Nova Scotia, in 1816 [*Nova Scotia Historical Quarterly* 3, 1973, no. 3, 191–6].

Nothing is known of William's architectural training, but he was presumably the Westmacott mentioned by Farington as Robert Smirke's clerk in 1819 [Diary, 19 Sept. 1819]. He exhibited at the Royal Academy from time to time between 1816 and 1848. His exhibited designs included a mausoleum to the memory of the poet James Thomson (1816), a cottage 'designed to be erected in Devonshire' (1817), a 'residence designed for a Russian nobleman' (1822), and 'Basket Lodge, a proposed residence for a gentleman in Hampshire' (1828). In 1839 he was among the competitors for the Ashmolean Museum at Oxford and for the Nelson Monument in Trafalgar Square. In the 1840s Westmacott became architect to the Committee of the Privy Council for Education and in that capacity designed National Schools in, e.g., Norfolk [Norfolk C.R.O. P/BG, 42, 54, 56, 122], and at Little Drayton (1851) in Shropshire [Shropshire C.R.O., 1564]. Towards the end of his life he was living in Hampshire, where he died in 1880, aged 87.

Westmacott's principal executed works appear to have been THE ROYAL VICTORIA ARCADE at RYDE, ISLE OF WIGHT, 1835–6, entrance altered 1856 [*Hampshire Advertiser*, 30 May 1835, and *Freemasons' Quarterly Review*, 1836, *ex inf.* Mr. R. F. Brinton; *Arch. Rev.* April 1972, 258], and ST. MARTIN'S MUSIC HALL, No. 89 LONG ACRE, LONDON, for John Hullah, 1847–50 [exhib. at R.A. 1846; *Builder* viii, 1850, 73] (H. R. Hitchcock, *Early Victorian Architecture in Britain*, 1954, ii, X 32). The former is classical in style, the latter Jacobean. In the R.I.B.A. Drawings Collection there are seven sketch-books containing drawings by various members of the Westmacott family, including a number by William Berners.

WESTON, WILLIAM, practised as an architect and builder at Gainsborough, where he is said to have designed the bridge over the R. Trent erected under an Act of 1787 and completed in 1791, though he is not mentioned in the incomplete minutes of the responsible committee in Nottingham

University Library [Ne C.4, 339, 358–9]. According to C. Moor's *History of Gainsborough*, 1904, 172, he was 'a man of great capacity', and later went to America, where he carried out important works for the government. He eventually returned to England, and lived in retirement at Lea, nr. Gainsborough. In his copy of the *Beauties of England and Wales*, now in the Library of the Society of Antiquaries, E. J. Willson noted that, besides designing the bridge, Weston 'also built two elegant small villas at Morton near Gainsborough'.

WETTEN, ROBERT GUNTER (*c.*1804–1868), was a pupil of P. F. Robinson. He exhibited occasionally at the Royal Academy and competed for the Houses of Parliament in 1835, submitting a Gothic design with a House of Lords resembling King's College Chapel at Cambridge. In 1829–30 he published *Designs for Villas in the Italian Style of Architecture, comprising designs for 6 different houses with descriptive text*. In 1837 he designed an undistinguished Gothic church, ST. JOHN'S, NEWPORT, ISLE OF WIGHT [J. Matthews, *St. John's Church, Newport*, 1988]. His only other recorded building appears to be PARHAM NEW HALL, SUFFOLK, for F. Corrance, 1851–2, which he exhibited at the R.A. in 1852. He practised in Westminster and died at Hanover Lodge, Kew Bridge, on 29 February 1868 [Principal Probate Registry, Calendar of Probates]. He was admitted to membership of the Florentine Academy in 1831.

WHARTON, SAMUEL, of Gray's Inn Square, London, was primarily a land surveyor. He was an 'honorary exhibitor' at the Royal Academy between 1810 and 1814. His designs included one for 'A National Edifice, extending from Carlton House to the site of St. James's Palace'.

WHEELER, JOHN, of Gloucester, was County Surveyor in the 1790s, and in that capacity completed the COUNTY GAOL at GLOUCESTER after the death of William Blackburn in 1790. He designed the BLUE COAT HOSPITAL, GLOUCESTER, a fine building erected in 1807 and demolished in 1889 [*A.P.S.D.*, *s.v.* 'Gloucester']. Wheeler also practised as a landscape-gardener, e.g. at THE MYNDE PARK, HEREFS., where he laid out the grounds for Thomas Symons in 1798 [N.L.W., Mynde Park, 2473].

WHEELER, JOSEPH (*c.*1775–1832), was an architect and builder of Cardiff, where he was sworn in as a capital burgess in 1817 [*Carmarthen Jnl.*, 17 Oct. 1817, *ex inf.* Mr. T. Lloyd]. He died at his daughter's house in Gloucester on 5 Jan. 1856, aged either 56 or 58, and was buried in St. Mary le Crypt churchyard, where there is a tombstone to his memory [*Gloucester Jnl.*, 21 Jan. 1832]. He had been in financial difficulties in 1827 [S.R.O., GD 152/53/1, letter from Lord Bute].

WHETTON, THOMAS (1754–1836), was a pupil of Sir William Chambers. He entered the Royal Academy Schools in 1771, was awarded the Silver Medal in 1771 and the Gold Medal in 1774. He exhibited at the Academy from 1774 to 1786. According to *A.P.S.D.* he rebuilt the premises on the east side of Berkeley Square occupied by Gunters the confectioners from about 1760 onwards. In 1788 he was paid 30 guineas for designs for the Council Room at the Liverpool Exchange, but they do not appear to have been executed [J. A. Picton, *Liverpool Municipal Records* ii, 1886, 265–6]. According to Redgrave's *Dictionary of Artists* (1878), he 'was allured from his profession by inheriting an ample fortune'. For many years he lived at Sunninghill in Berkshire, where he died on 18 July 1836, in his 83rd year.

WHICHCORD, JOHN (1790–1860), was born at Devizes, where his father practised as a surveyor. He was articled in 1806 to C. H. Masters of Bath, and subsequently entered the office of D. A. Alexander of London, who employed him at the London docks and at Maidstone Gaol, and to much of whose practice Whichcord eventually succeeded. Early in the 1820s he settled in Maidstone, where he became Surveyor to the County of Kent and also to the Medway Navigation Company, for whom he executed extensive hydraulic works, some tidal locks, and a number of bridges. For a time he was in partnership with an architect called John Walker, but from about 1845 he was assisted by his son John Whichcord, junior (1823–85), Fellow and in 1879–81 President of the R.I.B.A. He died at Maidstone on 10 June 1860, aged 70. A cast of a bust by E. W. Wyon is in the Maidstone Museum.

Whichcord was a competent architect but designed nothing of great distinction. His Holy Trinity Church at Maidstone (1826–8) is a dull classical building reminiscent of Smirke, but his later churches are mostly in a perfunctory Gothic style that betrays no sympathy with the ecclesiologists. His Royal Insurance Offices of 1827 have a handsome Italianate façade of considerable merit. His finest work is the grandly conceived Oakwood Hospital (1830), in a formal classical style.

[*A.P.S.D.*; *D.N.B.*; obituary in *Builder* xviii, 1860, 383; J. Newman, *The Buildings of Kent*, 1969, 106–7.]

WATERINGBURY CHURCH, KENT, enlarged north side, 1824–5, Gothic; rebuilt 1883–4 [I.C.B.S.].
MAIDSTONE, KENT, THE MARKETS and MITRE INN, *c.*1825 [*Topography of Maidstone*, Maidstone 1839, 22].
MAIDSTONE, KENT, HOLY TRINITY CHURCH, 1826–8, classical; altered 1878 [I.C.B.S.].
MAIDSTONE, KENT, THE KENT FIRE (now Royal Insurance) OFFICES, HIGH STREET, 1827 [*A.P.S.D.*].
MAIDSTONE, KENT, OAKWOOD HOSPITAL, 1830 [*Archaeologia Cantiana* lxxvii, 1962, 206].
MAIDSTONE, KENT, THE COUNTY LUNATIC ASYLUM, BARMING HEATH, 1830–3 [*A.P.S.D.*].
MAIDSTONE, KENT, THE WEST KENT INFIRMARY, MARSHAM STREET, 1832; since enlarged and altered [*Archaeologia Cantiana* lxxvii, 1962, 206].
MAIDSTONE, KENT, ROCKY HILL TERRACE, for 2nd Earl of Romney, *c.*1834 [*Topography of Maidstone*, Maidstone 1839, 102].
MAIDSTONE, KENT, THE CORN EXCHANGE, 1835 [*A.P.S.D.*; drawings in Maidstone Museum].
MAIDSTONE, KENT, ST. PETER'S CHAPEL, restored and enlarged, 1836–7, Gothic [F. Haslewood, *Memorials of Smarden*, Ipswich 1886, 61].
COWDEN CHURCH, KENT, added north aisle, 1837, Gothic [I.C.B.S.].
SEVENOAKS WEALD CHAPEL, KENT, enlarged 1839, Gothic [Kent Record Office, Herries MSS. U543/E11, *ex inf.* Mr. John Newman].
TOVIL CHURCH, KENT, 1839–41, Gothic; dem. 1986 [engraving in B.L., Add. MS. 32367].
DUNKIRK CHURCH, KENT, 1840, Gothic [I.C.B.S.].
PLATT CHURCH, KENT, with Walker, 1841–2, Gothic [*Civil Engineer and Architect's Jnl.* iv, 1841, 439].
BLINDLEY HEATH CHURCH, SURREY, with Walker, 1842, Gothic; chancel 1882 [Brayley, *History of Surrey* iv, 144].
EAST PECKHAM, KENT, HOLY TRINITY CHURCH, with Walker, 1842, Gothic [I.C.B.S.].
SISSINGHURST VICARAGE, KENT, with Walker, 1843 [C. C. R. Pile, *Cranbrook*, 1955, 97].
AYLESFORD, KENT, half-timbered houses for Charles Milner, with J. Whichcord, junior, 1846 [exhib. at R. A. 1846].
WEST WICKHAM CHURCH, KENT, restoration, with J. Whichcord, junior, 1847 [exhib. at R. A. 1847].
BARHAM PARSONAGE, KENT, for the Revd. Charles Oxenden, 1847–9 [*Archaeologia Cantiana* 96, 1980, 66].
PLAXTOL CHURCH, KENT, alterations including E. extension, with J. Whichcord, jr., 1852–3 [I.C.B.S.].
Numerous UNION WORKHOUSES in various parts of the country [*A.P.S.D.*].

WHITE, BENONI (*c.*1784–1833), was an architect of Devizes, where his father, Benoni White, senior, was in business as a builder. He died on 28 July 1833, aged 49, surviving his father by only a month [*Gent's Mag.* 1833 (ii), 189]. A third generation is represented by Benoni Thomas White (*c.*1808–51), to whom there is an inscription in St. James's churchyard, Devizes. He too appears to have been an architect. Benoni White (d. 1833) was the surveyor in charge of the repewing of ALL CANNINGS CHURCH, WILTS., in 1829 [I.C.B.S.]. His designs for the vicarage at WEST or BISHOP'S LAVINGTON, WILTS., 1830, are in the Salisbury Diocesan Records. Shortly before his death he made designs for rebuilding the body of ST. JAMES'S CHURCH, DEVIZES, which were carried out after his death by John Peniston of Salisbury (*q.v.*).

WHITE, CHARLES, an architect employed by the Board of Ordnance, exhibited at the Society of Artists in 1765, and at the Free Society of Artists between 1768 and 1783. The majority of his exhibits were of a topographical character, but they included a 'design for a town house for a person of distinction' (1769). In 1783 he showed 'a drawing of the entrance of the Dockyard at Portsmouth' and when Mrs. Lybbe Powys visited Portsmouth in 1792 with Lady Parker, it was 'Mr. White, Master of the Works', who showed them round [*Passages from the Diaries of Mrs. Lybbe Powys*, ed. Climenson, 1899, 267].

WHITE, EDWARD, was a builder, surveyor and architect at Margate, Kent, where he designed the Town Hall and Market Place in 1821 [Kidd's *Companion to the Isle of Thanet*, *c.*1830].

WHITE, FULLER (*c.*1719–1784?), of Weybridge, Surrey, was a carpenter by trade. From *c.*1755 to 1767 he was employed by the Earl of Lincoln, first at OATLANDS, nr. WEYBRIDGE, SURREY, and then at CLUMBER, NOTTS. Intending to erect 'some plain Buildings' at Clumber, the Earl 'judged Mr. White might be capable of conducting them & thereby save the expense of full Commission to a Regular Surveyor'. Building proceeded under White's direction from 1760 to 1767, but he proved to be either dishonest or incompetent and was first dismissed and then prosecuted for money owing to the Earl. He was also employed at BAUMBER CHURCH, LINCS., a church in the Earl's patronage which was remodelled in the Gothick style in the 1760s [D. J. Bradbury, *Clumber*, 1988, 3–4; Newcastle papers in Nottingham University Library, NeL 1098].

White is said to have designed the wooden bridge built at HAMPTON COURT in 1751–3 [H. Ripley, *History of Hampton*, 1884, 82], though there is no mention of him in the deeds relating to the construction of the bridge in the Surrey Record Office, and in 1771 he submitted designs for a wooden bridge across the Thames at Maidenhead [J. W. Walker, *History of Maidenhead*, 1931, 13–14]. In 1770 he received £210 for the 'repairs' and 'ornaments' of the churchyard at NEWBURY, BERKS., which probably included the erection of the two Gothick gateways, but it is not clear whether White designed them himself [H. Clifford Smith in *C. Life*, 24 March 1950, Correspondence; *Berks. Archl. Jnl.* 54, 1954–5, 65–6]. A monumental inscription in Weybridge churchyard records his death on 8 November 178[4?] in his 66th year.

WHITE, JOHN, was a baillie of Paisley, where he lived in Townhead. He held the office of Stampmaster and was founder and fourth president of the local Society for Reform of Manners. Among other buildings in Paisley he designed the HOSPITAL in HIGH STREET (dem.) and the TOLBOOTH, 1757 ['Semplis Scraps' in Paisley Library, *ex inf.* Mr. David Walker; W. M. Metcalfe, *History of Paisley*, 1909, 316, with illustration of Tolbooth]. The Tolbooth was rebuilt in 1821 and its steeple was demolished in 1870. White also designed the HIGH CHURCH, 1750–4, and its tower, 1770 [Robert Brown, *History of the High Church, Paisley*, Paisley 1880, 5–6, 11, 14; drawings of the roof construction among plans at Inveraray Castle].

WHITE, JOHN (*c.*1747–1813), was an able and successful surveyor who made a fortune out of property development in London. As surveyor to the Duke of Portland he was employed to lay out the Portland estate in Marylebone from about 1787 onwards. He himself was one of the principal speculators, and a survey of the estate made by him in 1797–9 (reproduced by A. T. Bolton in *The Architecture of R. and J. Adam* ii, 102) shows that he had been personally responsible for the erection of the houses on the west side of Harley Street between Weymouth Street and New Cavendish Street. Later he was concerned in the plans for the development of Marylebone Park, the greater part of which, leased to the Duke of Portland, was due to revert to the Crown in 1811. He submitted three plans for the layout of the park to John Fordyce, the Surveyor-General of Land Revenues, one of which (made in 1809) he published in 1813 together with an *Explanation of a Plan for the Improvement of Mary-le-bone Park*. One of its principal features was to be a 'Grand Crescent' approached by a continuation of Harley Street, with a new parish church designed by his son in the middle of the semicircle. Beyond there was to be a landscaped park surrounded by detached villas. White's proposals were set aside in favour of others by Nash, but his conception of a residential park (as opposed to a mere extension of urban London) was one which Nash took over and developed into the present Regent's Park.

White also had a considerable business as a builder and architect. He designed and built at least one large country house (Glevering Hall), and a list of other buildings with which he was concerned is given below. He occupied a house of his own erection in Marylebone, where he was active in local affairs, and built a country house for himself at Two Waters, nr. Hemel Hempstead in Hertfordshire. He married the daughter of Thomas Farnolls Pritchard, the Shrewsbury architect (*q.v.*), by whom he had two sons, John (*q.v.*) and Henry. He died in Marylebone on 21 November 1813, in his 67th year. His portrait in the R.I.B.A. Collection is illustrated in *R.I.B.A. Jnl.* xlix, 1942, 109, and there is a volume of his drawings and accounts in the same collection. [*A.P.S.D.*; *Gent's Mag.* 1813 (ii), 510; John Summerson, *John Nash*, 1935, 104, 109, 111, 118; Ann Saunders, *Regent's Park*, 1969, *passim.*]

LONDON, MARYLEBONE PARISH WORKHOUSE, 1755, dem. 1896, and the attached INFIRMARY, 1796–7, dem. 1881 [Thomas Smith, *Parish of St. Marylebone*, 1833, 271–3; R.I.B.A.D.].

CHISWICK HOUSE, MIDDLESEX, addition of wings for 5th Duke of Devonshire, 1788; dem. 1952. Although the wings are generally attributed to James Wyatt, e.g. by Neale, *Seats*, 2nd ser. v, 1829, there are drawings for them by White in R.I.B.A.D. pp. 27–31, and in 1837 the (R.)I.B.A. was told that the wings . . . were not added by

Wyatt, as generally supposed, but by Mr. White' [*Gent's Mag.* 1837 (ii), 1781].[1]

LONDON, MARYLEBONE, house for himself in New Road, opposite north end of Devonshire Place, 1791; dem. 1820 (drawing by Grimm in B. L., Add. MS. 15542, f. 139).

WOOLBEDING, nr. MIDHURST, SUSSEX, alterations for Lord Robert Spencer, 1791 [Arthur Oswald in *C. Life*, 15 Aug. 1947].

LONDON, No. 3 SLOANE TERRACE, work for David Thomas, 1792–3 [R.I.B.A.D., accounts, pp. 215 *et seq.*].

GLEVERING HALL, SUFFOLK, for Chaloner Arcedekne, 1792–4; enlarged by D. Burton 1834–5 [H. Davy, *Views of the Seats of Noblemen and Gentlemen in Suffolk*, 1827: 'from the plans of Mr. White'; R.I.B.A.D.].

FENGATE HOUSE, WEETING, NORFOLK, proposed alterations to farm-buildings, etc., 1801 [Norfolk Record Office, 13733].

WESTON PARK, STAFFS., repairs and improvements for 2nd Lord (1st Earl of) Bradford, 1802–8 [Weston muniments 3/13] (*C. Life*, 9, 16, 23 Nov. 1945).

BUXTON, DERBYSHIRE, block of houses known as THE SQUARE, 1806–7 [Ivan Hall, *Georgian Buxton*, Derbyshire Museum Service 1984, 39–40].

BUXTON, DERBYSHIRE ST. JOHN'S CHURCH, 1811-12 [drawings in B. L., Add. MS. 31323, I & J. signed 'John White & Son 1802 & 1811'].

TWO WATERS, nr. HEMEL HEMPSTEAD, HERTS., for himself; dem.

Works for Lady Bute 'at her New Offices, Green & Hot Houses, Garden, etc.', probably at BUTE HOUSE, PETERSHAM, SURREY (dem.) [R.I.B.A.D., pp. 201–12].

WHITE, JOHN (–1850), son of John White (d. 1813), was educated at Roy's Academy in Burlington Street, and afterwards assisted his father as surveyor to the Duke of Portland. He made a design for a double church 'upon a new principle accomodating a large number of persons', which he presented to the Marylebone vestry in 1812. It is illustrated in his pamphlet on the plans for Regent's Park. In 1807 he was appointed District Surveyor for St. Marylebone parish, a position which he retained for the remainder of his life. In 1845 he became the first chairman of the newly formed Association of District Surveyors. He was also a Commissioner of the Property Tax and on the Commission of Sewers for Westminster. After his father's death, White carried on his architectural practice, designing, in 1820, the premises of Smith's, the coachmakers, at 210 REGENT STREET [John Summerson, *John Nash*, 1935, 224]. He also desgined the EYRE ARMS TAVERN and ASSEMBLY ROOMS at ST. JOHN'S WOOD, and competed for London Bridge (1823) and the Houses of Parliament (1835). He published his designs for the former in a pamphlet *On Cementitious Architecture as applicable to the Construction of Bridges*, with an account of the first iron bridge designed by his grandfather, T. F. Pritchard, in 1775. In 1824 he took out a patent for a floating breakwater, of which he published an account entitled *An Essay on the Formation of Harbours of Refuge . . . by the Adoption of Moored Floating Constructions as Breakwaters*, 1840. He also published *Some Account of the Proposed Improvements of the Western Part of London by the Formation of the Regent's Park, etc.* (1814, 2nd ed. 1815), in which he described and illustrated the rival plans for the new park, including that made by his father in 1809. A letter illustrating the method suggested by him for lighting Benjamin West's picture gallery in Newman Street was printed in the *Builder* iii, 1845, 367. White married in 1805, and built himself a small house called Bridge House, on the north side of the canal at Westbourne Green, Paddington. He died in 1850, leaving a son, John Alfred White, who succeeded to his post as District Surveyor. [*A.P.S.D.*; W. L. Rutton, 'Westbourne Green', *Home Counties Magazine* ii, 1900, 277–8; R. M. Robbins, 'Some Designs for St. Marylebone Church', *London Topographical Record* xxiii, 1972.]

WHITE, THOMAS (*c.*1674–1748), of Worcester, was a carver and monumental mason whose claim to be considered as an architect rests on a passage in Nash's *History of Worcestershire* (1782). According to Nash, White was a native of Worcester and was apprenticed to 'a statuary and stonecutter in Piccadilly near Hyde Park Corner', after which 'Sir Chr. Wren took him with him to Rome, and placed him with a statuary there; in the intervals of his business, he by stealth made admeasurements of all the component parts of St. Peter's Church, and assisted Sir Chr. in modelling that of St. Paul's London. At his return to England Wren would have retained him for his foreman, to superintend the building of St. Paul's, but Mr. White having an estate in houses at Sidbury in Worcester, chose rather to retire to his native city, where he lived in great reputation as a master-builder and architect. He also occasionally exercised the art of sculpture, for he wrought the statue of Queen Anne which originally stood on a pedestal before the town

[1] There is, however, a design for a ceiling at Chiswick in the Wyatt album in the Metropolitan Museum at New York.

hall, and is now placed in a nich over the door of the modern building, for which the City of Worcester gave him his freedom. A better specimen of his skill was the Britannia in the tything of Whiston's; he also carved the bust of bishop Hough, in the east end of All Saints Church, and the bust of King George, over the gateway of Edgar's Tower, for which he is said to have taken only a promise to be invited yearly to the audit dinner. He is believed to have been the architect to several of the new churches, and at length at the request of the corporation he undertook to rebuild the town hall, which he performed so much to their satisfaction that they settled upon him a yearly pension for life of £30 a year. He never married, lived in easy circumstances, and died about the year 1738.'

Little of this account can be substantiated by documentary evidence, and parts of it are demonstrably inaccurate. Sir Christopher Wren was never in Italy, and there is no evidence that he employed White at St. Paul's or elsewhere.[1] White's will (P.C.C. 282 STRAHAN) shows that he died in 1748, not in 1738, and the *Worcester Postman* for 1713–14 proves that Nash was wrong in supposing that he never married, for it contains an advertisement in the name of 'Thomas White of the City of Worcester, Carver', disowning debts incurred by his wife Elinor.

That White was admitted a freeman of Worcester in return for making the statue of Queen Anne is, however, confirmed by a resolution of the City Chamber to that effect in 1709. There is, moreover, evidence that he was responsible for the elaborate carving that is the most striking feature of the Worcester Guildhall, for the great trophy in the pediment is signed by him and dated 1722. But there is no evidence that he designed the building itself, whose architect has yet to be identified.

The 'new churches' of which (according to Nash) White was 'believed to have been the architect' were those of St. Nicholas (1730–5), St. Swithin (1734–6), and All Saints (1738–42). St. Swithin's was designed and built by Thomas & Edward Woodward of Chipping Campden, All Saints probably by its builders, Richard Squire and William Davis. Only at St. Nicholas (where no documentation survives) may White perhaps have been involved in the design [D. Whitehead, 'The Georgian Churches of Worcester', *Trans. Worcs. Archl. Soc.* 13, 1992].

Outside Worcester the only building with which White can be associated is Castle Bromwich Church, Warwicks., which was remodelled at the expense of Sir John Bridgeman between 1726 and 1731. Among the Bridgeman papers at Weston Hall, Staffs., is the contract, dated 18 January 1724/5, whereby Thomas Clear *alias* Smith, of Castle Bromwich, mason, undertook to rebuild the tower of the church 'according to the form and module hereunto annexed', that is to say, in accordance with a crude elevation still attached to the document. The tower is surmounted by a panelled parapet with urns at the angles, and the contract specifies that the 'Battlements' 'are to be made and built of Stone so much as Mr. White of the City of Worcester, carver, shall think and say he reasonably deserves for the finishing the same' [G. W. Beard in *C. Life*, 20 July 1951]. This by no means proves that the church was designed by White, and it is significant that the clause in which his name appears is concerned solely with the value of ornamental masonry. The crude drawing is, moreover, in marked contrast to the very competent draughtsmanship of White's designs for two monuments in Blodwell Church, Shropshire, which survive in the Bridgeman muniments. These drawings are signed 'T. White, Worcester', but the monuments themselves (to Ursula, wife of Sir John Bridgeman, and her father Roger Mathews) are signed 'T. White, Salop.', which appears to indicate that the sculptor also had a yard at Shrewsbury. For a list of other monuments signed by White, see Gunnis's *Dictionary of British Sculptors*.

White died at Worcester in August 1748, and was buried at Kempsey, nr. Worcester, on the 26th of that month. According to a manuscript note in the Birmingham Reference Library copy of Green's *History of Worcester*, he was 74 years of age. In his will, dated 23 August 1748, he is described as 'Thomas White of the parish of St. Peter in the City of Worcester Statuary'. He left most of his property, which included a tenement in Prince Street, Westminster, to his servant, Mary Rudsbey.

[T. R. Nash, *History of Worcestershire* ii, 1782, Appendix, p. cxvi; V. Green, *History of Worcester* ii, 1796, 89–90; J. Chambers, *Biographical Illustrations of Worcester*, 1820, 344–6; J. Noake, 'The History of the Guildhall Worcester', *Associated Architectural Societies' Reports and Papers* xv, 1879–80; W. R. Buchanan-Dunlop, 'Thomas White of Worcester, Sculptor and Architect', *Trans.*

[1] Nash's statement may have been due to a confusion with another White who died on 13 Dec. 1764, aged 'near 90', and who is said to have 'conducted the curious woodwork in the dome of St. Paul's, a large part of Greenwich Hospital, and many other public buildings' [*Gent's Mag.*, 1764, 603].

Worcestershire Arch. Soc. N.S. xx, 1943, N.S. xxi, 1944, 64–5; Marcus Whiffen, 'A Note on Thomas White of Worcester', *Burlington Mag.* lxxxiv, May 1944, and lxxxviii, 1946, 76; Marcus Whiffen, 'White of Worcester', *C. Life*, 7 Dec. 1945; *Wren Soc.* iv, 17, xviii, 188–9, 203–4; information from Mr. B. Brotherton and Mr. D. Whitehead.]

WHITING, JOHN (1776–1846), a carpenter by trade, set up business in Ipswich in 1804, when he advertised his willingness to design houses. He was subsequently described as 'architect', and (by 1844) as 'County Surveyor'. In 1845 he went into partnership with Henry Woolnough (1820–62). The Norwich Diocesan Records show that he designed or altered a number of Suffolk parsonage houses, including those of ST. MARY QUAY, IPSWICH, in FOUNDATION STREET, 1822; CREETING ST. PETER, 1826; ST. MARY STOKE, IPSWICH, 1830; LITTLE GLEMHAM, 1834; NACTON, 1837; and HENLEY, 1837 [C. Brown *et al.*, *Dictionary of Architects of Suffolk Buildings 1800–1914*, 1991, 194].

WHITING, THOMAS (–1679), was a joiner by trade and was Master of the London Joiners' Company in 1677. He designed BREWERS' HALL, ADDLE LANE, LONDON, which was built in 1670–3 by John Caine, bricklayer (*q.v.*), 'according to the designe drawne by Mr. Whiting the Surveyor'. Whiting's 'Platforme of the Hall front' is preserved with the building accounts in the Guildhall Library (MS. 5502). The Hall is illustrated by R.C.H.M., *London* iv, 93–5. [H. L. Phillips, *Annals of the Joiners' Company*, 1915, 42, 128; will, P.C.C. 151 KING].

WHITLING, HENRY JOHN, practised at first from London, but Whitling is an old-established Cornish name, and several of his early commissions were from the south-western counties. In 1835 he was successful in the competition for a new Guildhall and Market House at Penzance, the design for which he exhibited at the Royal Academy, but the Municipal Reform Act intervened, and the new Corporation dropped Whitling's plans and instead adopted those of William Harris of Bristol. Whitling sued for damages and was paid £300 in compensation [P. A. S. Pool, *History of Penzance*, Penzance 1974, 135; *Architectural Mag.* ii, 1835, 138]. He also designed workhouses at BEAMINSTER and BRIDPORT in 1836 [*Architectural Mag.* iii, 1836, 532], and competed unsuccessfully for one at Bideford [*Trans. Devonshire Assoc.* 50, 1918, 552]. In 1839 another at RHAYADER in RADNORSHIRE was built to his designs [*Welshman*, 1 Feb. 1839, *ex inf.* Mr. T. Lloyd]. Early in the 1840s Whitling moved to Shrewsbury and designed the church of CWM-HEAD, nr. WISTASTOW, 1842–4, and in 1843 that of WALMLEY, nr. SUTTON COLDFIELD, WARWICKS., both in the neo-Norman style. At Cwm-Head he misled the incumbent into believing that his design had been approved by the Incorporated Church Building Society, and by 1844 he was reported to have left the country, 'having got into pecuniary difficulties', leaving the church at Walmley to be completed by D. R. Hill of Birmingham [I.C.B.S., files 2936, 3109, *ex inf.* the Revd. T. Parry]. In 1834 he had published *A Series of Original Designs for Shop Fronts.*

WHITMORE, Sir GEORGE (1775–1862), was the son of George Whitmore of Lower Slaughter Manor in Gloucestershire, and himself succeeded to the property on his father's death in 1794. In 1789 he entered the Royal Military Academy at Woolwich as a Gentleman Cadet, and in 1794 joined the Royal Engineers, in which he eventually rose to the rank of General. As a young officer he served at Gibraltar and from 1811 to 1829 was Commanding Officer of the Royal Engineers in Malta. He died in England on 2 April 1862.

In MALTA Whitmore designed the Doric portico of the MAIN GUARD in PALACE SQUARE, VALLETTA, and the NAVAL HOSPITAL at BIGHI, refitted parts of the interior of the GOVERNOR'S PALACE, altered the interior of the MANOEL THEATRE, and was responsible for completing the unfinished MONUMENT to SIR ALEXANDER BALL in the LOWER BARRACCA GARDEN. He also designed the monument to Col. Edwards (d. 1816) in the UPPER BARRACCA GARDEN. His designs (*c.*1825) for a Protestant Cathedral in the form of a Greek Cross with an Ionic portico were accepted by Lord Hastings as Governor, but did not proceed beyond the foundations.

While in Malta Whitmore went to Corfu at the behest of Sir Thomas Maitland, then Governor of Malta and high commissioner of the Ionian Islands, and there designed and built the PALACE OF ST. MICHAEL AND ST. GEORGE, 1819–24, and the circular temple known as SIR THOMAS MAITLAND'S MONUMENT, dated 1816 but not in fact built until 1821. These were notable as the first Greek Revival buildings on Greek territory, and show considerable scholarship and architectural ability. In 1822 Whitmore supervised the excavation of the archaic Greek temple at Cadachio in Corfu, and supplied an account of it for inclusion in the supplementary volume of *The Antiquities of Athens*, published in 1830.

It has been suggested that in Malta Whitmore took the credit for buildings that were actually designed by a talented Maltese artist and architect, Giorgio Pullicino, who was employed in his office as a draughtsman. Though Pullicino may have been a valuable assistant, Whitmore was himself a competent architectural draughtsman, and there is no reason to doubt his ability to design the neo-classical buildings of which (as his diary shows) he certainly considered himself to be the architect. In retirement he wrote a small MS. treatise on the designing of villas and their gardens, illustrated by his own elegant drawings, which remains among his papers in the Gloucestershire Record Office.

[Whitmore's MS. journals in the Glos. C.R.O., printed in part in *The General: The Travel Diaries of General Sir George Whitmore*, ed. Joan Johnson, 1987; *Giorgio Pullicino, Architect and Painter*, ed. J. Azzopardi, Mdina 1989; J. E. Dimacopoulos, 'Neo-classical preludes in Greece: George Whitmore's Architecture in Corfu', thesis submitted for the Diploma in Conservation Studies, York 1975; J. Dimacopolous, 'Whitmore of Corfu', *Arch. Rev.* Dec. 1979; S. Hourmouzios, 'An English Palace in Corfu', *C. Life*, 26 April 1962; Burke's *Landed Gentry*, *s.v.* 'Whitmore of Orsett Hall and Gumley'; monumental inscription in Lower Slaughter Church.]

WHITTAKER, the Revd. JOHN WILLIAM (?1790–1854), was a learned clergyman who had considerable knowledge in the fields of philology, geology and astronomy. He was vicar of Blackburn from 1822 until his death, and in 1825 married the eldest daughter of William Feilden of Feniscowles in Lancashire [*D.N.B.*]. The records of the Incorporated Church Building Society show that it was he who designed IMMANUEL CHURCH at FENISCOWLES in 1835–6 in a competent Gothic style. No other evidence of his architectural activities has so far come to light.

WHITTICKE, or **WHITTRICKE,** —, was employed by George Vernon in connection with the building of SUDBURY HALL, DERBYSHIRE, between 1660 and 1690. Vernon's account-book shows that in 1668 'Mr. Whitticke' was paid £100 for unspecified work or services, and that in September 1671 'Mr. Whittricke, surveyor' received the final instalment of a further payment of £11, but it is not clear what part, if any, he played in designing the house (illustrated in *C. Life*, 15–29 June 1935 and 10 June 1971).

See p. 1138

WHITTINGTON, WILLIAM (1769–1849), was a builder, surveyor and architect at Neath in Glamorganshire, of which town he was an Alderman. By 1828 he was surveyor of bridges for the county, and in that year OGMORE BRIDGE nr. BRIDGEND was built under his direction [*The Cambrian*, 19 July 1828]. He stated in 1836 that he had built NANTYGLO HOUSE, MONMOUTHSHIRE (dem.) for Joseph Bailey, *c.*1806 and GLANUSK PARK, BRECONSHIRE, for the same person, 1825–35, but he did not claim to have been the architect of either house and Glanusk was designed by Robert Lugar (*q.v.*) [N.L.W., Slebech 3964, p. 18]. In 1833 he certified the accounts for enlarging PENCERRIG HOUSE, RADNORSHIRE for Thomas Thomas [N.L.W., Pencerrig 325–8], and may have been responsible for the design. He also appears to have designed LAMPETER CHURCH, CARDIGANSHIRE, 1836–8 (rebuilt 1870) [I.C.B.S.] and ST. JOHN'S CHURCH, CLYDACH, GLAMORGANSHIRE, 1847, described as 'in the late Perpendicular style' [*The Cambrian*, 27 Feb. 1846]. Whittington died on 31 July 1849 after an accident [*The Cambrian* 3 and 10 Aug. 1849; information from Mr. Thomas Lloyd, to whom all references are due].

WHITTLE, JAMES (*c.*1742–1812), of Manchester, designed ST. JOHN'S, BLACKBURN, LANCS., a large classical church built in 1787–9, to which a tower was added in 1793, presumably by Whittle [*Leeds Intelligencer*, 24 May 1787, and Faculty for tower in Cheshire R.O., EDA 2/9, ff. 167–9, both *ex inf.* Dr. T. Friedman]. The demolished R.C. CHAPEL of ST. WILFRID at PRESTON, 1793, closely resembled St. John's. The recent death at Ardwick, nr. Manchester, of 'Mr. James Whittle, an eminent architect', was reported in *Gent's Mag.* Jan. 1813 (i), 87.

WHITWELL, THOMAS STEDMAN (1784–1840), was a native of Coventry. He was in London by 1806, when he began to exhibit at the Royal Academy, and in 1811 gave his address as the Architect's Office at the London Docks, where he was presumably employed as an assistant under D. A. Alexander. He attended Soane's lectures at the Royal Academy, and in 1813 offered his help in making the illustrative drawings and diagrams which accompanied them. This offer does not appear to have been accepted, and Whitwell was subsequently suspected of being the author of an attack on Soane which was printed in the *Guardian* of 20 May 1821, and also of the amusing but offensive article on 'The Sixth or Boeotian Order of Architecture', whose appearance in *Knight's Quarterly Magazine* for 1824 led Soane to institute legal proceedings against the publishers.

Whitwell's practice was chiefly in Birmingham and Coventry, where he designed a number of minor public buildings which have nearly all been demolished. In 1819 he made designs for a proposed development at Leamington Spa to be called 'Southville', of which a sketch was exhibited at the Royal Academy by W. Finley. The scheme included a church which was to be 'in dimension and external style, a facsimile of the Parthenon'. In 1825–6 Whitwell was involved in another utopian project, Robert Owen's Socialist community at New Harmony in Indiana. A model was made of his design of which he published a *Description* (London, 1830), and a bird's-eye view of the settlement drawn by him is in the National Library of Wales. His professional career was marred, if not ruined, by the collapse of the Brunswick Theatre in Whitechapel, whose iron roof fell only three days after its completion, with considerable loss of life. According, however, to the architect, the accident was due to 'an improper suspension of machinery and other heavy weights upon the tie-beams' rather than to any inherent defect in the construction. Whitwell died in Gray's Inn in May 1840. He had made a large collection of notes and sketches for a book to be called *Architectural Absurdities*, but it was not published and the MS. has been lost. He did, however, publish a tract *On warming and ventilating houses and buildings by means of large volumes of attempered air, as applied to some of the public edifices of the University of Cambridge; and illustrated by the case of the new fever-wards of Addenbrooke's Hospital in that town*, Cambridge 1834. The Gothic ticket of admission to Fonthill Abbey which he designed for the sale of 1823 is illustrated in *C. Life*, 25 April 1968.

[*A.P.S.D.*; B. Poole, *Coventry, its History and Antiquities*, 1870, 134; *Gent's Mag.* 1840 (ii), 107; *Builder* i, 1843, 272; A. T. Bolton, *The Portrait of Sir John Soane*, 1927, 143–4, 250, 374–81, S. Redgrave, *Dictionary of Artists of the English School*, 1878, 469; A. Bestor, *Backwoods Utopias*, Philadelphia 1970, 128–9, 169 n., 177, 214.]

BEECH HOUSE, BRANSGORE, HANTS., remodelled for J. P. Anderdon, 1816 [*Beauties of England and Wales*, Appendix to Introduction, 600].

BIRMINGHAM, THE NEW INDEPENDENT MEETING HOUSE, CARR'S LANE, 1819–20; refronted 1876; dem. *c.*1970 [exhib. at R. A. 1821].

COVENTRY, THE WEST ORCHARD CONGREGATIONAL CHAPEL, 1820; destroyed by bombing 1940 [*V.C.H. Warwicks.* viii, 389].

BIRMINGHAM, THE NEW LIBRARY (afterwards the Birmingham Joint Stock Bank), TEMPLE ROW WEST, 1820–1, Italianate [exhib. at R. A. 1820, 1821].

BRAMPTON PARK, HUNTS., for Lady Olivia Sparrow, 1821–2, Gothic; largely destroyed by fire 1907 [*A.P.S.D.*].

BIRMINGHAM, THE PANTECHNETHECA, NEW STREET (show-rooms), for Charles Jones, 1823; dem. [correspondence in the *Birmingham Chronicle* and *The Bazaar*, 1823] (J. Taylor, *The Architectural Medal*, 1978, No. 76a).

BIRMINGHAM, JONES'S GOLD AND SILVER MANUFACTORY, NEW STREET, 1823–4 [Birmingham Reference Library, 398204, f. 75].

COVENTRY, ST. MARY'S HALL, restoration, 1824 [*V.C.H. Warwicks.* viii, 143].

WARWICK, THE INDEPENDENT CHAPEL, COW LANE (now Brook Street), enlarged 1826 [J. N. Brewer, *The Warwick Guide*, n.d., 82].

LONDON, THE BRUNSWICK THEATRE, GOODMAN'S FIELDS, 1827–8; collapsed 1828 [*Companion to the Almanac*, 1828, 174].

COVENTRY, THE GAOL, *c.*1831; dem. 1860 [*V.C.H. Warwicks.* viii, 144].

WHITWORTH, JOHN (–1863), practised in Barnsley, where he died on 27 January 1863 [Principal Probate Registry, Calendar of Probates]. He added a S. aisle and chancel to CAWTHORNE CHURCH, YORKS. (W.R.), 1829 [I.C.B.S.], later largely rebuilt by G. F. Bodley, and a S. aisle to WOMBWELL CHURCH, YORKS. (W.R.), 1832–5 [I.C.B.S.].

WHYTE, DAVID A— (–1830), was a builder-architect living at Templeton, nr. Newtyle in Angus. Advertisements for contracts in the *Dundee Advertiser* show that he built a number of farmhouses in the neighbourhood between 1810 and 1830. His more important works were BANDIRRAN HOUSE, PERTHSHIRE, 1811, dem. *c.*1957; offices at AIRLIE CASTLE, ANGUS, for the 7th Earl of Airlie, 1813; GLENISLA MANSE, ANGUS, 1813 [S.R.O., HR 338/4]; KEITHICK HOUSE, nr. COUPAR ANGUS, PERTHSHIRE, for Dr. Wood, 1818–23, altered by D. Bryce 1839 [accounts at Keithick]; GLENISLA CHURCH, ANGUS, 1821 [S.R.O., RHP 7724]; and BALNABOTH HOUSE, ANGUS, reconstruction and offices, for the Hon. Donald Ogilvy, 1824–5 [S.R.O., GD 16/27/311]. [Information from Mr. David Walker.]

WICKHAM, WILLIAM (*c.*1750–), was a pupil of Edward Stevens, to whom he was apprenticed in 1767 [P.R.O., Apprenticeship Registers]. He was admitted to the Royal Academy Schools in 1770 at the age of

20, and was awarded the Silver Medal the same year. He exhibited at the Academy from 1772 to 1787, at first (1772) from Putney, then from various London addresses, and finally (1787) from Walworth. A set of designs by him for additions to Giles Hudson's house at Putney is in the Yale Center for British Art.

WICKINGS, WILLIAM (*c.*1757–1841), of Islington, was Surveyor to the County of Middlesex from 1805 to 1815. He designed the CHAPEL OF ST. MARY MAGDALENE, HOLLOWAY ROAD, ISLINGTON, an undistinguished classical building erected in 1812–14; altered 1895 and 1983 [S. Lewis, *History of Islington*, 1842, 254]. Wickings was President of the Surveyors' Club in 1807 and again in 1828, and gave the President's chain and badge in 1823. He died in Barnsbury Place, Islington, on 26 November 1841, aged 84 [*Gent's Mag.* 1842 (i), 112].

WIDDOWS, JOHN, designed the brick upper part of the tower of ST. OLAVE'S CHURCH, HART STREET, LONDON. On 10 March 1731/2, 'the Plan of Mr. John Widdows was approved off by the Gentlemen in Vestry', and on the completion of the work in 1732, it 'was agreed to make him a present of 20 guineas' for his 'care pains and trouble in attending from time to time as Surveyor during the Rebuilding of the Church Steeple' [Vestry Minutes in Guildhall Library, MS. 858/1].

WIGG, JOSEPH (*c.*1752–1824), Surveyor to the Inner Temple and Master of the Tylers' and Bricklayers' Company in 1819–20, was the founder of the firm of Wigg & Mansfield,[1] subsequently Wigg, Mansfield & Wigg, and eventually Wigg & Pownall, builders, surveyors and architects, whose premises were first at 10 North Place, Gray's Inn Lane and later at 7 Bedford Row. He was also Carpenter and from 1815 onwards Surveyor to the Society of Gray's Inn, for whom he designed the plain brick range of chambers known as VERULAM BUILDINGS in 1803. On his death in 1824 he was succeeded as Surveyor to Gray's Inn by his son George Wigg, who in 1825 designed the matching RAYMOND BUILDINGS on the west side of Gray's Inn gardens. In 1833 the Surveyorship of Gray's Inn passed to George's brother Francis Wigg (d. 1868), who in 1840–1 designed the Tudor Gothic LIBRARY (dem. 1941), and in 1842–3 (with George Pownall) the Jacobethan STAPLE INN BUILDINGS, HOLBORN, together with the lodge and gates between Staple Inn and Southampton Buildings. Wigg and Pownall also designed ST. CLEMENT'S CHAPEL, HASTINGS, SUSSEX, 1838, Gothic, dem. *c.*1970 [I.C.B.S.], and drawings exhibited at the Royal Academy in 1840–1 show that they competed for the Royal Exchange and for the Liverpool Assize Courts.

Under the names of 'Wigg, Son & Oliver' and 'Wigg, Oliver & Hudson', the firm continued at 7 Bedford Row up to the end of the century. It was evidently a successful one, for Francis Wigg left considerable property in Hertfordshire, including a country house at Frogmore in the parish of Aston, and Joseph's estate was valued at some £60,000 when he died on 26 February 1868. In 1852 he had founded almshouses at St. Stephen's near St. Albans, and it was presumably he who built the existing Victorian Gothic house at Frogmore.

[Gray's Inn Pension Books, vols. IV–VIII; *Gent's Mag.* 1824 (ii), 571; *V.C.H. Herts.* ii, 431–2; P.C.C. 698 ERSKINE; Principal Probate Registry, Calendar of Probates.].

WIGGENS, THOMAS, of Greenwich, won a premium from the Society of Arts in 1761 for his designs for a 'Temple of Fame' [Dossie, *Memoirs of Agriculture* iii, 1782, 420]. This was probably the Pantheon-like building for which drawings signed by Wiggens are in Sir John Soane's Museum (xlvii, 9, 3–5), together with a design for a new front for St. Stephen's Walbrook Church in the City of London. Wiggens, then under 25 years old, was probably the son of the Thomas Wiggens of Greenwich who in 1755 had been employed to survey the estates of Thomas Steavens in the Isle of Sheppey [*The Chirograph*, no. 9, Jan. 1940, 5]. In 1764 either he or his father designed the GREENWICH PARISH WORKHOUSE [Greenwich Vestry Minutes, 14 Dec. 1764, *ex inf.* Mr. Frank Kelsall]. In 1769 Thomas Wiggins of London competed for the Royal Exchange at Dublin [*Builder* xxvii, 1869, 781]. In 1770 he designed the CLOTHWORKERS' COMPANY'S

[1] James Mansfield was appointed Bricklayer to Gray's Inn in 1797, and in 1806 an advertisement to build a corn market and assembly rooms at Chepstow stated that plans might be seen at Mr. James Mansfield, John Street, Bedford Row (*Cambrian*, 22 Feb. 1806, *ex inf.* Mr. Thomas Lloyd). His son George Mansfield was evidently associated with Joseph Wigg in 1803, when he exhibited a drawing of Verulam Buildings at the R.A., and in the 1820s James Mansfield and Son and George Mansfield jr. were builders in Little James Street, Gray's Inn. In 1837 R. J. Mansfield exhibited at the R.A. from Wigg's office an elevation of 'Sopwell Hall proposed to be built near St. Albans'. Several members of the family were Masters of the Tylers's and Bricklayers' Company between 1827 and 1865.

ALMSHOUSES in FROG LANE, ISLINGTON [Clothworkers' Company's archives, *ex inf.* London Division, English Heritage]. With George Gibson he surveyed and condemned the old parish church of Lewisham, Kent, in 1773 [L. L. Duncan, *The Parish Church of St. Mary, Lewisham*, 1892, 12–16].

WIGHTWICK, GEORGE (1802–1872), was the only son of a country gentleman who lived first at Albrighton in Salop. and then at Alyn-Bank, nr. Mold in Flintshire, where George was born on 26 August 1802. His father was accidentally drowned in 1811. Four years later his mother married again and moved with her husband, a Mr. Damant, to London. George, who had begun his education at Wolverhampton Grammar School, was now sent to Lord's School at Tooting. In 1818 he was articled to Edward Lapidge but failed to secure admission to the Royal Academy Schools. On the termination of his pupilage in 1823, he obtained some desultory work by writing for a topographical dictionary and making drawings for Britton & Pugin's *Public Buildings of London*. Seeing no prospect of regular employment, he thought of abandoning architecture for the stage, but in 1825 his stepfather came to the rescue and gave him £100 to visit Italy. Here he worked industriously, making drawings which were to form the basis of his future publications. On his return in the following year he applied to Sir John Soane for employment, and for several months fulfilled the exacting duties of amanuensis and companion to the eccentric old gentleman, of whose person and dwelling he afterwards wrote a lively description (reprinted by A. T. Bolton in *The Portrait of Sir John Soane*, 395–410). But permanent employment still eluded him and in 1827, with the aid of a friendly loan, he published a volume of *Select Views of Roman Antiquities* in the hope of attracting prospective clients. This made a small profit, but failed to bring its author any commissions. It was followed by an unpublished play and a volume of essays entitled *The Life and Remains of Wilmot Warwick*, which the *Examiner* acknowledged as good enough for 'lassitude and a sofa'. In 1829, seeing no hope of establishing himself in London, Wightwick moved to Plymouth, where he soon built up a considerable local practice. He was invited by John Foulston, then about to retire, to enter into partnership with him, and in due course took his place as the leading architect in the western counties. In his own words:

> Houses, shops, terrace-rows, and other buildings in Plymouth, were committed to my superintendence: the stewards of the manor of Stoke Damerel (the late Mr. Cole and E. St. Aubyn, Esq.) retained me as architect to Devonport and its spreading suburb; and I made my entry into Cornwall as designer of a large residence, in the *then* Tudor style, at Liskeard. Mr friend, Dr. E. M., had put into my hands the first of my more important Plymouth works; and soon after its completion I removed into No. 3 Athenaeum Terrace, the 'important work' aforesaid. . . . Befriended also by the Revd. T. Phillpotts, my clerical connection so increased, that I had soon a half-dozen chapels, as many schools, and twice as many parsonage houses in hand. Then came the county 'great ones' and gentry, with their profitable requirements; and I was shortly busy, either in the construction of new, or the improvement of existing, buildings, varying in importance from the second-rate mansion to the lodge or cottage. . . . This indeed was my 'golden period', my clear receipts, before the establishment of income tax, averaging £1000 a year and in one year reaching £1800.

Like Foulston, Wightwick was eclectic in his choice of styles, and designed Gothic churches as well as classical public buildings and Italianate terraces. But his interest in ecclesiology was not sufficient to satisfy the High Church party which dominated the diocese of Exeter in the 1840s, and soon he began to lose his ecclesiastical patronage:

> My obstinate adherence to the principle of a peculiar form for the *auditorium* of a Protestant church, and to the necessity for modifying old Gothic design so as to adapt it to modern purposes,[1] lost me all prestige with my kind clerical employers. . . . Others were soon in the place which had very likely remained mine had I consented to be the mere draughtsman of the Diocesan Architectural Society; and from this time I declined as the leading practitioner in the south-western counties.

In 1851, seeing no prospect of recovering his former position, he gave up practice and retired to Clifton. In 1855 he moved to Portishead in Somerset, where he died on 9 July 1872. His first wife, the daughter of his stepfather by a former marriage, died in 1867, and in the following year he married Isabella, the daughter of Samuel Jackson, a water-colour painter of Clifton.

Wightwick is described as 'one of the best

[1] See Wightwick's letter on the subject in *Builder* iii, 1845, 16.

readers of Shakespeare's plays that ever read to the public . . . and much sought after as an entertainer of guests at . . . parties at country houses'. 'He possessed brilliant powers of conversation, with an unusual amount of wit, which made him a great favourite in society.' Writing came almost as naturally to him as drawing. In fact he may probably be regarded as the first English architectural journalist, contributing lightweight articles to *Fraser's Magazine* and the *New Monthly Magazine* as well as writing serious architectural criticism in *The Library of the Fine Arts* or Weale's *Quarterly Papers*. His first publication of 1827 was followed by 'Sketches by a Travelling Architect', published in *The Library of the Fine Arts* i–iv, 1831–2; *Remarks on Theatres*, 1832; *Nettleton's Guide to Plymouth, Stonehouse, Devonport and the Neighbouring Country*, 1836; *Sketches of a Practising Architect: A Selection of Vases, Chairs, Altars and Fragments from the Vatican*, 1837; an essay on the use of iron in architecture, printed in Loudon's *Architectural Magazine* iv, 1837; *The Palace of Architecture: a Romance of Art and History*, an elaborately illustrated survey of the historical styles aimed 'at the boudoir of the ladies' and designed 'to promote a just appreciation of Architecture in the minds of all who are susceptible of the Beautiful, the Poetical and the Romantic'; 'Ancient and Modern English Gothic Architecture', in Weale's *Quarterly Papers on Architecture* iii, 1845; *Hints to Young Architects*, 1846, 1847, 2nd ed. 1860, new ed. by Guillaume 1875, 1880; critical comments on Ruskin's *Seven Lamps of Architecture* in *The Architect and Building Operative*, 1849, 482 *et seq.*; and 'The Principles and Practice of Architectural Design', in the *Detached Essays* of the Architectural Publication Society, 1853. In 1858 he was awarded the Essay Medal of the R.I.B.A. for a 'Critical Study on the Architecture and Genius of Sir Christopher Wren'. His terms of employment were printed in *The Architect* ii, 1850, 28, and reprinted in *R.I.B.A. Jnt.* 1891, 61. His autobiography was published serially as 'The Life of an Architect', in *Bentley's Miscellany* xxxi–xxxv, 1852–4; xlii–xliii, 1857–8. He left his MS. lectures and a large collection of his drawings to the R.I.B.A. Library.

[*A.P.S.D.*; *D.N.B.*; A. T. Bolton, *The Portrait of Sir John Soane*, 1927, 393–413; J. Mordaunt Crook, 'Regency Architecture in the West Country', in *Journal of the Royal Society of Arts* cxix, 1971, 438–51.]

Drawings for nearly all the works listed below exist in the six volumes of Wightwick's drawings in the R.I.B.A. Collection, which appear to constitute a complete record of his work. If no other source is stated, it may be assumed that it is a drawing or drawings in the R.I.B.A. Collection.

PLYMOUTH AND DEVONPORT

ATHENAEUM TERRACE, 1832–4.

THE CRESCENT, terrace facing, *c.*1833.

OLD TOWN and TREVILLE STREETS, two houses and shop for Messrs. Dobb, Rundle & Brown, drapers, *c.*1833; dem. (G. Worsley, *Architectural Drawings of the Regency Period*, 1991, 152–3).

SUSSEX PLACE, 1833–6.

THE INDEPENDENT CHAPEL, NORLEY STREET, 1834; dem.

THE SOUTH DEVON AND EAST CORNWALL HOSPITAL, 1835–6 (*Architectural Mag.* iii, 1836, 566–9).

THE ESPLANADE, 1836.

THE TOWN HALL, 1839–40; dem. [*Civil Engineer and Architect's Jnl.* ii, 1839, 397].

HOLY TRINITY CHURCH, 1840–2, classical; dem.

THE DEVON AND CORNWALL FEMALE ORPHANAGE, LOCKYER STREET, 1841 [L. Jewitt, *History of Plymonth*, 1873, 438].

THE BAPTIST CHURCH, GEORGE STREET, 1845, classical.

GEORGE STREET, shops, *c.*1845 [*Companion to the Almanac*, 1847, 248].

THE ROYAL BRITISH FEMALE ORPHAN ASYLUM, STOKE DAMAREL, 1845–6.

CHRIST CHURCH, ETON PLACE, 1845–6; dem.

THE PUBLIC CEMETERY, 1847–8.

CONGREGATIONAL CHAPEL, COURTENAY STREET, façade in 'Anglo-Norman' style, 1847–8 (*Builder* vi, 1848, 499).

THE PUBLIC AND COTTONIAN LIBRARIES, enlarged and refronted, 1850; dem. (*Civil Engineer and Architect's Jnl.* xiii, 1850, 316; *The Architect and Building Gazette* ii, 1850, 426–7).

THE POST OFFICE, DEVONPORT, 1850 [*Architect and Building Gazette* ii, 1850, 223, 566–7, with plan and elevation].

THE MECHANICS' INSTITUTE, designed the interior, 1850 [*Architect and Building Gazette* ii, 1850, 318, with plan].

DEVON AND CORNWALL

LUXSTOWE, nr. LISKEARD, CORNWALL (now Council Offices), for William Glencross, 1831–2 (E. Twycross, *Mansions of England and Wales: Cornwall*, 1846).

CALLINGTON, CORNWALL, MARKET HOUSE and INN, for Alexander Baring, 1832–3; dem.

FALMOUTH, CORNWALL, ROYAL CORNWALL POLYTECHNIC HALL, 1835–6.

HAZELDON, nr. TAVISTOCK, DEVON, for C. V.

Bridgman, 1833–4, Tudor Gothic.

PENDREA, GULVAL, nr. PENZANCE, CORNWALL, a *cottage orné* for John Bedford, 1833–4.

HELSTON, CORNWALL, THE GUILDHALL, 1834 [*Architectural Mag.* ii, 1835, 44; drawings in Cornwall County Record Office].

HELSTON, CORNWALL, THE GRAMMAR SCHOOL, 1834.

HELSTON, CORNWALL, MONUMENT to H. M. Grylls, 1834, in form of Tudor Gothic gateway.

BRIXTON HOUSE, DEVON, new front, etc., for Henry Collins-Splatt, 1834.

BUDE CHURCH, CORNWALL, for Sir T. D. Acland, 1834–5, Gothic; enlarged 1876–7 (*Architectural Mag.* ii, 1835, 345–8).

HELSTON CHURCH, CORNWALL, restoration, 1837–8 [I.C.B.S.].

CREDITON CHURCH, DEVON, 'refitted and improved', 1838 [*Civil Engineer and Architect's Jnl.* i, 1837–8, 264].

TREVARNO, nr. HELSTON, CORNWALL, for C. W. Popham, 1839.

LAUNCESTON, CORNWALL, THE MARKETS, *c.*1840.

LANNER CHURCH, CORNWALL, 1840, Italianate.

LUPTON HOUSE, nr. BRIXHAM, DEVON, alterations for Sir J. B. Yarde Buller, Bart., *c.*1840.

MOUNT EDGCUMBE, CORNWALL, alterations and additions for 3rd Earl of Mount Edgcumbe, *c.*1840–4; little of Wightwick's work survived the bombing of 1941 and subsequent restoration (*C. Life*, 8 March 1902, 22–29 Dec. 1960).

PENDARVES, nr. CAMBORNE, CORNWALL, alterations to dining-room for E. W. W. Pendarves, 1841; dem. *c.*1955; and other buildings on the estate, for which see *Cornish Studies* 6, 1979 for 1978, 41–2.

PORTREATH CHURCH, CORNWALL, 1841, Gothic.

FLUSHING CHURCH, CORNWALL, 1841–2, 'Anglo-Norman'.

TRESLOTHAN CHURCH, CORNWALL, 1842, Gothic.

CADBURY CHURCH, DEVON, Gothic reredos, *c.*1842.

BODMIN, CORNWALL, COUNTY LUNATIC ASYLUM, additions, 1842 and 1847–8 [J. MacLean, *Deanery of Trigg Minor* i, 1873, 105].

BROWNSTON CHURCH, DEVON, 1844, Gothic.

CALVERLEIGH COURT, DEVON, for Joseph Chichester Nagle, 1844–5.

PENCARROW, CORNWALL, alterations for Sir William Molesworth, Bart., 1844–6, including Palladianizing of principal elevations, addition of porch, and formation of Music Room with shrine of Aphrodite [bound volume of drawings in Wightwick's hand and accounts in *British Almanac* for 1846, both at Pencarrow] (*C. Life*, 8–16 July 1954).

TREGENNA CASTLE, nr. ST. IVES, CORNWALL, enlarged for H. L. Stevens, 1845.

WATERMOUTH CASTLE, nr. ILFRACOMBE, DEVON, completion of interior and alterations to north front, for Arthur Basset, *c.*1845, Gothic.

TREGREHAN HOUSE, ST. BLAZEY, CORNWALL, alterations for Col. Edward Carlyon, including new S. front, 1848–9; Ionic colonnade dem. 1969 (E. Twycross, *Mansions of England & Wales: Cornwall*, 1846).

PENQUITE, GOLANT, CORNWALL, for Thomas Graham, 1848–9.

TRISTFORD HOUSE, DEVON, for Mrs. Wynne Pendarves, 1849, Tudor Gothic; enlarged *c.*1890.

PARSONAGES

Designs were made by Wightwick for the following Cornish parsonages, not all of which were necessarily built: GWENNAP, Tudor Gothic; LANREATH; LISKEARD, Tudor Gothic; MORVAH; PELYNT, Gothic; PROBUS, Tudor Gothic; ST. DOMINIC, Tudor Gothic; ST. IVES; SITHNEY; TRESLOTHAN; WENDRON.

WILCOX, EDWARD, was the son of Jonathan Wilcox (d. 1687), a master carpenter employed in rebuilding the church of St. Vedast, Foster Lane, in 1670–3. In 1676–8 Jonathan Wilcox was employed as surveyor by the commissioners appointed to lay out the Arundel estate in the Strand for Henry Howard, afterwards 6th Duke of Norfolk [Arundel Castle MS. MD 1514]. One of the commissioners was the architect William Winde, and in 1683 Winde employed Wilcox as master carpenter at Combe Abbey in Warwickshire. Winde's correspondence (Bodleian, MS. Gough Warwicks. 1) shows that Edward was left in charge of the business during his father's absence in Warwickshire. Both father and son were concerned in the building of ST. JAMES'S CHURCH, PICCADILLY, and in 1686 it was a design for the spire submitted by 'Mr. Wilcox' (probably the father) that was adopted by the Vestry in preference to one provided by Wren. This spire, a simple structure of wood covered with lead, was erected by Edward Wilcox in 1687, but had almost immediately to be dismantled owing to the appearance of cracks in the tower. Twelve years later, when the tower had been stabilized, it was decided to construct a new spire. Wilcox was asked to 'prepare some pretty design', but it is not clear whether the spire actually built (which survived until

1940) was his design or Wren's [*Survey of London* xxix, 32–8].

In 1689 Edward Wilcox contracted to perform the carpenter's work of the new stables and guard-house at Kensington Palace, and he was also employed in Hampton Court Gardens and at Dyrham Park, Glos., by William Talman. He was no doubt the 'Mr. Wilcocks' whose somewhat old-fashioned design for a new building at ALL SOULS COLLEGE, OXFORD, *c.*1710, is in the Clarke Collection at Worcester College [H. M. Colvin, *Catalogue of Architectural Drawings . . . in the Library of Worcester College*, 1964, pl. 52]. In 1721 the Duke of Chandos asked Wilcox to 'look over' the plans for his projected house in CAVENDISH SQUARE, LONDON, in order 'to reduce them into a less expensive compass', and invited him to 'undertake the whole care & conduct of the structure'. In the event the house was never built, but in *c.*1725 Wilcox built another house in the same square for the 1st Viscount Harcourt. The architect was Thomas Archer, but Wilcox modified his designs in execution, for there is an engraving by Rocque of the principal elevation, 'as it was drawn by Mr. Archer, but Built & Altered to what it now is by Edward Wilcox, Esq.' (see above, p. 77, and C. H. & M. I. Baker, *The Life and Circumstances of James Brydges, Duke of Chandos*, 1949, 267–8).

[*Wren Soc.* xx, 245; *Cal. Treas. Books and Papers 1702–14, passim.*]

WILDGOS, JOHN (1613–1672), was a member of the London Carpenters' Company, serving as a Warden in 1652, 1656 and 1658, and as Master in 1660. He was appointed one of the two City Viewers in 1655, and was among the 'former viewers of this Citty' who signed surveys made by Hooke, Mills and Oliver after the Great Fire. He was a Common Councilman for Portsoken Ward in 1659–60 and 1671–2.

In 1664 Wildgos designed the new gallery or Court Room at CARPENTERS' HALL, LONDON WALL (dem. 1867). This was a long narrow building extending south with a handsome pedimented façade facing the Company's garden on the east. In 1671 the windows of the hall itself were altered under his direction [E. B. Jupp & W. W. Pocock, *Historical Account of the Company of Carpenters*, 1887, 229–32, with illustration; cf. Shepherd, *London in the Nineteenth Century*, 1829, pl. 24].

After the Great Fire of 1666 Wildgos was involved in rebuilding the Halls of several of the City Companies. In 1666–8 he was responsible for the rebuilding of SALTERS' HALL (dem. 1823) [J. Steven Watson, *A History of the Salters' Company*, 1963, 81–2] (Brayley, *Beauties of England & Wales* x (ii), 1814, 373); in 1668 he made a 'draught or modell' for rebuilding the HALL OF THE COOPERS' COMPANY (dem. 1865), for which he was rewarded with a gift of five gold pieces [W. Foster, *Short History of the Coopers' Company*, Cambridge 1944, 76]; in 1668–70 he rebuilt the HALL OF THE PEWTERERS' COMPANY (dem. 1840), for which he made several 'draughts' [C. Welch, *History of the Pewterers' Company* ii, 1902, 137; accounts in Guildhall Library, MS. 7086/4]; and in 1669 he was paid £1 by the Scriveners' Company 'for draughts of the Hall', though the design adopted in 1670 appears to have been by William Young (*q.v.*) [Bodleian, MS. Rawlinson D. 734, ff. 20–5].

Wildgos died in May 1672, leaving considerable property to his family. His yard in Petticoat Lane went to his son John Wildgos, junior [P.C.C. 68 EURE; J. R. Woodhead, *The Rulers of London, 1660–1689*, 1965, 177].

The façade of Wildgos's addition to Carpenters' Hall and the arcaded entrance to Salters' Hall were both designs of some merit in which the simple classicism of the Restoration was tempered by some agreeable reminiscences of mannerism.

WILDS, AMON (1762–1833), was born in Hastings in January 1762. Originally established in Lewes, he moved to Brighton with his son, A. H. Wilds, in *c.*1815, and for some years carried on business as a builder in both towns simultaneously. He acted as Surveyor to the Town Commissioners of Brighton from 1825 to 1828, and was himself a Commissioner in 1832–3. He died in the latter year and was buried in St. Nicholas churchyard. The inscription on his tomb is given in J. A. Erredge's *History of Brighthelmston*, 1862, 107.

At Lewes Wilds rebuilt the nave of ALL SAINTS CHURCH in 1806, and soon afterwards designed and built Nos. 1–4 CASTLE PLACE. Nos. 2–3 were bought by Dr. Gideon Mantell, the geologist, and in 1819 were converted into a single house, whose porch has capitals designed in the form of fossil ammonites. The 'ammonite' capital was adopted by the firm and occurs on several buildings in Brighton designed by A. H. Wilds. He also designed the FIRE ENGINE HOUSE in the yard of the Star Inn in Fisher Street, 1817–18, demolished 1893 [W. H. Godfrey in *Sussex Notes and Queries* xv, May 1958, 4–6].

In Brighton Wilds designed WESTERN LODGE for Mrs. Sober *c.*1817, and RICHMOND TERRACE, which he built as a speculation in 1818. He presumably also designed the CONGREGATIONAL CHAPEL or ELIM FREE CHURCH in UNION STREET, which he built in 1820.

[Parish Register of All Saints, Hastings, *ex inf.* Mr. Derek Sherborne; A. Dale, *Fashionable Brighton*, 1847, *passim*; Michael Kearney, 'Ammonites in Architecture', *C. Life*, 27 Jan. 1983; Neil Bingham, *C. A. Busby*, 1991.]

WILDS, AMON HENRY (1784–1857), of Brighton, was the son and at first the partner of Amon Wilds (*q.v.*). In 1834, however, he entered into partnership with C. A. Busby (*q.v.*), in conjunction with whom he laid out the Kemp Town estate for T. R. Kemp, and took an active part in the development of Brighton as a seaside resort, designing many stuccoed crescents and terraces in the manner of John Nash. He was one of the Town Commissioners of Brighton from 1845 to 1848.

In 1827 the *Brighton Gazette* announced that Wilds was about to undertake extensive work at Chepstow on 'property belonging to the Duke of Beaufort, Mr. Jenkins and Mr. Stoke', and in 1829 that he had just returned from Limerick, where he was engaged upon 'some plans for the improvement and embellishment of that city' and a house for Sir Aubrey Hunter. Nine months later the same paper stated that he was 'shortly to commence large works in Wales and elsewhere'. In 1830 he was engaged in laying out a 'new town' on the Milton Park estate, nr. Gravesend, of which he exhibited a 'general view' at the Royal Academy. [A. Dale, *Fashionable Brighton*, 1947, *passim*; Neil Bingham, *C. A. Busby*, 1991, 62.]

Unless otherwise stated the following list of works is based on A. Dale's book cited above.

BRIGHTON

HOLY TRINITY CHAPEL, for Thomas Read Kemp, 1817; since altered and enlarged [*The Watering-Places of Great Britain and Fashionable Directory*, 1833, 30].

THE ROYAL PAVILION HOTEL, CASTLE SQUARE, alterations, 1820.

attributed: THE UNITARIAN CHAPEL, NEW ROAD, 1820.

attributed: Nos. 53–56 MONTPELIER ROAD.

Houses in KING'S ROAD between Middle Street and West Street, opened 1822.

KEMP TOWN (i.e. SUSSEX SQUARE, LEWES CRESCENT, ARUNDEL TERRACE and CHICHESTER TERRACE), for T. R. Kemp, 1823–*c.*1850, with C. A. Busby.

ORIENTAL PLACE and TERRACE, WEST CLIFF, 1825.

THE ROYAL NEWBURGH ASSEMBLY ROOMS, No. 31 CANNON PLACE (now flats), *c.*1825–33.

SILLWOOD PLACE, 1827.

SILLWOOD HOUSE (now Hotel), WEST CLIFF, for Sir David Scott, 1827–8.

WESTERN TERRACE (including his own house, Western Pavilion), *c.*1827.

HANOVER CRESCENT, *c.*1827.

ST. ALBAN'S HOUSE, REGENCY SQUARE, 1828–9.

PARK CRESCENT, 1829.

MONTPELIER CRESCENT, 1843–7.

VICTORIA TERRACE, HOVE (incomplete).

THE STEINE, No. 26.

THE VICTORIA FOUNTAIN on THE STEINE, 1846.

ELSEWHERE

CHEPSTOW, MONMOUTHSHIRE, proposed development for 6th Duke of Beaufort, Mr. Jenkins and Mr. Stoke, *c.*1827.

LIMERICK, IRELAND, a house for Sir Aubrey Hunter, 1829.

WORTHING, SUSSEX, PARK CRESCENT, *c.*1830 [exhib. at R.A. 1830–1].

CLANDON REGIS (dower house), CLANDON, SURREY, for 3rd Earl of Onslow, *c.*1830; rebuilt by Basil Champneys *c.*1890 [exhib. at R.A. 1830].

GRAVESEND, KENT, laid out MILTON PARK ESTATE (i.e. Berkeley Crescent, Harmer Street, etc.), *c.*1830.

GRAVESEND, KENT, THE CLIFTON BATHS, 1835; dem. [*Gent's Mag.* 1836 (i), 654].

GRAVESEND, KENT, refronted the TOWN HALL, 1836 [R. P. Cruden, *History of Gravesend*, 1843, 425].

WILKIE, ALEXANDER (*c.*1744–1811), 'Wright and Architect in this Burgh', is commemorated in Pittenweem Churchyard, Fife. He died on 18 June 1811, aged 67.

WILKINS, WILLIAM (1751–1815), born in Norwich in 1751, was the son of William Wilkins (*c.*1720–83), a plasterer and stucco worker of St. Benedict's parish. He was apprenticed to a London plasterer before entering into partnership with his father in 1773 (*Norwich Mercury*, 6 Nov. 1773). By the time of his father's death in 1783 he had acquired sufficient ability in draughtsmanship to advertise that, besides executing stucco and plasterwork 'in the very best manner', he also made 'Designs in Architecture . . . with Drawings of Buildings in Section, Elevation and Perspective' (*Ipswich Jnl.* 5 April 1783). Sir John Soane, who early in his career had carried out some alterations to Norwich Castle of which Wilkins disapproved, wrote of him as 'an able stuccadore who . . . had acquired some facility in drawings, and a smattering of Gothic lore, fancying himself an Architect' (*Professional Memoirs*, 1835, 20). Many of his architectural commissions were due to his friend Humphry Repton, who introduced him to prospective clients such as Lord Moira and Bartlett Gurney of Northrepps (for whom he designed a new house that was never built but is shown in Repton's Northrepps 'Red Book'). Repton's son, John Adey Repton, was later to become his pupil.

In 1799 Wilkins took a lease of the Norwich Theatre, of which he (and apparently his father before him) had for some years been one of the proprietors. He completely refitted the interior and added a colonnade at the east end before reopening the theatre, which, with its circuit, remained under his management until his death.

Wilkins was a Fellow of the Society of Antiquaries and had strong antiquarian interests. He wrote a number of papers on antiquarian and astronomical topics, including an 'Essay towards a History of the Venta Icenorum of the Romans and of Norwich Castle, with Remarks on the Architecture of the Anglo-Saxons and Normans', which was printed in *Archaeologia* xii, 1796, 132–80. Between 1782 and 1787 he exhibited at the Royal Academy several drawings and views of Norwich Cathedral, and between 1798 and 1800 John Adey Repton made, under his direction, an elaborate series of drawings of the Cathedral that was bought by the Society of Antiquaries and eventually published in facsimile in 1965. In Norwich Wilkins was one of the original members of a society of literati and intellectuals founded in 1785 and known as the 'United Friars'.

As a classical architect Wilkins designed nothing outstanding, but the fruits of his antiquarian studies are apparent in the Gothick fancies of Donington Hall and in his restoration of the upper part of St. Ethelbert's Gate at Norwich.

Towards the end of his life Wilkins moved to Cambridge, where he built himself a house. He died in London on 22 April 1815, in his 64th year. There is a tablet to his memory in St. Giles's Church, Cambridge. He had a very large family (thirty children altogether, according to William Daniell, though many died in infancy), the eldest of whom, William Wilkins, R.A., is noticed below. Another son, George, had a successful career in the Church, and a third, Henry, established himself as a builder at Bury St. Edmunds.

[*A.P.S.D.*; J. Chambers, *Norfolk Tour* ii, 1826, 1160–1; S. J. Wearing, *Georgian Norwich; its Builders*, 1926, 42–51; Dorothy Stroud, *Humphry Repton*, 1962, 38–9; Farington's Diary, 11 May 1808; *Gent's Mag.* 1815 (i), 474; C. B. Jewson, *The Jacobin City*, 1975, 145.]

SHELFORD, CAMBS., Mausoleum in the Camping Close for Thomas Wale, 1775; dem. 1845 [H. J. Wale, *My Grandfather's Pocket Book*, 1883, 5, 176, 179].

DONINGTON HALL, LEICS., for 2nd Earl of Moira (afterwards Marquess of Hastings), begun *c.*1790, date 1793 over front door, substantially complete by 1797 but chapel still under construction in 1802, externally Gothic [G. Richardson, *New Vitruvius Britannicus* ii, 1808, pls. 31–5; J. Brushe, 'Wilkins Senior's original designs for Donington Park as proposed by Repton', *Burlington Mag.* 121, 1979, 113–4] (*C. Life*, 22 March 1979].

NORWICH CASTLE, restoration, 1792–3 [*A.P.S.D.*].

STOKE EDITH, HEREFS., lodges at Hereford and Ledbury entrances to park and cottages in village, for Edward Foley, 1792–6 [drawings in Hereford C.R.O., B 30/1, nos. 11–12, etc.].

CALKE ABBEY, DERBYSHIRE, alterations and additions for Sir Henry Harpur, Bart., including Dining Room and Drawing Room, 1793–4, Library, 1804–5, portico, 1806–8, and lodges [H. Colvin, *Calke Abbey, Derbyshire*, 1985, 106–9, 122].

BRACONDALE LODGE, nr. NORWICH, NORFOLK, for Philip Martineau, *c.*1795; dem. *c.*1966 [D. Stroud, *Humphry Repton*, 1962, 66–7].

CAMBRIDGE, GONVILLE AND CAIUS COLLEGE, enlarged THE MASTER'S LODGE, 1795 [Willis & Clark, i, 202].

CAMBRIDGE, No. 38 NEWMARKET ROAD, for himself, *c.*1795 [R.C.H.M., *Cambridge*, 369].

HIGH LEGH HALL, CHESHIRE, stables, coachhouse, etc., for G. J. Legh, 1795–7; dem. 1963 [John Rylands Library, Manchester, correspondence among Legh muniments].

CAMBRIDGE, KING'S COLLEGE CHAPEL, minor repairs, 1798–1802 and 1811–12 [Willis & Clark, i, 531–2].

MILTON HOUSE, NORTHANTS., Gothic lodge for 4th Earl Fitzwilliam, *c.*1800 [*Gent's Mag.* 1801 (ii), 707].

CAMBRIDGE, NEWNHAM COTTAGE, QUEEN'S ROAD, for himself, *c.*1800 [R.C.H.M., *Cambridge*, 375–6].

NORWICH, THE THEATRE, reconstructed 1800; dem. [S. J. Wearing, *Georgian Norwich: its Builders*, 1926, 44–51].

THORESBY PARK, NOTTS., bridge for Lord Newark, *c.*1800 [J. H. Hodson, 'The building and alteration of the second Thoresby House, 1767–1804', *Thoroton Soc. Record Series* xxi, 1962, 18].

OXFORD, TRINITY COLLEGE, addition of attic storey to N. and W. sides of GARDEN QUADRANGLE, 1802 [Trinity College Archives,

Miscellanea, vol. 2, f. 18].

SOUTHWELL MINSTER, NOTTS., repaved choir and reroofed Chapter House, 1803; again reroofed 1880 [N. Summers, *A Prospect of Southwell*, 1974, 45].

PRESTWOLD HALL, LEICS., alterations for C. J. Packe, 1805 [C. Hussey in *C. Life*, 23 April 1959].

NORWICH CATHEDRAL, repaired interior after fire, 1806 [J. Britton, *History of the Cathedral Church of Norwich*, 1816].

GREAT YARMOUTH, NORFOLK, ST. NICHOLAS CHURCH, replaced spire, 1807; since removed [J. Preston, *Picture of Yarmouth*, Yarmouth 1819, 39].

COLCHESTER, ESSEX, THE NEW THEATRE, QUEEN STREET, 1811–12; destroyed by fire 1918 [Wearing, *op. cit.*, 51; G. O. Rickword, 'The Theatre Royal, Colchester 1812–1918', *Essex Review* 54, 1944, 22].

NORWICH, ST. ETHELBERT'S GATE, restoration of upper part, 1815 [J. T. MacNaughton-Jones, 'St. Ethelbert's Gate, Norwich', *Norfolk Archaeology* 34, 1966, 78, 81].

Note: It is clear from a lawsuit reported in *Norfolk Chronicle*, 8 Aug. 1818 that Wilkins was employed at Stanfield Hall, Norfolk, *c.*1815 as a plasterer only, the architect being W. Saul (*q.v.*). Unsigned drawings for alterations at HOLME PIERREPONT HALL, NOTTS., *c.*1790, are probably in Wilkins's hand.

WILKINS, WILLIAM (1778–1839), the eldest son of William Wilkins (*q.v.*), was born in Norwich on 31 August 1778. After receiving his early education at Norwich Grammar School, he entered Caius College, Cambridge, as a scholar in 1796, graduating B.A. as sixth wrangler in 1800. In the following year he was given a travelling scholarship which enabled him to spend four years in Greece, Asia Minor and Italy. During his absence he was elected (1803) a Fellow of Caius, and from 1804 to 1806 was Master of the Perse School (a sinecure regularly held by junior fellows of his college). His fellowship terminated on his marriage in 1811.

Simultaneously with his academic education Wilkins was being brought up by his father as an architect. While still an undergraduate he made measured drawings (now at Columbia University) of King's College Chapel which show his precocious ability as a draughtsman, and in 1799 he exhibited two drawings at the Royal Academy, one a view of the Gate of Honour at his own college, the other a 'Design for improving the seat of a nobleman in Nottinghamshire'. On his return from the Mediterranean in 1804 he immediately started practice in Cambridge, where he remained until about 1809, when he established an office in London (at first in Bedford Place, later in Weymouth Street).

Wilkins soon established himself as a leading protagonist of the Greek Revival. His earliest recorded work, Osberton House in Nottinghamshire, is notable for its Greek Doric portico, 'the first full-scale, pure Grecian portico in British domestic architecture'. This was followed by Downing College, where Wilkins's uncompromisingly Grecian design, backed by Thomas Hope, triumphed over James Wyatt's more old-fashioned neoclassicism. At the same time his similar design for Haileybury College was chosen by the Directors of the East India Company in preference to the one submitted by their own surveyor, Henry Holland. Other major buildings designed by Wilkins in the Grecian style were University College London, the Museum at York and the National Gallery in Trafalgar Square. In his domestic (as in most of his collegiate) work Wilkins bowed to the current fashion for Tudor Gothic, and only at Grange Park, Hampshire, was he able to persuade his client that a Greek temple could form a suitable residence for an English gentleman.

Like every architect of his time who sought for important commissions, Wilkins was obliged to enter for public competitions. In 1817, in conjunction with J. P. Gandy, he obtained the premium for the 'Waterloo Monument', with a design for an ornamental tower of three orders surrounded by a colonnade based on the Temple of the Sybils at Tivoli. This 'national monument', for which the estimate was £200,000, was to have stood at the north end of Portland Place, but was never built [*Gent's Mag.* 1817 (i), 624; *The Farington Diary*, ed. J. Greig, viii, 127]. In 1834 he competed for the Duke of York's column in Waterloo Place, and in 1835 for the Houses of Parliament. After the latter competition he wrote a pamphlet entitled *An Apology for the Design of the New Houses of Parliament marked Phil. Archimedes*, in which he criticized the plans of his rivals and attacked the decision of the committee. At Cambridge he had, in 1822, obtained the second prize for a design for the new Observatory, and in 1825, when the Fellows of St. John's College 'agreed to apply to Mr. Wilkins, Mr. Browne and Mr. Rickman' for designs for their new Court, it was the last-named whose plans they eventually adopted. In 1829 Wilkins was one of the four architects who were invited to submit designs for the proposed extension of the University Library. None was, however, adopted, and fresh designs were solicited from the same architects in the following year. Once more there was no agreement as to whose was the best design, and pamphlets were published in favour of those submitted by C. R. Cockerell and Messrs. Rickman & Hutchinson. Wilkins's design met with little favour, but he endeavoured to gain support by publishing an *Appeal to the Senate* in April 1831. In 1836, when the competition at last terminated in Cockerell's favour, none of the sixty-nine votes cast was in favour of Wilkins. Wilkins also competed without success for the Fitzwilliam Museum in 1835.

The circumstances in which Wilkins was chosen to be architect of the National Gallery are difficult to elucidate. He himself claimed that he had been the first to suggest that the site of the former Royal Mews should be used for the erection of a National Gallery. This was in 1831, when it was proposed to demolish the Mews and build shops on their site. Wilkins at once made designs for adapting the existing buildings for the purposes of a gallery. His scheme was brought to the notice of Lord Grey, the Prime Minister, who appointed a committee to consider it. The idea ultimately met with approval, and in March 1833 Parliament voted £50,000 for the erection of a new building to house both the Royal Academy, the Public Records, and the national collection of pictures. Designs were also submitted by John Nash and C. R. Cockerell, but there was no formal competition, and the whole affair was denounced as a 'job' in the *Spectator* and the *Literary Gazette*. The story that Nash and Cockerell submitted their designs in good time, but that Wilkins did not complete his until the last moment, when, urged by Samuel Rogers (a member of the committee), he 'sat up all night [and] sent one in [which was] instantly accepted against Cockerell and Nash', appears to be apocryphal.

Wilkins was an architect for whom scholarship was in some danger of inhibiting invention. Though his knowledge of antique sources was probably as wide as Cockerell's he lacked the latter's ability to assimilate and to synthesize. His was an architecture based essentially on archaeological investigation. It was a style more suited for public than for private buildings, and it was fortunate for Wilkins that the period after Waterloo was one of great public works which provided many opportunities for monumental architecture. In his handling of the Greek orders Wilkins showed more scholarship than Nash or Burton, and more sensibility than Smirke or Burn. But his architecture is effective in detail rather than in mass, and the National Gallery illustrates his characteristic inability to subordinate the parts to the whole. As a Gothic architect he specialized in the Tudor style which he used for both collegiate and country-house commissions. In Scotland Dalmeny House (with details derived from East Anglian manor houses such as East Barsham) provided a model that was imitated by William Burn and others. In England the pierced screen at King's Collge (originally intended to have been backed by a cloister) was a stroke of picturesque invention that shows what Wilkins could do when he was released from the shackles of classical scholarship.

Wilkins was elected F.S.A. in 1800 and to membership of the Society of Dilettanti in 1809. He was elected A.R.A. in 1824, R.A. in 1826, and F.R.S. in 1831. In May 1837 he was appointed Professor of Architecture in succession to Sir John Soane, but did not live to deliver any lectures. In 1824 he succeeded S. P. Cockerell as Surveyor to the East India Company. From his father Wilkins inherited the management of the Theatre Royal at Norwich (which he rebuilt), and he had a controlling interest in the theatres at Bury St. Edmunds, Cambridge, Colchester, Ipswich and Yarmouth. He was an enthusiastic patron of the theatre, and a portrait of him and his family in theatrical dress is reproduced in *R.I.B.A. Journal* xlvi, 1939, 914.

Very much a scholar, Wilkins was the author of several learned works on classical architecture, and as a commentator on Vitruvius he had the distinction of being the first to interpret the passage in Book III concerning *scamilli impares* in terms of a device for the correction of optical illusions in architecture (cf. *R.I.B.A. Journal*, 27 Aug. 1891, 424). His published works were 'An Account of the Prior's Chapel at Ely', in *Archaeologia* xiv, 1801; *The Antiquities of Magna Graecia*, Cambridge 1807, containing drawings of the temples at Syracuse, Agrigentum, Segesta and Paestum; 'John of Padua and Porta Honoris', in *Vetusta Monumenta* iv, 1809; *Atheniensia, or Remarks on the Topography and Buildings of Athens*, 1816; *The Civil Architecture of Vitruvius*, a translation with 41 plates, prefaced by a 'History of the Rise and Progress of Grecian Architecture', written anonymously by Lord Aberdeen, 1812; and *Prolusiones Architectonicae*, essays on Greek and Roman architecture, 1837. He was also the author of *A Letter to Lord Viscount Goderich on the Patronage of the Arts by the English Government*, 1832, a controversial pamphlet which was reprinted in the *Library of the Fine Arts* later the same year.

Wilkins died on 31 August 1839 at his house in Lensfield Road, Cambridge. He was buried in the crypt of Corpus Christi College

Chapel. A bust by E. H. Baily dated 1830 belongs to Trinity College, Cambridge, and is at present on loan to the Fitzwilliam Museum. John Hargrave Stevens was his pupil and Benjamin Ferrey was in his office for a time. Several drawings by him are in the R.I.B.A. Drawings Collection and the Yale Center for British Art.

[*A.P.S.D.*; *D.N.B.*; *Gent's Mag.* 1839 (ii), 426–7; *Civil Engineer and Architect's Jnl.* ii, 1839, 388; *The Architect*, 1886, 338–9; A. Beresford Pite, 'The Work of William Wilkins, R.A.', *R.I.B.A. Jnl.* 3rd ser. xl, 24 Dec. 1932; Gavin Walkley, 'William Wilkins', *C. Life*, 30 Dec. 1939; J. Mordaunt Crook, 'Haileybury and the Greek Revival. The Architecture of William Wilkins, R.A.', *The Haileyburian and I.S.C. Chronicle*, 1964; David Watkin, *Thomas Hope*, 1968; J. A. Venn, *Alumni Cantabrigienses*; Willis & Clark, ii, 278, iii, 97–117, 195; *History of the King's Works* vi, 1973, 461–70; John Harris, *Catalogue of British Drawings for Architecture, etc., in American Collections*, 1971, 276–8; R. W. Liscombe, *William Wilkins*, Cambridge 1980.]

PUBLIC BUILDINGS

THE EAST INDIA (now HAILEYBURY) COLLEGE, HERTS., 1806–9; enlarged 1874–5 [J. Mordaunt Crook, 'Haileybury and the Greek Revival', *The Haileyburian and I.S.C. Chronicle*, 1964].

CAMBRIDGE, DOWNING COLLEGE, 1807–20 [Willis & Clark ii, 761; C. M. Sicca, *Committed to Classicism: The Building of Downing College, Cambridge*, Cambridge 1987].

BATH, LOWER ASSEMBLY ROOMS, added Doric portico, 1808–9; rooms rebuilt by G. A. Underwood 1823–5, retaining the portico; dem. 1933 [exhib. at R.A. 1809] (*C. Life*, 21 Jan. 1933, 76].

DUBLIN, THE NELSON PILLAR, SACKVILLE (now O'CONNELL) STREET, 1808–9; dem. 1966 [exhib. at R.A. 1809].

CAMBRIDGE, THE PERSE SCHOOL, alterations to accommodate Fitzwilliam Collection, 1816; dem. 1868 [Willis & Clark, iii, 199].

GREAT YARMOUTH, NORFOLK, THE NELSON COLUMN, 1817–20 [exhib. at R.A. 1821]. See S. D. Kitson, *J. S. Cotman*, 1937, fig. 80, for Wilkins's original design for a column surmounted by a trireme supported by caryatides.

BATH, THE FREEMASONS' HALL (now Friends' Meeting House), YORK STREET, 1817–19 [W. Ison, *The Georgian Buildings of Bath*, 1948, 83–4].

CAMBRIDGE, KING'S COLLEGE, THE BRIDGE, 1819 [Willis & Clark, i, 573–4].

CAMBRIDGE, GREAT ST. MARY'S CHURCH, alterations to interior, 1819; mostly removed 1863 [Liscombe, *op. cit.*, 238; R.C.H.M. *Cambridge*, 279].

BURY ST. EDMUNDS, SUFFOLK, THE THEATRE, WEST GATE STREET, 1819 [S. Tymms, *Handbook to Bury St. Edmunds*, 1872, 83].

BURY ST. EDMUNDS, SUFFOLK, THE COUNTY GAOL, alterations, including addition of wings, in collaboration with John Orridge, the Governor (*q.v.*), *c.*1819 [J. Orridge, *Description of the Gaol at Bury St. Edmunds*, 1819, p. viii; Sir John Soane's Museum, J. Spiller's letters, nos. 79A, 82, 91].

NOTTINGHAM, ST. PAUL'S CHURCH, 1821–2; dem. 1925 [exhib. at R.A. 1821; J. Orange, *History of Nottingham* ii, 1840, 881].

NORWICH, THE SHIREHALL, 1822–3, Tudor Gothic; refaced 1913 [G. K. Blyth, *The Norwich Guide*, 1843, 82].

NORWICH, THE NEW NORFOLK GAOL, 1822–4 [Norfolk Record Office, QS Order Book C/S4/4].

LONDON, THE UNITED UNIVERSITY CLUB, PALL MALL EAST, with J. P. Gandy, 1822–6; attic storey added 1850–1; dem. 1902 [Britton & Pugin, *The Public Buildings of London* ii, 1828, 130–4].

CAMBRIDGE, TRINITY COLLEGE, THE NEW (KING'S) COURT, 1823–5, Tudor Gothic [Willis & Clark ii, 652–9].

CAMBRIDGE, CORPUS CHRISTI COLLEGE, NEW COURT, 1823–7, Gothic [Willis & Clark i, 302–4].

CAMBRIDGE, KING'S COLLEGE, NEW BUILDINGS and ENTRANCE SCREEN, 1824–8, Gothic [Willis & Clark i, 564–5; for the competition, see the catalogue of the *Exhibition of Designs for completing King's College, Cambridge*, 1823, and *Architect and Building News*, 23 June 1933].

ADDISCOMBE, SURREY, THE MILITARY SEMINARY, dining-room, barracks and other buildings, 1825–8; dem. 1861 [H. M. Vibart, *Addiscombe*, 1894, 29].

NORWICH, THE THEATRE, 1825–6; burnt 1934 [J. Chambers, *Norfolk Tour* iii, 1829, 1124–5].

HUNTINGDON, THE COUNTY GAOL, 1826–8 [J. Harris, *Catalogue of British Drawings for Architecture, etc., in American Collections*, 1971, 276; J. Gallier, *Autobiography of James Gallier*, Paris 1864, 15, 16].

LONDON, UNIVERSITY COLLEGE, GOWER STREET, assisted by J. P. Gandy, 1827–8 [exhib. at R.A. 1827, 1828; W. H. Leeds, *Supplement* to Britton & Pugin's *Public Buildings of London*, 1838, 77–88]. The library was designed by Prof. T. L. Donaldson, 1848–9, and the wings were completed later to the designs of Prof. T. Hayter Lewis and others.

YORK, THE PHILOSOPHICAL SOCIETY'S MUSEUM, 1827–30, executed under the superintendence of R. H. Sharp (*q.v.*) [*Gent's Mag.* 1827 (ii), 457; *Library of the Fine Arts* i, 1831, 172–3].

LONDON, ST. GEORGE'S HOSPITAL, HYDE PARK CORNER, 1828–9; enlarged 1859, 1868, etc.; converted into the Lanesborough Hotel, 1988–91 [W. H. Leeds, *Supplement* to Britton & Pugin's *Public Buildings of London*, 1838, 41–9].

LONDON, EAST INDIA HOUSE, LEADENHALL STREET, alterations, 1828; dem. 1861–2 [Britton & Pugin's *Public Buildings of London*, ed. Leeds, ii, 1838, 36].

LONDON, THE NATIONAL GALLERY, TRAFALGAR SQUARE, 1834–8 [W. H. Leeds, *Supplement* to Britton & Pugin's *Public Buildings of Leadon*, 1838, 56–76].

ALBURY, SURREY, THE CATHOLIC APOSTOLIC CHURCH, for William Drummond, Gothic; designed *c.*1837 in association with W. M. Brookes (*q.v.*), who completed the building after Wilkins's death [drawings in possession of the Trustees signed jointly by Wilkins and Brookes 1837–9: photos at N.M.R.].

DOMESTIC ARCHITECTURE

OSBERTON HALL, NOTTS., remodelled for F. F. Foljambe, *c.*1805; altered 1847–8 and 1872–80, when Wilkins's Greek Doric portico was removed [G. Richardson, *New Vitruvius Britannicus* ii, 1808, pls. 60–1].

GRANGE PARK, HANTS., remodelled for Henry Drummond, 1809 onwards; enlarged by C. R. Cockerell 1823–5 [J. M. Crook in *The Country Seat*, ed. Colvin & Harris, 1970, 220–8; J. Redmill in *C. Life*, 1 May 1975; Jane Geddes, 'The Grange, Northington', *Arch. Hist.* 26, 1983].

LONDON, ARGYLL HOUSE, ARGYLL STREET, internal decorations for 4th Earl of Aberdeen, 1809; dem. 1864–5 [B. L., Add. MS. 43230, ff. 31, 38].

BENTLEY PRIORY, MIDDLESEX, enlarged for 1st Marquess of Abercorn, *c.*1809–10; further work by R. Smirke 1815–18 [accounts in P.R.O., N. Ireland, IF/10, *ex inf.* Mr. Gervase Jackson-Stops].

PENTILLIE CASTLE, CORNWALL, for J. T. Coryton, *c.*1810, Tudor Gothic; partly dem. 1968 [*Cornwall Illustrated*, with text by J. Britton & E. W. Brayley, 1831, 16] (W. P. Wilkins, 'Pentillie Castle', *Arch. Rev.* June 1968).

DALMENY HOUSE, WEST LOTHIAN, for 4th Earl of Rosebery, 1814–17, Tudor Gothic [exhib. at R.A. 1817; J. P. Neale, *Views of Seats*, 1st ser. ii, 1819] (*Apollo*, June 1984, 400–5; *C. Life*, 17–24 Aug. 1989).

CAMBRIDGE, house in LENSFIELD ROAD, additions including portico, for himself, after 1811; dem. 1955.

STOURHEAD, WILTS., Grecian lodge for Sir R. Colt Hoare, 1816–17 [exhib. at R.A. 1817; payment in Stourhead archives, 1815].

TREGOTHNAN, nr. TRURO, CORNWALL, for 4th Viscount Falmouth, 1816–18, Tudor Gothic; enlarged by L. Vulliamy, 1842–6 [exhib. at R.A. 1817] (*C. Life*, 17–24 May 1956).

KESWICK HALL, NORFOLK, for Hudson Gurney, 1817–19; altered by Wilkins for Gurney, 1837; enlarged as Training College 1951 [C. H. Barham Johnson, *Keswick Hall*, Norwich 1957, 11–14; B.L., Add. MS. 23033, f. 87, engraving of house 'as altered by Wilkins in 1837'.]

DUNMORE PARK, STIRLINGSHIRE, for 5th Earl of Dunmore, 1820–2, Tudor Gothic; derelict since 1972 [exhib. at R.A. 1821; J. P. Neale, *Views of Seats*, 2nd ser. iii, 1826].

BYLAUGH HALL, NORFOLK, unexecuted design, 1822, Elizabethan style [R. W. Liscombe, 'Designs by William Wilkins for Bylaugh Hall, Norfolk', *Burlington Mag.* cxvi, July 1974].

KINGWESTON HOUSE, SOMERSET, portico for W. Dickinson, before 1828 [J. Britton, *Bath and Bristol*, 1829, 73; J. P. Neale, *Views of Seats*, 2nd ser., iv, 1828].

BROOKE HALL, NORFOLK, for the Revd. J. Holmes, 1827–30; dem. 1952–3 [B. B. Cooper, *The Life of Sir Astley Cooper* i, 1843, 64].

WILKINSON, GEORGE (*c.*1733–1820), was a builder-architect of Newcastle-under-Lyme, Staffordshire. When he died in April 1820, aged 67, the *Staffordshire Advertiser* wrote that 'This gentleman's architectural labours have contributed essential benefit to Newcastle, by them it has not only been considerably enlarged, but most of the erections which his public spirit led him to execute have been highly conducive to its present improved appearance.' So far his only identified work is the addition of bay windows (1783) and a service-wing (1793–7) to BETLEY COURT, STAFFS., for Sir Thomas Fletcher, Bart. [G. N. Brown, *This Old House*, Betley Court Gallery 1987, 20–3].

WILKINSON, GEORGE (1814–1890), was the son of W. A. Wilkinson, a carpenter and builder of Witney in Oxfordshire, and the elder brother of the Oxford architect William Wilkinson (1819–1901). In 1835 he won the competition for the workhouse at THAME, OXON. (now the Ryecote Wood College), and subsequently designed many other workhouses, including those at WITNEY and CHIPPING NORTON whose main blocks are built in the form of a cross, with a central lantern. He also designed the modest Italianate TOWN HALL at BAMPTON, OXON., in 1838. In about 1840 he went to Ireland as the chosen architect of the Poor Law Commissioners. There, besides many more workhouses, he designed the classical HARCOURT STREET RAILWAY STATION at DUBLIN, 1858–9, and made large additions to the COURTHOUSE at CASTLEBAR, CO. MAYO, 1860. He was the author of *Practical Geology and Ancient Architecture of Ireland*, 1845. He returned to England in about 1888, and died at Ryde House, Twickenham, on 4 October 1890. [Andrew Saint, 'Three Oxford Architects', *Oxoniensia* xxxv, 1970, 55–6; Witney Parish Register; Principal Probate Registry, Calendar of Probates.]

WILKINSON, NATHANIEL (–1764), was the best-known member of a family of master masons of Worcester. In 1713 the churchwardens of RIPPLE, WORCS., contracted with Thomas Wilkinson, of the parish of St. Helen's in Worcester, to take down the spire and part of the tower of their church and to rebuild the latter with 'rails and balisters, flower potts, fannes, and other handsome ornaments', some of which survived until 1937 [contract in Worcs. C.R.O.]. In 1716 Thomas Wilkinson was employed to take down the spire of ST. MARY'S CHURCH, LICHFIELD, STAFFS., as far as the battlements [MS. churchwardens' accounts]. He died in 1716, and was succeeded by his son Thomas, who was regularly employed on repairing the stonework of WORCESTER CATHEDRAL until his death in 1736. His place as cathedral mason was then taken by his son Nathaniel, who between 1748 and 1751 virtually rebuilt the north end of the north transept and paved the church with Painswick stone. He was well known as a 'spire-mender' and in 1751 built the exceptionally slender spire of ST. ANDREW'S CHURCH, which is one of the landmarks of Worcester. It stands on a tower 90 feet high and its apex is 245 feet from the ground. The celebrated spire of ROSS CHURCH, HEREFS., was repaired or rebuilt by Wilkinson, and he also constructed those of LEDBURY, in the same county (1732), MITCHELDEAN, GLOS. (? *c.*1733), and MONMOUTH. He died intestate on 28 September 1764, and was buried in St. Peter's Church, Worcester. His son, who bore the same name, followed his father's trade. [J. Chambers, *Biographical Illustrations of Worcester*, 1820, 352–3; J. Chambers, *General History of Worcester*, 1819, 131; J. Noake, *Notes and Queries for Worcestershire*, 1856, 41; J. Noake, *Worcestershire Scraps*, no. 8, p. 19; J. Noake, *The Monastery and Cathedral of Worcester*, 1866; C. Heath, *History of Monmouth*, 1804; information from Mr. D. Whitehead.]

WILKINSON, WILLIAM (*c.*1784–1830), practised as an architect at Mansfield Woodhouse, Notts., during the second and third decades of the nineteenth century. He was the author of a fantastic Gothic design for a 'National Mausoleum', presented to the Prince Regent in 1814, and now in the Royal Library at Windsor. In MANSFIELD he designed CARR BANK in 1805 for a Mr. Stanton and several houses in the CHESTERFIELD ROAD [A. S. Buxton, *Historic Mansfield* i, 1972 reprint, 103–4]. He also designed BARLOW VICARAGE, DERBYSHIRE, in 1819 [Bodleian Library, records of Queen Anne's Bounty], and in 1817 made a report on the steeple of CHESTERFIELD CHURCH which is printed in Hall's *History of Chesterfield*, 1839, 56–7. Wilkinson's death on 31 March 1830 at the age of 46 is recorded on a ledger-stone in Throapham Church, Yorkshire [*ex inf.* Mr. Donald Findlay].

WILLCOX, GEORGE H—, practised in Northampton, where he designed the classical NORTHAMPTON BATHS in ALBION PLACE (later the Victoria Dispensary and now the City Housing Department), 1836, and the Gothic ST. KATHARINE'S CHURCH, 1838–9, demolished 1950 [*Northampton Mercury*, 16 July 1836 and 12 Aug. 1837, *ex inf.* Mr. V. A. Hatley].

WILLDIG, JOHN (–1742), of Great Bolas, Shropshire, was a mason by trade. When GREAT BOLAS CHURCH was rebuilt in *c.*1726–9 Willdig was paid 15 guineas 'for his trouble in buying timber, and measuring the Joyner and Carpenters work, and drawing Draughts; and attending on the work and workmen even from the beginning to the end' [W. G. D. Fletcher, 'The Building of the Church of Great Bolas, 1726–9', *Trans. Shropshire Archl. Soc.* 4th. ser. x, 1925–6]. His burial in May 1742 is recorded in the parish register.

WILLIAMS, ARTHUR YATES (*c.*1809–1853), and his cousin George (1814–1898) were in partnership as architects in Liverpool from 1838 onwards. A. Y. Williams had previously been in partnership with Stephen Lane Edwards, in conjunction with whom he designed churches at Knotty Ash and

Accrington (above, p. 334). He died in July 1853, aged 44, and was buried in the churchyard of St. Nicholas', Halewood, which he had designed. George Williams, who was a pupil of Decimus Burton, continued to practise in Liverpool until 1880. He died in Virginia in 1898. Most of the Williamses' buildings in Lancashire have been demolished, but their handsome Athenaeum at Carlisle remains as a bank [information from Dr. Janet Gnosspelius; F. Boase, *Modern English Biography*, 1892, 889, for G. Williams].

DINGLE COTTAGE, LANCS., for James Yates (?), 1838 [E. Twycross, *The Mansions of England: Lancashire* iii, 1847, 55].

HALEWOOD, LANCS., ST. NICHOLAS' CHURCH, 1839; transepts added 1847, tower 1882 [James Eccles, *Centenary History of Halewood Parish Church*, *c.*1939].

ST. HELEN'S LANCS., THE TOWN HALL., 1839–40; dem. [*Civil Engineer and Architect's Jnl.* i, 1837–8, 296; T. C. Barker & J. R. Harris, *A Merseyside Town in the Industrial Revolution*, 1954].

ST. HELEN'S LANCS., ST. THOMAS'S CHURCH, 1839–40, Gothic; rebuilt 1890–1 and 1910 [*Civil Engineer and Architect's Jnl.* i, 1837–8, 296; *Gent's Mag.* 1840 (i), 82].

WATERLOO, LANCS., CHRIST CHURCH, 1839–41; rebuilt 1891–4 [*Civil Engineer and Architect's Jnl.* i, 1837–8, 88].

LIVERPOOL, ST. BARNABAS' CHURCH, 1840; dem. [*Civil Engineer and Architect's Jnl.* iii, 1840, 71].

CARLISLE, CUMBERLAND, THE ATHENAEUM (now Savings Bank), LOWTHER STREET, 1840 [Mannix & Whellan, *History, Gazetteer and Directory of Cumberland*, 1847, 140].

NEW BRIGHTON, WALLASEY, CHESHIRE, villa for J. C. Ewart, *c.*1842 [exhib. at Liverpool Society of Artists, 1842].

LIVERPOOL, PRINCE'S PARK, supervision of works under general direction of Sir Joseph Paxton, 1842–4 [S. Lewis, *Topographical Dictionary of England* iv, 1848, 386; G. F. Chadwick, *The Works of Sir Joseph Paxton*, 1961, 47].

LIVERPOOL, BRUNSWICK BUILDINGS, BRUNSWICK STREET, for J. C. Ewart, 1843, Italianate; dem. [*Companion to the Almanac*, 1843, 254–6, with illustration].

WILLIAMS, J—, exhibited a 'Design for a stable proposed to be built for T. Cholmondeley, Esq., M.P.', at the Royal Academy in 1807. His address (4 Marshall Street, London Road) differed from that of John Williams (*q.v.*).

WILLIAMS, JOHN (–1817), was a pupil of Thomas Hardwick, and subsequently teacher of military drawing at the Military Academy. All that is known of his architectural works is derived from the designs which he exhibited at the Royal Academy between 1799 and 1810. They included 'a villa intended to be erected in Carmarthenshire' (1802), another 'designed to be erected for the Duchess of Devonshire' (1803), and a third 'intended to be erected on Sydenham Common' (1804). He also made unexecuted designs 'for the village church at Bunney, Notts.' (1805), and for a chapel 'proposed to be erected on Sydenham Common' (1807). In 1812 he was awarded the first premium of £200 for a design for the penitentiary at Millbank, subsequently erected under the direction of Thomas Hardwick, but rebuilt by Smirke to a different design after the failure of the foundations. Williams died at his house in Jermyn Street, London, on 22 April 1817 [*A.P.S.D.*; *Builder* xxvi, 1868, 181, *Gent's Mag.* 1817 (i), 474].

WILLIAMSON, COLLEN (1727–1802), was a native of Dyke in Morayshire and a mason by trade. In 1761–2 he rebuilt or remodelled MOY HOUSE, MORAYSHIRE, for Sir Ludovic Grant, Bart., in an unsophisticated Scottish Georgian style [J. Macaulay, *The Classical Country House in Scotland 1660–1800*, 1987, 132–4]. In 1792 he emigrated to North America, where he was engaged as master mason to build the White House in Washington under the direction of James Hoban. He remained in this employment until 1795, when he was replaced by an Englishman called George Blagden. He died in America in 1802 [William Seale, *The President's House*, Washington 1986, i, 51, 57, 60, 68, 141].

WILLOUGHBY, JOHN RIVIS, held the post of Surveyor to the Corporation of York from 1833 until 1838, when he resigned [York Council Minutes, *ex inf.* Dr. E. A. Gee]. He was presumably the father of George Rivis Willoughby (1805–77), who practised in Louth from the 1840s onwards and who designed, *inter alia*, the church at HAUGHAM, LINCS., with a steeple imitating that of Louth, 1840–1 [S. Lewis, *Topographical Dictionary of England*, 1848, ii, 443–4].

WILLSFORD, THOMAS (1602–), a teacher of mathematics, was the author of *Architectonice, or The Art of Building*, 1659, a practical manual for the 'young surveyor' or architect [Eileen Harris, *British Architectural Books and Writers 1556–1785*, 1990, 478].

WILLSHIRE, RAYMOND (1785–1857), was first (1802–6) a pupil of Messrs. Middleton & Bailey of Lambeth, and later (*c.*1820–50) the partner of the latter. After Bailey's death in 1850 Willshire continued the practice in partnership with R. Parris. He died on 10 December 1857 [*Gent's Mag.* 1858 (i), 118]. In 1833 he was responsible for alterations to TEDDINGTON CHURCH, MIDDLESEX, including the addition of the chancel [I.C.B.S.].

WILLSON, ALEXANDER, is known only as the author of a rare publication entitled *The Antique and Modern Embellisher*, 1761, consisting of 40 plates of engraved designs for architectural ornament, on the title-page of which he is described as 'Architect, and Professor of Ornament' [Eileen Harris, *British Architectural Books and Writers 1556–1785*, 1990, 478–9].

WILLSON, EDWARD JAMES (1787–1854), was born at Lincoln on 21 June 1787. His father, William Willson (1745–1827), was a cabinet-maker and joiner by trade, but also described himself as a 'master-builder', and is said to have had an 'unusual knowledge of theoretical construction'.[1] The son had no regular architectural training, but worked for some time in his father's yard, and, by studying the cathedral and other ancient buildings in the city, acquired a considerable knowledge of Gothic architecture. This led to his employment by Dr. Bayley, the Archdeacon of Stow, for whom he rebuilt Messingham Church, and through whose influence he obtained a number of similar commissions in the diocese. In 1833 he was appointed County Surveyor and in that capacity restored the keep and walls of the Castle. For many years he was a member of the Lincoln City Council and served as Mayor in 1851–2.

Willson was an enthusiastic antiquary, with a wide knowledge of medieval English architecture and archaeology. He was the friend and collaborator of John Britton, whom he assisted in his *Architectural Antiquities* (1807–10) by writing the accounts of Boston and Barton-on-Humber Churches and of Beverley and Lincoln Minsters. Britton's *Cathedral Antiquities* (1814–35) and *Picturesque Antiquities of English Cities* (1830) also incorporate material supplied by Willson. He wrote the letterpress for the elder Pugin's *Specimens of Gothic Architecture* (1821–3) and for his *Examples of Gothic Architecture* (1828–34), compiling for the former a pioneer glossary of medieval technical terms. He made extensive topographical collections relating chiefly to Lincolnshire, and in 1841 delivered the opening address 'On Topography' which was published in the only volume of the *Trans. of the Lincolnshire Topographical Society*, 1843. He also took a prominent part in the Lincoln meeting of the Royal Archaeological Institute in 1848, contributing a paper on the bishop's palace which was printed in the volume of *Proceedings*. His library was sold at Lincoln on 21–23 November 1854, but his Lincolnshire collections are now in the Library of the Society of Antiquaries of London, of which he was a Fellow.

Willson was, for his time, a relatively careful and scholarly restorer of churches. In his own Gothic churches (usually built of yellow brick) he failed to translate antiquarian knowledge into effective design, but his classical R. C. chapel at Grantham has modest charm.

Willson died at Lincoln on 8 September 1854, aged 67, and was buried at Hainton. Like his parents, he was a Roman Catholic. He left two sons, one of whom, Thomas John Willson (1824–1903), became an architect and a Fellow of the Royal Institute of British Architects. There is a portrait of Willson in the Usher Art Gallery at Lincoln. [*A.P.S.D.*; *D.N.B.*; obituaries in *Builder* xiii, 1855, 4–5 (by John Britton), and *Gent's Mag.* 1855 (i), 321; Society of Antiquaries, Willson Collection, vol. iv.]

Unless otherwise stated the following list of works is based on the *D.N.B.* article, which incorporated information supplied by Willson's son.

MESSINGHAM CHURCH, LINCS., reconstructed for Archdeacon Bayley, 1817–18 [W. B. Stonehouse, *A Stow Visitation*, ed. N.S. Harding, 1940, 7–8, 52].

SAUNDBY CHURCH, NOTTS., repair or restoration, 1823; rebuilt by J. L. Pearson 1886–91.

WELTON-BY-LINCOLN CHURCH, LINCS., rebuilt nave and chancel, 1823–4 [Lincs. Record Office, parish records 7/1].

LINCOLN, No. 15 MINSTER YARD, rebuilt 1824 [*Associated Architectural Socs' Reports & Papers* 22, 1893, 6–8].

BLANKNEY HALL, LINCS., stables and offices for

[1] In Nov. 1729, Thomas Wilson, mason, contracted to rebuild Revesby Church, Lincs., for Joseph Banks [Banks papers in Lincolnshire Archives Office, HILL 22/7]. The original plan, section and elevation are preserved in the Banks Collection of drawings now in the Public Library at Lincoln (iii, 205). They are in the best style of eighteenth-century architectural draughtsmanship and were probably made by a London architect.

Charles Chaplin, 1825 [Lincs. Record Office, Heneage 8/2/5].

HAXEY CHURCH, LINCS., rebuilt N. aisle and N. chapel, 1825–6.

LOUTH CHURCH, LINCS., reroofed nave and aisles and rebuilt north porch, 1825–7 [R. W. Goulding, *Louth Parish Church*, 1916, 19].

NOTTINGHAM, ST. JOHN'S CHURCH (R.C.), for his brother, the Revd. R. W. Willson, afterwards Bishop of Hobart, *c.*1825–8; now secularized.

LINCOLN CATHEDRAL, the organ case, 1826, Gothic.

WEST RASEN CHURCH, LINCS., tower rebuilt and chancel reroofed [Lincs. Record Office, parish records, Add. 8].

EAST RETFORD, NOTTS., ST. SAVIOUR'S CHURCH, MOORGATE, 1828–30, Gothic [I.C.B.S.].

GRANTHAM, LINCS., ST. MARY'S CHURCH (R.C.), 1832.

LOUTH, LINCS., ST. MARY'S CHAPEL (R.C.), 1833, since enlarged.

HAINTON HALL and VILLAGE, LINCS., works for G. F. Heneage 1833 onwards, including stables, 1834–5, partly dem.; gamekeeper's house and dog-kennel, 1834–6; cottages, 1835 onwards; R.C. chapel in grounds, 1836, Gothic; the 'Heneage' public house, 1844–7; the School, 1846–7, Gothic; enlarged 1886; and minor alterations and additions to the Hall; also several farmhouses on the estate [Lincs. Record Office, Heneage papers, including plans of stables, chapel and school].

BUSLINGTHORPE CHURCH, LINCS., rebuilt 1835 [Kelly's *Directory of Lincolnshire*, 1885, 346].

LINCOLN CASTLE, restoration of keep, towers and walls, 1835–45 (see his *Report on the present state of the outward walls . . . of the Castle*, presented 1 Jan. 1835).

MELTON MOWBRAY, LEICS., ST. JOHN'S CHURCH (R.C)., THORPE END, 1840, Gothic.

HAINTON CHURCH, LINCS., reconstructed 1843–6 [*Ecclesiologist* ix, 1849, 138–9].

CABOURN, LINCS., THE PELHAM COLUMN, for 1st Earl of Yarborough, 1843–9.

STAUNTON-IN-THE VALE CHURCH, NOTTS., restoration, 1853.

WILLSON, THOMAS (*c.*1780–   ), was admitted to the Royal Academy Schools in 1800 at the age of 20. He obtained the Gold Medal the following year. His exhibits at the Royal Academy (1799–1831) included 'a Royal Military College, designed for the Emperor of Russia' (1805), 'a gentleman's house now building at Stockwell' (1805), and 'a national mausoleum to Naval and Military Heroes' (1815). In 1819–20 he led a party of emigrants to South Africa, but returned in 1822–3, having quarrelled with his companions, who accused him of deserting them [H. E. Hockley, *The Story of the British Settlers of 1820 in South Africa*, Cape Town 1957, 35, 40, 56, 251]. His exhibit at the Royal Academy in 1824 was 'a marine villa intended for Greenpoint, near Cape Town'. In 1831 he exhibited designs for a 'Pyramid Cemetery for the Metropolis' the base of which was to cover eighteen acres, 'which being multiplied by the several stages to be erected one above the other will generate nearly 1000 acres, self-created out of the void space overhead as the building progresses above the earth'. He failed, however, to interest the General Cemetery Company in the project, and twenty years later, having had no more success with the idea of a 'Victoria Pyramid Necropolis', thought of emigrating to Australia [Staffs. C.R.O., Gower papers, D 593 Q/1/6]. An engraved version of his design for the Pyramid Cemetery is in the Royal Library at Windsor, bound up with C. H. Tatham's designs for a Naval Monument. Willson was among the competitors for the Houses of Parliament in 1835.

WILSON, JOHN (–1764/5), was a master mason living at or near Sowerby in the West Riding of Yorkshire. Minutes in the Leeds Archives show that he designed and built SOWERBY CHURCH in 1761–3. It is a handsome classical building with a southern façade resembling that of Etty's Holy Trinity Church, Leeds. A payment in 1765 to Wilson's widow indicates that he died in that or the previous year.

WILSON, JOHN, was from 1815 to 1830 the leading architect in Guernsey, and during these years he designed a number of important buildings on the island, including the Greek Revival Church of St. James in St. Peter Port and the Tudor Gothic Elizabeth College. In 1828 he was appointed Surveyor to the Guernsey Board of Works. There is no record of his origins, unless he was the 'J. Wilson, junior', who exhibited architectural designs at the Royal Academy from London addresses in 1794–6, nor is it known why he left Guernsey soon after 1830. Besides the documented buildings listed below, several other houses in Guernsey (e.g. Bonamy, 1826, Summerland, Mount Durand, ?1828, Castle Carey, ?1829, and Grange Lodge, ?1830) can probably be attributed to him on stylistic grounds.

Several maps and plans made by Wilson while working in the Channel Islands are in the Public Record Office (MPD 22, MR 1363 and MPH 722). MPH 722 is a design for a Place d'Armes in Alderney in the distinctive style of draughtsmanship of an architect trained by the Royal Engineers. This suggests that Wilson may have been the John Wilson who was Clerk of Works at the Royal Arsenal, Woolwich, from 1839 until 1845, when he retired. This John Wilson, who died at Cardew Villa, Shirley, Milbrook, Hants., in January 1866, was a native of Cumberland and left some £12,000, to be laid out ultimately on the purchase of an estate in Cumberland for the benefit of a great-nephew of the same name.

[John Jacob, *Annals of Some of the British Norman Isles*, Paris 1830; B. Little, *St. Peter Port*, 1963; C. E. B. Brett, *Buildings in the Town and Parish of St. Peter Port*, National Trust of Guernsey 1975; C. E. B. Brett, 'A mysterious Guernsey architect', *C. Life*, 9 Nov. 1978; O. F. G. Hogg, *The Royal Arsenal* ii, 1963, 1107, 1228–9; Principal Probate Registry, will of John Wilson 1866.]

GUERNSEY

TORTEVAL CHURCH, 1816–17 [*Gazette de Guernesey*, 4 mai 1816; *Guernsey and Jersey Magazine* v, 1838, 275].

ST. PETER PORT, ST. JAMES'S CHURCH, 1817–18 [Brett, 42, No. 31].

ST. PETER PORT, THE MARKET HALL, 1822 [signed; Brett, 32, No. 8b].

ST. PETER PORT, THE ROYAL COURT HOUSE, alterations, 1822 [Brett, 36, No. 15].

ST. PETER PORT, THE TOWN CHURCH, alterations, 1823–6 [Brett, 25, No. 3].

ST. PETER PORT, SPRINGFIELD HOUSE, for Thomas Gosselin, *c.*1826–7 [Brett, 60, No. 49m].

ST. PETER PORT, ELIZABETH COLLEGE, 1826–9, Tudor Gothic [Brett, 44, No. 33].

ST. PETER PORT, LES ARCADES (former FISH MARKET), 1830 [Brett, 32, No. 8c].

ST. PETER PORT, FOUNTAIN STREET, *c.*1830 [Brett, 33, no. 6f].

WILSON, Sir WILLIAM (1641–1710), was a native of Leicester, and can probably be identified with William, son of William Wilson, baker, who was baptized in St. Nicholas Church, Leicester, on 16 May 1641. He appears to have served his apprenticeship with a statuary mason, and is said to have carved the statue of King Charles II which was set up on the west front of Lichfield Cathedral shortly before 1669, when Bishop Hacket's restoration was completed.[1] In 1670 he was employed as a carver at SUDBURY HALL, DERBYSHIRE, then being rebuilt by George Vernon, and executed, among other works, the elaborate sculpture of the entrance porch [C. Hussey in *C. Life* 15, 22, 29 June 1935]. In or about 1671 he executed the Wilbraham family monuments in WESTON CHURCH, STAFFS., for Lady Elizabeth Wilbraham, who recorded her bargain with the sculptor in her copy of Palladio's *First Book of Architecture* (trans. Godfrey Richards, 1663), preserved in the library at Weston Park [C. Hussey in *C. Life*, 9 Nov. 1945, 819]. He is also stated by Charles Deering, in his *Nottinghamia Vetus et Nova, or an Historical Account of Nottingham*, 1751, 186–7, to have carved the equestrian statue of William, Duke of Newcastle (d. 1676), on the north-east front of Nottingham Castle, which was completed in 1679. Soon afterwards, according to Deering, 'he was for a time spoiled for a statuary, because a Leicestershire [really a Warwickshire] widow lady, the Lady Pudsey, who was possessed of a very large jointure falling deeply in love with him, got him knighted and married him.' Jane Pudsey was the widow of Henry Pudsey of Langley, nr. Sutton Coldfield, Warwicks., who had died in 1677, and it has been plausibly suggested that his monument in Sutton Coldfield Church was executed by Wilson. The date of the marriage has not been established, but Wilson was knighted at Whitehall on 8 March 1681/2. An entry in Ashmole's diary shows that two days later he was 'admitted into the Fellowship of Freemasons' at Masons' Hall, London.

Between 1693 and 1697 Wilson supervised the erection of the FREE SCHOOL at APPLEBY, LEICS., for Sir John Moore. Moore was an Alderman of London and it was at his expense that the Writing School at Christ's Hospital was then in course of erection to the designs of Hawksmoor and Wren. Wren also prepared plans for Appleby School, which are among his drawings at All Souls College, Oxford (*Wren Soc.* xi, pls. liii–liv). They were to have been executed under the direction of Thomas Woodstock, a carpenter whom Wren had employed on many of the City churches. Wilson also offered his services as surveyor, but Moore hesitated to disoblige Wren by not employing Woodstock, although he believed Wilson 'to be an ingenious gentleman', whose advice would be valuable. When Woodstock died in 1694 Wilson at once took his place as surveyor in charge and proposed drastic alterations to Wren's design. Moore summoned him to London and (according to Wilson's own account) arranged an interview with Wren 'and shewed him my draughts of the Schoole, and asked his opinion of them. Sir

[1] The statue was taken down in 1877 and is now in the north-west tower; it is illustrated in *Wren Soc.* xi, pl. lix.

Christopher Wren did aprove of mine rather than his own'. The result was a building which, while it conformed to Wren's general plan, had, with its mullioned and transomed windows, the appearance of a Jacobean structure of the first half of the seventeenth century (*Wren Soc.* xi, pl. lv). In the end Moore found that the school cost more than he had anticipated, and Wilson had some difficulty in obtaining payment for his trouble as surveyor and for the statue of the founder which he had executed and set up in a pedimented niche in the main schoolroom [*Wren Soc.* xi, 84–107].

Both Wren and Wilson were concerned in the rebuilding of ST. MARY'S CHURCH at WARWICK after the fire of 1694, but the former's designs (*Wren Soc.* x, pls. 15–18) were not adopted, and it was under Wilson's direction that the rebuilding of the church was begun by William and Francis Smith in 1698. The tower was originally intended to stand on four piers inside the west end of the nave, but they proved inadequate to support its weight, and in 1700 the unfinished tower had to be taken down and a new one built on fresh foundations outside the west end 'according to Sir William Wilson's directions' [*The Great Fire of Warwick*, ed. M. Farr, Dugdale Soc. 1992, xxvi-xxvii]. Like the rest of the church, it exhibits a curious and rather awkward mixture of Gothic and classic motives.

Another building in which both Wren and Wilson were concerned was the stable at ARBURY HALL, WARWICKS., which was built by Richard Newdigate in *c.*1675. Wren was consulted, made a design for a 'porch' or doorway which is still preserved, and was presented with a pair of silver candlesticks costing £11 9s. But his design does not correspond to the doorway as built, and as Sir William Wilson was also paid £1 for a 'draught' of the porch, its ultimate form may have been due to him [*Wren Soc.* xii, 21 and and pl. xlix; Gordon Nares in *C. Life*, 8 Oct. 1953].

Soon after 1696 Wilson is said to have designed FOUR OAKS HALL, nr. SUTTON COLDFIELD, WARWICKS. (remodelled in the eighteenth century and dem. *c.*1900), for Lord Folliot of Ballyshannon, who had married Elizabeth, daughter and coheir of Henry Pudsey. This house, which had a rather old-fashioned roofline of curved and scrolled gables, is illustrated in *Wren Soc.* xi, pls. lxi–lxii. Two other buildings in Sutton Coldfield are attributed to Wilson because he is believed to have owned or occupied them both: the stables at LANGLEY HALL, *c.*1685, and MOAT HOUSE, a handsome house which he probably built for himself after his wife's death in 1697.

Wilson's later works as a sculptor included the statues over the porch of CASTLE BROMWICH HALL, WARWICKS., 1697 [G. W. Beard in *C. Life*, 18 March 1954, 780] and monuments in WINCHESTER CATHEDRAL (Sir John Clobery, d. 1687) and CHURCH GRESLEY CHURCH, DERBYSHIRE (Sir Thomas Gresley, d. 1699) [F. Madan, *The Gresleys of Drakelow*, 1899, 180–1]. Neither these nor a gauche elevation of baroque character in the archives at Melbourne Hall, inscribed 'alteration for Melbourne by Sr. Wm. Wilson', made probably in 1697, when he measured the foundations of that house for Thomas Coke, suggest that he was an artist of more than second-rate ability. He did, however, design an agreeable baroque CHAPEL at HALL GREEN, YARDLEY, nr. BIRMINGHAM, consecrated in May 1704 [D. Whitehead, 'Job Marston's Chapel', *Georgian Group Jnl.* 1992].

Lady Wilson died in 1697 and was buried at Sutton Coldfield. Her husband died there, at the age of 69, on 3 June 1710 and is commemorated by a monument now in the vestry. In his will he provided for a benefaction to the poor of St. Nicholas parish, Leicester. A portrait of him is reproduced in *Wren Soc.* xi, pl. lviii.

[*A.P.S.D.*; 'A Biographical Note on Sir William Wilson', *Wren Soc.* xi, 108–13; *History of the Forest and Chase of Sutton Coldfield*, 1860, 90, 101; R. Gunnis, *Dictionary of British Sculptors*, 1968.]

WINCKWORTH, JOHN (– *c.*1828), practised in Paddington, and latterly from Beaconsfield in Buckinghamshire, where his widow died in 1829, aged 68 [*Gent's Mag.* 1829 (i), 283]. He was at Beaconsfield when he made designs for Edward Willes for the interior of a library at NEWBOLD COMYN, WARWICKS., in 1821, and for alterations to a house at SHINFIELD, BERKS., in 1826 [Warwicks. C.R.O., CR 1247/40 and 47]. John Winckworth (*c.*1790–1848), a pupil of Henry Hakewill, who entered the Royal Academy Schools in 1812 and was awarded a Silver Medal by the Society of Arts in 1816, may have been his son.

WINDE, WILLIAM (–1722), was an architect of gentle birth, whose family had held lands at South Wootton in Norfolk since the sixteenth century. His grandfather, Sir Robert Winde, had been knighted by James I, and was Gentleman of the Privy Chamber to Charles I. He was with the King at Oxford during the siege of 1646 and forfeited part of his estate on account of his loyalty. He died in December 1652 and was buried in the church of St. Martin-in-the-Fields, London. Like so many royalists, his son Henry found refuge in

Holland, and it was stated in 1655 that he was then 'resident at Bergen-op-Zoom in Brabant and hath been constantly there in residence since 1647'. He 'died a Lieut.-Colonel in the service of the States of Holland' on 1 August 1658 and was buried in the Great Church at Bergen. According to George Vertue it was at Bergen-op-Zoom that his son William, the architect, was born, though the exact date of the event is unknown. It must, however, have taken place some years before 1647, for among the Montagu manuscripts there is a letter dated 8 April 1658, which shows that at that date Winde was already an Ensign in command of English troops at Bergen-op-Zoom. At the Restoration he evidently came to England to claim his patrimony, for it was on 15 August 1660 that he obtained the administration of his grandfather's estate. In 1661 he was made gentleman usher to Elizabeth, Queen of Bohemia (daughter of James I), and in September 1667 he bought a Cornet's commission in the King's Troop of the Royal Regiment of Horse. Although a cavalry officer, he evidently had some knowledge of military architecture, for in July 1667, when a squadron of Dutch ships lay in the Thames, he assisted in the fortification of Gravesend Reach. In his own words:

> Sir Godfrey Floyd being employed to fortify both the sides of the River at Gravesend and Tilbury: But he staying but one night Prince Rupert sending for him to Sheerness I was then left to fortify those Places on Gravesend and Tilbury side: I raised a new Platforme on the old Blockhouse which stands firm still, as also another on the top of the Leads for small Guns. His late Majesty and Sir Godfrey Floyd coming afterward to see these works were extreamly satisfied with them . . . .

In July 1676 Winde was promoted Lieutenant, and early in 1678 he was given the rank of Captain and sent to Jersey in command of his own troop of horse. He made a map of the island which, with 'several other Draughts', he sent to the King. According to his own account, he was to have superintended the fortification of the Channel Islands, but nothing was done owing to the death of the Governor, Sir Thomas Morgan, in 1679. In July Winde's troop was disbanded and he was recalled to England. He brought with him some additions to the map which he had made, and presented the King with a book 'with all the Castles, Landing-places and several views of the island set forth in Colours, and all done by my own hand, upon which his Majestie was pleased to say He never understood the Place till then and expressed great satisfaction'.[1] He was rewarded by a grant of the reversion of Major Martin Beckman's post of Second Engineer to the Ordnance (25 Sept. 1679). In 1680 he was ordered by the Commissioners of the Ordnance and Sir Bernard de Gomme, then Principal Engineer, 'to go to Portsmouth to look over the Fortifications, there having the year before been some failure in those works, which I readily undertook. But before I had received full instructions for that business, I was again sent for and ordered to go to Tangier as Comptroller of the Train of Artillery . . . but a Truce being made between that Garrison and the Enemy I went not.' Thus deprived once more of the opportunity of distinguishing himself as a military engineer, 'Captain' Winde (as he remained for the rest of his life) returned to the duties of a Lieutenant in the King's Troop. As such he took part in the Battle of Sedgemoor in June 1685, when 'he charged with the said Troop the Green Regiment of the Rebells and totally routed them taking a Colonel's Colours besides a Horse Colours.' But promotion still eluded him, despite the fact that he had the King's promise of preferment 'by the Rt. Honble the Marquis of Powis and the Earl of Craven' (who was his godfather)[2] and in 1685 and again in 1688 he addressed memorials to the King, representing that he was the oldest officer of his rank in the Regiment and had more than once been passed over in favour of others with less service to their credit.

The Revolution of 1688 must finally have extinguished Winde's hopes of military preferment, and for the remainder of his life he practised as an architect, designing country houses instead of fortifications, and directing masons and carpenters where before he had commanded troopers. It is possible that for his architectural training he was in some measure indebted to Sir Balthazar Gerbier, for it was to 'Master William Wine' that Gerbier addressed the last of the forty dedications with which he prefaced his *Counsel and Advise to All Builders*, 1663, and in it he refers to the study of military architecture upon which Winde had already embarked. When Gerbier died soon afterwards, it was Winde who took his place as architect of Lord Craven's new house at Hampstead Marshall in Berkshire. The original drawings, now in the Bodleian Library, show that work had started at least as early as 1662 and that the decoration of the interior was still in progress

[1] Winde's description of Jersey is probably to be identified with B.L., King's MS. 49.

[2] See Craven's will, in which he leaves £100 to 'Capt. William Winde Esqr. my Godson'.

as late as 1688. The drawings are by several hands and the formula 'This Draught allowed of by me, William Winde' shows that, like other architects of his time, Winde relied on his skilled artificers to submit their own designs for plaster-work, sculpture and joinery. Winde's correspondence with Lord Ashburnham and Lady Bridgeman shows that he was willing to bespeak pictures and other works of art for his clients, and there is evidence that he counted formal landscape-gardening among his accomplishments, for in one letter he recalled that 'When I was quartered in Kent and imployed in altering the Earle of Winchelsea's house of Eastwell . . . I transplanted trees of a considerable bigeness wch did very well & the same I did at Sr Charles Kemishe orchard at Rupera in Wales.'

The 'learned and ingenious Captain Wynne', as Colen Campbell calls him, must have been a figure of some importance in the artistic world of his day. He was a friend of Samuel Pepys, who left him a mourning ring in his will, and George Vertue gives details of pictures in his possession. He corresponded with Sir Hans Sloane and there is evidence that he was acquainted with Wren, for it was at the latter's house that Robert Hooke heard him talk of Dutch methods of walking on ice and of fortifications made of straw 'frozen together in a night or two by water thrown on them . . . and . . . secured from scaling by freezing the out sides in the same manner, and making them slippery'. In 1662 he became a Fellow of the Royal Society, but was expelled in 1685, apparently for failure to pay his subscription. He was the author of an unpublished *Cursus Mathematicus* in two volumes, of which the manuscript is now in the British Library (King's MSS. 266–7). It includes sections on Arithmetic, Geometry, Military Architecture, Cartography, Perspective, etc., and is dated 1688 on the title-page. Another manuscript containing mathematical and architectural notes by Winde is in the Inner Temple Library.

Although his recorded works are not numerous, Winde ranks with Hooke, May, Pratt and Talman as one of the principal English country-house architects of the late seventeenth century. At Hampstead Marshall he was completing another's work and his share in a building destroyed as long ago as 1718 is not easy to determine. But at Combe Abbey he followed the pattern of Pratt's Clarendon House. At Belton House (whose attribution to Winde is argued below) he did the same. At Ampthill (a similar house) he appears merely to have been consulted about the interior decoration after the shell had been completed. Cliveden and Buckingham House were houses of a different and architecturally a more advanced character, in which the hipped roof has given way to the balustraded attic. If Winde designed these two houses then he was one of the originators of an architectural formula that was to be much employed in the early eighteenth century. Buckingham House, in particular, was the prototype of many country houses with quadrant colonnades and flanking wings that were consciously modelled on the this well-known London mansion.[1] But the attribution of Cliveden to Winde rests solely on a muddled statement by George Vertue that may well be incorrect, and it is possible that at Buckingham House Talman had preceded Winde as architect (below, p. 1068). Other buildings by Winde remain to be identified. In May 1701 he told Lady Bridgeman that he intended shortly to visit an unnamed 'Building under my inspection in the Country', and the volume in the Inner Temple Library contains the dimensions of a proposed house for Major Knatchbull that has not been identified and was probably never built. The interiors of Winde's houses were handsomely fitted up with the help of the best contemporary craftsmen. Among those whom Winde regularly employed were Edward Pierce, the sculptor, Edward Goudge, the plasterer, and Jonathan and Edward Wilcox, carpenters. In 1688 he told Lady Bridgeman that Goudge had been 'imployed by mee this 6 or 7 yeares, is an excelent draufftsman and mackes all his desines hime sellfe.'

In 1676–8 Winde was one of the Commissioners appointed by Henry Howard, afterwards 6th Duke of Norfolk, to lay out the site of Arundel House in the Strand for building. Besides forming Arundel, Surrey and Norfolk Streets, and regulating their architecture, the Commissioners supervised the building of a mansion for the Duke, begun in 1677 but subsequently abandoned. To what extent Winde may have been personally responsible for the design of this house is not clear, as the only drawing for it mentioned in the Commissioners' minutes is a 'draught' by Edward Pierce for one of the fronts [Arundel Castle MS. MD 1514]. It is, however, possible that Winde himself designed Ham (afterwards Dorchester) House, Weybridge, for the Duke at this time.

Winde married Magdalen, daughter of Sir James Bridgeman and elder sister of Lady Howard of Escrick. 'Mrs. Magdalen Wind

[1] e.g. Wotton House, Bucks.; Gregories, nr. Beaconsfield; and Dunton Hall, Tydd St. Giles, Cambs. (dem. *c.*1755).

of the parish of St. Martin' was buried in Richmond Church, Surrey, on 8 January 1708/9, and is commemorated by an inscription on her sister's ledger-stone.[1] Her husband died in 1722 and was buried at St. Martin-in-the-Fields on 28 April. He left a son William, to whom administration was granted on 9 May. This son lived at Bexley in Kent and held the post of Chamberlain to Princess Sophia. When he died intestate in 1741 there was a sale of prints and drawings belonging to his father which was attended by George Vertue.[2] Vertue's account of the architectural drawings enables them to be identified as those now in the Bodleian Library (MSS. Gough Drawings a. 2–3). In the same library there is a volume (MS. Rawlinson B.143) containing a transcript of legal and other documents relating to the Winde family and its property, including William Winde's petitions to James II and a pedigree giving details of his father's death at Bergen-op-Zoom.

[J. Challenor-Smith, 'Captain William Winde, the Architect', *Genealogist*. N.S. xxxi, 1914–15, 243–4; C. Dalton, *English Army Lists and Commission Registers* i, 92, 190, 226, ii, 4, 120; *The Diary of Robert Hooke*, ed. H. W. Robinson & W. Adams, 1935, 113, 206, 401; Hist. MSS. Comm., *Manuscripts of Lord Montagu of Beaulieu, passim*; Walpole Society, *Vertue Note Books* i, 11, 84, 89, 91, 127, ii, 88, iv, 11, 111, 196; British Library, Add. MSS. 4063, ff. 56, 129–30, 4065, f. 88, 29557, ff. 43, 65; E. S. de Beer, 'The Earliest Fellows of the Royal Society', *Notes and Records of the Royal Society* vii, no. 2, 1950, 189.]

HAMPSTEAD MARSHALL, BERKS., completed house for 1st Earl of Craven after the death of Sir Balthazar Gerbier, *c.*1663–*c.*1688;[3] destroyed by fire 1718 (Thomas Strong, mason, Edward Pierce, carver, Edward Goudge, plasterer) [original designs in Bodleian Library, MS. Gough Drawings a. 2; British Museum Print Room 1881-6-11-154; and Soane Museum, Case 24, No. 68 (*Wren Soc.* xvii, pl. xxvii)]. (Surviving gate-piers are illustrated in *Arch. Rev.* xix, 1906, 155–64 and *C. Life*, 29 March 1913.)

CLIVEDEN HOUSE, BUCKS., for George Villiers, 2nd Duke of Buckingham (d. 1687), *c.*1676–8; wings added by Thomas Archer probably *c.*1705; house destroyed by fire 1795 [Walpole Soc., *Vertue Note Books* iv, 11, a source questioned by K. Downes, *English Baroque Architecture*, 1966, 69, but accepted by G. Jackson-Stops, 'The Cliveden Album', *Arch. Hist.* xix, 1976, 5–6] (*Vitruvius Britannicus* ii, 1717, pls. 70–4).

? HAM (afterwards DORCHESTER) HOUSE, WEYBRIDGE, SURREY, for 6th Duke of Norfolk, *c.*1677–8; dem. *c.*1830 [Arundel Castle MS. MD 1514 shows that in 1676–8 Winde was one of the Commissioners responsible for laying out the Arundel estate in the Strand for the Duke, and in the Inner Temple Library there is a sketch by Winde of 'the Roofe of the D: of Norfolk's at Waybridge'].

COMBE ABBEY, WARWICKS., rebuilt centre and N. wing for 1st Earl of Craven, 1682–88; N. wing dem. and much of interior dismantled 1932 (William Cooles, mason; Jonathan Wilcox, carpenter; John Syms, joiner; Edward Pierce, carver; Edward Goudge, plasterer) ['Letters & Papers relating to the rebuilding of Combe Abbey', ed. H. Colvin, *Walpole Soc.* l, 1984] (H. A. Tipping, *English Homes*, IV (i), 155–78).

attributed: DINGLEY HALL, NORTHANTS., rebuilt for Sir Edward Griffin, *c.*1684–88 [M. Binney in *C. Life*, 27 Nov. 1980: a stylistic attribution, supported by the fact that the joiner John Syms was employed both here and at Combe Abbey].

LONDON, POWIS (afterwards NEWCASTLE) HOUSE, LINCOLN'S INN FIELDS, for 1st Marquess of Powis, 1684–9; fitted up as the offices of the Great Seal after the Marquess's outlawry in 1690; refitted for the Duke of Newcastle 1715–17; divided 1771; rebuilt by Sir Edwin Lutyens 1930–1 [Walpole Soc., *Vertue Note Books* i, 127] (*Survey of London* iii, 110–18).

attributed: BELTON HOUSE, LINCS., for Sir John Brownlow, Bart., 1685–8 [stylistic attribution, based on close resemblance to Combe Abbey, and supported by the employment of Edward Goudge and Edward Wilcox]. A Chancery lawsuit [P.R.O., C8/527/2], shows that the mason William Stanton undertook to build the house 'by the great' in Feb. 1684/5, subcontracting the carpentry to Edward Wilcox. Accounts in the Brownlow papers in the Lincs. Record Office record payments to Stanton and Wilcox but do not mention the architect. Goudge's recent employment 'at Sir John Brownloe's' is mentioned in a letter

[1] 'In this Church also Lyes Buried Mrs. MAGDELEN WINDE, Eldest Sister of the said Lady Howard, with two of her children JOHN & MAGDELEN WINDE.'

[2] There is a copy of the Sale Catalogue in the B.L. (S.C. 266 (4)).

[3] The earliest of the Hampstead Marshall drawings is dated 1662, the latest 1688. One of them bears a note to the effect that the first floor was begun on 27 July 1664. Among the Montagu papers there is a pass, dated 17 July 1665, authorizing Winde to proceed to Hamstead Marshall in time of plague.

from Winde to Lady Bridgeman written in Feb. 1689/90. (H. A. Tipping, *English Homes* IV (i), 225–8; *C. Life*, 3, 10, 17 Sept. 1964; Oliver Hill & J. Cornforth, *English Country Houses: Caroline*, 1966, 192–202).

CASTLE BROMWICH HALL, WARWICKS., alterations to interior for Sir John and Lady Bridgeman, 1685–90 (Edward Pierce, carver; Edward Goudge, plasterer) [G. W. Beard in *C. Life*, 9 May 1952 and 'William Winde and interior design', *Arch. Hist.* 27, 1984].

EASTWELL PARK, KENT, alterations for the (2nd?) Earl of Winchilsea, probably *c.*1685 [mentioned in an undated letter from Winde to Lady Bridgeman].

LONDON, BUCKINGHAM HOUSE, ST. JAMES'S, for John Sheffield, 1st Duke of Buckingham, 1702–5; bought in 1762 by King George III, for whom the house was altered and enlarged by Sir William Chambers 1762–9; incorporated in the structure of Buckingham Palace, 1825–30. A summary of the cost in London University MS. 533, ff. 9–11, shows that John Fitch built the main structure by contract for £7000. Campbell says that this house was 'conducted by the learned and ingenious Capt. Wynne'. Elsewhere he uses the word 'conducted' in a sense different from 'designed'. Thus the Queen's gallery at Somerset House was 'taken from a Design of Inigo Jones, but conducted by another Hand', and Mr. Hudson's house at Sunbury was 'designed and conducted by Mr. Fort'. Winde may therefore have been carrying out another architect's design at Buckingham House; if so, that architect was probably William Talman (above, p. 950) [*Vitruvius Britannicus* i, 1715, pls. 43–4; *History of the King's Works*, v, 133–8; John Cornforth in *C. Life*, 12 July 1962].

AMPTHILL PARK, BEDS., advised 1st Lord Ashburnham on interior decoration (by Laguerre), iron work (by Tijou), and statues, 1706 [letterbook of Lord Ashburnham in West Sussex Record Office].

Note: On 17 Dec. 1689 Winde apologized to Lady Bridgeman for delay in answering a letter because of the arrival of Lord Craven's steward with workmen's bills 'from severall places, where his Lordship has buillte'. In addition to Hampstead Marshall and Combe Abbey, Lord Craven then owned Ashdown House, Berks., and Drury House, Drury Lane, London (dem. 1809). In August 1688 Winde refers in a letter to Goudge's work 'in a late building at Drury House'. It is likely that this was done under his supervision, as his address at this time was 'over against the Earl of Craven's house in Drury Lane'. In December 1697 Winde wrote that in the spring he was engaged 'to waite on the Duchess of Norfolk to Drayden in Northamptonshire and from thence withe the D. of Powis to the Read Castel', i.e. Powis Castle, Montgomeryshire.

WING, EDWARD (1683–1755), was a carpenter and master builder of Aynho in Northants. [Nicholas Cooper, *Aynho*, 1984, 166–8]. An account-book from Aynho Park, now in the County Record Office, shows that he was employed to rebuild AYNHO CHURCH in 1723–5, retaining the medieval tower. The building is chiefly remarkable as a rustic attempt to build something after the style of the churches erected in London under the 'Fifty New Churches' Act of 1711. Wing's designs, described as 'all of his own drawing', are preserved in the Diocesan Records. What is evidently another of Wing's 'draughts' is preserved among Browne Willis's manuscripts in the Bodleian Library (MS. Willis 34, f. 289). It corresponds with the church as built, except that the north and south doors are treated in a different manner.

Between 1724 and 1730, Wing was employed by Browne Willis to rebuild ST. MARTIN'S CHAPEL at FENNY STRATFORD, BUCKS. An engraving of the chapel, signed 'Ed. Wing de Aynhoe desig.', is preserved in the Bodleian Library. The traditional character of the design was, however, due to Browne Willis's antiquarian tastes. A south aisle was added in 1823, and in 1866 a new nave and chancel were built, the nave of Willis's chapel being retained as a north aisle. [Bodleian Library, MS. Willis 52; H. Roundell, 'Notes on the Life of Browne Willis', *Records of Bucks.* ii, 1870, 8.]

WING, JOHN (1728–1794), was the eldest son of John Wing of North Luffenham in Rutland and his first wife Elizabeth. Both his father, who died in 1752, and his grandfather Aaron Wing, who died in 1751 at the age of 85, were masons by trade. Aaron Wing was a nephew of Vincent Wing (1619–68), the astronomer and land surveyor, who also lived at North Luffenham, and a cousin of Tycho Wing (1696–1750) of Pickworth, the astrologer. Their common ancestor Jasper Wing, who died at North Luffenham in 1620, may well have been a mason also, since he mentions his tools in his will. He himself had come to North Luffenham from Great Ponton in Lincolnshire towards the end of the sixteenth century, and his Christian name seems to confirm the statement made by Vincent

Wing's biographer that the family was of Welsh origin.

John must have begun to assist his father at an early age, for a note in the parish register records that in March 1739/40 the dove-house over the porch of the rectory barn 'was made by John Wing Sen.[r] assisted by J. Wing Jun[r].' Subsequently he left North Luffenham for Hallaton in Leicestershire, a village with which his father had some connection, for in his will he had left a cottage there to his second wife Dorothy. In 1755 John Wing and Elizabeth Gibbins, 'both of this parish', were married at Hallaton, and Wing lived there for the greater part of his life. For the next quarter of a century he was the leading architect and stonemason in Leicestershire and designed some remarkable Gothic churches in that neighbourhood. As early as 1741 his father had rebuilt the tower and nave of GALBY CHURCH, LEICS., in a somewhat bizarre Gothic of his own devising, as recorded by J. Throsby in his *Select Views in Leicestershire* ii, 1790, 137. This was done at the expense of William Fortrey, a local squire, who in 1757 obtained a faculty to rebuild KING'S NORTON CHURCH, LEICS., to the designs of the younger Wing. Work began in 1760 and was completed in 1775.[1] The church is rectangular in plan, with closely spaced buttresses separating tall windows containing elaborate tracery of correct 'Early Decorated' character. The west tower was originally surmounted by a spire which was destroyed by lightning in 1850. Outside the east end of the church there is a handsome monument to Fortrey, who died in 1783.

A signed plan and elevation in an extra-illustrated copy of Nichols's *History of Leicestershire* in Leicester Central Reference Library show that in 1767 the body of CARLTON CURLIEU CHURCH, LEICS., was rebuilt in Gothic style to Wing's design at the expense of Sir John Palmer, Bart., and in 1788 Wing designed EAST CARLTON CHURCH, NORTHANTS., in a similar style for the same patron [J. P. Neale, *Views of Seats*, 1st ser. vi, 1823]. In 1769 he partly rebuilt the west tower of GREAT GLEN CHURCH, LEICS. [account for design and workmanship in parish records in Leics. C.R.O.], in 1772 he repaired 'the four middle windows in the spire' of ST. MARTIN'S CHURCH, LEICESTER [T. North, *Accounts of the Churchwardens of St. Martin's Leicester*, 1884, 225], and in 1774 he was paid £65 for repairing the steeple of BILLESDON CHURCH, LEICS. [*V.C.H. Leics.* v, 13].

Evidence for Wing's other architectural works comes chiefly from his pocket-books for the years 1775 and 1780, now in the County Record Office at Bedford [X 106/79–80]. Entries in the later pocket-book show that in 1780 he was building a bridge at Girtford near Sandy in Bedfordshire, and in 1781 he took a lease of a stone-quarry at Totternhoe in that county. Some time within the next few years he moved from Hallaton to Leicester, but eventually he left Leicestershire for Bedford, where he died on 24 June 1794, aged 65, and is commemorated by a tablet in the south aisle of St. Mary's Church. At Bedford Wing's business as an architect and mason was carried on by his eldest son John Wing (*q.v.*). His second son Moses (b. 1761) started business as a mason in Leicester in 1782, but died three years later at the age of 25. His third son Vincent (1763–1843) was apprenticed to a grocer in Melton Mowbray, and was the father of Vincent Wing (1803–79), also a grocer by trade, who inherited his grandfather's interest in Gothic architecture and contributed a number of papers on that subject to the first four volumes of the Leicestershire Archaeological Society's *Transactions*.

[*The Registers of North Luffenham*, ed. P. G. Dennis (Parish Register Soc., 1896); parish registers of Hallaton; wills in Peterborough Probate Registry; J. Gadbury, *A Brief Relation of the Life and Death of Mr. Vincent Wing*, 1670, 2; *A Pedigree of the Family of Wing* compiled by E. Green, 1886; W. Hartopp, *Register of the Freemen of Leicester 1770–1930*, 1933, 454; John Wing's pocket-books and other papers in the Bedfordshire County Record Office; *Trans. Leicestershire Arch. Soc.* v, 1882, 226; J. Brashe, 'Girtford Bridge and John Wing II', *Beds. Mag.* 15 (2), no. 114, Autumn 1975; information from Mrs. F. E. Skillington.]

WING, JOHN (1756–1826), was the eldest son of John Wing (*q.v.*) of Hallaton in Leicestershire, where he was born in July 1756. Early in the 1780s he moved from Leicestershire to Bedfordshire, where his father had recently acquired a stone-quarry at Totternhoe. He settled at Bedford, took over the quarry, and soon became the leading architect and builder in the county. He frequently acted as surveyor of bridges for the county and designed and built most of the public buildings in Bedford. He also made monuments, examples of which can be seen in the churches of Bedford, Flitton, Henlow,

[1] Dates recorded at the Archdeacon's Visitation in 1776 (Leicester Archdeaconry Records). A drawing of the tower and spire signed by Wing is in the Local Collection in Northampton Public Library. See also Throsby, *Select Views in Leicestershire* ii, 1790, 139.

Great Bowden (Leics.), Sandy, Aspley Guise, and Irthlingborough (Northants.).

Having in 1792 been admitted a burgess of Bedford, Wing became a prominent member of the corporation and held the office of Mayor on three occasions (in 1793, 1808 and 1817). In 1799 he married Elizabeth Tacy, by whom he had five sons. John (b. 1802) entered the Church and became vicar of St. Mary's Leicester. William Henry (b. 1803) died young. James Tacy (b. 1805) practised as an architect in Bedford and died at Sharnbrook in 1880.[1] Vincent (b. 1808) was apprenticed to an ironmonger at Melton Mowbray. Samuel (1812–65) became a solicitor in Bedford. John Wing died at Bedford on 2 December 1826, aged 70, and was buried in St. Mary's Church, where there is an inscription to his memory in the south aisle. [Wing family records in Bedford County Record Office; W. Hartopp, *Register of the Freemen of Leicester 1770–1930*, 581; L. N. Cottingham, *Plans etc. of King Henry VII's Chapel*, 1822, 11.]

BEDFORD

THE HOUSE OF INDUSTRY, 1795–6 [Bedford County Records, X 67/110] (engraved plan and elevation in Bodleian, Gough Maps 1, f. 3).

THE COUNTY GAOL, 1801 [*Report from the Committee of Aldermen appointed to visit Several Gaols in England*, 1816, 32].

THE INFIRMARY, 1802–3; rebuilt 1899 [infirmary minutes in Bedford County Record Office].

THE LUNATIC ASYLUM, 1809–12 [J. H. Matthiason, *Bedford and its Environs*, 1831, 119].

THE BRIDGE, 1811–13, widened 1938–40 ['Designed and executed by John Wing of Bedford', as recorded by an inscription on the parapet].

AVENUE HOUSE, AMPTHILL, BEDS., the COACH-HOUSE for John Morris, 1801 [Morris's House-Book, Sir Albert Richardson's Collection].

WINKS, CHARLES (–1839), was a builder from Ombersley in Worcestershire who became the estate architect at Trentham in Staffordshire in 1814. Besides his work on the Sutherland estate, he designed and built two Staffordshire churches, at FULFORD, 1825, Gothic, and HANFORD, 1827–8, rebuilt 1868 [both I.C.B.S.], and in 1829 designed a Gothic funerary chapel (dem. 1860) for the Kinnersley family at ASHLEY CHURCH, STAFFS. [faculty in Lichfield Joint Record Office]. He was also responsible for rebuilding CHAPEL CHORLTON CHURCH, STAFFS., in 1826–7, modifying plans originally made by James Trubshaw, jr. [I.C.B.S.]. His unexecuted design for a column in memory of the 1st Duke of Sutherland is in the Staffs. C.R.O., Gower papers, D 593/H/13/40; see also K 1/3/2.

WINTER, JAMES, was a Scottish architect and master mason. In 1743–4 he was employed by the 2nd Duke of Atholl to build a new stable-block at BLAIR CASTLE, PERTHSHIRE, and in 1747–58 to remodel the castle itself. His alterations to the exterior of the castle were destroyed in 1869, when the building was recastellated by David Bryce, and the interior was not his responsibility [Arthur Oswald in *C. Life*, 11 Nov. 1949]. A set of designs for remodelling the castle, marked 'By Mr. Winter 1743', remains at Blair, together with a design by him for an intended addition to Dunkeld House, Perthshire, dated 1744 [D.2.14 (9–12) and D.1.26]. In about 1750 Winter contracted for the masonry of STEWARTFIELD HOUSE, ROXBURGHSHIRE, for John Scot (designer unknown) [S.R.O., GD 237/213/3]. In 1756 he was named as arbitrator in connection with a dispute over the erection of the Town Hall and Steeple at Berwick-on-Tweed [Berwick Guild-Books, 14 Jan. 1756].

James was probably related to Thomas Winter, a foreman mason employed by William Adam at Floors Castle in 1726 [accounts at Floors], at Hamilton Church in 1731–4 [Duke of Hamilton's archives, TD 80/100/21], and probably at Aberuthven mausoleum in 1735 [S.R.O., GD 220/6/1384/30, no. 4], but Thomas Winter, a land surveyor and landscape-gardener active in Scotland in the 1730s and 1740s, was an Englishman brought from Norfolk in 1726 by Sir Archibald Grant of Monymusk [*Monymusk Papers*, ed. H. Hamilton, Scottish Historical Soc. 1945].

WINTER, THOMAS, of Nottingham, is described as a 'builder' in White's 1832 Directory. With the exception of the tower, WIDMERPOOL CHURCH, NOTTS., was rebuilt to his designs in 1831–2, and he repaired the tower in 1836–7 after damage by lightning [I.C.B.S.]. The church was again rebuilt 1888–95. In 1835 he made Gothic designs for rebuilding OLD DALBY OR DALBY-ON-THE-WOLDS CHURCH, LEICS., which were carried out in that or the following year [I.C.B.S.].

---

[1] His works included Pulloxhill Church, Beds., 1845–6, the village school at Tingrith, and the restoration of Aspley Guise Church.

A design by him for refronting WESTON COTTAGE, WESTON UNDERWOOD, DERBYSHIRE, dated 1831, is among the muniments at Kedleston Hall, and one for alterations to CLUMBER HOUSE, NOTTS., dated 1833, is in the R.I.B.A. Collection.

WINTON, GEORGE (*c.*1759–1822), is described as 'architect' on a large monument in St. Cuthbert's Churchyard, Edinburgh. He was a mason by trade, and was concerned in the building of houses in ALBANY STREET, ABERCROMBY PLACE, DUBLIN STREET and NORTHUMBERLAND STREET during the first decade of the nineteenth century [S.R.O., Edinburgh Sasines]. He died on 30 November 1822, aged 63.

WISHART, J—, exhibited at the Royal Academy between 1798 and 1808. From 1801 to 1808 his address was at the London Dock Office. His exhibits included a 'Design for a town hall and market place' (1799), 'A view of Sir G. Buggan's villa, and a remarkable rock, on Rustall Common, near Tunbridge Wells' (1802), 'The entrance from the River Thames into the London Docks at Bell-Dock' (1802), a 'design for a villa' (1804), and a 'design for a royal hospital' (1805).

WISHLADE, BENJAMIN (–1848), was born in Devonshire but moved to Kington in Herefordshire in 1806 and established himself there as a builder and surveyor. In KINGTON he built the TOWN HALL in a provincial Greek Revival style in 1820, the WORKHOUSE (now Kingswood House) in 1837, the NATIONAL SCHOOL, and 'many gentlemen's residences in the neighbourhood', including GRAVEL HILL VILLA for Morris Sayce, and PORTWAY VILLA for William Sayce in a Tudor Gothic style, 1833 [Parry, *History of Kington*, 1845, 23, 225–6]. The parish church was enlarged by him on the north side in 1829 [I.C.B.S.]. In Radnorshire, where he was County Surveyor, he was responsible for the GAOL at PRESTEIGNE, 1819–21, dem. 1897, for the suspension bridge over the R. Ithon at PEN-Y-BONT [W. K. Parker, 'Radnorshire Civic Buildings 1819–29', *Trans. Radnorshire Soc.* 50, 1980], and for rebuilding LLANFIHANGEL RHYDITHON CHURCH in 1838–9 [I.C.B.S.].

WITHENBURY or **WYTHINBURY,** JAMES (–1725), was a mason of Worcester, where, at the time of his death, he was also the proprietor of the 'King's Head' Inn [will in Worcester Probate Records]. The crudely drawn design which he made for HANBURY HALL, WORCS., in about 1700 is illustrated in *Country Life*, 4 January 1968, fig. 7. The marble monument to Bishop Lloyd in Fladbury Church, which Withenbury made in 1718, has been dismembered [A. Tindal Hart, *William Lloyd 1627–1717*, 1952, 258].

WOLFE, JOHN LEWIS (1798–1881), was the son of Lewis Wolfe, Comptroller of the Stationery Office [*Gent's Mag.* 1798 (i), 352]. He became a pupil of Joseph Gwilt and travelled on the Continent in 1816–18 and again in 1819–21. In 1820 he met Charles Barry in Rome and became his lifelong friend and architectural mentor. He was 'almost the only person' who knew Barry intimately, and to him the Revd. A. Barry was indebted for much of the information contained in the life of his father. For most of his life Wolfe appears to have enjoyed independent means, making it unnecessary for him to engage fully in architectural practice. In 1818 he exhibited a design for a museum at the Royal Academy, and in 1823 he competed for the new buildings at King's College, Cambridge. Fourteen of his notebooks, two sketch-books and several architectural designs in the Italian Renaissance style are in the R.I.B.A. MSS. and Drawings Collections [A. Barry, *Life and Works of Sir Charles Barry*, 1867, pp. v, 46–7; *R.I.B.A. Drawings Catalogue*; *T-Z*, 257–8].

WOOD, FREDERICK, exhibited at the Royal Academy between 1817 and 1839 and practised as an architect and surveyor from 28 Queen Street, Brompton, until soon after 1840. In 1838 he showed 'a view of a mansion lately built for a gentleman in the neighbourhood of London'. He competed for the Houses of Parliament in 1835, and for the Royal Exchange in 1839. Drawings in the estate office at Grimsthorpe show that he altered the kitchens of GRIMSTHORPE CASTLE, LINCS., in 1831.

WOOD, HENRY, was a London builder of Norfolk origin. In 1794–6 he built the mausoleum in Blickling Park to the designs of Joseph Bonomi [*Arch. Hist.* 34, 1991, 81], and he was presumably the architect called Wood to whose designs THORPE MARKET CHURCH, NORFOLK, was rebuilt in 1796 at the expense of the 1st Lord Suffield. It is a small Gothic building of flint with stone dressings [E. Bartell, *Observations on Cromer as a Watering Place*, 1800, 43].

WOOD, HENRY, was described as 'architect and statuary of London' when, in 1801, he bought the yard and business of William Paty of Bristol (*q.v.*). It was chiefly as a statuary mason that he worked in Bristol for the next thirty years, but in 1806–8 he designed and built MERTHYR MAWR, a small country house in GLAMORGANSHIRE, for Sir John Nicholl. [R. Gunnis, *Dictionary of British Sculptors*, 1968, 439; Hilary M. Thomas, *Merthyr Mawr House*, Glamorgan Archives Service, 1976] (*C. Life*, 1 Nov. 1984). He also designed the LOWER LODGE at ASHTON COURT, nr. BRISTOL soon after 1802 [T. Mowl & B. Earnshaw, *Trumpet at a Distant Gate*, 1985, 211].

WOOD, HENRY MOSES (1789–1867), practised in Nottingham from about 1810 onwards. His recorded works include ST. PETER'S CHURCH, RADFORD, NOTTS., 1810–12, in elementary Gothic [J. F. Sutton, *The Date Book for Nottingham*, 1852, 144]; DARLEY ABBEY CHURCH, DERBYSHIRE, 1818–19, a Gothic building of the Commissioners' type [S. Glover, *History of Derbyshire* ii(1), 1833, 350]; parsonages at SAWLEY, DERBYSHIRE, 1822–4 [Bodleian Library, records of Queen Anne's Bounty], RADCLIFFE-ON-TRENT, NOTTS., 1827 [Borthwick Institute, York, MGA 1827], CLIFTON, NOTTS., enlarged 1830 [*ibid.*, 1830/1], and COLSTON BASSETT, NOTTS., 1834 [*ibid.*, 1834/1]; the enlargement of DENTON HOUSE, nr. GRANTHAM, LINCS., for Sir W. Earle Welby, Bart., 1815 [plans reported to be in estate office] (J. P. Neale, *Views of Seats*, 1st ser. iii, 1820), and additions, including a new dining-room with Greek Revival façade to the street, to the JUDGES' LODGINGS or COUNTY HOUSE, HIGH PAVEMENT, NOTTINGHAM, 1833 [A. Henstock, 'County House, High Pavement, Nottingham', *Thoroton Society's Trans.* lxxviii, 1974, 63]. Wood was active as a land surveyor and was the author of a map of Nottingham, published in 1830. He died at Buxton on 28 September 1867, leaving two sons, Henry Walker Wood, who continued his practice in Nottingham, and Arthur Augustus Wood, a playwright [Principal Probate Registry, Calendar of Probates].

WOOD, JOHN (1704–1754), was born in Bath in 1704, baptized in St. James's Church on 26 August, and educated at the Blue Coat School. His father, George Wood, was a local builder of whom nothing is known beyond the fact that he was still working in Bath as late as 1727. John Wood's early life is obscure, but there is evidence that he was living in London in 1725–7 and that he was working in Yorkshire during the same period. He himself refers to 'engagements in London' which came to an end in the spring of 1727, and the St. Marylebone rate-books show that a John Wood was resident in Oxford Street between 1725 and 1727. He was, in fact, one of the principal builders on the Cavendish-Harley estate, then being laid out by the Earl of Oxford, to whom Wood was afterwards to dedicate his book on Stonehenge. The register of building leases (B.L., Add. MS. 18240) shows that between March 1723 and July 1730 he undertook to build five houses in Oxford Street, one in Margaret Street, and several more in Edward Street. He was also engaged in building in Cavendish Square, both for the Duke of Chandos and for Lord Bingley. The latter was erecting a large house on the west side of the Square, and Wood appears to have been acting as his surveyor. Lord Bingley had recently completed his country seat at Bramham Park in Yorkshire, and here Wood seems to have been employed in laying out the grounds, for there exists an engraved plan of the park signed 'Jo: Wood', and the volume of Wood's designs in Bath Reference Library contains a design for an aqueduct at Bramham. In his *Description of Bath*, published in 1742, Wood says that he was at Bramham Park 'about eighteen years ago', i.e. *c.*1724; he also states that it was while he was in Yorkshire in the summer of 1725 that he first began to plan the improvement of Bath, and that in the following year business 'called me twice into the North of England'. Further evidence of Wood's activity in the North comes in a letter written from Bath in 1749 by a Liverpool lady who reported (probably wrongly) that he had designed a house at Capesthorne in Cheshire early in the 1730s.[1]

By 1727, therefore, Wood had already gained an unusually wide experience of building operations for one still only in his 23rd year. In Marylebone he had seen how the speculative builder could be made to conform to a regular architectural scheme planned in advance, and he had been employed at at least one country house besides acting the parts of both builder and surveyor in London.

It was natural that Wood should sooner or later turn his attention to the improvement of his native city of Bath, then on the threshold of its Georgian prosperity. Acts had already been obtained to improve the roads leading to the city, 'to pave, clean and light' its streets, and to make the Avon navigable to Bristol; and so (to quote Wood's own account) 'when I found the Work was likely to go on, I began to turn my Thoughts towards the Improve-

[1] See S. A. Harris, 'Sarah Clayton's Letter and John Wood of Bath', *Trans. Hist. Soc. of Lancs. and Cheshire*, c, 1948, and A. H. & S. M. Gomme and S. A. Harris, 'Who Designed Capesthorne Hall?', *Ibid.* cxxi, 1969.

ment of the City by Building; and for this Purpose I procured a Plan of the Town, which was sent me into Yorkshire, in the summer of the Year 1725, where I, at my leisure Hours, formed one Design for the Ground, at the North West Corner of the City', belonging to Robert Gay, an eminent London surgeon who had been M.P. for Bath, and 'another for the Land, on the North East side of the Town and River' on the Earl of Essex's estate. These were alternative designs, for both included 'a grand Place of Assembly, to be called the Royal Forum of Bath; another Place, no less magnificent, for the Exhibition of Sports, to be called the Grand Circus; and a third Place, of equal State with either of the former, for the Practice of medicinal Exercises, to be called the Imperial Gymnasium of the City, from a Work of that kind, taking its Rise at first in Bath, during the Time of the Roman Emperors'. On his return to London Wood immediately communicated these ambitious proposals to the proprietors of the lands in question. They lay under consideration for a year while Wood completed his business in the North of England. But in November 1726 he became Gay's agent, with authority to enter into agreements with anyone willing to build a new street of houses known at first as Barton but eventually as Gay Street. In the following January he contracted with the Duke of Chandos to build a 'court of houses' on the site of St. John's Hospital, of which the Duke had acquired the lease, and on 10 March he undertook the execution of the Avon navigation scheme. Finding that the local builders were inefficient and antiquated in their methods, he procured masons from Yorkshire and carpenters, joiners and plasterers from London and elsewhere, 'and from time to time sent such as were necessary down to Bath to carry on the Buildings I had undertaken'. For the 'better execution' of the Avon scheme he employed labourers who had been engaged on the Chelsea waterworks, with the result that the cost of excavation was cut by a third.

In May 1727, having completed his engagements in London, Wood took up permanent residence in Bath, where he was soon involved in further schemes of building for Ralph Allen and Humphrey Thayer, the treasurers of the General Hospital. The death of George I in June 1727 caused a temporary setback to his building activities, for with the prospect of a general election Gay bowed to opinion in the city which was hostile to the creation of a New Town and withdrew his support for the continuation of Barton Street. Wood now produced a plan which put the rebuilding of the old town first, but this was rejected by the Corporation as 'chimerical'. Faced with the total failure of his scheme for erecting a new Bath, Wood decided on the bold step of becoming 'sole contractor' for a great residential square which was to be erected under his supervision and at his own risk. With this object he secured from Gay a ninety-nine years' lease of sufficient land upon which to build the east side of the Square. Further leases were granted between 1728 and 1734, and in 1736 Queen Square was completed as the first instalment of Wood's plan for a new Bath. Both in its design and in its mode of erection, the Square followed London precedent. Having marked out the site of the individual houses, Wood sub-leased them to owner-builders or building tradesmen, who were bound by their leases to follow his elevations, but left to plan and decorate the interiors as they chose. The effect (as in Cavendish and Grosvenor Squares) was 'to group ordinary town houses in such as way as to gain the effect of a single palace', and the existence of the local quarries enabled Wood's handsome Palladian façades to be carried out entirely in stone at reasonable cost. Encouraged by the success of the Square, Wood revived his schemes for a Circus and a Forum. The latter was actually begun in 1739 on the site of the Abbey Orchard, but the Parades and their connecting streets were the only portion of 'the Grand Place of Assembly to be called the Royal Forum of Bath' which was realized. The Circus, owing to the opposition of interested parties, was not begun until February 1754, within four months of Wood's death, and the greater part of it was erected under the superintendence of his son, John Wood the younger. As a residential unit it bore little resemblance to the 'Grand Circus for the exhibition of sports' of which Wood had dreamed in 1725, but architecturally it was highly effective, and the circus became a permanent feature of the English town-planning tradition.

As Bath became a place of fashionable resort so the celebrity of its architect spread, and Wood was invited to design public buildings in Bristol and Liverpool, as well as country houses in the neighbourhood of Bath itself. The most celebrated of these was Ralph Allen's great mansion at Prior Park, which he began in 1735. Owing to a quarrel with the owner, its completion was entrusted to Richard Jones, Allen's clerk of the works (*q.v.*), who altered the east wing in execution, destroying the symmetrical balance of Wood's design.

In 1741 Wood published a curious work entitled *The Origin of Building, or the Plagiarism of the Heathens Detected*, in which he endeavoured to prove that the development of classical architecture was anticipated in Biblical times and that the three primary orders had been divinely revealed to the Jews and exemplified in the Temple at Jerusalem. This thesis, which had first been put forward by G. B. Villalpanda in his Commentaries on Ezekiel, published in 1604, was apparently intended to vindicate classical architecture from the stigma of a pagan origin and thereby to justify its employment on religious as well as aesthetic grounds. In the following year Wood published *An Essay towards a Description of Bath* (2nd ed. 1749; reissued 1765), in which he allowed his imagination full scope, identifying the city of Bladud as the ancient seat of Apollo, and seeing in the megalithic circles at Stanton Drew a primitive version of the Temple of Jerusalem. Wood's other publications were *A Description of the Exchange of Bristol*, 1745, *Choir Gaure, vulgarly called Stonehenge, described, restored and explained*, 1747, and a *Dissertation Upon the Orders of Columns and their Appendages*, 1750. The work on Stonehenge was based on a survey which Wood had made for Lord Oxford in 1740 (now B.L., Harleian MSS. 7354, 7355). Its object was to demonstrate that the Wiltshire monument was 'a temple of the British Druids', and that the stone circles at Stanton Drew were its prototype.

Wood's fantasies (of which Freemasonry was another ingredient) were in part derived from Newton's *Chronology of Ancient Kingdoms Amended*, 1728, and applied to architecture some of the unconventional ideas which Newton had developed about the early history of religion. The Tabernacle of Moses, the Temple of Jerusalem, Stonehenge, and even medieval churches were seen by Wood as examples of a divinely ordained system of architecture independent of Rome and undreamt of by Vitruvius. These wildly unscholarly speculations from the lunatic fringe of English antiquarian thought had little influence on Wood's contemporaries, and in so far as he saw his own property developments in Bath as an opportunity to commemorate a mythical past, their architectural form was (as the names 'Forum' and 'Circus' imply) presumably intended to evoke an Imperial Roman rather than a British or Druidic image.

Wood died at his house on the south side of Queen Square on 23 May 1754, after 'a long and tedious illness', and was buried at Swainswick. He was in his 50th year. His speculations had been financially successful and he left substantial property to his wife Jane (who died in 1766), subject to annuities for his sons, John and Thayer Allen Wood, and his daughters, Jane and Elizabeth [P.C.C. 186 PINFOLD]. A volume containing some 80 architectural drawings by Wood is in the Bath Reference Library. It includes the plan of an unexecuted design for the Ranger's Lodge (later Viceregal Lodge) in Phoenix Park, Dublin.

[*A.P.S.D.*; *D.N.B.*; *Builder*, 1856, 386; 'Some Original Drawings by John Wood', *Architect and Building News*, 4 Nov. 1927; R. Wittkower, 'Federico Zuccari and John Wood of Bath', *Jnl. Warburg & Courtauld Institutes* v, 1943; W. Ison, *The Georgian Buildings of Bath*, 1948, 2nd ed. 1980; John Summerson, 'John Wood and the English Town-Planning Tradition', in *Heavenly Mansions*, 1949; C.H. & M.I. Collins Baker, *The Life of James Brydges, Duke of Chandos*, 1949, chaps. 12–13; W. S. Dakers, *John Wood and his Times* (a pamphlet, Bath 1954); B.L., Egerton MS. 3647, ff. 91, 105, etc. (Duke of Kingston's Bath estate records); Nottingham University Library, Manvers MS. 4184 (Bath lease book); B.L., Add. MSS. 18239–40 (Harley Estate records); Tim Mowl & Brian Earnshaw, *John Wood: Architect of Obsession*, 1988; Eileen Harris, 'John Wood's system of architecture', *Burlington Mag.* 131, 1989, *British Architectural Books and Writers 1566–1785*, 480–9; Simon Varey, *Space and the Eighteenth-Century English Novel*, Cambridge 1990, Part II].

BUILDINGS IN BATH

ST. JOHN'S HOSPITAL, CHAPEL COURT HOUSE and CHANDOS BUILDINGS, for 1st Duke of Chandos, 1727–30 [Baker, *op. cit.*, chap. 13].

LILLIPUT ALLEY, enlarged house for Philip Allen,[1] 1727–8 [described by Wood in his *Essay* as 'a sample for the greatest Magnificence that was ever proposed by me for our City Houses', but not accepted by Ison as Wood's own work].

LINDSEY'S (later WILTSHIRE'S) ASSEMBLY ROOMS, for Humphrey Thayer, 1728–30; dem. *c.*1820 [Ison, *op. cit.*].

QUEEN SQUARE and houses in WOOD STREET, JOHN STREET and OLD KING STREET, 1729–36 [Ison].

ST. MARY'S CHAPEL, QUEEN SQUARE, 1732–4; dem. *c.*1875 [Ison; plan and elevation by Wood in Bath City Art Gallery].

THE GENERAL (now ROYAL MINERAL WATER) HOSPITAL, 1738–42; attic storey added by

[1] Mr. Ison kindly informs me that there is evidence that this house was owned not, as generally supposed, by Ralph Allen, but by his brother Philip (d. 1765).

J. Palmer *c.*1793; extensions by Manners & Gill 1850–60 [Ison].

THE NORTH and SOUTH PARADES, with PIERREPONT and DUKE STREETS, 1740–3 [Ison].

GAY STREET, *c.*1750 onwards [Ison].

THE CIRCUS, begun 1754, completed by John Wood, junior [Ison].

BUILDINGS ELSEWHERE

BRAMHAM PARK, YORKS. (W.R.), work for 1st Lord Bingley, 1722–4, probably in connection with the formal garden layout, of which Wood published an engraved plan (B.L., *King's Maps* xlv, 16, and York Minster Library, Hailstone Collection). The dates are established by payments to Wood in Bingley's account at Hoare's bank published by G. W. Beard in *C. Life*, 11 Dec. 1958, 142. (*C. Life*, 12 June 1958).

TYBERTON COURT, HEREFS., completed interior for William Brydges, 1728; dem. 1952 [Mowl & Earnshaw, *op. cit.*, 56].

TYBERTON CHURCH, HEREFS., reredos for William Brydges, 1728–9 [B. A. Bailey, 'William Brydges and the rebuilding of Tyberton Church', *Trans. Woolhope Field Club* xxxvii, 1962; Mowl & Earnshaw, *op. cit.*, 57–9].

BRISTOL, ST. NICHOLAS CHURCH, structural repairs 1731; rebuilt 1763–9 [J. Latimer, *Annals of Bristol in the Eighteenth Century*, 1893, 179–80].

BELCOMBE COURT, nr. BRADFORD-ON-AVON, WILTS., for Francis Yerbury, 1734 [J. Wood, *Essay towards a Description of Bath*, 1749, 237–9] (*C. Life*, 22 Dec. 1950).

LLANDAFF CATHEDRAL, GLAMORGANSHIRE, constructed classical church within the ruined nave, 1734–52; dem. *c.*1850 [*Some Account of the Condition of the Fabric of Llandaff Cathedral from 1575 to the Present Time*, by the Bishop of Llandaff, 1860; N. Pevsner, 'John Wood at Llandaff', *Arch. Rev.* June 1954; E. T. Davies, 'John Wood's Italianate Temple', *Jnl. Historical Soc. of the Church in Wales* vi, 1956; D. R. Buttress, 'Llandaff Cathedral in the 18th and 19th Centuries', *ibid.* xvi, 1966; C. Stevenson, 'Solomon Engothicked: the Elder John Wood's Restoration of Llandaff Cathedral', *Art History* 6, no. 3, 1983].

PRIOR PARK, nr. BATH, for Ralph Allen, 1735–48. The east wing was completed by Richard Jones to a different design. In 1829 the mansion became a Roman Catholic college and the wings were remodelled by H. E. Goodridge. There was a fire in 1836, after which the interior of the main building was rebuilt by the same architect. The west pavilion was dem. in 1844 to make way for the chapel designed by J. J. Scoles [W. Ison, *The Georgian Buildings of Bath*, 1948, 135–44; drawings by Wood in volume in Bath Reference Library, ff. 43–56].

LILLIPUT CASTLE, LANSDOWN, nr. BATH, for Jeremiah Pierce, 1738; incorporated in Battlefields House 1802 [J. Wood, *op. cit.*, 234–7; drawings by Wood in volume in Bath Reference Library, ff. 23–4].

BRISTOL, THE EXCHANGE and MARKET, CORN STREET, 1741–3 [J. Wood, *A Description of the Exchange of Bristol*, 1745; volume of original drawings by Wood in Royal Academy Library (8516); W. Ison, *The Georgian Buildings of Bristol*, 1952, 95–105].

BATHFORD, SOMERSET, THE SPA, 1746; dem. [J. Wood, *Essay towards a Description of Bath*, 1749, 70].

TITANBARROW LOGIA (now WHITEHAVEN), KINGSDOWN ROAD, BATHFORD, nr. BATH, for Southwell Pigott, 1748–9 [J. Wood, *Essay towards a Description of Bath*, 1749, 239–40; contract and drawings by Wood in volume in Bath Reference Library, ff. 1–6].

LIVERPOOL, THE EXCHANGE (now TOWN HALL), 1749–54; interior destroyed by fire 1795 and rebuilt by J. Foster; dome and cupola added 1802, portico 1811 [J. A. Picton, *Liverpool Municipal Records, 1700–1835*, 1886, 158–9, 269–72] (*C. Life*, 23 July 1927).

WOOD, JOHN (1728–1781), the younger, son of John Wood of Bath, was christened in Bath Abbey on 25 February 1727/8. As a young man he evidently acted as his father's assistant, for in 1749, when the elder Wood designed the Exchange at Liverpool, he agreed 'to leave his son Mr. John Wood at Liverpoole during the summer season to superintend and carry on the said building', and a house in Liverpool was rented in the name of John Wood between 1750 and 1753. In July 1749 both he and his father were admitted freemen of Liverpool, and in 1751 he was elected a member of the Ugly Face Clubbe in that town. In the Club's minute-book his qualifications for membership are recorded in architectural terms. They read 'A stone colour'd complexion, a dimple in his Attick Story. The Pillasters of his face fluted. Tortoise-ey'd, a prominent nose. Wild grin, and face altogether resembling a badger, and finer tho' smaller than Sir Christopher Wren or Inigo Jones's.' After his father's death in 1754 Wood took his place as the leading architect in Bath, completing the building of the Circus and adding the Royal Crescent as the culmination of the great sequence of residential buildings begun by his father in 1727. Completed in 1775, the Crescent was the first (as well as the largest and grandest) of its kind, and was destined to find more imitators even than the neighbouring Circus. Wood's second masterpiece, the New Assembly Rooms, provided the city with a public building worthy of its domestic architecture, while his Hot Bath, built for the Corporation between 1773 and 1777, showed that its architect could design a small but complicated structure with as much success as the monumental Royal Crescent. The work of the younger Wood represents the climax of the Palladian tradition in Bath, and after his death the architectural initiative passed to those who, like Thomas Baldwin, looked for their inspiration to Robert Adam rather than to Palladio. John Wood died at Batheaston on 16 June 1781, and was buried in the family vault in Swainswick Church. He had been for many years a Justice of the Peace for the County of Somerset. He published *The Description of the Hot-Bath at Bath . . . together with the Plans, Elevations and Sections of the same: the Design of John Wood, Architect*, 1777, and *A Series of Plans, for Cottages or Habitations of the Labourer*, 1781, 2nd ed. 1792, 3rd ed. 1806, reprinted 1837, which shows a serious interest in working-class housing.

[*A.P.S.D.*; *D.N.B.*; *Registers of Bath Abbey*, Harleian Soc. i, 101; *Gent's Mag.* 1781, 295; J. A. Picton, *Liverpool Municipal Records, 1700–1835*, 1886, 158–9; S. A. Harris, 'Sarah Clayton's Letter and John Wood of Bath', *Trans. Historic Soc. of Lancs. and Cheshire*, c, 1948, 59, n. 3; W. Ison, *The Georgian Buildings of Bath*, 1948, 2nd ed. 1980; John Summerson, 'John Wood and the English Town Planning Tradition', in *Heavenly Mansions*, 1949; Eileen Harris, *British Architectural Books and Writers 1556–1785*, 1990, 489–91.]

BATH

THE ROYAL CRESCENT, 1767–75 [Ison, *op. cit.*].
BROCK STREET, *c.*1767 [Ison].
RIVERS STREET, *c.*1770 [Ison].
CATHERINE PLACE, *c.*1780 [Ison].
THE NEW ASSEMBLY ROOMS, 1769–71; interior restored after destruction by bombing 1942 [Ison].
attributed: ALFRED STREET, BENNETT STREET and RUSSELL STREET, 1772–6 [Ison].
MARGARET CHAPEL, BROCK STREET, for Cornelius Norton, *c.*1773, Gothic; secularized in the nineteenth century, and damaged by bombing 1942 [Ison].
THE HOT BATH (now THE OLD ROYAL BATHS), 1773–7 [Ison].

ELSEWHERE

BUCKLAND HOUSE, BERKS., for Sir Robert Throckmorton, 1755–8; enlarged by W. H. Romaine Walker 1910 [*Vitruvius Britannicus*, iv, 1767, pls. 90–3] (*C. Life*, 15–22 May 1915).
BITTON CHURCH, GLOS., designed reredos, etc., 1760–1 [H. T. Ellacombe, *History of the Parish of Bitton*, 1881, 5].
STANDLYNCH, now TRAFALGAR HOUSE, WILTS., added the wings for Henry Dawkins, 1766 [*Vitruvius Britannicus* v, 1771, pls. 78–81] (*C. Life*, 13–20 July 1945).
SALISBURY, WILTS., THE INFIRMARY, 1767–71 [R.C.H.M., *Salisbury* i, 52].
TREGENNA CASTLE, nr. ST. IVES, CORNWALL, for Samuel Stephens, 1773–4, castellated; enlarged by G. Wightwick 1845 [Lake's *Parochial History of Cornwall* ii, 1868, 262].
HARDENHUISH CHURCH, WILTS., for Benjamin Colbourne of Bath, consecrated 1779[1] [J. Britton, *Beauties of Wiltshire* iii, 1825, 162].
ST. IVES, CORNWALL, almshouses, before 1781 [J. Wood, *Plans for Labourers' Cottages*, 1792 ed., 24, 26, pl. iv].

WOOD, THOMAS (*c.*1644–1695), was a leading Oxford master mason and sculptor. He was the son of Richard Wood of Charlbury in Oxfordshire and was apprenticed at the age of 12 to William Byrd (*q.v.*). He was working on his own by 1675–6, when he was paid £4 14s. 4d. 'for carving of anticks etc.' in Adam de Brome's Chapel in St. Mary's Church, and £87 19s. 2d. for laying the marble paving in the chancel [T. G. Jackson, *Church of St. Mary the Virgin, Oxford*, 1897, 134–5]. In 1679 he undertook to perform the stonework of the BISHOP'S PALACE at CUDDESDON, OXON. (dem.), as sub-contractor to Richard Frogley, a master carpenter to whom Bishop Fell had 'set the whole work by the great'. Subsequent litigation between Frogley and Wood is described by Mrs. J. C. Cole, 'The Building of the Second Palace at Cuddesdon', *Oxoniensia* xxiv, 1959.

In 1678 Wood carved the monument to Francis Junius in St. George's Chapel, Windsor, which was erected at the expense of the University of Oxford, and in 1679–83 he was the master mason chosen to build the OLD ASHMOLEAN MUSEUM. A contemporary print by M. Burghers has the inscription 'T. Wood Archt.', and as the building accounts contain no payments for designs to anyone else, it is safe to assume that they were made by Wood

[1] Wood is said also to have designed Woolley Church, Somerset (1761), for Mrs. Elizabeth Parkins, but definite evidence appears to be lacking.

himself [C. E. Mallet, *History of the University of Oxford* ii, 1924, 435–6]. There are measured drawings of the building in *Details*, ed. R. R. Philips, i, 1909, 230–34.

In 1682 Wood designed a new parsonage house at Kingham, Oxon., for the rector, the Revd. William Dowdeswell, but his plans were rejected as too ambitious, and another master builder was employed to erect the existing rectory. Wood subsequently sued Dowdeswell for the value of his drawings, some of which were produced in evidence and are preserved among the records of the Vice-Chancellor's Court [University Archives, Vice-Chancellor's Court, 1688/9, Easter Term, 54].

In 1683–5 Wood rebuilt the west tower of DEDDINGTON CHURCH, OXON., in traditional Gothic style with battlements and pinnacles. It had fallen in 1634 and had been partly rebuilt during the next two years, but nothing more was done owing to the Civil War, and it was not until 1683 that the parishioners decided to complete the rebuilding. Wood contracted to perform the work for five or six hundred pounds [H. M. Colvin, *History of Deddington*, 1963, 105].

In October 1685 Wood was sent for by the Dean and Canons of WELLS CATHEDRAL to repair the roof of the nave of their church, which was 'in very great decay', and undertook to perform the necessary work for between £400 and £500 [Hist. MSS. Comm., *Wells* ii, 460–1]. The Dean at the time was Ralph Bathurst, President of Trinity College, Oxford.

Wood was an able provincial sculptor, and the Old Ashmolean Museum shows that he had some understanding of classical architecture. He died on 22 February 1694/5, in his 52nd year, and was buried in St. Michael's Church, Oxford, where there is a floor-slab to his memory. According to the inscription he 'was esteemed sufficiently qualifyed for better employments than those he was bound to by his education'.

[A. Wood, *Life and Times*, ed. Clark, iv, 75, 78; *Wren Soc.* xix, 94 n.; R. Gunnis, *Dictionary of British Sculptors*, 1968, 440; Mrs. J. C. Cole in *Oxoniensia* xiv, 1949, 68–9, xvii-xviii, 1952–3, 198, and xxix-xxx, 1964–5, 149; D. G. Vaisey, 'Thomas Wood and his Workshop', *Oxoniensia* xxxvi, 1971.]

WOOD, WILLIAM (1746–1818), a native of Germoe, Cornwall, began his career as the apprentice or foreman of John Bland, a builder of Truro. He eventually became the leading architect and builder in Truro and acted as surveyor for the Lemon estate there. His works in TRURO included the WORKHOUSE, 1780, and the ROYAL CORNWALL INFIRMARY, 1792–99 [C. T. Andrews, *The First Cornish Hospital*, Penzance 1975, 11–14]. In *c.*1770 pavilions were added to TREGREHAN HOUSE, ST. BLAZEY, CORNWALL, for Thomas Carlyon to Wood's designs [drawings at Tregrehan, *ex inf.* Mr. R. Hewlings]. Wood was declared bankrupt in 1783 and died in January 1818, aged 73 [*Gent's Mag.* 1783, 455; *West Briton and Cornwall Advertiser*, 9 Jan. 1818; Taunton MSS. at Royal Cornwall Institution; information from Mr. Edward Martin].

WOODHEAD, JOHN (–*c.*1838), practised in Doncaster, where he was the partner first of William Lindley (*q.v.*) and then of William Hurst (*q.v.*).

WOODING, RICHARD (–1809), was a London surveyor. In 1782 he was involved in speculative building in Spitalfields, and in 1789 he was one of the parties responsible for building THE OVAL in KENNINGTON [*Survey of London* xxvi, 21, 24, 107, xxvii, 112]. In 1792–3 he was the surveyor in charge of the rebuilding of WAX CHANDLERS' HALL, MAIDEN LANE (again rebuilt 1852–3) [Guildhall Library, MS. 9482/2]. In 1789, as 'Richard Wooding of Spitalfields, architect', he took an apprentice named John Smith [P.R.O., IR 1/34, p. 51].

WOODROFFE, EDWARD (*c.*1622–1675), held the post of Surveyor to the Dean and Chapter of Westminster from 22 October 1662 until his death in 1675.[1] After the Great Fire he was one of the three surveyors appointed to rebuild the City churches, the others being Sir Christopher Wren and Robert Hooke. There are several references to him in the parish records, but he remains a somewhat obscure figure in comparison with his more celebrated colleagues. Woodroffe also held the post of Assistant Surveyor of St. Paul's Cathdral and there are payments to him in the accounts for assisting Wren in the preparation of drawings, making contracts, measuring masons' work, etc., from 1668 onwards.[2] In 1670 he designed the houses

[1] The appointment of Edward Woodroffe as Surveyor is recorded in the Chapter Books on 22 Oct. 1662, but the payments in the Treasurer's Accounts from 1663 to 1671 are to *Robert* Woodroffe. Edward Woodroffe then appears in the accounts from 1672 until his death in 1675. There is no record of any fresh appointment in 1672.

[2] In Sept. 1673 a correspondent of Dean Sancroft wrote that 'Dr. Wren and Mr. Woodroof have been the week last past in the Convocation House, drawing the Lines of the Designe of the church upon the Table there, for the Joyner's Directions for making the new Modell' (*Wren Soc.* xiii, 51).

for the three Residentiary Canons in Amen Court. In conjunction with John Oliver he also reported on the cost of building the new Deanery in 1669, and in 1672 signed the contract on behalf of Dean Sancroft [*Wren Soc.* xiii, 52–6]. In 1673 new fittings in the choir of LINCOLN CATHEDRAL were to be made by a joiner 'according to Mr. Woodruff's designe' [contract in Lincs. Archives Office, D & C, Ciij 31/1/1].

Woodroffe died on 16 November 1675, in his 54th year, and was buried in the Cloisters of Westminster Abbey, where there was formerly a slab to his memory. In his will he is described as 'of St. Andrew's, Holborn, gentleman'. He may have been related to John Woodruff, a master mason of Windsor, who died in 1728 at the age of 58 [Westminster Abbey Muniments; J. Chester, *Westminster Abbey Registers* (Harleian Soc.), 163, 188; *Wren Soc.* xx, 252; J. Crull, *Antiquities of Westminster Abbey* ii, 1722, 185; J. Dart, *Westminster Abbey* ii, 1723, 138].

WOODS, JOSEPH (1776–1864), born at Stoke Newington on 24 August 1776, was the second son of Joseph Woods, a member of the Society of Friends. Owing to delicate health he left school early but nevertheless became proficient in Latin, Greek, Hebrew, French and Italian. At the age of 16 he was articled to a business at Dover but, preferring architecture, became a pupil of D. A. Alexander. He obtained admission to the Royal Academy Schools in 1798 and exhibited at the Academy between 1801 and 1815. Some of his exhibited designs were of a visionary character. In 1802 he showed a project for a stone bridge of a single span 600 feet wide over the Thames at London, of which he published an account in the *Monthly Magazine*, July 1802, 545–7, and in 1814 a design for a palace and public buildings extending continuously from Charing Cross to Westminster Bridge, a distance of 2500 feet. In 1803 he obtained the third premium in the competition for the conversion of the Parliament House at Dublin into a bank.

Wood's abilities lay in literary and scholarly pursuits rather than in practical architectural work, and as a practising architect he was not very successful. For his maternal uncle, Jonathan Hoare, he designed CLISSOLD HOUSE, CLISSOLD PARK, STOKE NEWINGTON, a severe neo-classical villa with a Greek Doric veranda (Pevsner, *London except the Cities of London and Westminster*, Buildings of England, 1952, pl. 45A). In 1811–12 he designed THE LONDON COMMERCIAL SALE ROOMS in MINCING LANE (dem.). The façade, in which he employed the order of the temple of Minerva Polias at Priene, is illustrated in Ackermann's *Repository of Arts*, 1813, 300. Owing to a miscalculation of the strength of some iron trusses there was a failure in the floor, which Woods was obliged to make good at his own expense, and soon afterwards he gave up architectural practice.

In 1806 Woods founded the London Architectural Society, of which he became the first president, and contributed papers on 'The Situation and Arrangement of Villas', 'Dilapidations' and 'Modern Theories of Taste' to the Society's *Essays* (1808–10). Having been invited to edit the remainder of Stuart and Revett's drawings of Grecian architecture, he issued the fourth volume of the *Antiquities of Athens* in 1816. During the years 1816–19 he travelled in France, Italy and Greece, and in 1825–6 he again visited the Continent, publishing in 1828 *Letters of an Architect from France, Italy, and Greece*, 2 vols. Having independent means, he was able in 1833 to retire to Lewes in Sussex. Here he devoted himself to botany, to which he made important contributions, publishing in 1850 his well-known *Tourists' Flora: A Descriptive Catalogue of the Flowering Plants and Ferns of the British Islands, France, Germany, Switzerland, Italy, and the Italian Islands*. He was a Fellow of the Linnean, Geological and Antiquarian Societies. He died at his home in Southover Crescent, Lewes, on 9 January 1864. There is an engraved portrait by Cotman, the original of which is in the Victoria and Albert Museum. Some of the drawings he made on the Continent are in the R.I.B.A. Collection.

[*Builder* xxi, 1863, 86, 112–13, xxii, 1864, 56; *R.I.B.A. Trans.* xv, 1863–4; *A.P.S.D.*; *D.N.B.*; M.A. Lower, *The Worthies of Sussex*, 1865, 312–14.]

WOODS, RICHARD (*c.*1716–1793), was primarily a land surveyor and landscape-gardener. A list of grounds improved by him is given by Hugh Prince, *Parks in England* (1967). This has since been extended by Fiona Cowell in articles in *Garden History* 14 (2), 1986 and 15 (1 and 2), 1987. He sometimes acted as an architect, chiefly of garden buildings, notably at WARDOUR CASTLE, WILTS., where he designed various ornamental buildings for the 8th Lord Arundell *c.*1766–71, and at IRNHAM HALL, LINCS., where he designed the stables (dem.) for the same nobleman in 1769–70, and at CANNON HALL, YORKSHIRE (W.R.), in 1760–1. His unexecuted designs for a Palladian mansion at Wardour are among the Arundell papers now in the Wiltshire Record Office. In the 1750s Woods was living at Chertsey in Surrey, but later he moved to

North Ockenden in Essex and ultimately to Ingrave in that county, where he died in May 1793, aged 77.

WOODSTOCK, THOMAS (–1694), was a master carpenter who was extensively employed by Sir Christopher Wren in rebuilding St. Paul's Cathedral and the City churches (see *Wren Soc.* x, 46–55, for details). According to Sir John Moore, to whom Woodstock had been recommended by Wren as a proper person to supervise the erection of his new School at Appleby, Leics., the Surveyor-General made 'use of Mr. Woodstock to oversee his workes and buildings in most places' [*Wren Soc.* xi, 87–9].

In the 1670s Woodstock was in partnership with William Clayton, a joiner, in various building enterprises in the City of London on behalf of the latter's brother, Sir Robert Clayton, and his business partner, John Morris. In 1672–5 Woodstock and Clayton carried out extensive works at Sir Robert Clayton's recently acquired country seat at MARDEN PARK, GODSTONE, SURREY (dem.) [Sir Robert Clayton's ledgers in Guildhall Library, London, MSS. 6428/1–3]. In 1677 Woodstock was consulted by Thomas Papillon, for whom he made a 'draft' for altering or rebuilding Acrise Place, Kent, which Papillon thought 'handome' but unduly expensive [Arthur Oswald in *C. Life*, 8 Aug. 1957, 261]. His opinion as to the best method of repairing the timber-framed tower of Harlow Church, Essex, is in the Bodleian Library, MS. Rawlinson B. 383, f. 330. In 1694 he was engaged as the architect of the proposed Danish Church in Wellclose Square, but his death in the summer of that year resulted in the commission being given to C. G. Cibber [H. Faber, *C. G. Cibber*, 1926, 63–4]. The contract whereby, on 15 December 1670, Thomas Woodstock and Nicholas Stapell contracted with George Ligoe to build on Fish Street Hill two houses 'of the third sort of building mentioned in the late Act of Parliament for the Rebuilding of the City of London' is preserved among the Guildhall Records [Deeds 94, 3].

WOODWARD, EDWARD (*c.*1697–1766) and his brother THOMAS (1699–1761) were master masons and quarry-owners of Chipping Campden in Gloucestershire. They were the sons of Thomas Woodward, who in 1719 took a lease of Westington Quarries for the lives of himself, his wife Mary and his third son Robert.[1] The only recorded works of Thomas Woodward the elder, who died in 1748 at the age of 76, are the repair of the spire of QUINTON CHURCH, WARWICKS., in 1712 [Warwicks. C.R.O., DR 468/21], and the rebuilding of the tower of BLOCKLEY CHURCH, WORCS. (now GLOS.), in 1725–7 [contract, with plan and elevation, among Northwick Park documents in Worcs. C.R.O., bdl. 31/1]. The tower is medieval in outline, with Gothic belfry windows copied from those of Chipping Campden Church.

Edward and Thomas Woodward worked in partnership in the 1730s. In March 1729/30 they contracted to rebuild ALCESTER CHURCH, WARWICKS., in accordance with a design formerly attached to the contract [Warwicks. C.R.O., DR 360/79/2, Box 11], but now lost. They were throughout to 'be under the advise direccion and Government . . . of Mr. Francis Smith [of Warwick] so as to do alter or amend anything of the said worke which hee shall think fitt to have done or altered'. It is probable, however, that they supplied the design themselves, and that Smith's functions were merely of a supervisory character. The church combines a classical interior with a Gothic exterior; its windows were remodelled in 1870–1, but their original form can be seen from the lithograph in *Notices of the Churches of Warwickshire* ii, 1858; the medieval tower was retained. The Woodwards' next contract was the rebuilding of the church of ST. JOHN THE BAPTIST at GLOUCESTER in 1732–4. Here there is no doubt that they were the designers as well as the builders, for in 1729 the churchwardens 'Payd the two Mr. Woodwards, for surveying, giving in an Estimation and draught of our church 10s. 6d.' The result was a handsome but rather unsophisticated classical building. St. John's was scarcely completed before the Woodwards had undertaken the rebuilding of ST. SWITHIN'S CHURCH, WORCESTER, a contract which necessitated their becoming freemen of the city in January 1734/5, on payment of a fine of £20. A brass plate over the west door records that 'This church was rebuilt by Ed. and Tho. Woodward in the year of our Lord 1736. Tho. Hoskyns, Tho. Wakeman, churchwardens.' The east front closely resembles that of St. John's, Gloucester, while the tower has ogee surrounds to the belfry windows which are derived from similar features on the tower of Chipping Campden Church. At about the

[1] Thomas (d. 1748) was the son of Thomas Woodward of Aston-sub-Edge, mason (d. 1 May 1716, aged 71), who was the son of Edward Woodward of Campden, mason (d. 13 May 1692). The first Thomas, disapproving of his son's second marriage, cut him off with a shilling and left his property in Aston-sub-Edge to his grandson Edward.

same time they reconstructed the nave of LLANDAFF CATHEDRAL in classical style to the designs of John Wood of Bath and carried out repairs to the bishop's palace at MATHERN in MONMOUTHSHIRE [D. R. Buttress, 'Llandaff Cathedral in the 18th and 19th Centuries', *Jnl. Historical Soc. of the Church in Wales* xvi, 1966].

Two early eighteenth-century Warwickshire country houses, FOXCOTE HALL (some three miles from Chipping Campden) and RADBROOKE MANOR, PRESTON-ON-STOUR, can be attributed to the Woodwards because their pedimented central features are essentially the same as those that decorate the east ends of their churches at Gloucester and Worcester. In both houses the *guttae* of the Doric order take the form of bells, an architectural idiosyncracy also found in the quadrant screen walls added to HONINGTON HALL, WARWICKS., for Joseph Townsend soon after 1737 [H. Colvin, 'Bell-*guttae* and the Woodwards of Chipping Campden', *Georgian Group Jnl.* 1993].

Thomas Woodward settled in Worcester and died there in November 1761 [Burial Register of St. Swithin's, Worcester]. In 1739 he rebuilt the nave of ST. MARY'S CHURCH, SWANSEA (dem. 1897) [D. G. Walker, *A Short History of the Parish Church of Swansea*, 1959, 12], and in 1745 he and Thomas Cook of Bewdley, joiner, undertook to build ST. ANNE'S CHURCH, BEWDLEY, in a classical style very similar to the Woodwards' other churches [Society of Antiquaries, Prattinton Miscellanea II/xiii]. A stone dislodged in 1950 was found to bear the name of 'Ric. Woodward Campden in Glos. 1745' – that is of Edward's son Richard (died 1755, aged 32), who was evidently working with his uncle at the time. Another stone inscribed with Richard Woodward's name and the date 1750 was found when the tower of FLADBURY CHURCH, WORCS., was repaired in *c.*1990, proving that the rebuilding of the upper part in 1750–2 with good Gothic detailing was the Woodwards' work.

Between 1750 and 1764[1] Edward Woodward was employed by the antiquary James West to reconstruct his house at ALSCOT, WARWICKS., and to remodel the neighbouring church of PRESTON-ON-STOUR (both illustrated in *C. Life*, 15, 22 and 29 May 1958). Letters and drawings preserved at Alscot Park show that in 1752 Woodward submitted designs for rebuilding the church in an elaborate Gothic style, with embattled parapets and crocketed pinnacles crowned by metal vanes.[1] The buttresses were to be ornamented by a series of shallow niches, and the tower was to be surmounted by a spire supported on flying buttresses, like that of St. Nicholas, Newcastle. In the event Woodward was merely allowed to remodel the existing church piecemeal, beginning with the chancel, which was rebuilt to the same dimensions as before, with three 'gothick' windows costing £90. The tower was strengthened by building up the staircase, and the nave was reconstructed with more Gothic windows 'like the great one' in the chancel. The result was much less elaborate than his original proposals, but it is none the less remarkable as one of the earliest Georgian Gothic churches, and as one known to have been designed by a mason with a traditional background and not by an architect like Henry Keene or an amateur like Sanderson Miller.

The rebuilding of Alscot Park was also carried out in the Gothic style, but here Woodward was working under the direction of Messrs. Shakespear & Phillips (*qq.v.*), London surveyors who provided drawings of a more sophisticated character than the rough 'draughts' of the Cotswold mason. Woodward did, however, submit designs of his own for various garden buildings, including an octagonal Gothic tower and an obelisk 70 feet high. The latter was apparently erected by him in 1757, but has since been destroyed.

In the churchyard at ILMINGTON, WARWICKS., four miles north-east of Chipping Campden, there is an elaborate Gothic monument which can hardly have been designed by anyone but Edward Woodward. It commemorates Samuel Sansom (d. 1750), and consists of a buttressed tomb-chest surmounted by a miniature tower and spire, complete with pinnacles and battlements very similar in character to those shown in Woodward's design for Preston Church. Other more conventional monumental tablets bearing the signature of Edward Woodward can be seen in several Cotswold churches, e.g. at Mickleton (Graves monument, 1721), Pebworth (Robert Martin, d. 1720), Alcester (John Brandis, d. 1724) and Blockley (Edward Croft and wife). The monument to his grandparents at Mickleton bears an inscription to the effect that it 'was made and erected by their Grandson Edw[d]. Woodward' and the family tomb in Chipping Campden churchyard was also 'built by him'. He him-

[1] The church was rebuilt between 1753 and 1757; work on the house began in about 1750 and was still in progress in 1764.

[1] Such metal vanes can actually be seen in the 1858 lithograph of Alcester Church, crowning the pinnacles of the nave as well as of the tower.

self died on 24 March 1766, aged 69, leaving a widow and three sons. Thomas (apparently his eldest son) was cut off with a shilling; Charles received a legacy of £50, leaving Edward as his principal legatee [P.C.C. 165 TYNDALL].

The account-book of the Hon. George Shirley of Ettington Park, Warwicks., contains a memorandum dated 27 July 1766, to the effect that 'Mr. Woodward promised to be at work at Eatington the 4th of Aug[t] and to finish the Venetian Windows, . . . in the Drawing room and . . . in the Bed-chamber over it.' This was presumably Edward Woodward, junior, of whom nothing more is known except that he was declared bankrupt in January 1777. It should be added that Rushen, in his *History of Campden*, states that the Woodwards are 'believed' to have built Bedfont House, an early eighteenth-century residence in the main street of their native town.

[P. C. Rushen, *History of Campden*, 1911, 38, 93–4, 136, 141; J. H. Bloom, *History of Preston-upon-Stour*, 1896; H. M. Colvin, 'Gothic Survival and Gothick Revival', *Arch. Rev.* March 1948; G. W. Beard & J. A. Piper, 'An Architectural Discovery', *C. Life*, 9 March 1951; *Gent's Mag.* 1777, 48; wills in Gloucester Probate Records.]

WOOLCOT, GEORGE (*c.*1785–1853), was a surveyor and builder of 54 Doughty Street, London, from about 1815 onwards. In the 1820s he was in partnership with Bryan Browning, in conjunction with whom he built Strensham Court, Worcs., to the designs probably of George Maddox, and York (now Lancaster) House, London, to those of Benjamin Wyatt (see p. 172). In 1824–5 Woolcot and Browning also built FILLONGLEY HALL, WARWICKS., for the Revd. Bowyer Adderley. This simple classical house, enlarged and embellished in 1840–1 to the designs of J. L. Ackroyd of Coventry, appears to have been designed by Woolcot [G. Jackson-Stops in *C. Life*, 20 July 1989]. Woolcot, 'late of Doughty Street and Muswell Hill', died in Westbourne Grove, Bayswater, on 8 March 1853, aged 68 [*Gent's Mag.* 1853 (i), 560].

WOOLER, JOHN, was an engineer and architect who was active in North Yorkshire and County Durham in the latter part of the eighteenth century. In 1763, when he was consulted about the harbour at Sunderland, he was described as 'Engineer at Whitby'. In 1768 he was paid 5 guineas by the Dean and Chapter of Durham for a plan of South Shields Market, and in 1777 he was invited to survey the Cathedral Church of Durham and make an estimate of the cost of repairing and beautifying it. In 1777 he also repaired the steeple of St. Nicholas's Church (now the Cathedral) at Newcastle.

In 1772 Wooler was the joint author with John Smeaton of a printed *Report relative to Tyne Bridge*, in which they considered the state of the old Tyne Bridge at Newcastle, and in 1775–81 he was associated with Robert Mylne in building the new Tyne Bridge, which stood until 1873. Responsibility for the bridge was shared between the Bishop of Durham and the Corporation of Newcastle. Mylne was employed by the former, Wooler by the latter. In 1775 Wooler was employed to consider the building of a new bridge across the Tyne at Hexham to replace one destroyed by a flood in 1771, but wisely concluded that 'whoever meddled with a bridge there, would burn their fingers', as indeed proved to be the case when the bridge designed by Smeaton was swept away in 1782.

[Durham Cathedral Chapter Acts; J. Sykes, *Local Records*, Newcastle 1865, i, 294, 300, 311; *Reports of the late John Smeaton*, 1812, i, 230, ii, 163, 252–60, iii, 267 *et seq.*; information from Prof. A. W. Skempton.]

WOOLFE, JOHN (–1793), was an Irishman, 'of a family of high respectability in the county of Kildare'. He was employed by James Paine as his clerk in the 1750s, and it was perhaps through Paine's agency that he obtained a post in the Office of Works as a 'labourer in trust'. In 1774 he was given the Clerkship of the Works at the Mews at Charing Cross. In the following year he was promoted to be Clerk of the Works at Whitehall, Westminster and St. James's, and in 1790 he succeeded Kenton Couse in the senior post of Examining Clerk.

Woolfe is best known as the joint author with James Gandon of the fourth and fifth volumes of *Vitruvius Britannicus*, which appeared under their names in 1767 and 1771, and constituted a valuable record of English architectural activity since the appearance of Colen Campbell's three volumes in the reign of George I. Unlike Campbell, Woolfe and Gandon had no architectural axe to grind, their purpose being 'not to reform English taste, but rather to celebrate its superiority' (Harris). According to Gandon's biographer, Woolfe 'was not of very active habits; hence the whole labour of preparing and bringing out the book rested with Mr. Gandon'. But as 84 of the plates were engraved from drawings by Woolfe and only 60 from drawings by Gandon, this statement is open to question.

As a practising architect Woolfe appears to have accomplished relatively little. With the exception of an unexecuted design for the addition of wings to Duff House, Fife (vol. v, pls. 58–60), not a single work of his own is illustrated in *Vitruvius Britannicus*, and the only buildings known to be by him are:

LONDON, FIFE HOUSE, WHITEHALL, altered or rebuilt for 2nd Earl of Fife, 1756–7; dem. 1869 [Fife papers, *ex inf.* Prof. A. A. Tait].

NORTHWICK PARK, GLOS., staircase and other alterations for Sir John Rushout, Bart., probably in the 1770s [C. R. Cockerell's diary, 25 Dec. 1821; cf. Northwick papers in Worcs. C.R.O., 2 plans for remodelling the house endorsed: 'Mr. Woolfe's plan for a house not executed'].

COLWORTH HOUSE, BEDS., addition of pediment and wings for William Lee, 1772–5; wings rebuilt *c.*1895 [Beds. C.R.O., Lee Antonie papers, UN 194–244].

DYFFRYN ALED, DENBIGHSHIRE, added wings and designed interior for Mrs. Meyrick, 1777; dem. *c.*1920 [Angus, *Select Views of Seats*, pl. xlviii, dated 1797].

WREST PARK, BEDS., altered N. front for Marchioness Grey, *c.*1790; dem. *c.*1840 [Note by Earl de Grey of Woolfe's employment in Beds. C.R.O., L 31/105; Woolfe is known to have been at Wrest in Dec. 1790].

LONDON, No. 67 (formerly 36) BROOK STREET, alterations for Miss Anne White, 1791 [*Survey of London* xl, 30].

Woolfe died at his house in Whitehall on 13 November 1793. His son John Woolfe, junior, had an architectural training and occupied a post as labourer in trust at Whitehall from 1787 until his death in 1806, but does not appear to have practised outside the Office of Works.

[*A.P.S.D.*; *D.N.B.*; *Gent's Mag.* 1793 (ii), 1060; T. Mulvany, *Life of James Gandon*, 1846, 18; *History of the King's Works* vi, 59, 673–4; Eileen Harris, *British Architectural Books and Writers 1556–1785*, 1990, 496–8].

WOOLLEY, JOHN (1810–1849), was the son of George Outram Woolley. He became a pupil of Robert Abraham and attended the R.A. Schools, exhibiting at the Academy between 1829 and 1831. Private means enabled him to devote his time more to the theory than to the practice of architecture, and his career was cut short by his early death. He was one of the original members of the Architectural Society and was elected a Fellow of the Institute of British Architects in 1842. [*Builder* vii, 1849, 451; *Gent's Mag.* 1849 (ii), 551; *R.I.B.A. Drawings Catalogue: T–Z*, 263.]

WORRALL, SAMUEL and JOHN, both of London, received £31 10s. in 1754 'for drawing three Plans, two Elevations and one Section for the new Town house and Steeple' at BERWICK-ON-TWEED, which was built by Joseph Dods between 1750 and 1755. It is Dods's name which appears on the building as 'Architect', but it seems clear that the design was supplied by the Worralls [J. Scott, *Berwick-on-Tweed*, 1887, 227; Corporation Guild-Books 1752–60, 73].

There were two London builders named Samuel Worrall. One, a mason, was Master of the Mason's Company in 1739. The other, a carpenter, played an important part in the Georgian development of Spitalfields, where he lived in Princelet Street. They were evidently related, for in 1735 the lease of a house in Spitalfields built by Samuel Worrall, carpenter, was assigned by Samuel Worrall, 'citizen and mason of London', to John Worrall of Spitalfields, carpenter [*Survey of London* xxvii, 182–3].

WORSLEY, THOMAS (1711–1778), of Hovingham Hall in Yorkshire, was a landowner, horse-breeder and amateur architect who was Surveyor of the Office of Works from 1760 until his death. He was educated at Eton, made the Grand Tour in 1735–7, and succeeded his father as the owner of Hovingham in 1750. Horses and architecture were his great interests in life. Horace Walpole calls him 'a creature of Lord Bute, and a kind of riding-master to the King'. It was Bute and George III who gave him the Surveyorship in 1760, and in the following year he was returned as M.P. for the Treasury borough of Orford. By 1760 the Surveyorship of the Works was essentially a political sinecure and the day-to-day administration fell on William Chambers as Comptroller, but until his health broke down in about 1770 Worsley kept himself well informed about the affairs of the Office over which he presided.

Worsley's interest in architecture went back to his boyhood, for among his drawings at Hovingham there is one of a Doric order made by him at Eton in 1728. Together with his friend Ralph Knight of Langold Park he made many architectural designs for his amusement, and was quite a competent draughtsman, but the stables at MARSKE HALL, nr. RICHMOND, YORKS. (N.R.), for John Hutton, *c.*1740, and HOVINGHAM HALL itself, which he rebuilt in the 1750s, appear to have been his only executed works of importance. The plan of Hovingham, by giving the manège, or riding-school, pride of place, pays tribute to Worsley's equestrian interests, but appears at the same time to have been intended to recall the plan of a Roman house as reconstructed by Palladio, and the elevations are well-designed Palladian compositions (*C. Life*, 10–17 Dec. 1927, 15 June 1961).

At Wallington, Northumberland, there is a design by Worsley for a gardener's house dated 1764. A design by him for a country house in the Avery Library at Columbia University is illustrated by John Harris, *Catalogue of British Drawings for Architecture, etc. in American Collections*, 1971, 278–9.

[Namier & Brooke, *The House of Commons 1754–70* iii, 1964, 659–61; *History of the King's Works* v, 76–7; J. Hunter, *South Yorkshire* i, 1828, 299; Giles Worsley, 'Thomas Worsley 1710–1778', unpublished B.A. thesis, Oxford 1982; Giles Worsley in *New Light on English Palladianism*, ed. C. Hind, Georgian Group Symposium, 1988, 64–9.]

WORTH, SAMUEL (1779–1870), was taken into partnership by Joseph Botham of Sheffield in 1826. Two years later he entered into a brief partnership with James Harrison (*q.v.*), in conjunction with whom he designed the MEDICAL SOCIETY'S buildings or SURGEONS' HALL in SURREY STREET, 1829 [S. Lewis, *Topographical Dictionary of England* iv, 1848, 62]. In 1832 he won the competition for the CUTLERS' HALL. The runner-up was B. B. Taylor (*q.v.*), who collaborated with him in designing the existing Grecian building in Church Street, enlarged in 1888, when the façade was duplicated. Worth's other principal works in Sheffield were the FREE WRITING-SCHOOL in TOWNHEAD STREET, 1827–8, the Doric Chapel, etc., for the GENERAL CEMETERY, 1836, and THE SHEFFIELD & HALLAMSHIRE BANK (now Midland Bank) in CHURCH STREET, 1838, altered *c.*1875 [R. E. Leader in *Jnl. Institute of Bankers* xxxviii, 1917, 240]. He also designed THE ROYAL HOTEL, WINSTER PLACE, BUXTON, DERBYSHIRE, for Andrew Brittlebank [Brittlebank papers in Derbyshire C.R.O., *ex inf.* M. Langham & C. Wells]. In about 1840 Worth took John Frith into partnership. J. B. Mitchell-Withers (1837–94) was his pupil. [R. E. Leader, *Surveyors and Architects of the Past in Sheffield*, 1903; *Architectural Mag.* iv, 1837, 81–2].

WREN, Sir CHRISTOPHER (1632–1723), was born at East Knoyle in Wiltshire on 20 October 1632. His father, the Revd. Christopher Wren, was Rector of Knoyle and a former Fellow of St. John's College, Oxford. He later became Dean of Windsor in succession to his brother Matthew, who had been consecrated Bishop of Hereford in 1634, was soon afterwards translated to Norwich, and died Bishop of Ely. Both Wren's father and his uncle were pillars of the High Church tradition, and it was in the atmosphere of conservative churchmanship that he was brought up. His first tutor was a clergyman, but later he was sent to Westminster School, where he became one of Dr. Busby's earliest pupils. After leaving Westminster in 1646, he spent some three years in London before going up to Wadham College, Oxford, as a Gentleman Commoner, probably in 1649, Meanwhile the outbreak of civil war had brought trouble to his family. His father's deanery was pillaged on two occasions, and his uncle, the Bishop of Ely, who had incurred the hostility of the extreme Puritan party, was imprisoned in the Tower. His father took refuge at Bletchingdon, nr. Oxford, where his son-in-law, William Holder, held the rectory. Holder, formerly a Fellow of Pembroke College, Cambridge, was a young man of considerable intellectual attainments, and according to Aubrey he was 'very helpful in the education of his brother-in-law . . . of whom he was as tender as if he had been his own child, whom he instructed first in geometrie and arithmetique'. At Oxford Wren came into contact with Dr. Charles Scarburgh, an eminent anatomist and mathematician, whom he assisted in his work, and with the group of scientific scholars who later formed the nucleus of the Royal Society. They included John Wilkins, the Warden of Wadham, Wallis, the mathematician, Boyle, the physicist, and Lawrence Rooke, the astronomer. In company with these eminent men, Wren made rapid progress in the new, experimental learning of which they were the pioneers. He assisted Scarburgh in his dissections and made pasteboard models demonstrating the working of the muscles in order to illustrate his friend's lectures at Surgeons' Hall. Scarburgh was a disciple of Harvey, the discoverer of the circulation of the blood, and later on Wren carried out an important experiment to show that fluids could be injected directly into the bloodstream of animals. He also made drawings of the brain which were published in Willis's *Cerebri Anatome* of 1664, and constructed a model of the human eye.

But anatomy was only one of Wren's scientific interests. At the age of 15 or 16 he had translated into Latin a tract on dialling by William Oughtred. Dialling was one of his father's hobbies, and it was probably through the sundial that Wren came to be interested in astronomy. Astronomy was to be his principal scientific occupation until the time when, as Surveyor of the King's Works and architect of St. Paul's Cathedral, his energies were to be largely absorbed by his architectural work. His first recorded invention was a *Panorganum Astronomicum*, or model showing the earth, sun and moon in their periodic relationships. At Oxford he received further encouragement from Seth Ward, then Professor of Astronomy, and from Sir Paul Neille, a wealthy amateur, who assisted him in his study of the planet Saturn. In addition to this strictly astronomical work, Wren concerned himself with related sciences such as physics and meteorology. In all these fields of 'philosophical' enquiry he distinguished himself by his skill in scientific demonstration and in devising appropriate apparatus to test his own and his friends' theories. Some of his inventions, like the transparent bee-hives 'built like castles and palaces' which he showed to Evelyn in 1654, were perhaps more ingenious than useful; but there were others which played an important part in the study of physics and astronomy, and it was this early interest in models and diagrams that was to give the experimental scientist his later facility in architectural design.

Wren took his B.A. degree on 18 March 1650/1, and his M.A. on 11 December 1653. In the latter year he became a Fellow of All Souls, where he continued his scientific studies until 1657, when he resigned to become Professor of Astronomy at Gresham College, London, in succession to Lawrence Rooke. In 1661 he returned to Oxford as Savilian Professor of Astronomy and received the degree of D.C.L. He was now, though only in his 29th year, at the height of his scientific fame: in the opinion of Robert Hooke, himself a brilliant experimentalist, 'there scarce ever met in one man, in so great a perfection, such a Mechanical Hand, and so Philosophical a Mind' (*Micrographia*, 1665). In 1660 the trials of his family had been terminated by the Restoration of Charles II, and the 'experimental philosophical clubbe' which had met in his rooms at Gresham College was about to be elevated into the Royal Society. The King himself was taking a personal interest in his scientific work and soon after the acquisition of Tangier in 1661 invited him to supervise its fortification, offering him at the same time the reversion of Sir John Denham's post as Surveyor-General of the Royal Works. This offer Wren declined on grounds of health, but there are indications that, in the intervals of scientific work, he was already turning his attention to architectural matters. In 1660 his exhibits at a scientific meeting included certain 'new designs tending to strength, convenience and beauty in building', and in 1663 he was consulted by the Commission for repairing St. Paul's Cathedral. Such activities – though they might take up more of the Savilian Professor's time than was thought fitting at Oxford – were in no way exceptional: architecture in the seventeenth century was not yet a profession, and several of Wren's acquaintances counted it among their intellectual diversions. For Evelyn it was 'the flower and crown as it were of all the sciences mathematical', and Wren, with his skill as a draughtsman and his fondness for model-making, was bound sooner or later to add it to his other accomplishments. His academic training gave him a ready understanding of the conventions of the Roman orders, and in 1663, when his uncle, the aged Bishop of Ely, asked him to design the new chapel of Pembroke College, Cambridge, the result was an entirely competent, if somewhat un-imaginative, essay in classical architecture. His second building of importance, the Sheldonian Theatre at Oxford, is equally academic in design, the prototype being an antique theatre of the kind represented in the Italian architectural treatises: but the novel construction of its roof attracted a great deal of attention and added much to Wren's reputation as an architect. Roman theatres were open to the sky, and the difficulty of covering his English reproduction without the inappropriate support of columns set Wren a problem in carpentry which he solved by means of an ingenious timber truss based on the researches of his friend and colleague Dr. Wallis, the Professor of Geometry.

The Sheldonian Theatre was followed by a new building for Trinity College, Oxford, and in 1665, when Wren made his only visit abroad, his purpose was not only to add to his scientific experience, but also 'to survey the most esteem'd Fabricks of Paris' and to observe the achievements of contemporary French artists and architects. Back in England, he applied himself once more to the problem of restoring St. Paul's, and had actually prepared an elaborate scheme for its repair when the Great Fire of London at once placed the old cathedral beyond hope of redemption and gave Wren a unique opportunity of exercising his talents as an architect. Within a few days of the disaster he had presented the King with a scheme for rebuilding the City in accordance with a regular plan. It soon became evident, however, that this was a Utopian project, for the survival of London as a commercial capital depended upon its immediate reconstruction, and this could only be done on the lines of the existing streets. Much could, however, be done to improve the City by replanning in detail, and in October 1666 the King appointed Wren, Pratt and May as his 'Commissioners' to join with three nominees of the City in order to make a survey of the destroyed area and to consider how it should best be rebuilt.[1] To this committee was due the drafting of the Rebuilding Act which was passed by Parliament in 1667, but the design of individual buildings was beyond its terms of reference, and the statement in *Parentalia* that Wren was appointed 'Surveyor-general and principal Architect for rebuilding the whole city' is incorrect. Indeed, it has been stated that the scheme for the Fleet Canal is the only part of 'the general secular rebuilding which can indisputably be attributed to Wren', and it is uncertain whether even the Monument can be regarded as his own design.

For the City churches, on the other hand, Wren was personally responsible: they were to be rebuilt out of a tax on the import of coal to London, and Wren was appointed 'to direct and order the dimensions, formes and Modells of the said Churches', with Robert Hooke and Edward Woodroffe 'as assistants, for the more expedite and secure performance of the same' (warrant of 17 May 1670: Guildhall Library, MS. 25540/1, pp. 1–2). Though the designing of more than fifty churches was clearly beyond the capacity of one man, and much of it must have been delegated to Hooke and Woodroffe (and later to Hawksmoor and Dickinson), Wren appears to have retained ultimate control, and it is significant that all the surviving drawings came from his office. One for the west front of St. Edmund, Lombard Street (*Wren Soc.* ix, pl. 15) in Hooke's hand bears the initials CW in the pediment to show that Wren had approved it. All the fifty-odd churches paid for out of the Coal Money were therefore rebuilt by Wren's authority and in accordance with his conception of Protestant church architecture, if not in every case to his personal design. The Coal Money paid only for the fabrics of the new churches: for their internal fittings and decoration the parishes were individually responsible and, although Wren's advice was often asked, the designs for galleries, altarpieces and the like were submitted by the craftsmen concerned and selected by the vestrymen on their own authority. The towers, on the other hand, were in every case a product of Wren's office, and display an astonishing variety of invention which is among his chief claims to greatness as an architect. Few of them were completed until the 1690s or even later, and they show an assurance in design which is often absent from the churches themselves.

The rebuilding of St. Paul's Cathedral was financed in the same way as that of the City churches. But the latter had first call on the Coal Money, and it was not until 1675 that work was actually begun on the new cathedral, with Wren as architect in charge. The design had, however, been under consideration ever since it became apparent (in 1668) that Old St. Paul's was incapable of repair. Wren himself favoured a centrally planned church of the type represented by the 'Great Model' of 1673. This indeed 'pleased persons of distinction, skilled in antiquity and architecture': but it did not find favour in ecclesiastical circles and suffered, moreover, from the disadvantage that it could not be built in stages. Wren, therefore, 'turned his thoughts to a cathedral form, as they called it, but so rectified as to reconcile the Gothick to a better manner of architecture'. The result was the 'Warrant Design' of 1675, in which the medieval plan was preserved beneath a classical dress. The design of the western portico and towers, and of the dome which took the place of a central tower, underwent many modifications as the work progressed, and in their final form the towers have a baroque character which owed something to the influence of Roman churches which Wren was able to study in engravings.

In March 1668/9 Wren became Surveyor-General of the King's Works in succession to Sir John Denham. Both John Webb and Hugh May had strong claims to this coveted post, and Wren's appointment was apparently due to the personal favour of Charles II. The parallel post of Comptroller at Windsor was, however, given to May, and as Webb was already in charge of the new Palace at Greenwich, the two most important works undertaken by Wren's department during the early years of his tenure of office were designed by others. But the surveyorship brought with it administrative responsibilities which were hardly compatible with academic routine, and in 1673 Wren resigned his professorship at Oxford. On 14 November the same year he received the honour of knighthood. In 1684, on the death of Hugh May, he succeeded to the latter's post at Windsor, and in 1696, when it was decided to complete Greenwich Palace as a Naval Hospital, Wren was appointed Surveyor. He was also one of the chief promoters of the Military Hospital at Chelsea, as well as being the architect of its buildings. In 1699 he was placed in charge of the repair of Westminster Abbey, for which money had been voted by Parliament, and made designs for a central tower which were not, however, executed. In addition to discharging these official duties, Wren was an active member of the Royal Society, of which

[1] For Wren's share in the rebuilding of London, see T. F. Reddaway, *The Rebuilding of London after the Great Fire*, 1940.

he was President for two years (1681–3), a member of the Council of the Hudson's Bay Company, and on two occasions a Member of Parliament, representing Plympton in 1685–7 and Weymouth in 1701–2. He was also one of the Commissioners for Building Fifty New Churches in London under the Act of 1711, and took an active part in its proceedings until the original commission was dissolved in 1715.

Despite his Tory connections, Wren survived the Whig Revolution of 1688 without loss of office. But his management of the Office of Works during his later years was somewhat lax, and in 1714 reforms were introduced by Lord Halifax, the First Lord of the Treasury. Wren retained the title of Surveyor, but authority was vested in a body of Commissioners, of whom he was one, and Vanbrugh as Comptroller became the leading figure in the Office. In 1718 this civilized arrangement was upset in order to provide a place of profit for William Benson (*q.v.*). Wren was dismissed and went into retirement at Hampton Court, where he had been allowed by Queen Anne to acquire a lease for life of the Surveyor's official residence on the Green. He had already given up the Surveyorship of Greenwich Hospital in 1716, and his Comptrollership at Windsor had come to an end the same year, when the nominally separate organization there was united with the Office of Works in London. Only the Surveyorships of St. Paul's Cathedral and Westminster Abbey remained in his possession when, 'having', in his own words, 'worn out (by God's Mercy) a long life in the Royal Service, and having made some Figure in the world', Wren died on 25 February 1723, at the age of 90. He was buried in the crypt of St. Paul's Cathedral, where a monument was later erected to his memory.

Wren's achievement as an architect cannot adequately be summarized within the compass of a dictionary. For forty years he was the acknowledged arbiter of English architectural taste, and his own output of buildings was greater than that of any other English architect of his time. Being a self-taught architect, his education as a designer was a continuing process, and in the course of his long life he was receptive to many ideas, native and foreign. French and Dutch architecture provided the main influences on his style in its formative years, but his approach to design was essentially empirical, and he showed his familiarity both with classical antiquity (as represented by Serlio, Palladio and others) and with Italian baroque buildings studied in engravings. His own works, ranging from the simple Renaissance classicism of Pembroke College Chapel to the Borrominesque spire of St. Vedast's Church, epitomize the whole history of English architecture during the fifty years after the Restoration. Even Gothic had its place in Wren's architectural vocabulary, to be used in situations (as at Christ Church, Oxford) where conformity to existing work authorized it. His capacity for brilliant improvisation is no less apparent in Tom Tower than it is in many of the London churches, where a variety of classical interiors of various kinds was ingeniously fitted into the awkwardly constricted spaces afforded by the irregular medieval sites. In designing the steeples Wren and his assistants were equally resourceful, creating a classical equivalent of the traditional medieval spire that was to become a characteristic feature of English church architecture until the nineteenth century. If the City churches were triumphs of improvisation, St. Paul's Cathedral was a long-meditated masterpiece. Though the final result is a major architectural achievement, the insistence of the clergy on a traditional cruciform plan robbed Wren of the opportunity to design a building in which the logic of classical design could be clearly and uncompromisingly expressed. St. Paul's is therefore in some ways a disappointing building. The dome and west towers compose splendidly from afar, but at close quarters the former is seen to be less satisfactorily related to the body of the building. Within there is much to admire in detail, but all Wren's ingenuity could not conceal an awkward inequality in the arches supporting the dome, and the interior as a whole lacks either the mystery latent in its Gothic plan or the baroque drama promised by its west front.

As a secular architect Wren's services were almost entirely monopolized by his royal masters. But circumstances proved fatal to all his major schemes for Winchester, Hampton Court, Greenwich and Whitehall, and it is only on paper that Wren's potentiality as a designer of palaces can be fully appreciated. At Winchester he envisaged, and almost completed, a building with a recessed centre like Le Vau's Versailles. Formally aligned on the west front of the Cathedral, it would have been a major monument of Anglo-French taste. At Greenwich the necessity of retaining the Queen's House frustrated a more elaborate design of the same sort, and left Wren dexterously to dignify an unresolved duality by means of two answering domes. The Whitehall scheme went through several revisions, but emerged at last as a vast and grandiose palace, linked by a long processional colonnade to a new Parliament House sharply distinguished by its antique

Roman dress from the baroque splendour of the Court.

Compared with these visions of grandeur, Wren's actual achievements at Chelsea Hospital, Whitehall Palace, Hampton Court and Kensington were relatively modest, and his share in the great country houses of the period was minimal. But his unrealized designs were not without their influence. Just as Winchester Palace was a child of Versailles, so the unfinished Winchester had its architectural progeny in the Garden Quadrangle of New College, Oxford (above, p. 204). More importantly, it is in Wren's first design for Greenwich Hospital, with quadrant colonnades linking the wings to a domed central block, that the genesis of Vanbrugh's Castle Howard must be sought, and incidentally it is to Wren's twin domes that Gandon's Dublin Custom House owes the form of its principal ornament. And many details of Wren's works, both secular and ecclesiastical, were of course imitated by the craftsmen who worked for him both in the Royal Works and in the City churches. Together with Hawksmoor and Dickinson, his personal assistants, these were the men who assimilated his ideas and reproduced them in their own buildings. If the conception of a 'school of Wren' has any validity, it is to be found in the work of men such as Matthew Banckes and Christopher Kempster (*qq.v.*), rather than in that of Wren's colleagues May, Pratt, Talman and Vanbrugh, each of whom developed his own forms of architural expression. This 'school' survived until the 1720s, when the Palladian group, led by Lord Burlington, captured the Office of Works and spread a new doctrine of classical correctitude which supplanted the pragmatic English baroque of Wren and his disciples.

In 1669 Wren married Faith, the daughter of Sir John Coghill of Bletchingdon, the Oxfordshire village where he spent much of his early life. There were two sons of the marriage, Gilbert, who died in infancy, and Christopher, who was born in February 1675, only a few months before his mother's death the following September. In 1677 Wren married again, his second wife being Jane, daughter of Lord Fitzwilliam of Lifford. By her he had a daughter Jane, who died unmarried in 1702, aged 26, and a son William, who survived his father, dying in 1738. Christopher Wren, junior (1675–1747), held the post of Chief Clerk of the King's Works from 1702 until 1716, when he was dismissed as a result of Lord Halifax's reforms. Although in *Vitruvius Britannicus* he is given the credit for having designed Marlborough House, he appears merely to have assisted his father, and nothing suggests that he had any genuine ability as an architect.[1] He made the collection of family documents which, as *Parentalia, or Memoirs of the Family of the Wrens*, was published by his son Stephen in 1750.[2] In 1715 he married, as his second wife, the widow of a Warwickshire gentleman, from whose family his father had purchased for him the estate of Wroxall Abbey in that county.[3] His death in 1747 resulted in the sale of his father's architectural drawings, the majority of which came eventually into the possession of All Souls College, Oxford. Others, purchased by the 3rd Duke of Argyll and subsequently in the Bute Collection, were dispersed by auction at Sotheby's in May 1951.

Of the numerous portraits of Wren in existence, the most authentic are: (i) the marble bust by Edward Pierce in the Ashmolean Museum, Oxford, dating probably from the 1670s; (ii) the portrait in the possession of the Royal Society by Closterman (*c.*1695); (iii) that in the Sheldonian Theatre at Oxford begun by Verrio (d. 1707) and completed by Thornhill and Kneller; (iv) the portrait in the National Portrait Gallery by Kneller, which is dated 1711; (v) an ivory plaque of Wren in old age attributed to Le Marchand and also in the National Portrait Gallery.

The chief sources for Wren's life and works are: (i) the family records published in *Parentalia*; (ii) the *Diary* of his friend and colleague Robert Hooke (*q.v.*); (iii) the records of the Royal Society; (iv) the official records of the Office of Works; (v) the *Calendars of Treasury Books* and *Papers*; and (vi) his own drawings, of which a catalogue is given in *Wren Soc.* xx.[4]

---

[1] Mr. Hugh Scrutton had in his possession a model for the east end of a church, inscribed in a contemporary hand, 'St. Paul Basilica. Submitted & rejected. Christopher Wren, Esq.' This probably represents a design submitted by the younger Wren to the Commissioners for Building Fifty New Churches under the Act of 1711.

[2] There are three manuscripts of this work, one in B.L., Add. MS. 25071 dated 1719, another at All Souls College (MS. 313) dated 1728 but containing later material, and a third at the Royal Society dated 1741 but probably begun earlier. For the 'heirloom' copy of the book in the R.I.B.A. Library, containing MS. additions, see L. Weaver in *R.I.B.A. Jnl.* xviii, 1911, 569.

[3] The conveyance, as enrolled in Chancery (P.R.O., C 54/5045, no. 3), shows that Wren paid £19,600 for the estate in August 1713. For this information I am indebted to Mr. Frank Kelsall.

[4] This does not include the drawings from the Bute Collection sold in 1951. The greater part was purchased by the National Art Collections Fund and divided between St. Paul's Cathedral Library,

There are several biographies of Wren, but the older lives (e.g. those by James Elmes, L. Phillimore, L. Milman and Sir Lawrence Weaver) have been rendered obsolete by the enterprise of the *Wren Society* (20 vols. 1924–43) in documenting Wren's works and in publishing his drawings and those of his contemporaries. The best modern studies of Wren are those by G. F. Webb (1937), John Summerson (1953), E. F. Sekler (1956), Margaret Whinney (1971) and Kerry Downes (1971 and 1982).

SELECT BIBLIOGRAPHY

R. A. Beddard, 'Wren's Mausoleum for Charles I', *Arch. Hist.* 27, 1984.

J. A. Bennett, 'Christopher Wren: the natural causes of beauty', *Arch. Hist.* 15, 1972.

J. A. Bennett, 'A Study of Parentalia, with two unpublished letters of Sir Christopher Wren', *Annals of Science* xxx, 1973.

J. A. Bennett, *The Mathematical Science of Sir Christopher Wren*, Cambridge 1982.

H. M. Colvin, J. Mordaunt Crook, Kerry Downes & John Newman, *The History of the King's Works* v, 1976.

Kerry Downes, 'Wren and Whitehall in 1664', *Burlington Mag.* Feb. 1971.

Kerry Downes, *Christopher Wren*, 1971.

Kerry Downes, *The Architecture of Wren*, 1982.

Kerry Downes, *Sir Christopher Wren*, catalogue of an exhibition at Whitechapel Art Gallery, 1982.

V. Fürst, *The Architecture of Sir Christopher Wren*, 1956.

S. B. Hamilton, 'The Place of Sir Christopher Wren in the History of Structural Engineering', *Newcomen Soc's Trans.* xiv, 1933–4.

Eileen Harris, *British Architectural Books and Writers, 1556–1785*, 1990, 503–8 (on *Parentalia*).

P. D. Harvey, 'A Signed Plan by Sir Christopher Wren', *British Museum Quarterly* xxv, 1963.

G. H. Huxley, 'The Geometrical Work of Sir Christopher Wren', *Scripta Mathematica* xxv, 1960.

Paul Jeffery, 'Wren's St. Mary, and other projects for Lincoln's Inn Fields', *Arch. Hist.* 31, 1988.

H. W. Jones, 'Sir Christopher Wren and Natural Philosophy: with a check list of his scientific activities', *Notes and Records of the Royal Society* xiii, 1958.

F. Kimball, 'Wren: some of his sources', *Arch. Rev.* lv, 1924.

W. T. Law, 'Notes on the Wren Pedigree', *Genealogist*, N.S. vi, 1889, 168–71.

Jane Lang, *Rebuilding St. Paul's after the Great Fire of London*, 1956.

T. F. Reddaway, *The Rebuilding of London after the Great Fire*, 1940.

J. W. Ryland, *Records of Wroxall Abbey and Manor*, 1903.

Sale Catalogues of Libraries of Eminent Persons, vol. iv, *Architects*, ed. D. J. Watkin, 1972, 1–43.

E. F. Sekler, *Wren and his Place in European Architecture*, 1956.

H. S. Smith, 'Pedigree of Wren', *Genealogist*, N.S. i, 1884, 262–6.

Sotheby & Co., *Catalogue of Architectural Drawings . . . by Sir Christopher Wren*, 23 May 1951.

John Summerson, 'The Mind of Wren', in *Heavenly Mansions and Other Essays on Architecture*, 1949.

John Summerson, *Sir Christopher Wren*, 1953.

John Summerson, 'Sir Christopher Wren, P.R.S.', *Notes and Records of the Royal Society* xv, 1960.

John Summerson, 'Drawings of London Churches in the Bute Collection: a catalogue', *Arch. Hist.* xiii, 1970.

Geoffrey Webb, *Wren*, 1937.

Margaret Whinney, 'Sir Christopher Wren's Visit to Paris', *Gazette des Beaux-Arts*, 6th ser. 51, 1958.

Margaret Whinney, *Wren*, 1971.

Stephen Wren, *Parentalia, or Memoirs of the Family of the Wrens*, 1750 (reprinted by the Gregg Press, 1965).

The Wren Memorial Volume, published by the R.I.B.A. 1923.

The Wren Society, 20 vols. 1924–43.

UNIVERSITY BUILDINGS

attributed: PEMBROKE COLLEGE CHAPEL, CAMBRIDGE, for his uncle Matthew Wren, Bishop of Ely, 1663–5; east end extended 1880 [Willis & Clark, i, 147; *Wren Soc.* v, 27–9, pl. xi] (R.C.H.M., *Cambridge*, 153–4).

THE SHELDONIAN THEATRE, OXFORD, 1664–9; roof reconstructed by G. Saunders 1802, cupola rebuilt by E. Blore 1838, restoration of stonework, etc., by W. Godfrey Allen 1959–60 [*Wren Soc.* v, pls. ii–iii, xix, 91–9; engravings of roof in R. Plot, *Natural History of Oxfordshire*, 1677, and S. Wren, *Parentalia*, 1750, 334–5; John Summerson, *The Sheldonian in its Time*, 1964; H. M. Colvin, *The Sheldonian Theatre and the*

---

the R.I.B.A. Collection (drawings of St. Stephen's Walbrook and other City churches), All Souls College, Oxford (elevation of design for Whitehall Palace), and the Victoria and Albert Museum (miscellaneous drawings).

Divinity School, 1964, 2nd ed. 1974].

ALL SOULS COLLEGE, OXFORD, SCREEN in CHAPEL, 1664 (the gift of Sir William Portman). One of Wren's designs for this work is illustrated in *Wren Soc.* v, pl. vii, but it does not represent the screen as executed (see elevation of 'Half the screen as made by S.r W.m Portman, before the whole was pulled down A.D. 1716' in Clarke Collection, Worcester College). In 1716 the screen was remodelled by Sir James Thornhill, who entirely altered the part above the cornice and converted Wren's pedimented doorway into an open archway [All Souls College Archives].

EMMANUEL COLLEGE, CAMBRIDGE, THE CHAPEL and GALLERY, 1668–73 [Willis & Clark, ii, 703–9; *Wren Soc.* v, 29–31, pl. xii] (R.C.H.M., *Cambridge*, 64–6).

TRINITY COLLEGE, OXFORD, THE GARDEN QUADRANGLE, built in three stages:

(1) North wing, 1668 (Thomas Strong, mason; Robert Minchin, carpenter).
(2) West wing, 1682.
(3) South Wing,[1] 1728 (William Townesend, mason).

In 1802 the walls were raised to create an attic storey and the original mansard roofs were removed. When the building was refaced in 1958–65 the proportions of the attic windows were altered and improved [*Wren Soc.* v, 14–16, pls. iv–v].

In 1692 Wren was shown the designs for the CHAPEL (possibly by Dean Aldrich), and wrote to the President that he had 'considered the designe you sent me of your chapel, which in the maine is very well, and I believe your worke is too far advanced to admitt of any advice: however, I have sent my thoughts which will be of use to the mason to form his mouldings' [*Wren Soc.* v, 15]. The Bursar's Accounts for 1692 (B.L., MS. Lansdowne 718) contain a payment of £2 3s. 'to Sir Christopher Wren's servant'.

ST. JOHN'S COLLEGE, OXFORD, SCREEN in CHAPEL, *c.*1670; destroyed 1843, when two Corinthian columns were incorporated in the staircase at Painswick House, Glos. [*Wren Soc.* ix, pl. 39; x, 129 n.].

MERTON COLLEGE, OXFORD, SCREEN in CHAPEL, 1671–3; dismantled *c.*1850, partly restored 1960 [J. R. L. Highfield, 'Alexander Fisher, Sir Christopher Wren and Merton College Chapel', *Oxoniensia* xxiv, 1959].

THE QUEEN'S COLLEGE, OXFORD, THE WILLIAMSON BUILDING, 1671–4; upper storey added *c.*1730 [*Cal. of State Papers, Domestic, 1671*, 4, 122; *ibid., 1671–2*, 369] (*V.C.H. Oxon.* iii, 125, plate).

[1] i.e. the north range of the Durham Quadrangle.

TRINITY COLLEGE, CAMBRIDGE, THE LIBRARY, 1676–84 [Willis & Clark, ii, 533–51; *Wren Soc.* v, 32–44, pls. xv-xxvi; H. Colvin, 'The Building and Design of the Library', in *The Wren Library*, ed. D. McKitterick, Cambridge 1995] (R.C.H.M., *Cambridge*, 236–41).

CHRIST CHURCH, OXFORD, TOM TOWER, 1681–2, Gothic [*Wren Soc.* v, 17–23, pl. viii; xix, pls. liv–lvi; W. D. Caröe, *Tom Tower, Christ Church, Oxford*, 1923].

BODLEIAN LIBRARY, OXFORD, repaired Divinity School and designed buttresses (removed 1960) on south side of Duke Humphrey's Library, 1701–3 [John Walker, *Oxoniana* iii, 1809, 16–27 (for Wren's letters); E. P. Warren, 'Sir Christopher Wren's Repair of the Divinity School and Duke Humphrey's Library', *Wren Memorial Volume*, 1923, 233–8; J. N. L. Myres, 'Recent Discoveries in the Bodleian Library', *Archaeologia* ci, 1967].

ROYAL PALACES, ETC.

ST. JAMES'S PALACE, repairs and alterations to the Queen's Catholic Chapel, for Queen Catherine of Braganza, 1682–4 [*History of the King's Works* v, 249–53].

WINCHESTER PALACE, for King Charles II, 1683–5; left unfinished at the King's death; used for the reception of French prisoners of war 1757–64 and 1778–85; occupied by French refugee clergy 1792–6; converted into barracks 1810; destroyed by fire 1894 [*Wren Soc.* vii, 11–69, pls. i–iv; *History of the King's Works* v, 304–13].

WINDSOR CASTLE, THE GUARD-HOUSE, 1685; dem. [*Wren Soc.* viii, 13–15; *History of the King's Works* v, 329].

WHITEHALL PALACE, new range containing CATHOLIC CHAPEL, COUNCIL CHAMBER and PRIVY GALLERY, for King James II, 1685–7; destroyed by fire 1698; THE QUEEN'S APARTMENT and TERRACE GARDEN, begun for Queen Mary of Modena, completed for Queen Mary II, 1688–93; destroyed by fire 1698 [*Wren Soc*, vii, 71–9, pls. vii, xiii–xxi; *History of the King's Works* v, 285–97]. Wren's unexecuted designs for a new palace after the fire of 1698 are illustrated in *Wren Soc.* viii.

HAMPTON COURT PALACE, rebuilt south and east ranges for King William III and Queen Mary II, 1689–94; interior of King's Apartment completed by W. Talman 1699 [*Wren Soc.* iv; *History of the King's Works* v, 156–65].

KENSINGTON PALACE, reconstructed for King William III and Queen Mary II, 1689–96 [*Wren Soc.* vii, 135–96 and plates; G. H.

Chettle & P. A. Faulkner, 'Sir Christopher Wren and Kensington Palace', *Jnl. British Archaeological Assn.*, 3rd ser. xiv, 1951; *History of the King's Works* v, 183–91].

WESTMINSTER PALACE, refitted interior of HOUSE OF COMMONS, 1692, widened galleries 1707 to accommodate Scottish members; altered by James Wyatt 1800, destroyed by fire 1834. For this, and other minor alterations to the palace for which Wren was responsible, see *History of the King's Works* v, 385–418.

ST. JAMES'S PALACE, range of STATE APARTMENTS for Queen Anne, 1703 [*History of the King's Works* v, 237–9].

PUBLIC BUILDINGS, ETC.

LONDON, THE CUSTOM HOUSE, 1669–71; reconstructed by Thomas Ripley 1718–25; destroyed by fire 1814 [*History of the King's Works* v, 345–8].

LONDON, THE MONUMENT (to the Fire of 1666), FISH STREET HILL, 1671–6. Hooke was actively concerned in the erection of the Column and, according to Aubrey's *Brief Lives*, he was its architect: but it is impossible to give either Hooke or Wren the sole credit for what seems to have been a work of collaboration. A drawing of the scaffolding used is given in *Civil Engineer and Architect's Jnl.* i, 267. [C. Welch, *The History of the Monument*, 1893; *Wren Soc.* v, 45–51, pls. xxxiv-xxxvii; xviii, 190–1, pls. xvii–xviii; M. I. Batten, 'The Architecture of Robert Hooke', *Walpole Soc.* xxv, 84; T. F. Reddaway, *The Rebuilding of London after the Great Fire*, 1940, 216 n.; and unpublished documents in Bodleian Library, MS. Rawlinson B.363.]

LONDON, DRURY LANE THEATRE, for Thomas Killigrew, 1672–4; remodelled by R. Adam 1775–6, rebuilt by H. Holland 1791–4 [R. Leacroft, 'Wren's Drury Lane', *Arch. Rev.* July 1950; *Wren Soc.* xii, pl. xxiii].

LINCOLN CATHEDRAL LIBRARY, built for Dean Honywood, 1674–5, according to Wren's 'directions' and 'Mr. Tompson's modell' [*Wren Soc.* xvii, 76–7, pls. lxv–lxvi] (measured drawings in *Builder* lxii, 1892, 259–63). Mr. Tompson was probably the London mason John Thompson (d. 1700), who worked under Wren at St. Paul's and elsewhere. The design may have been basically his, with guidance from Wren.

GREENWICH, THE ROYAL OBSERVATORY, 1675–6; new buildings added 1813–44 [*Wren Soc.* xix, 113–15, pls. lxviii–lxix].

? ABINGDON TOWN HALL, BERKS., 1678–80. There is no documentary evidence that this building was designed by Wren, but the attribution is possible on stylistic grounds, and in 1681, when recommending Christopher Kempster, the master mason, as one whom he had 'used in good workes', Wren mentioned that he 'wrought the Town-house at Abbington'. The fact that John Scarborough (*q.v.*) was employed as a measurer is also in favour of Wren's authorship [*Wren Soc.* v, 18, xix, 100–2; accounts in B.L., Add. MS. 28666, ff. 338–9] (measured drawings in *Details*, ed. R. R. Phillips, i, 1909, 69–71).

LONDON, MIDDLE TEMPLE, THE CLOISTERS in PUMP COURT, 1680–1; destroyed by bombing 1940–1. Nicholas Barbon prepared a 'model' for this building in 1679, but it was rejected in favour of ' a model drawn by Sir C. Wren' and, when the work was completed, John Foltrop the builder claimed £250 from the Society 'for his loss in materials about the foundations and for extraordinary charges in building the Cloisters according to Sir Christopher Wren's model and directions, over and above his agreement with Dr. Barbon' [*Middle Temple Records*, ed. C. H. Hopwood, iii, 1905, 1334–8]. Wren's original design (illustrated in *C. Life*, 28 May 1948, 1073) showed a cloister of seven arches, but this was increased in execution to eight.

LONDON, THE NAVY OFFICE, SEETHING LANE, 1682–3; dem. [T. F. Reddaway, 'Sir Christopher Wren's Navy Office', *Bull. Institute of Historical Research* xxx, 1957].

CHELSEA, THE ROYAL HOSPITAL, 1682–92 [*Wren Soc.* xix, 61–86, pls. xxx–xlvii; C. G. T. Dean, *The Royal Hospital, Chelsea*, 1950].

WINDSOR, BERKS., THE COURT HOUSE, supervised completion after the death of its builder, Sir Thomas Fitch (*q.v.*), in 1688 [Tighe & Davis, *Annals of Windsor* ii, 1858, 423]. The statue of Prince George of Denmark was presented by Wren's son Christopher in 1713, when he was elected M.P. for the borough.

ETON COLLEGE, BUCKS., THE UPPER SCHOOL, 1689–91 [in a letter to Samuel Pepys, written in 1694, John Evelyn states that it was Wren who had lately 'built the new schole . . . from the foundations': Evelyn's letter-book in Christ Church Library, Oxford, No. 693. Accounts printed in *Wren Soc.* xix, 108–10 show that Wren's 'servant' had been paid £1 1s. 6d. in 1686 when the former school threatened collapse, and that the master carpenter Matthew Banckes (*q.v.*) received £86 'for Surveying and Advising and Examining and Correcting the Workmen's Accounts'].

CHRIST'S HOSPITAL, LONDON. In 1692 Wren 'presented the draught of the New intended Writing Schoole', but there is evidence that the drawings were made by Hawksmoor, and those which are preserved in the All Souls Collection are in his hand. Sir John Moore's Writing School (1693–5; dem. 1902) may therefore be regarded either as a design by Wren worked out by Hawksmoor, or as an early work of the latter carried out under Wren's directions. There appears to be no evidence that Wren designed the Mathematical School (1682–3; dem. 1902), which seems to have been designed by Hooke or Oliver. [*Wren Soc.* xi, 60–80, pls. xliv–li, xvii, pl. xlvii; E. H. Pearce, *Christ's Hospital*, 1908, 151.]

APPLEBY, LEICS., SIR JOHN MOORE'S SCHOOL, 1693–7. The original designs were made by Wren but they were carried out by Sir William Wilson (*q.v.*), who completely altered their character in execution [*Wren Soc.* xi, 84 *et seq.*, pls. liii–liv].

? WILLIAMSBURG, VIRGINIA, U.S.A., WILLIAM AND MARY COLLEGE, 1695–9. According to Hugh Jones, *Present State of Virginia*, 1724, 26, the College was 'first modelled by Sir Christopher Wren, adapted to the Nature of the Country by the Gentlemen there'. The accounts show that workmen and materials were brought from England, and that Thomas Hadley was the surveyor in charge. Only part of the original scheme was completed in the 1690s. There was a fire in 1705, after which the college was rebuilt: it was restored in 1929–31 [J. D. Kornwolf, *The Colonial Campus of the College of William and Mary*, Williamsburg 1989].

GREENWICH, THE ROYAL HOSPITAL FOR SEAMEN, 1696 onwards. As Surveyor in charge from 1696 to 1716, Wren was responsible for the general layout, and personally designed the base wing on the west side of King Charles's Court (subsequently remodelled), the Great Hall, the twin domes and the colonnades. Though they were erected during his surveyorship, his responsibility for the design of the east range of Queen Anne's Court and the West and South Dormitories in King William's Court is doubtful. [*Wren Soc.* vi; J. H. V. Davies, 'The Dating of the Buildings of the Royal Hospital at Greenwich', *Archaeological Jnl.* cxiii, 1956.]

LONDON, THE ROYAL SOCIETY'S REPOSITORY, CRANE COURT, FLEET STREET, 1711–12; dem. *c.*1782 [J. A. Bennett, 'Wren's Last Building?' *Notes and Records of the Royal Society* xxvii, 1973].

DOMESTIC ARCHITECTURE

LONGLEAT HOUSE, WILTS., principal doorway for Sir James Thynne (d. 1670); replaced 1705 by the existing doorway, apparently designed by the French sculptor Claude David, and re-erected, with only one pair of columns instead of two, at the School House built by Lord Weymouth at WARMINSTER, WILTS., in 1707. Lord Weymouth himself consulted Wren when altering Longleat in 1683 [Longleat archives, Book 179 B, and Thynne Papers xxxiv, ff. 103, 109; R. Hope, 'Doorway by Wren', *Arch. Rev.* June 1966, 478–9].

ARBURY HALL, WARWICKS., design for a stable doorway for Richard Newdigate, 1674, either not executed or modified in execution by Sir William Wilson [above, p. 1064].

TRING MANOR HOUSE, HERTS., for Henry Guy, Gentleman of the Privy Chamber to King Charles II, probably *c.*1680; remodelled 1872 onwards: stated by Roger North to have been 'built by S[r] Chr. Wren' in his MS. treatise 'Of Building' [B.L., Add. MS. 32540, f. 48[v]]. The engraving in Chauncy's *Historical Antiquities of Hertfordshire*, 1700, is dedicated to Guy by John Oliver, Assistant Surveyor of St. Paul's Cathedral. For 18th-century survey plan and elevation in R.I.B.A.D. see Downes, *Architecture of Wren*, fig. 16.

THORESBY HOUSE, NOTTS. For Wren's involvement in the remodelling of 1685–7 see above, p. 951.

LONDON, BRIDGWATER SQUARE, BARBICAN, was built as a personal speculation by Wren and George Jackson of Chipping Warden on the site of Bridgwater House, which was destroyed by fire in 1687. They bought the site for £4400 in 1688. Those who took building plots included Nicholas Hawksmoor, William Emmett (bricklayer), Samuel Fulkes (mason), Henry Doogood (plasterer), Edward Strong (mason), John Smallwell (joiner), Thomas Hill (mason), Nicholas Goodwin (brickmaker), Richard Billinghurst (bricklayer) and Samuel Wing (ironmonger) [Guildhall Library, MS. 2461]. An earlier scheme for laying out the site for building had been made by Wren in 1673 on behalf of the Earl of Bridgwater, but was not carried out. The Royal Warrant [P.R.O., C 82/2441], dated 30 June 1673, states that Wren 'hath . . . made and framed a Draught mapp or chart of the Whole Designe'. The plan referred to is now P.R.O., MPA 22. The original houses in Bridgwater Square have all been demolished or rebuilt.

WINSLOW HALL, BUCKS., was probably designed by Wren for William Lowndes, Secretary of the Treasury, 1699–1702, as he examined and passed the workmen's bills, but the fact that he performed this service does not prove that he was the architect [*Wren Soc.* xvii, 54–75, pls. lviii–lxiv] (*C. Life*, 24 Aug. 1951).

LONDON, MARLBOROUGH HOUSE, ST. JAMES'S, for Sarah, Duchess of Marlborough, 1709–11. Although Christopher Wren, junior, is credited with the design by Campbell, *Vitruvius Britannicus* i, 1715, pls. 39–40, it is clear that he was merely assisting his father. There have been numerous alterations, including the addition of a low attic storey in 1771–3. A new entrance hall was added on the north side in 1860–2 when the house was the official residence of the Prince of Wales, and the attic storey was raised in 1880 [*Wren Soc.* vii, 225–9; David Green, *Blenheim Palace*, 1951, 248–9; A. Searle, 'Sir Christopher Wren and Marlborough House', *British Library Jnl.* 8 (i), 1982, 37–45] (R.C.H.M., *London* (*West*), 132–4).

CHURCHES

(excluding the churches in the City of London rebuilt after the Great Fire)

SALISBURY CATHEDRAL, WILTS., report for Dr. Seth Ward, Bishop of Salisbury, 1668: printed in *Wren Soc.* xi, 21–6, from *Parentalia*, 303–6; see also R. Rawlinson, *History of the Cathedral Church of Salisbury*, 1719, 1–21; designed bishop's throne and furniture for choir, 1671–3 [G. J. Elkington, 'Alexander Fort and Salisbury Cathedral', *Wilts. Archaeological Mag.* lvii, 1958, 56–63 and *ibid.* lxxvi, 1982, 116–17].

WESTMINSTER, ST. MARTIN-IN-THE-FIELDS CHURCH, designed cupola to surmount tower in 1672; dem. 1722 [*Survey of London* xx, 23, n., pls. 8–9].

INGESTRE CHURCH, STAFFS., may have been designed by Wren for Walter Chetwynd, who, like himself, was a Fellow of the Royal Society, 1673–6. The attribution is supported by an elevation for a lantern on a tower, inscribed 'Mr. Chetwin's Tower', which was sold with other Wren drawings in the Bute sale of 1951. The lantern was not, however, built, and the church could have been designed by someone else closely connected with Wren's office. (*Wren Soc.* xix, 57, pls. xv–xxiv).

ST. PAUL'S CATHEDRAL, LONDON, 1675–1710. Wren's designs are illustrated in *Wren Soc.* i–iii and xiii–xiv and by K. Downes, *Sir Christopher Wren: The Design of St. Paul's Cathedral*, 1988. An important drawing corresponding to the first model is described by Norbert Lynton in *Burlington Mag.* xcvii, 1955, 40–4. The transition from the 'Warrant' design to the executed structure is discussed by John Summerson in 'The Penultimate Design for St. Paul's Cathedral', *Burlington Mag.* March 1961. See also Summerson, 'J. H. Mansart, Sir Christopher Wren and the dome of St. Paul's Cathedral', *Burlington Mag.* 132, 1990. Jane Lang, *Rebuilding St. Paul's*, 1956, is a fully documented history of Wren's cathedral. A. F. E. Poley, *St. Paul's Cathedral*, 1927, contains a magnificent set of measured drawings.

WESTMINSTER, ST. JAMES'S CHURCH, PICCADILLY, 1676–84; wooden spire (perhaps designed by Edward Wilcox, *q.v.*) added 1687; church seriously damaged by bombing 1940 but restored by Sir Albert Richardson 1947–54 [*Survey of London* xxix, chap. iii and plates] (measured drawings in *Wren Soc.* ix, 30–2).

WESTMINSTER, ST. ANNE'S CHURCH, SOHO: Wren was one of the commissioners appointed to complete this church in 1685, and may have designed it when work began in 1677. But Talman was also concerned in 1685, and the authorship of the design remains uncertain. The church was reconstructed in 1830–1 and dem. 1953 after war-damage [*Survey of London* xxxiii, chap. x and plates].

WESTMINSTER, ST. CLEMENT DANES, STRAND, 1680–2; upper stage of tower added by James Gibbs 1719–20; semicircular porch on south side removed in nineteenth century; interior destroyed by bombing 1941 and restored by W. A. S. Lloyd 1957–8 [*Wren Soc.* ix, 21–2; x, 23–4, 108–11].

WINDSOR, ST. GEORGE'S CHAPEL, survey and repairs, 1681–2 [W. H. St. J. Hope, *History of Windsor Castle* ii, 386].

WESTMINSTER, ST. MARGARET'S CHURCH, advice in connection with erection of a gallery in the south aisle in 1682; destroyed 1877–82 [Vestry Minutes in Westminster City Library, 13 Jan. 1681/2: 'Sir Christopher Wren being this day present, at the desire of the Gentlemen of the Vestry, will assist them with his Advice, concerning the New Gallery designed to be Erected in the parish Church, and will Agree with the Artificers touching the same at as reasonable Rates as he can. And the Churchwardens are desired to attend the said Sr Christopher from time to time with the Artificers viz. – Noell Ansell Joyner and Bernard Angier Carpenter.']

LONDON, THE TEMPLE CHURCH, repaired fabric and refitted interior, 1682–3. Wren's altarpiece was removed in 1840 but replaced in 1954 [*Wren Soc.* x, (58)–(60)].

LONDON, THE FRENCH PROTESTANT CHURCH in THE SAVOY, enlarged 1686; dem. An engraved plan and elevation, accompanied by a licence, dated 24 Feb. 1685/6, to enlarge the church 'according to the Draught thereof made by our said Surveyor General', is in the P.R.O. (MPA 41) and is reproduced by R. Somerville, *The Savoy*, 1960, 66 [*History of the King's Works* v, 361].

WARWICK, ST. MARY'S CHURCH. For Wren's abortive designs for partially rebuilding this church before or after the fire of 1694, see *Wren Soc.* x, pls. 15–18 and Michael Farr, *The Great Fire of Warwick*, Dugdale Soc. 1992, xxiv–xxv.

AMPTHILL CHURCH, BEDS., approved design of a family pew for Lord Ashburnham, 1696; erected by Alexander Fort, joiner; dem. 1877 [R. Gunnis, 'A Storm about a Pew', *Bedfordshire Magazine* ii, no. 15, 1950–1; Lincoln Diocesan Registry, Fac. 9/3 and 17].

WESTMINSTER ABBEY, extensive repairs, 1698–1722 [*Wren Soc.* xi, 12–20, 27–32, pls. i–vi; E. Beresford Chancellor, 'Wren's Restoration of Westminster Abbey', *Connoisseur* lxxviii, 1927, 145]. In addition to the accounts summarized in *Wren Soc.* xi, 13–14, there is in the Bodleian Library a volume recording payments authorized by Wren from 1698 to 1713 (MS. Gough Westminster 1).

ELY CATHEDRAL, advice in connection with repairs to north transept in 1699–1702 [*Wren Soc.* xix, 148]. The doorway to the north transept was designed either by Wren or by Robert Grumbold, the contracting mason, who is known to have submitted a design.

THE LONDON CITY CHURCHES

With a few exceptions,[1] those City churches that were rebuilt after the Great Fire of 1666 were rebuilt under the direction of Wren with the assistance of Hooke and Woodroffe (d. 1675) (above, p. 1085). As products of Wren's office all of those listed below may therefore be included in the catalogue of Wren's architectural works, but not all of them were personally designed by him, and it must be emphasized that in most cases the fittings, and sometimes even the architectural details, were designed by the craftsmen employed, and that Wren often exercised only a very loose control over their execution. For this reason, the names of the principal craftsmen have been given in the following list whenever they are known. The building accounts, of which there are two sets, one in Guildhall Library, MSS. 25536–9, and the other in Bodleian Library, MSS. Rawlinson B. 387–9, are summarized from the latter source in *Wren Soc.* x, and extracts from the parish records are printed in vol. xix; in one or two cases it has been possible to supplement the information there given from parish records which were not available to the editors of the Wren Society. A large number of Wren's original designs for the City churches have been published by the Wren Society, but over fifty more drawings were sold at Sotheby's on 23 May 1951. For these see John Summerson, 'Drawings for the London City Churches', *R.I.B.A. Jnl.* Feb. 1952, and 'Drawings of London Churches in the Bute Collection: a catalogue', in *Architectural History* xiii, 1970.

In 1848–9 measured drawings of all but four of the churches then still in existence were published by John Clayton as *Plans Elevations and Sections of the Parochial Churches of Sir Chr. Wren*. The 60 plates comprised in this now rare work were reproduced in vol. ix of the *Wren Society. The Churches of London* by George Godwin, 2 vols., 1838–9, contains engravings by Le Keux showing many of the churches and their interiors before alteration or destruction. The valuable contemporary descriptions given by E. Hatton, *A New View of London*, 2 vols., 1708, are reprinted in *Wren Soc.* x, 15–44. Other works dealing wholly or in part with Wren's City churches are A. T. Taylor, *The Towers and Steeples designed by Sir Christopher Wren*, 1881; W. Niven, *London City Churches destroyed since 1800, or now threatened*, privately printed, 1887; G. H. Birch, *London Churches of the Seventeenth and Eighteenth Centuries*, 1896 (with superb photogravure plates); Philip Norman, *The London City Churches*, published by the London Society, 2nd ed. 1929; The Royal Commission on Historical Monuments' *Report* on London, vol. iv, *The City*, 1929; Miss E. Jeffries Davis, 'The Parish Churches of the City of London', *Jnl. Royal Society of Arts*

[1] St. Mary Aldermary was rebuilt by a private benefaction without recourse to the funds adminstered by Wren and his colleagues (see H. Colvin, 'The Church of St. Mary Aldermary and its rebuilding after the Great Fire of London', *Arch. Hist.* 24, 1981). St. Michael Cornhill also benefited substantially from a private benefaction and the rebuilding appears to have been carried out by the parish without architectural guidance from Wren (*Wren Soc.* xix, 45–6). St. Mary Woolnoth and St. Sepulchre Holborn were damaged but not destroyed and required only repairs.

lxxxiii, 9 Aug. 1935; Gerald Cobb, *The Old Churches of London*, 3rd ed. 1948; Elizabeth & Wayland Young, *Old London Churches*, 1956; and B. F. L. Clarke, *Parish Churches of London*, 1966.

ST. ALBAN, WOOD STREET, 1682–5; apse added and interior refitted by Sir Gilbert Scott 1859; destroyed by bombing 1940 except for tower. Sam. Fulkes, mason; Matthew Banckes, carpenter; William Cleer, joiner; John Grove and H. Doogood, plasterers. Much of the medieval fabric had survived the alterations of 1633–4 and the fire of 1666 and was incorporated by Wren in his rebuilding, which was Gothic in style.

ALL HALLOWS, LOMBARD STREET, 1686–94; repaired 1824 and 1871; internal alterations 1888; dem. 1939. John Thompson, mason; Charles King and John Evans, bricklayers; Thos. Woodstock, carpenter; William Cleer, Thomas Powell, William Grey and John Mitchell, joiners; John Miller and Saunders, carvers; H. Doogood, plasterer. The tower was re-erected as part of All Hallows, Twickenham (consecrated 1940), which contains the organ, monuments and other fittings.

ALL HALLOWS THE GREAT, UPPER THAMES STREET, 1677–83; the tower was rebuilt in 1876–7; dem. 1893–4. William Hammond, mason; Thos. Horn, bricklayer; Robert Day, carpenter; Thos. Powell and William Cleer, joiners; H. Doogood, John Grove and John Sherwood, plasterers. The fittings are now distributed between St. Margaret, Lothbury (screen and sounding-board), St. Michael, Paternoster Royal (candelabrum, etc.), All Hallows, Gospel Oak (communion table), and St. Paul's, Hammersmith (pulpit).

ALL HALLOWS, BREAD STREET or WATLING STREET, 1677–84; steeple completed 1697; dem. 1876–7. Sam. Fulkes, mason; John Longland, carpenter; William Cleer, joiner; H. Doogood and John Grove, plasterers. Some of the fittings were placed in the church of All Hallows, London Docks.

ST. ANDREW BY THE WARDROBE, 1685–93; west gallery inserted 1774; repaired by S. S. Teulon 1838; south front and tower altered by T. Garner *c.*1875; gutted by bombing 1940, restored by Marshall Sisson 1959–61. Nicholas Young, mason; Thomas Horn, bricklayer; John Longland and Israel Knowles, carpenters; Roger Davis, William Cleer and William Smith, joiners; Jonathan Maine, wood-carver; H. Doogood, plasterer.

ST. ANDREW, HOLBORN, 1684–90; tower completed 1703; internal alterations by J. H. Good, 1818, and in 1872 by S. S. Teulon, who exposed medieval features in lower part of tower, etc.; gutted by bombing 1941, restored by Mottistone & Paget, 1960. Edward Pierce and William Stanton, masons; John Longland, carpenter; Valentine Houseman, joiner; Edward Pierce, wood carver; Robert Dyer, plasterer.

ST. ANNE AND ST. AGNES, GRESHAM STREET, 1677–80; steeple added later *c.*1714; exterior rendered in cement by Charles Tyrrell 1820–1; alterations to interior by W. M. Brooks 1838–9, and by E. Christian 1888–9; damaged by bombing 1940 and subsequently restored. R. Walters and Wm. Hammond, masons; John Fitch, bricklayer; Ralph Cadman and Messrs. Cheltenham, Fuller and Page, joiners; John Sherwood, plasterer.

ST. ANTHOLIN, WATLING STREET, 1678–82; tower completed 1688; dem. 1875. Thos. Cartwright, mason; Edward Elder and Thomas Horn, bricklayers; John Longland and William Atwell, carpenters; William Cleer and William Grey, joiners; Jonathan Maine, carver; H. Doogood and John Grove, plasterers. The upper part of the spire, renewed *c.*1825, is preserved in a private garden at Forest Hill (*C. Life*, 26 Aug. 1939, 214). The reredos was removed to St. Antholin, Nunhead Row, Camberwell; the pulpit is in Blandford Church, Dorset.

ST. AUGUSTINE, WATLING STREET, 1680–3, spire completed 1695; interior altered by Sir A. Blomfield 1878; spire and most of church destroyed by bombing 1941; tower and restored spire remain incorporated in St. Paul's Cathedral choir school. Edward Strong, mason; Israel Knowles, carpenter; William Draper, joiner; Jonathan Maine, carver; John Combes, plasterer.

ST. BARTHOLOMEW, EXCHANGE, 1674–9; dem. 1840–1 for site of the Royal Exchange and 'Sun' Fire Office. John Thompson, mason; Robert Brown, bricklayer; Matthew Banckes, carpenter; William Cleer and T. Poultney, joiners; Henry Doogood and John Grove, plasterers. The new church of St. Bartholomew, Moor Lane, by C. R. Cockerell was 'in the style of the old one' and incorporated its fittings and some of its carved stonework. On its demolition in 1902 the reredos and carved door-cases were removed to a chapel in St. Giles', Cripplegate, where they were destroyed by bombing in 1940–1. Some panelling is at St. John's, Hendon, and the pulpit, font and altar-rails are at St. Bartholomew, Stamford Hill.

ST. BENET, GRACECHURCH STREET, 1681–6;

dem. 1867–8. Thos. Wise, mason; John Longland, carpenter; William Cleer and John Mitchell, joiners; H. Doogood and John Grove, plasterers. The pulpit is now in St. Olave, Hart Street.

ST. BENET, PAUL'S WHARF, 1677–83 (now the Welsh Church). Thomas and Edward Strong, masons; Israel Knowles, carpenter; William Cleer, joiner; H. Doogood and John Grove, plasterers.

ST. BENET FINK, THREADNEEDLE STREET, 1670–3; dem. 1842–4 for site of the Royal Exchange. Thos. Cartwright, mason; Nicholas Wood, bricklayer; Henry Blowes, carpenter; William Cleer and William Grey, joiners; Edward Pierce, carver; John Grove, plasterer. The organ (1714) is now in Malmesbury Abbey Church, the reredos and pulpit in Emanuel School Chapel, and a door-case in Lytes Cary House, Somerset.

ST. BRIDE, FLEET STREET, 1671–8; steeple 1701–3; interior destroyed by bombing 1940, and restored by W. Godfrey Allen 1955–7. Joshua Marshall and Sam. Fulkes, masons; Benjamin Leach, bricklayer; John Longland, carpenter; William Cleer and William Grey, joiners; William Emmett, wood carver; John Grove, plasterer. The spire was struck by lightning in 1764, after which the upper 84 feet were rebuilt by William Staines; it was again damaged by lightning in 1803. (W. H. Godfrey, *The Church of St. Bride, Fleet Street*, London Survey Monograph no. 15, 1944.)

CHRIST CHURCH, NEWGATE STREET, 1677–87; steeple completed 1704: the urns which formerly surmounted the colonnaded storey were removed before 1814 but restored in 1960; interior 'repaired and beautified' in 1834, and again in 1880; body of church destroyed by bombing 1940. John Shorthose and Richard Crooke, masons; Edward Elder and John How, bricklayers; John Longland, carpenter; Matthew Williams, joiner; H. Doogood, plasterer.

ST. CHRISTOPHER LE STOCKS, THREADNEEDLE STREET, 1670–1 (incorporating much of the medieval fabric); dem. 1781 for site of Bank of England. John Thompson, mason; Matthew Banckes, carpenter; William Grey, joiner; William Emmett, wood carver; John Grove, plasterer. The figures of Moses and Aaron from the altar-piece of this church are now in St. Margaret, Lothbury, the reredos in Great Bearsted Church, Essex, the pulpit in Canewdon Church, Essex.

ST. CLEMENT, EASTCHEAP, 1683–7; interior rearranged by Butterfield in 1872 and again in 1889; roof rebuilt 1925. Edward Strong, mason; Israel Knowles and William Grey, carpenters; T. Poultney, joiner; Jonathan Maine, carver; John Grove and H. Doogood, plasterers.

ST. DIONIS BACKCHURCH, FENCHURCH STREET, 1670–4; steeple completed 1684; dem. 1878–9. John Thompson, mason; William Taylour, Richard Reading, William Atwell, John Longland, carpenters; William Cleer and William Grey, joiners; H. Doogood and John Grove, plasterers. The altar, pulpit, font and other fittings are in St. Dionis, Fulham; the royal arms and some panelling in St. Dionis Hall, Lime Street. The monument to Sir Thomas Rawlinson was re-erected in Hawkshead Church, Lancs.

ST. DUNSTAN IN THE EAST, 1670–1 (incorporating shell of the old church); Gothic steeple 1697–9; nave and chancel rebuilt by D. Laing and W. Tite 1817–21; destroyed by bombing 1941 except steeple. James Flory, mason (of church); Ephraim Beauchamp, mason (of steeple); Thomas Lane, joiner.

ST. EDMUND KING AND MARTYR, LOMBARD STREET, 1670–9; spire completed after 1708; repaired 1833; urns removed from steeple *c.*1908; damaged by bombing 1917. Abraham Story, mason; Maurice Emmett, bricklayer; Geo. Choby and Henry Wilkins, carpenters; Thos. Whiting and Thos. Creecher, joiners; Daniel Morrice and John Sherwood, plasterers.

ST. GEORGE, BOTOLPH LANE, 1671–4; dem. 1903–4. Nicholas Young, mason; Thos. Horn, bricklayer; Robert Day, carpenter; Wm. Cleer, joiner; Simon Audrey, carver; John Grove and Henry Doogood, plasterers. The organ and pulpit are now in St. George's Church, Southall, the royal arms at St. Mary-at-Hill, and the altar-table at St. Silas, Pentonville.

ST. JAMES, GARLICK HILL, 1676–83; spire 1713–17; repaired 1838, when three windows on north side were blocked and four others opened at east end; decorated by B. Champneys 1886. Chr. Kempster, mason; Thos. Warren, bricklayer; Israel Knowles, carpenter; Wm. Cleer and J. Fuller, joiners; William Newman, carver; John Grove and H. Doogood, plasterers.

ST. LAWRENCE, JEWRY, 1671–7; north gallery removed by Sir A. Blomfield 1866–7; roof repaired 1892; gutted by bombing 1940; restored by Cecil Brown 1954–7. Edward Pierce, mason; Thomas Newman, bricklayer; John Longland, carpenter; Wm. Cleer and Richard Kedge, joiners; Thos. Mead, plasterer; Edward Pierce, wood carver.

ST. MAGNUS MARTYR, LOWER THAMES STREET,

1671–6; steeple completed 1705; damaged by fire 1760; in *c.*1765 the west ends of the north and south aisles were set back and a passage-way made through the tower in order to improve the approach to Old London Bridge; later the windows of the north aisle were reduced to circular form and the south aisle was partially rebuilt; there were internal alterations by E. I'Anson in 1893 and by Martin Travers in 1924. George Dowdeswell and John Thompson, masons; Robert Brown, bricklayer; Matthew Banckes, carpenter; Wm. Cleer, Wm. Grey and – Massey, joiners; John Grove and H. Doogood, plasterers.

ST. MARGARET, LOTHBURY, 1686–90; alterations by Bodley and Garner 1890–1. Sam. Fulkes, mason; John Longland, carpenter; Wm. Cleer, joiner; H. Doogood, plasterer.

ST. MARGARET PATTENS, 1684–7; spire 1699–1703; the lead vases which formerly decorated the spire have been removed. Sam. Fulkes, mason; John Evans, bricklayer; Thos. Woodstock, carpenter; Wm. Cleer, joiner; John Grove and H. Doogood, plasterers.

ST. MARTIN, LUDGATE, 1677–84. Nicholas Young, mason; Allan Garway and Thos. Horn, bricklayers; Henry Blowes, Robert Day, and Matthew Banckes, carpenters; Messrs. Poulden and Athey, William Grey, joiners; Wm. Emmett, carver; H. Doogood and John Grove, plasterers.

ST. MARY ABCHURCH, 1681–6; damaged by bombing 1940 and restored by W. Godfrey Allen. Chr. Kempster, mason; John Bridges and John Evans, bricklayers; Thos. Woodstock, carpenter; Thos. Creecher and Wm. Grey, joiners; Grinling Gibbons, carver (of altar-piece);[1] William Emmett, carver (of gallery, etc.); H. Doogood and John Grove, plasterers.

ST. MARY, ALDERMANBURY, 1670–6; repaired by W. Hillier 1777, when windows on north side were partly bricked up; re-roofed 1808–10; repaired by Chas. Tyrrell 1830; tracery inserted in windows and other alterations by Woodthorpe 1864; further alterations 1923; interior destroyed by bombing 1940; church demolished and re-erected at Westminster College, Fulton, Missouri, U.S.A., 1964–5. Joshua Marshall, mason; Matthew Banckes, carpenter; Wm. Cleer, joiner; Thos. Turnly and Richard Kedge, carvers; John Grove, plasterer.

ST. MARY ALDERMARY, BOW LANE, WATLING STREET, completion of Gothic tower, 1702–4.

ST. MARY MAGDALENE, OLD FISH STREET, 1683–5; gutted by fire 1886 and dem. 1887. Edward Strong, mason; Israel Knowles, carpenter; Richard Kedge, joiner; Jonathan Maine, carver; H. Doogood, plasterer.

ST. MARY AT HILL, THAMES STREET, 1670–4; in 1787–8 the tower and west end were rebuilt in brick to the designs of George Gwilt; in 1827–8 the body of the church was repaired and partly rebuilt by James Savage, who in 1848–9 refitted the interior after a fire, employing W. Gibbs Rogers to execute the wood-carving in seventeenth-century style. Joshua Marshall, mason; Thos. Lock, carpenter; Wm. Cleer, joiner; John Grove, plasterer.

ST. MARY SOMERSET, THAMES STREET, 1686–95; dem., except tower, 1871. Chr. Kempster, mason; John Evans, bricklayer; James Groves, carpenter; Chas. Hopson and Wm. Cleer, joiners; H. Doogood, plasterer. The fittings were removed to St. Mary's, Britannia Street, Hoxton, where they were destroyed by bombing in 1940/1.

ST. MARY LE BOW, CHEAPSIDE, 1671–3; steeple completed 1680; the upper part of the steeple was rebuilt by George Gwilt, junior, in 1818–20, when the upper columns were renewed in Aberdeen granite and the terminal feature reduced in height; the church was severely damaged by bombing in 1941, and restored by L. King, 1956–64. Thos. Cartwright, mason (of church); Thos. Cartwright and J. Thompson, masons (of steeple); Antony Tanner, bricklayer; Matthew Banckes, carpenter; Wm. Cleer and T. Whiting, joiners; John Grove and H. Doogood, plasterers.

ST. MATTHEW, FRIDAY STREET, 1681–5; dem. 1881. Edward Pierce, mason; Thos. Horn, bricklayer; John Longland, carpenter; Wm. Cleer and Richard Kedge, joiners; Edward Pierce, carver; H. Doogood and John Grove, plasterers. The altar-piece and door-cases are now in the hall of Polesden Lacey House, Surrey: the font and other furniture are at St. Andrew-by-the-Wardrobe.

ST. MICHAEL, BASSISHAW, 1676–9; dem. 1899. John Fitch and James Flory, masons; Edward Dale, carpenter; John Blinco, Robert Christmas and Francis Ragg, joiners; John Sherwood, plasterer. For the sale of the fittings, see *N. and Q.* 9th ser. v, 1900, 6: the plaster royal arms are now in the Museum of London.

ST. MICHAEL, CORNHILL, Gothic tower begun by Wren's office in 1715–17, but building

[1] For documentary evidence that Grinling Gibbons was the carver of the altar-piece, see R. M. La Porte-Payne, *A Short History of St. Mary Abchurch*, 1946, Appendix IV.

suspended owing to lack of funds, and completed by N. Hawksmoor to his own designs 1718–22.

ST. MICHAEL, CROOKED LANE, 1684–8; tower completed 1698; dem. 1831 to make way for approaches to London Bridge. Wm. Hammond, mason; John Evans, bricklayer; Matthew Banckes and Robert Day, carpenters; Wm. Cleer, John Mitchell and Thos. Creecher, joiners; H. Doogood and John Grove, plasterers. The pulpit, altar-piece, communion railing, and other fittings were offered for sale to the Commissioners for Building New Churches in 1832 (Church Commissioners, File 21744, 41/27 (Part 6)). Their fate is unknown.

ST. MICHAEL, PATERNOSTER ROYAL, COLLEGE HILL, 1686–94; steeple completed 1713; internal repairs by J. Elmes 1820; alterations by Butterfield 1866; damaged by bombing 1944, and restored by E. Davies. Edward Strong, mason; Thos. Denning, carpenter; Wm. Cleer, joiner; H. Doogood, plasterer.

ST. MICHAEL, QUEENHITHE, 1676–87; dem. 1876. James Flory and Sam. Fulkes, masons; Thos. Warren, bricklayer; Matthew Banckes, carpenter; Robert Layton, joiner; Jonathan Maine and William Newman, carvers; H. Doogood and John Grove, plasterers. Some of the fittings, including the pulpit, were removed to St. James, Garlick Hill; the organ is now in Christchurch, Chelsea.

ST. MICHAEL, WOOD STREET, 1670–5; repaired by W. M. Brooks in 1831, when the tower 'was thrown open to the body of the church'; interior altered 1888; dem. 1894. Thos. Wise, mason; Rich. Cobbett, bricklayer; Saml. Lime, carpenter; Gerrard Lens, joiner; Sherwood and Morrice, plasterers. The pulpit is now in St. Mark's, Kennington.

ST MILDRED, BREAD STREET, 1681–7; destroyed by bombing 1941. Edward Strong, mason; Thos. Horn, bricklayer; Israel Knowles, carpenter; Wm. Cleer and Roger Davis, joiners; H. Doogood and John Grove, plasterers.

ST. MILDRED, POULTRY, 1670–6, tower not completed until early eighteenth century, when parish asked for assistance from Fifty New Churches Fund; dem. 1872. Jasper Latham, mason; Morrice Emmett, bricklayer; Thos. Lock, carpenter; Wm. Cleer, joiner; H. Doogood and John Grove, plasterers. Some of the fittings were removed to St. Paul's, Clerkenwell, where they were destroyed by bombing in 1940/1.

ST. NICHOLAS, COLE ABBEY, 1671–7; interior rearranged 1873, but partially restored to its original state 1928–9; gutted by bombing 1941 and restored by Arthur Bailey. Thos. Wise, mason; Henry Blowes, carpenter; Wm. Cleer and Richard Kedge, joiners; John Sherwood and Edw. Martin, plasterers.

ST. OLAVE, OLD JEWRY, 1670–6; dem., except the tower, 1888–9. John Shorthose, mason; Matthew Banckes and Robert Day, carpenters; Thos. Whiting and Valentine Houseman, joiners; Richard Cleere, carver; John Grove, plasterer. The pulpit and font are at the church of St. Olave, Woodberry Down, the other fittings at St. Margaret, Lothbury.

ST. PETER, CORNHILL, 1675–81; internal alterations by J. D. Wyatt 1872. Joshua Marshall and Abraham Story, masons; Thos. Warren, bricklayer; Thos. Woodstock, carpenter; Wm. Cleer, Thomas Poultney and Thomas Athew, joiners; Edward Freeman and Richard Howes, carvers; H. Doogood and John Grove, plasterers.

ST. STEPHEN, COLEMAN STREET, 1674–6; much altered 1771–2, 1822 and 1892; dem. after damage by bombing 1940. Joshua Marshall, mason; Jos. Lemm and Ab. Williams, bricklayers; Robert Horton, carpenter; Wm. Cleer and Thos. Creecher, joiners; Wm. Newman, carver; Robert Horton and Thomas Burton, plasterers.

ST. STEPHEN, WALBROOK, 1672–9; repaired by James Peacock 1803–4; pews removed, octagonal pedestals of columns made square, and mosaic floor inserted by F. C. Penrose 18–; damaged by bombing 1941, restored 1951–4; Thomas Strong and Chr. Kempster, masons; John Longland, carpenter; Roger Davis, Stephen College and Thos. Creecher, joiners; Jonathan Maine and William Newman, carvers; H. Doogood and John Grove, plasterers.

ST. SWITHIN, CANNON STREET, 1677–85; Italianate tracery inserted in windows by E. Woodthorpe 1869; dem. after damage by bombing 1941. Joshua Marshall and Sam. Fulkes, masons; John Longland, carpenter; Wm. Cleer, joiner; Richard Cleere, wood carver; Edward Pierce, carver (of dial); H. Doogood and John Grove, plasterers.

ST. VEDAST, FOSTER LANE, 1695–9; steeple 1710–12; gutted by bombing 1940; restored by S. E. Dykes Bower 1960–3. Edward Strong, sr., mason, John Longland, carpenter, John Smallwell, joiner; Edward Strong, jr., mason of steeple.

WRIGHT, NATHANIEL (–1821) was a builder-architect in the City of London. He was a carpenter by trade and was Master of the Carpenters' Company in 1800. He served as a member of the City Lands Committee in 1778, and held the post of District Surveyor for the Northern District of the City of London from 1782 onwards. As a builder he was active in the development of Finsbury in the 1770s. As an architect he was responsible for the virtual rebuilding of ST. BOTOLPH'S CHURCH, ALDERSGATE, in 1789–91, in a style closely modelled on Dance's All Hallows, London Wall. The east front to Aldersgate Street dates, however, from 1830, when it was executed in Roman cement by Messrs. John Ward & Son, builders, of Jewin Street [Vestry Minutes and accounts in Guildhall Library, MSS. 3863/1–2 and 1455/6]. An ornamental pump in CORNHILL designed by Wright is illustrated in *European Magazine*, May 1800, and in the R.I.B.A. Drawings Collection there is an unexecuted design by him for offices at Wrotham Park, Middlesex.

Wright's will shows that he died possessed of considerable property. He lived for most of his life in Hatton Garden but had a country retreat at Godstone and died in Sloane Street on 24 April 1821. Samuel Acton (*q.v.*) was his nephew and pupil. [Dorothy Stroud, *George Dance*, 1971, 129; *Gent's Mag.* 1821 (i), 476; P.C.C. 309 MANSFIELD.]

WRIGHT, ROBERT (*c.*1661–1736), of Castor in Northamptonshire, was a successful master carpenter who also acted as an architect and became Surveyor to the Dean and Chapter of Peterborough. He was much employed at MILTON HOUSE, NORTHANTS., and is often mentioned in letters to the 1st Earl Fitzwilliam from his steward [Northants, Record Office, F(M) C, 637, 658, 712, etc.]. In 1688 he was reported to be putting the wooden balustrade on the roof of UFFINGTON HOUSE, nr. Stamford, for Charles Bertie, and the steward considered him, though 'very young', to be 'a very prettie ingenious workman and one that understands all things belonging to any building'. He had recently 'been at a seat of Lord Danby's [afterwards 1st Duke of Leeds] near Scarborough in Yorkshire, where hee has drawn his lordship the draught of a fine new house, it is a treble house & in the shell not unlike Thorp house'[1]. At MILTON Wright undertook in 1689 to build the new stable wing. The original design appears to have been made by John Sturges (*q.v.*) but was subsequently modified by someone else (possibly Wright himself), for an anonymous account dated 1692 contains charges for 'drawing of a new draught for the wing building' as well as for 'a draught drawn in prospecttive of the great house with the rest of the building adjacent to it'.[1] Two later drawings by him survive among the Fitzwilliam papers. One (map 1966) is a plan of a large new house for Milton on Palladian lines signed and dated 1723, the other (plan 150) is a 'Draft of a wing for Milton House to be joyned to the great House on the East side of the Great Garden' dated 1725, and shows a plain two-storey range that was not built. He also made an undated 'Draught of the Roof' of MARHOLM CHURCH, NORTHANTS., which is in the same collection (plan 56). In 1719 he made designs for rebuilding a house at THURLBY, nr. BOURNE, LINCS., apparently for a Mr. Denshire. His drawings and estimate for £269 4s. 6d. are among the Ancaster papers in the Lincolnshire Record Office (Ancaster 3/24/8/62).

In 1720 Wright contracted to build Blatherwycke Hall, Northants, for Henry O'Brien to the designs of Thomas Ripley for £3000 [Northants. Record Office, OBB 12]. In the contract he is described as 'timber-merchant', and in 1715 he had bought all the timber in Blatherwycke and Bulwick woods for £7420 [Northants. Record Office, XYZ 1247]. In 1726 he was one of the contractors who undertook to make the R. Nene navigable under an Act of 11 George I, cap. xix. The work had been completed up to Oundle by 1730 [*Nene Valley Drainage & Navigation, Statement of Facts*, London 1891, 4]. In 1734, as surveyor to the Dean and Chapter of Peterborough, Wright was directed to make a general survey of the fabric of the cathedral and other buildings [Peterborough Chapter Act Book 1704–1814, f. 83d].

Wright died at Castor on 6 December 1736, aged 75, and is commemorated by a monument at the west end of the church that describes him as 'a Person that with an Honest Industry Purchased a Plentifull Fortune with a Fair Character'. His will is P.C.C. 284 DERBY.

WRIGHT, ROBERT (–1839), practised in Edinburgh, where he designed, *inter alia*, Nos. 39–43 CASTLE STREET, 1793, MORNINGSIDE PLACE, 1823–4, villas in PILRIG STREET, 1824, and ST. BERNARD'S CHURCH SCHOOL, 1826 [J. Gifford, C. McWilliam & D. Walker, *Edinburgh*, Buildings of Scotland,

[1] This house was not built, and its intended site is uncertain. Lord Danby (formerly Sir Thomas Osborne) had land in several parts of Yorkshire. In 1673 he was described as 'of Wickmore' in the parish of Brafferton in the North Riding.

[1] Milton House plan 19 is a perspective of the new stables which may be by Wright. The building is illustrated in *C. Life*, 18 May 1961, where it is wrongly attributed to William Talman.

1984, 292, 351, 409, 622 and *Edinburgh Evening Courant*, 4 Sept. 1824]. He was presumably the 'Mr. Wright' who designed NETHERBYRES, BERWICKSHIRE, for Sir Samuel Brown in a picturesque gabled style in 1836 [payments for 'Drawing Plan for and supervising building of Mansion House' in S.R.O., GD 416/53/2]. He died on 28 September 1839, leaving a son, Robert Wright, who continued his practice [S.R.O., SC 70/1/60, p. 486].

WRIGHT, SAMUEL, 'Architect, Surveyor and Auctioneer' of Kidderminster, was probably the surveyor of the same name previously in practice in Knutsford. Drawings signed by him show that in 1798–9 he was responsible for alterations to SHAKENHURST, BAYTON, WORCS., where he designed the centre and the S. bow to match the existing N. bow [drawings at Shakenhurst].

WRIGHT, STEPHEN (–1780), entered the employment of the Office of Works in December 1746, when he became Clerk of the Works at Hampton Court. He appears to have been a clerk or assistant of William Kent, for the latter's will, dated 1748, contains a clause bequeathing 'unto Stephen Wright fifty pounds, and unto my servant who shall be living with me at the time of my decease ten pounds'. He is probably the 'Stephen' referred to in letters written by Kent to Lord Burlington in 1738–9 [*Arch. Rev.* lxiii, 1928, 180], and in 1749 he had in his possession a number of Kent's designs for public buildings which he offered to the Board of Works for £80. At what date he became a protégé of the Duke of Newcastle is uncertain, but there is abundant evidence that he enjoyed the Duke's patronage. When Thomas Ripley, the Comptroller of the Works, was reported to be dying in 1758, Wright at once wrote to Newcastle to beg for his post. Ripley's successor was Henry Flitcroft, but it was by Newcastle's 'immediate appointment' that Wright was preferred to the posts of Master Mason and Deputy Surveyor vacated by the new Comptroller. When Flitcroft fell ill in his turn in 1766, Wright again solicited the Duke's favour on his behalf, though on this occasion his application was premature, as Flitcroft lived until 1769 and Wright remained Master Mason for the remainder of his life. Newcastle employed Wright as his architect at Claremont, and in 1754 when, as Chancellor of Cambridge University, he gave £500 towards building a new front to the University Library, it was Wright's design which he forced on the unwilling Syndics.

Wright was, as might he expected from his association with Kent, essentially a Palladian architect, and his University Library façade at Cambridge is a most elegant composition in that style. His work at Milton Hall shows that, like Kent, he could also make attractive Gothic designs if called upon to do so – in this case by a Catholic client apparently anxious to emphasize the medieval associations of his religion.

Wright died on 28 September 1780, after 'a lingering tho' not very painful illness', and was buried in the churchyard at Hampton in Middlesex. [*A.P.S.D.*; *History of the King's Works* v, 89–90, 424 n.; P.C.C. 498 COLLINS.]

LONDON, No. 22 ARLINGTON STREET, completed house for the Hon. Henry Pelham after William Kent's death in 1748 [R.I.B.A. Library, MS. 'Expences relating to Building in Arlington Street'].

SUNBURY CHURCH, MIDDLESEX, 1751–2; remodelled in neo-Byzantine style by S. S. Teulon 1856 [a contemporary entry in the Parish Register records that 'The Designer and Surveyor was Mr. Wright of the Board of Works at Hampton Court; and the Builder Richard Jupp, City Builder'].

THE WHITE LODGE, RICHMOND NEW PARK, repairs and redecoration for Princess Amelia, 1751–2; addition of wings for Princess Amelia, before 1761 [*Vitruvius Britannicus* iv, 1767, pls. 1–4; *History of the King's Works* v, 232].

CLAREMONT HOUSE, SURREY, work for 1st Duke of Newcastle, 1752; dem. [MS. account-book of William Farmer, a plumber, among the parish records of Kingston-on-Thames, shows that his work at Claremont in this year was valued by 'Mr. Wright of Hampton Court'].

OATLANDS, SURREY, works for the Earl of Lincoln (afterwards 2nd Duke of Newcastle) 1750s onwards, chiefly garden buildings, including the grotto built 1765–7 and dem. 1948 [accounts in Nottingham University Library, Newcastle papers; T. Knox on the grotto in *Georgian Group Jnl.* 1992].

CAMBRIDGE, THE UNIVERSITY LIBRARY, 1754–8 [Willis & Clark, iii, 63–8; original drawing illustrated in *Builder*, 28 Sept. 1907] (R.C.H.M., *Cambridge*, pl. 71 and plan, p. 13).

ASHBURNHAM PLACE, SUSSEX, measured work for 2nd Earl of Ashburnham, and may have been concerned in design of new front, 1760–1; remodelled 1813–17; refaced 1853; dem. 1959 [C. Hussey in *C. Life*, 23 April 1953].

MILTON HALL, nr. STEVENTON, BERKS., Gothic chapel and library for Bryant Barrett,

1764–72 [Arthur Oswald in *C. Life*, 24 Dec. 1948].

CLUMBER HOUSE, NOTTS., for 2nd Duke of Newcastle, *c.*1768–78; centre rebuilt after a fire in 1879; dem. 1938. Wright also designed the bridge over the lake and various buildings on the estate [accounts in Nottingham University Library, Newcastle papers; Watts, *Seats of the Nobility & Gentry*, pl. xxix, 1781; original drawing for south front illustrated in Sotheby's Catalogue, 10 Dec. 1968, lot 101] (*C. Life*, 12–19 Sept. 1908; survey plans in R.I.B.A.D.).

NEWARK BRIDGE, NOTTS. (R. Trent), for 2nd Duke of Newcastle, 1775; footpaths added 1848 [accounts in Nottingham University Library, Newcastle papers].

NOTTINGHAM, THE BLACKAMOOR'S HEAD INN, enlarged for 2nd Duke of Newcastle, 1775 [*ibid.*].

BUSHEY VILLA, TEDDINGTON, MIDDLESEX (dem), is stated by W. Keane, *Beauties of Middlesex*, 1850, 103, to have been designed 'by Wright'.

WRIGHT, THOMAS (1711–1786), astronomer, landscape-gardener and architect, was born at Byers Green, nr. Bishop Auckland in Durham, where his father was a carpenter. By the age of 14 he was, in his own words, 'much in love with Mathematicks' and 'very much given to the Amusements of Drawing, Planning of Maps and Buildings'. After four unhappy years as a clockmaker's apprentice, he tried without much success to make a living by teaching mathematics and publishing almanacs. The Earl of Scarbrough's patronage eventually enabled him to gain some reputation as a writer on astronomy. In 1737 he published *Universal Vicissitudes of the Seasons*, in 1740 *The Use of the Globes* (commissioned by John Senex), in 1742 *Clavis Coelestis*, and in 1750 his best-known book, *An Original Theory or New Hypothesis of the Universe*, an ingeniously speculative work of little real scientific value. A visit to Ireland in 1746–7 resulted in *Louthiana, or an Introduction to the Antiquities of Ireland*, 1748. This was a pioneer work on its subject, and a product of the antiquarian interests which Wright pursued alongside astronomy.

As an architect and landscape-gardener Wright owed his commissions largely to a small circle of aristocratic friends and patrons, which included the Dukes of Beaufort, Kent and Portland, Viscount Midleton, the Earl of Essex, Lord Limerick, and the Ansons of Shugborough. Among the grounds which he embellished were those at Badminton, Beckett Park (Berks.), Culford, Oatlands, Stoke Gifford, Shugborough, Wallington and Wrest. In 1755 and 1758 he published two volumes of engravings entitled *Six Original Designs of Arbours* and *Six Original Designs of Grottos*. These were the first and only instalments of a projected *Universal Architecture*. They are notable both for the elegance of the engravings and for showing the buildings (for the first time in a work of this kind) in a natural setting. Many of Wright's executed works were mock castles, Gothick arbours, grottos and suchlike follies, often designed to be built of rustic materials such as rubble stonework, rough timber and thatch, and covered with honeysuckle, ivy and moss. His larger classical buildings were basically Palladian, but for their decoration he favoured a rococo style which found expression in elaborately decorated interiors and in projecting bows and other deviations from the correct Palladian canon. Nuthall Temple, his most important architectural work, was a much enlarged and elaborated version of Scamozzi's Rocca Pisana.

In 1762 Wright retired to Byers Green, where he built himself a small villa and decorated its interior with elaborate sequences of prints illustrating the faculties of human knowledge, human passions, etc. On a neighbouring hill he began the erection of an observatory in the form of a round tower, but died in 1786 before it was finished. In 1793 the *Gentleman's Magazine* published a memoir of Wright illustrated by an engraved portrait and the researches of Dr. Eileen Harris have been summarized in three articles in *Country Life*, 26 August, 2 and 9 Sept. 1971, and in her edition of his *Arbours and Grottos*, Scolar Press 1979. Wright's journal is B.L., Add. MS. 15627. Two sketch-books are known, one in the Victoria and Albert Museum, the other in the Avery Library at Columbia University. For the latter see Michael McCarthy in *Journal of Garden History* i, 1981. An unpublished design for a Gothic building on the Wentworth estate in Yorkshire is in Sheffield Archives, WWM, MP 93.

Unless otherwise stated, the following list of Wright's executed architectural works is based on Harris, 1979, where further unexecuted and attributed works are discussed. The temple at Blickling there illustrated was only sketched by Wright, not designed by him.

BEAUMONT LODGE, OLD WINDSOR, BERKS., design, probably not executed, for a new house for the Dowager Duchess of Kent, 1743.

SHUGBOROUGH, STAFFS., THE SHEPHERD'S

MONUMENT for Thomas Anson, and *attributed*, other garden buildings and the addition of single-storey wings to the house, 1748.

STOKE GIFFORD, GLOS., remodelled exterior for Norborne Berkeley, cr. Lord Botetort, 1749–53 and 1760–4 [T. Mowl in *Georgian Group Jnl.* 1992].

BADMINTON HOUSE, GLOS., picturesque buildings in the park for 4th Duke of Beaufort, including the Ragged Castle, Castle Barn, Root House and thatched cottages, *c.*1750–6.

attributed: BERKELEY CASTLE, DR. JENNER'S HUT for 4th Earl of Berkeley, *c.*1750/5.

NUTHALL TEMPLE, NOTTS., for Sir Charles Sedley, Bart., 1754–7; interior of hall stuccoed by Thomas Roberts of Oxford to his own designs, 1765 [Bucks. C.R.O., D/LE/11/2]; interior decoration by James Wyatt (*q.v.*); dem. 1929 [*Vitruvius Britannicus* iv, 1767, pls. 56–7] (*C. Life*, 28 April, 5 May 1923).

BYERS GREEN, nr. BISHOP AUCKLAND, CO. DURHAM, house for himself, 1756–7; dem. (description by Wright in *Gent's Mag.* 1793 (i), 213–16).

attributed: WORKSOP MANOR, NOTTS., Gothic farm for Mary, Duchess of Norfolk, 1757.

HORTON HOUSE, NORTHANTS., remodelled S. front for 2nd Earl of Halifax (d. 1772), *c.*1760; dem. 1936; and *attributed*: THE MENAGERIE.

attributed: HAMPTON COURT HOUSE, MIDDLESEX, the grotto for 2nd Earl of Halifax, *c.*1765 [Eileen Harris in *C. Life*, 5 Aug. 1982].

CODGER FORT (a folly), ROTHLEY, NORTHUMBERLAND, for Sir Walter Blackett of Wallington, *c.*1769.

attributed: BISHOP AUCKLAND CASTLE, CO. DURHAM, completion of S. range for Bishop John Egerton, *c.*1771, Gothic.

WESTERTON HILL, nr. BISHOP AUCKLAND, CO. DURHAM, Observatory for himself, *c.*1785, unfinished.

IRELAND, small house at TULLYMORE, CO. DOWN, for 3rd Earl of Clanbrassill *c.*1751; probably designed garden buildings for same at DUNDALK, 1746–7. At BELVEDERE HOUSE, CO. WESTMEATH, there is a folly derived from one of Wright's engraved designs for grottos.

WRIGHT, THOMAS (–1843), practised in Salford (Manchester). In 1818 he won the competition for the BLACKFRIARS BRIDGE over the R. Irwell at MANCHESTER, completed in 1820 [Thomas Rickman's diary, 13 May 1818], and so called because it followed the design of Robert Mylne's Blackfriars Bridge in London. He was the architect of the COUNTY GAOL at KIRKDALE, nr. LIVERPOOL, designed on a polygonal plan and built in 1821–2 [J. A. Picton, *Memorials of Liverpool* ii, 1875, 409; *Lancashire Illustrated in a Series of Views by R. Wallis*, 1829, 54–5]. He also designed the classical church of CHRIST CHURCH, SALFORD, 1830–1; steeple added by E. H. Shellard 1846; dem. 1958 [*Manchester Herald*, 6 May 1830]. He died on 6 July 1843 [will in Lancs. C.R.O.]. His unexecuted designs for a Sessions House at Preston (1824) are in the Lancashire C.R.O.

WRIGHTE, WILLIAM, 'Architect', was the author of *Grotesque Architecture or Rural Amusement, consisting of Plans, Elevations and Sections for Huts, Retreats, Summer and Winter Hermitages, Terminaries, Chinese, Gothic and Natural Grottos, Cascades, Mosques, Moresque Pavilions, Grotesque and Rustic Seats, Greenhouses, etc., many of which may be executed with Flints, Irregular Stones, Rude Branches and Roots of Trees*, 1767, 2nd ed. 1790, 3rd 1802, 4th 1815. This was a successful pattern-book, but nothing whatever is known about its author.

WYATT, BENJAMIN (1709–1772), was the founder of the Wyatt building business in Staffordshire, and the father of Samuel and James Wyatt (*qq.v.*). His family had long been yeoman farmers in the parish of Weeford, nr. Lichfield. He was one of the eight sons of John Wyatt of Thickbroom in that parish. His elder brother John (1700–66) was a master carpenter who submitted a design for rebuilding Westminster Bridge in 1737, but was best known as an inventor of spinning machinery. Another brother, Job, patented a machine for making screws, while a third, William, became agent to the Paget family at Beaudesert. Benjamin himself was a farmer and timber merchant who developed a successful business as a builder and architect. He was assisted by several of his seven sons, especially the eldest, William, who appears to have designed most of the buildings erected by 'Benjamin Wyatt and Sons' in the 1750s and 1760s.

The building which is said to have 'first brought Benjamin Wyatt and his family into repute' as architects and builders was SWINFEN HALL, STAFFS., built for Samuel Swynfen in 1755–8 in an old-fashioned baroque style reminiscent of Francis Smith [S. Shaw, *History of Staffordshire* ii, 1801, 30*, confirmed by building accounts in Staffs. C.R.O., D(W) 1738/E/1–7]. In 1758–61 Benjamin and his sons rebuilt EGGINTON HALL, DERBYSHIRE (subsequently altered, and dem. 1955), for Sir John Every, Bart., either to their own designs

THE WYATT FAMILY

showing the relationship of the principal members engaged in architecture and the allied trades

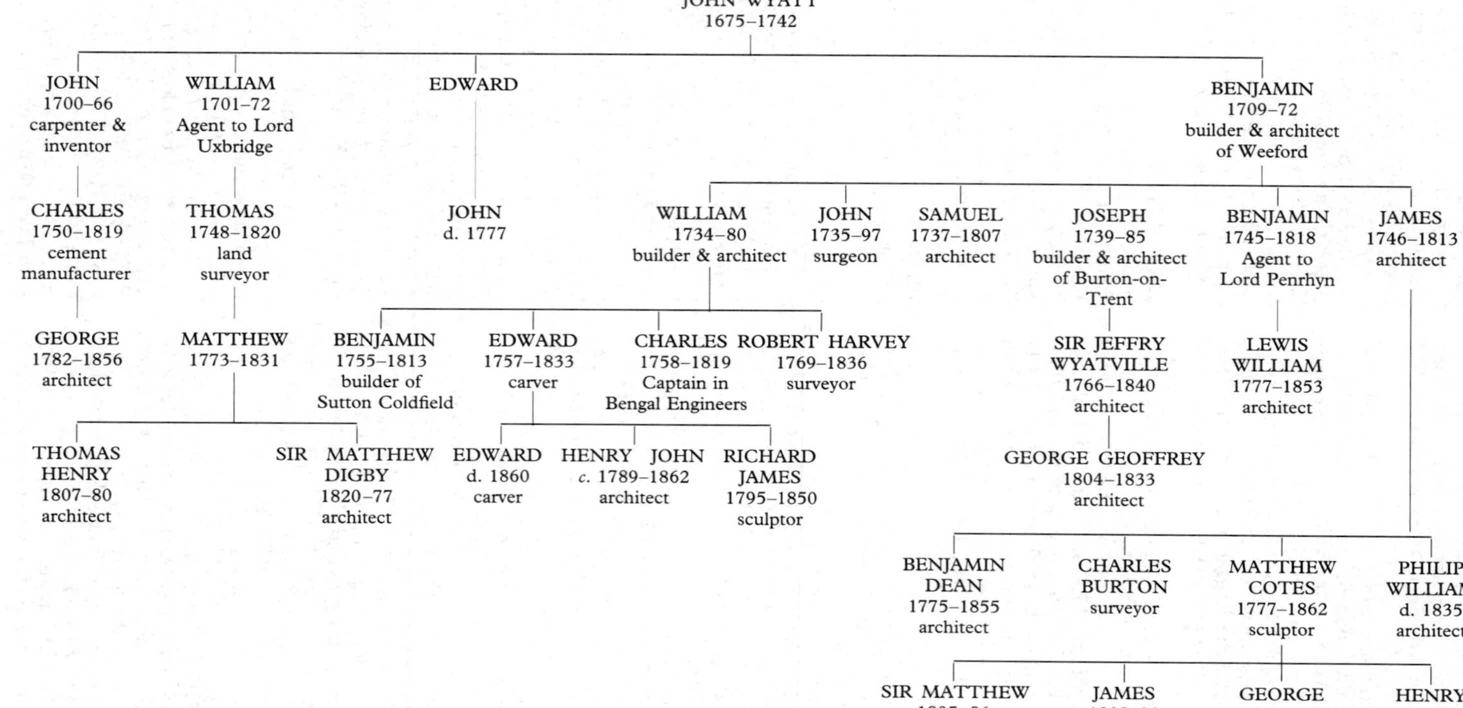

or to designs made a few years earlier by William Baker (*q.v.*) [Edward Saunders, 'Egginton Hall', *Derbyshire Life*, March 1974, 66]. One of their most important works was the construction of the SOHO MANUFACTORY at BIRMINGHAM (1765–6) for Matthew Boulton, who also employed them to complete his house at Soho, and did much to assist the younger members of the family in their subsequent careers. It was through Boulton that in 1766 William Wyatt began to make designs for the newly established GENERAL INFIRMARY at STAFFORD, which was built by the firm in 1769–72. William's 'plain and useful design' is represented in an engraving signed 'Benjamin Wyatt & Sons. Archit.' [B.L., *King's Maps* xxxviii, 46a]. In 1768–70 LEICESTER INFIRMARY was built by William Henderson (*q.v.*) under the direction of Benjamin Wyatt [see p. 488]. For the 9th Lord Paget (afterwards 1st Earl of Uxbridge) the Wyatts in 1770–2 built BURTON-ON-TRENT TOWN HALL, dem. 1883 (illustration in C. H. Underhill, *History of Burton on Trent*, 1941, 68), and in 1771–2 remodelled the interior of BEAUDESERT, STAFFS., dem. *c.*1935 [accounts in Staffs. Record Office, D(W) 1738, etc.]. For the design of the last work, which was partly in the Gothic style, the young James Wyatt was responsible, and his help may also explain the neo-classical influence apparent in the town hall at Burton.

Benjamin Wyatt died at Blackbrook Farm, Weeford, in July 1772. By his wife Mary Wright he had seven sons. William, the eldest, succeeded to his business, but died in 1780; John practised as a surgeon in London; Samuel, Joseph, Benjamin and James are all noticed separately below; Charles, the youngest, died in infancy.

[*A.P.S.D.*; *John Wyatt, Master Carpenter and Inventor*, 1885 (published anonymously, but by Laurence Jacob); *Weeford Parish Register* (Staffs. Parish Record Soc. 1955); D. Linstrum, *The Wyatt Family*, R.I.B.A. Drawings Catalogue, 1973, 7–8; J. M. Robinson, *The Wyatts*, 1979, chap. I.]

WYATT, BENJAMIN (1745–1818), the fifth son of Benjamin Wyatt of Weeford, was born on 14 January 1744/5. According to the inscription on his monument, he was 'for upwards of thirty years Chief Agent to the Penrhyn Estates' in North Wales. The first Lord Penrhyn was an enterprising landowner who made a fortune out of the Penrhyn slate quarries. Wyatt was concerned in several of his projects, including the building of Port Penrhyn and the construction of the railway from the quarries to the port. He was also responsible for a good deal of architectural work on the estate. An obituary in the *North Wales Gazette* mentions as 'monuments of his well-cultivated taste' the MARINE BATHS at PENRHYN, a villa for Lord Penrhyn at OGWEN BANK, and 'the characteristic order and embellishments of the Dairy Farm at Penanisarnant'. At BANGOR he designed a building for the CAERNARVONSHIRE AND ANGLESEY DISPENSARY (1809–10), now a private house, and the PENRHYN ARMS HOTEL, later the first home of the University College, but now demolished. Elsewhere he designed an inn at CAPEL CURIG and carried out alterations to ST. MARY'S CHAPEL, CAERNARVON, 1810–14.

Benjamin Wyatt lived at Lime Grove, nr. Bangor, in a house designed for him by his brother Samuel. He died on 5 January 1818, aged 73, and was buried in Llandegai Churchyard beneath a pyramid of slate. He left five sons, among whom were Lewis William (1777–1853), architect (*q.v.*), and James (1795–1882), of Bryngwynant, Beddgelert, who succeeded him as agent to Lord Penrhyn.

[*Gent's Mag.* 1818 (i), 89; L. W. Wyatt, *A Collection of Architectural Designs . . . executed upon the Estates of Lord Penrhyn*, 1800–1; W. Bingley, *North Wales*, 2nd ed. 1814, 106, 112, 293; *Cambria Depicta*, 1816, 111; P. B. Williams, *Tourist's Guide through the County of Caernarvon*, 1821, 32–8; R. Fenton, *Tours in Wales*, 1917, 237–40; *Trans. Caernarvonshire Hist. Soc.* xi, 1950, 61; will (P.C.C. 102 CRESSWELL); information from Prof. M. L. Clarke.]

WYATT, BENJAMIN (1755–1813), was the second son of John Wyatt (d. 1777) and a second cousin of Samuel and James Wyatt. He established himself at Sutton Coldfield in Warwickshire, where he died on 29 November 1813, aged 59. Although sometimes described as an architect in contemporary documents, he was mainly a builder, who appears generally to have relied on his architect relations for designs. Thus in 1803–5 he was obtaining drawing from Lewis Wyatt (then in James Wyatt's office) for alterations at Patshull House and for a house that he was building for Sir Charles Clarke at Wigginton, nr. Tamworth. It was he who rebuilt Weeford Church to James Wyatt's designs in 1803–4. In 1810 he was called in by the trustees for building CHRIST CHURCH, BIRMINGHAM, to complete that church after they became dissatisfied with its original architects, Charles Norton (*q.v.*) and William Whitmore.

[*Gent's Mag.* 1795 (ii), 877, 1814 (i), 304; Birmingham Probate Registry, Register of

Administrations, 25 Feb. 1814; William Salt Library, Stafford, M96.]

WYATT, BENJAMIN DEAN (1775–1855), the eldest son of James Wyatt, was born in London and educated at Westminster School. He matriculated at Christ Church, Oxford, in April 1795, but got into debt and went down in 1797 without taking a degree. In 1797 he went out to India to take up a secretarial appointment in the office of the East India Company at Calcutta, but finding his duties both more onerous and less remunerative than he had expected, resigned his post (18 Feb. 1802) and returned to England. In Calcutta he had worked for a time in the office of the Governor-General, Lord Wellesley, and it was this contact with the Wellesley family that led in 1807 to his appointment as secretary to Wellesley's younger brother Arthur, when the latter went to Dublin as Chief Secretary of Ireland in 1807. Two years later Wyatt returned to London and soon after began to practise as an architect from 22 Foley Place.

Although it was apparently not until 1809 that Wyatt decided to take up architecture as a career, he pursued it with such success that in 1811 he won the competition for rebuilding Drury Lane Theatre. When Joseph Farington asked Jeffry Wyatville 'how Benjamin Wyatt had acquired sufficient knowledge of Architecture to qualify him for such an undertaking', he was told that, after spending a period in his father's office, Benjamin 'had devoted his attention particularly to the study of a Theatre', and that, contrary to the general belief, he had received no assistance from his father: 'on the contrary, Wyatt was much displeased with Benjamin for offering a design as his younger brother Philip Wyatt had [also competed] for it', and had refused to have anything more to do with him when he won the commission. In 1811 Benjamin Wyatt published *Observations on the Principles of the Design for the Theatre now building in Drury Lane*, reissued in 1813 as *Observations on the Design for the Theatre Royal, Drury Lane, as executed in the year 1812*. The second edition was intended to refute 'a most unfounded and scandalous insinuation which appeared . . . in one of the weekly newspapers', that 'the design of the theatre was not his own, but had been copied without acknowledgement from one made by his cousin George Wyatt' (*q.v.*). Wyatt also exhibited a model of a 'superior design' at his house (Ackermann, *Repository of Arts* viii, 1812, 387).

In 1813 Benjamin Wyatt succeeded his father as Surveyor of Westminster Abbey, and for some years he enjoyed a successful London practice. In 1815–16 he made designs for a vast palace for Arthur Wellesley, now victor of Waterloo and Duke of Wellington. Conceived as a neo-classical Blenheim, this was never built, for the Duke decided to live at Stratfield Saye instead. The numerous surviving drawings show a grand but somewhat arid exterior of a familiar Wyatt type, but (as at Covent Garden) the interiors were to be handsomely decorated in a rich neo-classical style. It is the interiors rather than the exteriors of Wyatt's later buildings that are of most interest and merit, for at Crockford's Club and the three great London houses which he designed in collaboration with his brother Philip he achieved strikingly effective recreations of the French rococo style of the period of Louis XIV. Although Wyatt had visited France in 1815, the means by which he achieved this mastery of an intricate foreign style are by no means clear. All the drawings were, however, made in his office either by himself or his brother and their assistants (all of whom appear to have been of English nationality), and Wyatt's correspondence with the Duke of Sutherland shows that he was fully conversant with the techniques involved in fashioning *boiseries* and gilded stucco ornamentation in the French manner.

Wyatt's last important commission was the Duke of York's Column (1831–4). In 1827 he had resigned the surveyorship of Westminster Abbey, and in 1833 he was declared bankrupt. He died in Camden Town in 1855, leaving all his worldly goods to his 'good and faithful servant' Martha Turner. A portrait by S. Drummond, A.R.A., was engraved for the *European Magazine* of October 1812. W. G. Colman, A. D. Gough, John Harper, J. D. Paine and R. L. Roumieu were his pupils or assistants. Several of his drawings are in the R.I.B.A. Collection.

[*A.P.S.D.*; *London Gazette*, 1833 (i), 1032 (bankruptcy); P.R.O., P.C.C. 1855 register, f. 882 (will); Register of Births & Deaths, St. Pancras, June Quarter 1855 (death); Farington's Diary, 16 Oct. 1806, 9 July 1811, 2 Nov. 1812; G. F. R. Baker & A. H. Stenning, *The Record of Old Westminsters* ii, 1928, 1028; R. Stanley-Morgan, 'Benjamin Wyatt and his Noble Clients', *Arch. Rev.* cxlv, Feb. 1969; D. Linstrum, *The Wyatt Family*, R.I.B.A. Drawings Catalogue, 1973; D. Linstrum, 'The Waterloo Palace', *Arch. Rev.* clv, April 1974; J. M. Robinson, *The Wyatts*, 1979, 234–5; Canadian Centre for Architecture, *Architecture and its Image*, Montreal 1989, 171–2 (for the Waterloo palace).]

LONDON, THE THEATRE ROYAL., DRURY LANE, 1811–12; auditorium reconstructed by S. Beazley 1822, portico added 1831 [Britton

& Pugin, *Public Buildings of London* i, 1825, 227–61; *Gent's Mag.* 1811 (ii), 478; *European Mag.*, Oct. 1812, 260–4; *Builder* xiii, 1855, 437, 470; R. Carter, 'The Drury Lane Theatres of Henry Holland and B. D. Wyatt', *Jnl. Society of Architectural Historians* [of America] xxvi, 1967; Marcus Binney, 'The Theatre Royal, Drury Lane', *C. Life*, 10 Dec. 1970].

WESTMINSTER ABBEY, continued restoration of Henry VII's Chapel, 1813–22; restoration of rose window of S. transept, 1814; rearrangement of choir, etc., 1822–3 [J. P. Neale & E. W. Brayley, *Westminster Abbey* ii, 1823, 15, 270–1; J. M. Robinson, *op. cit.*].

WESTMINSTER SCHOOL, rebuilt exterior of Old School in stock brick, 1814 [L. E. Tanner, *Westminster School*, 1923, 37, 116].

DEVIZES, WILTS., THE MARKET CROSS, for 1st Viscount Sidmouth, 1814, Gothic [J. Waylen, *Chronicles of the Devizes*, 1839, 316].

MARESFIELD PARK, SUSSEX, remodelled for Sir John Shelley, Bart., 1816, Jacobean style; dem. after fire in 1921 [*The Diary of Frances Lady Shelley*, ed. R. Edgcumbe, ii, 1913, 67; T. W. Horsfield, *History of Sussex* i, 1835, 375–6].

WESTPORT, CO. MAYO, IRELAND, added wing containing library and gallery for 2nd Marquess of Sligo, 1819; destroyed by fire 1826 [drawings at Westport;[1] Mark Girouard in *C. Life*, 6 May 1965].

BELVOIR CASTLE, LEICS., interior decoration of principal rooms and Romanesque Mausoleum in grounds, for 5th Duke of Rutland, in collaboration with M. C. Wyatt, *c.*1820–30 [T. F. Dibdin, *Northern Tour* i, 1838, 73; I. Eller, *History of Belvoir Castle*, 1841, 349–53; C. Hussey in *C. Life*, 6, 13, 20, 27 Dec. 1956; C. Hussey, *English Country Houses: Late Georgian*, 1958, 122–39].

LONDON, YORK (afterwards STAFFORD, now LANCASTER) HOUSE, ST. JAMES'S, for Frederick Augustus, Duke of York, in collaboration with Philip Wyatt, 1825–7. This mansion was begun by R. Smirke in 1820, but he was dismissed in 1825, when the building was up to ground level, and fresh designs were made by Wyatt and put into execution. On the Duke's death in 1827 the incomplete shell was bought by the 2nd Marquess of Stafford (cr. Duke of Sutherland in 1833), whose son, on succeeding as 2nd Duke in 1833, added an attic storey and completed the interior. Wyatt made the designs for the latter, but the Duke and his agent evidently mistrusted him, for they insisted on employing Smirke as executant architect. The house was more or less complete by 1838, when Wyatt and the Duke fell out, and Charles Barry was employed to redesign the lantern and to decorate the staircase. [H. M. Colvin, 'The Architects of Stafford House', *Archi. Hist.* i, 1958; John Cornforth, 'Stafford House Revisited', *C. Life*, 7–14 Nov. 1968.]

LONDON, LONDONDERRY (formerly HOLDERNESSE) HOUSE, PARK LANE, reconstructed for 3rd Marquess of Londonderry, in collaboration with Philip Wyatt, 1825–8; dem. 1964 [*A.P.S.D.*; Arthur Oswald in *C. Life*, 10 July 1937].

LONDON, CROCKFORD'S CLUBHOUSE, Nos. 50–53 ST. JAMES'S STREET, in collaboration with Philip Wyatt, 1827; altered internally 1849 and refaced 1870–5 [J. Elmes, *Metropolitan Improvements*, 1831, 140–1].

LONDON, THE ORIENTAL CLUB, No. 18 HANOVER SQUARE, in collaboration with Philip Wyatt, 1827–8; enlarged by D. Burton 1852–4; dem. 1962 [*A.P.S.D.*; *A New Survey of London*, John Weale 1853, i, 304–5, with plan].

LONDON, APSLEY HOUSE, PICCADILLY, remodelled for 1st Duke of Wellington, in collaboration with Philip Wyatt, 1828–9 [*A.P.S.D.*]. Wyatt cased the house in Bath stone, added the Corinthian portico, and constructed the gallery in which the Waterloo Banquests were held until 1852.

LONDON, SPRING GARDENS, proposed alterations to basement of house for Lord Dover, 1831; dem. [P.R.O., MPE 839].

LONDON, CARLTON HOUSE TERRACE, interior of house (No. 6) for Marquess of Tavistock, 1831; remodelled 1889–90 [*A.P.S.D.*].

LONDON, THE DUKE OF YORK'S COLUMN, CARLTON GARDENS, 1831–4 [*Architectural Mag.* i, 1834, 192–201].

STRATFIELD SAYE, HANTS., alterations, including porch and conservatory, for 1st Duke of Wellington, 1838–40 [J. M. Robinson, *op. cit.*] (*C. Life*, 10 April 1975).

WYATT, CHARLES (1750–1819), of Bedford Row, London, was a son of John Wyatt (1700–66), the inventor, by his second wife Marabella. He was one of the original partners in the firm of Parker & Wyatt, manufacturers of the composition known at first as Parker's, sometimes as Wyatt's, and often as 'Roman' cement. It was patented in 1796 by James Parker of Northfleet, who obtained the raw material for its manufacture in the neighbourhood of the Isle of Sheppey. It had the

[1] These include an unexecuted design for a theatre at Westport by B. D. Wyatt, dated 1812 (illustrated by John Harris, 'The Wyatts at Westport', *Connoisseur* clxii, 1966, 224–7).

property of hardening under water and was extensively used in hydraulic works. It was also used as a stucco. After Charles Wyatt's death on 11 June 1819, in his 69th year, the manufacture was continued first by his son James (1779–1854) and then by the latter's cousin Walter Henry Wyatt (1781–1849). When he died the firm came to an end. A *Catalogue of Statues, Furniture, Vases, etc.* was published by 'Wyatt, Parker & Co.' in 1841. [*Gent's Mag.* 1819 (i), 589; G. R. Clarke, *History and Description of Ipswich*, 1830, 393; *A.P.S.D.*, *s.v.* 'Parker's Cement', 'Roman Cement' and 'Wyatt's Cement'.]

WYATT, CHARLES (1758–1819), was the son of James Wyatt's eldest brother William. He obtained a commission in the Bengal Engineers, and rose to the rank of Captain. From 1798 onwards he was employed by the Marquess Wellesley, Governor-General of India, to carry out various public works in Calcutta, and in that year it was his designs for the palatial Government House (1799–1804) that were preferred to those submitted by Edward Tiretta, architect to the East India Company. Wyatt's plans were based on James Paine's designs for Kedleston Hall, but with neo-classical detailing and other alterations which give the building a late rather than mid-Georgian character. Having made a modest fortune in India, Wyatt returned to England in 1804 and became M.P. for Sudbury, which he represented in two successive parliaments. After James Wyatt's death in 1813 Charles took over his house in Foley Place, where he died on 13 March 1819, aged 60. [S. Nilsson, *European Architecture in India 1750–1850*, 1968, 101–9, 110; *Gent's Mag.* 1819 (i), 377; correspondence in *C. Life*, 7 Jan. 1949, 1 Nov. 1956; will, P.C.C. ELLENBOROUGH, 2 April 1819; R. G. Thorne, *The House of Commons 1790–1820*. v, 1986, 657.]

WYATT, GEORGE (–1790), may have been a member of the Wyatt family whose pedigree is set out on page 1102, but his parentage has not so far been ascertained. The statement in the *Gentleman's Magazine* for 1790 that he was a brother of James Wyatt cannot be substantiated. He was a very successful builder in London, was Surveyor of Paving in the City in the 1770s, and for several years a Common Councillor for the ward of Farringdon Without. He was one of the proprietors of the Albion Mills built by Samuel Wyatt, and lived in the adjoining Albion Place. His niece, Elizabeth Smith, was the wife of Sir John Soane, and it was to the Soanes that Wyatt left all his considerable real property when he died on 23 February 1790. His business was carried on by Thomas Shepherd, his clerk, who died in 1792. [*Gent's Mag.* 1790 (i), 186, 1792 (i), 286; P.C.C. 111 BISHOP.]

WYATT, GEORGE (1782–1856), was the son of Charles Wyatt (d. 1819), the cement manufacturer. He became a pupil of James Wyatt, from whose office he exhibited student's work at the Royal Academy in 1798, 1799 and 1800. He subsequently practised as an architect, at first from Albany, Piccadilly,[1] and later from his father's house in Bedford Row. In 1812 he published *A Compendious Description of a Design for . . . erecting a Third Theatre in the Metropolis.* It was afterwards alleged in the press that Benjamin Dean Wyatt's plans for Drury Lane Theatre were based on these designs of George Wyatt's, an insinuation which Benjamin was at pains to deny in print (above, p. 1104). The list of buildings given below shows that George Wyatt was a competent designer in both neo-classical and Gothic styles, but he appears to have given up practice early to live in retirement on the profits of the family cement-works.

CULFORD HALL, SUFFOLK, curved Doric portico on entrance front for 2nd Marquess Cornwallis, 1806–8; since removed [signed drawing dated 1806 belonging to Lord Cadogan, *ex inf.* Dr. J. M. Robinson].

HOWICK HALL, NORTHUMBERLAND, remodelled north front for 2nd Earl Grey, 1808–9 [exhib. at R.A. 1809; Grey of Howick papers, Prior's Kitchen, Durham].

ROWTON CASTLE, SALOP., remodelled for Col. Richard Lyster, 1810–12, castellated [exhib. at R.A. as 'about to be' carried out in 1809, and as 'lately executed' in 1812].

DEVIZES, WILTS., castellated toll house on Bath Road, 1812 [exhib. at R.A. 1812].

TWIZELL HOUSE, nr. BELFORD, NORTHUMBERLAND, proposed alterations for P. J. Selby, exhibited at R.A. 1812; these probably included the Ionic portico; dem. *c.*1969.

BROME HALL, SUFFOLK, alterations for 2nd Marquess Cornwallis, 1815; dem. 1963 [letters in the Fitch Collection, Hartismere volume, Ipswich Public Library, *ex inf.* Dr. J. M. Robinson].

[1] He was at 2 Albany Court Yard from *c.*1809 to 1812. Lewis Wyatt succeeded him at the same address in 1813 and remained there until 1823. Although George and Lewis were evidently on friendly terms, their successive occupancy of the same premises affords no evidence that they were in practice together.

WYATT, HENRY JOHN (*c.*1789–1862), was one of the sons of Edward Wyatt (1757–1833), a second cousin of Samuel and James Wyatt. Edward was a successful carver and gilder with a shop in Oxford Street, and his younger son Richard James Wyatt (1795–1850) became a well-known sculptor. Henry John became a pupil of James Wyatt, attended the Royal Academy Schools, and won the Silver Medal in 1809.[1] He exhibited at the Academy from 1806 to 1828, and was still in practice in London in the 1840s in Sloane Terrace and later in Osnaburgh Street. Having retired to Sussex, he died on 20 July 1862, aged 73, and was buried in the family vault on the south side of the chancel of Merton Church, Surrey. His few recorded architectural works comprise ST. MARY'S CHURCH, HAMMERSMITH, 1812–13, remodelled 1883, dem. 1944 [exhib. at R.A. 1812]; a farm-house at BARCOMBE, SUSSEX, exhibited at the R.A. in 1823; and the houses (dem.) at the corner of GREAT GEORGE and DELAHAY STREETS, WESTMINSTER [*A.P.S.D.*].

Henry John Wyatt must not be confused with Henry Wyatt (d. 1899), fourth son of Matthew Cotes Wyatt, the sculptor. His practice was chiefly in Yorkshire, where he enlarged ALDBY PARK (E.R.), 1847–9, rebuilt NEWBY WISKE HALL, *c.*1850, and was responsible for a number of buildings in SCARBOROUGH, including the castellated SPA, 1837–9, destroyed by fire 1876. [Theakston's *Guide to Scarborough*, 1856; information from the late Miss Emily Wyatt; Aldby Park papers at Borthwick Institute, York.]

WYATT, JAMES (1746–1813), was the sixth son of Benjamin Wyatt of Weeford (*q.v.*). Very little is known about his boyhood, but some early signs of artistic ability must have led to the decision to send him to Italy. A member of the Bagot family of Blithfield, who was secretary to the Earl of Northampton's embassy to the Venetian Republic, appears to have offered or agreed to take James with him, and if so 1762 will have been the year of his arrival in Italy, where he is said to have spent six years, two in Venice (probably 1762–3) and four in Rome (probably 1764–7). In Venice he became a pupil of Antonio Visentini (d. 1782), under whom he made rapid progress as an architectural draughtsman. Little is known about his residence in Rome, but he is said to have caused some excitement by the intrepidity with which he made measured drawings of the dome of St. Peter's, 'lying on his back on a ladder slung horizontally, without cradle or side-rail, over a frightful void of 300 feet'.

Wyatt returned to England in or about 1768, and for the next few years worked in close association with the family firm, in particular with his elder brother Samuel. Although he brought with him a first-hand knowledge of both antique and renaissance architecture, the elegant neo-classical style displayed in nearly all the buildings which he designed in the course of the next few years owed much to that of Robert and James Adam, which he was probably able to study first-hand at Kedleston, where Samuel was master carpenter. Indeed a design by James for a large country house dated 1771 is clearly indebted to the south front of Kedleston, for it features the central bow originally envisaged by Paine with the simpler neo-classical treatment of the elevation substituted by Adam. Heaton Hall, Wyatt's first important country house, was also an elegant simplification of Paine's Kedleston. The building which made Wyatt's reputation was, however, not a country house but the Pantheon in Oxford Street, London. His brother John, a surgeon, was one of the shareholders, but the choice of a young and almost unknown architect appears to have been due to P. E. Turst, the owner of the site and the principal promoter of the project for a 'Winter Ranelagh'. When the Pantheon was opened in 1772 Turst's choice was endorsed by the fashionable public, and in a moment of enthusiasm Horace Walpole pronounced it to be 'the most beautiful edifice in England'. Externally it presented a conventional Palladian façade to the street, but the basilica-like hall, with its coffered dome, colonnaded aisles and apsidal ends, was something new in assembly rooms and brought its architect immediate celebrity. The design was exhibited at the Royal Academy, private commissions followed, and at the age of 26 Wyatt found himself a fashionable domestic architect and an Associate of the Royal Academy.

Though the conception of the Pantheon was no doubt entirely due to James Wyatt, its realization was a joint enterprise with his brother Samuel. From 1774 onwards, however, they conducted independent practices, and James soon outstripped his brother in celebrity, becoming in 1776 Surveyor to Westminster Abbey, in 1782 Architect to the Board of Ordnance, and in 1796 Surveyor-General and Comptroller of the Office of Works. The royal favour to which Wyatt owed the last appointment dated from 1793–5, when he had rebuilt Frogmore House for

[1] What are probably the drafts for his winning drawing (of the Admiralty Screen, Whitehall) are in Birmingham Reference Library (MS. 1542, Box 31, Bdl. 10).

Queen Charlotte. In 1793 Farington reported that George III had promised Wyatt the reversion of the surveyorship, and when Sir William Chambers died in 1796 Wyatt was duly given the post. As a royal architect he continued to give satisfaction by his works at Windsor and Kew, while his polished manners and polite accomplishments made him always welcome at Court. But as an administrator he was dilatory, negligent and irresponsible. Persistent neglect of his duties led in 1805 to his dismissal from the post of Deputy Surveyor of the Office of Woods and Forests, which he had held in plurality with the Works since 1799, and only royal favour can have prevented the Treasury from threatening him with dismissal from the Surveyor-Generalship itself. During the last decade of his regime the Office of Works was in a state of disarray, and from 1806 onwards various government enquiries were under way which, but for Wyatt's death, would inevitably have resulted in public disgrace. As it was, the Commissioners of Military Inquiry who investigated the confusion which he left behind him condemned not only the man but also the system which had permitted him to mismanage the royal Works for seventeen years. The reforms of 1814 were a direct consequence of Wyatt's incompetence: as Jeffry Wyatt later admitted, his uncle's 'neglect [had] destroyed the Office of Works as it was'.

The unbusinesslike habits which unfitted Wyatt for public office also bedevilled his private practice. At Rome he left the reputation of being an exceptionally talented student who 'did not apply sufficiently to his profession'. In England his early success brought him far more commissions than he could properly attend to. Between 1769 and 1813 he designed or altered several royal palaces, five cathedrals, seventeen other churches, eight colleges and well over a hundred country houses in England, Wales and Ireland.[1] It was more than even a well-organized office could easily manage, and Wyatt, despite numerous pupils and the delegation of some commissions to provincial architects like Potter of Lichfield, could not keep abreast of all the work he undertook. Already in 1776 reported to be 'as difficult of access as a Prime Minister', he became as time went on more and more capricious and inaccessible. When approached by a new client he would at first take the keenest interest in the commission, but when the work was about to begin he would lose interest in it and 'employ himself upon trifling professional matters which others could do'. This sort of conduct, so Jeffry Wyatt told Farington in 1806, had lost his uncle 'many great commissions'. Although he endeavoured to supplement his professional income by speculative building in London and by contracting for some of the country houses which he designed (notably Ragley), Wyatt's unbusiness-like methods were not calculated to make a success of such enterprises, and in 1806 William Porden told Farington that Wyatt lost two to three thousand pounds a year 'from mere neglect in respect of order in his accounts'. When he died (intestate) in 1813 he owed £900 to his principal draughtsman, John Dixon, and £3000 to the plasterer Bartoli. His house in Foley Place was mortgaged to the utmost, and his widow, left without means of support, depended for the rest of her life on a pension of £100 granted by Lord Liverpool.

Wyatt was an accomplished draughtsman whose 'wonderful command and facility of pencil' enabled him (according to Humphry Repton) to draw perfect circles and straight lines freehand. But his work lacked the consistency of a man dedicated to some definite aesthetic creed. He had, as Porden put it, 'no principles in his own Art', but drew on a wide variety of sources to produce a neo-classical architecture that began in the late Palladian tradition and ended with some acknowledgements to the Greek Revival. What he himself told George III was that 'there had been no regular architecture since Sir William Chambers – that when he came from Italy he found the public taste corrupted by the Adams, and he was obliged to comply with it.' Indeed he became almost as adept a purveyor of the Adam decorative style as the Adams themselves, and in 1773, when the Adams complained of imitators in the preface to their *Works*, Horace Walpole was quick to detect a hostile reference to Wyatt. Wyatt's decorative repertoire awaits detailed study, but in general his walls and ceilings are apt to be rather more sparsely ornamented than those designed by his rivals. Spatially, the Pantheon was undoubtedly his finest classical interior, but the ceiling of the hall at Heveningham is a brilliant exercise in interpenetrating forms which has no parallel in the Adams' work. Externally, the one consistent feature of Wyatt's domestic style is the prominent bow, often domed, which first appears in his drawing of 1771 and recurs in most of his classical houses. Like his brother Samuel he favoured

[1] Wyatt had a hand in several Irish houses in the 1770s, but his first recorded visit to Ireland was in 1785 (see *C. Life*, 21 Feb. 1963, 368, and a letter of 18 Sept. 1785 from Wyatt mentioning his impending journey to Ireland in an extra-illustrated copy of Lysons' *Environs* in the Yale Center for British Art, vi, f. 596).

crisp, clear-cut masonry with the minimum of ornamentation, but unlike Samuel, who preferred astylar façades, he often used an order to accentuate the central feature. The surviving houses that best exemplify these characteristics are Heaton, Bowden, Aston, Castle Coole and Dodington.

Despite his seventeen-year tenure of office as Surveyor of the Works, Wyatt had relatively few opportunities for public works on a large scale. His career as a govenment architect coincided with the Napoleonic Wars, and his death deprived him of participation in the metropolitan improvements of the Regency period. At Oxford (where he was the favoured architect from the 1770s onwards) there was no major commission to offer him, and at Cambridge his design for Downing College was defeated by a more doctrinaire neo-classicism than he was prepared to conform to.

It was, however, as a Gothic architect that Wyatt enjoyed a special celebrity. Every Georgian architect was called upon from time to time to produce designs in the medieval style, and Wyatt was by no means the first in the field. His success as a Gothicist was due partly to a better knowledge of authentic medieval prototypes than any of his predecessors had displayed, and partly to his success in recapturing the picturesque irregularity which was now seen to be an attractive and characteristic feature of medieval architecture. Of his earliest Gothic work at Beaudesert there appears to be no visual record, but at Sheffield Place, Sandleford Priory and Lee Priory, Wyatt displayed those qualities which were to win him the enthusiastic support of Horace Walpole. Here was something more convincing than the rococo Gothic of the previous generation, something that to Walpole's contemporaries seemed effectively to 'revive the long-forgotten beauties of Gothic architecture'. Soon Wyatt was the acknowledged expert in Gothic design. Shute Barrington, Bishop successively of Salisbury and Durham, gave him important ecclesiastical commissions, and the millionaire William Beckford employed him to design the fabulous Fonthill Abbey in Wiltshire. At Fonthill Wyatt attempted the sublime and perhaps achieved it. Fonthill was a rich man's folly that stood alone, but it ranks as the supreme example of ecclesiastical Gothic applied to secular purposes. Wycombe, Ashridge and Wilton were other works in the 'abbey' style, while Belvoir, Norris and Kew were experiments in the 'castle' style. At Belvoir a multiplicity of oriels, towers and turrets ensured a highly picturesque composition, but at Norris the same effect was achieved by the skilful use of simple castellated forms designed to be seen in silhouette, while at Kew Wyatt provided the prototype for a type of symmetrical castle that was to be taken up later by Smirke at Lowther and Eastnor. All these buildings were highly influential in the next generation, and establish Wyatt as a major figure in the history of the Picturesque.

As a restorer and improver of cathedrals, Wyatt's activities were, even in his own day, highly controversial. Here he was actuated by an essentially rationalist approach (akin to that expounded by Laugier) which saw merit in Gothic architecture, but sought to improve it by removing those accidental excrescences which are so characteristic of ancient buildings. Hence his advice at Salisbury to emphasize the unity of the thirteenth-century church by removing both external and internal obstructions and by levelling the Close; at Hereford to reduce the nave by one bay in order to give the central tower more centrality; and at Durham to pull the exterior together by demolishing the Galilee and crowning the central tower by a lantern and spire. At all three cathedrals bishop and chapter were generally sympathetic to Wyatt's proposals, but his programmes of 'improvement' were bitterly criticized by Richard Gough and John Carter in the *Gentleman's Magazine*, and the antiquarian opposition which they mobilized was instrumental in saving the Durham Galilee and the Neville screen. It was due in large measure to their persistent denunciations that in 1797 Wyatt experienced some difficulty in obtaining election to the Society of Antiquaries (black-balled in September, he was eventually admitted in December). The nineteenth century did not, however, forgive what the eighteenth had condoned, and Wyatt's reputation as the 'Destroyer' has lived on in antiquarian and ecclesiological circles almost to the present day. Although a better understanding of current aesthetic ideas helps to explain Wyatt's proposals, it is still difficult to regard his activities at Lichfield, Hereford, Salisbury and Durham otherwise than as those of an irresponsible meddler.

Wyatt became a full R.A. in 1785 and took an active part in the politics of the Academy. In 1803–4 he was the leader of an opposition party which eventually forced Benjamin West to resign the presidency. But the rebels had mistaken their man. Wyatt's ambitions were satisfied by his own election as President (1805) and he did nothing to implement the reforms which his party expected. 'He slept in committe, mumbled his speeches, and infuriated political patrons by his "old habits of delay". Within a year West was back in office. Wyatt had merely succeeded in making almost as many enemies in the Royal

Academy as he had in the Society of Antiquaries.' He was one of the original members of the Architects' Club founded in 1791, and sometimes presided over its meetings at the Thatched House Tavern.

Wyatt died on 4 September 1813. He was travelling over the Marlborough Downs with his friend and patron, Christopher Codrington of Dodington Park, when their carriage was involved in an accident. Wyatt's head struck the roof with great violence and he was killed instantaneously. His body was buried in Westminster Abbey. He left a widow and four sons, of whom the eldest, Benjamin Dean, and the youngest, Philip, are noticed separately. Matthew Cotes (1777–1862), the third son, became a well-known sculptor, whose best work is the bronze statue of George III in Cockspur Street. He was the father of Sir Matthew Wyatt, Lieutenant of the Queen's Gentlemen at Arms, of James Wyatt (d. 1893), a sculptor, and of Henry Wyatt (d. 1899), an architect who practised in Scarborough. Charles Burton, the second son, had a brief career as Surveyor-General of Crown Lands in Canada before he quarrelled with the Governor and was recalled to England, where he eventually entered the wine trade.

Wyatt's first London address was in Great Newport Street. In 1774 he moved to Newman Street, where he remained until 1783, when he took up residence at No. 42 Queen Anne Street East (later 1 Foley Place), which he had built for himself. He also had a country house at Hanworth in Middlesex.

The best portrait of Wyatt is that by Sir William Beechey at the Royal Academy. One by Ozias Humphrey, painted in 1793 and exhibited at the Royal Academy in 1795, was engraved by Singleton in 1796. One by his son Matthew Cotes, which was also engraved, now belongs to his descendants. The National Portrait Gallery has a bronze bust by Rossi, and there is a pencil portrait by George Dance in the Royal Academy Library. There is also a Wedgwood portrait medallion (example in Brooklyn Museum, U.S.A.). Wyatt's principal draughtsman was John Dixon (*q.v.*), who, according to Farington, had been with him from the time of the building of the Pantheon. He had many pupils, of whom the following is an incomplete list: Joseph Badger, junior, William Blogg, J. M. Gandy, J. P. Gandy, George Hadfield, Charles Humfrey, Henry Kitchen, William Newham, John Percy, Charles and William Porden, John Rawstorne, J. W. Sanderson, James Spiller, Thomas Taylor, Thomas and John Westmacott, and his own sons Benjamin and Philip Wyatt.

There is no *corpus* of drawings by Wyatt, but a number, from various sources, are in the R.I.B.A. Collection (see the *Catalogue* of Wyatt drawings by D. Linstrum, 1973). There is an album of designs for ceilings in the Metropolitan Museum at New York (see J. Harris, *Catalogue of British Drawings for Architecture, etc., in American Collections*, 1971) and another album of miscellaneous drawings is in the Victoria and Albert Museum. A third album was in the possession of the late Vicomte de Noailles (see *C. Life*, 5 Dec. 1947 and 2 July 1948).[1] For other drawings for particular buildings see Appendix A in D. Linstrum's *Catalogue* and the list of Wyatt's works in this *Dictionary*.

Miscellaneous letters and papers of James Wyatt are in the R.I.B.A. Collection (WY.1), the British Library (Egerton MS. 3515), the Victoria and Albert Museum (MS. 86ZZ.170), and Edinburgh University Library (La. II. 426/529).

[*A.P.S.D.*; *D.N.B.*; *Gent's Mag.* 1813 (ii), 296–7; *Universal Mag.* xx, 1813, 342–3; Farington's Diary, *passim*; biographical note in T.F. Hunt, *Architettura Campestre*, 1827, xiii–xvi; H. Repton's Reminiscences (B.L., Add. MS. 62112), f. 188; R. Turnor, *James Wyatt*, 1950 (a slight work); A. Dale, *James Wyatt*, 1956; J. M. Crook, 'The Surveyorship of James Wyatt 1796–1813' in *History of the King's Works* vi, 1973; D. Linstrum, Introduction to *The Wyatt Family*, R.I.B.A. Drawings Catalogue, 1973; J. M. Robinson, 'The Evolution of the Wyatt Style', *C. Life*, 20 Dec. 1973; Frances Fergusson, 'Wyatt's Chairs: rethinking the Adam Heritage', *Burlington Mag.* cxix, 1977; articles by J. M. Frew on Wyatt's cathedral restorations in *Jnl. Soc. of Architectural Historians* 38, 1979, and on his Gothic work in *ibid.* 41, 1982 and *Burlington Mag.* cxxv, 1984; J. M. Robinson, *The Wyatts*, 1979, 58–69, 239–46; C. M. Sicca, *Committed to Classicism: The Building of Downing College, Cambridge*, 1987.]

PUBLIC BUILDINGS, ETC.

LONDON, THE PANTHEON, OXFORD STREET, 1769–72; altered by Wyatt as a theatre for the Italian Opera 1790–1; destroyed by fire Jan. 1792; rebuilt to serve its original purpose as a 'Winter Ranelagh' in 1794–5, retaining Wyatt's original entrance-fronts to Oxford and Poland Streets; reconstructed by N. W. Cundy as the Pantheon Theatre 1811–12; remodelled by S. Smirke as the Pantheon Bazaar, 1833–4; closed

[1] A microfilm of the album is at the R.I.B.A. Drawings Collection.

1867 and converted into a wine-store; dem. 1937 [A. T. Bolton, 'The Pantheon', *London Topographical Record* xiii, 1923; *Survey of London* xxxi, chap. xiii].

EXETER, DEVON, THE SESSIONS HOUSE: Wyatt revised a design for the façade submitted by Messrs. Stowey & Jones (*q.v.*), eliminating the proposed pilasters and entablature and altering the proportions, 1773 [Devon County Records, File A5/166/22].

OXFORD, CHRIST CHURCH: CANTERBURY QUADRANGLE and GATEWAY, 1773–83; alterations to HALL, including staircase and panelling, 1801–4, Gothic; restoration of rooms in south-east corner of TOM QUADRANGLE after fire in March 1809 [R. Ackermann, *History of the University of Oxford* ii, 1814, 79; W. G. Hiscock, *A Christ Church Miscellany*, 1946, 204, 208–9].

OXFORD, WORCESTER COLLEGE, completed interior of HALL and CHAPEL after death of Henry Keene in 1776. The Hall was completed in 1784, the Chapel *c.*1790. W. Burges redecorated the Chapel in 1863–4, the Hall in 1877, but Wyatt's decoration in the latter was restored in 1966 [*V.C.H. Oxon.* iii, 308; H. M. Colvin, *Catalogue of Architectural Drawings . . . in the Library of Worcester College, Oxford*, 1964, 62].

OXFORD, THE RADCLIFFE OBSERVATORY, completion after death of Henry Keene, 1776–94. In 1773 the Trustees had ordered Keene to follow 'another Elevation' which was probably Wyatt's, and after his death they directed Keene's son to complete the building 'under the direction of Mr. Wyatt'. The globe surmounting the building bears an inscription giving the names of 'James Wyatt, Esq. R.A. Architect, James Pears Esq. Mayor of Oxford Builder & John Bacon Esq. R.A. Sculptor' [C. Hussey, 'The Radcliffe Observatory', *C. Life*, 10 May 1930].

OXFORD, ORIEL COLLEGE STABLES, ORIEL STREET, *c.*1778–9; dem. *c.*1873 [Christ Church archives, Canterbury account-book xxxiii, 6.3].

OXFORD, NEW COLLEGE: remodelled UPPER LIBRARY, 1778; re-roofed and ceiled HALL, 1786 (re-roofed by Sir Gilbert Scott 1865–6); re-roofed and refitted CHAPEL in Gothic style, 1789–94 (re-roofed and refitted by Scott 1877–81) [*V.C.H. Oxon*, iii, 147–9].

OXFORD, BRASENOSE COLLEGE, remodelled interior of LIBRARY, 1779–80 [*Brasenose Quatercentenary Monographs* iii, 1909, 34–5].

OXFORD, THE MUSIC SCHOOL, HOLYWELL, rearranged interior, 1780 [*The Magdalen College Register*, ed. Bloxam, ii, 1857, 222].

CHICHESTER, SUSSEX, interior of ASSEMBLY ROOMS at rear of Council Chamber, 1781–3 [J. Dallaway, *Western Division of Sussex* i, 1815, 170].

SWAFFHAM, NORFOLK, domed MARKET CROSS for 3rd Earl of Orford, 1783–4 [*Norfolk Chronicle*, 21 July 1781: 'the plan for a handsome market-cross is now making by that eminent architect, Mr. Wyatt, of Portland Street, London, to be erected . . . at Swaffham, at the sole expense of . . . the Earl of Orford', *ex inf.* Mr. David Cubitt].

PETWORTH, SUSSEX, THE COUNTY BRIDEWELL, 1785–8; altered by G. Moneypenny 1816; dem. 1835 [J. Dallaway, *Western Division of Sussex*, ed. Cartwright, ii (i), 1832, vii–x and plate].

ROMFORD, ESSEX, THE WORKHOUSE, 1786; dem. [Essex Record Office, D/DQ 75].

OXFORD, BODLEIAN LIBRARY, fitted up the room known as the AUCTARIUM, 1787; altered 1953 [Minutes of the Curators of the Bodleian Library, 1786–7].

attributed: LONDON, WHITE'S CLUB, ST. JAMES'S STREET, 1787–8; façade altered 1850 [*Survey of London* xxx, 452–3].

OXFORD, ORIEL COLLEGE, LIBRARY and COMMON ROOM, 1788–9 [J. Ingram, *Memorials of Oxford* i, 1837, 'Oriel College', 14].

LIVERPOOL, THE EXCHANGE (now TOWN HALL), enlarged by John Foster to Wyatt's designs, 1789–92; in 1795 the interior was destroyed by fire and rebuilt by Foster under Wyatt's direction. The dome and cupola were added in 1802, the portico in 1811 [J. A. Picton, *Liverpool Municipal Records 1700–1835*, 1886, 265-72] (*C. Life*, 23 July 1927).

OXFORD, MERTON COLLEGE, remodelled HALL in Gothic style, 1790–1; remodelled by Sir Gilbert Scott 1872–4 [J. Ingram, *Memorials of Oxford* i, 1837, 'Merton College', 12–13].

OXFORD, MAGDALEN COLLEGE, re-roofed CHAPEL, 1790–3 (altered by Cottingham 1830–2), and inserted plaster vault in HALL, 1790–5 (removed 1903) [*The Magdalen College Register*, ed. Bloxam, ii, 1857, clxxxvi–clxxxix, cxcv–ccii; T. S. R. Boase, 'An Oxford College and the Gothic Revival', *Jnl. Warburg and Courtauld Institutes* xviii, 1955].

LONDON, THE TOWER, buildings for Department of Ordnance, 1791–6 [Robinson, *op. cit.*, 243, citing *XVth Report of Commissioners of Military Enquiry*, 1811, 355].

OXFORD, BALLIOL COLLEGE, altered HALL and refitted LIBRARY with plaster Gothic vault, 1792–4 [J. Ingram, *Memorials of Oxford* i, 1837, 'Balliol College', 11–13; *V.C.H. Oxon.* iii, 92–3].

CARISBROOKE CASTLE, ISLE OF WIGHT, remodelled Governor's Lodgings for General Orde, *c.*1794 [J. M. Robinson, *op. cit.*, 240].

LONDON, WEEKS'S MUSEUM, TICHBORNE STREET, for Thomas Weeks, *c.*1795; dem. 1885 [by 'Wyatt': *Survey of London* xxxi, 54–5].

BIRMINGHAM, THE HEN AND CHICKENS HOTEL, NEW STREET, 1798; dem. [*Aris's Birmingham Gazette*, 26 March 1798].

RIPON, YORKS. (W.R.), THE TOWN HALL, 1798–9 [anon. *History of Ripon*, 1801, 58].

WESTMINSTER PALACE: cut away walls of HOUSE OF COMMONS to provide extra accommodation for the Irish members, 1800–1; fitted up Court of Requests for accommodation of HOUSE OF LORDS, 1800–1; reconstructed SPEAKER'S HOUSE, 1802–8; and constructed Gothic façade to offices on east side of OLD PALACE YARD; all destroyed by fire 1834 except Speaker's House, which was dem. 1842 [*History of the King's Works* vi, 517–19, 526, 532–4].

THE LAZARETTO, CHETNEY HILL, IWADE, KENT, 1800–6; dem. 1820 [*History of the King's Works* vi, 448–51].

ROYAL MILITARY ACADEMY, WOOLWICH, *c.*1800–6, castellated; damaged by fire 1873 [D. Lysons, *Environs of London* i (2), 1811, 596].

WOOLWICH, THE ROYAL ARTILLERY BARRACKS, additional BARRACKS and RIDING SCHOOL, 1802–8 [*A.P.S.D.*].

LONDON, HANOVER SQUARE CONCERT ROOM, altered 1803–4; dem. [Soane Museum, Soane's papers 7/J].

LIVERPOOL, LANCS., THE NEW EXCHANGE, in collaboration with John Foster (*q.v.*), 1803–9; dem. *c.*1863 [J. A. Picton, *Architectural History of Liverpool*, 1858, 11].

DERBY, THE ORDNANCE DEPOT (later used as a factory), 1804–5; dem. [R. Simpson, *Collection of Fragments illustrative of the History of Derby* i, 1826, 530].

LONDON, DORSET HOUSE, WHITEHALL, alterations to government offices, 1804–8; dem. 1845–6 [*History of the King's Works* vi, 550–1].

GREAT YARMOUTH, NORFOLK, THE NAVAL ARSENAL, 1806 [J. Chambers, *Norfolk Tour* i, 1829, 276].

LEWISHAM, KENT, ARMOURY MILLS, 1806 [Robinson, *op. cit.*, 242, citing *XVth Report of Commissioners of Military Enquiry*, 1811, 355].

SHREWSBURY, THE ARMOURY, 1806 [S. Lewis, *Topographical Dictionary of England* iv, 1831, 71].

LONDON, THE BANQUETING HOUSE (then CHAPEL ROYAL), WHITEHALL, added staircase at north end, 1808–9 [*History of the King's Works* vi, 545–6].

SANDHURST, BERKS., THE ROYAL MILITARY COLLEGE, built 1808–12, was based on a design by Wyatt made as early as 1801 (*Later Correspondence of George III*, ed. Aspinall, 3, 600), but carried out by John Sanders (*q.v.*) owing to Wyatt's negligence.

BADBY SCHOOL, NORTHANTS., for the Dowager Lady Knightley, *c.*1812, Gothic [G. Baker, *History of Northants* i, 1822, 257].

ECCLESIASTICAL WORKS

BURTON-ON-TRENT CHURCH, STAFFS., organcase, 1771; altered 1902 [signed drawing dated 1770 in R.I.B.A.D.].

LONDON, KENTISH TOWN EPISCOPAL CHAPEL (now PARISH CHURCH), LOWER CRAVEN PLACE, 1784–5; remodelled by J. H. Hakewill 1843–5 [T. Hope, *Observations on the Plans and Elevations by James Wyatt for Downing College, Cambridge*, 1804, 34; unsigned drawings in Hampstead Public Library, Heal Collection, A.5, 31, 32, 37].

LICHFIELD CATHEDRAL, STAFFS., survey, 1787, followed by repairs and improvements, 1788–93, including replacement of five divisions of vaulting in nave with plaster, rearrangement and refitting of choir, etc. The work was carried out by Joseph Potter (*q.v.*). It was all undone by Sir Gilbert Scott from 1856 onwards [J. Britton, *History of the Cathedral Church of Lichfield*, 1820; drawings by Wyatt in William Salt Library, Stafford, Staffordshire Views, vi, 102, 104, 105; J. Frew, 'James Wyatt at Lichfield Cathedral, 1787–92', *Jnl. S. Staffs. Archl. & Hist. Soc.* xix, 1977–8].

SALISBURY CATHEDRAL, WILTS., survey, 1787, and alterations to Cathedral, 1789–92, including destruction of north and south porches to transepts and of Hungerford and Beauchamp Chantries, rearrangement of interior, levelling of Close and demolition of detached belfry [W. Dodsworth, *A Guide to the Cathedral Church of Salisbury, with a particular account of the late Great Improvements made therein under the direction of James Wyatt, Esq.*, 1792; *Gent's Mag.* 1789 (ii), 873–4, 1042, 1064–6, 1194–6; J. Frew, 'James Wyatt's choir-screen at Salisbury Cathedral reconsidered', *Arch. Hist.* 27, 1984].

MANCHESTER, ST. PETER'S CHURCH, MOSLEY STREET, 1788–94; tower and spire added by F. Goodwin 1824; dem. 1906–7 [W. E. A. Axon, *Annals of Manchester*, 1886, 115–16].

HEREFORD CATHEDRAL, repairs following the collapse of the west tower and west end of the nave in 1786–7. Between 1788 and 1796 Wyatt rebuilt the west end of the nave, which was shortened by one bay, together with the whole of the nave triforium, clerestory and vault. He also remodelled the central tower. The west front was again rebuilt by J. O. Scott in 1904–8 [J. Britton, *History of the Cathedral Church of Hereford*, 1831; G. Marshall, *Hereford Cathedral*, Worcester *c.*1950].

MARCHWIEL CHURCH, DENBIGHSHIRE, steeple built at expense of Philip Yorke of Erddig, 1789 [John Jones, *Wrexham and its Neighbourhood*, 1868, 66; Erddig archives, payment of 15 gns. to 'Wyat' for 'plan of Church and monument' 1788, *ex inf.* Mr. Gervase Jackson-Stops].

EAST GRINSTEAD CHURCH, SUSSEX, 1789, Gothic; tower completed 1811–13 by J. T. Groves (*q.v.*) [W. H. Wills, *History of East Grinstead*, 1906, 66–7].

MILTON ABBAS, DORSET, restoration of ABBEY CHURCH for 1st Lord Milton, 1789–91 [J. Hutchins, *History of Dorset* iv, 1873, 405; *Diary and Letters of Fanny Burney*, ed. Dobson, v, 1904–5, 14]. (R.C.H.M., *Dorset* iii (2), 184–9).

attributed: MONGEWELL CHURCH, OXON., remodelled for Shute Barrington, Bishop of Durham, 1791, Gothic; altered 1880, now ruinous [Barrington was one of Wyatt's principal patrons, employing him at Salisbury, Durham and Bishop Auckland].

COVENTRY, WARWICKS., ST. MICHAEL'S CHURCH, repair of tower, carried out by Joseph Potter (*q.v.*), 1794 [T. Sharpe, *Illustrations of the History of St. Michael's Church, Coventry*, 1818, 48–9].

LONDON, LINCOLN'S INN CHAPEL, renewed roof and east window, 1795–6, Gothic [*The Black Books of Lincoln's Inn* iv, 53, 55–6, 58–60, 65; *The Farington Diary*, ed. J. Greig, i, 213].

DURHAM CATHEDRAL, survey, 1795, followed by repair of east end of Cathedral, 1797–1805, and controversial proposals for rearrangement of choir, demolition of Galilee, new central spire, etc., which were not carried out [R. A. Cordingley, 'Cathedral Innovations: James Wyatt at Durham Cathedral 1795–7', *Ancient Monuments Society's Trans.* N.S. iii, 1955].

BISHOP AUCKLAND, DURHAM, ST. ANNE'S CHAPEL in Market Place: the Gothic west tower built *c.*1800 by W. Atkinson (*q.v.*) and dem. 1847 with the rest of the chapel was probably based on a design made by Wyatt in 1796 [signed drawing in Newcastle Univ. Library cited by Robinson, *op. cit.*, 239].

AMLWCH CHURCH, ANGLESEY, Gothic, was probably based on a design made by Wyatt *c.*1790 but not carried out until 1800 owing to obstruction by the bishop [*A Letter to the Right Revd. Dr. Warren by Shôn Gwialan*, 1796, 61 *et seq.*, *ex inf.* Prof. M. L. Clarke].

ELY CATHEDRAL, CAMBS., repairs in association with J. T. Groves (*q.v.*), 1800–2 [above, p. 434; for Wyatt's report of 1796 see A. Gibbons, *Calendar of the Episcopal Records . . . at Ely*, 1891, 113].

WINDSOR, BERKS., ST. GEORGE'S CHAPEL, repairs to TOMB HOUSE (now ALBERT MEMORIAL CHAPEL), 1800–4, and formation of royal burial vault, 1804–10 [W. H. St. J. Hope, *Architectural History of Windsor Castle*, 1913, 408, 486, 489; *History of the King's Works* vi, 379].

ST. KEA CHURCH, CORNWALL, 1802, Gothic; dem. 1895 [W. Paraluna, *The Circle, or Historical Survey of Sixty Parishes in Cornwall*, 1819; Lake's *Parochial History of Cornwall*, 1867–73, ii, 318].

EGLWYS NEWYDD, HAFOD, CARDIGANSHIRE, for Thomas Johnes, 1803, Gothic; badly damaged by fire 1932 [B. H. Malkin, *The Scenery, etc., of S. Wales*, 1804; S. R. Meyrick, *History and Antiquities of the County of Cardigan*, 1810, 347].

WEEFORD CHURCH, STAFFS., 1803–4; Gothic; chancel rebuilt 1876 [correspondence about erection of church in William Salt Library, Stafford, MS. M. 96; variant drawings signed 'J.W.' 1803 and 1805 in Vestry].

WESTMINSTER ABBEY, arrangements for Handel Festival, 1784 [*Gent's Mag.* 1784 (i), 391–2; engraving in *European Mag.* May 1784]; rebuilt vault of central tower in Bernasconi's composition after fire of July 1803, destroyed by bombing 1941; directed refacing of Henry VII's Chapel by Thomas Gayfere (*q.v.*), 1809 onwards [J. P. Neale & E. W. Brayley, *Westminster Abbey* i, 1818, 'Henry VII's Chapel', 21–7, ii, 1823, 148].

DODINGTON CHURCH, GLOS., for Christopher Codrington, *c.*1800–5 [forms part of the outbuildings of Dodington Park, for which see below, p. 1118].

HANWORTH CHURCH, MIDDLESEX, designed 1808, built 1815–16 under the direction of B. D. Wyatt, Gothic; rebuilt by S. S. Teulon 1865 [Trustees' Minutes in G.L. Record Office, DRO 18/B3/1].

COUNTRY HOUSES, ETC.

GADDESDEN PLACE, GREAT GADDESDEN, HERTS., for Thomas Halsey, 1768–74; interior rebuilt after fire in 1905; wings dem. 1960 [J. E. Cussans, *History of Hertfordshire* iii, 1879, 121, and designs for ceilings in the Wyatt album in the Metropolitan

Museum]. Cussans says the house was completed in 1774, and the date 1768 is scratched on a wall. The conventional Palladian detailing should be compared with the exterior of the Pantheon as illustrated in *Survey of London* xxxii, pl. 20a.

FAWLEY COURT, BUCKS., interior decoration and ISLAND TEMPLE for Sambrooke Freeman, 1770–1 [*Passages from the Diary of Mrs. Lybbe Powys*, ed. Climenson, 1899, 145–8; G. Tyack, 'The Freemans of Fawley and their Buildings', *Records of Bucks.* 24, 1982, 139; Eileen Harris & J. M. Robinson, 'New Light on Wyatt at Fawley', *Arch. Hist.* 27, 1984; J. M. Robinson in *C. Life*, 4 July 1991].

HAGLEY HALL, STAFFS., octagonal drawing-room for Assheton Curzon, 1771; dem. *c.*1932 [ceiling exhib. at R.A. 1771; G. Beard, *Decorative Plasterwork in Great Britain*, 1975, 244].

BEAUDESERT, STAFFS., remodelling of interior for 1st Earl of Uxbridge, executed by Benjamin Wyatt & Sons, partly Gothic; Gothic hall altered by Joseph Potter 1826–31; dem. 1935 [H. Colvin, 'Beaudesert, Staffs.', *Trans. Ancient Monuments Soc.* N.S. 29, 1985].

HEATON HOUSE, LANCS., rebuilt for Sir Thomas Egerton, Bart., cr. Earl of Wilton, *c.*1772–8, E. Wing 1789 [exhib. at R.A. 1772] (*C. Life*, 29 Aug., 5 Sept. 1925; H. A. Tipping, *English Homes,* V (ii), 199–218; *Heaton Hall, Manchester: Bicentenary Exhibition*, 1972).

CRICHEL HOUSE, DORSET, interior of principal suite of rooms for Humphrey Sturt, 1772–80 [J. Cornforth, 'The Building of Crichel', *Arch. Hist.* 27, 1984](*C. Life*, 16, 23, 30 May 1925).

ERDDIG PARK, DENBIGHSHIRE, was consulted about the alterations carried out for Philip Yorke in 1773–4 [Erddig archives, *ex inf.* Mr. G. Jackson-Stops], and is credited with responsibility for them by J. Evans, *Beauties of England and Wales* xvii (i), 1812, 589, and *Cambrian Traveller's Guide*, 1813, 1161 (*C. Life*, 16–23 Aug. 1930, 6, 13 and 20 April 1978).

ALDWARK HALL, YORKS. (W.R.), designs for ceilings for Francis Foljambe, 1773–5; dem. 1899 [drawings in R.I.B.A. Collection (dated 1775), Wyatt Album in Metropolitan Museum (undated), and Pierpont Morgan Library (dated 1773)].

ABBEYLEIX, CO. LEIX, IRELAND, for 2nd Lord Knapton, 1773–6; exterior refaced by T. H. Wyatt 1859 [drawings by Wyatt in National Library of Ireland, LR 72884, and Metropolitan Museum, New York, Wyatt Album, no. 43] (T. U. Sadleir & P. L. Dickinson, *Georgian Mansions in Ireland*, 1915, 10–16; D. Guinness & W. Ryan, *Irish Houses and Castles*, 1971, 225–32; *C. Life*, 26 Sept. 1991).

SHARDELOES, nr. AMERSHAM, BUCKS., interior decoration, including library, for William Drake, 1773 onwards, and garden pavilion, 1785–6 [Bucks. C.R.O., Drake papers, D/Dr 5/43, 61, 69a; G. Eland, *Shardeloes Papers*, 1937, 135; John Harris in *Connoisseur*, 148, 1961, 269–75].

AUBREY HOUSE, NOTTING HILL, nr. LONDON, redecorated drawing-room for Lady Mary Coke, 1774 [*Letters and Journals of Lady Mary Coke* iv, 1896, 398–9, 438–9, 446] (*C. Life*, 2–9 May 1957).

HEATH LODGE, HAMPSTEAD, MIDDLESEX, for Mrs. Lessingham, 1775 [*V.C.H. Middlesex* ix, 69; T. J. Barratt, *Annals of Hampstead* 2, 201, 3, 286].

GUNTON HALL, NORFOLK, enlarged house and designed offices for Harbord Harbord, cr. Lord Suffield, 1775 [Anon, *History of Norfolk*, iii, 1781, 66; J. P. Neale, *Views of Seats*, 1st ser. iii, 1820].

COPPED HALL, ESSEX, internal alterations and redecoration for John Conyers, 1775–7; damaged by fire 1917 [drawings by Wyatt in Essex Record Office, D/DWE. 38–9; Brayley & Britton, *Beauties of England and Wales* v, 1803, 431] (*C. Life*, 29 Oct., 5 Nov. 1910).

HAMS HALL, WARWICKS., design for ceiling for C. B. Adderley, *c.*1775; dem. 1920 [Metropolitan Museum Album].

MILTON ABBEY, DORSET, decoration of rooms on first floor and bookcases in library for 1st Lord Milton, 1775–6 [drawings in R.I.B.A. Coll.; Arthur Oswald in *C. Life*, 28 July 1966].

SHEFFIELD PLACE, SUSSEX, remodelled for J. B. Holroyd, cr. Earl of Sheffield, *c.*1775–7, and further alterations, especially to south front, *c.*1780–90; Gothic [Holroyd papers in East Sussex Record Office, 5440/55, 58, and 63, *ex inf.* Dr. J. M. Frew; engraving dated 1779 in W. Watts, *Seats of the Nobility and Gentry*, showing first stage of work complete; W. Angus, *Seats of the Nobility and Gentry*, pl. xxvi, 1791, showing further additions].

BELTON HOUSE, LINCS., removed cupola and balustrade from roof (both restored 1872–93) and designed interiors of drawing-room (now library) and boudoir for 1st Lord Brownlow, 1776 [J. Britton, *Beauties of England and Wales* ix, 1807, 772] (*C. Life*, 17 Sept. 1964).

BURTON CONSTABLE, YORKS. (E.R.), interior of drawing-room, 1776, and the castellated Old Lodge, 1785–6, for William Constable [drawings at Burton Constable, nos. 9 and 12; G. Poulson, *History of Holderness* ii, 1841, 242; Geoffrey Webb in *C. Life*, 27 Aug., 3 Sept. 1932].

ARDBRACCAN HOUSE, CO. MEATH, IRELAND: Wyatt is credited by J. N. Brewer, *The Beauties of Ireland* ii, 1826, 189, with the design of the central block for Henry Maxwell, Bishop of Meath, 1776. Brewer says that the building was erected under the direction of the amateur architect, the Revd. Daniel Augustus Beaufort. Beaufort's surviving drawings suggest that he rather than Wyatt was the effective architect [C. C. Ellison, 'Remembering Dr. Beaufort', *Bull. Irish Georgian Soc.* xviii (i) 1975, 13–14].

DOWNHILL, CO. LONDONDERRY, IRELAND, is said to have been built *c.*1776–9 for Frederick Hervey, Bishop of Derry, by the Irish architect Michael Shanahan in accordance with a plan 'first made by Mr. James Wyatt of London'. That Wyatt had some share in the design is confirmed by references in the Hervey papers in the West Suffolk Record Office. The house was damaged by fire in 1851 and unroofed in 1950 [P. Rankin, *Irish Building Ventures of the Earl Bishop of Derry*, Ulster Architectural Heritage Soc. 1972, 15–17, and in *C. Life*, 8–15 July 1971].

HOTHFIELD PLACE, KENT, for 8th Earl of Thanet, 1776–80; dem. 1954 [design for a ceiling by Wyatt dated 1776 in Victoria & Albert Museum; A. Dale, *James Wyatt*, 1956, 43].

ROEHAMPTON GROVE (now Froebel Institute), PUTNEY, SURREY, new front block for Sir Joshua Vanneck, 1777; enlarged by W. Burn 1851 [E. W. Brayley, *History of Surrey* 1841–8, iii, 476].

NEW (ROUNDWAY) PARK, nr. DEVIZES, WILTS., for James Sutton, 1777–83; dem. 1955 [exhib. at R.A. 1784 by Wyatt's draughtsman Dixon as 'lately built by Mr. Wyatt'; payments to Wyatt in Sutton's accounts 1779 in Glos. C.R.O., D 1571/F. 641, p. 91; J. P. Neale, *Views of Seats*, 1st ser. v, 1822].

NUTHALL TEMPLE, NOTTS., interior decoration for Sir Charles Sedley, Bart., before 1778; dem. 1929 [three designs for ceilings inscribed 'Sir Charles Sedley' in Wyatt album, Metropolitan Museum; cf. *C. Life*, 25 April 1923, figs. 7, 9, 11].

BROOME PARK, KENT, decoration of saloon, etc., for Sir Henry Oxenden, Bart., 1778; only Wyatt's ceiling survives in saloon [W. Angus, *Seats*, pl. xviii, 1789; H. A. Tipping in *C. Life*, 6 July 1907].

BRYANSTON HOUSE, nr. BLANDFORD, DORSET, for H. B. Portman, 1778–*c.*1781; rebuilt by R. Norman Shaw 1890 [W. Watts, *Seats*, pl. lxxxiii, 1786].

KELMARSH HALL, NORTHANTS., design for interior decoration for William Hanbury, *c.*1778. A design for a dining-room ceiling by Wyatt is in the album in the Metropolitan Museum, but it is not known whether it was executed, as the interior of the house was entirely redecorated in 1928–9 (see *C. Life*, 25 Feb. 1933). Wyatt's design for gate-lodges, dated 1778, was carried out in 1965 by Col. C. Lancaster (see *Northants. Past and Present* iv, 1966–7, 16).

CHELSEA FARM (CREMORNE HOUSE), CHELSEA, MIDDLESEX, enlarged for 1st Viscount Cremorne, soon after 1778; dem. 1878 [T. Faulkner, *Chelsea* i, 1829, 65].

CURRAGHMORE, CO. WATERFORD, IRELAND, interiors of dining-room, staircase, library, etc., for 1st Marquess of Waterford, *c.*1778–80 [drawings in Wyatt album, Metropolitan Museum; Mark Girouard in *C. Life*, 14–21 Feb. 1963; for the date of Wyatt's work see diary of Revd. Daniel Augustus Beaufort quoted in *Bull. Irish Georgian Soc.* xviii (i), 1975, 28].

BLAGDON, NORTHUMBERLAND, stables and interior of dining-room, etc., for Sir Matthew White Ridley, Bart., 1778–91 [C. Hussey in *C. Life*, 18–25 July 1952].

BADGER HALL, SALOP., remodelled for Isaac Hawkins Browne, 1779–83; dem. 1952 [R.I.B.A.D.]. Wyatt's design for a 'pigeon-house' based on the Tower of the Winds at Athens was not executed.

RAGLEY HALL, WARWICKS., altered house and enlarged and remodelled stable-court for 1st Marquess of Hertford, 1779–1797 [Ragley papers in Warwicks. C.R.O., CR 114 A/194, 202, 203, 220/17–20, 195, 197; B.L., Egerton MS. 3515, f. 13]. The date of the portico is not clear, but it presumably formed part of Wyatt's works (*C. Life*, 22–29 March 1924, 1–8 May 1958).

NORTON PRIORY, CHESHIRE, remodelled for Sir Richard Brooke, Bart. (d. 1781) 'in his latter years'; dem. 1928 [B. Burke, *Visitation of Seats and Arms* ii, 1853, 171–2; F. H. Thompson in *Archaeological Jnl.* cxxiii, 1966, 62–8].

HARTWELL HOUSE, BUCKS., completed bridge (dem.) designed by H. Keene (*q.v.*), made designs for offices, and probably designed semi-circular vestibule, for Sir William Lee, Bart., 1780 [W. H. Smyth, *Addenda to the Ædes Hartwellianae*, 1864, 21; designs for offices in Bodleian, MS. Top. Gen. b. 55; G. Jackson-Stops in *C. Life*, 22 Nov. 1990].

HEVENINGHAM HALL, SUFFOLK, completed interior for Sir Gerard Vanneck, Bart., after dismissal of Sir Robert Taylor (*q.v.*), *c*.1780–4 [F. Shoberl, *Beauties of England and Wales* xiv, 1813, 360; C. Hussey, *English Country Houses: Mid Georgian*, 1956, 165–76].

HURSTBOURNE PARK, HANTS., for 2nd Earl of Portsmouth, *c*.1780–5; destroyed by fire 1870 [Harrison's *Views of Seats*, 1787, where it is stated to have been executed to Wyatt's designs by John Meadows, *q.v.*].

SANDLEFORD PRIORY, nr. NEWBURY, BERKS., remodelled for Mrs. Elizabeth Montagu, 1780–9, Gothic [S. Lysons, *Magna Britannia* i, 1806, 353; *Mrs. Montagu: her letters and friendships*, ed. R. Blunt, ii, 1923, 104, 108–9, 177, 201, 292].

WESTPORT, CO. MAYO, IRELAND, interior of dining-room, 1781, and design for greenhouse, 1796, for 1st Marquess of Sligo [Mark Girouard in *C. Life*, 29 April, 6 May 1965].

PISHIOBURY PARK, HERTS., remodelled for Jeremiah Milles, 1782–4, externally Gothic [J. P. Neale, *Views of Seats*, 1st ser. iv, 1821; J. Cussans, *History of Hertfordshire* i, 1870–3, 80].

MOUNT KENNEDY, CO. WICKLOW, IRELAND, for General Robert Cunninghame, cr. Lord Rossmore; built by T. Cooley *c*.1782 in accordance with designs made by Wyatt in 1772 [drawings in National Library of Ireland, LR 72884; J. Cornforth in *C. Life*, 28 Oct., 11 Nov. 1965].

MOUNT STEWART, CO. DOWN, IRELAND, designs for house and stables for 1st Marquess of Londonderry, 1783, probably not executed [Londonderry papers in P.R.O. N. Ireland at Belfast, D 654/H 1/1, p. 39, and drawings for stables in D 671/M71/4, *ex inf.* Prof. Alistair Rowan]. The existing house was built in the 1840s.

attributed: WETHERBY (or MICKLETHWAITE) GRANGE, YORKS. (W.R.), for Beilby Thompson, *c*.1784; dem. *c*.1962 [stylistic attribution, supported by a letter from John Carr to Beilby Thompson dated 9 Feb. 1784 about 'the alterations you have made to the great Mr. Wyatt's plan' (Leeds Archives, Lane-Fox deeds cxviii, 18). Alternative designs by Carr dated 1772 and 1783 exist in the same collection, but they were not adopted, and the house as built was a characteristic Wyatt design (H. Speight, *Lower Wharfedale*, 1902, 439).

SUDBOURNE HALL, SUFFOLK, for 1st Marquess of Hertford, *c*.1784; refaced in brick 1872–3; remodelled internally *c*.1905; dem. 1953 [F. Shoberl, *Beauties of England and Wales* xiv, 1813, 326] (*C. Life*, 23 Feb. 1901).

WYNNSTAY, DENBIGHSHIRE, alterations to south front begun for Sir Watkin Williams-Wynn, Bart., *c*.1785–9, but not completed owing to Wynn's death (1789); destroyed by fire 1858; also column in park to Wynn's memory, *c*.1790 [Peter Howell & T. W. Pritchard in *C. Life*, 30 March, 6 April 1972].

SLANE CASTLE, CO. MEATH, IRELAND, for 2nd Lord Conyngham, 1785–6, castellated; gutted by fire 1991 [A. Rowan, 'Georgian Castles in Ireland', *Bull. Irish Georgian Soc.* vii (i), 1964, 16–17; M. Oldlum in *C. Life*, 17, 24 July 1980].

FORNHAM HALL, SUFFOLK, for Sir Charles Kent, Bart., *c*.1785; dem. *c*.1951 [drawings by Wyatt in Victoria & Albert Museum and Wyatt album, Metropolitan Museum] (H. Davy, *Views of Seats in Suffolk*, 1827; H. R. Barker, *West Suffolk Illustrated*, 1907, 143–4).

LEE PRIORY, ICKHAM, KENT, remodelled for Thomas Barret, *c*.1785–90, Gothic; altered by Sir Gilbert Scott *c*.1865; dem. 1955 (portion of interior re-erected in Victoria & Albert Museum) [E. Hasted, *History of Kent* iii, 1790, 665; exhibited at R.A. 1785 by Dixon, Wyatt's draughtsman, as 'built from the designs of James Wyatt'; working drawings in Victoria & Albert Museum, 93 D.59] (*C. Life*, 30 May 1952, 1665–6).

THIRKLEBY PARK, YORKS. (N.R.), for Sir Thomas Frankland, Bart., *c*.1786–90; dem. 1927 [J. P. Neale, *Views of Seats*, 1st ser. v, 1822; signed drawings in R.I.B.A.D. dated 1787–92].

STANSTEAD HOUSE, SUSSEX, remodelled, with Joseph Bonomi, for Richard Barwell, 1786–91; destroyed by fire 1900 [J. Dallaway, *Western Division of Sussex* ii, 1815, 159].

CHEVENING HOUSE, KENT, refronted with pilasters and mathematical tiles for 3rd Earl Stanhope, 1786–96; Wyatt's work removed *c*.1970 [Stanhope papers at Chevening, 1046, accounts of A. Penberthey, 'Mr. Wyatt's building surveyor'] (*C. Life*, 17, 24 April, 1 May 1920, 11 June 1959).

GOODWOOD HOUSE, SUSSEX, works for 3rd Duke of Richmond, 1787 onwards, including the Kennels, 1787, the enlargement of the house, and various other buildings, including the dower house known as Molecombe, *c*.1790–1806 [F. Shoberl, *The Beauties of England and Wales* xiv, 1813, 69; W. H. Mason, *Goodwood*, 1839, 168] (*C. Life*, 9–16 July 1932).

attributed: ITCHENOR HOUSE, WEST ITCHENOR, SUSSEX, for 3rd Duke of Richmond, 1787 [attributed to Wyatt because of his employment by the Duke at Goodwood, and similarity to the dower house which he designed there].

GIDEA HALL, ESSEX, bridge in park and 'temple

for a cold-bath' for Richard Benyon, before 1788 [*Picturesque Views of Seats*, Harrison & Co., 1788]. The bridge survives in Raphael Park, Romford.

GREAT MILTON HOUSE, OXON., enlarged for Sir John Skynner, 1788 (or for the Hon. Richard Ryder, *c.*1806?) [Thomas Ellis, *Some Account of Great Milton*, Oxford 1819, 18; rainwater heads dated 1788].

BELMONT HOUSE, CLEHONGER, HEREFS., for John Matthews, 1788–90; largely rebuilt by E. W. Pugin *c.*1860 [J. Price, *Historical Account of the City of Hereford*, 1796, 191; E. W. Brayley & J. Britton, *Beauties of England & Wales*, vi, 1805, 586].

COBHAM HALL, KENT, works for 4th Earl of Darnley, including stables, 1789–90, pilasters, etc., in Gilt Hall, 1791–3, Gothic dairy, 1794–5, alterations to north wing, 1802–4, interiors of picture gallery and dining-room, 1805–10 [Darnley papers in Kent Record Office, *ex inf.* Dr. J. M. Frew; drawings formerly in Cambridge University School of Architecture]. There is no evidence of Wyatt's employment at Cobham before the early 1780s, when he designed the Mausoleum (below, p. 1121). He appears to have been first employed by the 4th Earl, who inherited in 1781, succeeding William Chambers and George Shakespear, the architects employed by the 3rd Earl in the 1760s and 1770s (cf. E. Wingfield-Stratford, *The Lords of Cobham Hall*, 1959, 259–60).

SYON HOUSE, MIDDLESEX, castellated stables, 1789–90, and iron bridge in park, 1790, for 2nd Duke of Northumberland [accounts for stables in Percy archives, Alnwick, U.III. 5(28), signed drawings for stables and bridge at Syon].

AMMERDOWN HOUSE, SOMERSET, for T. S. Jolliffe, 1789–93; enlarged 1857, 1877 and 1901 [C. Hussey in *C. Life*, 16 Feb., 2–9 March 1929; B. Little & A. Aldrich, *Ammerdown*, Ammerdown 1977].

STRAWBERRY HILL, TWICKENHAM, MIDDLESEX, the Offices for Horace Walpole, 1790, Gothic, following a design made by James Essex (d. 1784) [W. D. Lewis, 'The Genesis of Strawberry Hill', *Metropolitan Museum Studies* v (i), 1934, 82 and fig. 29].

ASTON HALL, nr. OSWESTRY, SALOP., for the Revd. J. R. Lloyd, 1789–93 [N.L.W., Aston Hall papers nos. 5234–5, Wyatt's account for drawings; N.M.R., photos of drawings by Wyatt sold in 1969].

LITTLE ASTON HALL, SHENSTONE, STAFFS., alterations and additions for William Tennant, probably *c.*1790; rebuilt 1857–9 [S. Shaw, *History of Staffordshire* ii, 1801, 52, with engraving].

GRESFORD LODGE, nr. WREXHAM, DENBIGHSHIRE, for John Parry, *c.*1790; dem. 1955–60 [J. Aikin, *Description of Country round Manchester*, 1795, 401].

SUFTON COURT, HEREFS., built for James Hereford, *c.*1790, is said to have been designed by 'Wyatt' by W. H. Cooke, *Collections towards the History of Herefordshire* iii, 1882, 73.

BIDBOROUGH RECTORY (now 'WYATTS'), KENT, *c.*1790 ['after a design of Mr. Wyatt's': E. Hasted, *History of Kent*, 2nd ed. v, 275].

NEWARK PARK, nr. WOTTON-UNDER-EDGE, GLOS., alterations, including south front, for Lewis Clutterbuck, *c.*1790, Gothic [J. & H. S. Storer, *Delineations of the County of Gloucester*, 1824].

HARTHAM PARK, PICKWICK, WILTS., for Lady James, 1790–5; enlarged 1858 and 1888 [J. Britton, *Beauties of Wiltshire* iii, 1825, 184, with engraving].

CASTLE COOLE, CO. FERMANAGH, IRELAND, for 1st Earl Belmore, 1790–7; offices added 1823 [G. Richardson, *New Vitruvius Britannicus* ii, 1808, pls. 65–70] (*C. Life*, 19–26 Dec. 1936).

FELBRIGG HALL, NORFOLK: Wyatt was employed by William Windham to carry out alterations between 1791 and 1804, but apparently did little except exasperate his client [*The Windham Papers*, ed. Earl of Rosebery, 1913, i, 182–3; ii, 229–30].

BROKE HALL, NACTON, SUFFOLK, rebuilt for Philip Broke, 1791–2, castellated [H. Repton, *Sketches and Hints on Landscape Gardening*, 1795, 18; drawing in Suffolk C.R.O. (I), HA 93/12/26] (J. P. Neale, *Views of Seats*, 1st ser. v, 1821; *C. Life*, 8 Aug. 1936, 158).

NEW HALL, NUNTON, WILTS., enlarged for J. T. Batt, 1792; destroyed by fire 1881 [J. Britton, *Beauties of Wiltshire* i, 1801, 114; B. Burke, *Visitation of Seats and Arms*, 2nd ser. ii, 1855, 127].

STOKE PARK, STOKE POGES, BUCKS., completed house for John Penn after death of R. Nasmith (*q.v.*), *c.*1793–7 [J. Penn, *An Historical and Descriptive Account of Stoke Park*, 1813, 60–1; drawings by Wyatt in B.L., Add. MS. 32450, E–H; Frances Fergusson, 'James Wyatt and John Penn: Architect and Patron at Stoke Park', *Arch. Hist.* 20, 1977].

SWINTON PARK, YORKS. (W.R.), decoration of drawing-room for William Danby, *c.*1793–4 [J. P. Neale, *Views of Seats*, 2nd ser. iv, 1828; J. Cornforth in *C. Life*, 14 April 1966].

FROGMORE HOUSE, nr. WINDSOR, BERKS., remodelled for Queen Charlotte, 1793–5; wings enlarged 1803–12 [R. Ackermann,

Repository of Arts, 3rd ser. i, 125–8; J. Hakewill, *History of Windsor*, 1813, 299–302; *History of the King's Works* vi, 326].

HENHAM HALL, SUFFOLK, for Sir John Rous, Bart., cr. Earl of Stradbroke, 1793–7; remodelled by E. M. Barry; dem. 1953 [H. Davy, *Views of Seats in Suffolk*, 1827; J. P. Neale, *Views of Seats*, 1st ser. iii, 1820; drawings in Suffolk Record Office].

BULBRIDGE HOUSE, WILTON, WILTS., remodelled for Lieut. Gen. Philip Goldsworthy, 1794 [C. Hussey in *C. Life*, 28 Feb., 7 March 1963].

LASBOROUGH PARK, nr. TETBURY, GLOS., for Edmund Estcourt, 1794, castellated [drawings by Wyatt preserved in house: see *C. Life*, 11 Feb. 1960, 279] (T. D. Fosbroke, *History of Gloucestershire* i, 1807, 410).

CROOME COURT, WORCS., ornamental buildings in grounds for 6th Earl of Coventry, 1794–1801, including the Panorama Tower (1801), a Gothic ruin in the woods, and the Doric lodge (dem. 1877) at the west entrance to the park [drawings by Wyatt in Estate Office, Croome; F. Grice, 'Park Ornaments of Croome', *Trans. Worcs. Archl. Soc.* 3rd ser. v, 1976].

ESCOT HOUSE, nr. HONITON, DEVON, alterations for Sir John Kennaway, Bart., *c.*1795; destroyed by fire 1808 [J. Britton & E. W. Brayley, *Beauties of England and Wales* iv, 1803, 301].

POWDERHAM CASTLE, DEVON, extensive alterations, including the Music Room, for 3rd Viscount Courtenay, 1794–6 [Mark Girouard in *C. Life*, 18 July 1963].

ALLESTREE HALL, DERBYSHIRE, for Bache Thornhill, 1795 [described as 'after a very clever plan of Wyatt's' by William Holbech of Farnborough, Warwicks., who visited the house in 1795 (MS. diary at Farnborough); plan signed by Wyatt and dated 1795 in Derbyshire County Museum Service, D.165].

CANWELL HALL, STAFFS., remodelled interior and added wings for Sir Robert Lawley, Bart., cr. Lord Wenlock, *c.*1795; dem. [S. Shaw, *History of Staffordshire* ii, 1801, 22*].

BISHOP AUCKLAND CASTLE, CO. DURHAM, extensive alterations for Bishop Shute Barrington, including Gothic screen and inner gateway and remodelling of principal rooms in Gothic style, *c.*1795 [drawings at Auckland Castle dated 1795; E. W. Brayley & J. Britton, *Beauties of England and Wales* v, 1803, 220–1; J. Cornforth in *C. Life*, 27 Jan., 3, 10 Feb. 1972].

WORSTEAD HALL, NORFOLK, for Sir Berney Brograve, Bart., *c.*1795–1800; dem. [J. P. Neale, *Views of Seats*, 1st ser. ii, 1819].

BOWDEN HOUSE, nr. LACOCK, WILTS., for B. Dickinson, 1796 [exhib. at R.A. 1796; G. Richardson, *New Vitruvius Britannicus* i, 1802, pls. 1–2] (Ralph Edwards, 'Bowden Park', *Connoisseur*, April 1961).

LONGFORD CASTLE, WILTS., designs and model for additional towers for 2nd Earl of Radnor, 1796 [accounts at Longford]. This was the beginning of the project for enlarging the house, afterwards carried out by D. A. Alexander in 1802–17 (*C. Life*, 12, 19, 26 Dec. 1931).

PLAS NEWYDD, ANGLESEY, remodelled for 1st Earl of Uxbridge, 1796 onwards, with Joseph Potter (*q.v.*) as executant architect, Gothic [R.I.B.A.D.; G. Jackson-Stops in *C. Life*, 24 June, 1 July, 16 Sept. 1976].

SOHO HOUSE, HANDSWORTH, BIRMINGHAM, remodelled for Matthew Boulton, 1796–8, completed by Samuel Wyatt [Tew MSS., Assay Office, Birmingham, *ex inf.* Dr. J. M. Robinson and drawings in Birmingham Reference Library Archives, MS. 1381].

FONTHILL ABBEY, WILTS., for William Beckford, 1796–1812, Gothic; tower collapsed 1825; remainder of house subsequently dem. except part of north wing [J. Rutter, *Delineations of Fonthill and its Abbey*, 1823; J. Britton, *Illustrations of Fonthill Abbey*, 1823; Boyd Alexander, *Life at Fonthill 1807–1822*, 1957; J. Wilton-Ely in *William Beckford Exhibition*, 1976, 35–57, and 'The Genesis and Evolution of Fonthill Abbey', *Arch. Hist.* 23, 1980].

BROADWAY, WORCS., the 'Saxon' tower on Broadway Hill, for 6th Earl of Coventry, *c.*1797 [drawings by Wyatt dated 1794 in Estate Office, Croome].

ACTON PARK, nr. WREXHAM, DENBIGHSHIRE, alterations for Sir Foster Cunliffe, Bart., completed 1797; dem. 1952 [Madame D'Arblay, *Memoirs of Dr. Burney* iii, 1832, 247] (J. P. Neale, *Views of Seats*, 2nd ser. v, 1829).

TRENTHAM HALL, STAFFS., said in 1797 to have been 'lately altered and enlarged by Wyatt' for 1st Marquess of Stafford; remodelled by Sir C. Barry 1834 onwards; dem. 1910 [*Diary and Letters of Madame D'Arblay*, ed. A. Dobson, v, 1905, 338].

PEPER HAROW, SURREY, conservatory for 4th Viscount Midleton, 1797; dem. probably in 1913 [E. W. Brayley, *History of Surrey* v, 1848, 232; drawing by Wyatt dated 1795 in collection of the late Sir Albert Richardson].

DODINGTON PARK, GLOS., for Christopher Codrington, 1798–1813 [exhib. at R.A. 1798; C. Hussey in *C. Life*, 22, 29 Nov. 1956; C. Hussey, *English Country Houses: Late Georgian*, 1958, 41–54].

NORRIS CASTLE, EAST COWES, ISLE OF WIGHT, for Lord Henry Seymour, 1799, castellated [E. W. Brayley & J. Britton, *Beauties of England and Wales* vi, 1805, 391; W. Cooke, *New Picture of the Isle of Wight*, 1808, 143; B. Burke, *Visitation of Seats* i (2), 1853, 89].

PENNSYLVANIA CASTLE, PORTLAND, DORSET, for John Penn, 1800, castellated [*D.N.B.*, *s.v.* 'Penn'; *Dorset Arch. Soc. Trans.* xxxvii, 1916, 248–51].

OTTERSHAW PARK, SURREY, entrance lodges for Edward Boehm, *c.*1800 [G. F. Prosser, *Illustrations of the County of Surrey*, 1828].

PURLEY HOUSE, BERKS., for the executors of Anthony Storer (d. 1799), who provided for its erection in his will, *c.*1800 [*Gent's Mag.* 1799 (ii), 626; D. & S. Lysons, *Magna Britannia* i, 1806, 325].

HANWORTH FARM, MIDDLESEX, for himself, *c.*1800; dem. Cary's *New Itinerary* of 1812 refers to Wyatt's country seat as 'Hanworth House', but it appears generally to have been known as 'Hanworth Farm' and stood about half a mile north-east of Hanworth Park.

BICTON LODGE, DEVON, completed house for 1st Lord Rolle (who succeeded to the property in 1797), *c.*1800; remodelled by W. Tapper 1908–9 [*The Copper-Plate Magazine* v, pl. ccx, 1800].

HINTON ST. GEORGE, SOMERSET, alterations and additions for 4th Earl Poulett, *c.*1800–5, Gothic [J. Soane, *Professional Memoirs*, 1835, 24; drawings by Wyatt in Yale Center for British Art dated 1801 and 1804] (J. P. Neale, *Views of Seats*, 2nd ser. iv, 1828).

CASSIOBURY PARK, HERTS., remodelled for 5th Earl of Essex, *c.*1800–5, castellated; dem. 1922 [J. Britton, *History . . . of Cassiobury Park*, 1837, 27] (*C. Life*, 17 Sept. 1910).

WINDSOR CASTLE, BERKS., remodelled royal apartments in Upper Ward for King George III, 1800–13, castellated Gothic; largely remodelled by Sir Jeffry Wyatville 1824–40 [W. H. St. J. Hope, *Architectural History of Windsor Castle*, 1913, 348–55; *History of the King's Works* vi, 375–9].

WILTON HOUSE, WILTS., restoration and additions for 11th Earl of Pembroke, including rebuilding of north and west fronts and erection of cloister, 1801–11, Gothic; north front remodelled by E. Warre 1913–15 [drawings at Wilton; J. Britton, *Beauties of England and Wales* xv, 1814, 336–7] (*C. Life*, 8 Aug. 1963 and 22 Aug., p. 439; *Arch. Hist.* 35, 1992, 111–12).

KEW PALACE, SURREY, for King George III, 1801–11, castellated Gothic; dem. 1827–8 [*History of the King's Works* vi, 356–8, fig. 7 and pl. 15].

THE WHITE LODGE, RICHMOND PARK, SURREY, alterations for benefit of 1st Viscount Sidmouth, 1801–6 [*History of the King's Works* vi, 355].

BELVOIR CASTLE, LEICS., remodelled for 5th Duke of Rutland, 1801–13, castellated Gothic; seriously damaged by fire 1816, after which the castle was restored under the direction of the amateur architect the Revd. J. Thoroton (d. 1820).[1] The north-east and north-west fronts are Thoroton's work, the south-east and south-west fronts Wyatt's [drawings in Belvoir muniments, maps 129, 130, 132; I. Eller, *History of Belvoir Castle*, 1841] (*C. Life*, 6, 13, 20, 27 Dec. 1956).

STOKE POGES VICARAGE, BUCKS., for John Penn, 1802–4, Gothic [J. Penn, *An Historical and Descriptive Account of Stoke Park*, 1813, 68].

WYCOMBE ABBEY, BUCKS., reconstructed for 1st Lord Carrington, *c.*1803–4, Gothic [D. & S. Lysons, *Magna Britannia* i, 1806, 676; *Passages from the Diaries of Mrs. Lybbe-Powys*, ed. Climenson, 1899, 356].

CRANBOURNE LODGE, WINDSOR, BERKS., remodelled for King George III, 1804–8; dem. 1830 [*History of the King's Works* vi, 394–5].

WEST DEAN PARK, SUSSEX, rebuilt for Sir James Peachey, Bart., cr. 1st Lord Selsey (d. 1808), *c.*1804–8, Gothic; completed by F. Sandys (*q.v.*); rebuilt 1893 [R. Ackermann, *Views of Seats* ii, 1830, 36–7] (J. P Neale, *Views of Seats*, 1st ser. iv, 1821; T. W. Horsfield, *History of Sussex* ii, 1835, 82).

SUNNINGHILL PARK, BERKS., alterations for G. H. Crutchley, probably soon after 1805; dem. 1947 [J. P. Neale, *Views of Seats*, 1st ser. iii, 1820].

BULSTRODE PARK, BUCKS., began reconstruction of west wing for 3rd Duke of Portland, *c.*1806–9, Gothic; not completed after Duke's death in 1809; rebuilt by B. Ferrey 1862 [*The Farington Diary* ed. J. Greig, vii, 34; J. Harris, 'Bulstrode', *Arch. Rev.* Nov. 1958].

ASHRIDGE PARK, HERTS., for 7th Earl of Bridgwater, 1808–13, completed by Sir Jeffry Wyatville 1813 onwards; Gothic [R.I.B.A.D.; inscription on brass plate in hall] (H. A. Tipping, *English Homes, VI* (i), 339–46).

attributed: ALTON ABBEY (later TOWERS), STAFFS., remodelling for 15th Earl of

[1] 'Of His architectural talents the new buildings erected at Belvoir Castle will be a lasting monument, for he participated in every plan connected with them, from their commencement in the year 1801, and during the latter years of his life he had the chief direction both in the design and execution of them' (inscription on monument in Bottesford Church).

Shrewsbury, 1811–13, Gothic; continued by William Hollins, Thomas Allason, A. W. N. Pugin and others [stylistic attribution; accounts in the Staffordshire Record Office show that work started in 1811, but no architect is named until Hollins in 1817, *ex inf.* Dr. J. M. Frew] (J. P. Neale, *Views of Seats* iii, 1820).

CHICKSANDS PRIORY, BEDS., alterations for Sir George Osborn, Bart., 1813–14, Gothic [I. D. Parry, *Select Illustrations of Bedfordshire*, 1827, 117; J. P. Neale, *Views of Seats*, 2nd ser. v, 1829].

ELVASTON HALL, DERBYSHIRE, rebuilt for 3rd Earl of Harrington, *c.*1815–19, by R. Walker (*q.v.*), to Gothic designs said to have been made by James Wyatt before his death [J. P. Neale, *Views of Seats*, 1st ser., vi, 1823].

SOPHIA LODGE, CLEWER, BERKS., remodelled for William Dawson, date uncertain, Gothic [R. Ackermann, *Repository of Arts*, 3rd ser. ii, 1823, 249–50].

FONTHILL HOUSE, WILTS., ceilings, etc. and fishing-lodge for William Beckford, date uncertain; house dem. *c.*1800 [J. Britton, *Beauties of Wiltshire* i, 1801, 212, 214, 246].

LONDON HOUSES

GROSVENOR SQUARE, No. 16, alterations for William Drake, *c.*1773–5, and new back staircase, 1789; dem. 1940 [Drake papers, Bucks. Record Office, D/Dr. 5/69, 71; 12/61] (*C. Life*, 2 July 1948).

PORTMAN SQUARE, Nos. 11–15 (north side), 1773–84, as a personal speculation [A. T. Bolton, *The Works of R. and J. Adam* ii, 1922, 81, 91].

DEVONSHIRE HOUSE, PICCADILLY, repairs and decoration for 5th Duke of Devonshire, 1776–90; dem. 1924–5 [household accounts at Chatsworth, *ex inf.* Dr. J. M. Robinson].

GROSVENOR SQUARE, No. 36 (later 41), remodelled for Peter Delmé, 1778–9; dem. 1962–5 [*A.P.S.D.*; designs for ceilings in Wyatt album, Metropolitan Museum].

CONDUIT STREET, No. 9, for Robert Vyner, 1779 [*A.P.S.D.*; B. Higgins, *Experiments . . . with . . . Calcareous Cements*, 1780, 216].

FOLEY PLACE (formerly QUEEN ANNE STREET EAST), No. 1, for himself, *c.*1780–3; dem. *c.*1928 [A. Dale, *James Wyatt*, 1956, 15–16] (A. E. Richardson & C. L. Gill, *London Houses 1660–1720*, 1911, pl. lxxii).

RICHMOND HOUSE, WHITEHALL, added staircase and two rooms for 3rd Duke of Richmond, 1782; destroyed by fire 1791 [H. Walpole, *Anecdotes of Painting* v, ed. F. W. Hilles & P. B. Daghlian, 1939, 161]; temporary theatre 1787 [Hist. MSS. Comm., *XVth Report*, Appendix, part vii, 281].

GROSVENOR SQUARE, No. 25 (later 28), designs for alterations for Sir Robert Rich, Bart., before 1785; dem. 1957 [bill for drawings in R.I.B.A. MS. and Archives Collection].

DOWNSHIRE HOUSE, No. 20 HANOVER SQUARE, interior decoration for 1st Marquess of Downshire, *c.*1789; since destroyed [design for ceiling for 'Lord Fairford now Marquis of Down' in Wyatt album, Metropolitan Museum].

BUCKINGHAM HOUSE, ST. JAMES'S, principal staircase for King George III, *c.*1800; dem. 1825 [*History of the King's Works* vi, 261].

ST. JAMES'S PLACE, No. 22, for Samuel Rogers, 1802–3; destroyed by bombing 1940 [*A.P.S.D.*; *Survey of London* xxx, 536–8].

CARLTON HOUSE, PALL MALL, repairs and redecoration of rooms in basement of garden front for the Prince of Wales, 1804–5; fitting up of additional library and strong room, 1812–13; dem. 1826 [*History of the King's Works* vi, 312–13, 315].

APSLEY HOUSE, PICCADILLY, repairs and redecoration for Marquess Wellesley, 1807; remodelled by B. D. Wyatt 1828–9 [Stratfield Saye papers cited by J. M. Robinson, *The Wyatts*, 1979, 242].

TOWN HOUSES ELSEWHERE

BRISTOL, design for CRESCENT in TYNDALL'S PARK, begun 1793 but never completed [W. Ison, *The Georgian Buildings of Bristol*, 1952, 26–7].

DUBLIN, LEINSTER HOUSE, decoration of picture gallery (now Senate Chamber) for 2nd Duke of Leinster, before 1794 [C. P. Curran, *Dublin Decorative Plasterwork*, 1967, 85 and pls. 171–2].

LEIDEN, HOLLAND, No. 19 RAPENBERG, ceiling for Johannes Meerman, 1788 [J. Harris, *Catalogue of British Drawings for Architecture, etc., in American Collections*, 1971, 300].

OXFORD, PHYSIC (BOTANIC) GARDEN, conversion of greenhouse into library and residence for Professor of Botany, 1789; enlarged by H. J. Underwood 1834 [T. W. M. Jaine in *Oxoniensia* xxxvi, 1971, 70].

MAUSOLEA AND MONUMENTS, ETC.

attributed: DARTREY (DAWSON'S GROVE), CO. MONAGHAN, Mausoleum for Thomas Dawson, 1st Viscount Cremorne, 1770 [drawings in National Library of Ireland attributed to Wyatt].

CHELTENHAM PARISH CHURCH, GLOS., tablet to Katherine A'Court, d. 1776, executed by

R. Westmacott [*The Torrington Diaries*, ed. C. B. Andrews, i, 1934, 123].

LICHFIELD CATHEDRAL, STAFFS., monument to David Garrick, d. 1779 [F. Calvert & W. West, *Picturesque Views of Staffordshire*, 1830, 3].

COBHAM HALL, KENT, Mausoleum for 4th Earl of Darnley, *c.*1783–4 [exhib. at R.A. 1783; drawings in Soane Museum].

BROCKLESBY PARK, LINCS., Mausoleum for 1st Lord Yarborough, 1786–94 [signed 'J. WYATT ESQR. ARCHT.'; exhib. at R.A. 1795; J. Lord, 'The Building of the Mausoleum at Brocklesby', *Church Monuments* vii, 1992] (*C. Life*, 3 March 1934).

SHRIVENHAM CHURCH, BERKS., monument to 2nd Viscount Barrington, d. 1793 [signed by Wyatt as architect and R. Westmacott as sculptor].

WILTON CHURCH, WILTS., monument to 10th Earl of Pembroke, d. 1794 [signed by Wyatt as architect and R. Westmacott as sculptor].

HALE CHURCH, HANTS., monument to Joseph May, d. 1796 [signed by Wyatt as architect and R. Westmacott as sculptor].

STOKE POGES CHURCHYARD, BUCKS., monument to Thomas Gray, erected 1799 [J. Penn, *An Historical and Descriptive Account of Stoke Park*, 1813, 61].

STOKE POGES PARK, BUCKS., column in memory of Sir Edward Coke, with statue by Rossi, 1800 [J. Penn, *An Historical and Descriptive Account of Stoke Park*, 1813, 61–2].

HAVERING CHURCH, ESSEX, monument to Sir John Smith Burges, Bart., d. 1803 [E. W. Brayley & J. Britton, *Beauties of England and Wales* v, 1803, 476].

WYATT, JEFFRY, *see* WYATVILLE, Sir JEFFRY.

WYATT, JOSEPH (1739–1785), the fourth son of Benjamin Wyatt of Weeford, was born on 9 October 1739. He practised as a mason and architect in Burton-on-Trent. In 1783 he made designs for rebuilding the church of BREEDON-ON-THE-HILL, LEICS., which was in disrepair, but it proved impossible to raise sufficient money to carry them out [B.L., Church Briefs, B. XXIV, 4]. The same difficulty prevented the execution of his designs for rebuilding GRESLEY CHURCH, DERBYSHIRE, for which a Brief was obtained in 1786, and his plans are still preserved among the Quarter Session Records at Derby [J. C. Cox, *Churches of Derbyshire* iii, 1877, 373 n.]. Wyatt, who died in 1785, was the father of Sir Jeffry Wyatville. He had the reputation of being a 'clever, but indolent' architect [*A.P.S.D.*]. A competently drawn design by him for a greenhouse for Sir Robert Wilmot of Osmaston Hall, nr. Derby, is among the Wilmot-Horton papers in the Derbyshire Record Office.

WYATT, LEWIS WILLIAM (1777–1853), was one of the sons of Benjamin Wyatt (d. 1818), agent to Lord Penrhyn. He was apprenticed first to his uncle Samuel, and then to his uncle James, and began practice on his own in about 1805. In 1804 he was, on his uncle James's recommendation, appointed Assistant Architect to the Board of Ordnance. In 1800 James gave him a place in the Office of Works as Labourer in Trust at Carlton House. In 1818 he was promoted to the Clerkship of the Works at the Tower of London, Somerset House, etc., and in 1829 was transferred to Hampton Court, but lost his post when the Office was reorganized in 1832.

Lewis Wyatt began to exhibit at the Royal Academy in 1795, showing in 1797 views of various buildings erected on the Penrhyn estates by his father and his uncle Samuel. These were published in 1800–1 as '*A Collection of Architectural Designs, rural and ornamental, executed . . . upon the Estates of the Right Hon. Lord Penrhyn in Caernarvonshire and Cheshire*, accurately delineated by L. W. Wyatt'. Lewis's earliest recorded works were designed in James Wyatt's office for execution by Benjamin Wyatt (d. 1813), who continued the family building business in Staffordshire (see below). When Samuel Wyatt died in 1807, Lewis completed two of his country-house commissions and succeeded to his practice in Cheshire.

Wyatt was primarily a country-house architect, his only public buildings of any consequence being the parish church at Stockport and the town hall at Basingstoke. In 1805 he was one of those who submitted designs for Downing College, Cambridge. Plans by James Wyatt were already under consideration but had been severely criticized by Thomas Hope, and it is possible that Lewis Wyatt's entry was an attempt to salvage the commission for the Wyatt family. It was, however, the Greek Revival designs of William Wilkins that were selected by the judges. In 1816 Wyatt published anonymously a *Prospectus of a Design for Various Improvements in the Metropolis*, in which he insisted on the need for a 'pre-arranged and well-organised plan' for the development of London, and advocated certain specific 'improvements', including the replanning of the West End so as to 'converge to a natural and appropriate focus in a palace for the sovereign'. This was to be on the site of Carlton House in St. James's

Park. Other proposals were for a crescent on the site of the present Trafalgar Square, facing a 'College of Arts and Sciences', and for a Thames embankment from Waterloo Bridge to Westminster. In 1827 he competed for St. George's Hospital, and in 1835 for the Houses of Parliament. His plans for the latter envisaged retaining as many of the buildings as had escaped the fire, and replacing those that had been destroyed in appropriate historical styles: 'Saxon' for the Painted Chamber, the 'Gothic of Edward III' for St. Stephen's Chapel, 'Plantagenet' for the two Houses, and 'Elizabethan' for the Speaker's house.

In his executed works Wyatt was eclectic in style. His best designs were in the neo-classical manner of his uncles Samuel and James (cf. Willey Hall and James Wyatt's Dodington Hall), but at Cranage Hall he tried the Tudor style, at Eaton Hall the Jacobean, and at Sherborne he reproduced the principal features of a sixteenth-century house with superimposed orders like Longleat. At Hackwood and Lyme his skill in incorporating and adapting earlier panelling and carving makes it difficult to decide precisely what is his and what is original, and at Hawkstone he showed the same expertise as his cousins Benjamin and Philip in recreating the *décor* of the age of Louis XIV. He had had the opportunity to study it on the spot, for he visited Paris in 1815 and again in 1825, when he was sent there to supervise repairs to the British Embassy. In 1820 he was given six months' leave by the Board of Works in order to visit Italy.

Wyatt gave up practice in about 1835. He had lost his Office of Works post in 1832 and the negligence of a clerk of works at Sherborne House in Gloucestershire had damaged his professional reputation by allowing defective workmanship which Wyatt was obliged to make good at considerable cost to himself. Fortunately the death of his father had left him well off and he was able to retire to Cliff Cottage, Puckpool, nr. Ryde in the Isle of Wight, where he died on 11 February 1853, aged 75. He left all his architectural drawings to his nephew Benjamin Wyatt Greenfield of Shirley, Hants. His excellent library and his small collection of Italian paintings were sold at Christie's on 1 June. Among the latter were several pictures 'purchased at Bologna, from the gallery of Count Marescalchi'. D. Harrison was a pupil.

[*A.P.S.D.*; *Gent's Mag.* 1853 (i), 670; *History of the King's Works* vi, 119, 633, 677; J. M. Robinson, *The Wyatts*, 1979, 140–56, 247–8; will in P.C.C. 1853, f. 241.]

PATSHULL HOUSE, STAFFS., supplied designs for alterations carried out by Benjamin Wyatt of Sutton Coldfield for Sir George Pigott, Bart., 1803–5 [William Salt Library, Stafford, Wyatt correspondence (M.96)].

WIGGINTON LODGE, nr. TAMWORTH, STAFFS., supplied designs for new house to be carried out by Benjamin Wyatt of Sutton Coldfield for Sir Charles Clarke, Bart., M.D., 1804 [William Salt Library, Stafford, Wyatt correspondence (M. 96)].

HEATON HOUSE, LANCS., works probably including orangery, Grand Lodge, library, chimney-stacks and alterations to N. front of house for 1st and 2nd Earls of Wilton, 1807–24 [*Heaton Hall, Manchester, Bicentenary Exhibition Catalogue*, 1972, 84, 86–7].

TATTON PARK, CHESHIRE, completion for Wilbraham Egerton of house begun by Samuel Wyatt (d. 1807) for William Egerton (d. 1806), 1807–16, including entrance to park from Knutsford and conservatory, 1818 [exhib. at R.A. 1811 and 1812; Arthur Oswald in *C. Life*, 16, 23, 30 July 1964; G. Jackson-Stops, *An English Arcadia*, National Trust 1991, 118–20].

HACKWOOD PARK, HANTS., completion for 2nd Lord Bolton of remodelling begun by Samuel Wyatt (d. 1807) for 1st Lord Bolton (d. 1807), 1807–13 and later [exhib. at R.A. 1810; R. Ackermann, *Repository of Arts*, 3rd ser., vi, 1825, 125–6] (*C. Life*, 17–24 May 1913, 10–17 Dec. 1987).

WONHAM MANOR, BETCHWORTH, SURREY, alterations for 1st Viscount Templetown, *c.*1805–10, Gothic [exhib. at R.A. 1810] (R. Ackermann, *Views of Country Seats* ii, 1830, 48).

MOUNT SHANNON, CO. LIMERICK, IRELAND, added portico for 2nd Earl of Clare, 1809, house gutted by fire 1922 (portico survives) [C. Fitzgibbon in *Quarterly Bull. Irish Georgian Soc.* xix, 1976, 14–19].

RODE HALL, CHESHIRE, alterations, including new dining-room, for Randle Wilbraham, 1810–12 [P. de Figueiredo & J. Treuherz, *Cheshire Country Houses*, 1988, 155–8].

STOKE HALL, EAST STOKE, NOTTS., enlarged for Sir Robert Bromley, Bart., 1812; altered 1923 [*A.P.S.D.*; A. Graves, *The Royal Academy of Arts* viii, 1905, 377. Both sources refer to a drawing, said to have been exhibited at the R.A. in 1812, which cannot, however, be found in the original R.A. catalogue for this year].

WILLEY HALL, SALOP., for Cecil Weld-Forester, cr. Lord Forester, 1813–15 [signed drawings in Shropshire Record Office and Avery Library, Columbia University, New York;

J. P. Neale, *Views of Seats*, 2nd ser. ii, 1825; C. Hussey, *English Country Houses: Late Georgian*, 1958, 115–21].

STOCKPORT PARISH CHURCH, CHESHIRE, rebuilt 1813–17, incorporating medieval chancel, Gothic [H. Heginbotham, *Stockport, Ancient and Modern* i, 1882, 217; exhib. at R.A. 1814; drawings in Soane Museum, xlvii, 10, 1–11].

LYME PARK, CHESHIRE, alterations for Thomas Legh, 1814–17, including addition of tower behind pediment on south front and remodelling of rooms on east front [exhib. at R.A. 1816; J. P. Neale, *Views of Seats*, 2nd ser. i, 1824; John Cornforth in *C. Life*, 26 Dec. 1974].

CUERDEN HALL, LANCS., enlarged for Robert Townley Parker, 1816–19 [E. Twycross, *The Mansions of England: Lancashire* i, 1847, 42; building accounts in Lancs. C.R.O., DDX 1564].

ROSTHERNE, CHESHIRE, school for Wilbraham Egerton, 1815, and addition of *cottage orné*, 1826 [J. M. Robinson, *op. cit.*, 248].

WINSLADE CHURCH, HANTS., rebuilt 1816–17 for 2nd Lord Bolton, Gothic [J. M. Robinson, *op. cit.*, 248].

OULTON HALL, CHESHIRE, altered interior, added terrace and designed stables for Sir John Grey-Egerton, Bart., *c.*1816–26; gutted by fire 1926 and since dem. [G. Ormerod, *History of Cheshire*, ed. Helsby, ii, 1882, 219].

WINSTANLEY HALL, LANCS., alterations for Meyrick Banckes, 1818–19 [drawings in Lancashire Record Office].

RADCLIFFE CHAPEL, nr. BURY, LANCS., for Countess Grosvenor, 1818–19, Gothic; rebuilt 1864–5 [by 'Mr. Wyatt': *Gent's Mag.* 1818 (i), 633].

BROME HALL, SUFFOLK, added bay window to Dining Room and designed offices for 2nd Marquess Cornwallis, 1819 [drawings sold at Christie's 24 March 1982].

DUNGENESS LIGHTHOUSE, KENT, repairs after damage by lightning, 1822 [J. M. Robinson, *op. cit.*, 247].

ST. ASAPH CATHEDRAL, FLINTSHIRE, ceiled nave and aisles with stucco, *c.*1822; removed 1865 [D. R. Thomas, *History of the Diocese of St. Asaph*, 1870, 207].

LONDON, Nos. 12–17 SUFFOLK STREET, *c.*1822–3. Wyatt built Nos. 12–14 as a personal speculation and lived in No. 13 from 1823 to 1829; Nos. 15–17 were built to his designs for John Holroyd [*Survey of London* xx, 93].

BOLTON HALL, YORKS. (N.R.), repairs and alterations for 2nd Lord Bolton, *c.*1823–4; gutted by fire 1902 [plans, *ex inf.* National Register of Archives, list 8638].

LONDON, MIDDLESEX HOSPITAL, minor alterations and repairs, 1823–9 [J. M. Robinson, *op. cit.*, 247].

BAKEWELL CHURCH, DERBYSHIRE, report on spire with Joseph Potter, 1824 [parish records].

ELSTREE CHURCH, HERTS., enlarged 1824; rebuilt 1853 by P. C. Hardwick [I.C.B.S.].

FLINTHAM HALL, NOTTS., library, offices and conservatory for Col. T. B. Hildyard, 1829; remodelled by T. Hine 1853–7 [drawings at Flintham Hall].

CRANAGE HALL, CHESHIRE, for Lawrence Armistead, 1828–9, Tudor [Ormerod, *History of Cheshire*, ed. Helsby, iii, 1882, 129].

EATON HALL, nr. CONGLETON, CHESHIRE, for G. C. Antrobus, 1829–31, Jacobean; dem. 1981 [P. de Figueiredo & J. Treuherz, *Cheshire Country Houses*, 1988, 233].

SHERBORNE HOUSE, GLOS., rebuilt for 2nd Lord Sherborne, 1829–34, reproducing the style of the seventeeth-century house [Dutton papers in Gloucestershire C.R.O., D678, F. 322] (*Connoisseur*, xxx, 1991).

BIBURY COURT, GLOS., minor alterations for 2nd Lord Sherborne, 1830 [*ibid.*].

LONDON, No. 53 LOWER GROSVENOR STREET, repairs for 2nd Lord Sherborne, 1832 [*ibid.*].

MAPLEDURHAM VICARAGE, OXON., alterations for Revd. Lord Augustus FitzClarence, 1832 [drawings in parish records, *ex inf.* Mr. D. Miles].

HAMPTON COURT, MIDDLESEX, house for Principal Stud Groom, 1832–3 [J. M. Robinson, op. cit., 247].

HAWKSTONE HALL, SALOP., drawing-room and other alterations and additions for Sir Rowland Hill, Bart., 1832–4 [Arthur Oswald in *C. Life*, 3 April 1958; Andor Gomme, 'The Building of Hawkstone Hall', *Archl. Jnl.* 141, 1984, 323–4].

BASINGSTOKE TOWN HALL, HANTS., 1833 [S. Lewis, *Topographical Dictionary of England* i, 1848, 169].

WYATT, Sir MATTHEW (1805–1886), was the eldest son of Matthew Cotes Wyatt (1777–1862), the sculptor. During the earlier part of his life he was active as an architect and speculative builder in London. In 1838–40, in partnership with John Howell, he built VICTORIA SQUARE to his own design. He then moved to Paddington, where he erected houses in STANHOPE TERRACE, WESTBOURNE and BATHURST STREETS, and the triangle of land bounded by CONNAUGHT STREET, SOUTHWICK STREET, HYDE PARK STREET and HYDE PARK SQUARE. He also built smaller houses, now demolished, in HOWLEY PLACE and PORTEUS ROAD on the Bishop of London's

Paddington estate. Many of his houses were built in partnership with his brother George Wyatt (d. 1880).

By the late 1840s Wyatt was living in affluence in Hyde Park Square and gave up active participation in building. He was knighted in 1848 after becoming an officer of the Honourable Corps of Gentlemen at Arms. [J. M. Robinson, *The Wyatts*, 1979, 200–1].

WYATT, PHILIP WILLIAM (–1835), was the fourth and youngest son of James Wyatt. He was educated privately before becoming a pupil in his father's office. Charming, lazy, feckless and improvident, he failed to make the most of his opportunities, and was frequently in financial difficulties, culminating in his imprisonment for debt in 1833. Throughout his life he was destined to be overshadowed by his elder brother Benjamin. In 1811, encouraged by his father, he competed for the Drury Lane Theatre, only to be defeated by Benjamin's rival plan. In 1813 he seized the opportunity of his brother's absence in Ireland to ride to Ragley in Warwickshire to announce his father's death to the Prince Regent at 3 o'clock in the morning, and to solicit his patronage, but the Prince merely 'returned a civil answer in a general way', and Philip failed to secure any of his father's posts. In 1814, no doubt hoping to attract clients, he exhibited a drawing at the Royal Academy, but relatively few commissions appear to have come his way, and in the 1820s he was acting as Benjamin's assistant or junior partner. As such he participated in the design of some important works, including York, Londonderry and Apsley Houses.

As an independent architect Philip's principal works were the classical Wynyard Park and the picturesque Gothic Conishead Priory, both buildings of some size and importance in their respective styles, though Conishead was only partly his, having been completed by George Webster to his own designs after Wyatt's dismissal in 1829.

In 1824 Wyatt was employed by Sir Frederick Trench to make designs for the Thames quay or embankment of which Trench was an enthusiastic promoter, but nothing came of this or of other schemes for the improvement of London for which he made drawings under Trench's directions.

[B.L., Add. MSS. 38256, ff. 14–19, 38265, ff. 194–5; P.R.O., PRIS 4/43, p. 11; *The Farington Diary*, ed. J. Greig, vii, 130, 205; Boyd Alexander, *Life at Fonthill*, 1957, 295–6; J. M. Robinson, *The Wyatts*, 1979, 101–5, 115–22, 243.]

GREAT YARMOUTH, NORFOLK, ST. NICHOLAS CHURCH, repairs 1813 [J. M. Robinson, *op. cit.*, 253; cf. J. Preston, *Picture of Yarmouth*, Yarmouth 1819, 39, 42].

LONDON, No. 40 UPPER BROOK STREET, redecorated for E. H. Ball Hughes, 1819 [Boyd Alexander, *op. cit.*, 296; *Reminiscences of Capt. Gronow*, ed. J. Raymond, 1964, 262].

LONDON, No. 10 ST. JAMES'S SQUARE, interior decoration for Earl of Blessington, in collaboration with M. C. Wyatt, 1821 [B.L., Egerton MS. 3515] (*Survey of London* xxix, 123, 130–2).

CONISHEAD PRIORY, LANCS., for T. R. Gale Braddyll, 1821–9, Gothic, completed by George Webster (*q.v.*) after Wyatt's dismissal in 1829 [R. Wallis, *Lancashire Illustrated*, 1829, 96].

WYNYARD PARK, CO. DURHAM, rebuilt for 3rd Marquess of Londonderry, 1822–30; interior partly destroyed by fire 1841 and restored by I. Bonomi & J. A. Cory 1842–4 [W. Fordyce, *History of Durham* ii, 1855, 322] (*C. Life* 28 Aug., 4 Sept. 1986).

BISHOPWEARMOUTH, CO. DURHAM, ST. THOMAS'S CHURCH, 1827–9, Gothic; dem. [W. Fordyce, *History of Durham* ii, 1855, 436].

SEAHAM HALL, CO. DURHAM, designs for alterations and lodges for 3rd Marquess of Londonderry, 1828, apparently not executed [J. M. Robinson, *op. cit.* 253 and cf. Pevsner & Williamson, *County Durham*, Buildings of England, 1983, 399 n].

MOUNT OSWALD, SOUTH ROAD, DURHAM, remodelled for Percival Wilkinson, 1829–30 [P. Meadows, 'Mount Oswald, Durham', *Durham Archl. Jnl.* 6, 1990].

RED HALL, HOUGHTON-LE-SKERNE, CO. DURHAM, for Capt. Robert Colling, 1830; dem. 1984 [B. Burke, *A Visitation of Seats and Arms* i, 1852, 116].

WEYMOUTH, DORSET, HOLY TRINITY CHURCH, 1834–6, Gothic, completed after Wyatt's death by his nephew Matthew Wyatt [R.C.H.M. *Dorset* ii (2), 334].

WYATT, SAMUEL (1737–1807), born on 8 September 1737, at Blackbrook Farm, Weeford, Staffs., was the third son of Benjamin Wyatt, builder and architect (*q.v.*). He was trained as a carpenter, and worked at first as a member of the family firm. In 1759 he was engaged first as master carpenter and then as clerk of the works at Kedleston Hall by Robert Adam. This appointment was to be of great importance in his career, for it brought him into contact with the leading neo-classical architect of the time, and gave him practical experience in the designing and construction of a major building. It was also at Kedleston that he met and in 1765 married Ann Sherwin, the daughter of Lord Scarsdale's land agent. In about 1768 he returned to Weeford, and in the following year he obtained his first architectural commission, a new drawing-room at Blithfield Hall, the seat of Sir William Bagot. Between 1769 and 1771 he was closely associated with his younger brother James in the design and construction of the Pantheon in Oxford Street, to whose complicated carpentry he applied the experience he had gained in executing the 'circular roofing' over the saloon at Kedleston, and it was James's designs that he and his brother William carried out when they remodelled the interior of Beaudesert in 1771–3. The death in 1772 of Benjamin Wyatt led to the break-up of the family firm, and in 1774 Samuel settled permanently in London. From the Duke of Portland he obtained the lease of a large house and timber-yard in Berwick Street, from which for nearly thirty years he was to conduct a highly successful business as architect, builder and timber-merchant.

As an architect Samuel Wyatt specialized in the designing of medium-sized country houses in an elegant and restrained neo-classical manner. Characteristic features of his houses were astylar elevations with prominent bowed projections, either domed (as at Doddington and Delamere) or duplicated (as at Belmont and Hurstmonceaux); oval or circular rooms ingeniously fitted into the plan; overarched tripartite windows; and the sparing use of Coade stone plaques as external decoration. Unlike his brother James he deviated little from his chosen neo-classical formulae, rarely using the Gothic style, and then only in exceptional circumstances (e.g. at Penrhyn).

Wyatt's spare neo-classical style was well adapted to utilitarian buildings, and he enjoyed a considerable reputation as a designer of model farm-buildings for improving landlords – notably at Holkham, where between 1780 and 1807 he built nearly fifty farms, barns, lodges, cottages, etc., for 'Coke of Norfolk'. A strong practical interest in building techniques led him to make extensive use of slate (from the Penrhyn quarries in North Wales managed by his brother Benjamin) for cladding and other purposes, and to experiment with cast-iron construction. It was he who in 1783–6 built the celebrated Albion Mills at Blackfriars. This was the first mill to be designed from the start to be powered by steam, and contained two of Boulton and Watt's double-acting rotative engines, each of 50 h.p. It was also one of the first large buildings to be founded on a structural raft. Its destruction by fire in March 1791 was a disaster which does nothing to impair Wyatt's credit as a structural innovator. In 1799 he was involved in the abortive scheme for a Thames tunnel, and in 1800 he took out a patent for building cast-iron bridges, warehouses, etc. In 1787–8 he designed and built twelve prefabricated wooden hospitals for use overseas. He was also the inventor of a 'sympathetic hinge', a device whereby both leaves of a double door are made to open simultaneously. He thought of himself as an engineer-architect rather than as an artist-architect like his brother James, and it is significant that he became a member of the Society for the Promotion of Arts, Manufactures and Commerce, and of the Smeatonian Society of Civil Engineers, but never exhibited at the Royal Academy, nor sought election to that body. Lacking his brother's social and artistic gifts, Samuel was characterized by Humphry Repton as 'slow, plodding, heavy in carriage, dull in conceiving the ideas of others and tedious in explaining his own'. But what he lacked in brilliance, he made up in competence and reliability, and unlike James, he died a wealthy man.

In 1792 Wyatt was appointed to his two principal public offices – the Surveyorship of Trinity House (Feb.) and the Clerkship of the Works at Chelsea Hospital (March). In October 1793 he succeeded John Vardy, junior, as Surveyor to the Mint, but was dismissed in December of the following year for inattention to his duties. His energies had perhaps been too much diverted to Ramsgate Harbour, of which he became Surveyor and Civil Engineer in March 1794. He died suddenly at Chelsea on 8 February 1807 at the age of 70, and was buried in the Hospital cemetery. He left no children. A portrait by Lemuel Abbott is in the Baker Museum of Furniture, Holland, Michigan, U.S.A. It shows him with four notebooks, inscribed 'Marston House', 'Pantheon 1772', 'Berechurch Hall' and 'Spring Gardens'. The group portrait of the Elder Brethren of Trinity House, painted by Gainsborough Dupont in 1793, shows Wyatt submitting his design for their building to the brethren (*Burlington Mag.*, July 1964, fig. 217). John Harvey (*q.v.*) and his nephew L. W. Wyatt (*q.v.*) were his principal pupils. Others were W. Atkinson (not the well-known architect of this name), R. Moreton (who was 'a relation of Mr. Godwin of Coalbrookdale') and W. Vierpyl.

[J. M. Robinson, *The Wyatts*, 1979, chap. iii and pp. 256–60; A. W. Skempton, 'Early Members of the Smeatonian Society of Civil Engineers', *Trans. Newcomen Soc.* xliv, 1971–2, 35; *Survey of London* xxxi, 233; Humphry

Repton's Autobiography, B.L., MS. 62112, f. 198.]

COUNTRY HOUSES, ETC.

BLITHFIELD HOUSE, STAFFS., additions and alterations, including drawing-room, for 1st Lord Bagot, 1769–70; remodelled in Gothic style *c.*1820–22 [J. M. Robinson, *op. cit.*, 256] (*C. Life*, 28 Oct., 4–11 Nov. 1954).

BERECHURCH HALL, ESSEX, alterations and additions for Sir Robert Smythe, Bart., *c.*1770; rebuilt 1881–2; dem. *c.*1960 [one of the books in Wyatt's portrait is labelled 'Berechurch Hall'].

attributed: DORFOLD HALL, CHESHIRE, alterations, including library, for James Tomkinson, 1771 [stylistic attribution, supported by a sheet of paper inscribed 'Henry Tomkinson Esq. Dorfold Hall' (*sic*) among Samuel Wyatt's drawings at Tatton Park] (*C. Life*, 31 Oct. 1908).

BOSTOCK HALL, CHESHIRE, probably completed interior for Edward Tomkinson, *c.*1775 [house said to be by 'Wyatt' by E. Twycross, *The Mansions of England* iv, 1850, 138].

attributed: WINNINGTON HALL, CHESHIRE, enlargement for Richard Pennant, cr. Lord Penrhyn, *c.*1775, and poultry house, *c.*1782–5 (dem.) [P. de Figueredo & J. Treuherz, *Cheshire Country Houses*, 1988, 198–202].

MARSTON HOUSE, MARSTON BIGOT, SOMERSET, work for 7th Earl of Cork & Orrery, probably including the addition of the wings dated 1777; interior of W. wing remodelled 1868 [one of the books in Wyatt's portrait is labelled 'Marston House'; cf. M. McGarvie, 'Marston House', *Procs. Somerset Archl. & Nat. Hist. Soc.* cxviii, 1974, 19].

BARON HILL, ANGLESEY, remodelled for 7th Viscount Bulkeley, 1776–9; gutted by fire 1836, now ruinous [drawings in Bodleian, MS. Top. Anglesey a.2] (W. Watts, *Views of Seats*, pl. xi, 1779).

DODDINGTON HALL, CHESHIRE, for Sir Thomas Broughton, Bart., 1777–98 [G. Richardson, *New Vitruvius Britannicus* i, 1802, pls. 57–60] (*C. Life*, 6–13 Feb. 1953). Wyatt also designed the Demesne Farm, for which his design is in the Cheshire Record Office [DDB/Q/3].

HERSTMONCEAUX PLACE, SUSSEX, additions for Francis Naylor, including south and east fronts, 1777 [J. Dallaway, *Discourses upon Architecture*, 1833, 330].

SANDON HALL, STAFFS., alterations to house for 1st Lord Harrowby, 1777–84; rebuilt by W. Burn 1851–55; also office court, and Park Farm [*Autobiography of Dudley, 1st Earl of Harrowby*, 1891, 12–13; Harrowby archives].

THORNDON HALL, ESSEX, completed interior for 9th Lord Petre, 1777–1801; destroyed by fire 1878; also Hatch Farm in the park [J. M. Robinson, *op. cit.*, 259].

MINCHENDEN HOUSE, SOUTHGATE, MIDDLESEX, addition of Drawing Room, etc. for 3rd Duke of Chandos, 1778; dem. 1853 [estimate and specification in Enfield Public Library, Groves Collection].

HOOTON HALL, CHESHIRE, for Sir William Stanley, Bart., 1778–88; remodelled in nineteenth century, dem. *c.*1935 [W. Watts, *Views of Seats*, pl. xxiii, 1780]. The fine lodges by Wyatt survive near the church at Childer Thornton.

TIXALL HALL, STAFFS., interior of south wing for the Hon. Thomas Clifford, *c.*1780–2; dem. 1927 [Sir T. & A. Clifford, *Description of Tixall*, 1817, 92].

HOLKHAM HALL, NORFOLK, numerous lodges, farm-houses, barns, cottages and other estate buildings for 1st Earl of Leicester, 1780–1807 [J. M. Robinson, 'Estate Buildings at Holkham', *C. Life*, 21–28 Nov. 1974].

MARBLE HILL HOUSE, TWICKENHAM, MIDDLESEX, repairs for 2nd Earl of Buckinghamshire, 1781 [M. P. G. Draper, *Marble Hill House*, 1970, 50].

BLICKLING HALL, NORFOLK, work for 2nd Earl of Buckinghamshire, probably including Orangery, 1782 [J. Maddison, *Blickling Hall*, National Trust 1987, 40, 65].

EGGINTON HALL, DERBYSHIRE, alterations, including addition of central bow, for Sir Edward Every, Bart., 1782–3; dem. 1955 [payments to 'Mr. Wyatt' cited by Edward Saunders, 'Egginton Hall', *Derbyshire Life*, March 1974].

PENRHYN CASTLE, CAERNARVONSHIRE, remodelled for Richard Pennant, cr. 1st Lord Penrhyn, 1782 onwards, Gothic; rebuilt by T. Hopper *c.*1825–44 [D. B. Hague in *C. Life*, 14 July, 1955, and *Caernarvonshire Archaeological Soc.'s Trans.* xx, 1959].

DELAMERE HOUSE, CHESHIRE, for George Wilbraham, 1784; dem. 1939 [by 'Wyatt' according to Ormerod, *History of Cheshire*, ed. Helsby, ii, 1882, 137] (E. Twycross, *The Mansions of England* iv, 1850, 112).

PORTSMOUTH DOCKYARD, HANTS., THE COMMISSIONER'S HOUSE, 1784–5 [G. Richardson, *New Vitruvius Britannicus* ii, 1808, pls. 17–22] (*C. Life*, 2–9 April 1964).

attributed: COTON HOUSE, CHURCHOVER, WARWICKS., for Abraham Grimes, *c.*1785 [stylistic attribution, combined with evidence that Wyatt visited a Mr. Grimes in Warwickshire in 1784: J. M. Robinson, *op. cit.*, 256].

TATTON PARK, CHESHIRE, for William Egerton, 1785–91; subsequently completed by L. W. Wyatt for Wilbraham Egerton [Ormerod, *History of Cheshire*, ed. Helsby, i, 1882, 445] (*C. Life*, 16, 23 and 30 July 1964).

HEATHFIELD HOUSE, HANDSWORTH, STAFFS., for James Watt, 1789–90; dem. 1927 [H. W. Dickinson, *James Watt*, 1935, 160–1; G. W. Beard, letter in *C. Life*, 6 March 1953, 667].

attributed: HEATON HOUSE, LANCS., The Music Room for Sir Thomas Egerton, Bart., later 1st Earl of Wilton, 1789–90 [frieze identical to that in Drawing Room at Tatton and organ case similar to Wyatt's unexecuted design for one at Tatton]. The stables (1777) may also be attributed to Wyatt (*C. Life*, 29 Aug., 5 Sept. 1925; *Heaton Hall Manchester: Bicentenary Exhibition 1772–1972*; J. Lomax, 'The first and second Earls of Wilton and . . . Heaton House', *Trans. Lancs. & Cheshire Antiqn. Soc.* 82, 1983).

EGHAM (RUNNYMEDE) PARK, EGHAM, SURREY, for David Jebb, 1789–92 [sale particulars 1805 in Surrey C.R.O., 54/61/5/2].

BELMONT HOUSE, KENT, reconstruction for Col. John Montresor, 1789–93 [C. Hussey in *C. Life*, 27 Jan. –3 Feb. 1955 and information from Dr. J. M. Robinson].

TEMPLE HOUSE, HURLEY, BERKS., for Thomas Williams, *c.*1790; dem. *c.*1930 [*The Farington Diary*, ed. J. Greig, iii, 103].

CULFORD HALL, SUFFOLK, remodelled for 1st Marquess Cornwallis, 1790–6; enlarged and altered 1894 [Wyatt is mentioned at architect in Repton's 'Red Book' of 1791–2, now in the Morton Arboretum Library, Lisle, Illinois, U.S.A.] (J. P. Neale, *Views of Seats*, 1st ser. vi, 1823).

SHUGBOROUGH, STAFFS., remodelled for Thomas Anson, cr. 1st Viscount Anson, 1790–8; also lodges, enlargement of stables and home farm, conversion of Tower of the Winds into a dairy, and two groups of cottages (one, known as 'The Ring', dem. *c.*1965), 1803–6 [accounts among Anson records in Staffs. Record Office; W. Pitt, *Topographical History of Staffordshire*, 1817, 90–1] (*C. Life*, 25 Feb., 11 March, 15–22 April 1954).

KINMEL PARK, DENBIGHSHIRE, for the Revd. Edward Hughes, 1790–1810; destroyed by fire 1841 [J. M. Robinson, *The Wyatts*, 257].

attributed: ST. ASAPH, FLINTSHIRE, THE BISHOP'S PALACE, for Bishop Lewis Bagot, 1791; W. front enlarged by E. Blore 1830–1 [stylistic attribution and Bagot connection].

DROPMORE, BUCKS., new façade with two bows for Lord Grenville, 1792–4 [J. M. Robinson, *op. cit.*, 256] (*C. Life*, 11–18 Oct. 1956).

SOMERLEY, nr. RINGWOOD, HANTS., for Daniel Hobson, 1792–5; additions by W. Burn & J. McVicar Anderson 1869–74 [C. Hussey in *C. Life*, 16, 23 and 30 Jan. 1958].

attributed: LIVERMERE PARK, SUFFOLK, addition of wings, etc., for N. Lee Acton, 1795–6; dem. 1887 [stylistic attribution] (J. P. Neale, *Views of Seats* vi, 1823).

SUNDRIDGE PARK, nr. BROMLEY, KENT, completion of house designed by John Nash and Humphry Repton for Sir Claude Scott, Bart., *c.*1800. Wyatt was responsible for the interior and the stables [S. Shaw, *History of Staffordshire* ii, 1801, Addenda, 16 and references cited on p. 692].

IGHTHAM COURT, KENT, repairs and alterations for Col. Richard James, 1801–7 [payment to Wyatt in James papers, Kent Record Office; Mark Girouard in *C. Life*, 26 June 1958].

WROTHAM RECTORY (now Court Lodge), KENT, for the Revd. George Moore, 1801–2 [C. Greenwood, *Epitome of County History: Kent*, 1838, 136].

LUTTERWORTH RECTORY, LEICS., for the Hon. and Revd. Henry Ryder, 1803 [drawings in Lincolnshire Record Office, MGA 39].

HURTS HALL, SAXMUNDHAM, SUFFOLK, for Charles Long, 1803; rebuilt 1893 [H. Davy, *Views of the Seats of Noblemen and Gentlemen in Suffolk*, 1827].

BUCKENHAM HALL, NORFOLK, alterations for 9th Lord Petre, 1803; dem. except the stables [J. M. Robinson, *op. cit.*, 256].

HACKWOOD PARK, HANTS., remodelled for 1st Lord Bolton, 1805–7, completed by L. W. Wyatt [J. M. Robinson, *op. cit.*, 256] (*C. Life*, 17–24 May 1913, 10–17 Dec. 1987).

PANSHANGER, HERTS., additions for 5th Earl Cowper, 1806–7, completed by W. Atkinson, who Gothicized Wyatt's addition; dem. 1953 [J. M. Robinson, *op. cit.*, 258] (*C. Life*, 11–18 Jan. 1936).

DIGSWELL HOUSE, HERTS., for the Hon. Spencer Cowper, *c.*1807 [Farington's Diary, 13 Feb. 1807].

LONDON: DOMESTIC ARCHITECTURE

PARK STREET, GROSVENOR SQUARE, No. 113 (later 13), internal alterations for 1st Lord Harrowby, 1774–6 [J. M. Robinson, *op. cit.*, 258].

PARK STREET, WESTMINSTER, No. 7 (now No. 14 QUEEN ANNE'S GATE), for Charles Towneley, 1775–6 [D. Cruickshank,

'Queen Anne's Cate', *Georgian Soc's Jnl.* 1992].

SPRING GARDENS, nr. CHARING CROSS, unidentified work, probably *c.*1775; dem. [one of the books in Wyatt's portrait is labelled 'Spring Gardens'].

NEW BOND STREET, alterations to house for 2nd Earl of Buckinghamshire, 1780 [J. Maddison, *Blickling Hall*, National Trust 1987, 40].

UPPER BROOK STREET, No. 36, alterations for Sir Edward Littleton, *c.*1781–4 [J. M. Robinson, *op. cit.*, 258].

attributed: OLD BURLINGTON STREET, No. 29, alterations, including porch, for Sir John Call, *c.*1785; dem. 1935 [*Survey of London* xxxii, 502 and pl. 80b].

UPPER BROOK STREET, No. 6, alterations for William Weddell, 1787; dem. 1936 [J. M. Robinson, *op. cit.*, 258; Jill Low, 'William Weddell's London House', *C. Life*, 27 Dec. 1979].

ST. JAMES'S SQUARE, No. 15 (LICHFIELD HOUSE), remodelled interior for Thomas Anson, cr. 1st Viscount Anson, 1791–4 [*Survey of London* xxix, 148–53].

CLEVELAND ROW, No. 4, for Lord Grenville, 1794–6 [J. M. Robinson, *op. cit.*, 257].

BRUTON STREET, No. 27, alterations for Lord Grey de Wilton (later Earl of Wilton), 1797 by 'Mr. Wyatt', presumably Samuel [J. Lomax in *Trans. Lancs, & Cheshire Antiq. Soc.* 82, 1983, 69].

GROSVENOR SQUARE, No. 10, alterations for Dowager Lady Petre, 1801–3; dem. 1864 [J. M. Robinson, *op. cit.*, 258].

GROSVENOR SQUARE, No. 40 (later 45), reconstructed for 10th Lord Petre, 1803–6; dem. 1938 [*Survey of London* xl, 159].

ST. JAMES'S SQUARE, No. 3, alterations for 3rd Earl of Hardwicke, 1806; dem. 1930 [correspondence sold at Sotheby's, 6 June 1968, wrongly attributed in the catalogue to James Wyatt] (*Survey of London* xl, 159).

PUBLIC AND INDUSTRIAL BUILDINGS

AMERSHAM CHURCH, BUCKS., repaired and refitted for William Drake, 1778–85; altered 1890 [Drake papers, Bucks. Record Office, D/DR/12/60–1].

BANGOR CATHEDRAL, probably the 'Mr. Wyatt' who rebuilt upper storey of Chapter House as library and registry, 1779 onwards, Gothic; dem. [M. L. Clarke, *Bangor Cathedral*, Cardiff 1969, 24; J. M. Robinson, *op. cit.*, 256].

BIRMINGHAM, THEATRE ROYAL, NEW STREET, new façade, 1780–2; dem. 1956 [signed drawing in B. L., *King's Maps* xlii, 82 l; minutes of proprietors in Birmingham Reference Library Archives, Lee Crowder 387] (*C. Life*, 11 Dec. 1915, 820).

SANDON CHURCH, STAFFS., refitted chancel for 1st Lord Harrowby, 1782; altered 1928 [F. E. Copleston, *Sandon Church Restorations*, 1929].

DEPTFORD, KENT, THE VICTUALLING YARD, a barn 1782; dem. [P.R.O., ADM 111/89].

LONDON, THE ALBION MILL, BLACKFRIARS, 1783–6; destroyed by fire 1791 [A. W. Skempton, 'Samuel Wyatt and the Albion Mill', *Arch. Hist.* xiv, 1971].

BIRMINGHAM, remodelled warehouse in Livery Street for Matthew Boulton, 1787–8; dem. 1950 [J. M. Robinson, *op. cit.*, 256].

LONDON, ST. MARY'S CHURCH, LAMBETH, alterations, 1787; altered 1851–2 [G. L. Record Office, DW/OP/1787/1–2].

DUNGENESS, KENT, LIGHTHOUSE for 1st Earl of Leicester, 1791 [J. M. Robinson, *op. cit.*, 256].

LONGSHIPS LIGHTHOUSE, CORNWALL, for Trinity House, 1792 [J. M. Robinson, *op. cit.*, 258].

DEPTFORD, KENT, TRINITY HOUSE ALMSHOUSES, alterations 1792–1803 [J. M. Robinson, *op. cit.*, 256].

STAFFORD, SHIRE HALL, joint design with John Harvey, 1794 [see p. 471].

LONDON, TRINITY HOUSE, TOWER HILL, 1793–6; gutted by bombing 1940, restored by A. E. Richardson 1953 [G. Richardson, *New Vitruvius Britannicus* i, 1802, pls. 22–3] (*C. Life*, 18 Jan. 1941, 22 Oct. 1953).

RAMSGATE HARBOUR, KENT, lighthouse, storehouse, harbour-master's house, gate-lodge, board room or pier house, etc., 1794–1805; all dem. [J. M. Robinson, 'Samuel Wyatt at Ramsgate', *Arch. Hist.* 16, 1973].

ST. AGNES LIGHTHOUSE, SCILLY ISLES, rebuilt top of lighthouse, 1806 [J. M. Robinson, *The Wyatts*, 259].

FLAMBOROUGH HEAD LIGHTHOUSE, YORKS. (E.R.), for Trinity House, 1806 [J. M. Robinson, *op. cit.*, 257].

LONDON, TRINITY ALMSHOUSES, MILE END ROAD, new Quadrangle, 1806; dem. *c.*1941 [J. M. Robinson, *op. cit.*, 258].

MARLOW, BUCKS., THE MARKET HOUSE (later Crown Inn), for Thomas Williams, 1807 [H. M. Colvin, 'Architectural History of Marlow', *Records of Bucks.* xv, 1947, 11].

WYATT, WILLIAM (1734–1783), *see* WYATT, BENJAMIN (1709–1772).

WYATVILLE, Sir JEFFRY (1766–1840), son of Joseph Wyatt of Burton-on-Trent, was born there on 3 August 1766. His mother died soon after his birth and his 'clever but indolent' father married again. The result was an unhappy childhood from which Jeffry tried unsuccessfully to escape by running away to sea. Eventually, however, he was apprenticed to his uncle Samuel Wyatt (*q.v.*), in whose London office he worked from 1784 or 1785 to 1791 or 1792. From 1786 onwards he exhibited regularly at the Royal Academy, and surviving drawings show that he had acquired considerable skill in architectural composition. In 1792 he transferred to the office of his more celebrated uncle James Wyatt, with whom he remained until 1799, when he entered into partnership with John Armstrong (d. 1803), a carpenter and building contractor with a successful business in Pimlico. This link with the building trade gave him a steady income while at the same time permitting him to develop a personal architectural practice. He soon became well known as a country-house architect with a large clientèle among the Whig aristocracy. Unlike his uncle James he was efficient, methodical and dependable, with a large and well-organized office in which by 1812 he was employing as many as ten clerks. When James died in 1813 Jeffry inherited some of his commissions (e.g. Bretby and Ashridge), and took his place as the principal representative of the Wyatt dynasty.

By the 1820s Jeffry Wyatt was one of the half-dozen leading English architects. On the back of a portrait painted about this time he complacently listed his principal employers, giving the names of four dukes, one marquess, seven earls and thirteen other landowners whose houses he had altered or rebuilt. In 1824 he was able to claim the supreme honour of royal patronage when he began the transformation of Windsor Castle for King George IV. Although extensively altered by Charles II, the Castle had, by the nineteenth century, become quite unfitted for the residence of the Sovereign, and in 1824 the sum of £150,000 was voted by the House of Commons for its improvement. A brief was drawn up by Sir Charles Long, the King's principal artistic adviser, and Jeffry Wyatt was invited to submit designs in company with the three architects of the Office of Works – Soane, Smirke and Nash. Wyatt's inclusion in this limited competition showed that he was highly regarded by the King and his mentor Long, and it was his designs – closely following Long's extremely detailed and specific brief – that were chosen. On 12 August 1824 the first stone was laid by George IV, who on the same day authorized the architect to call himself 'Wyatville' and to adopt the word 'Windsor' as his motto.[1] In 1828, on the completion of the royal apartments, Wyatville was knighted and granted a residence in the Winchester Tower, a privilege afterwards confirmed by William IV and Queen Victoria. As the work progressed the original estimates were far exceeded, and in 1830, when no less than £527,000 had been advanced, a select committee was appointed to enquire into the cost of completion. The committee found 'no reason to attribute the error of the original estimate to any want of due precaution on the part of the architect', and with the aid of further grants, totalling well over half a million pounds, the reconstruction of the Castle was finally completed soon after the accession of Queen Victoria in 1837. The Upper Ward was almost completely rebuilt on a large scale with a new 'George IV Gateway' forming a grand entrance on the south side. The State Apartments on the north side were reconstructed round a new Grand Staircase (subsequently replaced in 1866 by a new staircase designed by Salvin) and new and more convenient royal apartments were created on the east side facing the gardens. Externally Wyatville (following Long's directive) added greatly to the picturesque outline of the Castle by raising the Round Tower 33 feet, and so making of it a dominant feature round which to group the newly battlemented and machicolated towers. Wyatville's rehabilitation of Windsor Castle was not effected without much destruction of older buildings, including Hugh May's magnificently decorated State Apartments and the old royal chapel which had stood to the west of St. George's Hall since the twelfth century. But it fully achieved its main purpose in converting the old, scarcely habitable fortress into what the select committee of 1830 described as 'in all respects a fit residence for the Sovereign of this country'. At the command of George IV, Wyatville prepared a full account of the works carried out under his direction, which was eventually published in 1841 as *Illustrations of Windsor Castle by the late Sir Jeffry Wyatville, R.A.*, edited by his pupil Henry Ashton.

Wyatville was an able architect but scarcely a designer of genius. Best known as an expert purveyor of the picturesque country house, usually in a Tudor Gothic or 'Elizabethan' dress, he could also offer unexceptionable 'Grecian' elevations if required. But the latter

[1] According to *Gent's Mag.*, this was intended 'not merely as a personal compliment' but was done 'for the purpose of distinguishing and separating the Wyatt of that reign from his uncle, Mr. James Wyatt', who had been employed at Windsor in the preceding reign.

contributed nothing significant to the development of English neo-classical architecture, while only a readiness to advance stylistically into the sixteenth century distinguishes his Gothic houses from those of his uncle James. The general form of his greatest work – Windsor Castle – was to a large extent dictated by the detailed brief drawn up by Sir Charles Long, which Wyatville carried out in a workmanlike but not over-sensitive manner. The result was a masterpiece of Picturesque architecture that composes magnificently from almost any point of view, but does not bear inspection at close quarters, when Wyatville's coarse detailing and ubiquitous black ash mortar show a marked insensitivity to those variations in texture and profile that give life and interest to an ancient building.

Wyatville was elected A.R.A. in 1822 and R.A. in 1824. He had sought admission as an Associate as early as 1800, but there were objections to the election of an architect who was also in business as a builder, and he was allowed to remain a candidate for over twenty years before he was finally elected in 1822 at the age of 56. He was a Fellow of the Royal and Antiquarian Societies, and a member of the Saxon Ernestine Order, the Grand Cross of which was granted him by Queen Adelaide's brother, the Duke of Saxe-Meiningen, for whom he gave advice about the design of the castle at Landsberg and planned a ducal residence at Meiningen that was never built. His office and town residence were at 49 (now 39) Lower Brook Street, where he died on 18 February 1840 at the age of 73. He was buried in a vault at the east end of St. George's Chapel, Windsor. By his wife Sophia Powell (who died in 1810), he had two daughters and one son, George Geoffrey, who intended to follow his father's profession, but died in 1833 at the age of 29. Among his pupils or assistants were Henry Ashton, C. H. Basnett, Benjamin Baud, R. Carver, C. Chalkley, P. B. Cotes, W. J. Donthorn, J. Foster, W. Harris, Edward Haycock, H. Lester, Charles Parker, J. Sanderson and J. T. Wood. Michael Gandy was in his office from 1807 to 1840.

Wyatville is described as being 'of low stature and inelegant personal form' which was, however, redeemed by a lively expression. Throughout his life he retained a characteristic Midland accent and an engaging simplicity of manner. He got on well with royalty, but the fastidious C. R. Cockerell thought him, though 'good natured', 'no gentleman, vulgar minded . . . [and] a great boaster'. A list of portraits is given in Dr. Linstrum's book. The most important are the one by Sir Thomas Lawrence, painted in 1827–8, and the bust by Chantrey, carved *c.*1835–7, both at Windsor Castle.

[Obituary in *Gent's Mag.* 1840 (i), 545–9; *A.P.S.D.*; *D.N.B.*; D. Linstrum, *Sir Jeffry Wyatville*, 1972; D. Linstrum, *The Wyatt Family*, R.I.B.A. Drawings Catalogue, 1974; J. M. Robinson, *The Wyatts*, 1979, chap. v and pp. 271–4].

The following list of executed works may be supplemented by reference to the more elaborate 'Catalogue of Work' in Dr. Linstrum's biography, which gives additional references and includes some doubtful and unexecuted works not listed below. Illustrations of all Wyatville's principal buildings will be found in the same book.

WOOLLEY PARK, BERKS., remodelled for the Revd. P. Wroughton, 1799; wings added *c.*1860 [G. Richardson, *New Vitruvius Britannicus* ii, 1808, pls. 36–8; exhib. at R.A. 1799].

BLADON CASTLE, NEWTON SOLNEY, DERBYSHIRE, for Abraham Hoskins, 1801–5, castellated [apparently the building exhibited at the R.A. in 1799 as a 'villa at Bladon Hill . . . seat of Abraham Hoskins', and enlarged into a castellated house].

HILLFIELD LODGE (now CASTLE), nr. WATFORD, HERTS., for the Hon. George Villiers, *c.*1800–5, castellated [exhib. at R.A. 1805].

WOLLATON HALL, NOTTS., alterations and extensions for 6th Lord Middleton, *c.*1801 and 1823; Camellia House, 1822–3; Beeston and Lenton gateways to park, 1823–4; Elizabethan style [exhib. at R.A. 1804 and 1824; Linstrum, 255; Birmingham Reference Library, MS. 1056/249, order-book of Messrs. Jones & Clarke, conservatory manfrs., Nos. 293, 385 for the Camellia House].

STOCKTON HOUSE, WILTS., probably designed staircase for Henry Biggs, 1802 [*C. Life*, 21 Oct. 1905, 562; J. M. Robinson, *op. cit.*, 273].

LONDON, HOLDERNESSE (later LONDONDERRY) HOUSE, HERTFORD STREET, alterations for 6th Lord Middleton, 1802; remodelled by B. D. Wyatt 1825–8; dem. 1964 [Linstrum, 241].

NONSUCH PARK, SURREY, for Samuel Farmer, 1802–6, Tudor style; altered 1845 [exhib. at R.A. 1802–3].

GREATHAM HOSPITAL, CO. DURHAM, rebuilt at the expense of 7th Earl of Bridgwater, 1803–4, Tudor style [J. Dugdale, *The British Traveller* ii, 1819, 305].

BROWSHOLME HALL, YORKS. (W.R.), decoration of new gallery or drawing-room for T. L. Parker, 1805 [T. L. Parker, *A Description of*

Browsholme Hall, 1815, 8] (*C. Life*, 13 July 1935).

ABINGDON, BERKS., COUNTY BRIDEWELL (now recreation centre), 1805–11, built by Daniel Harris (*q.v.*) to Wyatville's designs [payment to Wyatville cited by Linstrum, 258; unsigned drawings in Berkshire Record Office, Q/AG/2/1; for Harris see *Report from the Committee of Aldermen appointed to visit Several Gaols in England* 1816, 25].

HYDE HALL, nr. SAWBRIDGEWORTH, HERTS., remodelled for 2nd Earl of Roden, 1806–7; also lodges to drive [Linstrum, 238].

LONGLEAT HOUSE, WILTS., alterations for 2nd Marquess of Bath, 1806–13, including reconstruction of north front, addition of Stable Court, a new principal staircase, and extensive internal alterations, chiefly in Elizabethan style; also Horningsham Lodge and estate buildings [Linstrum, 244–5] (*C. Life*, 29 April 1949).

ROCHE COURT, HANTS., castellated lodge for Sir J. S. W. Gardiner, Bart., 1808 [exhib. at R.A. 1808].

ROOD ASHTON HOUSE, nr. TROWBRIDGE, WILTS., enlarged for R. G. Long, 1808, Tudor style; altered by T. Hopper 1836 [exhib. at R.A. 1808].

LYPIATT PARK, GLOS., alterations and additions for Paul Wathen (later Sir Paul Baghot), 1809, Tudor Gothic; enlarged by T. H. Wyatt 1876 [exhib. at R.A. 1809].

THURLAND CASTLE, LANCS., design for chapel and entrance court for R. T. North, exhibited at R.A. 1809 and probably carried out as part of a general renovation; new drawing-room, etc., by G. Webster of Kendal, *c.*1827–9; extensive alterations after fire in 1879 [Linstrum, 249, where the reference to a design by Robert Walker is due to a mistake in Graves's catalogue of Royal Academy exhibitors, viii, 108].

BADMINTON HOUSE, GLOS., work for 6th Duke of Beaufort, including remodelling of interiors of drawing-room and library, new top light to staircase, and conservatory, 1809–11 [exhib. at R.A. 1811; accounts at Badminton] (*C. Life*, 2 Dec. 1939; 9 April 1987).

ENDSLEIGH, nr. MILTON ABBOT, DEVON, *cottage orné* for 6th Duke of Bedford, 1810 [exhib. at R.A. 1811; other references in Linstrum, 236] (*C. Life*, 3–10 Aug. 1961).

WYNNSTAY, DENBIGHSHIRE, round tower at Nant-y-Belan intended as cenotaph in memory of officers killed in Irish Rebellion of 1798, for Sir Watkin Williams-Wynn, Bart., *c.*1810 [S. Lewis, *Topographical Dictionary of Wales* ii, 1849, 372] (*C. Life*, 6 April 1972, 852, fig. 6).

BELTON HOUSE, LINCS., minor alterations to house, conservatory and dairy for 1st Earl Brownlow, *c.*1810 [exhib. at R.A. 1811; cf. Linstrum, 230 for drawings at Belton] (*C. Life*, 17 Sept. 1964; G. Jackson-Stops, *An English Arcadia*, National Trust 1991, 121–2).

LONDON, No. 5 GROSVENOR SQUARE, alterations and repairs for 6th Duke of Beaufort, 1810; dem. *c.*1961 [J. M. Robinson, *op. cit.*, 272].

LONDON, CHESTERFIELD HOUSE, SOUTH AUDLEY STREET, repairs costing £15,264 for 5th Earl of Chesterfield, 1811–13; dem. 1937 [account in Guildhall Library, MS. 3070 A].

CASSIOBURY PARK, HERTS., employed by 5th Earl of Essex after death of James Wyatt (1813), but uncertain precisely what he designed; house dem. 1922 [Linstrum, 234] (J. Britton, *Cassiobury Park*, 1837; *C. Life*, 17 Sept. 1910).

STUBTON HALL, LINCS., for Sir Robert Heron, Bart., 1813–14; portico and porch are later additions [inscription in house; exhib. at R.A. 1816].

BRETBY HALL, DERBYSHIRE, for 5th Earl of Chesterfield, *c.*1813–15, castellated. Designs had been made by James Wyatt before his death in 1813, but they were probably superseded by the designs for which Jeffry Wyatt was paid £108 2s. in 1819, some of which he exhibited at the R.A. in 1812 and 1813. According to J. Glover, *History of the County of Derby* ii, 1833, 163, the house 'was designed by Sir Jeffry Wyatville and Mr. Martin, the Earl's architect, and built under the direction of the latter', but was left unfinished after the Earl's death in 1815 [executors' accounts in Warwickshire C.R.O., CR 229/Box 14; cf. Linstrum, 231].

HINTON ST. GEORGE, SOMERSET, Gothic entrance and other works for 4th Earl Poulett, 1814–16 [exhib. at R.A. 1814].

FROME, SOMERSET, ST. JOHN'S CHURCH, designed Gothic screen to forecourt, and cased west front in ashlar, 1814; west front rebuilt 1862–4 [W. J. E. Bennett, *History of the Church of St. John of Frome*, 1866, 46–8].

ASHRIDGE PARK, HERTS., completion of and additions to the house (Gothic), lodges, farm-buildings, etc., for 7th Earl of Bridgwater, *c.*1814–17; the Bridgwater Column 1831–2 [inscription on brass plate in hall; exhib. at R.A. 1816–17; Linstrum, 228–9] (H. A. Tipping, *English Homes, VI* (i), 339–46).

DINTON HOUSE, nr. SALISBURY, WILTS., for William Wyndham, 1814–17 [drawings in R.I.B.A. Coll. illustrated by G. Worsley,

Architectural Drawings of the Regency Period, 1991, 66–71] (*C. Life*, 17 Dec. 1943).

TOWNELEY HALL, LANCS., remodelled S.E. wing and designed porch for Peregrine Towneley, *c.*1814–19 [Susan Bourne, *An Introduction to the Architecture of Towneley Hall*, 1979].

TREBARTHA HALL, NORTHILL, CORNWALL, alterations and additions for F. H. Rodd, 1815; dem. 1948 [plan in R.I.B.A. Coll.] (E. Twycross, *The Mansions of England: Cornwall*, 1846, 62; plans (not seen) in Cornwall Record Office, 49/1/131/1–10).

DENFORD HOUSE, BERKS., for William Hallett, *c.*1815; alterations by J. B. Papworth 1827–8; wings added 1939 [included in the list of Wyatville's works given by Ashton in his *Illustrations of Windsor Castle*].

BRETTON HALL, YORKS. (W.R.), enlarged and altered house and designed aviary, etc., for Col. T. R. Beaumont, *c.*1815 [exhib. at R.A. 1815; Arthur Oswald in *C. Life*, 21–28 May 1938; D. Linstrum, 'Two Wentworth Houses', *Leeds Arts Calendar*, no. 68, 1971].

BELTON CHURCH, LINCS., mortuary chapel for 1st Earl Brownlow, 1816 [exhib. at R.A. 1816].

MARSTON HOUSE, MARSTON BIGOT, SOMERSET, Ionic loggia for 8th Earl of Cork and Orrery, probably *c.*1817 when Wyatville wrote of going to Lord Cork's [Lord Cork is named as one of Wyatville's employers on the back of the portrait preserved in his family; M. McGarvie, 'Marston House', *Proceedings of the Somerset Archaeological and Nat. Hist. Soc.* cxviii, 1974, 20].

WOBURN ABBEY, BEDS., conversion of conservatory into sculpture gallery and addition of Temple of the Graces to contain group of 'The Graces' by Canova, for 6th Duke of Bedford, *c.*1816–18 [exhib. at R.A. 1818] (*C. Life*, 15 July 1965); Botanical House 1837 (dem.) and Araucaria House [Linstrum, 255; *History and Description of Woburn Abbey*, 1845, 180–1].

BANNER CROSS, ECCLESALL, nr. SHEFFIELD, YORKS. (W.R.), for General William Murray, 1817–21, castellated [Linstrum, 229].

LITTLE GADDESDEN CHURCH, HERTS., added south chapel to chancel, 1819, and probably designed south aisle, for the executors of 8th Earl of Bridgwater, 1830 [Linstrum, 240].

GOPSALL HALL, LEICS., entrance archway and probable alterations to house for the Hon. R. W. P. Curzon (later 1st Earl Howe), 1819; dem. 1951 [exhib. at R.A. 1819] (*Connoisseur* cxxviii, 1951).

TREBURSEY HOUSE, nr. LAUNCESTON, CORNWALL, for the Hon. William Eliot (later 2nd Earl of St. Germans), before 1820, Gothic [included in the list of Wyatville's works given by Ashton in his *Illustrations of Windsor Castle*; described as 'recently erected' by C. S. Gilbert, *Topography of Cornwall*, 1820, 492].

CHATSWORTH HOUSE, DERBYSHIRE, alterations and additions for 6th Duke of Devonshire, 1820–41, including the library, the north wing and tower, the north entrance archway, lodges and estate buildings [Francis Thompson, *A History of Chatsworth*, 1949; J. Cornforth in *C. Life*, 25 July, 1 Aug. 1968].

GREAT BERKHAMSTED CHURCH, HERTS., restorations, 1820 [*V.C.H. Herts.* ii, 174].

WOOLLEY PARK, YORKS. (W.R.), lodge and gateway to Sheffield road, for Godfrey Wentworth, 1820 [Linstrum, 225–6].

BISHOPSWOOD HOUSE, HEREFS., for John Partridge, *c.*1820, Gothic; destroyed by fire 1873 [Linstrum, 230–1].

CLAVERTON HOUSE, nr. BATH, SOMERSET, for John Vivian, *c.*1820 [included in the list of Wyatville's works given by Ashton in his *Illustrations of Windsor Castle*].

CAMBRIDGE, SIDNEY SUSSEX COLLEGE, remodelled 1821–2 and 1831–2, in Tudor Gothic style [exhib. at R.A. 1822 and 1832; Willis & Clark, ii, 741, 747–9] (R.C.H.M., *Cambridge* ii, 203 *et seq.*).

LONDON, No. 49 (later 50, now 39) LOWER BROOK STREET, remodelled for himself, 1821–3 [Linstrum, 23, 242–3].

MARBURY CHURCH, CHESHIRE, rebuilt chancel for 7th Earl of Bridgewater, 1822; altered 1891–2 [Linstrum, 245].

SANS SOUCI, LYTCHETT MINSTER, DORSET, greenhouse for Sir Claude Scott, Bart., 1822; dem. [exhib. at R.A. 1822].

WHITELEY WOOD HALL, nr. SHEFFIELD, YORKS. (W.R.), enlarged for William Silcock, 1822; dem. 1959 [exhib. at R.A. 1822; Linstrum, 251].

ALLENDALE HOUSE, WIMBORNE MINSTER, DORSET, for William Castleman, 1823 [included in the list of Wyatville's works given by Ashton in his *Illustrations of Windsor Castle*].

LONDON, BEDFORD LODGE, CAMPDEN HILL, alterations and additions for 6th Duke of Bedford, 1823 and 1835–6; dem. 1955 [*Survey of London*, xxxvii, 68–71].

WINDSOR GREAT PARK, ROYAL LODGE, alterations and additions for King George IV, 1823–30, Gothic; dem. 1830 except conservatory and dining-room, which form the nucleus of the existing building [Sir. O. Morshead, *George IV and Royal Lodge*, Brighton 1965; *History of the King's Works* vi, 399–401] (*C. Life*, 1 July 1939).

WINDSOR CASTLE, BERKS., remodelled Upper Ward and Round Tower for King George IV and King William IV, 1824–40 [H. Ashton, *Illustrations of Windsor Castle*, 1841; M. Gandy & B. Baud, *Architectural Illustrations of Windsor Castle*, 1842; Sir O. Morshead, *Windsor Castle*, 1957; *History of the King's Works* vi, 373–94; Linstrum, 252–3].

HASTINGS, SUSSEX, No. 14 MARINE PARADE, unspecified work for the Comte de Vandes, 1824 [*A.P.S.D.*; Linstrum, 237].

YESTER HOUSE, EAST LOTHIAN, keeper's lodge for 8th Marquess of Tweeddale, 1824 [exhib. at R.A. 1824].

SOMERHILL, nr. TONBRIDGE, KENT, interior of library in Jacobean style for James Alexander, *c.*1824; altered by Sir Herbert Baker in the 1930s [J. Britton, *Descriptive Sketches of Tunbridge Wells*, 1832, 121]. Further alterations to the house were carried out by Salvin in 1828–33.

LONDON, No. 10 GROSVENOR SQUARE, alterations for 2nd Lord (later 1st Earl of) Cawdor, *c.*1824; dem. 1865 [*Survey of London* xl, 126].

LONDON, SCOTT'S (now Westminster) BANK, No. 1A CAVENDISH SQUARE, new banking hall, etc., 1825; since altered [*A.P.S.D.*; Linstrum, 241].

WINDSOR GREAT PARK, rebuilt bridge over Virginia Water and constructed ornamental ruin known as 'Temple of Augustus', formed from classical fragments from Lepcis Magna, North Africa, 1826–9 [*History of the King's Works* vi, 396–7; G. E. Chambers, 'The Ruins at Virginia Water', *Berkshire Arch. Jnl.* liv, 1954–5].

LILLESHALL HALL, SALOP., for Lord Gower (later 2nd Duke of Sutherland), 1826–30, Elizabethan style [exhib. at R.A. 1829; Linstrum, 240].

GOLDEN GROVE, CARMARTHENSHIRE, for 2nd Lord (later 1st Earl of) Cawdor, 1826–37, Elizabethan style [exhib. at R.A. 1829; Linstrum, 236–7].

FORT BELVEDERE, WINDSOR GREAT PARK, alterations and additions for King George IV, 1828–9, castellated [*History of the King's Works* vi, 397: C. Hussey in *C. Life*, 19–26 Nov. 1959].

CHILLINGHAM CASTLE, NORTHUMBERLAND, work for 5th Earl of Tankerville, probably including alterations to hall and south wing and design of Village Lodge, *c.*1825–8 [*History of Northumberland* xiv, p. 336 *et seq.*; Tankerville papers in Northumberland Record Office; Linstrum, 234–5] (*C. Life*, 8 March 1913).

COBHAM HALL, KENT, repaired interior of north wing and designed Gothic entrance thereto, for 5th Earl of Darnley, who succeeded in 1831 and died in 1835 [C. Greenwood, *Epitome of County History: Kent*, 1838, 215].

KENSINGTON PALACE, LONDON, internal alterations, 1833 and 1835, including conversion of former kitchen into chapel [*History of the King's Works* vi, 347–8].

KEW GARDENS, SURREY, THE PANTHEON or KING WILLIAM'S TEMPLE, 1836–7 [Linstrum, 239; *History of the King's Works* vi, 441].

CADLAND, nr. SOUTHAMPTON, HANTS., enlarged and remodelled for A. R. Drummond, 1837–8; dem. 1953 [Linstrum, 137–40, 232–3].

RANGER'S LODGE, BUSHY PARK, MIDDLESEX, alterations, probably including conservatory, for Queen Adelaide, 1837–8 [Linstrum, 232].

KEW CHURCH, SURREY, enlarged at expense of King William IV, 1837–8 [E. W. Brayley, *Topographical History of Surrey*, 1841–8, iii, 153].

STACKPOLE COURT, PEMBROKESHIRE, remodelled for 1st Earl of Cawdor, 1839–40; dem. 1961 [S. Lewis, *Topographical Dictionary of Wales* ii, 1849, 373]; bridge 1832 [Linstrum, 248]. The works here were completed by H. Ashton, who presumably designed the surviving stables, dated 1844.

EASTBURY HOUSE, COMPTON, SURREY, additions for the Revd. Edward Fulham, who succeeded to the property in 1777 and died in 1832 [E. W. Brayley, *Topographical History of Surrey*, 1841–8, v, 225].

LEXHAM HALL, NORFOLK, additions for Col. F. W. Keppel; partly dem. after fire *c.*1950 [Linstrum, 240].

UNEXECUTED

Wyatville's most important unexecuted designs were for a PARLIAMENT HOUSE at QUEBEC, CANADA, 1812; a palatial mansion for Lord Yarborough at BROCKLESBY, LINCS., 1820; a mansion at TOTTENHAM PARK, WILTS., for 1st Marquess of Ailesbury, 1821; enlarging KINGSTON LACY, DORSET, for Henry Bankes, 1821; remodelling ST. JAMES'S PALACE, LONDON, for King William IV, 1831–5, and for a Royal Villa at MEININGEN, GERMANY, for the Duke of Saxe-Meiningen, 1835. The designs for Tottenham are in a bound volume among the Ailesbury muniments, those for Kingston Lacy at that house (National Trust). All the others are described and illustrated by Linstrum.

WYNN, THOMAS, 1st LORD NEWBOROUGH (1736–1807), was the son of Sir John Wynn, Bart., of Glynliffon, Caernarvonshire, whom he succeeded in

1773. He was educated at Queen's College, Cambridge, made the Grand Tour in 1758–60, and was a Member of Parliament from 1761 onwards. His support of the Government earned him an Irish peerage in 1776. His second marriage in 1786 to an Italian girl of 13 was characteristic of a somewhat eccentric and improvident career, in the course of which he occasionally acted as an amateur architect. According to R. E. Hunter, *A Short Account of the Isle of Thanet*, 1813, 63, Wynn designed KINGSGATE, KENT, an elaborate seaside villa begun in 1762 for Lord Holland as an English re-creation of Cicero's Formian villa at Baiae. Here he is said to have had the professional assistance of John Vardy (*q.v.*) [Hugh Honour in *C. Life*, 10 Dec. 1953]. For Holland's son, Charles James Fox, Wynn designed *c.*1805 a temple at ST. ANN'S HILL, CHERTSEY, SURREY, to display sculpture by Nollekens [G. H. Powell, *Reminiscences of the Table Talk of Samuel Rogers*, 1903, 57–8; letters sold at Sotheby's, 4 April 1949, lot 262]. This was the existing 'Temple of Friendship', which contained busts of Fox and his father by Nollekens [*Gardener's Mag.* 13, 1837, 113]. On his own estate at Glynliffon Wynn built at his own expense two forts against French invasion, one called 'Fort Belan' at the western entrance to the Menai Strait, the other 'Fort Williamsburg' on a hill in the park [L. Namier & J. Brooke, *History of Parliament: The Commons 1754–90* iii, 1964, 670–1].

WYNNE, JOHN, exhibited architectural designs at the Royal Academy in 1812–13 from 45 Paternoster Row, London. He was presumably the John Wynn whose designs for GREAT BERKHAMSTED RECTORY, HERTS., dated 1811, are in the Lincolnshire Record Office [MGA 63].

Y

YELLOWLEY, JOSEPH (–1828), was presumably a carpenter by trade, as he was Master of the Carpenters' Company in 1799 and again in the year of his death. He is described as an architect or surveyor in contemporary directories, and was President of the Surveyors' Club in 1810. He was employed by Whitbread's brewery and in 1812 planned docks in the Isle of Dogs [Middlesex County Records, D.P. 80, ex *inf.* Prof. M. H. Port].

YEMANS, or **YEOMANS,** JOHN, was a master bricklayer of Hampton-on-Thames, Middlesex. On 1 February 1699/1700, he contracted with William Lowndes to build the shell of WINSLOW HALL, BUCKS. The excellent brickwork of this house, which may have been designed by Wren, shows that Yemans was a highly competent workman [*Wren Soc.* xvii, 62–3]. In 1708 Yemans rebuilt the central tower of KINGSTON-ON-THAMES CHURCH, SURREY, 'according to the modell or Scheme drawn by him'. The former tower had been so badly damaged in the great storm of 1703 that it had had to be taken down soon afterwards [MS. Vestry Minutes]. Yemans's ledger, covering the years 1698–1711, is preserved among the Kingston Borough Records (D. IV, d. i). It shows that he lived at Hampton Wick and that he held office as churchwarden in 1699. In that year he carried out some minor alterations to the Earl of Rochester's house at Petersham, and in 1703–4 he did a good deal of work in connection with Mr. Hill's 'new building at Richmond', i.e. TRUMPETERS' HOUSE.

YENN, JOHN (1750–1821), the son of a City barber and wig-maker, was born on 8 March 1750. In 1764 he became a pupil of Sir William Chambers, and in 1769 was one of the first students admitted to the newly formed Royal Academy Schools. He was awarded the Gold Medal in 1771 for his design for a nobleman's villa (now in the R.I.B.A. Drawings Collection). Chambers employed him as a clerk of works at Somerset House from 1776 onwards, and was no doubt instrumental in obtaining for him the post of a labourer in trust in the Office of Works in 1777. In 1780 he became Clerk of the Works at Richmond New Park Lodge, and in 1782 was promoted to be Clerk of the Works at Buckingham House, Kensington Palace and the Royal Mews. In 1788 he succeeded Sir Robert Taylor as Surveyor of Greenwich Hospital.

Yenn was elected A.R.A. in 1774, and became a full academician in 1791. In 1796 he succeeded Chambers as Treasurer. He played an active part in Royal Academy politics and caused much trouble in 1803 by demanding an increase in the Treasurer's stipend. He incurred the dislike of Benjamin West, who told Farington that Yenn's 'watery eye' was a sure sign of treacherous character. Yenn was also a member of the Architects' Club from its foundation in 1791. He retired from the Office of Works in 1819 and died in Gloucester Place on 1 March 1821. His library was sold at Sotheby's on 30 April 1835 (B.L., SC.S 203(8)). A portrait in oils by J. F. Rigaud, painted in 1785, is at the Royal Academy, where there is also a pencil portrait by George Dance. The former portrait was engraved by

J. K. Sherwin. J. Fidler, George Meredith and Henry Hakewill were pupils.

Yenn's private practice was on a modest scale, and his executed buildings show him as a faithful disciple of his master Chambers.[1] His correct neo-classical style is best seen at Greenwich, where in 1811–14 he and H. H. Seward together rebuilt the west front of the King Charles block. His real distinction lay, however, in his brilliant architectural draughtsmanship. His exquisite coloured drawings, based on techniques of presentation learned in Chambers's office, are probably the finest made by any English architect of the eighteenth century. They show 'none of the leaning towards austerity that usually characterises neo-classicism'. On the contrary Yenn used his neo-classical repertoire with a lavish abandon that would have been more appropriate in the age of rococo. The principal collection of his drawings was given to the Royal Academy in 1865 by his daughter, Mrs. Thackeray. Other (though generally less spectacular) examples of Yenn's draughtsmanship are to be seen in the Victoria and Albert Museum, R.I.B.A. Drawings Collection, Minet Library at Camberwell, the Yale Center for British Art and the Memorial Library of the University of Delaware.

[*A.P.S.D.*; Farington's Diary, 13 Dec. 1794, 7 May 1795, 10 Dec. 1796, 19 Jan. 1804; P.R.O., Apprenticeship Registers, 1764; *History of the King's Works* vi; J. Harris, *Catalogue of British Drawings for Architecture, etc. in American Collections*, 1970, 310–17; *R.I.B.A. Drawings Catalogue: T–Z*, 278–9; *John Yenn, Draughtsman Extraordinary*, catalogue of exhibition at R.I.B.A. Drawings Coll. 1973; Marcus Binney, 'A Forgotten Pupil of Chambers', *C. Life*, 13 Sept. 1973.]

HADZOR HOUSE, nr. DROITWICH, WORCS., for Richard Amphlett, 1779; remodelled 1827 [exhib. at R.A. as 'now building' 1779].

EALING GROVE, MIDDLESEX, alterations and entrance lodges for 4th Duke of Marlborough, *c.*1780; dem. [exhib. at R.A. 1780; drawings in Delaware University Library].

LONDON, GRANTHAM HOUSE, WHITEHALL, alterations for 2nd Lord Grantham, probably *c.*1780; dem. *c.*1896 [drawings in Delaware University Library] (*Survey of London* xiii, 160–1).

LONDON, MARLBOROUGH HOUSE, ST. JAMES'S, decorations, etc., for 4th Duke of Marlborough, *c.*1784–5 [drawings in Delaware University Library; bill in B.L., Egerton MS. 2678, ff. 40–3].

SION HILL, ISLEWORTH, MIDDLESEX, alterations for 4th Duke of Marlborough, *c.*1784–5 [bill in B.L., Egerton MS. 2678, ff. 40–3].

BLENHEIM PALACE, OXON., THE TEMPLE OF HEALTH, 1789, and other minor works for 4th Duke of Marlborough [temple exhib. at R.A. 1791; drawings for temple and unexecuted designs for Ditchley Gate lodges in Delaware University Library; drawings for pier-glasses, fireplaces, etc. in Bodleian Library, MS. Top. Oxon. a. 37, ff. 143–7; other drawings, including unexecuted design for Rosamund's Well, in R.A. Library].

NORTH ASTON HALL, OXON., alterations for Oldfield Bowles, 1781–2; remodelled *c.*1850 [south front exhib. at R.A. 1782; drawings in Delaware University Library; working drawings in Bodleian Library, MS. Top. Oxon. a. 37, ff. 58–64].

WOODSTOCK CHURCH, OXON., rebuilt north aisle, 1783, Gothic; rebuilt by Sir A. W. Blomfield 1878. Yenn also made designs for rebuilding the tower, which were not executed but are preserved among the Oxford Diocesan Records in the C.R.O. [H. M. Colvin, 'The Rebuilding of Woodstock Church Tower, 1770–1786', *Oxfordshire Archaeological Soc.'s Report*, no. 87, 1949; drawings in Delaware University Library.]

LLANFYLLIN, MONTGOMERYSHIRE, THE TOWN HALL, *c.*1790; dem. 1960 [exhib. at R.A. 1791 as 'to be built', but said to have been built in 1789].

WARGRAVE HILL (now MANOR), WARGRAVE, BERKS., for Joseph Hill, *c.*1780–90; since enlarged [plans at Royal Academy] (E. B. Pope, *History of Wargrave*, Hitchin 1929, 59).

PUTNEY HEATH, SURREY, alterations to villa for Lady Polwarth, 1791–3 [Bedfordshire Record Office, L 31/282–4, and drawings in Minet Library, Camberwell].

PUTNEY HEATH, SURREY, alterations to Lady Grantham's house, 1792–3 [drawings in Minet Library, Camberwell].

WINDSOR CASTLE, BERKS., music room and dining-room in cast range of Upper Ward for King George III, 1795; dem. *c.*1825 [*History of the King's Works* vi, 374–5].

KENSINGTON PALACE, LONDON, alterations to the apartments of Edward, Duke of Kent, *c.*1800–10 [*History of the King's Works* vi, 340–1].

NEW YORK, AMERICA, design for a four-storey house made for a gentleman who intended

[1] In 1774 Chambers described Yenn as 'an ingenious faithful intelligent servant' who had lived with him for the past ten years, and who 'for two or three years past has managed a great part of my extensive business very much to my satisfaction' [B.L., Add. MS. 41135, f. 26].

to build a house in the city, but changed his mind, whereupon Yenn's designs were advertised for sale in the New York newspapers in 1804 [R. S. Gottesman, *The Arts and Crafts in New York, 1800–1804,* New York Historical Soc. 1965, 179].

LONDON, MELBOURNE, now DOVER, HOUSE, WHITEHALL, internal alterations for 1st Viscount Melbourne, 1805 [drawings at Royal Academy] (*Survey of London* xiv, chap. vi).

GREENWICH HOSPITAL, KENT, rebuilt west façade of King Charles Block, in association with H. H. Seward, 1811–14 [Hasted's *History of Kent: Hundred of Blackheath*, ed. Drake, 1886, 69].

YOUNG, JAMES, of London, was probably an Aberdonian, for in 1801 he made an unexecuted design for the Union Bridge that is now in the City Art Gallery, and in 1816 he was invited to compete for St. Andrew's Episcopal Church there [G. M. Fraser, 'Archibald Simpson and his times', *Aberdeen Weekly Jnl.* 25 April 1918]. An architect of this name was practising from 32 Percy Street, London, in 1827–8.

YOUNG, JOHN (–1679), was a prominent London master mason of the seventeenth century. Having been made 'sinisterly free' of the Weavers' Company, he regularized his position by transferring to the Masons' Company in 1637 and subsequently served as Warden and Master (1657). From 1638 onwards he did a good deal of work at the INNER TEMPLE [F. Inderwick, *Calendar of Inner Temple Records* ii, 246–7, 258, 263, 312–13, 321]. In 1638–40 he was, with Edmund Kinsman (*q.v.*) and James Holmes, one of the three London masons who contracted to build the tower of GOUDHURST CHURCH, KENT [*Archaeologia Cantiana* xxviii, 10–13]. In March 1649/50, as John Young, 'freemason in Blackfriars', he contracted to build the new church at BERWICK-ON-TWEED, 'conforme to his Moddell or draught', and performed his task to the satisfaction of three Scottish and three English masons who were employed to inspect the completed building in February 1652/3 [Berwick-on-Tweed Guild-books]. It was designed by Young in a mixture of Gothic and classical motifs somewhat reminiscent of the London church of St. Katherine Cree (1628–31). In the reign of Charles II, Young was employed as a mason at Greenwich Hospital, Mercers' Hall, Apothecaries' Hall and elsewhere. At APOTHECARIES' HALL, BLACKFRIARS LANE, he supplied in 1670 a 'draught' of the door-case to the hall incorporating the Company's arms, and built the stone stairs in the courtyard at his own cost in discharge of unpaid rent for the riverside premises (destroyed in the Great Fire) whose site he leased from the Company [Arthur Oswald in *C. Life*, 10 Oct. 1947].

Young died in March 1678/9, leaving two sons, Nicholas and John, both of whom followed their father's craft. Nicholas Young, who had several contracts for building Wren's City Churches, was Master of the Masons' Company in 1682. The date of his death has not been established, but he was still alive in 1700. His portrait is in Mr. Derek Sherborne's collection. John Young, junior, was Master of the Company in 1695 and died during his term of office.

[D. Knoop & G. P. Jones, *The London Mason in the Seventeenth Century*, 1935, 31; R. Gunnis, *Dictionary of British Sculptors*, 1968, 451–2; *Middle Temple Records*, ed. C. H. Hopwood, iii, 1460; Register of St. Anne's Blackfriars in Guildhall Library, MS. 4510/1].

YOUNG, JOHN (–1801), of Edinburgh, was a wright by trade, but is often described as 'architect' in contemporary sources. He was prominent among the builders of the New Town, taking five feus in 1767, and seventeen more between 1776 and 1795. Several houses in St. Andrew's Square were built by him, and he was the builder of Young Street in 1779–90. He was a member of the Town Council in 1790 and again in 1792 and 1793. He died on 26 July 1801. [A. J. Youngson, *The Making of Classical Edinburgh*, 1966, 84, 91, 101, 205; Town Council Minutes, 11 Aug. 1779 and 16 June 1806; *Scots Mag.*, 1801, 516].

YOUNG, WILLIAM, was Master of the Carpenters' Company in 1683. In 1670 he made a design for SCRIVENERS' HALL, NOBLE STREET, LONDON, that appears to have been the one carried out in 1671–5 [Bodleian Library, MS. Rawlinson D. 734, ff. 20–5]. The Hall was rebuilt in 1841 and 1870.

YOXALL, WILLIAM (1705–1770), was an architect of Nantwich in Cheshire. In 1731 he designed an altar-piece for NANTWICH CHURCH which was removed in 1855, and in 1742 he made a drawing of CREWE HALL, CHESHIRE, which was engraved [J. Partridge, *History of Nantwich*, 1774, 25; J. Hall, *History of Nantwich*, 1883, 219]. In 1762–3 he was employed to refit some of the rooms at CHIRK CASTLE, DENBIGHSHIRE, for Richard Myddelton. He proposed to ornament both the Drawing and Dining Rooms with a 'neat ornamental Gothick cornish', etc. [N.L.W., Myddelton papers, F. 7375 and Steward's Commonplace book, 1762–3]. His most important recorded work was CHESTER INFIRMARY, 1758–63 [Chester City Record Office, CR/60/2/43, *ex inf.* Dr. C. P. Lewis].

Addenda

FOSTER, JAMES

BRISTOL, ST JAMES'S CHURCH, S. porch, 1802–3, Gothic [Bristol R.O., P/St.J/Chw/36, *ex inf.* Mr D. Findlay].

FOSTER, JOHN

Add to bibliography: A. Jarvis, 'The interests and ethics of John Foster, Liverpool Dock Surveyor 1799–1824', *Trans. Historic Soc. Lancs. & Cheshire* 140, 1991.

HAMILTON, DAVID

GLASGOW, THE SHIP BANK, GLASSFORD STREET, *c.* 1825; dem. [*Glasgow Delineated*, 2nd ed. 1827, 83].

HARDWICK, PHILIP

CLIFTON HOUSE, nr. WORKINGTON, CUMBERLAND, for Richard Watts, 1824 [letter from Hardwick in Cumbria R.O., Carlisle, D/Pw/2/8].

LEVERTON, WILLIAM

Died at Forest Gate, Waltham, Essex, on 15 Jan. 1849, aged 91 [*Gent's Mag.* 1849 (i), 329].

MAUND, ANDREW

BRECON COUNTY GAOL, 1780–1 [D. Davies in *Brycheiniog* xxv, 1992–3, 85].

NIXSON, PAUL

Nixson was the younger brother of William Nixon (*q.v.*), but used the surname 'Nixson' [*ex inf.* Mr D. R. Perriam].

PAINE, JAMES

According to Arthur Young (*Tour through East of England*, ii, 1771, 241), YOUNGSBURY, nr. WARE, HERTS. (*c.* 1745), was 'built by Mr. Paine'.

SEPHTON, HENRY

attributed: OVER DARWEN CHURCH, LANCS, 1722; E. end rebuilt 1937–40 [closely resembles Sephton's Billinge Church].

TAYLOR, Sir ROBERT

CARMARTHEN, THE TOWN HALL, 1767 [E.I. Spence, *Summer Excursions* ii, 1809, 72].

WHITTICKE

Research by Ms Cherry Knott has shown that Whitticke was a land surveyor who played no part in designing Sudbury Hall.

Appendix A

SOME BUILDINGS ERECTED BEFORE 1840 TO THE DESIGNS OF VICTORIAN ARCHITECTS NOT INCLUDED IN THIS DICTIONARY

As one of the functions of this Dictionary is to serve as a work of reference for buildings erected between 1600 and 1840 it has seemed worth while to list below (and to index) the earlier works of some Victorian architects who do not qualify for biographical treatment. The list is limited to some of the more important buildings in this category and makes no claim to completeness.

BROWN, JOHN (*c.*1806–1876), of Norwich

STAMFORD, LINCS., ST. MICHAEL'S CHURCH, 1835–6, Gothic [G. Burton, *Chronology of Stamford*, 1846, 287].

SWAFFHAM, NORFOLK, THE SHIRE HALL, 1839 [C. Mackie, *Norfolk Annals* i, 1901, 375].

BUNNING, JAMES BUNSTONE (1802–1863)

LONDON, THE CITY OF LONDON SCHOOL, CHEAPSIDE, 1835–7, Gothic; dem. 1882 [exhib. at R.A. 1836] (W. Thornbury, *Old and New London* i, n.d., 379).

BURLISON, GEORGE (1807–1847), of Darlington

MIDDLESBROUGH, YORKS. (N.R.), CUSTOM HOUSE (originally EXCHANGE), NORTH STREET, 1836 [W. Lillie, *History of Middlesbrough*, 1968, 67].

BURT, HENRY (*c.*1804–1884), of Launceston

BODMIN, CORNWALL, THE ASSIZE COURT, 1837–8 [J. Maclean, *Deanery of Trigg Minor* i, 1873, 109].

CORDEROY, GEORGE (–1871)

WEYMOUTH, DORSET, THE TOWN HALL, 1836–7 [Weymouth Borough Archives].

CUNNINGHAM, JOHN (1799–1873), of Edinburgh and later of Liverpool

GREENLAW, BERWICKSHIRE, THE COURT HOUSE, 1829–31 [*The Architect's, Engineer's & Building Trades' Directory*, 1868, 107].

DERICK, JOHN MACDUFF (*c.*1806–1861)

BANBURY, OXON., ST. JOHN'S CHURCH (R.C.), 1835–6, Gothic [R. Gardner, *Gazetteer of The County of Oxford*, 1852, 417].

CHIPPING NORTON, OXON., HOLY TRINITY CHURCH (R.C.), 1836 [*London & Dublin Orthodox Jnl.* iv, 205].

ELLIOTT, JOHN (*c.*1812–1891), of Chichester

CHICHESTER, SUSSEX, THE CORN EXCHANGE, 1832 [*A.P.S.D.*, *s.v.* 'Chichester'].

GOODWOOD HOUSE, SUSSEX, completed E. wing for 5th Duke of Richmond, 1838–9 [W. H. Man, *Goodwood*, 1839, 122].

OVING, SUSSEX, almshouses, school and cottages for Miss Woods of Shopwyke, 1839, Tudor Gothic [Loudon, *Encyclopaedia of Cottage, Farm & Villa Architecture*, 1846, 1242–3]; also Vicarage, 1839 [W. Sussex R.O., Ep.I 41/34].

HENDERSON, JOHN (1804–1862), of Edinburgh

ARBROATH CHURCH, ANGUS, steeple, 1831 [*N.S.A.* xi, 81].

DUMFRIES, ST. MARY'S CHAPEL, 1837–8, Gothic [*A.P.S.D.*].

MONTROSE, ANGUS, THE MUSEUM, PANMURE PLACE, 1837 [*A.P.S.D.*].

EDINBURGH, MORNINGSIDE PARISH CHURCH, 1838, Romanesque [*A.P.S.D.*].

EDINBURGH, TRINITY EPISCOPAL CHAPEL, DEAN BRIDGE, 1838–9, Gothic [*A.P.S.D.*].

PANMURE, ANGUS, tower on Camustane Hill in honour of Lord Panmure, 1839 [*Forfarshire Illustrated*, 1843, 48].

HINDLE, WILLIAM JAMES (*c.*1811–1884), of Barnsley

BARNSLEY, YORKS. (W.R.), THE ODDFELLOWS' (now TEMPERANCE) HALL, PITT STREET, 1836–7 [R. Jackson, *History of Barnsley*, 1858, 136].

BARNSLEY, THE COMMERCIAL BUILDINGS, CHURCH STREET, 1837 [*ibid.*, 137].

JOHNSON, THOMAS (1794–1865), of Lichfield

STOKE-ON-TRENT, STAFFS., ST. PETER'S CHURCH, 1826–9, Gothic [I.C.B.S.].

NORCLIFFE HALL, CHESHIRE, for R. H. Greg, 1831, Tudor [*A.P.S.D.*].

LONGTON, STAFFS., ST. JAMES'S CHURCH, LANE END, 1832–4, Gothic [Port, 160–1].

MERE NEW HALL, CHESHIRE, for P. L. Brooke, 1834, Elizabethan; largely destroyed by fire *c.*1975 [*A.P.S.D.*].

HEATH HOUSE, TEAN, STAFFS., for J. B. Philips, 1836–40, Gothic [J. Cornforth in *C. Life*, 3 Jan. 1963].

CRESSBROOK HALL, nr. TIDESWELL, DERBYSHIRE, for Henry McConnell, *c.*1840, Elizabethan [*A.P.S.D.*].

LAMB, EDWARD BUCKTON (1806–1869)

LONDON, ST. PHILIP'S CHURCH, CLERKENWELL, 1831–2, Gothic; dem. 1938 [Port, 152–3].

CHEQUERS, BUCKS., alterations to N. front for Frankland Russell, 1837–8, Tudor Gothic [E. B. Lamb, *Studies in Ancient Domestic Architecture*, 1846].

MAIR, GEORGE JAMES JOHN (1810–1889)

NORTHWOOD HOUSE, WEST COWES, ISLE OF WIGHT, remodelled for George Henry Ward, 1838 onwards [exhib. at R.A. 1838, 1841, 1843, 1846; drawings (not as executed) in B.L., Add. MSS. 18157–8].

WELCOMBE HOUSE, nr. STRATFORD-ON-AVON, WARWICKS., for C. T. Warde, 1838; rebuilt 1869 [exhib. at R.A. 1838; plans in B.L., Add. MS. 18159, f. 18].

MOREING, CHARLES (*c.*1810–1885)

INGRESS ABBEY, GREENHITHE, KENT, for James Harmer, *c.*1832–4, Elizabethan [J. C. Loudon, *Architectural Mag.* i, 1834, 47; exhib. at R.A. 1832 and 1845].

NEVILL, JOSEPH (*c.*1811–1882), of Leamington and later of Abergavenny

LEAMINGTON, WARWICKS., CLARENCE TERRACE, *c.*1836 [*The Architect's, Engineer's and Building Trades' Directory*, 1868, 128].

NICHOLSON, WILLIAM ADAMS (1803–1853)

MANSFIELD, NOTTS., THE TOWN HALL, 1836 [*Builder* xi, 1853, 262].

BAYONS MANOR, TEALBY, LINCS., for Charles Tennyson D'Eyncourt, in collaboration with A. Salvin, 1836–40; dem. 1965 [T. R. Leach & R. Pacey, *Bayons Manor* (Lost Lincolnshire Houses, vol. 3, 1992)].

WRAGBY CHURCH, LINCS., rebuilt 1839, Gothic [*Builder* xi, 1853, 262].

PENNETHORNE, Sir JAMES (1801–1871)

SWITHLAND HALL, LEICS., for G. J. Danvers, afterwards 4th Earl of Lanesborough, 1834; wings added 1852 [G. Tyack, *Sir James Pennethorne*, 1992, 312–13].

LONDON, CHRIST CHURCH, ALBANY STREET, ST. PANCRAS (now Greek Orthodox Cathedral), 1836–7 [*ibid.*].

LONDON, HOLY TRINITY CHURCH, GRAY'S INN ROAD, HOLBORN, 1837–8; dem. 1931 [*ibid.*].

DILLINGTON HOUSE, nr. ILMINSTER, SOMERSET, remodelled for J. Lee Lee, 1838 [*ibid.*].

POYNTER, AMBROSE (1796–1886)

LONDON, ST. KATHARINE'S ROYAL HOSPITAL, REGENT'S PARK, 1826–8, Gothic [*History of the King's Works* vi, 479–80].

HODSOCK PRIORY, nr. WORKSOP, NOTTS., for Mrs. Chambers, 1829–33, Gothic [building accounts in Mellish papers, Nottingham University Library].

WARWICK CASTLE, reroofed and repaired Great Hall for 3rd Earl of Warwick, 1830–1, Gothic; destroyed by fire 1871 [exhib. at R.A. 1831; *V.C.H. Warwicks.* viii, 464].

SCOFTON-WITH-OSBERTON CHURCH, NOTTS., for G. S. Foljambe, 1833, neo-Norman [Charles Anderson, *Ancient Models: or, Hints on Church Building*, 2nd ed. 1841, 181–6, with plan and elevation].

CAMBRIDGE, CHRIST CHURCH, 1837–9, Tudor [Port, 140–1].

PUGIN, AUGUSTUS WELBY (1812–1852), all from Phoebe Stanton, *Pugin*, 1971, 196–7

ST. MARIE'S GRANGE, ALDERBURY, WILTS., for himself, 1835, Gothic; altered *c.*1875.

ALTON TOWERS, STAFFS., additions for 16th Earl of Shrewsbury, 1837 onwards, Gothic.

DERBY, ST. MARY'S CHURCH (R.C.), 1837–9, Gothic.

DUDLEY, WORCS., R.C. CHURCH, 1838–9, Gothic.

KEIGHLEY, YORKS. (W.R.), ST. ANNE'S CHURCH (R.C.), 1838, Gothic.

MACCLESFIELD, CHESHIRE, ST. ALBAN'S CHURCH (R.C.), 1839–41, Gothic.

SCARISBRICK HALL, LANCS., remodelled for Charles Scarisbrick, 1837–45, Gothic (*C. Life*, 13–20 March 1958).

READING, BERKS., ST. JAMES'S CHURCH (R.C.), 1837–40, neo-Norman; much altered.

SOLIHULL, WARWICKS., ST. AUGUSTINE'S CHURCH (R.C.), 1838, Gothic.

UTTOXETER, STAFFS., ST. MARY'S CHURCH (R.C.), 1838–9, Gothic; since remodelled.

RUMLEY, HENRY (–*c.*1858), of Bristol

UPHILL CASTLE, WESTON-SUPER-MARE, SOMERSET, *c.*1830, castellated [drawing in private possession, *ex inf.* Mr. J. Orbach].

BRISTOL, Nos. 1–9 QUEEN SQUARE, 1833 [W. Ison, *Georgian Buildings of Bristol*, 1952, 147].

FRENCHAY CHURCH, GLOS., 1834, Gothic [I.C.B.S.].

SALVIN, ANTHONY (1799–1881), all from J. Allibone, *Anthony Salvin*, 1988.

MAMHEAD, DEVON, rebuilt for Sir Robert Newman, Bart., 1825–38 (*C. Life*, 26 May, 2 June, 1955; C. Hussey, *English Country Houses: Late Georgian*, 1958, 193–205).

NORTHALLERTON VICARAGE (now Council Offices), YORKS. (N.R.), 1827–8, Tudor.

KILDALE HALL, nr. WHITBY, YORKS. (N.R.), alterations for R. B. Livesey, *c.*1827–31.

WROXHAM CHURCHYARD, NORFOLK, TRAFFORD MAUSOLEUM, 1828–9, Gothic.

MOREBY HALL, YORKS. (E.R.), for Henry Preston, 1828–33, Tudor (*C. Life*, 16 Feb. 1907).

BRANCEPETH CASTLE, CO. DURHAM, alterations to hall, etc., for William Russell, 1829.

ULVERSTON, LANCS., HOLY TRINITY CHURCH (now Sports Centre), 1829–31, Gothic.

NORTH SUNDERLAND CHURCH, NORTHUMBERLAND, 1830–33, neo-Norman.

NORWICH CATHEDRAL, restoration of S. transept, etc., 1830–4.

METHLEY HALL, YORKS. (W.R.), alterations and additions for 3rd Earl of Mexborough, 1830–6, Elizabethan; dem. 1963 (*C. Life*, 18 May 1907).

PARHAM HOUSE, SUSSEX, restoration for the Hon. Robert Curzon and his wife Baroness Zouche, 1830–6 (*C. Life*, 19 April 1902, 1, 15 June 1951).

HARLAXTON MANOR, LINCS., for Gregory de Ligne Gregory, 1831–7; completed by W. Burn 1838 onwards; Elizabethan (for illustrations see p. 189).

SKUTTERSKELFE HOUSE (formerly LEVEN GROVE), RUDBY, YORKS. (N.R.), for 10th Viscount Falkland, *c.*1831–8, classical.

COWESBY HALL, YORKS. (N.R.), for G. Lloyd, 1832–6, Elizabethan; rebuilt 1949.

SHILDON CHURCH, CO. DURHAM, 1833–4, Gothic; enlarged 1881–2, tower 1900.

RUNCTON HALL, NORTH RUNCTON, NORFOLK, for Daniel Gurney, 1834–5; dem. 1965.

NORWICH CASTLE, restoration, 1835–8.

KIMBERLEY HALL, NORFOLK, added quadrants connecting house to wings, for 2nd Lord Kimberley, 1835–8.

BURWARTON HALL, SALOP., for the Hon. G. F. Hamilton, 1835–9; enlarged by Salvin 1876–7, plain Italianate; altered *c.*1900 and reduced in size 1956–7 (*C. Life*, 17 March 1960).

CHALFONT HOUSE, BUCKS., alterations for John Hibbert, 1836, Gothic.

WOODLANDS, KENN, DEVON, new façade etc. for W. Ley, 1836.

DARLINGTON, CO. DURHAM, HOLY TRINITY CHURCH, 1836–8, Gothic; chancel added 1867.

DANESFIELD HOUSE, MARLOW, BUCKS., for C. Scott Murray, 1837–41; rebuilt 1899–1901 (F. O. Morris, *Picturesque Views of Seats* v, 1880, 77).

SCOTNEY CASTLE, KENT, for Edward Hussey, 1837–43, Elizabethan (*C. Life*, 6–13 Sept. 1956; C. Hussey, *English Country Houses: Late Georgian*, 1958, 220–9).

BURTONFIELD HOUSE, STAMFORD BRIDGE, YORKS. (E.R.), for C. A. Darley, 1838–40.

SMIRKE, SYDNEY (1797–1877)

CLUMBER HOUSE, NOTTS., library for 4th Duke of Newcastle, 1829–31; dem. 1938 [Nottingham University Library, Newcastle Papers, NeC 6132] (*C. Life*, 12 Sept. 1908).

OAKLEY PARK, nr. EYE, SUFFOLK, for Sir Edward Kerrison, Bart., *c.*1830; dem. *c.*1930 [*A.P.S.D.*] (*C. Life*, 4 Jan. 1908).

GUNNERSBURY HOUSE, MIDDLESEX, remodelled for Baroness Rothschild, *c.*1834 [*A.P.S.D.*].

THORNHAM HALL, SUFFOLK, remodelled for 4th Lord Henniker, 1837–8, Jacobean; dem. 1934 [*A.P.S.D.*] (H. R. Barker, *East Suffolk Illustrated*, 1908–9, 474).

CUSTOM HOUSES at BRISTOL, GLOUCESTER, NEWCASTLE and SHOREHAM, SUSSEX, *c.*1830–40 [J. M. Crook in *Seven Victorian Architects*, ed. Jane Fawcett, 1976, 152].

SPENCE, WILLIAM (*c.*1806–1883), of Glasgow

COULTERMAINS, LANARKSHIRE, for Adam Sim, 1838 [W. Hunter, *Biggar and the House of Fleming*, 1867, 588].

WARD, HENRY, of Stafford (–1899?)

STOKE-ON-TRENT, STAFFS., TOWN HALL, 1834 onwards [*V.C.H. Staffs.* viii, 182].

HOLMEBRIDGE CHURCH, YORKS. (W.R.), 1839–40, Gothic [I.C.B.S.].

WILSON, PATRICK (*c.*1798–1871), of Edinburgh

EDINBURGH, ARCHIBALD PLACE, terrace on W. side, begun 1824 [*Book of the Old Edinburgh Club* xviii, 1932, 161].

CAPRINGTON CASTLE, AYRSHIRE, remodelled for John Smith-Cunningham, *c.*1830 [*Edinburgh Evening Courant*, 30 April 1829; volume of signed drawings at Caprington, photos at N.M.R.S.].

WYATT, THOMAS HENRY (1807–1880)

LLANTARNAM ABBEY, MONMOUTHSHIRE, rebuilt for R. S. Blewitt, 1835, Elizabethan [exhib. at R.A. 1835].

NEWPORT, MONMOUTHSHIRE, ST. PAUL'S CHURCH, 1835, Gothic [exhib. at R.A. 1835].

MALPAS COURT, nr. NEWPORT, MONMOUTHSHIRE, for Thomas Prothero, 1836–8, Gothic [exhib. at R.A. 1838] (T. Nicholas, *The County Families of Wales* ii, 1875, 721).

Appendix B

NAMES INCLUDED IN PREVIOUS EDITIONS OF THIS DICTIONARY, BUT EXCLUDED FROM THE SECOND OR THIRD EDITIONS

C omitted as a craftsman only
I omitted as an architect practising in Ireland
O omitted as too obscure or unimportant for inclusion
V omitted as a Victorian architect, the bulk of whose practice was after 1840
X omitted as not an architect, or otherwise included in error.

1 INCLUDED IN THE FIRST EDITION BUT NOT IN THE SECOND OR THIRD EDITIONS

Acres, Jonathan	O
Adams, George	O
Ainger, Samuel	O
Akerman, John	O
Alcock, J—	O
Alderson, James	O
Allin, Nathaniel	O
Allingham, W—	O
Anderson, Robert	O
Andrews, George Townsend	V
Apsdell, —	O
Arnold, of Arnoll, —	O
Ashworth, Robert Holden	O
Atkey, W—	O
Atkinson, G—	O
Atkinson, James	X
Atkinson, William Lynn	O
Austin, —	O
Avis, Joseph	C
Baber, J—	O
Baker, Robert	O
Ball, John, senior	O
Ball, John, junior	O
Ballard, R—	V
Balls, Samuel Charles	X
Banckes, Henry	C
Banks, Mark	O
Barker, Robert	C
Barlow, Edward	O
Barlow, Henry Clark	X
Barnard, William	O
Barnes, T—	O
Barnes, William	V
Barr, James	V
Bartell, Edmund	X
Bartells, T—	O
Barton, T—	O
Bateman, Thomas	O
Baxter, J—	O
Bayles, James	O
Beadel, James	O
Beadnell, G—	O
Beatson, W—	V
Beaumont, Alfred	V
Bell, J— A—	V
Bell, John	O
Bell, W—	O
Belling, Lewis	O
Bennett, Alexander	O
Bennett, John	O
Bennett, Joseph B— H—	O
Best, G—	O
Bevan, R— and J—	O
Biers, H—	O
Birch, J— R—	O
Bird, W— S—	O
Bishop, E— W—	O
Bishop, John	O
Blackburn, C—	V
Bland, John	C
Blunt, Henry	V
Bower, G— T—	O
Bowerbank, Thomas	O
Brain, H—	X
Brewer, Peter	O
Bridge, Thomas	O
Bridger, James	O
Brock, G— R—	O
Brooks, S— H—	V
Brough, Benjamin	O
Brown, Henry	O
Brown, William	V
Browne, James	O
Bubb, W—	O
Buck, Peter	O
Buddle, Richard	O
Burcham, Samuel	O
Burgess, Henry	O
Burgess, Thomas	O
Burnett, William Suckling	O
Butcher, Thomas	O
Buxton, John	O
Carr, R—	O
Cartwright, U—	O
Cass, Christopher	C
Chambers, John	O
Chambers, T—	O
Chapman, R—	O
Child, Anthony	O
Churchill, John	C
Clark, John (of Spilsby)	O
Clark, Richard	O
Clark, R— G—	O
Cleare, Samuel	O
Clemence, J—	O

Cobden, T— I
Coley, Benjamin O
Comins, — O
Cooper, B— O
Cooper, Henry O
Corlass, Thomas O
Couldery, W— E— O
Courtney, H— F— T— V
Cox, J— O
Cox, Peter O
Crabtree, Samuel O
Creighton, J— O
Croshaw, C— W— O
Crouch, E— O
Crowe, J— O
Cumber, J— O
Curtis, Abraham O
Dade, Thomas O
Danvers, Samuel X
Davenport, John (d.1668) C
Davis, William C
Dean, W— O
Deane, Anthony See p. 297
D'Egville, James O
Delamaine, Edmund O
Denham, William C
Devall, John C
Docker, John O
Donne, J— O
Driffield, Robert O
Driffield, Thomas O
Duncombe, Nicholas O
Durant, Eustace C
Edwards, Henry O
Egenolf, G— O
Elland, R— O
Elmes, H— J— see p. 342
England, J— O
England, W— O
Farmer, John O
Fellow, John O
Fenning, H— O
Fentiman, — O
Fetherston, Thomas C
Field, T— O
Fieldwick, — O
Filer, Martin O
Flemming, John O
Foster, B— O
Fox, B— O
Foyster, H— S— O
Fradgley, — V
Francis, Frederick John V
Freeman, Thomas O
Fulling, Thomas O
Gammon, Leonard O
Gammon, Richard O
Garnett, R— O
Garrett, John O
Garrod, Thomas O
Gatton, Francis O
Gautrey, J— O
Gay, Robert O
Gittos, J— B— O
Glegg, T— O
Goodman, Francis O
Goodwin, John O
Grantham, William O
Gray, Edward O
Gray, Thomas C
Green, F— G— O
Grix, Henry O
Groom, A— J— O
Hague, T— O
Halford, Edward O
Hambley, — V
Hance, J— W— O
Hanson, John V
Harcourt, C— F— O
Harding, — X
Harding, Thomas O
Harrison, B— R— O
Harrison, D— O
Harrison, Gregory O
Harrison, James O
Harvey, Daniel C
Harvey, John (d. 1735) O
Haughton, Charles O
Hawkins, Edward O
Hawkins, George O
Healy, T— O
Heaton, William Draper O
Hele, John O
Hellis, Edward O
Heming, — O
Henman, Charles V
Herron, George O
Hewlett, Samuel O
Hicks, Jonathan C
Hicks, William O
Hilliar, J— O
Hinton, Thomas O
Hitchens, J— O
Hoare, George C
Hobbes, Thomas O
Hodskinson, J— X
Holden, Strickland O
Hollingsworth, Richard M— O
Hollins, Humphry C
Hooley, Thomas O
Hooper, Thomas C
Hopson, Sir Charles C
Horsenaile, Christopher C
Hughes, R— X
Hunt, Henry O
Hunt, John C
Hurdis, James O
Hurst, John C
Hutchins, S— or T— O
Inskipp, Walter O
Ives, G— E— O
Jackson, Benjamin C
Jackson, T— J— R— O
Jackson, William C
Jacques, John V
James, Richard C
Jennings, Richard C
Johnston, John X
Jones, Henry C
Jones, John O
Judge, George V
Kendall, George C
Kerison, Henry O
Kidd, Robert Charles O
Killock, — O
Kilpin, William O
Kimber, — O
King, John William Pusey O
Knight, John O
Knight, Thomas C
Kyffin, Alexander O
Kynaston, Thomas O
Langridge, William O
Lawrence, — O
Leach, George O
Lee, Abraham O
Lee, Henry C
Lee, John C
Legg, George V
Leicester, G— O— V
Leigh, William O
Lester, H— O
Lever, G— O
Lewington, John O
Lindegren, Nathaniel O
Lloyd, T— O
Loader, Thomas O
Lomas, W— O
Long, T— O
Lotan, J— O
Lovel, James O
Mair, George James John V
Mallison, F— O
Markes, A— O
Martin, Albinus X
Martin, John C
Maskrey, William and Bartholomew C
Matthews, John O
May, B— O
Meakin, — V
Mill, J— O
Miller, J— V
Mills, Charles O
Mills, Richard O
Mitchell, George O
Mole, William C

Monday, Thomas	C
Money, J—	O
Moreing, Charles	V
Morfitt, John	C
Morris, Thomas	O
Morrison, Robert	X
Morton, R—	O
Mulholland, John	O
Muschamp, John	C
Muspratt, Thomas	C
Mutleo, Robert	C
Naish, James	X
Naish, Thomas	O
Neagle, John	O
Negus, Francis	O
Nevill, Thomas	O
Newcombe, —	C
Newling, —	C
Newman, Robert	C
Newman, William	O
Nicholson, Samuel	O
Nicholson, William Adams	V
Norman, William	O
Olliphant, James	C
Pain, Ambrose	O
Palmer, G— H—	O
Parish, C—	V
Park, T—	O
Parker, R—	O
Parlby, James	O
Parrish, J—	O
Parry, H— B—	O
Pearce, Edmund	V
Pepper, C—	O
Percy, Thomas	V
Phillips, John	O
Pilkington, Thomas	V
Pilling, William	O
Pink, James	C
Piper, Frederick Magnus	O
Pitt, Charles	O
Plucknett, Thomas	O
Plumridge, W—	O
Pollden, R—	O
Ponsford, John	O
Porden, Charles	O
Poultney, Joseph	O
Powell, Richard	C
Pratt, G—	O
Pratt, J—	O
Proctor, J—	O
Provis, W— A—	X
Pullen, T— W—	O
Rampling, R— B—	V
Randle, Ephraim	O
Rawlinson, S— S—	V
Reed, John	C
Restall, W—	O
Richardson, W— H—	O
Riches, J—	O
Richley, Richard	O
Ride, John	see p.000
Ridley, W— J—	O
Roberts, E—	O
Robertson, W—	I
Robinson, George	O
Robinson, George James	O
Robinson, John	O
Robinson, John	O
Rogers, William	V
Rose, William	O
Rotherham, Thomas	O
Rowe, James	O
Ruck, T—	O
Russell, F— B—	O
Russell, George	O
Sadleir, Richard	O
Sanders, John	O
Sanderson, —	C
Santler, G—	O
Saunders, John	O
Scott, John	O
See, Thomas *see* Gee	
Seed, Brice	C
Shannon, M—	O
Sharp, John	O
Sheasby, Thomas	O
Shelston, J—	O
Shirley, Thomas	O
Short, William J—	V
Showbridge, John	O
Shrugg, James	C
Simes, Charles	O
Simmons, A—	O
Simmons, Henry	O
Slightholme, Thomas	O
Slingsby, Joseph	O
Smallwell, John	C
Smith, Richard	O
Smith, S—	X
Smith, William Alwell	O
Spray, Matthew	C
Spurrell, B—	O
Squirhill, David or Daniel	V
Stacey, —	C
Stakes, W—	O
Stallard, Henry	O
Stallwood, N—	O
Stanford, R—	O
Stanley, G—	X
Starkey, J—	O
Stayner, Thomas	C
Stead, Joseph	C
Stebbing, J— L—	O
Stokes, William	O
Story, Abraham	C
Stow, or Stowe, W—C—	V
Straphen, John	C
Stringer, James	O
Stutely, Martin Joseph	V
Swaine, George	O
Sword, Thomas	O
Tarte, J—	O
Taylor, Edward	O
Taylor, Thomas	O
Temple, J—	O
Thomas, Josiah	O
Thomas, M—	O
Thomas, William	O
Thompson, Henry Augustus	O
Thompson, Richard	C
Thomson, James William	O
Tildesley, Thomas	O
Tress, William	V
Tufnell, Capt. Edward	C
Tufnell, Samuel	C
Tufnell, William	C
Vierpyl, W—	O
Vyvyan, J—	I
Wadeson, Edward	O
Walker, Samuel D—	V
Walsh, Frederick	O
Waring, F—	O
Waterman, J—	O
Watson, T—	O
Watts, G—	O
Webb, E—	O
Webb, Thomas	C
Webb, West	O
Webb, William	O
Wells, J— S—	O
West, S—	O
White, S—	O
Whitehead, T—	O
Willoughby, Nicholas	C
Wilmot, John	O
Wilson, H—	O
Wilson, J—	O
Wilson, J—	O
Wise, Thomas	C
Wood, J— T—	O
Woodeson, Leonard	O
Woodgate, Robert	I
Woodward, R—	O
Woolcott, D— E—	O
Woolley, Samuel	O
Wright, C—	X
Wright, W—	O
Wyatt, Robert Harvey	O
Wyatt, Thomas	O
Wyatt William	O
Wyatville, George Geoffrey	O
Wynn, M—	O

2 INCLUDED IN THE SECOND EDITION BUT NOT IN THE THIRD EDITION

Appleton, Robert V
Baker, H— V
Billop, William O
Blechynden, Richard O
Brown, John V
Browne, Robert O
Carstairs, David C
Clarkson, John O
Clisby, T. W. O
Cook, Thomas (d. 1803) O
Cunningham, John V
Day, R— X
Dodds, Joseph C
Drew, Thomas O
Elliott, John V
Fisher, — (d. 1817) O
Foulon, John V
Gray, John V
Hering, Frederick V
Johnstone, John C
Julian, G. H. V
Leather, John O
Lock, Daniel X
Longworth, James O
Lovi. Fr. Walter X
Masters, George X
Nicol, W— X
Ponton, Alexander O
Poynter, Ambrose V
Reeves, Edward O
Rumley, Henry V
Sandford, George O
Scougal, David C
Shaw, John (17th century) O
Shearburn, William V
Shoubridge, William V
Smith, David V
Smith, William (d. 1786) O
Sperring, John O
Wale, James O
Westbrook, Samuel C
Young, John (d. 1877) V

Appendix C

PUBLIC OFFICES HELD BY ARCHITECTS 1600–1840

d. = died   r. = retired or resigned

ENGLAND

THE ADMIRALTY

Inspector of Repairs to the Admiralty and Surveyor of Works to the Victualling Office

The salary was £30. The office was abolished in 1800 (J. C. Sainty, *Admiralty Officials 1660–1870*, 1975, 76).

Benjamin Glanville	1731–1774 (d.)
James Arrow	1774–1785
S. P. Cockerell	1785–1800

Architect and Engineer to the Naval Works Department

This office was established in 1796 at a salary of £400. In 1807 it was transferred from the Admiralty to the Navy Board and renamed Assistant Civil Architect and Engineer to the Navy (J. C. Sainty, *Admiralty Officials 1660–1870*, 1975, 91).

Samuel Bunce	1796–1802 (d.)
Edward Holl	1804–1824 (d.)
G. L. Taylor	1824–1837 (r.)
Capt. H. R. Brandreth, R.E.	1836–1846 (r.)

THE BANK OF ENGLAND

Architects

Sir Robert Taylor	*c.*1764–1788 (d.)
Sir John Soane	1788–1833 (r.)
C. R. Cockerell	1833–1855 (r.)

BETHLEHEM HOSPITAL

Surveyors

Strickland Holden	–1765 (d.)
Williams—	*c.*1765–*c.*1780
William Hillyer	*c.*1780–1782 (d.)
Henry Holland	1782–1793 (r.)
James Lewis	1793–1816 (r.)
Philip Hardwick	1816–1837 (r.)
Sydney Smirke	1837–1861 (r.)

CHELSEA HOSPITAL

Clerks of the Works

A salary of £200 p.a. was paid from 1793 onwards (C. G. T. Dean, *The Royal Hospital, Chelsea*, 1950, 121, 316). The office was abolished in 1837.

Roger Hewitt	1691–1698 (r.)
Sir Charles Hopson	1698–1710 (d.)
Hugh Warren	1710–1728 (d.)
John Lane	1729–1753 (d.)
George Leach	1753–1755 (d.)
John Vardy	1756–1765 (d.)
Robert Adam	1765–1792 (d.)
Samuel Wyatt	1792–1807 (d.)
Sir John Soane	1807–1837 (d.)

COMMISSIONERS FOR BUILDING FIFTY NEW CHURCHES

Surveyors

Two Surveyors were appointed under the Act of 1711 at a salary of £200 each: Nicholas Hawksmoor and William Dickinson. Dickinson resigned in 1713, his place being taken by James Gibbs, who was superseded in 1715 by John James. Hawksmoor and James continued in charge until Midsummer 1733, when their appointments officially terminated, though both were paid 'for carrying on and finishing the works under their care' for some time afterwards.

COMMISSIONERS FOR BUILDING NEW CHURCHES (UNDER THE ACT OF 1818)

Architects

At first the Commissioners relied upon the three architects attached to H.M. Office of Works to examine and report upon the plans and estimates submitted, but in 1821 they were obliged, by increasing pressure of business, to appoint their own architect. The office was abolished on 1 Jan. 1857.

Edward Mawley	1821–1826 (d.)
J. H. Good	1826–1857

H.M. CUSTOMS

Surveyors of Buildings

The salary was £40 p.a. in the eighteenth century.

William Robinson	occurs 1752 onwards
William Rice	1768–1781 (r.)
William Pilkington	1781–1810 (r.)
David Laing	1810–1825 (dismissed)
vacant	1825–1830
John Taylor	1830–*c.*1841

EAST INDIA COMPANY

Surveyors

In 1752 the Company resolved to appoint a surveyor to supervise 'the work necessary to be done at this House and the Company's several warehouses'. At first the salary was £30 p.a. with a percentage for architectural work carried out under the Surveyor's direction, but it was increased to £60 in 1779, and Cockerell and Wilkins both received £500 p.a.

William Jones	1752–1757 (d.)
William Robinson	1757–1767 (d.)
Richard Jupp	1768–1799 (d.)
Henry Holland	1799–1806 (d.)
S. P. Cockerell	1806–1824 (r.)
William Wilkins	1824–1837 (r.)

Clerks of the Works

George Harrison	1837–*c.*1850
Arthur J. Green	*c.*1850–1855 (d.)

GREENWICH HOSPITAL

Surveyors

The salary was £200 a year. In 1821 the offices of Surveyor and Clerk of the Works were combined.

Sir Christopher Wren	1696–1716 (r.)
Sir John Vanbrugh	1716–1726 (d.)
Colen Campbell	1726–1729 (d.)
Thomas Ripley	1729–1758 (d.)
James Stuart	1758–1788 (d.)
Sir Robert Taylor	Feb.–Sept. 1788 (d.)
John Yenn	1788–1821 (d.)
H. H. Seward	1821–1823 (r.)

Clerks of the Works

John Scarborough	May–Nov. 1696 (d.)
Henry Symmonds	1696–1698 (d.)
Nicholas Hawksmoor[1]	1698–1735
John James[1]	1718–1746 (d.)
William Robinson	1746–1775 (d.)
Robert Mylne	1775–1782 (dismissed)
William Newton	1782–1790 (d.)
George Knight	1790–1810 (r.)
H. H. Seward	1810–1823 (r.)
Joseph Kay	1823–1847 (d.)

[1] Hawksmoor and James acted jointly from 1718 onwards (*Wren Soc.* vi, 31).

THE CITY OF LONDON

Clerks of the Works

The appointment was held by purchase, each Clerk of the Works having the right to nominate his successor in return for a substantial payment. He had no staff, but gave directions to the City Artificers, who had a monopoly of building work carried out for the Corporation. George Dance the elder discharged his duties in this regard by 'having all the artificers to meet him on a stated day once a week at the Moorgate Coffee-house, to receive his orders and instructions'. In 1771 his son obtained leave to appoint an Assistant Clerk of Works at his own expense, and nominated James Peacock, who was succeeded in 1814 by William Mountague. In 1848 the title was changed from 'Clerk of the City Works' to 'Architect of the City of London'. The following list gives the holders of the office from the Restoration onwards.

James Hayton	–1662 (r.)
Nicholas Duncomb	1662–1676 (r.)
Thomas Aylward	1676–1691 (r.)
John Noyes	1691–1692 (r.)
James Fell	1692–1693 (r.)
John Olley	1693–1711 (r.)
Isaac Olley	1711–1724 (d.)
George Smith	1724–1734 (dismissed)
George Dance, senior	1735–1768 (r.)
George Dance, junior	1768–1815 (r.)
William Mountague	1816–1843 (d.)

THE ROYAL MINT

Surveyors

The office was abolished in 1815, when the maintenance of the Mint was taken over by the Office of Works.

John Vardy	1749–1763 (r.)
John Vardy, junior	1763–1793 (r.)
Samuel Wyatt	1793–1794 (dismissed)
James Johnson	–1807 (d.)
Robert Smirke	1807–1815

THE ORDNANCE

The post of *Architect of the Ordnance* was created in 1719, at a time when the Ordnance Office was engaged in building forts in Scotland after the rebellion of 1715. It subsequently became more or less of a sinecure, and as such was held from 1762 to 1782 by the sons of Sir Charles Frederick, then Surveyor-General of the Ordnance. The salary was £120 p.a. The post was abolished in 1829. The following list of its occupants is based on the Ordnance records in the P.R.O., chiefly WO 48/68 and WO 54/203, 210, 212.

Andrews Jelfe	1719–1727
James Gibbs	1727–1754 (d.)
Capt. J. P. Desmaretz	1754–1762
Charles Frederick	1762–1777
Edward Boscawen Frederick	1778–1782
James Wyatt	1782–1813 (d.)
William Atkinson	1813–1829

THE ROYAL ACADEMY

Professors of Architecture

The Rules of the Royal Academy, drawn up at its foundation in 1768, provided that there should be a Professor of Architecture, 'who shall read annually Six Public Lectures, calculated to form the taste of the Students; to instruct them in the laws and principles of composition; and to point out to them the beauties and faults of celebrated productions'. His salary was to be £30 a year, and he was to 'continue in office during the King's pleasure'.

Thomas Sandby	1768–1798 (d.)
George Dance	1798–1805 (r.)
Sir John Soane	1806–1837 (d.)
William Wilkins	1837–1839 (d.)
C. R. Cockerell	1839–1857 (r.)

ST. PAUL'S CATHEDRAL

Surveyors

This post was in the gift of the Archbishop of Canterbury, the Bishop of London and the Lord Mayor. It is described by Farington (*Diary*, ed. J. Greig, vi, 268) as 'a place of honour, the salary only £70 a year', and should not be confused with the post of Surveyor to the Dean and Chapter of St. Paul's.

Sir Christopher Wren	1675–1723 (d.)
John James	1724–1746 (d.)
Henry Flitcroft	1746–1756
Stiff Leadbetter	1756–1766 (d.)
Robert Mylne	1766–1811 (d.)
S. P. Cockerell	1811–1819
C. R. Cockerell	1819–1852 (r.)

Assistant Surveyor

This post became redundant after the completion of the cathedral, and ceased to exist when John James succeeded Wren as Surveyor.

Edward Woodroffe	1668–1675 (d.)
John Oliver	1676–1701 (d.)
Thomas Bateman	1701–1715
John James	1715–1724 (promoted)

WESTMINSTER ABBEY

The Dean and Chapter of Westminster appointed an official, known as the 'College Surveyor', who looked after their urban property and made plans and surveys of their other estates when required. Until 1698, he was also in charge of the buildings of Westminster Abbey, but in that year Parliament granted an annual sum of money towards the repair and completion of the Abbey Church, and a new post of 'Surveyor to the Fabric' was created, together with a subordinate under-surveyorship. The under-surveyorship came to an end when Thomas Hinton became 'College Surveyor' in 1746, and in 1752 the latter office was merged with that of 'Surveyor to the Fabric'.

College Surveyors

William Mann	1598–1635 (d.)
William Ireland	1636–1638 (d.)
Adam Browne	1639–1655

John Sherman	1655–1660
Drew Sterrill	*c.*1660–1662 (d.)
Robert Woodroffe	1662–1671
Edward Woodroffe	1672–1675 (d.)
Thomas Plucknett	1675–1690
Robert Hooke	1691–
James Broughton	1697–1711 (d.)
William Dickinson	1711–1725 (d.)
John James	1725–1746 (d.)
Thomas Hinton	May–Aug. 1746 (d.)
Henry Keene	1746–1776 (d.)

Surveyors to the Fabric

Sir Christopher Wren	1699–1723 (d.)
Nicholas Hawksmoor	1723–1736 (d.)
John James	1736–1746 (d.)
James Horne	1746–1752 (r.)
Henry Keene	1752–1776 (d.)
James Wyatt	1776–1813 (d.)
Benjamin Dean Wyatt	1813–1827 (r.)
Edward Blore	1827–1849 (r.)

Under-Surveyors

James Broughton	1699–1711 (d.)
William Dickinson	1711–1725 (d.)
Thomas Hinton	1725–1746 (appointed College Surveyor)

H.M. OFFICE OF WOODS AND FORESTS

In 1795 the Treasury was persuaded that it would be advantageous if 'an experienced Architect should be appointed *Deputy Surveyor of His Majesty's Woods and Forests* for the purpose of preparing Plans & Estimates for Buildings & Repairs within the Department of the Surveyor General of H.M.'s Woods & Forests' (P.R.O., T 25/2, p. 387). The salary was £200 p.a. The office was abolished in 1815.

John Soane	1795–1799 (r.)
James Wyatt	1799–1805 (dismissed)
John Harvey	1805–1806 (dismissed)
John Nash James Morgan	1806–1815

H.M. OFFICE OF WORKS

For the history and constitution of the Office of Works see *The History of the King's Works*, ed. Colvin, in which full lists of officials will be found. Only the principal posts held by architects are given below.

Surveyors of the King's Works

William Spicer	1597–1604 (d.)
Sir David Cuningham	1604–1606
Simon Basil	1606–1615 (d.)
Inigo Jones	1615–1643 (ejected)
Edward Carter	1643–1653
(John Embree)	1653–1660 (ejected)

Sir John Denham	1660–1669 (d.)
Sir Christopher Wren	1669–1718 (dismissed)
William Benson	1718–1719 (dismissed)
Sir Thomas Hewett	1719–1726 (d.)
Hon. Richard Arundell, M.P.	1726–1737 (r.)
Hon. Henry Fox, M.P.	1737–1743 (r.)
Hon. Henry Finch, M.P.	1743–1760 (r.)
Thomas Worsley, M.P.	1760–1778 (d.)
Col. James Whitshed Keene, M.P.	1779–1782

Comptrollers of the King's Works

Simon Basil	1597–1606 (promoted)
Thomas Baldwin	1606–1641 (d.)
Francis Wethered	1641–1668 (d.)
Hugh May	1668–1684 (d.)
vacant	1684–1689
William Talman	1689–1702 (dismissed)
Sir John Vanbrugh	1702–1726 (d.)
Thomas Ripley	1726–1758 (d.)
Henry Flitcroft	1758–1769 (d.)
Sir William Chambers	1769–1782 (promoted)

Surveyors-General and Comptrollers of the King's Works

Sir William Chambers	1782–1796 (d.)
James Wyatt	1796–1813 (d.)

After Wyatt's death the Office of Works was reorganized with a non-professional *Surveyor-General of Works and Public Buildings*, Col. B. C. Stephenson, assisted by three 'Attached Architects' (John Nash, John Soane and Robert Smirke), who received a retaining fee and a percentage on work carried out under their direction. Stephenson had as his subordinate an *Assistant Surveyor and Cashier* (Robert Browne, 1814–1823, H. H. Seward, 1823–1832). This arrangement came to an end in 1832, when the Office of Works and the Office of Woods and Forests were combined under a body of Commissioners, with Seward as *Surveyor of Works and Buildings*. It was not until 1851 that the Office of Works became once more an independent institution, the ancestor of the modern Ministry of Works (later merged in the Department of the Environment).

Deputy Surveyors

Colen Campbell	1718–1719 (dismissed)
Westby Gill	1719–1735 (promoted)
William Kent	1735–1748 (d.)
Henry Flitcroft	1748–1758 (promoted)
Stephen Wright	1758–1780 (d.)
Sir Robert Taylor	1780–1782

Architects of the Works

Sir William Chambers	1761–1769 (promoted)
Robert Adam	1761–1769 (r.)
Sir Robert Taylor	1769–1777 (promoted)
James Adam	1769–1782
Thomas Sandby	1777–1780 (promoted)
James Paine	1780–1782

Secretaries to the Board of Works

Nicholas Hawksmoor	1715–1718 (dismissed)
Benjamin Benson	1718–1719 (dismissed)
John Hallam	1719–1726 (dismissed)
Nicholas Hawksmoor	1726–1736 (d.)
Isaac Ware	1736–1766 (d.)
William Robinson	1766–1775 (d.)
Kenton Couse	1775–1782

Master Masons

William Cure	1605–1632 (d.)
Nicholas Stone	1632–after 1640
Edward Marshall	1660–1673 (r.)
Joshua Marshall	1673–1678 (d.)
Thomas Wise	1678–1685 (d.)
John Oliver	1686–1701 (d.)
Benjamin Jackson	1701–1719 (d.)
Nicholas Dubois	1719–1735 (d.)
William Kent	1735–1748 (d.)
Henry Flitcroft	1748–1758 (promoted)
Stephen Wright	1758–1780 (d.)
Sir Robert Taylor	1780–1782

Master Carpenters

William Portington	1579–1629 (d.)
Richard Binding	1604–1611
Ralph Brice	–after 1640
John Davenport	1660–1668 (d.)
Richard Ryder	1668–1683 (d.)
Matthew Bancks, junior	1683–1706 (d.)
John Churchill	1706–1715 (d.)
Robert Barker	1718–1719 (dismissed)
Grinling Gibbons	1719–1721 (d.)
Thomas Ripley	1721–1726 (promoted)
William Kent	1726–1735 (promoted)
Westby Gill	1735–1746 (d.)
Henry Flitcroft	1746–1748 (promoted)
William Oram	1748–1777 (d.)
Sir Robert Taylor	1777–1780 (promoted)
Thomas Sandby	1780–1782

Comptrollers of the Works at Windsor Castle (from 1660)

Hartgill Baron	1660–1673 (d.)
Hugh May	1674–1684 (d.)
Sir Christopher Wren	1684–1716

SCOTLAND

THE SCOTTISH ROYAL WORKS

Until the Union (1707) the Scottish Master of Work was the equivalent of the English Surveyor of the King's Works, and at least two holders of the post (Sir William Bruce and James Smith) were practising architects as well as administrators. But after the Union the absence of a resident sovereign meant that there were few works to supervise, and the office became a sinecure (worth £400 p.a.). This situation lasted until the early nineteenth century. In 1808 the Edinburgh architect Robert Reid (*q.v.*) obtained a commission authorizing him to use the title of 'Architect and Surveyor to the King in Scotland', without any salary. When the then Master of Work, James Brodie, died in 1824, Reid succeeded in getting his office merged with his own, and in 1827 he became the head of a properly constituted Scottish Office of Works with a salary of £500 p.a. and a small staff. In 1831, however, Reid's department was made subordinate to the English Office of Works, and in 1840, when he retired, his post was abolished.

Masters of Work

David Cunningham of Robertland	1602–1607 (d.)
Sir James Murray of Kilbaberton	1607–1634 (d.)
Sir Anthony Alexander	1629–1637 (d.)
Henry Alexander (later 3rd Earl of Stirling)	1637–1641
Sir John Veitch of Dawyck	1641–
John Carmichael	1643–1644 (d.)
Sir Daniel Carmichael of Hyndford	1645–1649 (r.)
Sir Robert Montgomery	1649–
Sir William Moray of Dreghorn	1660–1668
vacant	1669–1670
Sir William Bruce of Balcaskie	1671–1678
David Maitland (acting)	1678–1682
James Smith	1683–1688
Sir Archibald Murray of Blackbarony	1689–1700 (d.)
James Scott of Logie, junior	1700–1704
Sir Francis Scott of Thirlestane	1704–1705
John Urquhart of Meldrum	1705–1714
John Campbell of Mamor	1705–1717
Sir John Anstruther of Anstruther	1717–1743
George Dundas	1743–1761
William Stewart of Hartwood	1761–1764
James Duff	1765–1768
Lt. Col. James Pringle	1768–1809 (d.)
James Brodie of Brodie	1809–1824 (d.)
Robert Reid	1824–1840 (r.)

THE CITY OF EDINBURGH

In 1720 Alexander McGill was appointed to the newly constituted post of City Architect at a salary of £50 p.a., but this was discontinued in 1725 as a measure of economy. An Overseer of Public Works was one of the City officials from at least the early eighteenth century until the office was discontinued in 1758, but its holders were clerks of the works rather than architects. The office of *Superintendent of Public Works* can be traced from 1786 onwards and was held by the following:

James Gordon	1786–1789 (r.)
William Sibbald	1790–1809 (d.)
John Paterson[1]	May–Dec. 1809
Thomas Bonnar	1809–1818 (dismissed)
Thomas Brown	1819–1847 (r.)

HERIOT'S HOSPITAL

George Heriot's Hospital was a major landowner in Edinburgh and appointed a *Superintendent of Property, Plans and Works*. The following holders of the office are given by William Stevens, *History of George Heriot's Hospital*, ed. Bedford, 1859, 311:

John Paterson[1]	1809–1810 (r.)
Thomas Bonnar	1810–*c.*1832 (d.)
Alexander Black	1833[2]–1858 (d.)

[1] This was John Paterson, civil engineer of Leith (d. 1823), not the architect of the same name.

[2] Stevens gives the date of his appointment as 1836, but in the *Edinburgh Almanac* he is listed as Superintendent from 1833 onwards.

Index of Persons

Note. The names of architects who are the subjects of entries in the text have not been indexed, nor, as a rule, have the names of members of their families.

Index of Places

I BRITISH ISLES

LONDON

LONDON

LONDON

LONDON

II OTHER COUNTRIES